Mergent's
HANDBOOK OF
COMMON STOCKS

Spring 2008

WILEY
Publishers Since 1807

MERGENT®

INTRODUCTION

Mergent's Handbook of Common Stocks provides quick and easy access to basic financial and business information on more than 900 stocks that are included in the Russell 1000, S&P 500, S&P 400 and Mergent's Dividend Achievers. The Tab Section provides one-line information on New York Stock Exchange companies.

The price charts, statistics, and analyses are presented in a format that provides the investor with the necessary perspective for acting on investment advice or suggestions. It also affords investors the opportunity to make investment decisions on their own.

Statistics and analyses are revised quarterly. Every effort is made to secure the most current operating results and dividend information available. In the case of year-end results, preliminary results are shown and analyzed as they are received. Full statistical presentations of annual report information are shown in the following edition. The schedule below describes the publication dates and company reporting periods usually covered in each edition.

The Winter Edition (published in January) covers quarterly reports and preliminary annual reports through September 30.

The Spring Edition (published in April) covers quarterly reports and preliminary annual reports through December 31.

The Summer Edition (published in July) covers quarterly reports and preliminary annual reports through March 31.

The Fall Edition (published in October) covers quarterly reports and preliminary annual reports through June 30.

Note: For various reasons, some companies may not report in time to meet our publication deadlines. Company reports received close to press time are shown in the Addenda. The remainder of late reports are published and analyzed in the next edition of the Handbook.

The special section on these opening pages contains a number of features, including a guide on how to use this book, a classification of companies by their major line of business based on their NAIC code, outstanding stock price movements by company, plus long-term charts on popular stock market averages. The Addenda provide the latest developments available just prior to publication but after the company reports have been completed.

TABLE OF CONTENTS

3a

HOW TO USE THIS BOOK

The presentation of historical data and analytical comments provides the answers to four basic questions for each company:

1. What does the company do?
   (See G.)
2. How has it done in the past?
   (See B, J.)
3. How is it doing now?
   (See C, D, H.)
4. How will it fare in the future?
   (See I.)

A. CAPSULE STOCK INFORMATION

shows where the stock is traded and its symbol, a recent price and price/earnings ratio, plus the yield afforded by the indicated dividend based on a recent price. The indicated dividend is the current annualized dividend based on the most recent price. Some companies are designated as Dividend Achievers. Dividend Achievers have, by *Mergent's* criteria, increased their cash dividend payments for at least ten consecutive years, adjusting for splits. The number of years of consecutive increases is given for each Dividend Achiever.

B. LONG-TERM PRICE CHART

illustrates the pattern of monthly stock price movements, fully adjusted for stock dividends and splits. The chart points out the degree of volatility in the price movement of the company's stock and what its long-term trend has been. It also shows how it has performed long-term relative to an initial investment in the S&P 500 Index equal to the price of the company's stock at the beginning of the period shown in the price chart. It indicates areas of price support and resistance, plus other technical points to be considered by the investor. The bars at the base of the long-term price chart indicate the monthly trading volume. Monthly trading

volume offers the individual an opportunity to recognize at what periods stock accumulation occurs and what percent of a company's outstanding shares are traded.

PRICE SCORES – Above each company's price/volume chart are its *Mergent's Price Scores*. These are basic measures of the stock's performance. Each stock is measured against the New York Stock Exchange Composite Index.

A score of 100 indicates that the stock did as well as the New York Stock Exchange Composite Index during the time period. A score of less than 100 means that the stock did not do as well; a score of more than 100 means that the stock outperformed the NYSE Composite Index. All stock prices are adjusted for splits and stock dividends. The time periods measured for each company conclude with the date of the recent price shown in the top line of each company's profile.

The *7 YEAR PRICE SCORE* mirrors the common stock's price growth over the previous seven years. The higher the price score, the better the relative performance. It is based on the ratio of the latest 12-month average price to the current seven-year average. This ratio is then indexed against the same ratio for the market as a whole (the New York Stock Exchange Composite Index), which is taken as 100.

The *12 MONTH PRICE SCORE* is a similar measurement but for a shorter period of time. It is based on the ratio of the latest two-month average price to the current 12-month average. As was done for the Long-Term Price Score, this ratio is also indexed to the same ratio for the market as a whole.

ILLUSTRATIVE, INC.

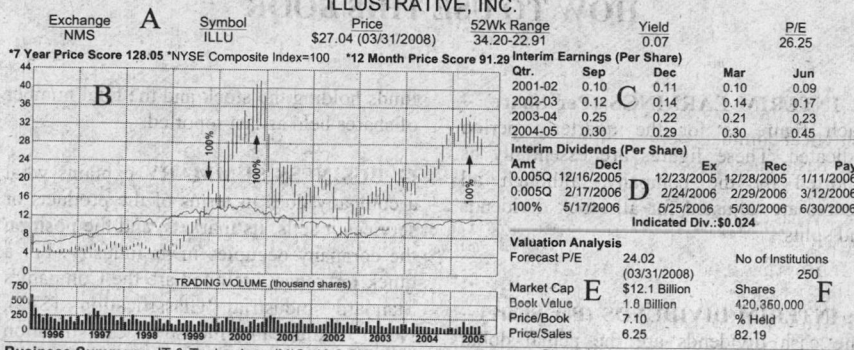

Exchange **A** NMS	Symbol ILLU	Price $27.04 (03/31/2008)	52Wk Range 34.20-22.91	Yield 0.07	P/E 26.25

*7 Year Price Score 128.05 *NYSE Composite Index=100 *12 Month Price Score 91.29

B

Interim Earnings (Per Share) **C**

Qtr.	Sep	Dec	Mar	Jun
2001-02	0.10	0.11	0.10	0.09
2002-03	0.12	0.14	0.14	0.17
2003-04	0.25	0.22	0.21	0.23
2004-05	0.30	0.29	0.30	0.45

Interim Dividends (Per Share) **D**

Amt	Decl	Ex	Rec	Pay
0.005Q	12/16/2005	12/23/2005	12/28/2005	1/11/2006
0.005Q	2/17/2006	2/24/2006	2/29/2006	3/12/2006
100%	5/17/2006	5/25/2006	5/30/2006	6/30/2006

Indicated Div.:$0.024

TRADING VOLUME (thousand shares)

Valuation Analysis **E** **F**

Forecast P/E	24.02 (03/31/2008)	No of Institutions	250
Market Cap	$12.1 Billion	Shares	420,360,000
Book Value	1.8 Billion	% Held	82.19
Price/Book	7.10		
Price/Sales	6.25		

Business Summary: IT & Technology (MIC: 10.2 SIC: 7372 NAIC: 511210) **G**

Illustrative offers a line of software and services for consumers, professionals and enterprises, in both public and private sectors. Co.'s digital imaging, design, and document technology platforms enable customers to create, manage and deliver content. Co. distributes its products through a network of distributors and dealers, value-added resellers, systems integrators, independent software vendors and original equipment manufacturers; direct to end users; and through Co.'s Web site. Co. also licenses its technology to major hardware manufacturers, software developers and service providers and offers integrated software services.

Recent Developments: **H** For the quarter ended Mar 31, 2008, net income was $149,778 thousand from net income of $109,401 thousand in the year-earlier quarter. Revenues were $496,029 thousand, up 21.0% from $410,085 thousand the year before. Operating income was $182,204 thousand versus an income of $141,839 thousand in the prior-year quarter, an increase of 28.5%. Total direct expense was $27,434 thousand versus $27,255 thousand in the prior-year quarter, an increase of 0.7%. Total indirect expense was $286,391 thousand versus $240,991 thousand in the prior-year quarter, an increase of 18.8%.

Prospects: **I** Co.'s results are benefiting from solid demand for its core financial sofware products across all its major geographic markets. Consequently, for the third quarter ended Dec 31 2007 Co. expects revenue of $430.0 million to $430.0 million, which represents 15.0% to 19.0% year-over-year growth, and earnings per share of $0.27 to $0.29. Also, Co. is targeting gross margin of about 85.0%, and operating margin of approximately 20.0% to 26.0%. Meanwhile, Co. continues to anticipate that its acquisition of FinSoftware, which was announced on May 31 2007, will close in October 2007.

Financial Data
(US$ in Thousands)

	6 Mos	3 Mos	06/30/2007	06/30/2006	06/30/2005	06/30/2004	06/30/2003	06/30/2002
Earnings Per Share **J**	1.03	0.96	0.91	0.55	0.40	0.41	0.56	0.46
Cash Flow Per Share	1.41	1.37	1.41	0.93	0.70	0.88	0.94	0.68
Tang Book Value Per Share	3.53	3.04	2.68	2.08	1.24	1.31	1.56	1.08
Dividends Per Share	0.025	0.025	0.025	0.025	0.025	0.025	0.025	0.025
Dividend Payout %	2.43	2.61	2.75	4.55	6.33	6.02	4.42	5.43
Income Statement								
Total Revenue	968,911	472,882	1,666,581	1,294,749	1,164,788	1,229,720	1,266,378	1,015,434
EBITDA	394,675	191,739	669,453	429,506	348,170	363,576	487,014	425,197
Depn & Amortn	30,082	14,954	60,808	49,014	63,481	56,645	43,275	50,770
Income Before Taxes	364,593	176,785	608,645	380,492	284,689	306,931	443,739	374,427
Income Taxes	62,921	24,891	158,247	114,148	93,290	101,287	155,931	136,676
Net Income	301,672	151,894	450,398	266,344	191,399	205,644	287,808	237,751
Average Shares	508,156	506,182	495,626	482,900	486,238	498,290	511,548	516,820
Balance Sheet								
Current Assets	1,999,568	1,699,939	1,551,029	1,329,028	814,172	767,364	877,912	623,015
Total Assets	2,421,216	2,122,810	1,958,632	1,555,045	1,051,610	930,623	1,069,416	803,859
Current Liabilities	517,924	484,188	451,408	436,530	377,289	313,651	314,605	267,629
Total Liabilities	551,313	498,245	535,155	454,245	377,289	313,651	316,872	291,650
Stockholders' Equity	1,869,903	1,624,565	1,423,477	1,100,800	674,321	616,972	752,544	512,209
Shares Outstanding	491,589	488,995	484,374	476,600	463,910	472,038	481,892	474,156
Statistical Record								
Return on Assets %	25.07	25.20	25.22	20.49	19.36	20.62	30.81	29.77
Return on Equity %	33.26	33.81	35.11	30.09	29.73	30.11	45.64	45.48
EBITDA Margin %	40.73	40.55	40.17	33.17	29.89	29.57	38.46	41.87
Net Margin %	31.14	32.12	27.03	20.57	16.43	16.72	22.73	23.41
Asset Turnover	0.87	0.90	0.93	1.00	1.18	1.23	1.36	1.27
Current Ratio	3.86	3.51	3.44	3.04	2.16	2.45	2.79	2.33
Price Range	34.20-19.85	32.45-17.20	31.48-17.20	22.91-12.40	21.49-8.35	38.34-11.42	41.63-13.77	19.14-4.67
P/E Ratio	33.20-19.27	33.81-17.91	34.59-18.90	41.66-22.55	53.72-20.88	93.52-27.85	74.33-24.58	41.61-10.16
Average Yield %	0.09	0.10	0.11	0.15	0.16	0.13	0.09	0.25

Address: 123 South Blvd., San Juan, CA 95102-1234 **K** Telephone: 444-555-0000 Fax: 444-555-0001	Web Site: www.illustrative.com Officers: Jack C. Warrick - Chmn. Chuck M. Norris - Vice Chmn.	Auditors: KPMG LLP Investor Contact: 444-555-0002 Transfer Agents: Computershare Investor Services LLC, Chicago, IL

HOW TO USE THIS BOOK

C. INTERIM EARNINGS (Per Share) – Each figure is for the quarterly period indicated. These figures are essentially as reported by the company, although all figures are adjusted for all stock dividends and splits.

D. INTERIM DIVIDENDS (Per Share) – The cash dividends are the actual dollar amounts declared by the company. No adjustments have been made for stock dividends and splits. **Ex-Dividend Date**: a stockholder must purchase the stock prior to this date in order to be entitled to the dividend. The **Record Date** indicates the date on which the shareholder had to have been a holder of record in order to qualify for the dividend. The **Payable Date** indicates the date the company paid or intends to pay the dividend. The cash amount shown in the first column is followed by a letter (example "Q" for quarterly) to indicate the frequency of the dividend. A notation of "Dividend payment suspended" indicates that dividend payments have been suspended within the most recent ten years.

Indicated Dividend This is the annualized amount (fully adjusted for splits) of the latest regular cash dividend. Companies with Dividend Reinvestment Plans are indicated here.

E. VALUATION ANALYSIS is a tool for evaluating a company's stock. Included are: Forecast Price/Earnings, Market Capitalization, Book Value, Price/Book and Price/Sales.

F. INSTITUTIONAL HOLDINGS – indicates the number of investment companies, insurance companies, mutual funds, bank trust and college endowment funds holding the stock and the total number of shares held as last reported.

G. BUSINESS SUMMARY explains what a company does in terms of the products or services it sells, its markets, and the position the company occupies in its industry. For a quick reference, included are the Company's Standard Industrial Classification (SIC), North American Industry Classification (NAIC) and Mergent's Industry Classification (MIC).

H. RECENT DEVELOPMENTS – This section captures what has happened in the most recent quarter for which results are available. It provides analysis of recently released sales and earnings figures, including special charges and credits, and may also include results by sector, expense trends and ratios, and other current information.

I. PROSPECTS – This section focuses on what is anticipated for the immediate future, as well as the outlook for the next few years, based on analysis by Mergent.

J. FINANCIAL DATA (fully adjusted for stock dividends and splits) is provided for at least the past seven fiscal years preceded by the most recent three-, six- and nine-month results if available.

Fiscal Years are the annual financial reporting periods as determined by each company. Annual prices and dividends are displayed based on the Company's fiscal year.

Per Share Data:

The Earnings Per Share figure is based on a trailing 12-month period. Earnings per share, and all per share figures, are adjusted for subsequent stock dividends and splits.

Cash Flow Per Share represents the annualized cash flow from operating activities (or for quarters, TTM cash flow

HOW TO USE THIS BOOK

from operating activities) divided by the average shares outstanding.

Tangible Book Value Per Share is calculated as stockholders equity (the value of common shares, paid-in capital and retained earnings) minus preferred stock and intangibles such as goodwill, patents and excess acquisition costs, divided by shares outstanding. It demonstrates the underlying cash value of each common share if the company were to be liquidated as of that date.

Dividends Per Share is the total of cash payments made per share to shareholders for the trailing 12-month period.

Dividend Payout % is the proportion of earnings available for common stock that is paid to common shareholders in the form of cash dividends. It is significant because it indicates what percentage of earnings is being reinvested in the business for internal growth.

EDITOR'S NOTE: TTM net income is net income for the last 365 days (normally four reported quarters) ended on the quarterly balance sheet date. Where that last 365 days does not exactly equate to the last four reported quarters the net income for any included partial quarter is adjusted on a pro-rata basis.

INCOME STATEMENT, BALANCE SHEET AND STATISTICAL RECORD

Includes pertinent earnings and balance sheet information essential to analyzing a corporation's performance. The comparisons provide the necessary historical perspective to intelligently review the various operating and financial trends. Generic definitions follow.

Income Statement:

Total Revenues consists of all revenues from operations.

EBITDA represents earnings before, interest, taxes, depreciation and amortization, and special items.

Depreciation and Amortization includes all non-cash charges such as depletion and amortization as well as depreciation.

Income Before Taxes is the remaining income *after* deducting all costs, expenses, property charges, interest etc. but *before* deducting income taxes.

Income Taxes includes the amount charged against earnings to provide for current and deferred income taxes.

Net Income consists of all revenues less all expenses (operating and non-operating), and is presented before preference and common dividends.

Average Shares Outstanding is the weighted average number of shares including common equivalent shares outstanding during the year, as reported by the corporation and fully adjusted for all stock dividends and splits. The use of *average shares* minimizes the distortion in *earnings per share* which could result from issuance of a large amount of stock or the

company's purchase of a large amount of its own stock during the year.

Balance Sheet:

Current Assets includes the short-term assets expected to be realized or consumed within one year. Normally includes cash and cash equivalents, short term investments, receivables, prepayments and inventories.

Total Assets represents all of the assets of the company, including tangible and intangible, and current and non-current.

Current Liabilities are all of the obligations of the company normally expected to be paid within one year. Includes bank overdrafts, short-term debt, payables and accruals.

HOW TO USE THIS BOOK

Long-Term Obligations are the total long-term debts (due beyond one year) reported by the company, including bonds, capital lease obligations, notes, mortgages, debentures, etc.

Total Liabilities represents all liabilities of the company, whether current or non-current.

Stockholders' Equity is the sum of all capital stock accounts – paid in capital (including additional premium), retained earnings, and all other capital balances.

Shares Outstanding is the number of shares outstanding as of the date of the company's quarterly/annual report, exclusive of treasury stock and adjusted for subsequent stock dividends and splits.

Statistical Record:

Return on Assets % represents the ratio of annualized net income (or for Mos, TTM net income) to average total assets. This ratio represents how effectively assets are being used to produce a profit.

Return on Equity % is the ratio of annualized net income (or for Mos, TTM net income) to average stockholders' equity, expressed as a percentage. This ratio illustrates how effectively the investment of the stockholders is being utilized to earn a profit.

EBITDA Margin % represents earnings before interest, taxes, depreciation and amortization as a percentage of total revenue.

Net Margin % is net income expressed as a percentage of total revenues.

Asset Turnover is annualized total revenue (or for Mos, TTM total revenue) divided by average total assets. A measure of efficiency for the use of assets.

Current Ratio represents current assets divided by current liabilities. The higher the figure the better the company is able to meet its current liabilities out of its current assets.

A key measure of liquidity for industrial companies.

Debt to Equity is the ratio of long-term obligations to stockholders' equity.

Price Ranges are based on each Company's fiscal year. Where actual stock sales did not take place, a range of lowest bid and highest asked prices is shown.

Price/Earnings Ratio is shown as a range. The figures are calculated by dividing the stock's highest price for the year and its lowest price by the year's earnings per share. Growth stocks tend to command higher P/Es than cyclical stocks.

Average Yield % is the ratio of annual dividends to the real average of the prices over the fiscal year.

EDITOR'S NOTE: In order to preserve the historical relationships between prices, earnings and dividends, figures are not restated to reflect subsequent events. Figures are presented in U.S. dollars unless otherwise indicated.

K. ADDITIONAL INFORMATION on each stock includes the officers of the company, investor relations contact, address, telephone number, web site and transfer agents.

OTHER DEFINITIONS

Factors Pertaining Especially to Real Estate Investment Trusts

Property Income is income from property rental and other associated activities.

Non-Property Income includes interest income and other income not from property activities.

HOW TO USE THIS BOOK

Factors Pertaining Especially to Utilities

Net Property, Plant & Equip is the cost of property, plant and equipment, less its accumulated depreciation.

PPE Turnover represents annualized total revenue (or for Mos, TTM total revenue) divided by average net property, plant and equipment.

Factors Pertaining Especially to Banks

Interest Income is all interest income, including income from loans and leases, securities and deposits.

Interest Expense is all interest expense, including from loans and leases, securities and deposits.

Net Interest Income is interest income less interest expense. This figure is presented before provision for losses.

Provision for Losses represents the amount charged against earnings to increase the provision made for losses on loans and leases.

Non-Interest Income is any income that is not interest-related. Such income could include trading revenue and gains on the sale of assets.

Non-Interest Expense is all expenses that are not interest related, including employment costs, office costs, marketing costs, etc.

Net Loans & Leases includes all loans and leases net of provisions for losses. May include commercial, agricultural, real estate, consumer and foreign loans.

Total Deposits are all time and demand deposits entrusted to a bank.

Net Interest Margin % is net interest income before provisions expressed as a percentage of total interest income. A key measure of bank profitability.

Efficiency Ratio % is non-interest expense expressed as a percentage of total revenue.

Loans to Deposits are net loans and leases divided by total deposits. A key measure of bank liquidity.

Factors Pertaining Especially to Insurance Companies

Premium Income is the amount of insurance premiums received from policyholders. This is the primary revenue source for insurance companies.

Benefits and Claims represents the payments made to policyholders under the terms of insurance contracts.

Loss Ratio % is benefits and claims expressed as a percentage of premium income. A key ratio of insurance company profitability.

ABBREVIATIONS AND SYMBOLS

A	Annual
ASE	American Stock Exchange
()	Deficit
(Div. Reinv. Plan)	Dividend Reinvestment Plan offered
E	Extra
M	Monthly
N/A	Not Applicable
N.M.	Not Meaningful
NYS	New York Stock Exchange
OTC	Over-The-Counter Market
Q	Quarterly
S	Semi-Annual
Sp	Special Dividend
U	Frequency Unknown

ANALYSIS OF STOCK PRICE MOVEMENTS BY COMPANY

For the three-month period beginning December 1, 2007 and ending February 29, 2008, the Dow Jones Industrial Average declined 8.24%, while the broader New York Stock Exchange Composite slid 9.07%. The Dow and NYSE began the period at 13,368.22 and 9,856.81, respectively. Both the Dow and NYSE would achieve their period highs of 13,850.92 and 10,140.47 on December 11. The indices period highs were driven by the prospect of lower interest rates from the Federal Reserve as well as a November jobs report that indicated stronger employment growth than some had anticipated. Conversely, the Dow dropped to its period low of 12,167.42 on January 22, while the NYSE reached its period low of 8,343.62 on January 23. Overall, the indices were negatively affected by investors' concerns regarding the general outlook for corporate profits in the event of a U.S. recession that some fear has been incited by the sharp slowdown in housing, related subprime mortgage problems, tightened credit for some businesses and households, and increased energy prices. In response to the uncertain economic and financial markets outlook, in January the Federal Reserve would lower its target for the federal-fund rate, charged on overnight loans between banks, twice within nine days to 3.0%. The Dow would close the three-month period at 12,266.39, while the NYSE would finish at 8,962.46.

Over the last twelve months, the best performing stock was The Mosaic Co., reflecting robust global demand for potash. The second-best price performer was *Consol Energy Inc.* Co. is benefiting from an increase in the average realized price per ton of coal as well as higher operating margins.

Range Resources Corp. was the third-best performing stock. Co. is experiencing solid production growth through a combination of drilling and additions from acquisitions. Also, Co. is benefiting from higher average realized prices for oil and gas.

The fourth-best performing stock was *EOG Resources, Inc.* Co. is experiencing higher natural gas deliveries. Also, Co. continues to drill numerous wells in large acreage plays, which in the aggregate it expects to contribute substantially to its production.

Massey Energy Co. was the fifth-best price performer. Co.'s results have benefited from higher shipments of metallurgical and industrial coal and higher coal sales prices.

The sixth-best performing stock was *Quicksilver Resources, Inc.* Co. is experiencing increased natural gas sales as a result of new wells placed into production, primarily in the Barnett Shale.

Ambac Financial Group, Inc. was the worst performing stock over the last twelve months. Poor credit market conditions continue to weigh on Co.'s operating results.

The second-worst performer was *MoneyGram International Inc.* During the the fourth quarter of 2007, Co. recorded $1.20 billion of other-than-temporary impairments in its investment portfolio.

Donnelley (R.H.) Corp. was the third-worst price performer. Co. lowered its 2008 outlook and now sees advertising sales decreasing in the mid single digits.

The fourth-worst performing stock was *PMI Group, Inc.* Co.'s operating results were significantly affected by the deterioration of the U.S. residential mortgage, housing, credit, and capital markets.

Radian Group, Inc. was the fifth-worst price performer. Operating results from Co.'s traditional mortgage insurance business are being hurt by the ongoing deteriorating domestic housing market.

The sixth-worst price performer was *Countrywide Financial Corp.* In January 2008, Co. entered into an agreement to be acquired by Bank of America Corporation.

HIGHEST-LOWEST

SHORT-TERM PRICE SCORES: COMPANY RANKINGS

25 HIGHEST

	SHORT-TERM PRICE SCORE♦	LONG-TERM PRICE SCORE♦	PRICE RANGE (52 Wks.)	RECENT PRICE
Mosaic Co.	182.3	...	117.06 - 26.85	102.60
Consol Energy Inc.	146.8	175.0	81.33 - 36.40	69.19
Range Resources Corp.	146.3	209.4	65.16 - 34.01	63.45
EOG Resources, Inc.	144.5	152.9	126.96 - 65.70	120.00
Massey Energy Co.	143.3	94.7	43.48 - 17.36	36.50
Quicksilver Resources, Inc.	142.8	165.0	38.15 - 18.94	36.53
Owens-Illinois, Inc.	140.9	174.0	57.97 - 26.12	56.43
Monsanto Co.	140.0	209.6	127.25 - 55.01	111.50
Cleveland-Cliffs Inc.	139.4	232.8	126.93 - 60.63	119.82
Hess Corp.	138.3	160.4	104.40 - 55.08	88.18
Southwestern Energy Co.	136.5	204.7	34.07 - 18.00	33.69
Flowserve Corp.	136.4	174.4	111.41 - 58.23	104.38
Arch Coal, Inc.	136.3	136.0	54.90 - 28.20	43.50
Foundation Coal Holdings Inc.	134.2	...	59.42 - 32.26	50.33
Denbury Resources, Inc.	133.8	207.3	32.67 - 15.02	28.55
Western Digital Corp.	133.7	149.6	33.99 - 16.50	27.04
AK Steel Holding Corp.	133.5	231.9	55.90 - 23.67	54.42
Helmerich & Payne, Inc.	133.4	136.6	47.42 - 29.07	46.87
MasterCard Inc.	131.6	...	224.98 - 106.9	222.99
Cimarex Energy Co.	131.3	...	56.00 - 34.40	54.74
Cabot Oil & Gas Corp.	131.1	171.4	53.41 - 31.55	50.84
Apache Corp.	129.6	143.1	120.82 - 71.26	120.82
W & T Offshore Inc.	127.6	...	38.84 - 21.19	34.11
Chesapeake Energy Corp.	126.8	152.0	49.00 - 31.54	46.15
Deere & Co.	126.6	158.8	94.69 - 52.24	80.44

25 LOWEST

Ambac Financial Group, Inc.	20.0	61.7	96.08 - 5.41	5.75
MoneyGram International Inc.	21.3	...	30.11 - 1.54	1.86
Donnelley (R.H.) Corp.	25.3	90.6	83.90 - 4.48	5.06
PMI Group, Inc.	29.3	59.7	50.07 - 5.12	5.82
Radian Group, Inc.	29.5	49.1	63.34 - 4.50	6.57
Countrywide Financial Corp.	31.8	66.5	41.31 - 4.09	5.50
MBIA Inc.	31.8	66.2	71.54 - 8.55	12.22
IndyMac Bancorp Inc.	39.8	50.4	36.66 - 4.36	4.96
MGIC Investment Corp.	42.9	48.8	66.53 - 10.04	10.53
Ruby Tuesday, Inc.	43.9	62.2	28.59 - 5.74	7.50
First Marblehead Corp.	44.0	...	44.43 - 7.41	7.46
Thornburg Mortgage Inc.	47.0	56.1	28.11 - 0.71	1.21
Owens Corning	47.7	...	6.25 - 1.05	1.35
Circuit City Stores, Inc.	48.9	56.5	19.11 - 3.60	3.98
Sprint Nextel Corp.	50.0	76.5	23.34 - 5.63	6.69
Westwood One, Inc.	50.8	14.7	8.16 - 1.51	2.10
US Airways Group Inc.	50.8	...	47.87 - 7.45	8.91
SLM Corp.	51.6	79.4	57.98 - 15.16	15.35
Harman Intl. Industries, Inc.	53.8	102.5	122.59 - 37.08	43.54
Washington Mutual Inc.	54.1	62.1	44.41 - 9.24	10.30
McClatchy Co.	55.3	30.4	32.24 - 8.66	10.70
Western Refining Inc.	56.2	...	65.16 - 13.07	13.47
Temple-Inland Inc.	56.4	110.4	38.53 - 12.10	12.72
Beazer Homes USA, Inc.	57.4	37.5	36.72 - 4.99	9.45
Talbots, Inc.	58.5	48.6	25.70 - 6.96	10.78

♦For definition see page 4a.

Ranking by Total Revenues

Based on most recent fiscal year-end figures.

Rank	Company Name	Revenues ($Mill)	Rank	Company Name	Revenues ($Mill)
1.	Exxon Mobil Corp.	404,552.0	26.	Altria Group Inc	73,801.0
2.	Wal-Mart Stores, Inc.	378,799.0	27.	Kroger Co.	70,235.0
3.	Chevron Corporation	220,904.0	28.	Boeing Co.	66,387.0
4.	Conocophillips	194,495.0	29.	AmerisourceBergen Corp.	66,074.3
5.	General Motors Corp	181,122.0	30.	Marathon Oil Corp.	65,207.0
6.	General Electric Co	172,738.0	31.	Target Corp	63,367.0
7.	Ford Motor Co.	172,455.0	32.	Merrill Lynch & Co Inc	62,675.0
8.	Citigroup Inc	159,229.0	33.	WellPoint Inc	61,134.3
9.	Bank of America Corp.	119,190.0	34.	Johnson & Johnson	61,095.0
10.	AT&T Inc	118,928.0	35.	Lehman Brothers Holdings	59,003.0
11.	Berkshire Hathaway Inc.	118,245.0	36.	Wachovia Corp	55,528.0
12.	JPMorgan Chase & Co.	116,353.0	37.	United Technologies Corp.	54,759.0
13.	American Intl Group	110,064.0	38.	Walgreen Co.	53,762.0
14.	Hewlett-Packard Co	104,286.0	39.	Wells Fargo & Co.	53,593.0
15.	Intl. Bus. Machines	98,786.0	40.	Dow Chemical Co.	53,513.0
16.	Valero Energy Corp.	95,327.0	41.	Metlife Inc	53,007.0
17.	Verizon Communications	93,469.0	42.	United Parcel Service Inc	49,692.0
18.	McKesson Corp.	92,977.0	43.	Pfizer Inc	48,418.0
19.	Goldman Sachs Group	87,968.0	44.	Lowe's Companies Inc	48,283.0
20.	Cardinal Health, Inc.	86,852.0	45.	Time Warner Inc	46,482.0
21.	Morgan Stanley	85,328.0	46.	Caterpillar Inc.	44,958.0
22.	Home Depot Inc	77,349.0	47.	Sunoco, Inc.	44,728.0
23.	Procter & Gamble Co.	76,476.0	48.	Medco Health Solutions	44,506.2
24.	CVS Caremark Corporation	76,329.5	49.	Archer Daniels Midland	44,018.0
25.	UnitedHealth Group Inc	75,431.0	50.	Freddie Mac	44,002.0

Ranking by Net Income

Based on most recent fiscal year-end figures.

Rank	Company Name	Net Income ($Mill)	Rank	Company Name	Net Income ($Mill)
1.	Exxon Mobil Corp.	40,610.0	26.	Disney (Walt) Co.	4,687.0
2.	General Electric Co	22,208.0	27.	UnitedHealth Group Inc	4,654.0
3.	Chevron Corporation	18,688.0	28.	Allstate Corp.	4,636.0
4.	JPMorgan Chase & Co.	15,365.0	29.	Wyeth	4,616.0
5.	Bank of America Corp.	14,982.0	30.	Travelers Companies Inc	4,601.0
6.	Berkshire Hathaway Inc.	13,213.0	31.	Home Depot Inc	4,395.0
7.	Wal-Mart Stores, Inc.	12,731.0	32.	Time Warner Inc	4,387.0
8.	AT&T Inc	11,951.0	33.	U.S. Bancorp	4,324.0
9.	Conocophillips	11,891.0	34.	Metlife Inc	4,317.0
10.	Goldman Sachs Group	11,599.0	35.	United Technologies Corp.	4,224.0
11.	Johnson & Johnson	10,576.0	36.	Lehman Brothers Holdings	4,192.0
12.	Intl. Bus. Machines	10,418.0	37.	3M Co	4,096.0
13.	Procter & Gamble Co.	10,340.0	38.	Boeing Co.	4,074.0
14.	Altria Group Inc	9,786.0	39.	American Express Co.	4,012.0
15.	Pfizer Inc	8,144.0	40.	Ingersoll-Rand Co. Ltd.	3,966.7
16.	Wells Fargo & Co.	8,057.0	41.	Marathon Oil Corp.	3,956.0
17.	Hewlett-Packard Co	7,264.0	42.	Anadarko Petroleum Corp	3,781.0
18.	Wachovia Corp	6,312.0	43.	Prudential Financial, Inc.	3,704.0
19.	American Intl. Group	6,200.0	44.	Citigroup Inc	3,617.0
20.	Coca-Cola Co	5,981.0	45.	Abbott Laboratories	3,606.3
21.	PepsiCo Inc.	5,658.0	46.	Devon Energy Corp.	3,606.0
22.	Verizon Communications	5,521.0	47.	Caterpillar Inc.	3,541.0
23.	Occidental Petroleum Corp	5,400.0	48.	Halliburton Company	3,499.0
24.	Valero Energy Corp.	5,234.0	49.	News Corp	3,426.0
25.	Schlumberger Ltd.	5,176.5	50.	WellPoint Inc	3,345.4

Ranking by Total Assets

Based on most recent fiscal year-end figures.

Rank	Company Name	Assets ($Mill)	Rank	Company Name	Assets ($Mill)
1.	Citigroup Inc	2,187,631.0	26.	Verizon Communications	186,959.0
2.	Bank of America Corp.	1,715,746.0	27.	SunTrust Banks, Inc.	179,573.9
3.	JPMorgan Chase & Co.	1,562,147.0	28.	Conocophillips	177,757.0
4.	Goldman Sachs Group	1,119,796.0	29.	Wal-Mart Stores, Inc.	163,514.0
5.	American Intl. Group	1,060,505.0	30.	Allstate Corp.	156,408.0
6.	Morgan Stanley	1,045,409.0	31.	SLM Corp.	155,565.0
7.	Merrill Lynch & Co Inc	1,020,050.0	32.	Principal Financial Group	154,520.2
8.	Fannie Mae	882,547.0	33.	Capital One Financial	150,590.4
9.	Freddie Mac	813,081.0	34.	National City Corp	150,374.0
10.	General Electric Co	795,337.0	35.	American Express Co.	149,830.0
11.	Wachovia Corp	782,896.0	36.	General Motors Corp	148,883.0
12.	Lehman Brothers Holdings	691,063.0	37.	Chevron Corporation	148,786.0
13.	Wells Fargo & Co.	575,442.0	38.	State Street Corp.	142,543.0
14.	Metlife Inc	558,562.0	39.	Regions Financial Corp	141,041.7
15.	Prudential Financial, Inc.	485,814.0	40.	PNC Financial Services Grp	138,920.0
16.	Bear Stearns Cos., Inc.	395,362.0	41.	Procter & Gamble Co.	138,014.0
17.	Hartford Financial Services	360,361.0	42.	Time Warner Inc	133,830.0
18.	Washington Mutual Inc.	327,913.0	43.	BB&T Corp.	132,618.0
19.	Ford Motor Co.	285,727.0	44.	Intl. Bus. Machines	120,431.0
20.	AT&T Inc	275,644.0	45.	Nationwide Financial Svcs	119,207.1
21.	Berkshire Hathaway Inc.	273,160.0	46.	Pfizer Inc	115,268.0
22.	Exxon Mobil Corp.	242,082.0	47.	Travelers Companies Inc	115,224.0
23.	U.S. Bancorp	237,615.0	48.	Genworth Financial Inc	114,315.0
24.	Countrywide Financial	211,730.1	49.	Ameriprise Financial Inc	109,230.0
25.	Lincoln National Corp.	191,435.0	50.	KeyCorp	99,983.0

Ranking by Market Capitalization

Based on most recent fiscal year-end figures and closing prices at 03/31/2008

Rank	Company Name	Market Cap ($Mill)	Rank	Company Name	Market Cap ($Mill)
1.	Exxon Mobil Corp.	452,505.3	26.	Goldman Sachs Group	65,780.1
2.	General Electric Co	369,569.6	27.	Disney (Walt) Co.	64,715.9
3.	AT&T Inc	231,168.3	28.	McDonald's Corp	64,227.2
4.	Procter & Gamble Co.	215,640.3	29.	Monsanto Co.	61,187.7
5.	Wal-Mart Stores, Inc.	208,320.9	30.	Occidental Petroleum	60,187.2
6.	Johnson & Johnson	183,750.9	31.	Lilly (Eli) & Co.	58,657.1
7.	Chevron Corporation	177,265.4	32.	CVS Caremark Corp	58,005.4
8.	Bank of America Corp.	168,404.9	33.	Boeing Co.	56,880.6
9.	Intl. Bus. Machines	159,391.9	34.	3M Co	56,011.5
10.	JPMorgan Chase & Co.	145,881.4	35.	U.S. Bancorp	55,974.5
11.	Berkshire Hathaway Inc.	144,254.2	36.	Wyeth	55,873.6
12.	Pfizer Inc	141,507.5	37.	Exelon Corp.	54,463.7
13.	Coca-Cola Co	141,462.6	38.	Medtronic, Inc.	54,320.8
14.	Conocophillips	119,002.4	39.	Wachovia Corp	53,513.6
15.	PepsiCo Inc.	115,649.2	40.	Morgan Stanley	50,597.1
16.	Hewlett-Packard Co	112,565.5	41.	United Parcel Service	50,553.2
17.	American Intl. Group	109,091.1	42.	American Express Co.	50,544.2
18.	Citigroup Inc	106,695.9	43.	Time Warner Inc	50,140.0
19.	Schlumberger Ltd.	104,200.9	44.	Caterpillar Inc.	49,789.3
20.	Verizon Communications	104,157.9	45.	Kraft Foods, Inc.	47,548.1
21.	Wells Fargo & Co.	95,937.1	46.	Home Depot Inc	47,270.3
22.	Genentech, Inc.	85,492.6	47.	Altria Group Inc	46,804.3
23.	Abbott Laboratories	85,247.4	48.	Devon Energy Corp.	46,363.2
24.	Merck & Co., Inc	82,172.7	49.	Mosaic Co	45,462.7
25.	United Technologies Corp.	67,548.1	50.	UnitedHealth Group	42,997.5

Ranking by Current Yield
Based on closing prices at 03/31/2008

Rank	Company Name	Yield %	Rank	Company Name	Yield %
1.	iStar Financial Inc	24.80	26.	Regions Financial Corp	7.70
2.	Entercom Communications	15.31	27.	Lee Enterprises, Inc.	7.59
3.	Altria Group Inc	13.51	28.	Comerica, Inc.	7.53
4.	Annaly Capital Management	12.53	29.	PNM Resources Inc	7.38
5.	HRPT Properties Trust	12.48	30.	Buckeye Partners, L.P.	7.27
6.	Bear Stearns Cos., Inc.	12.20	31.	Mack Cali Realty Corp	7.17
7.	Countrywide Financial	10.91	32.	Plains All American Pipeline	7.15
8.	MoneyGram International	10.75	33.	Universal Hlth Rlty Income	6.97
9.	Warner Music Group Corp	10.44	34.	Embarq Corp	6.86
10.	Brandywine Realty Trust	10.38	35.	KeyCorp	6.83
11.	Citizens Communications	9.53	36.	Bank of America Corp.	6.75
12.	Wachovia Corp (New)	9.48	37.	Great Plains Energy, Inc.	6.73
13.	CBL & Assoc. Properties	9.26	38.	Enterprise Products Partners	6.73
14.	Lexington Realty Trust	9.16	39.	McClatchy Co. (The)	6.73
15.	Hospitality Properties Trust	9.05	40.	Kinder Morgan Energy	6.73
16.	National City Corp	8.44	41.	Apartment Invest & Mgmt	6.70
17.	CIT Group, Inc.	8.44	42.	Ruby Tuesday, Inc.	6.67
18.	Duke Realty Corp.	8.42	43.	Developers Diversified Rlty	6.59
19.	Windstream Corp	8.37	44.	Media General, Inc.	6.56
20.	Colonial Properties Trust	8.32	45.	Leggett & Platt, Inc.	6.56
21.	Cedar Fair, L.P.	8.17	46.	Fidelity National Financial	6.55
22.	TEPPCO Partners, L.P.	8.06	47.	Asbury Automotive Group	6.54
23.	Liberty Property Trust	8.04	48.	Louisiana-Pacific Corp.	6.54
24.	Colonial BancGroup Inc.	7.89	49.	National Retail Properties	6.44
25.	Enbridge Energy Partners	7.89	50.	Realty Income Corp.	6.43

Ranking by Return on Equity
Based on most recent fiscal year-end figures.

Rank	Company Name	Return on Equity %	Rank	Company Name	Return on Equity %
1.	Clorox Co.	6,680.00	26.	Campbell Soup Co.	55.92
2.	Gartner, Inc.	335.74	27.	Frontier Oil Corp.	55.02
3.	ITT Educational Services	173.74	28.	Pitney Bowes Inc	54.64
4.	Windstream Corp	156.82	29.	Graco Inc.	53.24
5.	AutoZone, Inc.	136.88	30.	First Marblehead Corp	52.34
6.	Taubman Centers, Inc.	136.04	31.	MEMC Electronic Materials	51.61
7.	Owens-Illinois, Inc.	105.39	32.	Aeropostale Inc	50.87
8.	DST Systems Inc.	101.04	33.	Hercules Inc.	49.63
9.	Colgate-Palmolive Co.	93.99	34.	AMR Corp.	49.15
10.	Temple-Inland Inc.	88.15	35.	Halliburton Company	49.14
11.	Rockwell Automation	81.28	36.	Continental Airlines Inc	48.39
12.	Energizer Holdings, Inc.	74.20	37.	Kellogg Co	48.14
13.	Yum! Brands, Inc.	70.77	38.	McGraw-Hill Cos., Inc.	47.29
14.	Avon Products, Inc.	70.67	39.	Sotheby's	47.07
15.	Hanesbrands Inc	70.62	40.	Caterpillar Inc.	44.99
16.	Polaris Industries Inc.	65.61	41.	Nordstrom, Inc.	43.67
17.	Holly Corp.	63.05	42.	Coach, Inc.	42.95
18.	AK Steel Holding Corp.	60.03	43.	Rockwell Collins, Inc.	42.10
19.	Anheuser-Busch Cos.	59.67	44.	Schlumberger Ltd.	40.93
20.	Ingersoll-Rand Co. Ltd.	59.59	45.	Heinz (H.J.) Co.	40.50
21.	Boeing Co.	59.29	46.	MasterCard Inc	40.28
22.	Southern Copper Corp	58.99	47.	Allegheny Technologies	40.21
23.	Quicksilver Resources	58.32	48.	Eagle Materials Inc	40.10
24.	Goodyear Tire & Rubber	57.55	49.	Waddell & Reed Financial	40.07
25.	Waters Corp.	56.53	50.	Black & Decker Corp.	39.51

Ranking by High P/E Ratio
Based on closing prices at 03/31/2008

Rank	Company Name	P/E Ratio	Rank	Company Name	P/E Ratio
1.	Salesforce.Com Inc	385.80	26.	Simon Property Group	47.65
2.	American Tower Corp.	326.75	27.	USG Corp	46.61
3.	Las Vegas Sands Corp	223.15	28.	Saks, Inc.	41.57
4.	United Parcel Service	202.83	29.	Hershey Company	40.95
5.	KEMET Corp.	134.67	30.	Barr Pharmaceuticals	40.94
6.	ChoicePoint, Inc.	110.70	31.	Range Resources Corp	40.94
7.	Community Health Systems	101.73	32.	EastGroup Properties	40.75
8.	99 Cents Only Stores	98.90	33.	TETRA Technologies	40.62
9.	Corporate Office Properties	88.45	34.	IntercontinentalExchange	38.61
10.	St. Joe Co.	79.50	35.	Interpublic Group of Cos.	38.23
11.	Forest City Enterprises	76.67	36.	Kinder Morgan Energy	37.72
12.	Public Storage	76.40	37.	Diebold, Inc.	36.46
13.	Foundation Coal Holdings	71.90	38.	Arch Coal, Inc.	35.95
14.	Macerich Co.	69.57	39.	Janus Capital Group Inc	35.80
15.	Jarden Corp.	58.76	40.	Monsanto Co.	35.74
16.	Taubman Centers, Inc.	57.89	41.	Foot Locker, Inc.	35.67
17.	Pilgrim's Pride Corp.	57.80	42.	Alexandria Real Estate Eq.	35.25
18.	Tanger Factory Outlet Ctrs	53.43	43.	Iron Mountain Inc	35.25
19.	Southwestern Energy Co.	52.64	44.	Allergan, Inc	34.81
20.	ResMed Inc.	52.07	45.	Pall Corp.	33.08
21.	Peabody Energy Corp	52.04	46.	Thermo Fisher Scientific	33.05
22.	Hospira Inc	50.32	47.	Trane, Inc.	33.02
23.	Red Hat Inc	49.70	48.	Avon Products, Inc.	32.68
24.	Mosaic Co	47.94	49.	General Growth Properties	32.62
25.	Consol Energy Inc	47.72	50.	FMC Corp.	32.45

Ranking by Low P/E Ratio
Based on closing prices at 03/31/2008

Rank	Company Name	P/E Ratio	Rank	Company Name	P/E Ratio
1.	Temple-Inland Inc.	1.05	26.	SAFECO Corporation	6.30
2.	US Airways Group Inc	1.97	27.	Alaska Air Group, Inc.	6.33
3.	Qwest Communications Intl	2.94	28.	Gannett Co Inc	6.38
4.	Calpine Corp	3.28	29.	HCC Insurance Holdings	6.73
5.	Colonial Properties Trust	3.30	30.	RLI Corp.	6.78
6.	Ingersoll Rand Co. Ltd.	3.33	31.	DTE Energy Co.	6.82
7.	First Marblehead Corp	3.52	32.	Synovus Financial Corp.	6.91
8.	Western Refining Inc	3.82	33.	Mohawk Industries, Inc.	6.95
9.	Jones Apparel Group, Inc.	4.10	34.	Deluxe Corp.	6.96
10.	Continental Airlines Inc	4.63	35.	Travelers Companies Inc	6.97
11.	Altria Group Inc	4.81	36.	Westwood One, Inc.	7.00
12.	Beazer Homes USA, Inc.	4.97	37.	Chubb Corp	7.06
13.	AMR Corp.	5.04	38.	Sunoco, Inc.	7.07
14.	DST Systems Inc.	5.25	39.	Bear Stearns Cos., Inc.	7.09
15.	Marsh & McLennan Cos	5.29	40.	Owens-Illinois, Inc.	7.13
16.	Marshall & Ilsley Corp	5.35	41.	OfficeMax Inc	7.14
17.	Valero Energy Corp.	5.51	42.	ACE, Ltd.	7.19
18.	AmeriCredit Corp.	5.63	43.	Wesco International, Inc.	7.25
19.	United Rentals, Inc.	5.81	44.	Holly Corp.	7.26
20.	Boyd Gaming Corp.	5.85	45.	Trinity Industries, Inc.	7.30
21.	Frontier Oil Corp.	5.90	46.	Berkley (W. R.) Corp.	7.36
22.	Lee Enterprises, Inc.	5.99	47.	Tesoro Corporation	7.39
23.	Windstream Corp	6.16	48.	Westlake Chemical Corp	7.41
24.	Lehman Brothers Holdings	6.18	49.	Rockwell Automation, Inc.	7.46
25.	Allstate Corp.	6.19	50.	NACCO Industries Inc.	7.49

CLASSIFICATION BY INDUSTRY

Accommodation and Food Services
Accommodation
Choice Hotels International, Inc.
Host Hotels & Resorts Inc.
*Marriott International, Inc.
Park Place Entertainment Corp.
Wyndham Worldwide Corp.

Food Services and Drinking Places
Brinker International, Inc.
Burger King Holdings Inc.
*Darden Restaurants, Inc.
*McDonald's Corporation
Ruby Tuesday, Inc.
Tim Hortons Inc.
*Wendy's International, Inc.
*Yum! Brands, Inc.

Administrative & Support and Waste Management & Remediation Services
Administrative and Support Services
*Equifax Inc.
*Manpower Inc.
Mid Atlantic Medical Services
MPS Group, Inc.
Robert Half International, Inc.
*Rollins, Inc.

Waste Management and Remediation Services
Allied Waste Industries, Inc.
*Johnson Controls, Inc.
Republic Services, Inc.
*Waste Management, Inc.

Arts, Entertainment, and Recreation
Boyd Gaming Corp.
*Carnival Corp.
*Cedar Fair, L.P.
*Disney (Walt) Company (The)
GTECH Holdings Corp.
International Game Technology
Las Vegas Sands Corp.
MGM Mirage

Construction
ABM Industries Incorporated
*Beazer Homes USA, Inc.
*Boston Properties, Inc.
Centex Corporation
Dycom Industries, Inc.
Eagle Materials Inc.
EMCOR Group, Inc.
*Forest City Enterprises, Inc.
*Granite Construction Inc.
Halliburton Company
Horton (D.R.) Inc.

Hovnanian Enterprises, Inc.
Jacobs Engineering Group Inc.
KB Home
Lennar Corporation
M.D.C. Holdings, Inc.
Martin Marietta Materials, Inc.
*MDU Resources Group, Inc.
NVR Inc.
Owens Corning
Pulte Homes, Inc.
Quanta Services, Inc.
Ryland Group, Inc. (The)
Toll Brothers, Inc.

Educational Services
DeVry Inc.
ITT Educational Services, Inc.

Electric Power Generation
Calpine Corp.

Finance and Insurance
Commercial Banking
*BancorpSouth, Inc.
*Bank of America Corporation
*Bank of Hawaii Corporation
BankAtlantic Bancorp, Inc.
*BB&T Corporation
City National Corporation
*Colonial Bancgroup Inc.
*Comerica, Inc.
*Community Bank System, Inc.
Cullen/Frost Bankers, Inc.
*F.N.B. Corporation
*First Horizon National Corporation
*Hudson United Bancorp
*Irwin Financial Corp.
*J.P. Morgan Chase & Co.
*KeyCorp
*M&T Bank Corporation
Marshall & Ilsley Corp
*North Fork Bancorporation, Inc.
*Old National Bancorp
*PNC Financial Services Group
*Regions Financial Corp.
*State Street Corporation
*SunTrust Banks, Inc.
*Synovus Financial Corporation
*TCF Financial Corp.
*U.S. Bancorp
*UnionBanCal Corporation
*Valley National Bancorp
*Wachovia Corporation
*Wells Fargo & Company
*Wilmington Trust Corporation

Direct Health and Medical Insurance Carriers
*AFLAC Incorporated
*Aon Corporation
*CIGNA Corporation
 Conseco, Inc.
 Humana Inc.
 Pacificare Health Systems, Inc.
 Reinsurance Group of America
 UnitedHealth Group Inc.
*UnumProvident Corporation

Direct Life Insurance Carriers
 Assurant Inc.
*Genworth Financial Inc.
*Lincoln National Corporation
*Nationwide Financial Services
 Principal Financial Group, Inc.
*Protective Life Corporation
 Prudential Financial, Inc.
 Stancorp Financial Group, Inc.
*Torchmark Corporation

Direct Property and Casualty Insurance Carriers
 Allmerica Financial Corporation
*Allstate Corporation (The)
*American Financial Group, Inc.
 American International Group
 Berkley (W.R.) Corporation
 Berkshire Hathaway Inc.
*Chubb Corporation (The)
 CNA Financial Corporation
 Commerce Group, Inc.
 Hanover Insurance Group Inc.
 HCC Insurance Holdings, Inc.
 Horace Mann Educators Corp.
 Leucadia National Corporation
 Loews Corporation
 Markel Corporation
 Mercury General Corporation
 Progressive Corporation (The)
*RLI Corp.
 SAFECO Corporation
*The St Paul Travelers Companies Inc.
 Transatlantic Holdings, Inc.
*Unitrin, Inc.
 XL Capital Ltd.

Direct Title Insurance Carriers
 Alleghany Corporation
 Fidelity National Financial Inc.
*First American Corporation (The)

Insurance Agencies and Brokerages
 Aetna, Inc.
 Anthem, Inc.
 Brown & Brown, Inc.
 ChoicePoint Inc.

 Gallagher (Arthur J.) & Company
*Hartford Financial Services Group
 Hilb, Rogal & Hamilton Company
 Metlife, Inc.
 WellPoint Inc.

Mortgage and Nonmortgage Loan Brokers
*New York Community Bancorp, Inc.

Nondepository Credit Intermediation
*American Express Company
 AmeriCredit Corp.
 Ameriprise Financial Inc.
*Capital One Financial Corp.
*Countrywide Financial Corp.
 Discover Financial Services
 Fannie Mae
 First Marblehead Corp.
*Freddie Mac
*Morgan Stanley
 SLM Corporation
 Student Loan Corp. (The)
Real Estate Investment Trusts
 Alexandria Real Estate Equities, Inc.
 AMB Property Corporation
*Annaly Capital Management Inc.
 Apartment Investment & Mngmnt
 AvalonBay Communities, Inc.
*Brandywine Realty Trust
*BRE Properties, Inc.
 Camden Property Trust
 CB Richard Ellis Group Inc.
*CBL & Associates Properties
*Colonial Properties Trust
 Corporate Office Properties Trust
*Developers Diversified Realty
*Duke Realty Corporation
*EastGroup Properties, Inc.
*Equity Residential Prop. Trust
*Essex Property Trust, Inc.
*Federal Realty Investment Trust
*General Growth Properties, Inc.
*HCP, Inc.
*Highwoods Properties, Inc.
*Home Properties, Inc.
*Hospitality Properties Trust
*HRPT Properties Trust
*iStar Financial Inc.
*Kilroy Realty Corp.
*Kimco Realty Corp.
*Lexington Realty Trust
*Liberty Property Trust
*Macerich Company (The)
*Mack-Cali Realty Corporation
*National Retail Properties Inc.
 Plum Creek Timber Company
 Public Storage, Inc.
 Realty Income Corp.

*Regency Centers Corporation
*Shurgard Storage Centers, Inc.
*Simon Property Group, Inc.
 SL Green Realty Corp.
*Sovran Self Storage, Inc.
 Starwood Hotels & Resorts
*Tanger Factory Outlet Centers, Inc.
*Taubman Centers, Inc.
*Thornburg Mortgage, Inc.
*UDR Inc.
*Universal Health Realty Inc. Trust
*Ventas, Inc.
*Vornado Realty Trust
*Washington Real Est. Invst Trust
*Weingarten Realty Investors

Reinsurance Carriers
*ACE, Ltd.
 Ambac Financial Group, Inc.
*Marsh & McLennan Cos. Inc.
 MBIA Inc.
 MGIC Investment Corporation
*Old Republic International Corp.
 PMI Group, Inc. (The)
 Radian Group Inc.

Savings Institutions
 Astoria Financial Corp.
*Sovereign Bancorp, Inc.
*Washington Mutual, Inc.
*Webster Financial Corp.
**Securities, Commodity Contracts, and Other
Financial Investments and Related Activities**
 Bear Stearns Companies (The)
*Citigroup Inc.
 CME Group Inc.
 Eaton Vance Corporation
 Federated Investors, Inc.
*Franklin Resources, Inc.
 Goldman Sachs Group, Inc.
 IntercontinentalExchange Inc.
 Investment Technology Group Inc.
 Janus Capital Group, Inc.
 Jefferies Group, Inc.
 Legg Mason, Inc.
*Lehman Brothers Holdings Inc.
 MasterCard Inc.
*Merrill Lynch & Co., Inc.
 Raymond James Financial, Inc.
*Waddell & Reed Financial, Inc.
Other Financial Vehicles
 BlackRock, Inc.

Health Care and Social Assistance
 Apria Healthcare Group Inc.
 Brookdale Senior Living Inc.
 Community Health Systems, Inc.
 Coventry Health Care Inc.

DaVita Inc.
Health Management Associates
Health Net, Inc.
Kindred Healthcare, Inc.
Laboratory Corp. of America
*Tenet Healthcare Corporation
Universal Health Services, Inc.

Information
*Cable Networks, Program Distribution and
Internet Service Providers*
 Cablevision Systems Corp.
 Time Warner Cable Inc.
 Time Warner Inc.

*Information Services and Data Processing
Services*
 Affiliated Computer Services
 Alliance Data Systems Corp.
 Automatic Data Processing, Inc.
 Concord EFS, Inc.
 Donnelley (R.H.) Corp.
 DST Systems, Inc.
 Dun & Bradstreet Corp. (The)
*Electronic Data Systems Corp.
 Fair Isaac Corporation
 Getty Images, Inc.
 Imation Corporation
 IMS Health, Inc.
 NCR Corporation
 SRA International Inc.
 Total System Services, Inc.
 Western Union Co.

Motion Picture and Sound Recording Industries
 DreamWorks Animation SKG Inc.
 News Corp.
 Regal Entertainment Group
 Viacom Inc.
 Warner Music Group Corp.
 Westwood One, Inc.

Publishing Industries
*American Greetings Corporation
 Belo Corporation
 BMC Software, Inc.
*CA Inc.
*Gannett Co., Inc.
 Harte-Hanks, Inc.
 Lee Enterprises, Inc.
 McAfee Inc.
 McClatchy Company (The)
*McGraw-Hill Companies, Inc.
*Media General, Inc.
 Meredith Corporation
*New York Times Company
 Red Hat Inc.
*Reader's Digest Association, Inc.

Salesforce.Com Inc.
Scripps (E.W.) Company (The)
Sybase, Inc.
Washington Post Company
Wiley (John) & Sons Inc.

Radio and Television Broadcasting
Clear Channel Communications
Dolby Laboratories Inc.
Entercom Communications Corp.
Hearst-Argyle Television, Inc.

Telecommunications
American Tower Corporation
*CenturyTel, Inc.
Cincinnati Bell Inc.
*Citizens Communications Co.
Crown Castle International Corp.
*Embarq Corp.
Fidelity National Information Services Inc.
Neustar Inc.
Qwest Communications International
*Sprint Nextel Corporation
*Verizon Communications Inc.
Windstream Corp.

Management of Companies & Enterprises
*AT&T Inc.
IndyMac Bancorp, Inc.
*National City Corporation
*Temple-Inland Inc.
*Universal Corporation

Manufacturing
Beverage and Tobacco Product Manufacturing
*Altria Group, Inc.
*Anheuser-Busch Companies
*Brown-Forman Corporation
*Coca-Cola Company (The)
*Coca-Cola Enterprises Inc.
Constellation Brands, Inc.
Molson Coors Brewing Company
*Pepsi Bottling Group Inc.
*PepsiAmericas, Inc.
*PepsiCo Inc.
*Reynolds American Inc.
*UST, Inc.

Chemical Manufacturing
*3M Company
*Air Products & Chemicals, Inc.
*Albemarle Corporation
Alberto-Culver Company
*Avon Products, Inc.
*Ashland, Inc.
Blyth, Inc.
*Cabot Corporation
Charles River Laboratories Int.

Chemtura Corp.
*Church & Dwight Company, Inc.
*Clorox Company (The)
*Colgate-Palmolive Company
Cytec Industries, Inc.
*Dow Chemical Company
*du Pont (E.I.) de Nemours & Co.
*Eastman Chemical Company
*Eastman Kodak Company
*Ecolab, Inc.
*Estee Lauder Companies, Inc.
*Ferro Corp.
*Fuller (H.B.) Company
*Hercules Inc.
IMC Global, Inc.
*International Flavors & Fragrances
*Lubrizol Corporation
Monsanto Co.
Nalco Holding Co.
*Olin Corporation
*PPG Industries, Inc.
*Praxair, Inc.
*Procter & Gamble Company
*Rohm & Haas Company
*RPM International Inc.
Scotts Company (The)
*Sherwin-Williams Company
Smith International, Inc.
Stepan Co.
*Valspar Corporation (The)
Westlake Chemical Corp.

Computer and Electronic Product Manufacturing
Advanced Micro Devices, Inc.
Agilent Technologies, Inc.
*Allegheny Technologies Inc.
*Ametek, Inc.
Analog Devices, Inc.
*Applera Corp. – Applied Biosystems
*AVX Corporation
*Beckman Coulter, Inc.
Commscope, Inc.
*Corning Incorporated
Cypress Semiconductor Corp.
DRS Technologies Inc.
EMC Corporation
*Emerson Electric Co.
Fairchild Semiconductor Int'l.
Global Payments Inc.
Harman International Industries
*Harris Corporation
*Hewlett-Packard Company
*International Business Machines
International Rectifier Corp.
Jabil Circuit, Inc.
KEMET Corporation
L-3 Communications Holdings
Lexmark International, Inc.

LSI Corp
*Medtronic, Inc.
MEMC Electronic Materials, Inc.
Mettler-Toledo International Inc.
Micron Technology, Inc.
*Millipore Corporation
*Motorola, Inc.
National Semiconductor Corp.
Plantronics, Inc.
*Raytheon Company
*Rockwell Collins, Inc.
Teradyne, Inc.
Teradata Corp.
*Texas Instruments Inc.
Thermo Fisher Scientific Inc.
*Thomas & Betts Corporation
Unisys Corporation
Vishay Intertechnology, Inc.
Waters Corporation
Western Digital Corporation

Doll, Toy, and Game Manufacturing
*Hasbro, Inc.
*Mattel, Inc.

Electrical Equipment, Appliance, and Component Manufacturing
Amphenol Corp.
*Cooper Industries, Ltd.
*Eaton Corporation
Energizer Holdings, Inc.
General Cable Corp.
*General Electric Company
*Hubbell, Inc.
Jarden Corp.
*Rockwell Automation
*Smith (A.O.) Corporation
*Whirlpool Corporation

Fabricated Metal Product Manufacturing
Alliant Techsystems Inc.
*Ball Corporation
*Crane Co.
Crown Holdings, Inc.
Danaher Corporation
*Fortune Brands, Inc.
*Harsco Corporation
*Parker-Hannifin Corp.
Shaw Group Inc. (The)
*Snap-On Incorporated
*Stanley Works
*Timken Company (The)

Food Manufacturing
*Archer Daniels Midland Co.
*Campbell Soup Company
*ConAgra Foods, Inc.
Corn Products International Inc.

Dean Foods Company
Del Monte Foods Company
*General Mills, Inc.
*Heinz (H.J.) Company
*Hershey Foods Corporation
*Hormel Foods Corporation
*Kellogg Company
Kraft Foods, Inc.
*McCormick & Company, Inc.
Pilgrim's Pride Corp.
*Sara Lee Corporation
*Sensient Technologies Corp.
Smithfield Foods, Inc.
*Smucker (J.M.) Company
Tootsie Roll Industries, Inc.
*Tyson Foods, Inc.
*Wrigley (Wm.) Jr. Company

Furniture and Related Product Manufacturing
Furniture Brands International
HNI Corporation
*La-Z-Boy Incorporated
Leggett & Platt, Incorporated
*Masco Corporation
Steelcase Inc.

Machinery Manufacturing
AGCO Corporation
*Baker Hughes Inc.
*Brunswick Corporation
Cameron International Corp.
*Caterpillar Inc.
*Cummins Inc.
*Deere & Company
*Diebold, Inc.
*Donaldson Company, Inc.
*Dover Corporation
Dresser-Rand Group Inc.
Flowserve Corporation
FMC Corporation
FMC Technologies, Inc.
Gardner Denver, Inc.
*Graco Inc.
Grant Prideco Inc.
*IDEX Corporation
*ITT Industries Inc.
*Kennametal Inc.
*Manitowoc Company, Inc. (The)
Lennox International Inc.
NACCO Industries, Inc.
*Pall Corporation
*Pentair, Inc.
Roper Industries, Inc.
SPX Corporation
Terex Corporation
*Tennant Company
*Toro Co. (The)
*Trane, Inc.

arian Medical Systems, Inc.
*erox Corporation
*ork International Corporation

Medical Equipment and Supplies Manufacturing
Advanced Medical Optics Inc.
Bard (C.R.), Inc.
Baxter International Inc.
Becton, Dickinson and Company
Boston Scientific Corporation
Hill-Rom Holdings, Inc.
Mine Safety Appliances Company
ResMed Inc.
St. Jude Medical, Inc.
Steris Corporation
Stryker Corporation
*Teleflex Inc.
Zimmer Holdings, Inc.

Nonmetallic Mineral Product Manufacturing
Brink's Company (The)
Minerals Technologies Inc.
Owens-Illinois, Inc.
USG Corporation

Paper and Wood Product Manufacturing
*Avery Dennison Corporation
*Bemis Company, Inc.
*Boise Cascade Corporation
Glatfelter (P.H.) Company
*International Paper Company
*Kimberly-Clark Corporation
*Louisiana-Pacific Corporation
*MeadWestvaco Corporation
Packaging Corp. of America
*Potlatch Corporation
*Rayonier Inc.
*Sonoco Products Company
St. Joe Company (The)
Tenneco Inc.

Petroleum and Coal Products Manufacturing
*Chevron Corp.
*ConocoPhillips
*Exxon Mobil Corporation
Frontier Oil Corp.
*Hess Corp.
Holly Corp.
Murphy Oil Corporation
*Sunoco, Inc.
Tesoro Corporation
Valero Energy Corporation
Western Refining Inc.

Pharmaceutical Preparation Manufacturing
*Abbott Laboratories
*Allergan, Inc.
AmerisourceBergen Corporation

Barr Laboratories, Inc.
*Bristol-Myers Squibb Company
Edwards Lifesciences Corp.
Forest Laboratories, Inc.
Genentech, Inc.
Hospira Inc.
*Johnson & Johnson
King Pharmaceuticals, Inc.
*Lilly (Eli) & Company
Medicis Pharmaceutical Corp.
*Merck & Co., Inc.
*Mylan Laboratories Inc.
Par Pharmaceutical Companies, Inc.
*Pfizer Inc.
*Schering-Plough Corporation
Valeant Pharmaceuticals Internat.
Watson Pharmaceuticals, Inc.
*Wyeth

Plastics and Rubber Products Manufacturing
AptarGroup Inc.
Armstrong World Industry Inc.
*Carlisle Companies Incorporated
*Cooper Tire & Rubber Company
*Goodyear Tire & Rubber Co.
*Illinois Tool Works, Incorporated
*Myers Industries, Inc.
*Newell Rubbermaid Inc.
Pactiv Corporation
Sealed Air Corporation
Tupperware Brands Corporation
*West Pharmaceutical Services

Primary Metal Manufacturing
*AK Steel Holding Corporation
*Alcoa, Inc.
Carpenter Technology Corp.
Commercial Metals Co.
*Nucor Corporation
Precision Castparts Corp.
Titanium Metals Corp.
*United States Steel Corporation
*Worthington Industries, Inc.

Printing and Related Support Activities
Deluxe Corporation
*Donnelley (R.R.) & Sons Co.

Textiles, Apparel, and Leather Manufacturing
Coach, Inc.
GUESS ?, Inc.
Jones Apparel Group, Inc.
*Liz Claiborne, Inc.
Mohawk Industries, Inc.
*NIKE, Inc.
Phillips-Van Heusen Corp.
Polo Ralph Lauren Corporation
Timberland Co. (The)
*VF Corporation

Transportation Equipment Manufacturing
*ArvinMeritor, Inc.
 Autoliv, Inc.
*Boeing Company (The)
*BorgWarner Inc.
*Clarcor Inc.
*Federal Signal Corp.
*Ford Motor Company
 General Dynamics Corporation
*General Motors Corporation
*Goodrich Corporation
*Harley-Davidson, Inc.
*Honeywell International Inc.
*Lockheed Martin Corporation
*Modine Manufacturing Company
*Oshkosh Corp.
*Polaris Industries Inc.
 Sequa Corporation
*Textron Inc.
 Thor Industries, Inc.
 Trinity Industries, Inc.
 TRW Automotive Holdings Corp.
*United Technologies Corp.
*Visteon Corporation

Other Manufacturing
*Brady Corporation
 Callaway Golf Company
*Ingersoll-Rand Co. Ltd.

Mining
Activities Support for Mining
 BJ Services Company
 Diamond Offshore Drilling, Inc.
 ENSCO International Inc.
 EOG Resources, Inc.
 Helmerich & Payne, Inc.
*Marathon Oil Corporation
 Oceaneering International, Inc.
 Pride International, Inc.
 Rowan Companies, Inc.
 Schlumberger Ltd.
 Superior Energy Services, Inc.
 Transocean Inc.
 TETRA Technologies, Inc.
 Weatherford International, Ltd.

Mining (except Oil and Gas)
*Arch Coal, Inc.
 Cleveland-Cliffs Inc.
 CONSOL Energy Inc.
 Freeport-McMoRan Copper & Gold
 Foundation Coal Holdings Inc.
*Massey Energy Co.
 Mosaic Co. (The)
 Newmont Mining Corporation
 Peabody Energy Corp.
*Southern Copper Corp.

*Vulcan Materials Company

Oil and Gas Extraction
*Anadarko Petroleum Corp.
*Apache Corporation
 Atwood Oceanics, Inc.
 Cabot Oil & Gas Corp.
 Chesapeake Energy Corp.
 Cimarex Energy Co.
 Denbury Resources, Inc.
 Devon Energy Corporation
*Dynegy Inc.
*Enterprise Products Partners L.P.
 Forest Oil Corporation
*Kerr-McGee Corporation
 Nabors Industries Ltd.
 Newfield Exploration Co.
 Noble Corp.
 Noble Energy, Inc.
*Occidental Petroleum Corp.
 Pioneer Natural Resources Co.
 Plains Exploration & Production Co. L.P.
 Quicksilver Resources, Inc.
 Range Resources Corp.
 St. Mary Land & Exploration Co.
 Southwestern Energy Company
 Unit Corp.
 W & T Offshore Inc.
*XTO Energy, Inc.

Other Services
 ARAMARK Corporation
 Avis Budget Group Inc.
 Clear Channel Outdoor Holdings Inc.
 Corrections Corporation of America
*Regis Corporation
 Reliance Steel & Aluminum Co.
 Service Corporation International
 Weight Watchers International

Professional, Scientific, and Technical Services
 Agere Systems Inc.
*Block (H & R), Inc.
 Computer Sciences Corporation
 Convergys Corporation
 Covance Inc.
 Fluor Corporation
 Gartner Group, Inc.
 Hewitt Associates Inc.
*Interpublic Group of Companies
 Korn/Ferry International
 Moody's Corporation
 Navigant Consulting, Inc.
*Omnicom Group, Inc.
*PerkinElmer, Inc.
 Quest Diagnostics, Incorporated
 Valassis

Real Estate and Rental and Leasing
Real Estate
*ProLogis

Rental and Leasing Services
CIT Group Inc.
United Rentals, Inc.

Retail Trade
Building Material and Garden Equipment and Supplies Dealers
*Home Depot (The), Inc.
*Lowe's Companies, Inc.
Wesco International, Inc.

Clothing and Clothing Accessories Stores
Abercrombie & Fitch Co.
Aeropostale Inc.
American Eagle Outfitters, Inc.
Ann Taylor Stores Corp.
Cato Corp.
Chico's FAS, Inc.
*Foot Locker, Inc.
Gap, Inc. (The)
*Limited Brands
Nordstrom, Inc.
Payless ShoeSource Inc.
Talbots (The), Inc.
*Tiffany & Co.
TJX Companies, Inc. (The)

Furniture and Consumer Electronics
Best Buy Co., Inc.
Circuit City Stores, Inc.
GameStop Corp.
*Pier 1 Imports, Inc.
*RadioShack Corporation
Williams-Sonoma, Inc.

General Merchandise Stores
99 Cents Only Stores
Big Lots, Inc.
BJ's Wholesale Club, Inc.
Dillard's, Inc.
Family Dollar Stores, Inc.
Kohl's Corporation
Macys Inc.
Penney (J.C.) Company, Inc.
Saks Incorporated
*Target Corporation
*Wal-Mart Stores, Inc.

Southwest Airlines Co.
*Spectra Energy Corp.
TEPPCO Partners, L.P.
*Tidewater Inc.
*Union Pacific Corp.

Grocery Stores
Kroger Company (The)
*Ruddick Corporation
Safeway Inc.

Health and Personal Care Stores
*CVS/Caremark Corporation
*Longs Drug Stores Corporation
Medco Health Solutions, Inc.
*Omnicare, Inc.
*Rite Aid Corporation
*Walgreen Co.

Motor Vehicle and Parts Dealers
Advance Auto Parts, Inc.
Asbury Automotive Group, Inc.
AutoNation, Inc.
AutoZone, Inc.
Carmax Inc.
Group 1 Automotive, Inc.
Penske Automotive Group Inc.
Sonic Automotive, Inc.

Sporting Goods, Hobby, Book, and Music Stores and other
Barnes & Noble, Inc.
Borders Group, Inc.
Dick's Sporting Goods, Inc.
*Office Depot, Inc.
*OfficeMax Inc.
*Sotheby's Holdings, Inc.

Transportation and Warehousing
AirTran Holdings, Inc.
Alaska Air Group, Inc.
AMR Corporation
*Atmos Energy Corporation
*Buckeye Partners, L.P.
*Burlington Northern Santa Fe
Con-Way Inc.
Continental Airlines, Inc.
*CSX Corporation
*El Paso Corporation
Enbridge Energy Partners, L.P.
*FedEx Corporation
*GATX Corporation
Iron Mountain Incorporated
Kansas City Southern
Kirby Corp.
*Norfolk Southern Corporation
*OGE Energy Corp.
Overseas Shipholding Group
Plains All American Pipeline, L.P.
*Ryder System, Inc.
United Parcel Service, Inc.
US Airways Group Inc.
Western Gas Resources, Inc.
Williams Companies, Inc. (The)

Utilities

Utilities - Electric
AES Corporation (The)
Allegheny Energy, Inc.
*Alliant Energy Corporation
*Ameren Corporation
*American Electric Power Co.
*Aquila, Inc.
*Black Hills Corporation
*CenterPoint Energy, Inc.
*CMS Energy Corporation
*Consolidated Edison, Inc.
*Constellation Energy Group, Inc.
*Dominion Resources, Inc.
*DPL Inc.
*DTE Energy Co.
*Duke Energy Corporation
*Edison International
*Energy East Corporation
*Entergy Corporation
*Exelon Corporation
*FirstEnergy Corporation
*FPL Group, Inc.
*Great Plains Energy Incorporated
*Hawaiian Electric Industries, Inc.
*Idacorp, Inc.
*Integrys Energy Group Inc.
New Jersey Resources Corp.
*NiSource, Inc.
*Northeast Utilities
*NSTAR
*Pepco Holdings, Inc.
*PG&E Corporation
*Pinnacle West Capital Corp.
*PNM Resources, Inc.
*PPL Corporation
*Progress Energy, Inc.
*Public Service Enterprise Group
*Puget Energy, Inc.
Reliant Energy, Inc.
*SCANA Corporation
*Sierra Pacific Resources
*Southern Company (The)
*TECO Energy, Inc.
*Westar Energy, Inc.
*Wisconsin Energy Corporation
*Xcel Energy, Inc.

Utilities - Natural Gas
*AGL Resources Inc.

Airgas Inc.
*Energen Corporation
*Equitable Resources, Inc.
Kinder Morgan Energy Partner, L.P.
*National Fuel Gas Company
*NICOR Inc.
Northwest Natural Gas Co.
*Oneok Inc.
*Piedmont Natural Gas Company
*Questar Corporation
*Sempra Energy
*UGI Corporation
*Vectren Corporation
*WGL Holdings, Inc.

Utilities - Water
*American States Water Co.
*Aqua America, Inc.
*California Water Service Group
SJW Corp.

Wholesale Trade

Wholesale Trade, Durable Goods
Arrow Electronics, Inc.
*Avnet, Inc.
Ceridian Corporation
*Genuine Parts Company
Grainger (W.W.), Inc.
Hughes Supply, Inc.
*Ikon Office Solutions, Inc.
Ingram Micro Inc.
Lear Corporation
MSC Industrial Direct Co., Inc.
National-Oilwell, Inc.
*Owens & Minor, Inc.
*Pitney Bowes Inc.
*Weyerhaeuser Company
World Fuel Services Corp.

Wholesale Trade, Nondurable Goods
Cardinal Health, Inc.
*Crompton Corporation
*McKesson Corporation
*Supervalu Inc.
*Sysco Corporation

* Designates companies offering dividend reinvestment plans.

DOW JONES INDUSTRIAL AVERAGE
PRICES - EARNINGS - DIVIDENDS

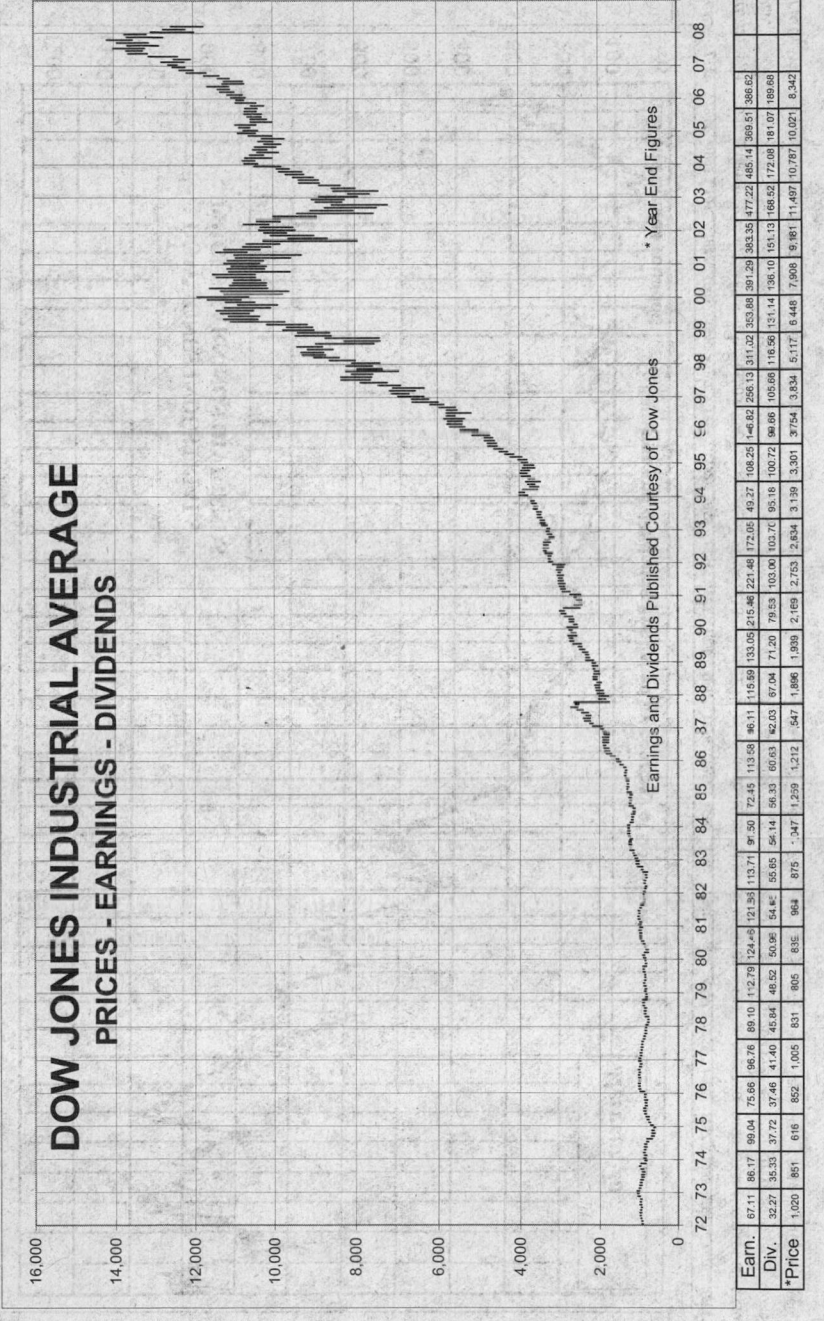

Earnings and Dividends Published Courtesy of Dow Jones

* Year End Figures

	72	73	74	75	76	77	78	79	80	81	82	83	84	85	86	87	88	89	90	91	92	93	94	95	96	97	98	99	00	01	02	03	04	05	06	07	08
Earn.	67.11	86.17	99.04	75.66	96.76	89.10	112.79	124.46	121.35	113.71	97.50	72.45	113.58	96.11	115.59	133.05	215.46	221.48	172.05	49.27	108.25	146.82	256.13	311.02	353.88	391.29	363.35	477.22	485.14	369.51	386.62						
Div.	32.27	35.33	37.72	37.46	41.40	45.84	48.52	50.98	54.86	56.14	56.33	60.63	62.03	67.04	71.20	79.53	103.00	103.70	95.18	100.72	105.66	118.56	131.14	136.10	151.13	168.52	172.08	181.07	189.68								
*Price	1,020	851	616	852	1,005	831	805	839	964	875	1,047	1,259	1,212	547	1,896	1,939	2,169	2,753	2,634	3,139	3,301	3,754	3,834	5,117	6,448	7,908	9,181	11,497	10,787	10,021	8,342						

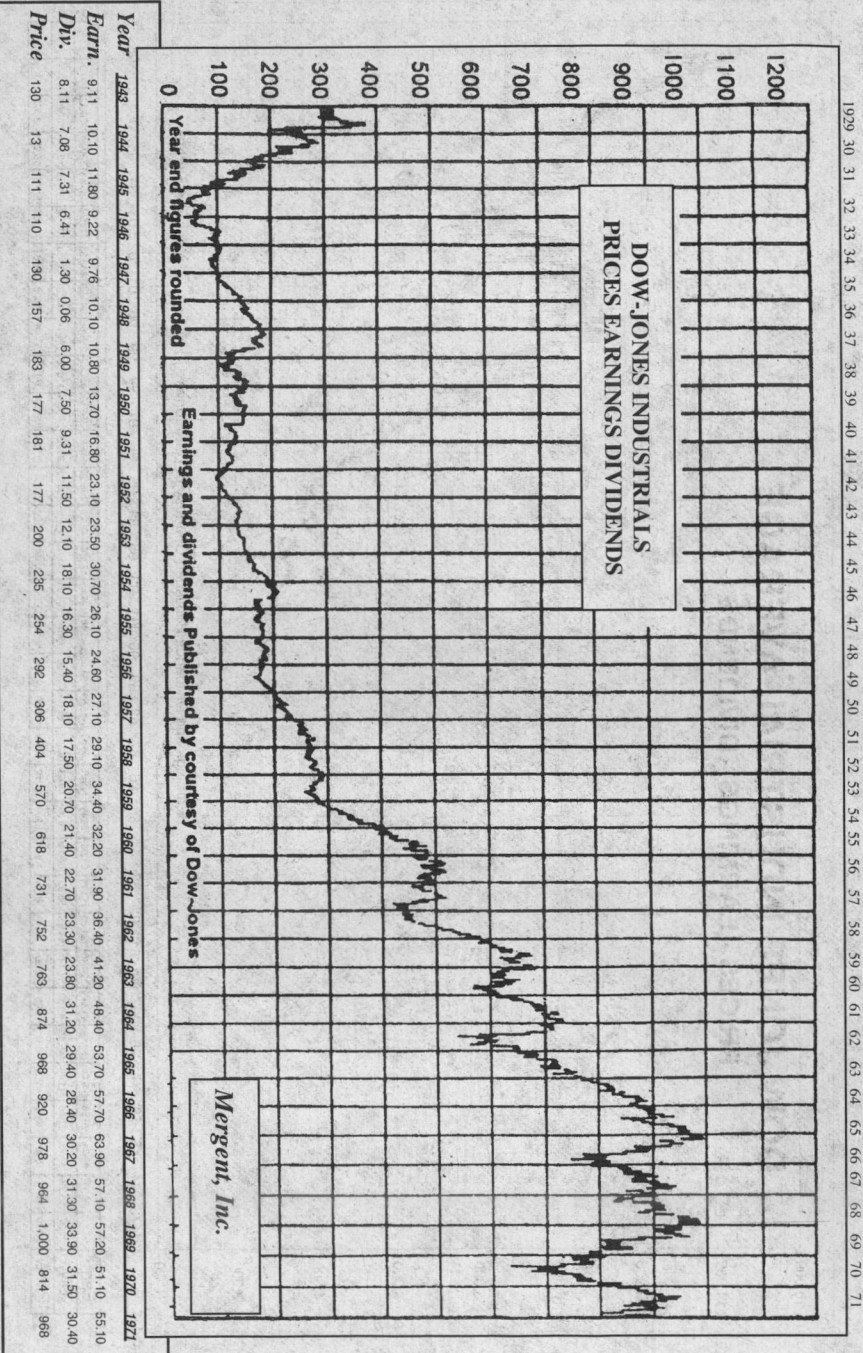

DOW-JONES INDUSTRIALS PRICES EARNINGS DIVIDENDS

Mergent, Inc.

Year end figures rounded

Earnings and dividends Published by courtesy of Dow-Jones

Year	Earn.	Div.	Price
1943	9.11	8.11	130
1944	10.10	7.08	13
1945	11.80	7.31	111
1946	9.22	6.41	110
1947	9.76	1.30	130
1948	10.10	0.06	157
1949	10.80	6.00	183
1950	13.70	7.50	177
1951	16.80	9.31	181
1952	23.10	11.50	177
1953	23.50	12.10	200
1954	30.70	18.10	235
1955	28.10	16.30	254
1956	24.60	18.10	292
1957	27.10	20.70	306
1958	29.10	21.40	404
1959	34.40	22.70	570
1960	32.20	23.30	618
1961	31.90	23.80	731
1962	36.40	31.20	752
1963	41.20	29.40	763
1964	48.40	28.40	874
1965	53.70	30.20	968
1966	57.70	31.30	920
1967	63.90	33.90	978
1968	57.10	31.50	964
1969	57.20	30.40	1,000
1970	51.10		814
1971	55.10		968

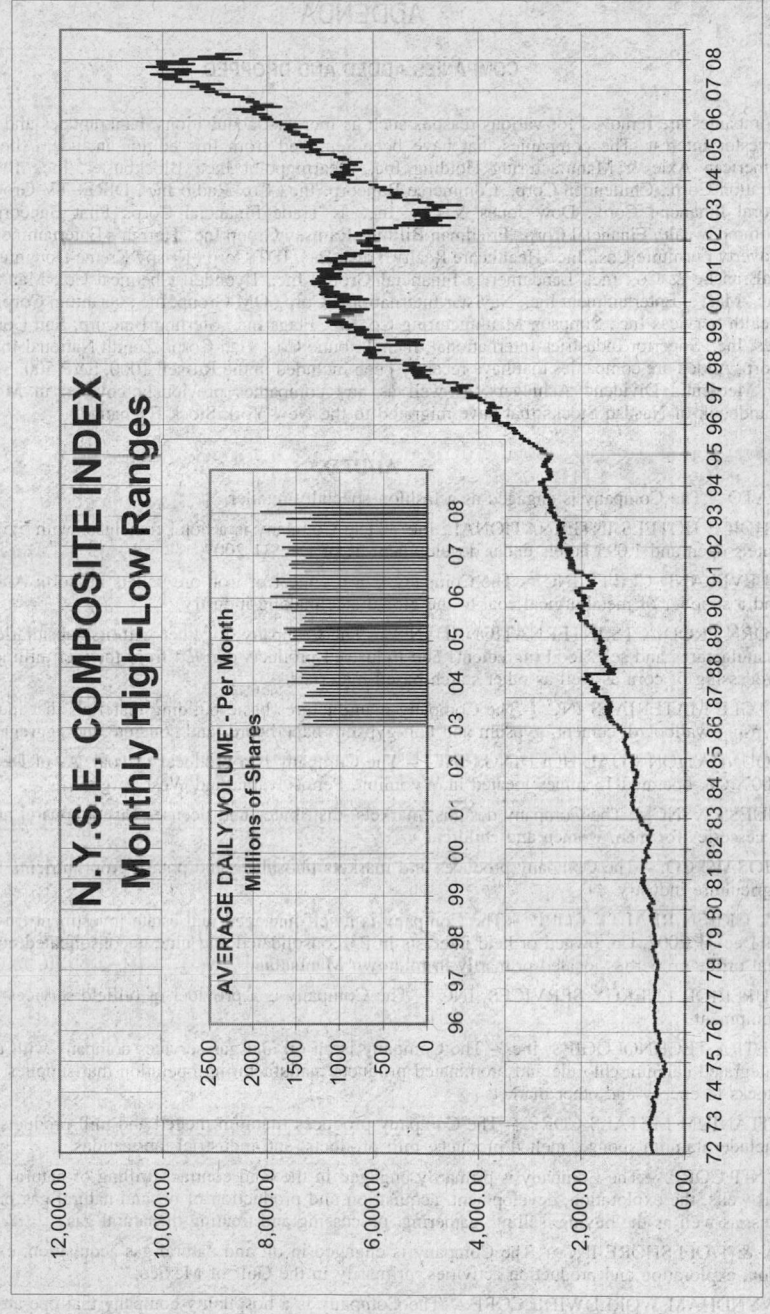

N.Y.S.E. COMPOSITE INDEX
Monthly High-Low Ranges

AVERAGE DAILY VOLUME - Per Month

Millions of Shares

ADDENDA

COMPANIES ADDED AND DROPPED

Companies are removed for various reasons such as mergers, acquisitions, bankruptcies and lack of investor interest. The companies that have been removed from this edition include: Allete Inc., American Axle & Manufacturing Holding Inc., Bearingpoint Inc., Blockbuster, Inc., Briggs & Stratton Corp., Chittenden Corp., Commerce Bancorp, Inc., Cox Radio Inc., DIRECTV Group Inc., Doral Financial Corp., Dow Jones & Co., Inc., E Trade Financial Corp., First Bancorp, First Commonwealth Financial Corp., Friedman Billings Ramsey Group Inc., Harrah's Entertainment, Inc., Haverty Furniture Cos., Inc., Healthcare Realty Trust, Inc., IDT Corp., Krispy Kreme Doughnuts Inc., LaBranche & Co., Inc., Landamerica Financial Group, Inc., Lyondell Chemical Co., Manor Care, Inc., Marvel Entertainment Inc., Navistar International Corp., OM Group, Inc., Quantum Corp., Sierra Health Services Inc., Simpson Manufacturing Co., Six Flags Inc., Sterling Bancorp, Sun Communities, Inc., Superior Industries International, Inc., Tribune Co., Viad Corp., Zenith National Insurance Corp. Added are companies that have recently been included in the Russell 1000, S&P 500, S&P 400 or Mergent's Dividend Achievers, as well as any companies previously covered in Mergent's Handbook of Nasdaq Stocks that have migrated to the New York Stock Exchange.

ADDED

CATO – The Company is engaged as a fashion specialty retailer.

CHOICE HOTELS INTERNATIONAL, Inc. – The Company is a hotel franchisor with 5,570 hotels open and 1,093 hotels under development as of Dec 31 2007.

CLEVELAND-CLIFFS INC. – The Company is a producer of iron ore pellets in North America and a supplier of metallurgical coal to the global steelmaking industry.

CORN PRODUCTS INTERNATIONAL INC. – The Company, together with its subsidiaries, manufactures and sells food ingredients and industrial products derived from the wet milling and processing of corn as well as other starch-based materials.

EAGLE MATERIALS INC. – The Company manufactures basic building materials that include gypsum wallboard, cement, gypsum and non-gypsum paperboard, and concrete and aggregates.

FOUNDATION COAL HOLDINGS INC. – The Company is a producer of coal. As of Dec 31 2007, Co. operated 13 mines located in Wyoming, Pennsylvania and West Virginia.

GUESS ?, INC. – The Company designs, markets, distributes and licenses casual apparel and accessories for men, women and children.

MOSAIC CO. – The Company produces and markets phosphate and potash crop nutrients for the agriculture industry.

SL GREEN REALTY CORP. – The Company is a self-managed real estate investment trust. As of Dec 31 2007, Co. owned or held interests in 23 consolidated and nine unconsolidated commercial office properties located primarily in midtown Manhattan.

SUPERIOR ENERGY SERVICES, INC. – The Company is a provider of oilfield services and equipment.

TETRA TECHNOLOGIES, Inc. – The Company is an oil and gas services company with an integrated calcium chloride and brominated products manufacturing operation that supplies feedstocks to energy and other markets.

TITANIUM METALS CORP. – The Company produces titanium melted and mill products, which include titanium sponge, melted products, mill products, and industrial fabrications.

UNIT CORP. – The Company is primarily engaged in the land contract drilling of natural gas and oil wells, the exploration, development, acquisition and production of oil and natural gas properties, as well as the buying, selling, gathering, processing and treating of natural gas.

W & T OFFSHORE INC. – The Company is engaged in oil and natural gas acquisition, exploitation, exploration and production activities, primarily in the Gulf of Mexico.

WYNDHAM WORLDWIDE CORP. – The Company is a hospitality company that operates in three segments: Lodging; Vacation Exchange and Rental; and Vacation Ownership.

ADDENDA (Continued)

RECENT AND PENDING STOCK DIVIDENDS AND SPLITS

Company	Amount	Ex-Div. Date	Date of Record	Payable Date
Alleghany Corp.	2%	3/28/08	4/1/08	4/25/08
Cleveland-Cliffs Inc.	2-for-1	5/16/08	5/1/08	5/15/08
Cummins, Inc.	2-for-1	1/3/08	12/21/07	1/2/08
Medco Health Solutions, Inc.	100%	1/25/08	1/10/08	1/24/08
New Jersey Resources Corp.	3-for-2	3/4/08	2/8/08	3/3/08
Public Service Enterprise Group Inc.	2-for1	2/5/08	1/25/08	2/4/08
Quicksilver Resources, Inc.	100%	2/1/08	1/18/08	1/31/08
Southwestern Energy Co.	2-for-1	3/26/08	3/14/08	3/25/08
Tootsie Roll Industries Inc.	3%	3/6/08	3/10/08	4/10/08
Valley National Bancorp	5%	5/7/08	5/9/08	5/23/08

RECENT DIVIDEND CHANGES

Company	Latest Dividend— Amount	Payable	Company	Latest Dividend— Amount	Payable
Increased			**Increased**		
Abbott Laboratories	0.36 Q	4/11/08	GATX Corp.	0.27 Q	2/27/08
Air Products & Chemicals	0.44 Q	3/28/08	General Dynamics Corp.	0.35 Q	4/9/08
Airgas Inc.	0.12 Q	3/11/08	General Mills, Inc.	0.40 Q	4/8/08
Albemarle Corp.	0.12 Q	3/12/08	Genuine Parts Co.	0.39 Q	3/5/08
Allstate Corp.	0.41 Q	3/12/08	Harte-Hanks, Inc.	0.08 Q	2/27/08
AMB Property Corp.	0.52 Q	4/2/08	Hasbro, Inc.	0.20 Q	4/29/08
American Greetings Corp.	0.12 Q	4/14/08	Holly Corp.	0.15 Q	3/17/08
Annaly Capital Management	0.48 Q	3/26/08	Integrys Energy Group Inc.	0.67 Q	2/27/08
AvalonBay Communities	0.89 Q	3/28/08	iStar Financial Inc.	0.87 Q	3/13/08
BlackRock, Inc.	0.78 Q	3/5/08	ITT Corporation	0.18 Q	3/5/08
BRE Properties, Inc.	0.56 Q	3/12/08	KeyCorp	0.38 Q	2/29/08
Camden Property Trust	0.70 Q	3/21/08	Kilroy Realty Corp	0.58 Q	3/27/08
CenturyTel, Inc.	0.07 Q	3/6/08	Kimberly-Clark Corp.	0.58 Q	3/5/08
Chubb Corp.	0.33 Q	3/26/08	Kroger Co.	0.09 Q	5/13/08
CIGNA Corp.	0.04 Q	3/7/08	Medicis Pharmaceutical	0.04 Q	3/28/08
CME Group Inc.	1.15 Q	3/6/08	Mercury General Corp.	0.58 Q	3/13/08
Coca-Cola Co.	0.38 Q	3/12/08	Meredith Corp.	0.22 Q	2/27/08
Coca-Cola Enterprises Inc.	0.07 Q	3/12/08	Nationwide Financial Svcs	0.29 Q	3/28/08
Colgate-Palmolive Co	0.40 Q	4/22/08	Nordstrom, Inc.	0.16 Q	2/27/08
Comerica, Inc.	0.66 Q	3/12/08	Nucor Corp.	0.32 Q	3/26/08
Constellation Energy Group	0.48 Q	3/6/08	NYSE Euronext	0.30 Q	6/11/08
Cooper Industries, Ltd.	0.25 Q	2/27/08	Old National Bancorp	0.23 Q	2/28/08
Corn Products International	0.12 Q	4/1/08	Owens & Minor, Inc.	0.20 Q	3/12/08
CSX Corp.	0.18 Q	5/28/08	Pall Corp.	0.13 Q	4/23/08
Developers Diversified Rlty	0.69 Q	3/18/08	Pepco Holdings Inc.	0.27 Q	3/6/08
Devon Energy Corp.	0.16 Q	3/13/08	Pepsi Bottling Group Inc.	0.17 Q	6/4/08
Dun & Bradstreet Corp	0.30 Q	2/27/08	PepsiAmericas, Inc.	0.14 Q	3/12/08
EastGroup Properties, Inc.	0.52 Q	3/18/08	PG&E Corp.	0.39 Q	3/27/08
Embarq Corp	0.69 Q	3/6/08	Piedmont Natural Gas Co.	0.26 Q	3/20/08
EOG Resources, Inc.	0.12 Q	4/14/08	PNC Financial Svcs. Grp.	0.66 Q	4/10/08
Essex Property Trust, Inc.	1.02 Q	3/27/08	PPL Corp.	0.34 Q	3/6/08
Family Dollar Stores, Inc.	0.13 Q	3/12/08	Praxair, Inc.	0.38 Q	3/5/08
Flowserve Corp.	0.25 Q	3/24/08	Procter & Gamble Co.	0.40 Q	4/16/08
Fluor Corp.	0.25 Q	3/5/08	Public Storage	0.55 Q	3/12/08
Foot Locker, Inc.	0.15 Q	4/16/08	Raytheon Co.	0.28 Q	3/28/08
FPL Group, Inc.	0.45 Q	2/27/08	Realty Income Corp.	0.14 Q	3/28/08
Fuller (H.B.) Company	0.07 Q	4/15/08	Reliance Steel & Aluminum	0.10 Q	3/5/08
Gallagher (Arthur J.) & Co.	0.32 Q	3/27/08	SCANA Corp	0.46 Q	3/6/08

ADDENDA (Continued)

Sealed Air Corp.	0.12 Q	3/5/08	**Decreased**			
Sempra Energy	0.35 Q	6/25/08	AK Steel Holding Corp.	0.05 Q	2/13/08
Sherwin-Williams Co.	0.35 Q	2/27/08	Ambac Financial Group, Inc.	0.07 Q	2/7/08
Smith International, Inc.	0.12 Q	3/12/08	Apache Corp.	0.10 Q	2/22/08
Sunoco, Inc.	0.30 Q	5/7/08	Brookdale Senior Living Inc.	0.25 Q	3/27/08
SunTrust Banks, Inc.	0.77 Q	2/27/08	Citigroup Inc.	0.32 Q	1/31/08
Tennant Co.	0.13 Q	2/27/08	Diamond Offshore Drilling	0.13 Q	2/13/08
The Gap, Inc.	0.09 Q	4/4/08	Fannie Mae	0.35 Q	1/29/08
Tim Hortons Inc.	0.09 Q	2/28/08	First Horizon National Corp	0.20 Q	3/12/08
TJX Companies, Inc.	0.11 Q	5/6/08	Furniture Brands Intl.	0.04 Q	2/7/08
Torchmark Corp.	0.14 Q	4/2/08	La-Z-Boy Inc.	0.04 Q	2/27/08
UST, Inc.	0.63 Q	3/12/08	Lexington Realty Trust	0.33 Q	3/27/08
Ventas, Inc.	0.51 Q	3/4/08	McDonald's Corp	0.38 Q	2/28/08
Waddell & Reed Financial	0.19 Q	4/2/08	National City Corp	0.21 Q	1/10/08
Waste Management, Inc.	0.27 Q	3/6/08	PMI Group, Inc.	0.01 Q	3/27/08
Weingarten Realty Investors	0.53 Q	3/5/08	Progressive Corp.	0.15 Q	1/17/08
Westar Energy Inc.	0.29 Q	3/5/08	Southern Copper Corp	1.40 Q	2/8/08
WGL Holdings, Inc.	0.36 Q	4/8/08	Temple-Inland Inc.	0.10 Q	2/27/08
Williams-Sonoma, Inc.	0.12 Q	4/23/08	Total System Services, Inc.	0.07 Q	3/18/08
Wolverine World Wide, Inc.	0.11 Q	3/28/08	Washingtong Mutual Inc.	0.15 Q	1/29/08
Wrigley (William) Jr. Co.	0.34 Q	4/11/08			

RECENT AND PENDING NAME CHANGES

Old	New
Hillenbrand Industries, Inc.	Hill-Rom Holdings, Inc.
Oshkosh Truck Corp.	Oshkosh Corp.

LATEST DEVELOPMENTS

BOEING, INC. – On Apr. 9, 2008, Co. announced a revised plan for first flight and initial deliveries of the 787 Dreamliner. Co.'s schedule now targets approximately 25 deliveries in 2009. First flight of the Dreamliner will move into the fourth quarter of 2008 rather than the end of the second quarter, and first delivery is now planned for the third quarter of 2009 instead of first quarter.

SUPERVALUE INC. – On Apr. 9, 2008, Co. announced the national launch of its Wild Harvest organic and natural brand. The new brand will be available beginning in April 2008 in the aisles of Co.'s family of grocery stores. The Wild Harvest brand will initially feature about 150 items. Longer term, Co. expects to offer approximately 250 to 300 products across various categories.

CONOCOPHILLIPS – On Apr. 8, 2008, Co. and BP PLC announced they have combined resources to start Denali - The Alaska Gas Pipeline. It is expected that the pipeline will move approximately 4.0 billion cubic feet of natural gas per day to markets. Co. and BP plan to spend $600.0 million to reach the first major project milestone, an open season, commencing before yearend 2010.

DEVON ENERGY CORP – On Apr. 8, 2008, Co. announced that it has agreed to sell its oil and gas business in the African nation of Equatorial Guinea to GEPetrol, the national oil company of Equatorial Guinea, for $2.20 billion. Co. expects closing to occur on or before May 30, 2008.

WASHINGTON MUTUAL INC.– On Apr. 8, 2008, Co. announced that it had entered into definitive agreements to raise an aggregate $7.00 billion through direct sale of equity securities to an investment vehicle managed by TPG Capital, and to other investors.

The 2008 Common Dividend Achievers

Companies listed below qualified for the 2008 Edition of Mergent's Dividend Achievers.
Also shown are total numbers of consecutive years of dividend growth.

Company Name	Years of Growth	Company Name	Years of Growth
3M Co	49	Commerce Bancorp, Inc.	16
Abbott Laboratories	35	Commerce Group Inc	13
ABM Industries, Inc.	43	Community Bank System, Inc.	16
AFLAC Inc.	25	Consolidated Edison Inc.	33
Air Products & Chemicals, Inc.	25	Corporate Office Properties Trust	10
Albemarle Corp.	13	Cullen/Frost Bankers, Inc.	14
Alexandria Real Estate Equities	10	Danaher Corp.	14
Allstate Corp.	14	Developers Diversified Realty Corp.	14
Altria Group Inc	42	Diebold, Inc.	54
Ambac Financial Group, Inc.	16	Donaldson Co. Inc.	12
American International Group Inc	22	Dover Corp	52
American States Water Co.	54	Duke Realty Corp.	14
Anheuser-Busch Cos., Inc.	33	EastGroup Properties, Inc.	15
AptarGroup Inc.	14	Eaton Vance Corp	26
Aqua America Inc	16	Ecolab, Inc.	15
Archer Daniels Midland Co.	33	Emerson Electric Co.	51
Astoria Financial Corp.	12	Energen Corp.	25
AT&T Inc	23	Energy East Corp.	10
Atmos Energy Corp.	20	Essex Property Trust, Inc.	13
Automatic Data Processing Inc.	32	Exxon Mobil Corp.	25
Avery Dennison Corp.	32	F.N.B. Corp	35
Avon Products, Inc.	17	Family Dollar Stores, Inc.	31
BancorpSouth Inc.	21	Federal Realty Invest. Trust	40
Bank of America Corp.	30	Forest City Enterprises, Inc.	13
Bank of Hawaii Corp	30	FPL Group, Inc.	12
BankAtlantic Bancorp, Inc.	11	Franklin Resources, Inc.	18
Bard (C.R.), Inc.	36	Fuller (H.B.) Company	40
BB&T Corp.	36	Gallagher (Arthur J.) & Co.	23
Beckman Coulter, Inc.	16	Gannett Co Inc	36
Becton, Dickinson and Co.	35	General Dynamics Corp.	16
Bemis Co Inc	24	General Electric Co	32
Black Hills Corporation	36	General Growth Properties, Inc.	14
Block (H & R), Inc.	10	Genuine Parts Co.	51
Brady Corp.	23	Grainger (W.W.) Inc.	36
Brown & Brown, Inc.	14	Harley-Davidson Inc	14
Brown-Forman Corp.	23	Harsco Corp.	13
Buckeye Partners, L.P.	12	Harte-Hanks, Inc.	12
California Water Service Group	40	Hartford Financial Services Group	11
Cardinal Health, Inc.	11	HCC Insurance Holdings, Inc.	11
Carlisle Companies Inc.	31	HCP, Inc.	22
Caterpillar Inc.	14	Helmerich & Payne Inc.	31
Cato Corp.	10	Hershey Company	33
CBL & Associates Properties, Inc.	12	Hilb Rogal & Hobbs Co	21
Cedar Fair, L.P.	20	Hillenbrand Industries, Inc.	37
CenturyTel, Inc.	34	HNI Corp	19
Chevron Corporation	20	Holly Corp.	14
Chubb Corp.	43	Home Depot Inc	20
Church & Dwight Co., Inc.	11	Home Properties Inc	13
Citigroup Inc	21	Hormel Foods Corp.	41
City National Corp.	13	Horton (D.R.) Inc.	10
Clarcor Inc.	27	Illinois Tool Works, Inc.	45
Clorox Co.	31	Integrys Energy Group Inc	49
Coca-Cola Co	45	International Business Machines Corp.	12
Colgate-Palmolive Co.	45	Irwin Financial Corp.	18
Colonial BancGroup Inc.	12	Johnson & Johnson	45
Comerica, Inc.	24	Johnson Controls Inc	32

The 2008 Common Dividend Achievers (Cont.)

Company Name	Years of Growth	Company Name	Years of Growth
KeyCorp	28	Realty Income Corp.	13
Kimberly-Clark Corp.	33	Regency Centers Corp.	13
Kimco Realty Corp.	15	RLI Corp.	31
Kinder Morgan Energy Partners, L.P.	11	Rohm & Haas Co.	30
La-Z-Boy Inc.	26	Roper Industries, Inc	15
Legg Mason, Inc.	24	RPM International Inc	34
Leggett & Platt, Inc.	36	Sherwin-Williams Co.	28
Lehman Brothers Holdings Inc	11	SJW Corp.	40
Lexington Realty Trust	13	Smith (A.O.) Corp	15
Liberty Property Trust	13	Sonoco Products Co.	24
Lilly (Eli) & Co.	40	Sovran Self Storage, Inc.	12
Lincoln National Corp.	24	Stanley Works	40
Lowe's Companies Inc	46	State Street Corp.	27
M & T Bank Corp	27	Stepan Co.	40
Macerich Co.	13	Stryker Corp.	15
Marshall & Ilsley Corp.	35	SunTrust Banks, Inc.	22
Martin Marietta Materials, Inc.	13	SUPERVALU INC	35
Masco Corp.	49	Synovus Financial Corp.	31
MBIA Inc.	20	Sysco Corp.	31
McCormick & Co., Inc.	21	Talbots, Inc.	13
McDonald's Corp	31	Tanger Factory Outlet Centers, Inc.	14
McGraw-Hill Cos., Inc.	34	Target Corp	36
MDU Resources Group Inc.	17	Taubman Centers, Inc.	11
Media General, Inc.	13	TCF Financial Corp.	16
Medtronic, Inc.	30	Teleflex Incorporated	30
Mercury General Corp.	21	Tennant Co.	35
Meredith Corp.	14	TEPPCO Partners, L.P.	15
Mine Safety Appliances Co	37	TJX Companies, Inc.	11
Myers Industries Inc.	31	Tootsie Roll Industries Inc	44
NACCO Industries Inc.	24	Total System Services, Inc.	10
National City Corp	15	Transatlantic Holdings, Inc.	17
National Fuel Gas Co.	36	U.S. Bancorp	36
National Retail Properties Inc	18	UDR, Inc.	22
Nationwide Financial Services Inc.	10	UGI Corp.	20
New Jersey Resources Corp	12	United Technologies Corp.	14
New York Times Co.	12	Universal Corp.	37
Nordstrom, Inc.	11	Universal Health Realty Inc. Trust	20
Northwest Natural Gas Co.	52	Valley National Bancorp	16
Nucor Corp.	35	Valspar Corp.	29
Old National Bancorp	24	Vectren Corp	32
Old Republic International Corp.	26	VF Corp.	35
Owens & Minor, Inc.	10	Vornado Realty Trust	14
Parker Hannifin Corp	51	Vulcan Materials Co.	15
Pentair, Inc.	31	Walgreen Co.	32
PepsiCo Inc.	36	Wal-Mart Stores, Inc.	32
Pfizer Inc	40	Washington Mutual Inc.	18
Piedmont Natural Gas Co., Inc.	28	Wash. Real Estate Invest. Trust	38
Pinnacle West Capital Corp.	14	Webster Financial Corp	15
Pitney Bowes Inc	24	Weingarten Realty Investors	19
Polaris Industries Inc.	12	Wells Fargo & Co.	20
PPG Industries, Inc.	36	West Pharmaceutical Services, Inc.	15
Praxair, Inc.	15	WGL Holdings, Inc.	31
Procter & Gamble Co.	54	Wiley (John) & Sons Inc.	14
Progress Energy Inc.	19	Wilmington Trust Corp.	26
ProLogis	13	Wolverine World Wide, Inc.	14
Protective Life Corp.	18	Wrigley (William) Jr. Co.	27
Questar Corp.	28		

ABBOTT LABORATORIES

Exchange	Symbol	Price	52Wk Range	Yield	P/E	Div Acheiver
NYS	ABT	$55.15 (3/31/2008)	60.50-50.03	2.61	23.87	35 Years

*7 Year Price Score 97.36 *NYSE Composite Index=100 *12 Month Price Score 106.32

Interim Earnings (Per Share)

Qtr.	Mar	Jun	Sep	Dec
2003	0.51	0.16	0.48	0.60
2004	0.52	0.40	0.51	0.62
2005	0.53	0.56	0.44	0.63
2006	0.56	0.40	0.46	(0.31)
2007	0.45	0.63	0.46	0.77

Interim Dividends (Per Share)

Amt	Decl	Ex	Rec	Pay
0.325Q	6/14/2007	7/11/2007	7/13/2007	8/15/2007
0.325Q	9/14/2007	10/11/2007	10/15/2007	11/15/2007
0.325Q	12/14/2007	1/11/2008	1/15/2008	2/15/2008
0.36Q	2/15/2008	4/11/2008	4/15/2008	5/15/2008

Indicated Div: $1.44 (Div. Reinv. Plan)

Valuation Analysis

		Institutional Holding	
Forecast P/E	16.10	No of Institutions	
	(1/10/2007)	1114	
Market Cap	$85.5 Billion	Shares	
Book Value	17.8 Billion	1,020,984,256	
Price/Book	4.81	% Held	
Price/Sales	3.30	66.17	

TRADING VOLUME (thousand shares)

Business Summary: Pharmaceuticals (MIC: 9.1 SIC: 2834 NAIC: 325412)

Abbott Laboratories is principally engaged in the discovery, development, manufacture and sale of a variety of health care products through four business segments: Pharmaceutical Products, Diagnostic Products, Nutritional Products, and Vascular Products. Co.'s primary products are prescription pharmaceuticals, nutritional products, vascular products and diagnostic testing products. In addition, Co. has a 50.0%-owned joint-venture, TAP Pharmaceutical Products Inc. with Takeda Pharmaceutical Company Ltd. of Japan, through which Co. develops, markets and sells pharmaceutical products such as Lupron®, Lupron Depot® and Prevacid® (lansoprazole), within the U.S., Puerto Rico and Canada.

Recent Developments: For the year ended Dec 31 2007, net income increased 110.1% to US$3.61 billion from US$1.72 billion in the prior year. Revenues were US$25.91 billion, up 15.3% from US$22.48 billion the year before. Operating income was US$4.58 billion versus US$2.04 billion in the prior year, an increase of 124.2%. Direct operating expenses rose 16.4% to US$11.42 billion from US$9.82 billion in the comparable period the year before. Indirect operating expenses decreased 6.6% to US$9.91 billion from US$10.62 billion in the equivalent prior-year period.

Prospects: Co.'s near-term outlook appears constructive. For instance, on Dec 20 2007, Co. has received marketing authorization from the European Commission for the use of HUMIRA® (adalimumab) as a treatment for moderate-to-severe plaque psoriasis in the European Union. Subsequently, on Jan 18 2007, Co. announced that it has also received U.S. Food and Drug Administration approval to market HUMIRA® as a treatment for adult patients with moderate to severe chronic plaque psoriasis. Meanwhile, Co. is forecasting earnings per share of $3.20 to $3.25 for full-year 2008 and earnings per share of $0.61 to $0.63 for the first quarter of 2008, both excluding specified items.

Financial Data

(US$ in Thousands)	12/31/2007	12/31/2006	12/31/2005	12/31/2004	12/31/2003	12/31/2002	12/31/2001	12/31/2000
Earnings Per Share	2.31	1.12	2.16	2.06	1.75	1.78	0.99	1.78
Cash Flow Per Share	3.36	3.44	3.25	2.75	2.40	2.68	2.30	2.00
Tang Book Value Per Share	1.24	N.M.	2.89	2.22	2.90	1.93	1.14	4.54
Dividends Per Share	1.270	1.160	1.085	1.025	0.970	0.915	0.820	0.740
Dividend Payout %	54.98	103.57	50.23	49.76	55.43	51.40	82.83	41.57
Income Statement								
Total Revenue	25,914,238	22,476,322	22,337,808	19,680,016	19,680,561	17,684,663	16,285,246	13,745,916
EBITDA	6,673,069	3,839,982	5,763,713	5,563,387	5,154,531	5,055,978	3,285,925	4,667,059
Income Before Taxes	4,469,648	2,276,370	4,619,920	4,125,600	3,734,417	3,673,413	1,883,148	3,816,407
Income Taxes	863,334	559,615	1,247,855	949,764	981,184	879,710	332,758	1,030,430
Net Income	3,606,314	1,716,755	3,372,065	3,235,851	2,753,233	2,793,703	1,550,390	2,785,977
Average Shares	1,560,057	1,536,724	1,564,103	1,570,611	1,571,869	1,573,293	1,565,963	1,565,579
Balance Sheet								
Current Assets	14,042,733	11,281,883	11,386,028	10,734,485	10,290,415	9,121,772	8,419,189	7,376,241
Total Assets	39,713,924	36,178,172	29,141,203	28,767,494	26,715,342	24,259,102	23,296,423	15,283,254
Current Liabilities	9,103,278	11,951,195	7,415,514	6,825,644	7,639,535	7,002,202	7,926,817	4,297,540
Long-Term Obligations	9,487,789	7,009,664	4,571,504	4,787,934	3,452,329	4,273,973	4,335,493	1,076,368
Total Liabilities	21,935,384	22,123,986	14,725,932	14,441,711	13,643,084	13,594,549	14,236,991	6,712,348
Stockholders' Equity	17,778,540	14,054,186	14,415,271	14,325,783	13,072,258	10,664,553	9,059,432	8,570,906
Shares Outstanding	1,549,910	1,537,243	1,539,234	1,560,023	1,564,517	1,563,068	1,554,530	1,545,934
Statistical Record								
Return on Assets %	9.50	5.26	11.65	11.63	10.80	11.75	8.04	18.68
Return on Equity %	22.66	12.06	23.47	23.56	23.20	28.33	17.59	34.73
EBITDA Margin %	25.75	17.08	25.80	28.27	26.19	28.59	20.18	33.95
Net Margin %	13.92	7.64	15.10	16.44	13.99	15.80	9.52	20.27
Asset Turnover	0.68	0.69	0.77	0.71	0.77	0.74	0.84	0.92
Current Ratio	1.54	0.94	1.54	1.57	1.35	1.30	1.06	1.72
Debt to Equity	0.53	0.50	0.32	0.33	0.26	0.40	0.48	0.13
Price Range	59.43-48.97	49.48-39.55	49.99-37.63	46.99-36.81	44.10-32.16	53.97-29.00	53.10-39.34	52.15-27.71
P/E Ratio	25.73-21.20	44.18-35.31	23.14-17.42	22.81-17.87	25.20-18.38	30.32-16.29	53.64-39.74	29.30-15.57
Average Yield %	2.33	2.58	2.47	2.47	2.51	2.13	1.75	1.90

Address: 100 Abbott Park Road, Abbott Park, IL 60064-6400 Telephone: 847-937-6100	Web Site: www.abbott.com Officers: Miles D. White - Chmn., C.E.O. Richard A. Gonzalez - Pres., C.O.O., Medical Products	Auditors: Deloitte & Touche LLP Investor Contact: 847-937-7300 Transfer Agents: EquiServe, Providence, RI

ABERCROMBIE & FITCH CO.

Exchange	Symbol	Price	52Wk Range	Yield	P/E
NYS	ANF	$73.14 (3/31/2008)	84.51-68.15	0.96	14.07

*7 Year Price Score 132.18 *NYSE Composite Index=100 *12 Month Price Score 106.56

TRADING VOLUME (thousand shares)

Interim Earnings (Per Share)

Qtr.	Apr	Jul	Oct	Jan
2003-04	0.26	0.35	0.51	0.95
2004-05	0.31	0.44	0.42	1.11
2005-06	0.45	0.63	0.79	1.79
2006-07	0.62	0.72	1.11	2.15
2007-08	0.65	0.88	1.29	2.38

Interim Dividends (Per Share)

Amt	Decl	Ex	Rec	Pay
0.175Q	5/23/2007	6/1/2007	6/5/2007	6/26/2007
0.175Q	8/23/2007	8/30/2007	9/4/2007	9/25/2007
0.175Q	11/21/2007	11/30/2007	12/4/2007	12/18/2007
0.175Q	2/15/2008	2/27/2008	2/29/2008	3/18/2008

Indicated Div: $0.70

Valuation Analysis — Institutional Holding

Forecast P/E	N/A
Market Cap	$6.3 Billion
Book Value	1.6 Billion
Price/Book	3.89
Price/Sales	1.68

No of Institutions 341
Shares 80,101,832
% Held 91.35

Business Summary: Retail - Apparel and Accessory Stores (MIC: 5.8 SIC: 5651 NAIC: 448140)

Abercrombie & Fitch, through its subsidiaries, is a specialty retailer that operates stores and websites selling casual sportswear apparel, including knit and woven shirts, graphic t-shirts, fleece, jeans and woven pants, shorts, sweaters, outerwear, personal care products and accessories for men, women and kids under the Abercrombie & Fitch, abercrombie, Hollister and RUEHL brands. Co. also operates stores under the Gilly Hicks brand offering bras, underwear, personal care products, sleepwear and at-home products for women. As of Feb 2 2008, Co. operated 1,035 stores in the U.S., Canada and the U.K.

Recent Developments: For the year ended Feb 2 2008, net income increased 12.7% to US$475.7 million from US$422.2 million in the prior year. Revenues were US$3.75 billion, up 13.0% from US$3.32 billion the year before. Operating income was US$740.5 million versus US$658.1 million in the prior year, an increase of 12.5%. Direct operating expenses rose 11.7% to US$1.24 billion from US$1.11 billion in the comparable period the year before. Indirect operating expenses increased 14.2% to US$1.77 billion from US$1.55 billion in the equivalent prior-year period.

Prospects: For the first half of the fiscal year ending Jan 31 2009, Co. expects net income per diluted share of $1.61 to $1.65, which is a 5.0% to 8.0% growth over the first half of fiscal 2007. Co. noted that the low end of the earnings guidance reflects a negative 1.0% comparable store sales estimate for the first half of fiscal 2008. For fiscal 2008, Co. expects to increase gross square-footage by approximately 11.0% with the addition of 110 new North American, non-flagship stores including four new Abercrombie & Fitch stores, 67 new Hollister Co. stores, 17 new abercrombie stores, six new RUEHL stores and 16 new Gilly Hicks stores as well as four new, non-flagship Hollister Co. stores in the U.K.

Financial Data

(US$ in Thousands)	02/02/2008	02/03/2007	01/28/2006	01/29/2005	01/31/2004	02/01/2003	02/02/2002	02/03/2001
Earnings Per Share	5.20	4.59	3.66	2.28	2.06	1.94	1.65	1.55
Cash Flow Per Share	9.40	6.50	5.22	4.61	2.92	2.99	2.36	1.49
Tang Book Value Per Share	18.78	15.92	11.34	7.78	9.21	7.71	6.02	4.28
Dividends Per Share	0.700	0.700	0.600	0.500	...	...	...	...
Dividend Payout %	13.46	15.25	16.39	21.93	...	...	...	...
Income Statement								
Total Revenue	3,749,847	3,318,158	2,784,711	2,021,253	1,707,810	1,595,757	1,364,853	1,237,604
EBITDA	886,795	769,761	634,417	420,655	398,238	369,542	312,613	284,383
Income Before Taxes	759,325	671,986	549,412	352,853	335,342	316,385	276,522	261,453
Income Taxes	283,628	249,800	215,426	136,477	130,240	121,450	107,850	103,320
Net Income	475,697	422,186	333,986	216,376	205,102	194,935	168,672	158,133
Average Shares	91,523	92,010	91,221	95,110	99,580	100,631	102,524	102,156
Balance Sheet								
Current Assets	1,140,255	1,092,078	947,084	652,277	752,655	601,156	405,195	303,562
Total Assets	2,567,598	2,248,067	1,789,718	1,347,501	1,199,163	994,822	770,546	587,516
Current Liabilities	543,113	510,627	491,554	413,865	280,002	211,470	163,579	154,562
Total Liabilities	949,285	842,770	794,601	678,375	327,906	245,295	175,112	164,816
Stockholders' Equity	1,618,313	1,405,297	995,117	669,326	871,257	749,527	595,434	422,700
Shares Outstanding	86,158	88,300	87,726	86,037	94,607	97,268	98,900	98,796
Statistical Record								
Return on Assets %	19.81	20.57	21.35	17.04	18.75	22.15	24.91	29.76
Return on Equity %	31.55	34.61	40.24	28.17	25.38	29.07	33.22	42.40
EBITDA Margin %	23.65	23.20	22.78	20.81	23.32	23.16	22.90	22.98
Net Margin %	12.69	12.72	11.99	10.71	12.01	12.22	12.36	12.78
Asset Turnover	1.56	1.62	1.78	1.59	1.56	1.81	2.02	2.33
Current Ratio	2.10	2.14	1.93	1.58	2.69	2.84	2.48	1.96
Price Range	84.51-68.15	81.51-50.95	73.14-44.36	52.13-25.54	33.11-23.49	33.30-15.57	45.98-16.60	30.18-8.19
P/E Ratio	16.25-13.11	17.76-11.10	19.98-12.12	22.86-11.20	16.07-11.40	17.16-8.03	27.87-10.06	19.47-5.28
Average Yield %	0.90	1.08	1.01	1.37	...	...	...	...

Address: 6301 Fitch Path, New Albany, OH 43054
Telephone: 614-283-6500

Web Site: www.abercrombie.com
Officers: Michael S. Jeffries - Chmn., C.E.O. Diane Chang - Sr. V.P., Sourcing

Auditors: PricewaterhouseCoopers LLP
Transfer Agents: First Chicago Trust Co. of New York

2

ABM INDUSTRIES, INC.

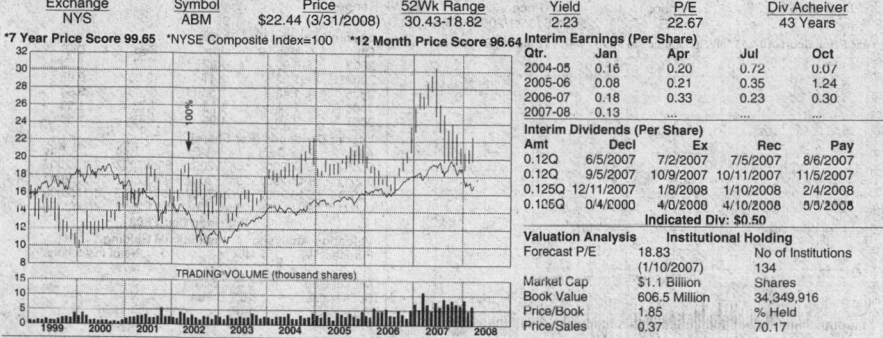

Exchange	Symbol	Price	52Wk Range	Yield	P/E	Div Acheiver
NYS	ABM	$22.44 (3/31/2008)	30.43-18.82	2.23	22.67	43 Years

*7 Year Price Score 99.65   *NYSE Composite Index=100   *12 Month Price Score 96.64

Interim Earnings (Per Share)

Qtr.	Jan	Apr	Jul	Oct
2004-05	0.16	0.20	0.72	0.07
2005-06	0.08	0.21	0.35	1.24
2006-07	0.18	0.33	0.23	0.30
2007-08	0.13	...	...	...

Interim Dividends (Per Share)

Amt	Decl	Ex	Rec	Pay
0.12Q	6/5/2007	7/2/2007	7/5/2007	8/6/2007
0.12Q	9/5/2007	10/9/2007	10/11/2007	11/5/2007
0.125Q	12/11/2007	1/8/2008	1/10/2008	2/4/2008
0.125Q	0/4/2000	4/0/2000	4/10/2008	5/5/2008

Indicated Div: $0.50

Valuation Analysis

		Institutional Holding	
Forecast P/E	18.83	No of Institutions	
	(1/10/2007)	134	
Market Cap	$1.1 Billion	Shares	
Book Value	606.5 Million	34,349,916	
Price/Book	1.85	% Held	
Price/Sales	0.37	70.17	

TRADING VOLUME (thousand shares)

Business Summary: Miscellaneous Business Services (MIC: 12.8 SIC: 7349 NAIC: 561790)

ABM Industries and its subsidiaries provide janitorial, parking, security, engineering and lighting services for commercial, industrial, institutional and retail facilities in the U.S. and British Columbia, Canada. Co. conducts business through a number of subsidiaries, which are grouped into five segments based on the nature of its business operations. The operating subsidiaries within each segment generally report to the same senior management. Referred to collectively as the ABM Family of Services, as of Oct 31 2007, the five segments were: Janitorial, Parking, Security, Engineering, and Lighting.

Recent Developments: For the quarter ended Jan 31 2008, net income decreased 26.9% to US$6.4 million from US$8.7 million in the year-earlier quarter. Revenues were US$922.6 million, up 31.1% from US$703.5 million the year before. Operating income was US$15.3 million versus US$13.5 million in the prior-year quarter, an increase of 13.7%. Direct operating expenses rose 32.2% to US$832.9 million from US$630.1 million in the comparable period the year before. Indirect operating expenses increased 24.1% to US$74.4 million from US$60.0 million in the equivalent prior-year period.

Prospects: For the fiscal year ending Oct 31 2008, Co. now anticipates earnings of $1.00 to $1.15 per diluted share, based on continued organic growth, the benefit of recent acquisitions and lower costs related to its infrastructure initiatives. In 2008, Co. is anticpating savings of about $28.0 million to $32.0 million through a reduction in workforce and back office functions, consolidation of facilities, as well as lower professional fees and other services. Meanwhile, Co. expects to attain operating margins for the Nov 14 2007 acquired OneSource Services, Inc. business along with other operations in its Janitorial segment and to realize annual cost saving of about $45.0 million to $50.0 million.

Financial Data
(US$ in Thousands)

	3 Mos	10/31/2007	10/31/2006	10/31/2005	10/31/2004	10/31/2003	10/31/2002	10/31/2001
Earnings Per Share	0.99	1.04	1.88	1.15	0.61	1.81	0.92	0.65
Cash Flow Per Share	1.30	1.10	2.66	0.76	0.69	1.23	2.26	1.38
Tang Book Value Per Share	N.M.	6.58	5.54	4.24	3.95	3.01	4.46	5.08
Dividends Per Share	0.485	0.480	0.440	0.420	0.400	0.380	0.360	0.330
Dividend Payout %	48.99	46.15	23.40	36.52	65.57	20.99	39.13	50.77
Income Statement								
Total Revenue	922,636	2,842,811	2,792,668	2,587,761	2,416,223	2,262,476	2,191,957	1,950,038
EBITDA	21,669	98,552	178,505	83,977	64,029	69,681	84,510	79,273
Depn & Amortn	6,336	...	...	...	...	...	...	...
Income Before Taxes	10,601	79,787	157,741	64,386	46,362	54,852	69,328	52,945
Income Taxes	4,237	27,347	64,536	20,832	15,889	18,454	22,600	20,119
Net Income	6,364	52,440	93,205	57,941	30,473	90,458	46,728	32,826
Average Shares	50,911	50,629	49,678	50,367	50,064	50,004	51,015	50,020
Balance Sheet								
Current Assets	680,508	642,890	631,741	521,453	486,088	500,648	437,785	465,541
Total Assets	1,628,332	1,120,673	1,016,274	903,710	842,524	795,983	704,939	683,100
Current Liabilities	386,163	289,744	319,285	275,074	254,428	256,691	227,090	235,999
Long-Term Obligations	316,000	...	...	...	...	...	...	942
Total Liabilities	1,021,860	514,915	475,027	427,784	400,363	351,947	318,269	321,923
Stockholders' Equity	606,472	605,758	541,247	475,926	442,161	444,036	386,670	361,177
Shares Outstanding	50,093	50,019	48,634	49,051	48,707	48,367	48,997	48,778
Statistical Record								
Return on Assets %	3.82	4.91	9.71	6.64	3.71	12.05	6.73	4.95
Return on Equity %	8.65	9.14	18.33	12.62	6.86	21.78	12.50	9.69
EBITDA Margin %	2.35	3.47	6.39	3.25	2.65	3.08	3.86	4.07
Net Margin %	0.69	1.84	3.34	2.24	1.26	4.00	2.13	1.68
Asset Turnover	2.34	2.66	2.91	2.96	2.94	3.01	3.16	2.94
Current Ratio	1.76	2.22	1.98	1.90	1.91	1.95	1.93	1.97
Debt to Equity	0.52	...	...	...	...	...	...	N.M.
Price Range	30.43-18.82	30.43-19.59	21.65-16.22	22.39-17.99	20.87-15.25	16.44-12.72	19.43-13.05	19.10-12.50
P/E Ratio	30.74-19.01	29.26-18.84	11.52-8.63	19.47-15.64	34.21-25.00	9.08-7.03	21.12-14.18	29.38-19.23
Average Yield %	2.02	1.96	2.38	2.15	2.20	2.56	2.23	2.08

Address: 160 Pacific Avenue, Suite 222, San Francisco, CA 94111 **Telephone:** 415-733-4000	**Web Site:** www.abm.com **Officers:** Martin H. Mandles - Chmn., Chief Admin. Officer Henrik C. Slipsager - Pres., C.E.O.	**Auditors:** KPMG LLP **Investor Contact:** 415-733-4000 **Transfer Agents:** Mellon Investor Services LLC, San Francisco, CA

3

ACE, LTD.

Exchange	Symbol	Price	52Wk Range	Yield	P/E
NYS	ACE	$55.06 (3/31/2008)	63.97-53.66	1.96	7.19

*7 Year Price Score 107.43 ***NYSE Composite Index=100** ***12 Month Price Score 103.30**

Interim Earnings (Per Share)

Qtr.	Mar	Jun	Sep	Dec
2003	0.90	1.32	1.22	1.55
2004	1.53	1.41	(0.05)	0.95
2005	1.48	1.58	(0.43)	0.64
2006	1.46	1.72	1.73	1.99
2007	2.10	1.93	1.95	1.68

Interim Dividends (Per Share)

Amt	Decl	Ex	Rec	Pay
0.27Q	5/17/2007	6/27/2007	6/29/2007	7/13/2007
0.27Q	8/17/2007	9/26/2007	9/30/2007	10/12/2007
0.27Q	11/16/2007	12/27/2007	12/31/2007	1/11/2008
0.27Q	2/27/2008	3/27/2008	3/31/2008	4/14/2008

Indicated Div: $1.08

Valuation Analysis **Institutional Holding**

Forecast P/E	N/A	No of Institutions
		N/A
Market Cap	$18.2 Billion	Shares
Book Value	16.7 Billion	N/A
Price/Book	1.09	% Held
Price/Sales	1.28	N/A

Business Summary: Insurance (MIC: 8.2 SIC: 6351 NAIC: 524130)

ACE is a holding company and, with its subsidiaries, Co. operates as a global property and casualty insurance and reinsurance organization that provides a range of products and services to commercial and individual customers in more than 140 countries and jurisdictions at Dec 31 2007. Co. operates through four business segments: Insurance - North American, which comprises its property and casualty operations in the U.S., Canada and Bermuda; Insurance - Overseas General, which comprises its network of retail insurance operations, and the wholesale insurance operations; Global Reinsurance, reinsurance operations comprising Bermuda, USA, Europe and Canada; and Life Insurance and Reinsurance.

Recent Developments: For the year ended Dec 31 2007, net income increased 11.8% to US$2.58 billion from US$2.31 billion in the prior year. Revenues were US$14.15 billion, up 6.2% from US$13.33 billion the year before. Net premiums earned were US$12.30 billion versus US$11.83 billion in the prior year, an increase of 4.0%.

Prospects: On Apr 1 2008, Co. completed its acquisition of 100.0% of the outstanding shares of Combined Insurance Company of America, a provider of specialty individual accident and supplemental health insurance products, and 14 of its subsidiaries from Aon Corp., for $2.56 billion. Co. believes that this purchase will add balance and capability to its existing accident and health business and will provide opportunity for future revenue and earnings growth. Looking ahead, while it remains focused on its strategy of sustaining growth in book value through a combination of underwriting and investment income, Co. believes that it is well positioned to manage through an increasingly difficult environment.

Financial Data
(US$ in Thousands)

	12/31/2007	12/31/2006	12/31/2005	12/31/2004	12/31/2003	12/31/2002	12/31/2001	12/31/2000
Earnings Per Share	7.66	6.91	3.31	3.83	5.01	0.19	(0.74)	2.31
Cash Flow Per Share	14.47	12.76	14.73	17.63	15.61	9.31	5.79	(1.93)
Tang Book Value Per Share	42.29	35.36	28.17	25.38	21.87	13.98	12.83	11.08
Dividends Per Share	1.060	0.980	0.900	0.820	0.740	0.660	0.580	0.500
Dividend Payout %	13.84	14.18	27.19	21.41	14.77	347.37	...	21.65
Income Statement								
Premium Income	12,297,000	11,825,000	11,748,000	11,136,474	9,602,383	6,830,504	5,917,177	4,534,763
Total Revenue	14,154,000	13,328,000	13,088,000	12,332,125	10,689,742	7,123,004	6,644,687	5,266,657
Benefits & Claims	7,519,000	7,193,000	8,714,000	7,886,247	6,298,479	5,064,628	4,953,685	2,936,065
Income Before Taxes	3,153,000	2,823,000	1,301,000	1,414,772	1,695,829	(39,139)	(202,418)	636,890
Income Taxes	575,000	522,000	273,000	275,683	278,347	(115,688)	(78,674)	93,908
Net Income	2,578,000	2,305,000	1,028,000	1,139,089	1,417,482	76,549	(146,414)	542,982
Average Shares	330,447	327,232	297,299	285,485	275,655	269,870	233,799	227,418
Balance Sheet								
Total Assets	72,090,000	67,135,000	62,440,000	56,342,436	49,552,793	43,450,937	37,186,764	31,689,526
Total Liabilities	55,413,000	52,857,000	50,628,000	46,506,624	40,717,997	36,751,201	30,769,007	25,958,265
Stockholders' Equity	16,677,000	14,278,000	11,812,000	9,835,812	8,834,796	6,388,686	6,106,707	5,420,211
Shares Outstanding	329,704	326,455	323,322	284,478	279,897	262,679	259,861	232,346
Statistical Record								
Return on Assets %	3.70	3.56	1.73	2.15	3.05	0.19	N.M.	1.75
Return on Equity %	16.66	17.67	9.50	12.17	18.62	1.23	N.M.	10.97
Loss Ratio %	61.14	60.83	74.17	70.81	65.59	74.15	83.72	64.75
Net Margin %	18.21	17.29	7.85	9.24	13.26	1.07	(2.20)	10.31
Price Range	63.97-53.22	61.16-48.18	56.57-38.70	45.74-33.15	41.42-23.75	44.82-23.32	41.25-20.50	43.56-14.69
P/E Ratio	8.35-6.95	8.85-6.97	17.09-11.69	11.94-8.66	8.27-4.74	235.89-122.74		18.86-6.36
Average Yield %	1.79	1.81	1.95	1.98	2.24	1.90	1.61	1.73

Address: 17 Woodbourne Avenue, Hamilton, HM 08	Web Site: www.acelimited.com	Auditors: PricewaterhouseCoopers LLP
Telephone: 441-295-5200 Fax: 441-292-8675	Officers: Brian Duperreault - Chmn. Evan G. Greenberg - Pres., C.E.O.	Investor Contact: 441-299-9283

4

ADVANCE AUTO PARTS INC

Exchange	Symbol	Price	52Wk Range	Yield	P/E
NYS	AAP	$34.05 (3/31/2008)	42.26-30.31	0.70	14.93

*7 Year Price Score N/A *NYSE Composite Index=100 *12 Month Price Score 101.95

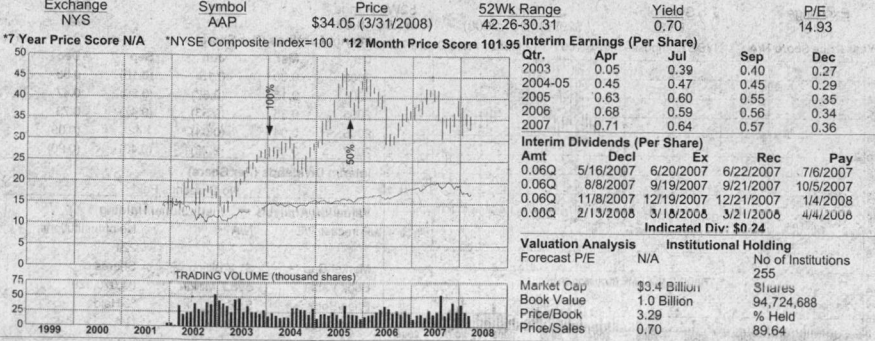

Interim Earnings (Per Share)

Qtr.	Apr	Jul	Sep	Dec
2003	0.05	0.39	0.40	0.27
2004-05	0.45	0.47	0.45	0.29
2005	0.63	0.60	0.55	0.35
2006	0.68	0.59	0.56	0.34
2007	0.71	0.64	0.57	0.36

Interim Dividends (Per Share)

Amt	Decl	Ex	Rec	Pay
0.06Q	5/16/2007	6/20/2007	6/22/2007	7/6/2007
0.06Q	8/8/2007	9/19/2007	9/21/2007	10/5/2007
0.06Q	11/8/2007	12/19/2007	12/21/2007	1/4/2008
0.00Q	2/13/2008	3/18/2008	3/21/2008	4/4/2008

Indicated Div: $0.24

Valuation Analysis

Forecast P/E	N/A
Market Cap	$3.4 Billion
Book Value	1.0 Billion
Price/Book	3.29
Price/Sales	0.70

Institutional Holding

No of Institutions	255
Shares	94,724,688
% Held	89.64

Business Summary: Retail - Automotive (MIC: 5.7 SIC: 5531 NAIC: 441310)

Advance Auto Parts is a retailer of automotive parts, accessories and maintenance items to do-it-yourself (DIY) and do-it-for-me (DIFM) customers in the U.S. Co. conducts its operations in two segments: Advance Auto Parts (AAP) and Autopart International (AI). The AAP segment is comprised of Co.'s store operations within the U.S., Puerto Rico and the Virgin Islands which operate under the trade names Advance Auto Parts, Advance Discount Auto Parts and Western Auto. The AI segment consists solely of the operations of Autopart International, Inc., which operate under the Autopart International trade name . As of Dec 29 2007, Co. operated a total of 3,153 AAP stores and 108 AI stores.

Recent Developments: For the year ended Dec 29 2007, net income increased 3.0% to US$238.3 million from US$231.3 million in the prior year. Revenues were US$4.84 billion, up 4.9% from US$4.62 billion the year before. Operating income was US$416.4 million versus US$403.4 million in the prior year, an increase of 3.2%. Direct operating expenses rose 4.5% to US$2.52 billion from US$2.42 billion in the comparable period the year before. Indirect operating expenses increased 5.9% to US$1.90 billion from US$1.80 billion in the equivalent prior-year period.

Prospects: For the fiscal year ending Dec 2008, Co. is expecting sales of $5.10 billion and earnings of about $2.55 per diluted share. This guidance is based on the prevailing economic environment where Co. believes it is prudent to forecast comparable store sales to be flat until its trends demonstrate sustainable improvement. In addition, Co.'s operating income as a percentage of sales should be about flat versus 2007, and its gross margin is expected to improve modestly from lower costs and gains from its logistics network. Co. also expects to open 100 new Advance Auto Parts stores and 15 new Autopart International stores, and to relocate 10 to 20 stores and close 10 to 15 stores during the year.

Financial Data

(US$ in Thousands)	12/29/2007	12/30/2006	12/31/2005	01/01/2005	01/03/2004	12/28/2002	12/29/2001	12/30/2000
Earnings Per Share	2.28	2.16	2.13	1.66	1.11	0.60	0.13	0.23
Cash Flow Per Share	3.96	3.15	3.01	2.39	3.20	2.32	1.21	1.23
Tang Book Value Per Share	9.72	9.20	7.88	6.67	5.70	4.37	2.94	1.84
Dividends Per Share	0.240	0.240	...	...	...	...	...	...
Dividend Payout %	10.53	11.11	...	...	...	...	...	...
Income Statement								
Total Revenue	4,844,404	4,616,503	4,264,971	3,770,297	3,493,696	3,287,883	2,517,639	2,288,022
EBITDA	564,943	545,864	531,865	431,776	347,134	312,112	176,216	173,798
Income Before Taxes	382,634	369,915	378,923	305,748	203,711	123,191	28,501	27,161
Income Taxes	144,317	138,597	144,198	117,721	78,424	47,799	11,312	10,535
Net Income	238,317	231,318	234,725	187,988	124,935	65,019	11,442	19,559
Average Shares	104,654	107,124	109,987	113,221	112,114	108,564	87,474	85,833
Balance Sheet								
Current Assets	1,682,825	1,611,973	1,547,940	1,377,427	1,226,454	1,185,472	1,135,848	897,775
Total Assets	2,805,566	2,682,681	2,542,149	2,201,962	1,983,071	1,965,225	1,950,615	1,356,360
Current Liabilities	1,225,928	1,113,420	1,141,464	961,125	853,945	722,576	693,749	579,192
Long-Term Obligations	505,062	477,173	406,040	438,300	422,780	724,832	932,022	576,964
Total Liabilities	1,781,771	1,651,827	1,622,378	1,479,647	1,351,827	1,496,869	1,662,044	1,200,089
Stockholders' Equity	1,023,795	1,030,854	919,771	722,315	631,244	468,356	288,571	156,271
Shares Outstanding	99,060	105,351	108,198	108,367	110,826	107,205	98,076	84,867
Statistical Record								
Return on Assets %	8.71	8.88	9.92	9.01	6.23	3.33	0.69	...
Return on Equity %	23.26	23.78	28.67	27.85	22.36	17.23	5.16	...
EBITDA Margin %	11.66	11.82	12.47	11.45	9.94	9.49	7.00	7.60
Net Margin %	4.92	5.01	5.50	4.99	3.58	1.98	0.45	0.85
Asset Turnover	1.77	1.77	1.80	1.81	1.74	1.68	1.53	...
Current Ratio	1.37	1.45	1.36	1.43	1.44	1.64	1.64	1.55
Debt to Equity	0.49	0.46	0.44	0.61	0.67	1.55	3.23	3.69
Price Range	42.26-30.31	44.61-28.70	47.29-28.17	30.61-22.10	27.68-12.53	20.62-13.63	15.68-13.23	...
P/E Ratio	18.54-13.29	20.65-13.29	22.20-13.22	18.44-13.31	24.93-11.29	34.37-22.72	120.64-101.79	...
Average Yield %	0.64	0.65	...	...	...	...	...	...

Address: 5008 Airport Road, Roanoke, VA 24012 Telephone: 540-362-4911	Web Site: www.advanceautoparts.com Officers: Lawrence P. Castellani - Chmn. Michael N. Coppola - Pres., C.E.O.	Auditors: Deloitte & Touche LLP Transfer Agents: Mellon Investor Services, LLC

5

ADVANCED MEDICAL OPTICS INC

Exchange	Symbol	Price	52Wk Range	Yield	P/E
NYS	EYE	$20.30 (3/31/2008)	42.90-18.83	N/A	N/A

*7 Year Price Score N/A   *NYSE Composite Index=100   *12 Month Price Score 79.42

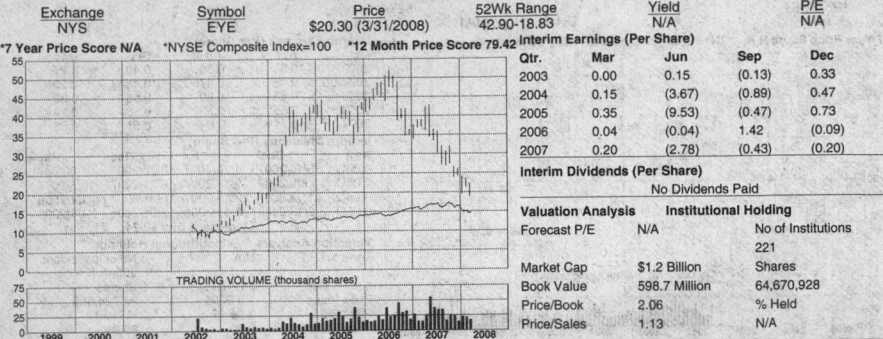

Interim Earnings (Per Share)

Qtr.	Mar	Jun	Sep	Dec
2003	0.00	0.15	(0.13)	0.33
2004	0.15	(3.67)	(0.89)	0.47
2005	0.35	(9.53)	(0.47)	0.73
2006	0.04	(0.04)	1.42	(0.09)
2007	0.20	(2.78)	(0.43)	(0.20)

Interim Dividends (Per Share)

No Dividends Paid

Valuation Analysis — **Institutional Holding**

Forecast P/E	N/A	No of Institutions 221
Market Cap	$1.2 Billion	Shares
Book Value	598.7 Million	64,670,928
Price/Book	2.06	% Held
Price/Sales	1.13	N/A

Business Summary: Medical Instruments & Equipment (MIC: 9.6 SIC: 3841 NAIC: 339112)

Advanced Medical Optics is engaged in the development, manufacture and marketing of medical devices for the eye. As of Dec 31 2007, Co. had three product lines: cataract / implant, laser vision correction, and eye care. In the cataract and implant market, Co. focuses on the four products required for cataract surgery: foldable intraocular lenses, implantation systems, phacoemulsification systems and viscoelastics. In the laser vision correction market, Co. markets lasers systems, diagnostic devices, treatment cards and disposable patient interfaces. Co.'s eye care product line provides a range of contact lens care products for use with most contact lenses.

Recent Developments: For the year ended Dec 31 2007, net loss amounted to US$192.9 million versus net income of US$79.5 million in the prior year. Revenues were US$1.09 billion, up 9.4% from US$997.5 million the year before. Operating loss was US$100.1 million versus an income of US$197.7 million in the prior year. Direct operating expenses rose 25.2% to US$475.0 million from US$379.3 million in the comparable period the year before. Indirect operating expenses increased 70.3% to US$715.9 million from US$420.4 million in the equivalent prior-year period.

Prospects: For 2008, Co. now expects revenues of $1.22 billion to $1.24 billion versus $1.23 billion to $1.25 billion previously. Co.'s estimate assumes a decline in its 2008 U.S. excimer procedures of approximately 10.0% and a more modest rate of growth for its U.S. femtosecond procedure and refractive intraocular lenses sales than previously expected. Separately, Co. has announced plans to reduce its fixed costs, including workforce reduction and plans to consolidate certain operations to improve its overall facility utilization. Hence, Co. expects savings of $4.0 million to $7.0 million in 2008 and annualized savings of approximately $10.0 million to $12.0 million upon full implementation.

Financial Data
(US$ in Thousands)

	12/31/2007	12/31/2006	12/31/2005	12/31/2004	12/31/2003	12/31/2002	12/31/2001	12/31/2000
Earnings Per Share	(3.22)	1.21	(8.28)	(3.89)	0.35	...	...	...
Cash Flow Per Share	0.87	3.55	0.38	1.19	1.65	...	...	...
Tang Book Value Per Share	N.M.	N.M.	N.M.	N.M.	N.M.	N.M.	3.92	...
Income Statement								
Total Revenue	1,090,846	997,496	920,673	742,099	601,453	538,087	543,095	570,573
EBITDA	(10,169)	245,686	(359,377)	(70,667)	57,033	74,082	101,731	101,842
Income Before Taxes	(179,953)	144,816	(440,297)	(121,216)	17,262	44,572	75,944	68,200
Income Taxes	12,996	65,345	12,900	8,154	6,905	18,662	20,594	19,020
Net Income	(192,949)	79,471	(453,197)	(129,370)	10,357	25,910	54,959	49,180
Average Shares	59,991	65,571	54,764	33,284	29,644	...	...	...
Balance Sheet								
Current Assets	523,111	478,143	479,005	376,825	252,492	274,494	210,552	228,942
Total Assets	2,748,336	2,013,897	1,980,722	1,076,534	461,345	463,206	377,466	404,655
Current Liabilities	342,594	217,453	260,116	193,923	115,301	108,204	85,551	87,165
Long-Term Obligations	1,543,230	851,105	500,000	550,643	233,611	277,559	75,809	100,364
Total Liabilities	2,149,600	1,297,906	970,660	800,264	368,153	397,522	163,536	189,396
Stockholders' Equity	598,736	715,991	1,010,062	276,270	93,192	65,684	213,930	215,259
Shares Outstanding	60,644	59,510	67,830	37,068	29,377	28,720	28,723	...
Statistical Record								
Return on Assets %	N.M.	3.98	N.M.	N.M.	2.24	6.16	14.05	...
Return on Equity %	N.M.	9.21	N.M.	N.M.	13.04	18.53	25.61	...
EBITDA Margin %	N.M.	24.63	N.M.	N.M.	9.48	13.77	18.73	17.85
Net Margin %	N.M.	7.97	N.M.	N.M.	1.72	4.82	10.12	8.62
Asset Turnover	0.46	0.50	0.60	0.96	1.30	1.28	1.39	...
Current Ratio	1.53	2.20	1.84	1.94	2.19	2.54	2.46	2.63
Debt to Equity	2.58	1.19	0.50	1.99	2.51	4.23	0.35	0.47
Price Range	42.90-23.82	52.04-34.77	44.26-32.84	42.95-19.65	20.17-11.50	12.16-8.15	...	...
P/E Ratio	...	43.01-28.74	...	...	57.63-32.86	...	...	...

Address: 1700 E. St. Andrew Place, Santa Ana, CA 92705 Telephone: 714-247-8200	Web Site: www.amo-inc.com Officers: William R. Grant - Chmn. James V. Mazzo - Pres., C.E.O.	Auditors: PricewaterhouseCoopers LLP Investor Contact: 714-247-8465 Transfer Agents: Mellon Investor Services, LLC, Ridgefield Park, NJ

ADVANCED MICRO DEVICES, INC.

Exchange	Symbol	Price	52Wk Range	Yield	P/E
NYS	AMD	$5.89 (3/31/2008)	15.84-5.53	N/A	N/A

*7 Year Price Score 56.10   *NYSE Composite Index=100   *12 Month Price Score 63.99

TRADING VOLUME (thousand shares)

Interim Earnings (Per Share)

Qtr.	Mar	Jun	Sep	Dec
2003	(0.42)	(0.40)	(0.09)	0.13
2004	0.12	0.09	0.12	(0.07)
2005	(0.04)	0.03	0.18	0.23
2006	0.38	0.18	0.27	(1.16)
2007	(1.11)	(1.09)	(0.71)	(3.14)

Interim Dividends (Per Share)

No Dividends Paid

Valuation Analysis

		Institutional Holding	
Forecast P/E	12.17	No of Institutions	
	(1/10/2007)	359	
Market Cap	$3.6 Billion	Shares	
Book Value	3.0 Billion	410,510,592	
Price/Book	1.19	% Held	
Price/Sales	0.59	73.98	

Business Summary: IT & Technology (MIC: 10.2 SIC: 3674 NAIC: 334413)

Advanced Micro Devices is a global semiconductor company that provides processing services for the computing, graphics and consumer electronics markets. Co. provides x86 microprocessors for the commercial and consumer markets, embedded microprocessors for commercial, commercial client and consumer markets and chipsets for desktop and notebook personal computers (PCs), professional workstations and servers; graphics, video and multimedia products for desktop and notebook computers, including home media PCs, professional workstations and servers; and products for consumer electronic devices such as mobile phones and digital televisions and technology for game consoles.

Recent Developments: For the year ended Dec 29 2007, net loss amounted to US$3.38 billion versus a net loss of US$166.0 million in the prior year. Revenues were US$6.01 billion, up 6.4% from US$5.65 billion the year before. Operating loss was US$2.87 billion versus a loss of US$47.0 million in the prior year. Direct operating expenses rose 31.3% to US$3.75 billion from US$2.86 billion in the comparable period the year before. Indirect operating expenses increased 80.5% to US$5.13 billion from US$2.84 billion in the equivalent prior-year period.

Prospects: For the fiscal quarter ending Mar 2008, Co. anticipates revenue to decrease in line with seasonality. Nevertheless, Co. remains encouraged with its near-term outlook as it continues to focus on its strategy to develop new products to address market and customer requirements. For instance, on Feb 27 2008, Co. announced collaboration with Microsoft® to combine Co.'s Opteron™ processors with Microsoft's Windows Server® 2008 to meet the demands of global digital economy and computing requirements of businesses of all sizes. Meanwhile, Co. expects to ship a higher volume of its quad-core Opteron processors, which it introduced in Aug 2007, during the first half of 2008.

Financial Data

(US$ in Thousands)	12/29/2007	12/31/2006	12/25/2005	12/26/2004	12/28/2003	12/29/2002	12/30/2001	12/31/2000
Earnings Per Share	(6.06)	(0.34)	0.40	0.25	(0.79)	(3.81)	(0.18)	2.89
Cash Flow Per Share	(0.56)	2.57	3.72	3.04	0.85	(0.26)	0.51	3.83
Tang Book Value Per Share	0.82	2.49	7.70	7.68	6.96	7.16	10.64	10.10
Income Statement								
Total Revenue	6,013,000	5,649,000	5,847,577	5,001,435	3,519,168	2,697,029	3,891,754	4,644,187
EBITDA	...	704,000	...	1,415,561	808,454	(472,475)	547,316	1,831,778
Income Before Taxes	...	(143,000)	...	96,994	(277,467)	(1,264,603)	(93,923)	1,251,899
Income Taxes	23,000	23,000	(6,642)	5,838	2,936	44,586	(14,463)	256,868
Net Income	(3,379,000)	(166,000)	165,483	91,156	(274,490)	(1,303,012)	(60,581)	983,026
Average Shares	558,000	492,000	440,776	371,066	346,934	342,334	332,407	350,000
Balance Sheet								
Current Assets	3,816,000	3,963,000	3,558,836	3,227,997	2,900,278	2,019,678	2,353,109	2,657,689
Total Assets	11,550,000	13,147,000	7,287,779	7,844,210	7,094,345	5,619,181	5,647,242	5,767,735
Current Liabilities	2,625,000	2,852,000	1,821,961	1,846,376	1,452,270	1,372,079	1,313,937	1,224,109
Long-Term Obligations	5,031,000	3,672,000	1,327,065	1,628,268	1,899,674	1,779,837	672,945	1,167,973
Total Liabilities	8,560,000	7,362,000	3,935,942	4,834,157	4,656,035	3,151,916	2,092,187	2,596,068
Stockholders' Equity	2,990,000	5,785,000	3,351,837	3,010,053	2,438,310	2,467,265	3,555,055	3,171,667
Shares Outstanding	606,000	547,000	435,526	391,738	350,252	344,528	334,192	314,137
Statistical Record								
Return on Assets %	N.M.	N.M.	2.19	1.22	N.M.	N.M.	N.M.	19.07
Return on Equity %	N.M.	N.M.	5.22	3.36	N.M.	N.M.	N.M.	37.55
EBITDA Margin %	...	12.46	...	28.30	22.97	N.M.	14.06	39.44
Net Margin %	N.M.	N.M.	2.83	1.82	N.M.	N.M.	N.M.	21.17
Asset Turnover	0.49	0.54	0.77	0.67	0.56	0.48	0.68	0.90
Current Ratio	1.45	1.39	1.95	1.75	2.00	1.47	1.79	2.17
Debt to Equity	1.68	0.63	0.40	0.54	0.78	0.72	0.19	0.37
Price Range	20.18-7.32	42.10-17.39	30.50-14.16	24.85-10.86	18.29-4.94	20.00-3.20	34.40-7.93	47.50-13.69
P/E Ratio	...	...	76.25-35.40	99.40-43.44	...	...	...	16.44-4.74

Address: One AMD Place, Sunnyvale, CA 94088-3453	Web Site: www.amd.com	Auditors: Ernst & Young LLP
Telephone: 408-749-4000	Officers: Hector de J. Ruiz - Chmn., Pres., C.E.O.	Transfer Agents: First National Bank of Boston, Boston, Ma
Fax: 408-982-6161	Robert R. Herb - Exec. V.P., Chief Sales & Mktg. Officer	

AEROPOSTALE INC

Exchange	Symbol	Price	52Wk Range	Yield	P/E
NYS	ARO	$27.11 (3/31/2008)	31.65-18.37	N/A	15.67

*7 Year Price Score N/A   *NYSE Composite Index=100   *12 Month Price Score 112.85

TRADING VOLUME (thousand shares)

Interim Earnings (Per Share)

Qtr.	Apr	Jul	Oct	Jan
2003-04	0.02	0.03	0.25	0.32
2004-05	0.07	0.13	0.37	0.41
2005-06	0.10	0.09	0.31	0.50
2006-07	0.10	0.11	0.41	0.71
2007-08	0.17	0.19	0.48	0.89

Interim Dividends (Per Share)

Amt	Decl	Ex	Rec	Pay
50%	3/11/2004	4/27/2004	4/12/2004	4/26/2004
50%	7/11/2007	8/22/2007	8/6/2007	8/21/2007

Valuation Analysis   Institutional Holding

Forecast P/E	N/A	No of Institutions 201
Market Cap	$1.8 Billion	Shares 55,463,976
Book Value	197.3 Million	% Held
Price/Book	9.16	N/A
Price/Sales	1.14	

Business Summary: Retail - Apparel and Accessory Stores (MIC: 5.8 SIC: 5621 NAIC: 448120)

Aeropostale is a mall-based, specialty retailer of casual apparel and accessories. Co. designs, markets and sells its own brand of merchandise primarily targeting 14 to 17 year-old young women and young men. Co. maintains control over its proprietary brands by designing and sourcing all of its merchandise. Co.'s products are sold only at its stores and online through its e-commerce website, www.aeropostale.com. Co. also operates Jimmy'Z Surf Co., Inc., a California lifestyle-oriented brand targeting young women and men aged 18 to 25. At Feb 2 2008, Co. operated 828 stores, consisting of 802 Aéropostale stores in 47 states, 12 Aéropostale stores in Canada, and 14 Jimmy'Z stores in 11 states.

Recent Developments: For the year ended Feb 2 2008, net income increased 21.1% to US$129.2 million from US$106.6 million in the prior year. Revenues were US$1.59 billion, up 12.6% from US$1.41 billion the year before. Operating income was US$202.5 million versus US$167.8 million in the prior year, an increase of 20.7%. Direct operating expenses rose 8.3% to US$1.04 billion from US$957.8 million in the comparable period the year before. Indirect operating expenses increased 21.9% to US$350.8 million from US$287.7 million in the equivalent prior-year period.

Prospects: For the fiscal year ending Feb 2009, Co. expects to attain earnings per share growth of approximately 18.0%, with expected net earnings for the first quarter of fiscal 2008 of $0.20 to $0.22 per share compared with $0.18 per share in the first quarter of fiscal 2007. Meanwhile, Co. plans to invest about $80.0 million in capital expenditures in fiscal 2008, primarily for the opening of 85 new Aéropostale stores in its new store format including 15 in Canada and its first three new stores in Puerto Rico. Co.'s capital expenditure plans also include about $10.0 million to remodel 18 existing stores to its new store format and about $20.0 million for other initiatives.

Financial Data

(US$ in Thousands)	02/02/2008	02/03/2007	01/28/2006	01/29/2005	01/31/2004	02/01/2003	02/02/2002	08/04/2001
Earnings Per Share	1.73	1.32	1.00	0.98	0.62	0.36	0.37	0.13
Cash Flow Per Share	2.31	2.18	1.76	1.64	1.26	0.68	...	0.27
Tang Book Value Per Share	2.96	4.01	3.48	2.84	2.22	1.61	0.83	0.36
Income Statement								
Total Revenue	1,590,883	1,413,208	1,204,347	964,212	734,868	550,904	284,040	304,767
EBITDA	231,321	190,933	153,738	145,848	96,090	57,740	50,626	21,437
Income Before Taxes	209,003	174,830	139,101	137,368	88,956	52,153	48,525	17,979
Income Taxes	79,806	68,183	55,147	53,256	34,702	20,863	19,888	7,065
Net Income	129,197	106,647	83,954	84,112	54,254	31,290	30,269	11,319
Average Shares	74,846	80,637	83,905	85,882	87,430	85,171	81,000	79,796
Balance Sheet								
Current Assets	284,687	398,793	339,339	279,487	212,447	144,789	89,780	72,695
Total Assets	514,169	581,164	503,951	405,819	307,048	223,032	146,927	121,128
Current Liabilities	197,387	164,798	126,353	96,994	71,568	57,998	51,599	61,885
Total Liabilities	316,893	269,048	219,161	167,568	121,355	95,073	77,120	85,795
Stockholders' Equity	197,276	312,116	284,790	238,251	185,693	127,959	60,190	26,290
Shares Outstanding	66,684	77,467	81,075	83,049	83,775	79,438	72,371	72,371
Statistical Record								
Return on Assets %	23.66	19.34	18.51	23.66	20.53	16.96	...	10.38
Return on Equity %	50.87	35.16	32.19	39.79	34.69	33.35	...	52.66
EBITDA Margin %	14.54	13.51	12.77	15.13	13.08	10.48	17.82	7.03
Net Margin %	8.12	7.55	6.97	8.72	7.38	5.68	10.66	3.71
Asset Turnover	2.91	2.56	2.65	2.71	2.78	2.99	...	2.79
Current Ratio	1.44	2.42	2.69	2.88	2.97	2.50	1.74	1.17
Price Range	31.65-18.37	24.51-14.28	23.31-12.21	22.50-13.54	15.13-4.40	12.65-2.38	...	...
P/E Ratio	18.30-10.62	18.57-10.82	23.31-12.21	22.96-13.82	24.40-7.09	35.14-6.60	...	...

Address: 1372 Broadway, 8th Floor, New York, NY 10018 Telephone: 646-485-5398	Web Site: www.aeropostale.com Officers: Julian R. Geiger - Chmn., C.E.O. John S. Mills - Pres., C.O.O.	Auditors: Deloitte & Touche LLP Transfer Agents: American Stock Transfer & Trust Company, New York, NY

AES CORP.

Exchange	Symbol	Price	52Wk Range	Yield	P/E
NYS	AES	$16.67 (3/31/2008)	23.90-15.98	N/A	N/A

*7 Year Price Score 109.54 *NYSE Composite Index=100 *12 Month Price Score 94.59

TRADING VOLUME (thousand shares)

Interim Earnings (Per Share)

Qtr.	Mar	Jun	Sep	Dec
2003	0.17	(0.22)	0.12	(0.74)
2004	0.08	0.06	0.21	0.25
2005	0.20	0.13	0.37	0.27
2006	0.52	0.25	(0.52)	0.12
2007	(0.67)	0.36	0.15	0.03

Interim Dividends (Per Share)

No Dividends Paid

Valuation Analysis		Institutional Holding	
Forecast P/E	15.01	No of Institutions	
	(1/10/2007)	389	
Market Cap	$11.2 Billion	Shares	
Book Value	3.2 Billion	541,745,664	
Price/Book	3.53	% Held	
Price/Sales	0.82	81.57	

Business Summary: Electricity (MIC: 7.1 SIC: 4911 NAIC: 221121)

AES is a global power holding company. Co. owned a portfolio of electricity generation and distribution businesses on five continents and in 28 countries, with generation capacity totaling approximately 43,000 megawatts and distribution networks serving over 11 million people as of Dec 31 2007. Co. has two main types of businesses: The Generation business, where it owns and/or operates power plants to generate and sell power to wholesale customers such as utilities and other intermediaries, and The Utilities business, where it owns and/or operates utilities to distribute, transmit and sell electricity to end-user customers in the residential, commercial, industrial and governmental sectors.

Recent Developments: For the year ended Dec 31 2007, income from continuing operations increased 181.3% to US$495.0 million from US$176.0 million a year earlier. Net loss amounted to US$95.0 million versus net income of US$247.0 million in the prior year. Revenues were US$13.59 billion, up 17.4% from US$11.58 billion the year before. Direct operating expenses rose 25.0% to US$10.18 billion from US$8.14 billion in the comparable period the year before. Indirect operating expenses increased 147.5% to US$787.0 million from US$318.0 million in the equivalent prior-year period.

Prospects: On Feb 5 2008, Co. announced an agreement to sell its interests in its Ekibastuz power plant and Maikuben West coal mine to Kazakhmys PLC, a producer of copper, for about $1.48 billion. The agreement reflects Co.'s focus on portfolio management and efforts to maintain its presence in the growing Kazakhstan market. Co. expects to close the sale in the second quarter of 2008. Meanwhile, in Feb 2008, Co. signed an agreement with National Power Corp., a state owned utility, to purchase a 600 megawatt coal-fired generation facility in Masinloc, Philippines for $930.0 million; and expects to close in Apr 2008. For 2008, Co. expects earnings from continuing operations of $2.43 per diluted share.

Financial Data

(US$ in Thousands)	12/31/2007	12/31/2006	12/31/2005	12/31/2004	12/31/2003	12/31/2002	12/31/2001	12/31/2000
Earnings Per Share	(0.14)	0.39	0.95	0.60	(0.67)	(6.51)	0.51	1.40
Cash Flow Per Share	3.53	3.65	3.31	2.44	2.65	2.68	3.18	1.04
Tang Book Value Per Share	1.85	1.97	0.34	0.41	N.M.	...	4.25	4.97
Income Statement								
Total Revenue	13,588,000	12,299,000	11,086,000	9,486,000	8,415,000	8,632,000	9,327,000	6,691,000
EBITDA	3,844,000	3,591,000	3,852,000	3,353,000	3,127,000	(95,000)	3,126,000	2,900,000
Income Before Taxes	1,614,000	1,299,000	1,458,000	884,000	640,000	(2,651,000)	802,000	1,019,000
Income Taxes	685,000	403,000	465,000	249,000	194,000	(27,000)	230,000	252,000
Net Income	(95,000)	261,000	630,000	386,000	(403,000)	(3,509,000)	273,000	641,000
Average Shares	678,000	672,000	664,600	646,400	597,900	538,900	543,500	473,100
Balance Sheet								
Current Assets	8,336,000	6,565,000	5,232,000	4,938,000	4,886,000	4,349,000	4,653,000	5,573,000
Total Assets	34,453,000	31,163,000	29,432,000	29,732,000	29,904,000	33,776,000	36,736,000	31,033,000
Current Liabilities	5,482,000	5,029,000	5,406,000	4,822,000	6,487,000	6,511,000	5,041,000	4,882,000
Long-Term Obligations	16,629,000	14,892,000	15,908,000	16,823,000	16,792,000	16,706,000	19,586,000	15,699,000
Total Liabilities	28,048,000	25,027,000	26,172,000	26,482,000	28,454,000	32,321,000	28,689,000	23,612,000
Stockholders' Equity	3,164,000	3,036,000	1,649,000	1,645,000	645,000	(341,000)	5,539,000	4,811,000
Shares Outstanding	670,339	665,126	655,882	650,093	626,000	558,000	533,000	481,000
Statistical Record								
Return on Assets %	N.M.	0.86	2.13	1.29	N.M.	N.M.	0.81	2.46
Return on Equity %	N.M.	11.14	38.25	33.62	N.M.	N.M.	5.28	17.17
EBITDA Margin %	28.29	29.20	34.75	35.35	37.16	N.M.	33.52	43.34
Net Margin %	N.M.	2.12	5.68	4.07	N.M.	N.M.	2.93	9.58
Asset Turnover	0.41	0.41	0.37	0.32	0.26	0.24	0.28	0.26
Current Ratio	1.52	1.31	0.97	1.02	0.75	0.67	0.92	1.14
Debt to Equity	5.26	4.91	9.65	10.23	26.03	...	3.54	3.26
Price Range	23.90-17.76	23.72-16.20	17.65-12.84	13.67-7.69	9.50-2.72	17.84-0.95	59.70-11.98	70.63-34.81
P/E Ratio	...	60.82-41.54	18.58-13.52	22.78-12.82	...	...	117.06-23.49	50.45-24.87

Address: 4300 Wilson Boulevard, Arlington, VA 22203 **Telephone:** 703-522-1315 **Fax:** 703-528-4510	**Web Site:** www.aes.com **Officers:** Richard Darman - Chmn. Paul T. Hanrahan - Pres., C.E.O.	**Auditors:** Ernst & Young LLP **Transfer Agents:** EquiServe Trust Co., N.A., Providence, RI

AETNA INC.

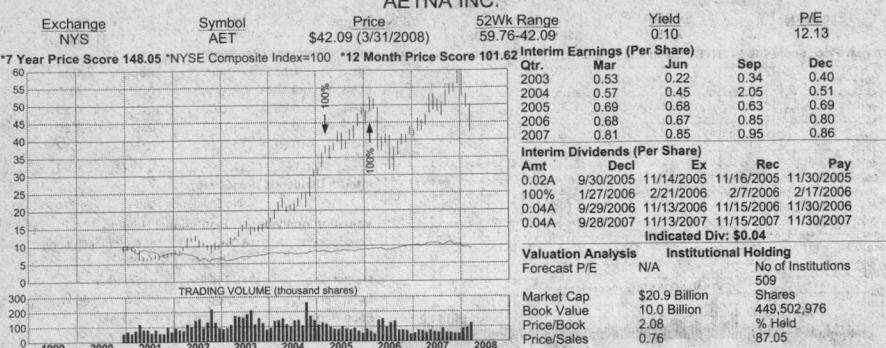

Exchange	Symbol	Price	52Wk Range	Yield	P/E
NYS	AET	$42.09 (3/31/2008)	59.76-42.09	0.10	12.13

*7 Year Price Score 148.05 *NYSE Composite Index=100 *12 Month Price Score 101.62

Interim Earnings (Per Share)

Qtr.	Mar	Jun	Sep	Dec
2003	0.53	0.22	0.34	0.40
2004	0.57	0.45	2.05	0.51
2005	0.69	0.68	0.63	0.69
2006	0.68	0.67	0.85	0.80
2007	0.81	0.85	0.95	0.86

Interim Dividends (Per Share)

Amt	Decl	Ex	Rec	Pay
0.02A	9/30/2005	11/14/2005	11/16/2005	11/30/2005
100%	1/27/2006	2/21/2006	2/7/2006	2/17/2006
0.04A	9/29/2006	11/13/2006	11/15/2006	11/30/2006
0.04A	9/28/2007	11/13/2007	11/15/2007	11/30/2007

Indicated Div: $0.04

Valuation Analysis

		Institutional Holding	
Forecast P/E	N/A	No of Institutions	
		509	
Market Cap	$20.9 Billion	Shares	
Book Value	10.0 Billion	449,502,976	
Price/Book	2.08	% Held	
Price/Sales	0.76	87.05	

Business Summary: Insurance (MIC: 8.2 SIC: 6324 NAIC: 524114)

Aetna is a health care benefits company. As of Dec 31 2007, Co. served about 36.7 million people with information and resources to help them make better informed decisions about their health care. Co. provides traditional and consumer-directed health insurance products and related services, including medical, pharmacy, dental, behavioral health, group life and disability plans and medical management capabilities. Co.'s customers include employer groups, individuals, college students, part-time and hourly workers, health plans, government-sponsored plans and expatriates. At such date, Co. operated through three business segments: Health Care, Group Insurance and Large Case Pensions.

Recent Developments: For the year ended Dec 31 2007, income from continuing operations increased 8.6% to US$1.83 billion from US$1.69 billion a year earlier. Net income increased 7.6% to US$1.83 billion from US$1.70 billion in the prior year. Revenues were US$27.60 billion, up 9.8% from US$25.15 billion the year before. Net premiums earned were US$23.48 billion versus US$21.11 billion in the prior year, an increase of 11.2%. Net investment income fell 1.3% to US$1.15 billion from US$1.16 billion a year ago.

Prospects: Going forward, Co. plans to grow the revenue in its Health Care segment via an increase membership, including efforts to reach customers via an integrated product approach in order to generate sales to new customers, as well as increased cross-sell penetration in its existing membership base and via targeted geographic marketing. In detail, Co. expects this membership growth to be a combination of both administrative services contract and Insured medical members. Meanwhile, for full-year 2008, Co. projects operating earnings to be $4.00 per share. Further, Co. expects its 2008 first quarter operating earnings to be $0.92 per share, reflecting growth of 14.0% over the same period in 2007.

Financial Data
(US$ in Thousands)

	12/31/2007	12/31/2006	12/31/2005	12/31/2004	12/31/2003	12/31/2002	12/31/2001	12/31/2000
Earnings Per Share	3.47	2.99	2.70	3.58	1.48	(4.12)	(0.49)	0.23
Cash Flow Per Share	4.06	3.09	3.27	2.37	0.61	0.51	(0.06)	2.69
Tang Book Value Per Share	8.46	7.46	8.57	8.42	6.14	4.69	4.51	4.25
Dividends Per Share	0.040	0.040	0.020	0.010	0.010	0.010	0.010	...
Dividend Payout %	1.15	1.34	0.74	0.28	0.68	...	...	...
Income Statement								
Premium Income	23,479,400	21,109,500	18,927,700	16,676,700	14,904,000	16,712,700	21,772,000	23,214,900
Total Revenue	27,599,600	25,145,700	22,491,900	19,904,100	17,976,400	19,878,700	25,190,800	26,818,900
Benefits & Claims	2,248,100	2,319,000	2,364,500	2,191,500	2,090,800	2,245,500	2,458,300	2,153,500
Income Before Taxes	2,796,400	2,586,600	2,547,400	1,898,900	1,441,600	544,800	(378,700)	(39,000)
Income Taxes	965,400	901,000	912,900	683,800	507,800	151,600	(87,200)	88,400
Net Income	1,831,000	1,701,700	1,634,500	2,245,100	933,800	(2,522,500)	(279,600)	127,100
Average Shares	527,000	569,100	604,900	628,000	632,400	611,600	572,800	565,200
Balance Sheet								
Total Assets	50,724,700	47,626,400	44,364,600	42,133,700	40,950,200	40,047,500	43,255,100	47,445,700
Total Liabilities	40,686,300	38,481,300	34,259,700	33,052,300	33,026,200	33,067,500	33,364,800	37,318,600
Stockholders' Equity	10,038,400	9,145,100	10,104,900	9,081,400	7,924,000	6,980,000	9,890,300	10,127,100
Shares Outstanding	496,300	516,000	566,500	586,011	610,094	599,864	577,063	570,474
Statistical Record								
Return on Assets %	3.72	3.70	3.78	5.39	2.31	N.M.	N.M.	0.25
Return on Equity %	19.09	17.68	17.04	26.33	12.53	N.M.	N.M.	1.22
Loss Ratio %	9.57	10.99	12.49	13.14	14.03	13.44	11.29	9.28
Net Margin %	6.63	6.77	7.27	11.28	5.19	(12.69)	(1.11)	0.47
Price Range	59.76-40.89	52.32-30.99	49.34-30.16	31.72-16.50	17.12-10.21	12.94-7.69	10.38-5.81	10.28-8.25
P/E Ratio	17.22-11.78	17.50-10.36	18.27-11.17	8.86-4.61	11.57-6.90	...	...	44.70-35.87
Average Yield %	0.08	0.09	0.05	0.04	0.07	0.10	0.13	...

Address: 151 Farmington Avenue, Hartford, CT 06156
Telephone: 860-273-0123

Web Site: www.aetna.com
Officers: John W. Rowe M.D. - Chmn., C.E.O.
Ronald A. Williams - Pres.

Auditors: KPMG LLP
Investor Contact: 860-273-7830
Transfer Agents: Computershare Trust Company, N.A., Providence, RI

AFFILIATED COMPUTER SERVICES, INC.

Exchange	Symbol	Price	52Wk Range	Yield	P/E
NYS	ACS	$50.11 (3/31/2008)	61.45-40.39	N/A	18.91

*7 Year Price Score 82.32   *NYSE Composite Index=100   *12 Month Price Score 105.02

TRADING VOLUME (thousand shares)

Interim Earnings (Per Share)

Qtr.	Sep	Dec	Mar	Jun
2004-05	0.72	0.73	0.88	0.86
2005-06	0.74	0.81	0.62	0.70
2006-07	0.59	0.72	0.82	0.37
2007-08	0.65	0.81	...	...

Interim Dividends (Per Share)

No Dividends Paid

Valuation Analysis

		Institutional Holding	
Forecast P/E	11.48	No of Institutions	
	(1/10/2007)	328	
Market Cap	$4.8 Billion	Shares	
Book Value	2.0 Billion	80,547,044	
Price/Book	2.35	% Held	
Price/Sales	0.81	81.43	

Business Summary: IT & Technology (MIC: 10.2 SIC: 7374 NAIC: 518210)

Affiliated Computer Services is engaged in the provision of business process outsourcing and information technology services to commercial and government clients. Co.'s Commercial segment provides business process outsourcing, information technology, systems integration and consulting services to healthcare providers and payors, manufacturers, retailers, wholesale distributors, utilities, entertainment companies, higher education institutions, financial institutions, insurance and transportation companies. Co.'s Government segment includes its relationship with the U.S. Department of Education, for which Co. services federal student loans, including their Direct Student Loan program.

Recent Developments: For the quarter ended Dec 31 2007, net income increased 13.2% to US$81.6 million from US$72.1 million in the year-earlier quarter. Revenues were US$1.51 billion, up 5.9% from US$1.43 billion the year before. Operating income was US$157.9 million versus US$150.3 million in the prior-year quarter, an increase of 5.0%. Direct operating expenses rose 5.8% to US$1.33 billion from US$1.26 billion in the comparable period the year before. Indirect operating expenses increased 20.5% to US$23.5 million from US$19.5 million in the equivalent prior-year period.

Prospects: On Jan 9 2008, Co. announced that it has acquired Syan Holdings Limited, a provider of information technology outsourcing services, for $60.0 million. The acquisition should strengthen Co.'s global information technology outsourcing (ITO) presence by adding a base of U.K. operations, including two data centers. Also, on Feb14 2008, Co. announced an agreement to acquire sds business services GmbH, a provider of data center, infrastructure services, and application-related services, for $67.0 million. The acquisition enhances Co.'s global ITO presence by providing information technology operations and capabilities in Germany. The acquisition is expected to close in Mar 2008.

Financial Data

(US$ in Thousands)	6 Mos	3 Mos	06/30/2007	06/30/2006	06/30/2005	06/30/2004	06/30/2003	06/30/2002
Earnings Per Share	2.65	2.56	2.49	2.87	3.19	3.83	2.20	1.76
Cash Flow Per Share	7.68	5.75	7.37	5.18	5.80	3.61	4.12	3.14
Tang Book Value Per Share	N.M.	N.M.	N.M.	N.M.	0.30	2.37	1.94	0.11
Income Statement								
Total Revenue	3,004,525	1,493,083	5,772,479	5,353,661	4,351,159	4,106,393	3,787,206	3,062,918
EBITDA	494,666	236,905	847,278	860,480	866,388	1,010,320	651,830	488,569
Depn & Amortn	185,182	90,824	...	...	...	...	...	...
Income Before Taxes	222,465	102,111	383,413	558,313	641,071	829,183	490,947	360,456
Income Taxes	74,725	35,967	130,323	199,507	225,126	299,340	184,105	130,860
Net Income	147,740	66,144	253,090	358,806	415,945	529,843	306,842	229,596
Average Shares	100,310	100,986	101,572	125,027	130,382	139,646	143,430	137,464
Balance Sheet								
Current Assets	1,890,927	1,910,238	1,810,534	1,529,263	1,244,097	1,044,424	979,498	874,489
Total Assets	6,031,621	6,079,006	5,982,429	5,502,437	4,850,838	3,907,242	3,698,705	3,403,567
Current Liabilities	960,496	922,022	970,872	825,105	838,114	637,570	557,476	485,913
Long-Term Obligations	2,364,855	2,353,097	2,342,272	1,614,032	750,355	372,439	498,340	708,233
Total Liabilities	3,981,689	3,916,205	3,916,261	3,046,219	2,012,410	1,316,755	1,269,517	1,308,147
Stockholders' Equity	2,049,932	2,162,801	2,066,168	2,456,218	2,838,428	2,590,487	2,429,188	2,095,420
Shares Outstanding	95,974	100,441	99,558	113,159	125,231	142,581	133,207	132,024
Statistical Record								
Return on Assets %	4.47	4.40	4.41	6.93	9.50	13.89	8.64	8.67
Return on Equity %	13.57	12.99	11.19	13.55	15.32	21.05	13.56	15.40
EBITDA Margin %	16.46	15.87	14.68	16.07	19.91	24.60	17.21	15.95
Net Margin %	4.92	4.43	4.38	6.70	9.56	12.90	8.10	7.50
Asset Turnover	1.00	1.00	1.01	1.03	0.99	1.08	1.07	1.16
Current Ratio	1.97	2.07	1.86	1.85	1.48	1.64	1.76	1.80
Debt to Equity	1.15	1.09	1.13	0.66	0.26	0.14	0.21	0.34
Price Range	61.45-40.39	61.45-47.45	61.45-48.00	63.46-46.74	60.76-46.85	57.46-43.00	56.17-33.88	56.75-35.48
P/E Ratio	23.19-15.24	24.00-18.54	24.68-19.28	22.11-16.29	19.05-14.69	15.00-11.23	25.53-15.40	32.24-20.16

Address: 2828 North Haskell, Dallas, TX 75204 **Telephone:** 214-841-6111 **Fax:** 214-841-8315	**Web Site:** www.acs-inc.com **Officers:** Darwin Deason - Chmn. Mark A. King - Pres., C.E.O.	**Auditors:** PricewaterhouseCoopers LLP **Investor Contact:** 214-841-8011

11

AFLAC INC.

Exchange	Symbol	Price	52Wk Range	Yield	P/E	Div Acheiver
NYS	AFL	$64.95 (3/31/2008)	65.55-47.34	1.48	19.62	25 Years

*7 Year Price Score 114.21 *NYSE Composite Index=100 *12 Month Price Score 117.23

Interim Earnings (Per Share)

Qtr.	Mar	Jun	Sep	Dec
2003	0.45	0.48	0.45	0.14
2004	0.61	0.51	0.58	0.82
2005	0.64	0.66	0.90	0.72
2006	0.74	0.81	0.73	0.66
2007	0.84	0.84	0.85	0.78

Interim Dividends (Per Share)

Amt	Decl	Ex	Rec	Pay
0.205Q	4/24/2007	5/16/2007	5/18/2007	6/1/2007
0.205Q	7/24/2007	8/15/2007	8/17/2007	9/4/2007
0.205Q	10/24/2007	11/14/2007	11/16/2007	12/3/2007
0.24Q	1/29/2008	2/15/2008	2/20/2008	3/3/2008

Indicated Div: $0.96 (Div. Reinv. Plan)

Valuation Analysis

		Institutional Holding	
Forecast P/E	12.19	No of Institutions	
	(1/10/2007)	617	
Market Cap	$31.6 Billion	Shares	
Book Value	8.8 Billion	302,908,864	
Price/Book	3.59	% Held	
Price/Sales	2.05	61.58	

Business Summary: Insurance (MIC: 8.2 SIC: 6321 NAIC: 524114)

AFLAC is a holding company that sells supplemental health and life insurance. At Dec 31 2007, Co.'s insurance operations were conducted via American Family Life Assurance Co. of Columbus, which operated in the U.S. (Aflac U.S.) and as a branch in Japan (Aflac Japan). Co.'s Aflac U.S. sells supplemental and life insurance products, including accident/disability, cancer expense, short-term disability, sickness and hospital indemnity, hospital intensive care, fixed-benefit dental, vision care and long-term care plans.. Co.'s Aflac Japan sells cancer, care, living benefit life, ordinary life insurance and general medical indemnity plans as well as medical/sickness riders and annuities.

Recent Developments: For the year ended Dec 31 2007, net income increased 10.2% to US$1.63 billion from US$1.48 billion in the prior year. Revenues were US$15.39 billion, up 5.3% from US$14.62 billion the year before. Net premiums earned were US$12.97 billion versus US$12.31 billion in the prior year, an increase of 5.4%. Net investment income rose 7.5% to US$2.33 billion from US$2.17 billion a year ago.

Prospects: For the full year of 2008, Co. is projecting growth in operating earnings of 13.0% to 15.0%, or $3.70 to $3.76 per diluted share, excluding the effect of the yen. Similarly, Co. remains encouraged by the outlook for the medical insurance market in Japan, given the continued cost pressure on Japan's health care system. Hence, Co.'s objective is to grow its Japan sales by 3.0% to 8.0%, which include the contributions from its new distribution channels, while profit margin is estimated to continue expanding. For its U.S. operations, Co. intends to improve total new annualized premium sales by 8.0% to 12.0%, while pretax operating profit margin is forecasted to remain relatively stable.

Financial Data
(US$ in Thousands)

	12/31/2007	12/31/2006	12/31/2005	12/31/2004	12/31/2003	12/31/2002	12/31/2001	12/31/2000
Earnings Per Share	3.31	2.95	2.92	2.52	1.52	1.55	1.28	1.26
Cash Flow Per Share	9.54	8.87	8.85	8.82	6.60	5.87	5.43	6.17
Tang Book Value Per Share	18.08	16.93	15.89	15.04	13.03	12.43	10.40	8.87
Dividends Per Share	0.800	0.550	0.440	0.380	0.300	0.230	0.193	0.165
Dividend Payout %	24.17	18.64	15.07	15.08	19.74	14.84	15.04	13.10
Income Statement								
Premium Income	12,973,000	12,314,000	11,990,000	11,302,000	9,921,000	8,595,000	8,061,000	8,239,000
Total Revenue	15,393,000	14,616,000	14,363,000	13,281,000	11,447,000	10,257,000	9,598,000	9,720,000
Benefits & Claims	9,285,000	9,016,000	8,890,000	8,482,000	7,529,000	6,589,000	6,303,000	6,618,000
Income Before Taxes	2,499,000	2,264,000	2,226,000	1,807,000	1,225,000	1,259,000	1,081,000	1,012,000
Income Taxes	865,000	781,000	743,000	508,000	430,000	438,000	394,000	325,000
Net Income	1,634,000	1,483,000	1,483,000	1,299,000	795,000	821,000	687,000	687,000
Average Shares	493,971	501,827	507,704	516,421	522,138	528,326	537,380	544,906
Balance Sheet								
Total Assets	65,805,000	59,805,000	56,361,000	59,326,000	50,964,000	45,058,000	37,860,000	37,232,000
Total Liabilities	57,010,000	51,464,000	48,434,000	51,753,000	44,318,000	38,664,000	32,435,000	32,538,000
Stockholders' Equity	8,795,000	8,341,000	7,927,000	7,573,000	6,646,000	6,394,000	5,425,000	4,694,000
Shares Outstanding	486,530	492,550	498,894	503,608	509,892	514,439	521,615	529,209
Statistical Record								
Return on Assets %	2.60	2.55	2.56	2.35	1.66	1.98	1.83	1.84
Return on Equity %	19.07	18.23	19.14	18.22	12.19	13.89	13.58	16.00
Loss Ratio %	71.57	73.22	74.15	75.05	75.89	76.66	78.19	80.33
Net Margin %	10.62	10.15	10.33	9.78	6.95	8.00	7.16	7.07
Price Range	62.90-45.64	49.30-42.46	49.60-35.70	42.23-34.95	36.67-30.08	33.17-23.12	34.83-23.01	36.53-17.19
P/E Ratio	19.00-13.79	16.71-14.39	16.99-12.23	16.76-13.87	24.13-19.79	21.40-14.92	27.21-17.98	28.99-13.64
Average Yield %	1.50	1.20	1.03	0.96	0.92	0.78	0.67	0.62

Address: 1932 Wynnton Road, Columbus, GA 31999	Web Site: www.aflac.com	Auditors: KPMG LLP
Telephone: 706-323-3431	Officers: Daniel P. Amos - Chmn., C.E.O. Kriss Cloninger III - Pres., C.F.O., Treas.	Investor Contact: 706-596-3264
Fax: 706-596-3488		Transfer Agents: AFLAC Incorporated, Columbus, GA

AGCO CORP.

Exchange	Symbol	Price	52Wk Range	Yield	P/E
NYS	AG	$59.88 (3/31/2008)	70.78-35.96	N/A	23.48

*7 Year Price Score 171.06 *NYSE Composite Index=100 *12 Month Price Score 126.28

TRADING VOLUME (thousand shares)

Interim Earnings (Per Share)

Qtr.	Mar	Jun	Sep	Dec
2003	0.17	0.21	0.22	0.39
2004	0.33	0.54	0.38	0.44
2005	0.23	0.47	0.31	(0.66)
2006	0.19	0.45	0.06	(1.40)
2007	0.26	0.67	0.80	0.82

Interim Dividends (Per Share)

Dividend Payment Suspended

Valuation Analysis		Institutional Holding	
Forecast P/E	13.58	No of Institutions	
	(1/10/2007)	203	
Market Cap	$5.5 Billion	Shares	
Book Value	2.0 Billion	105,217,088	
Price/Book	2.69	% Held	
Price/Sales	0.80	N/A	

Business Summary: Industrial Machinery and Equipment (MIC: 11.5 SIC: 3523 NAIC: 333111)

AGCO manufactures and distributes agricultural equipment and related replacement parts globally. Co. sells a range of agricultural equipment, including tractors, combines, self-propelled sprayers, hay tools, forage equipment and implements and a line of diesel engines. As of Dec 31 2007, Co.'s products were marketed under the AGCO®, Challenger®, Fendt®, Gleaner®, Hesston®, Massey Ferguson®, RoGator®, Spra-Coupe®, Sunflower®, Terra-Gator®, Valtra® and White™ Planters brand names. Co. also provides retail financing in the U.S., Canada, Brazil, Germany, France, the U.K., Australia, Ireland and Austria through its joint ventures with Coöperatieve Centrale Raiffeisen-Boerenleenbank B.A.

Recent Developments: For the year ended Dec 31 2007, net income amounted to US$246.3 million versus a net loss of US$64.9 million in the prior year. Revenues were US$6.83 billion, up 25.6% from US$5.44 billion the year before. Operating income was US$394.8 million versus US$68.9 million in the prior year, an increase of 473.0%. Direct operating expenses rose 25.1% to US$5.64 billion from US$4.51 billion in the comparable period the year before. Indirect operating expenses decreased 7.3% to US$796.2 million from US$858.9 million in the equivalent prior year period.

Prospects: For the full year of 2008, Co. is targeting net sales to grow by 11.0% to 13.0% over its 2007 levels, while earnings are forecasted to range from $2.75 to $3.00 per share. In addition, Co. expects worldwide industry retail sales of farm equipment to increase modestly from its 2007 levels, while farm income in North America is projected to be higher, driving increased demand in industry retail sales compared with 2007. However, Co. foresees operating margin improvement due to higher sales volumes and cost reduction efforts will be restrained by its investments in higher engineering expenses, a European information system initiative and new market development and distribution enhancements.

Financial Data
(US$ in Thousands)

	12/31/2007	12/31/2006	12/31/2005	12/31/2004	12/31/2003	12/31/2002	12/31/2001	12/31/2000
Earnings Per Share	2.55	(0.71)	0.35	1.71	0.98	(1.14)	0.33	0.06
Cash Flow Per Share	5.51	4.87	2.72	3.08	1.17	0.99	3.30	2.94
Tang Book Value Per Share	12.79	7.61	5.61	5.02	6.48	4.30	5.34	8.45
Dividends Per Share	...	...	...	...	...	...	0.010	0.040
Dividend Payout %	...	...	...	...	...	...	3.03	66.67
Income Statement								
Total Revenue	6,828,100	5,435,000	5,449,700	5,273,300	3,495,300	2,922,700	2,541,500	2,336,100
EBITDA	484,900	151,500	346,000	401,500	224,200	135,500	145,000	102,400
Income Before Taxes	327,300	(19,200)	160,100	224,400	98,300	25,800	14,700	(13,900)
Income Taxes	111,400	73,500	151,100	86,200	41,200	99,000	1,200	(7,600)
Net Income	246,300	(64,900)	31,600	158,800	74,400	(84,400)	22,600	3,500
Average Shares	96,600	90,800	90,700	95,600	75,600	74,200	68,500	59,700
Balance Sheet								
Current Assets	2,721,700	2,309,000	2,086,200	2,404,500	1,684,500	1,412,200	1,182,500	1,240,300
Total Assets	4,787,600	4,114,500	3,861,200	4,297,300	2,839,400	2,349,000	2,173,300	2,104,200
Current Liabilities	2,083,300	1,623,600	1,260,400	1,359,000	929,100	785,000	642,800	636,400
Long-Term Obligations	294,100	577,400	841,800	1,151,700	711,100	636,900	617,700	570,200
Total Liabilities	2,744,600	2,620,900	2,445,200	2,874,900	1,933,300	1,631,400	1,373,900	1,314,300
Stockholders' Equity	2,043,000	1,493,600	1,416,000	1,422,400	906,100	717,600	799,400	789,900
Shares Outstanding	91,609	91,177	90,508	90,394	75,409	75,197	72,311	59,589
Statistical Record								
Return on Assets %	5.53	N.M.	0.77	4.44	2.87	N.M.	1.06	0.16
Return on Equity %	13.93	N.M.	2.23	13.60	9.16	N.M.	2.84	0.43
EBITDA Margin %	7.10	2.79	6.35	7.61	6.41	4.64	5.71	4.38
Net Margin %	3.61	N.M.	0.58	3.01	2.13	N.M.	0.89	0.15
Asset Turnover	1.53	1.36	1.34	1.47	1.35	1.29	1.19	1.06
Current Ratio	1.31	1.42	1.66	1.77	1.81	1.80	1.84	1.95
Debt to Equity	0.14	0.39	0.59	0.81	0.78	0.89	0.77	0.72
Price Range	70.78-29.18	32.93-16.31	21.89-14.74	22.82-16.25	22.89-14.41	26.15-14.92	16.85-8.00	14.38-9.69
P/E Ratio	27.76-11.44	...	62.54-42.11	13.35-9.50	23.36-14.70	...	51.06-24.24	239.58-161.46
Average Yield %	...	...	...	...	...	...	0.09	0.35

Address: 4205 River Green Parkway, Duluth, GA 30096 Telephone: 770-813-9200 Fax: 770-813-6070	Web Site: www.agcocorp.com Officers: Martin Richenhagen - Pres., C.E.O. Andrew H. Beck - Sr. V.P., C.F.O.	Auditors: KPMG LLP Transfer Agents: SunTrust Bank Atlanta

AGILENT TECHNOLOGIES, INC.

Exchange	Symbol	Price	52Wk Range	Yield	P/E
NYS	A	$29.83 (3/31/2008)	40.40-29.22	N/A	19.63

*7 Year Price Score 106.36 *NYSE Composite Index=100 *12 Month Price Score 94.27

Interim Earnings (Per Share)

Qtr.	Jan	Apr	Jul	Oct
2004-05	0.21	0.19	0.21	0.04
2005-06	5.83	0.26	0.54	0.47
2006-07	0.36	0.30	0.45	0.46
2007-08	0.31	...	...	...

Interim Dividends (Per Share)

No Dividends Paid

Valuation Analysis — **Institutional Holding**

Forecast P/E	17.33	No of Institutions
	(1/10/2007)	446
Market Cap	$11.0 Billion	Shares
Book Value	3.2 Billion	296,425,920
Price/Book	3.46	% Held
Price/Sales	1.98	73.44

TRADING VOLUME (thousand shares)

Business Summary: Instruments and Related Products (MIC: 11.15 SIC: 3823 NAIC: 334513)

Agilent Technologies provides core bio-analytical and electronic measurement applications to the communications, electronics, life sciences and chemical analysis industries. Co.'s Electronic Measurement business provides electronic measurement instruments and systems monitoring, management and optimization tools for communications networks and services, software design tools and related services, while Co.'s Bio-Analytical Measurement business provides application-focused appliances that include instruments; software, consumables and services that enable customers to identify, quantify and analyze the physical and biological properties of substances and products.

Recent Developments: For the quarter ended Jan 31 2008, net income decreased 20.0% to US$120.0 million from US$150.0 million in the year-earlier quarter. Revenues were US$1.39 billion, up 8.8% from US$1.28 billion the year before. Operating income was US$134.0 million versus US$95.0 million in the prior-year quarter, an increase of 41.1%. Direct operating expenses rose 8.1% to US$637.0 million from US$589.0 million in the comparable period the year before. Indirect operating expenses increased 4.4% to US$622.0 million from US$596.0 million in the equivalent prior-year period.

Prospects: Despite the weakness in U.S. capital markets and the potential slowdown of the U.S. economy, Co. remains optimistic regarding its near-term outlook. Looking ahead, Co.'s continued focus will be to grow revenue in the electronic measurement and bio-analytical markets by increasing its presence in new markets, expanding its existing markets with new products and channels and through strategic acquisitions. In addition, Co. intends to continue to pursue profitable growth by expanding its footprint in core/adjacent markets while seeking revenue growth opportunities. Hence, for the fiscal quarter ended Apr 30 2008, Co. is projecting revenues to be in the range of $1.40 billion to $1.45 billion.

Financial Data
(US$ in Thousands)

	3 Mos	10/31/2007	10/31/2006	10/31/2005	10/31/2004	10/31/2003	10/31/2002	10/31/2001
Earnings Per Share	1.52	1.57	7.50	0.65	0.71	(4.35)	(2.22)	0.38
Cash Flow Per Share	2.37	2.46	1.47	1.82	1.37	(0.30)	(1.26)	(0.25)
Tang Book Value Per Share	6.34	6.75	7.79	7.38	6.42	5.09	8.44	9.95
Income Statement								
Total Revenue	1,393,000	5,420,000	4,973,000	5,139,000	7,181,000	6,056,000	6,010,000	8,396,000
EBITDA	187,000	780,000	688,000	395,000	732,000	(328,000)	(812,000)	257,000
Depn & Amortn	49,000	...	...	...	...	...	...	...
Income Before Taxes	147,000	670,000	627,000	254,000	440,000	(690,000)	(1,547,000)	(477,000)
Income Taxes	27,000	32,000	91,000	155,000	91,000	1,100,000	(525,000)	(71,000)
Net Income	120,000	638,000	3,307,000	327,000	349,000	(2,058,000)	(1,032,000)	174,000
Average Shares	382,000	406,000	441,000	500,000	490,000	473,000	465,000	458,000
Balance Sheet								
Current Assets	5,070,000	3,671,000	3,958,000	4,447,000	4,577,000	3,889,000	4,880,000	4,799,000
Total Assets	7,459,000	7,554,000	7,369,000	6,751,000	7,056,000	6,297,000	8,203,000	7,986,000
Current Liabilities	2,674,000	1,663,000	1,538,000	1,936,000	1,871,000	1,906,000	2,181,000	2,002,000
Long-Term Obligations	626,000	2,087,000	1,500,000	...	1,150,000	1,150,000	1,150,000	...
Total Liabilities	4,286,000	4,320,000	3,721,000	2,670,000	3,487,000	3,473,000	3,576,000	2,327,000
Stockholders' Equity	3,173,000	3,234,000	3,648,000	4,081,000	3,569,000	2,824,000	4,627,000	5,659,000
Shares Outstanding	368,000	370,000	408,000	503,600	487,000	476,000	467,000	461,000
Statistical Record								
Return on Assets %	8.30	8.55	46.84	4.74	5.21	N.M.	N.M.	2.12
Return on Equity %	17.80	18.54	85.57	8.55	10.89	N.M.	N.M.	3.19
EBITDA Margin %	13.42	14.39	13.83	7.69	10.19	N.M.	N.M.	3.06
Net Margin %	8.61	11.77	66.50	6.36	4.86	N.M.	N.M.	2.07
Asset Turnover	0.76	0.73	0.70	0.74	1.07	0.84	0.74	1.02
Current Ratio	1.90	2.21	2.57	2.30	2.45	2.04	2.24	2.40
Debt to Equity	0.20	0.65	0.41	...	0.32	0.41	0.25	...
Price Range	40.40-30.69	40.40-30.69	36.90-25.53	32.08-19.23	35.34-18.55	24.91-10.79	35.17-10.23	63.68-17.78
P/E Ratio	26.58-20.19	25.73-19.55	4.92-3.40	49.35-29.58	49.77-26.13	...	...	167.59-46.78

Address: 5301 Stevens Creek Blvd, Santa Clara, CA 95051 Telephone: 408-553-7777	Web Site: www.investor.agilent.com Officers: Edward W. Barnholt - Chmn. William P. Sullivan - Pres., C.E.O.	Auditors: PricewaterhouseCoopers LLP Investor Contact: 650-752-5329

AGL RESOURCES INC.

Exchange	Symbol	Price	52Wk Range	Yield	P/E
NYS	ATG	$34.32 (3/31/2008)	44.12-33.80	4.90	12.62

*7 Year Price Score 100.83 *NYSE Composite Index=100   *12 Month Price Score 98.82

Interim Earnings (Per Share)

Qtr.	Mar	Jun	Sep	Dec
2003	0.85	0.29	0.34	0.54
2004	1.00	0.33	0.31	0.64
2005	1.14	0.30	0.19	0.86
2006	1.41	0.25	0.46	0.60
2007	1.30	0.40	0.17	0.85

Interim Dividends (Per Share)

Amt	Decl	Ex	Rec	Pay
0.41Q	5/2/2007	5/16/2007	5/18/2007	6/1/2007
0.41Q	8/1/2007	8/15/2007	8/17/2007	9/1/2007
0.41Q	11/1/2007	11/14/2007	11/16/2007	12/1/2007
0.42Q	2/7/2008	2/13/2008	2/15/2008	3/1/2008

Indicated Div: $1.68

Valuation Analysis   **Institutional Holding**

Forecast P/E	14.36	No of Institutions
	(1/10/2007)	237
Market Cap	$2.6 Billion	Shares
Book Value	1.7 Billion	49,325,984
Price/Book	1.58	% Held
Price/Sales	1.05	63.44

Business Summary: Gas Utilities (MIC: 7.4 SIC: 4924 NAIC: 221210)

AGL Resources is a holding company that sells, distributes, transports and stores natural gas. At Dec 31 2007, Co.'s six utilities served over 2.2 million end-use customers. Co. is also involved in several related businesses, including retail natural gas marketing to end-use customers; natural gas asset management and related logistics activities for each of its utilities and for nonaffiliated companies; natural gas storage arbitrage and related activities; and the development and operation of high-deliverability natural gas storage assets. Co. also owns and operates a telecommunications business that constructs and operates conduit and fiber infrastructure in select metropolitan areas.

Recent Developments: For the year ended Dec 31 2007, net income decreased 0.5% to US$211.0 million from US$212.0 million in the prior year. Revenues were US$2.49 billion, down 4.8% from US$2.62 billion the year before. Operating income was US$489.0 million versus US$488.0 million in the prior year, an increase of 0.2%. Direct operating expenses declined 7.6% to US$1.37 billion from US$1.48 billion in the comparable period the year before. Indirect operating expenses decreased 2.3% to US$636.0 million from US$651.0 million in the equivalent prior-year period.

Prospects: On Jan 2 2008, Co.'s subsidiary, Golden Triangle Storage, Inc., announced that it has received an order from the Federal Energy Regulatory Commission granting it a Certificate of Public Convenience and Necessity to construct and operate its proposed underground natural gas storage project in the Beaumont, TX area, and approving market-based rates for the services it will provide. Initial commercial operations are slated to begin in late 2010 to early 2011, with construction on the first cavern expected to begin in Mar 2008 or Apr 2008. Separately, assuming normal weather and average volatility in natural gas prices, Co. expects its 2008 earnings to be between $2.75 and $2.85 per share.

Financial Data
(US$ in Thousands)

	12/31/2007	12/31/2006	12/31/2005	12/31/2004	12/31/2003	12/31/2002	12/31/2001	09/30/2001
Earnings Per Share	2.72	2.72	2.48	2.28	2.01	1.82	0.45	1.62
Cash Flow Per Share	4.88	4.56	1.01	4.32	1.94	5.09	(0.32)	1.83
Tang Book Value Per Share	16.24	15.30	13.86	13.44	11.92	9.42	9.24	8.99
Dividends Per Share	1.640	1.480	1.300	1.150	1.110	1.080	1.080	1.080
Dividend Payout %	60.29	54.41	52.42	50.44	55.22	59.34	240.00	66.67
Income Statement								
Total Revenue	2,494,000	2,621,000	2,718,000	1,832,000	983,700	868,900	201,000	1,049,300
EBITDA	607,000	602,000	552,000	413,000	389,500	336,100	85,500	327,000
Income Before Taxes	338,000	341,000	310,000	243,000	222,500	161,000	38,500	138,800
Income Taxes	127,000	129,000	117,000	90,000	86,800	58,000	13,600	49,900
Net Income	211,000	212,000	193,000	153,000	127,900	103,000	24,900	88,900
Average Shares	77,400	78,000	77,800	67,000	63,700	56,600	55,600	54,900
Balance Sheet								
Net PPE	3,566,000	3,436,000	3,271,000	3,178,000	2,352,400	2,194,200	2,085,200	2,058,900
Total Assets	6,268,000	6,147,000	6,251,000	5,640,000	3,977,800	3,742,000	3,454,300	3,368,100
Long-Term Obligations	1,674,000	1,622,000	1,615,000	1,623,000	730,800	767,000	797,000	845,000
Total Liabilities	4,607,000	4,538,000	4,752,000	4,255,000	2,807,200	2,804,700	2,546,200	2,476,800
Stockholders' Equity	1,661,000	1,609,000	1,499,000	1,385,000	945,300	710,100	690,100	671,400
Shares Outstanding	76,400	77,700	77,700	76,700	64,500	56,700	55,600	55,100
Statistical Record								
Return on Assets %	3.40	3.42	3.25	3.17	3.31	2.86	0.73	3.30
Return on Equity %	12.91	13.64	13.38	13.10	15.45	14.71	3.03	13.76
EBITDA Margin %	24.34	22.97	20.31	22.54	39.60	38.68	42.54	31.16
Net Margin %	8.46	8.09	7.10	8.35	13.00	11.85	12.39	8.47
PPE Turnover	0.71	0.78	0.84	0.66	0.43	0.41	0.09	0.57
Asset Turnover	0.40	0.42	0.46	0.38	0.25	0.24	0.06	0.39
Debt to Equity	1.01	1.01	1.08	1.17	0.77	1.08	1.15	1.26
Price Range	44.12-35.81	39.70-34.41	39.10-32.25	33.59-26.80	29.21-22.08	25.00-17.94	23.16-20.00	24.48-19.17
P/E Ratio	16.22-13.17	14.60-12.65	15.77-13.00	14.73-11.75	14.53-10.99	13.74-9.86	51.47-44.44	15.11-11.83
Average Yield %	4.09	4.04	3.65	3.87	4.26	4.74	5.04	4.92

Address: Ten Peachtree Place N.E., Atlanta, GA 30309
Telephone: 404-584-4000

Web Site: www.aglresources.com
Officers: D. Raymond Riddle - Interim Chmn., C.E.O.
Kevin P. Madden - Exec. V.P., External Affairs

Auditors: PricewaterhouseCoopers LLP
Investor Contact: 404-584-380
Transfer Agents: Computershare Trust Company, N.A., Providence, RI

AIR PRODUCTS & CHEMICALS, INC.

Exchange	Symbol	Price	52Wk Range	Yield	P/E	Div Acheiver
NYS	APD	$92.00 (3/31/2008)	103.08-73.69	1.91	19.17	25 Years

*7 Year Price Score 122.30 *NYSE Composite Index=100 *12 Month Price Score 110.46

TRADING VOLUME (thousand shares)

Interim Earnings (Per Share)

Qtr.	Dec	Mar	Jun	Sep
2004-05	0.72	0.75	0.82	0.79
2005-06	0.80	0.89	0.92	0.57
2006-07	1.03	1.02	1.28	1.31
2007-08	1.19	...	...	...

Interim Dividends (Per Share)

Amt	Decl	Ex	Rec	Pay
0.38Q	5/17/2007	6/28/2007	7/2/2007	8/13/2007
0.38Q	9/20/2007	9/27/2007	10/1/2007	11/12/2007
0.38Q	11/15/2007	12/28/2007	1/2/2008	2/11/2008
0.44Q	3/20/2008	3/28/2008	4/1/2008	5/12/2008

Indicated Div: $1.76 (Div. Reinv. Plan)

Valuation Analysis   **Institutional Holding**

Forecast P/E	15.48	No of Institutions
	(1/10/2007)	567
Market Cap	$19.7 Billion	Shares
Book Value	5.6 Billion	179,196,096
Price/Book	3.52	% Held
Price/Sales	1.96	82.79

Business Summary: Chemicals (MIC: 11.1 SIC: 2813 NAIC: 325120)

Air Products and Chemicals serves technology, energy, industrial and healthcare customers globally with a portfolio of products and services that include atmospheric gases, process and specialty gases, performance materials, equipment and services. Co. is a supplier of hydrogen and helium to growth markets such as semiconductor materials, refinery hydrogen, natural gas liquefaction, home healthcare and enhanced coatings and adhesives. As of Sep 30 2007, Co. served in over 40 countries internationally and operated through six business segments: Merchant Gases; Tonnage Gases; Electronics and Performance Materials; Equipment and Energy; Healthcare; and Chemicals.

Recent Developments: For the quarter ended Dec 31 2007, income from continuing operations increased 16.3% to US$257.0 million from US$221.0 million in the year-earlier quarter. Net income increased 14.5% to US$263.7 million from US$230.3 million in the year-earlier quarter. Revenues were US$2.47 billion, up 9.1% from US$2.27 billion the year before. Operating income was US$372.0 million versus US$317.4 million in the prior-year quarter, an increase of 17.2%. Direct operating expenses rose 8.4% to US$1.79 billion from US$1.65 billion in the comparable period the year before. Indirect operating expenses increased 4.1% to US$313.1 million from US$300.7 million in the equivalent prior-year period.

Prospects: On Feb 13 2007, Co. announced an agreement with Applied Process Technology, Inc., for exclusive rights to market HiPOx™ technology in the U.S. and Canada for municipal wastewater and drinking water applications, non-exclusive access to other geographic regions, and industrial wastewater and groundwater remediation applications. Separately, on Feb 1 2008, Co. completed the sale of its interests in its vinyl acetate ethylene polymers joint ventures to its partner, Wacker Chemie AG, for $265.0 million and full ownership in the Elkton, MD, and Piedmont, SC, production facilities and their related businesses. For the fiscal year ending Sep 2008, Co. expects earnings of $4.85 to $5.00 per share.

Financial Data

(US$ in Thousands)	3 Mos	09/30/2007	09/30/2006	09/30/2005	09/30/2004	09/30/2003	09/30/2002	09/30/2001
Earnings Per Share	4.80	4.64	3.18	3.08	2.64	1.78	2.36	2.12
Cash Flow Per Share	7.86	6.86	5.96	6.10	4.84	4.72	4.90	5.05
Tang Book Value Per Share	19.04	18.53	17.44	16.03	15.45	12.99	13.33	13.67
Dividends Per Share	1.520	1.480	1.340	1.250	1.040	0.880	0.820	0.780
Dividend Payout %	31.67	31.90	42.14	40.58	39.39	49.44	34.75	36.79
Income Statement								
Total Revenue	2,473,600	10,037,800	8,850,400	8,143,500	7,411,400	6,297,300	5,401,200	5,722,700
EBITDA	615,300	2,370,900	1,930,300	1,834,900	1,687,300	1,354,000	1,495,400	1,540,000
Depn & Amortn	218,000	...	...	...	...	...	...	...
Income Before Taxes	356,300	1,376,300	1,049,300	997,700	851,400	565,400	784,500	737,000
Income Taxes	93,200	301,200	271,200	263,300	226,600	147,200	240,800	219,000
Net Income	263,700	1,035,600	723,400	711,700	604,100	397,300	525,400	465,600
Average Shares	222,300	223,200	227,500	231,400	228,900	223,600	222,700	219,300
Balance Sheet								
Current Assets	2,863,800	2,858,400	2,612,600	2,414,700	2,416,900	2,067,900	1,909,300	1,684,800
Total Assets	13,014,300	12,659,500	11,180,700	10,408,800	10,040,400	9,431,900	8,495,000	8,084,100
Current Liabilities	2,224,600	2,422,700	2,323,400	1,943,200	1,705,600	1,581,200	1,256,200	1,352,400
Long-Term Obligations	3,415,600	2,976,500	2,280,200	2,052,900	2,113,600	2,168,600	2,041,000	2,027,500
Total Liabilities	7,227,800	6,986,600	6,078,700	5,652,200	5,427,500	5,461,300	4,850,200	4,860,300
Stockholders' Equity	5,603,000	5,495,600	4,924,000	4,575,500	4,444,000	3,782,500	3,460,400	3,105,800
Shares Outstanding	214,448	215,355	217,250	221,898	227,301	227,265	227,219	227,186
Statistical Record								
Return on Assets %	8.72	8.69	6.70	6.96	6.19	4.43	6.34	5.69
Return on Equity %	19.95	19.88	15.23	15.78	14.65	10.97	16.00	15.71
EBITDA Margin %	24.87	23.62	21.81	22.53	22.77	21.50	27.69	26.91
Net Margin %	10.66	10.32	8.17	8.74	8.15	6.31	9.73	8.14
Asset Turnover	0.82	0.84	0.82	0.80	0.76	0.70	0.65	0.70
Current Ratio	1.29	1.18	1.12	1.24	1.42	1.31	1.52	1.25
Debt to Equity	0.61	0.54	0.46	0.45	0.48	0.57	0.59	0.65
Price Range	103.08-69.11	97.82-66.69	69.23-53.33	65.14-52.31	55.00-44.50	48.64-37.49	53.05-36.82	48.00-32.94
P/E Ratio	21.48-14.40	21.08-14.37	21.77-16.77	21.15-16.98	20.83-16.86	27.33-21.06	22.48-15.60	22.64-15.54
Average Yield %	1.80	1.91	2.14	2.13	2.07	2.04	1.77	1.93

Address: 7201 Hamilton Boulevard, Allentown, PA 18195-1501	Web Site: www.airproducts.com	Auditors: KPMG LLP
Telephone: 610-481-4911	Officers: John P. Jones III - Chmn., Pres., C.E.O. Paul E. Huck - V.P., C.F.O.	Transfer Agents: American Stock Transfer & Trust Company, New York, NY
Fax: 610-481-5900		

AIRGAS INC.

*7 Year Price Score 139.92 *NYSE Composite Index=100 ***12 Month Price Score 106.07**

Interim Earnings (Per Share)
Qtr.	Jun	Sep	Dec	Mar
2004-05	0.29	0.30	0.30	0.32
2005-06	0.38	0.38	0.39	0.43
2006-07	0.48	0.49	0.40	0.55
2007-08	0.63	0.60	0.67	...

Interim Dividends (Per Share)
Amt	Decl	Ex	Rec	Pay
0.09Q	5/8/2007	6/13/2007	6/15/2007	6/29/2007
0.09Q	8/7/2007	9/12/2007	9/14/2007	9/28/2007
0.09Q	10/9/2007	12/12/2007	12/14/2007	12/31/2007
0.12Q	1/29/2008	3/11/2008	3/12/2008	3/31/2008

Indicated Div: $0.48

Valuation Analysis
		Institutional Holding	
Forecast P/E	15.11	No of Institutions	
	(1/10/2007)	249	
Market Cap	$2.7 Billion	Shares	
Book Value	1.4 Billion	59,793,584	
Price/Book	2.73	% Held	
Price/Sales	0.99	76.11	

TRADING VOLUME (thousand shares)

Business Summary: Machinery Supply Retail (MIC: 12.9 SIC: 5084 NAIC: 423830)

Airgas is a distributor of industrial, medical, and specialty gases, and welding equipment and supplies. Co. is also a distributor of safety products, a producer of nitrous oxide and dry ice, a liquid carbon dioxide producer in the Southeast region of the U.S., and a distributor of process chemicals, refrigerants, and ammonia products. Co. provides these products to its customer base through multiple sales channels including branch-based sales representatives, retail stores, strategic customer account programs, telesales, catalogs, e-business and independent distributors. Co. operates through two segments: Distribution and All Other Operations.

Recent Developments: For the quarter ended Dec 31 2007, net income increased 74.9% to US$56.8 million from US$32.5 million in the year-earlier quarter. Revenues were US$1.01 billion, up 28.0% from US$787.4 million the year before. Operating income was US$118.5 million versus US$85.3 million in the prior-year quarter, an increase of 38.8%. Direct operating expenses rose 26.9% to US$479.8 million from US$378.2 million in the comparable period the year before. Indirect operating expenses increased 26.5% to US$409.8 million from US$323.9 million in the equivalent prior-year period.

Prospects: Co. is expanding its operations via strategic acquisitions. For instance, on Feb 4 2008, Co. announced that it has acquired Merriam-Graves Corp., a distributor of industrial, medical, and specialty gases and related supplies operating in 25 locations in New England and New York. The acquired business generated $47.0 million in revenues in 2007. Separately, on Jan 3 2008, Co. announced that it has acquired Pima Welding Supply Inc., an industrial gas and welding supply distributor, which had annual sales of about $5.0 million in 2007. This acquisition provides Co. with an industrial cylinder fill plant and a retail store that should improve services to customers in the Tucson, AZ area.

Financial Data
(US$ in Thousands)	9 Mos	6 Mos	3 Mos	03/31/2007	03/31/2006	03/31/2005	03/31/2004	03/31/2003
Earnings Per Share	2.45	2.18	2.07	1.92	1.57	1.20	1.07	0.94
Cash Flow Per Share	6.55	5.05	4.78	4.08	4.73	2.97	2.86	2.76
Tang Book Value Per Share	3.71	4.26	3.26	2.93	4.59	3.76	2.22	1.93
Dividends Per Share	0.340	0.320	0.300	0.280	0.240	0.180	0.160	...
Dividend Payout %	13.88	14.68	14.49	14.58	15.29	15.00	14.95	...
Income Statement								
Total Revenue	2,930,427	1,922,382	915,099	3,205,051	2,829,610	2,411,409	1,895,468	1,786,964
EBITDA	474,444	311,978	151,506	464,849	388,995	311,242	258,019	235,523
Depn & Amortn	141,142	93,070	44,472	...	...	...	...	...
Income Before Taxes	265,132	173,910	86,526	257,144	208,037	148,413	127,706	109,304
Income Taxes	102,767	68,351	34,095	99,883	77,866	54,583	47,514	41,199
Net Income	159,135	102,329	51,720	154,416	123,531	92,022	80,192	68,105
Average Shares	84,605	84,209	83,630	82,566	81,152	77,000	74,700	72,300
Balance Sheet								
Current Assets	596,979	658,614	639,619	549,499	458,516	466,257	326,830	270,582
Total Assets	3,813,288	3,798,127	3,712,742	3,333,457	2,474,412	2,291,863	1,931,079	1,700,243
Current Liabilities	478,019	475,233	439,503	427,956	475,654	333,288	242,469	208,896
Long-Term Obligations	1,493,901	1,559,812	1,598,004	1,309,719	635,726	801,635	682,698	658,031
Total Liabilities	2,440,860	2,481,597	2,518,814	2,208,075	1,527,253	1,477,691	1,239,178	1,103,310
Stockholders' Equity	1,372,428	1,316,530	1,193,928	1,125,382	947,159	814,172	691,901	596,933
Shares Outstanding	82,318	82,072	79,226	78,668	77,277	76,111	75,689	72,405
Statistical Record								
Return on Assets %	6.18	5.53	5.36	5.32	5.18	4.36	4.40	3.99
Return on Equity %	16.55	15.17	15.32	14.90	14.03	12.22	12.41	12.38
EBITDA Margin %	16.19	16.23	16.56	14.50	13.75	12.91	13.61	13.18
Net Margin %	5.43	5.32	5.65	4.82	4.37	3.82	4.23	3.81
Asset Turnover	1.15	1.10	1.07	1.10	1.19	1.14	1.04	1.05
Current Ratio	1.25	1.39	1.46	1.28	0.96	1.40	1.35	1.30
Debt to Equity	1.09	1.18	1.34	1.16	0.67	0.98	0.99	1.10
Price Range	55.27-39.31	52.05-36.05	48.23-34.11	42.91-33.79	39.58-21.58	27.05-20.83	24.35-16.75	19.68-11.87
P/E Ratio	22.56-16.04	23.88-16.54	23.30-16.48	22.35-17.60	25.21-13.75	22.54-17.36	22.76-15.65	20.94-12.63
Average Yield %	0.74	0.75	0.75	0.73	0.82	0.76	0.82	...

Address: 259 North Radnor-Chester Road, Suite 100, Radnor, PA 19087-5283 **Telephone:** 610-687-5253 **Fax:** 610-687-1052	**Web Site:** www.airgas.com **Officers:** Peter McCausland - Chmn., Pres., C.E.O. Michael L. Molinini - Exec. V.P., C.O.O.	**Auditors:** KPMG LLP **Investor Contact:** 610-902-6205 **Transfer Agents:** The Bank of New York

AIRTRAN HOLDINGS, INC.

Exchange	Symbol	Price	52Wk Range	Yield	P/E
NYS	AAI	$6.60 (3/31/2008)	12.47-5.74	N/A	11.38

*7 Year Price Score 76.59   *NYSE Composite Index=100   *12 Month Price Score 82.19

Interim Earnings (Per Share)

Qtr.	Mar	Jun	Sep	Dec
2003	0.03	0.74	0.24	0.22
2004	0.05	0.18	(0.11)	0.02
2005	(0.09)	0.13	0.00	(0.01)
2006	(0.05)	0.32	(0.05)	(0.03)
2007	0.03	0.42	0.11	0.01

Interim Dividends (Per Share)

No Dividends Paid

Valuation Analysis

		Institutional Holding	
Forecast P/E	12.22	No of Institutions	
	(1/10/2007)	169	
Market Cap	$606.4 Million	Shares	
Book Value	446.3 Million	99,200,792	
Price/Book	1.36	% Held	
Price/Sales	0.26	N/A	

TRADING VOLUME (thousand shares)

Business Summary: Aviation (MIC: 1.1 SIC: 4512 NAIC: 481111)

AirTran Holdings conducts its operations through its wholly owned subsidiary, AirTran Airways, Inc. (AirTran Airways or Airways). AirTran Airways operates scheduled airline service primarily in short-haul markets in the eastern United States, with a majority of its flights originating and terminating at its hub in Atlanta, GA. Co. serves both the leisure and business traveler, and as of Jan 23 2008, operated 87 Boeing B717-200 (B717) and 50 Boeing B737-700 (B737) aircraft offering approximately 700 scheduled flights per day to 55 locations in the U.S. Co. serves or have announced service to 52 cities from Atlanta, 29 cities from Orlando, and 14 cities from Baltimore/Washington.

Recent Developments: For the year ended Dec 31 2007, net income increased 258.0% to US$52.7 million from US$14.7 million in the prior year. Revenues were US$2.31 billion, up 22.1% from US$1.89 billion the year before. Operating income was US$137.9 million versus US$40.9 million in the prior year, an increase of 237.5%. Direct operating expenses rose 16.6% to US$1.43 billion from US$1.23 billion in the comparable period the year before. Indirect operating expenses increased 18.7% to US$739.4 million from US$622.8 million in the equivalent prior-year period.

Prospects: Looking ahead, Co. plans to mitigate the continued high fuel costs by continuing to manage its costs. For example, Co. intends to grow its network by increasing the number of flights in its markets and adding new routes between cities already in its system and service to new cities. Specifically, Co. believes that the expansion of its network should allow it to build upon its existing infrastructure, which should reduce unit costs and improve productivity. Meanwhile, for 2008, Co. expects capacity as measured by available seat miles to increase by 10.0% to 11.0% from 2007. Also, Co. expects 2008 non-fuel unit operating costs per available seat mile to be flat to down 1.0% versus 2007.

Financial Data
(US$ in Thousands)

	12/31/2007	12/31/2006	12/31/2005	12/31/2004	12/31/2003	12/31/2002	12/31/2001	12/31/2000
Earnings Per Share	0.58	0.17	0.02	0.14	1.21	0.15	(0.04)	0.69
Cash Flow Per Share	1.99	0.83	0.74	0.45	1.77	0.09	1.41	1.05
Tang Book Value Per Share	4.53	3.87	3.63	3.51	3.23	0.25	N.M.	N.M.
Income Statement								
Total Revenue	2,309,983	1,893,355	1,450,544	1,041,422	918,040	733,370	665,164	624,094
EBITDA	179,210	69,426	31,163	45,773	135,159	51,048	66,993	107,229
Income Before Taxes	87,352	25,929	2,922	20,023	87,164	9,959	1,140	47,436
Income Taxes	34,669	10,415	1,200	7,768	(13,353)	(786)	3,240	...
Net Income	52,683	15,514	1,722	12,255	100,517	10,745	(2,757)	47,436
Average Shares	104,319	92,436	90,185	89,523	86,607	73,153	67,774	69,175
Balance Sheet								
Total Assets	2,048,466	1,601,584	1,158,909	905,731	808,364	473,450	497,816	546,255
Long-Term Obligations	958,218	724,265	401,367	300,134	241,821	199,713	254,772	365,412
Total Liabilities	1,602,116	1,218,754	806,989	571,695	506,151	421,565	464,409	538,395
Stockholders' Equity	446,350	382,830	351,920	334,036	302,213	51,885	33,407	7,860
Shares Outstanding	91,886	91,160	88,791	86,617	84,209	71,132	69,528	65,823
Statistical Record								
Return on Assets %	2.89	1.12	0.17	1.43	15.68	2.21	N.M.	9.34
Return on Equity %	12.71	4.22	0.50	3.84	56.77	25.20	N.M.	...
EBITDA Margin %	7.76	3.67	2.15	4.40	14.72	6.96	10.07	17.18
Net Margin %	2.28	0.82	0.12	1.18	10.95	1.47	(0.41)	7.60
Asset Turnover	1.27	1.37	1.41	1.21	1.43	1.51	1.27	1.23
Price Range	12.88-7.16	18.41-9.39	16.42-7.50	15.17-9.67	20.76-3.90	7.32-2.64	12.01-3.03	7.25-3.75
P/E Ratio	22.21-12.34	108.29-55.24	821.00-375.00	108.36-69.07	17.16-3.22	48.80-17.60	...	10.51-5.43

Address: 9955 AirTran Boulevard, Orlando, FL 32827 **Telephone:** 407-318-5600	**Web Site:** www.airtran.com **Officers:** Joseph B. Leonard - Chmn., C.E.O. Robert L. Forano - Pres., C.O.O.	**Auditors:** Ernst & Young LLP **Transfer Agents:** American Stock Transfer & Trust Co., Brooklyn, NY

AK STEEL HOLDING CORP.

Exchange	Symbol	Price	52Wk Range	Yield	P/E
NYS	AKS	$54.42 (3/31/2008)	55.90-23.67	N/A	15.73

*7 Year Price Score 231.93 *NYSE Composite Index=100 ***12 Month Price Score 133.49**

Interim Earnings (Per Share)

Qtr	Mar	Jun	Sep	Dec
2003	(0.38)	(0.72)	(2.56)	(1.51)
2004	1.52	0.85	0.76	(0.95)
2005	0.54	0.08	(0.26)	(0.37)
2006	0.06	0.26	0.23	(0.44)
2007	0.56	0.98	0.97	0.95

Interim Dividends (Per Share)

Dividend Payment Suspended

Valuation Analysis		Institutional Holding	
Forecast P/E	7.55	No of Institutions	
	(1/10/2007)	153	
Market Cap	$6.1 Billion	Shares	
Book Value	874.7 Million	116,344,376	
Price/Book	6.94	% Held	
Price/Sales	0.87	N/A	

Business Summary: Metal Works (MIC: 11.3 SIC: 3312 NAIC: 331111)

AK Steel Holding, through its wholly-owned subsidiary, AK Steel Corporation, is a producer of flat-rolled carbon, stainless and electrical steels and tubular products. As of Dec 31 2007, Co.'s operations consisted of seven steelmaking and finishing plants located in Indiana, Kentucky, Ohio and Pennsylvania. Co.'s operations also include AK Tube LLC, which further finishes flat-rolled carbon and stainless steel at two tube plants located in Ohio and Indiana into welded steel tubing used in the automotive, large truck and construction markets, and European trading companies that buy and sell steel and steel products.

Recent Developments: For the year ended Dec 31 2007, net income increased to US$387.7 million from US$12.0 million in the prior year. Revenues were US$7.00 billion, up 15.4% from US$6.07 billion the year before. Operating income was US$624.4 million versus US$65.6 million in the prior year, an increase of 851.8%. Direct operating expenses rose 8.6% to US$5.92 billion from US$5.45 billion in the comparable period the year before. Indirect operating expenses decreased 16.5% to US$459.6 million from US$550.7 million in the equivalent prior-year period.

Prospects: For the first quarter of 2008, Co. expects shipments to be comparable to its fourth quarter 2007 shipment level of 1,568,100 tons, with a 5.0% to 6.0% increase in average per-ton selling price compared with the fourth quarter 2007 level. The higher selling prices are expected to be partly offset by higher raw material costs, particularly in carbon scrap, purchased slabs, iron ore, and purchased coke. Accordingly, Co. expects to generate operating profit of about $100 per ton. Meanwhile, Co. noted that the outlook for grain-oriented electrical steel remains very strong, with demand continuing to grow for its energy efficient products used in power generation and distribution transformers.

Financial Data
(US$ in Thousands)

	12/31/2007	12/31/2006	12/31/2005	12/31/2004	12/31/2003	12/31/2002	12/31/2001	12/31/2000
Earnings Per Share	3.46	0.11	(0.02)	2.18	(5.17)	(4.67)	(0.87)	1.20
Cash Flow Per Share	6.34	0.62	2.55	2.06	(0.66)	2.88	1.56	3.00
Tang Book Value Per Share	7.51	3.44	1.30	0.92	...	3.02	7.42	11.03
Dividends Per Share	...	...	...	...	...	0.500	0.125	0.500
Dividend Payout %	...	...	...	...	...	...	...	41.67
Income Statement								
Total Revenue	7,003,000	6,069,000	5,647,400	5,217,300	4,041,700	4,289,000	3,994,100	4,611,500
EBITDA	838,500	289,700	329,700	135,900	(422,400)	(439,400)	231,800	594,200
Income Before Taxes	591,300	(3,100)	38,000	(193,300)	(773,000)	(802,900)	(146,700)	210,100
Income Taxes	203,600	(15,100)	38,800	(223,800)	(265,900)	(327,300)	(54,300)	77,700
Net Income	387,700	12,000	(2,300)	238,400	(560,400)	(502,400)	(92,400)	132,400
Average Shares	111,900	110,500	109,700	109,200	108,500	107,900	107,700	109,600
Balance Sheet								
Current Assets	2,426,800	2,547,500	2,246,400	2,106,800	1,358,000	1,699,700	1,547,800	1,521,800
Total Assets	5,197,400	5,517,600	5,487,900	5,452,700	5,025,600	5,399,700	5,225,800	5,239,800
Current Liabilities	972,900	931,500	903,400	746,700	778,900	860,300	954,400	890,300
Long-Term Obligations	652,700	1,115,200	1,114,900	1,109,700	1,197,800	1,259,900	1,324,500	1,387,600
Total Liabilities	4,322,700	5,100,600	5,267,400	5,255,300	5,078,400	4,870,400	4,192,500	3,920,500
Stockholders' Equity	874,700	417,000	220,500	197,400	(52,800)	529,300	1,033,300	1,319,300
Shares Outstanding	111,497	110,324	109,806	109,151	108,577	107,895	107,713	107,650
Statistical Record								
Return on Assets %	7.24	0.22	N.M.	4.54	N.M.	N.M.	N.M.	2.53
Return on Equity %	60.03	3.76	N.M.	328.84	N.M.	N.M.	N.M.	10.17
EBITDA Margin %	11.97	4.77	5.84	2.60	N.M.	N.M.	5.80	12.89
Net Margin %	5.54	0.20	N.M.	4.57	N.M.	N.M.	N.M.	2.87
Asset Turnover	1.31	1.10	1.03	0.99	0.78	0.81	0.76	0.88
Current Ratio	2.49	2.73	2.49	2.82	1.74	1.98	1.62	1.71
Debt to Equity	0.75	2.67	5.06	5.62	...	2.38	1.28	1.05
Price Range	53.21-16.39	17.03-7.74	17.94-6.30	15.96-3.98	8.43-1.91	14.50-6.49	14.50-7.80	20.06-7.94
P/E Ratio	15.38-4.74	154.82-70.36	...	7.32-1.83	...	...	...	16.72-6.61
Average Yield %	...	...	...	...	...	4.68	1.13	4.83

Address: 703 Curtis Street, Middletown, OH 45043 **Telephone:** 513-425-5000 **Fax:** 513-425-5220	**Web Site:** www.aksteel.com **Officers:** Robert H. Jenkins - Chmn. James L. Wainscott - Pres., C.E.O.	**Auditors:** Deloitte & Touche, LLP **Investor Contact:** 151-342-52888 **Transfer Agents:** Computershare Investor Services, LLC, Chicago, IL

ALASKA AIR GROUP, INC.

Exchange	Symbol	Price	52Wk Range	Yield	P/E
NYS	ALK	$19.62 (3/31/2008)	38.58-18.04	N/A	6.35

*7 Year Price Score 73.04   *NYSE Composite Index=100   *12 Month Price Score 99.11

Interim Earnings (Per Share)

Qtr.	Mar	Jun	Sep	Dec
2003	(2.12)	1.70	1.52	(0.60)
2004	(1.59)	(0.06)	2.94	(1.86)
2005	(2.39)	0.56	2.71	(0.94)
2006	(2.36)	1.38	(0.44)	(0.29)
2007	(0.26)	1.13	2.11	0.12

Interim Dividends (Per Share)

No Dividends Paid

Valuation Analysis		Institutional Holding	
Forecast P/E	7.91	No of Institutions	
	(1/10/2007)	174	
Market Cap	$746.6 Million	Shares	
Book Value	1.0 Billion	37,701,304	
Price/Book	0.73	% Held	
Price/Sales	0.21	93.57	

TRADING VOLUME (thousand shares)

Business Summary: Aviation (MIC: 1.1 SIC: 4512 NAIC: 481111)

Alaska Air Group is engaged in providing passenger air service through its two principal subsidiaries, Alaska Airlines, Inc. (Alaska) and Horizon Air Industries, Inc. (Horizon). In addition, Co. provides freight and mail services, primarily to and within the state of Alaska and on the West Coast. Through Alaska, Co. provides north/south service within the western U.S., Canada and Mexico, as well as passenger and cargo services to and within the state of Alaska. Through Horizon, Co. provides regional airline services in the Pacific Northwest, and serves a number of cities in six states and six cities in Canada. As of Dec 31 2007, Co.'s operating fleet consisted of 115 jet aircraft

Recent Developments: For the year ended Dec 31 2007, net income amounted to US$125.0 million versus a net loss of US$52.6 million in the prior year. Revenues were US$3.51 billion, up 5.1% from US$3.33 billion the year before. Operating income was US$212.0 million versus a loss of US$87.3 million in the prior year. Direct operating expenses rose 1.2% to US$1.51 billion from US$1.49 billion in the comparable period the year before. Indirect operating expenses decreased 7.5% to US$1.79 billion from US$1.93 billion in the equivalent prior-year period.

Prospects: For 2008, Co. is projecting mainline capacity growth at its Alaska Airlines Inc. subsidiary of about 3.0%, driven by the anticipated delivery of 17 new B737-800 aircraft in 2008 and the annualization of capacity additions deriving from 14 B737-800 aircrafts delivered in 2007. However, Co. foresees a 4.0% reduction of total system capacity at its Horizon Air Industries Inc. subsidiary, due to the forecasted reduction of several Q200 and the retirement of one CRJ700 aircrafts. Lastly, Co. expects Alaska's fleet size to increase by one aircraft in 2008 on a net basis. For the first quarter of 2008, Co. estimates capacity growth of 5.0% to 6.0% and 1.0% at Alaska and Horizon, respectively.

Financial Data
(US$ in Thousands)

	12/31/2007	12/31/2006	12/31/2005	12/31/2004	12/31/2003	12/31/2002	12/31/2001	12/31/2000
Earnings Per Share	3.09	(1.39)	(0.01)	(0.57)	0.51	(4.47)	(1.49)	(2.66)
Cash Flow Per Share	12.01	11.86	9.85	12.40	13.33	4.69	10.50	10.00
Tang Book Value Per Share	26.91	21.98	23.73	23.08	23.49	22.76	28.98	30.57
Income Statement								
Total Revenue	3,506,000	3,334,400	2,975,300	2,723,800	2,444,800	2,224,100	2,140,900	2,177,200
EBITDA	385,300	68,700	305,900	210,300	263,900	115,300	161,100	151,300
Income Before Taxes	201,600	(87,800)	137,200	(20,600)	29,000	(101,800)	(57,500)	(15,700)
Income Taxes	76,600	(35,200)	52,700	(5,300)	15,500	(34,600)	(18,000)	(2,300)
Net Income	125,000	(52,600)	(5,900)	(15,300)	13,500	(118,600)	(39,500)	(70,300)
Average Shares	40,424	37,939	33,917	26,859	26,730	26,546	26,499	26,440
Balance Sheet								
Total Assets	4,490,900	4,077,100	3,792,000	3,335,000	3,259,200	2,880,700	2,933,800	2,630,000
Long-Term Obligations	1,124,600	1,031,700	969,100	989,600	906,900	856,700	863,300	609,200
Total Liabilities	3,466,900	3,191,600	2,964,400	2,670,200	2,585,000	2,225,000	2,113,500	1,767,700
Stockholders' Equity	1,024,000	885,500	827,600	664,800	674,200	655,700	820,300	862,300
Shares Outstanding	38,050	40,293	33,454	27,126	26,761	26,573	26,528	26,457
Statistical Record								
Return on Assets %	2.92	N.M.	N.M.	N.M.	0.44	N.M.	N.M.	N.M.
Return on Equity %	13.09	N.M.	N.M.	N.M.	2.03	N.M.	N.M.	N.M.
EBITDA Margin %	10.99	2.06	10.28	7.72	10.79	5.18	7.52	6.95
Net Margin %	3.57	(1.58)	(0.20)	(0.56)	0.55	(5.33)	(1.85)	(3.23)
Asset Turnover	0.82	0.85	0.83	0.82	0.80	0.77	0.77	0.90
Price Range	44.47-21.80	44.56-30.05	37.36-26.57	33.49-18.88	31.67-15.66	33.73-14.11	34.00-17.70	36.06-20.75
P/E Ratio	14.39-7.06	...	...	...	62.10-30.71	...	...	...

Address: 19300 International Blvd., Seattle, WA 98188 Telephone: 206-392-5040	Web Site: www.alaskaair.com Officers: William S. Ayer - Chmn., Pres., C.E.O. Bradley D. Tilden - Exec. V.P., Fin., C.F.O.	Auditors: KPMG LLP Investor Contact: 206-433-3170 Transfer Agents: Computershare Investor Services

ALBEMARLE CORP.

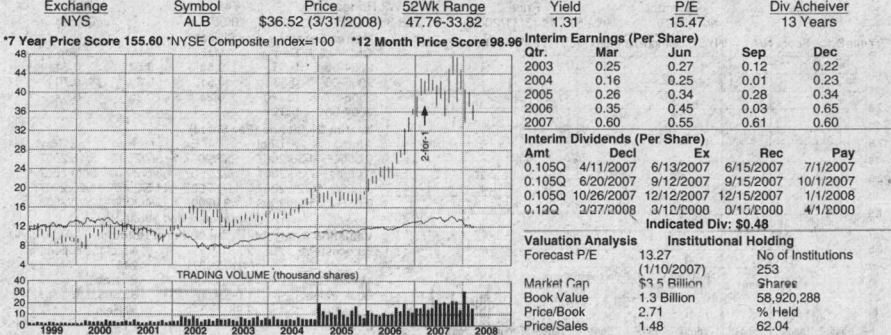

Exchange	Symbol	Price	52Wk Range	Yield	P/E	Div Acheiver
NYS	ALB	$36.52 (3/31/2008)	47.76-33.82	1.31	15.47	13 Years

*7 Year Price Score 155.60 *NYSE Composite Index=100 *12 Month Price Score 98.96

Interim Earnings (Per Share)

Qtr.	Mar	Jun	Sep	Dec
2003	0.25	0.27	0.12	0.22
2004	0.16	0.25	0.01	0.23
2005	0.26	0.34	0.28	0.34
2006	0.35	0.45	0.03	0.65
2007	0.60	0.55	0.61	0.60

Interim Dividends (Per Share)

Amt	Decl	Ex	Rec	Pay
0.105Q	4/11/2007	6/13/2007	6/15/2007	7/1/2007
0.105Q	6/20/2007	9/12/2007	9/15/2007	10/1/2007
0.105Q	10/26/2007	12/12/2007	12/15/2007	1/1/2008
0.12Q	2/27/2008	3/12/2000	0/15/2000	4/1/2000

Indicated Div: $0.48

Valuation Analysis   **Institutional Holding**

Forecast P/E	13.27	No of Institutions
	(1/10/2007)	253
Market Cap	$3.5 Billion	Shares
Book Value	1.3 Billion	58,920,288
Price/Book	2.71	% Held
Price/Sales	1.48	62.04

Business Summary: Chemicals (MIC: 11.1 SIC: 2821 NAIC: 325211)

Albemarle is a global producer of engineered specialty chemicals. Co.'s Polymer Additives segment consists of brominated, mineral and phosphorus flame retardants and other polymer additives such as curatives, antioxidants and stabilizers. The Catalysts segment includes refinery catalysts to reduce sulphur and other impurities from petroleum products and for cracking petroleum into higher-value products, such as fuels and petrochemical feedstock; and polyolefin catalysts used as co catalysts in the production of polyolefins. The Fine Chemicals segment produces performance chemicals; pharmachemicals; agrichemicals; and provides fine chemistry services and intermediates.

Recent Developments: For the year ended Dec 31 2007, net income increased 60.7% to US$229.7 million from US$143.0 million in the prior year. Revenues were US$2.34 billion, down 1.4% from US$2.37 billion the year before. Operating income was US$309.9 million versus US$177.5 million in the prior year, an increase of 74.6%. Direct operating expenses declined 5.7% to US$1.71 billion from US$1.82 billion in the comparable period the year before. Indirect operating expenses decreased 16.3% to US$312.6 million from US$373.3 million in the equivalent prior-year period.

Prospects: For 2008, Co. expects continued Asian and Middle East growth to compensate for slower market growth in the U.S. For example, Co. anticipates growth across its business segments to be driven by several factors, including the increasing demand for electrical and electronic equipment, as well as new construction and new product introductions. In addition, Co. expects that oil demand will remain strong and believes that it has the catalyst production capacity on line to meet this growth in demand for 2008 and 2009. Meanwhile, Co. is continuing to increase its presence in China with expansions underway that should help it grow flame retardants, antioxidants and fine chemicals during 2008.

Financial Data

(US$ in Thousands)	12/31/2007	12/31/2006	12/31/2005	12/31/2004	12/31/2003	12/31/2002	12/31/2001	12/31/2000
Earnings Per Share	2.36	1.47	1.21	0.65	0.85	0.86	0.73	1.09
Cash Flow Per Share	2.55	3.98	1.82	2.30	1.82	1.72	1.57	1.69
Tang Book Value Per Share	8.83	6.59	5.73	3.67	6.29	6.41	6.17	5.85
Dividends Per Share	0.420	0.345	0.310	0.292	0.282	0.270	0.260	0.230
Dividend Payout %	17.80	23.47	25.73	45.35	33.04	31.21	35.37	21.10
Income Statement								
Total Revenue	2,336,187	2,368,506	2,107,499	1,513,737	1,110,237	980,215	916,899	917,549
EBITDA	423,006	290,300	282,844	186,462	177,445	189,486	180,342	227,249
Income Before Taxes	277,819	133,386	123,438	71,844	88,055	103,813	97,196	147,501
Income Taxes	55,078	2,192	27,593	17,005	13,890	29,068	29,029	45,725
Net Income	229,690	142,969	114,867	54,839	71,945	74,745	68,167	101,776
Average Shares	97,216	97,136	95,496	85,054	84,292	86,274	93,048	93,212
Balance Sheet								
Current Assets	1,033,438	960,854	873,663	747,410	481,369	413,064	383,661	315,154
Total Assets	2,830,450	2,530,368	2,547,243	2,442,745	1,387,291	1,192,956	1,129,475	981,803
Current Liabilities	402,917	482,949	421,917	373,746	210,071	165,007	303,837	142,116
Long-Term Obligations	707,311	681,859	775,889	899,584	228,389	180,137	12,353	97,681
Total Liabilities	1,552,145	1,502,270	1,616,968	1,731,370	751,070	623,216	536,173	422,896
Stockholders' Equity	1,278,305	1,028,098	930,275	711,375	636,221	569,740	593,302	558,907
Shares Outstanding	94,734	94,860	93,499	83,796	82,306	83,384	90,996	91,647
Statistical Record								
Return on Assets %	8.57	5.63	4.60	2.86	5.58	6.44	6.46	10.49
Return on Equity %	19.92	14.60	13.99	8.12	11.93	12.85	11.83	19.34
EBITDA Margin %	18.11	12.26	13.42	12.32	15.98	19.33	19.67	24.77
Net Margin %	9.83	6.04	5.45	3.62	6.48	7.63	7.43	11.09
Asset Turnover	0.87	0.93	0.84	0.79	0.86	0.84	0.87	0.95
Current Ratio	2.61	1.99	2.07	2.00	2.29	2.50	1.26	2.22
Debt to Equity	0.55	0.66	0.83	1.26	0.36	0.32	0.02	0.17
Price Range	47.76-35.02	36.65-19.41	19.45-16.23	20.16-13.68	15.22-11.14	16.45-11.20	12.53-8.68	12.84-7.28
P/E Ratio	20.24-14.84	24.93-13.21	16.08-13.41	31.02-21.04	17.91-13.11	19.12-13.02	17.16-11.88	11.78-6.68
Average Yield %	1.02	1.34	1.70	1.83	2.09	1.92	2.36	2.20

Address: 330 South Fourth Street, P.O. Box 1335, Richmond, VA 23219 **Telephone:** 804-788-6000 **Fax:** 804-788-5688	**Web Site:** www.albemarle.com **Officers:** William M. Gottwald - Chmn. Floyd D. Gottwald Jr. - Vice-Chmn.	**Auditors:** PricewaterhouseCoopers LLP **Investor Contact:** 804-788-6096 **Transfer Agents:** National City Bank, Cleveland, OH

ALBERTO-CULVER CO

Exchange	Symbol	Price	52Wk Range	Yield	P/E
NYS	ACV	$27.41 (3/31/2008)	28.30-21.75	0.95	23.63

*7 Year Price Score N/A   *NYSE Composite Index=100   *12 Month Price Score 118.42

TRADING VOLUME (thousand shares)

Interim Earnings (Per Share)

Qtr.	Dec	Mar	Jun	Sep
2004-05	0.53	0.53	0.57	0.64
2005-06	0.56	0.61	0.33	0.70
2006-07	(0.06)	0.23	0.25	0.37
2007-08	0.31	...	...	...

Interim Dividends (Per Share)

Amt	Decl	Ex	Rec	Pay
0.055Q	4/30/2007	5/3/2007	5/7/2007	5/18/2007
0.055Q	7/30/2007	8/2/2007	8/6/2007	8/20/2007
0.055Q	10/29/2007	11/1/2007	11/5/2007	11/20/2007
0.065Q	1/28/2008	1/31/2008	2/4/2008	2/20/2008

Indicated Div: $0.26

Valuation Analysis / Institutional Holding

Forecast P/E	20.31 (1/10/2007)	No of Institutions	245
Market Cap	$2.7 Billion	Shares	67,303,336
Book Value	1.0 Billion	% Held	71.11
Price/Book	2.66		
Price/Sales	1.70		

Business Summary: Chemicals (MIC: 11.1 SIC: 2844 NAIC: 325620)

Alberto-Culver operates two consumer products divisions: Consumer Packaged Goods, which develops, manufactures, distributes and markets branded beauty care products as well as branded food and household products; as well as Cederroth International, which manufactures, markets and distributes beauty and health care products throughout Scandinavia and in Europe. At Sep 30 2007, Co.'s beauty and health care products included Alberto VO5, TRESemme, St. Ives, Just For Me and FDS feminine deodorant sprays. Co.'s Food and household products include Mrs. Dash salt-free seasoning blends, Molly McButter butter flavored sprinkles, SugarTwin sugar substitute, and Kleen Guard furniture polish.

Recent Developments: For the quarter ended Dec 31 2007, income from continuing operations increased to US$29.5 million from US$3,000 in the year-earlier quarter. Net income amounted to US$30.9 million versus a net loss of US$5.9 million in the year-earlier quarter. Revenues were US$400.7 million, up 14.1% from US$351.1 million the year before. Operating income was US$40.6 million versus a loss of US$1.6 million in the prior-year quarter. Direct operating expenses rose 11.6% to US$189.9 million from US$170.1 million in the comparable period the year before. Indirect operating expenses decreased 6.8% to US$170.1 million from US$182.6 million in the equivalent prior-year period.

Prospects: Co.'s top-line results are being positively affected by an increase in sales from both its Consumer Packaged Goods and Cederroth International divisions. Particularly, Co. is seeing an increase in sales in its Consumer Packaged Goods due to higher sales of TRESemme shampoos, conditioners and styling products. Meanwhile, as a result of the reorganization plan and other restructuring activities, Co. expects to recognize cost savings of $24.0 million on an annualized basis. Co. indicated that the vast majority of the cost savings amounts will affect advertising, marketing, selling and administrative expenses.

Financial Data

(US$ in Thousands)	3 Mos	09/30/2007	09/30/2006	09/30/2005	09/30/2004	09/30/2003	09/30/2002	09/30/2001
Earnings Per Share	1.16	0.80	2.20	2.27	1.54	1.80	1.55	1.27
Cash Flow Per Share	1.26	1.03	2.78	2.29	2.87	2.50	2.69	1.96
Tang Book Value Per Share	6.97	6.61	10.92	9.18	8.24	7.04	5.03	4.60
Dividends Per Share	0.220	25.165	0.490	0.445	0.105	0.405	0.352	0.323
Dividend Payout %	18.97	3,145.63	22.27	19.60	6.82	22.50	22.79	25.33
Income Statement								
Total Revenue	400,675	1,541,581	3,772,001	3,531,231	3,257,996	2,891,417	2,650,976	2,494,180
EBITDA	48,502	137,626	372,093	386,186	285,212	322,618	281,642	284,181
Depn & Amortn	7,896	...	...	...	...	...	...	...
Income Before Taxes	43,486	112,962	308,286	324,463	212,644	251,400	211,792	167,236
Income Taxes	13,982	31,735	102,965	113,562	70,874	89,247	74,127	56,860
Net Income	30,907	78,264	205,321	210,901	141,770	162,153	137,665	110,376
Average Shares	100,608	98,358	93,485	92,838	91,832	89,956	88,821	86,757
Balance Sheet								
Current Assets	885,685	857,538	1,428,801	1,189,624	1,118,433	1,165,489	984,217	876,949
Total Assets	1,519,862	1,487,560	2,582,597	2,302,123	2,058,780	1,945,609	1,729,491	1,516,501
Current Liabilities	396,268	416,050	590,848	535,930	532,434	465,509	460,447	390,303
Long-Term Obligations	2,743	2,077	122,322	124,084	121,246	320,587	320,181	321,183
Total Liabilities	492,766	503,789	823,668	770,501	745,074	883,480	867,032	780,492
Stockholders' Equity	1,017,213	973,364	1,729,781	1,531,622	1,313,706	1,062,129	862,459	736,009
Shares Outstanding	98,722	98,057	93,239	91,991	90,764	88,460	87,268	85,242
Statistical Record								
Return on Assets %	8.12	3.85	8.41	9.67	7.06	8.82	8.48	7.60
Return on Equity %	12.51	5.79	12.59	14.82	11.90	16.85	17.22	16.08
EBITDA Margin %	12.11	8.93	9.86	10.94	8.75	11.16	10.62	11.39
Net Margin %	7.71	5.08	5.44	5.97	4.35	5.61	5.19	4.43
Asset Turnover	1.12	0.76	1.54	1.62	1.62	1.57	1.63	1.72
Current Ratio	2.24	2.06	2.42	2.22	2.10	2.50	2.14	2.25
Debt to Equity	N.M.	N.M.	0.07	0.08	0.09	0.30	0.37	0.44
Price Range	25.99-21.75	25.77-17.85	...	...	...	...	...	...
P/E Ratio	22.41-18.75	32.21-22.31	...	...	...	...	...	...
Average Yield %	0.23	108.36	...	...	...	...	...	...

Address: 2525 Armitage Avenue, Melrose Park, IL 60160 Telephone: 708-450-3000 Fax: 708-450-3419	Web Site: www.alberto.com Officers: Carol L. Bernick - Chmn. Howard B. Bernick - Pres., C.E.O.	Auditors: KPMG LLP Investor Contact: 708-450-3117 Transfer Agents: The Corporation Trust Company, Wilmington, DE

ALCOA, INC.

Exchange	Symbol	Price	52Wk Range	Yield	P/E
NYS	AA	$36.06 (3/31/2008)	47.35-28.79	1.89	12.22

*7 Year Price Score 94.02   ***NYSE Composite Index=100**   ***12 Month Price Score 105.55**

Interim Earnings (Per Share)

Qtr.	Mar	Jun	Sep	Dec
2003	0.17	0.26	0.33	0.32
2004	0.41	0.46	0.32	0.30
2005	0.30	0.52	0.33	0.25
2006	0.69	0.85	0.61	0.41
2007	0.75	0.81	0.63	0.75

Interim Dividends (Per Share)

Amt	Decl	Ex	Rec	Pay
0.17Q	7/20/2007	8/1/2007	8/3/2007	8/25/2007
0.17Q	9/14/2007	10/31/2007	11/2/2007	11/25/2007
0.17Q	1/18/2008	2/6/2008	2/8/2008	2/25/2008
0.17Q	0/14/2000	4/00/2000	5/02/2000	5/25/2000

Indicated Div: $0.68

Valuation Analysis

Forecast P/E	10.10
	(1/10/2007)
Market Cap	$20.8 Billion
Book Value	16.0 Billion
Price/Book	1.86
Price/Sales	0.97

Institutional Holding

No of Institutions	617
Shares	703,415,296
% Held	80.90

TRADING VOLUME (thousand shares)

Business Summary: Metal Works (MIC: 11.3 SIC: 3353 NAIC: 331315)

Alcoa is engaged in the production and management of primary aluminum, fabricated aluminum, and alumina combined, through its active and growing participation in all major aspects of the industry: technology, mining, refining, smelting, fabricating, and recycling. Co.'s Nonaluminum products include precision castings, industrial fasteners, consumer products, food service and flexible packaging products, plastic closures, and electrical distribution systems for cars and trucks. As of Dec 31 2007, Co. operated through six segments: Alumina, Primary Metals, Flat-Rolled Products, Extruded and End Products, Engineered Solutions, and Packaging and Consumer.

Recent Developments: For the year ended Dec 31 2007, income from continuing operations increased 19.0% to US$2.57 billion from US$2.16 billion a year earlier. Net income increased 14.1% to US$2.56 billion from US$2.25 billion in the prior year. Revenues were US$30.75 billion, up 1.2% from US$30.38 billion the year before. Direct operating expenses rose 4.0% to US$24.25 billion from US$23.32 billion in the comparable period the year before. Indirect operating expenses increased 2.6% to US$3.92 billion from US$3.82 billion in the equivalent prior-year period.

Prospects: On Dec 21 2007, Co. announced that it has agreed to sell certain subsidiaries of its packaging and consumer businesses to New Zealand's Rank Group Ltd. for $2.70 billion, as part of its 2007 portfolio management plan. Co. also noted that it will continue to operate its flat-rolled can sheet product serving the packaging market. The transaction should close by the end of the first quarter of 2008. Meanwhile, on Feb 1 2008, Co. announced that it is partnering with Aluminum Corp. of China to acquire 12.0% of the UK common stock of Rio Tinto plc. Co. will contribute up to $1.20 billion in the total investment, which is expected to allow it to benefit from developments in the mining market.

Financial Data

(US$ in Thousands)	12/31/2007	12/31/2006	12/31/2005	12/31/2004	12/31/2003	12/31/2002	12/31/2001	12/31/2000
Earnings Per Share	2.95	2.57	1.40	1.49	1.08	0.49	1.05	1.81
Cash Flow Per Share	3.61	2.95	1.92	2.52	2.85	2.18	2.81	3.49
Tang Book Value Per Share	12.75	8.53	6.96	6.72	6.30	4.15	4.90	6.20
Dividends Per Share	0.680	0.600	0.600	0.600	0.600	0.600	0.600	0.500
Dividend Payout %	23.05	23.35	42.86	40.27	55.56	122.45	57.14	27.62
Income Statement								
Total Revenue	30,748,000	30,379,000	26,159,000	23,478,000	21,504,000	20,263,000	22,859,000	23,090,000
EBITDA	5,698,000	4,623,000	3,135,000	3,375,000	2,833,000	1,995,000	2,906,000	4,031,000
Income Before Taxes	4,491,000	3,432,000	1,933,000	2,204,000	1,669,000	925,000	1,641,000	2,812,000
Income Taxes	1,555,000	835,000	441,000	557,000	404,000	292,000	525,000	942,000
Net Income	2,564,000	2,248,000	1,233,000	1,310,000	938,000	420,000	908,000	1,484,000
Average Shares	869,000	875,000	876,900	877,400	856,600	849,800	866,600	823,200
Balance Sheet								
Current Assets	8,096,000	8,157,000	8,700,000	7,003,000	6,740,000	6,217,000	6,702,000	7,670,000
Total Assets	38,803,000	37,183,000	33,696,000	32,609,000	31,711,000	29,810,000	28,355,000	31,691,000
Current Liabilities	7,166,000	7,281,000	7,368,000	6,298,000	5,084,000	4,461,000	5,003,000	7,954,000
Long-Term Obligations	6,371,000	5,910,000	5,279,000	5,346,000	6,692,000	8,365,000	6,388,000	4,987,000
Total Liabilities	20,327,000	20,752,000	18,958,000	17,893,000	18,296,000	18,590,000	16,428,000	18,755,000
Stockholders' Equity	16,016,000	14,631,000	13,373,000	13,300,000	12,075,000	9,927,000	10,614,000	11,422,000
Shares Outstanding	827,401	867,739	870,268	870,980	868,490	844,819	847,581	865,517
Statistical Record								
Return on Assets %	6.75	6.34	3.72	4.06	3.05	1.44	3.02	6.07
Return on Equity %	16.73	16.05	9.25	10.30	8.53	4.09	8.24	16.68
EBITDA Margin %	18.53	15.22	11.98	14.38	13.17	9.85	12.71	17.46
Net Margin %	8.34	7.40	4.71	5.58	4.36	2.07	3.97	6.43
Asset Turnover	0.81	0.86	0.79	0.73	0.70	0.70	0.76	0.94
Current Ratio	1.13	1.26	1.19	1.19	1.33	1.42	1.36	0.95
Debt to Equity	0.40	0.40	0.39	0.40	0.55	0.84	0.60	0.44
Price Range	47.35-28.48	36.59-26.60	32.12-22.54	38.78-28.70	38.91-18.57	39.56-18.03	45.36-28.30	43.00-23.50
P/E Ratio	16.05-9.65	14.24-10.35	22.94-16.10	26.03-19.26	36.03-17.19	80.73-36.80	43.20-26.95	23.76-12.98
Average Yield %	1.86	1.99	2.14	1.82	2.30	2.02	1.62	1.57

Address: 390 Park Avenue, New York, NY 10022-4608	Web Site: www.alcoa.com	Auditors: PricewaterhouseCoopers LLP
Telephone: 212-836-2674	Officers: Alain J. P. Belda - Chmn., C.E.O. Richard B. Kelson - Exec. V.P., C.F.O.	Investor Contact: 212-836-2674
Fax: 412-553-4498		Transfer Agents: Computershare Trust Company, N.A.

ALEXANDRIA REAL ESTATE EQUITIES, INC.

Exchange	Symbol	Price	52Wk Range	Yield	P/E	Div Acheiver
NYS	ARE	$92.72 (3/31/2008)	111.54-86.13	3.36	35.25	10 Years

*7 Year Price Score 116.12 *NYSE Composite Index=100 *12 Month Price Score 102.82

TRADING VOLUME (thousand shares)

Interim Earnings (Per Share)

Qtr.	Mar	Jun	Sep	Dec
2003	0.63	0.65	1.12	0.69
2004	0.78	0.71	0.79	0.05
2005	0.55	0.58	0.56	0.53
2006	0.56	0.57	0.56	0.57
2007	0.52	0.73	0.68	0.70

Interim Dividends (Per Share)

Amt	Decl	Ex	Rec	Pay
0.76Q	6/18/2007	6/28/2007	7/2/2007	7/13/2007
0.76Q	9/19/2007	9/27/2007	10/1/2007	10/15/2007
0.78Q	12/13/2007	12/28/2007	1/2/2008	1/15/2008
0.78Q	3/20/2008	3/28/2008	4/1/2008	4/15/2008

Indicated Div: $3.12

Valuation Analysis

		Institutional Holding	
Forecast P/E	16.04 (1/10/2007)	No of Institutions	163
Market Cap	$2.9 Billion	Shares	29,710,560
Book Value	1.5 Billion	% Held	
Price/Book	1.95		N/A
Price/Sales	7.23		

Business Summary: Property, Real Estate & Development (MIC: 8.3 SIC: 6798 NAIC: 525930)

Alexandria Real Estate Equities is a real estate investment trust. Co. is engaged primarily in the ownership, operation, management, selective redevelopment, development and acquisition of properties for the life sciences industry. Co.'s properties are designed and improved for lease primarily to institutional, pharmaceutical, biotechnology, medical device, life science product, service, biodefense and translational research entities, as well as governmental agencies. As of Dec 31 2007, Co. had 166 properties, with 162 properties located in nine states in the U.S. and four properties located in Canada, with approximately 12.1 million rentable square feet of office/laboratory space.

Recent Developments: For the year ended Dec 31 2007, income from continuing operations increased 23.7% to US$85.2 million from US$68.9 million a year earlier. Net income increased 27.7% to US$93.7 million from US$73.4 million in the prior year. Revenues were US$405.4 million, up 30.4% from US$310.8 million the year before. Revenues from property income rose 30.6% to US$390.5 million from US$299.0 million in the corresponding earlier year.

Prospects: Co.'s near-term outlook appears encouraging, attributable to growth in both its top-and bottom-line result. Specifically, Co.'s top-line growth is being fueled by an increase in rental revenues, mainly from properties acquired. Going forward, Co. continues to pursue opportunities to acquire land for future development and will continue to initiate development projects. In addition, Co. intends to continue its biopharmaceutical international expansion opportunities particularly in Canada, Europe, and Asia. For 2008, Co. is updating its guidance and is projecting funds from operations per diluted share to be approximately $6.10 and earnings per diluted share to be approximately $3.27.

Financial Data
(US$ in Thousands)

	12/31/2007	12/31/2006	12/31/2005	12/31/2004	12/31/2003	12/31/2002	12/31/2001	12/31/2000
Earnings Per Share	2.63	2.25	2.22	2.33	3.10	2.24	1.64	1.52
Cash Flow Per Share	6.25	5.11	5.76	3.50	3.94	3.81	3.78	2.27
Tang Book Value Per Share	43.48	40.14	28.64	22.12	21.34	20.54	17.98	18.04
Dividends Per Share	3.040	2.860	2.720	2.520	2.200	2.000	1.810	1.290
Dividend Payout %	115.59	127.11	122.52	108.15	70.97	98.20	110.37	84.87
Income Statement								
Property Income	390,492	304,969	239,286	179,743	158,490	143,062	124,522	103,404
Non-Property Income	14,868	11,852	4,798	3,541	2,068	1,610	3,268	3,506
Total Revenue	405,360	316,821	244,084	183,284	160,558	144,672	127,790	106,910
Interest Expense	88,387	71,371	49,116	28,670	26,416	24,984	29,126	25,791
Net Income	93,724	73,416	63,433	60,195	59,643	40,032	30,277	26,009
Average Shares	30,004	25,524	21,316	19,658	19,247	17,859	16,208	14,699
Balance Sheet								
Total Assets	4,642,094	3,617,477	2,362,450	1,872,284	1,272,577	1,159,243	962,146	780,984
Long-Term Obligations	2,787,904	2,024,866	1,406,666	1,186,946	709,007	614,878	573,161	431,256
Total Liabilities	3,062,768	2,208,348	1,512,535	1,251,811	765,442	673,390	629,508	461,832
Stockholders' Equity	1,503,820	1,351,652	829,800	620,473	507,135	485,853	332,638	319,152
Shares Outstanding	31,603	29,012	22,441	19,594	19,264	18,973	16,354	15,548
Statistical Record								
Return on Assets %	2.27	2.46	3.00	3.82	4.91	3.77	3.47	3.64
Return on Equity %	6.56	6.73	8.75	10.65	12.01	9.78	9.29	8.92
Net Margin %	23.12	23.17	25.99	32.84	37.15	27.67	23.69	24.33
Price Range	113.41-86.13	104.79-82.36	85.70-62.87	74.90-51.65	58.90-39.95	49.34-38.50	41.93-35.54	38.50-29.13
P/E Ratio	43.12-32.75	46.57-36.60	38.60-28.32	32.15-22.17	19.00-12.89	22.03-17.19	25.57-21.67	25.33-19.16
Average Yield %	3.03	3.08	3.63	4.05	4.74	4.55	4.69	3.86

Address: 135 North Los Robles Avenue, Suite 250, Pasadena, CA 91101
Telephone: 626-578-0777

Officers: Jerry M. Sudarsky - Chmn. Joel S. Marcus - C.E.O.

Auditors: Ernst & Young LLP
Transfer Agents: American Stock Transfer & Trust Company

ALLEGHANY CORP.

Exchange	Symbol	Price	52Wk Range	Yield	P/E
NYS	Y	$341.50 (3/31/2008)	422.06-328.43	N/A	10.43

*7 Year Price Score 122.89 *NYSE Composite Index=100   *12 Month Price Score 98.98

Interim Earnings (Per Share)

Qtr.	Mar	Jun	Sep	Dec
2003	0.93	0.72	9.05	8.92
2004	7.46	5.85	(5.65)	6.49
2005	7.27	3.74	(11.04)	6.29
2006	7.06	8.75	5.70	7.78
2007	11.67	6.89	7.72	6.84

Interim Dividends (Per Share)

Amt	Decl	Ex	Rec	Pay
2%	3/4/2005	3/30/2005	4/1/2005	4/22/2005
2%	3/14/2006	3/30/2006	4/3/2006	4/28/2006
2%	2/28/2007	3/29/2007	4/2/2007	4/27/2007
2%	2/27/2008	3/28/2008	4/1/2008	4/26/2008

Valuation Analysis

		Institutional Holding	
Forecast P/E	N/A	No of Institutions	137
Market Cap	$2.8 Billion	Shares	
Book Value	2.8 Billion		5,482,390
Price/Book	1.02	% Held	
Price/Sales	1.98		67.37

Business Summary: Insurance (MIC: 8.2 SIC: 6331 NAIC: 524126)

Alleghany is engaged in the property and casualty and surety insurance business through its wholly-owned subsidiary Alleghany Insurance Holdings, LLC. (AIHL). AIHL's insurance business is conducted through its wholly-owned subsidiaries RSUI Group, Inc., Capitol Transamerica Corporation and Platte River Insurance Company, AIHL's majority-owned subsidiary, Darwin Professional Underwriters, Inc. and Employers Direct Insurance Company. AIHL's wholly-owned subsidiary, AIHL Re LLC, provides catastrophe reinsurance to RSUI. Co. also owns and manages properties in the Sacramento, CA region through its subsidiary Alleghany Properties, LLC.

Recent Developments: For the year ended Dec 31 2007, income from continuing operations increased 21.5% to US$305.3 million from US$251.2 million a year earlier. Net income increased 21.5% to US$305.3 million from US$251.2 million in the prior year. Revenues were US$1.43 billion, up 18.4% from US$1.21 billion the year before. Net premiums earned were US$1.16 billion versus US$1.01 billion in the prior year, an increase of 14.4%.

Prospects: Co.'s near-term outlook appears constructive despite lower net earnings primarily due to greater than expected losses incurred in its Capitol Transamerica Corp. subsidiary's property lines of business. However, Co.'s RSUI Group, Inc. and Darwin Professional Underwriters, Inc. subsidiaries reported an increase in underwriting profit primarily due to an increase in net premiums earned. In addition, Co.'s Employers Direct Insurance Co. (EDC) subsidiary, which was acquired in 2007, contributed to its results reflecting a reduction in EDC's reserves. Also, Co. is seeing higher net investment income as a result of solid operating cash flow and the net positive effect of the acquisition of EDC.

Financial Data
(US$ in Thousands)

	12/31/2007	12/31/2006	12/31/2005	12/31/2004	12/31/2003	12/31/2002	12/31/2001	12/31/2000
Earnings Per Share	32.75	29.13	6.26	14.14	19.67	6.62	27.30	7.95
Cash Flow Per Share	57.66	66.76	43.37	49.29	51.81	4.73	41.94	(13.61)
Tang Book Value Per Share	273.89	237.17	202.75	184.43	160.63	154.82	171.36	143.45
Income Statement								
Premium Income	1,155,221	1,010,129	849,653	805,417	430,914	125,649	...	365,568
Total Revenue	1,432,041	1,209,165	1,095,956	1,240,927	1,018,233	576,857	924,955	945,208
Benefits & Claims	550,329	498,954	747,967	540,569	250,202	100,508	...	392,006
Income Before Taxes	477,780	362,930	59,819	170,127	240,367	57,404	534,379	(12,144)
Income Taxes	157,901	106,109	13,842	52,179	77,989	2,591	103,816	(46,119)
Net Income	305,277	251,244	52,334	117,696	162,378	54,813	224,230	68,857
Average Shares	9,331	8,640	8,368	8,334	8,255	8,285	8,215	8,655
Balance Sheet								
Total Assets	6,733,046	6,178,740	5,913,731	4,427,725	3,568,040	2,134,382	1,875,005	2,707,616
Total Liabilities	3,939,171	3,755,494	4,045,404	2,671,625	2,005,218	755,040	484,423	1,542,542
Stockholders' Equity	2,793,875	2,423,246	1,868,327	1,756,100	1,562,822	1,379,342	1,390,582	1,165,074
Shares Outstanding	8,322	8,280	8,388	8,308	8,274	8,180	8,115	8,121
Statistical Record								
Return on Assets %	4.73	4.16	1.01	2.94	5.70	2.73	9.79	1.91
Return on Equity %	11.70	11.71	2.89	7.07	11.04	3.96	17.55	6.04
Loss Ratio %	47.64	49.40	88.03	67.12	58.06	79.99	...	107.23
Net Margin %	21.32	20.78	4.78	9.48	15.95	9.50	24.24	7.28
Price Range	422.06-340.78	349.87-253.75	301.54-246.16	276.93-199.51	202.91-138.92	170.93-153.84	195.01-159.28	175.39-138.21
P/E Ratio	12.89-10.41	12.01-8.71	48.17-39.32	19.59-14.11	10.32-7.06	25.82-23.24	7.14-5.83	22.06-17.39

Address: 7 Times Square Tower, 17TH Floor, New York, NY 10036 Telephone: 212-752-1356 Fax: 212-759-8149	Web Site: www.alleghanyfunds.com Officers: F. M. Kirby - Chmn. John J. Burns Jr. - Pres., C.E.O., C.O.O.	Auditors: KPMG LLP Transfer Agents: Computershare Investor Services LLC

ALLEGHENY ENERGY, INC.

Exchange	Symbol	Price	52Wk Range	Yield	P/E
NYS	AYE	$50.50 (3/31/2008)	64.99-46.74	N/A	20.78

*7 Year Price Score 145.57 *NYSE Composite Index=100 *12 Month Price Score 101.32

TRADING VOLUME (thousand shares)

Interim Earnings (Per Share)

Qtr.	Mar	Jun	Sep	Dec
2003	(0.46)	(1.82)	(0.40)	(0.11)
2004	0.25	(0.31)	(2.40)	1.14
2005	0.29	(0.12)	0.21	0.02
2006	0.67	0.18	0.65	0.38
2007	0.65	0.45	0.67	0.65

Interim Dividends (Per Share)

Dividend Payment Suspended

Valuation Analysis		Institutional Holding	
Forecast P/E	16.44	No of Institutions	
	(1/10/2007)	313	
Market Cap	$8.4 Billion	Shares	
Book Value	2.5 Billion	124,166,216	
Price/Book	3.33	% Held	
Price/Sales	2.55	75.51	

Business Summary: Electricity (MIC: 7.1 SIC: 4911 NAIC: 221121)

Allegheny Energy is a utility holding company. Co. operates mainly through its subsidiaries in two business segments: the Delivery and Services segment, which operates electric transmission and distribution systems in Pennsylvania, West Virginia, Maryland and Virginia, consisting of Co.'s Monongahela Power Company (Monongahela), excluding its generation operations, The Potomac Edison Company, and West Penn Power Company; and the Generation and Marketing segment, which owns, operates and manages electric generation facilities, consisting of Co.'s Allegheny Energy Supply Company, LLC, Allegheny Generating Company, and Monongahela's generation operations.

Recent Developments: For the year ended Dec 31 2007, income from continuing operations increased 29.3% to US$412.2 million from US$318.7 million a year earlier. Net income increased 29.1% to US$412.2 million from US$319.3 million in the prior year. Revenues were US$3.31 billion, up 5.9% from US$3.12 billion the year before. Operating income was US$817.3 million versus US$732.3 million in the prior year, an increase of 11.6%. Direct operating expenses rose 4.3% to US$2.00 billion from US$1.92 billion in the comparable period the year before. Indirect operating expenses increased 3.9% to US$488.8 million from US$470.3 million in the equivalent prior-year period.

Prospects: Looking ahead to 2008 and beyond, Co. believes that it is well-positioned for robust earnings growth, reflecting its continued focused on growing earnings by improving power plant performance, expanding its transmission system, and controlling costs. Separately, Co. estimates 2008 capital expenditures of $1.35 billion, primarily related to expenditures for its Trans-Allegheny Interstate Line Project, which has a target completion date of 2011, expenditures for other related transmission projects requested by PJM Interconnection, L.L.C., and constructions of the Scrubbers at its Fort Martin and Hatfield's Ferry generation facilities, which are both expected to be completed in 2009.

Financial Data

(US$ in Thousands)	12/31/2007	12/31/2006	12/31/2005	12/31/2004	12/31/2003	12/31/2002	12/31/2001	12/31/2000
Earnings Per Share	2.43	1.89	0.40	(1.83)	(2.80)	(5.04)	3.47	2.14
Cash Flow Per Share	5.75	4.65	3.14	3.90	2.92	2.59	2.78	4.82
Tang Book Value Per Share	12.97	10.36	7.98	6.94	8.72	12.05	16.48	13.80
Dividends Per Share	0.150	...	...	...	...	1.290	1.720	1.720
Dividend Payout %	6.17	...	...	...	...	...	49.57	80.37
Income Statement								
Total Revenue	3,307,020	3,121,489	3,037,887	2,756,121	2,472,432	2,988,487	10,378,931	4,011,852
EBITDA	1,132,240	1,033,483	909,952	952,541	229,827	(242,051)	...	...
Income Before Taxes	666,140	494,840	140,503	208,519	(558,378)	(850,156)	...	...
Income Taxes	250,805	173,543	64,771	79,669	(216,990)	(334,471)	245,067	184,801
Net Income	412,214	319,321	63,065	(310,598)	(354,979)	(632,690)	417,775	236,629
Average Shares	169,468	168,679	158,634	156,491	126,848	125,657	120,542	110,436
Balance Sheet								
Net PPE	7,196,580	6,512,893	6,277,428	6,303,018	7,453,477	6,882,574	6,853,015	5,539,338
Total Assets	9,906,589	8,552,446	8,558,812	9,045,140	10,171,896	10,600,279	11,167,552	7,697,017
Long-Term Obligations	3,982,712	3,409,993	3,640,910	4,564,552	5,159,920	154,998	3,235,730	2,559,510
Total Liabilities	7,357,996	6,437,338	6,817,528	7,595,706	8,568,580	8,572,931	8,353,592	5,882,336
Stockholders' Equity	2,535,352	2,080,395	1,695,295	1,353,816	1,515,859	1,931,507	2,709,969	1,740,681
Shares Outstanding	167,223	165,360	162,952	137,380	126,968	126,597	125,276	110,436
Statistical Record								
Return on Assets %	4.47	3.73	0.72	N.M.	N.M.	N.M.	4.43	3.24
Return on Equity %	17.86	16.91	4.14	N.M.	N.M.	N.M.	18.77	13.74
EBITDA Margin %	34.24	33.11	29.95	34.56	9.30	N.M.	...	...
Net Margin %	12.46	10.23	2.08	(11.27)	(14.36)	(21.17)	4.03	5.90
PPE Turnover	0.48	0.49	0.48	0.40	0.34	0.44	1.68	0.74
Asset Turnover	0.36	0.36	0.35	0.29	0.24	0.27	1.10	0.55
Debt to Equity	1.57	1.64	2.15	3.37	3.40	0.08	1.19	1.47
Price Range	64.99-44.40	46.03-32.00	32.05-18.48	20.11-12.03	12.95-4.82	43.53-3.80	54.79-33.25	48.19-24.00
P/E Ratio	26.74-18.27	24.35-16.93	80.13-46.20	...	...	...	15.79-9.58	22.52-11.21
Average Yield %	0.28	...	...	...	...	5.24	3.93	5.23

Address: 800 Cabin Hill Drive,	Web Site: www.alleghenyenergy.com	Auditors: Deloitte & Touche LLP
Greensburg, PA 15601	Officers: Paul J. Evanson - Chmn., Pres., C.E.O.	Investor Contact: 724-838-6895
Telephone: 724-837-3000	Jeffrey D. Serkes - Sr. V.P., C.F.O.	Transfer Agents: Mellon Investor Services LLC

ALLEGHENY TECHNOLOGIES, INC

Exchange	Symbol	Price	52Wk Range	Yield	P/E
NYS	ATI	$71.36 (3/31/2008)	118.78-65.44	1.01	9.83

*7 Year Price Score 208.30 *NYSE Composite Index=100   *12 Month Price Score 83.91

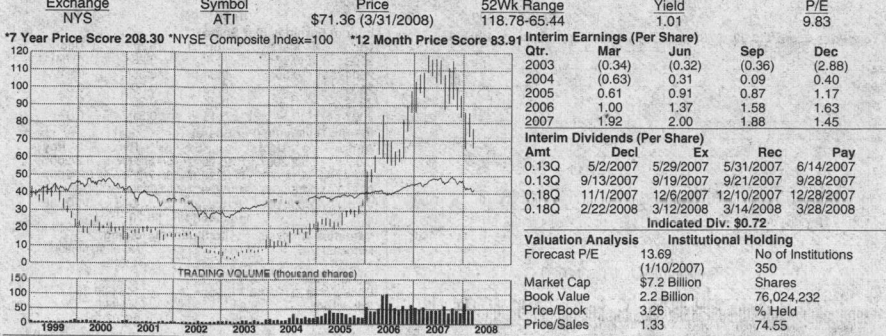

Interim Earnings (Per Share)

Qtr.	Mar	Jun	Sep	Dec
2003	(0.34)	(0.32)	(0.36)	(2.88)
2004	(0.63)	0.31	0.09	0.40
2005	0.61	0.91	0.87	1.17
2006	1.00	1.37	1.58	1.63
2007	1.92	2.00	1.88	1.45

Interim Dividends (Per Share)

Amt	Decl	Ex	Rec	Pay
0.13Q	5/2/2007	5/29/2007	5/31/2007	6/14/2007
0.13Q	9/13/2007	9/19/2007	9/21/2007	9/28/2007
0.18Q	11/1/2007	12/6/2007	12/10/2007	12/28/2007
0.18Q	2/22/2008	3/12/2008	3/14/2008	3/28/2008

Indicated Div: $0.72

Valuation Analysis / Institutional Holding

Valuation Analysis		Institutional Holding	
Forecast P/E	13.69	No of Institutions	
	(1/10/2007)	350	
Market Cap	$7.2 Billion	Shares	
Book Value	2.2 Billion	76,024,232	
Price/Book	3.26	% Held	
Price/Sales	1.33	74.55	

Business Summary: Metal Works (MIC: 11.3 SIC: 3317 NAIC: 331210)

Allegheny Technologies is a global producer for a range of specialty metals. As of Dec 31 2007, Co. conducted its businesses through three segments: Co.'s High Performance Metals segment produces, converts and distributes a range of alloys, primarily in long product forms such as ingot, billet, bar, rod, wire, and seamless tube. Co.'s Flat-Rolled Products segment produces, converts and distributes stainless steel, nickel-based alloys, and titanium and titanium-based alloys, in a variety of product forms. Co.'s Engineered Products segment's primary business includes the production of tungsten powder, tungsten heavy alloys, tungsten carbide materials, and tungsten carbide cutting tools.

Recent Developments: For the year ended Dec 31 2007, net income increased 30.1% to US$747.1 million from US$574.1 million in the prior year. Revenues were US$5.45 billion, up 10.5% from US$4.94 billion the year before. Operating income was US$1.15 billion versus US$900.9 million in the prior year, an increase of 27.9%. Direct operating expenses rose 7.0% to US$4.00 billion from US$3.74 billion in the comparable period the year before. Indirect operating expenses increased 0.5% to US$296.7 million from US$295.3 million in the equivalent prior year period.

Prospects: Looking ahead, Co. foresees demand from the commercial aerospace market to remain at a high level as it continues to see higher backlog from airframe and jet engine customers. In addition, Co. expects demand from the chemical process industry, oil and gas, and electrical energy markets to remain strong as the global infrastructure build and rebuild continues. Meanwhile, Co. anticipates capital expenditures for 2008 to be about $500.0 million, mainly for the completion of its ongoing capital projects as well as other potential growth capital projects, excluding the capital expansion underway at its STAL Precision Stainless Steel Co. Ltd. joint venture operations in Shanghai, China.

Financial Data

(US$ in Thousands)	12/31/2007	12/31/2006	12/31/2005	12/31/2004	12/31/2003	12/31/2002	12/31/2001	12/31/2000
Earnings Per Share	7.26	5.59	3.57	0.22	(3.89)	(0.82)	(0.31)	1.60
Cash Flow Per Share	6.98	3.18	2.31	0.28	1.01	2.53	1.53	1.68
Tang Book Value Per Share	19.82	12.71	6.11	2.30	N.M.	3.15	9.42	10.51
Dividends Per Share	0.570	0.430	0.280	0.240	0.240	0.660	0.800	0.800
Dividend Payout %	7.85	7.69	7.84	109.09	...	...	...	50.00
Income Statement								
Total Revenue	5,452,500	4,936,600	3,539,900	2,733,000	1,937,400	1,907,800	2,128,000	2,460,400
EBITDA	1,255,000	976,700	423,000	131,400	(177,900)	20,500	91,500	342,900
Income Before Taxes	1,147,300	869,200	307,100	19,800	(280,200)	(103,800)	(36,400)	208,800
Income Taxes	400,200	297,300	(54,700)	...	33,100	(38,000)	(11,200)	76,300
Net Income	747,100	571,900	359,800	19,800	(314,600)	(65,800)	(25,200)	132,300
Average Shares	102,960	102,380	100,800	90,500	80,800	80,600	80,300	80,300
Balance Sheet								
Current Assets	2,248,700	1,987,900	1,484,000	1,160,200	743,300	812,400	926,100	1,022,800
Total Assets	4,095,600	3,282,200	2,731,600	2,315,700	1,884,900	2,093,200	2,643,200	2,776,200
Current Liabilities	704,000	645,500	560,900	492,800	394,700	342,000	332,700	413,500
Long-Term Obligations	507,300	529,900	547,000	553,300	504,300	509,400	573,000	490,600
Total Liabilities	1,872,100	1,789,600	1,931,700	1,889,800	1,710,200	1,644,400	1,698,500	1,737,000
Stockholders' Equity	2,223,500	1,492,600	799,900	425,900	174,700	448,800	944,700	1,039,200
Shares Outstanding	101,586	101,201	98,200	95,782	80,654	80,634	80,314	80,339
Statistical Record								
Return on Assets %	20.25	19.02	14.26	0.94	N.M.	N.M.	N.M.	4.78
Return on Equity %	40.21	49.89	58.70	6.58	N.M.	N.M.	N.M.	11.80
EBITDA Margin %	23.02	19.78	11.95	4.81	N.M.	1.07	4.30	13.94
Net Margin %	13.70	11.58	10.16	0.72	N.M.	N.M.	N.M.	5.39
Asset Turnover	1.48	1.64	1.40	1.30	0.97	0.81	0.79	0.89
Current Ratio	3.19	3.08	2.65	2.35	1.88	2.38	2.78	2.47
Debt to Equity	0.23	0.36	0.68	1.30	2.89	1.14	0.61	0.47
Price Range	118.78-83.22	98.20-36.05	36.53-18.03	22.93-8.72	13.90-2.45	18.11-5.30	21.07-12.73	26.38-13.00
P/E Ratio	16.36-11.46	17.57-6.45	10.23-5.05	104.23-39.64	...	...	...	16.48-8.13
Average Yield %	0.56	0.66	1.08	1.55	3.78	5.41	4.68	3.97

Address: 1000 Six PPG Place, Pittsburgh, PA 15222-5479 Telephone: 412-394-2800 Fax: 412-394-2805	Web Site: www.alleghenytechnologies.com Officers: Robert P. Bozzone - Chmn. L. Patrick Hassey - Pres., C.E.O.	Auditors: Ernst & Young LLP Transfer Agents: Mellon Investor Services LLC, Jersey City, NJ

ALLERGAN, INC

Exchange	Symbol	Price	52Wk Range	Yield	P/E
NYS	AGN	$56.39 (3/31/2008)	68.69-54.61	0.35	34.81

*7 Year Price Score 113.00   *NYSE Composite Index=100   *12 Month Price Score 104.67

TRADING VOLUME (thousand shares)

Interim Earnings (Per Share)

Qtr.	Mar	Jun	Sep	Dec
2003	0.27	(0.41)	0.28	(0.34)
2004	0.30	0.34	0.35	0.41
2005	0.30	0.13	0.56	0.52
2006	(1.65)	0.24	0.35	0.47
2007	0.14	0.45	0.51	0.52

Interim Dividends (Per Share)

Amt	Decl	Ex	Rec	Pay
0.05Q	5/2/2007	5/16/2007	5/18/2007	6/8/2007
0.05Q	8/1/2007	8/15/2007	8/17/2007	9/7/2007
0.05Q	11/6/2007	11/7/2007	11/9/2007	11/30/2007
0.05Q	1/30/2008	2/13/2008	2/15/2008	3/7/2008

Indicated Div: $0.20

Valuation Analysis

		Institutional Holding	
Forecast P/E	N/A	No of Institutions	430
Market Cap	$17.3 Billion	Shares	
Book Value	3.7 Billion		148,682,384
Price/Book	4.61	% Held	
Price/Sales	4.38		96.70

Business Summary: Pharmaceuticals (MIC: 9.1 SIC: 2834 NAIC: 325412)

Allergan is a health care company that develops and markets specialty pharmaceutical and medical device products for the ophthalmic, neurological, medical aesthetics, medical dermatological, breast aesthetics, obesity intervention, urological and other specialty markets. Co. targets products and technologies related to specific disease areas such as glaucoma, retinal disease, dry eye, psoriasis, acne, movement disorders, neuropathic pain and genitourinary diseases. Co.'s products are sold to drug wholesalers, independent and chain drug stores, pharmacies, commercial optical chains, opticians, mass merchandisers, hospitals, group purchasing organizations and ambulatory surgery centers.

Recent Developments:
For the year ended Dec 31 2007, income from continuing operations was US$501.0 million compared with a loss of US$127.4 million a year earlier. Net income amounted to US$499.3 million versus a net loss of US$127.4 million in the prior year. Revenues were US$3.94 billion, up 28.6% from US$3.06 billion the year before. Operating income was US$719.4 million versus a loss of US$3.2 million in the prior year. Direct operating expenses rose 16.9% to US$673.2 million from US$575.7 million in the comparable period the year before. Indirect operating expenses increased 2.2% to US$2.55 billion from US$2.49 billion in the equivalent prior-year period.

Prospects:
For full-year 2008, Co. is targeting total product net sales of between $4.40 billion and $4.58 billion and total specialty pharmaceuticals net sales of between $3.53 billion and $3.62 billion. For the first quarter of 2008, Co. projects total product net sales between $1.04 billion and $1.07 billion. Separately, on Jan 30 2008, Co. announced the phased closure of its breast implant manufacturing facility at Arklow, Ireland and the transfer of production to its manufacturing plant in Costa Rica. Co. presently expects to incur restructuring and other transition related costs beginning in the first quarter of 2008 and continuing up through 2009 of between $60.0 million and $65.0 million.

Financial Data
(US$ in Thousands)

	12/31/2007	12/31/2006	12/31/2005	12/31/2004	12/31/2003	12/31/2002	12/31/2001	12/31/2000
Earnings Per Share	1.62	(0.44)	1.50	1.41	(0.20)	0.28	0.84	0.81
Cash Flow Per Share	2.60	2.54	1.62	2.08	1.67	0.18	1.37	1.35
Tang Book Value Per Share	0.54	0.76	5.24	3.91	2.39	2.95	3.24	2.81
Dividends Per Share	0.200	0.200	0.200	0.180	0.180	0.180	0.180	0.160
Dividend Payout %	12.35	...	13.29	12.77	...	63.16	21.43	19.88
Income Statement								
Total Revenue	3,938,900	3,063,300	2,319,200	2,045,600	1,771,400	1,425,300	1,745,500	1,625,500
EBITDA	912,500	153,300	664,900	616,200	39,600	147,400	412,700	386,500
Income Before Taxes	687,700	(19,500)	599,200	532,100	(29,500)	89,800	336,400	303,800
Income Taxes	186,200	107,500	192,400	154,000	22,200	25,100	109,100	88,100
Net Income	499,300	(127,400)	403,900	377,100	(52,500)	75,200	224,900	215,100
Average Shares	308,700	293,800	268,000	267,800	260,400	262,200	275,600	267,600
Balance Sheet								
Current Assets	2,124,200	2,130,300	1,825,600	1,376,000	928,200	1,200,200	1,325,300	1,326,300
Total Assets	6,579,300	5,767,100	2,850,500	2,257,000	1,754,900	1,806,600	2,046,200	1,971,000
Current Liabilities	715,700	658,100	1,044,000	459,600	383,400	403,600	490,000	432,500
Long-Term Obligations	1,590,200	1,606,400	57,500	570,100	573,300	526,400	520,600	584,700
Total Liabilities	2,840,700	2,624,000	1,283,600	1,140,800	1,036,300	998,300	1,068,800	1,097,200
Stockholders' Equity	3,738,600	3,143,100	1,566,900	1,116,200	718,600	808,300	977,400	873,800
Shares Outstanding	305,907	304,538	265,648	262,834	260,286	258,996	262,500	263,362
Statistical Record								
Return on Assets %	8.09	N.M.	15.82	18.75	N.M.	3.90	11.20	12.96
Return on Equity %	14.51	N.M.	30.11	40.99	N.M.	8.42	24.30	28.44
EBITDA Margin %	23.17	5.00	28.67	30.12	2.24	10.34	23.64	23.78
Net Margin %	12.68	N.M.	17.42	18.43	N.M.	5.28	12.88	13.23
Asset Turnover	0.64	0.71	0.91	1.02	0.99	0.74	0.87	0.98
Current Ratio	2.97	3.24	1.75	2.99	2.42	2.97	2.70	3.07
Debt to Equity	0.43	0.51	0.04	0.51	0.80	0.65	0.53	0.67
Price Range	68.45-52.91	61.51-46.81	54.97-34.53	46.03-33.84	40.76-28.48	36.15-24.77	44.92-29.62	47.24-21.89
P/E Ratio	42.25-32.66	...	36.65-23.02	32.65-24.00	...	129.11-88.48	53.47-35.27	58.32-27.02
Average Yield %	0.33	0.36	0.47	0.44	0.49	0.60	0.49	0.48

Address: 2525 Dupont Drive, P.O. Box 19534, Irvine, CA 92612-9534 Telephone: 714-246-4500 Fax: 714-246-6987	Web Site: www.allergan.com Officers: David E.I. Pyott - Chmn., Pres., C.E.O. Herbert W. Boyer - Vice-Chmn.	Auditors: Ernst & Young LLP Investor Contact: 714-246-4636 Transfer Agents: EquiServe Trust Company

ALLIANCE DATA SYSTEMS CORP.

Exchange	Symbol	Price	52Wk Range	Yield	P/E
NYS	ADS	$47.51 (3/31/2008)	80.72-42.48	N/A	23.40

*7 Year Price Score N/A   *NYSE Composite Index=100   *12 Month Price Score 78.28

Interim Earnings (Per Share)

Qtr.	Mar	Jun	Sep	Dec
2003	0.16	0.15	0.23	0.30
2004	0.39	0.33	0.31	0.19
2005	0.43	0.40	0.42	0.38
2006	0.69	0.55	0.60	0.48
2007	0.70	0.55	0.36	0.42

Interim Dividends (Per Share)

No Dividends Paid

Valuation Analysis

		Institutional Holding	
Forecast P/E	15.48	No of Institutions	
	(1/10/2007)	298	
Market Cap	$3.7 Billion	Shares	
Book Value	1.2 Billion	78,152,560	
Price/Book	3.13	% Held	
Price/Sales	1.63	98.21	

Business Summary: Miscellaneous Business Services (MIC: 12.8 SIC: 7389 NAIC: 522320)

Alliance Data Systems is a provider of data-driven and transaction-based marketing and customer loyalty services. As of Dec 31 2007, Co. operated in three reportable segments: Marketing Services, which provides loyalty programs, such as the AIR MILES® Reward Program and direct marketing services; Credit Services, which securitizes the credit card receivables that it underwrites from its private label retail card programs; and Transaction Services, which encompasses card processing, billing and payment processing and customer care for retailers, customer information system hosting, customer care and billing and payment processing for utilities and other processing-oriented businesses.

Recent Developments: For the year ended Dec 31 2007, net income decreased 13.5% to US$164.1 million from US$189.6 million in the prior year. Revenues were US$2.29 billion, up 14.6% from US$2.00 billion the year before. Operating income was US$344.3 million versus US$347.3 million in the prior year, a decrease of 0.9%. Direct operating expenses rose 13.7% to US$1.63 billion from US$1.43 billion in the comparable period the year before. Indirect operating expenses increased 45.7% to US$315.9 million from US$216.9 million in the equivalent prior-year period.

Prospects: Co.'s top-line results are being positively affected by higher revenue from its Marketing Services and Credit Services segments. Looking ahead, Co. intends to improve its position in loyalty programs by expanding the scope of its AIR MILES Reward Program and by developing stand-alone loyalty programs such as the Hilton HHonors Program and the Citi Thank You Network. Meanwhile, for full-year 2008, Co. remains optimistic in its ability to attain double-digit organic growth in operating results. Consequently, Co. is projecting earnings per diluted share to be approximately $4.30 per diluted share, a 15.0% growth rate over 2007.

Financial Data
(US$ in Thousands)

	12/31/2007	12/31/2006	12/31/2005	12/31/2004	12/31/2003	12/31/2002	12/31/2001	12/31/2000
Earnings Per Share	2.03	2.32	1.64	1.22	0.84	0.34	(0.18)	(0.60)
Cash Flow Per Share	7.29	5.88	1.33	4.37	1.61	1.72	2.63	1.83
Tang Book Value Per Share	N.M.	N.M.	N.M.	N.M.	0.93	0.37	0.19	N.M.
Income Statement								
Total Revenue	2,291,189	1,998,742	1,552,437	1,257,438	1,019,144	871,451	777,351	678,195
EBITDA	488,269	457,064	318,967	236,375	221,437	135,106	108,296	95,532
Income Before Taxes	274,752	306,269	222,126	164,319	108,982	47,416	3,995	(19,482)
Income Taxes	110,691	116,664	83,381	61,948	41,684	20,671	11,612	1,841
Net Income	164,061	189,605	138,745	102,371	67,298	26,203	(8,232)	(21,323)
Average Shares	80,811	81,686	84,637	84,040	80,313	76,696	64,555	47,538
Balance Sheet								
Current Assets	1,453,041	1,309,975	1,042,453	617,346	582,852	388,940	463,503	523,775
Total Assets	4,103,594	3,404,015	2,926,082	2,239,080	1,868,442	1,453,418	1,477,218	1,420,606
Current Liabilities	1,325,724	877,720	1,048,571	560,619	490,400	427,430	429,729	491,838
Long-Term Obligations	644,375	741,675	258,501	206,861	189,361	107,918	199,100	274,335
Total Liabilities	2,906,628	2,332,482	2,004,975	1,368,560	1,166,111	910,680	971,490	1,058,215
Stockholders' Equity	1,196,966	1,071,533	921,107	870,520	702,331	542,738	505,728	242,991
Shares Outstanding	78,762	79,654	80,405	82,347	79,625	74,938	73,987	47,545
Statistical Record								
Return on Assets %	4.37	5.99	5.37	4.97	4.05	1.79	N.M.	N.M.
Return on Equity %	14.46	19.03	15.49	12.98	10.81	5.00	N.M.	N.M.
EBITDA Margin %	21.31	22.87	20.55	18.80	21.11	15.50	13.93	14.09
Net Margin %	7.16	9.49	8.94	8.14	6.41	3.01	N.M.	N.M.
Asset Turnover	0.61	0.63	0.60	0.61	0.63	0.59	0.54	0.50
Current Ratio	1.10	1.49	0.99	1.10	1.19	0.91	1.08	1.06
Debt to Equity	0.54	0.69	0.28	0.24	0.27	0.20	0.39	1.13
Price Range	80.72-57.14	66.00-36.96	47.48-32.79	48.52-26.92	30.51-14.79	25.95-13.85	19.15-11.35	
P/E Ratio	39.76-28.15	28.45-15.93	28.95-19.99	39.77-22.07	36.32-17.61	76.32-40.74	...	...

Address: 17655 Waterview Parkway, Dallas, TX 75252 Telephone: 972-348-5100	Web Site: www.alliancedata.com Officers: J. Michael Parks - Chmn., C.E.O. Edward J. Heffernan - Exec. V.P., C.F.O.	Auditors: Deloitte & Touche LLP Transfer Agents: Computershare Trust Company, N.A., Providence, RI

ALLIANT ENERGY CORP.

Exchange	Symbol	Price	52Wk Range	Yield	P/E
NYS	LNT	$35.01 (3/31/2008)	45.74-34.39	4.00	9.26

*7 Year Price Score 108.92 *NYSE Composite Index=100 *12 Month Price Score 96.82

Interim Earnings (Per Share)

Qtr.	Mar	Jun	Sep	Dec
2003	(0.01)	0.35	0.94	0.44
2004	0.31	(0.12)	0.71	0.37
2005	0.02	(0.50)	0.96	(0.55)
2006	(0.01)	0.39	0.67	1.65
2007	0.55	0.43	1.08	1.73

Interim Dividends (Per Share)

Amt	Decl	Ex	Rec	Pay
0.318Q	4/13/2007	4/26/2007	4/30/2007	5/15/2007
0.318Q	7/13/2007	7/27/2007	7/31/2007	8/15/2007
0.318Q	10/12/2007	10/29/2007	10/31/2007	11/15/2007
0.35Q	1/18/2008	1/29/2008	1/31/2008	2/15/2008

Indicated Div: $1.40

Valuation Analysis

Forecast P/E	13.94
	(1/10/2007)
Market Cap	$3.9 Billion
Book Value	2.7 Billion
Price/Book	1.44
Price/Sales	1.12

Institutional Holding

No of Institutions	263
Shares	66,273,040
% Held	56.28

Business Summary: Electricity (MIC: 7.1 SIC: 4931 NAIC: 221122)

Alliant Energy is a public utility holding company for Interstate Power and Light Co. (IPL), Wisconsin Power and Light Co. (WPL), Resources and Corporate Services. IPL is a public utility engaged principally in the generation and distribution of electric energy; and the distribution and transportation of natural gas in selective markets in Iowa and Minnesota. WPL is a public utility engaged principally in the generation and distribution of electric energy; and the distribution and transportation of natural gas in selective markets in Wisconsin. Resources is the parent company for Co.'s non-regulated businesses. Corporate Services provides administrative services to Co. and its subsidiaries.

Recent Developments: For the year ended Dec 31 2007, net income increased 34.7% to US$425.3 million from US$315.7 million in the prior year. Revenues were US$3.44 billion, up 2.3% from US$3.36 billion the year before. Operating income was US$763.1 million versus US$493.5 million in the prior year, an increase of 54.6%. Direct operating expenses rose 1.0% to US$2.52 billion from US$2.50 billion in the comparable period the year before. Indirect operating expenses decreased 58.7% to US$152.6 million from US$369.6 million in the equivalent prior-year period.

Prospects: On Feb 6 2008, Co.'s Interstate Power and Light Company (IPL) subsidiary announced its acquisition of a 300 megawatt wind power farm in north central Iowa, near Hampton, IA from Iowa Winds, LLC. Co. expects the farm should produce up to 500 megawatts of emissions-free energy once completely developed. IPL expects developing 200 megawatts of wind power on the site beginning in 2009, to be commercially operable in 2010. In addition, Co. is pursuing needed baseload generation and has proposed the addition of the Sutherland Generating Station Unit 4 in Marshalltown, IA., which should be operational in 2013. For 2008, Co. expects earnings from continuing operations of $2.55 to $2.75 per share.

Financial Data
(US$ in Thousands)

	12/31/2007	12/31/2006	12/31/2005	12/31/2004	12/31/2003	12/31/2002	12/31/2001	12/31/2000
Earnings Per Share	3.78	2.69	(0.07)	1.28	1.81	1.18	2.14	5.03
Cash Flow Per Share	5.24	3.60	5.15	4.42	4.14	5.99	5.97	5.45
Tang Book Value Per Share	24.30	22.83	20.85	22.13	21.37	19.89	21.39	25.79
Dividends Per Share	1.270	1.150	1.050	1.013	1.000	2.000	2.000	2.000
Dividend Payout %	33.60	42.75	...	79.10	55.25	169.49	93.46	39.76
Income Statement								
Total Revenue	3,437,600	3,359,400	3,279,600	2,958,700	3,128,187	2,608,812	2,777,340	2,404,984
EBITDA	1,095,300	971,300	523,900	855,800	799,868	645,140	803,979	1,161,260
Income Before Taxes	680,500	541,300	3,500	294,600	231,528	112,377	245,070	620,770
Income Taxes	255,800	203,000	(52,900)	83,800	71,827	36,108	59,840	238,816
Net Income	425,300	315,700	(7,700)	145,500	183,543	106,881	172,362	398,662
Average Shares	112,521	117,190	116,793	113,701	101,544	90,959	80,636	79,193
Balance Sheet								
Net PPE	4,334,300	4,581,500	4,471,500	4,672,800	4,432,599	3,196,988	3,037,609	3,719,307
Total Assets	7,189,700	7,084,100	7,733,100	8,275,200	7,775,446	7,001,395	6,247,682	6,733,766
Long-Term Obligations	1,404,500	1,323,300	1,914,600	2,299,500	2,123,298	2,637,803	2,457,941	1,910,116
Total Liabilities	4,264,700	4,189,000	5,048,800	5,470,000	5,160,329	4,960,142	4,215,388	4,582,504
Stockholders' Equity	2,681,200	2,651,300	2,440,500	2,561,400	2,371,314	1,836,190	1,918,341	2,037,472
Shares Outstanding	110,359	116,126	117,035	115,741	110,962	92,304	89,682	79,010
Statistical Record								
Return on Assets %	5.96	4.26	N.M.	1.81	2.48	1.61	2.66	6.21
Return on Equity %	15.95	12.40	N.M.	5.88	8.72	5.69	8.71	18.96
EBITDA Margin %	31.86	28.91	15.97	28.92	25.57	24.73	28.95	48.29
Net Margin %	12.37	9.40	(0.23)	4.92	5.87	4.10	6.21	16.58
PPE Turnover	0.77	0.74	0.72	0.65	0.82	0.84	0.82	0.67
Asset Turnover	0.48	0.45	0.41	0.37	0.42	0.39	0.43	0.37
Debt to Equity	0.52	0.50	0.78	0.90	0.90	1.44	1.28	0.94
Price Range	45.74-35.81	39.70-28.50	30.39-25.88	28.80-23.76	24.94-15.12	30.86-14.39	33.10-27.99	34.63-26.02
P/E Ratio	12.10-9.47	14.76-10.59	...	22.50-18.56	13.78-8.35	26.15-12.19	15.47-13.08	6.88-5.17
Average Yield %	3.13	3.32	3.77	3.91	5.03	8.50	6.59	6.85

Address: 4902 N. Biltmore Lane, Madison, WI 53718-2132 **Telephone:** 608-458-3311 **Fax:** 608-458-4824	**Web Site:** www.alliantenergy.com **Officers:** Erroll B. Davis Jr. - Chmn. William D. Harvey - Pres., C.E.O., C.O.O.	**Auditors:** Deloitte & Touche LLP **Investor Contact:** 608-458-3267 **Transfer Agents:** Wells Fargo Shareowner Services, St. Paul, MN

ALLIANT TECHSYSTEMS INC.

Exchange	Symbol	Price	52Wk Range	Yield	P/E
NYS	ATK	$103.53 (3/31/2008)	119.85-88.50	N/A	16.73

*7 Year Price Score 121.10 *NYSE Composite Index=100 ***12 Month Price Score 107.08**

TRADING VOLUME (thousand shares)

Interim Earnings (Per Share)

Qtr.	Jun	Sep	Dec	Mar
2004-05	0.72	0.78	1.25	1.27
2005-06	0.99	1.07	1.26	0.77
2006-07	1.09	1.15	1.53	1.58
2007-08	1.50	1.44	1.65	...

Interim Dividends (Per Share)

Amt	Decl	Ex	Rec	Pay
3-for-2	5/9/2002	6/11/2002	5/17/2002	6/10/2002

Valuation Analysis **Institutional Holding**

Forecast P/E	11.99	No of Institutions
	(1/10/2007)	249
Market Cap	$3.4 Billion	Shares
Book Value	698.3 Million	31,487,034
Price/Book	4.85	% Held
Price/Sales	0.83	95.49

Business Summary: Aerospace & Defense (MIC: 1 SIC: 3764 NAIC: 332994)

Alliant Techsystems is a supplier of aerospace and defense products to the U.S. Government, allied nations, and prime contractors. Co. is also a supplier of ammunition and related accessories. Co.'s operating segments are Mission Systems, Ammunition Systems and Launch Systems. Mission Systems operates in four areas: Weapon Systems, Aerospace Systems, Space Systems, and Technical Services. Ammunition Systems develops and produces military ammunition and gun systems; civil ammunition and accessories; and propellant and energetic materials. Launch Systems produces rocket motor systems for human and cargo launch vehicles, conventional and strategic missiles, and missile defense interceptors.

Recent Developments: For the quarter ended Dec 30 2007, net income increased 13.9% to US$58.3 million from US$51.2 million in the year-earlier quarter. Revenues were US$1.05 billion, up 16.7% from US$903.8 million the year before. Operating income was US$110.6 million versus US$92.4 million in the prior-year quarter, an increase of 19.6%. Direct operating expenses rose 14.9% to US$842.2 million from US$732.7 million in the comparable period the year before. Indirect operating expenses increased 29.7% to US$102.1 million from US$78.7 million in the equivalent prior-year period.

Prospects: On Jan 8 2008, Co. announced its intent to acquire the Information Systems and Geospatial Information Services businesses from Canadian-based MacDonald, Dettwiler and Associates (MDA) for C$1.33 billion. Upon closure, which is slated to occur early in the fiscal quarter ending June 2008, Co. expects the purchase to substantially grow its domestic and international market position in space systems, as well as providing higher growth and earnings profile, and be neutral to earnings per share in fiscal 2009 ending Mar 2009 and accretive thereafter. For fiscal 2008 ending Mar 2008, Co. expects sales in excess of $4.1 billion and earnings of $6.25 to $6.35 per share, excluding MDA acquisition.

Financial Data

(US$ in Thousands)	9 Mos	6 Mos	3 Mos	03/31/2007	03/31/2006	03/31/2005	03/31/2004	03/31/2003
Earnings Per Share	6.19	6.06	5.77	5.32	4.11	4.03	4.14	3.16
Cash Flow Per Share	9.01	5.16	0.87	1.31	5.77	5.22	4.66	5.13
Income Statement								
Total Revenue	3,042,582	1,987,717	958,372	3,564,940	3,216,807	2,801,129	2,366,193	2,172,135
EBITDA	377,688	246,865	121,755	415,880	410,766	369,317	346,981	342,677
Depn & Amortn	60,553	40,286	20,251	...	...	...	...	...
Income Before Taxes	254,130	161,927	82,491	264,796	227,557	220,540	217,796	211,231
Income Taxes	91,800	58,084	29,913	80,217	73,271	66,549	55,041	82,384
Net Income	161,909	103,579	52,404	184,128	153,882	153,540	162,305	124,287
Average Shares	35,434	35,450	34,852	34,591	38,145	38,145	39,176	39,344
Balance Sheet								
Current Assets	1,185,450	1,154,295	1,156,240	1,029,018	1,019,451	833,414	805,605	712,316
Total Assets	3,140,347	3,097,245	3,107,572	2,874,682	2,901,980	3,015,810	2,833,329	2,479,264
Current Liabilities	1,068,571	1,051,409	524,500	503,272	670,944	431,740	428,391	428,053
Long-Term Obligations	999,000	1,050,000	1,555,000	1,455,000	1,096,000	1,131,353	1,076,000	820,856
Total Liabilities	2,442,028	2,472,144	2,449,084	2,316,801	2,273,622	2,329,451	2,269,129	2,001,340
Stockholders' Equity	698,319	625,101	658,488	557,881	628,358	686,359	564,200	477,924
Shares Outstanding	32,734	32,699	33,591	33,075	35,207	37,248	37,439	38,486
Statistical Record								
Return on Assets %	7.08	6.95	6.52	6.37	5.20	5.25	6.09	5.30
Return on Equity %	34.17	36.98	29.40	31.04	23.41	24.56	31.06	24.02
EBITDA Margin %	12.41	12.42	12.70	11.67	12.77	13.18	14.66	15.78
Net Margin %	5.32	5.21	5.47	5.16	4.78	5.48	6.86	5.72
Asset Turnover	1.33	1.30	1.22	1.23	1.09	0.96	0.89	0.93
Current Ratio	1.11	1.10	2.20	2.04	1.52	1.93	1.88	1.66
Debt to Equity	1.43	1.68	2.36	2.61	1.74	1.65	1.91	1.72
Price Range	119.85-78.21	112.84-76.03	101.82-75.61	90.19-74.78	78.93-67.66	73.93-54.40	60.09-47.20	75.55-43.00
P/E Ratio	19.36-12.63	18.62-12.55	17.65-13.10	16.95-14.06	19.20-16.46	18.34-13.50	14.51-11.40	23.91-13.61

Address: 5050 Lincoln Drive, Edina, MN 55436	**Web Site:** www.atk.com	**Auditors:** Deloitte & Touche LLP
Telephone: 952-351-3000	**Officers:** Paul David Miller - Chmn. Daniel J. Murphy Jr. - C.E.O.	**Investor Contact:** 952-351-3056
Fax: 952-351-3009		**Transfer Agents:** Mellon Investor Services LLC

ALLIED WASTE INDUSTRIES, INC.

Exchange	Symbol	Price	52Wk Range	Yield	P/E
NYS	AW	$10.81 (3/31/2008)	14.00-9.30	N/A	17.16

*7 Year Price Score 86.62   *NYSE Composite Index=100   ***12 Month Price Score 91.55**

Interim Earnings (Per Share)

Qtr.	Mar	Jun	Sep	Dec
2003	0.22	0.03	0.06	(2.57)
2004	(0.01)	(0.07)	0.12	0.04
2005	0.05	0.12	0.13	0.16
2006	0.08	0.08	0.17	0.00
2007	0.08	0.21	0.05	0.28

Interim Dividends (Per Share)

No Dividends Paid

Valuation Analysis / Institutional Holding

Valuation Analysis		Institutional Holding	
Forecast P/E	17.02	No of Institutions	268
	(1/10/2007)		
Market Cap	$4.0 Billion	Shares	
Book Value	3.9 Billion		335,739,040
Price/Book	1.03	% Held	
Price/Sales	0.66		91.02

Business Summary: Sanitation Services (MIC: 7.3 SIC: 4953 NAIC: 562219)

Allied Waste Industries is a non-hazardous solid waste management company. Co. provides collection, transfer, recycling and disposal services for residential, commercial and industrial customers in the U.S. As of Dec 31 2007, Co. served its customers through a network of 291 collection companies, 161 transfer stations, 161 active landfills and 53 recycling facilities in 124 markets within 37 states and Puerto Rico. Co. is a vertically integrated company that picks up waste from businesses and residences and disposes the waste in its own landfills. Co. generally provides collection services under direct agreements with its customers or pursuant to contracts with municipalities.

Recent Developments: For the year ended Dec 31 2007, income from continuing operations increased 98.8% to US$309.8 million from US$155.8 million a year earlier. Net income increased 70.0% to US$273.6 million from US$160.9 million in the prior year. Revenues were US$6.07 billion, up 2.7% from US$5.91 billion the year before. Operating income was US$1.06 billion versus US$954.6 million in the prior year, an increase of 10.6%. Direct operating expenses was unchanged at US$3.79 billion versus the comparable period the year before. Indirect operating expenses increased 5.0% to US$1.23 billion from US$1.17 billion in the equivalent prior-year period.

Prospects: Co.'s top-line growth is driven by higher average price as it continues to benefit from its ongoing implementation of its strategic pricing program, and higher diesel fuel costs. Meanwhile, Co. believes that it is well positioned for further results improvement in 2008 due to its strong market position, its progress in cost reduction initiatives, and its continuing initiatives to advance its strategic pricing, customer service and people development. For 2008, Co. is expecting revenue growth of approximately 1.5% to 3.0%, comprising price growth of 4.5%, partially offset by a potential decrease in annual volume of 1.5% to 3.0%; along with operating income of $1.15 billion to $1.19 billion.

Financial Data
(US$ in Thousands)

	12/31/2007	12/31/2006	12/31/2005	12/31/2004	12/31/2003	12/31/2002	12/31/2001	12/31/2000
Earnings Per Share	0.63	0.33	0.46	0.09	(2.27)	0.71	(0.07)	0.29
Cash Flow Per Share	2.89	2.58	2.18	2.06	3.85	5.43	4.77	4.24
Income Statement								
Total Revenue	6,068,700	6,028,800	5,734,800	5,362,000	5,247,700	5,517,306	5,565,260	5,707,485
EBITDA	1,570,100	1,495,200	1,407,000	686,200	1,501,700	985,810	1,853,241	1,977,580
Income Before Taxes	517,300	399,500	327,500	127,500	201,800	410,711	269,966	381,168
Income Taxes	207,100	238,500	133,900	72,200	88,700	183,614	190,834	237,540
Net Income	273,600	160,900	203,800	49,300	128,700	215,111	58,486	124,387
Average Shares	443,000	359,300	330,100	319,700	203,800	193,508	194,906	191,122
Balance Sheet								
Current Assets	1,158,200	1,047,700	920,400	922,600	1,285,600	1,072,087	1,198,486	1,271,703
Total Assets	13,948,700	13,811,000	13,625,600	13,493,900	13,860,900	13,928,922	14,347,093	14,513,634
Current Liabilities	2,247,100	1,532,700	1,575,500	1,756,700	1,567,800	1,449,793	1,433,535	1,599,752
Long-Term Obligations	6,085,600	6,674,000	6,853,200	7,429,200	7,984,500	8,718,642	9,237,503	9,635,124
Total Liabilities	10,044,500	10,212,100	10,186,200	10,889,000	11,343,200	11,992,920	12,592,270	12,745,975
Stockholders' Equity	3,904,200	3,598,900	3,439,400	2,604,900	2,517,700	689,098	585,779	697,832
Shares Outstanding	370,400	367,900	331,200	317,500	320,100	196,215	196,236	196,109
Statistical Record								
Return on Assets %	1.97	1.17	1.50	0.36	0.93	1.52	0.41	0.84
Return on Equity %	7.29	4.57	6.74	1.92	8.03	33.75	9.11	18.57
EBITDA Margin %	25.87	24.80	24.53	12.80	28.62	17.87	33.30	34.65
Net Margin %	4.51	2.67	3.55	0.92	2.45	3.90	1.05	2.18
Asset Turnover	0.44	0.44	0.42	0.39	0.38	0.39	0.39	0.39
Current Ratio	0.52	0.68	0.58	0.53	0.82	0.74	0.84	0.79
Debt to Equity	1.56	1.85	1.99	2.85	3.17	12.65	15.77	13.81
Price Range	14.00-10.75	14.26-8.53	9.28-6.95	14.36-8.00	13.99-7.75	14.43-5.80	19.74-9.10	14.56-5.38
P/E Ratio	22.22-17.06	43.21-25.85	20.17-15.11	159.56-88.89	...	20.32-8.17	...	50.22-18.53

Address: 18500 North Allied Way, Phoenix, AZ 85054 **Telephone:** 480-627-2700 **Fax:** 480-423-9424	**Web Site:** www.alliedwaste.com **Officers:** John J. Zillmer - Chmn., C.E.O. Thomas W. Ryan - Vice- Chmn., Exec. V.P.	**Auditors:** PricewaterhouseCoopers LLP **Transfer Agents:** American Stock Transfer & Trust Company

ALLSTATE CORP.

Exchange	Symbol	Price	52Wk Range	Yield	P/E	Div Acheiver
NYS	ALL	$48.06 (3/31/2008)	63.47-45.72	3.41	6.19	14 Years

*7 Year Price Score 92.61 ***NYSE Composite Index=100** ***12 Month Price Score 93.12**

Interim Earnings (Per Share)

Qtr.	Mar	Jun	Sep	Dec
2003	0.94	0.84	0.97	1.08
2004	1.34	1.47	0.09	1.64
2005	1.64	1.71	(2.36)	1.56
2006	2.19	1.89	1.83	1.93
2007	2.41	2.30	1.70	1.36

Interim Dividends (Per Share)

Amt	Decl	Ex	Rec	Pay
0.38Q	5/15/2007	5/30/2007	6/1/2007	7/2/2007
0.38Q	7/17/2007	8/29/2007	8/31/2007	10/1/2007
0.38Q	11/13/2007	11/28/2007	11/30/2007	1/2/2008
0.41Q	2/20/2000	3/12/2000	3/14/2000	4/1/2008

Indicated Div: $1.64 (Div. Reinv. Plan)

Valuation Analysis		Institutional Holding	
Forecast P/E	10.45	No of Institutions	
	(1/10/2007)	757	
Market Cap	$27.1 Billion	Shares	
Book Value	21.9 Billion	435,660,480	
Price/Book	1.24	% Held	
Price/Sales	0.74	70.41	

TRADING VOLUME (thousand shares)

Business Summary: Insurance (MIC: 8.2 SIC: 6331 NAIC: 524126)

Allstate is a holding company for Allstate Insurance Company. Co.'s business is conducted principally through Allstate Insurance Co., Allstate Life Insurance Co. as well as their subsidiaries. Co. is engaged, principally in the U.S., in the personal property and casualty insurance business as well as the life insurance, retirement and investment products business. As of Dec 31 2007, Co. provided insurance products to more than 17.0 million households through approximately 14,900 agents and financial specialists. Co. operates in four business segments: Allstate Protection, Allstate Financial, Discontinued Lines and Coverages, as well as Corporate and Other.

Recent Developments: For the year ended Dec 31 2007, net income decreased 7.2% to US$4.64 billion from US$4.99 billion in the prior year. Revenues were US$36.77 billion, up 2.7% from US$35.80 billion the year before. Net premiums earned were US$29.10 billion versus US$29.33 billion in the prior year, a decrease of 0.8%. Net investment income rose 4.2% to US$6.44 billion from US$6.18 billion a year ago.

Prospects: For the full year of 2008, Co. is targeting its Property-Liability combined ratio to be within the range of 87.0 to 89.0, excluding the effects of catastrophes and prior year reserve reestimates. The difference between 100.0% and the combined ratio represents underwriting income as a percentage of premiums earned. In addition, Co. is projecting premium written at its Allstate Protection segment to be slightly higher compared with its 2007 levels. Moreover, Co. is anticipating continued growth of its standard auto premiums written, driven mainly by increased policies in force resulting from improved agency effectiveness and further optimization in its advertising and higher average premium.

Financial Data
(US$ in Thousands)

	12/31/2007	12/31/2006	12/31/2005	12/31/2004	12/31/2003	12/31/2002	12/31/2001	12/31/2000
Earnings Per Share	7.77	7.84	2.64	4.54	3.83	1.60	1.60	2.95
Cash Flow Per Share	9.17	7.99	8.47	7.84	8.09	6.26	3.18	2.32
Tang Book Value Per Share	37.35	33.80	29.97	30.74	27.89	23.52	22.35	22.26
Dividends Per Share	1.520	1.400	1.280	1.120	0.930	0.840	0.760	0.680
Dividend Payout %	19.56	17.86	48.48	24.67	24.28	52.50	47.50	23.05
Income Statement								
Premium Income	29,099,000	29,333,000	29,088,000	28,061,000	26,981,000	25,654,000	24,427,000	24,076,000
Total Revenue	36,769,000	35,796,000	35,383,000	33,936,000	32,149,000	29,579,000	28,865,000	29,134,000
Benefits & Claims	19,256,000	17,587,000	22,790,000	19,461,000	19,283,000	19,427,000	19,203,000	19,585,000
Income Before Taxes	6,653,000	7,178,000	2,088,000	4,585,000	3,571,000	1,540,000	1,285,000	3,047,000
Income Taxes	2,017,000	2,185,000	323,000	1,230,000	846,000	65,000	73,000	795,000
Net Income	4,636,000	4,993,000	1,765,000	3,181,000	2,705,000	1,134,000	1,158,000	2,211,000
Average Shares	596,700	637,200	667,300	700,300	706,200	709,900	723,300	748,700
Balance Sheet								
Total Assets	156,408,000	157,554,000	156,072,000	149,725,000	134,142,000	117,426,000	109,175,000	104,808,000
Total Liabilities	134,557,000	135,708,000	135,886,000	127,902,000	113,577,000	99,788,000	91,779,000	86,607,000
Stockholders' Equity	21,851,000	21,846,000	20,186,000	21,823,000	20,565,000	17,438,000	17,196,000	17,451,000
Shares Outstanding	563,000	622,000	646,000	683,000	704,000	702,000	712,000	728,000
Statistical Record								
Return on Assets %	2.95	3.18	1.15	2.24	2.15	1.00	1.08	2.17
Return on Equity %	21.22	23.76	8.40	14.97	14.24	6.55	6.68	12.95
Loss Ratio %	66.17	59.96	78.35	69.35	71.47	75.73	78.61	81.35
Net Margin %	12.61	13.95	4.99	9.37	8.41	3.83	4.01	7.59
Price Range	65.36-49.22	65.92-50.42	62.33-49.67	51.76-42.71	43.03-30.68	41.32-31.56	45.21-31.02	44.00-17.75
P/E Ratio	8.41-6.33	8.41-6.43	23.61-18.81	11.40-9.41	11.23-8.01	25.82-19.72	28.26-19.39	14.92-6.02
Average Yield %	2.61	2.44	2.30	2.39	2.52	2.27	2.01	2.41

Address: 2775 Sanders Road, Northbrook, IL 60062-6127 **Telephone:** 800-574-3553	**Web Site:** www.allstate.com **Officers:** Edward M. Liddy - Chmn., C.E.O. Thomas J. Wilson - Pres., C.O.O.	**Auditors:** Deloitte & Touche LLP **Investor Contact:** 800-416-8803 **Transfer Agents:** Wells Fargo Bank, N.A., St. Paul, MN

ALTRIA GROUP INC

Exchange	Symbol	Price	52Wk Range	Yield	P/E	Div Acheiver
NYS	MO	$22.20 (3/31/2008)	24.43-20.10	13.51	4.81	42 Years

*7 Year Price Score 122.18 *NYSE Composite Index=100 *12 Month Price Score 110.12

Interim Earnings (Per Share)

Qtr.	Mar	Jun	Sep	Dec
2003	1.07	1.20	1.22	1.02
2004	1.07	1.27	1.29	0.94
2005	1.25	1.28	1.38	1.09
2006	1.65	1.29	1.36	1.40
2007	1.30	1.05	1.24	1.03

Interim Dividends (Per Share)

Amt	Decl	Ex	Rec	Pay
0.75Q	8/29/2007	9/12/2007	9/14/2007	10/10/2007
0.75Q	12/12/2007	12/21/2007	12/26/2007	1/10/2008
0.00Q	1/30/2008	3/31/2008	3/19/2008	3/28/2008
0.75Q	2/27/2008	3/17/2008	3/19/2008	4/10/2008

Indicated Div: $3.00 (Div. Reinv. Plan)

Valuation Analysis

Forecast P/E	14.64 (1/10/2007)
Market Cap	$46.8 Billion
Book Value	18.6 Billion
Price/Book	2.52
Price/Sales	0.63

Institutional Holding

No of Institutions	1145
Shares	1,525,058,432
% Held	72.62

Business Summary: Tobacco Products (MIC: 4.2 SIC: 2111 NAIC: 312221)

Altria Group is a holding company. Co., via its wholly owned subsidiaries, Philip Morris USA Inc., Philip Morris International Inc., and John Middleton, Inc., are engaged in the manufacture and sale of cigarettes and other tobacco products. Philip Morris Capital Corporation, another wholly owned subsidiary of Co., maintains a portfolio of controlled and direct finance leases. At Dec 31 2007, Co. held a 28.6% economic and voting interest in SABMiller Plc., which is engaged in the manufacture and sale of various beer products. As of Dec 31 2007, Co.'s reportable segments were U.S. tobacco; European Union; Eastern Europe, Middle East and Africa; Asia; Latin America; and Financial Services.

Recent Developments: For the year ended Dec 31 2007, income from continuing operations decreased 1.8% to US$9.16 billion from US$9.33 billion a year earlier. Net income decreased 18.6% to US$9.79 billion from US$12.02 billion in the prior year. Revenues were US$73.80 billion, up 10.1% from US$67.05 billion the year before. Operating income was US$13.24 billion versus US$12.89 billion in the prior year, an increase of 2.7%. Direct operating expenses rose 12.2% to US$52.30 billion from US$46.62 billion in the comparable period the year before. Indirect operating expenses increased 9.7% to US$8.27 billion from US$7.54 billion in the equivalent prior-year period.

Prospects: Co. expects stronger earnings per share growth in the second half of 2008. Meanwhile, on Dec 11 2007, Co. acquired John Middleton, Inc., a manufacturer of machine-made large cigars, from Bradford Holdings, Inc., for $2.90 billion. Notably, Co. projects the transaction to be modestly accretive to its 2008 earnings. Separately, on Jan 30 2008, Co.'s Board of Directors announced its plans to spin off all of its interest in Philip Morris International, Inc. (PMI), to its shareholders in a tax-free distribution, which is anticipated to be made on Mar 28 2008. Thus, Co. expects the PMI spin-off to provide solid growth prospects, while sharpen its focus on capital allocation and its market.

Financial Data

(US$ in Thousands)	12/31/2007	12/31/2006	12/31/2005	12/31/2004	12/31/2003	12/31/2002	12/31/2001	12/31/2000
Earnings Per Share	4.62	5.71	4.99	4.56	4.52	5.21	3.87	3.75
Cash Flow Per Share	4.91	6.51	5.34	5.31	5.33	5.03	4.08	4.87
Tang Book Value Per Share	2.66	N.M.	N.M.	N.M.	N.M.	N.M.	N.M.	N.M.
Dividends Per Share	3.050	3.320	3.060	2.820	2.640	2.440	2.220	2.020
Dividend Payout %	66.02	58.14	61.32	61.84	58.41	46.83	57.36	53.87
Income Statement								
Total Revenue	73,801,000	101,407,000	97,854,000	89,610,000	81,832,000	80,408,000	89,924,000	80,356,000
EBITDA	14,215,000	19,217,000	18,267,000	16,787,000	17,350,000	20,563,000	18,039,000	16,396,000
Income Before Taxes	13,020,000	16,536,000	15,435,000	14,004,000	14,760,000	18,098,000	14,284,000	13,960,000
Income Taxes	4,096,000	4,351,000	4,618,000	4,540,000	5,151,000	6,424,000	5,407,000	5,450,000
Net Income	9,786,000	12,022,000	10,435,000	9,416,000	9,204,000	11,102,000	8,560,000	8,510,000
Average Shares	2,116,000	2,105,000	2,090,000	2,063,000	2,038,000	2,129,000	2,210,000	2,272,000
Balance Sheet								
Current Assets	22,890,000	26,152,000	25,781,000	25,901,000	21,382,000	17,441,000	17,275,000	17,238,000
Total Assets	57,211,000	104,270,000	107,949,000	101,648,000	96,175,000	87,540,000	84,968,000	79,067,000
Current Liabilities	18,782,000	25,427,000	26,158,000	23,574,000	21,393,000	19,082,000	20,141,000	25,949,000
Long-Term Obligations	7,963,000	14,498,000	17,868,000	18,683,000	21,163,000	21,355,000	19,163,000	20,181,000
Total Liabilities	38,657,000	64,651,000	72,242,000	70,934,000	71,098,000	68,062,000	65,348,000	64,062,000
Stockholders' Equity	18,554,000	39,619,000	35,707,000	30,714,000	25,077,000	19,478,000	19,620,000	15,005,000
Shares Outstanding	2,107,676	2,097,080	2,084,264	2,059,527	2,037,263	2,039,259	2,152,503	2,208,897
Statistical Record								
Return on Assets %	12.12	11.33	9.96	9.49	10.02	12.87	10.44	12.09
Return on Equity %	33.64	31.92	31.43	33.66	41.32	56.79	49.44	56.00
EBITDA Margin %	19.26	18.95	18.67	18.73	21.20	25.57	20.06	20.40
Net Margin %	13.26	11.86	10.66	10.51	11.25	13.81	9.52	10.59
Asset Turnover	0.91	0.96	0.93	0.90	0.89	0.93	1.10	1.14
Current Ratio	1.22	1.03	0.99	1.10	1.00	0.91	0.86	0.66
Debt to Equity	0.43	0.37	0.50	0.61	0.84	1.10	0.98	1.34
Price Range	24.12-19.03	19.96-15.90	17.90-14.01	14.26-10.40	12.71-6.50	13.36-8.37	12.27-9.29	10.47-4.38
P/E Ratio	5.22-4.12	3.50-2.78	3.59-2.81	3.13-2.28	2.81-1.44	2.56-1.61	3.17-2.40	2.79-1.17
Average Yield %	14.28	18.65	19.38	23.32	27.59	22.08	20.29	31.63

Address: 120 Park Avenue, New York, NY 10017 **Telephone:** 917-663-4000	**Web Site:** www.altria.com **Officers:** Louis C. Camilleri - Chmn., C.E.O. André Calantzopoulos - Pres., C.E.O.	**Auditors:** PricewaterhouseCoopers LLP **Investor Contact:** 917-663-3460 **Transfer Agents:** First Chicago Trust Company, Jersey City, NJ

AMB PROPERTY CORP.

Exchange	Symbol	Price	52Wk Range	Yield	P/E
NYS	AMB	$54.42 (3/31/2008)	65.83-46.76	3.82	18.39

*7 Year Price Score 113.49 *NYSE Composite Index=100 *12 Month Price Score 97.60

Interim Earnings (Per Share)

Qtr.	Mar	Jun	Sep	Dec
2003	0.69	0.19	0.26	0.32
2004	0.19	0.22	0.35	0.66
2005	0.52	0.45	0.31	1.58
2006	0.26	0.80	0.33	0.91
2007	0.23	1.10	0.69	0.92

Interim Dividends (Per Share)

Amt	Decl	Ex	Rec	Pay
0.50Q	5/10/2007	7/3/2007	7/6/2007	7/16/2007
0.50Q	9/27/2007	10/3/2007	10/5/2007	10/15/2007
0.50Q	12/18/2007	12/19/2007	12/21/2007	1/7/2008
0.52Q	2/21/2008	4/2/2008	4/4/2008	4/15/2008

Indicated Div: $2.08

Valuation Analysis

		Institutional Holding	
Forecast P/E	16.03	No of Institutions	
	(1/10/2007)	260	
Market Cap	$5.4 Billion	Shares	
Book Value	2.8 Billion	78,180,232	
Price/Book	1.95	% Held	
Price/Sales	8.06	79.05	

TRADING VOLUME (thousand shares)

Business Summary: Property, Real Estate & Development (MIC: 8.3 SIC: 6798 NAIC: 525930)

AMB Property, through its controlling interest in its subsidiary, AMB Property, L.P., is engaged in acquiring, developing and operating industrial properties in distribution markets throughout Americas, Europe and Asia. Co.'s industrial properties include logistics facilities, centers or warehouses; distribution facilities, centers or warehouses; and High Throughput Distribution® facilities. As of Dec 31 2007, Co. owned or had investments in, on a consolidated basis or through unconsolidated co-investment ventures, properties and development projects expected to total about 147.7 million square feet in 45 markets in 14 countries.

Recent Developments: For the year ended Dec 31 2007, income from continuing operations increased 48.8% to US$242.6 million from US$163.0 million a year earlier. Net income increased 40.2% to US$314.3 million from US$224.1 million in the prior year. Revenues were US$669.7 million, down 5.9% from US$711.3 million the year before. Revenues from property income fell 4.1% to US$638.0 million from US$665.2 million in the corresponding earlier year.

Prospects: Co.'s 2008 outlook appears favorable, reflecting its development pipeline comprising approximately 17.8 million square feet globally, with an estimated total investment of $1.70 billion scheduled for delivery through 2009. Thus, for 2008, Co. reaffirms its previous FFO guidance of $3.85 to $4.05 per share and expects earnings per share of $2.80 to $3.00. Separately, on Jan 15 2008, Co. expanded its portfolio in the Inland Empire submarket of Los Angeles with the acquisition of a 902,000 square foot industrial facility fully-occupied by Wal-Mart Stores, Inc., which should add to Co.'s portfolio of distribution facilities in Southern California totaling more than 22.0 million square feet.

Financial Data

(US$ in Thousands)	12/31/2007	12/31/2006	12/31/2005	12/31/2004	12/31/2003	12/31/2002	12/31/2001	12/31/2000
Earnings Per Share	2.96	2.30	2.85	1.39	1.47	1.37	1.47	1.35
Cash Flow Per Share	2.47	3.83	3.52	3.57	3.35	3.47	3.43	3.11
Tang Book Value Per Share	25.61	21.67	20.28	18.83	19.12	19.36	19.76	19.87
Dividends Per Share	2.000	1.840	1.760	1.700	1.660	1.640	1.580	1.480
Dividend Payout %	67.57	80.00	61.75	122.30	112.93	119.71	107.48	109.63
Income Statement								
Property Income	637,964	683,794	632,207	652,794	601,700	588,522	568,066	464,164
Non-Property Income	31,707	46,102	43,942	12,895	13,337	27,321	32,779	13,543
Total Revenue	669,671	729,896	676,149	665,689	615,037	615,843	600,845	477,707
Interest Expense	126,945	165,230	149,492	157,852	146,773	147,101	128,985	90,270
Net Income	314,260	224,072	257,807	125,471	134,019	124,237	137,953	121,782
Average Shares	99,808	91,106	87,873	85,368	82,852	84,795	85,214	84,155
Balance Sheet								
Total Assets	7,262,403	6,713,512	6,802,739	6,386,943	5,420,666	4,992,494	4,760,893	4,425,626
Long-Term Obligations	3,494,844	3,437,415	3,401,561	3,257,191	2,574,257	2,235,361	2,135,664	1,836,276
Total Liabilities	3,801,040	3,709,295	3,665,305	3,519,477	2,761,352	2,417,077	2,274,265	1,983,318
Stockholders' Equity	2,763,952	2,166,657	1,916,299	1,671,140	1,666,899	1,684,150	1,752,342	1,767,930
Shares Outstanding	99,210	89,662	85,814	83,248	81,792	82,029	83,821	84,138
Statistical Record								
Return on Assets %	4.50	3.32	3.91	2.12	2.57	2.55	3.00	3.02
Return on Equity %	12.75	10.98	14.37	7.50	8.00	7.23	7.84	6.75
Net Margin %	46.93	30.70	38.13	18.85	21.79	20.17	22.96	25.49
Price Range	65.83-49.05	62.77-46.85	49.85-36.89	41.08-29.25	33.45-26.00	31.00-24.99	26.64-22.90	26.06-19.25
P/E Ratio	22.24-16.57	27.29-20.37	17.49-12.94	29.55-21.04	22.76-17.69	22.63-18.24	18.12-15.58	19.31-14.26
Average Yield %	3.42	3.43	4.17	4.77	5.75	5.89	6.37	6.50

Address: Pier 1, Bay 1, San Francisco, CA 94111
Telephone: 415-394-9000
Fax: 415-394-9001

Web Site: www.amb.com
Officers: Hamid R. Moghadam - Chmn., C.E.O. W. Blake Baird - Pres.

Auditors: PricewaterhouseCoopers LLP
Transfer Agents: Computershare Trust

AMBAC FINANCIAL GROUP, INC.

Exchange	Symbol	Price	52Wk Range	Yield	P/E	Div Acheiver
NYS	ABK	$5.75 (3/31/2008)	96.08-5.41	4.87	N/A	16 Years

*7 Year Price Score 61.72 *NYSE Composite Index=100 *12 Month Price Score 20.02

Interim Earnings (Per Share)

Qtr.	Mar	Jun	Sep	Dec
2003	1.27	1.48	1.45	1.45
2004	1.55	1.63	1.65	1.69
2005	1.66	1.69	1.61	1.90
2006	2.06	2.22	1.98	1.89
2007	2.02	1.67	(3.53)	(31.81)

Interim Dividends (Per Share)

Amt	Decl	Ex	Rec	Pay
0.18Q	5/8/2007	5/18/2007	5/22/2007	6/6/2007
0.21Q	7/25/2007	8/8/2007	8/10/2007	9/5/2007
0.21Q	10/24/2007	11/7/2007	11/12/2007	12/5/2007
0.07Q	1/29/2008	2/7/2008	2/11/2008	3/5/2008

Indicated Div: $0.28

Valuation Analysis | **Institutional Holding**

Valuation Analysis		Institutional Holding	
Forecast P/E	10.25	No of Institutions	
	(1/10/2007)	403	
Market Cap	$583.9 Million	Shares	
Book Value	2.3 Billion	101,899,136	
Price/Book	0.26	% Held	
Price/Sales	N/A	99.55	

Business Summary: Insurance (MIC: 8.2 SIC: 6351 NAIC: 524130)

Ambac Financial Group is a holding company. At Dec 31 2007, Co. had two reportable segments: Financial Guarantee, which provides financial guarantees, including credit derivatives for public finance, structured finance and other obligations; and Financial Services, which provides investment agreements, funding conduits, interest rate, total return and currency swaps, principally to clients of the financial guarantee business, which includes municipalities and other public entities, health care organizations, investor-owned utilities and asset-backed issuers. As of Dec 31 2007, Co. had $23.57 billion of total assets.

Recent Developments: For the year ended Dec 31 2007, net loss amounted to US$3.25 billion versus net income of US$875.9 million in the prior year. Revenues were US$4.21 billion, compared with US$1.83 billion the year before. Net premiums earned were US$841.5 million versus US$811.6 million in the prior year, an increase of 3.7%. Net investment income rose 10.7% to US$915.4 million from US$827.2 million a year ago.

Prospects: Co.'s outlook appears challenging, reflecting decreases in its top- and bottom-line results. Meanwhile, Co. expects the negative effect of the Assured Guaranty Re., Ltd., cede, which has taken place in early Dec 2007, on its full year 2008 premiums earned to be approximately $28.0 million. In addition, Co. anticipates making a number of changes to its business. Thus, Co. states that certain of its businesses in which it currently operate will be suspended or discontinued, and other businesses de-emphasized or subject to new limitations. Accordingly, Co. believes that these changes will result in lower revenues, credit enhancement production and net income relative to historical levels.

Financial Data

(US$ in Thousands)	12/31/2007	12/31/2006	12/31/2005	12/31/2004	12/31/2003	12/31/2002	12/31/2001	12/31/2000
Earnings Per Share	(31.56)	8.15	6.87	6.53	5.66	3.97	3.97	3.41
Cash Flow Per Share	9.18	8.47	9.30	8.64	9.42	7.60	6.36	4.57
Tang Book Value Per Share	22.45	58.49	50.85	46.13	39.71	34.20	28.26	24.60
Dividends Per Share	0.780	0.660	0.550	0.470	0.420	0.380	0.340	0.307
Dividend Payout %	...	8.10	8.01	7.20	7.42	9.57	8.56	8.99
Income Statement								
Premium Income	841,461	811,623	816,020	716,659	620,317	471,534	378,734	311,276
Total Revenue	(4,214,926)	1,832,104	1,661,707	1,406,708	1,272,208	971,818	724,920	621,310
Benefits & Claims	256,109	20,004	149,856	69,600	53,400	26,700	20,000	15,000
Income Before Taxes	(5,146,916)	1,210,213	1,022,764	976,782	849,589	564,190	568,727	482,124
Income Taxes	(1,898,759)	334,302	271,754	250,942	221,490	131,596	135,821	115,952
Net Income	(3,248,157)	875,911	751,010*	724,551	618,915	432,594	432,906	366,172
Average Shares	102,929	107,536	109,394	110,898	109,409	109,066	108,948	107,415
Balance Sheet								
Total Assets	23,565,011	20,267,813	19,725,140	18,585,258	16,747,314	15,355,538	12,267,695	10,120,300
Total Liabilities	21,285,118	14,083,624	14,352,933	13,560,801	12,492,756	11,730,359	9,284,007	7,524,186
Stockholders' Equity	2,279,893	6,184,189	5,372,207	5,024,457	4,254,558	3,625,179	2,983,688	2,596,114
Shares Outstanding	101,550	105,730	105,639	108,915	107,144	105,990	105,584	105,550
Statistical Record								
Return on Assets %	N.M.	4.38	3.92	4.09	3.86	3.13	3.87	3.40
Return on Equity %	N.M.	15.16	14.45	15.57	15.71	13.09	15.52	15.83
Loss Ratio %	30.44	2.46	18.36	9.71	8.61	5.66	5.28	4.82
Net Margin %	...	47.81	45.20	51.51	48.65	44.51	59.72	58.94
Price Range	96.08-21.79	89.78-74.17	82.39-62.20	84.42-64.04	72.19-44.51	69.69-49.90	63.43-45.50	58.31-26.13
P/E Ratio	...	11.02-9.10	11.99-9.05	12.93-9.81	12.75-7.86	17.55-12.57	15.98-11.46	17.10-7.66
Average Yield %	1.10	0.81	0.75	0.63	0.68	0.63	0.61	0.77

Address: One State Street Plaza, New York, NY 10004
Telephone: 212-668-0340
Fax: 212-509-9190

Web Site: www.ambac.com
Officers: Phillip B. Lassiter - Chmn. Howard C. Pfeffer - Vice-Chmn., Sr. Managing Dir., Public Fin., Investment & Fin. Serv.

Auditors: KPMG LLP
Investor Contact: 212-208-3333
Transfer Agents: Citibank, N.A., New York, NY

AMEREN CORP.

Exchange	Symbol	Price	52Wk Range	Yield	P/E
NYS	AEE	$44.04 (3/31/2008)	54.93-41.49	5.77	14.78

*7 Year Price Score 85.83   ***NYSE Composite Index=100**   ***12 Month Price Score 93.43**

Interim Earnings (Per Share)

Qtr.	Mar	Jun	Sep	Dec
2003	0.63	0.68	1.70	0.23
2004	0.55	0.65	1.20	0.40
2005	0.62	0.93	1.37	0.08
2006	0.34	0.60	1.42	0.29
2007	0.59	0.69	1.18	0.52

Interim Dividends (Per Share)

Amt	Decl	Ex	Rec	Pay
0.635Q	4/24/2007	6/4/2007	6/6/2007	6/29/2007
0.635Q	8/10/2007	9/4/2007	9/6/2007	9/28/2007
0.635Q	10/12/2007	12/3/2007	12/5/2007	12/31/2007
0.635Q	2/8/2008	3/3/2008	3/5/2008	3/31/2008

Indicated Div. 32.54

Valuation Analysis   **Institutional Holding**

Forecast P/E	13.09 (1/10/2007)	No of Institutions 370
Market Cap	$9.2 Billion	Shares 127,762,032
Book Value	6.8 Billion	% Held 61.94
Price/Book	1.36	
Price/Sales	1.22	

TRADING VOLUME (thousand shares)

Business Summary: Electricity (MIC: 7.1 SIC: 4931 NAIC: 221111)

Ameren is a public utility holding company. Through its subsidiaries, Co. operates rate-regulated electric generation, transmission and distribution businesses; rate-regulated natural gas transmission and distribution businesses; and non-rate-regulated electric generation businesses in Missouri and Illinois. As of Dec 31 2007, Co.'s subsidiaries included Union Electric Company (UE), Central Illinois Public Service Company (CIPS), CILCORP Inc. (CILCORP) and Illinois Power Company (IP). UE, CIPS, CILCO and IP develop and manage a portfolio of gas supply resources; all of which are responsible for the purchase and delivery of natural gas to their gas utility customers.

Recent Developments: For the year ended Dec 31 2007, net income increased 13.0% to US$618.0 million from US$547.0 million in the prior year. Revenues were US$7.55 billion, up 9.7% from US$6.88 billion the year before. Operating income was US$1.34 billion versus US$1.17 billion in the prior year, an increase of 14.4%. Indirect operating expenses increased 8.7% to US$6.20 billion from US$5.71 billion in the equivalent prior-year period.

Prospects: For 2008, Co. is expecting earnings of $2.68 to $3.08 per share, assuming normal weather for the year. For example, Co. estimates earnings growth in its rate regulated businesses to come from factors, such as the updating of existing customer rates to better reflect the investments in its electric and gas infrastructure. However, Co. expects earnings to be tempered by rising costs and investments, mainly in its regulated businesses. As such, Co. plans to mitigate such situation via several initiatives, including filing more frequent rate cases requesting moderate rate increases and improving the output of its non-rate-regulated electric generation business and related energy marketing.

Financial Data

(US$ in Thousands)	12/31/2007	12/31/2006	12/31/2005	12/31/2004	12/31/2003	12/31/2002	12/31/2001	12/31/2000
Earnings Per Share	2.98	2.66	3.02	2.84	3.25	2.60	3.40	3.33
Cash Flow Per Share	5.31	6.22	5.83	6.04	6.40	5.70	5.37	6.22
Tang Book Value Per Share	27.47	26.80	25.12	24.90	23.20	24.93	24.26	23.30
Dividends Per Share	2.540	2.540	2.540	2.540	2.540	2.540	2.540	2.540
Dividend Payout %	85.23	95.49	84.11	89.44	78.15	97.69	74.71	76.28
Income Statement								
Total Revenue	7,546,000	6,880,000	6,780,000	5,160,000	4,593,000	3,841,000	4,505,867	3,855,849
EBITDA	2,172,000	1,898,000	1,932,000	1,691,000	1,646,000	...	...	...
Income Before Taxes	986,000	869,000	1,000,000	812,000	807,000	...	...	...
Income Taxes	330,000	284,000	356,000	282,000	301,000	...	...	...
Net Income	618,000	547,000	606,000	530,000	524,000	382,000	468,545	457,094
Average Shares	207,400	205,600	200,800	186,400	161,100	146,100	137,320	137,215
Balance Sheet								
Net PPE	15,069,000	14,286,000	13,572,000	13,297,000	10,917,000	8,914,000	8,426,562	7,705,672
Total Assets	20,728,000	19,578,000	18,162,000	17,434,000	14,233,000	11,499,000	10,400,575	9,714,430
Long-Term Obligations	5,691,000	5,285,000	5,354,000	5,021,000	4,070,000	3,433,000	2,835,378	2,745,068
Total Liabilities	13,759,000	12,784,000	11,586,000	11,425,000	9,675,000	7,449,000	6,813,084	6,278,622
Stockholders' Equity	6,752,000	6,583,000	6,364,000	5,800,000	4,354,000	3,842,000	3,348,760	3,196,671
Shares Outstanding	208,300	206,600	204,700	195,200	162,900	154,100	138,045	137,215
Statistical Record								
Return on Assets %	3.07	2.90	3.40	3.34	4.07	3.49	4.66	4.83
Return on Equity %	9.27	8.45	9.96	10.41	12.79	10.62	14.32	14.50
EBITDA Margin %	28.78	27.59	28.50	32.77	35.84	...	...	...
Net Margin %	8.19	7.95	8.94	10.27	11.41	9.95	10.40	11.85
PPE Turnover	0.51	0.49	0.50	0.43	0.46	0.44	0.56	0.52
Asset Turnover	0.37	0.36	0.38	0.33	0.36	0.35	0.45	0.41
Debt to Equity	0.84	0.80	0.84	0.87	0.93	0.89	0.85	0.86
Price Range	54.93-47.54	55.12-48.04	56.29-47.72	50.15-40.78	46.49-37.95	45.13-36.55	45.19-37.10	46.81-27.81
P/E Ratio	18.43-15.95	20.72-18.06	18.64-15.80	17.66-14.36	14.30-11.68	17.36-14.06	13.29-10.91	14.06-8.35
Average Yield %	4.88	4.93	4.85	5.53	5.99	6.06	6.19	6.92

Address: 1901 Chouteau Avenue, St. Louis, MO 63103	Web Site: www.ameren.com	Auditors: PricewaterhouseCoopers LLP
Telephone: 314-621-3222	Officers: Gary L. Rainwater - Chmn., Pres., C.E.O.	Transfer Agents: Ameren Services Company, St. Louis, MO
Fax: 314-621-2888	Warner L. Baxter - Exec. V.P., C.F.O.	

AMERICAN EAGLE OUTFITTERS, INC.

Exchange	Symbol	Price	52Wk Range	Yield	P/E
NYS	AEO	$17.51 (3/31/2008)	31.18-16.47	2.28	9.62

*7 Year Price Score 130.35 *NYSE Composite Index=100 *12 Month Price Score 91.62

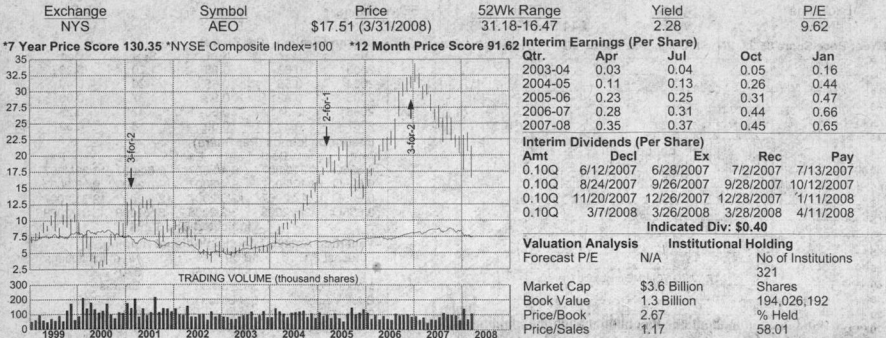

Interim Earnings (Per Share)

Qtr.	Apr	Jul	Oct	Jan
2003-04	0.03	0.04	0.05	0.16
2004-05	0.11	0.13	0.26	0.44
2005-06	0.23	0.25	0.31	0.47
2006-07	0.28	0.31	0.44	0.66
2007-08	0.35	0.37	0.45	0.65

Interim Dividends (Per Share)

Amt	Decl	Ex	Rec	Pay
0.10Q	6/12/2007	6/28/2007	7/2/2007	7/13/2007
0.10Q	8/24/2007	9/26/2007	9/28/2007	10/12/2007
0.10Q	11/20/2007	12/26/2007	12/28/2007	1/11/2008
0.10Q	3/7/2008	3/26/2008	3/28/2008	4/11/2008
			Indicated Div: $0.40	

Valuation Analysis | **Institutional Holding**

Forecast P/E	N/A	No of Institutions
		321
Market Cap	$3.6 Billion	Shares
Book Value	1.3 Billion	194,026,192
Price/Book	2.67	% Held
Price/Sales	1.17	58.01

Business Summary: Retail - Apparel and Accessory Stores (MIC: 5.8 SIC: 5651 NAIC: 448140)

American Eagle Outfitters is a retailer that operates under the the American Eagle Outfitters®, aerie™ by American Eagle and MARTIN + OSA™ brands. Co. designs, markets and sells merchandise targeting 15 to 25 year-olds. Co. also distributes merchandise via its e-commerce operation, ae.com, which provides additional sizes, colors and styles of AE® merchandise. Co.'s collection includes standards like jeans and graphic t-shirts as well as accessories, outerwear, footwear, basics and swimwear under its American Eagle Outfitters®, American Eagle® and AE® brand names. Co.'s MARTIN + OSA™ provides refined casual clothing and accessories, targeting 28 to 40 year-old women and men.

Recent Developments: For the year ended Feb 2 2008, income from continuing operations increased 3.3% to US$400.0 million from US$387.4 million a year earlier. Net income increased 3.3% to US$400.0 million from US$387.4 million in the prior year. Revenues were US$3.06 billion, up 9.3% from US$2.79 billion the year before. Operating income was US$598.8 million versus US$586.8 million in the prior year, an increase of 2.0%. Direct operating expenses rose 12.3% to US$1.63 billion from US$1.45 billion in the comparable period the year before. Indirect operating expenses increased 9.4% to US$824.4 million from US$753.6 million in the equivalent prior-year period.

Prospects: For the fiscal year ending Jan 31 2009, Co. intends to open about 80 stores, all of which will be 3,500 to 4,500 gross square feet. Additionally, Co. plans to open about 40 new AE® stores, 15 MARTIN + OSA stores, as well as remodel about 40 to 50 existing AE® stores. In this respect, Co. is projecting square footage growth to be approximately 10.0%. Meanwhile, for the third quarter ended May 2008, Co. continues to anticipate earnings to be in the range of $0.25 to $0.27 per share, versus earnings of $0.35 per share in the previous fiscal year, reflecting negative comparable store sales for the remainder of this fiscal quarter and a higher markdown rate compared with prior fiscal year.

Financial Data

(US$ in Thousands)	02/02/2008	02/03/2007	01/28/2006	01/29/2005	01/31/2004	02/01/2003	02/02/2002	02/03/2001
Earnings Per Share	1.82	1.70	1.26	0.95	0.28	0.41	0.48	0.43
Cash Flow Per Share	2.15	3.31	2.12	1.70	0.89	0.49	0.82	0.71
Tang Book Value Per Share	6.50	6.36	5.16	4.25	2.97	2.60	2.22	1.63
Dividends Per Share	0.375	0.275	0.183	0.040	...	...	...	...
Dividend Payout %	20.60	16.18	14.55	4.23	...	...	...	...
Income Statement								
Total Revenue	3,055,419	2,794,409	2,309,371	1,881,241	1,519,968	1,463,141	1,371,899	1,093,477
EBITDA	745,584	717,100	551,545	435,108	162,866	194,274	211,120	176,000
Income Before Taxes	636,381	629,067	476,967	366,835	106,585	143,613	169,245	152,800
Income Taxes	236,362	241,708	183,256	142,603	46,585	54,878	63,750	59,042
Net Income	400,019	387,359	294,153	213,343	60,000	88,735	105,495	93,758
Average Shares	220,280	228,384	233,031	225,366	216,621	218,349	221,391	216,396
Balance Sheet								
Current Assets	1,020,834	1,198,254	1,080,672	827,640	525,623	427,878	378,030	318,661
Total Assets	1,867,680	1,987,484	1,605,649	1,293,659	865,071	741,339	672,721	543,046
Current Liabilities	376,178	460,464	361,623	253,265	189,035	141,586	149,942	149,147
Long-Term Obligations	...	...	...	...	13,874	16,356	19,361	24,889
Total Liabilities	527,216	570,172	450,097	330,173	221,401	163,857	170,669	175,351
Stockholders' Equity	1,340,464	1,417,312	1,155,552	963,486	643,670	577,482	502,052	367,695
Shares Outstanding	204,480	221,284	221,896	224,232	213,573	213,141	215,718	211,257
Statistical Record								
Return on Assets %	20.81	21.21	20.35	19.82	7.49	12.58	17.40	20.55
Return on Equity %	29.09	29.62	27.84	26.62	9.85	16.48	24.33	29.18
EBITDA Margin %	24.40	25.66	23.88	23.13	10.72	13.28	15.39	16.10
Net Margin %	13.09	13.86	12.74	11.34	3.95	6.06	7.69	8.57
Asset Turnover	1.59	1.53	1.60	1.75	1.90	2.08	2.26	2.40
Current Ratio	2.71	2.60	2.99	3.27	2.78	3.02	2.52	2.14
Debt to Equity	...	...	...	...	0.02	0.03	0.04	0.07
Price Range	32.67-17.70	34.34-16.80	22.32-13.33	16.83-6.37	7.47-4.52	9.67-3.43	13.76-5.86	12.86-2.64
P/E Ratio	17.95-9.73	20.20-9.88	17.71-10.58	17.71-6.70	26.69-16.13	23.58-8.37	28.67-12.20	29.91-6.14
Average Yield %	1.46	1.10	1.03	0.36	...	...	...	...

Address: 150 Thorn Hill Drive, Warrendale, PA 15086-7528
Telephone: 724-776-4857
Fax: 724-776-6160

Web Site: www.ae.com
Officers: Jay L. Schottenstein - Chmn. Roger S. Markfield - Vice-Chmn., Pres.

Auditors: Ernst & Young LLP
Investor Contact: 724-776-4857
Transfer Agents: National City Bank, Cleveland, OH

AMERICAN ELECTRIC POWER COMPANY, INC.

Exchange	Symbol	Price	52Wk Range	Yield	P/E
NYS	AEP	$41.63 (3/31/2008)	50.95-40.23	3.94	15.31

*7 Year Price Score 99.10   *NYSE Composite Index=100   ***12 Month Price Score 98.50**

TRADING VOLUME (thousand shares)

Interim Earnings (Per Share)

Qtr.	Mar	Jun	Sep	Dec
2003	1.24	0.44	0.65	(1.99)
2004	0.70	0.25	1.34	0.45
2005	0.90	0.58	0.99	(0.39)
2006	0.96	0.44	0.67	0.46
2007	0.68	0.45	1.02	0.57

Interim Dividends (Per Share)

Amt	Decl	Ex	Rec	Pay
0.39Q	4/24/2007	5/8/2007	5/10/2007	6/8/2007
0.39Q	7/25/2007	8/8/2007	8/10/2007	9/10/2007
0.41Q	10/23/2007	11/7/2007	11/9/2007	12/10/2007
0.41Q	1/23/2008	2/6/2008	2/8/2008	3/10/2008

Indicated Div: $1.64

Valuation Analysis

		Institutional Holding	
Forecast P/E	13.34	No of Institutions	
	(1/10/2007)	484	
Market Cap	$16.7 Billion	Shares	
Book Value	10.1 Billion	277,999,136	
Price/Book	1.65	% Held	
Price/Sales	1.25	70.08	

Business Summary: Electricity (MIC: 7.1 SIC: 4911 NAIC: 221121)

American Electric Power Company is a public utility holding company. Co.'s electric utility operating companies provide generation, transmission and distribution services to customers in Arkansas, Indiana, Kentucky, Louisiana, Michigan, Ohio, Oklahoma, Tennessee, Texas, Virginia and West Virginia. At Dec 31 2007, Co. operated a portfolio of assets including about 38,000 megawatts of generating capacity; about 39,000 miles of transmission lines; 212,781 miles of distribution lines that deliver electricity to 5.2 million customers; and coal transportation assets, which include over 8,400 railcars, 2,650 barges, 52 towboats and a coal handling terminal with 20.0 million tons of annual capacity.

Recent Developments: For the year ended Dec 31 2007, income from continuing operations increased 15.3% to US$1.14 billion from US$992.0 million a year earlier. Net income increased 8.7% to US$1.09 billion from US$1.00 billion in the prior year. Revenues were US$13.38 billion, up 6.0% from US$12.62 billion the year before. Operating income was US$2.32 billion versus US$1.97 billion in the prior year, an increase of 18.0%. Direct operating expenses rose 6.3% to US$8.83 billion from US$8.31 billion in the comparable period the year before. Indirect operating expenses decreased 5.0% to US$2.23 billion from US$2.34 billion in the equivalent prior-year period.

Prospects: Co.'s outlook appears constructive. For instance, on Mar 3 2008, Co. announced that the Potomac-Appalachian Transmission Highline, its joint venture with Allegheny Energy Inc., has received approval from the Federal Energy Regulatory Commission for transmission incentives to support construction of the 290-mile transmission line from West Virginia to Maryland. The project cost is estimated at about $1.80 billion, with Co.'s share of the project estimated at about $600.0 million. Meanwhile, in view of the strong results from its wholesale marketing activities and earnings potential related to its regulatory plan, Co. has raised its 2008 ongoing earnings guidance to $3.10 to $3.30 per share.

Financial Data

(US$ in Thousands)	12/31/2007	12/31/2006	12/31/2005	12/31/2004	12/31/2003	12/31/2002	12/31/2001	12/31/2000
Earnings Per Share	2.72	2.53	2.08	2.75	0.29	(1.57)	3.01	0.83
Cash Flow Per Share	5.99	6.93	4.81	6.34	5.99	5.05	9.17	4.65
Tang Book Value Per Share	24.98	23.54	22.89	21.32	19.74	19.68	20.90	20.72
Dividends Per Share	1.580	1.500	1.420	1.400	1.650	2.400	2.400	2.400
Dividend Payout %	58.09	59.29	68.27	50.91	568.97	...	79.73	289.16
Income Statement								
Total Revenue	13,380,000	12,622,000	12,111,000	14,057,000	14,545,000	14,555,000	61,257,000	13,694,000
EBITDA	4,076,000	3,726,000	3,514,000	3,808,000	2,989,000	2,463,000	3,957,000	2,198,000
Income Before Taxes	1,657,000	1,477,000	1,453,000	1,699,000	880,000	235,000	1,572,000	899,000
Income Taxes	516,000	485,000	430,000	572,000	358,000	214,000	569,000	597,000
Net Income	1,089,000	1,002,000	814,000	1,089,000	110,000	(519,000)	971,000	267,000
Average Shares	400,198	396,483	391,000	396,000	385,000	332,000	322,000	322,000
Balance Sheet								
Net PPE	29,870,000	26,781,000	24,284,000	22,801,000	22,029,000	21,684,000	24,543,000	22,393,000
Total Assets	40,366,000	37,987,000	36,172,000	34,663,000	36,744,000	34,741,000	47,281,000	54,548,000
Long-Term Obligations	14,202,000	12,429,000	11,073,000	11,008,000	12,322,000	8,863,000	9,753,000	9,602,000
Total Liabilities	30,226,000	28,514,000	27,023,000	26,087,000	28,809,000	27,532,000	38,896,000	46,333,000
Stockholders' Equity	10,079,000	9,412,000	9,088,000	8,515,000	7,874,000	7,064,000	8,229,000	8,054,000
Shares Outstanding	400,426	396,674	393,718	395,858	395,016	338,835	322,235	322,019
Statistical Record								
Return on Assets %	2.78	2.70	2.30	3.04	0.31	N.M.	1.91	0.70
Return on Equity %	11.17	10.83	9.25	13.25	1.47	N.M.	11.93	4.08
EBITDA Margin %	30.46	29.52	29.01	27.09	20.55	16.92	6.46	16.05
Net Margin %	8.14	7.94	6.72	7.75	0.76	(3.57)	1.59	1.95
PPE Turnover	0.47	0.49	0.51	0.63	0.67	0.63	2.61	0.77
Asset Turnover	0.34	0.34	0.34	0.39	0.41	0.35	1.20	0.36
Debt to Equity	1.41	1.32	1.22	1.29	1.56	1.25	1.19	1.19
Price Range	50.95-41.86	42.93-32.31	40.25-32.50	35.23-29.01	31.04-19.94	48.06-17.69	51.11-39.81	48.00-26.06
P/E Ratio	18.73-15.39	16.97-12.77	19.35-15.62	12.81-10.55	107.03-68.76	...	16.98-13.23	57.83-31.40
Average Yield %	3.40	4.08	3.92	4.32	6.12	6.61	5.29	6.75

Address: 1 Riverside Plaza, Columbus, OH 43215-2373 Telephone: 614-716-1000 Fax: 614-223-1823	Web Site: www.aep.com Officers: Michael G. Morris - Chmn., Pres., C.E.O. Susan Tomasky - Exec. V.P., Policy, Fin., Strategic Planning, C.F.O.	Auditors: Deloitte & Touche LLP Investor Contact: 614-716-2885 Transfer Agents: EquiServe Trust Company, N.A., Providence, RI

AMERICAN EXPRESS CO.

Exchange	Symbol	Price	52Wk Range	Yield	P/E
NYS	AXP	$43.72 (3/31/2008)	65.55-40.04	1.65	13.01

*7 Year Price Score 101.53 *NYSE Composite Index=100 *12 Month Price Score 85.87

Interim Earnings (Per Share)

Qtr.	Mar	Jun	Sep	Dec
2003	0.53	0.59	0.59	0.59
2004	0.61	0.68	0.69	0.70
2005	0.75	0.81	0.82	0.59
2006	0.69	0.76	0.79	0.75
2007	0.87	0.88	0.90	0.71

Interim Dividends (Per Share)

Amt	Decl	Ex	Rec	Pay
0.15Q	5/22/2007	7/3/2007	7/6/2007	8/10/2007
0.15Q	9/25/2007	10/3/2007	10/5/2007	11/9/2007
0.18Q	11/19/2007	1/2/2008	1/4/2008	2/8/2008
0.18Q	3/31/2008	4/9/2008	4/11/2008	5/9/2008
			Indicated Div: $0.72	

Valuation Analysis

		Institutional Holding	
Forecast P/E	16.07	No of Institutions	
	(1/10/2007)	1084	
Market Cap	$50.6 Billion	Shares	
Book Value	11.0 Billion	977,163,456	
Price/Book	4.59	% Held	
Price/Sales	1.83	81.95	

Business Summary: Credit & Lending (MIC: 8.6 SIC: 6159 NAIC: 522298)

American Express is a payments, network and travel company. Co.'s products and services include charge and credit cards; Travelers Cheques and prepaid products; consumer travel services; business travel, corporate cards and other expense management products and services; network services and merchant acquisition and merchant processing for its network partners and proprietary payments businesses; and point-of-sale, back-office, and marketing products and services. These products and services are sold through various channels including direct mail, the Internet and direct response advertising. At Dec 31 2007, Co. had two segments: Global Consumer Group and Global Business-to-Business Group.

Recent Developments: For the year ended Dec 31 2007, income from continuing operations increased 12.1% to US$4.05 billion from US$3.61 billion a year earlier. Net income increased 8.2% to US$4.01 billion from US$3.71 billion in the prior year. Net interest income increased 29.4% to US$7.42 billion from US$5.73 billion in the prior year. Provision for loan losses was US$4.34 billion versus US$3.03 billion in the prior year, an increase of 43.5%. Non-interest income rose 4.6% to US$20.32 billion from US$19.42 billion, while non-interest expense advanced 4.9% to US$17.82 billion.

Prospects: On Feb 29 2008, Co. announced that it has sold its international banking subsidiary, American Express Bank Ltd. (AEB), to Standard Chartered PLC for about $823.0 million. Going forward, Co. expects to realize an additional amount representing the net asset value of American Express International Deposit Co. (AEIDC), a subsidiary that issues investment certificates to AEB's customers, which has been contracted to be sold to Standard Chartered 18 months after the close of the AEB sale, through a put/call agreement. At Dec 31 2007, the net asset value of the AEIDC business was $232.0 million. Meanwhile, Co. expects its reported earnings per share for 2008 to grow in the 4.0% to 6.0% range.

Financial Data
(US$ in Thousands)

	12/31/2007	12/31/2006	12/31/2005	12/31/2004	12/31/2003	12/31/2002	12/31/2001	12/31/2000
Earnings Per Share	3.36	2.99	2.97	2.68	2.30	2.01	0.98	2.07
Cash Flow Per Share	7.23	7.43	6.52	7.24	1.98	6.57	4.02	4.77
Tang Book Value Per Share	9.52	8.77	8.50	12.83	11.93	10.62	9.04	8.81
Dividends Per Share	0.600	0.540	0.480	0.320	0.380	0.400	0.320	0.315
Dividend Payout %	17.86	18.06	16.16	11.94	16.52	19.90	32.65	15.22
Income Statement								
Total Revenue	27,731,000	27,136,000	24,267,000	29,115,000	25,866,000	23,807,000	22,582,000	23,675,000
Income Before Taxes	5,566,000	5,328,000	4,248,000	4,951,000	4,247,000	3,727,000	1,596,000	3,908,000
Income Taxes	1,518,000	1,599,000	1,027,000	1,435,000	1,247,000	1,056,000	285,000	1,098,000
Net Income	4,012,000	3,707,000	3,734,000	3,445,000	2,987,000	2,671,000	1,311,000	2,810,000
Average Shares	1,196,000	1,238,000	1,258,000	1,285,000	1,298,000	1,330,000	1,336,000	1,360,000
Balance Sheet								
Total Assets	149,830,000	127,853,000	113,960,000	192,638,000	175,001,000	157,253,000	151,100,000	154,423,000
Total Liabilities	138,801,000	117,342,000	103,411,000	176,618,000	159,678,000	143,392,000	138,563,000	142,239,000
Stockholders' Equity	11,029,000	10,511,000	10,549,000	16,020,000	15,323,000	13,861,000	12,037,000	11,684,000
Shares Outstanding	1,158,000	1,199,000	1,241,000	1,249,000	1,284,000	1,305,000	1,331,000	1,326,000
Statistical Record								
Return on Assets %	2.89	3.07	2.44	1.87	1.80	1.73	0.86	1.85
Return on Equity %	37.25	35.20	28.11	21.92	20.47	20.63	11.05	25.73
Price Range	65.55-50.84	61.90-50.62	52.84-43.60	49.82-41.75	42.90-27.56	39.28-23.28	48.96-22.42	55.15-35.82
P/E Ratio	19.51-15.13	20.70-16.93	17.79-14.68	18.59-15.58	18.65-11.98	19.54-11.58	49.96-22.88	26.64-17.30
Average Yield %	1.01	0.99	1.00	0.71	1.05	1.24	0.95	0.67

Address: 200 Vesey Street, New York, NY 10285	Web Site: www.americanexpress.com	Auditors: PricewaterhouseCoopers LLP
Telephone: 212-640-2000	Officers: Kenneth I. Chenault - Chmn., C.E.O. Jonathan S. Linen - Vice-Chmn.	Transfer Agents: Mellon Investor Services LLC, Ridgefield Park, NJ

AMERICAN FINANCIAL GROUP, INC (HOLDING CO.)

Exchange	Symbol	Price	52Wk Range	Yield	P/E
NYS	AFG	$25.56 (3/31/2008)	36.26-24.39	1.96	8.25

*7 Year Price Score 109.27 *NYSE Composite Index=100   *12 Month Price Score 93.83

Interim Earnings (Per Share)

Qtr.	Mar	Jun	Sep	Dec
2003	0.24	0.29	0.39	1.82
2004	0.65	0.50	1.23	0.82
2005	0.54	0.69	(0.23)	0.73
2006	0.85	1.02	0.77	1.11
2007	0.92	0.54	0.93	0.70

Interim Dividends (Per Share)

Amt	Decl	Ex	Rec	Pay
0.10Q	7/2/2007	7/11/2007	7/13/2007	7/25/2007
0.10Q	10/1/2007	10/11/2007	10/15/2007	10/25/2007
0.125Q	1/1/2008	1/11/2008	1/15/2008	1/25/2008
0.125Q	4/1/2008	4/11/2008	4/15/2008	4/25/2008

Indicated Div: $0.50

Valuation Analysis   **Institutional Holding**

Forecast P/E	N/A	No of Institutions
		228
Market Cap	$2.9 Billion	Shares
Book Value	3.0 Billion	69,214,768
Price/Book	0.95	% Held
Price/Sales	0.66	57.76

TRADING VOLUME (thousand shares)

Business Summary: Insurance (MIC: 8.2 SIC: 6331 NAIC: 524126)

American Financial Group is a holding company that, through its subsidiaries, is engaged primarily in property and casualty insurance and in the sale of traditional fixed, indexed and variable annuities and a variety of supplemental insurance products. Co.'s property and casualty insurance segment reports in four Specialty sub-segments: Property and Transportation, Specialty Casualty, Specialty Financial and California Workers' Compensation. Co.'s annuity and supplemental insurance business markets traditional fixed, indexed and variable annuities and a variety of supplemental insurance products.

Recent Developments: For the year ended Dec 31 2007, net income decreased 15.5% to US$383.2 million from US$453.4 million in the prior year. Revenues were US$4.40 billion, up 3.6% from US$4.25 billion the year before. Net premiums earned were US$3.13 billion versus US$2.92 billion in the prior year, an increase of 7.1%.

Prospects: Co. continues to evaluate expansion in existing markets and opportunities in new specialty markets that meet its profitability objectives. For example, in Jan 2008, Co. acquired a majority interest in Marketform Group Ltd., an insurer in the non-U.S. medical malpractice market, and Strategic Comp Holdings, LLC, a provider of workers' compensation programs in the U.S., which are expected to contribute to continuing growth of its specialty property and casualty business. For 2008, Co. is targeting net written premium growth of 4.0% to 7.0%. Co. also expects strong underwriting profits; however, it is anticipating a modest decline in its specialty group's overall average renewal rates in 2008.

Financial Data
(US$ in Thousands)

	12/31/2007	12/31/2006	12/31/2005	12/31/2004	12/31/2003	12/31/2002	12/31/2001	12/31/2000
Earnings Per Share	3.10	3.75	1.75	3.21	2.75	0.81	(0.15)	(0.63)
Cash Flow Per Share	6.70	8.20	8.83	9.10	7.14	7.87	7.09	4.98
Tang Book Value Per Share	25.04	23.14	19.56	19.70	17.41	14.25	11.54	12.16
Dividends Per Share	0.400	0.367	0.333	0.333	0.333	0.333	0.667	0.667
Dividend Payout %	12.90	9.78	19.08	10.40	12.14	40.98	...	...
Income Statement								
Premium Income	3,126,400	2,917,800	2,737,503	2,461,667	2,241,093	2,708,247	2,874,060	2,725,333
Total Revenue	4,404,700	4,250,100	4,038,283	3,906,265	3,359,643	3,749,568	3,923,632	3,817,327
Benefits & Claims	2,149,500	2,109,600	2,317,225	1,994,631	1,898,830	2,360,936	2,587,733	2,415,639
Income Before Taxes	638,900	697,600	356,814	589,538	301,006	178,019	55,898	109,893
Income Taxes	225,800	235,700	115,843	186,089	(47,454)	17,880	10,078	29,041
Net Income	383,200	453,400	206,580	359,860	293,815	84,640	(14,840)	(56,035)
Average Shares	123,200	120,500	117,769	112,237	105,408	103,804	102,552	88,611
Balance Sheet								
Total Assets	25,807,500	25,101,100	22,815,992	22,559,527	20,197,258	19,504,826	17,401,681	16,415,541
Total Liabilities	22,661,500	21,888,300	20,097,340	19,909,394	17,933,538	17,307,954	15,448,572	14,358,978
Stockholders' Equity	3,046,100	2,928,900	2,457,542	2,430,547	2,076,161	1,725,848	1,498,379	1,548,530
Shares Outstanding	113,499	119,303	117,101	114,951	109,584	103,694	102,737	101,115
Statistical Record								
Return on Assets %	1.51	1.89	0.91	1.68	1.48	0.46	N.M.	N.M.
Return on Equity %	12.83	16.83	8.45	15.93	15.46	5.25	N.M.	N.M.
Loss Ratio %	68.75	72.30	84.65	81.03	84.73	87.18	90.04	88.64
Net Margin %	8.70	10.67	5.12	9.21	8.75	2.26	(0.38)	(1.47)
Price Range	36.50-25.57	36.35-24.83	25.92-18.68	21.49-17.63	17.73-12.17	19.98-12.83	20.20-12.49	19.08-12.33
P/E Ratio	11.77-8.25	9.69-6.62	14.81-10.67	6.70-5.49	6.45-4.42	24.67-15.84	...	...
Average Yield %	1.24	1.24	1.52	1.67	2.25	2.01	4.00	4.22

Address: One East Fourth Street, Cincinnati, OH 45202 Telephone: 513-579-2121 Fax: 513-579-0108	Web Site: www.amfnl.com Officers: Carl H. Lindner - Chmn., Co-C.E.O. S. Craig Lindner - Co-C.E.O.	Auditors: Ernst & Young LLP Investor Contact: 513-579-6739

AMERICAN GREETINGS CORP.

Exchange	Symbol	Price	52Wk Range	Yield	P/E
NYS	AM	$18.55 (3/31/2008)	28.98-17.12	2.59	17.67

*7 Year Price Score 92.23   *NYSE Composite Index=100   *12 Month Price Score 87.23

Interim Earnings (Per Share)

Qtr.	May	Aug	Nov	Feb
2004-05	0.06	0.10	0.78	0.28
2005-06	0.35	0.05	0.19	0.56
2006-07	0.24	(0.18)	0.83	(0.17)
2007-08	0.54	0.15	0.52	...

Interim Dividends (Per Share)

Amt	Decl	Ex	Rec	Pay
0.10Q	6/22/2007	7/5/2007	7/9/2007	7/19/2007
0.10Q	9/20/2007	10/3/2007	10/5/2007	10/15/2007
0.10Q	12/20/2007	1/2/2008	1/4/2008	1/14/2008
0.12Q	3/28/2008	4/14/2008	4/16/2008	4/28/2008

Indicated Div: $0.48

Valuation Analysis

		Institutional Holding	
Forecast P/E	N/A	No of Institutions	163
Market Cap	$968.0 Million	Shares	62,104,488
Book Value	1.0 Billion	% Held	
Price/Book	0.94	N/A	
Price/Sales	0.55		

Business Summary: Printing (MIC: 13.4 SIC: 2771 NAIC: 511191)

American Greetings designs, produces and sells greeting cards and other social expression products. Co.'s greeting cards, gift wrap, party goods, stationery and giftware are produced and sold in North America, including the U.S., Canada and Mexico, and throughout the world, such as in the U.K. and Australia. Also, Co.'s AG Interactive, Inc. subsidiary distributes social expression products, including e-mail greetings, personalized printable greeting cards and graphics, via digital and other electronic channels such as Web sites, Internet portals, instant messaging services and electronic mobile devices. At Feb 28 2007, Co. owned and operated 436 card and gift retail stores in North America.

Recent Developments: For the quarter ended Nov 23 2007, income from continuing operations decreased 37.3% to US$29.5 million from US$47.0 million in the year-earlier quarter. Net income decreased 41.6% to US$29.0 million from US$49.7 million in the year-earlier quarter. Revenues were US$485.7 million, down 6.8% from US$521.2 million the year before. Operating income was US$42.6 million versus US$73.9 million in the prior-year quarter, a decrease of 42.3%. Direct operating expenses declined 8.9% to US$223.3 million from US$245.2 million in the comparable period the year before. Indirect operating expenses increased 8.7% to US$219.8 million from US$202.1 million in the equivalent prior-year period.

Prospects: On Oct 25 2007, Co. announced the acquisition of Webshots, an online photo and video sharing site, for about $45.0 million. Also, on Nov 28 2007, Co. announced that it has entered into an agreement to acquire PhotoWorks, an online personal publishing company and photography site, for about $26.5 million, which is expected to close in late Jan 2008. Notably, Webshots should allow Co. to expand its offerings of online social expressions into the area of online photo sharing, and PhotoWorks should also allow Co. to further expand its social expression photo offering. Meanwhile, for the fiscal year ending Feb 2008, Co. expects earnings from continuing operations of $1.35 to $1.55 per share.

Financial Data

(US$ in Thousands)	9 Mos	6 Mos	3 Mos	02/28/2007	02/28/2006	02/28/2005	02/29/2004	02/28/2003
Earnings Per Share	1.05	1.35	1.02	0.71	1.16	1.25	1.40	1.63
Cash Flow Per Share	5.84	5.36	4.84	4.61	4.21	5.23	4.38	1.17
Tang Book Value Per Share	14.61	14.89	14.60	14.30	16.84	16.18	15.39	13.17
Dividends Per Share	0.380	0.360	0.340	0.320	0.320	0.120	...	...
Dividend Payout %	36.22	26.71	33.24	45.07	27.59	9.60	...	...
Income Statement								
Total Revenue	1,283,138	797,392	418,013	1,744,603	1,885,701	1,902,727	2,008,943	1,995,860
EBITDA	156,930	97,622	65,410	145,622	217,371	239,644	320,648	344,743
Depn & Amortn	36,002	23,919	11,989	...	...	...	...	...
Income Before Taxes	112,331	67,826	54,913	69,361	138,935	108,248	170,751	200,838
Income Taxes	43,495	28,478	24,291	26,096	48,810	37,698	66,081	79,732
Net Income	67,441	38,425	30,050	42,378	84,376	95,279	104,670	121,106
Average Shares	55,466	56,180	55,650	62,362	79,226	82,016	80,088	78,980
Balance Sheet								
Current Assets	808,341	796,023	767,717	799,281	1,162,142	1,281,639	1,176,968	1,234,488
Total Assets	1,868,483	1,802,513	1,773,167	1,778,214	2,218,962	2,535,628	2,484,013	2,584,120
Current Liabilities	455,843	370,813	338,160	373,000	584,040	487,667	422,963	699,397
Long-Term Obligations	200,975	200,988	223,800	223,915	300,516	486,099	665,874	726,531
Total Liabilities	838,564	749,227	735,528	765,640	998,937	1,148,848	1,216,473	1,506,656
Stockholders' Equity	1,029,919	1,053,286	1,037,639	1,012,574	1,220,025	1,386,780	1,267,540	1,077,464
Shares Outstanding	52,185	55,504	55,643	55,122	60,348	69,026	67,468	65,899
Statistical Record								
Return on Assets %	2.87	4.11	2.97	2.12	3.55	3.80	4.12	4.66
Return on Equity %	5.15	6.86	5.14	3.80	6.47	7.18	8.90	12.23
EBITDA Margin %	12.23	12.24	15.65	8.35	11.53	12.59	15.96	17.27
Net Margin %	5.26	4.82	7.19	2.43	4.47	5.01	5.21	6.07
Asset Turnover	0.90	0.96	0.91	0.87	0.79	0.76	0.79	0.77
Current Ratio	1.77	2.15	2.27	2.14	1.99	2.63	2.78	1.77
Debt to Equity	0.20	0.19	0.22	0.22	0.25	0.35	0.53	0.67
Price Range	28.98-22.30	28.98-22.30	26.13-20.72	25.04-20.66	27.70-20.39	27.91-19.43	22.85-12.95	22.97-12.56
P/E Ratio	27.60-21.24	21.47-16.52	25.62-20.31	35.27-29.10	23.88-17.58	22.33-15.54	16.32-9.25	14.09-7.71
Average Yield %	1.52	1.46	1.43	1.38	1.30	0.50	...	...

Address: One American Road, Cleveland, OH 44144-2398 Telephone: 216-252-7300 Fax: 216-255-6777	Web Site: www.americangreetings.com Officers: Morry Weiss - Chmn. Jeffrey M. Weiss - Pres., C.O.O.	Auditors: Ernst & Young LLP Investor Contact: 216-.25-2.4864 Transfer Agents: National City Bank, Cleveland, Ohio

AMERICAN INTERNATIONAL GROUP INC

Exchange	Symbol	Price	52Wk Range	Yield	P/E	Div Acheiver
NYS	AIG	$43.25 (3/31/2008)	72.65-39.80	1.85	18.10	22 Years

*7 Year Price Score 75.21   *NYSE Composite Index=100   *12 Month Price Score 81.74

Interim Earnings (Per Share)

Qtr.	Mar	Jun	Sep	Dec
2003	0.74	0.87	0.89	1.03
2004	1.01	1.09	0.95	0.64
2005	1.40	1.53	0.65	0.17
2006	1.22	1.21	1.61	1.32
2007	1.58	1.64	1.19	(2.01)

Interim Dividends (Per Share)

Amt	Decl	Ex	Rec	Pay
0.20Q	5/16/2007	9/5/2007	9/7/2007	9/21/2007
0.20Q	9/5/2007	12/5/2007	12/7/2007	12/21/2007
0.20Q	11/14/2007	3/5/2008	3/7/2008	3/21/2008
0.20Q	3/12/2008	6/4/2008	6/6/2008	6/20/2008

Indicated Div: $0.80

Valuation Analysis   **Institutional Holding**

Forecast P/E	10.44	No of Institutions
	(1/10/2008)	1290
Market Cap	$109.4 Billion	Shares
Book Value	95.8 Billion	1,777,085,440
Price/Book	1.14	% Held
Price/Sales	0.99	68.31

Business Summary: Insurance (MIC: 8.2 SIC: 6331 NAIC: 524126)

American International Group is a holding company which, through its subsidiaries, is engaged in an array of insurance and insurance related activities in the U.S. and abroad. Co.'s primary activities include both General Insurance and Life Insurance & Retirement Services operations as well as other significant activities including Financial Services and Asset Management. As of Dec 31 2007, Co.'s reportable segments by product or service line were General Insurance, Life Insurance & Retirement Services, Financial Services and Asset Management. As of the date above, Co. provided its products and services in more than 130 countries and jurisdictions.

Recent Developments: For the year ended Dec 31 2007, net income decreased 55.9% to US$6.20 billion from US$14.05 billion in the prior year. Revenues were US$110.06 billion, down 2.9% from US$113.39 billion the year before. Net premiums earned were US$79.30 billion versus US$74.21 billion in the prior year, an increase of 6.9%. Net investment income rose 9.8% to US$28.62 billion from US$26.07 billion a year ago.

Prospects: Looking ahead, Co. is projecting further price decline in its commercial lines during 2008. Thus, Co. intends to identify strategic opportunities and build new general insurance businesses through its product line distribution networks in the U.S. and globally while maintaining stringent underwriting discipline. Specifically, Co. plans to improve its Life Insurance & Retirement Services businesses through direct marketing channels as it anticipates the ageing population in the U.S. will provide growth potential for several of its products. Meanwhile, Co. expects the weakening U.S. housing market will continue to affect its United Guaranty Residential Insurance Co. subsidiary's results.

Financial Data

(US$ in Thousands)	12/31/2007	12/31/2006	12/31/2005	12/31/2004	12/31/2003	12/31/2002	12/31/2001	12/31/2000
Earnings Per Share	2.39	5.36	3.99	3.69	3.53	2.10	2.02	2.41
Cash Flow Per Share	13.61	2.62	9.68	13.62	13.85	7.15	2.94	2.55
Tang Book Value Per Share	34.15	35.77	30.13	27.73	24.39	20.32	19.94	16.98
Dividends Per Share	0.730	0.630	0.550	0.280	0.224	0.178	0.158	0.141
Dividend Payout %	30.54	11.75	13.78	7.59	6.35	8.48	7.82	5.84
Income Statement								
Premium Income	79,302,000	74,083,000	70,209,000	66,593,000	54,613,000	44,589,000	38,608,000	31,017,000
Total Revenue	110,064,000	113,194,000	108,905,000	97,987,000	81,303,000	67,482,000	55,911,000	42,440,000
Benefits & Claims	66,115,000	59,706,000	63,711,000	58,313,000	46,886,000	41,927,000	27,222,000	18,565,000
Income Before Taxes	8,943,000	21,687,000	15,213,000	14,950,000	13,908,000	8,142,000	8,139,000	8,349,000
Income Taxes	1,455,000	6,537,000	4,258,000	4,620,000	4,264,000	2,328,000	2,339,000	2,458,000
Net Income	6,200,000	14,048,000	10,477,000	9,731,000	9,274,000	5,519,000	5,363,000	5,636,000
Average Shares	2,598,000	2,623,000	2,627,000	2,637,000	2,628,000	2,634,000	2,650,000	2,343,000
Balance Sheet								
Total Assets	1,060,505,000	979,414,000	853,370,000	798,660,000	678,346,000	561,229,000	492,982,000	306,577,000
Total Liabilities	964,604,000	877,546,000	766,867,000	717,854,000	606,901,000	499,973,000	438,630,000	265,611,000
Stockholders' Equity	95,801,000	101,677,000	86,317,000	80,607,000	71,253,000	59,103,000	52,150,000	39,619,000
Shares Outstanding	2,529,584	2,601,196	2,596,647	2,596,423	2,608,447	2,609,600	2,615,432	2,332,713
Statistical Record								
Return on Assets %	0.61	1.53	1.27	1.31	1.50	1.05	1.34	1.96
Return on Equity %	6.28	14.95	12.55	12.78	14.23	9.92	11.69	15.41
Loss Ratio %	83.37	80.59	90.74	87.57	85.85	94.03	70.51	59.85
Net Margin %	5.63	12.41	9.62	9.93	11.41	8.18	9.59	13.28
Price Range	72.65-51.33	72.81-57.76	73.12-50.35	76.77-54.70	66.28-44.47	79.61-51.10	96.88-67.05	103.69-54.29
P/E Ratio	30.40-21.48	13.58-10.78	18.33-12.62	20.80-14.82	18.78-12.60	37.91-24.33	47.96-33.19	43.02-22.53
Average Yield %	1.09	0.96	0.90	0.40	0.39	0.27	0.19	0.17

Address: 70 Pine Street, New York, NY 10270
Telephone: 212-770-7000
Fax: 212-344-6828

Web Site: www.aig.com
Officers: Thomas R. Tizzio - Sr. Vice-Chmn., Gen. Insurance Edmund S. W. Tse - Sr. Vice-Chmn., Life Insurance

Auditors: PricewaterhouseCoopers LLP
Investor Contact: 212-770-6293
Transfer Agents: EquiServe Trust Company, N.A. Providence, RI

AMERICAN STATES WATER CO.

Exchange	Symbol	Price	52Wk Range	Yield	P/E	Div Acheiver
NYS	AWR	$36.00 (3/31/2008)	45.45-32.29	2.78	22.36	54 Years

*7 Year Price Score 104.12 *NYSE Composite Index=100 *12 Month Price Score 97.46

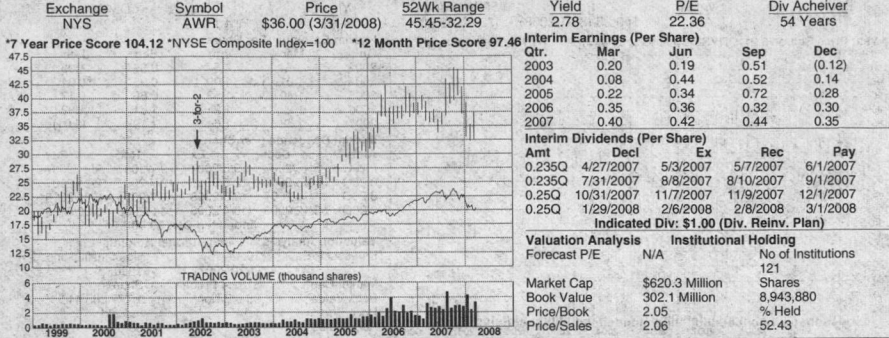

Interim Earnings (Per Share)

Qtr.	Mar	Jun	Sep	Dec
2003	0.20	0.19	0.51	(0.12)
2004	0.08	0.44	0.52	0.14
2005	0.22	0.34	0.72	0.28
2006	0.35	0.36	0.32	0.30
2007	0.40	0.42	0.44	0.35

Interim Dividends (Per Share)

Amt	Decl	Ex	Rec	Pay
0.235Q	4/27/2007	5/3/2007	5/7/2007	6/1/2007
0.235Q	7/31/2007	8/8/2007	8/10/2007	9/1/2007
0.25Q	10/31/2007	11/7/2007	11/9/2007	12/1/2007
0.25Q	1/29/2008	2/6/2008	2/8/2008	3/1/2008

Indicated Div: $1.00 (Div. Reinv. Plan)

Valuation Analysis / **Institutional Holding**

Forecast P/E	N/A	No of Institutions
		121
Market Cap	$620.3 Million	Shares
Book Value	302.1 Million	8,943,880
Price/Book	2.05	% Held
Price/Sales	2.06	52.43

TRADING VOLUME (thousand shares)

Business Summary: Water Utilities (MIC: 7.2 SIC: 4941 NAIC: 221310)

American States Water is the parent company of Golden State Water Company (GSWC), American States Utility Services, Inc. (ASUS), and Chaparral City Water Company (CCWC). GSWC is a public utility engaged in the purchase, production and distribution of water in California, which served about 254,546 water customers as of Dec 31 2007. GSWC also distributes electricity in one customer service area, which served around 23,273 electric customers at Dec 31 2007. CCWC is a public utility, which served approximately 13,488 customers in the town of Fountain Hills, AZ and a portion of the City of Scottsdale, AZ, at Dec 31 2007. ASUS provides water and wastewater services on a contract basis.

Recent Developments: For the year ended Dec 31 2007, net income increased 21.4% to US$28.0 million from US$23.1 million in the prior year. Revenues were US$301.4 million, up 12.2% from US$268.6 million the year before. Operating income was US$67.7 million versus US$56.6 million in the prior year, an increase of 19.7%. Direct operating expenses rose 6.2% to US$134.5 million from US$126.6 million in the comparable period the year before. Indirect operating expenses increased 16.1% to US$99.1 million from US$85.4 million in the equivalent prior-year period.

Prospects: On Feb 6 2008, Co. announced that the California Public Utilities Commission (CPUC) approved rate increases for the Region I water service area of its Golden State Water Company (GSWC) unit, retroactive to Jan 1 2008. At the same time, the CPUC approved rate increases for Region II and Region III of Co.'s customer service areas effective Jan 1 2008. The authorized rate increases will provide GSWC additional annual revenues of $6.4 million for Region I, $3.6 million for Region II and $3.0 million for Region III in 2008. The combined rate increases for Regions I, II and III are designed to generate about $13.0 million annually, based upon normalized sales levels approved by the CPUC.

Financial Data

(US$ in Thousands)	12/31/2007	12/31/2006	12/31/2005	12/31/2004	12/31/2003	12/31/2002	12/31/2001	12/31/2000
Earnings Per Share	1.61	1.33	1.57	1.18	0.78	1.34	1.33	1.27
Cash Flow Per Share	2.98	3.04	3.25	3.21	3.08	1.70	2.62	2.18
Tang Book Value Per Share	16.88	15.96	15.02	14.30	13.97	14.05	13.23	12.75
Dividends Per Share	0.955	0.910	0.900	0.888	0.884	0.871	0.867	0.857
Dividend Payout %	59.32	68.42	57.32	75.25	113.33	65.02	65.00	67.28
Income Statement								
Total Revenue	301,370	268,629	236,197	228,005	212,669	209,205	197,514	183,960
EBITDA	96,972	83,337	...	...	...	...	...	...
Income Before Taxes	48,820	38,762	...	...	...	...	...	...
Income Taxes	20,790	15,681	21,945	13,390	9,167	12,949	15,379	15,127
Net Income	28,030	23,081	26,766	18,541	11,892	20,339	20,447	18,086
Average Shares	17,177	17,101	16,809	15,663	15,227	15,157	15,256	14,116
Balance Sheet								
Net PPE	776,379	750,601	713,225	664,165	602,298	563,311	539,842	509,096
Total Assets	963,898	936,957	876,777	810,277	757,475	701,650	683,764	616,646
Long-Term Obligations	267,226	267,833	268,405	228,902	229,799	231,089	245,692	176,452
Total Liabilities	661,769	653,221	612,683	558,812	544,988	488,371	482,182	422,323
Stockholders' Equity	302,129	283,734	264,094	251,465	212,487	213,279	201,582	194,323
Shares Outstanding	17,231	17,049	16,797	16,752	15,212	15,180	15,119	15,113
Statistical Record								
Return on Assets %	2.95	2.55	3.17	2.36	1.63	2.94	3.14	3.14
Return on Equity %	9.57	8.43	10.38	7.97	5.59	9.81	10.33	10.17
EBITDA Margin %	32.18	31.02	...	...	...	...	...	...
Net Margin %	9.30	8.59	11.33	8.13	5.59	9.72	10.35	9.83
PPE Turnover	0.39	0.37	0.34	0.36	0.36	0.38	0.38	0.38
Asset Turnover	0.32	0.30	0.28	0.29	0.29	0.30	0.30	0.32
Debt to Equity	0.88	0.94	1.02	0.91	1.08	1.08	1.22	0.91
Price Range	45.45-33.82	42.39-30.78	34.06-24.64	26.78-21.37	28.71-21.80	28.85-21.01	25.32-19.35	24.75-17.00
P/E Ratio	28.23-21.01	31.87-23.14	21.69-15.69	22.69-18.11	36.81-27.95	21.53-15.68	19.04-14.55	19.49-13.39
Average Yield %	2.46	2.47	3.12	3.65	3.56	3.54	3.86	4.21

Address: 630 East Foothill Boulevard, San Dimas, CA 91773-1212 Telephone: 909-394-3600 Fax: 909-394-1382	Web Site: www.aswater.com Officers: Lloyd E. Ross - Chmn. Floyd E. Wicks - Pres., C.E.O.	Auditors: PricewaterhouseCoopers LLP Investor Contact: 909-394-3633 Transfer Agents: ChaseMellon Shareholder Services, L.L.C., Ridgefield Park, NJ.

AMERICAN TOWER CORP.

Exchange	Symbol	Price	52Wk Range	Yield	P/E
NYS	AMT	$39.21 (3/31/2008)	46.34-35.50	N/A	301.62

*7 Year Price Score 159.57 *NYSE Composite Index=100 *12 Month Price Score 101.37

Interim Earnings (Per Share)

Qtr.	Mar	Jun	Sep	Dec
2003	(0.47)	(0.53)	(0.25)	(0.22)
2004	(0.19)	(0.27)	(0.25)	(0.39)
2005	(0.14)	(0.14)	(0.06)	(0.25)
2006	(0.01)	0.02	0.01	0.04
2007	0.05	(0.05)	0.14	(0.02)

Interim Dividends (Per Share)

No Dividends Paid

Valuation Analysis		Institutional Holding	
Forecast P/E	57.60	No of Institutions	
	(1/10/2007)	396	
Market Cap	$15.7 Billion	Shares	
Book Value	3.0 Billion	418,232,160	
Price/Book	5.18	% Held	
Price/Sales	10.75	99.58	

TRADING VOLUME (thousand shares)

Business Summary: Communications (MIC: 10.1 SIC: 4899 NAIC: 517212)

American Tower is a holding company that provides wireless and broadcast communications sites. Co.'s main business is leasing of antenna space on multi-tenant communications sites to wireless service providers and radio and television broadcast companies. Co. also manages rooftop and tower sites for third parties, operates distributed antenna systems within buildings, and provides network development services that support its rental and management operations and the addition of new tenants and equipment on its sites. As at Dec 31 2007, Co.'s portfolio included 19,500 tower sites in the U.S. and 3,200 in Mexico and Brazil; as well as 150 in-building distributed antenna systems in the U.S.

Recent Developments: For the year ended Dec 31 2007, income from continuing operations increased 227.2% to US$92.7 million from US$28.3 million a year earlier. Net income increased 104.9% to US$56.3 million from US$27.5 million in the prior year. Revenues were US$1.46 billion, up 10.6% from US$1.32 billion the year before. Operating income was US$378.4 million versus US$283.9 million in the prior year, an increase of 33.3%. Direct operating expenses rose 4.7% to US$359.6 million from US$343.5 million in the comparable period the year before. Indirect operating expenses increased 4.2% to US$718.6 million from US$689.9 million in the equivalent prior-year period.

Prospects: While it remains focused on growing its site leasing business, Co. expects rental and management revenue to grow as it continues to utilize existing site capacity. For 2008, Co. is projecting rental and management segment revenue to be between $1.52 billion and $1.54 billion and network development services segment revenue of about $35.0 million to $50.0 million. In addition, Co. anticipates income from continuing operations of approximately $126.0 million to $143.0 million for 2008. Further, Co. plans to construct approximately 300 to 400 new sites in 2008, including in-building systems, and is budgeting capital expenditures of between approximately $185.0 million and $215.0 million.

Financial Data

(US$ in Thousands)	12/31/2007	12/31/2006	12/31/2005	12/31/2004	12/31/2003	12/31/2002	12/31/2001	12/31/2000
Earnings Per Share	0.13	0.06	(0.57)	(1.10)	(1.46)	(5.84)	(2.35)	(1.15)
Cash Flow Per Share	1.68	1.46	1.31	0.96	0.75	0.54	0.14	(0.15)
Tang Book Value Per Share	N.M.	0.88	0.74	N.M.	0.28	N.M.	1.85	2.06
Income Statement								
Total Revenue	1,456,594	1,317,385	944,786	706,660	715,144	788,420	1,134,191	735,275
EBITDA	894,326	801,067	535,143	331,246	340,830	193,832	133,907	180,213
Income Before Taxes	152,840	70,864	(127,474)	(314,137)	(308,628)	(379,403)	(566,881)	(249,946)
Income Taxes	59,809	41,768	4,003	(80,176)	(66,137)	(64,634)	(116,787)	(59,656)
Net Income	56,316	27,484	(171,590)	(247,587)	(303,417)	(1,141,879)	(450,094)	(194,628)
Average Shares	426,079	436,217	302,510	224,336	208,098	195,454	191,586	168,715
Balance Sheet								
Current Assets	245,674	486,022	225,878	309,037	411,515	536,253	522,207	471,152
Total Assets	8,130,457	8,613,219	8,768,220	5,085,972	5,332,488	5,662,203	6,829,723	5,660,679
Current Liabilities	317,378	569,629	453,216	332,205	294,778	670,294	342,714	297,786
Long-Term Obligations	4,283,467	3,289,109	3,451,276	3,155,228	3,283,603	3,194,537	3,549,375	2,457,045
Total Liabilities	5,105,023	4,224,712	4,231,846	3,608,938	3,602,342	3,906,313	3,946,590	2,767,303
Stockholders' Equity	3,022,092	4,384,916	4,526,580	1,470,953	1,711,547	1,740,323	2,869,196	2,877,030
Shares Outstanding	399,518	424,672	412,654	229,599	219,904	195,683	195,287	180,398
Statistical Record								
Return on Assets %	0.67	0.32	N.M.	N.M.	N.M.	N.M.	N.M.	N.M.
Return on Equity %	1.52	0.62	N.M.	N.M.	N.M.	N.M.	N.M.	N.M.
EBITDA Margin %	61.40	60.81	56.64	46.87	47.66	24.58	11.81	24.51
Net Margin %	3.87	2.09	N.M.	N.M.	N.M.	N.M.	N.M.	N.M.
Asset Turnover	0.17	0.15	0.14	0.14	0.13	0.13	0.18	0.17
Current Ratio	0.77	0.85	0.50	0.93	1.40	0.80	1.52	1.58
Debt to Equity	1.42	0.75	0.76	2.15	1.92	1.84	1.24	0.85
Price Range	46.34-37.18	38.27-27.30	28.09-16.46	18.55-10.34	12.00-3.53	10.22-0.71	41.00-5.98	54.81-29.00
P/E Ratio	356.46-286.00	637.83-455.00	...	...	...	...	...	...

Address: 116 Huntington Avenue, Boston, MA 02116	Web Site: www.americantower.com	Auditors: Deloitte & Touche LLP
Telephone: 617-375-7500	Officers: James D. Taiclet Jr. - Chmn., Pres., C.E.O. J. Michael Gearon Jr. - Vice-Chmn., Pres., American Tower International	Investor Contact: 617-375-7500
Fax: 617-375-7575		Transfer Agents: The Bank of New York, New York, NY

AMERICREDIT CORP.

Exchange	Symbol	Price	52Wk Range	Yield	P/E
NYS	ACF	$10.07 (3/31/2008)	28.23-9.56	N/A	5.63

*7 Year Price Score 64.96   *NYSE Composite Index=100   *12 Month Price Score 76.20

Interim Earnings (Per Share)

Qtr.	Sep	Dec	Mar	Jun
2004-05	0.43	0.39	0.46	0.48
2005-06	0.35	0.59	0.60	0.55
2006-07	0.54	0.74	0.80	0.67
2007-08	0.49	(0.17)	...	...

Interim Dividends (Per Share)

No Dividends Paid

Valuation Analysis / Institutional Holding

Valuation Analysis		Institutional Holding	
Forecast P/E	7.78	No of Institutions	
	(1/10/2007)	242	
Market Cap	$1.2 Billion	Shares	
Book Value	2.0 Billion	147,072,352	
Price/Book	0.58	% Held	
Price/Sales	N/A	N/A	

TRADING VOLUME (thousand shares)

Business Summary: Credit & Lending (MIC: 8.6 SIC: 6141 NAIC: 522291)

AmeriCredit is an independent auto finance company that operates in the automobile finance business. Co. purchases auto finance contracts generally without recourse from franchised and select independent automobile dealerships and, to a lesser extent, make loans directly to customers buying new and used vehicles and provide lease financing through Co.'s dealership network. Co. predominantly target consumers who are typically unable to obtain financing from banks, credit unions and manufacturer captive auto finance companies. Co. services its loan portfolio at regional centers using automated loan servicing and collection systems.

Recent Developments: For the quarter ended Dec 31 2007, net loss amounted to US$19.1 million versus net income of US$95.4 million in the year-earlier quarter. Provision for loan losses was US$356.5 million versus US$174.8 million in the prior-year quarter, an increase of 104.0%. Non-interest income rose 13.5% to US$653.3 million from US$575.6 million, while non-interest expense advanced 18.7% to US$111.8 million.

Prospects: Going forward, Co. expects to be challenged by the higher credit enhancement levels in its securitization transactions, credit deterioration in its portfolio, disruptions in the capital markets and weakening demand for securities guaranteed by insurance policies. As such, Co. implemented a revised operating plan in Jan 2008, which includes increasing the minimum credit score requirements for new loan originations and lowering its originations infrastructure. For fiscal year ending June 2008, Co. is projecting net income in a range of $170.0 million to $195.0 million and earnings of about $1.35 to $1.55 per share, as well as new loan origination volume of $6.50 billion to $7.00 billion.

Financial Data

(US$ in Thousands)	6 Mos	3 Mos	06/30/2007	06/30/2006	06/30/2005	06/30/2004	06/30/2003	06/30/2002
Earnings Per Share	1.79	2.70	2.73	2.08	1.73	1.42	0.15	3.87
Cash Flow Per Share	10.41	9.89	9.06	7.18	7.37	5.16	16.75	(4.42)
Tang Book Value Per Share	15.41	15.78	15.73	15.78	14.57	13.48	12.02	16.69
Income Statement								
Interest Income	...	...	2,142,470	1,641,125	1,217,696	927,592	613,225	339,430
Interest Expense	...	...	680,825	419,360	264,276	251,963	202,225	135,928
Net Interest Income	...	...	1,461,645	1,221,765	953,420	675,629	411,000	203,502
Provision for Losses	601,158	244,645	727,653	567,545	418,711	257,070	307,570	65,161
Non-Interest Income	1,305,928	652,674	197,453	170,213	233,150	288,244	368,056	850,802
Non-Interest Expense	222,189	110,420	399,378	339,198	315,460	341,687	437,000	424,131
Income Before Taxes	57,287	86,348	532,067	485,235	452,399	365,116	34,486	565,012
Income Taxes	14,558	24,529	171,818	179,052	166,490	138,133	13,277	217,529
Net Income	42,729	61,819	360,249	306,183	285,909	226,983	21,209	347,483
Average Shares	114,253	128,111	133,224	148,824	167,242	159,630	137,807	89,800
Balance Sheet								
Total Assets	18,149,312	18,428,223	17,811,020	13,067,865	10,947,038	8,824,579	8,108,029	4,224,931
Total Liabilities	16,172,174	16,417,830	15,735,870	11,058,979	8,825,122	6,699,467	6,227,400	2,792,615
Stockholders' Equity	1,977,138	2,010,393	2,075,150	2,008,886	2,121,916	2,125,112	1,880,629	1,432,316
Shares Outstanding	114,478	114,138	118,656	127,332	145,627	157,612	156,450	85,817
Statistical Record								
Return on Assets %	1.45	2.09	2.33	2.55	2.89	2.67	0.34	9.13
Return on Equity %	12.22	18.63	17.64	14.82	13.46	11.30	1.28	27.88
Net Interest Margin %	...	...	68.22	74.45	78.30	72.84	67.02	59.95
Efficiency Ratio %	...	...	17.07	18.73	21.74	28.10	44.53	35.63
Price Range	28.23-9.56	28.23-16.61	28.23-21.85	31.70-21.43	25.60-17.25	20.25-6.60	26.08-1.64	63.63-14.98
P/E Ratio	15.77-5.34	10.46-6.15	10.34-8.00	15.24-10.30	14.80-9.97	14.26-4.65	173.87-10.93	16.44-3.87

Address: 801 Cherry Street, Suite 3900, Fort Worth, TX 76102 **Telephone:** 817-302-7000 **Fax:** 817-336-9519	**Web Site:** www.americredit.com **Officers:** Clifton H. Morris Jr. - Chmn., C.E.O. Daniel E. Berce - Pres.	**Auditors:** Deloitte & Touche LLP **Investor Contact:** 817-302-7394 **Transfer Agents:** ChaseMellon Shareholder Services, Ridgefield Park, NJ

AMERIPRISE FINANCIAL INC

Exchange	Symbol	Price	52Wk Range	Yield	P/E
NYS	AMP	$51.85 (3/31/2008)	66.95-47.08	1.16	15.29

*7 Year Price Score N/A   ***NYSE Composite Index=100**   ***12 Month Price Score 96.20**

Interim Earnings (Per Share)

Qtr.	Mar	Jun	Sep	Dec
2005	0.74	0.63	0.50	0.45
2006	0.57	0.57	0.71	0.69
2007	0.68	0.81	0.83	1.07

Interim Dividends (Per Share)

Amt	Decl	Ex	Rec	Pay
0.15Q	3/15/2007	5/2/2007	5/4/2007	5/18/2007
0.15Q	7/25/2007	8/2/2007	8/6/2007	8/17/2007
0.15Q	10/24/2007	11/1/2007	11/5/2007	11/16/2007
0.15Q	1/24/2008	1/31/2008	2/4/2008	2/18/2008

Indicated Div: $0.60

Valuation Analysis

		Institutional Holding	
Forecast P/E	N/A	No of Institutions	510
Market Cap	$11.8 Billion	Shares	201,970,736
Book Value	7.8 Billion	% Held	84.43
Price/Book	1.51		
Price/Sales	1.33		

Business Summary: Wealth Management (MIC: 8.8 SIC: 6282 NAIC: 523930)

Ameriprise Financial is engaged in providing financial planning, products and services designed for its clients' cash and liquidity, asset accumulation, income, protection, and estate and wealth transfer needs. As of Dec 31 2007, Co. had about 2.8 million individual, business and institutional clients and a network of over 11,800 financial advisors and registered representatives. Its asset management, annuity, and auto and home protection products are also distributed outside of its affiliated financial advisors, through third party advisors and affinity relationships. Co. operates in five segments: Advice & Wealth Management; Asset Management; Annuities; Protection, and Corporate & Other.

Recent Developments: For the year ended Dec 31 2007, income from continuing operations increased 29.0% to US$814.0 million from US$631.0 million a year earlier. Net income increased 29.0% to US$814.0 million from US$631.0 million in the prior year. Revenues were US$8.91 billion, up 7.4% from US$8.29 billion the year before. Direct operating expenses rose 11.9% to US$2.08 billion from US$1.86 billion in the comparable period the year before. Indirect operating expenses increased 3.1% to US$5.81 billion from US$5.64 billion in the equivalent prior-year period.

Prospects: Co.'s near-term outlook appears satisfactory reflecting strong growth in its recent net income and revenue primarily as a result of an increase in its fee-based businesses driven by net inflows in wrap accounts and variable annuities, market appreciation and continued advisor productivity gains. Conversely, these gains are being partially offset by higher distribution expenses which reflect the higher levels of assets under management and overall business growth. Additionally, Co. is seeing a decrease in its net investment income attributable to a reduction in volume in annuity fixed accounts and certificates.

Financial Data
(US$ in Thousands)

	12/31/2007	12/31/2006	12/31/2005	12/31/2004	12/31/2003	12/31/2002
Earnings Per Share	3.39	2.54	2.32	...	...	...
Cash Flow Per Share	3.58	2.51	3.82	...	...	...
Tang Book Value Per Share	34.29	32.83	30.76	...	...	...
Dividends Per Share	0.560	0.440	...	...	...	...
Dividend Payout %	16.52	17.32	...	...	...	...
Income Statement						
Total Revenue	8,909,000	8,140,000	7,484,000	7,245,000	6,361,000	5,793,000
Income Before Taxes	1,016,000	797,000	745,000	1,173,000	941,000	925,000
Income Taxes	202,000	166,000	187,000	308,000	203,000	251,000
Net Income	814,000	631,000	574,000	794,000	725,000	674,000
Average Shares	239,900	248,500	247,200	...	...	...
Balance Sheet						
Total Assets	109,230,000	104,172,000	93,121,000	93,113,000	85,384,000	...
Total Liabilities	101,420,000	96,247,000	85,434,000	86,411,000	78,096,000	...
Stockholders' Equity	7,810,000	7,925,000	7,687,000	6,702,000	7,288,000	...
Shares Outstanding	227,747	241,391	249,875	...	...	...
Statistical Record						
Return on Assets %	0.76	0.64	0.62	0.89	...	...
Return on Equity %	10.35	8.08	7.98	11.32	...	...
Price Range	66.95-54.10	55.30-40.69	43.90-32.39	...	...	...
P/E Ratio	19.75-15.96	21.77-16.02	18.92-13.96	...	...	...
Average Yield %	0.93	0.95	...	...	...	...

Address: 707 2nd Avenue South, Minneapolis, MN 55402 **Telephone:** 612-671-3131	**Web Site:** www.ameriprise.com **Officers:** James M. Cracchiolo - Chmn., C.E.O. Walter S. Berman - Exec. Vice-Pres., C.F.O.	**Auditors:** Ernst & Young LLP **Transfer Agents:** The Bank of New York

AMERISOURCEBERGEN CORP.

Exchange	Symbol	Price	52Wk Range	Yield	P/E
NYS	ABC	$40.98 (3/31/2008)	54.69-39.09	0.73	16.13

*7 Year Price Score 105.31 *NYSE Composite Index=100 *12 Month Price Score 99.08

Interim Earnings (Per Share)

Qtr.	Dec	Mar	Jun	Sep
2004-05	0.30	0.45	0.46	0.10
2005-06	0.46	0.61	0.58	0.60
2006-07	0.63	0.68	0.69	0.51
2007-08	0.66	...	...	...

Interim Dividends (Per Share)

Amt	Decl	Ex	Rec	Pay
0.00Q	7/12/2007	8/1/2007	7/20/2007	7/31/2007
0.05Q	8/9/2007	8/16/2007	8/20/2007	9/4/2007
0.075Q	11/8/2007	11/15/2007	11/19/2007	12/3/2007
0.075Q	2/5/2008	2/13/2008	2/18/2008	3/3/2008

Indicated Div: $0.30

Valuation Analysis | **Institutional Holding**

Forecast P/E	16.71	No of Institutions
	(1/10/2007)	338
Market Cap	$6.7 Billion	Shares
Book Value	2.9 Billion	185,141,152
Price/Book	2.31	% Held
Price/Sales	0.10	97.72

Business Summary: Pharmaceuticals (MIC: 9.1 SIC: 5122 NAIC: 424210)

AmerisourceBergen is a pharmaceutical services company, with operations in the U.S., Canada and the U.K. Co. services both healthcare providers and pharmaceutical manufacturers in the pharmaceutical supply channel, and provides drug distribution and related services. In addition, Co.'s services include the distribution of branded and generic pharmaceuticals, over-the-counter healthcare products, home healthcare supplies and equipment, and related services; the provision of pharmaceuticals and pharmacy services to workers' compensation and specialty drug patient; and related services such as pharmaceutical packaging, pharmacy automation, supply management software and inventory management.

Recent Developments: For the quarter ended Dec 31 2007, net income decreased 10.1% to US$109.8 million from US$122.2 million in the year-earlier quarter. Revenues were US$17.37 billion, up 3.9% from US$16.73 billion the year before. Operating income was US$195.0 million versus US$208.9 million in the prior-year quarter, a decrease of 6.6%. Direct operating expenses rose 4.6% to US$16.87 billion from US$16.13 billion in the comparable period the year before. Indirect operating expenses decreased 19.0% to US$312.5 million from US$385.8 million in the equivalent prior-year period.

Prospects: For the fiscal year ending Sep 30 2008, Co. continues to anticipate earnings to be in the range of $2.77 to $2.95 per diluted share, representing growth of about 13.0% to 20.0% over earnings of $2.46 per share in prior fiscal year, excluding the $0.09 benefit from special items and the $0.08 contribution from PharMerica Long-Term Care. In addition, Co. now projects operating revenue growth of 7.0% to 9.0%, an increase from its previous estimate of 5.0% to 7.0%, primarily due to the expected growth of certain large institutional customers. Similarly, Co. is forecasting operating margin expansion in its Pharmaceutical Distribution Segment to be in the low single digit basis points range.

Financial Data

(US$ in Thousands)	3 Mos	09/30/2007	09/30/2006	09/30/2005	09/30/2004	09/30/2003	09/30/2002	09/30/2001
Earnings Per Share	2.54	2.50	2.25	1.24	2.03	1.95	1.58	1.05
Cash Flow Per Share	4.97	6.52	3.94	7.22	3.69	1.62	2.55	(0.35)
Tang Book Value Per Share	0.65	2.88	7.91	8.81	8.62	7.21	5.21	3.44
Dividends Per Share	0.225	0.200	0.100	0.050	0.050	0.050	0.050	...
Dividend Payout %	8.86	8.00	4.44	4.03	2.46	2.57	3.16	...
Income Statement								
Total Revenue	17,372,915	66,074,312	61,203,145	54,577,321	53,178,954	49,657,328	45,234,794	16,191,353
EBITDA	219,810	921,682	850,026	616,930	960,166	951,314	779,359	273,224
Depn & Amortn	25,557	...	...	...	...	...	...	...
Income Before Taxes	177,829	785,050	740,629	468,825	760,373	726,127	572,047	202,833
Income Taxes	68,009	291,282	272,617	176,903	291,983	284,898	227,106	77,731
Net Income	109,820	469,167	467,714	264,645	468,390	441,229	344,941	123,796
Average Shares	167,062	187,886	207,446	215,540	235,558	231,908	224,456	125,614
Balance Sheet								
Current Assets	8,838,836	8,714,300	9,210,407	7,987,692	8,295,389	8,858,518	8,349,637	7,512,502
Total Assets	12,611,757	12,310,064	12,783,920	11,381,174	11,654,003	12,040,125	11,213,012	10,291,245
Current Liabilities	8,311,511	7,857,036	7,459,188	6,052,096	6,103,908	6,256,102	6,099,517	5,532,453
Long-Term Obligations	1,250,284	1,227,298	1,093,931	951,479	1,157,111	1,722,724	1,756,494	1,597,295
Total Liabilities	9,726,575	9,210,344	8,642,763	7,100,817	7,314,958	8,034,808	7,896,674	7,178,065
Stockholders' Equity	2,885,182	3,099,720	4,141,157	4,280,357	4,339,045	4,005,317	3,316,338	2,838,564
Shares Outstanding	162,532	169,476	196,350	209,752	219,385	224,004	213,163	207,069
Statistical Record								
Return on Assets %	3.56	3.74	3.87	2.30	3.94	3.80	3.21	1.94
Return on Equity %	13.39	12.96	11.11	6.14	11.20	12.05	11.21	7.93
EBITDA Margin %	1.27	1.39	1.39	1.13	1.81	1.92	1.72	1.69
Net Margin %	0.63	0.71	0.76	0.48	0.88	0.89	0.76	0.76
Asset Turnover	5.20	5.27	5.07	4.74	4.48	4.27	4.21	2.54
Current Ratio	1.06	1.11	1.23	1.32	1.36	1.42	1.37	1.36
Debt to Equity	0.43	0.40	0.26	0.22	0.27	0.43	0.53	0.56
Price Range	54.69-42.83	54.69-43.16	47.15-35.61	38.05-24.48	31.97-24.21	36.35-22.69	39.91-26.73	34.42-19.74
P/E Ratio	21.53-16.86	21.88-17.26	20.95-15.83	30.69-19.74	15.75-11.93	18.64-11.63	25.26-16.92	32.78-18.80
Average Yield %	0.47	0.42	0.24	0.16	0.18	0.17	0.15	...

Address: 1300 Morris Drive, Suite 100, Chesterbrook, PA 19087-5594	Web Site: www.amerisourcebergen.com	Auditors: Ernst & Young LLP
Telephone: 610-727-7000	Officers: James R. Mellor - Chmn. Kurt J. Hilzinger - Pres., C.O.O.	Investor Contact: 610-727-7118
Fax: 610-647-0141		Transfer Agents: The Bank of New York

AMETEK, INC.

Exchange	Symbol	Price	52Wk Range	Yield	P/E
NYS	AME	$43.91 (3/31/2008)	47.91-33.73	0.55	20.71

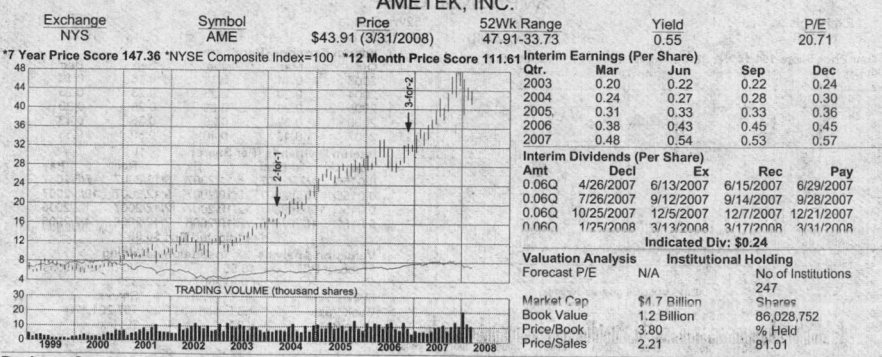

*7 Year Price Score 147.36 *NYSE Composite Index=100 *12 Month Price Score 111.61

Interim Earnings (Per Share)

Qtr.	Mar	Jun	Sep	Dec
2003	0.20	0.22	0.22	0.24
2004	0.24	0.27	0.28	0.30
2005	0.31	0.33	0.33	0.36
2006	0.38	0.43	0.45	0.45
2007	0.48	0.54	0.53	0.57

Interim Dividends (Per Share)

Amt	Decl	Ex	Rec	Pay
0.06Q	4/26/2007	6/13/2007	6/15/2007	6/29/2007
0.06Q	7/26/2007	9/12/2007	9/14/2007	9/28/2007
0.06Q	10/25/2007	12/5/2007	12/7/2007	12/21/2007
0.06Q	1/25/2008	3/13/2008	3/17/2008	3/31/2008

Indicated Div: $0.24

Valuation Analysis   **Institutional Holding**

Forecast P/E	N/A	No of Institutions
		247
Market Cap	$4.7 Billion	Shares
Book Value	1.2 Billion	86,028,752
Price/Book	3.80	% Held
Price/Sales	2.21	81.01

Business Summary: Electrical (MIC: 11.14 SIC: 3621 NAIC: 334513)

Ametek manufactures electronic instruments and electromechanical devices through its operations in North America, Europe, Asia, and South America. Co. markets its products worldwide through two operating groups, the Electronic Instruments Group (EIG) and the Electromechanical Group (EMG). EIG builds monitoring, testing, and calibration instruments and display devices for the process, aerospace, industrial and power markets. EMG is a supplier of electromechanical devices. EMG produces highly engineered electromechanical connectors for hermetic (moisture-proof) applications, specialty metals for niche markets, and brushless air-moving motors, blowers, and heat exchangers.

Recent Developments: For the year ended Dec 31 2007, net income increased 25.3% to US$228.0 million from US$181.9 million in the prior year. Revenues were US$2.14 billion, up 17.5% from US$1.82 billion the year before. Operating income was US$386.6 million versus US$309.0 million in the prior year, an increase of 25.1%. Direct operating expenses rose 15.4% to US$1.44 billion from US$1.25 billion in the comparable period the year before. Indirect operating expenses increased 18.3% to US$305.8 million from US$258.4 million in the equivalent prior-year period.

Prospects: On Feb 21 2008, Co. announced the acquisition of Drake Air, a provider of heat-transfer repair services to the commercial aerospace industry. The acquisition of Drake Air further expands Co.'s presence in the global aerospace maintenance, repair and overhaul services (MRO) industry. Notably, coupled with its acquisitions of Umeco Repair and Overhaul in Nov 2007, Southern Aeroparts in Dec 2006 and B&S Aircraft Parts in June 2007, the acquisition enhances Co.'s global MRO platform. For 2008, Co. expects revenue to increase in the low double digits on a percentage basis, with earnings of approximately $2.40 to $2.45 per diluted share, an increase of 13.0% to 16.0% over the 2007 level.

Financial Data
(US$ in Thousands)

	12/31/2007	12/31/2006	12/31/2005	12/31/2004	12/31/2003	12/31/2002	12/31/2001	12/31/2000
Earnings Per Share	2.12	1.71	1.33	1.09	0.87	0.83	0.66	0.70
Cash Flow Per Share	2.63	2.16	1.60	1.58	1.56	1.05	0.57	0.82
Tang Book Value Per Share	N.M.	N.M.	N.M.	N.M.	N.M.	0.26	N.M.	N.M.
Dividends Per Share	0.240	0.180	0.160	0.160	0.080	0.080	0.080	0.080
Dividend Payout %	11.32	10.53	12.06	14.72	9.23	9.64	12.12	11.37
Income Statement								
Total Revenue	2,136,850	1,819,290	1,434,457	1,232,318	1,091,622	1,040,542	1,019,289	1,024,660
EBITDA	435,975	351,782	276,549	234,031	191,577	181,029	158,725	178,598
Income Before Taxes	336,444	263,686	204,208	165,779	130,087	122,898	84,362	106,138
Income Taxes	108,424	81,752	63,565	53,068	42,272	39,200	18,251	37,606
Net Income	228,020	181,934	140,643	112,711	87,815	83,698	66,111	68,532
Average Shares	107,580	106,608	106,066	103,881	101,430	100,881	100,335	97,602
Balance Sheet								
Current Assets	952,204	684,063	556,307	461,940	382,066	350,569	379,347	303,100
Total Assets	2,745,700	2,130,876	1,780,600	1,420,352	1,214,847	1,030,006	1,029,289	858,988
Current Liabilities	640,750	480,900	405,792	272,838	289,231	261,420	336,150	297,655
Long-Term Obligations	666,953	518,267	475,309	400,177	317,674	279,636	303,434	233,616
Total Liabilities	1,504,993	1,164,204	975,048	760,770	685,717	609,825	694,231	578,150
Stockholders' Equity	1,240,707	966,672	805,552	659,582	529,130	420,181	335,058	280,838
Shares Outstanding	107,368	106,058	105,714	103,027	100,473	99,201	98,448	97,335
Statistical Record								
Return on Assets %	9.35	9.30	8.79	8.53	7.82	8.13	7.00	8.40
Return on Equity %	20.66	20.53	19.20	18.91	18.50	22.16	21.47	27.50
EBITDA Margin %	20.40	19.34	19.28	18.99	17.55	17.40	15.57	17.43
Net Margin %	10.67	10.00	9.80	9.15	8.04	8.04	6.49	6.69
Asset Turnover	0.88	0.93	0.90	0.93	0.97	1.01	1.08	1.26
Current Ratio	1.49	1.42	1.37	1.69	1.32	1.34	1.13	1.02
Debt to Equity	0.54	0.54	0.59	0.61	0.60	0.67	0.91	0.83
Price Range	47.91-30.94	33.69-26.79	29.64-22.67	23.91-15.37	16.27-9.90	13.55-8.78	11.33-7.40	8.98-5.33
P/E Ratio	22.60-14.59	19.70-15.66	22.29-17.04	21.93-14.10	18.71-11.38	16.32-10.58	17.17-11.21	12.83-7.62
Average Yield %	0.61	0.60	0.60	0.60	0.83	0.60	0.84	1.17

Address: 37 North Valley Road, Building 4, Paoli, PA 19301
Telephone: 610-647-2121
Fax: 610-647-0211

Web Site: www.ametek.com
Officers: Frank S. Hermance - Chmn., C.E.O. John J. Molinelli - Exec. V.P., C.F.O.

Auditors: Ernst & Young LLP
Investor Contact: 610-647-2121
Transfer Agents: American Stock Transfer and Trust Co., New York, NY

AMPHENOL CORP.

Exchange	Symbol	Price	52Wk Range	Yield	P/E
NYS	APH	$37.25 (3/31/2008)	47.16-32.84	0.16	19.20

*7 Year Price Score 151.14 *NYSE Composite Index=100 *12 Month Price Score 105.13

TRADING VOLUME (thousand shares)

Interim Earnings (Per Share)

Qtr.	Mar	Jun	Sep	Dec
2003	0.14	0.11	0.16	0.19
2004	0.20	0.23	0.23	0.26
2005	0.26	0.29	0.28	0.30
2006	0.32	0.29	0.36	0.43
2007	0.43	0.46	0.50	0.55

Interim Dividends (Per Share)

Amt	Decl	Ex	Rec	Pay
0.015Q	4/27/2007	6/11/2007	6/13/2007	7/5/2007
0.015Q	7/30/2007	9/10/2007	9/12/2007	10/3/2007
0.015Q	10/26/2007	12/10/2007	12/12/2007	1/2/2008
0.015Q	1/25/2008	3/10/2008	3/12/2008	4/2/2008

Indicated Div: $0.06

Valuation Analysis   **Institutional Holding**

Forecast P/E	18.86	No of Institutions
	(1/10/2007)	329
Market Cap	$6.7 Billion	Shares
Book Value	1.3 Billion	167,201,120
Price/Book	5.27	% Held
Price/Sales	2.34	93.90

Business Summary: Electrical (MIC: 11.14 SIC: 3678 NAIC: 334417)

Amphenol is a global designer, manufacturer and marketer of interconnect and cable products. The primary end markets for Co.'s products are communication systems for the converging technologies of voice, video and data communications; industrial applications including factory automation and motion control systems, medical and industrial instrumentation, mass transportation, natural resource exploration and automotive applications; and commercial aerospace and military applications. Co. sells its products through its own global sales force, independent manufacturers' representatives and a global network of electronics distributors.

Recent Developments: For the year ended Dec 31 2007, net income increased 38.1% to US$353.2 million from US$255.7 million in the prior year. Revenues were US$2.85 billion, up 15.4% from US$2.47 billion the year before. Operating income was US$552.9 million versus US$424.6 million in the prior year, an increase of 30.2%. Direct operating expenses rose 14.1% to US$1.92 billion from US$1.68 billion in the comparable period the year before. Indirect operating expenses increased 3.8% to US$377.3 million from US$363.6 million in the equivalent prior-year period.

Prospects: Notwithstanding uncertain market conditions, Co. is optimistic about continuing improvement in the short term and confident about the long term outlook for continued growth and profitability. Hence, based on relatively stable currency exchange rates, Co. expects to achieve revenues and earnings per share in 2008 of $3.10 billion to $3.18 billion and $2.18 to $2.25, respectively, representing an increase of 9.0% to 11.0% and 12.0% to 16.0% over 2007 revenues and earnings per share, respectively. For the first quarter of 2008, Co. expects revenues in the range of $740.0 million to $755.0 million and earnings per share in the range of $0.50 and $0.52, respectively.

Financial Data
(US$ in Thousands)

	12/31/2007	12/31/2006	12/31/2005	12/31/2004	12/31/2003	12/31/2002	12/31/2001	12/31/2000
Earnings Per Share	1.94	1.40	1.14	0.91	0.59	0.46	0.49	0.63
Cash Flow Per Share	2.17	1.62	1.30	1.18	0.93	0.77	0.71	0.92
Tang Book Value Per Share	0.97	N.M.	N.M.	N.M.	N.M.	N.M.	N.M.	N.M.
Dividends Per Share	0.060	0.060	0.060	...	...	...	...	...
Dividend Payout %	3.09	4.30	5.26	...	...	...	...	...
Income Statement								
Total Revenue	2,851,041	2,471,430	1,808,147	1,530,446	1,239,504	1,062,002	1,103,771	1,359,702
EBITDA	617,464	485,195	383,700	310,238	225,546	204,830	240,345	280,007
Income Before Taxes	500,984	373,272	307,968	247,441	157,561	122,662	135,355	173,218
Income Taxes	147,790	117,581	101,629	84,130	53,571	42,318	51,645	65,314
Net Income	353,194	255,691	206,339	163,311	103,990	80,344	83,710	107,904
Average Shares	182,503	183,347	180,943	179,473	176,263	173,782	171,988	171,515
Balance Sheet								
Current Assets	1,223,808	934,605	709,814	529,015	451,349	389,164	370,257	412,670
Total Assets	2,675,733	2,195,397	1,932,540	1,306,711	1,181,384	1,078,908	1,026,743	1,004,322
Current Liabilities	520,481	447,659	335,930	277,572	217,642	235,914	203,400	242,539
Long-Term Obligations	721,561	677,173	765,970	432,144	532,280	565,885	660,614	700,216
Total Liabilities	1,410,819	1,292,403	1,243,305	825,107	857,978	911,926	922,810	975,088
Stockholders' Equity	1,264,914	902,994	689,235	481,604	323,406	166,982	103,933	29,234
Shares Outstanding	178,840	178,265	178,623	175,783	175,371	170,286	169,200	166,747
Statistical Record								
Return on Assets %	14.50	12.39	12.74	13.09	9.20	7.63	8.24	11.69
Return on Equity %	32.58	32.12	35.25	40.46	42.41	59.31	125.72	...
EBITDA Margin %	21.66	19.63	21.22	20.27	18.20	19.29	21.77	20.59
Net Margin %	12.39	10.35	11.41	10.67	8.39	7.57	7.58	7.94
Asset Turnover	1.17	1.20	1.12	1.23	1.10	1.01	1.09	1.47
Current Ratio	2.35	2.09	2.11	1.91	2.07	1.65	1.82	1.70
Debt to Equity	0.57	0.75	1.11	0.90	1.65	3.39	6.36	23.95
Price Range	47.16-30.80	34.63-22.23	22.74-16.98	18.56-14.06	15.99-9.49	12.74-6.91	14.13-7.42	17.50-7.72
P/E Ratio	24.31-15.87	24.73-15.88	19.95-14.89	20.39-15.45	27.10-16.08	27.70-15.03	28.83-15.15	27.78-12.25
Average Yield %	0.16	0.21	0.29	...	...	...	...	...

Address: 358 Hall Avenue, Wallingford, CT 06492	**Web Site:** www.amphenol.com	**Auditors:** Deloitte & Touche LLP
Telephone: 203-265-8900	**Officers:** Martin H. Loeffler - Chmn., Pres., C.E.O.	**Transfer Agents:** EquiServe Trust Company, N.A.
Fax: 203-265-8746	Edward G. Jepsen - Exec. V.P., C.F.O.	

AMR CORP. (DE)

Exchange	Symbol	Price	52Wk Range	Yield	P/E
NYS	AMR	$9.02 (3/31/2008)	33.12-8.38	N/A	5.07

*7 Year Price Score 96.18   *NYSE Composite Index=100   *12 Month Price Score 63.07

Interim Earnings (Per Share)

Qtr.	Mar	Jun	Sep	Dec
2003	(6.68)	(0.47)	0.00	(0.68)
2004	(1.03)	0.03	(1.33)	(2.41)
2005	(1.00)	0.30	(0.93)	(3.63)
2006	(0.49)	1.14	0.06	0.07
2007	0.30	1.08	0.61	(0.20)

Interim Dividends (Per Share)

No Dividends Paid

Valuation Analysis		Institutional Holding	
Forecast P/E	0.42	No of Institutions	
	(1/10/2007)	301	
Market Cap	$2.2 Billion	Shares	
Book Value	2.7 Billion	205,694,752	
Price/Book	0.85	% Held	
Price/Sales	0.10	85.74	

Business Summary: Aviation (MIC: 1.1 SIC: 4512 NAIC: 481111)

AMR is engaged in the airline industry. Through its principal subsidiary, American Airlines, Inc. (American), Co. conducts and provides scheduled passenger airline. As of Dec 31 2007, American provided scheduled jet service to approximately 170 destinations throughout North America, the Caribbean, Latin America, Europe and Asia. In addition, AMR Eagle Holding Corporation, a wholly-owned subsidiary of Co., owns two regional airlines which do business as American Eagle Airlines, Inc. and Executive Airlines, Inc. As of Dec 31 2007, Co.'s owned and leased aircraft in operation included 294 AMR Eagle Aircrafts.

Recent Developments: For the year ended Dec 31 2007, net income increased 118.2% to US$504.0 million from US$231.0 million in the prior year. Revenues were US$22.94 billion, up 1.6% from US$22.56 billion the year before. Operating income was US$965.0 million versus US$1.06 billion in the prior year, a decrease of 9.0%. Direct operating expenses rose 4.1% to US$12.97 billion from US$12.46 billion in the comparable period the year before. Indirect operating expenses decreased 0.5% to US$9.00 billion from US$9.05 billion in the equivalent prior-year period.

Prospects: On Nov 28 2007, Co. announced its plans to sell its AMR Eagle subsidiary, which consists of American Eagle Airlines Inc. and Executive Airlines Inc., its wholly-owned regional carrier. Co. believes that the sale will enable its American Airlines subsidiary to concentrate on its mainline operations, while ensuring American Airlines' continued access to cost-competitive regional feed. Accordingly, Co. expects to complete the sale in 2008. Meanwhile, for full year 2008, Co. expects its mainline capacity to increase by 1.0%, with a 0.4% reduction in domestic capacity and a 3.3% increase in international capacity, and an increase of 8.6% in its mainline unit costs, as compared to full year 2007.

Financial Data
(US$ in Thousands)

	12/31/2007	12/31/2006	12/31/2005	12/31/2004	12/31/2003	12/31/2002	12/31/2001	12/31/2000
Earnings Per Share	1.78	0.98	(5.21)	(4.74)	(7.76)	(22.57)	(11.43)	5.03
Cash Flow Per Share	7.90	9.46	6.21	4.44	3.80	(7.12)	3.32	20.89
Tang Book Value Per Share	6.02	...	...	...	N.M.	N.M.	17.19	39.67
Income Statement								
Total Revenue	22,935,000	22,563,000	20,712,000	18,645,000	17,440,000	17,299,000	18,963,000	19,703,000
EBITDA	2,263,000	2,110,000	1,046,000	1,256,000	646,000	(1,966,000)	(1,068,000)	2,651,000
Income Before Taxes	504,000	231,000	(861,000)	(761,000)	(1,308,000)	(3,860,000)	(2,756,000)	1,287,000
Income Taxes	...	...	...	...	(80,000)	(1,337,000)	(994,000)	508,000
Net Income	504,000	231,000	(861,000)	(761,000)	(1,228,000)	(3,511,000)	(1,762,000)	813,000
Average Shares	299,000	264,000	165,000	161,000	158,000	156,000	154,000	162,000
Balance Sheet								
Total Assets	28,571,000	29,145,000	29,495,000	28,773,000	29,330,000	30,267,000	32,841,000	26,213,000
Long-Term Obligations	10,093,000	12,041,000	13,456,000	13,524,000	13,126,000	12,310,000	9,834,000	5,474,000
Total Liabilities	25,914,000	29,751,000	30,973,000	29,354,000	29,284,000	29,310,000	27,468,000	19,037,000
Stockholders' Equity	2,657,000	(606,000)	(1,478,000)	(581,000)	46,000	957,000	5,373,000	7,176,000
Shares Outstanding	249,398	222,224	182,732	161,155	159,582	156,089	154,484	152,062
Statistical Record								
Return on Assets %	1.75	0.79	N.M.	N.M.	N.M.	N.M.	N.M.	3.21
Return on Equity %	49.15	...	...	...	N.M.	N.M.	N.M.	11.55
EBITDA Margin %	9.87	9.35	5.05	6.74	3.70	N.M.	N.M.	13.45
Net Margin %	2.20	1.02	(4.16)	(4.08)	(7.04)	(20.30)	(9.29)	4.13
Asset Turnover	0.79	0.77	0.71	0.64	0.59	0.55	0.64	0.78
Price Range	40.66-14.03	34.10-18.76	22.71-7.83	17.38-6.49	14.90-1.41	29.05-3.15	43.75-16.49	39.19-21.09
P/E Ratio	22.84-7.88	34.80-19.14	...	...	...	...	...	7.79-4.19

Address: 4333 Amon Carter Blvd., Fort Worth, TX 76155
Telephone: 817-963-1234
Fax: 817-967-9641

Web Site: www.amrcorp.com
Officers: Gerard J. Arpey - Chmn., Pres., C.E.O. Daniel P. Garton - Exec. V.P., Mktg.

Auditors: Ernst & Young LLP
Investor Contact: 817-967-2970

51

ANADARKO PETROLEUM CORP

Exchange	Symbol	Price	52Wk Range	Yield	P/E
NYS	APC	$63.03 (3/31/2008)	67.05-43.68	0.57	7.80

*7 Year Price Score 122.27 *NYSE Composite Index=100 *12 Month Price Score 121.26

Interim Earnings (Per Share)

Qtr.	Mar	Jun	Sep	Dec
2003	0.81	0.60	0.55	0.58
2004	0.78	0.80	0.79	0.82
2005	1.02	1.06	1.25	1.86
2006	1.42	1.76	3.15	4.13
2007	0.23	1.39	1.07	0.32

Interim Dividends (Per Share)

Amt	Decl	Ex	Rec	Pay
0.09Q	5/16/2007	6/11/2007	6/13/2007	6/27/2007
0.09Q	8/7/2007	9/10/2007	9/12/2007	9/26/2007
0.09Q	11/7/2007	12/10/2007	12/12/2007	12/26/2007
0.09Q	2/12/2008	3/10/2008	3/12/2008	3/26/2008

Indicated Div: $0.36

Valuation Analysis

Forecast P/E	7.25
	(1/10/2007)
Market Cap	$29.5 Billion
Book Value	16.4 Billion
Price/Book	1.80
Price/Sales	1.86

Institutional Holding

No of Institutions	687
Shares	382,495,648
% Held	81.71

Business Summary: Oil and Gas (MIC: 14.2 SIC: 1311 NAIC: 211111)

Anadarko Petroleum is engaged in oil and gas exploration and production, with 2.43 billion barrels of oil equivalent of proved reserves as of Dec 31 2007. Co. markets natural gas, oil and natural gas liquids (NGLs) and owns and operates gas gathering and processing systems. In addition, Co. has hard minerals properties through non-operated joint ventures and royalty arrangements in several coal, trona and industrial mineral mines. Co.'s core areas of operation are located onshore in the U.S., the deepwater of the Gulf of Mexico and Algeria. As of Dec 31 2007, Co. had proved reserves of 8.50 trillion cubic feet of natural gas and 1.00 billion barrels of crude oil, condensate and NGLs.

Recent Developments: For the year ended Dec 31 2007, net income decreased 20.4% to US$3.78 billion from US$4.75 billion in the prior year. Revenues were US$15.89 billion, up 55.3% from US$10.23 billion the year before. Operating income was US$7.35 billion versus US$4.38 billion in the prior year, an increase of 67.7%. Direct operating expenses rose 50.3% to US$2.58 billion from US$1.72 billion in the comparable period the year before. Indirect operating expenses increased 44.4% to US$5.97 billion from US$4.13 billion in the equivalent prior-year period.

Prospects: For 2008, Co. is budgeting capital expenditures of about $4.50 billion to $4.70 billion, including approximately 20.0% for exploration activities. The capital budget reflects its commitment to accelerate its net risked captured resources in its asset base mainly to achieve double-digit production growth in the Rocky Mountain region; the development in deepwater Gulf of Mexico, including the start-up of the Blind Faith platform; driving toward first production at the Peregrino field offshore Brazil; and extending its deepwater exploration activities worldwide. In addition, Co. is projecting oil and natural gas production in a range of 205 to 210 million barrels of oil equivalent for 2008.

Financial Data

(US$ in Thousands)	12/31/2007	12/31/2006	12/31/2005	12/31/2004	12/31/2003	12/31/2002	12/31/2001	12/31/2000
Earnings Per Share	8.08	10.46	5.20	3.18	2.54	1.61	(0.38)	2.08
Cash Flow Per Share	6.24	10.64	8.82	6.40	6.09	4.43	6.64	4.16
Tang Book Value Per Share	23.83	21.95	21.06	16.67	14.16	10.81	9.71	10.40
Dividends Per Share	0.360	0.360	0.360	0.280	0.220	0.163	0.113	0.100
Dividend Payout %	4.46	3.44	6.93	8.81	8.64	10.12	...	4.81
Income Statement								
Total Revenue	15,892,000	10,187,000	7,100,000	6,067,000	5,122,000	3,860,000	8,369,000	5,686,000
EBITDA	10,261,000	6,869,000	5,439,000	4,276,000	3,524,000	2,544,000	930,000	2,144,000
Income Before Taxes	6,329,000	4,238,000	3,895,000	2,477,000	1,974,000	1,207,000	(390,000)	1,426,000
Income Taxes	2,559,000	1,442,000	1,424,000	871,000	729,000	376,000	(214,000)	602,000
Net Income	3,781,000	4,854,000	2,466,000	1,601,000	1,287,000	825,000	(188,000)	796,000
Average Shares	468,000	464,000	474,000	504,000	506,000	520,000	500,000	386,000
Balance Sheet								
Current Assets	4,516,000	4,614,000	2,916,000	2,502,000	1,324,000	1,280,000	1,201,000	1,894,000
Total Assets	48,481,000	58,844,000	22,588,000	20,192,000	20,546,000	18,248,000	16,771,000	16,590,000
Current Liabilities	5,257,000	16,758,000	2,403,000	1,993,000	1,715,000	1,861,000	1,801,000	1,676,000
Long-Term Obligations	11,151,000	11,520,000	3,555,000	3,671,000	5,058,000	5,171,000	4,638,000	3,984,000
Total Liabilities	32,117,000	43,931,000	11,537,000	10,907,000	11,947,000	11,276,000	10,406,000	9,804,000
Stockholders' Equity	16,364,000	14,913,000	11,051,000	9,285,000	8,599,000	6,972,000	6,365,000	6,786,000
Shares Outstanding	468,000	467,000	463,800	473,200	502,800	502,800	497,800	506,606
Statistical Record								
Return on Assets %	7.05	11.92	11.53	7.84	6.64	4.71	N.M.	7.67
Return on Equity %	24.18	37.39	24.25	17.86	16.53	12.37	N.M.	19.08
EBITDA Margin %	64.57	67.43	76.61	70.48	68.80	65.91	11.11	37.71
Net Margin %	23.79	47.65	34.73	26.39	25.13	21.37	N.M.	14.00
Asset Turnover	0.30	0.25	0.33	0.30	0.26	0.22	0.50	0.55
Current Ratio	0.86	0.28	1.21	1.26	0.77	0.69	0.67	1.13
Debt to Equity	0.68	0.77	0.32	0.40	0.59	0.74	0.73	0.59
Price Range	67.05-38.63	56.70-41.09	50.38-30.20	35.52-24.32	25.65-20.25	29.15-19.00	36.49-22.02	37.42-14.22
P/E Ratio	8.30-4.78	5.42-3.93	9.69-5.81	11.17-7.65	10.10-7.97	18.10-11.80	...	17.99-6.84
Average Yield %	0.72	0.75	0.88	0.96	0.98	0.67	0.39	0.40

Address: 1201 Lake Robbins Drive, The Woodlands, TX 77380-1046 Telephone: 832-636-1000	Web Site: www.anadarko.com Officers: James T. Hackett - Pres., C.E.O. James R. Larson - Sr. V.P., Fin., C.F.O.	Auditors: KPMG LLP Investor Contact: 832-636-1000 Transfer Agents: Mellon Investor Services LLC, South Hackensack, NJ

ANALOG DEVICES, INC.

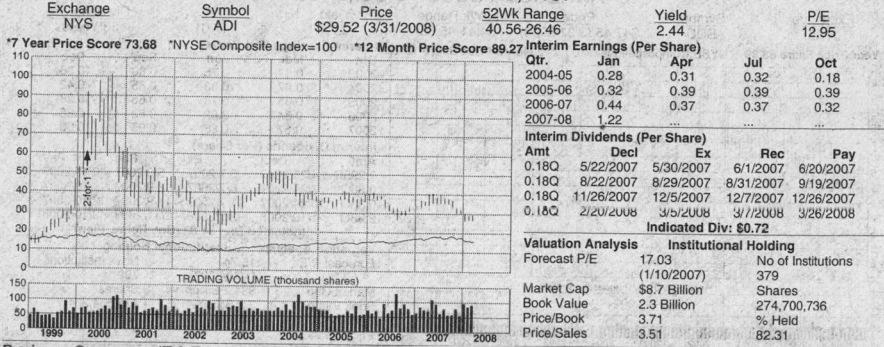

Exchange	Symbol	Price	52Wk Range	Yield	P/E
NYS	ADI	$29.52 (3/31/2008)	40.56-26.46	2.44	12.95

*7 Year Price Score 73.68   *NYSE Composite Index=100   *12 Month Price Score 89.27

Interim Earnings (Per Share)

Qtr.	Jan	Apr	Jul	Oct
2004-05	0.28	0.31	0.32	0.18
2005-06	0.32	0.39	0.39	0.39
2006-07	0.44	0.37	0.37	0.32
2007-08	1.22	...	...	...

Interim Dividends (Per Share)

Amt	Decl	Ex	Rec	Pay
0.18Q	5/22/2007	5/30/2007	6/1/2007	6/20/2007
0.18Q	8/22/2007	8/29/2007	8/31/2007	9/19/2007
0.18Q	11/26/2007	12/5/2007	12/7/2007	12/26/2007
0.18Q	2/20/2008	3/5/2008	3/7/2008	3/26/2008

Indicated Div: $0.72

Valuation Analysis

	Institutional Holding	
Forecast P/E	17.03	No of Institutions
	(1/10/2007)	379
Market Cap	$8.7 Billion	Shares
Book Value	2.3 Billion	274,700,736
Price/Book	3.71	% Held
Price/Sales	3.51	82.31

Business Summary: IT & Technology (MIC: 10.2 SIC: 3674 NAIC: 334413)

Analog Devices designs, manufactures and markets analog, mixed-signal and digital signal processing integrated circuits used in signal processing for industrial, communication, computer and consumer applications. Co. also serve the personal computer market with products that monitor and manage power usage, process signals used in flat panel displays and multimedia projectors, and enable enhanced audio. Co.'s products include converting real-world phenomena, such as temperature, motion, pressure, light and sound into electrical signals used in electronic equipments including industrial process control, defense electronics, cellular communications, computers, automobiles, and digital cameras.

Recent Developments: For the quarter ended Feb 2 2008, income from continuing operations decreased 22.1% to US$121.8 million from US$156.5 million in the year-earlier quarter. Net income increased 141.9% to US$370.7 million from US$153.2 million in the year-earlier quarter. Revenues were US$613.9 million, down 2.0% from US$626.3 million the year before. Operating income was US$145.9 million versus US$169.4 million in the prior year quarter, a decrease of 13.9%. Direct operating expenses rose 5.1% to US$238.1 million from US$226.6 million in the comparable period the year before. Indirect operating expenses decreased 0.2% to US$229.9 million from US$230.3 million in the equivalent prior-year period.

Prospects: Co. completed the sales of its CPU voltage regulation and PC thermal monitoring business for about $184.0 million, as well as it cellular handset radio and baseband chipset operations for $350.0 million on Jan 2 and Jan 11 2008, respectively. The divestments have improved Co.'s product portfolio by allowing it to focus on its signal processing technologies, leading to margin growth. For the fiscal quarter ending May 2008, Co. is encouraged with its product demand due to higher order rates and backlog. Thus, Co. is expecting revenue of $615.0 million to $640.0 million and diluted earnings per share from continuing operations of $0.39 to $0.42.

Financial Data

(US$ in Thousands)	3 Mos	11/03/2007	10/28/2006	10/29/2005	10/30/2004	11/01/2003	11/02/2002	11/03/2001
Earnings Per Share	2.28	1.50	1.48	1.08	1.45	0.78	0.28	0.93
Cash Flow Per Share	2.65	2.50	1.74	1.81	2.08	1.19	0.62	2.31
Tang Book Value Per Share	6.99	6.71	9.17	9.61	9.66	8.42	7.50	7.20
Dividends Per Share	0.720	0.700	0.561	0.320	0.200	...	...	...
Dividend Payout %	31.52	46.67	37.87	29.63	13.79	...	...	...
Income Statement								
Total Revenue	613,909	2,546,117	2,573,176	2,388,808	2,633,800	2,047,268	1,707,508	2,276,915
EBITDA	183,714	733,523	734,590	671,412	849,543	541,154	357,917	647,561
Depn & Amortn	37,974	...	...	...	...	...	...	...
Income Before Taxes	158,266	658,920	662,395	587,690	732,736	381,836	140,350	507,244
Income Taxes	36,418	158,444	113,661	172,903	161,998	83,555	35,051	150,867
Net Income	370,719	496,907	549,482	414,787	570,738	298,281	105,299	356,377
Average Shares	304,260	332,301	370,964	383,474	392,854	382,227	381,245	381,962
Balance Sheet								
Current Assets	2,099,405	1,978,995	3,011,302	3,732,456	3,528,611	2,885,716	3,624,225	3,434,919
Total Assets	3,134,943	2,971,949	3,986,851	4,583,211	4,720,083	4,092,877	4,980,191	4,884,863
Current Liabilities	711,425	548,051	490,943	818,923	567,002	463,477	483,635	527,948
Long-Term Obligations	...	...	...	...	...	...	1,274,487	1,206,038
Total Liabilities	795,690	633,808	550,841	891,710	920,511	804,803	2,080,175	2,041,837
Stockholders' Equity	2,339,253	2,338,141	3,435,793	3,691,501	3,799,572	3,288,074	2,900,016	2,843,026
Shares Outstanding	293,935	303,354	342,000	366,831	375,840	370,234	363,187	363,250
Statistical Record								
Return on Assets %	20.58	14.05	12.86	8.94	12.99	6.59	2.14	7.54
Return on Equity %	25.57	16.93	15.46	11.10	16.15	9.67	3.68	13.62
EBITDA Margin %	29.93	28.81	28.55	28.11	32.26	26.43	20.96	28.44
Net Margin %	60.39	19.52	21.35	17.36	21.67	14.57	6.17	15.65
Asset Turnover	0.71	0.72	0.60	0.51	0.60	0.45	0.35	0.48
Current Ratio	2.95	3.61	6.13	4.56				
Debt to Equity	...	...	...	...	...	0.23	6.23	7.49	6.51
Price Range	40.56-26.46	40.56-31.22	40.91-26.73	41.34-32.48	51.39-33.57	44.86-23.04	47.95-18.29	63.25-30.99
P/E Ratio	17.79-11.61	27.04-20.81	27.64-18.06	38.28-30.07	35.44-23.15	57.51-29.54	171.25-65.32	68.01-33.32
Average Yield %	2.05	1.96	1.61	0.87	0.45	...	0.44	0.42

Address: One Technology Way, Norwood, MA 02062-9106	Web Site: www.analog.com	Auditors: Ernst & Young LLP
Telephone: 781-329-4700	Officers: Ray Stata - Chmn. Jerald G. Fishman - Pres., C.E.O.	Investor Contact: 178-146-13282
Fax: 781-326-8703		Transfer Agents: EquiServe Trust Company, N.A., Providence, RI

ANHEUSER-BUSCH COS., INC.

Exchange	Symbol	Price	52Wk Range	Yield	P/E	Div Acheiver
NYS	BUD	$47.45 (3/31/2008)	54.41-45.68	2.78	17.01	33 Years

*7 Year Price Score 83.39 *NYSE Composite Index=100 *12 Month Price Score 101.07

Interim Earnings (Per Share)

Qtr.	Mar	Jun	Sep	Dec
2003	0.57	0.75	0.80	0.36
2004	0.67	0.83	0.85	0.42
2005	0.65	0.78	0.66	0.26
2006	0.64	0.82	0.82	0.25
2007	0.67	0.88	0.95	0.30

Interim Dividends (Per Share)

Amt	Decl	Ex	Rec	Pay
0.295Q	4/25/2007	5/7/2007	5/9/2007	6/11/2007
0.33Q	7/25/2007	8/7/2007	8/9/2007	9/10/2007
0.33Q	10/24/2007	11/7/2007	11/9/2007	12/10/2007
0.33Q	1/10/2008	2/7/2008	2/11/2008	3/10/2008

Indicated Div: $1.32 (Div. Reinv. Plan)

Valuation Analysis **Institutional Holding**

Forecast P/E	15.74	No of Institutions
	(1/10/2007)	792
Market Cap	$34.2 Billion	Shares
Book Value	3.2 Billion	474,554,304
Price/Book	10.86	% Held
Price/Sales	2.05	62.21

TRADING VOLUME (thousand shares)

Business Summary: Food (MIC: 4.1 SIC: 2082 NAIC: 312120)

Anheuser-Busch Companies is the holding company of Anheuser-Busch, Inc., which is engaged in the beer business. Co.'s beer is primarily sold under brand names including Budweiser, Michelob, Busch, Natural Light, and Natural Ice. As of Dec 31 2007, worldwide sales of Co.'s beer brands aggregated 128.4 million barrels. Additionally, Co. is engaged in the family entertainment industry, primarily through its wholly-owned subsidiary, Busch Entertainment Corporation, which owned nine theme parks as of Dec 31 2006. Also, Co. is engaged in packaging, malt and rice production, international beer, non-beer beverages, real estate development, and transportation services.

Recent Developments: For the year ended Dec 31 2007, net income increased 7.6% to US$2.12 billion from US$1.97 billion in the prior year. Revenues were US$16.69 billion, up 6.2% from US$15.72 billion the year before. Operating income was US$2.89 billion versus US$2.72 billion in the prior year, an increase of 6.4%. Direct operating expenses rose 6.6% to US$10.84 billion from US$10.17 billion in the comparable period the year before. Indirect operating expenses increased 4.3% to US$2.96 billion from US$2.83 billion in the equivalent prior-year period.

Prospects: Co. remains focused on its strategies to accelerate U.S. beer sales and profitability in 2008. Specifically, Co. plans to increase total media spending by 10.0% in 2008 and will focus its national media spending on fewer brands, emphasizing those like Budweiser and Bud Light that benefit the most from large scale media exposure. Co. is also focusing on productivity improvement and supply chain savings to mitigate commodity cost pressures in 2008. Notably, Co. has expanded its Blue Ocean brewery cost reduction initiative to drive additional cost savings and process improvements across all areas of its business. Thus, Co. is targeting earnings per share growth in the 7.0% to 10.0% range.

Financial Data (US$ in Thousands)	12/31/2007	12/31/2006	12/31/2005	12/31/2004	12/31/2003	12/31/2002	12/31/2001	12/31/2000
Earnings Per Share	2.79	2.53	2.35	2.77	2.48	2.20	1.89	1.69
Cash Flow Per Share	3.94	3.52	3.51	3.67	3.60	3.19	2.65	2.48
Tang Book Value Per Share	2.22	3.36	2.71	1.88	2.74	3.19	4.15	4.11
Dividends Per Share	1.250	1.130	1.030	0.930	0.830	0.750	0.690	0.630
Dividend Payout %	44.80	44.66	43.83	33.57	33.47	34.09	36.51	37.28
Income Statement								
Total Revenue	16,685,700	15,717,100	15,035,700	14,934,200	14,146,700	13,566,400	12,911,500	12,261,800
EBITDA	3,882,600	3,697,500	3,602,700	4,332,400	4,076,900	3,820,600	3,545,300	3,297,200
Income Before Taxes	2,422,700	2,276,900	2,191,500	2,999,400	2,824,300	2,623,600	2,377,600	2,179,900
Income Taxes	969,800	900,500	850,400	1,163,200	1,093,300	1,041,500	913,200	828,300
Net Income	2,115,300	1,965,200	1,839,200	2,240,300	2,075,900	1,933,800	1,704,500	1,551,600
Average Shares	757,100	777,000	782,600	808,500	837,000	878,900	901,600	919,700
Balance Sheet								
Current Assets	2,024,500	1,829,500	1,758,700	1,818,400	1,630,300	1,504,700	1,550,400	1,547,900
Total Assets	17,155,000	16,377,200	16,555,000	16,173,400	14,689,500	14,119,500	13,862,000	13,084,500
Current Liabilities	2,303,800	2,246,100	1,982,600	1,969,000	1,857,200	1,787,700	1,732,300	1,675,700
Long-Term Obligations	9,140,300	7,653,500	7,972,100	8,278,600	7,285,400	6,603,200	5,983,900	5,374,500
Total Liabilities	14,003,400	12,438,500	13,211,700	13,505,300	11,977,800	11,067,200	9,800,500	8,955,600
Stockholders' Equity	3,151,600	3,938,700	3,343,300	2,668,100	2,711,700	3,052,300	4,061,500	4,128,900
Shares Outstanding	721,300	766,100	777,700	785,000	813,100	846,600	879,100	903,600
Statistical Record								
Return on Assets %	12.62	11.93	11.24	14.48	14.41	13.82	12.65	12.03
Return on Equity %	59.67	53.97	61.19	83.06	72.03	54.37	41.62	38.44
EBITDA Margin %	23.27	23.53	23.96	29.01	28.82	28.16	27.46	26.89
Net Margin %	12.68	12.50	12.23	15.00	14.67	14.25	13.20	12.65
Asset Turnover	1.00	0.95	0.92	0.97	0.98	0.97	0.96	0.95
Current Ratio	0.88	0.81	0.89	0.92	0.88	0.84	0.89	0.92
Debt to Equity	2.90	1.94	2.38	3.10	2.69	2.16	1.47	1.30
Price Range	54.41-46.95	49.91-40.42	50.73-40.57	54.29-49.15	53.69-45.92	54.97-44.00	46.51-38.50	49.81-27.47
P/E Ratio	19.50-16.83	19.73-15.98	21.59-17.26	19.60-17.85	21.65-18.52	24.99-20.00	24.61-20.37	29.47-16.25
Average Yield %	2.46	2.48	2.25	1.80	1.65	1.49	1.62	1.62

Address: One Busch Place, St. Louis, MO 63118
Telephone: 314-577-2000
Fax: 314-577-2900

Web Site: www.anheuser-busch.com
Officers: August A. Busch III - Chmn. Keith M. Kasen - Chmn.

Auditors: PricewaterhouseCoopers LLP
Transfer Agents: Mellon Investor Services, LLC, Ridgefield Park, NJ

ANNALY CAPITAL MANAGEMENT INC

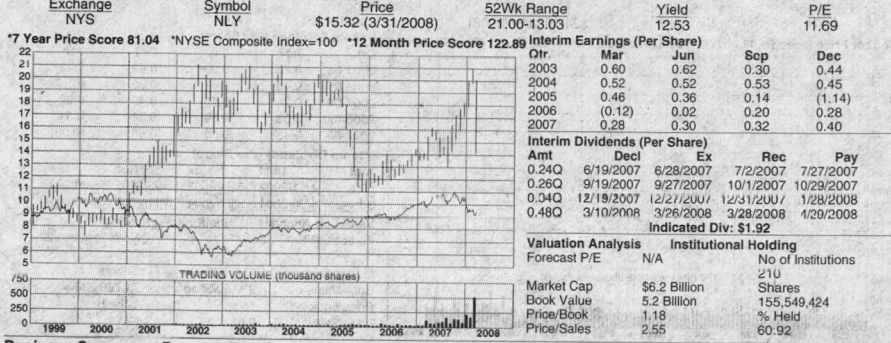

Exchange	Symbol	Price	52Wk Range	Yield	P/E
NYS	NLY	$15.32 (3/31/2008)	21.00-13.03	12.53	11.69

*7 Year Price Score 81.04 *NYSE Composite Index=100 *12 Month Price Score 122.89

Interim Earnings (Per Share)

Qtr	Mar	Jun	Sep	Dec
2003	0.60	0.62	0.30	0.44
2004	0.52	0.52	0.53	0.45
2005	0.46	0.36	0.14	(1.14)
2006	(0.12)	0.02	0.20	0.28
2007	0.28	0.30	0.32	0.40

Interim Dividends (Per Share)

Amt	Decl	Ex	Rec	Pay
0.24Q	6/19/2007	6/28/2007	7/2/2007	7/27/2007
0.26Q	9/19/2007	9/27/2007	10/1/2007	10/29/2007
0.04Q	12/19/2007	12/27/2007	12/31/2007	1/28/2008
0.48Q	3/10/2008	3/26/2008	3/28/2008	4/29/2008

Indicated Div: $1.92

Valuation Analysis

		Institutional Holding	
Forecast P/E	N/A	No of Institutions	210
Market Cap	$6.2 Billion	Shares	155,549,424
Book Value	5.2 Billion	% Held	
Price/Book	1.18		60.92
Price/Sales	2.55		

Business Summary: Property, Real Estate & Development (MIC: 8.3 SIC: 6798 NAIC: 525930)

Annaly Capital Management owns, manages, and finances a portfolio of investment securities, including mortgage pass-through certificates, collateralized mortgage obligations, agency callable debentures, and other securities representing interests in or obligations backed by pools of mortgage loans. In addition, Co. may acquire mortgage-backed securities backed by single family residential mortgage loans as well as securities backed by loans on multi-family, commercial or other real estate-related properties. As of Dec 31 2007, all of the mortgage-backed securities that Co. had acquired have been backed by single-family residential mortgage loans.

Recent Developments: For the year ended Dec 31 2007, net income increased 341.7% to US$414.4 million from US$93.8 million in the prior year. Revenues were US$2.42 billion, up 100.9% from US$1.20 billion the year before.

Prospects: Co.'s total net income has benefited from an increase in net interest income, gains on the sale of securities, a reduction in losses on other-than temporarily impaired securities, the increased asset base, and the increase in interest rate spread. However, Co. noted that although the extreme market turbulence that began in Aug 2007 has subsided, the fixed income market conditions remain volatile. Hence, Co. continues to monitor the market for evidence of changes in prepayment behavior. Separately, Co. continues to explore alternative business strategies, alternative investments and other strategic initiatives to complement its core business strategy of investing in investment securities.

Financial Data
(US$ in Thousands)

	12/31/2007	12/31/2006	12/31/2005	12/31/2004	12/31/2003	12/31/2002	12/31/2001	12/31/2000
Earnings Per Share	1.31	0.44	(0.19)	2.03	1.94	2.67	2.21	1.15
Cash Flow Per Share	1.77	1.32	2.30	3.52	3.85	3.68	2.41	1.01
Tang Book Value Per Share	12.43	11.36	10.42	12.24	11.96	12.77	11.15	9.34
Dividends Per Share	1.040	0.240	1.040	1.980	1.950	2.670	1.750	1.150
Dividend Payout %	79.39	54.55	...	97.54	100.52	100.00	79.19	100.00
Income Statement								
Interest Income	2,355,447	1,221,882	705,046	532,328	337,433	404,165	263,058	109,750
Interest Expense	1,926,465	1,055,013	568,560	270,116	182,004	191,758	168,055	92,902
Net Interest Income	428,982	166,869	136,486	262,212	155,429	212,407	95,002	16,849
Non-Interest Income	61,235	(19,191)	(100,711)	17,727	40,907	21,063	4,586	2,025
Non-Interest Expense	66,313	43,507	34,278	26,889	16,233	13,963	7,311	2,287
Income Before Taxes	423,904	101,678	1,497	253,050	...	...	...	...
Income Taxes	8,870	7,538	10,744	4,458	...	...	...	...
Net Income	414,384	93,816	(9,247)	248,592	180,103	219,507	92,278	16,587
Average Shares	306,263	167,746	122,475	118,459	93,031	82,282	41,857	14,377
Balance Sheet								
Total Assets	53,903,514	30,715,980	16,063,422	19,560,299	12,990,286	11,659,084	7,717,314	2,035,029
Total Liabilities	48,585,536	28,056,149	14,559,399	17,859,829	11,841,066	10,579,018	7,049,957	1,899,386
Stockholders' Equity	5,204,938	2,543,041	1,504,023	1,700,470	1,149,220	1,080,066	667,357	135,642
Shares Outstanding	401,822	205,345	123,684	121,263	96,074	84,569	59,826	14,522
Statistical Record								
Return on Assets %	0.98	0.40	N.M.	1.52	1.46	...	1.89	0.94
Return on Equity %	10.70	4.64	N.M.	17.40	16.16	...	22.98	13.85
Net Interest Margin %	18.21	13.66	19.36	49.26	46.06	52.55	36.11	15.35
Efficiency Ratio %	2.74	3.62	5.67	4.89	4.29	3.28	2.73	2.05
Price Range	18.18-13.03	14.42-11.34	20.00-10.94	21.13-16.11	21.10-15.65	21.15-15.56	17.01-8.75	9.50-7.25
P/E Ratio	13.88-9.95	32.77-25.77	...	10.41-7.94	10.88-8.07	7.92-5.83	7.70-3.96	8.26-6.30
Average Yield %	6.82	1.88	6.39	10.84	10.66	14.92	13.78	13.51

Address: 1211 Avenue of the Americas, Suite 2902, New York, NY 10036 **Telephone:** 212-696-0100 **Fax:** 212-696-9809	**Web Site:** www.annaly.com **Officers:** Michael A. J. Farrell - Chmn.,Pres., C.E.O. Wellington J. St. Claire - Vice-Chmn., Chief Invest. Officer	**Auditors:** Deloitte & Touche LLP **Investor Contact:** 888-826-6259 **Transfer Agents:** Mellon Investors Services, LLC, South Hakensack, NJ

ANN TAYLOR STORES CORP.

Exchange	Symbol	Price	52Wk Range	Yield	P/E
NYS	ANN	$24.18 (3/31/2008)	39.09-19.28	N/A	15.80

*7 Year Price Score 99.02   *NSYE Composite Index=100   *12 Month Price Score 83.54

Interim Earnings (Per Share)

Qtr.	Apr	Jul	Oct	Jan
2003-04	0.26	0.30	0.42	0.43
2004-05	0.43	0.41	0.20	(0.17)
2005-06	0.24	0.10	0.42	0.37
2006-07	0.53	0.59	0.54	0.31
2007-08	0.46	0.50	0.66	(0.08)

Interim Dividends (Per Share)

Amt	Decl	Ex	Rec	Pay
50%	4/11/2002	5/21/2002	5/2/2002	5/20/2002
3-for-2	4/30/2004	5/27/2004	5/11/2004	5/26/2004

Valuation Analysis

		Institutional Holding	
Forecast P/E	N/A	No of Institutions	209
Market Cap	$1.5 Billion	Shares	71,760,336
Book Value	839.5 Million	% Held	N/A
Price/Book	1.75		
Price/Sales	0.61		

Business Summary: Retail - Apparel and Accessory Stores (MIC: 5.8 SIC: 5621 NAIC: 448120)

AnnTaylor Stores is a national specialty retailer of women's apparel, shoes and accessories under the Ann Taylor, Ann Taylor Loft (LOFT) and Ann Taylor Factory brand names. Co.'s stores provide severalcareer and casual separates, dresses; tops, weekend wear, shoes and accessories, coordinated as part of a total wardrobing strategy. As of Feb 2 2008, Co. operated 929 retail stores in 46 states in the U.S., the District of Columbia and Puerto Rico, of which 349 were Ann Taylor stores, 512 were LOFT stores and 68 were Ann Taylor Factory stores. Co. sells its products through traditional retail stores and over the Internet at anntaylor.com and anntaylorLOFT.com or by phone at 1-800-DIAL-ANN.

Recent Developments: For the year ended Feb 2 2008, net income decreased 32.0% to US$97.2 million from US$143.0 million in the prior year. Revenues were US$2.40 billion, up 2.3% from US$2.34 billion the year before. Operating income was US$155.4 million versus US$223.8 million in the prior year, a decrease of 30.6%. Direct operating expenses rose 5.5% to US$1.15 billion from US$1.09 billion in the comparable period the year before. Indirect operating expenses increased 6.1% to US$1.10 billion from US$1.03 billion in the equivalent prior-year period.

Prospects: For the fiscal year ending Jan 31 2009, Co. is targeting earnings of $1.80 to $1.90 per diluted share, excluding one-time restructuring costs. Also, Co. is forecasting total net sales growth in the low single digits, with comparable store sales to be flat to slightly negative. Similarly, Co. is projecting total square footage decline of about 2.0%, reflecting a reduction of square footage associated with the 64 stores being closed in prior fiscal year, partially offset by the opening of about 50 to 55 new stores. Lastly, Co. is expecting restructuring program savings of about $20.0 million to $25.0 million, excluding anticipated one-time restructuring costs of $7.0 million to $10.0 million.

Financial Data
(US$ in Thousands)

	02/02/2008	02/03/2007	01/28/2006	01/29/2005	01/31/2004	02/01/2003	02/02/2002	02/03/2001
Earnings Per Share	1.53	1.98	1.13	0.88	1.42	1.15	0.44	0.78
Cash Flow Per Share	4.11	4.10	4.36	2.44	2.85	2.40	1.21	1.18
Tang Book Value Per Share	9.08	11.00	10.32	9.06	7.99	6.36	4.93	4.26
Income Statement								
Total Revenue	2,396,510	2,342,907	2,073,146	1,853,583	1,587,708	1,380,966	1,299,573	1,232,776
EBITDA	272,190	329,727	235,212	191,007	227,158	188,632	116,551	145,446
Income Before Taxes	161,040	238,781	138,261	106,354	168,288	131,407	54,662	93,398
Income Taxes	63,805	95,799	56,389	43,078	67,346	51,249	25,557	41,035
Net Income	97,235	142,982	81,872	63,276	100,942	80,158	29,105	52,363
Average Shares	63,452	72,107	72,270	72,933	73,144	72,451	65,490	70,247
Balance Sheet								
Current Assets	507,891	690,605	676,212	587,314	577,368	455,271	325,853	313,809
Total Assets	1,393,755	1,568,503	1,492,906	1,327,338	1,151,873	1,010,826	882,986	848,115
Current Liabilities	312,876	299,418	257,586	243,746	161,620	151,195	136,614	141,042
Long-Term Obligations	...	...	...	...	125,152	121,652	118,280	116,210
Total Liabilities	554,271	518,592	458,424	400,594	321,237	296,408	270,857	274,086
Stockholders' Equity	839,484	1,049,911	1,034,482	926,744	830,636	714,418	612,129	574,029
Shares Outstanding	60,879	69,373	72,491	70,632	68,067	67,322	66,098	64,850
Statistical Record								
Return on Assets %	6.58	9.19	5.82	5.12	9.36	8.49	3.37	6.39
Return on Equity %	10.32	13.50	8.37	7.22	13.10	12.12	4.92	9.46
EBITDA Margin %	11.36	14.07	11.35	10.30	14.31	13.66	8.97	11.80
Net Margin %	4.06	6.10	3.95	3.41	6.36	5.80	2.24	4.25
Asset Turnover	1.62	1.51	1.47	1.50	1.47	1.46	1.51	1.50
Current Ratio	1.62	2.31	2.63	2.41	3.57	3.01	2.39	2.22
Debt to Equity	...	...	...	...	0.15	0.17	0.19	0.20
Price Range	39.67-19.28	44.56-32.32	35.13-21.44	31.31-20.45	27.63-11.77	21.94-12.02	17.22-9.63	19.67-6.78
P/E Ratio	25.93-12.60	22.51-16.32	31.09-18.97	35.58-23.24	19.46-8.29	19.08-10.45	39.14-21.89	25.21-8.69

Address: 7 Times Square, New York, NY 10036 **Telephone:** 212-541-3300 **Fax:** 212-541-3379	**Web Site:** www.anntaylor.com **Officers:** Ronald W. Hovespian - Chmn. Kay Krill - Pres., C.E.O.	**Auditors:** Deloitte & Touche LLP **Investor Contact:** 212-541-3484 **Transfer Agents:** Mellon Investor Services, Jersey City, NJ

AON CORP.

Exchange	Symbol	Price	52Wk Range	Yield	P/E
NYS	AOC	$40.20 (3/31/2008)	50.08-37.94	1.49	14.94

*7 Year Price Score 111.41 *NYSE Composite Index=100 *12 Month Price Score 103.92

Interim Earnings (Per Share)

Qtr.	Mar	Jun	Sep	Dec
2003	0.48	0.46	0.36	0.67
2004	0.53	0.52	0.36	0.23
2005	0.59	0.57	0.36	0.65
2006	0.57	0.57	0.32	0.67
2007	0.66	0.75	0.64	0.64

Interim Dividends (Per Share)

Amt	Decl	Ex	Rec	Pay
0.15Q	4/13/2007	4/27/2007	5/1/2007	5/14/2007
0.15Q	7/20/2007	7/30/2007	8/1/2007	8/14/2007
0.15Q	10/11/2007	10/30/2007	11/1/2007	11/14/2007
0.15Q	1/18/2008	1/30/2008	2/1/2008	2/14/2008

Indicated Div: $0.60

Valuation Analysis

		Institutional Holding	
Forecast P/E	12.54	No of Institutions	
	(1/10/2007)	346	
Market Cap	$12.2 Billion	Shares	
Book Value	6.2 Billion	263,377,088	
Price/Book	1.97	% Held	
Price/Sales	1.64	88.27	

Business Summary: Insurance (MIC: 8.2 SIC: 6321 NAIC: 524114)

Aon is a holding company. Co.'s Risk and Insurance Brokerage Services segment acts as an advisor and insurance broker, and is engaged in risk management, and negotiating and placing insurance risk with insurance carriers through its global distribution network. Co.'s Consulting segment offers advice and services to clients for employee benefits, compensation, management consulting, communications, human resource outsourcing, strategic human resource consulting, and financial advisory and litigation consulting. Co.'s Insurance Underwriting segment provides specialty insurance products, including accident, health and life insurance.

Recent Developments: For the year ended Dec 31 2007, income from continuing operations increased 50.3% to US$672.0 million from US$447.0 million a year earlier. Net income increased 20.0% to US$864.0 million from US$720.0 million in the prior year. Revenues were US$7.47 billion, up 8.6% from US$6.88 billion the year before. Net investment income rose 36.2% to US$301.0 million from US$221.0 million a year ago.

Prospects: On Feb 22 2008, Co. announced a definitive agreement to acquire substantially all of Gallagher Re's U.S. and U.K. reinsurance brokerage business. As a result of this transaction, Co. will have a significant presence in the U.S. accident, and life markets with enhanced capabilities in the U.K. specialty, casualty and financial institutions business. This agreement includes an initial payment of approximately $30.0 million in cash and an additional payment for revenues generated in the 12 months. Meanwhile, Co. continues to focus on its global restructuring plan that is projected to deliver $50.0 million to $70.0 million of savings in 2008, and $175.0 million to $200.0 million in 2009.

Financial Data
(US$ in Thousands)

	12/31/2007	12/31/2006	12/31/2005	12/31/2004	12/31/2003	12/31/2002	12/31/2001	12/31/2000
Earnings Per Share	2.69	2.13	2.17	1.63	1.97	1.64	0.73	1.79
Cash Flow Per Share	4.33	3.05	2.75	3.69	4.13	4.42	2.08	2.83
Tang Book Value Per Share	3.56	1.80	2.48	0.76	N M	N M	N.M.	N.M.
Dividends Per Share	0.600	0.600	0.600	0.600	0.600	0.825	0.895	0.870
Dividend Payout %	22.30	28.17	27.65	36.81	30.46	50.30	122.60	48.60
Income Statement								
Premium Income	...	1,918,000	2,848,000	2,788,000	2,609,000	2,368,000	2,027,000	1,921,000
Total Revenue	7,471,000	8,954,000	9,837,000	10,172,000	9,810,000	8,822,000	7,676,000	7,375,000
Benefits & Claims	...	1,142,000	1,551,000	1,516,000	1,427,000	1,375,000	1,111,000	1,037,000
Income Before Taxes	1,074,000	920,000	965,000	880,000	1,110,000	793,000	399,000	854,000
Income Taxes	352,000	294,000	323,000	303,000	411,000	293,000	156,000	333,000
Net Income	864,000	720,000	737,000	546,000	628,000	466,000	203,000	474,000
Average Shares	323,000	342,100	341,500	336,600	317,800	283,000	272,000	263,000
Balance Sheet								
Total Assets	24,948,000	24,318,000	27,818,000	28,329,000	27,027,000	25,334,000	22,386,000	22,251,000
Total Liabilities	18,727,000	19,100,000	22,515,000	23,176,000	22,479,000	20,687,000	18,015,000	18,013,000
Stockholders' Equity	6,221,000	5,218,000	5,303,000	5,103,000	4,498,000	3,895,000	3,521,000	3,388,000
Shares Outstanding	304,300	299,600	321,200	316,800	313,600	310,300	247,700	256,100
Statistical Record								
Return on Assets %	3.51	2.76	2.63	1.97	2.40	1.95	0.91	2.18
Return on Equity %	15.11	13.69	14.16	11.34	14.96	12.57	5.88	14.68
Loss Ratio %	...	59.54	54.46	54.38	54.70	58.07	54.81	53.98
Net Margin %	11.56	8.04	7.49	5.37	6.40	5.28	2.64	6.43
Price Range	50.08-34.67	42.36-31.90	36.90-20.85	28.99-19.20	26.46-17.64	39.54-14.60	44.75-31.81	42.75-21.06
P/E Ratio	18.62-12.89	19.89-14.98	17.00-9.61	17.79-11.78	13.43-8.95	24.11-8.90	61.30-43.58	23.88-11.77
Average Yield %	1.43	1.65	2.17	2.35	2.72	3.02	2.50	2.71

Address: 200 E. Randolph Street, Chicago, IL 60601 Telephone: 312-381-1000	Web Site: www.aon.com Officers: Patrick G. Ryan - Chmn. Gregory C. Case - Pres., C.E.O.	Auditors: Ernst & Young LLP Transfer Agents: EquiServe Trust Company, N.A., Providence, RI

APACHE CORP.

Exchange	Symbol	Price	52Wk Range	Yield	P/E
NYS	APA	$120.82 (3/31/2008)	120.82-71.26	0.50	14.40

*7 Year Price Score 143.07 *NYSE Composite Index=100 *12 Month Price Score 129.56

Interim Earnings (Per Share)

Qtr.	Mar	Jun	Sep	Dec
2003	1.05	0.75	0.84	0.80
2004	1.06	1.13	1.31	1.53
2005	1.67	1.76	2.05	2.35
2006	1.97	2.17	1.94	1.56
2007	1.47	1.89	1.83	3.20

Interim Dividends (Per Share)

Amt	Decl	Ex	Rec	Pay
0.15Q	10/5/2007	10/18/2007	10/22/2007	11/23/2007
0.15Q	12/18/2007	1/17/2008	1/22/2008	2/22/2008
0.10Q	2/15/2008	2/22/2008	2/26/2008	3/18/2008
0.15Q	2/15/2008	4/18/2008	4/22/2008	5/22/2008
		Indicated Div: $0.60		

Valuation Analysis

		Institutional Holding	
Forecast P/E	8.29	No of Institutions	
	(1/10/2007)	745	
Market Cap	$40.2 Billion	Shares	
Book Value	15.4 Billion	272,149,088	
Price/Book	2.62	% Held	
Price/Sales	4.03	82.23	

Business Summary: Oil and Gas (MIC: 14.2 SIC: 1311 NAIC: 211111)

Apache is an energy company that explores for, develops and produces natural gas, crude oil and natural gas liquids (NGLs). In North America, Co.'s exploration and production interests are focused in the Gulf of Mexico, the Gulf Coast, East Texas, the Permian Basin, the Anadarko Basin and the Western Sedimentary Basin of Canada. Outside of North America, Co. has exploration and production interests onshore Egypt, offshore Western Australia, offshore the U.K. in the North Sea, and onshore Argentina. As of Dec 31 2007, Co. had total estimated proved reserves of 1.13 billion barrels of crude oil, condensate and NGLs and 7.90 trillion cubic feet of natural gas.

Recent Developments: For the year ended Dec 31 2007, net income increased 10.2% to US$2.81 billion from US$2.55 billion in the prior year. Revenues were US$9.98 billion, up 20.4% from US$8.29 billion the year before. Indirect operating expenses increased 24.0% to US$5.31 billion from US$4.28 billion in the equivalent prior-year period.

Prospects: For 2008, Co. expects to be actively drilling, and has set an exploration and development budget of about $4.60 billion, an increase of 9.0% from 2007. Notably, Co. estimates investing $900.0 million on drilling, recompletions, upgrades, production enhancement and seismic in the Gulf Coast, and expects to spend $660.0 million on drilling, recompletions and production enhancement in Central U.S. Meanwhile, on Jan 24 2008, Co. announced the first two discoveries from its 2008 exploration program, the Hydra-1X exploration well in Egypt's Western Desert, and the Brulimar-1 discovery on Australia's Northwest Shelf. Thus, in 2008, Co. plans to drill 282 wells in Egypt and 52 wells in Australia.

Financial Data

(US$ in Thousands)	12/31/2007	12/31/2006	12/31/2005	12/31/2004	12/31/2003	12/31/2002	12/31/2001	12/31/2000
Earnings Per Share	8.39	7.64	7.84	5.03	3.43	1.80	2.37	2.45
Cash Flow Per Share	17.09	13.07	13.17	9.88	8.39	4.65	6.72	5.60
Tang Book Value Per Share	45.33	39.01	31.06	24.18	19.25	15.33	13.63	12.07
Dividends Per Share	0.600	0.450	0.340	0.260	0.208	0.190	0.121	0.091
Dividend Payout %	7.15	5.89	4.34	5.17	6.05	10.58	5.12	3.70
Income Statement								
Total Revenue	9,977,858	8,288,779	7,584,244	5,332,577	4,190,299	2,559,873	2,777,126	2,283,904
EBITDA	7,020,403	5,967,840	5,742,007	4,004,191	3,112,778	1,833,848	2,071,279	1,896,591
Income Before Taxes	4,672,612	4,009,595	4,206,254	2,663,083	1,922,251	898,970	1,199,254	1,203,681
Income Taxes	1,860,254	1,457,144	1,582,524	993,012	827,004	344,641	475,855	-483,086
Net Income	2,812,358	2,552,451	2,623,730	1,668,754	1,121,885	554,329	723,399	713,056
Average Shares	334,596	333,211	333,749	330,477	325,330	304,612	303,246	288,093
Balance Sheet								
Current Assets	2,752,251	2,490,271	2,162,077	1,348,782	899,072	766,781	697,749	630,020
Total Assets	28,634,651	24,308,175	19,271,796	15,502,480	12,416,126	9,459,851	8,933,656	7,481,950
Current Liabilities	2,665,016	3,811,612	2,186,564	1,282,891	820,378	532,235	522,458	553,347
Long-Term Obligations	4,011,605	2,019,831	2,191,954	2,588,390	2,326,966	2,158,815	2,244,357	2,193,258
Total Liabilities	13,256,672	11,117,122	8,730,581	7,298,059	5,883,328	4,535,571	4,515,173	3,727,310
Stockholders' Equity	15,377,979	13,191,053	10,541,215	8,204,421	6,532,798	4,924,280	4,418,483	3,754,640
Shares Outstanding	332,927	330,737	330,121	327,457	324,497	302,506	287,916	285,596
Statistical Record								
Return on Assets %	10.62	11.71	15.09	11.92	10.26	6.03	8.81	10.95
Return on Equity %	19.69	21.51	27.99	22.58	19.58	11.87	17.70	22.14
EBITDA Margin %	70.36	72.00	75.71	75.09	74.29	71.64	74.58	83.04
Net Margin %	28.19	30.79	34.59	31.29	26.77	21.65	26.05	31.22
Asset Turnover	0.38	0.38	0.44	0.38	0.38	0.28	0.34	0.35
Current Ratio	1.03	0.65	0.99	1.05	1.10	1.44	1.34	1.14
Debt to Equity	0.26	0.15	0.21	0.32	0.36	0.44	0.51	0.58
Price Range	108.45-63.16	75.53-57.23	77.26-47.73	54.06-37.23	41.30-26.69	28.42-21.61	30.65-16.77	31.68-14.12
P/E Ratio	12.93-7.53	9.89-7.49	9.85-6.09	10.75-7.40	12.04-7.78	15.79-12.01	12.93-7.08	12.93-5.76
Average Yield %	0.73	0.67	0.53	0.58	0.64	0.74	0.52	0.40

Address: One Post Oak Central, 2000 Post Oak Boulevard, Suite 100, Houston, TX 77056-4400
Telephone: 713-296-6000
Fax: 713-296-6490

Web Site: www.apachecorp.com
Officers: Raymond Plank - Chmn. G. Steven Farris - Pres., C.E.O., C.O.O.

Auditors: Ernst & Young LLP
Investor Contact: 713-296-6662
Transfer Agents: Wells Fargo Bank N.A., South St. Paul, MN

APARTMENT INVESTMENT & MANAGEMENT CO.

Exchange	Symbol	Price	52Wk Range	Yield	P/E
NYS	AIV	$35.81 (3/31/2008)	58.88-30.73	6.70	N/A

*7 Year Price Score 84.41   *NYSE Composite Index=100   *12 Month Price Score 89.45

TRADING VOLUME (thousand shares)

Interim Earnings (Per Share)

Qtr.	Mar	Jun	Sep	Dec
2003	0.00	0.39	0.15	0.19
2004	(0.06)	(0.08)	1.48	0.54
2005	(0.22)	0.06	0.05	(0.07)
2006	0.63	0.17	(0.48)	0.69
2007	0.09	0.03	(0.22)	(0.26)

Interim Dividends (Per Share)

Amt	Decl	Ex	Rec	Pay
0.60Q	8/1/2007	8/15/2007	8/17/2007	8/31/2007
0.60Q	10/30/2007	11/14/2007	11/16/2007	11/30/2007
0.60Q	12/21/2007	12/27/2007	12/31/2007	1/30/2008
1.91Q	12/21/2007	12/21/2007	12/31/2007	1/30/2008

Indicated Div: $2.40

Valuation Analysis / Institutional Holding

Forecast P/E	N/A	No of Institutions
	(1/10/2007)	276
Market Cap	$3.4 Billion	Shares
Book Value	1.7 Billion	91,115,480
Price/Book	1.97	% Held
Price/Sales	2.00	93.38

Business Summary: Property, Real Estate & Development (MIC: 8.3 SIC: 6798 NAIC: 525930)

Apartment Investment and Management is a self-administered and self-managed real-estate investment trust engaged in the acquisition, ownership, management and redevelopment of apartment properties. As of Dec 31 2007, Co. owned or managed a real-estate portfolio of 1,169 apartment properties containing 203,040 apartment units located in 46 states, the District of Columbia and Puerto Rico. Co.'s property operations components are conventional and affordable. Co.'s conventional operations include 439 properties with 127,532 units, while its affordable operations include 312 properties with 37,104 units, with rents that are generally paid, in whole or part by a government agency.

Recent Developments: For the year ended Dec 31 2007, loss from continuing operations was US$48.1 million compared with a loss of US$42.5 million a year earlier. Net income decreased 83.1% to US$29.9 million from US$176.8 million in the prior year. Revenues were US$1.72 billion, up 7.5% from US$1.60 billion the year before. Revenues from property income rose 6.1% to US$1.65 billion from US$1.55 billion in the corresponding earlier year.

Prospects: Going forward, Co. remains focused on reinvesting in and upgrading its portfolio through property redevelopments. Hence, for the full-year of 2008, Co. is planning to invest between $250.0 million and $300.0 million in conventional redevelopment projects and it expects to invest approximately $72.0 million in affordable redevelopment projects. Meanwhile, excluding impairment and preferred redemption charges, for the first quarter of 2008, Co. is projecting funds from operations (FFO) to be in the range of $0.68 to $0.72 per share, while for the full-year of 2008, FFO is expected to range from $3.22 to $3.38 per share.

Financial Data

(US$ in Thousands)	12/31/2007	12/31/2006	12/31/2005	12/31/2004	12/31/2003	12/31/2002	12/31/2001	12/31/2000
Earnings Per Share	(0.36)	1.00	(0.18)	1.88	0.70	0.87	0.23	0.52
Cash Flow Per Share	4.67	5.56	3.79	3.91	4.63	5.80	6.82	5.91
Tang Book Value Per Share	10.68	15.66	17.82	20.73	21.36	23.66	20.01	23.32
Dividends Per Share	4.310	2.400	3.000	2.400	3.060	3.280	3.120	2.800
Dividend Payout %		240.00	...	127.66	437.14	377.01	1,356.52	538.46
Income Statement								
Property Income	1,647,429	1,642,300	1,484,174	1,434,114	1,445,796	1,405,684	1,297,764	1,051,000
Non-Property Income	73,755	48,694	37,349	34,801	70,487	100,550	165,800	39,382
Total Revenue	1,721,184	1,690,994	1,521,523	1,468,915	1,516,283	1,506,234	1,463,564	1,090,382
Interest Expense	422,130	408,075	367,860	366,617	372,746	339,737	315,860	269,026
Net Income	29,911	176,787	70,982	263,497	158,857	169,046	107,352	99,178
Average Shares	99,629	95,758	93,894	93,118	92,968	86,773	73,648	69,063
Balance Sheet								
Total Assets	10,606,532	10,289,775	10,016,751	10,072,241	10,113,362	10,316,601	8,322,536	7,699,874
Long-Term Obligations	7,456,725	6,805,093	6,284,243	5,973,353	6,084,288	6,233,727	4,760,842	4,031,375
Total Liabilities	8,301,787	7,552,287	6,865,240	6,580,240	6,756,652	6,687,573	5,104,603	4,694,200
Stockholders' Equity	1,749,704	2,339,892	2,716,103	3,008,160	2,860,657	3,163,387	2,716,390	2,501,657
Shares Outstanding	96,130	96,820	95,732	94,853	93,887	93,769	74,498	71,337
Statistical Record								
Return on Assets %	0.29	1.74	0.71	2.60	1.56	1.81	1.34	1.48
Return on Equity %	1.46	6.99	2.48	8.96	5.27	5.75	4.11	4.15
Net Margin %	1.74	10.45	4.67	17.94	10.48	11.22	7.33	9.10
Price Range	64.35-34.62	58.88-38.72	44.01-35.15	38.83-27.88	41.98-33.01	51.40-34.64	49.81-41.00	49.94-36.63
P/E Ratio	...	58.88-38.72	...	20.65-14.83	59.97-47.16	59.08-39.82	216.58-178.26	96.03-70.43
Average Yield %	8.66	4.95	7.80	7.22	8.28	7.57	6.90	6.58

Address: 4582 South Ulster Street Parkway, Suite 1100, Denver, CO 80237 Telephone: 303-757-8101 Fax: 303-759-3226	Web Site: www.aimco.com Officers: Terry Considine - Chmn., C.E.O. Paul J. McAuliffe - Exec. V.P., C.F.O., Investor Relations	Auditors: ERNST & YOUNG LLP Investor Contact: 303-691-4327 Transfer Agents: EquiServe, Providence, Rhode Island

APPLERA CORP.

Exchange	Symbol	Price	52Wk Range	Yield	P/E
NYS	ABI	$32.86 (3/31/2008)	37.14-27.99	0.52	18.67

*7 Year Price Score 102.78 *NYSE Composite Index=100 *12 Month Price Score 109.54

Interim Earnings (Per Share)

Qtr.	Sep	Dec	Mar	Jun
2004-05	(0.10)	0.10	(0.01)	1.18
2005-06	(0.02)	(0.06)	0.34	1.18
2006-07	(0.41)	0.38	0.33	0.61
2007-08	0.33	0.49	...	...

Interim Dividends (Per Share)

Amt	Decl	Ex	Rec	Pay
0.043Q	3/26/2007	5/30/2007	6/1/2007	7/2/2007
0.043Q	8/16/2007	8/30/2007	9/4/2007	10/1/2007
0.043Q	11/15/2007	11/29/2007	12/3/2007	1/2/2008
0.043Q	1/17/2008	2/28/2008	3/3/2008	4/1/2008

Indicated Div: $0.17

Valuation Analysis

		Institutional Holding	
Forecast P/E	N/A	No of Institutions	317
Market Cap	$8.1 Billion	Shares	163,799,696
Book Value	2.0 Billion	% Held	
Price/Book	4.14		89.24
Price/Sales	3.65		

TRADING VOLUME (thousand shares)

Business Summary: Instruments and Related Products (MIC: 11.15 SIC: 3826 NAIC: 334516)

Applera is a life sciences company comprised of two business segments: the Applied Biosystems group and the Celera Genomics group. Co.'s Applied Biosystems group serves the life science industry and research community by developing and marketing instrument-based systems, consumables, software, and services. Co.'s Celera Genomics group is primarily a molecular diagnostics business that is using proprietary genomics and proteomics discovery platforms to identify and validate novel diagnostic markers, and is developing diagnostic products based on these markers as well as other known markers.

Recent Developments: For the quarter ended Dec 31 2007, net income increased 16.3% to US$86.6 million from US$74.5 million in the year-earlier quarter. Revenues were US$601.4 million, up 11.0% from US$541.8 million the year before. Operating income was US$117.4 million versus US$90.2 million in the prior-year quarter, an increase of 30.1%. Direct operating expenses rose 2.9% to US$246.3 million from US$239.4 million in the comparable period the year before. Indirect operating expenses increased 12.0% to US$237.7 million from US$212.2 million in the equivalent prior-year period.

Prospects: Looking ahead to the fiscal year ending June 2008, Co.'s Applied Biosystems group is projecting mid single digit growth, supported by growth across all product categories with the exception of its other product lines, which it expects to decline. The Group also expects gross margin improvement in fiscal 2008 compared with fiscal 2007 gross margin of 55.3%, as well as anticipates an increase in operating margin in fiscal 2008 of approximately 200 basis points compared with operating margin of 17.2% in the prior year, excluding special items. For its Celera group, Co. is anticipating total reported revenues in the range of US$135.0 million to US$145.0 million for the full fiscal year.

Financial Data
(US$ in Thousands)

	6 Mos	3 Mos	06/30/2007	06/30/2006	06/30/2005	06/30/2004	06/30/2003	06/30/2002
Earnings Per Share	1.76	1.65	0.94	1.43	1.19	0.88	0.95	0.78
Cash Flow Per Share	1.84	1.63	1.30	1.05	0.80	0.70	0.70	0.77
Tang Book Value Per Share	5.77	6.21	7.66	7.19	8.45	7.97	8.07	7.70
Dividends Per Share	0.170	0.170	0.170	0.170	0.170	0.170	0.170	0.170
Dividend Payout %	9.66	10.30	18.09	11.89	14.29	19.32	17.89	21.79
Income Statement								
Total Revenue	1,118,035	516,673	2,132,493	1,949,390	1,845,140	1,825,193	1,777,232	1,701,218
EBITDA	245,609	100,899	256,114	257,912	238,983	204,450	194,433	24,086
Depn & Amortn	43,326	20,025	...	...	...	...	...	...
Income Before Taxes	217,346	91,687	223,222	215,254	173,343	129,487	105,577	(28,550)
Income Taxes	69,058	29,997	72,451	2,762	13,548	14,534	(12,903)	12,031
Net Income	148,288	61,690	159,300	212,492	159,795	125,581	102,080	(40,581)
Average Shares	516,800	268,800	268,500	266,900	272,400	280,800	281,886	281,489
Balance Sheet								
Current Assets	1,493,014	1,587,170	1,838,587	1,626,965	2,087,609	1,923,408	2,073,383	2,012,498
Total Assets	3,038,743	2,912,623	3,152,540	3,012,975	3,164,185	2,972,851	3,257,492	3,075,399
Current Liabilities	801,016	803,980	623,174	608,290	592,671	596,768	630,617	627,239
Long-Term Obligations	...	...	...	...	...	...	17,101	17,983
Total Liabilities	1,079,282	1,073,323	836,486	808,641	820,102	791,802	917,207	850,456
Stockholders' Equity	1,959,461	1,839,300	2,316,054	2,204,334	2,344,083	2,181,049	2,340,285	2,224,943
Shares Outstanding	247,022	247,554	262,594	261,735	272,663	268,774	285,121	283,793
Statistical Record								
Return on Assets %	9.92	9.88	5.17	6.88	5.21	4.02	3.22	N.M.
Return on Equity %	14.23	14.29	7.05	9.34	7.06	5.54	4.47	N.M.
EBITDA Margin %	21.97	19.53	12.01	13.23	12.95	11.20	10.94	1.42
Net Margin %	13.26	11.94	7.47	10.90	8.66	6.88	5.74	N.M.
Asset Turnover	0.74	0.74	0.69	0.63	0.60	0.58	0.56	0.57
Current Ratio	1.86	1.97	2.95	2.67	3.52	3.22	3.29	3.21
Debt to Equity	...	...	...	...	...	...	0.01	0.01
Price Range	37.14-27.99	38.27-27.99	38.27-27.99	32.88-19.61	22.68-18.05	23.82-18.24	24.06-14.10	40.17-15.71
P/E Ratio	21.10-15.90	23.19-16.96	40.71-29.78	22.99-13.71	19.06-15.17	27.07-20.73	25.33-14.84	51.50-20.14
Average Yield %	0.53	0.52	0.52	0.66	0.84	0.81	0.93	0.67

Address: 301 Merritt 7, Norwalk, CT 06851-1070	Web Site: www.applera.com	Auditors: PricewaterhouseCoopers LLP
Telephone: 203-840-2000	Officers: Tony L. White - Chmn., Pres., C.E.O. Kathy P. Ordoñez - Sr. V.P.	Investor Contact: 650-554-2479
Fax: 203-762-6000		Transfer Agents: EquiServe Trust Company, N.A., Providence, RI

APRIA HEALTHCARE GROUP INC.

Exchange	Symbol	Price	52Wk Range	Yield	P/E
NYS	AHG	$19.75 (3/31/2008)	34.22-18.41	N/A	10.13

*7 Year Price Score 78.27   *NYSE Composite Index=100   *12 Month Price Score 89.93

Interim Earnings (Per Share)

Qtr.	Mar	Jun	Sep	Dec
2003	0.50	0.53	0.54	0.58
2004	0.55	0.57	0.60	0.55
2005	0.51	0.06	0.38	0.42
2006	0.38	0.43	0.45	0.49
2007	0.44	0.47	0.48	0.56

Interim Dividends (Per Share)

No Dividends Paid

Valuation Analysis   **Institutional Holding**

Forecast P/E	14.50
	(1/10/2007)
Market Cap	$864.9 Million
Book Value	512.0 Million
Price/Book	1.69
Price/Sales	0.53

No of Institutions	174
Shares	47,475,632
% Held	N/A

Business Summary: Diagnostic Services (MIC: 9.5 SIC: 8082 NAIC: 621610)

Apria Healthcare Group provides home healthcare services through about 550 branch locations that serve patients in all 50 states in the U.S., as of Dec 31 2007. Co. has three service lines: home respiratory therapy, which provides oxygen systems, ventilators, sleep apnea equipment, nebulizers, respiratory medications and related clinical/administrative support services; home infusion therapy, which provides intravenous administration of anti-infectives, pain management, chemotherapy, nutrients, immune globulin, other medications and related services; and home medical equipment, which provides patient safety items, ambulatory and in-home equipment, such as wheelchairs and hospital beds.

Recent Developments: For the year ended Dec 31 2007, net income increased 15.9% to US$86.0 million from US$74.3 million in the prior year. Revenues were US$1.63 billion, up 7.6% from US$1.52 billion the year before. Operating income was US$158.5 million versus US$147.0 million in the prior year, an increase of 7.8%. Direct operating expenses rose 8.3% to US$565.0 million from US$521.6 million in the comparable period the year before. Indirect operating expenses increased 7.1% to US$908.3 million from US$848.1 million in the equivalent prior-year period.

Prospects: For the full year of 2008, Co. is projecting revenue growth of 33.0% to 35.0%, mainly due to higher revenue in its home infusion therapy service line, the Dec 3 2007 acquisition of Coram Inc. and increased sales volume in its home respiratory therapy service line. In addition, Co. is targeting net income to range from $2.04 to $2.14 per diluted share. Further, Co. now foresees the acquisition of Coram to be neutral to earnings, based upon recent performance and a strong start to the integration process. Looking ahead, Co. expects to continue to face pricing pressures from Medicare as well as from its managed care customers as these payers seek to lower costs by obtaining favorable pricing.

Financial Data
(US$ in Thousands)

	12/31/2007	12/31/2006	12/31/2005	12/31/2004	12/31/2003	12/31/2002	12/31/2001	12/31/2000
Earnings Per Share	1.95	1.75	1.37	2.27	2.15	2.08	1.79	1.06
Cash Flow Per Share	6.75	6.62	4.28	5.58	4.94	4.80	4.47	3.66
Tang Book Value Per Share	N.M.	N.M.	N.M.	N.M.	0.55	1.75	0.81	0.16
Income Statement								
Total Revenue	1,631,801	1,517,307	1,474,101	1,451,449	1,380,945	1,252,196	1,131,915	1,014,201
EBITDA	184,432	173,167	270,107	345,799	341,201	297,469	261,682	243,476
Income Before Taxes	138,037	118,237	107,370	178,305	186,573	167,952	117,542	98,141
Income Taxes	51,998	43,257	40,429	64,297	70,581	52,357	44,097	41,135
Net Income	86,039	74,980	66,941	114,008	115,992	115,595	71,917	57,006
Average Shares	44,140	42,935	48,985	50,180	54,066	55,455	55,778	54,022
Balance Sheet								
Current Assets	457,335	344,937	344,001	348,311	429,335	290,361	239,823	226,470
Total Assets	1,597,802	1,168,496	1,185,898	1,107,664	1,043,435	795,656	695,782	616,603
Current Liabilities	547,852	203,523	170,791	178,335	192,260	183,713	174,750	132,611
Long-Term Obligations	433,031	485,000	640,855	475,957	469,241	247,655	278,234	337,750
Total Liabilities	1,085,777	758,065	858,734	701,479	677,487	444,347	452,984	470,361
Stockholders' Equity	512,025	410,431	327,164	406,185	365,948	351,309	242,798	146,242
Shares Outstanding	43,794	42,789	42,250	48,608	51,107	54,897	54,604	53,067
Statistical Record								
Return on Assets %	6.22	6.37	5.84	10.57	12.61	15.50	10.96	9.13
Return on Equity %	18.65	20.33	18.26	29.45	32.34	38.91	36.97	51.28
EBITDA Margin %	11.30	11.41	18.32	23.82	24.71	23.76	23.12	24.01
Net Margin %	5.27	4.94	4.54	7.85	8.40	9.23	6.35	5.62
Asset Turnover	1.18	1.29	1.29	1.35	1.50	1.68	1.72	1.62
Current Ratio	0.83	1.69	2.01	1.95	2.23	1.58	1.37	1.71
Debt to Equity	0.85	1.18	1.96	1.17	1.28	0.70	1.15	2.31
Price Range	34.22-20.17	27.24-17.48	36.75-22.51	34.00-26.60	31.32-20.74	28.00-19.00	28.99-20.40	30.00-10.63
P/E Ratio	17.55-10.34	15.57-9.99	26.82-16.43	14.98-11.72	14.57-9.65	13.46-9.13	22.47-15.81	28.30-10.02

Address: 26220 Enterprise Court, Lake Forest, CA 92630-8405
Telephone: 949-639-2000
Fax: 949-639-2900

Web Site: www.apria.com
Officers: Ralph V. Whitworth - Chmn. Lawrence A. Mastrovich - Pres., C.O.O.

Auditors: Deloitte & Touche LLP
Transfer Agents: American Stock Transfer & Trust Co., New York, NY

APTARGROUP INC.

Exchange	Symbol	Price	52Wk Range	Yield	P/E	Div Acheiver
NYS	ATR	$38.93 (3/31/2008)	44.70-33.62	1.34	19.66	14 Years

7 Year Price Score 128.92 *NYSE Composite Index=100* **12 Month Price Score 104.95**

Interim Earnings (Per Share)

Qtr.	Mar	Jun	Sep	Dec
2003	0.27	0.29	0.26	0.27
2004	0.28	0.30	0.34	0.33
2005	0.30	0.41	0.34	0.34
2006	0.28	0.39	0.40	0.39
2007	0.41	0.52	0.56	0.50

Interim Dividends (Per Share)

Amt	Decl	Ex	Rec	Pay
0.13Q	4/18/2007	4/30/2007	5/2/2007	5/23/2007
0.13Q	7/18/2007	7/27/2007	7/31/2007	8/21/2007
0.13Q	10/17/2007	10/29/2007	10/31/2007	11/21/2007
0.13Q	1/17/2008	1/29/2008	1/31/2008	2/21/2008

Indicated Div: $0.52

Valuation Analysis | **Institutional Holding**

Forecast P/E	16.23	No of Institutions
	(1/10/2007)	199
Market Cap	$2.7 Billion	Shares
Book Value	1.1 Billion	31,704,752
Price/Book	2.37	% Held
Price/Sales	1.40	91.41

TRADING VOLUME (thousand shares)

Business Summary: Plastics (MIC: 11.7 SIC: 3089 NAIC: 326199)

AptarGroup is a global supplier of a range of dispensing systems for the personal care, fragrance/cosmetic, and pharmaceutical markets, as well as for the household and food/beverage markets. Co. has manufacturing facilities worldwide, including North America, Europe, Asia and South America. Co. operates through three reportable business segments: the Beauty & Home segment, which sells spray and lotion dispensing systems and accessories primarily to the personal care, fragrance/cosmetic and household markets; the Pharma segment, which sells dispensing systems to the pharmaceutical market; and the Closures segment, which sells closures to each market served by Co.

Recent Developments: For the year ended Dec 31 2007, income from continuing operations increased 35.6% to US$139.5 million from US$102.9 million a year earlier. Net income increased 37.7% to US$141.7 million from US$402.9 million in the prior year. Revenues were US$1.89 billion, up 18.2% from US$1.60 billion the year before. Operating income was US$210.7 million versus US$161.6 million in the prior year, an increase of 30.4%. Direct operating expenses rose 18.2% to US$1.28 billion from US$1.09 billion in the comparable period the year before. Indirect operating expenses increased 12.5% to US$397.7 million from US$353.5 million in the equivalent prior-year period.

Prospects: Looking ahead for 2008, Co. believes that the cost of raw materials, particularly resin and metal components, should continue to increase. Nevertheless, Co. is committed to passing theses cost increases along in its selling price where possible, and anticipates gains in productivity and costs savings to partially offset certain price declines and costs increases. Meanwhile, for the first quarter of 2008, Co. expects continuing demand for its dispensing systems to result in sales improvements across each of its business segments. At the same time, Co. is projecting diluted earnings per share of $0.46 to $0.49 per share compared to $0.41 per share recorded in the first quarter of 2007.

Financial Data

(US$ in Thousands)	12/31/2007	12/31/2006	12/31/2005	12/31/2004	12/31/2003	12/31/2002	12/31/2001	12/31/2000
Earnings Per Share	1.98	1.44	1.39	1.25	1.08	0.91	0.81	0.89
Cash Flow Per Share	3.98	2.83	2.76	2.52	1.93	2.15	1.80	1.81
Tang Book Value Per Share	12.88	10.39	8.71	9.40	8.38	6.06	4.50	4.27
Dividends Per Share	0.500	0.420	0.350	0.220	0.130	0.120	0.110	0.100
Dividend Payout %	25.25	29.27	25.27	17.53	12.04	13.19	13.66	11.24
Income Statement								
Total Revenue	1,892,167	1,601,385	1,380,009	1,296,608	1,114,689	926,691	891,986	883,481
EBITDA	334,035	275,683	250,335	237,427	210,022	179,111	175,689	186,109
Income Before Taxes	199,995	148,306	141,953	137,177	117,270	98,358	88,355	97,922
Income Taxes	60,488	45,410	41,919	43,890	37,591	31,711	29,447	33,256
Net Income	141,739	102,896	100,034	93,287	79,679	66,647	58,844	64,666
Average Shares	71,523	71,744	72,354	74,314	73,802	73,246	73,058	72,738
Balance Sheet								
Current Assets	1,003,445	762,820	605,291	661,229	602,454	447,196	374,915	407,549
Total Assets	1,911,950	1,592,012	1,357,319	1,374,026	1,264,343	1,047,671	915,327	952,239
Current Liabilities	565,189	400,185	320,762	276,861	283,220	162,688	154,151	203,102
Long-Term Obligations	146,711	168,877	144,541	142,581	125,196	219,182	239,387	252,752
Total Liabilities	792,932	645,612	547,931	500,829	481,292	453,204	446,123	511,699
Stockholders' Equity	1,119,018	946,400	809,388	873,197	783,051	594,467	469,204	440,540
Shares Outstanding	68,200	69,200	69,800	76,400	75,400	74,400	74,000	73,200
Statistical Record								
Return on Assets %	8.09	6.98	7.32	7.05	6.89	6.79	6.30	7.10
Return on Equity %	13.72	11.72	11.89	11.23	11.57	12.53	12.94	14.98
EBITDA Margin %	17.65	17.22	18.14	18.31	18.84	19.33	19.70	21.07
Net Margin %	7.49	6.43	7.25	7.19	7.15	7.19	6.60	7.32
Asset Turnover	1.08	1.09	1.01	1.01	0.98	0.94	0.96	0.97
Current Ratio	1.78	1.91	1.89	2.39	2.13	2.75	2.43	2.01
Debt to Equity	0.13	0.18	0.18	0.16	0.16	0.37	0.51	0.57
Price Range	44.70-29.10	30.88-23.65	27.50-23.72	27.22-18.69	19.74-13.26	19.35-12.56	18.45-13.69	15.00-9.94
P/E Ratio	22.58-14.70	21.44-16.42	19.78-17.06	21.77-14.95	18.28-12.27	21.26-13.80	22.78-16.90	16.85-11.17
Average Yield %	1.36	1.56	1.38	1.01	0.75	0.75	0.69	0.80

Address: 475 West Terra Cotta Avenue, Suite E, Crystal Lake, IL 60014	**Web Site:** www.aptargroup.com	**Auditors:** PricewaterhouseCoopers LLP
Telephone: 815-477-0424	**Officers:** King Harris - Chmn. Peter Pfeiffer - Vice-Chmn.	**Transfer Agents:** Mellon Investor Services, LLC, South Hackensack, NJ
Fax: 815-477-0481		

AQUA AMERICA INC

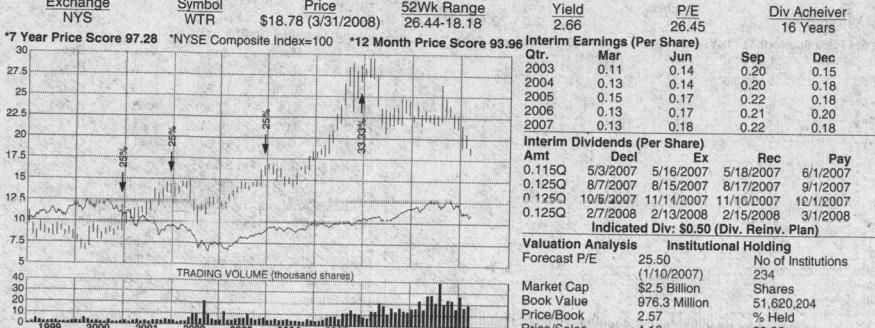

Exchange	Symbol	Price	52Wk Range	Yield	P/E	Div Acheiver
NYS	WTR	$18.78 (3/31/2008)	26.44-18.18	2.66	26.45	16 Years

*7 Year Price Score 97.28   *NYSE Composite Index=100   *12 Month Price Score 93.96

Interim Earnings (Per Share)

Qtr.	Mar	Jun	Sep	Dec
2003	0.11	0.14	0.20	0.15
2004	0.13	0.14	0.20	0.18
2005	0.15	0.17	0.22	0.18
2006	0.13	0.17	0.21	0.20
2007	0.13	0.18	0.22	0.18

Interim Dividends (Per Share)

Amt	Decl	Ex	Rec	Pay
0.115Q	5/3/2007	5/16/2007	5/18/2007	6/1/2007
0.125Q	8/7/2007	8/15/2007	8/17/2007	9/1/2007
0.125Q	10/5/2007	11/14/2007	11/16/2007	12/1/2007
0.125Q	2/7/2008	2/13/2008	2/15/2008	3/1/2008

Indicated Div: $0.50 (Div. Reinv. Plan)

Valuation Analysis   **Institutional Holding**

Forecast P/E	25.50	No of Institutions
	(1/10/2007)	234
Market Cap	$2.5 Billion	Shares
Book Value	976.3 Million	51,620,204
Price/Book	2.57	% Held
Price/Sales	4.16	39.00

Business Summary: Water Utilities (MIC: 7.2 SIC: 4941 NAIC: 221310)

Aqua America is a holding company. As of Dec 31 2007, Co.'s subsidiaries operated regulated utilities that provided water or wastewater services to about 3.0 million people in Pennsylvania, Ohio, North Carolina, Illinois, Texas, New Jersey, Florida, Indiana, Virginia, Maine, Missouri, New York and South Carolina. Co.'s key subsidiary, Aqua Pennsylvania, Inc. provided water or wastewater services to about one-half of its customers, located in the suburban areas north and west of the City of Philadelphia and in 23 other counties in Pennsylvania. Co. also provides water and wastewater services through operating and maintenance contracts with municipal authorities and other parties.

Recent Developments: For the year ended Dec 31 2007, net income increased 3.3% to US$95.0 million from US$92.0 million in the prior year. Revenues were US$602.5 million, up 12.9% from US$533.5 million the year before. Operating income was US$216.0 million versus US$205.5 million in the prior year, an increase of 5.1%. Indirect operating expenses increased 17.9% to US$386.5 million from US$327.9 million in the equivalent prior-year period.

Prospects: For 2008, Co. intends to file 21 additional rate requests proposing an aggregate of approximately $18.8 million of increased annual revenues. In addition, Co. noted that it has recently been awarded a rate increase in North Carolina plus cases and surcharges in other states designed to increase annual operating revenues by more than $3.0 million. Separately, Co. believes that utility acquisitions will continue to be its primary source of growth. Hence, Co. intends to continue to pursue acquisitions of municipally-owned and investor-owned water and wastewater systems of all sizes that provide services in areas adjacent to its existing service territories or in new service areas.

Financial Data
(US$ in Thousands)

	12/31/2007	12/31/2006	12/31/2005	12/31/2004	12/31/2003	12/31/2002	12/31/2001	12/31/2000
Earnings Per Share	0.71	0.70	0.71	0.64	0.59	0.58	0.52	0.48
Cash Flow Per Share	1.46	1.31	1.57	1.39	1.22	1.06	0.90	0.80
Tang Book Value Per Share	7.04	6.79	6.14	5.73	5.34	4.36	4.15	3.85
Dividends Per Share	0.480	0.444	0.399	0.367	0.364	0.323	0.303	0.282
Dividend Payout %	67.61	63.40	56.25	57.65	61.78	55.41	57.99	58.12
Income Statement								
Total Revenue	602,499	533,491	496,779	442,039	367,233	322,028	307,280	275,538
EBITDA	310,474	285,723	265,619	239,674	212,843	193,970	179,114	161,455
Income Before Taxes	155,542	152,250	148,069	132,131	116,718	109,252	99,087	86,995
Income Taxes	60,528	60,246	56,913	52,124	45,923	42,046	38,976	34,105
Net Income	95,014	92,004	91,156	80,007	70,795	67,206	60,111	52,890
Average Shares	133,602	131,774	129,206	125,709	118,993	115,385	114,591	109,022
Balance Sheet								
Net PPE	2,792,794	2,505,995	2,279,950	2,069,812	1,824,291	1,486,703	1,368,115	1,251,427
Total Assets	3,226,912	2,877,903	2,626,725	2,340,248	2,069,736	1,717,069	1,560,339	1,414,010
Long-Term Obligations	1,215,053	951,660	878,438	784,461	696,666	582,910	516,520	468,769
Total Liabilities	2,250,614	1,956,273	1,814,802	1,591,780	1,410,706	1,223,972	1,086,506	981,663
Stockholders' Equity	976,298	921,630	811,923	748,468	659,030	493,097	473,833	432,347
Shares Outstanding	133,400	132,325	128,970	127,179	123,452	113,194	113,977	111,824
Statistical Record								
Return on Assets %	3.11	3.34	3.67	3.62	3.74	4.10	4.04	3.91
Return on Equity %	10.01	10.61	11.68	11.34	12.29	13.90	13.27	13.17
EBITDA Margin %	51.53	53.56	53.47	54.22	57.96	60.23	58.29	58.60
Net Margin %	15.77	17.25	18.35	18.10	19.28	20.87	19.56	19.20
PPE Turnover	0.23	0.22	0.23	0.23	0.22	0.23	0.23	0.23
Asset Turnover	0.20	0.19	0.20	0.20	0.19	0.20	0.21	0.20
Debt to Equity	1.24	1.03	1.08	1.05	1.06	1.18	1.09	1.08
Price Range	26.44-21.20	29.59-20.61	28.97-17.61	18.44-14.18	16.69-11.83	14.99-9.77	14.54-9.60	11.91-6.48
P/E Ratio	37.24-29.86	42.27-29.44	40.80-24.80	28.82-22.16	28.28-20.04	25.84-16.84	27.96-18.46	24.81-13.50
Average Yield %	2.11	1.82	1.77	2.30	2.61	2.54	2.51	3.33

Address: 762 W. Lancaster Avenue, Bryn Mawr, PA 19010-3489 **Telephone:** 610-524-8000 **Fax:** 610-645-1061	**Web Site:** www.aquaamerica.com **Officers:** Nicholas DeBenedictis - Chmn., Pres. Roy H. Stahl - Exec. V.P., Sec., Gen. Couns.	**Auditors:** PricewaterhouseCoopers LLP **Transfer Agents:** BankBoston, N.A., Boston, MA

AQUILA INC (DE)

Exchange	Symbol	Price	52Wk Range	Yield	P/E
NYS	ILA	$3.21 (3/31/2008)	4.33-3.20	N/A	N/A

*7 Year Price Score 40.31   ***NYSE Composite Index=100**   ***12 Month Price Score 93.89**

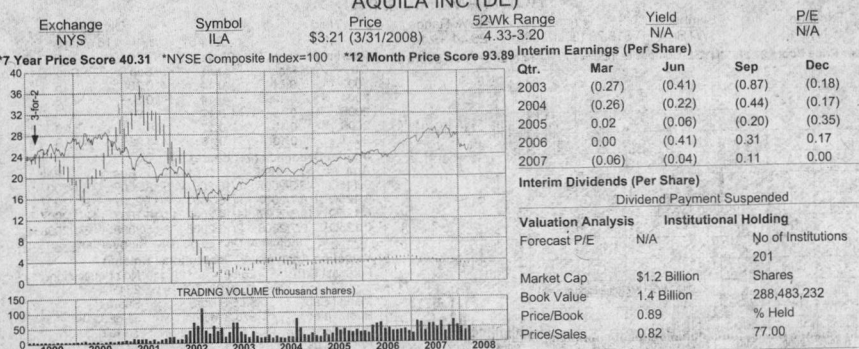

Interim Earnings (Per Share)

Qtr.	Mar	Jun	Sep	Dec
2003	(0.27)	(0.41)	(0.87)	(0.18)
2004	(0.26)	(0.22)	(0.44)	(0.17)
2005	0.02	(0.06)	(0.20)	(0.35)
2006	0.00	(0.41)	0.31	0.17
2007	(0.06)	(0.04)	0.11	0.00

Interim Dividends (Per Share)

Dividend Payment Suspended

Valuation Analysis		Institutional Holding	
Forecast P/E	N/A	No of Institutions	201
Market Cap	$1.2 Billion	Shares	288,483,232
Book Value	1.4 Billion	% Held	77.00
Price/Book	0.89		
Price/Sales	0.82		

Business Summary: Electricity (MIC: 7.1 SIC: 4911 NAIC: 221122)

Aquila is an integrated electric and natural gas utility. Co.'s business is organized into three business segments: Electric Utilities, which comprises regulated electric utility operations; Gas Utilities, which comprises regulated gas utility operations; and Merchant Services, which comprises remaining unregulated energy activities. As of Dec 31 2007, Co.'s Electric Utilities included 15,190 pole miles of electric transmission and distribution lines, and its Gas Utilities included 604 miles of intrastate gas transmission pipelines and 11,364 miles of gas distribution mains and service lines.

Recent Developments: For the year ended Dec 31 2007, loss from continuing operations was US$18.1 million compared with a loss of US$282.0 million a year earlier. Net loss amounted to US$5.4 million versus net income of US$23.9 million in the prior year. Revenues were US$1.47 billion, up 7.1% from US$1.37 billion the year before. Operating income was US$106.3 million versus a loss of US$222.6 million in the prior year. Direct operating expenses rose 2.2% to US$900.9 million from US$881.6 million in the comparable period the year before. Indirect operating expenses decreased 35.4% to US$459.4 million from US$710.6 million in the equivalent prior-year period.

Prospects: On Mar 10 2008, Co., Black Hills Corp, and Great Plains Energy, Inc. announced that the Kansas Corporation Commission has approved the proposed acquisition of Co.'s natural gas utility assets in Kansas by Black Hills, and the proposed acquisition of Co. by Great Plains Energy. As such, all necessary regulatory approvals pertaining to the Black Hills purchase of Co.'s utility properties have been obtained. To close the proposed transaction, Great Plains Energy and Co. needs to obtain approval from the Missouri Public Service Commission. Notably, the acquisition of Co. by Great Plains Energy and the sale of its assets to Black Hills are contingent upon the closing of the other transaction.

Financial Data
(US$ in Thousands)

	12/31/2007	12/31/2006	12/31/2005	12/31/2004	12/31/2003	12/31/2002	12/31/2001	12/31/2000
Earnings Per Share	(0.01)	0.06	(0.60)	(1.13)	(1.73)	(12.83)	2.42	2.21
Cash Flow Per Share	0.42	0.16	0.13	(1.35)	(0.68)	(1.84)	2.00	8.47
Tang Book Value Per Share	3.31	3.19	3.21	4.22	6.39	6.75	22.01	17.94
Dividends Per Share	...	...	...	...	...	0.775	1.200	1.200
Dividend Payout %	...	...	...	...	...	...	49.59	54.30
Income Statement								
Total Revenue	1,466,600	1,369,600	1,314,200	1,711,000	1,674,000	2,377,100	40,376,800	28,974,900
EBITDA	239,000	(85,300)	98,000	(153,800)	(45,900)	(1,370,400)	977,600	765,000
Income Before Taxes	(12,100)	(349,300)	(201,100)	(562,500)	(492,300)	(1,857,900)	481,600	325,000
Income Taxes	6,000	(67,300)	(43,100)	(213,300)	(141,700)	(135,100)	202,200	118,200
Net Income	(5,400)	23,900	(230,000)	(292,500)	(336,400)	(2,075,100)	279,400	206,800
Average Shares	375,680	375,450	363,300	251,350	194,750	161,720	115,710	93,750
Balance Sheet								
Current Assets	555,600	874,000	1,344,100	1,548,800	2,718,800	4,074,200	4,807,400	6,868,600
Total Assets	2,993,600	3,472,400	4,630,700	4,777,300	7,719,100	9,259,200	11,948,300	14,115,600
Current Liabilities	421,500	501,700	994,600	854,400	2,261,300	3,596,900	5,677,700	7,484,400
Long-Term Obligations	1,035,400	1,385,900	1,891,200	2,329,900	2,291,200	2,398,000	1,747,900	2,345,900
Total Liabilities	1,637,900	2,166,300	3,320,800	3,646,800	6,359,800	7,651,300	9,146,700	11,866,000
Stockholders' Equity	1,355,700	1,306,100	1,309,900	1,130,500	1,359,300	1,607,900	2,551,600	1,899,600
Shares Outstanding	375,905	374,521	373,603	241,739	195,252	193,775	115,941	100,310
Statistical Record								
Return on Assets %	N.M.	0.59	N.M.	N.M.	N.M.	N.M.	2.14	1.90
Return on Equity %	N.M.	1.83	N.M.	N.M.	N.M.	N.M.	12.55	12.04
EBITDA Margin %	16.30	N.M.	7.46	N.M.	N.M.	N.M.	2.42	2.64
Net Margin %	N.M.	1.75	N.M.	N.M.	N.M.	N.M.	0.69	0.71
Asset Turnover	0.45	0.34	0.28	0.27	0.20	0.22	3.10	2.67
Current Ratio	1.32	1.74	1.35	1.81	1.20	1.13	0.85	0.92
Debt to Equity	0.76	1.06	1.44	2.06	1.69	1.49	0.69	1.23
Price Range	4.75-3.48	4.78-3.60	4.13-3.20	4.75-2.34	4.25-1.12	26.70-1.58	37.55-22.48	31.00-15.31
P/E Ratio	...	79.67-60.00	...	...	...	...	15.52-9.29	14.03-6.93
Average Yield %	...	...	...	...	...	...	6.43	3.94	5.41

Address: 20 West Ninth Street, Kansas City, MO 64105	Web Site: www.aquila.com	Auditors: KPMG LLP
Telephone: 816-421-6600	Officers: Richard C. Green Jr. - Chmn., Pres., C.E.O.	Investor Contact: 816-421-6600
Fax: 816-467-3435	Keith G. Stamm - Sr. V.P., C.O.O.	Transfer Agents: UMB Bank, n.a., Kansas City, MO

ARCH COAL, INC.

Exchange	Symbol	Price	52Wk Range	Yield	P/E
NYS	ACI	$43.50 (3/31/2008)	54.90-28.20	0.64	35.95

*7 Year Price Score 136.03 *NYSE Composite Index=100 *12 Month Price Score 136.30

Interim Earnings (Per Share)

Qtr.	Mar	Jun	Sep	Dec
2003	(0.17)	(0.03)	0.09	0.21
2004	0.57	0.09	0.08	0.15
2005	0.04	0.01	0.13	(0.01)
2006	0.42	0.48	0.35	0.55
2007	0.20	0.26	0.19	0.56

Interim Dividends (Per Share)

Amt	Decl	Ex	Rec	Pay
0.07Q	4/26/2007	5/30/2007	6/1/2007	6/15/2007
0.07Q	8/3/2007	8/29/2007	8/31/2007	9/14/2007
0.07Q	10/25/2007	11/28/2007	11/30/2007	12/14/2007
0.07Q	2/21/2008	2/27/2008	2/29/2008	3/14/2008

Indicated Div: $0.28

Valuation Analysis

		Institutional Holding	
Forecast P/E	7.32	No of Institutions	
	(1/10/2007)	305	
Market Cap	$6.2 Billion	Shares	
Book Value	1.5 Billion	132,696,360	
Price/Book	4.07	% Held	
Price/Sales	2.58	N/A	

Business Summary: Coal Mining (MIC: 14.4 SIC: 1221 NAIC: 212111)

Arch Coal is a coal producer that is engaged in the mining, processing and marketing of bituminous and sub-bituminous coal with low sulfur content. Co. sells substantially all of its coal to power plants, steel mills and industrial facilities. As of Dec 31 2007, Co. operated 18 active mines at 11 mining complexes throughout the U.S. and estimates that its proven and probable coal reserves had an average heat value of approximately 10,000 British thermal units and an average sulfur content of approximately 0.71%. Co. operates through three segments, which are the Powder River Basin, the Western Bituminous region and the Central Appalachia region.

Recent Developments: For the year ended Dec 31 2007, net income decreased 33.0% to US$174.9 million from US$260.9 million in the prior year. Revenues were US$2.41 billion, down 3.5% from US$2.50 billion the year before. Operating income was US$229.6 million versus US$336.7 million in the prior year, a decrease of 31.8%. Direct operating expenses declined 1.1% to US$1.89 billion from US$1.91 billion in the comparable period the year before. Indirect operating expenses increased 16.5% to US$295.7 million from US$253.9 million in the equivalent prior-year period.

Prospects: Co. is optimistic that its domestic coal markets will continue to improve in 2008, driven by the strength of international coal markets, which should result in meaningful expansion in its operating margins and earnings per share in 2008. In particular, Co. estimates its 2008 diluted earnings of $2.00 to $2.50 per share, coupled with sales volume from company controlled operations of $135.0 million to $140.0 million tons, excluding all purchased coal from third parties. Additionally, excluding reserve additions, Co. targets its 2008 capital spending of $310.0 million to $340.0 million for development work at certain of its mining operations, including the continuing work at Black Thunder.

Financial Data

(US$ in Thousands)	12/31/2007	12/31/2006	12/31/2005	12/31/2004	12/31/2003	12/31/2002	12/31/2001	12/31/2000
Earnings Per Share	1.21	1.80	0.17	0.89	0.10	(0.03)	0.07	(0.17)
Cash Flow Per Share	2.32	2.16	2.00	1.31	1.55	1.68	1.50	1.77
Tang Book Value Per Share	10.42	9.32	8.03	8.39	6.41	4.54	4.67	1.45
Dividends Per Share	0.270	0.220	0.160	0.149	0.115	0.115	0.115	0.115
Dividend Payout %	22.31	12.22	91.43	16.71	121.05		153.33	...
Income Statement								
Total Revenue	2,413,644	2,500,431	2,508,773	1,907,168	1,435,488	1,534,139	1,488,728	1,404,621
EBITDA	469,406	537,574	294,023	349,083	102,449	204,029	239,960	275,496
Income Before Taxes	155,079	268,581	3,473	113,576	(2,870)	(21,562)	2,509	(16,736)
Income Taxes	(19,850)	7,650	(34,650)	(130)	(23,210)	(19,000)	(4,700)	(4,000)
Net Income	174,929	260,931	38,123	113,706	16,686	(2,562)	7,209	(12,736)
Average Shares	144,019	144,812	179,940	127,468	105,770	104,748	97,836	76,328
Balance Sheet								
Current Assets	521,145	487,277	729,564	730,857	513,645	291,713	289,456	277,890
Total Assets	3,594,599	3,320,814	3,051,440	3,256,535	2,387,649	2,182,808	2,203,559	2,232,614
Current Liabilities	556,515	440,806	513,188	375,054	276,638	253,914	239,643	315,446
Long-Term Obligations	1,085,579	1,122,595	971,755	1,001,323	700,022	740,242	775,565	1,102,014
Total Liabilities	2,062,913	1,955,220	1,867,199	2,176,709	1,699,614	1,647,945	1,632,817	2,012,740
Stockholders' Equity	1,531,686	1,365,594	1,184,241	1,079,826	688,035	534,863	570,742	219,874
Shares Outstanding	143,158	142,179	142,572	124,286	106,409	104,868	104,705	76,346
Statistical Record								
Return on Assets %	5.06	8.19	1.21	4.02	0.73	N.M.	0.33	N.M.
Return on Equity %	12.08	20.47	3.37	12.83	2.73	N.M.	1.82	N.M.
EBITDA Margin %	19.45	21.50	11.72	18.30	7.14	13.30	16.12	19.61
Net Margin %	7.25	10.44	1.52	5.96	1.16	N.M.	0.48	N.M.
Asset Turnover	0.70	0.78	0.80	0.67	0.63	0.70	0.67	0.61
Current Ratio	0.94	1.11	1.42	1.95	1.86	1.15	1.21	0.88
Debt to Equity	0.71	0.82	0.82	0.93	1.02	1.38	1.36	5.01
Price Range	44.93-27.42	54.94-26.45	40.34-16.82	19.11-13.31	15.94-8.18	12.20-7.49	18.84-6.66	7.22-2.41
P/E Ratio	37.13-22.66	30.52-14.69	237.26-98.91	21.48-14.95	159.35-81.75		... 269.07-95.09	...
Average Yield %	0.78	0.58	0.57	0.92	1.04	1.41	1.01	2.66

Address: One CityPlace Drive, Suite 300, St. Louis, MO 63141 **Telephone:** 314-994-2700 **Fax:** 314-994-2878	**Web Site:** www.archcoal.com **Officers:** James R. Boyd - Chmn. Steven F. Leer - Pres., C.E.O.	**Auditors:** Ernst & Young LLP **Investor Contact:** 314-994-2717 **Transfer Agents:** American Stock Transfer & Trust Company, New York, NY

ARCHER DANIELS MIDLAND CO.

Exchange	Symbol	Price	52Wk Range	Yield	P/E	Div Acheiver
NYS	ADM	$41.16 (3/31/2008)	47.09-32.09	1.26	11.97	33 Years

*7 Year Price Score 133.18 *NYSE Composite Index=100 *12 Month Price Score 124.72

Interim Earnings (Per Share)

Qtr.	Sep	Dec	Mar	Jun
2004-05	0.41	0.48	0.41	0.30
2005-06	0.29	0.56	0.53	0.62
2006-07	0.61	0.67	0.56	1.47
2007-08	0.68	0.73	...	...

Interim Dividends (Per Share)

Amt	Decl	Ex	Rec	Pay
0.115Q	5/3/2007	5/15/2007	5/17/2007	6/7/2007
0.115Q	8/1/2007	8/13/2007	8/15/2007	9/5/2007
0.115Q	11/8/2007	11/20/2007	11/23/2007	12/6/2007
0.13Q	2/5/2008	2/14/2008	2/19/2008	3/11/2008

Indicated Div: $0.52 (Div. Reinv. Plan)

Valuation Analysis **Institutional Holding**

Forecast P/E	N/A	No of Institutions
		526
Market Cap	$26.5 Billion	Shares
Book Value	12.3 Billion	424,630,976
Price/Book	2.15	% Held
Price/Sales	0.50	65.05

TRADING VOLUME (thousand shares)

Business Summary: Food (MIC: 4.1 SIC: 2075 NAIC: 311225)

Archer Daniels Midland is engaged in procuring, transporting, storing, processing and merchandising agricultural commodities and products. Co. operates three key segments: Oilseeds Processing, which processes oilseeds, such as soybeans, cottonseed, sunflower seeds, peanuts, and flaxseed into vegetable oils and meals; Corn Processing, which produces syrups, starches, dextros and sweeteners used in the food and beverage industry, as well as produces bioproducts such as alcohol and amino acids; and Agricultural Services, which buys, stores, cleans and transports agricultural commodities and resells these commodities as feed ingredients and raw materials for the agricultural processing industry.

Recent Developments: For the quarter ended Dec 31 2007, net income increased 7.2% to US$473.0 million from US$441.3 million in the year-earlier quarter. Revenues were US$16.50 billion, up 50.3% from US$10.98 billion the year before. Direct operating expenses rose 54.4% to US$15.55 billion from US$10.07 billion in the comparable period the year before. Indirect operating expenses increased 13.3% to US$338.0 million from US$298.2 million in the equivalent prior-year period.

Prospects: Co.'s near-term outlook appears to be favorable as it continues to experience a significant growth in oilseed processing sales, driven by an increase in average selling prices, and to a lesser extent, higher sales volumes. Specifically, Co. attributes the improvement in average selling prices to better global demand for protein and vegetable oil. In addition, Co. is seeing an escalation in corn processing sales, bolstered by the accelerating demand for sweeteners and starches. Moreover, Co.'s solid crushing margins and merchandising results in North and South America is being positively affected by the improving oilseed supplies and increasing demand for vegetable oil and soybean meal.

Financial Data
(US$ in Thousands)

	6 Mos	3 Mos	06/30/2007	06/30/2006	06/30/2005	06/30/2004	06/30/2003	06/30/2002
Earnings Per Share	3.44	3.38	3.30	2.00	1.59	0.76	0.70	0.78
Cash Flow Per Share	(3.62)	(1.53)	0.47	2.11	3.25	0.05	1.67	2.31
Tang Book Value Per Share	18.65	17.89	17.80	14.47	12.47	11.31	10.43	10.39
Dividends Per Share	0.460	0.445	0.430	0.370	0.320	0.270	0.240	0.198
Dividend Payout %	13.37	13.17	13.03	18.50	20.13	35.53	34.29	25.34
Income Statement								
Total Revenue	29,324,000	12,828,000	44,018,000	36,596,111	35,943,810	36,151,394	30,708,033	23,453,561
EBITDA	1,892,000	920,000	4,289,000	2,877,144	2,507,607	1,749,860	1,639,670	1,688,963
Depn & Amortn	360,000	185,000	...	...	...	...	...	...
Income Before Taxes	1,331,000	647,000	3,154,000	1,855,250	1,516,375	718,011	630,973	718,937
Income Taxes	418,000	206,000	992,000	543,180	471,990	223,301	179,828	207,844
Net Income	913,000	441,000	2,162,000	1,312,070	1,044,385	494,710	451,145	511,093
Average Shares	646,000	647,000	656,000	656,287	656,123	647,698	646,086	656,955
Balance Sheet								
Current Assets	22,660,000	19,018,000	15,122,000	11,826,277	9,710,701	10,338,996	8,421,857	7,363,231
Total Assets	33,490,000	29,392,000	25,118,000	21,269,030	18,598,105	19,368,821	17,182,879	15,416,273
Current Liabilities	14,561,000	11,526,000	7,868,000	6,164,767	5,366,864	6,750,237	5,147,472	4,719,297
Long-Term Obligations	5,233,000	4,733,000	4,752,000	4,050,323	3,530,140	3,739,875	3,872,287	3,111,294
Total Liabilities	21,166,000	17,572,000	13,865,000	11,462,150	10,164,633	11,670,605	10,113,682	8,661,452
Stockholders' Equity	12,324,000	11,820,000	11,253,000	9,806,880	8,433,472	7,698,216	7,069,197	6,754,821
Shares Outstanding	643,576	642,890	614,400	655,685	650,399	650,748	644,855	649,993
Statistical Record								
Return on Assets %	7.63	8.57	9.32	6.58	5.50	2.70	2.77	3.44
Return on Equity %	19.33	19.90	20.53	14.39	12.95	6.68	6.53	7.81
EBITDA Margin %	6.45	7.17	9.74	7.86	6.98	4.84	5.34	7.20
Net Margin %	3.11	3.44	4.91	3.59	2.91	1.37	1.47	2.18
Asset Turnover	1.81	1.85	1.90	1.84	1.89	1.97	1.88	1.58
Current Ratio	1.56	1.65	1.92	1.92	1.81	1.53	1.64	1.56
Debt to Equity	0.42	0.40	0.42	0.41	0.42	0.49	0.55	0.46
Price Range	47.09-30.70	39.87-30.70	44.00-30.70	45.25-20.56	25.32-15.43	17.59-12.08	14.28-10.54	15.60-12.00
P/E Ratio	13.69-8.92	11.80-9.08	13.33-9.30	22.63-10.28	15.92-9.70	23.14-15.89	20.40-15.06	20.00-15.38
Average Yield %	1.31	1.28	1.18	1.27	1.60	1.78	1.98	1.44

Address: 4666 Faries Parkway, Box 1470, Decatur, IL 62525 **Telephone:** 217-424-5200 **Fax:** 217-424-5381	**Web Site:** www.admworld.com **Officers:** G. Allen Andreas - Chmn., C.E.O., Acting Pres., Acting C.O.O. David J. Smith - Exec. V.P., Sec., Gen. Couns.	**Auditors:** Ernst & Young LLP **Investor Contact:** 217-424-4647 **Transfer Agents:** Hickory Point Bank & Trust, fsb, Decatur, IL

ARMSTRONG WORLD INDUSTRY INC

Exchange	Symbol	Price	52Wk Range	Yield	P/E
NYS	AWI	$35.66 (3/31/2008)	56.99-27.01	N/A	13.93

*7 Year Price Score N/A   *NYSE Composite Index=100   *12 Month Price Score 84.46

Interim Earnings (Per Share)

Qtr.	Mar	Jun	Sep	Sep
2007	0.46	0.91	0.85	0.34

Interim Dividends (Per Share)

Amt	Decl	Ex	Rec	Pay
4.50U	2/29/2008	3/7/2008	3/11/2008	3/31/2008

Valuation Analysis   . Institutional Holding

Forecast P/E	N/A	No of Institutiono
		75
Market Cap	$2.0 Billion	Shares
Book Value	2.4 Billion	15,507,962
Price/Book	0.83	% Held
Price/Sales	0.57	27.53

TRADING VOLUME (thousand shares)

1999 2000 2001 2002 2003 2004 2005 2006 2007 2008

Business Summary: Building & General Construction (MIC: 3.2 SIC: 3089 NAIC: 326199)

Armstrong World Industries is a global producer of flooring products and ceiling systems for use primarily in the construction and renovation of commercial, institutional and residential buildings. Through its U.S. operations and U.S. and international subsidiaries, Co. designs, manufactures and sells flooring products (primarily resilient and wood flooring) and ceiling systems (primarily mineral fiber, fiberglass and metal) around the world. Co.'s wood flooring products are principally sold under the brand names Bruce®, Hartco®, Robbins®, Timberland®, Armstrong;, HomerWood® and Capella®. Co. also designs, manufactures and sells kitchen and bathroom cabinets in the U.S.

Recent Developments: For the year ended Dec 31 2007, net income increased to US$145.3 million from US$2.2 million in the prior year. Revenues were US$3.55 billion, up 334.3% from US$817.3 million the year before. Operating income was US$296.7 million versus US$16.5 million in the prior year, an increase of. Direct operating expenses rose 306.6% to US$2.69 billion from US$660.4 million in the comparable period the year before. Indirect operating expenses increased 304.3% to US$567.7 million from US$140.4 million in the equivalent prior-year period.

Prospects: For 2008, Co. expects growth in Building Products' North American and European commercial markets to slow, to a low single digits decline and low single digits growth, respectively. At the same time, Co. sees North American commercial floor markets essentially flat, while the North American residential floor markets are expected to decrease between 10.0% and 15.0% due to an anticipated 25.0% decline in U.S. housing starts and expected mid-single-digit declines in renovation. On a consolidated basis, Co. expects that improved prices and increased manufacturing productivity will continue to offset cost inflation. Based on these factors, Co. expects 2008 sales of $3.50 billion to $3.65 billion.

Financial Data

(US$ in Thousands)	12/31/2007	12/31/2006	09/30/2006	12/31/2005	12/31/2004
Earnings Per Share	2.56	0.04	...	...	...
Cash Flow Per Share	10.27	1.27	...	...	...
Tang Book Value Per Share	30.81	26.65	...	...	...
Income Statement					
Total Revenue	3,549,700	817,300	2,608,600	3,326,600	3,279,100
EBITDA	452,000	52,700	2,257,200	253,600	109,700
Income Before Taxes	259,200	7,100	2,150,800	104,900	(49,200)
Income Taxes	106,400	3,800	726,600	(1,200)	21,400
Net Income	145,300	2,200	1,355,800	111,100	(79,700)
Average Shares	56,700	55,300			
Balance Sheet					
Current Assets	1,501,000	1,371,400		1,561,300	
Total Assets	4,649,900	4,170,700	...	4,606,000	
Current Liabilities	497,300	516,600		433,300	...
Long-Term Obligations	485,800	801,500		21,500	
Total Liabilities	2,212,700	2,006,000	...	5,925,900	...
Stockholders' Equity	2,437,200	2,164,700	...	(1,319,900)	
Shares Outstanding	56,828	56,091	...	40,485	
Statistical Record					
Return on Assets %	3.29	0.05	...	...	
Return on Equity %	6.31	0.52	...	...	
EBITDA Margin %	12.73	6.45	86.53	7.62	3.35
Net Margin %	4.09	0.27	51.97	3.34	N.M.
Asset Turnover	0.80	0.19	...	...	...
Current Ratio	3.02	2.65	...	3.60	...
Debt to Equity	0.20	0.37	...	...	...
Price Range	56.99-35.97	42.40-35.41	...	...	...
P/E Ratio	22.26-14.05	N.M.	...	...	...

Address: 2500 Columbia Ave., Lancaster, PA 17603 Telephone: 717-397-0611	Web Site: www.armstrong.com Officers: Michael D. Lockhart - Chmn., C.E.O. F. Nicholas Grasberger - Sr. Vice-Pres., C.F.O.	Auditors: KPMG LLP

ARROW ELECTRONICS, INC.

Exchange	Symbol	Price	52Wk Range	Yield	P/E
NYS	ARW	$33.65 (3/31/2008)	44.33-30.60	N/A	10.26

*7 Year Price Score 113.17 *NYSE Composite Index=100 *12 Month Price Score 93.19

Interim Earnings (Per Share)

Qtr.	Mar	Jun	Sep	Dec
2003	(0.01)	0.07	(0.06)	0.00
2004	0.27	0.55	0.52	0.39
2005	0.47	0.48	0.52	0.61
2006	0.66	0.76	0.70	1.04
2007	0.77	0.79	0.79	0.92

Interim Dividends (Per Share)

No Dividends Paid

Valuation Analysis | **Institutional Holding**

Forecast P/E	9.25	No of Institutions
	(1/10/2007)	247
Market Cap	$4.1 Billion	Shares
Book Value	3.6 Billion	116,258,192
Price/Book	1.16	% Held
Price/Sales	0.26	94.59

Business Summary: Retail - Appliances and Electrical (MIC: 5.10 SIC: 5065 NAIC: 423690)

Arrow Electronics is a provider of products, services, and applications to industrial and commercial users of electronic components and enterprise computing services and products. Co.'s products and services include materials planning, design services, programming and assembly services, inventory management, and online supply chain tools. As of Dec 31 2007, Co. consisted of two business segments; global components and global enterprise computing solutions, and has served as a supply channel partner for more than 700 suppliers and over 140,000 original equipment manufacturers, contract manufacturers, and commercial customers.

Recent Developments: For the year ended Dec 31 2007, net income increased 5.0% to US$407.8 million from US$388.3 million in the prior year. Revenues were US$15.98 billion, up 17.7% from US$13.58 billion the year before. Operating income was US$686.9 million versus US$606.2 million in the prior year, an increase of 13.3%. Direct operating expenses rose 18.7% to US$13.70 billion from US$11.55 billion in the comparable period the year before. Indirect operating expenses increased 12.2% to US$1.60 billion from US$1.43 billion in the equivalent prior-year period.

Prospects: For the first quarter of 2008, Co. expects sales of $3.93 billion to $4.23 billion, with global component sales of $2.78 billion and $2.98 billion and global enterprise computing solutions sales of $1.15 billion and $1.25 billion. Concurrently, Co. expects earnings per diluted share of $0.81 to $0.87, excluding any charges. Meanwhile, on Feb 11 2008, Co. has agreed to acquire ACI Electronics LLC, an independent distributor of electronic components used in defense and aerospace applications. The transaction should further bolster Co.'s position in the North American defense and aerospace marketplace, as well as expand its customer base and strengthen its relationships with key suppliers.

Financial Data

(US$ in Thousands)	12/31/2007	12/31/2006	12/31/2005	12/31/2004	12/31/2003	12/31/2002	12/31/2001	12/31/2000
Earnings Per Share	3.28	3.16	2.09	1.75	0.25	(6.04)	(0.75)	3.62
Cash Flow Per Share	6.91	0.99	3.42	1.65	2.91	6.69	17.05	(3.47)
Tang Book Value Per Share	14.43	14.42	11.00	10.49	5.76	4.85	5.43	6.88
Income Statement								
Total Revenue	15,984,992	13,577,112	11,164,196	10,646,113	8,679,313	7,390,154	10,127,604	12,959,250
EBITDA	784,063	679,821	535,413	473,859	256,184	248,920	234,557	880,945
Income Before Taxes	592,183	518,277	385,561	304,983	47,284	17,547	(109,294)	610,131
Income Taxes	180,697	128,457	131,248	96,436	21,206	6,166	(34,189)	248,195
Net Income	407,792	388,331	253,609	207,504	25,700	(610,482)	(73,826)	357,931
Average Shares	124,429	123,181	124,080	124,561	100,917	101,068	98,384	98,833
Balance Sheet								
Current Assets	5,589,395	4,895,621	4,517,474	4,027,533	3,769,647	3,333,735	3,471,386	5,764,210
Total Assets	8,059,860	6,669,572	6,044,917	5,509,101	5,332,988	4,667,605	5,358,984	7,604,541
Current Liabilities	2,987,374	2,504,110	2,331,878	1,666,388	1,640,624	1,462,393	1,046,985	2,570,876
Long-Term Obligations	1,223,337	976,774	1,138,981	1,465,880	2,016,627	1,807,113	2,441,983	3,027,671
Total Liabilities	4,508,000	3,673,013	3,672,031	3,314,915	3,827,657	3,432,356	3,592,523	5,690,793
Stockholders' Equity	3,551,860	2,996,559	2,372,886	2,194,186	1,505,331	1,235,249	1,766,461	1,913,748
Shares Outstanding	122,827	122,419	120,014	116,301	101,080	100,447	99,857	98,410
Statistical Record								
Return on Assets %	5.54	6.11	4.39	3.82	0.51	N.M.	N.M.	5.91
Return on Equity %	12.45	14.46	11.11	11.19	1.88	N.M.	N.M.	20.61
EBITDA Margin %	4.90	5.01	4.80	4.45	2.95	3.37	2.32	6.80
Net Margin %	2.55	2.86	2.27	1.95	0.30	N.M.	N.M.	2.76
Asset Turnover	2.17	2.14	1.93	1.96	1.74	1.47	1.56	2.14
Current Ratio	1.87	1.96	1.94	2.42	2.30	2.28	3.32	2.24
Debt to Equity	0.34	0.33	0.48	0.67	1.34	1.46	1.38	1.58
Price Range	44.33-32.70	36.65-26.00	33.25-21.71	28.46-20.84	24.15-11.65	32.61-9.14	32.75-19.11	44.69-20.88
P/E Ratio	13.52-9.97	11.60-8.23	15.91-10.39	16.26-11.91	96.60-46.60	...	...	12.34-5.77

Address: 50 Marcus Drive, Melville, NY 11747-4210	Web Site: www.arrow.com	Auditors: Ernst & Young LLP
Telephone: 631-847-2000	Officers: Daniel W. Duval - Chmn. William E. Mitchell - Pres., C.E.O.	Transfer Agents: Mellon Investor Services, Jersey City, NJ
Fax: 631-391-1640		

68

ARVINMERITOR, INC.

Exchange	Symbol	Price	52Wk Range	Yield	P/E
NYS	ARM	$12.51 (3/31/2008)	23.52-9.37	3.20	N/A

*7 Year Price Score 70.81 *NYSE Composite Index=100 *12 Month Price Score 80.46

Interim Earnings (Per Share)

Qtr.	Dec	Mar	Jun	Sep
2004-05	0.26	(0.48)	0.66	(0.28)
2005-06	0.49	0.64	0.29	(3.94)
2006-07	0.10	(1.34)	(0.99)	(0.87)
2007-08	(0.17)	...	...	...

Interim Dividends (Per Share)

Amt	Decl	Ex	Rec	Pay
0.10Q	4/27/2007	5/17/2007	5/21/2007	6/11/2007
0.10Q	7/27/2007	8/16/2007	8/20/2007	9/10/2007
0.10Q	11/13/2007	11/21/2007	11/26/2007	12/10/2007
0.10Q	1/25/2008	2/14/2008	2/19/2008	3/10/2008

Indicated Div: 60.40

Valuation Analysis / Institutional Holding

Forecast P/E	9.86	No of Institutions
	(1/10/2007)	171
Market Cap	$910.7 Million	Shares
Book Value	544.0 Million	79,844,088
Price/Book	1.67	% Held
Price/Sales	0.14	N/A

Business Summary: Automotive (MIC: 15.1 SIC: 3714 NAIC: 336350)

ArvinMeritor supplies integrated systems, modules and components serving commercial truck, trailer, light vehicle and specialty original equipment manufacturers and certain aftermarkets. Light Vehicle Systems supplies body systems, chassis systems and wheel products for passenger cars, all-terrain vehicles, light and medium trucks and sport utility vehicles. Commercial Vehicle Systems supplies drivetrain systems and components, including axles and drivelines, braking systems, suspension systems and ride control products for medium-and heavy-duty trucks, trailers and specialty vehicles, and to the commercial vehicle aftermarket.

Recent Developments: For the quarter ended Dec 31 2007, loss from continuing operations was US$1.0 million compared with income of US$10.0 million in the year-earlier quarter. Net loss amounted to US$12.0 million versus net income of US$7.0 million in the year-earlier quarter. Revenues were US$1.66 billion, up 6.1% from US$1.57 billion the year before. Operating income was US$28.0 million versus US$33.0 million in the prior-year quarter, a decrease of 15.2%. Direct operating expenses rose 4.7% to US$1.53 billion from US$1.46 billion in the comparable period the year before. Indirect operating expenses increased 43.7% to US$102.0 million from US$71.0 million in the equivalent prior-year period.

Prospects: Co.'s near-term outlook appears to be favorable. For the fiscal year ending Sep 30 2008, Co. is projecting sales from continuing operations to be in the range of $6.90 billion to $7.10 billion, due to continued growth outside the U.S. and favorable foreign exchange activities. In addition, Co. continues to anticipate earnings from continuing operations in the range of $1.40 to $1.60 per diluted share, before special items, assuming 2.2% U.S. Gross Domestic Product growth, and excludes gains or losses on divestitures and restructuring costs. Similarly, Co. expects to generate annualized saving of approximately $75.0 million from its ongoing Performance Plus profit improvement program.

Financial Data
(US$ in Thousands)

	3 Mos	09/30/2007	10/01/2006	10/02/2005	10/03/2004	09/28/2003	09/29/2002	09/30/2001
Earnings Per Share	(3.37)	(3.11)	(2.52)	0.17	(0.61)	2.00	1.59	0.53
Cash Flow Per Share	(2.81)	0.51	6.37	(0.47)	3.20	3.82	2.78	9.15
Tang Book Value Per Share	N.M.	N.M.	5.58	0.30	1.60	N.M.	N.M.	N.M.
Dividends Per Share	0.400	0.400	0.400	0.400	0.400	0.400	0.400	0.760
Dividend Payout %	...	...	...	235.29	...	20.00	25.16	143.40
Income Statement								
Total Revenue	1,663,000	6,449,000	9,195,000	8,903,000	8,033,000	7,788,000	6,882,000	6,805,000
EBITDA	71,000	106,000	(44,000)	213,000	362,000	427,000	536,000	440,000
Depn & Amortn	32,000	...	...	...	...	...	...	...
Income Before Taxes	12,000	(23,000)	(216,000)	31,000	179,000	213,000	235,000	63,000
Income Taxes	10,000	(8,000)	(56,000)	(5,000)	44,000	68,000	75,000	21,000
Net Income	(12,000)	(219,000)	(175,000)	12,000	(42,000)	136,000	107,000	35,000
Average Shares	71,900	70,500	69,300	69,900	68,600	67,900	67,200	66,100
Balance Sheet								
Current Assets	2,179,000	2,389,000	3,095,000	3,170,000	2,986,000	2,239,000	1,976,000	1,755,000
Total Assets	4,558,000	4,789,000	5,513,000	5,870,000	5,639,000	5,253,000	4,651,000	4,362,000
Current Liabilities	1,796,000	2,079,000	2,549,000	2,523,000	2,273,000	1,878,000	1,743,000	1,672,000
Long-Term Obligations	1,141,000	1,130,000	1,184,000	1,451,000	1,487,000	1,541,000	1,435,000	1,313,000
Total Liabilities	4,014,000	4,246,000	4,506,000	4,995,000	4,651,000	4,354,000	3,871,000	3,654,000
Stockholders' Equity	544,000	543,000	944,000	875,000	988,000	899,000	741,000	651,000
Shares Outstanding	72,800	72,600	70,600	70,300	69,500	68,500	67,900	65,600
Statistical Record								
Return on Assets %	N.M.	N.M.	N.M.	0.21	N.M.	2.75	2.38	0.77
Return on Equity %	N.M.	N.M.	N.M.	1.29	N.M.	16.63	15.42	4.85
EBITDA Margin %	4.27	1.64	N.M.	2.39	4.51	5.48	7.79	6.47
Net Margin %	N.M.	N.M.	N.M.	0.13	N.M.	1.75	1.55	0.51
Asset Turnover	1.30	1.26	1.62	1.55	1.45	1.58	1.53	1.50
Current Ratio	1.21	1.15	1.21	1.26	1.31	1.19	1.13	1.05
Debt to Equity	2.10	2.08	1.25	1.66	1.51	1.71	1.94	2.02
Price Range	23.52-9.37	23.52-13.91	17.63-12.90	22.72-11.81	26.10-16.57	21.25-12.77	32.15-14.60	21.75-9.50
P/E Ratio	...	...	...	133.65-69.47	...	10.63-6.38	20.22-9.18	41.04-17.92
Average Yield %	2.27	2.16	2.59	2.23	1.98	2.36	1.74	4.94

Address: 2135 West Maple Road, Troy, MI 48084-7186
Telephone: 248-435-1000
Fax: 248-435-1393

Web Site: www.arvinmeritor.com
Officers: Charles G. McClure Jr. - Chmn., Pres., C.E.O. Vernon G. Baker II - Sr. V.P., Gen. Couns.

Auditors: Deloitte & Touche LLP
Investor Contact: 248-655-2159
Transfer Agents: The Bank of New York

ASBURY AUTOMOTIVE GROUP, INC

Exchange	Symbol	Price	52Wk Range	Yield	P/E
NYS	ABG	$13.76 (3/31/2008)	29.82-12.19	N/A	8.99

*7 Year Price Score N/A   *NYSE Composite Index=100   *12 Month Price Score 77.58

Interim Earnings (Per Share)

Qtr.	Mar	Jun	Sep	Dec
2003	0.21	0.38	0.50	(0.63)
2004	0.32	0.45	0.37	0.39
2005	0.29	0.49	0.45	0.62
2006	0.37	0.56	0.51	0.34
2007	0.01	0.62	0.57	0.34

Interim Dividends (Per Share)

No Dividends Paid

Valuation Analysis

		Institutional Holding	
Forecast P/E	N/A	No of Institutions	
		116	
Market Cap	$434.6 Million	Shares	
Book Value	584.2 Million	24,153,048	
Price/Book	0.74	% Held	
Price/Sales	0.08	74.67	

Business Summary: Retail - Automotive (MIC: 5.7 SIC: 5599 NAIC: 441229)

Asbury Automotive Group is an automotive retailer operating 124 franchises at 93 dealership locations in 22 metropolitan markets within 11 states throughout the U.S. as of Dec 31 2007. Co.'s retail network is organized into primarily four regions of Florida, West, Mid-Atlantic and South, and includes nine locally branded dealership groups. Co. provides its customers a range of automotive products and services including; new and used vehicles and related financing; vehicle maintenance and repair services; replacement parts; arranging new and used vehicle financing; and arranging the sale of warranty, insurance and extended service contracts.

Recent Developments: For the year ended Dec 31 2007, income from continuing operations decreased 19.1% to US$54.3 million from US$67.1 million a year earlier. Net income decreased 16.1% to US$51.0 million from US$60.7 million in the prior year. Revenues were US$5.71 billion, up 0.3% from US$5.69 billion the year before. Operating income was US$181.4 million versus US$188.3 million in the prior year, a decrease of 3.7%. Direct operating expenses were unchanged at US$4.82 billion versus the comparable period the year before. Indirect operating expenses increased 3.8% to US$708.1 million from US$682.4 million in the equivalent prior-year period.

Prospects: Co. is experiencing a decrease in net income, reflecting a challenging environment for vehicle sales, both new and used, in the fourth quarter of 2007, with notable softness in its key Florida markets. Nevertheless, while retail market conditions are likely to remain difficult throughout 2008, Co. believes that its expense reduction effort should position it well for future growth. As a result, Co. expects diluted earnings per share from continuing operations of $1.80 to $2.00 for full year 2008, based on a range for U.S. new vehicle unit sales of between 15.3 million and 15.5 million for 2008, as well as a projected decrease in its same store used unit volumes of between 5.0% and 8.0%.

Financial Data
(US$ in Thousands)

	12/31/2007	12/31/2006	12/31/2005	12/31/2004	12/31/2003	12/31/2002	12/31/2001	12/31/2000
Earnings Per Share	1.53	1.78	1.86	1.53	0.46	1.15	0.80	...
Cash Flow Per Share	2.14	3.87	(1.24)	(0.32)	2.96	2.06	2.84	...
Tang Book Value Per Share	1.51	3.71	1.45	N.M.	0.91	0.75	N.M.	...
Dividends Per Share	0.850	0.400	...	...	...	...	...	...
Dividend Payout %	55.56	22.47	...	...	...	...	...	...
Income Statement								
Total Revenue	5,712,967	5,748,331	5,540,663	5,301,135	4,776,505	4,486,038	4,318,292	4,027,790
EBITDA	191,520	210,395	186,612	164,590	119,803	155,702	156,071	140,317
Income Before Taxes	84,823	107,700	95,758	84,108	41,066	76,604	51,853	42,178
Income Taxes	30,537	40,546	35,854	31,364	21,268	36,742	5,351	3,511
Net Income	50,955	60,749	61,081	50,073	15,187	38,085	43,829	28,927
Average Shares	33,340	34,067	32,896	32,674	32,715	33,073	34,022	...
Balance Sheet								
Current Assets	1,192,422	1,293,064	1,185,180	1,143,506	1,012,009	849,783	753,258	775,102
Total Assets	2,016,300	2,030,837	1,930,800	1,897,959	1,814,279	1,605,644	1,460,657	1,404,200
Current Liabilities	871,667	881,055	838,226	847,510	757,026	692,873	609,997	628,622
Long-Term Obligations	473,851	454,010	472,427	495,272	559,128	440,143	492,548	435,879
Total Liabilities	1,432,075	1,419,004	1,383,034	1,417,936	1,380,572	1,178,693	1,117,106	1,082,318
Stockholders' Equity	584,225	611,833	547,766	480,023	433,707	426,951	343,551	321,882
Shares Outstanding	31,581	33,534	32,848	32,577	32,431	33,227	34,000	...
Statistical Record								
Return on Assets %	2.52	3.07	3.19	2.69	0.89	2.48	3.06	...
Return on Equity %	8.52	10.48	11.89	10.93	3.53	9.89	13.17	...
EBITDA Margin %	3.35	3.66	3.37	3.10	2.51	3.47	3.61	3.48
Net Margin %	0.89	1.06	1.10	0.94	0.32	0.85	1.01	0.72
Asset Turnover	2.82	2.90	2.89	2.85	2.79	2.93	3.01	...
Current Ratio	1.37	1.47	1.41	1.35	1.34	1.23	1.23	1.23
Debt to Equity	0.81	0.74	0.86	1.03	1.29	1.03	1.43	1.35
Price Range	29.82-14.84	25.98-16.33	18.00-13.71	19.35-12.59	18.99-5.95	22.25-7.30	...	...
P/E Ratio	19.49-9.70	14.60-9.17	9.68-7.37	12.65-8.23	41.28-12.93	19.35-6.35	...	...
Average Yield %	3.69	1.94	...	...	...	...	...	...

Address: 622 Third Avenue, 37th Floor, New York, NY 10017 **Telephone:** 212-885-2500	**Web Site:** www.asburyauto.com **Officers:** Michael J. Durham - Chmn. Kenneth B. Gilman - Pres., C.E.O.	**Auditors:** Deloitte & Touche LLP **Investor Contact:** 212-885-2520 **Transfer Agents:** EquiServe Trust Company, N.A., Kansas City, MO

ASHLAND INC

Exchange	Symbol	Price	52Wk Range	Yield	P/E
NYS	ASH	$47.30 (3/31/2008)	66.50-42.08	2.33	13.99

*7 Year Price Score N/A   *NYSE Composite Index=100   *12 Month Price Score 89.63

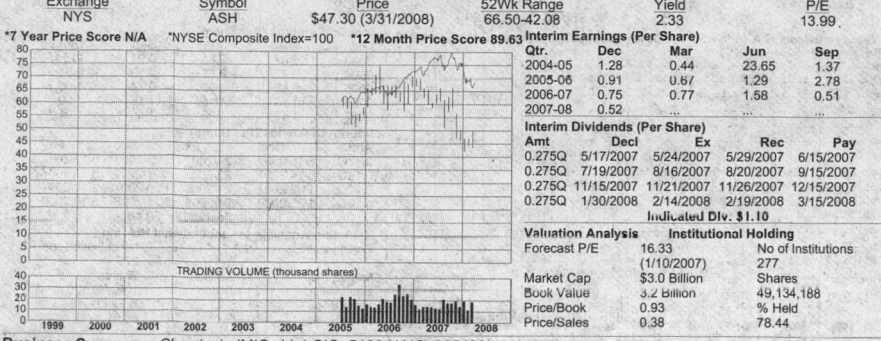

Interim Earnings (Per Share)

Qtr.	Dec	Mar	Jun	Sep
2004-05	1.28	0.44	23.65	1.37
2005-06	0.91	0.67	1.29	2.78
2006-07	0.75	0.77	1.58	0.51
2007-08	0.52	...	...	...

Interim Dividends (Per Share)

Amt	Decl	Ex	Rec	Pay
0.275Q	5/17/2007	5/24/2007	5/29/2007	6/15/2007
0.275Q	7/19/2007	8/16/2007	8/20/2007	9/15/2007
0.275Q	11/15/2007	11/21/2007	11/26/2007	12/15/2007
0.275Q	1/30/2008	2/14/2008	2/19/2008	3/15/2008

Indicated Div. $1.10

Valuation Analysis

		Institutional Holding	
Forecast P/E	16.33 (1/10/2007)	No of Institutions	277
Market Cap	$3.0 Billion	Shares	49,134,188
Book Value	3.2 Billion	% Held	78.44
Price/Book	0.93		
Price/Sales	0.38		

Business Summary: Chemicals (MIC: 11.1 SIC: 5169 NAIC: 325199)

Ashland has four business segments including: Ashland Performance Materials, which is a manufacturer and supplier of specialty chemicals and services to the building and construction, packaging and converting, transportation, marine and metal casting industries; Ashland Distribution, which distributes chemicals, plastics and resins in North America and plastics in Europe; Valvoline, which is a producer and marketer of automotive lubricants, chemicals, appearance products, antifreeze and filters; and Ashland Water Technologies, which is a supplier of chemical and non-chemical water treatment services for industrial, municipal and commercial facilities.

Recent Developments: For the quarter ended Dec 31 2007, income from continuing operations decreased 28.3% to US$38.0 million from US$53.0 million in the year-earlier quarter. Net income decreased 32.7% to US$33.0 million from US$49.0 million in the year-earlier quarter. Revenues were US$1.91 billion, up 5.7% from US$1.80 billion the year before. Operating income was US$46.0 million versus US$58.0 million in the prior-year quarter, a decrease of 20.7%. Direct operating expenses rose 6.7% to US$1.59 billion from US$1.49 billion in the comparable period the year before. Indirect operating expenses increased 5.5% to US$270.0 million from US$256.0 million in the equivalent prior-year period.

Prospects: Despite the difficult conditions in the North American building and construction and transportation markets, Co. is encouraged with its outlook as its Performance Materials business is expected continue to benefit from the increasing use of composites and adhesives in various markets and applications. Also, the selling price increases on lubricant products in Co.'s Valvoline business early in the second quarter of the fiscal year ending Sep 2008 should stabilize Valvoline's gross profit margin and help maintain solid operating results going forward. Furthermore, the selling prices increases in Co.'s Water Technologies business could boost its earnings in the latter half of the fiscal year.

Financial Data

(US$ in Thousands)	3 Mos	09/30/2007	09/30/2006	09/30/2005	09/30/2004	09/30/2003	09/30/2002	09/30/2001
Earnings Per Share	3.38	3.60	5.64	26.85	5.31	1.10	1.67	5.93
Cash Flow Per Share	6.17	3.14	2.08	0.51	2.98	3.56	2.72	12.01
Tang Book Value Per Share	44.93	44.08	41.58	42.32	30.46	25.44	24.29	24.61
Dividends Per Share	1.100	11.300	1.100	0.275	1.100	1.100	1.100	1.100
Dividend Payout %	32.54	313.89	19.50	1.02	20.72	100.00	65.87	18.55
Income Statement								
Total Revenue	1,905,000	7,834,000	7,277,000	9,860,000	8,781,000	7,865,000	7,792,000	8,547,000
EBITDA	92,000	343,000	272,000	2,071,000	849,000	464,000	551,000	1,091,000
Depn & Amortn	34,000	...	...	...	...	...	...	...
Income Before Taxes	58,000	259,000	212,000	1,803,000	548,000	138,000	200,000	681,000
Income Taxes	20,000	58,000	29,000	(202,000)	150,000	44,000	71,000	275,000
Net Income	33,000	230,000	407,000	2,004,000	378,000	75,000	117,000	417,000
Average Shares	64,000	64,000	72,000	75,000	71,000	69,000	70,000	70,000
Balance Sheet								
Current Assets	3,236,000	3,276,000	4,250,000	3,757,000	2,302,000	2,085,000	1,925,000	2,213,000
Total Assets	5,646,000	5,686,000	6,590,000	6,815,000	7,502,000	7,006,000	6,725,000	6,945,000
Current Liabilities	1,044,000	1,152,000	2,041,000	1,545,000	1,815,000	1,484,000	1,511,000	1,497,000
Long-Term Obligations	64,000	64,000	70,000	82,000	1,109,000	1,512,000	1,606,000	1,786,000
Total Liabilities	2,440,000	2,532,000	3,494,000	3,076,000	4,796,000	4,753,000	4,552,000	4,719,000
Stockholders' Equity	3,206,000	3,154,000	3,096,000	3,739,000	2,706,000	2,253,000	2,173,000	2,226,000
Shares Outstanding	62,902	63,000	67,000	73,000	72,000	68,000	68,000	69,000
Statistical Record								
Return on Assets %	3.87	3.75	6.07	27.99	5.20	1.09	1.71	6.08
Return on Equity %	7.03	7.36	11.91	62.19	15.20	3.39	5.32	19.90
EBITDA Margin %	4.83	4.38	3.74	21.00	9.67	5.90	7.07	12.76
Net Margin %	1.73	2.94	5.59	20.32	4.30	0.95	1.50	4.88
Asset Turnover	1.43	1.28	1.09	1.38	1.21	1.15	1.14	1.25
Current Ratio	3.10	2.84	2.08	2.43	1.27	1.40	1.27	1.48
Debt to Equity	0.02	0.02	0.02	0.02	0.41	0.67	0.74	0.80
Price Range	69.80-46.53	70.81-50.94	74.55-51.23	62.54-52.15	...	...	...	...
P/E Ratio	20.65-13.77	19.67-14.15	13.22-9.08	2.33-1.94	...	...	...	...
Average Yield %	1.81	17.77	1.76	0.46	...	...	...	...

Address: 50 E. RiverCenter Boulevard, Covington, KY 41012-0391 Telephone: 859-815-3333 Fax: 859-329-5188	Web Site: www.ashland.com Officers: James J. O'Brien - Chmn., C.E.O. J. Marvin Quin - Sr. V.P., C.F.O.	Auditors: Ernst & Young LLP Investor Contact: 859-815-4095 Transfer Agents: National City Bank, Cleveland, OH

ASSURANT INC

Exchange	Symbol	Price	52Wk Range	Yield	P/E
NYS	AIZ	$60.86 (3/31/2008)	69.74-47.50	0.79	11.31

*7 Year Price Score N/A   *NYSE Composite Index=100   *12 Month Price Score 113.02

Interim Earnings (Per Share)

Qtr.	Mar	Jun	Sep	Dec
2003	0.67	0.83	0.91	(0.71)
2004	0.73	0.67	0.53	0.61
2005	0.82	0.92	0.74	1.03
2006	1.23	1.16	1.18	1.99
2007	1.45	1.36	1.56	1.01

Interim Dividends (Per Share)

Amt	Decl	Ex	Rec	Pay
0.12Q	5/18/2007	5/24/2007	5/29/2007	6/12/2007
0.12Q	8/14/2007	8/23/2007	8/27/2007	9/11/2007
0.12Q	11/9/2007	11/21/2007	11/26/2007	12/10/2007
0.12Q	1/25/2008	2/21/2008	2/25/2008	3/10/2008

Indicated Div: $0.48

Valuation Analysis

		Institutional Holding	
Forecast P/E	N/A	No of Institutions	279
Market Cap	$7.2 Billion	Shares	106,279,120
Book Value	4.1 Billion	% Held	86.87
Price/Book	1.75		
Price/Sales	0.85		

TRADING VOLUME (thousand shares)

1999 2000 2001 2002 2003 2004 2005 2006 2007 2008

Business Summary: Insurance (MIC: 8.2 SIC: 6321 NAIC: 524113)

Assurant is a holding company that provides insurance products and related services in North America and selected international markets. Through its operating subsidiaries, Co. is engaged in providing creditor-placed homeowners insurance, manufactured housing homeowners insurance, debt protection administration, credit insurance, warranties and extended service contracts, individual health and small employer group health insurance, group dental insurance, group disability insurance, group life insurance and pre-funded funeral insurance. Co. has five segments: Assurant Solutions, Assurant Specialty Property, Assurant Health, Assurant Employee Benefits, and Corporate and Other.

Recent Developments: For the year ended Dec 31 2007, net income decreased 8.9% to US$653.7 million from US$717.4 million in the prior year. Revenues were US$8.45 billion, up 4.7% from US$8.07 billion the year before. Net premiums earned were US$7.41 billion versus US$6.84 billion in the prior year, an increase of 8.2%. Net investment income rose 8.5% to US$799.1 million from US$736.7 million a year ago.

Prospects: On Oct 1 2007, Co. announced that its U.K. affiliate has acquired Centrepoint Insurance Services Ltd., a distributor of buildings and contents and mortgage payment protection to financial intermediaries in the U.K. The acquisition, along with Co.'s Jul 2007 acquisition of Swansure Group, is expected to accelerate its growth in the U.K. mortgage market. The acquisition should dilute Co.'s earnings per share by less than 1.0% in 2008 and is expected to be accretive to earnings per share beginning in 2010. Going forward, Co. plans to utilize both its Centrepoint and Swansure acquisitions to grow its mortgage product portfolio, its distribution and its geographic footprint in the U.K.

Financial Data (US$ in Thousands)	12/31/2007	12/31/2006	12/31/2005	12/31/2004	12/31/2003	12/31/2002	12/31/2001
Earnings Per Share	5.38	5.57	3.50	2.53	1.70	(9.17)	0.90
Cash Flow Per Share	10.05	7.28	7.51	6.01	6.79	3.34	...
Tang Book Value Per Share	27.64	24.81	22.17	20.12	16.51	15.76	...
Dividends Per Share	0.460	0.300	0.310	0.210	1.660	0.380	1.000
Dividend Payout %	8.55	5.39	8.86	8.30	97.65	...	111.11
Income Statement							
Total Revenue	8,453,515	8,070,584	7,497,675	7,403,464	7,066,213	6,532,200	6,186,874
EBITDA	1,072,208	1,151,746	663,001	523,971	237,880	337,463	358,902
Income Before Taxes	1,011,040	1,095,742	655,608	535,928	259,357	370,397	205,644
Income Taxes	357,294	379,871	176,253	185,368	73,705	110,657	107,591
Net Income	653,746	717,418	479,355	350,560	185,652	(1,001,199)	98,053
Average Shares	121,436	128,812	136,945	138,467	109,222	109,222	109,222
Balance Sheet							
Current Assets	5,875,746	5,966,572	6,317,660	5,803,875	6,321,360	6,472,808	...
Total Assets	26,750,316	25,165,148	25,365,453	24,503,896	23,728,319	22,279,055	...
Current Liabilities	422,138	475,743	509,334	575,851	681,521	724,905	...
Long-Term Obligations	971,863	971,774	971,690	971,611	1,750,000	...	...
Total Liabilities	22,661,413	21,332,551	21,665,894	20,868,465	21,096,216	18,253,262	...
Stockholders' Equity	4,088,903	3,832,597	3,699,559	3,635,431	2,632,103	2,555,059	...
Shares Outstanding	117,808	122,618	130,591	139,766	109,222	109,222	109,222
Statistical Record							
Return on Assets %	2.52	2.84	1.92	1.45	0.81	...	...
Return on Equity %	16.51	19.05	13.07	11.16	7.16	...	...
EBITDA Margin %	12.68	14.27	8.84	7.08	3.37	5.17	5.80
Net Margin %	7.73	8.89	6.39	4.74	2.63	N.M.	1.58
Asset Turnover	0.33	0.32	0.30	0.31	0.31	...	...
Current Ratio	13.92	12.54	12.40	10.08	9.28	8.93	...
Debt to Equity	0.24	0.25	0.26	0.27	0.66	...	...
Price Range	69.74-47.50	56.47-43.23	44.50-29.85	31.00-23.70	...	...	...
P/E Ratio	12.96-8.83	10.14-7.76	12.71-8.53	12.25-9.37	...	...	...
Average Yield %	0.80	0.60	0.85	0.80	...	...	...

Address: One Chase Manhattan Plaza, 41st Floor, New York, NY 10005 Telephone: 212-859-7000	Web Site: www.assurant.com Officers: John Michael Palms - Chmn. Robert B. Pollock - Pres., C.O.O.	Auditors: PricewaterhouseCoopers LLP Investor Contact: 866-888-4219

ASTORIA FINANCIAL CORP.

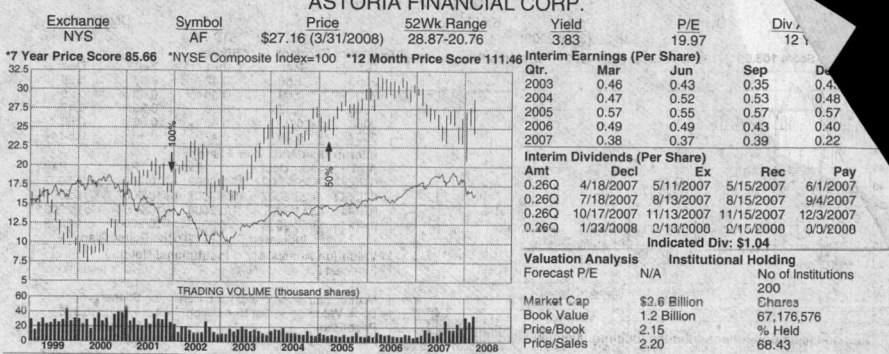

Exchange	Symbol	Price	52Wk Range	Yield	P/E	Div
NYS	AF	$27.16 (3/31/2008)	28.87-20.76	3.83	19.97	12

*7 Year Price Score 85.66   *NYSE Composite Index=100   *12 Month Price Score 111.46

Interim Earnings (Per Share)

Qtr.	Mar	Jun	Sep	De
2003	0.46	0.43	0.35	0.4
2004	0.47	0.52	0.53	0.48
2005	0.57	0.55	0.57	0.57
2006	0.49	0.49	0.43	0.40
2007	0.38	0.37	0.39	0.22

Interim Dividends (Per Share)

Amt	Decl	Ex	Rec	Pay
0.26Q	4/18/2007	5/11/2007	5/15/2007	6/1/2007
0.26Q	7/18/2007	8/13/2007	8/15/2007	9/4/2007
0.26Q	10/17/2007	11/13/2007	11/15/2007	12/3/2007
0.26Q	1/23/2008	2/13/2000	2/15/2000	0/0/2000

Indicated Div: $1.04

Valuation Analysis   **Institutional Holding**

Forecast P/E	N/A	No of Institutions
		200
Market Cap	$2.6 Billion	Shares
Book Value	1.2 Billion	67,176,576
Price/Book	2.15	% Held
Price/Sales	2.20	68.43

TRADING VOLUME (thousand shares)

Business Summary: Other Depository Banking (MIC: 8.5 SIC: 6035 NAIC: 522120)

Astoria Financial is the holding company of Astoria Federal Savings and Loan Association, and its consolidated subsidiaries. Co.'s primary business is attracting retail deposits from the general public and investing those deposits, together with funds generated from operations, principal repayments on loans and securities and borrowings, primarily in one-to-four family mortgage loans, multi-family mortgage loans, commercial real estate loans and mortgage-backed securities. Co. also invests in construction loans and other loans, U.S. government, government agency and government-sponsored enterprise, securities and other investments. As of Dec 31 2007, Co. had total assets of $21.72 billion.

Recent Developments: For the year ended Dec 31 2007, net income decreased 28.6% to US$124.8 million from US$174.9 million in the prior year. Net interest income decreased 14.6% to US$333.5 million from US$390.4 million in the prior year. Non-interest income fell 17.0% to US$75.8 million from US$91.4 million, while non-interest expense advanced 4.3% to US$231.3 million.

Prospects: The decrease in short-term interest rates has produced a more favorable interest rate environment for Co. going forward. This, Co. expects the yield curve to remain positively sloped and steepen further for 2008, resulting in improved opportunities for earnings growth and an expansion of net interest margin. Co. will also continue to capitalize on residential mortgage market opportunities that result in improved loan volumes and mortgage spreads. However, Co. expects its loan growth to be somewhat tempered due to the reduced number of states in which it will originate residential loans. Further, Co. will focus on deposit growth and may fund some of its loan growth with lower cost borrowings.

Financial Data

(US$ in Thousands)	12/31/2007	12/31/2006	12/31/2005	12/31/2004	12/31/2003	12/31/2002	12/31/2001	12/31/2000
Earnings Per Share	1.36	1.80	2.26	2.00	1.66	1.90	1.57	1.44
Cash Flow Per Share	2.30	2.29	2.68	2.56	3.13	1.26	1.64	1.60
Tang Book Value Per Share	10.58	10.33	10.94	10.59	10.11	10.58	9.69	8.50
Dividends Per Share	1.040	0.960	0.800	0.667	0.573	0.513	0.407	0.340
Dividend Payout %	76.47	53.33	35.40	33.33	34.54	27.02	25.96	23.61
Income Statement								
Interest Income	1,105,322	1,086,814	1,082,987	1,045,901	1,057,291	1,266,262	1,438,563	1,517,934
Interest Expense	771,794	696,429	604,207	575,335	677,753	801,838	969,189	1,010,918
Net Interest Income	333,528	390,385	478,780	470,566	379,538	464,424	469,374	507,016
Provision for Losses	2,500	...	...	...	...	2,307	4,028	4,014
Non-Interest Income	75,790	91,350	102,199	80,084	119,561	107,407	100,974	69,246
Non-Interest Expense	231,273	221,803	228,734	225,011	205,877	198,020	206,518	200,988
Income Before Taxes	175,545	259,932	352,245	325,639	293,222	371,495	345,190	350,695
Income Taxes	50,723	85,035	118,442	106,102	96,376	123,066	120,036	134,146
Net Income	124,822	174,897	233,803	219,537	196,846	248,429	222,860	216,549
Average Shares	92,092	97,280	103,408	109,806	115,942	127,379	138,261	146,152
Balance Sheet								
Net Loans & Leases	16,076,068	14,891,749	14,311,134	13,180,521	12,603,866	11,975,815	12,084,976	11,344,518
Total Assets	21,719,368	21,554,519	22,380,271	23,415,869	22,457,665	21,697,829	22,667,706	22,336,802
Total Deposits	13,049,438	13,224,024	12,810,455	12,323,257	11,186,594	11,067,196	10,903,693	10,071,687
Total Liabilities	20,508,024	20,338,765	21,030,044	22,046,105	21,061,134	20,143,831	21,000,120	20,698,639
Stockholders' Equity	1,211,344	1,215,754	1,350,227	1,369,764	1,396,531	1,553,998	1,542,586	1,513,163
Shares Outstanding	95,728	98,211	104,967	110,304	118,005	127,208	136,150	148,930
Statistical Record								
Return on Assets %	0.58	0.80	1.02	0.95	0.89	1.12	0.99	0.96
Return on Equity %	10.29	13.63	17.19	15.83	13.34	16.05	14.59	15.94
Net Interest Margin %	30.17	35.92	44.21	44.99	35.90	36.68	32.63	33.40
Efficiency Ratio %	19.58	18.83	19.30	19.98	17.49	14.42	13.41	12.66
Loans to Deposits	1.23	1.13	1.12	1.07	1.13	1.08	1.11	1.13
Price Range	30.29-23.00	31.79-27.32	30.21-24.11	28.04-22.47	25.48-15.49	23.37-14.57	21.00-16.19	18.15-7.38
P/E Ratio	22.27-16.91	17.66-15.18	13.37-10.67	14.02-11.23	15.35-9.33	12.30-7.67	13.38-10.31	12.60-5.12
Average Yield %	3.94	3.19	2.96	2.68	2.96	2.60	2.21	3.20

Address: One Astoria Federal Plaza, Lake Success, NY 11042-1085 **Telephone:** 516-327-3000 **Fax:** 516-327-7860	**Web Site:** www.astoriafederal.com **Officers:** George L. Engelke Jr. - Chmn., Pres., C.E.O. Monte N. Redman - Exec. V.P., C.F.O.	**Auditors:** KPMG LLP **Investor Contact:** 516-327-7877 **Transfer Agents:** Mellon Investor Services LLC, Ridgefield Park, NJ

AT&T INC

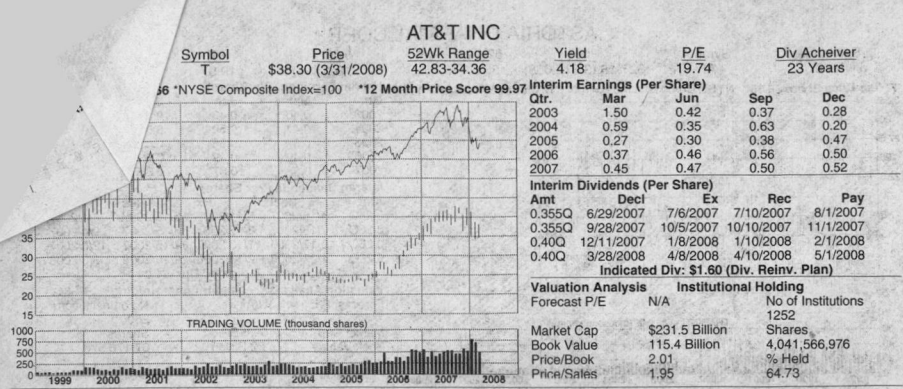

Symbol	Price	52Wk Range	Yield	P/E	Div Achiever
T	$38.30 (3/31/2008)	42.83-34.36	4.18	19.74	23 Years

56 *NYSE Composite Index=100   *12 Month Price Score 99.97

Interim Earnings (Per Share)

Qtr.	Mar	Jun	Sep	Dec
2003	1.50	0.42	0.37	0.28
2004	0.59	0.35	0.63	0.20
2005	0.27	0.30	0.38	0.47
2006	0.37	0.46	0.56	0.50
2007	0.45	0.47	0.50	0.52

Interim Dividends (Per Share)

Amt	Decl	Ex	Rec	Pay
0.355Q	6/29/2007	7/6/2007	7/10/2007	8/1/2007
0.355Q	9/28/2007	10/5/2007	10/10/2007	11/1/2007
0.40Q	12/11/2007	1/8/2008	1/10/2008	2/1/2008
0.40Q	3/28/2008	4/8/2008	4/10/2008	5/1/2008

Indicated Div: $1.60 (Div. Reinv. Plan)

TRADING VOLUME (thousand shares)

Valuation Analysis

		Institutional Holding	
Forecast P/E	N/A	No of Institutions	1252
Market Cap	$231.5 Billion	Shares	4,041,566,976
Book Value	115.4 Billion	% Held	64.73
Price/Book	2.01		
Price/Sales	1.95		

Business Summary: Communications (MIC: 10.1 SIC: 4813 NAIC: 517110)

AT&T is a holding company providing telecommunications services. As of Dec 31 2007, Co. was divided into four reportable segments: wireline, which consisted of three product-based categories: voice, data and other; wireless, which provided a range of nationwide wireless voice communications services in a variety of pricing plans, including postpaid and prepaid service plans; advertising & publishing, which included its directory operations that published Yellow and White Pages directories and sold directory and Internet-based advertising; and other, which included operations from Sterling, its business integration software and services subsidiary, as well as corporate and other operations.

Recent Developments: For the year ended Dec 31 2007, net income increased 62.5% to US$11.95 billion from US$7.36 billion in the prior year. Revenues were US$118.93 billion, up 88.6% from US$63.06 billion the year before. Operating income was US$20.40 billion versus US$10.29 billion in the prior year, an increase of 98.3%. Direct operating expenses rose 61.4% to US$46.06 billion from US$28.54 billion in the comparable period the year before. Indirect operating expenses increased 116.6% to US$52.47 billion from US$24.23 billion in the equivalent prior-year period.

Prospects: Looking ahead, Co. expects further ramp in consolidated revenue growth into the mid-single-digit range in 2008 with growth at mid-single-digit or better in the years following. Also, Co. anticipates continued mid-teens wireless service revenue growth in 2008 reflecting strong subscriber growth and continued robust growth in wireless data services. Meanwhile, on Feb 13 2008, Co. announced the completion of its acquisition of spectrum licenses covering 196 million people in 281 license areas from a subsidiary of Aloha Partners, L.P., a Delaware limited partnership. The addition of Aloha's spectrum will enhance Co.'s ability to continue to meet growing customer demand for mobile services.

Financial Data

(US$ in Thousands)	12/31/2007	12/31/2006	12/31/2005	12/31/2004	12/31/2003	12/31/2002	12/31/2001	12/31/2000
Earnings Per Share	1.94	1.89	1.42	1.77	2.56	1.69	2.13	2.32
Cash Flow Per Share	5.56	4.02	3.85	3.30	4.07	4.57	4.40	4.20
Tang Book Value Per Share	N.M.	N.M.	8.29	11.78	11.08	9.51	8.62	7.38
Dividends Per Share	1.470	1.350	1.290	1.250	1.367	1.066	1.023	1.005
Dividend Payout %	75.77	71.43	90.85	70.62	53.42	63.09	48.00	43.32
Income Statement								
Total Revenue	118,928,000	63,055,000	43,862,000	40,787,000	40,843,000	43,138,000	45,908,000	51,476,000
EBITDA	43,257,000	22,226,000	14,413,000	15,228,000	17,385,000	19,826,000	21,307,000	23,878,000
Income Before Taxes	18,204,000	10,881,000	5,718,000	7,165,000	8,901,000	10,457,000	11,357,000	12,888,000
Income Taxes	6,253,000	3,525,000	932,000	2,186,000	2,930,000	2,984,000	4,097,000	4,921,000
Net Income	11,951,000	7,356,000	4,786,000	5,887,000	8,505,000	5,653,000	7,242,000	7,967,000
Average Shares	6,169,999	3,902,000	3,379,000	3,322,000	3,329,000	3,348,000	3,396,000	3,433,000
Balance Sheet								
Net PPE	95,890,000	94,596,000	58,727,000	50,046,000	52,128,000	48,490,000	49,827,000	47,195,000
Total Assets	275,644,000	270,634,000	145,632,000	108,844,000	100,166,000	95,057,000	96,322,000	98,651,000
Long-Term Obligations	57,255,000	50,063,000	26,115,000	21,231,000	16,060,000	18,536,000	17,133,000	15,492,000
Total Liabilities	160,277,000	155,094,000	90,942,000	68,340,000	61,918,000	61,858,000	63,831,000	68,188,000
Stockholders' Equity	115,367,000	115,540,000	54,690,000	40,504,000	38,248,000	33,199,000	32,491,000	30,463,000
Shares Outstanding	6,043,544	6,238,745	3,876,884	3,300,912	3,305,236	3,318,000	3,354,216	3,386,709
Statistical Record								
Return on Assets %	4.38	3.53	3.76	5.62	8.71	5.91	7.43	8.74
Return on Equity %	10.35	8.64	10.06	14.91	23.81	17.21	23.01	27.79
EBITDA Margin %	36.37	35.25	32.86	37.34	42.57	45.96	46.41	46.39
Net Margin %	10.05	11.67	10.91	14.43	20.82	13.10	15.78	15.48
PPE Turnover	1.25	0.82	0.81	0.80	0.81	0.88	0.95	1.09
Asset Turnover	0.44	0.30	0.34	0.39	0.42	0.45	0.47	0.56
Debt to Equity	0.50	0.43	0.48	0.52	0.42	0.56	0.53	0.51
Price Range	42.83-33.81	35.75-24.45	25.77-22.10	27.59-23.00	31.19-19.34	40.17-20.10	52.38-37.38	58.50-35.44
P/E Ratio	22.08-17.43	18.92-12.94	18.15-15.56	15.59-12.99	12.18-7.55	23.77-11.89	24.59-17.55	25.22-15.27
Average Yield %	3.74	4.61	5.38	4.95	5.77	3.48	2.37	2.19

Address: 175 E. Houston St., San Antonio, TX 78205-2233	**Web Site:** www.att.com	**Auditors:** Ernst & Young LLP
Telephone: 210-821-4105	**Officers:** Edward E. Whitacre Jr. - Chmn., C.E.O.	**Investor Contact:** 210-351-3990
Fax: 210-351-3553	William M. Daley - Pres.	**Transfer Agents:** EquiServe Trust Company, N.A., Jersey City, NJ

ATMOS ENERGY CORP.

Exchange	Symbol	Price	52Wk Range	Yield	P/E	Div Acheiver
NYS	ATO	$25.50 (3/31/2008)	33.11-25.09	5.10	14.25	20 Years

*7 Year Price Score 89.32 *NYSE Composite Index=100 *12 Month Price Score 99.78

TRADING VOLUME (thousand shares)

Interim Earnings (Per Share)

Qtr.	Dec	Mar	Jun	Sep
2004-05	0.79	1.11	0.06	(0.22)
2005-06	0.88	1.10	(0.22)	0.07
2006-07	0.10	1.20	(0.15)	(0.08)
2007-08	0.82	...	...	...

Interim Dividends (Per Share)

Amt	Decl	Ex	Rec	Pay
0.32Q	5/2/2007	5/23/2007	5/25/2007	6/11/2007
0.32Q	8/2/2007	8/23/2007	8/27/2007	9/10/2007
0.325Q	11/7/2007	11/21/2007	11/26/2007	12/10/2007
0.325Q	2/5/2008	2/21/2008	2/25/2008	3/10/2008

Indicated Div: $1.30 (Div. Reinv. Plan)

Valuation Analysis **Institutional Holding**

Forecast P/E	15.27	No of Institutions
	(1/10/2007)	212
Market Cap	$2.3 Billion	Shares
Book Value	2.0 Billion	53,593,440
Price/Book	1.13	% Held
Price/Sales	0.39	60.50

Business Summary: Gas Utilities (MIC: 7.4 SIC: 4924 NAIC: 486210)

Atmos Energy is engaged primarily in the natural gas utility business as well as other natural gas nonutility businesses. As of Sep 30 2007, Co. distributed natural gas through sales and transportation arrangements to approximately 3.2 million residential, commercial, public authority and industrial customers through its six regulated natural gas distribution divisions, which covered service areas in 12 states. Co.'s primary service areas are located in Colorado, Kansas, Kentucky, Louisiana, Mississippi, Tennessee and Texas. Co.'s nonregulated businesses operate in 22 states and include its natural gas marketing operations as well as its pipeline, storage and other operations.

Recent Developments: For the quarter ended Dec 31 2007, net income decreased 9.2% to US$73.8 million from US$81.3 million in the year-earlier quarter. Revenues were US$1.66 billion, up 3.4% from US$1.60 billion the year before. Operating income was US$158.5 million versus US$171.2 million in the prior-year quarter, a decrease of 7.4%. Direct operating expenses rose 5.0% to US$1.29 billion from US$1.23 billion in the comparable period the year before. Indirect operating expenses increased 3.3% to US$211.1 million from US$204.4 million in the equivalent prior-year period.

Prospects: Co.'s near-term outlook appears mixed. On one hand, Co. is seeing a decline in performance at its natural gas marketing segment due to a decrease in delivered gas margins, reflecting the effects of a less volatile market. However, Co. is seeing improved performance at its natural gas distribution segment due to an increase in rates at the Mid-Tex Division, as well as in its Kentucky, Louisiana and Tennessee service areas. For the fiscal year ending Sep 2008, Co. is reaffirming its earnings guidance of $1.95 to $2.05 per diluted share, assuming lower contribution from the natural gas marketing segment and the continued execution of its rate strategy in the natural gas distribution segment.

Financial Data

(US$ in Thousands)	3 Mos	09/30/2007	09/30/2006	09/30/2005	09/30/2004	09/30/2003	09/30/2002	09/30/2001
Earnings Per Share	1.79	1.92	1.82	1.72	1.58	1.54	1.45	1.47
Cash Flow Per Share	4.98	6.29	3.86	4.93	5.00	1.07	7.20	2.18
Tang Book Value Per Share	14.40	13.75	11.13	10.74	14.25	11.35	9.19	12.43
Dividends Per Share	1.285	1.280	1.260	1.240	1.220	1.200	1.180	1.160
Dividend Payout %	71.79	66.67	69.23	72.09	77.22	77.92	81.38	78.91
Income Statement								
Total Revenue	1,657,510	5,898,431	6,152,363	4,973,326	2,920,037	2,799,916	950,849	1,442,275
EBITDA	206,952	606,875	569,464	529,472	301,314	279,225	237,931	206,939
Depn & Amortn	48,536	...	...	...	...	...	...	...
Income Before Taxes	121,599	262,584	236,890	218,018	137,765	126,371	94,836	89,458
Income Taxes	47,796	94,092	89,153	82,233	51,538	46,910	35,180	33,368
Net Income	73,803	168,492	147,737	135,785	86,227	71,688	59,656	56,090
Average Shares	89,608	87,745	81,390	79,012	54,416	46,496	41,250	38,247
Balance Sheet								
Net PPE	3,888,126	3,836,836	3,629,156	3,374,367	1,722,521	1,515,989	1,300,320	1,335,398
Total Assets	6,399,763	5,896,917	5,719,547	5,653,527	2,869,883	2,518,508	1,980,221	2,036,180
Long-Term Obligations	2,124,915	2,126,315	2,180,362	2,183,104	861,311	863,918	670,463	692,399
Total Liabilities	4,367,280	3,931,163	4,071,449	4,051,105	1,736,424	1,660,991	1,406,986	1,452,316
Stockholders' Equity	2,032,483	1,965,754	1,648,098	1,602,422	1,133,459	857,517	573,235	583,864
Shares Outstanding	89,906	89,326	81,739	80,539	62,799	51,475	41,675	40,791
Statistical Record								
Return on Assets %	2.55	2.90	2.60	3.19	3.19	3.19	2.97	3.31
Return on Equity %	8.15	9.32	9.09	9.93	8.64	10.02	10.31	11.49
EBITDA Margin %	12.49	10.29	9.26	10.65	10.32	9.97	25.02	14.35
Net Margin %	4.45	2.86	2.40	2.73	2.95	2.56	6.27	3.89
PPE Turnover	1.58	1.58	1.76	1.95	1.80	1.99	0.72	1.24
Asset Turnover	0.94	1.02	1.08	1.17	1.08	1.24	0.47	0.85
Debt to Equity	1.05	1.08	1.32	1.36	0.76	1.01	1.17	1.19
Price Range	33.11-26.11	33.11-26.47	29.11-25.79	29.76-24.85	26.86-23.68	25.45-20.70	24.46-18.37	26.25-19.31
P/E Ratio	18.50-14.59	17.24-13.79	15.99-14.17	17.30-14.45	17.00-14.99	16.53-13.44	16.87-12.67	17.86-13.14
Average Yield %	4.30	4.16	4.66	4.49	4.87	5.21	5.37	5.08

Address: Three Lincoln Centre, Suite 1800, 5430 LBJ Freeway, Dallas, TX 75240
Telephone: 972-934-9227
Fax: 972-855-3075

Web Site: www.atmosenergy.com
Officers: Robert W. Best - Chmn., Pres., C.E.O. John P. Reddy - Sr. V.P., C.F.O.

Auditors: Ernst & Young LLP
Transfer Agents: EquiServe Trust Company, Providence, RI

ATWOOD OCEANICS, INC.

Exchange	Symbol	Price	52Wk Range	Yield	P/E
NYS	ATW	$91.72 (3/31/2008)	104.77-58.17	N/A	18.72

*7 Year Price Score 185.44 *NYSE Composite Index=100 *12 Month Price Score 123.51

Interim Earnings (Per Share)

Qtr.	Dec	Mar	Jun	Sep
2004-05	0.28	0.15	0.19	0.22
2005-06	0.47	0.50	1.04	0.74
2006-07	0.67	1.01	1.00	1.69
2007-08	1.20	...	...	...

Interim Dividends (Per Share)

No Dividends Paid

Valuation Analysis — **Institutional Holding**

Forecast P/E	5.27	No of Institutions
	(1/10/2007)	146
Market Cap	$2.9 Billion	Shares
Book Value	654.8 Million	27,242,016
Price/Book	4.44	% Held
Price/Sales	6.84	87.61

TRADING VOLUME (thousand shares)

Business Summary: Oil and Gas (MIC: 14.2 SIC: 1381 NAIC: 213111)

Atwood Oceanics is engaged in the international offshore drilling and completion of exploratory and developmental oil and gas wells and related support, management and consulting services. Co.'s worldwide operations include eight offshore mobile drilling units located in six regions of the world offshore Southeast Asia, offshore Africa, offshore India, offshore Australia, the Black Sea and the U.S. Gulf of Mexico. The submersible RICHMOND is Co.'s only drilling unit working in U.S. waters. Co. supports its operations from its Houston headquarters and offices located in Vietnam, Australia, Malaysia, Egypt, Indonesia, Singapore and the United Kingdom.

Recent Developments: For the quarter ended Dec 31 2007, net income increased 82.8% to US$38.5 million from US$21.1 million in the year-earlier quarter. Revenues were US$111.0 million, up 25.1% from US$88.8 million the year before. Operating income was US$43.2 million versus US$24.5 million in the prior-year quarter, an increase of 76.1%. Direct operating expenses rose 4.0% to US$51.1 million from US$49.1 million in the comparable period the year before. Indirect operating expenses increased 10.8% to US$16.8 million from US$15.2 million in the equivalent prior-year period.

Prospects: On Jan 3 2008, Co. announced that its Atwood Oceanics Pacific Limited (AOPL) subsidiary has been awarded a contract by Chevron Australia Pty. Ltd. to provide a Mobile Offshore Semisubmersible Drilling Unit for a firm three year period. Thus, AOPL has executed a construction contract with Jurong Shipyard Pte. Ltd. to construct a Friede & Goldman ExD Millennium Semisubmersible Drilling Unit to provide the drilling rig, with delivery expected in 2011. Meanwhile, Co. estimates that its total capital expenditures for the last three quarters of fiscal year ending Sep 2008 to be $225.0 million, partially for the construction of its ATWOOD AURORA jack-up and the new semisubmersible drilling unit.

Financial Data

(US$ in Thousands)	3 Mos	09/30/2007	09/30/2006	09/30/2005	09/30/2004	09/30/2003	09/30/2002	09/30/2001
Earnings Per Share	4.90	4.37	2.74	0.83	0.27	(0.46)	1.01	0.98
Cash Flow Per Share	5.67	6.09	2.76	1.35	0.92	0.49	1.53	2.25
Tang Book Value Per Share	20.66	19.44	14.78	11.80	9.79	9.51	9.97	8.96
Income Statement								
Total Revenue	111,048	403,037	276,625	176,156	163,454	144,765	149,157	147,541
EBITDA	49,521	167,648	122,953	61,098	54,500	34,694	64,752	69,746
Depn & Amortn	6,326	...	...	...	...	...	...	...
Income Before Taxes	43,111	159,959	91,836	25,608	12,402	1,636	38,777	41,121
Income Taxes	4,562	20,935	5,714	(403)	4,815	14,438	10,492	13,775
Net Income	38,549	139,024	86,122	26,011	7,587	(12,802)	28,285	27,346
Average Shares	32,162	31,814	31,442	31,220	28,064	27,692	27,988	27,956
Balance Sheet								
Current Assets	272,052	216,179	147,673	92,053	92,966	76,012	71,813	45,721
Total Assets	796,879	717,724	593,829	495,694	498,936	522,674	444,530	353,878
Current Liabilities	51,311	57,630	61,365	56,159	60,053	49,949	24,416	20,664
Long-Term Obligations	50,000	...	28,000	54,000	145,000	181,000	115,000	60,000
Total Liabilities	142,053	101,869	134,935	133,557	227,347	259,207	168,397	106,242
Stockholders' Equity	654,826	615,855	458,894	362,137	271,589	263,467	276,133	247,636
Shares Outstanding	31,702	31,675	31,046	30,682	27,746	27,702	27,690	27,646
Statistical Record								
Return on Assets %	22.08	21.20	15.81	5.23	1.48	N.M.	7.09	8.20
Return on Equity %	27.54	25.87	20.98	8.21	2.83	N.M.	10.80	11.74
EBITDA Margin %	44.59	41.60	44.45	34.68	33.34	23.97	43.41	47.27
Net Margin %	34.71	34.49	31.13	14.77	4.64	N.M.	18.96	18.53
Asset Turnover	0.60	0.61	0.51	0.35	0.32	0.30	0.37	0.44
Current Ratio	5.30	3.75	2.41	1.64	1.55	1.52	2.94	2.21
Debt to Equity	0.08	...	0.06	0.15	0.53	0.69	0.42	0.24
Price Range	101.80-43.97	80.57-42.02	58.08-33.30	42.69-22.79	24.07-11.77	16.35-11.73	25.16-12.52	24.95-12.10
P/E Ratio	20.78-8.97	18.44-9.62	21.20-12.15	51.43-27.46	89.15-43.57	...	24.91-12.40	25.46-12.35

Address: 15835 Park Ten Place Drive, Houston, TX 77084 Telephone: 281-749-7800	Web Site: www.atwd.com Officers: John R. Irwin - Pres., C.E.O. James M. Holland - Sr. V.P., C.F.O., Sec.	Auditors: PricewaterhouseCoopers LLP Investor Contact: 713-492-2929 Transfer Agents: Continental Stock Transfer & Trust Company, New York, NY

AUTOLIV INC.

Exchange	Symbol	Price	52Wk Range	Yield	P/E
NYS	ALV	$50.20 (3/31/2008)	64.65-45.75	3.11	13.64

*7 Year Price Score 113.66 *NYSE Composite Index=100   *12 Month Price Score 96.77

Interim Earnings (Per Share)

Qtr.	Mar	Jun	Sep	Dec
2003	0.54	0.75	0.54	0.98
2004	0.80	0.94	0.72	1.00
2005	0.84	0.94	0.66	0.81
2006	1.13	1.00	1.48	1.28
2007	0.91	0.72	0.81	1.23

Interim Dividends (Per Share)

Amt	Decl	Ex	Rec	Pay
0.39Q	5/3/2007	8/7/2007	8/9/2007	9/6/2007
0.39Q	8/16/2007	11/6/2007	11/8/2007	12/6/2007
0.39Q	12/19/2007	2/5/2008	2/7/2008	3/6/2008
0.39Q	2/19/2008	5/6/2008	5/8/2008	6/5/2008

Indicated Div: $1.56

Valuation Analysis

		Institutional Holding	
Forecast P/E	12.24	No of Institutions	
	(1/10/2007)	250	
Market Cap	$3.7 Billion	Shares	
Book Value	2.3 Billion	60,272,280	
Price/Book	1.58	% Held	
Price/Sales	0.55	75.09	

TRADING VOLUME (thousand shares)

Business Summary: Automotive (MIC: 15.1 SIC: 3714 NAIC: 336399)

Autoliv is a supplier of automotive occupant safety restraint systems with a range of product offerings, including modules and components for passenger and driver-side airbags, side-impact airbag protection systems, seatbelts, steering wheels, safety seats and other safety systems and products. Co. has two operating segments: airbags/seatbelt products; and electronics/sensing products. As of Dec 31 2007, including joint venture operations, Co. had approximately 80 wholly or partially owned production facilities located in 29 countries, consisting of both component factories and assembly factories. Co.'s key markets are located throughout Europe, the U.S., Japan and Asia-Pacific.

Recent Developments: For the year ended Dec 31 2007, net income decreased 28.4% to US$287.9 million from US$402.3 million in the prior year. Revenues were US$6.77 billion, up 9.4% from US$6.19 billion the year before. Operating income was US$502.0 million versus US$520.0 million in the prior year, a decrease of 3.5%. Direct operating expenses rose 10.5% to US$5.44 billion from US$4.92 billion in the comparable period the year before. Indirect operating expenses increased 11.2% to US$828.6 million from US$745.2 million in the equivalent prior-year period.

Prospects: In 2008, Co. expects to ramp up production in its new Chinese manufacturing facilities, which should favorably affect its margins as capacity utilization rises. Co. also expects to benefit from higher vehicle production in Asia Pacific and Eastern Europe, and higher installation rates of side curtain airbags in North America and Europe. Also, Co. expects to offset the negative effects of an anticipated 5.0% decline in light vehicle production in North America and Western Europe through strong side curtain sales, and the step-up in sales of active seatbelts and seatbelt pretensioners. For 2008, Co. expects sales growth of 7.0%, and operating margin to improve to a level of 8.0% to 8.5%.

Financial Data

(US$ In Thousands)	12/31/2007	12/31/2006	12/31/2005	12/31/2004	12/31/2003	12/31/2002	12/31/2001	12/31/2000
Earnings Per Share	3.68	4.88	3.26	3.46	2.81	1.84	0.49	1.67
Cash Flow Per Share	10.02	6.82	5.37	7.20	5.56	5.19	2.72	2.63
Tang Book Value Per Share	7.99	9.07	7.61	10.08	7.29	3.70	1.94	1.75
Dividends Per Share	1.540	1.360	1.170	0.770	0.540	0.440	0.440	0.440
Dividend Payout %	41.85	27.87	35.89	22.25	19.22	23.91	89.80	26.35
Income Statement								
Total Revenue	6,769,000	6,118,000	6,204,900	6,143,900	5,300,800	4,443,400	3,991,000	4,116,100
EBITDA	829,200	824,000	828,700	821,000	717,100	583,400	483,600	612,900
Income Before Taxes	446,200	481,400	482,000	484,500	397,000	286,700	116,800	290,600
Income Taxes	150,300	58,900	173,200	149,000	120,200	94,600	59,800	117,200
Net Income	287,900	402,300	292,600	326,300	268,400	180,500	47,900	168,700
Average Shares	78,300	82,500	89,700	94,200	95,400	98,000	98,000	100,900
Balance Sheet								
Current Assets	2,095,200	2,098,400	2,162,500	2,190,800	1,839,400	1,533,800	1,363,600	1,310,000
Total Assets	5,303,400	5,110,800	5,065,200	5,354,100	4,894,300	4,294,800	4,004,300	4,067,800
Current Liabilities	1,663,300	1,531,600	1,764,300	1,799,300	1,366,900	1,189,800	914,400	1,255,900
Long-Term Obligations	1,040,300	887,700	757,100	667,100	846,200	842,700	1,037,100	737,400
Total Liabilities	2,904,100	2,622,800	2,683,400	2,717,700	2,492,300	2,248,100	2,129,000	2,157,700
Stockholders' Equity	2,349,100	2,402,900	2,316,100	2,636,400	2,402,000	2,046,700	1,875,300	1,910,100
Shares Outstanding	73,800	80,100	83,700	92,000	94,900	96,300	97,900	97,800
Statistical Record								
Return on Assets %	5.53	7.91	5.62	6.35	5.84	4.35	1.19	4.36
Return on Equity %	12.12	17.05	11.82	12.92	12.07	9.20	2.53	8.76
EBITDA Margin %	12.25	13.47	13.36	13.36	13.53	13.13	12.12	14.89
Net Margin %	4.25	6.58	4.72	5.31	5.06	4.06	1.20	4.10
Asset Turnover	1.30	1.20	1.19	1.20	1.15	1.07	0.99	1.06
Current Ratio	1.26	1.37	1.23	1.22	1.35	1.31	1.49	1.07
Debt to Equity	0.44	0.37	0.33	0.25	0.35	0.41	0.55	0.39
Price Range	64.65-52.67	60.72-47.53	51.80-41.10	48.80-37.65	38.24-18.79	25.65-17.20	21.42-13.90	31.44-14.94
P/E Ratio	17.57-14.31	12.44-9.74	15.89-12.61	14.10-10.88	13.61-6.69	13.94-9.35	43.71-28.37	18.82-8.94
Average Yield %	2.63	2.47	2.52	1.82	1.98	2.00	2.46	1.79

Address: World Trade Center, Klarabergsviadukten 70, Section E, Stockholm, SE-107 24	Web Site: www.autoliv.com	Auditors: Ernst & Young AB
Telephone: 858-720-600	Officers: S. Jay Stewart - Chmn. Lars Westerberg - Pres., C.E.O.	Transfer Agents: EquiServe Trust Company N.A., Providence, RI
Fax: 841-170-25		

AUTOMATIC DATA PROCESSING INC.

Exchange	Symbol	Price	52Wk Range	Yield	P/E	Div Acheiver
NYS	ADP	$42.39 (3/31/2008)	50.11-37.90	2.74	19.72	32 Years

*7 Year Price Score 89.25   *NYSE Composite Index=100   ***12 Month Price Score 95.01**

Interim Earnings (Per Share)

Qtr.	Sep	Dec	Mar	Jun
2004-05	0.35	0.42	0.57	0.44
2005-06	0.38	0.45	0.64	1.22
2006-07	0.46	0.54	0.70	0.35
2007-08	0.55	0.55	...	...

Interim Dividends (Per Share)

Amt	Decl	Ex	Rec	Pay
0.23Q	4/25/2007	6/13/2007	6/15/2007	7/1/2007
0.23Q	8/9/2007	9/12/2007	9/14/2007	10/1/2007
0.29Q	11/13/2007	12/12/2007	12/14/2007	1/1/2008
0.29Q	1/31/2008	3/12/2008	3/14/2008	4/1/2008

Indicated Div: $1.16

Valuation Analysis   **Institutional Holding**

Forecast P/E	16.77	No of Institutions
	(1/10/2007)	830
Market Cap	$22.1 Billion	Shares
Book Value	5.2 Billion	397,559,040
Price/Book	4.27	% Held
Price/Sales	2.67	72.25

Business Summary: IT & Technology (MIC: 10.2 SIC: 7374 NAIC: 518210)

Automatic Data Processing is a provider of business outsourcing services and integrated computing applications. Co.'s Employer Services segment provides a range of human resource information, payroll processing, tax and benefits administration products and services, including traditional and Web-based outsourcing applications. Co.'s Professional Employer Organization Services segment provides employment administration outsourcing services through a co-employment relationship. Co.'s Dealer Services segment provides integrated dealer management systems and business applications to automotive, heavy truck, and powersports vehicle retailers in the U.S., Canada, South Africa, Asia and Europe.

Recent Developments: For the quarter ended Dec 31 2007, income from continuing operations increased 17.6% to US$291.6 million from US$248.0 million in the year-earlier quarter. Net income decreased 2.2% to US$291.2 million from US$297.7 million in the year-earlier quarter. Revenues were US$2.15 billion, up 14.7% from US$1.87 billion the year before. Direct operating expenses rose 19.3% to US$979.8 million from US$821.5 million in the comparable period the year before. Indirect operating expenses increased 10.6% to US$188.4 million from US$170.3 million in the equivalent prior-year period.

Prospects: For the fiscal year ending June 30 2008, Co. continues to anticipate revenue growth in the range of 12.0% to 13.0%. In addition, Co. is projecting revenue growth of about 10.0% in its Employer Services segment, while top-line improvement in its Professional Employer Organization (PEO) Services segment is estimated to range from 19.0% to 20.0%. Also, Co. is targeting high single-digit to low double-digit new business sales growth worldwide for its Employer Services and PEO Services segments. Lastly, Co. expects to attain the high-end of its 18.0% to 21.0% forecasted growth in diluted earnings per share from continuing operations, despite the lower interest rates and economic volatility.

Financial Data

(US$ in Thousands)	6 Mos	3 Mos	06/30/2007	06/30/2006	06/30/2005	06/30/2004	06/30/2003	06/30/2002
Earnings Per Share	2.15	2.14	2.04	2.68	1.79	1.56	1.68	1.75
Cash Flow Per Share	2.67	2.66	2.36	3.15	2.46	2.35	2.61	2.48
Tang Book Value Per Share	4.00	3.68	3.93	5.21	4.55	4.23	4.57	5.25
Dividends Per Share	0.980	0.920	0.875	0.710	0.605	0.540	0.475	0.448
Dividend Payout %	45.58	42.99	42.89	26.49	33.80	34.62	28.27	25.57
Income Statement								
Total Revenue	4,142,100	1,992,000	7,800,000	8,881,500	8,499,100	7,754,942	7,147,017	7,004,263
EBITDA	980,700	450,300	1,787,800	2,037,900	2,039,900	1,867,276	1,822,307	1,968,539
Depn & Amortn	185,600	83,400	...	...	...	...	...	...
Income Before Taxes	822,100	381,500	1,623,500	1,743,000	1,677,900	1,494,530	1,645,200	1,786,970
Income Taxes	290,100	141,100	602,300	670,600	622,500	558,960	627,050	686,200
Net Income	588,500	297,400	1,138,700	1,554,000	1,055,400	935,570	1,018,150	1,100,770
Average Shares	530,400	536,200	557,900	580,300	590,000	598,749	605,917	630,579
Balance Sheet								
Current Assets	3,091,200	3,078,300	3,364,200	4,760,100	4,441,100	2,761,589	3,675,501	2,817,257
Total Assets	27,545,700	25,703,300	26,648,900	27,490,100	27,615,400	21,120,559	19,833,671	18,276,522
Current Liabilities	1,752,900	1,958,100	1,790,800	2,592,700	2,800,700	1,768,424	1,998,783	1,411,102
Long-Term Obligations	36,700	43,500	43,500	74,300	75,800	76,200	84,674	90,648
Total Liabilities	22,368,100	20,705,400	21,501,000	21,478,500	21,831,600	15,702,889	14,462,198	13,162,317
Stockholders' Equity	5,177,600	4,997,900	5,147,900	6,011,600	5,783,800	5,417,670	5,371,473	5,114,205
Shares Outstanding	521,400	526,100	535,800	561,400	580,200	587,115	594,839	616,317
Statistical Record								
Return on Assets %	3.96	4.54	4.21	5.64	4.33	4.56	5.34	6.09
Return on Equity %	21.15	21.74	20.41	26.35	18.84	17.30	19.42	22.43
EBITDA Margin %	23.68	22.61	22.92	22.95	24.00	24.08	25.50	28.10
Net Margin %	14.21	14.93	14.60	17.50	12.42	12.06	14.25	15.72
Asset Turnover	0.28	0.33	0.29	0.32	0.35	0.38	0.38	0.39
Current Ratio	1.76	1.57	1.88	1.84	1.59	1.56	1.84	2.00
Debt to Equity	0.01	0.01	0.01	0.01	0.01	0.01	0.02	0.02
Price Range	50.11-42.33	50.11-41.76	50.11-38.29	43.07-37.38	41.52-34.92	42.07-30.41	40.15-24.48	54.13-38.71
P/E Ratio	23.31-19.69	23.42-19.51	24.56-18.77	16.07-13.95	23.20-19.51	26.97-19.50	23.90-14.57	30.93-22.12
Average Yield %	2.12	2.03	1.99	1.76	1.57	1.48	1.45	0.94

Address: One ADP Boulevard,	**Web Site:** www.adp.com	**Auditors:** Deloitte & Touche LLP
Roseland, NJ 07068	**Officers:** Arthur F. Weinbach - Chmn., C.E.O. Gary	**Transfer Agents:** Mellon Investor
Telephone: 973-974-5000	C. Butler - Pres., C.O.O.	Services, Ridgefield Park, NJ
Fax: 973-974-5390		

AUTONATION, INC.

Exchange	Symbol	Price	52Wk Range	Yield	P/E
NYS	AN	$14.97 (3/31/2008)	22.81-12.30	N/A	10.77

*7 Year Price Score 86.61 *NYSE Composite Index=100 *12 Month Price Score 89.93

Interim Earnings (Per Share)

Qtr.	Mar	Jun	Sep	Dec
2003	0.63	0.37	0.38	0.28
2004	0.32	0.34	0.34	0.60
2005	0.36	0.73	0.48	0.28
2006	0.33	0.32	0.38	0.35
2007	0.37	0.37	0.37	0.29

Interim Dividends (Per Share)

No Dividends Paid

Valuation Analysis — **Institutional Holding**

Forecast P/E	11.05	No of Institutions	
	(1/10/2007)	225	
Market Cap	$2.7 Billion	Shares	
Book Value	3.5 Billion	181,177,904	
Price/Book	0.78	% Held	
Price/Sales	0.15	86.66	

TRADING VOLUME (thousand shares)

Business Summary: Retail - Automotive (MIC: 5.7 SIC: 5599 NAIC: 441229)

AutoNation, through its subsidiaries, is engaged in automotive retailing. As of Dec 31 2007, Co. owned and operated 322 new vehicle franchises from 244 stores located in major metropolitan markets, predominantly in the Sunbelt region of the U.S. Co. provides a range of automotive products and services, including new vehicles, used vehicles, vehicle maintenance and repair services, vehicle parts, extended service contracts, vehicle protection products and other aftermarket products. Co. also arranges financing for vehicle purchases through third-party finance sources.

Recent Developments: For the year ended Dec 31 2007, income from continuing operations decreased 12.9% to US$288.0 million from US$330.8 million a year earlier. Net income decreased 12.1% to US$278.7 million from US$316.9 million in the prior year. Revenues were US$17.69 billion, down 5.0% from US$18.63 billion the year before. Operating income was US$704.8 million versus US$791.7 million in the prior year, a decrease of 11.0%. Direct operating expenses declined 5.1% to US$14.85 billion from US$15.64 billion in the comparable period the year before. Indirect operating expenses decreased 2.4% to US$2.14 billion from US$2.19 billion in the equivalent prior year period.

Prospects: Looking ahead, Co. foresees that new vehicle retail market will continue to be challenging, primarily in California and Florida. Specifically, Co. anticipates that in 2008, the U.S. new vehicle industry sales will decline to the mid-15.0 million unit level from 16.1 million units in 2007. Nevertheless, Co. believes that the recent interest rates reduction from Federal Reserve could positively affect the automotive retail outlook in the second half of 2008. Meanwhile, Co. is projecting capital expenditures for the full year of 2008 to be approximately $110.0 million, excluding any acquisition-related spending, land purchased for future sites, or lease buy-outs, net of asset sales.

Financial Data
(US$ in Thousands)

	12/31/2007	12/31/2006	12/31/2005	12/31/2004	12/31/2003	12/31/2002	12/31/2001	12/31/2000
Earnings Per Share	1.39	1.38	1.85	1.59	1.67	1.19	0.69	0.91
Cash Flow Per Share	1.04	1.33	2.21	1.65	0.94	1.71	1.62	0.78
Tang Book Value Per Share	2.20	2.88	6.53	4.87	3.91	2.80	2.99	2.65
Income Statement								
Total Revenue	17,691,500	18,988,600	19,253,400	19,424,700	19,381,100	19,478,500	19,989,300	20,609,600
EBITDA	799,300	887,800	895,200	851,500	801,900	802,500	590,300	892,000
Income Before Taxes	459,300	542,100	622,900	606,600	591,000	618,000	400,800	525,000
Income Taxes	171,300	210,700	227,400	210,200	84,900	236,400	155,800	196,900
Net Income	278,700	316,900	496,500	433,600	479,200	381,600	232,300	329,900
Average Shares	200,000	229,300	268,000	272,500	287,000	321,500	335,200	361,400
Balance Sheet								
Current Assets	3,238,400	3,385,800	3,880,400	3,677,700	3,990,300	3,629,100	3,152,500	4,176,200
Total Assets	8,479,600	8,607,000	8,824,500	8,698,900	8,823,100	8,584,800	8,065,400	8,830,000
Current Liabilities	2,901,800	3,030,500	3,412,100	3,411,200	3,809,500	2,980,700	2,578,100	3,141,300
Long-Term Obligations	1,751,900	1,557,900	484,400	797,700	808,500	642,700	647,300	850,400
Total Liabilities	5,006,100	4,894,300	4,155,000	4,435,800	4,873,400	4,674,600	4,237,500	4,987,500
Stockholders' Equity	3,473,500	3,712,700	4,669,500	4,263,100	3,949,700	3,910,200	3,827,900	3,842,500
Shares Outstanding	180,356	206,752	262,232	264,262	269,713	333,505	321,713	348,085
Statistical Record								
Return on Assets %	3.26	3.64	5.67	4.94	5.51	4.58	2.75	3.57
Return on Equity %	7.76	7.56	11.12	10.53	12.19	9.86	6.06	7.79
EBITDA Margin %	4.52	4.68	4.65	4.38	4.14	4.12	2.95	4.33
Net Margin %	1.58	1.67	2.58	2.23	2.47	1.96	1.16	1.60
Asset Turnover	2.07	2.18	2.20	2.21	2.23	2.34	2.37	2.23
Current Ratio	1.12	1.12	1.14	1.08	1.05	1.22	1.22	1.33
Debt to Equity	0.50	0.42	0.10	0.19	0.20	0.16	0.17	0.22
Price Range	23.08-14.94	22.85-18.99	22.60-17.92	19.21-15.20	19.07-11.67	18.45-9.08	12.69-5.44	9.26-5.00
P/E Ratio	16.60-10.75	16.56-13.76	12.22-9.69	12.08-9.56	11.42-6.99	15.50-7.63	18.39-7.88	10.18-5.49

Address: 110 S.E. 6th Street, Ft. Lauderdale, FL 33301
Telephone: 954-769-6000
Fax: 954-779-3884

Web Site: www.autonation.com
Officers: Michael J. Jackson - Chmn., C.E.O. Michael E. Maroone - Pres., C.O.O.

Auditors: KPMG LLP
Transfer Agents: Computershare Investor Services, LLC, Chicago, IL

AUTOZONE, INC.

Exchange	Symbol	Price	52Wk Range	Yield	P/E
NYS	AZO	$113.83 (3/31/2008)	140.10-103.43	N/A	12.54

*7 Year Price Score 111.34 ***NYSE Composite Index=100** ***12 Month Price Score 103.22**

TRADING VOLUME (thousand shares)

Interim Earnings (Per Share)

Qtr.	Nov	Feb	Apr	Aug
2005			7.18	
2005-06	1.48	1.25	1.89	2.88
2006-07	1.73	1.45	2.17	3.20
Qtr.	Nov	Jan	Apr	Aug
2007-08	2.02	1.67	...	...

Interim Dividends (Per Share)

No Dividends Paid

Valuation Analysis

		Institutional Holding	
Forecast P/E	12.54	No of Institutions	
	(1/10/2007)	311	
Market Cap	$7.2 Billion	Shares	
Book Value	282.2 Million	67,898,016	
Price/Book	25.50	% Held	
Price/Sales	1.14	97.04	

Business Summary: Retail - Automotive (MIC: 5.7 SIC: 5531 NAIC: 441310)

AutoZone is a retailer of automotive parts and accessories, with most of its sales to do-it-yourself customers. Via its website, Co. sells diagnostic and repair information, auto and light truck parts, and accessories. As of Aug 25 2007, Co. operated 3,933 stores in the U.S. and Puerto Rico, and 123 in Mexico. Each store carries products for cars, sport utility vehicles, vans and light trucks, including new and remanufactured automotive hard parts, maintenance items, accessories and non-automotive products. Co. also has a commercial sales program that provides credit and prompt delivery of parts and other products to local, regional and national repair garages, dealers and service stations.

Recent Developments: For the quarter ended Feb 9 2008, net income increased 3.6% to US$106.7 million from US$103.0 million in the year-earlier quarter. Revenues were US$1.34 billion, up 3.0% from US$1.30 billion the year before. Operating income was US$196.9 million versus US$188.9 million in the prior-year quarter, an increase of 4.2%. Direct operating expenses rose 1.6% to US$671.4 million from US$661.1 million in the comparable period the year before. Indirect operating expenses increased 4.6% to US$470.9 million from US$450.3 million in the equivalent prior-year period.

Prospects: Co.'s near term outlook appears favourable, reflecting growth in its top- and bottom-line results. Further, Co. is seeing an increase in its gross margin primarily due to its ongoing category management efforts. Separately, on Mar 7 2008, Co. announced plans to open a new distribution center in Hazleton, PA. in order to enhance its supply chain capabilities. Further, the center is expected to distribute parts and products to Co.'s stores in surrounding states. The center should complete in the summer of 2008. In addition to its investment in the new center, for the fiscal year ending Aug 2008, Co. expects to invest in its new store development program and enhancements to existing stores.

Financial Data

(US$ in Thousands)	6 Mos	3 Mos	08/25/2007	08/26/2006	08/27/2005	08/28/2004	08/30/2003	08/31/2002
Earnings Per Share	9.08	8.86	8.53	7.50	7.18	6.56	5.34	4.00
Cash Flow Per Share	13.67	13.96	12.26	10.97	8.28	7.53	7.38	6.96
Tang Book Value Per Share	N.M.	N.M.	1.52	2.35	1.15	N.M.	0.90	3.87
Income Statement								
Total Revenue	2,794,899	1,455,655	6,169,804	5,948,355	5,710,882	5,637,025	5,457,123	5,325,510
EBITDA	513,638	277,482	1,216,396	1,150,949	1,113,604	1,109,827	1,027,545	889,263
Depn & Amortn	79,377	40,107	...	...	...	...	...	...
Income Before Taxes	377,611	209,313	936,150	902,036	873,221	905,902	833,007	691,148
Income Taxes	138,390	76,797	340,478	332,761	302,202	339,700	315,403	263,000
Net Income	239,221	132,516	595,672	569,275	571,019	566,202	517,604	428,148
Average Shares	63,740	65,444	69,844	75,859	79,508	86,350	96,963	107,111
Balance Sheet								
Current Assets	2,356,644	2,319,737	2,270,455	2,118,927	1,929,459	1,755,757	1,584,994	1,450,128
Total Assets	4,938,397	4,874,217	4,804,709	4,526,306	4,245,257	3,912,565	3,680,466	3,477,791
Current Liabilities	2,325,222	2,319,270	2,285,895	2,054,568	1,811,159	1,818,115	1,675,566	1,533,571
Long-Term Obligations	2,095,000	2,161,070	1,935,618	1,857,157	1,861,850	1,869,250	1,546,845	1,194,517
Total Liabilities	4,656,164	4,703,164	4,401,509	4,056,778	3,854,250	3,741,172	3,306,708	2,788,664
Stockholders' Equity	282,233	171,053	403,200	469,528	391,007	171,393	373,758	689,127
Shares Outstanding	63,220	63,178	65,960	71,082	76,539	79,628	88,708	99,268
Statistical Record								
Return on Assets %	12.71	12.77	12.80	13.02	14.04	14.95	14.50	12.19
Return on Equity %	147.54	170.91	136.88	132.67	203.62	208.29	97.66	54.16
EBITDA Margin %	18.38	19.06	19.72	19.35	19.50	19.69	18.83	16.70
Net Margin %	8.56	9.10	9.65	9.57	10.00	10.04	9.48	8.04
Asset Turnover	1.31	1.32	1.33	1.36	1.40	1.49	1.53	1.52
Current Ratio	1.01	1.00	0.99	1.03	1.07	0.97	0.95	0.95
Debt to Equity	7.42	12.63	4.80	3.96	4.76	10.91	4.14	1.73
Price Range	140.10-103.43	140.10-108.36	140.10-88.15	101.06-77.76	103.80-73.76	103.53-72.25	91.80-58.61	82.95-38.49
P/E Ratio	15.43-11.39	15.81-12.23	16.42-10.33	13.47-10.37	14.46-10.27	15.78-11.01	17.19-10.98	20.74-9.62

Address: 123 South Front Street, Memphis, TN 38103-3607 Telephone: 901-495-6500 Fax: 901-495-8300	Web Site: www.autozone.com Officers: J.R. Pitt Hyde III - Chmn. William C. Rhodes III - Pres., C.E.O.	Auditors: Ernst & Young LLP Transfer Agents: Computershare Investor Services

AVALONBAY COMMUNITIES, INC.

Exchange	Symbol	Price	52Wk Range	Yield	P/E
NYS	AVB	$96.52 (3/31/2008)	133.00-83.18	3.70	22.04

*7 Year Price Score 119.51 *NYSE Composite Index=100 *12 Month Price Score 93.61

Interim Earnings (Per Share)

Qtr.	Mar	Jun	Sep	Dec
2003	0.49	1.08	0.79	1.38
2004	0.32	0.46	0.60	1.53
2005	0.92	0.74	1.30	1.26
2006	1.49	0.90	0.57	0.98
2007	0.56	0.61	1.58	1.64

Interim Dividends (Per Share)

Amt	Decl	Ex	Rec	Pay
0.85Q	6/14/2007	6/27/2007	6/29/2007	7/16/2007
0.85Q	9/12/2007	9/26/2007	9/28/2007	10/15/2007
0.85Q	12/14/2007	12/27/2007	12/31/2007	1/15/2008
0.892Q	2/5/2008	3/28/2008	4/1/2008	4/16/2008

Indicated Div: $3.57

Valuation Analysis

		Institutional Holding	
Forecast P/E	56.57	No of Institutions	
	(1/10/2007)	272	
Market Cap	$7.5 Billion	Shares	
Book Value	3.0 Billion	72,169,184	
Price/Book	2.47	% Held	
Price/Sales	9.18	90.96	

Business Summary: Property, Real Estate & Development (MIC: 8.3 SIC: 6798 NAIC: 525930)

AvalonBay Communities is a real estate investment trust that is engaged in the development, redevelopment, acquisition, ownership and operation of multifamily communities in high barrier-to-entry markets of the U.S. Co.'s markets are located in the Northeast, Mid-Atlantic, Midwest, Pacific Northwest, and Northern and Southern California regions of the U.S. Co.'s real estate investments consist primarily of current operating apartment communities, communities in various stages of development and Development Rights. Co. has three reportable segments: Established Communities, Other Stabilized Communities and Development/Redevelopment Communities.

Recent Developments: For the year ended Dec 31 2007, income from continuing operations increased 51.5% to US$247.7 million from US$163.5 million a year earlier. Net income increased 34.4% to US$358.2 million from US$266.5 million in the prior year. Revenues were US$812.7 million, up 12.7% from US$721.4 million the year before.

Prospects: For full-year 2008, Co. expects earnings per share (EPS) to be in the range of $6.50 to $8.50. In addition, Co. expects funds from operations (FFO) per share to increase to a range of $4.90 to $5.20 compared with $4.61 for the year prior, resulting in an increase in FFO per share of approximately 9.5% at the mid-point of the range. Co. expects the increase in FFO per share to be driven mainly by growth in net operating income (NOI) from its Established Communities and other stabilized communities and an increase in NOI from its development and redevelopment. Separately, for the first quarter of 2008, Co. expects EPS of $0.58 to $0.62 with FFO per share to range from $1.23 to $1.27.

Financial Data
(US$ in Thousands)

	12/31/2007	12/31/2006	12/31/2005	12/31/2004	12/31/2003	12/31/2002	12/31/2001	12/31/2000
Earnings Per Share	4.38	3.57	4.21	2.92	3.73	2.23	3.12	2.53
Cash Flow Per Share	5.79	4.75	4.20	3.84	3.50	4.48	4.55	4.43
Tang Book Value Per Share	39.14	35.24	34.50	32.86	32.58	32.18	33.68	36.35
Dividends Per Share	3.400	3.120	2.840	2.800	2.800	2.800	2.560	2.240
Dividend Payout %	77.63	87.39	67.46	95.89	75.07	125.56	82.05	88.54
Income Statement								
Property Income	...	...	...	...	...	630,502	637,379	571,943
Non-Property Income	812,741	737,300	670,680	648,454	609,651	8,464	4,278	1,452
Total Revenue	812,741	737,300	670,680	648,454	609,651	638,966	641,657	573,395
Interest Expense	97,545	111,046	127,099	131,314	134,911	121,380	103,203	83,609
Net Income	358,160	278,399	322,378	219,745	271,525	173,618	248,997	210,604
Average Shares	70,856	75,586	74,769	73,354	70,203	70,674	69,781	68,140
Balance Sheet								
Total Assets	6,736,484	5,813,186	5,165,060	5,068,281	4,909,582	4,950,835	4,664,289	4,397,225
Long-Term Obligations	3,208,202	2,825,586	2,366,564	2,442,291	2,337,817	2,471,163	2,082,769	1,729,924
Total Liabilities	3,686,678	3,176,478	2,603,933	2,661,465	2,573,496	2,678,852	2,294,541	1,905,231
Stockholders' Equity	3,026,654	2,631,438	2,541,663	2,385,291	2,311,334	2,194,540	2,314,555	2,442,493
Shares Outstanding	77,318	74,668	73,663	72,582	70,937	68,202	68,713	67,191
Statistical Record								
Return on Assets %	5.71	5.07	6.30	4.39	5.51	3.61	5.50	4.91
Return on Equity %	12.66	10.76	13.09	9.33	12.05	7.70	10.47	8.73
Net Margin %	44.07	37.76	48.07	33.89	44.54	27.17	38.81	36.73
Price Range	148.52-91.56	134.00-91.44	92.65-66.05	75.30-46.90	49.55-35.39	52.65-36.72	51.90-42.65	50.25-33.19
P/E Ratio	33.91-20.90	37.54-25.61	22.01-15.69	25.79-16.06	13.28-9.49	23.61-16.47	16.63-13.67	19.86-13.12
Average Yield %	2.81	2.76	3.61	4.83	6.52	6.30	5.43	5.37

Address: 2900 Eisenhower Avenue, Suite 300, Alexandria, VA 22314
Telephone: 703-329-6300
Fax: 703-329-1459

Web Site: www.avalonbay.com
Officers: Bryce Blair - Chmn., C.E.O. Timothy J. Naughton - Pres., C.O.O.

Auditors: Ernst & Young LLP
Transfer Agents: The Bank of New York, New York, NY

AVERY DENNISON CORP.

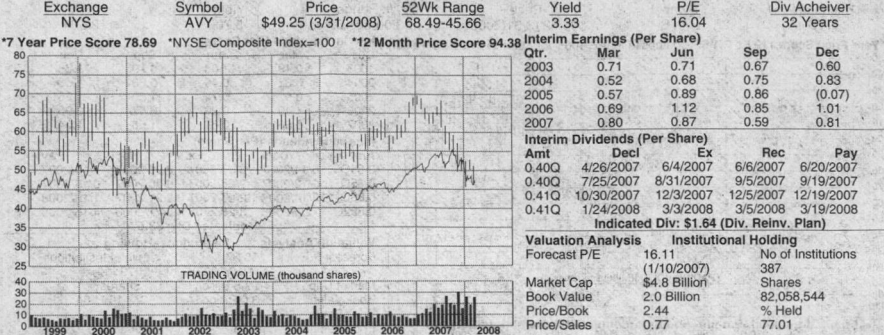

Exchange	Symbol	Price	52Wk Range	Yield	P/E	Div Achiever
NYS	AVY	$49.25 (3/31/2008)	68.49-45.66	3.33	16.04	32 Years

*7 Year Price Score 78.69 *NYSE Composite Index=100 *12 Month Price Score 94.38

Interim Earnings (Per Share)

Qtr.	Mar	Jun	Sep	Dec
2003	0.71	0.71	0.67	0.60
2004	0.52	0.68	0.75	0.83
2005	0.57	0.89	0.86	(0.07)
2006	0.69	1.12	0.85	1.01
2007	0.80	0.87	0.59	0.81

Interim Dividends (Per Share)

Amt	Decl	Ex	Rec	Pay
0.40Q	4/26/2007	6/4/2007	6/6/2007	6/20/2007
0.40Q	7/25/2007	8/31/2007	9/5/2007	9/19/2007
0.41Q	10/30/2007	12/3/2007	12/5/2007	12/19/2007
0.41Q	1/24/2008	3/3/2008	3/5/2008	3/19/2008

Indicated Div: $1.64 (Div. Reinv. Plan)

Valuation Analysis

		Institutional Holding	
Forecast P/E	16.11	No of Institutions	
	(1/10/2007)	387	
Market Cap	$4.8 Billion	Shares	
Book Value	2.0 Billion		82,058,544
Price/Book	2.44	% Held	
Price/Sales	0.77		77.01

TRADING VOLUME (thousand shares)

Business Summary: Paper Products (MIC: 11.11 SIC: 2672 NAIC: 322222)

Avery Dennison is primarily engaged in the production of pressure-sensitive materials, by which some of these materials are converted into labels and other products through embossing, printing, stamping and die-cutting, and some are sold in unconverted form as base materials, tapes and reflective sheeting. Co. also manufactures and sells a variety of office products and other converted products such as binders, organizing systems, markers, fasteners, business forms as well as tickets, tags and imprinting equipment for retail and apparel manufacturers. As of Dec 29 2007, Co. operated approximately 200 manufacturing and distribution facilities located in over 60 countries.

Recent Developments: For the year ended Dec 29 2007, income from continuing operations decreased 15.3% to US$303.5 million from US$358.5 million a year earlier. Net income decreased 18.7% to US$303.5 million from US$373.2 million in the prior year. Revenues were US$6.31 billion, up 13.1% from US$5.58 billion the year before. Direct operating expenses rose 13.6% to US$4.59 billion from US$4.04 billion in the comparable period the year before. Indirect operating expenses increased 22.2% to US$1.35 billion from US$1.10 billion in the equivalent prior-year period.

Prospects: For the full year of 2008, Co. is anticipating earnings of $3.80 to $4.20 per share, assuming reported revenue growth of 9.5% to 12.5%, including a 6.5% contribution from the June 15 2007 acquisition of Paxar Corp. and an estimated 2.0% to 3.0% benefit from currency translation. In addition, Co. is targeting total annual cost synergies related to the integration of Paxar Corp. to range from $60.0 million to $70.0 million. Similarly, Co. foresees that its ongoing restructuring and business restructuring initiatives to yield incremental savings of approximately $30.0 million, net of transition costs. Lastly, Co. expects price increases to at least partially offset raw material inflation.

Financial Data

(US$ in Thousands)	12/29/2007	12/30/2006	12/31/2005	01/01/2005	12/27/2003	12/28/2002	12/29/2001	12/30/2000
Earnings Per Share	3.07	3.66	2.25	2.78	2.68	2.59	2.47	2.84
Cash Flow Per Share	5.10	5.13	4.42	5.09	3.38	5.32	3.85	4.18
Tang Book Value Per Share	N.M.	8.84	7.42	6.45	4.53	2.53	4.70	3.93
Dividends Per Share	1.610	1.570	1.530	1.490	1.450	1.350	1.230	1.110
Dividend Payout %	52.44	42.90	68.00	53.60	54.10	52.12	49.80	39.08
Income Statement								
Total Revenue	6,307,800	5,575,900	5,473,500	5,340,900	4,762,600	4,206,900	3,803,300	3,893,500
EBITDA	609,900	623,500	568,300	561,600	514,200	517,600	515,800	583,200
Income Before Taxes	375,300	425,600	366,800	373,400	334,900	364,800	359,800	426,300
Income Taxes	71,800	73,100	75,000	93,700	92,100	107,600	116,400	142,800
Net Income	303,500	367,200	226,400	279,700	267,900	257,200	243,200	283,500
Average Shares	98,900	100,400	100,500	100,500	100,000	99,400	98,600	99,800
Balance Sheet								
Current Assets	2,058,300	1,655,400	1,558,300	1,542,400	1,440,900	1,215,500	982,500	982,400
Total Assets	6,244,800	4,293,600	4,203,900	4,399,300	4,105,300	3,652,400	2,819,200	2,699,100
Current Liabilities	2,477,600	1,698,800	1,525,600	1,387,300	1,496,000	1,296,100	951,300	800,700
Long-Term Obligations	1,145,000	501,600	723,000	1,007,200	887,700	837,200	626,700	772,900
Total Liabilities	4,255,400	2,613,100	2,692,000	2,850,600	2,786,600	2,596,000	1,889,800	1,871,000
Stockholders' Equity	1,989,400	1,680,500	1,511,900	1,548,700	1,318,700	1,056,400	929,400	828,100
Shares Outstanding	98,386	98,313	99,727	100,113	99,569	110,467	109,890	110,245
Statistical Record								
Return on Assets %	5.78	8.67	5.28	6.47	6.93	7.97	8.84	10.74
Return on Equity %	16.59	23.07	14.84	19.19	22.62	25.98	27.75	34.71
EBITDA Margin %	9.67	11.18	10.38	10.52	10.80	12.30	13.56	14.98
Net Margin %	4.81	6.59	4.14	5.24	5.63	6.11	6.39	7.28
Asset Turnover	1.20	1.32	1.28	1.24	1.23	1.30	1.38	1.48
Current Ratio	0.83	0.97	1.02	1.11	0.96	0.94	1.03	1.23
Debt to Equity	0.58	0.30	0.48	0.65	0.67	0.79	0.67	0.93
Price Range	69.67-49.69	69.11-55.09	62.53-50.30	65.78-54.90	63.51-47.75	69.49-52.86	60.24-44.39	78.00-43.31
P/E Ratio	22.69-16.19	18.88-15.05	27.79-22.36	23.66-19.75	23.70-17.82	26.83-20.41	24.39-17.97	27.46-15.25
Average Yield %	2.61	2.58	2.73	2.44	2.64	2.19	2.34	1.88

Address: 150 North Orange Grove Boulevard, Pasadena, CA 91103 **Telephone:** 626-304-2000 **Fax:** 626-792-7312	**Web Site:** www.averydennison.com **Officers:** Dean A. Scarborough - Pres., C.E.O. Robert G. van Schoonenberg - Exec. V.P., Sec., Gen. Couns.	**Auditors:** PricewaterhouseCoopers LLP **Investor Contact:** 626-304-2204 **Transfer Agents:** EquiServe Trust Company, N.A., Providence, RI

AVIS BUDGET GROUP INC

Exchange	Symbol	Price	52Wk Range	Yield	P/E
NYS	CAR	$10.62 (3/31/2008)	30.72-9.46	N/A	N/A

*7 Year Price Score 71.61 *NYSE Composite Index=100 *12 Month Price Score 60.31

Interim Earnings (Per Share)

Qtr.	Mar	Jun	Sep	Dec
2003	3.00	3.70	1.90	2.80
2004	4.20	6.60	5.60	3.30
2005	(0.80)	3.60	4.70	5.10
2006	0.70	(7.50)	(10.07)	0.06
2007	0.12	0.23	0.99	(10.22)

Interim Dividends (Per Share)

No Dividends Paid

Valuation Analysis **Institutional Holding**

Forecast P/E	11.20	No of Institutions
	(1/10/2007)	283
Market Cap	$1.1 Billion	Shares
Book Value	1.5 Billion	76,967,440
Price/Book	0.75	% Held
Price/Sales	0.18	76.00

Business Summary: Hospitality & Tourism (MIC: 5.1 SIC: 7514 NAIC: 532111)

Avis Budget Group is engaged in the global vehicle rental industry through its Avis and Budget brands. Co.'s Avis is a rental car supplier to the premium commercial and leisure segments of the travel industry and Budget is a rental car supplier to the price-conscious segments of the industry. As of Dec 31 2007, Co. had approximately 6,900 car and truck rental locations globally. Co. operates in three segments: domestic car rental, consisting of its Avis and Budget U.S. car rental operations; international car rental, consisting of its international Avis and Budget car rental operations; and truck rental, consisting of its Budget truck rental operations.

Recent Developments: For the year ended Dec 31 2007, loss from continuing operations was US$947.0 million compared with a loss of US$451.0 million a year earlier. Net loss amounted to US$916.0 million versus a net loss of US$1.99 billion in the prior year. Revenues were US$5.99 billion, up 5.2% from US$5.69 billion the year before. Indirect operating expenses increased 9.6% to US$6.98 billion from US$6.37 billion in the equivalent prior-year period.

Prospects: For full-year 2008, Co. estimates that its revenue will increase over 2007 revenue of $6.00 billion, excluding unusual items. Specifically, Co. expects domestic enplanements for determining on-airport rental volumes, will increase modestly amid a relatively weak macroeconomic environment in the first half of 2008. In addition, Co. expects that its domestic time and mileage revenue per rental day will increase and its domestic rental day volume will increase approximately 3.0% to 5.0%. Co. also expects incremental year-over-year revenue growth from Where2 GPS rentals and insurance replacement rentals. Co. further expects cost-saving efforts to contribute at least $40.0 million in 2008.

Financial Data

(US$ in Thousands)	12/31/2007	12/31/2006	12/31/2005	12/31/2004	12/31/2003	12/31/2002	12/31/2001	12/31/2000
Earnings Per Share	(8.88)	(19.82)	12.60	19.60	11.30	8.10	4.10	8.10
Cash Flow Per Share	16.62	2.50	31.87	52.40	70.82	12.34	32.04	19.08
Dividends Per Share	...	1.100	4.000	3.200	...	...	...	...
Dividend Payout %	...	...	31.75	16.33	...	...	...	...
Income Statement								
Total Revenue	5,986,000	5,689,000	18,236,000	19,785,000	18,192,000	14,088,000	8,950,000	3,930,000
EBITDA	657,000	790,000	3,107,000	5,222,000	4,800,000	3,908,000	2,927,000	1,452,000
Income Before Taxes	(992,000)	(677,000)	1,346,000	2,554,000	2,231,000	1,659,000	759,000	969,000
Income Taxes	(45,000)	(226,000)	474,000	728,000	745,000	556,000	235,000	309,000
Net Income	(916,000)	(1,994,000)	1,341,000	2,082,000	1,172,000	846,000	385,000	602,000
Average Shares	103,100	100,600	106,000	106,400	104,000	104,300	91,700	76,200
Balance Sheet								
Current Assets	1,218,000	1,806,000	3,426,000	3,865,000	4,478,000	3,358,000	6,492,000	2,384,000
Total Assets	12,474,000	13,271,000	34,104,000	42,555,000	39,037,000	35,897,000	33,452,000	14,516,000
Current Liabilities	1,104,000	1,884,000	5,717,000	6,332,000	7,335,000	5,863,000	10,290,000	3,467,000
Long-Term Obligations	7,383,000	7,083,000	13,588,000	19,410,000	18,994,000	18,315,000	13,836,000	2,432,000
Total Liabilities	11,009,000	10,828,000	22,813,000	29,860,000	28,851,000	26,207,000	26,009,000	9,684,000
Stockholders' Equity	1,465,000	2,443,000	11,291,000	12,695,000	10,186,000	9,315,000	7,068,000	2,774,000
Shares Outstanding	103,986	101,191	101,160	105,132	100,884	103,176	97,770	73,788
Statistical Record								
Return on Assets %	N.M.	N.M.	3.50	5.09	3.13	2.44	1.61	4.05
Return on Equity %	N.M.	N.M.	11.18	18.15	12.02	10.33	7.82	24.11
EBITDA Margin %	10.98	13.89	17.04	26.39	26.39	27.74	32.70	36.95
Net Margin %	N.M.	N.M.	7.35	10.52	6.44	6.01	4.30	15.32
Asset Turnover	0.47	0.24	0.48	0.48	0.49	0.41	0.37	0.26
Current Ratio	1.10	0.96	0.60	0.61	0.61	0.57	0.63	0.69
Debt to Equity	5.04	2.90	1.20	1.53	1.86	1.97	1.96	0.88
Price Range	30.72-12.62	24.40-17.30	30.57-21.96	31.80-25.40	28.29-13.30	25.36-11.47	27.31-12.21	33.70-10.78
P/E Ratio	...	...	2.43-1.74	1.62-1.30	2.50-1.18	3.13-1.42	6.66-2.98	4.16-1.33
Average Yield %	...	5.21	14.70	11.02	...	...	...	...

Address: 9 West 57th Street, New York, NY 10019 **Telephone:** 212-413-1800 **Fax:** 212-413-1924	**Web Site:** www.cendant.com **Officers:** Henry R. Silverman - Chmn., C.E.O. James E. Buckman - Vice-Chmn., Gen. Couns.	**Auditors:** Deloitte & Touche LLP **Investor Contact:** 212-413-1834

AVNET INC

Exchange	Symbol	Price	52Wk Range	Yield	P/E
NYS	AVT	$32.73 (3/31/2008)	44.33-29.43	N/A	10.39

*7 Year Price Score 130.78 *NYSE Composite Index=100 *12 Month Price Score 95.40

Interim Earnings (Per Share)

Qtr.	Sep	Dec	Mar	Jun
2004-05	0.30	0.36	0.34	0.39
2005-06	0.17	0.34	0.48	0.40
2006-07	0.44	0.67	0.70	0.82
2007-08	0.69	0.93	...	...

Interim Dividends (Per Share)

Dividend Payment Suspended

Valuation Analysis **Institutional Holding**

Forecast P/E	8.06	No of Institutions
	(1/10/2007)	274
Market Cap	$4.9 Billion	Shares
Book Value	3.8 Billion	142,720,976
Price/Book	1.30	% Held
Price/Sales	0.29	96.58

TRADING VOLUME (thousand shares)

Business Summary: Electrical (MIC: 11.14 SIC: 5065 NAIC: 423690)

Avnet is engaged in the industrial distribution of electronic components, enterprise computer and storage products and embedded subsystems. In particular, Co. distributes electronic components, computer products and software as received from its suppliers or with assembly by Co. Additionally, Co. provides engineering design, materials management and logistics services, system integration and configuration, and supply chain advisory services. At June 30 2007, Co. was comprised of two operating groups: Electronics Marketing and Technology Solutions. Co. markets and sells semiconductors, interconnect, passive and electromechanical devices.

Recent Developments: For the quarter ended Dec 29 2007, net income increased 43.5% to US$142.2 million from US$99.1 million in the year-earlier quarter. Revenues were US$4.75 billion, up 22.2% from US$3.89 billion the year before. Operating income was US$207.9 million versus US$163.8 million in the prior-year quarter, an increase of 26.9%. Direct operating expenses rose 22.3% to US$4.16 billion from US$3.40 billion in the comparable period the year before. Indirect operating expenses increased 17.8% to US$388.8 million from US$330.1 million in the equivalent prior-year period.

Prospects: For the fiscal quarter ended March 2008, Co. is projecting consolidated sales of $4.37 billion and $4.57 billion and earnings of $0.85 to $0.89 per share, excluding the amortization of intangible assets or integration charges related to acquisitions that have closed or will close in the third fiscal quarter of 2008. Separately, on Jan 10 2008, Co. announced a definitive agreement to acquire Azzurri Technology Ltd., a design-in distributor of semiconductors and embedded systems products with annual revenue of about $100.0 million. The transaction is expected to be immediately accretive to earnings, excluding minimal integration charges, and supports Co.'s long-term return on capital goals.

Financial Data

(US$ in Thousands)	6 Mos	3 Mos	06/30/2007	07/01/2006	07/02/2005	07/03/2004	06/27/2003	06/28/2002
Earnings Per Share	3.15	2.88	2.63	1.39	1.39	0.60	(0.39)	(5.61)
Cash Flow Per Share	3.71	4.71	4.91	(0.13)	3.84	0.53	5.47	8.26
Tang Book Value Per Share	14.38	14.44	13.34	10.46	9.95	8.79	8.16	8.04
Dividends Per Share	...	...	...	...	...	...	...	0.150
Income Statement								
Total Revenue	8,851,863	4,098,718	15,681,087	14,253,630	11,066,816	10,244,741	9,048,442	8,920,248
EBITDA	423,811	186,148	717,566	479,178	386,561	257,511	114,285	107,649
Depn & Amortn	27,710	13,522	...	...	...	...	...	...
Income Before Taxes	359,920	154,069	586,619	316,147	239,759	98,398	(79,405)	(120,813)
Income Taxes	112,177	48,532	193,552	111,600	71,520	25,501	(33,289)	(36,377)
Net Income	247,743	105,537	393,067	204,547	168,239	72,897	(46,116)	(664,931)
Average Shares	152,975	153,458	149,613	147,150	121,469	121,252	119,456	118,561
Balance Sheet								
Current Assets	5,943,446	5,482,505	5,488,845	4,467,462	3,782,967	3,483,986	3,126,090	3,205,532
Total Assets	8,027,951	7,367,674	7,355,119	6,215,693	5,098,215	4,863,651	4,499,551	4,681,954
Current Liabilities	2,954,562	2,528,680	2,776,985	2,438,324	1,717,518	1,644,993	1,306,050	1,276,836
Long-Term Obligations	1,177,055	1,156,008	1,155,990	918,810	1,183,195	1,196,160	1,278,399	1,565,836
Total Liabilities	4,260,108	3,792,507	3,954,474	3,384,510	3,001,182	2,910,225	2,667,029	2,877,444
Stockholders' Equity	3,767,843	3,575,167	3,400,645	2,831,183	2,097,033	1,953,426	1,832,522	1,804,510
Shares Outstanding	150,051	149,998	149,805	146,655	120,765	120,477	119,543	119,423
Statistical Record								
Return on Assets %	6.56	6.27	5.81	3.63	3.39	1.53	N.M.	N.M.
Return on Equity %	14.02	13.42	12.65	8.32	8.33	3.78	N.M.	N.M.
EBITDA Margin %	4.79	4.54	4.58	3.36	3.49	2.51	1.26	1.21
Net Margin %	2.80	2.57	2.51	1.44	1.52	0.71	N.M.	N.M.
Asset Turnover	2.34	2.33	2.32	2.53	2.23	2.15	1.98	1.70
Current Ratio	2.01	2.17	1.98	1.83	2.20	2.12	2.39	2.51
Debt to Equity	0.31	0.32	0.34	0.32	0.56	0.61	0.70	0.87
Price Range	44.33-25.70	44.33-19.45	43.62-16.77	27.10-19.21	22.80-15.77	26.35-12.39	21.99-5.96	29.06-17.59
P/E Ratio	14.07-8.16	15.39-6.75	16.59-6.38	19.50-13.82	16.40-11.35	43.92-20.65		
Average Yield %	...	...	...	...	...	...	...	0.63

Address: 2211 South 47th Street, Phoenix, AZ 85034 Telephone: 480-643-2000	Web Site: www.avnet.com Officers: Roy Vallee - Chmn., C.E.O. Raymond Sadowski - Sr. V.P., C.F.O., Asst. Sec.	Auditors: KPMG LLP

AVON PRODUCTS, INC.

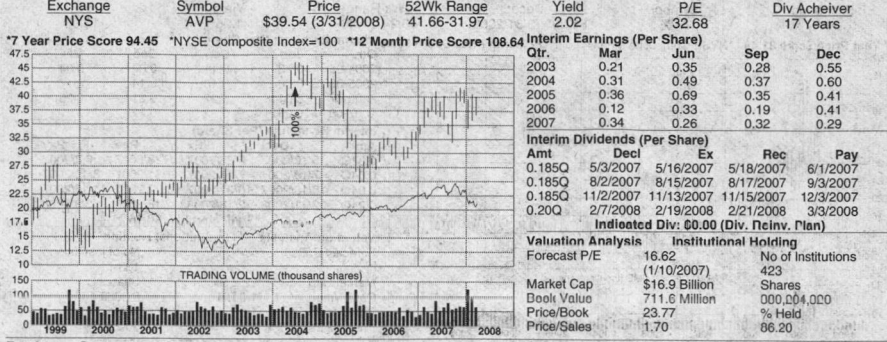

Exchange	Symbol	Price	52Wk Range	Yield	P/E	Div Acheiver
NYS	AVP	$39.54 (3/31/2008)	41.66-31.97	2.02	32.68	17 Years

*7 Year Price Score 94.45   *NYSE Composite Index=100   *12 Month Price Score 108.64

Interim Earnings (Per Share)

Qtr.	Mar	Jun	Sep	Dec
2003	0.21	0.35	0.28	0.55
2004	0.31	0.49	0.37	0.60
2005	0.36	0.69	0.35	0.41
2006	0.12	0.33	0.19	0.41
2007	0.34	0.26	0.32	0.29

Interim Dividends (Per Share)

Amt	Decl	Ex	Rec	Pay
0.185Q	5/3/2007	5/16/2007	5/18/2007	6/1/2007
0.185Q	8/2/2007	8/15/2007	8/17/2007	9/3/2007
0.185Q	11/2/2007	11/13/2007	11/15/2007	12/3/2007
0.20Q	2/7/2008	2/19/2008	2/21/2008	3/3/2008

Indicated Div: C0.00 (Div. Reinv. Plan)

Valuation Analysis

		Institutional Holding	
Forecast P/E	16.62	No of Institutions	
	(1/10/2007)	423	
Market Cap	$16.9 Billion	Shares	
Book Value	711.6 Million	000,004,0C0	
Price/Book	23.77	% Held	
Price/Sales	1.70	86.20	

TRADING VOLUME (thousand shares)

Business Summary: Consumer Products Manufacturing (MIC: 4 SIC: 2844 NAIC: 325620)

Avon Products is a global manufacturer and marketer of beauty and related products. As of Dec 31 2007, Co.'s products are categorized into three product categories: Beauty, which consists of cosmetics, fragrances, skin care and toiletries; Beauty Plus, which consists of fashion jewelry, watches, apparel and accessories; and Beyond Beauty, which consists of home products and gift and decorative products. Co.'s Health and Wellness products and mark., a global cosmetics brand that focuses on the market for young women, are also included among these three categories. Co.'s business is conducted primarily in one channel, direct selling; and operated throughout six regions.

Recent Developments: For the year ended Dec 31 2007, net income increased 11.1% to US$530.7 million from US$477.6 million in the prior year. Revenues were US$9.94 billion, up 13.4% from US$8.76 billion the year before. Operating income was US$872.7 million versus US$761.4 million in the prior year, an increase of 14.6%. Direct operating expenses rose 15.4% to US$3.94 billion from US$3.42 billion in the comparable period the year before. Indirect operating expenses increased 11.7% to US$5.12 billion from US$4.59 billion in the equivalent prior-year period.

Prospects: On Jan 8 2008, Co. announced the final initiatives of the restructuring program under its ongoing turnaround plan and expects to attain annualized savings of about $430.0 million upon by 2012, compared with its prior objective of $300.0 million. Specifically, Co. anticipates these savings to reach $300.0 million in 2009. Also, Co. now projects total costs to implement the restructuring initiatives to be about $530.0 million, of which about $70.0 million will be recorded in late 2009. Meanwhile, Co. continues to expect benefits from its Product Line Simplification initiative in the second half of 2008, and to reach an annualized run rate in excess of $200.0 million by the end of 2009.

Financial Data
(US$ in Thousands)

	12/31/2007	12/31/2006	12/31/2005	12/31/2004	12/31/2003	12/31/2002	12/31/2001	12/31/2000
Earnings Per Share	1.21	1.06	1.81	1.77	1.39	1.11	0.90	1.00
Cash Flow Per Share	1.36	1.78	1.92	1.86	1.58	1.20	1.59	0.68
Tang Book Value Per Share	1.66	1.79	1.76	2.02	0.79	...	...	...
Dividends Per Share	0.740	0.700	0.660	0.560	0.420	0.400	0.380	0.370
Dividend Payout %	61.16	66.04	36.46	31.64	30.22	36.04	42.46	37.19
Income Statement								
Total Revenue	9,938,700	8,763,900	8,149,600	7,747,800	6,876,000	6,228,300	5,994,500	5,714,600
EBITDA	1,050,500	917,000	1,291,100	1,343,000	1,161,500	1,022,000	846,400	864,300
Income Before Taxes	796,100	703,500	1,124,200	1,187,500	993,500	835,600	665,700	691,000
Income Taxes	262,800	223,400	269,700	330,600	318,900	292,300	230,900	201,700
Net Income	530,700	477,600	847,600	846,100	664,800	534,600	430,000	478,400
Average Shares	436,890	449,160	469,470	477,960	483,140	490,940	492,100	485,900
Balance Sheet								
Current Assets	3,515,400	3,334,400	2,920,900	2,506,400	2,226,100	2,048,200	1,889,100	1,545,700
Total Assets	5,716,200	5,238,200	4,763,300	4,148,100	3,562,300	3,327,500	3,193,100	2,826,400
Current Liabilities	3,053,400	2,550,100	2,501,600	1,525,500	1,587,700	1,975,500	1,461,000	1,359,300
Long-Term Obligations	1,167,900	1,170,700	766,500	866,300	877,700	767,000	1,236,300	1,108,200
Total Liabilities	5,004,600	4,447,800	3,969,100	3,197,900	3,191,000	3,455,200	3,267,700	3,042,200
Stockholders' Equity	711,600	790,400	794,200	950,200	371,300	(127,700)	(74,600)	(215,800)
Shares Outstanding	427,700	441,300	451,480	471,530	470,596	470,515	473,362	476,324
Statistical Record								
Return on Assets %	9.69	9.55	19.02	21.89	19.30	16.40	14.29	17.82
Return on Equity %	70.67	60.28	97.18	127.70	545.81	...	...	...
EBITDA Margin %	10.57	10.46	15.84	17.33	16.89	16.41	14.12	15.12
Net Margin %	5.34	5.45	10.40	10.92	9.67	8.58	7.17	8.37
Asset Turnover	1.81	1.75	1.83	2.00	2.00	1.91	1.99	2.13
Current Ratio	1.15	1.31	1.17	1.64	1.40	1.04	1.29	1.14
Debt to Equity	1.64	1.48	0.97	0.91	2.36	...	...	...
Price Range	41.66-31.97	33.88-27.06	45.07-24.71	46.14-30.86	34.67-24.58	28.48-21.86	24.80-18.39	24.78-12.69
P/E Ratio	34.43-26.42	31.96-25.53	24.90-13.65	26.07-17.44	24.95-17.68	25.66-19.69	27.55-20.43	24.78-12.69
Average Yield %	1.97	2.30	1.86	1.40	1.38	1.58	1.71	1.94

Address: 1345 Avenue of the Americas, New York, NY 10105-0196
Telephone: 212-282-5000
Fax: 212-282-6035

Web Site: www.avoncompany.com
Officers: Andrea Jung - Chmn., C.E.O. Susan J. Kropf - Pres., C.O.O.

Auditors: PricewaterhouseCoopers LLP
Investor Contact: 212-282-5320
Transfer Agents: EquiServe Trust Company, N.A. Providence, RI

AVX CORP.

Exchange	Symbol	Price	52Wk Range	Yield	P/E
NYS	AVX	$12.81 (3/31/2008)	18.24-11.86	1.25	13.92

*7 Year Price Score 81.49 *NYSE Composite Index=100 *12 Month Price Score 89.80

Interim Earnings (Per Share)

Qtr.	Jun	Sep	Dec	Mar
2004-05	0.13	0.11	0.04	0.04
2005-06	0.06	0.10	0.14	0.17
2006-07	0.21	0.22	0.21	0.25
2007-08	0.23	0.22	0.22	...

Interim Dividends (Per Share)

Amt	Decl	Ex	Rec	Pay
0.04Q	5/10/2007	5/23/2007	5/28/2007	6/8/2007
0.04Q	7/19/2007	7/27/2007	7/31/2007	8/13/2007
0.04Q	10/18/2007	10/31/2007	11/2/2007	11/16/2007
0.04Q	2/11/2008	2/13/2008	2/18/2008	3/3/2008

Indicated Div: $0.16

Valuation Analysis   **Institutional Holding**

Forecast P/E	N/A	No of Institutions 133
Market Cap	$2.2 Billion	Shares
Book Value	1.8 Billion	51,989,400
Price/Book	1.25	% Held
Price/Sales	1.38	30.25

Business Summary: Electrical (MIC: 11.14 SIC: 3678 NAIC: 334417)

AVX is a manufacturer and supplier of various passive electronic components and related products. Co.'s passive electronic component products, which store, filter or regulate electric energy, include ceramic and tantalum capacitors, film capacitors, varistors and non-linear resistors manufactured in its facilities throughout the world and passive components manufactured by Kyocera Corporation of Japan, Co.'s majority stockholder. Co. sells its products to customers in industries such as telecommunications, information technology hardware, automotive electronics, medical devices and instrumentation, industrial instrumentation, defense and aerospace electronic systems and consumer electronics.

Recent Developments: For the quarter ended Dec 31 2007, net income increased 3.3% to US$37.0 million from US$35.8 million in the year-earlier quarter. Revenues were US$429.5 million, up 13.6% from US$378.1 million the year before. Operating income was US$40.5 million versus US$43.1 million in the prior-year quarter, a decrease of 6.1%. Direct operating expenses rose 16.4% to US$355.7 million from US$305.5 million in the comparable period the year before. Indirect operating expenses increased 13.0% to US$33.3 million from US$29.5 million in the equivalent prior-year period.

Prospects: Co. believes that the industry demand for its products is in line with component manufacturing capacity, and as such, it expects a continued pricing environment with below normal annual price declines. Co. also expects to focus on cost reductions via process improvements and enhanced production capabilities, and to emphasize on the sales of improved electronic components to support existing electronic devices. Further, Co. expects its Sep 2007 acquisition of American Technical Ceramics Corp. to benefit its advanced component product group with offerings of additional components for its end-user's electronics, and to boost its sales growth for the rest of the fiscal year ending Mar 2008.

Financial Data

(US$ in Thousands)	9 Mos	6 Mos	3 Mos	03/31/2007	03/31/2006	03/31/2005	03/31/2004	03/31/2003
Earnings Per Share	0.92	0.91	0.91	0.89	0.47	0.32	(0.62)	(0.07)
Cash Flow Per Share	1.06	1.23	1.21	1.42	0.93	0.33	0.48	0.70
Tang Book Value Per Share	8.81	8.62	9.34	9.11	8.01	7.92	7.58	7.91
Dividends Per Share	0.158	0.155	0.153	0.150	0.150	0.150	0.150	0.150
Dividend Payout %	17.12	17.03	16.76	16.85	31.91	46.88	...	...
Income Statement								
Total Revenue	1,213,406	783,864	383,158	1,498,495	1,333,208	1,283,202	1,136,577	1,134,111
EBITDA	160,689	106,404	55,349	231,392	163,041	156,415	(48,978)	93,401
Depn & Amortn	39,184	24,229	12,036	...	...	...	...	...
Income Before Taxes	156,154	107,155	55,153	217,566	119,620	88,044	(131,671)	(10,438)
Income Taxes	42,535	30,555	15,994	63,701	37,868	32,312	(24,065)	2,000
Net Income	113,619	76,600	39,159	153,865	81,752	55,732	(107,606)	(12,438)
Average Shares	171,888	172,477	172,587	172,751	173,053	173,906	173,634	174,325
Balance Sheet								
Current Assets	1,432,544	1,391,660	1,495,935	1,421,395	1,203,772	1,118,136	1,101,979	1,077,957
Total Assets	2,053,171	2,030,121	1,935,781	1,899,536	1,675,208	1,689,749	1,667,877	1,700,513
Current Liabilities	227,824	229,633	197,978	207,360	171,030	196,572	214,890	185,557
Long-Term Obligations	1,145	4,773	...	...	...	...	...	...
Total Liabilities	296,866	304,159	256,379	264,257	227,099	250,498	281,333	237,357
Stockholders' Equity	1,756,305	1,725,962	1,679,402	1,635,279	1,448,109	1,439,251	1,386,544	1,463,156
Shares Outstanding	171,277	171,513	171,901	171,674	172,216	172,955	173,648	176,368
Statistical Record								
Return on Assets %	8.00	8.12	8.49	8.61	4.86	3.32	N.M.	N.M.
Return on Equity %	9.33	9.50	9.86	9.98	5.66	3.94	N.M.	N.M.
EBITDA Margin %	13.24	13.57	14.45	15.44	12.23	12.19	N.M.	8.24
Net Margin %	9.36	9.77	10.22	10.27	6.13	4.34	N.M.	N.M.
Asset Turnover	0.81	0.80	0.82	0.84	0.79	0.76	0.67	0.67
Current Ratio	6.29	6.06	7.56	6.85	7.04	5.69	5.13	5.81
Price Range	18.24-13.12	18.30-14.00	18.30-13.16	19.88-13.16	17.70-10.81	17.32-11.17	19.02-9.00	23.50-7.54
P/E Ratio	19.83-14.26	20.11-15.38	20.11-14.46	22.34-14.79	37.66-23.00	54.13-34.91	...	...
Average Yield %	1.00	0.97	0.96	0.94	1.11	1.15	1.08	1.15

Address: 801 17th Ave. S., Myrtle Beach, SC 29577	**Web Site:** www.avx.com	**Auditors:** PricewaterhouseCoopers LLP
Telephone: 843-448-9411	**Officers:** Benedict P. Rosen - Chmn. Yasuo Nishiguchi - Vice-Chmn.	**Investor Contact:** 843-448-9411
Fax: 843-448-6091		**Transfer Agents:** American Stock Transfer and Trust Company, New York, NY

BAKER HUGHES INC.

Exchange	Symbol	Price	52Wk Range	Yield	P/E
NYS	BHI	$68.50 (3/31/2008)	98.67-63.90	0.76	14.48

*7 Year Price Score 128.12 *NYSE Composite Index=100 *12 Month Price Score 91.18

TRADING VOLUME (thousand shares)

Interim Earnings (Per Share)

Qtr.	Mar	Jun	Sep	Dec
2003	0.13	0.24	(0.29)	0.30
2004	0.28	0.35	0.11	0.54
2005	0.53	0.64	0.65	0.75
2006	0.99	4.14	1.09	1.05
2007	1.17	1.09	1.22	1.26

Interim Dividends (Per Share)

Amt	Decl	Ex	Rec.	Pay
0.13Q	4/26/2007	5/3/2007	5/7/2007	5/18/2007
0.13Q	7/26/2007	8/2/2007	8/6/2007	8/17/2007
0.13Q	10/25/2007	11/1/2007	11/5/2007	11/16/2007
0.13Q	1/24/2008	1/31/2008	2/4/2008	2/15/2008

Indicated Div: $0.52

Valuation Analysis / **Institutional Holding**

Forecast P/E	10.81 (1/10/2007)	No of Institutions	554
Market Cap	$21.6 Billion	Shares	209,491,232
Book Value	0.0 Billion	% Held	90.40
Price/Book	3.43		
Price/Sales	2.07		

Business Summary: Oil and Gas (MIC: 14.2 SIC: 3533 NAIC: 333132)

Baker Hughes is a supplier of products and technology services and systems to the global oil and natural gas industry, including products and services for drilling, formation evaluation, completion and production of oil and natural gas wells. As of Dec 31 2007, Co. had two operating segments. The Drilling and Evaluation segment provides products and services used to drill and evaluate oil and natural gas wells. The Completion and Production segment provides equipment and services used from the completion phase through the productive life of oil and natural gas wells. Co. operates primarily in North and Latin America, Middle East and Asia Pacific, Europe, Africa, Russia and the Caspian.

Recent Developments: For the year ended Dec 31 2007, income from continuing operations decreased 36.9% to US$1.51 billion from US$2.40 billion a year earlier. Net income decreased 37.4% to US$1.51 billion from US$2.42 billion in the prior year. Revenues were US$10.43 billion, up 15.5% from US$9.03 billion the year before. Operating income was US$2.28 billion versus US$1.93 billion in the prior year, an increase of 17.8%. Direct operating expenses rose 16.5% to US$6.85 billion from US$5.88 billion in the comparable period the year before. Indirect operating expenses increased 7.2% to US$1.30 billion from US$1.22 billion in the equivalent prior-year period.

Prospects: For 2008, Co. foresees revenues outside North America to increase in a percentage range from the low to mid-teens over its 2007 levels. In addition, Co. anticipates revenue growth from North America to be no more than moderate. Similarly, Co. is projecting capital expenditures to be about $1.30 billion, excluding acquisitions and including $250.0 million to $300.0 million for infrastructure primarily outside of North America, with the balance used for normal, recurring items necessary to support the growth of its business and operations. For the first quarter of 2008, Co. is forecasting a sequential decline of $100.0 million in export shipments from its Completion and Production segment.

Financial Data
(US$ in Thousands)

	12/31/2007	12/31/2006	12/31/2005	12/31/2004	12/31/2003	12/31/2002	12/31/2001	12/31/2000
Earnings Per Share	4.73	7.27	2.57	1.58	0.38	0.50	1.30	0.31
Cash Flow Per Share	4.64	1.78	2.81	2.34	1.98	2.01	2.15	1.70
Tang Book Value Per Share	15.14	11.58	9.42	7.35	5.87	6.06	5.69	4.64
Dividends Per Share	0.520	0.520	0.475	0.460	0.460	0.460	0.460	0.460
Dividend Payout %	10.99	7.15	18.48	29.11	121.05	92.00	35.38	148.39
Income Statement								
Total Revenue	10,428,200	9,027,400	7,185,500	6,103,800	5,292,800	5,020,400	5,382,200	5,233,800
EBITDA	2,838,900	4,166,800	1,717,300	1,223,000	775,000	787,900	1,120,700	1,016,000
Income Before Taxes	2,256,700	3,736,800	1,279,200	780,500	328,200	380,400	661,800	236,000
Income Taxes	742,800	1,338,200	404,800	252,300	148,100	156,700	223,100	133,700
Net Income	1,513,900	2,419,000	878,400	528,600	128,900	168,900	438,000	102,300
Average Shares	320,100	332,600	341,500	335,600	335,900	337,900	337,400	332,900
Balance Sheet								
Current Assets	5,455,600	4,967,800	3,840,100	2,966,600	2,523,900	2,555,500	2,697,200	2,486,600
Total Assets	9,856,600	8,705,700	7,807,400	6,821,300	6,302,200	6,400,800	6,676,200	6,452,700
Current Liabilities	1,617,900	1,621,900	1,360,700	1,235,500	1,301,900	1,080,100	1,212,400	987,800
Long-Term Obligations	1,069,400	1,073,800	1,078,000	1,086,300	1,133,000	1,424,300	1,682,400	2,049,600
Total Liabilities	3,551,000	3,462,800	3,109,600	2,925,900	2,951,800	3,003,600	3,348,400	3,406,000
Stockholders' Equity	6,305,600	5,242,900	4,697,800	3,895,400	3,350,400	3,397,200	3,327,800	3,046,700
Shares Outstanding	315,400	319,900	341,500	336,600	332,000	335,800	336,000	333,700
Statistical Record								
Return on Assets %	16.31	29.30	12.01	8.03	2.03	2.58	6.67	1.51
Return on Equity %	26.22	48.67	20.44	14.55	3.82	5.02	13.74	3.34
EBITDA Margin %	27.22	46.16	23.90	20.04	14.64	15.69	20.82	19.41
Net Margin %	14.52	26.80	12.22	8.66	2.44	3.36	8.14	1.95
Asset Turnover	1.12	1.09	0.98	0.93	0.83	0.77	0.82	0.77
Current Ratio	3.37	3.06	2.82	2.40	1.94	2.37	2.22	2.52
Debt to Equity	0.17	0.20	0.23	0.28	0.34	0.42	0.51	0.67
Price Range	98.67-62.74	88.60-62.17	62.76-41.20	44.89-31.80	35.94-27.10	39.42-22.80	44.99-26.29	42.94-20.25
P/E Ratio	20.86-13.26	12.19-8.55	24.42-16.03	28.41-20.13	94.58-71.32	78.84-45.60	34.61-20.22	138.51-65.32
Average Yield %	0.66	0.71	0.93	1.19	1.49	1.42	1.42	1.41

Address: 2929 Allen Parkway, Suite 2100, Houston, TX 77019-2118 **Telephone:** 713-439-8600 **Fax:** 713-439-8699	**Web Site:** www.bakerhughes.com **Officers:** Chad C. Deaton - Chmn., C.E.O. James R. Clark - Pres., C.O.O.	**Auditors:** Deloitte & Touche LLP **Investor Contact:** 713-439-8039 **Transfer Agents:** Mellon Investor Services LLC, Jersey City, New Jersey, United States

BALL CORP

Exchange	Symbol	Price	52Wk Range	Yield	P/E
NYS	BLL	$45.94 (3/31/2008)	55.75-41.56	0.87	16.77

*7 Year Price Score 117.28 *NYSE Composite Index=100 *12 Month Price Score 97.93

Interim Earnings (Per Share)

Qtr.	Mar	Jun	Sep	Dec
2003	0.28	0.65	0.60	0.48
2004	0.41	0.80	0.90	0.50
2005	0.51	0.71	0.73	0.43
2006	0.43	1.26	0.97	0.49
2007	0.78	1.03	0.59	0.34

Interim Dividends (Per Share)

Amt	Decl	Ex	Rec	Pay
0.10Q	4/25/2007	5/30/2007	6/1/2007	6/15/2007
0.10Q	7/25/2007	8/30/2007	9/4/2007	9/18/2007
0.10Q	10/24/2007	11/29/2007	12/3/2007	12/17/2007
0.10Q	1/23/2008	2/28/2008	3/3/2008	3/17/2008

Indicated Div: $0.40

Valuation Analysis

		Institutional Holding	
Forecast P/E	12.38	No of Institutions	
	(1/10/2007)	258	
Market Cap	$4.6 Billion	Shares	
Book Value	1.3 Billion	78,036,944	
Price/Book	3.43	% Held	
Price/Sales	0.62	75.70	

TRADING VOLUME (thousand shares)

Business Summary: Metal Products (MIC: 11.4 SIC: 3411 NAIC: 332431)

Ball supplies metal and plastic packaging to the beverage, food and household products industries. Co.'s packaging products are produced for a variety of end uses and are manufactured in plants around the world. Co. also supplies aerospace and other technologies and services to governmental and commercial customers. As of Dec 31 2007, Co. had five reportable segments organized along a combination of product lines and geographic areas: metal beverage packaging, Americas; metal beverage packaging, Europe/Asia; metal food and household products packaging, Americas; plastic packaging, Americas; and aerospace and technologies.

Recent Developments: For the year ended Dec 31 2007, net income decreased 14.7% to US$281.3 million from US$329.6 million in the prior year. Revenues were US$7.39 billion, up 11.6% from US$6.62 billion the year before. Operating income was US$513.9 million versus US$581.3 million in the prior year, a decrease of 11.6%. Direct operating expenses rose 12.4% to US$6.23 billion from US$5.54 billion in the comparable period the year before. Indirect operating expenses increased 29.9% to US$649.3 million from US$499.8 million in the equivalent prior-year period.

Prospects: Co. is focused on developing and marketing new and existing products that meet the needs of its customers and consumer. Accordingly, Co. is installing a new 24-ounce can production line in its Monticello, Indiana, facility, expected to be operational in mid-2008. Co. will also focus on improving its food and household products packaging and plastic packaging segments, and aims to achieve in 2008 earnings greater than the $3.50 per diluted share attained in 2007. In 2009, Co. hopes to complete a project to upgrade and streamline its North American beverage can end manufacturing capabilities to generate productivity gains and cost reductions in its metal beverage packaging, Americas, segment.

Financial Data
(US$ in Thousands)

	12/31/2007	12/31/2006	12/31/2005	12/31/2004	12/31/2003	12/31/2002	12/31/2001	12/31/2000
Earnings Per Share	2.74	3.14	2.38	2.60	2.01	1.36	(0.93)	0.54
Cash Flow Per Share	6.65	3.88	5.19	4.82	3.26	4.02	2.92	1.52
Tang Book Value Per Share	N.M.	N.M.	N.M.	N.M.	N.M.	N.M.	1.27	1.71
Dividends Per Share	0.400	0.400	0.400	0.350	0.240	0.180	0.150	0.150
Dividend Payout %	14.60	12.74	16.81	13.46	11.94	13.28	...	28.04
Income Statement								
Total Revenue	7,389,700	6,621,500	5,751,200	5,440,200	4,977,000	3,858,900	3,686,100	3,664,700
EBITDA	794,900	833,900	676,000	754,000	666,300	460,200	127,100	368,200
Income Before Taxes	364,500	446,900	346,100	435,200	319,700	235,400	(113,700)	113,900
Income Taxes	95,700	131,600	99,300	139,200	100,100	83,900	(9,700)	42,800
Net Income	281,300	329,600	261,500	295,600	229,900	156,100	(99,200)	68,200
Average Shares	102,760	104,951	109,732	113,790	114,274	115,076	109,760	124,068
Balance Sheet								
Current Assets	1,842,900	1,761,300	1,225,800	1,245,600	923,500	1,224,500	793,500	969,300
Total Assets	6,020,600	5,840,900	4,343,400	4,477,700	4,069,600	4,132,400	2,313,600	2,649,800
Current Liabilities	1,513,100	1,454,300	1,176,000	996,300	861,100	1,068,900	574,700	659,100
Long-Term Obligations	2,181,800	2,270,400	1,473,300	1,537,700	1,579,300	1,854,000	949,100	1,011,600
Total Liabilities	4,677,000	4,674,500	3,503,000	3,384,700	3,255,600	3,633,900	1,799,800	1,952,500
Stockholders' Equity	1,342,500	1,165,400	835,300	1,086,600	807,800	492,900	504,100	682,400
Shares Outstanding	100,224	104,136	104,200	112,691	112,778	113,490	115,634	112,196
Statistical Record								
Return on Assets %	4.74	6.47	5.93	6.90	5.61	4.84	N.M.	2.53
Return on Equity %	22.43	32.95	27.21	31.12	35.35	31.31	N.M.	9.91
EBITDA Margin %	10.76	12.59	11.75	13.86	13.39	11.93	3.45	10.05
Net Margin %	3.81	4.98	4.55	5.43	4.62	4.05	N.M.	1.86
Asset Turnover	1.25	1.30	1.30	1.27	1.21	1.20	1.49	1.36
Current Ratio	1.22	1.21	1.04	1.25	1.07	1.15	1.38	1.47
Debt to Equity	1.63	1.95	1.76	1.42	1.96	3.76	1.88	1.48
Price Range	55.75-43.91	44.79-34.71	45.87-35.56	44.94-28.59	29.79-21.29	26.95-16.32	17.75-9.79	11.81-6.63
P/E Ratio	20.35-16.03	14.26-11.05	19.27-14.94	17.28-11.00	14.82-10.59	19.82-12.00	...	21.87-12.27
Average Yield %	0.80	0.99	1.01	0.97	0.91	0.80	1.16	1.76

Address: 10 Longs Peak Drive, Broomfield, CO 80021
Telephone: 303-469-3131
Fax: 303-460-2127

Web Site: www.ball.com
Officers: R. David Hoover - Chmn., Pres., C.E.O. Hanno C. Fiedler - Exec. V.P.

Auditors: PricewaterhouseCoopers LLP
Investor Contact: 303-460-3537
Transfer Agents: EquiServe Trust Company, N.A., Providence, RI

BANCORPSOUTH INC.

Exchange	Symbol	Price	52Wk Range	Yield	P/E	Div Acheiver
NYS	BXS	$23.16 (3/31/2008)	26.00-20.17	3.63	13.70	21 Years

*7 Year Price Score 87.86   *NYSE Composite Index=100   *12 Month Price Score 104.92

Interim Earnings (Per Share)

Qtr.	Mar	Jun	Sep	Dec
2003	0.50	0.37	0.43	0.37
2004	0.35	0.40	0.36	0.32
2005	0.40	0.33	0.29	0.45
2006	0.47	0.45	0.38	0.26
2007	0.42	0.43	0.44	0.39

Interim Dividends (Per Share)

Amt	Decl	Ex	Rec	Pay
0.21Q	4/25/2007	6/13/2007	6/15/2007	7/2/2007
0.21Q	7/25/2007	9/12/2007	9/14/2007	10/1/2007
0.21Q	10/10/2007	12/12/2007	12/14/2007	1/2/2008
0.21Q	1/23/2008	3/12/2008	3/14/2008	4/1/2008

Indicated Div: $0.84 (Div. Reinv. Plan)

Valuation Analysis

Forecast P/E	13.53
	(1/10/2007)
Market Cap	$1.9 Billion
Book Value	1.2 Billion
Price/Book	1.59
Price/Sales	1.85

Institutional Holding

No of Institutions	110
Shares	21,127,884
% Held	26.72

TRADING VOLUME (thousand shares)

Business Summary: Commercial Banking (MIC: 8.1 SIC: 6022 NAIC: 522110)

BancorpSouth is a financial holding company. Through its principal bank subsidiary, BancorpSouth Bank (the Bank), Co. conducts a general commercial banking, trust and insurance business through 295 offices in Mississippi, Tennessee, Alabama, Arkansas, Texas, Louisiana, Florida, and Missouri. The Bank operates investment services, credit insurance and insurance agency subsidiaries which engage in investment brokerage services and sales of other insurance products. Additionally, the Bank's trust department provides a variety of services. As of Dec 31 2007, Co. and its subsidiaries had total assets of $13.19 billion and total deposits of $10.06 billion.

Recent Developments: For the year ended Dec 31 2007, net income increased 10.2% to US$137.9 million from US$125.2 million in the prior year. Net interest income increased 9.6% to US$422.9 million from US$385.8 million in the prior year. Provision for loan losses was US$22.7 million versus US$8.6 million in the prior year, an increase of 164.6%. Non-interest income rose 12.5% to US$231.8 million from US$206.1 million, while non-interest expense advanced 8.9% to US$428.1 million.

Prospects: Co. remains encouraged to pursue its long-term goals in 2008, as it intends to continue to add new products and services, and expand into contiguous markets through de novo bank development and acquisition. For example, on Jan 4 2008, Co.'s BancorpSouth Insurance Services subsidiary announced that it has acquired the property and casualty lines of business of Arthur J. Gallagher, Risk Management Services, Inc. in Springfield, MO. Further, on Feb 4 2008, BancorpSouth Insurance Services announced that it has agreed to acquire JMG/IC Insurance Agency, Inc. in Nacogdoches, TX. Both of these acquisitions provide Co. with the opportunity to continue expanding its insurance brokerage business.

Financial Data

(US$ in Thousands)	12/31/2007	12/31/2006	12/31/2005	12/31/2004	12/31/2003	12/31/2002	12/31/2001	12/31/2000
Earnings Per Share	1.69	1.57	1.47	1.43	1.68	1.39	1.19	0.88
Cash Flow Per Share	1.39	1.57	2.40	1.39	3.12	2.10	1.15	1.65
Tang Book Value Per Share	11.44	11.16	10.58	10.34	10.38	10.40	9.92	9.39
Dividends Per Share	0.830	0.790	0.760	0.730	0.660	0.610	0.570	0.530
Dividend Payout %	49.11	50.32	51.70	51.05	39.29	43.88	47.90	60.23
Income Statement								
Interest Income	801,242	681,891	559,936	497,629	526,911	590,418	665,835	674,035
Interest Expense	378,343	296,092	204,379	163,837	175,805	218,892	331,093	346,883
Net Interest Income	422,899	385,799	355,557	333,792	351,106	371,526	334,742	327,152
Provision for Losses	22,696	8,577	24,467	17,485	25,130	29,411	22,259	26,166
Non-Interest Income	231,799	206,094	198,812	183,519	190,086	132,239	128,633	85,578
Non-Interest Expense	428,058	393,154	362,102	342,945	322,594	312,398	295,313	274,227
Income Before Taxes	203,944	190,162	167,800	156,881	193,468	161,956	145,803	112,337
Income Taxes	66,001	64,968	52,601	46,261	62,334	49,938	47,340	37,941
Net Income	137,943	125,194	115,199	110,620	131,134	112,018	98,463	74,396
Average Shares	81,845	79,542	78,597	77,378	78,164	80,481	82,979	84,811
Balance Sheet								
Net Loans & Leases	9,193,019	7,861,960	7,338,326	6,830,250	6,215,624	6,359,314	6,055,587	6,041,405
Total Assets	13,189,841	12,040,521	11,768,674	10,848,193	10,305,035	10,189,247	9,395,429	9,044,034
Total Deposits	10,064,099	9,710,578	9,607,258	9,059,091	8,599,128	8,548,918	7,856,840	7,480,920
Total Liabilities	11,993,215	11,013,936	10,791,508	9,931,765	9,436,129	9,381,424	8,590,026	8,254,458
Stockholders' Equity	1,196,626	1,026,585	977,166	916,428	868,906	807,823	805,403	789,576
Shares Outstanding	82,299	79,109	79,237	78,037	77,926	77,680	81,225	84,043
Statistical Record								
Return on Assets %	1.09	1.05	1.02	1.04	1.28	1.14	1.07	1.00
Return on Equity %	12.41	12.50	12.17	12.36	15.64	13.89	12.35	11.53
Net Interest Margin %	52.78	56.58	63.50	67.08	66.63	62.93	50.27	48.54
Efficiency Ratio %	41.44	44.27	47.72	50.35	44.99	43.23	37.17	36.10
Loans to Deposits	0.91	0.81	0.76	0.75	0.72	0.74	0.77	0.81
Price Range	27.51-21.60	28.50-22.08	24.99-20.01	25.22-19.82	24.45-17.72	22.00-16.30	17.00-12.88	17.13-11.88
P/E Ratio	16.28-12.78	18.15-14.06	17.00-13.61	17.64-13.86	14.55-10.55	15.83-11.73	14.29-10.82	19.46-13.49
Average Yield %	3.38	3.06	3.42	3.25	3.12	3.11	3.76	3.61

Address: One Mississippi Plaza, 201 South Spring Street, Tupelo, MS 38804 **Telephone:** 662-680-2000 **Fax:** 601-680-2570	**Web Site:** www.bancorpsouth.com **Officers:** Aubrey B. Patterson - Chmn., C.E.O. James V. Kelley - Pres., C.O.O.	**Auditors:** KPMG LLP **Transfer Agents:** SunTrust Bank, Atlanta, GA

BANK OF AMERICA CORP.

Exchange	Symbol	Price	52Wk Range	Yield	P/E	Div Acheiver
NYS	BAC	$37.91 (3/31/2008)	52.71-35.31	6.75	11.49	30 Years

*7 Year Price Score 90.16   *NYSE Composite Index=100   *12 Month Price Score 93.88

Interim Earnings (Per Share)

Qtr.	Mar	Jun	Sep	Dec
2003	0.80	0.90	0.96	0.91
2004	0.92	0.93	0.91	0.93
2005	1.14	1.06	1.02	0.82
2006	1.07	1.19	1.18	1.15
2007	1.16	1.28	0.82	0.05

Interim Dividends (Per Share)

Amt	Decl	Ex	Rec	Pay
0.56Q	4/25/2007	5/30/2007	6/1/2007	6/22/2007
0.64Q	7/25/2007	9/5/2007	9/7/2007	9/28/2007
0.64Q	10/24/2007	12/5/2007	12/7/2007	12/28/2007
0.64Q	1/23/2008	3/5/2008	3/7/2008	3/28/2008

Indicated Div: $2.56 (Div. Reinv. Plan)

Valuation Analysis

		Institutional Holding	
Forecast P/E	10.11 (1/10/2007)	No of Institutions	1387
Market Cap	$168.2 Billion	Shares	2,729,134,080
Book Value	146.8 Billion	% Held	
Price/Book	1.15		61.02
Price/Sales	1.41		

Business Summary: Commercial Banking (MIC: 8.1 SIC: 6021 NAIC: 522110)

Bank of America is a bank holding company and a financial holding company. Through its banking subsidiaries and various nonbanking subsidiaries throughout the U.S. and in selected international markets, Co. provides a range of banking and nonbanking financial services and products through three business segments: Global Consumer and Small Business Banking, Global Corporate and Investment Banking, and Global Wealth and Investment Management. As of Dec 31 2007, Co. operated in 32 states, the District of Columbia and more than 30 foreign countries. At Dec 31 2007, Co. had total assets of $1.72 trillion and total deposits of $805.20 billion.

Recent Developments: For the year ended Dec 31 2007, net income decreased 29.1% to US$14.98 billion from US$21.13 billion in the prior year. Net interest income decreased 0.5% to US$34.43 billion from US$34.59 billion in the prior year. Provision for loan losses was US$8.39 billion versus US$5.01 billion in the prior year, an increase of 67.4%. Non-interest income fell 16.1% to US$31.89 billion from US$37.99 billion, while non-interest expense advanced 4.0% to US$37.01 billion.

Prospects: Moving ahead, Co. will focus on investment banking and global markets with traditional strength to ensure continued growth. For instance, on Jan 15 2008, Co. announced several changes in its Global Markets and Global Investment Banking businesses, such as a decline in activities in certain of its structured products, the resizing of its international platform, and plans to sell its equity prime brokerage business. Separately, on Jan 11 2008, Co. entered into a definitive agreement to acquire Countrywide Financial Corp. for about $4.00 billion. This deal is expected to close early in the third quarter of 2008, and will be neutral to Co.'s earnings per share in 2008 and accretive in 2009.

Financial Data

(US$ in Thousands)	12/31/2007	12/31/2006	12/31/2005	12/31/2004	12/31/2003	12/31/2002	12/31/2001	12/31/2000
Earnings Per Share	3.30	4.59	4.04	3.69	3.56	2.96	2.09	2.26
Cash Flow Per Share	2.49	3.21	(3.05)	(1.05)	8.18	(3.95)	(4.02)	1.59
Tang Book Value Per Share	11.54	12.18	12.48	11.80	11.38	11.88	10.40	9.50
Dividends Per Share	2.400	2.120	1.900	1.700	1.440	1.220	1.140	1.030
Dividend Payout %	72.73	46.19	47.03	46.07	40.39	41.29	54.55	45.58
Income Statement								
Interest Income	87,304,000	78,585,000	58,626,000	43,227,000	31,643,000	32,161,000	38,293,000	43,258,000
Interest Expense	52,871,000	43,994,000	27,889,000	14,430,000	10,179,000	11,238,000	18,003,000	24,816,000
Net Interest Income	34,433,000	34,591,000	30,737,000	28,797,000	21,464,000	20,923,000	20,290,000	18,442,000
Provision for Losses	8,385,000	5,010,000	4,014,000	2,769,000	2,839,000	3,697,000	4,287,000	2,535,000
Non-Interest Income	31,886,000	37,989,000	26,438,000	22,220,000	17,363,000	14,201,000	14,823,000	14,514,000
Non-Interest Expense	37,010,000	35,597,000	28,681,000	27,027,000	20,127,000	18,436,000	20,709,000	18,633,000
Income Before Taxes	20,924,000	31,973,000	24,480,000	21,221,000	15,861,000	12,991,000	10,117,000	11,788,000
Income Taxes	5,942,000	10,840,000	8,015,000	7,078,000	5,051,000	3,742,000	3,325,000	4,271,000
Net Income	14,982,000	21,133,000	16,465,000	14,143,000	10,810,000	9,249,000	6,792,000	7,517,000
Average Shares	4,480,253	4,595,895	4,068,140	3,823,943	3,030,356	3,130,934	3,251,308	3,329,858
Balance Sheet								
Net Loans & Leases	864,756,000	697,474,000	565,746,000	513,211,000	365,300,000	335,904,000	322,278,000	385,355,000
Total Assets	1,715,746,000	1,459,737,000	1,291,803,000	1,110,457,000	736,445,000	660,458,000	621,764,000	642,191,000
Total Deposits	805,177,000	693,497,000	634,670,000	618,570,000	414,113,000	386,458,000	373,495,000	364,244,000
Total Liabilities	1,568,943,000	1,324,465,000	1,190,270,000	1,010,812,000	688,465,000	610,139,000	573,244,000	594,563,000
Stockholders' Equity	146,803,000	135,272,000	101,533,000	99,645,000	47,980,000	50,319,000	48,520,000	47,628,000
Shares Outstanding	4,437,885	4,458,151	3,999,688	4,046,546	2,882,286	3,001,382	3,118,594	3,227,264
Statistical Record								
Return on Assets %	0.94	1.54	1.37	1.53	1.55	1.44	1.07	1.18
Return on Equity %	10.62	17.85	16.37	19.11	21.99	18.72	14.13	16.29
Net Interest Margin %	39.44	44.02	52.43	66.62	67.83	65.06	52.99	42.63
Efficiency Ratio %	31.05	30.54	33.72	41.30	41.07	39.77	38.99	32.25
Loans to Deposits	1.07	1.01	0.89	0.83	0.88	0.87	0.86	1.06
Price Range	54.05-41.10	54.90-43.09	47.08-41.57	47.44-38.96	41.77-32.81	38.45-27.07	32.50-23.38	30.50-19.00
P/E Ratio	16.38-12.45	11.96-9.39	11.65-10.29	12.86-10.56	11.73-9.22	12.99-9.15	15.55-11.18	13.50-8.41
Average Yield %	4.84	4.27	4.23	3.99	3.82	3.61	3.98	4.23

Address: Bank of America Corporate Center, 100 N. Tryon Street, Charlotte, NC 28255 Telephone: 704-386-5681 Fax: 704-388-9278	Web Site: www.bankofamerica.com Officers: Kenneth D. Lewis - Chmn., C.E.O. Timothy J. Mayopoulos - Exec. V.P., Gen. Couns.	Auditors: PricewaterhouseCoopers LLP Investor Contact: 800-521-3984 Transfer Agents: Mellon Investor Services LLC, South Hackensack, NJ

BANK OF HAWAII CORP

Exchange	Symbol	Price	52Wk Range	Yield	P/E	Div Acheiver
NYS	BOH	$49.56 (3/31/2008)	54.85-43.07	3.55	13.43	30 Years

*7 Year Price Score 98.19   *NYSE Composite Index=100   *12 Month Price Score 103.89

Interim Earnings (Per Share)

Qtr.	Mar	Jun	Sep	Dec
2003	0.47	0.48	0.61	0.65
2004	0.69	0.79	0.78	0.82
2005	0.83	0.87	0.85	0.86
2006	0.87	0.73	0.93	0.99
2007	0.94	0.95	0.96	0.83

Interim Dividends (Per Share)

Amt	Decl	Ex	Rec	Pay
0.41Q	4/23/2007	5/29/2007	5/31/2007	6/14/2007
0.41Q	7/23/2007	8/29/2007	8/31/2007	9/14/2007
0.44Q	10/22/2007	11/28/2007	11/30/2007	12/14/2007
0.44Q	1/28/2008	2/27/2008	2/29/2008	3/14/2008

Indicated Div: $1.76 (Div. Reinv. Plan)

Valuation Analysis

		Institutional Holding	
Forecast P/E	N/A	No of Institutions	204
Market Cap	$2.4 Billion	Shares	32,292,780
Book Value	750.3 Million	% Held	64.94
Price/Book	3.21		
Price/Sales	2.86		

TRADING VOLUME (thousand shares)

Business Summary: Commercial Banking (MIC: 8.1 SIC: 6022 NAIC: 522110)

Bank of Hawaii is the bank holding company for Bank of Hawaii (the Bank). The Bank provides financial services and products mainly in Hawaii and the Pacific Islands. The Bank's subsidiaries include Bank of Hawaii Leasing, Inc., Bankoh Investment Services, Inc., Pacific Century Life Insurance Corporation, Triad Insurance Agency, Inc., Bank of Hawaii Insurance Services, Inc., Pacific Century Insurance Services, Inc., Bankoh Investment Partners, LLC, and Bank of Hawaii International, Inc. The Bank's subsidiaries provide equipment leasing, securities brokerage and investment services, and insurance and insurance agency services. As of Dec 31 2007, Co. had total assets of $10.47 billion.

Recent Developments: For the year ended Dec 31 2007, net income increased 1.9% to US$183.7 million from US$180.4 million in the prior year. Net interest income decreased 1.9% to US$395.0 million from US$402.6 million in the prior year. Provision for loan losses was US$15.5 million versus US$10.8 million in the prior year, an increase of 44.1%. Non-interest income rose 11.2% to US$240.5 million from US$216.2 million, while non-interest expense advanced 4.5% to US$335.4 million.

Prospects: Co.'s near-term outlook appears constructive. Co.'s strategy for growth is to focus on the Hawaii market with specific initiatives that include introducing new products, services and delivery processes, and enhanced services. In detail, Co. is seeing near-term growth opportunities within the area of investment services. In addition, Co. intends to focus on integration that involves products and services, financial capabilities, and delivery channels. In particular, Co. will continue to identify inter-segment operating efficiencies and developing new products, services and processes. Specifically, Co. intends to reduce redundant products and services that exist in multiple business units.

Financial Data
(US$ in Thousands)

	12/31/2007	12/31/2006	12/31/2005	12/31/2004	12/31/2003	12/31/2002	12/31/2001	12/31/2000
Earnings Per Share	3.69	3.52	3.41	3.08	2.21	1.70	1.46	1.42
Cash Flow Per Share	4.77	4.16	4.44	4.87	5.46	9.13	(3.28)	3.50
Tang Book Value Per Share	14.15	11.70	12.49	13.83	13.38	15.09	16.16	13.93
Dividends Per Share	1.670	1.520	1.360	1.230	0.870	0.730	0.720	0.710
Dividend Payout %	45.26	43.18	39.88	39.94	39.37	42.94	49.32	50.00
Income Statement								
Interest Income	601,875	572,672	506,442	455,014	442,521	516,538	828,262	1,057,493
Interest Expense	206,857	170,059	99,329	64,424	76,579	146,307	368,584	501,262
Net Interest Income	395,018	402,613	407,113	390,590	365,942	370,231	459,678	556,231
Provision for Losses	15,507	10,758	4,588	(10,000)	...	11,616	74,339	142,853
Non-Interest Income	240,487	216,176	209,314	205,094	198,720	199,921	452,619	263,429
Non-Interest Expense	335,407	320,962	327,642	334,440	357,875	370,835	597,616	496,430
Income Before Taxes	284,591	287,069	284,197	271,244	206,787	187,701	239,959	179,990
Income Taxes	100,888	106,710	102,636	97,905	71,592	66,521	122,164	66,329
Net Income	183,703	180,359	181,561	173,339	135,195	121,180	117,795	113,661
Average Shares	49,833	51,178	53,310	56,241	61,085	71,447	80,577	79,813
Balance Sheet								
Net Loans & Leases	6,502,204	6,544,111	6,095,361	5,897,776	5,637,306	5,256,269	5,950,248	9,168,140
Total Assets	10,472,942	10,571,815	10,187,038	9,766,191	9,461,647	9,516,418	10,627,797	14,013,816
Total Deposits	7,942,372	8,023,394	7,907,468	7,564,667	7,332,779	6,920,161	6,673,596	9,080,581
Total Liabilities	9,722,687	9,852,395	9,493,686	8,951,357	8,668,515	8,500,659	9,380,785	12,712,460
Stockholders' Equity	750,255	719,420	693,352	814,834	793,132	1,015,759	1,247,012	1,301,356
Shares Outstanding	48,589	56,827	51,276	54,960	54,928	63,015	73,218	79,612
Statistical Record								
Return on Assets %	1.75	1.74	1.82	1.80	1.42	1.20	0.96	0.80
Return on Equity %	25.00	25.53	24.08	21.50	14.95	10.71	9.24	9.02
Net Interest Margin %	65.63	70.30	80.39	85.84	82.69	71.68	55.50	52.60
Efficiency Ratio %	39.82	40.69	45.78	50.66	55.81	51.76	46.66	37.58
Loans to Deposits	0.82	0.82	0.77	0.78	0.77	0.76	0.89	1.01
Price Range	54.85-46.78	54.87-47.33	54.14-44.05	50.95-41.70	42.72-29.43	30.75-23.88	27.88-16.94	22.94-11.25
P/E Ratio	14.86-12.68	15.59-13.45	15.88-12.92	16.54-13.54	19.33-13.32	18.09-14.05	19.10-11.60	16.15-7.92
Average Yield %	3.21	2.96	2.76	2.68	2.54	2.62	3.13	4.26

Address: 130 Merchant Street, Honolulu, HI 96813 Telephone: 808-538-4727 Fax: 808-521-7602	Web Site: www.boh.com Officers: Allan R. Landon - Chmn., Pres., C.E.O. Alton T. Kuioka - Vice-Chair, Commercial Banking	Auditors: ERNST & YOUNG LLP Investor Contact: 808-537-8430 Transfer Agents: Computershare Investor Services, LLC, Canton, MA

BANKATLANTIC BANCORP, INC.

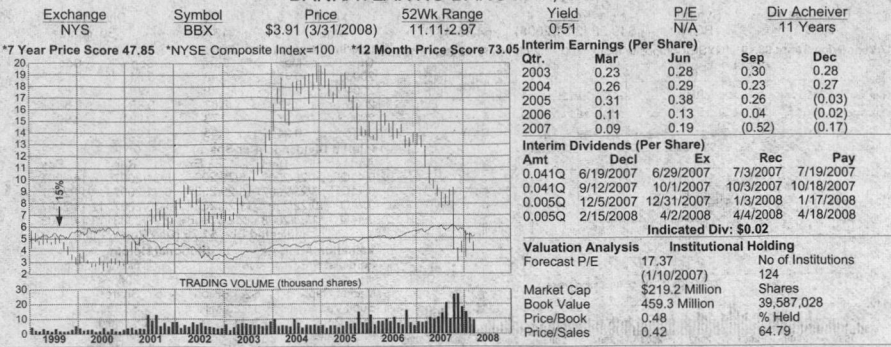

Exchange	Symbol	Price	52Wk Range	Yield	P/E	Div Acheiver
NYS	BBX	$3.91 (3/31/2008)	11.11-2.97	0.51	N/A	11 Years

*7 Year Price Score 47.85 *NYSE Composite Index=100 *12 Month Price Score 73.05

Interim Earnings (Per Share)

Qtr.	Mar	Jun	Sep	Dec
2003	0.23	0.28	0.30	0.28
2004	0.26	0.29	0.23	0.27
2005	0.31	0.38	0.26	(0.03)
2006	0.11	0.13	0.04	(0.02)
2007	0.09	0.19	(0.52)	(0.17)

Interim Dividends (Per Share)

Amt	Decl	Ex	Rec	Pay
0.041Q	6/19/2007	6/29/2007	7/3/2007	7/19/2007
0.041Q	9/12/2007	10/1/2007	10/3/2007	10/18/2007
0.005Q	12/5/2007	12/31/2007	1/3/2008	1/17/2008
0.005Q	2/15/2008	4/2/2008	4/4/2008	4/18/2008

Indicated Div: $0.02

Valuation Analysis   **Institutional Holding**

Forecast P/E	17.37	No of Institutions
	(1/10/2007)	124
Market Cap	$219.2 Million	Shares
Book Value	459.3 Million	39,587,028
Price/Book	0.48	% Held
Price/Sales	0.42	64.79

Business Summary: Other Depository Banking (MIC: 8.5 SIC: 6035 NAIC: 522120)

BankAtlantic Bancorp is a financial services holding company and owns BankAtlantic and its subsidiaries. As of Dec 31 2007, BankAtlantic provided traditional retail banking services and a range of business banking products and related financial services through a network of more than 100 branches or stores in southeast and central Florida and the Tampa Bay area, primarily in the metropolitan areas surrounding the cities of Miami, Ft. Lauderdale, West Palm Beach and Tampa, which are located in the Florida counties of Miami-Dade, Broward, Palm Beach, Hillsborough and Pinellas. At such date, Co. had total assets of about $6.38 billion, and total deposits of about $3.95 billion.

Recent Developments: For the year ended Dec 31 2007, loss from continuing operations was US$30.0 million compared with income of US$26.9 million a year earlier. Net loss amounted to US$22.2 million versus net income of US$15.4 million in the prior year. Net interest income decreased 10.7% to US$178.8 million from US$200.1 million in the prior year. Provision for loan losses was US$70.8 million versus US$8.6 million in the prior year, an increase of 726.2%. Non-interest income rose 6.5% to US$151.8 million from US$142.6 million, while non-interest expense advanced 5.7% to US$317.4 million.

Prospects: Looking ahead, while Co. remains committed to store expansion in the long-term, Co. has decided to reduce its new store openings in 2008 to the four originally planned for the first quarter of 2008. As part of this decision, on Mar 11 2008, Co.'s BankAtlantic subsidiary has reached an agreement to sell its five stores in the Orlando market to Mercantile Bank. The sale will allow Co. to focus on those markets where it has a greater retail presence. The transaction is expected to close in the second quarter of 2008, subject to receipt of regulatory approval. Meanwhile, Co. anticipates a decline in short term interest rates to result in core deposit growth during 2008.

Financial Data

(US$ in Thousands)	12/31/2007	12/31/2006	12/31/2005	12/31/2004	12/31/2003	12/31/2002	12/31/2001	12/31/2000
Earnings Per Share	(0.38)	0.25	0.92	1.11	1.08	0.81	0.65	0.54
Cash Flow Per Share	0.70	0.05	0.95	1.12	1.71	0.01	1.92	3.25
Tang Book Value Per Share	6.84	7.33	7.10	6.36	5.48	6.46	6.82	6.27
Dividends Per Share	0.128	0.158	0.146	0.136	0.128	0.120	0.112	0.076
Dividend Payout %	...	63.20	15.87	12.25	11.85	14.81	17.28	14.06
Income Statement								
Interest Income	371,633	367,177	360,405	260,555	261,849	309,770	325,618	327,891
Interest Expense	192,857	167,057	145,328	87,722	113,217	151,962	187,599	210,012
Net Interest Income	178,776	200,120	215,077	172,833	148,632	157,808	138,019	117,879
Provision for Losses	70,842	8,574	(6,615)	(5,109)	(547)	14,077	16,905	29,132
Non-Interest Income	151,832	142,616	341,099	344,789	281,714	248,318	123,273	116,164
Non-Interest Expense	317,350	300,186	470,111	412,053	368,872	334,480	190,376	177,207
Income Before Taxes	(57,584)	33,976	92,680	110,678	62,021	57,569	54,011	27,704
Income Taxes	(27,572)	7,097	33,498	39,910	23,424	15,876	22,736	11,607
Net Income	(22,200)	15,387	59,182	70,768	67,717	50,335	32,160	16,766
Average Shares	58,161	62,563	63,119	63,056	62,354	64,400	54,313	47,126
Balance Sheet								
Net Loans & Leases	4,520,101	4,586,607	4,624,772	4,599,048	3,686,153	3,372,630	2,774,238	2,853,804
Total Assets	6,378,817	6,495,662	6,471,411	6,356,777	4,831,549	5,421,011	4,654,486	4,617,300
Total Deposits	3,953,405	3,867,036	3,752,676	3,457,202	3,058,142	2,920,555	2,276,567	2,234,485
Total Liabilities	5,919,496	5,970,680	5,955,075	5,887,512	4,418,097	4,951,677	4,218,813	4,368,479
Stockholders' Equity	459,321	524,982	516,336	469,265	413,452	469,334	435,673	248,821
Shares Outstanding	56,072	61,033	60,760	60,090	59,272	58,317	58,079	31,704
Statistical Record								
Return on Assets %	N.M.	0.24	0.92	1.26	1.32	1.00	0.69	0.38
Return on Equity %	N.M.	2.96	12.01	15.99	15.34	11.12	9.40	6.90
Net Interest Margin %	48.11	54.50	59.68	66.33	56.76	50.94	42.39	35.95
Efficiency Ratio %	60.62	58.88	67.01	68.07	67.86	59.93	42.41	39.91
Loans to Deposits	1.14	1.19	1.23	1.33	1.21	1.15	1.22	1.28
Price Range	13.98-2.97	15.96-12.66	19.90-13.36	19.99-13.96	14.34-6.45	9.55-5.59	8.15-2.85	3.90-2.25
P/E Ratio	...	63.84-50.64	21.63-14.52	18.01-12.58	13.28-5.97	11.79-6.90	12.54-4.38	7.23-4.17
Average Yield %	1.51	1.10	0.88	0.80	1.23	1.58	2.04	2.47

Address: 2100 West Cypress Creek Road, Fort Lauderdale, FL 33309 **Telephone:** 954-940-5000	**Web Site:** www.bankatlanticbancorp.com **Officers:** Alan B. Levan - Chmn., Pres., C.E.O. John E. Abdo - Vice-Chmn.	**Auditors:** PricewaterhouseCoopers LLP **Investor Contact:** 954-940-5300 **Transfer Agents:** American Stock Transfer & Trust Co

BARD (C.R.), INC.

Exchange	Symbol	Price	52Wk Range	Yield	P/E	Div Acheiver
NYS	BCR	$96.40 (3/31/2008)	99.66-77.99	0.62	25.10	36 Years

*7 Year Price Score 127.21 *NYSE Composite Index=100 *12 Month Price Score 119.49

TRADING VOLUME (thousand shares)

Interim Earnings (Per Share)

Qtr.	Mar	Jun	Sep	Dec
2003	0.45	0.47	0.49	0.20
2004	0.68	0.55	0.95	0.65
2005	0.75	0.79	0.83	0.75
2006	0.76	0.76	0.82	0.21
2007	0.95	0.91	0.96	1.01

Interim Dividends (Per Share)

Amt	Decl	Ex	Rec	Pay
0.14Q	4/18/2007	4/26/2007	4/30/2007	5/11/2007
0.15Q	6/13/2007	7/19/2007	7/23/2007	8/3/2007
0.15Q	10/10/2007	10/18/2007	10/22/2007	11/2/2007
0.15Q	12/12/2007	1/16/2008	1/21/2008	2/1/2008

Indicated Div: $0.60 (Div. Reinv. Plan)

Valuation Analysis | **Institutional Holding**

Forecast P/E	19.06 (1/10/2007)	No of Institutions 382
Market Cap	$9.7 Billion	Shares
Book Value	1.8 Billion	87,760,848
Price/Book	5.23	% Held
Price/Sales	4.39	84.98

Business Summary: Health (MIC: 9 SIC: 3841 NAIC: 339112)

C. R. Bard is engaged in the design, manufacture, packaging, distribution and sale of medical, surgical, diagnostic and patient care devices. Co. provides four major product group categories: vascular, urology, oncology and surgical specialties. Co. develops, manufactures and markets a range of products for the peripheral vascular market. Co.'s urology products include Foley catheters and other urology products. Co.'s oncology products cover a range of devices used in the treatment and management of various cancers and other diseases and disorders. In addition, Co. provides surgical specialty products including meshes and fixation systems for hernia and other soft tissue repairs.

Recent Developments: For the year ended Dec 31 2007, income from continuing operations increased 29.2% to US$406.4 million from US$314.5 million a year earlier. Net income increased 49.4% to US$406.4 million from US$272.1 million in the prior year. Revenues were US$2.20 billion, up 11.2% from US$1.98 billion the year before. Direct operating expenses rose 12.6% to US$864.5 million from US$767.6 million in the comparable period the year before. Indirect operating expenses increased 2.0% to US$792.5 million from US$777.0 million in the equivalent prior-year period.

Prospects: Going forward, Co. remains focused on implementing its strategy of pursuing the acquisition of complementary businesses, technologies and products to facilitate its business. For example, on Jan 17 2008, Co. announced that it has acquired the assets of the LifeStent® product family from Edwards Lifesciences Corp. for a total transaction value of about $139.0 million. Co. believes that this transaction will further strengthen its existing portfolio of non-coronary stent and stent graft products. In addition, Co. expects this transaction to have a negligible effect on earnings in 2008 and be accretive thereafter, excluding the effect of a charge for purchased research and development.

Financial Data

(US$ in Thousands)	12/31/2007	12/31/2006	12/31/2005	12/31/2004	12/31/2003	12/31/2002	12/31/2001	12/31/2000
Earnings Per Share	3.84	2.55	3.12	2.82	1.60	1.47	1.38	1.04
Cash Flow Per Share	5.33	3.22	3.83	2.65	2.54	2.62	2.42	2.03
Tang Book Value Per Share	10.73	9.46	9.08	7.26	5.35	4.84	3.97	2.53
Dividends Per Share	0.580	0.540	0.500	0.470	0.450	0.430	0.420	0.410
Dividend Payout %	15.10	21.18	16.03	16.67	28.13	29.25	30.55	39.23
Income Statement								
Total Revenue	2,202,000	1,985,500	1,771,300	1,656,100	1,433,100	1,273,800	1,181,300	1,098,800
EBITDA	626,400	394,600	494,900	460,500	261,300	245,500	238,700	199,900
Income Before Taxes	577,300	347,600	449,600	414,200	223,200	211,000	204,900	154,000
Income Taxes	170,900	75,500	112,500	111,400	54,700	56,000	61,700	47,100
Net Income	406,400	272,100	337,100	302,800	168,500	155,000	143,200	106,900
Average Shares	105,900	106,900	108,000	107,200	105,200	105,600	104,001	102,443
Balance Sheet								
Current Assets	1,242,000	1,133,900	1,264,100	1,054,000	875,100	758,000	647,400	526,600
Total Assets	2,475,500	2,277,200	2,265,600	2,009,100	1,692,000	1,416,700	1,231,100	1,089,200
Current Liabilities	281,700	295,900	640,600	390,300	421,900	316,900	234,500	224,500
Long-Term Obligations	149,800	150,600	800	151,400	151,500	152,200	156,400	204,300
Total Liabilities	627,500	579,200	729,500	649,000	646,300	536,300	442,400	475,300
Stockholders' Equity	1,848,000	1,698,000	1,536,100	1,360,100	1,045,700	880,400	788,700	613,900
Shares Outstanding	100,191	103,155	104,012	104,672	103,509	103,205	104,767	101,817
Statistical Record								
Return on Assets %	17.10	11.98	15.77	16.32	10.84	11.71	12.34	9.62
Return on Equity %	22.92	16.83	23.28	25.10	17.50	18.57	20.42	17.94
EBITDA Margin %	28.45	19.87	27.94	27.81	18.23	19.27	20.21	18.19
Net Margin %	18.46	13.70	19.03	18.28	11.76	12.17	12.12	9.73
Asset Turnover	0.93	0.87	0.83	0.89	0.92	0.96	1.02	0.99
Current Ratio	4.41	3.83	1.97	2.70	2.07	2.39	2.76	2.35
Debt to Equity	0.08	0.09	N.M.	0.11	0.14	0.17	0.20	0.33
Price Range	95.05-77.25	85.43-61.00	72.79-61.36	64.58-40.20	40.63-27.41	32.25-23.13	32.26-21.00	27.34-17.63
P/E Ratio	24.75-20.12	33.50-23.92	23.33-19.67	22.90-14.26	25.39-17.13	21.94-15.73	23.37-15.21	26.29-16.95
Average Yield %	0.70	0.74	0.75	0.88	1.33	1.57	1.62	1.82

Address: 730 Central Avenue, Murray Hill, NJ 07974 Telephone: 908-277-8000 Fax: 908-277-8278	Web Site: www.crbard.com Officers: Timothy M. Ring - Chmn., C.E.O. John H. Weiland - Pres., C.O.O.	Auditors: KPMG LLP Investor Contact: 908-277-8413 Transfer Agents: EquiServe Trust Company, N.A., Providence, RI

BARNES & NOBLE INC

Exchange	Symbol	Price	52Wk Range	Yield	P/E
NYS	BKS	$30.65 (3/31/2008)	42.82-26.26	N/A	15.10

*7 Year Price Score 98.93 *NYSE Composite Index=100 *12 Month Price Score 92.00

TRADING VOLUME (thousand shares)

Interim Earnings (Per Share)

Qtr.	Apr	Jul	Oct	Jan
2003-04	(0.03)	0.20	0.14	1.76
2004-05	0.17	0.12	0.10	1.55
2005-06	0.13	0.18	0.00	1.70
2006-07	0.14	0.24	(0.04)	1.83
2007-08	(0.03)	0.26	0.07	1.72

Interim Dividends (Per Share)

No Dividends Paid

Valuation Analysis   **Institutional Holding**

Forecast P/E	N/A	No of Institutions
		217
Market Cap	$1.8 Billion	Shares
Book Value	1.1 Billion	45,364,240
Price/Book	1.72	% Held
Price/Sales	0.34	68.80

Business Summary: Retail - Miscellaneous (MIC: 5.11 SIC: 5942 NAIC: 451211)

Barnes & Noble is primarily engaged in the sale of trade books, mass market paperbacks, children's books, bargain books, magazines, music and movies direct to customers. As of Feb 2 2008, Co. operated 798 bookstores and a website. Of the 793 bookstores, 713 were operated primarily under the Barnes & Noble Booksellers trade name and 85 were operated mainly under the B. Dalton Bookseller trade name. Co. conducts the online part of its business through barnesandnoble.com llc, a seller of books on the Internet, while through Sterling Publishing Co., Inc., Co. is a general trade book publisher. Additionally, Co. owns about 74.0% interest in Calendar Club L.L.C., an operator of seasonal kiosks.

Recent Developments: For the year ended Feb 2 2008, net income decreased 9.8% to US$135.8 million from US$150.5 million in the prior year. Revenues were US$5.41 billion, up 2.8% from US$5.26 billion the year before. Operating income was US$208.1 million versus US$253.4 million in the prior year, a decrease of 17.9%. Direct operating expenses rose 4.1% to US$3.77 billion from US$3.62 billion in the comparable period the year before. Indirect operating expenses increased 3.4% to US$1.43 billion from US$1.38 billion in the equivalent prior-year period.

Prospects: For the fiscal year ending Jan 31 2009, Co. expects comparable store sales to be slightly positive, while earnings are estimated to range from $1.70 to $1.90 per share. In addition, Co. is forecasting capital expenditures to be in the range of $200.0 million to $210.0 million, primarily for its anticipated plan to open between 35 to 40 new Barnes & Noble stores, the maintenance of existing stores as well as system enhancements for the retail stores and the website. For the fiscal quarter ended May 2008, Co. expects comparable store sales to be slightly negative, while earnings are projected to range from $0.05 to $0.10 per share.

Financial Data

(US$ in Thousands)	02/02/2008	02/03/2007	01/28/2006	01/29/2005	01/31/2004	02/01/2003	02/02/2002	02/03/2001
Earnings Per Share	2.03	2.17	2.03	1.93	2.07	1.39	0.94	(0.81)
Cash Flow Per Share	6.85	4.09	7.42	7.74	7.74	4.97	6.91	1.23
Tang Book Value Per Share	12.13	12.51	11.37	11.39	9.64	9.12	7.96	6.43
Dividends Per Share	0.600	0.600	0.300	...	...	...	...	...
Dividend Payout %	29.56	27.65	14.78	...	...	...	...	...
Income Statement								
Total Revenue	5,410,828	5,261,254	5,103,004	4,873,595	5,951,015	5,269,335	4,870,390	4,375,804
EBITDA	388,026	425,776	424,223	402,114	462,384	350,899	269,853	124,356
Income Before Taxes	215,270	254,921	250,409	218,606	295,839	199,313	109,345	(32,997)
Income Taxes	76,917	102,606	102,042	94,001	120,554	80,223	45,378	18,969
Net Income	135,799	150,527	146,681	143,376	151,853	99,948	63,967	(51,966)
Average Shares	67,050	69,226	72,150	75,696	77,105	77,680	77,839	64,341
Balance Sheet								
Current Assets	1,965,681	1,922,440	1,860,176	1,970,010	2,193,489	1,886,868	1,590,994	1,455,253
Total Assets	3,249,826	3,196,798	3,164,132	3,301,528	3,507,294	2,995,427	2,623,220	2,557,476
Current Liabilities	1,590,167	1,496,998	1,512,668	1,325,582	1,441,841	1,231,448	1,140,228	935,075
Long-Term Obligations	...	...	...	245,000	300,000	300,000	449,000	666,900
Total Liabilities	2,163,053	2,021,273	2,038,234	2,126,644	2,020,348	1,766,686	1,735,110	1,779,799
Stockholders' Equity	1,074,720	1,164,865	1,115,841	1,165,942	1,259,659	1,027,790	888,110	777,677
Shares Outstanding	60,293	65,088	66,680	70,268	68,047	64,608	67,208	65,044
Statistical Record								
Return on Assets %	4.22	4.66	4.55	4.22	4.68	3.57	2.48	N.M.
Return on Equity %	12.16	12.99	12.89	11.85	13.31	10.46	7.70	N.M.
EBITDA Margin %	7.17	8.09	8.31	8.25	7.77	6.66	5.54	2.84
Net Margin %	2.51	2.86	2.87	2.94	2.55	1.90	1.31	N.M.
Asset Turnover	1.68	1.63	1.58	1.44	1.84	1.88	1.89	1.73
Current Ratio	1.24	1.28	1.23	1.49	1.52	1.53	1.40	1.56
Debt to Equity	...	...	...	0.21	0.24	0.29	0.51	0.86
Price Range	42.98-26.74	47.40-32.58	43.72-31.95	32.94-20.33	25.22-11.50	24.74-12.20	31.36-17.05	20.68-11.89
P/E Ratio	21.17-13.17	21.84-15.01	21.54-15.74	17.07-10.53	12.18-5.55	17.80-8.77	33.36-18.14	...
Average Yield %	1.61	1.51	0.79	...	...	...	...	...

Address: 122 Fifth Avenue, New York, NY 10011 **Telephone:** 212-633-3300 **Fax:** 212-366-5186	**Web Site:** www.barnesandnobleinc.com **Officers:** Leonard Riggio - Chmn. Stephen Riggio - Vice-Chmn., C.E.O.	**Auditors:** BDO Seidman, LLP **Transfer Agents:** The Bank of New York, New York, NY

BARR PHARMACEUTICALS INC

Exchange	Symbol	Price	52Wk Range	Yield	P/E
NYS	BRL	$48.31 (3/31/2008)	57.87-45.67	N/A	40.94

*7 Year Price Score 94.50   ***NYSE Composite Index=100**   ***12 Month Price Score 100.46**

TRADING VOLUME (thousand shares)

Interim Earnings (Per Share)

Qtr.	Mar	Jun	Sep	Dec
2007-08	0.11	0.41	0.36	0.30

Interim Dividends (Per Share)

Amt	Decl	Ex	Rec	Pay
50%	2/13/2004	3/16/2004	2/23/2004	3/15/2004

Valuation Analysis   **Institutional Holding**

Forecast P/E	11.44	No of Institutions	
	(1/10/2007)	342	
Market Cap	$5.2 Billion	Shares	
Book Value	1.9 Billion	86,165,504	
Price/Book	2.79	% Held	
Price/Sales	2.08	80.79	

Business Summary: Pharmaceuticals (MIC: 9.1 SIC: 2834 NAIC: 325412)

Barr Pharmaceuticals is a specialty pharmaceutical company. Co. develops, manufactures and markets generic and proprietary pharmaceutical products. Co.'s generic product portfolio includes solid oral dosage forms, injectables and cream/ointment products. At Dec 31 2007, Co. marketed for sale in the U.S., about 245 different dosage forms and strengths of about 120 different generic pharmaceutical products, including 25 oral contraceptive products; and in Europe and the rest of the world, approximately 1,025 generic pharmaceutical products. Co.'s products include SEASONIQUE®, PLAN B™ and PARAGARD® T 380A.

Recent Developments: For the year ended Dec 31 2007, income from continuing operations was US$142.1 million compared with a loss of US$336.4 million a year earlier. Net income amounted to US$128.4 million versus a net loss of US$338.2 million in the prior year. Revenues were US$2.50 billion, up 176.4% from US$904.8 million the year before. Operating income was US$312.6 million versus a loss of US$211.0 million in the prior year. Direct operating expenses rose 217.1% to US$1.17 billion from US$369.3 million in the comparable period the year before. Indirect operating expenses increased 36.2% to US$1.02 billion from US$746.5 million in the equivalent prior-year period.

Prospects: For 2008, Co. expects total revenues of $2.70 billion to $2.80 billion, including total product sales of $2.55 billion to $2.65 billion. Specifically, Co. expects sales of Kariva, its generic version of Mircette oral contraceptive, to decline in the second half of 2008 versus the first half of 2008, due to potential competition when the patent on its Mircette product expires in Oct 2008. Co. also expects that competition will continue to reduce selling prices, causing its generic oral contraceptives revenues to decrease; but anticipates the increase in sales of its SEASONIQUE, Plan B and ParaGard oral contraceptives to drive proprietary product sales growth of about 20.0% in 2008 over 2007.

Financial Data

(US$ in Thousands)	12/31/2007	12/31/2006	06/30/2006	06/30/2005	06/30/2004	06/30/2003	06/30/2002	06/30/2001
Earnings Per Share	1.18	(3.18)	3.12	2.03	1.15	1.62	2.06	0.74
Cash Flow Per Share	3.57	1.33	3.11	3.52	2.53	1.62	2.37	0.81
Tang Book Value Per Share	0.90	N.M.	11.54	10.81	9.18	8.03	6.39	4.59
Income Statement								
Total Revenue	2,500,582	916,403	1,314,465	1,047,399	1,309,088	902,864	1,188,984	509,686
EBITDA	631,177	(213,234)	566,565	360,710	223,374	280,561	348,780	104,402
Income Before Taxes	207,835	(304,279)	522,948	329,876	194,440	262,715	337,784	101,116
Income Taxes	64,546	34,505	186,471	114,888	71,337	95,149	125,405	38,629
Net Income	128,350	(338,155)	336,477	214,988	123,103	167,566	212,219	62,487
Average Shares	108,631	106,377	107,798	106,052	106,661	103,591	102,201	84,795
Balance Sheet								
Current Assets	1,750,185	2,087,999	1,108,982	993,356	878,246	847,504	637,668	436,774
Total Assets	4,761,627	4,961,862	1,921,419	1,482,846	1,333,269	1,180,937	888,554	543,394
Current Liabilities	779,331	1,211,893	187,319	212,970	207,645	274,787	177,455	151,560
Long-Term Obligations	1,781,692	1,937,215	7,431	15,493	32,355	34,027	42,634	24,899
Total Liabilities	2,857,152	3,455,536	230,463	248,876	291,223	312,942	222,022	177,752
Stockholders' Equity	1,866,321	1,465,228	1,690,956	1,233,970	1,042,046	867,995	666,532	365,642
Shares Outstanding	107,810	106,563	106,206	103,367	104,495	100,568	98,111	79,659
Statistical Record								
Return on Assets %	2.64	N.M.	19.77	15.27	9.77	16.19	29.64	12.92
Return on Equity %	7.71	N.M.	23.01	18.89	12.85	21.84	41.12	19.29
EBITDA Margin %	25.24	N.M.	43.10	34.44	17.06	31.07	29.33	20.48
Net Margin %	5.13	N.M.	25.60	20.53	9.40	18.56	17.85	12.26
Asset Turnover	0.51	0.19	0.77	0.74	1.04	0.87	1.66	1.05
Current Ratio	2.25	1.72	5.92	4.66	4.23	3.08	3.59	2.88
Debt to Equity	0.95	1.32	N.M.	0.01	0.03	0.04	0.06	0.07
Price Range	57.87-46.17	58.28-45.11	68.70-45.22	53.45-32.43	56.49-33.15	43.68-22.44	39.72-26.93	34.44-19.56
P/E Ratio	49.04-39.13	...	22.02-14.49	26.33-15.98	49.12-28.83	26.96-13.85	19.28-13.07	46.55-26.43

Address: 400 Chestnut Ridge Road, Woodcliff Lake, NJ 07677-7668
Telephone: 201-930-3300
Fax: 201-930-3330

Web Site: www.barrlabs.com
Officers: Bruce L. Downey - Chmn., C.E.O. Paul M. Bisaro - Pres., C.O.O.

Auditors: Deloitte & Touche LLP
Investor Contact: 180-022-77522
Transfer Agents: Continental Stock Transfer & Trust Company, New York, NY

BAXTER INTERNATIONAL INC.

Exchange	Symbol	Price	52Wk Range	Yield	P/E
NYS	BAX	$57.82 (3/31/2008)	64.91-50.16	1.50	22.15

*7 Year Price Score 111.88 *NYSE Composite Index=100 *12 Month Price Score 111.07

Interim Earnings (Per Share)

Qtr.	Mar	Jun	Sep	Dec
2003	0.35	0.06	0.43	0.61
2004	0.29	(0.28)	0.45	0.17
2005	0.36	0.51	0.18	0.46
2006	0.43	0.47	0.57	0.66
2007	0.61	0.65	0.61	0.74

Interim Dividends (Per Share)

Amt	Decl	Ex	Rec	Pay
0.168Q	5/2/2007	6/6/2007	6/10/2007	7/2/2007
0.168Q	7/31/2007	9/6/2007	9/10/2007	10/1/2007
0.218Q	11/13/2007	12/6/2007	12/10/2007	1/3/2008
0.218Q	2/12/2008	3/6/2008	3/10/2008	4/1/2008

Indicated Div: $0.87

Valuation Analysis

Forecast P/E	N/A
Market Cap	$36.6 Billion
Book Value	6.9 Billion
Price/Book	5.30
Price/Sales	3.25

Institutional Holding

No of Institutions	653
Shares	544,813,824
% Held	83.84

Business Summary: Medical Instruments & Equipment (MIC: 9.6 SIC: 3841 NAIC: 339112)

Baxter International operates through three primary business segments. Co.'s BioScience business manufactures recombinant and plasma-based proteins to treat hemophilia and other bleeding disorders; plasma-based therapies to treat immune deficiencies, alpha 1-antitrypsin deficiency, burns and shock, and other chronic and acute blood-related conditions; products for regenerative medicine, such as proteins used in hemostasis, wound-sealing and tissue regeneration; and vaccines. Co.'s Medication Delivery business manufactures products used in the delivery of fluids and drugs to patients, and its Renal business provides products to treat end-stage renal disease, or irreversible kidney failure.

Recent Developments: For the year ended Dec 31 2007, income from continuing operations increased 22.1% to US$1.71 billion from US$1.40 billion a year earlier. Net income increased 22.2% to US$1.71 billion from US$1.40 billion in the prior year. Revenues were US$11.26 billion, up 8.5% from US$10.38 billion the year before. Direct operating expenses rose 1.8% to US$5.74 billion from US$5.64 billion in the comparable period the year before. Indirect operating expenses increased 15.7% to US$3.35 billion from US$2.90 billion in the equivalent prior-year period.

Prospects: Co. continues to enhance its operations by advancing the programs in its research and development pipeline. For instance, Co. noted that it has initiated the U.S. Phase III clinical trials for its seasonal influenza vaccine candidate. This trial, which will include over 3,000 subjects, is anticipated to be completed by mid-2008. Co. also expects to report the final results of its double-blind, placebo-controlled phase II study of the use of GAMMAGARD in patients with Alzheimer's disease in the second quarter of 2008. For full-year 2008, Co. expects sales growth, excluding foreign exchange, of 5.0% to 6.0%, and earnings, excluding special items, of $3.10 to $3.18 per diluted share.

Financial Data (US$ in Thousands)	12/31/2007	12/31/2006	12/31/2005	12/31/2004	12/31/2003	12/31/2002	12/31/2001	12/31/2000
Earnings Per Share	2.61	2.13	1.52	0.63	1.45	1.26	1.00	1.24
Cash Flow Per Share	3.58	3.35	2.49	2.24	2.38	1.99	1.95	2.07
Tang Book Value Per Share	7.53	6.42	3.61	2.44	1.74	1.53	3.44	2.42
Dividends Per Share	0.720	0.582	0.582	0.582	0.582	0.582	0.582	0.582
Dividend Payout %	27.59	27.32	38.29	92.38	40.14	46.19	58.20	46.94
Income Statement								
Total Revenue	11,263,000	10,378,000	9,849,000	9,509,000	8,916,000	8,110,000	7,663,000	6,896,000
EBITDA	2,717,000	2,355,000	2,142,000	1,130,000	1,782,000	1,887,000	1,414,000	1,370,000
Income Before Taxes	2,114,000	1,746,000	1,444,000	430,000	1,150,000	1,397,000	964,000	946,000
Income Taxes	407,000	348,000	486,000	47,000	228,000	364,000	300,000	208,000
Net Income	1,707,000	1,397,000	956,000	388,000	881,000	778,000	612,000	740,000
Average Shares	654,000	656,000	629,000	618,000	606,000	618,000	609,000	598,000
Balance Sheet								
Current Assets	7,555,000	6,970,000	5,116,000	6,019,000	5,437,000	5,160,000	3,977,000	3,651,000
Total Assets	15,294,000	14,686,000	12,727,000	14,147,000	13,779,000	12,478,000	10,343,000	8,733,000
Current Liabilities	3,812,000	3,610,000	4,165,000	4,286,000	3,819,000	3,851,000	3,294,000	3,372,000
Long-Term Obligations	2,664,000	2,567,000	2,414,000	3,933,000	4,421,000	4,398,000	2,486,000	1,726,000
Total Liabilities	8,378,000	8,414,000	8,428,000	10,442,000	10,456,000	9,539,000	6,586,000	6,074,000
Stockholders' Equity	6,916,000	6,272,000	4,299,000	3,705,000	3,323,000	2,939,000	3,757,000	2,659,000
Shares Outstanding	633,637	650,478	624,897	617,925	611,301	599,504	598,893	586,000
Statistical Record								
Return on Assets %	11.39	10.19	7.11	2.77	6.71	6.82	6.42	8.03
Return on Equity %	25.89	26.43	23.89	11.01	28.14	23.24	19.08	24.57
EBITDA Margin %	24.12	22.69	21.75	11.88	19.99	23.27	18.45	19.87
Net Margin %	15.16	13.46	9.71	4.08	9.88	9.59	7.99	10.73
Asset Turnover	0.75	0.76	0.73	0.68	0.68	0.71	0.80	0.75
Current Ratio	1.98	1.93	1.23	1.40	1.42	1.34	1.21	1.08
Debt to Equity	0.39	0.41	0.56	1.06	1.33	1.50	0.66	0.65
Price Range	61.09-46.33	47.21-35.45	40.95-33.37	34.59-28.76	31.20-18.56	59.60-24.22	55.50-40.75	44.44-24.79
P/E Ratio	23.41-17.75	22.16-16.64	26.94-21.95	54.90-45.65	21.52-12.80	47.30-19.22	55.50-40.75	35.84-19.99
Average Yield %	1.31	1.42	1.56	1.85	2.19	1.35	1.20	1.64

Address: One Baxter Parkway, Deerfield, IL 60015-4633
Telephone: 847-948-2000
Fax: 847-948-2964

Web Site: www.baxter.com
Officers: Robert L. Parkinson Jr. - Chmn., C.E.O. John J. Greisch - V.P., C.F.O.

Auditors: PricewaterhouseCoopers LLP
Investor Contact: 847-948-3371
Transfer Agents: EquiServe Trust Company

BB&T CORP.

Exchange	Symbol	Price	52Wk Range	Yield	P/E	Div Acheiver
NYS	BBT	$32.06 (3/31/2008)	42.90-26.88	5.74	10.21	36 Years

*7 Year Price Score 78.64   *NYSE Composite Index=100   *12 Month Price Score 95.51

Interim Earnings (Per Share)

Qtr.	Mar	Jun	Sep	Dec
2003	0.69	0.67	0.21	0.56
2004	0.60	0.72	0.74	0.75
2005	0.71	0.70	0.80	0.78
2006	0.79	0.79	0.77	0.46
2007	0.77	0.83	0.80	0.74

Interim Dividends (Per Share)

Amt	Decl	Ex	Rec	Pay
0.46Q	6/26/2007	7/11/2007	7/13/2007	8/1/2007
0.46Q	8/21/2007	10/10/2007	10/12/2007	11/1/2007
0.46Q	12/11/2007	1/9/2008	1/11/2008	2/1/2008
0.46Q	2/26/2008	4/10/2008	4/14/2008	5/1/2008

Indicated Div: $1.84 (Div. Reinv. Plan)

Valuation Analysis

Forecast P/E	11.44 (1/10/2007)
Market Cap	$17.5 Billion
Book Value	12.6 Billion
Price/Book	1.39
Price/Sales	1.64

Institutional Holding

No of Institutions	431
Shares	154,825,392
% Held	28.57

Business Summary: Commercial Banking (MIC: 8.1 SIC: 6021 NAIC: 522110)

BB&T is a financial holding company. Co. conducts its operations primarily through its commercial bank subsidiary, Branch Banking and Trust Company, which provides a range of banking services to individuals and businesses, and provides loans and markets deposits to businesses and consumers. Co.'s operations also consist of several nonbank subsidiaries, which provide financial services products, including automobile lending, equipment financing, full-service securities brokerage, payroll processing, asset management and capital markets services. As of Dec 31 2007, Co. had total assets of $132.62 billion and total deposits of $86.77 billion.

Recent Developments: For the year ended Dec 31 2007, net income increased 13.5% to US$1.73 billion from US$1.53 billion in the prior year. Net interest income increased 4.6% to US$3.88 billion from US$3.71 billion in the prior year. Provision for loan losses was US$448.0 million versus US$240.0 million in the prior year, an increase of 86.7%. Non-interest income rose 10.0% to US$2.77 billion from US$2.52 billion, while non-interest expense advanced 3.4% to US$3.64 billion.

Prospects: Co. is progressing with its plans to increase the contribution of its non-interest revenue sources to 45.0% over the next five years. Notably, Co. is pursuing acquisitions of other financial services companies, including insurance agencies and other fee income producing businesses to expand its fee-based revenues. For instance, on Feb 28 2008, Co.'s BB&T Insurance Services announced plans to expand its Florida operation with the acquisition of Burkey Risk Services of metro Orlando, which provides risk management and employee benefits services. Co. expects the transaction to close in early Mar 2008. Meanwhile, Co. expects net charge-offs and non-performing assets to increase into 2008.

Financial Data

(US$ in Thousands)	12/31/2007	12/31/2006	12/31/2005	12/31/2004	12/31/2003	12/31/2002	12/31/2001	12/31/2000
Earnings Per Share	3.14	2.81	3.00	2.80	2.07	2.72	2.12	1.55
Cash Flow Per Share	1.92	1.44	3.22	5.49	7.47	1.73	0.21	0.62
Tang Book Value Per Share	11.86	11.04	11.76	11.33	10.92	12.04	13.50	11.91
Dividends Per Share	1.760	1.600	1.460	1.340	1.220	1.100	0.980	0.860
Dividend Payout %	56.05	56.94	48.67	47.86	58.94	40.44	46.23	55.48
Income Statement								
Interest Income	7,894,000	6,893,000	5,505,842	4,546,695	4,354,792	4,434,044	4,849,538	4,339,674
Interest Expense	4,014,000	3,185,000	1,980,969	1,198,472	1,272,787	1,686,584	2,415,053	2,322,046
Net Interest Income	3,880,000	3,708,000	3,524,873	3,348,223	3,082,005	2,747,460	2,434,485	2,017,628
Provision for Losses	448,000	240,000	217,263	249,269	248,000	263,700	224,318	127,431
Non-Interest Income	2,774,000	2,521,000	2,325,622	2,119,271	1,889,135	1,692,475	1,378,691	777,022
Non-Interest Expense	3,636,000	3,516,000	3,166,501	2,895,863	3,165,501	2,468,110	2,228,430	1,761,539
Income Before Taxes	2,570,000	2,473,000	2,466,731	2,322,362	1,617,030	1,700,697	1,360,428	905,680
Income Taxes	836,000	945,000	812,962	763,987	552,127	497,468	386,790	279,238
Net Income	1,734,000	1,528,000	1,653,769	1,558,375	1,064,903	1,303,009	973,638	626,442
Average Shares	551,755	543,890	551,379	556,041	514,082	478,792	459,269	398,915
Balance Sheet								
Net Loans & Leases	90,682,000	82,703,000	74,198,188	67,357,669	61,520,449	52,794,328	46,798,755	39,778,674
Total Assets	132,618,000	121,351,000	109,169,759	100,508,641	90,466,613	80,216,816	70,869,945	59,340,228
Total Deposits	86,766,000	80,971,000	74,281,799	67,699,337	59,349,785	51,280,016	44,733,275	38,014,501
Total Liabilities	119,986,000	109,606,000	98,040,645	89,634,167	80,531,882	72,828,902	64,719,736	54,554,303
Stockholders' Equity	12,632,000	11,745,000	11,129,114	10,874,474	9,934,731	7,387,914	6,150,209	4,785,925
Shares Outstanding	545,955	541,475	543,102	550,406	541,942	470,452	455,682	401,678
Statistical Record								
Return on Assets %	1.37	1.33	1.58	1.63	1.25	1.72	1.50	1.22
Return on Equity %	14.23	13.36	15.03	14.94	12.29	19.25	17.81	15.65
Net Interest Margin %	49.15	53.79	64.02	73.64	70.77	61.96	50.20	46.49
Efficiency Ratio %	34.08	37.35	40.43	43.44	49.75	38.94	35.78	34.43
Loans to Deposits	1.05	1.02	1.00	0.99	1.04	1.03	1.05	1.05
Price Range	44.15-30.67	44.63-38.37	43.77-37.08	43.25-33.33	39.66-31.15	39.23-31.26	38.48-31.42	38.25-22.00
P/E Ratio	14.06-9.77	15.88-13.65	14.59-12.36	15.45-11.90	19.16-15.05	14.42-11.49	18.15-14.82	24.68-14.19
Average Yield %	4.41	3.81	3.60	3.50	3.46	2.99	2.73	3.06

Address: 200 West Second Street, PO Box 1250, Winston-Salem, NC 27102-1250 **Telephone:** 336-733-2000 **Fax:** 336-671-2399	**Web Site:** www.BBT.com **Officers:** John A. Allison IV - Chmn., C.E.O. Christopher L. Henson - Sr. Exec. V.P., C.F.O.	**Auditors:** PricewaterhouseCoopers LLP **Investor Contact:** 336-733-3058 **Transfer Agents:** Branch Banking & Trust Company, Wilson, NC

BEAR STEARNS COS., INC. (THE)

Exchange	Symbol	Price	52Wk Range	Yield	P/E
NYS	BSC	$10.49 (3/31/2008)	158.39-4.81	12.20	6.90

*7 Year Price Score 95.81   *NYSE Composite Index=100   *12 Month Price Score 61.25

TRADING VOLUME (thousand shares)

Interim Earnings (Per Share)

Qtr.	Feb	May	Aug	Nov
2002-03	2.00	2.05	2.30	2.18
2003-04	2.57	2.49	2.09	2.60
2004-05	2.64	2.09	2.69	2.89
2005-06	3.54	3.72	3.02	3.99
2006-07	3.82	2.52	1.16	(6.02)

Interim Dividends (Per Share)

Amt	Decl	Ex	Rec	Pay
0.32Q	3/22/2007	4/13/2007	4/17/2007	4/27/2007
0.32Q	6/13/2007	7/13/2007	7/17/2007	7/27/2007
0.32Q	9/20/2007	10/12/2007	10/16/2007	10/26/2007
0.32Q	12/20/2007	1/11/2008	1/15/2008	1/25/2008

Indicated Div: $1.28

Valuation Analysis

		Institutional Holding	
Forecast P/E	10.75 (1/10/2007)	No of Institutions	466
Market Cap	$1.2 Billion	Shares	80,165,536
Book Value	11.8 Billion	% Held	67.35
Price/Book	0.10		
Price/Sales	0.07		

Business Summary: Finance Intermediaries & Services (MIC: 8.7 SIC: 6211 NAIC: 523120)

Bear Stearns Companies is a holding company. Through its subsidiaries, Co. is a global investment banking, securities and derivatives trading, clearance and brokerage firm operating in three principal segments: Capital Markets, Global Clearing Services and Wealth Management. Co.'s Capital Markets segment is comprised of its equities, fixed income and investment banking businesses operating. Co.'s Global Clearing Services segment provides trade execution, securities clearing services, custody, financing, securities lending, and technology applications. Co.'s Wealth Management segment is comprised of the Private Client Services and Asset Management areas.

Recent Developments: For the year ended Nov 30 2007, net income decreased 88.7% to US$233.0 million from US$2.05 billion in the prior year. Revenues were US$16.15 billion, down 2.4% from US$16.55 billion the year before. Direct operating expenses rose 39.4% to US$10.21 billion from US$7.32 billion in the comparable period the year before. Indirect operating expenses decreased 5.4% to US$5.75 billion from US$6.08 billion in the equivalent prior-year period.

Prospects: Co.'s results are being hurt by a significant decrease in its Capital Markets segment due primarily to a reduction in fixed income net revenues, owing mainly to the challenging U.S. mortgage and credit markets. At the same time, Co.'s Capital Markets results are being negatively affected by lower investment banking net revenues as a result of less favorable market conditions for fixed income underwriting, which resulted in a decline in revenues from high yield and high grade underwriting. In response, for 2008, Co. will focus its resources on the businesses with growth potential in existing environment, while streamlining its operations in areas with lower expected activity levels.

Financial Data

(US$ in Thousands)	11/30/2007	11/30/2006	11/30/2005	11/30/2004	11/30/2003	11/30/2002	11/30/2001	11/30/2000
Earnings Per Share	1.52	14.27	10.31	9.76	8.52	6.47	4.27	5.35
Cash Flow Per Share	85.60	(145.93)	(107.51)	(17.03)	(42.19)	(10.30)	45.94	(27.61)
Tang Book Value Per Share	101.25	100.25	91.50	82.31	67.58	56.88	48.26	44.54
Dividends Per Share	1.280	1.120	1.000	0.850	0.740	0.620	0.600	0.550
Dividend Payout %	84.21	7.85	9.70	8.71	8.69	9.58	14.05	10.28
Income Statement								
Interest Income	11,556,000	8,536,029	5,107,019	2,317,315	1,955,373	2,232,159	4,339,298	5,642,361
Commissions & Fees	2,649,000	2,496,437	2,237,667	2,326,724	1,982,538	1,944,454	1,888,856	2,229,091
Employee Costs	3,425,000	4,343,499	3,553,216	3,253,862	2,880,695	2,508,197	2,528,852	2,814,193
Interest Expense	10,206,000	7,324,254	4,141,653	1,609,019	1,400,953	1,762,580	3,793,998	4,800,891
Income Before Taxes	193,000	3,146,630	2,207,059	2,022,154	1,772,269	1,310,963	934,444	1,171,523
Income Taxes	(40,000)	1,092,759	744,882	677,421	615,863	432,618	309,479	398,340
Net Income	233,000	2,053,871	1,462,177	1,344,733	1,156,406	878,345	618,692	773,183
Average Shares	146,442	148,575	147,467	145,284	145,027	146,346	152,216	152,034
Balance Sheet								
Total Assets	395,362,000	350,432,595	292,635,233	255,949,894	212,168,110	184,854,423	185,530,228	171,166,473
Total Liabilities	383,569,000	338,303,211	281,843,801	246,959,022	204,135,522	177,909,840	179,139,201	165,012,185
Stockholders' Equity	11,793,000	12,129,384	10,791,432	8,990,872	7,470,088	6,382,083	5,628,527	5,654,288
Shares Outstanding	112,998	117,408	113,868	103,786	102,572	100,024	100,042	108,982
Statistical Record								
Return on Assets %	0.06	0.64	0.53	0.57	0.58	0.47	0.35	0.46
Return on Equity %	1.95	17.92	14.78	16.29	16.70	14.63	10.97	14.40
Net Interest Margin %	11.68	14.20	18.90	30.57	28.35	21.04	12.57	14.91
Price Range	171.51-91.04	158.60-110.50	114.41-93.09	98.55-71.00	82.55-58.65	67.39-51.92	64.04-42.06	72.13-36.94
P/E Ratio	112.84-59.89	11.11-7.74	11.10-9.03	10.10-7.27	9.69-6.88	10.42-8.02	15.00-9.85	13.48-6.90
Average Yield %	0.92	0.83	0.98	1.00	1.07	1.03	1.11	1.15

Address: 383 Madison Avenue, New York, NY 10179
Telephone: 212-272-2000
Fax: 212-272-4785

Web Site: www.bearstearns.com
Officers: James E. Cayne - Chmn., C.E.O. Alan D. Schwartz - Co-Pres., Co-C.O.O.

Auditors: Deloitte & Touche LLP
Investor Contact: 212-272-9251
Transfer Agents: Mellon Investor Services, L.L.C., Ridgefield Park, NJ

BEAZER HOMES USA, INC.

Exchange	Symbol	Price	52Wk Range	Yield	P/E
NYS	BZH	$9.45 (3/31/2008)	36.72-4.99	N/A	4.97

*7 Year Price Score 37.51   *NYSE Composite Index=100   *12 Month Price Score 57.38

Interim Earnings (Per Share)

Qtr.	Dec	Mar	Jun	Sep
2003-04	1.14	1.17	1.44	1.95
2004-05	1.57	(2.09)	2.50	3.63
2005-06	2.00	2.35	2.37	2.19
2006-07	(1.54)	(1.12)	...	...

Interim Dividends (Per Share)

Dividend Payment Suspended

Valuation Analysis

		Institutional Holding	
Forecast P/E	N/A	No of Institutions	176
Market Cap	$369.5 Million	Shares	41,327,856
Book Value	1.6 Billion	% Held	
Price/Book	0.23	N/A	
Price/Sales	0.08		

TRADING VOLUME (thousand shares)

Business Summary: Building & General Construction (MIC: 3.2 SIC: 1531 NAIC: 236117)

Beazer Homes USA designs, sells and builds single-family homes in the U.S. Co. has three product categories: Economy, Value and Style. Co.'s economy class homes are targeted primarily at entry-level buyers, and are intended to meet the needs of those buyers for whom price is the most important factor in the buying decision. Co.'s value category homes are targeted at entry-level and move-up buyers, and are intended to appeal to buyers who are more interested in style and features, but are still somewhat price focused. Co.'s style class homes are targeted at more affluent move-up buyers, and are intended to appeal to buyers who place greater emphasis on style and features.

Recent Developments: Co. is in the process of restating certain prior periods' financial statements including interim periods of fiscal 2007 and 2006. Other than cash balances, Co. does not expect to release financial data until the restatements are complete. Co. stated that it is working expeditiously to complete the restatements and report financial results for the year ended Sep 30 2007 and the quarter ended Dec 31 2007 as soon as practicable. Co. believes such restatements can be completed prior to May 15 2008.

Prospects: On Feb 1 2008, Co. announced that it will discontinue mortgage origination services through Beazer Mortgage Corporation effective immediately and has ended its related mortgage services relationship with Homebuilders Financial Network, LLC. Also, Co. will exit its homebuilding operations in Charlotte, NC, Cincinnati/Dayton, OH, Columbia, SC, Columbus, OH, and Lexington, KY. As of Dec 31 2007, Co. controlled approximately 58,000 lots, reflecting reductions of 6.0% and 31.0%, respectively from previously reported levels as of Sep 30 2007 and Dec 31 2006. As of Dec 31 2007, unsold finished homes and unsold homes under construction declined by 49.0% and 37.0%, respectively, from year-ago levels.

Financial Data

(US$ in Thousands)	6 Mos	3 Mos	09/30/2006	09/30/2005	09/30/2004	09/30/2003	09/30/2002	09/30/2001
Earnings Per Share	1.90	5.37	8.89	5.87	5.70	4.26	3.58	2.73
Cash Flow Per Share	5.84	1.36	(7.65)	(2.08)	(1.84)	(1.06)	1.88	(1.20)
Tang Book Value Per Share	37.90	38.98	40.64	33.17	23.80	18.27	14.16	13.03
Dividends Per Share	0.400	0.400	0.400	0.333	0.133	...	...	...
Dividend Payout %	21.05	7.45	4.50	5.68	2.34	...	...	...
Income Statement								
Total Revenue	1,629,309	803,014	5,462,003	4,995,353	3,907,109	3,177,408	2,641,173	1,805,177
EBITDA	(158,939)	(92,075)	639,271	520,508	402,330	298,749	211,512	133,203
Depn & Amortn	5,002	2,551	...	...	...	...	...	...
Income Before Taxes	(163,941)	(94,626)	613,214	499,334	386,575	285,529	202,059	123,950
Income Taxes	(61,846)	(35,620)	224,453	236,810	150,764	112,784	79,425	48,341
Net Income	(102,095)	(59,006)	388,761	262,524	235,811	172,745	122,634	74,876
Average Shares	38,427	38,280	44,345	45,634	41,403	40,542	34,245	27,468
Balance Sheet								
Current Assets	3,662,150	3,903,241	4,301,144	3,540,043	2,827,349	1,889,018	1,570,550	944,976
Total Assets	4,191,024	4,313,348	4,559,431	3,770,516	3,149,462	2,212,034	1,892,847	995,289
Current Liabilities	489,787	491,487	141,131	141,623	123,287	125,521	108,554	70,893
Long-Term Obligations	1,762,473	1,784,287	1,838,660	1,321,936	1,137,404	741,365	739,100	395,238
Total Liabilities	2,587,889	2,665,867	2,857,508	2,265,828	1,917,341	1,218,339	1,093,332	644,094
Stockholders' Equity	1,603,135	1,647,481	1,701,923	1,504,688	1,232,121	993,695	799,515	351,195
Shares Outstanding	39,100	39,154	38,889	41,701	41,191	40,628	38,686	25,871
Statistical Record								
Return on Assets %	2.23	5.87	9.33	7.59	8.77	8.42	8.49	8.84
Return on Equity %	5.81	15.06	24.25	19.18	21.13	19.27	21.31	24.09
EBITDA Margin %	N.M.	N.M.	11.70	10.42	10.30	9.40	8.01	7.38
Net Margin %	N.M.	N.M.	7.12	5.26	6.04	5.44	4.64	4.15
Asset Turnover	1.14	1.26	1.31	1.44	1.45	1.55	1.83	2.13
Current Ratio	7.48	7.94	30.48	25.00	22.93	15.05	14.47	13.33
Debt to Equity	1.10	1.08	1.08	0.88	0.92	0.75	0.92	1.13
Price Range	68.78-28.77	82.03-37.24	82.03-37.24	66.91-33.36	37.30-28,13	31.43-17.46	31.03-13.89	25.73-8.65
P/E Ratio	36.20-15.14	15.28-6.93	9.23-4.19	11.40-5.68	6.54-4.94	7.38-4.10	8.67-3.88	9.42-3.17
Average Yield %	0.89	0.77	0.70	0.65	0.40	...	...	...

Address: 1000 Abernathy Road, Suite 1200, Atlanta, GA 30328
Telephone: 770-829-3700

Web Site: www.beazer.com
Officers: Brian C. Beazer - Chmn. Ian J. McCarthy - Pres., C.E.O.

Auditors: Deloitte & Touche LLP
Investor Contact: 770-829-3700
Transfer Agents: American Stock Transfer & Trust Co., New York, NY

BECKMAN COULTER, INC.

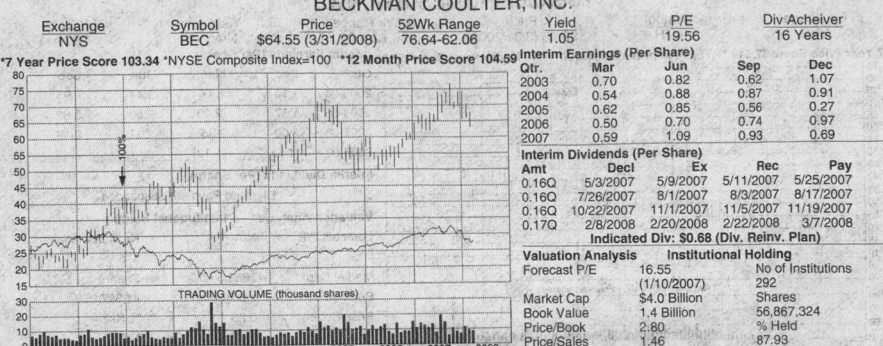

Exchange	Symbol	Price	52Wk Range	Yield	P/E	Div Acheiver
NYS	BEC	$64.55 (3/31/2008)	76.64-62.06	1.05	19.56	16 Years

*7 Year Price Score 103.34 *NYSE Composite Index=100 *12 Month Price Score 104.59

Interim Earnings (Per Share)

Qtr.	Mar	Jun	Sep	Dec
2003	0.70	0.82	0.62	1.07
2004	0.54	0.88	0.87	0.91
2005	0.62	0.85	0.56	0.27
2006	0.50	0.70	0.74	0.97
2007	0.59	1.09	0.93	0.69

Interim Dividends (Per Share)

Amt	Decl	Ex	Rec	Pay
0.16Q	5/3/2007	5/9/2007	5/11/2007	5/25/2007
0.16Q	7/26/2007	8/1/2007	8/3/2007	8/17/2007
0.16Q	10/22/2007	11/1/2007	11/5/2007	11/19/2007
0.17Q	2/8/2008	2/20/2008	2/22/2008	3/7/2008

Indicated Div: $0.68 (Div. Reinv. Plan)

Valuation Analysis

		Institutional Holding	
Forecast P/E	16.55	No of Institutions	
	(1/10/2007)	292	
Market Cap	$4.0 Billion	Shares	
Book Value	1.4 Billion	56,867,324	
Price/Book	2.80	% Held	
Price/Sales	1.46	87.93	

Business Summary: Instruments and Related Products (MIC: 11.15 SIC: 3826 NAIC: 334516)

Beckman Coulter is a biomedical testing company engaged in the manufacture of biomedical testing instrument systems, tests and supplies. Co. provides laboratory tools used to conduct basic research into the fundamental processes of human biology, to develop vaccines and drugs to treat disease, to conduct clinical trials and related research activities, and to perform various tasks from patient blood tests to diagnostic testing. Co. has four product areas, which include Chemistry Systems, Immunoassay Systems, Cellular Systems, and Discovery and Automation Systems. At Dec 31 2007, Co. marketed its products in more than 130 countries.

Recent Developments: For the year ended Dec 31 2007, income from continuing operations increased 32.6% to US$209.7 million from US$158.2 million a year earlier. Net income increased 13.1% to US$211.3 million from US$186.9 million in the prior year. Revenues were US$2.76 billion, up 9.2% from US$2.53 billion the year before. Operating income was US$272.4 million versus US$262.9 million in the prior year, an increase of 3.6%. Direct operating expenses rose 10.1% to US$1.47 billion in the comparable period the year before. Indirect operating expenses increased 9.5% to US$1.02 billion from US$934.1 million in the equivalent prior-year period.

Prospects: Co.'s near-term outlook appears favorable. Notably, for full-year 2008, Co. anticipates revenue growth to be in a range of 7.0% to 9.0%, operating margin to expand to around 12.5%, and earnings per diluted share to be between $3.50 and $3.65. Meanwhile, in the first quarter of 2008, Co. expects to commercialize its next chemistry / immunoassay work cell, the UniCel® DxC 880i, which is the first of four new work cells coming in 2008. Additionally, Co.'s new hematology system, the UniCel DxH, should be introduced at the end of 2008, and Co. also continues to make progress with the development of its DxN 'sample-to-result' instrument for molecular diagnostics.

Financial Data
(US$ in Thousands)

	12/31/2007	12/31/2006	12/31/2005	12/31/2004	12/31/2003	12/31/2002	12/31/2001	12/31/2000
Earnings Per Share	3.30	2.92	2.32	3.21	3.21	2.08	2.16	2.03
Cash Flow Per Share	6.35	5.16	6.74	4.32	3.68	5.12	4.57	3.55
Tang Book Value Per Share	5.05	1.38	4.68	6.19	2.99	N.M.	N.M.	N.M.
Dividends Per Share	0.640	0.600	0.560	0.480	0.400	0.350	0.340	0.325
Dividend Payout %	19.39	20.55	24.14	14.95	12.46	16.83	15.74	16.01
Income Statement								
Total Revenue	2,761,300	2,528,500	2,443,800	2,408,300	2,192,500	2,059,400	1,984,000	1,886,900
EBITDA	530,600	430,700	337,500	416,400	409,900	326,600	378,300	383,600
Income Before Taxes	292,700	215,200	165,600	278,200	272,800	178,900	205,000	181,900
Income Taxes	83,000	57,000	15,000	67,300	65,600	43,400	63,500	56,400
Net Income	211,300	186,900	150,600	210,900	207,200	135,500	138,400	125,500
Average Shares	64,066	63,971	64,861	65,773	64,493	65,060	64,011	61,800
Balance Sheet								
Current Assets	1,488,100	1,338,100	1,233,600	1,279,600	1,161,200	1,056,200	1,035,600	927,800
Total Assets	3,594,300	3,291,700	3,027,600	2,795,000	2,558,200	2,263,600	2,178,000	2,018,200
Current Liabilities	797,200	711,600	758,500	613,300	578,200	611,600	509,900	501,100
Long-Term Obligations	888,600	952,000	589,100	611,700	625,600	626,600	760,300	862,800
Total Liabilities	2,152,600	2,137,400	1,832,800	1,700,700	1,660,500	1,671,500	1,659,800	1,674,300
Stockholders' Equity	1,441,700	1,154,300	1,194,800	1,094,300	897,700	592,100	518,200	343,900
Shares Outstanding	62,500	61,000	62,400	61,600	62,000	61,000	61,200	59,700
Statistical Record								
Return on Assets %	6.14	5.92	5.17	7.86	8.59	6.10	6.60	6.06
Return on Equity %	16.28	15.91	13.16	21.12	27.82	24.41	32.11	43.78
EBITDA Margin %	19.22	17.03	13.81	17.29	18.70	15.86	19.07	20.33
Net Margin %	7.65	7.39	6.16	8.76	9.45	6.58	6.98	6.65
Asset Turnover	0.80	0.80	0.84	0.90	0.91	0.93	0.95	0.91
Current Ratio	1.87	1.88	1.63	2.09	2.01	1.73	2.03	1.85
Debt to Equity	0.62	0.82	0.49	0.56	0.70	1.06	1.47	2.51
Price Range	76.64-59.04	61.35-49.73	72.02-48.75	67.70-49.99	51.31-28.50	52.47-25.78	47.01-34.50	41.94-23.66
P/E Ratio	23.22-17.89	21.01-17.03	31.04-21.01	21.09-15.57	15.98-8.88	25.23-12.39	21.76-15.97	20.66-11.65
Average Yield %	0.94	1.07	0.91	0.84	0.98	0.84	0.83	1.00

Address: 4300 N. Harbor Boulevard, P.O. Box 3100, Fullerton, CA 92834-3100 **Telephone:** 714-871-4848 **Fax:** 714-773-8283	**Web Site:** www.beckmancoulter.com **Officers:** Scott Garrett - Pres., C.E.O. Arnold A. Pinkston - Sr. V.P., Gen. Couns.	**Auditors:** KPMG LLP **Investor Contact:** 714-773-7620 **Transfer Agents:** EquiServe Trust Company, N.A., Providence, RI

BECTON, DICKINSON AND CO.

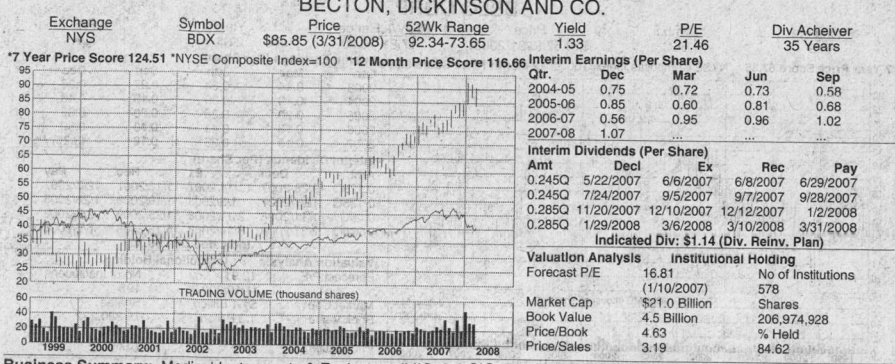

Exchange	Symbol	Price	52Wk Range	Yield	P/E	Div Acheiver
NYS	BDX	$85.85 (3/31/2008)	92.34-73.65	1.33	21.46	35 Years

*7 Year Price Score 124.51 *NYSE Composite Index=100 *12 Month Price Score 116.66

Interim Earnings (Per Share)

Qtr.	Dec	Mar	Jun	Sep
2004-05	0.75	0.72	0.73	0.58
2005-06	0.85	0.60	0.81	0.68
2006-07	0.56	0.95	0.96	1.02
2007-08	1.07	...	...	...

Interim Dividends (Per Share)

Amt	Decl	Ex	Rec	Pay
0.245Q	5/22/2007	6/6/2007	6/8/2007	6/29/2007
0.245Q	7/24/2007	9/5/2007	9/7/2007	9/28/2007
0.285Q	11/20/2007	12/10/2007	12/12/2007	1/2/2008
0.285Q	1/29/2008	3/6/2008	3/10/2008	3/31/2008

Indicated Div: $1.14 (Div. Reinv. Plan)

Valuation Analysis / Institutional Holding

Forecast P/E	16.81
	(1/10/2007)
Market Cap	$21.0 Billion
Book Value	4.5 Billion
Price/Book	4.63
Price/Sales	3.19

Institutional Holding
No of Institutions
578
Shares
206,974,928
% Held
84.62

Business Summary: Medical Instruments & Equipment (MIC: 9.6 SIC: 3841 NAIC: 339112)

Becton, Dickinson and Company manufactures and sells a range of medical supplies, devices, laboratory equipment and diagnostic products used by healthcare institutions, life science researchers, clinical laboratories, industry and the general public. Co.'s operations consist of three business segments: BD Medical, which produces an array of medical devices that are used in a range of healthcare settings; BD Diagnostics, which provides products for the collection and transport of diagnostic specimens and instrumentation for analysis across a range of infectious disease testing; and BD Biosciences, which produces research and clinical tools that facilitate the study of cells.

Recent Developments: For the quarter ended Dec 31 2007, income from continuing operations increased 106.7% to US$270.9 million from US$131.1 million in the year-earlier quarter. Net income increased 90.1% to US$271.5 million from US$142.9 million in the year-earlier quarter. Revenues were US$1.71 billion, up 13.6% from US$1.50 billion the year before. Operating income was US$362.7 million versus US$213.8 million in the prior-year quarter, an increase of 69.6%. Direct operating expenses rose 17.1% to US$829.8 million from US$708.9 million in the comparable period the year before. Indirect operating expenses decreased 11.3% to US$513.2 million from US$578.8 million in the equivalent prior-year period.

Prospects: For the fiscal year ending Sep 30 2008, Co. anticipates that earnings per share from continuing operations will increase by approximately 11.0% to 13.0% over its previous fiscal year's earnings from continuing operations of $3.84 per share. Specifically, Co.'s earnings guidance exclude the $0.48 in-process research and development charge related to the acquisitions of TriPath Imaging, Inc. in December 2006 and Plasso Technology, Ltd. on May 4 2007. Co. also anticipates higher resin and steel costs in fiscal 2008, as well as manufacturing start-up costs.

Financial Data
(US$ in Thousands)

	3 Mos	09/30/2007	09/30/2006	09/30/2005	09/30/2004	09/30/2003	09/30/2002	09/30/2001
Earnings Per Share	4.00	3.49	2.93	2.77	1.77	2.07	1.79	1.49
Cash Flow Per Share	5.87	5.05	4.36	4.87	4.35	3.56	3.24	3.03
Tang Book Value Per Share	13.58	12.82	11.18	9.36	8.01	6.63	4.95	5.35
Dividends Per Share	1.020	0.980	0.860	0.720	0.600	0.400	0.390	0.380
Dividend Payout %	25.50	28.08	29.35	25.99	33.90	19.32	21.79	25.50
Income Statement								
Total Revenue	1,705,767	6,359,708	5,834,827	5,414,681	4,934,745	4,527,940	4,033,069	3,754,302
EBITDA	478,595	1,597,494	1,342,257	1,300,866	1,035,487	1,003,889	901,204	937,864
Depn & Amortn	115,212	...	...	...	...	...	...	...
Income Before Taxes	366,572	1,203,945	1,034,957	1,004,854	752,868	709,706	628,589	576,750
Income Taxes	95,676	347,778	279,366	312,571	170,364	162,650	148,607	138,348
Net Income	271,518	890,033	752,200	722,263	467,402	547,056	479,982	401,652
Average Shares	253,116	254,810	256,554	260,712	263,337	263,635	268,183	268,833
Balance Sheet								
Current Assets	3,345,067	3,130,566	3,185,253	2,975,314	2,641,334	2,338,569	1,928,707	1,762,942
Total Assets	7,566,534	7,329,365	6,824,525	6,071,969	5,752,579	5,572,253	5,040,460	4,802,287
Current Liabilities	1,496,806	1,478,809	1,576,329	1,299,375	1,050,082	1,043,374	1,252,453	1,264,676
Long-Term Obligations	957,627	955,713	956,971	1,060,833	1,171,506	1,184,031	802,967	782,996
Total Liabilities	3,042,258	2,967,408	2,988,321	2,788,017	2,684,716	2,675,299	2,552,486	2,473,520
Stockholders' Equity	4,524,276	4,361,957	3,836,204	3,283,952	3,067,863	2,896,954	2,487,974	2,328,767
Shares Outstanding	244,055	243,837	245,468	247,684	249,334	251,133	255,529	259,236
Statistical Record								
Return on Assets %	14.17	12.58	11.67	12.22	8.23	10.31	9.75	8.63
Return on Equity %	24.10	21.71	21.13	22.74	15.63	20.32	19.93	18.75
EBITDA Margin %	28.06	25.12	23.00	24.02	20.98	22.17	22.35	24.98
Net Margin %	15.92	13.99	12.89	13.34	9.47	12.08	11.90	10.70
Asset Turnover	0.91	0.90	0.90	0.92	0.87	0.85	0.82	0.81
Current Ratio	2.23	2.12	2.02	2.29	2.52	2.24	1.54	1.39
Debt to Equity	0.21	0.22	0.25	0.32	0.38	0.41	0.32	0.34
Price Range	85.30-69.85	82.61-68.81	70.67-50.07	59.98-49.52	53.25-35.71	40.43-28.40	38.47-25.01	39.00-26.56
P/E Ratio	21.32-17.46	23.67-19.72	24.12-17.09	21.65-17.88	30.08-20.18	19.53-13.72	21.49-13.97	26.17-17.83
Average Yield %	1.31	1.30	1.40	1.30	1.31	1.17	1.14	1.12

Address: 1 Becton Drive, Franklin Lakes, NJ 07417-1880 **Telephone:** 201-847-6800 **Fax:** 201-847-6475	**Web Site:** www.bd.com **Officers:** Edward J. Ludwig - Chmn., Pres., C.E.O. John R. Considine - Exec. V.P., C.F.O.	**Auditors:** Ernst & Young LLP **Investor Contact:** 800-284-6845 **Transfer Agents:** EquiServe Trust Company, N.A., Jersey City, NJ

BELO CORP.

Exchange	Symbol	Price	52Wk Range	Yield	P/E
NYS	BLC	$10.57 (3/31/2008)	17.81-10.20	2.84	N/A

*7 Year Price Score 67.35   *NYSE Composite Index=100   *12 Month Price Score 88.68

Interim Earnings (Per Share)

Qtr.	Mar	Jun	Sep	Dec
2003	0.14	0.34	0.27	0.36
2004	0.19	0.39	0.10	0.46
2005	0.20	0.36	0.20	0.35
2006	0.16	0.41	0.19	0.50
2007	0.15	0.35	0.18	(3.26)

Interim Dividends (Per Share)

Amt	Decl	Ex	Rec	Pay
0.125Q	9/28/2007	11/14/2007	11/16/2007	12/7/2007
0.125Q	12/7/2007	1/8/2008	1/10/2008	1/25/2008
0.00Q	1/11/2008	2/11/2008	1/25/2008	2/8/2008
0.075Q	2/27/2008	5/14/2008	5/16/2008	6/6/2008
		Indicated Div: $0.30		

Valuation Analysis

		Institutional Holding	
Forecast P/E	12.91	No of Institutions	
	(1/10/2007)	197	
Market Cap	$1.1 Billion	Shares	
Book Value	1.3 Billion	75,380,232	
Price/Book	0.86	% Held	
Price/Sales	0.71	73.66	

Business Summary: Media (MIC: 13.1 SIC: 4833 NAIC: 515120)

Belo is a media company with various television broadcasting and newspaper publishing operations, including interactive media and cable news operations. At Dec 31 2006, Co. owned 20 television stations that reach 14.0% of U.S. television households, and managed one television station via a local marketing agreement. Co.'s primary daily newspapers are The Dallas Morning News, The Providence Journal, and The Press-Enterprise (Riverside, CA). Co. also owns two local and two regional cable news channels and holds ownership interests in two other cable news operations. Co. also offers various Internet-based products, operates over 30 Web sites and participates in several interactive alliances.

Recent Developments: For the year ended Dec 31 2007, net loss amounted to US$262.8 million versus net income of US$130.5 million in the prior year. Revenues were US$1.52 billion, down 4.6% from US$1.59 billion the year before. Operating loss was US$119.4 million versus an income of US$288.4 million in the prior year. Direct operating expenses declined 2.5% to US$606.8 million from US$622.6 million in the comparable period the year before. Indirect operating expenses increased 51.8% to US$1.03 billion from US$677.2 million in the equivalent prior-year period.

Prospects: For full-year 2008, Co. expects total revenues to be up in the mid-to-high single digits based on the strength of political in its markets. Specifically, Co. expects Internet revenue growth to be less than the rate experienced in 2007 but still to be up strong double-digits, while not expecting significant political revenue until the second half of 2008. Meanwhile, on Feb 8 2008, Co. announced that it has completed the spin-off of its newspaper businesses and related assets into a publicly-traded company called A. H. Belo Corporation, which should allow Co. to focus on opportunities that exist in its television businesses.

Financial Data
(US$ in Thousands)

	12/31/2007	12/31/2006	12/31/2005	12/31/2004	12/31/2003	12/31/2002	12/31/2001	12/31/2000
Earnings Per Share	(2.57)	1.26	1.12	1.13	1.11	1.15	(0.02)	1.29
Cash Flow Per Share	2.14	2.37	2.03	2.40	2.27	2.81	1.51	2.16
Dividends Per Share	0.500	0.450	0.400	0.380	0.340	0.300	0.300	0.280
Dividend Payout %	...	35.71	35.71	33.63	30.63	26.09	...	21.71
Income Statement								
Total Revenue	1,515,625	1,588,272	1,521,234	1,510,234	1,436,011	1,427,764	1,364,578	1,588,812
EBITDA	(6,654)	395,069	393,855	404,115	411,742	431,894	317,447	584,586
Income Before Taxes	(202,375)	203,683	206,960	215,801	209,460	213,454	21,763	266,834
Income Taxes	60,438	73,157	79,272	83,305	80,935	82,328	24,449	116,009
Net Income	(262,813)	130,526	127,688	132,496	128,525	131,126	(2,686)	150,825
Average Shares	102,245	103,882	113,552	117,272	115,487	113,638	109,816	117,198
Balance Sheet								
Current Assets	344,389	384,163	356,277	342,493	332,618	320,451	332,179	421,025
Total Assets	3,179,060	3,614,278	3,589,213	3,588,000	3,602,601	3,614,578	3,672,225	3,893,260
Current Liabilities	249,450	258,912	247,429	238,611	218,355	216,166	185,400	302,683
Long-Term Obligations	1,168,140	1,283,434	1,244,875	1,170,150	1,270,900	1,441,200	1,696,900	1,789,600
Total Liabilities	1,927,352	2,087,130	2,055,732	1,958,348	2,038,830	2,201,348	2,351,480	2,543,852
Stockholders' Equity	1,251,708	1,527,148	1,533,481	1,629,652	1,563,771	1,413,230	1,320,745	1,349,408
Shares Outstanding	102,259	102,296	107,734	114,333	115,024	112,758	110,382	109,853
Statistical Record								
Return on Assets %	N.M.	3.62	3.56	3.68	3.56	3.60	N.M.	3.82
Return on Equity %	N.M.	8.53	8.07	8.28	8.63	9.59	N.M.	10.98
EBITDA Margin %	N.M.	24.87	25.89	26.76	28.67	30.25	23.26	36.79
Net Margin %	N.M.	8.22	8.39	8.77	8.95	9.18	N.M.	9.49
Asset Turnover	0.45	0.44	0.42	0.42	0.40	0.39	0.36	0.40
Current Ratio	1.38	1.48	1.44	1.44	1.52	1.48	1.79	1.39
Debt to Equity	0.93	0.84	0.81	0.72	0.81	1.02	1.28	1.33
Price Range	17.81-12.82	18.30-12.15	20.98-16.61	23.59-16.97	22.83-15.07	19.43-14.63	15.95-12.29	15.94-9.84
P/E Ratio	...	14.52-9.64	18.73-14.83	20.87-15.01	20.56-13.58	16.89-12.72	...	12.36-7.63
Average Yield %	3.34	3.09	2.13	1.84	1.81	1.70	2.08	2.06

Address: P.O. Box 655237, Dallas, TX 75265-5237 **Telephone:** 214-977-6606 **Fax:** 214-977-6603	**Web Site:** www.belo.com **Officers:** Robert W. Decherd - Chmn., Pres., C.E.O. Dunia A. Shive - Exec. V.P., Media Oper.	**Auditors:** Ernst & Young LLP **Investor Contact:** 214-977-7095 **Transfer Agents:** EquiServe Trust Company, N.A., Providence, RI

BEMIS CO INC

*7 Year Price Score 87.44 ***NYSE Composite Index=100** ***12 Month Price Score 93.49**

Interim Earnings (Per Share)

Qtr.	Mar	Jun	Sep	Dec
2003	0.33	0.36	0.32	0.36
2004	0.40	0.42	0.41	0.44
2005	0.30	0.38	0.41	0.42
2006	0.35	0.46	0.45	0.39
2007	0.45	0.47	0.40	0.42

Interim Dividends (Per Share)

Amt	Decl	Ex	Rec	Pay
0.21Q	5/3/2007	5/16/2007	5/18/2007	6/1/2007
0.21Q	8/2/2007	8/15/2007	8/17/2007	9/4/2007
0.21Q	11/1/2007	11/14/2007	11/16/2007	12/3/2007
0.22Q	1/31/2008	2/13/2008	2/15/2008	3/3/2008

Indicated Div: $0.88 (Div. Reinv. Plan)

Valuation Analysis		Institutional Holding	
Forecast P/E	15.87	No of Institutions	
	(1/10/2007)	311	
Market Cap	$2.6 Billion	Shares	
Book Value	1.6 Billion	70,494,136	
Price/Book	1.64	% Held	
Price/Sales	0.70	67.40	

TRADING VOLUME (thousand shares)

Business Summary: Paper Products (MIC: 11.11 SIC: 2671 NAIC: 322221)

Bemis is a manufacturer of flexible packaging products and pressure sensitive materials, selling to customers primarily in the food industry throughout the U.S., Canada, South America, Europe, Asia Pacific and Mexico. Through its Flexible Packaging segment, Co. manufactures a range of consumer and industrial packaging such as multilayer flexible polymer film structures and laminates that are sold for food, medical and personal care products as well as non-food applications utilizing vacuum or modified atmosphere packaging. Co.'s Pressure Sensitive Materials segment manufactures pressure sensitive materials that are sold into label markets, graphic markets and technical markets.

Recent Developments: For the year ended Dec 31 2007, net income increased 3.0% to US$181.6 million from US$176.3 million in the prior year. Revenues were US$3.65 billion, up 0.3% from US$3.64 billion the year before. Direct operating expenses rose 1.0% to US$2.97 billion from US$2.94 billion in the comparable period the year before. Indirect operating expenses decreased 5.1% to US$390.1 million from US$410.9 million in the equivalent prior-year period.

Prospects: Going forward, Co. is projecting uncertain market conditions, as consumer budgets are being restrained by higher energy costs, higher food prices, and in some cases, increased housing-related costs associated with the ongoing mortgage market issues. Nevertheless, Co. expects to continue experiencing strong sales growth in 2008, primarily from the general food and consumer product markets and intends to begin shipping the new business awarded in 2007. In this respect, Co. is targeting earnings for the first quarter of 2008 to be in the range of $0.40 to $0.43 per diluted share. Meanwhile, Co. is forecasting earnings for the full year of 2008 to range from $1.78 to $1.88 per diluted share.

Financial Data

(US$ in Thousands)	12/31/2007	12/31/2006	12/31/2005	12/31/2004	12/31/2003	12/31/2002	12/31/2001	12/31/2000
Earnings Per Share	1.74	1.65	1.51	1.67	1.37	1.54	1.32	1.22
Cash Flow Per Share	3.94	3.33	2.63	2.53	2.93	2.71	3.01	1.97
Tang Book Value Per Share	8.12	7.31	6.29	7.48	5.81	4.11	4.39	4.76
Dividends Per Share	0.840	0.760	0.720	0.640	0.560	0.520	0.500	0.480
Dividend Payout %	48.28	46.06	47.68	38.32	40.88	33.77	37.88	39.34
Income Statement								
Total Revenue	3,649,281	3,639,363	3,473,950	2,834,394	2,635,018	2,369,038	2,293,104	2,164,583
EBITDA	445,306	439,054	427,928	425,549	367,440	386,246	351,572	319,632
Income Before Taxes	285,854	285,796	276,429	293,667	239,245	267,015	227,425	211,502
Income Taxes	104,300	109,500	113,900	113,700	92,100	101,500	87,100	80,900
Net Income	181,554	176,296	162,529	179,967	147,145	165,515	140,325	130,602
Average Shares	104,114	106,767	107,819	107,912	107,733	107,492	106,243	107,106
Balance Sheet								
Current Assets	1,136,943	1,093,712	987,810	873,767	751,906	721,655	586,897	639,959
Total Assets	3,191,396	3,039,009	2,964,600	2,486,743	2,292,932	2,256,650	1,922,974	1,888,643
Current Liabilities	534,550	555,455	474,320	375,143	315,586	325,853	238,182	495,097
Long-Term Obligations	775,456	722,211	790,107	533,886	583,399	718,277	595,249	437,952
Total Liabilities	1,590,138	1,537,808	1,587,553	1,175,904	1,148,802	1,293,236	1,034,698	1,088,316
Stockholders' Equity	1,562,332	1,472,016	1,349,355	1,307,866	1,138,733	958,974	886,148	798,757
Shares Outstanding	100,518	104,841	105,305	106,947	106,242	105,887	105,739	105,204
Statistical Record								
Return on Assets %	5.83	5.87	5.96	7.51	6.47	7.92	7.36	7.61
Return on Equity %	11.97	12.50	12.23	14.67	14.03	17.94	16.66	17.09
EBITDA Margin %	12.20	12.06	12.32	15.01	13.94	16.30	15.33	14.77
Net Margin %	4.98	4.84	4.68	6.35	5.58	6.99	6.12	6.03
Asset Turnover	1.17	1.21	1.27	1.18	1.16	1.13	1.20	1.26
Current Ratio	2.13	1.97	2.08	2.33	2.38	2.21	2.46	1.29
Debt to Equity	0.50	0.49	0.59	0.41	0.51	0.75	0.67	0.55
Price Range	36.23-25.85	34.82-28.49	31.36-23.44	29.31-23.48	25.53-19.89	29.04-19.94	26.08-14.41	19.25-12.03
P/E Ratio	20.82-14.86	21.10-17.27	20.77-15.52	17.55-14.06	18.64-14.52	18.85-12.95	19.76-10.91	15.78-9.86
Average Yield %	2.67	2.41	2.62	2.42	2.47	2.03	2.52	2.93

Address: One Neenah Center, 4th Floor, P.O. Box 669, Neenah, WI 54956-0669
Telephone: 920-727-4100

Web Site: www.bemis.com
Officers: John H. Roe - Chmn. Jeffrey H. Curler - Pres., C.E.O.

Auditors: PricewaterhouseCoopers LLP
Investor Contact: 920-727-4100
Transfer Agents: Wells Fargo Bank Minnesota, South St. Paul, MN

BERKLEY (W. R.) CORP.

Exchange	Symbol	Price	52Wk Range	Yield	P/E
NYS	BER	$27.69 (3/31/2008)	33.63-26.36	0.72	7.33

*7 Year Price Score 114.55 ***NYSE Composite Index=100** ***12 Month Price Score 100.97**

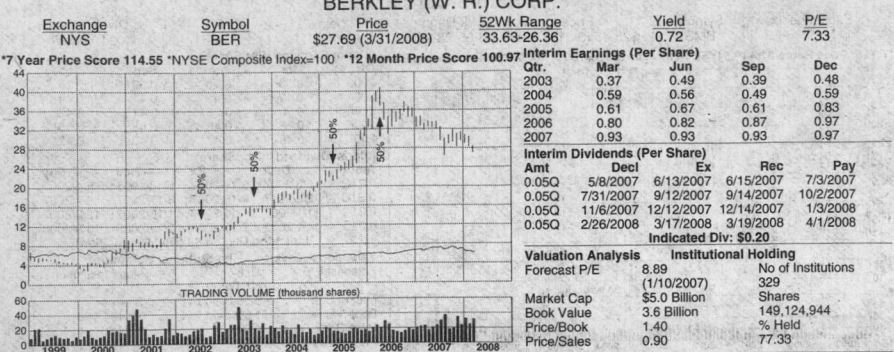

Interim Earnings (Per Share)

Qtr.	Mar	Jun	Sep	Dec
2003	0.37	0.49	0.39	0.48
2004	0.59	0.56	0.49	0.59
2005	0.61	0.67	0.61	0.83
2006	0.80	0.82	0.87	0.97
2007	0.93	0.93	0.93	0.97

Interim Dividends (Per Share)

Amt	Decl	Ex	Rec	Pay
0.05Q	5/8/2007	6/13/2007	6/15/2007	7/3/2007
0.05Q	7/31/2007	9/12/2007	9/14/2007	10/2/2007
0.05Q	11/6/2007	12/12/2007	12/14/2007	1/3/2008
0.05Q	2/26/2008	3/17/2008	3/19/2008	4/1/2008

Indicated Div: $0.20

Valuation Analysis		Institutional Holding	
Forecast P/E	8.89	No of Institutions	
	(1/10/2007)	329	
Market Cap	$5.0 Billion	Shares	
Book Value	3.6 Billion	149,124,944	
Price/Book	1.40	% Held	
Price/Sales	0.90	77.33	

Business Summary: Insurance (MIC: 8.2 SIC: 6331 NAIC: 524126)

W.R. Berkley is an insurance holding company. Co. operates in five segments of the property casualty insurance business: specialty lines of insurance, including excess and surplus lines, professional liability and commercial automobile; regional commercial property casualty insurance; alternative markets, including workers' compensation and self-insurance programs; reinsurance, including treaty, facultative and the Lloyd's of London business; and international. Co. conducts its specialty insurance and reinsurance operations nationwide, and its regional insurance operations mainly in the Midwest, Northeast, Southern (excluding Florida and Louisiana) and Mid Atlantic regions of the U.S.

Recent Developments: For the year ended Dec 31 2007, income from continuing operations decreased 100.0% to nil from US$699.5 million a year earlier. Net income increased 6.3% to US$743.6 million from US$699.5 million in the prior year. Revenues were US$5.55 billion, up 2.9% from US$5.39 billion the year before. Net premiums earned were US$4.66 billion versus US$4.69 billion in the prior year, a decrease of 0.6%. Net investment income rose 14.8% to US$672.7 million from US$586.2 million a year ago.

Prospects: Co.'s bottom-line results are benefiting from growth in its net investment income. Conversely, Co. is seeing a decline in its gross premiums written as compared with 2006. In particular, Co. is experiencing increasing competition and decreasing prices across most of its business segments, and it anticipates that this negative trend of growing competition and declining prices will continue in 2008. Furthermore, Co. believes that it is likely that investment returns will continue to be under pressure due to existing economic uncertainties and the shape of the yield curve.

Financial Data
(US$ in Thousands)

	12/31/2007	12/31/2006	12/31/2005	12/31/2004	12/31/2003	12/31/2002	12/31/2001	12/31/2000
Earnings Per Share	3.78	3.46	2.72	2.21	1.72	0.98	(0.62)	0.27
Cash Flow Per Share	7.83	8.15	9.03	8.55	7.48	5.58	1.03	(0.10)
Tang Book Value Per Share	19.23	16.95	13.08	10.82	8.64	6.85	5.15	4.69
Dividends Per Share	0.200	0.160	0.133	0.124	0.121	0.105	0.103	0.103
Dividend Payout %	5.29	4.62	4.90	5.63	7.06	10.67	...	37.41
Income Statement								
Premium Income	4,663,701	4,692,622	4,460,935	4,061,092	3,234,610	2,252,527	1,680,469	1,491,014
Total Revenue	5,553,639	5,394,831	4,996,839	4,512,235	3,630,108	2,566,084	1,941,797	1,781,287
Benefits & Claims	2,779,578	2,864,498	2,781,802	2,559,310	2,050,177	1,463,971	1,380,500	1,094,411
Income Before Taxes	1,057,634	988,645	770,537	638,513	489,304	259,433	(151,394)	40,851
Income Taxes	310,905	286,398	222,521	196,235	150,626	84,139	(56,661)	2,451
Net Income	743,646	699,518	544,892	438,105	337,220	175,045	(91,546)	36,238
Average Shares	196,698	201,961	200,425	198,407	195,891	178,615	154,684	131,579
Balance Sheet								
Total Assets	16,832,170	15,656,489	13,896,287	11,451,033	9,334,685	7,031,323	5,633,509	5,022,070
Total Liabilities	13,226,899	12,290,715	11,307,896	9,295,180	7,613,975	5,479,224	4,479,408	4,111,128
Stockholders' Equity	3,569,775	3,335,159	2,567,077	2,109,702	1,682,562	1,335,199	931,595	680,896
Shares Outstanding	180,320	192,771	191,264	189,613	187,959	186,379	168,280	129,885
Statistical Record								
Return on Assets %	4.58	4.73	4.30	4.20	4.12	2.76	N.M.	0.74
Return on Equity %	21.54	23.70	23.30	23.04	22.35	15.44	N.M.	5.68
Loss Ratio %	59.60	61.04	62.36	63.02	63.38	64.99	82.15	73.40
Net Margin %	13.39	12.97	10.90	9.71	9.29	6.82	(4.71)	2.03
Price Range	34.68-26.36	40.80-30.91	32.45-20.66	20.96-15.53	16.21-11.04	12.00-9.20	11.50-6.91	9.33-2.89
P/E Ratio	9.17-6.97	11.79-8.93	11.93-7.60	9.49-7.03	9.42-6.42	12.25-9.38	...	34.57-10.70
Average Yield %	0.64	0.45	0.54	0.67	0.86	0.97	1.17	2.06

Address: 475 Steamboat Road, Greenwich, CT 06830	Web Site: www.wrberkley.com	Auditors: KPMG LLP
Telephone: 203-629-3000	Officers: William R. Berkley - Chmn., Pres., C.E.O., C.O.O. Eugene G. Ballard - Sr. V.P., C.F.O., Treas.	Investor Contact: 203-629-3000
Fax: 203-629-3492		Transfer Agents: Wells Fargo Bank, N.A., South St. Paul, MN

BERKSHIRE HATHAWAY INC.

Exchange	Symbol	Price	52Wk Range	Yield	P/E
NYS	BRK A	$133400 (3/31/2008)	149200.00-107300.10	N/A	15.61

*7 Year Price Score 112.36 *NYSE Composite Index=100 *12 Month Price Score 119.17

TRADING VOLUME (thousand shares)

Interim Earnings (Per Share)

Qtr.	Mar	Jun	Sep	Dec
2003	1127.00	1452.00	1176.00	1554.00
2004	1008.00	834.00	739.00	2172.00
2005	886.00	941.00	-381.00	3331.00
2006	1501.00	1522.00	1797.00	2323.00
2007	1682.00	2018.00	2942.00	1904.00

Interim Dividends (Per Share)

No Dividends Paid

Valuation Analysis

		Institutional Holding	
Forecast P/E	N/A	No of Institutions	535
Market Cap	$2011.8 Billion	Shares	280,673
Book Value	120.7 Billion		
Price/Book	16.66	% Held	
Price/Sales	17.01		25.20

Business Summary: Insurance (MIC: 8.2 SIC: 6331 NAIC: 524126)

Berkshire Hathaway is a holding company owning subsidiaries engaged in a number of business activities. Co.'s insurance businesses are conducted on a primary and reinsurance basis. Additionally, Co. owns and operates a number of other businesses engaged in a variety of activities which include Utilities and Energy, Manufacturing, Service and Retailing, as well as Finance and Financial Products. Co.'s insurance and reinsurance activities are conducted through over 60 domestic and foreign-based insurance entities as of Dec 31 2007, providing insurance and reinsurance of property and casualty risks and also reinsure life, accident and health risks world-wide.

Recent Developments: For the year ended Dec 31 2007, net income increased 20.0% to US$13.21 billion from US$11.02 billion in the prior year. Revenues were US$118.25 billion, up 20.0% from US$98.54 billion the year before. Net premiums earned were US$31.78 billion versus US$23.96 billion in the prior year, an increase of 32.6%.

Prospects: On Dec 25 2007, Co. announced that it will purchase 60.0% of Marmon Holdings, Inc., for $4.50 billion, and will acquire the remaining 40.0% through staged acquisitions over a five to six year period for consideration to be based on the future earnings of Marmon. The acquisition is expected to close in the first quarter of 2008, subject to customary closing conditions, including regulatory approvals. Meanwhile, on Jan 14 2008, Co.'s finance and financial products business, CORT, has acquired Roomservice Group, as part of an expansion into the U.K. The acquisition demonstrates Co.'s commitment to developing its global network of furniture products and relocation services.

Financial Data
(US$ in Thousands)

	12/31/2007	12/31/2006	12/31/2005	12/31/2004	12/31/2003	12/31/2002	12/31/2001	12/31/2000
Earnings Per Share	8,548.00	7,144.00	5,538.00	4,753.00	5,309.00	2,795.00	521.00	2,185.00
Cash Flow Per Share	8,119.03	6,612.37	6,134.66	4,802.43	5,377.73	7,307.89	4,304.51	1,929.80
Tang Book Value Per Share	5,826.56	5,492.50	7,026.41	40,869.38	35,563.54	27,197.61	23,912.17	28,075.06
Income Statement								
Premium Income	31,783,000	23,964,000	21,997,000	21,085,000	21,493,000	19,182,000	17,905,000	19,343,000
Total Revenue	118,245,000	98,539,000	81,663,000	74,382,000	63,859,000	42,353,000	37,668,000	34,006,000
Benefits & Claims	22,796,000	14,686,000	17,116,000	14,823,000	14,927,000	15,269,000	18,398,000	17,332,000
Income Before Taxes	20,161,000	16,778,000	12,791,000	10,936,000	12,020,000	6,435,000	1,469,000	5,587,000
Income Taxes	6,594,000	5,505,000	4,159,000	3,569,000	3,805,000	2,134,000	620,000	2,018,000
Net Income	13,213,000	11,015,000	8,528,000	7,308,000	8,151,000	4,286,000	795,000	3,328,000
Average Shares	1,545	1,541	1,539	1,537	1,535	1,533	1,527	1,522
Balance Sheet								
Total Assets	273,160,000	248,437,000	198,325,000	188,874,000	180,559,000	169,544,000	162,752,000	135,792,000
Total Liabilities	149,759,000	137,756,000	106,025,000	102,216,000	102,218,000	104,116,000	103,453,000	72,799,000
Stockholders' Equity	120,733,000	108,419,000	91,484,000	85,900,000	77,596,000	64,037,000	57,950,000	61,724,000
Shares Outstanding	15,081	13,869	9,655	1,538	1,536	1,534	1,528	1,526
Statistical Record								
Return on Assets %	5.07	4.93	4.40	3.95	4.66	2.58	0.53	2.48
Return on Equity %	11.53	11.02	9.62	8.92	11.51	7.03	1.33	5.56
Loss Ratio %	71.72	61.28	77.81	70.30	69.45	79.60	102.75	89.60
Net Margin %	11.17	11.18	10.44	9.82	12.76	10.12	2.11	9.79
Price Range	149200-105100	113700-86100	91700-80500	95650-81400	84500-61200	78300-61500	75600-61400	71000-41300
P/E Ratio	17.45-12.30	15.92-12.05	16.56-14.54	20.12-17.13	15.92-11.53	28.01-22.00	145.11-117.85	32.49-18.90

Address: 1440 Kiewit Plaza, Omaha, NE 68131 Telephone: 402-346-1400	Web Site: www.berkshirehathaway.com Officers: Warren E. Buffett - Chmn., C.E.O. Charles T. Munger - Vice-Chmn.	Auditors: Deloitte & Touche LLP Transfer Agents: Wells Fargo Bank

BEST BUY INC

Exchange	Symbol	Price	52Wk Range	Yield	P/E
NYS	BBY	$41.46 (3/31/2008)	53.38-39.43	1.25	14.15

*7 Year Price Score 101.08 *NYSE Composite Index=100 *12 Month Price Score 100.40

Interim Earnings (Per Share)

Qtr.	May	Aug	Nov	Feb
2004-05	0.23	0.31	0.30	1.13
2005-06	0.34	0.37	0.28	1.28
2006-07	0.47	0.47	0.31	1.55
2007-08	0.39	0.55	0.53	...

Interim Dividends (Per Share)

Amt	Decl	Ex	Rec	Pay
0.10Q	6/20/2007	7/6/2007	7/10/2007	7/31/2007
0.13Q	9/19/2007	10/4/2007	10/9/2007	10/30/2007
0.13Q	12/19/2007	1/7/2008	1/9/2008	1/30/2008
0.13Q	4/3/2008	4/21/2008	4/23/2008	5/14/2008

Indicated Div: $0.52

Valuation Analysis / **Institutional Holding**

Forecast P/E	13.55 (1/10/2007)	No of Institutions 606
Market Cap	$17.4 Billion	Shares 346,112,992
Book Value	3.7 Billion	% Held 71.82
Price/Book	4.64	
Price/Sales	0.45	

TRADING VOLUME (thousand shares)

Business Summary: Retail - Appliances and Electrical (MIC: 5.10 SIC: 5731 NAIC: 443112)

Best Buy is a retailer of consumer electronics, home-office products, entertainment software, appliances and related services. Co. operates retail stores and commercial Web sites under the brand names Best Buy (BestBuy.com, BestBuyCanada.ca and BestBuy.com.cn), Five Star Appliance Co. (Five-Star.cn), Future Shop (FutureShop.ca), Geek Squad (GeekSquad.com and GeekSquad.ca), Magnolia Audio Video (MagnoliaAV.com), and Pacific Sales Kitchen and Bath Centers (PacificSales.com). As of Mar 3 2007, Co. operated 822 U.S. Best Buy stores, 20 Magnolia Audio Video stores, 14 Pacific Sales stores, 12 Geek Squad stores, 121 Future Shop stores, 47 Canada Best Buy stores, and 135 Five Star stores.

Recent Developments: For the quarter ended Dec 1 2007, net income increased 52.0% to US$228.0 million from US$150.0 million in the year-earlier quarter. Revenues were US$9.93 billion, up 17.2% from US$8.47 billion the year before. Operating income was US$351.0 million versus US$196.0 million in the prior-year quarter, an increase of 79.1%. Direct operating expenses rose 17.2% to US$7.59 billion from US$6.48 billion in the comparable period the year before. Indirect operating expenses increased 10.4% to US$1.99 billion from US$1.80 billion in the equivalent prior-year period.

Prospects: Co.'s near-term outlook appears encouraging reflecting strong increase in its net earnings. Specifically, results are benefiting from growth in its revenues, resulting primarily from new store openings and a comparable store sales gain, an unchanged gross profit rate and an improved selling, general and administrative expense rate. Accordingly, based on its solid 2008 third fiscal quarter results, Co. expects to deliver revenue of approximately $40.00 billion and diluted earnings per share within its previously announced guidance range of $3.10 to $3.20 for the full fiscal year ending Mar 2008. Notably, this range represents an average annual earnings growth rate of approximately 13.0%.

Financial Data
(US$ in Thousands)

	9 Mos	6 Mos	3 Mos	03/03/2007	02/25/2006	02/26/2005	02/28/2004	03/01/2003
Earnings Per Share	2.93	2.78	2.69	2.79	2.27	1.96	1.43	0.20
Cash Flow Per Share	6.35	4.29	4.20	3.60	3.47	3.78	2.92	1.55
Tang Book Value Per Share	6.11	5.35	10.61	10.82	9.60	7.91	5.97	4.70
Dividends Per Share	0.430	0.400	0.380	0.360	0.307	0.280	0.267	...
Dividend Payout %	14.70	14.39	14.13	12.90	13.51	14.29	18.60	...
Income Statement								
Total Revenue	26,605,000	16,677,000	7,927,000	35,934,000	30,848,000	27,433,000	24,547,000	20,946,000
EBITDA	1,535,000	1,012,000	445,000	2,528,000	2,100,000	1,901,000	1,689,000	1,320,000
Depn & Amortn	419,000	279,000	135,000	...	...	...	...	...
Income Before Taxes	1,063,000	703,000	303,000	2,130,000	1,721,000	1,443,000	1,296,000	1,014,000
Income Taxes	386,000	257,000	113,000	752,000	581,000	509,000	496,000	392,000
Net Income	670,000	442,000	192,000	1,377,000	1,140,000	984,000	705,000	99,000
Average Shares	430,800	456,200	491,500	496,200	504,800	504,900	492,000	487,200
Balance Sheet								
Current Assets	10,477,000	7,448,000	8,306,000	9,081,000	7,985,000	6,903,000	5,724,000	4,867,000
Total Assets	15,474,000	12,237,000	13,142,000	13,570,000	11,864,000	10,294,000	8,652,000	7,663,000
Current Liabilities	10,236,000	7,467,000	5,686,000	6,301,000	6,056,000	4,959,000	4,501,000	3,793,000
Long-Term Obligations	642,000	600,000	598,000	590,000	178,000	528,000	482,000	828,000
Total Liabilities	11,728,000	8,856,000	6,972,000	7,334,000	6,607,000	5,845,000	5,230,000	4,933,000
Stockholders' Equity	3,746,000	3,381,000	6,170,000	6,201,000	5,257,000	4,449,000	3,422,000	2,730,000
Shares Outstanding	419,484	417,777	473,898	480,655	485,098	492,513	486,972	482,949
Statistical Record								
Return on Assets %	8.98	10.92	10.81	10.65	10.32	10.42	8.67	1.32
Return on Equity %	29.66	30.52	22.80	23.65	23.56	25.07	22.98	3.78
EBITDA Margin %	5.77	6.07	5.61	7.04	6.81	6.93	6.88	6.30
Net Margin %	2.52	2.65	2.42	3.83	3.70	3.59	2.87	0.47
Asset Turnover	2.51	3.04	2.98	2.78	2.79	2.90	3.02	2.79
Current Ratio	1.02	1.00	1.46	1.44	1.32	1.39	1.27	1.28
Debt to Equity	0.17	0.18	0.10	0.10	0.03	0.12	0.14	0.30
Price Range	54.47-42.69	58.15-43.05	58.15-43.96	58.72-43.96	55.11-32.31	41.33-29.51	41.33-17.77	35.58-11.79
P/E Ratio	18.59-14.57	20.92-15.49	21.62-16.34	21.05-15.76	24.28-14.23	21.09-15.06	28.90-12.43	177.89-58.93
Average Yield %	0.90	0.81	0.76	0.69	0.70	0.70	0.79	0.87

Address: 7601 Penn Avenue South, Richfield , MN 55423-3645
Telephone: 612-291-1000
Fax: 612-292-4001

Web Site: www.bestbuy.com
Officers: Richard M. Schulze - Chmn. Bradbury H. Anderson - Vice-Chmn., C.E.O.

Auditors: DELOITTE & TOUCHE LLP
Investor Contact: 612-291-6147
Transfer Agents: EquiServe Trust Company, N.A., Providence, RI

BIG LOTS, INC.

Exchange	Symbol	Price	52Wk Range	Yield	P/E
NYS	BIG	$22.30 (3/31/2008)	35.60-12.62	N/A	14.39

*7 Year Price Score 126.39 *NYSE Composite Index=100   *12 Month Price Score 80.60

Interim Earnings (Per Share)

Qtr.	Apr	Jul	Oct	Jan
2003-04	0.09	(0.07)	(0.05)	0.73
2004-05	0.06	(0.06)	(0.28)	0.49
2005-06	0.07	(0.12)	(0.17)	0.13
2006-07	0.12	0.04	0.02	0.93
2007-08	0.26	0.22	0.14	0.93

Interim Dividends (Per Share)

No Dividends Paid

Valuation Analysis		Institutional Holding	
Forecast P/E	N/A	No of Institutions	
		240	
Market Cap	$1.8 Billion	Shares	
Book Value	638.5 Million	149,250,832	
Price/Book	2.89	% Held	
Price/Sales	0.40	N/A	

Business Summary: Retail - General (MIC: 5.2 SIC: 5331 NAIC: 452990)

Big Lots is a closeout broadline closeout retailer. Co. sources and purchases merchandise directly from manufacturers and other vendors at prices below those paid by traditional retailers. The majority of the merchandise sold by Co. is received and processed for retail sale and distributed to the retail locations from its closeout and furniture distribution centers. In addition to the merchandise distribution centers, Co. operates warehouses that distribute store fixtures and supplies. Co.'s merchandising categories include Consumables, Home, Furniture, Hardlines, Seasonal, and Other. As of Feb 2 2008, Co. operated a total of 1,353 stores in 47 states.

Recent Developments: For the year ended Feb 2 2008, income from continuing operations increased 34.2% to US$151.2 million from US$112.6 million a year earlier. Net income increased 27.7% to US$158.5 million from US$124.0 million in the prior year. Revenues were US$4.66 billion, down 1.8% from US$4.74 billion the year before. Operating income was US$236.5 million versus US$167.8 million in the prior year, an increase of 40.9%. Direct operating expenses declined 1.3% to US$2.82 billion from US$2.85 billion in the comparable period the year before. Indirect operating expenses decreased 6.9% to US$1.60 billion from US$1.72 billion in the equivalent prior-year period.

Prospects: For the fiscal year ending Jan 31 2009, Co. anticipates comparable store sales increase of approximately 1.0% to 2.0% with income from continuing operations in the range of $1.70 to $1.80 per diluted share. Further, Co. expects its capital expenditure requirement for fiscal 2008 to range between $90.0 million and $95.0 million, focusing on completing the installation of the new point-of-sale register system in its stores, development and licensing cost associated with its SAP for Retail software system implementation, the completion of approximately 40 additional store retrofits, approximately 20 new store openings, and other projects aimed at maintaining existing property and equipment.

Financial Data

(US$ in Thousands)	02/02/2008	02/03/2007	01/28/2006	01/29/2005	01/31/2004	02/01/2003	02/02/2002	02/03/2001
Earnings Per Share	1.55	1.11	(0.09)	0.21	0.69	0.66	(0.18)	(3.39)
Cash Flow Per Share	3.05	3.40	1.89	0.63	1.59	1.89	1.33	(2.72)
Tang Book Value Per Share	1.72	10.30	9.47	9.54	9.54	8.83	8.11	8.28
Dividends Per Share	...	...	...	...	...	...	0.010	...
Income Statement								
Total Revenue	4,656,302	4,743,048	4,429,905	4,375,072	4,174,383	3,868,550	3,433,321	3,277,088
EBITDA	324,819	266,684	141,490	169,494	221,962	228,161	41,727	247,756
Income Before Taxes	239,203	170,490	20,914	43,298	114,946	126,541	(47,461)	162,519
Income Taxes	88,023	57,872	5,189	12,887	24,051	49,984	(18,747)	64,195
Net Income	158,461	124,045	(10,088)	23,763	81,175	76,557	(20,234)	(380,652)
Average Shares	102,542	111,930	113,677	114,801	117,253	116,707	113,660	112,414
Balance Sheet								
Current Assets	891,110	1,149,047	993,754	1,034,782	1,167,600	1,069,167	991,074	1,100,567
Total Assets	1,443,815	1,720,526	1,625,497	1,733,584	1,784,688	1,642,271	1,533,209	1,585,396
Current Liabilities	500,344	474,232	436,523	412,513	463,586	410,907	321,874	324,994
Long-Term Obligations	163,700	...	5,500	159,200	204,000	204,000	204,000	268,000
Total Liabilities	805,329	590,823	546,773	658,094	668,628	616,090	605,676	657,584
Stockholders' Equity	638,486	1,129,703	1,078,724	1,075,490	1,116,060	1,026,181	927,533	927,812
Shares Outstanding	82,682	109,633	113,932	112,780	116,927	116,165	114,398	112,079
Statistical Record								
Return on Assets %	10.04	7.29	N.M.	1.35	4.75	4.84	N.M.	N.M.
Return on Equity %	17.97	11.05	N.M.	2.17	7.60	7.86	N.M.	N.M.
EBITDA Margin %	6.98	5.62	3.19	3.87	5.32	5.90	1.22	7.56
Net Margin %	3.40	2.62	N.M.	0.54	1.94	1.98	N.M.	N.M.
Asset Turnover	2.95	2.79	2.64	2.49	2.44	2.44	2.21	1.71
Current Ratio	1.78	2.42	2.28	2.51	2.52	2.60	3.09	3.39
Debt to Equity	0.26	...	0.01	0.15	0.18	0.20	0.22	0.29
Price Range	35.60-12.62	26.10-12.71	14.11-10.08	15.50-10.85	18.39-10.20	19.68-10.84	15.51-7.35	15.63-8.25
P/E Ratio	22.97-8.14	23.51-11.45	...	73.81-51.67	26.65-14.78	29.82-16.42	...	...
Average Yield %	...	...	...	...	...	...	0.09	...

Address: 300 Phillipi Road, P.O. Box 28512, Columbus, OH 43228-5311 **Telephone:** 614-278-6800 **Fax:** 614-278-6666	Web Site: www.biglots.com **Officers:** Steven S. Fishman - Chmn., Pres., C.E.O. Brad A. Waite - Exec. V.P., H.R., Loss Prevention	**Auditors:** Deloitte & Touche LLP **Investor Contact:** 614-278-6622 **Transfer Agents:** National City Bank, Cleveland, Ohio

BJ SERVICES CO.

Exchange	Symbol	Price	52Wk Range	Yield	P/E
NYS	BJS	$28.51 (3/31/2008)	30.78-20.56	0.70	11.68

*7 Year Price Score 90.52   *NYSE Composite Index=100   *12 Month Price Score 102.93

Interim Earnings (Per Share)

Qtr.	Dec	Mar	Jun	Sep
2005		1.38		
2005-06	0.48	0.62	0.67	0.75
2006-07	0.70	0.64	0.57	0.65
2007-08	0.58	...		

Interim Dividends (Per Share)

Amt	Decl	Ex	Rec	Pay
0.05Q	5/24/2007	6/13/2007	6/15/2007	7/13/2007
0.05Q	7/26/2007	9/11/2007	9/13/2007	10/12/2007
0.05Q	12/6/2007	12/14/2007	12/18/2007	1/11/2008
0.05Q	2/7/2008	3/12/2008	3/14/2008	4/15/2008

Indicated Div: $0.20

Valuation Analysis | **Institutional Holding**
Forecast P/E	7.70	No of Institutions
	(1/10/2007)	465
Market Cap	$8.4 Billion	Shares
Book Value	3.0 Billion	258,620,256
Price/Book	2.75	% Held
Price/Sales	1.70	88.20

Business Summary: Oil and Gas (MIC: 14.2 SIC: 1389 NAIC: 213112)

BJ Services is engaged in providing pressure pumping services and other oilfield services. Pressure pumping services consist of cementing and stimulation services used in the completion of new oil and natural gas wells and in remedial work on existing wells, both onshore and offshore. Oilfield services include completion tools, completion fluids, casing and tubular services, chemical services, and precommissioning, maintenance and turnaround services in the pipeline and process business, including pipeline inspection. As of Sep 30 2007, Co. had four business segments: U.S. and Mexico Pressure Pumping, International Pressure Pumping, Canada Pressure Pumping and the Oilfield Services Group.

Recent Developments: For the quarter ended Dec 31 2007, net income decreased 16.9% to US$172.2 million from US$207.1 million in the year-earlier quarter. Revenues were US$1.29 billion, up 8.5% from US$1.18 billion the year before. Operating income was US$252.6 million versus US$316.3 million in the prior-year quarter, a decrease of 20.2%. Direct operating expenses rose 20.5% to US$950.5 million from US$788.6 million in the comparable period the year before. Indirect operating expenses increased 3.9% to US$82.0 million from US$79.0 million in the equivalent prior-year period.

Prospects: For the second fiscal quarter ended Mar 2008, Co. expects relatively flat drilling activity with continued pricing pressures in the U.S. market at least until the latter part of 2008. However, Co. expects continued high demand for its services in a number of areas, mainly in gas shale areas in Arkansas, the Rockies and the Mid-Continent region, and it anticipates higher Gulf of Mexico activity mainly in the deep water area. Co. also expects Canadian drilling activity to increase as it enter the winter drilling season, and it expects its operating results to improve compared with prior quarter. For the second fiscal quarter of 2008, Co. is projecting earnings of $0.55 to $0.57 per share.

Financial Data
(US$ in Thousands)

	3 Mos	09/30/2007	09/30/2006	09/30/2005	09/30/2004	09/30/2003	09/30/2002	09/30/2001
Earnings Per Share	2.44	2.55	2.52	1.38	1.11	0.58	0.52	1.04
Cash Flow Per Share	2.64	2.87	2.64	1.69	1.65	1.03	1.10	1.58
Tang Book Value Per Share	7.06	6.47	4.16	4.94	3.73	2.43	1.74	2.78
Dividends Per Share	0.200	0.200	0.200	0.170	0.040	...	...	...
Dividend Payout %	8.20	7.84	7.94	12.32	3.62	...	...	...
Income Statement								
Total Revenue	1,285,065	4,802,409	4,367,864	3,243,186	2,600,986	2,142,877	1,865,796	2,233,520
EBITDA	312,636	1,352,974	1,338,488	789,878	656,721	409,692	364,580	644,865
Depn & Amortn	62,766				...	...	...	...
Income Before Taxes	242,482	1,112,848	1,172,083	653,347	520,737	275,672	252,694	529,181
Income Taxes	70,298	359,208	367,473	200,305	159,696	87,495	86,199	179,922
Net Income	172,184	753,640	804,610	453,042	361,041	188,177	166,495	349,259
Average Shares	295,284	295,916	318,820	329,115	326,828	322,514	321,472	334,160
Balance Sheet								
Current Assets	1,699,246	1,703,772	1,458,860	1,334,471	1,423,723	941,708	648,791	732,633
Total Assets	4,831,536	4,715,212	3,862,288	3,396,498	3,330,674	2,785,957	2,442,370	1,985,367
Current Liabilities	1,235,004	1,313,188	947,936	683,793	909,891	470,661	356,420	389,598
Long-Term Obligations	249,776	249,760	499,694	...	78,936	493,754	489,062	79,393
Total Liabilities	1,797,962	1,863,814	1,715,348	912,745	1,236,538	1,135,325	1,023,742	615,286
Stockholders' Equity	3,033,574	2,851,398	2,146,940	2,483,753	2,094,136	1,650,632	1,418,628	1,370,081
Shares Outstanding	292,977	291,735	293,193	323,410	323,737	316,612	313,590	320,968
Statistical Record								
Return on Assets %	16.36	17.57	22.17	13.47	11.77	7.20	7.52	18.53
Return on Equity %	26.78	30.16	34.75	19.79	19.23	12.26	11.94	27.50
EBITDA Margin %	24.33	28.17	30.64	24.36	25.25	19.12	19.54	28.87
Net Margin %	13.40	15.69	18.42	13.97	13.88	8.78	8.92	15.64
Asset Turnover	1.12	1.12	1.20	0.96	0.85	0.82	0.84	1.18
Current Ratio	1.38	1.30	1.54	1.95	1.56	2.00	1.82	1.88
Debt to Equity	0.08	0.09	0.23	...	0.04	0.30	0.34	0.06
Price Range	30.78-23.20	33.87-23.95	42.75-28.39	36.39-21.55	26.45-15.45	20.98-12.45	19.32-8.56	21.16-7.43
P/E Ratio	12.61-9.51	13.28-9.39	16.96-11.27	26.37-15.61	23.83-13.92	36.16-21.47	37.16-16.46	20.35-7.15
Average Yield %	0.74	0.70	0.57	0.65	0.19	...	...	...

Address: 4601 Westway Park Blvd., Houston, TX 77041	**Web Site:** www.bjservices.com	**Auditors:** Deloitte & Touche LLP
Telephone: 713-462-4239	**Officers:** J. W. Stewart - Chmn., Pres., C.E.O. Mark Airola - Chief Compliance Officer, Asst. Gen. Couns.	**Transfer Agents:** Bank of New York
Fax: 713-895-5603		

BJ'S WHOLESALE CLUB INC

Exchange	Symbol	Price	52Wk Range	Yield	P/E
NYS	BJ	$35.69 (3/31/2008)	39.00-26.80	N/A	18.78

*7 Year Price Score 89.98 ***NYSE Composite Index=100** ***12 Month Price Score 104.13**

Interim Earnings (Per Share)

Qtr.	Apr	Jul	Oct	Jan
2003-04	0.16	0.32	0.29	0.70
2004-05	0.23	0.40	0.33	0.67
2005-06	0.27	0.44	0.41	0.76
2006-07	0.23	0.39	0.28	0.18
2007-08	0.21	0.55	0.35	0.79

Interim Dividends (Per Share)

No Dividends Paid

Valuation Analysis   Institutional Holding

Forecast P/E	N/A	No of Institutions
		221
Market Cap	$2.2 Billion	Shares
Book Value	980.5 Million	59,346,356
Price/Book	2.20	% Held
Price/Sales	0.24	91.32

Business Summary: Retail - General (MIC: 5.2 SIC: 5331 NAIC: 452990)

BJ's Wholesale Club is a warehouse club operator in the eastern U.S. As of Feb 2 2008, Co. operated 177 warehouse clubs, 100 of which operated gasoline stations, in 16 states. Co.'s revenues are derived from the sale of food and general merchandise items, gasoline, and from membership fees. Co.'s food categories include frozen foods, fresh meat and dairy products, beverages, dry grocery, fresh produce and flowers, canned goods and household paper products, while its general merchandise includes consumer electronics, prerecorded media, small appliances, tires, jewelry, health and beauty aids, household needs, computer software, books, greeting cards, apparel, furniture, toys and other items.

Recent Developments: For the year ended Feb 2 2008, income from continuing operations increased 30.6% to US$121.4 million from US$93.0 million a year earlier. Net income increased 70.6% to US$122.9 million from US$72.0 million in the prior year. Revenues were US$9.01 billion, up 6.2% from US$8.48 billion the year before. Operating income was US$195.3 million versus US$144.4 million in the prior year, an increase of 35.3%. Direct operating expenses rose 6.5% to US$8.11 billion from US$7.62 billion in the comparable period the year before. Indirect operating expenses decreased 2.6% to US$698.4 million from US$716.8 million in the equivalent prior-year period.

Prospects: For 2008, Co. is projecting strong comparable club sales, slightly improved merchandise margins, better gasoline profitability and stringent expense control. In addition, Co. plans to continue its emphasis on growing its perishable businesses and expanding its assortment of organic fresh and frozen foods as well as natural meats and poultry. Similarly, Co. plans to enhance its perishable departments by installing more multi-deck refrigeration cases. Further, Co. anticipates that capital expenditures will total approximately $150.0 million to $170.0 million, based on plans to open 4 new clubs, as well as to increase capital spending on club renovations and Information Technology projects.

Financial Data
(US$ in Thousands)

	02/02/2008	02/03/2007	01/28/2006	01/29/2005	01/31/2004	02/01/2003	02/02/2002	02/03/2001
Earnings Per Share	1.90	1.08	1.87	1.63	1.47	1.84	1.11	1.77
Cash Flow Per Share	4.85	2.60	2.94	3.59	2.88	2.16	2.93	2.10
Tang Book Value Per Share	16.24	15.74	15.08	13.59	12.21	10.69	9.59	9.18
Income Statement								
Total Revenue	9,005,002	8,480,281	7,949,934	7,375,301	6,724,219	5,859,702	5,279,730	4,932,095
EBITDA	301,694	252,755	312,188	287,565	255,237	308,500	188,279	262,821
Income Before Taxes	199,033	150,140	211,123	189,468	168,113	235,680	130,533	213,823
Income Taxes	77,628	57,183	82,281	72,884	63,318	89,871	48,185	82,322
Net Income	122,861	72,016	128,533	114,401	102,866	130,866	82,348	131,501
Average Shares	64,557	66,387	68,755	70,131	69,815	71,120	73,981	74,380
Balance Sheet								
Current Assets	1,145,339	1,069,578	1,119,869	1,042,979	908,720	767,070	752,818	694,571
Total Assets	2,046,519	1,992,811	1,989,849	1,891,514	1,721,109	1,480,957	1,421,884	1,233,734
Current Liabilities	946,434	866,578	862,366	834,127	761,433	650,028	625,000	514,643
Long-Term Obligations	12,348	17,037	10,896	12,066	15,088	18,727	63,700	1,828
Total Liabilities	1,066,027	972,924	973,870	952,347	868,888	740,154	735,317	568,819
Stockholders' Equity	980,492	1,019,887	1,015,979	939,167	852,221	740,803	686,567	664,915
Shares Outstanding	60,382	64,780	67,392	69,089	69,789	69,284	71,593	72,462
Statistical Record								
Return on Assets %	6.10	3.56	6.64	6.35	6.44	9.04	6.22	11.21
Return on Equity %	12.32	6.96	13.18	12.81	12.95	18.39	12.22	20.83
EBITDA Margin %	3.35	2.98	3.93	3.90	3.80	5.26	3.57	5.33
Net Margin %	1.36	0.85	1.62	1.55	1.53	2.23	1.56	2.67
Asset Turnover	4.47	4.19	4.11	4.09	4.21	4.05	3.99	4.21
Current Ratio	1.21	1.23	1.30	1.25	1.19	1.18	1.20	1.35
Debt to Equity	0.01	0.02	0.01	0.01	0.02	0.03	0.09	N.M.
Price Range	39.00-26.80	32.48-25.38	33.75-25.85	31.04-20.29	27.18-9.38	47.35-15.40	56.97-40.35	42.95-26.75
P/E Ratio	20.53-14.11	30.07-23.50	18.05-13.82	19.04-12.45	18.49-6.38	25.73-8.37	51.32-36.35	24.27-15.11

Address: One Mercer Road, Natick, MA 01760	Web Site: www.bjs.com	Auditors: PricewaterhouseCoopers LLP
Telephone: 508-651-7400	Officers: Herbert J. Zarkin - Chmn. Michael T. Wedge - Pres., C.E.O.	Investor Contact: 508-651-6650
Fax: 508-651-6114		Transfer Agents: The Bank of New York

BLACK & DECKER CORP.

Exchange	Symbol	Price	52Wk Range	Yield	P/E
NYS	BDK	$66.10 (3/31/2008)	96.33-62.19	2.54	8.42

*7 Year Price Score 101.77 *NYSE Composite Index=100 *12 Month Price Score 89.53

Interim Earnings (Per Share)
Qtr.	Mar	Jun	Sep	Dec
2003	0.55	0.97	0.95	1.27
2004	1.09	1.50	1.37	1.63
2005	1.80	1.88	1.73	1.28
2006	1.45	1.98	1.74	1.39
2007	1.61	1.75	1.59	2.90

Interim Dividends (Per Share)
Amt	Decl	Ex	Rec	Pay
0.42Q	4/25/2007	6/13/2007	6/15/2007	6/29/2007
0.42Q	7/26/2007	9/12/2007	9/14/2007	9/28/2007
0.42Q	10/17/2007	12/12/2007	12/14/2007	12/28/2007
0.42Q	2/14/2008	3/12/2008	3/14/2008	3/28/2008

Indicated Div: $1.68

Valuation Analysis
Forecast P/E	10.31
	(1/10/2007)
Market Cap	$4.2 Billion
Book Value	1.5 Billion
Price/Book	2.85
Price/Sales	0.63

Institutional Holding
No of Institutions	
	351
Shares	
	57,862,700
% Held	
	88.21

Business Summary: Industrial Machinery and Equipment (MIC: 11.5 SIC: 3546 NAIC: 333991)

Black & Decker is a global manufacturer and marketer of power tools and accessories, hardware and home improvement products, and technology-based fastening systems. Co. operates in three reportable business segments: Power Tools and Accessories, including consumer and industrial power tools and accessories, lawn and garden tools, electric cleaning, automotive, and lighting products, and product service; Hardware and Home Improvement, including security hardware and plumbing products; and Fastening and Assembly Systems. As of Dec 31 2007, Co. operated 46 manufacturing facilities worldwide, including 30 located outside of the U.S. in 10 foreign countries.

Recent Developments: For the year ended Dec 31 2007, income from continuing operations increased 6.6% to US$518.1 million from US$486.1 million a year earlier. Net income increased 6.6% to US$518.1 million from US$486.1 million in the prior year. Revenues were US$6.56 billion, up 1.8% from US$6.45 billion the year before. Operating income was US$582.2 million versus US$740.4 million in the prior year, a decrease of 21.4%. Direct operating expenses rose 3.1% to US$4.34 billion from US$4.21 billion in the comparable period the year before. Indirect operating expenses increased 9.6% to US$1.64 billion from US$1.50 billion in the equivalent prior-year period.

Prospects: Despite the expectation of continued strong international momentum and new product pipeline, Co. anticipates organic sales to decline at a low single-digit rate in 2008 as compared to 2007, reflecting the continued weakness in key sectors of the U.S. economy, including lower residential construction. In addition, Co. expects operating income and margins in 2008 to be tempered by several factors, including the rising commodity, the change in China's value-added tax, and an increase in selling, general, and administrative expenses. Accordingly, Co. now projects diluted earnings of $1.10 and $1.20 per share for the first quarter of 2008 and $5.40 and $5.90 per share for full-year 2008.

Financial Data
(US$ in Thousands)	12/31/2007	12/31/2006	12/31/2005	12/31/2004	12/31/2003	12/31/2002	12/31/2001	12/31/2000
Earnings Per Share	7.85	6.55	6.69	5.59	3.75	2.84	1.33	3.34
Cash Flow Per Share	11.29	8.64	7.93	7.74	7.32	5.62	4.70	4.17
Tang Book Value Per Share	3.91	N.M.	5.27	4.56	0.96	N.M.	0.51	N.M.
Dividends Per Share	1.680	1.520	1.120	0.840	0.570	0.480	0.480	0.480
Dividend Payout %	21.40	23.21	16.74	15.03	15.20	16.90	36.09	14.37
Income Statement								
Total Revenue	6,563,200	6,447,300	6,523,700	5,398,400	4,482,700	4,394,000	4,333,100	4,560,800
EBITDA	749,000	893,100	1,015,300	768,900	559,500	493,000	399,000	672,200
Income Before Taxes	497,600	664,400	819,300	604,300	390,900	307,400	155,300	404,600
Income Taxes	(20,500)	178,300	275,300	163,200	103,700	77,700	47,300	122,600
Net Income	518,100	486,100	543,900	456,000	293,000	229,700	108,000	282,000
Average Shares	66,000	74,200	81,300	81,600	78,200	80,900	81,100	84,400
Balance Sheet								
Current Assets	2,839,500	2,703,400	3,347,400	2,927,200	2,203,000	2,193,900	1,892,300	1,962,000
Total Assets	5,410,900	5,247,700	5,816,600	5,530,800	4,222,500	4,130,500	4,014,200	4,089,700
Current Liabilities	1,880,800	1,779,600	2,264,000	1,792,600	1,312,100	1,453,400	1,070,600	1,632,300
Long-Term Obligations	1,179,100	1,170,300	1,030,300	1,200,600	915,600	927,600	1,191,400	798,500
Total Liabilities	3,952,200	4,084,100	4,293,000	3,972,100	3,376,000	3,530,900	3,263,200	3,397,300
Stockholders' Equity	1,458,700	1,163,600	1,523,600	1,558,700	846,500	599,600	751,000	692,400
Shares Outstanding	62,923	66,734	77,357	82,095	77,933	79,604	79,829	80,343
Statistical Record								
Return on Assets %	9.72	8.79	9.59	9.33	7.02	5.64	2.67	6.94
Return on Equity %	39.51	36.18	35.29	37.81	40.52	34.01	14.96	37.66
EBITDA Margin %	11.41	13.85	15.56	14.24	12.48	11.22	9.21	14.74
Net Margin %	7.89	7.54	8.34	8.45	6.54	5.23	2.49	6.18
Asset Turnover	1.23	1.17	1.15	1.10	1.07	1.08	1.07	1.12
Current Ratio	1.51	1.52	1.48	1.63	1.68	1.51	1.77	1.20
Debt to Equity	0.81	1.01	0.68	0.77	1.08	1.55	1.59	1.15
Price Range	96.33-69.50	93.69-66.14	92.95-76.18	89.19-48.25	49.65-33.76	50.00-35.50	46.37-29.01	52.25-28.44
P/E Ratio	12.27-8.85	14.30-10.10	13.89-11.39	15.96-8.63	13.24-9.00	17.61-12.50	34.86-21.81	15.64-8.51
Average Yield %	1.96	1.82	1.32	1.28	1.37	1.14	1.23	1.28

Address: 701 East Joppa Road, Towson, MD 21286 **Telephone:** 410-716-3900	**Web Site:** www.bdk.com **Officers:** Nolan D. Archibald - Chmn., Pres., C.E.O. Paul A. Gustafson - Exec. V.P.	**Auditors:** ERNST & YOUNG LLP **Investor Contact:** 410-716-3979 **Transfer Agents:** The Bank of New York, New York, NY

BLACK HILLS CORPORATION

Exchange	Symbol	Price	52Wk Range	Yield	P/E	Div Acheiver
NYS	BKH	$35.78 (3/31/2008)	44.90-34.93	3.91	13.55	36 Years

*7 Year Price Score 95.03 ***NYSE Composite Index=100** ***12 Month Price Score 98.58**

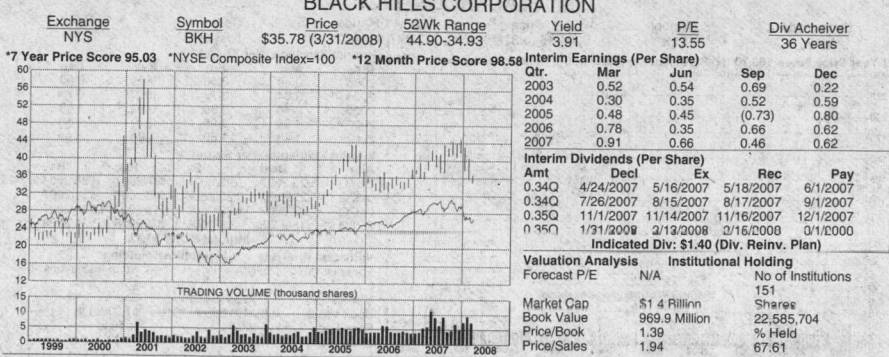

Interim Earnings (Per Share)

Qtr.	Mar	Jun	Sep	Dec
2003	0.52	0.54	0.69	0.22
2004	0.30	0.35	0.52	0.59
2005	0.48	0.45	(0.73)	0.80
2006	0.78	0.35	0.66	0.62
2007	0.91	0.66	0.46	0.62

Interim Dividends (Per Share)

Amt	Decl	Ex	Rec	Pay
0.34Q	4/24/2007	5/16/2007	5/18/2007	6/1/2007
0.34Q	7/26/2007	8/15/2007	8/17/2007	9/1/2007
0.35Q	11/1/2007	11/14/2007	11/16/2007	12/1/2007
0.35Q	1/31/2008	2/13/2008	2/16/2008	0/1/2008

Indicated Div: $1.40 (Div. Reinv. Plan)

Valuation Analysis

Forecast P/E	N/A
Market Cap	$1.4 Billion
Book Value	969.9 Million
Price/Book	1.39
Price/Sales	1.94

Institutional Holding

No of Institutions	151
Shares	22,585,704
% Held	
	67.61

Business Summary: Electricity (MIC: 7.1 SIC: 4911 NAIC: 221121)

Black Hills is an energy company operating in two business groups: utilities, and non-regulated energy. Co.'s utilities group consists of the Electric Utility segment, operating via its Black Hills Power (BHP) subsidiary; and Combination Electric and Gas Utility segment, which operates via its Cheyenne Light (CL) subsidiary. BHP generates, transmits and distributes electricity in South Dakota, Wyoming and Montana, while CL distributes electric and natural gas service in the Cheyenne, WY vicinity. Co. operates its non-regulated energy group via its Black Hills Energy subsidiary, which conducts its business through the oil and gas, power generation, coal mining, and energy marketing segments.

Recent Developments: For the year ended Dec 31 2007, income from continuing operations increased 35.2% to US$100.1 million from US$74.0 million a year earlier. Net income increased 21.9% to US$98.8 million from US$81.0 million in the prior year. Revenues were US$695.9 million, up 5.9% from US$656.9 million the year before. Operating income was US$179.6 million versus US$152.7 million in the prior year, an increase of 17.6%. Direct operating expenses declined 8.0% to US$260.0 million from US$282.4 million in the comparable period the year before. Indirect operating expenses increased 15.6% to US$256.4 million from US$221.8 million in the equivalent prior year period.

Prospects: For 2008, Co. expects earnings of $2.35 to $2.55 per share from continuing operations, excluding pre-close Aquila-related transaction costs of $0.10 to $0.20 per share to be expensed in early 2008. Further, Co. expects lower earnings from its coal mining segment as higher revenues from production and coal price increases should be offset by higher operating expenses. Nevertheless, Co. plans to focus on its producer, end-use origination, and gas storage and transportation services and a regional wholesale marketing strategy. Co. also expects improved earnings from its Oil and Gas segment due to higher oil and gas production as it focuses on its annual production growth target of 2.0% to 4.0%.

Financial Data

(US$ in Thousands)	12/31/2007	12/31/2006	12/31/2005	12/31/2004	12/31/2003	12/31/2002	12/31/2001	12/31/2000
Earnings Per Share	2.64	2.42	1.00	1.76	1.97	2.26	3.42	2.37
Cash Flow Per Share	6.81	7.83	5.34	4.21	5.59	8.16	6.99	3.36
Tang Book Value Per Share	24.32	22.03	20.49	20.37	19.55	15.42	14.67	10.45
Dividends Per Share	1.370	1.320	1.280	1.240	1.200	1.160	1.120	1.080
Dividend Payout %	51.89	54.55	128.00	70.45	60.91	51.33	32.75	45.57
Income Statement								
Total Revenue	695,914	656,882	1,391,644	1,121,701	1,250,052	423,919	1,558,558	1,623,836
EBITDA	279,614	247,386	176,095	222,442	219,209	206,360	234,106	150,610
Income Before Taxes	147,373	106,705	40,011	84,525	86,915	96,017	142,807	94,479
Income Taxes	45,641	33,802	18,299	26,704	29,920	29,662	50,544	30,358
Net Income	98,772	81,019	33,420	57,973	61,222	61,452	88,077	52,848
Average Shares	37,414	33,549	33,288	32,912	31,015	27,167	25,771	22,281
Balance Sheet								
Net PPE	1,823,534	1,646,367	1,435,398	1,445,732	1,442,422	1,476,263	1,238,224	794,281
Total Assets	2,472,866	2,244,676	2,119,960	2,056,163	2,063,225	2,035,169	1,658,767	1,320,320
Long-Term Obligations	564,372	628,340	670,193	733,581	868,459	618,862	415,798	307,092
Total Liabilities	1,503,011	1,454,635	1,381,081	1,320,398	1,353,478	1,500,006	1,143,603	1,037,974
Stockholders' Equity	969,855	790,041	738,879	735,765	709,747	535,163	515,164	282,346
Shares Outstanding	37,796	33,369	33,155	32,477	32,297	27,102	26,890	22,921
Statistical Record								
Return on Assets %	4.19	3.71	1.60	2.81	2.99	3.33	5.91	5.28
Return on Equity %	11.22	10.60	4.53	8.00	9.84	11.70	22.09	21.13
EBITDA Margin %	40.18	37.66	12.65	19.83	17.54	48.68	15.02	9.27
Net Margin %	14.19	12.33	2.40	5.17	4.90	14.50	5.65	3.25
PPE Turnover	0.40	0.43	0.97	0.77	0.86	0.31	1.53	2.57
Asset Turnover	0.30	0.30	0.67	0.54	0.61	0.23	1.05	1.62
Debt to Equity	0.58	0.80	0.91	1.00	1.22	1.16	0.81	1.09
Price Range	44.90-35.76	37.93-32.75	43.54-29.42	32.25-26.72	33.35-22.26	36.84-19.15	58.05-26.35	45.13-20.56
P/E Ratio	17.01-13.55	15.67-13.53	43.54-29.42	18.32-15.18	16.93-11.30	16.30-8.47	16.97-7.70	19.04-8.68
Average Yield %	3.41	3.79	3.51	4.17	4.08	3.99	2.86	4.17

Address: 625 Ninth Street, Rapid City, SD 57701	Web Site: www.blackhillscorp.com	Auditors: Deloitte & Touche LLP
Telephone: 605-721-1700	Officers: David R. Emery - Chmn., Pres., C.E.O.	Investor Contact: 605-721-2326
Fax: 605-721-2597	Thomas M. Ohlmacher - Pres., C.O.O., Wholesale Energy	Transfer Agents: Wells Fargo Shareowner Services

BLACKROCK, INC.

Exchange	Symbol	Price	52Wk Range	Yield	P/E
NYS	BLK	$204.18 (3/31/2008)	226.72-144.70	1.53	27.12

*7 Year Price Score 160.70 *NYSE Composite Index=100 *12 Month Price Score 121.24

Interim Earnings (Per Share)

Qtr.	Mar	Jun	Sep	Dec
2003	0.54	0.58	0.61	0.63
2004	0.84	0.73	(0.15)	0.75
2005	0.70	0.80	0.92	1.09
2006	1.06	0.95	0.28	1.58
2007	1.48	1.69	1.94	5.41

Interim Dividends (Per Share)

Amt	Decl	Ex	Rec	Pay
0.67Q	5/23/2007	6/5/2007	6/7/2007	6/25/2007
0.67Q	7/27/2007	8/29/2007	9/3/2007	9/24/2007
0.67Q	11/7/2007	11/29/2007	12/3/2007	12/24/2007
0.78Q	2/15/2008	3/5/2008	3/7/2008	3/24/2008

Indicated Div: $3.12

Valuation Analysis

Institutional Holding	
Forecast P/E	N/A
	No of Institutions
	157
Market Cap	$23.7 Billion
	Shares
Book Value	11.6 Billion
	57,936,636
Price/Book	2.04
	% Held
Price/Sales	4.89
	49.80

Business Summary: Finance Intermediaries & Services (MIC: 8.7 SIC: 6211 NAIC: 525990)

BlackRock is a publicly traded investment management firm, with $1.14 trillion of assets under management at Dec 31 2007. Co. provides investment management services to institutional clients and individual investors via various investment vehicles. Investment management services mainly consist of the management of fixed income, cash management and equity client accounts, management of open-end and closed-end mutual fund families and other non-U.S. equivalent retail products serving the institutional and retail markets, and management of alternative funds developed to serve various customer needs. Co. also provides risk management strategic advisory and enterprise investment system services.

Recent Developments: For the year ended Dec 31 2007, net income increased 208.5% to US$995.3 million from US$322.6 million in the prior year. Revenues were US$4.84 billion, up 130.9% from US$2.10 billion the year before. Operating income was US$1.29 billion versus US$471.8 million in the prior year, an increase of 174.2%. Indirect operating expenses increased 118.4% to US$3.55 billion from US$1.63 billion in the equivalent prior-year period.

Prospects: Despite the improvement in its results, Co. remains cautious with its near-term outlook due to the continued market volatility. For instance, Co. believes that the build-up of institutional liquidity assets experienced in the fourth quarter of 2007 may be temporary, as these assets are expected to be redeployed to longer-dated strategies as market conditions stabilize. In addition, while it expects demand for its advisory services to remain high through the volatile markets, demand may return to normal levels as market concerns ease. Further, Co. noted that returns on many major equity indices have declined from year-end 2007, which may negatively affect its revenue in future periods.

Financial Data
(US$ in Thousands)

	12/31/2007	12/31/2006	12/31/2005	12/31/2004	12/31/2003	12/31/2002	12/31/2001	12/31/2000
Earnings Per Share	7.53	3.87	3.50	2.17	2.36	2.04	1.65	1.35
Cash Flow Per Share	4.57	8.94	3.97	3.62	2.78	2.66	2.60	1.70
Tang Book Value Per Share	N.M.	N.M.	6.85	9.18	8.13	6.96	4.72	2.75
Dividends Per Share	2.680	1.680	1.200	1.000	0.400	...	...	...
Dividend Payout %	35.59	43.41	34.29	46.08	16.95	...	...	...
Income Statement								
Total Revenue	4,844,655	2,097,976	1,191,386	725,311	598,212	576,977	533,144	476,872
Income Before Taxes	1,822,719	528,233	375,755	200,438	250,902	223,948	180,991	149,917
Income Taxes	463,832	189,463	138,558	52,264	95,247	90,699	73,557	62,556
Net Income	995,272	322,602	233,908	143,141	155,402	133,249	107,434	87,361
Average Shares	132,088	83,358	66,875	65,960	65,860	65,307	64,926	64,590
Balance Sheet								
Total Assets	22,561,515	20,469,492	1,848,000	1,145,235	967,223	864,188	684,478	537,003
Total Liabilities	10,386,350	8,578,520	916,143	359,714	252,676	229,534	198,361	168,762
Stockholders' Equity	11,596,955	10,781,880	922,243	768,352	713,308	634,654	486,117	368,241
Shares Outstanding	116,059	116,408	64,000	63,665	64,096	64,916	64,465	63,997
Statistical Record								
Return on Assets %	4.63	2.89	15.63	13.52	16.97	17.21	17.59	17.70
Return on Equity %	8.89	5.51	27.67	19.27	23.06	23.78	25.15	26.86
Price Range	222.03-144.70	156.31-108.00	113.45-70.00	77.51-53.11	53.53-39.40	47.35-34.30	44.22-31.82	47.50-15.75
P/E Ratio	29.49-19.22	40.39-27.91	32.41-20.00	35.72-24.47	22.68-16.69	23.21-16.81	26.80-19.28	35.19-11.67
Average Yield %	1.59	1.21	1.42	1.52	0.86	...	...	...

Address: 40 East 52nd Street, New York, NY 10022 **Telephone:** 212-810-5300 **Fax:** 212-754-3123	**Web Site:** www.blackrock.com **Officers:** Laurence D. Fink - Chmn., C.E.O. Paul L. Audet - C.F.O., Managing Dir.	**Auditors:** Deloitte & Touche LLP **Transfer Agents:** Mellon Investor Services L.L.C., Ridgefield Park, NJ

BLOCK (H & R), INC.

Exchange	Symbol	Price	52Wk Range	Yield	P/E	Div Acheiver
NYS	HRB	$20.76 (3/31/2008)	23.89-17.00	2.75	N/A	10 Years

*7 Year Price Score 73.88   *NYSE Composite Index=100   *12 Month Price Score 101.31

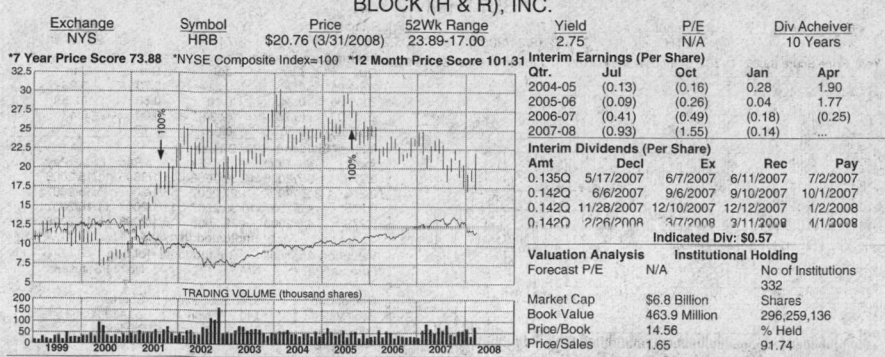

Interim Earnings (Per Share)

Qtr.	Jul	Oct	Jan	Apr
2004-05	(0.13)	(0.16)	0.28	1.90
2005-06	(0.09)	(0.26)	0.04	1.77
2006-07	(0.41)	(0.49)	(0.18)	(0.25)
2007-08	(0.93)	(1.55)	(0.14)	...

Interim Dividends (Per Share)

Amt	Decl	Ex	Rec	Pay
0.135Q	5/17/2007	6/7/2007	6/11/2007	7/2/2007
0.142Q	6/6/2007	9/6/2007	9/10/2007	10/1/2007
0.142Q	11/28/2007	12/10/2007	12/12/2007	1/2/2008
0.142Q	2/26/2008	3/7/2008	3/11/2008	4/1/2008

Indicated Div: $0.57

Valuation Analysis   **Institutional Holding**

Forecast P/E	N/A	No of Institutions
		332
Market Cap	$6.8 Billion	Shares
Book Value	463.9 Million	296,259,136
Price/Book	14.56	% Held
Price/Sales	1.65	91.74

Business Summary: Personal Services (MIC: 5.15 SIC: 7291 NAIC: 541213)

Block (H&R) is a financial services company. Co.'s Tax Services segment provides income tax return preparation as well as other services and products related to tax return preparation in the U.S., Canada and Australia. Co.'s Business Services segment is a national accounting, tax and business consulting firm under the RSM McGladrey name. Co.'s Consumer Financial Services segment provides brokerage services, along with investment planning and related financial advice through H&R Block Financial Advisors and full-service banking through H&R Block Bank. Co.'s mortgage operations provide home mortgage services through Option One Mortgage Corporation and H&R Block Mortgage Corporation.

Recent Developments: For the quarter ended Jan 31 2008, income from continuing operations decreased 57.7% to US$9.3 million from US$21.9 million in the year-earlier quarter. Net loss amounted to US$47.4 million versus a net loss of US$60.3 million in the year-earlier quarter. Revenues were US$972.6 million, up 4.4% from US$931.2 million the year before. Operating income was US$2.1 million versus US$31.0 million in the prior-year quarter, a decrease of 93.1%. Direct operating expenses rose 8.5% to US$701.4 million from US$646.3 million in the comparable period the year before. Indirect operating expenses increased 5.9% to US$269.0 million from US$254.0 million in the equivalent prior-year period.

Prospects: Co. is encouraged by its ongoing efforts to refocus its overall business and to tighten efficiency, as demonstrated by the Jan 2008 implementation of a program to reduce its expenses by approximately $110.0 million per year. This program includes Kansas City corporate support staff reduction reflecting Co.'s downsizing due to the exit from its mortgage business. Specifically, Co. expects reduced compensation expense of approximately $50.0 million per year, and Co. is seeking to eliminate about $60.0 million of non-compensation overhead expenses going forward. Separately, Co. continues to expect its retail client growth to be flat or an increase of 2.0% for the fiscal year ending Apr 2008.

Financial Data

(US$ in Thousands)	9 Mos	6 Mos	3 Mos	04/30/2007	04/30/2006	04/30/2005	04/30/2004	04/30/2003
Earnings Per Share	(2.87)	(2.91)	(1.85)	(1.33)	1.47	1.89	1.93	1.58
Cash Flow Per Share	(3.61)	(1.04)	(1.72)	(1.81)	1.78	1.55	2.61	1.92
Tang Book Value Per Share	N.M.	N.M.	N.M.	0.74	1.69	1.63	1.44	1.42
Dividends Per Share	0.555	0.547	0.540	0.530	0.485	0.430	0.390	0.350
Dividend Payout %	...	...	...	...	32.99	22.81	20.21	22.22
Income Statement								
Total Revenue	1,788,644	816,033	381,209	4,021,274	4,872,801	4,420,019	4,205,570	3,779,767
EBITDA	(293,337)	(330,823)	(145,910)	832,933	1,068,155	1,348,140	1,405,913	1,196,005
Depn & Amortn	107,989	75,246	37,075	...	...	...	...	...
Income Before Taxes	(403,197)	(407,316)	(183,580)	635,798	827,393	1,017,715	1,164,157	987,077
Income Taxes	(166,533)	(161,388)	(73,757)	261,461	336,985	381,858	459,901	407,013
Net Income	(852,209)	(804,851)	(302,580)	(433,653)	490,408	635,857	697,897	580,064
Average Shares	327,202	324,694	323,864	326,154	333,187	337,626	361,604	368,156
Balance Sheet								
Current Assets	8,131,347	3,981,033	2,888,591	3,454,292	2,823,947	3,070,634	2,961,299	2,747,361
Total Assets	11,575,211	7,106,771	6,868,070	7,499,493	5,989,135	5,539,283	5,380,026	4,603,905
Current Liabilities	7,670,603	3,876,151	4,710,363	5,176,352	2,893,436	2,208,920	2,472,043	1,897,196
Long-Term Obligations	2,917,411	2,144,012	519,803	519,807	417,539	923,073	545,811	822,302
Total Liabilities	11,111,279	6,562,491	5,786,708	6,084,994	3,841,336	3,562,912	3,483,017	2,940,196
Stockholders' Equity	463,932	544,280	1,081,362	1,414,499	2,147,799	1,976,371	1,897,009	1,663,709
Shares Outstanding	325,323	324,881	324,546	323,218	328,512	331,240	346,190	359,202
Statistical Record								
Return on Assets %	N.M.	N.M.	N.M.	N.M.	8.51	11.65	13.94	13.13
Return on Equity %	N.M.	N.M.	N.M.	N.M.	23.78	32.83	39.09	38.25
EBITDA Margin %	N.M.	N.M.	N.M.	20.71	21.92	30.50	33.43	31.64
Net Margin %	N.M.	N.M.	N.M.	N.M.	10.06	14.39	16.59	15.35
Asset Turnover	0.39	0.61	0.67	0.60	0.85	0.81	0.84	0.86
Current Ratio	1.06	1.03	0.61	0.67	0.98	1.39	1.20	1.45
Debt to Equity	6.29	3.94	0.48	0.37	0.19	0.47	0.29	0.49
Price Range	24.84-17.00	24.84-18.28	24.84-19.95	24.84-20.05	29.81-20.63	26.65-22.39	30.36-18.50	26.57-15.37
P/E Ratio	...	...	...	...	20.28-14.03	14.10-11.84	15.73-9.59	16.82-9.73
Average Yield %	2.63	2.46	2.40	2.34	1.93	1.77	1.64	1.64

Address: One H&R Block Way, Kansas City, MO 64105	**Web Site:** www.hrblock.com	**Auditors:** Deloitte & Touche LLP
Telephone: 816-854-3000	**Officers:** Mark A. Ernst - Chmn., Pres., C.E.O. Jeffery W. Yabuki - Exec. V.P., C.O.O.	**Investor Contact:** 800-869-9220Ext272
Fax: 816-932-8390		**Transfer Agents:** Mellon Investor Services LLC, Ridgefield Park, NJ

BLYTH, INC.

Exchange	Symbol	Price	52Wk Range	Yield	P/E
NYS	BTH	$19.72 (3/31/2008)	30.22-16.00	2.74	20.12

*7 Year Price Score 69.85   *NYSE Composite Index=100   *12 Month Price Score 98.84

Interim Earnings (Per Share)

Qtr.	Apr	Jul	Oct	Jan
2004-05	0.38	0.21	0.73	0.93
2005-06	0.24	0.10	0.56	(0.30)
2006-07	(0.75)	(2.24)	0.00	0.43
2007-08	0.30	0.08	0.17	...

Interim Dividends (Per Share)

Amt	Decl	Ex	Rec	Pay
0.27S	9/7/2006	10/30/2006	11/1/2006	11/15/2006
0.27S	3/27/2007	4/27/2007	5/1/2007	5/15/2007
0.27S	9/6/2007	10/30/2007	11/1/2007	11/15/2007
0.27S	4/8/2008	4/29/2008	5/1/2008	5/15/2008

Indicated Div: $0.54

Valuation Analysis

		Institutional Holding	
Forecast P/E	N/A	No of Institutions	122
Market Cap	$746.8 Million	Shares	28,479,232
Book Value	340.7 Million	% Held	72.48
Price/Book	2.19		
Price/Sales	0.64		

Business Summary: Consumer Accessories (MIC: 4.6 SIC: 3999 NAIC: 339999)

Blyth is a Home Expressions company engaging primarily in the home fragrance and decorative accessories industry. Co. designs, markets and distributes an array of candles, potpourri, decorative accessories, seasonal decorations and household convenience items, as well as tabletop lighting, accessories and chafing fuel for the Away-From-Home or foodservice trade, through its three primary business segments: the Direct Selling segment; the Wholesale segment; and the Catalog & Internet segment. Additionally, Co.'s sales and operations are conducted primarily in the U.S., Canada and Europe, with additional activity in Mexico, Australia and the Far East.

Recent Developments: For the quarter ended Oct 31 2007, income from continuing operations increased 240.4% to US$6.6 million from US$1.9 million in the year-earlier quarter. Net income amounted to US$6.6 million versus a net loss of US$221,000 in the year-earlier quarter. Revenues were US$285.9 million, down 4.0% from US$297.9 million the year before. Operating income was US$10.4 million versus US$4.7 million in the prior-year quarter, an increase of 122.9%. Direct operating expenses declined 11.7% to US$141.7 million from US$160.6 million in the comparable period the year before. Indirect operating expenses increased 0.8% to US$133.7 million from US$132.7 million in the equivalent prior-year period.

Prospects: On Apr 4 2008, Co. announced that it now expects earnings per share excluding restructuring charges to be in the range of $1.45 to $1.50 for its fiscal year ending Jan 2009. Co. attributes the projected results to lower earnings in PartyLite U.S. due to higher investment spending on promotions to drive sales and Consultant count growth and a higher effective tax rate. Including anticipated restructuring charges of about $0.05 per share related to its North American Wholesale home fragrance business, which is being realigned following the divestiture of the mass channel candle business in fiscal 2008, Co. anticipates reported earnings per share of between $1.40 and $1.45.

Financial Data

(US$ in Thousands)	9 Mos	6 Mos	3 Mos	01/31/2007	01/31/2006	01/31/2005	01/31/2004	01/31/2003
Earnings Per Share	0.98	0.81	(1.51)	(2.58)	0.60	2.22	1.88	1.83
Cash Flow Per Share	2.76	2.54	2.42	2.37	2.61	3.20	3.78	3.70
Tang Book Value Per Share	6.02	6.54	6.38	6.35	6.62	5.77	7.52	8.47
Dividends Per Share	0.540	0.540	0.540	0.500	0.440	0.360	0.280	0.220
Dividend Payout %	55.10	66.67	...	...	73.33	16.22	14.89	12.02
Income Statement								
Total Revenue	791,107	505,238	270,367	1,220,611	1,573,076	1,586,297	1,505,573	1,288,583
EBITDA	56,773	38,912	24,772	51,645	93,471	206,814	190,290	187,433
Depn & Amortn	22,341	14,435	7,568	...	...	...	...	...
Income Before Taxes	29,502	21,181	15,472	5,369	32,027	149,076	136,893	142,557
Income Taxes	7,940	6,223	3,713	2,664	7,775	52,922	50,377	53,032
Net Income	21,481	14,904	11,732	(103,173)	24,857	96,514	86,351	85,010
Average Shares	39,067	39,835	39,672	40,057	41,176	43,556	46,027	46,515
Balance Sheet								
Current Assets	490,190	484,258	492,061	479,918	648,993	514,131	606,739	472,437
Total Assets	770,459	768,644	781,857	774,638	1,116,520	1,075,820	1,127,963	886,658
Current Liabilities	153,109	121,111	140,668	140,100	209,852	201,959	206,199	153,623
Long-Term Obligations	210,374	210,575	210,772	214,792	344,921	271,573	275,743	165,079
Total Liabilities	429,737	397,031	417,153	410,945	622,696	554,471	538,993	347,194
Stockholders' Equity	340,722	371,613	364,704	363,693	493,824	521,349	588,970	539,464
Shares Outstanding	37,868	39,480	39,375	39,301	40,994	40,899	45,630	46,059
Statistical Record								
Return on Assets %	4.87	3.96	N.M.	N.M.	2.27	8.74	8.57	10.11
Return on Equity %	11.30	8.86	N.M.	N.M.	4.90	17.34	15.30	16.87
EBITDA Margin %	7.18	7.70	9.16	4.23	5.94	13.04	12.64	14.55
Net Margin %	2.72	2.95	4.34	N.M.	1.58	6.08	5.74	6.60
Asset Turnover	1.48	1.48	1.33	1.29	1.44	1.44	1.49	1.53
Current Ratio	3.20	4.00	3.50	3.43	3.09	2.55	2.94	3.08
Debt to Equity	0.62	0.57	0.58	0.59	0.70	0.52	0.47	0.31
Price Range	30.22-16.00	30.22-16.44	27.31-16.44	26.12-16.44	33.25-17.98	35.84-27.81	33.50-23.71	32.51-20.90
P/E Ratio	30.84-16.33	37.31-20.30	...	...	55.42-29.97	16.14-12.53	17.82-12.61	17.77-11.42
Average Yield %	2.32	2.32	2.52	2.35	1.69	1.13	1.00	0.80

Address: One East Weaver Street, Greenwich, CT 06831
Telephone: 203-661-1926
Fax: 203-661-1969

Web Site: www.blyth.com
Officers: Robert B. Goergen - Chmn., C.E.O. Robert H. Barghaus - V.P., C.F.O.

Auditors: Deloitte & Touche LLP
Investor Contact: 203-661-1926
Transfer Agents: EquiServe Trust Company, N.A., Providence, RI

BMC SOFTWARE, INC.

Exchange	Symbol	Price	52Wk Range	Yield	P/E
NYS	BMC	$32.52 (3/31/2008)	36.74-26.40	N/A	22.90

*7 Year Price Score 120.99 *NYSE Composite Index=100 *12 Month Price Score 111.64

Interim Earnings (Per Share)

Qtr.	Jun	Sep	Dec	Mar
2004-05	0.05	0.06	0.16	0.07
2005-06	(0.19)	0.19	0.22	0.24
2006-07	0.15	0.28	0.30	0.30
2007-08	0.28	0.39	0.45	...

Interim Dividends (Per Share)

No Dividends Paid

Valuation Analysis   **Institutional Holding**

Forecast P/E	21.35	No of Institutions
	(1/10/2007)	303
Market Cap	$6.3 Billion	Shares
Book Value	1.0 Billion	187,125,712
Price/Book	6.22	% Held
Price/Sales	3.72	91.74

Business Summary: IT & Technology (MIC: 10.2 SIC: 7372 NAIC: 511210)

BMC Software is an independent software vendor. Through its Business Service Management (BSM), Co. provides software applications that enable companies to manage their information technology (IT) infrastructure from a business perspective. Co.'s software applications include enterprise systems, applications, databases and service management. As of Mar 31 2007, Co. had two software business segments: Enterprise Service Management (ESM) and Mainframe Service Management (MSM) segments. ESM segment consists of its non-mainframe application as well as its core BSM products, including its remedy service management products, identity management and transaction management products.

Recent Developments: For the quarter ended Dec 31 2007, net income increased 39.9% to US$89.4 million from US$63.9 million in the year earlier quarter. Revenues were US$459.0 million, up 11.2% from US$412.9 million the year before. Operating income was US$106.5 million versus US$73.9 million in the prior-year quarter, an increase of 44.1%. Direct operating expenses rose 3.2% to US$101.7 million from US$98.5 million in the comparable period the year before. Indirect operating expenses increased 4.3% to US$250.8 million from US$240.5 million in the equivalent prior-year period.

Prospects: Co. is seeing growth in its revenues and upward momentum in profitability, which reflects its operational flexibility and the ability to scale the growth of its business, resulting in greater margin expansion. Meanwhile, Co. continues to strengthen its results by executing its strategy in capturing the growing demand for its Business Service Management applications, stabilize its mainframe segment and manage its operating expenses. Accordingly, for fiscal quarter ending Mar 2008, Co. expects revenue to be in the range of US$450.0 million to US$465.0 million. Additionally, Co. is anticipating its annual growth rate for fiscal 2008 revenue to be in the high single digits.

Financial Data

(US$ in Thousands)	9 Mos	6 Mos	3 Mos	03/31/2007	03/31/2006	03/31/2005	03/31/2004	03/31/2003
Earnings Per Share	1.42	1.27	1.16	1.03	0.47	0.34	(0.12)	0.20
Cash Flow Per Share	3.15	3.32	2.66	2.06	1.95	2.26	2.19	2.56
Tang Book Value Per Share	0.36	0.54	1.15	1.15	1.78	2.03	2.49	2.87
Income Statement								
Total Revenue	1,264,700	805,700	385,000	1,580,400	1,498,400	1,463,000	1,418,700	1,326,700
EBITDA	428,900	266,200	117,700	373,500	296,200	190,400	231,100	317,600
Depn & Amortn	110,300	72,800	35,600	...	...	...	...	...
Income Before Taxes	317,700	192,900	81,800	300,600	203,800	98,200	(29,400)	69,300
Income Taxes	92,900	57,500	24,600	84,700	101,800	22,900	(2,600)	21,300
Net Income	224,800	135,400	57,200	215,900	102,000	75,300	(26,800)	48,000
Average Shares	197,900	202,000	204,800	210,200	218,900	224,000	226,700	237,900
Balance Sheet								
Current Assets	1,706,600	1,718,300	1,789,900	1,789,500	1,506,400	1,440,400	1,424,900	1,098,200
Total Assets	3,148,100	3,147,500	3,242,000	3,260,000	3,210,900	3,298,300	3,044,800	2,845,500
Current Liabilities	1,182,400	1,162,300	1,171,100	1,232,900	1,202,400	1,085,100	986,900	838,800
Total Liabilities	2,139,600	2,118,300	2,154,700	2,210,900	2,112,100	2,036,500	1,829,600	1,462,100
Stockholders' Equity	1,008,500	1,029,200	1,087,300	1,049,100	1,098,800	1,261,800	1,215,200	1,383,400
Shares Outstanding	192,800	196,000	201,100	200,551	209,300	220,700	223,300	231,100
Statistical Record								
Return on Assets %	9.20	8.51	7.67	6.67	3.13	2.37	N.M.	1.74
Return on Equity %	27.57	25.15	22.91	20.10	8.64	6.08	N.M.	3.32
EBITDA Margin %	33.91	33.04	30.57	23.63	19.77	13.01	16.29	23.94
Net Margin %	17.77	16.81	14.86	13.66	6.81	5.15	N.M.	3.62
Asset Turnover	0.54	0.53	0.51	0.49	0.46	0.46	0.48	0.48
Current Ratio	1.44	1.48	1.53	1.45	1.25	1.33	1.44	1.31
Price Range	36.74-26.40	36.22-26.40	36.22-22.39	36.22-20.15	23.07-14.60	20.37-13.79	21.60-13.31	19.75-11.20
P/E Ratio	25.87-18.59	28.52-20.79	31.22-19.30	35.17-19.56	49.09-31.06	59.91-40.56	...	98.75-56.00

Address: 2101 CityWest Boulevard, Houston, TX 77042-2827
Telephone: 713-918-8800
Fax: 713-918-8000

Web Site: www.bmc.com
Officers: B. Garland Cupp - Chmn. Robert E. Beauchamp - Pres., C.E.O.

Auditors: Ernst & Young LLP
Investor Contact: 713-918-4525
Transfer Agents: Computershare Trust Company, N.A., Providence, RI

BOEING CO. (THE)

Exchange	Symbol	Price	52Wk Range	Yield	P/E
NYS	BA	$74.37 (3/31/2008)	107.23-72.45	2.15	14.09

*7 Year Price Score 125.37 *NYSE Composite Index=100 *12 Month Price Score 92.43

Interim Earnings (Per Share)

Qtr.	Mar	Jun	Sep	Dec
2003	(0.60)	(0.24)	0.32	1.41
2004	0.77	0.75	0.56	0.23
2005	0.66	0.70	1.26	0.58
2006	0.88	(0.21)	0.89	1.28
2007	1.13	1.35	1.44	1.36

Interim Dividends (Per Share)

Amt	Decl	Ex	Rec	Pay
0.35Q	4/30/2007	5/9/2007	5/11/2007	6/1/2007
0.35Q	6/25/2007	8/8/2007	8/10/2007	9/7/2007
0.35Q	10/29/2007	11/7/2007	11/9/2007	12/7/2007
0.40Q	12/10/2007	2/6/2008	2/8/2008	3/7/2008

Indicated Div: $1.60

Valuation Analysis

		Institutional Holding	
Forecast P/E	14.82	No of Institutions	
	(1/10/2007)	823	
Market Cap	$57.1 Billion	Shares	532,434,656
Book Value	9.0 Billion	% Held	
Price/Book	6.34	67.46	
Price/Sales	0.86		

Business Summary: Aviation (MIC: 1.1 SIC: 3721 NAIC: 336411)

Boeing is engaged in the design, development, manufacturing, sale and support of commercial jetliners, military aircraft, satellites, missile defense, human space flight and launch systems and services. As of Dec 31 2007, Co.'s business segments included: Commercial Airplanes; Boeing Capital Corporation; and Precision Engagement and Mobility Systems, Network and Space Systems, and Support Systems, which collectively were known as Integrated Defense Systems (IDS). Co.'s Other segment classification principally includes the activities of Connexion by BoeingSM, a broadband communications business; and Engineering, Operations and Technology, a research and development organization.

Recent Developments: For the year ended Dec 31 2007, income from continuing operations increased 84.0% to US$4.06 billion from US$2.21 billion a year earlier. Net income increased 83.9% to US$4.07 billion from US$2.22 billion in the prior year. Revenues were US$66.39 billion, up 7.9% from US$61.53 billion the year before. Operating income was US$5.83 billion versus US$3.01 billion in the prior year, an increase of 93.4%. Direct operating expenses rose 5.9% to US$53.40 billion from US$50.44 billion in the comparable period the year before. Indirect operating expenses decreased 11.4% to US$7.16 billion from US$8.08 billion in the equivalent prior-year period.

Prospects: For full-year 2008, Co. is lowering its revenue guidance to $67.00 billion to $68.00 billion from its prior estimate of $67.50 billion to $68.50 billion due to the rescheduling of initial 787 deliveries into 2009. However, Co. is raising its 2008 earnings per share guidance to $5.70 to $5.85 per share, from $5.55 to $5.75 per share, and is increasing its operating margin to 11.5% from 11.0%. Notably, these expectations are based on several factors which include the anticipated strong business performance at its Integrated Defense Systems and Boeing Commercial Airplanes segments, along with increasing commercial airplanes deliveries, and continued investment in new airplane development.

Financial Data

(US$ in Thousands)	12/31/2007	12/31/2006	12/31/2005	12/31/2004	12/31/2003	12/31/2002	12/31/2001	12/31/2000
Earnings Per Share	5.28	2.85	3.20	2.30	0.89	0.61	3.41	2.44
Cash Flow Per Share	12.62	9.73	8.88	4.27	4.82	5.44	4.67	6.89
Tang Book Value Per Share	4.99	N.M.	10.32	10.07	6.17	4.53	5.23	6.63
Dividends Per Share	1.400	1.200	1.000	0.770	0.680	0.680	0.680	0.560
Dividend Payout %	26.52	42.11	31.25	33.48	76.40	111.48	19.94	22.95
Income Statement								
Total Revenue	66,387,000	61,530,000	54,845,000	52,457,000	50,485,000	54,069,000	58,198,000	51,321,000
EBITDA	7,444,000	4,592,000	4,205,000	3,420,000	2,007,000	5,092,000	5,656,000	4,765,000
Income Before Taxes	6,118,000	3,194,000	2,819,000	1,960,000	550,000	3,180,000	3,564,000	2,999,000
Income Taxes	2,060,000	988,000	257,000	140,000	(168,000)	861,000	738,000	871,000
Net Income	4,074,000	2,215,000	2,572,000	1,872,000	718,000	492,000	2,827,000	2,128,000
Average Shares	772,500	787,600	802,900	813,000	808,900	808,400	829,300	871,300
Balance Sheet								
Current Assets	27,280,000	22,983,000	21,968,000	15,100,000	17,258,000	16,855,000	16,206,000	15,864,000
Total Assets	58,986,000	51,794,000	60,058,000	53,963,000	53,035,000	52,342,000	48,343,000	42,028,000
Current Liabilities	31,538,000	29,701,000	28,188,000	20,835,000	18,448,000	19,810,000	20,486,000	18,289,000
Long-Term Obligations	7,455,000	8,157,000	9,538,000	10,879,000	13,299,000	12,589,000	10,866,000	7,567,000
Total Liabilities	49,982,000	47,055,000	48,999,000	42,677,000	44,896,000	44,646,000	37,518,000	31,008,000
Stockholders' Equity	9,004,000	4,739,000	11,059,000	11,286,000	8,139,000	7,696,000	10,825,000	11,020,000
Shares Outstanding	768,043	788,738	800,170	832,183	841,482	840,035	837,580	875,484
Statistical Record								
Return on Assets %	7.36	3.96	4.51	3.49	1.36	0.98	6.26	5.43
Return on Equity %	59.29	28.04	23.02	19.22	9.07	5.31	25.88	18.88
EBITDA Margin %	11.21	7.46	7.67	6.52	3.98	9.42	9.72	9.28
Net Margin %	6.14	3.60	4.69	3.57	1.42	0.91	4.86	4.15
Asset Turnover	1.20	1.10	0.96	0.98	0.96	1.07	1.29	1.31
Current Ratio	0.86	0.77	0.78	0.72	0.94	0.85	0.79	0.87
Debt to Equity	0.83	1.72	0.86	0.96	1.63	1.64	1.00	0.69
Price Range	107.23-85.43	91.10-66.50	71.49-49.64	55.26-38.68	42.28-25.06	50.88-28.98	68.79-29.76	69.94-32.38
P/E Ratio	20.31-16.18	31.96-23.33	22.34-15.51	24.03-16.82	47.51-28.16	83.41-47.51	20.17-8.73	28.66-13.27
Average Yield %	1.48	1.50	1.61	1.62	2.04	1.71	1.31	1.14

Address: 100 North Riverside, Chicago, IL 60606-1596	Web Site: www.boeing.com	Auditors: Deloitte & Touche LLP
Telephone: 312-544-2000	**Officers:** W. James McNerney Jr. - Chmn., Pres., C.E.O. Laurette T. Koellner - Exec. V.P.	**Investor Contact:** 312-544-2660
Fax: 206-655-3987		**Transfer Agents:** EquiServe, Providence, RI

BORDERS GROUP, INC.

Exchange	Symbol	Price	52Wk Range	Yield	P/E
NYS	BGP	$5.87 (3/31/2008)	23.41-5.07	N/A	N/A

*7 Year Price Score 58.67   *NYSE Composite Index=100   *12 Month Price Score 62.94

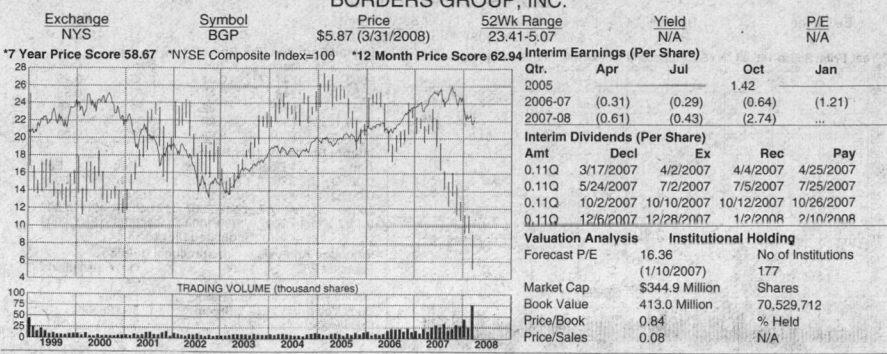

Interim Earnings (Per Share)

Qtr.	Apr	Jul	Oct	Jan
2005			1.42	
2006-07	(0.31)	(0.29)	(0.64)	(1.21)
2007-08	(0.61)	(0.43)	(2.74)	...

Interim Dividends (Per Share)

Amt	Decl	Ex	Rec	Pay
0.11Q	3/17/2007	4/2/2007	4/4/2007	4/25/2007
0.11Q	5/24/2007	7/2/2007	7/5/2007	7/25/2007
0.11Q	10/2/2007	10/10/2007	10/12/2007	10/26/2007
0.11Q	12/6/2007	12/28/2007	1/2/2008	2/10/2008

Valuation Analysis **Institutional Holding**

Forecast P/E	16.36	No of Institutions	
	(1/10/2007)	177	
Market Cap	$344.9 Million	Shares	
Book Value	413.0 Million		70,529,712
Price/Book	0.84	% Held	
Price/Sales	0.08	N/A	

Business Summary: Retail - Miscellaneous (MIC: 5.11 SIC: 5942 NAIC: 451211)

Borders Group operates book, music and movie superstores, and mall-based bookstores. As of Feb 3 2007, Co. operated 567 superstores under the Borders name, including 499 in the U.S., 41 in the U.K., 20 in Australia, three in Puerto Rico, two in New Zealand and one each in Singapore and Ireland. Co. also operated 564 mall-based and other bookstores under the Waldenbooks name in the U.S., and 30 bookstores under the Books etc. name in the U.K. Co. owned and operated Paperchase Products Ltd., a designer and retailer of stationery, cards and gifts. As of Feb 3 2007, Co. operated 99 Paperchase stores, mainly in the U.K. and added Paperchase shops to nearly 250 domestic Borders superstores.

Recent Developments: For the quarter ended Nov 3 2007, loss from continuing operations was US$41.7 million compared with a loss of US$34.4 million in the year-earlier quarter. Net loss amounted to US$161.1 million versus a net loss of US$39.1 million in the year-earlier quarter. Revenues were US$813.6 million, up 5.5% from US$771.0 million the year before. Operating loss was US$56.2 million versus a loss of US$48.0 million in the prior-year quarter. Direct operating expenses rose 6.6% to US$637.4 million from US$597.7 million in the comparable period the year before. Indirect operating expenses increased 5.0% to US$232.4 million from US$221.3 million in the equivalent prior-year period.

Prospects: Co.'s outlook seems constructive. For example, with the Sep 2007 sale of its U.K. and Ireland subsidiaries to a London-based private equity investor, Risk Capital Partners, Co. is able to focus investment and resources on its core U.S. superstore segment business going forward. Overall, Co. is encouraged by its progress with its strategic plan to drive a turnaround in the business, and thus, expects to deliver improved same-store sales results and profitability in the fiscal quarter ending Feb 2008 versus prior year's. Meanwhile, Co. plans to open eight additional domestic Borders superstores and two additional international Borders superstores for the rest of fiscal year ending Feb 2008.

Financial Data

(US$ in Thousands)	9 Mos	6 Mos	3 Mos	02/03/2007	01/28/2006	01/23/2005	01/25/2004	01/26/2003
Earnings Per Share	(4.92)	(2.85)	(2.73)	(2.44)	1.42	1.69	1.54	1.36
Cash Flow Per Share	1.13	2.02	1.64	0.76	2.40	2.94	2.89	2.36
Tang Book Value Per Share	6.34	9.08	9.55	10.29	12.52	13.00	13.40	11.86
Dividends Per Share	0.440	0.430	0.420	0.410	0.370	0.330	0.080	...
Dividend Payout %	...	...	...	...	26.06	19.53	5.19	...
Income Statement								
Total Revenue	2,473,800	1,842,500	885,800	4,113,500	4,079,200	3,903,000	3,731,000	3,513,000
EBITDA	(39,900)	(22,700)	(20,900)	(6,800)	294,900	329,600	309,700	291,000
Depn & Amortn	78,600	56,500	28,000	...	...	...	...	...
Income Before Taxes	(151,000)	(100,600)	(58,800)	(169,200)	159,100	207,600	196,900	181,300
Income Taxes	(60,800)	(39,600)	(22,900)	(17,900)	58,100	75,700	74,800	69,600
Net Income	(222,100)	(61,000)	(35,900)	(151,300)	101,000	131,900	120,000	111,700
Average Shares	58,800	58,800	58,600	61,900	71,088	77,900	77,900	82,033
Balance Sheet								
Current Assets	1,839,200	1,661,000	1,756,100	1,723,600	1,637,800	1,765,400	1,712,700	1,541,300
Total Assets	2,662,600	2,581,900	2,656,600	2,613,400	2,572,200	2,628,800	2,466,200	2,268,200
Current Liabilities	1,901,800	1,611,500	1,671,500	1,595,900	1,311,100	1,196,000	1,164,100	1,087,600
Long-Term Obligations	5,300	5,100	5,200	5,200	5,400	55,800	57,200	69,000
Total Liabilities	2,247,400	2,005,500	2,053,300	1,969,400	1,643,100	1,538,500	1,311,500	1,237,600
Stockholders' Equity	413,000	574,300	601,400	642,000	927,800	1,088,900	1,153,000	1,030,600
Shares Outstanding	58,751	58,827	58,740	58,476	64,149	73,875	78,273	78,731
Statistical Record								
Return on Assets %	N.M.	N.M.	N.M.	N.M.	3.83	5.19	5.08	5.04
Return on Equity %	N.M.	N.M.	N.M.	N.M.	9.88	11.80	11.02	11.31
EBITDA Margin %	N.M.	N.M.	N.M.	N.M.	7.23	8.44	8.30	8.28
Net Margin %	N.M.	N.M.	N.M.	N.M.	2.48	3.38	3.22	3.18
Asset Turnover	1.46	1.60	1.54	1.56	1.55	1.54	1.58	1.58
Current Ratio	0.97	1.03	1.05	1.08	1.25	1.48	1.47	1.42
Debt to Equity	0.01	0.01	0.01	0.01	0.01	0.05	0.05	0.07
Price Range	24.14-12.28	24.14-15.02	24.14-17.31	25.14-17.31	27.47-18.71	26.30-21.27	22.98-13.60	24.40-14.90
P/E Ratio	...	...	...	...	19.35-13.18	15.56-12.59	14.92-8.83	17.94-10.96
Average Yield %	2.25	2.07	2.02	1.89	1.56	1.41	0.44	...

Address: 100 Phoenix Drive, Ann Arbor, MI 48108-2202
Telephone: 734-477-1100
Fax: 734-477-4538

Web Site: www.bordersgroupinc.com
Officers: Gregory P. Josefowicz - Chmn., Pres., C.E.O. Michael G. Spinozzi - Exec. V.P., Chief Product Off.

Auditors: ERNST & YOUNG LLP
Transfer Agents: Computershare Trust Company, N.A., Providence, RI

BORG WARNER INC

Exchange	Symbol	Price	52Wk Range	Yield	P/E
NYS	BWA	$43.03 (3/31/2008)	52.85-37.03	1.02	17.56

*7 Year Price Score 146.03 ***NYSE Composite Index=100** ***12 Month Price Score 107.37**

Interim Earnings (Per Share)

Qtr.	Mar	Jun	Sep	Dec
2003	0.41	0.41	0.33	0.45
2004	0.46	0.48	0.40	0.59
2005	0.68	0.32	0.54	0.56
2006	0.53	0.60	0.34	0.35
2007	0.50	0.65	0.70	0.60

Interim Dividends (Per Share)

Amt	Decl	Ex	Rec	Pay
0.085Q	7/20/2007	7/30/2007	8/1/2007	8/15/2007
0.085Q	10/19/2007	10/30/2007	11/1/2007	11/15/2007
100%	11/14/2007	12/18/2007	12/6/2007	12/17/2007
0.11Q	11/14/2007	1/30/2008	2/1/2008	2/15/2008

Indicated Div: $0.44

Valuation Analysis · **Institutional Holding**

Forecast P/E	11.08 (1/10/2007)	No of Institutions 217
Market Cap	$5.0 Billion	Shares
Book Value	2.3 Billion	56,126,640
Price/Book	2.15	% Held
Price/Sales	0.94	96.82

Business Summary: Automotive (MIC: 15.1 SIC: 3714 NAIC: 336312)

Borg Warner is a global supplier of engineered systems and components, primarily for powertrain applications. As of Dec 31 2007, Co.'s products were designed to help improve vehicle performance, fuel efficiency, air quality and vehicle stability. These products are manufactured and sold worldwide, primarily to original equipment manufacturers (OEMs) of light-vehicles (passenger cars, sport-utility vehicles, vans and light-trucks). Co.'s products are also sold to OEMs of commercial trucks, buses and agricultural and off-highway vehicles. As of the date stated above, Co. operated manufacturing facilities serving customers in the Americas, Europe and Asia.

Recent Developments: For the year ended Dec 31 2007, net income increased 36.3% to US$288.5 million from US$211.6 million in the prior year. Revenues were US$5.33 billion, up 16.2% from US$4.59 billion the year before. Operating income was US$424.8 million versus US$274.6 million in the prior year, an increase of 54.7%. Direct operating expenses rose 17.2% to US$4.38 billion from US$3.74 billion in the comparable period the year before. Indirect operating expenses decreased 8.7% to US$525.1 million from US$575.3 million in the equivalent prior-year period.

Prospects: For 2008, Co. expects strong growth across its Europe and Asia operations, while anticipating its North American operations to remain focused on costs management in a weak vehicle production environment. Meanwhile, despite the moderate global vehicle production growth and the estimated lower sales in the U.S. market, Co. expects to achieve full-year 2008 sales growth in the range of 8.0% to 10.0%. Concurrently, Co. is projecting earnings of between $2.85 and $3.00 per share, which is an increase of 20.0% to 25.0% from 2007. Also, Co. expects 2008 operating margins to increase by 8.5% to 9.0% as a result of projected incremental income from net new business and its cost reductions plan.

Financial Data

(US$ in Thousands)	12/31/2007	12/31/2006	12/31/2005	12/31/2003	12/31/2003	12/31/2002	12/31/2001	12/31/2000
Earnings Per Share	2.45	1.83	2.09	1.93	1.60	(1.11)	0.63	0.89
Cash Flow Per Share	5.20	3.85	3.50	3.81	2.84	2.45	1.86	2.86
Tang Book Value Per Share	8.73	5.79	4.50	5.97	3.70	1.45	N.M.	N.M.
Dividends Per Share	0.340	0.320	0.280	0.250	0.180	0.150	0.150	0.150
Dividend Payout %	13.88	17.53	13.43	12.95	11.25	...	23.90	16.95
Income Statement								
Total Revenue	5,328,600	4,585,400	4,293,800	3,525,300	3,069,200	2,731,100	2,351,600	2,645,900
EBITDA	729,700	567,100	606,800	515,300	451,300	408,900	300,100	356,900
Income Before Taxes	430,400	270,300	314,200	308,600	256,700	233,800	106,100	148,800
Income Taxes	113,900	32,400	55,100	81,200	73,200	77,200	39,700	54,800
Net Income	288,500	211,600	239,600	218,300	174,900	(119,100)	66,400	94,000
Average Shares	117,840	115,942	114,796	113,074	109,208	107,416	105,852	105,948
Balance Sheet								
Current Assets	1,580,300	1,437,500	1,168,700	1,074,300	824,600	566,500	441,300	410,600
Total Assets	4,958,500	4,584,000	4,089,400	3,529,100	3,038,900	2,682,900	2,770,900	2,765,900
Current Liabilities	1,083,900	1,034,800	1,122,100	663,800	470,300	451,200	455,000	529,900
Long-Term Obligations	572,600	569,400	440,600	568,000	634,000	632,300	701,400	740,400
Total Liabilities	2,519,500	2,546,500	2,309,100	1,972,700	1,761,300	1,687,000	1,655,300	1,668,500
Stockholders' Equity	2,321,100	1,875,400	1,644,200	1,534,200	1,260,400	981,400	1,104,200	1,087,100
Shares Outstanding	116,128	115,386	114,268	112,714	110,314	106,320	105,460	104,900
Statistical Record								
Return on Assets %	6.05	4.88	6.29	6.63	6.11	N.M.	2.40	3.27
Return on Equity %	13.75	12.02	15.08	15.58	15.60	N.M.	6.06	8.74
EBITDA Margin %	13.69	12.37	14.13	14.62	14.70	14.97	12.76	13.49
Net Margin %	5.41	4.61	5.58	6.19	5.70	N.M.	2.82	3.55
Asset Turnover	1.12	1.06	1.13	1.07	1.07	1.00	0.85	0.92
Current Ratio	1.46	1.39	1.04	1.62	1.75	1.26	0.97	0.77
Debt to Equity	0.25	0.30	0.27	0.37	0.50	0.64	0.64	0.68
Price Range	52.85-29.30	33.65-26.75	30.81-22.63	27.09-19.23	21.33-11.02	17.13-9.86	13.63-9.12	11.03-7.52
P/E Ratio	21.57-11.96	18.39-14.61	14.74-10.83	14.03-9.96	13.33-6.89	...	21.63-14.48	12.39-8.44
Average Yield %	0.81	1.08	1.02	1.02	1.11	1.12	1.08	1.32	1.65

Address: 3850 Hamlin Road, Auburn Hills, MI 48326
Telephone: 248-754-9200

Web Site: www.borgwarner.com
Officers: Timothy M. Manganello - Chmn., C.E.O. Robin J. Adams - Exec. V.P., C.F.O., Chief Admin. Officer

Auditors: Deloitte & Touche LLP
Investor Contact: 248-754-0881
Transfer Agents: Mellon Investor Services L.L.C., Ridgefield Park, NJ

BOSTON PROPERTIES, INC.

Exchange	Symbol	Price	52Wk Range	Yield	P/E
NYS	BXP	$92.07 (3/31/2008)	119.47-82.10	2.95	8.42

*7 Year Price Score 124.19 *NYSE Composite Index=100   *12 Month Price Score 97.34

Interim Earnings (Per Share)

Qtr.	Mar	Jun	Sep	Dec
2003	1.91	0.64	0.57	0.60
2004	0.64	0.79	0.62	0.56
2005	0.55	1.43	0.50	1.35
2006	0.59	5.23	0.91	0.72
2007	6.99	0.84	1.99	1.10

Interim Dividends (Per Share)

Amt	Decl	Ex	Rec	Pay
0.68Q	9/17/2007	9/26/2007	9/28/2007	10/31/2007
0.68Q	12/18/2007	12/27/2007	12/31/2007	1/30/2008
5.98Q	12/18/2007	12/27/2007	12/31/2007	1/30/2008
0.00Q	0/17/2008	3/27/2008	3/31/2008	4/30/2008

Indicated Div: $2.72

Valuation Analysis

		Institutional Holding	
Forecast P/E	47.16	No of Institutions	371
	(1/10/2007)		
Market Cap	$11.0 Billion	Shares	122,251,728
Book Value	3.7 Billion	% Held	N/A
Price/Book	3.00		
Price/Sales	7.42		

Business Summary: Property, Real Estate & Development (MIC: 8.3 SIC: 6798 NAIC: 525930)

Boston Properties is a fully integrated self-administered and self-managed real estate investment trust engaged in the ownership and development of office properties in the U.S. Co.'s properties are concentrated in five markets: Boston, Washington D.C., midtown Manhattan, San Francisco and Princeton, NJ. At Dec 31 2007, Co. owned or had interests in 139 properties, totaling approximately 33.9 million net rentable square feet and structured parking for vehicles containing approximately 9.9 million square feet; with properties consisted of 135 office properties comprised of 115 Class A office properties and 20 Office/Technical properties, one hotel, and three retail properties.

Recent Developments: For the year ended Dec 31 2007, income from continuing operations increased 28.1% to US$1.10 billion from US$857.5 million a year earlier. Net income increased 51.6% to US$1.32 billion from US$873.6 million in the prior year. Revenues were US$1.48 billion, up 4.6% from US$1.42 billion the year before. Revenues from property income was unchanged at US$1.33 billion compared the corresponding earlier year.

Prospects: Looking ahead, Co. believes that it will benefit significantly from its development pipeline, of which it has entered 2008 with an active development program of approximately $2.10 billion. Further, Co. believes that its focus on new development should enhance its long-term return on equity and earnings growth as these developments are placed in-service in 2009, 2010 and 2011. Meanwhile, for full year 2008, Co. anticipates earnings in the range of $2.43 to $2.53 per diluted share and funds from operations of about $4.55 to $4.65 per diluted share, excluding future gains or losses or the effect on operating results from other possible future property acquisitions, dispositions or financings.

Financial Data
(US$ in Thousands)

	12/31/2007	12/31/2006	12/31/2005	12/31/2004	12/31/2003	12/31/2002	12/31/2001	12/31/2000
Earnings Per Share	10.94	7.46	3.86	2.61	3.71	4.66	2.19	2.01
Cash Flow Per Share	5.30	4.60	4.24	4.02	5.04	4.70	4.66	4.74
Tang Book Value Per Share	30.70	27.43	25.92	26.61	24.43	22.65	19.32	19.02
Dividends Per Share	8.700	8.120	5.190	2.580	2.500	2.410	2.270	2.040
Dividend Payout %	79.52	108.85	134.46	98.85	67.39	51.72	*103.65	101.49
Income Statement								
Property Income	1,334,219	1,344,034	1,339,033	1,293,292	1,219,165	1,173,785	1,007,610	858,942
Non-Property Income	148,070	133,552	98,602	107,173	90,463	61,038	25,368	20,411
Total Revenue	1,482,289	1,477,586	1,437,635	1,400,465	1,309,628	1,234,823	1,032,978	879,353
Interest Expense	205,007	298,260	308,091	306,170	299,436	271,685	223,389	...
Net Income	1,324,690	873,635	438,292	284,017	365,322	444,383	208,032	152,998
Average Shares	120,780	117,077	113,559	108,762	98,486	94,612	92,200	72,741
Balance Sheet								
Total Assets	11,192,637	9,695,022	8,902,368	9,063,228	8,551,100	8,427,203	7,253,510	6,226,470
Long-Term Obligations	5,492,166	4,600,937	4,826,254	5,011,814	5,004,720	5,147,220	4,314,942	3,414,891
Total Liabilities	6,869,920	5,848,288	5,245,754	5,340,827	5,320,804	5,423,032	4,554,697	3,601,028
Stockholders' Equity	3,668,825	3,223,226	2,917,346	2,936,073	2,400,163	2,159,590	1,754,073	1,647,727
Shares Outstanding	119,502	117,503	112,542	110,320	98,230	95,362	90,780	86,630
Statistical Record								
Return on Assets %	12.68	9.40	4.88	3.22	4.30	5.67	3.09	2.62
Return on Equity %	38.44	28.45	14.98	10.62	16.02	22.71	12.23	11.28
Net Margin %	89.37	59.13	30.49	20.28	27.90	35.99	20.14	17.40
Price Range	130.75-88.71	118.00-75.36	76.25-56.93	64.85-44.00	48.34-34.99	41.55-33.93	43.31-34.33	44.75-29.81
P/E Ratio	11.95-8.11	15.82-10.10	19.75-14.75	24.85-16.86	13.03-9.43	8.92-7.28	19.78-15.68	22.26-14.83
Average Yield %	8.03	8.58	7.69	4.84	5.97	6.33	5.82	5.48

Address: 111 Huntington Avenue, Boston, MA 02199 **Telephone:** 617-236-3300 **Fax:** 617-536-3128	**Web Site:** www.bostonproperties.com **Officers:** Mortimer B. Zuckerman - Chmn. Edward H. Linde - Pres., C.E.O.	**Auditors:** PricewaterhouseCoopers LLP **Investor Contact:** 617-236-3322 **Transfer Agents:** EquiServe Trust Comany, NA

BOSTON SCIENTIFIC CORP.

Exchange	Symbol	Price	52Wk Range	Yield	P/E
NYS	BSX	$12.87 (3/31/2008)	16.67-10.98	N/A	N/A

*7 Year Price Score 49.82   *NYSE Composite Index=100   *12 Month Price Score 99.28

TRADING VOLUME (thousand shares)

Interim Earnings (Per Share)

Qtr.	Mar	Jun	Sep	Dec
2003	0.12	0.13	0.15	0.16
2004	0.23	0.36	0.30	0.35
2005	0.42	0.24	(0.33)	0.40
2006	0.40	(3.21)	0.05	0.38
2007	0.08	0.08	(0.18)	(0.31)

Interim Dividends (Per Share)

No Dividends Paid

Valuation Analysis   **Institutional Holding**

Forecast P/E	17.81	No of Institutions
	(1/10/2007)	519
Market Cap	$19.2 Billion	Shares
Book Value	15.1 Billion	968,306,816
Price/Book	1.27	% Held
Price/Sales	2.30	65.33

Business Summary: Medical Instruments & Equipment (MIC: 9.6 SIC: 3841 NAIC: 339112)

Boston Scientific is a developer, manufacturer and marketer of medical devices that are used in a variety of interventional medical specialties including interventional cardiology, cardiac rhythm management, peripheral interventions, electrophysiology, neurovascular intervention, oncology, endoscopy, urology, gynecology and neuromodulation. Co.'s products are offered for sale mainly by three business groups: Cardiovascular, which includes its interventional cardiology, cardiac rhythm management and cardiovascular divisions; Endosurgery, which includes its oncology, endoscopy and urology/gynecology divisions; and Neuromodulation, which includes its auditory and pain management divisions.

Recent Developments: For the year ended Dec 31 2007, net loss amounted to US$495.0 million versus a net loss of US$3.58 billion in the prior year. Revenues were US$8.36 billion, up 6.9% from US$7.82 billion the year before. Operating loss was US$14.0 million versus a loss of US$2.95 billion in the prior year. Direct operating expenses rose 6.1% to US$2.34 billion from US$2.21 billion in the comparable period the year before. Indirect operating expenses decreased 29.6% to US$6.03 billion from US$8.56 billion in the equivalent prior-year period.

Prospects: On Feb 14 2008, Co. announced the divestiture of its Fluid Management and Venous Access businesses to Avista Capital Partners for $425.0 million. Separately, on Jan 7 2008, Co. announced the divestiture of its Cardiac Surgery and Vascular Surgery businesses to the Getinge Group of Sweden for $750.0 million. Collectively, in the first quarter of 2008, Co. expects to record after-tax charges of approximately $120.0 million and $240.0 million, respectively. These transactions reflect Co.'s initiative of divesting its five non-strategic businesses. Meanwhile, for the first quarter of 2008, Co. is projecting net sales of $1.96 billion to $2.08 billion and net income of $0.13 to $0.18 per share.

Financial Data
(US$ in Thousands)

	12/31/2007	12/31/2006	12/31/2005	12/31/2004	12/31/2003	12/31/2002	12/31/2001	12/31/2000
Earnings Per Share	(0.33)	(2.81)	0.75	1.24	0.56	0.45	(0.07)	0.46
Cash Flow Per Share	0.63	1.45	1.09	2.15	0.96	0.90	0.61	0.91
Tang Book Value Per Share	N.M.	N.M.	0.67	0.82	0.49	0.12	N.M.	0.33
Income Statement								
Total Revenue	8,357,000	7,821,000	6,283,000	5,624,000	3,476,000	2,919,000	2,673,000	2,664,000
EBITDA	940,000	(2,319,000)	1,295,000	1,833,000	885,000	825,000	471,000	869,000
Income Before Taxes	(569,000)	(3,535,000)	891,000	1,494,000	643,000	549,000	44,000	527,000
Income Taxes	(74,000)	42,000	263,000	432,000	171,000	176,000	98,000	154,000
Net Income	(495,000)	(3,577,000)	628,000	1,062,000	472,000	373,000	(54,000)	373,000
Average Shares	1,486,900	1,273,700	837,600	857,700	845,400	829,980	802,778	816,644
Balance Sheet								
Current Assets	5,921,000	4,901,000	2,631,000	3,289,000	1,880,000	1,208,000	1,106,000	992,000
Total Assets	31,197,000	31,096,000	8,196,000	8,170,000	5,699,000	4,450,000	3,974,000	3,427,000
Current Liabilities	3,250,000	2,630,000	1,479,000	2,605,000	1,393,000	923,000	831,000	819,000
Long-Term Obligations	7,933,000	8,895,000	1,864,000	1,139,000	1,172,000	847,000	973,000	574,000
Total Liabilities	16,100,000	15,798,000	3,914,000	4,145,000	2,837,000	1,983,000	1,959,000	1,492,000
Stockholders' Equity	15,097,000	15,298,000	4,282,000	4,025,000	2,862,000	2,467,000	2,015,000	1,935,000
Shares Outstanding	1,491,234	1,474,674	820,349	835,343	826,261	822,783	810,507	799,695
Statistical Record								
Return on Assets %	N.M.	N.M.	7.67	15.27	9.30	8.86	N.M.	10.63
Return on Equity %	N.M.	N.M.	15.12	30.76	17.71	16.64	N.M.	20.33
EBITDA Margin %	11.25	N.M.	20.61	32.59	25.46	28.26	17.62	32.62
Net Margin %	N.M.	N.M.	10.00	18.88	13.58	12.78	N.M.	14.00
Asset Turnover	0.27	0.40	0.77	0.81	0.68	0.69	0.72	0.76
Current Ratio	1.82	1.86	1.78	1.26	1.35	1.31	1.33	1.21
Debt to Equity	0.53	0.58	0.44	0.28	0.41	0.34	0.48	0.30
Price Range	18.59-11.47	26.48-14.65	35.55-22.95	45.81-32.12	36.76-19.84	22.11-10.56	13.84-6.75	14.16-6.13
P/E Ratio	...	...	47.40-30.60	36.94-25.90	65.64-35.42	49.12-23.46	...	30.77-13.32

Address: One Boston Scientific Place, Natick, MA 01760-1537	Web Site: www.bsci.com	Auditors: Ernst & Young LLP
Telephone: 508-650-8000	Officers: Peter M. Nicholas - Chmn. James R. Tobin - Pres., C.E.O., Dir.	Investor Contact: 508-650-8555
Fax: 508-647-2200		Transfer Agents: Mellon Investor Services LLC

BOYD GAMING CORP.

Exchange	Symbol	Price	52Wk Range	Yield	P/E
NYS	BYD	$20.00 (3/31/2008)	53.15-18.55	3.00	5.85

*7 Year Price Score 109.26 *NYSE Composite Index=100   *12 Month Price Score 61.14

TRADING VOLUME (thousand shares)

Interim Earnings (Per Share)

Qtr.	Mar	Jun	Sep	Dec
2003	0.25	0.07	0.12	0.19
2004	0.20	0.23	0.40	0.55
2005	0.45	0.54	0.36	0.25
2006	0.70	0.11	(0.15)	0.63
2007	2.46	0.25	0.36	0.35

Interim Dividends (Per Share)

Amt	Decl	Ex	Rec	Pay
0.15Q	4/26/2007	5/9/2007	5/11/2007	6/1/2007
0.15Q	8/1/2007	8/15/2007	8/17/2007	9/4/2007
0.15Q	10/31/2007	11/14/2007	11/16/2007	12/3/2007
0.15Q	2/7/2008	2/13/2008	2/18/2008	0/0/2000

Indicated Div: $0.60

Valuation Analysis / Institutional Holding

Forecast P/E	18.69 (1/10/2007)	No of Institutions 213
Market Cap	$1.8 Billion	Shares
Book Value	1.4 Billion	52,585,912
Price/Book	1.27	% Held
Price/Sales	0.88	60.31

Business Summary: Sporting & Recreational (MIC: 13.5 SIC: 7999 NAIC: 713210)

Boyd Gaming is a multi-jurisdictional gaming company. As of Dec 31 2007, Co. owned and operated 15 casino entertainment facilities located in eight distinct gaming markets in five states, with an aggregate of approximately 817,000 square feet of casino space, containing approximately 23,000 slot machines, 500 table games and 7,300 hotel rooms. Co. has gaming operations in Nevada, Illinois, Louisiana, Mississippi, Indiana and New Jersey. Co. operates through five segments: Las Vegas Locals, Downtown Las Vegas, Midwest and South, Stardust (which closed Nov 1 2006) and its 50.0% joint venture that owns a limited liability company that operates Borgata Hotel Casino & Spa in Atlantic City, NJ.

Recent Developments: For the year ended Dec 31 2007, net income increased 159.5% to US$303.0 million from US$116.8 million in the prior year. Revenues were US$2.00 billion, down 8.9% from US$2.19 billion the year before. Operating income was US$354.2 million versus US$404.7 million in the prior year, a decrease of 12.5%. Direct operating expenses declined 11.1% to US$1.06 billion from US$1.19 billion in the comparable period the year before. Indirect operating expenses decreased 2.2% to US$585.1 million from US$598.2 million in the equivalent prior-year period.

Prospects: Co. remains focused on the expansion projects at several of its properties. For instance, Co.'s $130.0 million expansion of the Blue Chip Casino Hotel in Michigan City, IN is on schedule for a Dec 2008 opening, and it is progressing with construction of The Water Club, its 800-room boutique hotel in Atlantic City, which should open in June 2008. Also, construction on Co.'s Echelon development continues to advance as foundation work is nearly complete for its hotels, which include Hotel Echelon, The Enclave and Shangri-La Las Vegas. Further, work on the Delano and the Mondrian hotels should begin in the second quarter of 2008, with Echelon projected to open in the third quarter of 2010.

Financial Data

(US$ in Thousands)	12/31/2007	12/31/2006	12/31/2005	12/31/2004	12/31/2003	12/31/2002	12/31/2001	12/31/2000
Earnings Per Share	3.42	1.30	1.60	1.42	0.62	0.61	0.40	1.01
Cash Flow Per Share	3.24	4.73	4.74	3.51	2.69	2.78	2.54	3.42
Tang Book Value Per Share	5.05	2.28	2.09	0.08	N.M.	N.M.	N.M.	N.M.
Dividends Per Share	0.585	0.530	0.460	0.320	0.150	...	...	...
Dividend Payout %	17.11	40.77	28.75	22.54	24.19	...	...	...
Income Statement								
Total Revenue	1,997,119	2,192,634	2,223,020	1,734,058	1,253,070	1,228,901	1,102,335	1,153,896
EBITDA	493,528	604,945	553,621	425,066	234,270	239,497	215,694	270,033
Income Before Taxes	184,935	246,839	245,099	187,099	65,815	76,964	41,932	102,057
Income Taxes	64,027	85,491	84,050	75,645	24,882	28,740	16,982	39,292
Net Income	303,035	116,778	144,610	111,454	40,933	40,012	24,950	62,765
Average Shares	88,608	89,593	90,507	78,235	66,163	66,125	62,360	62,278
Balance Sheet								
Current Assets	339,120	374,678	288,161	262,055	159,631	263,940	130,888	128,571
Total Assets	4,487,596	3,901,299	4,424,971	3,919,032	1,872,997	1,912,990	1,754,913	1,577,614
Current Liabilities	380,132	331,990	439,826	322,304	200,301	177,536	167,083	157,017
Long-Term Obligations	2,265,929	2,133,016	2,552,795	2,304,343	1,097,589	1,227,324	1,143,358	1,016,813
Total Liabilities	3,102,190	2,791,347	3,326,967	2,975,262	1,431,744	1,504,429	1,401,176	1,247,836
Stockholders' Equity	1,385,406	1,109,952	1,098,004	943,770	441,253	408,561	353,737	329,778
Shares Outstanding	87,747	87,105	89,286	87,537	64,980	64,761	62,363	62,234
Statistical Record								
Return on Assets %	7.22	2.81	3.47	3.84	2.16	2.18	1.50	4.14
Return on Equity %	24.29	10.58	14.17	16.05	9.63	10.50	7.30	20.98
EBITDA Margin %	24.71	27.59	24.90	24.51	18.70	19.49	19.57	23.40
Net Margin %	15.17	5.33	6.51	6.43	3.27	3.26	2.26	5.44
Asset Turnover	0.48	0.53	0.53	0.60	0.66	0.67	0.66	0.76
Current Ratio	0.89	1.13	0.66	0.81	0.80	1.49	0.78	0.82
Debt to Equity	1.64	1.92	2.32	2.44	2.49	3.00	3.23	3.08
Price Range	53.15-34.07	54.01-33.54	57.50-37.87	42.26-15.75	18.30-11.42	18.67-6.48	6.50-3.26	6.00-3.31
P/E Ratio	15.54-9.96	41.55-25.80	35.94-23.67	29.76-11.09	29.52-18.42	30.61-10.62	16.25-8.15	5.94-3.28
Average Yield %	1.31	1.24	0.95	1.22	1.01	...	...	...

Address: 2950 Industrial Road, Las Vegas, NV 89109 **Telephone:** 702-792-7200 **Fax:** 702-792-7266	Web Site: www.boydgaming.com **Officers:** William S. Boyd - Chmn., C.E.O. Marianne Boyd Johnson - Vice-Chmn., Sr. V.P.	**Auditors:** Deloitte & Touche LLP **Investor Contact:** 702-792-7212 **Transfer Agents:** Wells Fargo Shareowner Services, South St. Paul, MN

BRADY CORP.

Exchange	Symbol	Price	52Wk Range	Yield	P/E	Div Acheiver
NYS	BRC	$33.43 (3/31/2008)	43.78-28.58	1.79	15.55	23 Years

*7 Year Price Score 108.43 *NYSE Composite Index=100 *12 Month Price Score 94.87

Interim Earnings (Per Share)

Qtr.	Oct	Jan	Apr	Jul
2004-05	0.41	0.41	0.50	0.32
2005-06	0.60	0.43	0.61	0.43
2006-07	0.63	0.36	0.53	0.48
2007-08	0.66	0.48	...	...

Interim Dividends (Per Share)

Amt	Decl	Ex	Rec	Pay
0.14Q	5/16/2007	7/6/2007	7/10/2007	7/31/2007
0.15Q	9/11/2007	10/5/2007	10/10/2007	10/31/2007
0.15Q	11/16/2007	1/8/2008	1/10/2008	1/31/2008
0.15Q	2/19/2008	4/8/2008	4/10/2008	4/30/2008

Indicated Div: $0.60 (Div. Reinv. Plan)

Valuation Analysis

		Institutional Holding	
Forecast P/E	14.13 (1/10/2007)	No of Institutions	133
Market Cap	$1.8 Billion	Shares	44,920,448
Book Value	979.0 Million	% Held	83.27
Price/Book	1.86		
Price/Sales	1.26		

Business Summary: Consumer Accessories (MIC: 4.6 SIC: 3993 NAIC: 339950)

Brady manufactures and markets identification products and specialty materials globally. Co.'s major product categories focus on facility identification, safety and complimentary products for the Maintenance, Repair and Operations market as well as wire and people identification products. Product lines provided to original equipment manufacturers includes identification products for product identification, work in process identification, bar code labels and precision die-cut components for mobile telecommunications devices, hard disk drives, medical devices and supplies as well as automotive electronics. As of Jul 31 2007, Co. had 61 manufacturing and distribution facilities worldwide.

Recent Developments: For the quarter ended Jan 31 2008, net income increased 35.4% to US$26.7 million from US$19.7 million in the year-earlier quarter. Revenues were US$364.1 million, up 13.3% from US$321.3 million the year before. Operating income was US$42.4 million versus US$32.7 million in the prior-year quarter, an increase of 29.7%. Direct operating expenses rose 10.5% to US$189.1 million from US$171.1 million in the comparable period the year before. Indirect operating expenses increased 12.9% to US$132.6 million from US$117.4 million in the equivalent prior-year period.

Prospects: For the fiscal year ending Jul 31 2008, Co. continues to anticipate sales of $1.43 billion to $1.46 billion. Also, Co. is projecting earnings of $2.31 to $2.42 per diluted share, while net income is forecasted to range from $129.0 million to $135.0 million. Looking ahead, Co. plans to focus on integrating acquisitions and streamlining its business as well as restructure its Asia operations to emphasize on potential segments. Meanwhile, Co. is encouraged by the Mar 3 2008 acquisition of DAWG Inc., a provider of sorbents, spill-containment products, safety-storage cabinets, first-aid kits, and other products, which should expand its presence in the sorbents and spill containment market.

Financial Data

(US$ in Thousands)	6 Mos	3 Mos	07/31/2007	07/31/2006	07/31/2005	07/31/2004	07/31/2003	07/31/2002
Earnings Per Share	2.15	2.03	2.00	2.07	1.64	1.06	0.46	0.60
Cash Flow Per Share	3.43	2.90	2.52	2.32	2.43	1.79	1.19	1.18
Tang Book Value Per Share	1.13	0.97	0.07	0.45	1.89	1.69	4.47	4.61
Dividends Per Share	0.580	0.570	0.560	0.520	0.440	0.420	0.400	0.380
Dividend Payout %	26.98	28.08	28.00	25.12	26.83	39.44	87.91	63.33
Income Statement								
Total Revenue	744,258	380,134	1,362,631	1,018,436	816,447	671,219	554,866	516,962
EBITDA	132,838	72,624	228,718	194,063	150,643	91,748	50,347	59,847
Depn & Amortn	29,669	14,168	...	...	...	...	...	...
Income Before Taxes	89,702	51,736	151,928	144,688	115,418	70,327	32,455	43,135
Income Taxes	26,642	15,366	42,540	40,513	33,471	19,456	11,035	14,882
Net Income	63,060	36,370	109,388	104,175	81,947	50,871	21,420	28,253
Average Shares	55,228	55,121	54,741	50,385	49,859	47,812	46,754	46,679
Balance Sheet								
Current Assets	626,593	629,292	583,413	459,157	302,372	251,923	215,157	210,026
Total Assets	1,773,912	1,758,512	1,698,857	1,365,186	850,147	694,330	449,519	420,525
Current Liabilities	253,443	263,945	280,054	218,620	160,812	120,217	91,279	74,262
Long-Term Obligations	478,572	478,573	478,575	350,018	150,026	150,019	568	3,751
Total Liabilities	794,914	805,368	807,845	619,140	352,873	291,015	110,558	96,283
Stockholders' Equity	978,998	953,144	891,012	746,046	497,274	403,315	338,961	324,242
Shares Outstanding	54,571	54,386	54,125	53,727	49,245	48,160	46,618	46,242
Statistical Record								
Return on Assets %	7.23	7.01	7.14	9.40	10.61	8.87	4.92	6.95
Return on Equity %	13.25	12.85	13.36	16.76	18.20	13.67	6.46	9.01
EBITDA Margin %	17.85	19.10	16.79	19.06	18.45	13.67	9.07	11.58
Net Margin %	8.47	9.57	8.03	10.23	10.04	7.58	3.86	5.47
Asset Turnover	0.89	0.89	0.89	0.92	1.06	1.17	1.28	1.27
Current Ratio	2.47	2.38	2.08	2.10	1.88	2.10	2.36	2.83
Debt to Equity	0.49	0.50	0.54	0.47	0.30	0.37	N.M.	0.01
Price Range	43.78-29.44	43.78-30.91	40.52-30.91	41.83-27.01	35.40-21.11	23.10-15.90	17.70-12.89	20.30-13.65
P/E Ratio	20.36-13.69	21.57-15.23	20.26-15.46	20.21-13.05	21.59-12.87	21.79-15.00	38.48-28.02	33.83-22.75
Average Yield %	1.64	1.58	1.58	1.48	1.52	2.18	2.53	2.23

Address: 6555 West Good Hope Road, Milwaukee, WI 53223	Web Site: www.bradycorp.com	Auditors: Deloitte & Touche LLP
Telephone: 414-358-6600	Officers: Frank M. Jaehnert - Pres., C.E.O. David R. Hawke - Exec. V.P.	Investor Contact: 414-438-6940
Fax: 414-438-6910		Transfer Agents: Wells Fargo Bank Minnesota, N.A., St. Paul, MN

BRANDYWINE REALTY TRUST

Exchange	Symbol	Price	52Wk Range	Yield	P/E
NYS	BDN	$16.96 (3/31/2008)	33.79-15.70	10.38	30.84

*7 Year Price Score 74.27   *NYSE Composite Index=100   *12 Month Price Score 77.11

Interim Earnings (Per Share)

Qtr.	Mar	Jun	Sep	Dec
2003	0.30	0.29	0.37	0.44
2004	0.34	0.34	0.39	0.08
2005	0.13	0.12	0.24	0.12
2006	(0.05)	(0.15)	(0.02)	0.25
2007	0.19	(0.01)	0.00	0.36

Interim Dividends (Per Share)

Amt	Decl	Ex	Rec	Pay
0.44Q	6/12/2007	7/2/2007	7/5/2007	7/19/2007
0.44Q	9/12/2007	10/3/2007	10/5/2007	10/19/2007
0.44Q	12/11/2007	1/2/2008	1/4/2008	1/18/2008
0.44Q	3/12/2008	4/2/2008	4/4/2008	4/18/2008

Indicated Div: $1.76

Valuation Analysis		Institutional Holding	
Forecast P/E	N/A	No of Institutions	180
Market Cap	$1.5 Billion	Shares	
Book Value	1.7 Billion	90,862,960	
Price/Book	0.85	% Held	
Price/Sales	2.16	N/A	

TRADING VOLUME (thousand shares)

Business Summary: Property, Real Estate & Development (MIC: 8.3 SIC: 6798 NAIC: 525930)

Brandywine Realty Trust is a real estate investment trust involved in acquiring, developing, redeveloping, leasing and managing office and industrial properties. As of Dec 31 2007, Co. owned 216 office properties, 23 industrial facilities and one mixed-use property, containing an aggregate of approximately 24.9 million net rentable square feet. Co.'s properties are located in the surrounding Philadelphia, PA, Wilmington, DE, Southern and Central New Jersey, Richmond, VA, Metropolitan Washington, D.C., Austin, TX, and Oakland and Rancho Bernardo, CA. As of Dec 31 2007, Co. also managed approximately 14.5 million square feet of office and industrial properties for third parties.

Recent Developments: For the year ended Dec 31 2007, income from continuing operations was US$28.8 million compared with a loss of US$18.7 million a year earlier. Net income increased 438.6% to US$56.5 million from US$10.5 million in the prior year. Revenues were US$684.0 million, up 8.5% from US$630.3 million the year before. Revenues from property income rose 8.7% to US$658.2 million from US$605.3 million in the corresponding earlier year.

Prospects: For full-year 2008, Co. is forecasting funds from operations to be in the range of $2.46 to $2.56 per diluted share. In addition, Co. is projecting approximately $2.5 million to $3.0 million of incremental net operating income from five key ground-up developments namely South Lake, 2100 Franklin, Barton Creek, Metroplex I and 1200 Lenox Drive - and is targeting year-end occupancy for this group to be in a range of 30.0% to 35.0%. As for other income categories including termination fees, management income, interest income, income from joint ventures and certain other items, Co. is targeting a range of $30.0 million to $38.0 million compared with $47.0 million in 2007.

Financial Data

(US$ In Thousands)	12/31/2007	12/31/2006	12/31/2005	12/31/2004	12/31/2003	12/31/2002	12/31/2001	12/31/2000
Earnings Per Share	0.55	0.03	0.62	1.15	1.40	1.39	0.57	1.12
Cash Flow Per Share	2.52	2.70	2.24	3.20	3.22	3.34	3.97	2.85
Tang Book Value Per Share	17.53	18.30	18.28	18.92	18.63	19.49	19.87	21.20
Dividends Per Share	1.760	1.300	1.780	1.760	1.760	1.760	1.700	1.620
Dividend Payout %	320.00	4,333.33	287.10	153.04	125.71	126.62	298.25	144.64
Income Statement								
Property Income	658,154	640,406	377,581	313,203	294,700	286,962	300,031	279,966
Non-Property Income	25,818	22,395	13,879	10,389	10,959	9,768	10,794	7,118
Total Revenue	683,972	662,801	391,460	323,592	305,659	296,730	310,825	287,084
Interest Expense	167,171	175,784	74,363	55,061	57,835	63,522	66,385	64,746
Net Income	56,453	10,182	42,767	60,303	85,809	67,984	33,722	54,158
Average Shares	87,321	90,070	56,104	48,018	37,087	35,645	35,646	35,807
Balance Sheet								
Total Assets	5,214,099	5,508,263	2,805,745	2,633,984	1,855,776	1,919,288	1,960,203	1,825,440
Long-Term Obligations	3,100,969	3,152,230	1,521,384	1,306,669	867,659	1,004,729	1,009,165	866,202
Total Liabilities	3,386,745	3,486,346	1,663,022	1,444,116	950,431	1,097,793	1,108,213	923,961
Stockholders' Equity	1,743,235	1,897,926	1,104,864	1,147,002	770,988	686,443	708,156	756,505
Shares Outstanding	87,015	88,327	56,179	55,292	41,040	35,226	35,640	35,681
Statistical Record								
Return on Assets %	1.05	0.25	1.57	2.68	4.55	3.25	1.78	2.85
Return on Equity %	3.10	0.70	3.80	6.27	11.78	9.03	4.60	7.17
Net Margin %	8.25	1.58	10.92	18.64	28.07	21.23	10.85	18.17
Price Range	36.14-17.78	35.37-27.65	32.71-26.30	30.81-24.30	27.74-19.29	26.00-19.08	22.78-18.48	21.94-15.38
P/E Ratio	65.71-32.33	N.M.	52.76-42.42	26.79-21.13	19.81-13.78	18.71-13.73	39.96-32.42	19.59-13.73
Average Yield %	6.19	4.14	6.11	6.29	7.43	7.89	8.33	8.71

Address: 401 Plymouth Road, suite 500, Plymouth Meeting, PA 19462 **Telephone:** 610-325-5600 **Fax:** 610-325-5622	**Web Site:** www.brandywinerealty.com **Officers:** Anthony A. Nichols Sr. - Chmn. Gerard H. Sweeney - Pres., C.E.O.	**Auditors:** PricewaterhouseCoopers **Investor Contact:** 610-832-7702 **Transfer Agents:** Computershare, Providence, RI

BRE PROPERTIES, INC.

Exchange	Symbol	Price	52Wk Range	Yield	P/E
NYS	BRE	$45.56 (3/31/2008)	64.84-35.44	4.94	21.59

*7 Year Price Score 101.04 *NYSE Composite Index=100 *12 Month Price Score 91.74

Interim Earnings (Per Share)

Qtr.	Mar	Jun	Sep	Dec
2003	0.53	0.59	0.14	0.21
2004	0.27	0.27	0.20	0.48
2005	0.56	0.26	0.13	0.27
2006	0.14	1.33	0.22	0.25
2007	0.23	0.29	0.99	0.60

Interim Dividends (Per Share)

Amt	Decl	Ex	Rec	Pay
0.537Q	5/15/2007	6/13/2007	6/15/2007	6/29/2007
0.537Q	8/15/2007	9/12/2007	9/14/2007	9/28/2007
0.537Q	10/31/2007	12/12/2007	12/14/2007	12/31/2007
0.563Q	1/31/2008	3/12/2008	3/14/2008	3/31/2008

Indicated Div: $2.25

Valuation Analysis — **Institutional Holding**

Forecast P/E	33.80	No of Institutions
	(1/10/2007)	187
Market Cap	$2.3 Billion	Shares
Book Value	923.2 Million	43,918,184
Price/Book	2.52	% Held
Price/Sales	6.73	86.67

TRADING VOLUME (thousand shares)

Business Summary: Property, Real Estate & Development (MIC: 8.3 SIC: 6798 NAIC: 525930)

BRE Properties is a self-administered equity real estate investment trust, which is focused on the development, acquisition and management of multifamily apartment communities in six targeted metropolitan markets of the Western U.S. As of Dec 31 2007, Co.'s portfolio of real estate assets included: 77 wholly or majority owned stabilized multifamily communities, aggregating 21,808 units in California, Washington and Arizona; 13 stabilized multifamily communities owned through joint venture agreements, comprised of 4,080 apartment units; and 20 apartment communities in various stages of construction and development totaling 3,125 units.

Recent Developments: For the year ended Dec 31 2007, income from continuing operations decreased 8.0% to US$67.2 million from US$73.0 million a year earlier. Net income increased 6.6% to US$128.1 million from US$120.2 million in the prior year. Revenues were US$345.2 million, up 8.3% from US$318.6 million the year before. Revenues from property income rose 8.7% to US$330.8 million from US$304.4 million in the corresponding earlier year.

Prospects: For 2008, Co. is expecting Funds from Operations per share of $2.70 to $2.85, with anticipated same-store revenue growth of 3.5% to 5.0% and estimated same-store net operating income growth of between 3.5% and 5.0%. Concurrently, Co. projects earnings per share in the range of $1.15 to $1.30, excluding expected gains or losses related to property sales. Notably, this earnings guidance is based on several factors, including the expectation that its property operations in the San Francisco Bay area and Seattle should benefit from continued job growth, an absence of new apartment supply, and marginal impact from the existing subprime mortgage crisis and single-family housing recession.

Financial Data

(US$ in Thousands)	12/31/2007	12/31/2006	12/31/2005	12/31/2004	12/31/2003	12/31/2002	12/31/2001	12/31/2000
Earnings Per Share	2.11	1.96	1.22	1.21	1.48	1.91	1.69	0.81
Cash Flow Per Share	3.11	3.37	2.48	2.71	2.42	2.99	2.97	2.72
Tang Book Value Per Share	18.11	19.35	20.00	20.76	16.64	15.75	15.96	16.28
Dividends Per Share	2.150	2.050	2.000	1.950	1.950	1.950	1.860	1.700
Dividend Payout %	101.90	104.59	163.93	161.16	131.76	102.09	110.06	209.88
Income Statement								
Property Income	330,810	315,145	284,898	267,997	260,660	255,814	243,538	235,723
Non-Property Income	14,353	14,823	13,235	12,645	14,483	16,003	20,138	17,754
Total Revenue	345,163	329,968	298,133	280,642	275,143	271,817	263,676	253,477
Interest Expense	82,752	80,199	76,553	66,826	59,617	56,106	48,517	45,028
Net Income	128,081	120,195	80,948	73,541	83,128	95,809	83,377	41,303
Average Shares	51,780	52,150	51,790	50,825	47,445	47,770	48,510	48,270
Balance Sheet								
Total Assets	2,953,660	2,823,491	2,704,390	2,518,941	2,227,965	2,108,713	1,875,981	1,718,129
Long-Term Obligations	1,919,082	1,668,910	1,560,574	1,378,566	1,192,329	1,173,764	1,008,431	825,253
Total Liabilities	1,999,488	1,746,102	1,616,573	1,436,619	1,228,562	1,212,382	1,038,934	847,301
Stockholders' Equity	923,192	976,845	1,026,142	1,046,647	960,544	851,184	784,896	801,116
Shares Outstanding	50,968	50,484	51,312	50,418	49,992	45,870	45,807	45,895
Statistical Record								
Return on Assets %	4.43	4.35	3.10	3.09	3.83	4.81	4.64	2.40
Return on Equity %	13.48	12.00	7.81	7.31	9.18	11.71	10.51	5.07
Net Margin %	37.11	36.43	27.15	26.20	30.21	35.25	31.62	16.29
Price Range	71.77-39.97	66.30-47.21	47.37-34.90	42.31-30.75	34.84-28.34	34.25-27.38	32.90-26.75	33.63-21.38
P/E Ratio	34.01-18.94	33.83-24.09	38.83-28.61	34.97-25.41	23.54-19.15	17.93-14.34	19.47-15.83	41.51-26.40
Average Yield %	3.74	3.63	4.88	5.43	6.07	6.32	6.26	6.06

Address: 525 Market Street, 4th Floor, San Francisco, CA 94105-2712 Telephone: 415-445-6530	Web Site: www.breproperties.com Officers: Frank C. McDowell - Vice-Chmn., C.E.O. Constance B. Moore - Pres., C.O.O.	Auditors: Ernst & Young LLP Transfer Agents: Mellon Investor Services LLC, Jersey City, NJ

BRINKER INTERNATIONAL, INC.

Exchange	Symbol	Price	52Wk Range	Yield	P/E
NYS	EAT	$18.55 (3/31/2008)	34.16-15.32	2.37	9.37

*7 Year Price Score 62.98   *NYSE Composite Index=100   *12 Month Price Score 77.77

TRADING VOLUME (thousand shares)

Interim Earnings (Per Share)

Qtr.	Sep	Dec	Mar	Jun
2004-05	0.11	0.29	0.40	0.37
2005-06	0.24	0.33	0.50	0.56
2006-07	0.38	0.35	0.43	0.69
2007-08	0.34	0.52	...	...

Interim Dividends (Per Share)

Amt	Decl	Ex	Rec	Pay
0.09Q	5/31/2007	6/13/2007	6/15/2007	6/27/2007
0.09Q	8/23/2007	9/12/2007	9/14/2007	9/26/2007
0.11Q	11/1/2007	12/3/2007	12/5/2007	12/17/2007
0.11Q	1/31/2008	3/11/2008	3/13/2008	3/26/2008

Indicated Div: $0.44

Valuation Analysis

		Institutional Holding	
Forecast P/E	13.34 (1/10/2007)	No of Institutions	271
Market Cap	$1.9 Billion	Shares	118,266,112
Book Value	644.9 Million	% Held	96.69
Price/Book	2.91		
Price/Sales	0.46		

Business Summary: Hospitality & Tourism (MIC: 5.1 SIC: 5812 NAIC: 722110)

Brinker International owns, operates, develops and franchises four restaurant chains, which include: Chili's Grill & Bar, the Romano's Macaroni Grill, the Maggiano's Little Italy, and the On The Border Mexican Grill & Cantina. As of June 27, 2007, Co.'s system of Company-owned and franchised restaurants included 1,801 restaurants located in 49 states, and Washington, D.C. In addition, Co. has restaurants in the countries of Australia, Bahrain, Canada, Egypt, Ecuador, Germany, Guatemala, Indonesia, Japan, Kuwait, Lebanon, Malaysia, Mexico, Oman, Peru, Philippines, Puerto Rico, Qatar, Saudi Arabia, South Korea, Taiwan, United Arab Emirates, the U.K. and Venezuela.

Recent Developments: For the quarter ended Dec 26 2007, income from continuing operations increased 12.8% to US$46.2 million from US$41.0 million in the year-earlier quarter. Net income increased 23.3% to US$54.5 million from US$44.2 million in the year-earlier quarter. Revenues were US$868.2 million, down 3.5% from US$899.6 million the year before. Operating income was US$79.3 million versus US$66.7 million in the prior-year quarter, an increase of 18.9%. Direct operating expenses declined 1.7% to US$732.2 million from US$745.0 million in the comparable period the year before. Indirect operating expenses decreased 35.4% to US$56.8 million from US$87.8 million in the equivalent prior-year period.

Prospects: Co. expects its operational and financial strategies, including closing of underperforming locations and franchising of company-owned restaurants, to support its future performance. Thus, due to its Jan 2008 decision to close 25 underperforming restaurants, Co. estimates a charge related to the planned closures of $7.0 million to $9.0 million in continuing operations and $4.0 to $6.0 million in discontinued operations in the third fiscal quarter 2008. Co. also plans domestic and international franchise expansion as to attain at least 35.0% of franchise ownership of its brands by end of fiscal 2008 via a program of franchising company-owned Chili's, On The Border and Maggiano's restaurants.

Financial Data

(US$ in Thousands)	6 Mos	3 Mos	06/27/2007	06/28/2006	06/29/2005	06/30/2004	06/25/2003	06/26/2002
Earnings Per Share	1.98	1.81	1.85	1.62	1.15	1.05	1.13	1.01
Cash Flow Per Share	3.94	4.28	4.02	3.66	3.35	3.29	3.09	2.66
Tang Book Value Per Share	5.00	5.30	6.05	7.42	7.21	6.38	6.51	5.36
Dividends Per Share	0.380	0.360	0.337	0.200	...	...	...	...
Dividend Payout %	19.15	19.84	18.20	12.35	...	...	...	...
Income Statement								
Total Revenue	1,763,292	895,086	4,376,904	4,151,291	3,912,850	3,707,186	3,285,394	2,887,111
EBITDA	226,347	107,122	538,431	518,422	415,035	434,301	435,910	383,530
Depn & Amortn	77,624	38,535	...	...	...	...	...	...
Income Before Taxes	123,332	55,672	318,470	305,398	194,413	237,931	253,587	231,849
Income Taxes	38,570	17,136	88,421	91,448	34,194	83,970	84,951	79,136
Net Income	92,080	37,600	230,049	213,395	160,219	153,961	168,636	152,713
Average Shares	105,339	109,155	124,116	130,933	141,343	146,908	148,702	150,847
Balance Sheet								
Current Assets	595,335	642,502	364,181	242,310	240,179	400,920	166,467	141,954
Total Assets	2,317,642	2,313,783	2,318,021	2,221,779	2,156,124	2,211,791	1,943,290	1,783,336
Current Liabilities	621,680	501,967	525,082	497,375	419,917	379,162	310,211	302,220
Long-Term Obligations	884,414	952,995	826,918	500,515	406,505	639,291	353,785	426,679
Total Liabilities	1,672,753	1,617,433	1,512,932	1,145,947	1,055,842	1,185,718	803,040	806,240
Stockholders' Equity	644,889	696,350	805,089	1,075,832	1,100,282	1,026,073	1,140,250	977,096
Shares Outstanding	101,166	105,243	110,127	125,309	133,774	135,971	146,782	146,160
Statistical Record								
Return on Assets %	9.92	9.68	10.16	9.73	7.36	7.29	9.08	9.49
Return on Equity %	26.65	24.59	24.53	19.57	15.11	13.98	15.97	16.31
EBITDA Margin %	12.84	11.97	12.30	12.49	10.61	11.71	13.27	13.28
Net Margin %	5.22	4.20	5.26	5.12	4.09	4.15	5.13	5.29
Asset Turnover	1.74	1.86	1.93	1.90	1.80	1.76	1.77	1.80
Current Ratio	0.96	1.28	0.69	0.49	0.57	1.06	0.54	0.47
Debt to Equity	1.37	1.37	1.03	0.47	0.37	0.62	0.31	0.44
Price Range	35.50-19.00	48.02-26.21	48.02-28.82	42.86-35.35	41.85-29.49	39.54-29.60	36.68-25.12	35.45-22.45
P/E Ratio	17.93-9.60	26.53-14.48	25.96-15.58	26.46-21.82	36.39-25.64	37.66-28.19	32.46-22.23	35.10-22.23
Average Yield %	1.30	1.08	0.96	0.51	...	...	...	...

Address: 6820 LBJ Freeway, Dallas, TX 75240	Web Site: www.brinker.com	Auditors: KPMG LLP
Telephone: 972-980-9917	Officers: Douglas H. Brooks - Chmn., Pres., C.E.O.	Investor Contact: 972-980-9917
Fax: 972-770-9593	Charles M. Sonsteby - Exec. V.P., C.F.O.	Transfer Agents: Mellom Investor Services LLC., Dallas, TX

BRINKS CO (THE)

Exchange	Symbol	Price	52Wk Range	Yield	P/E
NYS	BCO	$67.18 (3/31/2008)	68.22-50.03	0.60	23.01

*7 Year Price Score 135.82 *NYSE Composite Index=100 *12 Month Price Score 114.06

Interim Earnings (Per Share)

Qtr.	Mar	Jun	Sep	Dec
2003	(0.03)	0.11	0.94	(0.48)
2004	0.47	0.34	0.68	0.70
2005	0.24	0.27	1.15	0.83
2006	6.92	0.62	0.56	2.73
2007	0.61	0.60	0.55	1.16

Interim Dividends (Per Share)

Amt	Decl	Ex	Rec	Pay
0.10Q	5/4/2007	5/11/2007	5/15/2007	6/1/2007
0.10Q	7/13/2007	7/20/2007	7/24/2007	9/4/2007
0.10Q	11/2/2007	11/13/2007	11/15/2007	12/3/2007
0.10Q	1/25/2008	2/1/2008	2/5/2008	3/3/2008

Indicated Div: $0.40

Valuation Analysis

Forecast P/E	N/A
Market Cap	$3.3 Billion
Book Value	1.0 Billion
Price/Book	3.11
Price/Sales	1.01

Institutional Holding

No of Institutions	180
Shares	39,796,104
% Held	82.05

Business Summary: Stone, Clay, Glass, and Concrete Products (MIC: 11.2 SIC: 4731 NAIC: 488510).

The Brinks Company is comprised of two segments. Brink's, Inc. offers services that include armored car transportation; automated teller machine replenishment and servicing; currency, deposit processing and cash management services, including Cash Logistics services; deploying and servicing safes and safe control devices, including its CompuSafe service; coin sorting and wrapping; integrated check and cash processing services; arranging the secure transportation of valuables; transporting, storing and destroying sensitive information, and guarding services, including airport security. Brink's Home Security offers security alarm monitoring services for residential and commercial properties.

Recent Developments: For the year ended Dec 31 2007, income from continuing operations increased 31.4% to US$148.6 million from US$113.1 million a year earlier. Net income decreased 76.6% to US$137.3 million from US$587.2 million in the prior year. Revenues were US$3.22 billion, up 15.2% from US$2.79 billion the year before. Operating income was US$274.0 million versus US$209.5 million in the prior year, an increase of 30.8%. Direct operating expenses rose 15.0% to US$2.45 billion from US$2.13 billion in the comparable period the year before. Indirect operating expenses increased 9.2% to US$494.2 million from US$452.5 million in the equivalent prior-year period.

Prospects: On Feb 25 2008, Co. announced that its board of directors has approved a strategic decision to spin-off its Brink's Home Security unit (BHS) into a separate publicly traded company. Co. will continue to operate Brink's, Incorporated, its secure transportation and cash management unit. The spin-off of BHS is expected to be completed in the fourth quarter of 2008. Meanwhile, Co.'s target for its Brink's, Incorporated subsidiary in 2008 is to deliver annual organic revenue growth in the high-single-digit percentage range with operating profit margins at or above 8.0%. Furthermore, Co. believes that it can deliver 10.0% or better increases in revenue and profit in 2008 at its BHS subsidiary.

Financial Data

(US$ in Thousands)	12/31/2007	12/31/2006	12/31/2005	12/31/2004	12/31/2003	12/31/2002	12/31/2001	12/31/2000
Earnings Per Share	2.92	11.64	2.50	2.20	0.55	0.48	0.31	(5.12)
Cash Flow Per Share	9.76	0.65	5.58	5.12	5.66	4.63	6.17	7.27
Tang Book Value Per Share	18.17	12.49	12.22	7.31	4.63	2.82	4.62	4.69
Dividends Per Share	0.362	0.212	0.100	0.100	0.100	0.100	0.100	0.100
Dividend Payout %	12.41	1.83	4.00	4.55	18.18	20.83	32.26	...
Income Statement								
Total Revenue	3,219,000	2,837,600	2,549,000	4,718,100	3,998,600	3,776,700	3,624,200	3,834,112
EBITDA	429,300	336,700	230,200	328,700	236,100	261,000	295,300	232,818
Income Before Taxes	273,600	204,300	91,800	161,500	73,900	110,200	73,200	4,629
Income Taxes	102,200	82,700	49,500	60,900	55,700	41,200	27,400	1,944
Net Income	137,300	587,200	142,400	121,500	29,400	26,100	16,600	(256,643)
Average Shares	47,000	50,500	57,000	55,300	53,200	52,400	51,400	50,146
Balance Sheet								
Current Assets	845,700	750,800	1,701,800	1,092,600	860,500	782,000	760,500	813,626
Total Assets	2,394,300	2,188,000	3,036,900	2,678,200	2,548,600	2,459,900	2,394,000	2,478,709
Current Liabilities	639,900	606,700	1,125,800	1,032,100	844,100	793,300	844,900	898,307
Long-Term Obligations	89,200	126,300	251,900	181,600	221,500	304,200	252,900	311,418
Total Liabilities	1,348,000	1,434,200	2,199,400	2,004,200	2,053,000	2,078,700	1,917,900	2,002,886
Stockholders' Equity	1,046,300	753,800	837,500	674,000	495,600	381,200	476,100	475,823
Shares Outstanding	48,400	48,500	58,700	56,700	54,300	54,300	54,300	51,778
Statistical Record								
Return on Assets %	5.99	22.48	4.98	4.64	1.17	1.08	0.68	N.M.
Return on Equity %	15.25	73.80	18.84	20.72	6.71	6.09	3.49	N.M.
EBITDA Margin %	13.34	11.87	9.03	6.97	5.90	6.91	8.15	6.07
Net Margin %	4.27	20.69	5.59	2.58	0.74	0.69	0.46	N.M.
Asset Turnover	1.40	1.09	0.89	1.80	1.60	1.56	1.49	1.55
Current Ratio	1.32	1.24	1.51	1.06	1.02	0.99	0.90	0.91
Debt to Equity	0.09	0.17	0.30	0.27	0.45	0.80	0.53	0.65
Price Range	68.22-54.05	65.10-48.00	48.76-30.49	39.91-22.61	23.21-12.36	28.31-17.74	25.20-16.88	22.00-10.94
P/E Ratio	23.36-18.51	5.59-4.12	19.50-12.20	18.14-10.28	42.20-22.47	58.98-36.96	81.29-54.45	...
Average Yield %	0.59	0.40	0.27	0.33	0.60	0.44	0.48	0.62

Address: 1801 Bayberry Court, P.O. Box 18100, Richmond, VA 23226-8100	**Web Site:** www.brinkscompany.com	**Auditors:** KPMG LLP
Telephone: 804-289-9600	**Officers:** Michael T. Dan - Chmn., Pres., C.E.O.	**Investor Contact:** 804-289-9708
Fax: 804-289-9770	James B. Hartough - V.P., Corp. Fin., Treas.	**Transfer Agents:** American Stock Transfer & Trust Company, New York, NY

BRISTOL-MYERS SQUIBB CO.

Exchange	Symbol	Price	52Wk Range	Yield	P/E
NYS	BMY	$21.30 (3/31/2008)	32.14-20.46	5.82	19.54

*7 Year Price Score 75.45   *NYSE Composite Index=100   *12 Month Price Score 87.14

TRADING VOLUME (thousand shares)

Interim Earnings (Per Share)

Qtr.	Mar	Jun	Sep	Dec
2003	0.39	0.45	0.45	0.29
2004	0.49	0.27	0.38	0.07
2005	0.27	0.50	0.49	0.25
2006	0.36	0.34	0.17	(0.07)
2007	0.35	0.36	0.43	(0.05)

Interim Dividends (Per Share)

Amt	Decl	Ex	Rec	Pay
0.28Q	6/12/2007	7/3/2007	7/6/2007	8/1/2007
0.28Q	9/11/2007	10/3/2007	10/5/2007	11/1/2007
0.31Q	12/6/2007	1/2/2008	1/4/2008	2/1/2008
0.31Q	3/4/2008	4/2/2008	4/4/2008	5/1/2008

Indicated Div: $1.24

Valuation Analysis

Forecast P/E	18.15
	(1/10/2007)
Market Cap	$41.8 Billion
Book Value	10.6 Billion
Price/Book	3.96
Price/Sales	2.16

Institutional Holding

No of Institutions	908
Shares	1,455,784,448
% Held	73.98

Business Summary: Pharmaceuticals (MIC: 9.1 SIC: 2834 NAIC: 325412)

Bristol-Myers Squibb is a biopharmaceutical and related health care products company. Co. is engaged in the discovery, development, licensing, manufacturing, marketing, distribution and sale of pharmaceuticals and related health care products. Co. has three reportable segments: Pharmaceuticals, Nutritionals and ConvaTec. The Pharmaceuticals segment consists of the global pharmaceutical/biotechnology and international consumer medicines business. The Nutritionals segment consists of Mead Johnson Nutritionals, primarily an infant formula and children's nutritionals business. The ConvaTec segment consists of ostomy, wound and skin care business.

Recent Developments: For the year ended Dec 31 2007, income from continuing operations increased 38.4% to US$1.97 billion from US$1.42 billion a year earlier. Net income increased 36.6% to US$2.17 billion from US$1.59 billion in the prior year. Revenues were US$19.35 billion, up 12.1% from US$17.26 billion the year before. Direct operating expenses rose 8.3% to US$6.22 billion from US$5.74 billion in the comparable period the year before. Indirect operating expenses increased 5.7% to US$10.03 billion from US$9.49 billion in the equivalent prior-year period.

Prospects: On Jan 8 2008, Co. announced that Avista Capital Partners, a private equity firm, has completed the acquisition of its Medical Imaging business unit, which is a supplier of medical imaging products for nuclear and ultrasound cardiovascular diagnostic imaging procedures, for approximately $525.0 million. The divestiture enables Co. to reinvest the proceeds on its pharmaceutical research, development and commercialization initiatives as it focuses on evolving into a BioPharma company. Meanwhile, for full year 2008, Co. is revising its earnings per share from continuing operations to $1.36 to $1.46 from $1.44 to $1.54, reflecting the effect from the sale of its Medical Imaging business.

Financial Data

(US$ in Thousands)	12/31/2007	12/31/2006	12/31/2005	12/31/2004	12/31/2003	12/31/2002	12/31/2001	12/31/2000
Earnings Per Share	1.09	0.81	1.52	1.21	1.59	1.07	2.67	2.36
Cash Flow Per Share	1.60	1.06	0.94	1.63	1.81	0.49	2.78	2.36
Tang Book Value Per Share	2.16	1.68	2.28	1.76	1.66	1.14	1.70	3.96
Dividends Per Share	1.120	1.120	1.120	0.840	1.120	1.400	1.100	0.980
Dividend Payout %	102.75	138.27	73.68	69.42	70.44	130.84	41.20	41.53
Income Statement								
Total Revenue	19,348,000	17,914,000	19,207,000	19,380,000	20,894,000	18,119,000	19,423,000	18,216,000
EBITDA	4,607,000	3,786,000	5,646,000	5,532,000	5,695,000	3,665,000	3,816,000	6,175,000
Income Before Taxes	3,534,000	2,635,000	4,516,000	4,418,000	4,694,000	2,647,000	2,986,000	5,478,000
Income Taxes	803,000	610,000	932,000	1,519,000	1,215,000	435,000	459,000	1,382,000
Net Income	2,165,000	1,585,000	3,000,000	2,388,000	3,106,000	2,066,000	5,245,000	4,711,000
Average Shares	1,980,000	1,963,000	1,983,000	1,976,000	1,950,000	1,942,000	1,965,000	1,997,000
Balance Sheet								
Current Assets	10,348,000	10,302,000	12,283,000	14,801,000	11,918,000	9,975,000	12,349,000	9,824,000
Total Assets	26,172,000	25,575,000	28,138,000	30,435,000	27,471,000	24,874,000	27,057,000	17,578,000
Current Liabilities	8,644,000	6,496,000	6,890,000	9,843,000	7,530,000	8,220,000	8,826,000	5,632,000
Long-Term Obligations	4,381,000	7,248,000	8,364,000	8,463,000	8,522,000	6,261,000	6,237,000	1,336,000
Total Liabilities	15,610,000	15,584,000	16,930,000	20,233,000	17,685,000	15,907,000	16,321,000	8,398,000
Stockholders' Equity	10,562,000	9,991,000	11,208,000	10,202,000	9,786,000	8,967,000	10,736,000	9,180,000
Shares Outstanding	1,962,000	1,967,000	1,957,000	1,947,000	1,939,983	1,936,829	1,935,620	1,953,535
Statistical Record								
Return on Assets %	8.37	5.90	10.24	8.23	11.87	7.96	23.50	27.08
Return on Equity %	21.07	14.95	28.02	23.83	33.13	20.97	52.67	52.71
EBITDA Margin %	23.81	21.13	29.40	28.54	27.26	20.23	19.65	33.90
Net Margin %	11.19	8.85	15.62	12.32	14.87	11.40	27.00	25.86
Asset Turnover	0.75	0.67	0.66	0.67	0.80	0.70	0.87	1.05
Current Ratio	1.20	1.59	1.78	1.50	1.58	1.21	1.40	1.74
Debt to Equity	0.41	0.73	0.75	0.83	0.87	0.70	0.58	0.15
Price Range	32.14-26.10	26.31-20.24	26.48-21.03	30.64-22.50	28.86-21.13	51.30-20.55	68.08-49.00	70.40-41.42
P/E Ratio	29.49-23.94	32.48-24.99	17.42-13.84	25.32-18.60	18.15-13.29	47.94-19.21	25.50-18.35	29.83-17.55
Average Yield %	3.89	4.64	4.62	3.34	4.44	4.41	1.88	1.77

Address: 345 Park Avenue, New York, NY 10154-0037
Telephone: 212-546-4000
Fax: 212-546-4020

Web Site: www.bms.com
Officers: James D. Robinson III - Chmn. Peter R. Dolan - C.E.O.

Auditors: PricewaterhouseCoopers LLP
Transfer Agents: Mellon Investor Services

BROOKDALE SENIOR LIVING INC

Exchange	Symbol	Price	52Wk Range	Yield	P/E
NYS	BKD	$23.90 (3/31/2008)	47.72-20.87	4.18	N/A

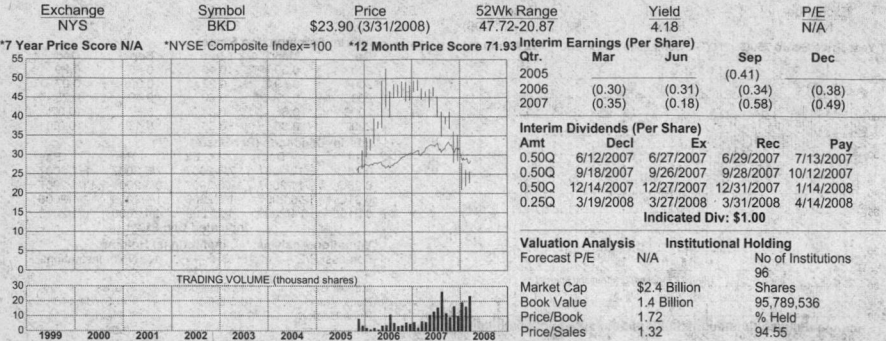

*7 Year Price Score N/A   *NYSE Composite Index=100   *12 Month Price Score 71.93

Interim Earnings (Per Share)

Qtr.	Mar	Jun	Sep	Dec
2005			(0.41)	
2006	(0.30)	(0.31)	(0.34)	(0.38)
2007	(0.35)	(0.18)	(0.58)	(0.49)

Interim Dividends (Per Share)

Amt	Decl	Ex	Rec	Pay
0.50Q	6/12/2007	6/27/2007	6/29/2007	7/13/2007
0.50Q	9/18/2007	9/26/2007	9/28/2007	10/12/2007
0.50Q	12/14/2007	12/27/2007	12/31/2007	1/14/2008
0.25Q	3/19/2008	3/27/2008	3/31/2008	4/14/2008

Indicated Div: $1.00

Valuation Analysis

Forecast P/E	N/A
Market Cap	$2.4 Billion
Book Value	1.4 Billion
Price/Book	1.72
Price/Sales	1.32

Institutional Holding

No of Institutions	96
Shares	95,789,536
% Held	94.55

Business Summary: Hospitals & Health Care (MIC: 9.3 SIC: 8051 NAIC: 623110)

Brookdale Senior Living is engaged as an operator of senior living facilities in the U.S. with 550 communities in 35 states at Dec 31 2007. As of such date, Co. operated four business segments: retirement centers, assisted living, continuing care retirement communities (CCRCs) and management services. As of the date stated above, Co. operated 87 retirement center communities with 15,990 units/beds, 409 assisted living communities with 21,087 units/beds, 32 CCRCs with 10,593 units/beds and 22 communities with 4,416 units/beds where it provides management services for third parties and affiliates.

Recent Developments: For the year ended Dec 31 2007, loss from continuing operations was US$162.0 million compared with a loss of US$108.1 million a year earlier. Net loss amounted to US$162.0 million versus a net loss of US$108.1 million in the prior year. Revenues were US$1.84 billion, up 40.4% from US$1.31 billion the year before. Operating loss was US$41.2 million versus a loss of US$44.7 million in the prior year. Indirect operating expenses increased 38.8% to US$1.88 billion from US$1.35 billion in the equivalent prior-year period.

Prospects: Looking ahead, Co. believes that several trends including the U.S. Census data assumption that individuals age 70 and older are expected to increase by 3.5 million through 2015 should result in the increase in the demand for senior living services. Meanwhile, reflecting the growing demand for senior living communities, Co. is planning to grow its future revenues through several initiatives including a combination of occupancy growth and monthly service fee increases. Thus, Co. expects to achieve annual growth in resident fees of 4.5% to 5.0% and anticipates holding annual cost to increase by 3.5%, which should result in annual same store Facility Operating Income growth of 7.5% to 8.0%.

Financial Data

(US$ in Thousands)	12/31/2007	12/31/2006	12/31/2005	09/30/2005	12/31/2004	12/31/2003	12/31/2002
Earnings Per Share	(1.60)	(1.34)	(0.41)	...	...	...	...
Cash Flow Per Share	1.97	1.06	0.15	...	...	...	...
Tang Book Value Per Share	8.18	11.33	8.69	...	...	...	...
Dividends Per Share	1.950	1.550	...	...	...	...	...
Income Statement							
Total Revenue	1,839,296	1,309,913	213,047	577,530	660,872	222,584	161,516
EBITDA	236,532	130,772	4,858	7,992	99,812	30,501	25,347
Income Before Taxes	(263,632)	(145,907)	(24,306)	(43,224)	(10,056)	(2,509)	20,383
Income Taxes	(101,260)	(38,491)	150	(247)	11,111	139	8,666
Net Income	(161,979)	(108,087)	(24,456)	(26,530)	(9,794)	(8,963)	6,455
Average Shares	101,511	80,842	59,710	...	...	...	...
Balance Sheet							
Current Assets	291,835	270,232	145,877	...	135,303	140,778	...
Total Assets	4,811,622	4,742,455	1,697,811	...	746,625	1,656,582	...
Current Liabilities	549,767	508,905	171,443	...	118,002	267,843	...
Long-Term Obligations	2,317,217	1,852,474	754,169	...	367,149	895,444	...
Total Liabilities	3,392,084	2,973,842	1,067,372	...	675,135	1,263,256	...
Stockholders' Equity	1,419,538	1,764,012	630,403	...	40,091	237,744	...
Shares Outstanding	101,941	101,260	65,006	...	...	...	...
Statistical Record							
EBITDA Margin %	12.86	9.98	2.28	1.38	15.10	13.70	15.69
Net Margin %	N.M.	N.M.	N.M.	N.M.	N.M.	N.M.	4.00
Asset Turnover	0.39	0.41	0.17	...	0.55	...	...
Current Ratio	0.53	0.53	0.85	...	1.15	0.53	...
Debt to Equity	1.63	1.05	1.20	...	9.16	3.77	...
Price Range	49.70-27.93	52.57-29.36	31.15-25.30	...	...	...	...
Average Yield %	4.69	3.67	...	...	...	...	...

Address: 330 North Wabash, Suite 1400, Chicago, IL 60611
Telephone: 312-977-3700

Web Site: www.brookdaleliving.com
Officers: Wesley R. Edens - Chmn. William B. Doniger - Vice-Chmn.

Auditors: Ernst & Young LLP
Investor Contact: 615-376-2412
Transfer Agents: American Stock Transfer & Trust Company

BROWN & BROWN, INC.

Exchange	Symbol	Price	52Wk Range	Yield	P/E	Div Acheiver
NYS	BRO	$17.38 (3/31/2008)	28.47-17.19	1.61	12.87	14 Years

*7 Year Price Score 93.25   *NYSE Composite Index=100   *12 Month Price Score 84.69

TRADING VOLUME (thousand shares)

Interim Earnings (Per Share)

Qtr.	Mar	Jun	Sep	Dec
2003	0.22	0.20	0.19	0.19
2004	0.27	0.23	0.22	0.22
2005	0.31	0.27	0.25	0.26
2006	0.36	0.32	0.29	0.26
2007	0.42	0.37	0.33	0.23

Interim Dividends (Per Share)

Amt	Decl	Ex	Rec	Pay
0.06Q	4/26/2007	5/7/2007	5/9/2007	5/23/2007
0.06Q	7/26/2007	8/6/2007	8/8/2007	8/22/2007
0.07Q	10/24/2007	11/5/2007	11/7/2007	11/21/2007
0.07Q	1/20/2000	2/4/2000	2/0/0000	2/20/2000

Indicated Div: $0.28

Valuation Analysis

		Institutional Holding	
Forecast P/E	17.18	No of Institutions	
	(1/10/2007)	234	
Market Cap	$2.4 Billion	Shares	
Book Value	1.1 Billion	89,263,648	
Price/Book	2.23	% Held	
Price/Sales	2.55	63.54	

Business Summary: Insurance (MIC: 8.2 SIC: 6411 NAIC: 524210)

Brown & Brown is an insurance agency, wholesale brokerage and service organization. Co. markets and sells to its customers insurance products and services, mainly in the property, casualty and employee benefits areas. Co. provides its customers with insurance contracts, as well as other targeted, customized risk management products and services. Co. is compensated for its services primarily by commissions paid by insurance companies and by fees paid by customers for certain services. As of Dec 31 2007, Co.'s activities were conducted in about 198 locations in 38 states that included Florida, New York, New Jersey, Texas, California, Georgia, Colorado, Illinois, and Virginia.

Recent Developments: For the year ended Dec 31 2007, net income increased 10.8% to US$191.0 million from US$172.4 million in the prior year. Revenues were US$959.7 million, up 9.3% from US$878.0 million the year before. Net investment income rose 165.7% to US$30.5 million from US$11.5 million a year ago.

Prospects: Co.'s outlook appears constructive, reflecting its recent efforts to expand its core business. For example, from Jan 1 2008 through Feb 28 2008, Co. acquired the assets and assumed certain liabilities of seven insurance intermediaries, two books of business (custom accounts) and the outstanding stock of one general insurance agency. The aggregate purchase price of these acquisitions was $71.1 million. In addition, Co. is planning to expand its operations in the U.K., while intending to continue to consider other international expansion opportunities. Meanwhile, for the first half of 2008, Co. is expecting continued competitive insurance pricing in the western U.S., mainly in Florida.

Financial Data
(US$ in Thousands)

	12/31/2007	12/31/2006	12/31/2005	12/31/2004	12/31/2003	12/31/2002	12/31/2001	12/31/2000
Earnings Per Share	1.35	1.22	1.08	0.93	0.80	0.61	0.42	0.29
Cash Flow Per Share	1.53	1.61	1.55	1.23	1.04	0.69	0.56	0.38
Tang Book Value Per Share	N.M.	N.M.	N.M.	N.M.	0.20	0.08	N.M.	0.17
Dividends Per Share	0.250	0.210	0.170	0.145	0.121	0.100	0.080	0.068
Dividend Payout %	18.52	17.21	15.74	15.59	15.16	16.39	18.82	23.28
Income Statement								
Total Revenue	959,667	878,004	785,807	646,934	551,040	455,742	365,029	209,706
Income Before Taxes	311,527	280,041	244,130	206,949	176,482	134,664	90,478	53,978
Income Taxes	120,568	107,691	93,579	78,106	66,160	49,271	34,834	20,792
Net Income	190,959	172,350	150,551	128,843	110,322	83,122	53,913	33,186
Average Shares	141,257	141,020	139,776	138,888	137,794	136,086	126,444	114,652
Balance Sheet								
Total Assets	1,960,659	1,807,952	1,608,660	1,249,517	865,854	754,349	488,737	276,719
Total Liabilities	863,201	878,607	844,316	625,192	367,819	362,759	313,452	154,808
Stockholders' Equity	1,097,458	929,345	764,344	624,325	498,035	391,590	175,285	121,911
Shares Outstanding	140,673	140,016	139,383	138,318	137,122	136,356	126,388	114,796
Statistical Record								
Return on Assets %	10.13	10.09	10.53	12.15	13.62	13.37	14.09	12.93
Return on Equity %	18.84	20.35	21.68	22.90	24.80	29.33	36.28	29.43
Price Range	28.96-23.10	35.23-27.42	31.24-21.30	23.30-16.04	18.72-13.65	18.07-12.37	15.40-7.72	8.86-3.91
P/E Ratio	21.45-17.11	28.88-22.48	28.93-19.72	25.05-17.25	23.40-17.06	29.61-20.28	36.68-18.39	30.55-13.47
Average Yield %	0.95	0.69	0.71	0.72	0.76	0.63	0.71	1.09

Address: 220 South Ridgewood Avenue, Daytona Beach, FL 32114 **Telephone:** 368-252-9601	**Web Site:** www.bbinsurance.com **Officers:** J. Hyatt Brown - Chmn., C.E.O. Jim W. Henderson - Pres., C.O.O., Asst. Treas.	**Auditors:** Deloitte & Touche LLP **Transfer Agents:** Wachovia Bank N.A., Charlotte, NC

BROWN-FORMAN CORP.

Exchange	Symbol	Price	52Wk Range	Yield	P/E	Div Acheiver
NYS	BF B	$66.22 (3/31/2008)	75.58-62.18	2.05	20.13	23 Years

*7 Year Price Score 107.30 *NYSE Composite Index=100 *12 Month Price Score 101.87

Interim Earnings (Per Share)
Qtr.	Jul	Oct	Jan	Apr
2004-05	0.42	0.84	0.78	0.47
2005-06	0.10	0.88	0.98	0.64
2006-07	0.76	1.00	0.85	0.54
2007-08	0.77	1.04	0.94	...

Interim Dividends (Per Share)
Amt	Decl	Ex	Rec	Pay
0.302Q	5/24/2007	6/4/2007	6/6/2007	7/1/2007
0.302Q	7/26/2007	8/30/2007	9/4/2007	10/1/2007
0.34Q	11/15/2007	12/3/2007	12/5/2007	1/1/2008
0.34Q	1/22/2008	3/3/2008	3/5/2008	4/1/2008

Indicated Div: $1.36

Valuation Analysis Institutional Holding
Forecast P/E	16.95	No. of Institutions
	(1/10/2007)	242
Market Cap	$8.1 Billion	Shares
Book Value	1.7 Billion	53,229,460
Price/Book	4.77	% Held
Price/Sales	3.20	80.33

Business Summary: Food (MIC: 4.1 SIC: 2084 NAIC: 312130)

Brown-Forman primarily manufactures, bottles, imports, exports and markets a variety of alcoholic beverage brands. Co. also manufactures and markets new and used oak barrels. As of Apr 30 2007, Co.'s primary beverage brands included, but not limited to, Jack Daniel's, Southern Comfort, Finlandia, Gentleman Jack, Amarula, Appleton Estate, Canadian Mist, Bel Arbor, Bonterra, Chambord, Don Eduardo, Fetzer, Bolla and Korbel. In the U.S., Co. sells spirits and wines either via wholesale distributors or directly to state governments in those states that control alcohol sales. Internationally, Co.'s key export markets are the U.K., Germany, Spain, Australia, France, South Africa, Canada and Japan.

Recent Developments: For the quarter ended Jan 31 2008, income from continuing operations increased 3.9% to US$115.9 million from US$111.6 million in the year-earlier quarter. Net income increased 10.4% to US$116.0 million from US$105.1 million in the year-earlier quarter. Revenues were US$672.4 million, up 15.5% from US$582.1 million the year before. Operating income was US$181.6 million versus US$168.8 million in the prior-year quarter, an increase of 7.6%. Direct operating expenses rose 23.1% to US$239.8 million from US$194.8 million in the comparable period the year before. Indirect operating expenses increased 14.9% to US$251.0 million from US$218.5 million in the equivalent prior-year period.

Prospects: Co. is benefiting from the January 2007 acquisition of Casa Herradura brands, favorable foreign exchange volatility, higher global consumer demand for Jack Daniel's Tennessee Whiskey and Finlandia Vodka, better demand for Gentleman Jack in the U.S., as well as continued growth for the Jack Daniel's & Cola ready-to-drink in Australia. However, these positive developments are being partially offset by softness for Southern Comfort and higher raw material costs. Meanwhile, for the fiscal year ending Apr 30 2008, Co. now anticipates earnings to range from $3.42 to $3.50 per diluted share, representing expected growth of 9.0% to 11.0% over its prior fiscal year's earnings of $3.14 per share.

Financial Data
(US$ in Thousands)	9 Mos	6 Mos	3 Mos	04/30/2007	04/30/2006	04/30/2005	04/30/2004	04/30/2003
Earnings Per Share	3.29	3.19	3.15	3.14	2.60	2.52	2.11	1.81
Cash Flow Per Share	3.86	3.62	3.30	2.89	2.83	3.25	2.51	1.80
Tang Book Value Per Share	2.56	2.98	1.96	1.78	8.52	5.69	4.30	2.43
Dividends Per Share	2.901	2.863	2.841	2.818	1.050	0.915	0.800	0.725
Dividend Payout %	88.22	89.65	90.07	89.87	40.45	36.31	37.91	39.94
Income Statement								
Total Revenue	1,975,100	1,302,700	587,100	2,218,000	1,976,000	2,312,000	2,213,000	2,060,000
EBITDA	588,100	393,800	168,200	646,000	607,000	548,000	463,000	433,000
Depn & Amortn	38,400	25,700	12,800	...	...	...	...	...
Income Before Taxes	517,200	344,700	144,300	586,000	559,000	476,000	388,000	373,000
Income Taxes	176,500	119,900	48,900	186,000	164,000	168,000	130,000	128,000
Net Income	340,700	224,600	95,300	389,000	320,000	308,000	258,000	245,000
Average Shares	123,974	124,534	124,434	124,201	121,986	122,507	121,986	135,126
Balance Sheet								
Current Assets	1,443,900	1,595,200	1,415,400	1,635,000	1,610,000	1,317,000	1,083,000	1,068,000
Total Assets	3,391,600	3,546,300	3,342,200	3,551,000	2,728,000	2,624,000	2,376,000	2,264,000
Current Liabilities	1,007,600	1,123,100	1,075,500	1,347,000	569,000	638,000	369,000	548,000
Long-Term Obligations	417,300	418,200	421,400	422,000	351,000	352,000	630,000	629,000
Total Liabilities	1,697,000	1,796,300	1,735,300	1,978,000	1,165,000	1,314,000	1,291,000	1,424,000
Stockholders' Equity	1,694,600	1,750,000	1,606,900	1,573,000	1,563,000	1,310,000	1,085,000	840,000
Shares Outstanding	122,043	123,427	123,493	123,237	122,465	121,888	121,588	121,134
Statistical Record								
Return on Assets %	11.43	12.24	12.81	12.39	11.96	12.32	11.09	11.45
Return on Equity %	23.37	22.64	24.25	24.81	22.28	25.72	26.73	22.78
EBITDA Margin %	29.78	30.23	28.65	29.13	30.72	23.70	20.92	21.02
Net Margin %	17.25	17.24	16.23	17.54	16.19	13.32	11.66	11.89
Asset Turnover	0.71	0.75	0.76	0.71	0.74	0.92	0.95	0.96
Current Ratio	1.43	1.42	1.32	1.21	2.83	2.06	2.93	1.95
Debt to Equity	0.25	0.24	0.26	0.27	0.22	0.27	0.58	0.75
Price Range	75.58-62.18	75.58-63.54	77.60-63.54	77.60-63.54	81.91-55.10	55.96-43.50	49.95-37.77	40.02-29.66
P/E Ratio	22.97-18.90	23.69-19.92	24.63-20.17	24.71-20.24	31.50-21.19	22.21-17.26	23.67-17.90	22.11-16.38
Average Yield %	4.18	4.16	4.10	4.01	1.62	1.89	1.85	2.04

Address: 850 Dixie Highway,	Web Site: www.brown-forman.com	Auditors: PricewaterhouseCoopers LLP
Louisville, KY 40210	Officers: Owsley Brown II - Chmn. Michael B.	Transfer Agents: National City Bank,
Telephone: 502-585-1100	Crutcher - Vice-Chmn., Sec., Gen. Couns.	Cleveland, OH
Fax: 502-774-7876		

BRUNSWICK CORP.

Exchange	Symbol	Price	52Wk Range	Yield	P/E
NYS	BC	$15.97 (3/31/2008)	34.80-14.87	3.76	12.88

*7 Year Price Score 63.47 *NYSE Composite Index=100 *12 Month Price Score 75.88

Interim Earnings (Per Share)

Qtr.	Mar	Jun	Sep	Dec
2003	0.04	0.59	0.41	0.42
2004	0.50	0.93	0.75	0.59
2005	0.96	1.15	0.89	0.90
2006	0.70	0.87	0.39	(0.55)
2007	0.50	0.63	0.02	0.08

Interim Dividends (Per Share)

Amt	Decl	Ex	Rec	Pay
0.60A	10/25/2004	11/18/2004	11/22/2004	12/15/2004
0.60A	10/26/2005	11/18/2005	11/22/2005	12/15/2005
0.60A	10/25/2006	11/22/2006	11/27/2006	12/15/2006
0.60A	10/24/2007	11/19/2007	11/21/2007	12/14/2007

Indicated Div: $0.60

Valuation Analysis

		Institutional Holding	
Forecast P/E	14.64	No of Institutions	
	(1/10/2007)	243	
Market Cap	$1.4 Billion	Shares	
Book Value	1.9 Billion	78,847,456	
Price/Book	0.74	% Held	
Price/Sales	0.25	86.91	

TRADING VOLUME (thousand shares)

Business Summary: Industrial Machinery and Equipment (MIC: 11.5 SIC: 3519 NAIC: 336612)

Brunswick is a global manufacturer and marketer of recreation products including boats, marine engines, fitness equipment and bowling and billiards equipment. As of Dec 31 2007, Co.'s products included fiberglass pleasure boats, luxury sportfishing convertibles and motoryachts, offshore fishing boats, marine parts and accessories; outboard, sterndrive and inboard engines, trolling motors, engine control systems; cardiovascular and strength training equipment, bowling equipment, billiards tables and accessories, Air Hockey tables and foosball tables. Co. also owns and operates Brunswick bowling centers in the U.S. and other countries, and retail billiards stores in the U.S.

Recent Developments: For the year ended Dec 31 2007, income from continuing operations decreased 69.8% to US$79.6 million from US$263.2 million a year earlier. Net income decreased 16.7% to US$111.6 million from US$133.9 million in the prior year. Revenues were US$5.67 billion, unchanged from the year before. Operating income was US$107.2 million versus US$341.2 million in the prior year, a decrease of 68.6%. Direct operating expenses rose 2.0% to US$4.53 billion from US$4.44 billion in the comparable period the year before. Indirect operating expenses increased 17.1% to US$1.04 billion from US$884.5 million in the equivalent prior-year period.

Prospects: For 2008, Co. expects lower domestic marine retail demand over 2007. Hence, Co. will focus on achieving appropriate levels of dealer inventories by reducing production of boats and marine engines. As a result, Co. expects its operating earnings and margins to be adversely affected by the reduction in marine retail demand and production declines. However, Co. expects sales to benefit from the introduction of new products and the continued growth of sales outside the U.S. Also, Co. expects sales in both the Fitness and Bowling and Billiards segments to increase due to new product launches at the Fitness segment and the continued roll-out of the Brunswick Zone XL model at Bowling and Billiards.

Financial Data

(US$ in Thousands)	12/31/2007	12/31/2006	12/31/2005	12/31/2004	12/31/2003	12/31/2002	12/31/2001	12/31/2000
Earnings Per Share	1.24	1.41	3.90	2.77	1.47	0.86	0.93	(1.08)
Cash Flow Per Share	3.50	3.35	4.44	4.33	4.33	4.59	3.77	2.89
Tang Book Value Per Share	11.07	9.75	9.99	7.84	6.77	5.90	5.78	6.40
Dividends Per Share	0.600	0.600	0.600	0.600	0.500	0.500	0.500	0.500
Dividend Payout %	48.39	42.55	15.38	21.66	34.01	58.14	53.76	...
Income Statement								
Total Revenue	5,671,200	5,665,000	5,923,800	5,229,300	4,128,700	3,711,900	3,370,800	3,811,900
EBITDA	316,400	521,500	696,200	581,200	392,700	353,300	345,500	539,700
Income Before Taxes	92,700	309,700	495,800	378,500	201,100	161,600	132,200	323,300
Income Taxes	13,100	46,500	110,400	108,700	65,900	58,100	47,500	121,100
Net Income	111,600	133,900	385,400	269,800	135,200	78,400	81,800	(95,800)
Average Shares	90,200	94,700	98,800	97,300	91,900	90,700	88,100	88,700
Balance Sheet								
Current Assets	2,114,300	2,078,400	2,235,000	2,098,700	1,715,200	1,660,200	1,400,900	1,831,800
Total Assets	4,365,600	4,450,300	4,621,500	4,346,400	3,602,500	3,407,100	3,157,500	3,396,500
Current Liabilities	1,296,200	1,293,200	1,305,200	1,253,800	1,101,800	1,005,600	902,700	1,247,900
Long-Term Obligations	727,400	725,700	723,700	728,400	583,800	589,500	600,200	601,800
Total Liabilities	2,472,700	2,578,500	2,642,700	2,634,100	2,279,500	2,305,300	2,046,600	2,329,400
Stockholders' Equity	1,892,900	1,871,800	1,978,800	1,712,300	1,323,000	1,101,800	1,110,900	1,067,100
Shares Outstanding	87,446	90,867	95,657	96,829	92,130	90,161	87,799	87,344
Statistical Record								
Return on Assets %	2.53	2.95	8.60	6.77	3.86	2.39	2.50	N.M.
Return on Equity %	5.93	6.95	20.88	17.73	11.15	7.09	7.51	N.M.
EBITDA Margin %	5.58	9.21	11.75	11.11	9.51	9.52	10.25	14.16
Net Margin %	1.97	2.36	6.51	5.16	3.27	2.11	2.43	N.M.
Asset Turnover	1.29	1.25	1.32	1.31	1.18	1.13	1.03	1.13
Current Ratio	1.63	1.61	1.71	1.67	1.56	1.65	1.55	1.47
Debt to Equity	0.38	0.39	0.37	0.43	0.44	0.54	0.54	0.56
Price Range	34.80-17.05	42.30-27.56	49.50-35.09	49.81-31.43	31.96-17.50	29.70-18.72	24.75-15.00	22.25-14.75
P/E Ratio	28.06-13.75	30.00-19.55	12.69-9.00	17.98-11.35	21.74-11.90	34.53-21.77	26.61-16.13	...
Average Yield %	2.13	1.74	1.39	1.46	2.05	2.08	2.43	2.70

Address: 1 North Field Court, Lake Forest, IL 60045-4811 **Telephone:** 847-735-4700 **Fax:** 847-735-4765	**Web Site:** www.brunswick.com **Officers:** George W. Buckley - Chmn., C.E.O. Peter B. Hamilton - Vice-Chmn.	**Auditors:** Ernst & Young LLP **Investor Contact:** 847-735-4204 **Transfer Agents:** Brunswick Shareholder Services, Lake Forest, IL

131

BUCKEYE PARTNERS, L.P.

Exchange	Symbol	Price	52Wk Range	Yield	P/E	Div Acheiver
NYS	BPL	$46.10 (3/31/2008)	55.49-44.29	7.27	15.21	12 Years

*7 Year Price Score 95.72   *NYSE Composite Index=100   *12 Month Price Score 102.51

Interim Earnings (Per Share)

Qtr.	Mar	Jun	Sep	Dec
2003	0.60	0.61	(0.89)	0.76
2004	0.69	0.69	0.71	0.66
2005	0.66	0.66	0.65	0.72
2006	0.59	0.61	0.69	0.75
2007	0.77	0.70	0.71	0.85

Interim Dividends (Per Share)

Amt	Decl	Ex	Rec	Pay
0.80Q	4/26/2007	5/3/2007	5/7/2007	5/31/2007
0.813Q	7/26/2007	8/2/2007	8/6/2007	8/31/2007
0.825Q	10/25/2007	11/1/2007	11/5/2007	11/30/2007
0.838Q	1/24/2008	2/1/2008	2/5/2008	2/29/2008

Indicated Div: $3.35

Valuation Analysis / Institutional Holding

Forecast P/E	N/A	No of Institutions
		147
Market Cap	$2.1 Billion	Shares
Book Value	N/A	7,434,932
Price/Book	N/A	% Held
Price/Sales	4.08	18.15

TRADING VOLUME (thousand shares)

Business Summary: Oil and Gas (MIC: 14.2 SIC: 4613 NAIC: 486910)

Buckeye Partners is primarily engaged in the transportation, terminalling and storage of refined petroleum products for key integrated oil companies, large refined products marketing companies and key end-users of petroleum products on a fee basis through facilities owned and operated by Co. Co. also operates pipelines owned by third parties under contracts with integrated oil and chemical companies and performs pipeline construction activities. As of Dec 31 2007, Co.'s facilities included approximately 5,400 miles of 6-inch to 24-inch diameter pipeline, 100 delivery points and 51 active bulk storage and terminal facilities with aggregate capacity of approximately 20.0 million barrels.

Recent Developments: For the year ended Dec 31 2007, net income increased 40.9% to US$155.4 million from US$110.2 million in the prior year. Revenues were US$519.3 million, up 12.5% from US$461.8 million the year before. Operating income was US$202.1 million versus US$177.1 million in the prior year, an increase of 14.1%. Direct operating expenses rose 13.2% to US$250.7 million from US$221.4 million in the comparable period the year before. Indirect operating expenses increased 5.2% to US$66.5 million from US$63.3 million in the equivalent prior-year period.

Prospects: On Jan 18 2008, Co. acquired Lodi Gas Storage, LLC, which owns two natural gas storage facilities located in northern California, including a facility known as Kirby Hills, for about $432.0 million. Accordingly, Co. expects to receive approval for the Kirby Hills Phase II expansion project in the first quarter of 2008. The expansion project, which is expected to be in service by the end of 2008, will provide an approximate incremental 12 billion cubic feet of working gas capacity. Meanwhile, on Feb 8 2008, Co. acquired Farm & Home Oil Company LLC, a regional distributor of refined petroleum products in eastern and central Pennsylvania and surrounding areas, for about $145.5 million.

Financial Data
(US$ in Thousands)

	12/31/2007	12/31/2006	12/31/2005	12/31/2004	12/31/2003	12/31/2002	12/31/2001	12/31/2000
Earnings Per Share	3.03	2.64	2.69	2.75	1.05	2.64	2.55	3.55
Cash Flow Per Share	4.70	3.80	3.84	3.30	3.81	3.43	2.99	2.87
Dividends Per Share	3.225	3.025	2.825	2.638	2.538	2.500	2.450	2.400
Dividend Payout %	106.44	114.58	105.02	95.91	241.67	94.70	96.08	67.61
Income Statement								
Net Income	155,356	110,240	99,958	82,962	30,154	71,902	69,402	96,331
Average Shares	42,101	39,202	37,145	30,151	28,748	27,228	27,193	27,138
Balance Sheet								
Total Assets	2,133,652	1,995,470	1,816,867	1,534,119	940,046	856,171	807,560	712,812
Total Liabilities	1,043,480	1,185,588	1,058,290	928,696	562,634	498,739	454,664	363,430
Shares Outstanding	45,962	39,697	38,162	34,525	28,966	27,182	27,164	27,090
Statistical Record								
Return on Assets %	7.52	5.78	5.97	6.69	3.36	8.64	9.13	13.85
Price Range	55.49-46.00	46.78-40.71	50.21-41.92	45.65-35.82	45.40-34.20	39.97-30.34	37.90-28.63	31.50-25.25
P/E Ratio	18.31-15.18	17.72-15.42	18.67-15.58	16.60-13.03	43.24-32.57	15.14-11.49	14.86-11.23	8.87-7.11
Average Yield %	6.35	6.94	6.22	6.34	6.47	6.79	7.09	8.74

Address: 5002 Buckeye Road, Emmaus, PA 18049 **Telephone:** 484-232-4000	**Web Site:** www.buckeye.com **Officers:** William H. Shea Jr. - Chmn., Pres., C.E.O. David J. Martinelli - Sr. V.P., Treas., Corp. Devel.	**Auditors:** Deloitte & Touche LLP **Investor Contact:** 800-422-2825

BURGER KING HOLDINGS INC

Exchange	Symbol	Price	52Wk Range	Yield	P/E
NYS	BKC	$27.66 (3/31/2008)	29.14-21.82	N/A	22.67

*7 Year Price Score N/A   *NYSE Composite Index=100   *12 Month Price Score 111.85

TRADING VOLUME (thousand shares)

Interim Earnings (Per Share)

Qtr.	Sep	Dec	Mar	Jun
2005-06	0.19	0.24	(0.11)	(0.09)
2006-07	0.30	0.28	0.25	0.26
2007-08	0.35	0.36	...	...

Interim Dividends (Per Share)

No Dividends Paid

Valuation Analysis

		Institutional Holding	
Forecast P/E	N/A	No. of Institutions	80
Market Cap	$3.7 Billion	Shares	
Book Value	789.0 Million		90,446,032
Price/Book	4.71	% Held	
Price/Sales	1.59		67.27

Business Summary: Hospitality & Tourism (MIC: 5.1 SIC: 5812 NAIC: 722211)

Burger King Holdings is the parent of Burger King Corporation, a corporation which franchises and operates fast food hamburger restaurants, under the Burger King® brand. As of Jun 30 2007, Co. owned or franchised a total of 11,283 restaurants in 69 countries and U.S. territories, of which 1,303 restaurants were company-owned and 9,980 were owned by Co.'s franchisees. Of these restaurants, 7,171 were located in the U.S. and 4,112 were located in Co.'s international markets. Co. operates in the fast food hamburger restaurant category of the restaurant industry. Co.'s restaurants feature flame-broiled hamburgers, chicken and other sandwiches, french fries, soft drinks and other food items.

Recent Developments: For the quarter ended Dec 31 2007, net income increased 28.9% to US$49.0 million from US$38.0 million in the year-earlier quarter. Revenues were US$613.0 million, up 9.7% from US$559.0 million the year before. Operating income was US$95.0 million versus US$75.0 million in the prior-year quarter, an increase of 26.7%. Direct operating expenses rose 7.7% to US$378.0 million from US$351.0 million in the comparable period the year before. Indirect operating expenses increased 5.3% to US$140.0 million from US$133.0 million in the equivalent prior-year period.

Prospects: For the fiscal year ending June 30 2008, Co. now anticipates earnings per share growth to be in excess of 15.0%. Going forward, Co. believes that continued improvement in the average restaurant sales of existing restaurants and strong sales at new restaurants, along with the closure of under-performing restaurants, will result in stronger operators throughout its system. Thus, Co. expects restaurant closures to continue to decline and restaurant openings to accelerate in most regions. Accordingly, Co. plans to expand its international platform, accelerate new restaurant development, focus on restaurant restructurings as well as implement marketing strategies and expand product offerings.

Financial Data

(US$ in Thousands)	6 Mos	3 Mos	06/30/2007	06/30/2006	06/30/2005	06/30/2004	06/30/2003
Earnings Per Share	1.22	1.14	1.08	0.24	0.44	0.05	0.23
Cash Flow Per Share	1.76	1.52	0.87	0.67	2.05	1.87	
Dividends Per Share	0.250	...	0.130	...	...	...	...
Dividend Payout %	20.49	...	12.04	...	...	...	...
Income Statement							
Total Revenue	1,215,000	602,000	2,234,000	2,048,000	1,940,000	1,754,000	906,000
EBITDA	235,000	117,000	379,000	241,000	225,000	136,000	118,000
Depn & Amortn	44,000	21,000	...	...	...	...	...
Income Before Taxes	159,000	80,000	223,000	80,000	78,000	9,000	40,000
Income Taxes	61,000	31,000	75,000	53,000	31,000	4,000	16,000
Net Income	98,000	49,000	148,000	27,000	47,000	5,000	24,000
Average Shares	137,912	137,700	136,800	114,690	106,910	106,061	104,692
Balance Sheet							
Current Assets	418,000	391,000	404,000	453,000	634,000	587,000	...
Total Assets	2,572,000	2,530,000	2,517,000	2,552,000	2,723,000	2,665,000	...
Current Liabilities	430,000	410,000	434,000	492,000	394,000	355,000	...
Long-Term Obligations	892,000	915,000	938,000	1,060,000	1,335,000	1,290,000	...
Total Liabilities	1,783,000	1,783,000	1,801,000	1,985,000	2,246,000	2,241,000	...
Stockholders' Equity	789,000	747,000	716,000	567,000	477,000	424,000	...
Shares Outstanding	134,439	135,162	135,217	133,058	106,734	106,349	...
Statistical Record							
Return on Assets %	6.72	6.35	5.84	1.02	1.74	...	...
Return on Equity %	23.55	23.33	23.07	5.17	10.43	...	...
EBITDA Margin %	19.34	19.44	16.97	11.77	11.60	7.75	13.02
Net Margin %	8.07	8.14	6.62	1.32	2.42	0.29	2.65
Asset Turnover	0.94	0.93	0.88	0.78	0.72	...	...
Current Ratio	0.97	0.95	0.93	0.92	1.61	1.65	...
Debt to Equity	1.13	1.22	1.31	1.87	2.80	3.04	...
Price Range	29.14-19.97	26.89-15.62	26.79-12.90	18.99-15.75	...	...	...
P/E Ratio	23.89-16.37	23.59-13.70	24.81-11.94	79.13-65.63	...	...	...
Average Yield %	0.25	0.27	0.66	...	...	...	...

Address: 5505 Blue Lagoon Drive, Miami, FL 33126
Telephone: 305-378-3000

Web Site: www.bk.com
Officers: Albert A. Magdall - Chmn.; James R. Shiring - Pres. & C.E.O.

Auditors: KPMG LLP
Investor Contact: 305-378-7696
Transfer Agents: The Bank of New York, New York, NY

BURLINGTON NORTHERN SANTA FE CORP.

Exchange	Symbol	Price	52Wk Range	Yield	P/E
NYS	BNI	$92.22 (3/31/2008)	95.34-76.27	1.39	18.08

*7 Year Price Score 138.14 *NYSE Composite Index=100 *12 Month Price Score 112.73

Interim Earnings (Per Share)

Qtr.	Mar	Jun	Sep	Dec
2003	0.50	0.54	0.55	0.61
2004	0.52	0.67	0.01	0.91
2005	0.83	0.96	1.09	1.13
2006	1.09	1.27	1.33	1.42
2007	0.96	1.20	1.48	1.46

Interim Dividends (Per Share)

Amt	Decl	Ex	Rec	Pay
0.25Q	4/19/2007	6/7/2007	6/11/2007	7/2/2007
0.32Q	7/19/2007	9/6/2007	9/10/2007	10/1/2007
0.32Q	10/18/2007	12/10/2007	12/12/2007	1/2/2008
0.32Q	2/13/2008	3/7/2008	3/11/2008	4/1/2008

Indicated Div: $1.28

Valuation Analysis   **Institutional Holding**

Forecast P/E	11.41	No of Institutions
	(1/10/2007)	618
Market Cap	$32.1 Billion	Shares
Book Value	11.1 Billion	270,614,880
Price/Book	2.88	% Held
Price/Sales	2.03	75.39

Business Summary: Rail Transport (MIC: 15.5 SIC: 4011 NAIC: 482111)

Burlington Northern Santa Fe is a holding company. Through its subsidiaries, Co. is primarily engaged in the freight rail transportation business from manufacturing, agricultural and natural resource industries. Co.'s freight business consists of consumer product international intermodal, domestic intermodal and automotive, while its industrial products consist of building products, construction products, petroleum products, chemicals and plastics products, and food and beverages. Co.'s agricultural products' freight business transports agricultural products, such as corn, wheat, soybeans, bulk foods and fertilizer.

Recent Developments: For the year ended Dec 31 2007, net income decreased 3.2% to US$1.83 billion from US$1.89 billion in the prior year. Revenues were US$15.80 billion, up 5.5% from US$14.99 billion the year before. Operating income was US$3.49 billion versus US$3.52 billion in the prior year, a decrease of 1.0%. Direct operating expenses rose 12.0% to US$7.25 billion from US$6.47 billion in the comparable period the year before. Indirect operating expenses increased 1.5% to US$5.07 billion from US$4.99 billion in the equivalent prior-year period.

Prospects: For 2008, Co. is expecting revenue growth in the high single digits on about flat unit volumes. Concurrently, Co. anticipates low double-digit growth in earnings per share, reflecting the expected revenue growth along with its ongoing focus on productivity. Meanwhile, on Feb 1 2008, Co. announced that it has acquired Diversified Freight Logistics, Inc. and Royal Cargo Line (together know as DFL), of Grapevine, TX. Co. noted that DFL, which is a global freight management company, will now operate as a division of its BNSF Logistics, an indirect, wholly-owned non-rail subsidiary, known as BNSF Logistics International that will provide air and ocean import and export and customs brokerage.

Financial Data

(US$ in Thousands)	12/31/2007	12/31/2006	12/31/2005	12/31/2004	12/31/2003	12/31/2002	12/31/2001	12/31/2000
Earnings Per Share	5.10	5.10	4.01	2.10	2.19	2.00	1.87	2.36
Cash Flow Per Share	9.91	8.61	7.02	6.41	6.19	5.57	5.67	5.61
Tang Book Value Per Share	32.05	29.05	25.59	24.71	22.87	21.11	20.35	19.10
Dividends Per Share	1.140	0.900	0.740	0.640	0.540	0.480	0.490	0.480
Dividend Payout %	22.35	17.65	18.45	30.48	24.66	24.00	26.20	20.34
Income Statement								
Total Revenue	15,802,000	14,985,000	12,987,000	10,946,000	9,413,000	8,979,000	9,208,000	9,205,000
EBITDA	4,761,000	4,607,000	3,960,000	2,694,000	2,561,000	2,575,000	2,554,000	2,933,000
Income Before Taxes	2,957,000	2,992,000	2,448,000	1,273,000	1,231,000	1,216,000	1,182,000	1,585,000
Income Taxes	1,128,000	1,105,000	917,000	482,000	454,000	456,000	445,000	605,000
Net Income	1,829,000	1,887,000	1,531,000	791,000	816,000	760,000	731,000	980,000
Average Shares	358,900	369,800	381,800	376,600	372,300	380,800	390,700	415,200
Balance Sheet								
Total Assets	33,583,000	31,643,000	30,304,000	28,925,000	26,939,000	25,767,000	24,721,000	24,375,000
Long-Term Obligations	7,735,000	6,912,000	6,698,000	6,051,000	6,440,000	6,641,000	6,363,000	6,614,000
Total Liabilities	22,439,000	21,247,000	20,796,000	19,614,000	18,444,000	17,835,000	16,872,000	16,895,000
Stockholders' Equity	11,144,000	10,396,000	9,508,000	9,311,000	8,495,000	7,932,000	7,849,000	7,480,000
Shares Outstanding	347,704	357,875	371,571	376,812	371,460	375,778	385,777	391,592
Statistical Record								
Return on Assets %	5.61	6.09	5.17	2.82	3.10	3.01	2.98	4.07
Return on Equity %	16.98	18.96	16.27	8.86	9.93	9.63	9.54	12.49
EBITDA Margin %	30.13	30.74	30.49	24.61	27.21	28.68	27.74	31.86
Net Margin %	11.57	12.59	11.79	7.23	8.67	8.46	7.94	10.65
Asset Turnover	0.48	0.48	0.44	0.39	0.36	0.36	0.38	0.38
Price Range	94.76-72.36	86.84-64.12	70.97-44.65	48.67-30.06	32.44-23.62	31.30-23.78	33.80-23.45	29.13-19.25
P/E Ratio	18.58-14.19	17.03-12.57	17.70-11.13	23.18-14.31	14.81-10.79	15.65-11.89	18.07-12.54	12.34-8.16
Average Yield %	1.36	1.19	1.37	1.77	1.93	1.73	1.70	2.02

Address: 2650 Lou Menk Drive, Fort Worth, TX 76131-2830 **Telephone:** 800-795-2673	**Web Site:** www.bnsf.com **Officers:** Matthew K. Rose - Chmn., Pres., C.E.O. Thomas N. Hund - Exec. V.P., C.F.O.	**Auditors:** PricewaterhouseCoopers LLP **Investor Contact:** 817-352-6452 **Transfer Agents:** EquiServe Trust Company, N.A., Jersey City, NJ

CA INC

Exchange	Symbol	Price	52Wk Range	Yield	P/E
NYS	CA	$22.50 (3/31/2008)	28.21-21.26	0.71	28.85

*7 Year Price Score 82.18   *NYSE Composite Index=100   *12 Month Price Score 100.52

Interim Earnings (Per Share)

Qtr.	Jun	Sep	Dec	Mar
2004-05	0.09	(0.16)	0.06	0.03
2005-06	0.15	0.07	0.10	(0.05)
2006-07	0.06	0.09	0.09	(0.03)
2007-08	0.24	0.26	0.31	...

Interim Dividends (Per Share)

Amt	Decl	Ex	Rec	Pay
0.04Q	6/12/2007	6/20/2007	6/22/2007	6/29/2007
0.04Q	8/22/2007	9/10/2007	9/12/2007	9/26/2007
0.04Q	11/29/2007	12/12/2007	12/14/2007	12/28/2007
0.04Q	2/26/2008	3/12/2008	3/14/2008	3/28/2008

Indicated Div. $0.10

Valuation Analysis

		Institutional Holding	
Forecast P/E	21.58	No of Institutions	
	(1/10/2007)	260	
Market Cap	$11.5 Billion	Shares	
Book Value	3.7 Billion	382,223,872	
Price/Book	3.11	% Held	
Price/Sales	2.73	72.48	

TRADING VOLUME (thousand shares)

Business Summary: IT & Technology (MIC: 10.2 SIC: 7372 NAIC: 511210)

CA is engaged in the business of developing, marketing, delivering and licensing of software products and services. Co. is considered an Independent Software Vendor (ISV). ISVs develop and license software products that can increase the capability of computer hardware platforms or operating systems sold by other vendors. Co.'s software helps its customers manage all of the people, processes, computers, networks and the range of technologies that make up their IT infrastructure. Co. has a portfolio of software products and services that span the areas of infrastructure management, security management, storage management and business service optimization.

Recent Developments: For the quarter ended Dec 31 2007, income from continuing operations increased 213.5% to US$163.0 million from US$52.0 million in the year-earlier quarter. Net income increased 226.0% to US$163.0 million from US$50.0 million in the year-earlier quarter. Revenues were US$1.10 billion, up 9.8% from US$1.00 billion the year before. Operating income was US$249.0 million versus US$95.0 million in the prior-year quarter, an increase of 162.1%. Direct operating expenses rose 6.4% to US$150.0 million from US$141.0 million in the comparable period the year before. Indirect operating expenses decreased 8.5% to US$701.0 million from US$766.0 million in the equivalent prior-year period.

Prospects: Co. expects its Nov 2007 agreement with HCL Technologies to establish a strategic partnership, in which HCL will assume all research and product development connected with its threat management security business, to be finalized in the fiscal quarter ending Mar 2008. Meanwhile, Co. projects its full fiscal 2008 total product and services bookings to grow at a percentage in the mid-teens over the prior year. In addition, Co. has increased its fiscal 2008 annual outlook, with total revenue of $4.25 billion to $4.28 billion, versus prior outlook of $4.15 billion to $4.20 billion, and earnings from continuing operations of $0.99 to $1.03 per share, versus prior $0.87 to $0.91 per share.

Financial Data

(US$ in Thousands)	9 Mos	6 Mos	3 Mos	03/31/2007	03/31/2006	03/31/2005	03/31/2004	03/31/2003
Earnings Per Share	0.78	0.56	0.39	0.22	0.27	0.02	0.04	(0.46)
Cash Flow Per Share	1.83	2.52	2.10	1.96	2.38	2.60	2.20	2.28
Dividends Per Share	...	...	...	0.160	0.120	0.080	0.080	0.080
Dividend Payout %	...	...	...	72.73	44.44	400.00	200.00	...
Income Statement								
Total Revenue	3,192,000	2,092,000	1,025,000	3,943,000	3,796,000	3,530,000	3,276,000	3,116,000
EBITDA	908,000	590,000	279,000	808,000	828,000	694,000	660,000	421,000
Depn & Amortn	204,000	135,000	68,000	...	...	...	...	...
Income Before Taxes	667,000	428,000	197,000	154,000	121,000	11,000	(54,000)	(363,000)
Income Taxes	238,000	162,000	68,000	33,000	(35,000)	(2,000)	(18,000)	(96,000)
Net Income	429,000	266,000	129,000	118,000	159,000	11,000	25,000	(267,000)
Average Shares	536,000	537,000	551,000	569,000	607,000	593,000	580,000	575,000
Balance Sheet								
Current Assets	2,867,000	2,567,000	2,668,000	3,101,000	2,648,000	3,954,000	3,358,000	3,565,000
Total Assets	10,144,000	9,922,000	10,067,000	10,585,000	10,438,000	11,082,000	10,679,000	11,054,000
Current Liabilities	3,421,000	3,358,000	3,584,000	3,714,000	3,377,000	3,664,000	2,455,000	2,974,000
Long-Term Obligations	2,216,000	2,218,000	2,220,000	2,572,000	1,810,000	1,810,000	2,298,000	2,298,000
Total Liabilities	6,460,000	6,422,000	6,720,000	6,895,000	5,758,000	6,242,000	5,961,000	6,691,000
Stockholders' Equity	3,684,000	3,500,000	3,347,000	3,690,000	4,680,000	4,840,000	4,718,000	4,363,000
Shares Outstanding	509,616	511,682	511,376	525,176	571,753	586,986	582,594	576,272
Statistical Record								
Return on Assets %	4.04	3.00	2.10	1.12	1.48	0.10	0.23	N.M.
Return on Equity %	11.19	8.35	5.35	2.82	3.34	0.23	0.55	N.M.
EBITDA Margin %	28.45	28.20	27.22	20.49	21.81	19.66	20.15	13.51
Net Margin %	13.44	12.72	12.59	2.99	4.19	0.31	0.76	N.M.
Asset Turnover	0.41	0.42	0.40	0.38	0.35	0.32	0.30	0.27
Current Ratio	0.84	0.76	0.74	0.83	0.78	1.08	1.37	1.20
Debt to Equity	0.60	0.63	0.66	0.70	0.39	0.37	0.49	0.53
Price Range	28.21-23.32	28.21-21.50	28.21-19.10	27.21-19.10	29.45-26.24	31.52-22.61	28.96-13.47	21.80-7.61
P/E Ratio	36.17-29.90	50.38-38.39	72.33-48.97	123.68-86.82	109.07-97.19	N.M.	724.00-336.75	...
Average Yield %	...	...	...	0.68	0.43	0.29	0.34	0.57

Address: One CA Plaza, Islandia, NY 11749	**Web Site:** www.ca.com	**Auditors:** KPMG LLP
Telephone: 631-342-6000	**Officers:** Kenneth D. Cron - Interim C.E.O. Kenneth V. Handal - Exec. V.P., Sec., Gen. Couns.	**Transfer Agents:** Mellon Investor Services, Ridgefield Park, NJ
Fax: 631-342-4854		

CABLEVISION SYSTEMS CORP.

Exchange	Symbol	Price	52Wk Range	Yield	P/E
NYS	CVC	$21.43 (3/31/2008)	38.52-21.20	N/A	28.96

*7 Year Price Score 89.35   *NYSE Composite Index=100   *12 Month Price Score 87.98

Interim Earnings (Per Share)

Qtr.	Mar	Jun	Sep	Dec
2003	(0.50)	0.56	(0.37)	(0.72)
2004	(0.42)	(0.65)	(0.22)	(1.07)
2005	(0.41)	0.77	(0.22)	0.19
2006	(0.21)	0.05	(0.21)	(0.09)
2007	(0.09)	1.08	(0.27)	0.02

Interim Dividends (Per Share)

No Dividends Paid

Valuation Analysis | **Institutional Holding**

Forecast P/E	N/A	No of Institutions
		255
Market Cap	$6.3 Billion	Shares
Book Value	N/A	200,037,840
Price/Book	N/A	% Held
Price/Sales	0.97	68.40

Business Summary: Media (MIC: 13.1 SIC: 4841 NAIC: 515210)

Cablevision Systems is a cable operator in the U.S. that operates cable programming networks, entertainment businesses and telecommunications companies. Through its Rainbow Media Holdings LLC subsidiary, Co. owns interests in and manages national and regional programming networks, the Madison Square Garden sports and entertainment businesses as well as cable television advertising sales companies. Through its Cablevision Lightpath Inc. subsidiary, Co. provides telephone services and Internet access to the business market. As of Dec 31 2007, Co. served approximately 3.1 million cable television subscribers in and around the New York City metropolitan area.

Recent Developments: For the year ended Dec 31 2007, income from continuing operations was US$23.7 million compared with a loss of US$142.0 million a year earlier. Net income amounted to US$218.5 million versus a net loss of US$126.5 million in the prior year. Revenues were US$6.48 billion, up 11.3% from US$5.83 billion the year before. Operating income was US$911.1 million versus US$588.9 million in the prior year, an increase of 54.7%. Indirect operating expenses increased 6.4% to US$5.57 billion from US$5.24 billion in the equivalent prior-year period.

Prospects: Co.'s results are benefiting from solid revenue growth across its segments. Meanwhile, Co. believes that the competition from other providers of high-speed Internet access, including digital subscriber line and fiber-based services offered by local telephone companies such as Verizon and AT&T together with its existing strong penetration in the high-speed data services business, should slow its growth in cable modem penetration in its Telecommunications Services segment from the growth rates it has previously experienced. Looking ahead, Co. seeks to grow its revenues in the Rainbow segment by increasing both the number of operators that carry its services and its viewing subscribers.

Financial Data

(US$ in Thousands)	12/31/2007	12/31/2006	12/31/2005	12/31/2004	12/31/2003	12/31/2002	12/31/2001	12/31/2000
Earnings Per Share	0.74	(0.45)	0.33	(2.36)	(1.04)	0.28	3.71	1.29
Cash Flow Per Share	3.26	3.39	3.28	2.13	1.59	1.33	(1.27)	0.71
Dividends Per Share	...	10.000	...	...	...	...	...	...
Income Statement								
Total Revenue	6,484,481	5,927,462	5,175,911	4,932,864	4,177,148	4,003,407	4,404,546	4,411,048
EBITDA	2,122,051	1,751,663	1,625,957	955,208	1,470,914	768,455	2,908,531	...
Income Before Taxes	102,845	(267,266)	(200,334)	(1,000,698)	(262,749)	(698,663)	1,195,465	...
Income Taxes	79,181	(134,217)	(79,401)	(333,696)	20,367	(137,814)	187,732	...
Net Income	218,456	(126,465)	94,300	(676,092)	(297,239)	90,112	1,007,733	229,253
Average Shares	294,604	283,627	281,936	287,085	285,486	331,959	177,172	173,913
Balance Sheet								
Current Assets	1,744,287	1,667,447	2,130,502	2,374,787	1,061,816	920,315	938,868	788,107
Total Assets	9,140,577	9,844,857	9,844,509	11,393,206	11,189,199	10,488,253	10,216,800	8,273,290
Current Liabilities	2,351,538	2,430,698	2,558,263	2,127,014	1,620,058	1,610,705	1,519,933	4,814,861
Long-Term Obligations	10,785,346	11,764,477	8,953,341	10,368,228	8,374,742	7,676,927	6,977,523	3,856,029
Total Liabilities	14,239,367	15,184,110	12,313,275	14,023,540	13,099,000	10,043,894	9,393,465	8,670,890
Stockholders' Equity	(5,098,790)	(5,339,253)	(2,468,766)	(2,630,334)	(1,989,802)	(1,723,832)	(1,585,906)	(2,529,879)
Shares Outstanding	294,272	292,380	289,428	287,803	286,809	280,134	270,092	174,921
Statistical Record								
Return on Assets %	2.30	N.M.	0.89	N.M.	N.M.	0.87	10.90	2.97
EBITDA Margin %	32.73	29.55	31.41	19.36	35.21	19.20	66.03	...
Net Margin %	3.37	N.M.	1.82	N.M.	N.M.	2.25	22.88	5.20
Asset Turnover	0.68	0.60	0.49	0.44	0.39	0.39	0.48	0.57
Current Ratio	0.74	0.69	0.83	1.12	0.66	0.57	0.62	0.16
Price Range	38.52-23.95	28.58-18.94	32.63-23.00	27.37-16.68	23.45-15.72	48.01-4.95	76.45-33.64	72.79-48.42
P/E Ratio	52.05-32.36	...	98.88-69.70	...	...	171.46-17.68	20.61-9.07	56.42-37.53
Average Yield %	...	41.04	...	...	...	...	...	...

Address: 1111 Stewart Avenue, Bethpage, NY 11714-3581 Telephone: 516-803-2300 Fax: 516-803-2273	Web Site: www.cablevision.com Officers: Charles F. Dolan - Chmn. William J. Bell - Vice-Chmn.	Auditors: KPMG LLP Investor Contact: 516-803-2270 Transfer Agents: Mellon Investor Services

CABOT CORP.

Exchange	Symbol	Price	52Wk Range	Yield	P/E
NYS	CBT	$28.00 (3/31/2008)	49.77-25.86	2.57	16.77

*7 Year Price Score 89.16 *NYSE Composite Index=100 *12 Month Price Score 80.90

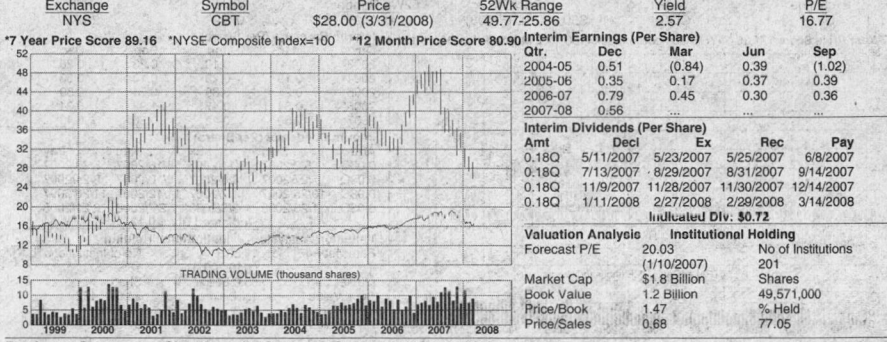

Interim Earnings (Per Share)

Qtr.	Dec	Mar	Jun	Sep
2004-05	0.51	(0.84)	0.39	(1.02)
2005-06	0.35	0.17	0.37	0.39
2006-07	0.79	0.45	0.30	0.36
2007-08	0.56	...	...	...

Interim Dividends (Per Share)

Amt	Decl	Ex	Rec	Pay
0.18Q	5/11/2007	5/23/2007	5/25/2007	6/8/2007
0.18Q	7/13/2007	8/29/2007	8/31/2007	9/14/2007
0.18Q	11/9/2007	11/28/2007	11/30/2007	12/14/2007
0.18Q	1/11/2008	2/27/2008	2/29/2008	3/14/2008

Indicated Div: $0.72

Valuation Analysis

		Institutional Holding	
Forecast P/E	20.03 (1/10/2007)	No of Institutions	201
Market Cap	$1.8 Billion	Shares	49,571,000
Book Value	1.2 Billion	% Held	77.05
Price/Book	1.47		
Price/Sales	0.68		

Business Summary: Chemicals (MIC: 11.1 SIC: 2895 NAIC: 325182)

Cabot is a global specialty chemicals and performance materials company. Co.'s principal products consists of rubber blacks, performance products, inkjet colorants, fumed metal oxides, aerogels, tantalum and related products as well as cesium formate drilling fluids. Co. is organized into four business segments: the Carbon Black Business, the Metal Oxides Business, the Supermetals Business and the Specialty Fluids Business. Co. has manufacturing facilities in the U.S. and more than 20 other countries. Therefore, Co. also manages its businesses on a regional basis and is organized into five business regions: North America, South America, Europe, Asia Pacific and China.

Recent Developments: For the quarter ended Dec 31 2007, income from continuing operations decreased 33.3% to US$36.0 million from US$54.0 million in the year-earlier quarter. Net income decreased 33.3% to US$36.0 million from US$54.0 million in the year-earlier quarter. Revenues were US$711.0 million, up 8.5% from US$655.0 million the year before. Operating income was US$44.0 million versus US$80.0 million in the prior-year quarter, a decrease of 45.0%. Direct operating expenses rose 17.4% to US$594.0 million from US$506.0 million in the comparable period the year before. Indirect operating expenses increased 5.8% to US$73.0 million from US$69.0 million in the equivalent prior-year period.

Prospects: Co.'s near-term outlook appears somewhat mixed. In detail, Co.'s results are being hurt by the escalating carbon black feedstock costs and the expiration of a favorable contract in its Supermetals Business. Going forward, Co. believes that the significant effect from the time lag of the feedstock related pricing adjustments in its supply contracts will continue to restrain its results in the volatile raw material costs environment. Nevertheless, Co. is encouraged by the recent volume growth in key geographic areas and market segments. In addition, Co. is seeing an improvement in consolidated net sales, driven by the positive effects of foreign currency translation on its selling prices.

Financial Data
(US$ in Thousands)

	3 Mos	09/30/2007	09/30/2006	09/30/2005	09/30/2004	09/30/2003	09/30/2002	09/30/2001
Earnings Per Share	1.67	1.90	1.28	(0.84)	1.82	1.14	1.50	1.66
Cash Flow Per Share	3.41	4.98	4.20	3.73	4.07	4.31	3.25	0.42
Tang Book Value Per Share	18.49	17.71	17.44	16.07	16.00	14.34	12.81	13.63
Dividends Per Share	0.720	0.720	0.640	0.640	0.600	0.540	0.520	0.480
Dividend Payout %	43.11	37.89	50.00		32.97	47.37	34.67	28.92
Income Statement								
Total Revenue	711,000	2,616,000	2,543,000	2,125,000	1,934,000	1,795,000	1,557,000	1,698,000
EBITDA	85,000	351,000	255,000	78,000	328,000	257,000	271,000	265,000
Depn & Amortn	42,000	...	...	...	...	...	...	...
Income Before Taxes	34,000	168,000	97,000	(93,000)	164,000	94,000	134,000	150,000
Income Taxes	6,000	38,000	9,000	(45,000)	39,000	17,000	30,000	42,000
Net Income	36,000	129,000	88,000	(48,000)	124,000	80,000	106,000	124,000
Average Shares	64,000	68,000	68,000	60,000	68,000	70,000	71,000	74,000
Balance Sheet								
Current Assets	1,367,000	1,275,000	1,255,000	1,248,000	1,173,000	1,140,000	959,000	968,000
Total Assets	2,760,000	2,636,000	2,534,000	2,374,000	2,426,000	2,308,000	2,067,000	1,919,000
Current Liabilities	591,000	547,000	505,000	433,000	372,000	352,000	286,000	291,000
Long-Term Obligations	505,000	503,000	459,000	463,000	506,000	516,000	495,000	419,000
Total Liabilities	1,431,000	1,442,000	1,338,000	1,275,000	1,235,000	1,229,000	1,090,000	969,000
Stockholders' Equity	1,243,000	1,194,000	1,196,000	1,099,000	1,191,000	1,079,000	977,000	950,000
Shares Outstanding	65,171	65,279	63,286	62,667	63,055	62,080	61,615	62,633
Statistical Record								
Return on Assets %	4.15	4.99	3.59	N.M.	5.22	3.66	5.32	6.12
Return on Equity %	8.87	10.79	7.67	N.M.	10.90	7.78	11.00	12.42
EBITDA Margin %	11.95	13.42	10.03	3.67	16.96	14.32	17.41	15.61
Net Margin %	5.06	4.93	3.46	N.M.	6.41	4.46	6.81	7.30
Asset Turnover	1.00	1.01	1.04	0.89	0.81	0.82	0.78	0.84
Current Ratio	2.31	2.33	2.49	2.88	3.15	3.24	3.35	3.33
Debt to Equity	0.41	0.42	0.38	0.42	0.42	0.48	0.51	0.44
Price Range	49.77-30.72	49.77-35.53	39.22-30.77	39.27-27.87	40.70-27.08	30.60-19.53	41.87-21.00	41.35-18.56
P/E Ratio	29.80-18.40	26.19-18.70	30.64-24.04	...	22.36-14.88	26.84-17.13	27.91-14.00	24.91-11.18
Average Yield %	1.71	1.64	1.86	1.88	1.77	2.08	1.68	1.51

Address: Two Seaport Lane, Suite 1300, Boston, MA 02210
Telephone: 617-345-0100
Fax: 617-242-6103

Web Site: www.cabot-corp.com
Officers: Kennett F. Burnes - Chmn., Pres., C.E.O. John A. Shaw - Exec. V.P., C.F.O.

Auditors: Deloitte & Touche LLP
Investor Contact: 617-345-0100
Transfer Agents: EqiServe Trust Company N.A., Providence, RI

CABOT OIL & GAS CORP.

Exchange	Symbol	Price	52Wk Range	Yield	P/E
NYS	COG	$50.84 (3/31/2008)	53.41-31.55	0.24	29.73

*7 Year Price Score 171.35 *NYSE Composite Index=100 *12 Month Price Score 131.13

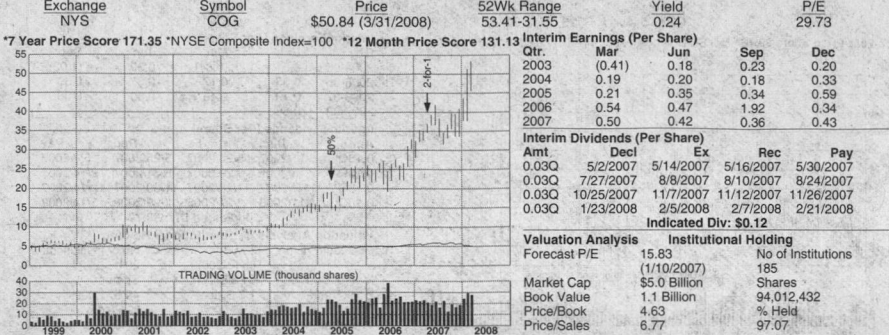

Interim Earnings (Per Share)

Qtr.	Mar	Jun	Sep	Dec
2003	(0.41)	0.18	0.23	0.20
2004	0.19	0.20	0.18	0.33
2005	0.21	0.35	0.34	0.59
2006	0.54	0.47	1.92	0.34
2007	0.50	0.42	0.36	0.43

Interim Dividends (Per Share)

Amt	Decl	Ex	Rec	Pay
0.03Q	5/2/2007	5/14/2007	5/16/2007	5/30/2007
0.03Q	7/27/2007	8/8/2007	8/10/2007	8/24/2007
0.03Q	10/25/2007	11/7/2007	11/12/2007	11/26/2007
0.03Q	1/23/2008	2/5/2008	2/7/2008	2/21/2008

Indicated Div: $0.12

Valuation Analysis

Forecast P/E	15.83
	(1/10/2007)
Market Cap	$5.0 Billion
Book Value	1.1 Billion
Price/Book	4.63
Price/Sales	6.77

Institutional Holding

No of Institutions	185
Shares	94,012,432
% Held	97.07

Business Summary: Oil and Gas (MIC: 14.2 SIC: 1311 NAIC: 211111)

Cabot Oil & Gas is an independent oil and gas company engaged in the development, exploitation and exploration of oil and gas properties in North America. In addition, Co. transports, stores, gathers and purchases natural gas for resale. Co.'s five principal areas of operation are the Appalachian Basin, the Gulf Coast, including south and east Texas and north Louisiana, the Rocky Mountains, the Anadarko Basin and the deep gas basin of Western Canada. As of Dec 31 2007, Co.'s proved reserves totaled approximately 1,616.00 billion cubic feet of natural gas equivalents, of which 97.0% was natural gas.

Recent Developments: For the year ended Dec 31 2007, net income decreased 47.9% to US$167.4 million from US$321.2 million in the prior year. Revenues were US$732.2 million, down 3.9% from US$762.0 million the year before. Operating income was US$274.7 million versus US$528.9 million in the prior year, a decrease of 48.1%. Direct operating expenses rose 0.5% to US$159.0 million from US$158.2 million in the comparable period the year before. Indirect operating expenses increased 298.6% to US$298.5 million from US$74.9 million in the equivalent prior-year period.

Prospects: In 2008, Co. plans to spend approximately $490.0 million on capital and exploration activities. Notably, Co. has budgeted approximately $189.0 million for capital and exploration expenditures in the east region, with plans to drill approximately 265 wells (258.5 net) primarily in West Virginia, including the Sissonville, Pineville, Logan-Holden-Dingess, Big Creek, Huff Creek and Hernshaw-Bullcreek fields. Also, Co. has budgeted approximately $209.0 million for capital and exploration expenditures in the Gulf Coast region, with plans to drill 69 wells (51.3 net) primarily in east Texas, including the Minden, County Line and Trawick fields.

Financial Data
(US$ in Thousands)

	12/31/2007	12/31/2006	12/31/2005	12/31/2004	12/31/2003	12/31/2002	12/31/2001	12/31/2000
Earnings Per Share	1.71	3.25	1.50	0.90	0.22	0.17	0.51	0.35
Cash Flow Per Share	4.77	3.69	3.73	2.79	2.51	1.73	2.76	1.44
Tang Book Value Per Share	10.98	9.82	6.18	4.69	3.78	3.67	3.62	2.77
Dividends Per Share	0.110	0.080	0.073	0.053	0.053	0.053	0.053	0.053
Dividend Payout %	6.43	2.46	4.91	5.95	24.62	32.00	10.46	15.09
Income Statement								
Total Revenue	732,170	761,988	682,797	530,408	509,391	353,756	447,042	368,651
EBITDA	401,483	639,480	344,692	241,967	137,945	120,289	155,168	118,258
Income Before Taxes	257,532	510,505	236,234	138,624	43,042	23,777	74,549	41,939
Income Taxes	90,109	189,330	87,789	50,246	15,063	7,674	27,465	16,467
Net Income	167,423	321,175	148,445	88,378	21,132	16,103	47,084	25,472
Average Shares	98,130	98,600	99,450	98,677	96,870	96,227	90,828	82,995
Balance Sheet								
Current Assets	221,413	315,682	230,312	194,679	121,396	93,121	84,987	110,269
Total Assets	2,208,594	1,834,491	1,495,370	1,210,956	1,024,201	1,054,871	1,069,031	735,634
Current Liabilities	252,266	251,027	218,584	196,889	154,701	123,024	110,240	118,108
Long-Term Obligations	330,000	220,000	320,000	250,000	270,000	365,000	393,000	253,000
Total Liabilities	1,138,337	889,293	895,159	755,294	659,004	704,214	722,479	493,129
Stockholders' Equity	1,070,257	945,198	600,211	455,662	365,197	350,657	346,552	242,505
Shares Outstanding	97,476	96,213	97,136	97,238	96,706	95,491	95,715	87,575
Statistical Record								
Return on Assets %	8.28	19.29	10.97	7.89	2.03	1.52	5.22	3.64
Return on Equity %	16.61	41.57	28.12	21.47	5.90	4.62	15.99	11.84
EBITDA Margin %	54.83	83.92	50.48	45.62	27.08	34.00	34.71	32.08
Net Margin %	22.87	42.15	21.74	16.66	4.15	4.55	10.53	6.91
Asset Turnover	0.36	0.46	0.50	0.47	0.49	0.33	0.50	0.53
Current Ratio	0.88	1.26	1.05	0.99	0.78	0.76	0.77	0.93
Debt to Equity	0.31	0.23	0.53	0.55	0.74	1.04	1.13	1.04
Price Range	41.88-28.06	32.85-19.21	25.77-13.89	16.13-9.59	10.09-7.58	8.73-6.13	11.40-5.57	10.58-4.73
P/E Ratio	24.49-16.41	10.11-5.91	17.18-9.26	17.92-10.65	45.85-34.44	51.37-36.08	22.35-10.92	30.24-13.51
Average Yield %	0.31	0.32	0.38	0.42	0.62	0.71	0.62	0.82

Address: 1200 Enclave Parkway, Houston, TX 77077
Telephone: 281-589-4600
Fax: 281-589-4653

Web Site: www.cabotog.com
Officers: Dan O. Dinges - Chmn., Pres., C.E.O.
Michael B. Walen - Sr. V.P., Exploration, Prodn.

Auditors: PricewaterhouseCoopers LLP
Investor Contact: 281-589-4993
Transfer Agents: The Bank of New York, New York, NY

CALIFORNIA WATER SERVICE GROUP (DE)

Exchange	Symbol	Price	52Wk Range	Yield	P/E	Div Acheiver
NYS	CWT	$38.15 (3/31/2008)	44.39-33.58	3.07	25.43	40 Years

*7 Year Price Score 95.71 *NYSE Composite Index=100 *12 Month Price Score 105.78

Interim Earnings (Per Share)

Qtr.	Mar	Jun	Sep	Dec
2003	(0.05)	0.30	0.53	0.42
2004	0.08	0.59	0.59	0.19
2005	0.03	0.41	0.71	0.31
2006	0.04	0.31	0.68	0.31
2007	0.07	0.37	0.67	0.39

Interim Dividends (Per Share)

Amt	Decl	Ex	Rec	Pay
0.29Q	4/25/2007	5/3/2007	5/7/2007	5/18/2007
0.29Q	8/1/2007	8/2/2007	8/6/2007	8/17/2007
0.29Q	10/25/2007	11/1/2007	11/5/2007	11/16/2007
0.292Q	1/23/2008	1/31/2008	2/4/2008	2/15/2008

Indicated Div: $1.17 (Div. Reinv. Plan)

Valuation Analysis

		Institutional Holding	
Forecast P/E	N/A	No of Institutions	100
Market Cap	$788.4 Million	Shares	8,335,861
Book Value	389.2 Million	% Held	40.35
Price/Book	2.03		
Price/Sales	2.15		

Business Summary: Water Utilities (MIC: 7.2 SIC: 4941 NAIC: 221310)

California Water Service Group is a holding company. Through its subsidiaries, Co. is engaged in the production, purchase, storage, treatment, testing, distribution and sale of water for domestic, industrial, public and irrigation uses, and for fire protection. In addition, Co. provides non-regulated water-related services under agreements with municipalities and other private companies including full water system operation, billing and meter reading services. As of Dec 31 2007, Co. provided its services to approximately 463,600 customers in 83 California communities; 15,800 customers in the Tacoma and Olympia areas; 7,500 customers in New Mexico; and 700 customers on the island of Maui.

Recent Developments: For the year ended Dec 31 2007, net income increased 21.8% to US$31.2 million from US$25.6 million in the prior year. Revenues were US$367.1 million, up 9.7% from US$334.7 million the year before. Operating income was US$44.2 million versus US$40.3 million in the prior year, an increase of 9.6%. Direct operating expenses rose 11.8% to US$195.4 million from US$174.7 million in the comparable period the year before. Indirect operating expenses increased 6.5% to US$127.5 million from US$119.7 million in the equivalent prior-year period.

Prospects: Going forward, Co. plans to continue to seek rate relief to recover its operating cost increases. For instance, Co. expects to receive decisions by July 2008 on the General Rate Cases filings for all of its centralized costs in addition to its three-year District General Rate Cases, which were submitted by its California Water Service Co. (Cal Water) subsidiary in 2007. Cal Water also plans to file advice letters in April and July 2008 to offset expected increases in purchased water and pump tax charges in some districts. Further, Cal Water is required to file an application in May 2008 for its cost of capital requirements under the California Public Utilities Commission's rate case plan.

Financial Data
(US$ in Thousands)

	12/31/2007	12/31/2006	12/31/2005	12/31/2004	12/31/2003	12/31/2002	12/31/2001	12/31/2000
Earnings Per Share	1.50	1.34	1.47	1.46	1.21	1.25	0.97	1.31
Cash Flow Per Share	2.42	3.22	4.69	3.13	2.80	2.20	2.54	2.28
Tang Book Value Per Share	18.66	18.31	15.98	15.66	14.44	13.12	12.95	13.13
Dividends Per Share	1.160	1.150	1.140	1.130	1.125	1.120	1.115	1.100
Dividend Payout %	77.33	85.82	77.55	77.40	92.98	89.60	114.95	83.97
Income Statement								
Total Revenue	367,082	334,717	320,728	315,567	277,128	263,151	246,820	244,806
Income Taxes	17,887	15,297	20,006	17,084	12,898	12,568	9,728	11,571
Net Income	31,159	25,580	27,223	26,026	19,417	19,073	14,965	19,963
Average Shares	20,689	18,925	18,402	17,674	15,893	15,185	15,285	15,173
Balance Sheet								
Net PPE	1,010,196	911,073	862,751	800,305	759,498	696,988	621,342	582,008
Total Assets	1,184,499	1,165,019	996,945	942,853	873,035	800,582	710,214	666,605
Long-Term Obligations	289,220	291,814	274,142	274,821	272,226	250,365	202,600	187,098
Total Liabilities	795,315	783,242	699,529	651,773	625,036	597,890	510,120	464,296
Stockholders' Equity	389,184	381,777	297,416	291,080	247,999	202,692	200,094	202,309
Shares Outstanding	20,666	20,657	18,390	18,367	16,932	15,182	15,182	15,146
Statistical Record								
Return on Assets %	2.65	2.37	2.81	2.86	2.32	2.52	2.17	3.17
Return on Equity %	8.08	7.53	9.25	9.63	8.62	9.47	7.44	10.40
Net Margin %	8.49	7.64	8.49	8.25	7.01	7.25	6.06	8.15
PPE Turnover	0.38	0.37	0.39	0.40	0.38	0.40	0.41	0.44
Asset Turnover	0.31	0.31	0.33	0.35	0.33	0.35	0.36	0.39
Debt to Equity	0.74	0.76	0.92	0.94	1.10	1.24	1.01	0.92
Price Range	44.54-34.46	45.36-33.72	41.90-32.12	37.70-26.19	30.97-23.65	26.69-21.60	28.60-23.38	30.94-21.69
P/E Ratio	29.69-22.97	33.85-25.16	28.50-21.85	25.82-17.94	25.60-19.55	21.35-17.28	29.48-24.10	23.62-16.56
Average Yield %	2.97	2.94	3.12	3.86	4.22	4.53	4.37	4.28

Address: 1720 North First Street, San Jose, CA 95112-4598 **Telephone:** 408-367-8200 **Fax:** 408-437-9185	**Web Site:** www.calwatergroup.com **Officers:** Robert W. Foy - Chmn. Peter C. Nelson - Pres., C.E.O.	**Auditors:** Deloitte & Touche LLP **Investor Contact:** 408-367-8200 **Transfer Agents:** State Street Bank and Trust Company, Boston, MA

139

CALLAWAY GOLF CO. (DE)

Exchange	Symbol	Price	52Wk Range	Yield	P/E
NYS	ELY	$14.68 (3/31/2008)	19.26-13.95	1.91	18.12

*7 Year Price Score 88.84   *NYSE Composite Index=100   *12 Month Price Score 100.32

TRADING VOLUME (thousand shares)

Interim Earnings (Per Share)

Qtr.	Mar	Jun	Sep	Dec
2003	0.64	0.52	0.03	(0.51)
2004	0.59	0.20	(0.53)	(0.42)
2005	0.27	0.27	(0.07)	(0.27)
2006	0.33	0.33	(0.18)	(0.15)
2007	0.48	0.53	0.02	(0.22)

Interim Dividends (Per Share)

Amt	Decl	Ex	Rec	Pay
0.07Q	6/5/2007	6/14/2007	6/18/2007	7/5/2007
0.07Q	8/23/2007	9/4/2007	9/6/2007	9/20/2007
0.07Q	11/30/2007	12/6/2007	12/10/2007	12/20/2007
0.07Q	2/21/2008	3/11/2008	3/13/2008	4/3/2008
			Indicated Div: $0.28	

Valuation Analysis — Institutional Holding

Valuation Analysis		Institutional Holding	
Forecast P/E	11.65	No of Institutions	
	(1/10/2007)	152	
Market Cap	$946.4 Million	Shares	
Book Value	568.2 Million	64,171,432	
Price/Book	1.67	% Held	
Price/Sales	0.84	87.73	

Business Summary: Consumer Accessories (MIC: 4.6 SIC: 3949 NAIC: 339920)

Callaway Golf designs, manufactures and sells golf clubs (drivers, fairway woods, irons, wedges and putters) and golf balls. Co. also sells golf accessories such as golf footwear, golf bags, golf gloves, golf headwear, golf towels and golf umbrellas. Also, Co. sells its products to golf retailers, sporting goods retailers and mass merchants, directly and through its wholly-owned subsidiaries, and to third party distributors in the U.S. and in over 100 countries around the world. Co. also sells pre-owned Callaway Golf products through its website, callawaygolfpreowned.com . In addition, Co. licenses its name for golf apparel, watches, rangefinders, practice aids, travel gear and eyewear..

Recent Developments: For the year ended Dec 31 2007, net income increased 134.4% to US$54.6 million from US$23.3 million in the prior year. Revenues were US$1.12 billion, up 10.5% from US$1.02 billion the year before. Operating income was US$90.2 million versus US$37.1 million in the prior year, an increase of 143.4%. Direct operating expenses rose 1.9% to US$631.4 million from US$619.8 million in the comparable period the year before. Indirect operating expenses increased 11.6% to US$403.0 million from US$361.0 million in the equivalent prior-year period.

Prospects: For the full year of 2008, Co. currently anticipates net sales to be in the range of $1.15 billion to $1.17 billion. In addition, Co. is forecasting capital expenditures to range from $50.0 million to $55.0 million, with approximately $15.0 million to support its building improvement and consolidation projects while the remaining amount will be utilized to support its ongoing operating requirements. Meanwhile, Co. intends to continue to implement its Gross Margin Improvement initiatives, which include improvements for the attainment of direct materials, indirect goods and services, its manufacturing and distribution process worldwide as well as its engineering and automation capabilities.

Financial Data

(US$ in Thousands)	12/31/2007	12/31/2006	12/31/2005	12/31/2004	12/31/2003	12/31/2002	12/31/2001	12/31/2000
Earnings Per Share	0.81	0.34	0.19	(0.15)	0.68	1.03	0.82	1.13
Cash Flow Per Share	2.29	0.26	1.02	0.13	1.80	2.09	1.43	1.30
Tang Book Value Per Share	6.13	5.92	5.97	5.88	6.27	5.57	5.05	5.38
Dividends Per Share	0.280	0.280	0.280	0.280	0.280	0.280	0.280	0.280
Dividend Payout %	34.57	82.35	147.37	...	41.18	27.18	34.15	24.78
Income Statement								
Total Revenue	1,124,591	1,017,907	998,093	934,564	814,032	792,064	816,163	837,627
EBITDA	126,762	71,364	54,176	27,641	113,901	152,654	137,211	178,290
Income Before Taxes	88,275	34,998	14,537	(23,713)	67,883	111,671	98,192	129,322
Income Taxes	33,688	11,708	1,253	(13,610)	22,360	42,225	39,817	47,366
Net Income	54,587	23,290	13,284	(10,103)	45,523	69,446	58,375	80,999
Average Shares	67,484	68,503	69,239	67,721	66,471	67,274	71,314	71,412
Balance Sheet								
Current Assets	496,581	493,200	438,590	393,732	383,462	369,027	354,691	342,469
Total Assets	856,963	845,947	764,498	735,737	748,566	679,845	647,602	630,934
Current Liabilities	223,548	223,455	140,205	120,798	130,160	109,161	101,874	109,306
Long-Term Obligations	...	...	...	26	154	...	3,160	...
Total Liabilities	286,755	266,843	168,450	149,420	159,183	136,458	133,253	119,190
Stockholders' Equity	568,230	577,117	596,048	586,317	589,383	543,387	514,349	511,744
Shares Outstanding	64,468	67,954	70,495	69,111	66,862	75,805	77,755	74,142
Statistical Record								
Return on Assets %	6.41	2.89	1.77	N.M.	6.37	10.46	9.13	12.95
Return on Equity %	9.53	3.97	2.25	N.M.	8.04	13.13	11.38	15.97
EBITDA Margin %	11.27	7.01	5.43	2.96	13.99	19.27	16.81	21.29
Net Margin %	4.85	2.29	1.33	N.M.	5.59	8.77	7.15	9.67
Asset Turnover	1.32	1.26	1.33	1.26	1.14	1.19	1.28	1.34
Current Ratio	2.22	2.21	3.13	3.26	2.95	3.38	3.48	3.13
Debt to Equity	...	...	...	N.M.	N.M.	...	0.01	...
Price Range	19.26-13.98	17.29-11.50	15.55-10.78	19.95-9.28	17.07-10.50	20.40-9.55	27.01-12.21	20.56-11.00
P/E Ratio	23.78-17.26	50.85-33.82	81.84-56.74	...	25.10-15.44	19.81-9.27	32.94-14.89	18.20-9.73
Average Yield %	1.67	1.95	2.04	1.97	1.97	1.80	1.49	1.77

Address: 2180 Rutherford Road, Carlsbad, CA 92008-8815 Telephone: 760-931-1771 Fax: 760-931-8013	Web Site: www.callawaygolf.com Officers: Ronald A. Drapeau - Chmn., C.E.O. Patrice Hutin - Pres., C.O.O.	Auditors: Deloitte & Touche LLP Investor Contact: 760-931-1771 Transfer Agents: Mellon Investor Services LLC, Ridgefield Park, NJ

CALPINE CORP

Exchange	Symbol	Price	52Wk Range	Yield	P/E
NYS	CPN	$18.42 (3/31/2008)	19.11-15.00	N/A	3.28

*7 Year Price Score N/A   *NYSE Composite Index=100   *12 Month Price Score N/A

Interim Earnings (Per Share)

Qtr.	Mar	Jun	Sep	Dec
2003	(0.14)	(0.06)	0.51	0.30
2004	(0.17)	(0.07)	0.03	(0.36)
2005	(0.38)	(0.66)	(0.45)	(19.95)
2006	(1.23)	(1.71)	0.00	(0.75)
2007	(0.96)	(1.04)	7.91	(0.29)

Interim Dividends (Per Share)

No Dividends Paid

Valuation Analysis

	Institutional Holding	
Forecast P/E	N/A	No of Institutions
		N/A
Market Cap	$8.8 Billion	Shares
Book Value	N/A	N/A
Price/Book	N/A	% Held
Price/Sales	1.11	N/A

TRADING VOLUME (thousand shares)

Business Summary: Electricity (MIC: 7.1 SIC: 4911 NAIC: 221122)

Calpine and its consolidated subsidiaries are engaged in the business of generating and selling of electricity and electricity-related products, through the operation of its portfolio of power generation facilities with all of its continuing operations located in the U.S. Co. markets electricity produced by its generating facilities to utilities and other third party purchasers while thermal energy produced by the gas-fired power cogeneration facilities is primarily sold to industrial users. Co. also has ownership interests in, and operates, gas-fired power generation and cogeneration facilities, geothermal power generation facilities, geothermal steam fields and gas pipelines in the U.S.

Recent Developments: For the quarter ended Sep 30 2007, net income increased to US$3.79 billion from US$2.0 million in the year-earlier quarter. Revenues were US$2.24 billion, up 3.8% from US$2.16 billion the year before. Operating income was US$367.0 million versus US$355.0 million in the prior-year quarter, an increase of 3.4%. Direct operating expenses rose 4.5% to US$1.83 billion from US$1.75 billion in the comparable period the year before. Indirect operating expenses decreased 18.2% to US$45.0 million from US$55.0 million in the equivalent prior-year period.

Prospects: Looking ahead, Co. expects the recently completed Original Debtor-in-possession Facility refinancing to support its efforts to emerge from Chapter 11. Subsequently, Co. intends to finalize and confirm a plan or plans of reorganization. For instance, on June 20 2007, Co. announced that it and certain of its subsidiaries have filed a Joint Plan of Reorganization and Disclosure Statement with the U.S. Bankruptcy Court for the Southern District of New York. Accordingly, Co. anticipates confirmation of the plan by the fourth quarter of 2007. Meanwhile, Co. remains focused to maximize its asset performance while utilizing growth and development opportunities.

Financial Data

(US$ in Thousands)	12/31/2007	12/31/2006	12/31/2005	12/31/2004	12/31/2003	12/31/2002	12/31/2001	12/31/2000
Earnings Per Share	5.62	(3.68)	(21.44)	(0.56)	0.71	0.33	1.87	1.10
Cash Flow Per Share	0.38	0.33	(1.53)	0.02	0.74	3.01	1.84	2.45
Tang Book Value Per Share	...	...	...	8.33	10.81	9.78	9.80	7.88
Income Statement								
Total Revenue	7,970,000	6,705,760	10,112,658	9,229,888	8,919,539	7,457,899	7,589,978	2,282,793
EBITDA	4,656,000	67,130	(8,549,267)	1,200,390	1,401,806	881,468	1,448,945	702,031
Income Before Taxes	2,147,000	(1,701,254)	(10,622,352)	(717,375)	109,619	29,996	986,323	543,638
Income Taxes	(546,000)	64,158	(741,398)	(276,549)	(134)	(19,096)	345,261	218,951
Net Income	2,693,000	(1,764,907)	(9,939,208)	(242,461)	282,022	118,618	648,105	323,452
Average Shares	479,478	479,136	463,567	430,775	396,219	362,533	317,919	280,776
Balance Sheet								
Net PPE	12,292,000	13,603,202	14,119,215	20,636,394	20,081,052	18,850,967	15,384,990	7,459,055
Total Assets	18,482,000	18,590,265	20,544,797	27,216,088	27,303,932	23,226,992	21,309,295	9,737,257
Long-Term Obligations	9,946,000	3,351,627	2,462,462	16,940,809	17,328,181	12,462,309	11,824,417	4,430,357
Total Liabilities	23,131,000	25,476,873	25,777,498	22,234,970	22,271,787	18,065,906	17,128,313	6,340,417
Stockholders' Equity	(4,652,000)	(7,152,900)	(5,508,085)	4,587,673	4,621,253	3,851,914	3,010,569	2,236,774
Shares Outstanding	479,314	529,764	569,081	536,509	415,010	380,816	307,058	283,715
Statistical Record								
Return on Assets %	14.53	N.M.	N.M.	N.M.	1.12	0.53	4.18	4.70
Return on Equity %	...	...	...	N.M.	6.66	3.46	24.70	20.15
EBITDA Margin %	58.42	1.00	N.M.	13.01	15.72	11.82	19.09	30.75
Net Margin %	33.79	(26.32)	(98.28)	(2.63)	3.16	1.59	8.54	14.17
PPE Turnover	0.62	0.48	0.58	0.45	0.46	0.44	0.66	0.44
Asset Turnover	0.43	0.34	0.42	0.34	0.35	0.33	0.49	0.33
Debt to Equity	...	...	...	3.69	3.75	3.24	3.93	1.98

Address: 50 West San Fernando Street, San Jose, CA 95113-2429	Web Site: www.calpine.com	Auditors: PrcewaterhouseCoopers LLP
Telephone: 408-995-5115	Officers: Kenneth T. Derr - Chmn., Acting C.E.O. Ann B. Curtis - Vice-Chmn., Exec. V.P., Corp. Sec.	Investor Contact: 408-995-5115
Fax: 408-995-0505		Transfer Agents: EquiServe Trust Company, N.A., Providence, RI

CAMDEN PROPERTY TRUST

Exchange	Symbol	Price	52Wk Range	Yield	P/E
NYS	CPT	$50.20 (3/31/2008)	75.32-42.18	5.58	20.00

*7 Year Price Score 95.61   *NYSE Composite Index=100   *12 Month Price Score 90.66

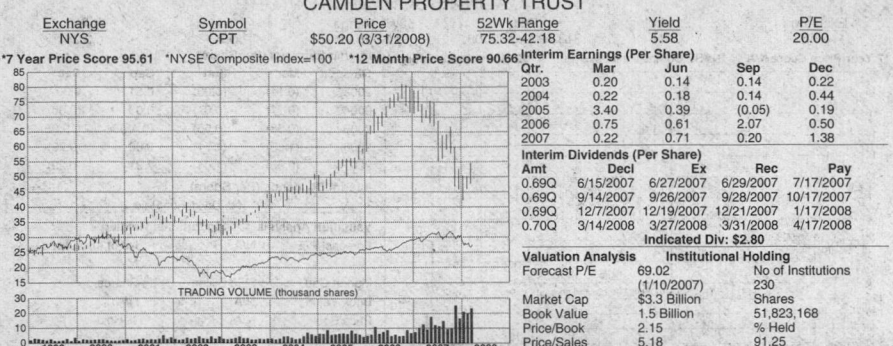

Interim Earnings (Per Share)

Qtr.	Mar	Jun	Sep	Dec
2003	0.20	0.14	0.14	0.22
2004	0.22	0.18	0.14	0.44
2005	3.40	0.39	(0.05)	0.19
2006	0.75	0.61	2.07	0.50
2007	0.22	0.71	0.20	1.38

Interim Dividends (Per Share)

Amt	Decl	Ex	Rec	Pay
0.69Q	6/15/2007	6/27/2007	6/29/2007	7/17/2007
0.69Q	9/14/2007	9/26/2007	9/28/2007	10/17/2007
0.69Q	12/7/2007	12/19/2007	12/21/2007	1/17/2008
0.70Q	3/14/2008	3/27/2008	3/31/2008	4/17/2008

Indicated Div: $2.80

Valuation Analysis

		Institutional Holding	
Forecast P/E	69.02 (1/10/2007)	No of Institutions	230
Market Cap	$3.3 Billion	Shares	51,823,168
Book Value	1.5 Billion	% Held	91.25
Price/Book	2.15		
Price/Sales	5.18		

Business Summary: Property, Real Estate & Development (MIC: 8.3 SIC: 6798 NAIC: 525930)

Camden Property Trust is a real estate investment trust. Through its subsidiaries, Co. owns, develops, constructs and manages multifamily apartment communities . As of Dec 31 2007, Co. owned interests in, operated or were developing 193 multifamily properties comprising 66,468 apartment homes located in 13 states. At such date, Co. also had 3,383 apartment homes under development at 11 of its multifamily properties, including 1,257 apartment homes at four multifamily properties owned through joint ventures, and two properties comprised of 391 apartment homes were designated as held for sale.

Recent Developments: For the year ended Dec 31 2007, income from continuing operations decreased 62.3% to US$47.1 million from US$125.0 million a year earlier. Net income decreased 36.2% to US$148.5 million from US$232.8 million in the prior year. Revenues were US$634.1 million, up 2.9% from US$616.1 million the year before. Revenues from property income rose 4.9% to US$609.1 million from US$580.6 million in the corresponding earlier year.

Prospects: Co. expects moderating growth for 2008. Notably, Co. projects its 2008 same-property net operating income growth of 2.25% to 3.25%, acquisitions of $200.0 million to $400.0 million, dispositions of $175.0 million to $380.0 million and new development starts of $200.0 million to $500.0 million. Thus, Co. estimates its full year 2008 funds from operations of $3.60 to $3.80 per diluted share and earnings per share of $0.44 to $0.66, excluding potential future gains on the sale of properties. Meanwhile, Co. believes that it has a solid development pipeline and it expects selective development of new apartment properties to continue to be significant to its portfolio growth over the near-term.

Financial Data

(US$ in Thousands)	12/31/2007	12/31/2006	12/31/2005	12/31/2004	12/31/2003	12/31/2002	12/31/2001	12/31/2000
Earnings Per Share	2.51	3.96	3.58	0.98	0.71	1.73	1.41	1.63
Cash Flow Per Share	3.84	4.09	3.86	3.85	3.51	4.57	4.98	4.29
Tang Book Value Per Share	23.40	26.68	22.56	15.20	15.68	17.05	18.88	25.55
Dividends Per Share	2.760	2.640	2.540	2.540	2.540	2.540	2.440	2.250
Dividend Payout %	109.96	66.67	70.95	259.18	357.75	146.82	173.05	138.04
Income Statement								
Property Income	609,080	599,430	524,090	410,107	403,579	396,505	403,620	391,141
Non-Property Income	25,002	35,530	44,491	21,124	12,961	14,478	24,595	12,398
Total Revenue	634,082	634,960	568,581	431,231	416,540	410,983	428,215	403,539
Interest Expense	116,281	118,344	111,548	79,214	75,414	71,499	69,841	69,036
Income Before Taxes	50,130	...	...	...	...	...	...	...
Income Taxes	3,052	...	...	...	...	...	...	...
Net Income	148,457	232,846	199,086	41,341	29,430	74,612	61,292	74,424
Average Shares	59,125	59,524	56,313	42,426	41,354	44,216	41,603	41,388
Balance Sheet								
Total Assets	4,890,760	4,586,050	4,487,799	2,629,364	2,625,561	2,609,899	2,449,665	2,430,881
Long-Term Obligations	2,828,095	2,330,976	2,633,091	1,576,405	1,509,677	1,427,016	1,207,047	1,138,117
Total Liabilities	3,139,495	2,628,183	2,895,873	1,731,282	1,644,291	1,569,717	1,325,335	1,244,371
Stockholders' Equity	1,531,313	1,734,356	1,370,903	738,515	784,885	839,453	918,251	974,183
Shares Outstanding	65,434	65,006	60,763	48,601	50,060	49,233	48,627	38,129
Statistical Record								
Return on Assets %	3.13	5.13	5.59	1.57	1.12	2.95	2.51	3.02
Return on Equity %	9.09	15.00	18.88	5.41	3.62	8.49	6.48	7.46
Net Margin %	23.41	36.67	35.01	9.59	7.07	18.15	14.31	18.44
Price Range	78.85-45.78	80.97-58.40	60.18-45.31	51.00-40.04	44.30-30.70	41.54-29.74	39.32-31.07	33.81-25.88
P/E Ratio	31.41-18.24	20.45-14.75	16.81-12.66	52.04-40.86	62.39-43.24	24.01-17.19	27.89-22.04	20.74-15.87
Average Yield %	4.22	3.67	4.86	5.60	6.97	7.14	6.98	7.74

Address: 3 Greenway Plaza, Suite 1300, Houston, TX 77046. **Telephone:** 713-354-2500 **Fax:** 713-354-2710	**Web Site:** www.camdenliving.com **Officers:** Richard J. Campo - Chmn., C.E.O. D. Keith Oden - Pres., C.O.O.	**Auditors:** Deloitte & Touche LLP **Transfer Agents:** American Stock Transfer and Trust Company, New York, NY

CAMERON INTERNATIONAL CORP

Exchange	Symbol	Price	52Wk Range	Yield	P/E
NYS	CAM	$41.64 (3/31/2008)	52.51-31.66	N/A	19.28

*7 Year Price Score 173.43 *NYSE Composite Index=100 *12 Month Price Score 106.87

TRADING VOLUME (thousand shares)

Interim Earnings (Per Share)

Qtr.	Mar	Jun	Sep	Dec
2003	0.04	0.09	0.16	0.03
2004	0.08	0.09	0.14	0.14
2005	0.13	0.17	0.22	0.23
2006	0.23	0.32	0.39	0.41
2007	0.44	0.54	0.66	0.53

Interim Dividends (Per Share)

Amt	Decl	Ex	Rec	Pay
100%	11/10/2005	12/16/2005	11/21/2005	12/15/2005
100%	10/2/2007	12/31/2007	12/17/2007	12/28/2007

Valuation Analysis / Institutional Holding

Forecast P/E	11.00	No of Institutions
	(1/10/2007)	331
Market Cap	$9.5 Billion	Shares
Book Value	2.1 Billion	100,073,136
Price/Book	4.54	% Held
Price/Sales	2.04	88.93

Business Summary: Oil and Gas (MIC: 14.2 SIC: 3533 NAIC: 333132)

Cameron International is a provider of flow equipment products, systems and services to oil, gas and process industries. Co.'s operations are organized into three business segments: Drilling & Production Systems, which provides systems and equipment used to control pressures, direct flows of oil and gas wells and separate oil and gas from impurities; Valves & Measurement, which provides valves and measurement systems used to control, direct and measure the flow of oil and gas as they are moved from individual wellheads through flow lines; and Compression Systems, which provides reciprocating and integrally geared centrifugal compression equipment and aftermarket parts and services.

Recent Developments: For the year ended Dec 31 2007, net income increased 57.6% to US$500.9 million from US$317.8 million in the prior year. Revenues were US$4.67 billion, up 24.7% from US$3.74 billion the year before. Direct operating expenses rose 24.7% to US$3.24 billion from US$2.60 billion in the comparable period the year before. Indirect operating expenses increased 9.6% to US$723.1 million from US$659.5 million in the equivalent prior-year period.

Prospects: For 2008, Co. expects earnings in the range of $2.45 to $2.55 per diluted share, excluding any charges related to the ongoing pension plan termination, reflecting the overall activity in the energy markets, its expectations for customer spending in the oil and gas markets, along with its continued efforts in controlling and reducing its operating costs. The expected growth in revenues and earnings also reflects Co.'s recent investments in machine tool upgrades, productivity improvements and new facilities. Meanwhile, Co. estimates that capital expenditures will total about $250.0 million to $270.0 million in 2008, primarily related to the new surface manufacturing facility in Romania.

Financial Data
(US$ in Thousands)

	12/31/2007	12/31/2006	12/31/2005	12/31/2004	12/31/2003	12/31/2002	12/31/2001	12/31/2000
Earnings Per Share	2.16	1.36	0.76	0.44	0.31	0.28	0.44	0.13
Cash Flow Per Share	2.06	2.41	1.59	0.91	0.47	0.82	0.58	0.10
Tang Book Value Per Share	5.95	4.74	4.18	3.67	3.80	3.37	2.91	2.69
Income Statement								
Total Revenue	4,666,368	3,742,907	2,517,847	2,092,845	1,634,346	1,538,100	1,563,678	1,386,709
EBITDA	810,817	583,689	340,303	228,639	164,127	162,491	231,297	137,132
Income Before Taxes	708,475	488,601	263,012	132,919	77,603	85,145	142,582	43,773
Income Taxes	207,615	170,785	91,882	38,504	20,362	24,676	44,237	16,113
Net Income	500,860	317,816	171,130	94,415	69,450	60,469	98,345	27,660
Average Shares	231,387	233,984	225,216	215,416	239,200	239,236	232,300	220,032
Balance Sheet								
Current Assets	3,071,931	2,907,652	1,728,056	1,205,324	1,147,701	1,017,861	964,986	687,986
Total Assets	4,730,819	4,350,750	3,098,562	2,356,430	2,140,685	1,997,670	1,875,052	1,493,873
Current Liabilities	1,692,876	1,628,212	921,861	528,260	679,919	374,810	377,771	346,031
Long-Term Obligations	745,128	745,408	444,435	458,355	204,061	462,942	459,142	188,060
Total Liabilities	2,635,855	2,609,311	1,503,799	1,128,183	1,003,962	956,367	951,771	651,594
Stockholders' Equity	2,094,964	1,741,439	1,594,763	1,228,247	1,136,723	1,041,303	923,281	842,279
Shares Outstanding	228,460	224,579	231,258	212,551	215,212	218,044	215,978	216,047
Statistical Record								
Return on Assets %	11.03	8.53	6.27	4.19	3.36	3.12	5.84	1.86
Return on Equity %	26.11	19.05	12.12	7.96	6.38	6.16	11.14	3.54
EBITDA Margin %	17.38	15.59	13.52	10.92	10.04	10.56	14.79	9.89
Net Margin %	10.73	8.49	6.80	4.51	4.25	3.93	6.29	1.99
Asset Turnover	1.03	1.00	0.92	0.93	0.79	0.79	0.93	0.93
Current Ratio	1.81	1.79	1.87	2.28	1.69	2.72	2.55	1.99
Debt to Equity	0.36	0.43	0.28	0.37	0.18	0.44	0.50	0.22
Price Range	52.51-24.93	28.75-19.28	21.25-12.88	14.05-10.28	13.81-10.45	14.82-9.22	18.25-7.29	20.97-10.92
P/E Ratio	24.31-11.54	21.14-14.18	27.96-16.95	31.93-23.35	44.55-33.71	52.95-32.92	41.48-16.56	161.30-84.01

Address: 1333 West Loop South, Suite 1700, Houston, TX 77027	Web Site: www.coopercameron.com	Auditors: Ernst & Young LLP
Telephone: 713-513-3300	Officers: Sheldon R. Erikson - Chmn., Pres., C.E.O. Franklin Myers - Sr. V.P., Fin., C.F.O.	Transfer Agents: EquiServe Trust Company N.A., Providence, RI
Fax: 713-513-3320		

CAMPBELL SOUP CO.

Exchange	Symbol	Price	52Wk Range	Yield	P/E
NYS	CPB	$33.95 (3/31/2008)	39.97-31.00	2.59	15.86

*7 Year Price Score 97.52   *NYSE Composite Index=100   *12 Month Price Score 96.45

Interim Earnings (Per Share)

Qtr.	Oct	Jan	Apr	Jul
2005			1.71	
2005-06	0.73	0.61	0.40	0.00
2006-07	0.72	0.72	0.55	0.17
2007-08	0.70	0.71	...	...

Interim Dividends (Per Share)

Amt	Decl	Ex	Rec	Pay
0.20Q	6/28/2007	7/5/2007	7/9/2007	7/30/2007
0.22Q	9/27/2007	10/4/2007	10/9/2007	10/29/2007
0.22Q	11/15/2007	12/27/2007	12/31/2007	1/28/2008
0.22Q	3/27/2008	4/3/2008	4/7/2008	4/28/2008

Indicated Div: $0.88

Valuation Analysis / **Institutional Holding**

Forecast P/E	18.81	No of Institutions
	(1/10/2007)	371
Market Cap	$12.7 Billion	Shares
Book Value	1.6 Billion	171,817,104
Price/Book	7.98	% Held
Price/Sales	1.59	44.06

Business Summary: Food (MIC: 4.1 SIC: 2032 NAIC: 311422)

Campbell Soup manufactures and markets convenience food products. Co.'s U.S. Soup, Sauces and Beverages segment provides condensed and ready-to-serve soups, broth and canned poultry, pasta and Mexican sauce, canned pasta, gravies and beans, meal kits, tomato juice as well as juice drinks. Co.'s Baking and Snacking segment provides cookies, crackers, and bakery and frozen products, while its International Soup and Sauces segment includes its soup, sauce and beverage business in Europe, Mexico, Latin America, the Asia Pacific region as well as Canada. Co.'s other segment distributes products such as soup, specialty entrees, beverage products, chocolates, as well as other prepared foods.

Recent Developments: For the quarter ended Jan 27 2008, income from continuing operations increased 1.2% to US$260.0 million from US$257.0 million in the year-earlier quarter. Net income decreased 3.9% to US$274.0 million from US$285.0 million in the year-earlier quarter. Revenues were US$2.22 billion, up 7.5% from US$2.06 billion the year before. Operating income was US$400.0 million versus US$399.0 million in the prior-year quarter, an increase of 0.3%. Direct operating expenses rose 9.6% to US$1.33 billion from US$1.21 billion in the comparable period the year before. Indirect operating expenses increased 8.2% to US$489.0 million from US$452.0 million in the equivalent prior-year period.

Prospects: On Dec 20 2007, Co. announced that it has signed an agreement to sell its Godiva Chocolatier business to Yildiz Holding A.S., which is the owner of the Ulker Group, a diversified food company based in Istanbul, Turkey, for $850.0 million. Accordingly, the closing of the transaction is anticipated to occur within the next several months and the divestiture is expected to sharpen Co.'s focus on its simple meals, baked snacks, and vegetable-based beverages businesses going forward. Meanwhile, for 2008, Co.'s capital expenditures are expected to be about $370.0 million, which will be used for, among others, the expansion of its U.S. beverage and its Pepperidge Farm bakery production capacity.

Financial Data

(US$ in Thousands)	6 Mos	3 Mos	07/29/2007	07/30/2006	07/31/2005	08/01/2004	08/03/2003	07/28/2002
Earnings Per Share	2.14	2.15	2.16	1.85	1.71	1.57	1.45	1.28
Cash Flow Per Share	2.10	2.20	1.75	3.02	2.43	1.81	2.09	2.49
Dividends Per Share	0.840	0.820	0.800	0.720	0.680	0.630	0.630	0.630
Dividend Payout %	39.29	38.18	37.04	38.92	39.77	40.13	43.45	49.22
Income Statement								
Total Revenue	4,403,000	2,298,000	7,867,000	7,343,000	7,548,000	7,109,000	6,678,000	6,133,000
EBITDA	966,000	499,000	1,576,000	1,440,000	1,489,000	1,375,000	1,348,000	1,303,000
Depn & Amortn	138,000	68,000	...	...	...	...	...	...
Income Before Taxes	744,000	389,000	1,149,000	1,001,000	1,030,000	947,000	924,000	798,000
Income Taxes	216,000	119,000	326,000	246,000	323,000	300,000	298,000	273,000
Net Income	544,000	270,000	854,000	766,000	707,000	647,000	595,000	525,000
Average Shares	386,000	388,000	396,000	414,000	413,000	412,000	411,000	411,000
Balance Sheet								
Current Assets	1,878,000	2,018,000	1,578,000	2,112,000	1,512,000	1,481,000	1,290,000	1,199,000
Total Assets	6,876,000	7,058,000	6,445,000	7,870,000	6,776,000	6,675,000	6,205,000	5,721,000
Current Liabilities	2,360,000	2,612,000	2,030,000	2,962,000	2,002,000	2,339,000	2,783,000	2,678,000
Long-Term Obligations	1,780,000	1,773,000	2,074,000	2,116,000	2,542,000	2,543,000	2,249,000	2,449,000
Total Liabilities	5,281,000	5,553,000	5,150,000	6,102,000	5,506,000	5,801,000	5,818,000	5,835,000
Stockholders' Equity	1,595,000	1,505,000	1,295,000	1,768,000	1,270,000	874,000	387,000	(114,000)
Shares Outstanding	375,000	378,000	379,000	402,000	408,000	408,000	410,000	410,000
Statistical Record								
Return on Assets %	11.82	11.88	11.96	10.49	10.54	10.07	9.82	9.04
Return on Equity %	54.11	60.31	55.92	50.57	66.13	102.90	428.85	...
EBITDA Margin %	21.94	21.71	20.03	19.61	19.73	19.34	20.19	21.25
Net Margin %	12.36	11.75	10.86	10.43	9.37	9.10	8.91	8.56
Asset Turnover	1.15	1.14	1.10	1.10	1.01	1.13	1.11	1.10	1.06
Current Ratio	0.80	0.77	0.78	0.71	0.76	0.63	0.46	0.45
Debt to Equity	1.12	1.18	1.60	1.20	2.00	2.91	5.81	...
Price Range	42.39-31.00	42.39-35.06	42.39-35.92	37.91-28.45	31.45-25.30	28.60-23.56	26.39-19.79	31.25-21.94
P/E Ratio	19.81-14.49	19.72-16.31	19.62-16.63	20.49-15.38	18.39-14.80	18.22-15.01	18.20-13.65	24.41-17.14
Average Yield %	2.24	2.24	2.08	2.23	2.38	2.38	2.74	2.28

Address: 1 Campbell Place, Camden, NJ 08103
Telephone: 856-342-4800
Fax: 856-342-3878

Web Site: www.campbellsoupcompany.com
Officers: Harvey Golub - Chmn. Douglas R. Conant - Pres., C.E.O.

Auditors: PricewaterhouseCoopers LLP
Investor Contact: 856-342-6428
Transfer Agents: EquiServe Trust Company, Providence, RI

CAPITAL ONE FINANCIAL CORP

Exchange	Symbol	Price	52Wk Range	Yield	P/E
NYS	COF	$49.22 (3/31/2008)	81.85-39.68	3.05	12.40

*7 Year Price Score 78.99 *NYSE Composite Index=100 *12 Month Price Score 84.53

Interim Earnings (Per Share)

Qtr.	Mar	Jun	Sep	Dec
2003	1.35	1.23	1.17	1.10
2004	1.84	1.65	1.97	0.76
2005	1.99	2.03	1.81	0.91
2006	2.86	1.78	1.89	1.09
2007	1.62	1.89	(0.21)	0.62

Interim Dividends (Per Share)

Amt	Decl	Ex	Rec	Pay
0.027Q	4/26/2007	5/8/2007	5/10/2007	5/21/2007
0.027Q	7/26/2007	8/8/2007	8/10/2007	8/20/2007
0.027Q	10/25/2007	11/7/2007	11/12/2007	11/23/2007
0.375Q	1/31/2008	2/7/2008	2/11/2008	2/20/2008
Indicated Div. $1.50				

Valuation Analysis

		Institutional Holding	
Forecast P/E	7.94	No of Institutions	
	(1/10/2007)	666	
Market Cap	$18.4 Billion	Shares	
Book Value	24.3 Billion	311,255,072	
Price/Book	0.76	% Held	
Price/Sales	0.96	75.81	

TRADING VOLUME (thousand shares)

Business Summary: Commercial Banking (MIC: 8.1 SIC: 6022 NAIC: 522110)

Capital One Financial is a holding company. Co.'s key subsidiaries include Capital One Bank (COB), which offers credit and debit card products, other lending products, and deposit products; Capital One, National Association, which offers a range of banking products and financial services to consumers, small businesses and commercial clients; and Superior Savings of New England, N.A., which focuses on telephone and media-based generation of deposits. Co. also offers its products outside of the U.S. mainly through Capital One Bank (Europe) plc, an indirect subsidiary of COB located in the U.K. and through a branch of COB in Canada. As of Dec 31 2007, Co. had total assets of $150.59 billion.

Recent Developments: For the year ended Dec 31 2007, net income decreased 35.0% to US$1.57 billion from US$2.41 billion in the prior year. Net interest income increased 28.3% to US$6.53 billion from US$5.09 billion in the prior year. Provision for losses was US$2.64 billion versus US$1.48 billion in the prior year, an increase of 78.6%. Non-interest income rose 15.0% to US$8.05 billion from US$7.00 billion, while non-interest expense advanced 16.3% to US$8.08 billion.

Prospects: Co.'s outlook appears somewhat challenging. For instance, Co. expects to remain cautious in underwriting both consumer and commercial loans in the present economic cycle within its Local Banking segment while anticipating that the intense competitive condition for deposits to continue in 2008. As a result, Co. expects loan growth rate and deposit growth rate in the low single digits in its Local Banking segment in 2008. Moreover, Co. is experiencing several challenges that may pressure results within its National Lending businesses, including weakening consumer credit and uncertainty regarding the consumer economy. Overall, for 2008, Co. projects revenue growth in the low single digits.

Financial Data

(US$ in Thousands)	12/31/2007	12/31/2006	12/31/2005	12/31/2004	12/31/2003	12/31/2002	12/31/2001	12/31/2000
Earnings Per Share	3.97	7.62	6.73	6.21	4.85	3.93	2.91	2.24
Cash Flow Per Share	33.34	10.91	14.01	19.16	9.02	10.35	6.04	7.09
Tang Book Value Per Share	30.74	28.30	33.99	33.98	25.75	20.44	15.33	9.94
Dividends Per Share	0.107	0.107	0.107	0.107	0.107	0.107	0.107	0.107
Dividend Payout %	2.69	1.40	1.58	1.72	2.20	2.71	3.67	4.76
Income Statement								
Interest Income	11,078,156	8,194,229	5,726,881	4,794,420	4,367,654	4,180,766	2,834,397	2,389,902
Interest Expense	4,548,311	3,094,599	2,046,639	1,791,442	1,582,565	1,461,654	1,171,007	801,017
Net Interest Income	6,529,845	5,099,630	3,680,242	3,002,978	2,785,089	2,719,112	1,663,390	1,588,885
Provision for Losses	2,636,502	1,476,438	1,491,072	1,220,852	1,517,497	2,149,328	989,836	718,170
Non-Interest Income	8,054,223	6,996,732	6,358,105	5,900,157	5,415,924	5,466,836	4,419,893	3,034,416
Non-Interest Expense	8,078,010	6,967,193	5,718,273	5,322,219	4,856,723	4,585,581	4,058,027	3,147,657
Income Before Taxes	3,869,556	3,652,731	2,829,002	2,360,064	1,826,793	1,451,039	1,035,420	757,171
Income Taxes	1,277,837	1,238,238	1,019,855	816,582	675,914	551,395	393,455	287,840
Net Income	1,570,332	2,414,493	1,809,147	1,543,482	1,135,842	899,644	641,965	469,634
Average Shares	395,545	317,023	268,908	248,767	234,103	228,744	220,576	209,449
Balance Sheet								
Net Loans & Leases	98,842,027	94,332,139	58,057,681	36,710,591	31,255,269	26,133,652	20,081,014	14,585,712
Total Assets	150,590,369	149,739,285	88,701,411	53,747,255	46,283,706	37,382,380	28,184,047	18,889,341
Total Deposits	82,990,462	85,770,892	47,933,267	25,636,802	22,416,332	17,325,965	12,838,968	8,379,025
Total Liabilities	126,296,257	124,504,079	74,572,497	45,359,066	40,231,895	32,759,209	24,860,569	16,926,827
Stockholders' Equity	24,294,112	25,235,206	14,128,914	8,388,189	6,051,811	4,623,171	3,323,478	1,962,514
Shares Outstanding	372,854	409,925	300,761	246,833	235,042	226,194	216,778	197,368
Statistical Record								
Return on Assets %	1.05	2.03	2.54	3.08	2.72	2.74	2.73	2.91
Return on Equity %	6.34	12.27	16.07	21.32	21.28	22.64	24.29	26.93
Net Interest Margin %	58.94	62.23	64.26	62.63	63.77	65.04	58.69	66.48
Efficiency Ratio %	42.22	45.86	47.32	49.77	49.64	47.53	55.94	58.03
Loans to Deposits	1.19	1.10	1.21	1.43	1.39	1.51	1.56	1.74
Price Range	83.61-45.66	89.92-69.88	88.01-70.65	84.21-60.23	64.12-25.38	65.75-24.70	72.06-39.95	71.75-33.06
P/E Ratio	21.06-11.50	11.80-9.17	13.08-10.50	13.56-9.70	13.22-5.23	16.73-6.28	24.76-13.73	32.03-14.76
Average Yield %	0.15	0.13	0.14	0.15	0.23	0.23	0.19	0.21

Address: 1680 Capital One Drive, Mclean, VA 22102 **Telephone:** 703-720-1000	**Web Site:** www.capitalone.com **Officers:** Richard D. Fairbank - Chmn., Pres., C.E.O. Nigel W. Morris - Vice-Chmn.	**Auditors:** Ernst & Young LLP **Investor Contact:** 703-720-1000 **Transfer Agents:** EquiServe Trust Company, N.A., Providence, RI

CARDINAL HEALTH, INC.

Exchange	Symbol	Price	52Wk Range	Yield	P/E	Div Acheiver
NYS	CAH	$52.51 (3/31/2008)	75.28-49.80	0.91	13.06	11 Years

*7 Year Price Score 82.05   *NYSE Composite Index=100   *12 Month Price Score 95.32

Interim Earnings (Per Share)

Qtr.	Sep	Dec	Mar	Jun
2004-05	0.49	0.49	0.84	0.59
2005-06	0.53	0.70	0.34	0.75
2006-07	0.66	1.80	0.05	2.26
2007-08	0.82	0.89	...	...

Interim Dividends (Per Share)

Amt	Decl	Ex	Rec	Pay
0.12Q	5/2/2007	6/27/2007	7/1/2007	7/15/2007
0.12Q	8/9/2007	9/27/2007	10/1/2007	10/15/2007
0.12Q	11/7/2007	12/27/2007	1/1/2008	1/15/2008
0.12Q	1/31/2008	3/28/2008	4/1/2008	4/15/2008
		Indicated Div: $0.48		

Valuation Analysis   Institutional Holding

Forecast P/E	12.96	No of Institutions	
	(1/10/2007)	504	
Market Cap	$18.8 Billion	Shares	
Book Value	7.1 Billion	337,604,512	
Price/Book	2.65	% Held	
Price/Sales	0.21	84.34	

Business Summary: Medical & Health Related Services (MIC: 12.5 SIC: 5122 NAIC: 424210)

Cardinal Health is a provider of products and services for the healthcare industry. As of June 30 2007, Co. had four segments: Healthcare Supply Chain Services - Pharmaceutical, which distributes branded and generic pharmaceutical products, over-the-counter healthcare products and consumer products; Healthcare Supply Chain Services - Medical, which distributes branded and private-label medical and laboratory products, as well as Co.'s own line of surgical and respiratory therapy products; Clinical Technologies and Services, which provides products and services to hospitals and other healthcare providers; and Medical Products Manufacturing, which manufactures medical and surgical products.

Recent Developments: For the quarter ended Dec 31 2007, income from continuing operations increased 3.0% to US$325.1 million from US$315.5 million in the year-earlier quarter. Net income decreased 56.1% to US$324.7 million from US$739.3 million in the year-earlier quarter. Revenues were US$23.28 billion, up 6.9% from US$21.78 billion the year before. Operating income was US$519.2 million versus US$511.9 million in the prior-year quarter, an increase of 1.4%. Direct operating expenses rose 7.0% to US$21.93 billion from US$20.48 billion in the comparable period the year before. Indirect operating expenses increased 6.0% to US$835.4 million from US$788.0 million in the equivalent prior-year period.

Prospects: Co. is seeing growth in three out of its four operating segments, and continues to expect overall improvement in its Healthcare Supply Chain Services Sector in the second half of the fiscal year ending June 2008. Meanwhile, within its Healthcare Supply Chain Services- Pharmaceutical segment, Co. has revised its fiscal 2008, citing the effect of anti-diversion measures for controlled substances, changes in its expectations for branded price increases and the generics market, and the effect of contract re-pricings. However, Co. still anticipates double-digit earnings per share growth for fiscal 2008 and aims to strengthen its business as it addresses the issues that have hampered its results.

Financial Data

(US$ in Thousands)	6 Mos	3 Mos	06/30/2007	06/30/2006	06/30/2005	06/30/2004	06/30/2003	06/30/2002
Earnings Per Share	4.02	4.93	4.77	2.33	2.41	3.35	3.10	2.30
Cash Flow Per Share	2.69	2.52	3.10	5.08	6.62	6.03	3.13	2.19
Tang Book Value Per Share	3.62	3.44	4.12	8.52	8.20	7.05	12.10	10.80
Dividends Per Share	0.450	0.420	0.390	0.270	0.150	0.120	0.105	0.100
Dividend Payout %	11.19	8.52	8.18	11.59	6.22	3.58	3.39	4.35
Income Statement								
Total Revenue	45,256,100	21,973,400	86,852,000	81,363,600	74,910,700	65,053,500	56,737,000	51,135,700
EBITDA	1,108,000	541,800	1,574,400	2,227,700	2,039,000	2,537,600	2,392,400	1,944,800
Depn & Amortn	191,900	94,900	...	...	...	...	...	...
Income Before Taxes	916,100	446,900	1,252,300	1,835,000	1,629,300	2,238,400	2,126,600	1,701,300
Income Taxes	287,800	143,700	412,600	590,300	582,600	713,700	714,700	575,000
Net Income	626,500	301,800	1,931,100	1,000,100	1,050,700	1,474,500	1,405,800	1,056,200
Average Shares	364,600	370,200	404,700	428,500	435,700	440,000	453,600	459,900
Balance Sheet								
Current Assets	14,721,800	14,333,200	14,544,500	14,776,700	13,442,700	13,057,900	13,249,600	11,906,600
Total Assets	23,466,800	22,998,100	23,153,800	23,374,100	22,059,200	21,369,100	18,521,400	16,438,000
Current Liabilities	11,410,500	11,114,000	11,459,700	11,372,800	10,105,000	9,369,400	7,314,400	6,810,400
Long-Term Obligations	3,396,500	3,347,500	3,457,300	2,599,700	2,319,900	2,834,700	2,471,900	2,207,000
Total Liabilities	16,358,700	15,929,900	15,776,900	14,883,400	13,466,200	13,392,800	10,763,300	10,045,000
Stockholders' Equity	7,108,100	7,068,200	7,376,900	8,490,700	8,593,000	7,976,300	7,758,100	6,393,000
Shares Outstanding	358,200	362,500	368,100	410,800	426,200	430,900	448,400	448,800
Statistical Record								
Return on Assets %	6.50	8.45	8.30	4.40	4.84	7.37	8.04	6.80
Return on Equity %	19.33	25.34	24.34	11.71	12.68	18.69	19.87	17.86
EBITDA Margin %	2.45	2.47	1.81	2.74	2.72	3.90	4.22	3.80
Net Margin %	1.38	1.37	2.22	1.23	1.40	2.27	2.48	2.07
Asset Turnover	3.76	3.79	3.73	3.58	3.45	3.25	3.25	3.29
Current Ratio	1.29	1.29	1.27	1.30	1.33	1.39	1.81	1.75
Debt to Equity	0.48	0.47	0.47	0.31	0.27	0.36	0.32	0.35
Price Range	75.28-56.47	75.28-61.83	75.28-61.83	75.34-57.28	70.05-37.65	75.98-54.75	71.16-49.08	76.60-60.80
P/E Ratio	18.73-14.05	15.27-12.54	15.78-12.96	32.33-24.58	29.07-15.62	22.68-16.34	22.95-15.83	33.30-26.43
Average Yield %	0.66	0.61	0.57	0.41	0.29	0.19	0.17	0.15

Address: 7000 Cardinal Place, Dublin, OH 43017	Web Site: www.cardinalhealth.com	Auditors: Ernst & Young, LLP
Telephone: 614-757-5000	Officers: Robert D. Walter - Chmn., C.E.O. George L. Fotiades - Pres., C.O.O.	Transfer Agents: Computershare
Fax: 614-717-6000		

CARLISLE COMPANIES INC.

Exchange	Symbol	Price	52Wk Range	Yield	P/E	Div Acheiver
NYS	CSL	$33.44 (3/31/2008)	49.96-29.96	1.73	9.72	31 Years

*7 Year Price Score 110.16   *NYSE Composite Index=100   *12 Month Price Score 91.35

TRADING VOLUME (thousand shares)

Interim Earnings (Per Share)

Qtr.	Mar	Jun	Sep	Dec
2003	0.28	0.47	0.40	0.30
2004	0.38	0.59	0.46	(0.16)
2005	0.45	0.56	0.32	0.39
2006	0.67	0.90	0.62	1.28
2007	0.59	0.85	1.31	0.69

Interim Dividends (Per Share)

Amt	Decl	Ex	Rec	Pay
0.135Q	5/2/2007	5/15/2007	5/17/2007	6/1/2007
0.145Q	8/1/2007	8/15/2007	8/17/2007	9/1/2007
0.145Q	11/7/2007	11/15/2007	11/19/2007	12/1/2007
0.145Q	2/5/2008	2/15/2008	2/20/2008	3/1/2008

Indicated Div: $0.58 (Div. Reinv. Plan)

Valuation Analysis

		Institutional Holding	
Forecast P/E	11.56	No of Institutions	
	(1/10/2007)	188	
Market Cap	$2.0 Billion	Shares	
Book Value	1.1 Billion	49,270,904	
Price/Book	1.81	% Held	
Price/Sales	0.70	80.76	

Business Summary: Rubber Products (MIC: 11.6 SIC: 3069 NAIC: 326211)

Carlisle Companies is a holding company. Co. manufactures and distributes a variety of products across a range of industries, which include roofing, construction, trucking, foodservice, industrial equipment, lawn and garden and aircraft manufacturing. Co. markets its products as a component supplier to original equipment manufacturers, distributors, as well as directly to end-users. As at Dec 31 2007, Co. managed its businesses under three operating groups: Construction Materials, Industrial Components and Diversified Components; and had five reportable segments: Construction Materials, Industrial Components, Specialty Products, Transportation Products, and General Industry.

Recent Developments: For the year ended Dec 31 2007, income from continuing operations increased 19.1% to US$213.0 million from US$178.8 million a year earlier. Net income decreased 0.7% to US$215.6 million from US$217.1 million in the prior year. Revenues were US$2.88 billion, up 12.4% from US$2.56 billion the year before. Direct operating expenses rose 12.7% to US$2.29 billion from US$2.04 billion in the comparable period the year before. Indirect operating expenses increased 18.2% to US$303.4 million from US$256.7 million in the equivalent prior-year period.

Prospects: On Jan 25 2008, Co. acquired Dinex International, Inc., a supplier of foodservice products, for $95.0 million. Hence, Dinex will operate within Co.'s FoodService Products business, and should complement Co.'s core foodservice product categories and supports its growth initiatives in the healthcare, educational, corrections and other institutional foodservice markets. Meanwhile, Co. has established a five year plan to achieve average sales growth target of 10.0% and a 15.0% operating income margin by 2012 through improved operating capabilities and strategic growth. For 2008, Co. expects organic sales growth to be at least equal to 2007, and operating margin to improve over the prior year.

Financial Data

(US$ in Thousands)	12/31/2007	12/31/2006	12/31/2005	12/31/2004	12/31/2003	12/31/2002	12/31/2001	12/31/2000
Earnings Per Share	3.44	3.46	1.71	1.27	1.44	0.47	0.41	1.57
Cash Flow Per Share	4.20	0.32	3.47	1.79	1.90	3.71	3.68	2.06
Tang Book Value Per Share	11.79	9.98	6.57	6.47	5.19	4.04	3.36	4.90
Dividends Per Share	0.560	0.520	0.480	0.450	0.435	0.425	0.410	0.380
Dividend Payout %	16.28	15.01	28.07	35.43	30.21	90.43	100.00	24.20
Income Statement								
Total Revenue	2,876,383	2,572,510	2,209,610	2,227,614	2,108,164	1,971,280	1,849,477	1,771,067
EBITDA	395,260	335,467	262,687	238,329	206,560	184,645	131,005	238,432
Income Before Taxes	319,342	255,317	193,558	170,340	131,733	110,500	37,925	150,865
Income Taxes	106,321	78,031	60,224	52,026	42,813	38,122	13,084	54,685
Net Income	215,637	215,689	106,365	79,612	88,920	28,625	24,841	96,180
Average Shares	62,630	62,236	62,156	62,818	61,726	61,166	60,900	61,198
Balance Sheet								
Current Assets	1,023,192	978,241	661,172	652,269	584,381	481,508	553,272	576,477
Total Assets	1,988,794	1,877,817	1,563,257	1,501,241	1,436,909	1,315,900	1,397,987	1,305,679
Current Liabilities	388,187	466,686	372,711	384,022	339,343	324,262	273,779	399,948
Long-Term Obligations	262,809	274,658	282,426	259,554	294,581	293,124	461,744	281,864
Total Liabilities	869,899	935,608	833,018	802,754	804,979	762,823	857,703	757,800
Stockholders' Equity	1,118,895	942,209	730,239	698,487	631,930	553,077	540,284	547,879
Shares Outstanding	60,603	61,450	60,714	61,792	61,983	61,195	60,526	60,502
Statistical Record								
Return on Assets %	11.15	12.54	6.94	5.40	6.46	2.11	1.84	8.04
Return on Equity %	20.92	25.79	14.89	11.94	15.01	5.24	4.57	18.70
EBITDA Margin %	13.74	13.04	11.89	10.70	9.80	9.37	7.08	13.46
Net Margin %	7.50	8.38	4.81	3.57	4.22	1.45	1.34	5.43
Asset Turnover	1.49	1.50	1.44	1.51	1.53	1.45	1.37	1.48
Current Ratio	2.64	2.10	1.77	1.70	1.72	1.48	2.02	1.44
Debt to Equity	0.23	0.29	0.39	0.37	0.47	0.53	0.85	0.51
Price Range	49.96-36.80	45.04-33.84	37.31-29.78	33.45-27.36	30.75-19.62	23.45-16.32	21.84-13.20	24.88-15.59
P/E Ratio	14.52-10.70	13.02-9.78	21.82-17.42	26.34-21.54	21.35-13.63	49.90-34.73	53.28-32.20	15.84-9.93
Average Yield %	1.28	1.30	1.43	1.49	1.87	2.12	2.33	1.86

Address: 13925 Ballantyne Corporate Place, Suite 400, Charlotte, NC 28277	**Web Site:** www.carlisle.com	**Auditors:** ERNST & YOUNG LLP
Telephone: 704-501-1100	**Officers:** Stephen P. Munn - Chmn. Richmond D. McKinnish - Pres., C.E.O.	**Investor Contact:** 704-501-1100
Fax: 704-501-1190		**Transfer Agents:** Computershare Investor Services, LLC., Chicago, IL

CARMAX INC.

Exchange	Symbol	Price	52Wk Range	Yield	P/E
NYS	KMX	$19.42 (3/31/2008)	27.40-16.63	N/A	20.88

*7 Year Price Score 119.48 *NYSE Composite Index=100 *12 Month Price Score 96.63

Interim Earnings (Per Share)

Qtr.	May	Aug	Nov	Feb
2004-05	0.17	0.14	0.09	0.14
2005-06	0.19	0.20	0.13	0.19
2006-07	0.27	0.25	0.21	0.20
2007-08	0.30	0.29	0.14	...

Interim Dividends (Per Share)

No Dividends Paid

Valuation Analysis

		Institutional Holding	
Forecast P/E	N/A	No of Institutions	287
Market Cap	$4.2 Billion	Shares	
Book Value	1.5 Billion		193,497,888
Price/Book	2.92	% Held	90.05
Price/Sales	0.53		

Business Summary: Retail - Automotive (MIC: 5.7 SIC: 5521 NAIC: 441120)

CarMax is a holding company. Through its subsidiaries, Co. is engaged as a retailer of used cars. In addition, Co. also provides a selection of used vehicles at fixed prices. Meanwhile, Co.'s sales process is designed to allow consumers the opportunity to shop for vehicles the same way they shop for items at other big-box retailers. Further, Co. also purchases, reconditions, and sells used vehicles as well as providing its customers with a range of related products and services, including the financing of vehicle purchases through CarMax Auto Finance. As of Feb 27 2007, Co. operated 77 used car superstores in 36 metropolitan markets and 81 retail stores.

Recent Developments: For the quarter ended Nov 30 2007, net income decreased 34.3% to US$29.8 million from US$45.4 million in the year-earlier quarter. Revenues were US$1.89 billion, up 6.6% from US$1.77 billion the year before. Direct operating expenses rose 6.7% to US$1.64 billion from US$1.54 billion in the comparable period the year before. Indirect operating expenses increased 25.0% to US$193.9 million from US$155.1 million in the equivalent prior-year period.

Prospects: For fiscal year ending Feb 29 2008, Co. is reducing its comparable store used unit sales guidance to approximately 2.0% while expecting earnings per share to be between $0.87 and $0.93 primarily as a result of the continued turmoil in the asset-backed credit markets and the resulting higher funding costs. Co. noted that such revised guidance are based on several assumptions, including an expectation that the increase in spreads experienced in the asset-backed commercial paper market will continue, at least in the near term. Meanwhile, during the 12 months ending Nov 30 2008, Co. plans to open 13 used car superstores which include eight production stores and five non-production stores.

Financial Data

(US$ in Thousands)	9 Mos	6 Mos	3 Mos	02/28/2007	02/28/2006	02/28/2005	02/29/2004	02/28/2003
Earnings Per Share	0.93	1.00	0.95	0.92	0.69	0.54	0.55	0.46
Cash Flow Per Share	0.71	1.01	0.76	0.64	0.58	0.22	0.72	0.35
Tang Book Value Per Share	6.66	6.48	6.11	5.77	4.57	3.84	3.28	2.69
Income Statement								
Total Revenue	6,154,964	4,269,664	2,147,134	7,465,656	6,259,967	5,260,262	4,597,691	3,969,944
EBITDA	296,413	235,308	116,672	357,900	266,729	204,776	205,653	171,647
Depn & Amortn	34,168	22,026	-10,835	...	...	...	...	...
Income Before Taxes	262,245	213,282	105,837	323,349	239,983	184,523	189,350	156,697
Income Taxes	102,049	82,932	40,482	124,752	91,928	71,595	72,900	61,895
Net Income	160,196	130,350	65,355	198,597	148,055	112,928	116,450	94,802
Average Shares	220,558	220,580	220,130	216,739	212,688	211,558	211,256	209,140
Balance Sheet								
Current Assets	1,212,237	1,132,716	1,188,327	1,150,516	941,738	864,956	773,481	708,745
Total Assets	2,109,392	1,977,790	1,977,150	1,885,573	1,489,247	1,293,013	1,037,017	917,617
Current Liabilities	510,088	423,614	502,942	512,022	363,315	329,331	242,398	248,103
Long-Term Obligations	27,280	27,361	33,469	33,744	134,787	128,419	100,000	100,000
Total Liabilities	655,063	566,957	648,781	638,198	529,509	492,037	356,264	363,048
Stockholders' Equity	1,454,329	1,410,833	1,328,369	1,247,375	959,738	800,976	680,753	554,569
Shares Outstanding	218,306	217,879	217,303	216,028	209,909	208,606	207,556	206,166
Statistical Record								
Return on Assets %	10.61	12.06	11.53	11.77	10.64	9.69	11.88	...
Return on Equity %	15.25	17.14	17.40	18.00	16.82	15.24	18.80	...
EBITDA Margin %	4.82	5.51	5.43	4.79	4.26	3.89	4.47	4.32
Net Margin %	2.60	3.05	3.04	2.66	2.37	2.15	2.53	2.39
Asset Turnover	4.21	4.38	4.30	4.42	4.50	4.52	4.69	...
Current Ratio	2.38	2.67	2.36	2.25	2.59	2.63	3.19	2.86
Debt to Equity	0.02	0.02	0.03	0.03	0.14	0.16	0.15	0.18
Price Range	29.25-18.88	29.25-18.77	29.25-14.91	29.25-14.91	16.80-12.37	17.69-9.22	19.63-6.33	16.65-6.76
P/E Ratio	31.45-20.30	29.25-18.77	30.78-15.70	31.79-16.21	24.35-17.93	32.76-17.08	35.68-11.50	36.20-14.70

Address: 12800 Tuckahoe Creek Parkway, Richmond, VA 23238	Web Site: www.carmax.com	Auditors: KPMG LLP
Telephone: 804-747-0422	Officers: Richard L. Sharp - Chmn. W. Austin Ligon - Pres., C.E.O.	Investor Contact: 804-935-4591
Fax: 804-747-5848		Transfer Agents: Wells Fargo Bank, N.A., South St. Paul, MN

CARNIVAL CORP.

CARNIVAL CORP.

Exchange	Symbol	Price	52Wk Range	Yield	P/E
NYS	CCL	$40.48 (3/31/2008)	51.33-36.48	3.95	14.06

*7 Year Price Score 90.57   *NYSE Composite Index=100   *12 Month Price Score 96.50

Interim Earnings (Per Share)

Qtr.	Feb	May	Aug	Nov
2004-05	0.42	0.47	1.36	0.43
2005-06	0.34	0.46	1.49	0.52
2006-07	0.35	0.48	1.67	0.44
2007-08	0.30	...	...	...

Interim Dividends (Per Share)

Amt	Decl	Ex	Rec	Pay
0.35Q	4/16/2007	5/16/2007	5/18/2007	6/8/2007
0.35Q	7/17/2007	8/22/2007	8/24/2007	9/14/2007
0.40Q	10/17/2007	11/20/2007	11/23/2007	12/14/2007
0.40Q	1/15/2008	2/20/2008	2/22/2008	3/14/2008

Indicated Div: $1.60

Valuation Analysis		Institutional Holding	
Forecast P/E	N/A	No of Institutions	
		424	
Market Cap	331.8 Billion	Shares	
Book Value	19.7 Billion	447,166,176	
Price/Book	1.61	% Held	
Price/Sales	2.36	71.74	

TRADING VOLUME (thousand shares)

Business Summary: Shipping (MIC: 15.3 SIC: 4489 NAIC: 483212)

Carnival is a global cruise and vacation company. Co. has a portfolio of 11 cruise brands providing cruise vacations in various vacation markets including North America, the U.K., Germany, southern Europe, Asia/Pacific and South America. The cruise brands are as follows: Carnival Cruise Lines, Princess Cruises, Costa Cruises, Holland America Lines, P&O Cruises, Cunard Line, AIDA Crusies, P&O Cruises Australia, Ocean Village, Ibero Cruises and The Yachts of Seabourn. At Jan 29 2008, Co. operated 85 cruise ships with passenger capacity of 158,352. In addition, Co. owns Holland America Tours and Princess Tours, the cruise/tour operators in the State of Alaska and the Yukon Territory of Canada.

Recent Developments: For the quarter ended Feb 29 2008, net income decreased 16.6% to US$236.0 million from US$283.0 million in the year-earlier quarter. Revenues were US$3.15 billion, up 17.3% from US$2.69 billion the year before. Operating income was US$312.0 million versus US$353.0 million in the prior-year quarter, a decrease of 11.6%. Direct operating expenses rose 25.0% to US$2.11 billion from US$1.69 billion in the comparable period the year before. Indirect operating expenses increased 12.7% to US$726.0 million from US$644.0 million in the equivalent prior-year period.

Prospects: Looking ahead to the fiscal year ending Nov 2008, Co. has revised its earnings per share guidance to a range of $3.00 to $3.20 compared with its previous guidance of $3.10 to $3.30, primarily as a result of higher fuel cost expectations. Meanwhile, Co. continues to enhance its business by expanding the number of cruise ships it operates. Notably, as of Jan 29 2008, Co. had signed agreements with three shipyards providing for the construction of 22 additional cruise ships scheduled to enter service between Apr 2008 and June 2012. These additions are expected to result in an increase in Co.'s passenger capacity of 51,338 lower berths going forward.

Financial Data
(US$ in Thousands)

	3 Mos	11/30/2007	11/30/2006	11/30/2005	11/30/2004	11/30/2003	11/30/2002	11/30/2001
Earnings Per Share	2.88	2.95	2.77	2.70	2.24	1.66	1.73	1.58
Cash Flow Per Share	4.87	5.13	4.54	4.23	4.00	2.69	2.50	2.12
Tang Book Value Per Share	18.78	17.60	17.10	15.47	13.85	11.83	11.48	10.13
Dividends Per Share	1.500	1.375	1.025	0.800	0.525	0.335	...	...
Dividend Payout %	52.00	46.61	37.00	29.63	23.44	20.18	...	...
Income Statement								
Total Revenue	3,152,000	13,033,000	11,839,000	11,087,000	9,727,000	6,718,000	4,368,269	4,535,751
EBITDA	615,000	3,825,000	3,593,000	3,534,000	2,980,000	1,976,000	...	...
Depn & Amortn	301,000	...	...	...	...	...	...	...
Income Before Taxes	226,000	2,424,000	2,318,000	2,330,000	1,901,000	1,223,000	...	...
Income Taxes	(10,000)	16,000	39,000	73,000	47,000	29,000	(56,562)	(12,257)
Net Income	236,000	2,408,000	2,279,000	2,257,000	1,854,000	1,194,000	1,015,941	926,200
Average Shares	814,000	828,000	836,000	853,000	851,000	724,000	388,036	586,862
Balance Sheet								
Current Assets	2,023,000	1,976,000	1,995,000	2,215,000	1,728,000	2,132,000	1,132,152	1,958,988
Total Assets	34,145,000	34,181,000	30,552,000	28,432,000	27,636,000	24,491,000	12,334,848	11,563,552
Current Liabilities	7,393,000	7,260,000	5,415,000	5,192,000	5,034,000	3,315,000	1,619,806	1,480,240
Long-Term Obligations	6,271,000	6,313,000	6,355,000	5,727,000	6,291,000	6,918,000	3,011,969	2,954,854
Total Liabilities	14,405,000	14,218,000	12,342,000	11,460,000	11,876,000	10,698,000	4,916,945	4,972,775
Stockholders' Equity	19,740,000	19,963,000	18,210,000	16,972,000	15,760,000	13,793,000	7,417,903	6,590,777
Shares Outstanding	786,000	850,000	794,000	807,000	804,000	798,000	586,788	586,171
Statistical Record								
Return on Assets %	7.30	7.44	7.73	8.05	7.09	6.48	8.50	8.66
Return on Equity %	12.38	12.62	12.96	13.79	12.51	11.26	14.50	14.87
EBITDA Margin %	19.51	29.35	30.35	31.88	30.64	29.41	...	...
Net Margin %	7.49	18.48	19.25	20.36	19.06	17.77	23.26	20.42
Asset Turnover	0.42	0.40	0.40	0.40	0.37	0.36	0.37	0.42
Current Ratio	0.27	0.27	0.37	0.43	0.34	0.64	0.70	1.32
Debt to Equity	0.32	0.32	0.35	0.34	0.40	0.50	0.41	0.45
Price Range	51.33-38.13	52.39-42.23	56.00-36.41	58.74-46.55	53.65-35.02	35.81-20.75	34.58-22.30	33.81-18.05
P/E Ratio	17.82-13.24	17.76-14.32	20.22-13.14	21.76-17.24	23.95-15.63	21.57-12.50	19.99-12.89	21.40-11.42
Average Yield %	3.26	2.89	2.20	1.52	1.17	1.13	...	...

Address: 3655 N.W. 87th Avenue, Miami, FL 33178-2428 Telephone: 305-599-2600	Web Site: www.carnivalcorp.com Officers: Micky Arison - Chmn., C.E.O. Richard D. Ames - Sr. V.P., Audit Services	Auditors: PricewaterhouseCoopers LLP Transfer Agents: ComputerShare Investor Services, Providence, RI

149

CARPENTER TECHNOLOGY CORP.

Exchange	Symbol	Price	52Wk Range	Yield	P/E
NYS	CRS	$55.97 (3/31/2008)	79.40-51.64	1.07	11.93

*7 Year Price Score 173.85 *NYSE Composite Index=100 *12 Month Price Score 102.41

Interim Earnings (Per Share)

Qtr.	Sep	Dec	Mar	Jun
2004-05	0.40	0.64	0.69	0.94
2005-06	0.77	0.82	1.16	1.28
2006-07	0.97	0.91	1.26	1.17
2007-08	1.12	1.14	...	...

Interim Dividends (Per Share)

Amt	Decl	Ex	Rec	Pay
0.15Q	8/21/2007	8/30/2007	9/4/2007	9/7/2007
0.15Q	10/16/2007	10/26/2007	10/30/2007	12/6/2007
100%	10/16/2007	11/16/2007	11/6/2007	11/15/2007
0.15Q	1/23/2008	2/1/2008	2/5/2008	3/6/2008

Indicated Div: $0.60

Valuation Analysis

		Institutional Holding	
Forecast P/E	9.03	No of Institutions	
	(1/10/2007)	228	
Market Cap	$2.7 Billion	Shares	
Book Value	935.4 Million	22,990,812	
Price/Book	2.91	% Held	
Price/Sales	1.35	89.72	

Business Summary: Metal Works (MIC: 11.3 SIC: 3312 NAIC: 331111)

Carpenter Technology is engaged in the manufacturing, fabrication, and distribution of specialty metals and engineered products. Co. primarily processes basic raw materials such as nickel, titanium, chromium, iron scrap and other metal alloying elements through various melting, hot forming and cold working facilities to produce finished products in the form of billet, bar, rod, wire, narrow strip, special shapes, and hollow forms in many sizes and finishes. Co. also produces certain metal powders and fabricated metal products. Co.'s operations are organized into four business units: Specialty Alloys Operations, Dynamet, Carpenter Powder Products, and Engineered Products.

Recent Developments: For the quarter ended Dec 31 2007, income from continuing operations increased 26.5% to US$57.7 million from US$45.6 million in the year-earlier quarter. Net income increased 16.6% to US$56.1 million from US$48.1 million in the year-earlier quarter. Revenues were US$446.4 million, up 6.1% from US$420.8 million the year before. Operating income was US$80.5 million versus US$59.0 million in the prior-year quarter, an increase of 36.4%. Direct operating expenses declined 0.2% to US$329.0 million from US$329.7 million in the comparable period the year before. Indirect operating expenses increased 15.0% to US$36.9 million from US$32.1 million in the equivalent prior-year period.

Prospects: On Dec 21 2007, Co. announced a definitive agreement to sell its ceramic operation, consisting of its Certech and Carpenter Advanced Ceramics business units, to The Morgan Crucible Company plc, a UK-based advanced materials company. The divestiture reflects Co.'s strategic decision to focus on global markets for specialty alloy products to further strengthen and grow its nickel-based alloy and titanium businesses. The transaction is valued at approximately $147.0 million and is expected to be completed early in 2008. Looking ahead to the second half of fiscal year ending June 2008, Co. expects continued strength in energy market sales and resumption in sales growth to the aerospace market.

Financial Data

(US$ in Thousands)	6 Mos	3 Mos	06/30/2007	06/30/2006	06/30/2005	06/30/2004	06/30/2003	06/30/2002
Earnings Per Share	4.69	4.46	4.32	4.04	2.69	0.75	(0.28)	(2.71)
Cash Flow Per Share	5.09	5.06	5.35	4.71	2.94	2.09	2.07	3.24
Tang Book Value Per Share	18.04	17.99	19.18	16.89	12.78	9.69	8.79	9.20
Dividends Per Share	0.563	0.525	0.487	0.300	0.204	0.165	0.289	0.660
Dividend Payout %	11.99	11.77	11.30	7.43	7.59	22.15	...	...
Income Statement								
Total Revenue	897,700	475,000	1,944,800	1,568,200	1,314,200	1,016,700	871,100	977,100
EBITDA	196,700	98,600	380,500	366,100	257,600	128,600	70,300	89,000
Depn & Amortn	25,100	12,400	...	...	...	...	...	...
Income Before Taxes	171,100	86,500	331,000	309,100	190,000	49,700	(22,900)	(13,300)
Income Taxes	57,500	28,800	103,800	97,300	54,500	13,700	(12,000)	(7,300)
Net Income	113,700	57,700	227,200	211,800	135,500	36,000	(10,900)	(118,300)
Average Shares	49,000	51,600	52,600	52,200	50,200	46,800	44,600	46,000
Balance Sheet								
Current Assets	1,057,300	1,121,200	1,255,700	999,300	731,600	491,800	369,300	375,900
Total Assets	1,848,900	1,899,500	2,025,700	1,887,900	1,653,400	1,456,200	1,399,900	1,479,500
Current Liabilities	312,900	335,500	366,200	271,400	249,100	230,100	149,900	210,800
Long-Term Obligations	300,000	300,300	299,500	333,100	333,700	332,700	378,900	375,800
Total Liabilities	913,500	942,700	958,000	941,600	929,200	918,200	925,300	971,200
Stockholders' Equity	935,400	956,800	1,067,700	946,300	724,200	538,000	474,600	508,300
Shares Outstanding	48,588	49,559	52,243	51,028	49,844	46,068	44,673	44,691
Statistical Record								
Return on Assets %	12.61	12.15	11.61	11.96	8.71	2.51	N.M.	N.M.
Return on Equity %	24.39	23.90	22.56	25.36	21.47	7.09	N.M.	N.M.
EBITDA Margin %	21.91	20.76	19.56	23.35	19.60	12.65	8.07	9.11
Net Margin %	12.67	12.15	11.68	13.51	10.31	3.54	N.M.	N.M.
Asset Turnover	1.05	1.05	0.99	0.89	0.85	0.71	0.61	0.62
Current Ratio	3.38	3.34	3.43	3.68	2.94	2.14	2.46	1.78
Debt to Equity	0.32	0.31	0.28	0.35	0.46	0.62	0.80	0.74
Price Range	79.40-48.65	74.03-48.65	68.27-45.34	69.88-25.64	35.00-15.65	17.45-7.42	14.15-4.79	15.07-10.38
P/E Ratio	16.93-10.37	16.60-10.91	15.80-10.49	17.30-6.35	13.01-5.82	23.27-9.90	...	...
Average Yield %	0.89	0.89	0.86	0.76	0.78	1.23	3.36	5.03

Address: P. O. Box 14662, Reading, PA 19610	**Web Site:** www.cartech.com	**Auditors:** PricewaterhouseCoopers LLP
Telephone: 610-208-2000	**Officers:** Robert J. Torcolini - Chmn., Pres., C.E.O.	**Investor Contact:** 610-208-2165
Fax: 610-208-2361	Terrence E. Geremski - Sr. V.P., Fin., C.F.O.	**Transfer Agents:** American Stock Transfer & Trust Company

CATERPILLAR INC.

Exchange	Symbol	Price	52Wk Range	Yield	P/E	Div Acheiver
NYS	CAT	$78.29 (3/31/2008)	86.98-62.47	1.84	14.58	14 Years

*7 Year Price Score 129.42   *NYSE Composite Index=100   *12 Month Price Score 104.38

Interim Earnings (Per Share)

Qtr.	Mar	Jun	Sep	Dec
2003	0.19	0.57	0.31	0.49
2004	0.58	0.78	0.70	0.78
2005	0.81	1.08	0.94	1.20
2006	1.20	1.52	1.14	1.31
2007	1.23	1.24	1.40	1.50

Interim Dividends (Per Share)

Amt	Decl	Ex	Rec	Pay
0.30Q	4/11/2007	4/19/2007	4/23/2007	5/19/2007
0.36Q	6/13/2007	7/18/2007	7/20/2007	8/20/2007
0.36Q	10/10/2007	10/18/2007	10/22/2007	11/20/2007
0.36Q	12/12/2007	1/17/2008	1/22/2008	2/20/2008

Indicated Div: $1.44 (Div. Reinv. Plan)

Valuation Analysis

		Institutional Holding	
Forecast P/E	10.09	No of Institutions	
	(1/10/2007)	864	
Market Cap	$48.9 Billion	Shares	
Book Value	8.9 Billion	413,362,752	
Price/Book	5.50	% Held	
Price/Sales	1.09	64.01	

Business Summary: Industrial Machinery and Equipment (MIC: 11.5 SIC: 3531 NAIC: 333120)

Caterpillar has three principal lines of business. Co.'s Machinery business designs, produces and sells construction, mining and forestry machinery, and designs, manufactures, remanufactures, maintains and services rail-related products. Co.'s Engines business designs, manufactures and sells engines for its machinery; electric power generation systems; on-highway vehicles and locomotives; marine, petroleum, construction, industrial agricultural and other applications; and related parts. Co.'s Financial Products business provides financing alternatives, loans and insurance services to customers and dealers for its machinery and engines, gas turbines and other equipment and marine vessels.

Recent Developments:
For the year ended Dec 31 2007, net income was unchanged at US$3.54 billion versus US$3.54 billion the prior year. Revenues were US$44.96 billion, up 8.3% from US$41.52 billion the year before. Operating income was unchanged at US$4.92 billion versus the prior year. Direct operating expenses rose 10.4% to US$32.63 billion from US$29.55 billion in the comparable period the year before. Indirect operating expenses increased 5.2% to US$7.41 billion from US$7.05 billion in the equivalent prior year period.

Prospects:
For 2008, Co. expects sales and revenues to be driven by strength in the economies outside North America, strong worldwide engine demand and a slight rebound in on-highway truck engine sales, which is anticipated to offset the ongoing weakness in the North American machinery market. Also, Co. plans to raise its research and development for new products and capital investment in order to accelerate its capacity globally, primarily with continuous focus on continuing its global deployment of the Caterpillar Production System with 6 Sigma. Hence, Co. is anticipating both sales and revenues to grow by about 5.0% to 10.0%, while profit per share is estimated to improve by 5.0% to 15.0%.

Financial Data
(US$ in Thousands)

	12/31/2007	12/31/2006	12/31/2005	12/31/2004	12/31/2003	12/31/2002	12/31/2001	12/31/2000
Earnings Per Share	5.37	5.17	4.04	2.88	1.56	1.15	1.16	1.51
Cash Flow Per Share	12.43	8.80	4.59	(5.81)	2.99	3.44	2.89	2.96
Tang Book Value Per Share	10.33	7.07	9.77	8.31	6.46	5.50	5.74	5.96
Dividends Per Share	1.320	1.100	0.910	0.780	0.710	0.700	0.690	0.665
Dividend Payout %	24.58	21.28	22.52	27.13	45.37	60.87	59.48	44.04
Income Statement								
Total Revenue	44,958,000	41,517,000	36,339,000	30,251,000	22,763,000	20,152,000	20,450,000	20,175,000
EBITDA	7,038,000	6,737,000	5,638,000	4,334,000	3,070,000	2,613,000	2,623,000	2,842,000
Income Before Taxes	4,953,000	4,861,000	3,901,000	2,707,000	1,477,000	1,114,000	1,169,000	1,528,000
Income Taxes	1,485,000	1,405,000	1,120,000	731,000	398,000	312,000	367,000	447,000
Net Income	3,541,000	3,537,000	2,854,000	2,035,000	1,099,000	798,000	805,000	1,053,000
Average Shares	659,500	683,500	705,800	707,400	702,800	693,800	694,200	697,795
Balance Sheet								
Current Assets	25,477,000	23,093,000	22,790,000	20,856,000	16,791,000	14,628,000	13,400,000	12,521,000
Total Assets	56,132,000	50,879,000	47,069,000	43,091,000	36,465,000	32,851,000	30,657,000	28,464,000
Current Liabilities	22,245,000	19,252,000	19,092,000	16,210,000	12,621,000	11,344,000	10,276,000	8,568,000
Long-Term Obligations	17,829,000	17,680,000	15,677,000	15,837,000	14,078,000	11,596,000	11,291,000	11,334,000
Total Liabilities	47,249,000	44,020,000	38,637,000	35,624,000	30,387,000	27,379,000	25,046,000	22,864,000
Stockholders' Equity	8,883,000	6,859,000	8,432,000	7,467,000	6,078,000	5,472,000	5,611,000	5,600,000
Shares Outstanding	623,986	645,808	670,867	685,873	687,524	688,510	686,752	686,793
Statistical Record								
Return on Assets %	6.62	7.22	6.33	5.10	3.17	2.51	2.72	3.81
Return on Equity %	44.99	46.26	35.90	29.97	19.03	14.40	14.36	18.98
EBITDA Margin %	15.65	16.23	15.52	14.33	13.49	12.97	12.83	14.09
Net Margin %	7.88	8.52	7.85	6.73	4.83	3.96	3.94	5.22
Asset Turnover	0.84	0.85	0.81	0.76	0.66	0.63	0.69	0.73
Current Ratio	1.15	1.20	1.19	1.29	1.33	1.29	1.30	1.46
Debt to Equity	2.01	2.58	1.86	2.12	2.32	2.12	2.01	2.02
Price Range	86.98-58.17	81.14-57.80	59.64-41.73	49.23-34.81	42.38-21.02	29.90-16.93	28.10-20.05	26.66-14.91
P/E Ratio	16.20-10.83	15.69-11.18	14.76-10.33	17.10-12.09	27.16-13.47	26.00-14.72	24.22-17.28	17.65-9.87
Average Yield %	1.82	1.60	1.79	1.96	2.34	2.91	2.84	3.44

Address: 100 NE Adams Street, Peoria, IL 61629-7310	**Web Site:** www.cat.com	**Auditors:** PricewaterhouseCoopers LLP
Telephone: 309-675-1000	**Officers:** James W. Owens - Chmn., C.E.O. David B. Burritt - V.P., C.F.O.	**Investor Contact:** 309-675-4549
Fax: 309-675-4332		**Transfer Agents:** Mellon Investor Services of South Hackensack, NJ

CATO CORP.

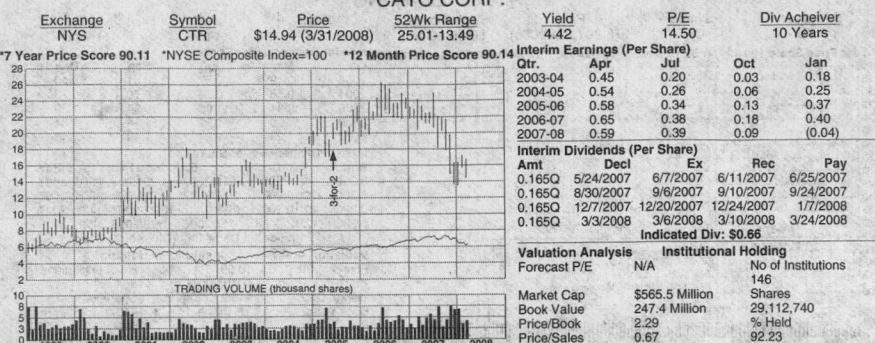

Exchange	Symbol	Price	52Wk Range	Yield	P/E	Div Acheiver
NYS	CTR	$14.94 (3/31/2008)	25.01-13.49	4.42	14.50	10 Years

*7 Year Price Score 90.11   *NYSE Composite Index=100   *12 Month Price Score 90.14

Interim Earnings (Per Share)

Qtr.	Apr	Jul	Oct	Jan
2003-04	0.45	0.20	0.03	0.18
2004-05	0.54	0.26	0.06	0.25
2005-06	0.58	0.34	0.13	0.37
2006-07	0.65	0.38	0.18	0.40
2007-08	0.59	0.39	0.09	(0.04)

Interim Dividends (Per Share)

Amt	Decl	Ex	Rec	Pay
0.165Q	5/24/2007	6/7/2007	6/11/2007	6/25/2007
0.165Q	8/30/2007	9/6/2007	9/10/2007	9/24/2007
0.165Q	12/7/2007	12/20/2007	12/24/2007	1/7/2008
0.165Q	3/3/2008	3/6/2008	3/10/2008	3/24/2008

Indicated Div: $0.66

Valuation Analysis   Institutional Holding

Forecast P/E	N/A		No of Institutions
			146
Market Cap	$565.5 Million	Shares	
Book Value	247.4 Million	29,112,740	
Price/Book	2.29	% Held	
Price/Sales	0.67	92.23	

Business Summary: Retail - Apparel and Accessory Stores (MIC: 5.8 SIC: 5621 NAIC: 448120)

Cato is engaged as a fashion specialty retailer for fashion and value conscious females. Co.'s stores provide an assortment of on-trend apparel and accessory items in junior/missy, plus sizes and girls sizes seven to 16 and emphasize color, product coordination and selection. Co. has two business segments: the operation of women's fashion specialty stores and a credit card division. As of Feb 2 2008, Co. operated 1,318 under the names Cato, Cato Fashions, Cato Plus, It's Fashion and It's Fashion Metro and are located primarily in strip shopping centers principally in the southeastern U.S.

Recent Developments: For the year ended Feb 2 2008, net income decreased 37.2% to US$32.3 million from US$51.5 million in the prior year. Revenues were US$846.4 million, down 3.4% from US$875.9 million the year before. Direct operating expenses declined 0.1% to US$572.3 million from US$572.7 million in the comparable period the year before. Indirect operating expenses increased 0.6% to US$224.9 million from US$223.5 million in the equivalent prior-year period.

Prospects: For the fiscal year ending Jan 31 2009, Co. is estimating comparable store sales to be down 3.0% to flat. Similarly, Co. is projecting net income to be in the range of $21.0 million to $27.0 million. Specifically, Co.'s net income guidance reflects the effects of closing 32 stores by end of this fiscal year, including the conversion of eight existing It's Fashion stores to the It's Fashion Metro format. In addition, Co. is targeting earnings to be in a range of $0.72 to $0.93 per diluted share, reflecting a decrease of 10.0% to 30.0% from previous fiscal year. Lastly, Co. intends to open 75 new stores, which include 30 new stores of an expanded version of It's Fashion division stores.

Financial Data
(US$ in Thousands)

	02/02/2008	02/03/2007	01/28/2006	01/29/2005	01/31/2004	02/01/2003	02/02/2002	02/03/2001
Earnings Per Share	1.03	1.62	1.41	1.11	0.89	1.18	1.11	1.02
Cash Flow Per Share	2.38	1.85	2.29	2.59	1.90	1.67	1.25	1.16
Tang Book Value Per Share	6.54	8.77	7.69	6.77	6.29	7.05	6.21	5.49
Dividends Per Share	0.645	0.580	0.507	0.457	0.420	0.390	0.353	0.283
Dividend Payout %	62.62	35.80	35.93	41.27	47.37	33.05	31.93	27.78
Income Statement								
Total Revenue	846,437	875,885	836,381	789,604	747,267	748,331	705,658	669,135
EBITDA	71,445	100,572	90,650	75,092	67,976	86,818	77,332	69,660
Income Before Taxes	49,233	79,631	70,375	54,695	49,277	71,839	66,286	60,042
Income Taxes	16,914	28,181	25,546	19,854	17,888	26,006	23,200	21,015
Net Income	32,319	51,450	44,829	34,841	31,389	45,833	43,086	39,027
Average Shares	31,513	31,815	31,789	31,478	35,339	38,921	38,832	38,197
Balance Sheet								
Current Assets	293,050	299,513	271,677	266,422	227,400	260,891	223,208	215,489
Total Assets	420,792	432,322	406,636	394,134	351,573	383,410	332,041	310,742
Current Liabilities	148,936	123,049	132,563	132,631	114,492	98,282	83,575	89,765
Long-Term Obligations	...	...	...	16,000	21,500	...	...	...
Total Liabilities	173,422	155,529	166,688	182,959	157,462	113,246	97,343	102,985
Stockholders' Equity	247,370	276,793	239,948	211,175	194,111	270,164	234,698	207,757
Shares Outstanding	37,852	31,552	31,219	31,205	30,870	38,343	37,796	37,872
Statistical Record								
Return on Assets %	7.60	12.07	11.23	9.37	8.56	12.85	13.44	12.87
Return on Equity %	12.37	19.59	19.93	17.24	13.56	18.21	19.53	19.37
EBITDA Margin %	8.44	11.48	10.84	9.51	9.10	11.60	10.96	10.41
Net Margin %	3.82	5.87	5.36	4.41	4.20	6.12	6.11	5.83
Asset Turnover	1.99	2.05	2.09	2.12	2.04	2.10	2.20	2.21
Current Ratio	1.97	2.43	2.05	2.01	1.99	2.65	2.67	2.40
Debt to Equity	...	...	...	0.08	0.11	...	...	...
Price Range	25.01-13.49	26.25-19.80	23.35-17.07	20.07-12.60	16.74-10.95	18.29-9.45	14.50-9.49	11.88-6.25
P/E Ratio	24.28-13.10	16.20-12.22	16.56-12.10	18.08-11.35	18.81-12.31	15.50-8.01	13.06-8.55	11.64-6.13
Average Yield %	3.18	2.50	2.50	3.00	3.08	2.80	2.98	3.54

Address: 8100 Denmark Road,	Web Site: www.catocorp.com	Auditors: PricewaterhouseCoopers LLP
Charlotte, NC 28273-5975	Officers: John P. Derham Cato - Chmn., Pres., C.E.O.	Transfer Agents: Wachovia Bank NA,
Telephone: 704-554-8510	Michael O. Moore - Exec. V.P., C.F.O., Sec.	Charlotte, NC
Fax: 704-551-7200		

CB RICHARD ELLIS GROUP INC

Exchange	Symbol	Price	52Wk Range	Yield	P/E
NYS	CBG	$21.64 (3/31/2008)	41.44-16.13	N/A	13.04

*7 Year Price Score N/A *NYSE Composite Index=100 *12 Month Price Score 76.92

Interim Earnings (Per Share)

Qtr.	Mar	Jun	Sep	Dec
2003	(0.01)	0.04	(0.16)	(0.05)
2004	(0.09)	0.01	0.05	0.31
2005	0.06	0.22	0.25	0.42
2006	0.16	0.27	0.39	0.52
2007	0.05	0.59	0.48	0.53

Interim Dividends (Per Share)

Amt	Decl	Ex	Rec	Pay
200%	5/2/2006	6/2/2006	5/15/2006	6/1/2006

Valuation Analysis **Institutional Holding**

Forecast P/E	N/A	No of Institutions	307
Market Cap	$4.4 Billion	Shares	
Book Value	988.5 Million	220,827,872	
Price/Book	4.41	% Held	
Price/Sales	0.72	96.94	

Business Summary: Property, Real Estate & Development (MIC: 8.3 SIC: 6519 NAIC: 531190)

CB Richard Ellis Group is a holding company that provides commercial real estate services under the CB Richard Ellis brand name. Through its subsidiaries, Co. is a global commercial real estate services firm offering a range of services to occupiers, owners, lenders and investors in office, retail, industrial, multi-family and other commercial real estate assets. Co.'s business is focused on several service competencies, including tenant representation, property/agency leasing, property sales, commercial property and corporate facilities management, valuation, real estate investment management, development services, commercial mortgage origination and servicing, and proprietary research.

Recent Developments: For the year ended Dec 31 2007, income from continuing operations increased 21.8% to US$387.9 million from US$318.6 million a year earlier. Net income increased 22.6% to US$390.5 million from US$318.6 million in the prior year. Revenues were US$6.03 billion, up 49.7% from US$4.03 billion the year before.

Prospects: On Feb 8 2008, Co. announced the acquisition of Eurisko Consulting SRL, a commercial real estate services company in Romania, for about $35.0 million. The acquisition strengthens Co.'s platform in the Central and Eastern Europe region. Meanwhile, reflecting its strategy of acquiring affiliate companies in global markets with high growth potential, on Feb 19 2008, Co. announced the acquisition of its affiliate company in Denmark, CB Richard Ellis Cederholm A/S, a commercial real estate services firm, for about $43.0 million. This transaction is a key building-block in the development and expansion of Co.'s operations across Scandinavia.

Financial Data
(US$ in Thousands)

	12/31/2007	12/31/2006	12/31/2005	12/31/2004	12/31/2003	12/31/2002	12/31/2001
Earnings Per Share	1.66	1.35	0.95	0.30	(0.23)	0.15	0.26
Cash Flow Per Share	2.84	1.63	1.62	0.89	0.42	0.52	...
Income Statement							
Total Revenue	6,034,249	4,032,027	2,910,641	2,365,096	1,630,074	1,170,277	562,828
EBITDA	828,195	619,677	446,798	224,265	132,817	130,676	74,930
Income Before Taxes	580,514	516,897	356,222	108,254	(40,980)	48,833	35,442
Income Taxes	192,643	198,326	138,881	43,529	(6,276)	30,106	18,016
Net Income	390,505	318,571	217,341	64,725	(34,704)	18,727	17,426
Average Shares	234,978	235,118	229,855	214,035	152,755	126,557	65,762
Balance Sheet							
Current Assets	2,360,830	2,212,013	1,292,947	863,695	838,982	345,940	
Total Assets	6,242,573	5,944,631	2,815,672	2,271,636	2,213,481	1,324,876	...
Current Liabilities	2,428,361	1,006,013	1,137,003	609,000	835,417	451,087	
Long-Term Obligations	1,991,857	2,232,857	549,156	600,884	791,420	499,004	...
Total Liabilities	4,990,417	4,684,854	2,015,163	1,705,763	1,873,896	1,067,920	
Stockholders' Equity	988,543	1,181,641	793,685	559,948	332,929	251,341	...
Shares Outstanding	201,594	227,474	221,353	213,094	181,757	118,957	...
Statistical Record							
Return on Assets %	6.41	7.27	8.54	2.88	N.M.	...	...
Return on Equity %	35.99	32.26	32.11	14.46	N.M.	...	...
EBITDA Margin %	13.72	15.37	15.35	9.48	8.15	11.17	13.31
Net Margin %	6.47	7.90	7.47	2.74	N.M.	1.60	3.10
Asset Turnover	0.99	0.92	1.14	1.05	0.92	...	...
Current Ratio	0.97	1.16	1.14	1.07	1.01	0.80	...
Debt to Equity	2.01	1.89	0.69	1.07	2.38	1.99	...
Price Range	41.44-18.38	33.83-20.10	19.82-10.61	11.30-6.07	...	...	...
P/E Ratio	24.96-11.07	25.06-14.89	20.86-11.16	37.68-20.22	...	...	...

Address: 865 South Figueroa Street, Suite 3400, Los Angeles, CA 90017 Telephone: 213-438-4880	Web Site: www.cbre.com Officers: Robert C. Blum - Chmn. Brett White - Pres.	Auditors: Deloitte & Touche LLP Transfer Agents: The Bank of New York

CBL & ASSOCIATES PROPERTIES, INC.

Exchange	Symbol	Price	52Wk Range	Yield	P/E	Div Acheiver
NYS	CBL	$23.53 (3/31/2008)	47.77-21.87	9.26	26:14	12 Years

*7 Year Price Score 88.00   *NYSE Composite Index=100   *12 Month Price Score 81.21

Interim Earnings (Per Share)

Qtr.	Mar	Jun	Sep	Dec
2003	0.37	0.34	0.33	0.96
2004	0.48	0.34	0.31	0.47
2005	0.39	0.32	0.92	0.39
2006	0.32	0.32	0.22	0.47
2007	0.26	0.17	0.26	0.20

Interim Dividends (Per Share)

Amt	Decl	Ex	Rec	Pay
0.505Q	6/8/2007	6/27/2007	6/29/2007	7/13/2007
0.505Q	9/7/2007	9/26/2007	9/28/2007	10/15/2007
0.545Q	11/6/2007	12/26/2007	12/28/2007	1/15/2008
0.545Q	2/28/2008	3/27/2008	3/31/2008	4/14/2008

Indicated Div: $2.18

Valuation Analysis

		Institutional Holding	
Forecast P/E	27.88	No of Institutions	
	(1/10/2007)	176	
Market Cap	$1.6 Billion	Shares	
Book Value	920.5 Million	59,043,532	
Price/Book	1.69	% Held	
Price/Sales	1.50	90.00	

Business Summary: Property, Real Estate & Development (MIC: 8.3 SIC: 6798 NAIC: 525930)

CBL & Associates Properties is a self-managed, self-administered real estate investment trust that owns, develops, acquires, leases, manages and operates regional malls and open-air and community shopping centers. At Dec 31 2007, Co. owned interests in 84 regional malls/open-air centers, 32 associated centers, 15 community centers and 19 office buildings; interests in four mall expansions, two associated/lifestyle centers, three community/open-air centers, a mixed-use center and an office building that are under construction, as well as options to acquire certain shopping center development sites; and mortgages on 16 properties that are secured by first mortgages or wrap-around mortgages.

Recent Developments: For the year ended Dec 31 2007, income from continuing operations decreased 22.0% to US$81.6 million from US$104.6 million a year earlier. Net income decreased 24.1% to US$89.1 million from US$117.5 million in the prior year. Revenues were US$1.04 billion, up 4.5% from US$995.5 million the year before. Revenues from property income rose 4.8% to US$1.02 billion from US$972.1 million in the corresponding earlier year.

Prospects: Co. expects results in 2008 to benefit from the expansions and improvements made to its existing portfolio in 2007, as well as new development projects that are scheduled to open in 2008. Contributions from the properties that Co. acquired in the fourth quarter of 2007 should also improve the overall growth profile of its portfolio. While monitoring the health of retailers, Co. will continue to focus on long-term growth. For 2008, Co. expects Funds from Operations of $3.46 to $3.56 per share. Co.'s estimate assumes same-center net operating income growth of 0.0% to 2.0%, excluding lease termination fees from both applicable periods, and assumes $0.12 to $0.16 of outparcel sales for 2008.

Financial Data
(US$ in Thousands)

	12/31/2007	12/31/2006	12/31/2005	12/31/2004	12/31/2003	12/31/2002	12/31/2001	12/31/2000
Earnings Per Share	0.90	1.33	2.03	1.61	2.00	1.25	1.05	1.19
Cash Flow Per Share	7.20	6.09	6.21	5.49	4.58	4.77	3.33	2.36
Tang Book Value Per Share	13.91	16.58	17.30	16.82	13.81	12.44	10.19	8.67
Dividends Per Share	2.060	1.877	1.766	1.494	1.345	1.160	1.065	1.020
Dividend Payout %	228.89	141.17	87.01	93.07	67.42	93.17	100.95	86.08
Income Statement								
Property Income	1,018,767	978,483	889,227	739,066	653,355	583,236	539,569	351,400
Non-Property Income	21,860	23,658	19,485	20,098	14,176	15,858	4,806	5,088
Total Revenue	1,040,627	1,002,141	908,712	759,164	667,531	599,094	544,375	356,488
Interest Expense	287,884	257,067	208,183	177,219	153,373	143,164	154,477	94,597
Income Taxes	8,390	5,902	...	...	...	...	...	...
Net Income	89,147	117,501	162,475	121,111	144,139	84,906	60,908	65,722
Average Shares	65,913	65,269	64,880	64,004	62,386	59,336	51,666	50,042
Balance Sheet								
Total Assets	8,105,047	6,518,810	6,352,322	5,204,500	4,264,310	3,795,114	3,372,851	2,115,565
Long-Term Obligations	5,869,318	4,564,535	4,341,055	3,371,679	2,738,102	2,402,079	2,315,955	1,424,337
Total Liabilities	6,264,202	4,874,504	4,661,325	3,583,743	2,899,579	2,553,411	2,419,662	1,502,565
Stockholders' Equity	920,548	1,084,856	1,081,522	1,054,151	837,300	741,190	522,088	434,825
Shares Outstanding	66,179	65,421	62,512	62,667	60,646	59,594	51,233	50,134
Statistical Record								
Return on Assets %	1.22	1.83	2.81	2.55	3.58	2.37	2.22	3.17
Return on Equity %	8.89	10.85	15.22	12.77	18.26	13.44	12.73	15.34
Net Margin %	8.57	11.72	17.88	15.95	21.59	14.17	11.19	18.44
Price Range	49.98-23.88	44.03-36.15	46.74-33.84	38.31-23.71	28.69-18.78	20.45-15.75	15.93-12.56	12.94-10.06
P/E Ratio	55.53-26.53	33.11-27.18	23.02-16.67	23.80-14.73	14.35-9.39	16.36-12.60	15.17-11.96	10.87-8.46
Average Yield %	5.44	4.60	4.45	5.01	5.80	6.32	7.37	8.69

Address: 2030 Hamilton Place Blvd., Suite 500, Chattanooga, TN 37421-6000 **Telephone:** 423-855-0001 **Fax:** 423-855-8662	**Web Site:** www.cblproperties.com **Officers:** Charles B. Lebovitz - Chmn., C.E.O. John N. Foy - Vice-Chmn., C.F.O., Treas.	**Auditors:** Deloitte & Touche LLP **Investor Contact:** 423-855-0001 **Transfer Agents:** SunTrust Bank, Atlanta, GA

CBS CORP

Exchange	Symbol	Price	52Wk Range	Yield	P/E
NYS	CBS A	$22.10 (3/31/2008)	34.97-21.57	4.52	12.77

*7 Year Price Score N/A ***NYSE Composite Index=100** ***12 Month Price Score 86.61**

Interim Earnings (Per Share)

Qtr.	Mar	Jun	Sep	Dec
2003	0.25	0.37	0.40	(0.22)
2004	0.41	0.43	(0.28)	(10.75)
2005	0.36	0.47	0.45	(10.25)
2006	0.30	1.02	0.41	0.43
2007	0.28	0.55	0.48	0.43

Interim Dividends (Per Share)

Amt	Decl	Ex	Rec	Pay
0.22Q	5/24/2007	5/31/2007	6/4/2007	7/1/2007
0.25Q	9/4/2007	9/12/2007	9/14/2007	10/1/2007
0.25Q	11/1/2007	11/28/2007	11/30/2007	1/1/2008
0.25Q	2/21/2008	2/29/2008	3/4/2008	4/1/2008

Indicated Div: $1.00

Valuation Analysis **Institutional Holding**

Forecast P/E	N/A	No of Institutions
		87
Market Cap	314.8 Billion	Shares
Book Value	21.5 Billion	10,158,717
Price/Book	0.69	% Held
Price/Sales	1.06	16.58

TRADING VOLUME (thousand shares)

1999 2000 2001 2002 2003 2004 2005 2006 2007 2008

Business Summary: Media (MIC: 13.1 SIC: 4833 NAIC: 515120)

CBS is a mass media company. Co.'s Television segment consists of CBS Television, comprised of several entities including, the CBS® Television Network, its 30 owned broadcast television stations, CBS Paramount Network Television, CBS Television Distribution, as well as its television production and syndication operations. Co.'s Radio segment owns and operates 140 radio stations in 30 U.S. markets through CBS Radio®. The outdoor segment displays advertising on media, while its Publishing segment consists of Simon & Schuster, which publishes and distributes consumer books under imprints such as Simon & Schuster®, Pocket Books®, Scribner® and Free Press®.

Recent Developments: For the year ended Dec 31 2007, income from continuing operations decreased 11.0% to US$1.23 billion from US$1.38 billion a year earlier. Net income decreased 24.9% to US$1.25 billion from US$1.66 billion in the prior year. Revenues were US$14.07 billion, down 1.7% from US$14.32 billion the year before. Operating income was US$2.62 billion versus US$2.61 billion in the prior year, an increase of 0.6%. Indirect operating expenses decreased 2.2% to US$11.45 billion from US$11.71 billion in the equivalent prior-year period.

Prospects: Despite the increased outdoor revenues due to increases in Europe and Asia, Co. is seeing a slight decrease in revenues resulting principally from several factors, including television and radio station divestitures as well as the non-renewal of several marginally profitable outdoor transit contracts. Meanwhile, Co. expects full-year 2008 operating income, excluding stock-based compensation expense, to increase by approximately 3.0% to 5.0% from $2.62 billion for 2007. Further, Co. is projecting 2008 capital expenditures in the range of $500.0 million to $550.0 million, principally reflecting increases for high-definition television upgrades and other information technology spending.

Financial Data

(US$ in Thousands)	12/31/2007	12/31/2006	12/31/2005	12/31/2004	12/31/2003	12/31/2002	12/31/2001	12/31/2000
Earnings Per Share	1.73	2.15	(8.98)	(10.19)	0.80	0.41	(0.13)	(0.67)
Cash Flow Per Share	3.06	2.47	4.48	2.12	2.01	1.78	2.03	1.89
Dividends Per Share	0.940	0.740	0.280	0.250	0.120	...	...	...
Dividend Payout %	54.34	34.42	...	...	15.00	...	...	...
Income Statement								
Total Revenue	14,072,900	14,320,200	14,536,400	22,525,900	26,585,300	24,605,700	23,222,800	20,043,700
EBITDA	2,947,396	3,025,600	(6,313,900)	(12,151,500)	4,622,200	5,512,300	2,668,700	2,207,200
Income Before Taxes	2,133,000	2,132,700	(7,511,700)	(13,655,000)	2,861,200	3,734,200	782,800	560,600
Income Taxes	821,500	652,200	808,100	1,378,600	1,599,000	1,448,900	922,500	729,800
Net Income	1,247,000	1,660,500	(7,089,100)	(17,462,200)	1,416,900	725,700	(223,500)	(816,100)
Average Shares	721,900	771,800	789,700	1,714,400	1,760,700	1,774,800	1,731,600	1,225,300
Balance Sheet								
Current Assets	6,030,900	8,144,100	6,795,500	7,493,500	7,736,300	7,166,800	7,206,400	7,832,400
Total Assets	40,430,200	43,508,800	43,029,600	68,002,300	89,848,500	89,754,200	90,809,900	82,646,100
Current Liabilities	4,404,600	4,399,500	5,378,600	6,879,500	7,584,800	7,341,100	7,561,700	7,758,200
Long-Term Obligations	7,068,600	7,027,300	7,153,200	9,649,200	9,683,200	10,205,200	10,823,700	12,473,800
Total Liabilities	18,957,800	19,986,300	21,292,600	25,978,000	26,643,500	27,266,400	28,093,100	34,679,200
Stockholders' Equity	21,472,400	23,522,500	21,737,000	42,024,300	63,205,000	62,487,800	62,716,800	47,966,900
Shares Outstanding	671,900	768,400	751,700	1,645,300	1,734,600	1,746,600	1,756,500	1,495,900
Statistical Record								
Return on Assets %	2.97	3.84	N.M.	N.M.	1.58	0.80	N.M.	N.M.
Return on Equity %	5.54	7.34	N.M.	N.M.	2.25	1.16	N.M.	N.M.
EBITDA Margin %	20.94	21.13	N.M.	N.M.	17.39	22.40	11.49	11.01
Net Margin %	8.86	11.60	N.M.	N.M.	5.33	2.95	N.M.	N.M.
Asset Turnover	0.34	0.33	0.26	0.28	0.30	0.27	0.27	0.37
Current Ratio	1.37	1.85	1.26	1.09	1.02	0.98	0.95	1.01
Debt to Equity	0.33	0.30	0.33	0.23	0.15	0.16	0.17	0.26
Price Range	34.97-25.78	31.95-23.96	26.70-25.05	...	...	...	...	...
P/E Ratio	20.21-14.90	14.86-11.14	...	...	...	...	...	...
Average Yield %	3.05	2.73	1.10	...	...	...	...	...

Address: 1515 Broadway, New York, NY 10036
Telephone: 212-258-6000

Web Site: www.viacom.com
Officers: Sumner M. Redstone - Chmn., C.E.O. Tom Freston - Co-Pres., Co-C.O.O.

Auditors: PricewaterhouseCoopers LLP

CEDAR FAIR, L.P.

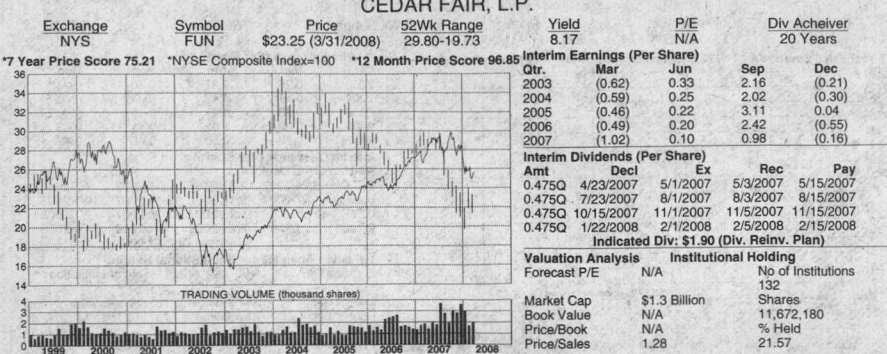

Exchange	Symbol	Price	52Wk Range	Yield	P/E	Div Acheiver
NYS	FUN	$23.25 (3/31/2008)	29.80-19.73	8.17	N/A	20 Years

*7 Year Price Score 75.21   *NYSE Composite Index=100   *12 Month Price Score 96.85

Interim Earnings (Per Share)

Qtr.	Mar	Jun	Sep	Dec
2003	(0.62)	0.33	2.16	(0.21)
2004	(0.59)	0.25	2.02	(0.30)
2005	(0.46)	0.22	3.11	0.04
2006	(0.49)	0.20	2.42	(0.55)
2007	(1.02)	0.10	0.98	(0.16)

Interim Dividends (Per Share)

Amt	Decl	Ex	Rec	Pay
0.475Q	4/23/2007	5/1/2007	5/3/2007	5/15/2007
0.475Q	7/23/2007	8/1/2007	8/3/2007	8/15/2007
0.475Q	10/15/2007	11/1/2007	11/5/2007	11/15/2007
0.475Q	1/22/2008	2/1/2008	2/5/2008	2/15/2008

Indicated Div: $1.90 (Div. Reinv. Plan)

Valuation Analysis — **Institutional Holding**

Forecast P/E	N/A	No of Institutions
		132
Market Cap	$1.3 Billion	Shares
Book Value	N/A	11,672,180
Price/Book	N/A	% Held
Price/Sales	1.28	21.57

Business Summary: Sporting & Recreational (MIC: 13.5 SIC: 7996 NAIC: 713110)

Cedar Fair is a publicly traded limited partnership managed by Cedar Fair Management, Inc. As of Dec 31 2007, Co. owned and operated 11 amusement parks, six outdoor water parks, one indoor water park and five hotels. Co.'s amusement parks include: Cedar Point, Sandusky, OH; Kings Island near Cincinnati, OH; Canada's Wonderland near Toronto, Canada; Dorney Park & Wildwater Kingdom, South Whitehall Township, PA; Valleyfair, Shakopee, MN; Michigan's Adventure located near Muskegon, MI; Kings Dominion near Richmond, VA; Carowinds in Charlotte, NC; Worlds of Fun, Kansas City, MO; Knott's Berry Farm, Buena Park, CA; and California's Great America, Santa Clara, CA.

Recent Developments: For the year ended Dec 31 2007, net loss amounted to US$4.5 million versus net income of US$87.5 million in the prior year. Revenues were US$987.0 million, up 18.7% from US$831.4 million the year before. Operating income was US$154.6 million versus US$219.5 million in the prior year, a decrease of 29.6%. Direct operating expenses rose 21.7% to US$511.7 million from US$420.5 million in the comparable period the year before. Indirect operating expenses increased 67.5% to US$320.7 million from US$191.4 million in the equivalent prior-year period.

Prospects: Co. remains committed to its long-term strategy of continuing to reinvest in improving its parks. Accordingly, for 2008, Co. is investing $88.0 million in capital improvements at its 18 properties, including the addition of roller coasters at Canada's Wonderland, Kings Dominion, Dorney Park, Knott's Berry Farm, and Michigan's Adventure, as well as the introduction of new water attractions at Carowinds and a new spinning ride at Great America. For full-year 2008, Co. anticipates revenues of about $990.0 million to $1.02 billion, reflecting improvements in attendance and in-park guest per capita spending across its parks, as well as accommodations revenues growth at its resort properties.

Financial Data
(US$ in Thousands)

	12/31/2007	12/31/2006	12/31/2005	12/31/2004	12/31/2003	12/31/2002	12/31/2001	12/31/2000
Earnings Per Share	(0.08)	1.59	2.93	1.47	1.67	1.39	1.13	1.50
Cash Flow Per Share	3.35	3.08	2.99	2.84	2.67	2.90	2.46	2.22
Dividends Per Share	1.895	1.870	1.830	1.790	1.740	1.650	1.580	1.502
Dividend Payout %		117.61	62.46	121.77	104.19	118.71	139.82	100.17
Income Statement								
Total Revenue	986,973	831,389	568,707	541,972	509,976	502,851	477,256	472,920
EBITDA	285,929	305,561	193,546	172,983	172,569	155,225	141,043	155,088
Income Before Taxes	9,738	126,564	111,576	97,030	103,806	88,576	74,414	94,159
Income Taxes	14,229	39,087	(49,276)	18,715	17,918	17,159	16,520	16,353
Net Income	(4,491)	87,477	160,852	78,315	85,888	71,417	57,894	77,806
Average Shares	54,200	54,872	54,950	53,315	51,334	51,263	51,113	51,679
Balance Sheet								
Current Assets	62,748	104,508	40,610	32,960	29,777	29,237	26,868	25,378
Total Assets	2,418,668	2,510,921	1,024,794	993,208	819,341	822,257	810,231	764,143
Current Liabilities	122,708	159,258	130,733	121,517	111,694	106,338	96,700	114,024
Long-Term Obligations	1,735,461	1,759,713	450,850	442,084	348,647	365,150	373,000	300,000
Total Liabilities	2,133,576	2,100,306	590,560	622,725	510,450	516,937	501,981	433,554
Shares Outstanding	54,248	54,092	53,797	53,480	50,673	50,549	50,514	50,813
Statistical Record								
Return on Assets %	N.M.	4.95	15.94	8.62	10.46	8.75	7.35	10.53
EBITDA Margin %	28.97	36.75	34.03	31.92	33.84	30.87	29.55	32.79
Net Margin %	N.M.	10.52	28.28	14.45	16.84	14.20	12.13	16.45
Asset Turnover	0.40	0.47	0.56	0.60	0.62	0.62	0.61	0.64
Current Ratio	0.51	0.66	0.31	0.27	0.27	0.27	0.28	0.22
Price Range	29.89-21.00	29.80-24.15	33.95-26.22	35.71-28.86	31.03-22.74	24.79-20.30	24.98-18.03	20.75-17.56
P/E Ratio	...	18.74-15.19	11.59-8.95	24.29-19.63	18.58-13.62	17.83-14.60	22.11-15.96	13.83-11.71
Average Yield %	7.07	6.86	5.97	5.69	6.51	7.10	7.50	8.05

Address: One Cedar Point Drive, Sandusky, OH 44870-5259
Telephone: 419-626-0830
Fax: 419-627-2234

Web Site: www.cedarfair.com
Officers: Richard L. Kinzel - Chmn., Pres., C.E.O.
Peter J. Crage - V.P., Fin., C.F.O.

Auditors: Deloitte & Touche LLP
Investor Contact: 419-627-2233
Transfer Agents: American Stock Transfer & Trust Company, New York, NY

CENTERPOINT ENERGY, INC

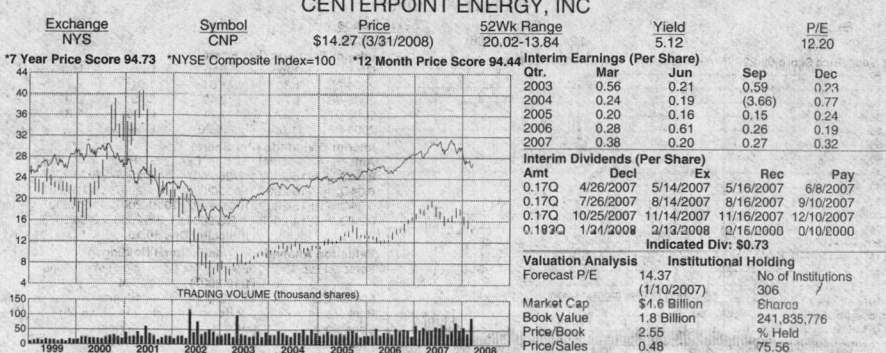

Exchange	Symbol	Price	52Wk Range	Yield	P/E
NYS	CNP	$14.27 (3/31/2008)	20.02-13.84	5.12	12.20

*7 Year Price Score 94.73 *NYSE Composite Index=100 *12 Month Price Score 94.44

Interim Earnings (Per Share)

Qtr.	Mar	Jun	Sep	Dec
2003	0.56	0.21	0.59	0.23
2004	0.24	0.19	(3.66)	0.77
2005	0.20	0.16	0.15	0.24
2006	0.28	0.61	0.26	0.19
2007	0.38	0.20	0.27	0.32

Interim Dividends (Per Share)

Amt	Decl	Ex	Rec	Pay
0.17Q	4/26/2007	5/14/2007	5/16/2007	6/8/2007
0.17Q	7/26/2007	8/14/2007	8/16/2007	9/10/2007
0.17Q	10/25/2007	11/14/2007	11/16/2007	12/10/2007
0.182Q	1/31/2008	2/13/2008	2/15/2008	0/10/2008

Indicated Div: $0.73

Valuation Analysis   **Institutional Holding**

Forecast P/E	14.37	No of Institutions
	(1/10/2007)	306
Market Cap	$4.6 Billion	Shares
Book Value	1.8 Billion	241,835,776
Price/Book	2.55	% Held
Price/Sales	0.48	75.56

TRADING VOLUME (thousand shares)

Business Summary: Electricity (MIC: 7.1 SIC: 4911 NAIC: 221122)

CenterPoint Energy is a public utility holding company. Co. operates through two indirect wholly-owned subsidiaries. CenterPoint Energy Houston Electric, LLC owns and operates Co.'s electric transmission and distribution business to retail electric providers serving about 2.0 million metered customers as of Dec 31 2007 in the Texas Gulf Coast area. CenterPoint Energy Resources Corp., together with its subsidiaries, owns and operates Co.'s local gas distribution companies, interstate pipelines and gas gathering systems, provides various ancillary services, and offers variable and fixed price physical natural gas supplies to commercial and industrial customers and electric and gas utilities.

Recent Developments: For the year ended Dec 31 2007, income from continuing operations decreased 7.6% to US$399.0 million from US$432.0 million a year earlier. Net income decreased 7.6% to US$399.0 million from US$432.0 million in the prior year. Revenues were US$9.62 billion, up 3.3% from US$9.32 billion the year before. Operating income was US$1.19 billion versus US$1.05 billion in the prior year, an increase of 13.4%. Indirect operating expenses increased 2.0% to US$8.44 billion from US$8.27 billion in the equivalent prior-year period.

Prospects: For 2008, Co. believes that it is well positioned to capitalize on opportunities in each of its businesses, and thus, projects earnings of $1.15 to $1.25 per diluted share, excluding the effect from acquisitions or divestitures, or the outcome of its regulated electric transmission and distribution utility operations true-up appeal. Meanwhile, Co.'s non-regulated natural gas marketing group, CenterPoint Energy Services, Inc., announced the completion of its transaction with Nordic Energy Services LLC in Jan 2008. The acquisition of Nordic Energy's commercial accounts substantially increases Co.'s presence in Indiana and highlights its overall growth strategy using targeted acquisitions.

Financial Data

(US$ in Thousands)	12/31/2007	12/31/2006	12/31/2005	12/31/2004	12/31/2003	12/31/2002	12/31/2001	12/31/2000
Earnings Per Share	1.17	1.33	0.75	(2.48)	1.58	(13.08)	3.35	1.56
Cash Flow Per Share	2.42	3.18	0.20	1.24	2.95	1.02	6.08	...
Tang Book Value Per Share	0.35	N.M.	N.M.	N.M.	N.M.	N.M.	16.29	...
Dividends Per Share	0.680	0.600	0.400	0.400	0.400	0.160	1.500	1.500
Dividend Payout %	58.12	45.11	53.33	...	25.32	...	44.78	96.15
Income Statement								
Total Revenue	9,623,000	9,319,000	9,722,000	8,510,428	9,760,124	7,922,498	10,656,357	10,374,202
EBITDA	1,413,000	1,279,000	996,000	926,111	1,464,688	1,905,508	1,927,470	1,737,324
Income Before Taxes	594,000	494,000	378,000	344,021	664,765	594,309	675,177	456,238
Income Taxes	195,000	62,000	153,000	138,306	216,301	208,026	328,252	234,196
Net Income	399,000	432,000	252,000	(904,704)	483,667	(3,920,234)	980,559	447,500
Average Shares	342,507	324,778	346,028	359,506	306,220	299,644	292,193	287,273
Balance Sheet								
Net PPE	9,740,000	9,204,000	8,492,000	8,186,393	11,811,536	11,409,369	11,199,505	...
Total Assets	17,872,000	17,633,000	17,116,000	18,161,957	21,376,664	19,634,279	31,266,363	...
Long-Term Obligations	8,364,000	7,802,000	8,568,000	7,193,016	10,783,064	9,194,320	4,919,737	...
Total Liabilities	16,062,000	16,077,000	15,820,000	17,056,455	19,437,197	17,506,189	23,822,696	...
Stockholders' Equity	1,810,000	1,556,000	1,296,000	1,105,502	1,760,557	1,421,950	6,737,923	...
Shares Outstanding	323,000	314,000	310,000	308,045	306,297	305,017	302,944	299,914
Statistical Record								
Return on Assets %	2.25	2.49	1.43	N.M.	2.36	N.M.	...	...
Return on Equity %	23.71	30.29	20.99	N.M.	30.40	N.M.	...	...
EBITDA Margin %	14.68	13.72	10.24	10.88	15.01	24.05	18.09	16.75
Net Margin %	4.15	4.64	2.59	(10.63)	4.96	(49.48)	9.20	4.31
PPE Turnover	1.02	1.05	1.17	0.85	0.84	0.70	...	...
Asset Turnover	0.54	0.54	0.55	0.43	0.48	0.31	...	...
Debt to Equity	4.62	5.01	6.61	6.51	6.12	6.47	0.73	...
Price Range	20.02-15.15	16.80-11.73	15.13-10.65	12.21-9.69	10.11-4.50	21.81-4.39	40.64-19.21	39.15-16.15
P/E Ratio	17.11-12.95	12.63-8.82	20.17-14.20	...	6.40-2.85	...	12.13-5.73	25.10-10.35
Average Yield %	3.87	4.42	3.13	3.68	4.83	1.22	5.26	5.79

Address: 1111 Louisiana Street, Houston, TX 77002
Telephone: 713-207-1111

Web Site: www.centerpointenergy.com
Officers: Milton Carroll - Chmn. David M. McClanahan - Pres., C.E.O.

Auditors: Deloitte & Touche LLP
Investor Contact: 713-207-6500
Transfer Agents: CenterPoint Energy Investor Services

CENTEX CORP.

Exchange	Symbol	Price	52Wk Range	Yield	P/E
NYS	CTX	$24.21 (3/31/2008)	48.86-18.28	0.66	N/A

*7 Year Price Score 62.22 *NYSE Composite Index=100 *12 Month Price Score 82.11

Interim Earnings (Per Share)

Qtr.	Jun	Sep	Dec	Mar
2004-05	1.35	1.61	1.91	2.77
2005-06	1.74	2.49	2.49	3.01
2006-07	1.27	1.11	(1.90)	1.67
2007-08	(1.05)	(5.26)	(7.94)	...

Interim Dividends (Per Share)

Amt	Decl	Ex	Rec	Pay
0.04Q	5/16/2007	5/25/2007	5/30/2007	6/20/2007
0.04Q	7/16/2007	7/30/2007	8/1/2007	8/22/2007
0.04Q	10/15/2007	10/29/2007	10/31/2007	11/21/2007
0.04Q	2/14/2008	3/3/2008	3/5/2008	3/26/2008

Indicated Div: $0.16

Valuation Analysis

		Institutional Holding	
Forecast P/E	32.42 (1/10/2007)	No of Institutions	304
Market Cap	$2.9 Billion	Shares	114,360,832
Book Value	3.2 Billion	% Held	95.75
Price/Book	0.90		
Price/Sales	0.35		

Business Summary: Building & General Construction (MIC: 3.2 SIC: 1531 NAIC: 236117)

Centex is a home building company. Co.'s principal operations are focused on residential and commercial construction and related activities, including mortgage financing. Co. operates in two principal business segments: Home Building and Financial Services. Home Building's operations involve the purchase and development of land or lots and the construction and sale of detached and attached single-family homes and land or lots. Financial Services' operations consist primarily of mortgage lending, title agency services and the sale of title insurance and other insurance products. These activities include mortgage origination and other related services for homes sold by Co.'s subsidiaries.

Recent Developments: For the quarter ended Dec 31 2007, loss from continuing operations was US$975.2 million compared with a loss of US$242.3 million in the year-earlier quarter. Net loss amounted to US$975.2 million versus a net loss of US$228.1 million in the year-earlier quarter. Revenues were US$1.91 billion, down 30.1% from US$2.73 billion the year before. Direct operating expenses declined 13.0% to US$2.53 billion from US$2.91 billion in the comparable period the year before. Indirect operating expenses decreased 47.7% to US$37.9 million from US$72.4 million in the equivalent prior-year period.

Prospects: Co.'s near-term outlook appears challenging. Co. anticipates that lower demand or prices for its homes or further disruption of the mortgage markets, would result in declines in sales of its homes, accumulation of unsold inventory and weaker margin, as well as potential additional land-related impairments and write-offs of deposits and pre-acquisition costs. Hence, Co. will continue to adjust its operations in response to market conditions by reducing its unsold inventory and land position while lowering its costs. Nevertheless, Co. believes that the fundamentals which support homebuyer demand in the long-term remain solid and the current market conditions will improve going forward.

Financial Data

(US$ in Thousands)	9 Mos	6 Mos	3 Mos	03/31/2007	03/31/2006	03/31/2005	03/31/2004	03/31/2003
Earnings Per Share	(12.58)	(6.54)	(0.17)	2.23	9.71	7.64	6.40	4.42
Cash Flow Per Share	17.78	16.09	9.24	7.87	(7.36)	(3.66)	5.57	(0.05)
Tang Book Value Per Share	25.70	34.08	39.16	40.79	39.25	31.53	22.79	19.13
Dividends Per Share	0.160	0.160	0.160	0.160	0.160	0.160	0.120	0.080
Dividend Payout %	...	...	...	7.17	1.65	2.09	1.88	1.81
Income Statement								
Total Revenue	6,063,504	4,157,417	1,941,415	12,014,567	14,399,669	12,859,695	10,363,391	9,117,241
EBITDA	(1,897,662)	(1,191,111)	(180,811)	162,568	1,958,562	1,632,028	1,250,690	908,064
Depn & Amortn	40,384	26,239	14,846	...	...	...	...	...
Income Before Taxes	(1,938,046)	(1,217,350)	(195,657)	102,773	1,895,493	1,573,769	1,149,064	794,851
Income Taxes	(187,690)	(442,182)	(64,322)	114,553	674,472	562,405	371,933	238,932
Net Income	(1,746,980)	(771,792)	(127,959)	268,366	1,289,313	1,011,364	827,686	555,919
Average Shares	122,787	122,301	121,469	120,537	132,749	132,397	129,392	126,116
Balance Sheet								
Current Assets	7,581,657	8,337,293	9,461,875	11,902,112	10,544,752	9,239,755	6,720,090	4,813,092
Total Assets	9,630,917	10,970,445	12,444,978	13,205,759	21,364,999	20,011,079	16,068,568	11,610,536
Current Liabilities	2,729,339	2,250,876	2,553,417	2,349,088	2,759,680	2,304,692	1,961,912	1,677,764
Long-Term Obligations	3,623,236	4,459,708	4,950,577	5,567,465	6,059,408	12,968,109	10,720,380	7,104,699
Total Liabilities	6,433,792	6,806,647	7,651,675	7,916,553	15,820,881	15,272,801	12,682,292	8,782,463
Stockholders' Equity	3,197,125	4,163,798	4,793,303	5,112,269	5,011,658	4,280,757	3,050,225	2,657,846
Shares Outstanding	118,239	117,481	116,749	119,969	122,103	127,729	122,660	119,478
Statistical Record								
Return on Assets %	N.M.	N.M.	N.M.	1.55	6.23	5.61	5.96	5.40
Return on Equity %	N.M.	N.M.	N.M.	5.30	27.75	27.59	28.92	23.29
EBITDA Margin %	N.M.	N.M.	N.M.	1.35	13.60	12.69	12.07	9.96
Net Margin %	N.M.	N.M.	N.M.	2.23	8.95	7.86	7.99	6.10
Asset Turnover	0.69	0.76	0.62	0.70	0.70	0.71	0.75	0.89
Current Ratio	2.78	3.70	3.71	5.07	3.82	4.01	3.43	2.87
Debt to Equity	1.13	1.07	1.03	1.09	1.21	3.03	3.51	2.67
Price Range	55.10-18.28	57.84-25.44	57.84-39.74	63.88-41.58	79.50-55.19	65.85-41.24	57.75-24.20	25.97-17.08
P/E Ratio	...	...	...	28.65-18.65	8.19-5.68	8.62-5.40	9.02-3.78	5.88-3.86
Average Yield %	0.42	0.35	0.32	0.31	0.24	0.31	0.30	0.35

Address: 2728 N. Harwood, Dallas, TX 75201-1516
Telephone: 214-981-5000

Web Site: www.centex.com
Officers: Timothy R. Eller - Chmn., Pres., C.E.O., C.O.O. Leldon E. Echols - Exec. V.P., C.F.O.

Auditors: Ernst & Young LLP
Transfer Agents: Mellon Investor Services LLC, Ridgefield Park, NJ

CENTURYTEL, INC.

Exchange	Symbol	Price	52Wk Range	Yield	P/E	Div Acheiver
NYS	CTL	$33.24 (3/31/2008)	49.52-33.05	0.81	8.94	34 Years

*7 Year Price Score 100.61   *NYSE Composite Index=100   *12 Month Price Score 89.31

Interim Earnings (Per Share)

Qtr.	Mar	Jun	Sep	Dec
2003	0.58	0.00	0.63	0.56
2004	0.58	0.60	0.63	0.62
2005	0.59	0.64	0.68	0.58
2006	0.55	1.26	0.65	0.62
2007	0.68	1.00	1.01	1.04

Interim Dividends (Per Share)

Amt	Decl	Ex	Rec	Pay
0.065Q	5/22/2007	5/31/2007	6/4/2007	6/15/2007
0.065Q	8/21/2007	8/30/2007	9/4/2007	9/17/2007
0.065Q	11/14/2007	11/23/2007	11/27/2007	12/10/2007
0.068Q	2/26/2008	3/6/2008	3/10/2008	3/24/2008

Indicated Div: $0.27 (Div. Reinv. Plan)

Valuation Analysis

		Institutional Holding	
Forecast P/E	17.02	No of Institutions	
	(1/10/2007)	313	
Market Cap	$3.6 Billion	Shares	
Book Value	3.4 Billion	100,675,024	
Price/Book	1.06	% Held	
Price/Sales	1.36	90.39	

Business Summary: Communications (MIC: 10.1 SIC: 4813 NAIC: 517110)

CenturyTel is an integrated communications company engaged primarily in providing an array of communications services, including local and long distance voice, Internet access and broadband services. Co. also provides fiber transport, local exchange carrier, security monitoring, and other communications and business information services. Co. conducts its operations in 25 states located in the continental U.S. As of Dec 31 2007, Co.'s local exchange telephone subsidiaries operated approximately 2.1 million telephone access lines, primarily in rural areas and small to mid-size cities in 24 states, with over 68.0% of these lines located in Missouri, Wisconsin, Alabama, Arkansas and Washington.

Recent Developments: For the year ended Dec 31 2007, net income increased 13.1% to US$418.4 million from US$370.0 million in the prior year. Revenues were US$2.66 billion, up 8.5% from US$2.45 billion the year before. Operating income was US$793.1 million versus US$665.5 million in the prior year, an increase of 19.2%. Indirect operating expenses increased 4.5% to US$1.86 billion from US$1.78 billion in the equivalent prior-year period.

Prospects: For full year 2008, Co. expects its operating revenues to decline as it continues to experience downward pressure primarily due to continued access line losses, reduced network access revenues and lower prior year revenue settlement amounts. Nevertheless, Co. expects such declines to be partially offset primarily due to increased demand for its Internet service offering and operating revenues contributed by its Apr 2007 acquisition of Madison River. Accordingly, Co. is targeting diluted earnings per share of $2.90 to $3.00. Meanwhile, for the first quarter 2008, Co. expects total revenues of $646.0 million to $656.0 million and diluted earnings per share of $0.69 to $0.73.

Financial Data

(US$ in Thousands)	12/31/2007	12/31/2006	12/31/2005	12/31/2004	12/31/2003	12/31/2002	12/31/2001	12/31/2000
Earnings Per Share	3.72	3.07	2.49	2.41	2.38	5.61	2.41	1.63
Cash Flow Per Share	9.42	7.21	7.37	6.95	7.44	5.62	4.73	4.00
Tang Book Value Per Share	N.M.	N.M.	0.90	N.M.	N.M.	N.M.	N.M.	N.M.
Dividends Per Share	0.260	0.250	0.240	0.230	0.220	0.210	0.200	0.190
Dividend Payout %	6.99	8.14	9.64	9.54	9.24	3.74	8.30	11.66
Income Statement								
Total Revenue	2,656,241	2,447,730	2,479,252	2,407,372	2,380,745	1,971,996	2,117,469	1,845,926
EBITDA	1,368,103	1,310,612	1,271,502	1,259,327	1,229,351	926,927	1,251,963	957,543
Income Before Taxes	618,942	591,149	537,770	547,372	531,959	293,456	553,056	386,185
Income Taxes	200,572	221,122	203,291	210,128	187,252	103,537	210,025	154,711
Net Income	418,370	370,027	334,479	337,244	344,707	801,624	343,031	231,474
Average Shares	113,094	122,229	136,087	142,144	144,700	142,879	142,307	141,864
Balance Sheet								
Net PPE	3,108,376	3,109,277	3,304,486	3,341,401	3,455,481	3,531,645	2,999,563	2,959,293
Total Assets	8,184,553	7,441,007	7,762,307	7,796,953	7,895,852	7,770,408	6,318,684	6,393,290
Long-Term Obligations	2,734,357	2,412,852	2,376,070	2,762,019	3,109,302	3,578,132	2,087,500	3,050,292
Total Liabilities	4,775,348	4,250,056	4,145,434	4,387,188	4,417,336	4,682,404	3,981,304	4,361,211
Stockholders' Equity	3,409,205	3,190,951	3,617,273	3,409,765	3,478,516	3,088,004	2,337,380	2,032,079
Shares Outstanding	108,491	113,253	131,074	132,373	144,364	142,955	141,232	140,667
Statistical Record								
Return on Assets %	5.35	4.87	4.30	4.29	4.40	11.38	5.40	4.16
Return on Equity %	12.68	10.87	9.52	9.77	10.50	29.55	15.70	11.90
EBITDA Margin %	51.51	53.54	51.29	52.31	51.64	47.00	59.13	51.87
Net Margin %	15.75	15.12	13.49	14.01	14.48	40.65	16.20	12.54
PPE Turnover	0.85	0.76	0.75	0.71	0.68	0.60	0.71	0.71
Asset Turnover	0.34	0.32	0.32	0.31	0.30	0.28	0.33	0.33
Debt to Equity	0.80	0.76	0.66	0.81	0.89	1.16	0.89	1.50
Price Range	49.52-40.30	43.79-32.84	36.28-30.26	35.49-26.33	36.63-25.51	35.20-22.18	39.00-26.18	47.38-24.50
P/E Ratio	13.31-10.83	14.26-10.70	14.57-12.15	14.73-10.93	15.39-10.72	6.27-3.95	16.18-10.86	29.06-15.03
Average Yield %	0.57	0.72	0.72	0.74	0.69	0.71	0.64	0.57

Address: 100 CenturyTel Drive, Monroe, LA 71203
Telephone: 318-388-9000
Fax: 318-789-8656

Web Site: www.centurytel.com
Officers: Glen F. Post III - Chmn., C.E.O. Karen A. Puckett - Pres., C.O.O.

Auditors: KPMG LLP
Investor Contact: 800-833-1188
Transfer Agents: Computershare Investor Services, LLC, Chicago, IL

CHARLES RIVER LABORATORIES INTERNATIONAL INC.

Exchange	Symbol	Price	52Wk Range	Yield	P/E
NYS	CRL	$58.94 (3/31/2008)	68.44-46.12	N/A	26.20

*7 Year Price Score 108.35 *NYSE Composite Index=100 *12 Month Price Score 112.53

Interim Earnings (Per Share)

Qtr.	Mar	Jun	Sep	Dec
2003	0.40	0.42	0.40	0.42
2004	0.36	0.52	0.51	0.29
2005	0.40	0.44	0.44	0.68
2006	(1.40)	0.36	(0.24)	0.48
2007	0.54	0.55	0.62	0.53

Interim Dividends (Per Share)
No Dividends Paid

Valuation Analysis

		Institutional Holding	
Forecast P/E	15.51	No of Institutions	
	(1/10/2007)	238	
Market Cap	$4.0 Billion	Shares	
Book Value	1.9 Billion	65,948,248	
Price/Book	2.16	% Held	
Price/Sales	3.26	98.53	

Business Summary: Miscellaneous Business Services (MIC: 12.8 SIC: 2836 NAIC: 325414)

Charles River Laboratories International is a provider of services that advance the drug discovery and development process. Co. has two reporting segments: Research Models and Services is engaged in production and sale of research models, principally genetically and virally defined purpose-bred rats and mice; Co.'s Preclinical Services provides in vivo and in vitro studies, supportive laboratory services, and strategic preclinical consulting and program management to support new drug development. As of Dec 31 2007, Co. operated approximately 60 facilities, including its production and warehousing facilities, throughout 15 countries worldwide.

Recent Developments: For the year ended Dec 29 2007, income from continuing operations increased 25.8% to US$157.6 million from US$125.2 million a year earlier. Net income amounted to US$154.4 million versus a net loss of US$55.8 million in the prior year. Revenues were US$1.23 billion, up 16.3% from US$1.06 billion the year before. Operating income was US$227.2 million versus US$188.2 million in the prior year, an increase of 20.7%. Direct operating expenses rose 15.4% to US$752.4 million from US$651.8 million in the comparable period the year before. Indirect operating expenses increased 14.9% to US$251.0 million from US$218.4 million in the equivalent prior-year period.

Prospects: Co.'s near-term outlook appears favorable, reflecting robust demand for its products and services. For 2008, Co. continues to project net sales growth in the range of 10.0% to 13.0%, while earnings are estimated to range from $2.59 to $2.69 per share. In addition, Co. expects its Preclinical Services segment to grow at a low- to mid-teens range, benefiting from the strong demand for outsourced development services and the addition of new capacity. Similarly, Co. anticipates its Research Models and Services segment to grow at a high-single-digit range, bolstered by broad-based segment growth, mainly in the North America research models, research model services and In Vitro businesses.

Financial Data
(US$ in Thousands)

	12/29/2007	12/30/2006	12/31/2005	12/25/2004	12/27/2003	12/28/2002	12/29/2001	12/30/2000
Earnings Per Share	2.25	(0.80)	1.96	1.68	1.64	1.06	0.80	(0.35)
Cash Flow Per Share	4.32	2.56	3.34	3.74	2.73	3.00	1.74	1.20
Tang Book Value Per Share	8.67	4.72	2.92	N.M.	7.18	5.01	4.51	2.09
Income Statement								
Total Revenue	1,230,626	1,058,385	1,122,228	766,917	613,723	554,629	465,630	306,585
EBITDA	312,122	271,740	283,300	207,355	168,900	147,474	117,958	84,002
Income Before Taxes	217,423	176,564	160,413	152,525	132,630	114,403	69,479	26,085
Income Taxes	59,400	49,738	16,576	61,156	51,063	43,572	27,095	7,837
Net Income	154,406	(55,783)	141,999	89,792	80,151	50,132	35,407	(11,224)
Average Shares	68,735	69,948	72,902	56,045	51,314	50,856	44,215	31,734
Balance Sheet								
Current Assets	607,864	501,093	419,322	510,306	370,888	278,092	210,154	119,737
Total Assets	2,805,537	2,557,544	2,538,209	2,626,835	799,554	701,344	571,362	410,608
Current Liabilities	302,528	259,331	311,412	349,115	114,351	113,369	98,532	64,320
Long-Term Obligations	484,998	547,084	260,217	605,980	185,683	192,484	155,867	202,500
Total Liabilities	941,570	953,110	701,478	1,144,538	324,755	325,401	268,864	280,351
Stockholders' Equity	1,860,467	1,595,211	1,827,013	1,472,505	464,623	357,376	289,510	116,927
Shares Outstanding	68,135	66,919	71,955	65,785	45,801	45,218	44,189	35,920
Statistical Record								
Return on Assets %	5.77	N.M.	5.41	5.26	10.71	7.90	7.23	N.M.
Return on Equity %	8.96	N.M.	8.47	9.30	19.56	15.54	17.47	N.M.
EBITDA Margin %	25.36	25.67	25.24	27.04	27.52	26.59	25.33	27.40
Net Margin %	12.55	N.M.	12.65	11.71	13.06	9.04	7.60	N.M.
Asset Turnover	0.46	0.42	0.43	0.45	0.82	0.87	0.95	0.78
Current Ratio	2.01	1.93	1.35	1.46	3.24	2.45	2.13	1.86
Debt to Equity	0.26	0.34	0.14	0.41	0.40	0.54	0.54	1.73
Price Range	67.35-43.24	50.56-33.92	52.71-41.76	48.87-33.77	38.55-24.75	40.98-27.80	37.40-18.00	34.00-20.50
P/E Ratio	29.93-19.22	...	26.89-21.31	29.09-20.10	23.51-15.09	38.66-26.23	46.75-22.50	...

Address: 251 Ballardvale Street,	Web Site: www.criver.com	Auditors: PricewaterhouseCoopers LLP
Wilmington, MA 01887	Officers: James C. Foster - Chmn., Pres., C.E.O.	Investor Contact: 978-658-6000
Telephone: 781-222-6000	Thomas F. Ackerman - Sr. V.P., C.F.O.	

CHEMTURA CORP

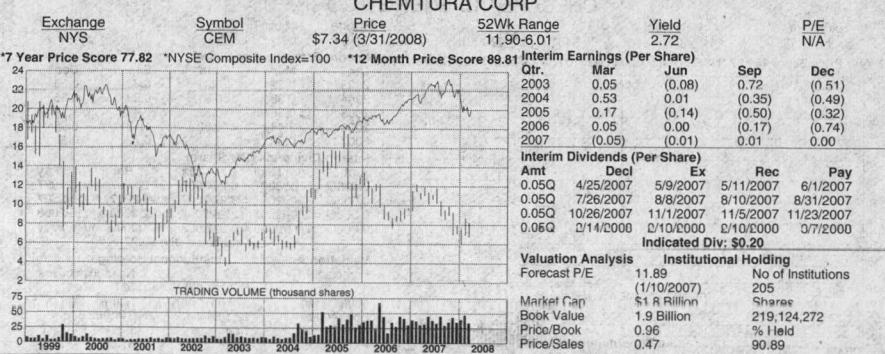

Exchange	Symbol	Price	52Wk Range	Yield	P/E
NYS	CEM	$7.34 (3/31/2008)	11.90-6.01	2.72	N/A

*7 Year Price Score 77.82   *NYSE Composite Index=100   *12 Month Price Score 89.81

Interim Earnings (Per Share)

Qtr.	Mar	Jun	Sep	Dec
2003	0.05	(0.08)	0.72	(0.51)
2004	0.53	0.01	(0.35)	(0.49)
2005	0.17	(0.14)	(0.50)	(0.32)
2006	0.05	0.00	(0.17)	(0.74)
2007	(0.05)	(0.01)	0.01	0.00

Interim Dividends (Per Share)

Amt	Decl	Ex	Rec	Pay
0.05Q	4/25/2007	5/9/2007	5/11/2007	6/1/2007
0.05Q	7/26/2007	8/8/2007	8/10/2007	8/31/2007
0.05Q	10/26/2007	11/1/2007	11/5/2007	11/23/2007
0.05Q	2/14/2000	2/10/2000	2/10/2000	3/7/2000

Indicated Div: $0.20

Valuation Analysis

		Institutional Holding	
Forecast P/E	11.89	No of Institutions	
	(1/10/2007)	205	
Market Cap	$1.8 Billion	Shares	
Book Value	1.9 Billion	219,124,272	
Price/Book	0.96	% Held	
Price/Sales	0.47	90.89	

TRADING VOLUME (thousand shares)

Business Summary: Chemicals (MIC: 11.1 SIC: 2869 NAIC: 424690)

Chemtura is a producer of specialty chemicals (including agricultural chemicals), polymer products, and a supplier of home pool and spa chemicals. Co.'s products are used in a variety of end-use markets, principally including transportation, construction, packaging, agriculture, lubricants, plastics for durable and non-durable goods, and personal care products. Most of Co.'s chemical products are sold to industrial manufacturing customers for use as additives, ingredients, or intermediates. Co.'s pool and spa chemicals are sold to dealers, distributors and major retailers.

Recent Developments: For the year ended Dec 31 2007, loss from continuing operations was US$45.0 million compared with a loss of US$273.0 million a year earlier. Net loss amounted to US$3.0 million versus a net loss of US$206.0 million in the prior year. Revenues were US$3.75 billion, up 8.4% from US$3.46 billion the year before. Operating income was US$59.0 million versus US$5.0 million in the prior year, an increase of. Direct operating expenses rose 10.0% to US$2.86 billion from US$2.60 billion in the comparable period the year before. Indirect operating expenses decreased 2.9% to US$826.0 million from US$851.0 million in the equivalent prior-year period.

Prospects: On Oct 31 2007, Co. has completed the sale of its optical monomers business to Acomon AG, an affiliate of Munich-based Auctus Management GmbH & Co. KG in an all-cash transaction for an undisclosed amount. Included in the transaction is Co.'s Ravenna, Italy manufacturing facility. Notably, proceeds from the sale will be used primarily for debt reduction. This deal should enable Co. to place greater focus on its core businesses and represents continued progress in its portfolio refinement and footprint optimization initiatives. Meanwhile, Co.'s focus remains on performance improvement despite challenges related to electronics, construction demand and continuing raw material cost pressure.

Financial Data

(US$ in Thousands)	12/31/2007	12/31/2006	12/31/2005	12/31/2004	12/31/2003	12/31/2002	12/31/2001	12/31/2000
Earnings Per Share	(0.01)	(0.85)	(1.05)	(0.30)	0.17	(2.45)	(1.10)	0.78
Cash Flow Per Share	0.62	1.04	(0.44)	0.32	(0.13)	1.78	1.64	1.54
Dividends Per Share	0.200	0.200	0.200	0.200	0.200	0.200	0.200	0.200
Dividend Payout %	...	...	...	...	117.65	...	...	25.64
Income Statement								
Total Revenue	3,747,000	3,722,707	2,986,608	2,549,762	2,185,043	2,546,872	2,718,798	3,038,430
EBITDA	321,000	199,247	148,651	121,128	70,987	257,539	106,831	444,821
Income Before Taxes	(41,000)	(117,383)	(119,652)	(83,399)	(154,753)	9,285	(188,606)	142,374
Income Taxes	4,000	135,625	65,198	(46,667)	(36,102)	(6,189)	(64,662)	53,101
Net Income	(3,000)	(205,517)	(186,640)	(34,590)	18,954	(283,507)	(123,944)	89,273
Average Shares	741,600	240,486	178,404	114,736	112,531	115,656	113,061	115,165
Balance Sheet								
Current Assets	1,381,000	1,385,790	1,341,600	996,338	810,454	777,144	818,074	1,076,095
Total Assets	4,416,000	4,399,406	4,986,003	2,678,709	2,529,182	2,840,815	3,232,188	3,528,327
Current Liabilities	681,000	887,976	975,689	709,169	701,245	681,490	682,618	715,463
Long-Term Obligations	1,058,000	1,063,360	1,309,603	862,251	754,018	1,261,847	1,392,833	1,479,394
Total Liabilities	2,563,000	2,720,502	3,210,606	2,349,729	2,226,473	2,640,932	2,684,647	2,774,351
Stockholders' Equity	1,853,000	1,678,904	1,775,397	328,980	302,709	199,883	547,541	753,976
Shares Outstanding	242,100	240,790	239,990	115,654	114,492	113,854	113,057	112,474
Statistical Record								
Return on Assets %	N.M.	N.M.	N.M.	N.M.	0.71	N.M.	N.M.	2.45
Return on Equity %	N.M.	N.M.	N.M.	N.M.	7.54	N.M.	N.M.	11.76
EBITDA Margin %	8.57	5.35	4.98	4.75	3.25	10.11	3.93	14.64
Net Margin %	N.M.	N.M.	N.M.	N.M.	0.87	N.M.	N.M.	2.94
Asset Turnover	0.85	0.79	0.78	0.98	0.81	0.84	0.80	0.84
Current Ratio	2.03	1.56	1.58	1.40	1.16	1.14	1.19	1.51
Debt to Equity	0.57	0.63	0.74	2.62	2.49	6.31	2.54	1.96
Price Range	12.19-6.98	13.48-7.79	17.82-9.92	11.80-5.36	7.56-3.68	12.90-5.68	12.19-6.27	13.94-7.06
P/E Ratio	...	...	...	...	44.47-21.65	...	...	17.87-9.05
Average Yield %	1.99	2.00	1.46	2.64	3.38	2.01	2.06	1.92

Address: 199 Benson Road,
Middlebury, CT 06749
Telephone: 203-573-2000

Web Site: www.cromptoncorp.com
Officers: Robert L. Wood - Chmn., Pres., C.E.O.
Karen O. Oscar - Exec. V.P., C.F.O.

Auditors: KPMG LLP
Investor Contact: 203-573-2000
Transfer Agents: Mellon Investor
Services LLC

CHESAPEAKE ENERGY CORP.

Exchange	Symbol	Price	52Wk Range	Yield	P/E
NYS	CHK	$46.15 (3/31/2008)	49.00-31.54	0.59	17.61

*7 Year Price Score 151.97 *NYSE Composite Index=100 *12 Month Price Score 126.75

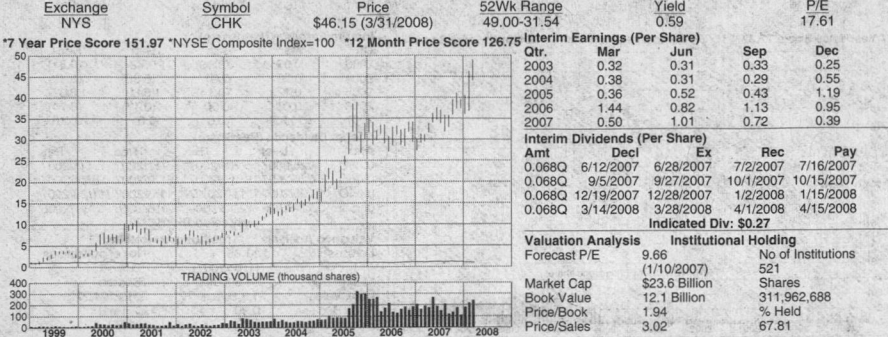

Interim Earnings (Per Share)

Qtr.	Mar	Jun	Sep	Dec
2003	0.32	0.31	0.33	0.25
2004	0.38	0.31	0.29	0.55
2005	0.36	0.52	0.43	1.19
2006	1.44	0.82	1.13	0.95
2007	0.50	1.01	0.72	0.39

Interim Dividends (Per Share)

Amt	Decl	Ex	Rec	Pay
0.068Q	6/12/2007	6/28/2007	7/2/2007	7/16/2007
0.068Q	9/5/2007	9/27/2007	10/1/2007	10/15/2007
0.068Q	12/19/2007	12/28/2007	1/2/2008	1/15/2008
0.068Q	3/14/2008	3/28/2008	4/1/2008	4/15/2008

Indicated Div: $0.27

Valuation Analysis

		Institutional Holding	
Forecast P/E	9.66 (1/10/2007)	No of Institutions	521
Market Cap	$23.6 Billion	Shares	311,962,688
Book Value	12.1 Billion	% Held	67.81
Price/Book	1.94		
Price/Sales	3.02		

Business Summary: Oil and Gas (MIC: 14.2 SIC: 1311 NAIC: 211111)

Chesapeake Energy is primarily engaged in the business of acquiring, exploring and developing properties for the production of crude oil and natural gas from underground reservoirs as well as the marketing of natural gas and oil for other working interest owners in properties it operates. Co.'s properties are mainly located in Oklahoma, Texas, Alabama, Arkansas, Louisiana, Kansas, Montana, Colorado, North Dakota, Nebraska, New Mexico, West Virginia, Kentucky, Ohio, New York, Maryland, Michigan, Mississippi, Pennsylvania, Tennessee, Utah, Virginia and Wyoming. As of Dec 31 2007, Co. had proved reserves of 10.879 trillion cubic feet of gas equivalent, of which 93.0% were natural gas.

Recent Developments: For the year ended Dec 31 2007, net income decreased 27.6% to US$1.45 billion from US$2.00 billion in the prior year. Revenues were US$7.80 billion, up 6.5% from US$7.33 billion the year before. Operating income was US$2.65 billion versus US$3.41 billion in the prior year, a decrease of 22.4%. Direct operating expenses rose 29.4% to US$950.0 million from US$734.0 million in the comparable period the year before. Indirect operating expenses increased 32.1% to US$4.20 billion from US$3.18 billion in the equivalent prior-year period.

Prospects: For 2008, Co. is projecting natural gas production of 851.00 billion cubic feet equivalent (bcfe) to 861.00 bcfe, an increase of 19.0% to 21.0% over its 2007 levels. Also, Co. is estimating investments for drilling, acreage acquisition, seismic and related capitalized internal costs to range from $5.90 billion to $6.50 billion. Meanwhile, Co. is in the process of forming a private partnership to own a non-operating interest in its midstream natural gas assets outside of Appalachia, which consist of natural gas gathering systems and processing assets. Co. anticipates raising $1.00 billion for a minority interest in the partnership and closing the transaction in the first half of 2008.

Financial Data

(US$ in Thousands)	12/31/2007	12/31/2006	12/31/2005	12/31/2004	12/31/2003	12/31/2002	12/31/2001	12/31/2000
Earnings Per Share	2.62	4.35	2.51	1.53	1.21	0.17	1.25	3.01
Cash Flow Per Share	10.82	12.15	7.47	5.71	4.48	2.59	3.41	2.43
Tang Book Value Per Share	21.85	20.32	12.42	8.57	5.45	3.99	3.75	1.84
Dividends Per Share	0.263	0.230	0.195	0.170	0.135	0.060	...	...
Dividend Payout %	10.02	5.29	7.77	11.11	11.16	35.29	...	...
Income Statement								
Total Revenue	7,800,000	7,325,595	4,665,290	2,709,268	1,717,432	737,751	969,051	627,952
EBITDA	4,744,000	5,026,152	2,663,942	1,588,122	1,043,173	414,697	719,313	391,274
Income Before Taxes	2,341,000	3,255,359	1,493,393	804,926	500,952	67,140	438,365	196,162
Income Taxes	890,000	1,252,036	545,091	289,771	190,360	26,854	174,959	(259,408)
Net Income	1,451,000	2,003,323	948,302	515,155	312,981	40,286	217,406	455,570
Average Shares	487,000	458,603	366,683	305,718	258,567	172,714	173,981	151,564
Balance Sheet								
Current Assets	1,396,000	1,153,869	1,183,397	567,540	342,404	435,317	361,383	166,926
Total Assets	30,734,000	24,417,167	16,118,462	8,244,509	4,572,291	2,875,608	2,286,768	1,440,426
Current Liabilities	2,761,000	1,889,809	1,964,088	963,953	513,156	265,552	173,381	162,701
Long-Term Obligations	10,950,000	7,375,548	5,489,742	3,075,109	2,057,713	1,651,198	1,329,453	944,845
Total Liabilities	18,604,000	13,165,696	9,944,139	5,081,626	2,839,481	1,967,733	1,519,361	1,127,194
Stockholders' Equity	12,130,000	11,251,471	6,174,323	3,162,883	1,732,810	907,875	767,407	313,232
Shares Outstanding	511,147	457,433	370,189	311,868	216,784	190,144	164,742	153,030
Statistical Record								
Return on Assets %	5.26	9.88	7.78	8.02	8.40	1.56	11.67	39.66
Return on Equity %	12.41	22.99	20.31	20.99	23.70	4.81	40.24	949.60
EBITDA Margin %	60.82	68.61	57.10	58.62	60.74	56.21	74.23	62.31
Net Margin %	18.60	27.35	20.33	19.01	18.22	5.46	22.43	72.55
Asset Turnover	0.28	0.36	0.38	0.42	0.46	0.29	0.52	0.55
Current Ratio	0.51	0.61	0.60	0.59	0.67	1.64	2.08	1.03
Debt to Equity	0.90	0.66	0.89	0.97	1.19	1.82	1.73	3.02
Price Range	41.06-27.30	35.04-27.02	38.86-15.22	18.13-11.90	13.95-7.40	8.55-5.15	10.97-4.99	10.25-2.06
P/E Ratio	15.67-10.42	8.06-6.21	15.48-6.06	11.85-7.78	11.53-6.12	50.29-30.29	8.78-3.99	3.41-0.69
Average Yield %	0.77	0.74	0.71	1.17	1.36	0.89	...	...

Address: 6100 North Western Avenue, Oklahoma City, OK 73118 Telephone: 405-848-8000 Fax: 405-483-0573	Web Site: www.chkenergy.com Officers: Aubrey K. McClendon - Chmn., C.E.O. Tom L. Ward - Pres., C.O.O., Dir.	Auditors: PricewaterhouseCoopers LLP Investor Contact: 405-848-8000 Transfer Agents: UMB Bank, N.A.

CHEVRON CORPORATION

Exchange	Symbol	Price	52Wk Range	Yield	P/E	Div Acheiver
NYS	CVX	$85.36 (3/31/2008)	94.86-74.83	2.72	9.73	20 Years

*7 Year Price Score 126.36 *NYSE Composite Index=100 ***12 Month Price Score 105.71**

TRADING VOLUME (thousand shares)

Interim Earnings (Per Share)

Qtr.	Mar	Jun	Sep	Dec
2003	0.91	0.75	1.01	0.81
2004	1.20	1.94	1.51	1.63
2005	1.28	1.76	1.64	1.86
2006	1.80	1.97	2.29	1.74
2007	2.18	2.52	1.75	2.32

Interim Dividends (Per Share)

Amt	Decl	Ex	Rec	Pay
0.58Q	4/25/2007	5/16/2007	5/18/2007	6/11/2007
0.58Q	7/25/2007	8/15/2007	8/17/2007	9/10/2007
0.58Q	10/31/2007	11/14/2007	11/16/2007	12/10/2007
0.50Q	1/00/2000	2/13/2008	2/15/2008	3/10/2008

Indicated Div: $2.32

Valuation Analysis   Institutional Holding

Forecast P/E	9.01	No of Institutions
	(1/10/2007)	1310
Market Cap	$170.4 Billion	Shares
Book Value	77.1 Billion	1,382,422,016
Price/Book	2.31	% Held
Price/Sales	0.81	64.07

Business Summary: Oil and Gas (MIC: 14.2 SIC: 2911 NAIC: 324110)

Chevron is an energy company engaged in petroleum operations, chemicals operations, mining operations of coal and other minerals, power generation and energy services. Co.'s operations consists of exploring for, developing and producing crude oil and natural gas; refining crude oil into finished petroleum products; marketing crude oil, natural gas and the products derived from petroleum; and transporting crude oil, natural gas and petroleum products. In addition, Co. is engaged in the manufacture and marketing of commodity petrochemicals, plastics for industrial uses, and fuel and lubricant oil additives through its chemical operations.

Recent Developments: For the year ended Dec 31 2007, net income increased 9.0% to US$18.69 billion from US$17.14 billion in the prior year. Revenues were US$220.90 billion, up 5.1% from US$210.12 billion the year before. Direct operating expenses rose 4.0% to US$133.31 billion from US$128.15 billion in the comparable period the year before. Indirect operating expenses increased 10.9% to US$55.43 billion from US$49.99 billion in the equivalent prior-year period.

Prospects: In 2008, Co. estimates capital and exploratory spending to be 15.0% higher at $22.90 billion, including $2.60 billion of spending by affiliates. About $17.50 billion, is budgeted for exploration and production activities, with $12.70 billion of this amount outside the U.S. Spending in 2008 is mainly targeted for exploratory prospects in the deepwater Gulf of Mexico and western Africa and development projects in Angola, Australia, Brazil, Indonesia, Kazakhstan, Nigeria, Thailand, the deepwater Gulf of Mexico, the Piceance Basin in Colorado and an oil sands project in Canada. Also, Co. projects its average global oil-equivalent production in 2008 to be about 2.65 million barrels per day.

Financial Data

(US$ in Thousands)	12/31/2007	12/31/2006	12/31/2005	12/31/2004	12/31/2003	12/31/2002	12/31/2001	12/31/2000
Earnings Per Share	8.77	7.80	6.54	6.28	3.48	0.54	1.54	3.98
Cash Flow Per Share	11.79	11.13	9.38	6.92	5.80	4.68	5.40	6.65
Tang Book Value Per Share	34.66	29.71	26.00	21.47	16.97	14.79	15.91	15.54
Dividends Per Share	2.260	2.010	1.750	1.530	1.430	1.400	1.325	1.300
Dividend Payout %	25.77	25.77	26.76	24.36	41.09	261.68	85.76	32.62
Income Statement								
Total Revenue	220,904,000	210,118,000	198,200,000	155,300,000	121,761,000	99,049,000	106,245,000	52,129,000
EBITDA	40,875,000	39,482,000	31,110,000	25,486,000	18,154,000	9,387,000	15,350,000	12,118,000
Income Before Taxes	32,167,000	31,976,000	25,197,000	20,551,000	12,770,000	4,156,000	8,291,000	9,270,000
Income Taxes	13,479,000	14,838,000	11,098,000	7,517,000	5,344,000	3,024,000	4,360,000	4,085,000
Net Income	18,688,000	17,138,000	14,099,000	13,328,000	7,230,000	1,132,000	3,288,000	5,185,000
Average Shares	2,132,000	2,197,000	2,155,000	2,122,000	2,120,000	2,126,000	2,125,800	1,302,200
Balance Sheet								
Current Assets	39,377,000	36,304,000	34,336,000	28,503,000	19,426,000	17,776,000	18,327,000	8,213,000
Total Assets	148,786,000	132,628,000	125,833,000	93,208,000	81,470,000	77,359,000	77,572,000	41,264,000
Current Liabilities	33,798,000	28,409,000	25,011,000	18,795,000	16,111,000	19,876,000	20,654,000	7,674,000
Long-Term Obligations	6,070,000	7,679,000	12,131,000	10,456,000	10,894,000	10,911,000	8,989,000	5,153,000
Total Liabilities	71,698,000	63,693,000	63,157,000	47,978,000	45,175,000	45,755,000	43,614,000	21,339,000
Stockholders' Equity	77,088,000	68,935,000	62,676,000	45,230,000	36,295,000	31,604,000	33,958,000	19,925,000
Shares Outstanding	2,090,433	2,164,558	2,232,687	2,107,120	2,138,295	2,136,273	2,134,441	1,282,120
Statistical Record								
Return on Assets %	13.28	13.26	12.87	15.22	9.10	1.46	5.53	12.62
Return on Equity %	25.60	26.04	26.13	32.61	21.30	3.45	12.20	27.45
EBITDA Margin %	18.50	18.79	15.70	16.41	14.91	9.48	14.45	23.25
Net Margin %	8.46	8.16	7.11	8.58	5.94	1.14	3.09	9.95
Asset Turnover	1.57	1.63	1.81	1.77	1.53	1.28	1.79	1.27
Current Ratio	1.17	1.28	1.37	1.52	1.21	0.89	0.89	1.07
Debt to Equity	0.08	0.11	0.19	0.23	0.30	0.35	0.26	0.26
Price Range	94.86-66.43	75.97-54.08	65.77-50.51	55.41-42.22	43.20-30.93	45.43-32.95	49.02-39.38	47.14-35.53
P/E Ratio	10.82-7.57	9.74-6.93	10.06-7.72	8.82-6.72	12.41-8.89	84.13-61.02	31.83-25.57	11.84-8.93
Average Yield %	2.74	3.19	3.04	3.20	4.04	3.51	2.98	3.07

Address: 6001 Bollinger Canyon Road, San Ramon, CA 94583-2324 Telephone: 925-842-1000 Fax: 415-894-6017	Web Site: www.chevron.com Officers: David J. O'Reilly - Chmn., C.E.O. Peter J. Robertson - Vice-Chmn.	Auditors: PricewaterhouseCoopers LLP Investor Contact: 925-842-5690 Transfer Agents: Mellon Investor Services LLC, Ridgefield Park, NJ

CHICO'S FAS INC

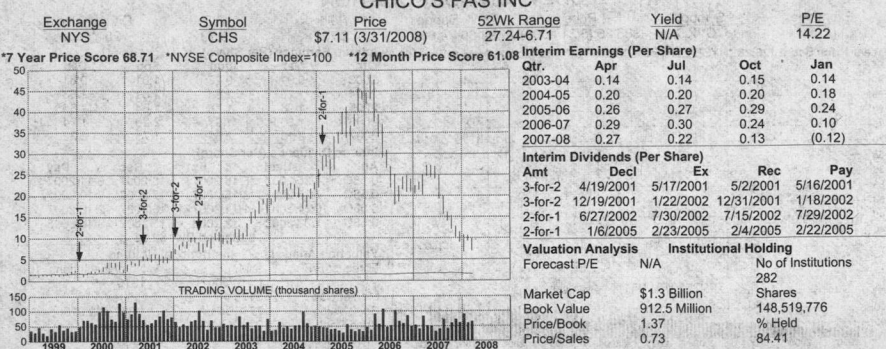

Exchange	Symbol	Price	52Wk Range	Yield	P/E
NYS	CHS	$7.11 (3/31/2008)	27.24-6.71	N/A	14.22

*7 Year Price Score 68.71 *NYSE Composite Index=100 *12 Month Price Score 61.08

Interim Earnings (Per Share)

Qtr.	Apr	Jul	Oct	Jan
2003-04	0.14	0.14	0.15	0.14
2004-05	0.20	0.20	0.20	0.18
2005-06	0.26	0.27	0.29	0.24
2006-07	0.29	0.30	0.24	0.10
2007-08	0.27	0.22	0.13	(0.12)

Interim Dividends (Per Share)

Amt	Decl	Ex	Rec	Pay
3-for-2	4/19/2001	5/17/2001	5/2/2001	5/16/2001
3-for-2	12/19/2001	1/22/2002	12/31/2001	1/18/2002
2-for-1	6/27/2002	7/30/2002	7/15/2002	7/29/2002
2-for-1	1/6/2005	2/23/2005	2/4/2005	2/22/2005

Valuation Analysis   **Institutional Holding**

Forecast P/E	N/A	No of Institutions
		282
Market Cap	$1.3 Billion	Shares
Book Value	912.5 Million	148,519,776
Price/Book	1.37	% Held
Price/Sales	0.73	84.41

Business Summary: Retail - Apparel and Accessory Stores (MIC: 5.8 SIC: 5621 NAIC: 448120)

Chico's FAS is a specialty retailer of a line of clothing, intimates, complementary accessories and other non-clothing gift items under the Chico's, White House|Black Market (WH|BM) and Soma Intimates (Soma) brand names. As of Mar 17 2008, Co. operated 1,045 retail stores in 49 states, the District of Columbia, the U.S. Virgin Islands and Puerto Rico. In addition, Co. has a separate outlet operation mainly to distribute its product line known as Additions by Chico's. Co.sells its products through traditional retail stores, catalog, and via the Internet.

Recent Developments: For the year ended Feb 2 2008, income from continuing operations decreased 47.8% to US$91.1 million from US$174.7 million a year earlier. Net income decreased 46.7% to US$88.9 million from US$166.6 million in the prior year. Revenues were US$1.71 billion, up 4.5% from US$1.64 billion the year before. Operating income was US$263.7 million versus US$263.7 million in the prior year, a decrease of 53.9%. Direct operating expenses rose 10.6% to US$745.3 million from US$673.7 million in the comparable period the year before. Indirect operating expenses increased 20.5% to US$847.6 million from US$703.5 million in the equivalent prior-year period.

Prospects: Looking ahead, Co. has revised its targeted new store openings for fiscal year ending Feb 2009 downward to about 35 to 40 net new stores, of which 17 to 20 are expected to be Chico's stores and 18 to 20 are expected to be White House | Black Market (WH|BM) stores. At the same time, Co. plans to close up to eight to 10 Chico's stores, six to eight WH|BM stores and four to six Soma stores. Also, Co. expects 31 to 33 relocations/expansions in fiscal 2008. Planned square footage growth for fiscal 2008 is estimated to be about 5.0% to 8.0%, slightly lower than its originally announced goal of a 10.0% increase. Meanwhile, Co. projects negative comparable store sales for the first half of 2008.

Financial Data
(US$ in Thousands)

	02/02/2008	02/03/2007	01/28/2006	01/29/2005	01/31/2004	02/01/2003	02/02/2002	02/03/2001
Earnings Per Share	0.50	0.93	1.06	0.78	0.57	0.39	0.25	0.17
Cash Flow Per Share	1.19	1.60	1.49	1.26	0.84	0.65	0.41	0.25
Tang Book Value Per Share	4.41	4.02	3.91	2.60	1.60	1.41	0.88	0.54
Income Statement								
Total Revenue	1,714,326	1,646,482	1,404,575	1,066,882	768,499	531,108	378,085	259,446
EBITDA	220,270	320,457	347,165	260,462	183,874	122,936	77,943	51,341
Income Before Taxes	139,160	261,679	306,549	226,703	161,662	107,676	68,043	45,772
Income Taxes	48,012	95,043	112,568	85,497	61,432	40,917	25,856	17,393
Net Income	88,875	166,636	193,981	141,206	100,230	66,759	42,187	28,379
Average Shares	176,355	178,452	182,407	180,149	176,284	172,064	167,556	163,330
Balance Sheet								
Current Assets	486,733	471,856	537,978	364,567	197,573	160,429	92,991	50,786
Total Assets	1,250,126	1,058,134	999,413	715,729	470,854	301,544	186,385	117,807
Current Liabilities	181,193	144,232	122,668	95,315	71,582	54,860	34,946	25,328
Long-Term Obligations	...	...	...	...	1,278	...	7,944	7,158
Total Liabilities	337,610	254,203	192,986	154,861	96,019	61,411	42,890	32,485
Stockholders' Equity	912,516	803,931	806,427	560,868	374,835	240,133	143,495	85,321
Shares Outstanding	176,245	175,749	181,726	178,961	175,074	170,564	163,162	157,464
Statistical Record								
Return on Assets %	7.72	15.94	22.68	23.87	26.02	27.44	27.81	29.68
Return on Equity %	10.38	20.36	28.45	30.26	32.69	34.90	36.98	40.47
EBITDA Margin %	12.85	19.46	24.72	24.41	23.93	23.15	20.62	19.79
Net Margin %	5.18	10.12	13.81	13.24	13.04	12.57	11.16	10.94
Asset Turnover	1.49	1.57	1.64	1.80	2.00	2.18	2.49	2.71
Current Ratio	2.69	3.27	4.39	3.82	2.76	2.92	2.66	2.01
Debt to Equity	...	...	...	...	N.M.	...	0.06	0.08
Price Range	27.24-6.71	48.90-17.80	45.85-24.81	26.33-16.95	19.50-8.54	11.52-6.73	7.53-3.53	4.58-0.98
P/E Ratio	54.48-13.42	52.58-19.14	43.25-23.41	33.76-21.74	34.21-14.99	29.53-17.26	30.12-14.11	26.92-5.76

Address: 11215 Metro Parkway, Fort Myers, FL 33966 Telephone: 239-277-6200 Fax: 239-277-5237	Web Site: www.chicos.com Officers: Marvin J. Gralnick - Chmn. Scott A. Edmonds - Pres., C.E.O.	Auditors: Ernst & Young LLP Transfer Agents: The Registrar and Transfer Company, Cransford, NJ

CHOICE HOTELS INTERNATIONAL, INC.

Exchange	Symbol	Price	52Wk Range	Yield	P/E
NYS	CHH	$34.11 (3/31/2008)	42.60-29.96	1.99	20.06

*7 Year Price Score 113.21 *NYSE Composite Index=100 *12 Month Price Score 97.69

Interim Earnings (Per Share)

Qtr.	Mar	Jun	Sep	Dec
2003	0.13	0.23	0.33	0.29
2004	0.15	0.27	0.36	0.30
2005	0.18	0.33	0.48	0.33
2006	0.26	0.36	0.69	0.36
2007	0.24	0.43	0.59	0.44

Interim Dividends (Per Share)

Amt	Decl	Ex	Rec	Pay
0.15Q	5/1/2007	7/3/2007	7/6/2007	7/20/2007
0.17Q	9/11/2007	10/3/2007	10/5/2007	10/19/2007
0.17Q	12/12/2007	1/2/2008	1/4/2008	1/18/2008
0.17Q	2/11/2008	4/2/2008	4/4/2008	4/18/2008

Indicated Div: $0.68

Valuation Analysis

Forecast P/E	22.57 (1/10/2007)
Market Cap	$2.1 Billion
Book Value	N/A
Price/Book	N/A
Price/Sales	3.44

Institutional Holding

No of Institutions	125
Shares	32,324,852
% Held	48.68

Business Summary: Hospitality & Tourism (MIC: 5.1 SIC: 7011 NAIC: 721110)

Choice Hotels International is a hotel franchisor with 5,570 hotels open and 1,093 hotels under development as of Dec 31 2007, representing 452,027 rooms open and 87,982 rooms under development in 49 states, the District of Columbia and 39 countries and territories outside the U.S. Co. franchises lodging properties under the proprietary brand names: Comfort Inn®, Comfort Suites®, Quality®, Clarion®, Sleep Inn®, Econo Lodge®, Rodeway Inn®, MainStay Suites®, Suburban Extended Stay Hotel®, Cambria Suites™ and Flag Hotels® Co. operates a single segment of franchising business and conducts its international franchise operations through direct and master franchising relationships.

Recent Developments: For the year ended Dec 31 2007, net income decreased 1.3% to US$111.3 million from US$112.8 million in the prior year. Revenues were US$615.5 million, up 14.0% from US$539.9 million the year before. Operating income was US$185.2 million versus US$166.6 million in the prior year, an increase of 11.1%. Direct operating expenses was unchanged at US$3.2 million versus the comparable period the year before. Indirect operating expenses increased 15.4% to US$427.1 million from US$370.1 million in the equivalent prior-year period.

Prospects: For 2008, Co. is projecting net domestic unit growth of about 5.0% and revenue per available room to grow by 3.0%. In addition, Co. is targeting the effective royalty rate to improve by 4 basis points. In addition, Co. intends to invest about $1.0 million to $3.0 million for marketing and reservation activities. Going forward, Co. will continue to improve its system hotels and utilize the domestic hotels under development to attain continued system growth. Also, Co. plans to improve its franchisees' revenues and overall profitability through national marketing campaigns, a central reservation system, property and yield management systems, better assurance levels and vendor relationships.

Financial Data
(US$ in Thousands)

	12/31/2007	12/31/2006	12/31/2005	12/31/2004	12/31/2003	12/31/2002	12/31/2001	12/31/2000
Earnings Per Share	1.70	1.68	1.32	1.08	0.98	0.76	0.16	0.40
Cash Flow Per Share	2.28	2.35	2.06	1.62	1.62	1.26	1.15	0.64
Dividends Per Share	0.620	0.540	0.468	0.412	...	...	...	...
Dividend Payout %	36.47	32.14	35.42	38.37	...	...	...	...
Income Statement								
Total Revenue	615,494	544,662	477,399	428,806	386,104	365,562	341,428	167,474
EBITDA	196,816	179,081	155,118	136,076	135,229	120,205	73,314	100,176
Income Before Taxes	173,886	155,278	130,742	114,524	112,407	95,818	45,417	69,582
Income Taxes	62,585	42,491	43,177	40,179	40,544	34,974	31,090	27,137
Net Income	111,301	112,787	87,565	74,345	71,863	60,844	14,327	42,445
Average Shares	65,331	67,050	66,336	69,000	73,348	80,114	89,144	106,506
Balance Sheet								
Current Assets	105,931	87,082	63,000	68,629	58,577	48,027	42,983	52,086
Total Assets	328,384	303,309	265,100	262,388	267,272	314,382	321,178	484,120
Current Liabilities	147,516	139,791	120,145	101,091	100,850	85,503	71,177	93,828
Long-Term Obligations	272,378	172,390	273,972	318,557	222,823	283,995	267,733	247,179
Total Liabilities	485,445	365,689	432,276	465,441	385,459	428,181	385,717	394,027
Stockholders' Equity	(157,061)	(62,380)	(167,176)	(203,053)	(118,187)	(113,799)	(64,539)	90,093
Shares Outstanding	62,091	66,355	65,219	64,624	69,491	74,326	83,995	86,919
Statistical Record								
Return on Assets %	35.24	39.69	33.20	28.00	24.71	19.15	3.56	8.92
Return on Equity %	...	...	...	...	...	...	112.13	54.37
EBITDA Margin %	31.98	32.88	32.49	31.73	35.02	32.88	21.47	59.82
Net Margin %	18.08	20.71	18.34	17.34	18.61	16.64	4.20	25.34
Asset Turnover	1.95	1.92	1.81	1.61	1.33	1.15	0.85	0.35
Current Ratio	0.72	0.62	0.52	0.68	0.58	0.56	0.60	0.56
Debt to Equity	...	...	...	...	...	...	...	2.74
Price Range	44.28-33.20	61.62-35.62	42.14-28.20	29.84-17.20	18.20-10.19	13.38-8.70	11.78-5.70	8.63-3.81
P/E Ratio	26.05-19.53	36.68-21.20	31.92-21.37	27.63-15.93	18.58-10.40	17.60-11.45	73.59-35.63	21.56-9.53
Average Yield %	1.63	1.16	1.45	1.70	...	...	...	...

Address: 10750 Columbia Pike, Silver Spring, MD 20901 **Telephone:** 301-592-5000	**Web Site:** www.choicehotels.com **Officers:** Stewart Bainum Jr. - Chmn. Charles A. Ledsinger - Pres., C.E.O.	**Auditors:** PricewaterhouseCoopers LLP **Transfer Agents:** Computershare Investor Services, Canton, MA

CHOICEPOINT, INC.

Exchange	Symbol	Price	52Wk Range	Yield	P/E
NYS	CPS	$47.60 (3/31/2008)	48.45-31.87	N/A	108.18

*7 Year Price Score 81.72 *NYSE Composite Index=100 ***12 Month Price Score 120.19**

Interim Earnings (Per Share)

Qtr.	Mar	Jun	Sep	Dec
2003	0.73	0.23	0.32	0.30
2004	0.37	0.40	0.43	0.43
2005	0.40	0.40	0.43	0.30
2006	0.34	0.40	(0.86)	0.28
2007	0.40	0.43	0.02	(0.42)

Interim Dividends (Per Share)

Amt	Decl	Ex	Rec	Pay
3-for-2	1/31/2001	3/8/2001	2/16/2001	3/7/2001
33%	4/25/2002	6/7/2002	5/16/2002	6/6/2002

Valuation Analysis — **Institutional Holding**

Forecast P/E	19.15	No of Institutions	
	(1/10/2007)	226	
Market Cap	$3.2 Billion	Shares	
Book Value	309.9 Million	65,707,304	
Price/Book	10.20	% Held	
Price/Sales	3.22	85.82	

Business Summary: IT & Technology (MIC: 10.2 SIC: 7374 NAIC: 518210)

ChoicePoint is a provider of identification and credential verification services. At Dec 31 2007, Co. had four segments: Insurance Services, which provides data, analytics, software and business information services to property and casualty personal and commercial insurance carriers; Screening and Authentication Services, which focuses on employment screenings, tenant screening, vital records and customer enrollment businesses; Business Services, which provides public information application primarily to banking, professional services, and government customers; and Marketing Services, which provides direct marketing and database software to the insurance and financial services industries.

Recent Developments: For the year ended Dec 31 2007, income from continuing operations increased 13.7% to US$63.0 million from US$55.4 million a year earlier. Net income increased 91.6% to US$32.4 million from US$16.9 million in the prior year. Revenues were US$982.0 million, up 2.3% from US$959.6 million the year before. Operating income was US$131.8 million versus US$106.6 million in the prior year, an increase of 23.6%. Direct operating expenses rose 2.3% to US$536.1 million from US$523.9 million in the comparable period the year before. Indirect operating expenses decreased 4.6% to US$314.1 million from US$329.1 million in the equivalent prior-year period.

Prospects: On Feb 21 2008, Co. announced an agreement, in which it will be acquired by Reed Elsevier Group Plc., a publisher and information provider, for $4.00 billion. Notably, Co. anticipates the transaction to close in the summer 2008. Meanwhile, on Feb 5 2008, Co. announced its acquisition of Optimal Decisions Group, which develops software to the insurance industry. Consequently, Co. expects the acquisition to expand its services to the Property and Casualty insurance market. For the year ending Dec 2008, Co. estimates its diluted earnings, excluding other operating charges, of $1.73 to $1.90 per share and internal revenue growth for its total continuing operations of 2.0% to 7.0%.

Financial Data
(US$ in Thousands)

	12/31/2007	12/31/2006	12/31/2005	12/31/2004	12/31/2003	12/31/2002	12/31/2001	12/31/2000
Earnings Per Share	0.44	0.20	1.53	1.62	1.58	1.01	0.58	0.52
Cash Flow Per Share	3.18	2.89	2.84	2.83	1.81	2.00	1.55	1.38
Tang Book Value Per Share	N.M.	N.M.	N.M.	N.M.	0.36	N.M.	N.M.	N.M.
Income Statement								
Total Revenue	981,955	1,054,992	1,057,914	918,713	795,746	791,562	655,967	593,533
EBITDA	195,538	206,440	313,816	303,124	231,680	238,991	179,020	143,672
Income Before Taxes	104,762	112,396	232,632	238,830	175,499	185,460	109,021	78,310
Income Taxes	41,773	43,621	91,976	90,875	67,391	71,217	58,687	34,488
Net Income	32,424	16,922	140,656	147,955	141,992	89,827	50,334	43,822
Average Shares	74,423	84,986	91,695	91,305	89,686	89,194	87,150	84,138
Balance Sheet								
Current Assets	419,985	317,519	272,238	218,377	203,952	205,335	212,670	178,329
Total Assets	1,214,850	1,346,092	1,462,976	1,287,476	1,021,284	979,010	832,392	704,439
Current Liabilities	288,567	309,997	270,584	223,668	178,481	202,696	284,689	106,339
Long-Term Obligations	530,000	315,028	80,035	17	1,835	97,059	2,390	141,638
Total Liabilities	878,158	679,105	442,102	303,817	230,789	356,403	347,571	303,370
Stockholders' Equity	309,922	666,987	1,020,874	983,659	790,495	622,607	484,821	401,069
Shares Outstanding	66,389	76,047	86,627	88,232	86,555	85,490	83,435	82,087
Statistical Record								
Return on Assets %	2.53	1.20	10.23	12.78	14.20	9.92	6.55	7.06
Return on Equity %	6.64	2.01	14.03	16.63	20.10	16.22	11.36	14.47
EBITDA Margin %	19.91	19.57	29.66	32.99	29.11	30.19	27.29	24.21
Net Margin %	3.30	1.60	13.30	16.10	17.84	11.35	7.67	7.38
Asset Turnover	0.77	0.75	0.77	0.79	0.80	0.87	0.85	0.96
Current Ratio	1.46	1.02	1.01	0.98	1.14	1.01	0.75	1.68
Debt to Equity	1.71	0.47	0.08	N.M.	N.M.	N.M.	N.M.	0.35
Price Range	43.95-35.51	46.30-30.50	47.85-36.73	46.34-36.39	41.90-29.99	47.83-29.76	38.76-23.18	32.78-16.25
P/E Ratio	99.89-80.70	231.50-152.50	31.27-24.01	28.60-22.46	26.52-18.98	47.36-29.47	66.83-39.96	63.04-31.25

Address: 1000 Alderman Drive, Alpharetta, GA 30005 **Telephone:** 770-752-6000 **Fax:** 770-752-6250	**Web Site:** www.choicepoint.com **Officers:** Derek V. Smith - Chmn., C.E.O. Douglas C. Curling - Pres., C.O.O.	**Auditors:** Deloitte & Touche LLP **Investor Contact:** 770-752-3369 **Transfer Agents:** SunTrust Banks, Inc., Atlanta, GA

CHUBB CORP.

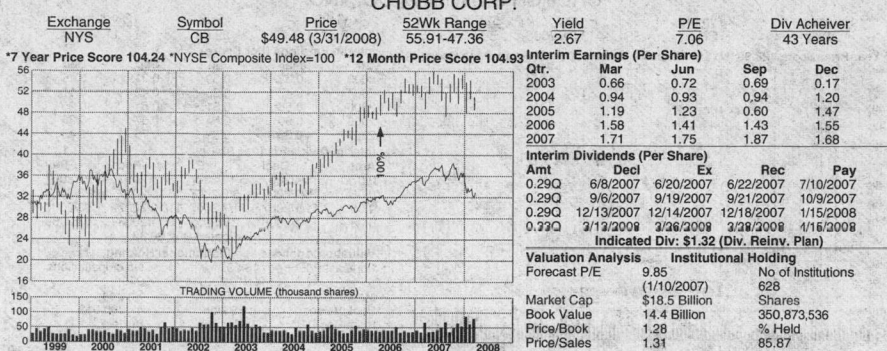

Exchange	Symbol	Price	52Wk Range	Yield	P/E	Div Acheiver
NYS	CB	$49.48 (3/31/2008)	55.91-47.36	2.67	7.06	43 Years

*7 Year Price Score 104.24 *NYSE Composite Index=100 *12 Month Price Score 104.93

Interim Earnings (Per Share)

Qtr.	Mar	Jun	Sep	Dec
2003	0.66	0.72	0.69	0.17
2004	0.94	0.93	0.94	1.20
2005	1.19	1.23	0.60	1.47
2006	1.58	1.41	1.43	1.55
2007	1.71	1.75	1.87	1.68

Interim Dividends (Per Share)

Amt	Decl	Ex	Rec	Pay
0.29Q	6/8/2007	6/20/2007	6/22/2007	7/10/2007
0.29Q	9/6/2007	9/19/2007	9/21/2007	10/9/2007
0.29Q	12/13/2007	12/14/2007	12/18/2007	1/15/2008
0.33Q	3/12/2008	3/26/2008	3/28/2008	4/16/2008

Indicated Div: $1.32 (Div. Reinv. Plan)

Valuation Analysis

Forecast P/E	9.85
	(1/10/2007)
Market Cap	$18.5 Billion
Book Value	14.4 Billion
Price/Book	1.28
Price/Sales	1.31

Institutional Holding

No of Institutions	628
Shares	350,873,536
% Held	85.87

TRADING VOLUME (thousand shares)

Business Summary: Insurance (MIC: 8.2 SIC: 6331 NAIC: 524126)

Chubb is a holding company with subsidiaries principally engaged in the property and casualty insurance business. Chubb Commercial Insurance provides a range of commercial insurance products, including coverage for multiple peril, casualty, workers' compensation and property and marine. Chubb Specialty Insurance provides a range of professional liability products for privately and publicly owned companies, financial institutions, professional firms and healthcare organizations. Chubb Personal Insurance provides products for individuals with fine homes and possessions who require more coverage choices and higher limits than standard insurance policies.

Recent Developments: For the year ended Dec 31 2007, net income increased 11.0% to US$2.81 billion in the prior year. Revenues were US$14.11 billion, up 0.7% from US$14.00 billion the year before. Net premiums earned were US$11.95 billion versus US$11.96 billion in the prior year, a decrease of 0.1%.

Prospects: Co.'s bottom line results are being positively affected by an increase in underwriting income in its property and casualty insurance business. In addition, Co. is seeing a slight overall growth in net written premiums in its insurance business reflecting its emphasis on underwriting discipline in an increasingly competitive market environment. Meanwhile, Co. expects overall premiums in its insurance business to be flat to modestly down in 2008 compared with 2007, with a modest increase for personal insurance and modest decreases for both commercial insurance and specialty insurance. Hence, Co. is projecting operating income per share to be in the range of $5.70 to $6.10 for 2008.

Financial Data

(US$ in Thousands)	12/31/2007	12/31/2006	12/31/2005	12/31/2004	12/31/2003	12/31/2002	12/31/2001	12/31/2000
Earnings Per Share	7.01	5.98	4.47	4.00	2.23	0.65	0.32	2.00
Cash Flow Per Share	8.11	8.10	9.47	10.74	9.39	6.99	2.93	2.76
Tang Book Value Per Share	37.31	32.57	28.56	25.07	21.43	18.67	17.81	18.56
Dividends Per Share	1.160	1.000	0.860	0.780	0.720	0.700	0.680	0.660
Dividend Payout %	16.55	16.72	19.24	19.48	32.29	108.53	215.87	32.92
Income Statement								
Premium Income	11,946,000	11,958,000	12,176,000	11,635,700	10,182,500	8,085,300	6,656,400	6,145,900
Total Revenue	14,107,000	14,003,000	14,082,300	13,177,200	11,394,000	9,140,300	7,754,000	7,251,500
Benefits & Claims	6,299,000	6,574,000	7,813,500	7,320,900	6,867,200	6,064,600	5,357,400	4,127,700
Income Before Taxes	3,937,000	3,525,000	2,447,000	2,068,200	933,600	168,400	(66,000)	851,000
Income Taxes	1,130,000	997,000	621,100	519,800	124,800	(54,500)	(177,500)	136,400
Net Income	2,807,000	2,528,000	1,825,900	1,548,400	808,800	222,900	111,500	714,600
Average Shares	400,300	422,400	408,400	386,400	362,600	345,800	351,600	356,600
Balance Sheet								
Total Assets	50,574,000	50,277,000	48,060,700	44,260,300	38,360,600	34,114,400	29,449,000	25,026,700
Total Liabilities	36,129,000	36,414,000	35,653,700	34,133,900	29,838,600	27,255,200	22,923,700	18,045,000
Stockholders' Equity	14,445,000	13,863,000	12,407,000	10,126,400	8,522,000	6,859,200	6,525,300	6,981,700
Shares Outstanding	374,649	411,276	418,076	385,353	375,926	342,403	340,142	349,838
Statistical Record								
Return on Assets %	5.57	5.14	3.96	3.74	2.23	0.70	0.41	2.93
Return on Equity %	19.83	19.25	16.21	16.56	10.52	3.33	1.65	10.75
Loss Ratio %	52.73	54.98	64.17	62.92	67.44	75.01	80.48	67.16
Net Margin %	19.90	18.05	12.97	11.75	7.10	2.44	1.44	9.85
Price Range	55.91-47.36	54.65-46.80	49.06-36.67	38.50-32.00	34.62-21.23	39.10-26.10	41.72-29.30	45.00-22.38
P/E Ratio	7.98-6.76	9.14-7.83	10.98-8.20	9.63-8.00	15.52-9.52	60.15-40.15	130.37-91.55	22.50-11.19
Average Yield %	2.20	1.99	2.02	2.23	2.42	2.13	1.91	1.93

Address: 15 Mountain View Road, P.O. Box 1615, Warren, NJ 07061-1615 **Telephone:** 908-903-2000 **Fax:** 908-903-2003	**Web Site:** www.chubb.com **Officers:** John D. Finnegan - Chmn., Pres., C.E.O. Michael O'Reilly - Vice-Chmn., C.F.O., Chief Invest. Officer	**Auditors:** Ernst & Young LLP **Transfer Agents:** EquiServe Trust Company, N.A., Jersey City, NJ

CHURCH & DWIGHT CO., INC.

Exchange	Symbol	Price	52Wk Range	Yield	P/E	Div Acheiver
NYS	CHD	$54.24 (3/31/2008)	56.93-43.25	0.59	22.05	11 Years

*7 Year Price Score 128.99 *NYSE Composite Index=100 *12 Month Price Score 113.55

TRADING VOLUME (thousand shares)

Interim Earnings (Per Share)

Qtr.	Mar	Jun	Sep	Dec
2003	0.33	0.39	0.31	0.25
2004	0.47	0.30	0.42	0.17
2005	0.56	0.51	0.51	0.25
2006	0.60	0.54	0.57	0.36
2007	0.66	0.59	0.75	0.46

Interim Dividends (Per Share)

Amt	Decl	Ex	Rec	Pay
0.07Q	5/4/2007	5/10/2007	5/14/2007	6/1/2007
0.08Q	8/2/2007	8/9/2007	8/13/2007	9/3/2007
0.08Q	11/1/2007	11/7/2007	11/12/2007	12/3/2007
0.08Q	2/1/2008	2/7/2008	2/11/2008	3/3/2008

Indicated Div: $0.32

Valuation Analysis / Institutional Holding

Valuation Analysis		Institutional Holding	
Forecast P/E	16.53 (1/10/2007)	No of Institutions	249
Market Cap	$3.6 Billion	Shares	47,960,912
Book Value	1.1 Billion	% Held	73.11
Price/Book	3.33		
Price/Sales	1.62		

Business Summary: Chemicals (MIC: 11.1 SIC: 2841 NAIC: 325611)

Church & Dwight produces, manufactures, and markets household, personal care and specialty products. Co.'s Consumer Domestic segment includes household products for deodorizing and cleaning, such as ARM & HAMMER baking soda and cat litter and SCRUB FREE and BRILLO cleaning products; and laundry products, such as XTRA and ARM & HAMMER laundry detergents, OXICLEAN pre-wash laundry additive and XTRA NICE'N FLUFFY fabric softeners. Co.'s Consumer International segment sells several personal care products, some of which use the same brands as its domestic product lines. Co.'s Specialty Products segment produces and sells sodium bicarbonate and animal nutrition and specialty cleaning products.

Recent Developments: For the year ended Dec 31 2007, net income increased 21.7% to US$169.0 million from US$138.9 million in the prior year. Revenues were US$2.22 billion, up 14.1% from US$1.95 billion the year before. Operating income was US$305.0 million versus US$252.1 million in the prior year, an increase of 21.0%. Direct operating expenses rose 14.2% to US$1.35 billion from US$1.18 billion in the comparable period the year before. Indirect operating expenses increased 10.6% to US$562.9 million from US$509.0 million in the equivalent prior-year period.

Prospects: Despite the continuing commodity cost challenges and a slowing economy, Co. is projecting earnings for the full year of 2008 to be about $2.77 per share, reflecting an increase of about 13.0% over its 2007 levels. Specifically, Co. expects the growth in earnings to be driven by solid organic revenue growth and gross margin expansion. Accordingly, Co. anticipates gross margin expansion by 100 basis points, due to the estimated benefits from the liquid laundry detergent concentration, the Orange Glo International business manufacturing integration, the February 2008 price increases on Trojan condoms and Arm & Hammer baking soda and cat litter, as well as its cost-reduction initiatives.

Financial Data

(US$ in Thousands)	12/31/2007	12/31/2006	12/31/2005	12/31/2004	12/31/2003	12/31/2002	12/31/2001	12/31/2000
Earnings Per Share	2.46	2.07	1.83	1.36	1.28	1.07	0.77	0.56
Cash Flow Per Share	3.78	2.87	2.98	3.14	1.95	1.92	0.71	1.78
Tang Book Value Per Share	N.M.	N.M.	N.M.	N.M.	0.98	0.92	0.31	2.62
Dividends Per Share	0.300	0.260	0.240	0.227	0.207	0.200	0.193	0.187
Dividend Payout %	12.20	12.56	13.11	16.67	16.15	18.75	25.22	33.33
Income Statement								
Total Revenue	2,220,940	1,945,661	1,736,506	1,462,062	1,056,874	1,047,149	1,080,864	795,725
EBITDA	380,488	318,853	263,230	207,939	171,686	152,956	113,235	80,471
Income Before Taxes	264,925	213,098	174,974	127,439	116,935	101,092	73,855	52,161
Income Taxes	95,900	74,171	52,068	38,631	35,974	34,402	26,871	18,315
Net Income	169,025	138,927	122,906	88,808	80,961	66,690	46,984	33,559
Average Shares	70,312	68,946	69,289	68,066	63,298	62,713	61,228	59,899
Balance Sheet								
Current Assets	735,353	556,070	494,438	493,796	289,222	285,436	293,207	162,527
Total Assets	2,532,490	2,334,154	1,962,117	1,877,998	1,119,617	988,241	949,085	455,632
Current Liabilities	457,789	444,404	409,710	357,539	232,054	191,167	196,016	149,138
Long-Term Obligations	707,311	792,925	635,261	754,706	331,149	352,488	406,564	20,136
Total Liabilities	1,452,225	1,470,317	1,265,239	1,317,968	681,123	640,595	666,782	220,982
Stockholders' Equity	1,080,265	863,837	696,878	560,030	438,494	347,646	282,303	234,650
Shares Outstanding	66,243	65,361	64,388	63,188	61,179	59,846	58,714	57,566
Statistical Record								
Return on Assets %	6.95	6.47	6.40	5.91	7.68	6.88	6.69	7.18
Return on Equity %	17.39	17.80	19.56	17.74	20.60	21.17	18.18	14.51
EBITDA Margin %	17.13	16.39	15.16	14.22	16.24	14.61	10.48	10.11
Net Margin %	7.61	7.14	7.08	6.07	7.66	6.37	4.35	4.22
Asset Turnover	0.91	0.91	0.90	0.97	1.00	1.08	1.54	1.70
Current Ratio	1.61	1.25	1.21	1.38	1.25	1.49	1.50	1.09
Debt to Equity	0.65	0.92	0.91	1.35	0.76	1.01	1.44	0.09
Price Range	56.93-43.25	43.38-32.96	39.04-32.29	33.62-25.78	27.65-18.73	23.93-17.27	18.96-13.21	18.21-9.88
P/E Ratio	23.14-17.58	20.96-15.92	21.33-17.64	24.72-18.96	21.60-14.63	22.36-16.14	24.62-17.15	32.51-17.63
Average Yield %	0.61	0.69	0.67	0.78	0.93	0.97	1.18	1.47

Address: 469 North Harrison Street, Princeton, NJ 08543-5297
Telephone: 609-683-5900
Fax: 609-497-7269

Web Site: www.churchdwight.com
Officers: Robert A. Davies III - Chmn. James R. Craigie - Pres., C.E.O.

Auditors: Deloitte & Touche LLP
Transfer Agents: Computershare Investor Services LLC

CIGNA CORP.

Exchange	Symbol	Price	52Wk Range	Yield	P/E
NYS	CI	$40.57 (3/31/2008)	56.36-38.76	0.10	10.48

*7 Year Price Score 128.83 *NYSE Composite Index=100 *12 Month Price Score 94.08

Interim Earnings (Per Share)

Qtr.	Mar	Jun	Sep	Dec
2003	0.56	(0.13)	0.46	0.69
2004	0.18	1.22	0.78	1.29
2005	1.09	1.83	0.67	0.58
2006	0.96	0.78	0.92	0.77
2007	0.98	0.68	1.28	0.93

Interim Dividends (Per Share)

Amt	Decl	Ex	Rec	Pay
200%	4/25/2007	6/5/2007	5/21/2007	6/4/2007
0.01A	7/25/2007	9/10/2007	9/12/2007	10/10/2007
0.01A	10/24/2007	12/11/2007	12/13/2007	1/10/2008
0.04A	2/27/2008	3/7/2008	3/11/2008	4/10/2008

Indicated Div: $0.04

Valuation Analysis

		Institutional Holding	
Forecast P/E	11.19	No of Institutions	
	(1/10/2007)	447	
Market Cap	$11.3 Billion	Shares	
Book Value	4.7 Billion	81,065,056	
Price/Book	2.39	% Held	
Price/Sales	0.64	83.17	

Business Summary: Insurance (MIC: 8.2 SIC: 6324 NAIC: 524114)

CIGNA is a holding company engaged in the provision of health care and related benefits offered primarily through the workplace. As of Dec 31 2007, Co. operated through six segments: Health Care, Disability and Life, International, Other Operations, and Run-off Reinsurance. Co.'s key product lines include health care products and services, group disability, life and accident insurance as well as disability and workers' compensation case management and related services. As of the date stated above, Co.'s products were marketed in all 50 states, the District of Columbia, Puerto Rico, the U.S. Virgin Islands and Canada.

Recent Developments: For the year ended Dec 31 2007, income from continuing operations decreased 3.4% to US$1.12 billion from US$1.16 billion a year earlier. Net income decreased 3.5% to US$1.12 billion from US$1.16 billion in the prior year. Revenues were US$17.62 billion, up 6.5% from US$16.55 billion the year before. Net investment income fell 6.8% to US$1.11 billion from US$1.20 billion a year ago.

Prospects: Co.'s 2008 outlook appears encouraging. Specifically, Co. expects full-year 2008 income from continuing operations, excluding realized investment results, the results of the guaranteed minimum income benefits (GMIB) business and special items, to be higher than the comparable 2007 amount due primarily to estimated earnings growth in its Health Care, Disability and Life, and International segments, tempered by lower earnings in its Run-off Reinsurance segment. Additionally, Co. anticipates that 2008 medical membership, excluding the affect of membership growth related to the pending acquisition of Great-West Healthcare, should increase by approximately 2.0% to 5.0%.

Financial Data

(US$ in Thousands)	12/31/2007	12/31/2006	12/31/2005	12/31/2004	12/31/2003	12/31/2002	12/31/2001	12/31/2000
Earnings Per Share	3.87	3.43	4.17	3.48	1.58	(0.94)	2.20	2.03
Cash Flow Per Share	4.74	1.94	1.88	3.50	5.51	3.16	2.45	3.50
Tang Book Value Per Share	10.60	8.87	10.28	9.05	6.87	5.37	7.65	7.75
Dividends Per Share	0.038	0.033	0.033	0.135	0.440	0.440	0.477	0.413
Dividend Payout %	0.99	0.97	0.80	3.88	27.79	...	19.42	20.39
Income Statement								
Total Revenue	17,623,000	16,547,000	16,684,000	18,176,000	18,808,000	19,348,000	19,115,000	19,994,000
Benefits & Claims	10,199,000	9,264,000	9,646,000	10,264,000	...	...	...	...
Income Before Taxes	1,631,000	1,731,000	1,793,000	2,375,000	903,000	(569,000)	1,497,000	1,497,000
Income Taxes	511,000	572,000	517,000	798,000	283,000	(172,000)	508,000	510,000
Net Income	1,115,000	1,155,000	1,625,000	1,438,000	668,000	(398,000)	989,000	987,000
Average Shares	288,332	336,984	389,418	413,652	421,818	446,061	450,108	479,430
Balance Sheet								
Total Assets	40,065,000	42,399,000	44,863,000	81,059,000	90,953,000	88,950,000	91,589,000	95,088,000
Total Liabilities	35,317,000	38,069,000	39,503,000	75,856,000	86,434,000	85,083,000	86,534,000	89,675,000
Stockholders' Equity	4,748,000	4,330,000	5,360,000	5,203,000	4,519,000	3,867,000	5,055,000	5,413,000
Shares Outstanding	279,588	292,417	363,573	396,021	421,773	418,110	424,659	456,015
Statistical Record								
Return on Assets %	2.70	2.65	2.58	1.67	0.74	N.M.	1.06	1.03
Return on Equity %	24.56	23.84	30.77	29.50	15.93	N.M.	18.90	17.03
Net Margin %	6.33	6.98	9.74	7.91	3.55	(2.06)	5.17	4.94
Price Range	56.33-42.65	44.42-29.58	39.77-26.20	27.40-17.68	19.40-13.07	36.94-12.03	42.83-23.87	45.00-20.40
P/E Ratio	14.56-11.02	12.95-8.62	9.54-6.28	7.87-5.08	12.28-8.27	...	19.47-10.85	22.17-10.05
Average Yield %	0.08	0.09	0.10	0.62	2.76	1.61	1.33	1.31

Address: Two Liberty Place, 1650 Market Street, Philadelphia, PA 19192 **Telephone:** 215-761-1000	**Web Site:** www.cigna.com **Officers:** H. Edward Hanway - Chmn., Pres., C.E.O. Michael W. Bell - Exec. V.P., C.F.O.	**Auditors:** PricewaterhouseCoopers LLP **Transfer Agents:** Mellon Investor Services, South Hackensack, NJ

CIMAREX ENERGY CO

Interim Earnings (Per Share)

Qtr.	Mar	Jun	Sep	Dec
2003	0.78	0.50	0.53	0.41
2004	0.70	0.85	0.91	1.12
2005	1.00	0.98	0.76	2.27
2006	1.29	0.98	1.11	0.70
2007	0.77	0.93	0.87	1.53

Interim Dividends (Per Share)

Amt	Decl	Ex	Rec	Pay
0.04Q	5/17/2007	8/13/2007	8/15/2007	9/3/2007
0.04Q	9/20/2007	11/13/2007	11/15/2007	12/3/2007
0.06Q	12/12/2007	2/13/2008	2/15/2008	3/3/2008
0.06Q	2/29/2008	5/13/2008	5/15/2008	6/2/2008

Indicated Div: $0.24

Valuation Analysis   **Institutional Holding**

Forecast P/E	N/A	No of Institutions
		265
Market Cap	$4.5 Billion	Shares
Book Value	3.3 Billion	62,736,800
Price/Book	1.39	% Held
Price/Sales	3.16	75.36

Business Summary: Oil and Gas (MIC: 14.2 SIC: 1311 NAIC: 211111)

Cimarex Energy is an independent oil and gas exploration and production company. As of Dec 31 2007, Co.'s operations were mainly located in Texas, Oklahoma, New Mexico, Kansas, Louisiana and Wyoming. Proved oil and gas reserves as of year-end 2007 totaled nearly 1.5 trillion cubic feet (Tcfe), consisting of 1.1 Tcf of gas and 58.3 million barrels of oil and natural gas liquids. Of total proved reserves, 76.0% were gas and 79.0% were classified as proved developed. Co. operates the wells that account for 82.0% of its total proved reserves and approximately 79.0% of production.

Recent Developments: For the year ended Dec 31 2007, net income increased 0.2% to US$346.5 million from US$345.7 million in the prior year. Revenues were US$1.43 billion, up 12.9% from US$1.27 billion the year before. Operating income was US$541.8 million versus US$517.6 million in the prior year, an increase of 4.7%. Indirect operating expenses increased 18.7% to US$889.4 million from US$749.5 million in the equivalent prior-year period.

Prospects: Co. outlook appears constructive, as reserves additions for 2007 totaled 311 billion cubic feet equivalent and replaced 189% of 2007 production. For 2008, Co. is projecting exploration and development capital expenditures of $1.10 billion to $1.30 billion. However, Co. noted that the actual amount invested will be highly dependent on commodity prices and rig rates. Mid-point 2008 projections by region are as follows: Mid-Contenent, $520.0 million; Permian, $450.0 million; Gulf Coast/GOM, $190.0 million; and Western/Other, $40.0 million. Co. sees full-year 2008 production of 465 to 485 million cubic feet equivalent per day, or 5.0% to 10.0% higher than 2007 after adjusting for property sales.

Financial Data
(US$ in Thousands)

	12/31/2007	12/31/2006	12/31/2005	12/31/2004	12/31/2003	12/31/2002	12/31/2001	09/30/2001
Earnings Per Share	4.09	4.11	4.90	3.59	2.22	1.31	0.17	352,530.00
Cash Flow Per Share	12.16	10.70	10.88	8.67	4.97	3.45	0.11	1,623,680.00
Tang Book Value Per Share	31.11	27.57	22.80	15.71	11.93	9.64	6.58	1,667,950.00
Dividends Per Share	0.160	0.160	...	...	...	...	...	...
Dividend Payout %	3.91	3.89	...	...	...	...	...	...
Income Statement								
Total Revenue	1,431,166	1,267,144	1,118,622	674,929	454,212	209,570	26,759	317,053
EBITDA	1,022,794	942,626	785,490	372,526	238,857	110,735	16,225	104,537
Income Before Taxes	544,625	544,324	516,455	246,318	148,169	61,379	7,253	54,838
Income Taxes	198,156	198,605	188,130	92,726	55,141	21,560	2,774	19,585
Net Income	346,469	345,719	328,325	153,592	94,633	39,819	4,479	35,253
Average Shares	84,632	84,090	67,000	42,763	42,640	30,317	26,591	100.00
Balance Sheet								
Current Assets	564,577	416,757	429,028	236,447	123,204	87,545	37,422	37,397
Total Assets	5,362,794	4,829,750	4,180,335	1,105,446	805,508	674,286	251,966	246,212
Current Liabilities	424,571	354,588	397,418	143,002	85,509	68,253	38,081	44,800
Long-Term Obligations	487,159	443,667	352,451	...	...	32,000	...	...
Total Liabilities	2,103,507	1,853,607	1,584,882	404,734	270,768	229,406	76,884	79,417
Stockholders' Equity	3,259,287	2,976,143	2,595,453	700,712	534,740	444,880	175,082	166,795
Shares Outstanding	82,541	82,883	82,377	41,729	41,063	41,410	26,591	100.00
Statistical Record								
Return on Assets %	6.80	7.67	12.42	16.03	12.79	8.60	1.33	13.25
Return on Equity %	11.11	12.41	19.92	24.80	19.32	12.85	1.94	19.60
EBITDA Margin %	71.47	74.39	70.22	55.19	52.59	52.84	60.63	32.97
Net Margin %	24.21	27.28	29.35	22.76	20.83	19.00	16.74	11.12
Asset Turnover	0.28	0.28	0.42	0.70	0.61	0.45	0.08	1.19
Current Ratio	1.33	1.18	1.08	1.65	1.44	1.28	0.98	0.83
Debt to Equity	0.15	0.15	0.14	...	...	0.07	...	...
Price Range	42.86-34.12	47.31-33.43	45.93-34.58	41.03-24.53	28.14-17.17	17.90-13.49	...	...
P/E Ratio	10.48-8.34	11.51-8.13	9.37-7.06	11.43-6.83	12.68-7.73	13.66-10.30	...	...
Average Yield %	0.42	0.40	...	...	...	...	...	...

Address: 1700 Lincoln Street, Suite 1800, Denver, CO 80203-4518	**Web Site:** www.cimarex.com	**Auditors:** KPMG LLP
Telephone: 303-295-3995	**Officers:** F. H. Merelli - Chmn., Pres., C.E.O. Thomas E. Jorden - Exec. V.P., Exploration	**Investor Contact:** 303-295-3995
Fax: 303-295-3494		**Transfer Agents:** Continental Stock Transfer & Trust Company

CINCINNATI BELL INC

Exchange	Symbol	Price	52Wk Range	Yield	P/E
NYS	CBB	$4.26 (3/31/2008)	6.14-3.75	N/A	17.75

*7 Year Price Score 65.60   *NYSE Composite Index=100   *12 Month Price Score 90.44

Interim Earnings (Per Share)

Qtr.	Mar	Jun	Sep	Dec
2003	0.55	1.13	0.18	3.47
2004	0.03	0.05	0.06	0.07
2005	(0.02)	(0.13)	(0.19)	0.05
2006	0.05	0.09	0.09	0.08
2007	0.08	0.09	0.09	(0.01)

Interim Dividends (Per Share)

No Dividends Paid

Valuation Analysis

		Institutional Holding	
Forecast P/E	N/A	No of Institutions	193
Market Cap	$1.1 Billion	Shares	
Book Value	N/A		223,352,736
Price/Book	N/A	% Held	
Price/Sales	0.78		90.25

Business Summary: Communications (MIC: 10.1 SIC: 4813 NAIC: 517110)

Cincinnati Bell is a local provider of data and voice communications services and equipment, as well as a regional provider of wireless and long distance communications services. Co. provides telecommunications service primarily on its owned local and wireless networks. Co. operates through three business segments: Wireline, which provides local voice, data, long-distance and other services; Wireless, which provides digital voice and data communications services through the operation of a Global System for Mobile Communications/General Packet Radio Service wireless network; and Technology Solutions, which provides outsourced telecommunications and information technology services.

Recent Developments:
For the year ended Dec 31 2007, net income decreased 15.2% to US$73.2 million from US$86.3 million in the prior year. Revenues were US$1.35 billion, up 6.2% from US$1.27 billion the year before. Operating income was US$282.4 million versus US$312.5 million in the prior year, a decrease of 9.6%. Direct operating expenses rose 7.3% to US$609.7 million from US$568.3 million in the comparable period the year before. Indirect operating expenses increased 17.3% to US$456.5 million from US$389.3 million in the equivalent prior-year period.

Prospects:
On Dec 31 2007, Co. purchased GramTel USA, Inc., a data center business in South Bend, IN with total floor capacity of 22,500 square feet, for $20.3 million. Separately, on Feb 1 2008, Co. finalized its acquisition of eGIX Inc., a privately held competitive service provider headquartered in Carmel, IN, for approximately $18.0 million plus certain additional, future performance-related payments. The acquisition of eGIX provides Co. with an immediate footprint in the small and medium-sized business market throughout Indiana and in Illinois. As a result of these strategic acquisitions, Co. is expecting revenue of approximately $1.40 billion and operating income of $326.0 million for 2008.

Financial Data

(US$ in Thousands)	12/31/2007	12/31/2006	12/31/2005	12/31/2004	12/31/2003	12/31/2002	12/31/2001	12/31/2000
Earnings Per Share	0.24	0.30	(0.30)	0.21	5.36	(19.38)	(1.36)	(1.82)
Cash Flow Per Share	1.25	1.36	1.31	1.22	1.37	0.88	1.19	1.56
Income Statement								
Total Revenue	1,348,600	1,270,100	1,209,600	1,207,100	1,557,800	2,155,900	2,350,500	2,050,100
EBITDA	435,600	459,700	348,900	491,300	821,100	(1,665,000)	356,600	81,200
Income Before Taxes	129,900	154,600	(10,200)	100,300	417,200	(2,325,500)	(366,400)	(542,100)
Income Taxes	56,700	68,300	54,300	36,100	(828,800)	105,700	(80,200)	(165,600)
Net Income	73,200	86,300	(64,500)	64,200	1,331,900	(4,222,300)	(286,200)	(377,100)
Average Shares	256,800	253,300	245,900	250,500	253,300	218,400	217,400	211,700
Balance Sheet								
Net PPE	933,700	818,800	800,400	851,100	898,800	867,900	3,059,500	2,966,200
Total Assets	2,019,600	2,013,800	1,863,300	1,958,700	2,073,500	1,467,600	6,312,000	6,477,600
Long-Term Obligations	2,001,900	2,065,900	2,073,400	2,111,100	2,274,500	2,354,700	2,702,000	2,507,000
Total Liabilities	2,687,200	2,805,400	2,572,800	2,544,000	2,713,200	3,572,000	4,197,900	4,022,300
Stockholders' Equity	(667,600)	(791,600)	(737,700)	(624,500)	(679,400)	(2,548,300)	1,678,400	2,021,500
Shares Outstanding	248,357	247,471	247,163	245,401	244,561	218,690	218,067	215,529
Statistical Record								
Return on Assets %	3.63	4.45	N.M.	3.18	75.23	N.M.	N.M.	N.M.
EBITDA Margin %	32.30	36.19	28.84	40.70	52.71	N.M.	15.17	3.96
Net Margin %	5.43	6.79	(5.33)	5.32	85.50	(195.85)	(12.18)	(18.39)
PPE Turnover	1.54	1.57	1.46	1.38	1.76	1.10	0.78	0.75
Asset Turnover	0.67	0.66	0.63	0.60	0.88	0.55	0.37	0.31
Debt to Equity	...	...	...	...	...	...	1.61	1.24
Price Range	6.14-4.26	5.14-3.45	4.71-3.51	5.89-3.26	7.25-3.51	10.55-1.15	28.75-7.79	40.50-20.00
P/E Ratio	25.58-17.75	17.13-11.50	...	28.05-15.52	1.35-0.65	...	...	...

Address: 201 East Fourth Street, Cincinnati, OH 45202 Telephone: 513-397-9900	Web Site: www.cincinnatibell.com Officers: Phillip R. Cox - Chmn. John F. Cassidy - Pres., C.E.O.	Auditors: Deloitte & Touche LLP Investor Contact: 513-397-1195 Transfer Agents: Fifth Third Bank, Cincinnati, OH

CIRCUIT CITY STORES, INC.

Exchange	Symbol	Price	52Wk Range	Yield	P/E
NYS	CC	$3.98 (3/31/2008)	19.11-3.60	4.02	N/A

*7 Year Price Score 56.51   *NYSE Composite Index=100   ***12 Month Price Score 48.92**

TRADING VOLUME (thousand shares)

Interim Earnings (Per Share)

Qtr.	May	Aug	Nov	Feb
2004-05	(0.03)	(0.06)	(0.03)	0.43
2005-06	(0.07)	0.01	0.06	0.78
2006-07	0.04	0.06	(0.09)	0.00
2007-08	(0.33)	(0.38)	(1.26)	

Interim Dividends (Per Share)

Amt	Decl	Ex	Rec	Pay
0.018Q	12/15/2005	12/28/2005	12/31/2005	1/16/2006
0.018Q	3/15/2006	3/29/2006	3/31/2006	4/17/2006
0.018Q	6/15/2006	6/28/2006	6/30/2006	7/17/2006
0.04Q	9/15/2006	9/27/2006	9/30/2006	10/16/2006

Indicated Div: $0.16

Valuation Analysis / Institutional Holding

Forecast P/E	N/A	No of Institutions
		269
Market Cap	$670.1 Million	Shares
Book Value	1.4 Billion	161,714,832
Price/Book	0.47	% Held
Price/Sales	0.06	92.03

Business Summary: Retail - Appliances and Electrical (MIC: 5.10 SIC: 5731 NAIC: 443112)

Circuit City Stores is a specialty retailer of consumer electronics, home office products, entertainment software, and related services. Co.'s domestic segment conducts business through its Circuit City stores in the U.S. and via the Web at www.circuitcity.com and www.firedog.com. As of Feb 28 2007, Co.'s domestic segment operated 642 Superstores and 12 other stores in 158 U.S. media markets. Co.'s international segment, which comprises the operations of InterTAN, Inc., conducts its business in Canada through stores and via the web at www.thesource.ca. As of Feb 28 2007, Co.'s international segment operated 509 company-owned stores, 296 dealer outlets, and one Battery Plus® store.

Recent Developments: For the quarter ended Nov 30 2007, loss from continuing operations was US$208.0 million compared with a loss of US$19.9 million in the year-earlier quarter. Net loss amounted to US$207.3 million versus a net loss of US$20.4 million in the year-earlier quarter. Revenues were US$2.96 billion, down 3.1% from US$3.06 billion the year before. Operating loss was US$142.4 million versus a loss of US$38.9 million in the prior-year quarter. Direct operating expenses rose 0.6% to US$2.40 billion from US$2.38 billion in the comparable period the year before. Indirect operating expenses decreased 0.9% to US$708.1 million from US$714.8 million in the equivalent prior-year period.

Prospects: For the fourth fiscal quarter ended Feb 2008, assuming that current sales and margin trends to continue, Co. expects to deliver a modest loss from continuing operations before income taxes driven by a pre-tax loss in its domestic segment. Meanwhile, Co. is progressing on its transformation initiatives, and as a result, it remains on track to reduce expenses by about $150.0 million in fiscal 2008, with estimated annual expense savings of $200.0 million expected to be realized beginning in fiscal 2009. Separately, Co. expects to open 61 to 63 incremental and relocated domestic segment Superstores in fiscal 2008, with about two-thirds of the openings to be in a 20,000 square foot format.

Financial Data

(US$ in Thousands)	9 Mos	6 Mos	3 Mos	02/28/2007	02/28/2006	02/28/2005	02/29/2004	02/28/2003
Earnings Per Share	...	...	...	(0.05)	0.77	0.31	(0.43)	0.40
Cash Flow Per Share	(0.06)	1.53	1.28	1.86	2.05	2.36	(0.64)	(1.06)
Tang Book Value Per Share	7.59	8.80	9.18	9.67	9.73	9.78	10.91	11.15
Dividends Per Share	0.160	0.040	0.058	0.075	0.080	0.070	0.070	0.070
Dividend Payout %	...	...	...	...	10.39	22.58	...	17.50
Income Statement								
Total Revenue	8,093,191	5,129,505	2,485,537	12,429,754	11,597,686	10,472,364	9,745,445	9,953,530
EBITDA	(221,234)	(121,575)	(38,026)	176,170	402,921	250,143	210,124	245,337
Depn & Amortn	141,183	98,492	50,143	...	...	...	...	...
Income Before Taxes	(350,834)	(210,639)	(82,475)	20,328	239,082	95,789	(1,240)	67,040
Income Taxes	(24,970)	(92,773)	(27,663)	30,510	87,970	35,878	(453)	25,475
Net Income	(324,748)	(117,402)	(54,566)	(8,281)	139,746	61,658	(89,269)	106,084
Average Shares	164,916	164,837	165,842	170,448	180,653	196,227	205,865	247,904
Balance Sheet								
Current Assets	3,772,775	2,847,132	2,668,283	2,883,512	2,833,341	2,685,715	2,919,061	3,102,910
Total Assets	4,999,615	4,037,508	3,827,914	4,007,283	4,069,044	3,789,382	3,633,000	3,799,117
Current Liabilities	2,979,776	1,862,028	1,598,503	1,714,029	1,622,330	1,263,846	1,176,703	1,280,069
Long-Term Obligations	51,538	50,710	48,961	50,487	51,985	11,522	22,691	11,254
Total Liabilities	3,560,953	2,400,459	2,127,725	2,216,039	2,114,411	1,701,948	1,409,039	1,457,542
Stockholders' Equity	1,438,662	1,637,049	1,700,189	1,791,244	1,954,633	2,087,434	2,223,961	2,341,575
Shares Outstanding	168,377	168,586	168,521	170,689	174,789	188,150	203,899	209,954
Statistical Record								
Return on Assets %	N.M.	N.M.	N.M.	N.M.	3.56	1.66	N.M.	2.54
Return on Equity %	N.M.	N.M.	N.M.	N.M.	6.91	2.86	N.M.	4.18
EBITDA Margin %	N.M.	N.M.	N.M.	1.42	3.47	2.39	2.16	2.46
Net Margin %	N.M.	N.M.	N.M.	N.M.	1.20	0.59	N.M.	1.07
Asset Turnover	2.33	2.96	3.10	3.08	2.95	2.82	2.62	2.39
Current Ratio	1.27	1.53	1.67	1.68	1.75	2.13	2.48	2.42
Debt to Equity	0.04	0.03	0.03	0.03	0.03	0.01	0.01	N.M.
Price Range	25.42-5.45	28.82-10.57	31.13-15.32	31.29-19.00	25.57-14.95	17.49-10.43	13.02-4.27	16.24-4.13
P/E Ratio	...	...	...	...	33.21-19.42	56.42-33.65	...	40.61-10.32
Average Yield %	0.27	0.21	0.25	0.30	0.43	0.51	0.79	0.66

Address: 9950 Mayland Drive, Richmond, VA 23233-1464 Telephone: 804-486-4000	Web Site: www.circuitcity.com Officers: W. Alan McCollough - Chmn., C.E.O. Philip J. Schoonover - Pres.	Auditors: KPMG LLP Transfer Agents: Wells Fargo Shareowner Services, South St. Paul, MN

CIT GROUP, INC.

Interim Earnings (Per Share)

Qtr.	Mar	Jun	Sep	Dec
2003	0.60	0.65	0.69	0.72
2004	0.88	0.82	0.86	0.94
2005	0.98	1.03	1.06	1.38
2006	1.12	1.16	1.44	1.28
2007	1.01	(0.70)	(0.24)	(0.68)

Interim Dividends (Per Share)

Amt	Decl	Ex	Rec	Pay
0.25Q	4/17/2007	5/11/2007	5/15/2007	5/30/2007
0.25Q	7/16/2007	8/13/2007	8/15/2007	8/30/2007
0.25Q	10/16/2007	11/13/2007	11/15/2007	11/30/2007
0.25Q	1/16/2008	2/13/2008	2/15/2008	2/20/2008

Indicated Div: $1.00

Valuation Analysis

		Institutional Holding	
Forecast P/E	9.72 (1/10/2007)	No of Institutions	391
Market Cap	$2.3 Billion	Shares	184,265,248
Book Value	7.0 Billion	% Held	95.23
Price/Book	0.32		
Price/Sales	0.32		

Business Summary: Credit & Lending (MIC: 8.6 SIC: 6153 NAIC: 532420)

CIT Group is a global commercial finance company that provides financing and leasing products and services to clients in over 30 industries, with a focus on commercial clients in the middle-market companies. Co.'s core industries include transportation, particularly aerospace and rail, and a range of manufacturing and retailing. Co. also serves the wholesaling, healthcare, communications, media and entertainment and various service-related industries, as well as provides financing to the student loan market. Co.'s product and service offerings include: asset based loans, secured lines of credit, import and export financing, acquisition and expansion financing, and project financing.

Recent Developments: For the year ended Dec 31 2007, net loss amounted to US$81.0 million versus net income of US$1.05 billion in the prior year. Net interest loss amounted to US$3.83 billion versus a net interest loss of US$2.87 billion in the prior year. Provision for loan losses was US$593.8 million versus US$222.2 million in the prior year, an increase of 167.2%. Non-interest income rose 23.4% to US$7.02 billion from US$5.69 billion, while non-interest expense advanced 140.9% to US$2.87 billion.

Prospects: In light of the challenging overall market conditions, Co. remains focused on capital discipline, portfolio management, strengthening balance sheet and increasing the value of the liquidating home lending portfolio. For 2008, Co. expects lower net finance revenue, with spread compression due to higher borrowing costs and reduced revenue from the Dell vendor relationship; and softness in other income due to low asset sale and syndication gains. However, Co. expects positive operating expense trends due to lower headcount and other cost savings initiatives. Co. continued its cost savings initiatives in the first quarter of 2008, and hence, expects to realize $60.0 million of annual savings.

Financial Data

(US$ in Thousands)	12/31/2007	12/31/2006	12/31/2005	12/31/2004	12/31/2003	12/31/2002	09/30/2002	09/30/2001
Earnings Per Share	(0.58)	5.00	4.44	3.50	2.66	0.67	(31.66)	0.86
Cash Flow Per Share	12.17	7.12	14.14	7.65	10.33	...	...	...
Tang Book Value Per Share	27.95	31.48	27.38	25.94	23.17	21.18	20.67	19.04
Dividends Per Share	1.000	0.800	0.610	0.520	0.480	0.120	...	...
Dividend Payout %	...	16.00	13.74	14.86	18.05	17.91	...	...
Income Statement								
Total Revenue	7,024,900	5,693,900	4,515,200	3,785,700	3,729,500	971,700	4,342,800	1,676,500
EBITDA	(230,100)	1,486,900	2,417,800	2,236,700	2,023,900	513,300	(5,073,200)	972,400
Income Before Taxes	(272,300)	1,412,000	1,416,600	1,237,900	937,300	236,000	(6,314,200)	451,100
Income Taxes	(194,400)	364,400	464,200	483,200	365,000	92,000	374,000	195,000
Net Income	(81,000)	1,046,000	949,100	...	(5,400)	...	...	...
Average Shares	191,412	203,111	210,734	215,054	213,143	...	...	...
Balance Sheet								
Current Assets	7,495,800	4,458,400	3,638,600	2,210,200	1,973,700	2,036,600	2,274,400	808,000
Total Assets	90,248,000	77,067,900	63,386,600	51,111,300	46,342,800	41,932,400	42,710,500	51,090,100
Current Liabilities	14,993,800	13,937,100	13,734,600	11,501,900	11,414,900	10,097,800	9,893,200	13,403,600
Long-Term Obligations	68,236,100	55,339,800	42,639,500	33,513,900	29,494,700	26,706,700	27,801,800	26,828,500
Total Liabilities	83,229,900	69,276,900	56,374,100	45,015,800	40,909,600	36,804,500	37,695,000	40,232,100
Stockholders' Equity	6,960,600	7,751,100	6,962,700	6,055,100	5,394,200	4,870,700	4,757,800	10,598,000
Shares Outstanding	189,925	198,295	199,110	210,440	211,805	211,805	211,573	211,573
Statistical Record								
Return on Assets %	N.M.	1.49	1.66	...	N.M.	...	...	...
Return on Equity %	N.M.	14.22	14.58	...	N.M.	...	...	...
EBITDA Margin %	N.M.	26.11	53.55	59.08	54.27	52.82	N.M.	58.00
Net Margin %	N.M.	18.37	21.02	...	N.M.	...	...	...
Asset Turnover	0.08	0.08	0.08	0.08	0.08	0.02	0.09	0.04
Current Ratio	0.50	0.32	0.27	0.19	0.17	0.20	0.23	0.06
Debt to Equity	9.80	7.14	6.12	5.53	5.47	5.48	5.84	2.53
Price Range	61.36-22.76	56.35-42.44	52.62-35.45	45.82-33.28	35.95-16.61	22.49-13.95	23.80-17.98	...
P/E Ratio	...	11.27-8.49	11.85-7.98	13.09-9.51	13.52-6.24	33.57-20.82	...	...
Average Yield %	2.15	1.56	1.40	1.37	1.92	0.64	...	...

Address: 505 Fifth Avenue, New York, NY 10017
Telephone: 212-771-0505

Web Site: www.cit.com
Officers: Jeffrey M. Peek - Chmn., C.E.O. Joseph M. Leone - Vice-Chmn., C.F.O.

Auditors: PricewaterhouseCoopers LLP
Investor Contact: 973-422-3284
Transfer Agents: The Bank of New York, New York, NY

CITIGROUP INC

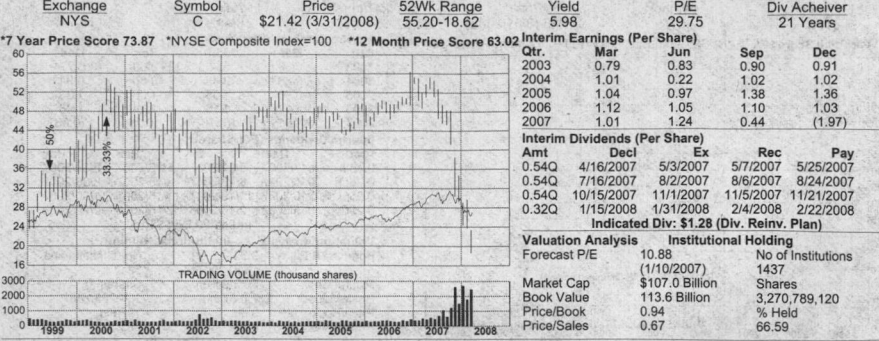

*7 Year Price Score 73.87   *NYSE Composite Index=100   *12 Month Price Score 63.02

Interim Earnings (Per Share)

Qtr.	Mar	Jun	Sep	Dec
2003	0.79	0.83	0.90	0.91
2004	1.01	0.22	1.02	1.02
2005	1.04	0.97	1.38	1.36
2006	1.12	1.05	1.10	1.03
2007	1.01	1.24	0.44	(1.97)

Interim Dividends (Per Share)

Amt	Decl	Ex	Rec	Pay
0.54Q	4/16/2007	5/3/2007	5/7/2007	5/25/2007
0.54Q	7/16/2007	8/2/2007	8/6/2007	8/24/2007
0.54Q	10/15/2007	11/1/2007	11/5/2007	11/21/2007
0.32Q	1/15/2008	1/31/2008	2/4/2008	2/22/2008

Indicated Div: $1.28 (Div. Reinv. Plan)

Valuation Analysis   Institutional Holding

Forecast P/E	10.88	No of Institutions
	(1/10/2007)	1437
Market Cap	$107.0 Billion	Shares
Book Value	113.6 Billion	3,270,789,120
Price/Book	0.94	% Held
Price/Sales	0.67	66.59

TRADING VOLUME (thousand shares)

Business Summary: Commercial Banking (MIC: 8.1 SIC: 6021 NAIC: 522110)

Citigroup is a global financial services holding company whose businesses provide a range of financial services to consumer and corporate customers. Co.'s activities are conducted through the Global Consumer Group (U.S. and International)- Credit Cards, Consumer Lending, Retail Distribution, Commercial Business, Consumer Finance and Retail Banking; Citi Markets & Banking - Securities and Banking, and Transaction Services; Global Wealth Management - Smith Barney, Private Bank, and Citigroup Investment Research; Citi Alternative Investments; and Corporate/Other business segments. As of Dec 31 2007, Co. had total assets of $2.19 trillion and total deposits of $826.23 billion.

Recent Developments: For the year ended Dec 31 2007, income from continuing operations decreased 83.0% to US$3.62 billion from US$21.25 billion a year earlier. Net income decreased 83.2% to US$3.62 billion from US$21.54 billion in the prior year. Net interest income increased 18.7% to US$46.94 billion from US$39.55 billion in the prior year. Provision for loan losses was US$17.42 billion versus US$6.74 billion in the prior year, an increase of 158.6%. Non-interest income fell 30.6% to US$34.76 billion from US$50.06 billion, while non-interest expense advanced 17.5% to US$62.57 billion.

Prospects: In 2008, Co.'s U.S. Consumer businesses will continue to focus on expanding its customer base, offering an integrated set of products and services, and utilizing previous acquisitions and prior strategic investments. Co.'s International Consumer businesses also expects to drive growth in loans, deposits and investment product sales from expanding its customer base through organic growth, investments in expanding the branch network, and the benefit from 2007 acquisitions. For instance, on Dec 1 2007, Co. announced that it has completed the acquisition of Bank of Overseas Chinese, a provider of corporate banking, consumer and wealth management products and services, for $427.0 million.

Financial Data

(US$ in Thousands)	12/31/2007	12/31/2006	12/31/2005	12/31/2004	12/31/2003	12/31/2002	12/31/2001	12/31/2000
Earnings Per Share	0.72	4.31	4.75	3.26	3.42	2.94	2.72	2.62
Cash Flow Per Share	(14.56)	(0.02)	6.28	(0.47)	(2.92)	5.13	5.28	0.54
Tang Book Value Per Share	9.95	14.14	12.76	11.72	10.75	9.70	15.57	12.84
Dividends Per Share	2.160	1.960	1.760	1.600	1.100	0.700	0.600	0.520
Dividend Payout %	300.00	45.48	37.05	49.08	32.16	23.81	22.06	19.85
Income Statement								
Interest Income	124,467,000	96,431,000	76,021,000	66,709,000	57,047,000	58,939,000	66,565,000	64,939,000
Premium Income	3,534,000	3,202,000	3,132,000	3,993,000	3,749,000	3,410,000	13,460,000	12,429,000
Interest Expense	77,531,000	56,943,000	36,676,000	22,086,000	17,271,000	21,248,000	31,965,000	36,638,000
Benefits & Claims	935,000	967,000	867,000	3,801,000	3,895,000	3,478,000	11,759,000	10,147,000
Income Before Taxes	1,701,000	29,639,000	29,433,000	24,182,000	26,333,000	20,537,000	21,897,000	21,143,000
Income Taxes	(2,201,000)	8,101,000	9,078,000	6,909,000	8,195,000	6,998,000	7,526,000	7,525,000
Net Income	3,617,000	21,538,000	24,589,000	17,046,000	17,853,000	15,276,000	14,126,000	13,519,000
Average Shares	4,995,299	4,986,099	5,160,399	5,207,399	5,193,599	5,166,199	5,146,999	5,122,199
Balance Sheet								
Total Assets	2,187,631,000	1,884,318,000	1,494,037,000	1,484,101,000	1,264,032,000	1,097,190,000	1,051,450,000	902,210,000
Total Liabilities	2,074,033,000	1,764,535,000	1,381,500,000	1,374,810,000	1,166,018,000	1,010,472,000	970,203,000	831,084,000
Stockholders' Equity	113,598,000	119,783,000	112,537,000	109,291,000	98,014,000	86,718,000	81,247,000	66,206,000
Shares Outstanding	4,994,581	4,911,993	4,980,223	5,194,642	5,156,949	5,140,681	5,118,688	5,022,221
Statistical Record								
Return on Assets %	0.18	1.28	1.65	1.24	1.51	1.42	1.45	1.67
Return on Equity %	3.10	18.54	22.17	16.40	19.33	18.19	19.16	23.27
Net Interest Margin %	37.71	40.95	51.76	66.89	69.72	63.95	51.98	43.58
Loss Ratio %	26.46	30.20	27.68	95.19	103.89	101.99	87.36	81.64
Price Range	55.25-29.29	56.41-45.05	49.78-43.05	52.29-42.56	49.00-31.42	48.55-25.21	52.57-33.95	54.97-33.61
P/E Ratio	76.74-40.68	13.09-10.45	10.48-9.06	16.04-13.06	14.33-9.19	16.51-8.57	19.33-12.48	20.98-12.83
Average Yield %	4.52	4.01	3.77	3.40	2.63	1.84	1.31	1.16

Address: 399 Park Avenue, New York, NY 10043
Telephone: 212-559-1000
Fax: 212-816-8913

Web Site: www.citigroup.com
Officers: Sanford I. Weill - Chmn. William R. Rhodes - Sr. Vice-Chmn.

Auditors: KPMG LLP
Transfer Agents: Mellon Investor Services, LLC, Ridgefield Park, NJ

CITIZENS COMMUNICATIONS CO

Exchange	Symbol	Price	52Wk Range	Yield	P/E
NYS	CZN	$10.49 (3/31/2008)	15.91-10.16	9.53	16.14

*7 Year Price Score 88.48   *NYSE Composite Index=100   *12 Month Price Score 87.26

Interim Earnings (Per Share)

Qtr.	Mar	Jun	Sep	Dec
2003	0.45	0.12	0.04	0.05
2004	0.15	0.08	(0.04)	0.05
2005	0.12	0.13	0.11	0.23
2006	0.15	0.31	0.40	0.20
2007	0.21	0.12	0.14	0.18

Interim Dividends (Per Share)

Amt	Decl	Ex	Rec	Pay
0.25Q	5/18/2007	6/6/2007	6/9/2007	6/29/2007
0.25Q	7/27/2007	9/5/2007	9/9/2007	9/28/2007
0.25Q	10/25/2007	12/5/2007	12/9/2007	12/31/2007
0.25Q	2/21/2008	3/6/2008	3/10/2008	3/31/2008

Indicated Div: $1.00

Valuation Analysis | **Institutional Holding**

Forecast P/E	20.07 (1/10/2007)	No of Institutions 332
Market Cap	$3.4 Billion	Shares
Book Value	997.9 Million	214,531,952
Price/Book	3.45	% Held
Price/Sales	1.50	63.33

Business Summary: Communications (MIC: 10.1 SIC: 4813 NAIC: 517110)

Citizens Communications is a communications company engaged in providing services to rural areas as well as to small and medium-sized towns and cities as an incumbent local exchange carrier (ILEC). As of Dec 31 2007, Co. operated in one reportable segment, Frontier, which provides both regulated and unregulated communications services to residential, business and wholesale customers. Co.'s Frontier services include local services, access services, long distance services, data and internet, directory services, wireless services and television services. As of Dec 31 2007, Co. operated as an ILEC in 24 states in the U.S.

Recent Developments: For the year ended Dec 31 2007, net income decreased 37.7% to US$214.7 million from US$344.6 million in the prior year. Revenues were US$2.29 billion, up 13.0% from US$2.03 billion the year before. Operating income was US$705.4 million versus US$644.5 million in the prior year, an increase of 9.5%. Direct operating expenses rose 14.6% to US$1.04 billion from US$904.4 million in the comparable period the year before. Indirect operating expenses increased 14.6% to US$545.9 million from US$476.5 million in the equivalent prior-year period.

Prospects: Co.'s improved top-line performance is mainly attributable to its Mar 2007 acquisition of Commonwealth Telephone Enterprises as well its Oct 2007 acquisition of Global Valley along with growth in data and internet services revenue, offset by declines in federal and state subsidies and a decline in basic access lines. Meanwhile, Co. believes that competition will continue to intensify in 2008 across all of its products and in all of its markets. Further, Co. expects to continue to lose access lines but to increase high-speed internet subscribers during 2008. Overall, Co. anticipates that continued loss of access lines coupled with increased competition could reduce its revenues in 2008.

Financial Data

(US$ in Thousands)	12/31/2007	12/31/2006	12/31/2005	12/31/2004	12/31/2003	12/31/2002	12/31/2001	12/31/2000
Earnings Per Share	0.65	1.06	0.60	0.23	0.64	(2.43)	(0.38)	(0.11)
Cash Flow Per Share	2.48	2.57	2.50	2.35	2.59	2.27	1.90	1.17
Tang Book Value Per Share	N.M.	N.M.	N.M.	N.M.	N.M.	N.M.	N.M.	4.09
Dividends Per Share	1.000	1.000	1.000	2.500	...	...	...	...
Dividend Payout %	153.85	94.34	166.67	1,086.96	...	...	...	...
Income Statement								
Total Revenue	2,288,015	2,025,367	2,162,479	2,192,980	2,444,938	2,669,332	2,456,993	1,802,358
EBITDA	1,269,164	1,203,420	1,165,370	1,037,263	1,207,309	(4,822)	939,141	524,980
Income Before Taxes	342,668	390,487	284,508	85,529	195,509	(1,231,640)	(72,521)	(49,993)
Income Taxes	128,014	136,479	84,340	13,379	67,216	(414,874)	(14,805)	(16,132)
Net Income	214,654	344,555	202,375	77,130	187,832	(682,897)	(89,682)	(28,391)
Average Shares	332,378	324,545	341,675	309,183	302,436	284,573	273,721	266,931
Balance Sheet								
Net PPE	3,335,244	2,983,504	3,186,465	3,338,300	3,525,640	3,690,056	4,512,038	3,509,767
Total Assets	7,256,069	6,791,205	6,412,109	6,668,419	7,689,110	8,146,742	10,553,600	6,955,006
Long-Term Obligations	4,736,897	4,460,755	3,999,376	4,266,998	4,195,629	4,957,361	5,534,906	3,062,289
Total Liabilities	6,258,170	5,733,173	5,370,300	5,306,179	6,273,927	6,974,603	8,607,458	5,235,005
Stockholders' Equity	997,899	1,058,032	1,041,809	1,362,240	1,415,183	1,172,139	1,946,142	1,720,001
Shares Outstanding	327,749	322,265	328,168	339,633	284,709	282,482	281,289	265,768
Statistical Record								
Return on Assets %	3.06	5.22	3.09	1.00	2.37	N.M.	N.M.	N.M.
Return on Equity %	20.88	32.82	16.84	5.18	14.52	N.M.	N.M.	N.M.
EBITDA Margin %	55.47	59.42	53.89	47.30	49.38	N.M.	38.22	29.13
Net Margin %	9.38	17.01	9.36	3.29	7.68	(25.58)	(3.65)	(1.58)
PPE Turnover	0.72	0.66	0.66	0.64	0.68	0.65	0.61	0.56
Asset Turnover	0.33	0.31	0.33	0.30	0.31	0.29	0.28	0.28
Debt to Equity	4.75	4.22	3.84	3.13	2.96	4.23	2.84	1.78
Price Range	15.91-12.05	14.83-12.02	13.92-12.09	14.75-11.73	13.30-9.08	11.33-4.60	15.70-8.34	18.88-12.69
P/E Ratio	24.48-18.54	13.99-11.34	23.20-20.15	64.13-51.00	20.78-14.19	...	...	...
Average Yield %	6.98	7.50	7.65	19.00	...	...	...	...

Address: Three High Ridge Park, Stamford, CT 06905-1390	Web Site: www.czn.net	Auditors: KPMG LLP
Telephone: 203-614-5600	Officers: Leonard Tow - Chmn., C.E.O. Scott N. Schneider - Vice-Chmn., Pres., C.O.O.	Transfer Agents: Illinois Stock Transfer Company, Chicago, IL
Fax: 203-614-4602		

CITY NATIONAL CORP. (BEVERLY HILLS, CA)

Exchange	Symbol	Price	52Wk Range	Yield	P/E	Div Acheiver
NYS	CYN	$49.46 (3/31/2008)	78.39-48.57	3.88	10.94	13 Years

*7 Year Price Score 88.75 *NYSE Composite Index=100 *12 Month Price Score 85.80

Interim Earnings (Per Share)

Qtr.	Mar	Jun	Sep	Dec
2003	0.87	0.93	1.05	0.87
2004	1.00	1.03	1.04	0.97
2005	1.09	1.13	1.17	1.21
2006	1.12	1.16	1.20	1.19
2007	1.15	1.19	1.22	0.96

Interim Dividends (Per Share)

Amt	Decl	Ex	Rec	Pay
0.46Q	4/27/2007	5/7/2007	5/9/2007	5/23/2007
0.46Q	7/25/2007	8/6/2007	8/8/2007	8/22/2007
0.46Q	10/24/2007	11/5/2007	11/7/2007	11/21/2007
0.48Q	1/24/2008	2/4/2008	2/6/2008	2/20/2008

Indicated Div: $1.92

Valuation Analysis

		Institutional Holding	
Forecast P/E	13.08	No of Institutions	
	(1/10/2007)	210	
Market Cap	$2.4 Billion	Shares	
Book Value	1.7 Billion	30,435,532	
Price/Book	1.44	% Held	
Price/Sales	1.99	63.89	

TRADING VOLUME (thousand shares)

Business Summary: Commercial Banking (MIC: 8.1 SIC: 6021 NAIC: 522110)

City National is a bank holding and financial holding company. Co. provides a range of banking, investing and trust services through its wholly-owned banking subsidiary, City National Bank, through 62 offices, including 15 full-service regional centers, in Southern California, the San Francisco Bay area, Nevada and New York City. Co. provides lending, deposit, cash management, international banking, equipment financing, and other products and services. Co. operates via three segments, Commercial and Private Banking, Wealth Management, and Other. As of Dec 31 2007, Co. had consolidated total assets of $15.89 billion, loan balances of $11.46 billion, and total deposits of $11.82 billion.

Recent Developments: For the year ended Dec 31 2007, net income decreased 4.6% to US$222.7 million from US$233.5 million in the prior year. Net interest income increased 0.4% to US$608.3 million from US$605.9 million in the prior year. Provision for loan losses was US$20.0 million versus a credit for loan losses of US$610,000 in the prior year. Non-interest income rose 25.1% to US$303.2 million from US$242.4 million, while non-interest expense advanced 11.2% to US$529.2 million.

Prospects: For full year 2008, Co. projects its earnings per share to decrease by 7.0% to 12.0% from its 2007 earnings of $4.62 per share. This guidance is a result of Co.'s expectation that the economy will grow at a nominal rate and that certain sectors, such as housing, will continue to put downward pressure on economic conditions. Furthermore, Co. anticipates moderate growth in loans and deposits as well as strong growth in non-interest income. Additionally, Co. expects that growth in net interest income will be somewhat constrained primarily attributable to lower interest rates, a slight increase in non-performing loans, and a moderate reduction in commercial real estate loans.

Financial Data

(US$ in Thousands)	12/31/2007	12/31/2006	12/31/2005	12/31/2004	12/31/2003	12/31/2002	12/31/2001	12/31/2000
Earnings Per Share	4.52	4.66	4.60	4.04	3.72	3.56	2.96	2.72
Cash Flow Per Share	2.75	2.99	5.83	4.23	5.71	3.72	3.06	3.98
Tang Book Value Per Share	23.54	25.13	23.61	21.27	18.65	17.42	14.81	11.50
Dividends Per Share	1.840	1.640	1.440	1.280	0.970	0.780	0.740	0.700
Dividend Payout %	40.71	35.19	31.30	31.68	26.08	21.91	25.00	25.74
Income Statement								
Interest Income	894,101	826,294	718,552	604,325	575,725	609,700	625,248	646,288
Interest Expense	285,829	220,405	106,125	58,437	61,110	94,444	191,094	239,772
Net Interest Income	608,272	605,889	612,427	545,888	514,615	515,256	434,154	406,516
Provision for Losses	20,000	(610)	...	...	29,000	67,000	35,000	21,500
Non-Interest Income	303,202	242,564	208,189	184,265	177,225	146,293	132,384	109,484
Non-Interest Expense	529,245	476,219	438,385	395,410	364,178	332,591	313,395	294,770
Income Before Taxes	353,373	366,886	376,556	329,751	294,623	261,958	218,143	199,730
Income Taxes	130,660	133,363	141,821	123,429	107,946	78,858	71,973	68,070
Net Income	222,713	233,523	234,735	206,322	186,677	183,100	146,170	131,660
Average Shares	49,290	50,063	51,062	51,074	50,198	51,389	49,376	48,393
Balance Sheet								
Net Loans & Leases	11,462,115	10,230,663	9,111,619	8,345,619	7,716,756	7,834,968	7,016,344	6,391,710
Total Assets	15,889,290	14,884,381	14,581,860	14,231,513	13,018,242	11,870,392	10,176,316	9,096,669
Total Deposits	11,822,505	12,172,816	12,138,472	11,986,915	10,937,063	9,839,698	8,131,202	7,408,670
Total Liabilities	14,202,007	13,365,041	13,099,501	12,856,616	11,772,942	10,760,433	9,285,739	8,353,021
Stockholders' Equity	1,655,607	1,490,915	1,458,008	1,348,535	1,219,256	1,109,959	890,577	743,648
Shares Outstanding	48,235	47,882	49,713	49,546	49,204	48,983	48,149	47,629
Statistical Record								
Return on Assets %	1.45	1.59	1.63	1.51	1.50	1.66	1.52	1.61
Return on Equity %	14.16	15.84	16.73	16.03	16.03	18.31	17.89	19.97
Net Interest Margin %	68.03	73.33	85.23	90.33	89.39	84.51	69.44	62.90
Efficiency Ratio %	44.20	44.55	47.30	50.14	48.37	43.99	41.37	39.00
Loans to Deposits	0.97	0.84	0.75	0.70	0.71	0.80	0.86	0.86
Price Range	78.39-59.10	78.00-63.69	75.60-66.88	70.75-57.93	64.00-39.25	56.14-40.40	49.38-33.91	40.75-25.88
P/E Ratio	17.34-13.08	16.74-13.67	16.43-14.54	17.51-14.34	17.20-10.55	15.77-11.35	16.68-11.46	14.98-9.51
Average Yield %	2.59	2.33	2.02	2.00	1.96	1.57	1.80	1.99

Address: City National Center, 400 North Roxbury Drive, Beverly Hills, CA 90210 **Telephone:** 310-888-6000 **Fax:** 310-888-6045	**Web Site:** www.cnb.com **Officers:** Bram Goldsmith - Chmn. Russell D. Goldsmith - Vice-Chmn., C.E.O.	**Auditors:** KPMG LLP **Investor Contact:** 310-888-6700 **Transfer Agents:** Continental Stock Transfer & Trust Co.

CLARCOR INC.

Exchange	Symbol	Price	52Wk Range	Yield	P/E	Div Acheiver
NYS	CLC	$35.55 (3/31/2008)	41.88-30.93	0.90	19.86	27 Years

*7 Year Price Score 117.90 *NYSE Composite Index=100 *12 Month Price Score 113.71

Interim Earnings (Per Share)

Qtr.	Feb	May	Aug	Nov
2004-05	0.25	0.33	0.40	0.48
2005-06	0.31	0.32	0.44	0.52
2006-07	0.32	0.41	0.53	0.53
2007-08	0.32	...	...	...

Interim Dividends (Per Share)

Amt	Decl	Ex	Rec	Pay
0.072Q	6/26/2007	7/11/2007	7/13/2007	7/27/2007
0.08Q	9/25/2007	10/10/2007	10/12/2007	10/26/2007
0.08Q	12/17/2007	1/9/2008	1/11/2008	1/25/2008
0.08Q	3/31/2008	4/9/2008	4/11/2008	4/25/2008

Indicated Div: $0.32 (Div. Reinv. Plan)

Valuation Analysis | **Institutional Holding**

Forecast P/E	17.40 (1/10/2007)	No of Institutions 167
Market Cap	$1.8 Billion	Shares 45,000,776
Book Value	608.3 Million	% Held
Price/Book	2.95	87.75
Price/Sales	1.86	

Business Summary: Industrial Machinery and Equipment (MIC: 11.5 SIC: 3714 NAIC: 336399)

Clarcor operates through three principal industry segments: Industrial/Environmental Filtration, Engine/ Mobile Filtration and Packaging. Co.'s Industrial/ Environmental segment manufactures and markets filtration products used in industrial and commercial processes, and in buildings and infrastructures of various types. Co.'s Engine/ Mobile segment sells filtration products used on engines and in mobile equipment applications, construction, industrial, mining and agricultural equipment. Co.'s consumer and industrial packaging products business manufactures a range of different types and sizes of containers and packaging specialties through its wholly-owned subsidiary, J. L. Clark, Inc.

Recent Developments: For the quarter ended Mar 1 2008, net income decreased 1.4% to US$16.1 million from US$16.4 million in the year-earlier quarter. Revenues were US$250.2 million, up 19.4% from US$209.5 million the year before. Operating income was US$27.7 million versus US$23.6 million in the prior-year quarter, an increase of 17.6%. Direct operating expenses rose 16.9% to US$173.6 million from US$148.6 million in the comparable period the year before. Indirect operating expenses increased 30.5% to US$48.8 million from US$37.4 million in the equivalent prior-year period.

Prospects: For the remainder of fiscal year ending Nov 30 2008, Co. is projecting sales growth and margin improvement, with international sales growth estimated to continue at a rate higher than its domestic growth rate. In addition, Co. believes that ongoing focus on cost reductions and price increases should offset the forecasted cost increases for energy and purchased materials. Also, Co. plans to continue to make capital investments to improve capability, increase manufacturing and distribution capacity, develop new filter media and products as well as implement new enterprise planning systems. Hence, Co. is anticipating earnings for fiscal 2008 to be in the range of $1.85 to $2.05 per share.

Financial Data
(US$ in Thousands)

	3 Mos	12/01/2007	12/02/2006	11/30/2005	11/30/2004	11/30/2003	11/30/2002	11/30/2001
Earnings Per Share	1.79	1.78	1.59	1.46	1.24	1.08	0.93	0.84
Cash Flow Per Share	2.76	2.74	1.23	1.73	1.46	1.75	1.71	1.29
Tang Book Value Per Share	5.69	7.68	7.21	6.10	5.48	4.90	3.87	3.20
Dividends Per Share	0.305	0.297	0.275	0.259	0.251	0.246	0.241	0.236
Dividend Payout %	17.01	16.71	17.30	17.72	20.26	22.91	26.08	28.13
Income Statement								
Total Revenue	250,181	921,191	904,347	873,974	787,686	741,358	715,563	666,964
EBITDA	35,358	153,289	149,107	138,717	118,272	107,483	97,583	97,200
Depn & Amortn	7,831	...	...	...	...	...	...	...
Income Before Taxes	24,230	130,509	126,941	117,922	99,060	86,059	71,450	65,734
Income Taxes	7,941	39,675	43,795	40,968	34,717	31,371	24,773	23,804
Net Income	16,149	90,659	82,710	76,393	63,997	54,552	46,601	41,893
Average Shares	51,211	50,885	52,176	52,215	51,506	50,745	50,343	49,784
Balance Sheet								
Current Assets	426,663	371,920	380,340	324,933	303,990	257,402	259,746	244,350
Total Assets	959,073	739,135	727,516	675,272	627,797	538,237	546,119	530,617
Current Liabilities	144,503	114,171	118,428	121,470	126,272	111,373	174,255	94,931
Long-Term Obligations	127,418	17,329	15,946	16,009	24,130	16,913	22,648	135,203
Total Liabilities	350,743	183,405	190,007	192,439	199,335	167,845	230,658	256,356
Stockholders' Equity	608,330	555,730	537,509	482,833	428,462	370,392	315,461	274,261
Shares Outstanding	50,491	49,218	51,082	51,594	51,223	50,618	49,837	49,252
Statistical Record								
Return on Assets %	10.67	12.40	11.73	11.73	10.95	10.06	8.66	8.11
Return on Equity %	15.59	16.63	16.12	16.77	15.98	15.91	15.80	16.23
EBITDA Margin %	14.13	16.64	16.49	15.87	15.02	14.50	13.64	14.57
Net Margin %	6.45	9.84	9.15	8.74	8.12	7.36	6.51	6.28
Asset Turnover	1.14	1.26	1.28	1.34	1.35	1.37	1.33	1.29
Current Ratio	2.95	3.26	3.21	2.68	2.41	2.31	1.49	2.57
Debt to Equity	0.21	0.03	0.03	0.03	0.06	0.05	0.07	0.49
Price Range	41.88-30.07	41.88-30.07	36.27-26.97	31.51-24.88	26.26-20.43	22.95-15.53	17.00-12.82	13.80-8.56
P/E Ratio	23.40-16.80	23.53-16.89	22.81-16.96	21.58-17.04	21.18-16.47	21.25-14.37	18.28-13.78	16.43-10.19
Average Yield %	0.86	0.86	0.87	0.94	1.12	1.31	1.61	1.94

Address: 840 Crescent Centre Drive, Suite 600, Franklin, TN 37067 **Telephone:** 615-771-3100	**Web Site:** www.clarcor.com **Officers:** Norman E. Johnson - Chmn., Pres., C.E.O. William B. Walker - Vice-Chmn.	**Auditors:** PricewaterhouseCoopers LLP **Transfer Agents:** First Chicago Trust Company of New York, Jersey City, NJ

CLEAR CHANNEL COMMUNICATIONS INC

Exchange	Symbol	Price	52Wk Range	Yield	P/E
NYS	CCU	$29.22 (3/31/2008)	38.56-26.92	N/A	15.46

*7 Year Price Score 76.94   *NYSE Composite Index=100   *12 Month Price Score 95.60

Interim Earnings (Per Share)

Qtr.	Mar	Jun	Sep	Dec
2003	0.12	0.41	1.03	0.30
2004	0.19	0.41	0.44	(7.79)
2005	0.09	0.40	0.38	0.85
2006	0.19	0.39	0.38	0.43
2007	0.21	0.48	0.56	0.64

Interim Dividends (Per Share)

Amt	Decl	Ex	Rec	Pay
0.188Q	2/21/2007	3/28/2007	3/31/2007	4/15/2007
0.188Q	4/19/2007	6/27/2007	6/30/2007	7/15/2007
0.188Q	7/27/2007	9/26/2007	9/30/2007	10/15/2007
0.188Q	12/3/2007	12/27/2007	12/31/2007	1/15/2008

Valuation Analysis   Institutional Holding

Forecast P/E	19.99	No of Institutions
(1/10/2007)		374
Market Cap	$14.5 Billion	Shares
Book Value	8.8 Billion	413,393,024
Price/Book	1.65	% Held
Price/Sales	2.13	83.32

Business Summary: Media (MIC: 13.1 SIC: 4832 NAIC: 515111)

Clear Channel Communications is a media company with three principal business segments: radio broadcasting, Americas outdoor advertising and international outdoor advertising. Co. also owns, programmes or sells airtime for 56 television stations, including 18 television stations distributed as digital multicast stations and owns a media representation firm. As of Dec 31 2007, Co. owned 1,005 radio stations and a national radio network operating in the U.S. In addition, Co. has equity interests in various international radio broadcasting companies. As of Dec 31 2007, Co. owned or operated approximately 209,000 Americas and 687,000 international outdoor advertising display faces.

Recent Developments: For the year ended Dec 31 2007, income from continuing operations increased 24.5% to US$772.1 million from US$620.0 million a year earlier. Net income increased 35.7% to US$938.5 million from US$691.5 million in the prior year. Revenues were US$6.82 billion, up 5.6% from US$6.46 billion the year before. Operating income was US$1.65 billion versus US$1.56 billion in the prior year, an increase of 5.7%. Direct operating expenses rose 8.0% to US$2.71 billion from US$2.51 billion in the comparable period the year before. Indirect operating expenses increased 2.9% to US$2.46 billion from US$2.39 billion in the equivalent prior-year period.

Prospects: Going forward, Co. is continuing to purchase, sell, or swap assets or businesses in order to maximize the efficiency of its portfolio. For instance, Co. continues to pursue the divesture of 187 non-core radio stations, which are no longer under a definitive asset purchase agreement. Accordingly, through Feb 13 2008, Co. had definitive asset purchase agreements for the sale of 12 additional non-core radio stations, which were part of the 187 non-core radio stations. Separately, Co. is progressing on its agreement under which CC Media Holdings, Inc. will acquire Co., for $39.20 per share, which is expected to close by the end of the first quarter of 2008.

Financial Data
(US$ in Thousands)

	12/31/2007	12/31/2006	12/31/2005	12/31/2004	12/31/2003	12/31/2002	12/31/2001	12/31/2000
Earnings Per Share	1.89	1.38	1.71	(6.75)	1.85	(25.56)	(1.93)	0.57
Cash Flow Per Share	3.13	3.68	2.57	3.04	2.73	2.88	1.03	1.78
Dividends Per Share	0.750	0.750	0.688	0.450	0.200	...	...	...
Dividend Payout %	39.68	54.35	40.20	...	10.81	...	...	...
Income Statement								
Total Revenue	6,816,909	7,066,957	6,610,418	9,418,459	8,930,899	8,421,055	7,970,003	5,345,306
EBITDA	2,264,691	2,339,347	2,152,968	2,425,946	2,984,745	2,271,731	1,873,560	2,497,706
Income Before Taxes	1,247,930	1,221,506	1,079,328	1,364,192	1,925,364	1,218,189	(1,248,997)	713,539
Income Taxes	428,753	500,817	426,336	518,393	779,773	493,366	(104,971)	464,731
Net Income	938,507	691,517	935,662	(4,038,169)	1,145,591	(16,053,703)	(1,144,026)	248,808
Average Shares	495,784	501,639	547,151	598,275	620,770	627,440	591,965	438,711
Balance Sheet								
Current Assets	2,294,583	2,205,730	2,248,409	2,269,922	2,185,682	2,123,495	1,941,299	2,343,217
Total Assets	18,805,528	18,890,179	18,703,376	19,927,949	28,352,693	27,672,153	47,603,142	50,056,461
Current Liabilities	2,813,277	1,663,846	2,107,313	2,184,552	1,892,719	3,010,639	2,959,857	2,128,550
Long-Term Obligations	5,214,988	7,326,700	6,155,363	6,962,560	6,921,348	7,382,090	7,967,713	10,100,028
Total Liabilities	10,008,037	10,847,838	9,876,914	10,439,871	12,798,754	13,462,061	17,867,079	19,709,288
Stockholders' Equity	8,797,491	8,042,341	8,826,462	9,488,078	15,553,939	14,210,092	29,736,063	30,347,173
Shares Outstanding	497,917	493,868	538,173	567,264	615,893	613,100	597,990	585,650
Statistical Record								
Return on Assets %	4.98	3.68	4.84	N.M.	4.09	N.M.	N.M.	0.74
Return on Equity %	11.15	8.20	10.22	N.M.	7.70	N.M.	N.M.	1.23
EBITDA Margin %	33.22	33.10	32.57	25.76	33.42	26.98	23.51	46.73
Net Margin %	13.77	9.79	14.15	N.M.	12.83	N.M.	N.M.	4.65
Asset Turnover	0.36	0.38	0.34	0.39	0.32	0.22	0.16	0.16
Current Ratio	0.82	1.33	1.07	1.04	1.15	0.71	0.66	1.10
Debt to Equity	0.59	0.91	0.70	0.73	0.44	0.52	0.27	0.33
Price Range	38.56-33.38	35.66-27.41	33.27-28.00	45.38-29.00	45.03-30.99	51.71-21.67	64.19-35.25	91.37-43.83
P/E Ratio	20.40-17.66	25.84-19.86	19.46-16.38	...	24.34-16.75	...	...	160.30-76.89
Average Yield %	2.05	2.46	2.22	1.24	0.52	...	...	...

Address: 200 East Basse Road, San Antonio, TX 78209	**Web Site:** www.clearchannel.com	**Auditors:** Ernst & Young LLP
Telephone: 210-822-2828	**Officers:** L. Lowry Mays - Chmn., C.E.O. Mark Pitman Mays - Pres., C.O.O.	**Investor Contact:** 210-822-2828
Fax: 210-822-2299		

CLEAR CHANNEL OUTDOOR HOLDINGS INC

Exchange	Symbol	Price	52Wk Range	Yield	P/E
NYS	CCO	$19.01 (3/31/2008)	29.78-19.01	N/A	27.55

*7 Year Price Score N/A   *NYSE Composite Index=100   *12 Month Price Score 92.32

TRADING VOLUME (thousand shares)

Interim Earnings (Per Share)

Qtr.	Mar	Jun	Sep	Dec
2005	(0.02)	0.06	0.03	0.12
2006	0.02	0.14	0.09	0.18
2007	0.05	0.19	0.15	0.30

Interim Dividends (Per Share)

No Dividends Paid

Valuation Analysis

Forecast P/E	N/A
Market Cap	$6.8 Billion
Book Value	2.0 Billion
Price/Book	3.41
Price/Sales	2.06

Institutional Holding

No of Institutions	97
Shares	39,837,832
% Held	N/A

Business Summary: Advertising, Marketing & PR (MIC: 12.4 SIC: 7312 NAIC: 541850)

Clear Channel Outdoor provides advertising through billboards, street furniture displays, transit displays and other out-of-home advertising displays, such as wallscapes, spectaculars, neons and mall displays, which it owns or operates in markets worldwide. Co.'s business consists of two reportable operating segments: Americas and International. Co.'s Americas reporting segment primarily consists of operations in the U.S., Canada and Latin America while its International reporting segment consists of operations in Europe, Asia, Africa and Australia. As of Dec 31 2007, Co. owned or operated approx. 897,000 advertising displays worldwide.

Recent Developments: For the year ended Dec 31 2007, net income increased 60.7% to US$246.0 million from US$153.1 million in the prior year. Revenues were US$3.28 billion, up 13.3% from US$2.90 billion the year before. Operating income was US$555.3 million versus US$445.5 million in the prior year, an increase of 24.6%. Direct operating expenses rose 14.5% to US$1.73 billion from US$1.51 billion in the comparable period the year before. Indirect operating expenses increased 5.8% to US$991.7 million from US$937.4 million in the equivalent prior-year period.

Prospects: Co. remains committed to investing in its outdoor assets with the objective of strengthening its ability to engage its audiences and better serve its base of global advertisers. For instance, on Nov 26 2007, Co. signed a comprehensive agreement with Qwikker, a provider of location-based mobile content distribution infrastructure, to build an interactive digital network to enable the delivery of mobile content over Bluetooth wireless technology. Specifically, Co. will deploy Qwikker technology within its global network of out-of-home advertising properties thus enabling the delivery of mobile content campaigns integrated with its traditional advertising displays.

Financial Data

(US$ in Thousands)	12/31/2007	12/31/2006	12/31/2005	12/31/2004	12/31/2003	12/31/2002
Earnings Per Share	0.69	0.43	0.19	...	...	...
Cash Flow Per Share	1.96	1.53	1.39	...	...	...
Tang Book Value Per Share	0.88	N.M.	0.00	...	...	...
Income Statement						
Income Before Taxes	411,892	290,667	122,929	70,032	(23,141)	(106,346)
Income Taxes	146,641	122,080	45,484	62,554	11,852	(50,638)
Net Income	245,990	153,072	61,573	(155,380)	(34,993)	(3,582,906)
Average Shares	355,806	352,262	319,921	...	...	...
Balance Sheet						
Total Assets	5,935,604	5,421,891	4,918,345	5,240,933	5,232,820	...
Total Liabilities	3,952,874	3,835,513	3,708,908	2,511,280	2,472,656	...
Stockholders' Equity	1,982,730	1,586,378	1,209,437	2,729,653	2,760,164	...
Shares Outstanding	355,493	354,565	350,237	...	...	...
Statistical Record						
Return on Assets %	4.33	2.96	1.21	N.M.	...	...
Return on Equity %	13.78	10.95	3.13	N.M.	...	...
Price Range	29.78-23.50	27.94-18.92	20.30-18.55	...	...	...
P/E Ratio	43.16-34.06	64.98-44.00	106.84-97.63	...	...	...

Address: 200 East Basse Road, San Antonio, TX 78209 **Telephone:** 210-832-3700	**Web Site:** www.clearchanneloutdoor.com **Officers:** L. Lowry Mays - Chmn. Paul J. Meyer - Pres., C.O.O. Mark P. Mays - C.E.O.	**Auditors:** Ernst & Young LLP **Transfer Agents:** The Bank of New York, New York, NY

CLEVELAND-CLIFFS INC.

Exchange	Symbol	Price	52Wk Range	Yield	P/E
NYS	CLF	$119.82 (3/31/2008)	126.93-60.63	0.58	23.31

*7 Year Price Score 232.83 *NYSE Composite Index=100 *12 Month Price Score 139.42

Interim Earnings (Per Share)

Qtr.	Mar	Jun	Sep	Dec
2003	0.05	(0.52)	(0.12)	(0.22)
2004	(0.04)	0.72	1.96	3.22
2005	0.46	1.79	1.53	1.19
2006	0.69	1.53	1.68	1.33
2007	0.62	1.66	1.08	1.77

Interim Dividends (Per Share)

Amt	Decl	Ex	Rec	Pay
0.125Q	7/11/2007	8/13/2007	8/15/2007	9/4/2007
0.125Q	11/13/2007	11/20/2007	11/23/2007	12/3/2007
0.175Q	1/18/2008	2/13/2008	2/15/2008	3/3/2008
2-for-1	3/11/2008	5/16/2008	5/1/2008	5/15/2008

Indicated Div: $0.70

Valuation Analysis / **Institutional Holding**

Forecast P/E	9.71 (1/10/2007)	No of Institutions 203
Market Cap	$5.3 Billion	Shares 48,181,584
Book Value	1.2 Billion	% Held
Price/Book	4.59	N/A
Price/Sales	2.35	

TRADING VOLUME (thousand shares)

Business Summary: Non-Precious Metals (MIC: 14.3 SIC: 1011 NAIC: 212299)

Cleveland-Cliffs is a global mining company. Co. is a producer of iron ore pellets in North America and a supplier of metallurgical coal to the global steelmaking industry. As of Dec 31 2007, Co. operated six iron ore mines in Michigan, Minnesota and Eastern Canada, and three coking coal mines in West Virginia and Alabama. Co. also owns 80.4% of Portman, an iron ore mining company in Australia, serving the Asian iron ore markets with direct-shipping fines and lump ore. Co. is organized into three reportable business segments: North America Iron Ore, North American Coal and Asia-Pacific Iron Ore.

Recent Developments: For the year ended Dec 31 2007, income from continuing operations decreased 3.6% to US$269.8 million from US$279.8 million a year earlier. Net income decreased 3.6% to US$270.0 million from US$280.1 million in the prior year. Revenues were US$2.28 billion, up 18.4% from US$1.92 billion the year before. Operating income was US$381.6 million versus US$365.7 million in the prior year, an increase of 4.3%. Direct operating expenses rose 20.3% to US$1.81 billion from US$1.51 billion in the comparable period the year before. Indirect operating expenses increased 66.5% to US$80.4 million from US$48.3 million in the equivalent prior-year period.

Prospects: Co.'s near-term outlook appears favorable, reflecting robust revenue growth in its North American Iron Ore segment. For 2008, Co. expects sales volume of North American Iron Ore of 23.0 million tons with revenue per ton of $76.00. In addition, Co. expects its North American Coal segment to sell 4.5 million tons of metallurgical coal with sales per ton of approximately $91.00. For its Asia-Pacific Iron Ore segment, Co. expects sales volume of 8.0 million tones with revenues per ton of approximately $88.00. For its Sonoma Coal Project Joint Venture, Co. expects shipments to begin in the first quarter of 2008 with sales volume of about 2.0 million tons and revenue per ton of $82.00 for 2008.

Financial Data

(US$ in Thousands)	12/31/2007	12/31/2006	12/31/2005	12/31/2004	12/31/2003	12/31/2002	12/31/2001	12/31/2000
Earnings Per Share	5.14	5.20	4.99	5.90	(0.80)	(4.66)	(0.57)	0.43
Cash Flow Per Share	6.96	10.18	11.84	(3.30)	1.04	1.01	0.17	0.67
Tang Book Value Per Share	26.10	18.23	14.55	9.52	5.06	1.17	9.22	9.93
Dividends Per Share	0.500	0.475	0.300	0.050	...	...	0.100	0.375
Dividend Payout %	9.73	9.13	6.02	0.85	...	...	...	86.71
Income Statement								
Total Revenue	2,275,200	1,921,700	1,739,500	1,206,700	857,700	617,100	387,600	455,000
EBITDA	490,500	457,500	411,500	304,200	(6,200)	(23,400)	(27,400)	42,200
Income Before Taxes	380,700	387,800	368,100	285,600	(35,200)	(57,300)	(53,600)	16,600
Income Taxes	84,100	90,900	84,800	(34,900)	(300)	9,100	(16,300)	(1,500)
Net Income	270,000	280,100	277,600	323,600	(32,700)	(188,300)	(22,900)	18,100
Average Shares	52,513	53,827	55,672	54,842	41,024	40,468	40,400	41,600
Balance Sheet								
Current Assets	754,600	782,300	636,000	733,800	313,300	300,500	362,700	248,000
Total Assets	3,075,800	1,939,700	1,746,700	1,161,100	895,200	730,100	825,000	727,800
Current Liabilities	399,600	374,900	362,700	257,100	225,900	204,800	189,800	102,200
Long-Term Obligations	440,000	...	...	...	...	35,000	70,000	70,000
Total Liabilities	1,659,600	935,800	850,900	534,600	646,900	630,900	424,900	301,900
Stockholders' Equity	1,163,700	745,800	651,600	424,000	228,100	79,300	374,200	402,000
Shares Outstanding	44,583	40,905	43,830	43,197	41,992	40,736	40,568	40,477
Statistical Record								
Return on Assets %	10.77	15.20	19.09	31.39	N.M.	N.M.	N.M.	2.56
Return on Equity %	28.28	40.09	51.62	98.98	N.M.	N.M.	N.M.	4.46
EBITDA Margin %	21.56	23.81	23.66	25.21	N.M.	N.M.	N.M.	9.27
Net Margin %	11.87	14.58	15.96	26.82	N.M.	N.M.	N.M.	3.98
Asset Turnover	0.91	1.04	1.20	1.17	1.06	0.79	0.50	0.64
Current Ratio	1.89	2.09	1.75	2.85	1.39	1.47	1.91	2.43
Debt to Equity	0.38	...	...	...	...	0.44	0.19	0.17
Price Range	104.75-46.41	54.13-31.72	48.76-23.93	26.78-9.90	13.43-3.75	7.25-4.04	5.55-3.49	7.78-4.95
P/E Ratio	20.38-9.03	10.41-6.10	9.77-4.80	4.54-1.68	...	...	...	18.10-11.52
Average Yield %	0.67	1.13	0.84	0.31	...	...	2.29	6.17

Address: 1100 Superior Avenue, Suite 1500, Cleveland, OH 44114-2544 **Telephone:** 216-694-5700 **Fax:** 216-694-4880	**Web Site:** www.cleveland-cliffs.com **Officers:** John S. Brinzo - Chmn., C.E.O. David H. Gunning - Vice-Chmn.	**Auditors:** Deloitte & Touche LLP **Transfer Agents:** Computershare, Providence, RI

CLOROX CO.

<table>
<tr><th>Exchange</th><th>Symbol</th><th>Price</th><th>52Wk Range</th><th>Yield</th><th>P/E</th><th>Div Acheiver</th></tr>
<tr><td>NYS</td><td>CLX</td><td>$56.64 (3/31/2008)</td><td>68.50-55.61</td><td>2.82</td><td>17.06</td><td>31 Years</td></tr>
</table>

*7 Year Price Score 96.15   *NYSE Composite Index=100   *12 Month Price Score 100.42

Interim Earnings (Per Share)

Qtr.	Sep	Dec	Mar	Jun
2004-05	0.57	3.68	0.76	1.09
2005-06	0.71	0.55	0.72	0.92
2006-07	0.73	0.62	0.84	1.07
2007-08	0.76	0.65	...	...

Interim Dividends (Per Share)

Amt	Decl	Ex	Rec	Pay
0.40Q	5/24/2007	7/25/2007	7/27/2007	8/15/2007
0.40Q	9/19/2007	10/29/2007	10/31/2007	11/15/2007
0.40Q	11/14/2007	1/24/2008	1/28/2008	2/15/2008
0.40Q	2/7/2008	4/23/2008	4/25/2008	5/15/2008

Indicated Div: $1.60 (Div. Reinv. Plan)

Valuation Analysis

Forecast P/E	15.55
	(1/10/2007)
Market Cap	$7.9 Billion
Book Value	N/A
Price/Book	N/A
Price/Sales	1.57

Institutional Holding

No of Institutions	440
Shares	115,020,448
% Held	76.04

Business Summary: Chemicals (MIC: 11.1 SIC: 2842 NAIC: 325612)

Clorox manufactures and markets consumer products. Co. has three business segments: Household Group–North America, Specialty Group and International. The products of the Household Group–North America segment include: laundry additives, home-care products, water-filtration systems and filters, professional products for institutional, janitorial, healthcare and food-service markets and auto-care products. The products of the Specialty Group segment include: plastic bags, wraps and containers, cat litter products, food products and charcoal products. The products of the International segment, which are for the Asia-Pacific and Latin America markets, include bleaches, sponges and insecticides.

Recent Developments: For the quarter ended Dec 31 2007, income from continuing operations increased 1.1% to US$92.0 million from US$91.0 million in the year-earlier quarter. Net income decreased 4.2% to US$92.0 million from US$96.0 million in the year-earlier quarter. Revenues were US$1.19 billion, up 7.7% from US$1.10 billion the year before. Direct operating expenses rose 10.6% to US$707.0 million from US$639.0 million in the comparable period the year before. Indirect operating expenses increased 7.7% to US$351.0 million from US$326.0 million in the equivalent prior-year period.

Prospects: For the fiscal year ending June 30 2008, Co. now anticipates sales growth in the range of 6.0% to 7.0%, including the anticipated benefit of the bleach business and the Burt's Bees acquisition on Nov 30, 2007. In addition, Co. is projecting earnings to be in the range of $3.20 to $3.35 per diluted share, compared with its prior earnings outlook of $3.33 to $3.50 per diluted share. Co. noted that its outlook is being updated to include anticipated dilution related to the Burt's Bees acquisition, additional restructuring-related charges associated with the decision to exit the private label food bag business, and an increase for the benefit of strong first-half 2008 operating results.

Financial Data

(US$ in Thousands)	6 Mos	3 Mos	06/30/2007	06/30/2006	06/30/2005	06/30/2004	06/30/2003	06/30/2002
Earnings Per Share	3.32	3.29	3.26	2.90	6.11	2.56	2.23	1.37
Cash Flow Per Share	5.51	5.14	4.68	3.47	4.53	4.24	3.68	3.78
Tang Book Value Per Share	...	...	N.M.	...	...	0.77	N.M.	0.24
Dividends Per Share	1.420	1.310	1.200	1.140	1.100	1.080	0.880	0.840
Dividend Payout %	42.77	39.82	36.81	39.31	18.00	42.19	39.46	61.31
Income Statement								
Total Revenue	2,425,000	1,239,000	4,847,000	4,644,000	4,388,000	4,324,000	4,144,000	4,061,000
EBITDA	400,000	222,000	1,018,000	935,000	964,000	1,028,000	965,000	668,000
Depn & Amortn	98,000	48,000	...	...	...	...	...	...
Income Before Taxes	302,000	174,000	743,000	653,000	729,000	840,000	802,000	498,000
Income Taxes	99,000	63,000	247,000	210,000	214,000	294,000	288,000	176,000
Net Income	203,000	111,000	501,000	444,000	1,096,000	549,000	493,000	322,000
Average Shares	141,026	146,127	153,935	153,001	179,176	214,371	220,692	234,704
Balance Sheet								
Current Assets	1,215,000	1,064,000	1,032,000	1,007,000	1,090,000	1,043,000	951,000	1,002,000
Total Assets	4,853,000	3,673,000	3,666,000	3,616,000	3,617,000	3,834,000	3,652,000	3,630,000
Current Liabilities	2,331,000	2,153,000	1,427,000	1,130,000	1,348,000	1,268,000	1,451,000	1,225,000
Long-Term Obligations	2,223,000	1,477,000	1,462,000	1,966,000	2,122,000	475,000	495,000	678,000
Total Liabilities	5,407,000	4,310,000	3,495,000	3,772,000	4,170,000	2,294,000	2,626,000	2,425,000
Stockholders' Equity	(554,000)	(637,000)	171,000	(156,000)	(553,000)	1,540,000	1,215,000	1,354,000
Shares Outstanding	138,856	138,505	151,256	151,298	151,683	212,988	213,676	223,009
Statistical Record								
Return on Assets %	11.70	13.87	13.76	12.28	29.42	14.63	13.54	8.45
Return on Equity %	...	...	6,680.00	...	222.09	39.75	38.38	19.79
EBITDA Margin %	16.49	17.92	21.00	20.13	21.97	23.77	23.29	16.45
Net Margin %	8.37	8.96	10.34	9.56	24.98	12.70	11.90	7.93
Asset Turnover	1.18	1.37	1.33	1.28	1.18	1.15	1.14	1.07
Current Ratio	0.52	0.49	0.72	0.89	0.81	0.82	0.66	0.82
Debt to Equity	...	...	8.55	...	...	0.31	0.41	0.50
Price Range	68.50-57.14	68.50-57.14	68.50-58.35	64.76-53.32	65.27-49.56	53.95-42.00	48.24-32.18	47.62-34.64
P/E Ratio	20.63-17.21	20.82-17.37	21.01-17.90	22.33-18.39	10.68-8.11	21.07-16.41	21.63-14.43	34.76-25.28
Average Yield %	2.23	2.05	1.89	1.96	1.93	2.26	2.07	2.07

<table>
<tr><td>Address: 1221 Broadway, Oakland, CA 94612-1888
Telephone: 510-271-7000
Fax: 510-832-1463</td><td>Web Site: www.thecloroxcompany.com
Officers: G. E. Johnston - Chmn., C.E.O. D. J. Heinrich - Sr. V.P., C.F.O.</td><td>Auditors: Ernst & Young LLP
Transfer Agents: EquiServe Trust Company N.A., Providence, RI</td></tr>
</table>

CME GROUP INC

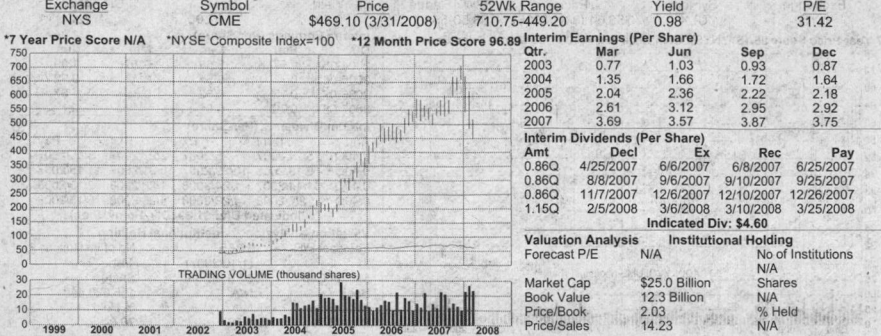

Exchange	Symbol	Price	52Wk Range	Yield	P/E
NYS	CME	$469.10 (3/31/2008)	710.75-449.20	0.98	31.42

*7 Year Price Score N/A   *NYSE Composite Index=100   *12 Month Price Score 96.89

Interim Earnings (Per Share)

Qtr.	Mar	Jun	Sep	Dec
2003	0.77	1.03	0.93	0.87
2004	1.35	1.66	1.72	1.64
2005	2.04	2.36	2.22	2.18
2006	2.61	3.12	2.95	2.92
2007	3.69	3.57	3.87	3.75

Interim Dividends (Per Share)

Amt	Decl	Ex	Rec	Pay
0.86Q	4/25/2007	6/6/2007	6/8/2007	6/25/2007
0.86Q	8/8/2007	9/6/2007	9/10/2007	9/25/2007
0.86Q	11/7/2007	12/6/2007	12/10/2007	12/26/2007
1.15Q	2/5/2008	3/6/2008	3/10/2008	3/25/2008

Indicated Div: $4.60

Valuation Analysis   Institutional Holding

Forecast P/E	N/A	No of Institutions
		N/A
Market Cap	$25.0 Billion	Shares
Book Value	12.3 Billion	N/A
Price/Book	2.03	% Held
Price/Sales	14.23	N/A

Business Summary: Finance Intermediaries & Services (MIC: 8.7 SIC: 6231 NAIC: 523210)

CME Group is the holding company of two futures exchanges: Chicago Mercantile Exchange Inc. and Board of Trade of the City of Chicago, Inc. Co. offers futures and options on futures based on U.S. interest rate yield curve, equity indexes, foreign exchange, agricultural commodities and alternative investments such as weather and real estate. Co.'s products are traded through CME Globex® electronic trading platform, its open outcry auction markets or through privately negotiated transactions that it clears. Co.'s customers consist of professional traders, financial institutions, individual and institutional investors, major corporations, manufacturers, producers and governments.

Recent Developments: For the year ended Dec 31 2007, net income increased 61.7% to US$658.5 million from US$407.3 million in the prior year. Revenues were US$1.76 billion, up 61.1% from US$1.09 billion the year before. Operating income was US$1.05 billion versus US$621.1 million in the prior year, an increase of 69.1%. Indirect operating expenses increased 50.5% to US$705.6 million from US$468.9 million in the equivalent prior-year period.

Prospects: Co. will continue to explore opportunities to position it to benefit from growth in key geographies via strategic investments, and to capitalize on opportunities in Asia and Latin America with diverse product offerings. For example, Co. is expanding its foreign exchange options product suite, and expects growth in the electronic execution of foreign exchange options on CME Globex® in 2008. Co. also expects higher trading volume from customers outside of the U.S. as it expands its global footprint in the foreign exchange market. Meanwhile, Co. is progressing with the integration of its Jul 2007 acquired CBOT Holdings, Inc., and expects annual expense savings of over $100.0 million in 2008.

Financial Data

(US$ in Thousands)	12/31/2007	12/31/2006	12/31/2005	12/31/2004	12/31/2003	12/31/2002	12/31/2001	12/31/2000
Earnings Per Share	14.93	11.60	8.81	6.38	3.60	3.13	2.37	(0.21)
Cash Flow Per Share	18.61	13.60	11.41	9.78	5.85	4.86	4.19	1.14
Tang Book Value Per Share	N.M.	42.91	32.24	23.70	17.10	13.71	7.83	...
Dividends Per Share	1.720	2.520	1.840	1.040	0.630	...	...	...
Dividend Payout %	11.52	21.72	20.89	16.30	17.50	...	...	...
Income Statement								
Total Revenue	1,756,101	1,089,947	920,518	733,789	536,041	453,177	387,153	226,552
EBITDA	1,233,933	745,055	576,600	424,584	259,141	202,738	152,004	25,406
Income Before Taxes	1,095,802	671,657	508,379	367,656	206,125	154,229	114,365	(8,083)
Income Taxes	437,269	264,309	201,522	148,101	83,993	60,162	46,063	(3,339)
Net Income	658,533	407,348	306,857	219,555	122,132	94,067	68,302	(5,909)
Average Shares	44,107	35,124	34,839	34,410	33,934	30,060	29,273	28,774
Balance Sheet								
Current Assets	4,987,055	4,030,252	3,783,422	2,694,865	4,723,379	3,215,131	1,946,110	267,432
Total Assets	20,306,197	4,306,505	3,969,394	2,857,466	4,872,636	3,355,016	2,068,881	381,444
Current Liabilities	4,076,063	2,755,354	2,829,927	2,025,623	4,287,975	2,889,494	1,801,845	198,294
Long-Term Obligations	...	...	...	...	...	2,328	6,650	6,063
Total Liabilities	8,000,560	2,787,413	2,850,710	2,044,869	4,309,641	2,908,877	1,818,512	217,773
Stockholders' Equity	12,305,637	1,519,092	1,118,684	812,597	562,995	446,139	250,369	163,671
Shares Outstanding	53,281	34,838	34,547	34,101	32,925	32,533	28,771	...
Statistical Record								
Return on Assets %	5.35	9.84	8.99	5.67	2.97	3.47	5.57	...
Return on Equity %	9.53	30.89	31.78	31.83	24.21	27.01	32.99	...
EBITDA Margin %	70.27	68.36	62.64	57.86	48.34	44.74	39.26	11.21
Net Margin %	37.50	37.37	33.34	29.92	22.78	20.76	17.64	N.M.
Asset Turnover	0.14	0.26	0.27	0.19	0.13	0.17	0.32	...
Current Ratio	1.22	1.46	1.34	1.33	1.10	1.11	1.08	1.35
Debt to Equity	...	...	...	...	...	0.01	0.03	0.04
Price Range	710.75-497.95	553.86-357.80	396.90-169.96	228.70-72.36	78.98-41.50	45.06-42.00	...	...
P/E Ratio	47.61-33.35	47.75-30.84	45.05-19.29	35.85-11.34	21.94-11.53	14.40-13.42	...	...
Average Yield %	0.30	0.54	0.68	0.77	1.02	...	...	...

Address: 20 South Wacker Drive, Chicago, IL 60606	**Web Site:** www.cme.com	**Auditors:** Ernst & Young LLP
Telephone: 312-930-1000	**Officers:** Terrence A. Duffy - Chmn. William R. Shepard - Vice-Chmn.	**Transfer Agents:** Computershare Investor Services, Chicago, IL
Fax: 312-466-4410		

CMS ENERGY CORP

Exchange	Symbol	Price	52Wk Range	Yield	P/E
NYS	CMS	$13.54 (3/31/2008)	18.93-13.35	2.66	N/A

*7 Year Price Score 94.75   *NYSE Composite Index=100   ***12 Month Price Score 94.06**

Interim Earnings (Per Share)
Qtr.	Mar	Jun	Sep	Dec
2003	0.51	(0.31)	(0.51)	(0.01)
2004	(0.07)	0.10	0.34	0.24
2005	0.74	0.12	(1.21)	(0.02)
2006	(0.12)	0.31	(0.47)	(0.15)
2007	(0.97)	0.15	0.34	(0.57)

Interim Dividends (Per Share)
Amt	Decl	Ex	Rec	Pay
0.05Q	4/24/2007	5/8/2007	5/10/2007	5/31/2007
0.05Q	7/20/2007	8/8/2007	8/10/2007	8/31/2007
0.05Q	10/26/2007	11/7/2007	11/9/2007	11/30/2007
0.09Q	1/25/2008	2/6/2008	2/8/2008	2/29/2008

Indicated Div: $0.36

Valuation Analysis
		Institutional Holding	
Forecast P/E	12.57	No of Institutions	
	(1/10/2007)	249	
Market Cap	$3.0 Billion	Shares	
Book Value	2.4 Billion	208,544,720	
Price/Book	1.26	% Held	
Price/Sales	0.47	93.41	

Business Summary: Electricity (MIC: 7.1 SIC: 4931 NAIC: 221119)

CMS Energy is an energy company operating primarily in Michigan. As of Dec 31 2007, Co. conducted its businesses through two principal subsidiaries. The Consumers Energy Company subsidiary provides electricity and/or natural gas to almost 6.5 million of Michigan's 10.0 million residents and serves customers in all 68 counties of Michigan's Lower Peninsula as of Dec 31 2007. The CMS Enterprises Company subsidiary is engaged primarily in domestic independent power production. Co. manages its businesses by the nature of services each provides and operates principally in three business segments: electric utility, gas utility, and enterprises.

Recent Developments: For the year ended Dec 31 2007, loss from continuing operations was US$126.0 million compared with a loss of US$133.0 million a year earlier. Net loss amounted to US$215.0 million versus a net loss of US$79.0 million in the prior year. Revenues were US$6.46 billion, up 5.5% from US$6.13 billion the year before. Operating income was US$1.0 million versus a loss of US$54.0 million in the prior year. Direct operating expenses rose 7.1% to US$5.56 billion from US$5.19 billion in the comparable period the year before. Indirect operating expenses decreased 8.8% to US$905.0 million from US$992.0 million in the equivalent prior-year period.

Prospects: For the full year of 2008, Co. is projecting project electric deliveries to decline one-quarter of a percent compared to its 2007 levels. This outlook assumes a small decline in industrial economic activity, the cancellation of one wholesale customer contract, and normal weather conditions throughout the year. In addition, Co. expects the transmission rates to increase by $42.0 million, attributable primarily to a 33.0% escalation in transmission rate at Michigan Electric Transmission Co., LLC. Meanwhile, Co. anticipates electric deliveries over the next five years to grow by 1.0% annually, excluding transactions with other wholesale market participants and other electric utilities.

Financial Data
(US$ in Thousands)	12/31/2007	12/31/2006	12/31/2005	12/31/2004	12/31/2003	12/31/2002	12/31/2001	12/31/2000
Earnings Per Share	(1.02)	(0.41)	(0.44)	0.64	(0.30)	(4.46)	(4.17)	0.32
Cash Flow Per Share	0.12	3.13	3.05	2.35	(1.67)	2.90	3.19	3.99
Tang Book Value Per Share	9.46	9.91	10.41	10.51	9.68	7.86	8.31	12.13
Dividends Per Share	0.200	...	...	...	...	1.090	1.460	1.460
Dividend Payout %	...	...	...	...	...	...	...	456.25
Income Statement								
Total Revenue	6,464,000	6,810,000	6,288,000	5,472,000	5,513,000	8,687,000	9,597,000	8,998,000
EBITDA	728,000	883,000	783,000	1,210,000	1,083,000	528,000	921,000	1,365,000
Income Before Taxes	(310,000)	(243,000)	(266,000)	122,000	15,000	(403,000)	(401,000)	104,000
Income Taxes	(195,000)	(158,000)	(168,000)	(5,000)	58,000	13,000	(73,000)	60,000
Net Income	(215,000)	(79,000)	(84,000)	121,000	(44,000)	(620,000)	(545,000)	36,000
Average Shares	222,644	219,900	211,800	174,100	150,400	139,000	130,800	113,100
Balance Sheet								
Net PPE	8,728,000	7,976,000	7,845,000	8,636,000	6,944,000	5,734,000	8,362,000	7,835,000
Total Assets	14,196,000	15,371,000	16,020,000	15,872,000	13,838,000	13,915,000	17,102,000	15,851,000
Long-Term Obligations	5,788,000	6,422,000	7,286,000	7,263,000	6,762,000	5,472,000	6,983,000	7,518,000
Total Liabilities	11,772,000	12,832,000	13,393,000	13,495,000	11,948,000	12,738,000	15,168,000	13,446,000
Stockholders' Equity	2,424,000	2,539,000	2,627,000	2,377,000	1,890,000	1,177,000	1,960,000	2,405,000
Shares Outstanding	225,146	222,783	220,497	194,997	161,100	144,100	132,989	121,201
Statistical Record								
Return on Assets %	N.M.	N.M.	N.M.	0.81	N.M.	N.M.	N.M.	0.23
Return on Equity %	N.M.	N.M.	N.M.	5.66	N.M.	N.M.	N.M.	1.46
EBITDA Margin %	11.26	12.97	12.45	22.11	19.64	6.08	9.60	15.17
Net Margin %	(3.33)	(1.16)	(1.34)	2.21	(0.80)	(7.14)	(5.68)	0.40
PPE Turnover	0.77	0.86	0.76	0.70	0.91	1.28	1.19	1.12
Asset Turnover	0.44	0.43	0.39	0.37	0.40	0.56	0.58	0.57
Debt to Equity	2.39	2.53	2.77	3.06	3.58	4.65	3.56	3.13
Price Range	18.93-15.48	16.95-12.46	16.71-9.81	10.53-7.90	10.59-3.49	24.62-5.79	31.75-19.89	31.69-16.44
P/E Ratio	...	...	...	16.45-12.34	...	...	...	99.02-51.37
Average Yield %	1.16	...	...	...	...	7.49	5.53	5.99

Address: One Energy Plaza, Jackson, MI 49201-2276
Telephone: 517-788-0550

Web Site: www.cmsenergy.com
Officers: Kenneth Whipple - Chmn. S. Kinnie Smith Jr. - Vice-Chmn., Gen. Couns.

Auditors: PricewaterhouseCoopers LLP
Investor Contact: 517-788-1868
Transfer Agents: Investor Services Department, Jackson, MI

CNA FINANCIAL CORP.

Exchange	Symbol	Price	52Wk Range	Yield	P/E
NYS	CNA	$25.79 (3/31/2008)	51.81-23.91	2.33	8.24

*7 Year Price Score 102.23 *NYSE Composite Index=100 *12 Month Price Score 76.60

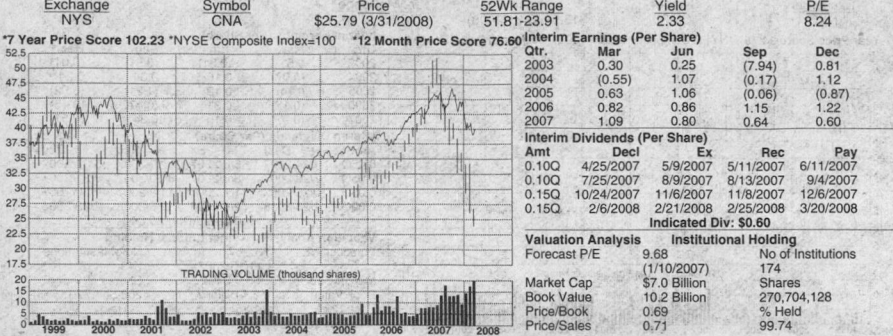

Interim Earnings (Per Share)

Qtr.	Mar	Jun	Sep	Dec
2003	0.30	0.25	(7.94)	0.81
2004	(0.55)	1.07	(0.17)	1.12
2005	0.63	1.06	(0.06)	(0.87)
2006	0.82	0.86	1.15	1.22
2007	1.09	0.80	0.64	0.60

Interim Dividends (Per Share)

Amt	Decl	Ex	Rec	Pay
0.10Q	4/25/2007	5/9/2007	5/11/2007	6/11/2007
0.10Q	7/25/2007	8/9/2007	8/13/2007	9/4/2007
0.15Q	10/24/2007	11/6/2007	11/8/2007	12/6/2007
0.15Q	2/6/2008	2/21/2008	2/25/2008	3/20/2008

Indicated Div: $0.60

Valuation Analysis

		Institutional Holding	
Forecast P/E	9.68	No of Institutions	
	(1/10/2007)	174	
Market Cap	$7.0 Billion	Shares	
Book Value	10.2 Billion	270,704,128	
Price/Book	0.69	% Held	
Price/Sales	0.71	99.74	

Business Summary: Insurance (MIC: 8.2 SIC: 6331 NAIC: 524126)

CNA Financial is an insurance holding company. Co.'s property and casualty insurance operations are conducted by Continental Casualty Company and The Continental Insurance Company. Co. serves a range of customers, including small, medium and large businesses, associations, professionals, and groups and individuals with several insurance and risk management products and services. Co.'s insurance products primarily include property and casualty coverages. Co.'s services include risk management, information services, warranty and claims administration. Co.'s core business, property and casualty insurance operations, is reported in two business segments: Standard Lines and Specialty Lines.

Recent Developments: For the year ended Dec 31 2007, income from continuing operations decreased 24.6% to US$857.0 million from US$1.14 billion a year earlier. Net income decreased 23.2% to US$851.0 million from US$1.11 billion in the prior year. Revenues were US$9.89 billion, down 4.7% from US$10.38 billion the year before. Net premiums earned were US$7.48 billion versus US$7.60 billion in the prior year, a decrease of 1.6%. Net investment income rose 0.9% to US$2.43 billion from US$2.41 billion a year ago.

Prospects: Co.'s recent lower net operating income from continuing operations is primarily due to lower net investment income and decreased current accident year underwriting results from its Standard Lines and Specialty Lines segments. However, Co. noted that these decreases were largely offset by favorable net prior year development in the fourth quarter of 2007 as compared with unfavorable net prior year development for the same period in 2006. Moving ahead, Co. believes that the continuing competitive market conditions will continue pressure on premium and income levels, and the expense ratio in both its Standard and Specialty Lines segments.

Financial Data
(US$ in Thousands)

	12/31/2007	12/31/2006	12/31/2005	12/31/2004	12/31/2003	12/31/2002	12/31/2001	12/31/2000
Earnings Per Share	3.13	4.05	0.76	1.47	(6.58)	0.68	(8.48)	6.61
Cash Flow Per Share	4.56	8.58	8.47	6.26	7.75	4.65	(3.09)	(7.46)
Tang Book Value Per Share	36.84	35.51	31.46	32.41	32.60	37.91	36.23	50.91
Dividends Per Share	0.350	...	...	...	...	...	...	...
Dividend Payout %	11.18	...	...	...	...	...	...	...
Income Statement								
Premium Income	7,484,000	7,603,000	7,569,000	8,209,000	9,214,000	10,213,000	9,365,000	11,474,000
Total Revenue	9,885,000	10,376,000	9,862,000	9,930,000	11,716,000	12,286,000	13,203,000	15,614,000
Income Before Taxes	1,222,000	1,650,000	162,000	497,000	(2,352,000)	341,000	(2,305,000)	1,810,000
Income Taxes	317,000	469,000	(105,000)	29,000	(913,000)	68,000	(743,000)	568,000
Net Income	851,000	1,108,000	264,000	441,000	(1,433,000)	155,000	(1,644,000)	1,214,000
Average Shares	271,800	262,300	256,000	256,000	227,000	223,600	194,000	183,600
Balance Sheet								
Total Assets	56,732,000	60,283,000	58,786,000	62,500,000	68,503,000	61,731,000	65,968,000	62,068,000
Total Liabilities	46,197,000	50,180,000	49,545,000	53,018,000	59,295,000	52,074,000	57,377,000	52,204,000
Stockholders' Equity	10,150,000	9,768,000	8,950,000	9,207,000	8,952,000	9,401,000	8,367,000	9,647,000
Shares Outstanding	271,662	271,108	256,001	255,953	223,617	223,608	223,596	183,263
Statistical Record								
Return on Assets %	1.45	1.86	0.44	0.67	N.M.	0.24	N.M.	1.96
Return on Equity %	8.55	11.84	2.91	4.84	N.M.	1.74	N.M.	13.03
Net Margin %	8.61	10.68	2.68	4.44	(12.23)	1.26	(12.45)	7.78
Price Range	51.81-32.70	40.27-29.88	34.91-25.84	30.49-22.17	26.90-19.00	30.86-22.32	39.90-24.35	41.44-24.75
P/E Ratio	16.55-10.45	9.94-7.38	45.93-34.00	20.74-15.08	...	45.38-32.82	...	6.27-3.74
Average Yield %	0.83	...	...	...	...	...	...	...

Address: 333 South Wabash Avenue, Chicago, IL 60604
Telephone: 312-822-5000
Fax: 312-822-6419

Web Site: www.cna.com
Officers: Bernard L. Hengesbaugh - Chmn. Stephen W. Lilienthal - C.E.O.

Auditors: Deloitte & Touche LLP
Investor Contact: 312-822-7757
Transfer Agents: EquiServe Trust Company, N.A.

COACH, INC.

Exchange	Symbol	Price	52Wk Range	Yield	P/E
NYS	COH	$30.15 (3/31/2008)	53.79-24.62	N/A	15.62

*7 Year Price Score 141.14 *NYSE Composite Index=100   *12 Month Price Score 80.61

Interim Earnings (Per Share)

Qtr.	Sep	Dec	Mar	Jun
2004-05	0.17	0.34	0.23	0.25
2005-06	0.24	0.45	0.28	0.31
2006-07	0.34	0.61	0.40	0.42
2007-08	0.41	0.69	...	...

Interim Dividends (Per Share)

Amt	Decl	Ex	Rec	Pay
2-for-1	5/2/2002	7/5/2002	6/19/2002	7/3/2002
2-for-1	8/7/2003	10/2/2003	9/17/2003	10/1/2003
2-for-1	1/25/2005	4/5/2005	3/21/2005	4/4/2005

Valuation Analysis   Institutional Holding

Forecast P/E	N/A	No of Institutions
		560
Market Cap	$10.6 Billion	Shares
Book Value	1.0 Billion	314,658,080
Price/Book	6.72	% Held
Price/Sales	3.61	85.00

Business Summary: Leather and Leather Products (MIC: 4.5 SIC: 3171 NAIC: 316992)

Coach is engaged in the design and market of modern American classic accessories. Co.'s primary product offerings include handbags, women's and men's accessories, footwear, outerwear, business cases, sunwear, watches, travel bags, jewelry and fragrance. Co.'s products are sold through its Direct-to-Consumer segment, which includes Company-operated stores in North America and Japan, its online store and its catalogs, as well as through its Indirect segment, which includes department store locations in the U.S., international department stores, freestanding retail locations and specialty retailers.

Recent Developments: For the quarter ended Dec 29 2007, income from continuing operations increased 17.6% to US$252.3 million from US$214.5 million in the year-earlier quarter. Net income increased 10.9% to US$252.3 million from US$227.5 million in the year earlier quarter. Revenues were US$978.0 million, up 21.4% from US$805.6 million the year before. Operating income was US$403.1 million versus US$340.7 million in the prior-year quarter, an increase of 18.3%. Direct operating expenses rose 30.6% to US$240.7 million from US$184.3 million in the comparable period the year before. Indirect operating expenses increased 19.1% to US$334.2 million from US$280.6 million in the equivalent prior-year period.

Prospects: For the fiscal year ending June 30 2008, Co. is targeting sales of at least $3.15 billion, reflecting an increase of at least 20.0% from the prior fiscal year, while earnings are estimated to be about $2.06 per diluted share, representing an improvement of about 22.0%. Co.'s guidance assumes sales of about $1.50 billion and earnings of $0.97 per share in the second half of fiscal 2008. In North America, Co. expects to open about 40 new retail stores, while 10 to 15 net new locations are being scheduled to open in Japan. Meanwhile, Co. will continue to invest in department store, distributor locations and corporate infrastructure while expanding its Jacksonville distribution center.

Financial Data

(US$ in Thousands)	6 Mos	3 Mos	06/30/2007	07/01/2006	07/02/2005	07/03/2004	06/28/2003	06/29/2002
Earnings Per Share	1.93	1.84	1.76	1.27	1.00	0.68	0.40	0.23
Cash Flow Per Share	2.41	2.22	2.11	1.58	1.44	1.19	0.62	0.31
Tang Book Value Per Share	3.79	4.74	4.52	2.57	2.07	2.00	1.11	0.67
Income Statement								
Total Revenue	1,654,735	676,718	2,612,456	2,111,501	1,710,423	1,321,106	953,226	719,403
EBITDA	690,960	263,486	1,074,284	829,719	678,843	487,319	273,993	159,129
Depn & Amortn	49,139	24,728	...	...	...	...	...	...
Income Before Taxes	667,385	253,754	1,034,670	797,227	637,570	447,657	244,821	133,336
Income Taxes	260,282	98,968	398,141	302,950	235,277	167,866	90,585	47,325
Net Income	407,123	154,806	663,665	494,277	388,652	261,748	146,628	85,827
Average Shares	366,569	379,285	377,356	388,495	390,191	385,558	371,684	363,808
Balance Sheet								
Current Assets	1,480,348	1,885,897	1,740,196	974,482	709,360	705,616	448,538	287,588
Total Assets	2,310,722	2,679,031	2,449,512	1,626,520	1,347,132	1,028,658	617,652	440,571
Current Liabilities	427,005	402,124	407,996	341,824	265,780	181,938	161,461	159,428
Long-Term Obligations	2,580	2,580	2,865	3,100	3,270	3,420	3,535	3,615
Total Liabilities	728,869	673,198	539,158	437,786	314,356	246,372	190,723	180,215
Stockholders' Equity	1,581,853	2,005,833	1,910,354	1,188,734	1,032,776	782,286	426,929	260,356
Shares Outstanding	352,310	372,529	372,521	369,830	378,429	379,236	366,018	357,814
Statistical Record								
Return on Assets %	33.41	31.88	32.65	33.34	32.81	31.28	27.79	24.61
Return on Equity %	47.00	43.42	42.95	44.62	42.94	42.59	42.79	42.12
EBITDA Margin %	41.76	38.94	41.12	39.30	39.69	36.89	28.74	22.12
Net Margin %	24.60	22.88	25.40	23.41	22.72	19.81	15.38	11.93
Asset Turnover	1.36	1.28	1.29	1.42	1.44	1.58	1.81	2.06
Current Ratio	3.47	4.69	4.27	2.85	2.67	3.88	2.78	1.80
Debt to Equity	N.M.	N.M.	N.M.	N.M.	N.M.	N.M.	0.01	0.01
Price Range	53.79-30.41	53.79-34.20	53.79-25.58	36.97-27.75	33.92-18.06	23.09-12.44	13.22-4.53	7.49-2.74
P/E Ratio	27.87-15.76	29.23-18.59	30.56-14.53	29.11-21.85	33.92-18.06	33.96-18.29	33.05-11.33	32.54-11.90

Address: 516 West 34th Street, New York, NY 10001

Telephone: 212-594-1850

Fax: 212-594-1682

Web Site: www.coach.com

Officers: Lew Frankfort - Chmn., C.E.O. Keith Monda - Pres., C.O.O.

Auditors: Deloitte & Touche LLP

Investor Contact: 212-629-2618

Transfer Agents: Mellon Investor Services

COCA-COLA CO (THE)

Exchange	Symbol	Price	52Wk Range	Yield	P/E	Div Acheiver
NYS	KO	$60.87 (3/31/2008)	65.56-48.52	2.50	23.68	45 Years

*7 Year Price Score 96.38   *NYSE Composite Index=100   *12 Month Price Score 112.01

Interim Earnings (Per Share)

Qtr.	Mar	Jun	Sep	Dec
2003	0.34	0.55	0.50	0.38
2004	0.46	0.65	0.39	0.50
2005	0.42	0.72	0.54	0.37
2006	0.47	0.78	0.62	0.29
2007	0.54	0.80	0.71	0.52

Interim Dividends (Per Share)

Amt	Decl	Ex	Rec	Pay
0.34Q	4/19/2007	6/13/2007	6/15/2007	7/1/2007
0.34Q	7/19/2007	9/12/2007	9/15/2007	10/1/2007
0.34Q	10/18/2007	11/28/2007	12/1/2007	12/15/2007
0.38Q	2/21/2008	3/12/2008	3/15/2008	4/1/2008

Indicated Div: $1.52 (Div. Reinv. Plan)

Valuation Analysis

		Institutional Holding	
Forecast P/E	17.60 (1/10/2007)	No of Institutions	1131
Market Cap	$141.1 Billion	Shares	1,486,067,200
Book Value	21.7 Billion	% Held	64.18
Price/Book	6.49		
Price/Sales	4.89		

Business Summary: Food (MIC: 4.1 SIC: 2086 NAIC: 312111)

Coca-Cola is a global manufacturer, distributor and marketer of nonalcoholic beverage concentrates and syrups. Co. also manufactures, distributes and markets some finished beverages. Co. primarily sells concentrates and syrups, as well as some finished beverages, to bottling and canning operations, distributors, fountain wholesalers and fountain retailers. As of Dec 31 2007, Co. owned or licensed more than 450 brands, including Coca-Cola, Diet Coke, Fanta and Sprite, and a variety of diet and light beverages, waters, juice and juice drinks, teas, coffees, and energy and sports drinks. Additionally, Co. has ownership interests in numerous joint ventures bottling and canning operations.

Recent Developments: For the year ended Dec 31 2007, net income increased 17.7% to US$5.98 billion from US$5.08 billion in the prior year. Revenues were US$28.86 billion, up 19.8% from US$24.09 billion the year before. Operating income was US$7.25 billion versus US$6.31 billion in the prior year, an increase of 15.0%. Direct operating expenses rose 27.5% to US$10.41 billion from US$8.16 billion in the comparable period the year before. Indirect operating expenses increased 16.5% to US$11.20 billion from US$9.62 billion in the equivalent prior-year period.

Prospects: For 2008, Co. now foresees net purchases of property, plant and equipment to range from $1.60 billion to $1.70 billion. Meanwhile, Co. plans to close its beverage concentrate manufacturing and distribution plant in Drogheda, Ireland by September 2008, which is expected to improve operating productivity and capacity utilization. Further, Co. intends to purchase the remaining 10.5% of Coca-Cola China Industries Ltd. by the end of 2008. Separately, on Feb 5 2008, Co. announced an agreement to acquire 40.0% interest in Honest Tea, Inc., a maker of certified organic beverages, which is in-line with its strategy of investing in key beverage businesses and potential beverages in North America.

Financial Data

(US$ in Thousands)	12/31/2007	12/31/2006	12/31/2005	12/31/2004	12/31/2003	12/31/2002	12/31/2001	12/31/2000
Earnings Per Share	2.57	2.16	2.04	2.00	1.77	1.23	1.60	0.88
Cash Flow Per Share	3.09	2.54	2.69	2.45	2.22	1.91	1.65	1.44
Tang Book Value Per Share	4.11	5.08	5.29	5.02	4.14	3.34	3.53	2.98
Dividends Per Share	1.360	1.240	1.120	1.000	0.880	0.800	0.720	0.680
Dividend Payout %	52.92	57.41	54.90	50.00	49.72	65.04	45.00	77.27
Income Statement								
Total Revenue	28,857,000	24,088,000	23,104,000	21,962,000	21,044,000	19,564,000	20,092,000	20,458,000
EBITDA	9,256,000	7,543,000	7,627,000	7,154,000	6,347,000	6,295,000	6,437,000	4,274,000
Income Before Taxes	7,873,000	6,578,000	6,690,000	6,222,000	5,495,000	5,499,000	5,670,000	3,399,000
Income Taxes	1,892,000	1,498,000	1,818,000	1,375,000	1,148,000	1,523,000	1,691,000	1,222,000
Net Income	5,981,000	5,080,000	4,872,000	4,847,000	4,347,000	3,050,000	3,969,000	2,177,000
Average Shares	2,331,000	2,350,000	2,393,000	2,429,000	2,462,000	2,483,000	2,487,000	2,487,000
Balance Sheet								
Current Assets	12,105,000	8,441,000	10,250,000	12,094,000	8,396,000	7,352,000	7,171,000	6,620,000
Total Assets	43,269,000	29,963,000	29,427,000	31,327,000	27,342,000	24,501,000	22,417,000	20,834,000
Current Liabilities	13,225,000	8,890,000	9,836,000	10,971,000	7,886,000	7,341,000	8,429,000	9,321,000
Long-Term Obligations	3,277,000	1,314,000	1,154,000	1,157,000	2,517,000	2,701,000	1,219,000	835,000
Total Liabilities	21,525,000	13,043,000	13,072,000	15,392,000	13,252,000	12,701,000	11,051,000	11,518,000
Stockholders' Equity	21,744,000	16,920,000	16,355,000	15,935,000	14,090,000	11,800,000	11,366,000	9,316,000
Shares Outstanding	2,318,000	2,318,000	2,369,000	2,409,339	2,441,531	2,470,979	2,486,228	2,484,762
Statistical Record								
Return on Assets %	16.33	17.11	16.04	16.48	16.77	13.00	18.35	10.23
Return on Equity %	30.94	30.53	30.18	32.20	33.58	26.33	38.38	23.06
EBITDA Margin %	32.08	31.31	33.01	32.57	30.16	32.18	32.04	20.89
Net Margin %	20.73	21.09	21.09	22.07	20.66	15.59	19.75	10.64
Asset Turnover	0.79	0.81	0.76	0.75	0.81	0.83	0.93	0.96
Current Ratio	0.92	0.95	1.04	1.10	1.06	1.00	0.85	0.71
Debt to Equity	0.15	0.08	0.07	0.07	0.18	0.23	0.11	0.09
Price Range	64.09-45.89	49.00-40.09	45.25-40.31	53.00-38.65	50.75-37.07	57.64-43.47	60.82-42.85	66.88-43.31
P/E Ratio	24.94-17.86	22.69-18.56	22.18-19.76	26.50-19.32	28.67-20.94	46.86-35.34	38.01-26.78	75.99-49.22
Average Yield %	2.53	2.83	2.62	2.15	2.00	1.61	1.48	1.23

Address: One Coca-Cola Plaza, Atlanta, GA 30313
Telephone: 404-676-2121
Fax: 404-676-6792

Web Site: www.coca-cola.com
Officers: E. Neville Isdell - Chmn., C.E.O. Gary P. Fayard - Exec. V.P., C.F.O.

Auditors: Ernst & Young LLP
Investor Contact: 404-676-5766
Transfer Agents: EquiServe Trust Company, N.A., Providence, RI

COCA-COLA ENTERPRISES INC.

Exchange	Symbol	Price	52Wk Range	Yield	P/E
NYS	CCE	$24.20 (3/31/2008)	26.89-20.29	1.16	16.58

*7 Year Price Score 92.08   *NYSE Composite Index=100   **12 Month Price Score 108.94

Interim Earnings (Per Share)

Qtr.	Mar	Jun	Sep	Dec
2003	0.06	0.56	0.56	0.27
2004	0.22	0.43	0.44	0.17
2005	0.10	0.70	0.40	(0.12)
2006	0.03	0.71	0.44	(3.59)
2007	0.03	0.56	0.55	0.32

Interim Dividends (Per Share)

Amt	Decl	Ex	Rec	Pay
0.06Q	4/24/2007	6/13/2007	6/15/2007	6/28/2007
0.06Q	7/23/2007	9/12/2007	9/14/2007	9/27/2007
0.06Q	10/24/2007	11/28/2007	11/30/2007	12/13/2007
0.07Q	2/12/2008	3/12/2008	3/14/2008	3/27/2008

Indicated Div: $0.28

Valuation Analysis / **Institutional Holding**

Forecast P/E	14.44	No of Institutions
	(1/10/2007)	248
Market Cap	$11.8 Billion	Shares
Book Value	5.7 Billion	218,714,528
Price/Book	2.07	% Hold
Price/Sales	0.56	45.58

Business Summary: Food (MIC: 4.1 SIC: 2086 NAIC: 312111)

Coca Cola Enterprises markets, produces and distributes its bottle and can nonalcoholic beverages, mostly those licensed through The Coca-Cola Company and its affiliates and joint ventures. Co. markets, produces and distributes its products to customers and consumers through license territories in 46 states in the U.S., the District of Columbia, the U.S. Virgin Islands, and the 10 provinces of Canada. Co. is also the sole licensed bottler for products of The Coca-Cola Company in Belgium, continental France, Great Britain, Luxembourg, Monaco, and the Netherlands. As of Dec 31 2007, Co. provided its service covering a market of about 414.0 million consumers throughout these territories.

Recent Developments: For the year ended Dec 31 2007, net income amounted to US$711.0 million versus a net loss of US$1.14 billion in the prior year. Revenues were US$20.94 billion, up 5.7% from US$19.80 billion the year before. Operating income was US$1.47 billion versus a loss of US$1.50 billion in the prior year. Direct operating expenses rose 7.4% to US$12.96 billion from US$12.07 billion in the comparable period the year before. Indirect operating expenses decreased 29.5% to US$6.51 billion from US$9.23 billion in the equivalent prior-year period.

Prospects: For full-year 2008, Co. continues to expect revenue to be in-line with its long-term objective of high single-digit growth, reflecting the favorable effect of the full year distribution of glacéau, FUZE, and Campbell, which create a mix effect as a result of their higher selling price per case. In addition, Co. expects volume growth in a low to mid single-digit range in both North America and Europe, driven by robust marketing and brand initiatives. Further, Co. expects operating income to increase at the high end of the long-term target range of 5.0% to 6.0%, with earnings per diluted share to be in line with the long-term objective of high single-digit growth.

Financial Data

(US$ in Thousands)	12/31/2007	12/31/2006	12/31/2005	12/31/2004	12/31/2003	12/31/2002	12/31/2001	12/31/2000
Earnings Per Share	1.46	(2.41)	1.08	1.26	1.46	1.07	(0.75)	0.54
Cash Flow Per Share	3.44	3.35	3.46	3.46	3.98	3.20	2.58	3.50
Tang Book Value Per Share	N.M.	N.M.	N.M.	N.M.	N.M.	N.M.	6.25	6.67
Dividends Per Share	0.240	0.240	0.160	0.160	0.160	0.160	0.160	0.160
Dividend Payout %	16.44	...	14.81	12.70	10.96	14.95	...	29.63
Income Statement								
Total Revenue	20,936,000	19,804,000	18,706,000	18,158,000	17,330,000	16,889,000	15,700,000	14,750,000
EBITDA	2,537,000	(473,000)	2,612,000	2,655,000	2,744,000	2,412,000	1,956,000	2,385,000
Income Before Taxes	841,000	(2,118,000)	790,000	818,000	972,000	705,000	(150,000)	333,000
Income Taxes	130,000	(975,000)	276,000	222,000	296,000	211,000	(131,000)	97,000
Net Income	711,000	(1,143,000)	514,000	596,000	676,000	494,000	(321,000)	236,000
Average Shares	488,000	475,000	476,000	473,000	461,000	458,000	432,000	429,000
Balance Sheet								
Current Assets	4,092,000	3,691,000	3,395,000	3,264,000	3,000,000	2,844,000	2,876,000	2,631,000
Total Assets	24,046,000	23,225,000	25,357,000	26,354,000	25,700,000	24,375,000	23,719,000	22,162,000
Current Liabilities	5,343,000	3,818,000	3,846,000	3,431,000	3,941,000	3,455,000	4,522,000	3,094,000
Long-Term Obligations	7,391,000	9,218,000	9,165,000	10,523,000	10,552,000	11,236,000	10,365,000	10,348,000
Total Liabilities	18,357,000	18,699,000	19,714,000	20,976,000	21,335,000	21,028,000	20,899,000	19,328,000
Stockholders' Equity	5,689,000	4,526,000	5,643,000	5,378,000	4,365,000	3,347,000	2,820,000	2,834,000
Shares Outstanding	486,953	479,690	473,795	469,650	455,754	449,700	445,115	418,068
Statistical Record								
Return on Assets %	3.01	N.M.	1.99	2.28	2.70	2.05	N.M.	1.05
Return on Equity %	13.92	N.M.	9.33	12.20	17.53	16.02	N.M.	8.17
EBITDA Margin %	12.12	N.M.	13.96	14.62	15.83	14.28	12.46	16.17
Net Margin %	3.40	N.M.	2.75	3.28	3.90	2.92	N.M.	1.60
Asset Turnover	0.89	0.82	0.72	0.70	0.69	0.70	0.68	0.66
Current Ratio	0.77	0.97	0.88	0.95	0.76	0.82	0.64	0.85
Debt to Equity	1.30	2.04	1.62	1.96	2.42	3.36	3.68	3.65
Price Range	26.89-20.01	22.46-18.88	23.74-18.62	29.02-18.62	23.02-17.05	24.46-16.13	23.64-14.09	29.19-14.63
P/E Ratio	18.42-13.71	...	21.98-17.24	23.03-14.78	15.77-11.68	22.86-15.07	...	54.05-27.08
Average Yield %	1.04	1.18	0.76	0.70	0.81	0.78	0.90	0.80

Address: 2500 Windy Ridge Parkway, Atlanta, GA 30339
Telephone: 770-989-3000
Fax: 770-989-3788

Web Site: www.cokecce.com
Officers: Lowry F. Kline - Chmn. John R. Alm - Pres., C.E.O.

Auditors: Ernst & Young LLP
Investor Contact: 770-989-3246
Transfer Agents: American Stock Transfer & Trust Co., New York, NY

COLGATE-PALMOLIVE CO.

Exchange	Symbol	Price	52Wk Range	Yield	P/E	Div Acheiver
NYS	CL	$77.91 (3/31/2008)	80.98-64.44	2.05	24.35	45 Years

*7 Year Price Score 99.83   *NYSE Composite Index=100   *12 Month Price Score 113.99

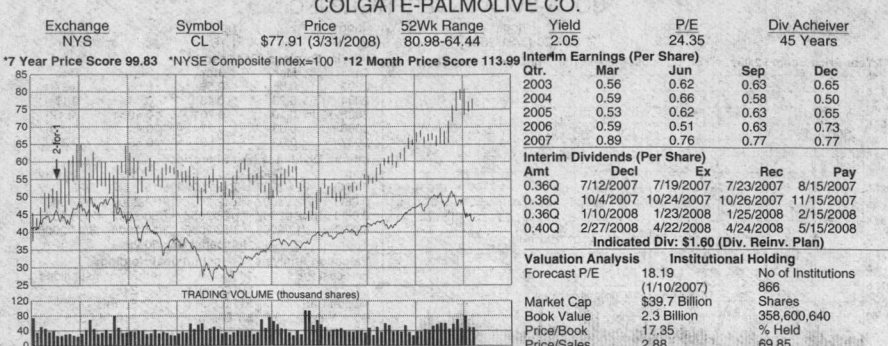

Interim Earnings (Per Share)

Qtr.	Mar	Jun	Sep	Dec
2003	0.56	0.62	0.63	0.65
2004	0.59	0.66	0.58	0.50
2005	0.53	0.62	0.63	0.65
2006	0.59	0.51	0.63	0.73
2007	0.89	0.76	0.77	0.77

Interim Dividends (Per Share)

Amt	Decl	Ex	Rec	Pay
0.36Q	7/12/2007	7/19/2007	7/23/2007	8/15/2007
0.36Q	10/4/2007	10/24/2007	10/26/2007	11/15/2007
0.36Q	1/10/2008	1/23/2008	1/25/2008	2/15/2008
0.40Q	2/27/2008	4/22/2008	4/24/2008	5/15/2008

Indicated Div: $1.60 (Div. Reinv. Plan)

Valuation Analysis

		Institutional Holding	
Forecast P/E	18.19	No of Institutions	
	(1/10/2007)	866	
Market Cap	$39.7 Billion	Shares	
Book Value	2.3 Billion	358,600,640	
Price/Book	17.35	% Held	
Price/Sales	2.88	69.85	

Business Summary: Chemicals (MIC: 11.1 SIC: 2844 NAIC: 325620)

Colgate-Palmolive manufactures and markets a variety of products in two business segments. The products in Oral, Personal and Home Care segment includes toothpaste, oral rinses and toothbrushes, bar and liquid hand soaps, shower gels, shampoos, conditioners, deodorants and antiperspirants, shave products, detergents, fabric conditioners, cleansers and cleaners and bleaches. The products in Pet Nutrition segment includes pet food products manufactured and marketed by Hill's Pet Nutrition. Trademarks include Colgate, Palmolive, Kolynos, Sorriso, Elmex, Mennen, Protex, Softsoap, Irish Spring, Ajax, Axion, Soupline, Suavitel, Tom's of Maine, Hill's Science Diet and Hill's Prescription Diet.

Recent Developments: For the year ended Dec 31 2007, net income increased 28.4% to US$1.74 billion from US$1.35 billion in the prior year. Revenues were US$13.79 billion, up 12.7% from US$12.24 billion the year before. Operating income was US$2.65 billion versus US$2.16 billion in the prior year, an increase of 22.8%. Direct operating expenses rose 9.1% to US$6.04 billion from US$5.54 billion in the comparable period the year before. Indirect operating expenses increased 12.2% to US$5.09 billion from US$4.54 billion in the equivalent prior-year period.

Prospects: For 2008, Co. anticipates solid top-line growth to be driven by new product pipeline with various marketing campaigns to support them. Also, Co. is projecting gross profit margin, excluding restructuring charges, to be up within its targeted range of 75 to 125 basis points, while earnings per share growth is expected to be in the double-digit range. For the first quarter of 2008, Co. plans to launch several products, including Colgate Total Advanced Whitening and Colgate Total Advanced Fresh toothpastes, Colgate 360 degree Deep Clean manual toothbrush, Colgate 360 degree Sonic Power battery toothbrush, Suavitel Aroma Sensations fabric conditioner and Mennen Speed Stick 24/7 deodorant.

Financial Data

(US$ in Thousands)	12/31/2007	12/31/2006	12/31/2005	12/31/2004	12/31/2003	12/31/2002	12/31/2001	12/31/2000
Earnings Per Share	3.20	2.46	2.43	2.33	2.46	2.19	1.89	1.70
Cash Flow Per Share	4.31	3.54	3.43	3.30	3.29	2.97	2.87	2.66
Dividends Per Share	1.400	1.250	1.110	0.960	0.900	0.720	0.675	0.630
Dividend Payout %	43.75	50.81	45.68	41.20	36.59	32.88	35.71	37.06
Income Statement								
Total Revenue	13,789,700	12,237,700	11,396,900	10,584,200	9,903,400	9,294,300	9,427,800	9,357,900
EBITDA	2,987,000	2,489,200	2,544,300	2,449,900	2,481,500	2,309,600	2,171,000	2,078,300
Income Before Taxes	2,496,500	2,001,800	2,079,000	2,002,400	2,041,900	1,870,300	1,668,700	1,567,200
Income Taxes	759,100	648,400	727,600	675,300	620,600	582,000	522,100	503,400
Net Income	1,737,400	1,353,400	1,351,400	1,327,100	1,421,300	1,288,300	1,146,600	1,063,800
Average Shares	543,700	550,500	556,500	569,300	578,800	589,100	607,700	627,300
Balance Sheet								
Current Assets	3,618,500	3,301,000	2,757,100	2,739,900	2,496,500	2,228,100	2,203,400	2,347,200
Total Assets	10,112,000	9,138,000	8,507,100	8,672,900	7,478,800	7,087,200	6,984,800	7,252,300
Current Liabilities	3,162,700	3,469,100	2,743,000	2,730,700	2,445,400	2,148,700	2,123,500	2,244,100
Long-Term Obligations	3,221,900	2,720,400	2,918,000	3,089,500	2,684,900	3,210,800	2,812,000	2,536,900
Total Liabilities	7,825,800	7,727,100	7,157,000	7,427,500	6,591,700	6,736,900	6,138,400	5,784,200
Stockholders' Equity	2,286,200	1,410,900	1,350,100	1,245,400	887,100	350,300	846,400	1,468,100
Shares Outstanding	509,034	512,658	516,170	526,625	533,697	536,001	550,722	566,655
Statistical Record								
Return on Assets %	18.05	15.34	15.73	16.39	19.52	18.31	16.11	14.46
Return on Equity %	93.99	98.04	104.13	124.12	229.72	215.31	99.08	64.26
EBITDA Margin %	21.66	20.34	22.32	23.15	25.06	24.85	23.03	22.21
Net Margin %	12.60	11.06	11.86	12.54	14.35	13.86	12.16	11.37
Asset Turnover	1.43	1.39	1.33	1.31	1.36	1.32	1.32	1.27
Current Ratio	1.14	0.95	1.01	1.00	1.02	1.04	1.04	1.05
Debt to Equity	1.41	1.93	2.16	2.48	3.03	9.17	3.32	1.73
Price Range	80.64-64.44	66.83-53.70	56.39-48.55	58.92-43.06	60.88-49.10	58.73-44.36	62.50-51.00	65.00-42.75
P/E Ratio	25.20-20.14	27.17-21.83	23.21-19.98	25.29-18.48	24.75-19.96	26.82-20.26	33.07-26.98	38.24-25.15
Average Yield %	2.02	2.09	2.13	1.82	1.64	1.33	1.19	1.13

Address: 300 Park Avenue, New York, NY 10022-7499 **Telephone:** 212-310-2000 **Fax:** 212-310-3284	**Web Site:** www.colgate.com **Officers:** Reuben Mark - Chmn., C.E.O. Javier G. Teruel - Vice-Chmn.	**Auditors:** PricewaterhouseCoopers LLP **Investor Contact:** 212-310-3072 **Transfer Agents:** EquiServe Trust Company, N.A., Providence, RI

COLLECTIVE BRANDS INC

Exchange	Symbol	Price	52Wk Range	Yield	P/E
NYS	PSS	$12.12 (3/31/2008)	35.72-11.85	N/A	18.65

*7 Year Price Score 96.53 *NYSE Composite Index=100 *12 Month Price Score 71.15

Interim Earnings (Per Share)

Qtr.	Apr	Jul	Oct	Jan
2003-04	0.21	0.08	(0.03)	(0.25)
2004-05	0.20	0.05	0.10	(0.38)
2005-06	0.45	0.29	0.32	(0.08)
2006-07	0.53	0.48	0.43	0.37
2007-08	0.59	0.38	0.39	(0.71)

Interim Dividends (Per Share)

Amt	Decl	Ex	Rec	Pay
3-for-1	2/28/2003	3/28/2003	3/13/2003	3/27/2003

Valuation Analysis **Institutional Holding**

Forecast P/E	N/A	No of Institutions
		N/A
Market Cap	$772.7 Million	Shares
Book Value	702.9 Million	N/A
Price/Book	1.10	% Held
Price/Sales	0.25	N/A

Business Summary: Retail - Apparel and Accessory Stores (MIC: 5.8 SIC: 5661 NAIC: 448210)

Collective Brands is a footwear specialty retailer. At Feb 2 2008, Co. operated a total of 4,552 retail stores in 15 countries and territories. Co.'s stores offer fashionable, quality, private and branded label footwear and accessories for women, men and children at affordable prices in a self-selection shopping format. Co.'s stores feature several designer and mainstream footwear brands including Abaete for Payless™, Airwalk®, American Eagle™, Champion®, and Dexter®. Co.'s Payless Domestic segment includes operations in the U.S, Guam and Saipan while its Payless International segment includes operations in Canada; Puerto Rico; the U.S. Virgin Islands as well as South and Central America.

Recent Developments: For the year ended Feb 2 2008, income from continuing operations decreased 65.9% to US$42.7 million from US$125.4 million a year earlier. Net income decreased 65.0% to US$42.7 million from US$122.0 million in the prior year. Revenues were US$3.04 billion, up 8.5% from US$2.80 billion the year before. Operating income was US$91.3 million versus US$166.4 million in the prior year, a decrease of 45.1%. Direct operating expenses rose 12.3% to US$2.04 billion from US$1.82 billion in the comparable period the year before. Indirect operating expenses increased 11.2% to US$899.6 million from US$809.3 million in the equivalent prior-year period.

Prospects: On Mar 11 2008, Co. announced plans to improve product distribution for its North American retail and wholesale customers by consolidating its five primary North American distribution centers into three U.S. centers. This business decision should allow Co. to utilize its distribution centers to ensure for a faster distribution of all its products to customers. In particular, Co. intends to shift the distribution of Robeez® product from its Burnaby, British Columbia distribution center to its Huntington, IN distribution center, and particularly to its new Eastern Distribution Center in Brookville, OH, which will begin operation in the spring of 2009.

Financial Data
(US$ in Thousands)

	02/02/2008	02/03/2007	01/28/2006	01/29/2005	01/31/2004	02/01/2003	02/02/2002	02/03/2001
Earnings Per Share	0.65	1.82	0.98	(0.03)	...	1.55	0.67	1.67
Cash Flow Per Share	3.00	3.43	3.35	3.80	3.11	1.93	2.33	2.92
Tang Book Value Per Share	N.M.	10.48	9.33	8.44	8.51	8.30	7.00	6.22
Income Statement								
Total Revenue	3,035,400	2,796,700	2,667,300	2,656,500	2,783,300	2,878,000	2,913,700	2,948,400
EBITDA	223,200	268,200	206,800	157,300	100,800	281,200	206,800	330,600
Income Before Taxes	59,000	169,900	106,400	44,700	(16,200)	158,900	71,800	203,000
Income Taxes	8,600	39,900	30,800	13,200	(9,100)	58,000	27,600	79,000
Net Income	42,700	122,000	66,400	(2,000)	(100)	105,800	45,400	120,600
Average Shares	65,387	66,974	67,854	68,020	68,020	68,121	67,776	72,162
Balance Sheet								
Current Assets	938,200	906,600	854,300	729,000	658,000	633,600	536,500	434,700
Total Assets	2,415,200	1,427,400	1,314,500	1,239,800	1,176,900	1,150,800	1,069,200	1,002,800
Current Liabilities	413,100	380,300	338,500	338,300	289,600	341,800	291,200	228,700
Long-Term Obligations	914,900	201,700	204,200	204,300	202,800	140,700	245,100	309,200
Total Liabilities	1,712,300	727,300	662,500	644,800	569,400	552,600	602,200	592,400
Stockholders' Equity	702,900	700,100	652,000	595,000	607,500	598,200	467,000	410,400
Shares Outstanding	63,752	64,996	67,305	67,191	67,991	67,946	66,758	65,964
Statistical Record								
Return on Assets %	2.23	8.76	5.21	N.M.	N.M.	9.56	4.39	11.42
Return on Equity %	6.10	17.75	10.68	N.M.	N.M.	19.92	10.38	21.30
EBITDA Margin %	7.35	9.59	7.75	5.94	3.62	9.77	7.10	11.21
Net Margin %	1.41	4.36	2.49	N.M.	N.M.	3.68	1.56	4.09
Asset Turnover	1.58	2.01	2.09	2.20	2.40	2.60	2.82	2.79
Current Ratio	2.27	2.38	2.52	2.16	2.28	1.85	1.84	1.90
Debt to Equity	1.30	0.29	0.31	0.34	0.33	0.24	0.52	0.75
Price Range	35.72-14.10	34.96-20.60	25.57-11.57	16.80-9.33	16.48-12.00	21.10-14.25	26.06-17.33	23.90-13.06
P/E Ratio	54.95-21.69	19.21-11.32	26.09-11.81	...	N.M.	13.61-9.19	38.90-25.86	14.31-7.82

Address: 3231 S.E. Sixth Avenue, Topeka, KS 66607-2207
Telephone: 785-233-5171
Fax: 785-295-6049

Web Site: www.paylessinfo.com
Officers: Howard R. Fricke - Chmn. Matthew E. Rubel - Pres., C.E.O.

Auditors: Deloitte & Touche LLP
Investor Contact: 785-295-6695
Transfer Agents: UMB Bank

COLONIAL BANCGROUP INC.

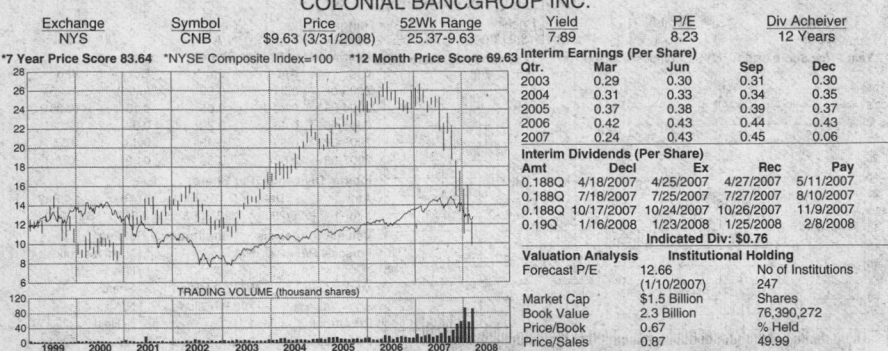

Exchange	Symbol	Price	52Wk Range	Yield	P/E	Div Acheiver
NYS	CNB	$9.63 (3/31/2008)	25.37-9.63	7.89	8.23	12 Years

*7 Year Price Score 83.64   *NYSE Composite Index=100   *12 Month Price Score 69.63

Interim Earnings (Per Share)

Qtr.	Mar	Jun	Sep	Dec
2003	0.29	0.30	0.31	0.30
2004	0.31	0.33	0.34	0.35
2005	0.37	0.38	0.39	0.37
2006	0.42	0.43	0.44	0.43
2007	0.24	0.43	0.45	0.06

Interim Dividends (Per Share)

Amt	Decl	Ex	Rec	Pay
0.188Q	4/18/2007	4/25/2007	4/27/2007	5/11/2007
0.188Q	7/18/2007	7/25/2007	7/27/2007	8/10/2007
0.188Q	10/17/2007	10/24/2007	10/26/2007	11/9/2007
0.19Q	1/16/2008	1/23/2008	1/25/2008	2/8/2008

Indicated Div: $0.76

Valuation Analysis

		Institutional Holding	
Forecast P/E	12.66	No of Institutions	
	(1/10/2007)	247	
Market Cap	$1.5 Billion	Shares	
Book Value	2.3 Billion	76,390,272	
Price/Book	0.67	% Held	
Price/Sales	0.87	49.99	

TRADING VOLUME (thousand shares)

Business Summary: Commercial Banking (MIC: 8.1 SIC: 6022 NAIC: 522110)

Colonial BancGroup is a bank holding company. Through its subsidiary, Colonial Bank, Co. conducts a general commercial banking business and provides various demand, savings and time deposit products as well as extensions of credit via personal, commercial and mortgage loans. Co. also provides treasury management services, electronic banking services and credit card and merchant services. Further, Co., through its Colonial Brokerage, Inc. subsidiary, provides full service and discount brokerage services and investment advice. As of Dec 31 2007, Co. had total assets of $25.98 billion and total deposits of $18.54 billion.

Recent Developments: For the year ended Dec 31 2007, net income decreased 31.9% to US$180.9 million from US$265.8 million in the prior year. Net interest income increased 0.8% to US$761.4 million from US$755.3 million in the prior year. Provision for loan losses was US$106.5 million versus US$22.1 million in the prior year, an increase of 380.8%. Non-interest income fell 1.6% to US$186.2 million from US$189.2 million, while non-interest expense advanced 7.7% to US$559.7 million.

Prospects: Co.'s outlook appears challenging, reflecting the compression in net interest margin primarily as a result of increased funding costs arising from increased deposit pricing and a shift in deposits towards higher rate certificates of deposit from no to low cost products, as well as a significant increase in loan loss provision due to the weakening economic conditions. However, Co. believes that by increasing its loan loss reserves, it should be well-positioned to handle the continued weakness in the housing sector. Meanwhile, Co. continues to focus on growing deposits throughout its market areas and monitor possible acquisitions of strong banks operating in high growth markets.

Financial Data

(US$ in Thousands)	12/31/2007	12/31/2006	12/31/2005	12/31/2004	12/31/2003	12/31/2002	12/31/2001	12/31/2000
Earnings Per Share	1.17	1.72	1.52	1.33	1.20	1.16	1.06	1.01
Cash Flow Per Share	1.46	(0.74)	(1.26)	(0.33)	1.32	(1.43)	1.13	3.76
Tang Book Value Per Share	7.63	9.05	8.02	7.47	7.06	6.58	6.52	6.19
Dividends Per Share	0.750	0.680	0.610	0.580	0.560	0.520	0.480	0.440
Dividend Payout %	64.10	39.53	40.13	43.61	46.67	44.83	45.28	43.56
Income Statement								
Interest Income	1,556,485	1,455,585	1,162,055	848,017	780,808	783,431	902,167	897,761
Interest Expense	795,111	700,318	452,833	263,501	274,165	322,261	480,238	507,870
Net Interest Income	761,374	755,267	709,222	584,516	506,643	461,170	421,929	389,891
Provision for Losses	106,450	22,142	26,838	26,994	37,378	35,980	39,573	29,680
Non-Interest Income	186,224	189,222	175,976	138,027	127,449	102,332	93,709	75,299
Non-Interest Expense	559,678	519,601	515,255	429,870	369,551	312,779	284,168	249,982
Income Before Taxes	268,486	402,746	343,105	265,679	227,163	214,743	191,897	185,528
Income Taxes	87,561	136,933	114,603	90,331	77,236	73,872	69,181	67,732
Net Income	180,925	265,813	228,502	175,348	149,927	140,025	122,103	112,731
Average Shares	154,391	154,810	150,790	132,315	125,289	120,648	115,881	111,472
Balance Sheet								
Net Loans & Leases	17,228,555	16,778,039	15,826,705	13,387,505	11,828,670	11,904,266	10,280,918	9,319,471
Total Assets	25,975,989	22,784,249	21,426,197	18,897,150	16,273,302	15,822,355	13,185,103	11,727,637
Total Deposits	18,544,267	16,091,054	15,483,449	11,646,612	9,768,592	9,319,735	8,322,979	8,143,017
Total Liabilities	23,409,360	20,726,914	19,493,506	17,503,535	15,094,997	14,750,919	12,320,329	10,970,785
Stockholders' Equity	2,273,571	2,057,335	1,932,691	1,393,615	1,178,305	1,071,436	864,774	756,852
Shares Outstanding	157,440	152,852	154,242	133,823	126,974	123,700	115,244	110,307
Statistical Record								
Return on Assets %	0.74	1.20	1.13	0.99	0.93	0.97	0.98	1.00
Return on Equity %	8.36	13.32	13.74	13.60	13.33	14.46	15.06	15.48
Net Interest Margin %	48.92	51.89	61.03	68.93	64.89	58.87	46.77	43.43
Efficiency Ratio %	32.12	31.59	38.51	43.60	40.69	35.31	28.53	25.69
Loans to Deposits	0.93	1.04	1.02	1.15	1.21	1.28	1.24	1.14
Price Range	26.69-13.27	26.97-23.53	25.74-19.76	22.45-16.52	17.47-10.75	16.11-11.01	14.98-10.75	11.25-8.31
P/E Ratio	22.81-11.34	15.68-13.68	16.93-13.00	16.88-12.42	14.56-8.96	13.89-9.49	14.13-10.14	11.14-8.23
Average Yield %	3.34	2.72	2.73	3.06	4.03	3.77	3.66	4.54

Address: 100 Colonial Bank Boulevard, Montgomery, AL 36117
Telephone: 334-676-5000
Fax: 334-240-5345

Web Site: www.colonialbank.com
Officers: Robert E. Lowder - Chmn., C.E.O. W. Flake Oakley IV - Pres.

Auditors: PricewaterhouseCoopers LLP
Transfer Agents: SunTrust Bank, Atlanta, GA

COLONIAL PROPERTIES TRUST (AL)

Exchange	Symbol	Price	52Wk Range	Yield	P/E
NYS	CLP	$24.05 (3/31/2008)	50.20-20.00	8.32	3.30

*7 Year Price Score 70.32   *NYSE Composite Index=100   *12 Month Price Score 78.05

Interim Earnings (Per Share)

Qtr.	Mar	Jun	Sep	Dec
2003	0.52	0.15	0.26	0.37
2004	0.50	0.24	0.18	0.54
2005	2.51	0.20	1.04	1.72
2006	0.12	0.62	0.32	2.86
2007	0.69	6.51	0.03	0.05

Interim Dividends (Per Share)

Amt	Decl	Ex	Rec	Pay
8.08E	6/4/2007	6/18/2007	6/14/2007	6/27/2007
0.68Q	7/25/2007	8/2/2007	8/6/2007	8/13/2007
0.50Q	10/24/2007	11/2/2007	11/6/2007	11/13/2007
0.50Q	1/31/2008	2/7/2008	2/11/2008	2/19/2008

Indicated Div: $2.00

Valuation Analysis

		Institutional Holding	
Forecast P/E	10.66	No of Institutions	
	(1/10/2007)	192	
Market Cap	$1.1 Billion	Shares	
Book Value	1.1 Billion	34,086,724	
Price/Book	1.00	% Held	
Price/Sales	2.83	73.67	

Business Summary: Property, Real Estate & Development (MIC: 8.3 SIC: 6798 NAIC: 525930)

Colonial Properties is a self-administered equity real estate investment trust. Co. owns, develops and operates multifamily, office and retail properties in the Sunbelt region of the U.S. Co.'s activities include full or partial ownership of about 200 properties as of Dec 31 2007, located in Alabama, Arizona, California, Florida, Georgia, Maryland, North Carolina, South Carolina, Tennessee, Texas, and Virginia, development of new properties, acquisition of existing properties, build-to-suit development, and the provision of management, leasing, and brokerage services for commercial real estate. Co. is the general partner of, and holds about 82.5% of the interests in Colonial Realty L.P.

Recent Developments: For the year ended Dec 31 2007, net income increased 74.9% to US$355.9 million from US$203.5 million in the prior year. Revenues were US$401.5 million, down 9.8% from US$445.4 million the year before. Revenues from property income fell 12.0% to US$352.0 million from US$399.8 million in the corresponding earlier year.

Prospects: For the full year of 2008, Co. is projecting earnings to be in the range of $1.20 to $1.50 per diluted share, while Funds From Operations are forecasted to range from $2.15 to $2.25 per diluted share. In addition, Co. is targeting multifamily same-property growth in net operating income in the range of 3.5% to 4.5%. Similarly, Co. is anticipating development spending of $350.0 million to $400.0 million, while total dispositions are estimated to range from $450.0 million to $500.0 million. Specifically, Co.'s expectations reflect reduced development spending across all property types, increased dispositions of multifamily assets and lower corporate general and administrative costs.

Financial Data

(US$ in Thousands)	12/31/2007	12/31/2006	12/31/2005	12/31/2004	12/31/2003	12/31/2002	12/31/2001	12/31/2000
Earnings Per Share	7.28	3.92	5.13	1.45	1.29	2.58	2.02	1.82
Cash Flow Per Share	2.14	3.78	4.05	4.98	5.52	6.41	6.57	4.96
Tang Book Value Per Share	24.16	32.22	32.76	21.92	22.80	23.53	24.19	21.88
Dividends Per Share	13.290	2.720	2.700	2.680	2.660	2.640	2.520	2.400
Dividend Payout %	182.55	69.39	52.63	184.83	206.20	102.33	124.75	131.87
Income Statement								
Property Income	351,972	446,502	451,515	309,151	308,001	303,764	293,837	283,587
Non-Property Income	49,545	49,581	43,928	28,259	26,241	26,102	22,488	18,723
Total Revenue	401,517	496,083	495,443	337,410	334,242	329,866	316,325	302,310
Interest Expense	90,390	126,640	130,636	78,933	66,666	65,265	71,397	71,855
Income Taxes	(15,831)	...	6,343	...	...	...	15	...
Net Income	355,901	203,480	219,641	54,618	52,265	73,377	55,609	49,390
Average Shares	47,009	46,020	38,462	27,462	25,232	22,408	20,792	21,249
Balance Sheet								
Total Assets	3,229,830	4,431,777	4,499,258	2,801,343	2,194,927	2,129,856	2,014,623	1,944,099
Long-Term Obligations	1,641,839	2,397,906	2,494,350	1,855,787	1,267,865	1,262,193	1,191,791	1,179,095
Total Liabilities	1,769,502	2,548,666	2,633,211	1,930,335	1,323,140	1,317,759	1,245,537	1,209,859
Stockholders' Equity	1,140,785	1,486,568	1,474,714	605,026	601,733	537,803	507,435	453,826
Shares Outstanding	47,216	46,144	45,014	27,599	26,394	22,850	20,976	20,742
Statistical Record								
Return on Assets %	9.29	4.56	6.02	2.18	2.42	3.54	2.81	2.60
Return on Equity %	27.09	13.74	21.12	9.03	9.17	14.04	11.57	10.44
Net Margin %	88.64	41.02	44.33	16.19	15.64	22.24	17.58	16.40
Price Range	50.20-21.35	51.69-43.22	47.90-35.55	42.44-33.93	40.31-30.77	38.95-31.15	31.60-25.20	28.63-22.69
P/E Ratio	6.90-2.93	13.19-11.03	9.34-6.93	29.27-23.40	31.25-23.85	15.10-12.07	15.64-12.48	15.73-12.47
Average Yield %	33.91	5.70	6.57	6.85	7.59	7.64	8.68	9.36

Address: 2101 Sixth Avenue North, Suite 750, Birmingham, AL 35203 Telephone: 205-250-8700 Fax: 205-250-8890	Web Site: www.colonialprop.com Officers: Thomas H. Lowder - Chmn., Pres., C.E.O. John P. Rigrish - Exec. V.P., Chief Admin. Officer	Auditors: PricewaterhouseCoopers LLP Transfer Agents: ComputerShare Investor Services, Providence, RI

COMERICA, INC.

Exchange	Symbol	Price	52Wk Range	Yield	P/E	Div Acheiver
NYS	CMA	$35.08 (3/31/2008)	63.72-35.06	7.53	7.92	24 Years

*7 Year Price Score 74.54 *NYSE Composite Index=100 *12 Month Price Score 82.96

Interim Earnings (Per Share)

Qtr.	Mar	Jun	Sep	Dec
2003	1.00	0.97	0.89	0.89
2004	0.92	1.10	1.13	1.21
2005	1.16	1.28	1.41	1.26
2006	1.18	1.22	1.23	1.85
2007	1.19	1.25	1.18	0.80

Interim Dividends (Per Share)

Amt	Decl	Ex	Rec	Pay
0.64Q	5/15/2007	6/13/2007	6/15/2007	7/1/2007
0.64Q	7/24/2007	9/12/2007	9/15/2007	10/1/2007
0.64Q	11/13/2007	12/12/2007	12/15/2007	1/1/2008
0.66Q	1/22/2008	3/12/2008	3/15/2008	4/1/2008

Indicated Div: $2.64 (Div. Reinv. Plan)

Valuation Analysis / **Institutional Holding**

Forecast P/E	11.24	No of Institutions
	(1/10/2007)	387
Market Cap	$5.3 Billion	Shares
Book Value	5.1 Billion	109,395,424
Price/Book	1.03	% Held
Price/Sales	1.14	69.39

TRADING VOLUME (thousand shares)

Business Summary: Commercial Banking (MIC: 8.1 SIC: 6021 NAIC: 522110)

Comerica is a financial holding company with total assets of approximately $62.33 billion and total deposits of approximately $44.28 billion as of Dec 31 2007. Co. delivers financial services in its four primary geographic markets: Midwest, consisting of Michigan, Ohio and Illinois; Western, consisting of the states of California, Arizona, Nevada, Colorado and Washington; Texas and Florida. Through its subsidiaries, Co. has aligned its operations into three major lines of business: The Business Bank, The Retail Bank, and Wealth & Institutional Management. In addition to the three major lines of business, the Finance Division is also reported as a segment.

Recent Developments: For the year ended Dec 31 2007, income from continuing operations decreased 12.8% to US$682.0 million from US$782.0 million a year earlier. Net income decreased 23.2% to US$686.0 million from US$893.0 million in the prior year. Net interest income increased 1.0% to US$2.00 billion from US$1.98 billion in the prior year. Provision for loan losses was US$212.0 million versus US$37.0 million in the prior year, an increase of 473.0%. Non-interest income rose 3.9% to US$888.0 million from US$855.0 million, while non-interest expense advanced 1.0% to US$1.69 billion.

Prospects: For the full year of 2008, Co. is projecting average loan growth to grow in the mid to high single-digit range, excluding Financial Services Division (FSD) loans, with flat growth in the Midwest market, high single-digit growth in the Western market and low double-digit growth in the Texas market. In addition, Co. is forecasting average earning asset growth in excess of average loan growth, while average FSD non interest-bearing deposits are estimated to range from $1.20 billion to $1.40 billion. Furthermore, Co. is targeting net interest margin to be in the range of 3.20% and 3.25%, based on a 50 basis point Federal Reserve rate cut in January 2008 and a 25 basis point cut in March 2008.

Financial Data

(US$ in Thousands)	12/31/2007	12/31/2006	12/31/2005	12/31/2004	12/31/2003	12/31/2002	12/31/2001	12/31/2000
Earnings Per Share	4.43	5.49	5.11	4.36	3.75	3.40	3.88	4.63
Cash Flow Per Share	6.63	6.09	5.07	5.96	7.55	7.02	5.63	5.07
Tang Book Value Per Share	34.12	32.70	31.11	29.95	29.20	28.30	27.15	23.94
Dividends Per Share	2.560	2.360	2.200	2.080	2.000	1.920	1.760	1.600
Dividend Payout %	57.79	42.99	43.05	47.71	53.33	56.47	45.36	34.56
Income Statement								
Interest Income	3,730,000	3,422,000	2,726,000	2,237,000	2,412,000	2,797,000	3,393,547	3,261,636
Interest Expense	1,727,000	1,439,000	770,000	427,000	486,000	665,000	1,291,209	1,602,785
Net Interest Income	2,003,000	1,983,000	1,956,000	1,810,000	1,926,000	2,132,000	2,102,338	1,658,851
Provision for Losses	212,000	37,000	(47,000)	64,000	377,000	635,000	236,000	145,000
Non-Interest Income	888,000	855,000	942,000	857,000	887,000	900,000	803,332	825,890
Non-Interest Expense	1,691,000	1,674,000	1,666,000	1,493,000	1,483,000	1,515,000	1,559,033	1,188,370
Income Before Taxes	988,000	1,127,000	1,279,000	1,110,000	953,000	882,000	1,110,637	1,151,371
Income Taxes	306,000	345,000	418,000	353,000	292,000	281,000	401,059	402,045
Net Income	686,000	893,000	861,000	757,000	661,000	601,000	709,578	749,326
Average Shares	155,000	162,000	169,000	174,000	176,000	177,000	177,665	156,398
Balance Sheet								
Net Loans & Leases	50,186,000	46,938,000	42,731,000	40,170,000	39,499,000	41,490,000	40,541,248	35,522,235
Total Assets	62,331,000	58,001,000	53,013,000	51,766,000	52,592,000	53,301,000	50,731,973	41,985,185
Total Deposits	44,278,000	44,927,000	42,431,000	40,936,000	41,463,000	41,775,000	37,570,379	27,168,012
Total Liabilities	57,214,000	52,848,000	47,945,000	46,661,000	47,482,000	48,354,000	45,924,509	37,977,919
Stockholders' Equity	5,117,000	5,153,000	5,068,000	5,105,000	5,110,000	4,947,000	4,807,464	4,007,266
Shares Outstanding	149,988	157,574	162,900	170,475	175,000	174,775	177,074	156,943
Statistical Record								
Return on Assets %	1.14	1.61	1.64	1.45	1.25	1.16	1.53	1.85
Return on Equity %	13.36	17.47	16.93	14.78	13.15	12.32	16.10	19.98
Net Interest Margin %	53.70	57.95	71.75	80.91	79.85	76.22	61.95	50.86
Efficiency Ratio %	36.62	39.14	45.42	48.25	44.95	40.98	37.15	29.07
Loans to Deposits	1.13	1.04	1.01	0.98	0.95	0.99	1.08	1.31
Price Range	63.72-40.89	60.07-50.70	63.21-53.46	63.46-51.02	56.31-37.61	65.30-35.53	64.95-44.66	60.31-33.81
P/E Ratio	14.38-9.23	10.94-9.23	12.37-10.46	14.56-11.70	15.02-10.03	19.21-10.45	16.74-11.51	13.03-7.30
Average Yield %	4.58	4.16	3.79	3.62	4.33	3.47	3.11	3.29

Address: Comerica Tower at Detroit Center, 500 Woodward Avenue, MC 3391, Detroit, MI 48226
Telephone: 313-222-9743
Fax: 313-222-6091

Web Site: www.comerica.com
Officers: Ralph W. Babb Jr. - Chmn., Pres., C.E.O. Elizabeth S. Acton - Exec. V.P., C.F.O.

Auditors: ERNST & YOUNG LLP
Investor Contact: 313-222-2840
Transfer Agents: Wells Fargo Shareowner Services, South St. Paul, MN

COMMERCE GROUP INC (MA)

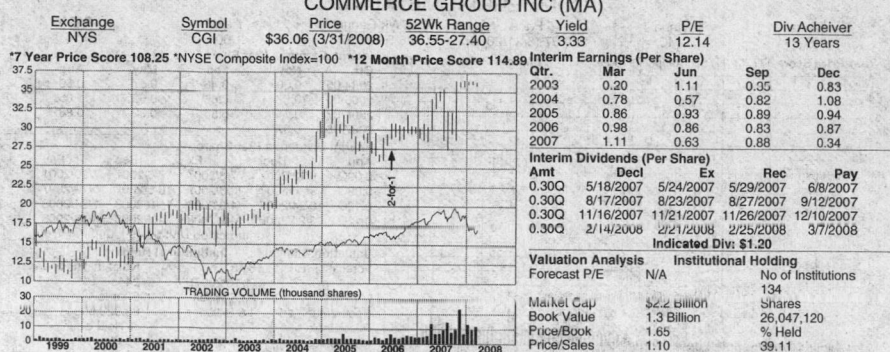

Exchange	Symbol	Price	52Wk Range	Yield	P/E	Div Acheiver
NYS	CGI	$36.06 (3/31/2008)	36.55-27.40	3.33	12.14	13 Years

*7 Year Price Score 108.25 *NYSE Composite Index=100 *12 Month Price Score 114.89

Interim Earnings (Per Share)

Qtr.	Mar	Jun	Sep	Dec
2003	0.20	1.11	0.35	0.83
2004	0.78	0.57	0.82	1.08
2005	0.86	0.93	0.89	0.94
2006	0.98	0.86	0.83	0.87
2007	1.11	0.63	0.88	0.34

Interim Dividends (Per Share)

Amt	Decl	Ex	Rec	Pay
0.30Q	5/18/2007	5/24/2007	5/29/2007	6/8/2007
0.30Q	8/17/2007	8/23/2007	8/27/2007	9/12/2007
0.30Q	11/16/2007	11/21/2007	11/26/2007	12/10/2007
0.30Q	2/14/2008	2/21/2008	2/25/2008	3/7/2008

Indicated Div: $1.20

Valuation Analysis

Forecast P/E	N/A
Market Cap	$2.2 Billion
Book Value	1.3 Billion
Price/Book	1.65
Price/Sales	1.10

Institutional Holding

No of Institutions	134
Shares	26,047,120
% Held	39.11

TRADING VOLUME (thousand shares)

Business Summary: Insurance (MIC: 8.2 SIC: 6331 NAIC: 524126)

Commerce Group provides personal and commercial property and casualty insurance primarily in Massachusetts, and in other states. Co.'s core product lines are personal automobile, homeowners, and commercial automobile insurance. Co. markets its products mainly through its network of independent agents in all states, except California and New York, where it uses agents and brokers. Co. writes insurance through its principal subsidiary, The Commerce Insurance Company. Co. also writes insurance through four other subsidiaries: Citation Insurance Company, Commerce West Insurance Company, American Commerce Insurance Company, and State-Wide Insurance Company.

Recent Developments: For the year ended Dec 31 2007, net income decreased 21.0% to US$190.9 million from US$241.5 million in the prior year. Revenues were US$1.98 billion, up 1.7% from US$1.95 billion the year before. Net premiums earned were US$1.82 billion versus US$1.76 billion in the prior year, an increase of 3.2%. Net investment income rose 11.3% to US$159.8 million from US$143.6 million a year ago.

Prospects: Co.'s results are being restrained by losses in net realized investment as a result of severe credit market declines, mainly in its preferred stock segment. In addition, Co. is seeing a decline in direct premiums written in its Massachusetts segment, primarily due to declines in its personal and commercial automobile business. Meanwhile, Co. is progressing on its agreement with MAPFRE, S.A. that provides for the acquisition of Co. by MAPFRE, which is expected to close late in the first quarter of 2008 or early in the second quarter of 2008, subject to the receipt of approvals in Massachusetts, as well as California, New York and Ohio, and to the approval of other standard conditions.

Financial Data
(US$ in Thousands)

	12/31/2007	12/31/2006	12/31/2005	12/31/2004	12/31/2003	12/31/2002	12/31/2001	12/31/2000
Earnings Per Share	2.97	3.55	3.61	3.25	2.50	0.71	1.38	1.94
Cash Flow Per Share	3.21	5.08	4.64	4.93	4.06	3.47	1.58	2.16
Tang Book Value Per Share	21.87	22.53	19.39	16.73	14.20	12.27	12.22	11.54
Dividends Per Share	1.200	0.975	0.735	0.655	0.635	0.615	0.595	0.575
Dividend Payout %	40.40	27.46	20.39	20.12	25.45	86.62	43.27	29.72
Income Statement								
Premium Income	1,816,967	1,760,700	1,709,924	1,638,833	1,445,628	1,210,040	1,043,652	954,483
Total Revenue	1,982,447	1,949,469	1,884,381	1,806,571	1,640,822	1,257,119	1,153,838	1,099,480
Benefits & Claims	1,171,431	1,068,414	1,050,186	1,044,840	1,070,147	909,769	777,543	686,157
Income Before Taxes	267,730	346,420	352,603	304,186	219,305	52,026	115,425	170,066
Income Taxes	75,275	103,994	107,768	89,003	58,068	17,063	23,194	38,306
Net Income	190,903	241,535	243,912	214,431	160,943	46,755	93,094	132,080
Average Shares	64,280	68,012	67,695	65,905	64,509	66,056	67,589	68,242
Balance Sheet								
Total Assets	3,914,687	4,110,869	3,927,010	3,610,396	3,164,231	2,382,688	2,140,082	2,075,614
Total Liabilities	2,583,700	2,600,639	2,615,984	2,489,114	2,247,630	1,588,530	1,327,808	1,292,665
Stockholders' Equity	1,316,924	1,503,271	1,305,069	1,116,156	912,211	790,052	812,274	781,881
Shares Outstanding	60,224	66,727	67,306	66,645	64,121	64,232	66,260	67,506
Statistical Record								
Return on Assets %	4.76	6.01	6.47	6.31	5.80	2.07	4.42	6.67
Return on Equity %	13.54	17.20	20.15	21.09	18.91	5.84	11.68	18.44
Loss Ratio %	64.47	60.68	61.42	63.76	74.03	75.19	74.50	71.89
Net Margin %	9.63	12.39	12.94	11.87	9.81	3.72	8.07	12.01
Price Range	36.55-27.40	32.00-25.86	34.85-26.79	31.06-19.70	20.47-16.15	21.02-14.74	20.02-12.32	15.41-11.63
P/E Ratio	12.31-9.23	9.01-7.29	9.65-7.42	9.56-6.06	8.19-6.46	29.61-20.76	14.51-8.92	7.94-5.99
Average Yield %	3.73	3.37	2.43	2.69	3.40	3.31	3.46	4.24

Address: 211 Main Street, Webster, MA 01570 Telephone: 508-943-9000	Web Site: www.commerceinsurance.com Officers: Arthur J. Remillard Jr. - Chmn., Pres., C.E.O. Gerald Fels - Exec. V.P., C.F.O.	Auditors: PricewaterhouseCoopers LLP Transfer Agents: EquiServe Trust Company N.A., Kansas City, MO

COMMERCIAL METALS CO.

Exchange	Symbol	Price	52Wk Range	Yield	P/E
NYS	CMC	$29.97 (3/31/2008)	36.59-23.57	1.60	10.74

*7 Year Price Score 177.73 *NYSE Composite Index=100* ***12 Month Price Score 102.87**

Interim Earnings (Per Share)

Qtr.	Nov	Feb	May	Aug
2004-05	0.60	0.46	0.57	0.69
2005-06	0.57	0.65	0.62	1.05
2006-07	0.71	0.54	0.82	0.86
2007-08	0.57	...	...	...

Interim Dividends (Per Share)

Amt	Decl	Ex	Rec	Pay
0.09Q	6/18/2007	7/3/2007	7/6/2007	7/20/2007
0.09Q	9/20/2007	10/3/2007	10/5/2007	10/19/2007
0.12Q	10/24/2007	1/8/2008	1/10/2008	1/24/2008
0.12Q	3/24/2008	4/2/2008	4/4/2008	4/18/2008

Indicated Div: $0.48

Valuation Analysis

Forecast P/E	8.43 (1/10/2007)	
Market Cap	$3.5 Billion	
Book Value	1.6 Billion	
Price/Book	2.19	
Price/Sales	0.41	

Institutional Holding

No of Institutions	244
Shares	85,923,608
% Held	72.69

TRADING VOLUME (thousand shares)

Business Summary: Metal Works (MIC: 11.3 SIC: 3312 NAIC: 331111)

Commercial Metals is engaged in manufacturing, recycling, marketing and distributing steel and metal products and related materials and services through a network of locations located throughout the U.S. and internationally. As of Aug 31 2007, Co. had five business segments: domestic mills, a network of steel mills; CMCZ, a Swiss steel mill subsidiary; domestic fabrication, operating steel reinforcing bar fabrication and construction-related product sales facilities; recycling, processing secondary metals for use as a raw material by manufacturers; and marketing and distribution, buying and selling primary and secondary metals, fabricated metals and other industrial products.

Recent Developments: For the quarter ended Nov 30 2007, income from continuing operations decreased 28.4% to US$65.0 million from US$90.7 million in the year-earlier quarter. Net income decreased 19.0% to US$69.2 million from US$85.4 million in the year-earlier quarter. Revenues were US$2.12 billion, up 11.8% from US$1.89 billion the year before. Direct operating expenses rose 15.6% to US$1.86 billion from US$1.61 billion in the comparable period the year before. Indirect operating expenses increased 16.5% to US$162.4 million from US$139.5 million in the equivalent prior-year period.

Prospects: For the quarter ending Feb 2008, Co.'s recycling business should benefit from higher ferrous scrap prices, while increasing ferrous scrap prices will likely cause a temporary margin squeeze in its nonferrous scrap business in the U.S. Co. also anticipates its business to be driven by the continued robust nonresidential construction activity in the U.S. and globally. Also, Co. believes higher international steel prices should continue to be sustainable due to China's recent significant reduction in steel exports. However, Co.'s fabrication shipments in the U.S. are likely to slow due to seasonal factors and there will likely be a subsequent margin squeeze due to rising steel prices.

Financial Data

(US$ in Thousands)	3 Mos	08/30/2007	08/31/2006	08/31/2005	08/31/2004	08/31/2003	08/31/2002	08/31/2001
Earnings Per Share	2.79	2.92	2.89	2.31	1.11	0.17	0.36	0.23
Cash Flow Per Share	3.20	3.92	1.98	1.70	0.43	0.14	0.88	1.85
Tang Book Value Per Share	13.35	12.74	10.05	7.47	5.38	4.53	4.39	4.16
Dividends Per Share	0.360	0.330	0.170	0.115	0.085	0.080	0.069	0.065
Dividend Payout %	12.90	11.30	5.88	4.97	7.69	48.48	19.23	28.11
Income Statement								
Total Revenue	2,116,004	8,329,016	7,555,924	6,592,697	4,768,327	2,875,885	2,479,926	2,441,216
EBITDA	129,722	648,188	639,871	519,643	282,991	91,597	124,717	106,572
Depn & Amortn	31,522	...	...	...	...	...	...	...
Income Before Taxes	98,200	540,883	554,493	443,033	211,947	30,394	63,138	39,300
Income Taxes	33,357	172,769	187,937	157,996	65,055	11,490	22,613	14,960
Net Income	69,164	355,431	356,347	285,781	132,021	18,904	40,525	24,340
Average Shares	120,372	121,681	123,459	123,380	119,377	114,422	113,101	105,283
Balance Sheet								
Current Assets	2,403,880	2,458,852	2,144,792	1,700,917	1,424,232	844,417	794,152	642,177
Total Assets	3,560,969	3,472,663	2,898,868	2,332,922	1,988,046	1,275,406	1,230,076	1,084,800
Current Liabilities	1,085,222	1,072,589	1,182,305	891,942	783,477	444,991	415,147	349,942
Long-Term Obligations	707,624	706,817	322,086	386,741	393,368	254,997	255,969	251,638
Total Liabilities	1,958,451	1,921,196	1,617,730	1,382,939	1,327,419	768,473	728,770	649,327
Stockholders' Equity	1,599,254	1,548,567	1,220,104	899,561	660,627	506,933	501,306	435,473
Shares Outstanding	116,921	118,566	117,881	116,261	117,111	111,978	114,073	104,628
Statistical Record								
Return on Assets %	10.58	11.19	13.62	13.23	8.07	1.51	3.50	2.16
Return on Equity %	23.25	25.75	33.62	36.63	22.55	3.75	8.65	5.69
EBITDA Margin %	6.13	7.78	8.47	7.88	5.93	3.19	5.03	4.37
Net Margin %	3.27	4.27	4.72	4.33	2.77	0.66	1.63	1.00
Asset Turnover	2.64	2.62	2.89	3.05	2.91	2.30	2.14	2.16
Current Ratio	2.22	2.29	1.81	1.91	1.82	1.90	1.91	1.84
Debt to Equity	0.44	0.46	0.26	0.43	0.60	0.50	0.51	0.58
Price Range	36.59-25.01	36.59-19.09	31.16-13.80	18.38-8.36	9.18-4.54	4.95-3.20	6.15-3.13	4.07-2.60
P/E Ratio	13.11-8.96	12.53-6.54	10.78-4.78	7.96-3.62	8.27-4.09	29.12-18.82	17.08-8.68	17.71-11.31
Average Yield %	1.17	1.04	0.79	0.90	1.20	1.94	1.47	1.98

Address: 6565 MacArthur Blvd, Suite 800, Irving, TX 75039 **Telephone:** 214-689-4300 **Fax:** 214-689-5886	**Web Site:** www.commercialmetals.com **Officers:** Stanley A. Rabin - Chmn., Pres., C.E.O. A. Leo Howell - V.P.	**Auditors:** Deloitte & Touche LLP **Transfer Agents:** Mellon Investor Services, LLC, Ridgefield Park, NJ

COMMSCOPE, INC.

Exchange	Symbol	Price	52Wk Range	Yield	P/E
NYS	CTV	$34.83 (3/31/2008)	63.41-34.63	N/A	12.53

*7 Year Price Score 168.19 *NYSE Composite Index=100 *12 Month Price Score 89.40

TRADING VOLUME (thousand shares)

Interim Earnings (Per Share)

Qtr.	Mar	Jun	Sep	Dec
2003	(0.05)	(0.87)	0.02	(0.29)
2004	(0.27)	1.37	0.27	(0.23)
2005	0.09	0.25	0.18	0.26
2006	0.19	0.65	0.61	0.38
2007	0.63	0.83	0.81	0.51

Interim Dividends (Per Share)

No Dividends Paid

Valuation Analysis   **Institutional Holding**

Forecast P/E	N/A	No of Institutions
		243
Market Cap	$2.3 Billion	Shares
Book Value	1.3 Billion	65,673,740
Price/Book	1.82	% Held
Price/Sales	1.21	N/A

Business Summary: Communications (MIC: 10.1 SIC: 3663 NAIC: 334220)

Commscope provides infrastructure applications for communications networks. Co., through Andrew Corporation, provides radio frequency subsystem applications for wireless networks. In addition, through its SYSTIMAX® and Uniprise® brands, Co. provides structured cabling systems for business enterprise applications. Co. also manufactures coaxial cable for broadband cable television networks and provides cabinets for digital subscriber line and Fiber-to-the-Node applications. Co. sells its products directly to end-user customers and to original equipment manufacturers as well as through a global network of distributors, system integrators and resellers.

Recent Developments: For the year ended Dec 31 2007, net income increased 57.4% to US$204.8 million from US$130.1 million in the prior year. Revenues were US$1.93 billion, up 18.9% from US$1.62 billion the year before. Operating income was US$286.5 million versus US$158.6 million in the prior year, an increase of 80.7%. Direct operating expenses rose 13.7% to US$1.34 billion from US$1.18 billion in the comparable period the year before. Indirect operating expenses increased 6.0% to US$302.5 million from US$285.5 million in the equivalent prior-year period.

Prospects: On Dec 27 2007, Co. acquired Andrew Corp. for approximately $2.65 billion. Notably, Co. expects the acquisition to expand its global service model and provide an opportunity to build upon complementary global product offerings. Meanwhile, Co. expects operating income to increase in 2008 primarily due to the increase in sales as a result of the Andrew acquisition and higher sales volumes and shifts in the mix of products sold to higher margin products in its legacy business. Specifically, Co. is targeting revenue to be in a range of $4.10 billion to $4.30 billion for 2008. However, Co. noted that volatile raw materials costs could have an adverse effect on operating margins.

Financial Data

(US$ in Thousands)	12/31/2007	12/31/2006	12/31/2005	12/31/2004	12/31/2003	12/31/2002	12/31/2001	12/31/2000
Earnings Per Share	2.78	1.84	0.78	1.15	(1.19)	(1.10)	0.52	1.60
Cash Flow Per Share	3.91	2.03	1.57	1.88	1.54	1.70	3.00	0.88
Tang Book Value Per Share	N.M.	8.77	5.39	3.96	5.02	6.03	7.20	3.98
Income Statement								
Total Revenue	1,930,763	1,623,946	1,337,165	1,152,696	373,260	598,467	738,498	950,026
EBITDA	334,694	215,465	134,504	61,225	24,919	21,192	99,729	178,533
Income Before Taxes	299,059	163,695	71,087	(6,308)	(13,989)	(21,288)	55,213	136,880
Income Taxes	94,218	52,187	21,109	(7,019)	(5,174)	(7,858)	20,426	51,993
Net Income	204,841	130,133	49,978	75,755	(70,560)	(67,152)	27,865	84,887
Average Shares	74,674	72,266	67,385	67,685	59,231	61,171	53,500	56,047
Balance Sheet								
Current Assets	2,231,390	807,800	589,262	448,093	330,672	258,459	245,868	289,663
Total Assets	5,106,571	1,302,473	1,102,181	1,030,579	739,781	772,668	889,005	721,182
Current Liabilities	998,221	183,243	176,942	156,673	50,036	44,488	46,743	80,559
Long-Term Obligations	2,348,157	271,100	284,300	297,300	183,300	183,300	191,918	225,316
Total Liabilities	3,826,563	563,369	580,156	581,116	284,075	255,133	282,491	346,662
Stockholders' Equity	1,280,008	739,104	522,025	449,463	455,706	517,535	606,514	374,520
Shares Outstanding	66,870	59,734	55,873	54,487	59,318	59,219	61,688	51,263
Statistical Record								
Return on Assets %	6.39	10.82	4.69	8.53	N.M.	N.M.	3.46	12.99
Return on Equity %	20.29	20.64	10.29	16.69	N.M.	N.M.	5.68	25.81
EBITDA Margin %	17.33	13.27	10.06	5.31	4.35	3.54	13.50	18.79
Net Margin %	10.61	8.01	3.74	6.57	N.M.	N.M.	3.77	8.94
Asset Turnover	0.60	1.35	1.25	1.30	0.76	0.72	0.92	1.45
Current Ratio	2.24	4.41	3.33	2.86	6.61	5.81	5.26	3.60
Debt to Equity	1.83	0.37	0.54	0.66	0.40	0.35	0.32	0.60
Price Range	63.41-28.98	35.61-20.35	20.89-14.01	22.52-15.96	16.80-7.00	23.35-6.12	26.21-15.00	48.00-16.00
P/E Ratio	22.81-10.42	19.35-11.06	26.78-17.96	19.58-13.88	...	...	50.40-28.85	30.00-10.00

Address: 1100 CommScope Place S.E., Hickory, NC 28602 **Telephone:** 828-324-2200 **Fax:** 828-328-3400	**Web Site:** www.commscope.com **Officers:** Frank M. Drendel - Chmn., C.E.O. Brian D. Garrett - Pres., C.O.O.	**Auditors:** Ernst & Young LLP **Transfer Agents:** Mellon Investor Services, LLC, Ridgefield Park, NJ

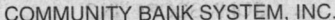

COMMUNITY BANK SYSTEM, INC.

Exchange	Symbol	Price	52Wk Range	Yield	P/E	Div Acheiver
NYS	CBU	$24.56 (3/31/2008)	26.06-17.09	3.42	17.30	16 Years

*7 Year Price Score 81.67 *NYSE Composite Index=100 *12 Month Price Score 121.39

Interim Earnings (Per Share)

Qtr.	Mar	Jun	Sep	Dec
2003	0.38	0.38	0.44	0.30
2004	0.38	0.40	0.45	0.41
2005	0.43	0.46	0.48	0.28
2006	0.31	0.33	0.36	0.26
2007	0.32	0.34	0.37	0.40

Interim Dividends (Per Share)

Amt	Decl	Ex	Rec	Pay
0.20Q	5/18/2007	6/13/2007	6/15/2007	7/10/2007
0.21Q	8/15/2007	9/12/2007	9/14/2007	10/10/2007
0.21Q	11/29/2007	12/12/2007	12/14/2007	1/10/2008
0.21Q	2/4/2008	3/12/2008	3/14/2008	4/10/2008

Indicated Div: $0.84 (Div. Reinv. Plan)

Valuation Analysis

Forecast P/E	N/A
Market Cap	$727.8 Million
Book Value	478.8 Million
Price/Book	1.52
Price/Sales	2.35

Institutional Holding

No of Institutions	104
Shares	14,745,938
% Held	48.90

TRADING VOLUME (thousand shares)

Business Summary: Commercial Banking (MIC: 8.1 SIC: 6021 NAIC: 522110)

Community Bank System is a single bank holding company. As of Dec 31 2007, Co., through its wholly-owned community banking subsidiary, Community Bank, N.A., operated 131 customer facilities throughout 25 counties of Upstate New York and five counties of Northeastern Pennsylvania, providing a range of commercial and retail banking services. In addition, Co., provides administration, consulting and actuarial services to sponsors of employee benefit plans through its subsidiary, Benefit Plans Administrative Services, Inc. As of Dec 31 2007, Co. had total assets of $4.70 billion and total deposits of $3.23 billion.

Recent Developments: For the year ended Dec 31 2007, net income increased 11.8% to US$42.9 million from US$38.4 million in the prior year. Net interest income increased 0.9% to US$136.0 million from US$134.8 million in the prior year. Provision for loan losses was US$2.0 million versus US$6.6 million in the prior year, a decrease of 69.6%. Non-interest income rose 8.1% to US$53.3 million from US$49.3 million, while non-interest expense advanced 11.7% to US$142.1 million.

Prospects: Co. intends to grow its branch network through a disciplined acquisition strategy and certain selective de novo expansions. Co. also plans to build its loan and deposit volume using both organic and acquisition strategies as well as increase its non-interest income through development of banking-related fee income, growth in existing financial services business units, and the acquisition of additional financial services and banking businesses. Also, Co. believes that its ongoing objective of lowering its overall funding costs by reducing higher cost time deposits, and focus on expanding core account relationships, should improve its net interest margin by about 10 basis points in 2008.

Financial Data

(US$ in Thousands)	12/31/2007	12/31/2006	12/31/2005	12/31/2004	12/31/2003	12/31/2002	12/31/2001	12/31/2000
Earnings Per Share	1.42	1.26	1.65	1.64	1.50	1.47	0.81	1.43
Cash Flow Per Share	1.69	2.44	2.39	2.85	2.78	2.24	1.92	1.94
Tang Book Value Per Share	7.51	7.17	7.77	7.90	7.37	7.33	4.87	6.32
Dividends Per Share	0.820	0.780	0.740	0.680	0.610	0.560	0.540	0.520
Dividend Payout %	57.75	61.90	44.85	41.46	40.80	38.23	66.67	36.49
Income Statement								
Interest Income	256,237	231,901	219,194	212,795	191,129	204,870	197,850	145,221
Interest Expense	120,263	97,092	75,572	61,752	59,301	77,020	101,195	74,012
Net Interest Income	135,974	134,809	143,622	151,043	131,828	127,850	96,655	71,208
Provision for Losses	2,004	6,585	8,534	8,750	11,195	12,222	7,097	7,182
Non-Interest Income	53,286	49,276	60,846	44,445	34,981	32,600	29,083	20,989
Non-Interest Expense	142,074	127,203	127,389	119,899	102,461	95,824	89,039	55,989
Income Before Taxes	45,182	50,297	68,545	66,839	53,153	52,404	29,602	29,027
Income Taxes	2,291	11,920	17,740	16,643	12,773	13,887	8,891	8,708
Net Income	42,891	38,377	50,805	50,196	40,380	38,517	19,129	20,319
Average Shares	30,232	30,392	30,838	30,670	27,034	26,334	23,650	14,271
Balance Sheet								
Net Loans & Leases	2,784,628	2,665,245	2,379,236	2,326,715	2,099,414	1,780,574	1,708,969	1,084,112
Total Assets	4,697,502	4,497,797	4,152,734	4,393,831	3,855,397	3,434,204	3,210,833	2,022,635
Total Deposits	3,228,464	3,168,299	2,984,768	2,928,978	2,725,488	2,505,356	2,545,970	1,457,730
Total Liabilities	4,218,718	4,036,269	3,695,139	3,919,203	3,450,569	3,109,166	2,942,853	1,883,260
Stockholders' Equity	478,784	461,528	457,595	474,628	404,828	325,038	267,980	139,376
Shares Outstanding	29,634	30,020	29,956	30,641	28,330	25,957	25,805	13,986
Statistical Record								
Return on Assets %	0.93	0.89	1.19	1.21	1.11	1.16	0.73	1.05
Return on Equity %	9.12	8.35	10.90	11.38	11.07	12.99	9.39	16.35
Net Interest Margin %	53.07	58.13	65.52	70.98	68.97	62.41	48.85	49.03
Efficiency Ratio %	45.90	45.24	45.49	46.61	45.31	40.35	39.24	33.69
Loans to Deposits	0.86	0.84	0.80	0.79	0.77	0.71	0.67	0.74
Price Range	23.61-17.09	24.85-18.90	28.25-21.42	28.35-19.25	25.13-15.55	17.01-13.07	14.82-12.45	13.02-10.13
P/E Ratio	16.63-12.04	19.72-15.00	17.12-12.98	17.29-11.74	16.75-10.37	11.57-8.89	18.30-15.37	9.10-7.08
Average Yield %	4.00	3.57	3.13	2.84	3.07	3.67	3.95	4.55

Address: 5790 Widewaters Parkway, DeWitt, NY 13214-1883 **Telephone:** 315-445-2282 **Fax:** 315-445-7347	**Web Site:** www.communitybankna.com **Officers:** James A. Gabriel - Chmn. Sanford A. Belden - Pres., C.E.O.	**Auditors:** PricewaterhouseCoopers LLP **Investor Contact:** 315-445-7300 **Transfer Agents:** ChaseMellon Shareholder Services, L.L.C., Ridgefield Park, NJ

COMMUNITY HEALTH SYSTEMS, INC.

Exchange	Symbol	Price	52Wk Range	Yield	P/E
NYS	CYH	$33.57 (3/31/2008)	43.04-27.86	N/A	104.91

*7 Year Price Score 92.99 *NYSE Composite Index=100 *12 Month Price Score 99.14

Interim Earnings (Per Share)

Qtr.	Mar	Jun	Sep	Dec
2003	0.33	0.30	0.31	0.35
2004	0.39	0.37	0.32	0.43
2005	0.39	0.43	0.46	0.51
2006	0.55	0.54	0.09	0.56
2007	0.58	0.57	0.11	(0.93)

Interim Dividends (Per Share)

No Dividends Paid

Valuation Analysis		Institutional Holding	
Forecast P/E	N/A	No of Institutions	
		262	
Market Cap	$3.2 Billion	Shares	
Book Value	1.7 Billion	92,276,112	
Price/Book	1.88	% Held	
Price/Sales	0.45	98.10	

Business Summary: Hospitals & Health Care (MIC: 9.3 SIC: 8062 NAIC: 622110)

Community Health Systems owns, leases and operates acute care hospitals that are the principal providers of primary healthcare services in non-urban communities in the U.S. Co. provides range of general hospital healthcare services to patients in the communities in which it is located. Services provided by Co.'s hospitals include emergency room services, general surgery, critical care, internal medicine, obstetrics and diagnostic services. Co. also owns physician practices, imaging centers, home health agencies and ambulatory surgery centers. At Dec 31 2007, Co. owned, leased or operated 115 hospitals, geographically diversified across 27 states, with an aggregate of 16,971 licensed beds.

Recent Developments: For the year ended Dec 31 2007, income from continuing operations decreased 66.3% to US$59.9 million from US$177.7 million a year earlier. Net income decreased 82.0% to US$30.3 million from US$168.3 million in the prior year. Revenues were US$7.13 billion, up 70.5% from US$4.18 billion the year before. Operating income was US$485.7 million versus US$385.1 million in the prior year, an increase of 26.1%. Indirect operating expenses increased 75.0% to US$6.64 billion from US$3.80 billion in the equivalent prior-year period.

Prospects: On Feb 29 2008, Co. announced the sale of nine hospitals to Capella Healthcare, Inc., a privately held, for-profit hospital company in Tennessee for $315.0 million. Meanwhile, for full-year 2008, Co. expects net operating revenues of $11.00 billion to $11.30 billion and income from continuing operations per diluted share of $2.25 to $2.45. Also, Co. plans to spend about $775.0 million to $800.0 million in 2008, including about $635.0 million to $650.0 million for renovation, equipment purchases and Information Technology conversion costs related with the former Triad hospitals, and about $140.0 million to $150.0 million for construction and equipment cost of the replacement hospitals.

Financial Data

(US$ in Thousands)	12/31/2007	12/31/2006	12/31/2005	12/31/2004	12/31/2003	12/31/2002	12/31/2001	12/31/2000
Earnings Per Share	0.32	1.75	1.79	1.51	1.30	1.00	0.50	0.14
Cash Flow Per Share	7.35	3.69	4.64	3.40	2.48	2.90	1.75	0.34
Tang Book Value Per Share	N.M.	4.12	3.26	0.30	1.97	1.87	1.17	N.M.
Income Statement								
Total Revenue	7,127,494	4,365,576	3,738,320	3,332,641	2,834,624	2,200,417	1,693,625	1,337,501
EBITDA	800,013	569,231	571,695	496,459	434,536	359,728	308,711	252,736
Income Before Taxes	102,900	278,161	310,920	260,223	219,678	178,650	94,495	27,742
Income Taxes	43,003	106,682	120,782	102,002	88,206	73,392	45,944	18,173
Net Income	30,289	168,263	167,544	151,433	131,472	99,984	44,743	9,569
Average Shares	94,642	96,332	98,579	105,863	108,094	108,378	90,251	69,187
Balance Sheet								
Current Assets	2,557,898	1,021,384	914,209	815,449	696,080	647,726	494,559	408,577
Total Assets	13,493,643	4,506,579	3,934,218	3,632,608	3,350,211	2,809,496	2,460,664	2,213,837
Current Liabilities	1,447,935	575,283	437,403	362,359	398,064	318,430	299,572	240,873
Long-Term Obligations	9,077,367	1,905,781	1,648,500	1,804,868	1,444,981	1,173,929	980,083	1,201,590
Total Liabilities	11,782,839	2,782,906	2,369,641	2,392,617	1,999,622	1,595,191	1,344,999	1,457,663
Stockholders' Equity	1,710,804	1,723,673	1,564,577	1,239,991	1,350,589	1,214,305	1,115,665	756,174
Shares Outstanding	95,635	94,050	93,564	87,616	98,681	98,829	98,469	86,137
Statistical Record								
Return on Assets %	0.34	3.99	4.43	4.33	4.27	3.79	1.91	0.46
Return on Equity %	1.76	10.23	11.95	11.66	10.25	8.58	4.78	1.94
EBITDA Margin %	11.22	13.04	15.29	14.90	15.33	16.35	18.23	18.90
Net Margin %	0.42	3.85	4.48	4.54	4.64	4.54	2.64	0.72
Asset Turnover	0.79	1.03	0.99	0.95	0.92	0.84	0.72	0.65
Current Ratio	1.76	1.78	2.09	2.25	1.75	2.03	1.65	1.70
Debt to Equity	5.31	1.11	1.05	1.46	1.07	0.97	0.88	1.59
Price Range	43.04-27.86	39.65-32.36	40.69-27.01	30.73-23.40	27.40-16.88	29.90-19.40	34.25-22.00	36.55-13.69
P/E Ratio	134.50-87.06	22.66-18.49	22.73-15.09	20.35-15.50	21.08-12.98	29.90-19.40	68.50-44.00	261.07-97.77

Address: 7100 Commerce Way, Suite 100, Brentwood, TN 37027	Web Site: www.chs.net	Auditors: Deloitte & Touche LLP
Telephone: 615-465-7000	Officers: Wayne T. Smith - Chmn., Pres., C.E.O. W. Larry Cash - Exec. V.P., C.F.O.	Transfer Agents: Mellon Investor Services LLC, Atlanta, GA

COMPUTER SCIENCES CORP.

Exchange	Symbol	Price	52Wk Range	Yield	P/E
NYS	CSC	$40.79 (3/31/2008)	61.79-38.49	N/A	11.96

*7 Year Price Score 92.34   *NYSE Composite Index=100   *12 Month Price Score 88.36

Interim Earnings (Per Share)

Qtr.	Jun	Sep	Dec	Mar
2004-05	0.58	0.68	0.82	2.14
2005-06	0.70	0.53	1.08	1.06
2006-07	(0.29)	0.53	0.65	1.31
2007-08	0.61	0.43	1.05	...

Interim Dividends (Per Share)

No Dividends Paid

Valuation Analysis		Institutional Holding	
Forecast P/E	12.30	No of Institutions	
	(1/10/2007)	378	
Market Cap	$6.7 Billion	Shares	
Book Value	5.6 Billion	155,123,248	
Price/Book	1.20	% Held	
Price/Sales	0.41	89.55	

Business Summary: IT & Technology (MIC: 10.2 SIC: 7373 NAIC: 541512)

Computer Sciences is engaged in providing information technology (IT) and business process outsourcing as well as professional services globally. Co.'s outsourcing services include operating all or a portion of a customer's technology infrastructure, including systems analysis, applications development, network operations, desktop computing and data center management. Co.'s IT and professional services include systems integration, consulting and other professional services. Co. also licenses enhanced software systems for the financial services markets and provides an array of end-to-end e-business applications that address the needs of key commercial and government clients.

Recent Developments: For the quarter ended Dec 28 2007, net income increased 57.7% to US$179.0 million from US$113.5 million in the year-earlier quarter. Revenues were US$4.16 billion, up 14.3% from US$3.64 billion the year before. Direct operating expenses rose 13.8% to US$3.30 billion from US$2.90 billion in the comparable period the year before. Indirect operating expenses increased 11.7% to US$547.3 million from US$489.9 million in the equivalent prior-year period.

Prospects: Co.'s outlook appears positive as it continues to receive new contract awards. For instance, on Feb 11 2008, Co. announced that it has been awarded a contract, valued at an estimated $482.0 million, to provide technical support services for the U.S. Air Force Air Education and Training Command at Vance Air Force Base in Enid, OK. Further, Co. expects its Jan 2008 acquisition of First Consulting Group to increase its healthcare and delivery capabilities, offerings and healthcare presence in the U.S., Europe and Asia. Hence, for the fiscal year ending Mar 2008, Co. is projecting revenue of $16.20 billion to $16.50 billion and earnings, excluding special items, of $3.75 to $3.85 per share.

Financial Data

(US$ in Thousands)	9 Mos	6 Mos	3 Mos	03/30/2007	03/31/2006	04/01/2005	04/02/2004	03/28/2003
Earnings Per Share	3.41	3.01	3.10	2.16	3.38	4.22	2.75	2.54
Cash Flow Per Share	9.26	8.27	7.95	8.98	8.38	10.27	8.81	6.68
Tang Book Value Per Share	2.35	2.76	8.98	10.60	15.15	12.61	7.26	4.39
Income Statement								
Total Revenue	12,015,100	7,855,100	3,837,900	14,856,600	14,615,600	14,058,600	14,767,600	11,346,500
EBITDA	1,589,200	972,200	468,400	1,894,700	2,072,000	2,001,600	1,945,600	1,603,400
Depn & Amortn	878,300	571,200	279,000	...	...	...	...	...
Income Before Taxes	607,600	341,300	169,700	607,000	821,100	715,400	746,900	611,600
Income Taxes	244,700	157,400	61,600	218,200	244,100	219,000	227,500	171,400
Net Income	362,900	183,900	108,100	388,800	634,000	810,200	519,400	440,200
Average Shares	169,793	175,264	177,445	179,733	187,695	191,799	188,700	173,119
Balance Sheet								
Current Assets	6,991,100	6,696,900	7,760,100	6,706,400	6,305,900	5,689,800	4,867,200	4,088,100
Total Assets	15,361,500	15,118,700	14,769,400	13,730,500	12,943,300	12,633,900	11,804,000	10,433,200
Current Liabilities	5,046,400	4,685,200	4,496,200	5,259,600	4,141,100	3,877,900	3,253,200	2,987,200
Long-Term Obligations	2,515,100	2,511,800	2,496,700	1,412,200	1,376,800	1,303,000	2,306,400	2,204,900
Total Liabilities	9,810,300	9,456,700	9,166,900	7,845,600	6,171,400	6,139,200	6,300,300	5,826,800
Stockholders' Equity	5,551,200	5,662,000	5,602,500	5,885,500	6,771,900	6,494,700	5,503,700	4,606,400
Shares Outstanding	163,638	169,394	174,471	173,317	187,250	191,206	187,841	186,757
Statistical Record								
Return on Assets %	4.21	3.84	3.97	2.92	4.97	6.65	4.60	4.64
Return on Equity %	10.14	9.14	9.23	6.16	9.58	13.54	10.11	10.73
EBITDA Margin %	13.23	12.38	12.20	12.75	14.18	14.24	13.17	14.13
Net Margin %	3.02	2.34	2.82	2.62	4.34	5.76	3.52	3.88
Asset Turnover	1.13	1.12	1.09	1.12	1.15	1.15	1.31	1.19
Current Ratio	1.39	1.43	1.73	1.28	1.52	1.47	1.50	1.37
Debt to Equity	0.45	0.44	0.45	0.24	0.20	0.20	0.42	0.48
Price Range	61.79-49.61	61.79-47.69	59.36-46.43	59.80-46.43	58.00-42.87	57.70-39.03	46.68-28.52	50.75-24.56
P/E Ratio	18.12-14.55	20.53-15.84	19.15-14.98	27.69-21.50	17.16-12.68	13.67-9.25	16.97-10.37	19.98-9.67

Address: 2100 East Grand Avenue, El Segundo, CA 90245	Web Site: www.csc.com	Auditors: Deloitte & Touche LLP
Telephone: 310-615-0311	Officers: Van B. Honeycutt - Chmn., C.E.O. Michael W. Laphen - Pres., C.O.O.	Investor Contact: 310-615-1700
Fax: 310-640-2648		Transfer Agents: Mellon Investor Sevices, S.Hackensack, NJ

CON-WAY INC

Exchange	Symbol	Price	52Wk Range	Yield	P/E
NYS	CNW	$49.48 (3/31/2008)	56.96-38.14	0.81	16.28

*7 Year Price Score 95.01   *NYSE Composite Index=100   *12 Month Price Score 107.42

Interim Earnings (Per Share)

Qtr.	Mar	Jun	Sep	Dec
2003	0.30	0.31	0.46	0.49
2004	0.45	0.64	(3.90)	0.57
2005	0.52	1.24	1.18	0.92
2006	0.81	1.30	1.24	1.64
2007	0.65	0.96	0.78	0.64

Interim Dividends (Per Share)

Amt	Decl	Ex	Rec	Pay
0.10Q	4/23/2007	5/11/2007	5/15/2007	6/15/2007
0.10Q	6/26/2007	8/10/2007	8/14/2007	9/14/2007
0.10Q	9/25/2007	11/9/2007	11/14/2007	12/14/2007
0.10Q	1/31/2008	2/12/2008	2/14/2008	3/14/2008

Indicated Div. $0.40

Valuation Analysis | **Institutional Holding**

Forecast P/E	10.90	No of Institutions
	(1/10/2007)	172
Market Cap	$2.2 Billion	Shares
Book Value	909.1 Million	42,486,072
Price/Book	2.46	% Held
Price/Sales	0.51	91.27

Business Summary: Road Transport (MIC: 15.2 SIC: 4213 NAIC: 484122)

Con-Way provide transportation, logistics, and supply chain management services for manufacturing, industrial, and retail customers. Co.'s principal business units operate in regional and transcontinental less-than-truckload and full-truckload freight transportation, truckload brokerage, global logistics management, and trailer manufacturing. As of Dec 31 2007, Co.'s Freight segment operated 340 freight service centers; its Logistics segment operated 64 warehouses in North America and an additional 66 warehouses outside of North America, and owned 278 trucks, tractors, and trailers; while its Truckload business units operated five terminals and owned about 2,600 tractors and 8,100 trailers.

Recent Developments: For the year ended Dec 31 2007, income from continuing operations decreased 43.5% to US$153.8 million from US$272.3 million a year earlier. Net income decreased 42.5% to US$152.9 million from US$266.1 million in the prior year. Revenues were US$4.39 billion, up 3.9% from US$4.22 billion the year before. Operating income was US$264.5 million versus US$401.8 million in the prior year, a decrease of 34.2%. Indirect operating expenses increased 7.9% to US$4.12 billion from US$3.82 billion in the equivalent prior-year period.

Prospects: Co.'s near-term outlook appears somewhat mixed. On one hand, Co. noted that the markets for its less-than-truckload and full-truckload services are expected to remain competitive throughout 2008. On the other hand, Co. is encouraged with the overall market for global logistics services, and expects its Menlo Worldwide subsidiary to be positioned for growth, due to its 2007 acquisitions in Asia, and particularly as multinational businesses increase their reliance on third-party logistics to enhance global supply chain efficiency. For full-year 2008, Co. expects earnings from continuing operations to be in a range of $3.40 to $3.80 per diluted share.

Financial Data

(US$ in Thousands)	12/31/2007	12/31/2006	12/31/2005	12/31/2004	12/31/2003	12/31/2002	12/31/2001	12/31/2000
Earnings Per Share	3.04	4.98	3.85	(2.15)	1.57	1.74	(8.26)	2.36
Cash Flow Per Share	8.25	8.86	4.17	7.50	4.49	0.10	6.30	3.35
Tang Book Value Per Share	5.36	13.22	14.71	11.77	7.87	5.71	3.99	12.16
Dividends Per Share	0.400	0.100	0.400	0.400	0.400	0.400	0.400	0.400
Dividend Payout %	13.16	2.01	10.39	...	25.48	22.99	...	16.95
Income Statement								
Total Revenue	4,387,363	4,221,478	4,169,590	3,712,379	5,104,332	4,762,119	4,862,731	5,572,377
EBITDA	458,430	574,852	522,904	414,858	344,843	337,489	(465,142)	489,175
Income Before Taxes	242,646	392,309	351,121	246,823	156,016	146,244	(695,933)	261,196
Income Taxes	88,871	119,978	121,873	96,378	63,992	32,035	(262,367)	109,880
Net Income	152,912	266,132	222,020	(115,000)	91,014	101,811	(394,591)	133,064
Average Shares	48,327	52,280	56,213	56,452	56,725	56,655	48,752	55,901
Balance Sheet								
Current Assets	855,478	1,090,484	1,444,047	1,514,895	1,316,679	1,268,488	1,327,846	1,240,335
Total Assets	3,017,680	2,301,889	2,480,572	2,496,401	2,749,852	2,739,761	2,990,020	3,244,941
Current Liabilities	681,492	559,802	631,496	712,831	809,595	873,054	883,975	958,909
Long-Term Obligations	955,722	557,723	581,469	601,344	536,314	557,610	565,815	534,649
Total Liabilities	2,108,584	1,561,110	1,569,654	1,719,034	1,806,044	1,896,763	2,226,933	2,058,019
Stockholders' Equity	909,096	740,779	910,918	777,367	818,808	717,998	638,087	1,061,922
Shares Outstanding	45,215	46,448	52,276	52,179	49,977	49,482	48,890	48,655
Statistical Record								
Return on Assets %	5.75	11.13	8.96	N.M.	3.35	3.55	N.M.	4.28
Return on Equity %	18.54	32.23	26.42	N.M.	11.98	15.02	N.M.	13.27
EBITDA Margin %	10.45	13.62	12.54	11.17	6.76	7.09	N.M.	8.78
Net Margin %	3.49	6.30	5.35	N.M.	1.80	2.14	N.M.	2.42
Asset Turnover	1.65	1.77	1.68	1.41	1.86	1.66	1.56	1.77
Current Ratio	1.26	1.95	2.29	2.13	1.63	1.45	1.50	1.29
Debt to Equity	1.05	0.75	0.64	0.77	0.65	0.78	0.89	0.50
Price Range	56.96-38.14	61.06-42.89	59.73-41.74	50.50-30.50	35.45-24.61	37.98-28.42	36.94-21.61	34.75-20.25
P/E Ratio	18.74-12.55	12.26-8.61	15.51-10.84	...	22.58-15.68	21.83-16.33	...	14.72-8.58
Average Yield %	0.82	0.20	0.81	1.01	1.31	1.24	...	1.45

Address: 2855 Campus Drive, Suite 300, San Mateo, CA 94403
Telephone: 650-378-5200

Web Site: www.cnf.com
Officers: W. Keith Kennedy Jr. - Chmn. Douglas W. Stotlar - Pres., C.E.O.

Auditors: KPMG LLP
Investor Contact: 800-340-6641
Transfer Agents: The Bank of New York, New York, NY

CONAGRA FOODS, INC.

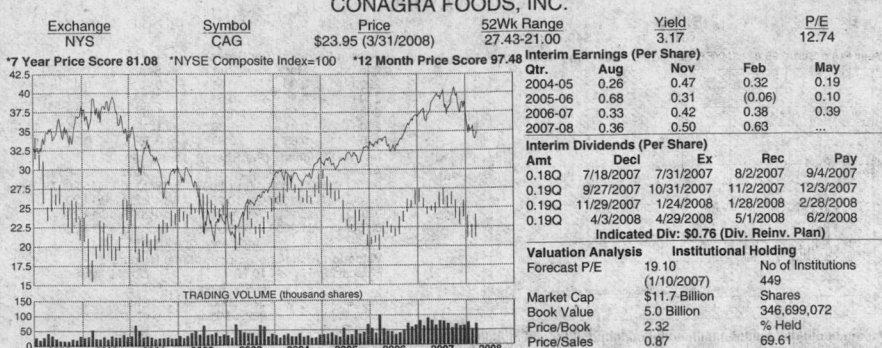

Exchange	Symbol	Price	52Wk Range	Yield	P/E
NYS	CAG	$23.95 (3/31/2008)	27.43-21.00	3.17	12.74

*7 Year Price Score 81.08   *NYSE Composite Index=100   *12 Month Price Score 97.48

Interim Earnings (Per Share)

Qtr.	Aug	Nov	Feb	May
2004-05	0.26	0.47	0.32	0.19
2005-06	0.68	0.31	(0.06)	0.10
2006-07	0.33	0.42	0.38	0.39
2007-08	0.36	0.50	0.63	...

Interim Dividends (Per Share)

Amt	Decl	Ex	Rec	Pay
0.18Q	7/18/2007	7/31/2007	8/2/2007	9/4/2007
0.19Q	9/27/2007	10/31/2007	11/2/2007	12/3/2007
0.19Q	11/29/2007	1/24/2008	1/28/2008	2/28/2008
0.19Q	4/3/2008	4/29/2008	5/1/2008	6/2/2008

Indicated Div: $0.76 (Div. Reinv. Plan)

Valuation Analysis

		Institutional Holding	
Forecast P/E	19.10	No of Institutions	
	(1/10/2007)	449	
Market Cap	$11.7 Billion	Shares	
Book Value	5.0 Billion	346,699,072	
Price/Book	2.32	% Held	
Price/Sales	0.87	69.61	

Business Summary: Food (MIC: 4.1 SIC: 2099 NAIC: 311999)

ConAgra Foods is a packaged food company serving a range of food customers. Co.'s Consumer Foods segment includes branded, private label and customized food products that are sold in various retail and foodservice channels. Co.'s Food and Ingredients segment includes commercially branded foods and ingredients, which are sold primarily to foodservice, food manufacturing and industrial customers. Co.'s Trading and Merchandising segment includes the sourcing, merchandising, trading, marketing and distribution of agricultural and energy commodities. Co.'s International Foods segment includes branded food products which are sold primarily in retail channels in North America, Europe and Asia.

Recent Developments: For the quarter ended Feb 24 2008, income from continuing operations increased 66.3% to US$310.1 million from US$186.5 million in the year-earlier quarter. Net income increased 60.5% to US$309.1 million from US$192.6 million in the year-earlier quarter. Revenues were US$3.53 billion, up 20.9% from US$2.92 billion the year before. Direct operating expenses rose 19.2% to US$2.56 billion from US$2.14 billion in the comparable period the year before. Indirect operating expenses increased 10.0% to US$556.7 million from US$506.3 million in the equivalent prior-year period.

Prospects: For the fiscal year ending May 25 2008, Co. is projecting earnings to be in the range of $1.80 to $1.85 per share, excluding items affecting comparability. Separately, on Mar 27 2008, Co. announced an agreement to divest its Foods Trading and Merchandising segment to the Ospraie Special Opportunities fund and other investors for approximately $2.10 billion, subject to certain adjustments. Co. believes that this transaction, which is in-line with its ongoing core food businesses growth initiatives, should help improve its results going forward. Closing of the sale is subject to satisfaction of customary closing conditions, including receipt of regulatory approvals and financing matters.

Financial Data

(US$ in Thousands)	9 Mos	6 Mos	3 Mos	05/27/2007	05/28/2006	05/29/2005	05/30/2004	05/25/2003
Earnings Per Share	1.88	1.63	1.55	1.51	1.03	1.23	1.66	1.46
Cash Flow Per Share	1.04	1.32	0.79	1.88	2.07	2.15	1.40	1.35
Tang Book Value Per Share	1.49	1.01	0.67	0.74	0.79	0.47	0.41	N.M.
Dividends Per Share	0.740	0.730	0.720	0.720	0.998	1.077	1.028	0.978
Dividend Payout %	39.27	44.66	46.34	47.68	96.84	87.60	61.90	66.95
Income Statement								
Total Revenue	9,995,000	6,466,600	2,955,600	12,028,200	11,908,800	14,752,600	14,522,100	19,839,200
EBITDA	1,252,000	757,400	326,400	1,351,100	1,266,600	1,511,000	1,503,600	...
Depn & Amortn	231,500	153,200	75,800	...	...	...	...	...
Income Before Taxes	1,020,500	604,200	250,600	1,005,100	955,400	1,158,000	1,151,300	...
Income Taxes	371,800	220,300	87,400	365,700	309,700	470,000	355,300	436,000
Net Income	729,300	420,200	175,400	764,600	533,800	641,500	879,800	774,800
Average Shares	490,600	490,700	492,800	507,100	520,200	520,200	530,700	530,700
Balance Sheet								
Current Assets	6,335,100	5,795,300	5,018,700	5,006,000	4,790,300	4,523,700	5,144,900	6,059,600
Total Assets	13,386,500	12,799,300	11,954,800	11,835,500	11,970,400	12,791,700	14,230,100	15,071,400
Current Liabilities	3,752,800	3,391,300	2,727,500	2,680,900	2,964,800	2,388,600	3,001,600	3,803,400
Long-Term Obligations	3,375,900	3,375,100	3,420,100	3,420,000	3,154,800	4,349,100	5,280,700	5,395,200
Total Liabilities	8,348,200	7,994,900	7,359,200	7,252,600	7,320,400	7,932,300	9,390,600	10,449,700
Stockholders' Equity	5,038,500	4,804,400	4,595,600	4,582,900	4,650,000	4,859,400	4,839,500	4,621,700
Shares Outstanding	487,608	487,396	487,155	489,779	510,861	518,101	521,194	536,765
Statistical Record								
Return on Assets %	7.20	6.42	6.47	6.44	4.32	4.76	5.91	5.08
Return on Equity %	19.03	16.92	16.67	16.61	11.26	13.26	18.30	17.40
EBITDA Margin %	12.53	11.71	11.04	11.23	10.64	10.24	10.35	...
Net Margin %	7.30	6.50	5.93	6.36	4.48	4.35	6.06	3.91
Asset Turnover	1.04	1.01	1.03	1.01	0.96	1.09	0.98	1.30
Current Ratio	1.69	1.71	1.84	1.87	1.62	1.89	1.71	1.59
Debt to Equity	0.67	0.70	0.74	0.75	0.68	0.89	1.09	1.17
Price Range	27.43-21.00	27.52-22.81	27.52-23.17	27.52-21.25	26.15-19.50	30.00-25.59	29.34-21.15	27.65-19.65
P/E Ratio	14.59-11.17	16.88-13.99	17.75-14.95	18.23-14.07	25.39-18.93	24.39-20.80	17.67-12.74	18.94-13.46
Average Yield %	2.99	2.86	2.82	2.94	4.48	3.96	4.10	4.06

Address: One ConAgra Drive, Omaha, NE 68102-5001 Telephone: 402-595-4000 Fax: 402-978-4447	Web Site: www.conagrafoods.com Officers: Gary M. Rodkin - Pres., C.E.O. Frank S. Sklarsky - Exec. V.P., C.F.O.	Auditors: KPMG LLP Investor Contact: 402-595-4154 Transfer Agents: Wells Fargo Shareowner Services, St. Paul, MN

CONOCOPHILLIPS

Exchange	Symbol	Price	52Wk Range	Yield	P/E
NYS	COP	$76.21 (3/31/2008)	90.17-67.74	2.47	10.56

*7 Year Price Score 135.03 *NYSE Composite Index=100 *12 Month Price Score 106.35

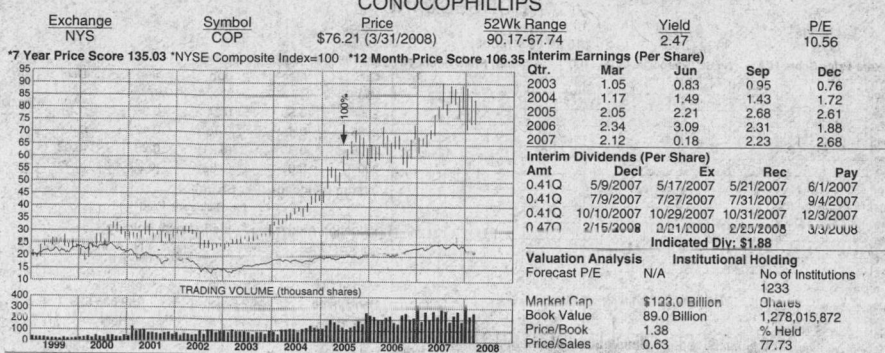

Interim Earnings (Per Share)

Qtr.	Mar	Jun	Sep	Dec
2003	1.05	0.83	0.95	0.76
2004	1.17	1.49	1.43	1.72
2005	2.05	2.21	2.68	2.61
2006	2.34	3.09	2.31	1.88
2007	2.12	0.18	2.23	2.68

Interim Dividends (Per Share)

Amt	Decl	Ex	Rec	Pay
0.41Q	5/9/2007	5/17/2007	5/21/2007	6/1/2007
0.41Q	7/9/2007	7/27/2007	7/31/2007	9/4/2007
0.41Q	10/10/2007	10/29/2007	10/31/2007	12/3/2007
0.47Q	2/15/2008	2/21/2008	2/25/2008	3/3/2008

Indicated Div: $1.88

Valuation Analysis · **Institutional Holding**

Forecast P/E	N/A	No of Institutions
		1233
Market Cap	$123.0 Billion	Shares
Book Value	89.0 Billion	1,278,015,872
Price/Book	1.38	% Held
Price/Sales	0.63	77.73

TRADING VOLUME (thousand shares)

Business Summary: Oil and Gas (MIC: 14.2 SIC: 2911 NAIC: 324110)

ConocoPhillips is an international integrated energy company. As of Dec 31 2007, Co. conducted its businesses in six operating segments. The Exploration and Production segment explores for, produces and markets crude oil, natural gas, and natural gas liquids. The Midstream segment gathers and processes natural gas, and fractionates and markets natural gas liquids. The Refining and Marketing segment purchases, refines, markets and transports crude oil and petroleum products. The LUKOIL Investment segment consists of Co.'s equity investment in OAO LUKOIL. The Chemicals segment manufactures and markets petrochemicals and plastics; and the Emerging Businesses segment develops new businesses.

Recent Developments: For the year ended Dec 31 2007, income from continuing operations decreased 23.5% to US$11.89 billion from US$15.55 billion a year earlier. Net income decreased 23.5% to US$11.89 billion from US$15.55 billion in the prior year. Revenues were US$194.50 billion, up 3.2% from US$188.52 billion the year before. Direct operating expenses rose 3.7% to US$134.11 billion from US$129.31 billion in the comparable period the year before. Indirect operating expenses increased 20.2% to US$37.02 billion from US$30.80 billion in the equivalent prior-year period.

Prospects: For the first quarter of 2008, Co. projects production from its Exploration & Production segment to be about 1.8 million barrels-of-oil-equivalent per day. In addition, Co. foresees the global refining crude oil capacity utilization rate at its downstream refining business to be in the mid-90.0% range. Also, Co. expects capital expenditures of about $6.44 billion for its U.S operations and about $7.89 billion for its International operations. Meanwhile, Co. is encouraged by the Jan 22 2008 acquisition of a 50.0% ownership stake in the Keystone Oil Pipeline, which should enable the integration of its upstream and downstream business while providing entry for potential Canadian production.

Financial Data

(US$ in Thousands)	12/31/2007	12/31/2006	12/31/2005	12/31/2004	12/31/2003	12/31/2002	12/31/2001	12/31/2000
Earnings Per Share	7.22	9.66	9.55	5.80	3.46	(0.30)	2.81	3.63
Cash Flow Per Share	15.12	13.57	12.65	8.63	6.87	5.15	6.08	7.86
Tang Book Value Per Share	36.40	30.50	26.34	19.17	13.33	10.30	14.06	11.93
Dividends Per Share	1.640	1.440	1.180	0.895	0.815	0.740	0.700	0.680
Dividend Payout %	22.71	14.91	12.36	15.43	23.59	...	24.87	18.73
Income Statement								
Total Revenue	194,495,000	188,523,000	183,364,000	136,916,000	105,097,000	57,224,000	26,868,000	21,227,000
EBITDA	31,570,000	35,617,000	27,800,000	18,167,000	11,822,000	4,387,000	4,693,000	4,948,000
Income Before Taxes	23,272,000	28,333,000	23,547,000	14,369,000	8,337,000	2,164,000	3,302,000	3,769,000
Income Taxes	11,381,000	12,783,000	9,907,000	6,262,000	3,744,000	1,450,000	1,659,000	1,907,000
Net Income	11,891,000	15,550,000	13,529,000	8,129,000	4,735,000	(295,000)	1,661,000	1,862,000
Average Shares	1,645,919	1,609,530	1,417,028	1,401,300	1,370,866	971,010	590,032	512,652
Balance Sheet								
Current Assets	24,735,000	25,066,000	19,612,000	15,021,000	11,192,000	10,903,000	4,363,000	2,606,000
Total Assets	177,757,000	164,781,000	106,999,000	92,861,000	82,455,000	76,836,000	35,217,000	20,509,000
Current Liabilities	26,882,000	26,431,000	21,359,000	15,586,000	14,011,000	12,816,000	4,542,000	3,492,000
Long-Term Obligations	20,289,000	23,091,000	10,758,000	14,370,000	16,340,000	18,917,000	8,645,000	7,521,000
Total Liabilities	87,601,000	80,933,000	53,059,000	49,033,000	47,247,000	46,318,000	20,227,000	13,766,000
Stockholders' Equity	88,983,000	82,646,000	52,731,000	42,723,000	34,366,000	29,517,000	14,340,000	6,093,000
Shares Outstanding	1,613,841	1,646,082	1,377,849	1,389,546	1,365,567	1,355,139	764,316	510,778
Statistical Record								
Return on Assets %	6.94	11.44	13.54	9.25	5.95	N.M.	5.96	10.40
Return on Equity %	13.86	22.97	28.35	21.03	14.82	N.M.	16.26	34.90
EBITDA Margin %	16.23	18.89	15.16	13.27	11.25	7.67	17.47	23.31
Net Margin %	6.11	8.25	7.38	5.94	4.51	N.M.	6.18	8.77
Asset Turnover	1.14	1.39	1.83	1.56	1.32	1.02	0.96	1.19
Current Ratio	0.92	0.95	0.92	0.96	0.80	0.85	0.96	0.75
Debt to Equity	0.23	0.28	0.20	0.34	0.48	0.64	0.60	1.23
Price Range	90.17-61.82	73.07-56.03	70.91-41.78	45.49-32.39	32.78-22.66	31.86-22.33	33.76-25.20	33.31-18.13
P/E Ratio	12.49-8.56	7.56-5.80	7.43-4.37	7.84-5.58	9.48-6.55	...	12.01-8.97	9.18-4.99
Average Yield %	2.14	2.26	2.05	2.35	3.02	2.71	2.45	2.60

Address: 600 North Dairy Ashford Road, Houston, TX 77079
Telephone: 281-293-1000
Fax: 281-661-7636

Web Site: www.conocophillips.com
Officers: James J. Mulva - Chmn., Pres., C.E.O. William B. Berry - Exec. V.P., Exploration & Prodn.

Auditors: Ernst & Young LLP
Transfer Agents: Mellon Investor Services

CONSECO INC

Exchange	Symbol	Price	52Wk Range	Yield	P/E
NYS	CNO	$10.20 (3/31/2008)	21.22-8.76	N/A	N/A

*7 Year Price Score N/A   *NYSE Composite Index=100   *12 Month Price Score 78.33

Interim Earnings (Per Share)

Qtr.	Mar	Jun	Sep	Dec
2003			0.67	
2004	0.50	0.34	0.36	0.48
2005	0.44	0.48	0.42	0.43
2006	0.35	(0.21)	0.26	(0.03)
2007	0.01	(0.38)	(0.29)	(0.43)

Interim Dividends (Per Share)

No Dividends Paid

Valuation Analysis

	Institutional Holding	
Forecast P/E	N/A	No of Institutions
		201
Market Cap	$1.9 Billion	Shares
Book Value	4.2 Billion	159,636,528
Price/Book	0.44	% Held
Price/Sales	0.41	N/A

TRADING VOLUME (thousand shares)

Business Summary: Insurance (MIC: 8.2 SIC: 6321 NAIC: 524114)

Conseco is a holding company for a group of insurance companies operating in the U.S. that develops, markets and administers supplemental health insurance, annuity, individual life insurance and other insurance products. Co. sells its products through three distribution channels: career agents, professional independent producers and direct marketing. Co. operates through three primary operating segments: Bankers Life, Conseco Insurance Group and Colonial Penn, which are defined on the basis of product distributions; a fourth segment comprised of other business in run-off; and corporate operations. As of Dec 31 2007, Co. had total assets of $33.51 billion.

Recent Developments: For the year ended Dec 31 2007, net loss amounted to US$179.9 million versus net income of US$106.0 million in the prior year. Revenues were US$4.57 billion, up 2.3% from US$4.47 billion the year before. Net premiums earned were US$3.17 billion versus US$2.99 billion in the prior year, an increase of 6.0%. Net investment income rose 2.0% to US$1.54 billion from US$1.51 billion a year ago.

Prospects: Moving forward, Co. expects maintaining strong growth at its Bankers Life and Colonial Penn segments and continuing to improve the focus and profitability mix of sales at its Conseco Insurance Group segment. Further, Co. intends to improve the performance of its long-term care business in its Other Business in Run-off segment by continuing to aggressively seek actuarially justified rate increases and by improving claims management. Also, Co. plans to complete the remediation project relating to its material weakness in internal controls while reducing its enterprise exposure to long-term care business.

Financial Data
(US$ in Thousands)

	12/31/2007	12/31/2006	12/31/2005	12/31/2004	12/31/2003	08/31/2003	12/31/2002	12/31/2001
Earnings Per Share	(1.12)	0.38	1.76	1.63	0.67	...	(22.67)	(1.24)
Cash Flow Per Share	4.06	6.14	7.69	7.90	4.39	...	3.75	3.92
Tang Book Value Per Share	22.94	26.58	25.42	21.41	8.22	...	...	1.62
Income Statement								
Premium Income	3,167,300	2,989,000	2,930,100	2,949,300	1,005,800	2,204,300	3,602,300	4,065,700
Total Revenue	4,572,300	4,467,400	4,326,500	4,330,000	1,505,500	3,202,200	4,418,300	8,108,100
Benefits & Claims	3,433,700	3,068,400	2,800,600	2,795,200	967,900	2,138,700	3,332,500	3,506,800
Income Before Taxes	(173,000)	152,300	503,400	454,100	149,500	2,172,200	(1,634,000)	(419,400)
Income Taxes	6,900	55,800	178,500	159,300	53,200	(13,500)	864,300	(115,800)
Net Income	(179,900)	96,500	324,900	294,800	96,300	2,201,700	(7,835,700)	(405,900)
Average Shares	173,374	152,509	185,040	155,930	143,486	...	345,807	338,145
Balance Sheet								
Total Assets	33,514,800	32,717,300	31,557,300	30,755,500	29,920,100	...	46,509,000	61,392,300
Total Liabilities	29,278,900	28,004,200	27,037,500	26,853,300	27,102,500	...	46,637,900	54,724,800
Stockholders' Equity	4,235,900	4,713,100	4,519,800	3,902,200	2,817,600	...	(2,050,400)	4,753,000
Shares Outstanding	184,652	152,165	151,513	151,057	100,115	...	346,007	344,743
Statistical Record								
Return on Assets %	N.M.	0.30	1.04	0.97	0.25	...	N.M.	N.M.
Return on Equity %	N.M.	2.09	7.72	8.75	25.10	...	N.M.	N.M.
Loss Ratio %	108.41	102.66	95.58	94.78	96.23	97.02	92.51	86.25
Net Margin %	(3.93)	2.16	7.51	6.81	6.40	68.76	(177.35)	(5.01)
Price Range	21.22-12.17	25.72-19.71	23.43-18.92	23.76-15.74	21.95-18.06	...	...	...
P/E Ratio	...	67.68-51.87	13.31-10.75	14.58-9.66	32.76-26.96	...	...	...

Address: 11825 N. Pennsylvania Street, Carmel, IN 46032 **Telephone:** 317-817-6100 **Fax:** 317-344-6452	**Web Site:** www.conseco.com **Officers:** William S. Kirsch - Pres., C.E.O. Russell M. Bostick - Exec. V.P., Chief Info. Officer	**Auditors:** PricewaterhouseCoopers LLP **Transfer Agents:** American Stock Transfer & Trust Company

CONSOL ENERGY INC

Exchange	Symbol	Price	52Wk Range	Yield	P/E
NYS	CNX	$69.19 (3/31/2008)	81.33-36.40	0.58	47.72

*7 Year Price Score 175.02 *NYSE Composite Index=100 *12 Month Price Score 146.81

Interim Earnings (Per Share)

Qtr.	Mar	Jun	Sep	Dec
2003	0.05	0.07	(0.04)	(0.13)
2004	0.63	0.14	(0.07)	0.37
2005	0.41	0.44	2.02	0.47
2006	0.67	0.57	0.27	0.69
2007	0.61	0.83	(0.03)	0.04

Interim Dividends (Per Share)

Amt	Decl	Ex	Rec	Pay
0.07Q	4/27/2007	5/4/2007	5/8/2007	5/29/2007
0.07Q	7/27/2007	8/7/2007	8/9/2007	8/27/2007
0.10Q	10/26/2007	11/5/2007	11/7/2007	11/23/2007
0.10Q	1/30/2008	2/5/2008	2/7/2008	2/22/2008

Indicated Div: $0.40

Valuation Analysis

		Institutional Holding	
Forecast P/E	9.44	No of Institutions	
	(1/10/2007)	316	
Market Cap	012.0 Billion	Shares	
Book Value	1.2 Billion	161,775,888	
Price/Book	10.39	% Held	
Price/Sales	3.35	88.63	

TRADING VOLUME (thousand shares)

Business Summary: Coal Mining (MIC: 14.4 SIC: 1221 NAIC: 212111)

Consol Energy is a multi-fuel energy producer and energy services provider mainly serving the electric power generation industry in the U.S. As of Dec 31 2007, Co. produced bituminous coal from 17 mining complexes in the U.S., including a fully consolidated, 49.0% owned, variable interest entity, and a 49.0% equity affiliate. Co.'s Coal unit is engaged in the mining, preparation and marketing of steam coal, sold mainly to power generators, and metallurgical coal, sold to metal and coke producers, while its Gas unit produces pipeline-quality methane gas for sale mainly to gas wholesalers. As of Dec 31 2007, Co. had an estimated 4.50 billion tons of proven and probable coal reserves.

Recent Developments: For the year ended Dec 31 2007, net income decreased 34.5% to US$267.8 million from US$408.9 million in the prior year. Revenues were US$3.76 billion, up 1.3% from US$3.72 billion the year before. Direct operating expenses rose 3.5% to US$2.59 billion from US$2.50 billion in the comparable period the year before. Indirect operating expenses increased 12.4% to US$747.7 million from US$665.0 million in the equivalent prior-year period.

Prospects: Despite a decline in total revenue mainly due to the lost sales of high value, metallurgical grade coal from the shutdown of its Buchanan Mine in Jul 2007, Co. is seeing an increase in average realized price per ton coupled with higher operating margins. Specifically, Co.'s growth in average realized price per ton is attributable to a general increase in market prices, while its growth in operating margins is fueled by higher average realized pricing and the idling of higher cost operations. Meanwhile, for full-year 2008, assuming its Buchanan Mine longwall production resumes on the first week of Mar 2008, Co. expects to produce 68.0 million to 72.0 million tons of coal.

Financial Data

(US$ in Thousands)	12/31/2007	12/31/2006	12/31/2005	12/31/2004	12/31/2003	12/31/2002	12/31/2001	06/30/2001
Earnings Per Share	1.45	2.20	3.13	1.09	(0.05)	0.07	0.01	1.17
Cash Flow Per Share	3.76	3.62	2.23	1.98	2.33	2.09	0.39	2.77
Tang Book Value Per Share	6.66	5.84	5.54	2.59	N.M.	1.03	1.73	2.23
Dividends Per Share	0.310	0.280	0.280	0.280	0.280	0.420	0.360	0.560
Dividend Payout %	21.38	12.73	8.95	25.69	...	560.00	11,200.00	48.07
Income Statement								
Total Revenue	3,762,197	3,715,171	3,810,449	2,776,749	2,222,466	2,183,598	1,081,198	2,368,415
EBITDA	758,191	850,930	921,018	367,867	215,658	232,396	106,008	500,799
Income Before Taxes	428,957	550,920	654,684	82,563	(33,507)	(40,423)	(19,620)	240,335
Income Taxes	136,137	112,430	64,339	(32,646)	(20,941)	(52,099)	(20,679)	56,685
Net Income	267,782	408,882	580,861	198,582	(7,798)	11,676	1,059	183,650
Average Shares	184,149	185,638	185,534	182,399	164,080	157,668	157,840	157,635
Balance Sheet								
Current Assets	683,155	914,496	998,500	470,169	470,840	622,837	570,254	565,861
Total Assets	6,208,090	5,663,332	5,087,652	4,195,611	4,318,978	4,293,160	4,297,594	3,894,971
Current Liabilities	1,016,397	740,124	803,922	705,485	824,599	814,433	640,748	933,973
Long-Term Obligations	488,925	492,745	438,367	425,760	441,912	488,431	472,669	231,028
Total Liabilities	4,993,671	4,597,181	4,062,296	3,726,590	4,028,341	4,131,113	4,026,035	3,543,324
Stockholders' Equity	1,214,419	1,066,151	1,025,356	469,021	290,637	162,047	271,559	351,647
Shares Outstanding	182,291	182,654	185,050	181,285	179,723	157,498	157,411	157,392
Statistical Record								
Return on Assets %	4.51	7.61	12.51	4.65	N.M.	0.27	0.02	4.73
Return on Equity %	23.48	39.10	77.74	52.14	N.M.	5.39	0.27	60.63
EBITDA Margin %	20.15	22.90	24.17	13.25	9.70	10.64	9.80	21.14
Net Margin %	7.12	11.01	15.24	7.15	N.M.	0.53	0.10	7.75
Asset Turnover	0.63	0.69	0.82	0.65	0.52	0.51	0.18	0.61
Current Ratio	0.67	1.24	1.24	0.67	0.57	0.76	0.89	0.61
Debt to Equity	0.40	0.46	0.43	0.91	1.52	3.01	1.74	0.66
Price Range	73.58-29.19	48.13-29.06	39.52-18.95	21.47-10.86	13.40-7.38	14.02-5.34	14.18-9.63	20.57-7.57
P/E Ratio	50.74-20.13	21.88-13.21	12.62-6.05	19.69-9.96	...	200.29-76.29	N.M.	17.59-6.47
Average Yield %	0.69	0.75	1.00	1.75	2.86	4.42	4.60	4.47

Address: Consol Plaza, 1800 Washington Road, Pittsburgh, PA 15241 Telephone: 412-831-4000 Fax: 412-831-4103	Web Site: Officers: John L. Whitmire - Chmn. J. Brett Harvey - Pres., C.E.O.	Auditors: ERNST & YOUNG LLP

CONSOLIDATED EDISON, INC.

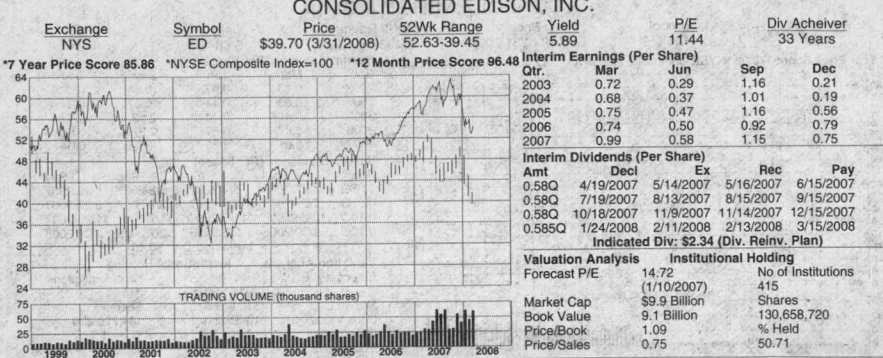

Exchange	Symbol	Price	52Wk Range	Yield	P/E	Div Acheiver
NYS	ED	$39.70 (3/31/2008)	52.63-39.45	5.89	11.44	33 Years

*7 Year Price Score 85.86 *NYSE Composite Index=100 *12 Month Price Score 96.48

Interim Earnings (Per Share)

Qtr.	Mar	Jun	Sep	Dec
2003	0.72	0.29	1.16	0.21
2004	0.68	0.37	1.01	0.19
2005	0.75	0.47	1.16	0.56
2006	0.74	0.50	0.92	0.79
2007	0.99	0.58	1.15	0.75

Interim Dividends (Per Share)

Amt	Decl	Ex	Rec	Pay
0.58Q	4/19/2007	5/14/2007	5/16/2007	6/15/2007
0.58Q	7/19/2007	8/13/2007	8/15/2007	9/15/2007
0.58Q	10/18/2007	11/9/2007	11/14/2007	12/15/2007
0.585Q	1/24/2008	2/11/2008	2/13/2008	3/15/2008

Indicated Div: $2.34 (Div. Reinv. Plan)

Valuation Analysis / **Institutional Holding**

Forecast P/E	14.72 (1/10/2007)	No. of Institutions 415
Market Cap	$9.9 Billion	Shares 130,658,720
Book Value	9.1 Billion	% Held 50.71
Price/Book	1.09	
Price/Sales	0.75	

Business Summary: Electricity (MIC: 7.1 SIC: 4931 NAIC: 221121)

Consolidated Edison is a holding company. Through its subsidiaries, Co. provides energy-related services. Con Edison of New York provides electric service in all of New York City (except part of Queens) and most of Westchester County, an approximately 660 square mile service area with a population of more than 9.0 million. It also provides gas service in Manhattan, the Bronx and parts of Queens and Westchester, and steam service in parts of Manhattan. Orange & Rockland Utilities, Inc. and its utility subsidiaries provide electric service in southeastern New York and in adjacent areas of northern New Jersey and eastern Pennsylvania, an approximately 1,350 square mile service area.

Recent Developments: For the year ended Dec 31 2007, income from continuing operations increased 25.0% to US$925.0 million from US$740.0 million a year earlier. Net income increased 26.1% to US$929.0 million from US$737.0 million in the prior year. Revenues were US$13.12 billion, up 9.7% from US$11.96 billion the year before. Operating income was US$1.40 billion versus US$1.22 billion in the prior year, an increase of 14.3%. Direct operating expenses rose 9.6% to US$9.31 billion from US$8.49 billion in the comparable period the year before. Indirect operating expenses increased 7.5% to US$2.42 billion from US$2.25 billion in the equivalent prior-year period.

Prospects: For the full year of 2008, Co. anticipates that the peak electric demand at both its Consolidated Edison Company of New York, Inc. (Con Edison of New York) and Orange and Rockland Utilities, Inc. (O&R) subsidiaries will be 13,775 megawatts (MW) and 1,645 MW, respectively. Over the next five years, Co. foresees that the average annual growth rate of the peak electric demand to be approximately 1.2% for Con Edison of New York and 2.5% for O&R. Thus, Co. is projecting total capital investment in 2008 to be approximately $2.60 billion for Con Edison of New York and $133.0 million for O&R, primarily to meet the growth in demand for electricity and electric, gas and steam reliability demands.

Financial Data

(US$ in Thousands)	12/31/2007	12/31/2006	12/31/2005	12/31/2004	12/31/2003	12/31/2002	12/31/2001	12/31/2000
Earnings Per Share	3.47	2.95	2.94	2.27	2.38	3.02	3.21	2.74
Cash Flow Per Share	5.84	5.43	3.25	5.58	5.97	7.07	6.36	4.51
Tang Book Value Per Share	34.83	32.09	30.68	29.86	29.15	25.40	24.21	26.39
Dividends Per Share	2.320	2.300	2.280	2.260	2.240	2.220	2.200	2.180
Dividend Payout %	66.86	77.97	77.55	99.56	94.12	73.51	68.54	79.56
Income Statement								
Total Revenue	13,120,000	12,137,000	11,690,000	9,758,000	9,827,000	8,481,860	9,633,962	9,431,391
Income Taxes	449,000	402,000	355,000	284,000	327,000	388,881	(21,922)	(10,622)
Net Income	929,000	737,000	719,000	537,000	528,000	646,036	682,242	582,835
Average Shares	267,300	250,300	244,700	236,400	221,800	214,049	212,919	212,186
Balance Sheet								
Net PPE	19,914,000	18,445,000	17,112,000	16,106,000	15,225,000	13,329,175	12,248,375	11,893,419
Total Assets	28,343,000	26,699,000	24,850,000	22,560,000	20,966,000	18,820,310	16,996,111	16,767,245
Long-Term Obligations	7,633,000	8,324,000	7,428,000	6,594,000	6,769,000	6,206,917	5,542,305	5,446,913
Total Liabilities	19,011,000	18,441,000	17,285,000	15,254,000	14,288,000	12,677,761	11,070,708	11,045,243
Stockholders' Equity	9,076,000	8,004,000	7,310,000	7,054,000	6,423,000	5,921,079	5,666,268	5,472,389
Shares Outstanding	248,814	234,245	222,075	219,303	202,629	213,932	212,146	188,816
Statistical Record								
Return on Assets %	3.38	2.86	3.03	2.46	2.65	3.61	4.04	3.60
Return on Equity %	10.88	9.63	10.01	7.95	8.55	11.15	12.25	10.68
Net Margin %	7.08	6.07	6.15	5.50	5.37	7.62	7.08	6.18
PPE Turnover	0.68	0.68	0.70	0.62	0.69	0.66	0.80	0.81
Asset Turnover	0.48	0.47	0.49	0.45	0.49	0.47	0.57	0.58
Debt to Equity	0.84	1.04	1.02	0.93	1.05	1.05	0.98	1.00
Price Range	52.63-43.65	49.13-41.40	49.24-41.41	45.59-37.26	45.99-37.00	45.10-33.58	42.18-32.38	39.25-26.19
P/E Ratio	15.17-12.58	16.65-14.03	16.75-14.09	20.08-16.41	19.32-15.55	14.93-11.12	13.14-10.09	14.32-9.56
Average Yield %	4.84	5.04	5.04	5.35	5.53	5.35	5.72	6.65

Address: 4 Irving Place, New York, NY 10003 **Telephone:** 212-460-4600 **Fax:** 212-475-0734	**Web Site:** www.conedison.com **Officers:** Eugene R. McGrath - Chmn., Pres. Joan S. Freilich - Vice-Chmn.	**Auditors:** PricewaterhouseCoopers LLP **Investor Contact:** 212-460-6611 **Transfer Agents:** The Bank of New York, New York, NY

CONSTELLATION BRANDS INC

Exchange	Symbol	Price	52Wk Range	Yield	P/E
NYS	STZ	$17.67 (3/31/2008)	25.99-17.66	N/A	13.59

*7 Year Price Score 95.04   *NYSE Composite Index=100   *12 Month Price Score 91.87

Interim Earnings (Per Share)

Qtr.	May	Aug	Nov	Feb
2004-05	0.23	0.34	0.41	0.20
2005-06	0.32	0.34	0.46	0.24
2006-07	0.36	0.28	0.45	0.29
2007-08	0.13	0.33	0.55	...

Interim Dividends (Per Share)

Amt	Decl	Ex	Rec	Pay
2-for-1	4/7/2005	5/16/2005	4/29/2005	5/13/2005

Valuation Analysis | **Institutional Holding**

Forecast P/E	11.43	No of Institutions
	(1/10/2007)	376
Market Cap	$3.8 Billion	Shares
Book Value	3.5 Billion	184,238,912
Price/Book	1.08	% Held
Price/Sales	0.95	87.50

TRADING VOLUME (thousand shares)

Business Summary: Food (MIC: 4.1 SIC: 2084 NAIC: 312130)

Constellation Brands is an international producer and marketer of beverage alcohol with a portfolio of brands across the wine, spirits and imported beer categories. Co. operates through three business segments: Constellation Wines, which sells wine brands across the table wine, sparkling wine and dessert wine categories; Constellation Spirits, which produces, bottles, imports and markets a line of distilled spirits; and Crown Imports, which has the exclusive right to import, market and sell Corona Extra, Corona Light, Coronita, Modelo Especial, Pacifico, Negra Modelo, St. Pauli Girl and Tsingtao brands in the U.S.

Recent Developments: For the quarter ended Nov 30 2007, net income increased 10.9% to US$119.6 million from US$107.8 million in the year-earlier quarter. Revenues were US$1.09 billion, down 27.1% from US$1.50 billion the year before. Operating income was US$198.3 million versus US$235.8 million in the prior-year quarter, a decrease of 15.9%. Direct operating expenses declined 33.4% to US$702.9 million from US$1.06 billion in the comparable period the year before. Indirect operating expenses decreased 7.5% to US$193.6 million from US$209.4 million in the equivalent prior-year period.

Prospects: For fiscal year ending Feb 29 2008, Co. expects earnings per share in the range of $1.06 to $1.11. Separately, on Dec 17 2007, Co. has completed its acquisition of the Fortune Brands, Inc. U.S. wine portfolio for $885.0 million, subject to closing adjustments. This acquisition reflects another significant step to expand its portfolio of fine wine in the luxury segments of the U.S. market. Overall, Co. expects the integration of the acquired wine business, realignment of its U.S. wine sales and marketing teams and portfolio rationalization to produce net cost savings of about $30.0 million annually by the end of fiscal 2010, with about $20.0 million estimated as savings in fiscal 2009.

Financial Data

(US$ in Thousands)	9 Mos	6 Mos	3 Mos	02/28/2007	02/28/2006	02/28/2005	02/29/2004	02/28/2003
Earnings Per Share	1.30	1.20	1.15	1.38	1.36	1.19	1.03	1.10
Cash Flow Per Share	2.08	1.89	0.96	1.37	1.97	1.49	1.69	1.31
Tang Book Value Per Share	N.M.	N.M.	N.M.	N.M.	N.M.	N.M.	0.43	0.39
Income Statement								
Total Revenue	2,888,600	1,793,800	901,200	5,216,400	4,603,448	4,087,638	3,552,429	2,731,612
EBITDA	731,300	418,300	182,700	943,300	795,115	673,376	591,127	500,472
Depn & Amortn	117,500	77,000	38,700	...	...	...	...	...
Income Before Taxes	365,000	174,900	64,300	535,300	477,258	431,974	344,397	334,936
Income Taxes	143,500	73,000	34,500	203,400	151,996	155,510	123,983	131,630
Net Income	221,500	101,900	29,800	331,900	325,262	276,464	220,414	203,306
Average Shares	462,673	219,300	233,439	239,772	238,707	233,060	213,896	185,492
Balance Sheet								
Current Assets	3,147,500	2,887,400	2,909,300	3,023,300	2,700,855	2,734,035	2,071,471	1,330,101
Total Assets	10,193,600	9,731,100	9,826,200	9,438,200	7,400,554	7,804,172	5,558,673	3,196,330
Current Liabilities	1,594,600	1,452,000	1,507,500	1,591,100	1,298,060	1,138,087	1,029,802	585,208
Long-Term Obligations	4,235,200	4,291,800	4,381,800	3,714,900	2,515,780	3,204,707	1,778,853	1,191,631
Total Liabilities	6,680,900	6,542,300	6,697,900	6,020,700	4,425,383	5,024,259	3,181,054	2,021,346
Stockholders' Equity	3,512,700	3,188,800	3,128,300	3,417,500	2,975,171	2,779,913	2,377,619	1,174,984
Shares Outstanding	215,597	215,073	215,336	234,869	223,034	219,022	213,256	181,522
Statistical Record								
Return on Assets %	2.91	2.92	3.16	3.94	4.28	4.14	5.02	6.49
Return on Equity %	8.53	8.81	8.84	10.38	11.30	10.72	12.37	19.08
EBITDA Margin %	25.32	23.32	20.27	18.08	17.27	16.47	16.64	18.32
Net Margin %	7.67	5.68	3.31	6.36	7.07	6.76	6.20	7.44
Asset Turnover	0.40	0.46	0.57	0.62	0.61	0.61	0.81	0.87
Current Ratio	1.97	1.99	1.93	1.90	2.08	2.40	2.01	2.27
Debt to Equity	1.21	1.35	1.40	1.09	0.85	1.15	0.75	1.01
Price Range	28.93-18.96	29.08-18.96	29.08-18.96	29.08-23.24	30.83-22.25	28.23-15.72	17.79-11.00	16.00-11.18
P/E Ratio	22.25-14.58	24.23-15.80	25.29-16.49	21.07-16.84	22.67-16.36	23.72-13.21	17.27-10.68	14.55-10.16

Address: 370 Woodcliff Drive, Suite 300, Fairport, NY 14450 **Telephone:** 585-218-3600 **Fax:** 585-394-4839	**Web Site:** www.cbrands.com **Officers:** Richard Sands - Chmn., C.E.O. Robert Sands - Pres., C.O.O.	**Auditors:** KPMG LLP **Investor Contact:** 888-922-2150 **Transfer Agents:** Mellon Investor Services, Ridgefield Park, NJ

CONSTELLATION ENERGY GROUP, INC.

Exchange	Symbol	Price	52Wk Range	Yield	P/E
NYS	CEG	$88.27 (3/31/2008)	107.13-79.25	2.16	19.62

*7 Year Price Score 146.64 *NYSE Composite Index=100 *12 Month Price Score 106.45

Interim Earnings (Per Share)

Qtr.	Mar	Jun	Sep	Dec
2003	(0.80)	0.58	1.15	0.71
2004	0.39	0.76	1.19	0.76
2005	0.68	0.68	1.03	1.09
2006	0.63	0.52	1.79	2.22
2007	1.07	0.64	1.38	1.42

Interim Dividends (Per Share)

Amt	Decl	Ex	Rec	Pay
0.435Q	5/18/2007	6/7/2007	6/11/2007	7/2/2007
0.435Q	7/20/2007	9/6/2007	9/10/2007	10/1/2007
0.435Q	10/18/2007	12/6/2007	12/10/2007	1/2/2008
0.477Q	1/30/2008	3/6/2008	3/10/2008	4/1/2008

Indicated Div: $1.91

Valuation Analysis / **Institutional Holding**

Forecast P/E	N/A	No of Institutions
		394
Market Cap	$15.8 Billion	Shares
Book Value	5.3 Billion	128,086,256
Price/Book	2.95	% Held
Price/Sales	0.74	71.16

TRADING VOLUME (thousand shares)

Business Summary: Electricity (MIC: 7.1 SIC: 4911 NAIC: 221119)

Constellation Energy is an energy company that manages its operations primarily through its merchant energy business and Baltimore Gas and Electric Company (BGE). Co.'s merchant energy business is a competitive provider of energy services, with facilities located throughout the U.S. and covering a variety of customers. BGE is a regulated electric transmission and distribution utility company and also a regulated gas distribution utility company with a service territory that covers the City of Baltimore and all or part of ten counties in central Maryland.

Recent Developments: For the year ended Dec 31 2007, income from continuing operations increased 9.9% to US$822.4 million from US$748.6 million a year earlier. Net income decreased 12.3% to US$821.5 million from US$936.4 million in the prior year. Revenues were US$21.19 billion, up 9.9% from US$19.28 billion the year before. Operating income was unchanged at US$1.33 billion versus the prior year. Direct operating expenses rose 10.7% to US$18.92 billion from US$17.10 billion in the comparable period the year before. Indirect operating expenses increased 9.7% to US$937.5 million from US$854.9 million in the equivalent prior-year period.

Prospects: Co. has reaffirmed its 2008 earnings outlook of $5.25 to $5.75 per share and expects to be in the middle to upper end of the range. For 2009, Co. now sees earnings growth of 15% to 20% over projected 2008 earnings. Separately, on Feb 12 2008, Co.'s UniStar Nuclear Energy joint venture announced it has notified the US Nuclear Regulatory Commission of its plans to submit a Combined License application in late 2008 for a potential advanced design nuclear reactor at its Nine Mile Point Nuclear Station in upstate New York. Also, Co. stated that it is working to be in a position to make a decision to break ground for a new reactor at its Calvert Cliffs site in southern Maryland at the end of 2008.

Financial Data

(US$ in Thousands)	12/31/2007	12/31/2006	12/31/2005	12/31/2004	12/31/2003	12/31/2002	12/31/2001	12/31/2000
Earnings Per Share	4.50	5.16	3.47	3.12	1.66	3.20	0.57	2.30
Cash Flow Per Share	5.15	2.93	3.53	6.30	6.49	6.21	3.57	5.66
Tang Book Value Per Share	28.46	24.66	26.74	25.99	23.18	22.73	23.48	20.95
Dividends Per Share	1.740	1.510	1.340	1.140	1.040	0.960	0.480	1.680
Dividend Payout %	38.67	29.26	38.62	36.54	62.65	30.00	84.21	73.04
Income Statement								
Total Revenue	21,193,200	19,284,900	17,132,000	12,549,700	9,703,000	4,703,000	3,928,300	3,878,500
EBITDA	2,016,700	1,973,400	1,723,900	1,752,000	1,685,400	1,664,700	828,000	1,371,600
Income Before Taxes	1,250,700	1,099,600	810,800	761,000	745,200	835,200	120,300	575,400
Income Taxes	428,300	351,000	204,100	172,200	269,500	309,600	37,900	230,100
Net Income	821,500	936,400	623,100	539,700	277,300	525,600	90,900	345,300
Average Shares	182,500	181,400	179,700	173,100	166,700	164,200	160,700	150,000
Balance Sheet								
Net PPE	9,767,100	9,222,100	10,066,700	10,086,600	9,601,500	7,957,100	7,700,400	6,644,000
Total Assets	21,945,700	21,801,600	21,473,900	17,347,100	15,800,700	14,128,900	14,077,600	12,384,600
Long-Term Obligations	4,660,500	4,222,300	4,369,300	4,813,200	5,039,200	4,613,900	2,712,500	3,159,300
Total Liabilities	16,415,500	17,002,300	16,368,400	12,430,200	11,470,200	10,076,600	10,044,000	9,041,600
Stockholders' Equity	5,340,200	4,609,300	4,915,500	4,726,900	4,140,500	3,862,300	3,843,600	3,153,000
Shares Outstanding	178,437	180,519	178,300	176,333	167,819	164,842	163,707	150,531
Statistical Record								
Return on Assets %	3.76	4.33	3.21	3.25	1.85	3.73	0.69	3.12
Return on Equity %	16.51	19.66	12.92	12.14	6.93	13.64	2.60	11.21
EBITDA Margin %	9.52	10.23	10.06	13.96	17.37	35.40	21.08	35.36
Net Margin %	3.88	4.86	3.64	4.30	2.86	11.18	2.31	8.90
PPE Turnover	2.23	2.00	1.70	1.27	1.11	0.60	0.55	0.64
Asset Turnover	0.97	0.89	0.88	0.76	0.65	0.33	0.30	0.35
Debt to Equity	0.87	0.92	0.89	1.02	1.22	1.19	0.71	1.00
Price Range	103.64-70.02	70.10-50.85	62.14-43.16	44.76-36.39	39.50-25.56	32.26-20.61	49.95-22.00	51.39-27.56
P/E Ratio	23.03-15.56	13.59-9.85	17.91-12.44	14.35-11.66	23.80-15.40	10.08-6.44	87.63-38.60	22.35-11.98
Average Yield %	1.99	2.59	2.47	2.85	3.19	3.46	1.33	4.63

Address: 750 E. Pratt Street, Baltimore, MD 21202	**Web Site:** www.constellationenergy.com	**Auditors:** PricewaterhouseCoopers LLP
Telephone: 410-783-2800	**Officers:** Mayo A. Shattuck III - Chmn., Pres., C.E.O. Thomas V. Brooks - Vice-Chmn.	**Investor Contact:** 410-783-3670
Fax: 410-234-5367		**Transfer Agents:** American Stock Transfer & Trust Company, New York, NY

CONTINENTAL AIRLINES INC

Exchange	Symbol	Price	52Wk Range	Yield	P/E
NYS	CAL	$19.23 (3/31/2008)	43.74-17.84	N/A	4.60

*7 Year Price Score 114.36 *NYSE Composite Index=100 *12 Month Price Score 85.62

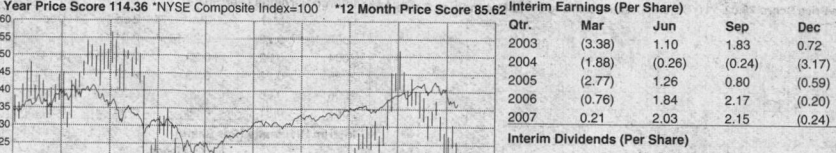

Interim Earnings (Per Share)

Qtr.	Mar	Jun	Sep	Dec
2003	(3.38)	1.10	1.83	0.72
2004	(1.88)	(0.26)	(0.24)	(3.17)
2005	(2.77)	1.26	0.80	(0.59)
2006	(0.76)	1.84	2.17	(0.20)
2007	0.21	2.03	2.15	(0.24)

Interim Dividends (Per Share)

No Dividends Paid

Valuation Analysis		Institutional Holding	
Forecast P/E	7.94	No of Institutions	
	(1/10/2007)	277	
Market Cap	$1.9 Billion	Shares	
Book Value	1.6 Billion	97,155,832	
Price/Book	1.22	% Held	
Price/Sales	0.13	N/A	

Business Summary: Aviation (MIC: 1.1 SIC: 4512 NAIC: 481111)

Continental Airlines is a U.S. air carrier engaged in transporting passengers, cargo and mail. Co., together with its wholly owned subsidiary, Continental Micronesia, Inc. (CMI) operates more than 2,900 daily departures. As of Dec. 31 2007, Co. flew to 134 domestic and 130 international destinations and offered additional connecting service through alliances with domestic and foreign carriers. Co. directly served 27 European cities, nine South American cities, Tel Aviv, Delhi, Mumbai, Hong Kong, Beijing, Tokyo, and provides service to Mexico and Central America, serving 41 cities. Through its Guam hub, CMI provides service in the western Pacific, including service to Japanese cities..

Recent Developments: For the year ended Dec 31 2007, net income increased 33.8% to US$459.0 million from US$343.0 million in the prior year. Revenues were US$14.23 billion, up 8.4% from US$13.13 billion the year before. Operating income was US$687.0 million versus US$468.0 million in the prior year, an increase of 46.8%. Direct operating expenses rose 8.0% to US$6.15 billion from US$5.69 billion in the comparable period the year before. Indirect operating expenses increased 6.1% to US$7.40 billion from US$6.97 billion in the equivalent prior-year period.

Prospects: Co.'s outlook appears encouraging. For instance, on Feb 20 2008, Co. reached agreement with The Boeing Company to order additional 27 aircraft, including eight new 777 and 19 new Next-Generation 737 (737NG) aircraft, bringing its total firm commitments to 111 new Boeing aircraft scheduled for delivery between Feb 20 2008 and the end of 2013. In addition to investing in new fuel efficient aircraft, Co. continues to enhance its existing fleet with fuel-saving technology. Separately, Co. has finalized two major supplier cost reduction initiatives in 2007 that, along with several other smaller initiatives, should reduce its costs by approximately $100.0 million annually when fully implemented.

Financial Data

(US$ in Thousands)	12/31/2007	12/31/2006	12/31/2005	12/31/2004	12/31/2003	12/31/2002	12/31/2001	12/31/2000
Earnings Per Share	4.18	3.30	(0.97)	(5.55)	0.58	(7.02)	(1.72)	5.45
Cash Flow Per Share	11.68	11.89	6.50	5.63	5.23	(1.21)	10.22	14.85
Tang Book Value Per Share	8.59	N.M.	N.M.	N.M.	N.M.	N.M.	2.03	1.35
Income Statement								
Total Revenue	14,232,000	13,128,000	11,208,000	9,744,000	8,870,000	8,402,000	8,969,000	9,899,000
EBITDA	804,000	662,000	305,000	320,000	995,000	125,000	546,000	1,080,000
Income Before Taxes	566,000	369,000	(68,000)	(440,000)	201,000	(615,000)	(114,000)	571,000
Income Taxes	107,000	...	...	(77,000)	114,000	(202,000)	(29,000)	222,000
Net Income	459,000	343,000	(68,000)	(363,000)	38,000	(451,000)	(95,000)	342,000
Average Shares	114,000	111,400	70,300	66,100	65,600	64,200	55,500	62,800
Balance Sheet								
Total Assets	12,105,000	11,308,000	10,529,000	10,545,000	10,649,000	10,740,000	9,791,000	9,201,000
Long-Term Obligations	4,366,000	4,859,000	5,057,000	5,167,000	5,558,000	5,222,000	4,198,000	3,374,000
Total Liabilities	10,555,000	10,961,000	10,303,000	10,279,000	9,857,000	9,720,000	8,387,000	7,349,000
Stockholders' Equity	1,550,000	347,000	226,000	266,000	792,000	767,000	1,161,000	1,160,000
Shares Outstanding	98,208	91,816	86,201	66,461	66,035	65,760	63,174	58,450
Statistical Record								
Return on Assets %	3.92	3.14	N.M.	N.M.	0.36	N.M.	N.M.	3.91
Return on Equity %	48.39	119.72	N.M.	N.M.	4.87	N.M.	N.M.	24.78
EBITDA Margin %	5.65	5.04	2.72	3.28	11.22	1.49	6.09	10.91
Net Margin %	3.23	2.61	(0.61)	(3.73)	0.43	(5.37)	(1.06)	3.45
Asset Turnover	1.22	1.20	1.06	0.92	0.83	0.82	0.94	1.13
Price Range	51.63-21.82	45.42-17.24	21.56-8.73	18.31-7.85	21.67-4.23	34.80-3.65	56.50-13.00	54.00-29.19
P/E Ratio	12.35-5.22	13.76-5.22	...	...	37.36-7.29	...	...	9.91-5.36

Address: 1600 Smith Street, Dept. HQSEO, Houston, TX 77002 Telephone: 713-324-2950	Web Site: www.continental.com Officers: Lawrence W. Kellner - Chmn., C.E.O. Jeffrey Smisek - Pres.	Auditors: Ernst & Young LLP Investor Contact: 713-324-5242 Transfer Agents: Mellon Investor Services LLC, Jersey City, NJ

CONVERGYS CORP.

Exchange	Symbol	Price	52Wk Range	Yield	P/E
NYS	CVG	$15.06 (3/31/2008)	27.24-13.86	N/A	12.24

*7 Year Price Score 78.02   *NYSE Composite Index=100   *12 Month Price Score 84.10

TRADING VOLUME (thousand shares)

Interim Earnings (Per Share)

Qtr.	Mar	Jun	Sep	Dec
2003	0.22	0.29	0.31	0.33
2004	0.22	0.20	0.21	0.14
2005	0.22	0.18	0.30	0.17
2006	0.26	0.28	0.32	0.31
2007	0.31	0.28	0.30	0.34

Interim Dividends (Per Share)

No Dividends Paid

Valuation Analysis

		Institutional Holding	
Forecast P/E	16.93	No of Institutions	
	(1/10/2007)	266	
Market Cap	$1.9 Billion	Shares	
Book Value	1.5 Billion	110,664,056	
Price/Book	1.27	% Held	
Price/Sales	0.68	80.98	

Business Summary: IT & Technology (MIC: 10.2 SIC: 7373 NAIC: 541512)

Convergys is engaged in the provision of relationship management services. Co. provides its clients with services to support their customers and employees. Co. has three segments: Customer Management, which provides outsourced customer care services as well as consulting services to in-house customer care operations; Information Management, which provides convergent rating, charging and billing systems for the global communications industry; and Human Resources Management, which provides human resource business process outsourcing (HR BPO) applications and learning systems.

Recent Developments: For the year ended Dec 31 2007, net income increased 2.0% to US$169.5 million from US$166.2 million in the prior year. Revenues were US$2.84 billion, up 2.0% from US$2.79 billion the year before. Operating income was US$244.8 million versus US$252.9 million in the prior year, a decrease of 3.2%. Direct operating expenses rose 4.7% to US$1.84 billion from US$1.75 billion in the comparable period the year before. Indirect operating expenses decreased 2.6% to US$761.6 million from US$782.1 million in the equivalent prior-year period.

Prospects: Looking ahead, Co. expects its Customer Management segment operating margin to be approximately 10.0% and revenue of $2.00 billion to $2.10 billion, or growth in the range of approximately 7.0% to 12.0% for 2008. Additionally, Co. estimates its Information Management segment revenues of approximately $625.0 million with an operating margin exceeding 15.0% for 2008. Also, Co. anticipates its HR Management segment revenues for 2008 to be approximately $250.0 million along with the return of an operating loss of less than $15.0 million. Overall, Co. continues to target its 2008 revenues in the range of $2.85 billion to $3.00 billion and earnings per diluted share of between $1.31 and $1.36.

Financial Data (US$ in Thousands)	12/31/2007	12/31/2006	12/31/2005	12/31/2004	12/31/2003	12/31/2002	12/31/2001	12/31/2000
Earnings Per Share	1.23	1.17	0.86	0.77	1.15	0.88	0.80	1.23
Cash Flow Per Share	1.57	2.55	1.66	1.38	2.49	2.64	1.98	1.17
Tang Book Value Per Share	4.57	3.85	3.13	2.62	2.60	2.54	3.08	2.41
Income Statement								
Total Revenue	2,844,300	2,789,800	2,582,100	2,487,700	2,288,800	2,286,200	2,320,600	2,162,500
EBITDA	393,000	410,100	381,900	324,900	402,500	392,500	451,200	510,700
Income Before Taxes	245,600	244,600	213,400	173,400	271,600	244,400	254,900	317,000
Income Taxes	76,100	78,400	90,800	61,900	100,000	98,500	116,100	122,300
Net Income	169,500	166,200	122,600	111,500	171,600	145,900	138,800	194,700
Average Shares	137,700	141,700	142,900	145,400	148,800	166,100	174,400	158,000
Balance Sheet								
Current Assets	861,600	930,200	849,000	592,800	419,500	418,200	523,100	481,100
Total Assets	2,564,200	2,540,300	2,411,400	2,208,100	1,810,200	1,619,500	1,742,900	1,779,500
Current Liabilities	426,900	595,900	617,800	577,400	542,700	462,000	492,400	359,000
Long-Term Obligations	259,300	259,600	297,500	302,200	58,800	4,600	3,600	290,700
Total Liabilities	1,042,500	1,085,200	1,056,300	922,800	666,700	493,200	516,300	667,000
Stockholders' Equity	1,521,700	1,455,100	1,355,100	1,285,300	1,143,500	1,126,300	1,226,600	1,112,500
Shares Outstanding	128,200	136,500	139,900	142,000	143,200	155,600	169,400	154,400
Statistical Record								
Return on Assets %	6.64	6.71	5.31	5.53	10.01	8.68	7.88	11.56
Return on Equity %	11.39	11.83	9.29	9.16	15.12	12.40	11.87	19.04
EBITDA Margin %	13.82	14.70	14.79	13.06	17.59	17.17	19.44	23.62
Net Margin %	5.96	5.96	4.75	4.48	7.50	6.38	5.98	9.00
Asset Turnover	1.11	1.13	1.12	1.23	1.33	1.36	1.32	1.28
Current Ratio	2.02	1.56	1.37	1.03	0.77	0.91	1.06	1.34
Debt to Equity	0.17	0.18	0.22	0.24	0.05	N.M.	N.M.	0.26
Price Range	27.24-15.49	24.54-15.55	17.78-12.58	19.48-12.42	20.60-11.35	37.96-12.60	49.99-24.80	55.13-28.00
P/E Ratio	22.15-12.59	20.97-13.29	20.67-14.63	25.30-16.13	17.91-9.87	43.14-14.32	62.49-31.00	44.82-22.76

Address: 201 East Fourth Street, Cincinnati, OH 45202 **Telephone:** 513-723-7000 **Fax:** 513-421-8624	**Web Site:** www.convergys.com **Officers:** James F. Orr - Chmn., C.E.O. David F. Dougherty - Pres., C.O.O.	**Auditors:** ERNST & YOUNG LLP **Investor Contact:** 513-723-7000 **Transfer Agents:** The Fifth Third Bank, Corporate Trust Services, Cincinnati, OH

COOPER INDUSTRIES, LTD.

Exchange	Symbol	Price	52Wk Range	Yield	P/E
NYS	CBE	$40.15 (3/31/2008)	58.72-36.97	2.49	10.76

*7 Year Price Score 125.41 *NYSE Composite Index=100 *12 Month Price Score 89.74

Interim Earnings (Per Share)

Qtr.	Mar	Jun	Sep	Dec
2003			0.79	
2004	0.41	0.45		0.00
2005	0.46	0.51	0.54	(0.65)
2006	0.57	0.53	0.69	0.69
2007	0.71	1.12	0.93	0.98

Interim Dividends (Per Share)

Amt	Decl	Ex	Rec	Pay
0.21Q	4/24/2007	5/29/2007	5/31/2007	7/2/2007
0.21Q	8/7/2007	8/29/2007	8/31/2007	10/1/2007
0.21Q	11/6/2007	11/28/2007	11/30/2007	1/2/2008
0.25Q	2/12/2008	2/27/2008	2/29/2008	4/1/2008

Indicated Div: $1.00

Valuation Analysis / **Institutional Holding**

Forecast P/E	14.03
	(1/10/2007)
Market Cap	$7.2 Billion
Book Value	2.8 Billion
Price/Book	2.54
Price/Sales	1.22

Institutional Holding	
No of Institutions	N/A
Shares	N/A
% Held	N/A
	N/A

TRADING VOLUME (thousand shares)

Business Summary: Electrical (MIC: 11.14 SIC: 3646 NAIC: 335122)

Cooper Industries operates in two business segments. The Electrical Products segment manufactures, markets and sells electrical and circuit protection products, including fittings, support systems, enclosures, wiring devices, plugs, receptacles, lighting fixtures, fuses, emergency lighting, fire detection systems and security products for use in residential, commercial and industrial construction, maintenance and repair applications. The Tools segment manufactures, markets and sells hand tools for industrial, construction and consumer markets; automated assembly systems for industrial markets; and electric and pneumatic industrial power tools for general industry applications.

Recent Developments: For the year ended Dec 31 2007, income from continuing operations increased 42.9% to US$692.3 million from US$484.3 million a year earlier. Net income increased 49.2% to US$692.3 million from US$464.0 million in the prior year. Revenues were US$5.90 billion, up 13.9% from US$5.18 billion the year before. Operating income was US$844.1 million versus US$694.1 million in the prior year, an increase of 21.6%. Direct operating expenses rose 12.7% to US$3.97 billion from US$3.52 billion in the comparable period the year before. Indirect operating expenses increased 12.4% to US$1.09 billion from US$969.0 million in the equivalent prior-year period.

Prospects: On Feb 11 2008, Co.'s subsidiary, Cooper Controls (U.K.) Limited has acquired more than 98.0% of the outstanding shares of The MTL Instruments Group plc, a company based in the U.K. for a total purchase price of about £144.3 million. Co. believes that this transaction will accelerate the growth of its Cooper Crouse-Hinds division within the global petrochemical and energy markets. Separately, for the first quarter of 2008, Co. expects earnings per share to increase 10.0% to 15.0% with revenue gains of 11.0% to 14.0%. For 2008, Co. expects earnings per share, excluding income tax accrual adjustments and legal matters, to increase 10.0% to 15.0%, with revenue gains of 10.0% to 13.0%.

Financial Data

(US$ in Thousands)	12/31/2007	12/31/2006	12/31/2005	12/31/2004	12/31/2003	12/31/2002	12/31/2001	12/31/2000
Earnings Per Share	3.73	2.48	0.86	1.79	0.79	1.14	1.22	1.90
Cash Flow Per Share	4.36	3.28	3.10	2.55	2.40	2.58	2.25	2.68
Tang Book Value Per Share	1.68	0.76	0.66	0.78	0.33	0.03	0.34	N.M.
Dividends Per Share	0.840	0.740	0.740	0.700	0.700	0.700	0.700	0.700
Dividend Payout %	22.52	29.90	85.55	39.11	88.61	61.40	57.38	36.84
Income Statement								
Total Revenue	5,903,100	5,184,600	4,730,400	4,462,900	4,061,400	3,960,500	4,209,500	4,459,900
EBITDA	995,400	810,900	670,800	614,200	513,400	476,400	587,500	824,600
Income Before Taxes	826,200	647,700	495,000	428,500	346,500	280,200	316,400	549,900
Income Taxes	133,900	163,400	103,900	88,700	72,200	66,500	55,100	192,500
Net Income	692,300	464,000	163,900	339,800	148,300	213,700	231,300	357,400
Average Shares	185,528	187,584	190,098	189,526	187,542	187,338	189,754	188,300
Balance Sheet								
Current Assets	2,303,000	2,193,700	2,131,100	2,218,600	1,960,800	1,689,000	1,651,200	1,735,100
Total Assets	6,133,500	5,374,800	5,215,100	5,340,800	4,965,300	4,687,900	4,611,400	4,789,300
Current Liabilities	1,635,100	1,499,300	1,161,100	1,827,600	1,021,900	959,500	1,106,100	1,173,600
Long-Term Obligations	909,900	702,800	1,002,900	698,600	1,336,700	1,280,700	1,107,000	1,300,800
Total Liabilities	3,291,600	2,899,500	3,009,900	3,054,300	2,847,100	2,685,500	2,588,200	2,885,100
Stockholders' Equity	2,841,900	2,475,300	2,205,200	2,286,500	2,118,200	2,002,400	2,023,200	1,904,200
Shares Outstanding	179,453	182,282	183,113	185,087	187,595	183,418	187,523	186,826
Statistical Record								
Return on Assets %	12.03	8.76	3.11	6.58	3.07	4.60	4.92	7.98
Return on Equity %	26.04	19.83	7.30	15.39	7.20	10.62	11.78	19.54
EBITDA Margin %	16.86	15.64	14.18	13.76	12.64	12.03	13.96	18.49
Net Margin %	11.73	8.95	3.46	7.61	3.65	5.40	5.49	8.01
Asset Turnover	1.03	0.98	0.90	0.86	0.84	0.85	0.90	1.00
Current Ratio	1.41	1.46	1.84	1.21	1.92	1.76	1.49	1.48
Debt to Equity	0.32	0.28	0.45	0.31	0.63	0.64	0.55	0.68
Price Range	58.72-44.67	47.75-36.94	37.48-31.11	34.13-25.78	29.35-17.03	22.98-13.98	30.13-15.93	22.97-15.09
P/E Ratio	15.74-11.98	19.25-14.90	43.58-36.18	19.06-14.40	37.15-21.56	20.16-12.26	24.69-13.05	12.09-7.94
Average Yield %	1.66	1.71	2.17	2.39	3.18	3.79	3.35	3.91

Address: 600 Travis, Suite 5800,	Web Site: www.cooperindustries.com	Auditors: Ernst & Young LLP
Houston, TX 77002	Officers: Kirk S. Hachigian - Chmn., Pres., C.E.O.	Investor Contact: 713-209-8610
Telephone: 713-209-8400	Terry A. Klebe - Sr. V.P., C.F.O.	Transfer Agents: Computershare Trust
Fax: 713-209-8996		Company, N.A., Canton, MA

COOPER TIRE & RUBBER CO.

Exchange	Symbol	Price	52Wk Range	Yield	P/E
NYS	CTB	$14.97 (3/31/2008)	28.02-13.69	2.81	7.84

*7 Year Price Score 94.86 *NYSE Composite Index=100 *12 Month Price Score 90.67

Interim Earnings (Per Share)

Qtr.	Mar	Jun	Sep	Dec
2003	0.21	0.17	0.24	0.38
2004	0.32	0.44	0.13	1.78
2005	0.07	(0.11)	(0.01)	(0.11)
2006	(0.08)	(0.34)	(0.41)	(0.45)
2007	0.33	0.28	0.48	0.82

Interim Dividends (Per Share)

Amt	Decl	Ex	Rec	Pay
0.105Q	5/1/2007	5/30/2007	6/1/2007	6/29/2007
0.105Q	8/3/2007	8/30/2007	9/4/2007	9/28/2007
0.105Q	11/15/2007	11/29/2007	12/3/2007	12/28/2007
0.105Q	2/27/2008	3/6/2008	3/10/2008	3/31/2008

Indicated Div: $0.42

Valuation Analysis / **Institutional Holding**

Forecast P/E	11.68
	(1/10/2007)
Market Cap	$893.1 Million
Book Value	792.3 Million
Price/Book	1.13
Price/Sales	0.30

No of Institutions 155
Shares 56,596,864
% Held 92.18

Business Summary: Rubber Products (MIC: 11.6 SIC: 3011 NAIC: 326211)

Cooper Tire & Rubber is engaged as a manufacturer of replacement tires. Co. focuses on the manufacture and sale of passenger and light truck replacement tires. In addition, Co. is engaged in manufacturing radial medium and bias light truck tires, as well as manufactures and sells motorcycle and racing tires. Co.'s North American Tire Operations segment produces passenger car and light truck tires, primarily for sale in the U.S. replacement market, while its International Tire Operations segment has manufacturing facilities in the U.K. and China, producing passenger car, light truck, racing, motorcycle tires, radial light and medium truck tires, and off-the-road tires.

Recent Developments: For the year ended Dec 31 2007, income from continuing operations was US$91.4 million compared with a loss of US$74.3 million a year earlier. Net income amounted to US$119.6 million versus a net loss of US$78.5 million in the prior year. Revenues were US$2.93 billion, up 13.9% from US$2.58 billion the year before. Operating income was US$134.4 million versus a loss of US$45.3 million in the prior year. Direct operating expenses rose 9.9% to US$2.62 billion from US$2.38 billion in the comparable period the year before. Indirect operating expenses decreased 24.0% to US$181.0 million from US$238.3 million in the equivalent prior-year period.

Prospects: Co. expects its turnaround efforts to continue in 2008. Specifically, Co. anticipates continued revenue growth and operational improvement in North America as it implements its Cooper Tire Lean Six Sigma operational excellence program and additional automation projects. Co.'s International operations will also continue to increase in scale and have the opportunity to begin improving margins due to the continued ramp up of its recently constructed greenfield joint venture in China and the added capacity in its other Chinese joint venture. Also, Co. expects continuing raw material price increases in 2008, and believes its price increases in each region will help to mitigate those effects.

Financial Data

(US$ in Thousands)	12/31/2007	12/31/2006	12/31/2005	12/31/2004	12/31/2003	12/31/2002	12/31/2001	12/31/2000
Earnings Per Share	1.91	(1.28)	(0.15)	2.68	1.00	1.51	0.25	1.31
Cash Flow Per Share	6.02	1.89	0.84	1.37	3.18	4.65	3.71	3.13
Tang Book Value Per Share	12.40	9.42	14.02	15.30	7.48	6.99	6.64	7.07
Dividends Per Share	0.420	0.420	0.420	0.420	0.420	0.420	0.420	0.420
Dividend Payout %	21.99	...	...	15.67	42.00	27.81	168.00	32.06
Income Statement								
Total Revenue	2,932,575	2,676,242	2,155,185	2,081,609	3,514,399	3,329,957	3,154,702	3,472,372
EBITDA	301,949	83,518	137,286	173,445	367,936	432,317	306,845	446,398
Income Before Taxes	116,030	(91,954)	(14,351)	35,006	114,110	177,197	29,158	160,156
Income Taxes	15,835	(9,727)	704	7,560	40,274	65,352	10,992	63,422
Net Income	119,570	(78,511)	(9,356)	201,347	73,836	111,845	18,166	96,734
Average Shares	62,712	61,338	63,653	75,185	74,203	74,024	72,558	73,584
Balance Sheet								
Current Assets	1,189,924	1,009,124	968,801	1,646,277	1,024,409	859,298	952,097	1,031,225
Total Assets	2,296,868	2,235,279	2,152,186	2,668,084	2,868,867	2,710,979	2,764,250	2,922,009
Current Liabilities	532,535	527,252	277,597	311,965	476,727	433,346	647,905	606,507
Long-Term Obligations	464,608	513,213	491,618	773,704	871,948	875,378	882,134	1,036,960
Total Liabilities	1,504,577	1,595,388	1,213,410	1,497,551	1,838,478	1,769,263	1,854,010	1,969,453
Stockholders' Equity	792,291	639,891	938,776	1,170,534	1,030,389	941,716	910,240	952,556
Shares Outstanding	59,661	61,379	61,321	71,139	73,964	73,557	72,599	72,543
Statistical Record								
Return on Assets %	5.28	N.M.	N.M.	7.25	2.65	4.09	0.64	3.40
Return on Equity %	16.70	N.M.	N.M.	18.25	7.49	12.08	1.95	10.01
EBITDA Margin %	10.30	3.12	6.37	8.33	10.47	12.98	9.73	12.86
Net Margin %	4.08	N.M.	N.M.	9.67	2.10	3.36	0.58	2.79
Asset Turnover	1.29	1.22	0.89	0.75	1.26	1.22	1.11	1.22
Current Ratio	2.23	1.91	3.49	5.28	2.15	1.98	1.47	1.70
Debt to Equity	0.59	0.80	0.52	0.66	0.85	0.93	0.97	1.09
Price Range	28.02-14.13	16.47-7.98	22.13-13.24	23.74-17.77	21.60-12.20	25.67-12.65	17.30-11.05	15.75-9.25
P/E Ratio	14.67-7.40	...	...	8.86-6.63	21.60-12.20	17.00-8.38	69.20-44.20	12.02-7.06
Average Yield %	2.02	3.43	2.37	1.99	2.53	2.27	3.04	3.60

Address: 701 Lima Avenue, Findlay, OH 45840	Web Site: www.coopertire.com	Auditors: ERNST & YOUNG LLP
Telephone: 419-423-1321	Officers: Thomas A. Dattilo - Chmn., Pres., C.E.O.	Investor Contact: 419-427-4768
Fax: 419-424-4305	Phillip G. Weaver - V.P., C.F.O.	Transfer Agents: Computershare Investor Services LLC, Chicago, IL

CORN PRODUCTS INTERNATIONAL INC

Exchange	Symbol	Price	52Wk Range	Yield	P/E
NYS	CPO	$37.14 (3/31/2008)	49.12-32.43	1.29	14.34

*7 Year Price Score 135.59 ***NYSE Composite Index=100** ***12 Month Price Score 98.76**

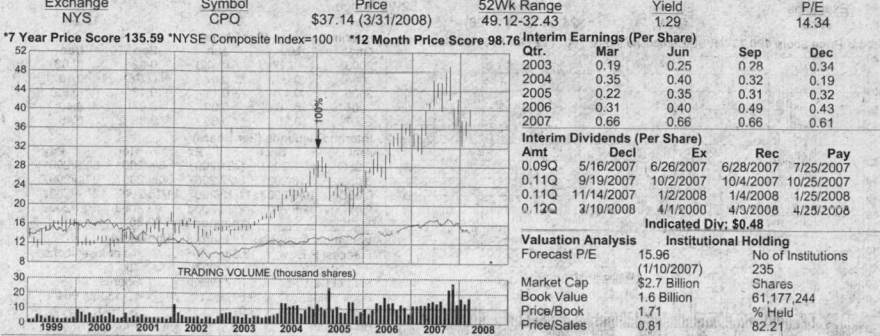

Interim Earnings (Per Share)

Qtr.	Mar	Jun	Sep	Dec
2003	0.19	0.25	0.28	0.34
2004	0.35	0.40	0.32	0.19
2005	0.22	0.35	0.31	0.32
2006	0.31	0.40	0.49	0.43
2007	0.66	0.66	0.66	0.61

Interim Dividends (Per Share)

Amt	Decl	Ex	Rec	Pay
0.09Q	5/16/2007	6/26/2007	6/28/2007	7/25/2007
0.11Q	9/19/2007	10/2/2007	10/4/2007	10/25/2007
0.11Q	11/14/2007	1/2/2008	1/4/2008	1/25/2008
0.12Q	3/10/2008	4/1/2008	4/3/2008	4/25/2008

Indicated Div: $0.48

Valuation Analysis / **Institutional Holding**

Forecast P/E	15.96	No of Institutions
	(1/10/2007)	235
Market Cap	$2.7 Billion	Shares
Book Value	1.6 Billion	61,177,244
Price/Book	1.71	% Held
Price/Sales	0.81	82.21

Business Summary: Food (MIC: 4.1 SIC: 2046 NAIC: 311221)

Corn Products International, together with its subsidiaries, manufactures and sells food ingredients and industrial products derived from the wet milling and processing of corn as well as other starch-based materials, such as tapioca. Co. operates in one business segment, corn refining, and is managed on a geographic basis that includes regional operations in North America, South America and Asia/Africa. Co.'s sweetener products include high fructose corn syrup, glucose corn syrups, high maltose corn syrups, caramel color, dextrose, maltodextrins and glucose and corn syrup solids. Co.'s starch-based products include both industrial and food-grade starches.

Recent Developments: For the quarter ended Sep 30 2007, net income increased 38.1% to US$51.1 million from US$37.0 million in the year-earlier quarter. Revenues were US$877.4 million, up 30.1% from US$674.2 million the year before. Operating income was US$88.0 million versus US$64.5 million in the prior-year quarter, an increase of 36.4%. Direct operating expenses rose 30.9% to US$735.7 million from US$562.0 million in the comparable period the year before. Indirect operating expenses increased 12.6% to US$53.7 million from US$47.7 million in the equivalent prior-year period.

Prospects: Co. is experiencing increases in its top-line results, as a result of an improved price/product mix, along with slightly higher volumes. In addition, Co.'s Dec 2006 acquisition of DEMSA and its Feb 2007 acquisition of GETEC and SPI Polyols also contributed to the increase in net sales. Moreover, Co. is seeing bottom-line growth reflecting an increase in operating income driven by improved results in North America and South America. Meanwhile, Co. continues to make progress on product channel expansions in countries such as Argentina, Columbia, Mexico, Pakistan and Thailand.

Financial Data

(US$ in Thousands)	12/31/2007	12/31/2006	12/31/2005	12/31/2004	12/31/2003	12/31/2002	12/31/2001	12/31/2000
Earnings Per Share	2.59	1.63	1.19	1.25	1.05	0.89	0.80	0.68
Cash Flow Per Share	3.45	3.10	3.28	2.26	3.28	2.89	2.42	2.99
Tang Book Value Per Share	15.99	12.77	11.53	9.93	8.18	7.67	8.11	9.17
Dividends Per Share	0.400	0.330	0.280	0.250	0.210	0.200	0.200	0.200
Dividend Payout %	15.44	20.25	23.53	20.00	19.91	22.60	25.00	29.63
Income Statement								
Total Revenue	3,391,000	2,621,000	2,360,000	2,283,000	2,102,000	1,871,000	1,887,000	1,865,000
EBITDA	468,000	339,000	286,000	280,000	275,000	220,000	229,000	237,000
Income Before Taxes	305,000	197,000	148,000	145,000	135,000	117,000	102,000	102,000
Income Taxes	102,000	69,000	55,000	43,000	49,000	42,000	36,000	36,000
Net Income	198,000	124,000	90,000	94,000	76,000	63,000	57,000	48,000
Average Shares	76,500	75,800	75,564	74,700	72,400	71,400	71,000	70,600
Balance Sheet								
Current Assets	1,089,000	837,000	685,000	661,000	547,000	485,000	555,000	555,000
Total Assets	3,103,000	2,662,000	2,389,000	2,367,000	2,210,000	2,015,000	2,227,000	2,339,000
Current Liabilities	674,000	517,000	424,000	462,000	394,000	347,000	675,000	486,000
Long-Term Obligations	519,000	480,000	471,000	480,000	452,000	516,000	312,000	453,000
Total Liabilities	1,479,000	1,288,000	1,150,000	1,253,000	1,232,000	1,187,000	1,370,000	1,379,000
Stockholders' Equity	1,605,000	1,330,000	1,210,000	1,081,000	911,000	828,000	857,000	960,000
Shares Outstanding	73,750	74,302	73,791	73,301	72,331	71,407	70,812	70,536
Statistical Record								
Return on Assets %	6.87	4.91	3.78	4.10	3.60	2.97	2.50	2.10
Return on Equity %	13.49	9.76	7.86	9.41	8.74	7.48	6.27	4.82
EBITDA Margin %	13.80	12.93	12.12	12.26	13.08	11.76	12.14	12.71
Net Margin %	5.84	4.73	3.81	4.12	3.62	3.37	3.02	2.57
Asset Turnover	1.18	1.04	0.99	0.99	1.00	0.88	0.83	0.82
Current Ratio	1.62	1.62	1.62	1.43	1.39	1.40	0.82	1.14
Debt to Equity	0.32	0.36	0.39	0.44	0.50	0.62	0.36	0.47
Price Range	49.12-30.79	37.21-23.68	30.14-18.05	27.75-17.23	17.94-13.68	17.63-12.38	18.43-12.25	16.38-9.88
P/E Ratio	18.97-11.89	22.83-14.53	25.33-15.17	22.20-13.78	17.09-13.02	19.80-13.91	23.03-15.31	24.08-14.52
Average Yield %	1.00	1.08	1.17	1.13	1.33	1.33	1.38	1.61

Address: 5 Westbrook Corporate Center, Westchester, IL 60154	Web Site: www.cornproducts.com	Auditors: KPMG LLP
Telephone: 708-551-2600	Officers: Samuel C. Scott III - Chmn., Pres., C.E.O. James W. Ripley - Sr. V.P., Planning, Info. Tech., Compliance	Investor Contact: 708-551-2592 Transfer Agents: The Bank of New York

CORNING, INC.

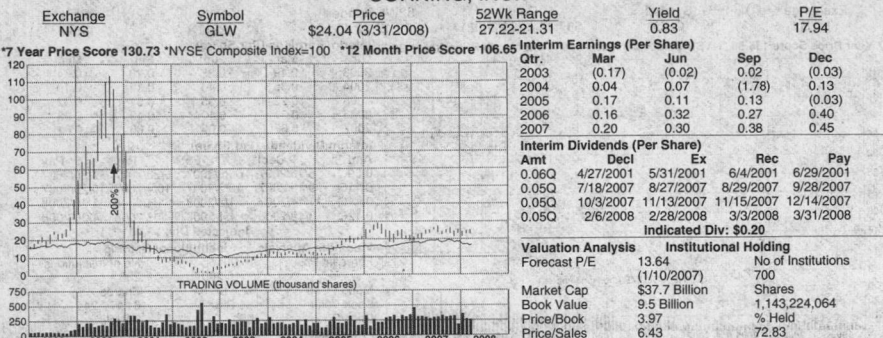

Exchange	Symbol	Price	52Wk Range	Yield	P/E
NYS	GLW	$24.04 (3/31/2008)	27.22-21.31	0.83	17.94

*7 Year Price Score 130.73 *NYSE Composite Index=100 *12 Month Price Score 106.65

Interim Earnings (Per Share)

Qtr.	Mar	Jun	Sep	Dec
2003	(0.17)	(0.02)	0.02	(0.03)
2004	0.04	0.07	(1.78)	0.13
2005	0.17	0.11	0.13	(0.03)
2006	0.16	0.32	0.27	0.40
2007	0.20	0.30	0.38	0.45

Interim Dividends (Per Share)

Amt	Decl	Ex	Rec	Pay
0.06Q	4/27/2001	5/31/2001	6/4/2001	6/29/2001
0.05Q	7/18/2007	8/27/2007	8/29/2007	9/28/2007
0.05Q	10/3/2007	11/13/2007	11/15/2007	12/14/2007
0.05Q	2/6/2008	2/28/2008	3/3/2008	3/31/2008

Indicated Div: $0.20

Valuation Analysis | **Institutional Holding**

Forecast P/E	13.64	No of Institutions
	(1/10/2007)	700
Market Cap	$37.7 Billion	Shares
Book Value	9.5 Billion	1,143,224,064
Price/Book	3.97	% Held
Price/Sales	6.43	72.83

TRADING VOLUME (thousand shares)

Business Summary: Metal Works (MIC: 11.3 SIC: 3357 NAIC: 334210)

Corning is a global, technology-based company that operates in four business segments. Co.'s Display Technologies segment manufactures glass substrates for active matrix liquid crystal displays (LCDs), which are used mainly in notebook computers, flat panel desktop monitors, and LCD televisions. Co.'s Telecommunications segment produces optical fiber and cable, and hardware and equipment products for the worldwide telecommunications industry, while the Life Sciences segment supplies laboratory products. Co.'s Environmental Products segment includes ceramic technologies and devices for emissions and pollution control in mobile and stationary applications, including filter products.

Recent Developments: For the year ended Dec 31 2007, net income increased 15.9% to US$2.15 billion from US$1.86 billion in the prior year. Revenues were US$5.86 billion, up 13.3% from US$5.17 billion the year before. Operating income was US$1.08 billion versus US$846.0 million in the prior year, an increase of 27.8%. Direct operating expenses rose 7.6% to US$3.11 billion from US$2.89 billion in the comparable period the year before. Indirect operating expenses increased 16.1% to US$1.67 billion from US$1.44 billion in the equivalent prior-year period.

Prospects: For the first quarter of 2008, Co. is projecting sales to be in the range of $1.59 billion to $1.62 billion, an improvement of more than 20.0% compared with the same period in 2007. In addition, Co. is targeting earnings to range from $0.41 to $0.43 per share, excluding special items, reflecting growth of about 50.0% over the same period in 2007. Similarly, Co. anticipates Liquid Crystal Display (LCD) glass volume to remain strong throughout the quarter, and to increase by 45.0% from the corresponding period in 2007. Meanwhile, for the full year of 2008, Co. expects global demand for LCD glass to grow 25.0% to 30.0%, representing an increase of more than 450.0 million square feet of glass.

Financial Data

(US$ in Thousands)	12/31/2007	12/31/2006	12/31/2005	12/31/2004	12/31/2003	12/31/2002	12/31/2001	12/31/2000
Earnings Per Share	1.34	1.16	0.38	(1.56)	(0.18)	(1.39)	(5.89)	0.48
Cash Flow Per Share	1.33	1.16	1.32	0.73	0.10	(0.31)	1.55	1.65
Tang Book Value Per Share	5.86	4.43	3.43	2.38	2.59	2.14	3.39	3.56
Dividends Per Share	0.100	...	...	...	...	...	0.120	0.240
Dividend Payout %	7.46	...	...	...	...	...	...	50.00
Income Statement								
Total Revenue	5,860,000	5,174,000	4,579,000	3,854,000	3,090,000	3,164,000	6,272,000	7,273,100
EBITDA	1,478,200	1,510,000	1,139,000	(1,218,100)	(120,000)	(1,921,000)	(4,946,000)	6,559,200
Income Before Taxes	1,291,000	961,000	572,000	(1,580,000)	(759,000)	(2,720,000)	(6,111,000)	691,400
Income Taxes	80,000	55,000	578,000	1,031,000	(254,000)	(726,000)	(452,000)	407,100
Net Income	2,150,000	1,855,000	585,000	(2,165,000)	(223,000)	(1,302,000)	(5,498,000)	422,000
Average Shares	1,603,000	1,594,000	1,535,000	1,386,000	1,274,000	1,030,000	933,000	879,300
Balance Sheet								
Current Assets	5,294,000	4,798,000	3,860,000	3,281,000	2,694,000	3,825,000	4,107,000	4,634,400
Total Assets	15,215,000	13,065,000	11,175,000	9,710,000	10,752,000	11,548,000	12,793,000	17,525,700
Current Liabilities	2,512,000	2,319,000	2,216,000	2,336,000	1,553,000	1,680,000	1,994,000	1,948,700
Long-Term Obligations	1,514,000	1,696,000	1,789,000	2,214,000	2,668,000	3,963,000	4,461,000	3,966,400
Total Liabilities	5,673,000	5,774,000	5,523,000	5,865,000	5,288,000	6,857,000	7,379,000	6,892,800
Stockholders' Equity	9,496,000	7,246,000	5,609,000	3,816,000	5,464,000	4,691,000	5,414,000	10,632,900
Shares Outstanding	1,568,000	1,565,000	1,536,000	1,408,000	1,343,000	1,197,000	921,000	924,100
Statistical Record								
Return on Assets %	15.21	15.31	5.60	N.M.	N.M.	N.M.	N.M.	3.58
Return on Equity %	25.68	28.86	12.41	N.M.	N.M.	N.M.	N.M.	6.55
EBITDA Margin %	25.23	29.18	24.87	N.M.	N.M.	N.M.	N.M.	90.18
Net Margin %	36.69	35.85	12.78	N.M.	N.M.	N.M.	N.M.	5.80
Asset Turnover	0.41	0.43	0.44	0.38	0.28	0.26	0.41	0.62
Current Ratio	2.11	2.07	1.74	1.40	1.73	2.28	2.06	2.38
Debt to Equity	0.16	0.23	0.32	0.58	0.49	0.84	0.82	0.37
Price Range	27.22-18.46	29.09-17.82	21.74-10.74	13.78-9.55	12.01-3.31	10.70-1.10	70.13-7.01	113.33-34.58
P/E Ratio	20.31-13.78	25.08-15.36	57.21-28.26	...	...	...	...	236.11-72.05
Average Yield %	0.42	...	...	...	...	...	0.57	0.33

Address: One Riverfront Plaza,	Web Site: www.corning.com	Auditors: PricewaterhouseCoopers LLP
Corning, NY 14831-0001	Officers: James R. Houghton - Chmn. James B. Flaws	Investor Contact: 607-974-9000
Telephone: 607-974-9000	- Vice-Chmn., C.F.O.	Transfer Agents: Computershare
Fax: 607-974-8688		Investor Services LLC, Chicago, IL

CORPORATE OFFICE PROPERTIES TRUST

Exchange	Symbol	Price	52Wk Range	Yield	P/E	Div Acheiver
NYS	OFC	$33.61 (3/31/2008)	48.55-26.76	4.05	86.18	10 Years

*7 Year Price Score 114.81 *NYSE Composite Index=100 *12 Month Price Score 89.24

Interim Earnings (Per Share)

Qtr.	Mar	Jun	Sep	Dec
2003	0.22	(0.30)	0.18	0.15
2004	0.14	0.13	0.12	0.15
2005	0.14	0.14	0.18	0.17
2006	0.15	0.13	0.33	0.08
2007	0.03	0.08	0.15	0.12

Interim Dividends (Per Share)

Amt	Decl	Ex	Rec	Pay
0.31Q	5/17/2007	6/27/2007	6/29/2007	7/17/2007
0.34Q	9/20/2007	9/26/2007	9/28/2007	10/16/2007
0.34Q	12/6/2007	12/27/2007	12/31/2007	1/15/2008
0.34Q	2/28/2008	3/27/2008	0/01/2000	4/15/2008

Indicated Div: $1.36

Valuation Analysis | **Institutional Holding**

Forecast P/E	N/A	No of Institutions
		163
Market Cap	$1.6 Billion	Shares
Book Value	822.6 Million	47,972,860
Price/Book	1.94	% Held
Price/Sales	3.88	N/A

Business Summary: Property, Real Estate & Development (MIC: 8.3 SIC: 6798 NAIC: 525930)

Corporate Office Properties Trust is an integrated and self-managed real estate investment trust that focuses on acquiring, developing, owning, managing and leasing suburban office properties in select markets and submarkets. As of Dec 31 2007, Co. owned 228 operating properties in Maryland, Virginia, Colorado, Texas, Pennsylvania and New Jersey containing 17.8 million rentable square feet; 19 office properties under construction or development that totals about 1.8 million square feet upon completion, one wholly owned office property totaling 74,749 square feet under redevelopment; and land parcels totaling 225 acres.

Recent Developments: For the year ended Dec 31 2007, income from continuing operations increased 2.9% to US$31.4 million from US$30.5 million a year earlier. Net income decreased 29.3% to US$34.8 million from US$49.2 million in the prior year. Revenues were US$410.2 million, up 16.0% from US$353.7 million the year before. Revenues from property income rose 17.4% to US$406.0 million from US$345.8 million in the corresponding earlier year.

Prospects: As of Dec 31 2007, Co. noted that it had construction underway on four wholly owned properties in Colorado Springs, three wholly owned properties in the Baltimore/Washington Corridor and two wholly owned properties in San Antonio, which it expects to be completed and begin generating rental revenue between 2008 and 2009. As a result, for 2008, Co. is updating its earnings per share guidance from $0.58 to $0.67 to a range of $0.62 to $0.69 per diluted share. In addition, Co. is revising its 2008 funds from operations (FFO) guidance from $2.40 to $2.49 to a range of $2.41 to $2.49 per diluted share, representing FFO growth of 8.0% to 11.0% compared with 2007 actual results.

Financial Data
(US$ in Thousands)

	12/31/2007	12/31/2006	12/31/2005	12/31/2004	12/31/2003	12/31/2002	12/31/2001	12/31/2000
Earnings Per Share	0.39	0.69	0.63	0.54	0.27	0.56	0.63	0.59
Cash Flow Per Share	2.96	2.73	2.57	2.54	2.54	2.77	2.53	1.86
Tang Book Value Per Share	15.07	13.68	12.31	12.33	13.42	12.22	12.78	9.49
Dividends Per Share	1.300	1.180	1.070	0.980	0.910	0.860	0.820	0.780
Dividend Payout %	333.33	171.01	169.84	181.48	337.04	153.57	130.16	132.20
Income Statement								
Property Income	406,023	353,501	324,268	239,591	203,288	147,995	125,546	108,993
Non-Property Income	4,151	7,902	4,877	3,885	2,875	3,888	3,864	...
Total Revenue	410,174	361,403	329,145	243,476	206,163	151,883	129,410	108,993
Interest Expense	85,708	74,225	58,895	46,694	41,079	39,067	32,773	30,454
Income Taxes	569	887	668	795	(124)	(242)	(269)	...
Net Income	34,784	49,227	39,031	37,032	30,877	23,301	19,922	15,134
Average Shares	47,630	43,262	38,997	34,982	28,021	24,547	21,623	19,213
Balance Sheet								
Total Assets	2,931,853	2,419,601	2,130,376	1,732,026	1,332,076	1,126,471	984,210	794,837
Long-Term Obligations	1,825,842	1,498,537	1,348,351	1,022,688	738,698	705,056	573,327	474,349
Total Liabilities	1,979,116	1,629,111	1,442,036	1,111,224	801,899	737,088	615,507	495,549
Stockholders' Equity	822,642	674,303	582,513	521,924	450,381	288,497	263,921	193,728
Shares Outstanding	47,366	42,897	39,927	36,842	29,397	23,606	20,648	20,409
Statistical Record								
Return on Assets %	1.30	2.16	2.02	2.41	2.51	2.21	2.24	1.99
Return on Equity %	4.65	7.83	7.07	7.60	8.36	8.44	8.71	7.82
Net Margin %	8.48	13.62	11.86	15.21	14.98	15.34	15.39	13.89
Price Range	56.00-30.97	51.20-36.24	36.90-25.35	29.35-19.47	22.14-13.59	14.59-11.85	12.50-9.10	10.00-7.63
P/E Ratio	143.59-79.41	74.20-52.52	58.57-40.24	54.35-36.06	82.00-50.33	26.05-21.16	19.84-14.44	16.95-12.92
Average Yield %	3.00	2.70	3.50	4.01	5.32	6.44	7.84	8.76

Address: 6711 Columbia Gateway Drive, Columbia, MD 21046
Telephone: 443-285-5400

Web Site: www.copt.com
Officers: Jay H. Shidler - Chmn. Randall M. Griffin - Pres., C.O.O.

Auditors: PricewaterhouseCoopers LLP
Investor Contact: 443-285-5450
Transfer Agents: Wells Fargo Bank, N.A., South St. Paul, MN

CORRECTIONS CORPORATION OF AMERICA

Exchange	Symbol	Price	52Wk Range	Yield	P/E
NYS	CXW	$27.52 (3/31/2008)	33.01-23.02	N/A	25.96

*7 Year Price Score 168.77 *NYSE Composite Index=100 *12 Month Price Score 98.82

TRADING VOLUME (thousand shares)

Interim Earnings (Per Share)

Qtr.	Mar	Jun	Sep	Dec
2003	0.19	0.11	0.18	0.69
2004	0.12	0.13	0.14	0.12
2005	(0.08)	0.12	0.17	0.19
2006	0.17	0.21	0.21	0.26
2007	0.26	0.26	0.26	0.27

Interim Dividends (Per Share)

Amt	Decl	Ex	Rec	Pay
3-for-2	...	9/14/2006	9/1/2006	9/13/2006
100%	6/7/2007	7/9/2007	6/29/2007	7/6/2007

Valuation Analysis

		Institutional Holding	
Forecast P/E	N/A	No of Institutions	212
Market Cap	$3.4 Billion	Shares	49,034,008
Book Value	1.2 Billion	% Held	79.87
Price/Book	2.80		
Price/Sales	2.32		

Business Summary: Miscellaneous Business Services (MIC: 12.8 SIC: 8744 NAIC: 561210)

Corrections Corporation of America owns and operates privatized correctional and detention facilities. At Dec 31 2007, Co. operated 65 correctional, detention and juvenile facilities, including 41 facilities that it owns, with a total design capacity of approximately 78,000 beds in 19 states and the District of Columbia. Also, Co. owned three additional correctional facilities that it leases to third-party operators. In addition to providing the fundamental residential services relating to inmates, Co.'s facilities provide a variety of rehabilitation and educational programs, including basic education, religious services, life skills and employment training and substance abuse treatment.

Recent Developments: For the year ended Dec 31 2007, income from continuing operations increased 26.6% to US$132.5 million from US$104.7 million a year earlier. Net income increased 26.7% to US$133.4 million from US$105.2 million in the prior year. Revenues were US$1.48 billion, up 11.7% from US$1.32 billion the year before. Operating income was US$266.3 million versus US$225.0 million in the prior year, an increase of 18.4%. Indirect operating expenses increased 10.3% to US$1.21 billion from US$1.10 billion in the equivalent prior-year period.

Prospects: Co. continues to move forward with its development and expansion efforts. For instance, construction of Co.'s new 3,060-bed La Palma Correctional Center in Eloy, AZ is scheduled to be completed in the second quarter of 2009 at an estimated total cost of $205.0 million. In addition, on Feb 22 2008, Co. announced plans to begin construction of a new 2,040-bed correctional center, Trousdale Correctional Center, which will be located in Trousdale County, TN, in the summer of 2008. The construction, which has an estimated total cost of about $143.0 million, should be completed in the fourth quarter of 2009. Meanwhile, Co. is targeting diluted earnings per share of $1.21 to $1.28 for 2008.

Financial Data

(US$ in Thousands)	12/31/2007	12/31/2006	12/31/2005	12/31/2004	12/31/2003	12/31/2002	12/31/2001	12/31/2000
Earnings Per Share	1.06	0.85	0.42	0.52	1.15	(0.17)	0.07	(18.90)
Cash Flow Per Share	2.05	1.44	1.33	1.19	2.10	1.22	1.27	(1.18)
Tang Book Value Per Share	9.71	8.47	7.57	7.53	6.93	5.93	5.24	5.54
Income Statement								
Total Revenue	1,478,837	1,331,088	1,192,640	1,148,258	1,036,737	962,838	980,791	310,278
EBITDA	349,216	297,277	206,789	235,269	226,165	198,747	229,257	(571,881)
Income Before Taxes	212,827	166,388	77,452	104,768	90,203	45,065	26,830	(778,909)
Income Taxes	80,312	61,149	26,888	42,126	(52,352)	(63,284)	1,136	(48,002)
Net Income	133,373	105,239	50,122	62,543	141,783	(7,916)	25,694	(730,782)
Average Shares	125,381	123,058	120,843	119,340	114,147	106,722	85,176	39,397
Balance Sheet								
Current Assets	340,663	391,242	320,131	302,288	293,178	254,347	216,331	238,687
Total Assets	2,485,740	2,250,860	2,086,313	2,023,078	1,959,028	1,874,071	1,971,280	2,176,992
Current Liabilities	214,731	164,382	173,312	172,265	159,626	185,966	976,720	275,499
Long-Term Obligations	975,677	975,968	963,800	999,113	1,002,282	932,905	171,591	1,137,976
Total Liabilities	1,263,765	1,201,179	1,169,682	1,207,084	1,183,563	1,140,073	1,224,119	1,488,977
Stockholders' Equity	1,221,975	1,049,681	916,631	815,994	775,465	733,998	747,161	688,015
Shares Outstanding	124,472	122,084	119,082	106,245	105,060	83,958	83,760	70,614
Statistical Record								
Return on Assets %	5.63	4.85	2.44	3.13	7.40	N.M.	1.24	N.M.
Return on Equity %	11.74	10.70	5.79	7.84	18.79	N.M.	3.58	N.M.
EBITDA Margin %	23.61	22.33	17.34	20.49	21.82	20.64	23.37	N.M.
Net Margin %	9.02	7.91	4.20	5.45	13.68	N.M.	2.62	N.M.
Asset Turnover	0.62	0.61	0.58	0.58	0.54	0.50	0.47	0.13
Current Ratio	1.59	2.38	1.85	1.75	1.84	1.37	0.22	0.87
Debt to Equity	0.80	0.93	1.05	1.22	1.29	1.27	0.23	1.65
Price Range	33.01-21.80	23.98-13.56	14.99-11.83	13.48-9.33	9.71-5.53	6.38-3.98	6.19-1.25	9.43-0.94
P/E Ratio	31.14-20.57	28.21-15.95	35.69-28.17	25.93-17.95	8.45-4.81	...	88.38-17.86	...

<table>
<tr><td>Address: 10 Burton Hills Boulevard, Nashville, TN 37215
Telephone: 615-263-3000</td><td>Web Site: www.correctionscorp.com
Officers: William F. Andrews - Chmn. John D. Ferguson - Pres., C.E.O.</td><td>Auditors: Ernst & Young LLP
Transfer Agents: American Stock Transfer and Trust Company, New York, NY</td></tr>
</table>

CONAGRA FOODS, INC.

Exchange
NYS

Symbol
CAG

*NYSE Composite Index=100

'7 Year Price Score 81.08

*12 Month Price Score 97.48

Price
$23.95 (3/31/2008)

52Wk Range
27.43-21.00

TRADING VOLUME (thousand shares)

Yield
3.17

P/E
12.74

Interim Earnings (Per Share)

Qtr.	Aug	Nov	Feb	May
2004-05	0.26	0.47	0.32	0.19
2005-06	0.68	0.31	(0.06)	0.50
2006-07	0.33	0.21	0.38	0.10
2007-08	0.36	0.50	0.63	0.39

Interim Dividends (Per Share)

Amt	Decl	Ex	Rec	Pay
0.18Q	7/18/2007	7/31/2007	8/2/2007	9/4/2007
0.19Q	9/27/2007	10/31/2007	11/2/2007	12/3/2007
0.19Q	11/29/2007	1/24/2008	11/2/2007	12/3/2007
0.19Q	4/3/2008	4/29/2008	5/1/2008	2/28/2008

Indicated Div: $0.76 (Div. Reinv. Plan)

Valuation Analysis

Forecast P/E

Market Cap	19.10 (1/10/2007)	Institutional Holding
Book Value	$11.7 Billion	No of Institutions 449
Price/Book	5.0 Billion	Shares 346,699,072
Price/Sales	2.32 / 0.87	% Held 69.61

Business Summary: Food (MIC: 4.1 SIC: 2099 NAIC: 311999)

ConAgra Foods is a packaged food company serving a range of food customers. Co.'s Consumer Foods segment includes branded, private label and customized food products that are sold in various retail and foodservice channels. Co.'s Food and Ingredients segment includes commercially branded foods and ingredients, which are sold primarily to foodservice channels. Co.'s Food and Ingredients segment includes Trading and Merchandising segment includes the sourcing, merchandising, trading, food manufacturing and distribution of agricultural and energy commodities. Co.'s International Foods segment includes branded food products which are sold primarily in retail channels in North America, Europe and Asia.

Recent Developments:
For the quarter ended Feb 24 2008, income from continuing operations increased 66.3% to US$310.1 million from US$186.5 million in the year-earlier quarter. Revenues were US$3.53 billion, up 20.9% from US$2.92 billion to US$309.1 million from US$192.6 million in the year-earlier quarter. Net income increased 60.5% to US$309.1 million from US$192.6 million in the year before. Indirect operating expenses rose 19.2% million from US$506.3 million in the equivalent prior-year period.

Prospects:
For the fiscal year ending May 25 2008, Co. is projecting earnings to be in the range of $1.80 to $1.85 per share, excluding items affecting comparability. Separately, on Mar 27 2008, Co. announced an agreement to divest its Foods Trading and Merchandising segment to the Ospraie Special Opportunities fund and other investors for approximately $2.10 billion, subject to certain adjustments. Co. believes that this transaction, which is in-line with its ongoing core food businesses growth initiatives, should help improve its results going forward. Closing of the sale is subject to satisfaction of customary closing conditions, including receipt of regulatory approvals and financing matters.

Financial Data
(US$ in Thousands)

	9 Mos	6 Mos	3 Mos	05/27/2007	05/28/2006	05/29/2005	05/30/2004	05/25/2003
Earnings Per Share	1.88	1.63	1.55	1.51	1.03	1.23	1.66	1.46
Cash Flow Per Share	1.04	1.32		1.88	2.07	2.15	1.40	1.35
Tang Book Value Per Share	1.49	1.01	0.79	0.74	0.79	0.47	0.41	N.M.
Dividends Per Share	0.740	0.730	0.67	0.720	0.998	1.077	1.028	0.978
Dividend Payout %	39.27	44.66	0.720	47.68	96.84	87.60	61.90	66.95
Income Statement			46.34					
Total Revenue	9,995,000	6,466,600	2,955,600					
EBITDA	1,252,000	757,400	326,400	12,208,200	11,908,800	14,752,600		19,839,200
Depn & Amortn	231,500	153,200	75,800	1,351,100	1,266,600	14,522,100		
Income Before Taxes	1,020,500	604,200	250,600			1,511,000	1,503,600	
Income Taxes	371,800	220,300	87,400	1,005,100				
Net Income	729,300	420,200	175,400	365,700	955,400			
Average Shares	490,600	490,700	492,800	764,600	309,700	1,158,000	1,111,300	
Balance Sheet				507,100	533,800	470,000	355,300	
Current Assets	6,333,100				520,200	641,500	879,800	436,000
Total Assets	13,386,700	5,795,300	5,006,000	4,790,300		520,200	530,700	774,800
Current Liabilities	3,761,000	12,709,300	11,954,800	11,835,500	4,523,700	5,144,900		530,700
Long-Term Obligations	3,375,900	3,391,300	2,727,500	11,970,400	2,680,900	12,791,700	6,059,600	
Total Liabilities	8,348,200	3,375,100	3,420,100	3,420,000	2,964,800	14,230,100	15,071,400	
Stockholders' Equity	5,038,500	7,994,900	7,359,200	7,252,600	3,154,800	3,001,600	3,803,400	
Shares Outstanding	487,608	4,804,400	4,595,600	4,582,900	7,320,400	5,280,700	5,395,200	
Statistical Record		487,396	487,155	489,779	4,650,000	9,390,600	4,839,500	
Return on Assets %	7.20				510,861	4,859,400	10,449,700	
Return on Equity %	19.03	6.42				518,101	521,194	
EBITDA Margin %	12.53	16.92	6.47					
Net Margin %	7.30	11.71	16.67	6.44				
Asset Turnover	1.04	6.50	11.04	16.61	4.32			
Current Ratio	1.69	1.01	5.93	11.23	11.26	4.76		
Debt to Equity	0.67	1.71	1.03	6.36	10.64	13.26	5.91	
Price Range	27.43-21.00	0.70	1.84	1.01	4.48	18.30	10.24	
P/E Ratio	14.59-11.17	27.52-22.23	0.74	0.75	1.87	0.96	4.35	10.35
Average Yield %	2.99	16.88-13.99	16.88-13.99	1.62	1.09	6.06		
	2.86	17.75-14.95	27.52-23.17	27.52-21.25	26.15-19.50	1.89	0.98	1.73
		2.82	18.23-14.07	25.39-18.93	30.00-25.59	29.34		
			2.94	4.48	24.39-20.80	17		
				3.96				

Address: One ConAgra Drive, Omaha, NE 68102-5001

Telephone: 402-595-4000

Fax: 402-978-4447

Web Site: www.conagrafoods.com

Officers: Gary M. Rodkin - Pres., C.E.O. Frank S. Sklarsky - Exec. V.P., C.F.O.

Auditors:
Investor Contact:
Transf

200

COVANCE INC.

Exchange	Symbol	Price	52Wk Range	Yield	P/E
NYS	CVD	$82.97 (3/31/2008)	96.13-59.02	N/A	30.62

*7 Year Price Score 148.14 *NYSE Composite Index=100 *12 Month Price Score 116.36

Interim Earnings (Per Share)

Qtr.	Mar	Jun	Sep	Dec
2003	0.28	0.29	0.31	0.32
2004	0.34	0.36	0.39	0.43
2005	0.45	0.46	0.49	0.47
2006	0.52	0.54	0.59	0.59
2007	0.60	0.64	0.69	0.78

Interim Dividends (Per Share)

No Dividends Paid

Valuation Analysis

		Institutional Holding	
Forecast P/E	19.08	No of Institutions	
	(1/10/2007)	286	
Market Cap	$5.3 Billion	Shares	
Book Value	1.1 Billion	55,039,920	
Price/Book	4.79	% Held	
Price/Sales	3.26	86.04	

Business Summary: Biotechnology (MIC: 9.2 SIC: 8731 NAIC: 541710)

Covance is a drug development services company providing a range of early-stage and late-stage product development services on a worldwide basis primarily to the pharmaceutical, biotechnology and medical device industries. Co. also provides laboratory testing services to the chemical, agrochemical and food industries. The services Co. provides constitutes two segments: early development services, which includes preclinical services and clinical pharmacology services; and late-stage development services, which includes central laboratory, clinical development, periapproval and market access services. As of Dec 31 2007, Co. maintained offices in more than 20 countries.

Recent Developments: For the year ended Dec 31 2007, net income increased 21.3% to US$175.9 million from US$145.0 million in the prior year. Revenues were US$1.63 billion, up 16.0% from US$1.41 billion the year before. Operating income was US$228.6 million versus US$193.2 million in the prior year, an increase of 18.3%. Direct operating expenses rose 16.3% to US$1.10 billion from US$948.0 million in the comparable period the year before. Indirect operating expenses increased 13.3% to US$300.1 million from US$264.8 million in the equivalent prior-year period.

Prospects: Co.'s outlook appears encouraging as it is seeing robust revenue growth and solid operating margins, reflecting strong demand for its early- and late-stage development service offerings. Accordingly, Co. experienced 20.6% growth in its backlog to US$2.68 billion at Dec 31 2007, which should support revenue growth. Accordingly, Co. continues to target low- to mid-teens revenue growth and a 20.0% year-over-year growth in earnings per share to $3.18 per diluted share. This forecast includes Co.'s sale of its centralized ECG business (Cardiac Safety Services), which Co. noted will remain in the base of the comparison year, will affect revenue growth in 2008 by approximately 350 basis points.

Financial Data

(US$ in Thousands)	12/31/2007	12/31/2006	12/31/2005	12/31/2004	12/31/2003	12/31/2002	12/31/2001	12/31/2000
Earnings Per Share	2.71	2.24	1.88	1.52	1.21	1.03	0.79	0.27
Cash Flow Per Share	4.60	4.00	2.91	2.60	2.27	2.12	1.13	0.85
Tang Book Value Per Share	15.69	12.57	10.68	9.33	8.11	6.19	4.86	3.19
Income Statement								
Total Revenue	1,631,516	1,406,058	1,250,454	1,056,397	974,210	924,697	855,877	868,087
EBITDA	302,808	250,413	221,855	186,590	161,716	133,706	132,909	98,222
Income Before Taxes	246,412	200,589	177,671	142,526	115,701	90,441	78,342	24,971
Income Taxes	72,934	57,179	58,786	45,532	40,021	26,658	30,442	9,735
Net Income	175,929	144,998	119,619	97,947	76,136	63,783	47,900	15,236
Average Shares	64,820	64,782	63,773	64,644	63,081	61,641	60,430	57,492
Balance Sheet								
Current Assets	770,057	639,566	546,710	508,954	449,854	345,386	324,493	353,012
Total Assets	1,560,185	1,297,678	1,056,603	924,685	807,625	677,003	612,028	771,091
Current Liabilities	358,160	289,704	252,728	219,126	189,824	214,435	226,783	451,722
Long-Term Obligations	...	...	...	...	...	...	15,000	17,224
Total Liabilities	449,997	374,383	324,832	286,999	243,644	245,336	267,083	505,340
Stockholders' Equity	1,110,188	923,295	731,771	637,686	563,981	431,667	344,945	265,751
Shares Outstanding	64,041	63,941	62,810	62,261	62,524	60,562	59,808	57,794
Statistical Record								
Return on Assets %	12.31	12.32	12.07	11.28	10.26	9.90	6.93	2.07
Return on Equity %	17.30	17.52	17.47	16.26	15.29	16.43	15.69	5.75
EBITDA Margin %	18.56	17.81	17.74	17.66	16.60	14.46	15.53	11.31
Net Margin %	10.78	10.31	9.57	9.27	7.82	6.90	5.60	1.76
Asset Turnover	1.14	1.19	1.26	1.22	1.31	1.43	1.24	1.18
Current Ratio	2.15	2.21	2.16	2.32	2.37	1.61	1.43	0.78
Debt to Equity	...	...	...	...	...	...	0.04	0.06
Price Range	90.17-58.49	68.00-49.15	52.96-35.86	41.40-26.25	27.55-16.90	24.63-12.71	25.30-10.56	16.25-6.88
P/E Ratio	33.27-21.58	30.36-21.94	28.17-19.07	27.24-17.27	22.77-13.97	23.91-12.34	32.03-13.37	60.19-25.46

Address: 210 Carnegie Center, Princeton, NJ 08540
Telephone: 609-452-4440
Fax: 609-452-9375

Web Site: www.covance.com
Officers: Christopher A. Kuebler - Chmn., C.E.O.
Joseph L. Herring - Pres., C.O.O.

Auditors: Ernst & Young LLP
Investor Contact: 609-452-4953
Transfer Agents: Computershare Investor Services LLC

COVENTRY HEALTH CARE INC.

Exchange	Symbol	Price	52Wk Range	Yield	P/E
NYS	CVH	$40.35 (3/31/2008)	62.36-40.31	N/A	10.14

*7 Year Price Score 132.02 *NYSE Composite Index=100   *12 Month Price Score 94.94

Interim Earnings (Per Share)

Qtr.	Mar	Jun	Sep	Dec
2003	0.37	0.47	0.49	0.50
2004	0.55	0.62	0.64	0.67
2005	0.73	0.79	0.81	0.77
2006	0.74	0.84	0.92	0.97
2007	0.76	0.96	1.08	1.18

Interim Dividends (Per Share)

Amt	Decl	Ex	Rec	Pay
50%	12/23/2003	2/2/2004	1/9/2004	1/30/2004
50%	8/31/2005	10/18/2005	10/3/2005	10/17/2005

Valuation Analysis   Institutional Holding

Forecast P/E	N/A	No of Institutions
		374
Market Cap	$6.2 Billion	Shares
Book Value	3.3 Billion	142,478,800
Price/Book	1.89	% Held
Price/Sales	0.63	89.34

Business Summary: Insurance (MIC: 8.2 SIC: 6324 NAIC: 524114)

Coventry Health Care is a managed health care company operating health plans, insurance companies, network rental/managed care services companies, and workers' compensation services companies. Co. provides risk and fee-based managed care products and services, including health maintenance organization, preferred provider organizations, point of service, Medicare Advantage, Medicare Prescription Drug Plans, Medicaid, Workers' Compensation and Network Rental to individuals, employer and government-funded groups, government agencies, and other insurance carriers and administrators. As of Dec 31 2007, Co. had 750,000 health plan members.

Recent Developments: For the year ended Dec 31 2007, net income increased 11.8% to US$626.1 million from US$560.0 million in the prior year. Revenues were US$9.88 billion, up 27.7% from US$7.73 billion the year before. Net premiums earned were US$8.69 billion versus US$6.86 billion in the prior year, an increase of 26.7%.

Prospects: Co. noted that it has closed an acquisition of a small behavioral health company on Feb 13 2008, which it expects to gain the benefits of in sourcing its behavioral health business in all of its markets over the next several years. In addition, Co. is pursuing a range of services for both life and dental products, and expects to move forward in these areas in 2008. For the first quarter of 2008, Co. expects total revenues to be $2.90 billion to $3.10 billion. Co. also expects earnings to be between $0.85 and $0.87 per diluted share, reflecting the effects of its Medicare Part D. As such, for full-year 2008, Co. anticipates that earnings to be between $4.42 and $4.58 per diluted share.

Financial Data

(US$ in Thousands)	12/31/2007	12/31/2006	12/31/2005	12/31/2004	12/31/2003	12/31/2002	12/31/2001	12/31/2000
Earnings Per Share	3.98	3.47	3.10	2.48	1.83	1.06	0.55	0.41
Cash Flow Per Share	3.74	6.72	5.09	3.42	2.44	1.57	1.24	0.79
Tang Book Value Per Share	0.89	5.92	3.21	6.60	4.57	2.85	2.86	2.31
Income Statement								
Total Revenue	9,879,531	7,733,756	6,611,246	5,311,969	4,535,143	3,576,905	3,147,245	2,604,910
EBITDA	1,283,785	1,117,258	918,351	574,085	430,321	250,293	160,582	129,094
Income Before Taxes	994,870	896,348	799,425	526,991	393,064	225,741	134,682	102,068
Income Taxes	368,776	336,303	297,786	189,874	142,919	80,138	51,153	40,728
Net Income	626,094	560,045	501,639	337,117	250,145	145,603	84,407	61,340
Average Shares	157,357	161,434	161,716	135,883	136,147	137,799	152,718	147,953
Balance Sheet								
Current Assets	1,846,701	2,134,382	1,325,702	973,027	533,967	424,275	578,518	506,500
Total Assets	7,158,791	5,665,107	4,895,172	2,340,600	1,981,736	1,643,440	1,451,273	1,239,036
Current Liabilities	1,749,821	1,651,989	1,270,227	931,820	854,880	800,712	751,545	632,163
Long-Term Obligations	1,662,021	750,500	760,500	170,500	170,500	175,000	...	...
Total Liabilities	3,857,312	2,712,105	2,340,469	1,128,174	1,052,738	997,403	762,194	638,606
Stockholders' Equity	3,301,479	2,953,002	2,554,703	1,212,426	928,998	646,037	689,079	600,430
Shares Outstanding	154,636	159,441	162,717	135,318	135,856	132,273	149,190	146,479
Statistical Record								
Return on Assets %	9.76	10.61	13.87	15.56	13.80	9.41	6.27	5.27
Return on Equity %	20.02	20.34	26.63	31.40	31.76	21.81	13.09	11.32
EBITDA Margin %	12.99	14.45	13.89	10.81	9.49	7.00	5.10	4.96
Net Margin %	6.34	7.24	7.59	6.35	5.52	4.07	2.68	2.35
Asset Turnover	1.54	1.46	1.83	2.45	2.50	2.31	2.34	2.24
Current Ratio	1.06	1.29	1.04	1.04	0.62	0.53	0.77	0.80
Debt to Equity	0.50	0.25	0.30	0.14	0.18	0.27	...	...
Price Range	62.36-49.44	61.24-44.78	60.20-34.54	36.01-25.63	29.23-11.28	16.69-8.85	11.28-6.11	12.97-3.00
P/E Ratio	15.67-12.42	17.65-12.90	19.42-11.14	14.52-10.33	15.97-6.16	15.74-8.30	20.51-11.11	31.64-7.32

Address: 6705 Rockledge Drive, Suite 900, Bethesda, MD 20817 Telephone: 301-581-0600 Fax: 301-493-0742	Web Site: www.coventryhealth.com Officers: Allen F. Wise - Chmn. Dale B. Wolf - C.E.O.	Auditors: Ernst & Young LLP Transfer Agents: Mellon Investor Services, LLC, Jersey City, NJ

CRANE CO.

Exchange	Symbol	Price	52Wk Range	Yield	P/E
NYS	CR	$40.35 (3/31/2008)	49.52-34.89	1.78	N/A

*7 Year Price Score 112.64 *NYSE Composite Index=100 *12 Month Price Score 101.76

Interim Earnings (Per Share)

Qtr.	Mar	Jun	Sep	Dec
2003	0.28	0.44	0.47	0.56
2004	0.37	0.52	(3.48)	0.78
2005	0.42	0.59	0.66	0.58
2006	0.61	0.71	0.74	0.61
2007	0.71	0.75	(3.29)	0.75

Interim Dividends (Per Share)

Amt	Decl	Ex	Rec	Pay
0.15Q	5/21/2007	5/29/2007	5/31/2007	6/8/2007
0.18Q	7/23/2007	8/29/2007	8/31/2007	9/11/2007
0.18Q	10/22/2007	11/28/2007	11/30/2007	12/10/2007
0.18Q	1/28/2008	2/27/2008	2/29/2008	3/10/2008

Indicated Div: $0.72

Valuation Analysis | **Institutional Holding**

Forecast P/E	11.01	No of Institutions
	(1/10/2007)	202
Market Cap	$2.4 Billion	Shares
Book Value	884.8 Million	39,343,952
Price/Book	2.74	% Held
Price/Sales	0.93	64.93

Business Summary: Metal Products (MIC: 11.4 SIC: 3492 NAIC: 336413)

Crane is a manufacturer of engineered industrial products, Co.'s Aerospace & Electronics segment comprises of two product groups: Aerospace and Electronics. The Engineered Materials segment manufactures mostly fiberglass reinforced plastic panels for the truck trailer and recreational vehicle markets, and industrial and commercial construction industries. The Merchandising Systems segment makes vending machines, coin changers and validators. Co. also operates Fluid Handling and Controls segments, the latter of which produces ride-leveling, air-suspension control valves for heavy trucks and trailers as well as ultra-rugged computers, and measurement and control systems.

Recent Developments: For the year ended Dec 31 2007, net loss amounted to US$62.3 million versus net income of US$165.9 million in the prior year. Revenues were US$2.62 billion, up 16.1% from US$2.26 billion the year before. Operating loss was US$107.7 million versus an income of US$247.9 million in the prior year. Direct operating expenses rose 16.4% to US$1.78 billion from US$1.53 billion in the comparable period the year before. Indirect operating expenses increased 96.7% to US$950.7 million from US$483.3 million in the equivalent prior-year period.

Prospects: For 2008, Co. has its increase its earnings guidance to a range of $3.45 to $3.60 per share, an increase of 8.0% to 13.0% compared with $3.19 per diluted share in 2007. In addition, Co. expects sales to increase 8.0% to approximately $2.80 billion, with growth in all its segments. Notably, Co. expects a 16.0% increase in operating profits in Fluid Handling reflecting solid global demand, represents approximately 43.0% of its sales. Also, Co. expects operating profits in its long-cycle Aerospace & Electronics businesses to increase 12.0% from continued strong demand and to benefit in the last half of 2008 as engineering investment slows from delivery of the 787 and A400M programs.

Financial Data

(US$ in Thousands)	12/31/2007	12/31/2006	12/31/2005	12/31/2004	12/31/2003	12/31/2002	12/31/2001	12/31/2000
Earnings Per Share	(1.04)	2.67	2.25	(1.78)	1.75	(0.19)	1.47	2.02
Cash Flow Per Share	3.88	2.98	3.04	1.87	2.74	3.31	3.30	2.47
Tang Book Value Per Share	N.M.	1.51	2.06	0.34	3.24	3.24	3.87	4.11
Dividends Per Share	0.660	0.550	0.450	0.400	0.400	0.400	0.400	0.400
Dividend Payout %	...	20.60	20.00	...	22.86	...	27.21	19.80
Income Statement								
Total Revenue	2,619,171	2,256,889	2,061,249	1,890,335	1,635,991	1,516,347	1,587,180	1,491,190
EBITDA	(36,440)	311,695	272,282	(90,659)	224,013	88,858	230,551	266,385
Income Before Taxes	(118,895)	239,334	196,523	(168,170)	151,164	24,453	135,817	190,360
Income Taxes	(56,553)	73,447	60,486	(62,749)	46,861	7,825	47,197	66,631
Net Income	(62,342)	165,887	136,037	(105,421)	104,303	(11,448)	88,620	123,729
Average Shares	60,037	62,103	60,413	59,251	59,716	59,728	60,355	61,399
Balance Sheet								
Current Assets	1,037,622	880,409	798,395	702,806	661,776	509,477	523,257	500,152
Total Assets	2,877,292	2,430,484	2,139,486	2,116,508	1,811,776	1,413,696	1,292,115	1,143,851
Current Liabilities	493,552	461,926	398,589	410,014	418,574	288,425	249,139	231,977
Long-Term Obligations	398,301	391,760	293,248	296,592	295,861	205,318	302,368	213,790
Total Liabilities	1,984,095	1,503,848	1,386,192	1,452,814	1,025,525	764,634	640,820	537,088
Stockholders' Equity	884,803	918,603	753,294	663,694	786,251	649,062	651,295	606,763
Shares Outstanding	60,161	60,472	60,408	59,203	59,676	59,447	59,689	60,426
Statistical Record								
Return on Assets %	N.M.	7.26	6.39	N.M.	6.47	N.M.	7.28	10.64
Return on Equity %	N.M.	19.84	19.20	N.M.	14.53	N.M.	14.09	21.00
EBITDA Margin %	N.M.	13.81	13.21	N.M.	13.69	5.86	14.53	17.86
Net Margin %	N.M.	7.35	6.60	N.M.	6.38	N.M.	5.58	8.30
Asset Turnover	0.99	0.99	0.97	0.96	1.01	1.12	1.30	1.28
Current Ratio	2.10	1.91	2.00	1.71	1.58	1.77	2.10	2.16
Debt to Equity	0.45	0.43	0.39	0.45	0.38	0.32	0.46	0.35
Price Range	49.52-35.79	45.34-35.60	37.15-25.48	34.33-25.95	30.75-15.23	28.95-18.08	31.80-20.48	29.06-18.63
P/E Ratio	...	16.98-13.33	16.51-11.32	...	17.57-8.70	...	21.63-13.93	14.39-9.22
Average Yield %	1.53	1.40	1.55	1.34	1.77	1.71	1.50	1.68

Address: 100 First Stamford Place, Stamford, CT 06092
Telephone: 203-363-7300
Fax: 203-363-7295

Web Site: www.craneco.com
Officers: Robert S. Evans - Chmn. Eric C. Fast - Pres., C.E.O.

Auditors: Deloitte & Touche LLP
Investor Contact: 888-272-6327
Transfer Agents: Computershare Trust Company N.A., Providence, RI

CROWN CASTLE INTERNATIONAL CORP

Exchange	Symbol	Price	52Wk Range	Yield	P/E
NYS	CCI	$34.49 (3/31/2008)	42.75-32.26	N/A	N/A

*7 Year Price Score 153.30 *NYSE Composite Index=100 *12 Month Price Score 102.14

Interim Earnings (Per Share)

Qtr.	Mar	Jun	Sep	Dec
2003	(0.38)	(0.47)	(0.50)	(0.73)
2004	(0.34)	(0.22)	2.02	(0.59)
2005	(0.62)	(1.09)	(0.17)	(0.19)
2006	(0.06)	(0.09)	(0.10)	(0.06)
2007	(0.18)	(0.13)	(0.26)	(0.30)

Interim Dividends (Per Share)

No Dividends Paid

Valuation Analysis

		Institutional Holding	
Forecast P/E	249.31	No of Institutions	
	(1/10/2007)	214	
Market Cap	$9.7 Billion	Shares	
Book Value	3.2 Billion	197,069,296	
Price/Book	3.08	% Held	
Price/Sales	7.03	69.69	

TRADING VOLUME (thousand shares)

Business Summary: Communications (MIC: 10.1 SIC: 4899 NAIC: 517212)

Crown Castle International is a holding company that owns, operates and leases towers and other communication structures, including certain rooftop installations for wireless communications. In addition, Co. provides certain network services relating to its towers, including initial antenna installations and subsequent augmentation, network design and site selection, site acquisition, site development and other services. As of Dec 31 2007, Co. owned, leased or managed 23,800 towers, including 22,400 towers in the U.S. and Puerto Rico and 1,400 towers in Australia.

Recent Developments: For the year ended Dec 31 2007, loss from continuing operations was US$222.8 million compared with a loss of US$47.6 million a year earlier. Net loss amounted to US$222.8 million versus a net loss of US$41.9 million in the prior year. Revenues were US$1.39 billion, up 75.8% from US$788.2 million the year before. Operating income was US$99.5 million versus US$121.4 million in the prior year, a decrease of 18.0%. Direct operating expenses rose 86.5% to US$509.1 million from US$273.0 million in the comparable period the year before. Indirect operating expenses increased 97.3% to US$776.9 million from US$393.8 million in the equivalent prior-year period.

Prospects: Looking ahead, as a result of the anticipated growth in the wireless communications industry, Co. believes that the demand for its towers will continue and result in organic growth of its revenues due to the co-location of additional tenants on its existing towers. Meanwhile, for full-year 2008, Co. is expecting site rental revenue of $1.28 billion to $1.29 billion and site rental gross margin in the range of $930.0 million to $940.0 million, assuming U.S. dollar to Australian dollar exchange rate of $0.85 and $0.83 to A$1.00. At the same time, Co. is projecting a net loss of between $0.42 and $0.06 per share, based on 280.3 million shares outstanding as of Dec 31 2007.

Financial Data

(US$ in Thousands)	12/31/2007	12/31/2006	12/31/2005	12/31/2004	12/31/2003	12/31/2002	12/31/2001	12/31/2000
Earnings Per Share	(0.87)	(0.30)	(2.07)	0.89	(2.09)	(1.16)	(2.08)	(1.48)
Cash Flow Per Share	1.25	1.33	0.94	0.30	1.20	0.96	0.62	0.92
Tang Book Value Per Share	N.M.	0.69	3.91	6.69	3.52	5.28	6.00	6.58
Income Statement								
Total Revenue	1,385,486	788,221	676,759	603,865	930,348	901,533	898,951	649,165
EBITDA	243,550	236,871	(111,964)	(28,482)	(62,266)	39,185	(22,504)	36,472
Income Before Taxes	(317,003)	(48,373)	(393,654)	(312,468)	(386,418)	(262,743)	(350,995)	(202,324)
Income Taxes	(94,039)	843	3,225	(5,370)	7,518	12,276	16,478	246
Net Income	(222,813)	(41,893)	(401,537)	235,110	(398,365)	(272,521)	(366,167)	(204,786)
Average Shares	279,937	207,245	217,759	221,693	216,947	218,020	214,246	178,588
Balance Sheet								
Current Assets	497,255	800,027	221,293	637,314	641,760	867,081	1,216,061	772,134
Total Assets	10,488,133	5,006,168	4,131,317	4,571,522	6,737,591	6,892,601	7,375,458	6,439,841
Current Liabilities	371,987	200,795	464,214	285,065	643,530	360,769	411,453	324,876
Long-Term Obligations	5,987,695	3,513,890	1,975,686	1,753,148	3,182,850	3,212,710	3,394,011	2,602,687
Total Liabilities	7,007,424	3,907,964	2,614,206	2,199,389	4,038,143	3,756,706	3,963,013	3,020,917
Stockholders' Equity	3,166,911	756,281	1,178,376	1,833,625	1,984,413	2,208,498	2,364,648	2,420,862
Shares Outstanding	282,507	202,080	214,188	224,064	220,758	215,983	218,804	198,912
Statistical Record								
Return on Assets %	N.M.	N.M.	N.M.	4.15	N.M.	N.M.	N.M.	N.M.
Return on Equity %	N.M.	N.M.	N.M.	12.28	N.M.	N.M.	N.M.	N.M.
EBITDA Margin %	17.58	30.05	N.M.	N.M.	N.M.	4.35	N.M.	5.62
Net Margin %	N.M.	N.M.	N.M.	38.93	N.M.	N.M.	N.M.	N.M.
Asset Turnover	0.18	0.17	0.16	0.11	0.14	0.13	0.13	0.13
Current Ratio	1.34	3.98	0.48	2.24	1.00	2.40	2.96	2.38
Debt to Equity	1.89	4.65	1.68	0.96	1.60	1.45	1.44	1.08
Price Range	42.75-30.66	35.45-26.90	28.25-15.53	17.33-11.00	12.96-3.26	11.49-1.02	29.63-7.51	42.44-22.44
P/E Ratio	...	...	...	19.47-12.36	...	...	...	...

Address: 510 Bering Drive, Suite 500, Houston, TX 77057-1457
Telephone: 713-570-3000
Fax: 713-570-3100

Web Site: www.crowncastle.com
Officers: J. Landis Martin - Chmn. John P. Kelly - Pres., C.E.O.

Auditors: KPMG LLP
Investor Contact: 713-570-3000
Transfer Agents: Mellon Investor Services LLC

CROWN HOLDINGS INC

Exchange	Symbol	Price	52Wk Range	Yield	P/E.
NYS	CCK	$25.16 (3/31/2008)	27.18-21.35	N/A	7.89

*7 Year Price Score 151.98 *NYSE Composite Index=100 *12 Month Price Score 106.93

TRADING VOLUME (thousand shares)

Interim Earnings (Per Share)

Qtr.	Mar	Jun	Sep	Dec
2003	(0.21)	0.43	0.04	(0.32)
2004	(0.11)	0.20	0.35	(0.17)
2005	(0.06)	0.16	0.45	(2.74)
2006	0.04	0.29	0.50	0.99
2007	0.10	0.53	0.56	2.01

Interim Dividends (Per Share)

Dividend Payment Suspended

Valuation Analysis **Institutional Holding**

Forecast P/E	N/A		No of Institutions
			217
Market Cap	$4.0 Billion		Shares
Book Value	15.0 Million		136,490,288
Price/Book	268.00		% Held
Price/Sales	0.52		83.57

Business Summary: Metal Products (MIC: 11.4 SIC: 3411 NAIC: 332431)

Crown Holdings is engaged in the design, manufacture and sale of packaging products for consumer goods. Co.'s primary products include steel and aluminum cans for food, beverage, household and other consumer products and metal caps and closures. These products are manufactured in Co.'s plants both within and outside the U.S. and are sold through its sales organization to the soft drink, food, citrus, brewing, household products, personal care and various other industries. Co.'s business is organized geographically within three divisions, Americas, European and Asia-Pacific. At Dec 31 2007, Co. operated 141 plants along with sales and service facilities throughout 41 countries

Recent Developments: For the year ended Dec 31 2007, income from continuing operations increased 54.4% to US$528.0 million from US$342.0 million a year earlier. Net income increased 70.9% to US$528.0 million from US$309.0 million in the prior year. Revenues were US$7.73 billion, up 10.7% from US$6.98 billion the year before. Direct operating expenses rose 10.0% to US$6.70 billion from US$6.09 billion in the comparable period the year before. Indirect operating expenses increased 48.3% to US$826.0 million from US$557.0 million in the equivalent prior-year period.

Prospects: Co.'s outlook appears to be favorable as it is seeing an increase in net sales primarily attributable to higher sales unit volumes and the pass-through of higher raw material costs. In addition, Co. noted that its beverage can growth initiatives in emerging markets remain on plan, and is positively contributing to results. Looking ahead, Co. expects the positive momentum to continue in 2008. Meanwhile, Co. expects to continue to add capacity in many of the growth markets around the world. Additionally, Co. remains focused on managing invested capital by continuing its efforts to reduce can and end diameter, lighten its cans, reduce non-metal costs and restructure production processes.

Financial Data
(US$ in Thousands)

	12/31/2007	12/31/2006	12/31/2005	12/31/2004	12/31/2003	12/31/2002	12/31/2001	12/31/2000
Earnings Per Share	3.19	1.82	(2.18)	0.30	(0.19)	(8.38)	(7.74)	(1.40)
Cash Flow Per Share	3.16	2.15	(0.74)	2.44	2.64	2.89	2.47	2.14
Dividends Per Share	...	...	...	...	...	...	...	1.000
Income Statement								
Total Revenue	7,727,000	6,982,000	6,908,000	7,199,000	6,630,000	6,792,000	7,187,000	7,289,000
EBITDA	430,000	565,000	(32,000)	469,000	445,000	230,000	55,000	278,000
Income Before Taxes	201,000	335,000	(314,000)	161,000	119,000	(145,000)	(444,000)	(217,000)
Income Taxes	(400,000)	(62,000)	(2,000)	82,000	95,000	30,000	528,000	(58,000)
Net Income	528,000	309,000	(362,000)	51,000	(32,000)	(1,205,000)	(972,000)	(174,000)
Average Shares	165,500	169,800	165,900	168,800	164,700	143,800	125,600	126,800
Balance Sheet								
Current Assets	2,234,000	2,062,000	1,845,000	2,343,000	2,122,000	2,024,000	2,422,000	2,913,000
Total Assets	6,979,000	6,358,000	6,545,000	8,125,000	7,773,000	7,505,000	9,620,000	11,159,000
Current Liabilities	2,083,000	1,956,000	1,943,000	2,080,000	2,036,000	2,270,000	2,506,000	2,261,000
Long-Term Obligations	3,354,000	3,420,000	3,192,000	3,796,000	3,709,000	3,388,000	4,475,000	5,049,000
Total Liabilities	6,964,000	6,903,000	6,781,000	7,848,000	7,633,000	7,592,000	8,816,000	9,050,000
Stockholders' Equity	15,000	(545,000)	(236,000)	277,000	140,000	(87,000)	804,000	2,109,000
Shares Outstanding	159,777	162,711	166,712	165,559	165,024	159,430	125,702	125,621
Statistical Record								
Return on Assets %	7.92	4.79	N.M.	0.64	N.M.	N.M.	N.M.	N.M.
Return on Equity %	...	...	N.M.	24.39	N.M.	N.M.	N.M.	N.M.
EBITDA Margin %	5.56	8.09	N.M.	6.51	6.71	3.39	0.77	3.81
Net Margin %	6.83	4.43	N.M.	0.71	N.M.	N.M.	N.M.	N.M.
Asset Turnover	1.16	1.08	0.94	0.90	0.87	0.79	0.69	0.64
Current Ratio	1.07	1.05	0.95	1.13	1.04	0.89	0.97	1.29
Debt to Equity	223.60	...	...	13.70	26.49	...	5.57	2.39
Price Range	27.18-21.10	21.51-14.77	20.26-12.42	14.02-8.13	9.50-4.61	12.25-2.54	9.63-0.92	23.63-3.13
P/E Ratio	8.52-6.61	11.82-8.12	...	46.73-27.10	...	...	...	...
Average Yield %	...	...	...	...	...	...	...	7.20

Address: One Crown Way,	Web Site: www.crowncork.com	Auditors: PricewaterhouseCoopers LLP
Philadelphia, PA 19154-4599	Officers: John W. Conway - Chmn., Pres., C.E.O.	Investor Contact: 215-552-3770
Telephone: 215-698-5100	Alan W. Rutherford - Vice-Chmn., Exec. V.P., C.F.O.	Transfer Agents: Wells Fargo Bank
Fax: 215-676-7245		Minnesota, N.A.

CSX CORP.

Exchange	Symbol	Price	52Wk Range	Yield	P/E
NYS	CSX	$56.07 (3/31/2008)	57.43-38.11	1.28	18.75

*7 Year Price Score 149.04 *NYSE Composite Index=100 *12 Month Price Score 121.65

Interim Earnings (Per Share)

Qtr.	Mar	Jun	Sep	Dec
2003	0.23	0.29	(0.24)	0.28
2004	0.07	0.28	0.28	0.13
2005	1.28	0.36	0.36	0.52
2006	0.53	0.83	0.71	0.75
2007	0.52	0.71	0.91	0.86

Interim Dividends (Per Share)

Amt	Decl	Ex	Rec	Pay
0.15Q	5/8/2007	8/29/2007	8/31/2007	9/14/2007
0.15Q	9/12/2007	11/28/2007	11/30/2007	12/14/2007
0.15Q	2/13/2008	2/27/2008	2/29/2008	3/14/2008
0.18Q	3/17/2008	5/28/2008	5/30/2008	6/13/2008

Indicated Div: $0.72

Valuation Analysis   Institutional Holding

Forecast P/E	11.87	No of Institutions	
	(1/10/2007)	477	
Market Cap	$22.0 Billion	Shares	
Book Value	8.7 Billion	341,524,480	
Price/Book	2.63	% Held	
Price/Sales	2.28	78.19	

Business Summary: Rail Transport (MIC: 15.5 SIC: 4011 NAIC: 482111)

CSX is a transportation company. Co.'s Surface Transportation business, which includes its rail and intermodal businesses, provides rail-based transportation services including traditional rail service and the transport of intermodal containers and trailers. As at Dec 28 2007, Co. operated two business segments: rail segment, which provides rail freight transportation over a network of approximately 21,000 route miles in 23 states, the District of Columbia and the Canadian provinces of Ontario and Quebec, and intermodal segment, which provides integrated rail and truck transportation services and operates a network of intermodal facilities across North America.

Recent Developments: For the year ended Dec 28 2007, income from continuing operations decreased 6.4% to US$1.23 billion from US$1.31 billion a year earlier. Net income increased 2.0% to US$1.34 billion from US$1.31 billion in the prior year. Revenues were US$10.03 billion, up 4.9% from US$9.57 billion the year before. Operating income was US$2.26 billion versus US$2.14 billion in the prior year, an increase of 5.5%. Direct operating expenses rose 2.7% to US$6.92 billion from US$6.74 billion in the comparable period the year before. Indirect operating expenses increased 24.2% to US$856.0 million from US$689.0 million in the equivalent prior-year period.

Prospects: Although certain markets such as the housing and automotive sectors are expected to remain weak, Co.'s outlook for 2008 appears to be favorable. Co. believes that it is well positioned to meet the growing transportation demand, and its environment remains strong and will support further improvements in the future. Thus, Co. expects performance for 2008 to be within its long-term financial targets of compounded annual growth rates for operating income of 10.0% to 12.0% and earnings per share of 15.0% to 17.0%. Co.'s surface transportation business is budgeting nearly $5.00 billion between 2008 and 2010 mainly for infrastructure investment to improve network reliability and recoverability.

Financial Data

(US$ in Thousands)	12/28/2007	12/29/2006	12/30/2005	12/31/2004	12/26/2003	12/27/2002	12/28/2001	12/29/2000
Earnings Per Share	2.99	2.82	2.52	0.76	0.57	1.00	0.69	1.34
Cash Flow Per Share	5.09	4.69	2.57	3.31	1.88	2.66	1.96	1.69
Tang Book Value Per Share	21.29	20.43	18.23	15.80	15.00	14.54	14.32	14.14
Dividends Per Share	0.540	0.330	0.215	0.200	0.200	0.200	0.400	0.600
Dividend Payout %	18.06	11.70	8.53	26.32	35.09	20.10	57.97	44.94
Income Statement								
Total Revenue	10,030,000	9,566,000	8,618,000	8,020,000	7,793,000	8,152,000	8,110,000	8,191,000
EBITDA	3,184,000	3,059,000	2,254,000	1,781,000	1,305,000	1,817,000	1,588,000	1,420,000
Income Before Taxes	1,932,000	1,841,000	1,036,000	637,000	265,000	723,000	448,000	277,000
Income Taxes	706,000	531,000	316,000	219,000	76,000	256,000	155,000	91,000
Net Income	1,336,000	1,310,000	1,145,000	339,000	246,000	424,000	293,000	565,000
Average Shares	448,280	465,934	456,048	450,060	428,792	427,024	424,818	422,628
Balance Sheet								
Total Assets	25,534,000	25,129,000	24,232,000	24,581,000	21,760,000	20,951,000	20,801,000	20,491,000
Long-Term Obligations	6,470,000	5,362,000	5,093,000	6,234,000	6,886,000	6,519,000	5,839,000	5,810,000
Total Liabilities	16,849,000	16,187,000	16,278,000	17,770,000	15,307,000	14,710,000	14,681,000	14,474,000
Stockholders' Equity	8,685,000	8,942,000	7,954,000	6,811,000	6,453,000	6,241,000	6,120,000	6,017,000
Shares Outstanding	407,864	437,763	436,406	431,058	430,142	429,372	427,376	425,476
Statistical Record								
Return on Assets %	5.29	5.32	4.70	1.44	1.16	2.04	1.42	2.75
Return on Equity %	15.20	15.55	15.55	5.03	3.89	6.88	4.84	9.62
EBITDA Margin %	31.74	31.98	26.15	22.21	16.75	22.29	19.58	17.34
Net Margin %	13.32	13.69	13.29	4.23	3.16	-5.20	3.61	6.90
Asset Turnover	0.40	0.39	0.35	0.34	0.37	0.39	0.39	0.40
Price Range	51.26-33.89	37.91-24.61	25.55-18.50	20.16-14.61	18.00-12.96	20.55-12.79	20.31-12.84	16.28-9.78
P/E Ratio	17.14-11.33	13.44-8.73	10.14-7.34	26.53-19.22	31.58-22.73	20.55-12.79	29.43-18.61	12.15-7.30
Average Yield %	1.27	1.04	0.99	1.21	1.31	1.19	2.34	4.97

Address: 500 Water Street, 15th floor, Jacksonville, FL 32202
Telephone: 904-359-3200

Web Site: www.csx.com
Officers: Michael J. Ward - Chmn., Pres., C.E.O.
Oscar Munoz - Exec. V.P., C.F.O.

Auditors: ERNST & YOUNG LLP
Transfer Agents: The Bank of New York, New York, NY

CULLEN/FROST BANKERS, INC.

Exchange	Symbol	Price	52Wk Range	Yield	P/E	Div Acheiver
NYS	CFR	$53.04 (3/31/2008)	55.81-45.38	3.02	14.94	14 Years

*7 Year Price Score 94.54   *NYSE Composite Index=100   *12 Month Price Score 109.69

Interim Earnings (Per Share)

Qtr.	Mar	Jun	Sep	Dec
2003	0.59	0.67	0.62	0.57
2004	0.62	0.65	0.68	0.72
2005	0.70	0.77	0.79	0.81
2006	0.83	0.86	0.88	0.84
2007	0.78	0.89	0.95	0.93

Interim Dividends (Per Share)

Amt	Decl	Ex	Rec	Pay
0.40Q	4/26/2007	5/30/2007	6/1/2007	6/15/2007
0.40Q	7/26/2007	8/29/2007	8/31/2007	9/14/2007
0.40Q	10/25/2007	11/28/2007	11/30/2007	12/14/2007
0.40Q	1/24/2008	2/27/2008	2/29/2008	3/14/2008
		Indicated Div: $1.60		

Valuation Analysis

		Institutional Holding	
Forecast P/E	N/A	No of Institutions	
		213	
Market Cap	$3.1 Billion	Shares	
Book Value	1.5 Billion	38,692,952	
Price/Book	2.11	% Held	
Price/Sales	3.00	64.64	

Business Summary: Commercial Banking (MIC: 8.1 SIC: 6021 NAIC: 522110)

Cullen/Frost Bankers is a financial holding company. Through its subsidiaries, Co. provides commercial and consumer banking services, as well as trust and investment management, investment banking, insurance brokerage, leasing, asset-based lending, treasury management and item processing services throughout various markets in Texas. Co. serves a range of industries including, among others, energy, manufacturing, services, construction, retail, telecommunications, healthcare, military and transportation. As of Dec 31 2007, Co. had consolidated total assets of $13.49 billion, and total deposits of $10.53 billion.

Recent Developments: For the year ended Dec 31 2007, net income increased 9.5% to US$212.1 million from US$193.6 million in the prior year. Net interest income increased 10.6% to US$518.7 million from US$469.2 million in the prior year. Provision for loan losses was US$14.7 million versus US$14.2 million in the prior year, an increase of 3.6%. Non-interest income rose 11.4% to US$268.2 million from US$240.7 million, while non-interest expense advanced 12.7% to US$462.4 million.

Prospects: Despite the challenging banking environment, Co. is benefiting from several of its previous strategic decisions, including its withdrawal from the residential mortgage business, and its exit from the indirect lending and credit card businesses. Meanwhile, Co. is continuing to expand in the Texas markets. For instance, on Dec 1 2007, Co. acquired Prime Benefits, Inc., an independent Austin-based insurance agency providing employee benefits to businesses. The acquisition should complement Co.'s insurance team in Austin, strengthen its employee benefits offerings, and also allow it to expand the benefits services it can offer its business customers in Austin.

Financial Data
(US$ in Thousands)

	12/31/2007	12/31/2006	12/31/2005	12/31/2004	12/31/2003	12/31/2002	12/31/2001	12/31/2000
Earnings Per Share	3.55	3.42	3.07	2.66	2.48	2.23	1.52	2.03
Cash Flow Per Share	3.41	(0.96)	2.52	2.49	3.93	5.34	1.91	2.48
Tang Book Value Per Share	15.66	13.61	14.65	13.59	12.65	11.40	11.58	11.14
Dividends Per Share	1.540	1.320	1.165	1.035	0.940	0.875	0.840	0.760
Dividend Payout %	43.38	38.60	37.95	38.91	37.90	39.24	55.26	37.44
Income Statement								
Interest Income	768,847	683,959	509,827	393,544	368,946	389,898	460,976	512,331
Interest Expense	250,110	214,796	118,561	62,106	55,188	75,865	144,759	189,568
Net Interest Income	518,737	469,163	391,266	331,438	313,758	314,033	316,217	322,763
Provision for Losses	14,660	14,150	10,250	2,500	10,544	22,546	40,031	14,103
Non-Interest Income	268,231	240,747	230,379	225,110	215,361	200,709	192,891	170,865
Non-Interest Expense	462,446	410,353	367,007	345,030	326,035	312,142	352,606	313,280
Income Before Taxes	309,862	285,407	244,388	209,018	192,540	180,054	116,471	166,245
Income Taxes	97,791	91,816	78,965	67,693	62,039	57,821	38,565	57,428
Net Income	212,071	193,591	165,423	141,325	130,501	116,986	80,916	108,817
Average Shares	59,713	56,642	53,803	53,140	52,658	52,423	53,348	53,657
Balance Sheet								
Net Loans & Leases	7,677,023	7,277,299	6,004,730	5,089,181	4,507,245	4,436,329	4,445,727	4,471,380
Total Assets	13,485,014	13,224,189	11,741,437	9,952,787	9,672,114	9,552,318	8,369,584	7,660,372
Total Deposits	10,529,673	10,387,909	9,146,394	8,105,678	8,068,857	7,628,143	7,098,007	6,499,690
Total Liabilities	12,007,926	11,847,306	10,759,201	9,130,392	8,902,110	8,848,528	7,774,665	7,087,346
Stockholders' Equity	1,477,088	1,376,883	982,236	822,395	770,004	703,790	594,919	573,026
Shares Outstanding	58,662	59,839	54,482	51,923	51,776	51,295	51,355	51,430
Statistical Record								
Return on Assets %	1.59	1.55	1.53	1.44	1.36	1.31	1.01	1.48
Return on Equity %	14.86	16.41	18.33	17.70	17.71	18.02	13.86	20.05
Net Interest Margin %	67.47	68.60	76.74	84.22	85.04	80.54	68.60	63.00
Efficiency Ratio %	44.59	44.38	49.58	55.77	55.80	52.85	53.93	45.86
Loans to Deposits	0.73	0.70	0.66	0.63	0.56	0.58	0.63	0.69
Price Range	56.84-48.10	59.44-52.26	56.05-42.45	49.00-38.90	41.00-29.40	40.04-29.40	41.19-23.84	43.19-19.63
P/E Ratio	16.01-13.55	17.38-15.28	18.26-13.83	18.42-14.62	16.53-11.85	17.96-13.18	27.10-15.68	21.27-9.67
Average Yield %	2.94	2.35	2.40	2.35	2.69	2.53	2.54	2.69

Address: 100 W. Houston Street, San Antonio, TX 78205	**Web Site:** www.frostbank.com	**Auditors:** Ernst & Young LLP
Telephone: 210-220-4011	**Officers:** Tom C. Frost - Sr. Chmn. Richard W. Evans Jr. - Chmn., C.E.O.	**Investor Contact:** 210-220-5632
Fax: 210-220-5578		**Transfer Agents:** Bank of New York, New York, NY

CUMMINS, INC.

Exchange	Symbol	Price	52Wk Range	Yield	P/E
NYS	CMI	$46.82 (3/31/2008)	70.08-36.31	1.07	12.65

*7 Year Price Score 199.55 *NYSE Composite Index=100   *12 Month Price Score 99.06

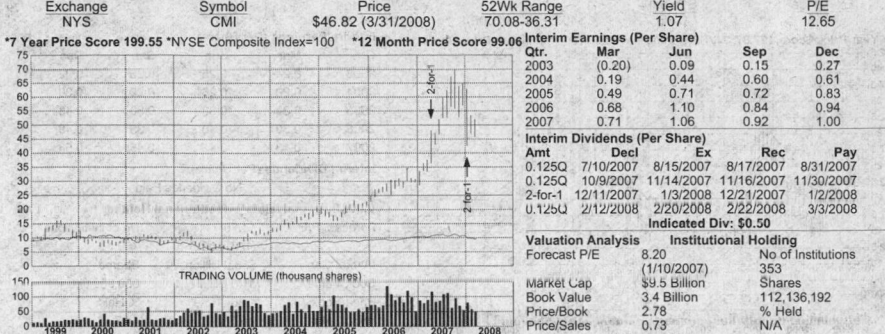

Interim Earnings (Per Share)

Qtr.	Mar	Jun	Sep	Dec
2003	(0.20)	0.09	0.15	0.27
2004	0.19	0.44	0.60	0.61
2005	0.49	0.71	0.72	0.83
2006	0.68	1.10	0.84	0.94
2007	0.71	1.06	0.92	1.00

Interim Dividends (Per Share)

Amt	Decl	Ex	Rec	Pay
0.125Q	7/10/2007	8/15/2007	8/17/2007	8/31/2007
0.125Q	10/9/2007	11/14/2007	11/16/2007	11/30/2007
2-for-1	12/11/2007	1/3/2008	12/21/2007	1/2/2008
0.125Q	2/12/2008	2/20/2008	2/22/2008	3/3/2008

Indicated Div: $0.50

Valuation Analysis   Institutional Holding

Forecast P/E	8.20	No of Institutions
	(1/10/2007)	353
Market Cap	$9.5 Billion	Shares
Book Value	3.4 Billion	112,136,192
Price/Book	2.78	% Held
Price/Sales	0.73	N/A

Business Summary: Industrial Machinery and Equipment (MIC: 11.5 SIC: 3519 NAIC: 333618)

Cummins designs, manufactures, distributes and services diesel and natural gas engines, electric power generation systems and engine-related component products, including filtration and exhaust aftertreatment, fuel systems, controls and air handling systems. Co. operates four segments: engine, which manufactures and markets a range of diesel and natural gas-powered engines under the Cummins brand name; power generation, which designs or manufactures components that make up power generation systems; components, which produces filters, fuel systems, aftertreatment systems, intake and exhaust systems; and distribution, which distributes Co.'s products and services to end-users.

Recent Developments: For the year ended Dec 31 2007, net income increased 3.4% to US$739.0 million from US$715.0 million in the prior year. Revenues were US$13.05 billion, up 14.8% from US$11.36 billion the year before. Operating income was US$1.16 billion versus US$1.13 billion in the prior year, an increase of 2.4%. Direct operating expenses rose 17.9% to US$10.49 billion from US$8.90 billion in the comparable period the year before. Indirect operating expenses increased 4.8% to US$1.40 billion from US$1.33 billion in the equivalent prior-year period.

Prospects: Despite the uncertainty that exists in the U.S. economy, Co. remains encouraged with its near-term outlook as it expects the North American truck engine markets to rebound somewhat from 2007. Co. also expects its Distribution segment to continue to grow to provide support for its products around the globe. Further, Co.'s Power Generation business is forecasted to remain strong in 2008, with demand being driven by global infrastructure needs, while its Components segment is forecasting improved profit performance, particularly in its Turbo Technologies and Emission Solutions businesses. Overall, for 2008, Co. expects sales to increase 12.0% from 2007 levels.

Financial Data

(US$ in Thousands)	12/31/2007	12/31/2006	12/31/2005	12/31/2004	12/31/2003	12/31/2002	12/31/2001	12/31/2000
Earnings Per Share	3.70	3.55	2.75	1.85	0.32	0.53	(0.67)	0.05
Cash Flow Per Share	4.08	4.41	4.30	3.63	1.01	1.25	0.94	2.53
Tang Book Value Per Share	14.20	11.12	7.56	5.18	3.00	2.42	4.12	5.93
Dividends Per Share	0.430	0.330	0.300	0.300	0.300	0.300	0.300	0.300
Dividend Payout %	11.62	9.29	10.90	16.24	94.49	56.34		600.00
Income Statement								
Total Revenue	13,048,000	11,362,000	9,918,000	8,438,000	6,296,000	5,853,000	5,681,000	6,597,000
EBITDA	1,481,000	1,428,000	1,177,000	773,000	354,000	347,000		316,000
Income Before Taxes	1,169,000	1,083,000	798,000	432,000	91,000	78,000		3,000
Income Taxes	381,000	324,000	216,000	56,000	12,000	(38,000)	(42,000)	(19,000)
Net Income	739,000	715,000	550,000	350,000	50,000	82,000	(102,000)	8,000
Average Shares	199,900	203,106	204,400	196,800	158,000	155,200	153,200	152,800
Balance Sheet								
Current Assets	4,815,000	4,488,000	3,916,000	3,273,000	2,130,000	1,982,000	1,635,000	1,830,000
Total Assets	8,195,000	7,465,000	6,885,000	6,527,000	5,126,000	4,837,000	4,335,000	4,500,000
Current Liabilities	2,711,000	2,399,000	2,218,000	2,197,000	1,391,000	1,329,000	970,000	1,223,000
Long-Term Obligations	555,000	647,000	1,213,000	1,299,000	1,380,000	999,000	915,000	1,032,000
Total Liabilities	4,493,000	4,409,000	4,796,000	4,918,000	4,054,000	3,904,000	3,227,000	3,092,000
Stockholders' Equity	3,409,000	2,802,000	1,864,000	1,401,000	949,000	841,000	1,025,000	1,336,000
Shares Outstanding	202,200	208,400	186,000	184,000	170,800	166,400	165,600	165,600
Statistical Record								
Return on Assets %	9.44	9.97	8.20	5.99	1.00	1.79	N.M.	0.17
Return on Equity %	23.80	30.65	33.69	29.71	5.59	8.79	N.M.	0.58
EBITDA Margin %	11.35	12.57	11.87	9.16	5.62	5.93		4.79
Net Margin %	5.66	6.29	5.55	4.15	0.79	1.40	N.M.	0.12
Asset Turnover	1.67	1.58	1.48	1.44	1.26	1.28	1.29	1.43
Current Ratio	1.78	1.87	1.77	1.49	1.53	1.49	1.69	1.50
Debt to Equity	0.16	0.23	0.65	0.93	1.45	1.19	0.89	0.77
Price Range	70.08-28.57	34.48-22.72	23.31-15.96	21.11-12.18	13.07-5.55	12.55-4.92	11.33-7.33	12.41-6.81
P/E Ratio	18.94-7.72	9.71-6.40	8.48-5.80	11.41-6.58	40.86-17.35	23.67-9.29		248.13-136.17
Average Yield %	0.86	1.17	1.52	1.87	3.20	3.52	3.14	3.46

Address: 500 Jackson Street,	Web Site: www.cummins.com	Auditors: PricewaterhouseCoopers LLP
Columbus, IN 47202-3005	Officers: Theodore M. Solso - Chmn., C.E.O. F.	Investor Contact: 812-377-3121
Telephone: 812-377-5000	Joseph Loughrey - Pres., C.O.O.	Transfer Agents: Wells Fargo
Fax: 812-377-4937		Shareownwer Services, St. Paul, MN

CVS CAREMARK CORPORATION

Exchange	Symbol	Price	52Wk Range	Yield	P/E
NYS	CVS	$40.51 (3/31/2008)	42.25-34.29	N/A	21.10

*7 Year Price Score 127.87 *NYSE Composite Index=100 *12 Month Price Score 111.17

Interim Earnings (Per Share)

Qtr.	Mar	Jun	Sep	Dec
2003	0.24	0.25	0.23	0.32
2004	0.29	0.28	0.22	0.30
2005	0.34	0.33	0.30	0.48
2006	0.39	0.40	0.33	0.49
2007	0.43	0.47	0.45	0.56

Interim Dividends (Per Share)

No Dividends Paid

Valuation Analysis / **Institutional Holding**

Forecast P/E	14.79	No of Institutions
	(1/10/2007)	760
Market Cap	$58.2 Billion	Shares
Book Value	31.3 Billion	689,032,640
Price/Book	1.86	% Held
Price/Sales	0.76	44.73

Business Summary: Retail - Miscellaneous (MIC: 5.11 SIC: 5912 NAIC: 446110)

CVS Caremark is engaged in the retail drugstore industry. Co. sells prescription drugs and an assortment of general merchandise, including over-the-counter drugs, beauty products and cosmetics, film and photofinishing services, seasonal merchandise, greeting cards and convenience foods through its CVS/pharmacy® retail stores and online through CVS.com®. Co. also provides pharmacy benefit management, mail order services and specialty pharmacy services through PharmaCare Management Services and PharmaCare Pharmacy® stores. As of Dec 29 2007, Co. operated 6,245 Retail Stores, 56 Specialty Pharmacy Stores, and 20 Specialty Mail Order Pharmacies.

Recent Developments: For the year ended Dec 29 2007, net income increased 92.6% to US$2.64 billion from US$1.37 billion in the prior year. Revenues were US$76.33 billion, up 74.2% from US$43.82 billion the year before. Operating income was US$4.79 billion versus US$2.44 billion in the prior year, an increase of 96.3%. Direct operating expenses rose 87.7% to US$60.22 billion from US$32.08 billion in the comparable period the year before. Indirect operating expenses increased 21.7% to US$11.31 billion from US$9.30 billion in the equivalent prior-year period.

Prospects: Co.'s net revenues are being positively affected by its Mar 2007 acquisition of Caremark Rx, Inc., which resulted in an increase in Pharmacy Services segment revenue and the inclusion of a full year of financial results and growth of the Standalone Drug Business, which resulted in an increase in Retail Pharmacy segment revenue. Additionally, Co. is experiencing higher gross profit primarily due to the integration with Caremark Rx, and increased utilization of generic drugs, which normally yield a higher gross profit rate than equivalent brand name drugs, in both its Retail Pharmacy and Pharmacy Services segments.

Financial Data

(US$ in Thousands)	12/29/2007	12/30/2006	12/31/2005	01/01/2005	01/03/2004	12/28/2002	12/29/2001	12/30/2000
Earnings Per Share	1.92	1.60	1.45	1.10	1.03	0.88	0.50	0.92
Cash Flow Per Share	2.44	2.13	1.99	1.15	1.21	1.54	0.87	1.00
Tang Book Value Per Share	N.M.	6.29	6.77	4.98	5.67	4.73	4.45	4.10
Dividends Per Share	0.049	0.155	0.145	0.133	0.115	0.115	0.115	0.115
Dividend Payout %	2.54	9.69	10.00	12.05	11.17	13.14	23.00	12.57
Income Statement								
Total Revenue	76,329,500	43,813,800	37,006,200	30,594,300	26,588,000	24,181,500	22,241,400	20,087,500
EBITDA	5,887,900	3,174,900	2,608,600	1,951,500	1,765,300	1,516,500	1,091,400	1,619,300
Income Before Taxes	4,358,700	2,225,800	1,909,000	1,396,400	1,375,500	1,155,800	709,600	1,243,400
Income Taxes	1,721,700	856,900	684,300	477,600	528,200	439,200	296,400	497,400
Net Income	2,637,000	1,368,900	1,224,700	918,800	847,300	716,600	413,200	746,000
Average Shares	1,371,800	853,200	841,600	830,800	815,400	810,600	816,600	816,000
Balance Sheet								
Current Assets	14,149,400	10,391,500	8,392,700	7,919,500	6,496,500	5,982,100	5,454,100	4,936,600
Total Assets	54,721,900	20,569,800	15,283,400	14,546,800	10,543,100	9,645,300	8,628,200	7,949,500
Current Liabilities	10,766,300	7,000,700	4,583,900	4,858,800	3,489,200	3,105,900	3,065,900	2,964,100
Long-Term Obligations	8,349,700	2,870,400	1,594,100	1,925,900	753,100	1,076,300	810,400	536,800
Total Liabilities	23,400,000	10,652,200	6,952,200	7,559,600	4,521,300	4,448,300	4,061,300	3,644,900
Stockholders' Equity	31,321,900	9,917,600	8,331,200	6,987,200	6,021,800	5,197,000	4,566,900	4,304,600
Shares Outstanding	1,436,457	825,737	814,308	801,918	790,768	786,142	781,774	784,644
Statistical Record								
Return on Assets %	7.02	7.66	8.23	7.34	8.26	7.86	5.00	9.83
Return on Equity %	12.82	15.04	16.03	14.16	14.86	14.72	9.34	18.74
EBITDA Margin %	7.71	7.25	7.05	6.38	6.64	6.27	4.91	8.06
Net Margin %	3.45	3.12	3.31	3.00	3.19	2.96	1.86	3.71
Asset Turnover	2.03	2.45	2.49	2.45	2.59	2.65	2.69	2.65
Current Ratio	1.31	1.48	1.83	1.63	1.86	1.93	1.78	1.67
Debt to Equity	0.27	0.29	0.19	0.28	0.13	0.21	0.18	0.12
Price Range	42.25-30.79	35.95-26.35	31.25-22.25	23.45-17.11	18.73-10.99	17.79-11.99	31.05-11.64	29.97-14.00
P/E Ratio	22.01-16.04	22.47-16.47	21.55-15.34	21.32-15.55	18.18-10.67	20.22-13.63	62.10-23.28	32.57-15.22
Average Yield %	0.13	0.51	0.53	0.65	0.79	0.78	0.52	0.54

Address: One CVS Drive, Woonsocket, RI 02895	**Web Site:** www.cvs.com	**Auditors:** Ernst & Young LLP
Telephone: 401-765-1500	**Officers:** Thomas M. Ryan - Chmn., Pres., C.E.O.	**Investor Contact:** 800-201-0938
Fax: 401-762-2137	David B. Rickard - Exec. V.P., C.F.O., Chief Admin. Officer	

CYPRESS SEMICONDUCTOR CORP.

Exchange	Symbol	Price	52Wk Range	Yield	P/E
NYS	CY	$23.61 (3/31/2008)	39.39-18.65	N/A	10.27

*7 Year Price Score 124.23 *NYSE Composite Index=100   *12 Month Price Score 87.71

Interim Earnings (Per Share)

Qtr.	Mar	Jun	Sep	Dec
2003	(0.27)	(0.10)	0.12	0.19
2004	0.16	0.13	0.02	(0.16)
2005	(0.53)	(0.12)	(0.04)	(0.01)
2006	0.05	0.04	0.06	0.10
2007	(0.01)	2.29	0.18	(0.03)

Interim Dividends (Per Share)

No Dividends Paid

Valuation Analysis   Institutional Holding

Forecast P/E	N/A	No of Institutions
		242
Market Cap	$3.8 Billion	Shares
Book Value	1.7 Billion	136,866,672
Price/Book	2.22	% Held
Price/Sales	2.39	90.04

Business Summary: IT & Technology (MIC: 10.2 SIC: 3674 NAIC: 334413)

Cypress Semiconductor designs, develops, manufactures and markets programmable applications for various markets including consumer, computation, data communications, automotive, and industrial. Co.'s offerings include Programmable System-on-Chip™ products, universal serial bus controllers, general-purpose programmable clocks and memories. In addition, Co. provides wired and wireless connectivity applications designed to enhance connectivity and performance in multimedia handsets. As of Dec 31 2007, Co.'s operations were divided into five reportable business segments: Consumer and Computation Division, Data Communications Division, Memory and Imaging Division, SunPower, and Other.

Recent Developments: For the year ended Dec 30 2007, net income increased 898.7% to US$394.3 million from US$39.5 million in the prior year. Revenues were US$1.60 billion, up 46.2% from US$1.09 billion the year before. Operating income was US$12.2 million versus US$26.9 million in the prior year, a decrease of 54.8%. Direct operating expenses rose 66.0% to US$1.05 billion from US$631.3 million in the comparable period the year before. Indirect operating expenses increased 23.8% to US$536.2 million from US$433.3 million in the equivalent prior-year period.

Prospects: Co.'s outlook appears favorable. Notably, Co. anticipates sales in China to triple over the next five years, led by demand for Programmable System-on-Chip™ mixed-signal arrays in electric bicycles, consumer electronics, white goods and handsets. Meanwhile, on Dec 19 2007, Co. announced a restructuring plan to exit its manufacturing facility located in Round Rock, TX. Under the plan, Co. will transition production from the Texas facility to its more cost-effective facility in Bloomington, MN as well as outside third-party foundries. Co. plans to continue operations at the Texas facility through the third quarter of 2008 and expects to complete the exit plan by the end of 2008.

Financial Data

(US$ in Thousands)	12/30/2007	12/31/2006	01/01/2006	01/02/2005	12/28/2003	12/29/2002	12/30/2001	12/31/2000
Earnings Per Share	2.30	0.25	(0.69)	0.17	(0.04)	(2.02)	(3.28)	2.03
Cash Flow Per Share	0.83	0.91	0.61	1.23	0.82	0.18	0.77	4.31
Tang Book Value Per Share	6.97	4.49	2.17	1.66	1.61	2.12	3.06	8.86
Income Statement								
Total Revenue	1,596,387	1,091,553	886,396	948,438	836,756	774,746	819,192	1,287,787
EBITDA	505,846	158,797	48,441	171,400	167,222	(37,522)	(221,267)	539,214
Income Before Taxes	398,277	52,710	(93,217)	(1,877)	(2,509)	(246,260)	(444,437)	370,170
Income Taxes	(314)	6,859	(1,339)	(26,575)	2,822	2,838	(32,680)	92,862
Net Income	394,300	39,482	(92,153)	24,698	(5,331)	(249,098)	(407,412)	277,308
Average Shares	171,836	179,271	133,188	134,592	121,509	123,112	124,135	144,228
Balance Sheet								
Current Assets	2,067,539	952,628	646,607	563,880	518,395	513,947	626,835	1,282,786
Total Assets	3,725,949	2,123,525	1,697,874	1,572,994	1,567,497	1,572,648	1,886,436	2,361,754
Current Liabilities	1,494,547	275,839	211,497	233,610	210,679	199,760	254,502	299,427
Long-Term Obligations	...	598,996	601,247	606,688	684,260	468,900	517,700	570,500
Total Liabilities	1,627,117	954,494	902,435	912,636	998,309	899,025	1,018,008	1,034,086
Stockholders' Equity	1,720,432	1,045,559	757,135	660,358	569,188	673,623	868,428	1,327,668
Shares Outstanding	161,648	144,844	137,036	128,493	120,483	123,743	121,495	125,659
Statistical Record								
Return on Assets %	13.52	2.07	N.M.	1.55	N.M.	N.M.	N.M.	15.99
Return on Equity %	28.59	4.39	N.M.	3.95	N.M.	N.M.	N.M.	27.45
EBITDA Margin %	31.69	14.55	5.46	18.07	19.98	N.M.	N.M.	41.87
Net Margin %	24.70	3.62	N.M.	2.60	N.M.	N.M.	N.M.	21.53
Asset Turnover	0.55	0.57	0.54	0.59	0.53	0.45	0.39	0.74
Current Ratio	1.38	3.45	3.06	2.41	2.46	2.57	2.46	4.28
Debt to Equity	...	0.57	0.79	0.92	1.20	0.70	0.60	0.43
Price Range	39.39-16.80	20.12-13.36	16.48-9.67	23.68-8.60	23.06-5.11	25.04-3.81	28.61-13.91	57.75-18.81
P/E Ratio	17.13-7.30	80.48-53.44	...	139.29-50.59	...	...	...	28.45-9.27

Address: 198 Champion Court, San Jose, CA 95134-1709
Telephone: 408-943-2600
Fax: 408-943-4730

Web Site: www.cypress.com
Officers: T. J. Rodgers - Pres., C.E.O. Brad W. Buss - Exec. V.P., Fin., Admin., C.F.O.

Auditors: PricewaterhouseCoopers LLP
Transfer Agents: EquiServe, L.P., Canton, MA

CYTEC INDUSTRIES, INC.

Exchange	Symbol	Price	52Wk Range	Yield	P/E
NYS	CYT	$53.85 (3/31/2008)	71.78-47.77	0.93	12.82

*7 Year Price Score 113.48 *NYSE Composite Index=100 *12 Month Price Score 99.51

Interim Earnings (Per Share)

Qtr.	Mar	Jun	Sep	Dec
2003	0.38	0.64	0.55	0.38
2004	0.78	0.72	0.23	1.09
2005	(0.16)	0.25	0.75	0.39
2006	0.79	1.00	0.51	1.71
2007	1.05	1.11	1.06	0.97

Interim Dividends (Per Share)

Amt	Decl	Ex	Rec	Pay
0.10Q	4/19/2007	5/8/2007	5/10/2007	5/25/2007
0.10Q	7/19/2007	8/8/2007	8/10/2007	8/27/2007
0.10Q	10/18/2007	11/7/2007	11/9/2007	11/26/2007
0.125Q	1/30/2008	2/7/2008	2/11/2008	2/25/2008

Indicated Div: $0.50

Valuation Analysis

		Institutional Holding	
Forecast P/E	12.19	No of Institutions	
	(1/10/2007)	188	
Market Cap	$2.6 Billion	Shares	
Book Value	1.9 Billion	37,907,636	
Price/Book	1.33	% Held	
Price/Sales	0.73	79.28	

Business Summary: Chemicals (MIC: 11.1 SIC: 2899 NAIC: 325998)

Cytec Industries is a specialty chemicals and materials company that develops, manufactures and sells products for a range of end markets, including aerospace, adhesives, automotive and industrial coatings, chemical intermediates, inks, mining, and plastics. Co. uses its technology and application development capability to create chemical and material applications that are formulated to perform specific functions for its customers. Co. has four business segments: Cytec Performance Chemicals; Cytec Surface Specialties; Cytec Engineered Materials; and Building Block Chemicals. As of Dec 31 2007, Co. had manufacturing and research facilities located in 18 countries.

Recent Developments: For the year ended Dec 31 2007, net income increased 5.8% to US$206.5 million in the prior year. Revenues were US$3.50 billion, up 5.2% from US$3.33 billion the year before. Operating income was US$324.1 million versus US$305.4 million in the prior year, an increase of 6.1%. Direct operating expenses rose 3.1% to US$2.75 billion from US$2.67 billion in the comparable period the year before. Indirect operating expenses increased 20.4% to US$426.8 million from US$354.5 million in the equivalent prior-year period.

Prospects: Despite the uncertain economic conditions and increased raw material costs, Co. is projecting 2008 diluted earnings per share in the range of $4.15 to $4.35 per share. For example, in its Cytec Surface Specialties segment, Co. is expecting 10.0% to 15.0% increase in operating earnings compared to 2007. Co. also estimates sales to increase by 4.0% in its Cytec Performance Chemicals segment, which should improve operating earnings by 10.0% versus 2007. Further, Co. expects 2008 sales and operating earnings to each grow by about 10.0% in 2008 for its Cytec Engineered Materials, as operating earnings for its Building Block Chemicals segment should be between $18.0 million and $20.0 million.

Financial Data

(US$ in Thousands)	12/31/2007	12/31/2006	12/31/2005	12/31/2004	12/31/2003	12/31/2002	12/31/2001	12/31/2000
Earnings Per Share	4.20	4.01	1.27	-2.84	1.93	1.96	1.71	4.15
Cash Flow Per Share	5.60	4.24	5.14	4.22	3.40	5.36	3.54	2.62
Tang Book Value Per Share	7.17	0.87	N.M.	12.48	8.87	6.43	6.58	5.77
Dividends Per Share	0.400	0.400	0.400	0.400	...	...	...	...
Dividend Payout %	9.52	9.98	31.50	14.08	...	...	...	...
Income Statement								
Total Revenue	3,503,800	3,329,500	2,925,700	1,721,300	1,471,800	1,346,200	1,387,100	1,492,500
EBITDA	505,500	469,800	264,600	273,900	235,000	212,900	224,400	401,400
Income Before Taxes	283,200	265,300	43,500	164,300	126,400	110,200	101,100	271,100
Income Taxes	76,700	69,200	(14,400)	38,200	35,400	30,900	34,900	93,500
Net Income	206,500	194,900	59,100	126,100	77,400	79,300	71,100	177,600
Average Shares	49,224	48,629	46,382	40,829	40,158	40,512	41,590	42,745
Balance Sheet								
Current Assets	1,276,100	1,153,400	1,122,600	904,800	711,400	604,800	509,900	567,800
Total Assets	4,061,700	3,831,500	3,810,500	2,226,100	2,025,900	1,751,500	1,650,400	1,719,400
Current Liabilities	686,900	611,900	625,900	496,700	336,500	430,800	282,000	358,900
Long-Term Obligations	705,300	900,400	1,225,500	300,100	416,200	216,000	314,700	311,200
Total Liabilities	2,131,800	2,261,400	2,572,400	1,319,600	1,270,500	1,128,600	1,013,500	1,103,200
Stockholders' Equity	1,929,900	1,570,100	1,238,100	906,500	755,400	622,900	636,900	616,200
Shares Outstanding	47,535	47,622	46,298	39,834	38,992	38,799	39,621	40,166
Statistical Record								
Return on Assets %	5.23	5.10	1.96	5.92	4.10	4.66	4.22	10.18
Return on Equity %	11.80	13.88	5.51	15.13	11.23	12.59	11.35	31.57
EBITDA Margin %	14.43	14.11	9.04	15.91	15.97	15.81	16.18	26.89
Net Margin %	5.89	5.85	2.02	7.33	5.26	5.89	5.13	11.90
Asset Turnover	0.89	0.87	0.97	0.81	0.78	0.79	0.82	0.86
Current Ratio	1.86	1.88	1.79	1.82	2.11	1.40	1.81	1.58
Debt to Equity	0.37	0.57	0.99	0.33	0.55	0.35	0.49	0.51
Price Range	71.78-53.83	62.40-45.89	54.25-39.52	51.73-32.97	38.76-25.98	33.58-19.34	38.31-21.27	39.94-22.50
P/E Ratio	17.09-12.82	15.56-11.44	42.72-31.12	18.21-11.61	20.08-13.46	17.13-9.87	22.40-12.44	9.62-5.42
Average Yield %	0.65	0.73	0.87	0.94	...	...	...	...

Address: Five Garret Mountain Plaza, West Paterson, NJ 07424 **Telephone:** 973-357-3100 **Fax:** 973-357-3061	**Web Site:** www.cytec.com **Officers:** D. Lilley - Chmn., Pres., C.E.O. J. P. Cronin - Exec. V.P., C.F.O.	**Auditors:** KPMG LLP **Investor Contact:** 973-357-3299 **Transfer Agents:** Mellon Investor Services

DANAHER CORP.

Exchange	Symbol	Price	52Wk Range	Yield	P/E	Div Acheiver
NYS	DHR	$76.03 (3/31/2008)	88.62-70.13	0.16	18.15	14 Years

*7 Year Price Score 123.49 *NYSE Composite Index=100 *12 Month Price Score 102.92

Interim Earnings (Per Share)

Qtr.	Mar	Jun	Sep	Dec
2003	0.33	0.40	0.44	0.53
2004	0.45	0.56	0.62	0.67
2005	0.58	0.70	0.70	0.78
2006	0.67	0.98	0.83	1.00
2007	0.78	0.96	1.48	0.97

Interim Dividends (Per Share)

Amt	Decl	Ex	Rec	Pay
0.03Q	5/24/2007	6/27/2007	6/29/2007	7/27/2007
0.03Q	9/14/2007	9/26/2007	9/28/2007	10/26/2007
0.03Q	12/5/2007	12/27/2007	12/31/2007	1/25/2008
0.00Q	2/21/2008	3/20/2008	3/28/2008	4/25/2008

Indicated Div: $0.12

Valuation Analysis

Forecast P/E	17.23
	(1/10/2007)
Market Cap	$24.2 Billion
Book Value	9.1 Billion
Price/Book	2.66
Price/Sales	2.19

Institutional Holding

No of Institutions	591
Shares	229,857,232
% Held	74.36

Business Summary: Instruments and Related Products (MIC: 11.15 SIC: 3823 NAIC: 334513)

Danaher operates four business segments: Professional Instrumentation, which provides professional and technical customers products and services for use in the performance of their work; Medical Technologies, which provides dentists, doctors, and scientific professionals products and services for use in the performance of their work; Industrial Technologies, which produces products and sub-systems that are usually incorporated by customers and systems integrators into production and packaging lines and by original equipment manufacturers into various end-products and systems; and Tools & Components, which produces mechanics' hand tools for the professional and do-it-yourself markets.

Recent Developments: For the year ended Dec 31 2007, income from continuing operations increased 9.4% to US$1.21 billion from US$1.11 billion a year earlier. Net income increased 22.1% to US$1.37 billion from US$1.12 billion in the prior year. Revenues were US$11.03 billion, up 16.5% from US$9.47 billion the year before. Operating income was US$1.74 billion versus US$1.50 billion in the prior year, an increase of 16.0%. Direct operating expenses rose 13.6% to US$5.99 billion from US$5.27 billion in the comparable period the year before. Indirect operating expenses increased 22.4% to US$3.30 billion from US$2.70 billion in the equivalent prior-year period.

Prospects: Co.'s recent results reflect continued strength in global economic conditions, mainly Europe and Asia, as well as North America. Meanwhile, Co. is encouraged by the Nov 21 2007 acquisition of Tektronix, Inc., which is expected to provide additional sales and earnings growth opportunities for its test and measurement business, both through the growth of existing products and services as well as through the potential acquisition of complementary businesses. For the full year of 2008, Co. is anticipating capital investment to exceed $200.0 million, primarily for increasing capacity, replacing equipment, supporting new product development and improving information technology systems.

Financial Data

(US$ in Thousands)	12/31/2007	12/31/2006	12/31/2005	12/31/2004	12/31/2003	12/31/2002	12/31/2001	12/31/2000
Earnings Per Share	4.19	3.48	2.76	2.30	1.69	0.94	1.00	1.12
Cash Flow Per Share	5.29	5.02	3.90	3.33	2.81	2.36	2.12	1.79
Tang Book Value Per Share	N.M.	N.M.	N.M.	N.M.	0.99	0.01	N.M.	0.28
Dividends Per Share	0.110	0.080	0.070	0.058	0.050	0.045	0.040	0.035
Dividend Payout %	2.63	2.30	2.54	2.50	2.97	4.79	3.98	3.14
Income Statement								
Total Revenue	11,025,917	9,596,404	7,984,704	6,889,301	5,293,876	4,577,232	3,782,444	3,777,777
EBITDA	2,009,201	1,735,210	1,441,640	1,261,261	979,431	830,687	680,401	701,870
Income Before Taxes	1,637,099	1,446,172	1,234,442	1,057,717	797,035	657,468	476,264	522,924
Income Taxes	423,101	324,143	336,642	311,717	260,201	223,327	178,599	198,711
Net Income	1,369,904	1,122,029	897,800	746,000	536,834	290,391	297,665	324,213
Average Shares	329,459	325,251	327,983	327,701	323,140	316,964	303,696	290,998
Balance Sheet								
Current Assets	4,049,767	3,394,902	2,945,019	2,918,690	2,942,151	2,387,266	1,874,615	1,474,306
Total Assets	17,471,935	12,864,151	9,163,109	8,493,893	6,890,050	6,029,145	4,820,483	4,031,679
Current Liabilities	2,899,853	2,459,556	2,268,586	2,202,286	1,380,021	1,265,312	1,017,294	1,018,540
Long-Term Obligations	3,395,764	2,422,861	857,771	925,535	1,284,498	1,197,422	1,119,333	713,557
Total Liabilities	8,386,247	6,219,491	4,082,759	3,874,211	3,243,341	3,019,546	2,591,897	2,089,346
Stockholders' Equity	9,085,688	6,644,660	5,080,350	4,619,682	3,646,709	3,009,599	2,228,586	1,942,333
Shares Outstanding	317,984	308,242	305,571	308,920	307,362	305,064	286,628	284,026
Statistical Record								
Return on Assets %	9.03	10.19	10.17	9.67	8.31	5.35	6.73	9.14
Return on Equity %	17.42	19.14	18.51	18.00	16.13	11.09	14.27	17.71
EBITDA Margin %	18.22	18.08	18.06	18.31	18.50	18.15	17.99	18.58
Net Margin %	12.42	11.69	11.24	10.83	10.14	6.34	7.87	8.58
Asset Turnover	0.73	0.87	0.90	0.89	0.82	0.84	0.85	1.06
Current Ratio	1.40	1.38	1.30	1.33	2.13	1.89	1.84	1.45
Debt to Equity	0.37	0.36	0.17	0.20	0.35	0.40	0.50	0.37
Price Range	88.62-69.88	74.98-54.30	58.07-48.56	58.64-43.99	45.98-30.23	37.66-26.62	33.84-22.77	34.34-18.56
P/E Ratio	21.15-16.68	21.55-15.60	21.04-17.59	25.50-19.13	27.20-17.88	40.07-28.32	33.84-22.77	30.66-16.57
Average Yield %	0.14	0.12	0.13	0.12	0.14	0.14	0.14	0.14

Address: 2099 Pennsylvania Avenue NW, 12th Floor, Washington, DC 20006-1813	Web Site: www.danaher.com	Auditors: Ernst & Young LLP
Telephone: 202-828-0850	**Officers:** Steven M. Rales - Chmn. Mitchell P. Rales - Exec. Chmn.	**Investor Contact:** 202-828-0850
Fax: 202-828-0860		**Transfer Agents:** SunTrust Bank

DARDEN RESTAURANTS, INC.

Exchange	Symbol	Price	52Wk Range	Yield	P/E
NYS	DRI	$32.55 (3/31/2008)	47.08-20.99	2.21	21.00

*7 Year Price Score 107.66 *NYSE Composite Index=100 *12 Month Price Score 85.47

Interim Earnings (Per Share)

Qtr.	Aug	Nov	Feb	May
2004-05	0.44	0.26	0.56	0.52
2005-06	0.53	0.35	0.67	0.60
2006-07	0.59	0.41	0.72	(0.36)
2007-08	0.72	0.30	0.88	...

Interim Dividends (Per Share)

Amt	Decl	Ex	Rec	Pay
0.18Q	6/19/2007	7/6/2007	7/10/2007	8/1/2007
0.18Q	9/18/2007	10/5/2007	10/10/2007	11/1/2007
0.18Q	12/18/2007	1/8/2008	1/10/2008	2/1/2008
0.18Q	3/18/2008	4/8/2008	4/10/2008	5/1/2008

Indicated Div: $0.72

Valuation Analysis | **Institutional Holding**

Forecast P/E	N/A	No of Institutions
		329
Market Cap	$4.6 Billion	Shares
Book Value	1.3 Billion	120,710,784
Price/Book	3.47	% Held
Price/Sales	0.76	85.38

Business Summary: Hospitality & Tourism (MIC: 5.1 SIC: 5812 NAIC: 722110)

Darden Restaurants is a casual dining restaurant company. As of March 2008, Co. owned and operated nearly 1,700 restaurants including Red Lobster, Olive Garden, LongHorn Steakhouse, The Capital Grille, Bahama Breeze and Seasons 52. Through its subsidiaries, Co. owns and operates all of its restaurants in the U.S. and Canada, and none of these restaurants are franchised. In Japan, Co. licenses Red Lobster restaurants to an unaffiliated Japanese corporation that operates the restaurants under an area development and franchise agreement.

Recent Developments: For the quarter ended Feb 24 2008, income from continuing operations decreased 1.8% to US$115.6 million from US$117.7 million in the year-earlier quarter. Net income increased 18.4% to US$126.0 million from US$106.4 million in the year-earlier quarter. Revenues were US$1.81 billion, up 25.0% from US$1.45 billion the year before. Direct operating expenses rose 27.4% to US$1.40 billion from US$1.10 billion in the comparable period the year before. Indirect operating expenses increased 31.8% to US$256.3 million from US$194.4 million in the equivalent prior-year period.

Prospects: Co.'s near-term outlook appears to be constructive. For the fiscal year ending May 29 2008, Co. continues to anticipate combined U.S. same- restaurant sales growth in the range of 2.0% to 3.0% for its Red Lobster, Olive Garden and LongHorn Steakhouse restaurant concepts. In addition, Co. now intends to open approximately 60 net new restaurants, including new restaurants at LongHorn Steakhouse and The Capital Grille through May 2008. As a result, Co. is targeting total sales growth to be in the range of 19.0% to 20.0%, compared with sales of $5.57 billion in the prior fiscal year. Lastly, Co. is forecasting earnings per share growth from continuing operations to range from 2.0% to 4.0%.

Financial Data

(US$ in Thousands)	9 Mos	6 Mos	3 Mos	05/27/2007	05/28/2006	05/29/2005	05/30/2004	05/25/2003
Earnings Per Share	1.55	1.38	1.50	1.35	2.16	1.78	1.36	1.31
Cash Flow Per Share	5.14	4.61	4.40	3.98	4.80	3.73	3.16	3.00
Tang Book Value Per Share	2.42	2.28	8.39	7.36	7.99	7.88	7.52	6.92
Dividends Per Share	0.77	0.59	0.64	0.460	0.40	0.080	0.080	...
Dividend Payout %	49.68	42.75	42.77	34.07	18.52	4.49	5.88	...
Income Statement								
Total Revenue	4,800,900	2,989,500	1,467,500	5,567,100	5,720,640	5,278,110	5,003,355	4,654,971
EBITDA	547,700	322,600	202,900	773,000	758,710	680,255	593,661	588,464
Depn & Amortn	179,700	111,500	51,000	...	...	...	...	...
Income Before Taxes	368,000	211,100	151,900	530,800	482,518	423,917	339,998	347,748
Income Taxes	101,800	60,400	45,300	153,700	144,324	133,311	108,536	115,488
Net Income	275,400	149,400	105,900	201,400	338,194	290,606	231,462	232,260
Average Shares	143,700	146,900	146,200	148,800	156,900	163,400	169,700	177,400
Balance Sheet								
Current Assets	540,000	631,300	552,600	545,400	377,607	407,266	346,307	325,629
Total Assets	4,725,600	4,754,400	2,931,800	2,880,800	3,010,170	2,937,771	2,780,348	2,664,633
Current Liabilities	1,242,500	1,302,800	995,100	1,074,400	1,026,078	1,044,607	683,481	639,909
Long-Term Obligations	1,695,300	1,686,100	491,000	491,600	494,653	350,318	653,349	658,086
Total Liabilities	3,412,400	3,452,600	1,741,700	1,786,300	1,780,407	1,664,752	1,534,578	1,468,442
Stockholders' Equity	1,313,200	1,301,800	1,190,100	1,094,500	1,229,763	1,273,019	1,245,770	1,196,191
Shares Outstanding	140,047	143,281	141,894	141,400	146,998	154,391	158,431	164,950
Statistical Record								
Return on Assets %	5.62	5.11	7.33	6.86	11.40	10.19	8.36	8.97
Return on Equity %	17.38	15.60	17.90	17.38	27.10	23.14	18.65	20.03
EBITDA Margin %	11.41	10.79	13.83	13.89	13.26	12.89	11.87	12.64
Net Margin %	5.74	5.00	7.22	3.62	5.91	5.51	4.63	4.99
Asset Turnover	1.52	1.45	1.87	1.90	1.93	1.85	1.81	1.80
Current Ratio	0.43	0.48	0.56	0.51	0.37	0.39	0.51	0.51
Debt to Equity	1.29	1.30	0.41	0.45	0.40	0.28	0.52	0.55
Price Range	47.08-20.99	47.08-38.32	47.08-35.24	45.88-33.29	42.75-28.80	32.80-19.40	25.37-18.39	27.40-16.80
P/E Ratio	30.37-13.54	34.12-27.77	31.39-23.49	33.99-24.66	19.79-13.33	18.43-10.90	18.65-13.52	20.92-12.82
Average Yield %	2.26	1.38	1.53	1.16	1.11	0.31	0.38	...

Address: 5900 Lake Ellenor Drive, Orlando, FL 32809 Telephone: 407-245-4000	Web Site: www.darden.com Officers: Joe R. Lee - Chmn. Andrew H. Madsen - Pres., C.O.O.	Auditors: KPMG LLP Transfer Agents: Wachovia Bank National Association

DAVITA INC.

Exchange	Symbol	Price	52Wk Range	Yield	P/E
NYS	DVA	$47.76 (3/31/2008)	66.53-42.48	N/A	13.45

*7 Year Price Score 128.20 *NYSE Composite Index=100   *12 Month Price Score 93.78

Interim Earnings (Per Share)

Qtr.	Mar	Jun	Sep	Dec
2003	0.35	0.37	0.30	0.59
2004	0.51	0.50	0.59	0.55
2005	0.55	0.51	0.53	0.62
2006	0.55	0.60	0.90	0.70
2007	0.72	1.17	0.88	0.79

Interim Dividends (Per Share)

Amt	Decl	Ex	Rec	Pay
3-for-2	5/17/2004	6/16/2004	6/1/2004	6/15/2004

Valuation Analysis   Institutional Holding

Forecast P/E	14.61	No of Institutions
	(1/10/2007)	287
Market Cap	$5.1 Billion	Shares
Book Value	1.7 Billion	94,027,040
Price/Book	2.95	% Held
Price/Sales	0.97	89.63

Business Summary: Diagnostic Services (MIC: 9.5 SIC: 8099 NAIC: 621999)

DaVita provides dialysis services for patients suffering from chronic kidney failure, also known as end stage renal disease (ESRD). As of Dec 31 2007, Co. operated or provided administrative services to about 1,359 outpatient dialysis centers in 43 states and the District of Columbia, serving about 107,000 patients on top of its acute inpatient dialysis services in about 700 hospitals. Co.'s other dialysis services include peritoneal dialysis, home based hemodialysis and hospital inpatient hemodialysis services. Co.'s other operations include various ancillary services and initiatives such as vascular access services, disease management services and ESRD clinical research programs.

Recent Developments: For the year ended Dec 31 2007, income from continuing operations increased 32.0% to US$381.8 million from US$289.3 million a year earlier. Net income increased 31.8% to US$381.8 million from US$289.7 million in the prior year. Revenues were US$5.26 billion, up 7.9% from US$4.88 billion the year before. Operating income was US$862.2 million versus US$739.4 million in the prior year, an increase of 16.6%. Direct operating expenses rose 5.9% to US$3.59 billion from US$3.39 billion in the comparable period the year before. Indirect operating expenses increased 8.1% to US$811.6 million from US$750.9 million in the equivalent prior-year period.

Prospects: Looking ahead, Co. continues to expect downward pressure from payors on its contracted commercial payment rates as a result of several factors, including general market conditions, recent and future consolidations among commercial payors, along with increased focus on dialysis services. For full-year 2008, Co. continues to project its operating income in the range of US$790.0 million to US$850.0 million, excluding the effect of any potential Medicare legislation, with expectation that operating income is more likely to be in the lower end of the range. Separately, Co. expects to open approximately the same number of centers in 2008 that it opened in 2007.

Financial Data

(US$ in Thousands)	12/31/2007	12/31/2006	12/31/2005	12/31/2004	12/31/2003	12/31/2002	12/31/2001	12/31/2000
Earnings Per Share	3.55	2.74	2.20	2.16	1.66	1.31	1.01	0.11
Cash Flow Per Share	5.03	5.02	4.82	4.24	3.11	3.17	2.17	2.51
Income Statement								
Total Revenue	5,264,151	4,880,662	2,973,918	2,298,595	2,016,418	1,854,632	1,650,753	1,486,302
EBITDA	1,078,139	925,760	590,402	500,962	429,781	432,488	418,585	273,177
Income Before Taxes	627,522	475,759	331,097	361,884	288,266	316,187	240,938	44,935
Income Taxes	245,744	186,430	123,675	139,630	112,475	129,500	104,600	27,960
Net Income	381,778	289,691	228,643	222,254	175,791	157,329	137,315	13,485
Average Shares	107,418	105,793	104,068	102,861	113,760	135,720	155,181	124,735
Balance Sheet								
Current Assets	1,976,250	1,709,496	1,654,408	868,720	605,058	544,526	474,664	397,875
Total Assets	6,943,960	6,491,816	6,279,762	2,511,959	1,945,530	1,775,693	1,662,683	1,596,632
Current Liabilities	1,086,496	1,112,172	989,733	441,735	362,820	292,601	298,681	249,527
Long-Term Obligations	3,683,887	3,730,380	4,085,435	1,322,468	1,117,002	1,311,252	811,190	974,006
Total Liabilities	5,211,710	5,245,892	5,429,153	1,988,825	1,638,659	1,705,429	1,159,046	1,247,264
Stockholders' Equity	1,732,250	1,245,924	850,609	523,134	306,871	70,264	503,637	349,368
Shares Outstanding	107,130	104,636	101,935	98,566	96,754	90,988	126,780	123,203
Statistical Record								
Return on Assets %	5.68	4.54	5.20	9.94	9.45	9.15	8.43	0.74
Return on Equity %	25.64	27.64	33.29	53.41	93.22	54.83	32.20	3.98
EBITDA Margin %	20.48	18.97	19.85	21.79	21.31	24.40	25.36	18.38
Net Margin %	7.25	5.94	7.69	9.67	8.72	8.48	8.32	0.91
Asset Turnover	0.78	0.76	0.68	1.03	1.08	1.08	1.01	0.81
Current Ratio	1.82	1.54	1.67	1.97	1.67	1.86	1.59	1.59
Debt to Equity	2.13	2.99	4.80	2.53	3.64	18.66	1.61	2.79
Price Range	66.53-51.54	60.27-47.59	53.59-39.26	39.62-25.33	26.67-13.01	17.42-12.97	16.30-9.73	11.67-1.71
P/E Ratio	18.74-14.52	22.00-17.37	24.36-17.85	18.34-11.73	16.06-7.84	13.30-9.90	16.14-9.64	106.06-15.53

Address: 21250 Hawthorne Blvd., Suite 800, Torrance, CA 90503-5517
Telephone: 310-792-2600
Fax: 310-792-8928

Web Site: www.davita.com
Officers: Kent J. Thiry - Chmn., C.E.O. Tom Kelly - Exec. V.P., Acting C.F.O.

Auditors: KPMG LLP
Investor Contact: 800-310-4872
Transfer Agents: The Bank of New York, New York, NY

DEAN FOODS CO.

Exchange	Symbol	Price	52Wk Range	Yield	P/E
NYS	DF	$20.09 (3/31/2008)	47.33-19.49	N/A	20.93

*7 Year Price Score 80.55   ***NYSE Composite Index=100**   ***12 Month Price Score 85.97**

Interim Earnings (Per Share)

Qtr.	Mar	Jun	Sep	Dec
2003	0.43	0.54	0.76	0.54
2004	0.43	0.47	0.25	0.63
2005	0.43	0.55	0.67	0.49
2006	0.37	0.21	0.51	0.52
2007	0.47	0.21	0.05	0.24

Interim Dividends (Per Share)

Amt	Decl	Ex	Rec	Pay
2-for-1	2/21/2002	4/24/2002	4/8/2002	4/24/2002
3-for-2	5/8/2003	6/10/2003	5/23/2003	6/9/2003
15.00SP	3/2/2007	4/3/2007	3/27/2007	4/2/2007

Valuation Analysis   Institutional Holding

Forecast P/E	15.65	No of Institutions
	(1/10/2007)	322
Market Cap	$2.7 Billion	Shares
Book Value	51.3 Million	104,218,320
Price/Book	51.82	% Held
Price/Sales	0.22	80.82

TRADING VOLUME (thousand shares)

Business Summary: Food (MIC: 4.1 SIC: 2024 NAIC: 311520)

Dean Foods is a food and beverage company. At Dec 31 2007, Co. had two reportable segments: the Dairy Group and WhiteWave Foods. Co.'s Dairy Group processes and distributes milk and various other dairy products in the U.S. under a range of local and regional brand names and under private labels. Co.'s WhiteWave Foods segment markets and sells a variety of dairy and dairy-related products, such as Silk® soymilk, Horizon Organic® milk and other dairy products, International Delight® coffee creamers, LAND O'LAKES® creamers and other fluid dairy products, and Rachel's Organic® organic yoghurt.

Recent Developments: For the year ended Dec 31 2007, net income decreased 41.7% to US$131.4 million from US$225.4 million in the prior year. Revenues were US$11.82 billion, up 17.1% from US$10.10 billion the year before. Operating income was US$553.6 million versus US$650.7 million in the prior year, a decrease of 14.9%. Direct operating expenses rose 23.5% to US$9.08 billion from US$7.36 billion in the comparable period the year before. Indirect operating expenses increased 4.5% to US$2.18 billion from US$2.09 billion in the equivalent prior-year period.

Prospects: Co. is seeing a decrease in earnings due to high dairy commodity costs and oversupply of organic milk that drove down realized prices at its WhiteWave Foods segment. For 2008, Co. expects that its results will continue to be driven primarily by swings in the dairy commodity markets, including the organic milk market. Co. noted that there is significant volatility in the pricing of conventional raw milk and anticipates volatility to continue in 2008, with conventional raw milk prices to decline in 2008 from the levels experienced in the fourth quarter of 2007. Nevertheless, Co. expects prices to remain high, and thus projects earnings per share to be at least $1.20 per share for 2008.

Financial Data

(US$ in Thousands)	12/31/2007	12/31/2006	12/31/2005	12/31/2004	12/31/2003	12/31/2002	12/31/2001	12/31/2000
Earnings Per Share	0.96	1.61	2.13	1.78	2.27	1.21	1.19	1.27
Cash Flow Per Share	2.69	4.19	3.82	3.40	3.60	4.86	3.67	3.51
Tang Book Value Per Share	N.M.	N.M.	N.M.	N.M.	N.M.	N.M.	11.20	7.32
Dividends Per Share	15.000	...	...	...	...	...	...	...
Dividend Payout %	N.M.	...	...	...	...	...	...	...
Income Statement								
Total Revenue	11,821,903	10,098,555	10,505,560	10,822,285	9,184,616	8,991,464	6,230,116	5,756,303
EBITDA	779,569	877,942	829,171	890,693	951,524	800,239	487,437	491,534
Income Before Taxes	214,469	455,713	438,896	462,376	573,526	420,785	230,763	233,965
Income Taxes	84,007	175,450	166,423	177,002	217,853	152,988	83,739	90,303
Net Income	131,353	225,414	327,531	285,374	355,703	175,416	109,830	118,719
Average Shares	137,291	139,762	153,438	160,704	160,695	163,163	110,676	110,013
Balance Sheet								
Current Assets	1,531,984	1,379,290	1,476,968	1,596,424	1,400,881	1,311,146	1,482,184	817,931
Total Assets	7,033,356	6,770,173	7,050,884	7,756,368	6,992,536	6,582,266	6,731,897	3,780,478
Current Liabilities	932,516	1,336,556	1,137,330	1,106,426	1,170,393	1,192,948	1,174,963	699,908
Long-Term Obligations	5,247,105	2,872,193	3,328,592	3,116,032	2,611,356	2,554,482	2,971,525	1,225,045
Total Liabilities	6,982,089	4,960,774	5,178,805	5,095,231	4,449,723	4,938,973	5,256,017	3,181,646
Stockholders' Equity	51,267	1,809,399	1,872,079	2,661,137	2,542,813	1,643,293	1,475,880	598,832
Shares Outstanding	132,236	128,371	134,209	149,222	154,993	132,961	131,809	81,856
Statistical Record								
Return on Assets %	1.90	3.26	4.42	3.86	5.24	2.64	2.09	3.68
Return on Equity %	14.12	12.25	14.45	10.94	16.99	11.25	10.59	20.02
EBITDA Margin %	6.59	8.69	7.89	8.23	10.36	8.90	7.82	8.54
Net Margin %	1.11	2.23	3.12	2.64	3.87	1.95	1.76	2.06
Asset Turnover	1.71	1.46	1.42	1.46	1.35	1.35	1.19	1.78
Current Ratio	1.64	1.03	1.30	1.44	1.20	1.10	1.26	1.17
Debt to Equity	102.35	1.59	1.78	1.17	1.03	1.55	2.01	2.05
Price Range	48.31-24.30	43.51-34.70	39.45-26.93	31.77-24.15	28.45-20.99	22.75-15.80	20.50-12.20	14.72-10.25
P/E Ratio	50.32-25.31	27.02-21.55	18.52-12.65	17.85-13.57	12.53-9.25	18.80-13.05	17.23-10.25	11.59-8.07
Average Yield %	45.25	...	...	...	...	...	...	...

Address: 2515 McKinney Avenue, Suite 1200, Dallas, TX 75201 **Telephone:** 214-303-3400 **Fax:** 214-528-9929	**Web Site:** www.deanfoods.com **Officers:** Gregg L. Engles - Chmn., C.E.O. Barry A. Fromberg - Exec. V.P., C.F.O.	**Auditors:** Deloitte & Touche LLP **Transfer Agents:** Computershare Investor Services

DEERE & CO.

Exchange	Symbol	Price	52Wk Range	Yield	P/E
NYS	DE	$80.44 (3/31/2008)	94.69-52.24	1.24	18.62

*7 Year Price Score 158.76 *NYSE Composite Index=100 *12 Month Price Score 126.57

Interim Earnings (Per Share)

Qtr.	Jan	Apr	Jul	Oct
2004-05	0.45	1.22	0.79	0.49
2005-06	0.50	1.56	0.93	0.61
2006-07	0.52	1.36	1.19	0.94
2007-08	0.83	...	...	...

Interim Dividends (Per Share)

Amt	Decl	Ex	Rec	Pay
0.25Q	8/29/2007	9/26/2007	9/28/2007	11/1/2007
100%	8/29/2007	12/4/2007	11/26/2007	12/3/2007
0.25Q	11/29/2007	12/27/2007	12/31/2007	2/1/2008
0.25Q	2/27/2008	3/27/2008	3/31/2008	5/1/2008

Indicated DIV: $1.00

Valuation Analysis

		Institutional Holding	
Forecast P/E	12.26	No of Institutions	
	(1/10/2007)	534	
Market Cap	$35.1 Billion	Shares	
Book Value	7.0 Billion	188,143,120	
Price/Book	4.98	% Held	
Price/Sales	1.41	82.94	

Business Summary: Industrial Machinery and Equipment (MIC: 11.5 SIC: 3523 NAIC: 333111)

Deere & Company engages in the manufacture and sale of agricultural and commercial equipment worldwide. Co.'s agricultural equipment segment manufactures and distributes farm equipment and service parts such as tractors and sprayers, while Co.'s commercial and consumer equipment segment manufactures and distributes equipment, products and service parts for commercial and residential uses. The construction and forestry segment manufactures, distributes to dealers and sells at retail a range of machines and service parts used in construction, earthmoving, material handling and timber harvesting. Co.'s credit segment primarily finances sales and leases of equipment by Co.'s dealers.

Recent Developments: For the quarter ended Jan 31 2008, net income increased 54.6% to US$369.1 million from US$238.7 million in the year-earlier quarter. Revenues were US$5.20 billion, up 17.5% from US$4.43 billion the year before. Direct operating expenses rose 14.0% to US$3.36 billion from US$2.95 billion in the comparable period the year before. Indirect operating expenses increased 20.2% to US$1.01 billion from US$842.5 million in the equivalent prior-year period.

Prospects: On Feb 29 2008, Co. announced that it has signed a definitive agreement to own 50.0% of Xuzhou Xuwa Excavator Machinery Co., Ltd., a subsidiary of Xuzhou Bohui Science and Technology Development CO. Ltd. in China, for undisclosed terms. Accordingly, Co. expects the transaction to expand its presence in the growing market for construction equipment. Meanwhile, Co. believes that it remains in position to benefit from positive global economic trends, such as growing demand for food and infrastructure, and the rising use of biofuels. For fiscal year ending Oct 2008, Co. is projecting equipment sales to increase by about 17.0% from its prior fiscal year, with net income of about $2.20 billion.

Financial Data
(US$ in Thousands)

	3 Mos	10/31/2007	10/31/2006	10/31/2005	10/31/2004	10/31/2003	10/31/2002	10/31/2001
Earnings Per Share	4.32	4.00	3.59	2.94	2.78	1.32	0.67	(0.14)
Cash Flow Per Share	5.99	6.14	2.08	2.50	2.34	3.20	3.94	2.37
Tang Book Value Per Share	12.98	13.17	13.92	12.13	10.93	5.91	4.75	6.57
Dividends Per Share	0.940	0.910	0.780	0.605	0.530	0.440	0.440	0.440
Dividend Payout %	21.78	22.75	21.73	20.61	19.06	33.33	66.17	...
Income Statement								
Total Revenue	5,201,000	24,082,200	22,147,800	21,930,500	19,986,100	15,534,600	13,947,000	13,292,900
EBITDA	1,026,300	4,571,100	3,882,700	3,553,300	3,326,800	1,910,800	1,593,800	1,088,900
Depn & Amortn	199,700	...	...	...	...	...	...	...
Income Before Taxes	531,500	2,675,500	2,173,800	2,155,800	2,113,700	971,300	602,700	(24,800)
Income Taxes	170,000	883,000	741,600	715,100	708,500	336,900	258,300	17,700
Net Income	369,100	1,821,700	1,693,800	1,446,800	1,406,100	643,100	319,200	(64,000)
Average Shares	444,200	455,000	471,600	492,800	506,200	486,600	481,800	473,600
Balance Sheet								
Current Assets	9,825,900	9,919,800	8,969,400	10,540,000	9,314,400	9,332,900	7,801,700	6,339,900
Total Assets	38,215,300	38,575,700	34,720,400	33,636,800	28,754,000	26,258,000	23,768,000	22,663,100
Current Liabilities	15,155,300	15,737,800	12,787,500	11,623,100	7,753,500	7,767,300	7,730,400	9,355,700
Long-Term Obligations	12,344,400	11,798,000	11,584,000	11,739,000	11,090,000	10,404,000	8,950,000	6,561,000
Total Liabilities	31,176,900	31,419,900	27,229,200	26,785,300	22,361,200	22,255,900	20,604,800	18,670,900
Stockholders' Equity	7,038,400	7,155,800	7,491,200	6,851,500	6,392,800	4,002,100	3,163,200	3,992,200
Shares Outstanding	436,035	439,636	454,466	473,743	493,718	487,042	477,789	474,663
Statistical Record								
Return on Assets %	5.40	4.97	4.96	4.64	5.10	2.57	1.37	N.M.
Return on Equity %	26.71	24.87	23.62	21.85	26.98	17.95	8.92	N.M.
EBITDA Margin %	19.73	18.98	17.53	16.20	16.65	12.30	11.43	8.19
Net Margin %	7.10	7.56	7.65	6.60	7.04	4.14	2.29	N.M.
Asset Turnover	0.69	0.66	0.65	0.70	0.72	0.62	0.60	0.62
Current Ratio	0.65	0.63	0.70	0.91	1.20	1.20	1.01	0.68
Debt to Equity	1.75	1.65	1.55	1.71	1.73	2.60	2.83	1.64
Price Range	94.69-50.14	77.45-42.41	45.67-30.34	37.21-28.58	37.42-28.80	30.31-18.98	24.89-18.50	23.31-17.30
P/E Ratio	21.92-11.61	19.36-10.60	12.72-8.45	12.66-9.72	13.46-10.36	22.96-14.38	37.15-27.60	...
Average Yield %	1.40	1.57	2.02	1.81	1.64	1.86	1.98	2.19

Address: One John Deere Place, Moline, IL 61265 **Telephone:** 309-765-8000 **Fax:** 309-765-9929	**Web Site:** www.johndeere.com **Officers:** Robert W. Lane - Chmn., Pres., C.E.O. Nathan J. Jones - Sr. V.P., C.F.O.	**Auditors:** Deloitte & Touche LLP **Investor Contact:** 309-765-4491 **Transfer Agents:** The Bank of New York, New York, NY

DEL MONTE FOODS CO.

Exchange	Symbol	Price	52Wk Range	Yield	P/E
NYS	DLM	$9.53 (3/31/2008)	12.75-7.83	N/A	16.15

*7 Year Price Score 83.21   *NYSE Composite Index=100   *12 Month Price Score 91.52

Interim Earnings (Per Share)

Qtr.	Jul	Oct	Jan	Apr
2004-05	0.04	0.20	0.23	0.09
2005-06	0.08	0.22	0.26	0.29
2006-07	0.03	0.11	0.23	0.18
2007-08	0.02	0.13	0.26	...

Interim Dividends (Per Share)

No Dividends Paid

Valuation Analysis

		Institutional Holding	
Forecast P/E	12.13	No of Institutions	
	(1/10/2007)	247	
Market Cap	$1.9 Billion	Shares	
Book Value	1.5 Billion	177,516,976	
Price/Book	1.28	% Held	
Price/Sales	0.52	87.92	

Business Summary: Food (MIC: 4.1 SIC: 2033 NAIC: 311421)

Del Monte Foods produces, distributes and markets branded and private label food and pet products for the U.S. retail market under several food brands which include Del Monte, StarKist, Contadina, S&W, College Inn and other brand names. Co.'s foods and snacks for pets include brand names such as Meow Mix, Kibbles 'n Bits, 9Lives, Milk-Bone, Pup-Peroni, Meaty Bone, Snausages and Pounce. The majority of Co.'s products are sold nationwide in channels serving retail markets, as well as the U.S. military, certain export markets, the foodservice industry and other food processors. Co. has two reportable segments: Consumer Products and Pet Products.

Recent Developments: For the quarter ended Jan 27 2008, income from continuing operations increased 18.2% to US$53.3 million from US$45.1 million in the year-earlier quarter. Net income increased 14.6% to US$53.3 million from US$46.5 million in the year-earlier quarter. Revenues were US$1.00 billion, up 10.4% from US$907.2 million the year before. Operating income was US$118.8 million versus US$110.5 million in the prior-year quarter, an increase of 7.5%. Direct operating expenses rose 14.4% to US$747.9 million from US$654.0 million in the comparable period the year before. Indirect operating expenses decreased 5.8% to US$134.4 million from US$142.7 million in the equivalent prior-year period.

Prospects: For the fourth quarter of the fiscal year ending Apr 2008, Co. expects sales growth of 6.0% to 8.0% and diluted earnings per share from continuing operations of $0.23 to $0.27. For the full fiscal year, Co. has raised its net sales growth target from a range of 5.0% to 7.0% to a range of 7.0% to 9.0% over fiscal 2007 net sales of $3.41 billion. The increase in net sales growth is driven by favorable merchandising during the Thanksgiving and holiday related promotion periods in the fiscal quarter ended Jan 2008, and the expectation of continued momentum in the near term. Co. has also reiterated its earnings per share from continuing operations guidance of $0.64 to $0.68 for the fiscal year.

Financial Data
(US$ in Thousands)

	9 Mos	6 Mos	3 Mos	04/29/2007	04/30/2006	05/01/2005	05/02/2004	04/27/2003
Earnings Per Share	0.59	0.56	0.54	0.55	0.83	0.56	0.78	0.76
Cash Flow Per Share	1.06	0.92	1.02	1.15	1.30	1.30	1.28	2.84
Dividends Per Share	0.160	0.160	0.160	0.160	0.080	...	...	...
Dividend Payout %	27.00	28.51	29.61	29.09	9.64	...	...	...
Income Statement								
Total Revenue	2,692,700	1,691,600	753,500	3,414,900	2,998,600	3,180,900	3,129,900	2,171,100
EBITDA	325,300	178,800	69,200	421,800	395,700	412,100	469,700	296,900
Depn & Amortn	78,500	51,900	25,700	...	...	...	...	...
Income Before Taxes	129,000	47,900	5,500	166,600	215,500	190,300	251,200	201,100
Income Taxes	45,500	17,700	2,000	53,600	78,500	71,700	90,500	67,600
Net Income	82,700	29,400	3,500	112,600	169,900	117,900	164,600	133,500
Average Shares	201,350	205,375	202,613	203,804	204,192	212,355	211,212	176,494
Balance Sheet								
Current Assets	1,393,600	1,564,900	1,309,800	1,216,500	1,617,100	1,318,400	1,225,700	1,139,400
Total Assets	4,703,200	4,882,800	4,639,000	4,561,500	3,622,900	3,530,600	3,459,700	3,544,900
Current Liabilities	699,400	866,400	634,500	559,900	511,200	390,000	434,300	444,500
Long-Term Obligations	1,922,200	1,932,100	1,942,000	1,951,900	1,242,500	1,304,400	1,369,500	1,635,300
Total Liabilities	3,239,900	3,413,600	3,185,500	3,109,300	2,308,900	2,270,000	2,330,800	2,595,500
Stockholders' Equity	1,463,300	1,469,200	1,453,500	1,452,200	1,314,000	1,260,600	1,128,900	949,400
Shares Outstanding	197,274	202,360	202,529	202,211	200,117	211,203	209,691	209,303
Statistical Record								
Return on Assets %	2.55	2.31	2.38	2.76	4.76	3.38	4.62	5.85
Return on Equity %	8.43	8.04	7.93	8.16	13.23	9.90	15.58	27.52
EBITDA Margin %	12.08	10.57	9.18	12.35	13.20	12.96	15.01	13.68
Net Margin %	3.07	1.74	0.46	3.30	5.67	3.71	5.26	6.15
Asset Turnover	0.77	0.73	0.76	0.84	0.84	0.91	0.88	0.95
Current Ratio	1.99	1.81	2.06	2.17	3.16	3.38	2.82	2.56
Debt to Equity	1.31	1.32	1.34	1.34	0.95	1.03	1.21	1.72
Price Range	12.75-8.52	12.75-10.19	12.75-10.05	12.05-10.05	12.03-9.88	11.62-9.90	11.62-7.87	11.96-7.12
P/E Ratio	21.61-14.44	22.77-18.20	23.61-18.61	21.91-18.27	14.49-11.90	20.75-17.68	14.90-10.09	15.74-9.37
Average Yield %	1.47	1.41	1.42	1.44	0.74	...	...	...

Address: One Market @ The Landmark, San Francisco, CA 94105	**Web Site:** www.delmonte.com	**Auditors:** KPMG LLP
Telephone: 415-247-3000	**Officers:** Richard G. Wolford - Chmn., Pres., C.E.O.	**Investor Contact:** 415-247-3382
Fax: 415-247-3565	David L. Meyers - Exec. V.P., Admin., C.F.O.	**Transfer Agents:** Bank of New York, New York, NY

DELUXE CORP.

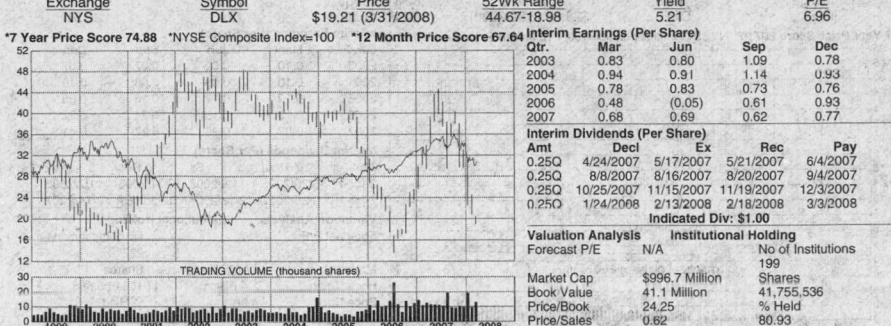

Exchange	Symbol	Price	52Wk Range	Yield	P/E
NYS	DLX	$19.21 (3/31/2008)	44.67-18.98	5.21	6.96

*7 Year Price Score 74.88 ***NYSE Composite Index=100** ***12 Month Price Score 67.64**

Interim Earnings (Per Share)

Qtr.	Mar	Jun	Sep	Dec
2003	0.83	0.80	1.09	0.78
2004	0.94	0.91	1.14	0.93
2005	0.78	0.83	0.73	0.76
2006	0.48	(0.05)	0.61	0.93
2007	0.68	0.69	0.62	0.77

Interim Dividends (Per Share)

Amt	Decl	Ex	Rec	Pay
0.25Q	4/24/2007	5/17/2007	5/21/2007	6/4/2007
0.25Q	8/8/2007	8/16/2007	8/20/2007	9/4/2007
0.25Q	10/25/2007	11/15/2007	11/19/2007	12/3/2007
0.25Q	1/24/2008	2/13/2008	2/18/2008	3/3/2008

Indicated Div: $1.00

Valuation Analysis

Forecast P/E	N/A
Market Cap	$996.7 Million
Book Value	41.1 Million
Price/Book	24.25
Price/Sales	0.62

Institutional Holding

No of Institutions	199
Shares	41,755,536
% Held	80.93

TRADING VOLUME (thousand shares)

Business Summary: Printing (MIC: 13.4 SIC: 2782 NAIC: 323118)

Deluxe utilizes direct marketing, a North American sales force, financial institution referrals, independent distributors and the internet to provide its customers a range of customized products and services: personalized printed items such as checks, forms, business cards, greeting cards, labels, and retail packaging supplies; promotional products and merchandising materials; fraud prevention and marketing services and financial institution customer loyalty and retention programs. Co. also sells personalized checks, accessories, stored value gift cards and other services directly to consumers. Co. has three segments: Small Business Services, Financial Services, and Direct Checks.

Recent Developments: For the year ended Dec 31 2007, income from continuing operations increased 42.7% to US$143.5 million from US$100.6 million a year earlier. Net income increased 42.2% to US$143.5 million from US$101.0 million in the prior year. Revenues were US$1.61 billion, down 2.0% from US$1.64 billion the year before. Operating income was US$267.5 million versus US$198.3 million in the prior year, an increase of 34.9%. Direct operating expenses declined 4.4% to US$586.6 million from US$613.3 million in the comparable period the year before. Indirect operating expenses decreased 9.2% to US$752.3 million from US$828.1 million in the equivalent prior-year period.

Prospects: Co. plans to invest in building out new products and key enablers such as e-commerce in the first half of 2008 to drive modest revenue growth during the latter half of the year. Co. is also pursuing cost reduction and business simplification initiatives, which is expected to reduce annual cost structure by at least $225.0 million, net of required investments, by end of 2009. For full-year 2008, Co. anticipates consolidated revenue of between $1.56 billion and $1.61 billion, with near flat revenue performance in 2008 as compared to 2007. Co. also expects earnings of between $3.00 and $3.20 per diluted share, and operating income to increase from 2007 due to its cost reduction initiatives.

Financial Data
(US$ in Thousands)

	12/31/2007	12/31/2006	12/31/2005	12/31/2004	12/31/2003	12/31/2002	12/31/2001	12/31/2000
Earnings Per Share	2.76	1.96	3.09	3.92	3.49	3.36	2.69	2.24
Cash Flow Per Share	4.76	4.69	3.53	6.12	3.33	4.09	3.96	3.50
Tang Book Value Per Share	N.M.	...	...	...	...	N.M.	N.M.	0.55
Dividends Per Share	1.000	1.300	1.600	1.480	1.480	1.480	1.480	1.480
Dividend Payout %	36.23	66.33	51.78	37.76	42.41	44.05	55.02	66.07
Income Statement								
Total Revenue	1,606,367	1,639,654	1,716,294	1,567,015	1,242,141	1,283,983	1,278,375	1,262,712
EBITDA	340,839	343,459	493,746	508,736	378,334	403,331	374,732	352,836
Income Before Taxes	217,654	142,541	250,734	316,873	299,380	340,722	297,534	273,429
Income Taxes	74,139	41,983	92,771	118,225	106,908	126,448	111,634	103,957
Net Income	143,515	100,954	157,521	197,991	192,472	214,274	185,900	161,936
Average Shares	51,932	51,230	50,936	50,549	55,228	63,747	69,115	72,420
Balance Sheet								
Current Assets	191,945	202,117	213,938	240,386	78,928	199,646	83,972	208,768
Total Assets	1,210,755	1,267,132	1,425,875	1,499,079	562,960	668,973	537,721	649,469
Current Liabilities	297,588	664,503	491,085	571,198	387,839	214,779	367,124	305,173
Long-Term Obligations	775,086	576,590	902,805	953,848	380,620	306,589	10,084	10,201
Total Liabilities	1,169,648	1,332,805	1,507,901	1,677,570	861,043	604,657	459,116	386,661
Stockholders' Equity	41,107	(65,673)	(82,026)	(178,491)	(298,083)	64,316	78,605	262,808
Shares Outstanding	51,887	51,519	50,735	50,265	50,173	61,445	64,101	72,555
Statistical Record								
Return on Assets %	11.58	7.50	10.77	19.15	31.25	35.51	31.32	19.67
Return on Equity %	...	...	...	...	...	299.85	108.90	47.49
EBITDA Margin %	21.22	20.95	28.77	32.47	30.46	31.41	29.31	27.94
Net Margin %	8.93	6.16	9.18	12.63	15.50	16.69	14.54	12.82
Asset Turnover	1.30	1.22	1.17	1.52	2.02	2.13	2.15	1.53
Current Ratio	0.65	0.30	0.44	0.42	0.20	0.93	0.23	0.68
Debt to Equity	18.86	...	...	...	...	4.77	0.13	0.04
Price Range	44.67-25.63	31.37-13.57	42.90-30.11	44.70-37.33	48.35-37.22	49.75-33.37	42.19-19.17	23.19-15.89
P/E Ratio	16.18-9.29	16.01-6.92	13.88-9.74	11.40-9.52	13.85-10.66	14.81-9.93	15.68-7.13	10.35-7.09
Average Yield %	2.79	5.85	4.19	3.60	3.51	3.37	4.99	7.78

Address: 3680 Victoria Street North, Shoreview, MN 55126-2966 **Telephone:** 651-483-7111 **Fax:** 651-483-7337	**Web Site:** www.deluxe.com **Officers:** Stephen P. Nachtsheim - Chmn. Ronald E. Eilers - Pres., Interim C.E.O., C.O.O.	**Auditors:** PricewaterhouseCoopers LLP **Transfer Agents:** Wells Fargo Shareowner Services, St. Paul, MN

DENBURY RESOURCES, INC. (DE)

Exchange	Symbol	Price	52Wk Range	Yield	P/E
NYS	DNR	$28.55 (3/31/2008)	32.67-15.02	N/A	28.55

*7 Year Price Score 207.27 *NYSE Composite Index=100 *12 Month Price Score 133.80

Interim Earnings (Per Share)

Qtr.	Mar	Jun	Sep	Dec
2003	0.10	0.02	0.07	0.07
2004	0.10	0.09	0.08	0.10
2005	0.13	0.17	0.16	0.23
2006	0.19	0.18	0.24	0.22
2007	0.07	0.25	0.27	0.41

Interim Dividends (Per Share)

Amt	Decl	Ex	Rec	Pay
2-for-1	10/20/2005	11/8/2005	10/31/2005	11/7/2005
2-for-1	9/25/2007	12/17/2007	12/5/2007	12/14/2007

Valuation Analysis   Institutional Holding

Forecast P/E	N/A	No of Institutions
		227
Market Cap	$7.0 Billion	Shares
Book Value	1.4 Billion	106,060,688
Price/Book	4.98	% Held
Price/Sales	7.19	88.04

Business Summary: Oil and Gas (MIC: 14.2 SIC: 1311 NAIC: 213112)

Denbury Resources is an independent oil and gas company engaged in the acquisition, development, operation and exploration of oil and natural gas properties in the Gulf Coast region of the U.S., primarily in Louisiana, Mississippi, Alabama, and Texas. Co. has four primary field offices located in Laurel, MS; McComb, MS; Brandon, MS; and Cleburne, TX. As of Dec 31 2007, Co. had proved reserves of 135.0 million barrels of oil and 358.6 million cubic feet of natural gas, or the equivalent of 194.7 million barrels of oil. As of the date stated above, Co. operated 683.4 net producing oil wells and 354.5 net producing natural gas wells.

Recent Developments: For the year ended Dec 31 2007, net income increased 25.0% to US$253.1 million from US$202.5 million in the prior year. Revenues were US$972.0 million, up 32.7% from US$732.3 million the year before. Direct operating expenses rose 37.4% to US$284.2 million from US$206.8 million in the comparable period the year before. Indirect operating expenses increased 50.2% to US$294.3 million from US$195.9 million in the equivalent prior-year period.

Prospects: Co.'s 2008 outlook appears encouraging, reflecting the existing commodity price environment as well as the political and environmental focus on sequestering carbon dioxide. Accordingly, Co. is increasing its 2008 production forecast by 1,500 barrel of oil equivalent per day (BOE/d) to 49,000 BOE/d, reflecting several factors which include the higher liquid recoveries from the Barnett Shale production during the fourth quarter of 2007 as well as its 2008 plan to drill 45 to 50 horizontal wells in that area. In addition, Co. anticipates production from its tertiary operations to increase from a 2007 average of 14,767 BOE/d to a projected 2008 range between 22,000 BOE/d and 25,000 BOE/d.

Financial Data

(US$ in Thousands)	12/31/2007	12/31/2006	12/31/2005	12/31/2004	12/31/2003	12/31/2002	12/31/2001	12/31/2000
Earnings Per Share	1.00	0.82	0.69	0.36	0.26	0.22	0.28	0.77
Cash Flow Per Share	2.38	1.98	1.62	0.77	0.92	0.75	0.94	0.52
Tang Book Value Per Share	5.74	4.60	3.20	2.40	1.94	1.71	1.65	1.18
Income Statement								
Total Revenue	971,950	731,536	560,392	382,972	333,014	285,152	285,111	181,651
EBITDA	589,314	478,739	346,843	219,367	174,861	164,551	152,719	111,147
Income Before Taxes	393,414	329,574	248,041	121,840	80,153	70,315	81,374	74,933
Income Taxes	140,267	127,117	81,570	39,392	26,212	23,520	24,824	(67,294)
Net Income	253,147	202,457	166,471	82,448	56,553	46,795	56,550	142,227
Average Shares	252,101	247,547	239,268	229,204	221,856	217,460	201,444	185,408
Balance Sheet								
Current Assets	240,359	183,269	299,183	172,846	108,155	128,464	103,278	97,990
Total Assets	2,771,077	2,139,837	1,505,069	992,706	982,621	895,292	789,988	457,379
Current Liabilities	264,633	200,398	154,064	82,906	126,574	95,879	79,938	38,786
Long-Term Obligations	680,330	514,173	379,461	227,581	298,203	344,889	334,769	199,000
Total Liabilities	1,366,699	1,033,778	771,407	451,034	561,419	528,495	440,820	241,214
Stockholders' Equity	1,404,378	1,106,059	733,662	541,672	421,202	366,797	349,168	216,165
Shares Outstanding	244,749	240,272	229,396	226,059	216,727	214,157	211,827	183,919
Statistical Record								
Return on Assets %	10.31	11.11	13.33	8.32	6.02	5.55	9.07	39.96
Return on Equity %	20.17	22.01	26.11	17.08	14.35	13.07	20.01	98.30
EBITDA Margin %	60.63	65.44	61.89	57.28	52.51	57.71	53.56	61.19
Net Margin %	26.05	27.68	29.71	21.53	16.98	16.41	19.83	78.30
Asset Turnover	0.40	0.40	0.45	0.39	0.35	0.34	0.46	0.51
Current Ratio	0.91	0.91	1.94	2.08	0.85	1.34	1.29	2.53
Debt to Equity	0.48	0.46	0.52	0.42	0.71	0.94	0.96	0.92
Price Range	30.15-13.03	18.30-12.07	12.81-6.21	7.29-3.42	3.56-2.60	2.93-1.60	2.92-1.52	2.75-0.92
P/E Ratio	30.15-13.03	22.32-14.73	18.57-9.01	20.24-9.50	13.69-9.98	13.31-7.27	10.43-5.42	3.57-1.20

Address: 5100 Tennyson Parkway, Suite 1200, Plano, TX 75024 **Telephone:** 972-673-2000 **Fax:** 972-673-2150	**Web Site:** www.denbury.com **Officers:** Ronald G. Greene - Chmn. Gareth Roberts - Pres., C.E.O.	**Auditors:** PricewaterhouseCoopers LLP **Investor Contact:** 972-673-2000 **Transfer Agents:** American Stock Transfer and Trust Company, New York, NY

DEVELOPERS DIVERSIFIED REALTY CORP.

Exchange	Symbol	Price	52Wk Range	Yield	P/E	Div Acheiver
NYS	DDR	$41.88 (3/31/2008)	66.25-32.92	6.59	22.64	14 Years

*7 Year Price Score 105.60 *NYSE Composite Index=100 *12 Month Price Score 86.77

Interim Earnings (Per Share)

Qtr.	Mar	Jun	Sep	Dec
2003	0.37	0.66	0.28	0.95
2004	0.46	0.77	0.30	0.72
2005	0.84	0.50	0.43	0.32
2006	0.33	0.59	0.45	0.44
2007	0.42	0.89	0.26	0.26

Interim Dividends (Per Share)

Amt	Decl	Ex	Rec	Pay
0.66Q	5/17/2007	6/18/2007	6/20/2007	7/3/2007
0.66Q	8/15/2007	9/20/2007	9/24/2007	10/2/2007
0.66Q	11/19/2007	12/19/2007	12/21/2007	1/8/2008
0.69Q	1/9/2008	3/18/2008	3/21/2008	4/8/2008

Indicated Div: $2.76

Valuation Analysis

Forecast P/E	15.24
	(1/10/2007)
Market Cap	$6.0 Billion
Book Value	3.0 Billion
Price/Book	1.67
Price/Sales	5.29

Institutional Holding

No of Institutions	272
Shares	96,829,488
% Held	76.38

TRADING VOLUME (thousand shares)

Business Summary: Property, Real Estate & Development (MIC: 8.3 SIC: 6798 NAIC: 525930)

Developers Diversified Realty is a self-administered and self-managed real estate investment trust primarily engaged in the business of acquiring, developing, redeveloping, owning, leasing as well as managing shopping and business centers. As of Feb 15 2008, Co.'s portfolio consisted of 709 shopping centers and seven business centers, which included 317 properties owned through unconsolidated joint ventures, as well as more than 1,600 acres of undeveloped land, of which approximately 600 acres were owned through joint ventures. These properties consist of shopping centers, enclosed malls and lifestyle centers.

Recent Developments: For the year ended Dec 31 2007, income from continuing operations increased 16.7% to US$186.8 million from US$160.0 million a year earlier. Net income increased 9.0% to US$276.0 million from US$253.3 million in the prior year. Revenues were US$944.9 million, up 21.9% from US$775.3 million the year before. Revenues from property income rose 20.6% to US$880.3 million from US$730.2 million in the corresponding earlier year.

Prospects: Looking ahead, Co.'s investment objective is to seek continued growth through strategic acquisition, development, redevelopment, renovation and expansion of potential real estate properties, primarily shopping centers. In addition, Co. expects to continue to divest assets that are not in-line with its long-term investment objectives, as part of its ongoing portfolio management and capital recycling initiatives to improve overall portfolio performance and operating efficiency. Meanwhile, Co. noted that its joint venture in Brazil is also developing a project located in Manaus, Brazil, whereby it will have a 47.4% ownership interest, at a projected cost of approximately $100.0 million.

Financial Data

(US$ in Thousands)	12/31/2007	12/31/2006	12/31/2005	12/31/2004	12/31/2003	12/31/2002	12/31/2001	12/31/2000
Earnings Per Share	1.85	1.81	2.08	2.24	2.27	1.16	1.17	1.31
Cash Flow Per Share	3.43	3.10	3.28	3.02	3.21	3.30	3.16	2.61
Tang Book Value Per Share	20.01	16.30	16.96	16.90	12.35	9.63	8.92	8.75
Dividends Per Share	2.640	2.360	2.160	1.940	1.690	1.520	1.480	1.440
Dividend Payout %	142.70	130.39	103.85	86.61	74.45	131.03	126.50	109.92
Income Statement								
Property Income	880,286	773,618	695,017	568,631	446,231	333,569	294,209	262,685
Non-Property Income	64,565	44,480	32,159	30,302	29,866	23,674	28,030	23,108
Total Revenue	944,851	818,098	727,176	598,933	476,097	357,243	322,239	285,793
Interest Expense	261,318	221,525	182,279	129,659	89,078	76,831	81,770	77,030
Income Taxes	(14,642)	(2,481)	342	1,469	...	...	...	...
Net Income	276,047	253,264	282,643	269,762	240,261	101,970	92,372	100,833
Average Shares	121,497	109,613	109,142	99,024	84,188	64,837	55,834	56,176
Balance Sheet								
Total Assets	9,089,816	7,179,753	6,862,977	5,583,547	3,941,151	2,776,852	2,497,207	2,332,021
Long-Term Obligations	5,591,014	4,248,812	3,891,001	2,718,690	2,083,131	1,498,798	1,308,301	1,227,575
Total Liabilities	6,090,991	4,683,570	4,292,696	3,029,228	2,327,081	1,831,291	1,663,193	1,312,469
Stockholders' Equity	2,998,825	2,496,183	2,570,281	2,554,319	1,614,070	945,561	834,014	783,750
Shares Outstanding	119,448	108,986	108,947	108,082	86,433	66,608	59,454	54,880
Statistical Record								
Return on Assets %	3.39	3.61	4.54	5.65	7.15	3.87	3.83	4.32
Return on Equity %	10.05	10.00	11.03	12.91	18.77	11.46	11.42	12.29
Net Margin %	29.22	30.96	38.87	45.04	50.46	28.54	28.67	35.28
Price Range	71.38-37.69	66.11-47.80	49.08-38.91	45.85-31.47	33.60-21.28	23.47-18.20	19.20-12.94	16.13-11.31
P/E Ratio	38.58-20.37	36.52-26.41	23.60-18.71	20.47-14.05	14.80-9.37	20.23-15.69	16.41-11.06	12.31-8.64
Average Yield %	4.68	4.34	4.88	5.17	6.12	7.10	8.86	10.51

Address: 3300 Enterprise Parkway, Beachwood, OH 44122 **Telephone:** 216-755-5500 **Fax:** 216-755-1500	**Web Site:** www.ddrc.com **Officers:** Scott A. Wolstein - Chmn., C.E.O. David M. Jacobstein - Pres., C.O.O.	**Auditors:** PricewaterhouseCoopers LLP **Transfer Agents:** National City Bank

DEVON ENERGY CORP.

Exchange	Symbol	Price	52Wk Range	Yield	P/E
NYS	DVN	$104.33 (3/31/2008)	107.59-70.11	0.61	13.04

7 Year Price Score 149.99 *NYSE Composite Index=100 *12 Month Price Score 125.98

Interim Earnings (Per Share)

Qtr.	Mar	Jun	Sep	Dec
2003	1.34	0.81	0.85	1.16
2004	1.00	1.01	1.03	1.35
2005	1.14	1.38	1.63	2.11
2006	1.56	1.92	1.57	1.29
2007	1.44	2.00	1.63	2.93

Interim Dividends (Per Share)

Amt	Decl	Ex	Rec	Pay
0.14Q	6/1/2007	6/13/2007	6/15/2007	6/29/2007
0.14Q	9/4/2007	9/12/2007	9/14/2007	9/28/2007
0.14Q	12/3/2007	12/12/2007	12/14/2007	12/28/2007
0.16Q	3/5/2008	3/13/2008	3/17/2008	3/31/2008
		Indicated Div: $0.64		

Valuation Analysis

Forecast P/E	N/A	Institutional Holding	
		No of Institutions	718
Market Cap	$46.3 Billion	Shares	344,636,288
Book Value	22.0 Billion	% Held	
Price/Book	2.11	% Held	77.54
Price/Sales	4.08		

Business Summary: Oil and Gas (MIC: 14.2 SIC: 1311 NAIC: 211111)

Devon Energy is engaged in oil and gas exploration, development and production, the transportation of oil, gas, and natural gas liquids (NGLs), and the processing of natural gas. Co. owns oil and gas properties principally in the U.S. and Canada and, to a lesser degree, various regions located outside North America, including Azerbaijan, Brazil, and China. Also, Co. has marketing and midstream operations in North America, including the marketing of natural gas, crude oil and NGLs, and the construction and operation of pipelines, storage and treating facilities and gas processing plants. As of Dec 31 2007, Co. had total proved reserves of 2,496 million barrels of oil equivalent.

Recent Developments: For the year ended Dec 31 2007, income from continuing operations increased 19.4% to US$3.15 billion from US$2.63 billion a year earlier. Net income increased 26.7% to US$3.61 billion from US$2.85 billion in the prior year. Revenues were US$11.36 billion, up 16.3% from US$9.77 billion the year before. Direct operating expenses declined 0.3% to US$340.0 million from US$341.0 million in the comparable period the year before. Indirect operating expenses increased 15.5% to US$6.90 billion from US$5.97 billion in the equivalent prior-year period.

Prospects: On Mar 6 2008, Co. announced that it has agreed to sell its oil and gas business in the African nation of Cote d'Ivoire to Afren plc for $205.0 million. The sale, which should close in the second quarter of 2008, is part of Co.'s plans to divest its operations in Egypt and West Africa to redeploy capital to the growth opportunities it developed onshore in North America and in the deepwater Gulf of Mexico, as well as to focus on its global operations in Brazil and China. Going forward, negotiations are under way for the sales of Co.'s remaining properties in Africa, which it expects to complete by mid 2008. Meanwhile, Co. expects its 2008 production to grow about 9.0% from its 2007 levels.

Financial Data

(US$ in Thousands)	12/31/2007	12/31/2006	12/31/2005	12/31/2004	12/31/2003	12/31/2002	12/31/2001	12/31/2000
Earnings Per Share	8.00	6.34	6.26	4.38	4.04	0.30	0.36	2.75
Cash Flow Per Share	14.95	13.56	12.25	9.96	9.01	5.66	7.37	6.34
Tang Book Value Per Share	35.64	26.43	20.65	16.61	11.81	3.50	4.30	11.61
Dividends Per Share	0.560	0.450	0.300	0.200	0.100	0.100	0.100	0.100
Dividend Payout %	7.00	7.10	4.79	4.57	2.48	32.79	27.78	3.64
Income Statement								
Total Revenue	11,362,000	10,578,000	10,741,000	9,189,000	7,352,000	4,316,000	3,075,000	2,784,103
EBITDA	7,082,000	6,454,000	7,276,000	6,069,000	4,559,000	1,643,000	1,020,000	1,879,821
Income Before Taxes	4,224,000	4,012,000	4,552,000	3,293,000	2,245,000	(134,000)	84,000	1,141,980
Income Taxes	1,078,000	1,189,000	1,622,000	1,107,000	514,000	(193,000)	30,000	411,638
Net Income	3,606,000	2,846,000	2,930,000	2,186,000	1,747,000	104,000	103,000	730,342
Average Shares	450,000	448,000	470,000	499,000	434,000	312,000	260,000	263,460
Balance Sheet								
Current Assets	3,914,000	3,212,000	4,206,000	3,583,000	2,364,000	1,064,000	1,081,000	934,137
Total Assets	41,456,000	35,063,000	30,273,000	29,736,000	27,162,000	16,225,000	13,184,000	6,860,478
Current Liabilities	3,657,000	4,645,000	2,934,000	3,100,000	2,071,000	1,042,000	919,000	628,987
Long-Term Obligations	6,924,000	5,568,000	5,957,000	7,031,000	8,580,000	7,562,000	6,589,000	2,048,836
Total Liabilities	19,450,000	17,621,000	15,411,000	16,062,000	16,106,000	11,572,000	9,925,000	3,582,874
Stockholders' Equity	22,006,000	17,442,000	14,862,000	13,674,000	11,056,000	4,653,000	3,259,000	3,277,604
Shares Outstanding	444,214	444,029	443,451	483,909	472,180	313,514	244,756	257,276
Statistical Record								
Return on Assets %	9.43	8.71	9.77	7.66	8.05	0.71	1.03	12.68
Return on Equity %	18.28	17.62	20.54	17.63	22.24	2.63	3.15	27.47
EBITDA Margin %	62.33	61.01	67.74	66.05	62.01	38.07	33.17	67.52
Net Margin %	31.74	26.90	27.28	23.79	23.76	2.41	3.35	26.23
Asset Turnover	0.30	0.32	0.36	0.32	0.34	0.29	0.31	0.48
Current Ratio	1.07	0.69	1.43	1.16	1.14	1.02	1.18	1.49
Debt to Equity	0.31	0.32	0.40	0.51	0.78	1.63	2.02	0.63
Price Range	93.50-63.28	74.03-49.10	70.18-36.60	41.42-26.64	28.95-21.43	26.38-17.77	33.15-15.57	32.00-15.84
P/E Ratio	11.69-7.91	11.68-7.74	11.21-5.85	9.46-6.08	7.17-5.30	87.93-59.23	92.08-43.26	11.64-5.76
Average Yield %	0.72	0.71	0.57	0.61	0.40	0.44	0.40	0.40

Address: 20 North Broadway, Suite 1500, Oklahoma City, OK 73102-8260 **Telephone:** 405-235-3611 **Fax:** 405-552-4550	**Web Site:** www.devonenergy.com **Officers:** J. Larry Nichols - Chmn., C.E.O. John Richels - Pres.	**Auditors:** KPMG LLP **Investor Contact:** 405-552-4526 **Transfer Agents:** Wachovia Bank, N.A., Charlotte, NC

DEVRY INC.

Exchange	Symbol	Price	52Wk Range	Yield	P/E
NYS	DV	$41.84 (3/31/2008)	59.80-27.98	0.29	29.89

*7 Year Price Score 127.15 *NYSE Composite Index=100 *12 Month Price Score 118.19

TRADING VOLUME (thousand shares)

Interim Earnings (Per Share)

Qtr.	Sep	Dec	Mar	Jun
2004-05	0.06	0.08	0.17	0.09
2005-06	0.07	0.15	0.22	0.17
2006-07	0.29	0.23	0.32	0.22
2007-08	0.37	0.49	...	...

Interim Dividends (Per Share)

Amt	Decl	Ex	Rec	Pay
0.05S	11/15/2006	12/18/2006	12/20/2006	1/15/2007
0.05S	5/14/2007	6/14/2007	6/18/2007	7/12/2007
0.06S	11/7/2007	12/12/2007	12/14/2007	1/4/2008

Indicated Div: $0.12

Valuation Analysis   **Institutional Holding**

Forecast P/E	18.02	No of Institutions
	(1/10/2007)	159
Market Cap	$3.0 Billion	Shares
Book Value	703.2 Million	59,083,984
Price/Book	4.25	% Held
Price/Sales	2.99	83.26

Business Summary: Vocational Education Services (MIC: 6.2 SIC: 8299 NAIC: 611519)

DeVry, through its wholly-owned subsidiaries, owns and operates: DeVry University, which provides undergraduate and graduate degree programs in technology, healthcare technology and business, as well as graduate degree programs in management; Ross University, which provides medical and veterinary medical education; Chamberlain College of Nursing, which provides several nursing degree and degree completion programs; and Becker Professional Review, which prepares candidates for the Certified Public Accountant and Chartered Financial Analyst professional certification examinations, and provides continuing professional education programs and seminars in accounting and finance.

Recent Developments: For the quarter ended Dec 31 2007, net income increased 118.4% to US$35.8 million from US$16.4 million in the year-earlier quarter. Revenues were US$273.7 million, up 16.2% from US$235.6 million the year before. Operating income was US$46.9 million versus US$21.8 million in the prior-year quarter, an increase of 115.4%. Direct operating expenses rose 2.7% to US$123.9 million from US$120.6 million in the comparable period the year before. Indirect operating expenses increased 10.4% to US$102.9 million from US$93.2 million in the equivalent prior-year period.

Prospects: Co.'s outlook appears to be encouraging, reflecting its focus on strategic initiatives of growing its total student population, opening new locations and diversifying into secondary education through its Oct 2007 acquisition of Advanced Academics, Inc. Meanwhile, Co. plans to invest in its technology infrastructure, marketing, recruiting, and student services to further enhance quality and support growth over the longer term although it is expected to add to costs and effect earnings in the near term. Meanwhile, Co. noted that its Chamberlain College of Nursing has received approval to establish new campuses in Phoenix, AZ, and Addison, IL, with classes scheduled to begin in March 2008.

Financial Data

(US$ in Thousands)	6 Mos	3 Mos	06/30/2007	06/30/2006	06/30/2005	06/30/2004	06/30/2003	06/30/2002
Earnings Per Share	1.40	1.14	1.07	0.61	0.40	0.82	0.87	0.95
Cash Flow Per Share	2.29	2.18	1.77	1.29	1.24	1.91	1.40	1.65
Tang Book Value Per Share	4.61	4.52	4.13	2.96	2.06	1.54	0.45	3.94
Dividends Per Share	0.110	0.100	0.100	...	...	...	...	...
Dividend Payout %	7.86	8.77	9.35	...	...	...	...	...
Income Statement								
Total Revenue	524,055	250,318	933,473	843,298	781,304	784,885	679,579	648,134
EBITDA	100,569	43,353	146,294	115,781	100,264	143,762	128,069	144,972
Depn & Amortn	19,734	9,451	...	...	...	...	...	...
Income Before Taxes	85,815	36,088	104,940	57,483	34,747	81,356	86,457	110,629
Income Taxes	23,167	9,253	28,752	14,430	8,013	23,295	33,459	43,574
Net Income	62,648	26,835	76,188	43,053	28,544	58,061	61,148	67,055
Average Shares	72,520	71,074	71,400	70,000	70,351	70,131	70,336	70,594
Balance Sheet								
Current Assets	368,257	353,729	218,985	228,073	242,338	208,875	169,687	117,827
Total Assets	996,332	952,540	844,113	872,482	910,035	884,132	856,644	467,628
Current Liabilities	246,933	246,925	165,875	211,269	186,722	156,649	138,511	103,692
Long-Term Obligations	...	...	...	65,000	175,000	215,000	275,000	...
Total Liabilities	293,167	286,564	202,147	307,875	402,111	405,875	440,977	114,082
Stockholders' Equity	703,165	665,976	641,966	564,607	507,924	478,257	415,667	353,546
Shares Outstanding	71,361	70,508	71,131	70,757	70,475	70,021	70,021	69,898
Statistical Record								
Return on Assets %	10.60	8.68	8.88	4.83	3.18	6.65	9.23	15.61
Return on Equity %	15.53	13.10	12.63	8.03	5.79	12.95	15.90	21.01
EBITDA Margin %	19.19	17.32	15.67	13.73	12.83	18.32	18.85	22.37
Net Margin %	11.95	10.72	8.16	5.11	3.65	7.40	9.00	10.35
Asset Turnover	1.04	1.02	1.09	0.95	0.87	0.90	1.03	1.51
Current Ratio	1.49	1.43	1.32	1.08	1.30	1.33	1.23	1.14
Debt to Equity	...	...	...	0.12	0.34	0.45	0.66	...
Price Range	59.80-26.46	38.32-21.60	35.76-19.90	25.95-17.65	27.42-14.22	32.20-22.01	26.20-13.58	39.99-22.84
P/E Ratio	42.71-18.90	33.61-18.95	33.42-18.60	42.54-28.93	68.55-35.55	39.27-26.84	30.11-15.61	42.09-24.04
Average Yield %	0.30	0.33	0.37	...	...	...	...	...

Address: One Tower Lane, Suite 1000, Oakbrook Terrace, IL 60181 **Telephone:** 630-571-7700 **Fax:** 630-571-0317	**Web Site:** www.devryinc.com. **Officers:** Dennis J. Keller - Chmn. Ronald L. Taylor - C.E.O.	**Auditors:** PricewaterhouseCoopers LLP **Investor Contact:** 630-574-1949 **Transfer Agents:** Computershares Investor Services, L.L.C., Chicago, IL

DIAMOND OFFSHORE DRILLING, INC.

Exchange	Symbol	Price	52Wk Range	Yield	P/E
NYS	DO	$116.40 (3/31/2008)	148.51-81.47	0.43	19.02

*7 Year Price Score 170.79 *NYSE Composite Index=100 *12 Month Price Score 115.86

Interim Earnings (Per Share)

Qtr.	Mar	Jun	Sep	Dec
2003	(0.17)	(0.13)	(0.09)	0.01
2004	(0.08)	(0.08)	0.02	0.08
2005	0.23	0.31	0.60	0.77
2006	1.06	1.27	1.19	1.60
2007	1.64	1.81	1.48	1.19

Interim Dividends (Per Share)

Amt	Decl	Ex	Rec	Pay
0.125Q	10/22/2007	10/31/2007	11/2/2007	12/3/2007
1.25Q	10/22/2007	10/31/2007	11/2/2007	12/3/2007
0.125Q	2/7/2008	2/13/2008	2/18/2008	3/3/2008
1.25Q	2/7/2008	2/13/2008	2/18/2008	3/3/2008

Indicated Div: $0.50

Valuation Analysis | **Institutional Holding**

Forecast P/E	5.81	No of Institutions	
	(1/10/2007)	284	
Market Cap	$16.2 Billion	Shares	
Book Value	2.9 Billion	131,576,512	
Price/Book	5.62	% Held	
Price/Sales	6.30	95.11	

Business Summary: Oil and Gas (MIC: 14.2 SIC: 1381 NAIC: 213111)

Diamond Offshore Drilling is a global offshore oil and gas drilling contractor with a fleet of 44 offshore rigs. At Dec 31 2007, Co.'s fleet consisted of 30 semisubmersibles, 13 jack-ups and a drillship. Co. provides a range of services in various markets, including the deep water, harsh environment, conventional semisubmersible and jack-up markets. Co. provides offshore drilling services to a customer base that includes independent oil and gas companies and government-owned oil companies. Principal markets for Co.'s offshore contract drilling services are the Gulf of Mexico, Europe, mainly the U.K. and Norway, the Mediterranean Basin, South America, Australia, Asia and Middle East.

Recent Developments: For the year ended Dec 31 2007, net income increased 19.8% to US$846.5 million from US$706.8 million in the prior year. Revenues were US$2.57 billion, up 25.1% from US$2.05 billion the year before. Operating income was US$1.22 billion versus US$940.4 million in the prior year, an increase of 30.1%. Direct operating expenses rose 24.5% to US$1.01 billion from US$812.1 million in the comparable period the year before. Indirect operating expenses increased 11.0% to US$333.0 million from US$300.1 million in the equivalent prior-year period.

Prospects: Co.'s near-term outlook appears to be constructive. In particular, Co. expects to experience strong worldwide demand for its mid-water and deepwater semisubmersible rigs in 2008. In this respect, Co. believes that the Gulf of Mexico (GOM) semisubmersible market will remain strong in 2008 as it continues to view these markets as under-supplied. In addition, Co. anticipates that the Brazilian as well as the Australia/Asia/Middle East and Mediterranean floater market will continue to remain robust throughout 2008. Meanwhile, Co. expects its additional Ocean Yorktown and Ocean Worker semisubmersible units to commence operations in Brazil by the second and third quarters of 2008, respectively.

Financial Data

(US$ in Thousands)	12/31/2007	12/31/2006	12/31/2005	12/31/2004	12/31/2003	12/31/2002	12/31/2001	12/31/2000
Earnings Per Share	6.12	5.12	1.91	(0.06)	(0.37)	0.47	1.26	0.53
Cash Flow Per Share	8.77	5.89	3.02	1.61	1.25	2.14	2.81	1.48
Tang Book Value Per Share	20.72	17.95	14.38	12.65	12.81	13.68	13.74	12.86
Dividends Per Share	5.750	2.000	0.375	0.250	0.438	0.500	0.500	0.500
Dividend Payout %	93.95	39.06	19.63	...	...	106.38	39.68	94.34
Income Statement								
Total Revenue	2,567,723	2,052,572	1,221,002	814,662	680,941	752,561	885,349	659,436
EBITDA	1,477,300	1,154,291	571,155	210,553	149,967	283,781	435,868	226,107
Income Before Taxes	1,246,537	966,332	356,395	(3,533)	(54,237)	96,174	272,365	110,867
Income Taxes	399,996	259,485	96,058	3,710	(5,823)	33,654	90,820	38,586
Net Income	846,541	706,847	260,337	(7,243)	(48,414)	62,520	173,823	72,281
Average Shares	138,945	138,781	141,351	129,021	130,253	140,713	149,294	145,050
Balance Sheet								
Current Assets	1,265,190	1,481,547	1,281,878	1,195,681	835,263	1,033,756	1,427,415	1,100,957
Total Assets	4,341,465	4,132,839	3,606,922	3,379,386	3,135,019	3,258,765	3,502,517	3,079,506
Current Liabilities	453,011	333,509	268,986	613,907	100,000	118,402	335,016	123,013
Long-Term Obligations	503,071	964,310	977,654	709,413	928,030	924,475	920,636	856,559
Total Liabilities	1,464,398	1,813,331	1,753,595	1,753,558	1,454,539	1,451,251	1,649,371	1,311,653
Stockholders' Equity	2,877,067	2,319,508	1,853,327	1,625,828	1,680,480	1,807,514	1,853,146	1,767,853
Shares Outstanding	138,870	129,216	128,925	128,567	130,336	130,336	132,053	133,150
Statistical Record								
Return on Assets %	19.98	18.27	7.45	N.M.	N.M.	1.85	5.28	2.50
Return on Equity %	32.58	33.88	14.97	N.M.	N.M.	3.42	9.60	3.99
EBITDA Margin %	57.53	56.24	46.78	25.85	22.02	37.71	49.23	34.29
Net Margin %	32.97	34.44	21.32	N.M.	N.M.	8.31	19.63	10.96
Asset Turnover	0.61	0.53	0.35	0.25	0.21	0.22	0.27	0.23
Current Ratio	2.79	4.44	4.77	1.95	8.35	8.73	4.26	8.95
Debt to Equity	0.17	0.42	0.53	0.44	0.55	0.51	0.50	0.48
Price Range	148.51-73.65	96.15-63.90	71.31-38.25	40.29-20.48	23.62-17.15	34.74-17.90	45.04-23.43	47.13-26.50
P/E Ratio	24.27-12.03	18.78-12.48	37.34-20.03	...	...	73.91-38.09	35.75-18.60	88.92-50.00
Average Yield %	5.85	2.54	0.71	0.92	2.18	1.91	1.47	1.35

Address: 15415 Katy Freeway,	Web Site: www.diamondoffshore.com	Auditors: Deloitte & Touche LLP
Houston, TX 77094	Officers: James S. Tisch - Chmn., C.E.O. Lawrence	Investor Contact: 281-492-5393
Telephone: 281-492-5300	R. Dickerson - Pres., C.O.O.	Transfer Agents: Mellon Investor
Fax: 281-492-5316		Services LLC, Jersey City, NJ

DICK'S SPORTING GOODS, INC

Exchange	Symbol	Price	52Wk Range	Yield	P/E
NYS	DKS	$26.78 (3/31/2008)	35.84-25.05	N/A	20.14

*7 Year Price Score N/A   *NYSE Composite Index=100   *12 Month Price Score 104.73

TRADING VOLUME (thousand shares)

Interim Earnings (Per Share)

Qtr.	Apr	Jul	Oct	Jan
2003-04	0.07	0.16	0.04	0.26
2004-05	0.11	0.17	(0.02)	0.40
2005-06	(0.07)	0.20	0.04	0.50
2006-07	0.11	0.23	0.07	0.60
2007-08	0.19	0.41	0.10	0.62

Interim Dividends (Per Share)

No Dividends Paid

Valuation Analysis   Institutional Holding

Forecast P/E	N/A	No of Institutions
		219
Market Cap	$3.0 Billion	Shares
Book Value	888.5 Million	44,481,968
Price/Book	3.35	% Held
Price/Sales	0.77	83.40

Business Summary: Retail - Sporting, Toys & Hobby (MIC: 5.12 SIC: 5941 NAIC: 451110)

Dick's Sporting Goods is a full-line sporting goods retailer offering an assortment of brand name sporting goods equipment, apparel and footwear in a specialty store environment. As of Feb 2 2008, Co. operated 340 Dick's stores, 79 Golf Galaxy stores and 15 Chick's stores, with approximately 21.1 million square feet, in 40 states, the majority of which are located throughout the eastern half of the U. S. Co. also provides a range of sporting goods and active apparel for the beginner, intermediate and enthusiast sports consumer. The merchandise offered by Co. includes apparel, footwear as well as hardlines, including hunting and fishing gear, sporting goods equipment and golf equipment.

Recent Developments: For the year ended Feb 2 2008, net income increased 37.7% to US$155.0 million from US$112.6 million in the prior year. Revenues were US$3.89 billion, up 24.9% from US$3.11 billion the year before. Operating income was US$268.8 million versus US$197.7 million in the prior year, an increase of 36.0%. Direct operating expenses rose 23.1% to US$2.73 billion from US$2.22 billion in the comparable period the year before. Indirect operating expenses increased 27.2% to US$889.2 million from US$699.0 million in the equivalent prior-year period.

Prospects: For the fiscal year ending Jan 31 2009, Co. is projecting earnings to be in the range of $1.49 to $1.54 per diluted share, representing an increase of about 12.0% to 16.0% over earnings per diluted share of $1.33 in the previous fiscal year. In addition, Co. is forecasting comparable store sales, excluding the Chick's Sporting Goods stores, to be flat to an increase of 1.0%. Similarly, Co. intends to open approximately 46 new Dick's Sporting Goods stores, 10 new Golf Galaxy stores and relocate one Dick's store. For the fiscal quarter ended April 2008, Co. is targeting earnings of $0.16 to $0.19 per diluted share, while comparable store sales are expected to decrease by 1.0% to 4.0%.

Financial Data
(US$ in Thousands)

	02/02/2008	02/03/2007	01/28/2006	01/29/2005	01/31/2004	02/01/2003	02/02/2002	02/03/2001
Earnings Per Share	1.33	1.01	0.68	0.65	0.53	0.47	0.33	0.12
Cash Flow Per Share	2.41	1.88	1.71	1.13	0.97	0.86	0.19	0.46
Tang Book Value Per Share	4.54	4.37	2.57	1.60	2.58	1.73	0.94	0.69
Income Statement								
Total Revenue	3,888,422	3,114,162	2,624,987	2,109,399	1,470,845	1,272,584	1,074,568	893,396
EBITDA	343,869	252,639	184,454	160,471	107,416	81,057	57,442	42,966
Income Before Taxes	257,527	187,685	121,634	114,841	88,031	63,773	39,119	26,578
Income Taxes	102,491	75,074	48,654	45,936	35,212	25,509	15,648	10,631
Net Income	155,036	112,611	72,980	68,905	52,819	38,264	23,471	8,643
Average Shares	116,504	110,790	107,958	105,042	100,300	81,916	71,472	74,008
Balance Sheet								
Current Assets	1,060,604	969,779	614,017	311,011	364,894	275,277	236,267	196,667
Total Assets	2,035,635	1,524,265	1,187,789	1,085,048	498,531	376,226	322,810	264,513
Current Liabilities	761,948	564,983	471,269	402,667	228,015	220,175	167,310	145,428
Long-Term Obligations	181,185	180,865	181,020	257,369	3,411	3,364	80,650	73,327
Total Liabilities	1,147,115	903,715	772,996	771,381	255,550	235,727	259,705	225,771
Stockholders' Equity	888,520	620,550	414,793	313,667	242,981	140,499	63,105	38,742
Shares Outstanding	111,145	106,170	100,552	97,659	94,321	80,992	67,307	55,858
Statistical Record								
Return on Assets %	8.73	8.17	6.44	8.73	12.11	10.98	8.01	...
Return on Equity %	20.60	21.40	20.09	24.83	27.62	37.69	46.22	...
EBITDA Margin %	8.84	8.11	7.03	7.61	7.30	6.37	5.35	4.81
Net Margin %	3.99	3.62	2.78	3.27	3.59	3.01	2.18	0.97
Asset Turnover	2.19	2.26	2.32	2.67	3.37	3.65	3.67	...
Current Ratio	1.40	1.54	1.30	1.32	1.60	1.25	1.41	1.35
Debt to Equity	0.20	0.29	0.44	0.82	0.01	0.02	1.28	1.89
Price Range	35.84-24.66	27.90-17.62	20.07-13.50	19.02-12.50	13.25-4.33	5.63-3.29	...	...
P/E Ratio	26.95-18.55	27.62-17.45	29.51-19.85	29.27-19.23	25.00-8.16	11.99-6.99	...	...

Address: 300 Industry Drive, RIDC Park West, Pittsburgh, PA 15275
Telephone: 724-273-3400

Web Site: www.dickssportinggoods.com
Officers: Edward W. Stack - Chmn., C.E.O. William J. Colombo - Pres., C.O.O.

Auditors: Deloitte & Touche LLP
Investor Contact: 412-809-0100
Transfer Agents: Wachovia Bank, National Association, Charlotte, NC

DIEBOLD, INC.

Exchange	Symbol	Price	52Wk Range	Yield	P/E	Div Acheiver
NYS	DBD	$37.55 (3/31/2008)	54.25-23.71	2.66	36.46	54 Years

*7 Year Price Score 77.09   *NYSE Composite Index=100   *12 Month Price Score 82.49

Interim Earnings (Per Share)

Qtr.	Mar	Jun	Sep	Dec
2004	0.40	0.60	0.67	0.87
2005	0.37	0.45	0.37	0.15
2006	0.18	0.26	0.45	0.41
2007	(0.09)	...	...	...

Interim Dividends (Per Share)

Amt	Decl	Ex	Rec	Pay
0.235Q	4/26/2007	5/9/2007	5/11/2007	6/1/2007
0.235Q	8/8/2007	8/22/2007	8/24/2007	9/7/2007
0.235Q	10/18/2007	11/14/2007	11/16/2007	12/7/2007
0.25Q	2/13/2008	2/21/2008	2/25/2008	3/7/2008

Indicated Div: $1.00 (Div. Reinv. Plan)

Valuation Analysis / Institutional Holding

Forecast P/E	19.33	No of Institutions
	(1/10/2007)	289
Market Cap	$2.5 Billion	Shares
Book Value	1.1 Billion	52,007,736
Price/Book	2.24	% Held
Price/Sales	0.85	79.15

TRADING VOLUME (thousand shares)

Business Summary: Office Equipment Supplies (MIC: 11.12 SIC: 3578 NAIC: 333313)

Diebold is engaged primarily in the sale, manufacture, installation and service of automated self-service transaction systems, electronic and physical security products, election systems and software. Co. specializes in technology that enables people worldwide to access services when, where and how they may choose. Co.'s segments comprises of three main sales channels: Diebold North America (DNA), Diebold International (DI) and Election Systems (ES) & Other. Co.'s primary customers include banks and financial institutions, as well as public libraries, government agencies, utilities and various retail outlets.

Recent Developments: On Mar 3 2008, Co. announced that as a result of discussions with the Office of the Chief Accountant of the SEC it will correct for that revenue previously recognized on a bill and hold basis by now recognizing that revenue upon customer acceptance of products at a customer location. Co.'s corrected method of recognizing revenue will be adopted retroactively by restating previously issued financial statements. Thus, Co. has concluded that its financial statements for the fiscal years ended Dec 31, 2006, 2005, 2004 and 2003; the quarterly data in each of the quarters for the years ended Dec 31, 2006 and 2005; and the quarter ended Mar 31, 2007, should no longer be relied upon.

Prospects: On Mar 2 2008, United Technologies Corporation (UTX) announced that it has made a proposal to acquire all the outstanding shares of Co. for $40.00 per share in cash. Subsequently, on Mar 3 2008, Co. rejected UTX's unsolicited proposal to acquire it. Separately, for full year 2008, Co. expects revenue growth of 6.0% to 8.0%. Specifically, Co. sees financial self-service revenue growth of 4.0% to 5.0% and security revenue growth of 6.0% to 7.0%. Also, election systems revenue, including Brazil, is anticipated to be in the range of $105.0 million to $115.0 million, while Brazilian lottery systems revenue is anticipated to be in the range of $10.0 million to $13.0 million.

Financial Data

(US$ in Thousands)	3 Mos	12/31/2006	12/31/2005	12/31/2004	12/31/2003	12/31/2002	12/31/2001	12/31/2000
Earnings Per Share	1.03	1.29	1.36	2.54	2.40	1.37	0.93	1.92
Cash Flow Per Share	2.98	3.76	1.66	3.22	2.90	2.27	2.16	2.04
Tang Book Value Per Share	9.56	9.62	11.11	11.84	11.24	9.32	8.79	8.94
Dividends Per Share	0.880	0.860	0.820	0.740	0.680	0.660	0.640	0.620
Dividend Payout %	85.44	66.67	60.29	29.13	28.33	48.18	68.82	32.29
Income Statement								
Total Revenue	628,444	2,906,232	2,587,049	2,380,910	2,109,673	1,940,163	1,760,297	1,743,608
EBITDA	28,431	230,283	231,001	354,583	330,609	306,526	157,960	257,939
Depn & Amortn	19,165	...	...	...	...	...	...	...
Income Before Taxes	(160)	124,449	138,251	268,943	257,023	218,551	99,839	204,357
Income Taxes	5,725	37,902	55,347	84,986	82,247	86,250	32,946	67,438
Net Income	(5,885)	86,547	96,746	183,957	174,776	99,154	66,893	136,919
Average Shares	66,156	66,885	70,966	72,534	72,924	72,297	71,783	71,479
Balance Sheet								
Current Assets	1,454,144	1,595,681	1,427,880	1,234,632	1,105,159	924,888	952,426	804,363
Total Assets	2,406,080	2,514,279	2,353,193	2,135,552	1,900,502	1,625,081	1,651,913	1,585,427
Current Liabilities	614,872	598,736	580,031	728,623	618,653	564,962	658,018	566,792
Long-Term Obligations	544,784	665,481	454,722	...	...	...	20,800	20,800
Total Liabilities	1,305,578	1,422,878	1,200,344	875,077	752,264	684,258	748,803	649,361
Stockholders' Equity	1,100,502	1,091,401	1,152,849	1,260,475	1,148,238	940,823	903,110	936,066
Shares Outstanding	65,722	65,595	68,721	71,592	72,649	72,111	71,356	71,547
Statistical Record								
Return on Assets %	2.76	3.56	4.31	9.09	9.91	6.05	4.13	9.47
Return on Equity %	6.09	7.71	8.02	15.23	16.73	10.75	7.27	15.34
EBITDA Margin %	4.52	7.92	8.93	14.89	15.67	15.80	8.97	14.79
Net Margin %	N.M.	2.98	3.74	7.73	8.28	5.11	3.80	7.85
Asset Turnover	1.18	1.19	1.15	1.18	1.20	1.18	1.09	1.21
Current Ratio	2.36	2.67	2.46	1.69	1.79	1.64	1.45	1.42
Debt to Equity	0.50	0.61	0.39	...	...	...	0.02	0.02
Price Range	48.25-37.48	46.93-37.01	57.58-33.37	56.06-44.85	57.43-33.94	42.41-31.00	41.00-25.96	34.56-21.63
P/E Ratio	46.84-36.39	36.38-28.69	42.34-24.54	22.07-17.66	23.93-14.14	30.96-22.63	44.09-27.91	18.00-11.26
Average Yield %	2.02	2.05	1.74	1.48	1.52	1.76	1.93	2.24

Address: 5995 Mayfair Road, North Canton, OH 44720-8077	Web Site: www.diebold.com	Auditors: KPMG LLP
Telephone: 330-490-4000	Officers: Walden W. O'Dell - Chmn., C.E.O. Thomas W. Swidarski - Pres., C.O.O.	Investor Contact: 330-490-5900
Fax: 330-588-3794		Transfer Agents: The Bank of New York, New York, NY

DILLARD'S INC.

Exchange	Symbol	Price	52Wk Range	Yield	P/E
NYS	DDS	$17.21 (3/31/2008)	39.90-14.79	0.93	25.31

*7 Year Price Score 90.55   ***NYSE Composite Index=100**   ***12 Month Price Score 74.09**

TRADING VOLUME (thousand shares)

Interim Earnings (Per Share)

Qtr.	Apr	Jul	Oct	Jan
2003-04	0.29	(0.60)	(0.19)	0.61
2004-05	0.64	(0.31)	(0.23)	1:30
2005-06	0.46	(0.15)	(0.03)	1.21
2006-07	0.77	0.20	0.17	1.92
2007-08	0.53	(0.31)	(0.15)	0.60

Interim Dividends (Per Share)

Amt	Decl	Ex	Rec	Pay
0.04Q	5/30/2007	6/27/2007	6/29/2007	8/1/2007
0.04Q	9/4/2007	9/26/2007	9/28/2007	11/1/2007
0.04Q	11/21/2007	12/27/2007	12/31/2007	2/4/2008
0.04Q	3/19/2008	3/27/2008	3/31/2008	5/1/2008

Indicated Div: $0.16

Valuation Analysis

		Institutional Holding	
Forecast P/E	N/A	No of Institutions	246
Market Cap	$1.3 Billion	Shares	78,735,104
Book Value	2.5 Billion	% Held	
Price/Book	0.51		98.24
Price/Sales	0.18		

Business Summary: Retail - General (MIC: 5.2 SIC: 5311 NAIC: 452111)

Dillard's operates a chain of retail department stores located primarily in the Southwest, Southeast and Midwest regions of the U.S. As of Feb 2 2008, Co. operated 326 stores in 29 states. Co. provides a selection of merchandise including apparel for women, men and children, accessories, cosmetics, home furnishings and other consumer goods. Co.'s major product categories include cosmetics, ladies' apparel and accessories, juniors' and children's apparel, men's apparel and accessories, shoes, and home and other. Co.'s customers may also purchase merchandise on-line at its website, www.dillards.com, which features on-line gift registries and other services.

Recent Developments: For the year ended Feb 2 2008, net income decreased 78.1% to US$53.8 million from US$245.6 million in the prior year. Revenues were US$7.37 billion, down 5.6% from US$7.81 billion the year before. Direct operating expenses declined 4.9% to US$4.79 billion from US$5.03 billion in the comparable period the year before. Indirect operating expenses decreased 0.3% to US$2.44 billion from US$2.45 billion in the equivalent prior-year period.

Prospects: For the fiscal quarter ended May 2008, Co. plans to close its 110,000 square feet store in Richmond, VA and its 124,000 square feet store in Greeley, CO, along with its distribution center in Louisville, KY. For the fiscal quarter ended November 2008, Co. plans to open a 145,000 square feet store in North Tampa, FL, a 126,000 square feet store in Anderson, SC, a 140,000 square feet store in Pearland, TX and a 200,000 square feet store in Kansas City, MO. For the fiscal year ending Jan 31 2009, Co. foresees capital expenditures to be about $215.0 million, mainly for the openings of nine locations, along with the store re-opening in Biloxi, MS, totaling about 1.3 million square feet.

Financial Data

(US$ in Thousands)	02/02/2008	02/03/2007	01/28/2006	01/29/2005	01/31/2004	02/01/2003	02/02/2002	02/03/2001
Earnings Per Share	0.68	3.05	1.49	1.41	0.11	(4.67)	0.85	(0.06)
Cash Flow Per Share	3.25	4.46	4.54	6.68	5.18	4.24	7.35	8.60
Tang Book Value Per Share	33.02	31.85	29.08	27.51	26.35	26.25	25.02	24.05
Dividends Per Share	0.160	0.160	0.160	0.160	0.160	0.160	0.160	0.160
Dividend Payout %	23.53	5.25	10.74	11.35	145.45	...	18.82	...
Income Statement								
Total Revenue	7,370,806	7,810,067	7,707,993	7,816,271	7,863,668	8,233,939	8,388,339	8,817,785
EBITDA	452,933	644,740	545,731	629,143	494,260	699,585	615,670	671,279
Income Before Taxes	60,518	253,842	135,785	184,551	15,994	211,100	111,571	140,860
Income Taxes	13,010	20,580	14,300	66,885	6,650	74,800	45,785	44,030
Net Income	53,761	245,646	121,485	117,666	9,344	(398,405)	71,798	(5,850)
Average Shares	79,103	80,475	81,661	83,717	83,900	85,316	84,020	91,171
Balance Sheet								
Current Assets	1,945,199	2,047,816	2,160,179	2,291,441	3,113,891	3,130,451	2,814,510	2,842,948
Total Assets	5,338,129	5,408,015	5,516,919	5,691,581	6,411,007	6,675,932	7,074,559	7,199,309
Current Liabilities	1,184,170	977,115	1,147,392	1,045,233	1,336,087	886,461	928,071	876,697
Long-Term Obligations	785,904	984,939	1,090,752	1,343,006	1,872,776	2,211,606	2,145,036	2,396,577
Total Liabilities	2,824,018	2,821,061	3,176,378	3,366,884	4,174,000	4,411,736	4,406,162	4,569,489
Stockholders' Equity	2,514,111	2,586,953	2,340,541	2,324,697	2,237,097	2,264,196	2,668,397	2,629,820
Shares Outstanding	75,166	80,141	79,294	83,205	83,490	84,757	83,887	85,000
Statistical Record								
Return on Assets %	1.00	4.42	2.17	1.95	0.14	N.M.	1.01	N.M.
Return on Equity %	2.11	9.81	5.22	5.17	0.42	N.M.	2.72	N.M.
EBITDA Margin %	6.14	8.26	7.08	8.05	6.29	8.50	7.34	7.61
Net Margin %	0.73	3.15	1.58	1.51	0.12	N.M.	0.86	N.M.
Asset Turnover	1.38	1.41	1.38	1.30	1.21	1.20	1.18	1.15
Current Ratio	1.64	2.10	1.87	2.19	2.26	3.53	3.03	3.24
Debt to Equity	0.31	0.38	0.47	0.58	0.84	0.98	0.80	0.91
Price Range	39.90-14.93	36.09-24.23	28.14-19.40	27.54-15.54	17.86-12.49	30.47-12.94	22.00-12.63	19.75-9.50
P/E Ratio	58.68-21.96	11.83-7.94	18.89-13.02	19.53-11.02	162.36-113.55	...	25.88-14.86	...
Average Yield %	0.58	0.53	0.68	0.76	1.09	0.74	0.89	1.16

Address: 1600 Cantrell Road, Little Rock, AR 72201 **Telephone:** 501-376-5200 **Fax:** 501-376-5917	**Web Site:** www.dillards.com **Officers:** William Dillard II - Chmn., C.E.O. Alex Dillard - Pres.	**Auditors:** Deloitte & Touche LLP **Investor Contact:** 501-376-5544 **Transfer Agents:** Registrar and Transfer Company, Cranford, NJ

DISCOVER FINANCIAL SERVICES

Exchange	Symbol	Price	52Wk Range	Yield	P/E
NYS	DFS	$16.37 (3/31/2008)	31.70-12.55	1.47	13.31

*7 Year Price Score N/A   *NYSE Composite Index=100   *12 Month Price Score N/A

Interim Earnings (Per Share)

No earnings information available

Interim Dividends (Per Share)

Amt	Decl	Ex	Rec	Pay
0.06Q	9/25/2007	10/3/2007	10/5/2007	10/23/2007
0.06Q	12/20/2007	12/31/2007	1/3/2008	1/22/2008
0.06Q	3/19/2008	4/1/2008	4/3/2008	4/22/2008

Indicated Div: $0.24

Valuation Analysis

		Institutional Holding	
Forecast P/E	N/A	No of Institutions	N/A
Market Cap	$7.8 Billion	Shares	N/A
Book Value	5.6 Billion	% Held	N/A
Price/Book	1.40		
Price/Sales	N/A	N/A	

TRADING VOLUME (thousand shares)

Business Summary: Credit & Lending (MIC: 8.6 SIC: 6141 NAIC: 522210)

Discover Financial Services is a credit card issuer and electronic payment services company. Co. is also engaged in payments processing, as Co. is one of only two credit card issuers with a U.S. payments network and the only issuer whose wholly-owned network operations include both credit and debit functionality. Co. issues credit cards in the United States under the Discover Card brand to various segments within the consumer and small business sectors. Co. manages the business activities in three segments: U.S. Card, International Card and Third-Party Payments.

Recent Developments: For the quarter ended Aug 31 2007, net income decreased 16.2% to US$202.2 million from US$241.4 million in the year-earlier quarter. Net interest income increased 0.5% to US$394.1 million from US$392.3 million in the year-earlier quarter. Provision for loan losses was US$211.6 million versus US$231.6 million in the prior-year quarter, a decrease of 8.7%. Non-interest income declined 4.9% to US$845.5 million compared with US$889.4 million the year before, while non-interest expense advanced 2.4% to US$698.8 million.

Prospects: On Oct 9 2007, Co. announced an issuer processor agreement with TSYS, a processor for bankcard issuers and merchant acquirers, in which TSYS will process prepaid and credit card transactions on Co.'s Discover Network business unit. This agreement should contribute to Discover Network's increased sales volume going forward. Separately, on Sep 20 2007, Co. and Chase Paymentech Solutions, LLC, a global payments firm and merchant acquirer, announced the integration of Discover Network card acceptance into Chase Paymentech's payments network for small- to mid-sized merchants, with the rollout of the full processing package to merchant customers scheduled to start in early 2008.

Financial Data

(US$ in Thousands)	11/30/2007	11/30/2006	11/30/2005	11/30/2004
Earnings Per Share	1.23	...	...	...
Cash Flow Per Share	4.27	...	...	...
Tang Book Value Per Share	10.98	5,039,867.00	4,278,405.00	...
Income Statement				
Income Before Taxes	945,196	1,582,305	924,256	1,218,907
Income Taxes	356,566	505,689	346,341	442,654
Net Income	588,630	1,076,616	577,915	776,253
Average Shares	478,878	...	...	...
Balance Sheet				
Total Assets	37,376,105	29,067,242	26,943,923	...
Total Liabilities	31,776,683	23,292,470	22,343,474	...
Stockholders' Equity	5,599,422	5,774,772	4,600,449	...
Shares Outstanding	477,762	1,000.00	1,000.00	...
Statistical Record				
Return on Assets %	1.77	...	...	...
Return on Equity %	10.35	...	...	...
Price Range	31.70-16.25	...	...	...
P/E Ratio	25.77-13.21	...	...	...

Address: 2500 Lake Cook Road, Riverwoods, IL 60015 **Telephone:** 224-405-0900	**Web Site:** www.discoverfinancial.com **Officers:** Dennis D. Dammerman - Chmn. Roger C. Hochschild - Pres., C.O.O. David W. Nelms - C.E.O.	**Auditors:** Deloitte and Touche LLP

DISNEY (WALT) CO. (THE)

Exchange	Symbol	Price	52Wk Range	Yield	P/E
NYS	DIS	$31.38 (3/31/2008)	35.86-28.12	N/A	15.01

*7 Year Price Score 104.45 *NYSE Composite Index=100 *12 Month Price Score 102.40

Interim Earnings (Per Share)

Qtr.	Dec	Mar	Jun	Sep
2004-05	0.35	0.34	0.41	0.13
2005-06	0.37	0.37	0.53	0.36
2006-07	0.79	0.44	0.57	0.44
2007-08	0.63	...	...	...

Interim Dividends (Per Share)

Dividend Payment Suspended

Valuation Analysis

		Institutional Holding	
Forecast P/E	17.56	No of Institutions	
	(1/10/2007)	960	
Market Cap	$60.6 Billion	Shares	
Book Value	30.4 Billion	1,374,689,920	
Price/Book	1.99	% Held	
Price/Sales	1.66	67.11	

Business Summary: Media (MIC: 13.1 SIC: 7313 NAIC: 541840)

Walt Disney is a global entertainment company. Co.'s Media Networks operates the ABC Television Network and ten owned television stations, the ESPN Radio Network, the Radio Disney Network as well as 46 owned radio stations. Co.'s Parks and Resorts segment owns and operates the Walt Disney World Resort in Florida and the Disneyland Resort in California. Co.'s Studio Entertainment segment produces and acquires live-action and animated motion pictures for global distribution. Co.'s Consumer Products segment licenses the name Walt Disney, as well as its characters and visual and literary properties, to various manufacturers, retailers, show promoters, and publishers.

Recent Developments: For the quarter ended Dec 29 2007, income from continuing operations decreased 25.4% to US$1.25 billion from US$1.68 billion in the year-earlier quarter. Net income decreased 26.5% to US$1.25 billion from US$1.70 billion in the year-earlier quarter. Revenues were US$10.45 billion, up 9.1% from US$9.58 billion the year before. Direct operating expenses rose 6.5% to US$8.42 billion from US$7.91 billion in the comparable period the year before. Indirect operating expenses amounted to nil compared with an income of US$1.05 billion in the equivalent prior-year period.

Prospects: On Feb 18 2008, Co. announced that it will increase its strategic investment to 32.1% in UTV Software Communications Ltd. (UTV) through its Walt Disney Company (Southeast Asia) Pte. Ltd. subsidiary. Co. believes that this transaction, which is worth about $200.0 million, will strengthen its entry into the Indian market through UTV and complements its improving Disney-branded businesses and long-held joint-venture in ESPN STAR Sports. Concurrent with this transaction, Co. will invest approximately $30.0 million for a 15.0% stake in UTV Global Broadcasting Ltd., while UTV will invest $60.0 million for a 75.0% stake. This transaction is subject to UTV shareholder and regulatory approvals.

Financial Data

(US$ in Thousands)	3 Mos	09/29/2007	09/30/2006	10/01/2005	09/30/2004	09/30/2003	09/30/2002	09/30/2001
Earnings Per Share	2.09	2.25	1.64	1.22	1.12	0.62	0.60	(0.02)
Cash Flow Per Share	2.91	2.70	3.03	2.10	2.13	1.42	1.12	1.43
Tang Book Value Per Share	3.02	3.15	3.10	3.24	3.15	2.01	1.78	4.03
Dividends Per Share	0.350	0.310	0.270	0.240	0.210	0.210	0.210	0.210
Dividend Payout %	16.76	13.78	16.46	19.67	18.75	33.87	35.00	...
Income Statement								
Total Revenue	10,452,000	35,510,000	34,285,000	31,944,000	30,752,000	27,061,000	25,329,000	25,269,000
EBITDA	2,634,000	9,809,000	7,475,000	5,923,000	5,566,000	4,124,000	3,232,000	3,037,000
Depn & Amortn	385,000	...	...	...	...	...	...	...
Income Before Taxes	2,033,000	7,725,000	5,447,000	3,987,000	3,739,000	2,254,000	2,190,000	1,283,000
Income Taxes	759,000	-2,874,000	1,890,000	1,241,000	1,197,000	789,000	853,000	1,059,000
Net Income	1,250,000	4,687,000	3,374,000	2,533,000	2,345,000	1,267,000	1,236,000	(158,000)
Average Shares	1,989,000	2,092,000	2,076,000	2,089,000	2,106,000	2,067,000	2,044,000	2,143,000
Balance Sheet								
Current Assets	13,268,000	11,314,000	9,562,000	8,845,000	9,369,000	8,314,000	7,849,000	7,029,000
Total Assets	62,772,000	60,928,000	59,998,000	53,158,000	53,902,000	49,988,000	50,045,000	43,699,000
Current Liabilities	12,383,000	11,391,000	10,210,000	9,168,000	11,059,000	8,669,000	7,819,000	6,219,000
Long-Term Obligations	12,785,000	12,166,000	11,135,000	10,531,000	9,734,000	10,987,000	12,825,000	8,940,000
Total Liabilities	32,392,000	30,175,000	28,178,000	26,948,000	27,821,000	26,197,000	26,600,000	21,027,000
Stockholders' Equity	30,380,000	30,753,000	31,820,000	26,210,000	26,081,000	23,791,000	23,445,000	22,672,000
Shares Outstanding	1,931,000	1,962,200	2,064,000	2,007,200	1,998,400	2,013,300	2,018,600	2,018,600
Statistical Record								
Return on Assets %	6.88	7.77	5.98	4.72	4.50	2.53	2.64	N.M.
Return on Equity %	13.53	15.02	11.66	9.66	9.38	5.36	5.36	N.M.
EBITDA Margin %	25.20	27.62	21.80	18.54	18.10	15.24	12.76	12.02
Net Margin %	11.96	13.20	9.84	7.93	7.63	4.68	4.88	N.M.
Asset Turnover	0.59	0.59	0.61	0.60	0.59	0.54	0.54	0.57
Current Ratio	1.07	0.99	0.94	0.96	0.85	0.96	1.00	1.13
Debt to Equity	0.42	0.40	0.35	0.40	0.37	0.46	0.55	0.39
Price Range	35.86-31.24	35.86-29.95	30.48-22.53	29.31-22.12	27.47-19.79	22.13-13.87	24.53-13.51	40.59-16.66
P/E Ratio	17.16-14.95	15.94-13.31	18.59-13.74	24.03-18.13	24.53-17.67	35.70-22.37	40.88-22.52	...
Average Yield %	1.03	0.92	1.00	0.92	0.90	1.15	1.05	-0.72

Address: 500 South Buena Vista Street, Burbank, CA 91521 Telephone: 818-560-1000	Web Site: www.disney.com Officers: George J. Mitchell - Chmn. Robert A. Iger - Pres., C.E.O.	Auditors: PricewaterhouseCoopers LLP Transfer Agents: Walt Disney Company, Glendale, CA

243

DOLBY LABORATORIES INC

Exchange	Symbol	Price	52Wk Range	Yield	P/E
NYS	DLB	$36.26 (3/31/2008)	52.73-31.37	N/A	25.72

*7 Year Price Score N/A   *NYSE Composite Index=100   *12 Month Price Score 118.19

Interim Earnings (Per Share)

Qtr.	Dec	Mar	Jun	Sep
2004-05	0.11	0.10	0.13	0.16
2005-06	0.16	0.25	0.17	0.22
2006-07	0.27	0.34	0.26	0.39
2007-08	0.42	...	...	...

Interim Dividends (Per Share)

No Dividends Paid

Valuation Analysis / **Institutional Holding**

Forecast P/E	N/A	No of Institutions
		134
Market Cap	$4.0 Billion	Shares
Book Value	867.2 Million	35,832,316
Price/Book	4.64	% Held
Price/Sales	7.61	32.90

TRADING VOLUME (thousand shares)

Business Summary: Communications (MIC: 10.1 SIC: 3663 NAIC: 334220)

Dolby Laboratories is engaged in delivering sound technologies that are designed to assist the entertainment creation process and enhance the entertainment experience. Co. delivers products, services and technologies at each stage of the entertainment chain, including content creation, content distribution and content playback. Co. conducts its business in two segments. Through the products and production services segment, Co. designs, manufactures and sells audio products for the motion picture, broadcast, music and video game industries. Through the technology licensing segment, Co. licenses its technologies to manufacturers of consumer electronics products and software developers.

Recent Developments: For the quarter ended Dec 28 2007, net income increased 59.5% to US$47.7 million from US$29.9 million in the year-earlier quarter. Revenues were US$150.2 million, up 43.8% from US$104.4 million the year before. Operating income was US$67.4 million versus US$39.3 million in the prior-year quarter, an increase of 71.6%. Direct operating expenses declined 5.6% to US$18.0 million from US$19.0 million in the comparable period the year before. Indirect operating expenses increased 40.6% to US$64.9 million from US$46.1 million in the equivalent prior-year period.

Prospects: For the fiscal year ending Sep 30 2008, Co. now anticipates revenues of $575.0 million to $615.0 million, net income in the range of $157.0 million to $167.0 million and earnings to range from $1.34 to $1.44 per diluted share. Looking ahead, Co. foresees that sales of products incorporating its technologies in potential economies, such as China and India, will increase as consumers in these geographical markets have more disposable income available to purchase entertainment products. Lastly, Co. believes that manufacturers from lower-cost manufacturing countries, including China, will increase production of consumer electronics and digital entertainment products to meet higher demand.

Financial Data
(US$ in Thousands)

	3 Mos	09/28/2007	09/29/2006	09/30/2005	09/24/2004	09/26/2003	09/27/2002
Earnings Per Share	1.41	1.26	0.80	0.50	0.43	0.36	...
Cash Flow Per Share	1.74	1.50	1.26	0.82	0.55	0.47	...
Tang Book Value Per Share	4.63	6.55	5.18	4.04	1.32	0.93	...
Income Statement							
Total Revenue	150,227	482,028	391,542	327,967	289,041	217,472	161,868
EBITDA	72,360	201,176	142,540	97,457	77,521	56,256	7,448
Depn & Amortn	5,246	...	...	...	...	...	...
Income Before Taxes	72,572	209,416	146,637	91,218	68,092	47,610	(198)
Income Taxes	24,607	65,131	55,833	37,330	27,321	16,079	11
Net Income	47,673	142,831	89,549	52,293	39,842	30,969	(105)
Average Shares	114,700	113,573	111,658	104,220	92,783	86,084	85,008
Balance Sheet							
Current Assets	629,184	733,418	572,632	454,188	144,757	105,592	...
Total Assets	1,126,631	991,697	739,288	586,277	261,866	202,707	...
Current Liabilities	173,572	143,204	92,854	72,794	64,476	51,379	...
Long-Term Obligations	9,209	9,691	10,893	12,124	13,580	14,548	...
Total Liabilities	237,422	172,262	125,089	106,874	101,339	92,802	...
Stockholders' Equity	867,178	797,156	594,288	461,139	143,327	93,775	...
Shares Outstanding	111,046	110,250	107,261	103,908	86,547	85,006	85,006
Statistical Record							
Return on Assets %	16.74	16.55	13.55	12.13	17.20	...	...
Return on Equity %	21.27	20.59	17.02	17.02	33.70	...	...
EBITDA Margin %	48.17	41.74	36.40	29.72	26.82	25.87	4.60
Net Margin %	31.73	29.63	22.87	15.94	13.78	14.24	N.M.
Asset Turnover	0.55	0.56	0.59	0.76	1.25	...	...
Current Ratio	3.62	5.12	6.17	6.24	2.25	2.06	...
Debt to Equity	0.01	0.01	0.02	0.03	0.09	0.16	...
Price Range	51.61-30.49	38.15-18.77	23.54-15.00	24.57-15.47	...	...	...
P/E Ratio	36.60-21.62	30.28-14.90	29.42-18.75	49.14-30.94	...	...	...

Address: 100 Potrero Avenue, San Francisco, CA 94103-4813 Telephone: 415-558-0200	Web Site: www.dolby.com Officers: Ray Dolby - Chmn. Bill Jasper - Pres., C.E.O.	Auditors: KPMG LLP Transfer Agents: EquiServe Trust Company, N.A.

DOMINION RESOURCES INC

Exchange	Symbol	Price	52Wk Range	Yield	P/E
NYS	D	$40.84 (3/31/2008)	48.99-39.05	3.87	10.53

*7 Year Price Score 100.69 *NYSE Composite Index=100 *12 Month Price Score 100.83

Interim Earnings (Per Share)

Qtr.	Mar	Jun	Sep	Dec
2003	0.82	0.38	(0.40)	(0.28)
2004	0.67	0.38	0.51	0.33
2005	0.63	0.48	0.02	0.37
2006	0.77	0.23	0.93	0.04
2007	0.65	(0.76)	3.62	0.59

Interim Dividends (Per Share)

Amt	Decl	Ex	Rec	Pay
0.355Q	8/8/2007	8/29/2007	8/31/2007	9/20/2007
0.395Q	10/19/2007	11/28/2007	11/30/2007	12/20/2007
2-for-1	10/29/2007	11/20/2007	11/9/2007	11/19/2007
0.395Q	1/25/2008	2/27/2008	2/29/2008	3/20/2008

Indicated Div: $1.58

Valuation Analysis

Forecast P/E	N/A
Market Cap	$23.6 Billion
Book Value	9.4 Billion
Price/Book	2.51
Price/Sales	1.50

Institutional Holding

No of Institutions	653
Shares	227,600,464
% Held	64.99

Business Summary: Electricity (MIC: 7.1 SIC: 4911 NAIC: 221121)

Dominion Resources operates through several subsidiaries, including: Virginia Electric and Power Company, which generates, transmits and distributes electricity for sale in Virginia and northeastern North Carolina; Dominion Energy, Inc., which engages in merchant generation, energy marketing and price risk management activities and natural gas exploration and production in the Appalachian basin of the U.S.; and Dominion Transmission, Inc., which operates a natural gas transmission pipeline and underground storage system in the Northeast, mid-Atlantic and Midwest states. As of Dec 31 2007, Co. had total proved oil and gas reserves of approximately 4,640 billion cubic feet equivalent.

Recent Developments: For the year ended Dec 31 2007, income from continuing operations increased 76.8% to US$2.71 billion from US$1.53 billion a year earlier. Net income increased 84.0% to US$2.54 billion from US$1.38 billion in the prior year. Revenues were US$15.67 billion, down 3.8% from US$16.30 billion the year before. Operating income was US$5.57 billion versus US$3.32 billion in the prior year, an increase of 67.8%. Direct operating expenses declined 9.2% to US$6.97 billion from US$7.68 billion in the comparable period the year before. Indirect operating expenses decreased 40.8% to US$3.14 billion from US$5.30 billion in the equivalent prior-year period.

Prospects. Co. continues to enhance its operations through strategic transactions with other entities. For instance, on Jan 24 2008, Co. announced that it has acquired a 50.0% interest in a joint venture with BP Alternative Energy Inc. (BP) to develop a wind-turbine facility in Benton County, IN. The facility should generate a total of 750 megawatts (Mw), of which 650 Mw will be jointly owned by Co. with BP. Co. expects the first phase of this project to be operating by the end of 2008, the second phase to begin operating in 2009. Accordingly, Co. is expecting operating earnings of $3.05 to $3.15 per share in 2008 and long-term annual operating earnings per share growth of at least 6.0% thereafter.

Financial Data

(US$ in Thousands)	12/31/2007	12/31/2006	12/31/2005	12/31/2004	12/31/2003	12/31/2002	12/31/2001	12/31/2000
Earnings Per Share	3.88	1.97	1.50	1.89	0.50	2.41	1.08	0.93
Cash Flow Per Share	(0.38)	5.73	3.83	4.30	3.71	4.36	4.82	2.85
Tang Book Value Per Share	9.21	11.44	8.79	10.48	9.60	9.09	7.85	7.10
Dividends Per Share	1.460	1.380	1.340	1.300	1.290	1.290	1.290	1.290
Dividend Payout %	37.63	70.23	89.33	68.78	258.00	53.53	120.00	139.46
Income Statement								
Total Revenue	15,674,000	16,482,000	18,041,000	13,972,000	12,078,000	10,218,000	10,558,000	9,260,000
EBITDA	7,186,000	5,242,000	4,129,000	4,320,000	3,729,000	4,248,000	3,135,000	2,826,000
Income Before Taxes	4,494,000	2,489,000	1,616,000	1,964,000	1,546,000	2,043,000	914,000	600,000
Income Taxes	1,783,000	920,000	597,000	700,000	397,000	681,000	370,000	183,000
Net Income	2,539,000	1,380,000	1,033,000	1,249,000	318,000	1,362,000	544,000	436,000
Average Shares	655,200	703,200	688,800	661,000	637,600	562,000	505,000	471,800
Balance Sheet								
Net PPE	21,352,000	29,382,000	28,940,000	26,716,000	25,850,000	20,257,000	18,681,000	14,849,000
Total Assets	39,123,000	49,269,000	52,660,000	45,446,000	44,186,000	37,909,000	34,369,000	29,348,000
Long-Term Obligations	13,235,000	14,791,000	14,653,000	15,507,000	15,776,000	12,060,000	12,119,000	10,101,000
Total Liabilities	29,432,000	36,076,000	42,006,000	33,763,000	33,391,000	26,042,000	24,485,000	21,461,000
Stockholders' Equity	9,406,000	12,913,000	10,397,000	11,426,000	10,538,000	10,213,000	8,368,000	6,992,000
Shares Outstanding	577,000	698,000	694,000	680,000	650,000	616,000	529,400	491,600
Statistical Record								
Return on Assets %	5.74	2.71	2.11	2.78	0.77	3.77	1.71	1.85
Return on Equity %	22.75	11.84	9.47	11.34	3.06	14.66	7.08	7.40
EBITDA Margin %	45.85	31.80	22.89	30.92	30.87	41.57	29.69	30.52
Net Margin %	16.20	8.37	5.73	8.94	2.63	13.33	5.15	4.71
PPE Turnover	0.62	0.57	0.65	0.53	0.52	0.52	0.63	0.72
Asset Turnover	0.35	0.32	0.37	0.31	0.29	0.28	0.33	0.39
Debt to Equity	1.41	1.15	1.41	1.36	1.50	1.18	1.45	1.44
Price Range	48.99-40.00	42.01-34.52	43.25-33.35	34.23-30.63	32.83-25.92	33.42-18.25	34.78-28.00	33.63-17.56
P/E Ratio	12.63-10.31	21.32-17.52	28.83-22.23	18.11-16.20	65.66-51.84	13.87-7.57	32.20-25.93	36.16-18.88
Average Yield %	3.33	3.60	3.58	4.05	4.33	4.44	4.14	5.32

Address: 120 Tredegar Street, Richmond, VA 23219 **Telephone:** 804-819-2000 **Fax:** 804-775-5819	**Web Site:** www.dom.com **Officers:** Thos E. Capps - Chmn., C.E.O. Thomas F. Farrell II - Pres., C.O.O.	**Auditors:** Deloitte & Touche LLP **Investor Contact:** 804-819-2150 **Transfer Agents:** Dominion Resources Services, Inc

DONALDSON CO. INC.

Exchange	Symbol	Price	52Wk Range	Yield	P/E	Div Acheiver
NYS	DCI	$40.28 (3/31/2008)	48.18-34.30	1.09	20.45	12 Years

*7 Year Price Score 114.49 *NYSE Composite Index=100 *12 Month Price Score 112.63

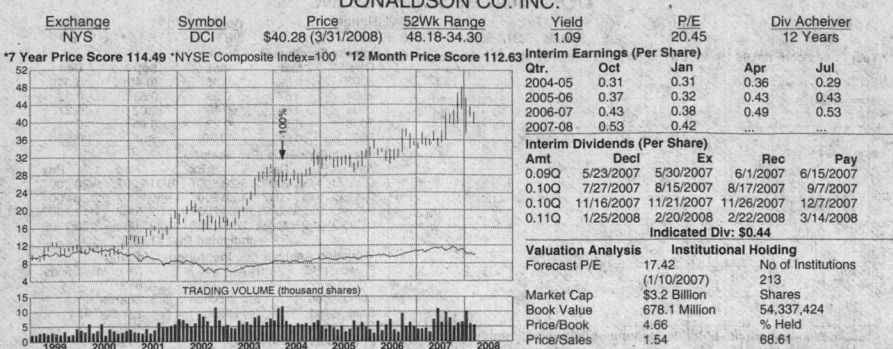

Interim Earnings (Per Share)

Qtr.	Oct	Jan	Apr	Jul
2004-05	0.31	0.31	0.36	0.29
2005-06	0.37	0.32	0.43	0.43
2006-07	0.43	0.38	0.49	0.53
2007-08	0.53	0.42	...	...

Interim Dividends (Per Share)

Amt	Decl	Ex	Rec	Pay
0.09Q	5/23/2007	5/30/2007	6/1/2007	6/15/2007
0.10Q	7/27/2007	8/15/2007	8/17/2007	9/7/2007
0.10Q	11/16/2007	11/21/2007	11/26/2007	12/7/2007
0.11Q	1/25/2008	2/20/2008	2/22/2008	3/14/2008

Indicated Div: $0.44

Valuation Analysis   **Institutional Holding**

Forecast P/E	17.42 (1/10/2007)	No of Institutions 213
Market Cap	$3.2 Billion	Shares
Book Value	678.1 Million	54,337,424
Price/Book	4.66	% Held
Price/Sales	1.54	68.61

Business Summary: Industrial Machinery and Equipment (MIC: 11.5 SIC: 3564 NAIC: 333412)

Donaldson is engaged in the manufacture of filtration systems and replacement parts. Co.'s product includes air and liquid filters, exhaust and emission control products for mobile equipment; in-plant air cleaning systems; compressed air purification systems; air intake systems for industrial gas turbines and filters for applications such as computer disk drives and semi-conductor processing. Co.'s products are manufactured at over 35 plants globally and through three of its joint ventures. As of Jul 31 2007, Co. had two reporting segments: Engine Products and Industrial Products, which were engaged in the design, manufacture and sale of systems to filter air and liquid and other products.

Recent Developments: For the quarter ended Jan 31 2008, net income increased 8.9% to US$34.1 million from US$31.3 million in the year-earlier quarter. Revenues were US$511.8 million, up 10.4% from US$463.7 million the year before. Operating income was US$50.6 million versus US$42.9 million in the prior-year quarter, an increase of 18.1%. Direct operating expenses rose 8.1% to US$348.6 million from US$322.5 million in the comparable period the year before. Indirect operating expenses increased 14.5% to US$112.6 million from US$98.3 million in the equivalent prior-year period.

Prospects: For the fiscal year ending Jul 31 2008, Co. now anticipates sales growth in its Engine Products segment to be in the range of 10.0% to 12.0%, while sales at its Industrial Products segment are forecasted to grow by 14.0% to 16.0%. Similarly, Co. is targeting sales of its Industrial Filtration and Special Applications Products to improve by 10.0% to 15.0%, while Gas Turbine Products sales are estimated to improve by about 20.0% to 30.0%. In addition, Co. is projecting operating margin of at least 11.0%, while operating income is estimated to increase by 14.0% to 19.0% over its prior fiscal year's level. Hence, Co. now expects earnings to be in the range of $2.00 to $2.10 per share.

Financial Data

(US$ in Thousands)	6 Mos	3 Mos	07/31/2007	07/31/2006	07/31/2005	07/31/2004	07/31/2003	07/31/2002
Earnings Per Share	1.97	1.93	1.83	1.55	1.27	1.18	1.05	0.95
Cash Flow Per Share	1.80	1.52	1.45	1.89	1.68	1.34	1.69	1.75
Tang Book Value Per Share	6.43	6.51	5.73	5.14	4.77	5.03	3.40	3.18
Dividends Per Share	0.380	0.370	0.360	0.320	0.235	0.205	0.175	0.155
Dividend Payout %	19.29	19.17	19.67	20.65	18.50	17.37	16.59	16.32
Income Statement								
Total Revenue	1,037,339	525,576	1,918,828	1,694,327	1,595,733	1,414,980	1,218,252	1,126,005
EBITDA	144,403	77,707	268,986	243,742	208,431	188,345	174,013	157,300
Depn & Amortn	27,967	14,059	...	...	...	...	...	...
Income Before Taxes	108,120	59,465	204,861	189,167	154,733	141,836	130,567	119,018
Income Taxes	30,727	16,142	54,144	56,860	44,179	35,519	35,253	32,135
Net Income	77,393	43,323	150,717	132,307	110,554	106,317	95,314	86,883
Average Shares	81,702	81,882	82,435	85,139	86,883	90,429	90,469	91,428
Balance Sheet								
Current Assets	752,318	732,037	673,644	561,405	618,822	557,380	454,705	456,484
Total Assets	1,427,278	1,393,279	1,319,017	1,124,067	1,111,773	1,001,609	881,997	850,131
Current Liabilities	461,259	443,701	458,944	359,869	354,202	275,524	214,076	272,790
Long-Term Obligations	176,910	149,667	129,004	100,495	103,302	70,856	105,156	105,019
Total Liabilities	749,226	703,134	694,319	577,265	587,157	452,316	434,604	467,510
Stockholders' Equity	678,052	690,145	624,698	546,802	524,616	549,293	447,393	382,621
Shares Outstanding	78,367	79,298	79,142	80,540	83,059	86,281	99,311	87,829
Statistical Record								
Return on Assets %	12.35	12.37	12.34	11.84	10.46	11.26	11.01	11.16
Return on Equity %	26.16	24.81	25.73	24.70	20.59	21.28	22.97	24.76
EBITDA Margin %	13.92	14.79	14.02	14.39	13.06	13.31	14.28	13.97
Net Margin %	7.46	8.24	7.85	7.81	6.93	7.51	7.82	7.72
Asset Turnover	1.57	1.56	1.57	1.52	1.51	1.50	1.41	1.45
Current Ratio	1.63	1.65	1.47	1.56	1.75	2.02	2.12	1.67
Debt to Equity	0.26	0.22	0.21	0.18	0.20	0.13	0.24	0.27
Price Range	48.18-34.30	42.86-33.87	38.55-32.00	35.93-28.70	33.97-25.24	30.52-23.63	24.41-15.43	22.30-13.47
P/E Ratio	24.46-17.41	22.21-17.55	21.07-17.49	23.18-18.52	26.75-19.87	25.87-20.02	23.25-14.70	23.47-14.17
Average Yield %	0.99	1.01	1.01	0.99	0.77	0.74	0.94	0.86

Address: 1400 West 94th Street, Minneapolis, MN 55431 **Telephone:** 952-887-3131 **Fax:** 952-887-3155	**Web Site:** www.donaldson.com **Officers:** William M. Cook - Chmn., Pres., C.E.O. James R. Giertz - Sr. V.P., Commercial & Industrial	**Auditors:** PricewaterhouseCoopers LLP **Investor Contact:** 952-887-3753 **Transfer Agents:** Wells Fargo Bank, N.A., South St. Paul, MN

DONNELLEY (R.H.) CORP.

Exchange	Symbol	Price	52Wk Range	Yield	P/E
NYS	RHD	$5.06 (3/31/2008)	83.90-4.48	N/A	7.78

*7 Year Price Score 90.63   *NYSE Composite Index=100   *12 Month Price Score 25.28

Interim Earnings (Per Share)

Qtr.	Mar	Jun	Sep	Dec
2003	(2.76)	(0.81)	(0.04)	0.05
2004	0.54	0.65	0.31	(0.36)
2005	(4.10)	0.44	0.62	(6.32)
2006	(0.76)	(1.15)	(0.51)	(0.72)
2007	0.22	0.34	0.25	(0.17)

Interim Dividends (Per Share)

Amt	Decl	Ex	Rec	Pay
0.01Q	4/24/2006	4/28/2006	5/2/2006	5/30/2006

Valuation Analysis   Institutional Holding

Forecast P/E	N/A	No of Institutions
		187
Market Cap	$347.9 Million	Shares
Book Value	1.8 Billion	79,550,384
Price/Book	0.19	% Held
Price/Sales	0.13	N/A

TRADING VOLUME (thousand shares)

Business Summary: Advertising, Marketing & PR (MIC: 12.4 SIC: 7319 NAIC: 541890)

R.H. Donnelley is a Yellow Pages and online commercial search company. Co publishes and distributes advertiser content utilizing three brands: Dex, Qwest, Embarq and AT&T. Co.'s Triple Play integrated marketing services suite includes: print Yellow Pages directories, its proprietary DexKnows.com online search site and the rest of the Internet via Dex Search Marketing® tools. Co.'s print directories provide local information to consumers, facilitating their search for products and services offered by local merchants. Co.'s online products and services provide merchants with additional methods to connect with consumers who are seeking to purchase products and services using the Internet.

Recent Developments: For the year ended Dec 31 2007, net income amounted to US$46.9 million versus a net loss of US$237.7 million in the prior year. Revenues were US$2.68 billion, up 41.1% from US$1.90 billion the year before. Operating income was US$905.0 million versus US$442.8 million in the prior year, an increase of 104.4%. Direct operating expenses rose 31.6% to US$450.3 million from US$342.1 million in the comparable period the year before. Indirect operating expenses increased 18.9% to US$1.33 billion from US$1.11 billion in the equivalent prior-year period.

Prospects: For 2008, Co. has lowered its outlook to reflect the softer economy and now expects net revenue of $2.60 billion to $2.70 billion as well as operating income of $820.0 million to $870.0 million. Co. also expects advertising sales to decrease in the mid single digits. Separately, Co. believes that over the next several years, references to print yellow pages directories may continue to gradually decrease as users may increasingly turn to digital and interactive media delivery devices for local commercial search information. Hence, Co. expects overall directory usage to grow, largely due to growth of Internet directory usage.

Financial Data
(US$ in Thousands)

	12/31/2007	12/31/2006	12/31/2005	12/31/2004	12/31/2003	12/31/2002	12/31/2001	12/31/2000
Earnings Per Share	0.65	(3.14)	(9.10)	1.15	(3.53)	1.40	1.61	3.83
Cash Flow Per Share	9.75	11.56	12.36	12.96	8.10	1.69	2.88	2.58
Dividends Per Share	...	0.010	...	...	...	...	...	...
Income Statement								
Total Revenue	2,680,299	1,895,921	956,631	603,116	256,445	73,806	76,739	141,287
EBITDA	1,369,914	766,442	460,387	358,396	159,828	151,780	122,239	249,303
Income Before Taxes	75,892	(322,229)	110,709	116,218	(85,971)	111,983	86,528	203,018
Income Taxes	29,033	(84,525)	43,176	45,906	(36,018)	44,806	36,272	77,556
Net Income	46,859	(237,704)	67,533	70,312	(49,953)	67,177	49,815	124,758
Average Shares	71,963	66,448	31,731	32,616	30,683	30,298	30,976	32,594
Balance Sheet								
Current Assets	1,467,191	1,532,225	565,845	623,309	284,591	1,968,674	11,010	90,949
Total Assets	10,089,093	16,147,468	3,867,824	3,978,922	2,538,734	2,223,375	295,981	365,284
Current Liabilities	1,778,731	2,009,218	738,818	623,797	299,613	34,041	44,584	46,862
Long-Term Obligations	9,998,474	10,020,521	2,978,615	2,965,331	2,042,547	2,075,470	283,904	347,526
Total Liabilities	14,266,357	14,326,712	3,825,090	3,744,826	2,396,756	2,190,516	407,294	473,794
Stockholders' Equity	1,822,736	1,820,756	(291,415)	17,985	(56,245)	(30,600)	(111,313)	(108,510)
Shares Outstanding	68,758	70,464	31,888	31,484	31,032	29,721	29,389	30,939
Statistical Record								
Return on Assets %	0.29	N.M.	1.72	2.15	N.M.	5.33	15.07	32.71
Return on Equity %	2.57	N.M.	...	...	...	...	...	...
EBITDA Margin %	51.11	40.43	48.13	59.42	62.32	205.65	159.29	176.45
Net Margin %	1.75	N.M.	7.06	11.66	N.M.	91.02	64.91	88.30
Asset Turnover	0.17	0.19	0.24	0.18	0.11	0.06	0.23	0.37
Current Ratio	0.82	0.76	0.77	1.00	0.95	57.83	0.99	1.93
Debt to Equity	5.49	5.50	...	164.88	...	...	...	...
Price Range	83.90-35.98	65.70-50.18	67.32-55.97	59.11-39.75	42.97-28.88	32.10-22.02	32.30-22.88	24.31-15.13
P/E Ratio	129.08-55.35	...	...	51.40-34.57	...	22.93-15.73	20.06-14.21	6.35-3.95
Average Yield %	...	0.02	...	...	...	...	...	...

Address: 1001 Winstead Drive, Cary, NC 27513	Web Site: www.rhd.com	Auditors: PricewaterhouseCoopers LLP
Telephone: 919-297-1600	Officers: David C. Swanson - Chmn., C.E.O. Peter J. McDonald - Pres., C.O.O.	Investor Contact: 914-933-3178
		Transfer Agents: The Bank of New York

DONNELLEY (R.R.) & SONS CO.

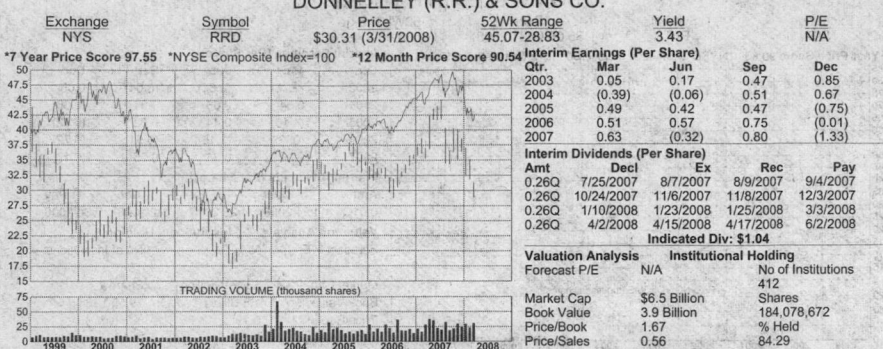

Exchange	Symbol	Price	52Wk Range	Yield	P/E
NYS	RRD	$30.31 (3/31/2008)	45.07-28.83	3.43	N/A

*7 Year Price Score 97.55 ***NYSE Composite Index=100** ***12 Month Price Score 90.54**

Interim Earnings (Per Share)

Qtr.	Mar	Jun	Sep	Dec
2003	0.05	0.17	0.47	0.85
2004	(0.39)	(0.06)	0.51	0.67
2005	0.49	0.42	0.47	(0.75)
2006	0.51	0.57	0.75	(0.01)
2007	0.63	(0.32)	0.80	(1.33)

Interim Dividends (Per Share)

Amt	Decl	Ex	Rec	Pay
0.26Q	7/25/2007	8/7/2007	8/9/2007	9/4/2007
0.26Q	10/24/2007	11/6/2007	11/8/2007	12/3/2007
0.26Q	1/10/2008	1/23/2008	1/25/2008	3/3/2008
0.26Q	4/2/2008	4/15/2008	4/17/2008	6/2/2008

Indicated Div: $1.04

Valuation Analysis — **Institutional Holding**

Forecast P/E	N/A	No of Institutions
		412
Market Cap	$6.5 Billion	Shares
Book Value	3.9 Billion	184,078,672
Price/Book	1.67	% Held
Price/Sales	0.56	84.29

Business Summary: Printing (MIC: 13.4 SIC: 2759 NAIC: 323119)

R.R. Donnelley & Sons is engaged as a full-service provider of print and related services, including document-based business process outsourcing. Co. provides its services in long and short run commercial printing, direct mail, financial printing, print fulfillment, forms and labels, logistics, digital printing, call centers, transactional print-and-mail, print management, online services, digital photography, color services, and content and database management to customers in the publishing, healthcare, advertising, retail, technology, financial services and other industries.

Recent Developments: For the year ended Dec 31 2007, loss from continuing operations was US$48.4 million compared with income of US$402.6 million a year earlier. Net loss amounted to US$48.9 million versus net income of US$400.6 million in the prior year. Revenues were US$11.59 billion, up 24.4% from US$9.32 billion the year before. Operating income was US$315.1 million versus US$750.7 million in the prior year, a decrease of 58.0%. Direct operating expenses rose 25.5% to US$8.53 billion from US$6.80 billion in the comparable period the year before. Indirect operating expenses increased 55.0% to US$2.74 billion from US$1.77 billion in the equivalent prior-year period.

Prospects: On Feb 27 2008, Co. announced an agreement to acquire Pro Line Printing, Inc., a producer of newspaper inserts, for $122.0 million. The purchase should expand Co.'s geographic footprint for offset printed tabloid inserts, provide production capacity, increase utilization at its other facilities, and be accretive to its earnings in the first full year of operations. Meanwhile, Co. expects net sales for 2008 to increase over 2007 due to increased volume and incremental sales from its acquisitions in 2007. Also, Co. expects to offset the rising paper, ink, and energy costs through savings from the integration of its recent acquisitions and its efforts to improve manufacturing productivity.

Financial Data

(US$ in Thousands)	12/31/2007	12/31/2006	12/31/2005	12/31/2004	12/31/2003	12/31/2002	12/31/2001	12/31/2000
Earnings Per Share	(0.22)	1.83	0.63	0.88	1.54	1.24	0.21	2.17
Cash Flow Per Share	5.39	4.18	4.41	4.05	3.13	3.62	4.70	6.04
Tang Book Value Per Share	N.M.	0.54	N.M.	3.81	5.14	4.51	3.92	5.06
Dividends Per Share	1.040	1.040	1.040	1.040	1.020	0.980	0.940	0.900
Dividend Payout %	...	56.83	165.08	118.18	66.23	79.03	447.62	41.47
Income Statement								
Total Revenue	11,587,100	9,316,600	8,430,200	7,156,400	4,787,162	4,754,937	5,297,760	5,764,335
EBITDA	917,000	1,203,600	867,500	828,200	587,995	590,923	524,800	914,025
Income Before Taxes	91,400	601,300	331,800	356,800	208,277	175,733	74,894	433,984
Income Taxes	136,500	196,000	237,400	92,600	31,768	33,496	49,906	167,084
Net Income	(48,900)	400,600	137,100	178,300	176,509	142,237	24,988	266,900
Average Shares	218,000	218,900	216,700	204,200	114,302	114,372	118,498	123,093
Balance Sheet								
Current Assets	3,521,300	2,517,000	2,621,700	2,600,600	999,510	866,439	940,194	1,206,449
Total Assets	12,086,700	9,635,800	9,373,700	8,553,700	3,188,950	3,151,772	3,400,017	3,914,202
Current Liabilities	2,765,200	1,611,800	1,814,100	1,487,300	883,582	954,730	984,290	1,190,561
Long-Term Obligations	3,601,900	2,358,600	2,365,400	1,581,200	752,497	752,870	881,318	739,190
Total Liabilities	8,179,400	5,511,100	5,649,500	4,567,100	2,205,798	2,237,178	2,511,610	2,681,654
Stockholders' Equity	3,907,300	4,124,700	3,724,200	3,986,600	983,152	914,594	888,407	1,232,548
Shares Outstanding	215,900	218,800	217,500	222,400	113,674	113,124	113,121	140,889
Statistical Record								
Return on Assets %	N.M.	4.21	1.53	3.03	5.57	4.34	0.68	6.85
Return on Equity %	N.M.	10.21	3.56	7.16	18.60	15.78	2.36	22.45
EBITDA Margin %	7.91	12.92	10.29	11.57	12.28	12.43	9.91	15.86
Net Margin %	N.M.	4.30	1.63	2.49	3.69	2.99	0.47	4.63
Asset Turnover	1.07	0.98	0.94	1.22	1.51	1.45	1.45	1.48
Current Ratio	1.27	1.56	1.45	1.75	1.13	0.91	0.96	1.01
Debt to Equity	0.92	0.57	0.64	0.40	0.77	0.82	0.99	0.60
Price Range	45.07-34.35	35.95-28.70	38.00-29.94	35.29-27.95	30.15-17.05	31.96-19.06	31.62-24.83	27.00-19.00
P/E Ratio	...	19.64-15.68	60.32-47.52	40.10-31.76	19.58-11.07	25.77-15.37	150.57-118.24	12.44-8.76
Average Yield %	2.68	3.15	3.03	3.32	4.29	3.70	3.33	3.88

Address: 111 South Wacker Drive, Chicago, IL 60606
Telephone: 312-326-8000
Fax: 312-326-8543

Web Site: www.rrdonnelley.com
Officers: Stephen M. Wolf - Chmn. Mark A. Angelson - C.E.O.

Auditors: Deloite & Touche LLP
Investor Contact: 312-326-8313
Transfer Agents: EquiServe Trust Company, N.A., Jersey City, NJ

DOVER CORP

Exchange	Symbol	Price	52Wk Range	Yield	P/E	Div Acheiver
NYS	DOV	$41.78 (3/31/2008)	54.44-35.55	1.91	12.82	52 Years

*7 Year Price Score 94.56   *NYSE Composite Index=100   *12 Month Price Score 95.58

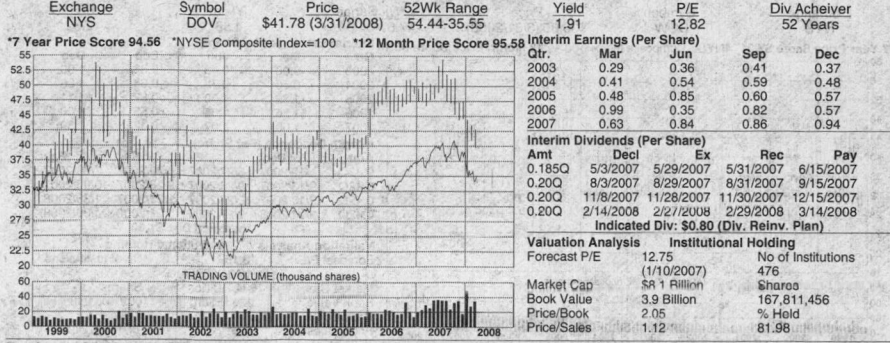

Interim Earnings (Per Share)

Qtr.	Mar	Jun	Sep	Dec
2003	0.29	0.36	0.41	0.37
2004	0.41	0.54	0.59	0.48
2005	0.48	0.85	0.60	0.57
2006	0.99	0.35	0.82	0.57
2007	0.63	0.84	0.86	0.94

Interim Dividends (Per Share)

Amt	Decl	Ex	Rec	Pay
0.185Q	5/3/2007	5/29/2007	5/31/2007	6/15/2007
0.20Q	8/3/2007	8/29/2007	8/31/2007	9/15/2007
0.20Q	11/8/2007	11/28/2007	11/30/2007	12/15/2007
0.20Q	2/14/2008	2/27/2008	2/29/2008	3/14/2008

Indicated Div: $0.80 (Div. Reinv. Plan)

Valuation Analysis   Institutional Holding

Forecast P/E	12.75 (1/10/2007)	No of Institutions 476
Market Cap	$8.1 Billion	Shares 167,811,456
Book Value	3.9 Billion	% Hold
Price/Book	2.05	81.98
Price/Sales	1.12	

Business Summary: Industrial Machinery and Equipment (MIC: 11.5 SIC: 3532 NAIC: 333131)

Dover owns and operates a global portfolio of manufacturing companies providing components and equipment, specialty systems and support services for a variety of applications in the industrial products, engineered systems, fluid management and electronic technologies markets. In addition, Co. provides engineering, testing and other services. Co.'s operating companies are based primarily in the U.S. and Europe in manufacturing and other operations throughout the world. As of Dec 31 2007, Co. reported its results in four business segments: Industrial Products, Engineered Systems, Fluid Management and Electronic Technologies, in addition to six core business platforms.

Recent Developments: For the year ended Dec 31 2007, income from continuing operations increased 10.3% to US$653.3 million from US$592.5 million a year earlier. Net income increased 17.7% to US$661.1 million from US$561.8 million in the prior year. Revenues were US$7.23 billion, up 14.2% from US$6.33 billion the year before. Operating income was US$980.7 million versus US$897.9 million in the prior year, an increase of 9.2%. Direct operating expenses rose 14.5% to US$4.60 billion from US$4.02 billion in the comparable period the year before. Indirect operating expenses increased 16.3% to US$1.64 billion from US$1.41 billion in the equivalent prior year period.

Prospects: Co.'s results are being driven primarily by solid performances in its Industrial Products segment, attributable to the acquisition of Paladin in August 2006 and the July 2007 acquisition of Hanmecson International. Looking ahead, Co. will continue to implement its strategic initiatives, which include realigning its operating structure into four industry segments with six business platforms, investing in potential add-on acquisitions as well as generating potential integration within its businesses. Hence, Co. is projecting earnings improvement for the full year of to be in excess of 10.0%, assuming a reasonably stable global economy, despite challenges in a few of its end-markets.

Financial Data
(US$ in Thousands)

	12/31/2007	12/31/2006	12/31/2005	12/31/2004	12/31/2003	12/31/2002	12/31/2001	12/31/2000
Earnings Per Share	3.26	2.73	2.50	2.02	1.44	(0.60)	1.22	2.54
Cash Flow Per Share	4.48	4.31	3.25	2.93	2.93	1.95	3.35	2.73
Tang Book Value Per Share	N.M.	N.M.	N.M.	2.16	2.70	2.65	1.97	1.79
Dividends Per Share	0.770	0.710	0.660	0.620	0.570	0.540	0.520	0.480
Dividend Payout %	23.62	26.01	26.40	30.69	39.58	...	42.62	18.90
Income Statement								
Total Revenue	7,226,089	6,511,623	6,078,380	5,488,112	4,413,296	4,183,664	4,459,695	5,400,717
EBITDA	1,221,640	1,101,354	891,513	774,281	585,367	495,523	533,677	1,064,194
Income Before Taxes	887,604	822,869	643,588	552,146	371,892	269,691	238,434	772,315
Income Taxes	234,331	219,541	169,135	143,006	86,676	58,542	71,595	239,108
Net Income	661,080	561,782	510,142	412,755	292,927	(121,261)	248,537	519,612
Average Shares	202,918	205,497	204,177	204,786	203,614	203,346	204,013	204,677
Balance Sheet								
Current Assets	2,544,238	2,271,506	1,975,925	2,149,947	1,849,640	1,638,001	1,654,928	1,974,849
Total Assets	8,069,770	7,626,658	6,573,032	5,792,179	5,133,752	4,437,385	4,602,202	4,892,116
Current Liabilities	1,681,003	1,433,980	1,207,454	1,355,976	910,801	696,938	819,171	1,604,640
Long-Term Obligations	1,452,003	1,480,491	1,344,173	753,063	1,003,915	1,030,299	1,033,243	631,846
Total Liabilities	4,123,597	3,815,636	3,243,509	2,673,497	2,391,081	2,042,762	2,082,663	2,450,541
Stockholders' Equity	3,946,173	3,811,022	3,329,523	3,118,682	2,742,671	2,394,623	2,519,539	2,441,575
Shares Outstanding	194,038	204,316	202,850	203,496	202,912	202,402	202,579	203,183
Statistical Record								
Return on Assets %	8.42	7.91	8.25	7.53	6.12	N.M.	5.24	11.48
Return on Equity %	17.04	15.73	15.82	14.05	11.40	N.M.	10.02	23.13
EBITDA Margin %	16.91	16.91	14.67	14.11	13.26	11.84	11.97	19.70
Net Margin %	9.15	8.63	8.39	7.52	6.64	N.M.	5.57	9.62
Asset Turnover	0.92	0.92	0.98	1.00	0.92	0.93	0.94	1.19
Current Ratio	1.51	1.58	1.64	1.59	2.03	2.38	2.02	1.23
Debt to Equity	0.37	0.39	0.40	0.24	0.37	0.43	0.41	0.26
Price Range	54.44-44.34	51.58-41.49	41.94-34.70	44.02-36.03	40.08-23.35	43.31-23.91	43.32-28.77	53.81-36.00
P/E Ratio	16.70-13.60	18.89-15.20	16.78-13.88	21.79-17.84	27.83-16.22	...	35.51-23.58	21.19-14.17
Average Yield %	1.57	1.49	1.69	1.56	1.76	1.63	1.39	1.07

Address: 280 Park Avenue, New York, NY 10017-1292
Telephone: 212-922-1640
Fax: 212-922-1656

Web Site: www.dovercorporation.com
Officers: Thomas L. Reece - Chmn. Ronald L. Hoffman - Pres., C.E.O.

Auditors: PricewaterhouseCoopers LLP
Investor Contact: 212-922-1640
Transfer Agents: Mellon Investor Services, Ridgefield Park, NJ

DOW CHEMICAL CO.

Exchange	Symbol	Price	52Wk Range	Yield	P/E
NYS	DOW	$36.85 (3/31/2008)	47.67-34.64	4.56	12.32

*7 Year Price Score 87.21   ***NYSE Composite Index=100**   ***12 Month Price Score 96.10**

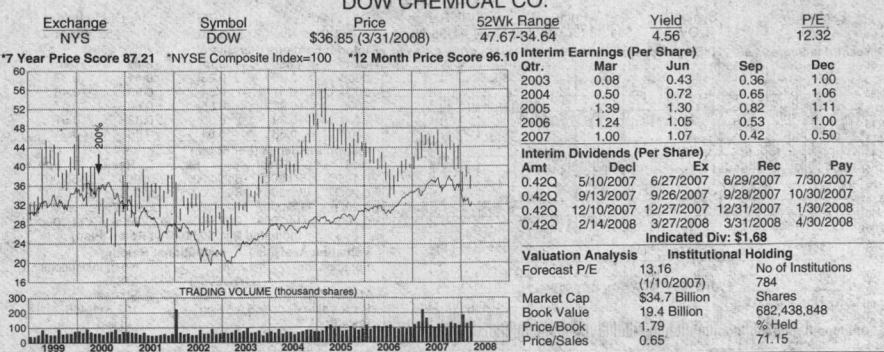

Interim Earnings (Per Share)

Qtr.	Mar	Jun	Sep	Dec
2003	0.08	0.43	0.36	1.00
2004	0.50	0.72	0.65	1.06
2005	1.39	1.30	0.82	1.11
2006	1.24	1.05	0.53	1.00
2007	1.00	1.07	0.42	0.50

Interim Dividends (Per Share)

Amt	Decl	Ex	Rec	Pay
0.42Q	5/10/2007	6/27/2007	6/29/2007	7/30/2007
0.42Q	9/13/2007	9/26/2007	9/28/2007	10/30/2007
0.42Q	12/10/2007	12/27/2007	12/31/2007	1/30/2008
0.42Q	2/14/2008	3/27/2008	3/31/2008	4/30/2008

Indicated Div: $1.68

Valuation Analysis   **Institutional Holding**

Forecast P/E	13.16	No of Institutions
	(1/10/2007)	784
Market Cap	$34.7 Billion	Shares
Book Value	19.4 Billion	682,438,848
Price/Book	1.79	% Held
Price/Sales	0.65	71.15

Business Summary: Chemicals (MIC: 11.1 SIC: 2821 NAIC: 325211)

Dow Chemical is engaged in the manufacture and sale of chemicals, plastic materials, agricultural and other products and services. Co. serves customers in approximately 160 countries and a range of markets, including food, transportation, health and medicine, personal and home care, and building and construction, among others. As of Dec 31 2007, Co. had 150 manufacturing sites in 37 countries and supplies approximately 3,100 products. As of Dec 31 2007, Co. cionducted its businesses through these operating segments: Performance Plastics; Performance Chemicals, Agricultural Sciences; Basic Plastics; Basic Chemicals; and Hydrocarbons and Energy.

Recent Developments: For the year ended Dec 31 2007, net income decreased 22.5% to US$2.89 billion from US$3.72 billion in the prior year. Revenues were US$53.51 billion, up 8.9% from US$49.12 billion the year before. Direct operating expenses rose 11.7% to US$46.40 billion from US$41.53 billion in the comparable period the year before. Indirect operating expenses increased 17.8% to US$3.88 billion from US$3.29 billion in the equivalent prior-year period.

Prospects: For the full year of 2008, Co. is projecting somewhat uncertain economic conditions in the U.S. Nevertheless, with majority of its sales occurred outside the U.S., Co. intends to attain growth in key regions, such as Brazil, Eastern Europe/Russia, India and China through its existing global footprint. For instance, on Dec 13 2007, Co. announced that it will form a 50/50 joint venture with Petrochemical Industries Co. of Kuwait to manufacture and market polyethylene, ethylenamines, ethanolamines, polypropylene, and polycarbonate. The transaction is subject to the completion of definitive agreements, customary conditions and regulatory approvals, and is anticipated to close in late 2008.

Financial Data

(US$ in Thousands)	12/31/2007	12/31/2006	12/31/2005	12/31/2004	12/31/2003	12/31/2002	12/31/2001	12/31/2000
Earnings Per Share	2.99	3.82	4.62	2.93	1.87	(0.37)	(0.43)	2.22
Cash Flow Per Share	4.70	4.32	4.64	2.83	4.11	2.32	1.98	1.79
Tang Book Value Per Share	15.99	13.95	12.14	9.01	5.79	4.19	7.58	10.77
Dividends Per Share	1.635	1.500	1.340	1.340	1.340	1.340	1.295	1.160
Dividend Payout %	54.68	39.27	29.00	45.73	71.66	...	...	52.25
Income Statement								
Total Revenue	53,513,000	49,124,000	46,307,000	40,161,000	32,632,000	27,609,000	27,805,000	23,008,000
EBITDA	6,714,000	7,357,000	8,922,000	6,442,000	4,303,000	1,831,000	1,808,000	4,468,000
Income Before Taxes	4,229,000	4,972,000	6,399,000	3,796,000	1,751,000	(622,000)	(613,000)	2,401,000
Income Taxes	1,244,000	1,155,000	1,782,000	877,000	(82,000)	(280,000)	(228,000)	823,000
Net Income	2,887,000	3,724,000	4,515,000	2,797,000	1,730,000	(338,000)	(385,000)	1,513,000
Average Shares	965,600	974,400	976,800	953,800	926,100	910,500	901,800	683,000
Balance Sheet								
Current Assets	18,654,000	17,209,000	17,404,000	15,890,000	13,002,000	11,681,000	10,308,000	9,260,000
Total Assets	48,801,000	45,581,000	45,934,000	45,885,000	41,891,000	39,562,000	35,515,000	27,645,000
Current Liabilities	12,445,000	10,601,000	10,663,000	10,506,000	9,534,000	8,856,000	8,125,000	7,873,000
Long-Term Obligations	7,581,000	8,036,000	9,186,000	11,629,000	11,763,000	11,659,000	9,266,000	4,865,000
Total Liabilities	29,412,000	28,516,000	30,610,000	33,615,000	32,716,000	31,936,000	25,522,000	18,459,000
Stockholders' Equity	19,389,000	17,065,000	15,324,000	12,270,000	9,175,000	7,626,000	9,993,000	9,186,000
Shares Outstanding	940,366	958,050	967,156	952,926	927,448	912,656	904,837	677,503
Statistical Record								
Return on Assets %	6.12	8.14	9.83	6.36	4.25	N.M.	N.M.	5.68
Return on Equity %	15.84	23.00	32.72	26.01	20.59	N.M.	N.M.	17.24
EBITDA Margin %	12.55	14.98	19.27	16.04	13.19	6.63	6.50	19.42
Net Margin %	5.39	7.58	9.75	6.96	5.30	N.M.	N.M.	6.58
Asset Turnover	1.13	1.07	1.01	0.91	0.80	0.74	0.88	0.86
Current Ratio	1.50	1.62	1.63	1.51	1.36	1.32	1.27	1.18
Debt to Equity	0.39	0.47	0.60	0.95	1.28	1.53	0.93	0.53
Price Range	47.67-39.27	44.93-33.54	56.42-40.63	51.02-36.86	42.00-25.16	36.75-24.50	39.58-29.45	46.67-23.38
P/E Ratio	15.94-13.13	11.76-8.78	12.21-8.79	17.41-12.58	22.46-13.45	...	...	21.02-10.53
Average Yield %	3.75	3.75	2.85	3.16	4.11	4.42	3.77	3.49

Address: 2030 Dow Center, Midland, MI 48674 Telephone: 989-636-1000 Fax: 989-636-3518	Web Site: www.dow.com Officers: William S. Stavropoulos - Chmn. Anthony J. Carbone - Vice-Chmn.	Auditors: Deloitte & Touche LLP Investor Contact: 989-636-8193

DPL INC.

Exchange	Symbol	Price	52Wk Range	Yield	P/E
NYS	DPL	$25.64 (3/31/2008)	31.91-24.58	4.29	13.64

*7 Year Price Score 96.37   *NYSE Composite Index=100   *12 Month Price Score 98.20

Interim Earnings (Per Share)

Qtr.	Mar	Jun	Sep	Dec
2003	0.44	0.28	0.62	(0.12)
2004	0.41	0.46	0.69	0.22
2005	0.58	0.17	0.20	0.41
2006	0.46	0.18	0.43	0.08
2007	0.47	0.49	0.53	0.39

Interim Dividends (Per Share)

Amt	Decl	Ex	Rec	Pay
0.26Q	4/27/2007	5/11/2007	5/15/2007	6/1/2007
0.26Q	7/27/2007	8/15/2007	8/17/2007	9/1/2007
0.26Q	10/30/2007	11/13/2007	11/15/2007	12/1/2007
0.275Q	1/29/2008	2/12/2008	2/14/2008	3/1/2008

Indicated Div: $1.10

Valuation Analysis   **Institutional Holding**

Forecast P/E	17.01	No of Institutions
	(1/10/2007)	221
Market Cap	$2.9 Billion	Shares
Book Value	895.6 Million	69,991,056
Price/Book	3.25	% Held
Price/Sales	1.92	61.88

TRADING VOLUME (thousand shares)

Business Summary: Electricity (MIC: 7.1 SIC: 4931 NAIC: 221121)

DPL is a regional electric energy and utility company. Through its principal subsidiary, The Dayton Power and Light Company (DP&L), Co. is primarily engaged in the generation, transmission and distribution of electricity in West Central Ohio. Electricity for DP&L's 24 county service area is primarily generated at eight coal-fired power plants and is distributed to more than 515,000 retail customers as of Dec 31 2007. DP&L also purchases retail peak load requirements from DPL Energy, LLC. In addition, DP&L sells any excess energy and capacity into the wholesale market. Principal industries served by Co. include automotive, food processing, paper, plastic manufacturing and defense.

Recent Developments: For the year ended Dec 31 2007, income from continuing operations increased 68.6% to US$211.8 million from US$125.6 million a year earlier. Net income increased 58.9% to US$221.8 million from US$139.6 million in the prior year. Revenues were US$1.52 billion, up 8.8% from US$1.39 billion the year before. Operating income was US$370.1 million versus US$281.0 million in the prior year, an increase of 31.7%. Direct operating expenses rose 21.1% to US$615.4 million from US$508.1 million in the comparable period the year before. Indirect operating expenses decreased 12.3% to US$530.2 million from US$604.4 million in the equivalent prior-year period.

Prospects. For the full year of 2008, Co. continues to anticipate earnings to be in the range of $1.90 to $2.10 per share. In addition, Co. is projecting construction additions to be approximately $205.0 million, mainly for its The Dayton Power and Light Company (DP&L) subsidiary's environmental compliance program, power plant equipment, as well as its transmission and distribution system. Similarly, Co. is forecasting construction additions of about $203.0 million for its DP&L subsidiary, related to environmental compliance program, power plant equipment, and its transmission and distribution system. Meanwhile, Co. is targeting earnings for full-year 2009 to range from $2.10 to $2.40 per share.

Financial Data

(US$ in Thousands)	12/31/2007	12/31/2006	12/31/2005	12/31/2004	12/31/2003	12/31/2002	12/31/2001	12/31/2000
Earnings Per Share	1.88	1.15	1.35	1.78	1.22	0.72	1.71	1.83
Cash Flow Per Share	2.95	2.75	2.60	1.10	2.92	2.63	2.60	1.68
Tang Book Value Per Share	7.69	6.30	8.14	8.25	7.13	6.56	6.49	6.98
Dividends Per Share	1.040	1.000	0.960	0.960	0.940	0.940	0.940	0.940
Dividend Payout %	55.32	86.96	71.11	53.93	77.05	130.56	54.97	51.37
Income Statement								
Total Revenue	1,515,700	1,393,500	1,284,900	1,199,900	1,191,000	1,186,400	1,199,600	1,436,900
EBITDA	560,900	457,000	491,600	647,900	584,600	474,600	648,000	733,700
Income Before Taxes	334,300	195,400	204,600	342,900	215,000	137,600	336,800	441,500
Income Taxes	122,500	69,800	79,900	125,600	83,500	50,300	121,300	156,600
Net Income	221,800	139,600	174,400	217,300	148,500	87,300	216,500	243,500
Average Shares	117,800	121,900	129,100	122,200	121,700	121,900	126,600	137,900
Balance Sheet								
Net PPE	2,777,000	2,559,300	2,572,900	2,530,100	2,373,900	2,502,700	2,482,300	2,267,000
Total Assets	3,566,600	3,612,200	3,791,700	4,165,500	4,444,700	4,176,100	4,253,500	4,436,000
Long-Term Obligations	1,541,500	1,551,800	1,677,100	2,117,300	1,954,700	2,142,400	2,150,800	1,758,500
Total Liabilities	2,671,000	2,877,200	2,730,700	3,098,500	3,519,400	3,323,400	3,409,500	3,520,700
Stockholders' Equity	895,600	735,000	1,061,000	1,067,000	925,300	852,800	844,000	915,300
Shares Outstanding	113,558	113,018	127,526	126,501	126,501	126,501	126,501	127,774
Statistical Record								
Return on Assets %	6.18	3.77	4.38	5.03	3.45	2.07	4.98	5.53
Return on Equity %	27.20	15.55	16.39	21.75	16.70	10.29	24.61	20.32
EBITDA Margin %	37.01	32.80	38.26	54.00	49.08	40.00	54.02	51.06
Net Margin %	14.63	10.02	13.57	18.11	12.47	7.36	18.05	16.95
PPE Turnover	0.57	0.54	0.50	0.47	0.47	0.48	0.51	0.63
Asset Turnover	0.42	0.38	0.32	0.28	0.28	0.28	0.28	0.33
Debt to Equity	1.72	2.11	1.58	1.98	2.11	2.51	2.55	1.92
Price Range	31.91-26.04	28.72-25.11	28.12-24.08	25.36-17.21	21.15-11.95	27.19-13.75	32.38-22.30	33.69-16.63
P/E Ratio	16.97-13.85	24.97-21.83	20.83-17.84	14.25-9.67	17.34-9.80	37.76-19.10	18.93-13.04	18.41-9.08
Average Yield %	3.58	3.69	3.68	4.72	5.95	4.53	3.52	3.81

Address: 1065 Woodman Drive, Dayton, OH 45432
Telephone: 937-224-6000
Fax: 937-224-6500

Web Site: www.dplinc.com
Officers: Robert D. Biggs - Exec. Chmn. W. August Hillenbrand - Vice-Chmn.

Auditors: KPMG LLP
Transfer Agents: EquiServe, Providence, RI

DREAMWORKS ANIMATION SKG INC

Exchange	Symbol	Price	52Wk Range	Yield	P/E
NYS	DWA	$25.78 (3/31/2008)	34.70-21.87	N/A	11.88

*7 Year Price Score N/A   *NYSE Composite Index=100   *12 Month Price Score 93.69

Interim Earnings (Per Share)

Qtr.	Mar	Jun	Sep	Dec
2004	(0.33)	1.89	0.18	2.87
2005	0.44	(0.04)	(0.01)	0.61
2006	0.12	0.13	0.10	(0.20)
2007	0.15	0.60	0.47	0.95

Interim Dividends (Per Share)

No Dividends Paid

Valuation Analysis   Institutional Holding

Forecast P/E	N/A	No of Institutions
		131
Market Cap	$2.5 Billion	Shares
Book Value	1.0 Billion	47,181,184
Price/Book	2.43	% Held
Price/Sales	3.23	45.57

TRADING VOLUME (thousand shares)

Business Summary: Movies & Film (MIC: 13.2 SIC: 7812 NAIC: 512110)

DreamWorks Animation SKG is principally engaged in developing and producing computer-generated (CG) animated feature films. Co. develops as well as produces animated films and characters in the theatrical, home entertainment, television, merchandising and licensing and other markets. Co. derives its revenue from feature films in theaters and in markets, such as home entertainment, as well as pay and free broadcast television. As of Dec 31 2007, Co. has released a total of 15 animated feature films, nine of which have been CG animated feature films, and one direct-to-video title.

Recent Developments: For the year ended Dec 31 2007, net income increased to US$218.4 million from US$15.1 million in the prior year. Revenues were US$767.2 million, up 94.3% from US$394.8 million the year before. Operating income was US$291.3 million versus a loss of US$1.1 million in the prior year. Direct operating expenses rose 17.4% to US$372.3 million from US$317.1 million in the comparable period the year before. Indirect operating expenses increased 31.4% to US$103.6 million from US$78.8 million in the equivalent prior-year period.

Prospects: For 2008, Co. expects full year results to be driven primarily by the release of Kung Fu Panda, which opens domestically on June 6 2008. However, Co. expects that a significant portion of its 2008 earnings will occur in the second half of the year after distribution and marketing costs for Kung Fu Panda have been recouped by its distributor. Also, Co.'s second film for 2008, the sequel to Madagascar, is set for release on Nov 7 2008, but is not expected to generate significant revenue for the year. Meanwhile, Co. intends to expand its franchises into new growth vehicles in 2008. Notably, Co. plans to release Shrek the Musical on Broadway on Dec 14 2008.

Financial Data
(US$ in Thousands)

	12/31/2007	12/31/2006	12/31/2005	12/31/2004	12/31/2003	12/31/2002	12/31/2001
Earnings Per Share	2.17	0.15	1.01	4.05	...	...	...
Cash Flow Per Share	1.50	1.05	3.61	(0.53)	...	...	...
Tang Book Value Per Share	10.24	9.65	8.84	7.70	...	...	...
Income Statement							
Total Revenue	767,178	394,842	462,316	1,078,160	300,986	434,324	661,144
EBITDA	213,060	47,430	112,016	445,392	(166,302)	(15,453)	91,703
Income Before Taxes	227,749	64,227	112,077	423,326	(182,800)	(22,876)	86,433
Income Taxes	9,385	49,102	7,492	90,326	1,839	2,191	1,434
Net Income	218,364	15,125	104,585	333,000	(187,161)	(25,067)	2,256
Average Shares	100,469	103,612	104,062	82,151	...	...	...
Balance Sheet							
Current Assets	1,124,497	1,133,217	1,084,792	970,825	562,313	630,611	...
Total Assets	1,327,784	1,280,469	1,313,176	1,200,003	677,124	675,012	...
Current Liabilities	235,721	124,310	169,534	152,917	187,904	179,836	...
Long-Term Obligations	70,547	119,950	194,531	217,200	498,723	318,189	...
Total Liabilities	306,268	244,260	364,065	370,117	686,627	498,025	...
Stockholders' Equity	1,018,575	1,033,268	946,170	826,945	(12,444)	176,987	...
Shares Outstanding	96,086	103,491	103,142	102,950	...	...	...
Statistical Record							
Return on Assets %	16.74	1.17	8.32	35.38	N.M.	...	...
Return on Equity %	21.28	1.53	11.80	81.54	N.M.	...	...
EBITDA Margin %	27.77	12.01	24.23	41.31	N.M.	N.M.	13.87
Net Margin %	28.46	3.83	22.62	30.89	N.M.	N.M.	0.34
Asset Turnover	0.59	0.30	0.37	1.15	0.45	...	...
Current Ratio	4.77	9.12	6.40	6.35	2.99	3.51	...
Debt to Equity	0.07	0.12	0.21	0.26	...	1.80	...
Price Range	34.70-22.95	29.87-20.30	41.09-22.52	41.98-35.51	...	...	...
P/E Ratio	15.99-10.58	199.13-135.33	40.68-22.30	10.37-8.77	...	...	...

Address: 1000 Flower Street, Glendale, CA 91201-3007 **Telephone:** 818-695-5000	**Web Site:** www.dreamworksanimation.com **Officers:** Roger A. Enrico - Chmn. Jeffrey Katzenberg - C.E.O.	**Auditors:** Ernst & Young LLP **Investor Contact:** 818-695-3900 **Transfer Agents:** The Bank of New York

DRESSER-RAND GROUP INC

Exchange	Symbol	Price	52Wk Range	Yield	P/E
NYS	DRC	$30.75 (3/31/2008)	43.48-27.47	N/A	24.60

*7 Year Price Score N/A   *NYSE Composite Index=100   *12 Month Price Score 95.98

TRADING VOLUME (thousand shares)

Interim Earnings (Per Share)

Qtr.	Mar	Jun	Sep	Dec
2004	...	...	...	0.00
2005	(0.04)	(0.03)	0.15	0.48
2006	0.14	0.13	0.27	0.38
2007	0.18	0.31	0.25	0.51

Interim Dividends (Per Share)

No Dividends Paid

Valuation Analysis   **Institutional Holding**

Forecast P/E	N/A	No of Institutions
		140
Market Cap	$2.6 Billion	Shares
Book Value	805.2 Million	69,826,264
Price/Book	3.26	% Held
Price/Sales	1.58	81.69

Business Summary: Industrial Machinery and Equipment (MIC: 11.5 SIC: 3511 NAIC: 333611)

Dresser-Rand Group is engaged in the design, manufacture, sale and servicing of turbo and reciprocating compressors, gas and steam turbines, gas expanders and associated control panels. Co.'s installed base of equipment includes such brand names as Dresser-Rand, Dresser-Clark, Ingersoll Rand, Worthington, Turbodyne, Terry, Coppus, Murray and Nadrowski. Additionally, as of Dec 31 2007, Co. provided a full range of aftermarket parts and services to this installed base through its global network of 27 service and support centers covering more than 140 countries.

Recent Developments: For the year ended Dec 31 2007, net income increased 35.4% to US$106.7 million from US$78.8 million in the prior year. Revenues were US$1.67 billion, up 10.9% from US$1.50 billion the year before. Operating income was US$197.1 million versus US$176.3 million in the prior year, an increase of 11.8%. Direct operating expenses rose 10.8% to US$1.22 billion from US$1.10 billion in the comparable period the year before. Indirect operating expenses increased 10.7% to US$251.8 million from US$227.4 million in the equivalent prior-year period.

Prospects: Co.'s outlook appears constructive, reflecting continued strong demand for rotating equipment and aftermarket parts and services. Notably, Co.'s backlog at the end of December 2007 of $1.86 billion was 46.7% higher than the backlog at the end of December 2006 of $1.27 billion. Co. stated that at Dec 31, 2007, 77.0% of the backlog of $1.86 billion was scheduled to ship in 2008. Accordingly, Co. expects its 2008 operating income to be in the range of $285.0 million to $315.0 million and its first quarter 2008 operating income to be in the range of 10.0% to 12.0% of the total year.

Financial Data

(US$ in Thousands)	12/31/2007	12/31/2006	12/31/2005	12/31/2004	10/29/2004	12/31/2003	12/31/2002
Earnings Per Share	1.25	0.92	0.56	0.13	...	...	...
Cash Flow Per Share	2.53	1.92	3.19	0.33	...	...	...
Income Statement							
Total Revenue	1,665,000	1,501,527	1,208,203	199,907	715,495	1,335,350	1,031,353
EBITDA	260,600	241,292	180,571	40,427	73,680	58,974	62,604
Income Before Taxes	167,600	137,316	52,554	14,504	54,121	31,803	28,006
Income Taxes	60,900	58,557	15,459	7,275	11,970	11,438	11,910
Net Income	106,700	78,759	37,095	7,229	42,151	20,365	16,096
Average Shares	85,586	85,453	66,547	53,793	...	...	...
Balance Sheet							
Current Assets	825,700	669,032	549,415	574,012	...	672,370	...
Total Assets	1,950,900	1,771,329	1,657,871	1,751,074	...	1,063,875	...
Current Liabilities	620,500	471,500	393,180	329,662	...	336,138	...
Long-Term Obligations	370,300	505,565	598,137	816,664	...	213	...
Total Liabilities	1,145,700	1,139,458	1,143,211	1,298,177	...	498,840	...
Stockholders' Equity	805,200	631,871	514,660	452,897	...	565,035	...
Shares Outstanding	85,477	85,477	85,476	54,219	...	...	...
Statistical Record							
Return on Assets %	5.73	4.59	2.18	0.51	...	...	...
Return on Equity %	14.85	13.74	7.67	1.42	...	...	...
EBITDA Margin %	15.65	16.07	14.95	20.22	10.30	4.42	6.07
Net Margin %	6.41	5.25	3.07	3.62	5.89	1.53	1.56
Asset Turnover	0.89	0.88	0.71	0.14	...	...	...
Current Ratio	1.33	1.42	1.40	1.74	...	2.00	...
Debt to Equity	0.46	0.80	1.16	1.80	...	N.M.	...
Price Range	43.48-22.97	27.94-18.60	25.99-19.80	...	...	...	...
P/E Ratio	34.78-18.38	30.37-20.22	46.41-35.36	...	...	...	...

Address: 1200 W. Sam Houston Parkway N., Houston, TX 77043 **Telephone:** 713-467-2221	**Web Site:** www.dresser-rand.com **Officers:** William E. Macaulay - Chmn. Vincent R. Volpe Jr. - Pres., C.E.O.	**Auditors:** PricewaterhouseCoopers LLP **Transfer Agents:** The Bank of New York

DRS TECHNOLOGIES INC

Exchange	Symbol	Price	52Wk Range	Yield	P/E
NYS	DRS	$58.28 (3/31/2008)	61.24-45.92	0.21	18.10

*7 Year Price Score 107.88 *NYSE Composite Index=100 *12 Month Price Score 110.72

Interim Earnings (Per Share)

Qtr.	Jun	Sep	Dec	Mar
2004-05	0.43	0.52	0.62	0.61
2005-06	0.49	0.66	0.69	0.83
2006-07	0.52	0.62	0.86	1.11
2007-08	0.04	1.04	1.03	...

Interim Dividends (Per Share)

Amt	Decl	Ex	Rec	Pay
0.03Q	5/11/2007	6/13/2007	6/15/2007	6/29/2007
0.03Q	8/10/2007	9/12/2007	9/14/2007	9/28/2007
0.03Q	11/9/2007	12/12/2007	12/14/2007	12/31/2007
0.03Q	2/8/2008	3/12/2008	3/14/2008	3/31/2008

Indicated Div: $0.12

Valuation Analysis

		Institutional Holding	
Forecast P/E	13.90	No of Institutions	
	(1/10/2007)	225	
Market Cap	$2.4 Billion	Shares	45,152,432
Book Value	1.6 Billion	% Held	
Price/Book	1.49	N/A	
Price/Sales	0.76		

Business Summary: Instruments and Related Products (MIC: 11.15 SIC: 3812 NAIC: 334511)

DRS Technologies is a supplier of defense electronic products, systems and military support services. Co. provides products and services to branches of the U.S. military, aerospace and defense prime contractors, government intelligence agencies, international military forces and industrial markets. Co. focuses on several areas, such as command and control, intelligence, surveillance, reconnaissance, power management, battlefield digitization, advanced communications and networks, military vehicle diagnostics, troop sustainment and technical support.

Recent Developments: For the quarter ended Dec 31 2007, net income increased 21.4% to US$42.6 million from US$35.1 million in the year-earlier quarter. Revenues were US$836.6 million, up 23.0% from US$680.4 million the year before. Operating income was US$91.7 million versus US$76.6 million in the prior-year quarter, an increase of 19.7%. Indirect operating expenses increased 23.4% to US$744.9 million from US$603.7 million in the equivalent prior-year period.

Prospects: Co.'s recent results have been positively affected by solid revenue growth, primarily driven by increased shipments of driver vision enhancement equipment and components for ground-based vehicles and increased demand for and services provided under the R2 program. Also, revenues increased due to higher shipments of thermal imaging systems and subsystems for long-range surveillance systems, thermal weapons sights and combat display workstations. As a result, Co. has raised its guidance for the fiscal year ending Mar 2008, expecting revenues of $3.18 billion to $3.23 billion, operating margin to be better than 10.0%, as well as diluted earnings of $3.24 to $3.31 per share.

Financial Data

(US$ in Thousands)	9 Mos	6 Mos	3 Mos	03/31/2007	03/31/2006	03/31/2005	03/31/2004	03/31/2003
Earnings Per Share	3.22	3.05	2.63	3.12	2.67	2.18	1.80	1.58
Cash Flow Per Share	6.20	5.52	5.49	4.90	5.30	5.11	4.22	2.82
Dividends Per Share	0.120	0.120	0.120	0.120	0.120	...	...	...
Dividend Payout %	3.73	3.93	4.56	3.85	4.49	...	...	...
Income Statement								
Total Revenue	2,356,009	1,519,399	735,630	2,821,113	1,735,532	1,308,600	1,001,250	675,762
EBITDA	271,104	159,457	49,284	383,896	243,824	184,469	133,936	83,520
Depn & Amortn	57,263	37,360	18,513	...	...	...	...	...
Income Before Taxes	131,137	66,220	2,620	188,594	135,050	105,123	81,101	57,450
Income Taxes	43,832	21,536	970	60,104	51,994	44,842	34,430	25,701
Net Income	87,305	44,684	1,650	127,060	81,494	60,677	44,720	30,171
Average Shares	41,469	41,360	41,253	40,778	30,576	27,833	24,777	19,073
Balance Sheet								
Current Assets	1,138,499	1,071,705	1,029,399	1,125,662	903,565	801,896	502,207	389,299
Total Assets	4,223,507	4,152,395	4,119,171	4,214,710	4,021,894	1,893,498	1,595,388	972,121
Current Liabilities	802,084	734,309	712,218	770,532	703,363	422,092	387,754	289,275
Long-Term Obligations	1,654,335	1,705,943	1,732,102	1,783,046	1,828,771	727,611	565,654	216,837
Total Liabilities	2,604,050	2,584,498	2,605,433	2,712,260	2,670,314	1,222,070	999,763	533,941
Stockholders' Equity	1,619,457	1,567,897	1,513,738	1,502,450	1,351,580	671,428	595,625	438,180
Shares Outstanding	41,358	41,189	41,081	40,673	39,912	27,472	27,063	22,421
Statistical Record								
Return on Assets %	3.17	3.03	2.62	3.09	2.76	3.48	3.47	3.84
Return on Equity %	8.65	8.43	7.43	8.90	8.06	9.58	8.63	8.68
EBITDA Margin %	11.51	10.49	6.70	13.61	14.05	14.10	13.38	12.36
Net Margin %	3.71	2.94	0.22	4.50	4.70	4.64	4.47	4.46
Asset Turnover	0.75	0.73	0.71	0.69	0.59	0.75	0.78	0.86
Current Ratio	1.42	1.46	1.45	1.46	1.28	1.90	1.30	1.35
Debt to Equity	1.02	1.09	1.14	1.19	1.35	1.08	0.95	0.49
Price Range	61.24-45.92	58.14-43.29	57.27-36.09	57.56-36.09	56.16-42.50	45.09-26.78	31.71-23.49	48.15-21.10
P/E Ratio	19.02-14.26	19.06-14.19	21.78-13.72	18.45-11.57	21.03-15.92	20.68-12.28	17.62-13.05	30.47-13.35
Average Yield %	0.22	0.23	0.24	0.24	0.24	...	...	...

Address: 5 Sylvan Way, Parsippany, NJ 07054	Web Site: www.drs.com	Auditors: KPMG LLP
Telephone: 973-898-1500	Officers: Mark S. Newman - Chmn., Pres., C.E.O.	Investor Contact: 973-898-1500
Fax: 973-898-4730	Richard A. Schneider - Exec. V.P., C.F.O.	Transfer Agents: Mellon Investor Services

DST SYSTEMS INC. (DE)

Exchange	Symbol	Price	52Wk Range	Yield	P/E
NYS	DST	$65.74 (3/31/2008)	88.23-65.15	N/A	5.32

*7 Year Price Score 121.56 *NYSE Composite Index=100 *12 Month Price Score 95.55

Interim Earnings (Per Share)

Qtr.	Mar	Jun	Sep	Dec
2003	0.43	0.44	0.45	1.45
2004	0.60	0.60	0.61	0.79
2005	0.61	2.11	1.97	0.72
2006	1.11	0.76	0.76	1.15
2007	0.90	1.01	9.62	0.98

Interim Dividends (Per Share)

No Dividends Paid

Valuation Analysis		Institutional Holding	
Forecast P/E	16.31	No of Institutions	
	(1/10/2007)	236	
Market Cap	$4.0 Billion	Shares	
Book Value	1.2 Billion	54,145,820	
Price/Book	3.45	% Held	
Price/Sales	1.74	82.17	

Business Summary: IT & Technology (MIC: 10.2 SIC: 7374 NAIC: 518111)

DST Systems is engaged in the business of providing information processing and software services and products. As of Dec 31 2007, Co. conducted its businesses through two operating segments. Co.'s Financial Services Segment provides information processing and computer software services and products using software systems primarily to mutual funds, investment managers, insurance companies, banks, brokers, financial planners, real estate partnerships, providers of healthcare plans, third party administrators, medical practice groups and healthcare providers. Co.'s Output Solutions Segment provides single source, integrated print and electronic statement and billing output applications.

Recent Developments: For the year ended Dec 31 2007, net income increased 220.5% to US$874.7 million from US$272.9 million in the prior year. Revenues were US$2.30 billion, up 3.0% from US$2.24 billion the year before. Operating income was US$343.9 million versus US$305.3 million in the prior year, an increase of 12.6%. Indirect operating expenses increased 1.5% to US$1.96 billion from US$1.93 billion in the equivalent prior-year period.

Prospects: Beginning in July 2008, Co. expects to derive revenues from non-traded Real Estate Investment Trust participant through the introduction of its TA2000 software system, which is slated to provide recordkeeping and accounting and clerical processing services as well as other related products. Also, Co. anticipates that the Jul 31 2007 acquisition of TASS, LLC and the conversion of subaccounts attained in the second quarter of 2007 should expand its existing mutual fund subaccounting capabilities and offerings. Meanwhile, as of Jan 21 2008, Co. had about 530,000 mutual fund shareowner accounts and about 7.1 million mutual fund subaccounts, which are expected to convert in throughout 2008.

Financial Data

(US$ in Thousands)	12/31/2007	12/31/2006	12/31/2005	12/31/2004	12/31/2003	12/31/2002	12/31/2001	12/31/2000
Earnings Per Share	12.35	3.78	5.39	2.59	2.77	1.72	1.81	1.67
Cash Flow Per Share	0.85	5.47	2.23	4.73	3.24	3.28	3.00	2.66
Tang Book Value Per Share	16.56	5.58	5.60	6.69	3.56	8.63	10.58	12.48
Income Statement								
Total Revenue	2,302,500	2,235,800	2,515,100	2,428,600	2,416,300	2,383,800	1,660,000	1,362,100
EBITDA	1,579,900	585,200	926,000	534,600	606,200	474,000	520,400	471,200
Income Before Taxes	1,389,200	378,500	703,000	322,000	430,100	316,600	353,500	336,700
Income Taxes	514,500	105,600	278,400	99,200	109,300	107,600	125,300	120,900
Net Income	874,700	272,900	424,600	222,800	320,800	209,000	228,200	215,800
Average Shares	70,700	72,100	78,700	86,100	116,000	121,700	126,000	129,400
Balance Sheet								
Current Assets	739,000	652,500	760,400	796,000	681,800	665,100	604,800	590,700
Total Assets	3,395,900	3,119,100	3,029,500	3,383,400	3,198,600	2,744,200	2,704,000	2,552,400
Current Liabilities	1,526,200	1,596,300	1,622,300	713,500	572,200	546,500	471,400	356,200
Long-Term Obligations	97,200	493,200	541,400	1,373,700	1,437,800	379,500	243,400	68,700
Total Liabilities	2,236,800	2,546,800	2,533,800	2,637,600	2,514,900	1,322,200	1,231,600	986,600
Stockholders' Equity	1,159,100	572,300	495,700	745,800	683,700	1,422,000	1,472,400	1,565,800
Shares Outstanding	60,800	65,700	71,700	80,200	83,900	119,600	120,400	121,800
Statistical Record								
Return on Assets %	26.85	8.88	13.24	6.75	10.80	7.67	8.68	8.82
Return on Equity %	101.04	51.10	68.40	31.09	30.47	14.44	15.02	14.21
EBITDA Margin %	68.62	26.17	36.82	22.01	25.09	19.88	31.35	34.59
Net Margin %	37.99	12.21	16.88	9.17	13.28	8.77	13.75	15.84
Asset Turnover	0.71	0.73	0.78	0.74	0.81	0.88	0.63	0.56
Current Ratio	0.48	0.41	0.47	1.12	1.19	1.22	1.28	1.66
Debt to Equity	0.08	0.86	1.09	1.84	2.10	0.27	0.17	0.04
Price Range	88.23-63.05	63.89-55.31	62.14-44.38	52.25-41.30	41.90-24.30	50.50-24.37	66.25-39.90	74.06-26.69
P/E Ratio	7.14-5.11	16.90-14.63	11.53-8.23	20.17-15.95	15.13-8.77	29.36-14.17	36.60-22.04	44.35-15.98

Address: 333 West 11th Street, Kansas City, MO 64105
Telephone: 816-435-1000
Fax: 816-435-8630

Web Site: www.dstsystems.com
Officers: Thomas A. McDonnell - Pres., C.E.O.
Thomas A. McCullough - Exec. V.P., C.O.O.

Auditors: PricewaterhouseCoopers LLP
Transfer Agents: Computershare Trust Company, N.A., Providence, RI

DTE ENERGY CO.

Exchange	Symbol	Price	52Wk Range	Yield	P/E
NYS	DTE	$38.89 (3/31/2008)	54.20-38.71	5.45	6.82

*7 Year Price Score 87.82 *NYSE Composite Index=100 *12 Month Price Score 92.75

Interim Earnings (Per Share)

Qtr.	Mar	Jun	Sep	Dec
2003	0.92	(0.23)	1.04	1.36
2004	1.09	0.20	0.54	0.65
2005	0.70	0.17	0.02	2.16
2006	0.76	(0.19)	1.06	0.79
2007	0.76	2.20	1.19	1.55

Interim Dividends (Per Share)

Amt	Decl	Ex	Rec	Pay
0.53Q	6/1/2007	6/14/2007	6/18/2007	7/15/2007
0.53Q	8/31/2007	9/17/2007	9/19/2007	10/15/2007
0.53Q	12/7/2007	12/13/2007	12/17/2007	1/15/2008
0.53Q	3/7/2008	3/17/2008	3/19/2008	4/15/2008

Indicated Div: $2.12

Valuation Analysis

Institutional Holding	
Forecast P/E	16.44
	(1/10/2007)
Market Cap	$6.3 Billion
Book Value	5.9 Billion
Price/Book	1.08
Price/Sales	0.75

No of Institutions
294
Shares
117,273,736
% Held
66.21

TRADING VOLUME (thousand shares)

Business Summary: Electricity (MIC: 7.1 SIC: 4911 NAIC: 221121)

DTE Energy is a holding company. As of Dec 31 2007, Co.'s utility operations consisted primarily of Detroit Edison, which is engaged in the generation, purchase, distribution and sale of electricity to 2.2 million customers in southeastern Michigan, and Michigan Consolidated Gas, which is engaged in the purchase, storage, transmission, distribution and sale of natural gas to 1.3 million customers throughout Michigan. Co. also has four non-utility segments that are involved in coal transportation and marketing, gas pipelines processing and storage, unconventional gas project development and production, power and industrial projects, and energy marketing and trading operations.

Recent Developments: For the year ended Dec 31 2007, income from continuing operations increased 102.3% to US$787.0 million from US$389.0 million a year earlier. Net income increased 124.2% to US$971.0 million from US$433.0 million in the prior year. Revenues were US$8.51 billion, up 4.3% from US$8.16 billion the year before. Operating income was US$1.64 billion versus US$1.06 billion in the prior year, an increase of 54.2%. Direct operating expenses rose 12.4% to US$6.45 billion from US$5.73 billion in the comparable period the year before. Indirect operating expenses decreased 68.8% to US$426.0 million from US$1.37 billion in the equivalent prior-year period.

Prospects: For 2008, Co. reiterates its operating earnings guidance of $2.70 to $3.10 per diluted share, reflecting robust financial condition from both its Detroit Edison and Michigan Consolidated Gas subsidiaries. Meanwhile, Co. is progressing on its non-utility monetization plan, which entails selling assets in select non-utility businesses that have grown to a sufficient size and scale. For instance, on Jan 15 2008, Co. closed the sale of a portion of its Barnett Shale gas properties near Dallas, TX, for $250.0 million. Thus, following the close of its Power & Industrial transaction targeted later in the first quarter of 2008, Co. expects total cash proceeds from this plan of $1.70 billion.

Financial Data

(US$ in Thousands)	12/31/2007	12/31/2006	12/31/2005	12/31/2004	12/31/2003	12/31/2002	12/31/2001	12/31/2000
Earnings Per Share	5.70	2.43	3.05	2.49	3.09	3.83	2.16	3.27
Cash Flow Per Share	6.66	8.23	5.72	5.75	5.66	5.94	5.30	7.59
Tang Book Value Per Share	23.22	21.00	20.88	19.98	19.10	14.61	18.13	28.15
Dividends Per Share	2.120	2.075	2.060	2.060	2.060	2.060	2.060	2.060
Dividend Payout %	37.19	85.39	67.54	82.73	66.67	53.79	95.37	63.00
Income Statement								
Total Revenue	8,506,000	9,022,000	9,022,000	7,114,000	7,041,000	6,749,000	7,849,000	5,597,000
EBITDA	2,589,000	1,817,000	1,831,000	1,603,000	1,557,000	1,851,000	1,482,000	1,571,000
Income Before Taxes	1,155,000	324,000	497,000	396,000	357,000	573,000	219,000	477,000
Income Taxes	364,000	137,000	202,000	165,000	(123,000)	(59,000)	(110,000)	9,000
Net Income	971,000	433,000	537,000	431,000	521,000	632,000	332,000	468,000
Average Shares	170,000	178,000	176,000	173,300	168,300	164,767	154,000	143,000
Balance Sheet								
Net PPE	11,408,000	11,451,000	10,830,000	10,491,000	10,324,000	9,813,000	9,543,000	7,387,000
Total Assets	23,754,000	23,785,000	23,335,000	21,297,000	20,753,000	19,238,000	19,228,000	12,662,000
Long-Term Obligations	6,971,000	7,474,000	7,080,000	7,606,000	7,669,000	7,514,000	7,654,000	4,062,000
Total Liabilities	17,853,000	17,936,000	17,566,000	15,749,000	15,466,000	14,402,000	14,365,000	4,730,000
Stockholders' Equity	5,853,000	5,849,000	5,769,000	5,548,000	5,287,000	4,565,000	4,589,000	4,015,000
Shares Outstanding	163,232	177,138	177,814	174,209	168,606	167,462	142,651	142,651
Statistical Record								
Return on Assets %	4.09	1.84	2.41	2.04	2.61	3.29	2.08	3.74
Return on Equity %	16.60	7.45	9.49	7.93	10.58	13.81	7.72	11.78
EBITDA Margin %	30.44	20.14	20.29	22.53	22.11	27.43	18.88	28.07
Net Margin %	11.42	4.80	5.95	6.06	7.40	9.36	4.23	8.36
PPE Turnover	0.74	0.81	0.85	0.68	0.70	0.70	0.93	0.77
Asset Turnover	0.36	0.38	0.40	0.34	0.35	0.35	0.49	0.45
Debt to Equity	1.19	1.28	1.23	1.37	1.45	1.65	1.67	1.01
Price Range	54.20-43.96	49.19-39.00	48.11-41.81	45.30-38.07	49.28-34.54	47.68-34.10	46.68-33.75	39.19-29.19
P/E Ratio	9.51-7.71	20.24-16.05	15.77-13.71	18.19-15.29	15.95-11.18	12.45-8.90	21.61-15.62	11.98-8.93
Average Yield %	4.35	4.87	4.56	5.04	5.27	4.78	4.97	6.09

Address: 2000 2nd Avenue, Room 2412, Detroit, MI 48226-1279 Telephone: 313-235-4000	Web Site: www.dteenergy.com Officers: Anthony F. Earley Jr. - Chmn., C.E.O. Stephen E. Ewing - Vice-Chmn.	Auditors: Deloitte & Touche LLP Transfer Agents: The Bank of New York, New York, NY

DU PONT (E.I.) DE NEMOURS & CO

Exchange	Symbol	Price	52Wk Range	Yield	P/E
NYS	DD	$46.76 (3/31/2008)	53.35-42.54	3.51	14.52

*7 Year Price Score 87.00 *NYSE Composite Index=100 *12 Month Price Score 103.37

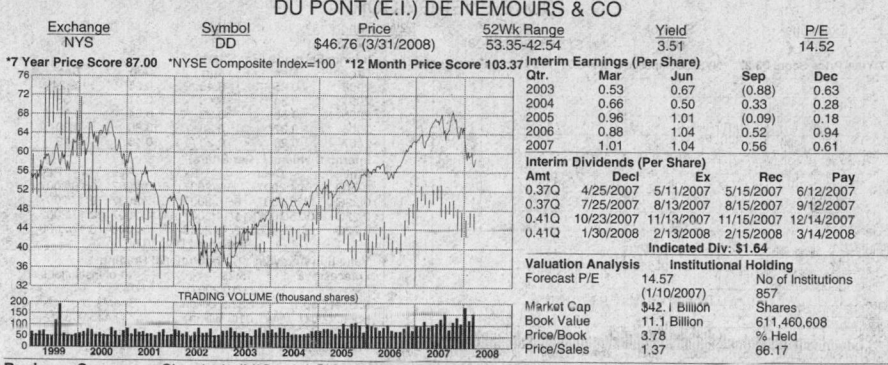

Interim Earnings (Per Share)

Qtr.	Mar	Jun	Sep	Dec
2003	0.53	0.67	(0.88)	0.63
2004	0.66	0.50	0.33	0.28
2005	0.96	1.01	(0.09)	0.18
2006	0.88	1.04	0.52	0.94
2007	1.01	1.04	0.56	0.61

Interim Dividends (Per Share)

Amt	Decl	Ex	Rec	Pay
0.37Q	4/25/2007	5/11/2007	5/15/2007	6/12/2007
0.37Q	7/25/2007	8/13/2007	8/15/2007	9/12/2007
0.41Q	10/23/2007	11/13/2007	11/15/2007	12/14/2007
0.41Q	1/30/2008	2/13/2008	2/15/2008	3/14/2008

Indicated Div: $1.64

Valuation Analysis **Institutional Holding**

Forecast P/E	14.57	No of Institutions
	(1/10/2007)	857
Market Cap	$42.1 Billion	Shares
Book Value	11.1 Billion	611,460,608
Price/Book	3.78	% Held
Price/Sales	1.37	66.17

Business Summary: Chemicals (MIC: 11.1 SIC: 2821 NAIC: 325211)

Du Pont (E.I.) de Nemours is engaged in science and technology in a range of disciplines, including biotechnology, electronics, materials science, safety and security and synthetic fibers. Co. operates globally, manufacturing a range of products for distribution and sale to many different markets, including the transportation, safety and protection, construction, motor vehicle, agriculture, home furnishings, medical electronics, communications, protective apparel and the nutrition and health markets. At Dec 31 2007, Co. is organized into: Agriculture & Nutrition; Coatings & Color Technologies; Electronic & Communication Technologies; Performance Materials; and Safety & Protection.

Recent Developments: For the year ended Dec 31 2007, net income decreased 5.1% to US$2.99 billion from US$3.15 billion in the prior year. Revenues were US$30.65 billion, up 5.8% from US$28.98 billion the year before. Direct operating expenses rose 5.5% to US$21.57 billion from US$20.44 billion in the comparable period the year before. Indirect operating expenses increased 2.5% to US$5.35 billion from US$5.21 billion in the equivalent prior-year period.

Prospects: Despite the continued weakness in U.S. housing and North American automotive markets and continued escalation of energy, ingredient and transportation costs, Co.'s 2008 outlook appears positive. In particular, Co. expects continued revenue growth in emerging markets and earnings growth across all of the growth platforms. In addition, Co. expects its results to be driven by several other factors, including new product acceleration, its pricing discipline efforts, as well as its continued cost and capital productivity gains across the company. Accordingly, Co. now projects earnings of $1.12 to $1.17 per share for the first quarter of 2008 and $3.35 to $3.55 per share for full-year 2008.

Financial Data

(US$ in Thousands)	12/31/2007	12/31/2006	12/31/2005	12/31/2004	12/31/2003	12/31/2002	12/31/2001	12/31/2000
Earnings Per Share	3.22	3.38	2.07	1.77	0.96	(1.11)	4.16	2.19
Cash Flow Per Share	4.68	4.05	2.59	3.23	2.60	2.06	2.33	4.85
Tang Book Value Per Share	6.64	4.99	4.24	6.25	4.63	4.38	7.30	4.50
Dividends Per Share	4.500	4.500	4.500	4.500	4.500	4.500	4.500	4.500
Dividend Payout %	139.75	133.14	217.39	254.24	468.75	...	108.17	205.48
Income Statement								
Total Revenue	30,653,000	28,982,000	28,491,000	27,995,000	27,730,000	24,522,000	25,370,000	29,202,000
EBITDA	5,327,000	4,940,000	4,916,000	2,789,000	1,727,000	3,639,000	8,598,000	5,307,000
Income Before Taxes	3,743,000	3,329,000	3,558,000	1,442,000	143,000	2,124,000	6,844,000	3,447,000
Income Taxes	748,000	196,000	1,468,000	(329,000)	(930,000)	185,000	2,467,000	1,072,000
Net Income	2,988,000	3,148,000	2,053,000	1,780,000	973,000	(1,103,000)	4,339,000	2,314,000
Average Shares	925,402	928,600	988,954	1,003,392	1,000,010	998,737	1,041,164	1,051,042
Balance Sheet								
Current Assets	13,160,000	12,870,000	12,422,000	15,211,000	18,462,000	13,459,000	14,801,000	11,656,000
Total Assets	34,131,000	31,777,000	33,250,000	35,632,000	37,039,000	34,621,000	40,319,000	39,426,000
Current Liabilities	8,541,000	7,940,000	7,463,000	7,939,000	13,043,000	7,096,000	8,067,000	9,255,000
Long-Term Obligations	5,955,000	6,013,000	6,783,000	5,548,000	4,301,000	5,647,000	5,350,000	6,658,000
Total Liabilities	22,553,000	21,914,000	23,853,000	23,145,000	26,761,000	23,135,000	23,443,000	25,747,000
Stockholders' Equity	11,136,000	9,422,000	8,907,000	11,377,000	9,781,000	9,063,000	14,452,000	13,299,000
Shares Outstanding	899,289	922,067	919,610	994,340	997,284	993,940	1,001,953	1,042,931
Statistical Record								
Return on Assets %	9.07	9.68	5.96	4.89	2.72	N.M.	10.88	5.75
Return on Equity %	29.07	34.35	20.24	16.78	10.33	N.M.	31.27	17.63
EBITDA Margin %	17.38	17.05	17.25	9.96	6.23	14.84	33.89	18.17
Net Margin %	9.75	10.86	7.21	6.36	3.51	N.M.	17.10	7.92
Asset Turnover	0.93	0.89	0.83	0.77	0.77	0.65	0.64	0.73
Current Ratio	1.54	1.62	1.66	1.92	1.42	1.90	1.83	1.26
Debt to Equity	0.53	0.64	0.76	0.49	0.44	0.62	0.37	0.50
Price Range	53.35-42.58	49.47-38.88	54.55-37.83	49.15-40.21	45.94-35.11	49.09-36.07	49.70-33.61	71.63-38.50
P/E Ratio	16.57-13.22	14.64-11.50	26.35-18.28	27.77-22.72	47.85-36.57	...	11.95-8.08	32.71-17.58
Average Yield %	9.13	10.53	9.97	10.31	10.85	10.40	10.37	9.19

Address: 1007 Market Street, Wilmington, DE 19898
Telephone: 302-774-1000
Fax: 302-774-0748

Web Site: www.dupont.com
Officers: Charles O. Holliday Jr. - Chmn., C.E.O.
Richard R. Goodmanson - Exec. V.P., C.O.O.

Auditors: PricewaterhouseCoopers LLP
Investor Contact: 302-774-4994
Transfer Agents: EquiServe Trust Company N.A., Providence, RI

DUKE ENERGY CORP

Exchange	Symbol	Price	52Wk Range	Yield	P/E
NYS	DUK	$17.85 (3/31/2008)	21.00-17.03	4.93	15.13

*7 Year Price Score 93.27   *NYSE Composite Index=100   *12 Month Price Score 102.10

Interim Earnings (Per Share)

Qtr.	Mar	Jun	Sep	Dec
2003	0.25	0.46	0.05	(2.24)
2004	0.34	0.46	0.41	0.33
2005	0.88	0.32	0.04	0.63
2006	0.37	0.28	0.60	0.30
2007	0.28	0.23	0.48	0.19

Interim Dividends (Per Share)

Amt	Decl	Ex	Rec	Pay
0.21Q	4/4/2007	5/9/2007	5/11/2007	6/18/2007
0.22Q	6/26/2007	8/15/2007	8/17/2007	9/17/2007
0.22Q	10/25/2007	11/14/2007	11/16/2007	12/17/2007
0.22Q	1/4/2008	2/13/2008	2/15/2008	3/17/2008

Indicated Div: $0.88

Valuation Analysis

		Institutional Holding	
Forecast P/E	15.79	No of Institutions	
	(1/10/2007)	747	
Market Cap	$22.5 Billion	Shares	739,443,008
Book Value	21.2 Billion	% Held	
Price/Book	1.06	58.82	
Price/Sales	1.77		

Business Summary: Gas Utilities (MIC: 7.4 SIC: 4923 NAIC: 221122)

Duke Energy is an energy company in the Americas. At Dec 31 2007, Co. operated the following business segments: U.S. Franchised Electric and Gas, which generates, transmits, distributes and sells electricity and transports and sells natural gas; Commercial Power, which owns, operates and manages non-regulated power plants; International Energy, which owns, operates and manages power generation facilities; and its 50.0% interest in the Crescent Resources joint venture. Co.'s principal customers for power and natural gas marketing and transportation services are industrial end-users, marketers, local distribution companies and utilities located throughout the U.S., Canada and Latin America.

Recent Developments: For the year ended Dec 31 2007, income from continuing operations increased 40.9% to US$1.52 billion from US$1.08 billion a year earlier. Net income decreased 19.5% to US$1.50 billion from US$1.86 billion in the prior year. Revenues were US$12.72 billion, up 19.9% from US$10.61 billion the year before. Operating income was US$2.49 billion versus US$1.82 billion in the prior year, an increase of 36.9%. Direct operating expenses rose 9.8% to US$7.83 billion from US$7.13 billion in the comparable period the year before. Indirect operating expenses increased 45.0% to US$2.40 billion from US$1.66 billion in the equivalent prior-year period.

Prospects: Co.'s outlook seems constructive, reflecting its focus on pursuing new supply options, pursuing low-carbon and no-carbon applications to meet future energy needs, and controlling costs. Also, Co. is encouraged by the execution of its expansion projects, including its new integrated gasification combined cycle plant at its Indiana Edwardsport Generating Station, and a new 800 megawatts coal unit at its existing Cliffside facility in North Carolina. Meanwhile, Co. is budgeting capital and investment expenditures of approximately $5.10 billion for 2008, with $3.90 billion to support its U.S. franchised electric and gas segment, which is expected to significantly contribute to future earnings.

Financial Data
(US$ in Thousands)

	12/31/2007	12/31/2006	12/31/2005	12/31/2004	12/31/2003	12/31/2002	12/31/2001	12/31/2000
Earnings Per Share	1.18	1.57	1.88	1.54	(1.48)	1.22	2.44	2.38
Cash Flow Per Share	2.55	3.20	3.00	4.43	4.35	5.42	5.99	3.02
Tang Book Value Per Share	12.55	13.54	13.65	12.85	10.74	12.51	14.10	11.49
Dividends Per Share	0.860	0.310	1.170	1.100	1.100	1.100	1.100	1.100
Dividend Payout %	72.88	19.75	62.23	71.43	...	90.16	45.08	46.22
Income Statement								
Total Revenue	12,720,000	15,184,000	16,746,000	22,503,000	22,529,000	15,663,000	59,503,000	49,318,000
EBITDA	4,615,000	6,140,000	6,687,000	5,158,000	1,655,000	4,454,000	5,379,000	5,055,000
Income Before Taxes	2,234,000	2,862,000	3,816,000	1,772,000	(1,712,000)	1,652,000	3,144,000	2,796,000
Income Taxes	712,000	843,000	1,283,000	540,000	(707,000)	618,000	1,150,000	1,020,000
Net Income	1,500,000	1,863,000	1,824,000	1,490,000	(1,323,000)	1,034,000	1,898,000	1,776,000
Average Shares	1,266,000	1,188,000	970,000	966,000	903,000	838,100	767,000	739,400
Balance Sheet								
Net PPE	31,110,000	41,447,000	29,200,000	33,506,000	34,986,000	36,219,000	28,415,000	24,469,000
Total Assets	49,704,000	68,700,000	54,723,000	55,470,000	56,203,000	60,966,000	48,375,000	58,176,000
Long-Term Obligations	9,498,000	18,118,000	14,547,000	16,932,000	20,622,000	20,221,000	12,321,000	11,019,000
Total Liabilities	28,505,000	42,598,000	38,284,000	39,029,000	42,455,000	46,022,000	35,686,000	48,120,000
Stockholders' Equity	21,199,000	26,102,000	16,439,000	16,441,000	13,748,000	14,944,000	12,689,000	10,056,000
Shares Outstanding	1,262,000	1,257,000	928,000	957,000	911,000	895,000	777,000	739,000
Statistical Record								
Return on Assets %	2.53	3.02	3.31	2.66	N.M.	1.89	3.56	3.87
Return on Equity %	6.34	8.76	11.09	9.84	N.M.	7.48	16.69	18.59
EBITDA Margin %	36.28	40.44	39.93	22.92	7.35	28.44	9.04	10.25
Net Margin %	11.79	12.27	10.89	6.62	(5.87)	6.60	3.19	3.60
PPE Turnover	0.35	0.43	0.53	0.66	0.63	0.48	2.25	2.16
Asset Turnover	0.21	0.25	0.30	0.40	0.38	0.29	1.12	1.07
Debt to Equity	0.45	0.69	0.88	1.03	1.50	1.35	0.97	1.10
Price Range	21.00-17.03	19.63-15.80	17.55-14.27	15.11-11.06	12.38-7.14	23.08-9.60	27.53-19.10	26.08-13.45
P/E Ratio	17.80-14.43	12.50-10.06	9.34-7.59	9.81-7.18	...	18.92-7.87	11.28-7.83	10.96-5.65
Average Yield %	4.45	1.80	7.27	8.58	10.87	6.61	4.75	5.72

Address: 526 South Church Street, Charlotte, NC 28202-1803 Telephone: 704-594-6200 Fax: 704-382-0230	Web Site: www.duke-energy.com Officers: Paul M. Anderson - Chmn., C.E.O. Fred J. Fowler - Pres., C.O.O.	Auditors: Deloitte & Touche LLP Investor Contact: 800-488-3853 Transfer Agents: Duke Energy, Charlotte, NC

DUKE REALTY CORP.

Exchange	Symbol	Price	52Wk Range	Yield	P/E	Div Achiever
NYS	DRE	$22.81 (3/31/2008)	44.66-21.23	8.42	14.72	14 Years

*7 Year Price Score 82.16   *NYSE Composite Index=100   *12 Month Price Score 78.35

Interim Earnings (Per Share)

Qtr.	Mar	Jun	Sep	Dec
2003	0.28	0.25	0.30	0.37
2004	0.23	0.24	0.30	0.29
2005	0.18	0.28	1.48	0.23
2006	0.08	0.16	0.45	0.37
2007	0.49	0.27	0.39	0.40

Interim Dividends (Per Share)

Amt	Decl	Ex	Rec	Pay
0.475Q	4/25/2007	5/10/2007	5/14/2007	5/31/2007
0.48Q	7/25/2007	8/10/2007	8/14/2007	8/31/2007
0.48Q	10/31/2007	11/9/2007	11/14/2007	11/30/2007
0.48Q	1/30/2008	2/12/2008	2/14/2008	2/29/2008

Indicated Div: $1.92 (Div. Reinv. Plan)

Valuation Analysis

		Institutional Holding	
Forecast P/E	N/A	No of Institutions	318
Market Cap	$3.3 Billion	Shares	
Book Value	2.8 Billion		101,552,312
Price/Book	1.21	% Held	
Price/Sales	2.85		74.21

Business Summary: Property, Real Estate & Development (MIC: 8.3 SIC: 6798 NAIC: 525930)

Duke Realty is a self-administered and self-managed real estate investment trust company. As of Dec 31 2007, Co.'s 726 rental properties encompassed approximately 121.1 million rentable square feet and were leased by more than 3,400 tenants whose businesses include manufacturing, retailing, wholesale trade, distribution and professional services. In addition, Co. owned or controlled more than 7,700 acres of unencumbered land ready for development. Through its service operations, Co. provides, on a fee basis, leasing, property and asset management, development, construction, build-to-suit, and other tenant-related services.

Recent Developments: For the year ended Dec 31 2007, income from continuing operations increased 5.2% to US$159.2 million from US$151.4 million a year earlier. Net income increased 36.9% to US$279.5 million from US$204.1 million in the prior year. Revenues were US$1.17 billion, up 1.2% from US$1.16 billion the year before. Revenues from property income rose 6.9% to US$794.5 million from US$743.5 million in the corresponding earlier year

Prospects: Co.'s outlook appears somewhat mixed. For instance, Co.'s pipeline totaled $2.00 billion, including $742.0 million of developments with an expected stabilized return of 9.0% that it plans to own indefinitely after completion; $1.00 billion of developments with an expected stabilized return of 8.4% that Co. plans to sell within about one year of completion; and a $183.0 million backlog of third-party construction volume with an average overall profit margin of 15.8%. However, Co. noted that the volatility in the capital markets has increased uncertainty in the business climate, and thus, has revised its 2008 funds from operations per share guidance to $2.60 to $2.90 from $2.80 to $3.00.

Financial Data

(US$ in Thousands)	12/31/2007	12/31/2006	12/31/2005	12/31/2004	12/31/2003	12/31/2002	12/31/2001	12/31/2000
Earnings Per Share	1.55	1.07	2.17	1.06	1.19	1.19	1.75	1.66
Cash Flow Per Share	2.33	2.04	2.86	2.67	2.72	4.25	3.34	3.53
Tang Book Value Per Share	13.72	12.15	13.33	15.18	15.57	16.11	16.56	16.45
Dividends Per Share	1.910	1.890	2.920	1.850	1.830	1.810	1.760	1.640
Dividend Payout %	123.23	176.64	134.56	174.53	153.78	152.10	100.57	98.80
Income Statement								
Property Income	794,488	780,671	676,634	744,065	706,722	684,311	691,958	697,270
Non-Property Income	375,611	412,762	459,753	421,934	343,074	268,319	341,695	97,355
Total Revenue	1,170,099	1,193,433	1,136,387	1,165,999	1,049,796	952,630	1,033,653	794,625
Interest Expense	168,358	179,007	120,369	135,130	129,160	117,073	113,830	133,948
Net Income	279,467	204,147	355,662	188,701	199,232	206,325	282,409	261,939
Average Shares	149,614	149,393	155,877	157,062	151,141	150,839	151,710	147,441
Balance Sheet								
Total Assets	7,661,981	7,238,595	5,647,560	5,896,643	5,561,249	5,348,823	5,330,033	5,460,036
Long-Term Obligations	4,316,460	3,961,845	2,600,651	2,518,704	2,335,536	2,106,285	1,814,856	1,973,215
Total Liabilities	4,828,265	4,578,159	3,012,196	2,875,661	2,681,706	2,424,002	2,149,834	2,311,829
Stockholders' Equity	2,750,033	2,503,583	2,452,798	2,825,869	2,666,749	2,616,180	2,785,009	2,712,890
Shares Outstanding	146,175	133,921	134,697	142,894	136,594	135,007	131,416	127,932
Statistical Record								
Return on Assets %	3.75	3.17	6.16	3.28	3.65	3.86	5.23	4.77
Return on Equity %	10.64	8.24	13.48	6.85	7.54	7.64	10.27	9.71
Net Margin %	23.88	17.11	31.30	16.18	18.98	21.66	27.32	32.96
Price Range	48.21-24.76	43.95-33.33	34.72-29.40	35.77-28.76	31.75-24.50	28.95-22.42	25.97-22.00	25.75-17.88
P/E Ratio	31.10-15.97	41.07-31.15	16.00-13.55	33.75-27.13	26.68-20.59	24.33-18.84	14.84-12.57	15.51-10.77
Average Yield %	5.19	5.10	9.05	5.68	6.53	7.15	7.36	7.45

Address: 600 East 96th Street, Suite 100, Indianapolis, IN 46240 Telephone: 317-808-6000 Fax: 317-808-6770	Web Site: www.dukerealty.com Officers: Thomas L. Hefner - Chmn., C.E.O. Dennis D. Oklak - Pres., C.O.O.	Auditors: KPMG LLP Investor Contact: 317-808-6005 Transfer Agents: American Stock Transfer & Trust Company, New York, NY

DUN & BRADSTREET CORP (DE)

Exchange	Symbol	Price	52Wk Range	Yield	P/E
NYS	DNB	$81.38 (3/31/2008)	106.63-81.02	1.47	16.31

*7 Year Price Score 129.58 ***NYSE Composite Index=100** ***12 Month Price Score 100.09**

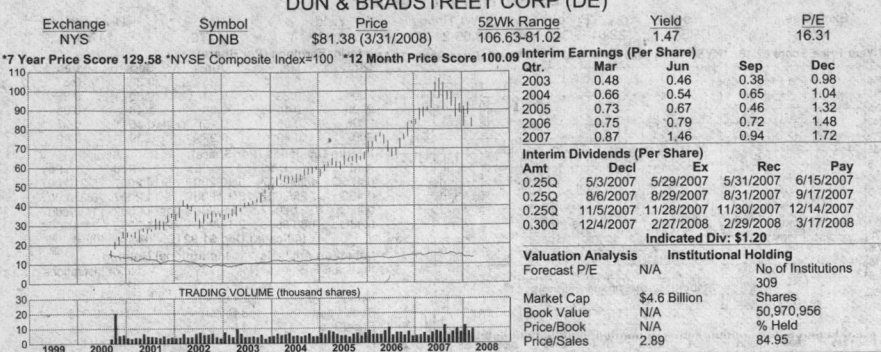

Interim Earnings (Per Share)

Qtr.	Mar	Jun	Sep	Dec
2003	0.48	0.46	0.38	0.98
2004	0.66	0.54	0.65	1.04
2005	0.73	0.67	0.46	1.32
2006	0.75	0.79	0.72	1.48
2007	0.87	1.46	0.94	1.72

Interim Dividends (Per Share)

Amt	Decl	Ex	Rec	Pay
0.25Q	5/3/2007	5/29/2007	5/31/2007	6/15/2007
0.25Q	8/6/2007	8/29/2007	8/31/2007	9/17/2007
0.25Q	11/5/2007	11/28/2007	11/30/2007	12/14/2007
0.30Q	12/4/2007	2/27/2008	2/29/2008	3/17/2008

Indicated Div: $1.20

Valuation Analysis | **Institutional Holding**

Forecast P/E	N/A	No of Institutions
		309
Market Cap	$4.6 Billion	Shares
Book Value	N/A	50,970,956
Price/Book	N/A	% Held
Price/Sales	2.89	84.95

Business Summary: Miscellaneous Business Services (MIC: 12.8 SIC: 7389 NAIC: 518111)

Dun & Bradstreet is engaged in providing commercial information and insight on businesses. Co. provides its customers with four service sets, including Risk Management Solutions™; Sales & Marketing Solutions™; E-Business Solutions™; and Supply Management Solutions™. As of Dec 31 2007, Co.'s global commercial database contained more than 125.0 million business records. Also, at Dec 31 2007, Co. managed its business through two business segments: U.S., which consists solely of its U.S. operations; and International, which consists of its operations in Canada, Europe, Asia Pacific and Latin America.

Recent Developments: For the year ended Dec 31 2007, income from continuing operations increased 22.6% to US$292.7 million from US$238.7 million a year earlier. Net income increased 23.8% to US$298.1 million from US$240.7 million in the prior year. Revenues were US$1.60 billion, up 8.4% from US$1.47 billion the year before. Operating income was US$425.6 million versus US$393.7 million in the prior year, an increase of 8.1%. Direct operating expenses rose 4.7% to US$430.4 million from US$410.9 million in the comparable period the year before. Indirect operating expenses increased 10.9% to US$743.2 million from US$670.3 million in the equivalent prior-year period.

Prospects: For the full year of 2008, Co. continues to anticipate revenue growth of 8.0% to 10.0%, excluding the effect of foreign translation. In addition, Co. is targeting operating income to grow by 11.0% to 13.0% and earnings to improve in the 14.0% to 16.0% range, excluding non-core gains and charges. Meanwhile, Co. noted that it has completed the acquisition of AllBusiness.com, Inc. for approximately $55.0 million on Dec 4 2007, which should strengthen its Internet capabilities while expanding its advertising-based revenue stream. Accordingly, Co. expects this transaction to generate approximately $10.0 million of incremental revenue in 2008 and to be accretive to its earnings in 2009.

Financial Data
(US$ in Thousands)

	12/31/2007	12/31/2006	12/31/2005	12/31/2004	12/31/2003	12/31/2002	12/31/2001	12/31/2000
Earnings Per Share	4.99	3.70	3.19	2.90	2.30	1.87	1.88	2.52
Cash Flow Per Share	6.76	4.82	3.91	3.79	3.21	2.86	2.73	0.29
Dividends Per Share	1.000	...	...	...	...	...	...	...
Dividend Payout %	20.04	...	...	...	...	...	...	...
Income Statement								
Total Revenue	1,599,200	1,531,300	1,443,600	1,414,000	1,386,400	1,275,600	1,308,800	1,417,600
EBITDA	509,800	435,200	413,000	398,600	358,800	339,900	363,200	267,600
Income Before Taxes	426,300	388,900	354,100	340,800	280,400	239,200	257,800	151,700
Income Taxes	135,800	146,800	133,600	129,200	106,200	94,100	101,100	78,100
Net Income	298,100	240,700	221,200	211,800	174,500	143,400	153,200	206,600
Average Shares	59,800	65,100	69,415	73,104	75,826	76,874	81,510	81,994
Balance Sheet								
Current Assets	718,300	645,000	759,300	762,100	730,800	614,200	580,200	538,600
Total Assets	1,658,800	1,360,100	1,613,400	1,635,500	1,624,700	1,527,700	1,431,200	1,423,600
Current Liabilities	910,000	805,500	1,029,100	713,600	735,900	718,100	662,700	743,100
Long-Term Obligations	724,800	458,900	100	300,000	299,900	299,900	299,600	...
Total Liabilities	2,095,300	1,756,600	1,535,800	1,581,300	1,576,300	1,546,500	1,452,100	1,474,600
Stockholders' Equity	(440,100)	(399,100)	77,600	54,200	48,400	(18,800)	(20,900)	(51,000)
Shares Outstanding	56,800	60,100	67,057	68,613	72,253	74,358	76,878	80,154
Statistical Record								
Return on Assets %	19.75	16.19	13.62	12.96	11.07	9.69	10.73	13.74
Return on Equity %	...	...	335.66	411.74	1,179.05	...	...	...
EBITDA Margin %	31.88	28.42	28.61	28.19	25.88	26.65	27.75	18.88
Net Margin %	18.64	15.72	15.32	14.98	12.59	11.24	11.71	14.57
Asset Turnover	1.06	1.03	0.89	0.87	0.88	0.86	0.92	0.94
Current Ratio	0.79	0.80	0.74	1.07	0.99	0.86	0.88	0.72
Debt to Equity	...	...	N.M.	5.54	6.20	...	...	...
Price Range	106.63-82.28	84.25-65.50	67.88-55.04	60.37-48.18	50.71-32.62	43.08-28.32	36.25-21.23	26.94-13.50
P/E Ratio	21.37-16.49	22.77-17.70	21.28-17.25	20.82-16.61	22.05-14.18	23.04-15.14	19.28-11.29	10.69-5.36
Average Yield %	1.07	...	...	...	...	...	...	...

Address: 103 JFK Parkway, Short hills, NJ 07078	**Web Site:** www.dnb.com	**Auditors:** PricewaterhouseCoopers LLP
Telephone: 973-921-5500	**Officers:** Steven W. Alesio - Chmn., Pres., C.E.O. Cynthia B. Hamburger - Sr. V.P., Customer Opers.	**Transfer Agents:** Computershare Trust Company, N.A., Providence, RI

DYCOM INDUSTRIES, INC.

Exchange	Symbol	Price	52Wk Range	Yield	P/E
NYS	DY	$12.01 (3/31/2008)	32.36-11.16	N/A	12.78

*7 Year Price Score 100.07 *NYSE Composite Index=100   *12 Month Price Score 61.55

TRADING VOLUME (thousand shares)

Interim Earnings (Per Share)

Qtr.	Oct	Jan	Apr	Jul
2004-05	0.32	0.15	0.28	(0.26)
2005-06	0.23	0.10	(0.16)	0.24
2006-07	0.24	0.14	0.31	0.35
2007-08	0.36	(0.08)	...	...

Interim Dividends (Per Share)

No Dividends Paid

Valuation Analysis

Institutional Holding		
Forecast P/E	19.06	No of Institutions
	(1/10/2007)	134
Market Cap	$492.6 Million	Shares
Book Value	454.6 Million	38,071,980
Price/Book	1.08	% Held
Price/Sales	0.40	93.64

Business Summary: Construction - Public Infrastructure (MIC: 3.1 SIC: 1623 NAIC: 237130)

Dycom Industries, through its subsidiaries, is a provider of specialty contracting services. These services are provided throughout the U.S. and include engineering, construction, maintenance and installation services to telecommunications providers, underground locating services to various utilities including telecommunications providers, and other construction and maintenance services to electric utilities and others. In addition, Co. maintains and installs underground natural gas transmission and distribution systems for gas companies. Additionally, Co. provides services on a limited basis in Canada.

Recent Developments: For the quarter ended Jan 26 2008, loss from continuing operations was US$3.1 million compared with income of US$5.6 million in the year-earlier quarter. Net loss amounted to US$3.2 million versus net income of US$5.6 million in the year-earlier quarter. Revenues were US$284.8 million, up 10.2% from US$258.3 million the year before. Direct operating expenses rose 17.6% to US$247.9 million from US$210.8 million in the comparable period the year before. Indirect operating expenses increased 10.4% to US$39.2 million from US$35.5 million in the equivalent prior-year period.

Prospects: Co.'s near-term outlook appears to be encouraging. In detail, Co. is experiencing solid revenue growth, driven primarily by an increase in specialty contracting services provided to telecommunications companies, higher revenues from construction and maintenance services provided to electric utilities and other customers as well as an improvement in underground facility locating services revenues. In this respect, for the fiscal quarter ended Apr 26 2008, Co. is projecting revenues from continuing operations to be in the range of $270.0 million to $295.0 million. In addition, Co. is forecasting earnings from continuing operations in the range of $0.08 to $0.13 per diluted share.

Financial Data
(US$ in Thousands)

	6 Mos	3 Mos	07/28/2007	07/29/2006	07/30/2005	07/31/2004	07/26/2003	07/27/2002
Earnings Per Share	0.94	1.16	1.03	0.43	0.49	1.20	0.36	(2.73)
Cash Flow Per Share	2.65	2.78	2.69	2.45	1.80	2.53	0.53	1.45
Tang Book Value Per Share	3.35	3.40	3.02	3.06	6.60	5.34	7.15	6.76
Income Statement								
Total Revenue	614,430	329,672	1,137,812	1,023,673	986,627	872,716	618,183	624,021
EBITDA	56,431	42,688	141,122	98,483	104,295	139,435	68,229	9,633
Depn & Amortn	29,729	14,411	...	...	...	...	...	...
Income Before Taxes	19,961	24,931	69,477	40,430	58,634	97,180	30,455	(26,590)
Income Taxes	7,837	9,674	27,275	22,250	34,320	38,547	13,306	9,508
Net Income	11,702	14,927	41,884	18,180	24,314	58,633	17,149	(123,027)
Average Shares	40,799	41,174	40,713	47,056	49,184	48,819	47,886	45,049
Balance Sheet								
Current Assets	285,948	312,117	292,437	254,508	341,079	276,033	305,473	256,736
Total Assets	788,418	815,353	789,764	690,015	696,709	651,835	536,543	514,553
Current Liabilities	120,566	126,699	127,252	111,794	118,712	102,478	70,734	70,551
Long-Term Obligations	152,119	167,786	163,509	150,009	4,179	7,094	20	30
Total Liabilities	333,819	357,062	345,133	300,560	146,899	132,874	86,203	83,256
Stockholders' Equity	454,599	458,291	444,631	389,455	549,810	518,961	450,340	431,297
Shares Outstanding	41,017	40,968	41,005	40,612	48,865	48,596	47,986	47,846
Statistical Record								
Return on Assets %	5.03	6.01	5.68	2.63	3.62	9.71	3.27	N.M.
Return on Equity %	8.93	11.02	10.07	3.88	4.56	11.90	3.90	N.M.
EBITDA Margin %	9.18	12.95	12.40	9.62	10.57	15.98	11.04	1.54
Net Margin %	1.90	4.53	3.68	1.78	2.46	6.72	2.77	N.M.
Asset Turnover	1.60	1.52	1.54	1.48	1.47	1.44	1.18	1.15
Current Ratio	2.37	2.46	2.30	2.54	2.88	2.69	4.32	3.64
Debt to Equity	0.33	0.37	0.37	0.39	0.01	0.01	N.M.	N.M.
Price Range	32.36-21.86	32.36-20.00	31.62-16.74	24.91-17.72	35.39-18.54	29.35-16.43	17.92-8.59	22.37-8.89
P/E Ratio	34.43-23.26	27.90-17.24	30.70-16.25	57.93-41.21	72.22-37.84	24.46-13.69	49.78-23.86	...

Address: 11770 US Highway 1, Suite 101, Palm Beach Gardens, FL 33408 **Telephone:** 561-627-7171 **Fax:** 561-627-7709	**Web Site:** www.dycomind.com **Officers:** Steven E. Nielsen - Chmn., Pres., C.E.O. Timothy Estes - Exec. V.P., C.O.O.	**Auditors:** Deloitte & Touche LLP **Investor Contact:** 561-627-7171 **Transfer Agents:** Wachovia Bank, N.A.

DYNEGY INC (DE)

Exchange	Symbol	Price	52Wk Range	Yield	P/E
NYS	DYN	$7.89 (3/31/2008)	10.65-6.44	N/A	22.54

*7 Year Price Score 68.15   *NYSE Composite Index=100   *12 Month Price Score 96.24

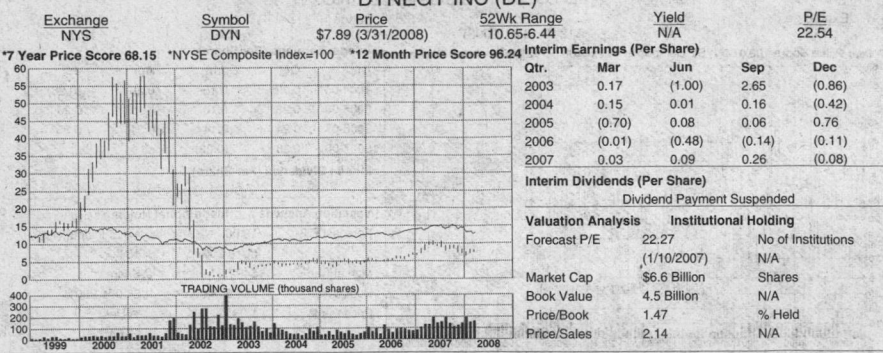

Interim Earnings (Per Share)

Qtr.	Mar	Jun	Sep	Dec
2003	0.17	(1.00)	2.65	(0.86)
2004	0.15	0.01	0.16	(0.42)
2005	(0.70)	0.08	0.06	0.76
2006	(0.01)	(0.48)	(0.14)	(0.11)
2007	0.03	0.09	0.26	(0.08)

Interim Dividends (Per Share)

Dividend Payment Suspended

Valuation Analysis   Institutional Holding

Forecast P/E	22.27	No of Institutions
	(1/10/2007)	N/A
Market Cap	$6.6 Billion	Shares
Book Value	4.5 Billion	N/A
Price/Book	1.47	% Held
Price/Sales	2.14	N/A

Business Summary: Electricity (MIC: 7.1 SIC: 4911 NAIC: 221122)

Dynegy is a holding company. Through its subsidiaries, Co. is primarily engaged in the production and sale of electric energy, capacity and ancillary services from its fleet of 29 operating power plants in 13 states totaling nearly 20,000 megawatt of generating capacity at Dec 31 2007. Co.'s customers include regional transmission organizations and independent system operators, integrated utilities, municipalities, electric cooperatives, transmission and distribution utilities, industrial customers, power marketers, financial participants such as banks and hedge funds, other power generators and commercial end-users. Co. operates through three business segments: Midwest, Northeast and West.

Recent Developments: For the year ended Dec 31 2007, income from continuing operations was US$116.0 million compared with a loss of US$321.0 million a year earlier. Net income amounted to US$264.0 million versus a net loss of US$333.0 million in the prior year. Revenues were US$3.10 billion, up 75.3% from US$1.77 billion the year before. Operating income was US$605.0 million versus US$105.0 million in the prior year, an increase of 476.2%. Direct operating expenses rose 77.2% to US$2.01 billion from US$1.14 billion in the comparable period the year before. Indirect operating expenses decreased 8.3% to US$485.0 million from US$529.0 million in the equivalent prior-year period.

Prospects: On Dec 13 2007, Co. sold a non-controlling ownership interest in Plum Point Energy Associates, LLC (PPEA), which represents about 125 megawatt (MW) of generating capacity in the Plum Point power generation facility under construction near Osceola, AR, to John Hancock Life Insurance Co. for about $82.0 million, net of non-recourse project debt. Upon closing, Co. continues to own a 37.0% interest in PPEA, representing approximately 140 MW of generating capacity, and continues in its role as administrative project manager. Separately, Co. expects the sale of its interest in the Calcasieu power generation facility to Entergy Gulf States, Inc. for about $57.0 million to close in early 2008.

Financial Data

(US$ in Thousands)	12/31/2007	12/31/2006	12/31/2005	12/31/2004	12/31/2003	12/31/2002	12/31/2001	12/31/2000
Earnings Per Share	0.35	(0.75)	0.21	(0.10)	1.35	(8.38)	1.90	1.48
Cash Flow Per Share	0.45	(0.42)	(0.08)	0.01	2.34	(0.07)	2.49	1.45
Tang Book Value Per Share	4.25	3.85	4.40	4.87	5.04	4.57	8.79	6.30
Dividends Per Share	...	...	...	...	...	0.150	0.300	0.247
Dividend Payout %	...	...	...	...	...	...	15.79	16.71
Income Statement								
Total Revenue	3,103,000	2,017,000	2,313,000	6,153,000	5,787,000	5,553,000	42,242,000	29,445,000
EBITDA	984,000	121,000	(526,000)	737,000	362,000	(1,610,000)	1,623,000	1,370,000
Income Before Taxes	267,000	(526,000)	(1,199,000)	(99,000)	(672,000)	(2,582,000)	915,000	762,000
Income Taxes	151,000	(168,000)	(395,000)	(89,000)	(198,000)	(627,000)	269,000	261,000
Net Income	264,000	(333,000)	103,000	(15,000)	(453,000)	(2,737,000)	648,000	501,000
Average Shares	752,000	509,000	513,000	504,000	423,000	418,000	340,000	315,000
Balance Sheet								
Current Assets	1,663,000	2,082,000	3,706,000	2,752,000	3,030,000	7,586,000	9,507,000	10,150,000
Total Assets	13,221,000	7,630,000	10,126,000	9,852,000	13,293,000	20,030,000	24,874,000	21,406,000
Current Liabilities	999,000	1,259,000	2,116,000	1,802,000	2,576,000	6,748,000	8,555,000	9,405,000
Long-Term Obligations	5,939,000	3,190,000	4,228,000	4,332,000	5,893,000	5,454,000	4,124,000	3,433,000
Total Liabilities	8,692,000	5,363,000	7,573,000	7,479,000	10,716,000	16,374,000	17,396,000	16,444,000
Stockholders' Equity	4,506,000	2,267,000	2,153,000	1,867,000	2,045,000	2,087,000	4,719,000	3,598,000
Shares Outstanding	840,370	498,241	400,306	380,224	375,562	370,062	355,218	332,651
Statistical Record								
Return on Assets %	2.53	N.M.	1.03	N.M.	N.M.	N.M.	2.80	3.58
Return on Equity %	7.80	N.M.	5.12	N.M.	N.M.	N.M.	15.58	20.36
EBITDA Margin %	31.71	6.00	N.M.	11.98	6.26	N.M.	3.84	4.65
Net Margin %	8.51	N.M.	4.45	N.M.	N.M.	N.M.	1.53	1.70
Asset Turnover	0.30	0.23	0.23	0.53	0.35	0.25	1.83	2.10
Current Ratio	1.66	1.65	1.75	1.53	1.18	1.12	1.11	1.08
Debt to Equity	1.32	1.41	1.96	2.32	2.88	2.61	0.87	0.95
Price Range	10.65-6.52	7.24-4.68	5.63-3.23	5.86-3.46	5.23-1.18	32.00-0.51	57.95-20.90	57.58-17.19
P/E Ratio	30.43-18.63	...	26.81-15.38	...	3.87-0.87	...	30.50-11.00	38.91-11.61
Average Yield %	...	...	...	...	...	1.36	0.68	0.65

Address: 1000 Louisiana, Suite 5800, Houston, TX 77002	Web Site: www.dynegy.com	Auditors: ERNST & YOUNG LLP
Telephone: 713-507-6400	Officers: Bruce A. Williamson - Chmn., C.E.O. Stephen A. Furbacher - Pres., C.O.O.	Transfer Agents: Mellon Investor Services LLC
Fax: 713-507-6888		

EAGLE MATERIALS INC

Exchange	Symbol	Price	52Wk Range	Yield	P/E
NYS	EXP	$35.55 (3/31/2008)	50.95-29.05	2.25	12.74

*7 Year Price Score 120.49 *NYSE Composite Index=100 *12 Month Price Score 95.52

TRADING VOLUME (thousand shares)

Interim Earnings (Per Share)

Qtr.	Jun	Sep	Dec	Mar
2004-05	0.41	0.54	0.47	0.50
2005-06	0.64	0.80	0.73	0.85
2006-07	1.16	1.32	0.83	0.76
2007-08	0.80	0.73	0.50	...

Interim Dividends (Per Share)

Amt	Decl	Ex	Rec	Pay
0.20Q	5/21/2007	6/18/2007	6/20/2007	7/20/2007
0.20Q	8/3/2007	10/3/2007	10/5/2007	11/5/2007
0.20Q	11/5/2007	12/19/2007	12/21/2007	1/21/2008
0.20Q	1/31/2008	3/18/2008	3/20/2008	4/18/2008

Indicated Div: $0.80

Valuation Analysis | **Institutional Holding**

Forecast P/E	N/A	No of Institutions
		214
Market Cap	$1.6 Billion	Shares
Book Value	434.7 Million	43,987,252
Price/Book	3.60	% Held
Price/Sales	1.97	91.02

Business Summary: Stone, Clay, Glass, and Concrete Products (MIC: 11.2 SIC: 3241 NAIC: 327310)

Eagle Materials manufactures basic building materials which include gypsum wallboard, cement, gypsum and non-gypsum paperboard, and concrete and aggregates. Co. operates in four segments: Gypsum Wallboard, Cement, Recycled Paperboard, and Concrete and Aggregates. These operations are conducted in the U.S., and include the mining of gypsum and the manufacture and sale of gypsum wallboard, the mining of limestone, the manufacture, production, distribution and sale of cement, the manufacture and sale of recycled paperboard to the gypsum wallboard industry and other paperboard converters, the sale of readymix concrete, and the mining and sale of aggregates (crushed stone, sand and gravel).

Recent Developments: For the quarter ended Dec 31 2007, net income decreased 45.3% to US$22.4 million from US$40.9 million in the year-earlier quarter. Revenues were US$173.0 million, down 19.2% from US$214.2 million the year before. Direct operating expenses declined 8.4% to US$140.8 million from US$153.8 million in the comparable period the year before. Indirect operating expenses decreased 23.5% to US$4.3 million from US$5.6 million in the equivalent prior-year period.

Prospects: Co. expects the low industry utilization rate and the soft residential construction will further hurt its operating results through fiscal year ending Mar 2009. Notably, Co. expects its recycled paperboard operations to be challenged by the low wallboard demand due to the reduction in residential construction. Co. also expects to the soft residential and infrastructure spending mainly in its northern California markets to depress its aggregate and concrete sales volumes. However, Co. believes it is well positioned to mitigate the effects of changing industry conditions given its low-cost, balanced mix of construction products and its geographical location in the sunbelt regions of the U.S.

Financial Data

(US$ in Thousands)	9 Mos	6 Mos	3 Mos	03/31/2007	03/31/2006	03/31/2005	03/31/2004	03/31/2003
Earnings Per Share	2.79	3.12	3.71	4.07	3.02	1.91	1.19	1.04
Cash Flow Per Share	3.10	4.11	4.11	4.94	3.58	2.85	2.02	2.18
Tang Book Value Per Share	8.29	7.89	9.88	9.93	7.89	7.65	7.08	7.97
Dividends Per Share	0.775	0.725	0.725	0.700	0.475	0.400	0.150	0.067
Dividend Payout %	27.78	23.24	19.54	17.20	15.73	20.94	180.67	6.43
Income Statement								
Total Revenue	604,705	431,700	221,237	922,401	859,702	616,541	502,622	501,257
EBITDA	185,463	136,894	71,629	349,154	285,344	195,246	138,959	132,994
Depn & Amortn	32,354	21,435	10,682	...	...	...	...	...
Income Before Taxes	139,778	107,824	57,463	304,288	241,066	158,089	102,123	86,613
Income Taxes	43,922	34,343	18,761	101,624	80,082	51,402	35,222	29,007
Net Income	95,856	73,481	38,702	202,664	160,984	106,687	66,901	57,606
Average Shares	44,596	47,336	48,594	49,787	53,330	55,883	56,209	55,570
Balance Sheet								
Current Assets	205,035	179,099	189,854	173,609	216,626	141,655	106,778	124,351
Total Assets	1,122,566	1,092,980	1,085,550	971,410	888,916	780,001	692,975	712,078
Current Liabilities	104,623	166,597	152,375	108,024	104,699	121,869	94,171	96,195
Long Term Obligations	400,000	320,000	200,000	200,000	200,000	54,000	58,700	55,590
Total Liabilities	687,842	673,339	541,005	425,364	424,178	294,633	253,953	232,246
Stockholders' Equity	434,724	419,641	544,545	546,046	464,738	485,368	439,022	479,832
Shares Outstanding	44,034	44,351	48,028	47,909	50,318	54,675	56,305	55,138
Statistical Record								
Return on Assets %	12.69	14.67	17.75	21.79	19.29	14.49	9.50	7.92
Return on Equity %	27.25	31.86	34.30	40.10	33.89	23.08	14.52	12.69
EBITDA Margin %	30.67	31.71	32.38	37.85	33.19	31.67	27.65	26.53
Net Margin %	15.85	17.02	17.49	21.97	18.73	17.30	13.31	11.49
Asset Turnover	0.76	0.81	0.86	0.99	1.03	0.84	0.71	0.69
Current Ratio	1.96	1.08	1.25	1.61	2.07	1.16	1.13	1.29
Debt to Equity	0.92	0.76	0.37	0.37	0.43	0.11	0.13	0.12
Price Range	50.95-33.95	50.95-32.20	50.74-32.20	74.30-32.20	63.76-25.08	28.88-19.62	20.37-12.00	15.00-10.57
P/E Ratio	18.26-12.17	16.33-10.32	13.68-8.68	18.26-7.91	21.11-8.31	15.12-10.27	17.11-10.08	14.43-10.16
Average Yield %	1.80	1.66	1.71	1.57	1.24	1.66	13.31	0.54

Address: 3811 Turtle Creek Blvd, Suite 1100, Dallas, TX 75219 **Telephone:** 214-432-2000 **Fax:** 214-432-2100	**Web Site:** www.eaglematerials.com **Officers:** Steven R. Rowley - C.E.O. Arthur R. Zunker Jr. - Sr. V.P., Finance & Treas.	**Auditors:** Ernst & Young LLP **Transfer Agents:** Mellon Investor Services LLC, Ridgefield Park, NJ

EASTGROUP PROPERTIES, INC.

Exchange	Symbol	Price	52Wk Range	Yield	P/E	Div Acheiver
NYS	EGP	$46.46 (3/31/2008)	51.60-39.44	4.48	40.75	15 Years

*7 Year Price Score 100.82 *NYSE Composite Index=100 *12 Month Price Score 104.43

Interim Earnings (Per Share)

Qtr.	Mar	Jun	Sep	Dec
2003	0.17	0.21	0.13	0.20
2004	0.21	0.22	0.32	0.24
2005	0.23	0.24	0.23	0.19
2006	0.25	0.22	0.23	0.47
2007	0.25	0.23	0.30	0.36

Interim Dividends (Per Share)

Amt	Decl	Ex	Rec	Pay
0.50Q	5/30/2007	6/13/2007	6/15/2007	6/29/2007
0.50Q	9/6/2007	9/14/2007	9/18/2007	9/28/2007
0.50Q	12/7/2007	12/14/2007	12/18/2007	12/31/2007
0.52Q	3/6/2008	3/18/2008	3/21/2008	3/31/2008

Indicated Div: $2.08 (Div. Reinv. Plan)

Valuation Analysis		Institutional Holding	
Forecast P/E	15.40	No of Institutions	
	(1/10/2007)	150	
Market Cap	$1.1 Billion	Shares	
Book Value	402.4 Million	18,788,144	
Price/Book	2.75	% Held	
Price/Sales	7.34	79.26	

Business Summary: Property, Real Estate & Development (MIC: 8.3 SIC: 6798 NAIC: 525930)

EastGroup Properties is a self-administered equity real estate investment trust focused on the development, acquisition and operation of industrial properties in major Sunbelt markets throughout the U.S. with an emphasis in the states of Florida, Texas, Arizona and California, the majority of which are clustered around major transportation features in supply constrained submarkets. Co. focuses on business distribution space for location sensitive tenants primarily in the 5,000 to 50,000 square foot range. As of Dec 31 2007, Co. owned 202 industrial properties and one office building with an additional 5.73 million square feet under development.

Recent Developments: For the year ended Dec 31 2007, income from continuing operations increased 27.5% to US$28.7 million from US$22.5 million a year earlier. Net income increased 1.7% to US$29.7 million from US$29.2 million in the prior year. Revenues were US$150.7 million, up 13.2% from US$133.1 million the year before. Revenues from property income rose 13.3% to US$150.6 million from US$133.0 million in the corresponding earlier year.

Prospects: For full-year 2008, Co. expects Funds from Operations per share of $3.20 to $3.30. In addition, Co. expects earnings per share of $1.01 to $1.11. Co.'s estimates are based on the assumptions of average occupancy of 93.5% to 95.5% and same property net operating income increase of 0.0% to 2.5%. Separately, Co. is under contract to purchase a portfolio of properties consisting of five buildings with 669,000 square feet in four different locations and 9.9 acres of developable land in Charlotte for a total purchase price of $41.9 million. Co. expects the acquisition to close in the first quarter of 2008 and to increase its total ownership in Charlotte to over 1.6 million square feet.

Financial Data
(US$ in Thousands)

	12/31/2007	12/31/2006	12/31/2005	12/31/2004	12/31/2003	12/31/2002	12/31/2001	12/31/2000
Earnings Per Share	1.14	1.17	0.89	0.98	0.70	0.84	1.51	1.68
Cash Flow Per Share	3.67	2.98	3.11	2.76	2.84	3.39	3.23	3.38
Tang Book Value Per Share	15.28	16.07	14.77	14.98	16.05	15.40	16.48	16.84
Dividends Per Share	2.000	1.960	1.940	1.920	1.900	1.880	1.800	1.580
Dividend Payout %	175.44	167.52	217.98	195.92	271.43	223.81	119.21	94.05
Income Statement								
Property Income	150,638	133,144	125,548	114,051	107,771	103,048	100,560	93,906
Non-Property Income	92	469	957	633	670	2,762	4,735	4,197
Total Revenue	150,730	133,613	126,505	114,684	108,441	105,810	105,295	98,103
Interest Expense	27,314	24,616	23,444	20,481	19,015	17,387	17,823	18,570
Net Income	29,734	29,234	22,191	23,327	20,445	23,626	34,182	36,512
Average Shares	23,781	22,692	21,892	21,088	18,194	16,237	16,046	15,798
Balance Sheet								
Total Assets	1,055,833	911,787	863,538	768,664	729,267	702,341	683,782	666,205
Long-Term Obligations	465,360	417,440	346,961	303,674	285,722	248,343	205,014	168,709
Total Liabilities	651,136	490,842	496,972	414,974	360,518	344,097	311,333	289,116
Stockholders' Equity	402,385	418,797	364,864	351,806	366,945	356,485	370,710	375,392
Shares Outstanding	23,808	23,701	22,030	21,059	20,853	16,104	15,912	15,849
Statistical Record								
Return on Assets %	3.02	3.29	2.72	3.11	2.86	3.41	5.06	5.61
Return on Equity %	7.24	7.46	6.19	6.47	5.65	6.50	9.16	9.78
Net Margin %	19.73	21.88	17.54	20.34	18.85	22.33	32.46	37.22
Price Range	57.40-39.44	56.09-43.06	46.60-35.64	38.59-28.01	32.90-23.88	26.35-22.40	23.90-20.19	23.88-17.56
P/E Ratio	50.35-34.60	47.94-36.80	52.36-40.04	39.38-28.58	47.00-34.11	31.37-26.67	15.83-13.37	14.21-10.45
Average Yield %	4.20	4.07	4.72	5.70	6.93	7.61	8.10	7.55

Address: 300 One Jackson Place, 188 East Capitol Street, Jackson, MS 39201
Telephone: 601-354-3555
Fax: 601-352-1441

Web Site: www.eastgroup.net
Officers: Leland R. Speed - Chmn. David H. Hoster II - Pres., C.E.O.

Auditors: KPMG LLP
Transfer Agents: EquiServe Trust Company, N.A.

EASTMAN CHEMICAL CO.

Exchange	Symbol	Price	52Wk Range	Yield	P/E
NYS	EMN	$62.45 (3/31/2008)	71.23-58.02	2.82	17.44

*7 Year Price Score 107.14 *NYSE Composite Index=100 *12 Month Price Score 107.05

TRADING VOLUME (thousand shares)

Interim Earnings (Per Share)

Qtr.	Mar	Jun	Sep	Dec
2003	0.27	0.46	(4.35)	0.12
2004	(0.07)	1.07	0.49	0.69
2005	2.00	2.51	1.50	0.80
2006	1.27	1.37	1.15	1.12
2007	0.91	1.22	0.24	1.20

Interim Dividends (Per Share)

Amt	Decl	Ex	Rec	Pay
0.44Q	5/3/2007	6/13/2007	6/15/2007	7/2/2007
0.44Q	8/2/2007	9/13/2007	9/17/2007	10/1/2007
0.44Q	12/6/2007	12/13/2007	12/17/2007	1/2/2008
0.44Q	2/21/2008	3/13/2008	3/17/2008	4/1/2008

Indicated Div: $1.76

Valuation Analysis

		Institutional Holding	
Forecast P/E	N/A	No of Institutions	
		280	
Market Cap	$5.0 Billion	Shares	
Book Value	2.1 Billion	71,975,096	
Price/Book	2.39	% Held	
Price/Sales	0.73	85.59	

Business Summary: Chemicals (MIC: 11.1 SIC: 2821 NAIC: 325211)

Eastman Chemical is a chemical company that manufactures and sells a portfolio of chemicals, plastics, and fibers globally through 13 manufacturing sites in eight countries as of Dec 31 2007. Co.'s operates its business through five operating segments: Coatings, Adhesives, Specialty Polymers, and Inks, which manufactures liquid vehicles, additives, specialty polymers, and other raw materials used in the production of paints and coatings, inks, adhesives, and other formulated products; Fibers, which supplies acetate tow and produces acetate yarn; Performance Chemicals and Intermediates; Performance Polymers; and Specialty Plastics which produces copolyesters and cellulosic plastics.

Recent Developments: For the year ended Dec 31 2007, income from continuing operations decreased 24.8% to US$321.0 million from US$427.0 million a year earlier. Net income decreased 26.7% to US$300.0 million from US$409.0 million in the prior year. Revenues were US$6.83 billion, up 0.8% from US$6.78 billion the year before. Operating income was US$504.0 million versus US$654.0 million in the prior year, a decrease of 22.9%. Direct operating expenses rose 2.2% to US$5.64 billion from US$5.51 billion in the comparable period the year before. Indirect operating expenses increased 12.6% to US$688.0 million from US$611.0 million in the equivalent prior-year period.

Prospects: For 2008, Co. projects earnings per share to be similar to 2007, excluding gains and charges in both periods related to strategic decisions and actions. For example, Co. expects its Coatings, Adhesives, Specialty Polymers, and Inks segment to maintain robust earnings at the low end of the 15.0% to 20.0% operating margin range. Also, Co. plans to improve the profitability of its polyethylene terephthalate (PET) product lines in the Performance Polymers segment via several initiatives, including the Dec 2007 sale of its underperforming PET manufacturing facilities and related businesses in the U.K. and the Netherlands for $330.0 million, which should close in the first quarter of 2008.

Financial Data
(US$ in Thousands)

	12/31/2007	12/31/2006	12/31/2005	12/31/2004	12/31/2003	12/31/2002	12/31/2001	12/31/2000
Earnings Per Share	3.58	4.91	6.81	2.18	(3.50)	0.79	(2.33)	3.94
Cash Flow Per Share	8.84	7.42	9.53	6.35	3.16	10.39	5.61	10.79
Tang Book Value Per Share	22.17	20.53	15.94	10.67	8.97	9.02	9.92	15.64
Dividends Per Share	1.760	1.770	1.760	1.760	1.760	1.760	1.760	1.760
Dividend Payout %	49.16	36.05	25.84	80.73	...	222.78	...	44.67
Income Statement								
Total Revenue	6,830,000	7,450,000	7,059,000	6,580,000	5,800,000	5,320,000	5,384,000	5,292,000
EBITDA	859,000	964,000	1,187,000	501,000	110,000	603,000	278,000	1,005,000
Income Before Taxes	470,000	576,000	783,000	64,000	(381,000)	84,000	(297,000)	452,000
Income Taxes	149,000	167,000	226,000	(106,000)	(108,000)	5,000	(118,000)	149,000
Net Income	300,000	409,000	557,000	170,000	(270,000)	61,000	(179,000)	303,000
Average Shares	83,900	83,200	81,800	78,300	77,100	77,100	76,800	77,000
Balance Sheet								
Current Assets	2,293,000	2,422,000	1,924,000	1,768,000	2,010,000	1,529,000	1,458,000	1,523,000
Total Assets	6,009,000	6,173,000	5,773,000	5,872,000	6,230,000	6,273,000	6,086,000	6,550,000
Current Liabilities	1,122,000	1,059,000	1,051,000	1,099,000	1,477,000	1,224,000	958,000	1,258,000
Long-Term Obligations	1,535,000	1,589,000	1,621,000	2,061,000	2,089,000	2,054,000	2,143,000	1,914,000
Total Liabilities	3,927,000	4,144,000	4,161,000	4,688,000	5,187,000	5,002,000	4,708,000	4,738,000
Stockholders' Equity	2,082,000	2,029,000	1,612,000	1,184,000	1,043,000	1,271,000	1,378,000	1,812,000
Shares Outstanding	79,670	83,530	81,531	79,213	77,244	77,346	76,979	76,743
Statistical Record								
Return on Assets %	4.93	6.85	9.57	2.80	N.M.	0.99	N.M.	4.70
Return on Equity %	14.59	22.47	39.84	15.23	N.M.	4.61	N.M.	16.92
EBITDA Margin %	12.58	12.94	16.82	7.61	1.90	11.33	5.16	18.99
Net Margin %	4.39	5.49	7.89	2.58	N.M.	1.15	N.M.	5.73
Asset Turnover	1.12	1.25	1.21	1.08	0.93	0.86	0.85	0.82
Current Ratio	2.04	2.29	1.83	1.61	1.36	1.25	1.52	1.21
Debt to Equity	0.74	0.78	1.01	1.74	2.00	1.62	1.56	1.06
Price Range	71.23-57.90	61.23-47.70	61.36-44.70	57.97-38.00	39.53-27.89	49.04-35.35	55.25-30.25	54.13-34.19
P/E Ratio	19.90-16.17	12.47-9.71	9.01-6.56	26.59-17.43	...	62.08-44.75	...	13.74-8.68
Average Yield %	2.74	3.29	3.26	3.88	5.26	4.15	3.95	3.97

Address: 100 N. Eastman Road, Kingsport, TN 37660	Web Site: www.eastman.com	Auditors: PricewaterhouseCoopers LLP
Telephone: 423-229-2000	Officers: J. Brian Ferguson - Chmn., C.E.O. James P. Rogers - Exec. V.P.	Investor Contact: 423-229-8692
Fax: 423-224-0208		Transfer Agents: American Stock Transfer & Trust Company, New York, NY

EASTMAN KODAK CO.

Exchange	Symbol	Price	52Wk Range	Yield	P/E
NYS	EK	$17.67 (3/31/2008)	29.68-16.62	2.83	7.52

*7 Year Price Score 67.97   *NYSE Composite Index=100   *12 Month Price Score 80.19

Interim Earnings (Per Share)

Qtr.	Mar	Jun	Sep	Dec
2003	0.04	0.39	0.42	0.06
2004	0.10	0.54	1.67	(0.37)
2005	(0.50)	(0.54)	(3.61)	(0.15)
2006	(1.04)	(0.98)	(0.13)	0.06
2007	(0.53)	2.00	0.13	0.75

Interim Dividends (Per Share)

Amt	Decl	Ex	Rec	Pay
0.25S	5/10/2006	5/30/2006	6/1/2006	7/18/2006
0.25S	10/17/2006	10/30/2006	11/1/2006	12/14/2006
0.25S	5/9/2007	5/30/2007	6/1/2007	7/16/2007
0.25S	10/16/2007	10/30/2007	11/1/2007	12/14/2007

Indicated Div: $0.50

Valuation Analysis   Institutional Holding

Forecast P/E	29.18	No of Institutions
	(1/10/2007)	302
Market Cap	$5.1 Billion	Shares
Book Value	3.0 Billion	320,325,792
Price/Book	1.68	% Held
Price/Sales	0.49	N/A

Business Summary: Consumer Accessories (MIC: 4.6 SIC: 3861 NAIC: 325992)

Eastman Kodak operates via three key segments: Consumer Digital Imaging Group, which provides a range of products and services for capturing, storing, printing and sharing images; Film Products Group, which provides consumers and entertainment imaging customers with film-related products and services; and Graphic Communications Group, which serves the creative, in-plant, data center, commercial printing, packaging, newspaper and digital service bureau market segments with a range of products that provide customers with a variety of applications for prepress equipment, workflow software, digital and traditional printing, document scanning and multi-vendor information technology services.

Recent Developments: For the year ended Dec 31 2007, loss from continuing operations was US$205.0 million compared with a loss of US$804.0 million a year earlier. Net income amounted to US$676.0 million versus a net loss of US$601.0 million in the prior year. Revenues were US$10.30 billion, down 2.5% from US$10.57 billion the year before. Operating loss was US$230.0 million versus a loss of US$476.0 million in the prior year. Direct operating expenses declined 4.6% to US$7.79 billion from US$8.16 billion in the comparable period the year before. Indirect operating expenses decreased 4.8% to US$2.75 billion from US$2.89 billion in the equivalent prior-year period.

Prospects: Going forward, Co. expects its 2004-2007 Restructuring Program, which includes total employment reductions in the range of 27,000 to 28,000 positions, to generate annual cost savings of approximately $1.68 billion, with the majority of these savings expected to be realized by the end of 2008. For the full-year 2008, on a continuing operations basis, Co. expects its total revenue growth to be flat to an increase of 2.0%. Co. also expects digital revenue growth of 7.0% to 10.0%, with 60.0% of these revenues to be generated by output businesses and 40.0% from capture businesses. Overall, Co. is targeting earnings from continuing operations of $250.0 million to $275.0 million for the year.

Financial Data

(US$ in Thousands)	12/31/2007	12/31/2006	12/31/2005	12/31/2004	12/31/2003	12/31/2002	12/31/2001	12/31/2000
Earnings Per Share	2.35	(2.09)	(4.73)	1.94	0.92	2.64	0.26	4.59
Cash Flow Per Share	1.09	3.33	4.20	4.06	5.74	7.56	7.11	3.21
Tang Book Value Per Share	3.51	N.M.	N.M.	6.58	5.53	6.28	6.69	8.54
Dividends Per Share	0.500	0.500	0.500	0.500	1.150	1.800	1.770	1.760
Dividend Payout %	21.28	...	...	25.77	125.00	68.18	680.77	38.34
Income Statement								
Total Revenue	10,301,000	13,274,000	14,268,000	13,517,000	13,317,000	12,835,000	13,234,000	13,994,000
EBITDA	547,000	1,187,000	847,000	1,104,000	1,150,000	1,937,000	1,246,000	3,199,000
Income Before Taxes	(256,000)	(346,000)	(766,000)	(94,000)	172,000	946,000	108,000	2,132,000
Income Taxes	(51,000)	254,000	689,000	(175,000)	(66,000)	153,000	32,000	725,000
Net Income	676,000	(601,000)	(1,362,000)	556,000	265,000	770,000	76,000	1,407,000
Average Shares	287,700	287,300	287,900	286,800	286,600	291,700	291,000	306,600
Balance Sheet								
Current Assets	6,053,000	5,557,000	5,781,000	5,648,000	5,455,000	4,534,000	4,683,000	5,491,000
Total Assets	13,659,000	14,320,000	14,921,000	14,737,000	14,818,000	13,369,000	13,362,000	14,212,000
Current Liabilities	4,446,000	4,971,000	5,489,000	4,990,000	5,307,000	5,377,000	5,354,000	6,215,000
Long-Term Obligations	1,289,000	2,714,000	2,764,000	1,852,000	2,302,000	1,164,000	1,666,000	1,166,000
Total Liabilities	10,630,000	12,932,000	12,954,000	10,926,000	11,554,000	10,592,000	10,468,000	10,784,000
Stockholders' Equity	3,029,000	1,388,000	1,967,000	3,811,000	3,264,000	2,777,000	2,894,000	3,428,000
Shares Outstanding	287,999	287,333	287,223	286,696	286,580	285,933	290,929	290,484
Statistical Record								
Return on Assets %	4.83	N.M.	N.M.	3.75	1.88	5.76	0.55	9.82
Return on Equity %	30.61	N.M.	N.M.	15.67	8.77	27.16	2.40	38.23
EBITDA Margin %	5.31	8.94	5.94	8.17	8.64	15.09	9.42	22.86
Net Margin %	6.56	N.M.	N.M.	4.11	1.99	6.00	0.57	10.05
Asset Turnover	0.74	0.91	0.96	0.91	0.94	0.96	0.96	0.98
Current Ratio	1.36	1.12	1.05	1.13	1.03	0.84	0.87	0.88
Debt to Equity	0.43	1.96	1.41	0.49	0.71	0.42	0.58	0.34
Price Range	29.68-21.72	29.73-19.09	34.76-20.95	34.26-24.80	40.24-20.50	38.22-25.86	49.21-24.65	66.25-36.44
P/E Ratio	12.63-9.24	...	...	17.66-12.78	43.74-22.28	14.48-9.80	189.27-94.81	14.43-7.94
Average Yield %	1.95	2.04	1.82	1.76	4.07	5.76	4.37	3.21

Address: 343 State Street, Rochester, NY 14650	Web Site: www.kodak.com	Auditors: PricewaterhouseCoopers LLP
Telephone: 585-724-4000	Officers: Daniel A. Carp - Chmn. Antonio M. Perez - Pres., C.E.O.	Transfer Agents: EquiServe Trust Company, N.A.
Fax: 716-724-0663		

EATON CORP.

Exchange	Symbol	Price	52Wk Range	Yield	P/E
NYS	ETN	$79.67 (3/31/2008)	102.55-77.55	2.51	12.03

*7 Year Price Score 122.80 *NYSE Composite Index=100 *12 Month Price Score 97.04

TRADING VOLUME (thousand shares)

Interim Earnings (Per Share)

Qtr.	Mar	Jun	Sep	Dec
2003	0.50	0.64	0.69	0.72
2004	0.85	1.03	1.09	1.16
2005	1.19	1.37	1.30	1.38
2006	1.36	1.64	1.62	1.60
2007	1.56	1.64	1.71	1.71

Interim Dividends (Per Share)

Amt	Decl	Ex	Rec	Pay
0.43Q	4/25/2007	5/3/2007	5/7/2007	5/25/2007
0.43Q	7/25/2007	8/2/2007	8/6/2007	8/24/2007
0.43Q	10/24/2007	11/1/2007	11/5/2007	11/23/2007
0.50Q	1/22/2008	1/31/2008	2/4/2008	2/22/2008
		Indicated Div: $2.00		

Valuation Analysis

		Institutional Holding	
Forecast P/E	11.13	No of Institutions	
	(1/10/2007)	437	
Market Cap	$11.6 Billion	Shares	
Book Value	5.2 Billion	116,310,424	
Price/Book	2.25	% Held	
Price/Sales	0.89	79.56	

Business Summary: Industrial Machinery and Equipment (MIC: 11.5 SIC: 3566 NAIC: 335999)

Eaton is a global industrial manufacturer. Co. is engaged in the business of providing electrical systems and components for power quality, distribution and control; fluid power systems and services for industrial, mobile and aircraft equipment; intelligent truck drivetrain systems for safety and fuel economy; and automotive engine air management systems, powertrain applications and specialty controls for performance, fuel economy and safety. As of Dec 31 2007, Co. conducted its businesses through four operating segments: Fluid Power, Electrical, Automotive and Truck. As of Dec 31 2007, Co. had sold its products in more than 150 countries.

Recent Developments: For the year ended Dec 31 2007, income from continuing operations increased 6.9% to US$959.0 million from US$897.0 million a year earlier. Net income increased 4.6% to US$994.0 million from US$950.0 million in the prior year. Revenues were US$13.03 billion, up 6.5% from US$12.23 billion the year before. Direct operating expenses rose 4.8% to US$9.38 billion from US$8.95 billion in the comparable period the year before. Indirect operating expenses increased 9.8% to US$2.47 billion from US$2.25 billion in the equivalent prior-year period.

Prospects: For the full year of 2008, Co. is projecting net income in the range of $7.25 to $7.75 per share, while operating income is estimated to range from $7.75 to $8.25 per share, excluding integration charges of its recent acquisitions. In addition, Co. expects to outgrow its end markets by about $275.0 million and foresees revenues to grow by about 25.0% over its 2007 levels. Separately, on Dec 20 2007, Co. announced plans for two electrical acquisitions in Europe and Asia Pacific for a total transaction value of approximately $2.23 billion. The transaction, which is expected to close in the first quarter of 2008, is subject to regulatory approvals and other customary closing conditions.

Financial Data

(US$ in Thousands)	12/31/2007	12/31/2006	12/31/2005	12/31/2004	12/31/2003	12/31/2002	12/31/2001	12/31/2000
Earnings Per Share	6.62	6.22	5.23	4.13	2.56	1.96	1.20	3.12
Cash Flow Per Share	7.88	9.53	7.56	5.46	5.91	6.37	5.51	3.60
Tang Book Value Per Share	N.M.	0.70	0.09	3.45	3.14	N.M.	0.29	N.M.
Dividends Per Share	1.720	1.480	1.240	1.080	0.920	0.880	0.880	0.880
Dividend Payout %	25.98	23.79	23.71	26.15	35.94	44.90	73.64	28.21
Income Statement								
Total Revenue	13,033,000	12,370,000	11,115,000	9,817,000	8,061,000	7,209,000	7,299,000	8,309,000
EBITDA	1,657,000	1,527,000	1,495,000	1,259,000	989,000	879,000	869,000	1,191,000
Income Before Taxes	1,041,000	989,000	996,000	781,000	508,000	399,000	278,000	552,000
Income Taxes	82,000	77,000	191,000	133,000	122,000	118,000	109,000	189,000
Net Income	994,000	950,000	805,000	648,000	386,000	281,000	169,000	453,000
Average Shares	150,300	177,900	154,000	157,100	150,500	143,400	141,000	145,200
Balance Sheet								
Current Assets	4,767,000	4,400,000	3,378,000	3,182,000	3,093,000	2,457,000	2,387,000	2,571,000
Total Assets	13,430,000	11,417,000	10,218,000	9,075,000	8,223,000	7,138,000	7,646,000	8,180,000
Current Liabilities	3,659,000	3,407,000	2,968,000	2,262,000	2,126,000	1,734,000	1,669,000	2,107,000
Long-Term Obligations	2,432,000	1,774,000	1,830,000	1,734,000	1,651,000	1,887,000	2,252,000	2,447,000
Total Liabilities	8,258,000	7,311,000	6,440,000	5,469,000	5,106,000	4,836,000	5,171,000	5,770,000
Stockholders' Equity	5,172,000	4,106,000	3,778,000	3,606,000	3,117,000	2,302,000	2,475,000	2,410,000
Shares Outstanding	146,000	146,300	148,500	153,300	153,000	141,200	139,000	136,600
Statistical Record								
Return on Assets %	8.00	8.78	8.34	7.47	5.03	3.80	2.14	5.44
Return on Equity %	21.43	24.10	21.80	19.22	14.25	11.76	6.92	17.95
EBITDA Margin %	12.71	12.34	13.45	12.82	12.27	12.19	11.91	14.33
Net Margin %	7.63	7.68	7.24	6.60	4.79	3.90	2.32	5.45
Asset Turnover	1.05	1.14	1.15	1.13	1.05	0.98	0.92	1.00
Current Ratio	1.30	1.29	1.21	1.41	1.45	1.42	1.43	1.22
Debt to Equity	0.47	0.43	0.48	0.48	0.53	0.82	0.91	1.02
Price Range	102.55-73.80	78.89-63.00	72.36-56.68	72.36-53.24	54.33-33.45	43.92-29.68	40.09-28.73	36.45-25.39
P/E Ratio	15.49-11.15	12.68-10.13	13.84-10.84	17.52-12.89	21.22-13.06	22.41-15.14	33.41-23.95	11.68-8.14
Average Yield %	1.92	2.08	1.94	1.75	2.16	2.36	2.49	2.89

Address: Eaton Center, 1111 Superior Avenue, Cleveland, OH 44114-2584	Web Site: www.eaton.com	Auditors: Ernst & Young LLP
Telephone: 216-523-5000	Officers: Alexander M. Cutler - Chmn., Pres., C.E.O. Richard H. Fearon - Exec. V.P., Chief Fin. & Planning Officer	Investor Contact: 883-286-647 Transfer Agents: EquiServeTrust Company, N.A.
Fax: 216-479-7092		

EATON VANCE CORP

Exchange	Symbol	Price	52Wk Range	Yield	P/E	Div Acheiver
NYS	EV	$30.51 (3/31/2008)	50.03-28.33	1.97	20.34	26 Years

*7 Year Price Score 136.04 *NYSE Composite Index=100 *12 Month Price Score 86.67

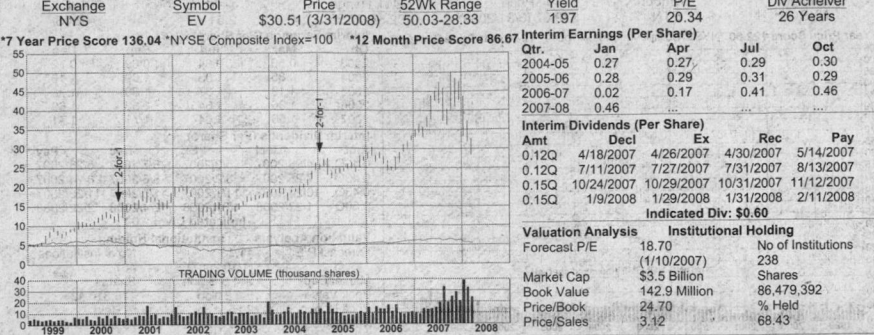

Interim Earnings (Per Share)

Qtr.	Jan	Apr	Jul	Oct
2004-05	0.27	0.27	0.29	0.30
2005-06	0.28	0.29	0.31	0.29
2006-07	0.02	0.17	0.41	0.46
2007-08	0.46	...	...	...

Interim Dividends (Per Share)

Amt	Decl	Ex	Rec	Pay
0.12Q	4/18/2007	4/26/2007	4/30/2007	5/14/2007
0.12Q	7/11/2007	7/27/2007	7/31/2007	8/13/2007
0.15Q	10/24/2007	10/29/2007	10/31/2007	11/12/2007
0.15Q	1/9/2008	1/29/2008	1/31/2008	2/11/2008

Indicated Div: $0.60

Valuation Analysis

Forecast P/E	18.70
	(1/10/2007)
Market Cap	$3.5 Billion
Book Value	142.9 Million
Price/Book	24.70
Price/Sales	3.12

Institutional Holding

No of Institutions	238
Shares	86,479,392
% Held	68.43

Business Summary: Wealth Management (MIC: 8.8 SIC: 6282 NAIC: 523930)

Eaton Vance is primarily engaged in the business of providing investment advisory and distribution services to mutual funds and other investment funds as well as investment management and counseling services to individual high-net-worth investors, family offices and institutional clients. Co.'s income investment products consists of an expanded duration and credit quality range, including both taxable and tax-free investments. Co.'s equity products provide a spectrum of investment objectives, risk profiles, income levels and geographic representation. As of Oct 31 2007, Co.'s total assets were $966.8 million and assets under management amounted to $161.7 billion.

Recent Developments: For the quarter ended Jan 31 2008, net income increased to US$57.9 million from US$2.6 million in the year-earlier quarter. Revenues were US$289.8 million, up 19.2% from US$243.2 million the year before. Operating income was US$99.2 million versus US$2.0 million in the prior-year quarter. Indirect operating expenses decreased 21.0% to US$190.6 million from US$241.2 million in the equivalent prior-year period.

Prospects: Co.'s near-term outlook appears to be promising. Specifically, Co. continues to experience growth in revenues, driven primarily by investment advisory and administration fees, due to an increase in average assets under management and the escalating average effective investment advisory and administration fee rates. In addition, Co. is seeing an improvement in distribution and underwriter fees, attributable to higher distribution plan payments as well as an improvement in underwriter fees and other distribution income. Lastly, Co. is benefiting from the escalating service fee revenues, resulting from an increase in average assets under management and private funds that pay service fees.

Financial Data
(US$ in Thousands)

	3 Mos	10/31/2007	10/31/2006	10/31/2005	10/31/2004	10/31/2003	10/31/2002	10/31/2001
Earnings Per Share	1.50	1.06	1.17	1.13	1.00	0.76	0.85	0.80
Cash Flow Per Share	2.63	2.14	2.06	0.82	0.87	0.32	0.97	1.02
Tang Book Value Per Share	0.04	0.76	2.89	2.51	2.37	2.06	1.92	1.40
Dividends Per Share	0.540	0.630	0.400	0.240	0.275	0.200	0.149	0.126
Dividend Payout %	36.00	59.43	34.19	21.24	27.64	26.49	17.50	15.78
Income Statement								
Total Revenue	289,796	1,084,100	862,194	753,175	661,813	523,133	522,985	486,372
Income Before Taxes	94,645	238,349	263,002	261,190	221,658	164,858	186,241	178,666
Income Taxes	37,023	93,200	102,245	97,500	79,797	57,700	65,184	62,469
Net Income	57,928	142,811	159,377	159,884	138,943	106,123	121,057	116,020
Average Shares	127,132	135,252	137,004	141,632	139,578	140,750	142,824	144,600
Balance Sheet								
Total Assets	831,390	966,831	668,195	702,544	743,566	658,702	616,619	675,301
Total Liabilities	680,636	729,439	162,165	242,971	226,190	234,734	242,919	373,210
Stockholders' Equity	142,860	229,168	496,485	454,953	449,506	416,277	372,302	301,126
Shares Outstanding	115,648	118,169	126,435	129,552	133,581	136,810	138,514	137,233
Statistical Record								
Return on Assets %	27.61	17.47	23.25	22.11	19.76	16.64	18.74	20.94
Return on Equity %	63.05	39.36	33.50	35.35	32.01	26.91	35.95	41.73
Price Range	50.03-32.93	50.03-29.87	31.10-24.14	27.30-21.80	21.81-16.46	17.80-11.70	20.36-11.98	19.10-11.16
P/E Ratio	33.35-21.95	47.20-28.18	26.58-20.63	24.16-19.29	21.81-16.46	23.42-15.39	23.95-14.09	23.88-13.95
Average Yield %	1.33	1.65	1.47	0.98	1.45	1.30	0.90	0.81

Address: The Eaton Vance Building, 255 State Street, Boston, MA 02109	**Web Site:** www.eatonvance.com	**Auditors:** Deloitte & Touche LLP
Telephone: 617-482-8260	**Officers:** James B. Hawkes - Chmn., Pres., C.E.O.	**Investor Contact:** 617-482-8260
Fax: 617-482-2396	Thomas E. Faust Jr. - Exec. V.P., Chief Investment Officer	**Transfer Agents:** EquiServe Trust Company, N.A., Kansas City, MO

ECOLAB, INC.

Exchange	Symbol	Price	52Wk Range	Yield	P/E	Div Acheiver
NYS	ECL	$43.43 (3/31/2008)	52.30-40.16	1.20	25.55	15 Years

*7 Year Price Score 114.15 *NYSE Composite Index=100 *12 Month Price Score 110.31

Interim Earnings (Per Share)

Qtr.	Mar	Jun	Sep	Dec
2003	0.21	0.25	0.33	0.26
2004	0.25	0.30	0.36	0.27
2005	0.29	0.33	0.40	0.21
2006	0.30	0.36	0.43	0.34
2007	0.35	0.44	0.46	0.45

Interim Dividends (Per Share)

Amt	Decl	Ex	Rec	Pay
0.115Q	5/4/2007	6/15/2007	6/19/2007	7/16/2007
0.115Q	8/3/2007	9/14/2007	9/18/2007	10/15/2007
0.13Q	12/6/2007	12/14/2007	12/18/2007	1/15/2008
0.13Q	2/22/2008	3/7/2008	3/11/2008	4/15/2008

Indicated Div: $0.52 (Div. Reinv. Plan)

Valuation Analysis

		Institutional Holding	
Forecast P/E	23.69	No of Institutions	
	(1/10/2007)	408	
Market Cap	$10.7 Billion	Shares	
Book Value	1.9 Billion	139,956,080	
Price/Book	5.54	% Held	
Price/Sales	1.96	56.14	

Business Summary: Chemicals (MIC: 11.1 SIC: 2842 NAIC: 325612)

Ecolab develops and markets products and services for the hospitality, foodservice, institutional and industrial markets. Co. operates in three business segments. The U.S. Cleaning and Sanitizing segment consists of seven business units and provides cleaning and sanitizing products and programs to U.S. markets. The U.S. Other Services segment consists of two business units and provides services for the detection, elimination and prevention of pests, as well as commercial equipment repair services for restaurants and other foodservice operators. The International segment operates about 70 countries outside U.S. through wholly-owned subsidiaries or through joint ventures with local partners.

Recent Developments: For the year ended Dec 31 2007, net income increased 15.9% to US$427.2 million from US$368.6 million in the prior year. Revenues were US$5.47 billion, up 11.7% from US$4.90 billion the year before. Operating income was US$667.3 million versus US$611.6 million in the prior year, an increase of 9.1%. Direct operating expenses rose 11.4% to US$2.69 billion from US$2.42 billion in the comparable period the year before. Indirect operating expenses increased 13.0% to US$2.11 billion from US$1.87 billion in the equivalent prior-year period.

Prospects: For the first quarter of 2008, Co. expects sales for both domestic and international operations, in fixed currencies, to increase over the corresponding period in 2007, while gross margins are forecasted to range from 49.0% to 50.0%, reflecting the effects of acquisitions. Going forward, Co. remains focused on making strategic acquisitions to improve its business. For instance, on Feb 4 2008, Co. announced that it has agreed to purchase Ecovation, Inc. for about $210.0 million. Accordingly, Co. anticipates this transaction, with projected 2008 sales in excess of $100.0 million, to be up to $0.01 dilutive to earnings per share in 2008, and show accretion building in 2009 and thereafter.

Financial Data

(US$ in Thousands)	12/31/2007	12/31/2006	12/31/2005	12/31/2004	12/31/2003	12/31/2002	12/31/2001	12/31/2000
Earnings Per Share	1.70	1.43	1.23	1.19	1.06	0.80	0.72	0.78
Cash Flow Per Share	3.23	2.49	2.31	2.26	2.04	1.64	1.43	1.23
Tang Book Value Per Share	1.33	1.67	2.00	1.33	1.14	0.83	0.41	1.77
Dividends Per Share	0.475	0.415	0.362	0.328	0.297	0.275	0.263	0.245
Dividend Payout %	27.94	29.02	29.47	27.52	28.07	34.38	36.21	31.41
Income Statement								
Total Revenue	5,469,600	4,895,814	4,534,832	4,184,933	3,761,819	3,403,585	2,354,723	2,264,313
EBITDA	958,400	872,442	788,632	769,345	716,475	607,606	481,169	491,575
Income Before Taxes	616,300	567,224	498,182	488,778	448,418	351,971	289,745	318,534
Income Taxes	189,100	198,609	178,701	178,290	171,070	140,081	117,408	129,495
Net Income	427,200	368,615	319,481	310,488	277,348	209,770	188,170	206,127
Average Shares	251,800	257,144	260,098	261,776	262,737	261,574	259,856	263,892
Balance Sheet								
Current Assets	1,717,300	1,853,557	1,421,666	1,279,066	1,150,340	1,015,937	929,583	600,568
Total Assets	4,722,800	4,419,365	3,796,628	3,716,174	3,228,918	2,878,429	2,525,000	1,714,011
Current Liabilities	1,518,300	1,502,730	1,119,357	939,547	851,942	866,350	827,952	532,034
Long-Term Obligations	599,900	557,058	519,374	645,445	604,441	539,743	512,280	234,377
Total Liabilities	2,787,100	2,739,135	2,147,418	2,153,655	1,933,492	1,778,678	1,644,648	957,004
Stockholders' Equity	1,935,700	1,680,230	1,649,210	1,562,519	1,295,426	1,099,751	880,352	757,007
Shares Outstanding	246,825	251,336	254,143	257,541	257,416	259,880	255,800	254,322
Statistical Record								
Return on Assets %	9.35	8.97	8.50	8.92	9.08	7.76	8.88	12.46
Return on Equity %	23.63	22.14	19.89	21.67	23.16	21.19	22.98	27.07
EBITDA Margin %	17.52	17.82	17.39	18.38	19.05	17.85	20.43	21.71
Net Margin %	7.81	7.53	7.05	7.42	7.37	6.16	7.99	9.10
Asset Turnover	1.20	1.19	1.21	1.20	1.23	1.26	1.11	1.37
Current Ratio	1.13	1.23	1.27	1.36	1.35	1.17	1.12	1.13
Debt to Equity	0.31	0.33	0.31	0.41	0.47	0.49	0.58	0.31
Price Range	52.30-40.16	46.19-33.85	36.76-31.06	35.26-26.22	27.91-23.36	25.07-18.36	21.97-15.48	22.34-14.13
P/E Ratio	30.76-23.62	32.30-23.67	29.89-25.25	29.63-22.03	26.33-22.04	31.34-22.96	30.51-21.51	28.65-18.11
Average Yield %	1.07	1.02	1.10	1.08	1.16	1.22	1.33	1.31

Address: 370 Wabasha Street North, St. Paul, MN 55102
Telephone: 651-293-2233
Fax: 612-225-3080

Web Site: www.ecolab.com
Officers: Douglas M. Baker Jr. - Pres., C.E.O. Steven L. Fritze - Exec. V.P., C.F.O.

Auditors: PricewaterhouseCoopers LLP
Investor Contact: 612-293-2809
Transfer Agents: EquiServe Trust Company, N.A., Providence, RI

EDISON INTERNATIONAL

Exchange	Symbol	Price	52Wk Range	Yield	P/E
NYS	EIX	$49.02 (3/31/2008)	59.76-48.15	2.49	14.81

*7 Year Price Score 142.38 *NYSE Composite Index=100 *12 Month Price Score 100.47

Interim Earnings (Per Share)

Qtr.	Mar	Jun	Sep	Dec
2003	0.17	0.07	1.65	0.61
2004	0.30	(1.15)	2.46	1.14
2005	0.61	0.61	1.39	0.82
2006	0.78	0.54	1.38	0.86
2007	1.01	0.28	1.39	0.64

Interim Dividends (Per Share)

Amt	Decl	Ex	Rec	Pay
0.29Q	4/26/2007	6/27/2007	6/29/2007	7/31/2007
0.29Q	9/6/2007	9/26/2007	9/28/2007	10/31/2007
0.305Q	12/14/2007	12/27/2007	12/31/2007	1/31/2008
0.305Q	2/28/2008	3/27/2008	3/31/2008	4/30/2008

Indicated Div: $1.22

Valuation Analysis   **Institutional Holding**

Forecast P/E	12.68	No of Institutions
	(1/10/2007)	375
Market Cap	$16.0 Billion	Shares
Book Value	8.4 Billion	233,187,504
Price/Book	1.89	% Held
Price/Sales	1.22	71.57

Business Summary: Electricity (MIC: 7.1 SIC: 4911 NAIC: 221122)

Edison International is engaged in the business of holding, for investment, the common stock of its subsidiaries. As of Dec 31 2007, Co.'s principal subsidiaries include: Southern California Edison Company, a electric utility that supplies electric energy to a 50,000 square-mile area of central, coastal and southern California; Edison Mission Energy, which is engaged in the business of owning or leasing, operating and selling energy and capacity from independent power production facilities; and Edison Capital, which has investments in energy and infrastructure projects worldwide and in affordable housing projects located throughout the U.S.

Recent Developments: For the year ended Dec 31 2007, net income decreased 7.0% to US$1.10 billion from US$1.18 billion in the prior year. Revenues were US$13.11 billion, up 3.9% from US$12.62 billion the year before. Operating income was US$2.51 billion versus US$2.49 billion in the prior year, an increase of 0.8%. Direct operating expenses rose 4.3% to US$9.34 billion from US$8.95 billion in the comparable period the year before. Indirect operating expenses increased 7.5% to US$1.27 billion from US$1.18 billion in the equivalent prior-year period.

Prospects: Co. is seeing a decrease in earnings as higher earnings at its Southern California Edison Co. (SCE) subsidiary primarily from the favorable resolution of a state tax issue in the 2006 period is offset by lower results at its Edison Mission Group (EMG) subsidiary, primarily due to lower earnings from Edison Capital and higher EMG corporate costs. For full-year 2008, Co. expects earnings per share of $3.61 to $4.01. Separately, SCE recently began construction of the Tehachapi Renewable Transmission Project, a wind transmission project capable of carrying 4,500 megawatts of electricity, in the U.S. Co. expects the first three segments of the project to be operational in early 2009.

Financial Data
(US$ in Thousands)

	12/31/2007	12/31/2006	12/31/2005	12/31/2004	12/31/2003	12/31/2002	12/31/2001	12/31/2000
Earnings Per Share	3.31	3.57	3.43	2.77	2.50	3.20	3.17	(5.84)
Cash Flow Per Share	9.79	11.02	6.79	4.89	10.14	7.14	9.12	4.22
Tang Book Value Per Share	25.92	23.66	20.30	18.57	13.86	11.59	8.10	7.43
Dividends Per Share	1.175	1.100	1.020	1.050	0.200	...	...	1.110
Dividend Payout %	35.50	30.81	29.74	37.91	8.00	...	...	...
Income Statement								
Total Revenue	13,113,000	12,622,000	11,852,000	10,199,000	12,135,000	11,488,000	11,436,000	11,717,000
EBITDA	2,662,000	2,592,000	2,657,000	1,365,000	2,326,000	2,922,000	5,723,000	(1,436,000)
Income Before Taxes	1,799,000	1,855,000	1,756,000	282,000	992,000	1,526,000	4,049,000	(2,992,000)
Income Taxes	492,000	582,000	457,000	(92,000)	213,000	391,000	1,647,000	(1,049,000)
Net Income	1,098,000	1,181,000	1,137,000	916,000	821,000	1,077,000	1,035,000	(1,943,000)
Average Shares	331,000	330,000	332,000	331,000	329,000	328,000	326,000	333,000
Balance Sheet								
Net PPE	22,309,000	20,269,000	18,588,000	17,397,000	20,288,000	15,170,000	14,427,000	17,903,000
Total Assets	37,562,000	36,261,000	34,791,000	33,269,000	34,962,000	33,284,000	36,774,000	35,100,000
Long-Term Obligations	9,016,000	9,101,000	8,833,000	9,678,000	11,787,000	11,557,000	12,674,000	12,150,000
Total Liabilities	27,908,000	27,366,000	27,156,000	26,778,000	28,933,000	27,064,000	31,824,000	31,152,000
Stockholders' Equity	8,444,000	7,709,000	6,615,000	6,049,000	5,383,000	4,437,000	3,272,000	2,420,000
Shares Outstanding	325,811	325,811	325,811	325,811	325,811	325,811	325,811	325,811
Statistical Record								
Return on Assets %	2.97	3.32	3.34	2.68	2.41	3.07	2.88	N.M.
Return on Equity %	13.59	16.49	17.96	15.98	16.72	27.94	36.37	N.M.
EBITDA Margin %	20.30	20.54	22.42	13.38	19.17	25.44	50.04	N.M.
Net Margin %	8.37	9.36	9.59	8.98	6.77	9.38	9.05	(16.58)
PPE Turnover	0.62	0.65	0.66	0.54	0.68	0.78	0.71	0.62
Asset Turnover	0.36	0.36	0.35	0.30	0.36	0.33	0.32	0.33
Debt to Equity	1.07	1.18	1.34	1.60	2.19	2.60	3.87	5.02
Price Range	59.76-42.94	46.95-38.32	48.92-30.71	32.43-21.53	21.98-11.06	19.50-7.85	15.94-8.25	29.50-14.94
P/E Ratio	18.05-12.97	13.15-10.73	14.26-8.95	11.71-7.77	8.79-4.42	6.09-2.45	5.03-2.60	...
Average Yield %	2.21	2.59	2.60	4.05	1.21	...	...	5.17

Address: 2244 Walnut Grove Avenue, Suite 369, Rosemead, CA 91770 Telephone: 626-302-2222 Fax: 626-302-9935	Web Site: www.edison.com Officers: John E. Bryson - Chmn., Pres., C.E.O. Tom McDaniel - Exec. V.P., C.F.O.	Auditors: PricewaterhouseCoopers LLP Transfer Agents: Wells Fargo Bank, N.A., South St. Paul, MN

EDWARDS LIFESCIENCES CORP

Exchange	Symbol	Price	52Wk Range	Yield	P/E
NYS	EW	$44.55 (3/31/2008)	52.76-42.59	N/A	23.82

*7 Year Price Score 105.96 *NYSE Composite Index=100 *12 Month Price Score 100.18

TRADING VOLUME (thousand shares)

Interim Earnings (Per Share)

Qtr.	Mar	Jun	Sep	Dec
2003	0.24	0.34	0.40	0.31
2004	(1.04)	0.41	0.20	0.44
2005	0.50	0.22	(0.07)	0.62
2006	0.73	0.58	0.45	0.34
2007	0.54	0.57	0.48	0.28

Interim Dividends (Per Share)

No Dividends Paid

Valuation Analysis   **Institutional Holding**

Forecast P/E	17.97	No of Institutions	
	(1/10/2007)	226	
Market Cap	$2.5 Billion	Shares	
Book Value	835.0 Million	51,031,224	
Price/Book	3.02	% Held	
Price/Sales	2.31	88.16	

Business Summary: Medical Instruments & Equipment (MIC: 9.6 SIC: 3842 NAIC: 339113)

Edwards Lifesciences is a provider of products and technologies that are designed to treat advanced cardiovascular disease. Co. focuses on providing products and technologies to address specific cardiovascular opportunities, including heart valve disease; critical care technologies; and peripheral vascular disease. Co.'s products and technologies to treat cardiovascular disease are categorized into five main areas: Heart Valve Therapy; Critical Care; Cardiac Surgery Systems; Vascular; and Other Distributed Products. At Dec 31 2007, Co.'s products included Carpentier Edwards PERIMOUNT pericardial valve, Swan-Ganz hemodynamic monitoring products, and Embol-X intra-aortic filtration system.

Recent Developments: For the year ended Dec 31 2007, net income decreased 13.4% to US$113.0 million from US$130.5 million in the prior year. Revenues were US$1.09 billion, up 5.2% from US$1.04 billion the year before. Direct operating expenses rose 1.2% to US$378.2 million from US$373.6 million in the comparable period the year before. Indirect operating expenses increased 16.0% to US$563.6 million from US$485.7 million in the equivalent prior-year period.

Prospects: Looking ahead, Co. is focusing on new product launches while progressing with its transcatheter heart valve platform. For instance, Co. plans to introduce additional product enhancements that will enable its FloTrac continuous cardiac output monitoring system, a minimally invasive cardiac monitoring technology, to address a wider range of patients. Further, Co. anticipates that it will obtain FDA approval for its PERIMOUNT Magna mitral valve by mid-2008. In view of this, Co. plans to introduce its enhanced aortic valve, the Magna Ease, in the U.S. in 2009. For full year 2008, Co. expects total sales of $1.16 billion to $1.21 billion, with earnings per diluted share of $2.32 and $2.40.

Financial Data

(US$ in Thousands)	12/31/2007	12/31/2006	12/31/2005	12/31/2004	12/31/2003	12/31/2002	12/31/2001	12/31/2000
Earnings Per Share	1.87	2.10	1.27	0.03	1.29	0.91	(0.19)	(4.81)
Cash Flow Per Share	3.67	3.95	2.30	3.02	2.07	2.04	1.71	2.34
Tang Book Value Per Share	6.40	5.12	3.61	2.32	3.63	2.39	0.96	N.M.
Income Statement								
Total Revenue	1,091,100	1,037,000	997,900	931,500	860,500	704,000	692,000	804,000
EBITDA	206,000	231,800	182,600	98,600	150,100	106,600	60,000	(174,000)
Income Before Taxes	149,800	172,300	116,700	30,100	92,800	56,000	(9,000)	(259,000)
Income Taxes	36,800	41,800	37,400	28,400	13,800	300	1,000	13,000
Net Income	113,000	130,500	79,300	1,700	79,000	55,700	(11,000)	(272,000)
Average Shares	62,700	63,900	62,300	62,000	61,100	61,300	59,000	58,400
Balance Sheet								
Current Assets	581,700	531,600	514,200	367,500	360,200	326,400	293,000	282,000
Total Assets	1,345,100	1,246,800	1,229,100	1,112,700	1,101,400	1,008,200	973,000	1,088,000
Current Liabilities	375,400	226,200	194,200	195,400	167,200	197,900	184,000	219,000
Long-Term Obligations	61,700	235,900	316,100	267,100	255,800	245,500	310,000	367,000
Total Liabilities	510,100	497,400	539,100	484,600	466,300	468,800	514,000	648,000
Stockholders' Equity	835,000	749,400	690,000	628,100	635,100	539,400	459,000	440,000
Shares Outstanding	56,600	57,700	59,524	59,438	59,480	60,177	59,327	58,668
Statistical Record								
Return on Assets %	8.72	10.54	6.77	0.15	7.49	5.62	N.M.	N.M.
Return on Equity %	14.26	18.13	12.03	0.27	13.45	11.16	N.M.	N.M.
EBITDA Margin %	18.88	22.35	18.30	10.59	17.44	15.14	8.67	N.M.
Net Margin %	10.36	12.58	7.95	0.18	9.18	7.91	N.M.	N.M.
Asset Turnover	0.84	0.84	0.85	0.84	0.82	0.71	0.67	0.64
Current Ratio	1.55	2.35	2.65	1.88	2.15	1.65	1.59	1.29
Debt to Equity	0.07	0.31	0.46	0.43	0.40	0.46	0.68	0.83
Price Range	52.76-45.96	48.31-41.35	46.76-39.47	42.26-29.61	32.52-24.44	29.53-18.57	28.76-16.88	26.25-13.00
P/E Ratio	28.21-24.58	23.00-19.69	36.82-31.08	N.M.	25.21-18.95	32.45-20.41	...	...

Address: One Edwards Way, Irvine, CA 92614 Telephone: 949-250-2500 Fax: 949-250-2525	Web Site: www.edwards.com Officers: Michael A. Mussallem - Chmn., C.E.O. Corinne H. Lyle - Corp. V.P., C.F.O., Treas.	Auditors: PricewaterhouseCoopers LLP Investor Contact: 949-250-2806 Transfer Agents: Computershare Investor Services

EL PASO CORP.

Exchange	Symbol	Price	52Wk Range	Yield	P/E
NYS	EP	$16.64 (3/31/2008)	18.43-14.66	0.96	10.88

*7 Year Price Score 75.00   *NYSE Composite Index=100   *12 Month Price Score 105.78

TRADING VOLUME (thousand shares)

Interim Earnings (Per Share)

Qtr.	Mar	Jun	Sep	Dec
2003	(0.66)	(1.99)	(0.24)	(0.33)
2004	(0.32)	0.03	(0.33)	(0.85)
2005	0.17	(0.38)	(0.50)	(0.26)
2006	0.49	0.21	0.18	(0.23)
2007	0.89	0.22	0.20	0.22

Interim Dividends (Per Share)

Amt	Decl	Ex	Rec	Pay
0.04Q	7/26/2007	9/5/2007	9/7/2007	10/1/2007
0.04Q	10/25/2007	12/5/2007	12/7/2007	1/7/2008
0.04Q	2/7/2008	3/5/2008	3/7/2008	4/1/2008
0.04Q	3/31/2008	6/4/2008	6/6/2008	7/1/2008

Indicated Div: $0.16

Valuation Analysis

		Institutional Holding	
Forecast P/E	11.22 (1/10/2007)	No of Institutions	402
Market Cap	$11.7 Billion	Shares	514,777,024
Book Value	5.3 Billion	% Held	73.56
Price/Book	2.21		
Price/Sales	2.51		

Business Summary: Gas Utilities (MIC: 7.4 SIC: 4922 NAIC: 486210)

El Paso is an energy company that operates in the regulated natural gas transmission and exploration and production sectors of the energy industry. Co. owns or have interests in North America interstate pipeline system that connects natural gas producing basins to its consuming markets. Co.'s exploration and production business is focused on the exploration for and the acquisition, development and production of natural gas, oil and natural gas liquids in the U.S., Brazil and Egypt. As at Dec 31 2007, Co. held an estimated 2.90 trillion cubic feet of proved natural gas and oil reserves, excluding its equity share in the proved reserves of an unconsolidated affiliate.

Recent Developments: For the year ended Dec 31 2007, income from continuing operations decreased 17.9% to US$436.0 million from US$531.0 million a year earlier. Net income increased 133.7% to US$1.11 billion from US$475.0 million in the prior year. Revenues were US$4.65 billion, up 8.6% from US$4.28 billion the year before. Operating income was US$1.65 billion versus US$1.43 billion in the prior year, an increase of 15.3%. Direct operating expenses rose 2.9% to US$245.0 million from US$238.0 million in the comparable period the year before. Indirect operating expenses increased 5.4% to US$2.76 billion from US$2.62 billion in the equivalent prior-year period.

Prospects: On Feb 7 2008, Co. closed on the previously announced acquisition of a 50.0% interest in the Gulf LNG Clean Energy Project, a liquefied natural gas terminal, for $294.0 million. The terminal, which is currently under construction in Pascagoula, MS, is expected to be placed in service in late 2011. Separately, for full-year 2008, Co. anticipates average daily production volumes of approximately 805 million cubic feet of natural gas equivalents per day (MMcfe/d) to 860 MMcfe/d, excluding approximately 65 MMcfe/d to 70 MMcfe/d from its equity investment in Four Star Oil and Gas Company. In addition, Co. is projecting earnings from continuing operations of $1.00 to $1.10 per share for 2008.

Financial Data

(US$ in Thousands)	12/31/2007	12/31/2006	12/31/2005	12/31/2004	12/31/2003	12/31/2002	12/31/2001	12/31/2000
Earnings Per Share	1.53	0.64	(0.98)	(1.48)	(3.23)	(2.62)	0.18	2.73
Cash Flow Per Share	2.59	3.10	0.41	2.05	3.90	0.78	8.16	(4.51)
Tang Book Value Per Share	6.47	4.93	3.38	4.68	5.36	11.69	17.63	15.20
Dividends Per Share	0.160	0.160	0.160	0.160	0.160	0.870	0.850	0.824
Dividend Payout %	10.46	25.00	...	...	...	...	472.22	30.18
Income Statement								
Total Revenue	4,648,000	4,281,000	4,017,000	5,874,000	6,711,000	12,194,000	57,475,000	21,950,000
EBITDA	2,779,000	2,659,000	1,381,000	1,825,000	1,794,000	1,021,000	...	...
Income Before Taxes	658,000	522,000	(991,000)	(777,000)	(1,200,000)	(1,784,000)	...	...
Income Taxes	222,000	(9,000)	(289,000)	25,000	(584,000)	(495,000)	182,000	286,000
Net Income	1,110,000	475,000	(606,000)	(948,000)	(1,928,000)	(1,467,000)	93,000	652,000
Average Shares	699,000	739,000	646,000	639,000	597,000	560,000	516,000	243,000
Balance Sheet								
Net PPE	19,354,000	16,678,000	19,135,000	18,812,000	18,594,000	23,610,000	24,591,000	11,659,000
Total Assets	24,579,000	27,261,000	31,838,000	31,383,000	37,084,000	46,224,000	48,171,000	27,445,000
Long-Term Obligations	12,483,000	13,329,000	17,023,000	18,241,000	20,275,000	16,307,000	13,184,000	5,949,000
Total Liabilities	18,734,000	23,044,000	28,418,000	27,577,000	32,163,000	34,427,000	34,802,000	21,818,000
Stockholders' Equity	5,280,000	4,186,000	3,389,000	3,439,000	4,474,000	8,377,000	9,356,000	3,569,000
Shares Outstanding	700,536	697,117	659,461	643,297	632,201	599,568	530,734	234,780
Statistical Record								
Return on Assets %	4.28	1.61	N.M.	N.M.	N.M.	N.M.	0.25	2.95
Return on Equity %	23.45	12.54	N.M.	N.M.	N.M.	N.M.	1.44	19.96
EBITDA Margin %	59.79	62.11	34.38	31.07	26.73	8.37	...	...
Net Margin %	23.88	11.10	(15.09)	(16.14)	(28.73)	(12.03)	0.16	2.97
PPE Turnover	0.26	0.24	0.21	0.31	0.32	0.51	3.17	2.00
Asset Turnover	0.18	0.14	0.13	0.17	0.16	0.26	1.52	0.99
Debt to Equity	2.36	3.18	5.02	5.30	4.53	1.95	1.41	1.67
Price Range	18.43-13.76	16.20-11.88	13.92-9.54	11.54-6.62	9.96-3.45	46.77-5.30	74.50-38.60	73.19-31.25
P/E Ratio	12.05-8.99	25.31-18.56	...	...	...	...	413.89-214.44	26.81-11.45
Average Yield %	1.00	1.16	1.40	1.96	2.20	3.62	1.51	1.63

Address: 1001 Louisiana Street, Houston, TX 77002 **Telephone:** 713-420-2600 **Fax:** 713-420-4417	**Web Site:** www.elpaso.com **Officers:** Ronald L. Kuehn Jr. - Chmn. Douglas L. Foshee - Pres., C.E.O.	**Auditors:** Ernst & Young LLP **Investor Contact:** 713-420-5855 **Transfer Agents:** Fleet National Bank c/o EquiServe, Providence, RI

ELECTRONIC DATA SYSTEMS CORP.

Exchange	Symbol	Price	52Wk Range	Yield	P/E
NYS	EDS	$16.65 (3/31/2008)	29.89-15.90	1.20	12.33

*7 Year Price Score 63.58   *NYSE Composite Index=100   *12 Month Price Score 82.57

Interim Earnings (Per Share)

Qtr.	Mar	Jun	Sep	Dec
2003	(0.26)	0.28	0.00	(0.79)
2004	(0.02)	0.54	(0.30)	0.11
2005	0.01	0.05	0.02	0.21
2006	0.05	0.20	0.24	0.41
2007	0.31	0.26	0.42	0.35

Interim Dividends (Per Share)

Amt	Decl	Ex	Rec	Pay
0.05Q	4/17/2007	5/11/2007	5/15/2007	6/11/2007
0.05Q	7/17/2007	8/13/2007	8/15/2007	9/10/2007
0.05Q	10/16/2007	11/13/2007	11/15/2007	12/10/2007
0.05Q	2/5/2008	2/15/2008	2/20/2008	3/10/2008

Indicated Div: $0.20

Valuation Analysis | **Institutional Holding**

Forecast P/E	16.50	No of Institutions
	(1/10/2007)	359
Market Cap	$8.5 Billion	Shares
Book Value	9.7 Billion	462,656,032
Price/Book	0.88	% Held
Price/Sales	0.38	89.93

TRADING VOLUME (thousand shares)

Business Summary: IT & Technology (MIC: 10.2 SIC: 7371 NAIC: 541511)

Electronic Data Systems is a technology services firm that provides its clients with a portfolio of related services worldwide within the categories of infrastructure, applications and business process outsourcing services. Co.'s services include the design, construction or management of computer networks, information systems, information processing facilities as well as business processes. As of Dec 31 2007, Co. served clients in the manufacturing, financial services, healthcare, communications, energy, transportation, and consumer and retail industries as well as governments around the world.

Recent Developments: For the year ended Dec 31 2007, income from continuing operations increased 46.1% to US$729.0 million from US$499.0 million a year earlier. Net income increased 52.3% to US$716.0 million from US$470.0 million in the prior year. Revenues were US$22.13 billion, up 4.1% from US$21.27 billion the year before. Operating income was US$1.13 billion versus US$816.0 million in the prior year, an increase of 38.7%. Direct operating expenses rose 1.9% to US$18.94 billion from US$18.58 billion in the comparable period the year before. Indirect operating expenses increased 10.3% to US$2.07 billion from US$1.87 billion in the equivalent prior-year period.

Prospects: For 2008, Co. will invest in improving its cost competitiveness, expanding its sales capabilities, growing its applications services business and improving its service quality and client satisfaction. Co. expects these initiatives to improve operating margin in 2009. In addition, Co. expects revenues to exceed $22.50 billion in 2008, representing growth of approximately 2.0%, including the effect of its Saber Government Solutions acquisition in 2007 but excluding the effect of currency exchange rates. Separately, Co. recently announced that, as the leader of the oneMeridian consortium, it has been awarded an eight-year information technology services deal worth approximately $1.00 billion.

Financial Data

(US$ in Thousands)	12/31/2007	12/31/2006	12/31/2005	12/31/2004	12/31/2003	12/31/2002	12/31/2001	12/31/2000
Earnings Per Share	1.35	0.89	0.28	0.32	(3.55)	2.28	2.81	2.40
Cash Flow Per Share	3.99	3.72	2.50	2.62	2.89	4.69	3.66	3.33
Tang Book Value Per Share	7.20	5.41	5.81	5.59	N.M.	3.22	3.06	4.53
Dividends Per Share	0.200	0.200	0.200	0.400	0.600	0.600	0.600	0.600
Dividend Payout %	14.81	22.47	71.43	125.00	...	26.32	21.35	25.00
Income Statement								
Total Revenue	22,134,000	21,268,000	19,757,000	20,669,000	21,476,000	21,502,000	21,543,000	19,226,800
EBITDA	2,560,000	2,157,000	1,961,000	(67,000)	1,575,000	3,226,000	3,928,000	3,440,700
Income Before Taxes	1,089,000	756,000	439,000	(388,000)	(389,000)	1,525,000	2,199,000	1,800,000
Income Taxes	360,000	257,000	153,000	(93,000)	(137,000)	518,000	812,000	656,700
Net Income	716,000	470,000	150,000	159,000	(1,690,000)	1,116,000	1,363,000	1,143,300
Average Shares	542,000	529,000	526,000	501,000	479,000	489,000	484,000	476,400
Balance Sheet								
Current Assets	8,445,000	8,257,000	8,502,000	8,479,000	6,823,000	9,385,000	7,374,000	6,166,700
Total Assets	19,224,000	17,954,000	17,087,000	17,744,000	18,280,000	18,880,000	16,353,000	12,700,300
Current Liabilities	4,916,000	5,234,000	5,048,000	5,256,000	7,473,000	6,129,000	4,367,000	4,318,300
Long-Term Obligations	3,209,000	2,965,000	2,939,000	3,168,000	3,488,000	4,148,000	4,692,000	2,585,600
Total Liabilities	9,533,000	10,058,000	9,575,000	10,304,000	12,566,000	11,858,000	9,907,000	7,561,600
Stockholders' Equity	9,691,000	7,896,000	7,512,000	7,440,000	5,714,000	7,022,000	6,446,000	5,138,700
Shares Outstanding	509,862	514,317	523,286	515,304	480,604	476,872	477,315	465,298
Statistical Record								
Return on Assets %	3.85	2.68	0.86	0.87	N.M.	6.33	9.38	9.04
Return on Equity %	8.14	6.10	2.01	2.40	N.M.	16.57	23.53	23.57
EBITDA Margin %	11.57	10.14	9.93	N.M.	7.33	15.00	18.23	17.90
Net Margin %	3.23	2.21	0.76	0.76	N.M.	5.19	6.33	5.95
Asset Turnover	1.19	1.21	1.13	1.14	1.16	1.22	1.48	1.52
Current Ratio	1.72	1.58	1.68	1.61	0.91	1.53	1.69	1.43
Debt to Equity	0.33	0.38	0.39	0.43	0.61	0.59	0.73	0.50
Price Range	29.89-19.37	27.98-22.60	24.78-18.68	25.22-15.79	24.56-14.45	68.55-11.27	71.88-53.12	75.00-39.00
P/E Ratio	22.14-14.35	31.44-25.39	88.50-66.71	78.81-49.34	...	30.07-4.94	25.58-18.90	31.25-16.25
Average Yield %	0.79	0.79	0.94	2.01	2.98	1.48	0.97	1.08

Address: 5400 Legacy Drive, Plano, TX 75024 -3199	Web Site: www.eds.com	Auditors: KPMG LLP
Telephone: 972-604-6000	Officers: Michael H. Jordan - Chmn., C.E.O. Jeffrey M. Heller - Pres.	Investor Contact: 888-610-1122
Fax: 972-605-6796		

273

EMBARQ CORP

Exchange	Symbol	Price	52Wk Range	Yield	P/E
NYS	EQ	$40.10 (3/31/2008)	65.06-38.93	6.86	9.03

*7 Year Price Score N/A   *NYSE Composite Index=100   *12 Month Price Score 84.79

TRADING VOLUME (thousand shares)

Interim Earnings (Per Share)

Qtr.	Mar	Jun	Sep	Dec
2005	0.00	0.00	0.00	0.00
2006	0.00	1.44	1.06	0.00
2007	1.05	1.15	1.01	1.23

Interim Dividends (Per Share)

Amt	Decl	Ex	Rec	Pay
0.625Q	4/25/2007	6/6/2007	6/8/2007	6/30/2007
0.625Q	8/16/2007	9/5/2007	9/7/2007	9/30/2007
0.625Q	10/15/2007	12/6/2007	12/10/2007	12/31/2007
0.688Q	1/9/2008	3/6/2008	3/10/2008	3/31/2008

Indicated Div: $2.75

Valuation Analysis   Institutional Holding

Forecast P/E	N/A	No of Institutions
		370
Market Cap	$6.1 Billion	Shares
Book Value	264.0 Million	128,133,696
Price/Book	23.25	% Held
Price/Sales	0.96	85.12

Business Summary: Communications (MIC: 10.1 SIC: 4813 NAIC: 517110)

Embarq provides, both directly and via wholesale and sales agency relationships, communications services consisting of local and long distance voice and data services, high-speed Internet access, satellite video, wireless and other communication related products and services to consumer and business customers primarily throughout 18 states. Co. also provides access to its local network and other wholesale communications services for customers and other carriers. Co.'s Logistics segment provides wholesale product distribution, logistics and configuration services. Co.'s Telecommunications segment provides voice, data, high-speed Internet, wireless, product and other products and services.

Recent Developments: For the year ended Dec 31 2007, net income decreased 12.9% to US$683.0 million from US$784.0 million in the prior year. Revenues were US$6.37 billion, up 0.0% from US$6.36 billion the year before. Operating income was US$1.50 billion versus US$1.54 billion in the prior year, a decrease of 2.6%. Direct operating expenses rose 0.2% to US$2.20 billion from US$2.19 billion in the comparable period the year before. Indirect operating expenses increased 1.4% to US$2.67 billion from US$2.63 billion in the equivalent prior-year period.

Prospects: Co.'s near-term outlook appears to be mixed. For the full year of 2008, Co. expects wireless dilution to improve by as much as 75.0% from the $77.0 million in 2007. In addition, Co. anticipates access line losses to be flat or slightly higher compared with the 434,000 line losses in 2007, based on an absolute basis. Similarly, Co. foresees revenues in its Telecommunications segment to decrease by 1.2% to 2.5% to the range of $5.75 billion to $5.83 billion, despite access line losses. Also, Co. foresees that the declining rate of its total voice revenues will increase due to the continuing access line losses but forecasts continued growth in special access and business data services.

Financial Data

(US$ in Thousands)	12/31/2007	12/31/2006	12/31/2005	12/31/2004	12/31/2003
Earnings Per Share	4.44	...	...	...	...
Cash Flow Per Share	10.69	...	...	...	...
Tang Book Value Per Share	1.55	...	...	...	...
Dividends Per Share	2.375	...	...	...	...
Dividend Payout %	53.49	...	...	...	...
Income Statement					
Total Revenue	6,365,000	6,363,000	6,254,000	6,139,000	6,159,000
EBITDA	2,564,000	2,585,000	2,534,000	2,560,000	2,597,000
Income Before Taxes	1,075,000	1,234,000	1,472,000	1,486,000	1,489,000
Income Taxes	392,000	450,000	578,000	569,000	569,000
Net Income	683,000	784,000	878,000	917,000	1,554,000
Average Shares	153,900	...	...	...	...
Balance Sheet					
Current Assets	986,000	1,023,000	1,072,000	1,054,000	...
Total Assets	8,901,000	9,091,000	9,221,000	9,329,000	...
Current Liabilities	1,198,000	1,264,000	1,084,000	1,084,000	...
Long-Term Obligations	5,779,000	6,421,000	1,123,000	1,125,000	...
Total Liabilities	8,637,000	9,559,000	4,369,000	4,369,000	...
Stockholders' Equity	264,000	(468,000)	4,852,000	4,960,000	...
Shares Outstanding	153,100	149,700	...	...	...
Statistical Record					
Return on Assets %	7.59	8.56	9.47	...	...
Return on Equity %	...	35.77	17.90	...	...
EBITDA Margin %	40.28	40.63	40.52	41.70	42.17
Net Margin %	10.73	12.32	14.04	14.94	25.23
Asset Turnover	0.71	0.69	0.67	...	...
Current Ratio	0.82	0.81	0.99	0.97	...
Debt to Equity	21.89	...	0.23	0.23	...
Price Range	65.06-47.66	52.94-39.33	...	...	...
P/E Ratio	14.65-10.73	...	...	...	...
Average Yield %	4.14	...	...	...	...

Address: 5454 West 110th Street, Overland Park, KS 66211 Telephone: 913-323-4637	Web Site: www.embarq.com Officers: Thomas A. Gerke - Pres., C.E.O. Gene M. Betts C.E.O.	Auditors: KPMG LLP Transfer Agents: UMB Bank, n.a., Kansas City, MO

EMC CORP. (MA)

Exchange	Symbol	Price	52Wk Range	Yield	P/E
NYS	EMC	$14.34 (3/31/2008)	25.39-14.09	N/A	18.62

*7 Year Price Score 105.45 *NYSE Composite Index=100 *12 Month Price Score 91.15

Interim Earnings (Per Share)

Qtr.	Mar	Jun	Sep	Dec
2003	0.02	0.04	0.07	0.10
2004	0.06	0.08	0.09	0.13
2005	0.11	0.12	0.17	0.07
2006	0.12	0.12	0.13	0.18
2007	0.15	0.16	0.23	0.24

Interim Dividends (Per Share)
No Dividends Paid

Valuation Analysis | Institutional Holding

Forecast P/E	N/A	No of Institutions	
		749	
Market Cap	$30.1 Billion	Shares	
Book Value	12.5 Billion	1,660,275,840	
Price/Book	2.41	% Held	
Price/Sales	2.28	79.10	

Business Summary: IT & Technology (MIC: 10.2 SIC: 3572 NAIC: 334112)

EMC develops, delivers and supports the information infrastructure technologies and applications. Co.'s Information Infrastructure business supports customers' information lifecycle management strategies and helps them build information infrastructures that store and protect the growing quantities of information. Co.'s Information Infrastructure business consists of three segments: Information Storage, Content Management and Archiving, and RSA Information Security. Co.'s VMware Virtual Infrastructure business provides virtualization applications that separate the operating system and application software from the underlying hardware to achieve improvements in manageability.

Recent Developments: For the year ended Dec 31 2007, net income increased 35.7% to US$1.67 billion from US$1.23 billion in the prior year. Revenues were US$13.23 billion, up 18.6% from US$11.16 billion the year before. Operating income was US$1.74 billion versus US$1.21 billion in the prior year, an increase of 44.0%. Direct operating expenses rose 14.8% to US$6.02 billion from US$5.24 billion in the comparable period the year before. Indirect operating expenses increased 16.3% to US$5.47 billion from US$4.71 billion in the equivalent prior-year period.

Prospects: On Feb 21 2008, Co. signed a definitive agreement to acquire Pi Corporation, a developer of software and provider of services for personal information management. The acquisition will be an all-cash transaction and is expected to be completed in the first quarter of 2008. Co. expects the acquisition to be dilutive by $0.01 per diluted share in 2008. Separately, on Mar 6 2008, Co. acquired Document Sciences Corporation, a provider of document output management and customer communications management software for approximately $85.8 million. Co. believes that this acquisition will extend its offerings, as well as adding communications services to improve its interactive content management.

Financial Data

(US$ in Thousands)	12/31/2007	12/31/2006	12/31/2005	12/31/2004	12/31/2003	12/31/2002	12/31/2001	12/31/2000
Earnings Per Share	0.77	0.54	0.47	0.36	0.22	(0.05)	(0.23)	0.79
Cash Flow Per Share	1.50	0.95	0.93	0.87	0.69	0.66	0.74	0.97
Tang Book Value Per Share	2.40	1.56	3.20	3.22	3.19	3.21	3.42	3.72
Income Statement								
Total Revenue	13,230,205	11,155,090	9,663,955	8,229,488	6,236,808	5,438,352	7,090,633	8,872,816
EBITDA	3,049,698	2,188,303	2,381,783	1,868,618	1,108,476	381,691	108,515	2,999,627
Income Before Taxes	2,059,569	1,390,018	1,652,243	1,185,030	571,023	(296,487)	(577,035)	2,441,198
Income Taxes	378,446	162,664	519,078	313,841	74,915	(177,781)	(69,323)	659,123
Net Income	1,665,668	1,223,982	1,133,165	871,189	496,108	(118,706)	(507,712)	1,707,073
Average Shares	2,157,873	2,286,304	2,432,382	2,450,570	2,237,656	2,206,294	2,211,273	2,245,203
Balance Sheet								
Current Assets	10,053,102	6,520,587	6,573,976	4,830,926	4,687,304	4,217,248	4,923,242	6,100,051
Total Assets	22,284,654	18,566,247	16,790,383	15,422,906	14,092,860	9,590,447	9,889,635	10,628,342
Current Liabilities	4,408,208	3,881,104	3,673,858	2,948,700	2,546,529	2,041,650	2,179,414	2,113,647
Long-Term Obligations	3,450,000	3,450,000	126,963	128,456	129,966	...	...	14,457
Total Liabilities	9,574,349	8,240,540	4,724,953	3,899,619	3,208,139	2,364,445	2,288,815	2,451,133
Stockholders' Equity	12,521,317	10,325,707	12,065,430	11,523,287	10,884,721	7,226,002	7,600,820	8,177,209
Shares Outstanding	2,102,187	2,122,339	2,384,147	2,404,969	2,414,739	2,185,375	2,220,382	2,195,489
Statistical Record								
Return on Assets %	8.15	6.92	7.04	5.89	4.19	N.M.	N.M.	19.97
Return on Equity %	14.58	10.93	9.61	7.75	5.48	N.M.	N.M.	27.07
EBITDA Margin %	23.05	19.62	24.65	22.71	17.77	7.02	1.53	33.81
Net Margin %	12.59	10.97	11.73	10.59	7.95	N.M.	N.M.	20.08
Asset Turnover	0.65	0.63	0.60	0.56	0.53	0.56	0.69	0.99
Current Ratio	2.28	1.68	1.79	1.64	1.84	2.07	2.26	2.89
Debt to Equity	0.28	0.33	0.01	0.01	0.01	...	...	N.M.
Price Range	25.39-12.93	14.58-9.65	14.87-11.47	15.59-9.37	14.49-6.14	17.37-3.83	78.37-11.00	101.29-47.09
P/E Ratio	32.97-16.79	27.00-17.87	31.64-24.40	43.31-26.03	65.86-27.91	...	...	128.21-59.61

Address: 176 South Street, Hopkinton, MA 01748	**Web Site:** www.emc.com	**Auditors:** PricewaterhouseCoopers LLP
Telephone: 508-435-1000	**Officers:** Michael C. Ruettgers - Chmn. Joseph M. Tucci - Pres., C.E.O.	**Investor Contact:** 508-293-7137
Fax: 508-435-5222		

EMCOR GROUP, INC.

Exchange	Symbol	Price	52Wk Range	Yield	P/E
NYS	EME	$22.21 (3/31/2008)	38.31-18.54	N/A	11.69

*7 Year Price Score 139.50 *NYSE Composite Index=100 *12 Month Price Score 84.50

TRADING VOLUME (thousand shares)

Interim Earnings (Per Share)

Qtr.	Mar	Jun	Sep	Dec
2003	0.05	0.13	0.11	0.04
2004	0.09	0.02	0.25	0.17
2005	0.03	0.13	0.48	0.30
2006	0.11	0.26	0.34	0.61
2007	0.18	0.39	0.57	0.75

Interim Dividends (Per Share)

No Dividends Paid

Valuation Analysis / **Institutional Holding**

Forecast P/E	17.00	No of Institutions
	(1/10/2007)	194
Market Cap	$1.4 Billion	Shares
Book Value	885.0 Million	34,118,864
Price/Book	1.64	% Held
Price/Sales	0.24	N/A

Business Summary: Building & General Construction (MIC: 3.2 SIC: 1731 NAIC: 238210)

EMCOR Group provides services to a range of commercial, industrial, utility and institutional customers through approximately 70 primary operating subsidiaries and joint venture entities. Co. is primarily focused on providing construction services relating to electrical and mechanical systems in facilities of all types and in providing services for the operation, maintenance and management of all aspects of such facilities, commonly referred to as facilities services. As of Dec 31 2007, Co.'s offices are located throughout the U.S., in Canada and in the U.K. Additionally, Co. also conducts its business through two joint-ventures in the United Arab Emirates.

Recent Developments: For the year ended Dec 31 2007, income from continuing operations increased 45.2% to US$124.0 million from US$85.4 million a year earlier. Net income increased 46.4% to US$126.8 million from US$86.6 million in the prior year. Revenues were US$5.93 billion, up 20.9% from US$4.90 billion the year before. Operating income was US$199.8 million versus US$111.8 million in the prior year, an increase of 78.8%. Direct operating expenses rose 20.1% to US$5.22 billion from US$4.35 billion in the comparable period the year before. Indirect operating expenses increased 14.2% to US$503.0 million from US$440.6 million in the equivalent prior-year period.

Prospects: Co. is continuing to build its presence in growth markets, such as oil and gas, healthcare and transportation that should be either independent of or countercyclical to broader economic trends. For example, on Jan 7 2008, Co. announced that it has acquired Redman Equipment & Manufacturing Company, a privately held aftermarket heat exchanger services provider. The acquisition should contribute to Co.'s growing presence in the industrial services market by facilitating it to extend its Ohmstede's integrated shop and service offerings to the West Coast markets. Meanwhile, Co. is expecting revenues of $6.30 billion to $6.50 billion and diluted earnings of $2.08 to $2.28 per share for 2008.

Financial Data

(US$ in Thousands)	12/31/2007	12/31/2006	12/31/2005	12/31/2004	12/31/2003	12/31/2002	12/31/2001	12/31/2000
Earnings Per Share	1.90	1.33	0.94	0.53	0.33	1.02	0.85	0.74
Cash Flow Per Share	4.02	3.31	2.30	0.89	0.02	2.60	1.57	2.18
Tang Book Value Per Share	1.06	6.03	5.06	4.33	3.68	3.11	6.17	3.96
Income Statement								
Total Revenue	5,927,152	5,021,036	4,714,547	4,747,880	4,534,646	3,968,051	3,419,854	3,460,204
EBITDA	235,445	135,153	99,247	64,542	69,687	130,551	106,882	95,026
Income Before Taxes	201,749	117,738	71,030	33,162	36,916	112,326	89,474	71,587
Income Taxes	77,706	30,484	9,738	(45)	16,295	49,424	39,462	31,498
Net Income	126,808	86,634	60,042	33,207	20,621	62,902	50,012	40,089
Average Shares	66,731	65,480	63,669	62,266	61,846	61,828	60,960	59,774
Balance Sheet								
Current Assets	1,935,790	1,662,413	1,389,803	1,425,571	1,389,156	1,334,935	1,217,324	1,138,760
Total Assets	2,871,643	2,089,023	1,778,941	1,817,969	1,795,247	1,758,491	1,349,664	1,261,864
Current Liabilities	1,514,223	1,208,348	1,045,316	1,162,373	1,178,457	1,179,875	854,261	852,387
Long-Term Obligations	223,453	1,239	1,406	1,332	561	905	848	115,878
Total Liabilities	1,986,602	1,378,714	1,163,505	1,255,608	1,273,891	1,268,621	927,731	1,028,361
Stockholders' Equity	885,041	710,309	615,436	562,361	521,356	489,870	421,933	233,503
Shares Outstanding	65,196	63,655	62,207	60,944	60,128	59,675	59,260	41,882
Statistical Record								
Return on Assets %	5.11	4.48	3.34	1.83	1.16	4.05	3.83	3.45
Return on Equity %	15.90	13.07	10.20	6.11	4.08	13.80	15.26	19.80
EBITDA Margin %	3.97	2.69	2.11	1.36	1.54	3.29	3.13	2.75
Net Margin %	2.14	1.73	1.27	0.70	0.45	1.59	1.46	1.16
Asset Turnover	2.39	2.60	2.62	2.62	2.55	2.55	2.62	2.98
Current Ratio	1.28	1.38	1.33	1.23	1.18	1.13	1.43	1.34
Debt to Equity	0.25	N.M.	N.M.	N.M.	N.M.	N.M.	N.M.	0.50
Price Range	38.31-23.52	31.31-17.79	18.06-10.54	11.72-8.62	13.68-8.32	15.90-11.04	12.04-6.17	6.84-4.39
P/E Ratio	20.16-12.38	23.54-13.37	19.21-11.21	22.12-16.25	41.46-25.22	15.59-10.82	14.16-7.26	9.25-5.93

Address: 301 Merritt Seven, Norwalk, CT 06851	**Web Site:** www.emcorgroup.com	**Auditors:** ERNST & YOUNG LLP
Telephone: 203-849-7800	**Officers:** Frank T. MacInnis - Chmn., Pres., C.E.O. Sheldon I. Cammaker - Exec. V.P., Sec., Gen. Couns.	**Investor Contact:** 203-849-7938
Fax: 203-849-7900		**Transfer Agents:** Bank of New York

EMERSON ELECTRIC CO.

Exchange	Symbol	Price	52Wk Range	Yield	P/E	Div Acheiver
NYS	EMR	$51.46 (3/31/2008)	58.32-41.85	2.33	18.25	51 Years

*7 Year Price Score 116.42 *NYSE Composite Index=100 *12 Month Price Score 108.97

Interim Earnings (Per Share)

Qtr.	Dec	Mar	Jun	Sep
2004-05	0.35	0.41	0.43	0.51
2005-06	0.48	0.53	0.59	0.65
2006-07	0.55	0.61	0.72	0.78
2007-08	0.71	...	...	...

Interim Dividends (Per Share)

Amt	Decl	Ex	Rec	Pay
0.263Q	5/1/2007	5/9/2007	5/11/2007	6/11/2007
0.263Q	8/7/2007	8/15/2007	8/17/2007	9/10/2007
0.30Q	11/6/2007	11/14/2007	11/16/2007	12/10/2007
0.30Q	2/5/2008	2/13/2008	2/15/2008	3/10/2008

Indicated Div: $1.20 (Div. Reinv. Plan)

Valuation Analysis

Forecast P/E	15.41
	(1/10/2007)
Market Cap	$40.5 Billion
Book Value	9.2 Billion
Price/Book	4.42
Price/Sales	1.75

Institutional Holding

No of Institutions	946
Shares	580,411,392
% Held	72.74

Business Summary: Electrical (MIC: 11.14 SIC: 3823 NAIC: 335312)

Emerson Electric is engaged in the design and supply of product technology and delivery of engineering services in industrial, commercial and consumer markets globally. Co. is organized into five business segments, based on the nature of the products and services rendered, namely Process Management, Industrial Automation, Network Power, Climate Technologies, and Appliance and Tools. As of Sep 30 2007, Co. had approximately 265 manufacturing locations worldwide, of which approximately 165 were located outside the U.S., primarily in Europe and to a lesser extent in Asia, Canada and Latin America.

Recent Developments: For the quarter ended Dec 31 2007, income from continuing operations increased 17.3% to US$522.0 million from US$445.0 million in the year-earlier quarter. Net income increased 27.0% to US$565.0 million from US$445.0 million in the year-earlier quarter. Revenues were US$5.64 billion, up 11.6% from US$5.05 billion the year before. Direct operating expenses rose 11.0% to US$3.62 billion from US$3.26 billion in the comparable period the year before. Indirect operating expenses increased 10.4% to US$1.19 billion from US$1.08 billion in the equivalent prior-year period.

Prospects: For the fiscal year ending Sep 30 2008, Co. is targeting earnings from continuing operations in the range of $2.95 to $3.05 per share, reflecting growth of 11.0% to 15.0%. This guidance is based on anticipated underlying sales growth in the range of 5.0% to 7.0%, reported sales growth in the range of 9.0% to 11.0%, and operating profit margin improvement of 40 to 60 basis points. Separately, on Jan 3 2008, Co. announced the sale of its Brooks Instrument unit to American Industrial Partners Capital Fund IV, L.P. for about $100.0 million. This transaction reflects Co.'s ongoing strategy to manage its business towards potential businesses that are strategic to its overall portfolio.

Financial Data
(US$ in Thousands)

	3 Mos	09/30/2007	09/30/2006	09/30/2005	09/30/2004	09/30/2003	09/30/2002	09/30/2001
Earnings Per Share	2.82	2.66	2.24	1.70	1.49	1.29	0.14	1.20
Cash Flow Per Share	3.96	3.80	3.08	2.64	2.64	2.07	2.17	2.01
Tang Book Value Per Share	2.24	2.99	2.66	2.34	2.36	1.80	0.99	1.11
Dividends Per Share	1.087	1.050	0.890	0.830	0.800	0.785	0.775	0.765
Dividend Payout %	38.56	39.47	39.73	48.82	53.69	60.62	534.48	63.75
Income Statement								
Total Revenue	5,637,000	22,572,000	20,133,000	17,305,000	15,615,000	13,958,000	13,824,000	15,479,600
EBITDA	998,000	3,923,000	3,438,000	2,858,000	2,561,000	2,179,000	2,339,000	2,601,400
Depn & Amortn	171,000	...	...	...	...	...	...	...
Income Before Taxes	778,000	3,107,000	2,684,000	2,149,000	1,852,000	1,414,000	1,565,000	1,588,600
Income Taxes	256,000	971,000	839,000	727,000	595,000	401,000	505,000	556,800
Net Income	565,000	2,136,000	1,845,000	1,422,000	1,257,000	1,089,000	122,000	1,031,800
Average Shares	796,300	803,900	824,400	837,800	844,400	841,800	841,800	859,000
Balance Sheet								
Current Assets	8,994,000	8,065,000	7,330,000	6,837,000	6,416,000	5,500,000	4,961,000	5,320,100
Total Assets	20,854,000	19,680,000	18,672,000	17,227,000	16,361,000	15,194,000	14,545,000	15,046,400
Current Liabilities	6,408,000	5,546,000	5,374,000	4,931,000	4,339,000	3,417,000	4,400,000	5,379,100
Long Term Obligations	3,197,000	3,372,000	3,128,000	3,128,000	3,136,000	3,733,000	2,990,000	2,255,600
Total Liabilities	11,680,000	10,908,000	10,518,000	9,827,000	9,123,000	8,734,000	8,804,000	8,932,400
Stockholders' Equity	9,174,000	8,772,000	8,154,000	7,400,000	7,238,000	6,460,000	5,741,000	6,114,000
Shares Outstanding	787,639	788,434	804,693	821,303	838,857	842,308	841,419	839,251
Statistical Record								
Return on Assets %	11.29	11.14	10.28	8.47	7.95	7.32	0.82	6.83
Return on Equity %	25.96	25.24	23.72	19.43	18.30	17.85	2.06	16.49
EBITDA Margin %	17.70	17.38	17.08	16.52	16.40	15.61	16.92	16.81
Net Margin %	10.02	9.46	9.16	8.22	8.05	7.80	0.88	6.67
Asset Turnover	1.16	1.18	1.12	1.03	0.99	0.94	0.93	1.02
Current Ratio	1.40	1.45	1.36	1.39	1.48	1.61	1.13	0.99
Debt to Equity	0.35	0.38	0.38	0.42	0.43	0.58	0.52	0.37
Price Range	58.32-41.85	53.37-41.10	43.73-33.97	35.94-30.68	34.23-26.32	28.40-21.21	32.76-21.60	39.41-22.90
P/E Ratio	20.68-14.84	20.06-15.45	19.52-15.16	21.14-18.04	22.97-17.67	22.01-16.44	233.96-154.29	32.84-19.08
Average Yield %	2.25	2.31	2.24	2.50	2.62	3.11	2.88	2.34

Address: 8000 W. Florissant Avenue, St. Louis, MO 63136 **Telephone:** 314-553-2000 **Fax:** 314-553-3527	**Web Site:** www.emerson.com **Officers:** David N. Farr - Chmn., C.E.O., Pres. Walter J. Galvin - Sr. Exec. V.P., C.F.O.	**Auditors:** KPMG LLP **Investor Contact:** 314-553-2197 **Transfer Agents:** EquiServe Trust Company, N.A., Providence, RI

ENBRIDGE ENERGY PARTNERS, L.P.

Exchange	Symbol	Price	52Wk Range	Yield	P/E
NYS	EEP	$47.55 (3/31/2008)	61.82-44.19	7.89	19.41

*7 Year Price Score 87.93   *NYSE Composite Index=100   *12 Month Price Score 99.77

Interim Earnings (Per Share)

Qtr.	Mar	Jun	Sep	Dec
2003	0.62	0.39	0.38	0.54
2004	0.50	0.56	0.39	0.61
2005	0.37	0.32	(0.32)	0.69
2006	1.12	0.96	1.03	0.51
2007	0.40	0.69	0.75	0.58

Interim Dividends (Per Share)

Amt	Decl	Ex	Rec	Pay
0.925Q	4/26/2007	5/3/2007	5/7/2007	5/15/2007
0.925Q	7/27/2007	8/2/2007	8/6/2007	8/14/2007
0.95Q	10/29/2007	11/2/2007	11/6/2007	11/14/2007
0.95Q	1/28/2008	2/4/2008	2/6/2008	2/14/2008

Indicated Div: $3.75

Valuation Analysis		Institutional Holding	
Forecast P/E	16.45	No of Institutions	151
	(1/10/2007)		
Market Cap	$4.3 Billion	Shares	11,871,978
Book Value	N/A	% Held	23.77
Price/Book	N/A		
Price/Sales	0.59		

Business Summary: Oil and Gas (MIC: 14.2 SIC: 4619 NAIC: 486990)

Enbridge Energy Partners owns and operates crude oil and liquid petroleum transportation and storage assets, natural gas gathering, treating, processing, transportation and marketing assets. The liquids segment includes Co.'s Lakehead, North Dakota and Mid-Continent systems. Co.'s natural gas segment includes the operations of natural gas gathering and transmission pipelines, and treating and processing plants. Co.'s marketing segment provides natural gas supply, transportation, balancing, storage and sales services. As of Dec 31 2007, Co. had about 5,000 miles of crude oil gathering and transportation lines and 28.9 million barrels of crude oil storage and terminaling capacity.

Recent Developments: For the year ended Dec 31 2007, income from continuing operations decreased 23.9% to US$216.9 million from US$284.9 million a year earlier. Net income decreased 12.4% to US$249.5 million from US$284.9 million in the prior year. Revenues were US$7.28 billion, up 11.9% from US$6.51 billion the year before. Operating income was US$318.8 million versus US$386.9 million in the prior year, a decrease of 17.6%. Direct operating expenses rose 13.2% to US$6.36 billion from US$5.62 billion in the comparable period the year before. Indirect operating expenses increased 20.0% to US$599.9 million from US$499.9 million in the equivalent prior-year period.

Prospects: Going forward, Co. is planning to develop new gathering, processing, transportation and storage assets to meet customer needs, by expanding capacity into new markets with favorable supply and demand fundamentals. Meanwhile, as part of its overall expansion program of approximately $5.00 billion covering 2007 through 2010, for full-year 2008, Co. is projecting capital expenditures to be approximately $1.40 billion, which includes $575.0 million for ongoing construction of the Southern Access Expansion, $215.0 million for start of construction for the Alberta Clipper Program, $540.0 million for other system enhancements, and $70.0 million for core maintenance activities.

Financial Data
(US$ in Thousands)

	12/31/2007	12/31/2006	12/31/2005	12/31/2004	12/31/2003	12/31/2002	12/31/2001	12/31/2000
Earnings Per Share	2.45	3.62	1.06	2.06	1.93	1.76	0.98	1.78
Cash Flow Per Share	5.37	4.58	4.30	4.36	2.77	5.47	4.05	4.05
Dividends Per Share	3.725	3.700	3.700	3.700	3.700	3.600	3.500	3.500
Dividend Payout %	152.04	102.21	349.06	179.61	191.71	204.55	357.14	196.63
Income Statement								
Income Before Taxes	222,000	...	...	...	...	...	39,400	...
Income Taxes	5,100	...	...	...	...	...	...	...
Net Income	249,500	284,900	89,200	138,200	114,700	78,100	38,900	60,200
Average Shares	86,300	70,200	62,100	56,100	47,700	36,700	30,200	28,900
Balance Sheet								
Total Assets	6,891,600	5,223,800	4,428,400	3,763,000	3,231,800	2,834,900	1,649,200	1,376,700
Total Liabilities	4,320,100	3,180,400	3,064,600	2,365,100	1,918,500	1,843,300	1,005,000	840,800
Shares Outstanding	90,789	77,595	65,556	59,111	44,078	35,226	32,966	28,902
Statistical Record								
Return on Assets %	4.12	5.90	2.18	3.94	3.68	3.48	2.57	4.30
Price Range	61.82-48.53	50.67-42.09	56.80-42.16	51.57-41.82	52.86-41.83	46.35-37.60	49.50-39.80	42.75-33.00
P/E Ratio	25.23-19.81	14.00-11.63	53.58-39.77	25.03-20.30	27.39-21.67	26.34-21.36	50.51-40.61	24.02-18.54
Average Yield %	6.97	8.02	7.15	7.66	7.82	8.34	7.79	9.14

Address: 1100 Louisiana Street, Suite 3300, Houston, TX 77002	Web Site: www.enbridgepartners.com	Auditors: PricewaterhouseCoopers LLP
Telephone: 888-650-8900	Officers: D. C. Tutcher - Pres. J. R. Bird - V.P. Liquids Transportation	Transfer Agents: Mellon Investor Services LLC, South Hackensack, NJ

ENERGEN CORP.

Exchange	Symbol	Price	52Wk Range	Yield	P/E	Div Achiever
NYS	EGN	$62.30 (3/31/2008)	69.18-49.10	0.77	14.56	25 Years

*7 Year Price Score 158.71 *NYSE Composite Index=100 ***12 Month Price Score 112.35**

Interim Earnings (Per Share)

Qtr.	Mar	Jun	Sep	Dec
2003	0.78	0.33	0.17	0.28
2004	0.82	0.30	0.19	0.43
2005	0.80	0.51	0.26	0.78
2006	1.18	0.67	0.56	1.31
2007	1.44	0.94	0.80	1.10

Interim Dividends (Per Share)

Amt	Decl	Ex	Rec	Pay
0.115Q	4/25/2007	5/11/2007	5/15/2007	6/1/2007
0.115Q	7/25/2007	8/13/2007	8/15/2007	9/4/2007
0.115Q	10/24/2007	11/13/2007	11/16/2007	12/3/2007
0.12Q	1/23/2008	2/13/2008	2/15/2008	3/3/2008

Indicated Div: $0.48 (Div. Reinv. Plan)

Valuation Analysis

	Institutional Holding	
Forecast P/E	11.94	No of Institutions
	(1/10/2007)	253
Market Cap	$4.4 Billion	Shares
Book Value	1.4 Billion	48,516,832
Price/Book	3.20	% Held
Price/Sales	3.07	67.05

TRADING VOLUME (thousand shares)

Business Summary: Gas Utilities (MIC: 7.4 SIC: 4924 NAIC: 221210)

Energen is an energy holding company engaged mainly in the development, acquisition, exploration and production of oil and gas in the continental U.S. (oil and gas operations) and in the purchase, distribution, and sale of natural gas principally in central and north Alabama (natural gas distribution). Co.'s two principal subsidiaries are Energen Resources Corporation (Energen Resources) and Alabama Gas Corporation (Alagasco). As of Dec 31 2007, Energen Resources' proved oil and gas reserves totaled 1,754 billion cubic feet equivalent. Also, as of Dec 31 2007, Alagasco's service territory is located in central and parts of north Alabama and included 177 cities and communities in 28 counties.

Recent Developments: For the year ended Dec 31 2007, income from continuing operations increased 13.0% to US$309.2 million from US$273.5 million a year earlier. Net income increased 13.0% to US$309.2 million from US$273.6 million in the prior year. Revenues were US$1.44 billion, up 2.9% from US$1.39 billion the year before. Operating income was US$522.0 million versus US$477.3 million in the prior year, an increase of 9.4%. Direct operating expenses declined 3.5% to US$651.9 million from US$675.3 million in the comparable period the year before. Indirect operating expenses increased 8.2% to US$261.2 million from US$241.4 million in the equivalent prior-year period.

Prospects: For 2008, Co. expects oil and gas capital spending of about $308.0 million, including $290.0 million for existing properties. Included in the $290.0 million is approximately $153.0 million for the development of identified proved undeveloped reserves. For 2009, Co. expects capital spending of about $271.0 million, including about $260.0 million for existing properties. Included in the $260.0 million is approximately $81.0 million for the development of identified proved undeveloped reserves. Separately, Co. is raising its 2008 earnings guidance by $0.30 to a new range of $3.95 to $4.35 per diluted share. For 2009, Co. expects earnings of $4.45 to $4.85 per diluted share.

Financial Data

(US$ in Thousands)	12/31/2007	12/31/2006	12/31/2005	12/31/2004	12/31/2003	12/31/2002	12/31/2001	09/30/2001
Earnings Per Share	4.28	3.73	2.35	1.75	1.55	1.01	0.06	1.09
Cash Flow Per Share	6.76	6.66	4.59	4.00	3.43	3.18	0.27	2.55
Tang Book Value Per Share	19.47	17.06	12.15	10.98	9.65	8.39	7.59	7.80
Dividends Per Share	0.460	0.440	0.400	0.378	0.365	0.355	0.345	0.343
Dividend Payout %	10.75	11.80	17.02	21.63	23.55	34.98	575.00	31.42
Income Statement								
Total Revenue	1,435,060	1,393,986	1,128,394	937,384	842,221	677,175	146,164	784,973
EBITDA	685,118	619,291	448,896	366,766	334,440	245,575	36,013	212,917
Income Before Taxes	476,641	428,553	270,377	203,063	174,393	91,095	195	83,872
Income Taxes	167,429	155,030	97,491	75,613	64,128	20,509	(3,384)	15,976
Net Income	309,233	273,570	173,012	127,463	110,654	68,639	3,658	67,896
Average Shares	72,180	73,278	73,714	73,117	71,133	67,676	62,554	62,167
Balance Sheet								
Net PPE	2,538,243	2,252,414	2,068,011	1,783,059	1,433,451	1,256,803	1,005,679	998,334
Total Assets	3,079,653	2,836,887	2,618,226	2,181,739	1,781,432	1,530,891	1,240,356	1,223,879
Long Term Obligations	562,365	582,490	683,236	612,891	552,842	512,954	544,133	544,110
Total Liabilities	1,700,995	1,634,818	1,725,548	1,378,073	1,082,400	948,081	766,151	743,112
Stockholders' Equity	1,378,658	1,202,069	892,678	803,666	699,032	582,810	474,205	480,767
Shares Outstanding	70,816	70,445	73,493	73,165	72,447	69,490	62,497	61,598
Statistical Record								
Return on Assets %	10.45	10.03	7.21	6.41	6.68	4.95	0.24	5.60
Return on Equity %	23.96	26.12	20.40	16.92	17.26	12.99	0.67	15.40
EBITDA Margin %	47.74	44.43	39.78	39.13	39.71	36.26	24.64	27.12
Net Margin %	21.55	19.63	15.33	13.60	13.14	10.14	2.50	8.65
PPE Turnover	0.60	0.65	0.59	0.58	0.63	0.60	0.12	0.82
Asset Turnover	0.49	0.51	0.47	0.47	0.51	0.49	0.10	0.65
Debt to Equity	0.41	0.48	0.77	0.76	0.79	0.88	1.15	1.13
Price Range	69.18-43.99	47.38-32.77	43.40-27.14	29.90-20.00	20.98-14.12	14.90-10.93	12.60-11.00	19.86-11.11
P/E Ratio	16.16-10.28	12.70-8.79	18.47-11.55	17.09-11.43	13.54-9.11	14.75-10.82	210.00-183.33	18.22-10.19
Average Yield %	0.83	1.13	1.16	1.60	2.14	2.76	2.91	2.27

Address: 605 Richard Arrington Jr. Blvd. N., Birmingham, AL 35203-2707 **Telephone:** 205-326-2700 **Fax:** 205-326-2704	**Web Site:** www.energen.com **Officers:** William Michael Warren Jr. - Chmn., Pres., C.E.O. Geoffrey C. Ketcham - Exec. V.P., C.F.O., Treas.	**Auditors:** PricewaterhouseCoopers LLP **Investor Contact:** 205-326-8421 **Transfer Agents:** EquiServe Trust Company, N.A., Providence, RI

ENERGIZER HOLDINGS, INC.

Exchange	Symbol	Price	52Wk Range	Yield	P/E
NYS	ENR	$90.48 (3/31/2008)	118.94-85.33	N/A	17.57

*7 Year Price Score 159.50 *NYSE Composite Index=100 ***12 Month Price Score 96.34**

TRADING VOLUME (thousand shares)

Interim Earnings (Per Share)

Qtr.	Dec	Mar	Jun	Sep
2004-05	1.62	0.78	0.73	0.75
2005-06	1.77	0.78	0.83	0.70
2006-07	2.08	1.14	1.06	1.21
2007-08	1.74	...	...	...

Interim Dividends (Per Share)
No Dividends Paid

Valuation Analysis / Institutional Holding

Valuation Analysis		Institutional Holding	
Forecast P/E	13.84	No of Institutions	
	(1/10/2007)	247	
Market Cap	$5.2 Billion	Shares	
Book Value	786.2 Million	43,550,536	
Price/Book	6.61	% Held	
Price/Sales	1.45	77.59	

Business Summary: Electrical (MIC: 11.14 SIC: 3692 NAIC: 335912)

Energizer Holdings is engaged in the manufacturing of primary batteries, flashlights and men's and women's wet-shave products. Co.'s subsidiaries manufacture and/or market primary lithium, alkaline and carbon zinc batteries, miniature batteries, specialty photo lithium batteries, rechargeable batteries, and flashlights and other lighting products. Through its Schick-Wilkinson Sword wet shave business, Co. manufactures and markets razor systems and disposable shave products for men and women, and shaving products such as lotions and shaving creams. Through its Oct 2007 acquisition of Playtex Products, Inc., Co. has three business categories: feminine care, skin care and infant care.

Recent Developments: For the quarter ended Dec 31 2007, net income decreased 16.1% to US$102.6 million from US$122.3 million in the year-earlier quarter. Revenues were US$1.19 billion, up 24.1% from US$959.2 million the year before. Direct operating expenses rose 29.4% to US$653.7 million from US$505.0 million in the comparable period the year before. Indirect operating expenses increased 40.0% to US$387.9 million from US$277.0 million in the equivalent prior-year period.

Prospects: For the fiscal year ending Sep 30 2008, Co. expects capital expenditures to be about $185.0 million, with increases in production related capital for existing businesses and planned spending for Playtex Products, Inc. For the rest of fiscal 2008, Co. foresees total material costs to increase by $10.0 million to $15.0 million. Thus, Co. recently raised the price on its U.S. rechargeable products by 8.5% to mitigate the accelerating costs related to these product lines. For the fiscal quarter ended Mar 31 2008, Co. anticipates total advertising and promotion for the Personal Care segment to increase to support the launch of its Quattro Trimmer product line while investing in its categories.

Financial Data

(US$ in Thousands)	3 Mos	09/30/2007	09/30/2006	09/30/2005	09/30/2004	09/30/2003	09/30/2002	09/30/2001
Earnings Per Share	5.15	5.51	4.14	3.90	3.21	1.93	2.01	(0.42)
Cash Flow Per Share	7.44	7.85	6.09	4.46	6.01	5.15	2.23	3.44
Tang Book Value Per Share	N.M.	N.M.	N.M.	N.M.	N.M.	1.99	6.71	5.42
Income Statement								
Total Revenue	1,189,900	3,365,100	3,076,900	2,989,800	2,812,700	2,232,500	1,739,700	1,694,200
EBITDA	148,300	640,400	552,000	566,400	504,600	349,000	356,900	144,500
Income Before Taxes	148,300	434,200	356,600	397,700	358,000	237,600	278,400	31,500
Income Taxes	45,700	112,800	95,700	111,300	90,600	67,700	92,000	70,500
Net Income	102,600	321,400	260,900	286,400	267,400	169,900	186,400	(39,000)
Average Shares	59,000	58,300	63,100	73,500	83,400	88,200	94,100	94,100
Balance Sheet								
Current Assets	2,020,800	2,011,400	1,635,100	1,464,000	1,376,700	1,243,100	887,900	783,300
Total Assets	5,919,000	3,553,000	3,132,600	2,960,300	2,915,700	2,732,100	1,588,100	1,497,600
Current Liabilities	1,503,200	1,122,900	926,900	838,100	907,900	727,500	534,600	495,200
Long-Term Obligations	2,694,000	1,372,000	1,625,000	1,295,000	1,059,600	913,600	160,000	225,000
Total Liabilities	5,132,800	2,899,100	2,920,200	2,507,200	2,333,500	1,924,100	883,300	889,700
Stockholders' Equity	786,200	653,900	212,400	453,100	582,200	808,000	704,800	607,900
Shares Outstanding	57,464	57,311	56,672	67,039	72,902	85,077	88,455	91,718
Statistical Record								
Return on Assets %	6.60	9.61	8.56	9.75	9.44	7.87	12.08	N.M.
Return on Equity %	54.64	74.20	78.41	55.33	38.36	22.46	28.40	N.M.
EBITDA Margin %	12.46	19.03	17.94	18.94	17.94	15.63	20.52	8.53
Net Margin %	8.62	9.55	8.48	9.58	9.51	7.61	10.71	N.M.
Asset Turnover	0.79	1.01	1.01	1.02	0.99	1.03	1.13	1.03
Current Ratio	1.34	1.79	1.76	1.75	1.52	1.71	1.66	1.58
Debt to Equity	3.43	2.10	7.65	2.86	1.82	1.13	0.23	0.37
Price Range	118.94-71.86	113.65-65.64	71.99-46.27	64.95-44.64	48.10-35.89	38.20-22.94	31.90-15.52	26.46-15.01
P/E Ratio	23.10-13.95	20.63-11.91	17.39-11.18	16.65-11.45	14.98-11.18	19.79-11.89	15.87-7.72	...

Address: 533 Maryville University Drive, St. Louis, MO 63141	Web Site: www.energizer.com	Auditors: PricewaterhouseCoopers LLP
Telephone: 314-985-2000	Officers: William P. Stiritz - Chmn. J. Patrick Mulcahy - Vice-Chmn.	Investor Contact: 314-982-2013
		Transfer Agents: Continental Stock Transfer & Trust Company, New York, NY

ENERGY EAST CORP.

Exchange	Symbol	Price	52Wk Range	Yield	P/E	Div Acheiver
NYS	EAS	$24.12 (3/31/2008)	27.90-22.37	5.14	14.98	10 Years

*7 Year Price Score 89.14   *NYSE Composite Index=100   *12 Month Price Score 106.50

Interim Earnings (Per Share)

Qtr.	Mar	Jun	Sep	Dec
2003	0.93	0.19	(0.04)	0.36
2004	0.82	0.26	0.11	0.37
2005	1.05	0.12	0.14	0.43
2006	0.90	0.19	0.14	0.52
2007	0.90	0.12	0.16	0.46

Interim Dividends (Per Share)

Amt	Decl	Ex	Rec	Pay
0.30Q	4/12/2007	4/19/2007	4/23/2007	5/15/2007
0.30Q	7/12/2007	7/19/2007	7/23/2007	8/15/2007
0.31Q	10/11/2007	10/18/2007	10/22/2007	11/15/2007
0.31Q	1/8/2008	1/16/2008	1/21/2008	2/15/2008

Indicated Div: $1.24

Valuation Analysis   **Institutional Holding**

Forecast P/E	15.73	No of Institutions
	(1/10/2007)	238
Market Cap	3.8 Billion	Shares
Book Value	3.2 Billion	80,141,056
Price/Book	1.19	% Held
Price/Sales	0.74	54.14

Business Summary: Electricity (MIC: 7.1 SIC: 4911 NAIC: 221121)

Energy East is a public utility holding company. Co.'s business consists of regulated electricity transmission and distribution operations in upstate New York and Maine and its regulated natural gas transportation, storage and distribution operations in upstate New York, Connecticut, Maine and Massachusetts. Additionally, Co.'s other businesses include retail energy marketing companies, a non-utility generating company, a Federal Energy Regulatory Commission regulated liquefied natural gas peaking plant, a natural gas delivery company, a propane air delivery company, telecommunications assets, a district heating and cooling system, and an energy consulting services company.

Recent Developments: For the year ended Dec 31 2007, net income decreased 3.3% to US$251.3 million from US$259.8 million in the prior year. Revenues were US$5.18 billion, down 1.0% from US$5.23 billion the year before. Operating income was US$615.0 million versus US$703.5 million in the prior year, a decrease of 12.6%. Direct operating expenses rose 0.9% to US$4.03 billion from US$3.99 billion in the comparable period the year before. Indirect operating expenses increased 0.1% to US$533.2 million from US$532.4 million in the equivalent prior-year period.

Prospects: Co.'s results are being negatively affected by several factors, including lower electric margins and increases in other operating and maintenance expense items. Looking ahead, Co. intends to augment its strategic focus of investing in the safety as well as the reliability of the transmission and distribution of electricity and natural gas by addressing several initiatives, which include investing in transmission to increase reliability, as well as meet new load growth and connect new, renewable generation to the network. Additionally, Co. intends to invest in its distribution infrastructure.

Financial Data

(US$ in Thousands)	12/31/2007	12/31/2006	12/31/2005	12/31/2004	12/31/2003	12/31/2002	12/31/2001	12/31/2000
Earnings Per Share	1.61	1.76	1.74	1.56	1.44	1.44	1.61	2.06
Cash Flow Per Share	3.30	2.58	3.40	2.31	3.31	3.13	1.16	1.99
Tang Book Value Per Share	10.62	9.05	9.12	7.52	7.11	6.53	7.57	6.49
Dividends Per Share	1.210	1.170	1.115	1.055	1.000	0.960	0.920	0.880
Dividend Payout %	75.16	66.48	64.08	67.63	69.44	66.67	57.14	42.72
Income Statement								
Total Revenue	5,178,108	5,230,665	5,298,543	4,756,692	4,593,819	4,008,918	3,759,787	2,959,520
EBITDA	1,028,144	1,142,063	1,098,600	1,132,183	1,032,584	800,656	763,295	711,388
Income Before Taxes	365,356	415,087	426,830	489,065	335,074	287,127	341,986	393,361
Income Taxes	114,058	155,255	169,997	251,444	127,687	98,524	154,379	156,682
Net Income	251,298	259,832	256,833	229,357	210,446	188,603	187,607	235,034
Average Shares	155,805	147,717	147,474	146,713	145,730	131,117	116,700	114,213
Balance Sheet								
Net PPE	6,158,494	5,948,023	5,783,454	5,662,168	5,778,109	4,801,839	3,626,432	3,632,928
Total Assets	11,878,709	11,562,401	11,487,708	10,796,113	11,306,432	10,269,879	7,269,232	7,003,633
Long-Term Obligations	3,877,029	3,726,709	3,667,065	3,797,685	3,994,096	3,351,959	2,471,278	2,346,814
Total Liabilities	8,647,029	8,673,462	8,590,403	8,118,184	8,643,013	7,348,305	5,099,682	5,243,787
Stockholders' Equity	3,207,093	2,864,347	2,872,674	2,631,258	2,572,324	2,460,612	1,781,177	1,716,522
Shares Outstanding	158,279	147,907	147,701	147,118	146,243	144,392	116,718	117,656
Statistical Record								
Return on Assets %	2.14	2.25	2.31	2.07	1.95	2.15	2.63	4.35
Return on Equity %	8.28	9.06	9.33	8.79	8.36	8.89	10.73	15.02
EBITDA Margin %	19.86	21.83	20.73	23.80	22.48	19.97	20.30	24.04
Net Margin %	4.85	4.97	4.85	4.82	4.58	4.70	4.99	7.94
PPE Turnover	0.86	0.89	0.93	0.83	0.87	0.95	1.04	1.02
Asset Turnover	0.44	0.45	0.48	0.43	0.43	0.46	0.53	0.55
Debt to Equity	1.21	1.30	1.28	1.44	1.55	1.36	1.39	1.37
Price Range	27.90-22.37	25.47-22.55	30.06-22.79	27.01-22.15	23.71-17.46	23.10-17.25	21.99-17.23	23.44-18.00
P/E Ratio	17.33-13.89	14.47-12.81	17.28-13.10	17.31-14.20	16.47-12.13	16.04-11.98	13.66-10.70	11.38-8.74
Average Yield %	4.72	4.82	4.29	4.33	4.79	4.58	4.68	4.22

Address: 52 Farm View Drive, New Gloucester, ME 04260-5116
Telephone:

Web Site: www.energyeast.com
Officers: Wesley W. von Schack - Chmn., Pres., C.E.O. Kenneth M. Jasinski - Exec. V.P., C.F.O.

Auditors: PricewaterhouseCoopers LLP
Transfer Agents: Mellon Investor Services LLC

ENSCO INTERNATIONAL INC.

Exchange	Symbol	Price	52Wk Range	Yield	P/E
NYS	ESV	$62.62 (3/31/2008)	65.90-49.53	0.16	9.30

*7 Year Price Score 124.49 *NYSE Composite Index=100 *12 Month Price Score 110.20

Interim Earnings (Per Share)

Qtr.	Mar	Jun	Sep	Dec
2003	0.15	0.21	0.19	0.17
2004	0.14	0.12	0.17	0.25
2005	0.28	0.46	0.50	0.69
2006	0.97	1.27	1.40	1.40
2007	1.54	1.72	1.82	1.65

Interim Dividends (Per Share)

Amt	Decl	Ex	Rec	Pay
0.025Q	5/22/2007	6/7/2007	6/11/2007	6/22/2007
0.025Q	8/29/2007	9/6/2007	9/10/2007	9/21/2007
0.025Q	11/6/2007	12/6/2007	12/10/2007	12/21/2007
0.025Q	2/28/2008	3/6/2008	3/10/2008	3/21/2008

Indicated Div: $0.10

Valuation Analysis — **Institutional Holding**

Forecast P/E	5.57 (1/10/2007)	No of Institutions 390
Market Cap	$9.0 Billion	Shares
Book Value	3.8 Billion	126,344,136
Price/Book	2.40	% Held
Price/Sales	4.20	84.30

TRADING VOLUME (thousand shares)

Business Summary: Oil and Gas (MIC: 14.2 SIC: 1381 NAIC: 213111)

ENSCO International is an offshore contract drilling company engaged in the exploration, development and production of oil and natural gas in domestic and international markets under contracts with major international, government-owned and independent oil and gas companies. Co.'s operations are concentrated in the North and South America, Europe/Africa, and Asia Pacific (which includes Asia, the Middle East, Australia, and New Zealand). As of Feb 15 2008, Co. owned and operated 44 jackup rigs, one ultra-deepwater semisubmersible rig and one barge rig. Co. also has four ultra-deepwater semisubmersible rigs under construction.

Recent Developments: For the year ended Dec 31 2007, income from continuing operations increased 30.8% to US$992.0 million from US$758.6 million a year earlier. Net income increased 28.9% to US$992.0 million from US$769.7 million in the prior year. Revenues were US$2.14 billion, up 18.2% from US$1.81 billion the year before. Operating income was US$1.22 billion versus US$1.02 billion in the prior year, an increase of 19.5%. Direct operating expenses rose 18.6% to US$684.1 million from US$576.7 million in the comparable period the year before. Indirect operating expenses increased 11.0% to US$243.8 million from US$219.6 million in the equivalent prior-year period.

Prospects: Co.'s outlook for 2008 appears encouraging. Specifically, Co. expects to benefit from its deepwater initiatives in 2008 as ENSCO 7500, its deepwater semisubmersible rig currently operating in the Gulf of Mexico, rolls to a significantly higher day rate. Consequently, ENSCO 8500, its ultra-deepwater semisubmersible rig is expected to commence its initial four-year contract in the Gulf of Mexico by late 2008 following completion of commissioning, mobilization and final outfitting. Furthermore, Co. noted that it has contracted approximately 85.0% of its international jackup rig days for 2008, and it is seeing some improvement in the U.S. Gulf of Mexico jackup market.

Financial Data

(US$ in Thousands)	12/31/2007	12/31/2006	12/31/2005	12/31/2004	12/31/2003	12/31/2002	12/31/2001	12/31/2000
Earnings Per Share	6.73	5.04	1.93	0.68	0.72	0.42	1.50	0.61
Cash Flow Per Share	8.47	6.20	2.34	1.71	1.96	1.49	3.08	1.00
Tang Book Value Per Share	23.74	18.97	14.32	12.18	11.55	10.85	9.93	8.82
Dividends Per Share	0.100	0.100	0.100	0.100	0.100	0.100	0.100	0.100
Dividend Payout %	1.49	1.98	5.18	14.71	13.89	23.81	6.67	16.39
Income Statement								
Total Revenue	2,143,800	1,813,500	1,046,900	768,000	790,800	698,100	817,400	533,800
EBITDA	1,421,700	1,194,100	573,800	322,800	323,200	249,100	451,000	237,200
Income Before Taxes	1,253,700	1,011,300	391,200	139,500	149,300	87,100	291,900	125,200
Income Taxes	261,700	252,700	107,300	36,000	42,100	27,800	84,600	39,800
Net Income	992,000	769,700	294,200	102,800	108,300	59,300	207,300	85,400
Average Shares	147,300	152,800	152,400	150,600	150,100	141,400	137,900	139,300
Balance Sheet								
Current Assets	1,129,300	987,200	578,400	493,700	543,300	387,500	461,300	288,700
Total Assets	4,968,800	4,334,400	3,617,900	3,322,000	3,183,000	3,061,500	2,323,800	2,108,000
Current Liabilities	503,500	384,900	231,400	215,800	187,400	198,300	149,300	117,100
Long-Term Obligations	291,400	308,500	475,400	527,100	549,900	547,500	462,400	422,200
Total Liabilities	1,216,800	1,118,400	1,084,700	1,140,100	1,101,900	1,094,500	883,600	779,100
Stockholders' Equity	3,752,000	3,216,000	2,533,200	2,181,900	2,081,100	1,967,000	1,440,200	1,328,900
Shares Outstanding	143,900	151,800	153,400	151,100	150,500	149,000	134,600	138,500
Statistical Record								
Return on Assets %	21.33	19.36	8.48	3.15	3.47	2.20	9.36	4.17
Return on Equity %	28.47	26.78	12.48	4.81	5.35	3.48	14.97	6.63
EBITDA Margin %	66.32	65.85	54.81	42.03	40.87	35.68	55.17	44.44
Net Margin %	46.27	42.44	28.10	13.39	13.69	8.49	25.36	16.00
Asset Turnover	0.46	0.46	0.30	0.24	0.25	0.26	0.37	0.26
Current Ratio	2.24	2.56	2.50	2.29	2.90	1.95	3.09	2.47
Debt to Equity	0.08	0.10	0.19	0.24	0.26	0.28	0.32	0.32
Price Range	65.90-46.50	57.89-37.57	50.28-29.79	33.75-25.08	30.90-24.01	35.36-21.04	44.44-13.20	42.50-21.25
P/E Ratio	9.79-6.91	11.49-7.45	26.05-15.44	49.63-36.88	42.92-33.35	84.19-50.10	29.63-8.80	69.67-34.84
Average Yield %	0.18	0.21	0.26	0.34	0.37	0.36	0.36	0.30

Address: 500 North Akard Street, Suite 4300, Dallas, TX 75201-3331 Telephone: 214-397-3000 Fax: 214-855-0300	Web Site: www.enscous.com Officers: Carl F. Thorne - Chmn., C.E.O. James W. Swent - Sr. V.P., C.F.O.	Auditors: KPMG LLP Investor Contact: 214-397-3000 Transfer Agents: American Stock Transfer and Trust Company

ENTERCOM COMMUNICATIONS CORP

Exchange	Symbol	Price	52Wk Range	Yield	P/E
NYS	ETM	$9.93 (3/31/2008)	29.28-9.69	15.31	N/A

*7 Year Price Score 42.56   *NYSE Composite Index=100   *12 Month Price Score 62.04

Interim Earnings (Per Share)

Qtr.	Mar	Jun	Sep	Dec
2003	0.18	0.37	0.41	0.42
2004	0.23	0.47	0.41	0.40
2005	0.34	0.53	0.48	0.16
2006	0.19	0.43	0.41	0.17
2007	(0.01)	(0.32)	0.37	(0.25)

Interim Dividends (Per Share)

Amt	Decl	Ex	Rec	Pay
0.38Q	5/7/2007	6/13/2007	6/15/2007	6/28/2007
0.38Q	8/1/2007	9/12/2007	9/14/2007	9/28/2007
0.38Q	11/8/2007	11/29/2007	12/3/2007	12/17/2007
0.38Q	2/12/2008	3/12/2008	3/14/2008	3/28/2008

Indicated Div: $1.52

Valuation Analysis | **Institutional Holding**

Forecast P/E	16.71	No of Institutions
	(1/10/2007)	137
Market Cap	$384.7 Million	Shares
Book Value	660.8 Million	25,397,768
Price/Book	0.58	% Held
Price/Sales	0.82	62.53

Business Summary: Media (MIC: 13.1 SIC: 4832 NAIC: 515112)

Entercom Communications is a radio broadcasting company operating 111 radio stations in 23 markets, including San Francisco, Boston, Seattle, Denver, Sacramento, Portland, Indianapolis, Kansas City, Milwaukee, Austin, Norfolk, Buffalo, New Orleans, Memphis, Providence, Greensboro, Greenville/Spartanburg, Rochester, Madison, Wichita, Wilkes-Barre/Scranton, Springfield and Gainesville/Ocala. Co.'s stations formats include news, talk, classic rock, adult contemporary alternative, oldies, jazz, and others. Co. also provides a range of geographical portfolio of radio stations and various radio stations formats for specific audiences to advertisers on a local, regional and national basis.

Recent Developments: For the year ended Dec 31 2007, loss from continuing operations was US$8.4 million compared with income of US$47.8 million a year earlier. Net loss amounted to US$8.4 million versus net income of US$48.0 million in the prior year. Revenues were US$468.4 million, up 6.5% from US$439.6 million the year before. Operating income was US$41.9 million versus US$126.3 million in the prior year, a decrease of 66.8%. Indirect operating expenses increased 36.1% to US$426.5 million from US$313.3 million in the equivalent prior-year period.

Prospects: Co. is encouraged with its recent operating performance reflecting growth in same station revenues and same station operating income. For full-year 2008, Co. anticipates that its capital expenditures will consist of $5.0 million incurred during the ordinary course of business and between $4.0 million and $6.0 million primarily for the consolidation and/or relocation of studio and office facilities in certain markets and the continued conversion to digital radio. Meanwhile, for the first quarter of 2008 Co. expects same station net revenues to decline in the mid-single digit range and same station operating expenses to decrease by approximately 1.0% as compared with same period in 2007.

Financial Data

(US$ in Thousands)	12/31/2007	12/31/2006	12/31/2005	12/31/2004	12/31/2003	12/31/2002	12/31/2001	12/31/2000
Earnings Per Share	(0.22)	1.19	1.50	1.50	1.39	(1.67)	0.38	1.04
Cash Flow Per Share	2.45	2.54	2.97	2.61	2.56	2.13	1.88	1.53
Dividends Per Share	1.520	1.520	...	...	...	...	...	...
Dividend Payout %	...	127.73	...	...	...	...	...	...
Income Statement								
Total Revenue	468,351	440,485	432,520	423,455	401,056	391,289	332,897	352,025
EBITDA	61,817	145,021	175,110	161,844	150,962	132,623	103,858	159,773
Income Before Taxes	(7,699)	83,676	127,585	123,523	115,212	93,353	30,028	79,050
Income Taxes	695	35,695	49,224	47,889	43,432	37,529	12,194	31,796
Net Income	(8,357)	47,981	78,361	75,634	71,780	(83,052)	17,268	47,254
Average Shares	38,229	40,704	46,221	50,334	51,607	49,765	45,994	45,613
Balance Sheet								
Current Assets	124,094	118,341	108,883	105,460	105,354	187,439	87,780	90,938
Total Assets	1,919,352	1,733,258	1,697,758	1,667,961	1,577,052	1,568,530	1,438,740	1,473,928
Current Liabilities	35,389	42,326	34,957	25,783	91,454	73,032	53,581	27,781
Long-Term Obligations	973,697	676,219	577,240	483,259	329,027	394,044	363,934	461,249
Total Liabilities	1,258,585	956,166	812,043	671,888	545,442	553,025	557,859	613,227
Stockholders' Equity	660,767	777,092	885,715	996,073	1,031,610	890,505	755,881	735,701
Shares Outstanding	38,740	40,426	42,881	48,635	51,431	49,859	45,353	45,239
Statistical Record								
Return on Assets %	N.M.	2.80	4.66	4.65	4.56	N.M.	1.19	3.28
Return on Equity %	N.M.	5.77	8.33	7.44	7.47	N.M.	2.32	6.63
EBITDA Margin %	13.20	32.92	40.49	38.22	37.64	33.89	31.20	45.39
Net Margin %	N.M.	10.89	18.12	17.86	17.90	N.M.	5.19	13.42
Asset Turnover	0.26	0.26	0.26	0.26	0.25	0.26	0.23	0.24
Current Ratio	3.51	2.80	3.11	4.09	1.15	2.57	1.64	3.27
Debt to Equity	1.47	0.87	0.65	0.49	0.32	0.44	0.48	0.63
Price Range	30.63-13.69	30.91-22.53	35.89-27.77	53.80-30.40	53.07-43.07	58.65-36.88	53.75-31.05	66.56-25.63
P/E Ratio	...	25.97-18.93	23.93-18.51	35.87-20.27	38.18-30.99	...	141.45-81.71	64.00-24.64
Average Yield %	6.44	5.62	...	...	...	...	...	...

Address: 401 City Avenue, Suite 409, Bala Cynwyd, PA 19004
Telephone: 610-660-5610
Fax: 610-660-5620

Web Site: www.entercom.com
Officers: Joseph M. Field - Chmn., C.E.O. David J. Field - Pres., C.O.O..

Auditors: PricewaterhouseCoopers LLP
Investor Contact: 610-660-5647

ENTERGY CORP.

Exchange	Symbol	Price	52Wk Range	Yield	P/E
NYS	ETR	$109.08 (3/31/2008)	126.07-95.98	2.75	19.48

*7 Year Price Score 133.93 *NYSE Composite Index=100 *12 Month Price Score 103.95

Interim Earnings (Per Share)

Qtr.	Mar	Jun	Sep	Dec
2003	1.73	0.89	1.57	(0.18)
2004	0.88	1.14	1.22	0.69
2005	0.79	1.33	1.65	0.44
2006	0.92	1.33	1.83	1.28
2007	1.03	1.32	2.30	0.97

Interim Dividends (Per Share)

Amt	Decl	Ex	Rec	Pay
0.75Q	7/30/2007	8/8/2007	8/10/2007	9/1/2007
0.75Q	10/26/2007	11/7/2007	11/9/2007	12/1/2007
0.75Q	1/25/2008	2/6/2008	2/8/2008	3/3/2008
0.75Q	4/8/2008	5/7/2008	5/9/2008	6/2/2008

Indicated Div: $3.00

Valuation Analysis

Forecast P/E	13.69
	(1/10/2007)
Market Cap	$21.1 Billion
Book Value	7.9 Billion
Price/Book	2.68
Price/Sales	1.83

Institutional Holding

No of Institutions	411
Shares	164,079,104
% Held	82.74

Business Summary: Electricity (MIC: 7.1 SIC: 4911 NAIC: 221113)

Entergy is an integrated energy company engaged primarily in electric power production and retail electric distribution operations. At Dec 31 2007, Co.'s Utility segment generated, transmitted, distributed, and sold electric power to 2.7 million utility customers in a four-state service territory that included portions of Arkansas, Mississippi, Texas, and Louisiana; as well as operated a small natural gas distribution business. Co.'s Non-Utility Nuclear segment owns and operates six nuclear power plants located in the northern U.S., and sells the electric power produced by those plants to wholesale customers. This business also provides services to other nuclear power plant owners.

Recent Developments: For the year ended Dec 31 2007, net income was unchanged at US$1.13 billion versus US$1.13 billion the prior year. Revenues were US$11.48 billion, up 5.1% from US$10.93 billion the year before. Operating income was US$2.06 billion versus US$1.81 billion in the prior year, an increase of 13.9%. Direct operating expenses declined 0.2% to US$7.92 billion from US$7.93 billion in the comparable period the year before. Indirect operating expenses increased 26.3% to US$1.51 billion from US$1.19 billion in the equivalent prior-year period.

Prospects: For 2008, Co. has reaffirmed its earnings guidance range of $6.50 to $6.90 per share on a business as usual basis, excluding expected expenses from its plan to spin-off its non-utility nuclear business and to enter into a nuclear services joint venture, which should be completed in the third quarter of 2008. Meanwhile, Co. expects the $66.0 million (including related investments) purchase of the Calcasieu plant, a 322 megawatt (MW) simple-cycle gas-fired power plant by its subsidiary, Entergy Gulf States Louisiana, to close in Mar 2008. Also, Co. expects the $210.0 million acquisition of the 789 MW gas-fired Ouachita power plant by its Entergy Arkansas, Inc. subsidiary to close in 2008.

Financial Data

(US$ in Thousands)	12/31/2007	12/31/2006	12/31/2005	12/31/2004	12/31/2003	12/31/2002	12/31/2001	12/31/2000
Earnings Per Share	5.60	5.36	4.19	3.93	4.01	2.64	3.23	2.97
Cash Flow Per Share	13.02	16.48	6.98	12.88	8.84	9.78	10.03	8.66
Tang Book Value Per Share	38.76	38.59	35.49	36.52	36.38	33.54	33.78	31.89
Dividends Per Share	2.580	2.160	2.160	1.890	1.600	1.340	1.275	1.215
Dividend Payout %	46.07	40.30	51.55	48.09	39.90	50.76	39.47	40.91
Income Statement								
Total Revenue	11,484,398	10,932,158	10,106,247	10,123,724	9,194,920	8,305,035	9,620,899	10,016,148
EBITDA	3,250,030	3,013,956	2,859,817	2,673,573	2,660,296	2,355,776	1,920,440	1,758,820
Income Before Taxes	1,649,266	1,576,142	1,527,836	1,298,957	1,303,461	917,010	1,182,718	1,189,836
Income Taxes	514,417	443,044	559,284	365,908	490,074	293,938	455,693	478,921
Net Income	1,134,849	1,132,602	923,758	933,049	950,467	623,072	750,507	710,915
Average Shares	202,780	211,452	214,441	231,193	231,146	227,303	224,733	228,541
Balance Sheet								
Net PPE	20,974,270	19,438,077	19,197,045	18,695,631	18,298,797	17,194,952	17,264,028	16,496,625
Total Assets	33,643,002	31,082,731	30,851,269	28,310,777	28,554,210	26,947,969	25,910,311	25,565,227
Long-Term Obligations	9,948,573	8,986,120	8,999,498	7,162,891	7,476,838	7,242,942	7,502,113	7,933,966
Total Liabilities	25,469,169	22,539,931	22,662,548	19,648,734	19,516,215	18,536,068	17,878,769	17,946,116
Stockholders' Equity	7,862,671	8,197,887	7,742,747	8,296,687	8,703,658	7,838,237	7,456,020	7,338,353
Shares Outstanding	193,120	202,667	207,529	216,829	228,897	222,421	220,732	219,604
Statistical Record								
Return on Assets %	3.51	3.66	3.12	3.27	3.42	2.36	2.92	2.92
Return on Equity %	14.13	14.21	11.52	10.95	11.49	8.15	10.15	9.58
EBITDA Margin %	28.30	27.57	28.30	26.41	28.93	28.37	19.96	17.56
Net Margin %	9.88	10.36	9.14	9.22	10.34	7.50	7.80	7.10
PPE Turnover	0.57	0.57	0.53	0.55	0.52	0.48	0.57	0.62
Asset Turnover	0.35	0.35	0.34	0.36	0.33	0.31	0.37	0.41
Debt to Equity	1.27	1.10	1.16	0.86	0.86	0.92	1.01	1.08
Price Range	124.15-90.45	93.28-67.67	78.43-64.88	68.16-50.68	57.14-42.85	46.70-33.18	44.48-33.66	43.25-16.69
P/E Ratio	22.17-16.15	17.40-12.63	18.72-15.48	17.34-12.90	14.25-10.69	17.69-12.57	13.77-10.42	14.56-5.62
Average Yield %	2.39	2.84	3.01	3.19	3.15	3.16	3.31	4.07

Address: 639 Loyola Avenue, New Orleans, LA 70113	Web Site: www.entergy.com	Auditors: Deloitte & Touche LLP
Telephone: 504-576-4000	Officers: Robert v. d. Luft - Chmn. J. Wayne Leonard - C.E.O.	Investor Contact: 504-576-4879
Fax: 504-576-4428		Transfer Agents: Mellon Investor Services, Ridgefield Park, NJ

ENTERPRISE PRODUCTS PARTNERS L.P.

Exchange	Symbol	Price	52Wk Range	Yield	P/E
NYS	EPD	$29.70 (3/31/2008)	33.33-28.00	6.73	30.94

*7 Year Price Score 101.34 *NYSE Composite Index=100 ***12 Month Price Score 105.51**

Interim Earnings (Per Share)

Qtr.	Mar	Jun	Sep	Dec
2003	0.19	0.14	(0.04)	0.13
2004	0.23	0.11	0.21	0.31
2005	0.25	0.14	0.29	0.22
2006	0.28	0.25	0.43	0.25
2007	0.20	0.26	0.20	0.30

Interim Dividends (Per Share)

Amt	Decl	Ex	Rec	Pay
0.475Q	4/16/2007	4/26/2007	4/30/2007	5/10/2007
0.482Q	7/17/2007	7/27/2007	7/31/2007	8/9/2007
0.49Q	10/16/2007	10/29/2007	10/31/2007	11/8/2007
0.50Q	1/15/2008	1/29/2008	1/31/2008	2/7/2008

Indicated Div: $2.00

Valuation Analysis

		Institutional Holding	
Forecast P/E	18.61	No of Institutions	
	(1/10/2007)	270	
Market Cap	$12.9 Billion	Shares	
Book Value	6.0 Billion	76,798,800	
Price/Book	2.15	% Held	
Price/Sales	0.76	17.76	

Business Summary: Oil and Gas (MIC: 14.2 SIC: 1311 NAIC: 211111)

Enterprise Products Partners is a North American midstream energy company providing a range of services to producers and consumers of natural gas, natural gas liquids (NGLs), crude oil and certain petrochemicals. In addition, Co. is engaged in the development of pipeline as well as other midstream infrastructure throughout the U.S. and the Gulf of Mexico. Co. conducts substantially all of its business through its wholly owned Enterprise Products Operating L.P. As of Dec 31 2006, Co. had four reportable segments: NGL Pipelines and Services; Onshore Natural Gas Pipelines and Services; Offshore Pipelines and Services; as well as Petrochemical Services.

Recent Developments: For the quarter ended Sep 30 2007, net income decreased 43.5% to US$117.6 million from US$208.3 million in the year-earlier quarter. Revenues were US$4.11 billion, up 6.2% from US$3.87 billion the year before. Operating income was US$210.8 million versus US$274.2 million in the prior-year quarter, a decrease of 23.1%. Direct operating expenses rose 8.7% to US$3.90 billion from US$3.58 billion in the comparable period the year before. Indirect operating expenses decreased 64.9% to US$4.8 million from US$13.6 million in the equivalent prior-year period.

Prospects: Co.'s outlook appears constructive. For instance, on Nov 14 2007, Co. announced that it has entered into agreements with Chevron U.S.A. Inc. to provide a comprehensive package of midstream services for Chevron's natural gas production in the Piceance Basin of northwest Colorado. Also, under the terms of a separate transportation and fractionation exchange agreement, Co. will receive Chevron's mixed natural gas liquids extracted at its Meeker facility and will utilize its integrated midstream network, which includes the Mid-America Pipeline (MAPL), to provide purity products to Chevron. Co. believes that these agreements will strengthen its position in the Piceance Basin area.

Financial Data

(US$ in Thousands)	12/31/2007	12/31/2006	12/31/2005	12/31/2004	12/31/2003	12/31/2002	12/31/2001	12/31/2000
Earnings Per Share	0.96	1.22	0.91	0.87	0.41	0.48	1.39	1.32
Cash Flow Per Share	3.67	2.84	1.65	1.42	2.12	2.12	2.03	2.68
Tang Book Value Per Share	10.34	11.00	10.69	10.38	6.06	4.51	5.36	8.96
Dividends Per Share	1.915	1.795	1.660	1.513	1.442	1.327	1.156	1.025
Dividend Payout %	199.48	147.13	182.42	173.85	351.83	276.56	83.48	77.65
Income Statement								
Total Revenue	16,950,125	13,990,969	12,256,959	8,321,202	5,346,431	3,584,783	3,179,727	3,073,139
EBITDA	892,659	868,471	1,089,164	621,913	382,167	294,134	...	...
Income Before Taxes	579,574	630,085	437,838	269,369	113,698	100,081	...	...
Income Taxes	15,257	21,323	8,362	3,761	5,293	1,634	...	...
Net Income	533,674	601,155	419,508	268,261	104,546	93,300	242,178	220,506
Average Shares	434,427	414,759	382,963	266,045	206,367	176,490	170,786	164,887
Balance Sheet								
Current Assets	2,537,885	1,922,158	1,971,447	1,440,723	687,183	637,568	518,775	381,392
Total Assets	16,608,007	13,989,718	12,591,016	11,315,461	4,802,814	4,230,272	2,431,193	1,951,521
Current Liabilities	3,044,683	1,984,921	1,890,271	1,585,879	1,096,876	721,356	409,216	586,379
Long-Term Obligations	6,906,145	5,295,590	4,833,781	4,266,236	1,899,548	2,231,463	855,278	404,000
Total Liabilities	10,476,358	7,509,485	6,911,707	5,986,676	3,096,861	3,029,368	1,284,271	1,015,562
Stockholders' Equity	6,009,352	6,351,058	5,565,813	5,222,310	1,671,604	1,188,681	1,135,391	926,554
Shares Outstanding	435,297	432,408	389,109	364,358	217,780	183,809	174,214	93,049
Statistical Record								
Return on Assets %	3.49	4.52	3.51	3.32	2.31	2.87	11.05	12.76
Return on Equity %	8.64	10.09	7.78	7.76	7.31	8.22	23.49	25.75
EBITDA Margin %	5.27	6.21	8.89	7.47	7.15	8.21	...	...
Net Margin %	3.15	4.30	3.42	3.22	1.96	2.66	7.62	7.18
Asset Turnover	1.11	1.05	1.03	1.03	1.18	1.08	1.45	1.78
Current Ratio	0.83	0.97	1.04	0.91	0.63	0.88	1.27	0.99
Debt to Equity	1.15	0.83	0.87	0.82	1.14	1.88	0.75	0.44
Price Range	33.33-28.00	29.80-23.90	27.70-23.47	25.86-20.00	24.70-18.01	25.35-16.25	25.98-13.44	15.81-9.13
P/E Ratio	34.72-29.17	24.43-19.59	30.44-25.79	29.72-22.99	60.24-43.93	52.81-33.85	18.69-9.67	11.98-6.91
Average Yield %	6.16	6.90	6.41	6.70	6.65	6.26	5.68	8.84

Address: 2727 North Loop West, Suite 700, Houston, TX 77008-1044
Telephone: 713-880-6500
Fax: 713-880-6668

Web Site: www.epplp.com
Officers: Dan L. Duncan - Chmn. O. S. Andras - Vice-Chmn.

Auditors: Deloitte & Touche LLP
Transfer Agents: Mellon Investor Services, LLC

EOG RESOURCES, INC.

Exchange	Symbol	Price	52Wk Range	Yield	P/E
NYS	EOG	$120.00 (3/31/2008)	126.96-65.70	0.40	27.46

*7 Year Price Score 152.87 *NYSE Composite Index=100 *12 Month Price Score 144.50

Interim Earnings (Per Share)

Qtr.	Mar	Jun	Sep	Dec
2003	0.55	0.46	0.50	0.30
2004	0.41	0.60	0.71	0.85
2005	0.83	1.02	1.40	1.88
2006	1.73	1.34	1.21	0.96
2007	0.88	1.24	0.82	1.44

Interim Dividends (Per Share)

Amt	Decl	Ex	Rec	Pay
0.09Q	4/24/2007	7/13/2007	7/17/2007	7/31/2007
0.09Q	9/6/2007	10/15/2007	10/17/2007	10/31/2007
0.09Q	12/11/2007	1/15/2008	1/17/2008	1/31/2008
0.12Q	2/7/2008	4/14/2008	4/16/2008	4/30/2008

Indicated Div: $0.48

Valuation Analysis | **Institutional Holding**

Forecast P/E	10.98	No of Institutions
	(1/10/2007)	405
Market Cap	$29.6 Billion	Shares
Book Value	7.0 Billion	220,453,392
Price/Book	4.23	% Held
Price/Sales	7.06	90.35

TRADING VOLUME (thousand shares)

Business Summary: Oil and Gas (MIC: 14.2 SIC: 1311 NAIC: 211111)

EOG Resources, together with its subsidiaries, explores for, develops, produces and markets natural gas and crude oil primarily in core producing basins in the U.S., Canada, offshore Trinidad, and the U.K. North Sea and, other selected international areas. At Dec 31 2007, Co.'s total estimated net proved reserves were 7,745 billion cubic feet equivalent (Bcfe), of which 6,669 billion cubic feet were natural gas reserves and 179 million barrels, or 1,076 Bcfe, were crude oil, condensate and natural gas liquids reserves. At such date, approximately 67.0% of Co.'s reserves (on a natural gas equivalent basis) were located in the U.S., 17.0% in Canada and 16.0% in Trinidad.

Recent Developments: For the year ended Dec 31 2007, net income decreased 16.2% to US$1.09 billion from US$1.30 billion in the prior year. Revenues were US$4.19 billion, up 7.1% from US$3.91 billion the year before. Operating income was US$1.65 billion versus US$1.90 billion in the prior year, a decrease of 13.4%. Direct operating expenses rose 34.6% to US$650.2 million from US$483.2 million in the comparable period the year before. Indirect operating expenses increased 24.0% to US$1.89 billion from US$1.53 billion in the equivalent prior-year period.

Prospects: Co. remains focused on expanding its North American drilling program. Accordingly, Co. expects to allocate higher amount of its domestic exploration and development expenditures to the Fort Worth Basin Barnett Shale and the Rocky Mountain operating area which includes the Uinta Basin and the North Dakota Bakken. In detail, Co. is budgeting 2008 exploration and development expenditures, excluding acquisitions, to be about $4.10 billion. As a result, Co. expects to increase overall production in 2008 by 15.0% over 2007 levels, with expected U.S. production growth of 19.0%, and a planned increase in crude oil and condensate and natural gas liquids production of 36.0% and 40.0%, respectively.

Financial Data

(US$ in Thousands)	12/31/2007	12/31/2006	12/31/2005	12/31/2004	12/31/2003	12/31/2002	12/31/2001	12/31/2000
Earnings Per Share	4.37	5.24	5.13	2.58	1.80	0.33	1.65	1.62
Cash Flow Per Share	11.88	10.66	9.92	6.16	5.76	2.90	5.17	4.13
Tang Book Value Per Share	28.33	22.76	17.42	11.97	8.95	6.64	6.48	5.28
Dividends Per Share	0.330	0.220	0.150	0.115	0.090	0.080	0.077	0.065
Dividend Payout %	7.55	4.20	2.92	4.47	5.00	24.62	4.70	4.01
Income Statement								
Total Revenue	4,190,791	3,904,415	3,620,213	2,271,225	1,744,675	1,095,036	1,654,887	1,489,895
EBITDA	2,743,191	2,772,888	2,681,901	1,493,543	1,154,430	577,362	1,068,954	1,064,589
Income Before Taxes	1,630,868	1,912,641	1,965,137	926,012	653,876	119,672	631,445	633,557
Income Taxes	540,950	612,756	705,561	301,157	216,600	32,499	232,829	236,626
Net Income	1,089,918	1,299,885	1,259,576	624,855	430,145	87,173	398,616	396,931
Average Shares	247,637	246,100	243,975	238,376	233,038	234,490	234,976	238,204
Balance Sheet								
Current Assets	1,292,039	1,350,080	1,563,238	586,803	396,014	394,792	272,421	394,427
Total Assets	12,088,907	9,402,160	7,753,320	5,798,923	4,749,015	3,814,006	3,414,044	3,000,815
Current Liabilities	1,474,170	1,255,012	1,172,041	632,204	476,519	276,351	310,847	369,678
Long-Term Obligations	1,185,000	733,442	858,992	1,077,622	1,108,872	1,145,132	855,969	859,000
Total Liabilities	5,098,813	3,802,489	3,437,028	2,853,499	2,525,634	2,141,611	1,771,358	1,619,890
Stockholders' Equity	6,990,094	5,599,671	4,316,292	2,945,424	2,223,381	1,672,395	1,642,686	1,380,925
Shares Outstanding	246,524	243,735	242,074	237,854	231,820	229,440	230,903	233,808
Statistical Record								
Return on Assets %	10.14	15.15	18.59	11.82	10.05	2.41	12.43	14.11
Return on Equity %	17.31	26.22	34.69	24.11	22.08	5.26	26.37	31.53
EBITDA Margin %	65.46	71.02	74.08	65.76	66.17	52.73	64.59	71.45
Net Margin %	26.01	33.29	34.79	27.51	24.65	7.96	24.09	26.64
Asset Turnover	0.39	0.46	0.53	0.43	0.41	0.30	0.52	0.53
Current Ratio	0.88	1.08	1.33	0.93	0.83	1.43	0.88	1.07
Debt to Equity	0.17	0.13	0.20	0.37	0.50	0.68	0.52	0.62
Price Range	91.02-59.96	84.81-57.36	80.84-32.48	37.91-21.45	23.61-18.00	21.89-15.47	26.78-13.32	28.22-6.94
P/E Ratio	20.83-13.72	16.19-10.95	15.76-6.33	14.70-8.31	13.11-10.00	66.32-46.86	16.23-8.07	17.42-4.28
Average Yield %	0.44	0.32	0.26	0.40	0.44	0.43	0.40	0.42

Address: 1111 Bagby, Sky Lobby 2,	Web Site: www.eogresources.com	Auditors: Deloitte & Touche LLP
Houston, TX 77002	Officers: Mark G. Papa - Chmn., C.E.O. Edmund P.	Investor Contact: 713-651-7000
Telephone: 713-651-7000	Segner III - Pres., Chief of Staff	Transfer Agents: EquiServe Trust Company, N.A.

EQUIFAX, INC.

Exchange	Symbol	Price	52Wk Range	Yield	P/E
NYS	EFX	$34.48 (3/31/2008)	46.26-32.43	0.46	17.07

*7 Year Price Score 102.79 *NYSE Composite Index=100 *12 Month Price Score 97.75

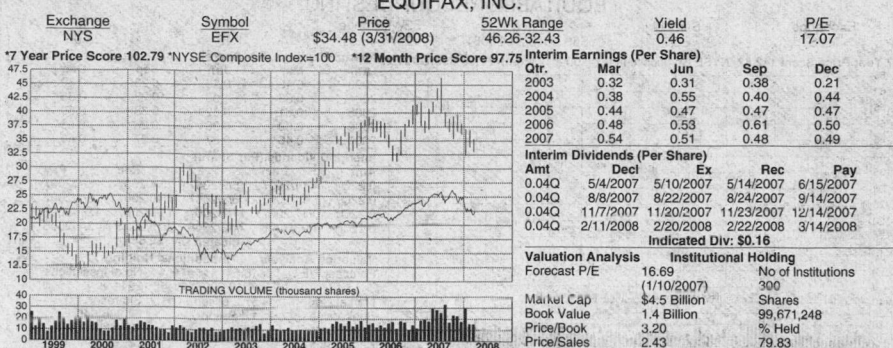

Interim Earnings (Per Share)

Qtr.	Mar	Jun	Sep	Dec
2003	0.32	0.31	0.38	0.21
2004	0.38	0.55	0.40	0.44
2005	0.44	0.47	0.47	0.47
2006	0.48	0.53	0.61	0.50
2007	0.54	0.51	0.48	0.49

Interim Dividends (Per Share)

Amt	Decl	Ex	Rec	Pay
0.04Q	5/4/2007	5/10/2007	5/14/2007	6/15/2007
0.04Q	8/8/2007	8/22/2007	8/24/2007	9/14/2007
0.04Q	11/7/2007	11/20/2007	11/23/2007	12/14/2007
0.04Q	2/11/2008	2/20/2008	2/22/2008	3/14/2008

Indicated Div: $0.16

Valuation Analysis

		Institutional Holding	
Forecast P/E	16.69	No of Institutions	
	(1/10/2007)	300	
Market Cap	$4.5 Billion	Shares	
Book Value	1.4 Billion	99,671,248	
Price/Book	3.20	% Held	
Price/Sales	2.43	79.83	

TRADING VOLUME (thousand shares)

Business Summary: Miscellaneous Business Services (MIC: 12.8 SIC: 7323 NAIC: 561450)

Equifax is a global provider of information solutions for businesses and consumers. Co.'s products and services are based on databases of consumer and business information derived from various types of credit, financial, public record, demographic and marketing data. Co.'s products and services include consumer information products, employment and income verification and products to consumers enabling them to monitor and protect their credit information. As of Dec 31 2007, Co. operated in five business segments: U.S. Consumer Information Solutions, TALX, North America Personal Solutions, North America Commercial Solutions and International.

Recent Developments: For the year ended Dec 31 2007, net income decreased 0.7% to US$272.7 million from US$274.5 million in the prior year. Revenues were US$1.84 billion, up 19.2% from US$1.55 billion the year before. Operating income was US$486.2 million versus US$436.1 million in the prior year; an increase of 11.5%. Direct operating expenses rose 20.1% to US$752.0 million from US$626.4 million in the comparable period the year before. Indirect operating expenses increased 25.0% to US$604.8 million from US$483.8 million in the equivalent prior-year period.

Prospects: For 2008, Co. expects its business segments, except its U.S. Consumer Information Solutions segment, to grow revenues over 2007 due to new products, new customers and growing volumes with its existing customers. Co. also plans to invest in unique data sources, pursue new vertical markets and expand into emerging markets. As a result, Co. expects consolidated revenue to grow by 9.0% to 12.0% in 2008. Separately, Co. recently reached a preliminary understanding with CRISIL Ltd, a ratings, research, risk and policy advisory company, and Tata Capital Ltd, both of India, to develop plans to create a credit information company in India; in line with its strategy to expand into new geographies.

Financial Data

(US$ in Thousands)	12/31/2007	12/31/2006	12/31/2005	12/31/2004	12/31/2003	12/31/2002	12/31/2001	12/31/2000
Earnings Per Share	2.02	2.12	1.86	1.76	1.21	1.29	0.88	1.68
Cash Flow Per Share	3.41	2.94	2.60	2.35	2.16	1.83	1.86	2.11
Dividends Per Share	0.160	0.160	0.150	0.110	0.080	0.080	0.225	0.370
Dividend Payout %	7.92	7.55	8.06	6.25	6.61	6.20	25.57	22.02
Income Statement								
Total Revenue	1,843,000	1,546,300	1,443,400	1,272,800	1,225,400	1,109,300	1,139,000	1,965,881
EBITDA	610,800	530,600	508,500	501,200	454,900	436,600	356,600	610,103
Income Before Taxes	424,600	415,900	390,700	385,200	283,100	314,900	202,600	385,369
Income Taxes	151,900	141,400	144,200	147,900	104,600	123,600	85,300	157,347
Net Income	272,700	274,500	246,500	234,700	164,900	178,000	122,500	228,022
Average Shares	135,100	129,400	132,200	133,500	136,700	138,500	139,000	136,016
Balance Sheet								
Current Assets	425,000	345,200	280,400	299,000	285,900	285,600	358,000	604,909
Total Assets	3,523,900	1,790,600	1,831,500	1,557,200	1,533,300	1,506,900	1,422,600	2,069,637
Current Liabilities	546,900	582,100	294,500	456,900	354,800	427,900	275,900	426,224
Long-Term Obligations	1,165,200	173,900	463,800	398,500	663,000	690,600	693,600	993,569
Total Liabilities	2,124,700	952,500	1,011,200	1,033,600	1,181,800	1,285,900	1,179,100	1,686,059
Stockholders' Equity	1,399,200	838,100	820,300	523,600	371,500	221,000	243,500	383,578
Shares Outstanding	129,700	124,700	129,200	129,400	132,700	135,700	136,200	135,835
Statistical Record								
Return on Assets %	10.26	15.16	14.55	15.05	10.78	12.15	7.02	11.63
Return on Equity %	24.38	33.10	36.68	52.30	55.66	76.64	39.07	75.90
EBITDA Margin %	33.14	34.31	35.23	39.38	37.12	39.36	31.31	31.03
Net Margin %	14.80	17.75	17.08	18.44	13.46	16.05	10.76	11.60
Asset Turnover	0.69	0.85	0.85	0.82	0.80	0.76	0.65	1.00
Current Ratio	0.78	0.59	0.95	0.66	0.81	0.67	1.30	1.42
Debt to Equity	0.83	0.21	0.57	0.76	1.78	3.12	2.85	2.59
Price Range	46.26-35.33	41.38-31.29	38.76-27.23	28.38-23.25	27.45-18.21	30.89-19.61	27.00-16.54	20.94-11.76
P/E Ratio	22.90-17.49	19.52-14.76	20.84-14.64	16.13-13.21	22.69-15.05	23.95-15.20	30.68-18.79	12.46-7.00
Average Yield %	0.40	0.44	0.44	0.43	0.35	0.32	1.06	2.38

Address: 1550 Peachtree Street, N.W., Atlanta, GA 30309
Telephone: 404-885-8000
Fax: 404-885-8682

Web Site: www.equifax.com
Officers: Thomas F. Chapman - Chmn. Mark E. Miller - Pres., C.O.O.

Auditors: Ernst & Young LLP
Investor Contact: 404-885-8000
Transfer Agents: Computershare Investor Services LLC, Providence, RI

EQUITABLE RESOURCES, INC.

Exchange	Symbol	Price	52Wk Range	Yield	P/E
NYS	EQT	$58.90 (3/31/2008)	63.74-46.51	1.49	28.05

*7 Year Price Score 142.82 *NYSE Composite Index=100 *12 Month Price Score 121.23

TRADING VOLUME (thousand shares)

Interim Earnings (Per Share)

Qtr.	Mar	Jun	Sep	Dec
2003	0.48	0.25	0.23	0.39
2004	0.55	1.03	0.28	0.35
2005	0.61	0.52	0.38	0.59
2006	0.59	0.36	0.26	0.59
2007	0.46	0.87	0.27	0.50

Interim Dividends (Per Share)

Amt	Decl	Ex	Rec	Pay
0.22Q	4/11/2007	5/2/2007	5/4/2007	6/1/2007
0.22Q	7/11/2007	8/8/2007	8/10/2007	9/1/2007
0.22Q	10/17/2007	11/7/2007	11/9/2007	12/1/2007
0.22Q	1/23/2008	2/13/2008	2/15/2008	3/1/2008

Indicated Div: $0.88

Valuation Analysis

		Institutional Holding	
Forecast P/E	16.54	No of Institutions	
	(1/10/2007)	291	
Market Cap	$7.2 Billion	Shares	
Book Value	1.1 Billion	94,296,640	
Price/Book	6.56	% Held	
Price/Sales	5.28	77.53	

Business Summary: Gas Utilities (MIC: 7.4 SIC: 4923 NAIC: 221210)

Equitable Resources is an integrated energy company, with an emphasis on Appalachian area natural gas activities, including production, gathering and processing, and distribution, transmission, storage and marketing. Co. and its subsidiaries offer energy (natural gas, and a limited amount of natural gas liquids and crude oil) products and services to wholesale and retail customers. Co. operates through two business segments: Equitable Supply and Equitable Utilities. In addition, Co.'s total proved reserves at Dec 31 2007 was 2,682 billion cubic feet of natural gas equivalents; 65.0% of which were proved developed.

Recent Developments: For the year ended Dec 31 2007, income from continuing operations increased 19.2% to US$257.5 million from US$216.0 million a year earlier. Net income increased 16.9% to US$257.5 million from US$220.3 million in the prior year. Revenues were US$1.36 billion, up 7.4% from US$1.27 billion the year before. Operating income was US$311.7 million versus US$372.5 million in the prior year, a decrease of 16.3%. Direct operating expenses rose 13.9% to US$554.5 million from US$504.3 million in the comparable period the year before. Indirect operating expenses increased 21.5% to US$475.3 million from US$391.1 million in the equivalent prior-year period.

Prospects: For 2008, Co. expects total sales of 80 billion cubic feet of natural gas equivalents (Bcfe) to 81 Bcfe with daily sales volumes of 235 million cubic feet of natural gas equivalents by the end of 2008, which is a 12.0% growth over the year end 2007 run rate. In addition, Co. expects to drill 250 to 300 horizontal wells in 2008 with continued investment in midstream infrastructure including the completion of the Big Sandy Pipeline and the Langley, KY, processing facility. Also, Co. plans to expand its market footprint in the Northeast and Mid-Atlantic gas sales markets, including the previously announced intent to jointly develop the Northeast Passage Project with Tennessee Gas Pipeline.

Financial Data

(US$ in Thousands)	12/31/2007	12/31/2006	12/31/2005	12/31/2004	12/31/2003	12/31/2002	12/31/2001	12/31/2000
Earnings Per Share	2.10	1.80	2.10	2.22	1.34	1.21	1.15	0.80
Cash Flow Per Share	3.52	5.16	(2.58)	1.43	0.98	1.69	1.01	2.77
Tang Book Value Per Share	8.98	7.78	2.96	6.74	7.33	5.83	6.17	4.86
Dividends Per Share	0.880	0.870	0.820	0.720	0.485	0.335	0.314	0.295
Dividend Payout %	41.90	48.33	39.05	32.43	36.19	27.80	27.28	36.88
Income Statement								
Total Revenue	1,361,406	1,267,910	1,253,724	1,191,609	1,047,277	1,069,068	1,764,491	1,652,218
EBITDA	559,349	472,905	549,576	556,533	380,933	339,845	355,670	338,011
Income Before Taxes	401,878	325,731	411,612	422,548	255,349	228,218	239,531	163,344
Income Taxes	144,395	109,706	153,038	142,694	81,792	77,592	87,723	57,171
Net Income	257,483	220,286	260,055	279,854	170,001	154,107	151,808	106,173
Average Shares	122,839	122,113	123,715	126,202	126,716	128,032	132,150	132,664
Balance Sheet								
Net PPE	2,919,491	2,377,471	2,083,205	1,879,787	1,766,782	1,561,815	1,414,277	1,419,429
Total Assets	3,936,971	3,256,911	3,342,285	3,196,546	2,939,892	2,436,891	2,518,747	2,455,850
Long-Term Obligations	753,500	753,500	763,434	617,769	632,147	447,000	271,250	287,789
Total Liabilities	2,839,499	2,310,631	2,987,817	2,321,874	1,974,552	1,533,252	1,547,593	1,637,155
Stockholders' Equity	1,097,472	946,280	354,468	874,672	965,340	778,639	846,154	693,695
Shares Outstanding	122,155	121,603	119,906	122,062	124,734	124,684	127,740	130,156
Statistical Record								
Return on Assets %	7.16	6.68	7.95	9.10	6.32	6.22	6.10	4.99
Return on Equity %	25.20	33.87	42.31	30.34	19.50	18.97	19.72	15.84
EBITDA Margin %	41.09	37.30	43.84	46.70	36.37	31.79	20.16	20.46
Net Margin %	18.91	17.37	20.74	23.49	16.23	14.42	8.60	6.43
PPE Turnover	0.51	0.57	0.63	0.65	0.63	0.72	1.25	1.25
Asset Turnover	0.38	0.38	0.38	0.39	0.39	0.43	0.71	0.78
Debt to Equity	0.69	0.80	2.15	0.71	0.65	0.57	0.32	0.41
Price Range	56.63-39.67	44.45-31.77	39.35-28.16	30.37-21.07	21.63-17.34	18.74-14.70	20.04-13.60	16.69-8.23
P/E Ratio	26.97-18.89	24.69-17.65	18.74-13.41	13.68-9.49	16.14-12.94	15.49-12.15	17.42-11.83	20.86-10.29
Average Yield %	1.77	2.37	2.45	2.88	2.47	1.95	1.89	2.37

Address: 225 North Shore Drive, Pittsburgh, PA 15212 Telephone: 412-553-5700 Fax: 412-553-5732	Web Site: www.eqt.com Officers: Murry S. Gerber - Chmn., Pres., C.E.O. David L. Porges - Vice-Chmn., Exec. V.P., Fin. & Admin.	Auditors: Ernst & Young LLP Investor Contact: 412-553-7833 Transfer Agents: Mellon Investor Services LLC

EQUITY RESIDENTIAL

Exchange	Symbol	Price	52Wk Range	Yield	P/E
NYS	EQR	$41.49 (3/31/2008)	51.84-32.72	4.65	12.24

*7 Year Price Score 95.95   *NYSE Composite Index=100   *12 Month Price Score 101.79

Interim Earnings (Per Share)

Qtr.	Mar	Jun	Sep	Dec
2003	0.41	0.41	0.41	0.32
2004	0.35	0.39	0.26	0.48
2005	0.74	0.44	0.86	0.74
2006	1.25	0.51	0.19	1.55
2007	0.40	0.95	1.62	0.46

Interim Dividends (Per Share)

Amt	Decl	Ex	Rec	Pay
0.463Q	5/24/2007	6/14/2007	6/18/2007	7/13/2007
0.463Q	8/17/2007	9/13/2007	9/17/2007	10/12/2007
0.482Q	12/13/2007	12/20/2007	12/24/2007	1/11/2008
0.482Q	2/19/2008	3/13/2008	3/17/2008	4/11/2008

Indicated Div: $1.93

Valuation Analysis

		Institutional Holding	
Forecast P/E	N/A	No of Institutions	302
Market Cap	$11.2 Billion	Shares	274,321,152
Book Value	5.1 Billion	% Held	93.30
Price/Book	2.21		
Price/Sales	5.49		

Business Summary: Property, Real Estate & Development (MIC: 8.3 SIC: 6798 NAIC: 525930)

Equity Residential is a real estate investment trust (REIT) focused on the acquisition, development and management of apartment properties. Co. is the general partner of, and as of Dec 31 2007, Co. owned an approximate 93.6% ownership interest in, ERP Operating Limited Partnership (the Operating Partnership). Co. is structured as an umbrella partnership REIT, under which all property ownership and business operations are conducted through the Operating Partnership and its subsidiaries. As of Dec 31 2007, Co., directly or indirectly through investments in title holding entities, owned all or a portion of 579 properties in 24 states and the District of Columbia consisting of 152,821 units.

Recent Developments: For the year ended Dec 31 2007, income from continuing operations increased 79.1% to US$93.0 million from US$51.9 million a year earlier. Net income decreased 7.8% to US$989.6 million from US$1.07 billion in the prior year. Revenues were US$2.04 billion, up 13.9% from US$1.79 billion the year before. Revenues from property income rose 13.9% to US$2.03 billion from US$1.78 billion in the corresponding earlier year.

Prospects: Looking ahead to 2008, while it remains cautious of the weakening economy and slowing job growth, Co.'s portfolio is 94.5% occupied as of Feb 5 2008. Thus, for full-year 2008, Co. expects to produce same-store revenue growth of 3.0% to 4.0%. Further, Co. expects funds from operations of $2.45 to $2.60 per share in 2008, assuming several factors, including higher same-store net operating income of approximately $30.0 million to $50.0 million, and the positive effect of the lease up of development and former condominium properties of approximately $25.0 million to $30.0 million. Moreover, Co. is estimating interest and other income will approximate $5.0 million to $10.0 million in 2008.

Financial Data
(US$ in Thousands)

	12/31/2007	12/31/2006	12/31/2005	12/31/2004	12/31/2003	12/31/2002	12/31/2001	12/31/2000
Earnings Per Share	3.39	3.50	2.79	1.48	1.55	1.18	1.36	1.67
Cash Flow Per Share	2.84	2.60	2.50	2.56	2.75	3.27	3.33	3.21
Tang Book Value Per Share	18.00	18.73	16.79	15.46	15.54	15.57	16.59	16.47
Dividends Per Share	1.750	1.750	1.750	1.750	1.750	1.750	1.750	1.750
Dividend Payout %	51.62	50.00	62.72	118.24	112.90	148.31	128.68	104.79
Income Statement								
Property Income	2,028,901	1,981,335	1,943,789	1,878,262	1,808,925	1,969,617	2,132,460	1,987,362
Non-Property Income	9,183	9,101	11,148	11,239	14,373	24,436	38,183	42,978
Total Revenue	2,038,084	1,990,436	1,954,937	1,889,501	1,823,298	1,994,053	2,170,643	2,030,340
Interest Expense	495,298	436,254	390,591	349,314	332,629	337,489	355,050	301,340
Net Income	989,022	1,072,844	861,793	472,329	543,847	421,313	473,585	549,451
Average Shares	302,233	315,579	310,785	303,871	297,041	297,969	295,552	291,266
Balance Sheet								
Total Assets	15,689,777	15,062,219	14,098,945	12,645,275	11,466,893	11,810,917	12,235,625	12,263,966
Long-Term Obligations	9,508,733	8,057,656	7,591,073	6,459,806	5,360,489	5,523,699	5,742,758	5,706,152
Total Liabilities	10,269,213	8,766,538	8,281,422	7,037,165	5,850,523	6,002,491	6,185,853	6,031,801
Stockholders' Equity	5,062,518	5,884,222	5,395,340	5,072,528	5,015,441	5,197,123	5,413,950	5,619,547
Shares Outstanding	269,554	293,551	289,536	285,076	277,643	271,095	265,232	265,232
Statistical Record								
Return on Assets %	6.44	7.36	6.44	3.91	4.67	3.50	3.87	4.57
Return on Equity %	18.08	19.02	16.47	9.34	10.65	7.94	8.58	9.85
Net Margin %	48.56	53.90	44.08	25.00	29.83	21.13	21.82	27.06
Price Range	56.35-34.24	54.73-39.99	41.99-31.20	36.57-27.29	30.05-23.24	30.90-21.91	30.35-24.82	28.59-19.53
P/E Ratio	16.62-10.10	15.64-11.43	15.05-11.18	24.71-18.44	19.39-14.99	26.19-18.57	22.32-18.25	17.12-11.70
Average Yield %	3.90	3.72	4.82	5.69	6.45	6.53	6.42	7.59

Address: Two North Riverside Plaza, Chicago, IL 60606 **Telephone:** 312-474-1300 **Fax:** 312-454-8703	**Web Site:** www.equityresidential.com **Officers:** Samuel Zell - Chmn. David J. Neithercut - Pres.	**Auditors:** Ernst & Young LLP **Investor Contact:** 312-466-3779 **Transfer Agents:** EquiServe Trust Company, NA Providence, RI

ESSEX PROPERTY TRUST, INC.

Exchange	Symbol	Price	52Wk Range	Yield	P/E	Div Acheiver
NYS	ESS	$113.98 (3/31/2008)	132.66-87.58	3.58	26.88	13 Years

*7 Year Price Score 113.42 *NYSE Composite Index=100 *12 Month Price Score 102.22

Interim Earnings (Per Share)

Qtr.	Mar	Jun	Sep	Dec
2003	0.48	0.50	0.43	0.28
2004	0.26	0.23	1.49	1.39
2005	1.13	1.64	0.35	0.19
2006	0.43	0.95	0.45	0.63
2007	1.46	0.39	0.39	2.03

Interim Dividends (Per Share)

Amt	Decl	Ex	Rec	Pay
0.93Q	6/7/2007	6/27/2007	6/29/2007	7/16/2007
0.93Q	9/18/2007	9/26/2007	9/28/2007	10/15/2007
0.93Q	12/7/2007	12/26/2007	12/28/2007	1/15/2008
1.02Q	2/27/2008	3/27/2008	3/31/2008	4/15/2008

Indicated Div: $4.08

Valuation Analysis

		Institutional Holding	
Forecast P/E	91.67	No of Institutions	
	(1/10/2007)	179	
Market Cap	$2.8 Billion	Shares	
Book Value	790.3 Million	24,164,530	
Price/Book	3.59	% Held	
Price/Sales	7.30	99.83	

TRADING VOLUME (thousand shares)

Business Summary: Property, Real Estate & Development (MIC: 8.3 SIC: 6798 NAIC: 525930)

Essex Property Trust operates as a self-administered and self-managed real estate investment trust. Co. is engaged primarily in the ownership, operation, management, acquisition, development and redevelopment of real estate. The majority of Co.'s real estate consists of apartment communities. As of Dec 31 2007, Co. owned or held an interest in 134 apartment communities, aggregating 27,489 units, located predominantly along the West Coast. Co.'s other properties included two recreational vehicle parks totaling 338 spaces, six office buildings that Co. primarily occupies and uses as office space, and one manufactured housing community containing 157 pads.

Recent Developments: For the year ended Dec 31 2007, income from continuing operations increased 26.2% to US$41.7 million from US$33.0 million a year earlier. Net income increased 84.3% to US$115.6 million from US$62.7 million in the prior year. Revenues were US$388.5 million, up 14.3% from US$339.8 million the year before. Revenues from property income rose 14.5% to US$383.4 million from US$334.8 million in the corresponding earlier year.

Prospects: Co. noted that it has 16 projects in various stages of development totaling 3,171 units, valued at $906.0 million. Notably, Co.'s Belmont Station, a 275-unit in downtown Los Angeles and Eastlake, a 127-unit located on Lake Union in Seattle, are nearing completion, and will begin leasing on-site in Apr 2008. Meanwhile, Co.'s 2008 acquisition plan is for an increase in new investments of $100.0 million. Thus, Co. will continue to concentrate its acquisitions efforts on the Seattle metropolitan area and the San Francisco Bay Area. For 2008, Co. expects fund from operations per diluted share will range from $5.85 to $6.15 and earnings per share will range from $1.85 to $2.15 per diluted share.

Financial Data

(US$ in Thousands)	12/31/2007	12/31/2006	12/31/2005	12/31/2004	12/31/2003	12/31/2002	12/31/2001	12/31/2000
Earnings Per Share	4.24	2.45	3.32	3.36	1.70	2.82	2.59	2.37
Cash Flow Per Share	7.78	6.93	5.41	5.30	4.81	4.63	5.36	5.04
Tang Book Value Per Share	30.76	25.08	24.14	24.58	24.74	23.41	20.98	21.27
Dividends Per Share	3.720	3.360	3.240	3.160	3.120	3.080	2.800	2.380
Dividend Payout %	87.74	137.14	97.59	94.05	183.53	109.22	108.11	100.42
Income Statement								
Property Income	383,433	343,044	316,340	283,483	222,868	177,265	183,482	167,771
Non-Property Income	5,090	5,030	10,951	...	11,582	22,857	22,152	10,969
Total Revenue	388,523	348,074	327,291	283,483	234,450	200,122	205,634	178,740
Interest Expense	80,995	72,898	73,614	63,023	42,751	35,012	39,105	30,384
Income Before Taxes	42,064	35,862	53,980	...	...	...	...	...
Income Taxes	400	525	2,538	...	...	...	...	...
Net Income	115,638	62,748	79,716	79,693	37,947	52,874	48,545	44,353
Average Shares	25,100	23,551	23,388	23,156	21,678	18,725	18,768	18,657
Balance Sheet								
Total Assets	2,980,323	2,485,840	2,239,290	2,217,217	1,728,564	1,619,734	1,329,458	1,281,849
Long-Term Obligations	1,657,691	1,411,554	1,354,918	1,316,984	832,229	804,063	638,660	595,535
Total Liabilities	1,762,133	1,491,599	1,425,109	1,385,810	895,064	865,890	691,379	652,044
Stockholders' Equity	790,318	612,209	580,967	591,277	589,701	491,314	386,599	391,675
Shares Outstanding	24,876	23,416	23,033	23,033	22,825	20,983	18,428	18,417
Statistical Record								
Return on Assets %	4.23	2.66	3.58	4.03	2.27	3.59	3.72	3.77
Return on Equity %	16.49	10.52	13.60	13.46	7.02	12.05	12.48	11.35
Net Margin %	29.76	18.03	24.36	28.11	16.19	26.42	23.61	24.81
Price Range	146.40-95.34	133.47-94.42	93.15-69.10	85.11-60.05	66.08-49.50	55.75-45.23	55.94-43.20	57.75-32.81
P/E Ratio	34.53-22.49	54.48-38.54	28.06-20.81	25.33-17.87	38.87-29.12	19.77-16.04	21.60-16.68	24.37-13.84
Average Yield %	3.08	2.95	3.92	4.55	5.36	6.11	5.67	5.36

Address: 925 East Meadow Drive, Palo Alto, CA 94303 Telephone: 650-494-3700 Fax: 650-494-8743	Web Site: www.expresspropertytrust.com Officers: George M. Marcus - Chmn. Keith R. Guericke - Vice-Chmn., Pres., C.E.O.	Auditors: KPMG LLP Investor Contact: 650-849-1600 Transfer Agents: Computershare Investor Services, LLC, Chicago, IL

EXELON CORP.

Exchange	Symbol	Price	52Wk Range	Yield	P/E
NYS	EXC	$81.27 (3/31/2008)	86.52-67.37	2.46	20.07

*7 Year Price Score 139.36 *NYSE Composite Index=100 *12 Month Price Score 109.08

Interim Earnings (Per Share)

Qtr.	Mar	Jun	Sep	Dec
2003	0.56	0.57	(0.16)	0.41
2004	0.61	0.78	0.85	0.53
2005	0.77	0.76	1.07	(1.24)
2006	0.59	0.95	(0.07)	0.87
2007	1.02	1.03	1.15	0.85

Interim Dividends (Per Share)

Amt	Decl	Ex	Rec	Pay
0.44Q	2/27/2007	5/11/2007	5/15/2007	6/11/2007
0.44Q	7/24/2007	8/13/2007	8/15/2007	9/10/2007
0.44Q	10/23/2007	11/13/2007	11/15/2007	12/10/2007
0.50Q	12/19/2007	2/13/2008	2/15/2008	3/10/2008

Indicated Div: $2.00

Valuation Analysis

		Institutional Holding	
Forecast P/E	13.10	No of Institutions	
	(1/10/2007)	615	
Market Cap	$53.7 Billion	Shares	
Book Value	10.1 Billion	440,722,112	
Price/Book	5.30	% Held	
Price/Sales	2.84	65.69	

Business Summary: Electricity (MIC: 7.1 SIC: 4931 NAIC: 221122)

Exelon is a utility services holding company. Co. operates via its subsidiaries, Exelon Generation Co. LLC, consisting of its owned and contracted electric generating facilities, wholesale energy marketing operations and retail sales operations; Commonwealth Edison Co., consisting of the purchase, and regulated retail and wholesale sale of electricity, and the distribution and transmission services to retail and wholesale customers in northern Illinois and the City of Chicago; and PECO Energy Co., consisting of the purchase and regulated retail sale of electricity, and the distribution and transmission services to retail customers in southeastern Pennsylvania and the City of Philadelphia.

Recent Developments: For the year ended Dec 31 2007, income from continuing operations increased 71.4% to US$2.73 billion from US$1.59 billion a year earlier. Net income increased 71.9% to US$2.74 billion from US$1.59 billion in the prior year. Revenues were US$18.92 billion, up 20.8% from US$15.66 billion the year before. Operating income was US$4.67 billion versus US$3.52 billion in the prior year, an increase of 32.6%. Direct operating expenses rose 31.1% to US$11.93 billion from US$9.10 billion in the comparable period the year before. Indirect operating expenses decreased 23.6% to US$2.32 billion from US$3.03 billion in the equivalent prior-year period.

Prospects: Co.'s near-term outlook appears encouraging, driven by recent improved generation margins and operating performance, including higher nuclear output and fleet capacity factors. For the full year of 2008, Co. is projecting earnings to be in the range of $3.70 to $4.10 per share, assuming normal weather. In addition, Co. is forecasting total capital expenditures to be about $3.12 billion, with $1.60 billion allocated for its Exelon Generation Company, LLC subsidiary, $1.00 billion for its Commonwealth Edison Company subsidiary, $394.0 million for its PECO Energy Company subsidiary as well as $122.0 million for corporate operations and Exelon Business Services Company, LLC subsidiary.

Financial Data (US$ in Thousands)	12/31/2007	12/31/2006	12/31/2005	12/31/2004	12/31/2003	12/31/2002	12/31/2001	12/31/2000
Earnings Per Share	4.05	2.35	1.36	2.78	1.38	2.22	2.21	1.44
Cash Flow Per Share	6.71	7.22	3.21	6.64	5.19	5.61	5.65	2.71
Tang Book Value Per Share	11.37	10.86	8.21	5.89	5.77	4.25	4.51	5.95
Dividends Per Share	1.760	1.600	1.600	1.255	0.960	0.880	0.910	0.454
Dividend Payout %	43.46	68.09	117.65	45.14	69.82	39.64	41.08	31.65
Income Statement								
Total Revenue	18,916,000	15,655,000	15,357,000	14,515,000	15,812,000	14,955,000	15,140,000	7,499,000
EBITDA	6,440,000	5,170,000	4,126,000	4,722,000	3,131,000	4,974,000	4,903,000	1,973,000
Income Before Taxes	4,172,000	2,796,000	1,895,000	2,512,000	1,124,000	2,668,000	2,347,000	907,000
Income Taxes	1,446,000	1,206,000	944,000	692,000	331,000	998,000	931,000	341,000
Net Income	2,736,000	1,592,000	923,000	1,864,000	905,000	1,440,000	1,428,000	586,000
Average Shares	676,000	676,000	676,000	669,000	658,000	650,000	644,000	408,000
Balance Sheet								
Net PPE	24,153,000	22,775,000	21,981,000	21,482,000	20,630,000	17,134,000	13,742,000	12,936,000
Total Assets	45,894,000	44,319,000	42,389,000	42,770,000	41,941,000	37,478,000	34,821,000	34,597,000
Long-Term Obligations	11,965,000	11,911,000	11,760,000	12,148,000	13,489,000	13,127,000	12,876,000	12,958,000
Total Liabilities	35,670,000	34,259,000	33,176,000	33,218,000	33,351,000	29,064,000	25,978,000	26,752,000
Stockholders' Equity	10,137,000	9,973,000	9,125,000	9,423,000	8,503,000	7,742,000	8,230,000	7,215,000
Shares Outstanding	660,879	670,000	666,409	664,188	656,365	646,625	642,013	340,957
Statistical Record								
Return on Assets %	6.07	3.67	2.17	4.39	2.28	3.98	4.11	2.45
Return on Equity %	27.21	16.67	9.95	20.74	11.14	18.03	18.49	12.81
EBITDA Margin %	34.05	33.02	26.87	32.53	19.80	33.26	32.38	26.31
Net Margin %	14.46	10.17	6.01	12.84	5.72	9.63	9.43	7.81
PPE Turnover	0.81	0.70	0.71	0.69	0.84	0.97	1.14	0.83
Asset Turnover	0.42	0.36	0.36	0.34	0.40	0.41	0.44	0.31
Debt to Equity	1.18	1.19	1.29	1.29	1.59	1.70	1.56	1.80
Price Range	86.18-59.18	63.46-51.54	56.92-42.03	44.70-31.29	33.18-23.41	28.46-20.18	34.90-20.52	35.42-16.81
P/E Ratio	21.28-14.61	27.00-21.93	41.85-30.90	16.08-11.26	24.04-16.97	12.82-9.09	15.79-9.29	24.60-11.68
Average Yield %	2.40	2.77	3.24	3.51	3.36	3.52	3.15	1.89

Address: 10 South Dearborn Street, P.O. Box 805379, Chicago, IL 60680-5379 Telephone: 312-394-7398	Web Site: www.exeloncorp.com Officers: John W. Rowe - Chmn., Pres., C.E.O. Pamela B. Strobel - Exec. V.P., Chief Admin. Officer	Auditors: PricewaterhouseCoopers LLP Investor Contact: 312-394-4321 Transfer Agents: Computershare Trust Company, N.A., Providence, RI

EXXON MOBIL CORP.

Exchange	Symbol	Price	52Wk Range	Yield	P/E	Div Acheiver
NYS	XOM	$84.58 (3/31/2008)	95.05-76.16	1.66	11.62	25 Years

*7 Year Price Score 128.16 *NYSE Composite Index=100 *12 Month Price Score 106.53

Interim Earnings (Per Share)

Qtr.	Mar	Jun	Sep	Dec
2003	1.05	0.62	0.55	1.01
2004	0.83	0.88	0.88	1.30
2005	1.22	1.20	1.58	1.71
2006	1.37	1.72	1.77	1.76
2007	1.62	1.83	1.70	2.13

Interim Dividends (Per Share)

Amt	Decl	Ex	Rec	Pay
0.35Q	4/25/2007	5/10/2007	5/14/2007	6/11/2007
0.35Q	7/25/2007	8/9/2007	8/13/2007	9/10/2007
0.35Q	10/31/2007	11/7/2007	11/9/2007	12/10/2007
0.35Q	1/30/2008	2/7/2008	2/11/2008	3/10/2008

Indicated Div: $1.40 (Div. Reinv. Plan)

Valuation Analysis

		Institutional Holding	
Forecast P/E	11.38	No of Institutions	
	(1/10/2007)	1469	
Market Cap	$455.2 Billion	Shares	
Book Value	121.8 Billion	3,020,861,440	
Price/Book	3.74	% Held	
Price/Sales	1.13	53.06	

TRADING VOLUME (thousand shares)

Business Summary: Oil and Gas (MIC: 14.2 SIC: 2911 NAIC: 324110)

ExxonMobil, through its affiliates, is primarily engaged in the energy business, involving exploration for, and production of, crude oil and natural gas, manufacture of petroleum products and transportation and sale of crude oil, natural gas and petroleum products. Co. manufactures and markets commodity petrochemicals, including olefins, aromatics, polyethylene and polypropylene plastics and a variety of specialty products. Co. also has interests in electric power generation facilities. Affiliates of Co. conduct research programs in support of these businesses. Co. has several divisions and hundreds of affiliates, many with names that include ExxonMobil, Exxon, Esso or Mobil.

Recent Developments: For the year ended Dec 31 2007, net income increased 2.8% to US$40.61 billion from US$39.50 billion in the prior year. Revenues were US$404.55 billion, up 7.1% from US$377.64 billion the year before. Direct operating expenses rose 9.3% to US$199.50 billion from US$182.55 billion in the comparable period the year before. Indirect operating expenses increased 5.7% to US$133.18 billion from US$125.98 billion in the equivalent prior-year period.

Prospects: On Feb 19 2008, Co. announced a new project to develop and produce hydrocarbon resources from the Point Thomson field on the Alaska North Slope. The project includes an investment of about $1.30 billion to begin a development and delineation drilling program in the winter of 2008-09 and to construct production facilities, pipelines, and infrastructures. Separately, on Jan 17 2008, Co. announced the completion and start-up of a $20.0 million compounding facility to supply polymers to the automotive, appliance and specialty consumer products industries, which should enhance its Chemical supply capabilities in North America while capitalizing on its global supply and technical capabilities.

Financial Data
(US$ in Thousands)

	12/31/2007	12/31/2006	12/31/2005	12/31/2004	12/31/2003	12/31/2002	12/31/2001	12/31/2000
Earnings Per Share	7.28	6.62	5.71	3.89	3.23	1.68	2.21	2.52
Cash Flow Per Share	9.43	8.34	7.68	6.24	4.30	3.15	3.33	3.29
Tang Book Value Per Share	22.62	19.87	18.13	15.90	13.69	11.13	10.74	10.21
Dividends Per Share	1.370	1.280	1.140	1.060	0.980	0.920	0.910	0.880
Dividend Payout %	18.82	19.34	19.96	27.25	30.34	54.76	41.18	34.92
Income Statement								
Total Revenue	404,552,000	377,635,000	370,680,000	298,035,000	246,738,000	204,506,000	213,488,000	232,748,000
EBITDA	83,124,000	79,472,000	70,181,000	51,646,000	41,220,000	26,218,000	32,356,000	35,800,000
Income Before Taxes	70,474,000	67,402,000	59,432,000	41,241,000	31,966,000	17,510,000	24,119,000	27,081,000
Income Taxes	29,864,000	27,902,000	23,302,000	15,911,000	11,006,000	6,499,000	9,014,000	11,091,000
Net Income	40,610,000	39,500,000	36,130,000	25,330,000	21,510,000	11,460,000	15,320,000	17,720,000
Average Shares	5,576,999	5,969,999	6,321,999	6,519,001	6,662,001	6,803,001	6,941,001	7,034,001
Balance Sheet								
Current Assets	85,963,000	75,777,000	73,342,000	60,377,000	45,960,000	38,291,000	35,681,000	40,399,000
Total Assets	242,082,000	219,015,000	208,335,000	195,256,000	174,278,000	152,644,000	143,174,000	149,000,000
Current Liabilities	58,312,000	48,817,000	46,307,000	42,981,000	38,386,000	33,175,000	30,114,000	38,191,000
Long-Term Obligations	7,183,000	6,645,000	6,220,000	5,013,000	4,756,000	6,655,000	7,099,000	7,280,000
Total Liabilities	120,320,000	105,171,000	97,149,000	93,500,000	84,363,000	78,047,000	70,013,000	78,243,000
Stockholders' Equity	121,762,000	113,844,000	111,186,000	101,756,000	89,915,000	74,597,000	73,161,000	70,757,000
Shares Outstanding	5,381,999	5,728,999	6,132,999	6,400,999	6,568,001	6,700,001	6,809,001	6,930,001
Statistical Record								
Return on Assets %	17.61	18.49	17.90	13.67	13.16	7.75	10.49	12.04
Return on Equity %	34.47	35.11	33.93	26.36	26.15	15.51	21.29	26.33
EBITDA Margin %	20.55	21.04	18.93	17.33	16.71	12.82	15.16	15.38
Net Margin %	10.04	10.46	9.75	8.50	8.72	5.60	7.18	7.61
Asset Turnover	1.75	1.77	1.84	1.61	1.51	1.38	1.46	1.58
Current Ratio	1.47	1.55	1.58	1.40	1.20	1.15	1.18	1.06
Debt to Equity	0.06	0.06	0.06	0.05	0.05	0.09	0.10	0.10
Price Range	95.05-69.86	78.73-56.65	64.98-49.49	51.97-40.10	41.00-31.82	44.38-30.27	45.77-35.83	47.22-35.53
P/E Ratio	13.06-9.60	11.89-8.56	11.38-8.67	13.36-10.31	12.69-9.85	26.42-18.02	20.71-16.21	18.74-14.10
Average Yield %	1.65	1.96	1.96	2.34	2.71	2.44	2.20	2.12

Address: 5959 Las Colinas Boulevard, Irving, TX 75039-2298	Web Site: www.exxonmobil.com	Auditors: PricewaterhouseCoopers LLP
Telephone: 972-444-1000	Officers: Lee R. Raymond - Chmn., C.E.O. R. W. Tillerson - Pres.	Transfer Agents: EquiServe Trust Company, N.A., Providence, RI
Fax: 972-444-1505		

F.N.B. CORP (PA)

Exchange	Symbol	Price	52Wk Range	Yield	P/E	Div Acheiver
NYS	FNB	$15.61 (3/31/2008)	17.91-13.29	6.15	13.57	35 Years

*7 Year Price Score 76.73   *NYSE Composite Index=100   *12 Month Price Score 99.50

Interim Earnings (Per Share)

Qtr.	Mar	Jun	Sep	Dec
2003	0.50	0.53	0.01	0.22
2004	0.34	0.32	0.31	0.31
2005	0.28	0.31	0.32	0.08
2006	0.27	0.28	0.29	0.29
2007	0.29	0.29	0.29	0.28

Interim Dividends (Per Share)

Amt	Decl	Ex	Rec	Pay
0.235Q	5/14/2007	5/30/2007	6/1/2007	6/15/2007
0.24Q	8/15/2007	8/29/2007	9/1/2007	9/15/2007
0.24Q	11/14/2007	11/28/2007	12/1/2007	12/15/2007
0.24Q	2/20/2008	2/28/2008	3/3/2008	3/15/2008

Indicated Div: $0.96 (Div. Reinv. Plan)

Valuation Analysis

Forecast P/E	N/A
Market Cap	$945.3 Million
Book Value	544.0 Million
Price/Book	1.74
Price/Sales	2.10

Institutional Holding

No of Institutions	100
Shares	21,357,704
% Held	35.36

TRADING VOLUME (thousand shares)

Business Summary: Commercial Banking (MIC: 8.1 SIC: 6021 NAIC: 522110)

F.N.B. is a financial holding company As of Dec 31 2007, Co. had four segments: Community Banking, Wealth Management, Insurance and Consumer Finance. Through its subsidiaries, Co. provides a range of financial services, mainly to consumers and small- to medium-sized businesses in its market areas. As of the date above, Co. had 155 Community Banking offices in Pennsylvania and Ohio and 54 Consumer Finance offices in those states and Tennessee. Through its Community Banking affiliate, Co. had six commercial loan production offices in Pennsylvania and Florida and one mortgage loan production office in Tennessee as of that date. As of Dec 31 2007, Co. had total assets of $6.09 billion.

Recent Developments: For the year ended Dec 31 2007, net income increased 3.0% to US$69.7 million from US$67.6 million in the prior year. Net interest income increased 3.2% to US$194.8 million from US$188.8 million in the prior year. Provision for loan losses was US$12.7 million versus US$10.4 million in the prior year, an increase of 21.9%. Non-interest income rose 2.9% to US$81.6 million from US$79.3 million, while non-interest expense advanced 3.2% to US$165.6 million.

Prospects: On Feb 15 2008, Co. announced that it has signed a definitive agreement to acquire Iron & Glass Bancorp, Inc. (IRGB) for about $86.1 million Co. believes that this transaction reflects its strategic focus to increase its market presence in Pittsburgh and throughout Allegheny County. Co. expects the transaction to be accretive to its earnings per share in the first full year of operation. Co. anticipates the transaction to be completed in the third quarter of 2008, pending regulatory and IRBG shareholder's approvals as well as other closing conditions. Meanwhile, Co. is progressing towards the acquisition of Omega Financial Corp. which is expected to close in the second quarter of 2008.

Financial Data
(US$ in Thousands)

	12/31/2007	12/31/2006	12/31/2005	12/31/2004	12/31/2003	12/31/2002	12/31/2001	12/31/2000
Earnings Per Share	1.15	1.14	0.98	1.29	1.25	1.34	1.52	1.62
Cash Flow Per Share	1.66	2.00	1.33	2.23	2.17	1.05	1.36	2.17
Tang Book Value Per Share	4.67	4.49	4.89	4.79	8.73	11.08	13.02	12.51
Dividends Per Share	0.950	0.940	0.925	0.920	0.930	0.810	0.526	...
Dividend Payout %	82.61	82.46	94.39	71.32	74.36	60.32	34.52	...
Income Statement								
Interest Income	368,890	342,422	297,189	254,448	423,313	426,784	296,693	290,936
Interest Expense	174,053	153,585	108,780	84,390	129,836	145,671	125,667	135,308
Net Interest Income	194,837	188,837	188,409	170,058	293,477	281,113	171,026	155,628
Provision for Losses	12,693	10,412	12,176	16,280	24,339	19,094	12,915	10,877
Non-Interest Income	81,609	79,275	57,947	78,141	130,571	120,873	82,799	73,045
Non-Interest Expense	165,611	160,514	137,075	142,587	315,523	289,444	174,830	137,501
Income Before Taxes	98,139	97,186	77,105	89,332	84,386	93,448	66,080	62,895
Income Taxes	33,912	34,219	21,847	27,537	25,397	30,113	21,508	20,119
Net Income	69,678	67,649	55,258	61,795	58,789	63,335	44,572	42,776
Average Shares	60,629	59,376	56,578	48,012	46,972	47,073	29,311	25,484
Balance Sheet								
Net Loans & Leases	4,297,066	4,204,524	3,703,080	3,344,813	5,650,924	5,176,275	3,162,982	2,924,378
Total Assets	6,088,021	6,007,592	5,590,326	5,027,009	8,308,310	7,090,232	4,129,087	3,886,548
Total Deposits	4,397,684	4,372,842	4,011,943	3,598,087	6,159,499	5,426,157	3,292,392	3,102,937
Total Liabilities	5,543,664	5,470,220	5,113,124	4,702,907	7,701,401	6,491,636	3,759,890	3,565,304
Stockholders' Equity	544,357	537,372	477,202	324,102	606,909	598,596	369,197	321,244
Shares Outstanding	60,554	60,394	57,419	50,058	46,313	46,055	28,346	25,541
Statistical Record								
Return on Assets %	1.15	1.17	1.04	0.92	0.76	1.13	1.11	1.12
Return on Equity %	12.88	13.34	13.79	13.24	9.75	13.09	12.91	13.95
Net Interest Margin %	52.82	55.15	63.40	66.83	69.33	65.87	57.64	53.49
Efficiency Ratio %	36.76	38.06	44.23	42.87	56.93	52.85	46.07	39.67
Loans to Deposits	0.98	0.96	0.92	0.93	0.92	0.95	0.96	0.94
Price Range	18.46-13.93	18.74-15.32	20.99-16.47	22.77-18.80	18.80-13.58	16.03-12.39	13.52-9.85	10.42-7.96
P/E Ratio	16.05-12.11	16.44-13.44	21.42-16.81	17.65-14.57	15.04-10.87	11.96-9.24	8.89-6.48	6.43-4.92
Average Yield %	5.70	5.62	4.95	4.40	5.75	5.62	4.46	...

Address: 2150 Goodlette Road North, Naples, FL 34102
Telephone: 239-262-7600

Web Site: www.fnbcorporation.com
Officers: Peter Mortensen - Chmn. Stephen J. Gurgovits - Pres., C.E.O.

Auditors: ERNST & YOUNG LLP
Investor Contact: 239-659-9894
Transfer Agents: F.N.B. Shareholder Services, Naples, FL

FAIR ISAAC CORP

Exchange	Symbol	Price	52Wk Range	Yield	P/E
NYS	FIC	$21.52 (3/31/2008)	40.55-20.83	0.37	12.73

*7 Year Price Score 82.00 *NYSE Composite Index=100 *12 Month Price Score 73.51

Interim Earnings (Per Share)

Qtr.	Dec	Mar	Jun	Sep
2004-05	0.36	0.45	0.53	0.52
2005-06	0.43	0.40	0.40	0.36
2006-07	0.52	0.37	0.42	0.51
2007-08	0.39	...	...	...

Interim Dividends (Per Share)

Amt	Decl	Ex	Rec	Pay
0.02Q	5/17/2007	5/25/2007	5/30/2007	6/13/2007
0.02Q	8/27/2007	9/6/2007	9/10/2007	9/26/2007
0.02Q	11/9/2007	12/3/2007	12/5/2007	12/19/2007
0.02Q	2/5/2008	2/15/2008	2/20/2008	3/5/2008

Indicated Div: $0.08

Valuation Analysis

		Institutional Holding	
Forecast P/E	N/A	No of Institutions	253
Market Cap	$1.1 Billion	Shares	52,371,336
Book Value	523.5 Million	% Held	91.69
Price/Book	2.03		
Price/Sales	1.31		

Business Summary: Miscellaneous Business Services (MIC: 12.8 SIC: 7389 NAIC: 541512)

Fair Isaac is engaged in providing analytical, credit scoring and credit account management products and services to banks, credit reporting agencies, credit card processing agencies, insurers, retailers, telecommunications providers, healthcare organizations and government agencies. Co.'s products and services consists of: analytics, which are designed to identify the risks and opportunities associated with individual clients, prospects and transactions, in order to detect patterns such as fraud; data management, profiling and text recognition; and software such as rules management systems that implement business rules, models and decision strategies.

Recent Developments: For the quarter ended Dec 31 2007, net income decreased 35.4% to US$20.2 million from US$31.2 million in the year-earlier quarter. Revenues were US$199.4 million, down 4.2% from US$208.2 million the year before. Operating income was US$33.2 million versus US$44.9 million in the prior-year quarter, a decrease of 26.0%. Direct operating expenses rose 7.6% to US$75.9 million from US$70.6 million in the comparable period the year before. Indirect operating expenses decreased 2.7% to US$90.2 million from US$92.8 million in the equivalent prior-year period.

Prospects: For the fiscal year ending Sep 2008, Co. expects revenues to be in the range of approximately $825.0 million to $835.0 million and earnings per diluted share to be in the range of approximately $1.80 to $1.90. However, Co. expects that pricing and competitive pressures will continue to adversely affect its Scoring Solutions segment revenues in fiscal 2008. Separately, on Jan 21 2008, Co. announced that it has acquired Dash Optimization, a provider of decision modeling and optimization software, for an aggregate cash purchase price of approximately $32.0 million. The acquisition is expected to strengthen Co.'s decision management portfolio and create growth opportunities.

Financial Data
(US$ in Thousands)

	3 Mos	09/30/2007	09/30/2006	09/30/2005	09/30/2004	09/30/2003	09/30/2002	09/30/2001
Earnings Per Share	1.69	1.82	1.59	1.86	1.41	1.41	0.32	0.89
Cash Flow Per Share	3.35	3.20	3.13	3.22	2.84	2.42	1.88	1.43
Tang Book Value Per Share	N.M.	N.M.	N.M.	0.03	1.31	4.26	5.97	5.21
Dividends Per Share	0.080	0.080	0.080	0.080	0.067	0.053	0.044	0.027
Dividend Payout %	4.73	4.40	5.03	4.30	4.73	3.77	13.89	3.01
Income Statement								
Total Revenue	199,385	822,236	825,365	798,671	706,206	629,295	392,418	329,148
EBITDA	42,718	199,127	201,304	248,897	224,714	219,850	79,028	101,925
Depn & Amortn	9,757	...	...	...	...	...	...	...
Income Before Taxes	31,090	149,662	159,192	194,088	168,815	172,140	53,098	76,853
Income Taxes	10,904	45,012	55,706	59,540	66,027	64,983	35,214	30,741
Net Income	20,186	104,650	103,486	134,548	102,788	107,157	17,884	46,112
Average Shares	51,200	57,548	65,125	73,584	73,032	75,973	56,325	51,883
Balance Sheet								
Current Assets	336,296	422,751	413,310	412,680	466,101	667,822	428,174	134,261
Total Assets	1,238,625	1,275,771	1,321,205	1,351,061	1,444,779	1,495,173	1,212,513	317,013
Current Liabilities	507,712	525,924	537,029	138,157	120,316	98,362	90,209	39,637
Long-Term Obligations	190,000	170,000	...	400,000	400,000	541,364	139,922	...
Total Liabilities	715,116	709,457	551,177	545,967	528,308	645,631	239,041	45,241
Stockholders' Equity	523,509	566,314	770,028	805,094	916,471	849,542	973,472	271,772
Shares Outstanding	49,464	51,064	59,369	63,836	69,579	69,867	75,997	50,934
Statistical Record								
Return on Assets %	7.29	8.06	7.75	9.62	6.97	7.92	2.34	16.52
Return on Equity %	15.31	15.66	13.14	15.63	11.61	11.76	2.87	19.59
EBITDA Margin %	21.42	24.22	24.39	31.16	31.82	34.94	20.14	30.97
Net Margin %	10.12	12.73	12.54	16.85	14.55	17.03	4.56	14.01
Asset Turnover	0.63	0.63	0.62	0.57	0.48	0.46	0.51	1.18
Current Ratio	0.66	0.80	0.77	2.99	3.87	6.79	4.75	3.39
Debt to Equity	0.36	0.30	...	0.50	0.44	0.64	0.14	...
Price Range	41.67-32.15	42.59-35.03	48.21-33.25	44.83-28.65	42.65-24.00	40.63-19.87	29.33-16.79	30.98-11.37
P/E Ratio	24.66-19.02	23.40-19.25	30.32-20.91	24.10-15.40	30.25-17.02	28.82-14.09	91.67-52.47	34.81-12.78
Average Yield %	0.21	0.21	0.20	0.23	0.19	0.17	0.18	0.14

Address: 901 Marquette Avenue, Suite 3200, Minneapolis, MN 55402-3232 **Telephone:** 612-758-5200	**Web Site:** www.fairisaac.com **Officers:** Thomas G. Grudnowski - Pres., C.E.O. Charles M. Osborne - V.P., C.F.O.	**Auditors:** DELOITTE & TOUCHE LLP **Investor Contact:** 415-491-7122 **Transfer Agents:** Mellon Investor Services, San Francisco, CA

FAIRCHILD SEMICONDUCTOR INTERNATIONAL, INC.

Exchange	Symbol	Price	52Wk Range	Yield	P/E
NYS	FCS	$11.92 (3/31/2008)	20.43-10.57	N/A	23.37

*7 Year Price Score 73.73   *NYSE Composite Index=100   *12 Month Price Score 76.29

TRADING VOLUME (thousand shares)

Interim Earnings (Per Share)

Qtr.	Mar	Jun	Sep	Dec
2003	(0.15)	(0.54)	(0.05)	0.05
2004	0.10	0.14	0.11	0.13
2005	(0.09)	(1.71)	(0.17)	(0.04)
2006	0.21	0.18	0.20	0.07
2007	0.05	0.03	0.16	0.27

Interim Dividends (Per Share)

No Dividends Paid

Valuation Analysis		Institutional Holding	
Forecast P/E	N/A	No of Institutions	
		190	
Market Cap	$1.5 Billion	Shares	
Book Value	1.2 Billion	119,893,072	
Price/Book	1.21	% Held	
Price/Sales	0.89	97.04	

Business Summary: IT & Technology (MIC: 10.2 SIC: 3674 NAIC: 334413)

Fairchild Semiconductor International is engaged in developing, manufacturing and selling power analog, power discrete and certain non-power semiconductor applications to a range of end market customers. Co. operates through three reportable segments: Analog Products, which designs, manufactures and markets analog and mixed signal integrated circuits for computing, consumer, communications, industrial and automotive applications; Functional Power, which designs, manufactures and markets power discrete semiconductors for computing, communications, industrial and automotive applications; and Standard Products, which designs, develops, manufactures and markets standard logic devices.

Recent Developments: For the year ended Dec 30 2007, net income decreased 23.3% to US$64.0 million from US$83.4 million in the prior year. Revenues were US$1.67 billion, up 1.2% from US$1.65 billion the year before. Operating income was US$102.3 million versus US$118.5 million in the prior year, a decrease of 13.7%. Direct operating expenses rose 2.2% to US$1.18 billion from US$1.15 billion in the comparable period the year before. Indirect operating expenses increased 2.6% to US$388.2 million from US$378.3 million in the equivalent prior-year period.

Prospects: Co. expects its 2007 Infrastructure Realignment Program to be largely completed by the 2008 second quarter and to affect about 97 manufacturing and non-manufacturing personnel. Accordingly, Co. is targeting annual cost savings from the employee separation of about $4.8 million beginning in the first quarter of 2008 and $1.2 million beginning in the second quarter of 2008. Co. is also expecting depreciation cost savings of $800,000 relating to the asset impairment charges. For the first quarter of 2008, Co. expects revenue to decline 2.0% to 6.0% and gross margin to be 100 to 150 basis points lower sequentially due to lower factory loadings and changes in variable compensation accruals.

Financial Data

(US$ in Thousands)	12/30/2007	12/31/2006	12/25/2005	12/26/2004	12/28/2003	12/29/2002	12/30/2001	12/31/2000
Earnings Per Share	0.51	0.67	(2.01)	0.48	(0.69)	(0.02)	(0.42)	2.69
Cash Flow Per Share	1.54	1.49	1.26	2.05	1.08	1.27	1.57	3.85
Tang Book Value Per Share	5.97	6.51	5.41	7.09	6.26	6.64	3.28	5.43
Income Statement								
Total Revenue	1,670,200	1,651,100	1,425,100	1,603,100	1,395,800	1,411,900	1,407,700	1,783,200
EBITDA	228,700	235,100	141,800	301,400	173,900	279,500	203,600	479,800
Income Before Taxes	82,100	98,800	(36,500)	72,800	(108,500)	(16,400)	(64,100)	270,700
Income Taxes	18,100	15,400	204,700	13,600	(27,000)	(13,900)	(22,400)	(2,400)
Net Income	64,000	83,400	(241,200)	59,200	(81,500)	(2,500)	(41,700)	273,100
Average Shares	126,300	124,400	120,200	123,500	117,500	108,100	99,600	101,400
Balance Sheet								
Current Assets	885,500	1,020,500	874,500	1,032,400	984,000	1,020,300	874,800	876,400
Total Assets	2,132,600	2,045,600	1,928,300	2,376,500	2,258,500	2,288,100	2,149,200	1,837,500
Current Liabilities	444,800	262,500	229,700	286,600	247,700	206,900	199,300	292,200
Long-Term Obligations	385,900	589,700	641,000	845,200	848,600	852,800	1,138,200	705,200
Total Liabilities	910,900	911,200	919,800	1,147,400	1,110,800	1,072,900	1,341,200	999,800
Stockholders' Equity	1,218,500	1,132,200	1,008,500	1,229,100	1,147,700	1,215,200	808,000	837,700
Shares Outstanding	124,134	122,729	120,529	119,577	118,285	117,005	99,965	99,324
Statistical Record								
Return on Assets %	3.07	4.13	N.M.	2.56	N.M.	N.M.	N.M.	18.06
Return on Equity %	5.46	7.67	N.M.	5.00	N.M.	N.M.	N.M.	51.13
EBITDA Margin %	13.69	14.24	9.95	18.80	12.46	19.80	14.46	26.91
Net Margin %	3.83	5.05	N.M.	3.69	N.M.	N.M.	N.M.	15.32
Asset Turnover	0.80	0.82	0.66	0.69	0.62	0.64	0.71	1.18
Current Ratio	1.99	3.92	3.81	3.60	3.97	4.93	4.39	3.00
Debt to Equity	0.32	0.52	0.64	0.69	0.74	0.70	1.41	0.84
Price Range	20.43-14.38	21.76-15.01	18.24-12.98	28.00-11.99	26.78-10.11	31.85-6.94	27.75-12.17	48.44-11.81
P/E Ratio	40.06-28.20	32.48-22.40	...	58.33-24.98	...	...	...	18.01-4.39

Address: 82 Running Hill Road, South Portland, ME 04106	Web Site: www.fairchildsemi.com	Auditors: KPMG LLP
Telephone: 207-775-8100	Officers: Kirk P. Pond - Chmn. Joseph R. Martin - Vice Chmn., Sr. Exec. V.P.	Transfer Agents: Computershare Trust Co., N.A., Canton, MA
Fax: 207-761-3415		

FAMILY DOLLAR STORES, INC.

Exchange	Symbol	Price	52Wk Range	Yield	P/E	Div Acheiver
NYS	FDO	$19.50 (3/31/2008)	35.23-15.85	2.56	12.26	31 Years

*7 Year Price Score 71.52   *NYSE Composite Index=100   *12 Month Price Score 81.85

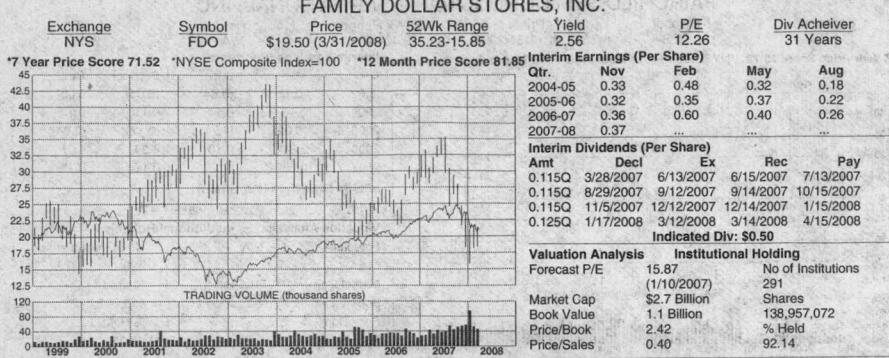

Interim Earnings (Per Share)

Qtr.	Nov	Feb	May	Aug
2004-05	0.33	0.48	0.32	0.18
2005-06	0.32	0.35	0.37	0.22
2006-07	0.36	0.60	0.40	0.26
2007-08	0.37	...	...	...

Interim Dividends (Per Share)

Amt	Decl	Ex	Rec	Pay
0.115Q	3/28/2007	6/13/2007	6/15/2007	7/13/2007
0.115Q	8/29/2007	9/12/2007	9/14/2007	10/15/2007
0.115Q	11/5/2007	12/12/2007	12/14/2007	1/15/2008
0.125Q	1/17/2008	3/12/2008	3/14/2008	4/15/2008

Indicated Div: $0.50

Valuation Analysis

	Institutional Holding	
Forecast P/E	15.87	No of Institutions
	(1/10/2007)	291
Market Cap	$2.7 Billion	Shares
Book Value	1.1 Billion	138,957,072
Price/Book	2.42	% Held
Price/Sales	0.40	92.14

Business Summary: Retail - General (MIC: 5.2 SIC: 5331 NAIC: 452990)

Family Dollar Stores is engaged in operating a chain of general merchandise retail discount stores, providing primarily low to lower-middle income consumers with a selection of merchandise, including consumables, home products, apparel and accessories, and electronics. As of Sep 1 2007, Co. operated more than 6,400 stores located in 44 states of the U.S. Co.'s store is between 7,500 and 9,500 square feet and generally serves customers who live within five miles of the store. Co.'s stores are located in urban, suburban, small town and rural markets.

Recent Developments: For the quarter ended Dec 1 2007, net income decreased 4.0% to US$51.9 million from US$54.1 million in the year-earlier quarter. Revenues were US$1.68 billion, up 5.2% from US$1.60 billion the year before. Operating income was US$85.1 million versus US$91.1 million in the prior-year quarter, a decrease of 6.6%. Direct operating expenses rose 5.7% to US$1.11 billion from US$1.05 billion in the comparable period the year before. Indirect operating expenses increased 6.3% to US$490.9 million from US$461.8 million in the equivalent prior-year period.

Prospects: For the fiscal year ending Aug 2008, Co. expects total sales to increase 2.0% to 3.0%. Co. also expects its comparable store sales to be flat or increase slightly and expects its gross margin to be pressured by a higher sales mix of lower-margin consumables. However, Co. believes that better purchase markups, lower inventory shrinkage, and its focus on expense control will partially offset these pressures. In addition, Co. expects to continue to invest in, among others, new store openings, store expansions, and its ongoing refrigerated cooler program for perishable goods in selected stores. Hence, Co. expects its earnings for the fiscal year to be between $1.56 and $1.64 per diluted share.

Financial Data
(US$ in Thousands)

	3 Mos	09/01/2007	08/26/2006	08/27/2005	08/28/2004	08/30/2003	08/31/2002	09/01/2001
Earnings Per Share	1.59	1.62	1.26	1.30	1.53	1.43	1.25	1.10
Cash Flow Per Share	2.91	2.74	2.92	1.80	2.21	1.72	2.34	0.95
Tang Book Value Per Share	8.05	8.19	8.04	8.64	8.13	7.61	6.66	5.57
Dividends Per Share	0.450	0.440	0.400	0.360	0.320	0.280	0.250	0.230
Dividend Payout %	28.24	27.16	31.75	27.69	20.92	19.58	20.00	20.91
Income Statement								
Total Revenue	1,683,043	6,834,305	6,394,772	5,824,808	5,281,888	4,750,171	4,162,652	3,665,362
EBITDA	123,198	532,693	451,942	457,528	512,098	478,040	418,636	366,107
Depn & Amortn	38,058	...	...	...	...	...	...	...
Income Before Taxes	82,614	381,896	311,144	342,795	414,215	389,725	341,621	298,422
Income Taxes	30,668	139,042	116,033	125,286	151,530	142,250	124,692	108,917
Net Income	51,946	242,854	195,111	217,509	262,685	247,475	216,929	189,505
Average Shares	141,324	149,599	155,124	167,092	171,624	173,354	174,049	172,774
Balance Sheet								
Current Assets	1,502,471	1,537,280	1,418,848	1,354,768	1,225,308	1,156,492	1,055,859	807,265
Total Assets	2,605,090	2,624,156	2,523,029	2,409,501	2,167,422	1,985,695	1,754,619	1,399,745
Current Liabilities	1,107,298	1,130,303	986,111	894,611	713,551	595,331	530,780	390,294
Long-Term Obligations	250,000	250,000	250,000	...	...	...	...	...
Total Liabilities	1,473,824	1,449,515	1,314,636	981,435	807,022	674,726	599,671	440,730
Stockholders' Equity	1,131,266	1,174,641	1,208,393	1,428,066	1,360,400	1,310,969	1,154,948	959,015
Shares Outstanding	140,527	143,344	150,210	165,262	167,396	172,208	173,329	172,035
Statistical Record								
Return on Assets %	9.05	9.28	7.93	9.53	12.72	13.27	13.79	14.11
Return on Equity %	19.70	20.05	14.84	15.64	19.78	20.13	20.58	21.22
EBITDA Margin %	7.32	7.79	7.07	7.85	9.70	10.06	10.06	9.99
Net Margin %	3.09	3.55	3.05	3.73	4.97	5.21	5.21	5.17
Asset Turnover	2.62	2.61	2.60	2.55	2.56	2.55	2.65	2.73
Current Ratio	1.36	1.36	1.44	1.51	1.72	1.94	1.99	2.07
Debt to Equity	0.22	0.21	0.21	...	...	...	...	...
Price Range	35.23-21.65	35.23-23.81	27.22-19.67	34.98-20.20	43.61-25.60	40.25-24.16	36.86-24.56	30.09-16.88
P/E Ratio	22.16-13.62	21.75-14.70	21.60-15.61	26.91-15.54	28.50-16.73	28.15-16.90	29.49-19.65	27.35-15.34
Average Yield %	1.52	1.45	1.68	1.28	0.92	0.87	0.80	0.96

Address: 10401 Old Monroe Road, Matthews, NC 28105 **Telephone:** 704-847-6961 **Fax:** 704-847-5534	**Web Site:** www.familydollar.com **Officers:** Howard R. Levine - Chmn., C.E.O. R. James Kelly - Vice-Chmn., C.F.O., Admin. Officer	**Auditors:** PricewaterhouseCoopers LLP **Transfer Agents:** Mellon Investor Services LLC, Ridgefield Park, NJ

FANNIE MAE

Exchange	Symbol	Price	52Wk Range	Yield	P/E
NYS	FNM	$26.32 (3/31/2008)	69.49-19.81	5.32	N/A

*7 Year Price Score 63.45   *NYSE Composite Index=100   *12 Month Price Score 62.03

Interim Earnings (Per Share)

Qtr.	Mar	Jun	Sep	Dec
2004			4.94	
Qtr.	Mar	Jun	Sep	Dec
2005	...	...	...	...
2006	1.94	1.97	(0.79)	4.14
2007	0.85	1.86	(1.56)	(3.80)

Interim Dividends (Per Share)

Amt	Decl	Ex	Rec	Pay
0.10Q	5/3/2007	5/16/2007	5/18/2007	5/25/2007
0.50Q	7/17/2007	7/27/2007	7/31/2007	8/27/2007
0.50Q	10/16/2007	10/29/2007	10/31/2007	11/26/2007
0.35Q	1/18/2008	1/29/2008	1/31/2008	2/25/2008

Indicated Div: $1.40

Valuation Analysis

		Institutional Holding	
Forecast P/E	10.03 (1/10/2007)	No of Institutions	590
Market Cap	$25.6 Billion	Shares	901,547,968
Book Value	44.0 Billion	% Held	
Price/Book	0.58		92.46
Price/Sales	0.59		

Business Summary: Credit & Lending (MIC: 8.6 SIC: 6111 NAIC: 522292)

Fannie Mae is engaged in providing funds to mortgage lenders through its purchases of mortgage assets, and issuing and guaranteeing mortgage-related securities that facilitate the flow of additional funds into the mortgage market. Co. also makes other investments that increase the supply of affordable housing. Co.'s customers include mortgage banking companies, investment banks, savings and loan associations, savings banks, commercial banks, credit unions, community banks, insurance companies, and state and local housing finance agencies. Co. is organized in three business segments: Single-Family Credit Guaranty, Housing and Community Development, and Capital Markets.

Recent Developments: For the year ended Dec 31 2007, net loss amounted to US$2.05 billion versus net income of US$4.06 billion in the prior year. Net interest income decreased 32.2% to US$4.58 billion from US$6.75 billion in the prior year. Co. reported a non-interest loss of US$1.41 billion versus non-interest income of US$1.73 billion last year, while non-interest expense declined 14.2% to US$2.65 billion.

Prospects: Looking ahead, Co. expects housing market weakness to continue in 2008, resulting in increased delinquencies, defaults and foreclosures on mortgage loans, and slower growth in U.S. residential mortgage debt outstanding. In response, Co. plans to prudently manage and preserve its capital, while building a solid mortgage credit book of business. Meanwhile, based on its market outlook, Co. expects that its credit losses and credit-related expenses will continue to grow during 2008, as will its guaranty fee income. Co. also believes that its single-family guaranty book of business will grow at a faster rate than the rate of overall growth in U.S. residential mortgage debt outstanding.

Financial Data

(US$ in Thousands)	12/31/2007	12/31/2006	12/31/2005	12/31/2004	12/31/2003	12/31/2002	12/31/2001	12/31/2000
Earnings Per Share	(2.63)	7.30	6.01	4.94	7.91	4.53	5.72	4.29
Cash Flow Per Share	44.14	32.61	80.56	...	19.98	12.24	14.70	12.44
Tang Book Value Per Share	27.82	33.33	31.11	30.74	18.83	13.76	15.86	18.58
Dividends Per Share	1.900	1.180	1.040	2.080	1.680	1.320	1.200	1.120
Dividend Payout %	...	16.16	17.30	42.11	21.24	29.14	20.98	26.11
Income Statement								
Interest Income	44,766,000	87,254,000	44,844,000	47,818,000	50,920,000	50,853,000	49,170,000	42,781,000
Interest Expense	40,185,000	73,750,000	33,339,000	29,737,000	37,351,000	40,287,000	41,080,000	37,107,000
Net Interest Income	4,581,000	13,504,000	11,505,000	18,081,000	13,569,000	10,566,000	8,090,000	5,674,000
Provision for Losses	...	...	...	...	100,000	128,000	(115,000)	(120,000)
Non-Interest Income	(1,411,000)	3,450,000	(1,142,000)	(9,464,000)	2,848,000	2,048,000	1,633,000	1,307,000
Non-Interest Expense	2,648,000	6,172,000	2,113,000	1,648,000	3,631,000	5,764,000	1,354,000	905,000
Income Before Taxes	(5,126,000)	9,126,000	7,571,000	3,999,000	10,413,000	6,048,000	8,291,000	5,982,000
Income Taxes	(3,091,000)	332,000	1,277,000	1,024,000	2,693,000	1,429,000	2,224,000	1,566,000
Net Income	(2,050,000)	8,118,000	6,347,000	4,967,000	7,905,000	4,619,000	5,894,000	4,448,000
Average Shares	973,000	1,944,000	998,000	973,000	981,000	997,000	1,006,000	1,009,000
Balance Sheet								
Net Loans & Leases	403,524,000	767,110,000	367,543,000	401,372,000	240,582,000	186,055,000	705,167,000	607,399,000
Total Assets	882,547,000	1,687,872,000	834,168,000	1,020,934,000	1,009,569,000	887,515,000	799,791,000	675,072,000
Total Liabilities	838,429,000	1,604,588,000	794,745,000	981,956,000	987,196,000	871,227,000	781,673,000	654,234,000
Stockholders' Equity	44,011,000	83,012,000	39,302,000	38,902,000	22,373,000	16,288,000	18,118,000	20,838,000
Shares Outstanding	974,104	1,944,221	970,532	969,075	970,000	989,000	997,000	999,000
Statistical Record								
Return on Assets %	N.M.	0.64	0.68	...	0.83	0.55	0.80	0.71
Return on Equity %	N.M.	13.27	16.23	...	40.89	26.85	30.26	23.06
Net Interest Margin %	10.23	15.48	25.66	37.81	26.65	20.78	16.45	13.26
Efficiency Ratio %	6.11	6.80	4.84	4.30	6.75	10.90	2.67	2.05
Price Range	69.49-28.25	61.65-46.37	71.27-41.62	79.88-63.40	75.37-58.93	83.15-59.54	87.49-72.95	87.81-48.38
P/E Ratio	...	8.45-6.35	11.86-6.93	16.17-12.83	9.53-7.45	18.36-13.14	15.30-12.75	20.47-11.28
Average Yield %	3.31	2.21	1.91	2.89	2.45	1.78	1.50	1.78

Address: 3900 Wisconsin Avenue, NW, Washington, DC 20016-2892 **Telephone:** 202-752-7000 **Fax:** 202-752-4934	**Web Site:** www.fanniemae.com **Officers:** Daniel H. Mudd - Pres., C.E.O. Julie St. John - Exec. V.P., Chief Tech. Officer	**Auditors:** Deloitte & Touche LLP **Investor Contact:** 202-752-7115 **Transfer Agents:** Equiserve Trust Company NA., Providence RI

FEDERAL REALTY INVESTMENT TRUST (MD)

Exchange	Symbol	Price	52Wk Range	Yield	P/E	Div Acheiver
NYS	FRT	$77.95 (3/31/2008)	95.19-64.48	3.13	22.59	40 Years

*7 Year Price Score 129.80 *NYSE Composite Index=100 *12 Month Price Score 98.06

TRADING VOLUME (thousand shares)

Interim Earnings (Per Share)

Qtr.	Mar	Jun	Sep	Dec
2003	0.26	0.29	0.44	0.67
2004	0.28	0.45	0.30	0.37
2005	0.40	0.41	0.52	0.60
2006	0.53	0.66	0.41	0.32
2007	0.41	0.47	0.41	2.15

Interim Dividends (Per Share)

Amt	Decl	Ex	Rec	Pay
0.575Q	5/2/2007	6/20/2007	6/22/2007	7/16/2007
0.61Q	8/1/2007	9/19/2007	9/21/2007	10/15/2007
0.61Q	10/31/2007	12/28/2007	1/2/2008	1/15/2008
0.61Q	2/12/2008	3/17/2008	3/19/2008	4/15/2008

Indicated Div: $2.44 (Div. Reinv. Plan)

Valuation Analysis

		Institutional Holding	
Forecast P/E	39.68 (1/10/2007)	No of Institutions	213
Market Cap	$4.6 Billion	Shares	49,979,176
Book Value	1.1 Billion	% Held	90.17
Price/Book	4.10		
Price/Sales	9.41		

Business Summary: Property, Real Estate & Development (MIC: 8.3 SIC: 6798 NAIC: 525930)

Federal Realty Investment Trust is an equity Real-Estate-Investment-Trust (REIT) focusing in the ownership, management, development and redevelopment of retail and mixed-use properties. As of Dec 31 2007, Co. owned or had a majority ownership interest in 82 community and neighborhood shopping centers and mixed-used properties, comprising of approximately 18.2 million square feet, located primarily in communities metropolitan markets in the Northeast and Mid-Atlantic regions of U.S., as well as California. In addition, Co. owned, through a joint venture in which it owns a 30.0% interest, seven retail real estate projects totaling approximately 1.0 million square feet as of Dec 31 2007.

Recent Developments: For the year ended Dec 31 2007, income from continuing operations increased 6.4% to US$96.4 million from US$90.6 million a year earlier. Net income increased 64.7% to US$195.5 million from US$118.7 million in the prior year. Revenues were US$485.9 million, up 13.6% from US$427.5 million the year before. Revenues from property income rose 13.9% to US$481.3 million from US$422.4 million in the corresponding earlier year.

Prospects: For 2008, Co. foresees its income from continuing operations to grow in comparison with its 2007 income from continuing operations, driven by increased earnings in its same-center portfolio and from properties under redevelopment as well as higher earnings as it expands through property acquisitions. In addition, Co. forecasts earnings to grow from the acquisition of neighborhood and community shopping centers in the East and West regions markets, as well as a reduction in earnings from selective dispositions. Hence, Co. is projecting Funds From Operations in the range of 3.89 to $3.94 per diluted share, while earnings are estimated to range from $2.08 to $2.13 per diluted share.

Financial Data

(US$ in Thousands)	12/31/2007	12/31/2006	12/31/2005	12/31/2004	12/31/2003	12/31/2002	12/31/2001	12/31/2000
Earnings Per Share	3.45	1.92	1.94	1.41	1.59	0.85	1.52	1.35
Cash Flow Per Share	3.82	3.45	3.32	3.15	2.58	2.86	2.77	2.73
Tang Book Value Per Share	18.84	14.17	12.10	12.57	11.31	9.40	8.92	9.31
Dividends Per Share	2.370	2.460	2.365	1.990	1.950	1.930	1.900	1.840
Dividend Payout %	68.70	128.13	121.91	141.13	122.64	227.06	125.00	136.30
Income Statement								
Property Income	481,332	445,927	404,960	389,359	352,497	313,678	293,912	271,749
Non-Property Income	4,560	5,095	5,370	4,915	5,379	5,156	6,590	7,532
Total Revenue	485,892	451,022	410,330	394,274	357,876	318,834	300,502	279,281
Interest Expense	111,365	102,808	88,566	85,058	75,232	65,054	69,313	66,418
Net Income	195,537	118,712	114,612	84,156	94,497	55,287	68,756	60,523
Average Shares	56,543	53,962	53,050	51,547	48,619	42,882	40,266	39,910
Balance Sheet								
Total Assets	2,989,297	2,688,606	2,350,852	2,266,896	2,143,435	1,999,378	1,837,978	1,621,079
Long-Term Obligations	1,427,640	1,587,906	1,073,388	979,006	949,357	1,003,212	935,625	809,200
Total Liabilities	1,842,847	1,882,337	1,556,812	1,457,408	1,422,479	1,325,725	1,212,572	1,105,504
Stockholders' Equity	1,114,632	784,078	774,847	790,534	691,374	644,287	592,388	467,654
Shares Outstanding	58,645	55,320	52,890	52,136	49,200	43,535	40,071	39,469
Statistical Record								
Return on Assets %	6.89	4.71	4.96	3.81	4.56	2.88	3.98	3.83
Return on Equity %	20.60	15.23	14.64	11.33	14.15	8.94	12.97	12.45
Net Margin %	40.24	26.32	27.93	21.34	26.40	17.34	22.88	21.67
Price Range	97.12-73.82	87.15-61.63	65.73-46.50	52.55-34.73	39.80-26.75	28.75-22.93	23.71-18.98	22.31-17.88
P/E Ratio	28.15-21.40	45.39-32.10	33.88-23.97	37.27-24.63	25.03-16.82	33.82-26.98	15.60-12.49	16.53-13.24
Average Yield %	2.76	3.40	4.17	4.57	5.81	7.32	9.03	9.13

Address: 1626 East Jefferson Street, Rockville, MD 20852-4041 **Telephone:** 301-998-8100 **Fax:** 301-998-3700	**Web Site:** www.federalrealty.com **Officers:** Mark Ordan - Chmn. Donald C. Wood - Pres., C.E.O., C.O.O.	**Auditors:** Grant Thornton LLP **Transfer Agents:** American Stock Transfer & Trust Company, New York, NY

298

FEDERAL SIGNAL CORP.

Exchange	Symbol	Price	52Wk Range	Yield	P/E
NYS	FSS	$13.96 (3/31/2008)	16.72-9.41	1.72	12.14

*7 Year Price Score 63.07   *NYSE Composite Index=100   *12 Month Price Score 95.30

TRADING VOLUME (thousand shares)

Interim Earnings (Per Share)

Qtr.	Mar	Jun	Sep	Dec
2003	0.14	0.20	0.21	0.24
2004	0.05	(0.14)	(0.08)	0.13
2005	0.00	0.23	0.21	(0.54)
2006	0.00	(0.04)	0.19	0.32
2007	0.64	0.23	0.09	0.18

Interim Dividends (Per Share)

Amt	Decl	Ex	Rec	Pay
0.06Q	4/24/2007	6/13/2007	6/15/2007	7/5/2007
0.06Q	7/24/2007	9/12/2007	9/14/2007	10/3/2007
0.06Q	10/23/2007	12/12/2007	12/14/2007	1/4/2008
0.06Q	2/22/2008	3/12/2008	3/14/2008	4/4/2008

Indicated Div: $0.24 (Div. Reinv. Plan)

Valuation Analysis / **Institutional Holding**

Forecast P/E	14.56	No of Institutions
	(1/10/2007)	130
Market Cap	$668.7 Million	Shares
Book Value	445.3 Million	35,079,308
Price/Book	1.50	% Held
Price/Sales	0.53	73.14

Business Summary: Automotive (MIC: 15.1 SIC: 3711 NAIC: 336211)

Federal Signal is engaged in the design and manufacture of products and integrated applications for municipal, governmental, industrial and airport customers. Co.'s portfolio of products includes safety and security systems, fire apparatus, aerial devices, street sweepers, industrial vacuums, waterblasters, sewer cleaners and consumable industrial tooling. As of Dec 31 2007, Co. and its subsidiaries operated manufacturing facilities in 38 plants in 14 countries around the world serving customers in approximately 100 countries in all regions of the world. In addition, Co. provides customer and dealer financing to support the sale of its vehicles.

Recent Developments: For the year ended Dec 31 2007, income from continuing operations decreased 13.4% to US$29.8 million from US$34.4 million a year earlier. Net income increased 141.9% to US$54.9 million from US$22.7 million in the prior year. Revenues were US$1.27 billion, up 4.7% from US$1.21 billion the year before. Operating income was US$64.1 million versus US$69.9 million in the prior year, a decrease of 8.3%. Direct operating expenses rose 4.7% to US$971.2 million from US$927.2 million in the comparable period the year before. Indirect operating expenses increased 8.5% to US$232.8 million from US$214.5 million in the equivalent prior-year period.

Prospects: Co. noted that the production slots for its Bronto aerial devices and Vactor sewer cleaners in 2008 are sold out and it is focusing on expanding these operations. In addition, Co. is optimistic that the diversity of its businesses and its cost containment actions of reducing expenses and scaling back on some initiatives in order to weather a possible economic downturn will position it well for earnings growth in 2008. Co. is also encouraged by the growth in international sales and expects an increasing portion of its revenues and profits to come from international sales for the foreseeable future. Separately, Co. noted that it is evaluating strategic alternatives for its E-ONE business.

Financial Data
(US$ in Thousands)

	12/31/2007	12/31/2006	12/31/2005	12/31/2004	12/31/2003	12/31/2002	12/31/2001	12/31/2000
Earnings Per Share	1.15	0.47	(0.10)	(0.05)	0.78	0.83	1.05	1.26
Cash Flow Per Share	1.37	0.62	1.51	1.09	1.57	...	2.10	1.41
Tang Book Value Per Share	N.M.	1.59	0.89	1.25	1.17	1.04	1.74	1.82
Dividends Per Share	0.240	0.240	0.240	0.400	0.700	0.800	0.780	0.760
Dividend Payout %	20.87	51.06	...	...	89.74	96.39	74.29	60.32
Income Statement								
Total Revenue	1,268,100	1,211,600	1,156,900	1,139,000	1,206,798	1,057,201	1,072,175	1,106,127
EBITDA	81,100	85,600	90,900	17,900	90,202	105,172	121,080	144,872
Income Before Taxes	34,000	42,700	46,300	(25,300)	46,017	61,102	64,454	84,414
Income Taxes	4,200	8,300	(1,000)	(12,600)	8,345	14,923	17,864	26,759
Net Income	54,900	22,700	(4,600)	(2,300)	37,303	38,195	47,373	57,537
Average Shares	47,900	48,000	48,200	48,100	47,984	...	45,443	45,521
Balance Sheet								
Current Assets	446,700	418,800	444,700	418,400	403,552	394,817	342,325	348,936
Total Assets	1,177,100	1,049,400	1,119,500	1,125,900	1,186,409	1,168,410	1,015,614	991,118
Current Liabilities	259,000	273,900	279,800	229,700	284,370	221,884	179,430	288,920
Long Term Obligations	378,100	309,300	362,600	394,100	395,477	481,566	446,595	316,932
Total Liabilities	731,800	663,000	743,200	713,200	763,359	769,601	655,305	633,687
Stockholders' Equity	445,300	386,400	376,300	412,700	422,509	398,065	359,436	357,431
Shares Outstanding	47,900	47,600	48,100	48,200	47,918	47,660	45,129	45,304
Statistical Record								
Return on Assets %	4.93	2.09	N.M.	N.M.	3.17	3.50	4.74	5.88
Return on Equity %	13.20	5.95	N.M.	N.M.	9.09	10.08	13.27	16.13
EBITDA Margin %	6.40	7.07	7.86	1.57	7.47	9.95	11.29	13.10
Net Margin %	4.33	1.87	N.M.	N.M.	3.09	3.61	4.44	5.20
Asset Turnover	1.14	1.12	1.03	0.98	1.02	0.97	1.07	1.13
Current Ratio	1.72	1.53	1.59	1.82	1.42	1.78	1.91	1.21
Debt to Equity	0.85	0.80	0.96	0.95	0.94	1.21	1.24	0.89
Price Range	16.84-10.93	19.35-12.94	17.68-13.98	20.43-15.96	20.70-13.67	26.75-16.16	24.50-17.25	23.88-14.88
P/E Ratio	14.64-9.50	41.17-27.53	...	...	26.54-17.53	32.23-19.47	23.33-16.43	18.95-11.81
Average Yield %	1.60	1.48	1.50	2.20	4.14	3.69	3.64	3.95

Address: 1415 West 22nd Street, Oak Brook, IL 60523-2004 **Telephone:** 630-954-2000 **Fax:** 630-954-2030	**Web Site:** www.federalsignal.com **Officers:** James C. Janning - Chmn. Robert D. Welding - Pres., C.E.O.	**Auditors:** Ernst & Young LLP **Investor Contact:** 630-954-2000 **Transfer Agents:** National City Bank, Cleveland, OH

FEDERATED INVESTORS INC (PA)

Exchange	Symbol	Price	52Wk Range	Yield	P/E
NYS	FII	$39.16 (3/31/2008)	44.39-31.44	2.15	18.47

*7 Year Price Score 97.88   *NYSE Composite Index=100   *12 Month Price Score 112.02

Interim Earnings (Per Share)

Qtr.	Mar	Jun	Sep	Dec
2003	0.43	0.44	0.46	0.39
2004	0.46	0.46	0.43	0.29
2005	0.06	0.35	0.59	0.48
2006	0.45	0.47	0.43	0.51
2007	0.50	0.54	0.57	0.52

Interim Dividends (Per Share)

Amt	Decl	Ex	Rec	Pay
0.21Q	4/26/2007	5/4/2007	5/8/2007	5/15/2007
0.21Q	7/26/2007	8/6/2007	8/8/2007	8/15/2007
0.21Q	10/29/2007	11/6/2007	11/8/2007	11/15/2007
0.21Q	1/24/2008	2/6/2008	2/8/2008	2/15/2008

Indicated Div: $0.84

Valuation Analysis

		Institutional Holding	
Forecast P/E	14.66 (1/10/2007)	No of Institutions	225
Market Cap	$4.0 Billion	Shares	65,763,276
Book Value	574.0 Million	% Held	63.51
Price/Book	6.94		
Price/Sales	3.53		

Business Summary: Wealth Management (MIC: 8.8 SIC: 6282 NAIC: 523930)

Federated Investors and its consolidated subsidiaries provide investment management products and related financial services. Co. sponsors, markets and provides investment-related services to various investment products, including mutual funds and separate accounts. As of Dec 31 2007, Co. provided investment advisory services to 148 Federated-sponsored funds as well as investment advisory services to $39.50 billion in separate account assets. Co.'s investment products are distributed in three principal markets: the wealth management and trust market, the broker/dealer market and the global institutional market. Co. had $301.62 billion in assets under management as of Dec 31 2007.

Recent Developments: For the year ended Dec 31 2007, income from continuing operations increased 13.8% to US$217.5 million from US$191.0 million a year earlier. Net income increased 10.0% to US$217.5 million from US$197.7 million in the prior year. Revenues were US$1.13 billion, up 15.2% from US$978.9 million the year before. Operating income was US$357.2 million versus US$308.5 million in the prior year, an increase of 15.8%. Indirect operating expenses increased 14.9% to US$770.5 million from US$670.4 million in the equivalent prior-year period.

Prospects: Co. is seeing an increase in revenues, primarily driven by higher revenue from average money market assets under management. Notably, Co. experienced increased asset inflows in its money market funds as a result of investors' increased concerns about risk and uncertainty in the financial markets and the Federal Reserve Bank interest rate cuts. Meanwhile, on Jan 7 2008, Co. announced the launch of Federated Kaufmann Large Cap Fund, an equity fund that seeks to provide capital appreciation by investing in the securities of companies in the U.S. and abroad. This complements the existing small- and mid-cap products and expands the $13.00 billion Federated Kaufmann franchise.

Financial Data
(US$ in Thousands)

	12/31/2007	12/31/2006	12/31/2005	12/31/2004	12/31/2003	12/31/2002	12/31/2001	12/31/2000
Earnings Per Share	2.12	1.86	1.48	1.64	1.71	1.74	1.40	1.27
Cash Flow Per Share	3.24	2.82	1.75	2.75	2.31	1.98	2.44	1.44
Tang Book Value Per Share	0.39	0.39	1.59	1.36	1.56	0.94	0.22	0.86
Dividends Per Share	0.810	0.690	0.575	0.414	0.297	0.217	0.175	0.139
Dividend Payout %	38.21	37.10	38.85	25.24	17.37	12.47	12.50	10.92
Income Statement								
Total Revenue	1,127,644	978,858	909,216	846,964	823,248	711,069	715,777	680,768
Income Before Taxes	346,678	304,767	280,011	289,264	299,600	315,714	269,603	242,522
Income Taxes	129,207	113,719	116,719	110,206	108,115	111,954	96,887	87,162
Net Income	217,471	197,729	160,283	181,179	191,485	203,760	168,447	155,360
Average Shares	102,606	106,288	108,252	110,410	112,059	117,304	119,992	122,295
Balance Sheet								
Total Assets	840,971	810,294	896,621	954,688	879,228	530,007	431,553	704,750
Total Liabilities	263,384	280,037	355,039	496,349	482,815	188,710	194,093	556,344
Stockholders' Equity	574,015	529,375	540,329	457,753	395,853	340,717	237,097	147,868
Shares Outstanding	101,758	103,863	107,042	107,008	108,664	112,560	115,369	117,129
Statistical Record								
Return on Assets %	26.34	23.17	17.32	19.70	27.18	42.38	29.65	22.49
Return on Equity %	39.42	36.97	32.12	42.33	51.99	70.53	87.51	116.20
Price Range	43.00-31.44	39.93-30.12	37.85-27.03	33.59-26.88	31.68-24.20	35.16-23.62	32.41-24.06	31.19-12.63
P/E Ratio	20.28-14.83	21.47-16.19	25.57-18.26	20.48-16.39	18.53-14.15	20.21-13.57	23.15-17.19	24.56-9.94
Average Yield %	2.14	1.99	1.84	1.38	1.08	0.72	0.60	0.64

Address: Federated Investors Tower, Pittsburgh, PA 15222-3779 Telephone: 412-288-1900 Fax: 412-288-2919	Web Site: www.federatedinvestors.com Officers: John F. Donahue - Chmn. John W. McGonigle - Vice-Chmn., Exec. V.P., Chief Legal Officer, Sec.	Auditors: Ernst & Young LLP Transfer Agents: Equiserve Trust Company,N.A.

FEDEX CORP

Exchange	Symbol	Price	52Wk Range	Yield	P/E
NYS	FDX	$92.67 (3/31/2008)	117.25-82.55	0.43	14.66

*7 Year Price Score 102.55 *NYSE Composite Index=100 *12 Month Price Score 94.57

TRADING VOLUME (thousand shares)

Interim Earnings (Per Share)

Qtr.	Aug	Nov	Feb	May
2004-05	1.08	1.15	1.03	1.46
2005-06	1.10	1.53	1.38	1.82
2006-07	1.53	1.64	1.35	1.96
2007-08	1.58	1.54	1.26	...

Interim Dividends (Per Share)

Amt	Decl	Ex	Rec	Pay
0.10Q	5/25/2007	6/7/2007	6/11/2007	7/2/2007
0.10Q	8/17/2007	9/6/2007	9/10/2007	10/1/2007
0.10Q	11/16/2007	12/10/2007	12/12/2007	1/2/2008
0.10Q	2/22/2008	3/7/2008	3/11/2008	4/1/2008

Indicated Div: $0.40

Valuation Analysis / Institutional Holding

Forecast P/E	12.74	No of Institutions
	(1/10/2007)	758
Market Cap	$28.7 Billion	Shares
Book Value	14.2 Billion	225,623,088
Price/Book	2.02	% Held
Price/Sales	0.77	73.30

Business Summary: Aviation (MIC: 1.1 SIC: 4513 NAIC: 492110)

FedEx provides a portfolio of transportation, e-commerce and business services through companies operating under the FedEx brand. These companies are included in four business segments, and represented by Federal Express Corp., an express transportation company; FedEx Ground Package System, Inc., a provider of small-package ground delivery services; FedEx Freight Corp., a U.S. provider of regional next-day and second-day and interregional less-than-truckload freight services; and FedEx Kinko's Office and Print Services, Inc., a provider of document services and business services.

Recent Developments: For the quarter ended Feb 29 2008, net income decreased 6.4% to US$393.0 million from US$420.0 million in the year-earlier quarter. Revenues were US$9.44 billion, up 9.8% from US$8.59 billion the year before. Operating income was unchanged at US$641.0 million versus the prior-year quarter. Direct operating expenses rose 15.6% to US$3.89 billion from US$3.37 billion in the comparable period the year before. Indirect operating expenses increased 7.0% to US$4.90 billion from US$4.58 billion in the equivalent prior-year period.

Prospects: For the fiscal quarter ended May 31 2008, Co. is projecting earnings $1.60 to $1.80 per diluted share, assuming no additional increases to current fuel prices and no further weakening in the economy. For the rest of fiscal 2008, Co. expects revenue growth rates to be restrained by high fuel prices and the continued weak U.S. economy are anticipated to lower demand for U.S. domestic express package and less-than-truckload freight services and constrain base yield growth in its transportation segments. Looking ahead, Co. foresees narrow earnings growth as an anticipated weak economic environment in the U.S., along with high fuel costs, will continue to limit demand for its services.

Financial Data

(US$ in Thousands)	9 Mos	6 Mos	3 Mos	05/31/2007	05/31/2006	05/31/2005	05/31/2004	05/31/2003
Earnings Per Share	6.32	6.43	6.53	6.48	5.83	4.72	2.76	2.74
Cash Flow Per Share	11.76	11.30	12.02	11.61	12.09	10.36	10.07	6.28
Tang Book Value Per Share	34.43	33.16	31.45	29.74	28.39	22.36	17.45	20.85
Dividends Per Share	0.390	0.380	0.370	0.360	0.320	0.280	0.220	0.200
Dividend Payout %	6.17	5.91	5.67	5.56	5.49	5.93	7.97	7.30
Income Statement								
Total Revenue	28,087,000	18,650,000	9,199,000	35,214,000	32,294,000	29,363,000	24,710,000	22,487,000
EBITDA	3,680,000	2,550,000	1,285,000	5,010,000	4,551,000	3,914,000	2,810,000	2,807,000
Depn & Amortn	1,447,000	955,000	473,000	...	...	...	...	...
Income Before Taxes	2,183,000	1,555,000	787,000	3,215,000	2,899,000	2,313,000	1,319,000	1,338,000
Income Taxes	817,000	582,000	293,000	1,199,000	1,093,000	864,000	481,000	508,000
Net Income	1,366,000	973,000	494,000	2,016,000	1,806,000	1,449,000	838,000	830,000
Average Shares	312,000	312,000	312,000	311,000	310,000	307,000	304,000	303,000
Balance Sheet								
Total Assets	24,596,000	24,347,000	23,906,000	24,000,000	22,690,000	20,404,000	19,134,000	15,385,000
Long-Term Obligations	2,006,000	2,007,000	2,007,000	2,007,000	1,592,000	2,427,000	2,837,000	1,709,000
Total Liabilities	10,404,000	10,587,000	10,685,000	11,344,000	11,179,000	10,816,000	11,098,000	8,097,000
Stockholders' Equity	14,192,000	13,760,000	13,221,000	12,656,000	11,511,000	9,588,000	8,036,000	7,288,000
Shares Outstanding	310,000	309,000	309,000	308,000	306,000	302,000	299,995	298,593
Statistical Record								
Return on Assets %	7.95	8.17	8.52	8.64	8.38	7.33	4.84	5.69
Return on Equity %	14.48	15.22	16.12	16.68	17.12	16.44	10.91	12.00
EBITDA Margin %	13.10	13.67	13.97	14.23	14.09	13.33	11.37	12.48
Net Margin %	4.86	5.22	5.37	5.72	5.59	4.93	3.39	3.69
Asset Turnover	1.50	1.48	1.50	1.51	1.50	1.49	1.43	1.54
Price Range	117.25-82.78	120.97-91.65	120.97-100.50	120.97-98.12	119.42-77.00	101.55-72.82	77.16-59.70	63.98-42.80
P/E Ratio	18.55-13.10	18.81-14.25	18.53-15.39	18.67-15.14	20.48-13.21	21.51-15.43	27.96-21.63	23.35-15.62
Average Yield %	0.38	0.35	0.33	0.33	0.33	0.33	0.32	0.38

Address: 942 South Shady Grove Road,	Web Site: www.fedex.com	Auditors: Ernst & Young LLP
Memphis, TN 38120	Officers: Fredrick W. Smith - Chmn., Pres., C.E.O.	Investor Contact: 901-818-7200
Telephone: 901-818-7500	Alan B. Graf Jr. - Exec. V.P., C.F.O.	
Fax: 901-346-1013		

FERRO CORP.

Business Summary: Chemicals (MIC: 11.1 SIC: 2851 NAIC: 325510)

Ferro produces specialty materials and chemicals that are sold to manufacturers who, in turn, make products for end-use markets. Co. produces inorganic specialty products such as glazes, frits, enamels, pigments, dinnerware decorations and other performance materials; organic specialty products, including polymer specialty materials, engineered plastic compounds, electrolytes, pharmaceutical active ingredients and specialty solvents; as well as electronic materials such as dielectrics, conductive pastes, metal powders and polishing materials. Co.'s products are mainly used in building and renovation, transportation, electronics, industrial products, packaging and pharmaceuticals.

Recent Developments: For the year ended Dec 31 2007, loss from continuing operations was US$94.3 million compared with income of US$21.1 million a year earlier. Net loss amounted to US$94.5 million versus net income of US$20.6 million in the prior year. Revenues were US$2.20 billion, up 8.0% from US$2.04 billion the year before. Direct operating expenses rose 10.0% to US$1.79 billion from US$1.63 billion in the comparable period the year before. Indirect operating expenses increased 41.5% to US$464.7 million from US$328.4 million in the equivalent prior-year period.

Prospects: For the first quarter of 2008, Co. is projecting sales of $550.0 million to $575.0 million, compared with sales of $530.0 million in the first quarter of 2007, reflecting an ongoing mix of business conditions in different regions. In addition, Co. is targeting earnings to range from $0.12 to $0.17 per share. Separately, on Dec 12 2007, Co. announced the Implementation of additional steps in the restructuring of its global Inorganic Specialties Group. These restructuring actions are part of Co.'s ongoing effort to reduce costs in its Inorganics manufacturing operations, including the reduction of annual manufacturing costs in Europe by $40.0 million to $50.0 million by the end of 2009.

Financial Data

(US$ in Thousands)	12/31/2007	12/31/2006	12/31/2005	12/31/2004	12/31/2003	12/31/2002	12/31/2001	12/31/2000
Earnings Per Share	(2.23)	0.44	0.35	0.55	0.43	1.79	1.04	1.92
Cash Flow Per Share	3.37	1.67	0.51	1.47	2.10	4.41	6.41	3.30
Tang Book Value Per Share	4.04	2.76	1.10	2.60	0.82	N.M.	N.M.	1.24
Dividends Per Share	0.580	0.580	0.580	0.580	0.580	0.580	0.580	0.580
Dividend Payout %	...	131.82	165.71	105.45	134.88	32.40	55.77	30.21
Income Statement								
Total Revenue	2,204,785	2,041,525	1,882,305	1,843,721	1,622,370	1,528,454	1,501,059	1,447,284
EBITDA	36,343	165,050	145,276	147,318	129,383	151,291	160,549	190,363
Income Before Taxes	(109,318)	25,588	24,072	31,192	24,243	48,580	61,466	116,615
Income Taxes	(15,064)	5,026	6,928	3,352	6,863	14,833	22,269	43,476
Net Income	(94,479)	20,090	16,276	24,925	19,551	73,723	39,197	73,139
Average Shares	42,926	42,422	42,309	42,235	41,090	41,008	37,118	37,663
Balance Sheet								
Current Assets	607,192	622,605	610,719	612,349	582,043	485,585	600,580	443,228
Total Assets	1,638,260	1,732,937	1,668,544	1,733,437	1,751,226	1,604,473	1,732,559	1,127,005
Current Liabilities	410,232	382,884	366,884	400,983	413,095	404,167	405,226	365,095
Long-Term Obligations	520,645	581,654	546,168	497,314	516,236	443,552	829,740	350,781
Total Liabilities	1,138,457	1,191,601	1,179,985	1,188,343	1,225,305	1,131,977	1,432,173	817,847
Stockholders' Equity	476,284	524,549	468,091	522,265	525,921	472,496	300,386	309,158
Shares Outstanding	43,578	42,865	52,313	42,138	41,457	40,516	34,336	34,164
Statistical Record								
Return on Assets %	N.M.	1.18	0.96	1.43	1.17	4.42	2.74	6.95
Return on Equity %	N.M.	4.05	3.29	4.74	3.92	19.08	12.86	24.07
EBITDA Margin %	1.65	8.08	7.72	7.99	7.97	9.90	10.70	13.15
Net Margin %	N.M.	0.98	0.86	1.35	1.21	4.82	2.61	5.05
Asset Turnover	1.31	1.20	1.11	1.06	0.97	0.92	1.05	1.38
Current Ratio	1.48	1.63	1.66	1.53	1.41	1.20	1.48	1.21
Debt to Equity	1.09	1.11	1.17	0.95	0.98	0.94	2.76	1.13
Price Range	25.99-17.89	21.56-14.09	23.50-16.33	27.44-18.48	27.21-19.32	30.55-21.47	26.11-19.79	23.88-17.63
P/E Ratio	...	49.00-32.02	67.14-46.66	49.89-33.60	63.28-44.93	17.07-11.99	25.11-19.03	12.43-9.18
Average Yield %	2.69	3.12	3.02	2.44	2.58	2.28	2.58	2.77

FIDELITY NATIONAL FINANCIAL INC

Exchange	Symbol	Price	52Wk Range	Yield	P/E
NYS	FNF	$18.33 (3/31/2008)	28.43-13.00	6.55	31.07

*7 Year Price Score N/A   *NYSE Composite Index=100   *12 Month Price Score 98.86

Interim Earnings (Per Share)

Qtr.	Mar	Jun	Sep	Dec
2005	0.48	0.93	0.00	0.00
2006	0.46	0.67	0.60	0.67
2007	0.37	0.38	0.03	(0.20)

Interim Dividends (Per Share)

Amt	Decl	Ex	Rec	Pay
0.30Q	4/25/2007	6/12/2007	6/14/2007	6/28/2007
0.30Q	7/26/2007	9/11/2007	9/13/2007	9/27/2007
0.30Q	10/24/2007	12/11/2007	12/13/2007	12/27/2007
0.30Q	1/30/2008	3/11/2008	3/13/2008	3/27/2008

Indicated Div: $1.20

Valuation Analysis

Forecast P/E	N/A
Market Cap	$4.1 Billion
Book Value	3.2 Billion
Price/Book	1.26
Price/Sales	0.74

Institutional Holding

No of Institutions	286
Shares	147,707,088
% Held	66.67

TRADING VOLUME (thousand shares)

1999 2000 2001 2002 2003 2004 2005 2006 2007 2008

Business Summary: Insurance (MIC: 8.2 SIC: 6361 NAIC: 524127)

Fidelity National Financial is a holding company that is a provider, through its subsidiaries, of title insurance, specialty insurance, claims management services, and information services. Co.'s title insurance underwriters include Fidelity National Title, Chicago Title, Ticor Title, Security Union Title, and Alamo Title. Co. also provides flood insurance, personal lines insurance, and home warranty insurance through its specialty insurance subsidiaries. Co. is also a provider of outsourced claims management services to corporate and public sector entities through Sedgwick CMS Holdings and a provider of information services through Ceridian Corp, both of which are minority-owned affiliates.

Recent Developments: For the year ended Dec 31 2007, net income decreased 70.4% to US$129.8 million from US$437.8 million in the prior year. Revenues were US$5.52 billion, down 41.5% from US$9.44 billion the year before. Net premiums earned were US$3.80 billion versus US$4.61 billion in the prior year, a decrease of 17.5%.

Prospects: In response to ongoing challenging Title business industry conditions, Co. intends to monitor operating metrics on a weekly basis and aggressively reduce headcount as order value declines while slowly adding headcount when volumes improve. Also, Co. noted that its business model is heavily weighted to variable incentive compensation, with bonus and commissions a large part of compensation. For its Title business, Co. has a minimum goal of an 8.0% to 10.0% pre-tax margin over a 12-month period. Meanwhile, Co. is striving to grow and expand its book in all three of its Specialty Insurance areas, which includes flood, personal lines and home warranty.

Financial Data

(US$ in Thousands)	12/31/2007	12/31/2006	12/31/2005	12/31/2004	12/31/2003
Earnings Per Share	0.59	2.39	3.11	...	...
Cash Flow Per Share	1.58	3.96	4.02	...	...
Tang Book Value Per Share	7.57	9.67	8.19	...	...
Income Statement					
Premium Income	3,800,458	4,606,200	4,948,966	4,718,217	4,700,750
Total Revenue	5,524,010	9,436,101	6,315,861	5,889,413	5,970,715
Benefits & Claims	653,876	486,334	354,710	259,402	248,834
Income Before Taxes	176,513	943,202	868,304	882,927	1,091,920
Income Taxes	46,776	350,871	327,351	323,598	407,736
Net Income	129,769	437,761	538,981	558,164	683,325
Average Shares	219,989	182,861	173,575	...	...
Balance Sheet					
Total Assets	7,556,414	7,259,559	5,900,533	5,074,091	...
Total Liabilities	4,258,458	3,729,147	3,416,158	2,393,384	...
Stockholders' Equity	3,244,088	3,474,368	2,480,037	2,676,756	...
Shares Outstanding	223,069	221,413	174,319	...	...
Statistical Record					
Return on Assets %	1.75	6.65	9.82	...	...
Return on Equity %	3.86	14.70	20.90	...	...
Loss Ratio %	17.21	10.56	7.17	5.50	5.29
Net Margin %	2.35	4.64	8.53	9.48	11.44
Price Range	28.43-13.49	25.60-18.03	26.00-20.30	...	...
P/E Ratio	48.19-22.86	10.71-7.54	8.36-6.53	...	...

Address: 601 Riverside Avenue, Jacksonville, FL 32204 Telephone: 904-854-8100	Web Site: www.fnf.com Officers: William P. Foley, II - Chmn. Frank P. Wiley - Vice-Chmn. Alan L. Stinson - C.E.O.	Auditors: KPMG LLP

FIDELITY NATIONAL INFORMATION SERVICES INC

Exchange	Symbol	Price	52Wk Range	Yield	P/E
NYS	FIS	$38.14 (3/31/2008)	57.67-36.31	0.52	13.34

*7 Year Price Score N/A *NYSE Composite Index=100 *12 Month Price Score 93.71

Interim Earnings (Per Share)

Qtr.	Mar	Jun	Sep	Dec
2003	0.18	0.35	0.40	0.47
2004	0.32	0.39	0.46	0.59
2005	0.37	0.75	0.37	0.57
2006	0.23	0.34	0.41	0.39
2007	0.30	0.75	1.25	0.56

Interim Dividends (Per Share)

Amt	Decl	Ex	Rec	Pay
0.05Q	4/24/2007	6/12/2007	6/14/2007	6/28/2007
0.05Q	7/24/2007	9/11/2007	9/13/2007	9/27/2007
0.05Q	10/23/2007	12/11/2007	12/13/2007	12/27/2007
0.05Q	2/13/2008	3/11/2008	3/13/2008	3/27/2008

Indicated Div: $0.20

Valuation Analysis

		Institutional Holding	
Forecast P/E	16.37 (1/10/2007)	No of Institutions	362
Market Cap	$7.4 Billion	Shares	138,198,544
Book Value	3.8 Billion	% Held	72.16
Price/Book	1.96		
Price/Sales	1.56		

TRADING VOLUME (thousand shares)

Business Summary: Credit & Lending (MIC: 8.6 SIC: 6159 NAIC: 522320)

Fidelity National Information Services is engaged in providing processing services, card issuer and transaction processing and mortgage-related services to financial institutions, mortgage lenders and servicers. As of Dec 31 2007, Co. operated through two reportable segments: Transaction Processing Services (TPS) and Lender Processing Services (LPS). The primary components of the TPS are Integrated Financial Solutions, Enterprise Solutions, and International, while the primary components of the LPS are Mortgage Processing and Information Services, which includes loan facilitation services, default management, and other information and outsourcing based services.

Recent Developments: For the year ended Dec 31 2007, income from continuing operations increased 111.9% to US$510.5 million from US$240.9 million a year earlier. Net income increased 116.6% to US$561.2 million from US$259.1 million in the prior year. Non-interest income rose 17.7% to US$4.76 billion from US$4.04 billion, while non-interest expense advanced 15.3% to US$4.01 billion.

Prospects: On Feb 28 2008, Co. announced the sale of its Certegy Gaming Services (CGS) for about $100.0 million in cash excluding CGS's payroll and personal check cashing services. The sale is expected to close in late Mar or early Apr 2008. Meanwhile, Co. noted that it is on track to complete the spin-off of its Lender Processing business by mid 2008. For full-year 2008, Co. expects capital expenditures of approximately $280.0 million to $300.0 million, mainly for equipment, purchased software and internally developed software. In addition, Co. expects 2008 revenue growth of 14.0% to 16.0%. For the first quarter of 2008, Co. is projecting earnings per diluted share to range from $0.42 to $0.45.

Financial Data

(US$ in Thousands)	12/31/2007	12/31/2006	12/31/2005	12/31/2004	12/31/2003	12/31/2002	12/31/2001	12/31/2000
Earnings Per Share	2.86	1.37	2.06	1.75	1.40	1.32	1.26	...
Cash Flow Per Share	2.40	2.66	2.08	2.30	2.12	1.86	1.51	...
Tang Book Value Per Share	N.M.	N.M.	3.10	0.59	0.58	N.M.	N.M.	...
Dividends Per Share	0.200	3.950	0.200	0.200	0.100	...	...	...
Dividend Payout %	6.99	288.32	9.71	11.43	7.14	...	...	...
Income Statement								
Total Revenue	4,758,016	4,132,602	1,117,141	1,039,506	1,015,464	1,007,968	851,123	778,562
EBITDA	1,563,507	1,025,253	251,454	234,604	204,207	192,118	197,850	191,166
Income Before Taxes	812,245	403,630	174,558	167,947	148,789	145,948	144,297	147,167
Income Taxes	300,530	150,150	68,927	62,071	55,052	55,964	56,276	57,609
Net Income	561,222	259,087	130,319	111,810	92,402	89,984	87,076	88,462
Average Shares	196,546	189,196	63,391	63,966	65,870	69,033	69,063	...
Balance Sheet								
Current Assets	1,829,495	1,300,539	444,902	408,717	321,628	312,000	282,906	199,207
Total Assets	9,794,583	7,630,560	972,435	922,209	785,047	702,141	697,573	502,445
Current Liabilities	1,254,214	880,515	233,562	290,338	244,093	250,930	221,936	160,251
Long-Term Obligations	4,003,383	2,947,840	227,881	273,968	222,399	214,200	230,000	...
Total Liabilities	5,999,210	4,474,846	513,165	622,146	523,908	503,698	485,708	172,921
Stockholders' Equity	3,781,179	3,142,744	459,270	300,063	261,139	198,443	211,865	323,618
Shares Outstanding	194,700	190,991	62,815	62,383	64,352	66,396	68,836	...
Statistical Record								
Return on Assets %	6.44	6.02	13.76	13.06	12.43	12.86	14.51	17.68
Return on Equity %	16.21	14.39	34.32	39.74	40.21	43.86	32.52	29.65
EBITDA Margin %	32.86	24.81	22.51	22.57	20.11	19.06	23.25	24.55
Net Margin %	11.80	6.27	11.67	10.76	9.10	8.93	10.23	11.36
Asset Turnover	0.55	0.96	1.18	1.21	1.37	1.44	1.42	1.56
Current Ratio	1.46	1.48	1.90	1.41	1.32	1.24	1.27	1.24
Debt to Equity	1.06	0.94	0.50	0.91	0.85	1.08	1.09	...
Price Range	57.67-40.34	44.16-33.74	41.29-32.78	39.65-31.44	35.03-21.65	44.13-18.08	35.45-23.90	...
P/E Ratio	20.16-14.10	32.23-24.63	20.04-15.91	22.66-17.97	25.02-15.46	33.43-13.70	28.13-18.97	...
Average Yield %	0.41	10.14	0.54	0.56	0.35	...	...	...

Address: 601 Riverside Avenue, Jacksonville, FL 32204 Telephone: 904-854-5000	Web Site: www.fidelityinfoservices.com Officers: Lee A. Kennedy - Chmn., C.E.O. Larry J. Towe - Pres., C.O.O.	Auditors: KPMG LLP Investor Contact: 904-854-3282 Transfer Agents: SunTrust Bank, Atlanta, Atlanta, Georgia

FIRST AMERICAN CORP (THE)

Exchange	Symbol	Price	52Wk Range	Yield	P/E
NYS	FAF	$33.94 (3/31/2008)	55.11-28.10	2.59	N/A

*7 Year Price Score 103.34 *NYSE Composite Index=100   *12 Month Price Score 93.57

Interim Earnings (Per Share)

Qtr.	Mar	Jun	Sep	Dec
2003	1.05	1.47	1.62	1.07
2004	0.62	1.27	1.17	0.76
2005	0.83	1.43	1.51	1.18
2006	0.71	0.26	0.92	1.06
2007	0.84	(0.68)	0.49	(0.69)

Interim Dividends (Per Share)

Amt	Decl	Ex	Rec	Pay
0.22Q	5/24/2007	6/27/2007	6/29/2007	7/16/2007
0.22Q	9/18/2007	9/26/2007	9/28/2007	10/15/2007
0.22Q	12/13/2007	12/27/2007	12/31/2007	1/15/2008
0.22Q	2/28/2008	3/27/2008	3/31/2008	4/15/2008

Indicated Div: $0.88

Valuation Analysis   **Institutional Holding**

Forecast P/E	N/A	No of Institutions
		261
Market Cap	33.1 Billion	Shares
Book Value	3.0 Billion	63,568,748
Price/Book	1.04	% Held
Price/Sales	0.38	65.68

TRADING VOLUME (thousand shares)

Business Summary: Insurance (MIC: 8.2 SIC: 6361 NAIC: 524127)

The First American is engaged in providing business information and related products and services. Co. has two primary business groups: the financial services group, which includes its title insurance and services segment and its specialty insurance segment; and the information technology group, which includes its mortgage information, property information and First Advantage segments. The First Advantage segment is comprised of Co.'s First Advantage Corporation subsidiary, which provides credit reports to the mortgage lending and automotive lending industries, and provides employer, corporate litigation as well as investigative services.

Recent Developments: For the year ended Dec 31 2007, net loss amounted to US$3.1 million versus net income of US$287.7 million in the prior year. Revenues were US$8.20 billion, down 3.8% from US$8.52 billion the year before.

Prospects: For 2008, Co. expects real estate and mortgage markets to remain difficult as the lack of secondary market activity and tightness of the credit markets continues to affect demand for its products. Nevertheless, Co. will remain focused on expense reductions, including further reducing personnel costs. Also, Co. expects non-real estate-related products and international title operations should continue to improve in 2008. Separately, on Feb 19 2008, Co. announced the acquisition of Verify Limited, an Asian Pacific employment screening company, by its Employer Services segment, which extends its services in Malaysia and China, and solidifies its international employment screening market.

Financial Data

(US$ in Thousands)	12/31/2007	12/31/2006	12/31/2005	12/31/2004	12/31/2003	12/31/2002	12/31/2001	12/31/2000
Earnings Per Share	(0.03)	2.92	4.97	3.83	5.22	2.92	2.27	1.24
Cash Flow Per Share	6.97	6.36	9.77	7.83	10.83	7.55	5.83	2.21
Tang Book Value Per Share	0.78	6.41	6.96	9.52	7.95	10.87	9.78	8.20
Dividends Per Share	0.880	0.720	0.720	0.600	0.500	0.340	0.270	0.240
Dividend Payout %		24.66	14.49	15.67	9.58	11.64	11.89	19.35
Income Statement								
Total Revenue	8,195,605	8,499,066	8,061,758	6,722,326	6,213,714	4,704,209	3,750,723	2,934,255
EBITDA	384,402	803,828	1,061,067	806,262	953,146	546,736	437,888	240,212
Income Before Taxes	152,063	596,903	903,628	677,284	838,722	449,907	329,540	153,876
Income Taxes	43,689	220,100	324,500	243,200	292,000	149,900	117,500	54,700
Net Income	(3,119)	287,676	485,266	349,099	451,022	234,367	167,268	82,223
Average Shares	94,649	98,653	97,795	91,895	87,775	82,567	75,834	66,050
Balance Sheet								
Current Assets	1,959,807	2,074,716	2,138,460	566,884	404,980	337,368	300,607	255,343
Total Assets	8,047,921	8,224,285	7,598,641	6,208,365	4,892,111	3,398,045	2,837,263	2,199,737
Current Liabilities	1,867,309	1,871,737	1,750,649	1,283,190	899,612	625,060	477,797	348,856
Long-Term Obligations	906,046	847,991	848,569	732,770	553,888	425,710	415,341	219,838
Total Liabilities	4,987,189	4,510,183	4,132,429	3,372,013	2,608,855	1,769,817	1,502,142	1,114,974
Stockholders' Equity	2,984,825	3,202,053	3,006,547	2,463,564	1,879,520	1,364,589	1,104,452	870,237
Shares Outstanding	91,830	96,484	95,860	90,058	78,826	73,636	68,694	63,887
Statistical Record								
Return on Assets %	N.M.	3.64	7.03	6.27	10.88	7.52	6.64	3.80
Return on Equity %	N.M.	9.27	17.74	16.03	27.81	18.98	16.94	9.73
EBITDA Margin %	4.69	9.46	13.16	11.99	15.34	11.62	11.67	8.19
Net Margin %	N.M.	3.38	6.02	5.19	7.26	4.98	4.46	2.80
Asset Turnover	0.97	1.07	1.17	1.21	1.50	1.51	1.49	1.36
Current Ratio	1.05	1.11	1.22	0.44	0.45	0.54	0.63	0.73
Debt to Equity	0.30	0.26	0.28	0.30	0.29	0.31	0.38	0.25
Price Range	55.11-30.07	46.95-36.10	49.02-31.31	35.14-24.60	30.64-21.72	23.10-16.54	34.91-16.51	32.88-10.69
P/E Ratio	...	16.08-12.36	9.86-6.30	9.17-6.42	5.87-4.16	7.91-5.66	15.38-7.27	26.51-8.62
Average Yield %	2.01	1.76	1.80	2.04	1.95	1.65	1.24	1.45

Address: 1 First American Way, Santa Ana, CA 92707-5913 **Telephone:** 714-854-3643	**Web Site:** www.firstam.com **Officers:** Parker S. Kennedy - Chmn., C.E.O. Craig I. DeRoy - Pres.	**Auditors:** PricewaterhouseCoopers LLP **Transfer Agents:** First American Trust, FSB

FIRST HORIZON NATIONAL CORP

Exchange	Symbol	Price	52Wk Range	Yield	P/E
NYS	FHN	$14.01 (3/31/2008)	41.20-14.01	5.71	N/A

*7 Year Price Score 58.87   *NYSE Composite Index=100   *12 Month Price Score 67.13

Interim Earnings (Per Share)

Qtr.	Mar	Jun	Sep	Dec
2003	0.91	0.90	0.91	0.90
2004	0.92	0.92	0.89	0.81
2005	0.85	0.80	0.90	0.85
2006	1.67	0.82	0.53	0.60
2007	0.55	0.17	(0.11)	(1.96)

Interim Dividends (Per Share)

Amt	Decl	Ex	Rec	Pay
0.45Q	4/18/2007	6/13/2007	6/15/2007	7/1/2007
0.45Q	7/18/2007	9/12/2007	9/14/2007	10/1/2007
0.45Q	10/16/2007	12/12/2007	12/14/2007	1/1/2008
0.20Q	1/17/2008	3/12/2008	3/14/2008	4/1/2008

Indicated Div: $0.80

Valuation Analysis

		Institutional Holding	
Forecast P/E	12.84	No of Institutions	
	(1/10/2007)	293	
Market Cap	$1.8 Billion	Shares	
Book Value	2.1 Billion	66,518,820	
Price/Book	0.83	% Held	
Price/Sales	0.56	53.07	

Business Summary: Commercial Banking (MIC: 8.1 SIC: 6021 NAIC: 522110)

First Horizon National is engaged in providing diversified financial services, including retail/commercial banking, mortgage banking, and capital markets through its principal subsidiary First Tennessee Bank, and its other banking-related subsidiaries. At Dec 31 2007, Co. had 216 financial centers (FCs) in six states: 187 FCs in 17 Tennessee counties; 11 FCs in Georgia; eight FCs in Mississippi; and 10 FCs in Texas. The 10 FC branches in Texas operating under the "First Horizon Bank" name were sold in Feb. 2008. At Dec 31 2007, Co. had total assets of $37.02 billion and $17.03 billion of total deposits.

Recent Developments: For the year ended Dec 31 2007, loss from continuing operations was US$174.9 million compared with income of US$250.8 million a year earlier. Net loss amounted to US$170.1 million versus net income of US$462.9 million in the prior year. Net interest income decreased 5.6% to US$940.6 million from US$996.9 million in the prior year. Provision for loan losses was US$272.8 million versus US$83.1 million in the prior year, an increase of 228.1%. Non-interest income fell 26.3% to US$859.9 million from US$1.17 billion, while non-interest expense advanced 5.8% to US$1.84 billion.

Prospects: Co. expects the residential commercial real estate, one-time close and home equity portfolios to contract in 2008 due to the challenging housing markets and its strategy to reduce real estate concentrations. Also, Co. expects commercial, financial and industrial loan growth to be modest with reduced demand. However, Co. expects net interest margin to remain stable as the steepening yield curve favorably affects the mortgage warehouse and lower-margin businesses. As part of its strategy to reduce its national real estate portfolio, Co. announced in Jan 2008 that it was discontinuing national homebuilder and commercial real estate lending through its First Horizon Construction Lending offices.

Financial Data

(US$ in Thousands)	12/31/2007	12/31/2006	12/31/2005	12/31/2004	12/31/2003	12/31/2002	12/31/2001	12/31/2000
Earnings Per Share	(1.35)	3.62	3.40	3.54	3.62	2.89	2.42	1.77
Cash Flow Per Share	0.90	13.07	3.97	(2.54)	18.79	(6.14)	(8.80)	3.75
Tang Book Value Per Share	5.75	4.71	4.78	6.33	7.06	8.41	4.99	4.03
Dividends Per Share	1.800	1.800	1.740	1.630	1.300	1.050	0.910	0.880
Dividend Payout %	...	49.72	51.18	46.05	35.91	36.33	37.60	49.72
Income Statement								
Interest Income	2,305,959	2,329,111	1,840,174	1,166,802	1,053,370	1,039,093	1,198,871	1,363,046
Interest Expense	1,365,317	1,332,174	856,147	310,491	247,586	286,581	512,596	764,695
Net Interest Income	940,642	996,937	984,027	856,311	805,784	752,512	686,275	598,351
Provision for Losses	272,765	83,129	67,678	48,348	86,698	92,184	93,493	67,353
Non-Interest Income	859,949	1,166,893	1,399,756	1,363,186	1,640,014	1,541,065	1,259,636	1,063,420
Non-Interest Expense	1,843,433	1,742,621	1,670,932	1,504,340	1,640,102	1,643,334	1,358,748	1,257,416
Income Before Taxes	(315,607)	338,080	645,173	666,809	718,998	558,059	493,670	337,002
Income Taxes	(140,231)	87,278	204,075	212,401	245,689	181,608	164,068	104,421
Net Income	(170,111)	462,914	438,000	454,408	473,309	376,451	318,209	232,581
Average Shares	125,843	127,917	128,950	128,436	130,876	130,221	131,537	131,663
Balance Sheet								
Net Loans & Leases	25,512,765	24,762,197	24,846,573	21,437,495	16,807,915	15,998,712	13,527,079	11,830,824
Total Assets	37,015,461	37,918,259	36,579,061	29,771,683	24,506,690	23,823,095	20,616,791	18,555,086
Total Deposits	17,032,285	20,213,232	23,437,770	19,782,167	15,679,971	15,713,903	13,606,334	12,188,691
Total Liabilities	34,584,588	35,160,599	33,971,476	27,730,242	22,615,920	21,987,523	18,994,842	17,032,502
Stockholders' Equity	2,135,596	2,462,390	2,312,311	2,040,983	1,890,318	1,691,180	1,477,762	1,384,156
Shares Outstanding	126,366	124,865	126,222	123,531	124,834	125,600	125,865	128,744
Statistical Record								
Return on Assets %	N.M.	1.24	1.32	1.67	1.96	1.69	1.62	1.26
Return on Equity %	N.M.	19.39	20.12	23.05	26.43	23.76	22.24	17.67
Net Interest Margin %	40.79	42.80	53.47	73.39	76.50	72.42	57.24	43.90
Efficiency Ratio %	58.23	49.85	51.57	59.46	60.89	63.69	55.27	51.82
Loans to Deposits	1.50	1.23	1.06	1.08	1.07	1.02	0.99	0.97
Price Range	45.13-18.00	42.76-37.20	44.55-35.13	48.01-41.59	47.98-35.94	40.45-30.05	37.25-27.38	29.06-16.06
P/E Ratio	...	11.81-10.28	13.10-10.33	13.56-11.75	13.25-9.93	14.00-10.40	15.39-11.31	16.42-9.07
Average Yield %	5.27	4.50	4.29	3.67	3.10	2.89	2.72	4.13

Address: 165 Madison Avenue, Memphis, TN 38103
Telephone: 901-523-4444
Fax: 901-523-4030

Web Site: www.firstTennessee.com
Officers: J. Kenneth Glass - Chmn., Pres., C.E.O.
John H. Hamilton - Exec. V.P., Product Mgmt. & Delivery Serv.

Auditors: KPMG LLP
Investor Contact: 901-523-4068
Transfer Agents: Wells Fargo Shareowner Services

FIRST MARBLEHEAD CORP

Exchange	Symbol	Price	52Wk Range	Yield	P/E
NYS	FMD	$7.46 (3/31/2008)	44.43-7.41	N/A	3.52

7 Year Price Score N/A *NYSE Composite Index=100* **12 Month Price Score 43.99**

TRADING VOLUME (thousand shares)

Interim Earnings (Per Share)

Qtr.	Sep	Dec	Mar	Jun
2004-05	(0.05)	0.75	0.47	0.43
2005-06	(0.05)	1.16	0.62	0.75
2006-07	1.49	0.85	0.75	0.83
2007-08	1.80	(1.26)	...	...

Interim Dividends (Per Share)

Amt	Decl	Ex	Rec	Pay
0.15Q	2/21/2007	3/1/2007	3/5/2007	3/12/2007
0.25Q	6/6/2007	6/14/2007	6/18/2007	6/25/2007
0.275Q	9/12/2007	9/20/2007	9/24/2007	9/28/2007
0.12Q	12/7/2007	12/13/2007	12/17/2007	12/21/2007

Valuation Analysis

		Institutional Holding	
Forecast P/E	N/A	No of Institutions	223
Market Cap	$697.5 Million	Shares	62,629,176
Book Value	921.0 Million	% Held	66.20
Price/Book	0.76		
Price/Sales	1.09		

Business Summary: Credit & Lending (MIC: 8.6 SIC: 6141 NAIC: 522291)

First Marblehead provides outsourcing services for private education lending. Co. focuses on private student loan programs for undergraduate, graduate and professional education, and, to a lesser degree, on continuing education programs, the primary and secondary school market, career training and study abroad programs. Co. is entitled to receive structural advisory fees and residuals for its services in connection with securitizations of loans generated by the loan programs that it facilitates. Co. also receives reimbursement for marketing coordination services and fees for administrative services it provides to the discrete trust vehicles that it forms for securitizations it facilitates.

Recent Developments: For the quarter ended Dec 31 2007, net loss amounted to US$117.7 million versus net income of US$81.2 million in the year-earlier quarter. Non-interest income was US$122.8 million versus US$197.8 million, while non-interest expense advanced 24.9% to US$73.7 million.

Prospects: On Apr 7 2008, The Education Resources Institute (TERI), a non-profit guarantor of private student loans, filed a voluntary petition for reorganization under Chapter 11 of the U.S. Bankruptcy Code. Co. noted that it has been in a strategic alliance with TERI since 2001, under which TERI has been the exclusive third-party provider of borrower default guarantees for its clients' private student loans. TERI also guarantees the loans held by The National Collegiate Student Loan Trusts (NCSLT), the series of trusts Co. uses in its securitization program. So, Co. is analyzing the implications of TERI's filing on its lenders, investors, borrowers, while working on securing an alternative guarantor.

Financial Data
(US$ in Thousands)

	6 Mos	3 Mos	06/30/2007	06/30/2006	06/30/2005	06/30/2004	06/30/2003	06/30/2002
Earnings Per Share	2.12	4.23	3.92	2.45	1.59	0.79	0.34	0.13
Cash Flow Per Share	(1.77)	0.65	2.07	0.52	1.11	0.38	0.22	0.04
Tang Book Value Per Share	9.13	10.49	8.95	6.04	4.27	2.83	0.57	0.15
Dividends Per Share	0.795	0.795	0.620	0.320	...	...	...	...
Dividend Payout %	37.50	18.79	15.82	13.04	...	...	...	...
Income Statement								
Total Revenue	257,152	379,962	880,704	563,572	417,977	199,260	91,356	41,259
EBITDA	95,378	286,883	644,091	393,203	280,968	132,663	57,922	20,628
Depn & Amortn	9,420	4,422	...	...	...	...	...	...
Income Before Taxes	85,958	282,461	627,765	383,754	277,089	128,801	54,013	17,536
Income Taxes	34,813	113,641	256,434	147,794	117,424	53,530	22,514	5,307
Net Income	51,145	168,820	371,331	235,960	159,665	75,271	31,499	12,229
Average Shares	93,500	93,796	94,043	96,258	100,206	95,273	92,341	93,403
Balance Sheet								
Current Assets	1,055,317	1,195,703	1,157,890	723,449	510,143	341,062	75,852	28,397
Total Assets	1,584,564	1,613,860	1,214,463	770,346	558,193	360,056	87,053	39,016
Current Liabilities	408,845	521,063	360,315	178,670	117,526	66,423	27,955	13,075
Long-Term Obligations	245,400	94,000	9,251	13,326	17,410	15,182	6,674	7,305
Total Liabilities	663,514	625,688	371,843	194,177	136,627	81,920	34,629	20,381
Stockholders' Equity	921,050	988,172	842,620	576,169	421,566	278,136	52,424	18,635
Shares Outstanding	93,501	93,498	93,342	94,563	97,349	95,962	79,778	76,682
Statistical Record								
Return on Assets %	15.22	30.92	37.42	35.52	34.78	33.58	49.97	...
Return on Equity %	23.62	47.32	52.34	47.30	45.64	45.42	88.65	...
EBITDA Margin %	37.09	75.50	73.13	69.77	67.22	66.58	63.40	50.00
Net Margin %	19.89	44.43	42.16	41.87	38.20	37.78	34.48	29.64
Asset Turnover	0.48	0.74	0.89	0.85	0.91	0.89	1.45	...
Current Ratio	2.58	2.29	3.21	4.05	4.34	5.13	2.71	2.17
Debt to Equity	0.27	0.10	0.01	0.02	0.04	0.05	0.13	0.39
Price Range	56.66-11.24	56.66-31.02	56.66-29.95	38.67-14.40	48.70-22.03	27.37-13.53	...	...
P/E Ratio	26.73-5.30	13.39-7.33	14.45-7.64	15.78-5.88	30.63-13.86	34.64-17.13	...	...
Average Yield %	2.09	1.85	1.45	1.33	...	...	...	...

Address: The Prudential Tower, 800 Boylston Street, 34th Floor, Boston, MA 02199-8157 **Telephone:** 617-638-2000	**Web Site:** www.firstmarblehead.com **Officers:** Daniel Maxwell Meyers - Chmn., Pres., C.E.O. Stephen E. Anbinder - Vice-Chmn.	**Auditors:** KPMG LLP **Transfer Agents:** EquiServe Trust Company, N.A.

307

Exchange	Symbol	Price	52Wk Range	Yield	P/E
NYS	FE	$68.62 (3/31/2008)	77.84-59.58	3.21	16.26

*7 Year Price Score 121.88 *NYSE Composite Index=100 *12 Month Price Score 110.43

Interim Earnings (Per Share)

Qtr.	Mar	Jun	Sep	Dec
2003	0.82	(0.20)	0.51	0.34
2004	0.53	0.62	0.91	0.61
2005	0.48	0.54	1.01	0.58
2006	0.67	0.91	1.40	0.84
2007	0.92	1.10	1.34	0.87

Interim Dividends (Per Share)

Amt	Decl	Ex	Rec	Pay
0.50Q	7/17/2007	8/3/2007	8/7/2007	9/1/2007
0.50Q	9/18/2007	11/5/2007	11/7/2007	12/1/2007
0.55Q	12/18/2007	2/5/2008	2/7/2008	3/1/2008
0.55Q	3/18/2008	5/5/2008	5/7/2008	6/1/2008

Indicated Div: $2.20

Valuation Analysis		Institutional Holding	
Forecast P/E	13.63	No of Institutions	
	(1/10/2007)	409	
Market Cap	$20.9 Billion	Shares	
Book Value	9.0 Billion	228,556,960	
Price/Book	2.33	% Held	
Price/Sales	1.63	71.60	

Business Summary: Electricity (MIC: 7.1 SIC: 4911 NAIC: 221122)

FirstEnergy's principal business is the holding, directly or indirectly, of all of the outstanding common stock of its eight principal electric utility operating subsidiaries: Ohio Edison Company, The Cleveland Electric Illuminating Company, The Toledo Edison Company, Pennsylvania Power Company, American Transmission Systems, Incorporated, Jersey Central Power & Light Company, Metropolitan Edison Company and Pennsylvania Electric Company. As of Dec 31 2007, Co.'s combined service areas covered approximately 36,100 square miles in Ohio, New Jersey and Pennsylvania, serving a combined population of approximately 11.3 million.

Recent Developments: For the year ended Dec 31 2007, income from continuing operations increased 4.1% to US$1.31 billion from US$1.26 billion a year earlier. Net income increased 4.4% to US$1.31 billion from US$1.25 billion in the prior year. Revenues were US$12.80 billion, up 11.3% from US$11.50 billion the year before. Operating income was US$2.82 billion versus US$2.61 billion in the prior year, an increase of 8.0%. Direct operating expenses rose 12.2% to US$8.10 billion from US$7.22 billion in the comparable period the year before. Indirect operating expenses increased 12.5% to US$1.89 billion from US$1.68 billion in the equivalent prior-year period.

Prospects: Looking ahead to 2008, Co. remains focused on its continued investment in projects to increase its generation capacity and energy production capability. For example, on Jan 29 2008, Co.'s FirstEnergy Generation Corp. subsidiary has agreed to purchase a partially complete natural gas combined- cycle plant in Fremont, OH, for $253.6 million. Upon completion of this facility, Co. expects to add 707 megawatts of generating capacity in Ohio. For 2008, Co. expects earnings growth to moderate compared with recent years, as higher fuel and purchase power expenses will continue to increase, while expecting incremental growth in distribution sales, and higher generation output compared with 2007.

Financial Data

(US$ in Thousands)	12/31/2007	12/31/2006	12/31/2005	12/31/2004	12/31/2003	12/31/2002	12/31/2001	12/31/2000
Earnings Per Share	4.22	3.81	2.61	2.67	1.39	2.14	2.81	2.69
Cash Flow Per Share	5.54	5.98	6.77	5.72	6.43	6.53	5.58	6.76
Tang Book Value Per Share	11.06	9.83	9.64	7.70	6.55	4.11	6.04	11.42
Dividends Per Share	2.000	1.800	1.668	1.500	1.500	1.500	1.500	1.500
Dividend Payout %	47.39	47.24	63.89	56.18	107.91	70.09	53.38	55.76
Income Statement								
Total Revenue	12,802,000	11,501,000	11,989,000	12,453,046	12,307,047	12,151,997	7,999,362	7,028,961
EBITDA	4,693,000	4,295,000	...	...	...	...	...	...
Income Before Taxes	2,192,000	2,053,000	...	...	...	...	...	...
Income Taxes	883,000	795,000	754,000	670,922	405,959	549,476	474,457	376,802
Net Income	1,309,000	1,254,000	861,000	878,175	422,764	629,280	646,447	598,970
Average Shares	310,000	327,000	330,000	328,982	304,972	294,421	230,430	222,444
Balance Sheet								
Net PPE	15,383,000	14,667,000	13,998,000	13,478,356	13,268,922	12,679,813	12,428,429	7,575,076
Total Assets	32,068,000	31,196,000	31,841,000	31,067,944	32,909,948	33,580,773	37,351,513	17,941,294
Long-Term Obligations	8,869,000	8,535,000	8,155,000	10,013,349	9,789,066	10,872,216	11,433,313	5,742,048
Total Liabilities	23,091,000	22,161,000	22,653,000	23,556,207	25,800,100	26,460,724	29,952,914	13,288,168
Stockholders' Equity	8,977,000	9,035,000	9,188,000	8,589,294	8,289,341	7,120,049	7,398,599	4,653,126
Shares Outstanding	304,835	319,205	329,836	329,836	329,836	297,636	297,636	224,531
Statistical Record								
Return on Assets %	4.14	3.98	2.74	2.74	1.27	1.77	2.34	3.30
Return on Equity %	14.53	13.76	9.69	10.38	5.49	8.67	10.73	12.96
EBITDA Margin %	36.66	37.34	...	...	...	...	...	...
Net Margin %	10.22	10.90	7.18	7.05	3.44	5.18	8.08	8.52
PPE Turnover	0.85	0.80	0.87	0.93	0.95	0.97	0.80	0.84
Asset Turnover	0.40	0.36	0.38	0.39	0.37	0.34	0.29	0.39
Debt to Equity	0.99	0.94	0.89	1.17	1.18	1.53	1.55	1.23
Price Range	74.76-57.90	61.31-48.20	52.73-38.26	43.15-35.20	38.50-27.65	38.65-25.05	36.88-25.81	31.88-18.19
P/E Ratio	17.72-13.72	16.09-12.65	20.20-14.66	16.16-13.18	27.70-19.89	18.06-11.71	13.12-9.19	11.85-6.76
Average Yield %	3.04	3.32	3.65	3.83	4.54	4.56	4.83	6.09

Address: 76 South Main Street, Akron, OH 44308-1890 Telephone: 800-736-3402 Fax: 330-384-3772	Web Site: www.firstenergycorp.com Officers: George M. Smart - Chmn. Anthony J. Alexander - Pres., C.E.O.	Auditors: PricewaterhouseCoopers LLP Investor Contact: 330-384-5500 Transfer Agents: FirstEnergy Securities Transfer Company, a subsidiary of FirstEnergy

FLOWSERVE CORP.

Exchange	Symbol	Price	52Wk Range	Yield	P/E
NYS	FLS	$104.38 (3/31/2008)	111.41-58.23	0.96	23.40

*7 Year Price Score 174.41 *NYSE Composite Index=100 *12 Month Price Score 136.39

Interim Earnings (Per Share)

Qtr.	Mar	Jun	Sep	Dec
2003	0.15	0.24	0.19	0.38
2004	0.19	0.11	0.11	0.08
2005	(0.07)	0.32	(0.19)	0.14
2006	0.24	0.57	0.50	0.71
2007	0.59	1.11	1.10	1.67

Interim Dividends (Per Share)

Amt	Decl	Ex	Rec	Pay
0.15Q	5/17/2007	6/25/2007	6/27/2007	7/11/2007
0.15Q	8/16/2007	9/24/2007	9/26/2007	10/10/2007
0.15Q	11/15/2007	12/21/2007	12/26/2007	1/9/2008
0.25Q	2/27/2008	3/24/2008	3/26/2008	4/9/2008

Indicated Div: $1.00

Valuation Analysis

		Institutional Holding	
Forecast P/E	12.24	No of Institutions	
	(1/10/2007)	184	
Market Cap	$5.9 Billion	Shares	
Book Value	1.3 Billion	53,596,160	
Price/Book	4.55	% Held	
Price/Sales	1.56	94.60	

TRADING VOLUME (thousand shares)

Business Summary: Industrial Machinery and Equipment (MIC: 11.5 SIC: 3561 NAIC: 333911)

Flowserve is a manufacturer and aftermarket service provider of flow control systems. Co. develops and manufactures precision-engineered flow control equipment such as, pumps, valves and seals, for critical service applications. Co.'s products and services are used in several industries, including petroleum, chemical, power generation and water treatment. As of Dec 31 2007, Co. operated in three business segments: the Flowserve Pump Division for engineered pumps, industrial pumps and related services; the Flow Control Division for industrial valves and related products and services; and the Flow Solutions Division for precision mechanical seals and related services.

Recent Developments: For the year ended Dec 31 2007, income from continuing operations increased 124.3% to US$255.8 million from US$114.0 million a year earlier. Net income increased 122.4% to US$255.8 million from US$115.0 million in the prior year. Revenues were US$3.76 billion, up 22.9% from US$3.06 billion the year before. Operating income was US$409.9 million versus US$239.6 million in the prior year, an increase of 71.1%. Direct operating expenses rose 22.5% to US$2.51 billion from US$2.05 billion in the comparable period the year before. Indirect operating expenses increased 9.1% to US$837.8 million from US$767.7 million in the equivalent prior-year period.

Prospects: Co.'s near-term outlook appears favorable. For full-year 2008, Co. expects revenues to increase over 2007, excluding currency fluctuations, due to continued economic strength in many of its geographic and core industrial markets. Co. has also reaffirmed its earnings per share estimate of $5.10 to $5.40. In addition, Co. expects its operating income to increase due to increased sales as well as a number of operational improvement programs and increased utilization of its facilities. However, Co. noted that the large proportion of original equipment business booked in 2007 by its Flowserve Pump Division may reduce gross profit margin as those products are shipped in 2008 and beyond.

Financial Data

(US$ in Thousands)	12/31/2007	12/31/2006	12/31/2005	12/31/2004	12/31/2003	12/31/2002	12/31/2001	12/31/2000
Earnings Per Share	4.46	2.02	0.21	0.43	0.96	1.02	(0.04)	0.35
Cash Flow Per Share	7.39	2.92	2.30	4.84	3.34	4.80	(1.24)	0.46
Tang Book Value Per Share	5.42	0.47	N.M.	N.M.	N.M.	N.M.	N.M.	N.M.
Dividends Per Share	0.600	...	...	...	...	...	...	...
Dividend Payout %	13.45	...	...	...	...	...	...	...
Income Statement								
Total Revenue	3,762,694	3,061,063	2,695,277	2,638,199	2,404,371	2,251,331	1,917,507	1,538,293
EBITDA	495,326	318,071	227,480	216,903	237,136	250,316	224,292	150,542
Income Before Taxes	360,068	187,276	83,272	59,624	73,835	92,070	25,629	23,184
Income Taxes	104,294	73,238	37,092	39,470	20,947	31,674	9,275	7,876
Net Income	255,774	115,032	11,835	24,200	52,888	53,025	(1,497)	13,241
Average Shares	57,289	56,905	56,690	55,650	55,250	52,193	38,719	37,842
Balance Sheet								
Current Assets	1,896,771	1,302,881	1,071,199	1,049,669	1,091,034	1,031,032	898,139	898,052
Total Assets	3,520,421	2,869,235	2,575,538	2,634,036	2,800,653	2,607,665	2,051,975	2,110,143
Current Liabilities	1,250,180	884,036	694,992	708,410	632,658	492,010	416,771	434,017
Long-Term Obligations	550,795	556,519	652,769	657,746	879,766	1,055,748	996,222	1,111,108
Total Liabilities	2,227,444	1,848,649	1,743,704	1,763,811	1,979,905	1,851,975	1,640,956	1,805,232
Stockholders' Equity	1,292,977	1,020,586	831,834	870,225	820,748	755,690	411,019	304,911
Shares Outstanding	56,309	56,022	55,974	55,468	54,839	54,850	44,792	37,436
Statistical Record								
Return on Assets %	8.01	4.23	0.45	0.89	1.96	2.28	N.M.	0.90
Return on Equity %	22.11	12.42	1.39	2.85	6.71	9.09	N.M.	4.31
EBITDA Margin %	13.16	10.39	8.44	8.22	9.86	11.12	11.70	9.79
Net Margin %	6.80	3.76	0.44	0.92	2.20	2.36	N.M.	0.86
Asset Turnover	1.18	1.12	1.03	0.97	0.89	0.97	0.92	1.04
Current Ratio	1.52	1.47	1.54	1.48	1.72	2.10	2.15	2.07
Debt to Equity	0.43	0.55	0.78	0.76	1.07	1.40	2.42	3.64
Price Range	101.00-48.98	60.75-40.91	39.56-23.70	27.79-18.89	22.62-10.70	34.90-7.90	32.90-19.33	23.00-10.56
P/E Ratio	22.65-10.98	30.07-20.25	188.38-112.86	64.63-43.93	23.56-11.15	34.22-7.75	...	65.71-30.18
Average Yield %	0.86	...	...	...	...	...	...	...

Address: 5215 North O'Connor Boulevard, Suite 2300, Irving, TX 75039	Web Site: www.flowserve.com	Auditors: PricewaterhouseCoopers LLP
Telephone: 972-443-6500	Officers: Lewis M. Kling - Pres., C.E.O. Mark A. Blinn - V.P., C.F.O.	Investor Contact: 972-443-6500
Fax: 972-443-6800		Transfer Agents: National City Bank, Cleveland, OH

FLUOR CORP.

Exchange	Symbol	Price	52Wk Range	Yield	P/E
NYS	FLR	$141.16 (3/31/2008)	168.09-90.05	0.71	24.13

*7 Year Price Score 162.16 *NYSE Composite Index=100 *12 Month Price Score 110.80

TRADING VOLUME (thousand shares)

Interim Earnings (Per Share)

Qtr.	Mar	Jun	Sep	Dec
2003	0.21	0.56	0.55	0.63
2004	0.57	0.54	0.57	0.57
2005	0.56	(0.19)	1.51	0.74
2006	1.00	0.74	0.31	0.90
2007	0.94	1.05	1.02	2.84

Interim Dividends (Per Share)

Amt	Decl	Ex	Rec	Pay
0.20Q	5/2/2007	6/5/2007	6/7/2007	7/3/2007
0.20Q	8/3/2007	9/4/2007	9/6/2007	10/2/2007
0.20Q	11/2/2007	12/4/2007	12/6/2007	1/3/2008
0.25Q	1/31/2008	3/5/2008	3/7/2008	4/2/2008

Indicated Div: $1.00

Valuation Analysis / **Institutional Holding**

Forecast P/E	N/A	No of Institutions
		323
Market Cap	$12.5 Billion	Shares
Book Value	2.3 Billion	80,671,944
Price/Book	5.50	% Held
Price/Sales	0.75	91.74

Business Summary: Construction - Public Infrastructure (MIC: 3.1 SIC: 1629 NAIC: 541330)

Fluor is a holding company that provides services on a global basis in the fields of engineering, procurement and construction management and project management. As of Dec 31 2007, Co. is divided into five principal operating segments: Oil & Gas, Industrial & Infrastructure, Government, Global Services and Power. In addition, Co.'s subsidiary, Fluor Constructors International, Inc., which is organized and operates separately from its business segments, provides management, construction and management services in the U.S. and Canada, both independently and as a subcontractor on projects in each of its segments.

Recent Developments: For the year ended Dec 31 2007, net income increased 102.4% to US$533.3 million from US$263.5 million in the prior year. Revenues were US$16.69 billion, up 18.6% from US$14.08 billion the year before. Direct operating expenses rose 17.5% to US$15.89 billion from US$13.52 billion in the comparable period the year before. Indirect operating expenses increased 8.4% to US$193.9 million from US$178.8 million in the equivalent prior-year period.

Prospects: On Mar 10 2008, Co. has been awarded a contract for engineering, procurement and construction for Total's Port Arthur, TX, refinery. Specifically, Co.'s scope of work includes building a coker, a desulfurization unit, a vacuum distillation unit and other related infrastructure. The full contract value of $1.90 billion will be booked in the first quarter of 2008. When commissioned in 2011, the refinery will convert heavy and process sour crude. Meanwhile, as a result of the strength of recent new business awards and stronger operating performance, Co. is raising its earnings guidance for 2008 to a range of $5.10 to $5.50 per share, from its previous range of $4.90 to $5.30 per share.

Financial Data
(US$ in Thousands)

	12/31/2007	12/31/2006	12/31/2005	12/31/2004	12/31/2003	12/31/2002	12/31/2001	12/31/2000
Earnings Per Share	5.85	2.95	2.62	2.25	1.95	2.03	0.25	(0.05)
Cash Flow Per Share	10.37	3.43	4.82	(1.00)	(3.77)	2.61	8.71	(0.63)
Tang Book Value Per Share	24.77	18.77	17.84	14.89	12.51	10.76	9.57	8.49
Dividends Per Share	0.800	0.800	0.640	0.640	0.640	0.640	0.640	...
Dividend Payout %	13.68	27.12	24.43	28.44	32.82	31.22	256.00	...
Income Statement								
Total Revenue	16,691,033	14,078,506	13,161,051	9,380,277	8,805,703	9,958,956	8,972,161	1,866,519
EBITDA	755,393	503,814	396,329	369,541	344,437	332,063	303,407	20,558
Income Before Taxes	649,093	381,990	299,582	281,158	267,981	260,524	185,320	(7,102)
Income Taxes	115,774	118,538	72,309	94,463	88,526	90,548	57,554	(3,079)
Net Income	533,319	263,452	227,273	186,695	157,450	163,615	19,410	(4,023)
Average Shares	91,089	89,196	86,656	82,795	80,539	79,853	79,187	74,098
Balance Sheet								
Current Assets	4,059,500	3,323,586	3,108,222	2,723,314	2,215,644	1,941,465	1,851,327	1,382,258
Total Assets	5,796,179	4,874,870	4,574,445	3,969,557	3,449,482	3,142,151	3,091,162	2,700,561
Current Liabilities	2,860,094	2,406,267	2,339,335	1,763,981	1,829,138	1,756,171	1,811,418	1,648,081
Long-Term Obligations	17,704	187,129	92,023	347,649	44,652	17,613	17,594	17,576
Total Liabilities	3,521,720	3,144,398	2,943,887	2,633,765	2,367,948	2,258,284	2,301,896	2,067,484
Stockholders' Equity	2,274,459	1,730,472	1,630,558	1,335,792	1,081,534	883,867	789,266	633,077
Shares Outstanding	88,682	88,041	87,088	84,538	82,102	80,188	80,106	74,609
Statistical Record								
Return on Assets %	10.00	5.58	5.32	5.02	4.78	5.25	0.67	N.M.
Return on Equity %	26.63	15.68	15.32	15.40	16.02	19.56	2.73	N.M.
EBITDA Margin %	4.53	3.58	3.01	3.94	3.91	3.33	3.38	1.10
Net Margin %	3.20	1.87	1.73	1.99	1.79	1.64	0.22	N.M.
Asset Turnover	3.13	2.98	3.08	2.52	2.67	3.20	3.10	0.42
Current Ratio	1.42	1.38	1.33	1.54	1.21	1.11	1.02	0.84
Debt to Equity	0.01	0.11	0.06	0.26	0.04	0.02	0.02	0.03
Price Range	168.09-75.92	101.95-74.40	78.15-50.37	54.54-36.84	40.54-27.18	44.57-20.94	62.65-31.82	33.19-27.06
P/E Ratio	28.73-12.98	34.56-25.22	29.83-19.23	24.24-16.37	20.79-13.94	21.74-10.21	250.60-127.28	...
Average Yield %	0.70	0.94	1.05	1.49	1.85	1.97	1.51	...

Address: One Enterprise Drive, Aliso Viejo, CA 92656	**Web Site:** www.fluor.com	**Auditors:** Ernst & Young LLP
Telephone: 949-349-2000	**Officers:** Alan L. Boeckmann - Chmn., C.E.O. H. Steven Gilbert - Sr. V.P., Human Res., Admin.	**Investor Contact:** 469-398-7221 **Transfer Agents:** Mellon Investor Services

310

FMC CORP.

Exchange	Symbol	Price	52Wk Range	Yield	P/E
NYS	FMC	$55.49 (3/31/2008)	59.41-36.94	N/A	32.45

*7 Year Price Score 153.91 *NYSE Composite Index=100 *12 Month Price Score 121.32

Interim Earnings (Per Share)

Qtr.	Mar	Jun	Sep	Dec
2003	0.03	0.30	(0.05)	0.09
2004	0.07	0.41	0.39	1.25
2005	0.83	0.40	(0.06)	0.32
2006	0.47	0.58	0.45	0.17
2007	0.58	0.11	0.48	0.53

Interim Dividends (Per Share)

No Dividends Paid

Valuation Analysis **Institutional Holding**

Forecast P/E	10.95	No of Institutions
	(1/10/2007)	211
Market Cap	$4.2 Billion	Shares
Book Value	1.1 Billion	32,764,104
Price/Book	3.92	% Held
Price/Sales	1.58	85.51

Business Summary: Chemicals (MIC: 11.1 SIC: 2812 NAIC: 325181)

FMC is a chemical company serving the agricultural, industrial and consumer markets. Co. operates through three segments: Agricultural Products, which focuses on insecticides that are designed to enhance crop yield and quality by controlling pests, and on herbicides, which are used to reduce the need for manual or mechanical weeding; Specialty Chemicals, which consists of Co.'s BioPolymer and lithium businesses and focuses on food ingredients; and Industrial Chemicals, which manufactures inorganic materials, including soda ash, hydrogen peroxide, specialty peroxygens and phosphorus chemicals.

Recent Developments: For the year ended Dec 31 2007, income from continuing operations increased 8.7% to US$156.7 million from US$144.1 million a year earlier. Net income increased 0.8% to US$132.4 million from US$131.3 million in the prior year. Revenues were US$2.63 billion, up 12.2% from US$2.35 billion the year before. Direct operating expenses rose 11.8% to US$1.83 billion from US$1.64 billion in the comparable period the year before. Indirect operating expenses increased 25.3% to US$574.8 million from US$458.6 million in the equivalent prior-year period.

Prospects: Despite the continuing affect of higher raw material costs, Co. continues to expect its agricultural products revenue growth of 5.0% to 10.0% due to the healthy global agricultural economy, new product introductions and increased demand for biofuels. Also, Co. expects its specialty chemicals revenue growth in the mid-single digits due higher volumes across the segment and higher selling prices in BioPolymer. Co. also expects industrial chemicals revenue growth of 5.0% to 10.0% due to higher volumes and selling prices across all businesses, mainly in soda ash. For 2008, Co. expects earnings before restructuring and other income and charges of $3.80 to $4.00 per diluted share.

Financial Data

(US$ in Thousands)	12/31/2007	12/31/2006	12/31/2005	12/31/2004	12/31/2003	12/31/2002	12/31/2001	12/31/2000
Earnings Per Share	1.71	1.67	1.49	2.14	0.38	0.96	(5.43)	1.75
Cash Flow Per Share	3.58	3.44	2.88	2.89	2.39	1.39	(3.37)	4.05
Tang Book Value Per Share	11.77	11.17	10.52	9.54	6.13	3.94	1.64	4.99
Dividends Per Share	0.405	0.360	...	...	...	...	...	...
Dividend Payout %	23.68	21.56	...	...	...	...	...	...
Income Statement								
Total Revenue	2,632,900	2,347,000	2,150,200	2,051,200	1,921,400	1,852,900	1,943,000	3,925,500
EBITDA	354,300	378,200	387,700	343,800	254,800	276,900	(283,000)	504,200
Income Before Taxes	185,700	213,500	193,300	131,100	38,000	86,500	(472,900)	222,600
Income Taxes	29,000	68,700	82,300	(44,500)	(1,800)	17,400	(166,600)	45,300
Net Income	132,400	132,000	116,600	160,700	10,300	65,800	(337,700)	110,600
Average Shares	77,599	79,076	78,372	74,702	71,182	68,686	62,104	63,152
Balance Sheet								
Current Assets	1,194,100	1,067,800	1,067,300	1,072,700	1,009,700	1,175,700	820,300	1,329,800
Total Assets	2,733,400	2,735,000	2,740,000	2,978,400	2,828,800	2,872,000	2,477,200	3,745,900
Current Liabilities	751,400	702,500	659,300	820,100	727,500	874,600	1,079,200	1,399,900
Long-Term Obligations	419,600	523,500	639,800	822,200	1,033,400	1,035,900	651,800	872,100
Total Liabilities	1,669,100	1,715,500	1,780,700	2,102,200	2,240,500	2,466,000	2,258,400	2,945,500
Stockholders' Equity	1,064,300	1,019,500	959,300	876,200	588,300	406,000	218,800	800,400
Shares Outstanding	75,129	76,635	77,031	74,057	70,522	70,144	62,610	61,289
Statistical Record								
Return on Assets %	4.84	4.82	4.08	5.50	0.93	2.46	N.M.	2.85
Return on Equity %	12.71	13.34	12.70	21.82	5.33	21.06	N.M.	14.29
EBITDA Margin %	13.46	16.11	18.03	16.76	13.26	14.94	N.M.	12.84
Net Margin %	5.03	5.62	5.42	7.81	1.38	3.55	N.M.	2.82
Asset Turnover	0.96	0.86	0.75	0.70	0.67	0.69	0.62	1.01
Current Ratio	1.59	1.52	1.62	1.31	1.39	1.34	0.76	0.95
Debt to Equity	0.39	0.51	0.67	0.94	1.76	2.55	2.98	1.09
Price Range	58.85-35.63	38.58-26.10	31.30-21.71	25.00-16.58	17.43-7.19	20.96-11.73	21.94-12.31	20.05-12.24
P/E Ratio	34.42-20.84	23.10-15.63	21.01-14.57	11.68-7.75	45.86-18.92	21.83-12.22	...	11.46-7.00
Average Yield %	0.91	1.13	...	...	...	...	...	...

Address: 1735 Market Street, Philadelphia, PA 19103	Web Site: www.fmc.com	Auditors: KPMG LLP
Telephone: 215-299-6000	**Officers:** William G. Walter - Chmn., Pres., C.E.O.	**Transfer Agents:** National City Bank,
Fax: 215-299-6618	W. Kim Foster - Sr. V.P., C.F.O.	Cleveland, OH

FMC TECHNOLOGIES, INC.

Exchange	Symbol	Price	52Wk Range	Yield	P/E
NYS	FTI	$56.89 (3/31/2008)	66.86-34.63	N/A	25.17

*7 Year Price Score N/A   *NYSE Composite Index=100   *12 Month Price Score 119.01

TRADING VOLUME (thousand shares)

Interim Earnings (Per Share)

Qtr.	Mar	Jun	Sep	Dec
2003	0.07	0.17	0.15	0.17
2004	0.10	0.17	0.16	0.41
2005	0.00	0.21	0.33	0.22
2006	0.34	0.47	0.44	0.73
2007	0.45	0.55	0.59	0.68

Interim Dividends (Per Share)

No Dividends Paid

Valuation Analysis

		Institutional Holding	
Forecast P/E	12.41	No of Institutions	
	(1/10/2007)	253	
Market Cap	$7.4 Billion	Shares	
Book Value	1.0 Billion	62,214,648	
Price/Book	7.20	% Held	
Price/Sales	1.59	92.09	

Business Summary: Oil and Gas (MIC: 14.2 SIC: 3533 NAIC: 333132)

FMC Technologies is engaged in providing technology systems for the energy industry and other industrial markets. Co. designs, manufactures and services systems and products such as subsea production and processing systems, surface wellhead production systems, high pressure fluid control equipment, measurement systems, and marine loading systems for the oil and gas industry. In addition, Co. produces food processing equipment for the food industry and specialized equipment to service the aviation industry. Co.'s business segments are Energy Systems (comprising Energy Production Systems and Energy Processing Systems), FoodTech and Airport Systems.

Recent Developments: For the year ended Dec 31 2007, net income increased 9.6% to US$302.8 million from US$276.3 million in the prior year. Revenues were US$4.62 billion, up 22.9% from US$3.76 billion the year before. Direct operating expenses rose 21.8% to US$3.65 billion from US$3.00 billion in the comparable period the year before. Indirect operating expenses increased 13.1% to US$511.7 million from US$452.6 million in the equivalent prior-year period.

Prospects: On Jan 2 2008, Co. received the award to supply deepwater subsea processing and production systems to Total Exploration & Production Angola. The award has a value of approximately US$980.0 million in revenue to Co. with deliveries for the project will be completed over a multi-year period and is expected to commence in 2009. Separately, on Dec 19 2007, Co. announced that it has increased its ownership stake in CDS Engineering BV, a provider of gas and liquids separation technology and equipment for both onshore and offshore applications and floating production systems, from 91.0% to 100.0%. For 2008, Co. expects diluted earnings per share from continuing operations of $2.75 to $2.85.

Financial Data
(US$ in Thousands)

	12/31/2007	12/31/2006	12/31/2005	12/31/2004	12/31/2003	12/31/2002	12/31/2001	12/31/2000
Earnings Per Share	2.26	1.97	0.75	0.84	0.56	(0.97)	0.27	0.46
Cash Flow Per Share	4.38	1.13	(0.22)	0.94	1.10	0.87	0.53	...
Tang Book Value Per Share	5.79	5.19	3.83	3.45	1.81	1.40	0.55	132,250.00
Income Statement								
Total Revenue	4,615,400	3,790,700	3,226,700	2,767,700	2,307,100	2,071,500	1,927,900	1,875,200
EBITDA	557,500	373,500	233,700	229,400	173,200	151,400	122,500	154,000
Income Before Taxes	464,000	296,000	162,300	159,000	106,600	90,300	63,500	90,600
Income Taxes	156,500	84,500	56,200	42,300	31,000	26,200	24,100	22,700
Net Income	302,800	276,300	106,100	116,700	75,600	(129,700)	34,700	67,900
Average Shares	133,800	140,400	141,600	138,600	133,800	133,648	131,846	...
Balance Sheet								
Current Assets	2,104,000	1,690,200	1,428,100	1,217,100	949,400	818,400	755,100	693,300
Total Assets	3,211,100	2,487,800	2,095,600	1,893,900	1,590,600	1,372,500	1,437,900	1,373,700
Current Liabilities	1,785,200	1,208,200	1,058,200	995,400	845,100	734,000	680,800	569,800
Long-Term Obligations	112,200	212,600	252,600	160,400	201,100	175,400	194,100	...
Total Liabilities	2,189,400	1,601,800	1,396,100	1,231,700	1,161,300	1,068,700	1,019,700	736,100
Stockholders' Equity	1,021,700	886,000	699,500	662,200	429,300	303,800	418,200	637,600
Shares Outstanding	129,300	134,600	136,200	137,394	132,400	131,000	130,010	2
Statistical Record								
Return on Assets %	10.63	12.06	5.32	6.68	5.10	N.M.	...	4.76
Return on Equity %	31.75	34.85	15.58	21.32	20.62	N.M.	...	9.96
EBITDA Margin %	12.08	9.85	7.24	8.29	7.51	7.31	6.35	8.21
Net Margin %	6.56	7.29	3.29	4.22	3.28	N.M.	1.80	3.62
Asset Turnover	1.62	1.65	1.62	1.58	1.56	1.47	...	1.31
Current Ratio	1.18	1.40	1.35	1.22	1.12	1.11	1.11	1.22
Debt to Equity	0.11	0.24	0.36	0.24	0.47	0.58	0.46	...
Price Range	66.86-27.75	35.66-22.50	21.89-14.53	17.23-11.52	12.27-9.09	11.80-7.23	11.00-5.66	...
P/E Ratio	29.58-12.28	18.10-11.42	29.19-19.37	20.51-13.71	21.90-16.22	...	40.74-20.94	...

Address: 1803 Gears Road, Houston, TX 77067 **Telephone:** 281-591-4000	**Web Site:** www.fmctechnologies.com **Officers:** Joseph H. Netherland - Chmn., Pres., C.E.O. Peter D. Kinnear - Exec. V.P.	**Auditors:** KPMG LLP **Investor Contact:** 281-591-4080 **Transfer Agents:** National City Bank, Cleveland, OH

FOOT LOCKER, INC.

Exchange	Symbol	Price	52Wk Range	Yield	P/E
NYS	FL	$11.77 (3/31/2008)	24.21-9.84	5.10	35.67

7 Year Price Score 69.82   *NYSE Composite Index=100*   **12 Month Price Score 79.48**

Interim Earnings (Per Share)

Qtr.	Apr	Jul	Oct	Jan
2003-04	0.26	0.24	0.41	0.47
2004-05	0.31	0.53	0.47	0.57
2005-06	0.37	0.28	0.42	0.61
2006-07	0.38	0.09	0.42	0.72
2007-08	0.11	(0.12)	(0.22)	0.55

Interim Dividends (Per Share)

Amt	Decl	Ex	Rec	Pay
0.125Q	5/30/2007	7/18/2007	7/20/2007	8/3/2007
0.125Q	8/13/2007	10/17/2007	10/19/2007	11/2/2007
0.125Q	11/14/2007	1/16/2008	1/18/2008	2/1/2008
0.15Q	2/20/2008	4/16/2008	4/18/2008	5/2/2008

Indicated Div: $0.60

Valuation Analysis

		Institutional Holding	
Forecast P/E	N/A	No of Institutions	260
Market Cap	$1.8 Billion	Shares	137,508,656
Book Value	2.3 Billion	% Held	88.90
Price/Book	0.80		
Price/Sales	0.33		

Business Summary: Retail - Apparel and Accessory Stores (MIC: 5.8 SIC: 5661 NAIC: 316213)

Foot Locker is a global retailer of athletic footwear and apparel. As of Feb 2 2008, Co. operated 3,785 primarily mall-based stores in the U.S., Canada, Europe and Asia Pacific, which includes Australia and New Zealand. Co., through its subsidiaries, operates in two reportable segments: Athletic Stores and Direct-to-Customers. The Athletic Stores segment serves as an athletic footwear and apparels retailer with formats including Foot Locker, Lady Foot Locker, Kids Foot Locker, Champs Sports and Footaction. The Direct-to-Customers segment reflects Footlocker.com, Inc., which sells, through its affiliates, including Eastbay, Inc., to customers through catalogs and Internet websites.

Recent Developments: For the year ended Feb 2 2008, net income decreased 79.7% to US$51.0 million from US$251.0 million in the prior year. Revenues were US$5.44 billion, down 5.4% from US$5.75 billion the year before. Direct operating expenses rose 0.1% to US$4.02 billion from US$4.01 billion in the comparable period the year before. Indirect operating expenses increased 8.5% to US$1.47 billion from US$1.36 billion in the equivalent prior-year period.

Prospects: Co.'s results are being hampered by significantly lower sales of its low-profile and casual footwear along with a softening in sales of branded and licensed apparel. For fiscal year ending Feb 2009, Co. expects comparable store sales to be relatively flat and net income in a range of $0.65 to $0.85 per share. Also, Co. estimates its fiscal 2008 capital spending to be about US$158.0 million, of which US$135.0 million relates to modernizations of existing stores and new store openings, and $23.0 million reflects the development of information systems and other support facilities. Meanwhile, Co. plans to open about 60 stores, remodel or relocate 200 stores, and close about 140 stores in 2008.

Financial Data
(US$ in Thousands)

	02/02/2008	02/03/2007	01/28/2006	01/29/2005	01/31/2004	02/01/2003	02/02/2002	02/03/2001
Earnings Per Share	0.33	1.60	1.68	1.88	1.39	1.05	0.64	(1.73)
Cash Flow Per Share	1.84	1.20	2.29	1.92	1.87	2.47	1.32	1.77
Tang Book Value Per Share	12.36	12.37	10.59	9.12	7.94	6.34	6.13	6.28
Dividends Per Share	0.500	0.395	0.315	0.255	0.150	0.030	...	...
Dividend Payout %	151.52	24.69	18.75	13.56	10.79	2.86	...	...
Income Statement								
Total Revenue	5,437,000	5,750,000	5,653,000	5,355,000	4,779,000	4,509,000	4,379,000	4,356,000
EBITDA	117,000	570,000	586,000	543,000	489,000	421,000	353,000	349,000
Income Before Taxes	(50,000)	392,000	405,000	374,000	324,000	246,000	175,000	176,000
Income Taxes	(99,000)	145,000	142,000	119,000	115,000	84,000	64,000	69,000
Net Income	51,000	251,000	264,000	293,000	207,000	153,000	92,000	(240,000)
Average Shares	155,600	156,800	157,600	157,100	152,900	150,800	146,900	139,100
Balance Sheet								
Current Assets	2,064,000	2,034,000	2,014,000	1,832,000	1,519,000	1,284,000	1,114,000	1,000,000
Total Assets	3,248,000	3,249,000	3,312,000	3,237,000	2,689,000	2,486,000	2,290,000	2,232,000
Current Liabilities	501,000	516,000	717,000	684,000	545,000	572,000	539,000	629,000
Long-Term Obligations	221,000	220,000	275,000	347,000	335,000	356,000	365,000	259,000
Total Liabilities	977,000	954,000	1,285,000	1,407,000	1,314,000	1,376,000	1,298,000	1,219,000
Stockholders' Equity	2,271,000	2,295,000	2,027,000	1,830,000	1,375,000	1,110,000	992,000	1,013,000
Shares Outstanding	154,474	155,703	155,504	156,091	143,952	141,075	139,911	138,491
Statistical Record								
Return on Assets %	1.57	7.53	8.08	9.92	8.02	6.42	4.08	N.M.
Return on Equity %	2.24	11.43	13.73	18.33	16.71	14.60	9.20	N.M.
EBITDA Margin %	2.15	9.91	10.37	10.14	10.23	9.34	8.06	8.01
Net Margin %	0.94	4.37	4.67	5.47	4.33	3.39	2.10	N.M.
Asset Turnover	1.68	1.72	1.73	1.81	1.85	1.89	1.94	1.81
Current Ratio	4.12	3.94	2.81	2.68	2.79	2.24	2.07	1.59
Debt to Equity	0.10	0.10	0.14	0.19	0.24	0.32	0.37	0.26
Price Range	24.21-9.84	27.32-21.27	29.58-19.00	27.17-20.07	25.64-9.52	17.84-8.49	18.98-10.60	16.38-5.31
P/E Ratio	73.36-29.82	17.07-13.29	17.61-11.31	14.45-10.68	18.45-6.85	16.99-8.09	29.66-16.56	...
Average Yield %	2.72	1.67	1.29	1.06	0.97	0.24	...	...

Address: 112 West 34th Street, New York, NY 10120	**Web Site:** www.footlocker-inc.com	**Auditors:** KPMG LLP
Telephone: 212-720-3700	**Officers:** Matthew D. Serra - Chmn., Pres., C.E.O.	**Transfer Agents:** The Bank of New York, New York, NY
Fax: 212-553-7026	Robert W. McHugh - Sr. V.P., C.F.O.	

FORD MOTOR CO. (DE)

Exchange	Symbol	Price	52Wk Range	Yield	P/E
NYS	F	$5.72 (3/31/2008)	9.64-5.11	N/A	N/A

7 Year Price Score 52.09   **NYSE Composite Index=100**   **12 Month Price Score 84.65**

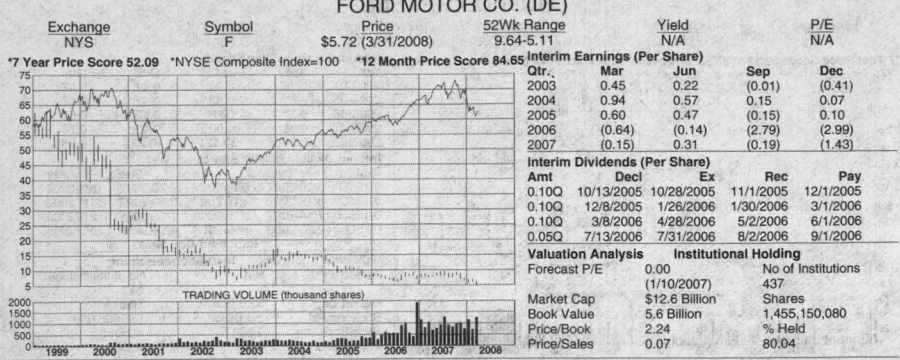

Interim Earnings (Per Share)

Qtr.	Mar	Jun	Sep	Dec
2003	0.45	0.22	(0.01)	(0.41)
2004	0.94	0.57	0.15	0.07
2005	0.60	0.47	(0.15)	0.10
2006	(0.64)	(0.14)	(2.79)	(2.99)
2007	(0.15)	0.31	(0.19)	(1.43)

Interim Dividends (Per Share)

Amt	Decl	Ex	Rec	Pay
0.10Q	10/13/2005	10/28/2005	11/1/2005	12/1/2005
0.10Q	12/8/2005	1/26/2006	1/30/2006	3/1/2006
0.10Q	3/8/2006	4/28/2006	5/2/2006	6/1/2006
0.05Q	7/13/2006	7/31/2006	8/2/2006	9/1/2006

Valuation Analysis   **Institutional Holding**

Forecast P/E	0.00	No of Institutions
	(1/10/2007)	437
Market Cap	$12.6 Billion	Shares
Book Value	5.6 Billion	1,455,150,080
Price/Book	2.24	% Held
Price/Sales	0.07	80.04

Business Summary: Automotive (MIC: 15.1 SIC: 3711 NAIC: 336111)

Ford Motor is a global automaker. Co.'s automotive sector manufactures and sells cars and trucks, as well as provides retail customers with a range of after-the-sale vehicle services and products through its dealer network and other channels, in areas such as maintenance and light repair, heavy repair, collision, vehicle accessories and extended service warranty. Co.'s financial services sector primarily includes Ford Motor Credit, which primarily includes vehicle-related financing, leasing and insurance. Co. also has an equity interest of approximately 33.4% in Mazda Motor Corp. at Dec 31 2007. As of Dec 31 2007, Co.'s vehicle brands include Ford, Mercury, Lincoln, and Volvo.

Recent Developments: For the year ended Dec 31 2007, loss from continuing operations was US$2.76 billion compared with a loss of US$12.63 billion a year earlier. Net loss amounted to US$2.72 billion versus a net loss of US$12.61 billion in the prior year. Revenues were US$172.46 billion, up 7.7% from US$160.07 billion the year before. Direct operating expenses declined 4.2% to US$142.59 billion from US$148.87 billion in the comparable period the year before. Indirect operating expenses increased 25.0% to US$24.24 billion from US$19.39 billion in the equivalent prior-year period.

Prospects: On Jan 23 2008, Co. and its subsidiary, Automotive Components Holdings, LLC (ACH), agreed to sell the ACH driveshaft business located in the ACH Monroe (Michigan) Plant to Neapco Drivelines, LLC. This transaction reflects Co.'s progress with its plans to sell or close essentially all of its ACH plants by the end of 2008, and to return to profitability in North America and in its automotive operations in 2009. Co. also remains committed to its plan to reduce annual North America operating costs by about $5.00 billion by the end of 2008 as compared with 2005. Accordingly, Co.'s total 2008 pre-tax results, although still projected at a loss, are expected to improve from its 2007 results.

Financial Data
(US$ in Thousands)

	12/31/2007	12/31/2006	12/31/2005	12/31/2004	12/31/2003	12/31/2002	12/31/2001	12/31/2000
Earnings Per Share	(1.38)	(6.72)	1.05	1.73	0.27	(0.54)	(3.02)	2.30
Cash Flow Per Share	4.23	1.67	8.03	12.34	11.04	10.24	12.57	22.84
Tang Book Value Per Share	1.61	...	3.68	4.60	2.40	N.M.	4.31	10.14
Dividends Per Share	...	0.250	0.400	0.400	0.400	0.400	1.050	0.300
Dividend Payout %	...	...	38.10	23.12	148.15	...	...	13.04
Income Statement								
Total Revenue	172,455,000	160,123,000	177,089,000	171,652,000	164,196,000	162,586,000	162,412,000	170,064,000
EBITDA	13,576,000	(907,000)	15,548,000	18,578,000	17,003,000	19,223,000	13,410,000	32,497,000
Income Before Taxes	(3,746,000)	(15,051,000)	1,996,000	4,853,000	1,370,000	953,000	(7,584,000)	8,234,000
Income Taxes	(1,294,000)	(2,646,000)	(512,000)	937,000	135,000	302,000	(2,151,000)	2,705,000
Net Income	(2,723,000)	(12,613,000)	2,024,000	3,487,000	495,000	(980,000)	(5,453,000)	3,467,000
Average Shares	1,978,000	1,877,000	2,135,000	2,126,000	1,843,000	1,829,000	1,810,000	1,504,000
Balance Sheet								
Current Assets	72,004,000	80,361,000	64,516,000	58,071,000	60,152,000	47,834,000	36,260,000	39,310,000
Total Assets	285,727,000	290,217,000	275,940,000	305,341,000	315,920,000	295,222,000	276,543,000	284,421,000
Current Liabilities	114,250,000	118,779,000	108,115,000	122,877,000	112,768,000	89,773,000	94,856,000	116,603,000
Long-Term Obligations	107,478,000	109,593,000	94,428,000	106,540,000	119,751,000	120,136,000	120,758,000	98,887,000
Total Liabilities	282,122,000	295,149,000	263,066,000	289,296,000	304,269,000	289,632,000	268,757,000	265,811,000
Stockholders' Equity	5,628,000	(3,465,000)	12,957,000	16,045,000	11,651,000	5,590,000	7,786,000	18,610,000
Shares Outstanding	2,207,002	1,862,538	1,908,000	1,908,000	1,831,388	1,831,219	1,806,608	1,835,050
Statistical Record								
Return on Assets %	N.M.	N.M.	0.70	1.12	0.16	N.M.	N.M.	1.23
Return on Equity %	N.M.	N.M.	13.96	25.11	5.74	N.M.	N.M.	14.98
EBITDA Margin %	7.87	N.M.	8.78	10.82	10.36	11.82	8.26	19.11
Net Margin %	N.M.	N.M.	1.14	2.03	0.30	N.M.	N.M.	2.04
Asset Turnover	0.60	0.57	0.61	0.55	0.54	0.57	0.58	0.61
Current Ratio	0.63	0.68	0.60	0.47	0.53	0.53	0.38	0.34
Debt to Equity	19.10	...	7.29	6.64	10.28	21.49	15.51	5.31
Price Range	9.64-6.70	9.19-6.19	14.71-7.65	17.10-12.70	16.79-6.60	18.19-7.15	30.71-14.93	54.80-22.13
P/E Ratio	...	...	14.01-7.29	9.88-7.34	62.19-24.44	...	...	23.83-9.62
Average Yield %	...	3.25	3.85	2.77	3.73	3.02	4.49	0.79

Address: One American Road, Dearborn, MI 48126-2798	**Web Site:** www.ford.com	**Auditors:** PricewaterhouseCoopers LLP
Telephone: 313-322-3000	**Officers:** William Clay Ford Jr. - Chmn., C.E.O. Greg C. Smith - Vice-Chmn., Exec. V.P.	**Transfer Agents:** First Chicago Trust Company of New York
Fax: 313-222-4177		

FOREST CITY ENTERPRISES, INC.

Exchange	Symbol	Price	52Wk Range	Yield	P/E	Div Acheiver
NYS	FCE A	$36.80 (3/31/2008)	72.23-34.47	0.87	72.16	13 Years

*7 Year Price Score 132.19 *NYSE Composite Index=100 *12 Month Price Score 74.90

Interim Earnings (Per Share)

Qtr.	Apr	Jul	Oct	Jan
2003-04	0.14	0.07	0.26	(0.05)
2004-05	0.07	0.34	0.36	0.06
2005-06	0.22	0.20	0.13	0.27
2006-07	0.52	0.07	0.45	0.67
2007-08	(0.17)	0.63	(0.11)	0.13

Interim Dividends (Per Share)

Amt	Decl	Ex	Rec	Pay
0.08Q	6/21/2007	8/30/2007	9/4/2007	9/18/2007
0.08Q	9/26/2007	11/29/2007	12/3/2007	12/17/2007
0.08Q	12/14/2007	2/28/2008	3/3/2008	3/17/2008
0.08Q	3/26/2008	5/29/2008	6/2/2008	6/17/2008

Indicated Div: $0.32

Valuation Analysis

	Institutional Holding	
Forecast P/E	N/A	No of Institutions
		163
Market Cap	$3.8 Billion	Shares
Book Value	972.1 Million	58,883,260
Price/Book	3.88	% Held
Price/Sales	2.91	76.45

Business Summary: Property, Real Estate & Development (MIC: 8.3 SIC: 6512 NAIC: 236220)

Forest City Enterprises is mainly engaged in the ownership, development, management and acquisition of commercial and residential real estate properties in 27 states and the District of Columbia. The Commercial Group owns, develops, acquires and operates regional malls, specialty/urban retail centers, office and life science buildings, hotels and mixed-use projects. The Residential Group owns, develops, acquires and operates residential rental properties, including upscale and middle market apartments as well as adaptive re-use developments. The Land Development Group acquires and sells both land and developed lots to residential, commercial and industrial customers.

Recent Developments: For the year ended Jan 31 2008, loss from continuing operations was US$13.2 million compared with income of US$30.7 million a year earlier. Net income decreased 70.4% to US$52.4 million from US$177.3 million in the prior year. Revenues were US$1.30 billion, up 15.3% from US$1.12 billion the year before.

Prospects: Co.'s near-term outlook appears to be constructive. For instance, on Jan 7 2008, Co. announced that its Forest City Land Group business unit and joint venture partner Covington Capital Corp. have completed the acquisition of more than 2,500 single-family home lots in the San Antonio, TX. Co. believes that this transaction complements its ongoing strategy of capitalizing existing market conditions to strategically acquire properties and land in potential markets. Meanwhile, for the fiscal year ending Jan 31 2009, Co. expects to begin work on an additional $1.40 billion of projects, resulting in an estimated $2.20 billion in projects under construction at the end of this fiscal year.

Financial Data

(US$ in Thousands)	01/31/2008	01/31/2007	01/31/2006	01/31/2005	01/31/2004	01/31/2003	01/31/2002	01/31/2001
Earnings Per Share	0.51	1.70	0.81	0.83	0.42	0.48	1.09	1.01
Cash Flow Per Share	2.66	3.05	3.40	3.74	1.49	2.16	0.85	2.28
Tang Book Value Per Share	7.89	10.07	8.78	7.99	7.49	7.11	6.70	5.06
Dividends Per Share	0.300	0.260	0.220	0.290	0.150	0.110	0.088	0.073
Dividend Payout %	58.82	15.29	27.16	34.73	35.71	22.68	8.14	7.28
Income Statement								
Property Income	1,295,620	1,168,835	1,200,775	1,041,851	898,339	791,806	738,508	658,369
Non-Property Income	...	...	...	...	123,249	135,744	168,062	136,416
Total Revenue	1,295,620	1,168,835	1,200,775	1,041,851	1,021,588	927,550	906,570	794,785
Interest Expense	328,887	293,803	273,115	248,328	198,122	177,237	178,580	182,544
Income Before Taxes	(3,415)	79,838	114,538	102,476	77,052	81,998	159,957	117,348
Income Taxes	3,004	34,412	23,238	37,326	28,799	31,826	63,487	22,312
Net Income	52,425	177,251	83,519	85,206	42,669	48,831	103,029	91,637
Average Shares	102,261	104,454	102,603	101,846	101,144	100,357	94,773	91,000
Balance Sheet								
Total Assets	10,251,597	8,981,604	7,990,341	7,289,260	5,895,072	5,077,209	4,417,646	4,030,470
Long-Term Obligations	7,408,384	6,321,399	5,930,506	5,480,023	4,162,938	3,451,241	2,959,552	2,905,204
Total Liabilities	8,929,964	7,580,692	6,993,243	6,388,962	5,097,687	4,292,171	3,687,256	3,495,744
Stockholders' Equity	972,116	1,025,811	894,382	804,525	748,911	705,972	662,513	456,636
Shares Outstanding	102,589	101,882	101,844	100,702	99,972	99,311	98,927	90,193
Statistical Record								
Return on Assets %	0.55	2.09	1.09	1.29	0.78	1.03	2.44	2.33
Return on Equity %	5.25	18.46	9.83	10.94	5.87	7.14	18.41	21.68
Net Margin %	4.05	15.16	6.96	8.18	4.18	5.26	11.36	11.53
Price Range	72.23-35.38	61.58-37.79	40.71-28.98	29.18-25.00	26.00-15.48	20.14-14.50	20.45-13.63	13.86-8.33
P/E Ratio	141.63-69.37	36.22-22.23	50.26-35.78	35.15-30.12	61.90-36.85	41.95-30.21	18.76-12.51	13.72-8.25
Average Yield %	0.52	0.52	0.63	1.08	0.74	0.63	0.54	0.66

Address: Terminal Tower, 50 Public Square, Suite 1100, Cleveland, OH 44113
Telephone: 216-621-6060
Fax: 216-362-2692

Web Site: www.forestcity.net
Officers: Albert B. Ratner - Co-Chmn. Samuel H. Miller - Co-Chmn., Treas.

Auditors: PricewaterhouseCoopers LLP
Transfer Agents: National City Bank, Cleveland, Ohio

FOREST LABORATORIES, INC.

Exchange	Symbol	Price	52Wk Range	Yield	P/E
NYS	FRX	$40.01 (3/31/2008)	55.25-35.44	N/A	22.60

*7 Year Price Score 74.57   *NYSE Composite Index=100   *12 Month Price Score 102.07

Interim Earnings (Per Share)

Qtr.	Jun	Sep	Dec	Mar
2004-05	0.60	0.79	0.70	0.16
2005-06	0.62	0.59	0.57	0.29
2006-07	0.62	0.75	0.78	(0.73)
2007-08	0.83	0.71	0.96	...

Interim Dividends (Per Share)

No Dividends Paid

Valuation Analysis

		Institutional Holding	
Forecast P/E	15.18	No of Institutions	
	(1/10/2007)	386	
Market Cap	$12.5 Billion	Shares	
Book Value	3.5 Billion	303,520,000	
Price/Book	3.53	% Held	
Price/Sales	3.34	95.49	

TRADING VOLUME (thousand shares)

Business Summary: Pharmaceuticals (MIC: 9.1 SIC: 2834 NAIC: 325412)

Forest Laboratories is engaged in the development, manufacture and sale of both branded and generic forms of drug products which require a physician's prescription, as well as non-prescription pharmaceutical products sold over-the-counter. Co.'s products include those developed by Co. and those acquired from other pharmaceutical companies and integrated into its marketing and distribution systems. As of Mar 31 2007, Co.'s products included Lexapro®, Namenda® (memantine HCl), Benicar® (olmesartan medoxomil), Benicar HCT, Campral® (acamprosate calcium), Celexa®, Tiazac®, Sudocrem®, Colomycin®, Infaco® and Exorex®.

Recent Developments: For the quarter ended Dec 31 2007, net income increased 20.6% to US$301.8 million from US$250.3 million in the year-earlier quarter. Revenues were US$998.2 million, up 11.8% from US$893.0 million the year before. Direct operating expenses rose 9.2% to US$213.5 million from US$195.5 million in the comparable period the year before. Indirect operating expenses increased 3.5% to US$393.9 million from US$380.7 million in the equivalent prior-year period.

Prospects: Co.'s outlook seems positive. For example, on Jan 22 2008, Co. entered into an agreement with a pharmaceutical company, Novexel, S.A. to develop, manufacture and commercialize Novexel's novel intravenous beta lactamase inhibitor, NXL 104 with its ceftaroline as a combination product in North America. Co. plans to initiate Phase I studies of the ceftaroline/NXL 104 combination in fiscal 2009. Meanwhile, Co. is raising its earnings guidance for fiscal year ending Mar 31 2008 to $3.35 to $3.45 per diluted share from $3.10 to $3.20 per share, excluding the effect of the one-time licensing payment made to Microbia in the fiscal second quarter for development and marketing rights to linaclotide.

Financial Data

(US$ in Thousands)	9 Mos	6 Mos	3 Mos	03/31/2007	03/31/2006	03/31/2005	03/31/2004	03/31/2003
Earnings Per Share	1.77	1.59	1.63	1.41	2.08	2.25	1.95	1.66
Cash Flow Per Share	2.54	2.46	2.77	2.79	1.78	2.54	1.71	2.02
Tang Book Value Per Share	10.72	10.03	9.64	8.93	7.69	8.21	8.03	5.66
Income Statement								
Total Revenue	2,845,476	1,847,234	928,274	3,441,785	2,962,390	3,159,639	2,680,274	2,245,806
EBITDA	1,047,415	644,664	355,115	809,024	954,609	1,241,401	959,013	872,130
Depn & Amort	34,988	23,075	11,317	...	...	...	...	...
Income Before Taxes	1,012,427	621,589	343,798	708,844	869,512	1,184,755	936,822	820,569
Income Taxes	217,264	128,183	75,636	254,741	160,998	345,950	200,948	198,581
Net Income	795,163	493,406	268,162	454,103	708,514	838,805	735,874	621,988
Average Shares	313,107	316,852	321,921	322,781	340,321	372,090	376,779	373,702
Balance Sheet								
Current Assets	2,864,614	2,702,914	2,658,946	2,422,717	2,207,187	2,708,022	2,916,234	2,255,333
Total Assets	4,281,966	4,048,280	3,978,030	3,653,372	3,119,840	3,705,002	3,862,736	2,918,107
Current Liabilities	565,329	578,441	592,125	627,608	420,967	563,690	604,754	564,397
Total Liabilities	757,494	754,437	745,785	628,559	422,031	572,617	606,872	566,289
Stockholders' Equity	3,524,472	3,293,843	3,232,245	3,024,813	2,697,809	3,132,385	3,255,864	2,351,818
Shares Outstanding	311,365	313,467	318,247	319,552	321,340	347,643	369,527	363,472
Statistical Record								
Return on Assets %	13.98	13.70	14.24	13.41	20.76	22.17	21.65	25.54
Return on Equity %	16.67	16.51	17.09	15.87	24.30	26.26	26.17	31.28
EBITDA Margin %	36.81	34.90	38.26	23.51	32.22	39.29	35.78	38.83
Net Margin %	27.94	26.71	28.89	13.19	23.92	26.55	27.46	27.70
Asset Turnover	0.94	0.98	0.97	1.02	0.87	0.84	0.79	0.92
Current Ratio	5.07	4.67	4.49	3.86	5.24	4.80	4.82	4.00
Price Range	57.84-35.44	57.84-35.99	57.84-38.38	57.84-36.29	47.93-32.93	75.20-36.47	77.59-42.00	55.50-33.00
P/E Ratio	32.68-20.02	36.38-22.64	35.48-23.55	41.02-25.74	23.04-15.83	33.42-16.21	39.79-21.54	33.43-19.88

Address: 909 Third Avenue, New York, NY 10022
Telephone: 212-421-7850
Fax: 212-750-9152

Web Site: www.frx.com
Officers: Howard Solomon - Chmn., C.EO. Kenneth E. Goodman - Pres., C.O.O.

Auditors: BDO Seidman, LLP
Transfer Agents: ChaseMellon Shareholder Services, L.L.C., Ridgefield Park, NJ

FOREST OIL CORP.

Exchange	Symbol	Price	52Wk Range	Yield	P/E
NYS	FST	$48.96 (3/31/2008)	51.71-33.46	N/A	22.46

*7 Year Price Score 136.70 *NYSE Composite Index=100 *12 Month Price Score 116.47

Interim Earnings (Per Share)

Qtr.	Mar	Jun	Sep	Dec
2003	0.80	0.48	0.54	(0.06)
2004	0.35	0.50	0.53	0.73
2005	0.63	0.83	0.05	0.91
2006	0.06	0.90	1.21	0.49
2007	0.11	1.08	0.65	0.27

Interim Dividends (Per Share)

No Dividends Paid

Valuation Analysis

		Institutional Holding	
Forecast P/E	N/A	No of Institutions	
		223	
Market Cap	$4.3 Billion	Shares	
Book Value	2.4 Billion	58,020,716	
Price/Book	1.79	% Held	
Price/Sales	3.99	92.08	

TRADING VOLUME (thousand shares)

1999 2000 2001 2002 2003 2004 2005 2006 2007 2008

Business Summary: Oil and Gas (MIC: 14.2 SIC: 1311 NAIC: 211111)

Forest Oil engaged in the acquisition, exploration, development and production of natural gas and liquids in North America as well as selected international locations. Co. operates in five business units: the Western U.S., Southern U.S., Alaska, Canada and International as well as geographical segments including the U.S., Canada and International. As of Dec 31 2007, Co.'s total estimated proved reserves, which amounted to 2.10 trillion cubic feet of natural gas equivalent, and producing properties were all located in North America with approximately 85.0% of its estimated proved oil and gas reserves were in the U.S., approximately 12.0% in Canada and approximately 3.0% were in Italy.

Recent Developments: For the year ended Dec 31 2007, income from continuing operations increased 1.9% to US$169.3 million from US$166.1 million a year earlier. Net income increased 0.5% to US$169.3 million from US$168.5 million in the prior year. Revenues were US$1.08 billion, up 32.2% from US$820.0 million the year before. Operating income was US$388.0 million versus US$272.8 million in the prior year, an increase of 42.2%. Direct operating expenses rose 14.9% to US$222.7 million from US$193.9 million in the comparable period the year before. Indirect operating expenses increased 34.0% to US$473.2 million from US$353.2 million in the equivalent prior year period.

Prospects: For 2008, Co. expects total net sales volumes will be 183 billions of cubic feet equivalen (Bcfe) to 190 Bcfe or an annual increase of 3.0% to 11.0%. Meanwhile, Co. expects to continue its development and exploitation activities on its North American assets for which it expects continued production growth in 2008. Thus, Co. expects its exploration and development expenditures for 2008 to be $900.0 million to $1.00 billion, in which most of its capital budget will be directed to its drilling programs in the Buffalo Wallow field in Texas Panhandle, the Deep Basin in Alberta, Canada, McAllen Ranch fields in South Texas, the Cotton Valley in East Texas, and the Arkoma Basin in Arkansas.

Financial Data

(US$ in Thousands)	12/31/2007	12/31/2006	12/31/2005	12/31/2004	12/31/2003	12/31/2002	12/31/2001	12/31/2000
Earnings Per Share	2.18	2.66	2.41	2.11	1.75	0.44	2.11	2.64
Cash Flow Per Share	9.31	6.79	10.24	9.95	7.72	4.05	10.45	6.60
Tang Book Value Per Share	24.28	21.39	25.48	23.51	22.14	19.32	19.48	17.41
Income Statement								
Total Revenue	1,083,892	819,992	1,072,045	912,898	657,178	475,694	1,018,379	913,058
EBITDA	735,201	595,651	675,008	610,899	428,107	276,899	466,667	410,940
Income Before Taxes	231,701	256,983	244,926	201,870	144,864	38,803	188,931	136,674
Income Taxes	62,395	90,903	93,358	78,744	54,636	14,317	79,577	6,066
Net Income	169,306	168,502	151,568	122,551	88,351	21,276	103,743	130,608
Average Shares	77,751	63,431	62,878	58,089	50,353	48,207	49,282	47,977
Balance Sheet								
Current Assets	361,374	261,000	315,925	283,468	215,360	160,471	201,965	238,828
Total Assets	5,695,548	3,189,072	3,645,546	3,122,505	2,683,548	1,924,681	1,796,369	1,752,378
Current Liabilities	738,382	263,941	522,916	323,615	273,109	191,675	240,298	239,937
Long-Term Obligations	1,503,035	1,204,709	1,769,614	1,777,638	929,971	767,219	594,178	622,234
Total Liabilities	3,283,737	1,755,066	1,961,024	2,539,177	1,497,750	1,003,470	872,426	893,412
Stockholders' Equity	2,411,811	1,434,006	1,684,522	1,472,147	1,185,798	921,211	923,943	858,966
Shares Outstanding	88,379	62,998	62,687	59,693	53,555	47,024	46,744	48,229
Statistical Record								
Return on Assets %	3.81	4.93	4.48	4.21	3.83	1.14	5.85	10.21
Return on Equity %	8.80	10.81	9.60	9.20	8.39	2.31	11.64	22.11
EBITDA Margin %	67.83	72.64	62.96	66.92	65.14	58.21	45.82	45.01
Net Margin %	15.62	20.55	14.14	13.42	13.44	4.47	10.19	14.30
Asset Turnover	0.24	0.24	0.32	0.31	0.29	0.26	0.57	0.71
Current Ratio	0.49	0.99	0.60	0.88	0.79	0.84	0.84	1.00
Debt to Equity	0.62	0.84	1.05	1.21	0.78	0.83	0.64	0.72
Price Range	51.66-28.96	39.64-28.15	36.27-19.73	22.79-15.72	19.66-13.39	21.67-14.01	24.98-15.71	24.70-9.71
P/E Ratio	23.70-13.28	14.90-10.58	15.05-8.19	10.80-7.45	11.23-7.65	49.25-31.85	11.84-7.44	9.36-3.68

Address: 707 Seventeenth Street, Suite 3600, Denver, CO 80202 **Telephone:** 303-812-1400 **Fax:** 303-812-1400	**Web Site:** www.forestoil.com **Officers:** Forrest E. Hoglund - Chmn. H. Craig Clark - Pres., C.E.O.	**Auditors:** Ernst & Young LLP **Transfer Agents:** Mellon Investor Services LLC, Jersey City, NJ

FORTUNE BRANDS INC

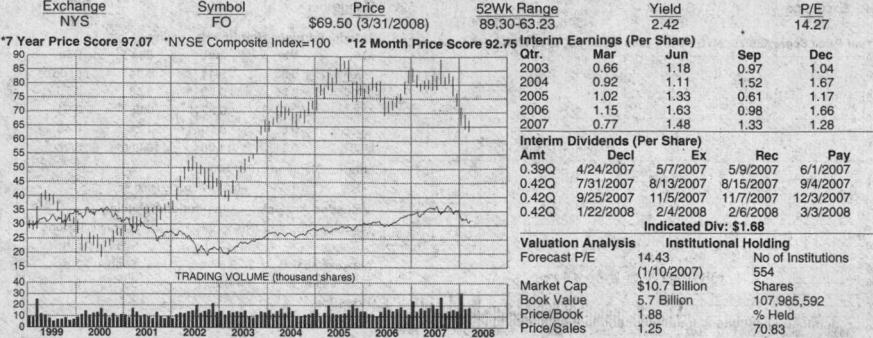

Exchange	Symbol	Price	52Wk Range	Yield	P/E
NYS	FO	$69.50 (3/31/2008)	89.30-63.23	2.42	14.27

*7 Year Price Score 97.07 *NYSE Composite Index=100 *12 Month Price Score 92.75

Interim Earnings (Per Share)

Qtr.	Mar	Jun	Sep	Dec
2003	0.66	1.18	0.97	1.04
2004	0.92	1.11	1.52	1.67
2005	1.02	1.33	0.61	1.17
2006	1.15	1.63	0.98	1.66
2007	0.77	1.48	1.33	1.28

Interim Dividends (Per Share)

Amt	Decl	Ex	Rec	Pay
0.39Q	4/24/2007	5/7/2007	5/9/2007	6/1/2007
0.42Q	7/31/2007	8/13/2007	8/15/2007	9/4/2007
0.42Q	9/25/2007	11/5/2007	11/7/2007	12/3/2007
0.42Q	1/22/2008	2/4/2008	2/6/2008	3/3/2008

Indicated Div: $1.68

Valuation Analysis

Forecast P/E	14.43
	(1/10/2007)
Market Cap	$10.7 Billion
Book Value	5.7 Billion
Price/Book	1.88
Price/Sales	1.25

Institutional Holding

No of Institutions	554
Shares	107,985,592
% Held	70.83

Business Summary: Metal Products (MIC: 11.4 SIC: 3433 NAIC: 333414)

Fortune Brands, Inc. is a holding company with subsidiaries that are engaged in the manufacture, production and sale of consumer branded products worldwide in the following markets: spirits, home & hardware, and golf products. Home and hardware brands include Aristokraft, Omega, Kitchen Craft, Schrock, Diamond, HomeCrest, Decorá and Kemper. Spirit and wine brands include Jim Beam, Maker's Mark, Sauza, Canadian Club, DeKuyper, Laphroaig, Courvoisier, Gilbey's, and others. Golf brands include Titleist, Pinnacle, Cobra, Scotty Cameron, FootJoy and others. Co.'s products are sold primarily in the U.S., Canada, Europe (primarily the U.K, Germany, France and Spain), Australia and Mexico.

Recent Developments: For the year ended Dec 31 2007, income from continuing operations decreased 7.7% to US$749.5 million from US$812.1 million a year earlier. Net income decreased 8.1% to US$762.6 million from US$830.1 million in the prior year. Revenues were US$8.56 billion, up 0.5% from US$8.52 billion the year before. Operating income was US$1.38 billion versus US$1.45 billion in the prior year, a decrease of 4.9%. Direct operating expenses rose 1.9% to US$5.08 billion from US$4.98 billion in the comparable period the year before. Indirect operating expenses increased 1.0% to US$2.11 billion from US$2.09 billion in the equivalent prior-year period.

Prospects: Co. plans to continue growing its spirits and golf brands, and to continue surpassing the home products industry. Accordingly, for 2008, Co. is targeting operating income before charges to be up at a mid-to-high-single-digit rate for its Spirits segment, operating income before charges in Home & Hardware segment to be down at a mid-single-digit-to-mid-teens rate, as well as operating income before charges to be up modestly, reflecting increased investment in brand building and international growth opportunities in its Golf segment. Overall, Co. expects earnings per share before charges or gains to be in the range of up at a low-single-digit rate to down at a high-single-digit rate.

Financial Data

(US$ in Thousands)	12/31/2007	12/31/2006	12/31/2005	12/31/2004	12/31/2003	12/31/2002	12/31/2001	12/31/2000
Earnings Per Share	4.87	5.42	4.13	5.23	3.86	3.41	2.49	(0.88)
Cash Flow Per Share	6.31	6.59	5.51	5.44	5.43	5.27	4.24	2.99
Tang Book Value Per Share	N.M,	N.M.	N.M.	N.M.	N.M.	N.M.	2.06	0.89
Dividends Per Share	1.620	1.500	1.380	1.260	1.140	1.020	0.970	0.930
Dividend Payout %	33.26	27.68	33.41	24.09	29.53	29.91	38.96	...
Income Statement								
Total Revenue	8,563,100	8,769,000	7,061,200	7,320,900	6,214,500	5,677,700	5,678,700	5,844,500
EBITDA	1,693,700	1,795,200	1,307,100	1,391,300	1,140,100	994,100	807,400	409,400
Income Before Taxes	1,120,200	1,209,100	926,100	1,085,600	884,400	756,200	491,900	38,900
Income Taxes	346,300	311,100	324,500	283,000	289,200	214,200	94,400	176,600
Net Income	762,600	830,100	621,100	783,800	579,200	525,600	386,000	(137,700)
Average Shares	156,500	153,000	150,500	149,900	150,300	154,000	155,300	157,600
Balance Sheet								
Current Assets	3,780,900	3,930,100	3,192,700	2,641,900	2,281,600	1,903,100	1,969,600	2,264,500
Total Assets	13,956,900	14,668,300	13,201,500	7,883,600	7,444,900	5,822,200	5,300,900	5,764,100
Current Liabilities	2,093,900	2,515,400	2,817,900	2,036,000	2,133,500	1,514,700	1,258,440	2,039,900
Long-Term Obligations	3,942,700	5,034,900	4,889,900	1,239,500	1,242,600	841,700	950,300	1,151,800
Total Liabilities	7,712,900	9,380,600	9,181,100	4,300,600	4,355,900	3,110,100	2,807,400	3,628,200
Stockholders' Equity	5,685,500	4,728,000	3,645,600	3,209,600	2,719,500	2,313,200	2,102,700	2,135,900
Shares Outstanding	153,913	151,909	146,290	144,285	146,264	146,990	147,997	153,508
Statistical Record								
Return on Assets %	5.33	5.96	5.89	10.20	8.73	9.45	6.98	N.M.
Return on Equity %	14.65	19.83	18.12	26.37	23.02	23.80	18.21	N.M.
EBITDA Margin %	19.78	20.47	18.51	19.00	18.35	17.51	14.22	7.00
Net Margin %	8.91	9.47	8.80	10.71	9.32	9.26	6.80	N.M.
Asset Turnover	0.60	0.63	0.67	0.95	0.94	1.02	1.03	0.96
Current Ratio	1.81	1.56	1.13	1.30	1.07	1.26	1.57	1.11
Debt to Equity	0.69	1.06	1.34	0.39	0.46	0.36	0.45	0.54
Price Range	89.30-72.36	85.35-68.88	90.00-70.68	74.23-62.98	67.26-38.29	54.26-35.24	37.82-27.34	31.10-18.29
P/E Ratio	18.34-14.86	15.75-12.71	21.79-17.11	14.19-12.04	17.42-9.92	15.91-10.34	15.19-10.98	...
Average Yield %	2.01	1.96	1.71	1.82	2.24	2.20	2.93	3.77

Address: 520 Lake Cook Road, Deerfield, IL 60015-5611 Telephone: 847-484-4400 Fax: 847-478-0073	Web Site: www.fortunebrands.com Officers: Norman H. Wesley - Chmn., C.E.O. Mark Hausberg - Sr. V.P., Fin., Treas.	Auditors: PricewaterhouseCoopers LLP Investor Contact: 847-484-4410 Transfer Agents: Bank of New York, New York, NY

FOUNDATION COAL HOLDINGS INC

Exchange	Symbol	Price	52Wk Range	Yield	P/E
NYS	FCL	$50.33 (3/31/2008)	59.42-32.26	0.40	71.90

*7 Year Price Score N/A   *NYSE Composite Index=100   *12 Month Price Score 134.18

Interim Earnings (Per Share)

Qtr.	Mar	Jun	Sep	Dec
2005	0.41	0.44	0.46	0.61
2006	0.67	0.46	0.00	(0.46)
2007	0.53	(0.08)	0.04	0.21

Interim Dividends (Per Share)

Amt	Decl	Ex	Rec	Pay
0.05Q	5/22/2007	6/13/2007	6/15/2007	6/28/2007
0.05Q	9/13/2007	9/19/2007	9/23/2007	9/28/2007
0.05Q	12/13/2007	12/19/2007	12/23/2007	12/28/2007
0.05Q	2/12/2008	3/11/2008	3/13/2008	3/27/2008

Indicated Div: $0.20

Valuation Analysis

		Institutional Holding	
Forecast P/E	N/A	No of Institutions	168
Market Cap	$2.3 Billion	Shares	43,940,560
Book Value	336.3 Million	% Held	97.41
Price/Book	6.73		
Price/Sales	1.52		

Business Summary: Coal Mining (MIC: 14.4 SIC: 1221 NAIC: 212111)

Foundation Coal Holdings is a producer of coal. As of Dec 31 2007, Co. operated 13 mines located in Wyoming, Pennsylvania and West Virginia. As of this date, Co. had approximately 1.6 billion tons of proven and probable coal reserves. Co. is also involved in marketing coal produced by others to supplement its own production and, through blending, provides its customers with coal qualities beyond those available from its own production. Co. is primarily a supplier of steam coal to U.S. utilities for use in generating electricity. Co. also sells steam coal to industrial plants and metallurgical coal to steel producers.

Recent Developments: For the year ended Dec 31 2007, net income increased 3.8% to US$32.6 million from US$31.4 million in the prior year. Revenues were US$1.49 billion, up 1.3% from US$1.47 billion the year before. Operating income was US$74.6 million versus US$96.9 million in the prior year, a decrease of 23.0%. Direct operating expenses rose 1.9% to US$1.13 billion from US$1.11 billion in the comparable period the year before. Indirect operating expenses increased 8.0% to US$283.5 million from US$262.5 million in the equivalent prior-year period.

Prospects: Co.'s near term outlook is supported by the growing global demand for coal. For 2008, Co. projects total revenue of $1.60 billion to $1.65 billion, net income of $50.0 million to $70.0 million and earnings per diluted share of $1.05 to $1.55. Based on its committed and priced planned shipments as of Jan 25 2008, Co. expects its committed and priced tonnage from its Eastern mines, encompassing Northern Appalachia and Central Appalachia, to realize $46.99, $44.62 and $17.24 per ton in 2008, 2009 and 2010, respectively. Co. also expects its committed and priced tonnage from the Powder River Basin to realize $9.95, $10.18, $10.55 and $10.85 per ton in 2008, 2009, 2010 and 2011, respectively.

Financial Data

(US$ in Thousands)	12/31/2007	12/31/2006	12/31/2005	12/31/2004
Earnings Per Share	0.70	0.67	1.92	0.58
Cash Flow Per Share	5.34	4.97	4.13	...
Tang Book Value Per Share	7.48	6.56	7.59	6.21
Dividends Per Share	0.200	0.200	0.180	...
Dividend Payout %	28.57	29.85	9.38	...
Income Statement				
Income Before Taxes	24,493	35,250	135,364	28,077
Income Taxes	(8,114)	3,831	46,461	13,600
Net Income	32,607	31,419	88,903	14,477
Average Shares	46,422	46,813	46,275	25,018
Balance Sheet				
Total Assets	1,908,164	1,949,580	2,008,120	2,545,230
Total Liabilities	1,571,827	1,651,767	1,668,870	2,288,467
Stockholders' Equity	336,337	297,813	339,250	256,763
Shares Outstanding	44,991	45,432	44,685	41,362
Statistical Record				
Return on Assets %	1.69	1.59	3.90	...
Return on Equity %	10.28	9.86	29.83	...
Price Range	52.60-29.93	55.86-29.15	38.98-20.00	23.38-21.50
P/E Ratio	75.14-42.76	83.37-43.51	20.30-10.42	40.31-37.07
Average Yield %	0.52	0.51	0.62	...

Address: 999 Corporate Boulevard, Suite 300, Linthicum Heights, MD 21090 Telephone: 410-689-7500	Web Site: www.foundationcoal.com Officers: William E. Macaulay - Chmn. James F. Roberts - Pres., C.E.O.	Auditors: Ernst & Young LLP Transfer Agents: The Bank of New York, New York, NY

FPL GROUP, INC.

Exchange	Symbol	Price	52Wk Range	Yield	P/E	Div Acheiver
NYS	FPL	$62.74 (3/31/2008)	72.56-54.92	2.84	19.19	12 Years

*7 Year Price Score 127.92 *NYSE Composite Index=100 *12 Month Price Score 106.38

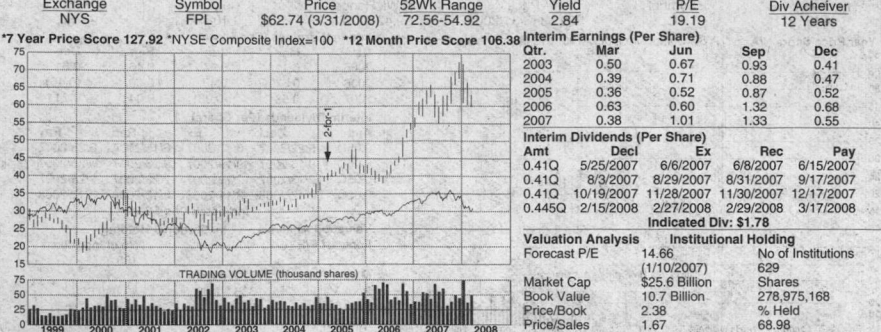

Interim Earnings (Per Share)

Qtr.	Mar	Jun	Sep	Dec
2003	0.50	0.67	0.93	0.41
2004	0.39	0.71	0.88	0.47
2005	0.36	0.52	0.87	0.52
2006	0.63	0.60	1.32	0.68
2007	0.38	1.01	1.33	0.55

Interim Dividends (Per Share)

Amt	Decl	Ex	Rec	Pay
0.41Q	5/25/2007	6/6/2007	6/8/2007	6/15/2007
0.41Q	8/3/2007	8/29/2007	8/31/2007	9/17/2007
0.41Q	10/19/2007	11/28/2007	11/30/2007	12/17/2007
0.445Q	2/15/2008	2/27/2008	2/29/2008	3/17/2008
		Indicated Div: $1.78		

Valuation Analysis

			Institutional Holding	
Forecast P/E	14.66		No of Institutions	
	(1/10/2007)		629	
Market Cap	$25.6 Billion		Shares	
Book Value	10.7 Billion		278,975,168	
Price/Book	2.38		% Held	
Price/Sales	1.67		68.98	

Business Summary: Electricity (MIC: 7.1 SIC: 4911 NAIC: 221121)

FPL Group is a holding company whose operations are conducted primarily through its wholly-owned subsidiary Florida Power & Light Company (FPL) and its wholly-owned indirect subsidiary FPL Energy, LLC (FPL Energy). FPL, a rate-regulated public utility, supplied electric service to approximately 4.5 million customer accounts throughout most of the east and lower west coasts of Florida, as of Dec 31 2007. FPL Energy invests in independent power projects through both controlled and consolidated entities and non-controlling ownership interests in joint ventures essentially all of which are accounted for under the equity method.

Recent Developments: For the year ended Dec 31 2007, net income increased 2.4% to US$1.31 billion from US$1.28 billion in the prior year. Revenues were US$15.26 billion, down 2.8% from US$15.71 billion the year before. Operating income was US$2.28 billion versus US$2.10 billion in the prior year, an increase of 8.9%. Direct operating expenses declined 4.2% to US$10.51 billion from US$10.97 billion in the comparable period the year before. Indirect operating expenses decreased 6.6% to US$2.47 billion from US$2.65 billion in the equivalent prior-year period.

Prospects: Co. continues to expect solid growth from its FPL Energy, LLC subsidiary, driven by new wind projects, as well as an expected increase in contribution from merchant assets and asset acquisitions. For instance, FPL Energy expects to add at least 1,100 megawatts of new wind projects to its portfolio in 2008, with construction already underway on a number of projects representing more than 700 megawatts that are expected to reach commercial operation by the end of 2008. However, the near-term outlook at Co.'s Florida Power & Light Company subsidiary appears somewhat uncertain due to the slowdown in customer and revenue growth, and the expectation of continued cost pressures.

Financial Data

(US$ in Thousands)	12/31/2007	12/31/2006	12/31/2005	12/31/2004	12/31/2003	12/31/2002	12/31/2001	12/31/2000
Earnings Per Share	3.27	3.23	2.29	2.46	2.50	1.37	2.31	2.07
Cash Flow Per Share	9.03	6.35	4.07	7.37	6.35	6.76	5.76	2.86
Tang Book Value Per Share	26.35	24.49	21.52	20.24	18.93	17.46	17.09	15.91
Dividends Per Share	1.640	1.500	1.420	1.300	1.200	1.160	1.120	1.080
Dividend Payout %	50.15	46.44	62.01	52.95	48.00	84.98	48.48	52.17
Income Statement								
Total Revenue	15,263,000	15,710,000	11,846,000	10,522,000	9,630,000	8,311,000	8,475,000	7,082,000
EBITDA	3,809,000	3,731,000	3,159,000	2,852,000	2,758,000	2,158,000	2,467,000	2,350,000
Income Before Taxes	1,680,000	1,678,000	1,157,000	1,154,000	1,261,000	939,000	1,160,000	1,040,000
Income Taxes	368,000	397,000	272,000	267,000	368,000	244,000	379,000	336,000
Net Income	1,312,000	1,281,000	885,000	887,000	890,000	473,000	781,000	704,000
Average Shares	400,600	396,500	385,700	361,600	356,400	346,600	337,800	340,000
Balance Sheet								
Net PPE	28,652,000	24,499,000	22,463,000	21,226,000	20,297,000	14,304,000	11,662,000	9,934,000
Total Assets	40,123,000	35,991,000	33,004,000	28,333,000	26,935,000	19,790,000	17,463,000	15,300,000
Long-Term Obligations	11,280,000	9,591,000	8,039,000	8,027,000	8,723,000	5,790,000	4,858,000	3,976,000
Total Liabilities	29,388,000	26,061,000	24,505,000	20,796,000	19,963,000	13,174,000	11,222,000	9,481,000
Stockholders' Equity	10,735,000	9,930,000	8,499,000	7,537,000	6,972,000	6,616,000	6,241,000	5,819,000
Shares Outstanding	407,344	405,404	394,854	372,351	368,000	366,000	352,000	351,532
Statistical Record								
Return on Assets %	3.45	3.71	2.89	3.20	3.81	2.54	4.77	4.89
Return on Equity %	12.70	13.90	11.04	12.19	13.10	7.36	12.95	12.30
EBITDA Margin %	24.96	23.75	26.67	27.11	28.64	25.97	29.11	33.18
Net Margin %	8.60	8.15	7.47	8.43	9.24	5.69	9.22	9.94
PPE Turnover	0.57	0.67	0.54	0.51	0.56	0.64	0.78	0.74
Asset Turnover	0.40	0.46	0.39	0.38	0.41	0.45	0.52	0.49
Debt to Equity	1.05	0.97	0.95	1.07	1.25	0.88	0.78	0.68
Price Range	72.56-53.85	55.10-38.03	47.84-36.03	37.98-30.48	33.91-27.10	32.45-23.15	35.13-25.95	36.25-18.41
P/E Ratio	22.19-16.47	17.06-11.77	20.89-15.73	15.44-12.39	13.57-10.84	23.69-16.90	15.21-11.23	17.51-8.89
Average Yield %	2.66	3.42	3.42	3.89	3.88	4.06	3.87	4.10

Address: 700 Universe Boulevard, Juno Beach, FL 33408-0420	Web Site: www.fplgroup.com	Auditors: Deloitte & Touche LLP
Telephone: 561-694-4000	Officers: Lewis Hay III - Chmn., Pres., C.E.O. Moray P. Dewhurst - V.P., Fin., C.F.O.	Transfer Agents: ComputerShare Investor Services, Chicago, IL
Fax: 561-694-4620		

FRANKLIN RESOURCES, INC.

Exchange	Symbol	Price	52Wk Range	Yield	P/E	Div Acheiver
NYS	BEN	$96.99 (3/31/2008)	143.95-87.22	0.82	12.97	18 Years

*7 Year Price Score 138.55 *NYSE Composite Index=100   *12 Month Price Score 87.22

TRADING VOLUME (thousand shares)

Interim Earnings (Per Share)

Qtr.	Dec	Mar	Jun	Sep
2004-05	0.92	0.85	1.00	1.28
2005-06	1.21	0.74	1.41	1.49
2006-07	1.67	1.73	1.86	1.77
2007-08	2.12	...	...	...

Interim Dividends (Per Share)

Amt	Decl	Ex	Rec	Pay
0.15Q	6/19/2007	6/27/2007	6/29/2007	7/13/2007
0.15Q	9/19/2007	10/2/2007	10/4/2007	10/12/2007
0.20Q	12/14/2007	12/26/2007	12/28/2007	1/11/2008
0.20Q	3/4/2008	3/26/2008	3/28/2008	4/11/2008

Indicated Div: $0.80 (Div. Reinv. Plan)

Valuation Analysis

Forecast P/E	16.59
	(1/10/2007)
Market Cap	$23.3 Billion
Book Value	7.0 Billion
Price/Book	3.32
Price/Sales	3.60

Institutional Holding

No of Institutions	482
Shares	117,312,792
% Held	46.25

Business Summary: Wealth Management (MIC: 8.8 SIC. 6282 NAIC: 523930)

Franklin Resources provides investment management, fund administration, shareholder services, transfer agency, underwriting, distribution, custodial, trustee and other fiduciary services (collectively investment management and related services) to the Franklin, Templeton, Mutual Series, Bissett, Fiduciary Trust and Darby funds, institutional, high net-worth and other investment accounts and products, collectively called its sponsored investment products. Services to Co.'s sponsored investment products are provided under contracts that set forth the level and nature of the fees to be charged for these services. As of Sep 30 2007, Co. had $645.90 billion in assets under its management.

Recent Developments: For the quarter ended Dec 31 2007, net income increased 21.4% to US$518.3 million from US$426.8 million in the year-earlier quarter. Revenues were US$1.69 billion, up 18.1% from US$1.43 billion the year before. Operating income was US$635.7 million versus US$508.1 million in the prior-year quarter, an increase of 25.1%. Indirect operating expenses increased 14.1% to US$1.05 billion from US$919.7 million in the equivalent prior-year period.

Prospects: Co. is experiencing robust growth in operating revenues, driven primarily by an increase in Investment Management Fees. Specifically, Co. is benefiting from improvement in simple monthly average assets under management and growth in its effective investment management fee rate, resulting from a shift in simple monthly average assets from fixed-income products towards equity products. In addition, Co. is seeing higher assets under management, primarily due to favorable market and excess sales over redemptions. Looking ahead, Co. expects to focus on its core strategies of expanding its assets under management and related operations globally, while closely managing its costs.

Financial Data
(US$ in Thousands)

	3 Mos	09/30/2007	09/30/2006	09/30/2005	09/30/2004	09/30/2003	09/30/2002	09/30/2001
Earnings Per Share	7.48	7.03	4.86	4.06	2.80	1.97	1.65	1.91
Cash Flow Per Share	5.49	6.72	5.01	4.35	3.78	2.16	2.82	2.19
Tang Book Value Per Share	20.67	21.49	18.57	14.39	12.23	9.31	8.69	7.63
Dividends Per Share	0.650	0.570	0.360	2.400	0.415	0.295	0.275	0.195
Dividend Payout %	8.69	8.11	7.41	59.11	14.82	14.97	16.67	10.21
Income Statement								
Total Revenue	1,685,591	6,205,769	5,050,726	4,310,098	3,438,208	2,624,448	2,518,532	2,354,843
Income Before Taxes	709,480	2,465,301	1,835,566	1,420,855	993,866	700,203	578,275	637,790
Income Taxes	191,164	692,363	567,998	363,224	291,981	197,373	145,552	153,069
Net Income	518,316	1,772,938	1,267,368	1,057,631	706,664	502,830	432,723	484,721
Average Shares	244,147	252,118	261,745	262,561	252,152	254,681	262,054	253,663
Balance Sheet								
Total Assets	9,672,751	9,943,250	9,499,859	8,893,927	8,228,135	6,970,749	6,422,738	6,265,650
Total Liabilities	2,621,858	2,569,571	2,719,335	3,133,436	3,045,262	2,660,641	2,155,792	2,287,754
Stockholders' Equity	7,012,891	7,332,275	6,684,728	5,684,384	5,106,784	4,310,108	4,266,946	3,977,896
Shares Outstanding	239,729	245,469	253,249	252,744	249,680	245,931	258,555	260,797
Statistical Record								
Return on Assets %	19.28	18.24	13.78	12.35	9.27	7.51	6.82	9.40
Return on Equity %	26.39	25.30	20.50	19.60	14.97	11.73	10.50	13.96
Price Range	143.95-109.29	143.95-103.87	105.79-78.24	84.34-55.76	60.05-43.56	46.80-28.18	44.13-30.97	47.83-31.90
P/E Ratio	19.24-14.61	20.48-14.78	21.77-16.10	20.77-13.73	21.45-15.56	23.76-14.30	26.75-18.77	25.04-16.70
Average Yield %	0.51	0.46	0.39	3.38	0.80	0.80	0.73	0.47

Address: One Franklin Parkway, San Mateo, CA 94403 **Telephone:** 650-312-2000 **Fax:** 650-312-3655	**Web Site:** www.franklinresources.com **Officers:** Charles B. Johnson - Chmn. Harmon E. Burns - Vice-Chmn.	**Auditors:** PricewaterhouseCoopers LLP **Investor Contact:** 800-632-2350 **Transfer Agents:** Bank of New York

FREDDIE MAC

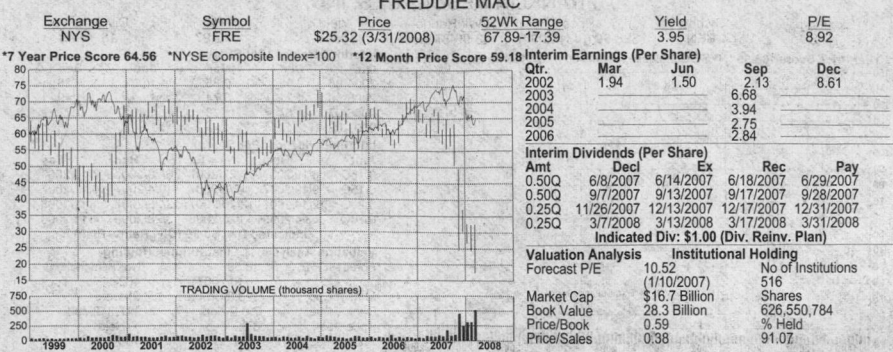

Exchange	Symbol	Price	52Wk Range	Yield	P/E
NYS	FRE	$25.32 (3/31/2008)	67.89-17.39	3.95	8.92

*7 Year Price Score 64.56   *NYSE Composite Index=100   *12 Month Price Score 59.18

Interim Earnings (Per Share)

Qtr.	Mar	Jun	Sep	Dec
2002	1.94	1.50	2.13	8.61
2003			6.68	
2004			3.94	
2005			2.75	
2006			2.84	

Interim Dividends (Per Share)

Amt	Decl	Ex	Rec	Pay
0.50Q	6/8/2007	6/14/2007	6/18/2007	6/29/2007
0.50Q	9/7/2007	9/13/2007	9/17/2007	9/28/2007
0.25Q	11/26/2007	12/13/2007	12/17/2007	12/31/2007
0.25Q	3/7/2008	3/13/2008	3/17/2008	3/31/2008

Indicated Div: $1.00 (Div. Reinv. Plan)

Valuation Analysis

		Institutional Holding	
Forecast P/E	10.52 (1/10/2007)	No of Institutions	516
Market Cap	$16.7 Billion	Shares	626,550,784
Book Value	28.3 Billion	% Held	91.07
Price/Book	0.59		
Price/Sales	0.38		

Business Summary: Credit & Lending (MIC: 8.6 SIC: 6111 NAIC: 522292)

Freddie Mac is a stockholder-owned company chartered by Congress in 1970 to stabilize the nation's residential mortgage markets and expand opportunities for homeownership and affordable rental housing. Co. purchases mortgages and bundle them into mortgage-related securities that can be sold to investors. Co. also purchases mortgage loans and mortgage-related securities for its investments portfolio. Co. finances its purchases for its investments portfolio and manages associated interest-rate and other market risks primarily by issuing a variety of debt instruments and entering into derivative contracts in the capital markets.

Recent Developments: For the year ended Dec 31 2006, net income increased 3.8% to US$2.21 billion from US$2.13 billion in the prior year. Net interest income decreased 9.5% to US$5.82 billion from US$6.43 billion in the prior year. Non-interest income rose 359.8% to US$915.0 million from US$199.0 million, while non-interest expense advanced 1.1% to US$3.05 billion.

Prospects: Co.'s operating results are being negatively affected by weakening house prices and deteriorating credit conditions. In response, Co. stated that it has begun raising prices, tightened its credit standards and enhanced its risk management practices. Furthermore, Co. believes that the market shift towards fixed rate originations and improved pricing and credit standards should strengthen its position it the weakness in credit markets begins to improve. However, the exact timing of this improvement is unknown. Meanwhile, remediation of the material weaknesses and significant deficiencies in its financial reporting process continues to be a top corporate priority for Co. in 2007.

Financial Data

(US$ in Thousands)	12/31/2006	12/31/2005	12/31/2004	12/31/2003	12/31/2002	12/31/2001	12/31/2000	12/31/1999
Earnings Per Share	2.84	2.75	3.94	6.68	14.18	5.64	3.40	2.96
Cash Flow Per Share	13.54	8.88	75.02	6.52	24.53	25.61	20.95	(17.82)
Tang Book Value Per Share	33.56	32.60	38.82	39.03	38.87	15.50	16.81	11.98
Dividends Per Share	1.910	1.520	1.200	1.040	0.880	0.800	0.680	0.600
Dividend Payout %	67.25	55.27	30.46	15.57	6.21	14.18	20.00	20.27
Income Statement								
Interest Income	43,087,000	36,327,000	35,603,000	37,098,000	38,476,000	34,288,000	28,350,000	22,753,000
Interest Expense	37,270,000	29,899,000	26,566,000	26,509,000	26,564,000	28,808,000	25,512,000	20,213,000
Net Interest Income	5,817,000	6,428,000	9,037,000	10,589,000	11,912,000	5,480,000	2,838,000	2,540,000
Provision for Losses	...	...	...	...	...	45,000	40,000	60,000
Non-Interest Income	915,000	199,000	(3,039,000)	(259,000)	7,782,000	1,885,000	1,619,000	1,515,000
Non-Interest Expense	3,047,000	3,013,000	2,371,000	2,221,000	1,865,000	1,020,000	883,000	834,000
Income Before Taxes	2,103,000	2,556,000	3,727,000	7,018,000	14,803,000	6,300,000	3,534,000	3,161,000
Income Taxes	(108,000)	367,000	790,000	2,202,000	4,713,000	1,927,000	995,000	943,000
Net Income	2,211,000	2,130,000	2,937,000	4,816,000	10,090,000	4,147,000	2,547,000	2,223,000
Average Shares	682,664	693,511	691,521	688,675	695,116	696,876	696,448	700,211
Balance Sheet								
Net Loans & Leases	700,543,000	709,384,000	664,468,000	660,357,000	589,722,000	494,259,000	385,117,000	322,569,000
Total Assets	813,081,000	806,222,000	795,284,000	803,449,000	752,249,000	617,340,000	459,297,000	386,684,000
Total Liabilities	784,264,000	778,082,000	762,359,000	770,033,000	718,610,000	598,367,000	443,865,000	374,602,000
Stockholders' Equity	28,301,000	27,191,000	31,416,000	31,487,000	31,330,000	15,373,000	14,837,000	11,525,000
Shares Outstanding	661,254	692,717	690,606	688,573	687,376	695,304	692,584	695,091
Statistical Record								
Return on Assets %	0.27	0.27	0.37	0.62	1.47	0.77	0.60	0.63
Return on Equity %	7.97	7.27	9.31	15.33	43.21	27.45	19.27	19.88
Net Interest Margin %	13.50	17.69	25.38	28.54	30.96	15.98	10.01	11.16
Efficiency Ratio %	6.92	8.25	7.28	6.03	4.03	2.82	2.95	3.44
Price Range	71.23-55.80	73.70-54.60	73.70-56.93	64.73-47.35	68.60-53.98	70.79-60.00	69.00-37.69	64.63-45.75
P/E Ratio	25.08-19.65	26.80-19.85	18.71-14.45	9.69-7.09	4.84-3.81	12.55-10.64	20.29-11.08	21.83-15.46
Average Yield %	3.00	2.40	1.88	1.88	1.41	1.22	1.41	1.08

Address: 8200 Jones Branch Drive, McLean, VA 22102-3110 **Telephone:** 571-382-4732	**Web Site:** www.freddiemac.com **Officers:** Richard F. Syron - Chmn., C.E.O. Eugene M. McQuade - Pres., C.O.O.	**Auditors:** PricewaterhouseCoopers LLP **Investor Contact:** 800-373-3343 **Transfer Agents:** EquiServe Trust Company, N.A., Jersey City, NJ

FREEPORT-MCMORAN COPPER & GOLD INC.

Exchange	Symbol	Price	52Wk Range	Yield	P/E
NYS	FCX	$96.22 (3/31/2008)	117.86-66.73	1.82	12.83

*7 Year Price Score 174.03 *NYSE Composite Index=100 *12 Month Price Score 113.29

Interim Earnings (Per Share)

Qtr.	Mar	Jun	Sep	Dec
2003	0.33	0.37	0.29	0.00
2004	(0.10)	(0.30)	0.10	1.15
2005	0.70	0.91	0.86	2.19
2006	1.23	1.74	1.67	1.99
2007	2.02	2.62	1.87	0.92

Interim Dividends (Per Share)

Amt	Decl	Ex	Rec	Pay
0.313Q	6/28/2007	7/12/2007	7/16/2007	8/1/2007
0.313Q	9/27/2007	10/11/2007	10/15/2007	11/1/2007
0.438Q	12/27/2007	1/11/2008	1/15/2008	2/1/2008
0.438Q	3/27/2008	4/11/2008	4/15/2008	5/1/2008

Indicated Div: $1.75

Valuation Analysis / **Institutional Holding**

Forecast P/E	7.86	No of Institutions	
	(1/10/2007)	473	
Market Cap	$36.9 Billion	Shares	
Book Value	18.2 Billion	202,020,464	
Price/Book	2.02	% Held	
Price/Sales	2.18	52.88	

Business Summary: Non-Precious Metals (MIC: 14.3 SIC: 1021 NAIC: 212234)

Freeport-McMoran Copper & Gold is engaged in copper, gold and molybdenum mining and production. Co. has six operating copper mines in North America: Morenci, Bagdad, Sierrita and Safford in Arizona, and Chino and Tyrone in New Mexico, as well as one operating molybdenum mine, Henderson in Colorado. Co. has four operating copper mines in South America, of which Co. owns a 53.56% interest in Cerro Verde, 80.0% interests in Candelaria and Ojos del Salado, and a 51.0% interest in El Abra, in Chile. Co. owns 90.64% of PT Freeport Indonesia, including 9.36% owned through its wholly owned subsidiary, PT Indocopper Investama. Co. also has a 57.75% interest in the Tenke Fungurume project in Africa.

Recent Developments: For the year ended Dec 31 2007, income from continuing operations increased 101.9% to US$2.94 billion from US$1.46 billion a year earlier. Net income increased 104.3% to US$2.98 billion from US$1.46 billion in the prior year. Revenues were US$16.94 billion, up 192.5% from US$5.79 billion the year before. Operating income was US$6.56 billion versus US$2.87 billion in the prior year, an increase of 128.5%. Direct operating expenses rose 255.0% to US$9.77 billion from US$2.75 billion in the comparable period the year before. Indirect operating expenses increased 261.5% to US$611.0 million from US$169.0 million in the equivalent prior-year period.

Prospects: For 2008, Co.'s expects consolidated sales volumes of about 4.30 billion pounds of copper, 1.3 million ounces of gold and 75.0 million pounds of molybdenum. Specifically, for the first quarter of 2008, Co. expects sales volumes of about 885.0 million pounds of copper, 170 thousand ounces of gold and 19.0 million pounds of molybdenum. Further, due to mine sequencing at Grasberg and the ramp-up of production at Safford, Co. expects higher second-half 2008 production, with about 56.0% of consolidated copper sales and 72.0% of consolidated gold sales. Meanwhile, Co. plans to expand its production profile and advance its development projects in Congo, Americas and Indonesia going forward.

Financial Data

(US$ in Thousands)	12/31/2007	12/31/2006	12/31/2005	12/31/2004	12/31/2003	12/31/2002	12/31/2001	12/31/2000
Earnings Per Share	7.50	6.63	4.67	0.85	0.97	0.87	0.53	0.26
Cash Flow Per Share	18.26	9.79	8.61	1.87	3.67	3.54	3.54	3.34
Tang Book Value Per Share	20.06	6.83	3.98	0.36	4.23	...	...	...
Dividends Per Share	1.375	4.750	2.500	1.100	0.270	...	...	...
Dividend Payout %	18.33	71.64	53.53	129.41	27.84	...	...	...
Income Statement								
Total Revenue	16,939,000	5,790,500	4,179,118	2,371,866	2,212,165	1,910,462	1,838,866	1,868,610
EBITDA	7,910,000	3,133,997	2,427,685	937,396	1,027,791	893,346	816,260	762,142
Income Before Taxes	6,133,000	2,825,871	2,036,938	574,384	583,775	449,662	358,776	273,240
Income Taxes	2,400,000	1,201,175	915,068	330,680	338,053	245,518	202,979	159,573
Net Income	2,977,000	1,456,509	995,127	202,267	181,660	164,654	113,025	76,987
Average Shares	397,000	221,498	220,470	184,923	159,102	146,418	144,938	134,519
Balance Sheet								
Current Assets	5,903,000	2,151,037	2,022,382	1,459,947	1,100,133	637,980	548,270	569,122
Total Assets	40,661,000	5,389,802	5,550,206	5,086,995	4,718,366	4,192,193	4,211,929	3,950,741
Current Liabilities	3,869,000	972,449	1,368,978	697,562	631,782	537,873	628,427	633,912
Long-Term Obligations	7,180,000	660,999	1,002,598	1,873,692	2,075,934	1,961,278	2,133,180	1,987,731
Total Liabilities	21,188,000	2,944,701	3,707,212	3,923,346	3,942,382	3,925,367	4,107,485	3,912,810
Stockholders' Equity	18,234,000	2,445,101	1,842,994	1,163,649	775,984	266,826	104,444	37,931
Shares Outstanding	383,000	196,965	186,806	178,990	183,367	144,909	143,975	144,041
Statistical Record								
Return on Assets %	12.93	26.63	18.71	4.11	4.08	3.92	...	1.91
Return on Equity %	28.79	67.93	66.20	20.80	34.84	88.70	...	65.39
EBITDA Margin %	46.70	54.12	58.09	39.52	46.46	46.76	44.39	40.79
Net Margin %	17.57	25.15	23.81	8.53	8.21	8.62	6.15	4.12
Asset Turnover	0.74	1.06	0.79	0.48	0.50	0.45	...	0.46
Current Ratio	1.53	2.21	1.48	2.09	1.74	1.19	0.87	0.90
Debt to Equity	0.39	0.27	0.54	1.61	2.68	7.35	20.42	52.40
Price Range	117.86-50.49	72.09-43.75	55.36-32.06	44.45-28.40	46.24-16.01	20.80-10.48	16.98-8.31	21.19-6.75
P/E Ratio	15.71-6.73	10.87-6.60	11.85-6.87	52.29-33.41	47.67-16.51	23.91-12.05	32.04-15.68	81.49-25.96
Average Yield %	1.68	8.36	5.98	3.00	1.01	...	...	...

Address: 1615 Poydras Street, New Orleans, LA 70112
Telephone: 504-582-4000
Fax: 504-582-1847

Web Site: www.fcx.com
Officers: James R. Moffett - Chmn., C.E.O. B. M. Rankin Jr. - Vice-Chmn.

Auditors: Ernst & Young LLP
Transfer Agents: Mellon Investor Services LLC

FRONTIER OIL CORP.

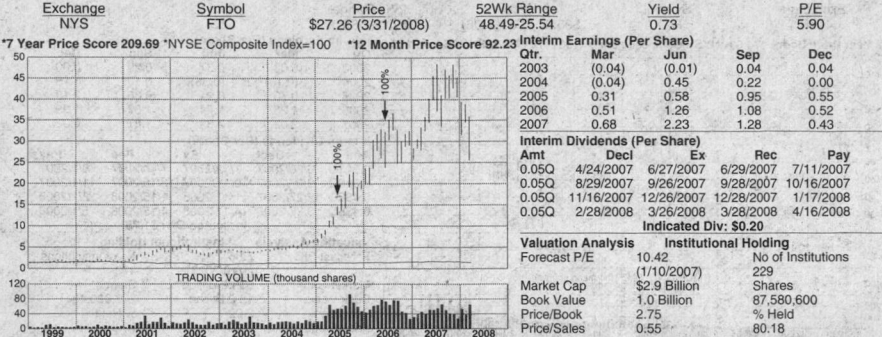

Exchange	Symbol	Price	52Wk Range	Yield	P/E
NYS	FTO	$27.26 (3/31/2008)	48.49-25.54	0.73	5.90

*7 Year Price Score 209.69 *NYSE Composite Index=100 *12 Month Price Score 92.23

Interim Earnings (Per Share)

Qtr.	Mar	Jun	Sep	Dec
2003	(0.04)	(0.01)	0.04	0.04
2004	(0.04)	0.45	0.22	0.00
2005	0.31	0.58	0.95	0.55
2006	0.51	1.26	1.08	0.52
2007	0.68	2.23	1.28	0.43

Interim Dividends (Per Share)

Amt	Decl	Ex	Rec	Pay
0.05Q	4/24/2007	6/27/2007	6/29/2007	7/11/2007
0.05Q	8/29/2007	9/26/2007	9/28/2007	10/16/2007
0.05Q	11/16/2007	12/26/2007	12/28/2007	1/17/2008
0.05Q	2/28/2008	3/26/2008	3/28/2008	4/16/2008

Indicated Div: $0.20

Valuation Analysis | **Institutional Holding**

Forecast P/E	10.42	No of Institutions
(1/10/2007)		229
Market Cap	$2.9 Billion	Shares
Book Value	1.0 Billion	87,580,600
Price/Book	2.75	% Held
Price/Sales	0.55	80.18

Business Summary: Oil and Gas (MIC: 14.2 SIC: 2911 NAIC: 324110)

Frontier Oil is an energy company engaged in crude oil refining and the wholesale marketing of refined petroleum products. Co. purchases crude oil to be refined and markets refined petroleum products including various grades of gasoline, diesel, jet fuel, asphalt and other by-products. Co. operates refineries in Cheyenne, WY and El Dorado, KS with a total annual average crude oil capacity of 162,000 barrels per day as of Dec 31 2007. Co. markets its products in the Rocky Mountain region and the Plains States of Colorado, Wyoming, Montana, Utah, Kansas, Oklahoma, Nebraska, Iowa, Missouri, North Dakota and South Dakota.

Recent Developments: For the year ended Dec 31 2007, net income increased 31.6% to US$499.1 million from US$379.3 million in the prior year. Revenues were US$5.19 billion, up 8.2% from US$4.80 billion the year before. Operating income was US$755.8 million versus US$574.2 million in the prior year, an increase of 31.6%. Direct operating expenses rose 5.1% to US$4.34 billion from US$4.13 billion in the comparable period the year before. Indirect operating expenses decreased 0.6% to US$93.2 million from US$93.7 million in the equivalent prior-year period.

Prospects: Co.'s near-term outlook appears favorable, reflecting increases in average diesel crack spread and average gasoline crack spread while light/heavy crude oil differentials improved. Looking ahead, Co.'s 2008 capital projects at the Cheyenne Refinery include the $117.0 million coker expansion, with the coke handling portion to be completed in early 2008 thus increasing the amount of higher margin projects, and the new amine unit expected to cost $20.5 million. Co.'s projects at its El Dorado Refinery include the $151.0 million crude unit and vacuum tower expansion expected to be online in the spring of 2008, and the $60.0 million coke drum replacement project to be completed by mid-2008.

Financial Data

(US$ in Thousands)	12/31/2007	12/31/2006	12/31/2005	12/31/2004	12/31/2003	12/31/2002	12/31/2001	12/31/2000
Earnings Per Share	4.62	3.37	2.40	0.64	0.03	0.01	1.00	0.34
Cash Flow Per Share	4.02	3.06	3.25	1.66	(0.06)	0.49	1.33	0.60
Tang Book Value Per Share	9.88	7.02	3.94	2.21	1.60	1.61	1.64	0.77
Dividends Per Share	0.180	0.110	0.575	0.055	0.050	0.050	0.037	...
Dividend Payout %	3.90	3.26	23.96	8.63	166.67	500.00	3.75	...
Income Statement								
Total Revenue	5,188,740	4,795,953	4,001,162	2,861,716	2,170,503	1,813,750	1,888,401	2,045,157
EBITDA	847,138	647,852	491,379	182,799	64,466	56,138	189,490	93,662
Income Before Taxes	768,873	580,114	443,251	112,103	6,188	2,088	135,726	39,281
Income Taxes	269,748	200,837	168,216	42,339	2,956	1,060	28,073	2,075
Net Income	499,125	379,277	272,532	69,764	3,232	1,028	107,653	37,206
Average Shares	107,970	112,512	113,636	109,604	107,964	107,736	107,540	111,156
Balance Sheet								
Current Assets	1,031,023	939,216	748,075	378,679	284,813	308,970	261,370	272,519
Total Assets	1,863,848	1,523,925	1,201,509	754,400	642,297	628,877	581,746	588,213
Current Liabilities	501,513	459,698	485,811	281,418	246,192	200,717	152,306	228,909
Long-Term Obligations	150,000	150,000	150,000	150,000	168,689	207,966	208,880	239,583
Total Liabilities	825,234	748,071	756,450	514,287	473,020	460,619	412,542	506,789
Stockholders' Equity	1,038,614	775,854	445,059	240,113	169,277	168,258	169,204	81,424
Shares Outstanding	104,956	110,344	112,698	108,124	105,515	104,556	103,274	106,269
Statistical Record								
Return on Assets %	29.47	27.83	27.87	9.96	0.51	0.17	18.40	6.69
Return on Equity %	55.02	62.13	79.55	33.99	1.92	0.61	85.91	56.17
EBITDA Margin %	16.33	13.51	12.28	6.39	2.97	3.10	10.03	4.58
Net Margin %	9.62	7.91	6.81	2.44	0.15	0.06	5.70	1.82
Asset Turnover	3.06	3.52	4.09	4.09	3.41	3.00	3.23	3.68
Current Ratio	2.06	2.04	1.54	1.35	1.16	1.54	1.72	1.19
Debt to Equity	0.14	0.19	0.34	0.62	1.00	1.24	1.23	2.94
Price Range	48.49-25.65	36.75-19.81	22.79-6.13	6.67-4.04	4.49-3.50	5.64-2.69	4.88-1.64	2.27-1.30
P/E Ratio	10.50-5.55	10.91-5.88	9.49-2.55	10.41-6.31	149.75-116.83	564.50-268.75	4.88-1.64	6.66-3.81
Average Yield %	0.47	0.39	4.16	1.06	1.24	1.21	1.17	...

Address: 10000 Memorial Drive, Suite 600, Houston, TX 77024-3411
Telephone: 713-688-9600
Fax: 713-688-0610

Web Site: www.frontieroil.com
Officers: James R. Gibbs - Chmn., Pres., C.E.O.
Michael C. Jennings - Exec. V.P., C.F.O.

Auditors: Deloitte & Touche LLP
Transfer Agents: Wells Fargo Shareowner Services, St. Paul, MN

FULLER (H.B.) COMPANY

Exchange	Symbol	Price	52Wk Range	Yield	P/E	Div Acheiver
NYS	FUL	$20.41 (3/31/2008)	31.35-17.99	1.29	13.52	40 Years

*7 Year Price Score 121.12 *NYSE Composite Index=100   ***12 Month Price Score 91.00**

TRADING VOLUME (thousand shares)

Interim Earnings (Per Share)

Qtr.	Feb	May	Aug	Nov
2004-05	0.11	0.28	0.27	0.40
2005-06	0.26	0.33	0.40	1.24
2006-07	0.34	0.44	0.46	0.43
2008-09	0.32	...	...	...

Interim Dividends (Per Share)

Amt	Decl	Ex	Rec	Pay
0.065Q	7/12/2007	7/24/2007	7/26/2007	8/9/2007
0.065Q	10/4/2007	10/16/2007	10/18/2007	11/1/2007
0.065Q	1/24/2008	2/5/2008	2/7/2008	2/21/2008
0.066Q	4/3/2008	4/15/2008	4/17/2008	5/1/2008

Indicated Div: $0.26 (Div. Reinv. Plan)

Valuation Analysis

		Institutional Holding	
Forecast P/E	14.30 (1/10/2007)	No of Institutions	179
Market Cap	$1.1 Billion	Shares	51,459,532
Book Value	765.7 Million	% Held	84.97
Price/Book	1.46		
Price/Sales	0.89		

Business Summary: Chemicals (MIC: 11.1 SIC: 2891 NAIC: 325520)

H.B. Fuller manufactures and markets adhesives and specialty chemical products. Co.'s business is reported in four operating segments: North America, Europe, Latin America and Asia Pacific, with adhesives as the main business component of each of the operating segments. The adhesives business components produce and supply industrial and performance adhesives products for applications in various markets, including assembly, such as woodworking and appliances; converting that includes packaging, corrugated, tape and label, and graphic arts; nonwoven, including disposable diapers, feminine care and adult incontinence products; and footwear.

Recent Developments: For the quarter ended Mar 31 2008, income from continuing operations decreased 2.5% to US$18.2 million from US$18.7 million in the year-earlier quarter. Net income decreased 12.5% to US$18.2 million from US$20.8 million in the year-earlier quarter. Revenues were US$322.6 million, down 3.2% from US$333.4 million the year before. Direct operating expenses declined 1.1% to US$231.1 million from US$233.7 million in the comparable period the year before. Indirect operating expenses decreased 9.2% to US$65.0 million from US$71.6 million in the equivalent prior-year period.

Prospects: For the fiscal year ending Dec 1 2008, Co. continues to anticipate earnings in the range of $1.76 and $1.86 per diluted share. Going forward, Co. intends to continue to make strategic investments, improve its top line results while managing the overall profitability of its operations to attain its near-and-long term objectives. For instance, Co. plans to open a regional technology center in Shanghai, China, which should help drive growth in the Asia Pacific region. Co. believes that the new center will focus on reactive chemistry while promoting product development and localization of initiatives in key market segments. Co. expects the center to be operation before the end of fiscal 2008.

Financial Data

(US$ in Thousands)	3 Mos	12/01/2007	12/02/2006	12/03/2005	11/27/2004	11/29/2003	11/30/2002	12/01/2001
Earnings Per Share	1.51	1.68	2.23	1.05	0.61	0.68	0.49	0.79
Cash Flow Per Share	1.84	2.35	3.20	2.15	2.17	1.06	1.47	1.61
Tang Book Value Per Share	7.71	7.92	6.84	8.33	7.62	7.26	6.30	6.19
Dividends Per Share	0.258	0.256	0.249	0.241	0.229	0.224	0.219	0.214
Dividend Payout %	17.09	15.24	11.15	22.87	37.20	33.15	44.64	27.23
Income Statement								
Total Revenue	322,648	1,400,258	1,472,391	1,512,193	1,409,606	1,287,331	1,256,210	1,274,059
EBITDA	39,479	180,630	144,963	135,651	103,549	104,218	97,203	117,871
Depn & Amortn	11,690	...	...	...	...	...	...	...
Income Before Taxes	24,861	136,887	100,031	82,401	48,298	50,808	40,312	63,470
Income Taxes	7,210	37,712	23,682	21,000	14,713	14,307	12,973	19,833
Net Income	18,213	102,173	134,213	61,576	35,603	38,619	28,176	44,439
Average Shares	57,492	60,991	60,065	58,476	57,818	57,399	57,202	56,660
Balance Sheet								
Current Assets	601,648	635,950	669,094	582,434	553,650	448,492	408,874	403,873
Total Assets	1,329,313	1,364,602	1,478,471	1,107,557	1,135,359	1,007,588	961,439	966,173
Current Liabilities	246,745	297,835	342,442	261,858	293,449	200,026	214,846	204,163
Long-Term Obligations	177,000	137,000	224,000	112,001	138,149	161,047	161,763	203,001
Total Liabilities	563,572	565,609	700,679	523,114	582,300	498,250	513,109	532,147
Stockholders' Equity	765,741	798,993	777,792	584,443	553,059	509,338	448,330	434,026
Shares Outstanding	54,640	57,436	59,931	58,369	57,282	56,870	56,724	56,561
Statistical Record								
Return on Assets %	6.72	7.21	10.41	5.40	3.33	3.93	2.93	4.51
Return on Equity %	11.59	13.00	19.76	10.65	6.72	8.09	6.40	10.63
EBITDA Margin %	12.24	12.90	9.85	8.97	7.35	8.10	7.74	9.25
Net Margin %	5.64	7.30	9.12	4.07	2.53	3.00	2.24	3.49
Asset Turnover	0.93	0.99	1.14	1.33	1.32	1.31	1.31	1.29
Current Ratio	2.44	2.14	1.95	2.22	1.89	2.24	1.90	1.98
Debt to Equity	0.23	0.17	0.29	0.19	0.25	0.32	0.36	0.47
Price Range	31.35-17.99	31.35-24.11	27.54-15.65	17.93-12.73	15.10-12.42	14.75-10.00	16.25-12.27	15.48-8.30
P/E Ratio	20.76-11.91	18.66-14.35	12.35-7.02	17.08-12.12	24.75-20.36	21.69-14.71	33.16-25.04	19.59-10.50
Average Yield %	0.99	0.94	1.14	1.60	1.67	1.83	1.53	1.85

Address: 1200 Willow Lake Boulevard, St. Paul, MN 55110-5101 **Telephone:** 651-236-5900 **Fax:** 651-236-5161	**Web Site:** www.hbfuller.com **Officers:** Albert P. L. Stroucken - Chmn., Pres., C.E.O. John A. Feenan - Sr. V.P., C.F.O.	**Auditors:** KPMG LLP **Investor Contact:** 651-236-5150 **Transfer Agents:** Wells Fargo Shareowner Services, Minnesota, MN

FURNITURE BRANDS INTERNATIONAL INC.

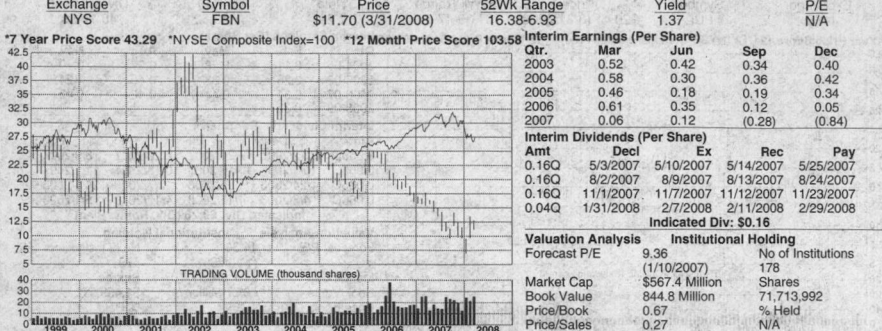

Exchange	Symbol	Price	52Wk Range	Yield	P/E
NYS	FBN	$11.70 (3/31/2008)	16.38-6.93	1.37	N/A

*7 Year Price Score 43.29   *NYSE Composite Index=100   *12 Month Price Score 103.58

Interim Earnings (Per Share)

Qtr.	Mar	Jun	Sep	Dec
2003	0.52	0.42	0.34	0.40
2004	0.58	0.30	0.36	0.42
2005	0.46	0.18	0.19	0.34
2006	0.61	0.35	0.12	0.05
2007	0.06	0.12	(0.28)	(0.84)

Interim Dividends (Per Share)

Amt	Decl	Ex	Rec	Pay
0.16Q	5/3/2007	5/10/2007	5/14/2007	5/25/2007
0.16Q	8/2/2007	8/9/2007	8/13/2007	8/24/2007
0.16Q	11/1/2007	11/7/2007	11/12/2007	11/23/2007
0.04Q	1/31/2008	2/7/2008	2/11/2008	2/29/2008
		Indicated Div: $0.16		

Valuation Analysis

		Institutional Holding	
Forecast P/E	9.36	No of Institutions	
	(1/10/2007)	178	
Market Cap	$567.4 Million	Shares	
Book Value	844.8 Million	71,713,992	
Price/Book	0.67	% Held	
Price/Sales	0.27	N/A	

Business Summary: Furniture and Fixtures (MIC: 11.10 SIC: 2519 NAIC: 337125)

Furniture Brands is a designer, manufacturer, sourcer, and retailer of home furnishings. Co. markets through a range of retail channels, from mass merchant stores to single-branded and independent dealers to specialized interior designers. Co. designs, manufactures, sources, markets and distributes: case goods, consisting of bedroom, dining room and living room furniture; stationary upholstery products, consisting of sofas, loveseats, sectionals and chairs; occasional furniture, consisting of wood, metal and glass tables, accent pieces, home entertainment centers and home office furniture; recliners, motion furniture and sleep sofas; and decorative accessories and accent pieces.

Recent Developments: For the year ended Dec 31 2007, loss from continuing operations was US$51.2 million compared with income of US$49.9 million a year earlier. Net loss amounted to US$45.6 million versus net income of US$55.1 million in the prior year. Revenues were US$2.08 billion, down 11.8% from US$2.36 billion the year before. Operating income was US$53.3 million versus an income of US$75.5 million in the prior year. Direct operating expenses declined 10.1% to US$1.67 billion from US$1.85 billion in the comparable period the year before. Indirect operating expenses increased 8.6% to US$469.4 million from US$432.3 million in the equivalent prior-year period.

Prospects: On Jan 7 2008, Co. announced initiatives to consolidate its distribution center operations and customs compliance efforts, and rollout consolidated container-direct deliveries to larger retailers, which should enable it to coordinate manufacturing and distribution; as well as the establishment of Furniture Brands (Hangzhou) Co., Ltd., which should strengthen its presence in Asia and enable it to improve delivery and reduce product development lead times. Meanwhile, for 2008, Co. expects sales of $1.90 billion to $2.00 billion and diluted net earnings per share of $0.40 to $0.60, excluding its Hickory Business Furniture subsidiary, which it plans to divest in the first quarter of 2008.

Financial Data

(US$ in Thousands)	12/31/2007	12/31/2006	12/31/2005	12/31/2004	12/31/2003	12/31/2002	12/31/2001	12/31/2000
Earnings Per Share	(0.94)	1.13	1.18	1.66	1.68	2.11	1.13	2.10
Cash Flow Per Share	3.16	(0.55)	3.64	1.96	3.09	2.03	3.67	2.66
Tang Book Value Per Share	10.62	11.55	11.11	11.36	10.96	9.24	7.18	5.92
Dividends Per Share	0.640	0.640	0.600	0.525	0.125	...	...	...
Dividend Payout %	...	56.64	50.85	31.63	7.44	...	...	...
Income Statement								
Total Revenue	2,082,056	2,418,175	2,386,774	2,447,430	2,367,738	2,397,709	1,891,313	2,116,239
EBITDA	(16,794)	132,667	146,549	205,869	218,813	254,202	164,601	259,941
Income Before Taxes	(80,478)	80,922	91,994	142,640	149,224	184,424	87,694	165,997
Income Taxes	(29,261)	25,867	30,558	51,073	54,651	65,593	29,664	57,574
Net Income	(45,649)	55,055	61,436	91,567	94,573	118,831	58,030	105,901
Average Shares	48,446	48,753	52,103	55,219	56,255	56,386	51,324	50,442
Balance Sheet								
Current Assets	899,854	941,174	931,668	908,125	886,052	849,459	778,715	691,581
Total Assets	1,463,078	1,558,203	1,582,224	1,587,759	1,578,259	1,567,402	1,503,489	1,304,838
Current Liabilities	187,399	188,556	213,485	197,010	182,819	197,364	175,295	143,118
Long-Term Obligations	280,000	300,800	301,600	302,400	303,200	374,800	454,400	462,000
Total Liabilities	618,312	647,488	678,272	630,276	611,357	697,887	743,830	720,933
Stockholders' Equity	844,766	910,715	903,952	957,483	966,902	869,515	759,659	583,905
Shares Outstanding	48,498	48,336	49,667	53,216	55,946	55,649	54,612	49,675
Statistical Record								
Return on Assets %	N.M.	3.51	3.88	5.77	6.01	7.74	4.13	8.14
Return on Equity %	N.M.	6.07	6.60	9.49	10.30	14.59	8.64	19.96
EBITDA Margin %	N.M.	5.49	6.14	8.41	9.24	10.60	8.70	12.28
Net Margin %	N.M.	2.28	2.57	3.74	3.99	4.96	3.07	5.00
Asset Turnover	1.38	1.54	1.51	1.54	1.51	1.56	1.35	1.63
Current Ratio	4.80	4.99	4.36	4.61	4.85	4.30	4.44	4.83
Debt to Equity	0.33	0.33	0.33	0.32	0.31	0.43	0.60	0.79
Price Range	17.67-9.62	25.07-16.05	25.05-16.60	34.97-21.00	29.33-18.17	42.30-19.02	32.41-18.25	22.00-14.06
P/E Ratio	...	22.19-14.20	21.23-14.07	21.07-12.65	17.46-10.82	20.05-9.01	28.68-16.15	10.48-6.70
Average Yield %	4.71	3.05	2.87	1.97	0.52	...	...	...

Address: 101 South Hanley Road, St. Louis, MO 63105-3493	Web Site: www.furniturebrands.com	Auditors: KPMG LLP
Telephone: 314-863-1100	Officers: Wilbert G. Holliman - Chmn. Lynn Chipperfield - Sr. V.P., Chief Admin. Officer	Transfer Agents: American Stock Transfer & Trust Company
Fax: 314-863-5306		

GALLAGHER (ARTHUR J.) & CO.

Exchange	Symbol	Price	52Wk Range	Yield	P/E	Div Achiever
NYS	AJG	$23.62 (3/31/2008)	31.08-23.24	5.42	16.52	23 Years

*7 Year Price Score 74.75   *NYSE Composite Index=100   *12 Month Price Score 97.05

Interim Earnings (Per Share)

Qtr.	Mar	Jun	Sep	Dec
2003	0.13	0.39	0.52	0.53
2004	0.41	0.49	0.57	0.51
2005	(0.80)	0.54	0.52	0.02
2006	0.17	0.37	0.51	0.25
2007	0.20	0.44	0.54	0.25

Interim Dividends (Per Share)

Amt	Decl	Ex	Rec	Pay
0.31Q	5/15/2007	6/27/2007	6/29/2007	7/16/2007
0.31Q	7/19/2007	9/26/2007	9/28/2007	10/15/2007
0.31Q	10/18/2007	12/27/2007	12/31/2007	1/15/2008
0.32Q	1/25/2008	3/27/2008	3/31/2008	4/15/2008

Indicated Div: $1.28

Valuation Analysis

		Institutional Holding	
Forecast P/E	15.88	No of Institutions	
	(1/10/2007)	228	
Market Cap	$2.2 Billion	Shares	
Book Value	715.5 Million	76,924,688	
Price/Book	3.04	% Held	
Price/Sales	1.34	78.21	

TRADING VOLUME (thousand shares)

Business Summary: Insurance (MIC: 8.2 SIC: 6411 NAIC: 524210)

Arthur J. Gallagher & Co. provides insurance brokerage and third-party claims settlement and administration services to entities in the U.S. and abroad. Co. has three operating segments: Brokerage, which primarily comprised of retail and wholesale brokerage operations; Risk Management, which provides contract claim settlement and administration services; and Financial Services, which manages Co.'s interests in tax-advantaged and clean-energy investments as well as its equity ownership. As of Dec 31 2007, Co. operated through a network of 200 sales and service offices in the U.S. and 12 countries and correspondent brokers and consultants in 100 countries.

Recent Developments: For the year ended Dec 31 2007, income from continuing operations increased 20.4% to US$154.6 million from US$128.4 million a year earlier. Net income increased 8.0% to US$138.8 million from US$128.5 million in the prior year. Revenues were US$1.62 billion, up 10.4% from US$1.47 billion the year before.

Prospects: Co. is focused on expense controls in light of a soft market. Notably, in the near-term, Co. expects to reduce its existing back office workforce by about 400 positions primarily through attrition. Co. has also adopted changes to other workforce related costs such as travel, entertainment, perquisites, and compensation that are expected to reduce its ongoing annualized costs. Meanwhile, Co. expects to complete the sale of its global reinsurance operations in early 2008. Co. also plans to sell its wholesale brokerage operation in Ireland in 2008. While the sale is expected to reduce Co.'s revenues, it should have a positive effect on Co.'s brokerage segment's earnings and pretax margins.

Financial Data
(US$ in Thousands)

	12/31/2007	12/31/2006	12/31/2005	12/31/2004	12/31/2003	12/31/2002	12/31/2001	12/31/2000
Earnings Per Share	1.43	1.31	0.32	1.99	1.57	1.41	1.39	1.05
Cash Flow Per Share	2.63	1.08	2.01	3.02	2.54	1.71	1.54	1.73
Tang Book Value Per Share	N.M.	3.40	3.67	4.20	4.40	4.44	3.60	3.75
Dividends Per Share	1.240	1.200	1.120	1.000	0.720	0.600	0.520	0.460
Dividend Payout %	86.71	91.60	350.00	50.25	45.86	42.55	37.41	43.81
Income Statement								
Total Revenue	1,623,300	1,534,000	1,483,900	1,480,300	1,263,800	1,101,222	910,043	740,596
Income Before Taxes	200,100	153,100	(2,800)	235,500	193,300	185,342	141,853	125,394
Income Taxes	45,500	24,600	(31,400)	47,000	47,100	55,603	16,597	37,618
Net Income	138,800	128,500	30,800	188,500	146,200	129,739	125,256	87,776
Average Shares	97,100	98,400	96,100	94,500	93,300	91,861	90,127	83,924
Balance Sheet								
Total Assets	3,556,800	3,420,100	3,389,500	3,237,900	2,901,600	2,463,574	1,471,823	1,062,298
Total Liabilities	2,841,300	2,556,000	2,620,400	2,476,900	2,282,500	1,935,419	1,100,210	747,926
Stockholders' Equity	715,500	864,100	769,100	761,000	619,100	528,155	371,613	314,372
Shares Outstanding	92,000	98,400	95,700	92,100	90,000	88,548	85,111	79,497
Statistical Record								
Return on Assets %	3.98	3.77	0.93	6.12	5.45	6.59	9.89	8.99
Return on Equity %	17.57	15.74	4.03	27.24	25.49	28.84	36.52	31.44
Price Range	31.08-24.19	31.76-24.56	32.68-26.50	33.96-27.06	32.65-23.45	36.86-22.10	38.30-22.00	33.66-11.75
P/E Ratio	21.73-16.92	24.24-18.75	102.13-82.81	17.07-13.60	20.80-14.94	26.14-15.67	27.55-15.83	32.05-11.19
Average Yield %	4.39	4.32	3.87	3.17	2.63	1.94	1.77	2.13

Address: Two Pierce Place, Itasca, IL 60143-3141 Telephone: 630-773-3800 Fax: 630-285-4000	Web Site: www.ajg.com Officers: Robert E. Gallagher - Chmn. J. Patrick Gallagher Jr. - Pres., C.E.O.	Auditors: Ernst & Young LLP Transfer Agents: Computershare Investor Services, Chicago, IL

GAMESTOP CORP

Exchange	Symbol	Price	52Wk Range	Yield	P/E
NYS	GME	$51.71 (3/31/2008)	63.30-32.64	N/A	29.55

*7 Year Price Score N/A   *NYSE Composite Index=100   *12 Month Price Score 108.65

Interim Earnings (Per Share)

Qtr.	Apr	Jul	Oct	Jan
2003-04	0.06	0.06	0.09	0.33
2004-05	0.06	0.07	0.11	0.30
2005-06	0.10	0.07	(0.02)	0.67
2006-07	0.07	0.02	0.09	0.82
2007-08	0.15	0.13	0.31	1.15

Interim Dividends (Per Share)

Amt	Decl	Ex	Rec	Pay
2-for-1	2/12/2007	3/19/2007	2/20/2007	3/16/2007

Valuation Analysis

		Institutional Holding	
Forecast P/E	N/A	No of Institutions	243
Market Cap	$8.3 Billion	Shares	115,625,024
Book Value	1.9 Billion	% Held	76.23
Price/Book	4.47		
Price/Sales	1.17		

Business Summary: Retail - Appliances and Electrical (MIC: 5.10 SIC: 5734 NAIC: 443120)

GameStop is a retailer of video game products and personal computer (PC) entertainment software. Co. sells new and used video game hardware, video game software and accessories, as well as PC entertainment software, and related accessories and other merchandise. As of Feb 2 2008, Co. operated 5,264 stores in the U.S., Australia, Canada and Europe, primarily under the names GameStop and EB Games. Co. also operates the electronic commerce websites www.gamestop.com and www.ebgames.com. In addition, Co. is engaged in publishing Game Informer, a multi-platform video game magazine in the U.S. with approximately 2.9 million subscribers as of Feb 2 2008.

Recent Developments: For the year ended Feb 2 2008, net income increased 82.2% to US$288.3 million from US$158.3 million in the prior year. Revenues were US$7.09 billion, up 33.4% from US$5.32 billion the year before. Operating income was US$501.4 million versus US$333.7 million in the prior year, an increase of 50.3%. Direct operating expenses rose 37.2% to US$5.28 billion from US$3.85 billion in the comparable period the year before. Indirect operating expenses increased 15.3% to US$1.31 billion from US$1.14 billion in the equivalent prior-year period.

Prospects: For fiscal year ending Jan 31 2009, Co.'s sales are projected to grow between 19.0% and 21.0%, with comparable store sales growth ranging from 10.0% to 12.0%, driven by a strong lineup of video game title releases across all platforms while diluted earnings per share are expected to range from $2.25 to $2.34, reflecting an increase of between 25.0% and 30.0% over fiscal 2007. Also, Co. plans to open between 575 and 600 stores worldwide in fiscal 2008. Looking further ahead, Co. expects earnings per share to grow at least 25.0% within fiscal year ending Jan 2010 based on its growing global retail footprint, continued expansion of the video game industry and the broadening consumer base.

Financial Data
(US$ in Thousands)

	02/02/2008	02/03/2007	01/28/2006	01/29/2005	01/31/2004	02/01/2003	02/02/2002	02/03/2001
Earnings Per Share	1.75	1.00	0.81	0.53	0.53	0.44	0.09	(0.17)
Cash Flow Per Share	3.19	2.78	2.52	1.34	0.62	0.83	1.09	(0.01)
Tang Book Value Per Share	2.86	N.M.	N.M.	2.19	2.41	2.02	...	...
Income Statement								
Total Revenue	7,093,962	5,318,900	3,091,783	1,842,806	1,578,838	1,352,791	1,121,138	756,697
EBITDA	620,107	437,796	260,936	136,598	133,644	109,866	64,384	27,811
Income Before Taxes	441,056	254,296	159,922	98,911	105,188	87,701	14,635	(17,797)
Income Taxes	152,765	96,046	59,138	37,985	41,721	35,297	7,675	(5,836)
Net Income	288,291	158,250	100,784	60,926	63,467	52,404	6,960	(11,961)
Average Shares	164,844	158,284	124,972	115,592	119,528	120,838	78,794	72,018
Balance Sheet								
Current Assets	1,794,717	1,440,341	1,121,265	423,988	472,752	416,453	236,704	138,435
Total Assets	3,775,891	3,349,584	3,015,119	914,983	898,924	803,909	606,843	509,757
Current Liabilities	1,260,557	1,087,057	887,674	313,895	283,850	246,771	205,597	140,161
Long-Term Obligations	574,473	843,723	963,463	24,347	...	...	399,623	385,148
Total Liabilities	1,913,445	1,973,706	1,900,406	371,972	304,891	255,234	610,828	530,367
Stockholders' Equity	1,862,446	1,375,878	1,114,713	543,011	594,033	548,675	(3,985)	(20,610)
Shares Outstanding	161,007	152,305	145,594	101,656	113,396	114,118	72,018	72,018
Statistical Record								
Return on Assets %	8.11	4.89	5.14	6.74	7.47	7.45	1.25	N.M.
Return on Equity %	17.85	12.50	12.19	10.75	11.14	19.29	...	...
EBITDA Margin %	8.74	8.23	8.44	7.41	8.46	8.12	5.74	3.68
Net Margin %	4.06	2.98	3.26	3.31	4.02	3.87	0.62	N.M.
Asset Turnover	2.00	1.64	1.58	2.04	1.86	1.92	2.01	1.82
Current Ratio	1.42	1.32	1.26	1.35	1.67	1.69	1.15	0.99
Debt to Equity	0.31	0.61	0.86	0.04	...	...	...	...
Price Range	63.30-25.57	29.01-18.34	19.59-9.30	11.75-7.27	9.46-3.79	12.11-4.25	...	...
P/E Ratio	36.17-14.61	29.01-18.34	24.19-11.48	22.17-13.72	17.85-7.16	27.51-9.66	...	...

Address: 625 Westport Parkway, Grapevine, TX 76051
Telephone: 817-424-2000
Web Site: www.gamestop.com
Officers: R. Richard Fontaine - Chmn., C.E.O. Daniel A. DeMatteo - Vice-Chmn., C.O.O.
Auditors: BDO SEIDMAN, LLP
Investor Contact: 817-424-2000
Transfer Agents: Bank of New York

GANNETT CO INC

Exchange	Symbol	Price	52Wk Range	Yield	P/E	Div Achiever
NYS	GCI	$29.05 (3/31/2008)	59.79-28.43	5.51	6.43	36 Years

*7 Year Price Score 53.01   *NYSE Composite Index=100   *12 Month Price Score 76.74

Interim Earnings (Per Share)

Qtr.	Mar	Jun	Sep	Dec
2003	0.93	1.20	1.03	1.31
2004	1.00	1.30	1.18	1.45
2005	1.05	1.37	1.22	1.43
2006	0.99	1.31	1.11	1.50
2007	0.90	1.56	1.01	1.06

Interim Dividends (Per Share)

Amt	Decl	Ex	Rec	Pay
0.31Q	4/24/2007	6/6/2007	6/8/2007	7/2/2007
0.40Q	7/24/2007	9/12/2007	9/14/2007	10/1/2007
0.40Q	10/23/2007	12/12/2007	12/14/2007	1/2/2008
0.40Q	2/27/2008	3/5/2008	3/7/2008	4/1/2008

Indicated Div: $1.60 (Div. Reinv. Plan)

Valuation Analysis — **Institutional Holding**

Forecast P/E	11.33	No of Institutions	532
	(1/10/2007)	Shares	191,142,272
Market Cap	$6.7 Billion	% Held	81.40
Book Value	9.0 Billion		
Price/Book	0.74		
Price/Sales	0.90		

TRADING VOLUME (thousand shares)

Business Summary: Media (MIC: 13.1 SIC: 2711 NAIC: 511110)

Gannett is a news and information company. In the U.S., Co. published 85 daily newspapers and nearly 900 non-daily publications as of Dec 31 2007. Co. also operates Web sites providing news, information and advertising that is customized for the market served and integrated with its publishing operations. Co.'s newspaper publishing operations in the U.K., operating as Newsquest, included locally integrated Web sites, classified business Web sites, 17 paid-for daily newspapers, and almost 300 non-daily publications as of Dec 31 2007. In broadcasting, Co. operated 23 television stations in the U.S. with a market reach of more than 20.0 million households as of Dec 31 2007.

Recent Developments: For the year ended Dec 30 2007, income from continuing operations decreased 14.3% to US$975.6 million from US$1.14 billion a year earlier. Net income decreased 9.1% to US$1.06 billion from US$1.16 billion in the prior year. Revenues were US$7.44 billion, down 5.2% from US$7.85 billion the year before. Operating income was US$1.65 billion versus US$1.90 billion in the prior year, a decrease of 13.3%. Direct operating expenses declined 4.7% to US$4.16 billion from US$4.37 billion in the comparable period the year before. Indirect operating expenses increased 3.3% to US$1.62 billion from US$1.57 billion in the equivalent prior-year period.

Prospects: Looking ahead, Co. expects strong advertising demand from local, state and national political and election activity in 2008 and it expects solid ad demand from Summer Olympics coverage on its NBC stations. In addition, Co. anticipates lower operating costs in 2008, reflecting savings from headcount reductions and centralization of operations, partially offset by potentially higher price-driven newsprint expense. Meanwhile, Co. expects capital expenditures of approximately $175.0 million for 2008, including approximately $11.0 million for land and buildings or renovation of existing facilities, $141.0 million for machinery and equipment, and $23.0 million for vehicles and other assets.

Financial Data
(US$ in Thousands)

	12/30/2007	12/31/2006	12/25/2005	12/26/2004	12/28/2003	12/29/2002	12/30/2001	12/31/2000
Earnings Per Share	4.52	4.90	5.05	4.92	4.46	4.31	3.12	6.41
Cash Flow Per Share	5.79	6.16	5.86	6.01	5.30	3.88	4.96	1.85
Dividends Per Share	1.420	1.200	1.120	1.040	0.980	0.940	0.900	0.860
Dividend Payout %	31.42	24.49	22.18	21.14	21.97	21.81	28.85	13.42
Income Statement								
Total Revenue	7,439,460	8,033,354	7,598,939	7,381,283	6,711,115	6,422,249	6,344,245	6,222,318
EBITDA	1,983,406	2,279,475	2,298,734	2,375,506	2,205,909	2,129,883	2,031,552	2,176,774
Income Before Taxes	1,448,877	1,719,482	1,817,855	1,995,386	1,840,313	1,764,528	1,370,597	1,608,840
Income Taxes	473,300	558,700	606,600	678,200	629,100	604,400	539,400	636,900
Net Income	1,055,612	1,160,782	1,244,654	1,317,186	1,211,213	1,160,128	831,197	1,719,077
Average Shares	233,710	236,756	246,256	267,590	271,872	269,286	266,833	268,118
Balance Sheet								
Current Assets	1,343,711	1,532,019	1,463,071	1,370,695	1,223,261	1,133,079	1,178,198	1,302,336
Total Assets	15,887,727	16,223,804	15,743,396	15,399,251	14,706,239	13,733,014	13,096,101	12,980,411
Current Liabilities	962,163	1,116,948	1,096,341	1,005,450	961,837	958,625	1,127,737	1,174,001
Long-Term Obligations	4,098,538	5,210,021	5,438,273	4,607,743	3,834,511	4,547,265	5,080,025	5,747,856
Total Liabilities	6,850,289	7,817,230	8,147,658	7,143,888	6,190,819	6,821,219	7,360,179	7,877,001
Stockholders' Equity	9,017,159	8,382,263	7,570,562	8,164,002	8,422,981	6,911,795	5,735,922	5,103,410
Shares Outstanding	230,202	234,743	238,045	254,344	272,417	267,909	265,797	264,271
Statistical Record								
Return on Assets %	6.59	7.14	8.02	8.77	8.54	8.67	6.39	15.38
Return on Equity %	12.17	14.32	15.86	15.93	15.84	18.40	15.38	34.75
EBITDA Margin %	26.66	28.38	30.25	32.18	32.87	33.16	32.02	34.98
Net Margin %	14.19	14.45	16.38	17.84	18.05	18.06	13.10	27.63
Asset Turnover	0.46	0.49	0.49	0.49	0.47	0.48	0.49	0.56
Current Ratio	1.40	1.37	1.33	1.36	1.27	1.18	1.04	1.11
Debt to Equity	0.45	0.62	0.72	0.56	0.46	0.66	0.89	1.13
Price Range	63.11-35.30	64.80-51.67	82.41-59.19	91.00-78.99	88.93-67.68	79.87-63.39	71.10-55.55	81.56-48.69
P/E Ratio	13.96-7.81	13.22-10.54	16.32-11.72	18.50-16.05	19.94-15.17	18.53-14.71	22.79-17.80	12.72-7.60
Average Yield %	2.76	2.08	1.53	1.22	1.27	1.28	1.40	1.41

Address: 7950 Jones Branch Drive, McLean, VA 22107	Web Site: www.gannett.com	Auditors: Ernst & Young LLP
Telephone: 703-854-6000	Officers: Douglas H. McCorkindale - Chmn., Pres., C.E.O. Gracia C. Martore - Sr. V.P., C.F.O.	Investor Contact: 703-854-6918 Transfer Agents: Wells Fargo Bank Minnesota, N.A., St. Paul, MN

GARDNER DENVER, INC.

Exchange	Symbol	Price	52Wk Range	Yield	P/E
NYS	GDI	$37.10 (3/31/2008)	45.80-28.70	N/A	9.76

*7 Year Price Score 145.66 *NYSE Composite Index=100 *12 Month Price Score 105.07

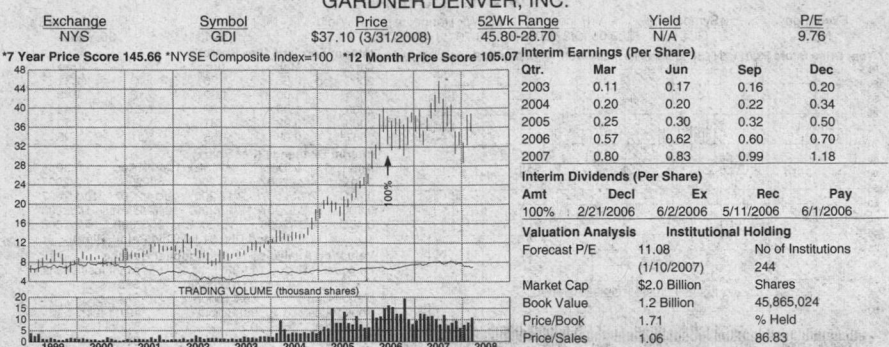

Interim Earnings (Per Share)

Qtr.	Mar	Jun	Sep	Dec
2003	0.11	0.17	0.16	0.20
2004	0.20	0.20	0.22	0.34
2005	0.25	0.30	0.32	0.50
2006	0.57	0.62	0.60	0.70
2007	0.80	0.83	0.99	1.18

Interim Dividends (Per Share)

Amt	Decl	Ex	Rec	Pay
100%	2/21/2006	6/2/2006	5/11/2006	6/1/2006

Valuation Analysis

		Institutional Holding	
Forecast P/E	11.08	No of Institutions	
	(1/10/2007)	244	
Market Cap	$2.0 Billion	Shares	
Book Value	1.2 Billion	45,865,024	
Price/Book	1.71	% Held	
Price/Sales	1.06	86.83	

Business Summary: Industrial Machinery and Equipment (MIC: 11.5 SIC: 3561 NAIC: 333911)

Gardner Denver designs, manufactures and markets compressor and vacuum products and fluid transfer products. Co.'s Compressor and Vacuum Products segment designs, manufactures, markets and services the following products for industrial and commercial applications: rotary screw, reciprocating, sliding vane air compressors; positive displacement, centrifugal and side channel blowers; and liquid ring pumps. Co.'s Fluid Transfer Products segment designs, manufactures, markets and services pumps, water jetting systems and related aftermarket parts used in oil and natural gas well drilling, servicing and production and in industrial cleaning and maintenance.

Recent Developments: For the year ended Dec 31 2007, net income increased 54.3% to US$205.1 million from US$132.9 million in the prior year. Revenues were US$1.87 billion, up 12.0% from US$1.67 billion the year before. Operating income was US$291.5 million versus US$234.3 million in the prior year, an increase of 24.4%. Direct operating expenses rose 11.5% to US$1.25 billion from US$1.12 billion in the comparable period the year before. Indirect operating expenses increased 4.3% to US$328.4 million from US$315.0 million in the equivalent prior-year period.

Prospects: Co. remains optimistic that orders for compressor and vacuum products will remain robust through the first half of 2008, driven by demand in Europe and Asia for original equipment manufacturer applications and engineered products, as well as marine and European mobile applications. However, the rate of order growth in the second half of 2008 is expected to slow slightly, reflecting an anticipated downturn in the European economy's rate of growth. For full-year 2008, based on several factors including its current economic outlook and existing backlog, Co. is raising its diluted earnings per share outlook range to $3.20 to $3.40, representing a 13.0% decrease from 2007.

Financial Data
(US$ in Thousands)

	12/31/2007	12/31/2006	12/31/2005	12/31/2004	12/31/2003	12/31/2002	12/31/2001	12/31/2000
Earnings Per Share	3.80	2.49	1.37	0.96	0.64	0.61	0.70	0.60
Cash Flow Per Share	3.41	3.19	2.41	2.02	1.44	1.66	1.42	1.01
Tang Book Value Per Share	5.00	N.M.	N.M.	N.M.	1.55	0.37	N.M.	0.71
Income Statement								
Total Revenue	1,868,844	1,669,176	1,214,552	739,539	439,530	418,158	419,770	379,358
EBITDA	353,155	252,824	133,966	74,187	44,924	42,966	52,250	45,775
Income Before Taxes	268,360	200,615	95,644	52,286	30,358	28,827	34,683	29,894
Income Taxes	63,256	67,707	28,693	15,163	9,715	9,225	12,659	11,210
Net Income	205,104	132,908	66,951	37,123	20,643	19,602	22,024	18,684
Average Shares	54,043	53,460	48,890	38,754	32,624	32,083	31,566	30,978
Balance Sheet								
Current Assets	701,528	579,718	586,267	385,522	287,809	178,436	201,135	179,916
Total Assets	1,905,607	1,750,231	1,715,060	1,028,609	589,733	472,842	488,688	403,881
Current Liabilities	312,202	326,344	313,844	239,018	100,956	78,321	84,577	68,243
Long-Term Obligations	263,987	383,459	542,641	280,256	165,756	112,663	160,230	115,808
Total Liabilities	745,894	897,701	1,056,771	623,133	323,828	249,919	289,960	232,733
Stockholders' Equity	1,159,713	852,530	658,289	405,476	265,905	222,923	198,728	171,148
Shares Outstanding	53,546	52,625	51,998	39,895	32,234	31,884	31,381	30,742
Statistical Record								
Return on Assets %	11.22	7.67	4.88	4.58	3.89	4.08	4.93	4.76
Return on Equity %	20.39	17.59	12.59	11.03	8.45	9.30	11.91	11.51
EBITDA Margin %	18.90	15.15	11.03	10.03	10.22	10.28	12.45	12.07
Net Margin %	10.97	7.96	5.51	5.02	4.70	4.69	5.25	4.93
Asset Turnover	1.02	0.96	0.89	0.91	0.83	0.87	0.94	0.97
Current Ratio	2.25	1.78	1.87	1.61	2.85	2.28	2.38	2.64
Debt to Equity	0.23	0.45	0.82	0.69	0.62	0.51	0.81	0.68
Price Range	45.80-30.55	40.25-24.30	25.72-16.52	18.90-11.94	12.50-8.32	13.95-7.17	11.99-8.56	10.65-7.13
P/E Ratio	12.05-8.04	16.16-9.76	18.77-12.06	19.69-12.43	19.53-13.01	22.87-11.75	17.13-12.24	17.75-11.88

Address: 1800 Gardner Expressway, Quincy, IL 62301 **Telephone:** 217-222-5400 **Fax:** 217-224-7814	**Web Site:** www.gardnerdenver.com **Officers:** Ross J. Centanni - Chmn., Pres., C.E.O. Tracy D. Pagliara - V.P., Admin., Sec., Gen. Couns.	**Auditors:** KPMG LLP **Transfer Agents:** National City Bank, Cleveland, OH

GARTNER, INC.

Exchange	Symbol	Price	52Wk Range	Yield	P/E
NYS	IT	$19.34 (3/31/2008)	28.22-14.36	N/A	28.44

*7 Year Price Score 131.78 *NYSE Composite Index=100   *12 Month Price Score 91.44

Interim Earnings (Per Share)

Qtr.	Mar	Jun	Sep	Dec
2003	(0.02)	0.13	0.07	0.05
2004	0.00	0.08	0.00	0.04
2005	(0.13)	(0.01)	(0.02)	0.13
2006	0.07	0.16	0.08	0.19
2007	0.08	0.13	0.11	0.36

Interim Dividends (Per Share)

No Dividends Paid

Valuation Analysis		Institutional Holding	
Forecast P/E	19.70	No of Institutions	
	(1/10/2007)	172	
Market Cap	$1.9 Billion	Shares	
Book Value	17.5 Million	101,999,296	
Price/Book	109.46	% Held	
Price/Sales	1.61	98.00	

Business Summary: Accounting & Management Consulting Services (MIC: 12.2 SIC: 8741 NAIC: 561110)

Gartner is a provider of research and analysis on information technology (IT), computer hardware, software, communications, and related technology industries. As of Dec 31 2007, Co. provided coverage of the IT industry to approximately 10,000 client organizations. Co. serves a global client base consisting primarily of chief information officers (CIOs) and other senior IT and business executives from various enterprises, government agencies and the investment community. The findings from Co.'s research are delivered through its three business segments: Research, Consulting, and Events.

Recent Developments: For the year ended Dec 31 2007, net income increased 26.4% to US$73.6 million from US$58.2 million in the prior year. Revenues were US$1.19 billion, up 12.2% from US$1.06 billion the year before. Operating income was US$133.1 million versus US$103.3 million in the prior year, an increase of 28.9%. Direct operating expenses rose 7.9% to US$545.3 million from US$505.3 million in the comparable period the year before. Indirect operating expenses increased 13.1% to US$510.8 million from US$451.7 million in the equivalent prior-year period.

Prospects: For full-year 2008, Co. expects total revenue of $1.30 billion to $1.33 billion with earnings per share of $0.90 to $1.00. By segment, Co. expects research revenue of $770.0 million to $780.0 million, consulting revenue of $335.0 million to $345.0 million, events revenue of $190.0 million to $194.0 million, and other revenue of $5.0 million to $6.0 million. However, due to the completion of divestiture of its Vision Events business on Feb 29 2008, Co. has reduced its full-year 2008 projections for revenue and earnings per share by approximately $21.0 million and $0.02, respectively. Co. noted that the divestiture is consistent with its strategy to focus on content driven event formats.

Financial Data

(US$ in Thousands)	12/31/2007	12/31/2006	12/31/2005	12/31/2004	12/31/2003	12/31/2002	09/30/2002	09/30/2001
Earnings Per Share	0.68	0.50	(0.02)	0.13	0.26	(0.18)	0.47	(0.77)
Cash Flow Per Share	1.43	0.94	0.24	0.39	1.50	0.01	1.74	0.86
Tang Book Value Per Share	N.M.	N.M.	N.M.	N.M.	1.11	...	...	...
Income Statement								
Total Revenue	1,189,198	1,060,321	989,004	893,821	858,446	229,814	907,174	952,042
EBITDA	162,706	136,606	52,236	64,116	91,257	(3,087)	139,080	64,623
Income Before Taxes	114,161	85,872	5,438	34,462	35,556	(20,022)	73,601	(9,392)
Income Taxes	40,608	27,680	7,875	17,573	11,863	(5,604)	25,025	(9,172)
Net Income	73,553	58,192	(2,437)	16,889	23,693	(14,418)	48,578	(66,203)
Average Shares	108,328	116,203	112,253	126,326	92,579	81,379	130,882	85,862
Balance Sheet								
Current Assets	337,190	484,033	462,119	487,845	549,477	459,265	455,033	448,821
Total Assets	1,133,210	1,039,793	1,026,617	861,194	917,264	827,403	824,850	839,002
Current Liabilities	876,012	803,883	642,768	529,198	491,133	457,877	437,342	527,514
Long-Term Obligations	157,500	150,000	180,000	150,000	...	351,539	346,300	326,200
Total Liabilities	1,115,712	1,013,475	880,029	731,146	541,518	856,104	829,740	873,520
Stockholders' Equity	17,498	26,318	146,588	130,048	375,746	(28,701)	(4,890)	(34,518)
Shares Outstanding	99,031	104,064	114,334	111,765	129,999	80,509	82,012	83,664
Statistical Record								
Return on Assets %	6.77	5.63	N.M.	1.89	2.72	N.M.	5.84	N.M.
Return on Equity %	335.74	67.31	N.M.	6.66	13.65	...	...	N.M.
EBITDA Margin %	13.68	12.88	5.28	7.17	10.63	N.M.	15.33	6.79
Net Margin %	6.19	5.49	N.M.	1.89	2.76	N.M.	5.35	N.M.
Asset Turnover	1.09	1.03	1.05	1.00	0.98	0.22	1.09	1.03
Current Ratio	0.64	0.60	0.72	0.92	1.12	1.00	1.04	0.85
Debt to Equity	9.00	5.70	1.23	1.15	...	...	...	...
Price Range	28.22-16.38	20.75-13.01	14.09-8.16	13.38-11.00	13.52-6.86	10.51-6.11	13.48-7.75	12.31-5.97
P/E Ratio	41.50-24.09	41.50-26.02	...	102.92-84.62	52.00-26.38	...	28.68-16.49	...

Address: 56 Top Gallant Road, Stamford, CT 06902-7700 Telephone: 203-964-0096	Web Site: www.gartner.com Officers: Michael D. Fleisher - Chmn., Pres. Gene Hall - C.E.O.	Auditors: KPMG LLP Transfer Agents: American Stock Transfer & Trust Company, New York, NY

GATX CORP.

*7 Year Price Score 104.25 *NYSE Composite Index=100 *12 Month Price Score 94.82

Interim Earnings (Per Share)

Qtr.	Mar	Jun	Sep	Dec
2003	0.04	0.50	0.46	0.56
2004	0.46	0.71	0.78	1.12
2005	0.52	0.63	0.61	(2.05)
2006	0.83	0.70	(0.13)	0.61
2007	0.62	0.77	1.62	0.80

Interim Dividends (Per Share)

Amt	Decl	Ex	Rec	Pay
0.24Q	4/27/2007	6/13/2007	6/15/2007	6/30/2007
0.24Q	7/27/2007	9/12/2007	9/14/2007	9/30/2007
0.24Q	10/26/2007	12/12/2007	12/14/2007	12/31/2007
0.27Q	2/1/2008	2/27/2008	2/29/2008	3/31/2008
		Indicated Div: $1.08		

Valuation Analysis

		Institutional Holding	
Forecast P/E	N/A	No of Institutions	205
Market Cap	$1.9 Billion	Shares	54,878,516
Book Value	1.1 Billion	% Held	N/A
Price/Book	1.63		
Price/Sales	1.39		

Business Summary: Rail Transport (MIC: 15.5 SIC: 4741 NAIC: 488210)

GATX leases, operates and manages long-lived, widely used assets in the rail, marine and industrial equipment markets. Co. has three business segments: Rail, Specialty and American Steamship Company (ASC). Co.'s Rail business is engaged in leasing tank and freight railcars and locomotives in North America and Europe. Co.'s Specialty business is primarily focused on providing leasing and related remarketing and asset management services in the marine and industrial equipment markets. In addition, Co.'s ASC business operates a fleet of self-unloading marine vessels on the Great Lakes and is engaged in the waterborne transportation of dry bulk commodities.

Recent Developments: For the year ended Dec 31 2007, income from continuing operations increased 22.7% to US$185.8 million from US$151.4 million a year earlier. Net income increased 80.9% to US$203.7 million from US$112.6 million in the prior year. Revenues were US$1.35 billion, up 9.5% from US$1.23 billion the year before. Indirect operating expenses increased 10.0% to US$959.5 million from US$872.4 million in the equivalent prior-year period.

Prospects: For 2008, Co. expects earnings per diluted share of $3.15 to $3.35, and expects a modest decline in consolidated segment profit; with profit to decline marginally at both its Rail and Specialty segment, but estimates higher profit at its American Steamship Company segment. Separately, Co. recently entered into a series of agreements with the Providence and Worcester Railroad Co. (P&W), through which it has become the supplier of substantially all of P&W's railcar needs. Co. will initially lease to P&W railcars worth about $35.0 million over 2008 and 2009, and has acquired a portion of P&W's existing railcar fleet and invested about $5.5 million in exchange for a 5.0% equity interest in P&W.

Financial Data

(US$ in Thousands)	12/31/2007	12/31/2006	12/31/2005	12/31/2004	12/31/2003	12/31/2002	12/31/2001	12/31/2000
Earnings Per Share	3.76	2.00	(0.29)	3.04	1.56	...	3.51	1.37
Cash Flow Per Share	6.81	5.75	5.68	6.09	8.31	8.99	7.33	9.37
Tang Book Value Per Share	21.82	20.58	18.50	19.93	16.13	15.07	16.79	16.25
Dividends Per Share	0.960	0.840	0.800	0.800	1.280	1.280	1.240	1.200
Dividend Payout %	25.53	42.00	...	26.32	82.05	...	35.33	87.59
Income Statement								
Total Revenue	1,346,000	1,229,100	1,134,600	1,231,400	1,312,400	1,322,700	1,521,400	1,390,800
EBITDA	587,300	529,000	349,600	596,900	624,600	631,700	671,400	630,900
Income Before Taxes	258,600	226,100	(27,800)	226,700	102,900	39,000	5,600	53,500
Income Taxes	72,800	75,600	(12,700)	68,200	26,000	10,000	(1,900)	22,700
Net Income	203,700	111,700	(14,300)	169,600	76,900	300	172,900	66,600
Average Shares	55,400	62,101	50,106	60,002	49,222	49,177	49,202	48,753
Balance Sheet								
Current Assets	572,600	775,700	608,400	553,400	1,066,000	1,534,800	1,836,900	1,684,500
Total Assets	4,725,600	4,644,000	5,244,400	5,612,900	6,080,600	6,428,300	6,109,700	6,263,700
Current Liabilities	366,900	182,000	234,400	450,300	370,700	426,600	658,900	1,016,200
Long-Term Obligations	2,112,400	2,192,300	2,815,600	3,060,000	3,823,900	4,212,800	3,788,500	3,752,300
Total Liabilities	3,576,100	3,481,000	4,222,100	4,532,000	5,191,700	5,626,700	5,227,900	5,474,200
Stockholders' Equity	1,149,500	1,163,000	1,022,300	1,080,900	888,900	801,600	881,800	789,500
Shares Outstanding	47,899	51,997	50,618	49,530	49,246	49,048	48,756	48,599
Statistical Record								
Return on Assets %	4.35	2.26	N.M.	2.89	1.23	0.00	2.79	1.10
Return on Equity %	17.62	10.22	N.M.	17.17	9.10	0.04	20.69	8.17
EBITDA Margin %	43.63	43.04	30.81	48.47	47.59	47.76	44.13	45.36
Net Margin %	15.13	9.09	N.M.	13.77	5.86	0.02	11.36	4.79
Asset Turnover	0.29	0.25	0.21	0.21	0.21	0.21	0.25	0.23
Current Ratio	1.56	4.26	2.60	1.23	2.88	3.60	2.79	1.66
Debt to Equity	1.84	1.89	2.75	2.83	4.30	5.26	4.30	4.75
Price Range	52.25-34.80	48.15-35.99	41.52-26.34	30.05-20.51	28.68-13.68	35.55-16.45	49.19-25.68	49.88-28.56
P/E Ratio	13.90-9.26	24.07-18.00	...	9.88-6.75	18.38-8.77	N.M.	14.01-7.32	36.41-20.85
Average Yield %	2.13	2.03	2.30	3.12	6.41	4.69	3.26	3.16

Address: 500 West Monroe Street, Chicago, IL 60661 **Telephone:** 312-621-6200 **Fax:** 312-621-6648	**Web Site:** www.gatx.com **Officers:** Ronald H. Zech - Chmn. Brian A. Kenney - Pres., C.E.O.	**Auditors:** Ernst & Young LLP **Investor Contact:** 312-621-6262 **Transfer Agents:** Mellon Investor Services LLC, Jersey City, NJ

GENENTECH, INC.

Exchange	Symbol	Price	52Wk Range	Yield	P/E
NYS	DNA	$81.18 (3/31/2008)	83.40-66.27	N/A	31.34

*7 Year Price Score 112.71 *NYSE Composite Index=100 *12 Month Price Score 109.10

Interim Earnings (Per Share)

Qtr.	Mar	Jun	Sep	Dec
2003	0.14	0.13	0.14	0.12
2004	0.17	0.16	0.21	0.20
2005	0.27	0.27	0.33	0.31
2006	0.39	0.49	0.53	0.56
2007	0.66	0.70	0.64	0.59

Interim Dividends (Per Share)

Amt	Decl	Ex	Rec	Pay
100%	3/3/2004	5/13/2004	4/28/2004	5/12/2004

Valuation Analysis / Institutional Holding

Forecast P/E	26.39	No of Institutions	
	(1/10/2007)	626	
Market Cap	$85.4 Billion	Shares	
Book Value	11.9 Billion	407,145,792	
Price/Book	7.17	% Held	
Price/Sales	7.28	38.66	

TRADING VOLUME (thousand shares)

Business Summary: Pharmaceuticals (MIC: 9.1 SIC: 2834 NAIC: 325412)

Genentech is a biotechnology company that develops, manufactures and commercializes biotherapeutics. In addition, Co. manufactures and commercializes biotechnology products, and receives royalties from companies that are licensed to market products based on its technology. As of Dec 31 2007, Co.'s products included Avastin for the treatment of first- or second-line metastatic cancer of the colon or rectum, Rituxan for the treatment of relapsed or refractory, low-grade or follicular, CD20 antibody-positive, B-cell non-Hodgkin's lymphoma, and Herceptin for use as an adjuvant treatment of node-positive breast cancer. Co. has a U.S.-based marketing, sales and distribution organization

Recent Developments: For the year ended Dec 31 2007, net income increased 31.0% to US$2.77 billion from US$2.11 billion in the prior year. Revenues were US$11.72 billion, up 26.3% from US$9.28 billion the year before. Operating income was US$4.23 billion versus US$3.15 billion in the prior year, an increase of 34.2%. Direct operating expenses rose 33.0% to US$1.57 billion from US$1.18 billion in the comparable period the year before. Indirect operating expenses increased 19.7% to US$5.92 billion from US$4.95 billion in the equivalent prior-year period.

Prospects: For 2008, Co. will continue to invest in the 20 new molecular entities in clinical development and expects new data from Rituxan® for multiple sclerosis and lupus and Avastin® in combination with Tarceva® for advanced non-small cell lung cancer. Separately, on Feb 22 2008, Co. announced the FDA approval for Avastin® (bevacizumab), in combination with paclitaxel chemotherapy, for the treatment of patients who have not received chemotherapy for metastatic HER2-negative breast cancer. Co. also noted that it has shared the results from a second Phase III trial (AVADO) with the FDA, and expects results from a third Phase III trial (RIBBON I) in first-line metastatic breast cancer in late 2008.

Financial Data

(US$ in Thousands)	12/31/2007	12/31/2006	12/31/2005	12/31/2004	12/31/2003	12/31/2002	12/31/2001	12/31/2000
Earnings Per Share	2.59	1.97	1.18	0.73	0.53	0.06	0.14	(0.07)
Cash Flow Per Share	3.07	2.03	2.24	1.13	1.20	0.57	0.46	0.18
Tang Book Value Per Share	8.71	7.30	5.30	4.58	4.19	3.00	3.32	2.80
Income Statement								
Total Revenue	11,724,000	9,284,000	6,633,372	4,621,157	3,300,327	2,719,246	2,212,277	1,736,356
EBITDA	4,724,000	3,654,000	2,291,044	1,489,537	1,117,455	304,704	711,077	466,977
Income Before Taxes	4,426,000	3,403,000	2,012,849	1,219,416	897,506	29,749	282,986	3,973
Income Taxes	1,657,000	1,290,000	733,858	434,600	287,324	(34,038)	127,112	20,414
Net Income	2,769,000	2,113,000	1,278,991	784,816	562,527	63,787	150,236	(74,241)
Average Shares	1,069,000	1,073,000	1,080,949	1,079,209	1,057,620	1,048,816	1,070,582	1,044,358
Balance Sheet								
Current Assets	8,753,000	5,704,000	4,418,779	3,122,757	2,756,830	2,082,784	2,209,352	1,788,811
Total Assets	10,940,000	14,042,000	12,140,879	9,403,395	8,736,171	6,777,319	7,134,847	6,711,813
Current Liabilities	3,918,000	2,157,000	1,659,832	1,243,266	873,031	646,660	651,755	448,681
Long-Term Obligations	2,402,000	2,204,000	2,083,024	412,250	412,250	...	...	149,692
Total Liabilities	7,035,000	5,364,000	4,677,295	2,621,205	2,215,873	1,438,435	1,215,028	1,037,610
Stockholders' Equity	11,905,000	9,478,000	7,469,584	6,782,190	6,520,298	5,338,884	5,919,819	5,674,203
Shares Outstanding	1,052,000	1,053,000	1,053,712	1,047,126	1,049,484	1,025,620	1,056,626	1,050,953
Statistical Record								
Return on Assets %	16.39	15.66	11.87	8.63	7.25	0.92	2.17	N.M.
Return on Equity %	25.90	24.94	17.95	11.77	9.49	1.13	2.59	N.M.
EBITDA Margin %	40.29	39.36	34.54	32.23	33.86	11.21	32.14	26.89
Net Margin %	23.62	22.76	19.28	16.98	17.04	2.35	6.79	N.M.
Asset Turnover	0.69	0.69	0.62	0.51	0.43	0.39	0.32	0.26
Current Ratio	2.23	2.64	2.66	2.75	3.16	3.22	3.39	3.99
Debt to Equity	0.20	0.23	0.28	0.06	0.06	...	...	0.03
Price Range	89.05-66.57	94.66-75.93	99.66-44.08	66.00-42.87	47.58-16.13	27.23-12.75	40.00-19.32	58.63-23.06
P/E Ratio	34.38-25.70	48.05-38.54	84.46-37.36	90.40-58.73	89.76-30.43	453.75-212.50	285.71-138.04	...

Address: 1 DNA Way, South San Francisco, CA 94080-4990 Telephone: 650-225-1000 Fax: 650-225-8326	Web Site: www.gene.com Officers: Arthur D. Levinson Ph.D. - Chmn., C.E.O. Susan D. Desmond-Hellmann M.D. - Pres., Product Devel.	Auditors: Ernst & Young LLP Investor Contact: 650-225-1034 Transfer Agents: EquiServe, LP

GENERAL CABLE CORP. (DE)

Exchange	Symbol	Price	52Wk Range	Yield	P/E
NYS	BGC	$59.07 (3/31/2008)	83.90-50.65	N/A	15.46

*7 Year Price Score 230.73 *NYSE Composite Index=100 *12 Month Price Score 97.54

TRADING VOLUME (thousand shares)

Interim Earnings (Per Share)

Qtr.	Mar	Jun	Sep	Dec
2003	0.00	0.09	0.06	(0.32)
2004	(0.09)	0.09	0.15	0.59
2005	0.18	0.23	0.07	(0.08)
2006	0.41	0.80	0.71	0.67
2007	0.71	1.15	1.11	0.83

Interim Dividends (Per Share)

Dividend Payment Suspended

Valuation Analysis — **Institutional Holding**

Forecast P/E	12.80	No of Institutions
	(1/10/2007)	213
Market Cap	$3.1 Billion	Shares
Book Value	651.3 Million	55,751,920
Price/Book	4.76	% Held
Price/Sales	0.67	N/A

Business Summary: Metal Works (MIC: 11.3 SIC: 3357 NAIC: 335929)

General Cable develops, designs, manufactures, markets, distributes and installs copper, aluminum and fiber optic wire and cable products. Co. has three operating and reportable segments based on geographic regions: North America, Europe and North Africa, and Rest of World, which consists of operations in Latin America, Sub-Saharan Africa, Middle East and Asia Pacific. At Dec 31 2007, Co. manufactured its product lines in 45 facilities and sold its products worldwide through its global operations. Co.'s trademarks include General Cable®, Anaconda®, BICC®, Carol®, GenSpeed®, Helix/HiTemp®, NextGen®, and Silec®, Polyrad® Phelps Dodge International Corporation® and Co.'s triad symbol.

Recent Developments: For the year ended Dec 31 2007, net income increased 54.2% to US$208.6 million from US$135.3 million in the prior year. Revenues were US$4.61 billion, up 25.9% from US$3.67 billion the year before. Operating income was US$366.1 million versus US$235.9 million in the prior year, an increase of 55.2%. Direct operating expenses rose 23.7% to US$3.95 billion from US$3.19 billion in the comparable period the year before. Indirect operating expenses increased 26.2% to US$296.6 million from US$235.1 million in the equivalent prior-year period.

Prospects: Co.'s recent results benefited from its exposure to global electrical infrastructure markets, the recent acquisition of Phelps Dodge International Corp., as well as favorable foreign exchange translation. Looking ahead, Co. expects to see returns over the next several years from its investments in submarine power cables, long-haul submarine fiber optic communications systems, high voltage underground cable systems, and products for the oil and gas industry. Separately, Co.'s Norddeutsche Seekablewerke GmbH subsidiary has recently been awarded a submarine power contract by BARD Engineering GmbH, for more than $30.0 million related to the construction of a wind farm in the North Sea.

Financial Data

(US$ in Thousands)	12/31/2007	12/31/2006	12/31/2005	12/31/2004	12/31/2003	12/31/2002	12/31/2001	12/31/2000
Earnings Per Share	3.82	2.60	0.41	0.75	(0.16)	(0.73)	(0.06)	(0.79)
Cash Flow Per Share	4.53	1.88	2.94	0.32	(0.43)	1.86	2.63	0.06
Tang Book Value Per Share	5.60	8.26	5.79	5.03	3.51	1.84	3.19	3.94
Dividends Per Share	...	...	...	...	...	0.150	0.200	0.200
Income Statement								
Total Revenue	4,614,800	3,665,100	2,380,800	1,970,700	1,538,400	1,453,900	1,651,400	2,697,800
EBITDA	400,900	286,700	149,000	90,700	80,600	46,300	147,400	95,500
Income Before Taxes	307,800	200,200	61,000	19,400	(1,900)	(28,000)	58,100	(40,900)
Income Taxes	99,400	64,900	-21,800	(18,100)	2,900	(9,900)	20,600	(14,500)
Net Income	208,600	135,300	39,200	37,900	(4,800)	(24,000)	(2,000)	(26,400)
Average Shares	54,600	52,000	41,900	50,300	33,600	33,000	33,100	33,600
Balance Sheet								
Current Assets	2,577,600	1,734,300	1,069,500	764,600	589,100	532,900	572,300	864,300
Total Assets	3,798,000	2,218,700	1,523,200	1,220,800	1,049,500	973,300	1,005,300	1,319,200
Current Liabilities	1,865,500	995,200	690,900	466,600	352,500	382,100	402,400	489,000
Long-Term Obligations	897,900	685,100	445,200	373,800	338,100	411,100	421,000	611,900
Total Liabilities	3,071,900	1,784,300	1,229,900	919,400	809,400	912,400	900,400	1,190,700
Stockholders' Equity	651,300	434,400	293,300	301,400	240,100	60,900	104,900	128,500
Shares Outstanding	52,430	52,002	49,520	39,335	38,908	33,135	32,838	32,649
Statistical Record								
Return on Assets %	6.93	7.23	2.86	3.33	N.M.	N.M.	N.M.	N.M.
Return on Equity %	38.43	37.19	13.18	13.96	N.M.	N.M.	N.M.	N.M.
EBITDA Margin %	8.69	7.82	6.26	4.60	5.24	3.18	8.93	3.54
Net Margin %	4.52	3.69	1.65	1.92	N.M.	N.M.	N.M.	N.M.
Asset Turnover	1.53	1.96	1.74	1.73	1.52	1.47	1.42	1.86
Current Ratio	1.38	1.74	1.55	1.64	1.67	1.39	1.42	1.77
Debt to Equity	1.38	1.58	1.52	1.24	1.41	6.75	4.01	4.76
Price Range	83.90-42.36	45.10-19.90	20.66-11.14	14.01-6.97	10.18-3.21	14.80-2.28	18.55-4.69	12.88-4.44
P/E Ratio	21.96-11.09	17.35-7.65	50.39-27.17	18.68-9.29	...	...	...	...
Average Yield %	...	...	...	...	...	1.91	1.60	2.60

Address: 4 Tesseneer Drive, Highland Heights, KY 41076-9753 **Telephone:** 859-572-8000 **Fax:** 859-572-8458	**Web Site:** www.generalcable.com **Officers:** John E. Welsh III - Non-Exec. Chmn. Gregory B. Kenny - Pres., C.E.O.	**Auditors:** Deloitte & Touche LLP **Investor Contact:** 859-572-8000 **Transfer Agents:** Mellon Investor Services LLC, Ridgefield Park, NJ

GENERAL DYNAMICS CORP.

Exchange	Symbol	Price	52Wk Range	Yield	P/E	Div Achiever
NYS	GD	$83.37 (3/31/2008)	94.00-74.24	1.68	16.41	16 Years

*7 Year Price Score 121.35 *NYSE Composite Index=100 *12 Month Price Score 108.54

TRADING VOLUME (thousand shares)

Interim Earnings (Per Share)

Qtr.	Mar	Jun	Sep	Dec
2003	0.56	0.61	0.66	0.70
2004	0.67	0.75	0.80	0.83
2005	0.83	0.85	0.92	1.00
2006	0.92	1.56	1.08	1.00
2007	1.06	1.26	1.34	1.43

Interim Dividends (Per Share)

Amt	Decl	Ex	Rec	Pay
0.29Q	6/6/2007	7/3/2007	7/6/2007	8/10/2007
0.29Q	8/1/2007	10/3/2007	10/5/2007	11/9/2007
0.29Q	12/5/2007	1/16/2008	1/18/2008	2/8/2008
0.35Q	3/5/2008	4/9/2008	4/11/2008	5/9/2008

Indicated Div: $1.40

Valuation Analysis

		Institutional Holding	
Forecast P/E	14.38	No of Institutions	
	(1/10/2007)	642	
Market Cap	$33.7 Billion	Shares	
Book Value	11.8 Billion	320,232,096	
Price/Book	2.86	% Held	
Price/Sales	1.24	78.93	

Business Summary: Shipping (MIC: 15.3 SIC: 3731 NAIC: 336611)

General Dynamics is engaged in the provision of products and services in business aviation; combat vehicles, weapons systems and munitions; shipbuilding design and construction; and information systems, technologies and services. Co.'s Aerospace group designs, manufactures and services mid-size and large-cabin business-jet aircraft. Co.'s Combat Systems group design, develop, produce and support tracked and wheeled military vehicles, weapons systems and munitions. Co.'s Marine Systems group designs, builds and supports submarines and surface ships. Co.'s Information Systems and Technology group provide technologies, products and services for government and commercial clients.

Recent Developments: For the year ended Dec 31 2007, income from continuing operations increased 21.6% to US$2.08 billion from US$1.71 billion a year earlier. Net income increased 11.6% to US$2.07 billion from US$1.86 billion in the prior year. Revenues were US$27.24 billion, up 13.2% from US$24.06 billion the year before. Operating income was US$3.11 billion versus US$2.63 billion in the prior year, an increase of 18.6%. Direct operating expenses rose 12.5% to US$24.13 billion from US$21.44 billion in the comparable period the year before.

Prospects: For the full year of 2008, Co. is projecting sales in its Aerospace group to grow by 13.0% to 15.0%. In addition, Co. plans to deliver 157 new aircraft, an increase of 14.0% over its 2007 level. For the Combat Systems group, Co. is targeting sales growth of about 9.0% to 10.0%, with operating margins improving 30 to 50 basis points over 2007. For the Marine Systems group, Co. is targeting sales growth of 3.0% to 4.0% with margins improving by about 10 to 20 basis points over 2007. Also, Co. is forecasting sales in its Information Systems and Technology group to increase by 5.0% to 6.0%. Therefore, Co. is anticipating 2008 earnings to be in the range of $5.55 to $5.65 per diluted share.

Financial Data

(US$ in Thousands)	12/31/2007	12/31/2006	12/31/2005	12/31/2004	12/31/2003	12/31/2002	12/31/2001	12/31/2000
Earnings Per Share	5.08	4.56	3.61	3.04	2.52	2.26	2.33	2.24
Cash Flow Per Share	7.23	5.27	5.12	4.50	4.36	2.79	2.74	2.67
Tang Book Value Per Share	4.59	0.25	1.40	N.M.	N.M.	2.81	1.92	3.21
Dividends Per Share	1.100	0.890	0.780	0.700	0.630	0.590	0.550	0.510
Dividend Payout %	21.65	19.52	21.61	22.99	25.00	26.11	23.66	22.77
Income Statement								
Total Revenue	27,240,000	24,063,000	21,244,000	19,178,000	16,617,000	13,829,000	12,163,000	10,356,000
EBITDA	3,685,000	3,145,000	2,560,000	2,259,000	1,747,000	1,842,000	1,751,000	1,548,000
Income Before Taxes	3,047,000	2,527,000	2,100,000	1,785,000	1,372,000	1,584,000	1,424,000	1,262,000
Income Taxes	967,000	817,000	632,000	582,000	375,000	533,000	481,000	361,000
Net Income	2,072,000	1,856,000	1,461,000	1,227,000	1,004,000	917,000	943,000	901,000
Average Shares	408,100	406,827	404,848	402,934	398,304	405,704	405,814	402,601
Balance Sheet								
Current Assets	12,298,000	9,880,000	9,173,000	7,287,000	6,394,000	5,098,000	4,893,000	3,551,000
Total Assets	25,733,000	22,376,000	19,591,000	17,544,000	16,183,000	11,731,000	11,069,000	7,987,000
Current Liabilities	9,164,000	7,824,000	6,907,000	5,374,000	5,616,000	4,582,000	4,579,000	2,901,000
Long-Term Obligations	2,118,000	2,774,000	2,781,000	3,291,000	3,296,000	718,000	724,000	162,000
Total Liabilities	13,965,000	12,549,000	11,446,000	10,355,000	10,262,000	6,532,000	6,541,000	4,167,000
Stockholders' Equity	11,768,000	9,827,000	8,145,000	7,189,000	5,921,000	5,199,000	4,528,000	3,820,000
Shares Outstanding	403,979	405,800	400,363	402,066	395,932	401,986	401,492	401,004
Statistical Record								
Return on Assets %	8.61	8.85	7.87	7.26	7.19	8.04	9.90	11.40
Return on Equity %	19.19	20.65	19.06	18.67	18.06	18.85	22.59	25.71
EBITDA Margin %	13.53	13.07	12.05	11.78	10.51	13.32	14.40	14.95
Net Margin %	7.61	7.71	6.88	6.40	6.04	6.63	7.75	8.70
Asset Turnover	1.13	1.15	1.14	1.13	1.19	1.21	1.28	1.31
Current Ratio	1.34	1.26	1.33	1.36	1.14	1.11	1.07	1.22
Debt to Equity	0.18	0.28	0.34	0.46	0.56	0.14	0.16	0.04
Price Range	94.00-73.95	77.69-56.80	60.53-49.38	54.91-43.05	45.20-26.18	55.29-37.28	47.49-30.50	39.00-18.50
P/E Ratio	18.50-14.56	17.04-12.46	16.77-13.68	18.06-14.16	17.93-10.39	24.46-16.50	20.38-13.09	17.41-8.26
Average Yield %	1.35	1.33	1.41	1.44	1.72	1.34	1.43	1.76

Address: 2941 Fairview Park Drive, Suite 100, Falls Church, VA 22042-4513 **Telephone:** 703-876-3000 **Fax:** 703-876-3125	**Web Site:** www.generaldynamics.com **Officers:** Nicholas D. Chabraja - Chmn., C.E.O. Michael W. Toner - Exec. V.P., Group Exec., Marine Systems	**Auditors:** KPMG LLP **Investor Contact:** 703-876-3195 **Transfer Agents:** EquiServe Trust Company, N.A., Jersey City, NJ

GENERAL ELECTRIC CO

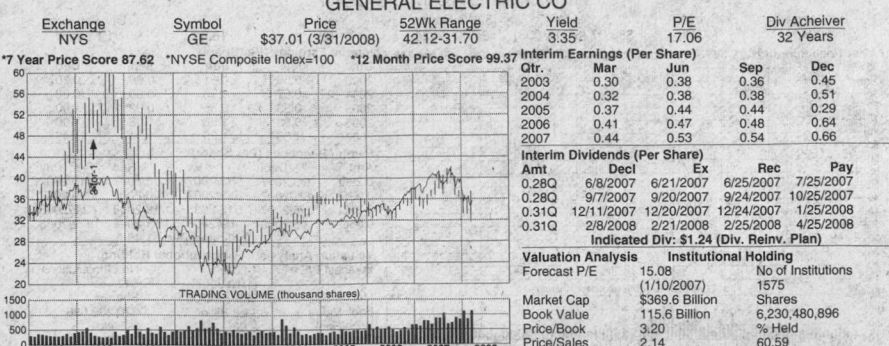

Exchange	Symbol	Price	52Wk Range	Yield	P/E	Div Acheiver
NYS	GE	$37.01 (3/31/2008)	42.12-31.70	3.35	17.06	32 Years

*7 Year Price Score 87.62   *NYSE Composite Index=100   *12 Month Price Score 99.37

Interim Earnings (Per Share)

Qtr.	Mar	Jun	Sep	Dec
2003	0.30	0.38	0.36	0.45
2004	0.32	0.38	0.38	0.51
2005	0.37	0.44	0.44	0.29
2006	0.41	0.47	0.48	0.64
2007	0.44	0.53	0.54	0.66

Interim Dividends (Per Share)

Amt	Decl	Ex	Rec	Pay
0.28Q	6/8/2007	6/21/2007	6/25/2007	7/25/2007
0.28Q	9/7/2007	9/20/2007	9/24/2007	10/25/2007
0.31Q	12/11/2007	12/20/2007	12/24/2007	1/25/2008
0.31Q	2/8/2008	2/21/2008	2/25/2008	4/25/2008

Indicated Div: $1.24 (Div. Reinv. Plan)

Valuation Analysis

	Institutional Holding	
Forecast P/E	15.08	No of Institutions
	(1/10/2007)	1575
Market Cap	$369.6 Billion	Shares
Book Value	115.6 Billion	6,230,480,896
Price/Book	3.20	% Held
Price/Sales	2.14	60.59

Business Summary: Electrical (MIC: 11.14 SIC: 3699 NAIC: 335999)

General Electric is a technology, media, and financial services corporation. With products and services ranging from aircraft engines, power generation, water processing, and security technology to medical imaging, business and consumer financing, media content and industrial products, Co. serves customers in more than 100 countries and employs more than 300,000 people worldwide. As of Dec 31 2007, Co. conducted its businesses through six operating segments which are: Infrastructure, Commercial Finance, GE Money, Healthcare, NBC Universal and Industrial.

Recent Developments: For the year ended Dec 31 2007, income from continuing operations increased 15.9% to US$22.47 billion from US$19.38 billion a year earlier. Net income increased 7.1% to US$22.21 billion from US$20.74 billion in the prior year. Revenues were US$172.74 billion, up 13.8% from US$151.84 billion the year before. Direct operating expenses rose 14.0% to US$104.93 billion from US$92.01 billion in the comparable period the year before. Indirect operating expenses increased 13.1% to US$40.30 billion from US$35.64 billion in the equivalent prior-year period.

Prospects: For the full year of 2008, Co. is projecting continuing earnings to be about $2.42 per share, an increase of about 10.0% over its 2007 level. Meanwhile, for the first quarter of 2008, Co. is anticipating continuing earnings in the range of $0.50 to $0.53 per share, reflecting growth of 4.0% to 10.0%, while net earnings are forecasted to range from $0.49 to $0.52 per share, representing an improvement of 11.0% to 18.0%. Separately, on Feb 4 2008, Co. acquired most of Merrill Lynch and Co., Inc.'s wholly-owned middle-market commercial finance business, Merrill Lynch Capital. This acquisition of over $12.00 billion in assets should strengthen Co.'s Commercial Finance business.

Financial Data

(US$ in Thousands)	12/31/2007	12/31/2006	12/31/2005	12/31/2004	12/31/2003	12/31/2002	12/31/2001	12/31/2000
Earnings Per Share	2.17	2.00	1.54	1.59	1.49	1.41	1.37	1.27
Cash Flow Per Share	4.51	2.96	3.56	3.50	3.02	2.96	3.24	2.29
Tang Book Value Per Share	1.83	2.52	2.64	2.55	2.40	1.76	2.33	2.32
Dividends Per Share	1.150	1.030	0.910	0.820	0.770	0.730	0.660	0.570
Dividend Payout %	53.00	51.50	59.09	51.57	51.68	51.77	48.18	44.88
Income Statement								
Total Revenue	172,738,000	163,391,000	149,702,000	152,363,000	134,187,000	131,698,000	125,913,000	129,853,000
EBITDA	36,876,000	33,778,000	30,667,000	31,722,000	26,860,000	24,889,000	26,790,000	26,182,000
Income Before Taxes	26,598,000	24,620,000	22,129,000	20,106,000	19,904,000	18,891,000	19,701,000	18,446,000
Income Taxes	4,130,000	3,954,000	3,854,000	3,513,000	4,315,000	3,758,000	5,573,000	5,711,000
Net Income	22,208,000	20,829,000	16,353,000	16,593,000	15,002,000	14,118,000	13,684,000	12,735,000
Average Shares	10,218,000	10,394,000	10,611,000	10,445,000	10,075,000	10,028,000	10,052,000	10,057,000
Balance Sheet								
Current Assets	50,903,000	39,630,000	34,336,000	39,339,000	32,148,000	28,838,000	27,237,000	25,509,000
Total Assets	795,337,000	697,239,000	673,342,000	750,330,000	647,483,000	575,244,000	495,023,000	437,006,000
Current Liabilities	246,113,000	220,514,000	204,927,000	206,280,000	176,530,000	181,827,000	198,904,000	156,112,000
Long-Term Obligations	319,015,000	260,804,000	212,281,000	213,161,000	170,004,000	140,632,000	79,806,000	82,132,000
Total Liabilities	671,774,000	577,347,000	555,934,000	623,663,000	562,523,000	506,065,000	434,984,000	381,578,000
Stockholders' Equity	115,559,000	112,314,000	109,354,000	110,284,000	79,180,000	63,706,000	54,824,000	50,492,000
Shares Outstanding	9,987,599	10,277,373	10,484,268	10,586,358	10,063,120	9,969,894	9,925,938	9,932,006
Statistical Record								
Return on Assets %	2.98	3.04	2.30	2.37	2.45	2.64	2.94	3.02
Return on Equity %	19.49	18.79	14.89	17.47	21.00	23.82	25.99	27.30
EBITDA Margin %	21.35	20.67	20.49	20.82	20.02	18.90	21.28	20.16
Net Margin %	12.86	12.75	10.92	10.89	11.18	10.72	10.87	9.81
Asset Turnover	0.23	0.24	0.21	0.22	0.22	0.25	0.27	0.31
Current Ratio	0.21	0.18	0.17	0.19	0.18	0.16	0.14	0.16
Debt to Equity	2.76	2.32	1.94	1.93	2.15	2.21	1.46	1.63
Price Range	42.12-34.09	38.15-32.11	37.18-32.68	37.48-29.18	32.11-22.17	41.55-22.00	53.40-30.37	60.00-41.71
P/E Ratio	19.41-15.71	19.07-16.06	24.14-21.22	23.57-18.35	21.55-14.88	29.47-15.60	38.98-22.17	47.24-32.84
Average Yield %	3.04	3.00	2.58	2.49	2.75	2.34	1.52	1.10

Address: 3135 Easton Turnpike, Fairfield, CT 06828-0001
Telephone: 203-373-2211
Fax: 203-373-3131

Web Site: www.ge.com
Officers: Jeffrey R. Immelt - Chmn., C.E.O. William M. Castell - Vice-Chmn.

Auditors: KPMG LLP
Investor Contact: 203-373-2816
Transfer Agents: GE Share Owner Services, c/o The Bank of New York, New York, NY

GENERAL GROWTH PROPERTIES, INC. (DE)

Exchange	Symbol	Price	52Wk Range	Yield	P/E	Div Acheiver
NYS	GGP	$38.17 (3/31/2008)	65.72-31.65	5.24	32.35	14 Years

*7 Year Price Score 119.39 *NYSE Composite Index=100 *12 Month Price Score 80.49

Interim Earnings (Per Share)

Qtr.	Mar	Jun	Sep	Dec
2003	0.24	0.23	0.29	1.12
2004	0.27	0.23	0.29	0.42
2005	0.06	0.01	(0.03)	0.28
2006	0.10	(0.11)	(0.03)	0.29
2007	0.94	0.03	(0.04)	0.24

Interim Dividends (Per Share)

Amt	Decl	Ex	Rec	Pay
0.45Q	7/5/2007	7/13/2007	7/17/2007	7/31/2007
0.50Q	10/4/2007	10/15/2007	10/17/2007	10/31/2007
0.50Q	1/7/2008	1/15/2008	1/17/2008	1/31/2008
0.50Q	4/4/2008	4/14/2008	4/16/2008	4/30/2008

Indicated Div: $2.00 (Div. Reinv. Plan)

Valuation Analysis

Forecast P/E	N/A
Market Cap	$9.3 Billion
Book Value	1.5 Billion
Price/Book	6.39
Price/Sales	2.85

Institutional Holding

No of Institutions	329
Shares	201,427,168
% Held	82.63

Business Summary: Property, Real Estate & Development (MIC: 8.3 SIC: 6798 NAIC: 525930)

General Growth Properties is a self-administered and self-managed real estate investment trust. Co.'s business is focused in two main areas: Retail and Other, which includes the operation, development and management of retail and other rental property, mainly shopping centers; and Master Planned Communities, which includes the development and sale of land, mainly in community development projects in and around Columbia, MD; Summerlin, NV; and Houston, TX. At Dec 31 2007, Co. had ownership interest in or management responsibility for over 200 regional shopping malls in 45 states. Also, Co. owned non-controlling interests in international joint ventures in Brazil, Turkey and Costa Rica.

Recent Developments: For the year ended Dec 31 2007, income from continuing operations increased 379.2% to US$288.0 million from US$60.1 million a year earlier. Net income increased 385.8% to US$288.0 million from US$59.3 million in the prior year. Revenues were US$3.26 billion, unchanged from the year before. Revenues from property income rose 10.8% to US$2.88 billion from US$2.60 billion in the corresponding earlier year.

Prospects: For full-year 2008, Co. anticipates that its Master Planned Communities segment will be tempered by several factors that include the weakening of the housing market and the estimated continued lower demand at its Las Vegas and Maryland communities. Meanwhile, Co. expects 2008 core funds from operations (FFO), which exclude real estate property net operating income from its master planned communities segment and its provision for income taxes, to be in the range of $3.58 to $3.61 per share, an increase of 20.5% to 21.5% from 2007. The significant increase in core FFO per share for 2008 reflects the elimination of certain 2007 non-recurring items.

Financial Data
(US$ in Thousands)

	12/31/2007	12/31/2006	12/31/2005	12/31/2004	12/31/2003	12/31/2002	12/31/2001	12/31/2000
Earnings Per Share	1.18	0.24	0.32	1.21	1.22	0.98	0.43	0.73
Cash Flow Per Share	2.90	3.38	3.54	3.41	2.88	2.47	1.31	1.98
Tang Book Value Per Share	4.39	5.34	6.32	9.13	7.69	6.39	6.37	5.98
Dividends Per Share	1.850	1.680	1.490	1.260	1.020	0.890	0.747	0.680
Dividend Payout %	156.78	700.00	465.63	104.13	83.61	90.51	175.00	93.58
Income Statement								
Property Income	2,882,491	2,602,487	2,494,851	1,588,496	1,150,315	871,559	713,316	682,109
Non-Property Income	379,310	653,796	578,565	214,349	120,413	108,907	90,393	16,658
Total Revenue	3,261,801	3,256,283	3,073,416	1,802,845	1,270,728	980,466	803,709	698,767
Interest Expense	1,174,097	1,117,437	1,031,241	472,185	278,543	218,935	214,277	218,075
Income Taxes	(294,160)	98,084	50,616	2,383	...	...	...	...
Net Income	287,954	59,273	75,553	267,852	263,411	209,238	92,310	137,948
Average Shares	244,538	242,054	238,469	220,829	215,079	212,553	158,721	156,288
Balance Sheet								
Total Assets	28,814,319	25,241,445	25,307,019	25,718,625	9,582,897	7,280,822	5,646,807	5,284,104
Long-Term Obligations	24,282,139	20,521,967	20,418,875	20,310,947	6,649,490	4,592,311	3,398,207	3,244,126
Total Liabilities	26,884,779	23,046,785	22,737,865	22,621,032	7,008,664	4,900,850	3,570,562	3,478,028
Stockholders' Equity	1,456,696	1,664,079	1,932,918	2,143,150	1,670,409	1,196,525	1,183,386	938,418
Shares Outstanding	243,898	242,066	239,196	234,724	217,293	187,191	185,771	156,843
Statistical Record								
Return on Assets %	1.07	0.23	0.30	1.51	3.12	3.24	1.69	2.69
Return on Equity %	18.45	3.30	3.71	14.01	18.38	17.59	8.70	14.74
Net Margin %	8.83	1.82	2.46	14.86	20.73	21.34	11.49	19.74
Price Range	67.00-40.55	55.70-42.36	47.86-31.64	36.63-25.51	27.89-16.09	17.33-12.91	13.39-11.00	12.06-8.94
P/E Ratio	56.78-34.36	232.08-176.50	149.56-98.88	30.27-21.08	22.86-13.19	17.69-13.17	31.15-25.58	16.52-12.24
Average Yield %	3.36	3.50	3.70	4.07	4.78	5.71	6.10	6.47

Address: 110 North Wacker Drive, Chicago, IL 60606 Telephone: 312-960-5000 Fax: 312-960-5475	Web Site: www.generalgrowth.com Officers: Matthew Bucksbaum - Chmn. Robert Michaels - Pres., C.O.O.	Auditors: Deloitte & Touche LLP Transfer Agents: Mellon Investor Services, LLC, South Hackensack, NJ

GENERAL MILLS, INC.

Exchange	Symbol	Price	52Wk Range	Yield	P/E
NYS	GIS	$59.88 (3/31/2008)	61.47-52.86	2.67	15.68

*7 Year Price Score 94.33 ***NYSE Composite Index=100** ***12 Month Price Score 105.52**

Interim Earnings (Per Share)

Qtr.	Aug	Nov	Feb	May
2004-05	0.47	0.97	0.58	1.14
2005-06	0.64	0.97	0.68	0.61
2006-07	0.74	1.08	0.74	0.63
2007-08	0.81	1.14	1.23	...

Interim Dividends (Per Share)

Amt	Decl	Ex	Rec	Pay
0.39Q	6/25/2007	7/6/2007	7/10/2007	8/1/2007
0.39Q	9/24/2007	10/5/2007	10/10/2007	11/1/2007
0.39Q	12/10/2007	1/8/2008	1/10/2008	2/1/2008
0.40Q	3/10/2008	4/8/2008	4/10/2008	5/1/2008

Indicated Div: $1.60

Valuation Analysis

	Institutional Holding	
Forecast P/E	15.59 (1/10/2007)	No of Institutions 672
Market Cap	$20.1 Billion	Shares
Book Value	5.9 Billion	258,590,720
Price/Book	3.38	% Held
Price/Sales	1.51	74.66

Business Summary: Food (MIC: 4.1 SIC: 2043 NAIC: 311230)

General Mills manufactures and markets branded, packaged, consumer foods and operates in the consumer foods industry. Co. also supplies branded and unbranded food products to the foodservice and commercial baking industries. Co.'s product categories are ready-to-eat cereals, refrigerated yogurt, ready-to-serve soup, dry dinners, shelf stable and frozen vegetables, refrigerated and frozen dough products, dessert and baking mixes, frozen pizza and pizza snacks, grain, fruit, and savory snacks, microwave popcorn, and organic products including soup, granola bars, and cereal. As of May 27 2007, these products were manufactured by Co. in 18 countries and marketed in more than 100 countries.

Recent Developments: For the quarter ended Feb 24 2008, net income increased 60.8% to US$430.1 million from US$267.5 million in the year-earlier quarter. Revenues were US$3.41 billion, up 11.5% from US$3.05 billion the year before. Operating income was US$695.4 million versus US$486.1 million in the prior-year quarter, an increase of 43.1%. Direct operating expenses rose 3.5% to US$2.05 billion from US$1.98 billion in the comparable period the year before. Indirect operating expenses increased 12.5% to US$658.8 million from US$585.6 million in the equivalent prior-year period.

Prospects: Co.'s near-term outlook appears encouraging, reflecting continued strong demand for its products across global markets. For the fiscal quarter ended May 31 2008, Co. expects input costs to be above its previous fiscal year's levels. Also, Co. plans to make strong investments in consumer marketing activities, in order to help drive continued net sales momentum through the fourth fiscal quarter of 2008 and into fiscal 2009. In this respect, Co. now anticipates earnings for the fiscal year ending May 31 2008 to be in the range of $3.45 to $3.47 per share, excluding an estimated $0.30 of non-cash commodity and tax items, versus earnings per share of $3.18 in the previous fiscal year.

Financial Data
(US$ in Thousands)

	9 Mos	6 Mos	3 Mos	05/27/2007	05/28/2006	05/29/2005	05/30/2004	05/25/2003
Earnings Per Share	3.82	3.33	3.27	3.18	2.90	3.08	2.75	2.43
Cash Flow Per Share	4.55	5.03	5.10	5.10	4.96	4.62	3.83	4.43
Dividends Per Share	1.540	1.520	1.480	1.440	1.340	1.240	1.100	1.100
Dividend Payout %	40.33	45.62	45.29	45.28	46.21	40.26	40.00	45.27
Income Statement								
Total Revenue	10,181,000	6,775,400	3,072,000	12,442,000	11,640,000	11,244,000	11,070,000	10,506,000
EBITDA	2,241,300	1,432,800	618,300	2,476,000	2,390,000	2,713,000	2,416,000	2,228,000
Depn & Amortn	348,700	235,600	108,200	...	...	...	...	...
Income Before Taxes	1,560,800	968,000	396,800	1,631,000	1,567,000	1,815,000	1,509,000	1,316,000
Income Taxes	531,000	338,600	130,300	560,000	541,000	664,000	528,000	460,000
Net Income	1,109,500	679,400	288,900	1,144,000	1,090,000	1,240,000	1,055,000	917,000
Average Shares	349,700	342,400	344,900	360,000	379,000	409,000	384,000	378,000
Balance Sheet								
Current Assets	3,958,300	3,843,900	3,478,100	3,054,000	3,176,000	3,055,000	3,215,000	3,179,000
Total Assets	19,266,800	19,081,500	18,477,900	18,184,000	18,207,000	18,066,000	18,448,000	18,227,000
Current Liabilities	6,141,100	6,223,100	7,505,400	5,845,000	6,138,000	4,184,000	2,757,000	3,444,000
Long-Term Obligations	3,600,700	3,599,100	3,003,800	3,218,000	2,415,000	4,255,000	7,410,000	7,516,000
Total Liabilities	13,097,700	13,159,700	13,776,900	11,726,000	11,299,000	11,257,000	12,901,000	13,752,000
Stockholders' Equity	5,926,800	5,679,500	4,458,700	5,319,000	5,772,000	5,676,000	5,248,000	4,175,000
Shares Outstanding	335,000	336,000	321,100	340,000	356,000	369,000	379,000	370,000
Statistical Record								
Return on Assets %	7.05	6.21	6.31	6.30	6.03	6.81	5.66	5.29
Return on Equity %	22.48	20.95	23.88	20.69	19.09	22.76	22.03	23.73
EBITDA Margin %	22.01	21.15	20.13	19.90	20.53	24.13	21.82	21.21
Net Margin %	10.90	10.03	9.40	9.19	9.36	11.03	9.53	8.73
Asset Turnover	0.70	0.68	0.68	0.69	0.64	0.62	0.59	0.61
Current Ratio	0.64	0.62	0.46	0.52	0.52	0.73	1.17	0.92
Debt to Equity	0.61	0.63	0.67	0.61	0.42	0.75	1.41	1.80
Price Range	61.47-52.86	61.47-54.84	61.47-52.16	60.97-49.45	52.09-44.68	53.36-43.30	49.66-43.86	48.00-38.40
P/E Ratio	16.09-13.84	18.46-16.47	18.80-15.95	19.17-15.55	17.96-15.41	17.32-14.06	18.06-15.95	19.75-15.80
Average Yield %	2.67	2.63	2.59	2.58	2.76	2.59	2.38	2.50

Address: Number One General Mills Boulevard, Minneapolis, MN 55426-1347 **Telephone:** 763-764-7600 **Fax:** 763-764-7384	**Web Site:** www.generalmills.com **Officers:** Stephen W. Sanger - Chmn., C.E.O. James A. Lawrence - Exec. V.P., C.F.O., International	**Auditors:** KPMG LLP **Investor Contact:** 763-764-2607 **Transfer Agents:** Wells Fargo Bank Minnesota, N.A., St. Paul, MN

GENERAL MOTORS CORP

Exchange	Symbol	Price	52Wk Range	Yield	P/E
NYS	GM	$19.05 (3/31/2008)	42.64-17.83	5.25	N/A

*7 Year Price Score 63.55   *NYSE Composite Index=100   *12 Month Price Score 82.26

TRADING VOLUME (thousand shares)

Interim Earnings (Per Share)

Qtr.	Mar	Jun	Sep	Dec
2003	2.71	1.58	0.00	2.15
2004	2.25	2.36	0.78	(0.44)
2005	(1.95)	(0.51)	(2.89)	(11.95)
2006	0.78	(5.97)	(0.16)	1.85
2007	0.11	1.56	(68.85)	(1.27)

Interim Dividends (Per Share)

Amt	Decl	Ex	Rec	Pay
0.25Q	5/1/2007	5/9/2007	5/11/2007	6/9/2007
0.25Q	8/7/2007	8/15/2007	8/17/2007	9/10/2007
0.25Q	11/6/2007	11/14/2007	11/16/2007	12/10/2007
0.25Q	2/5/2008	2/13/2008	2/15/2008	3/10/2008

Indicated Div: $1.00

Valuation Analysis

		Institutional Holding	
Forecast P/E	7.64	No of Institutions	
	(1/10/2007)	383	
Market Cap	$10.8 Billion	Shares	
Book Value	N/A	529,819,328	
Price/Book	N/A	% Held	
Price/Sales	0.06	93.65	

Business Summary: Automotive (MIC: 15.1 SIC: 3711 NAIC: 336111)

General Motors is primarily engaged in the worldwide development, production and marketing of cars, trucks and parts. Co. develops, manufactures and markets its vehicles worldwide through its four automotive regions: GM North America, GM Europe, GM Latin America/Africa/Mid-East and GM Asia Pacific. Co.'s total worldwide car and truck deliveries were 9.4 million as of Dec 31 2007. In addition, Co. also sells cars and trucks to fleet customers, including daily rental car companies, commercial fleet customers, leasing companies and governments. As of Dec 31 2007, Co. operated through two businesses, consisting of Automotive as well as Financing and Insurance Operations.

Recent Developments: For the year ended Dec 31 2007, loss from continuing operations was US$43.30 billion compared with a loss of US$2.42 billion a year earlier. Net loss amounted to US$38.73 billion versus a net loss of US$1.98 billion in the prior year. Revenues were US$181.12 billion, down 11.9% from US$205.60 billion the year before. Operating loss was US$4.39 billion versus a loss of US$5.82 billion in the prior year. Direct operating expenses declined 12.7% to US$169.00 billion from US$193.54 billion in the comparable period the year before. Indirect operating expenses decreased 7.7% to US$16.51 billion from US$17.89 billion in the equivalent prior-year period.

Prospects: Despite the uncertainty in the U.S. market, Co. continues to anticipate improved pre-tax automotive earnings in 2008 versus 2007, mainly driven by continued strong performance in potential markets. In addition, Co. is projecting improvements in automotive revenue, better pricing, encouraging material cost performance and continued reductions in structural cost as a percentage of revenue in 2008. Meanwhile, Co. estimates that should the U.S. market volume returns to favorable levels in 2009 and beyond, which would represent an increase of 1.0 million units, the change would generate additional pre-tax income to Co. in the range of approximately $1.00 billion to $1.50 billion annually.

Financial Data

(US$ in Thousands)	12/31/2007	12/31/2006	12/31/2005	12/31/2004	12/31/2003	12/31/2002	12/31/2001	12/31/2000
Earnings Per Share	(68.45)	(3.50)	(18.69)	4.95	7.14	3.35	1.77	6.68
Cash Flow Per Share	13.66	(20.78)	(29.83)	23.05	13.55	30.55	16.64	33.84
Tang Book Value Per Share	...	...	18.14	40.35	36.49	N.M.	N.M.	10.80
Dividends Per Share	1.000	1.000	2.000	2.000	2.000	2.000	2.000	2.000
Dividend Payout %	...	...	...	40.40	28.01	59.70	112.99	29.94
Income Statement								
Total Revenue	181,122,000	207,349,000	192,604,000	193,517,000	185,524,000	186,763,000	177,260,000	184,632,000
EBITDA	(3,351,000)	7,024,000	(20,000)	13,116,000	15,130,000	15,018,000	14,426,000	20,575,000
Income Before Taxes	(6,253,000)	(4,947,000)	(16,931,000)	1,192,000	2,981,000	2,080,000	1,518,000	7,164,000
Income Taxes	37,162,000	(2,785,000)	(5,878,000)	(911,000)	731,000	533,000	768,000	2,393,000
Net Income	(38,732,000)	(1,978,000)	(10,567,000)	2,805,000	3,822,000	1,736,000	601,000	4,452,000
Average Shares	566,000	566,000	565,000	1,557,000	1,669,000	1,481,500	1,442,000	1,291,000
Balance Sheet								
Current Assets	60,403,000	64,480,000	99,414,000	91,213,000	86,261,000	63,956,000	47,186,000	42,312,000
Total Assets	148,883,000	186,192,000	476,078,000	479,603,000	448,507,000	370,782,000	323,969,000	303,100,000
Current Liabilities	70,338,000	69,036,000	117,963,000	129,013,000	32,930,000	104,084,000	129,373,000	142,298,000
Long-Term Obligations	38,292,000	42,505,000	202,177,000	207,174,000	271,756,000	134,272,000	104,638,000	65,704,000
Total Liabilities	184,363,000	190,443,000	460,442,000	451,480,000	422,932,000	363,134,000	303,516,000	272,079,000
Stockholders' Equity	(37,094,000)	(5,441,000)	14,597,000	27,726,000	25,268,000	6,814,000	19,707,000	30,175,000
Shares Outstanding	566,059	565,670	565,518	565,132	561,997	1,518,732	1,436,549	1,423,468
Statistical Record								
Return on Assets %	N.M.	N.M.	N.M.	0.60	0.93	0.50	0.19	1.54
Return on Equity %	...	N.M.	N.M.	10.56	23.83	13.09	2.41	17.47
EBITDA Margin %	N.M.	3.39	N.M.	6.78	8.16	8.04	8.14	11.14
Net Margin %	N.M.	N.M.	N.M.	1.45	2.06	0.93	0.34	2.41
Asset Turnover	1.08	0.63	0.40	0.42	0.45	0.54	0.57	0.64
Current Ratio	0.86	0.93	0.84	0.71	2.62	0.61	0.36	0.30
Debt to Equity	...	...	13.85	7.47	10.75	19.71	5.31	2.18
Price Range	42.64-24.89	36.19-18.90	40.30-18.61	55.00-37.04	53.70-29.92	68.02-31.01	67.04-40.10	93.63-48.81
P/E Ratio	...	...	...	11.11-7.48	7.52-4.19	20.30-9.26	37.88-22.66	14.02-7.31
Average Yield %	3.08	3.68	6.40	4.50	5.17	4.07	3.73	2.89

Address: 300 Renaissance Center, P.O. Box 300, Detroit, MI 48265-3000 **Telephone:** 313-556-5000 **Fax:** 313-556-5108	**Web Site:** www.gm.com **Officers:** G. Richard Wagoner Jr. - Chmn., C.E.O. John M. Devine - Vice-Chmn., C.F.O.	**Auditors:** Deloitte & Touche LLP **Investor Contact:** 212-418-6270 **Transfer Agents:** BankBoston c/o Boston EquiServe Trust Co., Boston, MA

GENUINE PARTS CO.

Exchange	Symbol	Price	52Wk Range	Yield	P/E	Div Acheiver
NYS	GPC	$40.22 (3/31/2008)	51.43-39.15	3.88	13.50	51 Years

*7 Year Price Score 97.58   *NYSE Composite Index=100   *12 Month Price Score 95.12

Interim Earnings (Per Share)

Qtr.	Mar	Jun	Sep	Dec
2003	0.39	0.52	0.51	0.49
2004	0.57	0.58	0.56	0.54
2005	0.61	0.63	0.63	0.63
2006	0.66	0.70	0.71	0.70
2007	0.71	0.76	0.76	0.75

Interim Dividends (Per Share)

Amt	Decl	Ex	Rec	Pay
0.365Q	4/23/2007	6/6/2007	6/8/2007	7/2/2007
0.365Q	8/20/2007	9/5/2007	9/7/2007	10/1/2007
0.365Q	11/19/2007	12/5/2007	12/7/2007	1/2/2008
0.39Q	2/19/2008	3/5/2008	3/7/2008	4/1/2008

Indicated Div: $1.56 (Div. Reinv. Plan)

Valuation Analysis — **Institutional Holding**

Forecast P/E	14.17	No of Institutions
	(1/10/2007)	355
Market Cap	$6.7 Billion	Shares
Book Value	2.7 Billion	126,236,880
Price/Book	2.46	% Held
Price/Sales	0.62	74.04

Business Summary: Retail - Automotive (MIC: 5.7 SIC: 5013 NAIC: 423120)

Genuine Parts is a service organization that distributes automotive replacement parts, industrial replacement parts, office products and electrical/electronic materials. Co.'s Automotive Parts Group distributes automotive replacement parts and accessory items. The Industrial Parts Group distributes industrial replacement parts and related supplies in the U.S. and Canada. The Office Products Group is engaged in the wholesale distribution of office and other business related products that are used in the daily operation of businesses, schools, offices and institutions. The Electrical/Electronic Materials Group distributes materials to electrical and electronic manufacturers in North America.

Recent Developments: For the year ended Dec 31 2007, net income increased 6.5% to US$506.3 million from US$475.4 million in the prior year. Revenues were US$10.84 billion, up 3.7% from US$10.46 billion the year before. Direct operating expenses rose 3.7% to US$7.63 billion from US$7.35 billion in the comparable period the year before. Indirect operating expenses increased 3.1% to US$2.38 billion from US$2.31 billion in the equivalent prior-year period.

Prospects: For 2008, Co. will remain focused on driving sales growth, controlling costs and improving its operating margins across its four segments; and believes that its operating performance for the second half of 2008 will be slightly stronger than the first half of 2006. Accordingly, for full year 2008, Co. projects revenue growth of 5.0% to 8.0% for both its Industrial and the Electrical/ Electronic product group, revenue growth of 2.0% to 5.0% in its Automotive Parts group, and revenue growth of 1.0% to 4.0% in its Office Products group, thus resulting in total revenue growth of 3.0% to 6.0%. With that, Co. estimates net income growth of 4.0% to 7.0% and earnings per share of $3.12 to $3.22.

Financial Data

(US$ in Thousands)	12/31/2007	12/31/2006	12/31/2005	12/31/2004	12/31/2003	12/31/2002	12/31/2001	12/31/2000
Earnings Per Share	2.98	2.76	2.50	2.25	1.91	(0.16)	1.71	2.20
Cash Flow Per Share	3.79	2.53	2.53	3.17	2.31	1.56	1.93	1.79
Tang Book Value Per Share	15.86	14.59	15.21	14.21	12.95	11.88	10.97	10.50
Dividends Per Share	1.460	1.350	1.250	1.200	1.180	1.160	1.140	1.100
Dividend Payout %	48.99	48.91	50.00	53.33	61.78	...	66.67	50.00
Income Statement								
Total Revenue	10,843,195	10,457,942	9,783,050	9,097,267	8,449,300	8,258,927	8,220,668	8,369,857
EBITDA	935,774	875,915	774,593	698,126	640,756	675,887	581,806	739,053
Income Before Taxes	816,745	770,916	709,064	635,919	571,743	605,736	496,013	646,750
Income Taxes	310,406	295,511	271,630	240,367	218,101	238,236	198,866	261,427
Net Income	506,339	475,405	437,434	395,552	334,101	(27,590)	297,147	385,323
Average Shares	170,135	172,486	175,007	175,660	174,480	175,104	173,633	175,327
Balance Sheet								
Current Assets	4,053,012	3,835,127	3,806,882	3,633,484	3,417,626	3,335,775	3,146,212	3,019,481
Total Assets	4,774,069	4,496,984	4,771,538	4,455,247	4,116,497	4,019,843	4,206,646	4,142,114
Current Liabilities	1,547,976	1,198,768	1,249,104	1,132,715	1,016,931	1,069,718	919,181	988,313
Long-Term Obligations	263,707	512,248	500,000	500,000	625,108	674,796	835,580	770,581
Total Liabilities	2,057,353	1,946,993	2,077,581	1,910,870	1,804,214	1,889,834	1,861,523	1,881,308
Stockholders' Equity	2,716,716	2,549,991	2,693,957	2,544,377	2,312,283	2,130,009	2,345,123	2,260,806
Shares Outstanding	166,065	170,530	173,032	174,964	174,045	174,380	173,473	172,389
Statistical Record								
Return on Assets %	10.92	10.26	9.48	9.20	8.21	N.M.	7.12	9.52
Return on Equity %	19.23	18.13	16.70	16.24	15.04	N.M.	12.90	17.32
EBITDA Margin %	8.63	8.38	7.92	7.67	7.58	8.18	7.08	8.83
Net Margin %	4.67	4.55	4.47	4.35	3.95	N.M.	3.61	4.60
Asset Turnover	2.34	2.26	2.12	2.12	2.08	2.01	1.97	2.07
Current Ratio	2.62	3.20	3.05	3.21	3.36	3.12	3.42	3.06
Debt to Equity	0.10	0.20	0.19	0.20	0.27	0.32	0.36	0.34
Price Range	51.43-46.30	48.02-40.26	46.50-40.98	44.06-32.13	33.66-27.43	38.08-27.64	37.44-24.26	26.44-18.63
P/E Ratio	17.26-15.54	17.40-14.59	18.60-16.39	19.58-14.28	17.62-14.36	...	21.89-14.19	12.02-8.47
Average Yield %	2.98	3.09	2.87	3.20	3.74	3.48	3.78	4.98

Address: 2999 Circle 75 Parkway, Atlanta, GA 30339	Web Site: www.genpt.com	Auditors: Ernst & Young LLP
Telephone: 770-953-1700	Officers: Larry L. Prince - Chmn. Thomas C. Gallagher - Pres., C.E.O.	Investor Contact: 770-953-1700
Fax: 770-956-2211		Transfer Agents: Sun Trust Bank, Atlanta, GA

GENWORTH FINANCIAL INC

Exchange	Symbol	Price	52Wk Range	Yield	P/E
NYS	GNW	$22.64 (3/31/2008)	36.51-20.59	1.77	8.29

*7 Year Price Score N/A   *NYSE Composite Index=100   *12 Month Price Score 84.78

Interim Earnings (Per Share)

Qtr.	Mar	Jun	Sep	Dec
2003			2.21	
2004	0.56	0.55	0.55	0.00
2005	0.65	0.60	0.64	0.00
2006	0.70	0.68	0.65	0.81
2007	0.71	0.84	0.76	0.41

Interim Dividends (Per Share)

Amt	Decl	Ex	Rec	Pay
0.09Q	5/15/2007	7/10/2007	7/12/2007	7/27/2007
0.10Q	9/21/2007	10/10/2007	10/12/2007	10/29/2007
0.10Q	11/30/2007	1/9/2008	1/11/2008	1/28/2000
0.10Q	3/19/2008	4/9/2008	4/11/2008	4/28/2008

Indicated Div: $0.40

Valuation Analysis   Institutional Holding

Forecast P/E	N/A	No of Institutions
		366
Market Cap	$9.9 Billion	Shares
Book Value	13.5 Billion	432,569,440
Price/Book	0.73	%, Held
Price/Sales	0.89	98.14

Business Summary: Insurance (MIC: 8.2 SIC: 6311 NAIC: 524113)

Genworth Financial is a financial security company serving the homeownership, life security, wealth management and retirement security needs. As of Dec 31 2007, Co. had three operating segments. The Retirement and Protection segment offers a variety of protection, wealth accumulation, retirement income and institutional products. The International segment provides mortgage insurance products in Canada, Australia, New Zealand, Mexico, Japan and multiple European countries. The U.S. Mortgage Insurance offers mortgage insurance products predominantly insuring prime-based, individually underwritten residential mortgage loans, also known as flow mortgage insurance in the U.S.

Recent Developments: For the year ended Dec 31 2007, income from continuing operations decreased 10.1% to US$1.15 billion from US$1.28 billion a year earlier. Net income decreased 8.1% to US$1.22 billion from US$1.33 billion in the prior year. Revenues were US$11.13 billion, up 8.2% from US$10.29 billion the year before. Net premiums earned were US$6.33 billion versus US$5.80 billion in the prior year, an increase of 9.1%. Net investment income rose 9.2% to US$4.14 billion from US$3.79 billion a year ago.

Prospects: Co. remains cautious on its 2008 outlook, given the accelerating downturn in the U.S. housing market, slowing global economies and a shifting interest rate environment. Co. also expects to continue to experience lower sales and persistency in term life insurance policies, as it maintains pricing discipline in the competitive pricing condition. However, Co. believes that the higher demand for private mortgage insurance, higher interest rates and persistency, and its ongoing growth strategy will lead to growth in insurance in-force and related net earned premiums. For 2008, in view of current trends, Co. expects operating earnings per share to be at the lower end of $2.65 to $3.15 range.

Financial Data

(US$ in Thousands)	12/31/2007	12/31/2006	12/31/2005	12/31/2004	12/31/2003	12/31/2002	12/31/2001
Earnings Per Share	2.73	2.83	2.82	2.36	2.21	...	...
Cash Flow Per Share	10.90	...	7.32	11.20	7.59	...	...
Tang Book Value Per Share	23.15	24.27	23.52	21.69	26.00	...	...
Dividends Per Share	0.370	0.315	0.270	0.065	...	...	...
Dividend Payout %	13.55	11.13	10.71	2.75	...	...	...
Income Statement							
Premium Income	6,330,000	6,487,000	6,297,000	6,559,000	6,703,000	6,107,000	6,012,000
Total Revenue	11,125,000	11,029,000	10,504,000	11,057,000	11,671,000	11,229,000	11,101,000
Income Before Taxes	1,606,000	1,918,000	1,798,000	1,638,000	1,382,000	1,791,000	1,821,000
Income Taxes	452,000	594,000	577,000	493,000	413,000	111,000	390,000
Net Income	1,220,000	1,328,000	1,221,000	1,157,000	1,081,000	1,174,000	1,396,000
Average Shares	447,600	469,400	484,600	490,500	489,500	...	...
Balance Sheet							
Total Assets	114,315,000	110,871,000	105,292,000	103,878,000	103,431,000	117,357,000	...
Total Liabilities	100,837,000	97,541,000	91,982,000	91,012,000	87,631,000	100,605,000	...
Stockholders' Equity	13,478,000	13,330,000	13,310,000	12,866,000	15,800,000	16,752,000	...
Shares Outstanding	436,000	443,000	471,000	489,600	489,528	...	...
Statistical Record							
Return on Assets %	1.08	...	1.17	1.11	0.98	...	...
Return on Equity %	9.10	...	9.33	8.05	6.64	...	...
Net Margin %	10.97	12.04	11.62	10.46	9.26	10.46	12.58
Price Range	37.00-23.33	36.24-31.78	34.98-25.72	27.25-19.47	...	...	...
P/E Ratio	13.55-8.55	12.81-11.23	13.88-10.21	11.55-8.25	...	...	...
Average Yield %	1.16	0.93	0.90	0.28	...	...	...

Address: 6620 West Broad Street, Richmond, VA 23230 **Telephone:** 804-281-6000	Web Site: www.genworth.com **Officers:** Michael D. Fraizer - Chmn., Pres, C.E.O. Richard P. McKenney - Sr. V.P., C.F.O.	**Auditors:** KPMG LLP **Transfer Agents:** The Bank of New York

GETTY IMAGES, INC.

Exchange	Symbol	Price	52Wk Range	Yield	P/E
NYS	GYI	$32.00 (3/31/2008)	52.00-21.94	N/A	15.24

*7 Year Price Score 63.62   ***NYSE Composite Index=100**   ***12 Month Price Score 89.04**

TRADING VOLUME (thousand shares)

Interim Earnings (Per Share)

Qtr.	Mar	Jun	Sep	Dec
2003	0.23	0.23	0.16	0.49
2004	0.43	0.41	0.44	0.44
2005	0.54	0.53	0.60	0.64
2006	0.61	0.35	0.62	0.51
2007	0.63	0.56	0.43	0.48

Interim Dividends (Per Share)

No Dividends Paid

Valuation Analysis

		Institutional Holding	
Forecast P/E	15.08	No of Institutions	
	(1/10/2007)	200	
Market Cap	$1.9 Billion	Shares	
Book Value	1.4 Billion	48,349,544	
Price/Book	1.33	% Held	
Price/Sales	2.22	80.89	

Business Summary: Advertising, Marketing & PR (MIC: 12.4 SIC: 7336 NAIC: 541430)

Getty Images provides a variety of visual content, including creative or "stock" imagery, stock footage, editorial imagery (news, sports, entertainment and archival imagery), illustrations and related services. Co. also offers music for use in advertising, communications, television programming and feature films. Co.'s products are licensed through company-owned offices, a global network of delegates, who act as sales agents in countries where Co. does not have wholly-owned offices, and distributors. As of Dec 31 2007, Co.'s contents are available through websites, including www.gettyimages.com, www.punchstock.com, www.istockphoto.com, and www.wireimage.com and www.pumpaudio.com.

Recent Developments: For the year ended Dec 31 2007, net income decreased 3.5% to US$125.9 million from US$130.4 million in the prior year. Revenues were US$857.6 million, up 6.3% from US$806.6 million the year before. Operating income was US$196.3 million versus US$198.1 million in the prior year, a decrease of 0.9%. Direct operating expenses rose 10.3% to US$228.2 million from US$206.8 million in the comparable period the year before. Indirect operating expenses increased 7.8% to US$433.1 million from US$401.7 million in the equivalent prior-year period.

Prospects: On Feb 25 2008, Co. entered into a definitive agreement to be acquired by affiliates of the private equity firm Hellman & Friedman LLC in a transaction valued at approximately $2.40 billion, including the assumption of existing debt. Under the terms of the agreement, Co.'s stockholders will receive $34.00 in cash for each outstanding share of common stock they own. Co. expects the transaction to close in the second quarter of 2008. Separately, for the first quarter of 2008, Co. expects revenue of approximately $220.0 million and diluted earnings per share of $0.45 and expects revenue of approximately $900.0 million and diluted earnings per share of $2.00 to $2.10 for full-year 2008.

Financial Data

(US$ in Thousands)	12/31/2007	12/31/2006	12/31/2005	12/31/2004	12/31/2003	12/31/2002	12/31/2001	12/31/2000
Earnings Per Share	2.10	2.11	2.28	1.72	1.11	0.39	(1.84)	(3.40)
Cash Flow Per Share	4.20	4.43	4.18	3.42	2.85	1.99	0.88	0.76
Tang Book Value Per Share	1.31	2.88	6.23	6.92	3.77	0.86	N.M.	N.M.
Income Statement								
Total Revenue	857,591	806,589	733,729	622,427	523,196	463,011	450,985	484,846
EBITDA	288,024	270,282	284,372	228,184	154,779	125,864	56,843	15,714
Income Before Taxes	201,634	204,676	230,654	174,039	87,716	36,087	(98,662)	(164,151)
Income Taxes	75,763	74,248	80,951	67,389	23,699	14,619	(3,350)	5,567
Net Income	125,871	130,428	149,703	106,650	64,017	21,468	(95,312)	(169,334)
Average Shares	60,053	61,711	65,744	62,031	57,496	55,455	51,723	49,708
Balance Sheet								
Current Assets	504,489	487,025	645,663	631,862	407,509	212,589	150,641	204,025
Total Assets	2,012,155	1,714,384	1,663,085	1,451,584	1,224,084	1,025,055	993,081	1,100,636
Current Liabilities	480,846	133,201	396,645	113,780	115,083	111,078	137,366	142,662
Long-Term Obligations	...	265,000	...	265,000	265,011	244,739	256,215	274,427
Total Liabilities	584,227	466,147	420,125	388,472	388,278	357,102	393,581	417,089
Stockholders' Equity	1,427,928	1,248,237	1,242,960	1,063,112	835,806	667,953	599,500	683,547
Shares Outstanding	59,568	59,096	62,265	60,735	57,325	53,887	51,924	50,806
Statistical Record								
Return on Assets %	6.76	7.72	9.61	7.95	5.69	2.13	N.M.	N.M.
Return on Equity %	9.41	10.47	12.98	11.20	8.51	3.39	N.M.	N.M.
EBITDA Margin %	33.59	33.51	38.76	36.66	29.58	27.18	12.60	3.24
Net Margin %	14.68	16.17	20.40	17.13	12.24	4.64	N.M.	N.M.
Asset Turnover	0.46	0.48	0.47	0.46	0.46	0.46	0.43	0.47
Current Ratio	1.05	3.66	1.63	5.55	3.54	1.92	1.10	1.43
Debt to Equity	...	0.21	...	0.25	0.32	0.37	0.43	0.40
Price Range	56.06-26.65	90.29-41.65	93.98-64.85	69.30-47.50	50.74-25.80	38.11-13.80	37.00-9.29	60.50-23.47
P/E Ratio	26.70-12.69	42.79-19.74	41.22-28.44	40.29-27.62	45.71-23.24	97.72-35.38	...	...

Address: 601 N. 34th Street, Seattle, WA 98103	Web Site: www.gettyimages.com	Auditors: PricewaterhouseCoopers LLP
Telephone: 206-925-5000	Officers: Mark H. Getty - Chmn. Mark Torrance - Vice-Chmn.	Investor Contact: 206-925-5000
Fax: 206-925-5001		Transfer Agents: The Bank of New York, New York, NY

GLATFELTER

Exchange	Symbol	Price	52Wk Range	Yield	P/E
NYS	GLT	$15.11 (3/31/2008)	17.02-13.04	2.38	10.79

*7 Year Price Score 82.19   *NYSE Composite Index=100   *12 Month Price Score 104.55

Interim Earnings (Per Share)

Qtr.	Mar	Jun	Sep	Dec
2003	0.61	0.01	(0.15)	(0.17)
2004	0.83	(0.04)	0.05	0.43
2005	0.14	0.04	0.08	0.61
2006	(0.27)	(0.46)	0.12	0.34
2007	0.07	0.04	0.17	1.11

Interim Dividends (Per Share)

Amt	Decl	Ex	Rec	Pay
0.09Q	6/20/2007	7/3/2007	7/6/2007	8/1/2007
0.09Q	9/12/2007	10/3/2007	10/8/2007	11/1/2007
0.09Q	12/19/2007	1/4/2008	1/8/2008	2/1/2008
0.09Q	3/5/2008	4/4/2008	4/8/2008	5/1/2008

Indicated Div: $0.36

Valuation Analysis

		Institutional Holding	
Forecast P/E	10.73	No of Institutions	
	(1/10/2007)	131	
Market Cap	$002.1 Million	Shares	
Book Value	476.1 Million	42,861,240	
Price/Book	1.43	% Held	
Price/Sales	0.59	94.26	

Business Summary: Paper Products (MIC: 11.11 SIC: 2621 NAIC: 322121)

Glatfelter is a manufacturer of specialty papers and engineered products. Co.'s North America-based Specialty Papers business unit focuses on papers for the production of hardbound books and other book publishing needs, and for the envelope and converting applications, as well as products for digital imaging, transfer, casting, release, postal, playing card and other niche specialty applications. Co.'s Europe-based Composite Fibers business unit focuses on products such as paper for tea bags and coffee pods/pads and filters, decorative laminates used for furniture and flooring, and metallized products used in the labeling of beer bottles.

Recent Developments: For the year ended Dec 31 2007, net income amounted to US$63.5 million versus a net loss of US$12.2 million in the prior year. Revenues were US$1.16 billion, up 16.1% from US$997.1 million the year before. Operating income was US$118.8 million versus US$94,000 in the prior year, an increase of. Direct operating expenses rose 12.3% to US$1.00 billion from US$891.8 million in the comparable period the year before. Indirect operating expenses decreased 64.4% to US$37.5 million from US$105.2 million in the equivalent prior-year period.

Prospects: Looking ahead to 2008, while the economic growth in the U.S. is likely to slow further, Co. remains optimistic that the continued execution of its optimization and growth strategies will further strengthen its operations and improve efficiencies in both of its businesses. For the first quarter of 2008, in its Specialty Papers business, Co. expects volume to improve slightly versus prior year quarter and selling prices to be slightly higher than prior quarter. Co. also expects average selling prices and volumes in its Composite Fibers business to be higher than prior year quarter. However, Co. expects the higher selling prices to be offset by higher input costs, mainly fiber and energy.

Financial Data
(US$ in Thousands)

	12/31/2007	12/31/2006	12/31/2005	12/31/2004	12/31/2003	12/31/2002	12/31/2001	12/31/2000
Earnings Per Share	1.40	(0.27)	0.87	1.27	0.29	0.86	0.16	1.04
Cash Flow Per Share	2.23	(0.64)	0.97	0.90	1.07	1.71	1.50	2.44
Tang Book Value Per Share	9.89	8.66	9.80	9.56	8.48	8.57	8.27	8.79
Dividends Per Share	0.360	0.360	0.360	0.360	0.440	0.875	0.700	0.700
Dividend Payout %	25.71	...	41.38	28.35	151.72	101.74	437.50	67.31
Income Statement								
Total Revenue	1,157,768	997,137	589,199	553,477	543,233	553,637	652,539	739,812
EBITDA	175,024	49,114	121,858	153,734	88,894	117,827	56,708	114,709
Income Before Taxes	93,934	(22,228)	60,140	90,763	20,416	59,065	11,720	68,603
Income Taxes	30,462	(9,992)	21,531	34,661	7,430	21,470	4,762	24,603
Net Income	63,472	(12,236)	38,609	56,102	12,661	37,595	6,958	44,000
Average Shares	45,422	44,584	44,313	44,023	43,760	43,791	42,846	42,483
Balance Sheet								
Current Assets	373,412	375,039	233,557	198,432	171,702	176,380	240,428	286,624
Total Assets	1,287,067	1,225,643	1,044,977	1,052,270	1,027,019	957,028	960,724	1,013,191
Current Liabilities	197,556	193,290	139,878	104,007	112,470	97,948	209,315	119,184
Long-Term Obligations	301,041	375,295	184,000	207,277	248,469	218,709	152,593	300,245
Total Liabilities	810,999	837,275	612,665	631,900	655,588	583,195	607,255	640,488
Stockholders' Equity	476,068	388,368	432,312	420,370	371,431	373,833	353,469	372,703
Shares Outstanding	45,141	44,821	44,132	43,949	43,782	43,644	42,750	42,390
Statistical Record								
Return on Assets %	5.05	N.M.	3.68	5.38	1.28	3.92	0.70	4.35
Return on Equity %	14.69	N.M.	9.06	14.13	3.40	10.34	1.92	12.01
EBITDA Margin %	15.12	4.93	20.68	27.78	16.36	21.28	8.69	15.51
Net Margin %	5.48	N.M.	6.55	10.14	2.33	6.79	1.07	5.95
Asset Turnover	0.92	0.88	0.56	0.53	0.55	0.58	0.66	0.73
Current Ratio	1.89	1.94	1.60	1.91	1.53	1.80	1.15	2.40
Debt to Equity	0.63	0.97	0.43	0.49	0.67	0.59	0.43	0.81
Price Range	17.83-13.16	19.69-13.13	15.28-11.08	15.47-10.64	15.37-9.75	19.20-10.65	16.37-11.80	14.56-9.88
P/E Ratio	12.74-9.40	...	17.56-12.74	12.18-8.38	53.00-33.62	22.33-12.38	102.31-73.75	14.00-9.50
Average Yield %	2.39	2.32	2.68	2.87	3.53	5.70	4.92	6.17

Address: 96 South George Street, Suite 500, York, PA 17401 Telephone: 717-225-4711 Fax: 717-846-7208	Web Site: www.glatfelter.com Officers: George H. Glatfelter II - Chmn., C.E.O. John C. van Roden Jr. - Sr. V.P., C.F.O.	Auditors: Deloitte & Touche LLP Transfer Agents: Mellon Investor Services, LLC

GLOBAL PAYMENTS, INC.

Exchange	Symbol	Price	52Wk Range	Yield	P/E
NYS	GPN	$41.36 (3/31/2008)	47.56-35.75	0.19	22.48

*7 Year Price Score 114.67 *NYSE Composite Index=100 *12 Month Price Score 104.34

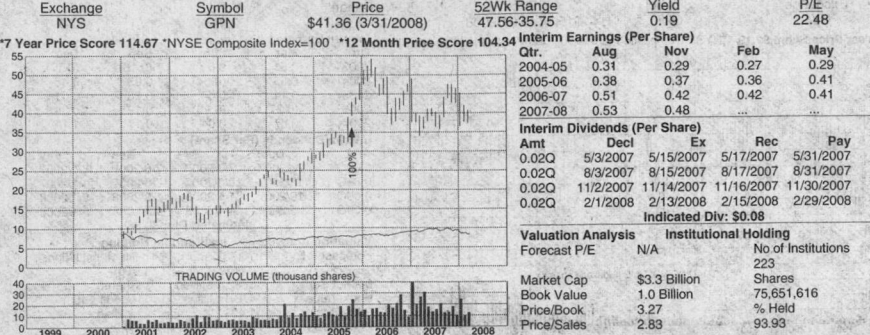

Interim Earnings (Per Share)

Qtr.	Aug	Nov	Feb	May
2004-05	0.31	0.29	0.27	0.29
2005-06	0.38	0.37	0.36	0.41
2006-07	0.51	0.42	0.42	0.41
2007-08	0.53	0.48	...	...

Interim Dividends (Per Share)

Amt	Decl	Ex	Rec	Pay
0.02Q	5/3/2007	5/15/2007	5/17/2007	5/31/2007
0.02Q	8/3/2007	8/15/2007	8/17/2007	8/31/2007
0.02Q	11/2/2007	11/14/2007	11/16/2007	11/30/2007
0.02Q	2/1/2008	2/13/2008	2/15/2008	2/29/2008

Indicated Div: $0.08

Valuation Analysis

Forecast P/E	N/A
Market Cap	$3.3 Billion
Book Value	1.0 Billion
Price/Book	3.27
Price/Sales	2.83

Institutional Holding

No.of Institutions	223
Shares	75,651,616
% Held	93.93

Business Summary: Miscellaneous Business Services (MIC: 12.8 SIC: 7389 NAIC: 522320)

Global Payments is a processing and consumer money transfer company. Co. enables merchants, multinational corporations, financial institutions, consumers, government agencies and other profit and non-profit business enterprises to facilitate payments to purchase goods and services. Co. serves as an intermediary in the exchange of information and funds that must occur between parties so that a payment transaction can be completed. Co. operates in two business segments: merchant services and money transfer; through which it provides various products. Co. markets its products and services throughout the U.S., Canada, Europe and the Asia-Pacific region.

Recent Developments: For the quarter ended Nov 30 2007, net income increased 12.7% to US$38.3 million from US$34.0 million in the year-earlier quarter. Revenues were US$308.8 million, up 18.4% from US$260.7 million the year before. Operating income was US$58.4 million versus US$52.3 million in the prior-year quarter, an increase of 11.7%. Direct operating expenses rose 10.2% to US$116.5 million from US$105.8 million in the comparable period the year before. Indirect operating expenses increased 30.4% to US$133.8 million from US$102.6 million in the equivalent prior-year period.

Prospects: Moving ahead, Co. is continuing to grow its domestic and international presence, build its independent sales organization sales channel, boost customer service, assess opportunities for profitable growth through acquisitions, pursue enhanced products and services for its customers, and improve its existing business model. For the fiscal year ending May 31 2008, Co. anticipates consolidated revenues to range from $1.25 billion to $1.26 billion, reflecting growth of 18.0% to 19.0% over fiscal 2007. Also, Co. expects earnings to range from $1.95 to $1.97 per diluted share for fiscal 2008, excluding the effect of future significant acquisitions, restructuring charges and operating tax item.

Financial Data
(US$ in Thousands)

	6 Mos	3 Mos	05/31/2007	05/31/2006	05/31/2005	05/31/2004	05/31/2003	05/31/2002
Earnings Per Share	1.84	1.78	1.75	1.53	1.17	0.80	0.70	0.32
Cash Flow Per Share	2.86	2.57	2.38	2.98	2.98	1.22	0.48	2.19
Tang Book Value Per Share	4.48	3.98	4.09	2.70	0.39	N.M.	0.91	0.04
Dividends Per Share	0.080	0.080	0.080	0.080	0.080	0.080	0.080	0.080
Dividend Payout %	4.35	4.49	4.57	5.23	6.87	10.00	11.35	25.40
Income Statement								
Total Revenue	619,756	310,980	1,061,523	908,056	784,331	629,320	516,084	462,826
EBITDA	152,376	83,291	...	242,020	199,217	135,249	117,144	94,034
Depn & Amortn	20,978	13,795	...	...	...	...	...	...
Income Before Taxes	131,398	69,496	...	201,520	153,917	99,749	85,144	64,463
Income Taxes	44,806	23,783	73,436	67,522	53,351	37,306	31,844	24,624
Net Income	81,888	43,575	142,985	125,524	92,896	62,443	53,300	23,840
Average Shares	80,506	81,907	81,822	82,149	79,760	77,910	75,648	76,018
Balance Sheet								
Current Assets	510,017	424,097	444,429	348,406	189,990	203,204	128,203	79,457
Total Assets	1,302,749	1,185,378	1,200,629	1,018,678	853,505	832,895	484,234	431,418
Current Liabilities	189,124	142,070	142,877	149,655	182,803	286,072	62,861	97,005
Long-Term Obligations	...	...	...	...	746	12,947	3,251	4,711
Total Liabilities	283,310	227,149	227,920	235,459	258,815	360,343	94,567	109,889
Stockholders' Equity	1,003,756	943,617	957,776	770,223	578,350	449,422	366,426	296,288
Shares Outstanding	79,470	79,392	80,877	79,813	78,195	76,136	74,264	73,574
Statistical Record								
Return on Assets %	12.33	12.97	12.89	13.41	11.02	9.46	11.64	5.36
Return on Equity %	15.97	16.44	16.55	18.62	18.08	15.27	16.09	8.40
EBITDA Margin %	24.59	26.78	...	26.65	25.40	21.49	22.70	20.32
Net Margin %	13.21	14.01	13.47	13.82	11.84	9.92	10.33	5.15
Asset Turnover	0.96	0.99	0.96	0.97	0.93	0.95	1.13	1.04
Current Ratio	2.70	2.99	3.11	2.33	1.04	0.71	2.04	0.82
Debt to Equity	...	...	...	...	N.M.	0.03	0.01	0.02
Price Range	49.05-34.06	49.05-34.06	49.48-34.06	54.18-31.57	34.65-20.91	25.57-15.98	18.23-11.23	19.21-11.53
P/E Ratio	26.66-18.51	27.56-19.13	28.27-19.46	35.41-20.63	29.62-17.88	31.96-19.97	26.05-16.05	60.03-36.02
Average Yield %	0.20	0.20	0.19	0.19	0.29	0.38	0.55	0.49

Address: 10 Glenlake Parkway, North Tower, Atlanta, GA 30328-3473
Telephone: 770-829-8000

Web Site: www.globalpaymentsinc.com
Officers: Paul R. Garcia - Chmn., Pres., C.E.O. James G. Kelly - Sr. Exec. V.P., C.F.O.

Auditors: Deloitte & Touche LLP
Transfer Agents: SunTrust Bank

GOLDMAN SACHS GROUP, INC.

Exchange	Symbol	Price	52Wk Range	Yield	P/E
NYS	GS	$166.87 (3/31/2008)	247.92-151.02	0.84	7.97

*7 Year Price Score 135.56 *NYSE Composite Index=100   *12 Month Price Score 92.57

Interim Earnings (Per Share)

Qtr.	Feb	May	Aug	Nov
2004-05	2.94	1.71	3.25	3.32
2005-06	5.08	4.78	3.26	6.57
2006-07	6.67	4.93	6.13	6.98
2007-08	3.23	...	...	...

Interim Dividends (Per Share)

Amt	Decl	Ex	Rec	Pay
0.35Q	6/14/2007	7/27/2007	7/31/2007	8/30/2007
0.35Q	9/20/2007	10/25/2007	10/29/2007	11/26/2007
0.35Q	12/18/2007	1/25/2008	1/29/2008	2/28/2008
0.35Q	3/18/2008	4/25/2008	4/29/2008	5/29/2008

Indicated Div: $1.40

Valuation Analysis

		Institutional Holding	
Forecast P/E	10.21	No of Institutions	
	(1/10/2007)	919	
Market Cap	$65.8 Billion	Shares	
Book Value	42.6 Billion	287,967,360	
Price/Book	1.54	% Held	
Price/Sales	0.79	70.50	

Business Summary: Finance Intermediaries & Services (MIC: 8.7 SIC: 6282 NAIC: 523110)

Goldman Sachs Group is a global investment banking, securities and investment management firm that provides a range of services worldwide to various client base that includes corporations, financial institutions, governments and individuals. Co.'s activities are divided into three segments: Investment Banking, which is composed of Financial Advisory and Underwriting; Trading and Principal Investments, which consists of Fixed Income, Currency and Commodities, Equities, and Principal Investments; and Asset Management and Securities Services. As of Nov 30 2007, Co. operated offices in over 25 countries.

Recent Developments: For the quarter ended Feb 29 2008, net income decreased 52.7% to US$1.51 billion from US$3.20 billion in the year-earlier quarter. Revenues were US$18.63 billion, down 16.4% from US$22.28 billion the year before. Direct operating expenses rose 7.8% to US$10.29 billion from US$9.55 billion in the comparable period the year before. Indirect operating expenses decreased 21.3% to US$6.19 billion from US$7.87 billion in the equivalent prior-year period.

Prospects: Co.'s near-term outlook appears to be constructive, attributable to an increase in net revenues in its trading and principal investments. Specifically, the increase in Co.'s trading and principal investments is being driven by higher net revenues in equities and fixed income, currency and commodities. In addition, Co. is seeing higher net revenues in its investment banking, reflecting an increase in financial advisory net revenues due to increased client activity. Moreover, Co.'s net revenues in asset management and securities services are benefiting from an increase in management and other fees and higher customer balances in securities lending and margin lending.

Financial Data

(US$ in Thousands)	3 Mos	11/30/2007	11/24/2006	11/25/2005	11/26/2004	11/28/2003	11/29/2002	11/30/2001
Earnings Per Share	20.94	24.73	19.69	11.21	8.92	5.87	4.03	4.26
Cash Flow Per Share	(172.75)	(154.95)	(106.34)	(26.03)	(68.85)	(32.14)	(20.39)	(29.29)
Tang Book Value Per Share	86.97	88.58	65.43	48.15	42.02	35.20	40.18	38.28
Dividends Per Share	1.400	1.400	1.300	1.000	1.000	0.740	0.480	0.480
Dividend Payout %	6.68	5.66	6.60	8.92	11.21	12.61	11.91	11.27
Income Statement								
Interest Income	11,245,000	45,968,000	35,186,000	21,250,000	11,914,000	10,751,000	11,269,000	16,620,000
Interest Expense	10,294,000	41,981,000	31,688,000	18,153,000	8,888,000	7,600,000	8,868,000	15,327,000
Net Interest Income	951,000	3,987,000	3,498,000	3,097,000	3,026,000	3,151,000	2,401,000	1,293,000
Non-Interest Income	7,384,000	42,000,000	34,167,000	22,141,000	17,925,000	12,872,000	11,585,000	14,518,000
Non-Interest Expense	6,192,000	28,383,000	23,105,000	16,965,000	14,275,000	11,578,000	10,733,000	12,115,000
Income Before Taxes	2,143,000	17,604,000	14,560,000	8,273,000	6,676,000	4,445,000	3,253,000	3,696,000
Income Taxes	632,000	6,005,000	5,023,000	2,647,000	2,123,000	1,440,000	1,139,000	1,386,000
Net Income	1,511,000	11,599,000	9,537,000	5,626,000	4,553,000	3,005,000	2,114,000	2,310,000
Average Shares	453,500	461,200	477,400	500,200	510,500	511,900	525,100	541,800
Balance Sheet								
Total Assets	1,189,006,000	1,119,796,000	838,201,000	706,804,000	531,379,000	403,799,000	355,574,000	312,218,000
Total Deposits	26,961,000	15,370,000	...	...	...	...	...	...
Total Liabilities	1,146,377,000	1,076,996,000	802,415,000	678,802,000	506,300,000	382,167,000	336,571,000	293,987,000
Stockholders' Equity	42,629,000	42,800,000	35,786,000	28,002,000	25,079,000	21,632,000	19,003,000	18,231,000
Shares Outstanding	394,473	390,682	412,666	437,170	480,959	473,014	472,941	476,229
Statistical Record								
Return on Assets %	0.93	1.17	1.24	0.91	0.98	0.79	0.63	0.76
Return on Equity %	24.54	29.04	29.98	21.26	19.55	14.83	11.39	13.08
Net Interest Margin %	8.46	8.67	9.94	14.57	25.40	29.31	21.31	7.78
Efficiency Ratio %	33.24	32.27	33.32	39.10	47.84	49.01	46.96	38.91
Price Range	247.92-164.90	247.92-164.90	202.29-125.13	134.08-95.50	109.05-83.86	96.98-62.85	96.75-59.28	118.62-65.75
P/E Ratio	11.84-7.87	10.03-6.67	10.27-6.36	11.96-8.52	12.23-9.40	16.52-10.71	24.01-14.71	27.85-15.43
Average Yield %	0.67	0.66	0.85	0.91	1.04	0.92	0.61	0.53

Address: 85 Broad Street, New York, NY 10004	**Web Site:** www.gs.com	**Auditors:** PricewaterhouseCoopers LLP
Telephone: 212-902-1000	**Officers:** Henry M. Paulson Jr. - Chmn., C.E.O.	**Investor Contact:** 212-357-2674
Fax: 212-902-3000	Robert S. Kaplan - Vice-Chmn.	**Transfer Agents:** Mellon Investor Services LLC, Jersey City, NJ

GOODRICH CORP.

Exchange	Symbol	Price	52Wk Range	Yield	P/E
NYS	GR	$57.51 (3/31/2008)	75.47-51.64	1.56	15.21

*7 Year Price Score 138.49 *NYSE Composite Index=100 *12 Month Price Score 102.81

Interim Earnings (Per Share)

Qtr.	Mar	Jun	Sep	Dec
2003	0.25	0.12	0.29	0.19
2004	0.38	0.32	0.41	0.30
2005	0.47	0.61	0.49	0.56
2006	1.60	0.64	0.80	0.77
2007	0.78	0.98	0.99	1.03

Interim Dividends (Per Share)

Amt	Decl	Ex	Rec	Pay
0.20Q	4/24/2007	5/31/2007	6/4/2007	7/2/2007
0.20Q	7/24/2007	8/30/2007	9/4/2007	10/1/2007
0.225Q	10/23/2007	11/29/2007	12/3/2007	1/2/2008
0.225Q	2/19/2008	2/28/2008	3/3/2008	4/1/2008
		Indicated Div: $0.90		

Valuation Analysis | **Institutional Holding**

Forecast P/E	13.29	No of Institutions
	(1/10/2007)	307
Market Cap	$7.2 Billion	Shares
Book Value	2.6 Billion	106,184,808
Price/Book	2.78	% Held
Price/Sales	1.12	84.69

Business Summary: Aviation (MIC: 1.1 SIC: 3728 NAIC: 336413)

Goodrich is engaged in supplying components, systems and services to the commercial and general aviation airplane markets. In addition, Co. is a supplier of systems and products to the global defense and space markets. Co.'s business is conducted on a global basis with manufacturing, service and sales undertaken in various locations throughout the world. Co.'s products and services are principally sold to customers in North America, Europe and Asia. As of Dec 31 2007, Co. conducted its businesses in three operating segments: The Actuation and Landing Systems, The Nacelles and Interior Systems and The Electronic Systems.

Recent Developments: For the year ended Dec 31 2007, income from continuing operations increased 3.8% to US$496.0 million from US$478.0 million a year earlier. Net income increased 0.1% to US$482.6 million from US$482.1 million in the prior year. Revenues were US$6.39 billion, up 11.8% from US$5.72 billion the year before. Operating income was US$881.3 million versus US$639.8 million in the prior year, an increase of 37.7%. Direct operating expenses rose 8.2% to US$4.48 billion from US$4.14 billion in the comparable period the year before. Indirect operating expenses increased 9.8% to US$1.03 billion from US$935.9 million in the equivalent prior-year period.

Prospects: For the full year of 2008, Co. is projecting sales to be in the range of $7.10 billion to $7.20 billion, while net income is expected to range from $4.15 to $4.30 per diluted share. In addition, Co. is anticipating large commercial airplane original equipment sales to increase by about 20.0%, while sales of regional, business and general aviation airplane original equipment are expected to grow by approximately 13.0%. Lastly, Co. is forecasting large commercial, regional, business and general aviation airplane aftermarket sales to improve by 8.0% to 10.0%, while defense and space sales of both original equipment and aftermarket products and services are estimated to grow by 5.0% to 8.0%.

Financial Data (US$ in Thousands)	12/31/2007	12/31/2006	12/31/2005	12/31/2004	12/31/2003	12/31/2002	12/31/2001	12/31/2000
Earnings Per Share	3.78	3.81	2.13	1.43	0.85	1.14	2.76	3.04
Cash Flow Per Share	4.75	2.22	2.84	3.49	4.71	5.20	3.71	2.19
Tang Book Value Per Share	5.84	1.10	N.M.	N.M.	N.M.	N.M.	4.67	3.48
Dividends Per Share	0.825	0.800	0.800	0.800	0.800	0.875	1.100	1.100
Dividend Payout %	21.83	21.00	37.56	55.94	94.12	76.75	39.86	36.18
Income Statement								
Total Revenue	6,392,200	5,878,300	5,396,500	4,724,500	4,382,900	3,910,200	4,184,500	4,363,800
EBITDA	1,082,800	823,100	714,700	562,000	437,800	526,700	539,200	759,400
Income Before Taxes	716,900	462,000	363,100	199,300	69,200	269,600	281,700	461,400
Income Taxes	220,900	(19,200)	119,300	43,400	22,800	93,200	94,300	156,700
Net Income	482,600	482,100	263,600	172,200	100,400	117,900	289,200	325,900
Average Shares	127,800	126,400	124,000	120,300	118,200	105,500	106,900	109,100
Balance Sheet								
Current Assets	3,548,800	3,007,500	2,425,400	2,356,800	2,087,100	2,008,100	1,921,300	3,080,300
Total Assets	7,534,000	6,901,200	6,454,000	6,217,500	5,889,900	5,989,600	4,638,100	5,717,500
Current Liabilities	1,742,600	1,632,600	1,614,600	1,564,500	1,400,900	1,554,200	1,158,600	2,147,300
Long-Term Obligations	1,562,900	1,721,700	1,742,100	1,899,400	2,136,600	2,129,000	1,307,200	1,316,200
Total Liabilities	4,954,600	4,924,500	4,981,000	4,874,600	4,696,400	4,931,300	3,151,700	4,217,100
Stockholders' Equity	2,579,400	1,976,700	1,473,000	1,342,900	1,193,500	932,900	1,361,400	1,226,600
Shares Outstanding	124,610	124,950	123,106	119,143	117,725	117,061	101,697	102,330
Statistical Record								
Return on Assets %	6.69	7.22	4.16	2.84	1.69	2.22	5.59	5.82
Return on Equity %	21.18	27.95	18.72	13.54	9.44	10.28	22.35	25.80
EBITDA Margin %	16.94	14.00	13.24	11.90	9.99	13.47	12.89	17.40
Net Margin %	7.55	8.20	4.88	3.64	2.29	3.02	6.91	7.47
Asset Turnover	0.89	0.88	0.85	0.78	0.74	0.74	0.81	0.78
Current Ratio	2.04	1.84	1.50	1.51	1.49	1.29	1.66	1.43
Debt to Equity	0.61	0.87	1.18	1.41	1.79	2.28	0.96	1.07
Price Range	75.47-45.31	46.52-37.48	45.82-30.33	33.55-26.75	30.09-13.51	32.85-14.38	42.62-16.47	41.24-21.19
P/E Ratio	19.97-11.99	12.21-9.84	21.51-14.24	23.46-18.71	35.40-15.89	28.82-12.61	15.44-5.97	13.56-6.97
Average Yield %	1.38	1.91	2.00	2.63	3.77	3.62	3.43	3.41

Address: Four Coliseum Centre, 2730 West Tyvola Road, Charlotte, NC 28217 **Telephone:** 704-423-7000 **Fax:** 704-423-7075	**Web Site:** www.goodrich.com **Officers:** Marshall O. Larsen - Chmn., Pres., C.E.O. Terrence G. Linnert - Exec. V.P., Human Res. & Admin, Gen. Couns.	**Auditors:** Ernst & Young LLP **Investor Contact:** 704-423-5517 **Transfer Agents:** The Bank of New York

GOODYEAR TIRE & RUBBER CO.

Exchange	Symbol	Price	52Wk Range	Yield	P/E
NYS	GT	$25.80 (3/31/2008)	36.63-23.49	N/A	9.74

*7 Year Price Score 140.30   *NYSE Composite Index=100   *12 Month Price Score 95.50

Interim Earnings (Per Share)

Qtr.	Mar	Jun	Sep	Dec
2003	(0.93)	(0.42)	(0.60)	(2.68)
2004	(0.44)	0.14	0.21	0.70
2005	0.35	0.34	0.70	(0.23)
2006	0.37	0.01	(0.27)	(2.02)
2007	(0.96)	0.26	2.75	0.21

Interim Dividends (Per Share)

Dividend Payment Suspended

Valuation Analysis   Institutional Holding

Forecast P/E	9.60	No of Institutions
	(1/10/2007)	282
Market Cap	$6.2 Billion	Shares
Book Value	2.9 Billion	169,168,976
Price/Book	2.17	% Held
Price/Sales	0.32	93.85

Business Summary: Rubber Products (MIC: 11.6 SIC: 3011 NAIC: 326211)

Goodyear Tire & Rubber is engaged in the development, manufacture, marketing and distribution of tires as well as rubber-related chemicals for a range of applications. Additionally, Co. is engaged as an operator of commercial truck service and tire retreading centers. As of Dec 31 2007, Co. manufactured its products in 64 manufacturing facilities in 25 countries, including the U.S. At such date, Co. operated its business through five segments: North American Tire; European Union Tire; Eastern Europe, Middle East and Africa Tire (Eastern Europe Tire); Latin American Tire, and Asia Pacific Tire.

Recent Developments: For the year ended Dec 31 2007, income from continuing operations was US$139.0 million compared with a loss of US$373.0 million a year earlier. Net income amounted to US$602.0 million versus a net loss of US$330.0 million in the prior year. Revenues were US$19.64 billion, up 4.8% from US$18.75 billion the year before. Direct operating expenses rose 1.2% to US$15.92 billion from US$15.74 billion in the comparable period the year before. Indirect operating expenses decreased 1.6% to US$2.81 billion from US$2.86 billion in the equivalent prior-year period.

Prospects: For 2008, Co. expects its North America consumer original equipment (OE) volume to be down 2.0% to 4.0%, as its commercial OE volume should be up 20.0% to 30.0% due to a recovery in demand following weak 2007 industry volumes reflecting regulations regarding new commercial vehicle emission standards. Co. also anticipates both North American consumer and commercial replacement volumes to be flat to up 2.0%. Concurrently, in Europe, Co. expects consumer OE volume to be up 2.0% to 4.0% and estimates commercial OE volume to be up 5.0% to 10.0%. Further, Co. expects European consumer replacement volume to be flat to up 1.0% as its commercial replacement volume should be up 1.0% to 2.0%.

Financial Data

(US$ in Thousands)	12/31/2007	12/31/2006	12/31/2005	12/31/2004	12/31/2003	12/31/2002	12/31/2001	12/31/2000
Earnings Per Share	2.65	(1.86)	1.16	0.63	(4.58)	(6.62)	(1.27)	0.25
Cash Flow Per Share	0.52	3.16	5.03	4.09	(1.73)	4.05	7.92	3.24
Tang Book Value Per Share	8.20	...	N.M.	N.M.	...	N.M.	14.06	18.49
Dividends Per Share	...	...	...	...	0.480	0.480	1.020	1.200
Dividend Payout %	...	...	...	...	...	...	...	480.00
Income Statement								
Total Revenue	19,644,000	20,258,000	19,723,000	18,370,400	15,119,000	13,850,000	14,147,200	14,417,100
EBITDA	1,445,000	834,000	1,547,000	1,371,900	273,800	807,400	612,600	957,800
Income Before Taxes	464,000	(224,000)	489,000	322,700	(689,900)	(17,900)	(273,000)	58,800
Income Taxes	255,000	106,000	250,000	207,900	112,200	1,087,900	(69,400)	18,500
Net Income	602,000	(330,000)	228,000	114,800	(802,100)	(1,105,800)	(203,600)	40,300
Average Shares	231,717	177,253	208,730	192,258	175,314	167,020	159,955	158,764
Balance Sheet								
Current Assets	10,172,000	10,179,000	8,680,000	8,631,700	6,988,100	5,226,700	5,233,000	5,467,200
Total Assets	17,191,000	17,029,000	15,627,000	16,533,300	15,005,500	13,146,600	13,512,900	13,568,000
Current Liabilities	4,664,000	4,666,000	4,811,000	5,113,100	3,685,500	4,071,400	3,326,500	4,225,900
Long-Term Obligations	4,329,000	6,563,000	4,742,000	4,449,100	4,826,200	2,989,000	3,203,600	2,349,600
Total Liabilities	14,341,000	17,787,000	15,554,000	16,460,500	15,018,600	12,496,000	10,648,900	10,065,000
Stockholders' Equity	2,850,000	(758,000)	73,000	72,800	(13,100)	650,600	2,864,000	3,503,000
Shares Outstanding	240,122	178,218	176,509	175,619	175,326	175,307	163,165	157,603
Statistical Record								
Return on Assets %	3.52	N.M.	1.42	0.73	N.M.	N.M.	N.M.	0.30
Return on Equity %	57.55	...	312.76	383.54	N.M.	N.M.	N.M.	1.13
EBITDA Margin %	7.36	4.12	7.84	7.47	1.81	5.83	4.54	6.64
Net Margin %	3.06	N.M.	1.16	0.62	N.M.	N.M.	N.M.	0.28
Asset Turnover	1.15	1.24	1.23	1.16	1.07	1.04	1.04	1.08
Current Ratio	2.18	2.18	1.80	1.69	1.90	1.28	1.58	1.29
Debt to Equity	1.52	...	64.96	61.11	...	4.59	1.12	0.67
Price Range	36.63-22.67	20.22-9.86	18.49-11.38	15.01-7.09	8.10-3.57	28.31-6.60	31.64-17.72	29.88-15.60
P/E Ratio	13.82-8.55	...	15.94-9.81	23.83-11.25	...	...	...	119.50-62.40
Average Yield %	...	...	...	...	7.84	2.81	4.15	5.31

Address: 1144 East Market Street, Akron, OH 44316-0001	**Web Site:** www.goodyear.com	**Auditors:** PricewaterhouseCoopers LLP
Telephone: 330-796-2121	**Officers:** Robert J. Keegan - Chmn., Pres., C.E.O.	**Transfer Agents:** EquiServe Trust
Fax: 330-796-4099	Richard J. Kramer - Exec. V.P., C.F.O.	Company, N.A., Providence, RI

GRACO INC.

Exchange	Symbol	Price	52Wk Range	Yield	P/E
NYS	GGG	$36.26 (3/31/2008)	46.07-32.37	2.04	15.63

*7 Year Price Score 103.73 *NYSE Composite Index=100 *12 Month Price Score 99.08

Interim Earnings (Per Share)

Qtr.	Mar	Jun	Sep	Dec
2003	0.25	0.35	0.33	0.31
2004	0.32	0.43	0.41	0.40
2005	0.38	0.51	0.44	0.46
2006	0.51	0.60	0.54	0.52
2007	0.50	0.66	0.60	0.57

Interim Dividends (Per Share)

Amt	Decl	Ex	Rec	Pay
0.165Q	6/14/2007	7/12/2007	7/16/2007	8/1/2007
0.165Q	9/28/2007	10/18/2007	10/22/2007	11/7/2007
0.185Q	12/7/2007	1/17/2008	1/22/2008	2/6/2008
0.185Q	2/15/2008	4/17/2008	4/21/2008	5/7/2008

Indicated Div: $0.74

Valuation Analysis

Forecast P/E	14.56
	(1/10/2007)
Market Cap	$2.2 Billion
Book Value	244.7 Million
Price/Book	9.18
Price/Sales	2.67

Institutional Holding

No of Institutions	221
Shares	54,075,888
% Held	81.14

Business Summary: Industrial Machinery and Equipment (MIC: 11.5 SIC: 3561 NAIC: 333911)

Graco is engaged in the provision of fluid handling applications used to spray, dispense, measure and move fluids and semi-solids in a range of applications throughout the manufacturing, processing, construction and maintenance industries gloablly. Co.'s Industrial segment markets equipment and services to customers who manufacture, assemble, repair and refinish products. Co.'s Contractor segment markets a line of airless paint and texture sprayers, accessories and spare parts to professional and semi-professional painters in the construction and maintenance industries. Co.'s Lubrication segment focuses on pumps, applicators and accessories for the motor vehicle lubrication market.

Recent Developments: For the year ended Dec 28 2007, net income increased 2.0% to US$152.8 million from US$149.8 million in the prior year. Revenues were US$841.3 million, up 3.0% from US$816.5 million the year before. Operating income was US$232.5 million versus US$226.0 million in the prior year, an increase of 2.9%. Direct operating expenses rose 3.0% to US$393.9 million from US$382.5 million in the comparable period the year before. Indirect operating expenses increased 3.4% to US$214.9 million from US$208.0 million in the equivalent prior-year period.

Prospects: For the full year of 2008, Co. anticipates that the challenging economic conditions in the U.S. will most likely to persist, primarily in markets related to the housing industry. Nevertheless, Co. remains optimistic in growing its sales, net income and earnings, driven mainly by the expected ongoing solid sales activity outside of U.S. Also, Co. will continue to invest in new products while exploring opportunities for strategic acquisitions. In detail, on Dec 3 2007, Co. announced a definitive agreement to acquire GlasCraft Inc. for approximately $35.0 million. The transaction, which is expected to be completed in the first quarter of 2008, is subject to customary closing conditions.

Financial Data

(US$ in Thousands)	12/28/2007	12/29/2006	12/30/2005	12/31/2004	12/26/2003	12/27/2002	12/28/2001	12/29/2000
Earnings Per Share	2.32	2.17	1.80	1.55	1.23	1.05	0.92	1.01
Cash Flow Per Share	2.73	2.30	2.23	1.75	1.59	1.35	1.29	1.17
Tang Book Value Per Share	2.19	3.20	2.87	3.08	2.17	3.28	2.28	1.62
Dividends Per Share	0.660	0.580	0.520	1.873	0.220	0.196	0.178	0.166
Dividend Payout %	28.45	26.73	28.89	120.85	17.84	18.68	19.32	16.45
Income Statement								
Total Revenue	841,339	816,468	731,702	605,032	535,098	487,048	472,819	494,373
EBITDA	260,934	251,358	214,224	179,087	147,143	130,419	117,207	125,487
Income Before Taxes	228,836	224,366	189,354	160,781	127,913	111,725	97,466	105,908
Income Taxes	76,000	74,600	63,500	52,100	41,200	36,100	32,200	35,800
Net Income	152,836	149,766	125,854	108,681	86,713	75,625	65,266	70,108
Average Shares	65,984	68,977	69,862	70,251	70,416	72,307	70,832	69,536
Balance Sheet								
Current Assets	248,832	238,983	213,898	227,226	256,106	240,524	155,497	143,742
Total Assets	536,724	511,603	445,630	371,714	397,390	355,850	276,113	237,976
Current Liabilities	125,877	128,929	111,581	96,773	187,947	80,214	73,253	81,841
Long-Term Obligations	107,060	...	...	...	...	...	...	18,050
Total Liabilities	292,050	180,599	157,946	140,877	227,580	110,444	102,373	127,121
Stockholders' Equity	244,674	331,004	287,684	230,837	169,810	245,406	173,740	110,855
Shares Outstanding	61,963	66,804	68,387	68,979	69,060	71,299	70,004	68,423
Statistical Record								
Return on Assets %	29.24	31.38	30.88	27.80	23.09	24.00	25.46	29.66
Return on Equity %	53.24	48.55	48.68	53.38	41.88	36.18	45.99	80.90
EBITDA Margin %	31.01	30.79	29.28	29.60	27.50	26.78	24.79	25.38
Net Margin %	18.17	18.34	17.20	17.96	16.21	15.53	13.80	14.18
Asset Turnover	1.61	1.71	1.80	1.55	1.42	1.55	1.84	2.09
Current Ratio	1.98	1.85	1.92	2.35	1.36	3.00	2.12	1.76
Debt to Equity	0.44	...	...	...	...	...	...	0.16
Price Range	46.07-36.25	48.95-36.48	40.68-31.83	37.70-26.43	26.99-17.12	20.32-15.27	17.16-10.82	12.30-8.59
P/E Ratio	19.86-15.63	22.56-16.81	22.60-17.68	24.32-17.05	21.95-13.92	19.36-14.54	18.65-11.76	12.17-8.51
Average Yield %	1.66	1.39	1.44	6.07	0.99	1.09	1.31	1.69

Address: 88 - 11th Avenue Northeast, Minneapolis, MN 55413-1894 Telephone: 612-623-6000 Fax: 612-623-6777	Web Site: www.graco.com Officers: L. R. Mitau - Chmn. David A. Roberts - Pres., C.E.O.	Auditors: Deloitte & Touche LLP Investor Contact: 612-623-6659 Transfer Agents: Wells Fargo Bank,N.A.

GRAINGER (W.W.) INC.

Exchange	Symbol	Price	52Wk Range	Yield	P/E	Div Acheiver
NYS	GWW	$76.39 (3/31/2008)	98.45-71.60	1.83	15.46	36 Years

*7 Year Price Score 113.59 ***NYSE Composite Index=100** ***12 Month Price Score 96.51**

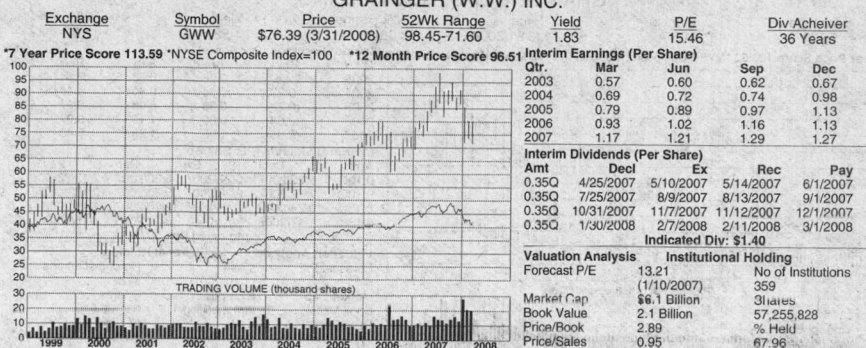

TRADING VOLUME (thousand shares)

1999 2000 2001 2002 2003 2004 2005 2006 2007 2008

Interim Earnings (Per Share)

Qtr.	Mar	Jun	Sep	Dec
2003	0.57	0.60	0.62	0.67
2004	0.69	0.72	0.74	0.98
2005	0.79	0.89	0.97	1.13
2006	0.93	1.02	1.16	1.13
2007	1.17	1.21	1.29	1.27

Interim Dividends (Per Share)

Amt	Decl	Ex	Rec	Pay
0.35Q	4/25/2007	5/10/2007	5/14/2007	6/1/2007
0.35Q	7/25/2007	8/9/2007	8/13/2007	9/1/2007
0.35Q	10/31/2007	11/7/2007	11/12/2007	12/1/2007
0.35Q	1/30/2008	2/7/2008	2/11/2008	3/1/2008

Indicated Div: $1.40

Valuation Analysis

		Institutional Holding	
Forecast P/E	13.21 (1/10/2007)	No of Institutions	359
Market Cap	$6.1 Billion	3harcs	
Book Value	2.1 Billion	57,255,828	
Price/Book	2.89	% Held	
Price/Sales	0.95	67.96	

Business Summary: Engineering Services (MIC: 12.1 SIC: 5063 NAIC: 423610)

W.W. Grainger is a supplier of facilities maintenance and other related products. Co. has three operating segments: Grainger Branch-based, which provides customers with products for facility maintenance and other product needs through logistics networks which are configured for product availability; Acklands - Grainger Branch-based, which distributes tools, fasteners, safety supplies, instruments, welding and shop equipment, and many other items; and Lab Safety Supply, Inc., which is a direct marketer of safety and other industrial products to U.S. and Canadian businesses through the distribution of multiple catalogs and other marketing materials distributed to targeted markets.

Recent Developments: For the year ended Dec 31 2007, net income increased 9.6% to US$420.1 million from US$383.4 million in the prior year. Revenues were US$6.42 billion, up 9.1% from US$5.88 billion the year before. Operating income was US$670.7 million versus US$578.1 million in the prior year, an increase of 16.0%. Direct operating expenses rose 8.1% to US$3.81 billion from US$3.53 billion in the comparable period the year before. Indirect operating expenses increased 8.8% to US$1.93 billion from US$1.78 billion in the equivalent prior-year period.

Prospects: For 2008, Co. expects total capital expenditures to range from $175.0 million to $200.0 million. Accordingly, Co. intends to invest in its market expansion program and information technology enhancements, with spending planned of: $50.0 million to $60.0 million for U.S. market expansion; $25.0 million to $30.0 million for supply chain infrastructure; $20.0 million to $30.0 million for information technology; and $15.0 million to $25.0 million for international expansion. In addition, Co. plans to add an additional 50,000 products to further supplement its Industrial Supply's product lines in 2008. Meanwhile, Co. is projecting 2008 earnings per share to be in the range of $5.65 to $6.00.

Financial Data

(US$ in Thousands)	12/31/2007	12/31/2006	12/31/2005	12/31/2004	12/31/2003	12/31/2002	12/31/2001	12/31/2000
Earnings Per Share	4.94	4.24	3.78	3.13	2.46	2.24	1.84	2.05
Cash Flow Per Share	5.69	4.97	4.83	4.49	4.34	3.30	5.48	2.98
Tang Book Value Per Share	23.47	23.40	23.48	20.44	18.20	16.59	15.09	14.08
Dividends Per Share	1.340	1.110	0.920	0.785	0.735	0.715	0.695	0.670
Dividend Payout %	27.13	26.18	24.34	25.08	29.88	31.92	37.77	32.68
Income Statement								
Total Revenue	6,418,014	5,883,654	5,526,636	5,049,785	4,667,014	4,643,898	4,754,317	4,977,044
EBITDA	804,709	702,021	630,437	541,407	474,011	492,915	408,336	461,000
Income Before Taxes	681,861	603,023	532,674	445,139	381,090	397,837	297,280	331,595
Income Taxes	261,741	219,624	186,350	158,216	154,119	162,349	122,750	138,692
Net Income	420,120	383,399	346,324	286,923	226,971	211,567	174,530	192,903
Average Shares	85,044	90,523	91,588	91,673	92,394	94,303	94,727	94,223
Balance Sheet								
Current Assets	1,800,817	1,862,086	1,997,868	1,754,713	1,633,413	1,484,947	1,392,611	1,483,002
Total Assets	3,094,028	3,046,088	3,107,921	2,809,573	2,624,678	2,437,448	2,331,246	2,459,601
Current Liabilities	826,403	706,323	726,964	662,434	706,640	586,266	553,811	747,324
Long-Term Obligations	4,895	4,895	4,895	...	4,895	119,693	118,219	125,258
Total Liabilities	995,920	868,473	818,945	741,603	779,543	769,750	728,057	922,215
Stockholders' Equity	2,098,108	2,177,615	2,288,976	2,067,970	1,845,135	1,667,698	1,603,189	1,537,386
Shares Outstanding	79,459	84,067	89,715	90,597	91,020	91,568	93,344	93,932
Statistical Record								
Return on Assets %	13.68	12.46	11.71	10.53	8.97	8.87	7.29	7.66
Return on Equity %	19.65	17.17	15.90	14.62	12.92	12.94	11.11	12.75
EBITDA Margin %	12.54	11.93	11.41	10.72	10.16	10.61	8.59	9.26
Net Margin %	6.55	6.52	6.27	5.68	4.86	4.56	3.67	3.88
Asset Turnover	2.09	1.91	1.87	1.85	1.84	1.95	1.98	1.98
Current Ratio	2.18	2.64	2.75	2.65	2.31	2.53	2.51	1.98
Debt to Equity	N.M.	N.M.	N.M.	...	N.M.	0.07	0.07	0.08
Price Range	98.45-69.34	79.73-60.62	71.97-52.29	66.62-45.17	53.11-41.93	59.27-39.82	48.52-30.23	56.00-24.63
P/E Ratio	19.93-14.04	18.80-14.30	19.04-13.83	21.28-14.43	21.59-17.04	26.46-17.78	26.37-16.43	27.32-12.01
Average Yield %	1.58	1.56	1.48	1.46	1.56	1.42	1.72	1.75

Address: 100 Grainger Parkway, Lake Forest, IL 60045-5201 **Telephone:** 847-535-1000 **Fax:** 847-535-0878	**Web Site:** www.grainger.com **Officers:** Richard L. Keyser - Chmn., C.E.O. James T. Ryan - Exec. V.P., Mktg., Sales, & Services	**Auditors:** Ernst & Young LLP **Investor Contact:** 847-535-1000 **Transfer Agents:** BankBoston, N.A. c/o EquiServe, Boston, MA

GRANITE CONSTRUCTION INC.

Exchange	Symbol	Price	52Wk Range	Yield	P/E
NYS	GVA	$32.71 (3/31/2008)	73.38-27.04	1.59	12.07

*7 Year Price Score 126.52 *NYSE Composite Index=100 *12 Month Price Score 70.35

Interim Earnings (Per Share)

Qtr.	Mar	Jun	Sep	Dec
2003	0.25	0.26	0.63	0.34
2004	(0.23)	0.34	0.80	0.48
2005	(0.20)	0.36	0.98	0.87
2006	(0.03)	0.80	1.10	0.07
2007	(0.05)	1.05	1.28	0.43

Interim Dividends (Per Share)

Amt	Decl	Ex	Rec	Pay
0.10Q	5/22/2007	6/27/2007	6/30/2007	7/13/2007
0.10Q	7/19/2007	9/26/2007	9/30/2007	10/15/2007
0.13Q	10/24/2007	12/18/2007	12/20/2007	1/15/2008
0.13Q	1/17/2008	3/27/2008	3/31/2008	4/15/2008

Indicated Div: $0.52

Valuation Analysis   **Institutional Holding**

Forecast P/E	17.44	No of Institutions
	(1/10/2007)	178
Market Cap	$1.3 Billion	Shares
Book Value	700.2 Million	33,435,510
Price/Book	1.84	% Held
Price/Sales	0.47	79.94

Business Summary: Construction - Public Infrastructure (MIC: 3.1 SIC: 1611 NAIC: 237310)

Granite Construction is a heavy civil construction contractor in the U.S., serving both public and private sector clients. Within the public sector, Co. primarily focuses on infrastructure projects including the construction of roads, highways, bridges, dams, tunnels, canals, mass transit facilities and airport infrastructure. Within the private sector, Co. performs site preparation and infrastructure services for residential development, commercial and industrial buildings, plants and other facilities. Co. also owns and leases substantial aggregate reserves, along with a number of construction materials processing plants as well as heavy construction equipment fleets.

Recent Developments: For the year ended Dec 31 2007, net income increased 39.2% to US$112.1 million from US$80.5 million in the prior year. Revenues were US$2.74 billion, down 7.8% from US$2.97 billion the year before. Operating income was US$174.9 million versus US$88.6 million in the prior year, an increase of 97.3%. Direct operating expenses declined 13.0% to US$2.33 billion from US$2.67 billion in the comparable period the year before. Indirect operating expenses increased 13.9% to US$235.9 million from US$207.1 million in the equivalent prior-year period.

Prospects: Co. is optimistic about its 2008 opportunities, as it expects to see continued earnings improvement in its Granite East business, while attaining gross margins in the low teens led by a robust backlog of work and improved execution. Co. is also planning to pursue several projects in three Granite East regions in 2008. Notably, Co. expects that its share of total revenue on a joint venture project to construct a transportation hub at the World Trade Center, NY to exceed $300.0 million. Meanwhile, despite the continued downturn in the residential construction market, Co. remains encouraged by the long-term outlook for its Granite West division as the housing market is expected to recover.

Financial Data

(US$ in Thousands)	12/31/2007	12/31/2006	12/31/2005	12/31/2004	12/31/2003	12/31/2002	12/31/2001	12/31/2000
Earnings Per Share	2.71	1.94	2.02	1.39	1.48	1.21	1.24	1.38
Cash Flow Per Share	5.75	6.35	3.61	1.96	1.93	2.60	3.13	1.89
Tang Book Value Per Share	17.75	16.60	14.91	13.23	12.16	11.03	10.19	9.24
Dividends Per Share	0.430	0.400	0.400	0.400	0.400	0.320	0.320	0.307
Dividend Payout %	15.87	20.62	19.80	28.78	27.03	26.45	25.81	22.22
Income Statement								
Total Revenue	2,737,914	2,969,604	2,641,352	2,136,212	1,844,491	1,764,742	1,547,994	1,348,325
EBITDA	259,993	162,577	209,428	162,623	171,324	146,319	134,510	140,703
Income Before Taxes	198,394	113,017	142,311	94,924	97,525	82,739	81,497	92,870
Income Taxes	65,470	38,678	41,413	28,477	35,304	29,951	30,969	37,055
Net Income	112,065	80,509	83,150	57,007	60,504	49,279	50,528	55,815
Average Shares	41,389	41,471	41,249	41,031	40,808	40,723	40,711	40,409
Balance Sheet								
Current Assets	1,127,513	1,083,205	976,948	825,338	618,651	547,895	586,916	411,628
Total Assets	1,786,418	1,632,838	1,472,230	1,277,954	1,060,410	983,819	929,684	711,142
Current Liabilities	729,945	763,443	609,147	469,411	348,704	327,499	338,503	231,577
Long-Term Obligations	268,417	78,576	124,415	148,503	126,708	132,380	131,391	63,891
Total Liabilities	1,062,748	922,762	817,443	702,690	544,647	513,632	511,182	333,378
Stockholders' Equity	700,199	694,544	621,560	550,474	504,891	454,869	418,502	377,764
Shares Outstanding	39,450	41,833	41,682	41,612	41,528	41,257	41,089	40,881
Statistical Record								
Return on Assets %	6.55	5.19	6.05	4.86	5.92	5.15	6.16	8.00
Return on Equity %	16.07	12.23	14.19	10.77	12.61	11.28	12.69	15.78
EBITDA Margin %	9.50	5.47	7.93	7.61	9.29	8.29	8.69	10.44
Net Margin %	4.09	2.71	3.15	2.67	3.28	2.79	3.26	4.14
Asset Turnover	1.60	1.91	1.92	1.82	1.80	1.84	1.89	1.93
Current Ratio	1.54	1.42	1.60	1.76	1.77	1.67	1.73	1.78
Debt to Equity	0.38	0.11	0.20	0.27	0.25	0.29	0.31	0.17
Price Range	73.38-32.68	63.29-37.06	39.61-22.50	27.87-17.33	24.25-13.89	25.30-13.98	30.50-19.33	20.50-11.75
P/E Ratio	27.08-12.06	32.62-19.10	19.61-11.14	20.05-12.47	16.39-9.39	20.91-11.55	24.60-15.59	14.86-8.51
Average Yield %	0.78	0.84	1.33	1.78	2.16	1.57	1.31	1.85

Address: 585 W. Beach Street, Box 50085, Watsonville, CA 95077-5085 Telephone: 831-724-1011	Web Site: www.graniteconstruction.com Officers: David H. Watts - Chmn. William G. Dorey - Pres., C.E.O.	Auditors: PricewaterhouseCoopers LLP Investor Contact: 831-761-4741 Transfer Agents: Registrar and Transfer Company, Cranford, NJ

GRANT PRIDECO INC

Exchange	Symbol	Price	52Wk Range	Yield	P/E
NYS	GRP	$49.22 (3/31/2008)	59.44-45.26	N/A	12.27

*7 Year Price Score 157.43 *NYSE Composite Index=100 *12 Month Price Score 101.82

Interim Earnings (Per Share)

Qtr.	Mar	Jun	Sep	Dec
2003	0.03	0.03	0.06	(0.08)
2004	0.09	0.02	0.15	0.19
2005	0.29	0.20	0.37	0.60
2006	0.69	0.79	0.95	1.07
2007	1.01	1.04	0.96	1.01

Interim Dividends (Per Share)

No Dividends Paid

Valuation Analysis | **Institutional Holding**

Forecast P/E	8.34	No of Institutions
	(1/10/2007)	317
Market Cap	$6.1 Billion	Shares
Book Value	1.7 Billion	110,081,936
Price/Book	3.58	% Held
Price/Sales	3.21	86.03

Business Summary: Oil and Gas (MIC: 14.2 SIC: 3533 NAIC: 333132)

Grant Prideco is engaged in drill stem technology development and drill pipe manufacturing, sales and service; and in drill bit technology, manufacturing, sales and service. Co. also provides several packages of large-bore tubular products and services. Co. operates under three segments, Drilling Products and Services, ReedHycalog and Other. Co.'s drill stem and drill bit products are used to drill oil and gas wells while its tubular technology and services are used in drilling and completing oil and gas wells. As of Dec 31 2007, Co.'s customers included oil and gas drilling contractors, major, independent and state-owned oil and gas companies as well as other oilfield service companies.

Recent Developments: For the year ended Dec 31 2007, income from continuing operations increased 18.3% to US$478.2 million from US$404.1 million a year earlier. Net income increased 11.8% to US$519.2 million from US$464.6 million in the prior year. Revenues were US$1.91 billion, up 23.1% from US$1.55 billion the year before. Operating income was US$580.7 million versus US$470.7 million in the prior year, an increase of 23.4%. Direct operating expenses rose 22.7% to US$975.4 million from US$794.6 million in the comparable period the year before. Indirect operating expenses increased 23.7% to US$352.5 million from US$284.9 million in the equivalent prior-year period.

Prospects: On Dec 17 2008, Co. announced that it has entered into a definitive agreement to be acquired by National Oilwell Varco, Inc. Upon completion of the transaction, each of Co.'s stockholders will receive 0.4498 of a share of National Oilwell Varco's common stock and $23.20 in cash for each share of Co.'s common stock, subject to various conditions including approval of Co.'s stockholders and customary regulatory approvals. Co. anticipates the transaction to close late in the first quarter or early second quarter of 2008. Meanwhile, Co. is progressing with the pending divestiture of its tubular businesses to Vallourec S.A, which is expected to close in the second quarter of 2008.

Financial Data

(US$ in Thousands)	12/31/2007	12/31/2006	12/31/2005	12/31/2004	12/31/2003	12/31/2002	12/31/2001	12/31/2000
Earnings Per Share	4.01	3.50	1.45	0.44	0.04	0.06	0.25	(0.15)
Cash Flow Per Share	3.81	3.02	1.53	0.92	0.66	1.07	0.37	(0.30)
Tang Book Value Per Share	9.39	5.89	3.97	2.16	1.43	1.29	2.18	1.84
Income Statement								
Total Revenue	1,908,634	1,835,693	1,349,997	945,643	838,456	639,748	740,127	498,481
EBITDA	762,206	736,546	364,413	186,855	102,835	81,523	108,285	26,997
Income Before Taxes	689,218	670,160	288,633	101,746	12,932	23,325	44,718	(21,850)
Income Taxes	201,088	195,215	89,680	31,710	4,526	7,228	15,651	(7,365)
Net Income	519,236	464,584	189,004	55,266	5,190	6,634	28,090	(16,485)
Average Shares	129,610	132,674	130,467	126,091	123,101	117,834	110,884	109,000
Balance Sheet								
Current Assets	1,320,627	947,446	726,255	596,767	510,863	522,431	392,363	377,033
Total Assets	2,350,704	2,022,067	1,540,284	1,344,466	1,262,061	1,315,349	915,598	892,564
Current Liabilities	342,002	307,339	246,646	195,501	166,255	181,979	186,181	178,585
Long-Term Obligations	176,095	237,212	217,484	377,773	426,853	478,846	205,024	219,104
Total Liabilities	640,903	659,184	544,129	638,925	655,947	726,477	446,631	461,061
Stockholders' Equity	1,709,801	1,362,883	996,155	705,541	606,114	588,872	468,967	431,503
Shares Outstanding	124,475	127,689	130,003	123,899	120,715	120,473	109,125	108,492
Statistical Record								
Return on Assets %	23.75	26.08	13.10	4.23	0.40	0.59	...	N.M.
Return on Equity %	33.80	39.39	22.21	8.40	0.87	1.25	...	N.M.
EBITDA Margin %	39.93	40.12	26.99	19.76	12.26	12.74	14.63	5.42
Net Margin %	27.20	25.31	14.00	5.84	0.62	1.04	3.80	N.M.
Asset Turnover	0.87	1.03	0.94	0.72	0.65	0.57	...	0.61
Current Ratio	3.86	3.08	2.94	3.05	3.07	2.87	2.11	2.11
Debt to Equity	0.10	0.17	0.22	0.54	0.70	0.81	0.44	0.51
Price Range	59.44-35.90	54.50-33.30	46.82-18.11	22.25-13.00	14.74-10.01	16.50-8.35	24.04-5.68	25.88-14.13
P/E Ratio	14.82-8.95	15.57-9.51	32.29-12.49	50.57-29.55	368.50-250.25	275.00-139.17	96.16-22.72	...

Address: 1330 Post Oak Blvd., Suite 2700, Houston, TX 77056	Web Site: www.grantprideco.com	Auditors: Ernst & Young LLP
Telephone: 832-681-8000	Officers: Michael McShane - Chmn., Pres., C.E.O.	Transfer Agents: American Stock Transfer & Trust Company, New York, NY
Fax: 832-297-8525	William G. Chunn - Exec. V.P., Oper.	

GREAT PLAINS ENERGY, INC.

Exchange	Symbol	Price	52Wk Range	Yield	P/E
NYS	GXP	$24.65 (3/31/2008)	33.18-24.35	6.73	13.32

*7 Year Price Score 82.68 *NYSE Composite Index=100 *12 Month Price Score 96.32

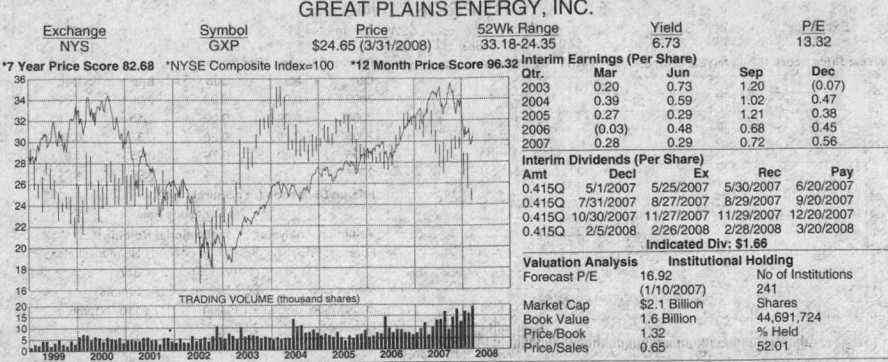

Interim Earnings (Per Share)

Qtr.	Mar	Jun	Sep	Dec
2003	0.20	0.73	1.20	(0.07)
2004	0.39	0.59	1.02	0.47
2005	0.27	0.29	1.21	0.38
2006	(0.03)	0.48	0.68	0.45
2007	0.28	0.29	0.72	0.56

Interim Dividends (Per Share)

Amt	Decl	Ex	Rec	Pay
0.415Q	5/1/2007	5/25/2007	5/30/2007	6/20/2007
0.415Q	7/31/2007	8/27/2007	8/29/2007	9/20/2007
0.415Q	10/30/2007	11/27/2007	11/29/2007	12/20/2007
0.415Q	2/5/2008	2/26/2008	2/28/2008	3/20/2008
		Indicated Div: $1.66		

Valuation Analysis

Valuation Analysis		Institutional Holding	
Forecast P/E	16.92 (1/10/2007)	No of Institutions	241
Market Cap	$2.1 Billion	Shares	44,691,724
Book Value	1.6 Billion	% Held	52.01
Price/Book	1.32		
Price/Sales	0.65		

Business Summary: Industrial Machinery and Equipment (MIC: 11.5 SIC: 3568 NAIC: 333613)

Great Plains Energy is a public utility holding company. As of Dec 31 2007, Co.'s operations were organized into two reportable segments. Co.'s Kansas City Power & Light Company segment is engaged in the generation, transmission, distribution and sale of electricity, serving about 506,000 customers located in all or portions of 24 counties in western Missouri and eastern Kansas. Co.'s Strategic Energy segment provides retail electricity supply services by entering into power supply contracts to supply electricity to its end-use customers as well as strategic planning, consulting and billing and scheduling services in the natural gas and electricity markets, serving about 109,000 accounts.

Recent Developments: For the year ended Dec 31 2007, income from continuing operations increased 24.8% to US$159.2 million from US$127.6 million a year earlier. Net income increased 24.8% to US$159.2 million from US$127.6 million in the prior year. Revenues were US$3.27 billion, up 22.1% from US$2.68 billion the year before. Operating income was US$319.8 million versus US$235.4 million in the prior year, an increase of 35.9%. Direct operating expenses rose 22.7% to US$2.56 billion from US$2.09 billion in the comparable period the year before. Indirect operating expenses increased 9.4% to US$382.4 million from US$349.6 million in the equivalent prior-year period.

Prospects: For the full year of 2008, Co. is projecting capital expenditure at its Kansas City Power & Light Company (KCP&L) utility to be approximately $724.7 million, excluding allowance for funds used to finance construction, with allocations of about $553.0 million for generating facilities, $16.0 million for nuclear fuel, $125.7 million for distribution and transmission facilities as well as $30.0 million for other facilities. Meanwhile, Co. is progressing towards the acquisition of Aquila, Inc., which is anticipated to close by the first half of 2008. In addition, KCP&L expects the ongoing environmental upgrading at its Iatan No. 1 generating units to be fully completed by the end of 2008.

Financial Data

(US$ in Thousands)	12/31/2007	12/31/2006	12/31/2005	12/31/2004	12/31/2003	12/31/2002	12/31/2001	12/31/2000
Earnings Per Share	1.85	1.61	2.15	2.49	2.07	1.99	(0.42)	2.54
Cash Flow Per Share	3.91	3.96	5.59	5.22	5.58	5.38	4.51	3.13
Tang Book Value Per Share	18.18	16.70	16.37	15.35	13.82	13.58	12.59	14.88
Dividends Per Share	1.660	1.660	1.660	1.660	1.660	1.660	1.660	1.660
Dividend Payout %	89.73	103.11	77.21	66.67	80.19	83.42	...	65.35
Income Statement								
Total Revenue	3,267,100	2,675,349	2,604,882	2,464,018	2,149,496	1,861,882	1,461,918	1,115,868
EBITDA	533,000	431,577	459,071	482,489	448,976	439,582	215,699	412,732
Income Before Taxes	232,700	177,384	212,139	227,386	209,127	177,473	(75,957)	181,797
Income Taxes	71,500	47,822	39,691	54,451	55,514	48,285	(35,914)	53,166
Net Income	159,200	127,630	162,310	180,811	144,923	126,188	(24,171)	158,704
Average Shares	85,200	78,170	74,700	72,092	69,248	62,623	61,864	61,864
Balance Sheet								
Net PPE	3,444,500	3,066,201	2,765,726	2,734,450	2,700,934	2,604,069	2,623,714	2,527,790
Total Assets	4,826,700	4,335,660	3,833,726	3,798,901	3,665,287	3,506,739	3,464,402	3,293,891
Long-Term Obligations	1,102,900	607,510	1,140,880	956,460	1,158,345	974,335	778,686	1,041,847
Total Liabilities	3,219,800	2,954,744	2,571,299	2,618,307	2,668,993	2,528,269	2,645,687	2,333,539
Stockholders' Equity	1,606,900	1,380,916	1,262,427	1,180,594	996,294	978,470	818,715	960,352
Shares Outstanding	86,234	80,351	74,740	74,365	69,255	69,196	61,908	61,908
Statistical Record								
Return on Assets %	3.48	3.12	4.25	4.83	4.04	3.62	N.M.	5.04
Return on Equity %	10.66	9.66	13.29	16.57	14.68	14.04	N.M.	16.98
EBITDA Margin %	16.31	16.13	17.62	19.58	20.89	23.61	14.75	36.99
Net Margin %	4.87	4.77	6.23	7.34	6.74	6.78	(1.65)	14.22
PPE Turnover	1.00	0.92	0.95	0.90	0.81	0.71	0.57	0.46
Asset Turnover	0.71	0.65	0.68	0.66	0.60	0.53	0.43	0.35
Debt to Equity	0.69	0.44	0.90	0.81	1.16	1.00	0.95	1.08
Price Range	33.18-26.99	32.80-27.33	32.63-27.27	35.29-28.17	32.60-21.77	26.60-16.62	27.35-23.50	29.00-21.25
P/E Ratio	17.94-14.59	20.37-16.98	15.18-12.68	14.17-11.31	15.75-10.52	13.37-8.35	...	11.42-8.37
Average Yield %	5.48	5.61	5.45	5.36	5.99	7.35	6.59	6.55

Address: 1201 Walnut Street, P.O. Box 418679, Kansas City, MO 64106-2124 **Telephone:** 816-556-2200 **Fax:** 816-556-2924	Web Site: www.greatplainsenergy.com **Officers:** Michael J. Chesser - Chmn., C.E.O. William H. Downey - Pres., C.O.O.	Auditors: Deloitte & Touche LLP **Transfer Agents:** UMB Bank, n.a., Kansas City, MO

GROUP 1 AUTOMOTIVE, INC.

Exchange	Symbol	Price	52Wk Range	Yield	P/E
NYS	GPI	$23.48 (3/31/2008)	43.30-20.33	2.39	8.10

*7 Year Price Score 78.05 *NYSE Composite Index=100 ***12 Month Price Score 81.20**

Interim Earnings (Per Share)

Qtr.	Mar	Jun	Sep	Dec
2003	0.64	0.86	0.92	0.84
2004	0.45	0.67	(0.42)	0.47
2005	(0.07)	0.75	0.88	0.66
2006	0.91	1.00	1.10	0.61
2007	0.72	1.01	0.90	0.27

Interim Dividends (Per Share)

Amt	Decl	Ex	Rec	Pay
0.14Q	5/17/2007	5/30/2007	6/1/2007	6/15/2007
0.14Q	8/8/2007	8/29/2007	9/1/2007	9/15/2007
0.14Q	11/8/2007	11/28/2007	12/1/2007	12/15/2007
0.14Q	2/26/2008	3/5/2008	3/7/2008	3/17/2008

Indicated Div: $0.56

Valuation Analysis

Forecast P/E	10.74 (1/10/2007)
Market Cap	$542.5 Million
Book Value	684.5 Million
Price/Book	0.79
Price/Sales	0.08

Institutional Holding

No of Institutions	168
Shares	29,181,300
% Held	N/A

TRADING VOLUME (thousand shares)

Business Summary: Retail - Automotive (MIC: 5.7 SIC: 5511 NAIC: 441110)

Group 1 Automotive is engaged in the automotive retail industry. As of Dec 31 2007, Co. owned and operated 142 franchises at 104 dealership locations and 26 collision centers. Through its operating subsidiaries, Co. markets and sells a range of automotive products and services including new and used vehicles and related financing, vehicle maintenance and repair services, replacement parts, and warranty, insurance and extended service contracts. Co.'s operations are mainly located in metropolitan areas in Alabama, California, Florida, Georgia, Kansas, Louisiana, Massachusetts, Mississippi, New Hampshire, New Jersey, New Mexico, New York, Oklahoma, South Carolina and Texas.

Recent Developments: For the year ended Dec 31 2007, net income decreased 23.1% to US$68.0 million from US$88.4 million in the prior year. Revenues were US$6.39 billion, up 5.1% from US$6.08 billion the year before. Operating income was US$180.6 million versus US$204.7 million in the prior year, a decrease of 11.7%. Direct operating expenses rose 5.4% to US$5.40 billion from US$5.12 billion in the comparable period the year before. Indirect operating expenses increased 7.3% to US$815.7 million from US$760.1 million in the equivalent prior-year period.

Prospects: Looking ahead to full year 2008, Co. expects earnings to be in a range of $2.95 to $3.25 per share, based on an anticipated 3.0% to 5.0% decline in same-store revenues. Notably, this guidance does not include the effect of future acquisitions, as well as potential one-time charges related to divestitures and associated exit costs expected to be in the range of $10.0 million to $15.0 million as Co. anticipates further disposition of underperforming franchises. Meanwhile, Co. has set a target of acquiring franchises with approximately $300.0 million in estimated annual revenues in 2008.

Financial Data

(US$ in Thousands)	12/31/2007	12/31/2006	12/31/2005	12/31/2004	12/31/2003	12/31/2002	12/31/2001	12/31/2000
Earnings Per Share	2.90	3.62	2.24	1.18	3.26	2.80	2.59	1.88
Cash Flow Per Share	0.16	2.21	13.31	3.60	3.57	3.21	4.32	4.46
Tang Book Value Per Share	N.M.	0.68	3.74	0.23	5.67	3.36	4.84	N.M.
Dividends Per Share	0.560	0.550	...	...	...	...	...	...
Dividend Payout %	19.31	15.19	...	...	...	...	...	...
Income Statement								
Total Revenue	6,392,997	6,083,484	5,969,590	5,435,033	4,518,560	4,214,364	3,996,374	3,586,146
EBITDA	202,786	224,552	186,978	110,270	162,344	148,518	146,936	134,900
Income Before Taxes	106,023	139,348	108,407	47,952	113,072	107,282	89,422	65,826
Income Taxes	38,071	50,958	38,138	20,171	36,946	40,217	33,980	25,014
Net Income	67,952	88,390	54,251	27,781	76,126	67,065	55,442	40,812
Average Shares	23,406	24,446	24,229	23,493	23,346	23,968	21,415	21,709
Balance Sheet								
Current Assets	1,260,084	1,178,012	1,105,828	1,205,215	930,923	903,038	661,932	720,539
Total Assets	2,505,297	2,113,955	1,833,618	1,947,220	1,488,165	1,423,765	1,054,425	1,099,553
Current Liabilities	1,069,531	940,958	968,632	1,049,762	654,393	809,283	507,219	665,770
Long-Term Obligations	674,838	428,639	158,074	156,747	230,178	83,222	95,499	140,393
Total Liabilities	1,820,816	1,421,115	1,206,825	1,380,046	970,056	980,348	662,182	852,137
Stockholders' Equity	684,481	692,840	626,793	567,174	518,109	443,417	392,243	247,416
Shares Outstanding	23,105	24,261	24,016	23,309	22,451	22,240	22,686	19,765
Statistical Record								
Return on Assets %	2.94	4.48	2.87	1.61	5.23	5.41	5.15	4.19
Return on Equity %	9.87	13.40	9.08	5.11	15.83	16.05	17.33	16.98
EBITDA Margin %	3.17	3.69	3.13	2.03	3.59	3.52	3.68	3.76
Net Margin %	1.06	1.45	0.91	0.51	1.68	1.59	1.39	1.14
Asset Turnover	2.77	3.08	3.16	3.16	3.10	3.40	3.71	3.68
Current Ratio	1.18	1.25	1.14	1.15	1.42	1.12	1.31	1.08
Debt to Equity	0.99	0.62	0.25	0.28	0.44	0.19	0.24	0.57
Price Range	54.51-23.71	63.18-32.02	32.72-24.04	38.25-26.68	40.05-20.11	50.15-18.92	34.50-8.19	16.50-8.13
P/E Ratio	18.80-8.18	17.45-8.85	14.61-10.73	32.42-22.61	12.29-6.17	17.91-6.76	13.32-3.16	8.78-4.32
Average Yield %	1.44	1.12	...	...	...	...	...	...

Address: 950 Echo Lane, Suite 100, Houston, TX 77024 **Telephone:** 713-647-5700 **Fax:** 713-647-5858	**Web Site:** www.group1auto.com **Officers:** Earl J. Hesterberg - Pres., C.E.O. Scott L. Thompson - Exec. V.P., C.F.O., Treas.	**Auditors:** Ernst & Young LLP **Transfer Agents:** Mellon Investor Services LLC, Dallas, TX

GUESS ?, INC.

Exchange	Symbol	Price	52Wk Range	Yield	P/E
NYS	GES	$40.47 (3/31/2008)	54.98-32.59	0.79	20.34

*7 Year Price Score 237.56 ***NYSE Composite Index=100** ***12 Month Price Score 94.20**

Interim Earnings (Per Share)

2007-08	0.38	0.40	0.62	0.59

Interim Dividends (Per Share)

Amt	Decl	Ex	Rec	Pay
0.06Q	6/5/2007	6/18/2007	6/20/2007	7/6/2007
0.08Q	9/4/2007	9/17/2007	9/19/2007	10/5/2007
0.08Q	12/4/2007	12/17/2007	12/19/2007	1/4/2008
0.08Q	3/19/2008	3/31/2008	4/2/2008	4/18/2008
		Indicated Div: $0.32		

Valuation Analysis

		Institutional Holding	
Forecast P/E	N/A	No of Institutions	
		168	
Market Cap	$3.8 Billion	Shares	
Book Value	657.0 Million	59,200,752	
Price/Book	5.81	% Held	
Price/Sales	2.18	31.76	

Business Summary: Apparel (MIC: 4.4 SIC: 2331 NAIC: 315212)

Guess? designs, markets, distributes and licenses casual apparel and accessories for men, women and children. Co.'s apparel is marketed under various trademarks including GUESS, GUESS?, GUESS U.S.A., GUESS Jeans, GUESS? and Triangle Design, Question Mark and Triangle Design, a stylized G, GUESS Kids, Baby GUESS, YES, G by GUESS, GUESS by MARCIANO and MARCIANO. Co.'s line of collections includes jeans, pants, skirts, dresses, shorts, blouses, shirts, and jackets. Co. also grant licenses to manufacture and distribute a range of products that complement its apparel lines, including eyewear, watches, handbags, footwear, leather apparel, swimwear, fragrance and other fashion accessories.

Recent Developments: For the year ended Feb 2 2008, net income increased to US$186.5 million from US$8.0 million in the prior year. Revenues were US$1.75 billion, up from US$136.0 million the year before. Operating income was US$309.1 million versus US$12.5 million in the prior year, an increase of. Direct operating expenses rose to US$957.1 million from US$80.2 million in the comparable period the year before. Indirect operating expenses increased to US$483.6 million from US$43.3 million in the equivalent prior-year period.

Prospects: For the fiscal year ending Jan 31 2009, Co. expects consolidated net revenues to range from $1.97 billion to $2.05 billion, operating margin of about 17.7%, and diluted earnings per share of $2.35 to $2.45. Looking ahead, Co. remains focused on the globalization of its brand, by continuing to expand both domestically and internationally. Thus, Co.'s capital expenditures for fiscal 2009 are planned at approximately $137.0 million, excluding estimated lease incentives, primarily for retail store expansion of approximately 60 stores in the U.S. and Canada, store remodeling programs, expansion in Europe and Asia, investments in information systems and improvements in other infrastructure.

Financial Data

(US$ in Thousands)	02/02/2008	02/03/2007	12/31/2006	12/31/2005	12/31/2004	12/31/2003	12/31/2002	12/31/2001
Earnings Per Share	1.99	0.09	1.34	0.66	0.33	0.09	(0.13)	0.07
Cash Flow Per Share	1.91	0.83	1.53	1.62	0.92	0.72	0.34	0.82
Tang Book Value Per Share	6.40	4.26	4.18	2.98	2.37	1.94	1.93	2.05
Dividends Per Share	0.280	...	...	...	...	...	...	...
Dividend Payout %	14.07	...	...	...	...	...	...	...
Income Statement								
Total Revenue	1,749,916	135,952	1,185,184	936,092	729,262	636,585	583,139	677,620
EBITDA	357,938	17,285	235,554	136,449	91,189	55,570	30,278	64,369
Income Before Taxes	311,463	12,720	195,997	97,695	50,713	12,786	(16,832)	10,742
Income Taxes	124,099	4,885	72,715	38,882	21,147	5,500	(5,550)	4,500
Net Income	186,472	7,980	123,168	58,813	29,566	7,286	(11,282)	6,242
Average Shares	93,695	93,120	92,074	90,118	89,088	87,116	86,784	87,916
Balance Sheet								
Current Assets	814,739	563,467	558,892	410,777	271,023	210,644	188,987	189,036
Total Assets	1,186,228	843,322	836,925	633,374	424,304	362,765	349,532	362,463
Current Liabilities	388,291	279,529	283,896	217,226	132,799	110,875	167,561	93,773
Long-Term Obligations	18,724	17,336	18,018	40,054	41,396	54,161	1,480	80,119
Total Liabilities	523,265	399,991	401,113	345,081	203,727	179,983	183,252	184,539
Stockholders' Equity	656,974	438,724	431,060	288,293	220,577	182,782	166,280	177,924
Shares Outstanding	94,337	93,105	92,088	89,938	88,355	87,345	86,153	86,785
Statistical Record								
Return on Assets %	18.43	10.20	16.75	11.12	7.49	2.05	N.M.	1.60
Return on Equity %	34.13	19.70	34.24	23.12	14.62	4.17	N.M.	3.54
EBITDA Margin %	20.45	12.71	19.87	14.58	12.50	8.73	5.19	9.50
Net Margin %	10.66	5.87	10.39	6.28	4.05	1.14	N.M.	0.92
Asset Turnover	1.73	1.74	1.61	1.77	1.85	1.79	1.64	1.73
Current Ratio	2.10	2.02	1.97	1.89	2.04	1.90	1.13	2.02
Debt to Equity	0.03	0.04	0.04	0.14	0.19	0.30	0.01	0.45
Price Range	54.98-32.59	37.42-32.35	32.55-17.18	18.45-5.99	9.70-5.59	7.55-1.66	4.54-1.75	4.34-2.41
P/E Ratio	27.63-16.38	415.83-359.44	24.29-12.82	27.95-9.08	29.39-16.92	83.89-18.44	...	62.07-34.38
Average Yield %	0.63	...	...	...	...	...	...	...

Address: 1444 South Alameda Street, Los Angeles, CA 90021 **Telephone:** 213-765-3100 **Fax:** 213-744-7838	**Web Site:** www.guess.com **Officers:** Maurice Marciano - Co-Chmn., Co-C.E.O. Paul Marciano - Co-Chmn., Co-C.E.O.	**Auditors:** KPMG LLP **Investor Contact:** 213-765-5578

HALLIBURTON COMPANY

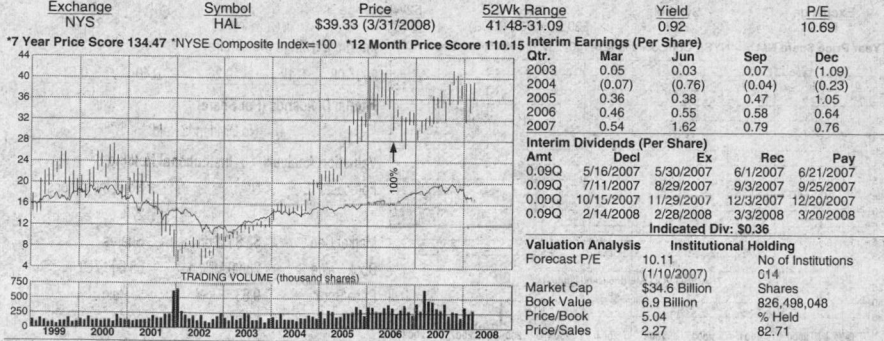

Exchange	Symbol	Price	52Wk Range	Yield	P/E
NYS	HAL	$39.33 (3/31/2008)	41.48-31.09	0.92	10.69

*7 Year Price Score 134.47 *NYSE Composite Index=100 *12 Month Price Score 110.15

Interim Earnings (Per Share)

Qtr.	Mar	Jun	Sep	Dec
2003	0.05	0.03	0.07	(1.09)
2004	(0.07)	(0.76)	(0.04)	(0.23)
2005	0.36	0.38	0.47	1.05
2006	0.46	0.55	0.58	0.64
2007	0.54	1.62	0.79	0.76

Interim Dividends (Per Share)

Amt	Decl	Ex	Rec	Pay
0.09Q	5/16/2007	5/30/2007	6/1/2007	6/21/2007
0.09Q	7/11/2007	8/29/2007	9/3/2007	9/25/2007
0.00Q	10/15/2007	11/29/2007	12/3/2007	12/20/2007
0.09Q	2/14/2008	2/28/2008	3/3/2008	3/20/2008

Indicated Div: $0.36

Valuation Analysis

		Institutional Holding	
Forecast P/E	10.11	No of Institutions	
	(1/10/2007)	014	
Market Cap	$34.6 Billion	Shares	
Book Value	6.9 Billion	826,498,048	
Price/Book	5.04	% Held	
Price/Sales	2.27	82.71	

TRADING VOLUME (thousand shares)

Business Summary: Oil and Gas (MIC: 14.2 SIC: 1389 NAIC: 213112)

Halliburton is a global provider of a range of discrete and integrated services and products to the energy industry. Co. serves the upstream oil and gas industry throughout the lifecycle of the reservoir: from locating hydrocarbons and managing geological data, to drilling and formation evaluation, well construction and completion, and optimizing production through the life of the field. As of Dec 31 2007, Co. operated in two business segments: Completion and Production, which delivers cementing, stimulation, intervention, and completion services; and Drilling and Evaluation, which provides field and reservoir modeling, drilling, evaluation, and precise well-bore placement products.

Recent Developments: For the year ended Dec 31 2007, income from continuing operations increased 15.9% to US$2.52 billion from US$2.18 billion a year earlier. Net income increased 49.0% to US$3.50 billion from US$2.35 billion in the prior year. Revenues were US$15.26 billion, up 17.8% from US$12.96 billion the year before. Operating income was US$3.50 billion versus US$3.25 billion in the prior year, an increase of 7.8%. Direct operating expenses rose 22.3% to US$11.53 billion from US$9.43 billion in the comparable period the year before. Indirect operating expenses decreased 15.1% to US$241.0 million from US$284.0 million in the equivalent prior-year period.

Prospects: Co. anticipates an average price decline for its U.S. land stimulation work in the mid- to upper-single digits in the first quarter of 2008 over the fourth quarter of 2007. Co. will partially mitigate this by growth in its other service lines, resulting in a more balanced portfolio, and by capitalizing on the trend towards unconventional plays and horizontal drilling. However, Co. expects prices to stabilize in the latter half of 2008, as equipment additions decelerate, and its customers try to meet their drilling plans. Also, Co. will continue to invest in infrastructure, capital, and technology primarily in the eastern hemisphere, and plans to open a technology center in Singapore in 2008.

Financial Data

(US$ in Thousands)	12/31/2007	12/31/2006	12/31/2005	12/31/2004	12/31/2003	12/31/2002	12/31/2001	12/31/2000
Earnings Per Share	3.68	2.23	2.27	(1.11)	(0.94)	(1.16)	0.94	0.56
Cash Flow Per Share	2.99	3.61	0.69	1.06	(0.89)	1.81	1.20	(0.06)
Tang Book Value Per Share	6.90	6.61	3.43	3.55	2.14	3.25	4.65	3.90
Dividends Per Share	0.345	0.300	0.250	0.250	0.250	0.250	0.250	0.250
Dividend Payout %	9.38	13.45	11.01	...	...	...	26.60	44.64
Income Statement								
Total Revenue	15,264,000	22,576,000	20,994,000	20,466,000	16,271,000	12,572,000	13,046,000	11,944,000
EBITDA	4,073,000	3,989,000	3,139,000	1,345,000	1,239,000	358,000	1,605,000	959,000
Income Before Taxes	3,460,000	3,449,000	2,492,000	651,000	612,000	(228,000)	954,000	335,000
Income Taxes	907,000	1,144,000	79,000	241,000	234,000	80,000	384,000	129,000
Net Income	3,499,000	2,348,000	2,358,000	(979,000)	(820,000)	(998,000)	809,000	301,000
Average Shares	950,000	1,054,000	1,038,000	882,000	874,000	864,000	860,000	892,000
Balance Sheet								
Current Assets	7,573,000	11,183,000	9,327,000	9,962,000	7,919,000	5,560,000	5,573,000	5,568,000
Total Assets	13,135,000	16,820,000	15,010,000	15,796,000	15,463,000	12,844,000	10,966,000	10,103,000
Current Liabilities	2,411,000	4,727,000	4,437,000	7,064,000	6,542,000	3,272,000	2,908,000	3,826,000
Long-Term Obligations	2,627,000	2,786,000	2,813,000	3,593,000	3,415,000	1,181,000	1,403,000	1,049,000
Total Liabilities	6,175,000	8,997,000	8,493,000	11,756,000	12,816,000	9,286,000	6,214,000	6,175,000
Stockholders' Equity	6,866,000	7,376,000	6,372,000	3,932,000	2,547,000	3,558,000	4,752,000	3,928,000
Shares Outstanding	880,000	998,000	1,028,000	884,000	878,000	872,000	868,000	854,000
Statistical Record								
Return on Assets %	23.36	14.75	15.31	N.M.	N.M.	N.M.	7.68	4.80
Return on Equity %	49.14	34.16	45.77	N.M.	N.M.	N.M.	18.64	12.16
EBITDA Margin %	26.68	17.67	14.95	6.57	7.61	2.85	12.30	8.03
Net Margin %	22.92	10.40	11.23	N.M.	N.M.	N.M.	6.20	4.19
Asset Turnover	1.02	1.42	1.36	1.31	1.15	1.06	1.24	1.14
Current Ratio	3.14	2.37	2.10	1.41	1.21	1.70	1.92	1.46
Debt to Equity	0.38	0.38	0.44	0.91	1.34	0.33	0.30	0.27
Price Range	41.48-28.27	41.66-26.57	34.70-18.79	20.68-13.00	13.56-8.89	10.50-4.55	24.60-6.00	27.34-16.69
P/E Ratio	11.27-7.68	18.68-11.91	15.29-8.28	...	...	...	26.17-6.38	48.83-29.80
Average Yield %	1.00	0.87	0.97	1.57	2.22	3.20	1.51	1.16

Address: 5 Houston Center, 1401 McKinney, Suite 2400, Houston, TX 77010	Web Site: www.halliburton.com	Auditors: KPMG LLP
	Officers: David J. Lesar - Chmn., Pres., C.E.O. C. Christpher Gaut - Exec. V.P., C.F.O.	Investor Contact: 888-669-3920
Telephone: 713-759-2600		Transfer Agents: Mellon Investor Services

HANESBRANDS INC

Exchange	Symbol	Price	52Wk Range	Yield	P/E
NYS	HBI	$29.20 (3/31/2008)	32.75-21.73	N/A	22.46

*7 Year Price Score N/A   *NYSE Composite Index=100   *12 Month Price Score 105.76

Interim Earnings (Per Share)

2007-08	0.12	0.26	0.40	0.51

Interim Dividends (Per Share)

No Dividends Paid

Valuation Analysis   **Institutional Holding**

Forecast P/E	N/A	No of Institutions
		273
Market Cap	$2.8 Billion	Shares
Book Value	288.9 Million	65,606,780
Price/Book	9.63	% Held
Price/Sales	0.62	68.08

TRADING VOLUME (thousand shares)

Business Summary: Apparel (MIC: 4.4 SIC: 2389 NAIC: 313312)

Hanesbrands is a consumer goods company with a portfolio of apparel brands, including Hanes™, Champion™, C9 by Champion™, Playtex™, Bali™, L'eggs™, Just My Size™, barely there™, Wonderbra™, Beefy-T™, Outer Banks™ and Duofold™. Co. designs, manufactures, sources and sells a range of apparel such as t-shirts, bras, panties, men's underwear, kids' underwear, socks, hosiery, casualwear and activewear. Co.'s business is organized into four operating segments, which includes innerwear, outerwear, hosiery and international. Co. sells its products primarily through retailers, including mass merchants, department stores and national chains.

Recent Developments: For the year ended Dec 29 2007, net income increased 70.1% to US$126.1 million from US$74.1 million in the prior year. Revenues were US$4.47 billion, up 98.8% from US$2.25 billion the year before. Operating income was US$388.6 million versus US$190.1 million in the prior year, an increase of 104.4%. Direct operating expenses rose 98.3% to US$3.03 billion from US$1.53 billion in the comparable period the year before. Indirect operating expenses increased 98.5% to US$1.05 billion from US$530.3 million in the equivalent prior-year period.

Prospects: Co.'s outlook appears solid, reflecting increased overall net sales due to growth in sales volume in Hanes™ brand casualwear and sock sales, Champion™ brand activewear sales and Bali™ brand intimate apparel sales, as well as double-digit gains in the hosiery and international segments driven by core hosiery product strength and growth in the European casualwear business. Overall, Co. believes that its strategic initiatives of investing in core brands, its continuing effort to improve operating efficiencies and lowering costs should position it to achieve long term growth goals. Also, Co. expects to continue to add new manufacturing capacity in Central America, the Caribbean Basin and Asia.

Financial Data

(US$ in Thousands)	12/29/2007	12/30/2006	07/01/2006	07/02/2005	07/03/2004
Earnings Per Share	1.30	0.77	...	...	...
Cash Flow Per Share	3.75	0.94	...	...	...
Income Statement					
Total Revenue	4,474,537	2,250,473	4,472,832	4,683,683	4,632,741
EBITDA	515,010	256,085	547,804	477,371	539,514
Income Before Taxes	184,126	111,920	416,320	345,516	400,872
Income Taxes	57,999	37,781	93,827	127,007	(48,680)
Net Income	126,127	74,139	322,493	218,509	449,552
Average Shares	96,741	96,620	...	...	...
Balance Sheet					
Current Assets	2,094,334	2,071,180	3,755,812	3,125,740	3,214,674
Total Assets	3,439,483	3,435,620	4,891,075	4,237,154	4,402,758
Current Liabilities	688,982	611,181	1,611,954	1,581,233	1,569,454
Long-Term Obligations	2,315,250	2,484,000	2,786	6,188	7,200
Total Liabilities	3,150,579	3,366,349	1,661,941	1,634,792	1,605,388
Stockholders' Equity	288,904	69,271	3,229,134	2,602,362	2,797,370
Shares Outstanding	95,232	96,312	...	...	...
Statistical Record					
Return on Assets %	3.68	1.29	7.09	5.07	...
Return on Equity %	70.62	3.71	11.09	8.12	...
EBITDA Margin %	11.51	11.38	12.25	10.19	11.65
Net Margin %	2.82	3.29	7.21	4.67	9.70
Asset Turnover	1.31	0.39	0.98	1.09	...
Current Ratio	3.04	3.39	2.33	1.98	2.05
Debt to Equity	8.01	35.86	N.M.	N.M.	N.M.
Price Range	32.75-24.04	24.71-18.00	...	...	...
P/E Ratio	25.19-18.49	32.09-23.38	...	...	...

Address: 1000 East Hanes Mill Road, Winston-Salem, NC 27105
Telephone: 336-519-4400

Web Site: www.hanesbrands.com
Officers: William J. Nictakis - Pres., C.C.O Richard A. Noll - C.E.O.

Auditors: PricewaterhouseCoopers LLP

HANOVER INSURANCE GROUP INC

Exchange	Symbol	Price	52Wk Range	Yield	P/E
NYS	THG	$41.14 (3/31/2008)	49.76-40.14	0.97	8.52

*7 Year Price Score 96.54   *NYSE Composite Index=100   *12 Month Price Score 104.59

Interim Earnings (Per Share)

Qtr.	Mar	Jun	Sep	Dec
2003	0.70	0.46	0.21	0.26
2004	0.23	0.60	0.33	1.18
2005	0.86	1.34	(10.51)	2.29
2006	0.75	0.99	0.65	0.89
2007	1.22	1.14	1.03	1.44

Interim Dividends (Per Share)

Amt	Decl	Ex	Rec	Pay
0.25A	10/23/2001	11/1/2001	11/5/2001	11/20/2001
0.25A	10/18/2005	11/23/2005	11/28/2005	12/12/2005
0.30A	10/17/2006	11/24/2006	11/28/2006	12/12/2006
0.40A	10/17/2007	11/26/2007	11/28/2007	12/12/2007

Indicated Div: $0.40

Valuation Analysis   **Institutional Holding**

Forecast P/E	N/A	No of Institutions
		195
Market Cap	$2.1 Billion	Shares
Book Value	2.3 Billion	37,833,652
Price/Book	0.93	% Held
Price/Sales	0.76	73.79

TRADING VOLUME (thousand shares)

Business Summary: Insurance (MIC: 8.2 SIC: 6331 NAIC: 524126)

Hanover Insurance Group is a holding company. Co.'s business includes insurance products and services in three property and casualty operating segments. Co.'s Personal Lines segment includes personal automobile, homeowners and other personal coverages, while its Commercial Lines segment includes commercial multiple peril, commercial automobile, workers' compensation and other commercial coverages, such as bonds and inland marine business. In addition, Co.'s Other Property and Casualty segment consists of Opus Investment Management, Inc., which markets investment management services to institutions, pension funds and other organizations, and Amgro, Inc., its financing business.

Recent Developments: For the year ended Dec 31 2007, income from continuing operations increased 24.8% to US$239.2 million from US$191.7 million a year earlier. Net income increased 48.6% to US$253.1 million from US$170.3 million in the prior year. Revenues were US$2.79 billion, up 5.4% from US$2.64 billion the year before. Net premiums earned were US$2.40 billion versus US$2.25 billion in the prior year, an increase of 6.7%. Net investment income rose 1.6% to US$324.0 million from US$318.9 million a year ago.

Prospects: Going forward, Co. remains focused on expanding its product offerings in specialty businesses. For instance, on Jan 14 2008, Co. announced that it has entered into a definitive agreement to acquire Verlan Holdings, Inc., a provider of insurance to manufacturers and distributors of chemical-related products. The transaction, which is expected to close before the end of the first quarter of 2008, is subject to regulatory reviews and approvals, as well as the approval of the shareholders of Verlan Holdings Inc. Meanwhile, Co. anticipates that continued growth from Connections® Auto and the recent agencies appointments to contribute to premium improvement in its Personal Lines business.

Financial Data
(US$ in Thousands)

	12/31/2007	12/31/2006	12/31/2005	12/31/2004	12/31/2003	12/31/2002	12/31/2001	12/31/2000
Earnings Per Share	4.83	3.27	(6.02)	2.34	1.63	(5.79)	(0.06)	3.70
Cash Flow Per Share	1.42	0.81	2.86	2.67	(3.29)	0.83	11.34	2.97
Tang Book Value Per Share	41.95	36.75	33.95	41.57	39.47	36.69	45.20	45.71
Dividends Per Share	0.400	0.300	0.250	...	...	...	0.250	0.250
Dividend Payout %	8.28	9.17	...	...	...	...	...	6.76
Income Statement								
Premium Income	2,404,800	2,254,600	2,198,200	2,288,600	2,282,300	2,320,100	2,254,700	2,068,900
Total Revenue	2,786,800	2,644,100	2,624,300	3,111,000	3,263,600	3,316,600	3,311,800	3,087,900
Benefits & Claims	...	...	...	...	...	...	68,300	...
Income Before Taxes	348,400	279,400	71,300	186,700	79,500	(521,200)	(59,400)	218,600
Income Taxes	109,200	87,700	(5,200)	4,200	(7,400)	(234,800)	(75,500)	2,700
Net Income	253,100	170,300	(325,200)	125,300	86,900	(306,100)	(3,100)	199,900
Average Shares	52,400	52,200	54,000	53,700	53,200	52,900	53,100	54,000
Balance Sheet								
Total Assets	9,815,600	9,856,600	10,634,000	23,719,200	25,112,500	26,578,900	30,336,100	31,588,000
Total Liabilities	7,516,600	7,857,400	8,682,700	21,379,700	22,892,300	24,206,700	27,645,000	28,878,900
Stockholders' Equity	2,299,000	1,999,200	1,951,300	2,339,500	2,220,200	2,072,200	2,391,100	2,409,100
Shares Outstanding	51,800	51,100	53,700	53,200	53,000	52,900	52,900	52,700
Statistical Record								
Return on Assets %	2.57	1.66	N.M.	0.51	0.34	N.M.	N.M.	0.64
Return on Equity %	11.78	8.62	N.M.	5.48	4.05	N.M.	N.M.	8.58
Loss Ratio %	...	...	...	...	...	...	3.03	...
Net Margin %	9.08	6.44	(12.39)	4.03	2.66	(9.23)	(0.09)	6.47
Price Range	49.76-41.14	54.11-41.17	42.11-30.27	38.25-25.45	31.29-9.84	50.33-7.16	67.25-38.17	72.50-35.31
P/E Ratio	10.30-8.52	16.55-12.59	...	16.35-10.88	19.20-6.04	...	...	19.59-9.54
Average Yield %	0.87	0.64	0.67	...	...	...	0.49	0.45

Address: 440 Lincoln Street, Worcester, MA 01653
Telephone: 508-855-1000
Fax: 508-853-6332

Web Site: www.allmerica.com
Officers: Michael P. Angelini - Chmn. Frederick H. Eppinger Jr. - Pres., C.E.O.

Auditors: PricewaterhouseCoopers LLP
Transfer Agents: Computershare Limited Providence, RI

HARLEY-DAVIDSON INC

Exchange	Symbol	Price	52Wk Range	Yield	P/E	Div Acheiver
NYS	HOG	$37.50 (3/31/2008)	65.55-34.68	3.20	10.03	14 Years

*7 Year Price Score 78.38   *NYSE Composite Index=100   *12 Month Price Score 80.70

Interim Earnings (Per Share)

Qtr.	Mar	Jun	Sep	Dec
2003	0.61	0.66	0.62	0.60
2004	0.68	0.83	0.77	0.71
2005	0.77	0.84	0.96	0.84
2006	0.86	0.91	1.20	0.97
2007	0.74	1.14	1.07	0.79

Interim Dividends (Per Share)

Amt	Decl	Ex	Rec	Pay
0.25Q	4/28/2007	6/7/2007	6/11/2007	6/19/2007
0.30Q	9/13/2007	9/27/2007	10/1/2007	10/11/2007
0.30Q	12/11/2007	12/19/2007	12/21/2007	12/28/2007
0.30Q	2/13/2008	3/3/2008	3/5/2008	3/18/2008

Indicated Div: $1.20 (Div. Reinv. Plan)

Valuation Analysis   **Institutional Holding**

Forecast P/E	14.35	No of Institutions
	(1/10/2007)	588
Market Cap	$8.9 Billion	Shares
Book Value	2.4 Billion	211,954,736
Price/Book	3.76	% Held
Price/Sales	1.46	82.32

Business Summary: Automotive (MIC: 15.1 SIC: 3751 NAIC: 336991)

Harley-Davidson is the parent company for Harley-Davidson Motor Co. (HDMC), Buell Motorcycle Co. (Buell) and Harley-Davidson Financial Services (HDFS). Through HDMC, Co. produces heavyweight motorcycles that comprise five families of motorcycles: Touring, Dyna™, Softail®, Sportster® and VRSC™. Through Buell, Co. produces sport motorcycles, including eight twin-cylinder XB models, a liquid-cooled engine motorcycle and the single-cylinder Buell® Blast®. HDFS provides wholesale and retail financing and insurance programs mainly to Harley-Davidson/Buell dealers and customers. Co. also provides a line of related motorcycle parts, accessories, apparel and general merchandise within HDMC and Buell.

Recent Developments: For the year ended Dec 31 2007, net income decreased 10.5% to US$933.8 million from US$1.04 billion in the prior year. Revenues were US$6.14 billion, down 0.7% from US$6.19 billion the year before. Operating income was US$1.43 billion versus US$1.60 billion in the prior year, a decrease of 10.7%. Direct operating expenses rose 2.0% to US$3.82 billion from US$3.74 billion in the comparable period the year before. Indirect operating expenses increased 6.4% to US$900.7 million from US$846.4 million in the equivalent prior-year period.

Prospects: For 2008, Co. expect the U.S. economy to continue to be challenging, and as a result, it plans to ship fewer Harley-Davidson® motorcycles than it expects its worldwide dealer network to sell, with 68,000 to 72,000 motorcycles scheduled to be shipped during the first quarter of the year. In view of that, Co. is anticipating moderate revenue growth, lower operating margin, as well as diluted earnings per share growth rate of 4.0% to 7.0% compared with 2007. Meanwhile, Co. expects to increase its capital expenditures for 2008 to a range of $240.0 million to $260.0 million, primarily driven by higher investments in manufacturing capabilities and its product program activities.

Financial Data

(US$ in Thousands)	12/31/2007	12/31/2006	12/31/2005	12/31/2004	12/31/2003	12/31/2002	12/31/2001	12/31/2000
Earnings Per Share	3.74	3.93	3.41	3.00	2.50	1.90	1.43	1.13
Cash Flow Per Share	3.20	2.88	3.43	3.28	3.10	2.58	2.50	1.86
Tang Book Value Per Share	9.70	10.45	11.05	10.73	9.63	7.21	5.64	4.47
Dividends Per Share	1.060	0.810	0.625	0.405	0.195	0.135	0.115	0.098
Dividend Payout %	28.34	20.61	18.33	13.50	7.80	7.11	8.04	8.63
Income Statement								
Total Revenue	6,143,044	6,185,577	5,673,832	5,320,452	4,903,733	4,302,470	3,544,959	2,943,543
EBITDA	1,629,733	1,810,922	1,670,667	1,570,497	1,339,865	1,045,064	809,038	664,321
Income Before Taxes	1,447,819	1,624,240	1,487,759	1,379,486	1,166,035	885,827	673,455	548,556
Income Taxes	513,976	581,087	528,155	489,720	405,107	305,610	235,709	200,843
Net Income	933,843	1,043,153	959,604	889,766	760,928	580,217	437,746	347,713
Average Shares	249,882	265,273	281,035	296,852	304,470	305,158	306,248	307,470
Balance Sheet								
Current Assets	3,467,314	3,550,633	3,145,237	3,266,272	2,729,127	2,066,586	1,665,264	1,297,264
Total Assets	5,656,606	5,532,150	5,255,209	5,483,293	4,923,088	3,861,217	3,118,495	2,436,404
Current Liabilities	1,905,079	1,595,677	873,112	1,172,696	955,773	990,052	716,110	497,743
Long-Term Obligations	980,000	870,000	1,000,000	800,000	670,000	380,000	380,000	355,000
Total Liabilities	3,281,115	2,775,413	2,171,604	2,264,822	1,965,396	1,628,302	1,362,212	1,030,749
Stockholders' Equity	2,375,491	2,756,737	3,083,605	3,218,471	2,957,692	2,232,915	1,756,283	1,405,655
Shares Outstanding	238,485	258,052	274,001	294,310	301,510	302,662	302,789	302,070
Statistical Record								
Return on Assets %	16.69	19.34	17.87	17.05	17.32	16.63	15.76	15.25
Return on Equity %	36.39	35.72	30.45	28.73	29.32	29.09	27.69	27.02
EBITDA Margin %	26.53	29.28	29.45	29.52	27.32	24.29	22.82	22.57
Net Margin %	15.20	16.86	16.91	16.72	15.52	13.49	12.35	11.81
Asset Turnover	1.10	1.15	1.06	1.02	1.12	1.23	1.28	1.29
Current Ratio	1.82	2.23	3.60	2.79	2.86	2.09	2.33	2.61
Debt to Equity	0.41	0.32	0.32	0.25	0.23	0.17	0.22	0.25
Price Range	73.85-44.96	75.50-47.96	62.18-44.40	62.97-46.00	52.45-35.95	57.00-42.83	55.66-35.19	50.00-29.63
P/E Ratio	19.75-12.02	19.21-12.20	18.23-13.02	20.99-15.33	20.98-14.38	30.00-22.54	38.92-24.61	44.25-26.22
Average Yield %	1.83	1.41	1.18	0.71	0.44	0.27	0.25	0.24

Address: 3700 West Juneau Avenue, P.O. Box 653, Milwaukee, WI 53201-0653 **Telephone:** 414-342-4680 **Fax:** 414-343-4621	**Web Site:** www.harley-davidson.com **Officers:** Jeffrey L. Bleustein - Chmn. James A. McCaslin - Pres., C.O.O.	**Auditors:** Ernst & Young LLP **Transfer Agents:** Computershare Investor Services, LLC, Chicago, IL

HARMAN INTERNATIONAL INDUSTRIES, INC.

Exchange	Symbol	Price	52Wk Range	Yield	P/E
NYS	HAR	$43.54 (3/31/2008)	122.59-37.08	0.11	11.22

*7 Year Price Score 102.50 *NYSE Composite Index=100 *12 Month Price Score 53.76

Interim Earnings (Per Share)

Qtr.	Sep	Dec	Mar	Jun
2004-05	0.48	0.92	0.90	1.01
2005-06	0.79	1.07	0.94	0.95
2006-07	0.85	1.22	1.07	1.58
2007-08	0.55	0.68	...	...

Interim Dividends (Per Share)

Amt	Decl	Ex	Rec	Pay
0.013Q	5/1/2007	5/7/2007	5/9/2007	5/23/2007
0.013Q	7/30/2007	8/6/2007	8/8/2007	8/22/2007
0.013Q	10/30/2007	11/6/2007	11/8/2007	11/21/2007
0.013Q	1/23/2008	2/4/2008	2/6/2008	2/20/2008

Indicated Div: $0.05

Valuation Analysis / Institutional Holding

Valuation Analysis		Institutional Holding	
Forecast P/E	14.80	No of Institutions	
	(1/10/2007)	310	
Market Cap	$2.6 Billion	Shares	
Book Value	1.2 Billion	62,424,968	
Price/Book	2.13	% Held	
Price/Sales	0.69	95.30	

Business Summary: Electrical (MIC: 11.14 SIC: 3651 NAIC: 334310)

Harman International is engaged in the development, manufacture and marketing of audio products and electronic systems. Co.'s businesses are organized into three segments: Automotive, which designs, manufactures and markets audio, electronic and infotainment systems for vehicle applications mainly to be installed as original equipment by automotive manufacturers; Consumer, which designs, manufactures and markets audio, video and electronic systems for home, mobile and multimedia applications; and Professional, which designs, manufactures and markets loudspeakers and electronic systems used by audio professionals in concert halls, stadiums, airports, houses of worship and other public spaces.

Recent Developments: For the quarter ended Dec 31 2007, net income decreased 47.3% to US$42.9 million from US$81.4 million in the year-earlier quarter. Revenues were US$1.07 billion, up 14.4% from US$931.7 million the year before. Operating income was US$60.8 million versus US$115.7 million in the prior-year quarter, a decrease of 47.4%. Direct operating expenses rose 24.9% to US$764.5 million from US$612.1 million in the comparable period the year before. Indirect operating expenses increased 17.8% to US$240.3 million from US$203.9 million in the equivalent prior year period.

Prospects: Going forward, Co. anticipates performance to be mitigated by lower portable navigation devices margins, product mix, and higher engineering and material costs due to several new infotainment platform launches, as well as pricing pressures. Thus, Co. is implementing strategic initiatives to optimize its global footprint in the automotive sector. For example, Co. has recently accelerated its restructuring initiatives with the announcement of the closure of its automotive manufacturing facilities in Northridge, California and Martinsville, Indiana. Co. noted that this initiative should improve cost structure while shifting some resources to other sites in both mature and emerging markets.

Financial Data

(US$ in Thousands)	6 Mos	3 Mos	06/30/2007	06/30/2006	06/30/2005	06/30/2004	06/30/2003	06/30/2002
Earnings Per Share	3.88	4.42	4.72	3.75	3.31	2.27	1.55	0.85
Cash Flow Per Share	3.12	2.43	3.30	6.03	6.25	7.31	3.87	2.89
Tang Book Value Per Share	13.49	17.79	16.71	12.82	10.74	9.43	6.66	5.03
Dividends Per Share	0.030	0.050	0.050	0.050	0.050	0.050	0.050	0.050
Dividend Payout %	1.29	1.13	1.06	1.33	1.51	2.20	3.23	5.88
Income Statement								
Total Revenue	2,012,572	946,962	3,551,144	3,247,897	3,030,889	2,711,374	2,228,519	1,826,188
EBITDA	172,531	74,919	510,867	519,163	464,518	350,759	253,637	199,247
Depn & Amortn	71,904	34,149	...	...	...	...	...	...
Income Before Taxes	96,310	39,360	382,205	376,187	335,337	227,520	142,471	90,177
Income Taxes	18,233	3,657	70,186	121,877	102,489	69,637	37,043	22,602
Net Income	79,409	36,529	313,963	255,295	232,848	157,883	105,428	57,513
Average Shares	62,882	66,363	66,449	68,105	70,399	69,487	68,048	67,806
Balance Sheet								
Current Assets	1,326,347	1,319,246	1,233,153	1,249,357	1,183,293	1,204,035	967,624	876,763
Total Assets	2,650,109	2,621,827	2,508,868	2,354,661	2,187,203	1,988,810	1,703,658	1,480,280
Current Liabilities	681,280	720,698	815,981	869,001	729,070	662,354	487,410	433,471
Long-Term Obligations	580,454	182,460	57,661	179,466	330,791	387,616	497,759	470,424
Total Liabilities	1,411,423	1,045,717	1,014,827	1,126,497	1,126,255	1,113,814	1,047,873	953,651
Stockholders' Equity	1,238,686	1,576,110	1,494,041	1,228,164	1,060,948	874,996	655,785	526,629
Shares Outstanding	60,535	65,250	65,238	66,064	66,662	66,090	65,219	65,046
Statistical Record								
Return on Assets %	10.15	12.10	12.91	11.24	11.15	8.53	6.62	4.35
Return on Equity %	19.92	21.09	23.07	22.31	24.06	20.57	17.83	12.11
EBITDA Margin %	8.57	7.91	14.39	15.98	15.33	12.94	11.38	10.91
Net Margin %	3.95	3.86	8.84	7.86	7.68	5.82	4.73	3.15
Asset Turnover	1.51	1.51	1.46	1.43	1.45	1.46	1.40	1.38
Current Ratio	1.95	1.83	1.51	1.44	1.62	1.82	1.99	2.02
Debt to Equity	0.47	0.12	0.04	0.15	0.31	0.44	0.76	0.89
Price Range	122.59-70.31	122.59-80.31	122.59-76.32	115.85-79.92	130.72-70.25	91.00-39.32	39.79-19.14	30.32-15.45
P/E Ratio	31.60-18.12	27.74-18.17	25.97-16.17	30.89-21.31	39.49-21.22	40.09-17.32	25.67-12.35	35.68-18.17
Average Yield %	0.05	0.05	0.05	0.05	0.05	0.08	0.17	0.22

Address: 1101 Pennsylvania Avenue, N.W., Suite 1010, Washington, DC 20004 **Telephone:** 202-393-1101 **Fax:** 202-393-3064	**Web Site:** www.harman.com **Officers:** Sidney Harman - Chmn. Bernard A. Girod - Vice-Chmn., C.E.O.	**Auditors:** KPMG LLP **Transfer Agents:** Mellon Investor Services, Los Angeles, CA

HARRIS CORP.

Exchange	Symbol	Price	52Wk Range	Yield	P/E
NYS	HRS	$48.53 (3/31/2008)	65.82-45.87	1.24	13.01

*7 Year Price Score 143.85 *NYSE Composite Index=100 ***12 Month Price Score 96.90**

Interim Earnings (Per Share)

Qtr.	Sep	Dec	Mar	Jun
2004-05	0.29	0.33	0.40	0.44
2005-06	0.36	0.22	0.52	0.61
2006-07	0.60	0.67	1.52	0.64
2007-08	0.73	0.83	...	...

Interim Dividends (Per Share)

Amt	Decl	Ex	Rec	Pay
0.11Q	4/27/2007	5/25/2007	5/30/2007	6/13/2007
0.15Q	8/27/2007	9/4/2007	9/6/2007	9/17/2007
0.15Q	10/26/2007	11/20/2007	11/23/2007	12/7/2007
0.15Q	2/22/2008	2/29/2008	3/4/2008	3/14/2008
		Indicated Div: $0.60		

Valuation Analysis

		Institutional Holding	
Forecast P/E	N/A	No of Institutions	380
Market Cap	$6.6 Billion	Shares	
Book Value	2.2 Billion	115,765,776	
Price/Book	2.98	% Held	
Price/Sales	1.36	86.34	

Business Summary: Instruments and Related Products (MIC: 11.15 SIC: 3812 NAIC: 334511)

Harris is an international communications and information technology company serving government and commercial markets. Co. is focused on developing assured communications™ products, systems and services for global markets, including government communications, RF communications, broadcast communications and wireless transmission network systems. Co. generally sells directly to its customers, the largest of which is the U.S. Government and its prime contractors. Co.'s four business segments include: Government Communications Systems, RF Communications, Broadcast Communications and Harris Stratex Networks, Inc.

Recent Developments: For the quarter ended Dec 28 2007, net income increased 21.6% to US$114.3 million from US$94.0 million in the year-earlier quarter. Revenues were US$1.32 billion, up 29.7% from US$1.02 billion the year before. Direct operating expenses rose 32.8% to US$908.2 million from US$683.7 million in the comparable period the year before. Indirect operating expenses increased 24.5% to US$226.1 million from US$181.6 million in the equivalent prior-year period.

Prospects: Co.'s outlook seems positive, reflecting recent top line growth across all of its operating segments, particularly in its RF Communications tactical radio business. Overall, given the growing order rates, and robust U.S. and international opportunities pipeline, Co. expects an increase in backlog for the rest of fiscal year ending June 2008. Further, Co. believes that strong markets, new products, and global market share expansion should drive double-digit growth in fiscal 2009. For fiscal 2008, Co. expects revenue of $5.20 billion to $5.30 billion, with organic revenue growth of 11.0% to 13.0% above fiscal 2007, and earnings of $3.35 to $3.45 per diluted share.

Financial Data

(US$ in Thousands)	6 Mos	3 Mos	06/29/2007	06/30/2006	07/01/2005	07/02/2004	06/27/2003	06/28/2002
Earnings Per Share	3.73	3.57	3.43	1.71	1.46	1.00	0.45	0.63
Cash Flow Per Share	3.29	3.39	3.32	2.52	2.28	2.01	1.15	1.57
Tang Book Value Per Share	1.98	1.50	N.M.	3.90	5.79	7.95	7.19	7.04
Dividends Per Share	0.520	0.480	0.440	0.320	0.240	0.200	0.160	0.100
Dividend Payout %	13.95	13.46	12.83	18.71	16.44	20.10	35.56	16.00
Income Statement								
Total Revenue	2,548,200	1,230,500	4,243,000	3,474,800	3,000,600	2,518,600	2,092,700	1,875,800
EBITDA	433,300	207,600	823,600	503,900	386,300	253,400	165,300	193,600
Depn & Amortn	84,200	41,900	...	...	...	...	...	...
Income Before Taxes	323,800	152,600	660,800	380,800	298,400	180,000	90,100	125,100
Income Taxes	110,100	52,800	190,900	142,900	96,200	54,300	30,600	42,500
Net Income	214,500	100,200	480,400	237,900	202,200	132,800	59,500	82,600
Average Shares	137,600	137,900	141,100	141,600	141,300	133,800	132,800	132,600
Balance Sheet								
Current Assets	1,960,000	1,870,100	1,828,800	1,428,400	1,317,600	1,553,800	1,357,700	1,153,500
Total Assets	4,551,200	4,450,800	4,406,000	3,142,300	2,457,400	2,225,800	2,080,300	1,858,500
Current Liabilities	1,021,400	1,409,800	1,638,100	752,100	590,200	542,800	495,500	425,600
Long-Term Obligations	832,500	408,100	408,900	699,500	401,400	401,400	401,600	283,000
Total Liabilities	2,009,900	1,978,200	2,175,300	1,480,200	1,018,300	947,000	897,100	708,600
Stockholders' Equity	2,208,900	2,143,100	1,903,800	1,662,100	1,439,100	1,278,800	1,183,200	1,149,900
Shares Outstanding	135,438	135,939	129,577	132,842	132,940	132,688	132,782	132,684
Statistical Record								
Return on Assets %	13.31	13.02	12.76	8.52	8.66	6.07	3.03	4.34
Return on Equity %	25.86	25.64	27.02	15.38	14.92	10.61	5.11	7.31
EBITDA Margin %	17.00	16.87	19.41	14.50	12.87	10.06	7.90	10.32
Net Margin %	8.42	8.14	11.32	6.85	6.74	5.27	2.84	4.40
Asset Turnover	1.24	1.19	1.13	1.24	1.28	1.15	1.07	0.99
Current Ratio	1.92	1.33	1.12	1.90	2.23	2.86	2.74	2.71
Debt to Equity	0.38	0.19	0.21	0.42	0.28	0.31	0.34	0.25
Price Range	65.82-46.68	61.59-40.06	55.57-38.17	49.66-31.11	34.78-21.78	25.38-14.61	18.34-12.15	19.25-12.89
P/E Ratio	17.65-12.51	17.25-11.22	16.20-11.13	29.04-18.19	23.83-14.92	25.38-14.61	40.76-27.00	30.56-20.45
Average Yield %	0.95	0.97	0.94	0.76	0.82	0.99	1.17	0.61

Address: 1025 W. NASA Boulevard, Melbourne, FL 32919 Telephone: 321-727-9100 Fax: 321-724-3973	Web Site: www.harris.com Officers: Howard L. Lance - Chmn., Pres., C.E.O. Bryan R. Roub - Sr. V.P., C.F.O.	Auditors: Ernst & Young LLP Transfer Agents: Mellon Investor Services LLC, Ridgefield Park, NJ

HARSCO CORP.

Exchange	Symbol	Price	52Wk Range	Yield	P/E	Div Achiever
NYS	HSC	$55.38 (3/31/2008)	65.75-44.72	1.41	15.69	13 Years

*7 Year Price Score 151.82 *NYSE Composite Index=100 *12 Month Price Score 109.31

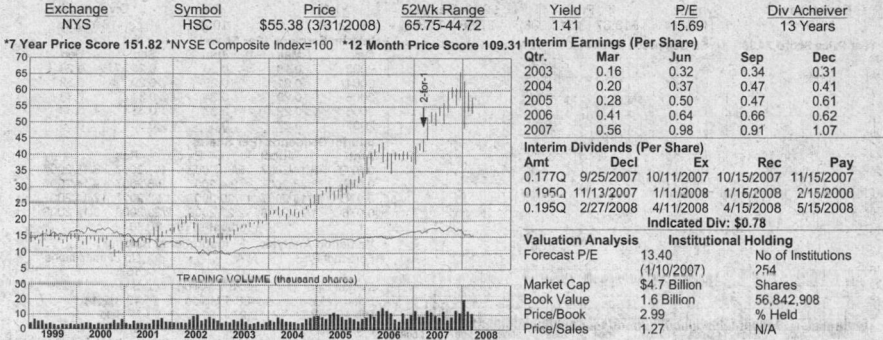

Interim Earnings (Per Share)

Qtr.	Mar	Jun	Sep	Dec
2003	0.16	0.32	0.34	0.31
2004	0.20	0.37	0.47	0.41
2005	0.28	0.50	0.47	0.61
2006	0.41	0.64	0.66	0.62
2007	0.56	0.98	0.91	1.07

Interim Dividends (Per Share)

Amt	Decl	Ex	Rec	Pay
0.177Q	9/25/2007	10/11/2007	10/15/2007	11/15/2007
0.195Q	11/13/2007	1/11/2008	1/16/2008	2/15/2000
0.195Q	2/27/2008	4/11/2008	4/15/2008	5/15/2008

Indicated Div: $0.78

Valuation Analysis   Institutional Holding

Forecast P/E	13.40	No of Institutions
	(1/10/2007)	254
Market Cap	$4.7 Billion	Shares
Book Value	1.6 Billion	56,842,908
Price/Book	2.99	% Held
Price/Sales	1.27	N/A

Business Summary: Metal Products (MIC: 11.4 SIC: 3441 NAIC: 332312)

Harsco is a provider of industrial services and engineered products. As of Dec 31 2007, Co.'s operations were divided into two reportable segments: Access Services and Mill Services, plus an all other category labeled Minerals & Rail Services and Products. The Access Services segment provides rental scaffolding, shoring, forming and other access applications to the global construction services industry. The Mill Services segment is a global provider of on-site, outsourced mill services to the global steel and metals industries. The All Other Category includes the Excell Minerals, Reed Minerals, Harsco Track Technologies, IKG Industries, Patterson-Kelley and Air-X-Changers Divisions.

Recent Developments: For the year ended Dec 31 2007, income from continuing operations increased 36.9% to US$255.1 million from US$186.4 million a year earlier. Net income increased 52.5% to US$299.5 million from US$196.4 million in the prior year. Revenues were US$3.69 billion, up 21.9% from US$3.03 billion the year before. Operating income was US$457.8 million versus US$344.3 million in the prior year, an increase of 33.0%. Direct operating expenses rose 21.9% to US$2.69 billion from US$2.20 billion in the comparable period the year before. Indirect operating expenses increased 14.0% to US$544.9 million from US$478.1 million in the equivalent prior-year period.

Prospects: For the full year of 2008, Co. now anticipates earnings from continuing operations to be in the range of $3.40 to $3.50 per share, reflecting an increase from its previous earnings guidance of $3.35 to $3.45 per share, as well as an improvement of approximately 15.0% over its 2007 earnings from continuing operations of $3.01 per diluted share, based on the mid-point of the new range. In addition, Co. anticipates strong end-market demand in its Access Services business to continue in most of the major geographic regions that it currently serves. Further, Co. believes that its recent restructuring and optimization efforts in its Mill Services business will result in margin improvements.

Financial Data

(US$ in Thousands)	12/31/2007	12/31/2006	12/31/2005	12/31/2004	12/31/2003	12/31/2002	12/31/2001	12/31/2000
Earnings Per Share	3.53	2.33	1.86	1.46	1.13	1.11	0.90	1.21
Cash Flow Per Share	5.60	4.88	3.79	3.28	3.23	3.14	3.02	3.24
Tang Book Value Per Share	7.78	5.30	4.25	5.81	4.52	3.30	4.16	3.83
Dividends Per Share	0.710	0.650	0.600	0.550	0.525	0.500	0.480	0.470
Dividend Payout %	20.11	27.96	32.26	37.80	46.67	45.25	53.63	38.84
Income Statement								
Total Revenue	3,688,160	3,423,293	2,766,210	2,502,059	2,118,516	1,976,732	2,108,474	2,004,741
EBITDA	765,267	611,643	467,087	394,348	343,148	331,995	338,294	351,807
Income Before Taxes	382,439	301,892	230,269	171,239	135,902	136,699	113,795	148,591
Income Taxes	117,745	97,523	64,771	49,034	41,708	42,740	36,982	46,805
Net Income	299,492	196,398	156,657	121,211	92,217	90,106	71,725	96,803
Average Shares	84,724	84,430	84,160	83,196	81,946	81,360	80,132	80,044
Balance Sheet								
Current Assets	1,345,337	1,231,622	1,101,023	924,924	764,351	702,402	716,067	726,415
Total Assets	3,905,430	3,326,423	2,975,804	2,389,756	2,138,035	1,999,297	2,090,766	2,180,948
Current Liabilities	873,970	910,775	748,403	578,397	495,075	473,850	474,674	536,179
Long-Term Obligations	1,012,087	864,817	905,859	594,747	584,425	605,613	720,197	774,450
Total Liabilities	2,339,311	2,180,059	1,981,910	1,475,566	1,361,047	1,354,757	1,404,593	1,506,769
Stockholders' Equity	1,566,119	1,146,364	993,894	914,190	776,988	644,540	686,173	674,179
Shares Outstanding	84,459	84,037	83,566	82,862	81,732	81,078	79,969	79,610
Statistical Record								
Return on Assets %	8.28	6.23	5.84	5.34	4.46	4.41	3.36	5.03
Return on Equity %	22.08	18.35	16.42	14.30	12.97	13.54	10.55	14.58
EBITDA Margin %	20.75	17.87	16.89	15.76	16.20	16.80	16.04	17.55
Net Margin %	8.12	5.74	5.66	4.84	4.35	4.56	3.40	4.83
Asset Turnover	1.02	1.09	1.03	1.10	1.02	0.97	0.99	1.04
Current Ratio	1.54	1.35	1.47	1.60	1.54	1.48	1.51	1.35
Debt to Equity	0.65	0.75	0.91	0.65	0.75	0.94	1.05	1.15
Price Range	65.75-37.21	44.01-34.28	34.70-24.97	28.00-20.18	22.14-13.87	22.00-12.43	17.95-11.91	15.88-8.84
P/E Ratio	18.63-10.54	18.89-14.71	18.66-13.42	19.18-13.83	19.59-12.27	19.82-11.20	19.95-13.23	13.12-7.31
Average Yield %	1.37	1.65	2.02	2.38	2.96	2.98	3.29	3.61

Address: 350 Poplar Church Road, Camp Hill, PA 17011 Telephone: 717-763-7064 Fax: 717-763-6424	Web Site: www.harsco.com Officers: Derek C. Hathaway - Chmn., Pres., C.E.O. D. H. Butler - Sr. V.P.	Auditors: PricewaterhouseCoopers LLP Investor Contact: 717-975-5677 Transfer Agents: Mellon Investor Services

HARTE-HANKS, INC.

Exchange	Symbol	Price	52Wk Range	Yield	P/E	Div Acheiver
NYS	HHS	$13.67 (3/31/2008)	27.56-13.38	2.19	10.85	12 Years

*7 Year Price Score 74.38   *NYSE Composite Index=100   *12 Month Price Score 82.47

Interim Earnings (Per Share)

Qtr.	Mar	Jun	Sep	Dec
2003	0.18	0.26	0.26	0.28
2004	0.21	0.29	0.29	0.32
2005	0.29	0.34	0.34	0.38
2006	0.29	0.37	0.35	0.39
2007	0.27	0.31	0.30	0.39

Interim Dividends (Per Share)

Amt	Decl	Ex	Rec	Pay
0.07Q	5/14/2007	5/30/2007	6/1/2007	6/15/2007
0.07Q	8/28/2007	9/4/2007	9/6/2007	9/14/2007
0.07Q	11/15/2007	11/29/2007	12/3/2007	12/14/2007
0.075Q	1/29/2008	2/27/2008	2/29/2008	3/14/2008

Indicated Div: $0.30

Valuation Analysis

Forecast P/E N/A

Institutional Holding

Market Cap	$928.7 Million
Book Value	408.5 Million
Price/Book	2.27
Price/Sales	0.80

No of Institutions 167
Shares 43,319,116
% Held 57.80

Business Summary: Advertising, Marketing & PR (MIC: 12.4 SIC: 7331 NAIC: 541860)

Harte-Hanks is a direct and targeted marketing company that provides direct marketing services and shopper advertising to local, regional, national and international consumer and business-to-business marketers. Co.'s direct marketing services are targeted to specific industries or markets with services and software products tailored to each industry or market. Co.'s Shoppers unit owns, operates and distributes shopper publications, which are weekly advertising publications delivered free to households and businesses in a particular geographic area. As of Dec 31 2007, Co. published 1,077 individual shopper editions each week distributed to zones with circulation of about 12,000 each.

Recent Developments: For the year ended Dec 31 2007, net income decreased 17.1% to US$92.6 million from US$111.8 million in the prior year. Revenues were US$1.16 billion, down 1.8% from US$1.18 billion the year before. Operating income was US$164.9 million versus US$186.1 million in the prior year, a decrease of 11.4%. Direct operating expenses declined 7.1% to US$402.8 million from US$433.6 million in the comparable period the year before. Indirect operating expenses increased 5.3% to US$595.2 million from US$565.0 million in the equivalent prior-year period.

Prospects: Looking ahead, Co. believes that in the long term it will continue to benefit from marketing and advertising expenditures being moved from other advertising media to the targeted media space, the results of which can be more effectively tracked, enabling measurement of the return on marketing investment. Nonetheless, Co. is not expecting improvement in revenue from its Shoppers segment in year 2008 given the existing difficult economic environments of the real estate and associated financing markets in California and Florida. Separately, on Jan 28 2008, Co. announced its acquisition of Mason Zimbler Limited, a digital marketing agency based in the U.K., servicing the technology sector.

Financial Data

(US$ in Thousands)	12/31/2007	12/31/2006	12/31/2005	12/31/2004	12/31/2003	12/31/2002	12/31/2001	12/31/2000
Earnings Per Share	1.26	1.39	1.34	1.11	0.97	0.96	0.82	0.79
Cash Flow Per Share	1.97	1.85	1.74	1.77	1.40	1.53	1.61	1.09
Tang Book Value Per Share	N.M.	N.M.	0.51	1.31	1.32	1.03	1.22	1.15
Dividends Per Share	0.280	0.240	0.200	0.160	0.120	0.098	0.080	0.067
Dividend Payout %	22.22	17.27	14.93	14.41	12.37	10.24	9.76	8.47
Income Statement								
Total Revenue	1,162,886	1,184,688	1,134,993	1,030,461	944,576	908,777	917,928	960,773
EBITDA	200,294	219,382	219,584	192,416	174,625	181,012	183,936	180,195
Income Before Taxes	151,137	179,248	186,479	162,968	143,905	147,350	132,438	136,859
Income Taxes	58,497	67,456	72,021	65,400	56,543	56,605	52,754	54,973
Net Income	92,640	111,792	114,458	97,568	87,362	90,745	79,684	81,886
Average Shares	73,703	80,646	85,406	87,806	89,982	94,872	97,174	104,479
Balance Sheet								
Current Assets	265,680	279,975	253,704	250,497	217,297	198,612	202,807	235,873
Total Assets	951,926	969,285	889,663	828,353	759,130	736,732	771,049	807,105
Current Liabilities	180,108	171,236	175,347	182,192	134,072	121,761	121,774	149,964
Long-Term Obligations	259,125	205,000	62,000	...	5,000	16,300	48,312	65,370
Total Liabilities	543,414	475,809	328,317	256,554	203,532	204,199	218,683	256,102
Stockholders' Equity	408,512	493,476	561,346	571,799	555,598	532,533	552,366	551,003
Shares Outstanding	67,936	75,214	81,488	84,981	87,492	90,204	93,212	97,028
Statistical Record								
Return on Assets %	9.64	12.03	13.32	12.26	11.68	12.04	10.10	10.36
Return on Equity %	20.54	21.20	20.20	17.26	16.06	16.73	14.44	14.47
EBITDA Margin %	17.22	18.52	19.35	18.67	18.49	19.92	20.04	18.76
Net Margin %	7.97	9.44	10.08	9.47	9.25	9.99	8.68	8.52
Asset Turnover	1.21	1.27	1.32	1.29	1.26	1.21	1.16	1.22
Current Ratio	1.48	1.64	1.45	1.37	1.62	1.63	1.67	1.57
Debt to Equity	0.63	0.42	0.11	...	0.01	0.03	0.09	0.12
Price Range	28.65-15.65	30.00-23.00	30.98-25.24	26.87-21.50	22.13-17.33	22.30-16.18	18.78-13.73	18.75-13.29
P/E Ratio	22.74-12.42	21.58-16.55	23.12-18.84	24.21-19.37	22.81-17.87	23.23-16.85	22.90-16.74	23.73-16.82
Average Yield %	1.18	0.90	0.73	0.67	0.63	0.50	0.51	0.42

Address: 200 Concord Plaza Drive, San Antonio, TX 78216	**Web Site:** www.harte-hanks.com	**Auditors:** KPMG LLP
Telephone: 210-829-9000	**Officers:** Larry D. Franklin - Chmn. Houston H. Harte - Vice-Chmn.	**Investor Contact:** 210-829-9140
Fax: 210-829-9403		**Transfer Agents:** Computershare Trust Company, N.A.

HARTFORD FINANCIAL SERVICES GROUP INC.

Exchange	Symbol	Price	52Wk Range	Yield	P/E	Div Acheiver
NYS	HIG	$75.77 (3/31/2008)	106.02-66.05	2.80	8.20	11 Years

*7 Year Price Score 103.54 *NYSE Composite Index=100 *12 Month Price Score 87.30

Interim Earnings (Per Share)

Qtr.	Mar	Jun	Sep	Dec
2003	(5.46)	1.88	1.20	1.70
2004	1.93	1.46	1.66	2.08
2005	2.21	1.98	1.76	1.50
2006	2.34	1.52	2.39	2.44
2007	2.71	1.96	2.68	1.89

Interim Dividends (Per Share)

Amt	Decl	Ex	Rec	Pay
0.50Q	5/17/2007	5/30/2007	6/1/2007	7/2/2007
0.50Q	7/19/2007	8/30/2007	9/4/2007	10/1/2007
0.53Q	10/18/2007	11/29/2007	12/3/2007	1/2/2008
0.53Q	2/21/2008	2/28/2008	3/3/2008	4/1/2008

Indicated Div: $2.12

Valuation Analysis   **Institutional Holding**

Forecast P/E	8.99	No of Institutions	
	(1/10/2007)	824	
Market Cap	$23.8 Billion	Shares	
Book Value	19.2 Billion	283,512,128	
Price/Book	1.24	% Held	
Price/Sales	0.92	88.54	

Business Summary: Insurance (MIC: 8.2 SIC: 6411 NAIC: 524210)

Hartford Financial Services is an insurance and financial services company. Co. has two major operations. Through its Life operations, Co. provides retail and institutional investment products, life insurance for wealth protection, accumulation and transfer needs, group benefits products, as well as fixed and variable annuity products. Through its Property & Casualty operations, Co. provides workers' compensation, property, automobile, liability, umbrella, specialty casualty, marine, livestock and fidelity and surety coverage, professional liability coverage, homeowners and home-based business coverage, and insurance-related services. At Dec 31 2007, Co. had total assets of $360.36 billion.

Recent Developments: For the year ended Dec 31 2007, net income increased 7.4% to US$2.95 billion from US$2.75 billion in the prior year. Revenues were US$25.92 billion, down 2.2% from US$26.50 billion the year before. Net premiums earned were US$15.62 billion versus US$15.02 billion in the prior year, an increase of 4.0%. Net investment income fell 17.7% to US$5.36 billion from US$6.52 billion a year ago.

Prospects: For 2008, Co. expects its core earnings estimate of $9.80 to $10.20 per diluted share, which is based on several assumptions, including the expectation that the U.S. equity markets will produce an annualized return of 9.0%, and an anticipated pre-tax underwriting loss of $160.0 million from other operations in property and casualty. Meanwhile, Co. believes the market for retirement products continues to expand as individuals increasingly save and plan for retirement. Thus, in Dec 2007, Co. announced three Retirement Plans acquisitions, which should increase its Retirement Plans segment's scale and grow its offering to serve additional markets, customers and retirement plans' types.

Financial Data

(US$ in Thousands)	12/31/2007	12/31/2006	12/31/2005	12/31/2004	12/31/2003	12/31/2002	12/31/2001	12/31/2000
Earnings Per Share	9.24	8.69	7.44	7.12	(0.33)	3.97	2.10	4.34
Cash Flow Per Share	18.94	18.26	12.52	8.99	14.30	10.62	9.69	10.62
Tang Book Value Per Share	55.69	33.07	45.03	42.55	35.00	35.31	29.81	32.98
Dividends Per Share	2.030	1.700	1.170	1.130	1.090	1.050	1.010	0.970
Dividend Payout %	21.97	19.56	15.73	15.87	...	26.45	48.10	22.35
Income Statement								
Premium Income	15,619,000	15,023,000	14,359,000	13,566,000	11,891,000	10,301,000	9,409,000	8,941,000
Total Revenue	25,916,000	26,500,000	27,083,000	22,693,000	18,733,000	15,907,000	15,147,000	14,703,000
Income Before Taxes	4,005,000	3,602,000	2,985,000	2,523,000	(550,000)	1,068,000	354,000	...
Income Taxes	1,056,000	857,000	711,000	385,000	(459,000)	68,000	(195,000)	390,000
Net Income	2,949,000	2,745,000	2,274,000	2,115,000	(91,000)	1,000,000	507,000	974,000
Average Shares	319,100	315,900	305,600	297,000	272,400	251,800	241,400	224,400
Balance Sheet								
Total Assets	360,361,000	326,710,000	285,557,000	259,735,000	225,853,000	182,043,000	181,238,000	171,532,000
Total Liabilities	341,157,000	307,834,000	270,232,000	245,497,000	214,214,000	171,309,000	172,225,000	164,068,000
Stockholders' Equity	19,204,000	18,876,000	15,325,000	14,238,000	11,639,000	10,734,000	9,013,000	7,464,000
Shares Outstanding	313,842	323,315	302,152	294,208	283,379	255,240	245,536	226,290
Statistical Record								
Return on Assets %	0.86	0.90	0.83	0.87	N.M.	0.55	0.29	0.57
Return on Equity %	15.49	16.05	15.38	16.30	N.M.	10.13	6.15	15.02
Net Margin %	11.38	10.36	8.40	9.32	(0.49)	6.29	3.35	6.62
Price Range	106.02-85.44	93.61-79.24	89.00-65.51	69.31-53.29	59.03-32.30	69.97-37.38	70.46-50.10	79.31-29.38
P/E Ratio	11.47-9.25	10.77-9.12	11.96-8.81	9.73-7.48	...	17.62-9.42	33.55-23.86	18.27-6.77
Average Yield %	2.13	1.99	1.55	1.77	2.26	1.87	1.57	1.70

Address: Hartford Plaza, Hartford, CT 06115-1900 **Telephone:** 860-547-5000 **Fax:** 860-720-6097	**Web Site:** www.thehartford.com **Officers:** Ramani Ayer - Chmn., Pres., C.E.O. David M. Johnson - Exec. V.P., C.F.O.	**Auditors:** Deloitte & Touche LLP **Transfer Agents:** The Bank of New York, New York

HASBRO, INC.

Exchange	Symbol	Price	52Wk Range	Yield	P/E
NYS	HAS	$27.90 (3/31/2008)	33.02-21.73	2.87	14.16

*7 Year Price Score 114.63 *NYSE Composite Index=100 *12 Month Price Score 101.23

Interim Earnings (Per Share)

Qtr.	Mar	Jun	Sep	Dec
2003	0.01	0.06	0.38	0.43
2004	0.03	0.06	0.45	0.42
2005	(0.02)	0.13	0.47	0.48
2006	(0.03)	0.07	0.58	0.61
2007	0.19	0.03	0.95	0.81

Interim Dividends (Per Share)

Amt	Decl	Ex	Rec	Pay
0.16Q	5/24/2007	7/30/2007	8/1/2007	8/15/2007
0.16Q	10/4/2007	10/30/2007	11/1/2007	11/15/2007
0.16Q	12/6/2007	1/30/2008	2/1/2008	2/15/2008
0.20Q	2/7/2008	4/29/2008	5/1/2008	5/15/2008

Indicated Div: $0.80

Valuation Analysis

		Institutional Holding	
Forecast P/E	18.09	No of Institutions	
	(1/10/2007)	273	
Market Cap	$4.1 Billion	Shares	
Book Value	1.4 Billion	138,202,528	
Price/Book	2.92	% Held	
Price/Sales	1.06	85.92	

TRADING VOLUME (thousand shares)

Business Summary: Consumer Accessories (MIC: 4.6 SIC: 3944 NAIC: 339932)

Hasbro provides children's and family leisure time and entertainment products and services. Co.'s brands include PLAYSKOOL, TRANSFORMERS, MY LITTLE PONY, SUPER SOAKER, MILTON BRADLEY, PARKER BROTHERS, and WIZARDS OF THE COAST. Co.'s offerings encompass a variety of games, including traditional board, card, hand-held electronic, trading card, roleplaying, plug and play and DVD games, as well as electronic learning aids and puzzles. Toy offerings include boys' action figures, vehicles and playsets, girls' toys, electronic toys, plush products, preschool toys and infant products, children's consumer electronics, electronic interactive products, creative play and toy related specialty products.

Recent Developments: For the year ended Dec 30 2007, net income increased 44.7% to US$333.0 million from US$230.1 million in the prior year. Revenues were US$3.84 billion, up 21.8% from US$3.15 billion the year before. Operating income was US$519.4 million versus US$376.4 million in the prior year, an increase of 38.0%. Direct operating expenses rose 20.9% to US$1.58 billion from US$1.30 billion in the comparable period the year before. Indirect operating expenses increased 18.4% to US$1.74 billion from US$1.47 billion in the equivalent prior-year period.

Prospects: Co.'s outlook appears to be promising. For instance, Co.'s STAR WARS product sales are expected to be supported by the release of animated television programming and animated motion picture in 2008. Moreover, Co. will expand its brand portfolio in 2008 by launching new products, such as its customizable version of TRIVIAL PURSUIT, and its VIRTUAL INTERACTIVE PET segment, which includes a doll that will allow the consumer access to a website to customize their pets as well as access to games and other features. Meanwhile, on Jan 25 2008, Co. announced that it has acquired privately-held Cranium, Inc., which develops and markets CRANIUM branded games and related products, for $77.5 million.

Financial Data

(US$ in Thousands)	12/30/2007	12/31/2006	12/25/2005	12/26/2004	12/28/2003	12/29/2002	12/30/2001	12/31/2000
Earnings Per Share	1.97	1.29	1.09	0.96	0.88	(0.98)	0.35	(0.82)
Cash Flow Per Share	3.87	1.89	2.79	2.04	2.62	2.75	2.17	0.91
Tang Book Value Per Share	2.95	3.34	3.61	3.00	1.32	0.08	N.M.	N.M.
Dividends Per Share	0.600	0.450	0.330	0.210	0.120	0.120	0.120	0.240
Dividend Payout %	30.46	34.88	30.28	21.88	13.64	...	34.29	...
Income Statement								
Total Revenue	3,837,557	3,151,481	3,087,627	2,997,510	3,138,657	2,816,230	2,856,339	3,787,215
EBITDA	623,547	488,093	521,582	437,966	460,649	365,425	425,786	152,656
Income Before Taxes	462,382	341,474	310,913	260,088	244,064	104,088	96,199	(225,986)
Income Taxes	129,379	111,419	98,838	64,111	69,049	29,030	35,401	(81,355)
Net Income	333,003	230,055	212,075	195,977	157,664	(170,674)	59,732	(144,631)
Average Shares	171,205	181,043	197,436	196,048	178,484	185,063	173,018	176,437
Balance Sheet								
Current Assets	1,888,240	1,718,315	1,830,195	1,718,222	1,509,263	1,431,624	1,368,618	1,580,213
Total Assets	3,237,063	3,096,905	3,301,143	3,240,660	3,163,376	3,142,881	3,368,979	3,828,459
Current Liabilities	887,671	905,893	910,726	1,148,611	930,055	966,850	758,591	1,239,812
Long-Term Obligations	709,723	494,917	495,619	302,698	686,871	857,274	1,165,649	1,167,838
Total Liabilities	1,851,971	1,559,015	1,577,667	1,600,936	1,758,136	1,951,515	2,016,115	2,501,053
Stockholders' Equity	1,385,092	1,537,890	1,723,476	1,639,724	1,405,240	1,191,366	1,352,864	1,327,406
Shares Outstanding	145,207	160,620	177,949	177,315	175,499	173,169	172,958	172,441
Statistical Record								
Return on Assets %	10.54	7.08	6.50	6.14	5.01	N.M.	1.66	N.M.
Return on Equity %	22.85	13.88	12.65	12.91	12.18	N.M.	4.47	N.M.
EBITDA Margin %	16.25	15.49	16.89	14.61	14.68	12.98	14.91	4.03
Net Margin %	8.68	7.30	6.87	6.54	5.02	N.M.	2.09	N.M.
Asset Turnover	1.22	0.97	0.95	0.94	1.00	0.87	0.80	0.90
Current Ratio	2.13	1.90	2.01	1.50	1.62	1.48	1.80	1.27
Debt to Equity	0.51	0.32	0.29	0.18	0.49	0.72	0.86	0.88
Price Range	33.02-25.71	27.43-17.49	22.11-18.56	23.33-17.00	22.48-11.21	16.97-10.06	18.22-10.31	18.94-9.13
P/E Ratio	16.76-13.05	21.26-13.56	20.28-17.03	24.30-17.71	25.55-12.74	...	52.06-29.46	...
Average Yield %	2.05	2.11	1.63	1.08	0.70	0.84	0.82	1.73

Address: 1027 Newport Avenue, P.O. Box 1059, Pawtucket, RI 02862-1059
Telephone: 401-431-8697
Fax: 401-727-5544

Web Site: www.hasbro.com
Officers: Alan G. Hassenfeld - Chmn. Alfred J. Verrecchia - Pres., C.E.O.

Auditors: KPMG LLP
Transfer Agents: Computershare Trust Company, N.A., Providence, RI

HAWAIIAN ELECTRIC INDUSTRIES, INC.

Exchange	Symbol	Price	52Wk Range	Yield	P/E
NYS	HE	$23.87 (3/31/2008)	26.65-20.51	5.19	23.17

*7 Year Price Score 77.46   *NYSE Composite Index=100   ***12 Month Price Score 106.92**

Interim Earnings (Per Share)

Qtr.	Mar	Jun	Sep	Dec
2003	0.33	0.29	0.41	0.50
2004	0.40	0.14	0.53	0.31
2005	0.30	0.34	0.46	0.46
2006	0.40	0.33	0.40	0.20
2007	0.08	0.21	0.24	0.49

Interim Dividends (Per Share)

Amt	Decl	Ex	Rec	Pay
0.31Q	5/4/2007	5/11/2007	5/15/2007	6/13/2007
0.31Q	8/7/2007	8/16/2007	8/20/2007	9/11/2007
0.31Q	11/2/2007	11/13/2007	11/15/2007	12/11/2007
0.31Q	2/21/2008	2/28/2008	3/3/2008	3/11/2008

Indicated Div: $1.24

Valuation Analysis

		Institutional Holding	
Forecast P/E	14.91	No of Institutions	185
	(1/10/2007)		
Market Cap	$2.0 Billion	Shares	27,300,668
Book Value	1.3 Billion	% Held	33.51
Price/Book	1.56		
Price/Sales	0.79		

Business Summary: Electricity (MIC: 7.1 SIC: 4911 NAIC: 221122)

Hawaiian Electric Industries is a holding company engaged in the electric utility, banking and other businesses operating primarily in the State of Hawaii. Co.'s subsidiary, Hawaiian Electric Company, Inc. and its operating subsidiaries, Maui Electric Company, Limited and Hawaii Electric Light Company, Inc., are regulated electric public utilities providing electric public utility service on the islands of Oahu, Maui, Lanai, Molokai and Hawaii, which islands collectively include approximately 95.0% of Hawaii's population. Co. also provides a range of banking and other financial services to consumers and businesses through its bank subsidiary, American Savings Bank, F.S.B.

Recent Developments: For the year ended Dec 31 2007, income from continuing operations decreased 21.5% to US$84.8 million from US$108.0 million a year earlier. Net income decreased 21.5% to US$84.8 million from US$108.0 million in the prior year. Revenues were US$2.54 billion, up 3.1% from US$2.46 billion the year before. Operating income was US$203.7 million versus US$239.4 million in the prior year, a decrease of 14.9%. Direct operating expenses rose 4.9% to US$2.32 billion from US$2.21 billion in the comparable period the year before. Indirect operating expenses increased 14.4% to US$15.5 million from US$13.5 million in the equivalent prior-year period.

Prospects: Co.'s bottom-line results are benefiting from higher net income in its electric utility operations, partly due to the favorable effect of interim rate relief for all its three utilities. However, Co. is seeing lower kilowatthour sales due in part to lower consumption by commercial customers. Meanwhile, in its banking operation, Co. is experiencing higher net interest income driven by higher balances on loans. In addition, Co.'s net interest margin is increasing as the yields on earning assets increased more than the overall cost of its liabilities. Going forward, Co. expects to see an increase in loan loss provisions, particularly as the economy begins to slow.

Financial Data

(US$ in Thousands)	12/31/2007	12/31/2006	12/31/2005	12/31/2004	12/31/2003	12/31/2002	12/31/2001	12/31/2000
Earnings Per Share	1.03	1.33	1.56	1.38	1.52	1.62	1.24	0.70
Cash Flow Per Share	2.64	3.53	2.70	3.06	3.19	3.37	3.84	4.01
Tang Book Value Per Share	14.29	13.38	13.92	13.88	13.12	12.89	11.63	11.21
Dividends Per Share	1.240	1.240	1.240	1.240	1.240	1.240	1.240	1.240
Dividend Payout %	120.39	93.23	79.49	89.86	81.31	76.54	100.40	177.14
Income Statement								
Total Revenue	2,536,418	2,460,904	2,215,564	1,924,057	1,781,316	1,653,701	1,727,277	1,719,024
EBITDA	366,820	395,816	416,794	416,378	400,192	393,339	371,915	263,624
Income Before Taxes	131,057	171,055	201,344	200,219	182,415	181,909	165,903	66,986
Income Taxes	46,278	63,054	73,900	92,480	64,367	63,692	58,157	21,242
Net Income	84,779	108,001	126,689	109,652	114,178	118,217	93,705	15,744
Average Shares	82,419	81,373	81,200	79,719	74,974	72,954	67,884	65,374
Balance Sheet								
Net PPE	2,743,410	2,647,490	2,542,776	2,422,303	2,311,888	2,079,325	2,067,503	2,091,345
Total Assets	10,293,916	9,891,209	9,951,577	9,610,627	9,201,158	8,876,503	8,517,943	8,469,322
Long-Term Obligations	3,052,768	2,701,770	2,078,493	2,154,966	2,081,473	2,282,522	2,178,521	2,337,983
Total Liabilities	8,984,196	8,761,676	8,700,654	8,365,277	7,877,721	7,595,797	7,353,872	7,395,018
Stockholders' Equity	1,275,427	1,095,240	1,216,630	1,210,945	1,089,031	1,046,300	929,665	839,059
Shares Outstanding	83,431	81,461	80,983	80,687	75,837	73,618	71,200	65,982
Statistical Record								
Return on Assets %	0.84	1.09	1.30	1.16	1.26	1.36	0.99	0.54
Return on Equity %	7.15	9.34	10.44	9.51	10.69	11.97	9.47	5.41
EBITDA Margin %	14.46	16.08	18.81	21.64	22.47	23.79	21.53	15.34
Net Margin %	3.34	4.39	5.72	5.70	6.41	7.15	4.85	2.66
PPE Turnover	0.94	0.95	0.89	0.81	0.81	0.80	0.83	0.82
Asset Turnover	0.25	0.25	0.23	0.20	0.20	0.19	0.20	0.20
Debt to Equity	2.39	2.47	1.71	1.78	1.91	2.18	2.34	2.79
Price Range	27.43-20.51	28.93-25.78	29.76-24.71	29.54-23.07	23.91-19.45	24.33-17.73	20.54-16.84	18.75-13.91
P/E Ratio	26.63-19.91	21.75-19.38	19.08-15.84	21.41-16.72	15.73-12.80	15.02-10.94	16.56-13.58	26.79-19.87
Average Yield %	5.16	4.58	4.64	4.76	5.72	5.69	6.58	7.54

Address: 900 Richards Street, Honolulu, HI 96813 Telephone: 808-543-5662 Fax: 808-543-7966	Web Site: www.hei.com Officers: Robert F. Clarke - Chmn., Pres., C.E.O. Eric K. Yeaman - V.P., C.F.O., Treas.	Auditors: KPMG LLP Transfer Agents: Continental Stock Transfer & Trust Company, New York, NY

HCC INSURANCE HOLDINGS, INC.

Exchange	Symbol	Price	52Wk Range	Yield	P/E	Div Acheiver
NYS	HCC	$22.69 (3/31/2008)	34.24-21.77	1.94	6.71	11 Years

*7 Year Price Score 99.32   *NYSE Composite Index=100   *12 Month Price Score 89.93

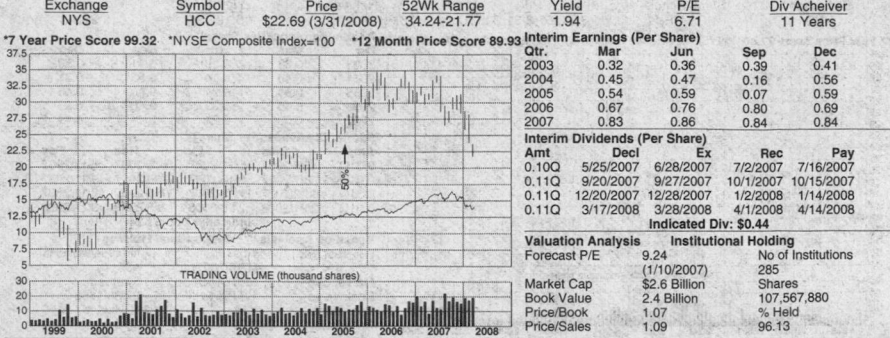

Interim Earnings (Per Share)

Qtr.	Mar	Jun	Sep	Dec
2003	0.32	0.36	0.39	0.41
2004	0.45	0.47	0.16	0.56
2005	0.54	0.59	0.07	0.59
2006	0.67	0.76	0.80	0.69
2007	0.83	0.86	0.84	0.84

Interim Dividends (Per Share)

Amt	Decl	Ex	Rec	Pay
0.10Q	5/25/2007	6/28/2007	7/2/2007	7/16/2007
0.11Q	9/20/2007	9/27/2007	10/1/2007	10/15/2007
0.11Q	12/20/2007	12/28/2007	1/2/2008	1/14/2008
0.11Q	3/17/2008	3/28/2008	4/1/2008	4/14/2008

Indicated Div: $0.44

Valuation Analysis

		Institutional Holding	
Forecast P/E	9.24	No of Institutions	
	(1/10/2007)	285	
Market Cap	$2.6 Billion	Shares	
Book Value	2.4 Billion	107,567,880	
Price/Book	1.07	% Held	
Price/Sales	1.09	96.13	

Business Summary: Insurance (MIC: 8.2 SIC: 6331 NAIC: 524126)

HCC Insurance Holdings provides property and casualty, surety, and group life, accident and health insurance coverages and related agency and reinsurance brokerage services to commercial customers and individuals. Co. operates primarily in the U.S., the U.K., Spain, Bermuda, Belgium and Ireland. Co. underwrites both on a primary basis, where it insures a risk in exchange for a premium, and on a reinsurance basis, where it insures all or a portion of another insurance company's risk in exchange for all or a portion of the premium. Co. markets its products both directly to customers and through a network of independent and affiliated brokers, producers, agents and third party administrators.

Recent Developments: For the year ended Dec 31 2007, income from continuing operations increased 15.5% to US$395.4 million from US$342.3 million a year earlier. Net income increased 15.5% to US$395.4 million from US$342.3 million in the prior year. Revenues were US$2.39 billion, up 15.1% from US$2.08 billion the year before. Net premiums earned were US$1.99 billion versus US$1.71 billion in the prior year, an increase of 16.1%. Net investment income rose 35.1% to US$206.5 million from US$152.8 million a year ago.

Prospects: For the full year 2008, Co. is projecting net earnings to be in the range of $2.90 to $3.20 per share, versus its 2007 earnings guidance of $3.10 to $3.25 per share, assuming net written premium of $2.00 billion, total revenue of $2.30 billion, a combined ratio of 85.0%, and average fully diluted shares outstanding of 118.5 million. Going forward, Co. will continue to explore potential acquisition opportunities to expand and strengthen its existing lines of business. For instance, on Jan 3 2008, Co. announced the acquisition of MultiNational Underwriters, LLC (MNU) for a total transaction value of about $42.0 million. Co. expects MNU to write more than $40.0 million in premium in 2008.

Financial Data
(US$ in Thousands)

	12/31/2007	12/31/2006	12/31/2005	12/31/2004	12/31/2003	12/31/2002	12/31/2001	12/31/2000
Earnings Per Share	3.38	2.93	1.79	1.65	1.49	1.12	0.34	0.71
Cash Flow Per Share	6.44	5.87	5.92	6.86	5.56	1.88	1.21	1.76
Tang Book Value Per Share	14.46	11.64	10.48	8.62	6.88	5.85	4.72	3.49
Dividends Per Share	0.420	0.375	0.282	0.213	0.187	0.170	0.163	0.147
Dividend Payout %	12.43	12.80	15.74	12.96	12.56	15.18	48.04	20.75
Income Statement								
Premium Income	1,985,086	1,709,189	1,369,988	1,010,692	738,272	505,521	342,787	267,647
Total Revenue	2,388,373	2,075,295	1,644,342	1,283,154	941,964	669,382	505,461	466,167
Benefits & Claims	1,183,947	1,011,856	921,197	645,230	488,652	306,491	267,390	198,470
Income Before Taxes	585,870	509,834	278,747	240,753	166,734	163,179	60,383	92,646
Income Taxes	190,441	167,549	85,647	81,732	59,857	57,351	30,186	37,202
Net Income	395,429	342,285	195,860	163,025	143,561	105,828	30,197	53,431
Average Shares	116,997	116,736	109,437	98,826	96,574	94,404	89,428	75,933
Balance Sheet								
Total Assets	8,074,645	7,630,132	7,026,066	5,933,437	4,864,296	3,704,151	3,219,120	2,742,976
Total Liabilities	5,634,280	5,587,329	5,332,370	4,609,772	3,817,376	2,821,244	2,455,667	2,213,541
Stockholders' Equity	2,440,365	2,042,803	1,693,696	1,323,665	1,046,920	882,907	763,453	529,435
Shares Outstanding	115,069	111,731	110,803	102,057	95,946	93,537	92,157	75,517
Statistical Record								
Return on Assets %	5.04	4.67	3.02	3.01	3.35	3.06	1.01	1.98
Return on Equity %	17.64	18.32	12.98	13.72	14.88	12.86	4.67	10.80
Loss Ratio %	59.64	59.20	67.24	63.84	66.19	60.63	78.00	74.15
Net Margin %	16.56	16.49	11.91	12.71	15.24	15.81	5.97	11.46
Price Range	34.24-26.57	35.09-28.58	32.86-21.34	23.04-18.63	21.29-14.99	19.15-13.19	19.34-13.67	17.96-7.38
P/E Ratio	10.13-7.86	11.98-9.75	18.36-11.92	13.96-11.29	14.29-10.06	17.10-11.77	56.88-40.20	25.29-10.39
Average Yield %	1.37	1.18	1.07	1.01	0.99	1.01	0.96	1.24

Address: 13403 Northwest Freeway, Houston, TX 77040-6094 **Telephone:** 713-690-7300 **Fax:** 713-462-2401	**Web Site:** www.hcc.com **Officers:** Stephen L. Way - Chmn., Pres., C.E.O. Edward H. Ellis Jr. - Exec. V.P., C.F.O., Chief Acctg. Officer	**Auditors:** PricewaterhouseCoopers LLP **Transfer Agents:** Wachovia Bank N.A.

HCP, INC.

Exchange	Symbol	Price	52Wk Range	Yield	P/E	Div Acheiver
NYS	HCP	$33.81 (3/31/2008)	37.03-25.76	5.38	12.48	22 Years

*7 Year Price Score 99.87   *NYSE Composite Index=100   *12 Month Price Score 103.86

Interim Earnings (Per Share)

Qtr.	Mar	Jun	Sep	Dec
2003	0.18	0.17	0.30	0.32
2004	0.31	0.27	0.22	0.31
2005	0.28	0.28	0.29	0.26
2006	0.38	0.26	0.52	1.49
2007	0.68	0.32	1.53	0.18

Interim Dividends (Per Share)

Amt	Decl	Ex	Rec	Pay
0.445Q	4/25/2007	5/3/2007	5/7/2007	5/18/2007
0.445Q	7/26/2007	8/2/2007	8/6/2007	8/21/2007
0.445Q	10/25/2007	11/1/2007	11/5/2007	11/19/2007
0.455Q	1/28/2008	2/5/2008	2/7/2008	2/21/2008

Indicated Div: $1.82 (Div. Reinv. Plan)

Valuation Analysis

		Institutional Holding	
Forecast P/E	47.05 (1/10/2007)	No of Institutions	N/A
Market Cap	$7.3 Billion	Shares	
Book Value	4.1 Billion	N/A	
Price/Book	1.79	% Held	
Price/Sales	7.46	N/A	

Business Summary: Property, Real Estate & Development (MIC: 8.3 SIC: 6798 NAIC: 525930)

HCP is a self-administered real estate investment trust, which together with its consolidated subsidiaries, invests primarily in real estate serving the healthcare industry in the U.S. Co. acquires healthcare facilities and leases them to healthcare providers and provides mortgage financing secured by healthcare facilities. Co.'s portfolio includes investments in: senior housing that consists of independent living facilities, assisted living facilities and continuing care retirement communities; medical office buildings; hospitals; skilled nursing facilities; and other healthcare facilities, including laboratory and office buildings.

Recent Developments: For the year ended Dec 31 2007, income from continuing operations increased 103.1% to US$160.8 million from US$79.2 million a year earlier. Net income increased 41.1% to US$589.0 million from US$417.5 million in the prior year. Revenues were US$982.5 million, up 83.7% from US$534.9 million the year before. Revenues from property income rose 75.4% to US$905.1 million from US$516.0 million in the corresponding earlier year.

Prospects: Looking ahead, Co. expects that the healthcare industry will continue to face increased regulation and pressure in the areas of fraud, waste and abuse, cost control, healthcare management and provision of services, as well as continuing cost control initiatives and reform efforts generally. On the positive side, Co. believes that its 2007 mezzanine loan investment will make a greater contribution to its interest income during 2008. Meanwhile, for full-year 2008, Co. is projecting net income applicable to common shares in the range of $2.02 to $2.10 per diluted shares. Concurrently, Co. anticipates 2008 funds from operations to range between $2.26 and $2.34 per diluted common share.

Financial Data

(US$ in Thousands)	12/31/2007	12/31/2006	12/31/2005	12/31/2004	12/31/2003	12/31/2002	12/31/2001	12/31/2000
Earnings Per Share	2.71	2.66	1.12	1.11	0.97	0.96	0.89	1.06
Cash Flow Per Share	2.18	2.25	2.09	2.06	2.06	1.94	1.86	2.01
Tang Book Value Per Share	14.50	12.74	7.90	8.49	8.82	8.46	8.62	8.55
Dividends Per Share	1.780	1.700	1.680	1.670	1.660	1.630	1.550	1.470
Dividend Payout %	65.68	63.91	150.00	150.45	171.13	168.91	174.16	138.03
Income Statement								
Property Income	905,076	...	...	388,631	348,649	331,737	310,602	306,830
Non-Property Income	77,433	619,087	477,276	40,053	51,534	27,839	21,858	22,977
Total Revenue	982,509	619,087	477,276	428,684	400,183	359,576	332,460	329,807
Interest Expense	357,024	213,304	107,201	89,136	90,749	77,952	78,489	86,747
Net Income	589,015	417,547	173,057	160,040	160,605	137,900	121,100	133,700
Average Shares	209,254	149,226	135,560	133,362	126,130	116,294	107,950	102,200
Balance Sheet								
Total Assets	12,521,772	10,012,749	3,597,265	3,102,634	3,035,957	2,748,417	2,431,153	2,398,703
Long-Term Obligations	7,510,907	6,202,015	1,956,946	1,486,206	1,407,284	1,333,848	1,057,752	1,158,928
Total Liabilities	8,078,792	6,556,948	2,048,215	1,561,411	1,595,340	1,467,528	1,184,429	1,254,148
Stockholders' Equity	4,103,709	3,294,036	1,399,766	1,419,442	1,440,617	1,280,889	1,246,724	1,144,555
Shares Outstanding	216,818	198,599	136,193	133,658	131,039	118,939	112,773	101,747
Statistical Record								
Return on Assets %	5.23	6.14	5.17	5.49	5.48	5.30	5.02	5.48
Return on Equity %	15.92	17.79	12.28	11.79	11.65	10.87	10.13	11.38
Net Margin %	59.95	67.45	36.26	39.43	39.63	38.21	36.45	40.56
Price Range	41.88-25.76	36.88-25.37	28.68-23.45	29.09-21.68	25.63-16.68	22.43-18.11	19.51-14.78	15.25-11.84
P/E Ratio	15.45-9.51	13.86-9.54	25.61-20.94	26.21-19.53	26.42-17.19	23.36-18.86	21.92-16.61	14.39-11.17
Average Yield %	5.26	5.85	6.43	6.43	8.01	8.00	8.87	10.77

Address: 3760 Kilroy Airport Way, Suite 300, Long Beach, CA 90806 **Telephone:** 562-733-5100	**Web Site:** www.hcpi.com **Officers:** Kenneth B. Roath - Chmn. James F. Flaherty III - Pres., C.E.O.	**Auditors:** Ernst & Young LLP **Investor Contact:** 949-221-0600 **Transfer Agents:** The Bank of New York, New York, NY

HEALTH MANAGEMENT ASSOCIATES, INC.

Exchange	Symbol	Price	52Wk Range	Yield	P/E
NYS	HMA	$5.29 (3/31/2008)	11.48-4.84	N/A	10.80

*7 Year Price Score 32.50   *NYSE Composite Index=100   *12 Month Price Score 76.41

Interim Earnings (Per Share)

Qtr.	Dec	Mar	Jun	Sep
2005			0.31	
Qtr.	Mar	Jun	Sep	Dec
2006	0.36	0.32	0.31	(0.23)
2007	0.27	0.05	0.12	0.05

Interim Dividends (Per Share)

Amt	Decl	Ex	Rec	Pay
0.06Q	5/2/2006	5/10/2006	5/12/2006	6/5/2006
0.06Q	8/1/2006	8/9/2006	8/11/2006	9/5/2006
0.06Q	10/31/2006	11/8/2006	11/10/2006	12/5/2006
10.00Q	1/17/2007	3/2/2007	2/27/2007	3/1/2007

Valuation Analysis   **Institutional Holding**

Forecast P/E	N/A	No of Institutions 302
Market Cap	$1.3 Billion	Shares
Book Value	81.0 Million	236,470,752
Price/Book	15.86	% Held
Price/Sales	0.29	97.67

Business Summary: Hospitals & Health Care (MIC: 9.3 SIC: 8062 NAIC: 622110)

Health Management Associates owns and operates general acute care hospitals in non-urban communities. As of Dec 31 2007, Co. operated 59 hospitals with a total of 8,458 licensed beds. Co.'s services include general surgery, internal medicine, obstetrics, emergency room care, radiology, oncology, diagnostic care, coronary care and pediatric services. Co. also provides outpatient services such as one-day surgery, laboratory, x-ray, respiratory therapy, cardiology and physical therapy. In addition, some of Co.'s hospitals provide specialty services in, among other areas, cardiology, neuro-surgery, oncology, computer-assisted tomography scanning, and magnetic resonance imaging.

Recent Developments: For the year ended Dec 31 2007, income from continuing operations decreased 35.1% to US$117.9 million from US$181.8 million a year earlier. Net income decreased 34.4% to US$119.9 million from US$182.7 million in the prior year. Revenues were US$4.39 billion, up 8.4% from US$4.05 billion the year before. Operating income was US$408.0 million versus US$340.8 million in the prior year, an increase of 19.7%. Indirect operating expenses increased 7.4% to US$3.98 billion from US$3.71 billion in the equivalent prior-year period.

Prospects: Co.'s near-term outlook appears constructive. Specifically, Co. believes that its recent implementations of corrective methods at certain hospitals to improve operating trends and its continued addition of physicians and medical equipment, coupled with improving demographics, will yield increased hospital surgical volume, emergency room visits and admissions. Also, Co. continues to improve its emergency room and diagnostic imaging services to meet the needs of the communities that its hospitals served. For full-year 2008, Co. expects diluted earnings per share from continuing operations to be between $0.40 and $0.50 on anticipated net revenue of between $4.50 billion and $4.70 billion.

Financial Data

(US$ in Thousands)	12/31/2007	12/31/2006	12/31/2005	09/30/2005	09/30/2004	09/30/2003	09/30/2002	09/30/2001
Earnings Per Share	0.49	0.75	0.31	1.42	1.32	1.13	0.97	0.76
Cash Flow Per Share	1.33	1.86	0.37	2.30	1.88	1.40	1.47	1.19
Tang Book Value Per Share	N.M.	6.19	5.87	5.89	5.05	5.16	4.24	4.08
Dividends Per Share	10.000	0.240	0.180	0.160	0.080	0.080	...	...
Dividend Payout %	2,040.82	32.00	58.06	11.27	6.06	7.08	...	...
Income Statement								
Total Revenue	4,392,086	4,056,599	917,186	3,588,822	3,205,885	2,560,576	2,262,601	1,879,801
EBITDA	636,555	541,684	170,056	720,459	661,395	568,600	500,990	411,597
Income Before Taxes	187,496	302,173	125,185	565,286	526,480	458,736	405,662	320,951
Income Taxes	69,587	117,107	48,679	211,629	201,381	175,312	159,226	125,973
Net Income	119,879	182,749	75,541	353,077	325,099	283,424	246,436	194,978
Average Shares	245,119	243,340	244,697	248,976	246,826	255,884	260,641	264,351
Balance Sheet								
Current Assets	1,066,107	1,012,004	1,010,282	988,155	941,594	1,093,336	695,786	565,231
Total Assets	4,643,919	4,490,952	4,091,224	3,988,171	3,507,288	2,979,487	2,364,317	1,941,577
Current Liabilities	597,646	472,021	931,795	1,068,857	320,131	272,963	273,743	188,087
Long-Term Obligations	3,566,355	1,297,047	619,179	366,649	925,518	924,713	650,159	428,990
Total Liabilities	4,562,891	2,084,830	1,827,049	1,698,712	1,529,278	1,342,412	1,017,565	687,928
Stockholders' Equity	81,028	2,406,122	2,264,175	2,289,459	1,978,010	1,637,075	1,346,752	1,253,649
Shares Outstanding	242,866	240,707	240,648	244,785	243,481	240,205	238,567	245,435
Statistical Record								
Return on Assets %	2.62	4.26	1.59	9.42	10.00	10.61	11.45	10.50
Return on Equity %	9.64	7.83	2.84	16.55	17.94	19.00	18.95	17.08
EBITDA Margin %	14.49	13.35	18.54	20.08	20.63	22.21	22.14	21.90
Net Margin %	2.73	4.50	8.24	9.84	10.14	11.07	10.89	10.37
Asset Turnover	0.96	0.95	0.19	0.96	0.99	0.96	1.05	1.01
Current Ratio	1.78	2.14	1.08	0.92	2.94	4.01	2.54	3.01
Debt to Equity	44.01	0.54	0.27	0.16	0.47	0.56	0.48	0.34
Price Range	21.35-5.80	22.75-19.27	23.61-20.99	26.61-18.95	26.29-19.00	22.80-16.69	22.87-16.53	22.31-13.96
P/E Ratio	43.57-11.84	30.33-25.69	76.16-67.71	18.74-13.35	19.92-14.39	20.18-14.77	23.58-17.04	29.36-18.37
Average Yield %	94.17	1.16	0.80	0.68	0.36	0.42	...	...

Address: 5811 Pelican Bay Boulevard, Suite 500, Naples, FL 34108-2710 Telephone: 239-598-3131	Web Site: www.hma-corp.com Officers: William J. Schoen - Chmn. Joseph V. Vumbacco - Vice-Chmn., C.E.O.	Auditors: Ernst & Young LLP Transfer Agents: Wachovia Bank, N.A., Charlotte, NC

HEALTH NET, INC.

Exchange	Symbol	Price	52Wk Range	Yield	P/E
NYS	HNT	$30.80 (3/31/2008)	58.75-30.50	N/A	18.12

*7 Year Price Score 116.89 ***NYSE Composite Index=100** ***12 Month Price Score 88.25**

TRADING VOLUME (thousand shares)

Interim Earnings (Per Share)

Qtr.	Mar	Jun	Sep	Dec
2003	0.57	0.63	(0.02)	0.80
2004	0.13	0.36	0.64	(0.75)
2005	0.19	0.47	0.67	0.66
2006	0.65	0.65	0.76	0.72
2007	0.77	0.80	(0.93)	1.03

Interim Dividends (Per Share)

No Dividends Paid

Valuation Analysis   Institutional Holding

Forecast P/E	11.50	No of Institutions
	(1/10/2007)	265
Market Cap	$3.4 Billion	Shares
Book Value	1.0 Billion	107,339,912
Price/Book	1.81	% Held
Price/Sales	0.24	95.91

Business Summary: Insurance (MIC: 8.2 SIC: 6324 NAIC: 524114)

Health Net is a managed care organization. As of Dec 31 2007, Co.'s health plans and government contracts subsidiaries provide health benefits through its health maintenance organizations, insured preferred provider organizations (PPOs) and point of service (POS) plans, to approximately 6.6 million individuals in all 50 states and the District of Columbia through group, individual, Medicare, Medicaid, TRICARE and Veterans Affairs programs. Co.'s subsidiaries also provide managed health care products related to behavioral health and prescription drugs. Co. also owns health and life insurance companies licensed to sell exclusive provider organization, PPO, POS and indemnity products.

Recent Developments: For the year ended Dec 31 2007, net income decreased 41.2% to US$193.7 million from US$329.3 million in the prior year. Revenues were US$14.11 billion, up 9.3% from US$12.91 billion the year before. Net premiums earned were US$11.44 billion versus US$10.36 billion in the prior year, an increase of 10.3%. Net investment income rose 8.2% to US$120.2 million from US$111.0 million a year ago.

Prospects: Looking ahead for full-year 2008, Co. expects that its general & administrative (G&A) ratio should further decrease, as it implements its G&A repositioning strategy in order to achieve greater cost savings and become more competitive. As a result, Co. anticipates earnings for the first quarter of 2008 to be approximately $0.67 per diluted share with estimated G&A ration of 10.7%. Consequently, Co. believes that its G&A ratios in subsequent quarters during 2008 should average less than 10.0%. Further, Co. is projecting full-year 2008 earnings per diluted share in the range of $4.14 to $4.17, with 38.0% of earnings per diluted share occurring during the first half of 2008.

Financial Data
(US$ in Thousands)

	12/31/2007	12/31/2006	12/31/2005	12/31/2004	12/31/2003	12/31/2002	12/31/2001	12/31/2000
Earnings Per Share	1.70	2.78	1.99	0.38	1.98	1.82	0.69	1.33
Cash Flow Per Share	5.44	2.41	1.69	(0.49)	3.27	3.38	4.44	2.98
Tang Book Value Per Share	9.20	8.38	7.38	4.74	4.80	4.35	2.94	1.61
Income Statement								
Total Revenue	14,108,271	12,908,350	11,940,533	11,646,393	11,064,702	10,201,543	10,064,460	9,076,555
EBITDA	401,886	504,388	409,958	111,704	575,648	426,687	236,045	368,646
Income Before Taxes	358,904	478,797	376,264	67,416	516,971	356,495	137,350	262,747
Income Taxes	165,207	149,484	146,479	24,812	193,891	118,928	50,821	99,124
Net Income	193,697	329,313	229,785	42,604	234,030	228,626	86,529	163,623
Average Shares	113,829	118,310	115,641	113,038	118,278	126,004	125,186	123,453
Balance Sheet								
Current Assets	3,701,104	3,217,846	2,911,618	2,492,314	2,412,480	2,372,404	2,341,943	2,399,554
Total Assets	4,933,055	4,297,022	3,940,722	3,653,194	3,549,276	3,466,677	3,359,647	3,670,116
Current Liabilities	2,312,017	2,109,503	1,839,076	1,861,156	1,773,705	1,702,050	1,755,526	1,811,081
Long-Term Obligations	510,434	300,000	387,954	397,760	398,963	398,821	593,860	766,450
Total Liabilities	3,057,473	2,518,057	2,351,647	2,380,314	2,255,051	2,157,628	2,394,135	2,608,985
Stockholders' Equity	1,875,582	1,778,965	1,589,075	1,272,880	1,294,225	1,309,049	1,165,512	1,061,131
Shares Outstanding	110,299	117,508	114,716	111,277	113,427	120,642	123,685	122,800
Statistical Record								
Return on Assets %	4.20	8.00	6.05	1.18	6.67	6.51	2.39	4.43
Return on Equity %	10.60	19.56	16.06	3.31	17.98	18.48	7.77	16.72
EBITDA Margin %	2.85	3.91	3.43	0.96	5.20	4.18	2.35	4.06
Net Margin %	1.37	2.55	1.92	0.37	2.12	2.24	0.86	1.80
Asset Turnover	3.06	3.13	3.14	3.23	3.15	2.90	2.78	2.46
Current Ratio	1.60	1.53	1.58	1.34	1.36	1.39	1.33	1.32
Debt to Equity	0.27	0.17	0.24	0.31	0.31	0.30	0.51	0.72
Price Range	58.75-46.12	53.24-37.21	52.58-28.02	33.46-22.23	35.62-23.06	29.65-20.61	25.63-16.13	26.88-7.69
P/E Ratio	34.56-27.13	19.15-13.38	26.42-14.08	88.05-58.50	17.99-11.65	16.29-11.32	37.14-23.38	20.21-5.78

Address: 21650 Oxnard Street, Woodland Hills, CA 91367
Telephone: 818-676-6000
Fax: 818-676-6000

Web Site: www.healthnet.com
Officers: Jay M. Gellert - Pres., C.E.O. B. Curtis Westen - Sr. V.P., Sec., Gen. Couns.

Auditors: Deloitte & Touche LLP
Investor Contact: 818-676-6978
Transfer Agents: Wells Fargo Bank, N.A., St. Paul, MN

HEARST-ARGYLE TELEVISION INC.

Exchange	Symbol	Price	52Wk Range	Yield	P/E
NYS	HTV	$20.63 (3/31/2008)	27.87-17.85	1.36	29.90

*7 Year Price Score 78.04   *NSE Composite Index=100   *12 Month Price Score 100.79

Interim Earnings (Per Share)

Qtr.	Mar	Jun	Sep	Dec
2003	0.11	0.29	0.24	0.36
2004	0.19	0.37	0.32	0.41
2005	0.14	0.68	0.13	0.12
2006	0.14	0.27	0.18	0.47
2007	0.05	0.18	0.10	0.36

Interim Dividends (Per Share)

Amt	Decl	Ex	Rec	Pay
0.07Q	5/3/2007	7/2/2007	7/5/2007	7/15/2007
0.07Q	9/26/2007	10/3/2007	10/5/2007	10/15/2007
0.07Q	12/10/2007	1/2/2008	1/5/2008	1/15/2008
0.07Q	3/27/2008	4/2/2008	4/5/2008	4/15/2008
		Indicated Div: $0.28		

Valuation Analysis

		Institutional Holding	
Forecast P/E	N/A	No of Institutions	
		95	
Market Cap	$1.9 Billion	Shares	
Book Value	2.0 Billion	21,401,102	
Price/Book	0.99	% Held	
Price/Sales	2.56	22.94	

Business Summary: Media (MIC: 13.1 SIC: 4833 NAIC: 515120)

Hearst-Argyle Television and its subsidiaries own and operate television stations in the U.S. At Dec 31 2007, Co. owned or managed 29 television stations reaching 20.4 million, or 18.1%, of television households in the U.S. Also, Co. owns and operates 26 network-affiliated television stations, as well as provides management services to two network-affiliated stations and one independent television station and two radio stations owned by The Hearst Corp. in exchange for management fees. Co.'s programming includes three main components: programs produced by networks with which it is affiliated; programs that it produces at its stations; and first-run syndicated programs that it acquires.

Recent Developments: For the year ended Dec 31 2007, net income decreased 34.5% to US$64.7 million from US$98.7 million in the prior year. Revenues were US$755.7 million, down 3.8% from US$785.4 million the year before. Operating income was US$176.2 million versus US$228.8 million in the prior year, a decrease of 23.0%. Indirect operating expenses increased 4.1% to US$579.6 million from US$556.6 million in the equivalent prior-year period.

Prospects: For 2008, Co. is anticipating growth in respect of total revenues, operating income and net income compared to 2007, driven by expected strong political spending and third-quarter Olympics revenue. At the same time, Co. expects its prospects to be positively affected by its existing local ratings performance momentum as well as the progress of its continued effort to expand its digital platforms, which now include 16 digital multicast channels and 12-mobile-enabled Websites. However, Co. is concern that existing economic stability, with recession and inflation threats, as well as a weaker jobs climate, should somewhat temper the expected growth until such time as its economy stabilizes.

Financial Data

(US$ in Thousands)	12/31/2007	12/31/2006	12/31/2005	12/31/2004	12/31/2003	12/31/2002	12/31/2001	12/31/2000
Earnings Per Share	0.69	1.06	1.08	1.30	1.00	1.15	0.32	0.47
Cash Flow Per Share	1.45	2.16	1.41	2.10	1.93	2.23	1.81	2.04
Dividends Per Share	0.280	0.280	0.280	0.180	0.060	...	...	...
Dividend Payout %	40.58	26.42	25.93	13.85	6.00	...	...	...
Income Statement								
Total Revenue	755,738	785,402	706,883	779,879	686,775	721,311	641,876	747,281
EBITDA	231,442	285,391	228,983	333,075	275,182	291,268	344,356	378,738
Income Before Taxes	105,451	156,650	104,134	200,294	136,530	174,218	57,662	78,908
Income Taxes	38,207	58,410	3,917	76,352	42,309	66,201	27,101	36,438
Net Income	64,656	98,723	100,217	123,942	94,221	108,017	31,087	44,925
Average Shares	94,299	93,353	93,214	101,406	92,990	92,550	92,000	92,457
Balance Sheet								
Current Assets	246,317	258,685	337,726	306,506	284,672	216,196	209,947	232,285
Total Assets	3,958,976	3,958,088	3,832,359	3,842,140	3,799,087	3,762,925	3,779,705	3,817,989
Current Liabilities	230,411	250,254	217,570	137,908	130,418	130,679	131,640	123,748
Long-Term Obligations	837,131	911,143	911,191	1,016,242	1,088,595	973,378	1,160,205	1,448,492
Total Liabilities	2,006,577	2,075,281	2,010,900	2,077,052	2,126,705	1,983,663	2,113,091	2,373,613
Stockholders' Equity	1,952,399	1,882,807	1,821,459	1,753,837	1,672,382	1,579,262	1,466,614	1,444,376
Shares Outstanding	93,847	93,188	92,651	92,855	92,766	92,364	91,827	91,925
Statistical Record								
Return on Assets %	1.63	2.53	2.61	3.24	2.49	2.86	0.82	1.16
Return on Equity %	3.37	5.33	5.61	7.22	5.80	7.09	2.14	3.13
EBITDA Margin %	30.62	36.34	32.39	42.71	40.07	40.38	53.65	50.68
Net Margin %	8.56	12.57	14.18	15.89	13.72	14.98	4.84	6.01
Asset Turnover	0.19	0.20	0.18	0.20	0.18	0.19	0.17	0.19
Current Ratio	1.07	1.03	1.55	2.22	2.18	1.65	1.59	1.88
Debt to Equity	0.43	0.48	0.50	0.58	0.65	0.62	0.79	1.00
Price Range	27.87-17.85	26.04-20.00	26.38-23.33	28.95-22.63	27.61-20.11	27.49-18.90	24.25-16.70	29.06-17.13
P/E Ratio	40.39-25.87	24.57-18.87	24.43-21.60	22.27-17.41	27.61-20.11	23.90-16.43	75.78-52.19	61.84-36.44
Average Yield %	1.15	1.20	1.12	0.70	0.25	...	...	...

Address: 888 Seventh Avenue, New York, NY 10106 **Telephone:** 212-887-6800 **Fax:** 212-887-6875	**Web Site:** www.hearstargyle.com **Officers:** Victor F. Ganzi - Chmn. David J. Barrett - Pres., C.E.O.	**Auditors:** Deloitte & Touche LLP **Transfer Agents:** Computershare Investor Services

HEINZ (H.J.) CO.

Exchange	Symbol	Price	52Wk Range	Yield	P/E
NYS	HNZ	$46.97 (3/31/2008)	48.62-41.90	3.24	18.21

*7 Year Price Score 96.27 *NYSE Composite Index=100 *12 Month Price Score 104.85

Interim Earnings (Per Share)

Qtr.	Jul	Oct	Jan	Apr
2004-05	0.55	0.56	0.43	0.59
2005-06	0.45	0.60	0.35	0.50
2006-07	0.58	0.57	0.66	0.55
2007-08	0.63	0.71	0.68	...

Interim Dividends (Per Share)

Amt	Decl	Ex	Rec	Pay
0.38Q	5/31/2007	6/21/2007	6/25/2007	7/10/2007
0.38Q	8/15/2007	9/19/2007	9/21/2007	10/10/2007
0.38Q	11/14/2007	12/19/2007	12/21/2007	1/10/2008
0.38Q	3/12/2008	3/10/2008	0/24/2000	4/10/2008

Indicated Div: $1.52 (Div. Reinv. Plan)

Valuation Analysis

Forecast P/E	16.65
	(1/10/2007)
Market Cap	$14.8 Billion
Book Value	2.0 Billion
Price/Book	7.40
Price/Sales	1.51

Institutional Holding

No of Institutions	560
Shares	223,390,752
% Held	68.77

Business Summary: Food (MIC: 4.1 SIC: 2033 NAIC: 311421)

H. J. Heinz and its subsidiaries manufacture and market a line of processed food products worldwide. Co.'s primary products include ketchup, condiments and sauces, frozen food, soups, beans and pasta meals, infant food as well as other processed food products. Co.'s segments are organized by geographical area, which includes North American Consumer Products, U.S. Foodservice, Europe, Asia/Pacific and Rest of World. Some of Co.'s primary food processing factories and major trademarks in North America include Heinz, Classico, Quality Chef Foods, Jack Daniel's, Catelli, Wyler's, Heinz Bell 'Orto, Bella Rossa, Chef Francisco, Dianne's, Ore-Ida, Tater Tots, Bagel Bites and Poppers.

Recent Developments: For the quarter ended Jan 30 2008, net income decreased 0.2% to US$218.5 million from US$219.0 million in the year-earlier quarter. Revenues were US$2.61 billion, up 13.8% from US$2.30 billion the year before. Operating income was US$406.1 million versus US$376.3 million in the prior-year quarter, an increase of 7.9%. Direct operating expenses rose 16.1% to US$1.68 billion from US$1.44 billion in the comparable period the year before. Indirect operating expenses increased 11.3% to US$529.4 million from US$475.8 million in the equivalent prior-year period.

Prospects: Co.'s results reflect improved sales, supported by favorable pricing and foreign exchange translation rates, as well as volume increase in its Asia/Pacific business, combined with solid growth in its Europe, North American Consumer Products and U.S. Foodservice segments. While it expects continued inflationary increases in commodity costs for the remainder of the fiscal year ending Apr 2008, Co. believes that strong sales growth, price increases, ongoing productivity improvements and its geographic diversity will help to mitigate these increases. As a result, Co. expects earnings per share for the full fiscal year to be in a range of $2.60 to $2.62, reflecting growth of 9.0% to 10.0%.

Financial Data
(US$ in Thousands)

	9 Mos	6 Mos	3 Mos	05/02/2007	05/03/2006	04/27/2005	04/28/2004	04/30/2003
Earnings Per Share	2.58	2.56	2.42	2.36	1.89	2.13	2.29	1.60
Cash Flow Per Share	3.62	3.21	3.19	3.24	3.12	3.33	3.56	2.59
Dividends Per Share	1.490	1.460	1.430	1.400	1.200	1.140	1.080	1.485
Dividend Payout %	57.81	57.11	59.18	59.32	63.49	53.52	47.16	92.81
Income Statement								
Total Revenue	7,382,527	4,771,664	2,248,285	9,001,630	8,643,438	8,912,297	8,414,538	8,236,836
EBITDA	1,386,133	909,436	427,689	1,681,997	1,240,405	1,515,721	1,591,008	1,296,342
Depn & Amortn	214,327	141,154	69,625	...	...	...	...	...
Income Before Taxes	922,291	602,933	279,715	1,124,399	693,461	1,058,614	1,168,551	868,731
Income Taxes	271,428	170,602	74,421	332,797	250,700	322,792	389,618	313,372
Net Income	650,863	432,331	205,294	785,746	645,603	752,699	804,273	566,285
Average Shares	321,381	321,903	325,477	332,468	342,121	353,450	354,372	354,144
Balance Sheet								
Current Assets	3,610,826	3,447,684	2,874,593	3,019,002	2,703,935	3,645,576	3,610,796	3,284,320
Total Assets	10,828,660	10,763,929	9,924,771	10,033,026	9,737,767	10,577,714	9,877,189	9,224,751
Current Liabilities	2,769,365	2,845,229	2,668,759	2,505,106	2,018,231	2,587,068	2,469,068	1,926,134
Long-Term Obligations	4,765,452	4,585,131	4,136,065	4,413,641	4,357,013	4,121,984	4,537,980	4,776,143
Total Liabilities	8,828,678	8,758,348	8,062,477	8,191,343	7,688,944	7,975,145	7,983,000	8,025,594
Stockholders' Equity	1,999,982	2,005,581	1,862,294	1,841,683	2,048,823	2,602,573	1,894,189	1,199,157
Shares Outstanding	315,149	316,918	319,145	321,779	330,757	347,677	351,957	351,448
Statistical Record								
Return on Assets %	7.91	7.96	8.14	7.97	6.25	7.38	8.44	5.82
Return on Equity %	39.65	39.37	39.70	40.50	27.31	33.57	52.14	38.92
EBITDA Margin %	18.78	19.06	19.02	18.69	14.35	17.01	18.91	15.74
Net Margin %	8.82	9.06	9.13	8.73	7.47	8.45	9.56	6.88
Asset Turnover	0.93	0.91	0.94	0.91	0.84	0.87	0.88	0.85
Current Ratio	1.30	1.21	1.08	1.21	1.34	1.41	1.46	1.71
Debt to Equity	2.38	2.29	2.22	2.40	2.13	1.58	2.40	3.98
Price Range	48.62-42.10	48.15-41.98	48.15-40.69	48.15-39.94	42.25-33.53	39.20-34.57	38.95-29.71	38.91-27.31
P/E Ratio	18.84-16.32	18.81-16.40	19.90-16.81	20.40-16.92	22.35-17.74	18.40-16.23	17.01-12.97	24.32-17.07
Average Yield %	3.23	3.18	3.18	3.20	3.31	3.06	3.09	4.56

Address: 600 Grant Street, Pittsburgh, PA 15219
Telephone: 412-456-5700
Fax: 412-456-6128

Web Site: www.heinz.com
Officers: William R. Johnson - Chmn., Pres., C.E.O.
Arthur B. Winkleblack - Exec. V.P., C.F.O.

Auditors: PricewaterhouseCoopers LLP
Investor Contact: 412-456-1048
Transfer Agents: Mellon Investor Services LLC, Ridgefield Park, NJ

371

HELMERICH & PAYNE, INC.

Exchange	Symbol	Price	52Wk Range	Yield	P/E	Div Acheiver
NYS	HP	$46.87 (3/31/2008)	47.42-29.07	0.38	11.08	31 Years

*7 Year Price Score 136.55 *NYSE Composite Index=100 *12 Month Price Score 133.41

Interim Earnings (Per Share)

Qtr.	Dec	Mar	Jun	Sep
2004-05	0.39	0.22	0.28	0.34
2005-06	0.48	0.61	0.75	0.93
2006-07	1.06	1.02	1.09	1.10
2007-08	1.02	...	...	...

Interim Dividends (Per Share)

Amt	Decl	Ex	Rec	Pay
0.045Q	6/7/2007	8/13/2007	8/15/2007	9/4/2007
0.045Q	9/6/2007	11/13/2007	11/15/2007	12/3/2007
0.045Q	...	2/13/2008	2/15/2008	3/3/2008
0.045Q	...	5/13/2008	5/15/2008	6/2/2008
		Indicated Div: $0.18		

Valuation Analysis   **Institutional Holding**

Forecast P/E	5.77	No of Institutions
	(1/10/2007)	283
Market Cap	$4.9 Billion	Shares
Book Value	1.9 Billion	80,432,704
Price/Book	2.54	% Held
Price/Sales	2.86	77.91

TRADING VOLUME (thousand shares)

Business Summary: Oil and Gas (MIC: 14.2 SIC: 1381 NAIC: 213111)

Helmerich & Payne is a holding company. Co. is engaged in contract drilling of oil and gas wells for others. Co.'s contract drilling business is composed of three segments: U.S. land drilling conducted primarily in Oklahoma, California, Texas, Wyoming, Colorado, Louisiana, Mississippi, Alabama, Arkansas, New Mexico, and North Dakota; U.S. offshore platform drilling in the Gulf of Mexico, California, Trinidad and Equatorial Guinea; and international drilling in which Co. operates in Venezuela, Ecuador, Colombia, Argentina, Bolivia, Tunisia, and Chile. Co. is also engaged in the ownership, development, and operation of commercial real estate, and these operations are conducted in Tulsa, OK.

Recent Developments: For the quarter ended Dec 31 2007, net income decreased 2.7% to US$107.8 million from US$110.8 million in the year-earlier quarter. Revenues were US$456.7 million, up 18.2% from US$386.4 million the year before. Operating income was US$168.6 million versus US$146.7 million in the prior-year quarter, an increase of 15.0%. Indirect operating expenses increased 20.1% to US$288.0 million from US$239.7 million in the equivalent prior-year period.

Prospects: Despite challenging spot market dayrates, Co.'s near-term outlook appears constructive. In detail, Co. plans to construct 11 additional FlexRigs® to operate under long-term contracts for three exploration and production companies. Specifically, the four new FlexRigs® to operate in the U.S. are scheduled to be deployed in the Barnett Shale during the fiscal quarter ended June 30, 2008. Meanwhile, Co. expects the seven new international FlexRigs® to be completed and mobilized at the rate of one per month beginning in the fourth fiscal quarter of 2008 with five of the seven rigs are projected to operate under five-year term contracts and the remaining two under three-year term contracts.

Financial Data

(US$ in Thousands)	3 Mos	09/30/2007	09/30/2006	09/30/2005	09/30/2004	09/30/2003	09/30/2002	09/30/2001
Earnings Per Share	4.23	4.27	2.77	1.23	0.04	0.17	0.63	1.42
Cash Flow Per Share	5.16	5.43	2.83	2.08	1.34	0.96	1.52	2.78
Tang Book Value Per Share	18.47	17.54	13.30	10.39	9.06	9.15	8.95	10.30
Dividends Per Share	0.180	0.180	0.169	0.165	0.161	0.160	0.153	0.150
Dividend Payout %	4.26	4.22	6.09	13.47	358.33	91.43	24.21	10.56
Income Statement								
Total Revenue	456,663	1,629,658	1,224,813	800,726	620,928	515,284	510,928	826,854
EBITDA	213,246	846,521	549,208	321,599	102,435	116,635	153,789	323,889
Depn & Amortn	43,984	...	...	...	...	...	...	...
Income Before Taxes	164,431	690,353	440,981	212,657	8,000	33,942	91,220	235,102
Income Taxes	60,146	250,984	154,391	87,463	4,365	14,649	40,573	93,027
Net Income	107,830	449,261	293,858	127,606	4,359	17,873	63,517	144,254
Average Shares	105,615	105,128	106,091	104,066	101,666	101,192	100,690	101,544
Balance Sheet								
Current Assets	541,282	498,964	428,691	499,797	245,886	197,531	178,751	331,412
Total Assets	3,058,789	2,885,369	2,134,712	1,663,350	1,406,844	1,415,835	1,227,313	1,364,507
Current Liabilities	231,199	226,612	264,548	89,481	59,903	88,618	72,899	121,221
Long-Term Obligations	485,000	445,000	175,000	200,000	200,000	200,000	100,000	50,000
Total Liabilities	1,144,770	1,069,853	752,820	584,112	492,734	498,584	332,143	338,030
Stockholders' Equity	1,914,019	1,815,516	1,381,892	1,079,238	914,110	917,251	895,170	1,026,477
Shares Outstanding	103,605	103,484	103,869	103,869	100,890	100,280	100,021	99,705
Statistical Record								
Return on Assets %	16.74	17.90	15.47	8.31	0.31	1.35	4.90	10.99
Return on Equity %	26.47	28.10	23.88	12.80	0.47	1.97	6.61	14.56
EBITDA Margin %	46.70	51.94	44.84	40.16	16.50	22.64	30.10	39.17
Net Margin %	23.61	27.57	23.99	15.94	0.70	3.47	12.43	17.45
Asset Turnover	0.64	0.65	0.64	0.52	0.44	0.39	0.39	0.63
Current Ratio	2.34	2.20	1.62	5.59	4.10	2.23	2.45	2.73
Debt to Equity	0.25	0.25	0.13	0.19	0.22	0.22	0.11	0.05
Price Range	40.28-23.06	36.43-21.75	39.95-22.02	30.56-13.83	15.31-11.89	16.17-11.79	15.71-9.20	21.42-8.69
P/E Ratio	9.52-5.45	8.53-5.09	14.42-7.95	24.85-11.24	382.63-297.13	95.12-69.32	24.93-14.60	15.08-6.12
Average Yield %	0.57	0.61	0.56	0.80	1.20	1.17	1.24	1.05

Address: 1437 South Boulder Avenue, Suite 1400, Tulsa, OK 74119-3623 **Telephone:** 918-742-5531 **Fax:** 918-742-0237	**Web Site:** www.hpinc.com **Officers:** W. H. Helmerich III - Chmn. Hans C. Helmerich - Pres., C.E.O.	**Auditors:** Ernst & Young LLP **Investor Contact:** 918-742-5531 **Transfer Agents:** UMB Bank, Kansas City, MO

HERCULES INC.

Exchange	Symbol	Price	52Wk Range	Yield	P/E
NYS	HPC	$18.29 (3/31/2008)	22.06-15.65	1.09	11.72

*7 Year Price Score 114.46 *NYSE Composite Index=100 *12 Month Price Score 101.05

Interim Earnings (Per Share)

Qtr.	Mar	Jun	Sep	Dec
2003	(0.14)	0.29	0.17	0.10
2004	0.24	0.04	(0.47)	0.45
2005	0.04	0.08	0.22	(0.72)
2006	0.13	(0.47)	0.31	2.17
2007	0.64	0.30	0.37	0.25

Interim Dividends (Per Share)

Amt	Decl	Ex	Rec	Pay
0.05Q	7/23/2007	9/26/2007	9/28/2007	10/19/2007
0.05Q	11/15/2007	12/26/2007	12/28/2007	1/18/2008
0.05Q	2/21/2008	3/26/2008	3/28/2008	4/18/2008

Indicated Div: $0.20

Valuation Analysis **Institutional Holding**

Forecast P/E	N/A	No of Institutions 242
Market Cap	$2.1 Billion	Shares
Book Value	478.0 Million	106,635,504
Price/Book	4.36	% Held
Price/Sales	0.98	91.60

Business Summary: Chemicals (MIC: 11.1 SIC: 2899 NAIC: 325998)

Hercules is a manufacturer and marketer of specialty chemicals and related services for a range of business, consumer and industrial applications. Co.'s principal products are chemicals used by the paper industry to increase paper and paperboard performance and improve the manufacturing process; water-soluble polymers; and specialty resins. Co.'s primary markets include pulp and paper; paints and adhesives; construction materials; food, pharmaceutical and personal care; and industrial specialties, including oilfield and general industrial. Co. operates on a global scale, with primary operations in North America, Europe, Asia and Latin America.

Recent Developments: For the year ended Dec 31 2007, income from continuing operations decreased 10.4% to US$170.9 million from US$190.8 million a year earlier. Net income decreased 25.1% to US$178.9 million from US$238.7 million in the prior year. Revenues were US$2.14 billion, up 5.0% from US$2.04 billion the year before. Operating income was US$264.2 million versus US$248.6 million in the prior year, an increase of 6.3%. Direct operating expenses rose 4.6% to US$1.41 billion from US$1.34 billion in the comparable period the year before. Indirect operating expenses increased 5.2% to US$466.3 million from US$443.3 million in the equivalent prior-year period.

Prospects: Looking ahead, while conditions are expected to remain challenging in the North American coatings and construction markets, Co. expects volume growth and profitability to continue in its Aqualon segment as availability and utilization of expanded capacity increases into 2008. Further, Co. also expects its Paper Technologies and Ventures (PTV) segment to continue to sustain growth in certain markets, mainly in non-Western Europe and South America. PTV is also continuing on its new product launch strategy with an emphasis on developing higher-margin products to improve the overall sales mix. Thus, for 2008, Co. expects to continue to deliver double-digit ongoing earnings per share growth.

Financial Data

(US$ in Thousands)	12/31/2007	12/31/2006	12/31/2005	12/31/2004	12/31/2003	12/31/2002	12/31/2001	12/31/2000
Earnings Per Share	1.56	2.14	(0.38)	0.25	0.42	(5.65)	(0.54)	0.91
Cash Flow Per Share	2.62	1.56	1.28	1.12	0.21	(1.99)	1.01	0.65
Dividends Per Share	0.100	...	...	...	...	...	...	0.620
Dividend Payout %	6.41	...	...	...	...	...	...	68.13
Income Statement								
Total Revenue	2,136,200	2,035,300	2,068,800	1,997,000	1,846,000	1,705,000	2,620,000	3,152,000
EBITDA	298,900	152,300	132,600	221,000	307,000	123,000	397,000	535,000
Income Before Taxes	151,300	3,200	(45,300)	29,000	95,000	(55,000)	23,000	164,000
Income Taxes	(20,300)	(192,200)	(7,200)	2,000	21,000	(4,000)	72,000	66,000
Net Income	178,900	238,700	(41,100)	27,000	45,000	(616,000)	(58,000)	98,000
Average Shares	115,100	111,300	108,700	109,000	107,900	109,100	108,200	107,400
Balance Sheet								
Current Assets	814,300	984,500	843,400	772,000	870,000	907,000	812,000	1,022,000
Total Assets	2,678,400	2,808,500	2,568,800	2,710,000	2,766,000	2,693,000	5,049,000	5,309,000
Current Liabilities	534,200	629,600	512,400	477,000	457,000	616,000	917,000	922,000
Long-Term Obligations	762,300	959,700	1,092,300	1,210,000	1,326,000	738,000	1,959,000	2,342,000
Total Liabilities	2,178,300	2,552,900	2,593,500	2,613,000	2,700,000	2,192,000	3,713,000	3,871,000
Stockholders' Equity	478,000	242,900	(24,700)	97,000	66,000	(123,000)	712,000	816,000
Shares Outstanding	113,998	116,028	112,737	112,141	110,991	109,369	108,787	107,542
Statistical Record								
Return on Assets %	6.52	8.88	N.M.	0.98	1.65	N.M.	N.M.	1.74
Return on Equity %	49.63	218.79	N.M.	33.04	...	N.M.	N.M.	11.64
EBITDA Margin %	13.99	7.48	6.41	11.07	16.63	7.21	15.15	16.97
Net Margin %	8.37	11.73	N.M.	1.35	2.44	N.M.	N.M.	3.11
Asset Turnover	0.78	0.76	0.78	0.73	0.68	0.44	0.51	0.56
Current Ratio	1.52	1.56	1.65	1.62	1.79	1.47	0.92	1.11
Debt to Equity	1.59	3.95	...	12.47	20.09	...	2.75	2.87
Price Range	22.06-17.49	19.52-11.03	15.24-10.20	15.09-9.99	12.40-7.60	13.68-8.67	19.94-6.94	27.88-11.63
P/E Ratio	14.14-11.21	9.12-5.15	...	60.36-39.96	29.52-18.10	...	...	30.63-12.77
Average Yield %	0.51	...	...	...	...	...	...	3.77

Address: Hercules Plaza, 1313 North Market Street, Wilmington, DE 19894-0001 **Telephone:** 302-594-5000 **Fax:** 302-594-5400	**Web Site:** www.herc.com **Officers:** John K. Wulff - Chmn. Craig A. Rogerson - Pres., C.E.O.	**Auditors:** BDO Seidman, LLP **Investor Contact:** 800-441-9274 **Transfer Agents:** Mellon Investor Services LLC, Jersey City, NJ

HERSHEY COMPANY (THE)

Exchange	Symbol	Price	52Wk Range	Yield	P/E	Div Acheiver
NYS	HSY	$37.67 (3/31/2008)	56.22-34.04	3.16	40.51	33 Years

*7 Year Price Score 80.76 *NYSE Composite Index=100 *12 Month Price Score 88.19

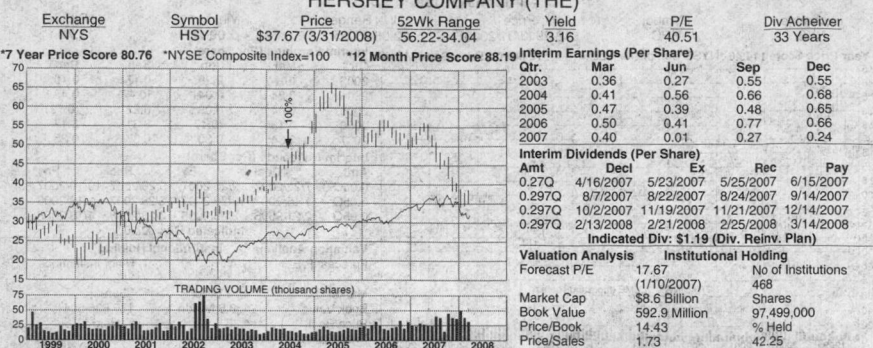

Interim Earnings (Per Share)

Qtr.	Mar	Jun	Sep	Dec
2003	0.36	0.27	0.55	0.55
2004	0.41	0.56	0.66	0.68
2005	0.47	0.39	0.48	0.65
2006	0.50	0.41	0.77	0.66
2007	0.40	0.01	0.27	0.24

Interim Dividends (Per Share)

Amt	Decl	Ex	Rec	Pay
0.27Q	4/16/2007	5/23/2007	5/25/2007	6/15/2007
0.297Q	8/7/2007	8/22/2007	8/24/2007	9/14/2007
0.297Q	10/2/2007	11/19/2007	11/21/2007	12/14/2007
0.297Q	2/13/2008	2/21/2008	2/25/2008	3/14/2008

Indicated Div: $1.19 (Div. Reinv. Plan)

Valuation Analysis

		Institutional Holding	
Forecast P/E	17.67	No of Institutions	
	(1/10/2007)	468	
Market Cap	$8.6 Billion	Shares	
Book Value	592.9 Million	97,499,000	
Price/Book	14.43	% Held	
Price/Sales	1.73	42.25	

Business Summary: Food (MIC: 4.1 SIC: 2064 NAIC: 311340)

Hershey is a North American manufacturer of chocolate and sugar confectionery products. Co.'s product groups include confectionery and snack products; gum and mint refreshment products; and food and beverage enhancers such as baking ingredients, peanut butter, toppings and beverages. Co. also provides a range of products specifically developed to address the nutritional interests of health-conscious consumers. Co.'s five operating segments comprise geographic regions including the U.S., Canada, Mexico, Brazil and other international locations, such as Japan, Korea, the Philippines, India and China. Co. markets its confectionery products in approximately 50 countries worldwide.

Recent Developments: For the year ended Dec 31 2007, net income decreased 61.7% to US$214.2 million from US$559.1 million in the prior year. Revenues were US$4.95 billion, up 0.1% from US$4.94 billion the year before. Operating income was US$458.8 million versus US$992.6 million in the prior year, a decrease of 53.8%. Direct operating expenses rose 7.7% to US$3.32 billion from US$3.08 billion in the comparable period the year before. Indirect operating expenses increased 34.0% to US$1.17 billion from US$875.0 million in the equivalent prior-year period.

Prospects: For 2008, Co. expects continued higher input and operating costs and greater levels of competitive activity. In response, Co. intends to offset such situation through several efforts, including the implementation of its productivity and cost savings plan. Also, Co. will continue to stabilize its business performance in the U.S., while focusing on growth in Asia, particularly China and India. For example, Co. will focus on its Reese's, Hershey's and Kisses brands, and plans to introduce Hershey's Bliss™, Signatures packaged candy and Starbucks® branded chocolates. Meanwhile, Co. is expecting total net sales growth of 3.0% to 4.0% and diluted earnings of $1.43 to $1.53 per share for 2008.

Financial Data

(US$ in Thousands)	12/31/2007	12/31/2006	12/31/2005	12/31/2004	12/31/2003	12/31/2002	12/31/2001	12/31/2000
Earnings Per Share	0.93	2.34	1.99	2.30	1.73	1.47	0.75	1.21
Cash Flow Per Share	3.40	3.07	1.89	3.13	2.26	2.29	2.59	1.50
Tang Book Value Per Share	N.M.	0.18	1.63	2.03	3.29	3.55	2.16	2.57
Dividends Per Share	1.135	1.030	0.930	0.835	0.723	0.630	0.583	0.540
Dividend Payout %	122.04	44.02	46.73	36.30	41.76	42.86	77.67	44.63
Income Statement								
Total Revenue	4,946,716	4,944,230	4,835,974	4,429,248	4,172,551	4,120,317	4,557,241	4,220,976
EBITDA	769,752	1,192,469	1,078,943	1,091,842	976,923	876,195	603,128	798,614
Income Before Taxes	340,242	876,502	772,926	835,644	732,827	637,565	343,541	546,639
Income Taxes	126,088	317,441	279,682	244,765	267,875	233,987	136,385	212,096
Net Income	214,154	559,061	493,244	590,879	457,584	403,578	207,156	334,543
Average Shares	231,449	239,071	248,292	256,827	264,532	275,429	275,392	276,730
Balance Sheet								
Current Assets	1,426,574	1,417,812	1,408,940	1,182,441	1,131,569	1,263,618	1,167,541	1,295,348
Total Assets	4,247,113	4,157,565	4,295,236	3,797,531	3,582,540	3,480,551	3,247,430	3,447,764
Current Liabilities	1,618,770	1,453,538	1,518,223	1,285,382	585,810	546,846	606,444	766,901
Long-Term Obligations	1,279,965	1,248,128	942,755	690,602	968,499	851,800	876,972	877,654
Total Liabilities	3,623,593	3,474,142	3,274,160	2,708,229	2,302,674	2,108,848	2,100,226	2,272,728
Stockholders' Equity	592,922	683,423	1,021,076	1,089,302	1,279,866	1,371,703	1,147,204	1,175,036
Shares Outstanding	227,049	230,263	240,524	246,587	259,059	268,440	332,145	272,563
Statistical Record								
Return on Assets %	5.10	13.23	12.19	15.97	12.96	12.00	6.19	9.82
Return on Equity %	33.56	65.60	46.74	49.74	34.51	32.04	17.84	29.35
EBITDA Margin %	15.56	24.12	22.31	24.65	23.41	21.27	13.23	18.92
Net Margin %	4.33	11.31	10.20	13.34	10.97	9.79	4.55	7.93
Asset Turnover	1.18	1.17	1.20	1.20	1.18	1.22	1.36	1.24
Current Ratio	0.88	0.98	0.93	0.92	1.93	2.31	1.93	1.69
Debt to Equity	2.16	1.83	0.92	0.63	0.76	0.62	0.76	0.75
Price Range	56.22-38.25	57.00-49.34	66.65-53.14	56.58-37.42	39.26-30.65	39.74-28.68	34.66-28.50	32.81-18.88
P/E Ratio	60.45-41.13	24.36-21.09	33.49-26.70	24.60-16.27	22.69-17.72	27.04-19.51	46.21-38.00	27.12-15.60
Average Yield %	2.34	1.94	1.55	1.82	2.05	1.86	1.85	2.20

Address: 100 Crystal A Drive, Hershey, PA 17033
Telephone: 717-534-4200
Fax: 717-531-6161

Web Site: www.hersheys.com
Officers: Richard H. Lenny - Chmn., Pres., C.E.O.
David J. West - Sr. V.P., C.F.O.

Auditors: KPMG LLP
Investor Contact: 800-539-0291
Transfer Agents: Mellon Investor Services, LLC, Ridgefield Park, NJ

HESS CORP

Exchange	Symbol	Price	52Wk Range	Yield	P/E
NYS	HES	$88.18 (3/31/2008)	104.40-55.08	0.45	15.36

*7 Year Price Score 160.39 *NYSE Composite Index=100 *12 Month Price Score 138.27

Interim Earnings (Per Share)

Qtr.	Mar	Jun	Sep	Dec
2003	0.66	0.94	0.55	0.22
2004	0.92	0.95	0.58	0.74
2005	0.71	0.96	0.87	1.44
2006	2.21	1.79	0.94	1.14
2007	1.17	1.75	1.23	1.59

Interim Dividends (Per Share)

Amt	Decl	Ex	Rec	Pay
0.10Q	6/6/2007	6/13/2007	6/15/2007	6/29/2007
0.10Q	9/5/2007	9/12/2007	9/14/2007	9/28/2007
0.10Q	12/5/2007	12/17/2007	12/19/2007	1/2/2008
0.10Q	3/5/2008	3/13/2008	3/17/2008	3/31/2008
			Indicated Div: $0.40	

Valuation Analysis

		Institutional Holding	
Forecast P/E	9.14	No of Institutions	
	(1/10/2007)	387	
Market Cap	$29.3 Billion	Shares	
Book Value	9.8 Billion	250,035,584	
Price/Book	2.89	% Held	
Price/Sales	0.89	79.37	

Business Summary: Oil and Gas (MIC: 14.2 SIC: 2911 NAIC: 324110)

Hess is a global integrated energy company that operates in two segments, Exploration and Production (E&P) and Marketing and Refining (M&R). The E&P segment explores for, develops, produces, purchases, transports and sells crude oil and natural gas. The M&R segment manufactures, purchases, transports, trades and markets refined petroleum products, natural gas and electricity. In addition, Co. owns 50.0% of a refinery joint venture in the U.S. Virgin Islands, and another refining facility, terminals and retail gasoline stations, most of which include convenience stores, located on the East Coast of the U.S. At Dec 31 2007, Co.'s proved reserves totaled 1.33 billion barrels of oil equivalent.

Recent Developments: For the year ended Dec 31 2007, net income decreased 4.6% to US$1.83 billion from US$1.92 billion in the prior year. Revenues were US$31.92 billion, up 11.2% from US$28.72 billion the year before. Direct operating expenses rose 13.4% to US$22.57 billion from US$19.91 billion in the comparable period the year before. Indirect operating expenses increased 18.6% to US$5.65 billion from US$4.76 billion in the equivalent prior-year period.

Prospects: For 2008, Co. expects total production of 380,000 barrels of oil equivalent per day (boepd) to 390,000 boepd. Going forward, Co. is progressing on its development projects, which include the expansion of offshore facilities and installation of wellhead platforms at Block A-18 of the Joint Development Area of Malaysia and Thailand, with full Phase 2 production expected in the second half of 2008, as well as the development of the Ujung Pangkah crude oil project, with production from Phase 2 oil project expected to commence in 2009. As such, Co. anticipates $4.40 billion in 2008 capital and exploratory expenditures, of which $4.30 billion relates to Exploration & Production operations.

Financial Data

(US$ in Thousands)	12/31/2007	12/31/2006	12/31/2005	12/31/2004	12/31/2003	12/31/2002	12/31/2001	12/31/2000
Earnings Per Share	5.74	6.07	3.98	3.19	2.37	(0.83)	3.42	3.79
Cash Flow Per Share	11.21	12.55	6.75	7.07	5.95	7.43	7.42	6.88
Tang Book Value Per Share	26.67	21.77	18.97	16.74	16.13	12.23	14.60	14.59
Dividends Per Share	0.400	0.100	0.400	0.400	0.400	0.400	0.400	0.200
Dividend Payout %	6.97	1.65	10.05	12.54	16.88	...	11.71	5.27
Income Statement								
Total Revenue	31,924,000	28,720,000	23,255,000	17,126,000	14,480,000	12,093,000	13,613,000	12,277,000
EBITDA	5,280,000	5,264,000	3,251,000	2,528,000	1,834,000	1,269,000	2,405,000	2,386,000
Income Before Taxes	3,704,000	4,040,000	2,226,000	1,558,000	781,000	(51,000)	1,438,000	1,672,000
Income Taxes	1,872,000	2,124,000	984,000	588,000	314,000	167,000	524,000	649,000
Net Income	1,832,000	1,916,000	1,242,000	977,000	643,000	(218,000)	914,000	1,023,000
Average Shares	319,312	315,667	312,105	306,258	271,026	264,561	264,093	269,634
Balance Sheet								
Current Assets	6,926,000	5,848,000	5,290,000	4,335,000	3,186,000	2,756,000	3,946,000	4,115,000
Total Assets	26,131,000	22,404,000	19,115,000	16,312,000	13,983,000	13,262,000	13,369,000	10,274,000
Current Liabilities	8,024,000	6,739,000	6,447,000	4,697,000	2,669,000	2,553,000	3,718,000	3,538,000
Long-Term Obligations	3,918,000	3,745,000	3,759,000	3,785,000	3,868,000	4,976,000	5,283,000	1,985,000
Total Liabilities	16,357,000	14,293,000	12,829,000	10,715,000	8,643,000	9,013,000	10,462,000	6,391,000
Stockholders' Equity	9,774,000	8,111,000	6,286,000	5,597,000	5,340,000	4,249,000	4,907,000	3,883,000
Shares Outstanding	320,600	315,018	279,198	275,145	269,604	267,579	267,387	266,232
Statistical Record								
Return on Assets %	7.55	9.23	7.01	6.43	4.72	N.M.	7.13	11.33
Return on Equity %	20.49	26.62	20.90	17.82	13.41	N.M.	20.80	29.48
EBITDA Margin %	16.54	18.33	13.98	14.76	12.67	10.49	17.67	19.43
Net Margin %	5.74	6.67	5.34	5.70	4.44	N.M.	6.71	8.33
Asset Turnover	1.32	1.38	1.31	1.13	1.06	0.84	1.06	1.36
Current Ratio	0.86	0.87	0.82	0.92	1.19	1.08	1.06	1.16
Debt to Equity	0.40	0.46	0.60	0.68	0.72	1.17	1.08	0.51
Price Range	104.40-47.31	56.02-38.50	46.46-26.33	30.97-17.72	19.02-13.86	28.07-16.56	29.97-18.05	25.35-16.08
P/E Ratio	18.19-8.24	9.23-6.34	11.67-6.62	9.71-5.56	8.02-5.85	...	8.76-5.28	6.69-4.24
Average Yield %	0.65	0.21	1.09	1.61	2.47	1.75	1.64	0.96

Address: 1185 Avenue of the Americas, New York, NY 10036
Telephone: 212-997-8500
Fax: 212-536-8390

Web Site: www.hess.com
Officers: John B. Hess - Chmn., C.E.O. J. Barclay Collins II - Exec. V.P., Gen. Couns.

Auditors: Ernst & Young LLP
Investor Contact: 212-536-8593
Transfer Agents: Bank of New York

HEWITT ASSOCIATES INC

Exchange	Symbol	Price	52Wk Range	Yield	P/E
NYS	HEW	$39.77 (3/31/2008)	40.12-28.94	N/A	N/A

*7 Year Price Score N/A   *NYSE Composite Index=100   *12 Month Price Score 122.51

Interim Earnings (Per Share)

Qtr.	Dec	Mar	Jun	Sep
2004-05	0.28	0.23	0.31	0.37
2005-06	0.29	0.29	(1.88)	0.22
2006-07	0.27	0.12	0.43	(2.44)
2007-08	0.59	...	...	...

Interim Dividends (Per Share)

No Dividends Paid

Valuation Analysis | **Institutional Holding**

Forecast P/E	N/A	No of Institutions
		137
Market Cap	$4.1 Billion	Shares
Book Value	935.3 Million	73,421,712
Price/Book	4.38	% Held
Price/Sales	1.34	66.20

Business Summary: Accounting & Management Consulting Services (MIC: 12.2 SIC: 8742 NAIC: 541612)

Hewitt Associates is a global provider of human resources outsourcing and consulting services in 33 countries. Co. assists clients generating value from their employees by addressing challenges presented by their people, workforce performance, and human resources operations. Co. operates three business segments: Benefits Outsourcing, Human Resource Business Process Outsourcing and Consulting, which help clients develop, implement, and deliver strategies and programs that ensure human resources business process design, administration, and technologies as well as manage human elements necessary to acquire, develop, motivate, and retain the talent required to meet business objectives.

Recent Developments: For the quarter ended Dec 31 2007, net income increased 112.7% to US$63.9 million from US$30.1 million in the year-earlier quarter. Revenues were US$819.0 million, up 9.8% from US$746.1 million the year before. Operating income was US$108.9 million versus US$46.5 million in the prior-year quarter, an increase of 134.1%. Indirect operating expenses increased 1.5% to US$710.1 million from US$699.5 million in the equivalent prior-year period.

Prospects: For the fiscal year ending Sep 30 2008, Co. continues to anticipate total net revenue growth in the mid-single digit range. In addition, Co. is projecting underlying operating income of $300.0 million to $315.0 million, while underlying earnings are forecasted to range from $1.70 to $1.80 per share. Co.'s expectations exclude the anticipated real estate charges of $35.0 million to $45.0 million and the expected one-time gain on the divestiture of its Cyborg business in the fiscal quarter ended Mar 31 2008. Separately, on Jan 16 2008, Co. announced plans to divest its Cyborg business to Vista Equity Partners, in-line with its strategy to restructure its human resource outsourcing services.

Financial Data
(US$ in Thousands)

	3 Mos	09/30/2007	09/30/2006	09/30/2005	09/30/2004	09/30/2003	09/30/2002	09/30/2001
Earnings Per Share	(1.30)	(1.62)	(1.08)	1.19	1.25	0.97	(0.27)	...
Cash Flow Per Share	4.13	4.03	3.54	3.11	2.50	2.94	2.94	...
Tang Book Value Per Share	4.19	4.88	4.24	2.26	3.87	2.32	1.64	2.93
Income Statement								
Total Revenue	818,992	2,990,326	2,857,161	2,898,450	2,262,227	2,031,293	1,750,079	1,502,093
EBITDA	149,897	55,475	96,220	385,961	341,369	292,411	333,843	292,844
Depn & Amortn	41,348	...	...	...	...	...	...	...
Income Before Taxes	113,403	(124,718)	(59,570)	220,515	207,859	160,641	223,426	183,182
Income Taxes	49,456	50,362	56,368	85,783	85,015	66,364	33,053	...
Net Income	63,947	(175,080)	(115,938)	134,732	122,844	94,277	190,373	183,182
Average Shares	109,494	107,866	107,642	113,105	97,950	96,832	85,301	...
Balance Sheet								
Current Assets	1,351,732	1,479,859	1,244,833	1,000,883	901,053	743,230	579,616	454,222
Total Assets	2,638,622	2,755,538	2,767,678	2,657,340	1,807,974	1,597,806	1,219,346	701,357
Current Liabilities	860,300	944,551	815,712	679,541	483,393	453,014	383,168	246,905
Long-Term Obligations	231,793	233,465	254,852	299,169	201,235	218,754	235,913	172,446
Total Liabilities	1,703,311	1,717,526	1,511,309	1,345,983	948,621	907,745	686,781	441,986
Stockholders' Equity	935,311	1,038,012	1,256,369	1,311,357	859,353	690,061	532,565	259,371
Shares Outstanding	102,997	107,126	110,822	108,178	98,579	90,217	98,457	88,507
Statistical Record								
Return on Assets %	N.M.	N.M.	N.M.	6.03	7.19	6.69	19.82	26.08
Return on Equity %	N.M.	N.M.	N.M.	12.41	15.81	15.42	48.08	72.97
EBITDA Margin %	18.30	1.86	3.37	13.32	15.09	14.40	19.08	19.50
Net Margin %	7.81	N.M.	N.M.	4.65	5.43	4.64	10.88	12.20
Asset Turnover	1.12	1.08	1.05	1.30	1.32	1.44	1.82	2.14
Current Ratio	1.57	1.57	1.53	1.47	1.86	1.64	1.51	1.84
Debt to Equity	0.25	0.22	0.20	0.23	0.23	0.32	0.44	0.66
Price Range	38.70-25.76	35.05-23.80	30.17-20.20	32.27-24.15	35.53-23.72	35.20-20.70	31.01-21.53	...
P/E Ratio	...	...	...	27.12-20.29	28.42-18.98	36.29-21.34	...	...

Address: 100 Half Day Road, Lincolnshire, IL 60069
Telephone: 847-295-5000
Fax: 847-295-7634

Web Site: www.hewitt.com
Officers: Dale L. Gifford - Chmn., C.E.O. Dan A. DeCanniere - C.F.O.

Auditors: Ernst & Young LLP
Investor Contact: 888-439-6397
Transfer Agents: EquiServe Trust Company, N.A., Providence, RI

HEWLETT-PACKARD CO

Exchange	Symbol	Price	52Wk Range	Yield	P/E
NYS	HPQ	$45.66 (3/31/2008)	53.41-40.31	0.70	15.64

*7 Year Price Score 138.27 *NYSE Composite Index=100 *12 Month Price Score 104.72

TRADING VOLUME (thousand shares)

Interim Earnings (Per Share)

Qtr.	Jan	Apr	Jul	Oct
2004-05	0.32	0.33	0.03	0.14
2005-06	0.42	0.66	0.48	0.61
2006-07	0.55	0.65	0.66	0.81
2007-08	0.80	...	...	...

Interim Dividends (Per Share)

Amt	Decl	Ex	Rec	Pay
0.08Q	5/18/2007	6/11/2007	6/13/2007	7/5/2007
0.08Q	7/20/2007	9/10/2007	9/12/2007	10/3/2007
0.08Q	11/19/2007	12/10/2007	12/12/2007	1/2/2008
0.08Q	1/18/2008	3/10/2008	3/12/2008	4/2/2008

Indicated Div: $0.32

Valuation Analysis

		Institutional Holding	
Forecast P/E	14.47	No of Institutions	
	(1/10/2007)	1006	
Market Cap	$114.8 Billion	Shares	
Book Value	37.9 Billion	2,071,214,464	
Price/Book	3.03	% Held	
Price/Sales	1.07	77.39	

Business Summary: IT & Technology (MIC: 10.2 SIC: 3571 NAIC: 334111)

Hewlett-Packard provides individual consumers, small- and medium-sized businesses and large enterprises with products and services that include: personal computing and other access devices; imaging and printing-related products and services; enterprise information technology infrastructure, including enterprise storage and server technology; and multi-vendor customer services, including technology support and maintenance, consulting and integration and outsourcing services. Co. operates through seven business segments. Enterprise Storage and Servers; HP Services; HP Software; the Personal Systems Group; the Imaging and Printing Group; HP Financial Services; and Corporate Investments.

Recent Developments: For the quarter ended Jan 31 2008, net income increased 37.9% to US$2.13 billion from US$1.55 billion in the year-earlier quarter. Revenues were US$28.47 billion, up 13.5% from US$25.08 billion the year before. Operating income was US$2.61 billion versus US$1.84 billion in the prior-year quarter, an increase of 41.8%. Direct operating expenses rose 12.3% to US$21.50 billion from US$19.14 billion in the comparable period the year before. Indirect operating expenses increased 6.1% to US$4.36 billion from US$4.10 billion in the equivalent prior-year period.

Prospects: Co. remains focused on expanding its operations via strategic acquisitions. For instance, in the fiscal first quarter ending Jan 2008, Co. completed three acquisitions for about $266.0 million. Subsequently, in Mar 2008, Co. completed the acquisition of Exstream Software, LLC, a privately-held enterprise software provider. Co. expects Exstream's technology, when combined with its document output management and printing market, should help businesses design, manage and publish structured and unstructured content via print and online. Meanwhile, for fiscal year ending Oct 2008, Co. is targeting diluted earnings per share of $3.26 to $3.30 on revenues of $113.50 billion to $114.00 billion.

Financial Data

(US$ in Thousands)	3 Mos	10/31/2007	10/31/2006	10/31/2005	10/31/2004	10/31/2003	10/31/2002	10/31/2001
Earnings Per Share	2.92	2.68	2.18	0.82	1.15	0.83	(0.36)	0.21
Cash Flow Per Share	5.01	3.66	4.08	2.79	1.68	1.99	2.18	1.32
Tang Book Value Per Share	4.82	4.91	6.57	6.04	6.06	6.08	5.36	6.81
Dividends Per Share	0.320	0.320	0.320	0.320	0.320	0.320	0.320	0.320
Dividend Payout %	10.96	11.94	14.68	39.02	27.83	38.55	...	152.38
Income Statement								
Total Revenue	28,467,000	104,286,000	91,658,000	86,696,000	79,905,000	73,061,000	56,588,000	45,226,000
EBITDA	3,434,000	11,860,000	9,495,000	5,865,000	6,599,000	5,451,000	1,050,000	2,071,000
Depn & Amortn	749,000	...	...	...	...	...	...	...
Income Before Taxes	2,685,000	9,177,000	7,191,000	3,543,000	4,196,000	2,888,000	(1,052,000)	702,000
Income Taxes	552,000	1,913,000	993,000	1,145,000	699,000	349,000	(129,000)	78,000
Net Income	2,133,000	7,264,000	6,198,000	2,398,000	3,497,000	2,539,000	(903,000)	408,000
Average Shares	2,655,000	2,716,000	2,852,000	2,909,000	3,055,000	3,063,000	2,499,000	1,974,000
Balance Sheet								
Current Assets	44,626,000	47,402,000	48,264,000	43,334,000	42,901,000	40,996,000	36,075,000	21,305,000
Total Assets	88,572,000	88,699,000	81,981,000	77,317,000	76,138,000	74,708,000	70,710,000	32,584,000
Current Liabilities	36,658,000	39,260,000	35,850,000	31,460,000	28,588,000	26,630,000	24,310,000	13,964,000
Long-Term Obligations	5,099,000	4,997,000	2,490,000	3,392,000	4,623,000	6,494,000	6,035,000	3,729,000
Total Liabilities	50,628,000	50,173,000	43,837,000	40,141,000	38,574,000	36,962,000	34,448,000	18,631,000
Stockholders' Equity	37,944,000	38,526,000	38,144,000	37,176,000	37,564,000	37,746,000	36,262,000	13,953,000
Shares Outstanding	2,514,000	2,580,000	2,732,000	2,837,000	2,911,000	3,043,000	3,043,733	1,939,000
Statistical Record								
Return on Assets %	9.24	8.51	7.78	3.13	4.62	3.49	N.M.	1.23
Return on Equity %	20.66	18.95	16.46	6.42	9.26	6.86	N.M.	2.90
EBITDA Margin %	12.06	11.37	10.36	6.77	8.26	7.46	1.86	4.58
Net Margin %	7.49	6.97	6.76	2.77	4.38	3.48	N.M.	0.90
Asset Turnover	1.27	1.22	1.15	1.13	1.06	1.00	1.10	1.36
Current Ratio	1.22	1.21	1.35	1.38	1.50	1.54	1.48	1.53
Debt to Equity	0.13	0.13	0.07	0.09	0.12	0.17	0.17	0.27
Price Range	53.41-38.67	52.87-38.22	39.87-28.04	29.20-18.76	26.12-16.50	23.52-14.85	23.53-11.16	47.44-14.50
P/E Ratio	18.29-13.24	19.73-14.26	18.29-12.86	35.61-22.88	22.71-14.35	28.34-17.89	...	225.89-69.05
Average Yield %	0.69	0.72	0.98	1.40	1.52	1.69	1.82	1.13

Address: 3000 Hanover Street, Palo Alto, CA 94304
Telephone: 650-857-1501

Web Site: www.hp.com
Officers: Mark Hurd - Pres., C.E.O. Robert P. Wayman - Exec. V.P., C.F.O.

Auditors: Ernst & Young LLP
Investor Contact: 866-438-4771
Transfer Agents: ComputerShare Investor Services, Chicago, IL

HIGHWOODS PROPERTIES, INC.

Exchange	Symbol	Price	52Wk Range	Yield	P/E
NYS	HIW	$31.07 (3/31/2008)	43.84-26.67	5.47	23.72

*7 Year Price Score 97.45   *NYSE Composite Index=100   *12 Month Price Score 92.59

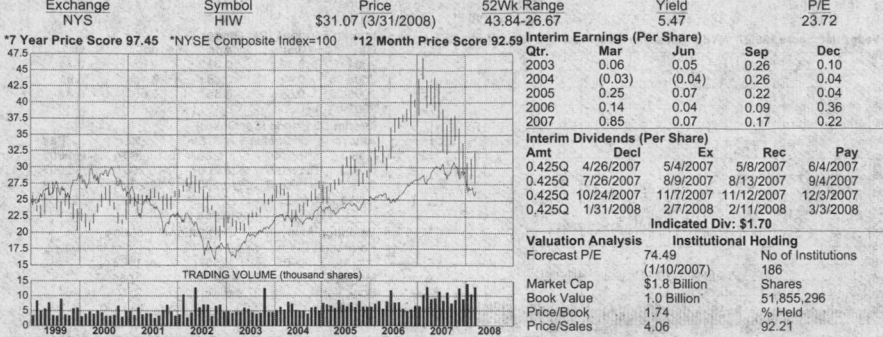

Interim Earnings (Per Share)

Qtr.	Mar	Jun	Sep	Dec
2003	0.06	0.05	0.26	0.10
2004	(0.03)	(0.04)	0.26	0.04
2005	0.25	0.07	0.22	0.04
2006	0.14	0.04	0.09	0.36
2007	0.85	0.07	0.17	0.22

Interim Dividends (Per Share)

Amt	Decl	Ex	Rec	Pay
0.425Q	4/26/2007	5/4/2007	5/8/2007	6/4/2007
0.425Q	7/26/2007	8/9/2007	8/13/2007	9/4/2007
0.425Q	10/24/2007	11/7/2007	11/12/2007	12/3/2007
0.425Q	1/31/2008	2/7/2008	2/11/2008	3/3/2008

Indicated Div: $1.70

Valuation Analysis   **Institutional Holding**

Forecast P/E	74.49	No of Institutions
	(1/10/2007)	186
Market Cap	$1.8 Billion	Shares
Book Value	1.0 Billion	51,855,296
Price/Book	1.74	% Held
Price/Sales	4.06	92.21

Business Summary: Property, Real Estate & Development (MIC: 8.3 SIC: 6798 NAIC: 525930)

Highwoods Properties is a self-administered and self-managed equity real estate investment trust that is engaged in the leasing, management, development, construction and other customer-related services for its properties and for third parties. Co. conducts substantially all of its activities through Highwoods Realty Limited Partnership. As of Dec 31 2007, Co. owned or had an interest in 378 in-service office, industrial and retail properties, encompassing about 33.9 million square feet and 527 rental residential units. Co.'s properties and development land are located in Florida, Georgia, Iowa, Kansas, Maryland, Mississippi, Missouri, North Carolina, South Carolina, Tennessee and Virginia.

Recent Developments: For the year ended Dec 31 2007, income from continuing operations increased 51.0% to US$55.4 million from US$36.7 million a year earlier. Net income increased 68.8% to US$90.7 million from US$53.7 million in the prior year. Revenues were US$437.1 million, up 6.8% from US$409.3 million the year before. Revenues from property income rose 7.1% to US$434.5 million from US$405.6 million in the corresponding earlier year.

Prospects: On Dec 17 2007, Co. announced that it has exited Columbia, SC through the sale of its remaining assets in that market for gross proceeds of $23.6 million. Over the next three years, Co. expects to sell $300.0 million to $600.0 million of its non-core properties. The proceeds from these asset sales will be used mainly to fund Co.'s development pipeline and/or make acquisitions. Meanwhile, assuming year end 2008 occupancy of 92.0% to 93.0% and same property net operating income growth of 1.5% to 2.5%, Co. is projecting 2008 funds from operations to be in the range of $2.56 to $2.72 per diluted share, excluding any gains or impairments associated with depreciable property dispositions.

Financial Data
(US$ in Thousands)

	12/31/2007	12/31/2006	12/31/2005	12/31/2004	12/31/2003	12/31/2002	12/31/2001	12/31/2000
Earnings Per Share	1.31	0.62	0.58	0.20	0.47	1.17	1.83	1.70
Cash Flow Per Share	2.86	2.67	2.87	3.23	2.88	3.79	4.57	4.32
Tang Book Value Per Share	15.51	16.19	17.29	18.41	20.82	22.10	23.22	23.98
Dividends Per Share	1.700	1.700	1.700	1.700	1.860	2.340	2.310	2.250
Dividend Payout %	129.77	274.19	293.10	850.00	395.74	200.00	126.23	132.35
Income Statement								
Property Income	434,469	413,159	404,848	457,746	422,062	454,220	506,850	543,383
Non-Property Income	2,590	3,639	5,853	6,978	...	...	33,765	23,048
Total Revenue	437,059	416,798	410,701	464,724	422,062	454,220	540,615	566,431
Interest Expense	100,337	100,766	107,708	120,026	114,271	110,527	108,501	112,827
Net Income	90,745	53,744	62,458	41,577	55,695	93,461	131,211	133,487
Average Shares	61,547	61,362	53,732	60,024	53,409	53,485	54,571	59,347
Balance Sheet								
Total Assets	2,926,955	2,844,853	2,908,978	3,239,658	3,326,809	3,395,369	3,648,286	3,701,602
Long-Term Obligations	1,677,058	1,500,659	1,505,770	1,637,883	1,558,758	1,528,720	1,719,230	1,587,019
Total Liabilities	1,834,824	1,657,396	1,633,225	1,757,818	1,670,530	1,649,334	1,839,465	1,696,843
Stockholders' Equity	1,022,033	1,107,731	1,181,619	1,368,110	1,491,029	1,557,472	1,605,640	1,791,545
Shares Outstanding	57,167	56,211	54,028	53,813	53,474	53,400	52,891	58,124
Statistical Record								
Return on Assets %	3.14	1.87	2.03	1.26	1.66	2.65	3.57	3.45
Return on Equity %	8.52	4.70	4.90	2.90	3.65	5.91	7.72	7.23
Net Margin %	20.76	12.89	15.21	8.95	13.20	20.58	24.27	23.57
Price Range	46.95-28.89	41.31-29.20	31.75-24.40	27.95-20.85	26.02-20.00	29.36-18.70	26.67-23.45	27.19-20.25
P/E Ratio	35.84-22.05	66.63-47.10	54.74-42.07	139.75-104.25	55.36-42.55	25.09-15.98	14.57-12.81	15.99-11.91
Average Yield %	4.47	4.88	6.03	6.84	8.18	9.42	9.18	9.66

Address: 3100 Smoketree Court, Suite 600, Raleigh, NC 27604
Telephone: 919-872-4924
Fax: 919-431-1439

Web Site: www.highwoods.com
Officers: O. Temple Sloan Jr. - Chmn. Edward J. Fritsch - Pres., C.E.O.

Auditors: Deloitte & Touche LLP
Transfer Agents: American Stock Transfer & Trust Co., Brooklyn, NY

HILB ROGAL & HOBBS CO

Exchange	Symbol	Price	52Wk Range	Yield	P/E	Div Acheiver
NYS	HRH	$31.47 (3/31/2008)	50.75-29.76	1.65	14.91	21 Years

*7 Year Price Score 92.03 ***NYSE Composite Index=100** ***12 Month Price Score 84.27**

Interim Earnings (Per Share)

Qtr.	Mar	Jun	Sep	Dec
2003	0.51	0.52	0.50	0.53
2004	0.67	0.56	0.58	0.42
2005	0.76	0.44	(0.19)	0.54
2006	0.71	0.57	0.53	0.58
2007	0.69	0.60	0.53	0.30

Interim Dividends (Per Share)

Amt	Decl	Ex	Rec	Pay
0.13Q	5/1/2007	6/13/2007	6/15/2007	6/29/2007
0.13Q	7/17/2007	9/12/2007	9/14/2007	9/28/2007
0.13Q	11/13/2007	12/12/2007	12/14/2007	12/31/2007
0.13Q	2/12/2008	3/12/2008	3/14/2008	3/31/2008

Indicated Div: $0.52

Valuation Analysis **Institutional Holding**

Forecast P/E	14.95	No of Institutions
	(1/10/2007)	141
Market Cap	$1.2 Billion	Shares
Book Value	683.2 Million	34,988,504
Price/Book	1.69	% Held
Price/Sales	1.45	95.85

Business Summary: Insurance (MIC: 8.2 SIC: 6411 NAIC: 524210)

Hilb Rogal & Hobbs is a holding company. Through its subsidiaries, Co. is engaged as an insurance and risk management intermediary between its clients and insurance companies that underwrite client risks. Co. assists clients in managing their risks in areas such as property and casualty, executive and employee benefits and other areas of specialized exposure. Co. also advises clients on risk management and employee benefits and provides claims management and loss control consulting services. Co.'s client base ranges from personal to national accounts and is primarily comprised of middle-market and major commercial and industrial accounts.

Recent Developments: For the year ended Dec 31 2007, net income decreased 10.2% to US$78.1 million from US$87.0 million in the prior year. Revenues were US$799.7 million, up 12.5% from US$710.8 million the year before.

Prospects: Co.'s recent results have been hampered by lower property and casualty premium rates, and one underperforming acquisition, Glencairn, which closed in Jan 2007, partly offset by growth in revenue from acquisitions. Nonetheless, Co. has taken cost actions to improve Glencairn's performance, and believes that Glencairn is on track to achieve accretive results. Meanwhile, Co. continues to execute on its acquisition program. For instance, on Feb 1 2008, Co. announced the acquisition of Talty Insurance Agency, Inc., which provides property and casualty and employee benefits coverage. Talty will move into Co.'s new Greenwood Village, CO location, which is slated to be completed on Apr 1 2008.

Financial Data
(US$ in Thousands)

	12/31/2007	12/31/2006	12/31/2005	12/31/2004	12/31/2003	12/31/2002	12/31/2001	12/31/2000
Earnings Per Share	2.11	2.39	1.55	2.23	2.06	2.01	1.07	0.77
Cash Flow Per Share	3.13	3.49	2.80	3.19	3.19	2.51	2.27	1.83
Dividends Per Share	0.510	0.475	0.450	0.407	0.367	0.357	0.347	0.338
Dividend Payout %	24.17	19.87	29.03	18.27	17.84	17.79	32.48	43.83
Income Statement								
Total Revenue	799,664	710,845	673,885	619,603	563,647	452,726	330,267	262,119
Income Before Taxes	130,990	141,412	92,907	137,977	124,901	103,257	56,730	39,737
Income Taxes	52,865	54,381	36,707	56,563	49,947	42,082	24,381	17,610
Net Income	78,125	87,031	56,200	81,414	74,954	63,119	32,349	21,802
Average Shares	37,060	36,369	36,314	36,402	26,204	29,010	27,411	29,183
Balance Sheet								
Total Assets	1,817,426	1,438,147	1,329,767	1,277,999	1,049,227	833,024	499,301	353,371
Total Liabilities	1,134,223	834,778	783,510	770,843	614,960	522,376	356,500	265,149
Stockholders' Equity	683,203	603,369	546,257	507,156	434,267	310,648	142,801	88,222
Shares Outstanding	36,749	36,312	35,955	35,886	35,446	33,484	28,310	26,560
Statistical Record								
Return on Assets %	4.80	6.29	4.31	6.98	7.96	9.78	7.59	6.48
Return on Equity %	12.14	15.14	10.67	17.25	20.12	28.72	28.00	27.28
Price Range	50.75-40.23	44.83-36.22	39.55-32.10	38.75-31.49	43.85-28.34	45.40-27.75	31.08-16.97	20.97-12.91
P/E Ratio	24.05-19.07	18.76-15.15	25.52-20.71	17.38-14.12	21.29-13.76	22.59-13.81	29.05-15.86	27.23-16.76
Average Yield %	1.15	1.18	1.26	1.16	1.12	0.93	1.56	1.98

Address: 4951 Lake Brook Drive, Suite 500, Glen Allen, VA 23060-9272 **Telephone:** 804-747-6500 **Fax:** 804-747-6046	**Web Site:** www.hrh.com **Officers:** Martin L. Vaughan III - Chmn., C.E.O. Michael Dinkins - Exec. V.P., C.F.O.	**Auditors:** Ernst & Young LLP **Investor Contact:** 804-747-6500 **Transfer Agents:** Mellon Investor Services, LLC, Ridgefield Park, NJ

HILL-ROM HOLDINGS, INC.

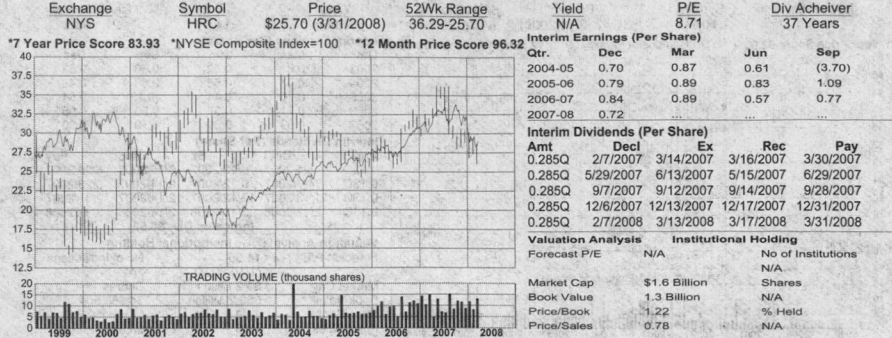

Exchange	Symbol	Price	52Wk Range	Yield	P/E	Div Acheiver
NYS	HRC	$25.70 (3/31/2008)	36.29-25.70	N/A	8.71	37 Years

*7 Year Price Score 83.93   *NYSE Composite Index=100   *12 Month Price Score 96.32

Interim Earnings (Per Share)

Qtr.	Dec	Mar	Jun	Sep
2004-05	0.70	0.87	0.61	(3.70)
2005-06	0.79	0.89	0.83	1.09
2006-07	0.84	0.89	0.57	0.77
2007-08	0.72	...	...	...

Interim Dividends (Per Share)

Amt	Decl	Ex	Rec	Pay
0.285Q	2/7/2007	3/14/2007	3/16/2007	3/30/2007
0.285Q	5/29/2007	6/13/2007	5/15/2007	6/29/2007
0.285Q	9/7/2007	9/12/2007	9/14/2007	9/28/2007
0.285Q	12/6/2007	12/13/2007	12/17/2007	12/31/2007
0.285Q	2/7/2008	3/13/2008	3/17/2008	3/31/2008

Valuation Analysis   **Institutional Holding**

Forecast P/E	N/A	No of Institutions
		N/A
Market Cap	$1.6 Billion	Shares
Book Value	1.3 Billion	N/A
Price/Book	1.22	% Held
Price/Sales	0.78	N/A

TRADING VOLUME (thousand shares)

Business Summary: Hospitals & Health Care (MIC: 9.3 SIC: 5047 NAIC: 423450)

Hillenbrand Industries is a holding company for its two operating businesses serving the health care and funeral services industries in the U.S. and abroad. Hill-Rom is manufacturer and provider of medical technologies and related services for the health care industry, including patient support systems, non-invasive therapeutic products for a variety of acute and chronic medical conditions, medical equipment rentals and health information technology applications. Batesville Casket serves the funeral services industry and is a manufacturer of caskets and cremation-related products.

Recent Developments: For the quarter ended Dec 31 2007, net income decreased 13.7% to US$44.8 million from US$51.9 million in the year-earlier quarter. Revenues were US$504.3 million, up 4.4% from US$483.2 million the year before. Operating income was US$62.9 million versus US$79.1 million in the prior-year quarter, a decrease of 20.5%. Direct operating expenses rose 6.1% to US$285.4 million from US$269.0 million in the comparable period the year before. Indirect operating expenses increased 15.5% to US$156.0 million from US$135.1 million in the equivalent prior-year period.

Prospects: For the fiscal year ending Sep 2008, Co. is targeting consolidated revenue of $2.10 billion to $2.16 billion. In addition, Co. is projecting total revenue at its Hill-Rom subsidiary in the range of $1.43 billion to $1.48 billion, while total revenue at its Batesville Casket Co. subsidiary is estimated to range from $668.0 million to $686.0 million. In addition, Co. is forecasting total net income in the range of $189.0 million to $206.0 million, while earnings are anticipated to range from $3.00 to $3.28 per share. Meanwhile, Co. is encouraged by the progress towards the planned separation of its medical technology and funeral services businesses scheduled for the end of March 2008.

Financial Data
(US$ in Thousands)

	3 Mos	09/30/2007	09/30/2006	09/30/2005	09/30/2004	09/30/2003	09/30/2002	12/01/2001
Earnings Per Share	2.95	3.07	3.59	(1.52)	1.75	2.22	(0.16)	2.71
Cash Flow Per Share	4.89	4.62	0.47	3.88	5.58	6.06	6.31	7.10
Tang Book Value Per Share	11.68	11.19	9.12	6.00	8.81	15.79	12.72	13.24
Dividends Per Share	1.140	1.138	1.130	1.120	1.080	1.000	0.977	0.840
Dividend Payout %	38.64	37.05	31.48	...	61.71	45.05	...	31.00
Income Statement								
Total Revenue	504,300	2,023,700	1,962,900	1,938,100	1,829,000	2,042,000	1,757,000	2,107,000
EBITDA	104,000	421,000	469,100	(97,500)	387,000	374,000	43,000	246,000
Depn & Amortn	29,000	...	...	...	...	...	...	...
Income Before Taxes	69,400	291,500	339,000	(115,900)	308,000	282,000	(35,000)	223,000
Income Taxes	24,600	100,900	117,500	(19,600)	120,000	100,000	(25,000)	53,000
Net Income	44,800	190,600	221,200	(94,100)	110,000	138,000	(10,000)	170,000
Average Shares	62,403	62,115	61,576	61,774	62,725	62,184	62,921	62,814
Balance Sheet								
Current Assets	941,700	894,400	763,900	890,500	739,000	708,000	958,000	868,000
Total Assets	2,165,000	2,117,000	1,952,200	2,229,200	1,992,000	5,412,000	5,442,000	5,049,000
Current Liabilities	331,900	339,600	325,200	669,000	313,000	367,000	551,000	320,000
Long-Term Obligations	351,500	348,600	347,000	350,700	360,000	155,000	322,000	305,000
Total Liabilities	858,400	839,200	820,500	1,265,200	896,000	4,253,000	4,443,000	4,023,000
Stockholders' Equity	1,306,600	1,277,800	1,131,700	964,000	1,096,000	1,159,000	999,000	1,026,000
Shares Outstanding	62,230	61,991	61,415	61,263	61,953	61,814	61,702	62,466
Statistical Record								
Return on Assets %	8.81	9.37	10.58	N.M.	2.96	2.54	N.M.	3.53
Return on Equity %	14.82	15.82	21.11	N.M.	9.73	12.79	N.M.	18.36
EBITDA Margin %	20.62	20.80	23.90	N.M.	21.16	18.32	2.45	11.68
Net Margin %	8.88	9.42	11.27	N.M.	6.01	6.76	N.M.	8.07
Asset Turnover	0.98	0.99	0.94	0.92	0.49	0.38	0.40	0.44
Current Ratio	2.84	2.63	2.35	1.33	2.36	1.93	1.74	2.71
Debt to Equity	0.27	0.27	0.31	0.36	0.33	0.13	0.32	0.30
Price Range	36.29-28.01	36.29-29.34	31.18-24.19	30.59-25.07	37.75-26.75	30.99-25.22	35.48-26.21	31.24-23.59
P/E Ratio	12.30-9.50	11.82-9.56	8.68-6.74	...	21.57-15.29	13.96-11.36	...	11.53-8.70
Average Yield %	3.58	3.51	4.15	3.96	3.34	3.63	3.15	3.00

Address: 1069 State Route 46 East,	Web Site: www.hillenbrand.com	Auditors: PricewaterhouseCoopers LLP
Batesville, IN 47006-8835	Officers: Ray J. Hillenbrand - Chmn. Rolf A. Classon	Investor Contact: 812-934-8400
Telephone: 812-934-7000	- Vice-Chmn., Interim C.E.O.	Transfer Agents: Computershare
Fax: 812-934-7364		Investor Services, Chicago, IL

HNI CORP

Exchange	Symbol	Price	52Wk Range	Yield	P/E	Div Acheiver
NYS	HNI	$26.89 (3/31/2008)	47.81-26.89	3.20	10.46	19 Years

*7 Year Price Score 79.57   *NYSE Composite Index=100   *12 Month Price Score 86.39

Interim Earnings (Per Share)

Qtr.	Mar	Jun	Sep	Dec
2003	0.27	0.35	0.59	0.47
2004	0.38	0.44	0.65	0.50
2005	0.47	0.63	0.73	0.67
2006	0.55	0.56	0.72	0.63
2007	0.43	0.57	0.76	0.82

Interim Dividends (Per Share)

Amt	Decl	Ex	Rec	Pay
0.195Q	5/8/2007	5/16/2007	5/18/2007	6/1/2007
0.195Q	8/7/2007	8/15/2007	8/17/2007	8/31/2007
0.195Q	11/9/2007	11/15/2007	11/19/2007	11/30/2007
0.215Q	2/13/2008	2/20/2008	2/22/2008	2/29/2008

Indicated Div: $0.86

Valuation Analysis   **Institutional Holding**

Forecast P/E	14.34 (1/10/2007)	No of Institutions	135
Market Cap	$1.2 Billion	Shares	24,352,400
Book Value	458.9 Million	% Held	
Price/Book	2.63		50.82
Price/Sales	0.47		

Business Summary: Furniture and Fixtures (MIC: 11.10 SIC: 2522 NAIC: 337214)

HNI is engaged in providing office furniture and hearth products. Co. designs, manufactures, and markets a range of office furniture in four basic categories: storage; seating; office systems; and desks and related products. Co.'s office furniture product offering is sold to dealers, wholesalers, retail superstores, end-user customers, and federal, state, and local governments. Co.'s office furniture products are sold under its HON®, Allsteel®, Maxon®, Gunlocke®, Pauli®, Whitehall®, basyx™, and Lamex® brands, as well as private labels. Co.'s hearth products includes gas, electric, and wood burning fireplaces, inserts, stoves, facings, and accessories.

Recent Developments: For the year ended Dec 29 2007, income from continuing operations decreased 7.6% to US$119.9 million from US$129.7 million a year earlier. Net income decreased 2.4% to US$120.4 million from US$123.4 million in the prior year. Revenues were US$2.57 billion, down 4.1% from US$2.68 billion the year before. Operating income was US$193.7 million versus US$206.4 million in the prior year, a decrease of 6.2%. Direct operating expenses declined 5.0% to US$1.66 billion from US$1.75 billion in the comparable period the year before. Indirect operating expenses decreased 1.2% to US$712.1 million from US$720.5 million in the equivalent prior-year period.

Prospects: Co. expects its office furniture business to continue to slow during the fiscal year ending Jan 2008. In response, Co. hopes to increase its investment in growth opportunities and position for the market recovery by improving its selling capabilities and launching new products. Co. will also work to offset the market softness and increased investment by focusing on its structural cost and streamlining its businesses. Meanwhile, Co. expects the housing market to decline in fiscal 2008 and pressure both revenue and profit in its hearth products segment; but plans to mitigate these conditions by streamlining its operations and positioning itself for long-term growth once conditions stabilize.

Financial Data

(US$ in Thousands)	12/29/2007	12/30/2006	12/31/2005	01/01/2005	01/03/2004	12/28/2002	12/29/2001	12/30/2000
Earnings Per Share	2.57	2.45	2.50	1.97	1.68	1.55	1.26	1.77
Cash Flow Per Share	6.25	3.20	3.69	3.41	2.39	3.45	3.87	3.42
Tang Book Value Per Share	4.51	5.10	6.78	8.04	8.89	7.79	6.45	5.97
Dividends Per Share	0.780	0.720	0.620	0.560	0.520	0.500	0.480	0.440
Dividend Payout %	30.35	29.39	24.80	28.43	30.95	32.26	38.10	24.86
Income Statement								
Total Revenue	2,570,472	2,679,803	2,450,572	2,093,447	1,755,728	1,692,622	1,792,438	2,046,286
EBITDA	261,831	275,919	281,060	253,636	227,358	215,762	217,123	267,759
Income Before Taxes	176,726	193,232	214,709	178,869	150,931	140,554	116,261	165,964
Income Taxes	57,141	63,670	77,295	65,287	52,826	49,194	41,854	59,747
Net Income	120,378	123,375	137,420	113,582	98,105	91,360	74,407	106,217
Average Shares	46,925	50,374	55,033	57,577	58,545	59,040	59,087	60,140
Balance Sheet								
Current Assets	489,072	501,174	486,598	374,579	462,122	405,054	319,657	330,141
Total Assets	1,206,976	1,226,359	1,140,271	1,021,657	1,021,826	1,020,552	961,891	1,022,470
Current Liabilities	384,461	358,542	358,174	266,250	245,816	298,680	230,443	264,868
Long-Term Obligations	281,091	285,974	103,869	3,645	4,126	9,837	80,830	128,285
Total Liabilities	748,068	730,440	546,327	352,494	311,937	373,659	369,211	449,128
Stockholders' Equity	458,908	495,919	593,944	669,163	709,889	646,893	592,680	573,342
Shares Outstanding	44,834	47,905	51,848	55,303	58,238	58,373	58,672	59,796
Statistical Record								
Return on Assets %	9.92	10.45	12.75	11.15	9.45	9.24	7.52	11.04
Return on Equity %	25.28	22.70	21.82	16.52	14.23	14.78	12.80	19.82
EBITDA Margin %	10.19	10.30	11.47	12.12	12.95	12.75	12.11	13.09
Net Margin %	4.68	4.60	5.61	5.43	5.59	5.40	4.15	5.19
Asset Turnover	2.12	2.27	2.27	2.05	1.69	1.71	1.81	2.13
Current Ratio	1.27	1.41	1.36	1.41	1.88	1.36	1.39	1.25
Debt to Equity	0.61	0.58	0.17	0.01	0.01	0.02	0.14	0.22
Price Range	51.61-34.87	61.55-38.81	61.53-38.89	45.71-35.40	43.87-24.67	30.64-23.37	28.82-19.96	27.81-16.00
P/E Ratio	20.08-13.57	25.12-15.84	24.61-15.56	23.20-17.97	26.11-14.68	19.77-15.08	22.87-15.84	15.71-9.04
Average Yield %	1.85	1.47	1.22	1.24	1.39	1.57	1.83	1.95	1.87

Address: 408 East Second Street, Muscatine, IA 52761-0071
Telephone: 563-264-7400
Fax: 563-264-7217

Web Site: www.hnicorp.com
Officers: Stan A. Askren - Chmn., C.E.O., Pres.
David C. Burdakin - Exec. V.P.

Auditors: PricewaterhouseCoopers LLP
Investor Contact: 563-272-7400
Transfer Agents: Computershare Investor Services, LLC, Chicago, IL

HOLLY CORP.

Exchange	Symbol	Price	52Wk Range	Yield	P/E	Div Acheiver
NYS	HOC	$43.41 (3/31/2008)	79.87-39.00	1.38	7.26	14 Years

*7 Year Price Score 203.98 *NYSE Composite Index=100 *12 Month Price Score 88.85

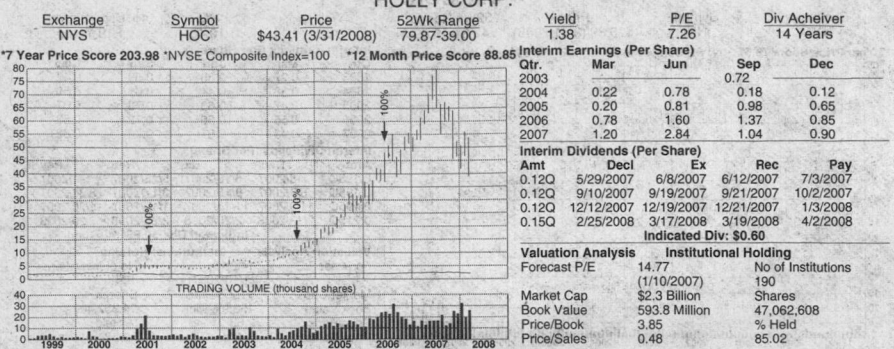

Interim Earnings (Per Share)

Qtr.	Mar	Jun	Sep	Dec
2003			0.72	
2004	0.22	0.78	0.18	0.12
2005	0.20	0.81	0.98	0.65
2006	0.78	1.60	1.37	0.85
2007	1.20	2.84	1.04	0.90

Interim Dividends (Per Share)

Amt	Decl	Ex	Rec	Pay
0.12Q	5/29/2007	6/8/2007	6/12/2007	7/3/2007
0.12Q	9/10/2007	9/19/2007	9/21/2007	10/2/2007
0.12Q	12/12/2007	12/19/2007	12/21/2007	1/3/2008
0.15Q	2/25/2008	3/17/2008	3/19/2008	4/2/2008
			Indicated Div: $0.60	

Valuation Analysis | **Institutional Holding**

Forecast P/E	14.77
	(1/10/2007)
Market Cap	$2.3 Billion
Book Value	593.8 Million
Price/Book	3.85
Price/Sales	0.48

No of Institutions	190
Shares	47,062,608
% Held	85.02

Business Summary: Oil and Gas (MIC: 14.2 SIC: 2911 NAIC: 324110)

Holly is an independent petroleum refiner producing light products such as gasoline, diesel fuel and jet fuel. Co.'s operations are organized into one business division, the refining business, which includes the Navajo Refinery in Artesia, NM; the Woods Cross Refinery, located just north of Salt Lake City, UT; and Holly Asphalt Company, which manufactures and markets asphalt products from various terminals in Arizona, New Mexico, Texas and northern Mexico. As of Dec 31 2007, Co. owned 900 miles of crude gathering pipelines, 67 crude oil trucks and 67 trailers as well as over 600,000 barrels of related tankage, and a 45.0% interest in Holly Energy Partners, L.P.

Recent Developments: For the year ended Dec 31 2007, net income increased 25.3% to US$334.1 million from US$266.6 million in the prior year. Revenues were US$4.79 billion, up 19.1% from US$4.02 billion the year before. Operating income was US$466.3 million versus US$361.9 million in the prior year, an increase of 28.9%. Direct operating expenses rose 19.5% to US$4.00 billion from US$3.35 billion in the comparable period the year before. Indirect operating expenses increased 3.2% to US$321.9 million from US$311.9 million in the equivalent prior-year period.

Prospects: On Feb 26 2008, Co. announced an agreement for the sale of certain pipeline and tankage assets to Holly Energy Partners, L.P. (HEP) for $180.0 million. Specifically, this agreement provides for consideration to Co. of $171.0 million in cash and HEP common units valued at about $9.0 million. Meanwhile, Co. is making substantial progress on both its Woods Cross and Navajo Refinery expansion and crude flexibility capital projects. These projects, expected to be completed at the end of the third quarter of 2008 and during 2009, respectively, remain on budget. Furthermore, Co.'s Salt Lake City to Las Vegas joint venture pipeline, expected to be operational in mid 2009, also remains on budget.

Financial Data

(US$ in Thousands)	12/31/2007	12/31/2006	12/31/2005	12/31/2004	12/31/2003	12/31/2002	07/31/2002	07/31/2001
Earnings Per Share	5.98	4.58	2.65	1.30	0.72	0.09	0.50	1.19
Cash Flow Per Share	7.71	4.30	4.07	2.63	1.14	(0.10)	0.68	1.74
Tang Book Value Per Share	11.29	8.43	6.42	5.43	4.33	3.68	3.67	3.26
Dividends Per Share	0.460	0.290	0.190	0.145	0.110	0.108	0.102	0.092
Dividend Payout %	7.69	6.33	7.17	11.11	15.28	126.47	20.40	7.76
Income Statement								
Total Revenue	4,791,742	4,023,217	3,212,745	2,246,373	1,403,244	448,637	888,906	1,142,130
EBITDA	528,897	415,090	310,430	178,102	112,312	20,842	80,020	151,689
Income Before Taxes	499,444	383,501	268,413	138,469	74,359	8,517	50,896	121,895
Income Taxes	165,316	136,603	101,424	54,590	28,306	3,114	18,867	48,445
Net Income	334,128	266,566	167,658	83,879	46,053	5,403	32,029	73,450
Average Shares	55,850	58,210	63,244	64,340	64,064	63,608	63,884	61,548
Balance Sheet								
Current Assets	1,034,621	806,852	775,929	572,906	336,406	254,347	278,844	284,130
Total Assets	1,663,945	1,237,869	1,142,900	982,713	708,892	515,793	502,930	490,429
Current Liabilities	818,080	559,393	577,367	424,264	364,667	241,902	218,971	226,399
Long-Term Obligations	...	...	...	25,000	8,571	17,143	25,714	34,286
Total Liabilities	893,725	607,370	608,523	485,247	425,808	287,299	273,750	288,695
Stockholders' Equity	593,794	466,094	377,351	339,916	268,609	228,494	228,556	201,734
Shares Outstanding	52,616	55,316	58,752	62,589	62,056	62,071	62,245	61,922
Statistical Record								
Return on Assets %	23.03	22.39	15.78	9.89	7.52	0.76	6.45	15.39
Return on Equity %	63.05	63.21	46.75	27.49	18.53	1.77	14.89	44.34
EBITDA Margin %	11.04	10.32	9.66	7.93	8.00	4.65	9.00	13.28
Net Margin %	6.97	6.63	5.22	3.73	3.28	1.20	3.60	6.43
Asset Turnover	3.30	3.38	3.02	2.65	2.29	0.63	1.79	2.39
Current Ratio	1.26	1.44	1.34	1.35	0.92	1.05	1.27	1.25
Debt to Equity	...	...	...	0.07	0.03	0.08	0.11	0.17
Price Range	79.87-45.65	55.68-28.38	32.35-12.69	14.22-6.80	7.50-5.00	5.75-3.75	5.29-3.67	6.24-1.50
P/E Ratio	13.36-7.63	12.16-6.20	12.21-4.79	10.93-5.23	10.41-6.94	63.83-41.67	10.57-7.33	5.25-1.26
Average Yield %	0.75	0.68	0.83	1.48	1.72	2.36	2.27	3.29

Address: 100 Crescent Court, Suite 1600, Dallas, TX 75201-6915 **Telephone:** 214-871-3555 **Fax:** 214-871-3566	**Web Site:** www.hollycorp.com **Officers:** C. Lamar Norsworthy III - Chmn., C.E.O. Matthew P. Clifton - Pres.	**Auditors:** ERNST & YOUNG LLP **Transfer Agents:** American Stock Transfer & Trust Company, New York, NY

HOME DEPOT INC

Exchange	Symbol	Price	52Wk Range	Yield	P/E	Div Achiever
NYS	HD	$27.97 (3/31/2008)	40.94-24.71	3.22	11.80	20 Years

*7 Year Price Score 71.13   *NYSE Composite Index=100   *12 Month Price Score 90.52

Interim Earnings (Per Share)

Qtr.	Apr	Jul	Oct	Jan
2003-04	0.39	0.56	0.50	0.42
2004-05	0.49	0.70	0.60	0.48
2005-06	0.57	0.82	0.72	0.61
2006-07	0.70	0.90	0.73	0.47
2007-08	0.53	0.81	0.60	0.43

Interim Dividends (Per Share)

Amt	Decl	Ex	Rec	Pay
0.225Q	5/23/2007	6/5/2007	6/7/2007	6/21/2007
0.225Q	8/16/2007	8/28/2007	8/30/2007	9/13/2007
0.225Q	11/15/2007	11/27/2007	11/29/2007	12/13/2007
0.225Q	2/28/2008	3/11/2008	3/13/2008	3/27/2008

Indicated Div: $0.90 (Div. Reinv. Plan)

Valuation Analysis

		Institutional Holding	
Forecast P/E	10.20	No of Institutions	
	(1/10/2007)	1193	
Market Cap	$47.0 Billion	Shares	
Book Value	17.7 Billion	1,348,485,376	
Price/Book	2.67	% Held	
Price/Sales	0.61	68.47	

TRADING VOLUME (thousand shares)

Business Summary: Retail - Hardware (MIC: 5.6 SIC: 5211 NAIC: 444110)

The Home Depot is a home improvement retailer that provides an array of building materials, home improvement and lawn and garden products and related services. Co. also operates EXPO Design Center (EXPO) stores, which provides products and services related to design and renovation projects. As of Feb 3 2008, Co. operated a total of 2,234 stores, which included 1,950 The Home Depot stores, 34 EXPO stores, five Yardbirds stores and two The Home Depot Design Center stores in the U.S., which include the territories of Puerto Rico, the Virgin Islands and Guam; as well as 165 The Home Depot stores in Canada, 66 The Home Depot stores in Mexico and 12 The Home Depot stores in China.

Recent Developments: For the year ended Feb 3 2008, income from continuing operations decreased 20.1% to US$4.21 billion from US$5.27 billion a year earlier. Net income decreased 23.7% to US$4.39 billion from US$5.76 billion in the prior year. Revenues were US$77.35 billion, down 2.1% from US$79.02 billion the year before. Operating income was US$7.24 billion versus US$8.87 billion in the prior year, a decrease of 18.3%. Direct operating expenses declined 2.1% to US$51.35 billion from US$52.48 billion in the comparable period the year before. Indirect operating expenses increased 6.1% to US$18.76 billion from US$17.68 billion in the equivalent prior-year period.

Prospects: For the full year of 2008, Co. continues to believe that the residential construction and home improvement market will remain soft. In this respect, for the fiscal year ending Feb 1 2009, Co. is projecting total sales to decline in the range of 4.0% to 5.0%, while operating margin is anticipated to decrease by 170 to 210 basis points. In addition, Co. is forecasting negative comparable store sales in the mid to high single digit range, while gross margin expansion is estimated to be flat to slightly positive. Similarly, Co. foresees earnings per share from continuing operation to be lower by 19.0% to 24.0%. Lastly, Co. expects to open 55 new store openings with five store relocations.

Financial Data

(US$ in Thousands)	02/03/2008	01/28/2007	01/29/2006	01/30/2005	02/01/2004	02/02/2003	02/03/2002	01/28/2001
Earnings Per Share	2.37	2.79	2.72	2.26	1.88	1.56	1.29	1.10
Cash Flow Per Share	3.05	3.74	3.04	3.14	2.87	2.06	2.51	1.21
Tang Book Value Per Share	9.77	9.50	11.12	10.42	9.56	8.39	7.53	6.32
Dividends Per Share	0.900	0.675	0.400	0.325	0.260	0.210	0.170	0.160
Dividend Payout %	37.97	24.19	14.71	14.38	13.83	13.46	13.18	14.55
Income Statement								
Total Revenue	77,349,000	90,837,000	81,511,000	73,094,000	64,816,000	58,247,000	53,553,000	45,738,000
EBITDA	9,148,000	11,559,000	10,942,000	9,245,000	7,922,000	6,733,000	5,696,000	4,792,000
Income Before Taxes	6,620,000	9,308,000	9,282,000	7,912,000	6,843,000	5,872,000	4,957,000	4,217,000
Income Taxes	2,410,000	3,547,000	3,444,000	2,911,000	2,539,000	2,208,000	1,913,000	1,636,000
Net Income	4,395,000	5,761,000	5,838,000	5,001,000	4,304,000	3,664,000	3,044,000	2,581,000
Average Shares	1,856,000	2,062,000	2,147,000	2,216,000	2,289,000	2,344,000	2,353,000	2,352,000
Balance Sheet								
Current Assets	14,674,000	18,000,000	15,346,000	14,190,000	13,328,000	11,917,000	10,361,000	7,777,000
Total Assets	44,324,000	52,263,000	44,482,000	38,907,000	34,437,000	30,011,000	26,394,000	21,385,000
Current Liabilities	12,706,000	12,931,000	12,901,000	10,529,000	9,554,000	8,035,000	6,501,000	4,385,000
Long-Term Obligations	11,383,000	11,643,000	2,672,000	2,148,000	856,000	1,321,000	1,250,000	1,545,000
Total Liabilities	26,610,000	27,233,000	17,573,000	14,749,000	12,030,000	10,209,000	8,312,000	6,381,000
Stockholders' Equity	17,714,000	25,030,000	26,909,000	24,158,000	22,407,000	19,802,000	18,082,000	15,004,000
Shares Outstanding	1,690,000	1,970,000	2,124,000	2,185,000	2,257,000	2,293,000	2,345,888	2,323,747
Statistical Record								
Return on Assets %	8.95	11.94	14.04	13.67	13.39	13.03	12.54	13.46
Return on Equity %	20.23	22.24	22.93	21.54	20.45	19.40	18.10	18.93
EBITDA Margin %	11.83	12.72	13.42	12.65	12.22	11.56	10.64	10.48
Net Margin %	5.68	6.34	7.16	6.84	6.64	6.29	5.68	5.64
Asset Turnover	1.58	1.88	1.96	2.00	2.02	2.07	2.21	2.38
Current Ratio	1.15	1.39	1.19	1.35	1.40	1.48	1.59	1.77
Debt to Equity	0.64	0.47	0.10	0.09	0.04	0.07	0.07	0.10
Price Range	41.76-24.71	43.81-33.13	43.95-35.09	43.79-32.88	37.52-20.70	52.07-20.53	53.45-32.80	68.50-34.88
P/E Ratio	17.62-10.43	15.70-11.87	16.16-12.90	19.38-14.55	19.96-11.01	33.38-13.16	41.43-25.43	62.27-31.70
Average Yield %	2.57	1.77	1.00	0.86	0.83	0.60	0.37	0.31

Address: 2455 Paces Ferry Road N.W., Atlanta, GA 30339-4024
Telephone: 770-433-8211
Fax: 770-431-2707

Web Site: www.homedepot.com
Officers: Robert L. Nardelli - Chmn. Pres., C.E.O. Carol B. Tome - Exec. V.P., C.F.O.

Auditors: KPMG LLP
Transfer Agents: EquiServe Trust Company, N.A., Providence, RI

HOME PROPERTIES INC

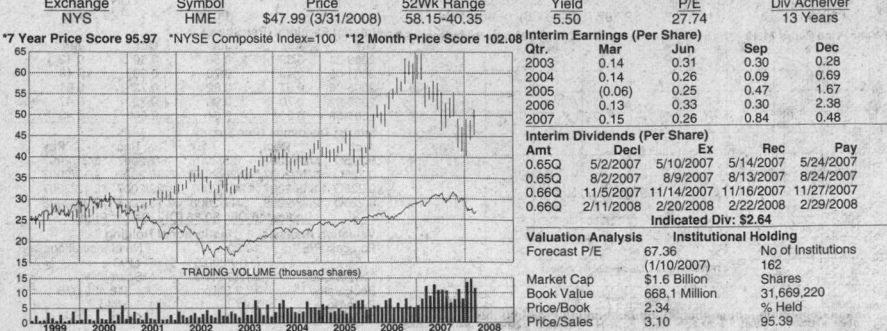

Exchange	Symbol	Price	52Wk Range	Yield	P/E	Div Acheiver
NYS	HME	$47.99 (3/31/2008)	58.15-40.35	5.50	27.74	13 Years

*7 Year Price Score 95.97 *NYSE Composite Index=100 *12 Month Price Score 102.08

Interim Earnings (Per Share)

Qtr.	Mar	Jun	Sep	Dec
2003	0.14	0.31	0.30	0.28
2004	0.14	0.26	0.09	0.69
2005	(0.06)	0.25	0.47	1.67
2006	0.13	0.33	0.30	2.38
2007	0.15	0.26	0.84	0.48

Interim Dividends (Per Share)

Amt	Decl	Ex	Rec	Pay
0.65Q	5/2/2007	5/10/2007	5/14/2007	5/24/2007
0.65Q	8/2/2007	8/9/2007	8/13/2007	8/24/2007
0.66Q	11/5/2007	11/14/2007	11/16/2007	11/27/2007
0.66Q	2/11/2008	2/20/2008	2/22/2008	2/29/2008

Indicated Div: $2.64

Valuation Analysis   **Institutional Holding**

Forecast P/E	67.36 (1/10/2007)	No of Institutions 162
Market Cap	$1.6 Billion	Shares 31,669,220
Book Value	668.1 Million	% Held 95.39
Price/Book	2.34	
Price/Sales	3.10	

Business Summary: Property, Real Estate & Development (MIC: 8.3 SIC: 6798 NAIC: 525930)

Home Properties is a self-administered and self-managed real estate investment trust that owns, operates, acquires, develops and rehabilitates apartment communities. Co.'s properties are regionally focused in select Northeast, Mid-Atlantic, and Southeast Florida markets of the U.S. Co. conducts its business through Home Properties, L.P. in which Co. held a 70.8% partnership interest as of Dec 31 2007. Co., as of Dec 31 2007, operated 125 communities with 38,646 apartment units. Of these, 37,496 units in 123 communities are owned outright, 868 units in one community are managed and partially owned by Co. as general partner, and 282 units in one community are managed for other owners.

Recent Developments: For the year ended Dec 31 2007, income from continuing operations increased 14.7% to US$30.1 million from US$26.3 million a year earlier. Net income decreased 44.3% to US$61.5 million from US$110.5 million in the prior year. Revenues were US$505.2 million, up 14.8% from US$440.2 million the year before. Revenues from property income rose 15.4% to US$502.1 million from US$435.0 million in the corresponding earlier year.

Prospects: Co. continues to benefit from gains related to the disposition of properties that have reached their potential. For instance, on Feb 1 2008, Co. closed the sale of five apartment communities in Long Island, NY, which should result in a gain before the allocation of minority interest of about $16.6 million in the first quarter of 2008. For full year 2008, Co.'s core properties revenue growth guidance is 3.8%, with rental rates projected to grow 3.1%, and economic occupancies expected to grow 0.2%. Also, Co.'s property other income is expected to grow, led by higher utility recovery income. At the same time, Co. is expecting funds from operations of $3.31 to $3.47 per share for the year.

Financial Data
(US$ in Thousands)

	12/31/2007	12/31/2006	12/31/2005	12/31/2004	12/31/2003	12/31/2002	12/31/2001	12/31/2000
Earnings Per Share	1.73	3.15	2.33	1.18	1.03	0.96	2.11	1.41
Cash Flow Per Share	4.91	4.98	4.16	4.82	4.99	5.51	6.71	6.15
Tang Book Value Per Share	20.49	21.01	19.14	19.48	20.53	20.67	21.10	19.50
Dividends Per Share	2.610	2.570	2.530	2.490	2.450	2.410	2.310	2.160
Dividend Payout %	150.87	81.59	108.58	211.02	237.86	251.04	109.48	153.19
Income Statement								
Property Income	502,101	448,763	441,197	455,023	429,618	392,620	362,233	310,249
Non-Property Income	3,087	5,229	2,604	3,307	4,886	2,942	5,290	8,799
Total Revenue	505,188	453,992	443,801	458,330	434,504	395,562	367,523	319,048
Interest Expense	119,383	106,773	97,898	90,506	85,110	77,314	66,446	56,792
Net Income	61,544	110,485	81,512	47,022	41,798	44,939	64,506	41,456
Average Shares	33,794	33,337	32,328	33,314	29,575	26,335	22,227	20,755
Balance Sheet								
Total Assets	3,216,423	3,240,418	2,977,870	2,816,796	2,513,317	2,456,266	2,063,789	1,871,888
Long-Term Obligations	1,989,289	1,924,313	1,850,483	1,702,722	1,380,696	1,335,807	992,858	832,783
Total Liabilities	2,269,301	2,202,259	1,997,789	1,785,599	1,441,510	1,396,963	1,052,606	882,083
Stockholders' Equity	668,061	755,617	656,812	720,422	741,263	726,242	620,596	569,528
Shares Outstanding	32,600	33,103	31,184	32,625	31,966	27,027	24,010	21,565
Statistical Record								
Return on Assets %	1.91	3.55	2.81	1.76	1.68	1.99	3.28	2.45
Return on Equity %	8.65	15.64	11.84	6.42	5.70	6.67	10.84	7.75
Net Margin %	12.18	24.34	18.37	10.26	9.62	11.36	17.55	12.99
Price Range	64.65-41.53	63.52-41.70	46.27-36.05	43.92-36.85	40.92-31.19	37.94-28.90	33.14-26.13	31.56-25.56
P/E Ratio	37.37-24.01	20.17-13.24	19.86-15.47	37.22-31.23	39.73-30.28	39.52-30.10	15.71-12.38	22.38-18.13
Average Yield %	4.91	4.76	6.17	6.23	6.76	7.16	7.81	7.68

Address: 850 Clinton Square, Rochester, NY 14604
Telephone: 585-546-4900
Fax: 585-546-5433

Web Site: www.homeproperties.com
Officers: Norman P. Leenhouts - Co-Chmn. Nelson B. Leenhouts - Co-Chmn.

Auditors: PricewaterhouseCoopers LLP
Investor Contact: 716-546-4900
Transfer Agents: Mellon Investor Services LLC, Ridgefield Park, NJ

HONEYWELL INTERNATIONAL, INC.

Exchange	Symbol	Price	52Wk Range	Yield	P/E
NYS	HON	$56.42 (3/31/2008)	61.77-46.15	1.95	17.85

*7 Year Price Score 119.79 *NYSE Composite Index=100 *12 Month Price Score 108.00

Interim Earnings (Per Share)

Qtr.	Mar	Jun	Sep	Dec
2003	0.30	0.37	0.40	0.47
2004	0.34	0.42	0.43	0.30
2005	0.42	0.36	0.55	0.61
2006	0.52	0.63	0.66	0.71
2007	0.66	0.78	0.81	0.91

Interim Dividends (Per Share)

Amt	Decl	Ex	Rec	Pay
0.25Q	4/23/2007	5/16/2007	5/18/2007	6/8/2007
0.25Q	7/27/2007	8/16/2007	8/20/2007	9/10/2007
0.25Q	10/26/2007	11/16/2007	11/20/2007	12/10/2007
0.275Q	2/14/2008	2/25/2008	2/27/2008	3/10/2008

Indicated Div: $1.10

Valuation Analysis

		Institutional Holding	
Forecast P/E	13.61	No of Institutions	
	(1/10/2007)	760	
Market Cap	$42.1 Billion	Shares	
Book Value	9.2 Billion	615,305,536	
Price/Book	4.57	% Held	
Price/Sales	1.22	76.92	

Business Summary: Automotive (MIC: 15.1 SIC: 3714 NAIC: 336399)

Honeywell International is a technology and manufacturing company, serving customers worldwide with aerospace products and services, control, sensing and security technologies for buildings, homes and industry, turbochargers, automotive products, specialty chemicals, electronic and improved materials, and process technology for refining and petrochemicals. Co. manages its business operations through four businesses that are reported as operating segments: Aerospace, Automation and Control Solutions, Specialty Materials and Transportation Systems. Co. is engaged in manufacturing, sales, service and research and development mainly in the U.S., Europe, Canada, Asia and Latin America.

Recent Developments: For the year ended Dec 31 2007, income from continuing operations increased 17.6% to US$2.44 billion from US$2.08 billion a year earlier. Net income increased 17.3% to US$2.44 billion from US$2.08 billion in the prior year. Revenues were US$34.59 billion, up 10.3% from US$31.37 billion the year before. Direct operating expenses rose 9.1% to US$26.30 billion from US$24.10 billion in the comparable period the year before. Indirect operating expenses increased 8.4% to US$4.57 billion from US$4.21 billion in the equivalent prior-year period.

Prospects: Despite outlook for softer global economic conditions in 2008, Co. expects sales in the range of $36.10 billion to 36.70 billion, an increase of 5.0% to 7.0%, with earnings per share in the range of $3.65 to $3.80, an increase of 16.0% to 21.0% versus 2007. Looking ahead to 2008, Co. is focusing on several areas, including attaining sales growth and manufacturing capability through global expansion, especially focused on emerging regions in China, India and the Middle East. Meanwhile, Co. expects to launch commercial diesel and passenger vehicle gasoline engines programs in Europe beginning in 2009, which is estimated to add about $95.0 million in annual revenues at full production.

Financial Data

(US$ In Thousands)	12/31/2007	12/31/2006	12/31/2005	12/31/2004	12/31/2003	12/31/2002	12/31/2001	12/31/2000
Earnings Per Share	3.16	2.52	1.94	1.49	1.54	(0.27)	(0.12)	2.05
Cash Flow Per Share	5.12	3.91	2.88	2.62	2.55	2.90	2.46	2.48
Tang Book Value Per Share	N.M.	0.09	1.95	4.70	4.46	2.52	3.45	4.72
Dividends Per Share	1.000	0.907	0.825	0.750	0.750	0.750	0.750	0.750
Dividend Payout %	31.65	36.01	42.53	50.34	48.70	...	...	36.59
Income Statement								
Total Revenue	34,589,000	31,367,000	27,653,000	25,601,000	23,103,000	22,274,000	23,652,000	25,023,000
EBITDA	4,533,000	3,872,000	3,376,000	2,661,000	2,570,000	70,000	902,000	3,874,000
Income Before Taxes	3,321,000	2,798,000	2,323,000	1,680,000	1,640,000	(945,000)	(422,000)	2,398,000
Income Taxes	877,000	720,000	742,000	399,000	296,000	(725,000)	(323,000)	739,000
Net Income	2,444,000	2,083,000	1,655,000	1,281,000	1,324,000	(220,000)	(99,000)	1,659,000
Average Shares	774,227	826,278	852,334	862,333	862,095	870,292	812,273	809,460
Balance Sheet								
Current Assets	13,685,000	12,304,000	11,962,000	12,820,000	11,523,000	10,195,000	9,894,000	10,661,000
Total Assets	33,805,000	30,941,000	32,294,000	31,062,000	29,344,000	27,559,000	24,226,000	25,175,000
Current Liabilities	11,941,000	10,135,000	10,430,000	8,739,000	6,783,000	6,574,000	6,220,000	7,214,000
Long-Term Obligations	5,419,000	3,909,000	3,082,000	4,069,000	4,961,000	4,719,000	4,731,000	3,941,000
Total Liabilities	24,583,000	21,221,000	21,040,000	19,810,000	18,615,000	18,634,000	15,056,000	15,468,000
Stockholders' Equity	9,222,000	9,720,000	11,254,000	11,252,000	10,729,000	8,925,000	9,170,000	9,707,000
Shares Outstanding	746,553	800,591	829,483	850,013	862,330	854,493	814,966	807,291
Statistical Record								
Return on Assets %	7.55	6.59	5.22	4.23	4.65	N.M.	N.M.	6.79
Return on Equity %	25.81	19.86	14.71	11.62	13.47	N.M.	N.M.	18.08
EBITDA Margin %	13.11	12.34	12.21	10.39	11.12	0.31	3.81	15.48
Net Margin %	7.07	6.64	5.98	5.00	5.73	N.M.	N.M.	6.63
Asset Turnover	1.07	0.99	0.87	0.85	0.81	0.86	0.96	1.02
Current Ratio	1.15	1.21	1.15	1.47	1.70	1.55	1.59	1.48
Debt to Equity	0.59	0.40	0.27	0.36	0.46	0.53	0.52	0.41
Price Range	61.77-44.13	45.46-35.84	39.30-33.21	38.11-31.75	33.43-20.73	40.76-19.20	53.50-23.59	59.88-33.00
P/E Ratio	19.55-13.97	18.04-14.22	20.26-17.12	25.58-21.31	21.71-13.46	...	...	29.21-16.10
Average Yield %	1.84	2.23	2.23	2.13	2.81	2.38	1.91	1.63

Address: 101 Columbia Road, Morris Township, NJ 07962	**Web Site:** www.honeywell.com	**Auditors:** PricewaterhouseCoopers LLP
Telephone: 973-455-2000	**Officers:** David M. Cote - Chmn., C.E.O. Adriane M. Brown - Pres., C.E.O., Transportation System	**Investor Contact:** 973-455-4732
Fax: 973-455-4807		**Transfer Agents:** American Stock Transfer & Trust Co., New York, NY

HORACE MANN EDUCATORS CORP.

Exchange	Symbol	Price	52Wk Range	Yield	P/E
NYS	HMN	$17.48 (3/31/2008)	22.59-16.22	2.40	9.40

*7 Year Price Score 87.23   *NYSE Composite Index=100   ***12 Month Price Score 96.32**

Interim Earnings (Per Share)

Qtr.	Mar	Jun	Sep	Dec
2003	0.19	0.05	(0.34)	0.54
2004	0.51	0.44	(0.30)	0.60
2005	0.57	0.72	0.02	0.35
2006	0.50	0.61	0.43	0.64
2007	0.52	0.52	0.41	0.41

Interim Dividends (Per Share)

Amt	Decl	Ex	Rec	Pay
0.105Q	5/23/2007	6/13/2007	6/15/2007	6/29/2007
0.105Q	9/11/2007	9/19/2007	9/21/2007	9/28/2007
0.105Q	12/11/2007	12/19/2007	12/21/2007	12/31/2007
0.105Q	3/5/2008	3/13/2008	3/17/2008	3/31/2008

Indicated Div: $0.42

Valuation Analysis   **Institutional Holding**

Forecast P/E	N/A	No of Institutions
		136
Market Cap	$738.4 Million	Shares
Book Value	693.3 Million	42,756,624
Price/Book	1.07	% Held
Price/Sales	0.83	99.14

Business Summary: Insurance (MIC: 8.2 SIC: 6331 NAIC: 524126)

Horace Mann Educators is an insurance holding company. Through its subsidiaries, Co. markets and underwrites personal lines of property and casualty and life insurance and retirement annuities primarily to educators and other employees of public schools and their families in the U.S. Co.'s primary insurance subsidiaries are Horace Mann Insurance Company, Teachers Insurance Company and Horace Mann Life Insurance Company, each of which is an Illinois corporation; Horace Mann Property & Casualty Insurance Company, a California corporation; and Horace Mann Lloyds, an insurance company in Texas. At Dec 31 2007, Co. had total assets of $6.30 billion and investment portfolio totaling $4.20 billion.

Recent Developments: For the year ended Dec 31 2007, net income decreased 16.1% to US$82.8 million from US$98.7 million in the prior year. Revenues were US$887.0 million, up 0.1% from US$885.8 million the year before. Net premiums earned were US$654.3 million versus US$653.9 million in the prior year, an increase of 0.1%. Net investment income rose 7.1% to US$223.8 million from US$209.0 million a year ago.

Prospects: For full-year 2008, Co. is targeting net income before realized investment gains and losses of between $1.70 and $1.90 per share. In detail, Co.'s projection anticipates modest increase in property and casualty combined ratios, pressured by recent, industry-wide claims frequency trends, a moderate decline in annuity and life profit margins, following a year of strong, double-digit earnings growth in 2007 and in anticipation of continued volatility in the financial markets. Meanwhile, Co.'s bottom-line results are being negatively affected by higher property and casualty average loss costs per policy that exceeded the growth in average premium per policy for the present accident period.

Financial Data
(US$ in Thousands)

	12/31/2007	12/31/2006	12/31/2005	12/31/2004	12/31/2003	12/31/2002	12/31/2001	12/31/2000
Earnings Per Share	1.86	2.19	1.67	1.25	0.44	0.28	0.63	0.51
Cash Flow Per Share	4.67	4.32	3.85	3.90	2.75	4.04	3.66	3.04
Tang Book Value Per Share	15.16	13.90	12.03	11.84	10.67	10.53	9.17	8.29
Dividends Per Share	0.420	0.420	0.420	0.420	0.420	0.420	0.420	0.420
Dividend Payout %	22.58	19.18	25.15	33.60	95.45	150.00	66.67	82.35
Income Statement								
Premium Income	654,257	653,922	664,939	674,704	643,536	625,233	615,242	598,714
Total Revenue	887,005	873,807	869,412	878,349	853,748	771,874	804,490	781,204
Benefits & Claims	408,490	388,735	442,717	484,410	518,978	450,866	475,583	466,048
Income Before Taxes	117,071	140,293	94,044	69,757	19,179	7,665	28,342	9,721
Income Taxes	34,283	41,585	16,771	13,444	204	(3,668)	2,755	(11,120)
Net Income	82,788	98,708	77,273	56,313	18,975	11,333	25,587	20,841
Average Shares	44,610	45,773	47,884	47,346	42,904	41,199	40,877	40,966
Balance Sheet								
Total Assets	6,259,313	6,329,687	5,840,607	5,371,902	4,972,988	4,512,289	4,489,026	4,420,580
Total Liabilities	5,566,035	5,672,606	5,260,016	4,795,696	4,442,513	3,983,447	4,029,836	3,992,587
Stockholders' Equity	693,278	657,081	580,591	576,206	530,475	528,842	459,190	427,993
Shares Outstanding	42,240	43,091	42,972	42,846	42,721	42,691	40,735	40,517
Statistical Record								
Return on Assets %	1.32	1.62	1.38	1.09	0.40	0.25	0.57	0.48
Return on Equity %	12.26	15.95	13.36	10.15	3.58	2.29	5.77	5.02
Loss Ratio %	62.44	59.45	66.58	71.80	80.64	72.11	77.30	77.84
Net Margin %	9.33	11.30	8.89	6.41	2.22	1.47	3.18	2.67
Price Range	22.59-16.35	20.79-16.22	20.60-16.01	19.28-13.97	16.75-12.50	23.95-13.70	22.09-15.30	21.88-12.44
P/E Ratio	12.15-8.79	9.49-7.41	12.34-9.59	15.42-11.18	38.07-28.41	85.54-48.93	35.06-24.29	42.89-24.39
Average Yield %	2.06	2.27	2.25	2.51	2.88	2.28	2.23	2.61

Address: 1 Horace Mann Plaza, Springfield, IL 62715-0001 **Telephone:** 217-789-2500 **Fax:** 217-788-5137	**Web Site:** www.horacemann.com **Officers:** Joseph J. Melone - Chmn. Louis G. Lower II - Pres., C.E.O.	**Auditors:** KPMG LLP **Transfer Agents:** American Stock Transfer & Trust Co. New York, NY

HORMEL FOODS CORP.

Exchange	Symbol	Price	52Wk Range	Yield	P/E	Div Achiever
NYS	HRL	$41.66 (3/31/2008)	42.20-31.76	1.78	18.27	41 Years

*7 Year Price Score 101.73 *NYSE Composite Index=100 *12 Month Price Score 115.63

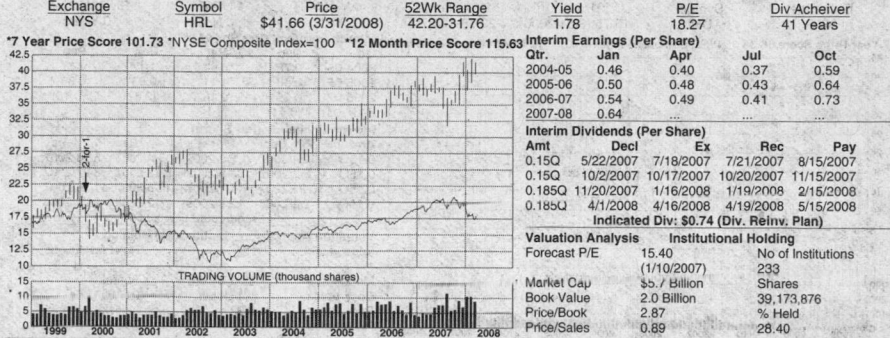

Interim Earnings (Per Share)

Qtr.	Jan	Apr	Jul	Oct
2004-05	0.46	0.40	0.37	0.59
2005-06	0.50	0.48	0.43	0.64
2006-07	0.54	0.49	0.41	0.73
2007-08	0.64	...	...	...

Interim Dividends (Per Share)

Amt	Decl	Ex	Rec	Pay
0.15Q	5/22/2007	7/18/2007	7/21/2007	8/15/2007
0.15Q	10/2/2007	10/17/2007	10/20/2007	11/15/2007
0.185Q	11/20/2007	1/16/2008	1/19/2008	2/15/2008
0.185Q	4/1/2008	4/16/2008	4/19/2008	5/15/2008

Indicated Div: $0.74 (Div. Reinv. Plan)

Valuation Analysis **Institutional Holding**

Forecast P/E	15.40	No of Institutions
	(1/10/2007)	233
Market Cap	$5.7 Billion	Shares
Book Value	2.0 Billion	39,173,876
Price/Book	2.87	% Held
Price/Sales	0.89	28.40

TRADING VOLUME (thousand shares)

Business Summary: Food (MIC: 4.1 SIC: 2011 NAIC: 311611)

Hormel Foods is engaged in the production of a range of meat and food products and the marketing of those products throughout the U.S. and internationally. Although pork and turkey remain the major raw materials for its products, Co. has emphasized for several years the manufacture and distribution of branded, consumer packaged items rather than the commodity fresh meat business. As of Oct 28 2007, Co. operated in five segments: grocery products, refrigerated foods, Jennie-O Turkey store, Specialty foods and all other. Co.'s meat products are sold fresh, frozen, cured, smoked, cooked, and canned.

Recent Developments: For the quarter ended Jan 27 2008, net income increased 17.1% to US$88.2 million from US$75.3 million in the year-earlier quarter. Revenues were US$1.62 billion, up 7.8% from US$1.50 billion the year before. Operating income was US$151.0 million versus US$119.8 million in the prior-year quarter, an increase of 26.0%. Direct operating expenses rose 6.5% to US$1.22 billion from US$1.14 billion in the comparable period the year before. Indirect operating expenses increased 4.8% to US$251.1 million from US$239.7 million in the equivalent prior-year period.

Prospects: Co.'s near-term outlook appears to be mixed. Specifically, Co. foresees that higher grain input and fuel costs for the remainder of fiscal year ending Oct 31 2008 will affect its Jennie-O Turkey Store and portions of its Refrigerated Foods business. Nevertheless, Co. believes that the anticipated lower hog input costs, price increases, and manufacturing efficiencies will help to offset these higher costs. Thus, Co. is targeting earnings for fiscal 2008 to range from $2.30 to $2.40 per share. Lastly, Co. estimates its fiscal 2008 fixed asset expenditures to range from $145.0 million to $150.0 million as several expansion projects are planned to address the demand for its key products.

Financial Data
(US$ in Thousands)

	3 Mos	10/28/2007	10/29/2006	10/30/2005	10/30/2004	10/25/2003	10/26/2002	10/27/2001
Earnings Per Share	2.28	2.17	2.05	1.82	1.65	1.33	1.35	1.30
Cash Flow Per Share	3.19	2.46	2.38	3.11	2.09	1.83	2.36	2.32
Tang Book Value Per Share	8.94	8.30	8.04	6.77	6.43	5.36	5.41	4.45
Dividends Per Share	0.635	0.600	0.560	0.520	0.450	0.420	0.390	0.370
Dividend Payout %	27.90	27.65	27.32	28.57	27.27	31.58	28.89	28.46
Income Statement								
Total Revenue	1,621,165	6,193,032	5,745,481	5,413,997	4,779,875	4,200,328	3,910,314	4,124,112
EBITDA	179,091	636,402	589,021	557,234	486,452	413,861	409,631	418,807
Depn & Amortn	33,060	...	...	...	...	...	...	...
Income Before Taxes	139,311	469,837	430,543	404,886	364,565	289,331	293,970	285,014
Income Taxes	51,130	167,945	144,404	151,427	132,902	103,552	104,648	102,573
Net Income	88,181	301,892	286,139	253,459	231,663	185,779	189,322	182,441
Average Shares	137,666	139,151	139,561	139,577	140,179	139,710	140,292	140,125
Balance Sheet								
Current Assets	1,279,357	1,231,725	1,141,671	1,041,084	1,029,403	823,974	962,170	883,281
Total Assets	3,431,258	3,393,650	3,060,306	2,822,406	2,533,968	2,393,121	2,220,196	2,162,698
Current Liabilities	582,578	664,777	585,014	583,172	461,366	441,969	410,111	420,203
Long-Term Obligations	350,000	350,005	350,054	350,430	361,510	395,273	409,648	462,407
Total Liabilities	1,462,407	1,508,867	1,257,394	1,247,830	1,134,720	1,140,386	1,104,941	1,166,817
Stockholders' Equity	1,968,851	1,884,783	1,802,912	1,574,576	1,399,248	1,252,735	1,115,255	995,881
Shares Outstanding	135,677	135,677	137,339	137,843	137,875	138,596	138,411	138,663
Statistical Record								
Return on Assets %	9.69	9.38	9.75	9.46	9.25	8.08	8.66	9.62
Return on Equity %	16.39	16.42	16.99	17.05	17.19	15.73	17.98	19.57
EBITDA Margin %	11.05	10.28	10.25	10.29	10.18	9.85	10.48	10.16
Net Margin %	5.44	4.87	4.98	4.68	4.85	4.42	4.84	4.42
Asset Turnover	1.94	1.92	1.96	2.02	1.91	1.83	1.79	2.17
Current Ratio	2.20	1.85	1.95	1.79	2.22	1.86	2.35	2.10
Debt to Equity	0.18	0.19	0.19	0.22	0.26	0.32	0.37	0.46
Price Range	41.70-31.76	39.49-31.76	38.02-31.70	33.08-27.58	31.63-23.80	24.98-20.18	28.03-20.50	26.39-16.75
P/E Ratio	18.29-13.93	18.20-14.64	18.55-15.46	18.18-15.15	19.17-14.42	18.78-15.17	20.76-15.19	20.30-12.88
Average Yield %	1.71	1.62	1.61	1.69	1.60	1.85	1.58	1.73

Address: 1 Hormel Place, Austin, MN 55912-3680
Telephone: 507-437-5611
Fax: 507-437-5489

Web Site: www.hormel.com
Officers: Joel W. Johnson - Chmn., C.E.O. Jeffrey M. Ettinger - Pres., C.O.O.

Auditors: Ernst & Young LLP
Investor Contact: 507-437-5007
Transfer Agents: Wells Fargo Bank Minnesota, N.A., South St. Paul, MN

HORTON (D.R.) INC.

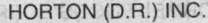

Exchange	Symbol	Price	52Wk Range	Yield	P/E	Div Acheiver
NYS	DHI	$15.75 (3/31/2008)	23.75-10.27	3.81	N/A	10 Years

*7 Year Price Score 66.38   *NYSE Composite Index=100   *12 Month Price Score 98.70

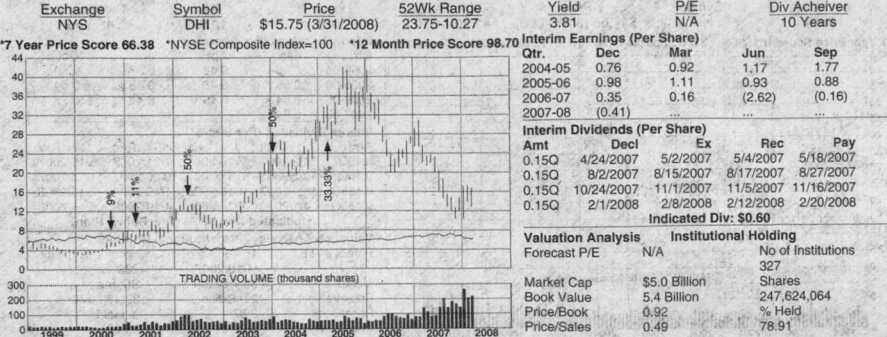

Interim Earnings (Per Share)

Qtr.	Dec	Mar	Jun	Sep
2004-05	0.76	0.92	1.17	1.77
2005-06	0.98	1.11	0.93	0.88
2006-07	0.35	0.16	(2.62)	(0.16)
2007-08	(0.41)	...	...	...

Interim Dividends (Per Share)

Amt	Decl	Ex	Rec	Pay
0.15Q	4/24/2007	5/2/2007	5/4/2007	5/18/2007
0.15Q	8/2/2007	8/15/2007	8/17/2007	8/27/2007
0.15Q	10/24/2007	11/1/2007	11/5/2007	11/16/2007
0.15Q	2/1/2008	2/8/2008	2/12/2008	2/20/2008

Indicated Div: $0.60

Valuation Analysis   **Institutional Holding**

Forecast P/E	N/A	No of Institutions
		327
Market Cap	$5.0 Billion	Shares
Book Value	5.4 Billion	247,624,064
Price/Book	0.92	% Held
Price/Sales	0.49	78.91

Business Summary: Building & General Construction (MIC: 3.2 SIC: 1531 NAIC: 236117)

D.R. Horton is a national homebuilder. Co. constructs and sells single-family homes, designed principally for first-time and move-up homebuyers, through its operating divisions in 27 states and 83 metropolitan markets of the United States, primarily under the name of D.R. Horton, America's Builder. Co.'s homebuilding operations generate most of their revenues from the sale of completed homes, with a lesser amount from the sale of land and lots. Co. also builds attached homes, such as town homes, duplexes, triplexes and condominiums. Co.'s financial services segment generates revenues from originating and selling mortgages and collecting fees for title insurance agency and closing services.

Recent Developments: For the quarter ended Dec 31 2007, net loss amounted to US$128.8 million versus net income of US$109.7 million in the year-earlier quarter. Revenues were US$1.74 billion, down 39.2% from US$2.87 billion the year before. Direct operating expenses declined 27.6% to US$1.71 billion from US$2.36 billion in the comparable period the year before. Indirect operating expenses decreased 28.2% to US$239.5 million from US$333.6 million in the equivalent prior-year period.

Prospects: Looking ahead, Co. believes that the housing market conditions will be challenging and may deteriorate further as inventory levels of both new and existing homes remains high while pricing continues to be competitive. Notably, the lending requirement continues to be more restrictive, while buyers continued to approach the home buying decision cautiously. Thus, Co. will continue to focus on reducing inventory and managing costs while adjusting its inventories to the ongoing housing demand. Meanwhile, Co. will closely monitor its products, pricing and other operational strategies in its California region, and will modify product offerings and pricing to improve its sales in this region.

Financial Data
(US$ in Thousands)

	3 Mos	09/30/2007	09/30/2006	09/30/2005	09/30/2004	09/30/2003	09/30/2002	09/30/2001
Earnings Per Share	(3.03)	(2.27)	3.90	4.62	3.09	2.06	1.44	1.12
Cash Flow Per Share	5.14	4.32	(3.81)	(1.99)	(1.36)	1.43	(0.34)	(0.24)
Tang Book Value Per Share	16.89	17.44	18.75	15.28	11.02	8.08	5.78	3.81
Dividends Per Share	0.600	0.600	0.440	0.308	0.215	0.135	0.097	0.060
Dividend Payout %	...	...	11.28	6.66	6.96	6.57	6.72	5.40
Income Statement								
Total Revenue	1,742,600	11,296,500	15,051,300	13,863,700	10,840,800	8,728,100	6,738,831	4,455,514
EBITDA	(186,400)	(856,600)	2,085,900	2,452,500	1,644,300	1,061,461	693,657	449,147
Depn & Amortn	16,500	...	...	...	...	...	...	...
Income Before Taxes	(202,900)	(951,200)	1,987,100	2,378,600	1,582,900	1,008,162	647,507	407,797
Income Taxes	(74,100)	(238,700)	753,800	908,100	607,800	382,207	242,815	152,924
Net Income	(128,800)	(712,500)	1,233,300	1,470,500	975,100	625,955	404,692	257,009
Average Shares	315,000	314,100	316,200	318,100	315,210	305,250	282,569	230,282
Balance Sheet								
Current Assets	8,715,400	9,613,100	12,179,000	9,636,600	7,085,400	5,665,200	4,447,413	3,043,657
Total Assets	10,401,000	11,556,300	14,820,700	12,514,800	8,985,200	7,279,377	6,017,527	3,652,190
Current Liabilities	358,600	954,000	2,174,000	2,070,200	946,600	397,978	391,355	182,641
Long-Term Obligations	3,724,200	3,989,000	4,886,900	3,660,100	3,006,500	2,565,145	2,486,976	1,701,689
Total Liabilities	4,948,800	5,901,000	8,262,700	6,951,200	4,858,100	4,112,216	3,726,719	2,393,079
Stockholders' Equity	5,414,100	5,586,900	6,452,900	5,360,400	3,960,700	3,031,260	2,269,863	1,250,247
Shares Outstanding	314,976	314,914	313,246	312,938	306,861	303,466	292,277	292,277
Statistical Record								
Return on Assets %	N.M.	N.M.	9.02	13.68	11.96	9.42	8.37	8.10
Return on Equity %	N.M.	N.M.	20.88	31.55	27.82	23.62	22.99	23.16
EBITDA Margin %	N.M.	N.M.	13.86	17.69	15.17	12.16	10.29	10.08
Net Margin %	N.M.	N.M.	8.19	10.61	8.99	7.17	6.01	5.77
Asset Turnover	0.85	0.86	1.10	1.29	1.33	1.31	1.39	1.40
Current Ratio	24.30	10.08	5.60	4.65	7.49	14.23	11.36	16.66
Debt to Equity	0.69	0.71	0.76	0.68	0.76	0.85	1.10	1.36
Price Range	30.86-10.41	30.86-12.81	41.39-20.00	42.11-20.71	26.79-16.35	16.43-8.03	14.37-6.79	9.93-4.82
P/E Ratio	...	...	10.61-5.13	9.11-4.48	8.67-5.29	7.98-3.90	9.98-4.72	8.86-4.31
Average Yield %	3.11	2.69	1.47	0.97	0.98	1.16	0.88	0.85

Address: 301 Commerce Street, Suite 500, Fort Worth, TX 76102 **Telephone:** 817-390-8200	**Web Site:** www.drhorton.com **Officers:** Donald R. Horton - Chmn. Donald J. Tomnitz - Vice-Chmn., Pres., C.E.O.	**Auditors:** Ernst & Young LLP **Investor Contact:** 817-390-8200 **Transfer Agents:** American Stock Transfer & Trust Co., New York, NY

HOSPIRA INC

Exchange	Symbol	Price	52Wk Range	Yield	P/E
NYS	HSP	$42.77 (3/31/2008)	44.51-37.61	N/A	50.32

*7 Year Price Score N/A   *NYSE Composite Index=100 *12 Month Price Score 111.10

Interim Earnings (Per Share)

Qtr.	Mar	Jun	Sep	Dec
2004	0.42	0.80	0.39	0.31
2005	0.49	0.44	0.37	0.16
2006	0.49	0.34	0.35	0.30
2007	(0.19)	0.20	0.37	0.47

Interim Dividends (Per Share)

No Dividends Paid

Valuation Analysis		Institutional Holding	
Forecast P/E	N/A	No of Institutions	390
Market Cap	$6.8 Billion	Shares	111,514,680
Book Value	1.7 Billion	% Held	71.50
Price/Book	3.89		
Price/Sales	1.97		

TRADING VOLUME (thousand shares)

Business Summary: Pharmaceuticals (MIC: 9.1 SIC: 2834 NAIC: 325412)

Hospira is a global specialty pharmaceutical and medication delivery company that is focused on products that improve the productivity, safety and efficacy of patient care in the acute care setting. Co. is engaged in the development, manufacture and marketing of specialty injectable pharmaceuticals and medication delivery systems that deliver drugs and intravenous fluids. Co. provides contract manufacturing services to pharmaceutical and biotechnology companies for formulation development, filling and finishing of injectable pharmaceuticals. Co.'s products are used by hospitals and alternate site providers, such as clinics, home healthcare providers and long-term care facilities.

Recent Developments: For the year ended Dec 31 2007, net income decreased 42.5% to US$136.8 million from US$237.7 million in the prior year. Revenues were US$3.44 billion, up 27.8% from US$2.69 billion the year before. Operating income was US$302.6 million versus US$339.6 million in the prior year, a decrease of 10.9%. Direct operating expenses rose 29.3% to US$2.26 billion from US$1.75 billion in the comparable period the year before. Indirect operating expenses increased 45.3% to US$871.3 million from US$599.7 million in the equivalent prior-year period.

Prospects: Co.'s outlook appears encouraging. For example, on Dec 19 2007, Co. announced that the European Commission has authorized it to market Retacrit™, for the treatment of anemia associated with chronic renal failure and chemotherapy. Subsequently, Co. began the launch of Retacrit™ in the European Union, beginning with Germany in early 2008. Meanwhile, on Feb 27 2008, Co. announced the launch of irinotecan hydrochloride injection in the U.S., for patients with colon or rectal cancer whose disease has recurred or progressed following therapy with other treatments. As such, for full-year 2008, Co. expects net sales growth to be 6.0% to 8.0%, with diluted earnings per share of $2.05 to $2.15.

Financial Data
(US$ in Thousands)	12/31/2007	12/31/2006	12/31/2005	12/31/2004	12/31/2003	12/31/2002
Earnings Per Share	0.85	1.48	1.46	1.92	1.67	1.58
Cash Flow Per Share	3.51	2.70	3.59	2.47	2.36	...
Tang Book Value Per Share	N.M.	8.03	7.57	5.75	...	...
Income Statement						
Total Revenue	3,436,238	2,688,505	2,626,696	2,645,036	2,623,737	2,602,550
EBITDA	594,468	495,364	491,590	573,444	505,088	486,148
Income Before Taxes	187,786	324,697	322,075	411,520	359,121	352,426
Income Taxes	51,028	87,018	86,437	109,968	98,758	105,728
Net Income	136,758	237,679	235,638	301,552	260,363	246,698
Average Shares	160,164	160,424	161,634	157,160	156,043	156,043
Balance Sheet						
Current Assets	1,841,020	1,522,890	1,561,165	1,198,325	1,041,350	...
Total Assets	5,084,666	2,847,587	2,789,182	2,342,790	2,250,163	...
Current Liabilities	794,289	606,226	596,236	536,194	359,601	...
Long-Term Obligations	2,184,385	702,044	695,285	698,841	...	...
Total Liabilities	3,339,442	1,486,498	1,461,315	1,358,871	796,699	...
Stockholders' Equity	1,745,224	1,361,089	1,327,867	983,919	1,453,464	...
Shares Outstanding	158,611	155,884	161,668	156,970	...	...
Statistical Record						
Return on Assets %	3.45	8.43	9.18	13.10	...	...
Return on Equity %	8.81	17.68	20.39	24.68	...	...
EBITDA Margin %	17.30	18.43	18.72	21.68	19.25	18.68
Net Margin %	3.98	8.84	8.97	11.40	9.92	9.48
Asset Turnover	0.87	0.95	1.02	1.15	...	...
Current Ratio	2.32	2.51	2.62	2.23	2.90	...
Debt to Equity	1.25	0.52	0.52	0.71	...	...
Price Range	44.51-33.85	47.63-31.17	44.88-28.45	33.91-24.35	...	...
P/E Ratio	52.36-39.82	32.18-21.06	30.74-19.49	17.66-12.68	...	...

Address: 275 North Field Drive, Lake Forest, IL 60045
Telephone: 224-212-2000

Web Site: www.hospira.com
Officers: David A. Jones - Chmn. Christopher B. Begley - C.E.O.

Auditors: Deloitte & Touche LLP
Transfer Agents: ComputerShare Investor Services, Providence, RI

HOSPITALITY PROPERTIES TRUST

Exchange	Symbol	Price	52Wk Range	Yield	P/E
NYS	HPT	$34.02 (3/31/2008)	47.80-30.40	9.05	10.40

*7 Year Price Score 86.56   *NYSE Composite Index=100   *12 Month Price Score 96.74

Interim Earnings (Per Share)

Qtr.	Mar	Jun	Sep	Dec
2003	0.46	0.43	0.43	2.24
2004	0.36	0.43	0.43	0.50
2005	0.40	0.30	0.40	0.65
2006	0.46	0.47	0.47	0.80
2007	0.43	0.50	1.52	0.81

Interim Dividends (Per Share)

Amt	Decl	Ex	Rec	Pay
0.76Q	7/2/2007	7/10/2007	7/12/2007	8/16/2007
0.77Q	10/10/2007	10/17/2007	10/19/2007	11/15/2007
0.77Q	1/3/2008	1/10/2008	1/14/2008	2/15/2008
0.77Q	4/1/2008	4/11/2008	4/15/2008	5/15/2008

Indicated Div: $3.08

Valuation Analysis

		Institutional Holding	
Forecast P/E	10.40	No of Institutions	
	(1/10/2007)	280	
Market Cap	$3.2 Billion	Shares	
Book Value	2.8 Billion	59,278,712	
Price/Book	1.15	% Held	
Price/Sales	2.48	63.17	

Business Summary: Property, Real Estate & Development (MIC: 8.3 SIC: 6798 NAIC: 525930)

Hospitality Properties Trust is a real estate investment trust that invests in hotels. As of Dec 31 2007, Co. owned 292 hotels with 43,223 rooms or suites, and 185 travel centers located in 44 states in the U.S., Canada and Puerto Rico. At Dec 31 2007, Co.'s hotels are operated as Courtyard by Marriott®, Candlewood Suites®, Staybridge Suites®, Residence Inn by Marriott®, Crowne Plaza Hotels & Resorts®, Hyatt Place™, AmeriSuites®, InterContinental Hotels & Resorts®, Marriott Hotels and Resorts®, Radisson® Hotels & Resorts, TownePlace Suites by Marriott®, Country Inns & Suites by Carlson®, Holiday Inn Hotels & Resorts®, SpringHill Suites by Marriott®, or Park Plaza® Hotels & Resorts.

Recent Developments: For the year ended Dec 31 2007, income from continuing operations increased 45.6% to US$227.8 million from US$156.5 million a year earlier. Net income increased 95.8% to US$331.0 million from US$169.0 million in the prior year. Revenues were US$1.29 billion, up 25.7% from US$1.02 billion the year before. Revenues from property income rose 162.6% to US$316.8 million from US$120.6 million in the corresponding earlier year.

Prospects: Co.'s near-term outlook appears encouraging. For instance, Co.'s hotel operating revenues are benefiting from increased revenues at its managed hotels and its Apr 2006 acquisition of four managed hotels. In detail, Co.'s revenues are increasing at most of its managed hotels due to higher average daily room rates. Furthermore, Co. is seeing an increase in hotels rental income as a result of Co. funding of improvements at certain of its leased hotels in 2006 and 2007 that resulted in increases in the annual minimum rents due to Co. Meanwhile, Co. remains focused to complete significant renovations at 20 hotels in its combination management agreements or leases in the first half of 2008.

Financial Data (US$ in Thousands)	12/31/2007	12/31/2006	12/31/2005	12/31/2004	12/31/2003	12/31/2002	12/31/2001	12/31/2000
Earnings Per Share	3.27	2.20	1.75	1.72	3.57	2.15	2.12	2.24
Cash Flow Per Share	4.17	3.71	3.47	3.35	3.51	3.36	3.48	3.33
Tang Book Value Per Share	25.52	27.40	24.64	23.85	23.81	23.81	24.51	24.98
Dividends Per Share	3.030	2.940	2.170	2.880	3.600	2.860	2.820	2.770
Dividend Payout %	92.66	133.64	124.00	167.44	100.84	133.02	133.02	123.66
Income Statement								
Total Revenue	1,285,479	1,039,415	834,412	645,368	552,801	348,706	303,877	263,023
EBITDA	451,986	...	...	...	...	...	...	...
Income Before Taxes	230,008	...	...	...	...	...	...	...
Income Taxes	2,191	...	...	...	...	...	...	...
Net Income	330,968	169,039	129,903	127,091	238,213	142,202	131,956	126,271
Average Shares	93,109	73,279	69,866	66,503	62,576	62,538	58,986	56,466
Balance Sheet								
Current Assets	51,535	580,619	47,631	54,405	62,183	54,144	78,875	51,907
Total Assets	5,679,307	3,957,463	3,114,607	2,689,425	2,761,601	2,403,756	2,354,964	2,220,909
Current Liabilities	178,777	190,557	190,185	228,265	221,703	272,029	265,700	258,150
Long-Term Obligations	2,579,391	1,199,830	960,372	697,505	826,126	473,965	464,781	464,748
Total Liabilities	2,892,873	1,509,923	1,259,152	1,003,552	1,116,073	758,736	750,445	737,969
Stockholders' Equity	2,786,434	2,447,540	1,855,455	1,685,873	1,645,528	1,645,020	1,604,519	1,482,940
Shares Outstanding	93,892	86,284	71,920	67,203	62,587	62,547	62,515	56,472
Statistical Record								
Return on Assets %	6.87	4.78	4.48	4.65	9.22	5.98	5.77	5.70
Return on Equity %	12.65	7.86	7.34	7.61	14.48	8.75	8.55	8.39
EBITDA Margin %	35.16	...	...	...	...	...	...	...
Net Margin %	25.75	16.26	15.57	19.69	43.09	40.78	43.42	48.01
Asset Turnover	0.27	0.29	0.29	0.24	0.21	0.15	0.13	0.12
Current Ratio	0.29	3.05	0.25	0.24	0.28	0.20	0.30	0.20
Debt to Equity	0.93	0.49	0.52	0.41	0.50	0.29	0.29	0.31
Price Range	48.84-32.22	48.19-38.12	43.12-36.19	43.96-33.90	39.44-26.14	34.21-26.27	28.12-19.64	23.67-17.40
P/E Ratio	14.94-9.85	21.90-17.33	24.64-20.68	25.56-19.71	11.05-7.32	15.91-12.22	13.26-9.26	10.57-7.77
Average Yield %	7.24	6.97	5.48	7.24	11.64	9.16	11.25	13.38

Address: 400 Centre Street, Newton, MA 02458 Telephone: 617-964-8389 Fax: 617-969-5730	Web Site: www.hptreit.com Officers: John G. Murray - Pres., C.O.O. Mark L. Kleifges - C.F.O., Treas.	Auditors: Ernst & Young LLP Transfer Agents: Wells Fargo Bank NA

HOST HOTELS & RESORTS INC

Exchange	Symbol	Price	52Wk Range	Yield	P/E
NYS	HST	$15.92 (3/31/2008)	27.04-15.57	5.03	11.97

*7 Year Price Score 109.83 *NYSE Composite Index=100 *12 Month Price Score 85.08

Interim Earnings (Per Share)

Qtr.	Mar	Jun	Sep	Dec
2003	(0.16)	(0.09)	(0.35)	0.54
2004	(0.12)	0.02	(0.17)	0.16
Qtr.	**Mar**	**Jun**	**Aug**	**Dec**
2005	(0.01)	0.22	(0.03)	0.19
2006	0.44	0.62	0.07	0.36
2007	0.35	0.27	0.18	0.54

Interim Dividends (Per Share)

Amt	Decl	Ex	Rec	Pay
0.20Q	9/17/2007	9/26/2007	9/30/2007	10/15/2007
0.20Q	12/17/2007	12/27/2007	12/31/2007	1/15/2008
0.20Q	12/17/2007	12/27/2007	12/31/2007	1/15/2008
0.20Q	3/17/2008	3/27/2008	3/31/2008	4/15/2008

Indicated Div: $0.80

Valuation Analysis

Forecast P/E	N/A
Market Cap	$8.3 Billion
Book Value	5.4 Billion
Price/Book	1.52
Price/Sales	1.53

Institutional Holding

No of Institutions	337
Shares	510,821,056
% Held	97.53

TRADING VOLUME (thousand shares)

Business Summary: Property, Real Estate & Development (MIC: 8.3 SIC: 6798 NAIC: 525930)

Host Hotels & Resorts is a lodging real estate investment trust company. Co. owns properties and conducts its operations through Host Hotels & Resorts, L.P., of which Co. is the sole general partner and in which it holds approximately 97.0% of the partnership interests, at Dec 31 2007. Also, as of Feb 25 2008, Co. owned, or had controlling interests in, 128 luxury and upper upscale, hotel lodging properties located throughout the U.S., Toronto and Calgary, Canada, Mexico City, Mexico and Santiago, Chile operated primarily under the Marriott®, Ritz-Carlton®, Hyatt®, Fairmont®, Four Seasons®, Hilton®, Westin®, Sheraton®, W®, St. Regis®, Swissôtel®, Delta®, and Luxury Collection® brand names.

Recent Developments: For the year ended Dec 31 2007, income from continuing operations increased 87.1% to US$550.0 million from US$294.0 million a year earlier. Net income decreased 1.5% to US$727.0 million from US$738.0 million in the prior year. Revenues were US$5.43 billion, up 12.7% from US$4.81 billion the year before. Revenues from property income rose 0.8% to US$120.0 million from US$119.0 million in the corresponding earlier year.

Prospects: Co. believes that the underlying lodging fundamentals related to its portfolio are likely to weaken in 2008. Hence, for 2008, Co. expects comparable hotel revenue per available room to increase about 2.0% to 4.0%, which is lower than prior year's revenue growth rate. Co. also expects operating profit margins to decrease about 130 basis points to 60 basis points. In addition, Co. expects earnings in the range of $1.05 to $1.14 per diluted share, with net income of $568.0 million to $622.0 million. Meanwhile, Co. is progressing on its capital expenditures and investment projects in an effort to expand its properties, with total investments for 2008 expected to be about $650.0 million.

Financial Data

(US$ in Thousands)	12/31/2007	12/31/2006	12/31/2005	12/31/2004	12/31/2003	12/31/2002	12/31/2001	12/31/2000
Earnings Per Share	1.33	1.48	0.38	(0.12)	(0.07)	(0.19)	0.08	0.03
Cash Flow Per Share	1.92	1.83	1.45	1.06	1.33	1.48	0.96	2.18
Tang Book Value Per Share	10.26	9.83	6.03	5.87	5.61	4.82	4.83	5.54
Dividends Per Share	1.000	0.760	0.410	0.050	...	...	0.780	0.910
Dividend Payout %	75.19	51.35	107.89	...	...	...	975.00	144.44
Income Statement								
Property Income	120,000	119,000	111,000	107,000	112,000	101,000	128,000	1,390,000
Non-Property Income	5,306,000	4,769,000	3,770,000	3,533,000	3,336,000	3,579,000	3,626,000	83,000
Total Revenue	5,426,000	4,888,000	3,881,000	3,640,000	3,448,000	3,680,000	3,754,000	1,473,000
Interest Expense	422,000	450,000	443,000	483,000	491,000	466,000	460,000	433,000
Income Before Taxes	553,000	314,000	162,000	(71,000)	(71,000)	(23,000)	61,000	61,000
Income Taxes	3,000	5,000	24,000	(10,000)	(12,000)	6,000	8,000	(98,000)
Net Income	727,000	738,000	166,000	...	14,000	(16,000)	51,000	156,000
Average Shares	554,700	483,800	355,500	337,300	281,000	263,000	288,400	289,000
Balance Sheet								
Total Assets	11,812,000	11,808,000	8,245,000	8,421,000	8,592,000	8,316,000	8,338,000	8,396,000
Long-Term Obligations	5,625,000	5,878,000	5,370,000	5,523,000	5,486,000	5,638,000	5,602,000	5,322,000
Total Liabilities	6,155,000	6,373,000	5,683,000	5,818,000	5,762,000	6,008,000	6,044,000	6,015,000
Stockholders' Equity	5,441,000	5,222,000	2,417,000	2,395,000	2,136,000	1,610,000	1,609,000	1,421,000
Shares Outstanding	521,100	521,100	361,000	350,300	320,300	263,700	263,200	221,300
Statistical Record								
Return on Assets %	6.16	7.36	1.99	...	0.17	N.M.	0.61	1.87
Return on Equity %	13.64	19.32	6.90	...	0.75	N.M.	3.37	10.63
Net Margin %	13.40	15.10	4.28	...	0.41	(0.43)	1.36	10.59
Price Range	28.71-16.71	25.60-18.95	19.05-15.49	17.30-11.37	12.32-6.10	12.05-7.75	13.89-6.45	12.94-8.06
P/E Ratio	21.59-12.56	17.30-12.80	50.13-40.76	...	...	...	173.63-80.63	20.54-12.80
Average Yield %	4.28	3.41	2.23	0.38	...	...	6.90	8.93

Address: 6903 Rockledge Drive, Suite 1500, Bethesda, MD 20817 Telephone: 240-744-1000 Fax: 240-380-6338	Web Site: www.hosthotels.com Officers: Richard E. Marriott - Chmn. Christopher J. Nassetts - Pres., C.E.O.	Auditors: KPMG LLP Transfer Agents: EquiServe Trust Company, NA Providence , RI

HOVNANIAN ENTERPRISES, INC.

Exchange	Symbol	Price	52Wk Range	Yield	P/E
NYS	HOV	$10.60 (3/31/2008)	25.95-4.80	N/A	N/A

*7 Year Price Score 39.15   *NYSE Composite Index=100   *12 Month Price Score 78.88

TRADING VOLUME (thousand shares)

Interim Earnings (Per Share)

Qtr.	Jan	Apr	Jul	Oct
2004-05	1.25	1.62	1.76	2.53
2005-06	1.25	1.55	1.15	(1.81)
2006-07	(0.91)	(0.49)	(1.27)	(7.44)
2007-08	(2.07)	...	...	...

Interim Dividends (Per Share)

Amt	Decl	Ex	Rec	Pay
100%	3/8/2004	3/29/2004	3/19/2004	3/26/2004

Valuation Analysis   **Institutional Holding**

Forecast P/E	N/A	No of Institutions
		165
Market Cap	$662.5 Million	Shares
Book Value	1.2 Billion	47,768,328
Price/Book	0.56	% Held
Price/Sales	0.14	N/A

Business Summary: Building & General Construction (MIC: 3.2 SIC: 1531 NAIC: 236117)

Hovnanian Enterprises is engaged in designing, constructing, marketing and selling single-family detached homes, attached townhomes and condominiums, mid-rise and high-rise condominiums, urban infill and active adult homes in planned residential developments. Co. consists of two operating groups: homebuilding and financial services. Co.'s financial services group provides mortgage loans and title services to its homebuilding customers. As of Oct 31 2007, Co. offered homes for sale in 431 communities in 47 markets in 19 states throughout the United States.

Recent Developments: For the quarter ended Jan 31 2008, net loss amounted to US$130.9 million versus a net loss of US$54.6 million in the year-earlier quarter. Revenues were US$1.09 billion, down 6.2% from US$1.17 billion the year before. Direct operating expenses rose 11.6% to US$1.13 billion from US$1.02 billion in the comparable period the year before. Indirect operating expenses decreased 43.3% to US$124.3 million from US$219.0 million in the equivalent prior-year period.

Prospects: Looking ahead, Co. foresees that its operating results will continue to be affected by the ongoing challenging market conditions. In response, Co. intends to shorten its land pipeline, reduce production volumes while balancing home price and profitability with sales pace. Also, Co. is delaying planned land purchases and renegotiating land prices while reducing its total number of controlled lots owned and under option. In addition, Co. is lowering the number of speculative homes put into production. Thus, Co. expects minimal investment in new land parcels throughout the fiscal year ending Oct 31 2008 despite its intention to continue purchasing strategic land positions.

Financial Data (US$ in Thousands)	3 Mos	10/31/2007	10/31/2006	10/31/2005	10/31/2004	10/31/2003	10/31/2002	10/31/2001
Earnings Per Share	(11.27)	(10.11)	2.14	7.16	5.35	3.92	2.14	1.15
Cash Flow Per Share	3.41	0.98	(10.36)	(0.38)	(3.03)	(3.14)	4.09	0.69
Tang Book Value Per Share	16.22	18.48	26.03	24.48	16.93	11.32	7.86	6.74
Income Statement								
Total Revenue	1,093,701	4,798,921	6,148,235	5,348,417	4,160,403	3,201,857	2,551,106	1,741,963
EBITDA	(163,148)	(466,559)	302,811	835,744	584,884	426,612	233,131	118,282
Depn & Amortn	5,646	...	...	...	...	...	...	...
Income Before Taxes	(168,794)	(646,966)	233,106	780,585	549,772	411,518	226,625	106,354
Income Taxes	(37,851)	(19,847)	83,573	308,738	201,091	154,138	88,347	42,668
Net Income	(130,943)	(627,119)	149,533	471,847	348,681	257,380	137,696	63,686
Average Shares	63,358	63,079	64,838	65,549	65,133	65,538	64,310	55,584
Balance Sheet								
Current Assets	3,892,171	3,995,202	4,627,739	3,887,730	2,667,413	1,831,950	1,377,848	832,784
Total Assets	4,325,066	4,540,548	5,480,035	4,719,955	3,156,267	2,332,371	1,678,128	1,064,258
Current Liabilities	375,775	505,850	441,115	457,752	212,812	168,831	50,754	50,884
Long-Term Obligations	2,365,478	2,114,148	2,369,721	1,770,607	1,256,792	1,013,382	761,755	508,339
Total Liabilities	3,084,799	3,155,017	3,405,387	2,747,349	1,805,305	1,418,116	1,115,579	688,612
Stockholders' Equity	1,184,746	1,321,803	1,942,163	1,791,357	1,192,394	819,712	562,549	375,646
Shares Outstanding	62,502	62,216	61,810	61,659	61,086	60,097	61,105	55,753
Statistical Record								
Return on Assets %	N.M.	N.M.	2.93	11.98	12.67	12.84	10.04	6.57
Return on Equity %	N.M.	N.M.	8.01	31.63	34.56	37.24	29.35	19.93
EBITDA Margin %	N.M.	N.M.	4.93	15.63	14.06	13.32	9.14	6.79
Net Margin %	N.M.	N.M.	2.43	8.82	8.38	8.04	5.40	3.66
Asset Turnover	0.98	0.96	1.21	1.36	1.51	1.60	1.86	1.80
Current Ratio	10.36	7.90	10.49	8.49	12.53	10.85	27.15	16.37
Debt to Equity	2.00	1.60	1.22	0.99	1.05	1.24	1.35	1.35
Price Range	36.98-4.80	38.01-9.99	54.29-25.04	73.19-38.00	48.31-29.33	41.28-14.36	20.00-5.58	9.60-3.59
P/E Ratio	...	...	25.37-11.70	10.22-5.31	9.03-5.48	10.53-3.66	9.35-2.61	8.35-3.13

Address: 110 West Front Street, P.O. Box 500, Red Bank, NJ 07701 **Telephone:** 732-747-7800	**Web Site:** www.khov.com **Officers:** Kevork S. Hovnanian - Chmn. Ara K. Hovnanian - Pres., C.E.O.	**Auditors:** Ernst & Young LLP **Investor Contact:** 732-747-7800 **Transfer Agents:** National City Bank, Cleveland, OH

HRPT PROPERTIES TRUST

Exchange	Symbol	Price	52Wk Range	Yield	P/E
NYS	HRP	$6.73 (3/31/2008)	12.69-6.62	12.48	24.04

*7 Year Price Score 74.48 *NYSE Composite Index=100 *12 Month Price Score 82.69

Interim Earnings (Per Share)

Qtr.	Mar	Jun	Sep	Dec
2003	0.12	0.12	0.09	0.17
2004	0.22	0.13	0.14	0.17
2005	0.12	0.20	0.13	0.15
2006	0.63	0.11	0.11	0.10
2007	0.08	0.08	0.08	0.04

Interim Dividends (Per Share)

Amt	Decl	Ex	Rec	Pay
0.21Q	7/5/2007	7/23/2007	7/25/2007	8/24/2007
0.21Q	10/4/2007	10/19/2007	10/23/2007	11/21/2007
0.21Q	1/3/2008	1/16/2008	1/18/2008	2/22/2008
0.21Q	4/4/2008	4/21/2008	4/23/2008	5/23/2008

Indicated Div: $0.84

Valuation Analysis

		Institutional Holding	
Forecast P/E	N/A	No of Institutions	210
Market Cap	$1.5 Billion	Shares	147,329,152
Book Value	2.9 Billion	% Held	69.81
Price/Book	0.52		
Price/Sales	1.81		

Business Summary: Property, Real Estate & Development (MIC: 8.3 SIC: 6798 NAIC: 525930)

HRPT Properties Trust is a real estate investment trust. Co.'s primary business is the ownership and operation of real estate, including office and industrial buildings as well as leased industrial land. As of Dec 31 2007, Co. owned 535 properties for a total investment of $6.20 billion at cost. Co.'s portfolio included 366 office properties with 35.3 million square feet of space, and 169 industrial properties with 29.1 million square feet of space. Co.'s 169 industrial and other properties included approximately 17.0 million square feet of leased industrial and commercial lands in Oahu, HI.

Recent Developments: For the year ended Dec 31 2007, income from continuing operations decreased 50.8% to US$121.8 million from US$247.5 million a year earlier. Net income decreased 50.4% to US$124.3 million from US$250.6 million in the prior year. Revenues were US$840.0 million, up 5.6% from US$795.5 million the year before.

Prospects: Co. is being hurt by lower net income due to the 2006 sale of the Senior Housing and Hospitality Properties common shares. However, Co. is seeing increased rental income due to higher rental income from its Oahu, HI, Metro Boston, MA and its Other Markets segment. Meanwhile, Co. continues to believe that the existing leasing market conditions in some areas where its properties are located may lead to modest increases in effective rents. Also, Co. expects the recent rises in fuel prices to cause continued higher operating costs, but remains positive that the affect of such increases should be partially offset by pass through of operating cost increases to tenants pursuant to lease terms.

Financial Data
(US$ in Thousands)

	12/31/2007	12/31/2006	12/31/2005	12/31/2004	12/31/2003	12/31/2002	12/31/2001	12/31/2000
Earnings Per Share	0.28	0.94	0.60	0.66	0.50	0.61	0.51	1.08
Cash Flow Per Share	1.27	1.36	1.14	1.18	1.47	1.39	1.11	1.17
Tang Book Value Per Share	9.85	10.22	10.30	10.29	10.71	11.20	11.36	11.59
Dividends Per Share	0.840	0.840	0.840	0.820	0.800	0.800	0.800	1.040
Dividend Payout %	300.00	89.36	140.00	124.24	160.00	131.15	156.86	96.30
Income Statement								
Property Income	840,010	795,821	710,758	603,229	500,316	413,790	387,561	400,976
Non-Property Income	...	...	...	...	411	3,176	6,611	4,030
Total Revenue	840,010	795,821	710,758	603,229	500,727	416,966	394,172	405,006
Interest Expense	171,571	165,894	143,663	118,212	101,144	86,360	87,075	100,074
Income Before Taxes	12,206	...	...	...	...	...	...	...
Income Taxes	395	...	...	...	...	...	...	...
Net Income	124,255	250,580	164,984	162,829	114,446	106,763	82,804	142,272
Average Shares	243,554	216,524	197,831	176,157	136,270	128,817	130,253	131,937
Balance Sheet								
Total Assets	5,859,332	5,575,949	5,327,167	4,813,330	4,013,244	3,206,340	2,805,426	2,900,143
Long-Term Obligations	2,774,160	2,397,231	2,520,156	2,355,031	1,876,821	1,215,977	1,097,217	1,302,950
Total Liabilities	2,956,449	2,625,181	2,681,681	2,506,136	2,001,593	1,280,067	1,148,926	1,370,931
Stockholders' Equity	2,902,883	2,950,768	2,645,486	2,307,194	2,011,651	1,926,273	1,656,500	1,529,212
Shares Outstanding	225,444	210,051	209,860	177,316	142,773	128,825	128,808	131,948
Statistical Record								
Return on Assets %	2.17	4.60	3.25	3.68	3.17	3.55	2.90	4.85
Return on Equity %	4.25	8.96	6.66	7.52	5.81	5.96	5.20	9.30
Net Margin %	14.79	31.49	23.21	26.99	22.86	25.60	21.01	35.13
Price Range	13.54-7.48	12.74-10.44	13.16-10.20	12.96-8.85	10.30-8.18	9.37-7.19	9.93-7.73	10.35-6.14
P/E Ratio	48.36-26.71	13.55-11.11	21.93-17.00	19.64-13.41	20.60-16.36	15.36-11.79	19.46-15.17	9.58-5.68
Average Yield %	7.99	7.33	7.02	7.65	8.78	9.39	9.48	14.05

Address: 400 Centre Street, Newton, MA 02458-2076
Telephone: 617-332-3990
Fax: 617-332-2261

Web Site: www.hrpreit.com
Officers: John A. Mannix - Pres., C.O.O. John C. Popeo - C.F.O., Treas., Sec.

Auditors: Ernst & Young LLP
Investor Contact: 617-332-3990
Transfer Agents: Wells Fargo Shareowner Services, St. Paul, MN

HUBBELL INC.

Exchange	Symbol	Price	52Wk Range	Yield	P/E
NYS	HUB A	$47.65 (3/31/2008)	61.15-46.20	2.77	13.61

*7 Year Price Score 107.46 *NYSE Composite Index=100 *12 Month Price Score 99.34

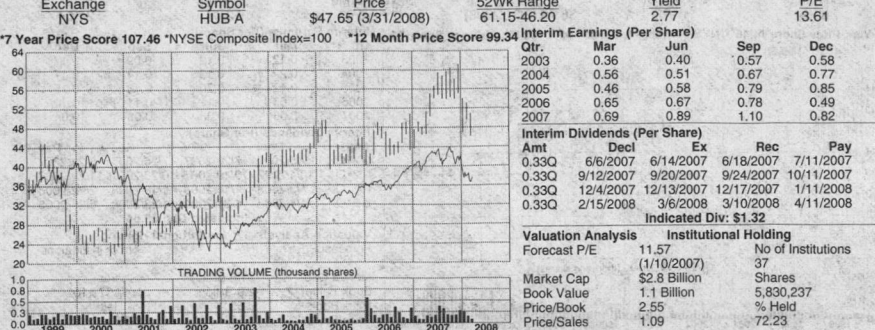

Interim Earnings (Per Share)

Qtr.	Mar	Jun	Sep	Dec
2003	0.36	0.40	0.57	0.58
2004	0.56	0.51	0.67	0.77
2005	0.46	0.58	0.79	0.85
2006	0.65	0.67	0.78	0.49
2007	0.69	0.89	1.10	0.82

Interim Dividends (Per Share)

Amt	Decl	Ex	Rec	Pay
0.33Q	6/6/2007	6/14/2007	6/18/2007	7/11/2007
0.33Q	9/12/2007	9/20/2007	9/24/2007	10/11/2007
0.33Q	12/4/2007	12/13/2007	12/17/2007	1/11/2008
0.33Q	2/15/2008	3/6/2008	3/10/2008	4/11/2008

Indicated Div: $1.32

Valuation Analysis — **Institutional Holding**

Forecast P/E	11.57	No of Institutions
	(1/10/2007)	37
Market Cap	$2.8 Billion	Shares
Book Value	1.1 Billion	5,830,237
Price/Book	2.55	% Held
Price/Sales	1.09	72.23

TRADING VOLUME (thousand shares)

Business Summary: Electrical (MIC: 11.14 SIC: 3644 NAIC: 335932)

Hubbell operates through three segments: Electrical, which sells wiring device products, lighting fixtures and controls, fittings, switches and outlet boxes, enclosures, wire management products and voice and data signal processing components; Power, which manufactures various transmission, distribution, substation and telecommunications products, including aluminum transformer equipment mounts, arresters, hot line taps, line construction materials, and pole line hardware; and Industrial Technology, which manufactures high voltage test and measurement equipment, industrial controls and communications systems used in the commercial, industrial and telecommunications markets.

Recent Developments: For the year ended Dec 31 2007, net income increased 31.8% to US$208.3 million from US$158.1 million in the prior year. Revenues were US$2.53 billion, up 5.0% from US$2.41 billion the year before. Operating income was US$299.4 million versus US$233.9 million in the prior year, an increase of 28.0%. Direct operating expenses rose 2.3% to US$1.80 billion from US$1.76 billion in the comparable period the year before. Indirect operating expenses increased 3.2% to US$436.4 million from US$422.9 million in the equivalent prior-year period.

Prospects: Despite a slowing U.S. economy and a continuing decline in the residential marketplace in 2008, Co. expects sales growth of 4.0% to 6.0%, a 100 basis point improvement in operating margin, and earnings per diluted share of $3.70 to $3.90. Going forward, Co. expects to pursue potential acquisitions that should expand its electrical component businesses. For example, on Jan 14 2008, Co. announced the acquisition of a lighting business, the Kurt Versen Company, for $100.0 million. The acquisition expands Co.'s Hubbel Lighting subsidiary's package of 16 lighting brands. The acquisition is expected to add about $72.0 million in annual net sales, and will be accretive to Co.'s 2008 results.

Financial Data

(US$ in Thousands)	12/31/2007	12/31/2006	12/31/2005	12/31/2004	12/31/2003	12/31/2002	12/31/2001	12/31/2000
Earnings Per Share	3.50	2.59	2.67	2.51	1.91	1.38	0.82	2.25
Cash Flow Per Share	5.70	2.32	3.02	3.04	4.09	3.04	3.40	2.02
Tang Book Value Per Share	10.63	9.62	10.58	10.09	8.41	7.25	7.98	8.64
Dividends Per Share	1.320	1.320	1.320	1.320	1.320	1.320	1.320	1.310
Dividend Payout %	37.71	50.97	49.44	52.59	69.11	95.65	160.98	58.22
Income Statement								
Total Revenue	2,533,900	2,414,300	2,104,900	1,993,000	1,770,700	1,587,800	1,312,200	1,424,100
EBITDA	362,000	292,300	285,400	266,800	228,700	194,600	124,300	258,900
Income Before Taxes	284,200	221,500	215,700	197,300	155,500	127,000	55,800	184,300
Income Taxes	75,900	63,400	50,600	42,600	40,400	18,400	7,500	46,100
Net Income	208,300	158,100	165,100	154,700	115,100	83,200	48,300	138,200
Average Shares	59,500	61,100	61,800	61,600	60,100	59,700	58,900	61,300
Balance Sheet								
Current Assets	788,000	814,400	820,100	892,400	709,300	596,300	508,300	620,000
Total Assets	1,863,400	1,751,500	1,667,000	1,642,400	1,499,400	1,410,300	1,205,400	1,454,500
Current Liabilities	419,500	382,300	360,500	409,300	288,400	254,700	283,900	489,400
Long-Term Obligations	199,400	199,300	199,200	199,100	298,800	298,700	99,800	99,700
Total Liabilities	780,800	736,000	668,900	698,100	669,700	666,100	468,900	685,000
Stockholders' Equity	1,082,600	1,015,500	998,100	944,300	829,700	744,200	736,500	769,500
Shares Outstanding	57,927	60,178	61,090	61,214	60,278	59,241	58,719	58,757
Statistical Record								
Return on Assets %	11.52	9.25	9.98	9.82	7.91	6.36	3.63	9.66
Return on Equity %	19.86	15.70	17.00	17.39	14.63	11.24	6.41	16.96
EBITDA Margin %	14.29	12.11	13.56	13.39	12.92	12.26	9.47	18.18
Net Margin %	8.22	6.55	7.84	7.76	6.50	5.24	3.68	9.70
Asset Turnover	1.40	1.41	1.27	1.27	1.22	1.21	0.99	1.00
Current Ratio	1.88	2.13	2.27	2.18	2.46	2.34	1.79	1.27
Debt to Equity	0.18	0.20	0.20	0.21	0.36	0.40	0.14	0.13
Price Range	61.15-43.61	50.82-40.10	49.65-39.25	48.36-36.92	42.84-26.95	35.00-25.26	29.65-23.59	28.13-21.56
P/E Ratio	17.47-12.46	19.62-15.48	18.60-14.70	19.27-14.71	22.43-14.11	25.36-18.30	36.16-28.77	12.50-9.58
Average Yield %	2.47	2.94	3.02	3.17	3.81	4.27	4.83	5.26

Address: 584 Derby-Milford Road, Orange, CT 06477-4024
Telephone: 203-799-4100
Fax: 203-799-4333

Web Site: www.hubbell.com
Officers: Timothy H. Powers - Chmn., Pres., C.E.O.
W. Robert Murphy - Sr. Group V.P.

Auditors: PricewaterhouseCoopers LLP
Transfer Agents: Mellon Investors Services LLC, Ridgefield Park, NJ

HUMANA INC.

Exchange	Symbol	Price	52Wk Range	Yield	P/E
NYS	HUM	$44.86 (3/31/2008)	86.98-40.88	N/A	9.14

*7 Year Price Score 163.59 *NYSE Composite Index=100 *12 Month Price Score 102.31

TRADING VOLUME (thousand shares)

Interim Earnings (Per Share)

Qtr.	Mar	Jun	Sep	Dec
2003	0.20	0.43	0.38	0.40
2004	0.41	0.50	0.52	0.29
2005	0.67	0.51	0.30	0.39
2006	0.50	0.53	0.95	0.92
2007	0.42	1.28	1.78	1.43

Interim Dividends (Per Share)

No Dividends Paid

Valuation Analysis		Institutional Holding	
Forecast P/E	11.28	No of Institutions	
	(1/10/2007)	332	
Market Cap	$7.6 Billion	Shares	
Book Value	4.0 Billion	143,738,032	
Price/Book	1.89	% Held	
Price/Sales	0.30	86.21	

Business Summary: Insurance (MIC: 8.2 SIC: 6324 NAIC: 524114)

Humana is a health benefits company engaged in providing a range of health and supplemental benefit plans for employer groups, government benefit programs, and individuals. At Dec 31 2007, Co. managed its business with two segments: Government and Commercial. The Government segment consists of beneficiaries of government benefit programs, and includes three lines of business: Medicare, Military, and Medicaid. The Commercial segment consists of members enrolled in Co.'s medical and specialty products marketed to employer groups and individuals. At Dec 31 2007, Co. had about 11.5 million members in its medical benefit plans, as well as about 6.8 million members in its specialty products.

Recent Developments: For the year ended Dec 31 2007, net income increased 71.0% to US$833.7 million from US$487.4 million in the prior year. Revenues were US$25.29 billion, up 18.1% from US$21.42 billion the year before. Net premiums earned were US$24.43 billion versus US$20.73 billion in the prior year, an increase of 17.9%.

Prospects: For 2008, Co. projects revenues of US$28.0 billion to US$30.0 billion and diluted earnings per common share of $5.35 to $5.55. Co. also expects its Medicare Advantage membership to continue to grow, adding 200,000 to 250,000 members by 2008. Meanwhile, on Feb 25 2008, Co. announced it has agreed to purchase the Medicare Advantage contract and related assets associated with the Las Vegas, NV individual SecureHorizons Medicare Advantage health maintenance organization (HMO) business of UnitedHealth Group, for $185.0 million. The transaction is forecast to increase Co.'s Medicare Advantage HMO membership by over 25,000 with members largely residing in Clark and Nye counties in Nevada.

Financial Data
(US$ in Thousands)

	12/31/2007	12/31/2006	12/31/2005	12/31/2004	12/31/2003	12/31/2002	12/31/2001	12/31/2000
Earnings Per Share	4.91	2.90	1.87	1.72	1.41	0.85	0.70	0.54
Cash Flow Per Share	7.34	10.28	5.87	2.16	2.60	1.97	0.91	0.24
Tang Book Value Per Share	13.91	10.46	7.41	7.52	6.54	5.09	4.33	3.37
Income Statement								
Premium Income	24,434,347	20,729,182	14,001,591	12,689,432	11,825,283	10,930,397	9,938,961	10,395,000
Total Revenue	25,289,989	21,416,537	14,418,127	13,104,325	12,226,311	11,261,181	10,194,886	10,514,000
Income Before Taxes	1,289,300	762,085	421,714	415,850	344,716	209,934	183,080	114,000
Income Taxes	455,616	274,662	113,231	135,838	115,782	67,179	65,909	24,000
Net Income	833,684	487,423	308,483	280,012	228,934	142,755	117,171	90,000
Average Shares	169,820	167,996	165,374	162,456	161,960	167,801	167,308	166,931
Balance Sheet								
Total Assets	12,879,074	10,127,496	6,869,614	5,657,617	5,293,323	4,600,030	4,403,638	4,167,000
Total Liabilities	8,850,137	7,073,610	4,395,509	3,567,493	3,457,374	2,993,556	2,895,689	2,807,000
Stockholders' Equity	4,028,937	3,053,886	2,474,105	2,090,124	1,835,949	1,606,474	1,507,949	1,360,000
Shares Outstanding	170,018	166,606	163,216	160,266	161,890	162,972	168,811	169,066
Statistical Record								
Return on Assets %	7.25	5.74	4.92	5.10	4.63	3.17	2.73	1.98
Return on Equity %	23.54	17.63	13.52	14.23	13.30	9.17	8.17	6.83
Net Margin %	3.30	2.28	2.14	2.14	1.87	1.27	1.15	0.86
Price Range	78.46-52.25	67.97-41.60	55.29-29.10	30.02-15.55	23.29-8.68	17.09-9.87	14.94-8.58	15.38-4.75
P/E Ratio	15.98-10.64	23.44-14.34	29.57-15.56	17.45-9.04	16.52-6.16	20.11-11.61	21.34-12.26	28.47-8.80

Address: 500 West Main Street, Louisville, KY 40202
Telephone: 502-580-1000
Fax: 502-580-1441

Web Site: www.humana.com
Officers: David A. Jones Jr. - Chmn. Michael B. McCallister - Pres., C.E.O.

Auditors: PricewaterhouseCoopers LLP
Transfer Agents: National City Bank, Cleveland, OH

IDACORP, INC.

Exchange	Symbol	Price	52Wk Range	Yield	P/E
NYS	IDA	$32.11 (3/31/2008)	36.38-29.19	3.74	17.26

*7 Year Price Score 83.73 *NYSE Composite Index=100 *12 Month Price Score 102.08

Interim Earnings (Per Share)

Qtr.	Mar	Jun	Sep	Dec
2003	(0.08)	(0.02)	1.22	0.10
2004	0.51	0.34	0.68	0.36
2005	0.55	0.22	0.56	0.17
2006	0.60	0.47	1.03	0.42
2007	0.56	0.42	0.65	0.23

Interim Dividends (Per Share)

Amt	Decl	Ex	Rec	Pay
0.30Q	4/19/2007	5/3/2007	5/7/2007	5/30/2007
0.30Q	7/19/2007	8/2/2007	8/6/2007	8/30/2007
0.30Q	10/18/2007	11/1/2007	11/5/2007	11/30/2007
0.30Q	1/17/2008	2/1/2008	2/5/2008	2/29/2008
			Indicated Div: $1.20	

Valuation Analysis

		Institutional Holding	
Forecast P/E	14.98	No of Institutions	
	(1/10/2007)	182	
Market Cap	$1.4 Billion	Shares	
Book Value	1.2 Billion	28,360,598	
Price/Book	1.20	% Held	
Price/Sales	1.65	66.26	

Business Summary: Electricity (MIC: 7.1 SIC: 4911 NAIC: 221111)

IDACORP is a holding company. Co.'s principal operating subsidiary, Idaho Power Company (IPC), is an electric utility engaged in the generation, transmission, distribution, sale and purchase of electric energy in southern Idaho and eastern Oregon. IPC holds franchises in 71 cities in Idaho and nine cities in Oregon. As of Dec 31 2007, IPC supplied electric energy to about 482,000 general business customers. Co.'s other subsidiaries include: IDACORP Financial Services, a holder of affordable housing and other real estate investments; Ida-West Energy, an operator of hydroelectric generation projects; and IDACORP Energy, a marketer of energy commodities.

Recent Developments: For the year ended Dec 31 2007, income from continuing operations decreased 17.8% to US$82.3 million from US$100.1 million a year earlier. Net income decreased 23.3% to US$82.3 million from US$107.4 million in the prior year. Revenues were US$879.4 million, down 5.1% from US$926.3 million the year before. Operating income was US$152.1 million versus US$169.7 million in the prior year, a decrease of 10.4%. Direct operating expenses declined 3.1% to US$703.0 million from US$725.3 million in the comparable period the year before. Indirect operating expenses decreased 22.2% to US$24.3 million from US$31.3 million in the equivalent prior-year period.

Prospects: Co. is focused on additional initiatives designed to recover its financial and operating costs of new facilities and system improvements. As such, Co. plans to for recover the investment and operating costs of its subsidiary, Idaho Power Company's 170-megawatt natural gas-fired peaking plant expected to go on line in Apr 2008; the power cost adjustment mechanism in Oregon; and the potential for general rate case filings in both Idaho and Oregon. Meanwhile, for 2008, Co. expects Idaho Power hydroelectric generation capacity of 7.0 million Megawatt per hour (MWh) to 9.0 million MWh. and non-regulated subsidiary earnings per share from continuing operations of $0.05 to $0.10.

Financial Data

(US$ in Thousands)	12/31/2007	12/31/2006	12/31/2005	12/31/2004	12/31/2003	12/31/2002	12/31/2001	12/31/2000
Earnings Per Share	1.86	2.51	1.50	1.90	1.22	1.63	3.35	3.72
Cash Flow Per Share	1.83	3.97	3.82	5.06	8.15	9.21	(0.21)	3.55
Tang Book Value Per Share	26.14	24.95	23.35	23.14	21.79	22.18	22.36	21.01
Dividends Per Share	1.200	1.200	1.200	1.200	1.695	1.860	1.860	1.860
Dividend Payout %	64.52	47.81	80.00	63.16	138.93	114.11	55.52	50.00
Income Statement								
Total Revenue	879,394	926,291	859,488	844,491	823,002	928,800	5,648,000	1,019,353
EBITDA	279,712	299,068	260,876	230,721	216,031	197,348	372,000	375,665
Income Before Taxes	96,003	115,452	76,581	48,213	25,459	10,525	190,000	210,701
Income Taxes	13,731	15,377	12,920	(24,770)	(21,119)	(51,147)	65,000	70,818
Net Income	82,339	107,403	63,661	72,983	46,578	61,672	125,000	139,883
Average Shares	44,291	42,874	42,279	38,361	38,186	37,729	37,387	37,556
Balance Sheet								
Net PPE	2,616,552	2,419,080	2,314,259	2,209,462	2,088,319	1,906,498	1,886,000	1,805,036
Total Assets	3,653,308	3,445,130	3,364,126	3,234,172	3,101,726	3,252,638	3,642,000	4,639,258
Long-Term Obligations	1,156,880	928,648	1,023,580	979,549	945,834	898,676	843,000	864,114
Total Liabilities	2,445,993	2,320,947	2,338,875	2,225,886	2,237,445	2,377,811	2,771,000	3,818,447
Stockholders' Equity	1,207,315	1,124,183	1,025,251	1,008,286	864,281	874,827	871,000	820,811
Shares Outstanding	45,062	43,833	42,417	42,217	38,206	38,017	37,562	37,567
Statistical Record								
Return on Assets %	2.32	3.15	1.93	2.30	1.47	1.79	3.02	3.83
Return on Equity %	7.06	9.99	6.26	7.77	5.36	7.07	14.78	17.73
EBITDA Margin %	31.81	32.29	30.35	27.32	26.25	21.25	6.59	36.85
Net Margin %	9.36	11.59	7.41	8.64	5.66	6.64	2.21	13.72
PPE Turnover	0.35	0.39	0.38	0.39	0.41	0.49	3.06	0.57
Asset Turnover	0.25	0.27	0.26	0.27	0.26	0.27	1.36	0.28
Debt to Equity	0.96	0.83	1.00	0.97	1.09	1.03	0.97	1.05
Price Range	39.09-30.49	40.12-29.88	32.00-26.53	32.80-25.48	30.00-21.09	40.82-21.36	47.50-34.10	50.88-26.00
P/E Ratio	21.02-16.39	15.98-11.90	21.33-17.69	17.26-13.41	24.59-17.29	25.04-13.10	14.18-10.18	13.68-6.99
Average Yield %	3.54	3.39	4.10	4.08	6.68	6.05	4.88	4.87

Address: 1221 W. Idaho Street, Boise, ID 83702-5627 Telephone: 208-388-2200	Web Site: www.idacorpinc.com Officers: Jon H. Miller - Chmn. Jan B. Packwood - Pres., C.E.O.	Auditors: Deloitte & Touche LLP Investor Contact: 208-388-2664 Transfer Agents: Wells Fargo Shareowner Services, South St. Paul, MN

IDEX CORPORATION

Exchange	Symbol	Price	52Wk Range	Yield	P/E
NYS	IEX	$30.69 (3/31/2008)	41.50-28.78	1.56	16.24

*7 Year Price Score 120.60 *NYSE Composite Index=100   *12 Month Price Score 92.32

Interim Earnings (Per Share)

Qtr.	Mar	Jun	Sep	Dec
2003	0.17	0.23	0.22	0.21
2004	0.23	0.29	0.29	0.30
2005	0.30	0.37	0.36	0.36
2006	0.37	0.43	0.57	0.44
2007	0.45	0.51	0.47	0.47

Interim Dividends (Per Share)

Amt	Decl	Ex	Rec	Pay
0.12Q	6/25/2007	7/12/2007	7/16/2007	7/31/2007
0.12Q	9/25/2007	10/11/2007	10/15/2007	10/31/2007
0.12Q	12/11/2007	1/11/2008	1/15/2008	1/31/2008
0.12Q	4/8/2008	4/11/2008	4/15/2008	4/30/2008

Indicated Div: $0.48

Valuation Analysis

		Institutional Holding	
Forecast P/E	14.67	No of Institutions	188
	(1/10/2007)		
Market Cap	$2.5 Billion	Shares	50,171,832
Book Value	1.2 Billion	% Held	
Price/Book	2.15		93.21
Price/Sales	1.84		

Business Summary: Industrial Machinery and Equipment (MIC: 11.5 SIC: 3561 NAIC: 333911)

IDEX manufactures an array of engineered industrial products sold to customers in a variety of industries globally in four business segments. The Fluid & Metering Technologies segment consists of Banjo, Liquid Controls, Pulsafeeder, Versa-Matic, Viking Pump and Warren Rupp units. The Health & Science Technologies segment includes Eastern Plastics, Gast Manufacturing, Micropump, Rheodyne and Sclvex. The Dispensing Equipment segment is comprised of FAST & Fluid Management and Fluid Management. The Fire & Safety/Diversified Products segment includes Hale Products fire suppression and rescue tools businesses, as well as the BAND-IT engineered clamping business.

Recent Developments: For the year ended Dec 31 2007, income from continuing operations increased 16.6% to US$155.9 million from US$133.7 million a year earlier. Net income increased 5.8% to US$155.1 million from US$146.7 million in the prior year. Revenues were US$1.36 billion, up 17.6% from US$1.15 billion the year before. Operating income was US$255.1 million versus US$217.2 million in the prior year, an increase of 17.4%. Direct operating expenses rose 16.6% to US$790.2 million from US$677.5 million in the comparable period the year before. Indirect operating expenses increased 20.4% to US$313.4 million from US$260.2 million in the equivalent prior-year period.

Prospects: For full-year 2008, Co. expects Fluid and Metering Technologies segment to be driven by continued strong global investment in the infrastructure-related markets and process control industries. Accordingly, Co. expects 2008 total revenue growth to range at 13.0% to 15.0%, with organic revenue growth of 4.0% to 6.0%, acquisitions of 6.0% and foreign currency translation of 3.0% and earnings per share in the range of $2.10 to $2.18 compared to $1.90 in the prior year. Meanwhile, on Jan 2 2008, Co. announced that it has completed the acquisition of ADS, LLC, a provider of metering technology and flow monitoring services for the water and wastewater markets, for approximately $160.0 million.

Financial Data

(US$ in Thousands)	12/31/2007	12/31/2006	12/31/2005	12/31/2004	12/31/2003	12/31/2002	12/31/2001	12/31/2000
Earnings Per Share	1.89	1.81	1.39	1.12	0.83	0.74	0.47	0.92
Cash Flow Per Share	2.46	2.01	1.88	1.89	1.53	1.52	1.58	1.38
Tang Book Value Per Share	N.M.	N.M.	1.29	N.M.	0.18	N.M.	N.M.	N.M.
Dividends Per Share	0.460	0.380	0.320	0.284	0.249	0.249	0.249	0.249
Dividend Payout %	24.34	20.96	23.08	25.40	29.87	33.53	53.33	27.05
Income Statement								
Total Revenue	1,358,631	1,154,940	1,043,275	928,297	797,920	742,014	726,947	704,276
EBITDA	297,015	248,658	214,002	180,170	140,816	130,354	118,466	154,251
Income Before Taxes	235,164	201,893	168,928	133,877	96,670	83,895	53,431	101,026
Income Taxes	79,200	68,171	59,125	47,471	34,318	29,783	20,721	37,581
Net Income	155,145	146,671	109,803	86,406	62,352	54,112	32,710	63,445
Average Shares	82,006	80,970	79,080	77,022	74,958	73,086	69,855	68,922
Balance Sheet								
Current Assets	637,138	417,908	347,501	261,238	224,496	221,260	214,903	232,089
Total Assets	1,989,594	1,670,821	1,244,180	1,186,292	960,739	931,050	838,804	758,854
Current Liabilities	198,953	187,252	153,296	148,255	115,681	108,332	87,338	177,811
Long-Term Obligations	448,901	353,770	156,899	225,317	176,546	241,051	291,820	153,809
Total Liabilities	826,871	691,549	421,170	472,687	368,637	424,259	437,692	384,352
Stockholders' Equity	1,162,723	979,272	823,010	713,605	592,102	506,791	401,112	374,502
Shares Outstanding	81,579	80,545	79,190	76,231	74,419	73,206	69,217	68,081
Statistical Record								
Return on Assets %	8.48	10.06	9.04	8.03	6.59	6.11	4.09	8.45
Return on Equity %	14.49	16.28	14.29	13.20	11.35	11.92	8.43	17.99
EBITDA Margin %	21.86	21.53	20.51	19.41	17.65	17.57	16.30	21.90
Net Margin %	11.42	12.70	10.52	9.31	7.81	7.29	4.50	9.01
Asset Turnover	0.74	0.79	0.86	0.86	0.84	0.84	0.91	0.94
Current Ratio	3.20	2.23	2.27	1.76	1.94	2.04	2.46	1.31
Debt to Equity	0.39	0.36	0.19	0.32	0.30	0.48	0.73	0.41
Price Range	41.50-30.74	35.43-27.16	30.13-24.65	27.13-17.76	18.60-11.81	17.61-11.56	16.50-11.40	15.89-10.25
P/E Ratio	21.96-16.26	19.57-15.01	21.68-17.73	24.23-15.85	22.40-14.23	23.80-15.63	35.11-24.25	17.27-11.14
Average Yield %	1.28	1.23	1.18	1.31	1.61	1.67	1.79	1.86

Address: 630 Dundee Road, Suite 400, Northbrook, IL 60062 Telephone: 847-498-7070 Fax: 847-498-3940	Web Site: www.idexcorp.com Officers: Dennis K. Williams - Chmn., Pres., C.E.O. Dominic A. Romeo CPA - V.P., C.F.O.	Auditors: Deloitte & Touche LLP Investor Contact: 847-498-7070 Transfer Agents: National City Bank, Cleveland, OH

IKON OFFICE SOLUTIONS, INC.

Exchange	Symbol	Price	52Wk Range	Yield	P/E
NYS	IKN	$7.60 (3/31/2008)	16.05-6.78	2.11	9.16

*7 Year Price Score 92.23   *NYSE Composite Index=100   *12 Month Price Score 65.67

Interim Earnings (Per Share)

Qtr.	Dec	Mar	Jun	Sep
2004-05	0.12	0.00	0.17	0.11
2005-06	0.21	0.19	0.20	0.20
2006-07	0.21	0.24	0.23	0.23
2007-08	0.13	...	...	...

Interim Dividends (Per Share)

Amt	Decl	Ex	Rec	Pay
0.04Q	5/1/2007	5/17/2007	5/21/2007	6/10/2007
0.04Q	7/26/2007	8/23/2007	8/27/2007	9/10/2007
0.04Q	10/25/2007	11/15/2007	11/19/2007	12/10/2007
0.04Q	1/24/2008	2/14/2008	2/19/2008	3/10/2008

Indicated Div: $0.16

Valuation Analysis

Institutional Holding		
Forecast P/E	15.76	No of Institutions
	(1/10/2007)	145
Market Cap	$710.6 Million	Shares
Book Value	1.4 Billion	121,683,360
Price/Book	0.51	% Held
Price/Sales	0.17	96.32

TRADING VOLUME (thousand shares)

Business Summary: IT & Technology (MIC: 10.2 SIC: 5045 NAIC: 423430)

Ikon Office Solutions is an independent channel for document management systems and services. Co. provides document management services, including professional services, on-site and off-site managed services, customized workflow softwares and enhanced support through its worldwide service professionals. Co. also provides document management services, including digital copying and printing, professional services, managed on-site services and off-site legal document services, customer services as well as lease financing. As of Sep 30 2007, Co. had over 400 locations throughout North America and Western Europe.

Recent Developments: For the quarter ended Dec 31 2007, net income decreased 45.2% to US$15.0 million from US$27.3 million in the year-earlier quarter. Revenues were US$998.1 million, down 1.0% from US$1.01 billion the year before. Operating income was US$37.8 million versus US$49.0 million in the prior-year quarter, a decrease of 22.9%. Direct operating expenses declined 1.9% to US$658.2 million from US$670.8 million in the comparable period the year before. Indirect operating expenses increased 4.9% to US$302.1 million from US$288.1 million in the equivalent prior-year period.

Prospects: For the fiscal year ending Sep 2008, Co. expects revenue to be flat, reflecting an improving equipment trend, flat Customer Service & Supplies, and growth in Managed & Professional Services. Earnings are forecast in the range of $0.92 to $0.98 per diluted share, excluding the restructuring charge taken in prior quarter. As reported, Co. expects diluted earnings per share of $0.88 to $0.94. Looking ahead, Co. has initiated several actions to improve equipment revenue and profitability, including working with its vendors to improve pricing and promotions. Co. is also taking steps to reduce its cost and expense structure by about $25.0 million, which should benefit results in fiscal 2008.

Financial Data
(US$ in Thousands)

	3 Mos	09/30/2007	09/30/2006	09/30/2005	09/30/2004	09/30/2003	09/30/2002	09/30/2001
Earnings Per Share	0.83	0.91	0.80	0.43	0.60	0.75	0.99	0.11
Cash Flow Per Share	1.42	1.35	0.74	(0.05)	(2.57)	3.03	3.33	2.89
Tang Book Value Per Share	0.69	3.21	3.02	2.16	3.09	2.58	2.08	0.97
Dividends Per Share	0.160	0.160	0.160	0.160	0.160	0.160	0.160	0.160
Dividend Payout %	19.28	17.58	20.00	37.21	26.67	21.33	16.16	145.45
Income Statement								
Total Revenue	998,055	4,168,344	4,228,249	4,377,305	4,649,820	4,710,912	4,827,502	5,273,479
EBITDA	56,407	274,976	269,584	230,526	264,412	347,864	424,636	315,737
Depn & Amortn	18,624	...	...	...	...	...	...	...
Income Before Taxes	26,948	163,434	157,918	104,950	123,986	186,373	239,200	67,796
Income Taxes	11,975	48,947	51,669	31,755	32,432	70,356	88,866	53,791
Net Income	14,973	114,487	106,202	60,666	91,554	116,017	150,334	15,205
Average Shares	114,586	126,342	132,941	157,691	169,282	167,802	155,084	144,408
Balance Sheet								
Current Assets	1,220,523	1,364,288	1,379,574	1,727,914	2,084,740	2,662,498	2,626,430	2,514,637
Total Assets	3,142,717	3,278,081	3,231,699	3,831,819	4,537,907	6,639,507	6,472,618	6,290,992
Current Liabilities	683,227	681,523	757,700	937,340	1,256,943	2,237,376	2,167,684	2,265,126
Long-Term Obligations	903,726	757,533	657,583	953,463	1,164,725	1,982,558	2,090,178	1,965,716
Total Liabilities	1,751,907	1,567,267	1,545,566	2,261,475	2,812,297	5,004,055	4,937,672	4,895,414
Stockholders' Equity	1,390,810	1,710,814	1,686,133	1,570,344	1,725,610	1,635,452	1,534,946	1,395,578
Shares Outstanding	93,494	117,570	128,929	135,750	142,133	146,368	144,024	141,776
Statistical Record								
Return on Assets %	3.20	3.52	3.01	1.45	1.63	1.77	2.36	0.24
Return on Equity %	6.59	6.74	6.52	3.68	5.43	7.32	10.26	1.07
EBITDA Margin %	5.65	6.60	6.38	5.27	5.69	7.38	8.80	5.99
Net Margin %	1.50	2.75	2.51	1.39	1.97	2.46	3.11	0.29
Asset Turnover	1.30	1.28	1.20	1.05	0.83	0.72	0.76	0.83
Current Ratio	1.79	2.00	1.82	1.84	1.66	1.19	1.21	1.11
Debt to Equity	0.65	0.44	0.39	0.61	0.67	1.21	1.36	1.41
Price Range	17.08-10.62	17.08-12.43	14.33-9.69	12.02-8.65	13.17-7.31	9.26-6.40	14.24-6.65	9.80-2.31
P/E Ratio	20.58-12.80	18.77-13.66	17.91-12.11	27.95-20.12	21.95-12.18	12.35-8.53	14.38-6.72	89.09-21.02
Average Yield %	1.13	1.13	1.30	1.55	1.45	2.09	1.52	2.86

Address: 70 Valley Stream Parkway, Malvern, PA 19355	Web Site: www.ikon.com	Auditors: PricewaterhouseCoopers LLP
Telephone: 610-296-8000	Officers: Matthew J. Espe - Chmn., Pres., C.E.O. Robert F. Woods - Sr. V.P., C.F.O.	Investor Contact: 610-408-7196 Transfer Agents: National City Bank, Cleveland, OH

ILLINOIS TOOL WORKS, INC.

Exchange	Symbol	Price	52Wk Range	Yield	P/E	Div Acheiver
NYS	ITW	$48.23 (3/31/2008)	60.00-46.27	2.32	14.35	45 Years

*7 Year Price Score 103.51   *NYSE Composite Index=100   *12 Month Price Score 98.11

Interim Earnings (Per Share)

Qtr.	Mar	Jun	Sep	Dec
2003	0.32	0.45	0.44	0.46
2004	0.47	0.58	0.55	0.60
2005	0.53	0.65	0.71	0.71
2006	0.65	0.81	0.78	0.77
2007	0.71	0.90	0.89	0.86

Interim Dividends (Per Share)

Amt	Decl	Ex	Rec	Pay
0.21Q	5/4/2007	6/27/2007	6/30/2007	7/16/2007
0.28Q	8/3/2007	9/26/2007	9/30/2007	10/15/2007
0.28Q	10/25/2007	12/27/2007	12/31/2007	1/14/2008
0.28Q	2/8/2008	3/27/2008	3/31/2008	4/14/2008

Indicated Div: $1.12 (Div. Reinv. Plan)

Valuation Analysis

		Institutional Holding	
Forecast P/E	12.82	No of Institutions	
	(1/10/2007)	679	
Market Cap	$25.6 Billion	Shares	
Book Value	9.4 Billion	462,971,904	
Price/Book	2.73	% Held	
Price/Sales	1.58	82.85	

Business Summary: Industrial Machinery and Equipment (MIC: 11.5 SIC: 3566 NAIC: 333612)

Illinois Tool Works is a manufacturer of industrial products and equipment. Co. has eight business segments: Industrial Packaging that produces steel, plastic and paper products; Power Systems & Electronics that produces equipment and consumables related with power conversion; Transportation that produces components for transportation-related applications; Construction Products that produces tools for construction applications; Food Equipment that produces commercial food equipment; Decorative Surfaces that produces decorative surfacing materials; Polymers & Fluids that produces adhesives and sealants; and All Other, which produces products such as plastic packaging and metal fasteners.

Recent Developments: For the year ended Dec 31 2007, Income from continuing operations increased 8.7% to US$1.83 billion from US$1.68 billion a year earlier. Net income increased 8.9% to US$1.87 billion from US$1.72 billion in the prior year. Revenues were US$16.17 billion, up 17.2% from US$13.80 billion the year before. Operating income was US$2.62 billion versus US$2.39 billion in the prior year, an increase of 10.0%. Direct operating expenses rose 17.6% to US$10.46 billion from US$8.89 billion in the comparable period the year before. Indirect operating expenses increased 22.4% to US$3.09 billion from US$2.53 billion in the equivalent prior-year period.

Prospects: On Jan 7 2008, Co. has acquired the assets of Peerless Machinery Corp., a manufacturer and supplier of mixers, bread dividers, dough handlers, and other food processing equipment based in Sidney, OH. This acquisition will help support the continued growth of Co.'s food equipment group, specifically in the wholesale baking industry. Meanwhile, Co. is forecasting a full-year 2008 diluted income per share from continuing operations range of $3.47 to $3.61, assuming total company revenue growth range of 6.0% to 10.0%. For the first quarter of 2008, Co. is forecasting income per share from continuing operations of $0.72 to $0.78, assuming total company revenue growth range of 8.0% to 11.0%.

Financial Data

(US$ in Thousands)	12/31/2007	12/31/2006	12/31/2005	12/31/2004	12/31/2003	12/31/2002	12/31/2001	12/31/2000
Earnings Per Share	3.36	3.01	2.60	2.19	1.66	1.16	1.31	1.58
Cash Flow Per Share	4.50	3.65	3.23	2.53	2.23	2.10	2.22	1.86
Tang Book Value Per Share	6.92	6.94	6.89	7.59	8.22	6.56	5.41	4.78
Dividends Per Share	0.980	0.750	0.610	0.520	0.470	0.450	0.420	0.380
Dividend Payout %	29.17	24.92	23.46	23.69	28.31	38.96	31.94	24.13
Income Statement								
Total Revenue	16,170,611	14,055,049	12,921,792	11,731,425	10,035,623	9,467,740	9,292,791	9,983,577
EBITDA	3,184,401	2,943,859	2,623,780	2,396,308	1,922,705	1,790,193	1,669,032	1,948,078
Income Before Taxes	2,580,979	2,445,246	2,181,569	1,999,405	1,576,114	1,433,560	1,230,849	1,478,180
Income Taxes	754,900	727,500	686,700	659,800	535,900	501,750	428,400	520,200
Net Income	1,869,862	1,717,746	1,494,869	1,338,694	1,023,680	712,592	805,659	957,980
Average Shares	556,030	569,892	575,434	609,702	617,500	616,090	612,612	605,828
Balance Sheet								
Current Assets	6,165,655	5,206,405	4,111,605	4,322,198	4,783,202	3,878,809	3,163,244	3,329,061
Total Assets	15,525,862	13,880,439	11,445,643	11,351,934	11,193,321	10,623,101	9,822,349	9,603,456
Current Liabilities	2,960,285	2,636,584	2,000,731	1,850,971	1,488,903	1,567,162	1,518,158	1,817,610
Long-Term Obligations	1,888,839	955,610	958,321	921,098	920,360	1,460,381	1,267,141	1,549,038
Total Liabilities	6,174,537	4,862,931	3,898,748	3,724,324	3,319,035	3,974,030	3,781,611	4,202,469
Stockholders' Equity	9,351,325	9,017,508	7,546,895	7,627,610	7,874,286	6,649,071	6,040,738	5,400,987
Shares Outstanding	530,096	558,749	561,627	584,456	617,272	613,165	609,852	610,897
Statistical Record								
Return on Assets %	12.72	13.57	13.11	11.84	9.38	6.97	8.29	10.24
Return on Equity %	20.36	20.74	19.70	17.22	14.10	11.23	14.08	18.70
EBITDA Margin %	19.69	20.95	20.31	20.43	19.16	18.91	17.96	19.51
Net Margin %	11.56	12.22	11.57	11.41	10.20	7.53	8.67	9.60
Asset Turnover	1.10	1.11	1.13	1.04	0.92	0.93	0.96	1.07
Current Ratio	2.08	1.97	2.06	2.34	3.21	2.48	2.08	1.83
Debt to Equity	0.20	0.11	0.13	0.12	0.12	0.22	0.21	0.29
Price Range	60.00-45.89	53.29-42.00	47.15-39.43	47.99-36.71	42.08-27.57	38.69-27.86	35.60-24.57	34.16-25.53
P/E Ratio	17.86-13.66	17.70-13.95	18.13-15.17	21.92-16.76	25.35-16.61	33.35-24.02	27.18-18.76	21.62-16.16
Average Yield %	1.82	1.61	1.42	1.18	1.39	1.33	1.34	1.30

Address: 3600 West Lake Avenue, Glenview, IL 60026-1215 Telephone: 847-724-7500	Web Site: www.itw.com Officers: W. James Farrell - Chmn. Frank S. Ptak - Vice-Chmn.	Auditors: Deloitte & Touche LLP Investor Contact: 847-657-4104 Transfer Agents: Computershare Investor Service, L.L.C., Chicago, IL

IMATION CORP.

Exchange	Symbol	Price	52Wk Range	Yield	P/E
NYS	IMN	$22.74 (3/31/2008)	41.83-17.95	2.81	N/A

*7 Year Price Score 66.57   *NYSE Composite Index=100   *12 Month Price Score 88.97

Interim Earnings (Per Share)

Qtr.	Mar	Jun	Sep	Dec
2003	0.59	0.53	0.45	0.68
2004	0.59	0.19	0.27	(0.21)
2005	0.92	0.62	0.48	0.53
2006	0.55	0.40	0.53	0.69
2007	0.44	(0.04)	0.24	(2.00)

Interim Dividends (Per Share)

Amt	Decl	Ex	Rec	Pay
0.16Q	5/2/2007	6/13/2007	6/15/2007	6/29/2007
0.16Q	8/2/2007	9/12/2007	9/14/2007	9/28/2007
0.16Q	11/7/2007	12/12/2007	12/14/2007	12/28/2007
0.16Q	2/6/2008	3/12/2008	3/14/2008	3/31/2008

Indicated Div: $0.64

Valuation Analysis

Forecast P/E	N/A
Market Cap	$873.2 Million
Book Value	1.1 Billion
Price/Book	0.83
Price/Sales	0.42

Institutional Holding

No of Institutions	178
Shares	30,255,384
% Held	86.29

TRADING VOLUME (thousand shares)

Business Summary: Electrical (MIC: 11.14 SIC: 3695 NAIC: 334613)

Imation is engaged in the development, manufacturing, sourcing, marketing and distribution of removable data storage media products and accessories. Furthermore, Co. provides removable data storage media products designed to capture, create, protect, preserve and retrieve digital assets. As of Dec 31 2007, Co. sold these products in approximately 100 countries around the world and under brand names such as Imation, Memorex and TDK Life on Record. Additionally, Co. sells a variety of consumer video, audio and home electronic products, primarily in North America and principally under the Memorex brand name.

Recent Developments: For the year ended Dec 31 2007, loss from continuing operations was US$50.4 million compared with income of US$75.2 million a year earlier. Net loss amounted to US$50.4 million versus net income of US$76.4 million in the prior year. Revenues were US$2.06 billion, up 30.1% from US$1.58 billion the year before. Operating loss was US$33.0 million versus an income of US$108.2 million in the prior year. Direct operating expenses rose 37.5% to US$1.71 billion from US$1.24 billion in the comparable period the year before. Indirect operating expenses increased 64.4% to US$387.9 million from US$235.9 million in the equivalent prior-year period.

Prospects: Co. estimates that its cost reduction restructuring program is expected to result in $25.0 million to $30.0 million in annualized cost savings once the program is fully implemented, which is intended to counteract the effect of declining gross margins, while incurring $35.0 million to $40.0 million in restructuring charges over two years related to this program. For full year 2008, Co. is targeting revenue of $2.40 billion, representing growth of approximately 16.0% over 2007. Co. also targets operating income of $95.0 million to $105.0 million including restructuring charges of $4.0 million to $6.0 million. Accordingly, Co. expects diluted earnings per share of $1.51 to $1.68.

Financial Data

(US$ in Thousands)	12/31/2007	12/31/2006	12/31/2005	12/31/2004	12/31/2003	12/31/2002	12/31/2001	12/31/2000
Earnings Per Share	(1.36)	2.17	2.54	0.84	2.26	2.11	(0.05)	(0.13)
Cash Flow Per Share	2.36	2.82	2.59	3.65	2.28	3.45	3.68	5.46
Tang Book Value Per Share	16.34	18.53	24.21	22.30	22.33	20.55	18.13	18.21
Dividends Per Share	0.620	0.540	0.460	0.380	0.240	...	...	...
Dividend Payout %	...	24.88	18.11	45.24	10.62	...	...	...
Income Statement								
Total Revenue	2,062,000	1,584,700	1,258,100	1,219,300	1,163,500	1,066,700	1,176,500	1,234,900
EBITDA	7,300	138,600	134,100	104,300	156,500	144,000	36,300	83,700
Income Before Taxes	(34,600)	111,800	106,700	53,200	122,100	112,600	(6,800)	(26,300)
Income Taxes	15,800	36,600	24,900	10,900	40,300	39,400	(5,100)	(25,300)
Net Income	(50,400)	76,400	87,900	29,900	82,000	75,100	(1,700)	(4,400)
Average Shares	37,000	35,200	34,600	35,600	36,300	35,600	34,800	35,100
Balance Sheet								
Current Assets	1,118,600	876,900	888,200	786,000	838,400	842,200	756,900	686,200
Total Assets	1,751,000	1,382,900	1,146,200	1,110,600	1,172,800	1,119,900	1,053,700	987,900
Current Liabilities	630,900	391,600	245,100	275,200	297,200	310,000	347,200	291,100
Long-Term Obligations	21,300	...	...	...	...	...	...	...
Total Liabilities	697,200	436,600	290,900	323,800	352,500	381,400	398,000	325,400
Stockholders' Equity	1,053,800	946,300	855,300	786,800	820,300	738,500	655,700	662,500
Shares Outstanding	38,400	35,000	34,500	33,700	35,400	35,500	35,300	35,200
Statistical Record								
Return on Assets %	N.M.	6.04	7.79	2.61	7.15	6.91	N.M.	N.M.
Return on Equity %	N.M.	8.48	10.71	3.71	10.52	10.77	N.M.	N.M.
EBITDA Margin %	0.35	8.75	10.66	8.55	13.45	13.50	3.09	6.78
Net Margin %	N.M.	4.82	6.99	2.45	7.05	7.04	N.M.	N.M.
Asset Turnover	1.32	1.25	1.11	1.07	1.01	0.98	1.15	1.16
Current Ratio	1.77	2.24	3.62	2.86	2.82	2.72	2.18	2.36
Debt to Equity	0.02	...	...	...	...	...	...	...
Price Range	48.50-19.38	48.81-37.50	46.44-30.52	43.62-29.81	40.80-32.25	42.25-21.07	25.40-14.94	33.56-14.19
P/E Ratio	...	22.49-17.28	18.28-12.02	51.93-35.49	18.05-14.27	20.02-9.99	...	...
Average Yield %	1.86	1.27	1.19	1.05	0.67	...	...	...

Address: 1 Imation Place, Oakdale, MN 55128-3414	**Web Site:** www.imation.com	**Auditors:** PricewaterhouseCoopers LLP
Telephone: 651-704-4000	**Officers:** Bruce A. Henderson - Chmn., C.E.O. Frank P. Russomanno - Exec. V.P., C.O.O.	**Transfer Agents:** PricewaterhouseCoopers LLP
Fax: 800-537-4675		

IMS HEALTH, INC.

Exchange	Symbol	Price	52Wk Range	Yield	P/E
NYS	RX	$21.01 (3/31/2008)	32.95-20.87	0.57	17.81

*7 Year Price Score 92.05   *NYSE Composite Index=100   *12 Month Price Score 89.90

TRADING VOLUME (thousand shares)

Interim Earnings (Per Share)

Qtr.	Mar	Jun	Sep	Dec
2003	1.71	0.23	0.29	0.28
2004	0.34	0.27	0.28	0.31
2005	0.13	0.41	0.30	0.38
2006	0.56	0.30	0.34	0.33
2007	0.43	0.36	0.29	0.10

Interim Dividends (Per Share)

Amt	Decl	Ex	Rec	Pay
0.03Q	4/17/2007	4/27/2007	5/1/2007	6/8/2007
0.03Q	7/17/2007	7/30/2007	8/1/2007	9/7/2007
0.03Q	10/16/2007	10/26/2007	10/30/2007	12/7/2007
0.03Q	2/12/2008	2/27/2008	3/1/2008	3/28/2008

Indicated Div: $0.12

Valuation Analysis

		Institutional Holding	
Forecast P/E	N/A	No of Institutions	378
Market Cap	$4.0 Billion	Shares	170,510,464
Book Value	N/A	% Held	87.38
Price/Book	N/A		
Price/Sales	1.83		

Business Summary: IT & Technology (MIC: 10.2 SIC: 7374 NAIC: 518210)

IMS Health is a global provider of market intelligence to the pharmaceutical and healthcare industries. Co. offers products and services for company's clients' day-to-day operations, including portfolio optimization capabilities; launch and brand management solutions; sales force effectiveness innovations; managed markets and consumer health offerings; and consulting and services solutions that are intended to improve return on investment and the delivery of healthcare worldwide. Co.'s information products are developed to meet client needs by using data secured from a worldwide network of suppliers in more than 100 countries.

Recent Developments: For the year ended Dec 31 2007, net income decreased 25.8% to US$234.0 million from US$315.5 million in the prior year. Revenues were US$2.19 billion, up 11.9% from US$1.96 billion the year before. Operating income was US$393.3 million versus US$444.2 million in the prior year, a decrease of 11.5%. Direct operating expenses rose 12.9% to US$958.5 million from US$848.8 million in the comparable period the year before. Indirect operating expenses increased 26.3% to US$840.8 million from US$665.6 million in the equivalent prior-year period.

Prospects: For the full year of 2008, Co. is projecting constant-dollar revenue growth to be in the range of 6.0% to 9.0%, along with constant-dollar operating income growth at or above 6.0% to 9.0%. In addition, Co. is forecasting earnings in the range of $1.70 to $1.76 per diluted share. Separately, on Jan 4 2008, Co. announced plans to strengthen its account management and business development capabilities, streamline consulting practice areas, and redeploy resources to accelerate the implementation of business process outsourcing services. Once fully implemented, Co. anticipates that these actions will generate approximately $55.0 million to $60.0 million of annual savings beginning in 2009.

Financial Data

(US$ in Thousands)	12/31/2007	12/31/2006	12/31/2005	12/31/2004	12/31/2003	12/31/2002	12/31/2001	12/31/2000
Earnings Per Share	1.18	1.53	1.22	1.20	2.58	0.93	0.62	0.40
Cash Flow Per Share	2.39	1.76	1.33	1.71	1.53	1.31	1.10	0.51
Dividends Per Share	0.120	0.120	0.080	0.080	0.080	0.080	0.080	0.080
Dividend Payout %	10.17	7.84	6.56	6.67	3.10	8.60	12.90	20.00
Income Statement								
Total Revenue	2,192,571	1,958,588	1,754,791	1,569,045	1,381,761	1,428,097	1,332,923	1,424,359
EBITDA	505,598	600,799	571,591	519,653	410,631	492,173	261,985	366,621
Income Before Taxes	349,595	448,745	454,253	414,439	324,323	423,510	183,801	261,313
Income Taxes	115,555	133,234	170,162	129,181	165,954	130,404	38,415	140,412
Net Income	234,040	315,511	284,091	285,422	638,945	266,115	185,426	170,816
Average Shares	198,672	206,598	232,484	237,705	247,263	286,663	300,147	300,038
Balance Sheet								
Current Assets	840,173	693,293	821,010	936,519	778,929	827,264	656,845	568,517
Total Assets	2,244,204	1,906,594	1,973,020	1,890,706	1,644,338	1,618,528	1,367,554	1,243,007
Current Liabilities	634,544	542,874	549,048	554,121	836,625	678,583	635,491	827,156
Long-Term Obligations	1,203,209	975,406	611,431	626,670	152,050	325,000	150,000	...
Total Liabilities	2,183,015	1,772,275	1,458,100	1,533,016	1,352,908	1,216,912	1,004,169	1,004,125
Stockholders' Equity	(40,315)	33,909	415,055	255,714	189,577	222,256	218,366	103,540
Shares Outstanding	191,227	200,678	227,970	229,129	238,339	281,065	294,088	291,339
Statistical Record								
Return on Assets %	11.28	16.27	14.71	16.10	39.16	17.82	14.21	8.95
Return on Equity %	...	140.55	84.71	127.85	310.29	120.79	115.21	40.35
EBITDA Margin %	23.06	30.68	32.57	33.12	29.72	34.46	19.65	25.74
Net Margin %	10.67	16.11	16.19	18.19	46.24	18.63	13.91	8.48
Asset Turnover	1.06	1.01	0.91	0.89	0.85	0.96	1.02	1.05
Current Ratio	1.32	1.28	1.50	1.69	0.93	1.22	1.03	0.69
Debt to Equity	...	28.77	1.47	2.45	0.80	1.46	0.69	...
Price Range	32.95-22.25	29.48-23.99	28.47-22.22	26.60-20.90	25.01-14.17	22.45-13.25	30.20-18.99	28.56-14.33
P/E Ratio	27.92-18.86	19.27-15.68	23.34-18.21	22.17-17.42	9.69-5.49	24.14-14.25	48.71-30.63	71.41-35.83
Average Yield %	0.42	0.45	0.32	0.33	0.43	0.44	0.31	0.40

Address: 901 Main Avenue, Suite 612, Norwalk, CT 06851-1187
Telephone: 203-845-5200
Fax: 203-845-5299

Web Site: www.imshealth.com
Officers: David M. Thomas - Exec. Chmn. David R. Carlucci - Pres., C.E.O.

Auditors: PricewaterhouseCoopers LLP
Investor Contact: 203-845-5237
Transfer Agents: American Stock Transfer and Trust Company

401

INTERCONTINENTALEXCHANGE INC

Exchange	Symbol	Price	52Wk Range	Yield	P/E
NYS	ICE	$130.50 (3/31/2008)	194.50-115.90	N/A	38.50

*7 Year Price Score N/A   *NYSE Composite Index=100   *12 Month Price Score 93.18

Interim Earnings (Per Share)

Qtr.	Mar	Jun	Sep	Dec
2005	0.17	(0.13)	0.05	(0.48)
2006	0.33	0.52	0.73	0.81
2007	0.80	0.75	0.93	0.90

Interim Dividends (Per Share)

No Dividends Paid

Valuation Analysis		Institutional Holding	
Forecast P/E	N/A	No of Institutions	
		218	
Market Cap	$9.1 Billion	Shares	
Book Value	1.5 Billion	52,951,308	
Price/Book	6.16	% Held	
Price/Sales	15.84	76.91	

TRADING VOLUME (thousand shares)

Business Summary: Finance Intermediaries & Services (MIC: 8.7 SIC: 6231 NAIC: 523210)

IntercontinentalExchange owns and operates an Internet-based, global electronic marketplace for facilitating trading in futures and over-the-counter (OTC) commodities and derivative financial products. Co. has three operating segments: OTC, futures and market data. In its OTC markets, Co. offers trading in over-the-counter, or off-exchange, derivative contracts, including contracts that provide for the physical delivery of an underlying commodity. In its futures markets, Co. offers trading in standardized derivative contracts on its regulated exchanges. Through its market data segment, Co. offers market data services and products for both futures and OTC market participants and observers.

Recent Developments: For the year ended Dec 31 2007, net income increased 67.9% to US$240.6 million from US$143.3 million in the prior year. Revenues were US$574.3 million, up 83.0% from US$313.8 million the year before. Operating income was US$353.6 million versus US$204.6 million in the prior year, an increase of 72.8%. Indirect operating expenses increased 102.2% to US$220.7 million from US$109.2 million in the equivalent prior-year period.

Prospects: On Jan 31 2008, Co. announced that it has entered into an agreement to acquire YellowJacket Software, Inc (YellowJacket), a financial technology firm that operates an electronic trade negotiation platform. The acquisition is not expected to be material to Co.'s operating results in the first half of 2008. Co. expects to complete the acquisition in Feb 2008. Separately, for full-year 2008, Co. expects capital expenditures to range from $36.0 million to $40.0 million, including $10.0 million to $12.0 million for leasehold improvements relating to the relocation and expansion of its London office, which houses futures, over-the-counter, clearing and market data staff and operations.

Financial Data
(US$ in Thousands)

	12/31/2007	12/31/2006	12/31/2005	12/31/2004	12/31/2003	12/31/2002
Earnings Per Share	3.39	2.40	(0.39)	0.40	0.36	0.36
Cash Flow Per Share	4.17	2.58	0.94	0.76	0.50	...
Tang Book Value Per Share	N.M.	6.42	2.82	0.87	0.37	...
Income Statement						
Income Before Taxes	358,434	212,543	59,995	33,722	19,866	52,445
Income Taxes	117,822	69,275	19,585	11,773	6,489	17,739
Net Income	240,612	143,268	40,410	21,949	13,377	34,706
Average Shares	70,980	59,599	53,218	53,062	54,639	54,850
Balance Sheet						
Total Assets	2,796,345	493,211	265,770	207,518	214,879	...
Total Liabilities	1,319,489	38,743	33,147	57,787	28,603	...
Stockholders' Equity	1,476,856	454,468	232,623	132,149	101,194	...
Shares Outstanding	69,711	58,125	55,511	52,865	52,862	...
Statistical Record						
Return on Assets %	14.63	37.75	17.08	10.36	...	...
Return on Equity %	24.92	41.70	22.16	18.76	...	...
Price Range	194.50-115.72	113.21-36.90	39.25-31.97	...	...	...
P/E Ratio	57.37-34.14	47.17-15.38	...	...	...	...

Address: 2100 RiverEdge Parkway, Suite 500, Atlanta, GA 30328 Telephone: 770-857-4700 Fax: 770-857-4755	Web Site: www.theice.com Officers: Jeffery C Sprecher - Chmn., C.E.O. Charles A. Vice - Pres., C.O.O.	Auditors: Ernst & Young LLP Transfer Agents: Computershare Investor Services

INDYMAC BANCORP INC

Exchange	Symbol	Price	52Wk Range	Yield	P/E
NYS	IMB	$4.96 (3/31/2008)	36.66-4.36	N/A	N/A

*7 Year Price Score 50.36 *NYSE Composite Index=100 *12 Month Price Score 39.78

Interim Earnings (Per Share)

Qtr.	Mar	Jun	Sep	Dec
2003	0.66	0.75	0.87	0.75
2004	0.70	0.38	0.78	0.87
2005	1.01	1.26	1.18	1.08
2006	1.18	1.49	1.19	0.95
2007	0.70	0.60	(2.77)	(6.82)

Interim Dividends (Per Share)

Amt	Decl	Ex	Rec	Pay
0.50Q	1/25/2007	2/6/2007	2/8/2007	3/8/2007
0.50Q	4/26/2007	5/8/2007	5/10/2007	6/7/2007
0.50Q	7/27/2007	8/7/2007	8/9/2007	9/6/2007
0.25Q	11/6/2007	11/13/2007	11/15/2007	12/6/2007

Valuation Analysis **Institutional Holding**

Forecast P/E	11.01	No of Institutions
	(1/10/2007)	239
Market Cap	$401.2 Million	Shares
Book Value	1.3 Billion	73,743,216
Price/Book	0.30	% Held
Price/Sales	0.20	N/A

Business Summary: Other Depository Banking (MIC: 8.5 SIC: 6035 NAIC: 551112)

IndyMac Bancorp is the holding company for IndyMac Bank, F.S.B., and operates through two main segments. The Mortgage Banking segment's core activities are loan production, loan sales, and the performance of its servicing functions, with product offering that includes adjustable-rate mortgages and fixed-rate mortgages. The Thrift segment mainly invests in single-family residential mortgage loans, construction financing for single-family residences or lots provided directly to individual customers; as well as mortgage-backed securities. As of Dec 31 2007, Co. had total assets of $32.73 billion and total deposits of $17.82 billion.

Recent Developments: For the year ended Dec 31 2007, net loss amounted to US$614.8 million versus net income of US$342.9 million in the prior year. Net interest income increased 7.6% to US$566.7 million from US$526.7 million in the prior year. Provision for loan losses was US$395.5 million versus US$20.0 million in the prior year, an increase of. Non-interest income was US$167.6 million versus US$840.0 million, while non-interest expense advanced 23.5% to US$975.4 million.

Prospects: In light of the deterioration of the housing and mortgage markets, Co. expects non-performing assets to be 7.5% to 8.0% of assets in the second half of 2008, compared to 4.61% of assets at Dec 31 2007. Nonetheless, for 2008, Co. expects a $1.10 billion reduction in its credit provisions/costs from 2007, given the reserves it established in 2007. Co. also expects to reduce its annualized operating costs year-over-year, excluding real estate owned costs, by $264.0 million. Also, Co.'s new, more government sponsored enterprises -oriented mortgage production business is projected to make $85.0 million after-tax in 2008. Overall, Co. expects a small profit of about $13.0 million in 2008.

Financial Data

(US$ in Thousands)	12/31/2007	12/31/2006	12/31/2005	12/31/2004	12/31/2003	12/31/2002	12/31/2001	12/31/2000
Earnings Per Share	(8.78)	4.82	4.54	2.74	3.01	2.41	1.84	1.69
Cash Flow Per Share	(100.90)	(109.34)	(72.20)	(86.00)	8.10	(15.74)	(19.35)	(12.66)
Tang Book Value Per Share	N.M.	1.28	5.46	8.74	9.51	9.39	8.09	7.69
Dividends Per Share	1.750	1.880	1.560	1.210	0.550	...	...	...
Dividend Payout %	...	39.00	34.36	44.16	18.27	...	...	...
Income Statement								
Interest Income	2,187,707	1,751,016	1,069,538	767,608	575,841	477,104	544,940	438,403
Interest Expense	1,620,965	1,224,295	649,644	362,546	264,904	267,816	340,941	283,355
Net Interest Income	566,742	526,721	419,894	405,062	310,937	209,288	203,999	155,048
Provision for Losses	395,548	19,993	9,978	8,170	19,700	16,154	22,022	15,974
Non-Interest Income	(167,630)	839,975	695,794	407,482	416,902	382,172	317,540	198,024
Non-Interest Expense	975,411	790,083	606,981	522,078	425,457	345,146	283,748	177,761
Income Before Taxes	(971,847)	556,620	498,729	282,296	282,682	230,160	216,547	141,080
Income Taxes	(380,060)	212,567	196,998	111,567	111,379	86,767	89,974	59,254
Net Income	(614,808)	342,929	300,226	170,522	171,303	143,393	116,388	117,926
Average Shares	74,261	71,118	66,060	62,152	56,926	59,592	63,191	69,787
Balance Sheet								
Net Loans & Leases	20,182,317	19,398,274	14,253,937	11,195,325	10,022,433	6,189,331	5,076,049	3,983,127
Total Assets	32,734,468	29,495,316	21,452,299	16,825,644	13,240,391	9,574,454	7,497,311	5,740,204
Total Deposits	17,815,243	10,898,006	7,671,924	5,743,479	4,350,773	3,140,502	3,238,864	797,935
Total Liabilities	30,899,330	27,467,048	19,926,198	15,561,673	12,222,960	8,724,489	6,535,886	5,012,311
Stockholders' Equity	1,343,824	2,028,268	1,526,101	1,263,971	1,017,431	849,965	845,138	727,893
Shares Outstanding	80,885	73,017	64,246	61,995	56,760	54,829	60,366	62,176
Statistical Record								
Return on Assets %	N.M.	1.35	1.57	1.13	1.50	1.68	1.76	2.48
Return on Equity %	N.M.	19.30	21.52	14.91	18.35	16.92	14.80	15.12
Net Interest Margin %	25.91	30.08	39.26	52.77	54.00	43.87	37.44	35.37
Efficiency Ratio %	48.29	30.49	34.38	44.43	42.86	40.17	32.90	27.93
Loans to Deposits	1.13	1.78	1.86	1.95	2.30	1.97	1.57	4.99
Price Range	45.19-5.89	50.11-37.61	46.08-33.10	37.82-29.41	30.83-17.75	26.75-16.57	29.59-21.62	29.50-10.50
P/E Ratio	...	10.40-7.80	10.15-7.29	13.80-10.73	10.24-5.90	11.10-6.88	16.08-11.75	17.46-6.21
Average Yield %	6.78	4.37	4.03	3.65	2.32	...	...	...

Address: 888 East Walnut Street, Pasadena, CA 91101	**Web Site:** www.indymacbank.com	**Auditors:** Ernst & Young LLP
Telephone: 626-535-5901	**Officers:** Michael W. Perry - Chmn., C.E.O. Scott Keys - Exec. V.P., C.F.O.	**Transfer Agents:** The Bank of New York, New York, NY
Fax: 626-229-6005		

INGERSOLL-RAND CO. LTD.

Exchange	Symbol	Price	52Wk Range	Yield	P/E
NYS	IR	$44.58 (3/31/2008)	55.99-36.77	1.62	3.32

*7 Year Price Score 114.66 *NYSE Composite Index=100 *12 Month Price Score 93.61

Interim Earnings (Per Share)

Qtr.	Mar	Jun	Sep	Dec
2003	0.45	0.41	0.44	0.57
2004	0.51	0.81	0.68	1.48
2005	0.64	0.83	0.75	0.87
2006	0.76	0.95	0.76	0.72
2007	0.70	3.17	0.92	8.61

Interim Dividends (Per Share)

Amt	Decl	Ex	Rec	Pay
0.18Q	8/1/2007	8/13/2007	8/15/2007	9/4/2007
0.18Q	10/8/2007	11/8/2007	11/13/2007	12/3/2007
0.18Q	2/6/2008	2/13/2008	2/15/2008	3/3/2008
0.18Q	4/2/2008	5/13/2008	5/15/2008	6/2/2008

Indicated Div: $0.72

Valuation Analysis

Forecast P/E	10.11
	(1/10/2007)
Market Cap	$12.2 Billion
Book Value	7.9 Billion
Price/Book	1.54
Price/Sales	1.39

Institutional Holding

No of Institutions	N/A
Shares	N/A
% Held	N/A

Business Summary: Industrial Machinery and Equipment (MIC: 11.5 SIC: 3569 NAIC: 333999)

Ingersoll-Rand Company operates through three key business segments: Climate Control Technologies, which designs, manufactures, sells and services transport temperature control units; refrigerated display merchandisers, beverage coolers, auxiliary power units and walk-in storage coolers and freezers; Industrial Technologies, which designs, manufactures, sells and services compressed air systems, tools, fluid and material handling, golf and utility vehicles and energy generation systems; and Security Technologies, which designs, manufactures, sells and services mechanical and electronic security products, biometric access control systems and security and scheduling software.

Recent Developments: For the year ended Dec 31 2007, income from continuing operations decreased 4.2% to US$733.1 million from US$765.0 million a year earlier. Net income increased 284.2% to US$3.97 billion from US$1.03 billion in the prior year. Revenues were US$8.76 billion, up 9.1% from US$8.03 billion the year before. Operating income was US$1.06 billion versus US$998.5 million in the prior year, an increase of 5.9%. Direct operating expenses rose 8.7% to US$6.27 billion from US$5.77 billion in the comparable period the year before. Indirect operating expenses increased 13.1% to US$1.43 billion from US$1.27 billion in the equivalent prior-year period.

Prospects: On Dec 17 2007, Co. announced that it has signed a definitive agreement to acquire Trane Inc., a global provider of indoor climate control systems and services, for about $9.50 billion. This transaction is expected to close in the second quarter of 2008. Coupled with its expectation of slow growth in North America and Western Europe and continued brisk growth in Eastern Europe, Asia and Latin America in 2008, Co. is anticipating revenue growth of 6.0% to 7.0% for the year, with 2.0% related to currency. In addition, excluding the one-time charges for its Trane acquisition, Co.'s full year earnings from continuing operations are forecasted to be in a range of $3.80 to $3.90 per share.

Financial Data
(US$ in Thousands)

	12/31/2007	12/31/2006	12/31/2005	12/31/2004	12/31/2003	12/31/2002	12/31/2001	12/31/2000
Earnings Per Share	13.43	3.20	3.09	3.48	1.87	(0.51)	0.74	2.06
Cash Flow Per Share	3.08	3.04	2.40	2.17	0.70	1.77	1.82	2.39
Tang Book Value Per Share	11.70	0.21	1.47	2.54	N.M.	N.M.	N.M.	N.M.
Dividends Per Share	0.720	0.680	0.570	0.440	0.360	0.340	...	...
Dividend Payout %	5.36	21.25	18.45	12.66	19.25	...	...	...
Income Statement								
Total Revenue	8,763,100	11,409,300	10,546,900	9,393,600	9,876,200	8,951,300	9,682,000	8,798,200
EBITDA	1,176,300	1,622,500	1,597,800	1,295,700	1,058,200	823,900	858,800	1,380,000
Income Before Taxes	937,500	1,300,000	1,257,800	968,200	687,700	387,700	243,300	829,300
Income Taxes	204,400	231,700	204,700	138,400	94,200	20,300	(2,900)	283,100
Net Income	3,966,700	1,032,500	1,054,200	1,218,700	644,500	(173,500)	246,200	669,400
Average Shares	295,300	323,100	341,300	350,800	344,800	340,400	332,600	324,821
Balance Sheet								
Current Assets	7,700,700	4,095,900	4,248,200	4,609,700	3,538,600	4,112,400	3,187,800	3,322,800
Total Assets	14,376,200	12,145,900	11,756,400	11,414,600	10,664,900	10,809,600	11,063,700	10,528,500
Current Liabilities	3,235,700	3,613,600	3,199,700	2,876,900	3,053,000	3,798,100	2,851,000	3,966,600
Long-Term Obligations	712,700	905,200	1,184,300	1,267,600	1,518,600	2,092,100	2,900,700	1,540,100
Total Liabilities	6,468,300	6,741,100	5,994,400	5,680,800	6,171,600	7,331,400	7,147,100	6,630,800
Stockholders' Equity	7,907,900	5,404,800	5,762,000	5,733,800	4,493,300	3,478,200	3,916,600	3,495,200
Shares Outstanding	272,613	306,762	360,740	356,754	348,907	338,457	336,006	321,133
Statistical Record								
Return on Assets %	29.91	8.64	9.10	11.01	6.00	N.M.	2.28	7.05
Return on Equity %	59.59	18.49	18.34	23.77	16.17	N.M.	6.64	20.30
EBITDA Margin %	13.42	14.22	15.15	13.79	10.71	9.20	8.87	15.69
Net Margin %	45.27	9.05	10.00	12.97	6.53	N.M.	2.54	7.61
Asset Turnover	0.66	0.95	0.91	0.85	0.92	0.82	0.90	0.93
Current Ratio	2.38	1.13	1.33	1.60	1.16	1.08	1.12	0.84
Debt to Equity	0.09	0.17	0.21	0.22	0.34	0.60	0.74	0.44
Price Range	55.99-38.75	47.63-35.29	43.66-35.40	41.00-30.48	34.02-17.61	27.08-14.92	24.98-15.51	28.63-15.25
P/E Ratio	4.17-2.89	14.88-11.03	14.13-11.46	11.78-8.76	18.19-9.42	...	33.75-20.96	13.90-7.40
Average Yield %	1.48	1.69	1.46	1.29	1.44	1.57	...	...

Address: Clarendon House, 2 Church Street, Hamilton, 07677
Telephone: 295-283-8

Web Site: www.irco.com
Officers: Herbert L. Henkel - Chmn., Pres., C.E.O. Timothy R. McLevish - Sr. V.P., C.F.O.

Auditors: PricewaterhouseCoopers LLP
Transfer Agents: The Bank of New York, New York, NY

INGRAM MICRO INC.

Exchange	Symbol	Price	52Wk Range	Yield	P/E
NYS	IM	$15.83 (3/31/2008)	22.02-14.97	N/A	10.15

*7 Year Price Score 94.29   *NYSE Composite Index=100   *12 Month Price Score 90.57

TRADING VOLUME (thousand shares)

Interim Earnings (Per Share)

Qtr.	Mar	Jun	Sep	Dec
2003	0.07	0.08	0.53	0.30
2004	0.24	0.16	0.49	0.49
2005	0.26	0.26	0.29	0.51
2006	0.36	0.32	0.34	0.53
2007	0.21	0.30	0.41	0.64

Interim Dividends (Per Share)

No Dividends Paid

Valuation Analysis | **Institutional Holding**
Forecast P/E	11.45	No of Institutions
	(1/10/2007)	213
Market Cap	$2.7 Billion	Shares
Book Value	3.4 Billion	131,721,072
Price/Book	0.80	% Held
Price/Sales	0.08	77.61

Business Summary: IT & Technology (MIC: 10.2 SIC: 5045 NAIC: 423430)

Ingram Micro is an information technology (IT) wholesale distributor that provides sales, marketing, and logistics services for the IT industry worldwide. As of Dec 31 2007, Co. had local sales offices and representatives in 34 countries. Co. provides over 1,400 suppliers access to a global customer base of about 170,000 resellers including value-added resellers, corporate resellers, direct marketers, retailers, Internet-based resellers, and government. Co. owns or is the licensee of various trademarks and service marks, including Ingram Micro, the Ingram Micro logo, V7 (Video Seven), VentureTech Network, AVAD and SymTech. As of Dec 29 2007, Co. had 114 distribution centers worldwide.

Recent Developments: For the year ended Dec 29 2007, net income increased 3.8% to US$275.9 million from US$265.8 million in the prior year. Revenues were US$35.05 billion, up 11.8% from US$31.36 billion the year before. Operating income was US$446.4 million versus US$422.4 million in the prior year, an increase of 5.7%. Direct operating expenses rose 11.7% to US$33.14 billion from US$29.67 billion in the comparable period the year before. Indirect operating expenses increased 15.8% to US$1.46 billion from US$1.26 billion in the equivalent prior-year period.

Prospects: In Jan 2008, Co. acquired the assets of privately owned Paradigm Distribution Ltd., a key distributor in the UK of mobile data and automatic identification and data capture / point-of-sale (AIDC/POS) technologies to service providers and system integrators, expanding its reach to distribution of mobile data and AIDC/POS services in Europe, Middle East and Africa. Meanwhile, Co. remains focused on its expansion in the mobile convergence market as it believes that it is positioned to benefit from the robust demand for smart handheld and converged devices. Thus, for the first quarter of 2008, Co. expects net income of $0.36 to $0.40 per diluted share on revenues of $8.75 billion to $9.00.

Financial Data

(US$ in Thousands)	12/29/2007	12/30/2006	12/31/2005	01/01/2005	01/03/2004	12/28/2002	12/29/2001	12/30/2000
Earnings Per Share	1.56	1.56	1.32	1.38	0.98	(1.81)	0.04	1.52
Cash Flow Per Share	1.67	0.31	0.03	2.53	(0.62)	1.59	1.95	5.78
Tang Book Value Per Share	15.57	13.44	11.09	10.59	10.72	9.30	9.12	9.87
Income Statement								
Total Revenue	35,047,089	31,357,477	28,808,312	25,462,071	22,613,017	22,459,265	25,186,933	30,715,149
EBITDA	504,705	474,145	410,983	351,088	217,827	128,593	170,283	573,257
Income Before Taxes	385,238	367,333	301,937	263,276	115,794	8,998	15,935	362,509
Income Taxes	109,330	101,567	85,031	43,375	(33,407)	3,329	6,588	138,756
Net Income	275,908	265,766	216,906	219,901	149,201	(275,192)	6,737	226,173
Average Shares	176,951	170,875	164,331	159,680	152,308	152,145	150,047	148,640
Balance Sheet								
Current Assets	7,920,667	6,746,073	6,071,298	6,082,162	4,968,093	4,600,386	4,456,846	5,770,084
Total Assets	8,975,001	7,704,307	7,034,990	6,926,737	5,474,162	5,144,354	5,302,007	6,608,982
Current Liabilities	5,087,611	4,467,781	4,105,484	4,313,213	3,340,108	3,186,869	3,139,617	4,117,965
Long-Term Obligations	387,500	270,714	455,650	346,183	239,909	241,052	205,304	502,844
Total Liabilities	5,548,059	4,783,832	4,596,392	4,685,927	3,601,213	3,508,365	3,434,709	4,734,590
Stockholders' Equity	3,426,942	2,920,475	2,438,598	2,240,810	1,872,949	1,635,989	1,867,298	1,874,392
Shares Outstanding	172,942	169,408	162,366	158,737	151,963	150,778	149,024	146,207
Statistical Record								
Return on Assets %	3.32	3.62	3.12	3.56	2.76	N.M.	0.11	3.05
Return on Equity %	8.72	9.95	9.30	10.72	8.37	N.M.	0.36	11.81
EBITDA Margin %	1.44	1.51	1.43	1.38	0.96	0.57	0.68	1.87
Net Margin %	0.79	0.85	0.75	0.86	0.66	N.M.	0.03	0.74
Asset Turnover	4.21	4.27	4.14	4.12	4.19	4.31	4.24	4.14
Current Ratio	1.56	1.51	1.48	1.41	1.49	1.44	1.42	1.40
Debt to Equity	0.11	0.09	0.19	0.15	0.13	0.15	0.11	0.27
Price Range	22.02-18.10	21.00-16.64	20.00-14.66	20.80-11.93	16.00-9.52	18.70-10.30	17.36-10.81	20.94-10.50
P/E Ratio	14.12-11.60	13.46-10.67	15.15-11.11	15.07-8.64	16.33-9.71	...	434.00-270.31	13.77-6.91

Address: 1600 E. St. Andrew Place, Santa Ana, CA 92705 **Telephone:** 714-566-1000 **Fax:** 714-566-7604	**Web Site:** www.ingrammicro.com **Officers:** Gregory M. E. Spierkel - Pres., C.E.O. Kevin M. Murai - Pres., C.O.O.	**Auditors:** PricewaterhouseCoopers LLP **Transfer Agents:** Computershare Trust Company, N.A., Providence, RI

INTEGRYS ENERGY GROUP INC

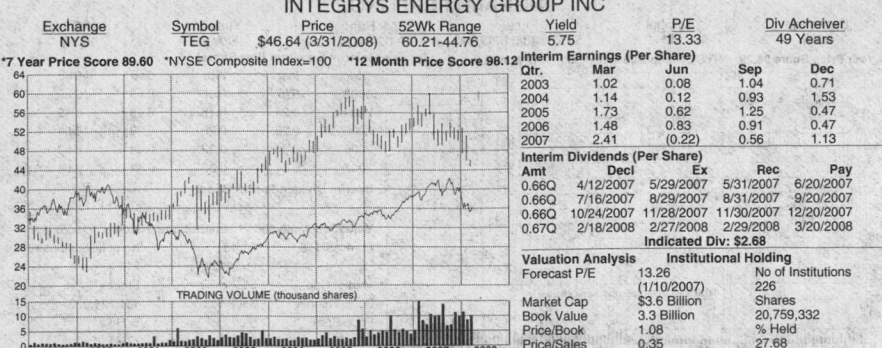

Exchange	Symbol	Price	52Wk Range	Yield	P/E	Div Acheiver
NYS	TEG	$46.64 (3/31/2008)	60.21-44.76	5.75	13.33	49 Years

*7 Year Price Score 89.60   *NYSE Composite Index=100   *12 Month Price Score 98.12

Interim Earnings (Per Share)

Qtr.	Mar	Jun	Sep	Dec
2003	1.02	0.08	1.04	0.71
2004	1.14	0.12	0.93	1.53
2005	1.73	0.62	1.25	0.47
2006	1.48	0.83	0.91	0.47
2007	2.41	(0.22)	0.56	1.13

Interim Dividends (Per Share)

Amt	Decl	Ex	Rec	Pay
0.66Q	4/12/2007	5/29/2007	5/31/2007	6/20/2007
0.66Q	7/16/2007	8/29/2007	8/31/2007	9/20/2007
0.66Q	10/24/2007	11/28/2007	11/30/2007	12/20/2007
0.67Q	2/18/2008	2/27/2008	2/29/2008	3/20/2008

Indicated Div: $2.68

Valuation Analysis

		Institutional Holding	
Forecast P/E	13.26	No of Institutions	
	(1/10/2007)	226	
Market Cap	$3.6 Billion	Shares	
Book Value	3.3 Billion	20,759,332	
Price/Book	1.08	% Held	
Price/Sales	0.35	27.68	

Business Summary: Electricity (MIC: 7.1 SIC: 4931 NAIC: 221121)

Integrys Energy Group is a holding company for regulated utility and non-regulated business units. As of Dec 31 2007, Co.'s primary wholly owned subsidiaries included Wisconsin Public Service Corporation, Upper Peninsula Power Company, Michigan Gas Utilities Corporation, Minnesota Energy Resources Corporation, The Peoples Gas Light and Coke Company, North Shore Gas Company, and Integrys Energy Services. Of these subsidiaries, six subsidiaries are regulated electric and/or natural gas utilities and one subsidiary, Integrys Energy Services, is a nonregulated energy supply and services company.

Recent Developments: For the year ended Dec 31 2007, income from continuing operations increased 19.5% to US$181.1 million from US$151.6 million a year earlier. Net income increased 60.1% to US$254.4 million from US$158.9 million in the prior year. Revenues were US$10.29 billion, up 49.4% from US$6.89 billion the year before. Operating income was US$367.4 million versus US$249.2 million in the prior year, an increase of 47.4%. Direct operating expenses rose 49.3% to US$9.64 billion from US$6.46 billion in the comparable period the year before. Indirect operating expenses increased 55.0% to US$282.5 million from US$182.2 million in the equivalent prior-year period.

Prospects: Co. remains its long-term diluted earnings per share growth rate target at 6.0% to 8.0% on an average annualized basis, as it continues to manage its portfolio of businesses to attain long-term growth in its utility and non-regulated operations. Notably, Co. expects its 2008 earnings of $3.33 to $3.78 per diluted share, excluding the effect of mark-to-market activity on derivative instruments. Meanwhile, on Feb 11 2008, Co.'s Wisconsin Public Service Corp. subsidiary filed a request with the Public Service Commission of Wisconsin to increase electric rates about $0.90 per month for typical residential customers so as to recover $13.4 million of additional fuel and related costs in 2008.

Financial Data (US$ in Thousands)	12/31/2007	12/31/2006	12/31/2005	12/31/2004	12/31/2003	12/31/2002	12/31/2001	12/31/2000
Earnings Per Share	3.50	3.67	4.07	3.72	2.85	3.42	2.74	2.53
Cash Flow Per Share	3.33	1.72	1.63	6.48	1.89	6.12	5.07	5.31
Tang Book Value Per Share	29.97	28.35	32.76	29.30	27.39	24.43	22.73	20.21
Dividends Per Share	0.583	2.280	2.240	2.200	2.160	2.120	2.080	2.040
Dividend Payout %	16.66	62.13	55.04	59.14	75.79	61.99	75.91	80.63
Income Statement								
Total Revenue	10,292,400	6,890,700	6,962,700	4,890,600	4,321,300	2,674,900	2,675,500	1,951,574
EBITDA	452,600	313,800	271,500	230,900	186,700	246,000	141,300	146,635
Income Before Taxes	267,100	196,600	208,800	186,200	144,300	137,300	85,500	76,109
Income Taxes	86,000	45,000	46,700	30,000	33,700	24,800	4,800	6,005
Net Income	254,400	158,900	160,500	142,800	97,800	112,500	80,700	70,104
Average Shares	71,800	42,400	38,700	37,600	33,200	31,700	28,300	26,463
Balance Sheet								
Net PPE	4,463,800	2,534,800	2,049,400	2,002,600	1,828,700	1,610,200	1,463,600	1,198,324
Total Assets	11,234,400	6,861,700	5,455,200	4,445,600	4,292,300	3,207,900	2,870,000	2,816,142
Long-Term Obligations	2,265,100	1,287,200	867,100	865,700	871,900	824,400	727,800	659,972
Total Liabilities	7,947,500	5,277,000	4,099,900	3,302,700	3,238,000	2,324,000	2,053,000	2,172,197
Stockholders' Equity	3,286,900	1,584,700	1,355,300	1,142,900	1,054,300	833,900	767,000	593,945
Shares Outstanding	76,330	43,375	39,807	37,259	36,621	32,040	31,496	26,851
Statistical Record								
Return on Assets %	2.81	2.58	3.24	3.26	2.61	3.70	2.84	3.02
Return on Equity %	10.44	10.81	12.85	12.96	10.36	14.05	11.86	11.84
EBITDA Margin %	4.40	4.55	3.90	4.72	4.32	9.20	5.28	7.51
Net Margin %	2.47	2.31	2.31	2.92	2.26	4.21	3.02	3.59
PPE Turnover	2.94	3.01	3.44	2.55	2.51	1.74	2.01	1.66
Asset Turnover	1.14	1.12	1.41	1.12	1.15	0.88	0.94	0.84
Debt to Equity	0.69	0.81	0.64	0.76	0.83	0.99	0.95	1.11
Price Range	60.21-49.06	57.43-47.63	59.40-47.84	50.32-43.52	46.77-37.12	42.45-31.52	36.55-31.82	38.69-22.81
P/E Ratio	17.20-14.02	15.65-12.98	14.59-11.75	13.53-11.70	16.41-13.02	12.41-9.22	13.34-11.61	15.29-9.02
Average Yield %	1.09	4.43	4.10	4.68	5.27	5.55	6.08	6.89

Address: 130 East Randolph Drive, Chicago, IL 60601	Web Site: www.integrysgroup.com	Auditors: Deloitte & Touche LLP
Telephone: 312-228-5400	Officers: Larry L. Weyers - Chmn., Pres., C.E.O. Thomas P. Meinz - Exec. V.P., Public Affairs	Investor Contact: 920-433-1857
		Transfer Agents: American Stock Transfer & Trust Company, New York, NY

INTERNATIONAL BUSINESS MACHINES CORP.

Exchange	Symbol	Price	52Wk Range	Yield	P/E	Div Acheiver
NYS	IBM	$115.14 (3/31/2008)	119.60-94.29	1.39	16.04	12 Years

*7 Year Price Score 95.24   *NYSE Composite Index=100   *12 Month Price Score 111.24

Interim Earnings (Per Share)

Qtr.	Mar	Jun	Sep	Dec
2003	0.79	0.97	1.02	1.55
2004	0.95	1.16	1.06	1.79
2005	0.84	1.12	0.94	1.97
2006	1.08	1.30	1.45	2.30
2007	1.21	1.55	1.68	2.76

Interim Dividends (Per Share)

Amt	Decl	Ex	Rec	Pay
0.40Q	4/24/2007	5/8/2007	5/10/2007	6/9/2007
0.40Q	7/31/2007	8/8/2007	8/10/2007	9/10/2007
0.40Q	10/30/2007	11/7/2007	11/9/2007	12/10/2007
0.40Q	1/29/2008	2/6/2008	2/8/2008	3/10/2008

Indicated Div: $1.60

Valuation Analysis

		Institutional Holding	
Forecast P/E	13.28	No of Institutions	
	(1/10/2007)	1249	
Market Cap	$159.5 Billion	Shares	
Book Value	28.5 Billion	889,945,920	
Price/Book	5.60	% Held	
Price/Sales	1.61	59.11	

Business Summary: IT & Technology (MIC: 10.2 SIC: 3571 NAIC: 334111)

International Business Machines is a worldwide information technology company which primarily provides a variety of business products and services through the utilization of information technology. Co.'s primary operations comprise a Global Technology Services segment, which primarily reflects Internet Technology infrastructure services and business process services; a Global Business Services segment, which primarily reflects professional services and application outsourcing services; a Software segment, which consists primarily of middleware and operating systems software; a Systems and Technology that provides business applications; and a Global Financing segment.

Recent Developments: For the year ended Dec 31 2007, income from continuing operations increased 10.6% to US$10.42 billion from US$9.42 billion a year earlier. Net income increased 9.8% to US$10.42 billion from US$9.49 billion in the prior year. Revenues were US$98.79 billion, up 8.1% from US$91.42 billion the year before. Direct operating expenses rose 7.4% to US$57.06 billion from US$53.13 billion in the comparable period the year before. Indirect operating expenses increased 7.0% to US$28.21 billion from US$26.37 billion in the equivalent prior-year period.

Prospects: Going forward, Co. will continue to pursue acquisitions to expand its capabilities. For instance, on Jan 31 2008, Co. announced that it completed the acquisition of Cognos, a publicly-held company based in Ottawa, Ontario, Canada, for a total transaction value of approximately $5.00 billion. Specifically, Co. believes that this transaction will accelerate its global Information on Demand initiative to unlock the business value of information. Separately, on Jan 23 2008, Co. announced that it is expanding its business event processing software portfolio by acquiring AptSoft Corporation, a privately-held software company. Co. expects this transaction to close in the first quarter of 2008.

Financial Data

(US$ in Thousands)	12/31/2007	12/31/2006	12/31/2005	12/31/2004	12/31/2003	12/31/2002	12/31/2001	12/31/2000
Earnings Per Share	7.18	6.11	4.87	4.93	4.32	2.06	4.35	4.44
Cash Flow Per Share	11.31	9.81	9.32	9.17	8.46	8.10	8.23	5.25
Tang Book Value Per Share	8.72	8.93	13.97	11.86	11.54	10.03	12.40	10.63
Dividends Per Share	1.500	1.100	0.780	0.700	0.630	0.590	0.550	0.510
Dividend Payout %	20.89	18.00	16.02	14.20	14.58	28.64	12.64	11.49
Income Statement								
Total Revenue	98,786,000	91,424,000	91,134,000	96,293,000	89,131,000	81,186,000	85,866,000	88,396,000
EBITDA	19,736,000	18,042,000	17,327,000	16,902,000	15,568,000	12,048,000	16,011,000	17,246,000
Income Before Taxes	14,489,000	13,317,000	12,226,000	12,028,000	10,874,000	7,524,000	10,953,000	11,534,000
Income Taxes	4,071,000	3,901,000	4,232,000	3,580,000	3,261,000	2,190,000	3,230,000	3,441,000
Net Income	10,418,000	9,492,000	7,934,000	8,430,000	7,583,000	3,579,000	7,723,000	8,093,000
Average Shares	1,450,570	1,553,535	1,627,632	1,708,872	1,756,090	1,730,941	1,771,230	1,812,118
Balance Sheet								
Current Assets	53,177,000	44,660,000	45,661,000	46,970,000	44,998,000	41,652,000	42,461,000	43,880,000
Total Assets	120,431,000	103,234,000	105,748,000	109,183,000	104,457,000	96,484,000	88,313,000	88,349,000
Current Liabilities	44,310,000	40,091,000	35,152,000	39,798,000	37,900,000	34,550,000	35,119,000	36,406,000
Long-Term Obligations	23,039,000	13,780,000	15,425,000	14,828,000	16,986,000	19,986,000	15,963,000	18,371,000
Total Liabilities	91,962,000	74,728,000	72,650,000	79,436,000	76,593,000	73,702,000	64,699,000	67,725,000
Stockholders' Equity	28,470,000	28,506,000	33,098,000	29,747,000	27,864,000	22,782,000	23,614,000	20,624,000
Shares Outstanding	1,385,234	1,506,482	1,573,979	1,645,592	1,694,508	1,722,366	1,723,193	1,762,899
Statistical Record								
Return on Assets %	9.32	9.08	7.38	7.87	7.55	3.87	8.74	9.18
Return on Equity %	36.57	30.82	25.25	29.19	29.95	15.43	34.92	39.24
EBITDA Margin %	19.98	19.73	19.01	17.55	17.47	14.84	18.65	19.51
Net Margin %	10.55	10.38	8.71	8.75	8.51	4.41	8.99	9.16
Asset Turnover	0.88	0.87	0.85	0.90	0.89	0.88	0.97	1.00
Current Ratio	1.20	1.11	1.30	1.18	1.19	1.21	1.21	1.21
Debt to Equity	0.81	0.48	0.47	0.50	0.61	0.88	0.68	0.89
Price Range	119.60-90.90	97.20-73.57	98.58-72.01	100.19-82.21	93.98-75.18	125.60-55.07	123.89-84.81	133.63-81.56
P/E Ratio	16.66-12.66	15.91-12.04	20.24-14.79	20.32-16.68	21.75-17.40	60.97-26.73	28.48-19.50	30.10-18.37
Average Yield %	1.42	1.32	0.93	0.77	0.74	0.70	0.51	0.46

Address: One New Orchard Road, Armonk, NY 10504 **Telephone:** 914-499-1900 **Fax:** 914-765-4190	**Web Site:** www.ibm.com **Officers:** Samuel J. Palmisano - Chmn., Pres., C.E.O. Nicholas M. Donofrio - Sr. V.P., Tech. & Mfg. Group	**Auditors:** PricewaterhouseCoopers LLP **Investor Contact:** 888-421-8860 **Transfer Agents:** EquiServe Trust Company, N.A., Providence, RI

INTERNATIONAL FLAVORS & FRAGRANCES INC.

Exchange	Symbol	Price	52Wk Range	Yield	P/E
NYS	IFF	$44.05 (3/31/2008)	54.20-39.48	2.09	15.62

*7 Year Price Score 105.15 *NYSE Composite Index=100 *12 Month Price Score 95.03

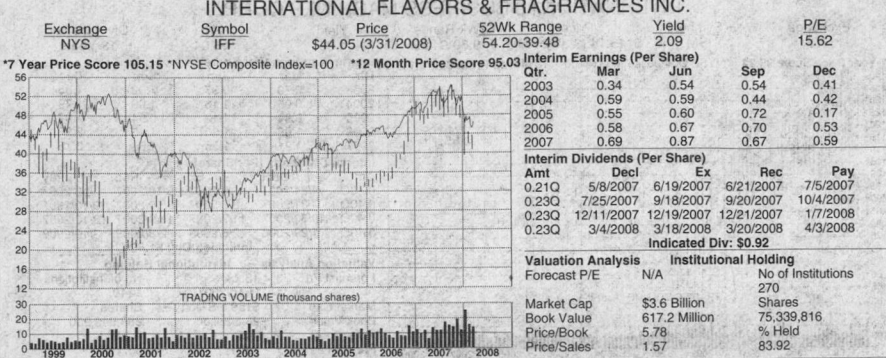

Interim Earnings (Per Share)

Qtr.	Mar	Jun	Sep	Dec
2003	0.34	0.54	0.54	0.41
2004	0.59	0.59	0.44	0.42
2005	0.55	0.60	0.72	0.17
2006	0.58	0.67	0.70	0.53
2007	0.69	0.87	0.67	0.59

Interim Dividends (Per Share)

Amt	Decl	Ex	Rec	Pay
0.21Q	5/8/2007	6/19/2007	6/21/2007	7/5/2007
0.23Q	7/25/2007	9/18/2007	9/20/2007	10/4/2007
0.23Q	12/11/2007	12/19/2007	12/21/2007	1/7/2008
0.23Q	3/4/2008	3/18/2008	3/20/2008	4/3/2008

Indicated Div: $0.92

Valuation Analysis

		Institutional Holding	
Forecast P/E	N/A	No of Institutions	270
Market Cap	$3.6 Billion	Shares	75,339,816
Book Value	617.2 Million	% Held	83.92
Price/Book	5.78		
Price/Sales	1.57		

Business Summary: Chemicals (MIC: 11.1 SIC: 2869 NAIC: 325199)

International Flavors & Fragrances produces flavor and fragrance products designed to impart or improve flavor or fragrance in various consumer products. Co. mainly sells its fragrance products to manufacturers of perfumes, cosmetics, personal care products, hair care products, deodorants, soaps, detergents and air care products. Co. also sells its flavor products mainly to manufacturers of prepared foods, beverages, dairy foods, pharmaceuticals and confectionery products as well as the food service industry. Co. has 31 manufacturing facilities in the U.S., Great Britain, Ireland, the Netherlands, Spain, Argentina, Brazil, Mexico, Australia, China, India, Indonesia, Japan and Singapore.

Recent Developments: For the year ended Dec 31 2007, net income increased 9.1% to US$247.1 million from US$226.5 million in the prior year. Revenues were US$2.28 billion, up 8.6% from US$2.10 billion the year before. Direct operating expenses rose 9.3% to US$1.32 billion from US$1.21 billion in the comparable period the year before. Indirect operating expenses increased 6.8% to US$593.1 million from US$555.1 million in the equivalent prior-year period.

Prospects: Co.'s results are benefiting from increased sales across its segments. Specifically, Co.'s flavors business unit is being driven by new wins and increased volume on Europe and the emerging markets of Asia and Latin America. Also, Co.'s fragrance business unit is encouraged by increases in ingredient sales and functional, offset by a decline in fine fragrance. Meanwhile, Co. is continuing to anticipate a net annual cost savings of around $4.0 million beginning in 2008 due to the 2007 amendment to its U.S. salaried qualified and non-qualified pension plans, along with the recent introduction of an enhanced defined contribution plan for those employees affected by the pension curtailment.

Financial Data

(US$ in Thousands)	12/31/2007	12/31/2006	12/31/2005	12/31/2004	12/31/2003	12/31/2002	12/31/2001	12/31/2000
Earnings Per Share	2.82	2.48	2.04	2.05	1.83	1.84	1.20	1.22
Cash Flow Per Share	3.63	2.91	1.89	3.13	2.88	2.57	1.90	2.66
Tang Book Value Per Share	N.M.	1.78	1.54	1.28	N.M.	N.M.	N.M.	N.M.
Dividends Per Share	0.880	0.765	0.730	0.685	0.630	0.600	0.600	1.290
Dividend Payout %	31.21	30.85	35.78	33.41	34.43	32.61	50.00	105.74
Income Statement								
Total Revenue	2,276,638	2,095,390	1,993,393	2,033,653	1,901,520	1,809,249	1,843,766	1,462,795
EBITDA	453,007	428,564	362,072	396,000	367,058	387,911	381,694	278,543
Income Before Taxes	328,684	313,282	246,188	281,002	251,860	266,417	187,777	184,127
Income Taxes	81,556	86,782	53,122	84,931	79,263	90,473	71,775	61,122
Net Income	247,128	226,500	193,066	196,071	172,597	175,944	116,002	123,005
Average Shares	87,633	91,369	94,826	95,418	94,419	95,873	96,819	101,093
Balance Sheet								
Current Assets	1,190,478	1,079,803	1,191,274	961,370	902,672	866,749	896,361	1,018,940
Total Assets	2,726,788	2,478,904	2,638,196	2,363,294	2,306,892	2,232,694	2,268,051	2,489,033
Current Liabilities	538,896	446,771	1,202,696	399,522	526,045	359,497	560,214	1,179,017
Long-Term Obligations	1,060,168	791,443	131,281	668,969	690,231	1,007,085	939,404	417,402
Total Liabilities	2,109,591	1,573,736	1,722,849	1,452,807	1,564,261	1,658,016	1,743,881	1,857,774
Stockholders' Equity	617,197	905,168	915,347	910,487	742,631	574,678	524,170	631,259
Shares Outstanding	80,995	89,417	92,714	94,672	93,729	94,254	94,764	97,426
Statistical Record								
Return on Assets %	9.49	8.85	7.72	8.37	7.60	7.82	4.88	6.31
Return on Equity %	32.47	24.88	21.15	23.66	26.20	32.02	20.08	16.47
EBITDA Margin %	19.90	20.45	18.16	19.47	19.30	21.44	20.70	19.04
Net Margin %	10.85	10.81	9.69	9.64	9.08	9.72	6.29	8.41
Asset Turnover	0.87	0.82	0.80	0.87	0.84	0.80	0.78	0.75
Current Ratio	2.21	2.42	0.99	2.41	1.72	2.41	1.60	0.86
Debt to Equity	1.72	0.87	0.14	0.73	0.93	1.75	1.79	0.66
Price Range	54.20-46.00	49.80-32.84	42.84-31.95	43.05-33.25	36.57-29.66	37.32-27.42	31.45-20.21	37.63-15.13
P/E Ratio	19.22-16.31	20.08-13.24	21.00-15.66	21.00-16.22	19.98-16.21	20.28-14.90	26.21-16.84	30.84-12.40
Average Yield %	1.76	2.01	1.96	1.82	1.96	1.83	2.31	4.63

Address: 521 West 57th Street, New York, NY 10019 **Telephone:** 212-765-5500 **Fax:** 212-708-7132	**Web Site:** www.iff.com **Officers:** Richard A. Goldstein - Chmn., C.E.O. D. Wayne Howard - Exec. V.P., Global Oper.	**Auditors:** PricewaterhouseCoopers LLP **Transfer Agents:** Wachovia Bank, National Association Shareholder Services Group

INTERNATIONAL GAME TECHNOLOGY

*7 Year Price Score 111.52 *NYSE Composite Index=100 *12 Month Price Score 116.74

Interim Earnings (Per Share)

Qtr.	Dec	Mar	Jun	Sep
2004-05	0.33	0.26	0.32	0.29
2005-06	0.34	0.35	0.33	0.18
2006-07	0.35	0.38	0.41	0.37
2007-08	0.36	...	...	...

Interim Dividends (Per Share)

Amt	Decl	Ex	Rec	Pay
0.13Q	6/25/2007	7/5/2007	7/9/2007	7/23/2007
0.14Q	9/25/2007	10/4/2007	10/9/2007	10/23/2007
0.14Q	12/10/2007	12/20/2007	12/24/2007	1/7/2008
0.14Q	2/26/2008	3/17/2008	3/19/2008	4/2/2008

Indicated Div: $0.56

Valuation Analysis / **Institutional Holding**

Forecast P/E	25.49	No of Institutions	
	(1/10/2007)	437	
Market Cap	$12.7 Billion	Shares	
Book Value	1.4 Billion	278,559,200	
Price/Book	9.17	% Held	
Price/Sales	4.82	82.35	

Business Summary: Consumer Accessories (MIC: 4.6 SIC: 3999 NAIC: 713120)

International Game Technology is a global company engaged in the design, manufacture, and marketing of computerized gaming equipment, network systems, licensing and services. Co. provides a range of electronic gaming equipment and network systems, as well as related services, parts, game theme conversions, and intellectual property licensing. Co. supplies its gaming products directly to the customer or through distributors in certain jurisdictions. In addition, Co. offers equipment contract financing for certain customers and development financing loans to select customers for new or expanding gaming facilities.

Recent Developments: For the quarter ended Dec 31 2007, net income decreased 6.0% to US$113.7 million from US$121.0 million in the year earlier quarter. Revenues were US$645.8 million, up 0.5% from US$642.3 million the year before. Operating income was US$195.7 million versus US$185.2 million in the prior-year quarter, an increase of 5.7%. Direct operating expenses declined 3.8% to US$279.3 million from US$290.3 million in the comparable period the year before. Indirect operating expenses increased 2.4% to US$170.8 million from US$166.8 million in the equivalent prior-year period.

Prospects: On Feb 22 2008, Co. and WMS Industries Inc., a gaming applications provider, signed an agreement that provides for a non-exclusive cross-license of each other's intellectual property and patents to realize the benefits of server-based gaming for their customers in an open architecture environment. The agreement accelerates the introduction of new applications such as Co.'s sb™ (server-based) Service Window. Going forward, Co. expects to benefit from new market opportunities, further gaming expansion outside of North America and new contribution channels enabled by network systems and table gaming initiatives. Co. also expects the first floor-wide deployment of its sb™ applications in 2009.

Financial Data

(US$ in Thousands)	3 Mos	09/30/2007	09/30/2006	09/30/2005	09/30/2004	09/30/2003	09/28/2002	09/29/2001
Earnings Per Share	1.52	1.51	1.20	1.20	1.34	1.11	0.79	0.70
Cash Flow Per Share	2.28	2.49	1.85	2.11	1.79	1.24	1.50	0.67
Tang Book Value Per Share	0.08	0.29	2.06	1.56	1.97	1.41	0.54	0.40
Dividends Per Share	0.540	0.520	0.500	0.480	0.300	0.175	...	...
Dividend Payout %	35.53	34.44	41.67	40.00	22.39	15.77	...	...
Income Statement								
Total Revenue	645,800	2,621,400	2,511,700	2,379,400	2,484,752	2,128,137	1,847,568	1,199,209
EBITDA	214,800	880,800	814,900	731,300	870,576	821,477	683,486	455,040
Depn & Amortn	19,200	...	...	...	...	...	...	...
Income Before Taxes	188,100	804,800	746,900	681,200	653,416	598,544	444,171	339,472
Income Taxes	74,400	296,600	273,300	244,700	225,003	223,257	167,453	125,537
Net Income	113,700	508,200	473,600	436,500	488,677	390,727	271,165	213,935
Average Shares	318,400	336,100	355,800	370,200	370,892	351,316	344,196	306,100
Balance Sheet								
Current Assets	1,306,600	1,287,000	1,375,700	1,437,200	1,509,704	2,078,228	1,195,022	967,674
Total Assets	4,280,700	4,167,500	3,902,700	3,864,400	3,872,964	4,185,241	3,315,818	1,923,439
Current Liabilities	608,900	691,500	1,246,600	1,217,600	560,009	945,081	511,059	370,899
Long-Term Obligations	1,617,100	1,503,000	200,000	200,000	791,848	1,146,759	971,375	984,742
Total Liabilities	2,901,000	2,714,800	1,860,700	1,958,700	1,896,315	2,497,753	1,874,011	1,627,326
Stockholders' Equity	1,379,700	1,452,700	2,042,000	1,905,700	1,976,649	1,687,478	1,433,144	296,113
Shares Outstanding	314,600	316,900	334,200	338,200	346,090	345,542	347,305	291,729
Statistical Record								
Return on Assets %	10.97	12.59	12.20	11.28	12.10	10.36	10.38	12.10
Return on Equity %	30.00	29.08	23.99	22.49	26.60	24.91	31.45	109.26
EBITDA Margin %	33.26	33.60	32.44	30.73	35.04	38.60	36.99	37.95
Net Margin %	17.61	19.39	18.86	18.34	19.67	18.36	14.68	17.84
Asset Turnover	0.57	0.65	0.65	0.62	0.62	0.56	0.71	0.68
Current Ratio	2.15	1.86	1.10	1.18	2.70	2.20	2.34	2.61
Debt to Equity	1.17	1.03	0.10	0.10	0.40	0.68	0.68	3.33
Price Range	48.26-34.21	48.26-34.21	41.66-25.93	36.67-24.22	46.82-28.09	28.87-16.31	17.76-10.28	16.33-8.20
P/E Ratio	31.75-22.51	31.96-22.66	34.72-21.61	30.56-20.18	34.94-20.96	26.01-14.69	22.48-13.01	23.33-11.72
Average Yield %	1.32	1.27	1.45	1.60	0.84	0.81	...	...

Address: 9295 Prototype Drive, Reno, NV 89521	**Web Site:** www.igt.com	**Auditors:** Deloitte & Touche LLP
Telephone: 775-448-7777	**Officers:** G. Thomas Baker - Chmn. Thomas J. Matthews - C.E.O.	**Investor Contact:** 775-448-0880
Fax: 775-448-0719		**Transfer Agents:** The Bank of New York, New York, NY

INTERNATIONAL PAPER CO.

Exchange	Symbol	Price	52Wk Range	Yield	P/E
NYS	IP	$27.20 (3/31/2008)	41.46-26.68	3.68	10.07

*7 Year Price Score 75.80 *NYSE Composite Index=100 *12 Month Price Score 95.09

Interim Earnings (Per Share)

Qtr.	Mar	Jun	Sep	Dec
2003	0.09	0.19	0.25	0.10
2004	0.15	0.40	(1.13)	0.51
2005	0.16	0.16	2.03	(0.15)
2006	(2.52)	0.24	0.42	4.08
2007	0.97	0.44	0.51	0.77

Interim Dividends (Per Share)

Amt	Decl	Ex	Rec	Pay
0.25Q	5/7/2007	5/16/2007	5/18/2007	6/15/2007
0.25Q	7/10/2007	8/13/2007	8/15/2007	9/17/2007
0.25Q	10/9/2007	11/14/2007	11/16/2007	12/14/2007
0.25Q	1/8/2008	2/13/2008	2/15/2008	3/14/2008

Indicated Div: $1.00

Valuation Analysis

Forecast P/E	13.39
	(1/10/2007)
Market Cap	$11.6 Billion
Book Value	8.7 Billion
Price/Book	1.33
Price/Sales	0.53

Institutional Holding

No of Institutions	441
Shares	403,997,984
% Held	89.26

Business Summary: Paper Products (MIC: 11.11 SIC: 2621 NAIC: 322121)

International Paper is a global paper and packaging company with a North American merchant distribution system, with primary markets and manufacturing operations in North America, Europe, Latin America, Russia, Asia and North Africa. Co. distributes printing, packaging, graphic arts, maintenance and industrial products principally through over 273 distribution branches located primarily in the U.S. As of Dec 31 2007, Co. owned or managed approximately 300,000 acres of forestlands in the U.S., approximately 250,000 acres in Brazil and had, through licenses and forest management agreements, harvesting rights on government-owned forestlands in Russia.

Recent Developments: For the year ended Dec 31 2007, income from continuing operations decreased 5.2% to US$1.22 billion from US$1.28 billion a year earlier. Net income increased 11.2% to US$1.17 billion from US$1.05 billion in the prior year. Revenues were US$21.89 billion, down 0.5% from US$22.00 billion the year before. Direct operating expenses declined 1.2% to US$16.06 billion from US$16.25 billion in the comparable period the year before. Indirect operating expenses increased 90.3% to US$3.88 billion from US$2.04 billion in the equivalent prior-year period.

Prospects: For the first quarter of 2008, Co. expects steady demand for North American printing papers and packaging although a greater than expected economic downturn in 2008 could negatively affect sales volumes and earnings. Co. also expects slight increases in paper and packaging price realizations from its announced price increases. However, Co. expects higher planned maintenance expenses and increases in wood, energy and transportation costs. Hence, excluding the effect of projected reduced earnings from land sales and the addition of equity earnings contributions from its recent investment in Ilim Holding S.A. in Russia, Co. expects lower 2008 first-quarter earnings over the 2007 fourth quarter.

Financial Data
(US$ in Thousands)

	12/31/2007	12/31/2006	12/31/2005	12/31/2004	12/31/2003	12/31/2002	12/31/2001	12/31/2000
Earnings Per Share	2.70	2.18	2.21	(0.07)	0.63	(1.83)	(2.50)	0.32
Cash Flow Per Share	4.40	2.57	3.11	4.90	3.80	4.35	3.55	5.39
Tang Book Value Per Share	11.81	11.10	6.75	6.69	6.01	4.31	7.78	11.89
Dividends Per Share	1.000	1.000	1.000	1.000	1.000	1.000	1.000	1.000
Dividend Payout %	37.04	45.87	45.25	...	158.73	...	...	312.50
Income Statement								
Total Revenue	21,890,000	21,995,000	24,097,000	25,548,000	25,179,000	24,976,000	26,363,000	28,180,000
EBITDA	1,951,000	3,709,000	1,179,000	1,489,000	1,112,000	1,154,000	1,534,000	3,455,000
Income Before Taxes	1,654,000	3,188,000	586,000	746,000	346,000	371,000	(1,265,000)	723,000
Income Taxes	415,000	1,889,000	(285,000)	206,000	(92,000)	(54,000)	(270,000)	117,000
Net Income	1,168,000	1,050,000	1,100,000	(35,000)	302,000	(880,000)	(1,204,000)	142,000
Average Shares	433,000	488,700	509,700	488,400	481,100	483,000	481,600	450,000
Balance Sheet								
Current Assets	6,735,000	8,637,000	7,409,000	9,319,000	9,337,000	7,738,000	8,312,000	10,455,000
Total Assets	24,159,000	24,034,000	28,771,000	34,217,000	35,525,000	33,792,000	37,158,000	42,109,000
Current Liabilities	3,842,000	4,641,000	4,844,000	4,872,000	6,803,000	4,579,000	5,374,000	7,413,000
Long-Term Obligations	6,353,000	6,531,000	11,023,000	14,132,000	13,450,000	13,042,000	12,457,000	12,648,000
Total Liabilities	15,487,000	16,071,000	20,420,000	25,963,000	27,288,000	26,418,000	26,867,000	30,075,000
Stockholders' Equity	8,672,000	7,963,000	8,351,000	8,254,000	8,237,000	7,374,000	10,291,000	12,034,000
Shares Outstanding	425,120	453,496	490,389	487,495	481,500	479,100	481,600	481,500
Statistical Record								
Return on Assets %	4.85	3.98	3.49	N.M.	0.87	N.M.	N.M.	0.39
Return on Equity %	14.04	12.87	13.25	N.M.	3.87	N.M.	N.M.	1.27
EBITDA Margin %	8.91	16.86	4.89	5.83	4.42	4.62	5.82	12.26
Net Margin %	5.34	4.77	4.56	N.M.	1.20	N.M.	N.M.	0.50
Asset Turnover	0.91	0.83	0.77	0.73	0.73	0.70	0.67	0.78
Current Ratio	1.75	1.86	1.53	1.91	1.37	1.69	1.55	1.41
Debt to Equity	0.73	0.82	1.32	1.71	1.63	1.77	1.21	1.05
Price Range	41.46-31.66	37.61-30.80	42.01-27.15	44.98-37.80	43.12-33.44	46.05-31.45	42.63-32.36	58.63-26.81
P/E Ratio	15.36-11.73	17.25-14.13	19.01-12.29	...	68.44-53.08	...	...	183.20-83.79
Average Yield %	2.78	2.95	2.98	2.40	2.66	2.52	2.63	2.71

Address: 6400 Poplar Avenue, Memphis, TN 38197 **Telephone:** 901-419-9000	**Web Site:** www.internationalpaper.com **Officers:** John V. Faraci - Chmn., C.E.O. Robert M. Amen - Pres.	**Auditors:** Deloitte & Touche LLP **Transfer Agents:** Mellon Investor Services LLC., Ridgefield Park, NJ

INTERNATIONAL RECTIFIER CORP.

Exchange	Symbol	Price	52Wk Range	Yield	P/E
NYS	IRF	$21.50 (3/31/2008)	39.50-20.63	N/A	9.60

*7 Year Price Score 71.19   *NYSE Composite Index=100   *12 Month Price Score 77.64

TRADING VOLUME (thousand shares)

Interim Earnings (Per Share)

Qtr.	Sep	Dec	Mar	Jun
2003-04	0.25	0.25	0.39	0.42
2004-05	0.53	0.55	0.48	0.36
2005-06	0.36	0.34	0.36	0.42
2006-07	0.47	0.99	...	...

Interim Dividends (Per Share)

No Dividends Paid

Valuation Analysis   Institutional Holding

Forecast P/E	15.83	No of Institutions	
	(1/10/2007)	227	
Market Cap	$1.6 Billion	Shares	
Book Value	1.8 Billion	62,849,340	
Price/Book	0.89	% Held	
Price/Sales	1.21	86.67	

Business Summary: IT & Technology (MIC: 10.2 SIC: 3674 NAIC: 334413)

International Rectifier designs, manufactures and markets power management products using power semiconductors. Power semiconductors convert power from an electrical outlet, a battery or an alternator running off an internal combustion engine into power for a range of electrical and electronic systems and equipment. Co.'s products are used in end-markets, including computers, communications networking, consumer electronics, energy-saving appliances, lighting, satellites, launch vehicles, aircraft and automotive diesel injection. In addition, Co. licenses its intellectual property to third parties.

Recent Developments: The Audit Committee of Co.'s Board of Directors has determined that Co.'s financial statements for its fiscal quarters ended Sep 30 2003 through Dec 31 2006 and for its fiscal years ended June 30 2004 through June 30 2006 should not be relied upon. The Audit Committee also found material weaknesses in internal control over financial reporting for such periods and that management's report on internal control over financial reporting for the fiscal years ended June 30 2005 and June 30 2006 contained in its public reports should not be relied upon. Consequently, Co. is unable to file its quarterly report for the period ended Sep 30 2007 on Form 10-Q within the prescribed time period.

Prospects: On Oct 2 2007, Co. announced the following internal initiatives: shifted reporting of the internal audit function to the Audit Committee of the board of directors and the general counsel; appointed a lead independent director; appointed a Special Committee of the board to advise and support the acting C.E.O.; evaluating independent third party consulting firms to document and assess the design effectiveness of processes and controls; revamped its hotline process and placed it under the internal audit function; changed reporting relationships at its Japan subsidiary; and added interim processes to help assure adherence to proper revenue recognition policies at the Japan subsidiary.

Financial Data

(US$ in Thousands)	6 Mos	3 Mos	06/30/2006	06/30/2005	06/30/2004	06/30/2003	06/30/2002	06/30/2001
Earnings Per Share	2.24	1.59	1.49	1.91	1.31	(1.40)	0.75	1.35
Cash Flow Per Share	2.63	2.18	2.26	3.27	2.48	2.02	0.81	3.32
Tang Book Value Per Share	22.03	20.40	19.69	18.52	15.61	13.11	13.64	14.13
Income Statement								
Total Revenue	643,455	344,243	1,171,118	1,174,424	1,060,500	864,443	720,229	978,585
EBITDA	140,442	67,412	228,296	253,981	177,219	(69,805)	123,218	167,712
Depn & Amortn	41,232	21,506	...	...	...	...	...	...
Income Before Taxes	103,538	48,410	158,750	184,068	118,284	(126,198)	65,811	118,381
Income Taxes	23,868	14,281	51,594	46,608	28,514	(36,559)	17,111	30,732
Net Income	106,078	34,129	107,156	137,460	89,770	(89,639)	48,700	87,649
Average Shares	72,854	72,630	71,753	77,089	68,363	63,982	65,271	64,800
Balance Sheet								
Current Assets	1,252,334	1,075,645	1,075,456	1,062,376	953,210	874,839	729,254	1,209,181
Total Assets	2,672,767	2,552,804	2,505,023	2,223,544	2,017,006	1,821,852	1,813,182	1,746,462
Current Liabilities	824,427	794,026	254,650	224,896	215,036	211,733	170,267	195,975
Long Term Obligations	81,263	81,805	617,540	547,259	560,019	579,379	566,841	552,751
Total Liabilities	918,379	894,153	900,691	798,341	812,794	809,613	754,537	766,805
Stockholders' Equity	1,754,388	1,658,651	1,604,332	1,425,203	1,204,212	1,012,239	1,058,645	979,657
Shares Outstanding	72,514	72,159	71,987	66,826	66,358	64,185	63,698	63,132
Statistical Record								
Return on Assets %	6.58	4.79	4.53	6.48	4.66	N.M.	2.74	6.32
Return on Equity %	9.99	7.35	7.07	10.46	8.08	N.M.	4.78	9.61
EBITDA Margin %	21.83	19.58	19.49	21.63	16.71	N.M.	17.11	17.14
Net Margin %	16.49	9.91	9.15	11.70	8.46	N.M.	6.76	8.96
Asset Turnover	0.52	0.52	0.50	0.55	0.55	0.48	0.40	0.71
Current Ratio	1.52	1.35	4.22	4.72	4.43	4.13	4.28	6.17
Debt to Equity	0.05	0.05	0.38	0.38	0.47	0.57	0.54	0.56
Price Range	48.54-32.38	48.54-27.86	55.82-27.86	49.64-31.39	56.25-26.82	28.53-11.12	49.69-24.75	67.78-28.00
P/E Ratio	21.67-14.46	30.53-17.52	37.46-18.70	25.99-16.43	42.94-20.47	...	66.25-33.00	50.21-20.74

Address: 233 Kansas Street, El Segundo, CA 90245 **Telephone:** 310-726-8000 **Fax:** 310-322-3332	**Web Site:** www.irf.com **Officers:** Eric Lidow - Chmn. Alexander Lidow - C.E.O.	**Auditors:** PricewaterhouseCoopers LLP **Investor Contact:** 310-726-8512 **Transfer Agents:** Mellon Investor Services, South Hackensack, NJ

INTERPUBLIC GROUP OF COMPANIES INC.

Exchange	Symbol	Price	52Wk Range	Yield	P/E
NYS	IPG	$8.41 (3/31/2008)	12.97-7.40	N/A	32.35

*7 Year Price Score 53.17   *NYSE Composite Index=100   *12 Month Price Score 90.29

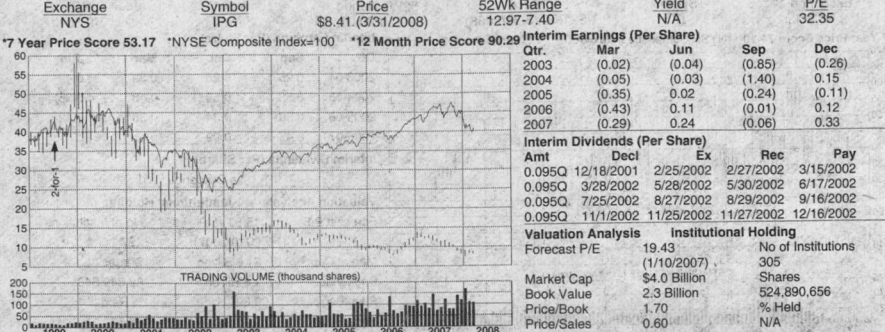

Interim Earnings (Per Share)

Qtr.	Mar	Jun	Sep	Dec
2003	(0.02)	(0.04)	(0.85)	(0.26)
2004	(0.05)	(0.03)	(1.40)	0.15
2005	(0.35)	0.02	(0.24)	(0.11)
2006	(0.43)	0.11	(0.01)	0.12
2007	(0.29)	0.24	(0.06)	0.33

Interim Dividends (Per Share)

Amt	Decl	Ex	Rec	Pay
0.095Q	12/18/2001	2/25/2002	2/27/2002	3/15/2002
0.095Q	3/28/2002	5/28/2002	5/30/2002	6/17/2002
0.095Q	7/25/2002	8/27/2002	8/29/2002	9/16/2002
0.095Q	11/1/2002	11/25/2002	11/27/2002	12/16/2002

Valuation Analysis   Institutional Holding

Forecast P/E	19.43	No of Institutions
	(1/10/2007)	305
Market Cap	$4.0 Billion	Shares
Book Value	2.3 Billion	524,890,656
Price/Book	1.70	% Held
Price/Sales	0.60	N/A

TRADING VOLUME (thousand shares)

Business Summary: Advertising, Marketing & PR (MIC: 12.4 SIC: 7311 NAIC: 541810)

Interpublic Group of Companies is engaged as an advertising and marketing services company. Co. has three global brands that provide applications for clients, including McCann Worldgroup (McCann), Draftfcb, and Lowe Worldwide (Lowe), as well as its domestic and media agencies. McCann provides communications tools and resources worldwide. Draftfcb is a modern agency model for clients seeking certain marketing programs. Lowe is engaged as a creative agency that operates in the global advertising markets. Co. also has two global media agencies, Initiative and Universal McCann, which provide media planning and buying, market intelligence and return-on-marketing investment analysis services.

Recent Developments: For the year ended Dec 31 2007, net income amounted to US$167.6 million versus a net loss of US$31.7 million in the prior year. Revenues were US$6.55 billion, up 5.9% from US$6.19 billion the year before. Operating income was US$344.3 million versus US$106.0 million in the prior year, an increase of 224.8%. Indirect operating expenses increased 2.1% to US$6.21 billion from US$6.08 billion in the equivalent prior-year period.

Prospects: Looking ahead, Co. will continue to evaluate strategic opportunities to grow and to increase its ownership interests in existing investments, mainly to develop the digital and marketing services components of its business and to expand its presence in potential markets, including Brazil, Russia, India and China. In addition, Co. will focus on improving its operating margin through several initiatives, such as improving its financial systems and back-office processing, reducing organizational challenges and divesting non-core and underperforming businesses as well as enhancing its real estate utilization. Thus, Co. remains optimistic in generating operating margin of 8.5% to 9.0% in 2008.

Financial Data
(US$ in Thousands)

	12/31/2007	12/31/2006	12/31/2005	12/31/2004	12/31/2003	12/31/2002	12/31/2001	12/31/2000
Earnings Per Share	0.26	(0.19)	(0.68)	(1.34)	(1.17)	0.26	(1.37)	1.15
Cash Flow Per Share	0.65	0.02	(0.05)	1.09	1.30	2.32	0.40	0.99
Dividends Per Share	...	...	...	...	...	0.380	0.380	0.370
Dividend Payout %	...	...	...	...	...	146.15	...	32.17
Income Statement								
Total Revenue	6,554,200	6,190,800	6,274,300	6,387,000	5,863,400	6,203,600	6,726,800	5,625,845
EBITDA	640,500	360,900	135,500	315,500	69,000	681,700	48,500	1,066,558
Income Before Taxes	235,700	(5,000)	(186,600)	(267,000)	(269,000)	265,400	(524,300)	657,906
Income Taxes	58,900	18,700	81,900	262,200	254,000	140,300	(43,900)	273,034
Net Income	167,600	(31,700)	(262,900)	(558,200)	(451,700)	99,500	(505,300)	358,658
Average Shares	503,100	428,100	424,800	415,300	385,500	381,300	369,000	312,653
Balance Sheet								
Current Assets	7,685,800	7,208,800	7,497,400	7,636,700	7,349,700	6,322,300	6,467,200	6,026,053
Total Assets	12,458,100	11,864,100	11,945,200	12,272,300	12,234,500	11,793,700	11,514,700	10,238,222
Current Liabilities	7,120,600	6,663,000	6,856,500	7,563,200	6,624,500	7,089,800	6,433,900	6,106,080
Long-Term Obligations	2,044,100	2,248,600	2,183,000	113,600	2,191,700	1,817,700	2,480,600	1,505,061
Total Liabilities	10,125,900	9,923,500	9,999,900	10,543,300	9,628,600	9,693,700	9,535,400	8,191,866
Stockholders' Equity	2,332,200	1,940,600	1,945,300	1,718,300	2,605,900	2,100,000	1,979,300	2,046,356
Shares Outstanding	471,200	468,600	429,900	424,700	418,100	386,200	378,500	314,672
Statistical Record								
Return on Assets %	1.38	N.M.	N.M.	N.M.	N.M.	0.85	N.M.	3.77
Return on Equity %	7.84	N.M.	N.M.	N.M.	N.M.	4.88	N.M.	19.47
EBITDA Margin %	9.77	5.83	2.16	4.94	1.18	10.99	0.72	18.96
Net Margin %	2.56	N.M.	N.M.	N.M.	N.M.	1.60	N.M.	6.38
Asset Turnover	0.54	0.52	0.52	0.52	0.49	0.53	0.62	0.59
Current Ratio	1.08	1.08	1.09	1.01	1.11	0.89	1.01	0.99
Debt to Equity	0.88	1.16	1.12	0.07	0.84	0.87	1.25	0.74
Price Range	13.81-8.10	12.35-7.86	13.68-9.14	17.19-10.51	16.41-8.01	34.89-11.25	47.19-19.30	57.69-33.06
P/E Ratio	53.12-31.15	...	...	...	...	134.19-43.27	...	50.16-28.75
Average Yield %	...	...	...	...	...	1.62	1.20	0.88

Address: 1114 Avenue of the Americas, New York, NY 10036 **Telephone:** 212-704-1200	**Web Site:** www.interpublic.com **Officers:** Michael I. Roth - Chmn., C.E.O. David A. Bell - Co-Chmn.	**Auditors:** PricewaterhouseCoopers LLP **Transfer Agents:** Mellon Investor Services, Inc.

INVESTMENT TECHNOLOGY GROUP INC.

Exchange	Symbol	Price	52Wk Range	Yield	P/E
NYS	ITG	$46.18 (3/31/2008)	49.45-36.58	N/A	18.62

*7 Year Price Score 108.63 *NYSE Composite Index=100 *12 Month Price Score 117.50

Interim Earnings (Per Share)

Qtr.	Mar	Jun	Sep	Dec
2003	0.14	0.25	0.24	0.27
2004	0.19	0.22	0.25	0.30
2005	0.31	0.41	0.37	0.50
2006	0.60	0.63	0.49	0.49
2007	0.55	0.60	0.65	0.67

Interim Dividends (Per Share)

Amt	Decl	Ex	Rec	Pay
3-for-2	11/13/2001	12/10/2001	11/23/2001	12/7/2001

Valuation Analysis   Institutional Holding

Forecast P/E	N/A	No of Institutions
		206
Market Cap	$2.0 Billion	Shares
Book Value	704.3 Million	39,247,344
Price/Book	2.85	% Held
Price/Sales	2.75	88.15

Business Summary: Finance Intermediaries & Services (MIC: 8.7 SIC: 6211 NAIC: 523999)

Investment Technology Group is an agency brokerage and technology firm. Co. has three reportable segments: U.S. Operations; International Operations and Canadian operations. Co.'s U.S. Operations segment provides trading, trade order management, connectivity and research services to institutional investors, plan sponsors, brokers, alternative investment funds and money managers in the U.S. Co.'s Canadian Operations segment provides trading, as well as connectivity and research services. Co.'s International Operations segment includes its trading, connectivity and research service businesses in Europe, Australia, Hong Kong and Japan, as well as a research and development facility in Israel.

Recent Developments: For the year ended Dec 31 2007, net income increased 13.5% to US$111.1 million from US$97.9 million in the prior year. Revenues were US$731.0 million, up 21.9% from US$599.5 million the year before. Indirect operating expenses increased 23.9% to US$542.1 million from US$437.5 million in the equivalent prior year period.

Prospects: Co.'s improved top-line results is due to higher U.S. commission revenue driven by volume growth, which is offsetting the negative effect of price competition for trade executions that continues to exert downward pressure on the revenues earned per share for shares traded in the U.S. equity markets. Also, Co. is seeing strong increase in its Canadian commission revenues and in its International Operations revenues. Looking ahead, Co. expects further growth in its International operations as it expands and globalizes its product line, including Triton, ITG Triton X and ITG Algorithms, development of new versions of existing products, and the further development of Macgregor products.

Financial Data
(US$ in Thousands)

	12/31/2007	12/31/2006	12/31/2005	12/31/2004	12/31/2003	12/31/2002	12/31/2001	12/31/2000
Earnings Per Share	2.48	2.21	1.60	0.96	0.89	1.51	1.62	1.35
Cash Flow Per Share	(2.48)	3.40	2.70	0.72	1.32	1.65	2.62	1.55
Tang Book Value Per Share	4.59	3.21	6.09	6.49	6.10	5.63	5.95	4.75
Income Statement								
Total Revenue	730,999	599,484	408,161	334,486	333,992	387,581	377,407	310,405
Income Before Taxes	188,868	161,964	109,096	66,592	69,701	127,253	136,112	112,996
Income Taxes	77,761	64,041	41,410	25,609	27,748	53,443	57,217	49,403
Net Income	111,107	97,923	67,686	40,983	41,953	73,810	78,895	63,593
Average Shares	44,784	44,289	42,391	42,841	47,016	49,003	48,689	47,328
Balance Sheet								
Total Assets	2,100,887	1,462,312	1,016,334	612,458	649,848	594,254	418,478	281,712
Total Liabilities	1,396,592	854,278	554,028	241,957	288,545	237,745	100,534	71,296
Stockholders' Equity	704,295	608,034	462,306	370,501	361,303	356,509	317,944	210,416
Shares Outstanding	43,462	43,809	42,773	41,950	44,740	47,530	48,641	47,425
Statistical Record								
Return on Assets %	6.24	7.90	8.31	6.48	6.74	14.58	22.54	27.50
Return on Equity %	16.93	18.30	16.25	11.17	11.69	21.89	29.86	38.90
Price Range	48.51-36.58	58.01-34.97	40.75-16.72	20.00-11.98	24.27-11.06	54.15-21.31	43.56-24.63	33.79-18.29
P/E Ratio	19.56-14.75	26.25-15.82	25.47-10.45	20.83-12.48	27.27-12.43	35.86-14.11	26.89-15.20	25.03-13.55

Address: 380 Madison Avenue, New York, NY 10017
Telephone: 212-588-4000
Fax: 212-444-6490

Web Site: www.itginc.com
Officers: Raymond L. Killian Jr. - Chmn., Pres., C.E.O. Angelo Bulone - Sr. V.P., Contr.

Auditors: KPMG LLP
Investor Contact: 212-444-6160
Transfer Agents: Computershare Trust Company N.A., Providence, RI

IRON MOUNTAIN INC

Exchange	Symbol	Price	52Wk Range	Yield	P/E
NYS	IRM	$26.44 (3/31/2008)	38.54-24.54	N/A	34.79

*7 Year Price Score 117.47 *NYSE Composite Index=100 *12 Month Price Score 105.01

Interim Earnings (Per Share)

Qtr.	Mar	Jun	Sep	Dec
2003	0.11	0.10	0.07	0.15
2004	0.12	0.11	0.09	0.15
2005	0.11	0.13	0.18	0.13
2006	0.13	0.19	0.13	0.18
2007	0.17	0.19	0.25	0.14

Interim Dividends (Per Share)

Amt	Decl	Ex	Rec	Pay
50%	12/5/2001	1/2/2002	12/17/2001	12/31/2001
50%	5/27/2004	7/1/2004	6/15/2004	6/30/2004
50%	12/7/2006	1/3/2007	12/18/2006	12/29/2006

Valuation Analysis   Institutional Holding

Forecast P/E	N/A	No of Institutions 214
Market Cap	$5.3 Billion	Shares
Book Value	1.8 Billion	186,838,160
Price/Book	2.96	% Held
Price/Sales	1.94	94.08

Business Summary: Miscellaneous Business Services (MIC: 12.8 SIC: 4225 NAIC: 541690)

Iron Mountain is engaged in the provision of information protection and storage services. Specifically, Co. offers records management and data protection services to a range of customer base including commercial, legal, banking, healthcare, accounting, insurance, entertainment and government organizations. Co.'s operations can be divided into three service categories: records management, data protection and recovery, and information destruction. As of Dec 31 2007, Co. provided services to more than 100,000 corporate clients throughout North America, Europe, Latin America and Asia Pacific; and operated over 1,000 records management facilities.

Recent Developments: For the year ended Dec 31 2007, net income increased 18.8% to US$153.1 million from US$128.9 million in the prior year. Revenues were US$2.73 billion, up 16.2% from US$2.35 billion the year before. Operating income was US$454.7 million versus US$407.2 million in the prior year, an increase of 11.7%. Direct operating expenses rose 17.3% to US$1.26 billion from US$1.07 billion in the comparable period the year before. Indirect operating expenses increased 16.8% to US$1.02 billion from US$868.9 million in the equivalent prior-year period.

Prospects: Co. remains focused on driving incremental revenues by acquiring new customer relationships and increasing business with new and existing customers, and selling additional products and services such as secure shredding and digital data protection to generate internal revenue growth. Co. also intends to continue to make acquisitions and investments in information protection and storage services businesses outside the U.S. and Canada. For full-year 2008, Co. is targeting 10.0% to 13.0% revenue growth, and expects revenue of $3.00 billion to $3.08 billion, with internal revenue growth of 7.0% to 9.0%. Also, Co. expects operating income of between $471.0 million and $499.0 million in 2008.

Financial Data

(US$ in Thousands)	12/31/2007	12/31/2006	12/31/2005	12/31/2004	12/31/2003	12/31/2002	12/31/2001	12/31/2000
Earnings Per Share	0.76	0.64	0.56	0.48	0.44	0.30	(0.24)	(0.15)
Cash Flow Per Share	2.42	1.89	1.92	1.57	1.50	1.34	0.85	0.88
Income Statement								
Total Revenue	2,730,035	2,350,342	2,078,155	1,817,589	1,501,329	1,318,497	1,171,116	986,371
EBITDA	706,272	633,012	572,475	519,759	442,029	371,342	285,132	229,348
Income Before Taxes	223,024	224,218	197,018	166,735	156,989	119,949	(8,131)	(18,032)
Income Taxes	69,010	93,795	81,484	69,574	66,730	49,295	26,036	9,125
Net Income	153,094	128,863	111,099	94,191	84,637	58,292	(44,057)	(27,825)
Average Shares	202,062	200,463	198,105	196,764	195,115	193,659	188,248	179,296
Balance Sheet								
Current Assets	822,396	679,721	554,168	501,154	471,583	367,040	309,317	236,668
Total Assets	6,307,921	5,209,521	4,766,140	4,442,387	3,892,099	3,230,655	2,859,906	2,659,096
Current Liabilities	765,677	638,647	591,996	515,463	584,745	427,962	359,009	314,053
Long-Term Obligations	3,232,848	2,605,711	2,503,526	2,438,587	1,974,147	1,662,365	1,460,843	1,314,342
Total Liabilities	4,512,466	3,656,248	3,396,011	3,223,819	2,825,985	2,285,794	1,973,947	1,734,638
Stockholders' Equity	1,795,455	1,553,273	1,370,129	1,218,568	1,066,114	944,861	885,959	924,458
Shares Outstanding	200,693	199,109	197,494	194,726	192,544	191,361	189,662	186,569
Statistical Record								
Return on Assets %	2.66	2.58	2.41	2.25	2.38	1.91	N.M.	N.M.
Return on Equity %	9.14	8.82	8.58	8.22	8.42	6.37	N.M.	N.M.
EBITDA Margin %	25.87	26.93	27.55	28.60	29.44	28.16	24.35	23.25
Net Margin %	5.61	5.48	5.35	5.18	5.64	4.42	N.M.	N.M.
Asset Turnover	0.47	0.47	0.45	0.43	0.42	0.43	0.42	0.49
Current Ratio	1.07	1.06	0.94	0.97	0.81	0.86	0.86	0.75
Debt to Equity	1.80	1.68	1.83	2.00	1.85	1.76	1.65	1.42
Price Range	38.54-25.54	29.85-22.94	29.81-18.01	23.37-17.43	17.92-13.80	14.91-9.52	13.52-9.78	11.65-8.65
P/E Ratio	50.71-33.61	46.65-35.84	53.24-32.17	48.68-36.31	40.72-31.36	49.70-31.75	...	...

Address: 745 Atlantic Ave., Boston, MA 02111 **Telephone:** 617-535-4766 **Fax:** 617-350-7881	**Web Site:** www.ironmountain.com **Officers:** C. Richard Reese - Chmn., C.E.O. Robert Brennan - Pres., C.O.O.	**Auditors:** Deloitte & Touche LLP **Investor Contact:** 617-535-4799 **Transfer Agents:** The Bank of New York, New York, NY

IRWIN FINANCIAL CORP. (COLUMBUS, IN)

Exchange	Symbol	Price	52Wk Range	Yield	P/E	Div Acheiver
NYS	IFC	$5.31 (3/31/2008)	18.47-4.56	N/A	N/A	18 Years

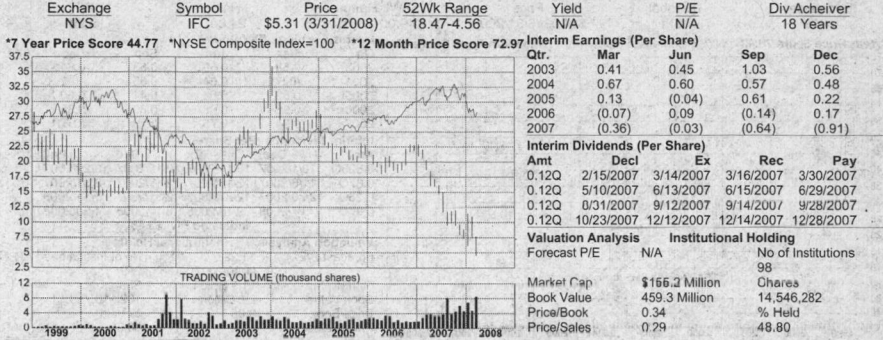

*7 Year Price Score 44.77   *NYSE Composite Index=100   *12 Month Price Score 72.97

Interim Earnings (Per Share)

Qtr.	Mar	Jun	Sep	Dec
2003	0.41	0.45	1.03	0.56
2004	0.67	0.60	0.57	0.48
2005	0.13	(0.04)	0.61	0.22
2006	(0.07)	0.09	(0.14)	0.17
2007	(0.36)	(0.03)	(0.64)	(0.91)

Interim Dividends (Per Share)

Amt	Decl	Ex	Rec	Pay
0.12Q	2/15/2007	3/14/2007	3/16/2007	3/30/2007
0.12Q	5/10/2007	6/13/2007	6/15/2007	6/29/2007
0.12Q	8/31/2007	9/12/2007	9/14/2007	9/28/2007
0.12Q	10/23/2007	12/12/2007	12/14/2007	12/28/2007

Valuation Analysis

Forecast P/E	N/A
Market Cap	$166.2 Million
Book Value	459.3 Million
Price/Book	0.34
Price/Sales	0.29

Institutional Holding

No of Institutions	98
Shares	14,546,282
% Held	48.80

Business Summary: Commercial Banking (MIC: 8.1 SIC: 6022 NAIC: 522110)

Irwin Financial is a bank holding company which is engaged primarily in the extension of credit to consumers and small businesses as well as providing the ongoing servicing of those customer accounts. Through its subsidiaries, Co. operates three primary lines of business: commercial banking through Irwin Union Bank & Trust Company and Irwin Union Bank, F.S.B.; commercial finance through Irwin Commercial Finance Corporation; as well as home equity lending through Irwin Home Equity Corporation. Also, Co. is engaged in conducting part of its finance line of business in Canadian markets. As of Dec 31 2007, Co. had $6.17 billion in assets and $3.33 billion in deposits.

Recent Developments: For the year ended Dec 31 2007, net loss amounted to US$54.7 million versus net income of US$1.7 million in the prior year. Net interest income increased 1.9% to US$262.4 million from US$257.4 million in the prior year. Provision for loan losses was US$135.0 million versus US$35.1 million in the prior year, an increase of 284.6%. Non-interest income fell 38.6% to US$27.4 million from US$44.6 million, while non-interest expense declined 5.2% to US$199.8 million.

Prospects: In view of the challenging market conditions, Co. has three principal financial goals for 2008. These include returning to profitability; managing its balance sheet to maintain strong capital and good liquidity; and managing its credit relationships and servicing and collections platforms to minimize its credit loss exposures. Co. noted that over the past several quarters it has focused on constraining balance sheet growth and reducing overall operating expenses, while strengthening its credit underwriting, servicing, collections, and risk management areas. Also, Co. has added substantially to loss reserves. Collectively, these actions should better position Co. for the year ahead.

Financial Data

(US$ in Thousands)	12/31/2007	12/31/2006	12/31/2005	12/31/2004	12/31/2003	12/31/2002	12/31/2001	12/31/2000
Earnings Per Share	(1.94)	0.05	0.66	2.32	2.45	1.89	2.00	1.67
Cash Flow Per Share	14.64	34.94	(8.81)	0.55	21.38	(24.11)	(12.84)	(4.87)
Tang Book Value Per Share	15.22	17.35	17.90	17.67	15.36	12.98	10.84	8.97
Dividends Per Share	0.480	0.440	0.400	0.320	0.280	0.270	0.260	0.240
Dividend Payout %	...	880.00	60.61	13.79	11.43	14.29	13.00	14.37
Income Statement								
Interest Income	513,029	482,128	422,258	344,303	370,984	311,442	268,233	184,530
Interest Expense	250,636	224,689	156,368	92,225	99,099	97,795	121,084	93,534
Net Interest Income	262,393	257,439	265,890	252,078	271,885	213,647	147,149	90,996
Provision for Losses	134,988	35,101	26,852	14,195	47,583	43,996	17,505	5,403
Non-Interest Income	27,384	44,621	120,486	287,050	329,299	257,433	271,391	211,711
Non-Interest Expense	199,767	210,688	331,555	407,235	435,199	340,853	327,420	237,962
Income Before Taxes	(44,978)	56,271	27,969	117,698	118,402	86,231	73,615	59,342
Income Taxes	(20,848)	18,870	8,982	47,794	45,585	33,398	28,624	23,676
Net Income	(54,673)	1,727	18,987	69,904	72,817	53,328	45,516	35,666
Average Shares	29,353	29,690	28,841	31,278	30,850	29,675	24,173	21,593
Balance Sheet								
Net Loans & Leases	5,557,509	5,401,235	5,732,599	4,296,708	3,980,664	4,079,189	2,619,221	1,801,581
Total Assets	6,166,105	6,237,958	6,646,524	5,239,341	4,988,359	4,884,722	3,439,795	2,422,429
Total Deposits	3,325,488	3,551,516	3,898,993	3,395,263	2,899,662	2,694,344	2,309,018	1,443,330
Total Liabilities	5,706,805	5,707,456	6,134,190	4,736,697	4,556,099	4,523,311	3,207,472	2,232,504
Stockholders' Equity	459,300	530,502	512,334	502,644	432,260	360,555	232,323	189,925
Shares Outstanding	29,226	29,736	28,618	28,452	28,134	27,771	21,305	21,025
Statistical Record								
Return on Assets %	N.M.	0.03	0.32	1.36	1.48	1.28	1.55	1.73
Return on Equity %	N.M.	0.33	3.74	14.91	18.37	17.99	21.56	20.37
Net Interest Margin %	51.15	53.40	62.97	73.21	73.29	68.60	54.86	49.31
Efficiency Ratio %	36.97	40.00	61.09	64.50	62.15	59.92	60.68	60.05
Loans to Deposits	1.67	1.52	1.47	1.27	1.37	1.51	1.13	1.25
Price Range	22.94-7.35	22.94-18.01	28.39-19.72	35.95-23.20	31.99-16.10	20.36-13.90	27.50-14.51	21.38-13.50
P/E Ratio	...	458.80-360.20	43.02-29.88	15.50-10.00	13.06-6.57	10.77-7.35	13.75-7.25	12.80-8.08
Average Yield %	3.32	2.17	1.81	1.18	1.20	1.58	1.22	1.52

Address: 500 Washington Street, Columbus, IN 47201
Telephone: 812-376-1909
Fax: 812-376-1709

Web Site: www.irwinfinancial.com
Officers: William I. Miller - Chmn., C.E.O. Thomas D. Washburn - Exec. V.P.

Auditors: PricewaterhouseCoopers LLP
Investor Contact: 812-376-1909
Transfer Agents: Mellon Investor Services, LLC, Ridgefield Park, NJ

ISTAR FINANCIAL INC

Exchange	Symbol	Price	52Wk Range	Yield	P/E
NYS	SFI	$14.03 (3/31/2008)	49.00-13.76	24.80	9.29

*7 Year Price Score 76.43   *NYSE Composite Index=100   *12 Month Price Score 63.47

Interim Earnings (Per Share)

Qtr.	Mar	Jun	Sep	Dec
2003	0.58	0.59	0.63	0.64
2004	(0.50)	0.64	0.65	1.02
2005	0.52	0.58	0.41	0.60
2006	0.66	0.68	0.80	0.65
2007	0.64	0.75	0.73	(0.61)

Interim Dividends (Per Share)

Amt	Decl	Ex	Rec	Pay
0.825Q	10/1/2007	10/11/2007	10/15/2007	10/29/2007
0.87Q	11/6/2007	12/13/2007	12/17/2007	12/31/2007
0.25Q	12/20/2007	12/27/2007	12/31/2007	1/14/2008
0.87Q	3/7/2008	3/13/2008	3/17/2008	4/30/2008

Indicated Div: $3.48

Valuation Analysis

		Institutional Holding	
Forecast P/E	11.22	No of Institutions	
	(1/10/2007)	259	
Market Cap	$1.9 Billion	Shares	
Book Value	2.9 Billion	102,110,768	
Price/Book	0.65	% Held	
Price/Sales	1.32	80.59	

TRADING VOLUME (thousand shares)

1999 2000 2001 2002 2003 2004 2005 2006 2007 2008

Business Summary: Property, Real Estate & Development (MIC: 8.3 SIC: 6798 NAIC: 525930)

iStar Financial is a finance company focused on the commercial real estate industry. Co. provides custom-tailored financing to private and corporate owners of real estate, including senior and mezzanine real estate debt, senior and mezzanine corporate capital, corporate net lease financing and equity. Co. has two primary lines of business: lending business, which is comprised of senior and mezzanine real estate loans that typically range in size from $20.0 million to $150.0 million, and have maturities generally ranging from three to 10 years; and corporate tenant leasing business that provides capital to corporations and other owners who control facilities leased to single creditworthy customers.

Recent Developments: For the year ended Dec 31 2007, net income decreased 36.2% to US$239.0 million from US$374.8 million in the prior year. Revenues were US$1.43 billion, up 48.5% from US$959.9 million the year before. Revenues from property income rose 6.1% to US$324.2 million from US$305.6 million in the corresponding earlier year.

Prospects: On Feb 19 2008, Co. announced that one of its timber investments, TimberStar Southwest, has entered into an agreement to sell about 900,000 acres of timberland for about $1.70 billion. TimberStar Southwest is a joint venture between its subsidiary TimberStar and equity investors MSD Capital, York Capital Management and Perry Capital. Upon completion of this deal in the second quarter of 2008, Co. expects to receive approximately $400.0 million of net proceeds. For 2008, Co. expects earnings per common share of $4.00 to $4.50, assuming minimal net asset growth in 2008 as well as its asset management focus on maximizing long-term returns rather than minimizing near-term earnings effect.

Financial Data

(US$ in Thousands)	12/31/2007	12/31/2006	12/31/2005	12/31/2004	12/31/2003	12/31/2002	12/31/2001	12/31/2000
Earnings Per Share	1.51	2.79	2.11	1.83	2.43	1.93	2.19	2.10
Cash Flow Per Share	4.43	3.78	4.59	3.29	3.37	3.88	3.07	2.25
Tang Book Value Per Share	20.59	23.05	21.53	22.03	22.53	20.64	20.46	20.86
Dividends Per Share	3.595	3.080	2.930	2.790	2.650	2.520	2.450	2.400
Dividend Payout %	238.08	110.39	138.86	152.46	109.05	130.57	111.87	114.29
Income Statement								
Interest Income	998,008	575,598	406,668	353,799	304,394	255,631	254,119	268,011
Interest Expense	627,720	429,807	313,053	231,027	194,999	185,375	170,121	173,891
Net Interest Income	370,288	145,791	93,615	122,772	109,395	70,256	83,998	94,120
Provision for Losses	185,000	14,000	2,250	9,000	7,500	8,250	7,000	6,500
Non-Interest Income	427,570	404,595	391,836	340,625	302,155	270,093	230,057	203,811
Non-Interest Expense	433,013	198,290	159,495	244,546	114,443	110,023	76,168	75,893
Net Income	238,958	374,827	287,913	260,447	292,157	215,270	229,912	217,586
Average Shares	127,792	116,219	113,703	112,464	104,101	92,649	88,234	86,151
Balance Sheet								
Net Loans & Leases	10,501,541	5,909,172	4,314,200	3,788,340	3,393,635	...	...	...
Total Assets	15,848,298	11,059,995	8,532,296	7,220,237	6,660,590	5,611,697	4,378,560	4,034,775
Total Deposits	19,849	23,581	...	...	...	...	...	...
Total Liabilities	12,894,869	8,034,394	6,052,114	4,745,749	4,240,256	3,583,816	2,588,132	2,240,666
Stockholders' Equity	2,899,481	2,986,863	2,446,671	2,455,242	2,415,228	2,025,300	1,787,778	1,787,885
Shares Outstanding	133,929	126,565	113,209	111,432	107,215	98,114	87,387	85,726
Statistical Record								
Return on Assets %	1.78	3.83	3.66	3.74	4.76	4.31	5.47	5.53
Return on Equity %	8.12	13.80	11.75	10.67	13.16	11.29	12.86	12.09
Net Interest Margin %	37.10	25.33	23.02	34.70	35.94	27.48	33.05	35.12
Efficiency Ratio %	30.37	20.23	19.97	35.22	18.87	20.93	15.73	16.09
Loans to Deposits	529.07	250.59	...	...	...	...	...	...
Price Range	52.54-25.45	48.59-35.55	45.26-35.36	45.57-34.50	40.00-27.05	31.45-24.59	28.46-19.19	22.44-16.63
P/E Ratio	34.79-16.85	17.42-12.74	21.45-16.76	24.90-18.85	16.46-11.13	16.30-12.74	13.00-8.76	10.68-7.92
Average Yield %	8.83	7.63	7.22	6.91	7.75	8.99	9.82	12.40

Address: 1114 Avenue of the Americas, New York, NY 10036
Telephone: 212-930-9400
Fax: 212-930-9494

Web Site: www.istarfinancial.com
Officers: Jay Sugarman - Chmn., C.E.O. Jay S. Nydick - Pres.

Auditors: PricewaterhouseCoopers LLP
Investor Contact: 212-930-9400
Transfer Agents: Equiserve, Inc., Jersey City, NJ

ITT CORPORATION

Exchange	Symbol	Price	52Wk Range	Yield	P/E
NYS	ITT	$51.81 (3/31/2008)	72.80-51.67	1.35	12.86

*7 Year Price Score 119.01 *NYSE Composite Index=100 *12 Month Price Score 95.44

Interim Earnings (Per Share)

Qtr.	Mar	Jun	Sep	Dec
2003	0.46	0.53	0.58	0.57
2004	0.47	0.59	0.58	0.65
2005	0.62	0.73	1.00	(0.44)
2006	0.83	0.75	0.77	0.75
2007	0.76	1.16	1.25	0.86

Interim Dividends (Per Share)

Amt	Decl	Ex	Rec	Pay
0.14Q	5/8/2007	5/16/2007	5/18/2007	7/1/2007
0.14Q	8/3/2007	8/22/2007	8/24/2007	10/1/2007
0.14Q	10/9/2007	11/14/2007	11/16/2007	1/1/2008
0.175Q	2/15/2008	3/5/2008	3/7/2008	4/1/2008
			Indicated Div: $0.70	

Valuation Analysis

		Institutional Holding	
Forecast P/E	15.37 (1/10/2007)	No of Institutions	431
Market Cap	$9.4 Billion	Shares	135,664,992
Book Value	3.9 Billion	% Held	74.63
Price/Book	2.38		
Price/Sales	1.04		

Business Summary: Industrial Machinery and Equipment (MIC: 11.5 SIC: 3561 NAIC: 333996)

ITT is engaged in the design and manufacture of engineered products and the provision of related services. Co.'s Fluid Technology segment is a global provider of fluid systems and applications for the Wastewater, Residential & Commercial Water, Industrial & BioPharm as well as Advanced Water Treatment markets. Co.'s Defense Electronics & Services segment develops, manufactures, and supports electronic systems and components for worldwide defense and commercial markets. Co.'s Motion & Flow Control segment provides products and services for the areas of communications, industrial, transportation, military/aerospace, commercial aircraft, computer, consumer, as well as RV/marine.

Recent Developments: For the year ended Dec 31 2007, income from continuing operations increased 26.7% to US$633.0 million from US$499.7 million a year earlier. Net income increased 27.7% to US$742.1 million from US$581.1 million in the prior year. Revenues were US$9.00 billion, up 15.3% from US$7.81 billion the year before. Operating income was US$977.2 million versus US$801.0 million in the prior year, an increase of 22.0%. Direct operating expenses rose 14.5% to US$6.44 billion from US$5.62 billion in the comparable period the year before. Indirect operating expenses increased 14.6% to US$1.59 billion from US$1.39 billion in the equivalent prior-year period.

Prospects: For 2008, Co. is targeting revenues of $11.13 billion to $11.28 billion and earnings of $3.80 to $3.95 per share. Specifically, Co. is targeting revenues in the Defense Electronics & Services business segment of $5.95 billion to $6.00 billion, driven by growth in the Advanced Engineering & Sciences and Systems divisions and the integration of the Dec 20 2007 acquired EDO Corp. Also, Co. anticipates revenues in its Fluid Technology business segment in the range of $3.68 billion to $3.73 billion, due to the improving Water & Wastewater and Industrial Process businesses, while revenues in the Motion & Flow Control business segment is expected to range from $1.53 billion to $1.58 billion.

Financial Data

(US$ in Thousands)	12/31/2007	12/31/2006	12/31/2005	12/31/2004	12/31/2003	12/31/2002	12/31/2001	12/31/2000
Earnings Per Share	4.03	3.10	1.91	2.29	2.15	2.03	1.52	1.47
Cash Flow Per Share	4.42	4.24	4.04	2.86	3.12	3.27	2.70	2.35
Tang Book Value Per Share	N.M.	1.64	1.38	N.M.	0.78	N.M.	N.M.	N.M.
Dividends Per Share	0.560	0.440	0.360	0.340	0.320	0.300	0.300	0.300
Dividend Payout %	13.90	14.19	18.85	14.85	14.92	14.78	19.67	20.41
Income Statement								
Total Revenue	9,003,300	7,807,900	7,427,300	6,764,100	5,626,600	4,985,300	4,675,700	4,829,400
EBITDA	1,149,200	982,600	677,000	836,500	708,600	712,600	608,300	696,900
Income Before Taxes	898,500	727,300	448,100	610,000	530,700	508,800	333,400	419,900
Income Taxes	265,500	227,600	133,700	172,500	139,800	128,900	116,700	155,400
Net Income	742,100	581,100	359,500	432,300	403,000	379,900	216,700	264,500
Average Shares	184,000	187,400	188,500	188,800	188,200	187,200	181,200	180,000
Balance Sheet								
Current Assets	4,929,800	3,347,700	2,772,000	2,329,200	2,105,500	1,700,500	1,458,800	1,506,300
Total Assets	11,552,700	7,430,000	7,063,400	7,276,700	5,937,600	5,389,600	4,508,400	4,611,400
Current Liabilities	5,456,300	2,759,400	2,560,400	2,445,800	1,686,600	1,730,200	1,896,600	2,232,700
Long-Term Obligations	483,000	500,400	516,300	542,800	460,900	492,200	456,400	408,400
Total Liabilities	7,607,900	4,565,200	4,340,000	4,933,700	4,089,900	4,252,300	3,132,600	3,400,200
Stockholders' Equity	3,944,800	2,864,800	2,723,400	2,343,000	1,847,700	1,137,300	1,375,800	1,211,200
Shares Outstanding	181,490	183,016	184,637	184,578	184,542	183,649	177,572	175,830
Statistical Record								
Return on Assets %	7.82	8.02	5.01	6.53	7.13	7.68	6.07	5.77
Return on Equity %	21.80	20.80	14.19	20.58	27.06	30.23	21.39	22.83
EBITDA Margin %	12.76	12.58	9.12	12.37	12.59	14.29	13.01	14.43
Net Margin %	8.24	7.44	4.84	6.39	7.18	7.62	5.92	5.48
Asset Turnover	0.95	1.08	1.04	1.02	0.99	1.01	1.03	1.05
Current Ratio	0.90	1.21	1.08	0.95	1.25	0.98	0.77	0.67
Debt to Equity	0.12	0.17	0.19	0.23	0.25	0.43	0.33	0.34
Price Range	72.80-56.65	57.96-45.50	57.48-40.24	43.20-35.66	37.10-25.34	35.30-23.63	25.65-18.30	19.56-11.63
P/E Ratio	18.06-14.06	18.70-14.68	30.09-21.07	18.86-15.57	17.26-11.79	17.39-11.64	16.88-12.04	13.31-7.91
Average Yield %	0.87	0.85	0.74	0.86	1.03	0.96	1.35	1.89

Address: 4 West Red Oak Lane, White Plains, NY 10604	**Web Site:** www.itt.com	**Auditors:** Deloitte & Touche LLP
Telephone: 914-641-2000	**Officers:** Steven R. Loranger - Chmn., Pres., C.E.O. George E. Minnich - Sr. V.P., C.F.O.	**Investor Contact:** 914-641-2030
Fax: 914-696-2950		**Transfer Agents:** Bank of New York, New York, NY

ITT EDUCATIONAL SERVICES, INC.

Exchange	Symbol	Price	52Wk Range	Yield	P/E
NYS	ESI	$45.93 (3/31/2008)	130.47-45.93	N/A	12.38

*7 Year Price Score 161.08 *NYSE Composite Index=100 *12 Month Price Score 66.28

TRADING VOLUME (thousand shares)

Interim Earnings (Per Share)

Qtr.	Mar	Jun	Sep	Dec
2003	0.19	0.21	0.34	0.52
2004	0.19	0.30	0.39	0.72
2005	0.32	0.48	0.73	0.81
2006	0.45	0.55	0.77	0.96
2007	0.66	0.87	0.98	1.20

Interim Dividends (Per Share)

Amt	Decl	Ex	Rec	Pay
100%	5/13/2002	6/6/2002	5/28/2002	6/5/2002

Valuation Analysis

	Institutional Holding	
Forecast P/E	17.60	No of Institutions
	(1/10/2007)	202
Market Cap	$1.8 Billion	Shares
Book Value	70.6 Million	41,311,168
Price/Book	25.84	% Held
Price/Sales	2.10	N/A

Business Summary: Schools and Universities (MIC: 6.1 SIC: 8222 NAIC: 611210)

ITT Educational Services is a for-profit provider of post-secondary degree programs through 97 institutes located in throughout 34 states in the U.S. Co. designs its education programs, after consultation with employers, to help graduates prepare for careers in various fields involving their areas of study. In addition, all of Co.'s institutes are authorized by the applicable education authorities of the states in which they operate and recruit; and are accredited by an accrediting commission recognized by the U.S. Department of Education. As of Dec 31 2007, Co. was providing diploma, associate, bachelor and master degree programs to approximately 53,000 students.

Recent Developments: For the year ended Dec 31 2007, net income increased 27.9% to US$151.6 million from US$118.5 million in the prior year. Revenues were US$869.5 million, up 14.7% from US$757.8 million the year before. Operating income was US$242.0 million versus US$181.5 million in the prior year, an increase of 33.3%. Direct operating expenses rose 0.5% to US$358.6 million from US$356.9 million in the comparable period the year before. Indirect operating expenses increased 22.6% to US$268.9 million from US$219.4 million in the equivalent prior-year period.

Prospects: Looking ahead into 2008, Co. anticipates that its quarterly marketing expenditures will increase in the range of 10.0% to 15.0%, versus its 2007 levels. Nevertheless, Co. remains optimistic regarding its near-term outlook. In detail, Co. is projecting earnings to be in the range of $4.50 to $4.60 per share, following the consideration of the current student financing environment. Also, Co. intends to open six to eight new locations in 2008. Meanwhile, Co. is developing several new degree programs of study in technology and non-technology areas at both the associate and bachelor degree levels. Co. plans to begin offering one or more of these new programs online and in residence in 2008.

Financial Data
(US$ in Thousands)

	12/31/2007	12/31/2006	12/31/2005	12/31/2004	12/31/2003	12/31/2002	12/31/2001	12/31/2000
Earnings Per Share	3.71	2.72	2.33	1.61	1.27	0.94	0.70	0.51
Cash Flow Per Share	4.43	3.84	3.34	2.97	3.37	2.77	1.00	1.18
Tang Book Value Per Share	1.78	2.53	6.75	5.11	3.22	1.97	1.69	1.38
Income Statement								
Total Revenue	869,508	757,764	688,003	617,834	522,856	464,946	410,551	347,524
EBITDA	265,280	203,164	192,110	141,631	117,706	89,426	70,133	56,234
Income Before Taxes	244,486	189,627	174,291	123,382	96,516	70,993	54,314	44,422
Income Taxes	92,894	71,111	64,579	48,119	37,658	27,139	20,600	16,937
Net Income	151,592	118,516	109,712	75,263	58,858	43,854	33,714	24,709
Average Shares	40,883	43,629	47,112	46,808	46,280	46,793	48,216	48,370
Balance Sheet								
Current Assets	349,823	380,952	437,008	372,781	256,646	173,266	134,210	92,570
Total Assets	540,953	560,320	592,491	493,389	363,270	247,707	195,399	150,896
Current Liabilities	291,924	284,505	251,139	233,101	202,337	142,495	108,393	79,926
Long-Term Obligations	150,000	150,000	...	...	...	...	...	...
Total Liabilities	470,395	456,375	283,897	258,315	217,146	158,683	117,211	86,210
Stockholders' Equity	70,558	103,945	308,594	235,074	146,124	89,024	78,188	64,686
Shares Outstanding	39,693	41,039	45,691	45,993	45,430	45,082	46,320	46,993
Statistical Record								
Return on Assets %	27.53	20.56	20.21	17.52	19.27	19.79	19.47	17.48
Return on Equity %	173.74	57.46	40.36	39.38	50.06	52.45	47.19	40.25
EBITDA Margin %	30.51	26.81	27.92	22.92	22.51	19.23	17.08	16.18
Net Margin %	17.43	15.64	15.95	12.18	11.26	9.43	8.21	7.11
Asset Turnover	1.58	1.31	1.27	1.44	1.71	2.10	2.37	2.46
Current Ratio	1.20	1.34	1.74	1.60	1.27	1.22	1.24	1.16
Debt to Equity	2.13	1.44	...	...	...	...	...	...
Price Range	130.47-68.24	70.79-56.00	62.46-42.88	59.46-28.29	56.03-23.26	26.25-14.50	22.70-9.28	14.09-6.00
P/E Ratio	35.17-18.39	26.03-20.59	26.81-18.40	36.93-17.57	44.12-18.31	27.92-15.43	32.43-13.26	27.63-11.76

Address: 13000 North Meridian Street, Carmel, IN 46032-1404 **Telephone:** 317-706-9200 **Fax:** 317-594-4382	**Web Site:** www.itt-tech.edu **Officers:** Rene R. Champagne - Chmn., C.E.O. Kevin M. Modany - Pres., C.O.O.	**Auditors:** PricewaterhouseCoopers LLP

JABIL CIRCUIT, INC.

Exchange	Symbol	Price	52Wk Range	Yield	P/E
NYS	JBL	$9.46 (3/31/2008)	25.32-9.03	N/A	21.02

*7 Year Price Score 62.39 *NYSE Composite Index=100 *12 Month Price Score 68.68

Interim Earnings (Per Share)

Qtr.	Nov	Feb	May	Aug
2004-05	0.27	0.22	0.29	0.34
2005-06	0.37	0.32	0.30	(0.22)
2006-07	0.20	0.07	0.03	0.05
2007-08	0.30	...	...	...

Interim Dividends (Per Share)

No Dividends Paid

Valuation Analysis — Institutional Holding

Forecast P/E	12.16	No of Institutions
	(1/10/2007)	332
Market Cap	$2.0 Billion	Shares
Book Value	2.6 Billion	168,005,072
Price/Book	0.77	% Held
Price/Sales	0.16	79.56

Business Summary: Electrical (MIC: 11.14 SIC: 3672 NAIC: 334412)

Jabil Circuit is engaged as a provider of electronic manufacturing services and applications. Co. provides electronics and mechanical design, production, product management and after-market services to companies in the aerospace, automotive, computing, consumer, defense, industrial, instrumentation, medical, networking, peripherals, storage, as well as telecommunications industries. As of Aug 31 2007, Co.'s key customers included Cisco Systems, Inc., EMC Corporation, Hewlett-Packard Company, International Business Machines Corporation, Network Appliance, NEC Corporation, Nokia Corporation, Royal Philips Electronics, Tellabs, Inc., and Valeo S.A.

Recent Developments: For the quarter ended Nov 30 2007, net income increased 49.8% to US$62.0 million from US$41.4 million in the year-earlier quarter. Revenues were US$3.37 billion, up 4.5% from US$3.22 billion the year before. Operating income was US$98.9 million versus US$61.1 million in the prior-year quarter, an increase of 61.9%. Direct operating expenses rose 3.2% to US$3.13 billion from US$3.03 billion in the comparable period the year before. Indirect operating expenses increased 7.6% to US$140.8 million from US$130.9 million in the equivalent prior-year period.

Prospects: For the second fiscal quarter ending Feb 2008, Co. targets net revenue to be in the range of $3.00 billion to $3.10 billion, with an estimated core operating margin range of 2.2% to 2.4%. Additionally, loss per share is estimated to be $(0.03) to $0.01 per diluted share. Further, for the fiscal year ending Aug 31 2008, Co. targets net revenue to range from $13.00 billion to $13.40 billion, with full year core operating income estimated to range from 3.1% to 3.6% or $400.0 million to $480.0 million. Co. is also targeting earnings for fiscal 2008 to be in the range of $0.69 to $0.99 per diluted share, including amortizations of intangibles, stock-based compensation and related charges.

Financial Data
(US$ in Thousands)

	3 Mos	08/31/2007	08/31/2006	08/31/2005	08/31/2004	08/31/2003	08/31/2002	08/31/2001
Earnings Per Share	0.45	0.35	0.77	1.12	0.81	0.21	0.17	0.59
Cash Flow Per Share	2.83	0.90	2.16	2.91	2.25	1.33	2.81	0.95
Tang Book Value Per Share	6.09	5.73	7.91	8.22	7.29	6.06	6.63	6.43
Dividends Per Share	0.280	0.280	0.140	...	...	...	...	...
Dividend Payout %	62.22	80.00	18.18	...	...	...	...	...
Income Statement								
Total Revenue	3,367,947	12,290,592	10,265,447	7,524,386	6,252,897	4,729,482	3,545,466	4,330,655
EBITDA	160,694	405,798	428,612	507,533	431,354	271,523	236,363	319,182
Depn & Amortn	66,269	...	...	...	...	...	...	...
Income Before Taxes	71,892	94,513	225,116	276,372	197,513	36,954	44,756	166,148
Income Taxes	9,631	21,401	60,598	44,525	30,613	(6,053)	10,041	47,631
Net Income	62,001	73,236	164,518	231,847	166,900	43,007	34,715	118,517
Average Shares	206,605	206,072	212,740	207,326	205,849	202,103	200,782	202,223
Balance Sheet								
Current Assets	4,021,079	3,666,293	3,678,965	2,685,935	2,182,675	2,093,947	1,588,344	1,446,798
Total Assets	6,734,039	6,295,232	5,411,730	4,077,762	3,329,356	3,244,743	2,547,906	2,357,578
Current Liabilities	3,243,562	2,990,847	2,701,334	1,568,129	1,159,084	1,263,218	593,382	504,775
Long-Term Obligations	758,775	760,477	329,520	326,580	305,194	297,018	354,668	361,667
Total Liabilities	4,148,003	3,843,539	3,117,249	1,942,045	1,510,016	1,656,269	1,040,940	943,502
Stockholders' Equity	2,576,923	2,443,011	2,294,481	2,135,217	1,819,340	1,588,476	1,506,966	1,414,076
Shares Outstanding	209,531	204,574	202,931	204,492	201,298	199,345	197,950	196,871
Statistical Record								
Return on Assets %	1.51	1.25	3.47	6.26	5.06	1.48	1.42	5.42
Return on Equity %	3.80	3.09	7.43	11.73	9.77	2.78	2.38	8.83
EBITDA Margin %	4.77	3.30	4.18	6.75	6.90	5.74	6.67	7.37
Net Margin %	1.84	0.60	1.60	3.08	2.67	0.91	0.98	2.74
Asset Turnover	2.00	2.10	2.16	2.03	1.90	1.63	1.45	1.98
Current Ratio	1.24	1.23	1.36	1.71	1.88	1.66	2.68	2.87
Debt to Equity	0.29	0.31	0.14	0.15	0.17	0.19	0.24	0.26
Price Range	29.18-16.95	31.05-20.07	43.31-22.07	32.75-20.36	32.35-19.48	28.15-11.53	30.71-14.96	65.84-18.12
P/E Ratio	64.84-37.67	88.71-57.34	56.25-28.66	29.24-18.18	39.94-24.05	134.05-54.90	180.65-88.00	111.60-30.71
Average Yield %	1.20	1.12	0.42	...	...	...	...	...

Address: 10560 Dr. Martin Luther King, Jr. Street North, St. Petersburg, FL 33716 Telephone: 727-577-9749 Fax: 727-579-8529	Web Site: www.jabil.com Officers: William D. Morean - Chmn. Timothy L. Main - Pres., C.E.O.	Auditors: KPMG LLP Investor Contact: 727-803-3349 Transfer Agents: EquiServe Trust Company

JACOBS ENGINEERING GROUP, INC.

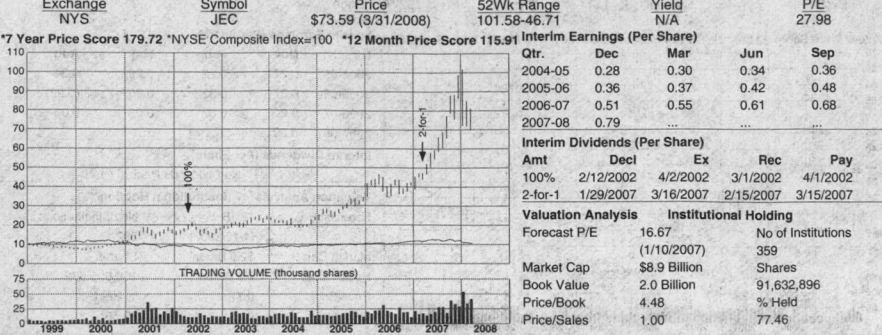

Exchange	Symbol	Price	52Wk Range	Yield	P/E
NYS	JEC	$73.59 (3/31/2008)	101.58-46.71	N/A	27.98

*7 Year Price Score 179.72 *NYSE Composite Index=100 *12 Month Price Score 115.91

Interim Earnings (Per Share)

Qtr.	Dec	Mar	Jun	Sep
2004-05	0.28	0.30	0.34	0.36
2005-06	0.36	0.37	0.42	0.48
2006-07	0.51	0.55	0.61	0.68
2007-08	0.79	...	...	...

Interim Dividends (Per Share)

Amt	Decl	Ex	Rec	Pay
100%	2/12/2002	4/2/2002	3/1/2002	4/1/2002
2-for-1	1/29/2007	3/16/2007	2/15/2007	3/15/2007

Valuation Analysis   **Institutional Holding**

Forecast P/E	16.67	No of Institutions
	(1/10/2007)	359
Market Cap	$8.9 Billion	Shares
Book Value	2.0 Billion	91,632,896
Price/Book	4.48	% Held
Price/Sales	1.00	77.46

Business Summary: Construction - Public Infrastructure (MIC: 3.1 SIC: 1629 NAIC: 236210)

Jacobs Engineering Group is engaged as a professional services firm. Co. provides technical, professional and construction services to industrial, commercial and governmental clients worldwide. Co. provides project services such as engineering, design, architectural and similar services, as well as process, scientific, and systems consulting services; operations and maintenance services; and construction services. Co. focuses its services on markets that include oil and gas exploration and production; various national government programs; pharmaceuticals; chemicals and polymers; infrastructure; technology and manufacturing; consumer products; and pulp and paper, among others.

Recent Developments: For the quarter ended Dec 31 2007, net income increased 60.6% to US$98.4 million from US$61.3 million in the year-earlier quarter. Revenues were US$2.47 billion, up 22.5% from US$2.02 billion the year before. Operating income was US$141.3 million versus US$94.4 million in the prior-year quarter, an increase of 49.7%. Direct operating expenses rose 19.3% to US$2.08 billion from US$1.75 billion in the comparable period the year before. Indirect operating expenses increased 39.3% to US$246.7 million from US$177.1 million in the equivalent prior-year period.

Prospects: Co.'s near term prospects appear favorable. Notably, in view of recent positive industry trends, favorable new business prospects and continuing backlog growth, Co. stated that it should continue to track above its target of 15.0% average annual. As a result, for the fiscal year ending Sep 2008, Co. expects earnings in the range of $2.95 to $3.25. Separately, on Jan 15 2007, Co. announced that it has received a contract from the U.S. Army to provide test and evaluation support to the Aberdeen Test Center at Aberdeen Proving Ground, MD. The contract, which consists of a base year and four one-year options, has a maximum potential value of $492.0 million.

Financial Data

(US$ in Thousands)	3 Mos	09/30/2007	09/30/2006	09/30/2005	09/30/2004	09/30/2003	09/30/2002	09/30/2001
Earnings Per Share	2.63	2.35	1.64	1.28	1.13	1.14	0.99	0.81
Cash Flow Per Share	2.20	3.04	1.92	1.41	0.78	1.34	1.48	0.14
Tang Book Value Per Share	9.80	9.92	7.18	4.74	3.60	4.00	2.73	2.55
Income Statement								
Total Revenue	2,471,817	8,473,970	7,421,270	5,635,001	4,594,235	4,615,601	4,555,661	3,956,993
EBITDA	167,091	492,567	345,836	285,716	233,078	234,185	208,978	185,145
Depn & Amortn	16,665	...	...	...	...	...	...	...
Income Before Taxes	153,705	448,642	305,287	236,059	198,424	196,939	168,754	138,206
Income Taxes	55,335	161,512	108,404	85,039	69,449	68,929	59,064	50,446
Net Income	98,370	287,130	196,883	151,020	128,975	128,010	109,690	87,760
Average Shares	124,078	122,226	120,374	117,380	114,866	112,784	110,792	108,992
Balance Sheet								
Current Assets	2,287,360	2,278,078	1,817,961	1,337,431	1,083,513	970,097	974,903	946,159
Total Assets	3,667,418	3,389,421	2,853,884	2,353,721	2,071,044	1,670,510	1,673,984	1,557,040
Current Liabilities	1,366,182	1,276,434	1,041,195	785,095	685,914	611,414	740,417	700,659
Long-Term Obligations	36,523	40,450	77,673	89,632	78,758	17,806	85,732	164,308
Total Liabilities	1,676,638	1,545,759	1,430,670	1,213,079	1,066,017	828,427	984,371	965,239
Stockholders' Equity	1,990,780	1,843,662	1,423,214	1,140,642	1,005,027	842,083	689,613	591,801
Shares Outstanding	121,231	120,221	117,991	116,259	113,397	111,672	109,530	107,489
Statistical Record								
Return on Assets %	9.77	9.20	7.56	6.83	6.88	7.65	6.79	5.97
Return on Equity %	18.58	17.58	15.36	14.08	13.93	16.71	17.12	16.14
EBITDA Margin %	6.76	5.81	4.66	5.07	5.07	5.07	4.59	4.68
Net Margin %	3.98	3.39	2.65	2.68	2.81	2.77	2.41	2.22
Asset Turnover	2.69	2.71	2.85	2.55	2.45	2.76	2.82	2.69
Current Ratio	1.67	1.78	1.75	1.70	1.58	1.59	1.32	1.35
Debt to Equity	0.02	0.02	0.05	0.08	0.08	0.02	0.12	0.28
Price Range	98.70-38.62	77.16-36.24	46.46-29.65	33.70-18.95	24.85-18.61	24.24-13.15	21.29-14.60	18.84-9.53
P/E Ratio	37.53-14.68	32.83-15.42	28.33-18.08	26.33-14.80	21.99-16.46	21.26-11.53	21.51-14.75	23.25-11.77

Address: 1111 South Arroyo Parkway, Pasadena, CA 91105 **Telephone:** 626-578-3500 **Fax:** 626-578-6967	**Web Site:** www.jacobs.com **Officers:** Noel G. Watson - Chmn., C.E.O. Craig L. Martin - Pres.	**Auditors:** Ernst & Young LLP **Investor Contact:** 818-449-2171

JANUS CAPITAL GROUP INC

Exchange	Symbol	Price	52Wk Range	Yield	P/E
NYS	JNS	$23.27 (3/31/2008)	36.80-21.07	0.17	35.80

*7 Year Price Score 115.46 *NYSE Composite Index=100 ***12 Month Price Score 93.27**

Interim Earnings (Per Share)

Qtr.	Mar	Jun	Sep	Dec
2003	0.17	0.21	0.22	3.54
2004	(0.08)	0.56	0.22	0.03
2005	0.09	0.12	0.15	0.05
2006	0.17	0.15	0.15	0.20
2007	0.19	0.27	0.07	0.12

Interim Dividends (Per Share)

Amt	Decl	Ex	Rec	Pay
0.04A	5/13/2004	7/13/2004	7/15/2004	7/30/2004
0.04A	5/10/2005	7/13/2005	7/15/2005	7/29/2005
0.04A	4/25/2006	5/11/2006	5/15/2006	5/31/2006
0.04A	5/2/2007	5/16/2007	5/18/2007	5/31/2007

Indicated Div: $0.04

Valuation Analysis / Institutional Holding

Forecast P/E	19.38	No of Institutions
	(1/10/2007)	279
Market Cap	$3.9 Billion	Shares
Book Value	1.7 Billion	178,257,472
Price/Book	2.25	% Held
Price/Sales	3.46	93.95

Business Summary: Wealth Management (MIC: 8.8 SIC: 6282 NAIC: 523930)

Janus Capital Group provides investment management, administration, distribution and related services to individual and institutional investors through mutual funds, subadvised relationships and separate accounts in both domestic and international markets. Co. provides investment advisory services through its primary subsidiaries: Janus Capital Management LLC and Enhanced Investment Technologies, LLC. Co.'s sales organization capabilities are segmented into four distribution channels: retail, U.S. intermediary, U.S. Institutional and International. As of Dec 31 2007, Co. had total assets under management of approximately $206.70 billion.

Recent Developments: For the year ended Dec 31 2007, income from continuing operations increased 38.2% to US$192.0 million from US$138.9 million a year earlier. Net income decreased 12.9% to US$116.3 million from US$133.6 million in the prior year. Revenues were US$1.12 billion, up 19.4% from US$935.8 million the year before. Operating income was US$349.3 million versus US$238.9 million in the prior year, an increase of 46.2%. Indirect operating expenses increased 10.2% to US$767.7 million from US$696.9 million in the equivalent prior-year period.

Prospects: Co.'s outlook seems favorable, reflecting improvement in its results from operations with growth in earnings per share and an increase in operating margin driven by strong investment performance and positive flows. Notably, Co.'s increase in investment management fees and average assets under management are driven primarily by market appreciation and investment performance combined with positive long-term net inflows. In addition, Co. is seeing an increase in performance fee revenue primarily due to fees earned on mutual funds. Moreover, Co. is encouraged by its progress in expanding its global and alternative product lineup and its investments in advisory and institutional distribution.

Financial Data
(US$ in Thousands)

	12/31/2007	12/31/2006	12/31/2005	12/31/2004	12/31/2003	12/31/2002	12/31/2001	12/31/2000
Earnings Per Share	0.65	0.66	0.40	0.73	4.14	0.38	1.31	2.90
Cash Flow Per Share	1.65	1.49	1.25	(0.04)	1.14	1.27	2.28	3.28
Tang Book Value Per Share	N.M.	N.M.	0.88	1.43	1.00	N.M.	1.46	4.04
Dividends Per Share	0.040	0.040	0.040	0.040	0.040	0.050	0.040	0.010
Dividend Payout %	6.15	6.06	10.00	5.48	0.97	13.16	3.05	0.34
Income Statement								
Total Revenue	1,117,000	1,026,700	953,100	1,010,800	994,700	1,144,800	1,555,700	2,248,100
Income Before Taxes	322,900	230,100	...	265,600	884,600	319,500	620,000	1,202,400
Income Taxes	116,400	81,900	67,900	92,200	(65,400)	231,800	217,700	427,000
Net Income	116,300	133,600	87,800	169,500	949,900	84,700	302,300	663,700
Average Shares	178,600	203,500	219,100	231,900	229,500	224,200	224,424	225,423
Balance Sheet								
Total Assets	3,564,100	3,537,900	3,628,500	3,767,600	4,332,200	3,321,700	3,391,600	1,581,000
Total Liabilities	1,824,400	1,213,700	1,031,500	1,028,000	1,667,900	1,810,200	2,005,000	449,900
Stockholders' Equity	1,723,500	2,306,400	2,581,200	2,734,500	2,661,200	1,508,000	1,363,300	1,057,800
Shares Outstanding	166,287	193,479	216,035	234,436	239,200	222,544	222,101	218,909
Statistical Record								
Return on Assets %	3.28	3.73	2.37	4.17	24.82	2.52	12.16	...
Return on Equity %	5.77	5.47	3.30	6.27	45.57	5.90	24.97	...
Price Range	36.80-19.43	24.15-15.80	19.93-12.99	17.70-12.73	18.55-9.86	28.91-9.08	46.00-18.55	53.94-32.50
P/E Ratio	56.62-29.89	36.59-23.94	49.83-32.48	24.25-17.44	4.48-2.38	76.08-23.89	35.11-14.16	18.60-11.21
Average Yield %	0.15	0.20	0.26	0.26	0.28	0.27	0.13	0.02

Address: 100 Fillmore Street, Denver, CO 64105. Telephone: 303-333-3863	Web Site: www.janus.com Officers: Steve L. Scheid - Chmn., C.E.O. Mark B. Whiston - Vice-Chmn., Pres.	Auditors: Deloitte & Touche LLP Investor Contact: 303-394-7311

421

JARDEN CORP.

Exchange	Symbol	Price	52Wk Range	Yield	P/E
NYS	JAH	$21.74 (3/31/2008)	44.89-19.85	N/A	57.21

*7 Year Price Score 117.43 *NYSE Composite Index=100   *12 Month Price Score 77.24

Interim Earnings (Per Share)

Qtr.	Mar	Jun	Sep	Dec
2003	0.13	0.30	0.46	0.01
2004	0.18	0.38	0.53	(0.09)
2005	(0.51)	0.12	0.40	0.03
2006	0.09	0.20	0.78	0.52
2007	0.02	0.23	0.28	(0.16)

Interim Dividends (Per Share)

Amt	Decl	Ex	Rec	Pay
2-for-1	5/6/2002	6/4/2002	5/20/2002	6/3/2002
3-for-2	10/30/2003	11/28/2003	11/12/2003	11/26/2003
3-for-2	6/9/2005	7/12/2005	6/20/2005	7/11/2005

Valuation Analysis / **Institutional Holding**

Forecast P/E	N/A	No of Institutions 191
Market Cap	$1.7 Billion	Shares
Book Value	1.5 Billion	73,357,224
Price/Book	1.09	% Held
Price/Sales	0.36	N/A

TRADING VOLUME (thousand shares)

Business Summary: Plastics (MIC: 11.7 SIC: 3089 NAIC: 326199)

Jarden is a provider of niche consumer products. As of Dec 31 2007, Co. operated three primary business segments: Outdoor Solutions, with consumer active lifestyle products for use outside the home or away from the home under brand names including Campingaz® and Coleman®; Consumer Solutions, with consumer products such as coffeemakers, bedding, heating pads, air cleaning products, personal and animal grooming products under brand names including FoodSaver® and Rival®; and Branded Consumables, with branded consumer products such as arts and crafts paint brushes, children's card games, firelogs and home safety equipment under brand names including Aviator®, Bernardin®, Bicycle® and Crawford®.

Recent Developments: For the year ended Dec 31 2007, net income decreased 73.5% to US$28.1 million from US$106.0 million in the prior year. Revenues were US$4.66 billion, up 21.2% from US$3.85 billion the year before. Operating income was US$232.0 million versus US$300.6 million in the prior year, a decrease of 22.8%. Direct operating expenses rose 21.1% to US$3.52 billion from US$2.90 billion in the comparable period the year before. Indirect operating expenses increased 41.9% to US$910.7 million from US$641.7 million in the equivalent prior-year period.

Prospects: Co. is seeing higher net sales supported by its recent acquisitions of K2 Inc. and Pure Fishing, Inc., offset by decreases in the domestic Coleman business due to inventory reduction initiatives at certain mass retailers. Co. noted that its diversity, whether by geographic region or breadth of products and price points, continues to be a key part of its strategy to mitigate risk and drive long term growth. Hence, Co. expects to grow top-line organically despite the macroeconomic challenges in 2008. Also, Co. expects its K2 acquisition to provide margin expansion and top-line growth opportunities in 2008 and expects to invest in new products to capitalize on its portfolio of brands.

Financial Data

(US$ in Thousands)	12/31/2007	12/31/2006	12/31/2005	12/31/2004	12/31/2003	12/31/2002	12/31/2001	12/31/2000
Earnings Per Share	0.38	1.59	0.22	0.99	0.90	1.12	(2.98)	0.17
Cash Flow Per Share	4.24	3.61	4.55	1.71	2.17	2.22	1.39	0.67
Tang Book Value Per Share	N.M.	N.M.	N.M.	N.M.	N.M.	N.M.	0.68	0.14
Income Statement								
Total Revenue	4,660,100	3,846,300	3,189,066	838,609	587,381	368,199	304,978	348,556
EBITDA	312,700	367,000	237,633	115,258	86,495	75,110	(95,348)	39,919
Income Before Taxes	66,600	188,000	95,668	68,475	52,266	52,498	(125,719)	7,065
Income Taxes	38,500	82,000	34,952	26,041	20,488	16,189	(40,443)	2,402
Net Income	28,100	106,000	60,716	42,434	31,778	36,309	(85,429)	4,922
Average Shares	73,300	66,500	54,700	42,682	35,296	32,382	28,633	28,723
Balance Sheet								
Current Assets	2,550,200	1,563,700	1,464,447	335,062	347,119	172,730	71,574	94,380
Total Assets	5,868,100	3,882,600	3,524,608	1,042,381	759,674	366,765	161,303	308,739
Current Liabilities	1,280,400	724,100	714,527	153,691	105,080	71,173	63,539	71,405
Long-Term Obligations	2,449,500	1,421,800	1,455,050	470,560	369,870	200,838	56,375	95,065
Total Liabilities	4,329,500	2,625,200	2,520,762	708,430	509,769	290,001	126,174	189,495
Stockholders' Equity	1,538,600	1,257,400	1,003,846	333,951	249,905	76,764	35,129	118,221
Shares Outstanding	76,800	71,600	68,066	42,438	40,510	32,334	28,791	28,536
Statistical Record								
Return on Assets %	0.58	2.86	2.66	4.70	5.64	13.75	N.M.	1.52
Return on Equity %	2.01	9.38	9.08	14.50	19.46	64.90	N.M.	4.07
EBITDA Margin %	6.71	9.54	7.45	13.74	14.73	20.40	N.M.	11.45
Net Margin %	0.60	2.76	1.90	5.06	5.41	9.86	N.M.	1.41
Asset Turnover	0.96	1.04	1.40	0.93	1.04	1.39	1.30	1.07
Current Ratio	1.99	2.16	2.05	2.18	3.30	2.43	1.13	1.32
Debt to Equity	1.59	1.13	1.45	1.41	1.48	2.62	1.60	0.80
Price Range	44.89-23.09	38.37-23.83	41.41-28.33	29.29-18.23	19.00-10.31	12.14-3.38	3.56-2.43	5.56-2.22
P/E Ratio	118.13-60.76	24.13-14.99	188.23-128.76	29.59-18.41	21.11-11.46	10.84-3.02	...	32.68-13.07

Address: 555 Theodore Fremd Avenue, Rye, NY 10580 **Telephone:** 914-967-9400	**Web Site:** www.jarden.com **Officers:** Martin E. Franklin - Chmn., C.E.O. Ian G. H. Ashken - Vice-Chmn., C.F.O., Sec.	**Auditors:** PricewaterhouseCoopers LLP **Transfer Agents:** National City Bank, Cleveland, OH

JEFFERIES GROUP, INC.

Exchange	Symbol	Price	52Wk Range	Yield	P/E
NYS	JEF	$16.13 (3/31/2008)	32.94-14.70	3.10	16.63

*7 Year Price Score 110.01 *NYSE Composite Index=100   *12 Month Price Score 75.52

TRADING VOLUME (thousand shares)

Interim Earnings (Per Share)

Qtr.	Mar	Jun	Sep	Dec
2003	0.13	0.16	0.17	0.25
2004	0.26	0.25	0.26	0.28
2005	0.28	0.27	0.28	0.34
2006	0.41	0.32	0.32	0.38
2007	0.42	0.45	0.26	(0.15)

Interim Dividends (Per Share)

Amt	Decl	Ex	Rec	Pay
0.125Q	4/17/2007	5/11/2007	5/15/2007	6/15/2007
0.125Q	7/18/2007	8/13/2007	8/15/2007	9/14/2007
0.125Q	10/15/2007	11/13/2007	11/15/2007	12/14/2007
0.125Q	1/22/2008	2/13/2008	2/15/2008	3/14/2008
		Indicated Div: $0.50		

Valuation Analysis

		Institutional Holding	
Forecast P/E	12.86	No of Institutions	
	(1/10/2007)	185	
Market Cap	$2.0 Billion	Shares	
Book Value	1.8 Billion	77,286,776	
Price/Book	1.14	% Held	
Price/Sales	0.74	62.46	

Business Summary: Finance Intermediaries & Services (MIC: 8.7 SIC: 6211 NAIC: 523110)

Jefferies Group and its subsidiaries operate as an investment bank and institutional securities firm serving companies and their investors. Co. provides these companies capital markets, mergers and acquisitions, restructuring and other financial advisory services, and provides investors research and trade execution in equity, equity-linked, high yield and investment grade fixed income securities, as well as commodities and derivatives. In addition, Co. provides asset management services and products to institutions and other investors. As of Dec 31 2007, Co. operated in two business segments, Capital Markets and Asset Management.

Recent Developments: For the year ended Dec 31 2007, net income decreased 29.7% to US$144.7 million from US$205.8 million in the prior year. Revenues were US$2.72 billion, up 38.5% from US$1.96 billion the year before. Direct operating expenses rose 127.6% to US$1.15 billion from US$505.6 million in the comparable period the year before. Indirect operating expenses increased 19.2% to US$1.32 billion from US$1.11 billion in the equivalent prior-year period.

Prospects: Notwithstanding the reduction in its bottom-line performance, Co. is seeing increases in its net revenues. Specifically, Co. attributes its net revenues growth primarily to the increase in its investment banking revenues, along with higher equity product revenues, partially offset by a decrease in its fixed income, excluding high yield, and commodities revenues, as well as reduction in its asset management fees and investment income (loss) from managed funds. In addition, Co. is experiencing growth in its interest income, mainly as a result of higher stock borrowing, securities purchased under agreements to resell activities and increases in interest rates.

Financial Data
(US$ in thousands)

	12/31/2007	12/31/2006	12/31/2005	12/31/2004	12/31/2003	12/31/2002	12/31/2001	12/31/2000
Earnings Per Share	0.97	1.42	1.16	1.03	0.71	0.57	0.57	0.56
Cash Flow Per Share	(3.04)	(1.26)	2.35	(2.40)	1.39	(1.68)	1.16	(0.48)
Tang Book Value Per Share	11.39	11.07	9.17	7.89	6.51	5.32	5.27	4.64
Dividends Per Share	0.500	0.450	0.255	0.180	0.105	0.050	0.050	0.050
Dividend Payout %	51.55	31.69	21.98	17.48	14.79	8.81	8.77	8.85
Income Statement								
Interest Income	1,174,883	528,882	304,053	134,450	102,403	92,027	131,408	172,124
Interest Expense	1,150,805	505,606	293,173	140,394	97,102	80,087	114,709	144,460
Net Interest Income	24,078	23,276	10,880	(5,944)	5,301	11,940	16,699	27,664
Non-Interest Income	1,544,012	1,434,326	1,193,820	1,064,189	824,313	662,749	653,583	589,739
Non-Interest Expense	1,322,356	1,108,948	936,293	831,256	685,081	570,997	567,630	522,010
Income Before Taxes	245,734	348,654	268,407	226,989	144,533	103,692	102,652	95,393
Income Taxes	93,178	137,541	104,089	83,955	52,851	41,121	43,113	40,412
Net Income	144,665	205,750	157,443	131,366	84,051	62,571	59,539	54,981
Average Shares	153,807	147,531	135,568	127,816	118,532	110,040	104,528	97,340
Balance Sheet								
Total Assets	29,793,817	17,899,882	12,780,931	13,824,628	10,992,283	6,898,691	5,344,737	3,957,869
Total Liabilities	28,032,273	16,318,795	11,494,081	12,785,495	10,153,912	6,270,174	4,779,081	3,499,422
Stockholders' Equity	1,761,544	1,581,087	1,286,850	1,039,133	838,371	628,517	565,656	458,447
Shares Outstanding	124,453	119,546	116,220	114,578	113,404	107,808	107,343	98,753
Statistical Record								
Return on Assets %	0.61	1.34	1.18	1.06	0.94	1.02	1.28	1.60
Return on Equity %	8.66	14.35	13.54	13.96	11.46	10.48	11.63	12.83
Net Interest Margin %	2.05	4.40	3.58	N.M.	5.18	12.97	12.71	16.07
Efficiency Ratio %	48.64	56.49	62.51	69.35	73.93	75.55	72.31	68.52
Price Range	32.94-22.65	34.43-23.09	23.89-16.90	21.47-14.19	16.75-8.29	12.78-8.40	10.60-6.47	7.95-4.80
P/E Ratio	33.96-23.35	24.25-16.26	20.59-14.57	20.84-13.78	23.59-11.68	22.41-14.75	18.60-11.36	14.20-8.57
Average Yield %	1.83	1.60	1.28	1.02	0.82	0.46	0.61	0.82

Address: 520 Madison Avenue, 12th Floor, New York, NY 10022
Telephone: 212-284-2550

Web Site: www.jefco.com
Officers: Richard B. Handler - Chmn., C.E.O. John C. Shaw Jr. - Pres., C.O.O.

Auditors: KPMG LLP
Investor Contact: 203-708-5975
Transfer Agents: American Stock Transfer & Trust Company

JOHNSON CONTROLS INC

Exchange	Symbol	Price	52Wk Range	Yield	P/E	Div Acheiver
NYS	JCI	$33.80 (3/31/2008)	44.42-31.05	1.54	15.36	32 Years

*7 Year Price Score 139.24 *NYSE Composite Index=100 *12 Month Price Score 99.46

Interim Earnings (Per Share)

Qtr.	Dec	Mar	Jun	Sep
2004-05	0.29	0.35	0.44	0.49
2005-06	0.28	0.28	0.57	0.61
2006-07	0.27	0.38	0.66	0.77
2007-08	0.39	...	...	...

Interim Dividends (Per Share)

Amt	Decl	Ex	Rec	Pay
3-for-1	7/25/2007	10/3/2007	9/14/2007	10/2/2007
0.11Q	7/25/2007	9/12/2007	9/14/2007	10/2/2007
0.13Q	11/14/2007	12/12/2007	12/14/2007	1/3/2008
0.13Q	1/23/2008	3/12/2008	3/14/2008	4/2/2008

Indicated Div: $0.52 (Div. Reinv. Plan)

Valuation Analysis

		Institutional Holding	
Forecast P/E	12.44	No of Institutions	
	(1/10/2007)	516	
Market Cap	$20.1 Billion	Shares	
Book Value	9.1 Billion	146,361,472	
Price/Book	2.21	% Held	
Price/Sales	0.56	74.49	

Business Summary: Automotive (MIC: 15.1 SIC: 2531 NAIC: 336360)

Johnson Controls operates in three primary businesses. The Building Efficiency business is engaged in designing, producing, marketing and installing Heating, Ventilation, & Air Conditioning (HVAC) equipment and building control systems that monitor, automate and integrate critical building operating equipment and conditions. The Automotive Experience is engaged in providing seating, instrument panel, overhead, floor console and door systems. The Power Solutions business services both automotive original equipment manufacturers and the general vehicle battery aftermarket by providing improved battery technology, coupled with systems engineering, marketing and enhanced services.

Recent Developments: For the quarter ended Dec 31 2007, income from continuing operations increased 39.9% to US$235.0 million from US$168.0 million in the year-earlier quarter. Net income increased 45.1% to US$235.0 million from US$162.0 million in the year-earlier quarter. Revenues were US$9.48 billion, up 15.5% from US$8.21 billion the year before. Direct operating expenses rose 14.6% to US$8.18 billion from US$7.14 billion in the comparable period the year before. Indirect operating expenses increased 16.9% to US$1.02 billion from US$872.0 million in the equivalent prior-year period.

Prospects: For the fiscal year ending Sep 30 2008, Co. continues to anticipate revenues increasing by 10.0% to $38.00 billion, while earnings from continuing operations are forecasted to improve by about 18.0% to a range of $2.45 to $2.50 per diluted share. For the fiscal quarter ended Mar 31 2008, Co. is targeting earnings from continuing operations to be in the range of $0.46 to $0.48 per diluted share, reflecting an increase from $0.37 per diluted share in the prior year, excluding non-recurring tax benefits. In addition, Co. is expecting strong earnings increases in all three of its businesses. Meanwhile, Co. intends to launch its lithium-ion battery systems for hybrid vehicles by late 2008.

Financial Data

(US$ in Thousands)	3 Mos	09/30/2007	09/30/2006	09/30/2005	09/30/2004	09/30/2003	09/30/2002	09/30/2001
Earnings Per Share	2.20	2.09	1.74	1.56	1.41	1.20	1.06	0.85
Cash Flow Per Share	3.27	3.24	2.43	1.61	2.64	1.43	1.86	1.87
Tang Book Value Per Share	3.44	3.37	1.10	3.52	1.94	1.27	0.75	1.17
Dividends Per Share	0.460	0.440	0.373	0.333	0.300	0.240	0.220	0.207
Dividend Payout %	20.88	21.05	21.41	21.37	21.23	20.00	20.79	24.27
Income Statement								
Total Revenue	9,484,000	34,624,000	32,235,000	27,479,400	26,553,400	22,646,000	20,103,400	18,427,200
EBITDA	496,000	2,339,000	2,091,000	1,747,200	1,922,300	1,718,800	1,632,800	1,493,000
Depn & Amortn	191,000	...	...	...	...	...	...	...
Income Before Taxes	305,000	1,607,000	1,138,000	1,003,400	1,212,100	1,057,500	1,006,000	867,100
Income Taxes	64,000	300,000	63,000	205,100	315,700	327,800	347,600	335,500
Net Income	235,000	1,252,000	1,028,000	909,400	817,500	682,900	600,500	478,300
Average Shares	602,900	599,200	589,800	582,900	577,800	567,600	564,600	558,000
Balance Sheet								
Current Assets	10,229,000	10,872,000	9,264,000	7,138,800	6,376,800	5,620,300	4,946,200	4,544,000
Total Assets	23,803,000	24,105,000	21,921,000	16,144,400	15,090,800	13,127,300	11,165,300	9,911,500
Current Liabilities	9,252,000	9,920,000	8,146,000	6,841,400	6,601,600	5,584,100	4,806,200	4,579,700
Long-Term Obligations	3,249,000	3,255,000	4,166,000	1,577,500	1,630,600	1,776,600	1,826,600	1,394,800
Total Liabilities	14,733,000	15,198,000	14,566,000	10,086,300	9,884,500	8,866,000	7,665,600	6,926,100
Stockholders' Equity	9,070,000	8,907,000	7,355,000	6,058,100	5,206,300	4,261,300	3,499,700	2,985,400
Shares Outstanding	593,770	593,766	587,321	578,612	570,962	540,932	533,280	524,993
Statistical Record								
Return on Assets %	5.76	5.44	5.40	5.82	5.78	5.62	5.70	4.95
Return on Equity %	15.92	15.40	15.33	16.15	17.22	17.60	18.52	17.20
EBITDA Margin %	5.23	6.76	6.49	6.36	7.24	7.59	8.12	8.10
Net Margin %	2.48	3.62	3.19	3.31	3.08	3.02	2.99	2.60
Asset Turnover	1.56	1.50	1.69	1.76	1.88	1.86	1.91	1.91
Current Ratio	1.11	1.10	1.14	1.04	0.97	1.01	1.03	0.99
Debt to Equity	0.36	0.37	0.57	0.26	0.31	0.42	0.52	0.47
Price Range	44.42-28.25	42.12-23.98	30.00-20.09	21.51-17.64	20.30-15.77	16.78-11.75	15.51-10.92	13.59-7.95
P/E Ratio	20.19-12.84	20.15-11.47	17.24-11.55	13.64-11.31	14.40-11.18	13.98-9.79	14.63-10.30	15.99-9.35
Average Yield %	1.28	1.33	1.51	1.71	1.62	1.71	1.61	1.88

Address: 5757 North Green Bay Avenue, P.O. Box 591, Milwaukee, WI 53201 Telephone: 414-524-1200 Fax: 414-524-3200	Web Site: www.johnsoncontrols.com Officers: John M. Barth - Chmn., Pres., C.E.O. Stephen A. Roell - Vice-Chmn., Exec. V.P.	Auditors: PricewaterhouseCoopers LLP Investor Contact: 414-524-2363 Transfer Agents: Firstar Trust Company, Milwaukee, WI

JOHNSON & JOHNSON

Exchange	Symbol	Price	52Wk Range	Yield	P/E	Div Acheiver
NYS	JNJ	$64.87 (3/31/2008)	68.40-59.77	2.56	17.87	45 Years

*7 Year Price Score 86.69   *NYSE Composite Index=100   *12 Month Price Score 106.53

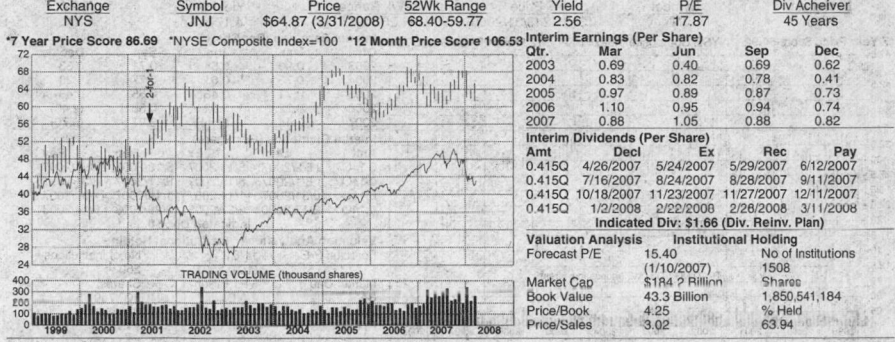

Interim Earnings (Per Share)

Qtr.	Mar	Jun	Sep	Dec
2003	0.69	0.40	0.69	0.62
2004	0.83	0.82	0.78	0.41
2005	0.97	0.89	0.87	0.73
2006	1.10	0.95	0.94	0.74
2007	0.88	1.05	0.88	0.82

Interim Dividends (Per Share)

Amt	Decl	Ex	Rec	Pay
0.415Q	4/26/2007	5/24/2007	5/29/2007	6/12/2007
0.415Q	7/16/2007	8/24/2007	8/28/2007	9/11/2007
0.415Q	10/18/2007	11/23/2007	11/27/2007	12/11/2007
0.415Q	1/2/2008	2/22/2008	2/26/2008	3/11/2008

Indicated Div: $1.66 (Div. Reinv. Plan)

Valuation Analysis   **Institutional Holding**

Forecast P/E	15.40	No of Institutions
	(1/10/2007)	1508
Market Cap	$184.2 Billion	Shares
Book Value	43.3 Billion	1,850,541,184
Price/Book	4.25	% Held
Price/Sales	3.02	63.94

TRADING VOLUME (thousand shares)

Business Summary: Health (MIC: 9 SIC: 2834 NAIC: 325412)

Johnson & Johnson is engaged in the research and development, manufacture and sale of a range of products in the health care field. As of Dec 31 2007, Co. operated through three segments. Co.'s Consumer segment includes a range of products used in the baby and child care, skin care, oral and wound care and women's health care fields, as well as nutritional and over-the-counter pharmaceutical products. Co.'s Pharmaceutical segment includes a range of products used in therapeutics areas. Co.'s Medical Devices and Diagnostics segment includes a range of products used primarily in the professional fields by physicians, nurses, therapists, hospitals, diagnostic laboratories and clinics.

Recent Developments: For the year ended Dec 30 2007, net income decreased 4.3% to US$10.58 billion from US$11.05 billion in the prior year. Revenues were US$61.10 billion, up 14.6% from US$53.32 billion the year before. Direct operating expenses rose 17.9% to US$17.75 billion from US$15.06 billion in the comparable period the year before. Indirect operating expenses increased 18.2% to US$29.68 billion from US$25.12 billion in the equivalent prior-year period.

Prospects: On Jan 21 2008, Co. announced that the U.S. FDA has granted accelerated approval to the anti-HIV medication INTELENCE tablets, a non-nucleoside reverse transcriptase inhibitor (NNRTI) to show antiviral activity in treatment-experienced adult patients with HIV resistant to a NNRTI and other antiretroviral agents. Separately, Co. is projecting earnings for 2008 to range from $4.39 to $4.44 per share, excluding the effects of in-process research and development charges or other special items. Meanwhile, Co.'s Pharmaceuticals segment plans to reduce its cost by consolidating certain operations, while continuing to invest in recently launched products and its late-stage pipeline of new products.

Financial Data

(US$ in Thousands)	12/30/2007	12/31/2006	01/01/2006	01/02/2005	12/28/2003	12/29/2002	12/30/2001	12/31/2000
Earnings Per Share	3.63	3.73	3.46	2.84	2.40	2.16	1.84	1.70
Cash Flow Per Share	5.30	4.87	4.00	3.69	3.58	2.73	2.93	2.37
Tang Book Value Per Share	5.12	3.67	8.64	6.72	5.17	4.53	4.97	4.15
Dividends Per Share	1.620	1.455	1.275	1.095	0.925	0.795	0.700	0.620
Dividend Payout %	44.63	39.01	36.85	38.56	38.54	36.81	38.04	36.47
Income Statement								
Total Revenue	61,095,000	53,324,000	50,514,000	47,348,000	41,862,000	36,298,000	33,004,000	29,139,000
EBITDA	15,871,000	16,015,000	15,244,000	14,933,000	12,192,000	10,900,000	9,200,000	7,904,000
Income Before Taxes	13,283,000	14,587,000	13,656,000	12,838,000	10,308,000	9,291,000	7,898,000	6,622,000
Income Taxes	2,707,000	3,534,000	3,245,000	4,329,000	3,111,000	2,694,000	2,230,000	1,822,000
Net Income	10,576,000	11,053,000	10,411,000	8,509,000	7,197,000	6,597,000	5,668,000	4,800,000
Average Shares	2,910,700	2,961,000	3,012,500	3,003,500	3,008,100	3,054,100	3,099,300	2,834,800
Balance Sheet								
Current Assets	29,945,000	22,975,000	31,394,000	27,320,000	22,995,000	19,266,000	18,473,000	15,450,000
Total Assets	80,954,000	70,556,000	58,025,000	53,317,000	48,263,000	40,556,000	38,488,000	31,321,000
Current Liabilities	19,837,000	19,161,000	12,635,000	13,927,000	13,448,000	11,449,000	8,044,000	7,140,000
Long-Term Obligations	7,074,000	2,014,000	2,017,000	2,565,000	2,955,000	2,022,000	2,217,000	2,037,000
Total Liabilities	37,635,000	31,238,000	20,154,000	21,504,000	21,394,000	17,859,000	14,255,000	12,513,000
Stockholders' Equity	43,319,000	39,318,000	37,871,000	31,813,000	26,869,000	22,697,000	24,233,000	18,808,000
Shares Outstanding	2,840,223	2,893,230	2,974,478	2,971,023	2,967,973	2,968,295	3,047,215	2,781,874
Statistical Record								
Return on Assets %	14.00	17.24	18.75	16.48	16.25	16.74	16.28	15.92
Return on Equity %	25.67	28.72	29.96	28.53	29.12	28.19	26.41	27.49
EBITDA Margin %	25.98	30.03	30.18	31.54	29.12	30.03	27.88	27.13
Net Margin %	17.31	20.73	20.61	17.97	17.19	18.17	17.17	16.47
Asset Turnover	0.81	0.83	0.91	0.92	0.95	0.92	0.95	0.97
Current Ratio	1.51	1.20	2.48	1.96	1.71	1.68	2.30	2.16
Debt to Equity	0.16	0.05	0.05	0.08	0.11	0.09	0.09	0.11
Price Range	68.40-59.77	69.10-56.80	69.40-60.04	63.76-49.50	58.67-48.73	65.49-41.85	60.97-41.63	52.53-34.25
P/E Ratio	18.84-16.47	18.53-15.23	20.06-17.35	22.45-17.43	24.45-20.30	30.32-19.38	33.14-22.62	30.90-20.15
Average Yield %	2.53	2.34	1.97	1.96	1.76	1.38	1.35	1.39

Address: One Johnson & Johnson Plaza, New Brunswick, NJ 08933 **Telephone:** 732-524-0400 **Fax:** 732-214-0332	**Web Site:** www.jnj.com **Officers:** William C. Weldon - Chmn., C.E.O. Robert J. Darretta - Vice-Chmn., C.F.O.	**Auditors:** PricewaterhouseCoopers LLP **Investor Contact:** 735-524-2455 **Transfer Agents:** EquiServe Trust Company, N.A., Providence, RI

JONES APPAREL GROUP, INC.

Exchange	Symbol	Price	52Wk Range	Yield	P/E
NYS	JNY	$13.42 (3/31/2008)	34.26-12.77	4.17	4.37

*7 Year Price Score 54.92   *NYSE Composite Index=100   *12 Month Price Score 72.64

Interim Earnings (Per Share)

Qtr.	Mar	Jun	Sep	Dec
2003	0.90	0.54	0.71	0.33
2004	0.73	0.61	0.77	0.28
2005	0.71	0.46	0.65	0.48
2006	0.22	0.32	0.56	(2.40)
2007	0.44	(0.44)	3.97	(0.70)

Interim Dividends (Per Share)

Amt	Decl	Ex	Rec	Pay
0.14Q	5/2/2007	5/16/2007	5/18/2007	6/1/2007
0.14Q	8/1/2007	8/15/2007	8/17/2007	8/31/2007
0.14Q	10/31/2007	11/14/2007	11/16/2007	11/30/2007
0.14Q	2/13/2008	2/27/2008	2/29/2008	3/14/2008

Indicated Div: $0.56

Valuation Analysis   **Institutional Holding**

Forecast P/E	11.81	No of Institutions	
	(1/10/2007)	260	
Market Cap	$1.1 Billion	Shares	
Book Value	2.0 Billion	102,759,352	
Price/Book	0.57	% Held	
Price/Sales	0.30	94.72	

TRADING VOLUME (thousand shares)

Business Summary: Apparel (MIC: 4.4 SIC: 2331 NAIC: 315232)

Jones Apparel Group is a designer, marketer and wholesaler of branded apparel, footwear and accessories. Co. also markets directly to customers through its specialty retail stores and value-based stores. Co.'s brands include Jones New York, Nine West, Anne Klein, Gloria Vanderbilt, Kasper, Bandolino, Easy Spirit, Evan-Picone, l.e.i., Energie, Enzo Angiolini, Joan & David, Mootsies Tootsies, Sam & Libby, Napier, Judith Jack and Le Suit. Co. also markets costume jewelry under the Givenchy brand and footwear under the Dockers Women brand. Co. has four reportable segments: wholesale better apparel, wholesale moderate apparel, wholesale footwear and accessories, and retail.

Recent Developments: For the year ended Dec 31 2007, income from continuing operations was US$45.9 million compared with a loss of US$175.0 million a year earlier. Net income amounted to US$311.1 million versus a net loss of US$144.1 million in the prior year. Revenues were US$3.85 billion, down 5.8% from US$4.09 billion the year before. Operating loss was US$27.0 million versus a loss of US$220.0 million in the prior year. Direct operating expenses declined 2.4% to US$2.61 billion from US$2.67 billion in the comparable period the year before. Indirect operating expenses decreased 22.4% to US$1.27 billion from US$1.63 billion in the equivalent prior-year period.

Prospects: Co. is cautiously optimsitic of its outlook for 2008, given the existing challenges and uncertainty in the overall general economic conditions. Conversely, Co. expects to benefit from its turnaround and recovery initiatives, including enhancing its product offerings, streamlining of its supply chain and distribution networks, as well as disposing several of its marginally profitable businesses. Notably, Co. is progressing with the closure of distribution centers in view of its cost reduction efforts and other restructuring actions, with one additional distribution center scheduled to close in 2008, and plans to remain focused on its review of cost structure for additional improvements.

Financial Data
(US$ in Thousands)

	12/31/2007	12/31/2006	12/31/2005	12/31/2004	12/31/2003	12/31/2002	12/31/2001	12/31/2000
Earnings Per Share	3.07	(1.30)	2.30	2.39	2.48	2.36	1.82	2.48
Cash Flow Per Share	1.60	3.83	3.62	3.73	3.57	5.59	4.56	2.84
Tang Book Value Per Share	4.75	1.30	N.M.	N.M.	0.98	0.66	0.03	0.16
Dividends Per Share	0.560	0.500	0.440	0.360	0.160	...	...	...
Dividend Payout %	18.24	...	19.13	15.06	6.45	...	...	...
Income Statement								
Total Revenue	3,848,500	4,742,800	5,074,200	4,649,700	4,375,300	4,340,900	4,073,100	4,142,700
EBITDA	79,800	(39,600)	603,200	641,200	681,800	680,400	572,600	692,600
Income Before Taxes	(58,500)	(199,500)	425,300	482,900	527,000	533,500	399,800	503,100
Income Taxes	(104,400)	(53,500)	151,000	181,100	198,400	201,200	163,600	201,200
Net Income	311,100	(144,100)	274,300	301,800	328,600	318,500	236,200	301,900
Average Shares	101,300	110,600	119,200	126,500	136,500	139,000	133,700	121,900
Balance Sheet								
Current Assets	1,294,100	1,278,600	1,284,300	1,296,200	1,455,900	1,318,200	1,141,000	1,181,700
Total Assets	3,236,600	3,787,000	4,577,800	4,550,800	4,187,700	3,852,600	3,373,500	2,979,200
Current Liabilities	395,600	615,400	836,500	683,900	629,000	427,300	378,200	886,800
Long-Term Obligations	777,700	788,600	789,800	1,016,600	835,100	978,100	976,600	576,200
Total Liabilities	1,239,800	1,575,400	1,911,400	1,896,900	1,649,900	1,549,100	1,468,100	1,502,000
Stockholders' Equity	1,996,800	2,211,600	2,666,400	2,653,900	2,537,800	2,303,500	1,905,400	1,477,200
Shares Outstanding	85,300	107,900	115,900	122,200	126,200	128,400	125,700	120,100
Statistical Record								
Return on Assets %	8.86	N.M.	6.01	6.89	8.17	8.82	7.44	10.43
Return on Equity %	14.78	N.M.	10.31	11.59	13.57	15.13	13.97	22.15
EBITDA Margin %	2.07	N.M.	11.89	13.79	15.58	15.67	14.06	16.72
Net Margin %	8.08	N.M.	5.41	6.49	7.51	7.34	5.80	7.29
Asset Turnover	1.10	1.13	1.11	1.06	1.09	1.20	1.28	1.43
Current Ratio	3.27	2.08	1.54	1.90	2.31	3.08	3.02	1.33
Debt to Equity	0.39	0.36	0.30	0.38	0.33	0.42	0.51	0.39
Price Range	35.24-15.99	35.78-28.10	37.06-26.74	39.74-33.46	36.98-26.80	41.31-27.07	47.21-24.65	35.00-20.56
P/E Ratio	11.48-5.21	...	16.11-11.63	16.63-14.00	14.91-10.81	17.50-11.47	25.94-13.54	14.11-8.29
Average Yield %	2.14	1.55	1.42	0.99	0.52	...	...	...

Address: 1411 Broadway, New York, NY 10018
Telephone: 212-642-3860

Web Site: www.jny.com
Officers: Sidney Kimmel - Chmn. Peter Boneparth - Pres., C.E.O.

Auditors: BDO Seidman, LLP
Investor Contact: 212-642-3860
Transfer Agents: Bank of New York, New York, NY

JPMORGAN CHASE & CO.

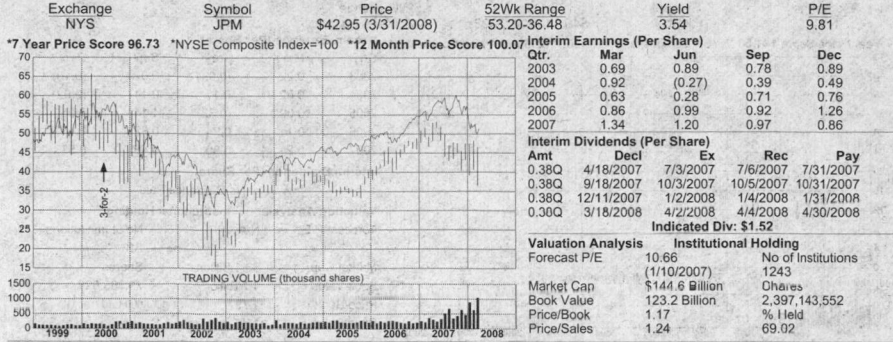

Exchange	Symbol	Price	52Wk Range	Yield	P/E
NYS	JPM	$42.95 (3/31/2008)	53.20-36.48	3.54	9.81

*7 Year Price Score 96.73   ***NYSE Composite Index=100**   ***12 Month Price Score 100.07**

Interim Earnings (Per Share)
Qtr.	Mar	Jun	Sep	Dec
2003	0.69	0.89	0.78	0.89
2004	0.92	(0.27)	0.39	0.49
2005	0.63	0.28	0.71	0.76
2006	0.86	0.99	0.92	1.26
2007	1.34	1.20	0.97	0.86

Interim Dividends (Per Share)
Amt	Decl	Ex	Rec	Pay
0.38Q	4/18/2007	7/3/2007	7/6/2007	7/31/2007
0.38Q	9/18/2007	10/3/2007	10/5/2007	10/31/2007
0.38Q	12/11/2007	1/2/2008	1/4/2008	1/31/2008
0.30Q	3/18/2008	4/2/2008	4/4/2008	4/30/2008

Indicated Div: $1.52

Valuation Analysis
Forecast P/E	10.66
	(1/10/2007)
Market Cap	$144.6 Billion
Book Value	123.2 Billion
Price/Book	1.17
Price/Sales	1.24

Institutional Holding
No of Institutions	1243
Shares	2,397,143,552
% Held	69.02

Business Summary: Commercial Banking (MIC: 8.1 SIC: 6021 NAIC: 522110)

JPMorgan Chase & Co. is a financial-holding company with $1.56 trillion in assets as of Dec 31 2007. Co.'s principal bank subsidiaries are JPMorgan Chase Bank, National Association, a national banking association with branches in 17 states, and Chase Bank USA, National Association, a national association that is Co.'s credit card-issuing bank. Co.'s principal nonbank subsidiary is J.P. Morgan Securities Inc., its U.S. investment banking firm. Co.'s activities are organized into six business segments: Investment Bank, Retail Financial Services, Card Services, Commercial Banking, Treasury & Securities Services, and Asset Management.

Recent Developments: For the year ended Dec 31 2007, income from continuing operations increased 12.6% to US$15.37 billion from US$13.65 billion a year earlier. Net income increased 6.4% to US$15.37 billion from US$14.44 billion in the prior year. Net interest income increased 24.3% to US$26.41 billion from US$21.24 billion in the prior year. Provision for loan losses was US$6.86 billion versus US$3.27 billion in the prior year, an increase of 109.9%. Non-interest income rose 10.3% to US$44.97 billion from US$40.76 billion, while non-interest expense advanced 7.4% to US$41.70 billion.

Prospects: Looking ahead, Co. anticipates a lower level of growth globally and in the U.S. during 2008 and increased credit costs in all businesses. Accordingly, Co. expects home equity losses for the first quarter of 2008 to be approximately $450.0 million and net charge-offs to potentially double from this level by the fourth quarter of 2008, and the net charge-off rate for its Card Services segment to grow to approximately 4.50% of managed loans in the first half of 2008 and to approximately 5.00% by the end of 2008. Furthermore, Co estimates the net loss in its Treasury and Other Corporate segments on a combined basis to be approximately $50.0 million to $100.0 million per quarter over time.

Financial Data
(US$ in Thousands)	12/31/2007	12/31/2006	12/31/2005	12/31/2004	12/31/2003	12/31/2002	12/31/2001	12/31/2000
Earnings Per Share	4.38	4.04	2.38	1.55	3.24	0.80	0.80	2.86
Cash Flow Per Share	(32.48)	(14.29)	(6.94)	(7.82)	7.27	(12.67)	(1.58)	(7.24)
Tang Book Value Per Share	18.77	16.11	14.02	13.34	14.76	14.21	12.54	12.96
Dividends Per Share	1.440	1.360	1.360	1.360	1.360	1.360	1.340	1.233
Dividend Payout %	32.88	33.66	57.14	87.74	41.98	170.00	167.50	43.12
Income Statement								
Interest Income	71,387,000	59,107,000	45,200,000	30,595,000	23,444,000	25,284,000	32,181,000	36,643,000
Interest Expense	44,981,000	37,865,000	25,369,000	13,834,000	11,107,000	13,758,000	21,379,000	27,131,000
Net Interest Income	26,406,000	21,242,000	19,831,000	16,761,000	12,337,000	11,526,000	10,802,000	9,512,000
Provision for Losses	6,864,000	3,270,000	3,483,000	2,544,000	1,540,000	4,331,000	3,185,000	1,377,000
Non-Interest Income	44,966,000	40,195,000	34,702,000	26,336,000	20,919,000	18,088,000	18,248,000	23,472,000
Non-Interest Expense	41,703,000	38,281,000	38,833,000	34,359,000	21,688,000	22,764,000	23,299,000	22,824,000
Income Before Taxes	22,805,000	19,886,000	12,215,000	6,194,000	10,028,000	2,519,000	2,566,000	8,733,000
Income Taxes	7,440,000	6,237,000	3,732,000	1,728,000	3,309,000	856,000	847,000	3,006,000
Net Income	15,365,000	14,444,000	8,483,000	4,466,000	6,719,000	1,663,000	1,694,000	5,727,000
Average Shares	3,508,000	3,573,900	3,557,300	2,850,600	2,055,000	2,009,000	1,972,400	1,969,000
Balance Sheet								
Net Loans & Leases	510,140,000	475,848,000	412,058,000	394,794,000	214,995,000	211,014,000	212,920,000	212,385,000
Total Assets	1,562,147,000	1,351,520,000	1,198,942,000	1,157,248,000	770,912,000	758,800,000	693,575,000	715,348,000
Total Deposits	740,728,000	638,788,000	554,991,000	521,456,000	326,492,000	304,753,000	293,650,000	279,365,000
Total Liabilities	1,438,926,000	1,235,730,000	1,091,731,000	1,051,595,000	724,758,000	716,494,000	651,926,000	672,460,000
Stockholders' Equity	123,221,000	115,790,000	107,211,000	105,653,000	46,154,000	42,306,000	41,099,000	42,338,000
Shares Outstanding	3,367,383	3,461,684	3,486,689	3,556,191	2,042,620	1,998,706	1,973,400	1,928,490
Statistical Record								
Return on Assets %	1.05	1.13	0.72	0.46	0.88	0.23	0.24	1.02
Return on Equity %	12.86	12.95	7.97	5.87	15.19	3.99	4.06	17.32
Net Interest Margin %	36.99	35.94	43.87	54.78	52.62	45.59	33.57	25.96
Efficiency Ratio %	35.84	38.55	48.60	60.35	48.89	52.49	46.20	38.00
Loans to Deposits	0.69	0.74	0.74	0.76	0.66	0.69	0.73	0.76
Price Range	53.20-40.46	48.95-38.05	40.20-33.27	43.01-35.19	37.30-20.75	39.14-15.45	55.98-30.82	65.67-36.88
P/E Ratio	12.15-9.24	12.12-9.42	16.89-13.98	27.75-22.70	11.51-6.40	48.92-19.31	69.97-38.52	22.96-12.89
Average Yield %	3.02	3.10	3.77	3.52	4.35	4.71	3.10	2.50

Address: 270 Park Avenue, New York, NY 10017-2070	**Web Site:** www.jpmorganchase.com	**Auditors:** PricewaterhouseCoopers LLP
Telephone: 212-270-6000	**Officers:** William B. Harrison Jr. - Chmn., C.E.O.	**Transfer Agents:** Mellon Investor Services LLC
Fax: 212-270-1648	Michael J. Cavanagh - Exec. V.P., C.F.O.	

KANSAS CITY SOUTHERN

Exchange	Symbol	Price	52Wk Range	Yield	P/E
NYS	KSU	$40.11 (3/31/2008)	42.50-29.50	N/A	25.55

*7 Year Price Score 141.56 *NYSE Composite Index=100 *12 Month Price Score 112.11

Interim Earnings (Per Share)

Qtr.	Mar	Jun	Sep	Dec
2003	0.22	(0.03)	0.02	(0.10)
2004	0.02	0.11	0.14	(0.02)
2005	0.09	(0.33)	1.14	0.05
2006	0.11	0.24	0.32	0.41
2007	0.21	0.30	0.48	0.57

Interim Dividends (Per Share)

No Dividends Paid

Valuation Analysis **Institutional Holding**

Forecast P/E	N/A	No of Institutions
		213
Market Cap	$3.1 Billion	Shares
Book Value	1.7 Billion	79,365,520
Price/Book	1.79	% Held
Price/Sales	1.77	N/A

Business Summary: Rail Transport (MIC: 15.5 SIC: 4011 NAIC: 482111)

Kansas City Southern is a holding company with principal operations in rail transportation. Co., along with its subsidiaries and affiliates, owns and operates a North American rail network strategically focused on the north/south freight corridor that connects commercial and industrial markets in the central U.S. with certain industrial cities in Mexico. Co.'s principal subsidiary, The Kansas City Southern Railway Company (KCSR), serves a ten-state region in the midwest and southern parts of the U.S. and has a short north/south rail route between Kansas City, Missouri, and several ports along the Gulf of Mexico in Alabama, Louisiana, Mississippi and Texas.

Recent Developments: For the year ended Dec 31 2007, net income increased 41.2% to US$153.8 million from US$108.9 million in the prior year. Revenues were US$1.74 billion, up 5.0% from US$1.66 billion the year before. Operating income was US$362.4 million versus US$304.3 million in the prior year, an increase of 19.1%. Direct operating expenses declined 0.0% to US$637.9 million from US$638.0 million in the comparable period the year before. Indirect operating expenses increased 3.5% to US$742.5 million from US$717.4 million in the equivalent prior-year period.

Prospects: Despite the expected challenge as a result of the uncertain economy, Co. believes that new business coming on-line both in the U.S. and Mexico, together with the continued strong pricing, should allow for volume growth in most commodity areas and revenue growth across-the-board. In addition, Co. expects full-year 2008 consolidated revenue growth to be in the high single digits and anticipates several factors, including price increases and intermodal growth originating at its port of Lázaro Cárdenas, to be key drivers for future growth. Meanwhile, Co. plans to acquire 30 new locomotives for U.S. operations through a leveraged lease arrangement at a cost of approximately $65.0 million.

Financial Data

(US$ in Thousands)	12/31/2007	12/31/2006	12/31/2005	12/31/2004	12/31/2003	12/31/2002	12/31/2001	12/31/2000
Earnings Per Share	1.57	1.08	1.10	0.25	0.10	0.91	0.50	6.42
Cash Flow Per Share	5.03	3.59	2.37	2.27	1.09	1.66	1.30	1.36
Tang Book Value Per Share	6.55	3.59	0.66	15.92	15.22	12.05	11.38	10.96
Dividends Per Share	1.000	1.000	1.000	1.000	1.000	1.000	1.000	1.000
Dividend Payout %	63.69	92.59	90.91	400.00	1,000.00	109.89	200.00	15.58
Income Statement								
Total Revenue	1,742,800	1,659,700	1,352,000	639,500	581,300	566,200	577,300	572,200
EBITDA	538,200	476,800	337,200	145,900	111,200	170,500	144,700	143,700
Income Before Taxes	221,300	154,600	76,000	48,000	500	64,100	33,900	21,800
Income Taxes	67,100	45,400	(7,100)	23,600	(2,800)	6,900	2,800	(3,600)
Net Income	153,800	108,900	100,900	24,400	12,200	57,200	30,700	380,500
Average Shares	97,616	92,386	92,747	63,983	61,725	62,318	60,984	58,390
Balance Sheet								
Total Assets	4,928,200	4,637,300	4,423,600	2,440,600	2,152,900	2,008,800	2,010,900	1,944,500
Long-Term Obligations	1,105,000	...	...	...	...	...	...	...
Total Liabilities	3,201,900	1,423,100	1,333,500	760,300	675,700	683,300	718,900	662,700
Stockholders' Equity	1,726,300	1,582,400	1,426,200	1,024,500	963,700	752,900	680,300	643,400
Shares Outstanding	76,975	75,920	73,412	63,270	62,175	61,103	59,243	58,140
Statistical Record								
Return on Assets %	3.22	2.40	2.94	1.06	0.59	2.85	1.55	15.08
Return on Equity %	9.30	7.24	8.23	2.45	1.42	7.98	4.64	39.39
EBITDA Margin %	30.88	28.73	24.94	22.81	19.13	30.11	25.06	25.11
Net Margin %	8.82	6.56	7.46	3.82	2.10	10.10	5.32	66.50
Asset Turnover	0.36	0.37	0.39	0.28	0.28	0.28	0.29	0.23
Price Range	42.50-28.37	30.00-22.32	25.56-16.09	17.75-12.67	14.81-10.75	17.35-12.00	16.75-9.50	10.13-4.23
P/E Ratio	27.07-18.07	27.78-20.67	23.24-14.63	71.00-50.68	148.10-107.50	19.07-13.19	33.50-19.00	1.58-0.66
Average Yield %	2.85	3.85	4.82	6.73	8.14	6.78	7.41	14.98

Address: 427 West 12th Street, Kansas City, MO 64105
Telephone: 816-983-1303
Fax: 816-556-0297

Web Site: www.kcsouthern.com
Officers: Michael R. Haverty - Chmn., Pres., C.E.O.
Gerald K. Davies - Exec. V.P., C.O.O.

Auditors: KPMG LLP
Investor Contact: 816-983-1551
Transfer Agents: UMB Bank, n.a., Kansas City, MO

KB HOME

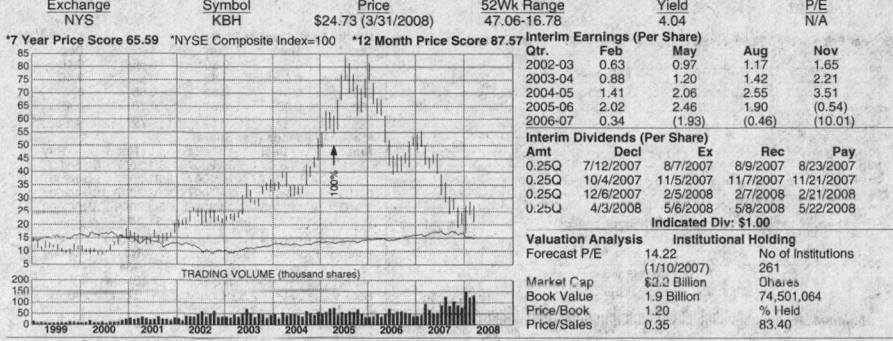

Exchange	Symbol	Price	52Wk Range	Yield	P/E
NYS	KBH	$24.73 (3/31/2008)	47.06-16.78	4.04	N/A

*7 Year Price Score 65.59 *NYSE Composite Index=100 *12 Month Price Score 87.57

Interim Earnings (Per Share)

Qtr.	Feb	May	Aug	Nov
2002-03	0.63	0.97	1.17	1.65
2003-04	0.88	1.20	1.42	2.21
2004-05	1.41	2.06	2.55	3.51
2005-06	2.02	2.46	1.90	(0.54)
2006-07	0.34	(1.93)	(0.46)	(10.01)

Interim Dividends (Per Share)

Amt	Decl	Ex	Rec	Pay
0.25Q	7/12/2007	8/7/2007	8/9/2007	8/23/2007
0.25Q	10/4/2007	11/5/2007	11/7/2007	11/21/2007
0.25Q	12/6/2007	2/5/2008	2/7/2008	2/21/2008
0.25Q	4/3/2008	5/6/2008	5/8/2008	5/22/2008

Indicated Div: $1.00

Valuation Analysis

Forecast P/E 14.22 (1/10/2007)
Market Cap $3.2 Billion
Book Value 1.9 Billion
Price/Book 1.20
Price/Sales 0.35

Institutional Holding

No of Institutions 261
Shares 74,501,064
% Held 83.40

TRADING VOLUME (thousand shares)

Business Summary: Building & General Construction (MIC: 3.2 SIC: 1531 NAIC: 236115)

KB Home is a builder of single-family homes, townhomes and condominiums in markets across the U.S. Co.'s four homebuilding segments offer a variety of homes designed primarily for first-time, first move-up and active adult buyers, including attached and detached single-family homes, townhomes and condominiums. Co.'s financial services segment derives from mortgage banking, title and insurance services offered to Co.'s homebuyers. Mortgage banking services are provided through Countrywide KB Home Loans, a joint venture operated by Countrywide Financial Corporation that offers a variety of loan programs to serve the needs of Co.'s homebuyers.

Recent Developments: For the year ended Nov 30 2007, loss from continuing operations was US$1.41 billion compared with income of US$392.9 million a year earlier. Net loss amounted to US$929.4 million versus net income of US$482.4 million in the prior year. Revenues were US$6.42 billion, down 31.6% from US$9.38 billion the year before. Direct operating expenses declined 11.0% to US$6.83 billion from US$7.67 billion in the comparable period the year before. Indirect operating expenses decreased 17.0% to US$932.5 million from US$1.12 billion in the equivalent prior year period.

Prospects: Co.'s 2008 outlook appears challenging,reflecting the oversupply of homes available for sale relative to demand in 2007. Also, Co. expects that the negative operational and financial pressures due to the housing market contraction will continue. At the same time, Co. believes that its intention to further reduce its active communities in 2008, in addition to its 2007 reduction of weaker markets, will have a negative affect on its year-over-year net order net results. Nevertheless, Co. expects to mitigate such situations through several of its continued efforts which include streamlining its costs structure and aligning its organization with anticipated reduced delivery volumes.

Financial Data

(US$ in Thousands)	11/30/2007	11/30/2006	11/30/2005	11/30/2004	11/30/2003	11/30/2002	11/30/2001	11/30/2000
Earnings Per Share	(12.04)	5.82	9.53	5.70	4.40	3.58	2.75	2.62
Cash Flow Per Share	15.48	9.08	(0.65)	(1.43)	5.87	4.30	0.61	0.83
Tang Book Value Per Share	19.91	30.09	27.50	19.35	14.67	11.25	8.95	5.27
Dividends Per Share	1.000	1.000	0.750	0.500	0.150	0.150	0.150	0.150
Dividend Payout %	...	17.18	7.87	8.77	3.41	4.20	5.45	5.73
Income Statement								
Total Revenue	6,416,526	11,003,792	9,441,650	7,052,684	5,850,554	5,030,816	4,574,184	3,930,858
EBITDA	(1,456,664)	734,795	1,334,130	755,801	597,522	517,135	407,172	365,667
Income Before Taxes	(1,460,770)	698,051	1,296,021	717,702	553,464	469,250	324,517	297,660
Income Taxes	(46,000)	215,700	453,600	236,800	182,700	154,900	110,300	87,700
Net Income	(929,414)	482,351	842,421	480,902	370,764	314,350	214,217	209,960
Average Shares	77,172	82,856	88,425	84,356	84,246	87,908	77,838	80,138
Balance Sheet								
Current Assets	4,933,414	7,753,186	6,854,056	5,042,150	3,671,399	3,507,008	3,275,554	2,431,544
Total Assets	5,705,956	9,014,464	7,746,920	5,835,956	4,235,859	4,025,540	3,692,866	2,828,921
Current Liabilities	699,851	1,071,265	892,727	794,075	586,245	521,341	479,568	322,672
Long Term Obligations	2,161,794	3,125,803	2,463,814	2,048,247	1,393,005	1,688,706	1,706,009	1,403,202
Total Liabilities	3,855,269	6,091,716	4,895,249	3,780,275	2,643,008	2,751,189	2,600,385	2,174,162
Stockholders' Equity	1,850,687	2,922,748	2,851,671	2,055,681	1,592,851	1,274,351	1,092,481	654,759
Shares Outstanding	89,525	89,374	94,884	93,376	93,257	95,948	100,754	85,898
Statistical Record								
Return on Assets %	N.M.	5.76	12.40	9.52	8.98	8.15	6.57	7.62
Return on Equity %	N.M.	16.71	34.33	26.29	25.86	26.56	24.52	31.45
EBITDA Margin %	N.M.	6.68	14.13	10.72	10.21	10.28	8.90	9.30
Net Margin %	N.M.	4.38	8.92	6.82	6.34	6.25	4.68	5.34
Asset Turnover	0.87	1.31	1.39	1.40	1.42	1.30	1.40	1.43
Current Ratio	7.05	7.24	7.68	6.35	6.26	6.73	6.83	7.54
Debt to Equity	1.17	1.07	0.86	1.00	0.87	1.33	1.56	2.14
Price Range	55.64-18.92	81.66-39.03	84.40-43.95	45.70-30.53	35.87-20.54	26.45-16.69	18.53-12.45	16.19-8.44
P/E Ratio	...	14.03-6.71	8.86-4.61	8.02-5.36	8.15-4.67	7.39-4.66	6.74-4.53	6.18-3.22
Average Yield %	2.52	1.79	1.17	1.38	0.55	0.66	0.99	1.33

Address: 10990 Wilshire Boulevard, Los Angeles, CA 90024
Telephone: 310-231-4000
Fax: 310-231-4222

Web Site: www.kbhome.com
Officers: Bruce Karatz - Chmn., C.E.O. Jeffrey T. Mezger - Exec. V.P., C.O.O.

Auditors: Ernst & Young LLP
Investor Contact: 310-231-4000
Transfer Agents: Mellon Investor Services, LLC, South Hackensack, NJ

KELLOGG CO

Exchange	Symbol	Price	52Wk Range	Yield	P/E
NYS	K	$52.56 (3/31/2008)	56.41-47.50	2.36	19.04

*7 Year Price Score 102.69 *NYSE Composite Index=100 *12 Month Price Score 103.36

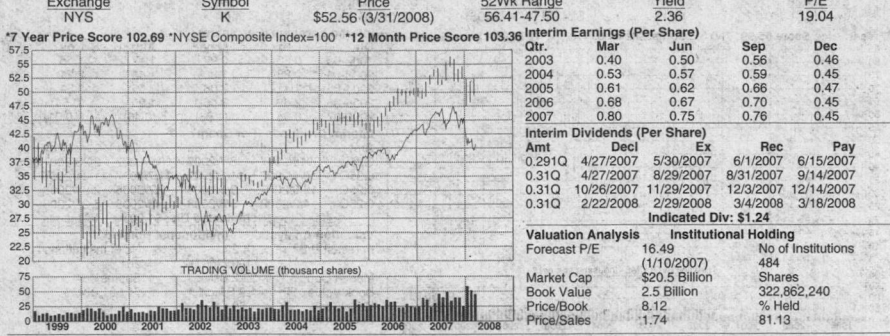

Interim Earnings (Per Share)

Qtr.	Mar	Jun	Sep	Dec
2003	0.40	0.50	0.56	0.46
2004	0.53	0.57	0.59	0.45
2005	0.61	0.62	0.66	0.47
2006	0.68	0.67	0.70	0.45
2007	0.80	0.75	0.76	0.45

Interim Dividends (Per Share)

Amt	Decl	Ex	Rec	Pay
0.291Q	4/27/2007	5/30/2007	6/1/2007	6/15/2007
0.31Q	4/27/2007	8/29/2007	8/31/2007	9/14/2007
0.31Q	10/26/2007	11/29/2007	12/3/2007	12/14/2007
0.31Q	2/22/2008	2/29/2008	3/4/2008	3/18/2008

Indicated Div: $1.24

Valuation Analysis / **Institutional Holding**

Forecast P/E	16.49 (1/10/2007)	No of Institutions	484
Market Cap	$20.5 Billion	Shares	322,862,240
Book Value	2.5 Billion	% Held	81.13
Price/Book	8.12		
Price/Sales	1.74		

Business Summary: Food (MIC: 4.1 SIC: 2043 NAIC: 311230)

Kellogg is engaged in the manufacture and marketing of ready-to-eat cereal and convenience foods, such as cookies, crackers, toaster pastries, cereal bars, fruit snacks, frozen waffles and veggie foods. As of Feb 22 2008, Co. manufactured these products in 18 countries and marketed them in more than 180 countries. Co.'s cereal products are generally marketed under the Kellogg's name and are sold principally to the grocery trade through direct sales forces for resale to consumers. In addition, Co. markets its convenience foods under brands such as Kellogg's, Keebler, Cheez-It, Murray, Austin and Famous Amos to supermarkets in the U.S.

Recent Developments: For the year ended Dec 29 2007, net income increased 9.9% to US$1.10 billion from US$1.00 billion in the prior year. Revenues were US$11.78 billion, up 8.0% from US$10.91 billion the year before. Operating income was US$1.87 billion versus US$1.77 billion in the prior year, an increase of 5.8%. Direct operating expenses rose 8.5% to US$6.60 billion from US$6.08 billion in the comparable period the year before. Indirect operating expenses increased 8.2% to US$3.31 billion from US$3.06 billion in the equivalent prior-year period.

Prospects: For 2008, Co. reaffirms its earnings guidance of $2.92 to $2.97 per share, which is in line with its long-term earnings growth at a high single-digit rate. In addition, Co. expects internal sales growth to be in the mid single-digits, slightly exceeding its low single-digit growth target, as a result of recent pricing initiatives and improved products. This higher-than-targeted sales growth will support Co.'s target of a mid single-digit operating profit growth. Meanwhile, in an effort to expand its presence in Eastern Europe, on Jan 17 2008, Co. announced that it has acquired The United Bakers Group, a producer of cereal, cookie, and cracker products in Russia, for $117.0 million.

Financial Data

(US$ in Thousands)	12/29/2007	12/30/2006	12/31/2005	01/01/2005	12/27/2003	12/28/2002	12/31/2001	12/31/2000
Earnings Per Share	2.76	2.51	2.36	2.14	1.92	1.75	1.16	1.45
Cash Flow Per Share	3.81	3.56	2.78	2.93	2.88	2.47	2.79	2.17
Tang Book Value Per Share	N.M.	N.M.	N.M.	N.M.	N.M.	N.M.	N.M.	1.21
Dividends Per Share	1.202	1.137	1.060	1.010	1.010	1.010	1.010	0.990
Dividend Payout %	43.55	45.30	44.92	47.20	52.60	57.71	87.07	68.28
Income Statement								
Total Revenue	11,776,000	10,906,700	10,177,200	9,613,900	8,811,500	8,304,100	8,853,300	6,954,700
EBITDA	2,238,000	2,131,700	2,117,200	2,084,500	1,926,700	1,885,400	1,701,800	1,310,800
Income Before Taxes	1,547,000	1,471,600	1,425,100	1,365,900	1,169,500	1,144,300	804,100	867,700
Income Taxes	444,000	466,500	444,700	475,300	382,400	423,400	322,100	280,000
Net Income	1,103,000	1,004,100	980,400	890,600	787,100	720,900	473,600	587,700
Average Shares	400,000	400,400	415,600	416,400	410,500	411,500	407,200	405,600
Balance Sheet								
Current Assets	2,717,000	2,427,000	2,196,500	2,121,800	1,797,200	1,763,400	1,902,000	1,606,800
Total Assets	11,397,000	10,714,000	10,574,500	10,790,400	10,230,800	10,219,300	10,368,600	4,896,300
Current Liabilities	4,044,000	4,020,200	3,162,800	2,846,000	2,766,000	3,014,900	2,207,600	2,492,600
Long-Term Obligations	3,270,000	3,053,000	3,702,600	3,892,600	4,265,400	4,519,400	5,619,000	709,200
Total Liabilities	8,871,000	8,645,000	8,290,800	8,533,200	8,787,600	9,324,200	9,497,100	3,998,800
Stockholders' Equity	2,526,000	2,069,000	2,283,700	2,257,200	1,443,200	895,100	871,500	897,500
Shares Outstanding	390,051	397,697	405,329	413,022	409,699	407,852	406,611	405,638
Statistical Record								
Return on Assets %	10.00	9.46	9.20	8.34	7.72	7.06	6.21	12.08
Return on Equity %	48.14	46.26	43.30	47.36	67.51	82.29	53.54	68.52
EBITDA Margin %	19.00	19.54	20.80	21.68	21.87	22.70	19.22	18.85
Net Margin %	9.37	9.21	9.63	9.26	8.93	8.68	5.35	8.45
Asset Turnover	1.07	1.03	0.96	0.90	0.86	0.81	1.16	1.43
Current Ratio	0.67	0.60	0.69	0.75	0.65	0.58	0.86	0.64
Debt to Equity	1.29	1.48	1.62	1.72	2.96	5.05	6.45	0.79
Price Range	56.41-48.89	50.79-42.64	46.46-42.41	45.24-37.20	37.80-28.02	36.89-29.35	33.56-25.00	31.31-21.00
P/E Ratio	20.44-17.71	20.24-16.99	19.69-17.97	21.14-17.38	19.69-14.59	21.08-16.77	28.93-21.55	21.59-14.48
Average Yield %	2.29	2.40	2.37	2.44	3.02	3.00	3.55	3.83

Address: One Kellogg Square, P.O. Box 3599, Battle Creek, MI 49016-3599
Telephone: 269-961-2000
Fax: 616-961-2871

Web Site: www.kelloggcompany.com
Officers: James M. Jenness - Chmn., C.E.O. A.D. David Mackay - Pres., C.O.O.

Auditors: PricewaterhouseCoopers LLP
Investor Contact: 269-961-2800
Transfer Agents: Wells Fargo Bank, N.A., St. Paul, MN

KEMET CORP.

Exchange	Symbol	Price	52Wk Range	Yield	P/E
NYS	KEM	$4.04 (3/31/2008)	9.00-3.96	N/A	134.67

*7 Year Price Score 50.42   *NYSE Composite Index=100   *12 Month Price Score 75.58

TRADING VOLUME (thousand shares)

Interim Earnings (Per Share)

Qtr.	Jun	Sep	Dec	Mar
2004-05	(0.02)	(0.09)	(0.45)	0.00
2005-06	0.04	(0.02)	0.02	(0.03)
2006-07	0.01	0.01	0.06	0.00
2007-08	0.08	0.05	(0.10)	...

Interim Dividends (Per Share)

No Dividends Paid

Valuation Analysis   **Institutional Holding**

Forecast P/E	N/A	No of Institutions
		158
Market Cap	$339.3 Million	Shares
Book Value	572.0 Million	80,739,664
Price/Book	0.59	% Held
Price/Sales	0.44	96.42

Business Summary: Electrical (MIC: 11.14 SIC: 3675 NAIC: 334414)

KEMET is engaged in the business of manufacturing a line of capacitors, including tantalum, multilayer ceramic and solid aluminum. Co. produces surface-mount capacitors, which are attached directly to the circuit board without lead wires, and leaded capacitors, which are attached to the circuit board using lead wires. Co.'s products are sold to original equipment manufacturers (OEMs) in a range of industries including the computer, communications, automotive, military, consumer and aerospace industries. Co. also sells an increasing number of its products to Electronics Manufacturing Services providers, which also serve OEMs in these industries, as well as to electronics distributors.

Recent Developments: For the quarter ended Dec 31 2007, net loss amounted to US$8.2 million versus net income of US$5.3 million in the year-earlier quarter. Revenues were US$228.7 million, up 38.2% from US$165.5 million the year before. Operating loss was US$1.6 million versus an income of US$6.2 million in the prior-year quarter. Direct operating expenses rose 47.9% to US$188.6 million from US$127.5 million in the comparable period the year before. Indirect operating expenses increased 31.1% to US$41.7 million from US$31.8 million in the equivalent prior-year period.

Prospects: On Jan 28 2008, Co. announced a cost savings initiative that involves the reduction of certain workforce in its U.S. and Mexico operations, as well as the relocation of some processes to China from Mexico and the US. Accordingly, Co. expects to generate an annualized cost reduction of about $16.0 million in the fiscal ending Mar 31 2008. Also, Co. is reducing certain workforce and plans to close its Vergato factory as part of its restructuring plans in Italy, while consolidating its Towcester operations with other facilities. Collectively, Co. expects these restructuring initiatives to generate an annualized savings of about $18.0 million by the end of fiscal year ending Mar 31 2009.

Financial Data
(US$ in Thousands)

	9 Mos	6 Mos	3 Mos	03/31/2007	03/31/2006	03/31/2005	03/31/2004	03/31/2003
Earnings Per Share	0.03	0.19	0.15	0.08	...	(2.01)	(1.30)	(0.65)
Cash Flow Per Share	0.12	0.19	0.01	0.26	...	...	0.44	0.51
Tang Book Value Per Share	4.57	5.73	5.70	5.79	5.41	5.44	7.39	8.72
Income Statement								
Total Revenue	608,942	380,248	183,119	658,714	490,106	425,338	433,882	447,332
EBITDA	49,039	11,033	18,582	8,739	(11,112)	(171,993)	(155,703)	(87,113)
Depn & Amortn	38,136	...	12,096	...	...	...	...	...
Income Before Taxes	7,162	9,565	5,747	7,460	(12,100)	(172,209)	(158,328)	(87,894)
Income Taxes	4,170	(1,577)	(1,310)	563	(12,475)	1,885	(46,353)	(31,906)
Net Income	2,892	11,042	7,032	6,897	375	(174,094)	(111,975)	(55,988)
Average Shares	83,984	84,176	84,117	85,797	80,779	86,518	86,412	86,167
Balance Sheet								
Current Assets	571,201	485,316	445,350	486,897	374,663	270,569	409,044	547,784
Total Assets	1,236,896	947,511	940,352	943,526	748,318	758,097	969,808	1,101,010
Current Liabilities	308,072	147,385	144,473	147,801	105,324	85,990	95,313	84,249
Long-Term Obligations	300,455	224,848	224,450	238,744	80,000	100,000	100,000	100,000
Total Liabilities	664,918	391,181	388,599	407,768	235,615	242,894	285,330	307,735
Stockholders' Equity	571,978	556,330	551,222	535,758	512,703	515,203	684,478	793,275
Shares Outstanding	83,989	83,974	83,931	83,751	86,879	86,563	86,468	86,239
Statistical Record								
Return on Assets %	0.28	1.90	1.54	0.82	...	...	N.M.	N.M.
Return on Equity %	0.56	3.06	2.50	1.32	...	...	N.M.	N.M.
EBITDA Margin %	8.05	2.90	10.15	1.33	N.M.	N.M.	N.M.	N.M.
Net Margin %	0.47	2.90	3.84	1.05	0.08	N.M.	N.M.	N.M.
Asset Turnover	0.71	0.81	0.78	0.78	...	...	0.42	0.39
Current Ratio	1.85	3.29	3.08	3.29	3.56	3.15	4.29	6.50
Debt to Equity	0.53	0.40	0.41	0.45	0.16	0.19	0.15	0.13
Price Range	9.00-5.86	9.00-6.05	9.22-6.89	11.45-6.89	9.48-6.12	14.94-7.58	16.62-7.69	22.08-6.29
P/E Ratio	300.00-195.33	47.37-34.00	61.47-45.93	143.13-86.13	N.M.	...	...	...

Address: 2835 Kemet Way, Simpsonville, SC 29681
Telephone: 864-963-6300
Fax: 864-963-6322

Web Site: www.kemet.com
Officers: Frank G. Brandenberg - Chmn. James P. McClintock - Pres., C.O.O.

Auditors: KPMG LLP
Investor Contact: 864-963-6300

KENNAMETAL INC.

Exchange	Symbol	Price	52Wk Range	Yield	P/E
NYS	KMT	$29.43 (3/31/2008)	45.60-27.43	1.63	11.63

*7 Year Price Score 123.56 *NYSE Composite Index=100 *12 Month Price Score 86.15

Interim Earnings (Per Share)

Qtr.	Sep	Dec	Mar	Jun
2004-05	0.30	0.37	0.40	0.49
2005-06	0.36	0.40	0.41	2.07
2006-07	0.39	0.39	0.66	0.79
2007-08	0.44	0.64	...	...

Interim Dividends (Per Share)

Amt	Decl	Ex	Rec	Pay
0.105Q	7/25/2007	8/3/2007	8/7/2007	8/22/2007
0.12Q	10/24/2007	11/5/2007	11/7/2007	11/19/2007
100%	10/24/2007	12/19/2007	12/4/2007	12/18/2007
0.12Q	1/23/2008	2/1/2008	2/5/2008	2/20/2008

Indicated Div: $0.48

Valuation Analysis   **Institutional Holding**

Forecast P/E	N/A	No of Institutions
		204
Market Cap	$2.3 Billion	Shares
Book Value	1.6 Billion	34,455,520
Price/Book	1.45	% Held
Price/Sales	0.89	89.18

Business Summary: Industrial Machinery and Equipment (MIC: 11.5 SIC: 3541 NAIC: 333512)

Kennametal supplies tooling, components and materials consumed in production processes. Co. develops and manufactures metalworking tools and wear-resistant parts using a specialized type of powder metallurgy. Co. also manufactures a line of toolholders, toolholding systems and rotary cutting tools. Moreover, Co. manufactures tungsten carbide products used in engineered applications, mining and highway construction, and other similar applications. Co. manufactures and markets engineered components with a proprietary metal cladding technology and provides engineered component process technology and materials that focus on component deburring, polishing and producing controlled radii.

Recent Developments: For the quarter ended Dec 31 2007, income from continuing operations increased 49.4% to US$50.1 million from US$33.6 million in the year-earlier quarter. Net income increased 66.9% to US$50.1 million from US$30.1 million in the year-earlier quarter. Revenues were US$647.4 million, up 13.7% from US$569.3 million the year before. Operating income was US$69.4 million versus US$55.9 million in the prior-year quarter, an increase of 24.2%. Direct operating expenses rose 14.9% to US$426.5 million from US$371.2 million in the comparable period the year before. Indirect operating expenses increased 6.5% to US$151.5 million from US$142.3 million in the equivalent prior-year period.

Prospects: For the rest of its fiscal year ending June 2008, Co. believes that the European market will remain favorable, and that business conditions will be strong in developing economies. However, Co. anticipates that the softness in the North American market will persist. Thus, Co. expects total fiscal 2008 sales growth of 11.0% to 12.0%, including organic sales growth of 3.0% to 4.0%. Co. noted that this growth rate is slightly lower than previously expected due to its outlook for more moderate expansion in global demand. For the third quarter of fiscal 2008, Co. expects total sales growth of 12.0% to 13.0%, including organic sales growth of 2.0% to 3.0%, and earnings per share of $0.72 to $0.75.

Financial Data

(US$ in Thousands)	6 Mos	3 Mos	06/30/2007	06/30/2006	06/30/2005	06/30/2004	06/30/2003	06/30/2002
Earnings Per Share	2.53	2.27	2.22	3.24	1.56	1.01	0.26	(3.35)
Cash Flow Per Share	3.01	3.55	2.59	0.25	2.74	2.48	2.58	2.49
Tang Book Value Per Share	9.38	8.99	8.34	8.77	4.20	4.71	3.49	4.97
Dividends Per Share	0.435	0.420	0.410	0.380	0.340	0.340	0.340	0.340
Dividend Payout %	17.19	18.46	18.47	11.73	21.73	33.66	133.33	...
Income Statement								
Total Revenue	1,262,499	615,076	2,385,493	2,329,628	2,304,167	1,971,441	1,758,957	1,583,742
EBITDA	181,318	87,011	367,152	555,508	281,898	202,547	154,499	165,307
Depn & Amortn	45,717	21,794	...	...	...	...	...	...
Income Before Taxes	119,271	57,418	249,496	447,719	184,277	110,674	34,290	59,051
Income Taxes	32,337	21,667	70,469	172,902	61,394	35,500	14,300	18,900
Net Income	85,025	34,879	174,243	256,283	119,291	73,578	18,130	(211,908)
Average Shares	78,647	79,068	78,546	79,102	76,112	72,946	70,958	63,254
Balance Sheet								
Current Assets	1,063,345	1,050,889	1,016,502	1,086,857	831,062	796,945	764,679	637,384
Total Assets	2,726,656	2,653,507	2,606,227	2,435,272	2,092,337	1,938,663	1,779,092	1,523,611
Current Liabilities	472,368	461,835	487,237	462,199	428,658	489,382	336,347	262,100
Long-Term Obligations	385,991	368,927	361,399	409,508	386,485	313,400	514,842	387,887
Total Liabilities	1,143,083	1,103,007	1,104,136	1,125,281	1,102,015	1,035,279	1,038,635	798,978
Stockholders' Equity	1,563,297	1,531,378	1,484,467	1,295,365	972,862	887,152	721,577	713,962
Shares Outstanding	77,038	77,842	77,972	77,214	76,254	73,266	70,946	69,620
Statistical Record								
Return on Assets %	7.76	7.13	6.91	11.32	5.92	3.95	1.10	N.M.
Return on Equity %	13.56	12.54	12.54	22.60	12.83	9.12	2.53	N.M.
EBITDA Margin %	14.36	14.15	15.39	23.85	12.23	10.27	8.78	10.44
Net Margin %	6.73	5.67	7.30	11.00	5.18	3.73	1.03	N.M.
Asset Turnover	0.99	0.98	0.95	1.03	1.14	1.06	1.07	0.95
Current Ratio	2.25	2.28	2.09	2.35	1.94	1.63	2.27	2.43
Debt to Equity	0.25	0.24	0.24	0.32	0.40	0.35	0.71	0.54
Price Range	45.60-28.59	44.27-28.15	41.18-25.06	33.52-22.50	26.29-20.27	22.90-16.80	17.93-13.73	21.49-14.86
P/E Ratio	18.03-11.30	19.50-12.40	18.55-11.29	10.34-6.94	16.85-12.99	22.67-16.63	68.94-52.79	...
Average Yield %	1.16	1.21	1.31	1.39	1.47	1.68	2.11	1.78

Address: 1600 Technology Way, P.O. Box 231, Latrobe, PA 15650-0231
Telephone: 724-539-5000
Fax: 724-539-4710

Web Site: www.kennametal.com
Officers: Markos I. Tambakeras - Chmn., Pres., C.E.O. R. Daniel Bagley - V.P., Corp. Strategy & MSSG Global Mktg.

Auditors: PricewaterhouseCoopers LLP
Investor Contact: 724-539-6559
Transfer Agents: Mellon Investor Services, LLC, Ridgefield Park, NJ

KEYCORP

Exchange	Symbol	Price	52Wk Range	Yield	P/E	Div Acheiver
NYS	KEY	$21.95 (3/31/2008)	38.58-20.50	6.83	9.46	28 Years

*7 Year Price Score 80.56 ***NYSE Composite Index=100** ***12 Month Price Score 82.92**

Interim Earnings (Per Share)

Qtr.	Mar	Jun	Sep	Dec
2003	0.51	0.53	0.53	0.55
2004	0.59	0.58	0.61	0.52
2005	0.64	0.70	0.67	0.72
2006	0.70	0.75	0.76	0.36
2007	0.87	0.84	0.54	0.07

Interim Dividends (Per Share)

Amt	Decl	Ex	Rec	Pay
0.365Q	5/10/2007	5/24/2007	5/29/2007	6/15/2007
0.365Q	7/20/2007	8/24/2007	8/28/2007	9/14/2007
0.365Q	11/15/2007	11/23/2007	11/27/2007	12/14/2007
0.375Q	12/20/2007	2/29/2008	3/4/2008	3/14/2008

Indicated Div: $1.50 (Div. Reinv. Plan)

Valuation Analysis

Forecast P/E	11.84 (1/10/2007)
Market Cap	$8.5 Billion
Book Value	7.7 Billion
Price/Book	1.10
Price/Sales	1.08

Institutional Holding

No of Institutions	457
Shares	221,717,232
% Held	56.00

Business Summary: Commercial Banking (MIC: 8.1 SIC: 6021 NAIC: 522110)

KeyCorp is a bank holding company. Through its subsidiaries, Co. provides retail and commercial banking, commercial leasing, investment management, consumer finance, and investment banking products and services to individual, corporate and institutional clients through two major business groups: Community Banking and National Banking. Also, Co.'s bank and trust company subsidiaries provide personal and corporate trust services, personal financial services, access to mutual funds, cash management services, investment banking and capital markets products, and international banking services. At Dec 31 2007, Co. had total assets of around $100.00 billion and total deposits of $63.10 billion.

Recent Developments: For the year ended Dec 31 2007, income from continuing operations decreased 21.1% to US$941.0 million from US$1.19 billion a year earlier. Net income decreased 12.9% to US$919.0 million from US$1.06 billion in the prior year. Net interest income decreased 1.6% to US$2.77 billion from US$2.82 billion in the prior year. Provision for loan losses was US$529.0 million versus US$150.0 million in the prior year, an increase of 252.7%. Non-interest income rose 4.8% to US$2.23 billion from US$2.13 billion, while non-interest expense advanced 3.1% to US$3.25 billion.

Prospects: For 2008, Co. expects net interest margin of around 3.30%; a low- to mid-single digit percentage growth in loans, excluding acquired balances; a low single digit percentage growth in core deposits; and a low single digit percentage growth in expenses, excluding the 2007 charges for Co.'s liability to Visa Inc. and for losses on lending-related commitments. Separately, on Jan 2 2008, Co. has completed its acquisition of U.S.B. Holding Co., Inc. the holding company for Union State Bank, headquartered in Orangeburg, NY. This transaction will add $3.00 billion in assets and 31 branches to Co.'s Hudson Valley/Metro NY District.

Financial Data

(US$ in Thousands)	12/31/2007	12/31/2006	12/31/2005	12/31/2004	12/31/2003	12/31/2002	12/31/2001	12/31/2000
Earnings Per Share	2.32	2.57	2.73	2.30	2.12	2.27	0.31	2.30
Cash Flow Per Share	(0.50)	2.48	5.30	3.95	2.97	3.43	3.99	3.65
Tang Book Value Per Share	16.39	15.99	15.05	13.91	13.88	13.35	11.85	12.42
Dividends Per Share	1.460	1.380	1.300	1.240	1.220	1.200	1.180	1.170
Dividend Payout %	62.93	53.70	47.62	53.91	57.55	52.86	380.65	48.70
Income Statement								
Interest Income	5,644,000	5,380,000	4,617,000	3,818,000	3,970,000	4,366,000	5,627,000	6,277,000
Interest Expense	2,875,000	2,565,000	1,827,000	1,181,000	1,245,000	1,617,000	2,802,000	3,547,000
Net Interest Income	2,769,000	2,815,000	2,790,000	2,637,000	2,725,000	2,749,000	2,825,000	2,730,000
Provision for Losses	529,000	150,000	143,000	185,000	501,000	553,000	1,350,000	490,000
Non-Interest Income	2,229,000	2,127,000	2,078,000	1,746,000	1,760,000	1,769,000	1,775,000	2,191,000
Non-Interest Expense	3,248,000	3,149,000	3,137,000	2,810,000	2,742,000	2,653,000	2,941,000	2,917,000
Income Before Taxes	1,221,000	1,643,000	1,588,000	1,388,000	1,242,000	1,312,000	259,000	1,517,000
Income Taxes	380,000	450,000	459,000	434,000	339,000	336,000	102,000	515,000
Net Income	919,000	1,055,000	1,129,000	954,000	903,000	976,000	132,000	1,002,000
Average Shares	395,823	410,222	414,014	415,430	426,157	430,703	429,573	435,573
Balance Sheet								
Net Loans & Leases	74,359,000	68,519,000	68,893,000	67,326,000	61,305,000	61,005,000	61,632,000	65,904,000
Total Assets	99,983,000	92,337,000	93,126,000	90,739,000	84,487,000	85,202,000	80,938,000	87,270,000
Total Deposits	63,099,000	59,116,000	58,765,000	57,842,000	50,858,000	49,346,000	44,795,000	48,649,000
Total Liabilities	92,237,000	84,634,000	85,528,000	83,622,000	77,518,000	78,367,000	74,783,000	80,647,000
Stockholders' Equity	7,746,000	7,703,000	7,598,000	7,117,000	6,969,000	6,835,000	6,155,000	6,623,000
Shares Outstanding	388,792	399,153	406,623	407,569	416,494	423,943	424,005	423,254
Statistical Record								
Return on Assets %	0.96	1.14	1.23	1.09	1.06	1.17	0.16	1.17
Return on Equity %	11.90	13.79	15.34	13.51	13.08	15.03	2.07	15.36
Net Interest Margin %	49.06	52.32	60.43	69.07	68.64	62.96	50.20	43.49
Efficiency Ratio %	41.25	41.95	46.86	50.50	47.85	43.24	40.00	34.44
Loans to Deposits	1.18	1.16	1.17	1.16	1.21	1.24	1.38	1.35
Price Range	39.79-21.91	38.60-33.13	34.83-30.81	34.46-28.43	29.32-22.52	29.00-21.30	28.44-20.75	28.25-15.69
P/E Ratio	17.15-9.44	15.02-12.89	12.76-11.29	14.98-12.36	13.83-10.62	12.78-9.38	91.73-66.94	12.28-6.82
Average Yield %	4.32	3.78	3.94	3.97	4.71	4.66	4.75	5.36

Address: 127 Public Square, Cleveland, OH 44114-1306 **Telephone:** 216-689-6300 **Fax:** 216-689-3595	**Web Site:** www.key.com **Officers:** Henry L. Meyer III - Chmn., Pres., C.E.O. Thomas C. Stevens - Vice-Chmn., Chief Admin. Officer, Sec.	**Auditors:** Ernst & Young LLP **Transfer Agents:** Computershare Investor Services, Chicago, IL

KILROY REALTY CORP

Exchange	Symbol	Price	52Wk Range	Yield	P/E
NYS	KRC	$49.11 (3/31/2008)	76.92-44.81	4.72	15.35

*7 Year Price Score 110.40 *NYSE Composite Index=100 *12 Month Price Score 84.51

Interim Earnings (Per Share)

Qtr.	Mar	Jun	Sep	Dec
2003	0.40	0.49	0.72	0.17
2004	0.21	0.28	0.36	0.08
2005	0.44	(0.05)	0.49	(0.06)
2006	0.46	0.58	0.98	0.27
2007	0.51	0.40	0.28	2.01

Interim Dividends (Per Share)

Amt	Decl	Ex	Rec	Pay
0.555Q	5/17/2007	6/27/2007	6/29/2007	7/18/2007
0.555Q	9/12/2007	9/26/2007	9/28/2007	10/18/2007
0.555Q	12/6/2007	12/27/2007	12/31/2007	1/18/2008
0.58Q	2/12/2008	3/27/2008	3/31/2008	4/18/2008

Indicated Div: $2.32

Valuation Analysis

		Institutional Holding	
Forecast P/E	N/A	No of Institutions	163
Market Cap	$1.6 Billion	Shares	
Book Value	693.3 Million		32,411,304
Price/Book	2.32	% Held	
Price/Sales	6.23		99.12

Business Summary: Property, Real Estate & Development (MIC: 8.3 SIC: 6798 NAIC: 525930)

Kilroy Realty is a real estate investment trust, which owns, operates, develops, and acquires Class A suburban office and industrial real estate in key suburban submarkets, primarily in Southern California. As of Dec 31 2007, Co.'s stabilized portfolio of operating properties was comprised of 86 office buildings (Office Properties) and 43 industrial buildings (Industrial Properties), which included an aggregate of approximately 8.1 million and 3.9 million rentable square feet, respectively. Also as of Dec 31 2007, the Office Properties were approximately 93.7% leased to 314 tenants, and the Industrial Properties were approximately 94.7% leased to 64 tenants.

Recent Developments: For the year ended Dec 31 2007, income from continuing operations increased 1.6% to US$40.6 million from US$39.9 million a year earlier. Net income increased 39.0% to US$113.8 million from US$81.9 million in the prior year. Revenues were US$258.5 million, up 7.0% from US$241.5 million the year before.

Prospects: Going forward, Co. will continue to pursue redevelopment opportunities in its strategic submarkets. For instance, Co. recently acquired a 23-acre development site entitled for 500,000 square feet of office space for about $88.0 million, increasing its future development pipeline to just over 116 acres, representing future development potential in excess of 2.0 million square feet of space. Meanwhile, Co. has four new office buildings totaling about 395,000 square feet, representing an estimated investment of about $161.0 million. Also, Co. has two redevelopment projects underway totaling just under 211,000 square feet, representing an incremental investment of about $26.0 million.

Financial Data
(US$ in Thousands)

	12/31/2007	12/31/2006	12/31/2005	12/31/2004	12/31/2003	12/31/2002	12/31/2001	12/31/2000
Earnings Per Share	3.20	2.30	0.84	0.93	1.78	1.45	1.40	1.75
Cash Flow Per Share	4.56	1.97	4.04	3.81	3.49	3.48	3.90	2.78
Tang Book Value Per Share	17.45	17.06	13.73	15.10	16.00	16.05	16.07	16.67
Dividends Per Share	2.220	2.120	2.040	1.980	1.980	1.980	1.920	1.800
Dividend Payout %	69.38	92.17	242.86	212.90	111.24	136.55	137.14	102.86
Income Statement								
Property Income	258,472	251,244	241,715	221,399	227,786	198,903	202,404	180,677
Non-Property Income	...	...	...	...	...	3,192	7,241	6,436
Total Revenue	258,472	251,244	241,715	221,399	227,786	202,095	209,645	187,113
Interest Expense	37,502	43,541	39,153	37,647	33,385	35,640	41,679	39,109
Income Before Taxes	48,281	51,662	11,628	37,688	66,689	47,312	61,526	67,450
Net Income	113,822	81,864	33,819	29,939	49,612	40,312	38,431	46,846
Average Shares	32,526	31,389	28,710	28,422	27,737	27,722	27,372	26,754
Balance Sheet								
Total Assets	2,068,720	1,799,352	1,674,474	1,599,215	1,512,635	1,506,602	1,457,229	1,457,169
Long-Term Obligations	1,107,002	879,198	842,282	801,441	761,048	762,037	714,587	723,688
Total Liabilities	1,263,481	1,011,790	1,031,106	912,534	838,226	845,934	799,055	789,010
Stockholders' Equity	693,292	674,296	519,268	552,692	489,870	439,971	440,628	441,425
Shares Outstanding	32,765	32,398	28,970	28,548	28,209	27,419	27,426	26,475
Statistical Record								
Return on Assets %	5.89	4.71	2.07	1.92	3.29	2.72	2.64	3.36
Return on Equity %	16.65	13.72	6.31	5.73	10.67	9.16	8.71	10.22
Net Margin %	44.04	32.58	13.99	13.52	21.78	19.95	18.33	25.04
Price Range	89.80-52.66	83.42-63.45	63.71-38.95	43.85-30.62	33.55-20.74	29.64-20.25	29.10-23.41	29.13-19.44
P/E Ratio	28.06-16.46	36.27-27.59	75.85-46.37	47.15-32.92	18.85-11.65	20.44-13.97	20.79-16.72	16.64-11.11
Average Yield %	3.19	2.90	4.30	5.51	7.41	7.90	7.34	7.42

Address: 12200 W. Olympic Boulevard, Suite 200, Los Angeles, CA 90064
Telephone: 310-481-8400
Fax: 310-481-6501

Web Site: www.kilroyrealty.com
Officers: John B. Kilroy Sr. - Chmn. John B. Kilroy Jr. - Pres., C.E.O.

Auditors: Deloitte & Touche LLP
Transfer Agents: Mellon Investor Services, LLC, Ridgefield Park, NJ

KIMBERLY-CLARK CORP.

Exchange	Symbol	Price	52Wk Range	Yield	P/E	Div Acheiver
NYS	KMB	$64.55 (3/31/2008)	71.98-62.99	3.59	15.78	33 Years

*7 Year Price Score 90.53 *NYSE Composite Index=100 *12 Month Price Score 102.35

Interim Earnings (Per Share)

Qtr.	Mar	Jun	Sep	Dec
2003	0.78	0.82	0.83	0.91
2004	0.91	0.90	0.89	0.91
2005	0.93	0.88	0.68	0.79
2006	0.60	0.82	0.79	1.04
2007	0.98	1.00	1.04	1.06

Interim Dividends (Per Share)

Amt	Decl	Ex	Rec	Pay
0.53Q	4/26/2007	6/6/2007	6/8/2007	7/3/2007
0.53Q	8/1/2007	9/5/2007	9/7/2007	10/2/2007
0.53Q	11/14/2007	12/5/2007	12/7/2007	1/3/2008
0.58Q	2/21/2008	3/5/2008	3/7/2008	4/2/2008
Indicated Div: $2.32 (Div. Reinv. Plan)				

Valuation Analysis

Forecast P/E	15.21
	(1/10/2007)
Market Cap	$27.2 Billion
Book Value	5.2 Billion
Price/Book	5.20
Price/Sales	1.49

Institutional Holding

No of Institutions	784
Shares	354,780,640
% Held	77.73

TRADING VOLUME (thousand shares)

Business Summary: Paper Products (MIC: 11.11 SIC: 2679 NAIC: 322299)

Kimberly-Clark is engaged in the manufacturing and marketing of a range of health and hygiene products around the world. Most of these products are made from natural or synthetic fibers using technologies in fibers, nonwovens and absorbency. Co. operates through the following four global business segments: Personal Care; Consumer Tissue; K-C Professional & Other; as well as Health Care. Co.'s products are sold under brands such as Huggies, Pull Ups, Little Swimmers, GoodNites, Kotex, Lightdays, Depend, Poise, Kleenex, Scott, Cottonelle, Viva, Andrex, Scottex, Hakle, Page, Kimberly-Clark, WypAll, Kimtech, Kleenguard, Kimcare, Ballard as well as other brand names.

Recent Developments: For the year ended Dec 31 2007, net income increased 21.6% to US$1.82 billion from US$1.50 billion in the prior year. Revenues were US$18.27 billion, up 9.1% from US$16.75 billion the year before. Operating income was US$2.62 billion versus US$2.10 billion in the prior year, an increase of 24.5%. Direct operating expenses rose 7.7% to US$12.56 billion from US$11.66 billion in the comparable period the year before. Indirect operating expenses increased 3.6% to US$3.09 billion from US$2.98 billion in the equivalent prior-year period.

Prospects: For 2008, Co. is expecting earnings of $4.32 to $4.51 per diluted share, as well as net sales growth of 5.0% to 7.0%, as foreign currency effects should benefit sales comparisons by at least 1.0%. At the same time, Co. continues to make progress with its cost reduction plan announced in Jul 2005, which calls for streamlining manufacturing and administrative operations mainly in North America and Europe. Specifically, Co. anticipates a net workforce reduction of about 10.0% by the end of 2008, with about 24 manufacturing facilities expected to be sold, closed or streamlined. Co. expects this plan to generate annual pretax savings of at least $350.0 million by 2009.

Financial Data

(US$ in Thousands)	12/31/2007	12/31/2006	12/31/2005	12/31/2004	12/31/2003	12/31/2002	12/31/2001	12/31/2000
Earnings Per Share	4.09	3.25	3.28	3.61	3.33	3.22	3.02	3.31
Cash Flow Per Share	5.50	5.63	4.88	5.49	5.15	4.69	4.26	3.94
Tang Book Value Per Share	5.42	7.10	6.22	8.13	8.21	6.65	7.10	7.04
Dividends Per Share	2.120	1.960	1.800	1.600	1.360	1.200	1.120	1.080
Dividend Payout %	51.83	60.31	54.88	44.32	40.84	37.27	37.09	32.63
Income Statement								
Total Revenue	18,266,000	16,746,900	15,902,600	15,083,200	14,348,000	13,566,300	14,524,400	13,982,000
EBITDA	3,356,000	2,968,800	2,976,100	3,148,300	3,065,700	3,182,400	3,077,800	3,307,200
Income Before Taxes	2,317,500	1,844,900	1,968,900	2,203,400	2,157,000	2,297,400	2,164,400	2,436,000
Income Taxes	536,500	469,200	438,400	483,900	514,200	666,600	645,700	758,500
Net Income	1,822,900	1,499,500	1,568,300	1,800,200	1,694,200	1,674,600	1,609,900	1,800,600
Average Shares	445,600	461,000	477,400	499,200	508,600	520,000	533,200	543,800
Balance Sheet								
Current Assets	6,096,600	5,269,700	4,783,100	4,961,900	4,438,100	4,273,900	3,922,200	3,789,900
Total Assets	18,439,700	17,067,000	16,303,200	17,018,000	16,779,900	15,585,800	15,007,600	14,479,800
Current Liabilities	4,928,600	5,015,800	4,642,900	4,537,200	3,918,700	4,038,300	4,168,300	4,573,900
Long-Term Obligations	4,393,900	2,276,000	2,594,900	2,298,000	2,733,700	2,844,000	2,424,000	2,000,600
Total Liabilities	12,211,400	10,176,200	9,987,600	9,665,600	9,445,700	9,382,000	8,822,300	8,712,500
Stockholders' Equity	5,223,700	6,097,400	5,558,200	6,629,500	6,766,300	5,650,300	5,646,900	5,767,300
Shares Outstanding	420,921	455,619	461,489	482,903	501,589	510,800	521,000	533,400
Statistical Record								
Return on Assets %	10.27	8.99	9.41	10.62	10.47	10.95	10.92	13.16
Return on Equity %	32.20	25.73	25.74	26.80	27.29	29.65	28.21	33.07
EBITDA Margin %	18.37	17.73	18.71	20.87	21.37	23.46	21.19	23.65
Net Margin %	9.98	8.95	9.86	11.94	11.81	12.34	11.08	12.88
Asset Turnover	1.03	1.00	0.95	0.89	0.89	0.89	0.99	1.02
Current Ratio	1.24	1.05	1.03	1.09	1.13	1.06	0.94	0.83
Debt to Equity	0.84	0.37	0.47	0.35	0.40	0.50	0.43	0.35
Price Range	71.98-65.76	68.13-57.07	68.15-55.97	66.98-55.52	58.10-42.66	65.34-45.28	70.58-51.36	70.59-44.61
P/E Ratio	17.60-16.08	20.96-17.56	20.78-17.06	18.56-15.38	17.45-12.81	20.29-14.06	23.37-17.01	21.33-13.48
Average Yield %	3.06	3.17	2.88	2.56	2.76	2.28	1.86	1.85

Address: 351 Phelps Drive, Irving, TX 75038	Web Site: www.kimberly-clark.com	Auditors: Deloitte & Touche LLP
Telephone: 972-281-1200	Officers: Thomas J. Falk - Chmn., Pres., C.E.O. Mark A. Buthman - Sr. V.P., C.F.O.	Investor Contact: 972-281-1478
		Transfer Agents: EquiServe Trust Company, N.A., Providence, RI

KIMCO REALTY CORP.

Exchange	Symbol	Price	52Wk Range	Yield	P/E	Div Achiever
NYS	KIM	$39.17 (3/31/2008)	49.55-30.47	4.08	23.74	15 Years

*7 Year Price Score 117.59 *NYSE Composite Index=100 *12 Month Price Score 95.42

Interim Earnings (Per Share)

Qtr.	Mar	Jun	Sep	Dec
2003	0.32	0.23	0.40	0.36
2004	0.30	0.30	0.34	0.32
2005	0.36	0.35	0.36	0.45
2006	0.40	0.43	0.36	0.51
2007	0.59	0.49	0.29	0.28

Interim Dividends (Per Share)

Amt	Decl	Ex	Rec	Pay
0.36Q	6/15/2007	7/2/2007	7/5/2007	7/16/2007
0.40Q	7/24/2007	10/1/2007	10/3/2007	10/15/2007
0.40Q	12/17/2007	12/28/2007	1/2/2008	1/15/2008
0.40Q	3/17/2008	4/2/2008	4/4/2008	4/15/2008

Indicated Div: $1.60 (Div. Reinv. Plan)

Valuation Analysis / **Institutional Holding**

Forecast P/E	16.57 (1/10/2007)	No of Institutions 364
Market Cap	$9.9 Billion	Shares
Book Value	3.9 Billion	176,473,328
Price/Book	2.54	% Held
Price/Sales	14.53	70.26

TRADING VOLUME (thousand shares)

Business Summary: Property, Real Estate & Development (MIC: 8.3 SIC: 6798 NAIC: 525930)

Kimco Realty, its subsidiaries, affiliates and related real estate joint ventures are engaged principally in the operation of neighborhood and community shopping centers which are anchored generally by discount department stores, supermarkets or drugstores. In addition, Co. provides property management services for shopping centers owned by affiliated entities, various real estate joint ventures and unaffiliated third parties. As of Dec 31 2007, Co. had interests in 1,973 properties, totaling approximately 183.0 million square feet of gross leasable area located in 45 states, Canada, Mexico, Puerto Rico and Chile.

Recent Developments: For the year ended Dec 31 2007, income from continuing operations increased 4.8% to US$359.2 million from US$342.8 million a year earlier. Net income increased 3.4% to US$442.8 million from US$428.3 million in the prior year. Revenues were US$681.6 million, up 16.0% from US$587.5 million the year before.

Prospects: For 2008, Co. is projecting Funds From Operations to be in the range of $2.70 to $2.78 per diluted share and growth in same-store net operating income is expected to be approximately 4.0%. Meanwhile, Co. noted that as of Dec 31 2007, it had in progress a total of 60 ground-up development projects including 27 merchant building projects, nine U.S. ground-up development projects, and 24 ground-up development projects located throughout Mexico. Hence, for 2008, Co. expects capital commitment for development projects to be approximately $200.0 million to $250.0 million, while capital commitment for redevelopment projects is expected to be approximately $90.0 million to $110.0 million.

Financial Data

(US$ in Thousands)	12/31/2007	12/31/2006	12/31/2005	12/31/2004	12/31/2003	12/31/2002	12/31/2001	12/31/2000
Earnings Per Share	1.65	1.70	1.52	1.25	1.31	1.08	1.08	0.95
Cash Flow Per Share	2.64	1.90	1.81	1.63	1.44	1.34	1.49	1.35
Tang Book Value Per Share	15.40	13.42	10.46	9.94	9.65	9.11	9.14	8.99
Dividends Per Share	1.520	1.380	1.270	1.160	1.095	1.050	0.980	0.907
Dividend Payout %	92.12	81.18	83.55	92.43	83.59	97.22	90.74	95.10
Income Statement								
Property Income	681,553	593,880	522,545	516,967	479,664	450,829	468,616	459,407
Total Revenue	681,553	593,880	522,545	516,967	479,664	450,829	468,616	459,407
Interest Expense	213,674	172,888	127,711	107,726	102,709	86,896	...	...
Income Before Taxes	78,034	164,199	185,917	226,397	200,889	261,474	255,914	...
Income Taxes	(44,490)	4,387	430	3,919	1,516	12,904	19,376	...
Net Income	442,830	428,259	363,628	297,137	307,879	245,668	236,538	205,025
Average Shares	257,058	244,615	230,868	227,144	217,540	211,938	202,326	187,306
Balance Sheet								
Total Assets	9,097,816	7,869,280	5,534,636	4,749,597	4,603,925	3,756,878	3,384,779	3,171,348
Long-Term Obligations	1,084,650	838,898	543,791	509,697	468,698	274,732	292,829	245,413
Total Liabilities	4,755,083	4,077,079	3,024,578	2,406,306	2,368,162	1,755,610	1,486,320	1,453,242
Stockholders' Equity	3,894,574	3,366,959	2,387,214	2,236,400	2,135,846	1,907,328	1,890,084	1,704,339
Shares Outstanding	252,803	250,870	228,059	224,852	221,247	209,203	206,705	189,434
Statistical Record								
Return on Assets %	5.22	6.39	7.07	6.34	7.36	6.88	7.22	6.62
Return on Equity %	12.20	14.89	15.73	13.55	15.23	12.94	13.16	12.36
Net Margin %	64.97	72.11	69.59	57.48	64.19	54.49	50.48	44.63
Price Range	53.41-35.30	46.88-32.73	33.25-26.20	29.47-20.27	22.93-15.25	16.81-14.01	17.00-13.63	14.88-11.02
P/E Ratio	32.37-21.39	27.58-19.25	21.88-17.23	23.58-16.22	17.50-11.64	15.56-12.97	15.74-12.62	15.66-11.60
Average Yield %	3.46	3.52	4.33	4.75	5.70	6.68	6.43	6.90

Address: 3333 New Hyde Park Road, Suite 100, New Hyde Park, NY 11042
Telephone: 516-869-9000
Fax: 516-869-9001

Web Site: www.kimcorealty.com
Officers: Milton Cooper - Chmn., C.E.O. Michael J. Flynn - Vice-Chmn., Pres., C.O.O.

Auditors: PricewaterhouseCoopers LLP
Investor Contact: 516-869-7288
Transfer Agents: The Bank of New York, New York, NY

KINDER MORGAN ENERGY PARTNERS, L.P.

Exchange	Symbol	Price	52Wk Range	Yield	P/E	Div Acheiver
NYS	KMP	$54.69 (3/31/2008)	59.35-48.63	6.73	N/A	11 Years

*7 Year Price Score 98.45   *NYSE Composite Index=100   *12 Month Price Score 114.68

Interim Earnings (Per Share)

Qtr.	Mar	Jun	Sep	Dec
2003	0.52	0.48	0.49	0.51
2004	0.52	0.51	0.59	0.60
2005	0.54	0.50	0.57	(0.03)
2006	0.53	0.53	0.40	0.59
2007	0.33	0.36	0.24	0.52

Interim Dividends (Per Share)

Amt	Decl	Ex	Rec	Pay
0.83Q	4/18/2007	4/26/2007	4/30/2007	5/15/2007
0.85Q	7/18/2007	7/27/2007	7/31/2007	8/14/2007
0.88Q	10/17/2007	10/29/2007	10/31/2007	11/14/2007
0.92Q	1/16/2008	1/29/2008	1/31/2008	2/14/2008

Indicated Div: $3.68

Valuation Analysis

	Institutional Holding	
Forecast P/E	18.96	No of Institutions
	(1/10/2007)	317
Market Cap	$13.6 Billion	Shares
Book Value	N/A	30,099,908
Price/Book	N/A	% Held
Price/Sales	1.47	18.49

TRADING VOLUME (thousand shares)

Business Summary: Gas Utilities (MIC: 7.4 SIC: 4922 NAIC: 486210)

Kinder Morgan Energy Partners is a pipeline transportation and energy storage company. As of Dec 31 2007, Co. owned an interest or operated over 25,000 miles of pipelines and approximately 165 terminals; its pipelines transported natural gas, gasoline, crude oil, carbon dioxide and other products, and its terminals store petroleum products and chemicals and handle bulk materials like coal and petroleum coke Co. is also a provider of carbon dioxide for oil recovery projects in North America. Co. operates through five segments: Products Pipelines, Natural Gas Pipelines, CO2, Terminals, and Trans Mountain.

Recent Developments: For the year ended Dec 31 2007, income from continuing operations decreased 57.9% to US$416.4 million from US$989.8 million a year earlier. Net income decreased 41.2% to US$590.3 million from US$1.00 billion in the prior year. Revenues were US$9.22 billion, up 1.9% from US$9.05 billion the year before. Operating income was US$807.7 million versus US$1.29 billion in the prior year, a decrease of 37.5%. Direct operating expenses rose 1.1% to US$7.07 billion from US$6.99 billion in the comparable period the year before. Indirect operating expenses increased 74.8% to US$1.34 billion from US$765.5 million in the equivalent prior-year period.

Prospects: Looking ahead, Co. expects to invest approximately $3.30 billion in expansion capital expenditures in 2008 including its share of capital spending for both the Rockies Express and Midcontinent Express natural gas pipeline projects, which should help drive earnings growth in 2009 and beyond. Separately, on Jan.16 2008, Co. announced that it plans to invest approximately $56.0 million to construct a petroleum coke terminal at the BP refinery located in Whiting, IN, which will handle approximately 2.2 million tons of petroleum coke per year from a coker unit BP plans to construct to process heavy crude oil from Canada. Notably, the facility is expected to be in service in mid-year 2011.

Financial Data
(US$ in Thousands)

	12/31/2007	12/31/2006	12/31/2005	12/31/2004	12/31/2003	12/31/2002	12/31/2001	12/31/2000
Earnings Per Share	(0.09)	2.04	1.58	2.22	2.00	1.96	1.56	1.34
Cash Flow Per Share	7.35	5.60	6.08	5.85	4.15	5.06	3.78	2.38
Dividends Per Share	3.390	3.230	3.070	2.810	2.575	2.360	2.075	1.600
Dividend Payout %	...	158.33	194.30	126.58	128.75	120.41	133.01	119.85
Income Statement								
Total Revenue	9,217,700	8,954,583	9,787,128	7,932,861	6,624,322	4,237,057	2,946,676	816,442
EBITDA	1,431,600	1,742,079	1,451,070	1,338,387	1,116,467	977,736	781,261	476,391
Income Before Taxes	487,400	991,191	836,688	851,304	710,503	623,660	458,716	292,282
Income Taxes	71,000	19,048	24,461	19,726	16,631	15,203	16,373	13,934
Net Income	590,300	972,143	812,227	831,578	697,337	608,377	442,343	278,348
Average Shares	236,900	224,914	212,429	197,038	185,494	172,186	154,110	126,212
Balance Sheet								
Net PPE	11,591,300	9,445,471	8,864,584	8,168,680	7,091,558	6,244,242	5,082,612	3,306,305
Total Assets	15,177,800	12,246,394	11,923,462	10,552,942	9,139,182	8,353,576	6,732,666	4,625,210
Long-Term Obligations	6,608,100	4,426,962	5,319,356	4,852,563	4,438,142	3,826,489	2,231,574	1,255,453
Total Liabilities	10,742,100	8,224,741	8,309,722	6,656,422	5,628,255	4,937,647	3,573,632	2,508,143
Shares Outstanding	247,966	230,431	220,237	207,008	189,039	180,910	165,804	129,716
Statistical Record								
Return on Assets %	4.30	8.04	7.23	8.42	7.97	8.07	7.79	7.07
EBITDA Margin %	15.53	19.45	14.83	16.87	16.85	23.08	26.51	58.35
Net Margin %	6.40	10.86	8.30	10.48	10.53	14.36	15.01	34.09
PPE Turnover	0.88	0.98	1.15	1.04	0.99	0.75	0.70	0.28
Asset Turnover	0.67	0.74	0.87	0.80	0.76	0.56	0.52	0.21
Price Range	56.96-47.46	50.88-43.15	54.18-42.95	49.27-38.33	49.69-34.25	38.65-28.00	39.05-26.13	28.16-18.56
P/E Ratio	...	24.94-21.15	34.29-27.18	22.19-17.27	24.84-17.13	19.72-14.29	25.03-16.75	21.01-13.85
Average Yield %	6.48	6.96	6.25	6.33	6.43	7.09	6.08	7.47

Address: 500 Dallas Street, Suite 1000, Houston, TX 77002
Telephone: 713-369-9000

Web Site: www.kindermorgan.com
Officers: Richard D. Kinder - Chmn., C.E.O. Michael C. Morgan - Pres.

Auditors: PricewaterhouseCoopers LLP
Investor Contact: 713-369-9490
Transfer Agents: Equiserve Trust Company, N.A.

KINDRED HEALTHCARE INC

Exchange	Symbol	Price	52Wk Range	Yield	P/E
NYS	KND	$21.87 (3/31/2008)	28.28-17.42	N/A	N/A

*7 Year Price Score N/A *NYSE Composite Index=100 *12 Month Price Score 106.60

Interim Earnings (Per Share)

Qtr.	Mar	Jun	Sep	Dec
2003	(0.38)	(1.25)	0.34	(0.86)
2004	0.32	0.52	0.37	0.46
2005	0.83	1.43	0.36	0.59
2006	0.58	0.69	0.07	0.55
2007	0.20	(1.52)	(0.23)	0.39

Interim Dividends (Per Share)

Amt	Decl	Ex	Rec	Pay
2-for-1	...	5/28/2004	5/10/2004	5/27/2004
0.00U	7/12/2007	8/1/2007	7/20/2007	7/31/2007

Valuation Analysis   Institutional Holding

Forecast P/E	N/A	No of Institutions
		140
Market Cap	$838.5 Million	Shares
Book Value	862.1 Million	43,967,896
Price/Book	0.97	% Held
Price/Sales	0.20	N/A

TRADING VOLUME (thousand shares)

Business Summary: Hospitals & Health Care (MIC: 9.3 SIC: 8059 NAIC: 623110)

Kindred Healthcare is a healthcare services company that through its subsidiaries operates hospitals, nursing centers and a contract rehabilitation services business across the United States. At Dec 31 2007, Co.'s hospital division operated 84 long-term acute care hospitals (6,567 licensed beds) in 24 states. Additionally, Co.'s health services division operated 228 nursing centers (29,106 licensed beds) in 27 states. Co. also operated a contract rehabilitation services business that provides rehabilitative services primarily in long-term care settings.

Recent Developments: For the year ended Dec 31 2007, income from continuing operations decreased 54.7% to US$34.7 million from US$76.7 million a year earlier. Net loss amounted to US$46.9 million versus net income of US$78.7 million in the prior year. Revenues were US$4.22 billion, up 2.2% from US$4.13 billion the year before. Indirect operating expenses increased 3.7% to US$4.15 billion from US$4.00 billion in the equivalent prior-year period.

Prospects: Going forward, Co. continues with its ongoing development activities. For instance, Co. remains focus on the completion of seven new hospital projects, which is already underway, as well as selective opportunities to broaden its nursing center and Peoplefirst Rehabilitation businesses. Meanwhile, with regard to its efforts to divest unprofitable facilities, Co. expects to sell the remaining eight facilities for $13.0 million to $23 million in 2008. For 2008, Co. has reaffirmed its earnings guidance and now expects consolidated revenues to be approximate $4.20 billion and net income from continuing operations of $49.0 million to $53.0 million or $1.25 to $1.35 per diluted share.

Financial Data

(US$ in Thousands)	12/31/2007	12/31/2006	12/31/2005	12/31/2004	12/31/2003	12/31/2002	12/31/2001	03/31/2001
Earnings Per Share	(1.17)	1.92	3.20	1.67	(2.15)	0.96	1.42	6.59
Cash Flow Per Share	4.21	3.32	7.05	7.47	3.42	7.16	4.60	2.07
Tang Book Value Per Share	18.60	19.27	21.45	18.51	15.58	15.39	13.65	...
Income Statement								
Total Revenue	4,220,266	4,266,661	3,923,999	3,531,223	3,284,019	3,357,822	2,329,019	752,409
EBITDA	238,567	274,328	336,851	256,891	184,560	154,222	162,449	82,330
Income Before Taxes	66,021	117,808	214,777	145,386	85,109	61,715	83,792	49,685
Income Taxes	31,301	46,569	86,147	59,463	35,655	28,389	36,450	500
Net Income	(46,870)	78,711	144,909	70,580	(75,336)	34,753	51,655	471,976
Average Shares	39,983	40,923	45,239	42,403	35,048	36,002	36,516	71,656
Balance Sheet								
Current Assets	1,013,647	1,002,561	944,964	874,343	843,087	920,316	831,973	...
Total Assets	2,079,552	2,016,127	1,760,561	1,593,293	1,585,414	1,644,178	1,508,874	...
Current Liabilities	629,942	606,998	620,627	577,766	577,880	582,156	515,126	...
Long-Term Obligations	291,574	130,090	26,323	32,544	139,397	162,008	212,269	...
Total Liabilities	1,217,428	1,020,549	890,025	873,508	987,849	1,012,550	918,393	...
Stockholders' Equity	862,124	995,578	870,536	719,785	597,565	631,628	590,481	...
Shares Outstanding	38,339	39,978	37,331	37,189	36,340	35,298	35,366	...
Statistical Record								
Return on Assets %	N.M.	4.17	8.64	4.43	N.M.	2.20	3.63	...
Return on Equity %	N.M.	8.44	18.22	10.69	N.M.	5.69	65.54	...
EBITDA Margin %	5.65	6.43	8.58	7.27	5.62	4.59	6.97	10.94
Net Margin %	N.M.	1.84	3.69	2.00	N.M.	1.03	2.22	62.73
Asset Turnover	2.06	2.26	2.34	2.22	2.03	2.13	1.64	...
Current Ratio	1.61	1.65	1.52	1.51	1.46	1.58	1.62	...
Debt to Equity	0.34	0.13	0.03	0.05	0.23	0.26	0.36	...
Price Range	28.19-17.42	24.53-15.55	32.34-19.09	23.56-17.60	20.45-4.23	20.04-4.62	25.06-11.95	...
P/E Ratio	...	12.78-8.10	10.11-5.97	14.11-10.54	...	20.88-4.81	17.64-8.42	...

Address: 680 South Fourth Street, Louisville, KY 40202-2412 Telephone: 502-596-7300	**Web Site:** www.kindredhealthcare.com **Officers:** Edward L. Kuntz - Chmn. Paul J. Diaz - Pres., C.E.O.	**Auditors:** PricewaterhouseCoopers LLP **Transfer Agents:** National City Bank., Cleveland OH

KING PHARMACEUTICALS, INC.

Exchange	Symbol	Price	52Wk Range	Yield	P/E
NYS	KG	$8.70 (3/31/2008)	21.67-8.50	N/A	11.60

*7 Year Price Score 61.94   *NYSE Composite Index=100   *12 Month Price Score 74.62

TRADING VOLUME (thousand shares)

Interim Earnings (Per Share)

Qtr.	Mar	Jun	Sep	Dec
2003	(0.03)	(0.15)	0.44	0.18
2004	(0.46)	(0.26)	(0.03)	0.06
2005	0.29	0.08	0.50	(0.39)
2006	0.21	0.46	0.37	0.15
2007	0.48	0.26	(0.17)	0.18

Interim Dividends (Per Share)

No Dividends Paid

Valuation Analysis		Institutional Holding	
Forecast P/E	10.41	No of Institutions	
	(1/10/2007)	291	
Market Cap	$2.1 Billion	Shares	
Book Value	2.5 Billion		241,245,520
Price/Book	0.85	% Held	
Price/Sales	1.00		99.20

Business Summary: Pharmaceuticals (MIC: 9.1 SIC: 2834 NAIC: 325412)

King Pharmaceuticals is a pharmaceutical company that researches, develops, manufactures, markets and sells primarily branded prescription pharmaceutical products for general/family practitioners, internal medicine physicians, cardiologists, endocrinologists, psychiatrists, neurologists, pain specialists, sleep specialists, and hospitals across the U.S. and in Puerto Rico. Co.'s pharmaceutical products can be divided into the following therapeutic areas, cardiovascular/metabolic, neuroscience, hospital/acute care and other. In addition, Co. manufactures third-party pharmaceutical products under contracts with a variety of pharmaceutical and biotechnology companies.

Recent Developments: For the year ended Dec 31 2007, income from continuing operations decreased 36.5% to US$183.2 million from US$288.6 million a year earlier. Net income decreased 36.7% to US$183.0 million from US$288.9 million in the prior year. Revenues were US$2.14 billion, up 7.5% from US$1.99 billion the year before. Operating income was US$227.5 million versus US$402.5 million in the prior year, a decrease of 43.5%. Direct operating expenses rose 35.0% to US$566.5 million from US$419.8 million in the comparable period the year before. Indirect operating expenses increased 15.2% to US$1.34 billion from US$1.17 billion in the equivalent prior-year period.

Prospects: Co. continues to advance its research and development projects. For instance, Co.'s collaboration partner, Pain Therapeutics, plans to file the New Drug Application for REMOXY™ to treat chronic pain with the U.S. FDA in the second quarter of 2008. Also, Co. expects the pivotal Phase III clinical trial program for ACUROX™ to treat acute pain to be completed in the second half of 2008. Meanwhile, Co. expects net sales from branded pharmaceutical products in 2008 decline from 2007 due to projected lower net sales of Altace®, as a third party entered the market with a generic substitute for Altace® capsules in Dec 2007 and additional third parties are likely to enter the market in 2008.

Financial Data

(US$ in Thousands)	12/31/2007	12/31/2006	12/31/2005	12/31/2004	12/31/2003	12/31/2002	12/31/2001	12/31/2000
Earnings Per Share	0.75	1.19	0.49	(0.66)	0.44	0.74	0.93	0.29
Cash Flow Per Share	2.77	1.92	2.15	1.08	1.81	1.87	1.21	0.83
Tang Book Value Per Share	6.51	5.41	3.66	1.83	0.68	2.90	3.51	0.87
Income Statement								
Total Revenue	2,136,882	1,988,500	1,772,881	1,304,364	1,521,388	1,128,335	872,262	620,243
EBITDA	392,065	552,440	318,920	110,696	312,298	317,658	420,545	258,725
Income Before Taxes	250,818	424,312	178,115	(58,034)	177,089	267,663	370,870	191,684
Income Taxes	67,600	135,730	61,485	(7,412)	71,233	85,143	138,006	87,103
Net Income	182,981	288,949	117,833	(160,288)	105,856	182,520	217,936	64,509
Average Shares	244,179	242,798	241,002	241,175	241,576	243,098	233,906	217,771
Balance Sheet								
Current Assets	1,819,654	1,673,473	1,247,789	1,127,063	946,303	1,261,702	1,237,559	317,243
Total Assets	3,426,822	3,329,531	2,965,242	2,924,156	3,177,734	2,750,660	2,506,611	1,282,395
Current Liabilities	453,085	617,796	971,460	688,930	668,849	369,964	151,443	105,082
Long-Term Obligations	400,000	400,000	...	345,000	345,000	345,093	346,397	99,005
Total Liabilities	916,065	1,040,925	991,820	1,075,366	1,135,554	819,477	598,327	294,662
Stockholders' Equity	2,510,757	2,288,606	1,973,422	1,848,790	2,042,180	1,931,183	1,908,284	987,733
Shares Outstanding	245,937	243,151	241,802	241,706	241,190	240,624	247,692	227,731
Statistical Record								
Return on Assets %	5.42	9.18	4.00	N.M.	3.57	6.94	11.50	6.16
Return on Equity %	7.63	13.56	6.17	N.M.	5.33	9.51	15.05	11.32
EBITDA Margin %	18.35	27.78	17.99	8.49	20.53	28.15	48.21	41.71
Net Margin %	8.56	14.53	6.65	N.M.	6.96	16.18	24.99	10.40
Asset Turnover	0.63	0.63	0.60	0.43	0.51	0.43	0.46	0.59
Current Ratio	4.02	2.71	1.28	1.64	1.41	3.41	8.17	3.02
Debt to Equity	0.16	0.17	...	0.19	0.17	0.18	0.18	0.10
Price Range	21.67-9.93	19.87-15.74	17.32-7.55	19.96-10.37	17.94-9.69	42.13-15.35	46.05-25.79	40.45-15.75
P/E Ratio	28.89-13.24	16.70-13.23	35.35-15.41	...	40.77-22.02	56.93-20.74	49.52-27.73	139.49-54.31

Address: 501 Fifth Street, Bristol, TN 37620	Web Site: www.kingpharm.com	Auditors: PricewaterhouseCoopers LLP
Telephone: 423-989-8000	Officers: Ted G. Wood - Chmn. Brian A. Markison - Pres., C.E.O.	Investor Contact: 423-989-8125
Fax: 423-274-8677		Transfer Agents: American Stock Transfer & Trust Company, New York, NY

KIRBY CORP.

Exchange	Symbol	Price	52Wk Range	Yield	P/E
NYS	KEX	$57.00 (3/31/2008)	57.00-35.00	N/A	24.89

*7 Year Price Score 147.83 *NYSE Composite Index=100 *12 Month Price Score 123.11

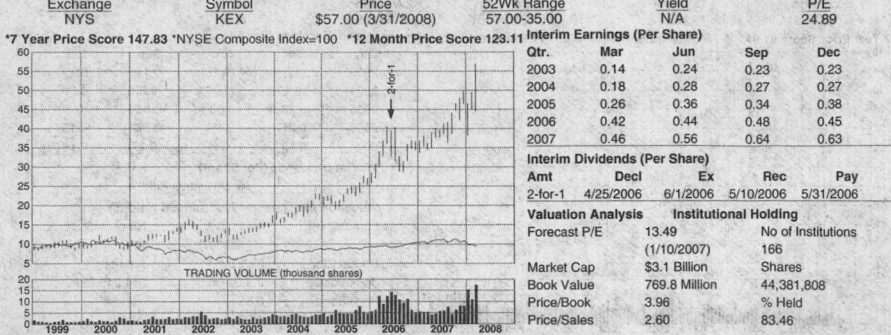

Interim Earnings (Per Share)

Qtr.	Mar	Jun	Sep	Dec
2003	0.14	0.24	0.23	0.23
2004	0.18	0.28	0.27	0.27
2005	0.26	0.36	0.34	0.38
2006	0.42	0.44	0.48	0.45
2007	0.46	0.56	0.64	0.63

Interim Dividends (Per Share)

Amt	Decl	Ex	Rec	Pay
2-for-1	4/25/2006	6/1/2006	5/10/2006	5/31/2006

Valuation Analysis — **Institutional Holding**

Forecast P/E	13.49	No of Institutions
	(1/10/2007)	166
Market Cap	$3.1 Billion	Shares
Book Value	769.8 Million	44,381,808
Price/Book	3.96	% Held
Price/Sales	2.60	83.46

Business Summary: Shipping (MIC: 15.3 SIC: 4449 NAIC: 483211)

Kirby, through its subsidiaries, conducts operations in two business segments: marine transportation and diesel engine services. Co.'s marine transportation segment is engaged in the inland transportation of petrochemicals, black oil products, refined petroleum products and agricultural chemicals by tank barges, and, to a lesser extent, the offshore transportation of dry-bulk cargoes by barge. Co.'s diesel engine services segment is engaged in the overhaul and repair of diesel engines and reduction gears, and related parts sales in three core markets: the marine market, the power generation market and the railroad market.

Recent Developments: For the year ended Dec 31 2007, net income increased 29.2% to US$123.3 million from US$95.5 million in the prior year. Revenues were US$1.17 billion, up 19.1% from US$984.2 million the year before. Operating income was US$220.8 million versus US$169.4 million in the prior year, an increase of 30.4%. Direct operating expenses rose 16.5% to US$735.4 million from US$631.3 million in the comparable period the year before. Indirect operating expenses increased 17.9% to US$216.4 million from US$183.5 million in the equivalent prior-year period.

Prospects: Looking ahead, Co. expects to continue to see strong demand for the transportation services of the marine transportation segment. Also, Co. projects that the diesel engine services segment will continue to perform well, with strong service activity and direct parts sales. For 2008, Co. expects net earnings in a range of $2.55 to $2.70 per share. In addition, Co. is budgeting capital expenditures of $150.0 million to $160.0 million, including $80.0 million for new tank barge and towboat construction. Co. noted that the new construction will consist of 26 barges with a total capacity of 570,000 barrels and five 1800 horsepower towboats, and expects delivery throughout 2008 and early 2009.

Financial Data

(US$ in Thousands)	12/31/2007	12/31/2006	12/31/2005	12/31/2004	12/31/2003	12/31/2002	12/31/2001	12/31/2000
Earnings Per Share	2.29	1.79	1.34	0.98	0.83	0.56	0.81	0.69
Cash Flow Per Share	4.45	2.87	2.83	2.58	2.32	1.51	2.02	1.70
Tang Book Value Per Share	10.10	7.71	7.26	5.52	4.43	3.47	3.00	2.09
Income Statement								
Total Revenue	1,172,625	984,218	795,722	675,319	613,474	535,403	566,884	512,644
EBITDA	307,375	240,615	183,002	148,292	133,953	104,540	136,408	129,933
Income Before Taxes	199,832	154,202	111,122	79,909	65,997	45,493	67,126	57,812
Income Taxes	76,491	58,751	42,341	30,365	25,079	18,047	27,523	23,699
Net Income	123,341	95,451	68,781	49,544	40,918	27,446	39,603	34,113
Average Shares	53,764	53,304	51,562	50,314	49,012	48,788	48,540	49,132
Balance Sheet								
Current Assets	267,343	249,592	186,276	139,650	131,779	119,468	113,247	118,466
Total Assets	1,430,475	1,271,119	1,025,548	904,675	854,961	791,758	754,471	749,268
Current Liabilities	191,420	166,867	139,821	104,390	98,868	91,245	97,057	97,037
Long-Term Obligations	296,015	309,518	200,032	217,436	255,040	265,665	249,402	288,037
Total Liabilities	660,645	639,124	488,006	469,440	482,829	468,447	453,449	486,619
Stockholders' Equity	769,830	631,995	537,542	435,235	372,132	323,311	301,022	262,649
Shares Outstanding	53,531	52,983	51,942	49,712	48,634	48,014	48,030	47,764
Statistical Record								
Return on Assets %	9.13	8.31	7.13	5.62	4.97	3.55	5.27	4.53
Return on Equity %	17.60	16.32	14.14	12.24	11.77	8.79	14.05	13.54
EBITDA Margin %	26.21	24.45	23.00	21.96	21.84	19.53	24.06	25.35
Net Margin %	10.52	9.70	8.64	7.34	6.67	5.13	6.99	6.65
Asset Turnover	0.87	0.86	0.82	0.77	0.75	0.69	0.75	0.68
Current Ratio	1.40	1.50	1.33	1.34	1.33	1.31	1.17	1.22
Debt to Equity	0.38	0.49	0.37	0.50	0.69	0.82	0.83	1.10
Price Range	49.93-33.65	40.56-25.73	27.61-19.00	22.98-15.36	17.44-11.07	16.43-10.48	14.18-9.32	12.31-8.63
P/E Ratio	21.80-14.69	22.66-14.37	20.60-14.18	23.44-15.67	21.01-13.34	29.33-18.71	17.50-11.51	17.84-12.50

Address: 55 Waugh Drive, Suite 1000, Houston, TX 77007	Web Site: www.kirbycorp.com	Auditors: KPMG LLP
Telephone: 713-435-1000	Officers: C. Berdon Lawrence - Chmn. Joseph H. Pyne - Pres., C.E.O.	Transfer Agents: EquiServe Trust Company, N.A.
Fax: 713-435-1010		

KOHL'S CORP.

Exchange	Symbol	Price	52Wk Range	Yield	P/E
NYS	KSS	$42.89 (3/31/2008)	78.89-38.33	N/A	12.65

*7 Year Price Score 81.53   *NYSE Composite Index=100   *12 Month Price Score 82.61

TRADING VOLUME (thousand shares)

Interim Earnings (Per Share)

Qtr.	Apr	Jul	Oct	Jan
2003-04	0.32	0.33	0.35	0.72
2004-05	0.33	0.45	0.42	0.92
2005-06	0.36	0.54	0.45	1.08
2006-07	0.48	0.69	0.68	1.46
2007-08	0.64	0.83	0.61	1.30

Interim Dividends (Per Share)

No Dividends Paid

Valuation Analysis		Institutional Holding	
Forecast P/E	13.25	No of Institutions	
	(1/10/2007)	543	
Market Cap	$13.3 Billion	Shares	
Book Value	6.1 Billion	292,207,616	
Price/Book	2.18	% Held	
Price/Sales	0.81	90.99	

Business Summary: Retail - General (MIC: 5.2 SIC: 5311 NAIC: 452111)

Kohl's is engaged in the business of operating family-oriented, department stores that sell moderately priced apparel, footwear and accessories for women, men and children; soft home products such as sheets and pillows; and housewares. In addition, Co. provides on-line shopping on its website that provides key items, family apparel and home merchandise as well as furniture and certain electronics. Co. also features fashion in apparel and home that would appeal to classic, updated and contemporary customers. As of Feb 2 2008, Co. operated 929 stores in 47 states and handled its merchandise through nine distribution centers.

Recent Developments: For the year ended Feb 2 2008, net income decreased 2.2% to US$1.08 billion from US$1.11 billion in the prior year. Revenues were US$16.47 billion, up 5.6% from US$15.60 billion the year before. Operating income was US$1.80 billion versus US$1.81 billion in the prior year, a decrease of 0.6%. Direct operating expenses rose 5.4% to US$10.46 billion from US$9.92 billion in the comparable period the year before. Indirect operating expenses increased 9.1% to US$4.21 billion from US$3.86 billion in the equivalent prior-year period.

Prospects: For the fiscal year ending Jan 31 2009, Co. is forecasting earnings of $3.15 to $3.50 per diluted share, based on several factors such as total sales increase of 5.0% to 8.0%, comparable store sales decrease of flat to 3.0% and a gross margin increase of flat to 20 basis points. In addition, Co. foresees that selling, general and administrative expenses will increase by 9.0% to 10.0%. Similarly, Co. plans to open about 70 to 75 new stores. Also, Co. intends to launch several brands such as Jumping Beans, Bobby Flay, FILA Sport, Abbey Dawn and the expansion of ELLE. Meanwhile, for the fiscal quarter ended May 2008, Co. is targeting earnings to range from $0.50 to $0.54 per diluted share.

Financial Data

(US$ in Thousands)	02/02/2008	02/03/2007	01/28/2006	01/29/2005	01/31/2004	02/01/2003	02/02/2002	02/03/2001
Earnings Per Share	3.39	3.31	2.43	2.12	1.72	1.87	1.45	1.10
Cash Flow Per Share	3.89	9.18	2.57	2.78	2.23	1.99	1.63	1.11
Tang Book Value Per Share	18.95	16.74	16.62	13.78	11.60	9.85	7.78	6.21
Income Statement								
Total Revenue	16,473,734	15,544,184	13,402,217	11,700,619	10,282,094	9,120,287	7,488,654	6,151,996
EBITDA	2,257,648	2,203,316	1,756,007	1,525,810	1,270,780	1,292,174	987,074	763,598
Income Before Taxes	1,742,061	1,774,445	1,345,790	1,174,250	950,373	1,034,374	799,864	605,114
Income Taxes	658,210	665,764	503,830	443,870	359,221	390,993	304,188	232,966
Net Income	1,083,851	1,108,681	841,960	730,380	591,152	643,381	495,676	372,148
Average Shares	320,087	334,771	346,772	344,773	344,907	346,728	341,041	338,075
Balance Sheet								
Current Assets	3,723,889	3,401,040	4,266,052	3,643,437	3,024,839	3,284,094	2,464,044	1,921,897
Total Assets	10,560,082	9,041,177	9,153,038	7,979,299	6,698,450	6,315,503	4,929,586	3,855,154
Current Liabilities	1,771,448	1,918,658	1,746,453	1,456,058	1,122,357	1,507,992	879,971	723,297
Long-Term Obligations	2,051,875	1,010,057	1,046,104	1,103,441	1,075,973	1,058,784	1,095,420	803,081
Total Liabilities	4,458,479	3,437,782	3,195,700	3,012,571	2,507,111	2,803,586	2,138,180	1,652,515
Stockholders' Equity	6,101,603	5,603,395	5,957,338	4,966,728	4,191,339	3,511,917	2,791,406	2,202,639
Shares Outstanding	310,468	320,986	345,088	343,345	340,141	337,322	335,138	332,167
Statistical Record								
Return on Assets %	11.09	11.99	9.86	9.98	9.11	11.47	11.32	10.82
Return on Equity %	18.57	18.87	15.46	15.99	15.39	20.47	19.91	18.83
EBITDA Margin %	13.70	14.17	13.10	13.04	12.36	14.17	13.18	12.41
Net Margin %	6.58	7.13	6.28	6.24	5.75	7.05	6.62	6.05
Asset Turnover	1.69	1.68	1.57	1.60	1.58	1.63	1.71	1.79
Current Ratio	2.10	1.77	2.44	2.50	2.70	2.18	2.80	2.66
Debt to Equity	0.34	0.19	0.18	0.22	0.26	0.30	0.39	0.36
Price Range	78.89-38.33	73.97-44.33	58.64-43.03	53.20-40.96	64.49-41.20	77.75-49.45	71.82-43.30	71.00-34.53
P/E Ratio	23.27-11.31	22.35-13.39	24.13-17.71	25.09-19.32	37.49-23.95	41.58-26.44	49.53-29.86	64.55-31.39

Address: N56 W17000 Ridgewood Drive, Menomonee Falls, WI 53051-5660 **Telephone:** 262-703-7000 **Fax:** 262-703-6373	Web Site: www.kohls.com **Officers:** R. Lawrence Montgomery - Chmn., C.E.O. Kevin Mansell - Pres.	**Auditors:** Ernst & Young LLP **Transfer Agents:** The Bank of New York, New York, NY

KORN/FERRY INTERNATIONAL (DE)

Exchange	Symbol	Price	52Wk Range	Yield	P/E
NYS	KFY	$16.90 (3/31/2008)	26.89-14.00	N/A	12.16

*7 Year Price Score 105.19 *NYSE Composite Index=100 *12 Month Price Score 87.27

Interim Earnings (Per Share)

Qtr.	Jul	Oct	Jan	Apr
2004-05	0.20	0.21	0.23	0.28
2005-06	0.27	0.25	0.37	0.44
2006-07	0.31	0.31	0.33	0.29
2007-08	0.36	0.37	0.37	...

Interim Dividends (Per Share)

No Dividends Paid

Valuation Analysis **Institutional Holding**

Forecast P/E	13.85	No of Institutions
	(1/10/2007)	152
Market Cap	$783.7 Million	Shares
Book Value	465.3 Million	39,645,180
Price/Book	1.68	% Held
Price/Sales	0.97	92.86

TRADING VOLUME (thousand shares)

Business Summary: Human Resources Services (MIC: 12.6 SIC: 7361 NAIC: 541612)

Korn/Ferry International is a provider of executive search, outsourced recruiting, and leadership development services. Co. provides executive search services for board level, chief executive, and other senior executive positions to clients in consumer, financial services, industrial, life sciences, and technology industries. Co.'s leadership services include succession planning, management and team development, competency modeling, executive coaching, onboarding, merger integration, cultural change, and executive compensation consulting. Co.'s clients include public and private companies, middle-market and emerging growth companies, as well as government and non profit organizations.

Recent Developments: For the quarter ended Jan 31 2008, net income increased 10.4% to US$16.3 million from US$14.7 million in the year-earlier quarter. Revenues were US$212.1 million, up 22.2% from US$173.5 million the year before. Operating income was US$21.2 million versus US$21.4 million in the prior-year quarter, a decrease of 1.1%. Indirect operating expenses increased 25.5% to US$190.9 million from US$152.1 million in the equivalent prior-year period.

Prospects: Co. is seeing an improvement in its fee revenue due to revenue growth across all its segments. Specifically, in the Executive Recruitment segment, Co.'s fee revenue is being driven by an increase in the number of search engagements opened as well as an increase in the average fee billed per search engagement. In addition, fee revenue for Co.'s Futurestep business is being positively affected by higher average fee billed per engagement resulting from continued strategic emphasis on larger outsourced recruiting solutions. For the quarter ending Apr 2008, Co. expects fee revenue of $195 million to $210.0 million and diluted earnings per share is likely to be in the range of $0.34 to $0.38.

Financial Data

(US$ in Thousands)	9 Mos	6 Mos	3 Mos	04/30/2007	04/30/2006	04/30/2005	04/30/2004	04/30/2003
Earnings Per Share	1.39	1.35	1.29	1.24	1.32	0.90	0.13	(0.63)
Cash Flow Per Share	2.20	1.63	1.69	2.57	2.02	2.28	0.82	0.65
Tang Book Value Per Share	6.69	6.41	6.34	6.16	5.20	3.66	2.16	1.90
Income Statement								
Total Revenue	615,192	403,101	196,277	689,201	551,769	476,377	350,703	338,466
EBITDA	89,145	60,128	30,193	101,951	96,270	77,577	27,599	4,290
Depn & Amortn	7,701	4,889	2,350	...	...	...	...	...
Income Before Taxes	77,749	52,792	26,611	82,499	77,024	58,678	7,666	(22,637)
Income Taxes	29,753	20,400	10,434	30,164	19,594	20,251	3,218	2,040
Net Income	50,465	34,209	17,100	55,498	59,430	38,620	5,403	(22,902)
Average Shares	44,303	45,841	47,063	46,938	47,270	46,229	39,202	37,576
Balance Sheet								
Current Assets	473,235	422,326	409,966	464,760	394,500	304,468	182,712	161,635
Total Assets	795,662	743,821	713,136	761,491	635,491	534,168	394,686	369,013
Current Liabilities	220,344	180,212	152,613	229,489	176,291	158,397	94,418	88,962
Long-Term Obligations	...	...	...	...	45,147	44,949	44,400	41,364
Total Liabilities	330,319	290,037	259,684	328,536	311,740	281,266	213,804	192,952
Stockholders' Equity	465,343	453,784	453,452	432,955	323,751	252,902	180,882	166,455
Shares Outstanding	46,374	46,615	48,336	47,174	41,201	39,888	38,170	37,590
Statistical Record								
Return on Assets %	8.47	8.96	9.05	7.95	10.16	8.32	1.41	N.M.
Return on Equity %	15.17	15.55	15.19	14.67	20.61	17.81	3.10	N.M.
EBITDA Margin %	14.49	14.92	15.38	14.79	17.45	16.28	7.87	1.27
Net Margin %	8.20	8.49	8.71	8.05	10.77	8.11	1.54	N.M.
Asset Turnover	1.06	1.10	1.11	0.99	0.94	1.03	0.92	0.91
Current Ratio	2.15	2.34	2.69	2.03	2.24	1.92	1.94	1.82
Debt to Equity	...	...	...	...	0.14	0.18	0.25	0.25
Price Range	26.89-14.00	26.89-16.33	26.89-17.96	24.51-17.86	21.36-14.35	21.61-13.07	16.58-6.74	11.60-5.70
P/E Ratio	19.35-10.07	19.92-12.10	20.84-13.92	19.77-14.40	16.18-10.87	24.01-14.52	127.54-51.85	...

Address: 1900 Avenue of the Stars, Suite 2600, Los Angeles, CA 90067
Telephone: 310-552-1834
Fax: 310-553-8640

Web Site: www.kornferry.com
Officers: Paul C. Reilly - Chmn., C.E.O. Gary D. Burnison - Exec. V.P., C.F.O., C.O.O.

Auditors: Ernst & Young LLP
Investor Contact: 310-556-8550
Transfer Agents: Mellon Investor Services, South Hackensack, NJ

KRAFT FOODS, INC.

Exchange	Symbol	Price	52Wk Range	Yield	P/E
NYS	KFT	$31.01 (3/31/2008)	36.74-28.81	3.48	19.14

*7 Year Price Score N/A   *NYSE Composite Index=100   *12 Month Price Score 100.02

Interim Earnings (Per Share)

Qtr.	Mar	Jun	Sep	Dec
2003	0.49	0.55	0.47	0.50
2004	0.33	0.41	0.46	0.36
2005	0.42	0.28	0.40	0.45
2006	0.61	0.41	0.45	0.38
2007	0.43	0.44	0.38	0.37

Interim Dividends (Per Share)

Amt	Decl	Ex	Rec	Pay
0.25Q	6/15/2007	6/26/2007	6/28/2007	7/6/2007
0.27Q	8/28/2007	9/6/2007	9/10/2007	10/5/2007
0.27Q	12/7/2007	12/21/2007	12/26/2007	1/4/2008
0.27Q	2/22/2008	3/12/2008	3/14/2008	4/4/2008

Indicated Div: $1.08

Valuation Analysis

		Institutional Holding	
Forecast P/E	14.94	No of Institutions	
	(1/10/2007)	312	
Market Cap	$47.6 Billion	Shares	
Book Value	27.3 Billion	216,587,568	
Price/Book	1.74	% Held	
Price/Sales	1.28	7.00	

Business Summary: Food (MIC: 4.1 SIC: 2099 NAIC: 311999)

Kraft Foods is a holding company engaged in the manufacture and marketing of packaged food products, which include snacks, beverages, cheese, snacks, convenient meals and various packaged grocery products. Co. operates through two units: Kraft North America Commercial and Kraft International. Co.'s Kraft North America Commercial operates in the U.S. and Canada, and manages its operations primarily by product category. Co.'s Kraft International Commercial manages its operations by geographic region. As of Dec 31 2007, Co. had operations in operations in more than 70 countries and sold its products in over 150 countries.

Recent Developments: For the year ended Dec 31 2007, income from continuing operations decreased 15.4% to US$2.59 billion from US$3.06 billion a year earlier. Net income decreased 15.4% to US$2.59 billion from US$3.06 billion in the prior year. Revenues were US$37.24 billion, up 8.4% from US$34.36 billion the year before. Operating income was US$4.33 billion versus US$4.52 billion in the prior year, a decrease of 4.2%. Direct operating expenses rose 12.4% to US$24.65 billion from US$21.94 billion in the comparable period the year before. Indirect operating expenses increased 4.6% to US$8.26 billion from US$7.90 billion in the equivalent prior-year period.

Prospects: On Nov 15 2007, Co. announced that it has agreed to merge its Post cereal business, including its Post brands, four manufacturing facilities and certain manufacturing equipment, into Ralcorp Holdings, Inc. after a tax-free distribution to its shareholders. The transaction, which represents proceeds of $2.60 billion to Co. and its stockholders, should close in mid-2008 and allow it to own 54.0% of the new Ralcorp. For 2008, Co. projects diluted earnings per share of $1.56 and organic net revenue growth of at least 4.0%. Notably, the guidance reflects Co.'s expectation for cumulative annualized savings to reach $1.20 billion, of which $1.00 billion will be realized by the end of 2008.

Financial Data
(US$ in Thousands)

	12/31/2007	12/31/2006	12/31/2005	12/31/2004	12/31/2003	12/31/2002	12/31/2001	12/31/2000
Earnings Per Share	1.62	1.85	1.55	1.55	2.01	1.96	1.17	1.38
Cash Flow Per Share	2.77	2.26	2.06	2.34	2.39	2.15	2.07	2.23
Dividends Per Share	1.040	0.960	0.870	0.770	0.660	0.560	0.260	...
Dividend Payout %	64.20	51.89	56.13	49.68	32.84	28.57	22.22	...
Income Statement								
Total Revenue	37,241,000	34,356,000	34,113,000	32,168,000	31,010,000	29,723,000	33,875,000	26,532,000
EBITDA	5,217,000	5,417,000	5,631,000	5,491,000	6,824,000	6,830,000	6,526,000	5,046,000
Income Before Taxes	3,727,000	4,016,000	4,116,000	3,946,000	5,346,000	5,267,000	3,447,000	3,415,000
Income Taxes	1,137,000	951,000	1,209,000	1,274,000	1,866,000	1,869,000	1,565,000	1,414,000
Net Income	2,590,000	3,060,000	2,632,000	2,665,000	3,476,000	3,394,000	1,882,000	2,001,000
Average Shares	1,594,000	1,655,000	1,693,000	1,714,000	1,728,000	1,736,000	1,610,000	1,455,000
Balance Sheet								
Current Assets	10,737,000	8,254,000	8,153,000	9,722,000	8,124,000	7,456,000	7,006,000	7,152,000
Total Assets	67,993,000	55,574,000	57,628,000	59,928,000	59,285,000	57,100,000	55,798,000	52,071,000
Current Liabilities	17,086,000	10,473,000	8,724,000	9,078,000	7,861,000	7,169,000	8,875,000	7,590,000
Long-Term Obligations	12,902,000	7,081,000	8,475,000	9,723,000	11,591,000	12,976,000	13,134,000	24,102,000
Total Liabilities	40,698,000	27,019,000	28,035,000	30,017,000	30,755,000	31,268,000	32,320,000	38,023,000
Stockholders' Equity	27,295,000	28,555,000	29,593,000	29,911,000	28,530,000	25,832,000	23,478,000	14,048,000
Shares Outstanding	1,533,777	1,635,972	1,669,880	1,705,355	1,721,937	1,730,619	1,735,000	1,455,000
Statistical Record								
Return on Assets %	4.19	5.41	4.48	4.46	5.97	6.01	3.49	4.84
Return on Equity %	9.27	10.52	8.85	9.10	12.79	13.77	10.03	14.51
EBITDA Margin %	14.01	15.77	16.51	17.07	22.01	22.98	19.26	19.02
Net Margin %	6.95	8.91	7.72	8.28	11.21	11.42	5.56	7.54
Asset Turnover	0.60	0.61	0.58	0.54	0.53	0.53	0.63	0.64
Current Ratio	0.63	0.79	0.93	1.07	1.03	1.04	0.79	0.94
Debt to Equity	0.47	0.25	0.29	0.33	0.41	0.50	0.56	1.72
Price Range	36.74-30.20	36.30-27.48	35.61-27.90	35.93-29.56	39.20-26.99	43.84-33.01	35.39-29.94	...
P/E Ratio	22.68-18.64	19.62-14.85	22.97-18.00	23.18-19.07	19.50-13.43	22.37-16.84	30.25-25.59	...
Average Yield %	3.11	2.98	2.77	2.39	2.14	1.45	0.80	...

Address: Three Lakes Drive, Northfield, IL 60093-2753 **Telephone:** 847-646-2000 **Fax:** 847-646-6005	**Web Site:** www.kraft.com **Officers:** Roger K. Deromedi - C.E.O. David Brearton - Sr. V.P., Bus. Process Simplification & Corp. Contr.	**Auditors:** PricewaterhouseCoopers LLP **Transfer Agents:** EquiServe Trust Co., NA, Providence, RI

KROGER CO.

Exchange	Symbol	Price	52Wk Range	Yield	P/E
NYS	KR	$25.40 (3/31/2008)	31.41-24.25	1.42	15.03

*7 Year Price Score 106.98 *NYSE Composite Index=100 *12 Month Price Score 99.17

Interim Earnings (Per Share)

Qtr.	May	Aug	Oct	Jan
2004-05	0.35	0.19	0.19	(0.87)
2005-06	0.40	0.27	0.25	0.39
2006-07	0.42	0.29	0.30	0.53
2007-08	0.47	0.38	0.37	0.47

Interim Dividends (Per Share)

Amt	Decl	Ex	Rec	Pay
0.075Q	6/29/2007	8/13/2007	8/15/2007	9/1/2007
0.075Q	9/20/2007	11/13/2007	11/15/2007	12/1/2007
0.075Q	1/18/2008	2/13/2008	2/15/2008	3/1/2008
0.09Q	3/13/2008	5/13/2008	5/15/2008	6/1/2008

Indicated Div: $0.36

Valuation Analysis   Institutional Holding

Forecast P/E	N/A	No of Institutions
		418
Market Cap	$16.8 Billion	Shares
Book Value	4.9 Billion	583,412,672
Price/Book	3.43	% Held
Price/Sales	0.24	82.22

TRADING VOLUME (thousand shares)

Business Summary: Retail - Food & Beverage (MIC: 5.3 SIC: 5411 NAIC: 445110)

Kroger is a retailer that operates retail food and drug stores, multi-department stores, jewelry stores, and convenience stores throughout the U.S. These stores are operated under banners such as Kroger, Ralphs, Fred Meyer, Food 4 Less, King Soopers, Smith's, Fry's, Fry's Marketplace, Dillons, QFC and City Market. In addition, Co. manufactures and processes some of the food for sale in its supermarkets. As of Feb 2 2008, Co. operated, either directly or through its subsidiaries, 2,486 supermarkets and multi-department stores, of which 696 had fuel centers, and in addition to the supermarkets, also operated 782 convenience stores and 394 jewelry stores.

Recent Developments: For the year ended Feb 2 2008, net income increased 5.9% to US$1.18 billion from US$1.12 billion in the prior year. Revenues were US$70.24 billion, up 6.2% from US$66.11 billion the year before. Operating income was US$2.30 billion versus US$2.24 billion in the prior year, an increase of 2.9%. Direct operating expenses rose 7.3% to US$53.78 billion from US$50.12 billion in the comparable period the year before. Indirect operating expenses increased 2.9% to US$14.16 billion from US$13.76 billion in the equivalent prior-year period.

Prospects: For fiscal year ending Jan 31 2009, Co. estimates earnings of $1.83 to $1.90 per diluted share, reflecting earnings per share growth of about 8.0% to12.0% due to strong identical sales and a slight improvement in non-fuel operating margins. Notably, fiscal 2008 identical supermarket sales growth is expected to be in the range of 3.0% to 5.0%, excluding fuel sales. Also, Co.'s anticipated capital investment of $2.00 billion to $2.20 billion in fiscal 2008, excluding acquisitions, is focused on improving store operations and reducing merchandising costs. Lastly, 2008 total food store square footage is expected to grow about 2.0% to 2.5% before acquisitions and operational closings.

Financial Data

(US$ in Thousands)	02/02/2008	02/03/2007	01/28/2006	01/29/2005	01/31/2004	02/01/2003	02/02/2002	02/03/2001
Earnings Per Share	1.69	1.54	1.31	(0.14)	0.42	1.52	1.26	1.04
Cash Flow Per Share	3.75	3.23	3.04	3.17	2.97	4.10	2.93	2.73
Tang Book Value Per Share	4.18	3.87	3.04	1.85	1.18	0.36	N.M.	N.M.
Dividends Per Share	0.290	0.195	...	...	...	...	...	...
Dividend Payout %	17.16	12.66	...	...	...	...	...	...
Income Statement								
Total Revenue	70,235,000	66,111,000	60,553,000	56,434,000	53,791,000	51,760,000	50,098,000	49,000,000
EBITDA	3,657,000	3,508,000	3,300,000	2,103,000	2,583,000	3,660,000	3,435,000	3,191,000
Income Before Taxes	1,827,000	1,748,000	1,525,000	290,000	770,000	1,973,000	1,711,000	1,508,000
Income Taxes	646,000	633,000	567,000	390,000	455,000	740,000	668,000	628,000
Net Income	1,181,000	1,115,000	958,000	(100,000)	315,000	1,205,000	1,043,000	877,000
Average Shares	698,000	723,000	731,000	736,000	754,000	791,000	825,000	846,000
Balance Sheet								
Current Assets	7,114,000	6,755,000	6,466,000	6,406,000	5,619,000	5,566,000	5,512,000	5,416,000
Total Assets	22,299,000	21,215,000	20,482,000	20,491,000	20,184,000	20,102,000	19,087,000	18,190,000
Current Liabilities	8,689,000	7,581,000	6,715,000	6,316,000	5,586,000	5,608,000	5,485,000	5,591,000
Long-Term Obligations	6,529,000	6,154,000	6,678,000	7,900,000	8,116,000	8,222,000	8,412,000	8,210,000
Total Liabilities	17,385,000	16,292,000	16,092,000	16,951,000	16,173,000	16,252,000	15,585,000	15,101,000
Stockholders' Equity	4,914,000	4,923,000	4,390,000	3,540,000	4,011,000	3,850,000	3,502,000	3,089,000
Shares Outstanding	663,000	705,000	723,000	728,000	743,000	758,000	894,000	815,000
Statistical Record								
Return on Assets %	5.44	5.26	4.69	N.M.	1.57	6.17	5.61	4.77
Return on Equity %	24.08	23.56	24.23	N.M.	8.04	32.87	31.74	29.90
EBITDA Margin %	5.21	5.31	5.45	3.73	4.80	7.07	6.86	6.51
Net Margin %	1.68	1.69	1.58	N.M.	0.59	2.33	2.08	1.79
Asset Turnover	3.24	3.12	2.96	2.78	2.68	2.65	2.70	2.67
Current Ratio	0.82	0.89	0.96	1.01	1.01	0.99	1.00	0.97
Debt to Equity	1.33	1.25	1.52	2.23	2.02	2.14	2.40	2.66
Price Range	31.41-24.80	25.85-18.27	20.62-15.27	19.46-14.73	19.60-12.13	23.48-11.41	27.36-19.92	27.06-14.19
P/E Ratio	18.59-14.67	16.79-11.86	15.74-11.66	...	46.67-28.88	15.45-7.51	21.71-15.81	26.02-13.64
Average Yield %	1.05	0.90	...	...	...	...	...	...

Address: 1014 Vine Street, Cincinnati, OH 45202	**Web Site:** www.kroger.com	**Auditors:** PricewaterhouseCoopers LLP
Telephone: 513-762-4000	**Officers:** David B. Dillon - Chmn., C.E.O. W. Rodney McMullen - Vice-Chmn.	**Investor Contact:** 513-762-4969
Fax: 513-762-1400		**Transfer Agents:** Bank of New York, New York, NY

444

L-3 COMMUNICATIONS HOLDINGS, INC.

Exchange	Symbol	Price	52Wk Range	Yield	P/E
NYS	LLL	$109.34 (3/31/2008)	114.69-87.81	1.10	18.28

*7 Year Price Score 122.77 *NYSE Composite Index=100 *12 Month Price Score 113.23

Interim Earnings (Per Share)

Qtr.	Mar	Jun	Sep	Dec
2003	0.50	0.53	0.74	0.94
2004	0.67	0.81	0.93	0.92
2005	0.86	0.99	1.11	1.25
2006	1.13	0.40	1.31	1.38
2007	1.29	1.49	1.56	1.64

Interim Dividends (Per Share)

Amt	Decl	Ex	Rec	Pay
0.25Q	4/24/2007	5/14/2007	5/16/2007	6/15/2007
0.25Q	7/10/2007	8/14/2007	8/16/2007	9/17/2007
0.26Q	10/9/2007	11/14/2007	11/16/2007	12/17/2007
0.30Q	2/5/2008	2/14/2008	2/19/2008	3/17/2008
		Indicated Div: $1.20		

Valuation Analysis

		Institutional Holding	
Forecast P/E	13.00	No of Institutions	
	(1/10/2007)	557	
Market Cap	$13.6 Billion	Shares	
Book Value	6.0 Billion	105,625,896	
Price/Book	2.27	% Held	
Price/Sales	0.97	84.54	

Business Summary: Communications (MIC: 10.1 SIC: 3663 NAIC: 334220)

L-3 Communications Holdings is a system contractor in aircraft modernization and maintenance, Command, Control, Communications, Intelligence, Surveillance and Reconnaissance (C3ISR) systems, and government services. Co.'s customers include the U.S. Department of Defense and its contractors, the U.S. Department of Homeland Security, U.S. Government intelligence agencies, aerospace and defense contractors, allied foreign government ministries of defense, commercial customers, and other U.S. federal, state and local government agencies. Co. has four segments: C3ISR, Government Services, Aircraft Modernization and Maintenance, and Specialized Products.

Recent Developments: For the year ended Dec 31 2007, net income increased 43.7% to US$756.1 million from US$526.1 million in the prior year. Revenues were US$13.96 billion, up 11.9% from US$12.48 billion the year before. Operating income was US$1.45 billion versus US$1.11 billion in the prior year, an increase of 30.4%. Direct operating expenses rose 11.7% to US$12.51 billion from US$11.20 billion in the comparable period the year before. Indirect operating expenses decreased 100.0% to nil from US$168.2 million in the equivalent prior-year period.

Prospects: Going forward, Co. expects to continue to generate modest improvements in operating margin as it expects to increase sales faster than indirect costs, reduce indirect costs, and improve its overall contract performance, including general and administrative costs. Accordingly, for full-year 2008, Co. is raising its net sales guidance from US$14.00 billion to US$14.20 billion to about US$14.20 billion to 14.40 billion, and diluted earnings per share guidance from US$6.41 to US$6.55 to about US$6.48 to US$6.62. Specifically, Co. expects its Government Services segment sales to be $4.00 billion to US$4.10 billion, and its Specialized Products segment sales to be US$5.10 billion to US$5.20 billion.

Financial Data

(US$ in Thousands)	12/31/2007	12/31/2006	12/31/2005	12/31/2004	12/31/2003	12/31/2002	12/31/2001	12/31/2000
Earnings Per Share	5.98	4.22	4.20	3.33	2.71	1.93	1.48	1.19
Cash Flow Per Share	10.17	8.73	7.13	5.74	4.75	3.66	2.31	1.70
Dividends Per Share	1.000	0.750	0.500	0.400	...	...	...	...
Dividend Payout %	16.72	17.77	11.90	12.01	...	...	...	...
Income Statement								
Total Revenue	13,960,500	12,476,900	9,444,700	6,896,997	5,061,594	4,011,229	2,347,422	1,910,061
EBITDA	1,687,900	1,319,200	1,150,500	868,180	669,896	535,954	355,580	298,596
Income Before Taxes	1,174,100	824,600	788,300	596,688	433,813	330,210	186,222	134,079
Income Taxes	418,000	298,500	279,800	214,808	156,173	117,885	70,764	51,352
Net Income	756,100	526,100	508,500	381,880	277,640	178,097	115,458	82,727
Average Shares	126,500	124,800	121,200	117,372	106,068	97,413	85,438	69,906
Balance Sheet								
Current Assets	4,763,100	3,929,800	3,643,500	2,800,324	1,937,702	1,639,374	1,238,585	829,570
Total Assets	14,390,700	13,286,700	11,909,100	7,780,765	6,492,890	5,242,308	3,335,433	2,463,544
Current Liabilities	2,581,700	2,376,400	1,854,300	1,175,840	924,212	696,639	524,277	468,669
Long-Term Obligations	4,559,100	4,566,300	4,644,000	2,203,717	2,458,785	1,847,752	1,315,252	1,095,000
Total Liabilities	8,314,700	7,896,500	7,337,200	3,903,468	3,842,183	2,966,865	2,051,644	1,770,975
Stockholders' Equity	5,988,900	5,305,900	4,490,700	3,799,761	2,574,496	2,202,202	1,213,892	692,569
Shares Outstanding	124,174	125,237	120,372	115,681	97,077	94,577	78,496	67,213
Statistical Record								
Return on Assets %	5.46	4.18	5.17	5.34	4.73	4.15	3.98	4.03
Return on Equity %	13.39	10.74	12.27	11.95	11.62	10.43	12.11	12.93
EBITDA Margin %	12.09	10.57	12.18	12.59	13.23	13.36	15.15	15.63
Net Margin %	5.42	4.22	5.38	5.54	5.49	4.44	4.92	4.33
Asset Turnover	1.01	0.99	0.96	0.96	0.86	0.94	0.81	0.93
Current Ratio	1.84	1.65	1.96	2.39	2.10	2.35	2.36	1.77
Debt to Equity	0.76	0.86	1.03	0.58	0.96	0.84	1.08	1.58
Price Range	114.69-80.02	86.95-66.58	84.52-65.23	76.87-49.80	51.60-35.60	65.98-41.09	48.23-31.24	38.78-17.84
P/E Ratio	19.18-13.38	20.60-15.78	20.12-15.53	23.08-14.95	19.04-13.14	34.19-21.29	32.59-21.11	32.59-14.99
Average Yield %	1.04	0.95	0.67	0.64	...	...	...	...

Address: 600 Third Avenue, New York, NY 10016 **Telephone:** 212-697-1111 **Fax:** 212-867-5249	**Web Site:** www.L-3Com.com **Officers:** Frank C. Lanza - Chmn., C.E.O. Robert V. LaPenta - Pres., C.F.O.	**Auditors:** PricewaterhouseCoopers LLP **Investor Contact:** 212-697-1111 **Transfer Agents:** Computershare Trust Company, Canton, MA

LA-Z-BOY INC.

Exchange	Symbol	Price	52Wk Range	Yield	P/E	Div Acheiver
NYS	LZB	$8.34 (3/31/2008)	12.78-5.46	1.92	N/A	26 Years

*7 Year Price Score 43.70 *NYSE Composite Index=100 *12 Month Price Score 100.07

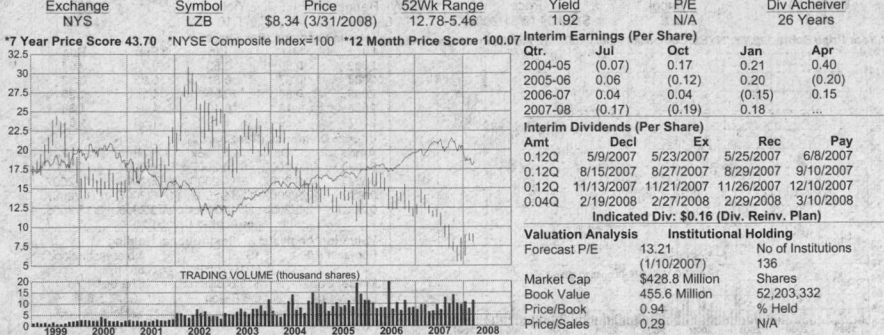

Interim Earnings (Per Share)

Qtr.	Jul	Oct	Jan	Apr
2004-05	(0.07)	0.17	0.21	0.40
2005-06	0.06	(0.12)	0.20	(0.20)
2006-07	0.04	0.04	(0.15)	0.15
2007-08	(0.17)	(0.19)	0.18	...

Interim Dividends (Per Share)

Amt	Decl	Ex	Rec	Pay
0.12Q	5/9/2007	5/23/2007	5/25/2007	6/8/2007
0.12Q	8/15/2007	8/27/2007	8/29/2007	9/10/2007
0.12Q	11/13/2007	11/21/2007	11/26/2007	12/10/2007
0.04Q	2/19/2008	2/27/2008	2/29/2008	3/10/2008

Indicated Div: $0.16 (Div. Reinv. Plan)

Valuation Analysis

		Institutional Holding	
Forecast P/E	13.21 (1/10/2007)	No of Institutions	136
Market Cap	$428.8 Million	Shares	52,203,332
Book Value	455.6 Million	% Held	
Price/Book	0.94	N/A	
Price/Sales	0.29		

Business Summary: Chemicals (MIC: 11.1 SIC: 2511 NAIC: 337121)

La-Z-Boy is a manufacturer of reclining-chair and upholstered furniture. Co. also manufactures and imports casegoods (wood) furniture products from outside the U.S. for resale in North America. As of Apr 28,2007, Co. operated within three segments: the Upholstery Group, the Casegoods Group, and the Retail Group. The operating units in the Upholstery Group are Bauhaus, England, La-Z-Boy, U.K., and La-Z-Boy while the operating units in the Casegoods Group are American Drew, Hammary, Kincaid, and Lea. The Retail Group consists of 70 company-owned La-Z-Boy Furniture Galleries® stores located in nine markets ranging from the Midwest to the East Coast of the U.S. and southeastern Florida.

Recent Developments: For the quarter ended Jan 26 2008, income from continuing operations increased 31.4% to US$9.1 million from US$6.9 million in the year-earlier quarter. Net income amounted to US$9.5 million versus a net loss of US$7.8 million in the year-earlier quarter. Revenues were US$373.1 million, down 7.8% from US$404.8 million the year before. Operating income was US$3.1 million versus US$9.5 million in the prior-year quarter, a decrease of 67.4%. Direct operating expenses declined 9.2% to US$264.4 million from US$291.3 million in the comparable period the year before. Indirect operating expenses increased 1.4% to US$105.5 million from US$104.1 million in the equivalent prior-year period.

Prospects: Co. anticipates the furniture industry will continue to be affected by the overall macroeconomic environment. Accordingly, Co. expects its sales to be down 4.0% to 8.0%, coupled with earnings per share of $0.06 to $0.14 for the second half of fiscal 2008, excluding the $6.0 million make-whole provision related to its credit refinancing, restructuring charges, income from anti-dumping monies, or any further effect from discontinued operations. Meanwhile, Co. plans to open four New Generation format La-Z-Boy Furniture Galleries® stores, of which one will be a new store and three will be store remodels or relocations, and will close one in the quarter ending Apr 2008.

Financial Data

(US$ in Thousands)	9 Mos	6 Mos	3 Mos	04/28/2007	04/29/2006	04/30/2005	04/24/2004	04/26/2003
Earnings Per Share	(0.03)	(0.36)	(0.13)	0.08	(0.06)	0.71	(0.11)	0.63
Cash Flow Per Share	1.33	1.08	0.36	0.65	1.74	0.87	2.49	2.19
Tang Book Value Per Share	7.72	7.69	7.87	8.18	8.39	8.17	8.19	8.36
Dividends Per Share	0.480	0.480	0.480	0.480	0.440	0.440	0.400	0.400
Dividend Payout %	...	...	...	600.00	...	61.97	...	63.49
Income Statement								
Total Revenue	1,082,911	709,830	344,396	1,617,302	1,916,777	2,048,381	1,998,876	2,111,830
EBITDA	17,445	(3,899)	(5,268)	64,327	50,207	92,150	62,653	196,202
Depn & Amortn	18,506	12,313	6,220	...	...	...	...	...
Income Before Taxes	(7,426)	(20,429)	(13,585)	29,858	9,433	53,379	22,288	154,997
Income Taxes	(4,359)	(8,235)	(5,043)	10,090	12,474	20,284	19,760	58,899
Net Income	(9,117)	(18,628)	(8,694)	4,139	(3,041)	37,185	(5,796)	36,316
Average Shares	51,590	51,410	51,380	51,606	51,801	52,138	53,679	57,435
Balance Sheet								
Current Assets	501,481	483,996	492,893	540,798	584,559	638,365	653,674	679,494
Total Assets	838,778	825,917	835,395	878,691	971,174	1,026,357	1,047,496	1,123,066
Current Liabilities	170,809	197,341	191,879	228,210	228,410	228,724	283,321	214,587
Long-Term Obligations	146,415	110,774	111,238	111,714	173,368	213,549	181,807	222,371
Total Liabilities	383,165	371,673	366,488	393,343	460,829	499,071	525,168	513,127
Stockholders' Equity	455,613	454,244	468,907	485,348	510,345	527,286	522,328	609,939
Shares Outstanding	51,417	51,416	51,379	51,377	51,782	52,225	52,031	55,027
Statistical Record								
Return on Assets %	N.M.	N.M.	N.M.	0.45	N.M.	3.53	N.M.	3.19
Return on Equity %	N.M.	N.M.	N.M.	0.83	N.M.	6.97	N.M.	5.50
EBITDA Margin %	1.61	N.M.	N.M.	3.98	2.62	4.50	3.13	9.29
Net Margin %	N.M.	N.M.	N.M.	0.26	N.M.	1.82	N.M.	1.72
Asset Turnover	1.73	1.73	1.82	1.75	1.92	1.94	1.85	1.85
Current Ratio	2.94	2.45	2.57	2.37	2.56	2.79	2.31	3.17
Debt to Equity	0.32	0.24	0.24	0.23	0.34	0.40	0.35	0.36
Price Range	14.89-5.46	14.89-6.94	15.46-10.29	16.37-11.30	17.04-10.67	21.31-11.84	24.12-18.90	30.20-16.45
P/E Ratio	...	...	...	204.63-141.25	...	30.01-16.68	...	47.94-26.11
Average Yield %	4.67	4.18	3.78	3.60	3.11	2.82	2.88	1.73

Address: 1284 North Telegraph Road, Monroe, MI 48162-3390 Telephone: 734-242-1444 Fax: 734-241-4422	Web Site: www.lazboy.com Officers: Patrick H. Norton - Chmn. Kurt L. Darrow - Pres., C.E.O.	Auditors: PricewaterhouseCoopers LLP Investor Contact: 734-241-4414 Transfer Agents: EquiServe Trust Company, N.A., Providence, RI

446

LABORATORY CORP. OF AMERICA HOLDINGS

Exchange	Symbol	Price	52Wk Range	Yield	P/E
NYS	LH	$73.68 (3/31/2008)	81.40-67.94	N/A	18.75

*7 Year Price Score 123.66 *NYSE Composite Index=100 ***12 Month Price Score 108.23**

Interim Earnings (Per Share)

Qtr.	Mar	Jun	Sep	Dec
2003	0.51	0.60	0.58	0.55
2004	0.61	0.66	0.66	0.48
2005	0.67	0.74	0.66	0.64
2006	0.76	0.87	0.81	0.81
2007	0.98	1.05	0.92	0.98

Interim Dividends (Per Share)

No Dividends Paid

Valuation Analysis — **Institutional Holding**

Forecast P/E	17.27	No of Institutions
	(1/10/2007)	480
Market Cap	$8.2 Billion	Shares
Book Value	1.7 Billion	119,858,456
Price/Book	4.74	% Held
Price/Sales	2.01	97.92

TRADING VOLUME (thousand shares)

Business Summary: Diagnostic Services (MIC: 9.5 SIC: 8071 NAIC: 621511)

Laboratory Corporation of America is an independent clinical laboratory. As of Dec 31 2007, Co. had a network of 37 primary laboratories and over 1,600 patient service centers along with a network of branches and STAT laboratories, which are laboratories that have the ability to perform certain routine tests quickly and report the results to the physician immediately. Through its network of laboratories, Co. offers a range of clinical laboratory tests which are used by the medical profession in routine testing, patient diagnosis, and in the monitoring and treatment of disease. Co. has also developed specialty testing businesses, such as oncology testing and diagnostic genetics.

Recent Developments: For the year ended Dec 31 2007, net income increased 10.5% to US$476.8 million from US$431.6 million in the prior year. Revenues were US$4.07 billion, up 13.3% from US$3.59 billion the year before. Operating income was US$777.0 million versus US$697.1 million in the prior year, an increase of 11.5%. Direct operating expenses rose 15.3% to US$2.38 billion from US$2.06 billion in the comparable period the year before. Indirect operating expenses increased 9.8% to US$914.2 million from US$832.3 million in the equivalent prior-year period.

Prospects: On Jan 24 2008, Co. announced a definitive agreement to acquire Tandem Labs, a contract research organization specializing in advanced mass spectrometry, immunoanalytical support, pharmacokinetics, and pharmacodynamics for the pharmaceutical and biotechnology industries. The acquisition, which complements its clinical trials business, further enhances Co.'s position in the laboratory and drug development industries. The transaction is expected to close in the first quarter of 2008, subject to regulatory approval. For 2008, Co. is projecting revenue growth of 13.0% to 14.3%, and diluted earnings per share of $4.74 to $4.90, excluding any share repurchase activity after Dec 31 2007.

Financial Data

(US$ in Thousands)	12/31/2007	12/31/2006	12/31/2005	12/31/2004	12/31/2003	12/31/2002	12/31/2001	12/31/2000
Earnings Per Share	3.93	3.24	2.71	2.45	2.22	1.77	1.27	0.81
Cash Flow Per Share	6.08	5.10	4.30	3.85	3.92	3.12	2.28	2.61
Tang Book Value Per Share	N.M.	N.M.	N.M.	1.04	0.27	2.67	0.83	0.08
Income Statement								
Total Revenue	4,068,200	3,590,800	3,327,600	3,084,800	2,939,400	2,507,700	2,199,800	1,919,300
EBITDA	1,021,700	923,700	824,900	790,200	716,900	549,600	460,900	334,200
Income Before Taxes	802,300	720,900	640,700	615,300	540,400	432,300	332,300	207,600
Income Taxes	325,500	289,300	254,500	252,300	219,400	177,700	149,600	95,500
Net Income	476,800	431,600	386,200	363,000	321,000	254,600	179,500	112,100
Average Shares	121,300	134,700	144,900	150,700	144,776	144,197	141,077	96,299
Balance Sheet								
Current Assets	937,500	887,000	707,300	740,000	657,900	396,700	624,500	511,700
Total Assets	4,368,200	4,000,800	3,875,800	3,600,900	3,414,900	2,611,800	1,929,600	1,666,900
Current Liabilities	967,900	930,900	888,100	300,800	757,600	228,800	201,200	311,900
Long-Term Obligations	1,077,500	605,000	604,800	892,200	360,700	521,500	508,900	353,700
Total Liabilities	2,642,900	2,023,700	1,990,100	1,601,600	1,519,000	1,000,100	844,200	789,500
Stockholders' Equity	1,725,300	1,977,100	1,885,700	1,999,300	1,895,900	1,611,700	1,085,400	877,400
Shares Outstanding	111,000	122,200	126,500	136,200	143,333	147,741	141,107	139,478
Statistical Record								
Return on Assets %	11.39	10.96	10.33	10.32	10.65	11.21	9.98	6.86
Return on Equity %	25.76	22.35	19.88	18.59	18.30	18.88	18.29	21.24
EBITDA Margin %	25.11	25.72	24.79	25.62	24.39	21.92	20.95	17.41
Net Margin %	11.72	12.02	11.61	11.77	10.92	10.15	8.16	5.84
Asset Turnover	0.97	0.91	0.89	0.88	0.98	1.10	1.22	1.18
Current Ratio	0.97	0.95	0.79	2.46	0.87	2.61	3.10	1.64
Debt to Equity	0.62	0.31	0.32	0.45	0.19	0.32	0.47	0.40
Price Range	81.40-66.95	73.94-53.68	54.58-44.93	50.00-36.80	37.10-23.24	51.98-19.19	45.40-27.95	45.00-8.13
P/E Ratio	20.71-17.04	22.82-16.57	20.14-16.58	20.41-15.02	16.71-10.47	29.37-10.84	35.75-22.01	55.56-10.03

Address: 358 South Main Street, Burlington, NC 27215	Web Site: www.labcorp.com	Auditors: PricewaterhouseCoopers LLP
Telephone: 336-584-5171	Officers: Thomas P. Mac Mahon - Chmn., Pres., C.E.O. William B. Hayes - Exec. V.P., C.F.O., Treas.	Investor Contact: 336-436-4879 Transfer Agents: American Stock Transfer & Trust Company, Brooklyn, NY

LAS VEGAS SANDS CORP

Exchange	Symbol	Price	52Wk Range	Yield	P/E
NYS	LVS	$73.64 (3/31/2008)	144.56-71.85	N/A	223.15

*7 Year Price Score N/A   *NYSE Composite Index=100   *12 Month Price Score 91.39

Interim Earnings (Per Share)

Qtr.	Mar	Jun	Sep	Dec
2004	0.15	1.42	(0.26)	0.21
2005	0.02	0.24	0.23	0.31
2006	0.34	-0.31	0.27	0.32
2007	0.26	0.10	(0.14)	0.11

Interim Dividends (Per Share)
No Dividends Paid

Valuation Analysis   Institutional Holding

Forecast P/E	N/A	No of Institutions
		243
Market Cap	$26.2 Billion	Shares
Book Value	2.3 Billion	104,044,864
Price/Book	11.57	% Held
Price/Sales	8.87	29.33

TRADING VOLUME (thousand shares)

1999 2000 2001 2002 2003 2004 2005 2006 2007 2008

Business Summary: Hospitality & Tourism (MIC: 5.1 SIC: 7011 NAIC: 721120)

Las Vegas Sands owns and operates The Venetian Resort Hotel Casino (The Venetian), The Palazzo Resort Hotel Casino (The Palazzo), The Sands Expo and Convention Center (The Sands Expo Center) and The Congress Center in Las Vegas, Nevada, and the Sands Macao and The Venetian Macao Resort Hotel (The Venetian Macao) in Macao, China. As of Dec 31 2007, Co. focused its principal operating and developmental activities in three geographic areas: Las Vegas, Macao and Singapore. Las Vegas operations consist of The Venetian, including The Sands Expo Center and The Congress Center, and The Palazzo, while Macao operations consist of the Sands Macao, The Venetian Macao and other ancillary operations.

Recent Developments: For the year ended Dec 31 2007, net income decreased 73.6% to US$116.7 million from US$442.0 million in the prior year. Revenues were US$2.95 billion, up 31.9% from US$2.24 billion the year before. Operating income was US$330.0 million versus US$574.1 million in the prior year, a decrease of 42.5%. Direct operating expenses rose 50.0% to US$1.75 billion from US$1.16 billion in the comparable period the year before. Indirect operating expenses increased 75.4% to US$874.7 million from US$498.7 million in the equivalent prior-year period.

Prospects: Co. continues to progress towards its construction activities, including the Cotai Strip™ development in Macau, with construction of its second property on the Cotai Strip. In particular, Co. expects the total cost to build its developments on the Cotai Strip to be about $12.00 billion, which includes the cost of constructing The Venetian Macao. At the same time, Co. continues to make progress on its construction and other development activities of the Marina Bay Sands, which remains on track for an opening in late 2009, in Singapore. In particular, Co. anticipates that the cost to design, develop and construct the Marina Bay Sands will be in excess of $4.00 billion.

Financial Data

(US$ in Thousands)	12/31/2007	12/31/2006	12/31/2005	12/31/2004	12/31/2003	12/31/2002	12/31/2001
Earnings Per Share	0.33	1.24	0.80	1.52	54.51	(9.71)	6.45
Cash Flow Per Share	1.03	(0.56)	1.67	1.14	112.36	71.16	...
Tang Book Value Per Share	6.36	5.85	4.54	3.72	132.84	82.26	...
Dividends Per Share	...	...	...	0.440	3.440	...	...
Dividend Payout %	...	...	...	28.95	6.31	...	...
Income Statement							
Total Revenue	2,950,567	2,236,859	1,740,912	1,197,056	691,754	623,336	586,973
EBITDA	558,713	693,883	450,913	688,108	...	...	...
Income Before Taxes	138,279	504,246	287,936	481,447	...	...	...
Income Taxes	21,591	62,243	4,250	(13,736)	...	...	...
Net Income	116,688	442,003	283,686	495,183	66,634	(11,844)	7,874
Average Shares	355,789	355,264	354,526	326,848	1,222	1,220	1,220
Balance Sheet							
Current Assets	1,379,086	1,093,557	644,706	1,405,126	272,739	212,239	...
Total Assets	11,466,517	7,126,458	3,879,739	3,601,478	1,917,035	1,606,762	...
Current Liabilities	1,493,273	734,648	460,368	612,560	223,366	161,494	...
Long-Term Obligations	7,517,997	4,136,152	1,625,901	1,485,064	1,525,116	1,343,762	...
Total Liabilities	9,206,243	5,051,304	2,270,201	2,285,477	1,754,927	1,506,378	...
Stockholders' Equity	2,260,274	2,075,154	1,609,538	1,316,001	162,108	100,384	...
Shares Outstanding	355,271	354,492	354,179	354,160	1,220	1,220	1,145
Statistical Record							
Return on Assets %	1.26	8.03	7.58	17.90	3.78	...	...
Return on Equity %	5.38	23.99	19.39	66.82	50.77	...	...
EBITDA Margin %	18.94	31.02	25.90	57.48	...	...	...
Net Margin %	3.95	19.76	16.30	41.37	9.63	N.M.	1.34
Asset Turnover	0.32	0.41	0.47	0.43	0.39	...	...
Current Ratio	0.92	1.49	1.40	2.29	1.22	1.31	...
Debt to Equity	3.33	1.99	1.01	1.13	9.41	13.39	...
Price Range	144.56-72.83	97.00-38.68	50.79-29.69	53.00-46.56	...	...	...
P/E Ratio	438.06-220.70	78.23-31.19	63.49-37.11	34.87-30.63	...	...	...
Average Yield %	...	...	...	0.91	...	...	...

Address: 3355 Las Vegas Boulevard South, Las Vegas, NV 89109 Telephone: 702-414-1000	Web Site: www.lasvegassands.com Officers: Sheldon G. Adelson - Chmn., C.E.O., Treas. William P. Weidner - Pres., C.O.O.	Auditors: PricewaterhouseCoopers LLP Transfer Agents: American Stock Transfer and Trust Company

LAUDER (ESTEE) COS., INC. (THE)

Exchange	Symbol	Price	52Wk Range	Yield	P/E
NYS	EL	$45.85 (3/31/2008)	51.48-38.04	1.20	20.47

*7 Year Price Score 92.46   *NYSE Composite Index=100   *12 Month Price Score 106.19

TRADING VOLUME (thousand shares)

Interim Earnings (Per Share)

Qtr.	Sep	Dec	Mar	Jun
2004-05	0.41	0.60	0.46	0.30
2005-06	0.26	0.38	0.28	0.21
2006-07	0.27	0.99	0.45	0.45
2007-08	0.20	1.14	...	...

Interim Dividends (Per Share)

Amt	Decl	Ex	Rec	Pay
0.40A	11/3/2004	12/8/2004	12/10/2004	12/28/2004
0.40A	11/10/2005	12/7/2005	12/9/2005	12/28/2005
0.50A	10/25/2006	12/6/2006	12/8/2006	12/27/2006
0.55A	11/9/2007	12/5/2007	12/7/2007	12/27/2007

Indicated Div: $0.55

Valuation Analysis   Institutional Holding

Forecast P/E	N/A	No of Institutions 338
Market Cap	$8.9 Billion	Shares
Book Value	1.4 Billion	103,339,248
Price/Book	6.45	% Held
Price/Sales	1.19	50.01

Business Summary: Chemicals (MIC: 11.1 SIC: 2844 NAIC: 325620)

Estée Lauder Companies is a manufacturer and marketer of skin care, makeup, fragrance and hair care products. Co. sells its products principally through limited distribution channels to complement the images related to its brands. These channels include over 20,000 points of sale and consist primarily of upscale department stores and perfumeries, specialty retailers, pharmacies, salons and spas. Co.'s products are also sold in freestanding company-owned stores and spas, its authorized retailer websites, stores on cruise ships, television direct marketing, in-flight and duty-free shops and self-select outlets. At June 30 2007, Co.'s products were sold in over 135 countries and territories.

Recent Developments: For the quarter ended Dec 31 2007, income from continuing operations increased 7.6% to US$224.4 million from US$208.5 million in the year-earlier quarter. Net income increased 7.7% to US$224.4 million from US$208.4 million in the year-earlier quarter. Revenues were US$2.31 billion, up 16.0% from US$1.99 billion the year before. Operating income was US$370.5 million versus US$332.4 million in the prior-year quarter, an increase of 11.5%. Direct operating expenses rose 15.9% to US$578.5 million from US$499.0 million in the comparable period the year before. Indirect operating expenses increased 17.3% to US$1.36 billion from US$1.16 billion in the equivalent prior-year period.

Prospects: Despite a slowdown in consumer spending in the U.S., Co. believes that it could achieve its profit objectives through ongoing cost containment efforts and expense control. For the fiscal year ending June 30 2008, Co.'s net sales are forecasted to grow between 7.0% and 9.0% in constant currency, driven by an increase in sales in hair care and skin care products, followed by makeup and fragrance products, while geographic region net sales growth in constant currency is expected to be led by Europe, the Middle East and Africa, followed by Asia/Pacific and the Americas. Overall, Co. continues to forecast diluted earnings per share to be in a range of $2.28 to $2.40 for the fiscal year.

Financial Data
(US$ in Thousands)

	6 Mos	3 Mos	06/30/2007	06/30/2006	06/30/2005	06/30/2004	06/30/2003	06/30/2002
Earnings Per Share	2.24	2.09	2.16	1.12	1.78	1.48	1.26	0.70
Cash Flow Per Share	3.71	3.09	3.24	3.30	2.13	2.93	2.36	2.17
Tang Book Value Per Share	2.45	1.67	2.23	4.29	4.09	4.35	2.91	3.23
Dividends Per Share	0.550	0.500	0.500	0.400	0.400	0.300	0.200	0.200
Dividend Payout %	24.55	23.92	23.15	35.71	22.47	20.27	15.87	28.57
Income Statement								
Total Revenue	4,018,900	1,710,100	7,037,500	6,463,800	6,336,300	5,790,400	5,117,600	4,743,700
EBITDA	570,300	136,900	957,100	818,000	917,300	835,700	669,900	503,400
Depn & Amortn	121,900	59,000	...	...	...	...	...	...
Income Before Taxes	411,700	59,500	711,000	393,800	706,700	616,900	487,000	331,600
Income Taxes	144,000	21,100	255,200	259,700	291,300	232,600	160,500	114,400
Net Income	263,500	39,100	449,200	244,200	406,100	342,100	319,800	191,900
Average Shares	196,500	197,200	207,800	217,400	228,600	231,600	234,700	241,100
Balance Sheet								
Current Assets	2,614,000	2,527,800	2,239,400	2,176,900	2,302,600	2,199,200	1,844,900	1,927,600
Total Assets	4,737,200	4,612,900	4,125,700	3,784,100	3,885,800	3,708,100	3,349,900	3,416,500
Current Liabilities	1,714,700	1,771,500	1,500,700	1,438,200	1,497,700	1,322,000	1,053,600	959,600
Long-Term Obligations	1,073,300	1,062,400	1,028,100	431,800	451,100	461,500	283,600	403,900
Total Liabilities	3,336,300	3,368,000	2,905,400	2,136,400	2,177,200	1,959,100	1,554,000	1,594,600
Stockholders' Equity	1,374,000	1,223,400	1,199,000	1,622,300	1,692,800	1,733,500	1,423,600	1,461,900
Shares Outstanding	193,429	192,989	194,328	211,761	220,304	227,527	227,456	237,602
Statistical Record								
Return on Assets %	10.16	10.05	11.36	6.37	10.70	9.67	9.45	5.78
Return on Equity %	29.84	30.58	31.84	14.73	23.70	21.61	22.17	13.64
EBITDA Margin %	14.19	8.01	13.60	12.66	14.48	14.43	13.09	10.61
Net Margin %	6.56	2.29	6.38	3.78	6.41	5.91	6.25	4.05
Asset Turnover	1.70	1.67	1.78	1.69	1.67	1.64	1.51	1.43
Current Ratio	1.52	1.43	1.49	1.51	1.54	1.66	1.75	2.01
Debt to Equity	0.78	0.87	0.86	0.27	0.27	0.27	0.20	0.28
Price Range	51.48-40.09	51.48-39.19	51.48-34.94	41.84-30.71	48.80-37.00	48.78-32.88	35.94-25.75	43.45-29.51
P/E Ratio	22.98-17.90	24.63-18.75	23.83-16.18	37.36-27.42	27.42-20.79	32.96-22.22	28.52-20.44	62.07-42.16
Average Yield %	1.22	1.13	1.17	1.08	0.92	0.76	0.67	0.57

Address: 767 Fifth Avenue, New York, NY 10153 Telephone: 212-572-4200	Web Site: www.elcompanies.com Officers: Leonard A. Lauder - Chmn. William P. Lauder - Pres., C.E.O.	Auditors: KPMG LLP Transfer Agents: Mellon Investor Services LLC, Pittsburgh, PA

LEAR CORP.

Exchange	Symbol	Price	52Wk Range	Yield	P/E
NYS	LEA	$25.91 (3/31/2008)	40.58-22.82	N/A	8.39

*7 Year Price Score 64.32 *NYSE Composite Index=100 *12 Month Price Score 93.63

Interim Earnings (Per Share)

Qtr.	Mar	Jun	Sep	Dec
2003	1.01	1.54	1.10	1.90
2004	1.30	1.65	1.32	1.51
2005	0.23	(0.66)	(11.17)	(8.97)
2006	0.26	(0.10)	(1.10)	(9.38)
2007	0.64	1.58	0.52	0.35

Interim Dividends (Per Share)

Amt	Decl	Ex	Rec	Pay
0.25Q	8/3/2005	8/17/2005	8/19/2005	9/6/2005
0.25Q	11/10/2005	11/22/2005	11/25/2005	12/12/2005
0.25Q	2/9/2006	2/22/2006	2/24/2006	3/13/2006

Dividend Payment Suspended

Valuation Analysis / **Institutional Holding**

Forecast P/E	12.96 (1/10/2007)	No of Institutions	192
Market Cap	$2.0 Billion	Shares	91,336,616
Book Value	1.1 Billion	% Held	
Price/Book	1.83	N/A	
Price/Sales	0.13		

Business Summary: Furniture and Fixtures (MIC: 11.10 SIC: 2531 NAIC: 423120)

Lear is an automotive supplier, and provides automotive seat and electrical distribution systems, and select electronic products. Co. supplies to automotive manufacturers, such as Ford, BMW, Fiat, Chrysler, Daimler and Porsche. Co. conducts its business in two product operating segments: seating, and electrical and electronic. The seating segment includes seat systems and the components thereof. The electrical and electronic segment includes electrical distribution systems and electronic products, primarily wire harnesses, junction boxes, terminals and connectors, various electronic control modules, as well as audio sound systems and in-vehicle television and video entertainment systems.

Recent Developments: For the year ended Dec 31 2007, net income amounted to US$241.5 million versus a net loss of US$707.5 million in the prior year. Revenues were US$16.00 billion, down 10.3% from US$17.84 billion the year before. Direct operating expenses declined 12.2% to US$14.85 billion from US$16.91 billion in the comparable period the year before. Indirect operating expenses decreased 11.5% to US$574.7 million from US$649.6 million in the equivalent prior-year period.

Prospects: For full year 2008, Co. expects net sales of about $15.00 billion, reflecting the addition of new business globally and the positive effect of foreign exchange, which should more than offset lower vehicle production and unfavorable platform mix in North America. Further, Co. targets income before interest, other expense, income taxes, restructuring costs and other special items of $660.0 million to $700.0 million. Co.'s guidance assumes, among other factors, an exchange rate of euro1.45, expectations for industry vehicle production of about 14.4 million units in North America and 20.1 million units in Europe, and production for the Domestic Three to be down about 9.0% in North America.

Financial Data

(US$ in Thousands)	12/31/2007	12/31/2006	12/31/2005	12/31/2004	12/31/2003	12/31/2002	12/31/2001	12/31/2000
Earnings Per Share	3.09	(10.31)	(20.57)	5.77	5.55	0.19	0.40	4.17
Cash Flow Per Share	6.08	4.16	8.35	9.87	8.79	8.34	12.97	11.52
Dividends Per Share	...	0.250	1.000	0.800	0.200	...	...	...
Dividend Payout %	...	...	...	13.86	3.60	...	...	...
Income Statement								
Total Revenue	15,995,000	17,838,900	17,089,200	16,960,000	15,746,700	14,424,600	13,624,700	14,072,800
EBITDA	819,300	(51,400)	(552,000)	1,084,900	1,042,800	992,000	757,300	1,192,600
Income Before Taxes	323,200	(653,400)	(1,128,600)	564,300	534,400	480,500	110,400	484,200
Income Taxes	89,900	54,900	194,300	128,000	153,700	157,000	68,700	197,300
Net Income	241,500	(707,500)	(1,381,500)	422,200	380,500	13,000	26,300	274,700
Average Shares	78,214	68,607	67,166	74,727	68,533	67,057	65,305	65,840
Balance Sheet								
Current Assets	3,718,000	3,890,300	3,846,400	4,372,000	3,375,400	2,507,700	2,366,800	2,828,000
Total Assets	7,800,400	7,850,500	8,288,400	9,944,400	8,571,000	7,483,000	7,579,200	8,375,500
Current Liabilities	3,603,900	3,887,300	4,106,700	4,647,900	3,582,100	3,045,200	3,182,800	3,371,600
Long-Term Obligations	2,344,600	2,434,500	2,243,100	1,866,900	2,057,200	2,132,800	2,293,900	2,852,100
Total Liabilities	6,709,700	7,248,500	7,177,400	7,214,300	6,313,500	5,820,700	6,020,100	6,774,700
Stockholders' Equity	1,090,700	602,000	1,111,000	2,730,100	2,257,500	1,662,300	1,559,100	1,600,800
Shares Outstanding	77,189	76,251	67,186	67,416	68,533	65,737	64,253	63,554
Statistical Record								
Return on Assets %	3.09	N.M.	N.M.	4.55	4.74	0.17	0.33	3.21
Return on Equity %	28.53	N.M.	N.M.	16.88	19.41	0.81	1.66	17.87
EBITDA Margin %	5.12	N.M.	N.M.	6.40	6.62	6.88	5.56	8.47
Net Margin %	1.51	N.M.	N.M.	2.49	2.42	0.09	0.19	1.95
Asset Turnover	2.04	2.21	1.87	1.83	1.96	1.92	1.71	1.64
Current Ratio	1.03	1.00	0.94	0.94	0.94	0.82	0.74	0.84
Debt to Equity	2.15	4.04	2.02	0.68	0.91	1.28	1.47	1.78
Price Range	40.62-27.37	34.01-16.01	61.01-27.09	68.88-49.73	63.12-33.06	52.49-33.15	42.14-24.42	35.44-19.94
P/E Ratio	13.15-8.86	...	...	11.94-8.62	11.37-5.96	276.26-174.47	105.35-61.05	8.50-4.78
Average Yield %	...	...	2.55	1.36	0.42	...	...	...

Address: 21557 Telegraph Road, Southfield, MI 48033	Web Site: www.lear.com	Auditors: Ernst & Young LLP
Telephone: 248-447-1500	Officers: Robert E. Rossiter - Chmn., C.E.O. James H. Vandenberghe - Vice-Chmn.	Transfer Agents: The Bank of New York
Fax: 248-447-7782		

LEE ENTERPRISES, INC.

Exchange	Symbol	Price	52Wk Range	Yield	P/E
NYS	LEE	$10.01 (3/31/2008)	30.77-9.52	7.59	5.99

*7 Year Price Score 41.10 *NYSE Composite Index=100 *12 Month Price Score 68.07

Interim Earnings (Per Share)

Qtr.	Dec	Mar	Jun	Sep
2004-05	0.60	0.40	0.41	0.29
2005-06	0.50	0.32	0.50	0.24
2006-07	0.58	0.26	0.49	0.44
2007-08	0.48	...	...	...

Interim Dividends (Per Share)

Amt	Decl	Ex	Rec	Pay
0.18Q	5/17/2007	5/30/2007	6/1/2007	7/2/2007
0.18Q	8/6/2007	8/29/2007	8/31/2007	10/1/2007
0.19Q	11/14/2007	11/29/2007	12/3/2007	1/2/2008
0.19Q	2/20/2008	2/28/2008	3/3/2008	4/1/2008

Indicated Div: $0.76

Valuation Analysis   Institutional Holding

Forecast P/E	14.67	No of Institutions
	(1/10/2007)	161
Market Cap	$466.6 Million	Shares
Book Value	1.1 Billion	36,459,808
Price/Book	0.43	% Held
Price/Sales	0.42	79.18

Business Summary: Media (MIC: 13.1 SIC: 2711 NAIC: 511110)

Lee Enterprises is a provider of local news, information and advertising in primarily midsize markets, with 51 daily newspapers and a joint interest in five others, online sites and more than 300 weekly newspapers and specialty publications in 23 states as of Sep 30 2007. In addition, Co.'s online activities include websites supporting each of its daily newspapers and certain of its other publications. Co. also owns 82.5% of an Internet service company, INN Partners, L.C., which provides online infrastructure and online publishing services for more than 1,500 daily and weekly newspapers and shoppers. Co. also offers commercial printing services.

Recent Developments: For the quarter ended Dec 31 2007, income from continuing operations decreased 17.9% to US$21.8 million from US$26.5 million in the year-earlier quarter. Net income decreased 17.0% to US$22.1 million from US$26.7 million in the year-earlier quarter. Revenues were US$279.9 million, down 6.2% from US$298.5 million the year before. Operating income was US$53.7 million versus US$63.8 million in the prior-year quarter, a decrease of 15.8%. Direct operating expenses declined 18.8% to US$25.1 million from US$30.9 million in the comparable period the year before. Indirect operating expenses decreased 1.4% to US$201.1 million from US$203.8 million in the equivalent prior-year period.

Prospects: Co.'s near term outlook appears challenging, reflecting recent unfavorable trends in print classified advertising revenue as well as declining newspaper circulation. Specifically, Co. is experiencing decreased advertising lineage across its Retail, National and Classified sectors, driven in part by the soft housing market nationally and lower automotive classified advertising. On a positive note, Co.'s online advertising continues to grow meaningfully, due to rate increases and expanded cross-selling with its print publications. In addition, Co. began selling online employment advertising on Yahoo! Hot Jobs during the three months ended Mar 31 2007.

Financial Data
(US$ In Thousands)

	3 Mos	09/30/2007	09/30/2006	09/30/2005	09/30/2004	09/30/2003	09/30/2002	09/30/2001
Earnings Per Share	1.67	1.77	1.56	1.70	1.91	1.75	1.85	7.13
Cash Flow Per Share	3.58	3.70	4.34	3.56	2.91	3.17	2.62	2.45
Tang Book Value Per Share	N.M.	N.M.	N.M.	N.M.	N.M.	N.M.	N.M.	8.43
Dividends Per Share	0.730	0.720	0.720	0.720	0.720	0.680	0.680	0.680
Dividend Payout %	43.71	40.68	46.15	42.35	37.70	38.86	36.76	9.54
Income Statement								
Total Revenue	279,856	1,127,661	1,128,648	860,859	683,324	656,741	525,896	441,153
EBITDA	57,680	292,440	298,062	217,433	194,287	183,554	155,879	108,007
Depn & Amortn	23,031	...	...	...	...	...	...	...
Income Before Taxes	34,649	116,123	112,107	121,391	134,661	121,523	111,059	92,434
Income Taxes	12,254	34,146	39,740	44,353	48,192	43,462	30,030	32,977
Net Income	22,126	80,999	70,832	76,878	86,071	78,041	81,975	314,228
Average Shares	45,769	45,804	45,546	45,348	45,092	44,316	44,351	44,089
Balance Sheet								
Current Assets	167,663	148,972	184,412	184,870	92,857	89,885	104,027	537,677
Total Assets	3,246,229	3,260,963	3,329,809	3,445,200	1,403,844	1,471,377	1,463,830	1,000,397
Current Liabilities	290,709	251,557	200,323	159,663	105,481	134,551	108,749	125,139
Long-Term Obligations	1,288,046	1,346,630	1,510,459	1,706,024	202,000	268,600	394,700	161,800
Total Liabilities	2,149,530	2,174,521	2,339,184	2,508,790	527,001	619,221	722,574	318,453
Stockholders' Equity	1,096,699	1,086,442	990,625	936,410	876,843	802,156	741,256	681,944
Shares Outstanding	46,611	46,187	45,881	45,493	45,217	44,621	44,311	44,038
Statistical Record								
Return on Assets %	2.34	2.46	2.09	3.17	6.08	5.41	6.65	35.98
Return on Equity %	7.26	7.80	7.35	8.48	10.22	10.11	11.52	58.35
EBITDA Margin %	20.61	25.93	26.41	25.26	28.43	27.95	29.64	24.48
Net Margin %	7.91	7.18	6.28	8.93	12.60	11.88	15.59	71.23
Asset Turnover	0.34	0.34	0.33	0.36	0.48	0.46	0.43	0.51
Current Ratio	0.58	0.59	0.92	1.16	0.88	0.67	0.96	4.30
Debt to Equity	1.17	1.24	1.52	1.82	0.23	0.33	0.53	0.24
Price Range	35.51-13.81	35.51-14.73	42.91-23.23	48.65-39.97	49.70-38.67	40.49-30.23	39.76-29.02	34.70-25.25
P/E Ratio	21.26-8.27	20.06-8.32	27.51-14.89	28.62-23.51	26.02-20.25	23.14-17.27	21.49-15.69	4.87-3.54
Average Yield %	3.22	2.77	2.24	1.64	1.59	1.94	1.93	2.20

Address: 201 N. Harrison Street, Suite 600, Davenport, IA 52801	**Web Site:** www.lee.net	**Auditors:** Deloitte & Touche LLP
Telephone: 563-383-2100	**Officers:** Mary E. Junck - Chmn., Pres., C.E.O.	**Investor Contact:** 563-383-2163
Fax: 563-326-2972	Rosanne M. Cheeseman - V.P., Sales & Mktg.	

LEGG MASON, INC.

Exchange	Symbol	Price	52Wk Range	Yield	P/E	Div Achiever
NYS	LM	$55.98 (3/31/2008)	105.87-52.72	1.71	11.64	24 Years

*7 Year Price Score 99.52   *NYSE Composite Index=100   *12 Month Price Score 83.34

Interim Earnings (Per Share)

Qtr.	Jun	Sep	Dec	Mar
2004-05	0.76	0.81	0.98	0.98
2005-06	0.93	0.99	5.80	0.85
2006-07	1.08	1.00	1.21	1.19
2007-08	1.32	1.23	1.07	...

Interim Dividends (Per Share)

Amt	Decl	Ex	Rec	Pay
0.24Q	4/23/2007	6/8/2007	6/12/2007	7/9/2007
0.24Q	7/19/2007	9/25/2007	9/27/2007	10/15/2007
0.24Q	10/16/2007	12/3/2007	12/5/2007	12/31/2007
0.24Q	1/29/2008	3/4/2008	3/6/2008	4/7/2008

Indicated Div: $0.96

Valuation Analysis

		Institutional Holding	
Forecast P/E	15.67	No of Institutions	
	(1/10/2007)	466	
Market Cap	$7.4 Billion	Shares	
Book Value	7.0 Billion	108,510,120	
Price/Book	1.06	% Held	
Price/Sales	1.58	81.22	

Business Summary: Finance Intermediaries & Services (MIC: 8.7 SIC: 6211 NAIC: 523120)

Legg Mason is a global asset management company. Through its subsidiaries, Co. provides investment management and related services to institutional and individual clients, company-sponsored mutual funds and other investment vehicles. In addition, Co. provides these products and services directly and through various financial intermediaries. As of June 30 2007, Co. divided its business into three operating divisions: Managed Investments; Institutional; and Wealth Management. Within each of its divisions, Co. provides its services through a number of asset managers, each of which is an individual business that generally markets its products and services under its own brand name.

Recent Developments: For the quarter ended Dec 31 2007, income from continuing operations decreased 11.2% to US$154.6 million from US$174.1 million in the year-earlier quarter. Net income decreased 11.5% to US$154.6 million from US$174.6 million in the year-earlier quarter. Revenues were US$1.19 billion, up 4.7% from US$1.13 billion the year before. Operating income was US$342.0 million versus US$263.4 million in the prior-year quarter, an increase of 29.8%. Indirect operating expenses decreased 2.9% to US$844.7 million from US$869.6 million in the equivalent prior-year period.

Prospects: Co.'s near-term outlook appears to be challenging, due to the continuous volatility of the U.S. and global economies, attributable primarily to disruptions in the credit markets, driven by the subprime mortgage crisis, a weaker U.S. dollar, slow job growth, and increased oil prices. Nevertheless, Co.'s investment managers remain focused on expanding its business into new markets, launching new products, and building new distribution relationships, as exhibited by the launching of Global Fund in China through a distribution partnership with Citibank China. Specifically, Co. believes that this development is in-line with its ongoing global growth strategy.

Financial Data
(US$ in Thousands)

	9 Mos	6 Mos	3 Mos	03/31/2007	03/31/2006	03/31/2005	03/31/2004	03/31/2003
Earnings Per Share	4.81	4.95	4.72	4.48	8.80	3.53	2.71	1.85
Cash Flow Per Share	5.48	6.57	5.99	6.42	4.52	3.98	1.88	3.09
Tang Book Value Per Share	0.38	N.M.	N.M.	N.M.	N.M.	7.91	6.50	3.32
Dividends Per Share	0.930	0.900	0.870	0.810	0.690	0.550	0.373	0.287
Dividend Payout %	19.33	18.18	18.43	18.08	7.84	15.58	13.79	15.47
Income Statement								
Total Revenue	3,564,963	2,378,319	1,205,968	4,343,675	2,645,212	2,489,552	2,004,267	1,615,382
Income Before Taxes	836,759	589,767	305,570	1,043,854	715,462	658,707	472,309	308,321
Income Taxes	313,483	221,164	114,590	397,612	275,595	250,276	181,701	117,412
Net Income	523,061	368,479	191,015	646,818	1,144,168	408,431	297,764	190,909
Average Shares	144,018	144,627	144,778	144,386	130,279	117,074	110,769	103,140
Balance Sheet								
Total Assets	10,561,401	10,080,904	9,686,186	9,604,488	9,302,490	8,219,472	7,262,981	6,067,450
Total Liabilities	3,527,715	3,233,542	2,925,722	3,062,998	3,452,374	5,926,326	5,703,371	4,819,493
Stockholders' Equity	7,033,686	6,847,362	6,760,464	6,541,490	5,850,116	2,293,146	1,559,610	1,247,957
Shares Outstanding	132,750	132,007	132,863	131,776	129,709	106,683	99,823	97,241
Statistical Record								
Return on Assets %	6.92	7.39	7.19	6.84	13.06	5.28	4.46	3.18
Return on Equity %	10.37	10.96	10.63	10.44	28.10	21.20	21.15	16.37
Price Range	109.65-68.48	109.65-77.84	109.65-82.30	126.10-82.30	136.40-70.20	84.12-48.97	63.22-32.49	37.98-25.44
P/E Ratio	22.80-14.24	22.15-15.73	23.23-17.44	28.15-18.37	15.50-7.98	23.83-13.87	23.33-11.99	20.53-13.75
Average Yield %	1.02	0.94	0.90	0.82	0.64	0.86	0.75	0.89

Address: 100 Light Street, Baltimore, MD 21202	Web Site: www.leggmason.com	Auditors: PricewaterhouseCoopers LLP
Telephone: 410-539-0000	Officers: Raymond A. Mason - Chmn., Pres., C.E.O.	Investor Contact: 410-539-0000
Fax: 410-539-8010	Timothy C. Scheve - Sr. Exec. V.P.	Transfer Agents: Wachovia Bank, N.A., Charlotte, NC

LEGGETT & PLATT, INC.

Exchange	Symbol	Price	52Wk Range	Yield	P/E	Div Acheiver
NYS	LEG	$15.25 (3/31/2008)	24.62-14.88	6.56	N/A	36 Years

*7 Year Price Score 69.46   *NYSE Composite Index=100   *12 Month Price Score 90.89

TRADING VOLUME (thousand shares)

Interim Earnings (Per Share)

Qtr.	Mar	Jun	Sep	Dec
2003	0.25	0.24	0.26	0.30
2004	0.32	0.39	0.41	0.33
2005	0.37	0.41	0.28	0.24
2006	0.33	0.45	0.45	0.38
2007	0.41	0.33	0.37	(1.17)

Interim Dividends (Per Share)

Amt	Decl	Ex	Rec	Pay
0.18Q	5/9/2007	6/13/2007	6/15/2007	7/13/2007
0.18Q	8/9/2007	9/12/2007	9/14/2007	10/15/2007
0.25Q	11/13/2007	12/12/2007	12/14/2007	1/15/2008
0.25Q	2/21/2008	3/12/2008	3/14/2008	4/15/2008

Indicated Div: $1.00

Valuation Analysis / Institutional Holding

Forecast P/E	12.18	No.of,Institutions
	(1/10/2007)	295
Market Cap	$2.6 Billion	Shares
Book Value	2.1 Billion	128,116,944
Price/Book	1.21	% Held
Price/Sales	0.60	72.22

Business Summary: Furniture and Fixtures (MIC: 11.10 SIC: 2519 NAIC: 337121)

Leggett & Platt is engaged in designing and producing a range of components and products that are used in homes, offices, retail stores and automobiles. Co.'s products include manufactured components for residential furniture and bedding, adjustable beds, carpet underlay, retail store fixtures and point-of-purchase displays, office furniture, drawn steel wire, automotive seat support and lumbar systems, and machinery for wire forming, sewing, and quilting. As of Dec 31 2007, Co.'s operations were organized into 22 business units, which are divided into 10 groups under four segments: Residential Furnishings, Commercial Fixturing & Components; Industrial Materials; and Specialized Product.

Recent Developments: For the year ended Dec 31 2007, income from continuing operations decreased 78.4% to US$51.0 million from US$235.6 million a year earlier. Net loss amounted to US$11.2 million versus net income of US$300.3 million in the prior year. Revenues were US$4.31 billion, down 0.6% from US$4.33 billion the year before. Operating income was US$177.5 million versus US$382.2 million in the prior year, a decrease of 53.6%. Direct operating expenses declined 0.4% to US$3.51 billion from US$3.52 billion in the comparable period the year before. Indirect operating expenses increased 45.4% to US$621.1 million from US$427.2 million in the equivalent prior-year period.

Prospects: For full year 2008, Co. is targeting earnings from continuing operations of $0.95 to $1.30 per share, excluding potential earnings from discontinued operations as well as possible gains or losses from the divestitures. In addition, Co. is forecasting sales from continuing operations to be about $4.20 billion. Specifically, Co.'s sales outlook reflects the planned elimination of about $100.0 million of revenue by end of 2008, with minimal acquisition revenue and overall flat sales from operations other than Store Fixtures. Meanwhile, Co. expects to generate proceeds of about $400.0 million from its divestiture activities in 2008.

Financial Data

(US$ in Thousands)	12/31/2007	12/31/2006	12/31/2005	12/31/2004	12/31/2003	12/31/2002	12/31/2001	12/31/2000
Earnings Per Share	(0.06)	1.61	1.30	1.45	1.05	1.17	0.94	1.32
Cash Flow Per Share	3.42	2.57	2.33	1.75	2.01	2.29	2.68	2.21
Tang Book Value Per Share	5.74	5.72	5.55	6.37	5.62	5.36	4.81	4.58
Dividends Per Share	0.780	0.670	0.630	0.580	0.540	0.500	0.480	0.420
Dividend Payout %	...	41.61	48.46	40.00	51.43	42.74	51.06	31.82
Income Statement								
Total Revenue	4,306,400	5,505,400	5,299,300	5,085,500	4,388,200	4,271,800	4,113,800	4,276,300
EBITDA	357,700	657,400	567,300	638,900	530,700	575,400	587,700	688,200
Income Before Taxes	128,400	434,800	356,200	422,600	315,100	363,500	297,300	418,600
Income Taxes	77,400	134,500	104,900	137,200	109,200	130,400	109,700	154,500
Net Income	(11,200)	300,300	251,300	285,400	205,900	233,100	187,600	264,100
Average Shares	179,827	186,832	193,574	196,875	196,953	199,795	200,434	200,388
Balance Sheet								
Current Assets	1,834,400	1,894,100	1,763,300	2,064,800	1,819,400	1,488,000	1,421,900	1,405,300
Total Assets	4,072,500	4,265,300	4,052,600	4,197,200	3,889,700	3,501,100	3,412,900	3,373,200
Current Liabilities	799,600	691,200	738,000	959,600	625,900	598,000	457,000	476,600
Long-Term Obligations	1,000,600	1,060,000	921,600	779,400	1,012,200	808,600	977,600	988,400
Total Liabilities	1,939,800	1,914,200	1,803,600	1,884,100	1,775,700	1,524,200	1,546,300	1,579,400
Stockholders' Equity	2,132,700	2,351,100	2,249,000	2,313,100	2,114,000	1,976,900	1,866,600	1,793,800
Shares Outstanding	168,725	178,000	182,576	190,886	192,102	194,498	196,298	196,097
Statistical Record								
Return on Assets %	N.M.	7.22	6.09	7.04	5.57	6.74	5.53	8.29
Return on Equity %	N.M.	13.06	11.02	12.86	10.07	12.13	10.25	15.31
EBITDA Margin %	8.31	11.94	10.71	12.56	12.09	13.47	14.29	16.09
Net Margin %	N.M.	5.45	4.74	5.61	4.69	5.46	4.56	6.18
Asset Turnover	1.03	1.32	1.28	1.25	1.19	1.24	1.21	1.34
Current Ratio	2.29	2.74	2.39	2.15	2.91	2.49	3.11	2.95
Debt to Equity	0.47	0.45	0.41	0.34	0.48	0.41	0.52	0.55
Price Range	24.62-17.27	26.96-22.39	29.44-18.55	30.56-21.35	23.57-17.40	27.16-18.90	24.23-17.00	22.25-14.25
P/E Ratio	...	16.75-13.91	22.65-14.27	21.08-14.72	22.45-16.57	23.21-16.15	25.78-18.09	16.86-10.80
Average Yield %	3.59	2.76	2.47	2.25	2.58	2.13	2.26	2.35

Address: No. 1 Leggett Road, Carthage, MO 64836	Web Site: www.leggett.com	Auditors: PricewaterhouseCoopers LLP
Telephone: 417-358-8131	Officers: Felix E. Wright - Chmn., C.E.O. David S. Haffner - Pres., C.O.O.	Investor Contact: 417-358-8131
Fax: 417-358-8449		Transfer Agents: U.M.B. Bank, Kansas City, MO

LEHMAN BROTHERS HOLDINGS INC

Exchange	Symbol	Price	52Wk Range	Yield	P/E	Div Achiever
NYS	LEH	$37.64 (3/31/2008)	81.30-31.75	1.81	6.18	11 Years

*7 Year Price Score 106.32 *NYSE Composite Index=100 *12 Month Price Score 84.69

Interim Earnings (Per Share)

Qtr.	Feb	May	Aug	Nov
2004-05	1.46	1.13	1.47	1.38
2005-06	1.83	1.69	1.57	1.72
2006-07	1.96	2.21	1.54	1.55
2007-08	0.81	...	...	...

Interim Dividends (Per Share)

Amt	Decl	Ex	Rec	Pay
0.15Q	4/26/2007	5/11/2007	5/15/2007	5/23/2007
0.15Q	8/1/2007	8/13/2007	8/15/2007	8/24/2007
0.15Q	10/30/2007	11/13/2007	11/15/2007	11/23/2007
0.17Q	1/29/2008	2/13/2008	2/15/2008	2/22/2008

Indicated Div: $0.68

Valuation Analysis

		Institutional Holding	
Forecast P/E	N/A	No of Institutions	652
Market Cap	$20.8 Billion	Shares	
Book Value	24.8 Billion		346,551,328
Price/Book	0.84	% Held	
Price/Sales	0.36		65.07

Business Summary: Finance Intermediaries & Services (MIC: 8.7 SIC: 6211 NAIC: 523110)

Lehman Brothers Holdings serves the financial needs of corporations, governments and municipalities, institutional clients and high-net-worth individuals worldwide. Co. provides an array of equities and fixed income sales, trading and research, investment banking, asset management, private investment management and private equity. Co. is a member of all principal securities and commodities exchanges in the U.S., as well as NASD, Inc., and holds memberships or associate memberships on several principal international securities and commodities exchanges, including the London, Tokyo, Hong Kong, Frankfurt, Paris, Milan and Australian. At Nov 30 2007, Co. had total assets of $691.06 billion.

Recent Developments: For the quarter ended Feb 29 2008, net income decreased 57.3% to US$489.0 million from US$1.15 billion in the year-earlier quarter. Revenues were US$12.37 billion, down 10.3% from US$13.80 billion the year before. Direct operating expenses rose 1.3% to US$8.86 billion from US$8.75 billion in the comparable period the year before. Indirect operating expenses decreased 15.1% to US$2.84 billion from US$3.35 billion in the equivalent prior-year period.

Prospects: For full-year 2008, Co. anticipates that global economic growth will be lower than 2007. In particular, Co. expects mergers and acquisitions (M&A) volumes to decline by 20.0% as compared to 2007, but believes that cross-border and international activity will continue to increase. Also, Co. expects lower returns for its equity capital markets during 2008, and anticipates global fixed income origination to decline as a result of securitizations and M&A. Furthermore, Co. believes that the U.S. growth rate in 2008 will decrease, reflecting the continued strain in the capital markets due to several factors which include the extended period of construction declines and housing price cuts.

Financial Data

(US$ in Thousands)	3 Mos	11/30/2007	11/30/2006	11/30/2005	11/30/2004	11/30/2003	11/30/2002	11/30/2001
Earnings Per Share	6.09	7.26	6.81	5.43	3.95	3.17	1.74	2.19
Cash Flow Per Share	(76.26)	(84.34)	(66.99)	(13.46)	(19.80)	5.18	49.83	13.74
Tang Book Value Per Share	32.15	32.47	27.62	22.92	18.77	16.06	17.37	15.98
Dividends Per Share	0.620	0.600	0.480	0.400	0.320	0.240	0.180	0.140
Dividend Payout %	10.19	8.26	7.05	7.36	8.10	7.56	10.37	6.39
Income Statement								
Interest Income	9,635,000	41,693,000	30,284,000	19,043,000	11,032,000	9,942,000	11,728,000	16,470,000
Interest Expense	8,863,000	39,746,000	29,126,000	17,790,000	9,674,000	8,640,000	10,626,000	15,656,000
Net Interest Income	772,000	1,947,000	1,158,000	1,253,000	1,358,000	1,302,000	1,102,000	814,000
Non-Interest Income	2,735,000	17,310,000	16,425,000	13,377,000	10,218,000	7,345,000	5,053,000	5,922,000
Non-Interest Expense	2,844,000	13,244,000	11,678,000	9,801,000	8,058,000	6,111,000	4,676,000	4,988,000
Income Before Taxes	663,000	...	...	...	...	...	...	...
Income Taxes	174,000	1,821,000	1,945,000	1,569,000	1,125,000	765,000	368,000	437,000
Net Income	489,000	4,192,000	4,007,000	3,260,000	2,369,000	1,699,000	975,000	1,255,000
Average Shares	572,800	568,300	578,400	587,200	581,400	519,800	522,400	530,600
Balance Sheet								
Total Assets	786,035,000	691,063,000	503,545,000	410,063,000	357,168,000	312,061,000	260,336,000	247,816,000
Total Deposits	28,829,000	29,363,000	21,412,000	...	...	...	...	...
Total Liabilities	761,203,000	668,573,000	484,354,000	393,269,000	342,248,000	297,577,000	250,684,000	238,647,000
Stockholders' Equity	24,832,000	22,490,000	19,191,000	16,794,000	14,920,000	13,174,000	8,942,000	8,459,000
Shares Outstanding	551,384	531,887	533,368	542,874	548,318	533,358	462,262	475,068
Statistical Record								
Return on Assets %	0.52	0.70	0.88	0.85	0.71	0.59	0.38	0.53
Return on Equity %	15.71	20.11	22.27	20.56	16.82	15.36	11.21	15.46
Net Interest Margin %	8.01	4.67	3.82	6.58	12.31	13.10	9.40	4.94
Efficiency Ratio %	22.99	22.45	25.00	30.23	37.92	35.35	27.86	22.28
Price Range	81.30-50.99	85.80-51.57	78.55-59.42	66.42-41.63	44.75-33.83	37.90-25.18	34.76-21.30	42.86-23.32
P/E Ratio	13.35-8.37	11.82-7.10	11.53-8.73	12.23-7.67	11.33-8.56	11.96-7.94	19.98-12.24	19.57-10.65
Average Yield %	0.95	0.85	0.69	0.80	0.82	0.75	0.60	0.41

Address: 745 Seventh Avenue, New York, NY 10019 Telephone: 212-526-7000 Fax: 212-526-3738	Web Site: www.lehman.com Officers: Richard S. Fuld Jr. - Chmn., C.E.O. Thomas A. Russo - Vice-Chmn., Chief Legal Officer	Auditors: Ernst & Young LLP Investor Contact: 212-526-0858 Transfer Agents: The Bank of New York

LENNAR CORP.

Exchange	Symbol	Price	52Wk Range	Yield	P/E
NYS	LEN	$18.81 (3/31/2008)	46.50-12.99	3.40	N/A

*7 Year Price Score 57.46 *NYSE Composite Index=100 *12 Month Price Score 70.94

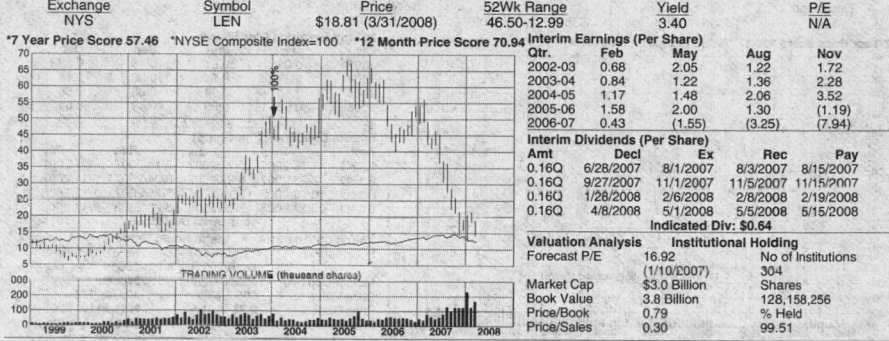

Interim Earnings (Per Share)

Qtr.	Feb	May	Aug	Nov
2002-03	0.68	2.05	1.22	1.72
2003-04	0.84	1.22	1.36	2.28
2004-05	1.17	1.48	2.06	3.52
2005-06	1.58	2.00	1.30	(1.19)
2006-07	0.43	(1.55)	(3.25)	(7.94)

Interim Dividends (Per Share)

Amt	Decl	Ex	Rec	Pay
0.16Q	6/28/2007	8/1/2007	8/3/2007	8/15/2007
0.16Q	9/27/2007	11/1/2007	11/5/2007	11/15/2007
0.16Q	1/28/2008	2/6/2008	2/8/2008	2/19/2008
0.16Q	4/8/2008	5/1/2008	5/5/2008	5/15/2008

Indicated Div: $0.64

Valuation Analysis

	Institutional Holding	
Forecast P/E	16.92	No of Institutions
	(1/10/2007)	304
Market Cap	$3.0 Billion	Shares
Book Value	3.8 Billion	128,158,256
Price/Book	0.79	% Held
Price/Sales	0.30	99.51

Business Summary: Building & General Construction (MIC: 3.2 SIC: 1521 NAIC: 236115)

Lennar is engaged in homebuilding and provision of financial services. Co.'s homebuilding operations include the construction and sale of single-family attached and detached homes, and to a lesser extent multi-level residential buildings, as well as the purchase, development and sale of residential land. As of Nov 30 2007, Co. has grouped its homebuilding activities into three reportable segments. Homebuilding East, Homebuilding Central and Homebuilding West. Co.'s financial services reportable segment provides mortgage financing, title insurance, closing services and other ancillary services (including high-speed Internet and cable television).

Recent Developments: For the year ended Nov 30 2007, loss from continuing operations was US$1.94 billion compared with income of US$593.9 million a year earlier. Net loss amounted to US$1.94 billion versus net income of US$593.9 million in the prior year. Revenues were US$10.19 billion, down 37.4% from US$16.27 billion the year before. Direct operating expenses declined 16.7% to US$12.64 billion from US$15.17 billion in the comparable period the year before. Indirect operating expenses decreased 10.4% to US$173.2 million from US$193.3 million in the equivalent prior-year period.

Prospects: For the near-term, Co. expects a continued decline in the market conditions, and is continuing to reduce home starts and adjust pricing to meet deteriorating housing market conditions in order to keep inventories low and its balance sheet positioned for future growth. Concurrently, Co. will continue to reduce the number of joint ventures and net recourse indebtedness exposure related to joint ventures by re-evaluating all of its joint ventures arrangements, mainly those ventures with recourse indebtedness. On a positive note, Co. believes that factors including its robust balance sheet and its construction costs reduction efforts will enable it mitigate such situation going forward.

Financial Data
(US$ in Thousands)

	11/30/2007	11/30/2006	11/30/2005	11/30/2004	11/30/2003	11/30/2002	11/30/2001	11/30/2000
Earnings Per Share	(12.31)	3.69	8.23	5.70	4.65	3.86	3.00	1.82
Cash Flow Per Share	2.82	3.51	2.08	1.75	3.94	1.60	0.47	4.15
Tang Book Value Per Share	23.52	34.81	32.09	25.94	20.68	17.17	12.96	9.79
Dividends Per Share	0.640	0.640	0.573	0.512	0.144	0.025	0.025	0.025
Dividend Payout %	...	17.34	6.96	8.99	3.09	0.65	0.83	1.37
Income Statement								
Total Revenue	10,186,781	16,266,662	13,866,971	10,504,899	8,907,619	7,319,802	6,029,301	4,706,968
EBITDA	(3,024,317)	992,660	2,239,252	1,592,353	1,282,965	948,098	748,093	431,088
Income Before Taxes	(3,081,081)	942,649	2,159,694	1,519,067	1,207,054	875,709	679,423	375,635
Income Taxes	(1,140,000)	348,780	815,284	573,448	455,663	330,580	261,578	146,498
Net Income	(1,941,081)	593,869	1,355,155	945,619	751,391	545,129	417,845	229,137
Average Shares	157,718	161,371	165,522	167,340	163,352	142,852	141,158	128,998
Balance Sheet								
Current Assets	5,538,717	8,676,984	9,095,001	6,617,827	4,917,769	4,017,172	3,264,899	2,631,481
Total Assets	9,102,747	12,408,266	12,541,225	9,165,280	6,775,432	5,755,633	4,714,426	3,777,914
Current Liabilities	504,068	1,093,793	1,737,032	...	...	...	...	...
Long-Term Obligations	2,836,873	2,613,503	2,592,772	2,021,014	1,552,217	1,585,309	1,505,255	1,254,650
Total Liabilities	5,252,100	6,651,501	7,211,571	5,112,308	3,511,658	3,526,476	3,055,164	2,549,334
Stockholders' Equity	3,822,119	5,701,372	5,251,411	4,052,972	3,263,774	2,229,157	1,659,262	1,228,580
Shares Outstanding	159,887	158,156	157,560	156,230	157,836	129,826	128,030	125,462
Statistical Record								
Return on Assets %	N.M.	4.76	12.49	11.83	11.99	10.41	9.84	7.83
Return on Equity %	N.M.	10.84	29.13	25.78	27.36	28.04	28.94	21.66
EBITDA Margin %	N.M.	6.10	16.15	15.16	14.40	12.95	12.41	9.16
Net Margin %	N.M.	3.65	9.77	9.00	8.44	7.45	6.93	4.87
Asset Turnover	0.95	1.30	1.28	1.31	1.42	1.40	1.42	1.61
Current Ratio	10.99	7.93	5.24	...	...	...	...	...
Debt to Equity	0.74	0.46	0.49	0.50	0.48	0.71	0.91	1.02
Price Range	56.11-14.49	65.95-40.07	68.27-44.27	56.01-40.99	49.20-22.18	28.80-16.92	22.55-14.42	15.78-7.05
P/E Ratio	...	17.87-10.86	8.30-5.38	9.83-7.19	10.58-4.77	7.46-4.38	7.52-4.81	8.67-3.87
Average Yield %	1.67	1.24	0.99	1.11	0.45	0.10	0.14	0.25

Address: 700 Northwest 107th Avenue, Miami, FL 33172	Web Site: www.lennar.com	Auditors: Deloitte & Touche LLP
Telephone: 305-559-4000	Officers: Robert J. Strudler - Chmn. Stuart A. Miller - Pres., C.E.O.	Transfer Agents: ComputerShare Investor Services, Providence, RI
Fax: 305-227-7115		

LENNOX INTERNATIONAL INC

Exchange	Symbol	Price	52Wk Range	Yield	P/E
NYS	LII	$35.97 (3/31/2008)	41.50-30.51	1.56	14.80

*7 Year Price Score 133.17 *NYSE Composite Index=100 *12 Month Price Score 111.85

Interim Earnings (Per Share)

Qtr.	Mar	Jun	Sep	Dec
2003	0.04	0.51	0.46	0.39
2004	(3.28)	0.54	0.30	0.13
2005	0.10	0.64	0.68	0.68
2006	0.28	0.85	0.49	0.64
2007	0.12	0.85	0.88	0.59

Interim Dividends (Per Share)

Amt	Decl	Ex	Rec	Pay
0.13Q	4/30/2007	5/14/2007	5/16/2007	6/1/2007
0.13Q	7/23/2007	8/22/2007	8/24/2007	9/11/2007
0.14Q	12/10/2007	12/26/2007	12/28/2007	1/18/2008
0.14Q	3/14/2008	3/26/2008	3/28/2008	4/11/2008
Indicated Div: $0.56				

Valuation Analysis

Institutional Holding	
Forecast P/E	11.52
	(1/10/2007)
Market Cap	$2.2 Billion
Book Value	808.5 Million
Price/Book	2.76
Price/Sales	0.60

No of Institutions
153
Shares
40,046,972
% Held
59.31

Business Summary: Purpose Machinery (MIC: 11.13 SIC: 3585 NAIC: 333415)

Lennox International is a global provider of climate control applications. Co. designs, manufactures and markets a range of products for the heating, ventilation, air conditioning and refrigeration markets. Co.'s products and services, which include furnaces, air conditioners, heat pumps, packaged heating and cooling systems, are sold through multiple distribution channels under brand names such as Lennox®, Armstrong Air™, Ducane™, Bohn®, Larkin™, Advanced Distributor Products®, Service Experts® and others. As of Dec 31 2007, Co. operated through four business segments, namely Residential Heating and Cooling; Commercial Heating and Cooling; Service Experts, and Refrigeration.

Recent Developments: For the year ended Dec 31 2007, net income increased 1.8% to US$169.0 million from US$166.0 million in the prior year. Revenues were US$3.75 billion, up 0.9% from US$3.72 billion the year before. Operating income was US$265.7 million versus US$223.3 million in the prior year, an increase of 19.0%. Direct operating expenses declined 2.1% to US$2.70 billion from US$2.76 billion in the comparable period the year before. Indirect operating expenses increased 6.8% to US$786.9 million from US$736.7 million in the equivalent prior-year period.

Prospects: For 2008, Co. continues to target revenue growth of 2.0% to 5.0% and earnings of $2.73 to $2.88 per share. Meanwhile, Co. plans to close its Lynwood, CA operations and consolidate its U.S. factory-built fireplace manufacturing operations in Union City, TN by the end of the second quarter of 2008, and to close its refrigeration operations in Danville, IL and combine certain of its Danville functions in Tifton, GA and Stone Mountain, GA in the first quarter of 2009. Co. also plans to shift the manufacturing lines for certain of its products to a new facility in Saltillo, Mexico, with initial production expected in the second quarter of 2008, ramping up to full production by early 2010.

Financial Data

(US$ in Thousands)	12/31/2007	12/31/2006	12/31/2005	12/31/2004	12/31/2003	12/31/2002	12/31/2001	12/31/2000
Earnings Per Share	2.43	2.26	2.11	(2.24)	1.40	(3.23)	(0.75)	1.05
Cash Flow Per Share	3.59	2.86	3.56	0.93	0.97	2.93	3.77	4.37
Tang Book Value Per Share	8.79	8.41	8.03	3.91	2.24	0.53	N.M.	0.06
Dividends Per Share	0.530	0.460	0.410	0.385	0.380	0.380	0.380	0.380
Dividend Payout %	21.81	20.35	19.43	...	27.14	...	...	36.19
Income Statement								
Total Revenue	3,749,700	3,671,100	3,366,200	2,982,700	3,085,100	3,025,767	3,119,691	3,247,357
EBITDA	313,800	267,100	287,800	6,800	206,900	183,174	81,283	241,552
Income Before Taxes	258,200	218,400	235,000	(63,000)	129,700	94,680	(44,396)	100,950
Income Taxes	89,200	52,400	83,000	30,500	45,300	35,879	(1,998)	41,892
Net Income	169,000	166,000	150,700	(134,400)	84,400	(190,423)	(42,398)	59,058
Average Shares	69,400	73,500	73,700	60,000	60,400	58,882	56,225	56,277
Balance Sheet								
Current Assets	1,070,700	1,018,400	1,047,200	844,700	845,500	675,055	713,365	901,210
Total Assets	1,814,600	1,719,800	1,737,600	1,518,600	1,726,600	1,521,718	1,793,988	2,055,031
Current Liabilities	684,200	651,100	656,500	584,000	615,300	537,461	554,546	589,920
Long-Term Obligations	166,700	96,800	108,000	268,100	337,300	356,747	465,163	627,550
Total Liabilities	1,006,100	915,400	943,200	1,045,700	1,142,400	1,067,328	1,137,697	1,309,916
Stockholders' Equity	808,500	804,400	794,400	472,900	584,200	452,799	654,640	743,057
Shares Outstanding	62,052	67,155	71,035	63,323	61,203	60,029	57,709	57,035
Statistical Record								
Return on Assets %	9.56	9.60	9.26	N.M.	5.20	N.M.	N.M.	3.15
Return on Equity %	20.96	20.77	23.78	N.M.	16.28	N.M.	N.M.	8.78
EBITDA Margin %	8.37	7.28	8.55	0.23	6.71	6.05	2.61	7.44
Net Margin %	4.51	4.52	4.48	N.M.	2.74	N.M.	N.M.	1.82
Asset Turnover	2.12	2.12	2.07	1.83	1.90	1.83	1.62	1.73
Current Ratio	1.56	1.56	1.60	1.45	1.37	1.26	1.29	1.53
Debt to Equity	0.21	0.12	0.14	0.57	0.58	0.79	0.71	0.84
Price Range	41.50-29.41	34.54-21.44	30.32-18.70	20.49-14.00	17.59-12.05	18.00-9.70	12.06-7.69	14.88-6.88
P/E Ratio	17.08-12.10	15.28-9.49	14.37-8.86	...	12.56-8.61	...	...	14.17-6.55
Average Yield %	1.55	1.41	1.66	1.75	2.24	2.57	3.82	3.70

Address: 2140 Lake Park Blvd., Richardson, TX 75080 Telephone: 972-497-5000 Fax: 972-497-5292	Web Site: www.lennoxinternational.com Officers: John W. Norris Jr. - Chmn. Robert E. Schjerven - C.E.O.	Auditors: KPMG LLP Investor Contact: 972-497-6670 Transfer Agents: Mellon Investor Services, South Hackensack, NJ

456

LEUCADIA NATIONAL CORP.

Exchange	Symbol	Price	52Wk Range	Yield	P/E
NYS	LUK	$45.22 (3/31/2008)	51.62-29.33	0.55	21.53

*7 Year Price Score 161.18 *NYSE Composite Index=100 *12 Month Price Score 116.61

Interim Earnings (Per Share)

Qtr.	Mar	Jun	Sep	Dec
2003	(0.08)	0.09	0.31	0.20
2004	(0.06)	0.16	0.33	0.22
2005	0.01	5.51	0.47	1.13
2006	0.36	0.17	0.27	0.05
2007	0.04	0.12	0.02	1.92

Interim Dividends (Per Share)

Amt	Decl	Ex	Rec	Pay
0.125A	12/7/2005	12/19/2005	12/21/2005	12/30/2005
100%	5/16/2006	6/15/2006	5/30/2006	6/14/2006
0.25A	12/7/2006	12/14/2006	12/18/2006	12/29/2006
0.25A	12/4/2007	12/13/2007	12/17/2007	12/28/2007

Indicated Div: $0.25

Valuation Analysis / **Institutional Holding**

Forecast P/E	N/A	No of Institutions
		266
Market Cap	$10.1 Billion	Shares
Book Value	5.6 Billion	113,068,520
Price/Book	1.81	% Held
Price/Sales	8.71	52.26

Business Summary: Communications (MIC: 10.1 SIC: 4822 NAIC: 517110)

Leucadia National is a diversified holding company engaged in various businesses, including manufacturing, real estate activities, medical product development, winery operations and residual banking and lending activities that are in run-off. Co. also owns equity interests in operating businesses and investment partnerships which are accounted for under the equity method of accounting, including gaming entertainment, land based contract oil and gas drilling, real estate activities and development of a copper mine in Spain. At Dec 31 2007, Co.'s business consists of five key operations: manufacturing; gaming entertainment; domestic real estate; medical product development; and winery.

Recent Developments: For the year ended Dec 31 2007, income from continuing operations increased 270.5% to US$480.8 million from US$129.8 million a year earlier. Net income increased 155.7% to US$484.3 million from US$189.4 million in the prior year. Revenues were US$1.15 billion, up 33.9% from US$862.7 million the year before. Direct operating expenses rose 95.0% to US$753.5 million from US$386.5 million in the comparable period the year before. Indirect operating expenses increased 33.9% to US$458.5 million from US$342.4 million in the equivalent prior year period.

Prospects: Looking ahead, Co. expects its real estate brokerage business to continue to be negatively affected by the depressed real estate market. Also, in its manufacturing operations, Co. estimates its Conwed Plastics, LLC's revenue to be tempered by those markets related to housing, which should offset its performance in the packaging market. Further, Co. expects its housing starts and 2008 revenue for Idaho Timber, LLC to continue to be hurt by the abundance of existing homes available for sale in the market. However, Co. will continue to maximize its gross margins and pre-tax results by focusing on several efforts, including developing new higher margin products and improving costs control.

Financial Data

(US$ in Thousands)	12/31/2007	12/31/2006	12/31/2005	12/31/2004	12/31/2003	12/31/2002	12/31/2001	12/31/2000
Earnings Per Share	2.10	0.85	7.13	0.67	0.52	0.96	(0.05)	0.70
Cash Flow Per Share	(0.08)	0.42	1.49	0.32	(0.13)	0.33	(0.14)	(0.88)
Tang Book Value Per Share	24.67	17.72	16.55	10.49	9.74	8.51	7.20	7.26
Dividends Per Share	0.250	0.250	0.125	0.125	0.083	0.083	0.083	0.083
Dividend Payout %	11.90	29.41	1.75	18.66	15.92	8.68	...	11.96
Income Statement								
Total Revenue	1,154,895	862,672	1,041,147	2,262,111	556,375	241,805	375,298	715,487
EBITDA	(14,645)	157,820	327,659	291,201	27,070	(25,328)	59,040	242,451
Income Before Taxes	(57,088)	133,820	138,163	55,285	(34,029)	(41,525)	53,673	193,302
Income Taxes	(559,771)	41,771	(1,131,082)	(20,192)	(44,201)	(144,865)	(16,640)	72,730
Net Income	484,294	189,399	1,636,041	145,500	97,054	161,623	(7,508)	116,008
Average Shares	234,653	231,884	231,274	214,942	185,103	167,001	165,927	166,587
Balance Sheet								
Current Assets	1,720,133	1,366,209	2,228,615	2,039,949	1,350,363	826,022	993,049	1,370,179
Total Assets	8,126,622	5,303,824	5,260,884	4,800,403	4,397,164	2,541,778	2,577,239	3,143,637
Current Liabilities	459,950	326,653	474,396	659,237	657,328	132,181	223,754	385,056
Long-Term Obligations	2,004,145	974,646	986,718	1,483,504	1,154,878	233,073	343,276	374,523
Total Liabilities	2,535,156	1,391,567	1,583,007	2,523,475	2,245,435	898,744	1,268,522	1,826,284
Stockholders' Equity	5,570,492	3,893,275	3,661,914	2,258,653	2,134,161	1,534,525	1,195,453	1,204,241
Shares Outstanding	222,574	216,351	216,058	215,200	212,470	174,805	165,954	165,890
Statistical Record								
Return on Assets %	7.21	3.59	32.52	3.16	2.80	6.31	N.M.	3.72
Return on Equity %	10.23	5.01	55.27	6.61	5.29	11.84	N.M.	9.95
EBITDA Margin %	N.M.	18.29	31.47	12.87	4.87	N.M.	15.73	33.89
Net Margin %	41.93	21.95	157.14	6.43	17.44	66.84	N.M.	16.21
Asset Turnover	0.17	0.16	0.21	0.49	0.16	0.09	0.13	0.23
Current Ratio	3.74	4.18	4.70	3.12	2.05	6.25	4.44	3.56
Debt to Equity	0.36	0.25	0.27	0.66	0.54	0.15	0.29	0.31
Price Range	51.62-26.61	32.16-23.77	24.41-16.41	23.41-15.23	15.37-10.97	13.31-9.32	11.81-8.79	12.31-7.00
P/E Ratio	24.58-12.67	37.84-27.97	3.42-2.30	34.95-22.74	29.55-21.09	13.86-9.71	...	17.59-10.00
Average Yield %	0.66	0.90	0.63	0.70	0.66	0.73	0.79	1.01

Address: 529 East South Temple, Salt Lake City, UT 84102-1089 **Telephone:** 801-521-1000 **Fax:** 212-598-4869	**Web Site:** www.leucadia.com **Officers:** Ian M. Cumming - Chmn. Joseph S. Steinberg - Pres.	**Auditors:** PricewaterhouseCoopers LLP **Investor Contact:** 212-460-1900 **Transfer Agents:** American Stock Transfer & Trust Company, New York, NY

LEXINGTON REALTY TRUST

Exchange	Symbol	Price	52Wk Range	Yield	P/E	Div Acheiver
NYS	LXP	$14.41 (3/31/2008)	21.65-13.04	9.16	18.71	13 Years

*7 Year Price Score 78.10   *NYSE Composite Index=100   *12 Month Price Score 87.68

Interim Earnings (Per Share)

Qtr.	Mar	Jun	Sep	Dec
2003	0.29	0.06	0.24	0.30
2004	0.24	0.27	0.19	0.09
2005	0.11	0.22	0.08	(0.08)
2006	0.04	0.41	(0.42)	(0.20)
2007	(0.05)	0.34	0.12	0.38

Interim Dividends (Per Share)

Amt	Decl	Ex	Rec	Pay
0.375Q	9/17/2007	9/26/2007	9/28/2007	10/15/2007
0.375Q	12/17/2007	12/27/2007	12/31/2007	1/15/2008
2.10SP	12/24/2007	12/27/2007	12/31/2007	1/15/2008
0.33Q	2/21/2008	3/27/2008	3/31/2008	4/15/2008

Indicated Div: $1.32

Valuation Analysis | **Institutional Holding**

Forecast P/E	N/A	No of Institutions
		180
Market Cap	$879.9 Million	Shares
Book Value	939.1 Million	53,989,052
Price/Book	0.94	% Held
Price/Sales	2.04	76.87

TRADING VOLUME (thousand shares)

Business Summary: Property, Real Estate & Development (MIC: 8.3 SIC: 6798 NAIC: 525930)

Lexington Realty Trust is a self-managed and self-administered real estate investment trust that acquires, owns, and manages a portfolio of net leased office and industrial properties. In addition, Co. acquires and hold investments in loan assets and debt securities related to real estate, which are primarily acquired through a 50.0% owned co-investment program. As of Dec 31 2007, Co. had ownership interests in approximately 280 consolidated real estate assets, located in 42 states and the Netherlands and containing an aggregate of approximately 45.5 million net rentable square feet of space, approximately 95.6% of which is subject to a lease.

Recent Developments: For the year ended Dec 31 2007, loss from continuing operations was US$10.8 million compared with a loss of US$7.9 million a year earlier. Net income increased 891.2% to US$76.9 million from US$7.8 million in the prior year. Revenues were US$431.7 million, up 131.3% from US$186.7 million the year before. Revenues from property income rose 129.6% to US$418.2 million from US$182.1 million in the corresponding earlier year.

Prospects: For the full year of 2008, Co. continues to anticipate Funds From Operations to be in the range of $1.56 to $1.64 per share. Specifically, Co.'s guidance is based on several factors such as the second closing of its specialty property co-investment program with Inland American Real Estate Trust for approximately $335.0 million of properties on or before Mar 31 2008 as well as the dispositions of $156.3 million of properties under contract and continued sale of primarily non-core properties under favorable prices. However, Co.'s outlook excludes any gains or impairments from property dispositions, as well as any one-time, non-recurring charges or credits that may occur during the year.

Financial Data

(US$ in Thousands)	12/31/2007	12/31/2006	12/31/2005	12/31/2004	12/31/2003	12/31/2002	12/31/2001	12/31/2000
Earnings Per Share	0.77	(0.17)	0.33	0.80	0.88	1.09	0.77	1.10
Cash Flow Per Share	4.43	2.07	2.26	1.95	2.11	2.15	2.28	2.41
Tang Book Value Per Share	0.75	6.19	10.27	12.03	12.02	11.09	9.89	8.78
Dividends Per Share	3.600	2.058	1.440	1.400	1.340	1.320	1.270	1.220
Dividend Payout %	467.53	...	436.36	175.00	152.27	121.10	164.94	110.91
Income Statement								
Property Income	418,180	202,836	191,767	146,340	111,658	93,884	78,402	76,824
Non-Property Income	13,567	4,555	5,365	4,885	8,862	6,735	4,460	3,181
Total Revenue	431,747	207,391	197,132	151,225	120,520	100,619	82,862	80,005
Income Before Taxes	(74,392)	(3,476)	13,933	41,860	34,812	...	...	27,967
Income Taxes	3,374	(238)	(150)	1,181	...	...	...	...
Net Income	76,851	7,753	32,695	44,807	33,649	30,595	18,062	21,952
Average Shares	64,910	52,163	49,902	52,048	39,493	32,602	19,862	24,714
Balance Sheet								
Total Assets	5,265,163	4,624,857	2,160,232	1,697,086	1,207,411	902,471	822,153	668,377
Long-Term Obligations	2,312,422	2,123,174	1,139,971	765,144	455,940	460,517	445,771	345,505
Total Liabilities	3,560,229	2,599,672	1,207,550	793,037	564,534	508,840	469,403	400,502
Stockholders' Equity	939,071	1,122,444	891,310	847,290	579,848	332,976	266,713	174,885
Shares Outstanding	61,064	69,051	52,155	48,621	40,682	30,030	24,507	17,151
Statistical Record								
Return on Assets %	1.55	0.23	1.70	3.08	3.19	3.55	2.42	3.30
Return on Equity %	7.46	0.77	3.76	6.26	7.37	10.20	8.18	12.45
Net Margin %	17.80	3.74	16.59	29.63	27.92	30.41	21.80	27.44
Price Range	22.22-14.52	22.78-19.63	25.19-20.37	23.23-17.30	20.85-15.63	16.75-14.25	15.56-11.94	12.25-9.00
P/E Ratio	28.86-18.86	...	76.33-61.73	29.04-21.63	23.69-17.76	15.37-13.07	20.21-15.50	11.14-8.18
Average Yield %	19.60	9.72	6.39	6.70	7.41	8.40	9.13	11.11

Address: One Penn Plaza, Suite 4015,	Web Site: www.lxp.com	Auditors: KPMG LLP
New York, NY 10119-4015	Officers: E. Robert Roskind - Chmn. T. Wilson Eglin	Transfer Agents: Mellon Investor
Telephone: 212-692-7200	- Pres., C.E.O., C.O.O.	Services LLC, Jersey City, NJ

LEXMARK INTERNATIONAL, INC.

Exchange	Symbol	Price	52Wk Range	Yield	P/E
NYS	LXK	$30.72 (3/31/2008)	62.01-28.02	N/A	9.78

*7 Year Price Score 54.10   *NYSE Composite Index=100   *12 Month Price Score 87.08

Interim Earnings (Per Share)

Qtr.	Mar	Jun	Sep	Dec
2003	0.73	0.77	0.79	1.05
2004	0.91	1.02	1.17	1.18
2005	0.96	0.64	0.59	0.71
2006	0.78	0.74	0.85	0.90
2007	0.95	0.67	0.48	1.04

Interim Dividends (Per Share)

No Dividends Paid

Valuation Analysis		Institutional Holding	
Forecast P/E	16.20	No of Institutions	
	(1/10/2007)	339	
Market Cap	$2.9 Billion	Shares	
Book Value	1.3 Billion	107,439,120	
Price/Book	2.28	% Held	
Price/Sales	0.58	N/A	

Business Summary: Office Equipment Supplies (MIC: 11.12 SIC: 3577 NAIC: 334119)

Lexmark International develops, manufactures and supplies printing and imaging devices for offices and homes. Co.'s products include laser printers, inkjet printers, multifunction devices, and associated supplies and services. Co. also sells dot matrix printers for printing single and multi-part forms by business users. Co. is primarily managed along its business and consumer market segments. Co. distributes its products via its distributor and reseller network and retail outlets worldwide. Also, Co. sells its products through several alliances and original equipment manufacturer arrangements such as Dell and International Business Machines Corporation.

Recent Developments: For the year ended Dec 31 2007, net income decreased 11.1% to US$300.8 million from US$338.4 million in the prior year. Revenues were US$4.97 billion, down 2.6% from US$5.11 billion the year before. Operating income was US$321.3 million versus US$442.5 million in the prior year, a decrease of 27.4%. Direct operating expenses declined 1.5% to US$3.41 billion from US$3.46 billion in the comparable period the year before. Indirect operating expenses increased 3.2% to US$1.24 billion from US$1.20 billion in the equivalent prior-year period.

Prospects: For the first quarter of 2008, Co. expects revenue to be down in the mid- to high-single digit percentage range, with earnings in the range of $0.66 to $0.76 per share. Meanwhile, Co. is progressing on its 2007 restructuring plan, which is expected to be largely completed by the end of 2008, and to generate savings of about $40.0 million in 2008, and $60.0 million annually beginning in 2009. Separately, as part of its strategy to increase its focus on higher- usage segments of the inkjet market, on Mar 4 2008, Co. introduced a new line of inkjet printers and all-in-one devices focused toward the home and student user.

Financial Data

(US$ in Thousands)	12/31/2007	12/31/2006	12/31/2005	12/31/2004	12/31/2003	12/31/2002	12/31/2001	12/31/2000
Earnings Per Share	3.14	3.27	2.91	4.28	3.34	2.79	2.05	2.13
Cash Flow Per Share	5.92	6.53	4.76	5.96	5.84	6.35	1.51	3.70
Tang Book Value Per Share	13.50	10.67	12.77	16.32	12.78	8.57	8.25	6.11
Income Statement								
Total Revenue	4,973,900	5,108,100	5,221,500	5,313,800	4,754,700	4,356,400	4,142,800	3,807,000
EBITDA	520,600	638,100	685,700	866,900	742,000	642,800	458,200	500,400
Income Before Taxes	349,500	459,300	553,700	746,500	593,500	495,600	317,800	396,400
Income Taxes	48,700	120,900	197,400	177,800	154,300	128,900	44,200	111,000
Net Income	300,800	338,400	356,300	568,700	439,200	366,700	273,600	285,400
Average Shares	95,800	103,500	122,300	132,900	131,400	131,600	133,800	134,300
Balance Sheet								
Current Assets	2,066,800	1,830,000	2,169,600	3,000,900	2,443,800	1,794,800	1,493,100	1,243,700
Total Assets	3,121,100	2,849,000	3,330,100	4,124,300	3,450,400	2,808,100	2,449,900	2,073,200
Current Liabilities	1,497,300	1,324,000	1,233,700	1,467,700	1,183,300	1,099,000	931,100	979,000
Long-Term Obligations	...	149,800	149,600	149,500	149,300	149,200	149,100	148,900
Total Liabilities	1,842,800	1,813,800	1,901,400	2,041,400	1,807,400	1,726,500	1,374,000	1,296,200
Stockholders' Equity	1,278,300	1,035,200	1,428,700	2,082,900	1,643,000	1,081,600	1,075,900	777,000
Shares Outstanding	94,700	97,000	111,900	127,600	128,600	126,200	130,400	127,086
Statistical Record								
Return on Assets %	10.08	10.95	9.56	14.97	14.04	13.95	12.10	15.08
Return on Equity %	26.00	27.47	20.29	30.44	32.24	33.99	29.53	39.64
EBITDA Margin %	10.47	12.49	13.13	16.31	15.61	14.76	11.06	13.14
Net Margin %	6.05	6.62	6.82	10.70	9.24	8.42	6.60	7.50
Asset Turnover	1.67	1.65	1.40	1.40	1.52	1.66	1.83	2.01
Current Ratio	1.38	1.38	1.76	2.04	2.07	1.64	1.60	1.27
Debt to Equity	...	0.14	0.10	0.07	0.09	0.14	0.14	0.19
Price Range	72.40-32.85	74.13-45.01	86.10-39.69	96.53-76.32	78.64-57.41	67.27-42.47	69.66-41.13	130.75-29.50
P/E Ratio	23.06-10.46	22.67-13.76	29.59-13.64	22.55-17.83	23.54-17.19	24.11-15.22	33.98-20.06	61.38-13.85

Address: One Lexmark Centre Drive, Lexington, KY 40550	Web Site: www.lexmark.com	Auditors: PricewaterhouseCoopers LLP
Telephone: 859-232-2000	Officers: Paul J. Curlander - Chmn., C.E.O. Paul A. Rooke - Exec. V.P.	Investor Contact: 859-232-5568
Fax: 859-232-3120		Transfer Agents: The Bank of New York

LIBERTY PROPERTY TRUST

Exchange	Symbol	Price	52Wk Range	Yield	P/E	Div Acheiver
NYS	LRY	$31.11 (3/31/2008)	50.24-25.85	8.04	17.28	13 Years

*7 Year Price Score 79.38   *NYSE Composite Index=100   *12 Month Price Score 87.21

Interim Earnings (Per Share)

Qtr.	Mar	Jun	Sep	Dec
2003	0.53	0.57	0.49	0.46
2004	0.45	0.44	0.46	0.53
2005	0.52	0.51	0.58	1.21
2006	1.01	0.76	0.52	0.67
2007	0.43	0.57	0.41	0.39

Interim Dividends (Per Share)

Amt	Decl	Ex	Rec	Pay
0.62Q	6/19/2007	6/27/2007	7/1/2007	7/15/2007
0.625Q	9/17/2007	9/27/2007	10/1/2007	10/15/2007
0.625Q	12/18/2007	12/27/2007	1/1/2008	1/15/2008
0.625Q	3/17/2008	3/28/2008	4/1/2008	4/15/2008
		Indicated Div: $2.50		

Valuation Analysis

		Institutional Holding	
Forecast P/E	24.94	No of Institutions	
	(1/10/2007)	255	
Market Cap	$2.8 Billion	Shares	
Book Value	1.8 Billion	86,939,640	
Price/Book	1.55	% Held	
Price/Sales	4.08	95.12	

Business Summary: Property, Real Estate & Development (MIC: 8.3 SIC: 6798 NAIC: 525930)

Liberty Property Trust is a self-administered and self-managed real estate investment trust. Co. provides leasing, property management, development, acquisition and other tenant-related services for its industrial and office properties. Co.'s industrial properties consist of a range of warehouse, distribution, service, assembly, light manufacturing and research and development facilities. Co.'s office properties are multi-story and single-story office buildings located principally in suburban mixed-use developments or office parks. At Dec 31 2007, Co. owned and operated 353 industrial and 296 office properties totaling 62.1 million square feet.

Recent Developments: For the year ended Dec 31 2007, income from continuing operations decreased 11.5% to US$125.9 million from US$142.2 million a year earlier. Net income decreased 38.2% to US$164.8 million from US$266.6 million in the prior year. Revenues were US$698.7 million, up 13.0% from US$618.4 million the year before.

Prospects: For 2008, Co. believes that straight line rents on renewal and replacement leases will on average be 0.0% to 2.0% greater than rents on expiring leases and expects average occupancy for its Properties in Operation to not increase or decrease by more than 1.0% compared with 2007. In addition, Co. expects wholly owned property acquisitions of $100.0 million to $200.0 million and that certain of the acquired properties will be either vacant or underleased. Co. also expects to dispose of $250.0 million to $350.0 million of operating properties. For its joint venture capital activity, Co. expects property acquisitions by existing joint ventures of $200.0 million to $250.0 million.

Financial Data
(US$ in Thousands)

	12/31/2007	12/31/2006	12/31/2005	12/31/2004	12/31/2003	12/31/2002	12/31/2001	12/31/2000
Earnings Per Share	1.80	2.95	2.82	1.88	2.05	2.02	2.15	2.17
Cash Flow Per Share	4.22	3.86	4.14	3.45	3.32	3.93	4.27	3.56
Tang Book Value Per Share	20.52	20.59	19.34	18.63	18.61	17.69	17.68	17.59
Dividends Per Share	2.490	2.470	2.450	2.430	2.410	2.380	2.320	2.180
Dividend Payout %	138.33	83.73	86.88	129.26	117.56	117.82	107.91	100.46
Income Statement								
Property Income	698,747	666,719	680,730	655,355	625,032	597,430	580,308	528,589
Non-Property Income	...	...	...	...	...	8,599	6,857	4,374
Total Revenue	698,747	666,719	680,730	655,355	625,032	606,029	587,165	532,963
Interest Expense	129,301	119,584	129,617	123,352	123,907	116,625	112,006	108,295
Income Before Taxes	147,613	155,336	163,368	168,413	171,051	...	...	...
Income Taxes	(709)	288	14,827	1,820	2,326	...	...	...
Net Income	164,831	266,574	249,351	161,443	163,610	161,665	166,537	159,271
Average Shares	91,803	90,492	88,376	86,024	79,868	76,272	73,580	68,173
Balance Sheet								
Total Assets	5,638,749	4,910,911	4,497,529	4,162,827	3,834,008	3,627,061	3,552,825	3,396,355
Long-Term Obligations	3,021,129	2,387,938	2,249,178	2,133,171	1,885,866	1,866,187	1,753,131	1,703,896
Total Liabilities	3,429,107	2,741,580	2,535,214	2,358,702	2,081,444	2,067,033	1,935,009	1,876,781
Stockholders' Equity	1,837,021	1,871,604	1,709,182	1,596,259	1,544,897	1,351,589	1,423,422	1,320,805
Shares Outstanding	91,567	90,913	88,356	85,675	83,012	76,425	73,661	68,212
Statistical Record								
Return on Assets %	3.12	5.67	5.76	4.03	4.39	4.50	4.79	4.88
Return on Equity %	8.89	14.89	15.09	10.25	11.30	11.65	12.14	12.15
Net Margin %	23.59	39.98	36.63	24.63	26.18	26.68	28.36	29.88
Price Range	53.91-28.16	52.35-41.32	45.80-38.19	45.47-35.05	38.90-29.31	35.17-27.60	31.10-25.75	28.97-22.00
P/E Ratio	29.95-15.64	17.75-14.01	16.24-13.54	24.19-18.64	18.98-14.30	17.41-13.66	14.47-11.98	13.35-10.14
Average Yield %	5.81	5.35	5.87	6.04	7.10	7.60	8.15	8.50

Address: 500 Chesterfield Parkway, Malvern, PA 19355	Web Site: www.libertyproperty.com	Auditors: Ernst & Young LLP
Telephone: 610-648-1700	Officers: William P. Hankowsky - Chmn., Pres., C.E.O., Chief Invest. Officer George J. Alburger Jr. - Exec. V.P., C.F.O.	Investor Contact: 610-648-1704
Fax: 610-644-4129		Transfer Agents: EquiServe Trust Company, N. A.

LILLY (ELI) & CO.

Exchange	Symbol	Price	52Wk Range	Yield	P/E	Div Acheiver
NYS	LLY	$51.59 (3/31/2008)	60.56-47.81	3.64	19.04	40 Years

*7 Year Price Score 71.13 *NYSE Composite Index=100 *12 Month Price Score 98.86

Interim Earnings (Per Share)

Qtr.	Mar	Jun	Sep	Dec
2003	0.38	0.64	0.66	0.69
2004	0.37	0.60	0.69	0.00
2005	0.68	(0.23)	0.73	0.64
2006	0.77	0.76	0.80	0.12
2007	0.47	0.61	0.85	0.78

Interim Dividends (Per Share)

Amt	Decl	Ex	Rec	Pay
0.425Q	4/16/2007	5/11/2007	5/15/2007	6/8/2007
0.425Q	6/21/2007	8/13/2007	8/15/2007	9/10/2007
0.425Q	10/15/2007	11/13/2007	11/15/2007	12/10/2007
0.47Q	12/17/2007	2/13/2008	2/15/2008	3/10/2008

Indicated Div: $1.88 (Div. Reinv. Plan)

Valuation Analysis

	Institutional Holding
Forecast P/E 14.15	No of Institutions
(1/10/2007)	843
Market Cap $68.6 Billion	Shares
Book Value 13.7 Billion	817,914,368
Price/Book 4.28	% Held
Price/Sales 3.14	72.12

Business Summary: Pharmaceuticals (MIC: 9.1 SIC: 2834 NAIC: 325412)

Eli Lilly is engaged primarily in the discovery, development, manufacture, and sale of pharmaceutical products. Co.'s principal products are: Neurosciences products, which includes Zyprexa®, Strattera®, Prozac®, Cymbalta® and Symbyax®; Endocrinology products, including Humalog®, Humalog Mix 75/25®, and Humalog Mix 50/50™, Humulin®, Actos®, Byetta®, Evista®, Humatrope®, and Forteo®; Oncology products, including Gemzar® and Alimta®, Cardiovascular products, including Cialis®, ReoPro® and Xigris®; and other pharmaceutical products, including Vancocin® and Ceclor® . Co. also has an animal health segment.

Recent Developments: For the year ended Dec 31 2007, net income increased 10.9% to US$2.95 billion from US$2.66 billion in the prior year. Revenues were US$18.63 billion, up 18.8% from US$15.69 billion the year before. Direct operating expenses rose 19.8% to US$4.25 billion from US$3.55 billion in the comparable period the year before. Indirect operating expenses increased 18.6% to US$10.63 billion from US$8.96 billion in the equivalent prior-year period.

Prospects: For 2008, Co. expects modest improvement in gross margin as a percent of sales, driven mainly by manufacturing expenses growing more slowly than sales. Total operating expenses are also estimated to grow slower than sales, with growth in the mid-single digits. Marketing, selling and administrative expenses are expected to grow in the low-single digits, driven by investments in prasugrel, Cymbalta, Evista for invasive breast cancer risk reduction, Humalog and Byetta, offset by decreases in other areas. Research and development expenses are expected to grow in the high- single to low-double digits. Lastly, Co.'s 2008 earnings per share are projected to be in the range of $3.80 to $3.95.

Financial Data
(US$ in Thousands)

	12/31/2007	12/31/2006	12/31/2005	12/31/2004	12/31/2003	12/31/2002	12/31/2001	12/31/2000
Earnings Per Share	2.71	2.45	1.81	1.66	2.37	2.50	2.55	2.79
Cash Flow Per Share	4.73	3.66	1.76	2.64	3.39	1.92	3.40	3.44
Tang Book Value Per Share	9.88	9.70	9.55	9.65	8.69	7.37	6.32	5.37
Dividends Per Share	1.700	1.600	1.520	1.420	1.340	1.240	1.120	1.040
Dividend Payout %	62.73	65.31	83.98	85.54	56.54	49.60	43.92	37.28
Income Statement								
Total Revenue	18,633,500	15,691,000	14,645,300	13,857,900	12,582,500	11,077,500	11,542,500	10,862,200
EBITDA	4,937,700	4,219,800	3,443,900	3,539,400	3,810,200	3,950,700	4,007,000	4,294,500
Income Before Taxes	3,876,800	3,418,000	2,717,500	2,941,900	3,261,700	3,457,700	3,552,100	3,858,700
Income Taxes	923,800	755,300	715,900	1,131,800	700,900	749,800	742,700	800,900
Net Income	2,953,000	2,662,700	1,979,600	1,810,100	2,560,800	2,707,900	2,780,000	3,057,800
Average Shares	1,090,750	1,087,190	1,092,150	1,088,936	1,082,230	1,085,088	1,090,793	1,097,725
Balance Sheet								
Current Assets	12,256,900	9,694,400	10,795,800	12,835,800	8,758,700	7,804,100	6,938,900	7,943,000
Total Assets	26,787,800	21,955,400	24,580,800	24,867,000	21,678,100	19,042,000	16,434,100	14,690,800
Current Liabilities	5,268,300	5,085,500	5,716,300	7,593,700	5,550,600	5,063,500	5,203,000	4,960,700
Long-Term Obligations	1,593,500	3,494,400	5,763,500	4,491,900	4,687,800	4,358,200	3,132,100	2,633,700
Total Liabilities	13,123,400	10,974,700	13,788,900	13,947,100	11,913,300	10,768,400	9,330,100	8,643,900
Stockholders' Equity	13,664,400	10,980,700	10,791,900	10,919,900	9,764,800	8,273,600	7,104,000	6,046,900
Shares Outstanding	1,134,313	1,131,668	1,130,137	1,131,942	1,123,725	1,122,443	1,123,348	1,125,560
Statistical Record								
Return on Assets %	12.12	11.44	8.01	7.76	12.58	15.27	17.86	22.16
Return on Equity %	23.96	24.46	18.24	17.45	28.39	35.22	42.28	55.14
EBITDA Margin %	26.50	26.89	23.52	25.54	30.28	35.66	34.72	39.54
Net Margin %	15.85	16.97	13.52	13.06	20.35	24.45	24.08	28.15
Asset Turnover	0.76	0.67	0.59	0.59	0.62	0.62	0.74	0.79
Current Ratio	2.33	1.91	1.89	1.69	1.58	1.54	1.33	1.60
Debt to Equity	0.34	0.32	0.53	0.41	0.48	0.53	0.44	0.44
Price Range	60.56-49.09	58.86-50.41	60.44-49.76	76.26-50.44	73.89-53.70	80.69-48.15	91.50-72.59	108.56-54.50
P/E Ratio	22.35-18.11	24.02-20.58	33.39-27.49	45.94-30.39	31.18-22.66	32.28-19.26	35.88-28.47	38.91-19.53
Average Yield %	3.07	2.90	2.76	2.15	2.11	1.91	1.40	1.32

Address: Lilly Corporate Center, Indianapolis, IN 46285	**Web Site:** www.lilly.com	**Auditors:** Ernst & Young LLP
Telephone: 317-276-2000	**Officers:** Sidney Taurel - Chmn., C.E.O. John C. Lechleiter Ph.D. - Pres., C.O.O.	**Investor Contact:** 317-276-2506
Fax: 317-276-6331		**Transfer Agents:** Norwest Shareowner Services, South St. Paul, MN

LIMITED BRANDS INC.

Exchange	Symbol	Price	52Wk Range	Yield	P/E
NYS	LTD	$17.10 (3/31/2008)	29.30-14.51	3.51	9.05

*7 Year Price Score 87.61   *NYSE Composite Index=100   *12 Month Price Score 81.40

TRADING VOLUME (thousand shares)

Interim Earnings (Per Share)

Qtr.	Apr	Jul	Oct	Jan
2003-04	0.19	0.19	0.25	0.73
2004-05	0.19	0.31	0.16	0.81
2005-06	0.06	0.27	(0.03)	1.36
2006-07	0.25	0.28	0.06	1.09
2007-08	0.13	0.67	0.03	1.04

Interim Dividends (Per Share)

Amt	Decl	Ex	Rec	Pay
0.15Q	5/22/2007	5/29/2007	5/31/2007	6/15/2007
0.15Q	8/10/2007	8/28/2007	8/30/2007	9/14/2007
0.15Q	11/12/2007	11/27/2007	11/29/2007	12/14/2007
0.15Q	2/4/2008	2/26/2008	2/28/2008	3/14/2008

Indicated Div: $0.60

Valuation Analysis / Institutional Holding

Forecast P/E	N/A	No of Institutions
		389
Market Cap	$5.9 Billion	Shares
Book Value	2.2 Billion	314,281,696
Price/Book	2.67	% Held
Price/Sales	0.58	78.64

Business Summary: Retail - Apparel and Accessory Stores (MIC: 5.8 SIC: 5621 NAIC: 448120)

Limited Brands sells women's intimate apparel, apparel, beauty and personal care products and accessories under various trade names through its retail stores and catalogue direct response channels. Co.'s Victoria's Secret segment sells women's intimate as well as other apparel, personal care and beauty products and accessories under the Victoria's Secret and La Senza brand. Co.'s Bath & Body Works segment sells personal care, beauty and home fragrance products marketed under the Bath & Body Works, C.O. Bigelow and White Barn Candle Company brands. As of Feb 2 2008, Co. operated a total of 2,926 retail stores.

Recent Developments: For the year ended Feb 2 2008, net income increased 6.2% to US$718.0 million from US$676.0 million in the prior year. Revenues were US$10.13 billion, down 5.0% from US$10.67 billion the year before. Operating income was US$1.11 billion versus US$1.18 billion in the prior year, a decrease of 5.6%. Direct operating expenses declined 1.0% to US$6.59 billion from US$6.66 billion in the comparable period the year before. Indirect operating expenses decreased 14.3% to US$2.43 billion from US$2.84 billion in the equivalent prior-year period.

Prospects: Looking ahead into fiscal year ending Jan 31 2009, Co. expects its earnings per share to be in the range of $1.35 to $1.55. Further, Co. anticipates spending approximately $575.0 million to $600.0 million for capital expenditures in 2008 with the majority relating to opening new stores and remodeling and improving existing stores. Particularly, Co. expects to open approximately 175 new stores and to close approximately 40 stores. Notably, Co.'s new stores will be mainly Victoria's Secret and Bath & Body Works. Meanwhile, for first fiscal quarter of 2008, Co. is estimating earnings to be in the range of $0.05 to $0.10, compared with $0.13 per share for the first fiscal quarter of 2007.

Financial Data

(US$ in Thousands)	02/02/2008	02/03/2007	01/28/2006	01/29/2005	01/31/2004	02/01/2003	02/02/2002	02/03/2001
Earnings Per Share	1.89	1.68	1.66	1.47	1.36	0.96	1.19	0.96
Cash Flow Per Share	2.05	1.49	2.69	1.99	2.05	1.56	2.27	1.77
Tang Book Value Per Share	N.M.	1.60	1.69	1.31	6.78	5.93	6.04	5.44
Dividends Per Share	0.600	0.600	0.600	1.710	0.400	0.300	0.300	0.300
Dividend Payout %	31.75	35.71	36.14	116.33	29.41	31.25	25.21	31.25
Income Statement								
Total Revenue	10,134,000	10,671,000	9,699,000	9,408,000	8,934,000	8,445,000	9,363,000	10,104,606
EBITDA	1,612,000	1,490,000	1,288,000	1,477,000	1,448,000	1,148,000	1,215,000	1,088,295
Income Before Taxes	1,129,000	1,097,000	957,000	1,116,000	1,166,000	837,000	904,000	758,905
Income Taxes	411,000	422,000	291,000	411,000	449,000	341,000	385,000	331,000
Net Income	718,000	676,000	683,000	705,000	717,000	502,000	519,000	427,905
Average Shares	380,000	403,000	411,000	479,000	526,000	522,000	435,000	443,048
Balance Sheet								
Current Assets	2,919,000	2,771,000	2,784,000	2,684,000	4,433,000	3,606,000	2,682,000	2,067,798
Total Assets	7,437,000	7,093,000	6,346,000	6,089,000	7,873,000	7,246,000	4,719,000	4,088,122
Current Liabilities	1,374,000	1,709,000	1,575,000	1,451,000	1,392,000	1,259,000	1,319,000	1,000,185
Long-Term Obligations	2,905,000	1,665,000	1,669,000	1,646,000	648,000	547,000	250,000	400,000
Total Liabilities	5,218,000	4,138,000	3,875,000	3,754,000	2,607,000	2,386,000	1,975,000	1,771,667
Stockholders' Equity	2,219,000	2,955,000	2,471,000	2,335,000	5,266,000	4,860,000	2,744,000	2,316,455
Shares Outstanding	346,000	398,000	395,000	407,000	518,000	523,000	429,000	425,943
Statistical Record								
Return on Assets %	9.91	9.90	11.02	10.13	9.51	8.41	11.82	10.30
Return on Equity %	27.83	24.51	28.50	18.60	14.20	13.24	20.57	18.86
EBITDA Margin %	15.91	13.96	13.28	15.70	16.21	13.59	12.98	10.77
Net Margin %	7.09	6.33	7.04	7.49	8.03	5.94	5.54	4.23
Asset Turnover	1.40	1.56	1.56	1.35	1.19	1.42	2.13	2.43
Current Ratio	2.12	1.62	1.77	1.85	3.18	2.86	2.03	2.07
Debt to Equity	1.31	0.56	0.68	0.70	0.12	0.11	0.09	0.17
Price Range	29.67-15.05	32.10-22.93	25.12-18.81	27.83-18.56	18.39-11.05	22.25-12.20	19.77-9.42	27.75-14.59
P/E Ratio	15.70-7.96	19.11-13.65	15.13-11.33	18.93-12.63	13.52-8.13	23.18-12.71	16.61-7.92	28.91-15.20
Average Yield %	2.53	2.25	2.70	8.06	2.56	1.77	1.98	1.42

Address: Three Limited Parkway, Columbus, OH 43230	**Web Site:** www.LimitedBrands.com	**Auditors:** Ernst & Young LLP
Telephone: 614-415-7000	**Officers:** Leslie H. Wexner - Chmn., C.E.O. Leonard A. Schlesinger - Vice-Chmn., C.O.O.	**Investor Contact:** 614-479-7000
Fax: 614-479-7440		**Transfer Agents:** The Bank of New York, New York, NY

LINCOLN NATIONAL CORP. (ID)

Exchange	Symbol	Price	52Wk Range	Yield	P/E	Div Acheiver
NYS	LNC	$52.00 (3/31/2008)	74.46-46.59	3.19	11.74	24 Years

*7 Year Price Score 101.62 *NYSE Composite Index=100 *12 Month Price Score 89.49

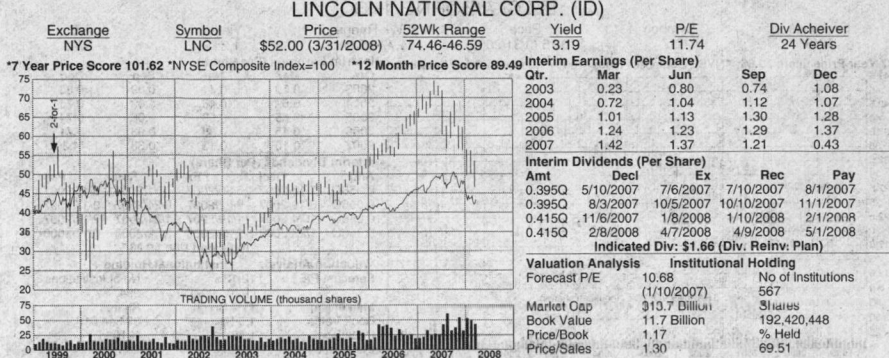

Interim Earnings (Per Share)

Qtr.	Mar	Jun	Sep	Dec
2003	0.23	0.80	0.74	1.08
2004	0.72	1.04	1.12	1.07
2005	1.01	1.13	1.30	1.28
2006	1.24	1.23	1.29	1.37
2007	1.42	1.37	1.21	0.43

Interim Dividends (Per Share)

Amt	Decl	Ex	Rec	Pay
0.395Q	5/10/2007	7/6/2007	7/10/2007	8/1/2007
0.395Q	8/3/2007	10/5/2007	10/10/2007	11/1/2007
0.415Q	11/6/2007	1/8/2008	1/10/2008	2/1/2008
0.415Q	2/8/2008	4/7/2008	4/9/2008	5/1/2008

Indicated Div: $1.66 (Div. Reinv. Plan)

Valuation Analysis   **Institutional Holding**

Forecast P/E   10.68   No of Institutions
(1/10/2007)   567
Market Cap $13.7 Billion   Shares
Book Value   11.7 Billion   192,420,448
Price/Book   1.17   % Held
Price/Sales   1.30   69.51

Business Summary: Insurance (MIC: 8.2 SIC: 6311 NAIC: 524113)

Lincoln National is a holding company, which operates multiple insurance and investment management businesses through subsidiary companies. Co. sells a range of wealth protection, accumulation and retirement income products and services. These products include institutional and/or retail fixed and indexed annuities, variable annuities, universal life insurance, variable universal life insurance, term life insurance, mutual funds and managed accounts. At Dec 31 2007, Co. provided products and services in four operating businesses: Individual Markets, Employer Markets, Investment Management and Lincoln UK.

Recent Developments: For the year ended Dec 31 2007, income from continuing operations increased 2.0% to US$1.32 billion from US$1.30 billion a year earlier. Net income decreased 7.7% to US$1.22 billion from US$1.32 billion in the prior year. Revenues were US$10.59 billion, up 18.2% from US$8.96 billion the year before. Net premiums earned were US$1.95 billion versus US$1.41 billion in the prior year, an increase of 38.3%. Net investment income rose 10.1% to US$4.38 billion from US$3.98 billion a year ago.

Prospects: Looking ahead into 2008, Co. expects the volatility in the capital markets and the low interest rate environment to continue, which should create challenges for its products that generate investment margin profits, such as fixed annuities and universal life insurance. Also, Co. anticipates continued competitive pressures in the life insurance and annuity marketplace and regulatory inspection of the life and annuity industry, which may lead to higher product costs. In response, Co. plans to significantly invest in expanding its distribution in each of its core Individual Markets, Investment Management and Employer Markets businesses while focusing on financial and execution discipline.

Financial Data
(US$ in Thousands)

	12/31/2007	12/31/2006	12/31/2005	12/31/2004	12/31/2003	12/31/2002	12/31/2001	12/31/2000
Earnings Per Share	4.43	5.13	4.72	3.95	2.85	0.49	3.05	3.19
Cash Flow Per Share	7.23	12.08	5.62	6.29	5.89	2.68	6.64	10.35
Tang Book Value Per Share	28.66	27.92	23.89	22.26	18.77	15.62	14.11	11.06
Dividends Per Share	3.000	3.000	3.000	3.000	3.000	3.000	3.000	3.000
Dividend Payout %	67.72	58.48	63.56	75.95	105.26	612.24	98.36	94.04
Income Statement								
Premium Income	1,945,000	1,406,000	308,398	298,904	280,951	315,943	1,704,002	1,813,111
Total Revenue	10,594,000	9,063,000	5,487,938	5,371,274	5,283,881	4,635,462	6,380,638	6,851,507
Benefits & Claims	2,698,000	4,170,000	2,365,620	2,303,652	2,428,523	2,859,505	3,409,740	3,557,160
Income Before Taxes	1,874,000	1,811,000	1,074,644	1,035,658	1,047,563	1,674	764,139	836,291
Income Taxes	553,000	495,000	243,589	304,147	280,408	(89,966)	158,362	214,898
Net Income	1,215,000	1,316,000	831,055	707,009	511,936	91,590	590,211	621,393
Average Shares	273,905	256,169	176,144	179,017	179,441	183,396	193,303	194,920
Balance Sheet								
Total Assets	191,435,000	178,494,000	124,787,566	116,219,265	106,744,868	93,133,422	98,001,304	99,844,059
Total Liabilities	179,717,000	166,293,000	118,403,177	110,043,676	100,933,243	87,837,155	92,737,820	94,889,975
Stockholders' Equity	11,718,000	12,201,000	6,384,389	6,175,589	5,811,625	5,296,267	5,263,484	4,954,084
Shares Outstanding	264,233	275,752	174,820	173,557	178,212	177,307	186,943	190,748
Statistical Record								
Return on Assets %	0.66	0.87	0.69	0.63	0.51	0.10	0.60	0.61
Return on Equity %	10.16	14.16	13.23	11.76	9.22	1.73	11.55	13.45
Loss Ratio %	138.71	296.59	767.07	770.70	864.39	905.07	200.10	196.19
Net Margin %	11.47	14.52	15.14	13.16	9.69	1.98	9.25	9.07
Price Range	74.46-56.16	66.46-52.20	53.89-41.95	49.95-40.17	41.32-25.17	53.50-25.17	52.55-39.10	56.13-23.19
P/E Ratio	16.81-12.68	12.96-10.18	11.42-8.89	12.65-10.17	14.50-8.83	109.18-51.37	17.23-12.82	17.59-7.27
Average Yield %	4.54	5.12	6.26	6.60	8.65	7.34	6.46	7.43

Address: Centre Square, West Tower, 1500 Market Street, 39th Floor, Philadelphia, PA 19102-2112 Telephone: 215-448-1400	Web Site: www.lfg.com Officers: Jon A. Boscia - Chmn., C.E.O. Casey J. Trumble - Sr. V.P.	Auditors: Ernst & Young LLP Investor Contact: 215-448-1422 Transfer Agents: First Chicago Trust Company of New York, Jersey City, NJ

LIZ CLAIBORNE, INC.

Exchange	Symbol	Price	52Wk Range	Yield	P/E
NYS	LIZ	$18.15 (3/31/2008)	44.77-16.04	1.24	N/A

*7 Year Price Score 70.66   *NYSE Composite Index=100   *12 Month Price Score 69.10

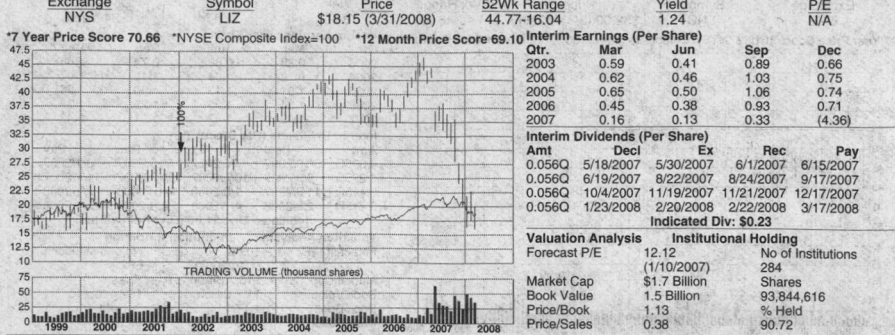

Interim Earnings (Per Share)

Qtr.	Mar	Jun	Sep	Dec
2003	0.59	0.41	0.89	0.66
2004	0.62	0.46	1.03	0.75
2005	0.65	0.50	1.06	0.74
2006	0.45	0.38	0.93	0.71
2007	0.16	0.13	0.33	(4.36)

Interim Dividends (Per Share)

Amt	Decl	Ex	Rec	Pay
0.056Q	5/18/2007	5/30/2007	6/1/2007	6/15/2007
0.056Q	6/19/2007	8/22/2007	8/24/2007	9/17/2007
0.056Q	10/4/2007	11/19/2007	11/21/2007	12/17/2007
0.056Q	1/23/2008	2/20/2008	2/22/2008	3/17/2008

Indicated Div: $0.23

Valuation Analysis / Institutional Holding

Forecast P/E	12.12	No of Institutions
	(1/10/2007)	284
Market Cap	$1.7 Billion	Shares
Book Value	1.5 Billion	93,844,616
Price/Book	1.13	% Held
Price/Sales	0.38	90.72

Business Summary: Apparel (MIC: 4.4 SIC: 2339 NAIC: 315239)

Liz Claiborne is engaged primarily in the design and marketing of a portfolio of branded women's and men's apparel, accessories and fragrance products. As of Dec 29 2007, Co. operated a total of 433 specialty retail stores under its trademarks, comprised of 284 retail stores within the U.S. and 149 retail stores outside of the U.S. (primarily in Western Europe and Canada). As of Dec 29 2007, Co. operated a total of 680 concession stores in Europe. Co. operates in two reportable segments: Direct Brands; and Partnered Brands. Co. also licenses to third parties the right to produce and market products bearing certain Company-owned trademarks.

Recent Developments: For the year ended Dec 29 2007, loss from continuing operations was US$370.0 million compared with income of US$220.9 million a year earlier. Net loss amounted to US$372.8 million versus net income of US$254.7 million in the prior year. Revenues were US$4.58 billion, down 1.4% from US$4.64 billion the year before. Operating loss was US$425.8 million versus an income of US$381.5 million in the prior year. Direct operating expenses rose 1.2% to US$2.41 billion from US$2.38 billion in the comparable period the year before. Indirect operating expenses increased 37.9% to US$2.59 billion from US$1.88 billion in the equivalent prior-year period.

Prospects: On Jan 17 2008, in an effort to improve the sales and earnings engine in its Partnered Brands segment for 2009, Co. announced that it entered into a license agreement with Kohl's, naming Kohl's as the exclusive retailer for its DANA BUCHMAN brand. As a result, Co. expects to close its existing DANA BUCHMAN operations in the first half of 2008 and launch its DANA BUCHMAN line in Kohl's stores no later than the first quarter of 2009. Meanwhile, in order to improve results of its wholesale-based Partnered Brands, Co. recently announced design agreements with Isaac Mizrahi for its Liz Claiborne brand and John Bartlett for its Claiborne men's business, both for 2009.

Financial Data
(US$ in Thousands)

	12/29/2007	12/30/2006	12/31/2005	01/01/2005	01/03/2004	12/28/2002	12/29/2001	12/30/2000
Earnings Per Share	(3.74)	2.46	2.94	2.85	2.55	2.16	1.83	1.72
Cash Flow Per Share	2.75	3.87	4.15	4.24	3.59	4.01	3.17	2.52
Tang Book Value Per Share	5.18	6.86	7.74	7.13	6.73	5.43	5.71	5.45
Dividends Per Share	0.225	0.225	0.225	0.225	0.225	0.225	0.225	0.225
Dividend Payout %	...	9.15	7.65	7.89	8.82	10.42	12.30	13.12
Income Statement								
Total Revenue	4,577,251	4,994,318	4,847,753	4,632,828	4,241,115	3,717,503	3,448,522	3,104,141
EBITDA	(268,094)	581,837	650,584	627,982	573,881	483,965	429,697	387,380
Income Before Taxes	(472,460)	406,536	491,278	480,197	438,391	362,446	300,089	288,430
Income Taxes	(102,440)	151,851	173,912	166,628	158,698	131,281	108,032	103,835
Net Income	(372,798)	254,685	317,366	313,569	279,693	231,165	192,057	184,595
Average Shares	99,800	103,483	107,919	109,886	109,619	107,196	105,051	107,494
Balance Sheet								
Current Assets	1,564,841	1,470,117	1,456,537	1,509,141	1,348,401	1,203,171	1,106,026	910,576
Total Assets	3,268,467	3,495,768	3,152,036	3,029,752	2,606,999	2,296,318	1,951,255	1,512,159
Current Liabilities	770,385	673,922	607,739	637,601	526,642	590,980	447,314	357,904
Long-Term Obligations	836,883	570,469	417,833	484,516	440,303	377,725	387,345	269,219
Total Liabilities	1,749,143	1,362,527	1,146,434	1,204,443	1,019,180	1,002,527	886,973	673,142
Stockholders' Equity	1,515,564	2,129,981	2,002,706	1,811,789	1,577,971	1,286,361	1,056,161	834,285
Shares Outstanding	94,742	103,156	104,985	108,734	109,571	107,035	105,224	102,418
Statistical Record								
Return on Assets %	N.M.	7.68	10.30	11.16	11.22	10.91	11.12	12.66
Return on Equity %	N.M.	12.36	16.69	18.55	19.21	19.79	20.37	21.32
EBITDA Margin %	N.M.	11.65	13.42	13.56	13.53	13.02	12.46	12.48
Net Margin %	N.M.	5.10	6.55	6.77	6.59	6.22	5.57	5.95
Asset Turnover	1.36	1.51	1.57	1.65	1.70	1.76	2.00	2.13
Current Ratio	2.03	2.18	2.40	2.37	2.56	2.04	2.47	2.54
Debt to Equity	0.55	0.27	0.21	0.27	0.28	0.29	0.37	0.32
Price Range	46.64-20.15	44.34-34.06	43.71-34.56	42.21-33.20	38.82-26.31	32.65-24.22	27.14-18.63	23.59-15.63
P/E Ratio	...	18.02-13.85	14.87-11.76	14.81-11.65	15.22-10.32	15.12-11.21	14.83-10.18	13.72-9.08
Average Yield %	0.63	0.58	0.57	0.60	0.68	0.77	0.93	1.12

Address: 1441 Broadway, New York, NY 10018
Telephone: 212-354-4900

Web Site: www.lizclaiborne.com
Officers: Paul R. Charron - Chmn., C.E.O. Trudy F. Sullivan - Exec. V.P.

Auditors: Deloitte & Touche LLP
Transfer Agents: First Chicago Trust Company of New York, Jersey City, NJ

LOCKHEED MARTIN CORP.

Exchange	Symbol	Price	52Wk Range	Yield	P/E
NYS	LMT	$99.30 (3/31/2008)	112.25-91.36	1.69	13.99

*7 Year Price Score 125.70 *NYSE Composite Index=100 *12 Month Price Score 109.81

Interim Earnings (Per Share)

Qtr.	Mar	Jun	Sep	Dec
2003	0.55	0.54	0.48	0.77
2004	0.65	0.66	0.69	0.83
2005	0.83	1.02	0.96	1.29
2006	1.34	1.34	1.46	1.68
2007	1.60	1.82	1.80	1.89

Interim Dividends (Per Share)

Amt	Decl	Ex	Rec	Pay
0.35Q	4/26/2007	5/30/2007	6/1/2007	6/22/2007
0.35Q	6/28/2007	8/30/2007	9/4/2007	9/28/2007
0.42Q	9/27/2007	11/29/2007	12/3/2007	12/28/2007
0.42Q	1/24/2008	2/28/2008	3/3/2008	3/28/2008
		Indicated Div: $1.68		

Valuation Analysis

Forecast P/E	14.20 (1/10/2007)	Institutional Holding	
		No of Institutions	572
Market Cap	$40.6 Billion	Shares	375,958,240
Book Value	9.8 Billion	% Held	88.99
Price/Book	4.14		
Price/Sales	0.97		

TRADING VOLUME (thousand shares)

Business Summary: Defense (MIC: 1.2 SIC: 3761 NAIC: 336414)

Lockheed Martin primarily researches, designs, develops, manufactures, integrates, operates and manages technology systems, products and services. Co. serves customers in domestic and international defense and civil markets, with its key customers being agencies of the U.S. Government. As of Dec 31 2007, Co. operated in four primary business segments: Aeronautics, Electronic Systems, Information Systems & Global Services, and Space Systems. As a systems-integrator Co.'s products and services range from electronics and information systems, including integrated net-centric installations, to missiles, aircraft, and spacecraft.

Recent Developments: For the year ended Dec 31 2007, net income increased 19.9% to US$3.03 billion from US$2.53 billion in the prior year. Revenues were US$41.86 billion, up 5.7% from US$39.62 billion the year before. Operating income was US$4.53 billion versus US$3.77 billion in the prior year, an increase of 20.1%. Direct operating expenses rose 4.0% to US$37.63 billion from US$36.19 billion in the comparable period the year before. Indirect operating income amounted to US$293.0 million compared with an income of US$336.0 million in the equivalent prior-year period.

Prospects: For 2008, Co. has raised its outlook for net sales and segment operating profit mainly due to volume and performance in its Aeronautics segment. Accordingly, Co. is projecting net sales of $41.80 billion to $42.80 billion versus prior guidance of $41.25 billion to $42.75 billion, and segment operating profit of $4.72 billion to $4.84 billion versus prior guidance of $4.66 billion to $4.79 billion. Co. is also raising its diluted earnings per share guidance to $7.05 to $7.25 from prior guidance of $6.95 to $7.15. Meanwhile, on Dec 20 2007, Co. acquired PercepTek, Inc., provider of autonomous software technologies, which should bolster its capabilities in unmanned systems and surveillance.

Financial Data

(US$ in Thousands)	12/31/2007	12/31/2006	12/31/2005	12/31/2004	12/31/2003	12/31/2002	12/31/2001	12/31/2000
Earnings Per Share	7.10	5.80	4.10	2.83	2.34	1.11	(2.42)	(1.29)
Cash Flow Per Share	10.19	8.84	7.25	6.58	4.05	5.14	4.27	5.02
Dividends Per Share	1.470	1.250	1.050	0.910	0.580	0.440	0.440	0.440
Dividend Payout %	20.70	21.55	25.61	32.16	24.79	39.64	...	...
Income Statement								
Total Revenue	41,862,000	39,620,000	37,213,000	35,526,000	31,824,000	26,578,000	23,990,000	25,329,000
EBITDA	5,346,000	4,717,000	3,691,000	2,745,000	2,628,000	1,716,000	1,711,000	2,173,000
Income Before Taxes	4,368,000	3,592,000	2,616,000	1,664,000	1,532,000	577,000	188,000	286,000
Income Taxes	1,335,000	1,063,000	791,000	398,000	479,000	44,000	109,000	710,000
Net Income	3,033,000	2,529,000	1,825,000	1,266,000	1,053,000	500,000	(1,046,000)	(519,000)
Average Shares	427,100	436,400	445,700	447,100	450,000	452,000	431,300	400,800
Balance Sheet								
Current Assets	10,940,000	10,164,000	10,529,000	8,953,000	9,401,000	10,626,000	10,778,000	11,239,000
Total Assets	28,926,000	28,231,000	27,744,000	25,554,000	26,175,000	25,758,000	27,654,000	30,349,000
Current Liabilities	9,871,000	9,553,000	9,428,000	8,566,000	8,893,000	9,821,000	9,689,000	10,175,000
Long-Term Obligations	4,303,000	4,405,000	4,784,000	5,104,000	6,072,000	6,217,000	7,422,000	9,065,000
Total Liabilities	19,121,000	21,347,000	19,877,000	18,533,000	19,419,000	19,893,000	21,211,000	23,189,000
Stockholders' Equity	9,805,000	6,884,000	7,867,000	7,021,000	6,756,000	5,865,000	6,443,000	7,160,000
Shares Outstanding	409,000	421,000	432,000	438,000	446,500	455,709	441,000	431,000
Statistical Record								
Return on Assets %	10.61	9.04	6.85	4.88	4.06	1.87	N.M.	N.M.
Return on Equity %	36.35	34.29	24.52	18.33	16.69	8.12	N.M.	N.M.
EBITDA Margin %	12.77	11.91	9.92	7.73	8.26	6.46	7.13	8.58
Net Margin %	7.25	6.38	4.90	3.56	3.31	1.88	N.M.	N.M.
Asset Turnover	1.46	1.42	1.40	1.37	1.23	1.00	0.83	0.84
Current Ratio	1.11	1.06	1.12	1.05	1.06	1.08	1.11	1.11
Debt to Equity	0.44	0.64	0.61	0.73	0.90	1.06	1.15	1.27
Price Range	112.25-91.36	92.95-63.55	65.40-53.29	61.62-43.82	58.85-41.13	71.43-46.24	49.92-31.73	35.85-16.63
P/E Ratio	15.81-12.87	16.03-10.96	15.95-13.00	21.77-15.48	25.15-17.58	64.35-41.66	...	...
Average Yield %	1.46	1.59	1.71	1.75	1.20	0.75	1.11	1.69

Address: 6801 Rockledge Drive, Bethesda, MD 20817-1877
Telephone: 301-897-6000
Fax: 301-897-6083

Web Site: www.lockheedmartin.com
Officers: Robert J. Stevens - Chmn., Pres., C.E.O.
Christopher E. Kubasik - Exec. V.P., C.F.O.

Auditors: Ernst & Young LLP
Transfer Agents: Computershare Trust Company, N.A., Providence, RI

LOEWS CORP.

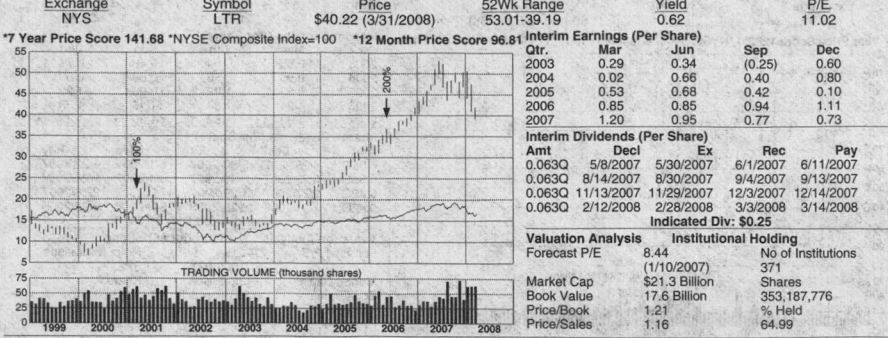

Exchange	Symbol	Price	52Wk Range	Yield	P/E.
NYS	LTR	$40.22 (3/31/2008)	53.01-39.19	0.62	11.02

*7 Year Price Score 141.68 *NYSE Composite Index=100 *12 Month Price Score 96.81

Interim Earnings (Per Share)

Qtr.	Mar	Jun	Sep	Dec
2003	0.29	0.34	(0.25)	0.60
2004	0.02	0.66	0.40	0.80
2005	0.53	0.68	0.42	0.10
2006	0.85	0.85	0.94	1.11
2007	1.20	0.95	0.77	0.73

Interim Dividends (Per Share)

Amt	Decl	Ex	Rec	Pay
0.063Q	5/8/2007	5/30/2007	6/1/2007	6/11/2007
0.063Q	8/14/2007	8/30/2007	9/4/2007	9/13/2007
0.063Q	11/13/2007	11/29/2007	12/3/2007	12/14/2007
0.063Q	2/12/2008	2/28/2008	3/3/2008	3/14/2008

Indicated Div: $0.25

Valuation Analysis

Forecast P/E	8.44
	(1/10/2007)
Market Cap	$21.3 Billion
Book Value	17.6 Billion
Price/Book	1.21
Price/Sales	1.16

Institutional Holding

No of Institutions	371
Shares	353,187,776
% Held	64.99

Business Summary: Insurance (MIC: 8.2 SIC: 6331 NAIC: 524126)

Loews is a holding company. At Dec 31 2007, Co. was engaged in commercial property and casualty insurance via its 89.0% owned CNA Financial Corp. subsidiary; production and sale of cigarettes via its 100.0% owned Lorillard, Inc. subsidiary; operation of offshore oil and gas drilling rigs via its 51.0% owned Diamond Offshore Drilling, Inc. subsidiary; exploration, production and sale of natural gas and natural gas liquids through its 100.0% owned HighMount Exploration & Production LLC subsidiary; operation of natural gas transmission pipeline systems via its 70.0% owned Boardwalk Pipeline Partners, LP subsidiary; and hotel operations via its 100.0% owned Loews Hotels Holding Corp. subsidiary.

Recent Developments: For the year ended Dec 31 2007, income from continuing operations decreased 0.8% to US$2.48 billion from US$2.50 billion a year earlier. Net income was unchanged at US$2.49 billion versus US$2.49 billion the prior year. Revenues were US$18.38 billion, up 3.8% from US$17.70 billion the year before. Net premiums earned were US$7.48 billion versus US$7.60 billion in the prior year, a decrease of 1.6%. Net investment income fell 0.7% to US$2.89 billion from US$2.91 billion a year ago.

Prospects: On Dec 17 2007, Co. announced plans to spin-off its ownership interest in Lorillard, Inc. to holders of its Carolina Group stock and Loews common stock, as a result of which the Carolina Group, and all of the Carolina Group stock, would be eliminated and Lorillard would become a separate publicly traded company. The spin-off should be completed in mid-2008. Separately, in Jan 2008, Co. closed the sale of Bulova Corp. to Citizen Watch Co., Ltd., which should result in a pretax gain of about $105.0 million. Meanwhile, Co. expects competitive market conditions to put ongoing pressure on premium and income levels at both the Standard and Specialty lines of its CNA Financial Corp. subsidiary.

Financial Data
(US$ in Thousands)

	12/31/2007	12/31/2006	12/31/2005	12/31/2004	12/31/2003	12/31/2002	12/31/2001	12/31/2000
Earnings Per Share	3.65	3.75	1.72	1.88	(1.30)	1.37	(1.01)	3.15
Cash Flow Per Share	10.60	3.10	6.04	5.06	5.00	3.18	0.92	(0.78)
Tang Book Value Per Share	30.66	29.77	22.95	21.35	19.31	19.88	16.23	18.27
Dividends Per Share	0.250	0.237	0.200	0.200	0.200	0.200	0.192	0.167
Dividend Payout %	6.85	6.33	11.63	10.64	...	14.60	...	5.30
Income Statement								
Premium Income	7,482,000	7,603,100	7,568,600	8,205,000	9,209,800	10,209,900	9,361,400	11,471,700
Total Revenue	18,380,000	17,911,000	16,017,800	15,242,300	16,461,000	17,495,400	19,417,200	21,337,800
Benefits & Claims	6,009,000	6,046,200	6,998,700	6,445,600	9,915,600	8,392,000	11,382,800	9,831,100
Income Before Taxes	4,575,000	4,472,100	1,846,500	1,822,000	(1,378,400)	1,647,100	(813,100)	3,205,900
Income Taxes	1,481,000	1,450,700	490,400	533,800	(534,100)	582,200	(175,400)	1,106,900
Net Income	2,489,000	2,491,300	1,211,600	1,231,300	(610,700)	912,000	(589,100)	1,876,700
Average Shares	536,000	553,540	557,970	556,500	556,350	562,770	585,984	596,198
Balance Sheet								
Total Assets	76,079,000	76,880,900	70,675,600	73,749,500	77,880,900	70,519,600	75,251,100	70,877,100
Total Liabilities	54,590,000	57,482,800	55,524,600	59,883,800	65,155,000	57,389,100	63,628,400	57,478,100
Stockholders' Equity	17,591,000	16,501,800	13,092,100	12,183,300	11,054,300	11,235,200	9,649,300	11,191,100
Shares Outstanding	529,683	544,203	557,540	556,753	556,341	556,323	574,479	591,684
Statistical Record								
Return on Assets %	3.25	3.38	1.68	1.62	N.M.	1.25	N.M.	2.67
Return on Equity %	14.60	16.84	9.59	10.57	N.M.	8.73	N.M.	17.68
Loss Ratio %	80.31	79.52	92.47	78.56	107.66	82.19	121.59	85.70
Net Margin %	13.54	13.91	7.56	8.08	(3.71)	5.21	(3.03)	8.80
Price Range	53.01-40.37	41.92-30.75	32.60-22.46	23.59-16.43	16.48-12.81	20.60-12.63	23.87-13.92	17.46-6.67
P/E Ratio	14.52-11.06	11.18-8.20	18.95-13.06	12.55-8.74	...	15.04-9.22	...	5.54-2.12
Average Yield %	0.53	0.66	0.74	1.01	1.37	1.16	1.03	1.46

Address: 667 Madison Avenue, New York, NY 10021-8087 **Telephone:** 212-521-2000 **Fax:** 212-521-2498	**Web Site:** www.loews.com **Officers:** Preston R. Tisch - Chmn. James S. Tisch - Pres., C.E.O.	**Auditors:** DELOITTE & TOUCHE LLP **Transfer Agents:** Mellon Investor Services LLC, Ridgefield Park, NJ

466

LONGS DRUG STORES CORP.

Exchange	Symbol	Price	52Wk Range	Yield	P/E
NYS	LDG	$42.46 (3/31/2008)	58.37-39.06	1.32	16.85

*7 Year Price Score 123.92 *NYSE Composite Index=100   *12 Month Price Score 97.52

Interim Earnings (Per Share)

Qtr.	Apr	Jul	Oct	Jan
2003-04	0.16	0.14	0.14	0.35
2004-05	0.25	0.09	0.17	0.47
2005-06	0.34	0.44	0.23	0.92
2006-07	0.41	0.50	0.33	0.71
2007-08	0.34	0.69	0.51	0.98

Interim Dividends (Per Share)

Amt	Decl	Ex	Rec	Pay
0.14Q	5/22/2007	5/24/2007	5/29/2007	7/10/2007
0.14Q	8/21/2007	8/24/2007	8/28/2007	10/10/2007
0.14Q	11/13/2007	11/23/2007	11/27/2007	1/10/2008
0.14Q	3/4/2000	3/7/2008	3/11/2008	4/14/2008

Indicated Div: $0.56

Valuation Analysis

		Institutional Holding	
Forecast P/E	N/A	No of Institutions	167
Market Cap	$1.5 Billion	Shares	29,242,622
Book Value	827.9 Million		
Price/Book	1.86	% Held	78.05
Price/Sales	0.29		

Business Summary: Retail - Miscellaneous (MIC: 5.11 SIC: 5912 NAIC: 446110)

Longs Drug Stores, through its wholly owned subsidiary, Longs Drug Stores California, Inc., operates retail drug stores on the West Coast of the U.S. and in Hawaii, primarily under the names Longs, Longs Drugs, Longs Drug Stores and Longs Pharmacy. In addition to prescription drugs, Co.'s core front-end merchandise categories include over-the-counter medications, health and beauty products, cosmetics, photo and photo processing, convenience food and beverage items and greeting cards. In addition, Co. sells merchandise in non core categories such as housewares, automotive and sporting goods. Co. also operates a mail order pharmacy business.

Recent Developments: For the year ended Jan 31 2008, income from continuing operations increased 24.5% to US$98.9 million from US$79.5 million a year earlier. Net income increased 29.2% to US$96.2 million from US$74.5 million in the prior year. Revenues were US$5.26 billion, up 5.8% from US$4.97 billion the year before. Operating income was US$164.6 million versus US$131.6 million in the prior year, an increase of 25.0%. Direct operating expenses rose 3.7% to US$3.61 billion from US$3.48 billion in the comparable period the year before. Indirect operating expenses increased 9.3% to US$1.48 billion from US$1.36 billion in the equivalent prior-year period.

Prospects: Co.'s near-term outlook appears to be constructive. For the fiscal year ending Jan 29 2009, Co. is projecting total revenues from continuing operations to increase by 5.0% to 7.0%, while total retail drug store sales are anticipated to grow by 1.0% to 3.0%, compared with its prior fiscal year's level. In addition, Co. estimates that same-store sales on a comparable basis will accelerate by 1.0% to 3.0%, compared with its previous fiscal year's level. Given these revenue expectations, Co. is forecasting income from continuing operations to be in the range of $3.02 to $3.12 per diluted share. Similarly, Co. plans to open or relocate approximately 20 to 30 stores and remodel up to 40 stores.

Financial Data

(US$ in Thousands)	01/31/2008	01/25/2007	01/26/2006	01/27/2005	01/29/2004	01/30/2003	01/31/2002	01/25/2001
Earnings Per Share	2.52	1.95	1.93	0.97	0.79	0.18	1.25	1.19
Cash Flow Per Share	5.76	4.93	5.46	4.88	3.29	1.14	5.31	5.13
Tang Book Value Per Share	19.65	19.15	18.26	17.07	16.66	16.34	15.75	14.70
Dividends Per Share	0.560	0.560	0.560	0.560	0.560	0.560	0.560	0.560
Dividend Payout %	22.22	28.72	29.02	57.73	70.89	311.11	44.80	47.06
Income Statement								
Total Revenue	5,262,565	5,097,052	4,670,303	4,607,873	4,526,524	4,426,273	4,304,734	4,027,132
EBITDA	261,181	211,848	210,230	155,751	142,996	135,415	167,474	159,844
Income Before Taxes	156,800	116,439	118,301	57,138	46,022	44,644	75,265	74,284
Income Taxes	57,909	41,978	44,417	20,578	16,258	13,317	28,097	29,400
Net Income	96,201	74,461	73,884	36,560	29,764	6,702	47,168	44,884
Average Shares	38,232	38,181	39,290	37,591	37,151	30,223	37,731	37,843
Balance Sheet								
Current Assets	963,189	883,789	783,367	700,579	736,515	662,661	604,414	608,141
Total Assets	1,846,716	1,687,668	1,504,144	1,411,163	1,442,112	1,352,071	1,411,591	1,353,667
Current Liabilities	730,075	650,561	592,453	465,040	562,938	420,098	447,754	448,694
Long-Term Obligations	193,316	128,211	70,078	156,046	114,558	181,429	198,774	198,060
Total Liabilities	1,018,791	872,111	736,266	684,026	728,191	635,601	690,018	669,872
Stockholders' Equity	827,925	815,557	767,878	727,137	713,921	716,470	721,573	683,795
Shares Outstanding	36,204	37,406	37,216	37,418	37,544	38,501	37,977	37,367
Statistical Record								
Return on Assets %	5.36	4.68	5.08	2.57	2.14	0.49	3.36	3.43
Return on Equity %	11.52	9.43	9.91	5.09	4.17	0.93	6.60	6.49
EBITDA Margin %	4.96	4.16	4.50	3.38	3.16	3.06	3.89	3.97
Net Margin %	1.83	1.46	1.58	0.79	0.66	0.15	1.10	1.11
Asset Turnover	2.93	3.20	3.21	3.24	3.25	3.21	3.06	3.08
Current Ratio	1.32	1.36	1.32	1.51	1.31	1.58	1.53	1.36
Debt to Equity	0.23	0.16	0.09	0.21	0.16	0.25	0.28	0.29
Price Range	58.37-41.62	48.36-34.29	45.97-25.88	27.80-17.75	25.10-13.44	32.09-19.66	31.81-20.40	24.88-16.56
P/E Ratio	23.16-16.52	24.80-17.58	23.82-13.41	28.66-18.30	31.77-17.01	178.28-109.22	25.45-16.32	20.90-13.92
Average Yield %	1.10	1.28	1.44	2.42	2.89	2.25	2.24	2.70

Address: 141 North Civic Drive, Walnut Creek, CA 94596
Telephone: 925-937-1170
Fax: 925-210-6886

Web Site: www.longs.com
Officers: Warren F. Bryant - Chmn., Pres., C.E.O. Steven F. McCann - Exec. V.P., C.F.O., Treas.

Auditors: Deloitte & Touche LLP
Investor Contact: 925-979-3979
Transfer Agents: Mellon Investor Services LLC

LOUISIANA-PACIFIC CORP.

Exchange	Symbol	Price	52Wk Range	Yield	P/E
NYS	LPX	$9.18 (3/31/2008)	21.05-8.53	6.54	N/A

*7 Year Price Score 75.69   *NYSE Composite Index=100   *12 Month Price Score 73.54

Interim Earnings (Per Share)

Qtr.	Mar	Jun	Sep	Dec
2003	0.01	(0.16)	1.17	1.53
2004	0.98	1.75	0.98	0.12
2005	0.91	0.90	1.53	0.81
2006	0.79	0.52	0.09	(0.23)
2007	(0.36)	(0.22)	(0.65)	(0.50)

Interim Dividends (Per Share)

Amt	Decl	Ex	Rec	Pay
0.15Q	5/7/2007	5/15/2007	5/17/2007	6/1/2007
0.15Q	8/6/2007	8/15/2007	8/17/2007	8/31/2007
0.15Q	11/5/2007	11/14/2007	11/16/2007	11/30/2007
0.15Q	2/4/2008	2/13/2008	2/15/2008	3/3/2008

Indicated Div: $0.60

Valuation Analysis		Institutional Holding	
Forecast P/E	0.00	No of Institutions	
	(1/10/2007)	224	
Market Cap	$946.3 Million	Shares	
Book Value	1.8 Billion	97,349,200	
Price/Book	0.52	% Held	
Price/Sales	0.56	93.30	

Business Summary: Wood Products (MIC: 11.9 SIC: 2493 NAIC: 321219)

Louisiana-Pacific is engaged in the manufacturing and distribution of building products for home construction, repair and remodeling, and manufactured housing. As of Dec 31 2007, Co. operated 24 facilities in the U.S. and Canada as well as one facility in Chile. Co. operates in three segments: Oriented Strand Board (OSB), which manufactures and distributes OSB structural panel products.; Siding, which provides SmartSide® siding products and related accessories as well as hardboard siding and accessories; and Engineered Wood Products, which manufactures and distributes I-joists and laminated veneer lumber and other related products.

Recent Developments: For the year ended Dec 31 2007, loss from continuing operations was US$155.3 million compared with income of US$133.9 million a year earlier. Net loss amounted to US$179.9 million versus net income of US$123.7 million in the prior year. Revenues were US$1.70 billion, down 22.1% from US$2.19 billion the year before. Operating loss was US$266.4 million versus an income of US$124.0 million in the prior year. Direct operating expenses declined 6.2% to US$1.67 billion from US$1.78 billion in the comparable period the year before. Indirect operating expenses increased 6.6% to US$303.7 million from US$284.8 million in the equivalent prior-year period.

Prospects: Looking ahead, Co. will continue to enhance its position in the oriented strand board (OSB) business through several initiatives, including expanding its capacity to meet growing OSB demand through internal growth in existing facilities and selected acquisitions. For example, on Dec 20 2007, Co. announced that it has signed a Memorandum of Understanding with Masisa S.A. Chile to acquire a 75.0% ownership interest in the OSB manufacturing assets in Brazil. Co. believes that the venture should allow it to accelerate its progress toward its goal of growing its global business. Also, Co. noted that it is opening a second OSB and siding mill in Lautaro, Chile, in the first quarter of 2008.

Financial Data

(US$ in Thousands)	12/31/2007	12/31/2006	12/31/2005	12/31/2004	12/31/2003	12/31/2002	12/31/2001	12/31/2000
Earnings Per Share	(1.73)	1.17	4.15	3.84	2.56	(0.59)	(1.64)	(0.13)
Cash Flow Per Share	(0.09)	1.75	4.72	5.54	4.83	0.85	1.42	0.79
Tang Book Value Per Share	15.00	17.18	16.66	13.48	8.60	5.78	7.48	9.28
Dividends Per Share	0.600	0.600	0.475	0.300	...	...	0.240	0.560
Dividend Payout %	...	51.28	11.45	7.81	...	...	...	...
Income Statement								
Total Revenue	1,704,900	2,235,100	2,598,900	2,849,400	2,300,200	1,942,700	2,359,700	2,932,800
EBITDA	(235,300)	203,400	519,700	719,100	569,800	174,000	(59,100)	209,300
Income Before Taxes	(270,600)	154,000	536,400	699,400	515,200	(20,900)	(289,100)	(18,200)
Income Taxes	(133,400)	24,200	61,300	279,700	233,100	4,300	(112,400)	(11,500)
Net Income	(179,900)	123,700	455,500	420,700	272,500	(62,000)	(171,600)	(13,800)
Average Shares	103,700	105,500	109,700	109,600	106,500	104,600	104,400	104,100
Balance Sheet								
Current Assets	1,075,900	1,504,000	1,797,200	1,604,100	1,325,200	491,300	493,100	654,100
Total Assets	3,229,300	3,436,400	3,598,000	3,450,600	3,204,400	2,773,100	3,016,800	3,374,700
Current Liabilities	488,600	264,900	346,100	440,000	289,600	273,300	309,500	378,200
Long-Term Obligations	485,800	644,600	734,800	622,500	1,020,500	1,070,100	1,152,000	1,183,800
Total Liabilities	1,409,800	1,369,000	1,555,100	1,682,800	1,880,500	1,767,100	1,935,900	2,079,500
Stockholders' Equity	1,819,500	2,067,400	2,042,900	1,767,800	1,310,900	1,006,000	1,080,900	1,295,200
Shares Outstanding	103,081	104,229	105,780	110,141	106,462	104,584	104,578	104,360
Statistical Record								
Return on Assets %	N.M.	3.52	12.92	12.61	9.12	N.M.	N.M.	N.M.
Return on Equity %	N.M.	6.02	23.91	27.26	23.52	N.M.	N.M.	N.M.
EBITDA Margin %	N.M.	9.10	20.00	25.24	24.77	8.96	N.M.	7.14
Net Margin %	N.M.	5.53	17.53	14.76	11.85	N.M.	N.M.	N.M.
Asset Turnover	0.51	0.64	0.74	0.85	0.77	0.67	0.74	0.85
Current Ratio	2.20	5.68	5.19	3.65	4.58	1.80	1.59	1.73
Debt to Equity	0.27	0.31	0.36	0.35	0.78	1.06	1.07	0.91
Price Range	23.33-13.51	29.45-18.26	28.55-22.86	27.99-17.88	19.10-7.30	12.48-5.40	13.84-5.80	15.38-7.06
P/E Ratio	...	25.17-15.61	6.88-5.51	7.29-4.66	7.46-2.85	...	...	...
Average Yield %	3.18	2.59	1.86	1.25	...	...	2.41	5.08

Address: 414 Union Street, Suite 2000, Nashville, TN 37219 **Telephone:** 615-986-5600 **Fax:** 615-986-5666	**Web Site:** www.lpcorp.com **Officers:** E. Gary Cook - Chmn. Richard W. Frost - Exec., V.P., Commodity Prods, Procurement & Engrg.	**Auditors:** Deloitte & Touche LLP **Transfer Agents:** Computershare Trust Company, N.A., Providence, RI

LOWE'S COMPANIES INC

Exchange	Symbol	Price	52Wk Range	Yield	P/E	Div Acheiver
NYS	LOW	$22.94 (3/31/2008)	32.99-20.31	1.39	12.33	46 Years

*7 Year Price Score 84.55   *NYSE Composite Index=100   *12 Month Price Score 91.94

TRADING VOLUME (thousand shares)

Interim Earnings (Per Share)

Qtr.	Apr	Jul	Oct	Jan
2003-04	0.27	0.38	0.28	0.25
2004-05	0.28	0.45	0.33	0.30
2005-06	0.37	0.53	0.41	0.44
2006-07	0.53	0.60	0.46	0.40
2007-08	0.48	0.67	0.43	0.28

Interim Dividends (Per Share)

Amt	Decl	Ex	Rec	Pay
0.08Q	5/25/2007	7/18/2007	7/20/2007	8/3/2007
0.08Q	8/20/2007	10/17/2007	10/19/2007	11/2/2007
0.08Q	11/19/2007	1/16/2008	1/18/2008	2/1/2008
0.08Q	3/24/2008	4/16/2008	4/18/2008	5/2/2008

Indicated Div: $0.32 (Div. Reinv. Plan)

Valuation Analysis

		Institutional Holding	
Forecast P/E	11.16	No of Institutions	
	(1/10/2007)	824	
Market Cap	$33.4 Billion	Shares	
Book Value	16.1 Billion	1,217,199,872	
Price/Book	2.08	% Held	
Price/Sales	0.69	80.59	

Business Summary: Retail - Furniture & Home Furnishings (MIC: 5.9 SIC: 5211 NAIC: 444110)

Lowe's Companies is engaged in retailing home improvement products, with focus on retail do-it-yourself (DIY) customers, do-it-for-me (DIFM) customers who utilize its installation services, and Commercial Business Customers. Co. provides a range of products and services for home decorating, maintenance, repair, remodeling, and property maintenance. In additions, Co. also carries certain brands for categories like lighting, flooring, home style and organization, tools and others. These band names are Premier™, Kobalt®, Portfolio®, Harbor Breeze®, Reliabilt®, Perfect Flame™, Top-Choice® Lumber and Utilitech™. As of Feb 1 2008, Co. operated 1,534 stores throughout the U.S. and Canada.

Recent Developments: For the year ended Feb 1 2008, net income decreased 9.5% to US$2.81 billion from US$3.11 billion in the prior year. Revenues were US$48.28 billion, up 2.9% from US$46.93 billion the year before. Direct operating expenses rose 2.7% to US$31.56 billion from US$30.73 billion in the comparable period the year before. Indirect operating expenses increased 9.1% to US$12.22 billion from US$11.20 billion in the equivalent prior-year period.

Prospects: For the fiscal year ending Jan 30 2008, Co. intends to open about 120 stores, reflecting total annual square footage growth of about 8.0%. In addition, Co. foresees total sales to increase about 3.0% but anticipates total comparable store sales to decline 5.0% to 6.0%, with store opening costs expected to be about $109.0 million. Hence, Co. is projecting earnings to be in the range of $1.50 to $1.58 per diluted share. For the fiscal quarter ended May 2 2008, Co. is targeting total sales growth of 2.0% but foresees comparable store sales to decline 5.0% to 7.0%. Thus, Co. is forecasting earnings of $0.38 to $0.42 per diluted share. Also, Co. plans to open approximately 21 new stores.

Financial Data

(US$ in Thousands)	02/01/2008	02/02/2007	02/03/2006	01/28/2005	01/30/2004	01/31/2003	02/01/2002	02/02/2001
Earnings Per Share	1.86	1.99	1.73	1.36	1.17	0.93	0.65	0.53
Cash Flow Per Share	2.94	2.94	2.43	1.96	1.94	1.74	1.05	0.73
Tang Book Value Per Share	11.04	10.31	9.14	7.45	6.55	5.31	4.30	3.58
Dividends Per Share	0.290	0.180	0.110	0.075	0.055	0.043	0.039	0.035
Dividend Payout %	15.59	9.05	6.36	5.55	4.70	4.59	5.96	6.64
Income Statement								
Total Revenue	48,283,000	46,927,000	43,243,000	36,464,000	30,838,000	26,491,000	22,111,108	18,778,559
EBITDA	5,975,000	6,235,000	5,557,000	4,456,000	3,779,000	3,004,000	2,158,353	1,690,951
Income Before Taxes	4,511,000	4,998,000	4,506,000	3,536,000	2,998,000	2,359,000	1,624,251	1,281,440
Income Taxes	1,702,000	1,893,000	1,735,000	1,360,000	1,136,000	888,000	600,989	471,569
Net Income	2,809,000	3,105,000	2,771,000	2,176,000	1,877,000	1,471,000	1,023,262	809,871
Average Shares	1,510,000	1,566,000	1,606,000	1,616,000	1,612,000	1,600,000	1,589,194	1,537,900
Balance Sheet								
Current Assets	8,686,000	8,314,000	7,831,000	6,974,000	6,687,000	5,568,000	4,920,392	4,175,013
Total Assets	30,869,000	27,767,000	24,682,000	21,209,000	19,042,000	16,109,000	13,736,219	11,375,754
Current Liabilities	7,751,000	6,539,000	5,832,000	5,719,000	4,368,000	3,578,000	3,016,830	2,928,585
Long-Term Obligations	5,576,000	4,325,000	3,499,000	3,060,000	3,678,000	3,736,000	3,734,011	2,697,669
Total Liabilities	14,771,000	12,042,000	10,343,000	9,674,000	8,733,000	7,807,000	7,061,777	5,880,869
Stockholders' Equity	16,098,000	15,725,000	14,339,000	11,535,000	10,309,000	8,302,000	6,674,442	5,494,885
Shares Outstanding	1,458,000	1,524,500	1,568,200	1,547,600	1,574,600	1,563,800	1,551,428	1,532,968
Statistical Record								
Return on Assets %	9.61	11.87	11.88	10.84	10.71	9.88	8.17	7.82
Return on Equity %	17.70	20.71	21.07	19.98	20.23	19.70	16.86	15.64
EBITDA Margin %	12.37	13.29	12.85	12.22	12.25	11.34	9.76	9.00
Net Margin %	5.82	6.62	6.41	5.97	6.09	5.55	4.63	4.31
Asset Turnover	1.65	1.79	1.85	1.82	1.76	1.78	1.77	1.81
Current Ratio	1.12	1.27	1.34	1.22	1.53	1.56	1.63	1.43
Debt to Equity	0.35	0.28	0.24	0.27	0.36	0.45	0.56	0.49
Price Range	34.93-20.31	34.65-26.37	34.70-25.75	30.13-23.25	30.02-17.00	24.05-16.75	23.75-12.50	15.88-9.36
P/E Ratio	18.78-10.92	17.41-13.25	20.06-14.88	22.15-17.09	25.66-14.53	25.86-18.01	36.54-19.23	29.95-17.66
Average Yield %	1.01	0.59	0.36	0.28	0.23	0.20	0.22	0.30

Address: 1000 Lowe's Boulevard, Mooresville, NC 28117 Telephone: 704-758-1000	Web Site: www.lowes.com Officers: Robert A. Niblock - Chmn., Pres., C.E.O. Larry D. Stone - Sr. Exec. V.P., Oper., Merchandising/Mkt.	Auditors: Deloitte & Touche LLP Investor Contact: 704-758-2033 Transfer Agents: EquiServe Trust Company, NA, Canton, MA

LSI CORP

Exchange	Symbol	Price	52Wk Range	Yield	P/E
NYS	LSI	$4.95 (3/31/2008)	10.23-3.88	N/A	N/A

*7 Year Price Score 58.20   *NYSE Composite Index=100   ***12 Month Price Score 82.40**

Interim Earnings (Per Share)

Qtr.	Mar	Jun	Sep	Dec
2003	(0.33)	(0.43)	(0.08)	0.02
2004	0.02	0.02	(0.73)	(0.52)
2005	0.01	0.06	(0.19)	0.10
2006	0.03	0.13	0.11	0.15
2007	0.07	(0.50)	(0.20)	(3.09)

Interim Dividends (Per Share)

No Dividends Paid

Valuation Analysis   **Institutional Holding**

Forecast P/E	17.32	No of Institutions
	(1/10/2007)	317
Market Cap	$3.4 Billion	Shares
Book Value	2.5 Billion	352,277,120
Price/Book	1.36	% Held
Price/Sales	1.29	45.74

Business Summary: IT & Technology (MIC: 10.2 SIC: 3674 NAIC: 334413)

LSI designs, develops, manufactures and markets semiconductors and storage systems. As of Dec 31 2007, Co. operated in two segments: Semiconductor, which designs, develops and markets integrated circuits for storage and networking applications, including custom products for a specific application defined by the customer and standard products for market applications that are sold to multiple customers; and Storage Systems, which designs, manufactures and sells enterprise storage systems, including open storage area network systems and storage products. Co. markets its products primarily to original equipment manufacturers that sell products to its target end customers.

Recent Developments: For the year ended Dec 31 2007, net loss amounted to US$2.49 billion versus net income of US$169.6 million in the prior year. Revenues were US$2.60 billion, up 31.4% from US$1.98 billion the year before. Operating loss was US$2.49 billion versus an income of US$158.3 million in the prior year. Direct operating expenses rose 46.7% to US$1.70 billion from US$1.16 billion in the comparable period the year before. Indirect operating expenses increased 410.6% to US$3.40 billion from US$664.9 million in the equivalent prior-year period.

Prospects: Co. is seeing an increase in revenue primarily due to the acquisition of Agere Systems Inc. in Apr 2007. Specifically, Co.'s Semiconductor segment benefited from the Agere acquisition while its Storage segment benefited from increased sales due to higher than expected seasonal demand. Meanwhile, Co. noted that with new design wins across its storage and networking areas, it is confident that it is well positioned for growth as these designs ramp to production in the future. For the first quarter of 2008, Co. projects revenue in the range of $620.0 million to $650.0 million with net loss per share in the range of $0.09 to $0.01. In addition, Co. expects gross margin of 36.0% to 40.0%.

Financial Data
(US$ in Thousands)

	12/31/2007	12/31/2006	12/31/2005	12/31/2004	12/31/2003	12/31/2002	12/31/2001	12/31/2000
Earnings Per Share	(3.87)	0.42	(0.01)	(1.21)	(0.82)	(0.79)	(2.84)	0.70
Cash Flow Per Share	0.46	0.62	0.64	0.24	0.50	0.41	0.34	1.81
Tang Book Value Per Share	1.12	2.24	1.66	1.38	2.39	2.80	3.15	5.96
Income Statement								
Total Revenue	2,603,643	1,982,148	1,919,250	1,700,164	1,693,070	1,816,938	1,784,923	2,737,667
EBITDA	(2,165,927)	271,673	197,824	(229,124)	35,066	188,202	(348,588)	866,397
Income Before Taxes	(2,475,489)	185,321	20,923	(439,499)	(284,386)	(290,404)	(1,030,355)	379,750
Income Taxes	11,326	15,682	26,540	24,000	24,000	1,750	(39,198)	142,959
Net Income	(2,486,819)	169,638	(5,623)	(463,531)	(308,547)	(292,440)	(991,955)	236,600
Average Shares	641,823	405,163	390,135	384,070	377,781	370,529	349,280	354,337
Balance Sheet								
Current Assets	2,192,558	1,635,737	1,620,119	1,365,287	1,390,037	1,626,053	1,768,968	2,072,240
Total Assets	4,396,390	2,852,144	2,796,066	2,874,001	3,447,901	4,142,737	4,625,772	4,197,487
Current Liabilities	762,456	526,771	742,769	396,280	391,251	397,811	509,985	626,934
Long-Term Obligations	717,967	350,000	350,000	781,846	865,606	1,241,217	...	...
Total Liabilities	1,911,145	956,171	1,167,879	1,255,696	1,397,953	1,835,876	2,140,020	1,693,608
Stockholders' Equity	2,484,996	1,895,738	1,627,950	1,618,046	2,042,450	2,300,355	2,479,885	2,498,137
Shares Outstanding	680,595	403,680	394,015	387,490	381,491	375,096	368,446	321,523
Statistical Record								
Return on Assets %	N.M.	6.01	N.M.	N.M.	N.M.	N.M.	N.M.	6.37
Return on Equity %	N.M.	9.63	N.M.	N.M.	N.M.	N.M.	N.M.	10.84
EBITDA Margin %	N.M.	13.71	10.31	N.M.	2.07	10.36	N.M.	31.65
Net Margin %	N.M.	8.56	N.M.	N.M.	N.M.	N.M.	N.M.	8.64
Asset Turnover	0.72	0.70	0.68	0.54	0.45	0.41	0.40	0.74
Current Ratio	2.88	3.11	2.18	3.45	3.55	4.09	3.47	3.31
Debt to Equity	0.29	0.18	0.21	0.48	0.42	0.54	...	...
Price Range	10.48-5.26	11.66-7.46	10.48-5.02	11.45-4.03	11.96-3.97	18.58-4.14	24.99-10.80	88.25-16.43
P/E Ratio	...	27.76-17.76	...	...	...	...	...	126.07-23.47

Address: 1621 Barber Lane, Milpitas, CA 95035 **Telephone:** 408-433-8000 **Fax:** 408-433-3220	**Web Site:** www.lsilogic.com **Officers:** Abhi Y. Talwalkar - Pres., C.E.O. Bryon Look - Exec. V.P., C.F.O.	**Auditors:** PricewaterhouseCoopers LLP **Transfer Agents:** Computershare Trust Company, NA, Providence, RI

LUBRIZOL CORP

Exchange	Symbol	Price	52Wk Range	Yield	P/E
NYS	LZ	$55.51 (3/31/2008)	69.53-48.98	2.16	13.71

*7 Year Price Score 122.34 *NYSE Composite Index=100 ***12 Month Price Score 99.99**

TRADING VOLUME (thousand shares)

Interim Earnings (Per Share)

Qtr.	Mar	Jun	Sep	Dec
2003	0.50	0.57	0.47	0.21
2004	0.72	0.08	0.61	0.26
2005	0.71	0.87	0.70	0.46
2006	(0.22)	0.74	0.73	0.27
2007	1.02	1.16	1.02	0.86

Interim Dividends (Per Share)

Amt	Decl	Ex	Rec	Pay
0.30Q	4/23/2007	5/8/2007	5/10/2007	6/8/2007
0.30Q	6/26/2007	8/8/2007	8/10/2007	9/10/2007
0.30Q	9/25/2007	11/7/2007	11/9/2007	12/10/2007
0.30Q	12/11/2007	2/6/2008	2/8/2008	3/10/2008

Indicated Div: $1.20

Valuation Analysis

		Institutional Holding	
Forecast P/E	12.45	No of Institutions	254
	(1/10/2007)		
Market Cap	$3.8 Billion	Shares	55,585,788
Book Value	2.0 Billion	% Held	80.37
Price/Book	1.95		
Price/Sales	0.84		

Business Summary: Chemicals (MIC: 11.1 SIC: 2869 NAIC: 325199)

Lubrizol is a specialty chemical company that produces and supplies technologies in the global transportation, industrial and consumer markets. Co. produces additives, ingredients, resins and compounds that are used in a range of applications, and are sold into markets such as engine oils, specialty driveline lubricants and metalworking fluids, as well as in markets such as personal care and over-the-counter pharmaceutical products and performance coatings and inks. Co's specialty materials products are also used in the construction, sporting goods, medical products, and automotive industries. Co. produces products with brand names such as Anglamol®, Carbopol®, Estane® and TempRite®.

Recent Developments: For the year ended Dec 31 2007, income from continuing operations increased 57.6% to US$283.4 million from US$179.8 million a year earlier. Net income increased 173.6% to US$283.4 million from US$103.6 million in the prior year. Revenues were US$4.50 billion, up 11.3% from US$4.04 billion the year before. Direct operating expenses rose 10.9% to US$3.38 billion from US$3.05 billion in the comparable period the year before. Indirect operating expenses increased 0.6% to US$666.9 million from US$662.8 million in the equivalent prior-year period.

Prospects: For full-year 2008, Co. plans to boost its earnings prospects via new product introductions, geographic expansion, product mix management, cost reduction initiatives and appropriate pricing actions. Thus, Co. expects 2008 earnings to be in the range of $4.15 to $4.40 per diluted share, up 9.0% from 2007. Specifically, Co. anticipates that volume growth in its Lubrizol Additives segment will be in the range of breakeven to 1.0%, as volume growth for its Lubrizol Advanced Materials segment is expected to increase by approximately 5.0%. In addition, Co. expects 2008 selling, technical, administrative and research expenses to be slightly less than 14.0% of revenues, down from 14.2% in 2007.

Financial Data
(US$ in Thousands)

	12/31/2007	12/31/2006	12/31/2005	12/31/2004	12/31/2003	12/31/2002	12/31/2001	12/31/2000
Earnings Per Share	4.05	1.52	2.75	1.67	1.75	2.29	1.83	2.22
Cash Flow Per Share	6.88	4.87	5.33	5.88	3.77	4.75	3.82	4.25
Tang Book Value Per Share	5.84	4.47	0.35	N.M.	13.22	12.78	11.86	11.34
Dividends Per Share	1.160	1.040	1.040	1.040	1.040	1.040	1.040	1.040
Dividend Payout %	28.64	68.42	37.82	62.28	59.43	45.41	56.83	46.85
Income Statement								
Total Revenue	4,499,000	4,040,800	4,042,700	3,159,500	2,052,123	1,983,867	1,844,644	1,775,780
EBITDA	624,200	505,800	551,700	373,600	250,809	292,820	257,035	289,440
Income Before Taxes	399,000	265,100	274,900	146,600	129,071	180,388	139,949	170,348
Income Taxes	115,600	83,300	93,600	53,100	38,297	54,116	45,833	52,339
Net Income	283,400	105,600	189,300	93,500	90,774	118,487	94,116	118,009
Average Shares	70,000	69,300	68,800	56,000	51,884	51,794	51,494	53,220
Balance Sheet								
Current Assets	1,847,300	1,836,300	1,572,300	1,598,000	937,848	909,779	756,724	727,908
Total Assets	4,643,800	4,386,200	4,366,300	4,566,300	1,942,316	1,860,137	1,662,319	1,659,490
Current Liabilities	884,700	632,000	664,900	657,300	299,477	307,741	259,214	282,246
Long-Term Obligations	1,223,900	1,538,000	1,662,900	1,964,100	386,726	384,845	388,111	378,783
Total Liabilities	2,630,100	2,626,100	2,748,100	2,989,200	937,730	937,497	856,550	874,739
Stockholders' Equity	1,951,300	1,707,400	1,567,200	1,523,500	953,305	869,252	773,192	752,281
Shares Outstanding	68,383	69,020	68,043	66,778	51,588	51,457	51,152	51,307
Statistical Record								
Return on Assets %	6.28	2.41	4.24	2.87	4.77	6.73	5.67	7.04
Return on Equity %	15.49	6.45	12.25	7.53	9.96	14.43	12.34	15.26
EBITDA Margin %	13.87	12.52	13.65	11.82	12.22	14.76	13.93	16.30
Net Margin %	6.30	2.61	4.68	2.96	4.42	5.97	5.10	6.65
Asset Turnover	1.00	0.92	0.91	0.97	1.08	1.13	1.11	1.06
Current Ratio	2.09	2.91	2.36	2.43	3.13	2.96	2.92	2.58
Debt to Equity	0.63	0.90	1.06	1.29	0.41	0.44	0.50	0.50
Price Range	69.53-49.07	50.25-38.35	44.00-35.25	37.36-29.86	34.23-26.92	35.84-26.21	37.08-24.44	33.50-18.56
P/E Ratio	17.17-12.12	33.06-25.23	16.00-12.82	22.37-17.88	19.56-15.38	15.65-11.45	20.26-13.35	15.09-8.36
Average Yield %	1.93	2.37	2.54	3.09	3.33	3.25	3.31	4.33

Address: 29400 Lakeland Boulevard, Wickliffe, OH 44092-2298 **Telephone:** 440-943-4200 **Fax:** 440-943-5337	Web Site: www.lubrizol.com **Officers:** James L. Hambrick - Chmn., Pres., C.E.O. Joseph W. Bauer - V.P., Gen. Couns.	Auditors: Deloitte & Touche LLP **Transfer Agents:** American Stock Transfer & Trust Company, New York, NY

M & T BANK CORP

Exchange	Symbol	Price	52Wk Range	Yield	P/E	Div Acheiver
NYS	MTB	$80.48 (3/31/2008)	113.62-71.59	3.48	13.53	27 Years

*7 Year Price Score 82.83   *NYSE Composite Index=100   *12 Month Price Score 92.55

Interim Earnings (Per Share)

Qtr.	Mar	Jun	Sep	Dec
2003	1.23	1.10	1.28	1.36
2004	1.30	1.53	1.56	1.61
2005	1.62	1.69	1.64	1.78
2006	1.77	1.87	1.85	1.88
2007	1.57	1.95	1.83	0.61

Interim Dividends (Per Share)

Amt	Decl	Ex	Rec	Pay
0.60Q	4/18/2007	5/30/2007	6/1/2007	6/29/2007
0.70Q	7/18/2007	8/30/2007	9/4/2007	9/28/2007
0.70Q	11/20/2007	12/13/2007	12/17/2007	12/31/2007
0.70Q	2/20/2008	2/27/2008	2/29/2008	3/31/2008

Indicated Div: $2.80 (Div. Reinv. Plan)

Valuation Analysis   **Institutional Holding**

Forecast P/E	14.10	No of Institutions
	(1/10/2007)	311
Market Cap	$8.8 Billion	Shares
Book Value	6.5 Billion	72,651,312
Price/Book.	1.36	% Held
Price/Sales	1.97	66.20

Business Summary: Commercial Banking (MIC: 8.1 SIC: 6022 NAIC: 522110)

M&T Bank is a holding company. Through its M&T Bank and M&T Bank, N.A. subsidiaries, Co. provides individuals, corporations and other businesses, and institutions with commercial and retail banking services, including loans and deposits, trust, mortgage banking, asset management, insurance and other financial services. As of Dec 31 2007, Co. had 704 banking offices located throughout New York State, Pennsylvania, Maryland, Delaware, New Jersey, Virginia, West Virginia and the District of Columbia, plus a branch in George Town, Cayman Islands. As of Dec 31, 2007, Co. also had total assets amounted $64.88 billion and total deposits amounted $41.27 billion.

Recent Developments: For the year ended Dec 31 2007, net income decreased 22.0% to US$654.3 million from US$839.2 million in the prior year. Net interest income increased 1.8% to US$1.85 billion from US$1.82 billion in the prior year. Provision for loan losses was US$192.0 million versus US$80.0 million in the prior year, an increase of 140.0%. Non-interest income fell 10.8% to US$933.0 million from US$1.05 billion, while non-interest expense advanced 4.9% to US$1.63 billion.

Prospects: Co.'s results reflect the ongoing turmoil in the residential real estate market and the challenges from lenders in the sub-prime residential mortgage lending market. Nevertheless, Co. remains optimistic regarding its near-term outlook. For instance, Co. is encouraged by the Dec 7 2007 acquisition of 13 First Horizon branches from First Horizon National Corp. as well as the Nov 30 2007 acquisition of Partners Trust Financial Group, Inc. Accordingly, Co. signed an agreement to divest three branch offices in Binghamton, NY with deposits of about $95.0 million as a condition by regulators for the approval of the Partners Trust acquisition. Co. expects this transaction to close in 2008.

Financial Data

(US$ in Thousands)	12/31/2007	12/31/2006	12/31/2005	12/31/2004	12/31/2003	12/31/2002	12/31/2001	12/31/2000
Earnings Per Share	5.95	7.37	6.73	6.00	4.95	5.07	3.82	3.44
Cash Flow Per Share	12.34	4.86	2.62	6.14	10.94	6.90	1.61	4.29
Tang Book Value Per Share	27.68	28.33	25.56	23.08	21.42	21.36	17.84	16.10
Dividends Per Share	2.600	2.250	1.750	1.600	1.200	1.050	1.000	0.625
Dividend Payout %	43.70	30.53	26.00	26.67	24.24	20.71	26.18	18.17
Income Statement								
Interest Income	3,544,813	3,314,093	2,788,694	2,298,732	2,126,565	1,842,099	2,101,885	1,772,784
Interest Expense	1,694,576	1,496,552	994,351	564,160	527,810	594,514	943,597	918,597
Net Interest Income	1,850,237	1,817,541	1,794,343	1,734,572	1,598,755	1,247,585	1,158,288	854,187
Provision for Losses	192,000	80,000	88,000	95,000	131,000	122,000	103,500	38,000
Non-Interest Income	932,989	1,045,852	949,718	942,969	831,095	511,931	477,426	324,672
Non-Interest Expense	1,627,689	1,551,751	1,485,142	1,516,018	1,448,180	921,032	948,318	694,453
Income Before Taxes	963,537	1,231,642	1,170,919	1,066,523	850,670	716,484	583,896	446,406
Income Taxes	309,278	392,453	388,736	344,002	276,728	231,392	205,821	160,250
Net Income	654,259	839,189	782,183	722,521	573,942	485,092	378,075	286,156
Average Shares	110,012	113,918	116,232	120,406	115,932	95,663	99,024	83,171
Balance Sheet								
Net Loans & Leases	47,262,123	42,297,349	39,692,982	37,771,613	35,158,377	25,291,312	24,762,752	22,368,111
Total Assets	64,875,639	57,064,905	55,146,406	52,938,721	49,826,081	33,174,525	31,450,196	28,949,456
Total Deposits	41,266,188	39,910,503	37,100,174	35,429,473	33,114,944	21,664,923	21,580,400	20,232,673
Total Liabilities	58,390,383	50,783,810	49,270,020	47,209,107	44,108,871	29,992,702	28,510,745	26,248,971
Stockholders' Equity	6,485,256	6,281,095	5,876,386	5,729,614	5,717,210	3,181,823	2,939,451	2,700,485
Shares Outstanding	109,852	110,216	112,059	115,227	120,106	92,028	93,683	93,244
Statistical Record								
Return on Assets %	1.07	1.50	1.45	1.40	1.38	1.50	1.25	1.11
Return on Equity %	10.25	13.81	13.48	12.59	12.90	15.85	13.41	12.69
Net Interest Margin %	52.20	54.84	64.34	75.46	75.18	67.73	55.11	48.18
Efficiency Ratio %	36.35	35.59	39.73	46.77	48.96	39.13	36.77	33.11
Loans to Deposits	1.15	1.06	1.07	1.07	1.06	1.17	1.15	1.11
Price Range	124.74-79.31	124.21-106.45	112.28-96.93	108.01-83.37	98.55-75.69	89.94-68.00	81.23-61.09	68.00-36.40
P/E Ratio	20.96-13.33	16.85-14.44	16.68-14.40	18.00-13.90	19.91-15.29	17.74-13.41	21.26-15.99	19.77-10.58
Average Yield %	2.43	1.92	1.67	1.69	1.39	1.30	1.39	1.34

Address: One M&T Plaza, Buffalo, NY 14203	**Web Site:** www.mtb.com	**Auditors:** PricewaterhouseCoopers LLP
Telephone: 716-842-5445	**Officers:** Robert G. Wilmers - Chmn. Carl L. Campbell - Vice-Chmn.	**Transfer Agents:** Registrar and Transfer Company, Cranford, NJ
Fax: 716-842-5177		

MACERICH CO. (THE)

Exchange	Symbol	Price	52Wk Range	Yield	P/E	Div Acheiver
NYS	MAC	$70.27 (3/31/2008)	97.69-58.91	4.55	70.27	13 Years

*7 Year Price Score 118.87 *NYSE Composite Index=100 *12 Month Price Score 90.23

Interim Earnings (Per Share)

Qtr.	Mar	Jun	Sep	Dec
2003	0.37	0.55	0.69	0.45
2004	0.31	0.29	0.29	0.51
2005	0.30	0.11	0.07	0.39
2006	0.11	0.36	0.66	2.06
2007	0.04	0.19	0.24	0.54

Interim Dividends (Per Share)

Amt	Decl	Ex	Rec	Pay
0.71Q	4/27/2007	5/16/2007	5/18/2007	6/8/2007
0.71Q	7/30/2007	8/17/2007	8/21/2007	9/7/2007
0.80Q	10/26/2007	11/13/2007	11/15/2007	12/7/2007
0.80Q	2/9/2008	2/20/2008	2/22/2008	3/7/2008

Indicated Div: $3.20

Valuation Analysis

		Institutional Holding	
Forecast P/E	53.39	No of Institutions	
	(1/10/2007)	219	
Market Cap	$5.1 Billion	Shares	
Book Value	1.3 Billion	72,001,888	
Price/Book	3.87	% Held	
Price/Sales	5.67	N/A	

TRADING VOLUME (thousand shares)

1999 2000 2001 2002 2003 2004 2005 2006 2007 2008

Business Summary: Property, Real Estate & Development (MIC: 8.3 SIC: 6798 NAIC: 525930)

Macerich is a self-administered and self-managed real estate investment trust engaged in the acquisition, ownership, development, redevelopment, management and leasing of regional and community shopping centers located throughout the U.S. As of Dec 31 2007, Co. is the sole general partner of, and owns a majority of the ownership interests in, The Macerich Partnership, L.P., a Delaware limited partnership. Additionally, as of such date, The Macerich Partnership owned or had an ownership interest in 74 regional shopping centers and 20 community shopping centers aggregating approximately 80.7 million square feet of gross leasable area.

Recent Developments: For the year ended Dec 31 2007, net income decreased 61.7% to US$96.5 million from US$252.4 million in the prior year. Revenues were US$896.4 million, up 8.0% from US$829.7 million the year before. Revenues from property income rose 7.7% to US$861.6 million from US$799.7 million in the corresponding earlier year.

Prospects: Co.'s outlook appears constructive, reflecting the continued execution of its redevelopment and development pipeline. For example, Co. anticipates opening the balance of its SanTan Village project, which includes Dick's Sporting Goods, Best Buy, Barnes & Noble and up to 13 restaurants, in phases throughout 2008. Additionally, Co. noted that it has recently received full entitlements to proceed with plans for a development of Santa Monica Place, a regional center which is projected for completion in fall 2009. Meanwhile, for full-year 2008, Co. is expecting diluted earnings in the range of $1.28 to $1.43 per share and diluted funds from operations of between $5.00 and $5.15 per share.

Financial Data

(US$ in Thousands)	12/31/2007	12/31/2006	12/31/2005	12/31/2004	12/31/2003	12/31/2002	12/31/2001	12/31/2000
Earnings Per Share	1.00	3.19	0.88	1.40	2.09	1.62	1.72	1.11
Cash Flow Per Share	4.54	2.99	3.97	3.31	4.88	5.52	4.16	3.55
Tang Book Value Per Share	17.29	20.54	11.92	14.30	15.34	15.49	10.27	10.78
Dividends Per Share	2.930	2.750	2.630	2.480	2.320	2.220	2.140	2.060
Dividend Payout %	293.00	86.21	298.86	177.14	111.00	137.04	124.42	185.59
Income Statement								
Property Income	861,603	799,727	743,104	528,099	468,255	366,883	323,038	311,919
Non-Property Income	34,765	29,929	24,281	19,169	17,749	12,041	11,535	8,173
Total Revenue	896,368	829,656	767,385	547,268	486,004	378,924	334,573	320,092
Interest Expense	263,726	274,667	249,910	146,327	132,512	122,934	109,646	108,447
Income Taxes	(470)	33	(2,031)	...	...	...	...	...
Net Income	96,540	252,358	71,686	91,633	128,034	81,382	77,723	56,929
Average Shares	84,760	88,058	73,573	73,099	75,198	50,066	44,963	45,050
Balance Sheet								
Total Assets	8,171,134	7,562,163	7,178,944	4,637,096	4,145,593	3,662,080	2,294,502	2,337,242
Long-Term Obligations	5,762,958	4,993,879	5,424,730	3,230,120	2,682,599	2,291,908	1,523,660	1,550,935
Total Liabilities	6,156,060	5,298,454	5,732,806	3,403,314	2,855,559	2,395,449	1,584,226	1,607,134
Stockholders' Equity	1,312,634	1,542,305	827,108	913,533	953,485	797,798	348,954	362,272
Shares Outstanding	72,311	71,567	59,941	58,785	57,902	51,490	33,981	33,612
Statistical Record								
Return on Assets %	1.23	3.42	1.21	2.08	3.28	2.73	3.36	2.39
Return on Equity %	6.76	21.30	8.24	9.79	14.62	14.19	21.86	11.56
Net Margin %	10.77	30.42	9.34	16.74	26.34	21.48	23.23	17.79
Price Range	103.32-70.63	87.00-67.90	71.19-53.28	64.66-39.75	44.50-28.82	31.48-26.30	26.60-18.75	24.75-18.44
P/E Ratio	103.32-70.63	27.27-21.29	80.90-60.55	46.19-28.39	21.29-13.79	19.43-16.23	15.47-10.90	22.30-16.61
Average Yield %	3.40	3.71	4.21	4.86	6.46	7.59	9.26	9.69

Address: 401 Wilshire Boulevard, Suite 700, Santa Monica, CA 90401
Telephone: 310-394-6000
Fax: 310-395-2791

Web Site: www.macerich.com
Officers: Mace Siegel - Chmn. Dana K. Anderson - Vice-Chmn.

Auditors: Deloitte & Touche LLP
Transfer Agents: Computershare Trust Company, N.A., Providence, RI

MACK CALI REALTY CORP

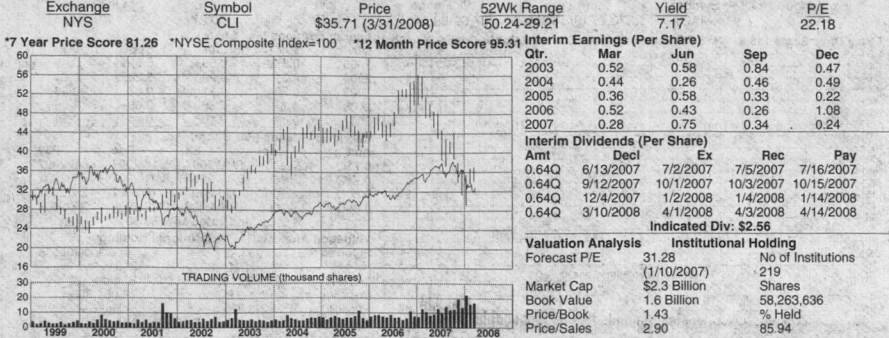

Exchange	Symbol	Price	52Wk Range	Yield	P/E
NYS	CLI	$35.71 (3/31/2008)	50.24-29.21	7.17	22.18

*7 Year Price Score 81.26   *NYSE Composite Index=100   *12 Month Price Score 95.31

Interim Earnings (Per Share)

Qtr.	Mar	Jun	Sep	Dec
2003	0.52	0.58	0.84	0.47
2004	0.44	0.26	0.46	0.49
2005	0.36	0.58	0.33	0.22
2006	0.52	0.43	0.26	1.08
2007	0.28	0.75	0.34	0.24

Interim Dividends (Per Share)

Amt	Decl	Ex	Rec	Pay
0.64Q	6/13/2007	7/2/2007	7/5/2007	7/16/2007
0.64Q	9/12/2007	10/1/2007	10/3/2007	10/15/2007
0.64Q	12/4/2007	1/2/2008	1/4/2008	1/14/2008
0.64Q	3/10/2008	4/1/2008	4/3/2008	4/14/2008

Indicated Div: $2.56

Valuation Analysis   **Institutional Holding**

Forecast P/E	31.28	No of Institutions
	(1/10/2007)	219
Market Cap	$2.3 Billion	Shares
Book Value	1.6 Billion	58,263,636
Price/Book	1.43	% Held
Price/Sales	2.90	85.94

Business Summary: Property, Real Estate & Development (MIC: 8.3 SIC: 6798 NAIC: 525930)

Mack Cali Realty is a real estate investment trust that owns and operates a real estate portfolio comprised of Class A office and office/flex properties located primarily in the Northeast. At Dec 31 2007, Co. owned or had interests in 294 properties plus developable land (collectively, the Properties). The Properties aggregate approximately 33.7 million square feet, which are comprised of 283 buildings, primarily office and office/flex buildings totaling approximately 33.3 million square feet, six industrial/warehouse buildings totaling approximately 387,400 square feet, two retail properties totaling approximately 17,300 square feet, one hotel and two parcels of land leased to others.

Recent Developments: For the year ended Dec 31 2007, income from continuing operations decreased 13.6% to US$73.1 million from US$84.7 million a year earlier. Net income decreased 23.6% to US$110.5 million from US$144.7 million in the prior year. Revenues were US$808.4 million, up 10.4% from US$732.0 million the year before. Revenues from property income rose 10.7% to US$786.3 million from US$710.4 million in the corresponding earlier year.

Prospects: On Feb 1 2008, Co. announced 55,245 square feet of lease renewals at its Westchester properties, such as Montefiore Medical Center, Citigroup Global Markets, Inc. and Cablevision Lightpath Inc, as part of its ongoing effort to build long-term tenant relationships. Meanwhile, for 2008, Co. expects the general downturn in its markets during the recent years to lead to continued decline in effective rental rates on new and renewed leases, and increases in vacancy rates and tenant installation costs, such as concessions. Separately, Co. is lowering its net income guidance to $0.66 to $0.82 per diluted share, as it continues to expect funds from operations of $3.40 to $3.56 per diluted share.

Financial Data
(US$ in Thousands)

	12/31/2007	12/31/2006	12/31/2005	12/31/2004	12/31/2003	12/31/2002	12/31/2001	12/31/2000
Earnings Per Share	1.61	2.28	1.51	1.65	2.43	2.43	2.32	3.10
Cash Flow Per Share	3.88	3.79	3.95	3.94	3.82	3.85	4.70	3.09
Tang Book Value Per Share	24.67	23.88	23.96	24.90	25.52	25.37	25.26	24.64
Dividends Per Share	2.560	2.530	2.520	2.520	2.520	2.490	2.450	1.770
Dividend Payout %	159.01	110.96	166.89	152.73	103.70	102.47	105.60	57.10
Income Statement								
Property Income	786,280	723,184	625,784	575,860	567,403	549,474	562,640	549,681
Non-Property Income	22,070	17,125	17,621	13,131	18,843	20,140	21,708	26,472
Total Revenue	808,350	740,309	643,405	588,991	586,246	569,614	584,348	576,153
Interest Expense	126,672	136,357	119,337	109,649	116,311	107,823	112,003	105,394
Net Income	110,466	144,666	95,488	102,453	143,053	139,722	131,659	185,338
Average Shares	82,500	77,901	74,189	68,743	65,990	65,427	64,775	73,070
Balance Sheet								
Total Assets	4,593,202	4,422,889	4,247,502	3,850,165	3,749,570	3,796,429	3,746,770	3,676,977
Long-Term Obligations	2,211,735	2,159,959	2,126,181	1,702,300	1,628,584	1,752,372	1,700,150	1,628,512
Total Liabilities	2,492,797	2,412,762	2,335,396	1,877,096	1,779,983	1,912,199	1,867,938	1,774,239
Stockholders' Equity	1,642,555	1,527,907	1,511,287	1,545,111	1,541,488	1,454,194	1,432,588	1,453,290
Shares Outstanding	65,558	62,925	62,019	61,038	59,420	57,318	56,712	58,980
Statistical Record								
Return on Assets %	2.45	3.34	2.36	2.69	3.79	3.70	3.55	5.06
Return on Equity %	6.97	9.52	6.25	6.62	9.55	9.68	9.12	12.77
Net Margin %	13.67	19.54	14.84	17.39	24.40	24.53	22.53	32.17
Price Range	56.28-31.38	55.10-42.58	48.02-40.67	47.00-35.20	41.75-27.35	35.59-27.91	31.92-25.58	28.75-22.88
P/E Ratio	34.96-19.49	24.17-18.68	31.80-26.93	28.48-21.33	17.18-11.26	14.65-11.49	13.76-11.03	9.27-7.38
Average Yield %	5.78	5.26	5.72	5.99	7.28	7.82	8.63	6.74

Address: 343 Thornall Street, Edison, NJ 08837-2206 **Telephone:** 732-590-1000 **Fax:** 732-205-8237	**Web Site:** www.mack-cali.com **Officers:** William L. Mack - Chmn. Mitchell E. Hersh - C.E.O.	**Auditors:** PricewaterhouseCoopers LLP **Transfer Agents:** Computershare Trust Company, N.A., Providence, RI

MACYS INC

Exchange	Symbol	Price	52Wk Range	Yield	P/E
NYS	M	$23.06 (3/31/2008)	46.31-21.31	2.25	11.71

*7 Year Price Score 97.32 ***NYSE Composite Index=100** ***12 Month Price Score 81.71**

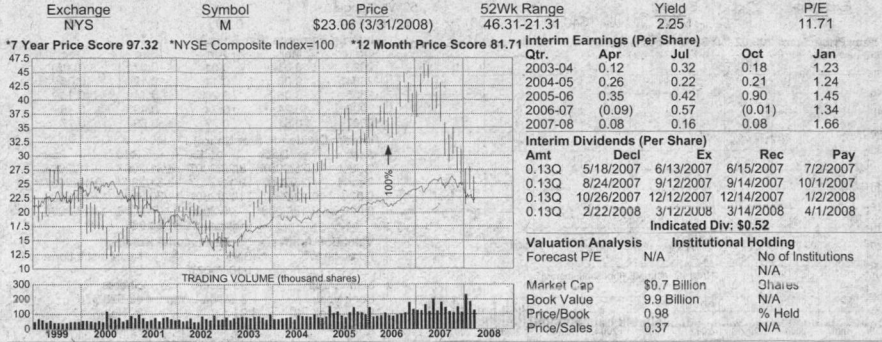

Interim Earnings (Per Share)

Qtr.	Apr	Jul	Oct	Jan
2003-04	0.12	0.32	0.18	1.23
2004-05	0.26	0.22	0.21	1.24
2005-06	0.35	0.42	0.90	1.45
2006-07	(0.09)	0.57	(0.01)	1.34
2007-08	0.08	0.16	0.08	1.66

Interim Dividends (Per Share)

Amt	Decl	Ex	Rec	Pay
0.13Q	5/18/2007	6/13/2007	6/15/2007	7/2/2007
0.13Q	8/24/2007	9/12/2007	9/14/2007	10/1/2007
0.13Q	10/26/2007	12/12/2007	12/14/2007	1/2/2008
0.13Q	2/22/2008	3/12/2008	3/14/2008	4/1/2008

Indicated Div: $0.52

Valuation Analysis   **Institutional Holding**

Forecast P/E	N/A	No of Institutions	N/A
Market Cap	$0.7 Billion	Shares	
Book Value	9.9 Billion	N/A	
Price/Book	0.98	% Held	
Price/Sales	0.37	N/A	

Business Summary: Retail - General (MIC: 5.2 SIC: 5311 NAIC: 452111)

Macys is engaged in operation of retail stores, selling a range of merchandise including men's, women's and children's apparel and accessories, cosmetics, home furnishings and other consumer goods. Most of Co.'s stores are located at urban or suburban sites, mainly in densely populated areas across the U.S. In addition, Co. conducts electronic commerce and direct-to-customer mail catalog businesses under the names macys.com, bloomingdales.com and Bloomingdale's By Mail. Co. also provides an on line bridal registry to customers. As of Feb 2 2008, Co. operated over 853 retail stores in 45 states, the District of Columbia, Guam and Puerto Rico under the names Macy's and Bloomingdale's.

Recent Developments: For the year ended Feb 2 2008, income from continuing operations decreased 8.0% to US$909.0 million from US$988.0 million a year earlier. Net income decreased 10.3% to US$893.0 million from US$995.0 million in the prior year. Revenues were US$26.31 billion, down 2.4% from US$26.97 billion the year before. Operating income was US$1.86 billion versus US$1.84 billion in the prior year, an increase of 1.5%. Direct operating expenses declined 3.2% to US$15.68 billion from US$16.20 billion in the comparable period the year before. Indirect operating expenses decreased 1.8% to US$8.77 billion from US$8.94 billion in the equivalent prior-year period.

Prospects: On Feb 6 2008, Co. announced its plan to combine its Minneapolis-based Macy's North organization into New York based Macy's East, its St. Louis-based Macy's Midwest organization into Atlanta-based Macy's South and its Seattle-based Macy's Northwest organization into San Francisco-based Macy's West. These moves, which are expected to be completed in the second quarter of 2008, should reduce Co.'s selling, general and administrative expenses by about $60.0 million in 2008. Meanwhile, for the fiscal year ending Jan 2009, Co. expects same store sales to be in the range of a decline 1.0% to growth of 1.5% and earnings per share on a diluted basis of $1.85 to $2.15, excluding one-time costs.

Financial Data

(US$ in Thousands)	02/02/2008	02/03/2007	01/28/2006	01/29/2005	01/31/2004	02/01/2003	02/02/2002	02/03/2001
Earnings Per Share	1.97	1.81	3.24	1.93	1.86	2.06	(0.69)	(0.45)
Cash Flow Per Share	5.01	6.73	4.59	4.32	4.32	2.97	3.53	3.09
Tang Book Value Per Share	N.M.	4.36	5.34	16.54	14.85	13.46	12.15	12.46
Dividends Per Share	0.518	0.507	0.385	0.265	0.188	...	...	...
Dividend Payout %	26.27	28.04	11.88	13.73	10.11	...	...	...
Income Statement								
Total Revenue	26,313,000	26,970,000	22,390,000	15,630,000	15,264,000	15,435,000	15,651,000	18,407,000
EBITDA	3,136,000	3,052,000	3,382,000	2,143,000	2,054,000	2,028,000	1,800,000	1,290,000
Income Before Taxes	1,320,000	1,446,000	2,044,000	1,116,000	1,084,000	1,048,000	780,000	113,000
Income Taxes	411,000	458,000	671,000	427,000	391,000	410,000	262,000	297,000
Net Income	893,000	995,000	1,406,000	689,000	693,000	818,000	(276,000)	(184,000)
Average Shares	451,800	547,700	434,600	356,400	373,200	397,400	399,700	409,600
Balance Sheet								
Current Assets	6,324,000	7,422,000	10,145,000	7,510,000	7,452,000	7,154,000	7,280,000	8,700,000
Total Assets	27,789,000	29,550,000	33,168,000	14,885,000	14,550,000	14,441,000	15,044,000	17,012,000
Current Liabilities	5,360,000	6,359,000	7,590,000	4,301,000	3,883,000	3,601,000	3,714,000	4,869,000
Long-Term Obligations	9,087,000	7,847,000	8,860,000	2,637,000	3,151,000	3,408,000	3,859,000	4,374,000
Total Liabilities	17,882,000	17,296,000	19,649,000	8,718,000	8,610,000	8,679,000	9,480,000	11,190,000
Stockholders' Equity	9,907,000	12,254,000	13,519,000	6,167,000	5,940,000	5,762,000	5,564,000	5,822,000
Shares Outstanding	419,745	496,900	546,800	334,200	357,000	380,400	401,600	395,200
Statistical Record								
Return on Assets %	3.12	3.12	5.87	4.69	4.79	5.56	N.M.	N.M.
Return on Equity %	8.08	7.60	14.32	11.41	11.88	14.48	N.M.	N.M.
EBITDA Margin %	11.92	11.32	15.10	13.71	13.46	13.14	11.50	7.01
Net Margin %	3.39	3.69	6.28	4.41	4.54	5.30	N.M.	N.M.
Asset Turnover	0.92	0.85	0.93	1.06	1.06	1.05	0.98	1.04
Current Ratio	1.18	1.17	1.34	1.75	1.92	1.99	1.96	1.79
Debt to Equity	0.92	0.64	0.66	0.43	0.53	0.59	0.69	0.75
Price Range	46.51-21.31	44.95-33.25	38.65-27.65	29.18-21.56	25.09-11.96	22.00-12.82	24.63-13.30	22.75-11.75
P/E Ratio	23.61-10.82	24.83-18.37	11.93-8.53	15.12-11.17	13.49-6.43	10.68-6.22	...	...
Average Yield %	1.53	1.33	1.16	1.06	0.97	...	...	...

Address: 151 West 34th Street, New York, NY 10001	Web Site: www.federated-fds.com	Auditors: KPMG LLP
Telephone: 212-494-1601	Officers: Terry J. Lundgren - Chmn., Pres., C.E.O. Thomas G. Cody - Vice-Chmn., Legal, H.R., Internal Audit & External Affairs	Investor Contact: 513-579-7780
Fax: 212-494-1838		Transfer Agents: Bank of New York, New York, NY

MANITOWOC CO., INC.

Exchange	Symbol	Price	52Wk Range	Yield	P/E
NYS	MTW	$40.80 (3/31/2008)	50.98-32.01	0.20	15.45

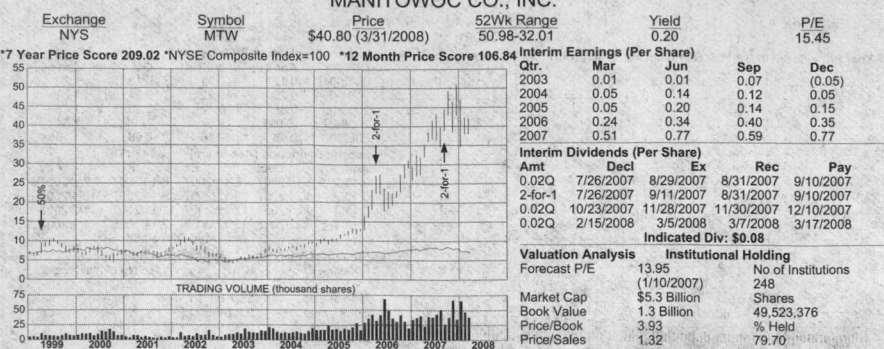

*7 Year Price Score 209.02 ***NYSE Composite Index=100** ***12 Month Price Score 106.84**

Interim Earnings (Per Share)

Qtr.	Mar	Jun	Sep	Dec
2003	0.01	0.01	0.07	(0.05)
2004	0.05	0.14	0.12	0.05
2005	0.05	0.20	0.14	0.15
2006	0.24	0.34	0.40	0.35
2007	0.51	0.77	0.59	0.77

Interim Dividends (Per Share)

Amt	Decl	Ex	Rec	Pay
0.02Q	7/26/2007	8/29/2007	8/31/2007	9/10/2007
2-for-1	7/26/2007	9/11/2007	8/31/2007	9/10/2007
0.02Q	10/23/2007	11/28/2007	11/30/2007	12/10/2007
0.02Q	2/15/2008	3/5/2008	3/7/2008	3/17/2008

Indicated Div: $0.08

Valuation Analysis

		Institutional Holding	
Forecast P/E	13.95 (1/10/2007)	No of Institutions	248
Market Cap	$5.3 Billion	Shares	49,523,376
Book Value	1.3 Billion	% Held	79.70
Price/Book	3.93		
Price/Sales	1.32		

Business Summary: Industrial Machinery and Equipment (MIC: 11.5 SIC: 3531 NAIC: 333120)

Manitowoc Company is an industrial manufacturer of cranes, foodservice equipment and mid-size commercial, research and military ships. Co.'s crane business designs, produces and markets a line of crawler cranes, mobile telescopic cranes, tower cranes and boom trucks. Co.'s foodservice business designs, produces and markets full product lines of ice making machines, walk-in and reach-in refrigerator/freezers, fountain beverage delivery systems and other foodservice refrigeration products. Co.'s marine service business offers new construction, ship repair and maintenance services for freshwater and saltwater vessels from two shipyards and one top-side repair yard on the U.S. Great Lakes.

Recent Developments: For the year ended Dec 31 2007, income from continuing operations increased 100.4% to US$333.6 million from US$166.5 million a year earlier. Net income increased 102.6% to US$336.7 million from US$166.2 million in the prior year. Revenues were US$4.01 billion, up 36.5% from US$2.93 billion the year before. Operating income was US$501.9 million versus US$302.4 million in the prior year, an increase of 66.0%. Direct operating expenses rose 35.3% to US$3.09 billion from US$2.29 billion in the comparable period the year before. Indirect operating expenses increased 18.8% to US$409.7 million from US$344.9 million in the equivalent prior-year period.

Prospects: For 2008, Co. expects expansion projects in its crane segment in North America, Europe, and Asia to support revenue growth of over 20.0% from 2007 levels. Co. also expects its foodservice sales to increase at a percentage rate in the mid-single digits, in spite of industry estimates for slowing sales growth. Further, in its marine segment, Co. is anticipating a robust backlog of commercial work and continued improvement in operating earnings, and believes that it is well-positioned to capitalize on existing and pending government contracts. Thus, Co. now expects 2008 earnings per share, excluding any unusual items, of $3.20 to $3.40, up 19.0% and 27.0% from its outstanding 2007 results.

Financial Data

(US$ in Thousands)	12/31/2007	12/31/2006	12/31/2005	12/31/2004	12/31/2003	12/31/2002	12/31/2001	12/31/2000
Earnings Per Share	2.64	1.33	0.54	0.36	0.03	(0.20)	0.47	0.60
Cash Flow Per Share	1.91	2.40	0.89	0.53	1.42	0.94	1.10	0.63
Tang Book Value Per Share	4.85	1.23	N.M.	N.M.	N.M.	N.M.	N.M.	N.M.
Dividends Per Share	0.075	0.070	0.070	0.070	0.070	0.070	0.075	0.075
Dividend Payout %	2.84	5.28	13.08	19.58	215.38	...	16.13	12.50
Income Statement								
Total Revenue	4,005,000	2,933,300	2,254,097	1,964,101	1,593,186	1,406,577	1,116,580	873,272
EBITDA	587,400	363,500	191,133	159,984	127,897	149,821	150,526	128,681
Income Before Taxes	463,000	244,900	73,858	49,129	22,606	62,780	79,689	96,120
Income Taxes	129,400	78,400	14,772	9,335	4,069	22,601	30,817	35,852
Net Income	336,700	166,200	65,800	39,138	3,549	(20,502)	45,548	60,268
Average Shares	127,489	125,571	123,052	109,508	106,811	103,127	98,193	100,491
Balance Sheet								
Current Assets	1,575,600	1,142,700	953,383	845,961	646,089	647,164	331,090	223,507
Total Assets	2,868,700	2,219,500	1,961,777	1,928,136	1,602,581	1,577,123	1,080,812	642,530
Current Liabilities	1,074,600	935,400	690,254	652,680	545,224	460,398	296,161	239,490
Long-Term Obligations	217,500	264,300	474,000	512,236	567,084	623,547	446,522	137,668
Total Liabilities	1,518,800	1,445,000	1,418,449	1,409,207	1,304,157	1,282,008	817,017	408,761
Stockholders' Equity	1,349,900	774,500	543,328	518,929	298,424	295,115	263,795	233,769
Shares Outstanding	129,880	124,243	121,450	119,798	106,288	96,212	96,212	97,037
Statistical Record								
Return on Assets %	13.23	7.95	3.38	2.21	0.22	N.M.	5.29	10.25
Return on Equity %	31.70	25.22	12.39	9.55	1.20	N.M.	18.31	25.80
EBITDA Margin %	14.67	12.39	8.48	8.15	8.03	10.65	13.48	14.74
Net Margin %	8.41	5.67	2.92	1.99	0.22	N.M.	4.08	6.90
Asset Turnover	1.57	1.40	1.16	1.11	1.00	1.06	1.30	1.49
Current Ratio	1.47	1.22	1.38	1.30	1.18	1.41	1.12	0.93
Debt to Equity	0.16	0.34	0.87	0.99	1.90	2.11	1.69	0.59
Price Range	50.98-25.93	31.09-12.86	13.30-8.57	9.80-6.90	7.94-4.20	10.93-5.75	8.20-5.70	8.61-4.48
P/E Ratio	19.31-9.82	23.37-9.67	24.63-15.88	27.22-19.16	264.58-139.83	...	17.45-12.12	14.35-7.47
Average Yield %	0.20	0.31	0.64	0.85	1.27	0.85	1.08	1.11

Address: 2400 South 44th Street, Manitowoc, WI 54221-0066 **Telephone:** 920-684-4410 **Fax:** 920-652-9778	**Web Site:** www.manitowoc.com **Officers:** Terry D. Growcock - Chmn., C.E.O. Carl J. Laurino - Sr. V.P., C.F.O., Treas.	**Auditors:** PricewaterhouseCoopers LLP **Investor Contact:** 920-652-1731 **Transfer Agents:** Computershare Trust Company, NA., Providence, RI

MANPOWER INC. (WI)

Exchange	Symbol	Price	52Wk Range	Yield	P/E
NYS	MAN	$56.26 (3/31/2008)	95.05-48.83	1.32	9.82

*7 Year Price Score 116.94 *NYSE Composite Index=100 *12 Month Price Score 86.50

Interim Earnings (Per Share)

Qtr.	Mar	Jun	Sep	Dec
2003	0.19	0.37	0.56	0.62
2004	0.43	0.56	0.89	0.68
2005	0.35	0.70	0.87	0.99
2006	0.59	0.91	1.16	1.89
2007	0.69	1.86	1.57	1.63

Interim Dividends (Per Share)

Amt	Decl	Ex	Rec	Pay
0.27S	4/25/2006	6/1/2006	6/5/2006	6/14/2006
0.32S	10/31/2006	12/1/2006	12/5/2006	12/15/2006
0.32S	5/2/2007	6/1/2007	6/5/2007	6/14/2007
0.37S	10/23/2007	12/3/2007	12/5/2007	12/14/2007

Indicated Div: $0.74

Valuation Analysis		Institutional Holding	
Forecast P/E	15.02	No of Institutions	
	(1/10/2007)	317	
Market Cap	$4.5 Billion	Shares	
Book Value	2.7 Billion	83,834,624	
Price/Book	1.68	% Held	
Price/Sales	0.22	98.44	

TRADING VOLUME (thousand shares)

Business Summary: Human Resources Services (MIC: 12.6 SIC: 7363 NAIC: 561330)

Manpower is engaged in the employment services industry. As of Dec 31 2007, Co. had nearly 4,500 offices in 80 countries and territories. Co.'s five major brands, Manpower, Manpower Professional, Elan, Jefferson Wells and Right Management, provide a range of services for the employment and business cycle that includes permanent, temporary and contract recruitment, employee assessment and selection, training, outplacement, outsourcing, consulting and professional services. Co. operates through both branch and/or franchise offices located in the U.S., France, Europe, Middle East and Africa, Canada, Australia, Japan, and Mexico.

Recent Developments: For the year ended Dec 31 2007, income from continuing operations increased 58.6% to US$484.7 million from US$305.7 million a year earlier. Net income increased 21.8% to US$484.7 million from US$398.0 million in the prior year. Revenues were US$20.50 billion, up 16.7% from US$17.56 billion the year before. Operating income was US$825.4 million versus US$532.1 million in the prior year, an increase of 55.1%. Direct operating expenses rose 15.5% to US$16.65 billion from US$14.42 billion in the comparable period the year before. Indirect operating expenses increased 15.7% to US$3.02 billion from US$2.61 billion in the equivalent prior-year period.

Prospects: Co.'s near-term outlook appears favorable. Specifically, Co. attributed its improved top- and bottom-line results to its performance in Europe, Asia and the emerging markets coupled with solid results from its Right Management business. Hence, for the first quarter of 2008, Co. expects diluted net earnings per share of $0.78 to $0.82 and expects revenues to increase by 15.0% to 17.0%. In addition, Co. expects gross profit margin of 17.7% to 17.9%. Separately, on Jan 10 2008, Co. acquired Clarendon Parker Middle East FZ LLC, a recruitment provider in the Middle East, for an undisclosed amount. Co. expects this acquisition to strengthen its market position in the Middle East.

Financial Data

(US$ in Thousands)	12/31/2007	12/31/2006	12/31/2005	12/31/2004	12/31/2003	12/31/2002	12/31/2001	12/31/2000
Earnings Per Share	5.73	4.54	2.87	2.59	1.74	1.46	1.62	2.22
Cash Flow Per Share	5.20	4.17	3.03	2.10	2.88	2.98	1.79	2.07
Tang Book Value Per Share	15.76	13.88	10.19	9.71	9.36	5.89	4.38	6.50
Dividends Per Share	0.690	0.590	0.470	0.300	0.200	0.200	0.200	0.200
Dividend Payout %	12.04	13.00	16.38	11.58	11.49	13.70	12.35	9.01
Income Statement								
Total Revenue	20,500,300	17,562,500	16,080,400	14,930,000	12,184,500	10,610,900	10,483,800	10,842,800
EBITDA	919,200	606,500	526,400	499,800	325,400	294,100	306,900	359,700
Income Before Taxes	791,200	481,900	394,700	369,500	222,100	188,000	197,900	265,200
Income Taxes	306,500	176,200	134,600	123,800	84,400	74,800	73,400	94,000
Net Income	484,700	398,000	260,100	245,700	137,700	113,200	124,500	171,200
Average Shares	84,600	87,700	91,100	96,800	79,300	77,700	77,000	77,100
Balance Sheet								
Current Assets	5,214,800	4,682,000	3,841,700	4,017,500	3,237,100	2,653,300	2,314,400	2,396,700
Total Assets	7,224,400	6,514,100	5,568,400	5,843,100	4,384,900	3,701,700	3,238,600	3,041,600
Current Liabilities	3,255,500	2,881,600	2,580,500	2,601,900	1,877,900	1,562,300	1,290,600	1,522,200
Long-Term Obligations	874,800	791,200	475,000	676,100	829,600	799,000	811,100	491,600
Total Liabilities	4,555,100	4,039,900	3,421,800	3,669,100	3,074,600	2,701,800	2,424,300	2,301,200
Stockholders' Equity	2,669,300	2,474,200	2,146,600	2,174,000	1,310,300	999,900	814,300	740,400
Shares Outstanding	79,872	85,070	87,372	90,290	78,659	77,098	76,128	75,772
Statistical Record								
Return on Assets %	7.06	6.59	4.56	4.79	3.41	3.26	3.96	5.93
Return on Equity %	18.85	17.23	12.04	14.06	11.92	12.48	16.02	24.55
EBITDA Margin %	4.48	3.45	3.27	3.35	2.67	2.77	2.93	3.32
Net Margin %	2.36	2.27	1.62	1.65	1.13	1.07	1.19	1.58
Asset Turnover	2.98	2.91	2.82	2.91	3.01	3.06	3.34	3.75
Current Ratio	1.60	1.62	1.49	1.54	1.72	1.70	1.79	1.57
Debt to Equity	0.33	0.32	0.22	0.31	0.63	0.80	1.00	0.66
Price Range	95.05-56.20	76.77-46.14	48.65-38.55	50.77-38.71	47.54-27.50	42.97-25.00	37.56-24.35	39.81-26.75
P/E Ratio	16.59-9.81	16.91-10.16	16.95-13.43	19.60-14.95	27.32-15.80	29.43-17.12	23.19-15.03	17.93-12.05
Average Yield %	0.92	0.96	1.07	0.65	0.54	0.56	0.64	0.58

Address: 100 Manpower Place, Milwaukee, WI 53212	Web Site: www.manpower.com	Auditors: Deloitte & Touche LLP
Telephone: 414-961-1000	**Officers:** Jeffery A. Joerres - Chmn., Pres., C.E.O.	**Transfer Agents:** Mellon Investor
Fax: 414-332-0796	Michael J. Van Handel - Exec. V.P., C.F.O., Sec.	Services, L.L.C., South Hackensack, NJ

MARATHON OIL CORP.

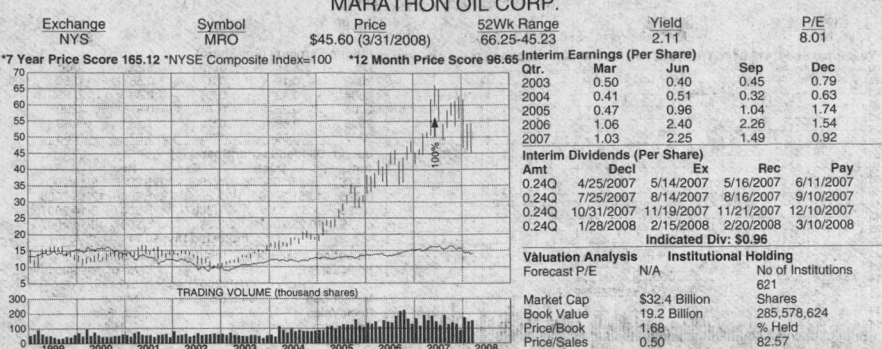

*7 Year Price Score 165.12 *NYSE Composite Index=100   *12 Month Price Score 96.65

Interim Earnings (Per Share)

Qtr.	Mar	Jun	Sep	Dec
2003	0.50	0.40	0.45	0.79
2004	0.41	0.51	0.32	0.63
2005	0.47	0.96	1.04	1.74
2006	1.06	2.40	2.26	1.54
2007	1.03	2.25	1.49	0.92

Interim Dividends (Per Share)

Amt	Decl	Ex	Rec	Pay
0.24Q	4/25/2007	5/14/2007	5/16/2007	6/11/2007
0.24Q	7/25/2007	8/14/2007	8/16/2007	9/10/2007
0.24Q	10/31/2007	11/19/2007	11/21/2007	12/10/2007
0.24Q	1/28/2008	2/15/2008	2/20/2008	3/10/2008

Indicated Div: $0.96

Valuation Analysis

		Institutional Holding	
Forecast P/E	N/A	No of Institutions	621
Market Cap	$32.4 Billion	Shares	285,578,624
Book Value	19.2 Billion	% Held	82.57
Price/Book	1.68		
Price/Sales	0.50		

Business Summary: Oil and Gas (MIC: 14.2 SIC: 2911 NAIC: 324110)

Marathon Oil is engaged in global exploration, production and marketing of liquid hydrocarbons and natural gas; mining, extraction and transportation of bitumen from oil sands deposits in Alberta, Canada, and upgrading of the bitumen for the production and marketing of synthetic crude oil and by-products; domestic refining, marketing and transportation of crude oil and petroleum products, mainly in the Midwest, upper Great Plains, Gulf Coast and southeastern regions of the U.S.; and global marketing and transportation of products manufactured from natural gas. At Dec 31 2007, Co.'s net proved liquid hydrocarbon and natural gas reserves totaled about 1.225 billion barrels of oil equivalent.

Recent Developments: For the year ended Dec 31 2007, income from continuing operations decreased 20.4% to US$3.95 billion from US$4.96 billion a year earlier. Net income decreased 24.4% to US$3.96 billion from US$5.23 billion in the prior year. Revenues were US$65.21 billion, down 0.4% from US$65.45 billion the year before. Operating income was US$6.64 billion versus US$8.97 billion in the prior year, a decrease of 26.0%. Direct operating expenses rose 15.8% to US$49.10 billion from US$42.42 billion in the comparable period the year before. Indirect operating expenses decreased 32.7% to US$9.46 billion from US$14.07 billion in the equivalent prior-year period.

Prospects: For 2008, Co. projects capital budget of $7.99 billion, reflecting a 67.0% growth over 2007 spending, mainly to grow its refining capacity through the Garyville refinery expansion, which should grow the refinery's crude oil throughput capacity by 180.0 million barrels per day when completed in late 2009 while enabling the refinery to provide an additional 7.5 million gallons of clean transportation fuels to the market each day. Co. is also allocating its 2008 budget for further development of its Canadian oil sands assets, expanding its Detroit refinery, funding its ongoing exploration activities and developing existing fields, including new developments in Angola and the Gulf of Mexico.

Financial Data

(US$ in Thousands)	12/31/2007	12/31/2006	12/31/2005	12/31/2004	12/31/2003	12/31/2002	12/31/2001	12/31/2000
Earnings Per Share	5.69	7.25	4.22	1.87	2.13	0.83	0.61	0.69
Cash Flow Per Share	9.45	7.67	6.65	5.53	4.45	3.88	5.88	5.05
Tang Book Value Per Share	22.59	18.73	13.90	11.18	9.18	7.57	7.98	7.86
Dividends Per Share	0.920	0.765	0.610	0.515	0.480	0.460	0.460	...
Dividend Payout %	16.17	10.55	14.45	27.61	22.54	55.42	75.41	...
Income Statement								
Total Revenue	65,207,000	65,449,000	63,673,000	49,907,000	41,234,000	31,720,000	33,066,000	33,859,000
EBITDA	8,423,000	10,476,000	6,267,000	3,395,000	2,970,000	2,402,000	3,480,000	2,393,000
Income Before Taxes	6,849,000	8,979,000	4,781,000	1,984,000	1,596,000	925,000	2,077,000	914,000
Income Taxes	2,901,000	4,022,000	1,730,000	727,000	584,000	389,000	759,000	482,000
Net Income	3,956,000	5,234,000	3,032,000	1,261,000	1,321,000	516,000	157,000	432,000
Average Shares	695,000	722,054	718,162	676,506	620,652	619,902	619,020	623,522
Balance Sheet								
Current Assets	10,587,000	10,096,000	9,383,000	8,867,000	6,040,000	4,479,000	4,411,000	4,985,000
Total Assets	42,746,000	30,831,000	28,498,000	23,423,000	19,482,000	17,812,000	16,129,000	15,232,000
Current Liabilities	11,260,000	8,061,000	8,154,000	5,253,000	4,207,000	3,659,000	3,468,000	4,012,000
Long-Term Obligations	6,084,000	3,061,000	3,698,000	4,057,000	4,085,000	4,410,000	3,432,000	1,937,000
Total Liabilities	23,523,000	15,706,000	16,358,000	12,622,000	11,396,000	12,730,000	11,189,000	10,387,000
Stockholders' Equity	19,223,000	14,607,000	11,705,000	8,111,000	6,075,000	5,082,000	4,940,000	4,845,000
Shares Outstanding	710,000	695,541	733,941	693,394	620,843	619,746	618,790	616,532
Statistical Record								
Return on Assets %	10.75	17.64	11.68	5.86	7.08	3.04	1.00	2.79
Return on Equity %	23.39	39.78	30.60	17.73	23.68	10.30	3.21	8.93
EBITDA Margin %	12.92	16.01	9.84	6.80	7.20	7.57	10.52	7.07
Net Margin %	6.07	8.00	4.76	2.53	3.20	1.63	0.47	1.28
Asset Turnover	1.77	2.21	2.45	2.32	2.21	1.87	2.11	2.18
Current Ratio	0.94	1.25	1.15	1.69	1.44	1.22	1.27	1.24
Debt to Equity	0.32	0.21	0.32	0.50	0.67	0.87	0.69	0.40
Price Range	66.25-41.72	48.78-32.62	35.41-17.86	21.07-15.39	16.68-10.10	15.01-9.50	16.72-12.64	14.91-10.63
P/E Ratio	11.64-7.33	6.73-4.50	8.39-4.23	11.26-8.23	7.83-4.74	18.08-11.45	27.41-20.72	21.60-15.40
Average Yield %	1.69	1.90	2.28	2.87	3.68	3.64	3.17	...

Address: 5555 San Felipe Road, Houston, TX 77056-2723	Web Site: www.marathon.com	Auditors: PricewaterhouseCoopers LLP
Telephone: 713-629-6600	Officers: Thomas J. Usher - Chmn. Clarence P. Cazalot Jr. - Pres., C.E.O.	Investor Contact: 713-296-4114 Transfer Agents: National City Bank

MARKEL CORP (HOLDING CO)

Exchange	Symbol	Price	52Wk Range	Yield	P/E
NYS	MKL	$439.97 (3/31/2008)	545.50-408.98	N/A	10.83

*7 Year Price Score 122.41 *NYSE Composite Index=100 *12 Month Price Score 101.82

TRADING VOLUME (thousand shares)

Interim Earnings (Per Share)

Qtr.	Mar	Jun	Sep	Dec
2003	3.70	5.97	(1.68)	4.53
2004	4.29	5.99	1.40	4.73
2005	7.47	5.95	(11.31)	12.28
2006	7.67	9.11	10.47	12.16
2007	9.88	12.15	9.26	9.36

Interim Dividends (Per Share)

No Dividends Paid

Valuation Analysis

	Institutional Holding	
Forecast P/E 14.69	No of Institutions	
(1/10/2007)	194	
Market Cap $4.4 Billion	Shares	
Book Value 2.6 Billion	7,100,057	
Price/Book 1.66	% Held	
Price/Sales 1.76	72.17	

Business Summary: Insurance (MIC: 8.2 SIC: 6331 NAIC: 524126)

Markel markets and underwrites specialty insurance products and programs for niche markets. Co.'s Essex Excess and Surplus Lines unit writes through Markel Essex Excess and Surplus Lines, Markel Shand Professional/Products Liability, Markel Brokered Excess and Surplus Lines and Markel Southwest Underwriters. In the Specialty Admitted segment, Co. writes business via the Markel Specialty Program Insurance, Markel American Specialty Personal and Commercial Lines and Markel Global Marine and Energy. Co.'s London Insurance Market segment consists of Markel International, which writes specialty property, casualty, professional liability and marine insurance on a direct and reinsurance basis.

Recent Developments: For the year ended Dec 31 2007, net income increased 3.4% to US$405.7 million from US$392.5 million in the prior year. Revenues were US$2.48 billion, down 1.4% from US$2.52 billion the year before. Net premiums earned were US$2.12 billion versus US$2.18 billion in the prior year, a decrease of 3.1%.

Prospects: Looking ahead, Co. plans to address the softening insurance market conditions by continuing to focus on several areas, such as customer service, new product development, geographic expansion and increased marketing efforts. Meanwhile, in its Markel Global Marine and Energy underwriting unit, Co. has added two additional product lines that will begin producing volume in 2008. Notably, Co.'s marine program will offer marine liability, brown water hull, protection and indemnity, cargo and package coverages for maritime-related businesses, while its onshore energy casualty program will provide primary, excess and umbrella casualty coverages to small to mid-sized onshore energy facilities.

Financial Data

(US$ in Thousands)	12/31/2007	12/31/2006	12/31/2005	12/31/2004	12/31/2003	12/31/2002	12/31/2001	12/31/2000
Earnings Per Share	40.64	39.40	14.80	16.41	12.52	7.65	(14.73)	(3.99)
Cash Flow Per Share	51.03	52.69	56.10	69.94	64.16	51.64	19.27	12.86
Tang Book Value Per Share	230.62	195.78	139.38	133.72	104.09	81.13	72.61	47.66
Income Statement								
Premium Income	2,117,294	2,184,381	1,938,461	2,053,887	1,864,251	1,549,016	1,206,684	938,543
Total Revenue	2,483,256	2,519,005	2,200,148	2,262,058	2,091,904	1,770,195	1,397,412	1,094,483
Benefits & Claims	1,096,203	1,132,579	1,299,983	1,308,343	1,269,522	1,114,610	1,049,421	731,531
Income Before Taxes	571,958	553,401	186,000	224,045	181,584	117,693	(182,198)	(51,806)
Income Taxes	166,289	160,899	38,085	58,633	58,107	42,369	(56,481)	(24,214)
Net Income	405,669	392,502	147,915	165,412	123,477	75,324	(125,717)	(27,592)
Average Shares	9,981	10,034	10,171	10,190	9,861	9,852	8,534	6,920
Balance Sheet								
Total Assets	10,134,419	10,088,131	9,814,098	9,397,586	8,532,233	7,408,560	6,440,628	5,473,153
Total Liabilities	7,493,257	7,791,738	8,108,665	7,741,083	7,149,954	6,249,449	5,355,520	4,720,781
Stockholders' Equity	2,641,162	2,296,393	1,705,433	1,656,503	1,382,279	1,159,111	1,085,108	752,372
Shares Outstanding	9,956	9,994	9,798	9,847	9,846	9,832	9,819	7,330
Statistical Record								
Return on Assets %	4.01	3.94	1.54	1.84	1.55	1.09	N.M.	N.M.
Return on Equity %	16.43	19.62	8.80	10.86	9.72	6.71	N.M.	N.M.
Loss Ratio %	51.77	51.85	67.06	63.70	68.10	71.96	86.97	77.94
Net Margin %	16.34	15.58	6.72	7.31	5.90	4.26	(9.00)	(2.52)
Price Range	545.50-458.91	481.50-319.50	367.91-307.69	364.00-253.51	279.00-202.40	221.00-171.50	210.15-160.88	181.00-113.50
P/E Ratio	13.42-11.29	12.22-8.11	24.86-20.79	22.18-15.45	22.28-16.17	28.89-22.42	...	...

Address: 4521 Highwoods Parkway, Glen Allen, VA 23060-6148	Web Site: www.markelcorp.com	Auditors: KPMG LLP
Telephone: 804-747-0136	Officers: Alan I. Kirshner - Chmn., C.E.O. Anthony F. Markel - Pres., C.O.O.	Investor Contact: 800-446-6671
Fax: 804-965-1600		Transfer Agents: Wachovia Bank, N.A.

MARRIOTT INTERNATIONAL, INC.

Exchange	Symbol	Price	52Wk Range	Yield	P/E
NYS	MAR	$34.36 (3/31/2008)	51.87-31.49	0.87	19.63

*7 Year Price Score 113.16 *NYSE Composite Index=100 *12 Month Price Score 92.55

Interim Earnings (Per Share)

Qtr.	Mar	Jun	Sep	Dec
2003	0.24	0.26	0.19	0.34
2004	0.23	0.34	0.28	0.40
2005	0.30	0.29	0.33	0.53
2006	0.14	0.43	0.33	0.51
2007	0.44	0.51	0.33	0.46

Interim Dividends (Per Share)

Amt	Decl	Ex	Rec	Pay
0.075Q	4/27/2007	6/19/2007	6/21/2007	7/20/2007
0.075Q	8/2/2007	9/4/2007	9/6/2007	10/23/2007
0.075Q	11/8/2007	12/4/2007	12/6/2007	1/9/2008
0.075Q	2/7/2008	4/1/2008	4/3/2008	5/1/2008

Indicated Div: $0.30

Valuation Analysis

		Institutional Holding	
Forecast P/E	19.84	No of Institutions	
	(1/10/2007)	421	
Market Cap	$12.3 Billion	Shares	
Book Value	1.4 Billion	223,475,968	
Price/Book	8.59	% Held	
Price/Sales	0.94	57.60	

Business Summary: Hospitality & Tourism (MIC: 5.1 SIC: 7011 NAIC: 721110)

Marriott International is a worldwide operator and franchisor of hotels and related lodging facilities. Co.'s operations are grouped into the following five business segments: North American Full-Service Lodging, North American Limited Service Lodging, International Lodging, Luxury Lodging, and Timeshare. Co. develops, operates and franchises hotels and corporate housing properties under 15 separate brand names, and it develops, operates and markets timeshare, fractional ownership and residential properties under four separate brand names. As of Dec 28 2007, Co. franchised 2,999 lodging properties worldwide, with 535,093 rooms.

Recent Developments: For the year ended Dec 28 2007, income from continuing operations decreased 2.1% to US$697.0 million from US$712.0 million a year earlier. Net income increased 14.5% to US$696.0 million from US$608.0 million in the prior year. Revenues were US$12.99 billion, up 8.3% from US$12.00 billion the year before. Operating income was US$1.19 billion versus US$1.09 billion in the prior year, an increase of 9.3%. Direct operating expenses rose 7.8% to US$11.03 billion from US$10.23 billion in the comparable period the year before. Indirect operating expenses increased 13.4% to US$768.0 million from US$677.0 million in the equivalent prior-year period.

Prospects: For 2008, Co. expects worldwide systemwide comparable revenue per available room (REVPAR) and North American company-operated comparable REVPAR to increase 3.0% to 5.0%. Also, Co. expects total fee revenue of approximately $1.49 billion to $1.52 billion, an increase of 4.0% to 6.0%, assuming modest increases in North American house profit margins and roughly 30,000 new room openings. At its timeshare segment, Co. expects results to total $300.0 million to $315.0 million, roughly flat with 2007, as timeshare sales and services revenue are expected to decline while timeshare contract sales are expected to increase. Overall, Co. is targeting earnings per share of $2.00 to $2.10 for 2008.

Financial Data

(US$ in Thousands)	12/28/2007	12/29/2006	12/30/2005	12/31/2004	01/02/2004	01/03/2003	12/28/2001	12/29/2000
Earnings Per Share	1.75	1.41	1.45	1.24	1.02	0.55	0.46	0.94
Cash Flow Per Share	2.07	2.41	1.94	1.97	0.91	1.06	0.82	1.77
Tang Book Value Per Share	N.M.	2.88	4.52	5.86	5.17	4.57	3.56	2.98
Dividends Per Share	0.287	0.240	0.200	0.165	0.147	0.138	0.128	0.117
Dividend Payout %	16.43	17.02	13.84	13.31	14.39	25.00	27.72	12.43
Income Statement								
Total Revenue	12,990,000	12,160,000	11,550,000	10,099,000	9,014,000	8,441,000	10,152,000	10,017,000
EBITDA	1,480,000	1,264,000	928,000	773,000	629,000	660,000	680,000	1,061,000
Income Before Taxes	1,137,000	997,000	717,000	654,000	488,000	471,000	370,000	757,000
Income Taxes	441,000	286,000	94,000	100,000	(43,000)	32,000	134,000	278,000
Net Income	696,000	608,000	669,000	596,000	502,000	277,000	236,000	479,000
Average Shares	397,300	430,200	462,400	481,000	490,800	509,200	513,400	508,000
Balance Sheet								
Current Assets	3,572,000	3,314,000	2,010,000	1,946,000	1,235,000	1,744,000	2,130,000	1,415,000
Total Assets	8,942,000	8,588,000	8,530,000	8,668,000	8,177,000	8,296,000	9,107,000	8,237,000
Current Liabilities	2,876,000	2,522,000	1,992,000	2,356,000	1,770,000	2,207,000	1,802,000	1,917,000
Long-Term Obligations	2,790,000	1,818,000	1,681,000	836,000	1,391,000	1,553,000	2,815,000	2,016,000
Total Liabilities	7,513,000	5,970,000	5,278,000	4,587,000	4,339,000	4,723,000	5,629,000	4,970,000
Stockholders' Equity	1,429,000	2,618,000	3,252,000	4,081,000	3,838,000	3,573,000	3,478,000	3,267,000
Shares Outstanding	357,100	389,500	411,800	451,600	462,400	471,800	481,400	482,000
Statistical Record								
Return on Assets %	7.96	7.12	7.80	7.10	6.11	3.13	2.73	6.17
Return on Equity %	34.49	20.77	18.30	15.09	13.58	7.73	7.02	15.56
EBITDA Margin %	11.39	10.39	8.03	7.65	6.98	7.82	6.70	10.59
Net Margin %	5.36	5.00	5.79	5.90	5.57	3.28	2.32	4.78
Asset Turnover	1.49	1.42	1.35	1.20	1.10	0.95	1.17	1.29
Current Ratio	1.24	1.31	1.01	0.83	0.70	0.79	1.18	0.74
Debt to Equity	1.95	0.69	0.52	0.20	0.36	0.43	0.81	0.62
Price Range	51.87-31.49	48.10-33.03	35.26-29.05	31.77-20.40	23.39-14.43	23.17-13.23	24.84-14.48	21.34-13.31
P/E Ratio	29.64-17.99	34.11-23.42	24.32-20.03	25.63-16.45	22.93-14.14	42.13-24.05	54.00-31.47	22.71-14.16
Average Yield %	0.65	0.64	0.62	0.67	0.76	0.75	0.61	0.66

Address: 10400 Fernwood Road, Bethesda, MD 20817 **Telephone:** 301-380-3000	**Web Site:** www.marriott.com **Officers:** J. W. Marriott Jr. - Chmn., C.E.O. John W. Marriott III - Vice-Chmn.	**Auditors:** Ernst & Young LLP **Transfer Agents:** Equiserve Trust Company, N.A.

MARSH & McLENNAN COMPANIES INC.

Exchange	Symbol	Price	52Wk Range	Yield	P/E
NYS	MMC	$24.35 (3/31/2008)	33.19-24.06	3.29	5.38

*7 Year Price Score 57.63   *NYSE Composite Index=100   *12 Month Price Score 100.62

Interim Earnings (Per Share)

Qtr.	Mar	Jun	Sep	Dec
2003	0.81	0.66	0.65	0.69
2004	0.83	0.73	0.04	(1.27)
2005	0.25	0.31	0.12	0.07
2006	0.75	0.31	0.31	0.40
2007	0.47	0.31	3.60	0.22

Interim Dividends (Per Share)

Amt	Decl	Ex	Rec	Pay
0.19Q	5/17/2007	7/3/2007	7/6/2007	8/15/2007
0.19Q	9/19/2007	10/11/2007	10/15/2007	11/15/2007
0.20Q	1/17/2008	1/24/2008	1/28/2008	2/15/2000
0.20Q	3/19/2008	4/4/2008	4/8/2008	5/15/2008

Indicated Div: $0.80

Valuation Analysis

Forecast P/E	14.11
	(1/10/2007)
Market Cap	$12.7 Billion
Book Value	7.8 Billion
Price/Book	1.62
Price/Sales	1.12

Institutional Holding

No of Institutions	443
Shares	431,947,584
% Held	78.14

Business Summary: Insurance (MIC: 8.2 SIC: 6411 NAIC: 524210)

Marsh & McLennan Companies is a professional services firm. Through its subsidiaries, Co. provides clients with advice and services in the areas of risk, strategy and human capital through three operating segments: Risk and Insurance Services, which includes risk management activities as well as insurance and reinsurance broking and services; Consulting, which includes human resource consulting and related outsourcing and investment services, and specialized management and economic consulting services; and Risk Consulting and Technology, which includes risk consulting and related investigative, quantitative, intelligence, financial, security and technology services.

Recent Developments: For the year ended Dec 31 2007, income from continuing operations decreased 14.9% to US$538.0 million from US$632.0 million a year earlier. Net income increased 150.0% to US$2.48 billion from US$990.0 million in the prior year. Revenues were US$11.35 billion, up 7.6% from US$10.55 billion the year before.

Prospects: Co.'s top line results are being positively affected by higher revenue in its Consulting, and Risk Consulting and Technology segments. Specifically, Co.'s Consulting revenue is increasing due to revenue growth throughout its retirement and investment, health and benefits, outsourcing, and talent operations. In addition, Co. is seeing an increase in Risk Consulting and Technology revenue, primarily due to higher revenue in its technology operations due to an acquisition and robust growth in background screening. Looking ahead, Co. expects revenue from its Marsh & McLennan Risk Capital Holdings subsidiary to continue to be lower in 2008 compared with 2007.

Financial Data
(US$ in Thousands)

	12/31/2007	12/31/2006	12/31/2005	12/31/2004	12/31/2003	12/31/2002	12/31/2001	12/31/2000
Earnings Per Share	4.53	1.76	0.74	0.33	2.81	2.45	1.70	2.05
Cash Flow Per Share	(0.43)	1.60	0.74	3.92	3.50	2.37	2.50	2.50
Tang Book Value Per Share	0.12	N.M.	N.M.	N.M.	N.M.	N.M.	N M	N.M.
Dividends Per Share	0.760	0.680	0.680	0.990	1.490	1.090	1.030	0.950
Dividend Payout %	16.78	38.64	91.89	300.00	53.02	44.49	60.77	46.34
Income Statement								
Total Revenue	11,350,000	11,921,000	11,652,000	12,159,000	11,588,000	10,440,000	9,943,000	10,157,000
Income Before Taxes	847,000	1,219,000	571,000	450,000	2,335,000	2,133,000	1,590,000	1,955,000
Income Taxes	295,000	388,000	192,000	259,000	770,000	717,000	599,000	733,000
Net Income	2,475,000	990,000	404,000	176,000	1,540,000	1,365,000	974,000	1,181,000
Average Shares	546,000	557,000	543,000	535,000	548,000	557,000	572,000	568,000
Balance Sheet								
Total Assets	17,359,000	18,137,000	17,892,000	18,337,000	15,053,000	13,855,000	13,293,000	13,769,000
Total Liabilities	9,537,000	12,318,000	12,532,000	13,281,000	9,602,000	8,837,000	8,120,000	8,541,000
Stockholders' Equity	7,822,000	5,819,000	5,360,000	5,056,000	5,451,000	5,018,000	5,173,000	5,228,000
Shares Outstanding	520,392	551,913	545,583	526,809	526,736	538,199	548,654	552,052
Statistical Record								
Return on Assets %	13.95	5.50	2.23	1.05	10.65	10.06	7.20	8.79
Return on Equity %	36.29	17.71	7.76	3.34	29.42	26.79	18.73	25.06
Price Range	33.19-24.20	32.73-24.77	33.09-26.93	49.30-24.10	54.74-38.52	56.85-35.53	58.56-40.25	67.44-36.50
P/E Ratio	7.33-5.34	18.60-14.07	44.72-36.39	149.39-73.03	19.48-13.71	23.20-14.50	34.45-23.68	32.90-17.80
Average Yield %	2.66	2.34	2.28	2.36	3.17	2.23	2.04	1.75

Address: 1166 Avenue Of The Americas, New York, NY 10036
Telephone: 212-345-5000
Fax: 212-345-4809

Web Site: www.mmc.com
Officers: Michael G. Cherkasky - Pres., C.E.O. Sandra S. Wijnberg - Sr. V.P., C.F.O.

Auditors: Deloitte & Touche LLP
Transfer Agents: The Bank of New York, New York, NY

MARSHALL & ILSLEY CORP

Exchange	Symbol	Price	52Wk Range	Yield	P/E	Div Acheiver
NYS	MI	$23.20 (3/31/2008)	34.50-21.71	5.34	5.35	35 Years

*7 Year Price Score N/A   *NYSE Composite Index=100   *12 Month Price Score N/A

Interim Earnings (Per Share)

No earnings information available

Interim Dividends (Per Share)

Amt	Decl	Ex	Rec	Pay
0.31Q	10/18/2007	11/28/2007	11/30/2007	12/14/2007
0.31Q	2/21/2008	2/28/2008	3/3/2008	3/14/2008

Indicated Div: $1.24

Valuation Analysis | **Institutional Holding**

Forecast P/E	N/A	No of Institutions
		N/A
Market Cap	$6.1 Billion	Shares
Book Value	7.0 Billion	N/A
Price/Book	0.87	% Held
Price/Sales	1.39	N/A

Business Summary: Commercial Banking (MIC: 8.1 SIC: 6021 NAIC: 522110)

Marshall & Ilsley is a bank holding company with total assets of $59.85 billion and deposits of $35.19 billion at Dec 31 2007. Co.'s key activities consist of banking and wealth management services. Banking services, lending and accepting deposits from commercial banking and community banking customers are provided via Co.'s key bank, M&I Marshall & Ilsley Bank (M&I Bank), Southwest Bank, which is headquartered in St. Louis, MO, M&I Bank FSB, a federal savings bank subsidiary of Co. in Las Vegas, and an asset-based lending subsidiary based in Minneapolis, MN. Co.'s wealth management services include trust, brokerage and insurance services, and investment management and advisory services.

Recent Developments: For the year ended Dec 31 2007, income from continuing operations decreased 23.3% to US$496.9 million from US$647.7 million a year earlier. Net income increased 42.5% to US$1.15 billion from US$807.8 million in the prior year. Net interest income increased 7.2% to US$1.62 billion from US$1.51 billion in the prior year. Provision for loan losses was US$319.8 million versus US$50.6 million in the prior year, an increase of 532.5%. Non-interest income rose 25.3% to US$729.1 million from US$581.7 million, while non-interest expense advanced 21.4% to US$1.31 billion.

Prospects: On Jan 2 2008, Co. acquired Indianapolis-based First Indiana Corporation for about $530.2 million, resulting in First Indiana's 32 offices becoming branches of Co.'s M&I bank subsidiary in Feb 2008. Meanwhile, Co. believes that continued pricing competition for loan products, increased funding costs and the elevated levels of nonperforming loans will result in a modest net interest margin compression in 2008. However, Co. expects its Nov 2007 separation from its former subsidiary, Metavante Corp., to drive earnings per share growth by enabling it to provide resources for organic growth, fund strategic initiatives within its businesses and pursue opportunities in new markets going forward.

Financial Data

(US$ in Thousands)	12/31/2007	12/31/2006	12/31/2005
Earnings Per Share	4.34	3.17	2.99
Cash Flow Per Share	3.66	3.39	...
Tang Book Value Per Share	19.83	17.92	...
Dividends Per Share	1.200	1.050	0.930
Dividend Payout %	27.65	33.12	31.10
Income Statement			
Total Revenue	4,398,231	3,835,920	2,862,651
EBITDA	774,248	1,016,200	913,865
Income Before Taxes	710,580	955,149	864,783
Income Taxes	213,641	307,435	278,124
Net Income	1,150,936	807,838	706,190
Average Shares	265,480	254,584	236,031
Balance Sheet			
Current Assets	1,955,428	1,491,086	...
Total Assets	59,848,596	56,230,257	...
Current Liabilities	43,667,736	41,051,507	...
Long-Term Obligations	8,207,406	8,026,155	...
Total Liabilities	52,815,867	50,078,886	...
Stockholders' Equity	7,032,729	6,151,371	...
Shares Outstanding	263,486	255,469	...
Statistical Record			
Return on Assets %	1.98	...	...
Return on Equity %	17.46	...	...
EBITDA Margin %	17.60	26.49	31.92
Net Margin %	26.17	21.06	24.67
Asset Turnover	0.08	...	...
Current Ratio	0.04	0.04	...
Debt to Equity	1.17	1.30	...
Price Range	34.50-26.36	...	...
P/E Ratio	7.95-6.07	...	...
Average Yield %	3.99	...	...

Address: 770 North Water Street, Milwaukee, WI 53202 Telephone: 414-765-7801	Web Site: www.micorp.com Officers: Dennis J. Kuester - Chmn., Sub. Off. Mark F. Furlong - Pres., C.E.O.	Auditors: DELOITTE & TOUCHE LLP

MARTIN MARIETTA MATERIALS, INC.

Exchange	Symbol	Price	52Wk Range	Yield	P/E	Div Acheiver
NYS	MLM	$106.17 (3/31/2008)	168.77-95.67	1.30	17.52	13 Years

*7 Year Price Score 157.50 *NYSE Composite Index=100 ***12 Month Price Score 88.31**

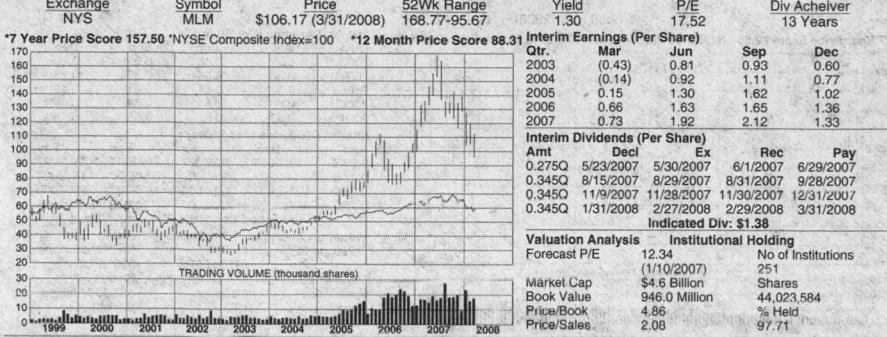

Interim Earnings (Per Share)

Qtr.	Mar	Jun	Sep	Dec
2003	(0.43)	0.81	0.93	0.60
2004	(0.14)	0.92	1.11	0.77
2005	0.15	1.30	1.62	1.02
2006	0.66	1.63	1.65	1.36
2007	0.73	1.92	2.12	1.33

Interim Dividends (Per Share)

Amt	Decl	Ex	Rec	Pay
0.275Q	5/23/2007	5/30/2007	6/1/2007	6/29/2007
0.345Q	8/15/2007	8/29/2007	8/31/2007	9/28/2007
0.345Q	11/9/2007	11/28/2007	11/30/2007	12/31/2007
0.345Q	1/31/2008	2/27/2008	2/29/2008	3/31/2008
Indicated Div: $1.38				

Valuation Analysis | **Institutional Holding**

Forecast P/E	12.34	No of Institutions
	(1/10/2007)	251
Market Cap	$4.6 Billion	Shares
Book Value	946.0 Million	44,023,584
Price/Book	4.86	% Held
Price/Sales	2.08	97.71

Business Summary: Earth & Rock Mining (MIC: 14.5 SIC: 1481 NAIC: 213115)

Martin Marietta Materials is a producer of aggregates for the construction industry, including infrastructure, commercial, agricultural, and residential. As of Dec 31 2007, Co.'s aggregates, asphalt products, and ready mixed concrete are sold and shipped from a network of approximately 287 quarries, underground mines, distribution facilities, and plants in 28 states, Canada, and the Bahamas Co. operates through four reportable business segments: the Mideast Group, Southeast Group, and West Group, comprising the Aggregates business, and the Specialty Products segment, which manufactures and markets magnesia-based chemical products, dolomitic lime, and structural composite products.

Recent Developments: For the year ended Dec 31 2007, income from continuing operations increased 7.0% to US$262.5 million from US$245.4 million a year earlier. Net income increased 7.1% to US$262.7 million from US$245.4 million in the prior year. Revenues were US$2.21 billion, up 0.7% from US$2.19 billion the year before. Operating income was US$433.0 million versus US$390.5 million in the prior year, an increase of 10.9%. Direct operating expenses declined 1.8% to US$1.64 billion from US$1.67 billion in the comparable period the year before. Indirect operating expenses increased 2.4% to US$137.9 million from US$134.7 million in the equivalent prior-year period.

Prospects: Looking ahead, Co. expects 2008 to be a challenging year reflecting the uncertainty prevalent in the U.S. economy. However, Co. expects that demand for aggregate products in the infrastructure and commercial construction markets to be solid. Further, Co. expects that magnesia-based chemicals products demand to steadily increase in its Specialty Products segment as industries focus on clean air, clean water, and other green initiatives. Accordingly, Co. estimates that 2008 aggregates volumes will range from growth of 1.0% to a decline of 3.0% and the rate of price increase will be in a range from 5.5% to 7.5%. Lastly, Co. projects net earnings of $6.25 to $7.00 per diluted share for 2008.

Financial Data

(US$ in Thousands)	12/31/2007	12/31/2006	12/31/2005	12/31/2004	12/31/2003	12/31/2002	12/31/2001	12/31/2000
Earnings Per Share	6.06	5.29	4.08	2.66	1.91	1.77	2.19	2.39
Cash Flow Per Share	9.27	7.44	6.83	5.53	5.67	4.18	5.28	4.54
Tang Book Value Per Share	8.35	14.99	12.81	11.99	10.83	9.70	8.55	9.70
Dividends Per Share	1.240	1.010	0.860	0.760	0.690	0.580	0.560	0.540
Dividend Payout %	20.46	19.09	21.08	28.57	36.13	32.77	25.57	22.59
Income Statement								
Total Revenue	2,207,141	2,206,401	2,004,243	1,759,613	1,711,453	1,692,437	1,718,050	1,517,517
EBITDA	589,811	532,232	448,895	359,849	324,324	326,994	359,866	347,089
Income Before Taxes	378,580	350,444	268,047	184,722	142,131	144,270	158,439	168,821
Income Taxes	116,073	106,640	72,534	56,543	41,047	46,455	53,077	56,794
Net Income	262,749	245,422	192,666	129,163	93,623	86,305	105,362	112,027
Average Shares	43,347	46,367	47,279	48,534	49,136	48,858	48,066	46,948
Balance Sheet								
Current Assets	626,010	592,354	602,041	624,253	621,519	526,149	496,232	425,001
Total Assets	2,683,805	2,506,421	2,433,316	2,355,852	2,330,093	2,258,530	2,224,580	1,841,439
Current Liabilities	306,616	315,072	200,122	203,813	220,164	197,827	192,037	189,113
Long-Term Obligations	848,186	579,308	709,159	713,661	717,073	733,471	797,385	601,580
Total Liabilities	1,737,814	1,252,449	1,259,631	1,202,425	1,200,246	1,175,520	1,202,368	978,153
Stockholders' Equity	945,991	1,253,972	1,173,685	1,153,427	1,129,847	1,083,010	1,022,212	863,286
Shares Outstanding	43,318	44,851	45,727	47,306	48,670	48,847	48,559	46,783
Statistical Record								
Return on Assets %	10.12	9.94	8.05	5.50	4.08	3.85	5.18	6.23
Return on Equity %	23.89	20.22	16.56	11.28	8.46	8.20	11.18	13.65
EBITDA Margin %	26.72	24.12	22.40	20.45	18.95	19.32	20.95	22.87
Net Margin %	11.90	11.12	9.61	7.34	5.47	5.10	6.13	7.38
Asset Turnover	0.85	0.89	0.84	0.75	0.75	0.76	0.85	0.84
Current Ratio	1.24	1.88	3.01	3.06	2.82	2.66	2.58	2.25
Debt to Equity	0.90	0.46	0.60	0.62	0.63	0.68	0.78	0.70
Price Range	168.77-99.93	112.37-76.39	79.93-50.01	53.66-41.66	47.78-26.15	48.12-27.45	51.27-36.00	54.25-32.25
P/E Ratio	27.85-16.49	21.24-14.44	19.59-12.26	20.17-15.66	25.02-13.69	27.19-15.51	23.41-16.44	22.70-13.49
Average Yield %	0.92	1.11	1.32	1.66	1.97	1.56	1.27	1.27

Address: 2710 Wycliff Road, Raleigh, NC 27607-3033	Web Site: www.martinmarietta.com	Auditors: Ernst & Young LLP
Telephone: 919-781-4550	Officers: Stephen P. Zelnak Jr. - Chmn., Pres., C.E.O. Philip J. Sipling - Exec. V.P.	Transfer Agents: American Stock Transfer & Trust Company, New York, NY
Fax: 919-783-4552		

MASCO CORP.

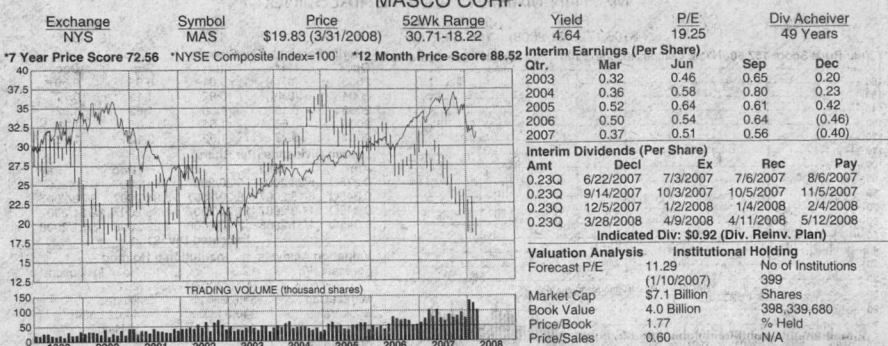

Exchange	Symbol	Price	52Wk Range	Yield	P/E	Div Achiever
NYS	MAS	$19.83 (3/31/2008)	30.71-18.22	4.64	19.25	49 Years

*7 Year Price Score 72.56   ***NYSE Composite Index=100**   ***12 Month Price Score 88.52**

Interim Earnings (Per Share)

Qtr.	Mar	Jun	Sep	Dec
2003	0.32	0.46	0.65	0.20
2004	0.36	0.58	0.80	0.23
2005	0.52	0.64	0.61	0.42
2006	0.50	0.54	0.64	(0.46)
2007	0.37	0.51	0.56	(0.40)

Interim Dividends (Per Share)

Amt	Decl	Ex	Rec	Pay
0.23Q	6/22/2007	7/3/2007	7/6/2007	8/6/2007
0.23Q	9/14/2007	10/3/2007	10/5/2007	11/5/2007
0.23Q	12/5/2007	1/2/2008	1/4/2008	2/4/2008
0.23Q	3/28/2008	4/9/2008	4/11/2008	5/12/2008

Indicated Div: $0.92 (Div. Reinv. Plan)

Valuation Analysis

		Institutional Holding	
Forecast P/E	11.29	No of Institutions	
	(1/10/2007)	399	
Market Cap	$7.1 Billion	Shares	
Book Value	4.0 Billion	398,339,680	
Price/Book	1.77	% Held	
Price/Sales	0.60	N/A	

Business Summary: Wood Products (MIC: 11.9 SIC: 2434 NAIC: 337110)

Masco is engaged in the manufacture, distribution, and installation of home improvement and building products, with an emphasis on brand name consumer products and services. These products and services are sold to the home improvement and new home construction markets through mass merchandisers, hardware stores, home centers, builders, distributors and other outlets for consumers and contractors. As of Dec 31 2007, Co. operated through five business segments: Cabinets and Related Products; Plumbing Products; Installation and Other Services; Decorative Architectural Products; and Other Specialty Products.

Recent Developments: For the year ended Dec 31 2007, income from continuing operations decreased 16.9% to US$397.0 million from US$478.0 million a year earlier. Net income decreased 20.9% to US$386.0 million from US$488.0 million in the prior year. Revenues were US$11.77 billion, down 7.5% from US$12.72 billion the year before. Operating income was US$959.0 million versus US$1.14 billion in the prior year, a decrease of 15.9%. Direct operating expenses declined 7.1% to US$8.56 billion from US$9.21 billion in the comparable period the year before. Indirect operating expenses decreased 4.8% to US$2.25 billion from US$2.37 billion in the equivalent prior-year period.

Prospects: For 2008, Co. anticipates a further decline in housing starts, a continued softness in sales of existing homes, as well as ongoing decline in consumer spending for home improvement products and moderation in the demand for certain of its international products. As a result, for 2008, Co. estimates its sales to decline high-single to low-double digits compared with 2007, and its earnings to be in a range of $0.85 to $1.15 per share. Meanwhile, Co. plans to sell several of its European business units that are not core to its long-term growth strategy. The dispositions, which should generate proceeds of more than $140.0 million, are expected to be completed by the end of 2008.

Financial Data
(US$ in Thousands)

	12/31/2007	12/31/2006	12/31/2005	12/31/2004	12/31/2003	12/31/2002	12/31/2001	12/31/2000
Earnings Per Share	1.03	1.22	2.19	1.96	1.64	1.15	0.42	1.31
Cash Flow Per Share	3.44	3.07	3.26	3.26	2.97	2.53	2.10	1.66
Tang Book Value Per Share	N.M.	0.54	0.88	1.54	1.35	1.31	1.30	2.78
Dividends Per Share	0.910	0.860	0.780	0.660	0.580	0.545	0.525	0.490
Dividend Payout %	88.35	70.49	35.62	33.67	35.37	47.39	125.00	37.40
Income Statement								
Total Revenue	11,770,000	12,778,000	12,642,000	12,074,000	10,936,000	9,419,400	8,358,000	7,243,000
EBITDA	1,266,000	1,378,000	1,882,000	1,958,000	1,702,000	1,462,440	773,860	1,262,630
Income Before Taxes	770,000	900,000	1,412,000	1,518,000	1,216,000	1,031,000	300,700	893,400
Income Taxes	336,000	412,000	518,000	569,000	463,000	348,900	102,200	301,700
Net Income	386,000	488,000	940,000	893,000	806,000	589,700	198,500	591,700
Average Shares	373,000	400,000	430,000	456,000	491,000	514,100	474,900	451,800
Balance Sheet								
Current Assets	3,808,000	5,115,000	5,123,000	4,402,000	3,804,000	3,949,770	2,626,920	2,308,160
Total Assets	10,907,000	12,325,000	12,559,000	12,541,000	12,149,000	12,050,430	9,183,330	7,744,000
Current Liabilities	1,908,000	3,389,000	2,894,000	2,147,000	2,099,000	1,932,450	1,236,560	1,078,050
Long-Term Obligations	3,966,000	3,533,000	3,915,000	4,187,000	3,848,000	4,316,470	3,627,630	3,018,240
Total Liabilities	6,882,000	7,854,000	7,711,000	7,118,000	6,693,000	6,756,590	5,063,500	4,317,940
Stockholders' Equity	4,025,000	4,471,000	4,848,000	5,423,000	5,456,000	5,293,840	4,119,830	3,426,060
Shares Outstanding	358,900	383,890	419,040	446,720	458,380	488,890	459,050	444,750
Statistical Record								
Return on Assets %	3.32	3.92	7.49	7.21	6.66	5.55	2.35	8.21
Return on Equity %	9.09	10.47	18.30	16.37	15.00	12.53	5.26	17.98
EBITDA Margin %	10.76	10.78	14.89	16.22	15.56	15.53	9.26	17.43
Net Margin %	3.28	3.82	7.44	7.40	7.37	6.26	2.37	8.17
Asset Turnover	1.01	1.03	1.01	0.98	0.90	0.89	0.99	1.00
Current Ratio	2.00	1.51	1.77	2.05	1.81	2.04	2.12	2.14
Debt to Equity	0.99	0.79	0.81	0.77	0.71	0.82	0.88	0.88
Price Range	33.93-20.94	33.20-26.00	38.03-27.37	36.80-26.02	28.31-16.82	29.08-17.68	26.49-18.00	25.69-14.81
P/E Ratio	32.94-20.33	27.21-21.31	17.37-12.50	18.78-13.28	17.26-10.26	25.29-15.37	63.07-42.86	19.61-11.31
Average Yield %	3.38	2.93	2.43	2.13	2.50	2.24	2.24	2.46

Address: 21001 Van Born Road, Taylor, MI 48180	**Web Site:** www.masco.com	**Auditors:** PricewaterhouseCoopers LLP
Telephone: 313-274-7400	**Officers:** Richard A. Manoogian - Chmn., C.E.O.	**Investor Contact:** 313-274-7400
Fax: 313-792-4177	Alan H. Barry - Pres., C.O.O.	**Transfer Agents:** Bank of New York, New York, NY

MASSEY ENERGY CO.

Exchange	Symbol	Price	52Wk Range	Yield	P/E
NYS	MEE	$36.50 (3/31/2008)	43.48-17.36	0.55	31.20

*7 Year Price Score 94.68 *NYSE Composite Index=100 *12 Month Price Score 143.26

TRADING VOLUME (thousand shares)

Interim Earnings (Per Share)

Qtr.	Mar	Jun	Sep	Dec
2003	(0.23)	(0.03)	(0.05)	(0.23)
2004	(0.03)	0.16	0.03	0.02
2005	0.59	0.44	0.28	(2.64)
2006	0.07	0.04	0.30	0.10
2007	0.40	0.43	0.27	0.07

Interim Dividends (Per Share)

Amt	Decl	Ex	Rec	Pay
0.04Q	5/22/2007	6/22/2007	6/26/2007	7/10/2007
0.04Q	8/14/2007	9/21/2007	9/25/2007	10/9/2007
0.05Q	11/13/2007	12/20/2007	12/24/2007	1/8/2008
0.05Q	2/19/2008	3/20/2008	3/25/2008	4/8/2008

Indicated Div: $0.20

Valuation Analysis

Forecast P/E	N/A
Market Cap	$2.9 Billion
Book Value	784.0 Million
Price/Book	3.72
Price/Sales	1.21

Institutional Holding

No of Institutions	193
Shares	84,286,352
% Held	N/A

Business Summary: Coal Mining (MIC: 14.4 SIC: 1221 NAIC: 212111)

Massey Energy produces, processes and sells bituminous coal of steam and metallurgical grades, primarily of a low sulfur content. Customers for Co.'s steam coal product include primarily electric power utility companies who use coal as fuel for their steam-powered generators. Customers for Co.'s metallurgical coal include primarily steel producers who use coal to produce coke, which is in turn used as a raw material in the steel manufacturing process. At Jan 31 2008, Co. operated 47 mines, including 35 underground (one of which employs both room and pillar and longwall mining) and 12 surface (with eight highwall miners in operation) in West Virginia, Kentucky and Virginia.

Recent Developments: For the year ended Dec 31 2007, net income increased 129.6% to US$94.1 million from US$41.0 million in the prior year. Revenues were US$2.41 billion, up 8.7% from US$2.22 billion the year before. Operating income was US$179.7 million versus US$111.0 million in the prior year, an increase of 61.9%. Direct operating expenses rose 5.0% to US$2.15 billion from US$2.05 billion in the comparable period the year before. Indirect operating expenses increased 38.4% to US$83.2 million from US$60.1 million in the equivalent prior-year period.

Prospects: For 2008, Co. projects produced coal shipments to be between 41.5 million and 43.0 million tons. Looking further ahead to 2009, Co. expects total shipments to be in a range of 44.0 million to 46.0 million tons. Meanwhile, Co.'s two-year internal expansion and cost reduction plan, which began in the fourth quarter of 2007, anticipates developing net additional annual production of 8.0 million tons in 2010 versus 2007, with the ramp up expected to occur during 2008 and 2009. Notably, these new tons will be weighted towards metallurgical coal production, which Co. believes should be cost advantaged versus existing comparable quality competitor production.

Financial Data

(US$ in Thousands)	12/31/2007	12/31/2006	12/31/2005	12/31/2004	12/31/2003	12/31/2002	12/31/2001	10/31/2001
Earnings Per Share	1.17	0.50	(1.33)	0.18	(0.54)	(0.44)	(0.20)	(0.01)
Cash Flow Per Share	4.94	2.65	3.54	3.00	0.21	1.65	0.22	2.74
Tang Book Value Per Share	9.81	8.60	10.26	10.16	10.05	10.73	...	11.62
Dividends Per Share	0.170	0.160	0.160	0.160	0.160	0.160	0.160	0.160
Dividend Payout %	14.53	32.00	...	88.89	...	...	...	...
Income Statement								
Total Revenue	2,413,523	2,219,854	2,204,258	1,766,644	1,553,424	1,630,095	246,443	1,253,756
EBITDA	425,714	341,544	213,616	270,806	178,953	181,042	11,983	197,979
Income Before Taxes	129,503	45,024	(75,410)	(5,643)	(60,651)	(57,520)	(23,524)	(8,757)
Income Taxes	35,405	3,408	26,228	(19,495)	(28,318)	(24,946)	(8,723)	(7,707)
Net Income	94,098	40,977	(101,638)	13,852	(40,212)	(32,574)	(14,801)	(1,030)
Average Shares	80,654	81,386	76,390	76,450	74,592	74,442	74,131	73,858
Balance Sheet								
Current Assets	887,394	799,728	1,044,447	790,698	702,522	509,841	...	455,104
Total Assets	2,860,671	2,740,696	2,986,412	2,650,905	2,376,738	2,241,433	...	2,268,666
Current Liabilities	367,862	354,537	373,730	332,302	259,274	573,263	...	540,171
Long-Term Obligations	1,102,672	1,102,324	1,102,582	900,195	784,327	286,000	...	300,000
Total Liabilities	2,076,667	2,043,405	2,145,428	1,874,032	1,617,782	1,433,220	...	1,102,316
Stockholders' Equity	784,004	697,291	840,984	776,873	758,956	808,212	...	866,350
Shares Outstanding	79,943	81,066	81,939	76,430	75,508	75,317	...	74,543
Statistical Record								
Return on Assets %	3.36	1.43	N.M.	0.55	N.M.	...	...	N.M.
Return on Equity %	12.70	5.33	N.M.	1.80	N.M.	...	...	N.M.
EBITDA Margin %	17.64	15.39	9.69	15.33	11.52	11.11	4.86	15.79
Net Margin %	3.90	1.85	N.M.	0.78	N.M.	N.M.	N.M.	N.M.
Asset Turnover	0.86	0.78	0.78	0.70	0.67	...	...	0.57
Current Ratio	2.41	2.26	2.79	2.38	2.71	0.89	...	0.84
Debt to Equity	1.41	1.58	1.31	1.16	1.03	0.35	...	0.35
Price Range	37.18-17.36	43.85-19.63	55.50-31.86	36.11-19.10	21.45-7.78	22.22-4.84	20.73-16.20	28.20-8.65
P/E Ratio	31.78-14.84	87.70-39.26	...	200.94-106.11	...	...	...	...
Average Yield %	0.66	0.51	0.36	0.61	1.30	1.39	0.87	0.89

Address: Massey Energy Company,	Web Site: www.masseyenergyco.com	Auditors: Ernst & Young LLP
P.O. Box 26765, Richmond, VA 23261	Officers: Don L. Blankenship - Chmn., Pres., C.E.O.	Investor Contact: 866-814-6512
Telephone: 804-788-1800	Baxter F. Phillips Jr. - Exec. V.P., Chief Admin.	Transfer Agents: Mellon Investor
Fax: 804-788-1870	Officer	Services LLC, Ridgefield Park, NJ

MASTERCARD INC

Exchange	Symbol	Price	52Wk Range	Yield	P/E
NYS	MA	$222.99 (3/31/2008)	224.98-106.96	0.27	27.87

*7 Year Price Score N/A   *NYSE Composite Index=100   *12 Month Price Score 131.62

Interim Earnings (Per Share)

Qtr.	Mar	Jun	Sep	Dec
2005	0.93	0.89	0.79	0.30
2006	1.27	(2.30)	1.42	0.30
2007	1.57	1.85	2.31	2.27

Interim Dividends (Per Share)

Amt	Decl	Ex	Rec	Pay
0.15Q	6/7/2007	6/29/2007	7/3/2007	8/10/2007
0.15Q	9/6/2007	10/17/2007	10/19/2007	11/9/2007
0.15Q	12/6/2007	1/9/2008	1/11/2008	2/11/2008
0.15Q	2/5/2008	4/7/2008	4/9/2008	5/9/2008

Indicated Div: $0.60

Valuation Analysis   **Institutional Holding**

Forecast P/E	N/A	No of Institutions 205
Market Cap	$29.3 Billion	Shares
Book Value	3.0 Billion	62,854,092
Price/Book	9.67	% Held
Price/Sales	7.20	46.53

Business Summary: Miscellaneous Business Services (MIC: 12.8 SIC: 7389 NAIC: 525990)

MasterCard is a global payment applications company that provides a range of services in support of the credit, debit and related payment programs of over 25,000 financial institutions, as of Dec 31 2007. Co. manages a family of payment card brands, including MasterCard®, MasterCard Electronic™, Maestro® and Cirrus®, which Co. licenses to its customers. As part of managing these brands, Co. also implements and enforces rules and standards surrounding the use of its payment card system. Cardholder and merchant relationships are managed principally by Co.'s customers.

Recent Developments: For the year ended Dec 31 2007, net income increased to US$1.09 billion from US$50.2 million in the prior year. Revenues were US$4.07 billion, up 22.3% from US$3.33 billion the year before. Operating income was US$1.11 billion versus US$229.5 million in the prior year, an increase of 382.8%. Indirect operating expenses decreased 4.4% to US$2.96 billion from US$3.10 billion in the equivalent prior-year period.

Prospects: Moving forward, Co. plans to expand its existing customer base in targeted geographies and higher-growth segments of the global payments industry, enhancing its merchant relationships, as well as continuing to invest in its brands. In addition, Co. intends to pursue incremental payment processing opportunities globally. Meanwhile, Co. believes that the trend within the global payments industry from paper-based forms of payment, such as cash and checks, toward electronic forms of payment, such as cards will create opportunities for continued growth of its business. Over the long-term, Co. anticipates higher volume of business by investing in strong customer relationships.

Financial Data

(US$ in Thousands)	12/31/2007	12/31/2006	12/31/2005	12/31/2004	12/31/2003
Earnings Per Share	8.00	0.37	2.67	2.38	(3.86)
Cash Flow Per Share	5.71	4.80	2.73	3.43	...
Tang Book Value Per Share	18.79	13.90	6.99	4.28	...
Dividends Per Share	0.600	0.180	...	...	...
Dividend Payout %	7.50	48.65	...	...	...
Income Statement					
Total Revenue	4,067,599	3,326,074	2,937,628	2,593,330	2,230,851
EBITDA	1,685,500	354,999	537,023	479,688	(464,435)
Income Before Taxes	1,671,432	294,172	407,338	323,700	(611,520)
Income Taxes	585,546	243,982	140,619	85,640	(220,778)
Net Income	1,085,886	50,190	266,719	238,060	(385,793)
Average Shares	135,695	135,779	100,000	100,000	100,000
Balance Sheet					
Current Assets	4,591,741	3,577,229	2,227,898	1,902,796	...
Total Assets	6,260,041	5,082,470	3,700,544	3,264,670	...
Current Liabilities	2,363,342	1,811,590	1,556,703	1,301,362	...
Long-Term Obligations	149,824	229,668	229,489	229,569	...
Total Liabilities	3,228,114	2,713,491	2,526,776	2,285,098	...
Stockholders' Equity	3,027,307	2,364,359	1,169,148	974,952	...
Shares Outstanding	131,271	134,969	100,000	100,000	100,000
Statistical Record					
Return on Assets %	19.15	1.14	7.66	...	...
Return on Equity %	40.28	2.84	24.88	...	...
EBITDA Margin %	41.44	10.67	18.28	18.50	N.M.
Net Margin %	26.70	1.51	9.08	9.18	N.M.
Asset Turnover	0.72	0.76	0.84	...	...
Current Ratio	1.94	1.97	1.43	1.46	...
Debt to Equity	0.05	0.10	0.20	0.24	...
Price Range	223.20-96.41	105.48-43.90	...	...	...
P/E Ratio	27.90-12.05	285.08-118.65	...	...	...
Average Yield %	0.42	0.27	...	...	...

Address: 2000 Purchase Street, Purchase, NY 10577 **Telephone:** 914-249-2000	**Web Site:** www.mastercardintl.com **Officers:** Richard Haythornthewaite - Chmn Alan J. Heuer - Vice-Chmn. Robert W. Selander - Pres., C.E.O.	**Auditors:** PricewaterhouseCoopers LLP **Transfer Agents:** Mellon Investor Services LLC

MATTEL INC

Exchange	Symbol	Price	52Wk Range	Yield	P/E
NYS	MAT	$19.90 (3/31/2008)	29.65-16.65	3.77	12.92

*7 Year Price Score 94.29   *NYSE Composite Index=100   *12 Month Price Score 95.73

Interim Earnings (Per Share)

Qtr.	Mar	Jun	Sep	Dec
2003	0.07	0.05	0.61	0.49
2004	0.02	0.06	0.61	0.67
2005	0.02	(0.23)	0.55	0.68
2006	0.08	0.10	0.62	0.74
2007	0.03	0.06	0.61	0.86

Interim Dividends (Per Share)

Amt	Decl	Ex	Rec	Pay
0.45A	11/18/2004	12/1/2004	12/3/2004	12/17/2004
0.50A	11/18/2005	11/30/2005	12/2/2005	12/16/2005
0.65A	11/17/2006	11/29/2006	12/1/2006	12/15/2006
0.75A	11/16/2007	11/28/2007	11/30/2007	12/14/2007

Indicated Div: $0.75

Valuation Analysis

Forecast P/E	14.70
	(1/10/2007)
Market Cap	$7.2 Billion
Book Value	2.3 Billion
Price/Book	3.12
Price/Sales	1.20

Institutional Holding

No of Institutions	360
Shares	339,645,408
% Held	86.39

Business Summary: Consumer Accessories (MIC: 4.6 SIC: 3942 NAIC: 339931)

Mattel designs, manufactures and markets a variety of toy products worldwide through sales to retailers and wholesalers and directly to consumers. Co.'s portfolio of brands and products are grouped in the following categories: Mattel Girls & Boys brands, which includes, among others, Barbie® fashion dolls and accessories, Disney Classics, Pixel Chix®, High School Musical, Hot Wheels®, Matchbox®, and Tyco® R/C vehicles and playsets, Fisher-Price Brands, which includes, among others, Fisher-Price®, Sesame Street®, BabyGear™, and Winnie the Pooh; and American Girl Brands, which includes including Just Like You® and Bitty Baby®.

Recent Developments: For the year ended Dec 31 2007, net income increased 1.2% to US$600.0 million from US$592.9 million in the prior year. Revenues were US$5.97 billion, up 5.7% from US$5.65 billion the year before. Operating income was US$730.1 million versus US$728.8 million in the prior year, an increase of 0.2%. Direct operating expenses rose 5.1% to US$3.19 billion from US$3.04 billion in the comparable period the year before. Indirect operating expenses increased 8.7% to US$2.05 billion from US$1.88 billion in the equivalent prior-year period.

Prospects: Looking ahead, Co. expects to face a challenging environment as retailers tightly manage inventory. Co. also expects to be challenged by higher costs for commodities, labor and quality testing. However, Co. is seeing several opportunities in 2008, as it introduces a line-up of toys based on entertainment properties. Notably, Co. plans to introduce new products for entertainment properties such as Warner Bros. Pictures' upcoming Batman™: The Dark Knight and Speed Racer movies, as well as DreamWorks Animation's movie, Kung Fu Panda™. Co. also continues to exploit content within its core brands, such as the planed launch of a full-length animated Barbie®: Mariposa™ in spring 2008.

Financial Data

(US$ in Thousands)	12/31/2007	12/31/2006	12/31/2005	12/31/2004	12/31/2003	12/31/2002	12/31/2001	12/31/2000
Earnings Per Share	1.54	1.53	1.01	1.35	1.22	0.52	0.68	(1.01)
Cash Flow Per Share	1.46	2.29	1.15	1.36	1.38	2.65	1.76	1.30
Tang Book Value Per Share	3.49	3.95	3.51	3.92	3.49	2.96	1.46	0.62
Dividends Per Share	0.750	0.650	0.500	0.450	0.400	0.050	0.050	0.270
Dividend Payout %	48.70	42.48	49.50	33.33	32.79	9.62	7.35	...
Income Statement								
Total Revenue	5,970,090	5,650,156	5,179,016	5,102,786	4,960,100	4,885,340	4,804,062	4,669,942
EBITDA	913,147	905,405	869,319	936,813	986,284	909,598	898,794	686,792
Income Before Taxes	703,398	683,756	652,049	696,254	740,854	621,497	430,010	225,424
Income Taxes	103,405	90,829	235,030	123,531	203,222	166,455	119,090	55,747
Net Income	500,993	592,977	417,019	572,723	537,632	230,101	298,919	(430,969)
Average Shares	390,612	386,422	411,039	423,093	442,231	441,292	436,166	427,126
Balance Sheet								
Current Assets	2,592,936	2,850,138	2,412,500	2,637,150	2,394,856	2,388,964	2,092,596	1,751,497
Total Assets	4,805,455	4,955,884	4,372,313	4,756,492	4,510,950	4,459,659	4,540,561	4,313,397
Current Liabilities	1,570,429	1,582,520	1,463,185	1,727,171	1,467,746	1,648,753	1,596,981	1,502,407
Long-Term Obligations	550,000	635,714	525,000	400,000	589,130	640,070	1,020,919	1,242,396
Total Liabilities	2,498,713	2,522,910	2,270,580	2,370,680	2,294,729	2,480,947	2,802,103	2,910,299
Stockholders' Equity	2,306,742	2,432,974	2,101,733	2,385,812	2,216,221	1,978,712	1,738,458	1,403,098
Shares Outstanding	361,400	384,300	388,600	415,400	428,500	430,500	430,900	426,000
Statistical Record								
Return on Assets %	12.29	12.71	9.14	12.33	11.99	5.11	6.75	N.M.
Return on Equity %	25.32	26.15	18.59	24.82	25.63	12.38	19.03	N.M.
EBITDA Margin %	15.30	16.02	16.79	18.36	19.88	18.62	18.71	14.71
Net Margin %	10.05	10.49	8.05	11.22	10.84	4.71	6.22	N.M.
Asset Turnover	1.22	1.21	1.13	1.10	1.11	1.09	1.09	0.99
Current Ratio	1.65	1.80	1.65	1.53	1.63	1.45	1.31	1.17
Debt to Equity	0.24	0.26	0.25	0.17	0.27	0.32	0.59	0.89
Price Range	29.65-18.97	23.80-14.78	21.42-14.53	19.50-15.98	23.05-18.80	22.20-15.75	19.75-13.70	15.00-9.06
P/E Ratio	19.25-12.32	15.56-9.66	21.21-14.39	14.44-11.84	18.89-15.41	42.69-30.29	29.04-20.15	...
Average Yield %	3.06	3.53	2.75	2.49	1.97	0.26	0.29	2.26

Address: 333 Continental Boulevard, El Segundo, CA 90245-5012
Telephone: 310-252-2000
Fax: 310-252-3671

Web Site: www.mattel.com
Officers: Robert A. Eckert - Chmn., C.E.O. Ellen L. Brothers - Exec. V.P., Pres., American Girl Brands

Auditors: PricewaterhouseCoopers LLP
Investor Contact: 310-252-2702
Transfer Agents: Computershare Trust Company, N.A.

MBIA INC.

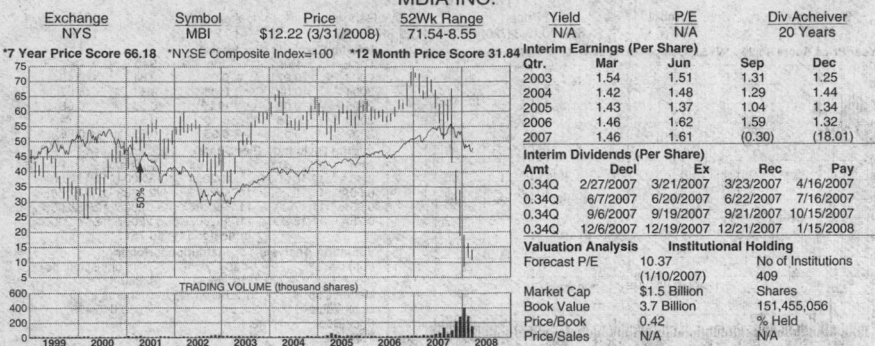

Exchange	Symbol	Price	52Wk Range	Yield	P/E	Div Acheiver
NYS	MBI	$12.22 (3/31/2008)	71.54-8.55	N/A	N/A	20 Years

*7 Year Price Score 66.18   *NYSE Composite Index=100   *12 Month Price Score 31.84

Interim Earnings (Per Share)

Qtr.	Mar	Jun	Sep	Dec
2003	1.54	1.51	1.31	1.25
2004	1.42	1.48	1.29	1.44
2005	1.43	1.37	1.04	1.34
2006	1.46	1.62	1.59	1.32
2007	1.46	1.61	(0.30)	(18.01)

Interim Dividends (Per Share)

Amt	Decl	Ex	Rec	Pay
0.34Q	2/27/2007	3/21/2007	3/23/2007	4/16/2007
0.34Q	6/7/2007	6/20/2007	6/22/2007	7/16/2007
0.34Q	9/6/2007	9/19/2007	9/21/2007	10/15/2007
0.34Q	12/6/2007	12/19/2007	12/21/2007	1/15/2008

Valuation Analysis

Forecast P/E 10.37 (1/10/2007)
Market Cap $1.5 Billion
Book Value 3.7 Billion
Price/Book 0.42
Price/Sales N/A

Institutional Holding

No of Institutions 409
Shares 151,455,056
% Held
N/A

Business Summary: Insurance (MIC: 8.2 SIC: 6351 NAIC: 524130)

MBIA provides financial guarantee insurance and other credit protection, as well as investment management services to public finance and structured finance issuers and investors and capital market participants on a global basis. Co.'s financial guarantee insurance provides an unconditional and irrevocable guarantee of the payment of the principal of, and interest or other amounts owing on, insured obligations when due or, in the event that Co. has the right, at its discretion, to accelerate insured obligations upon default or otherwise, upon such acceleration by Co, In addition, Co. conducts its business through its subsidiaries, MBIA Insurance Corporation and MBIA Asset Management, LLC.

Recent Developments: For the year ended Dec 31 2007, loss from continuing operations was US$1.92 billion compared with income of US$813.2 million a year earlier. Net loss amounted to US$1.92 billion versus net income of US$819.3 million in the prior year. Revenues were negative US$282.6 million, compared with US$2.70 billion the year before. Net premiums earned were US$824.0 million versus US$824.6 million in the prior year, a decrease of 0.1%. Net investment income rose 22.5% to US$2.18 billion from US$1.78 billion a year ago.

Prospects: On Feb 25 2008, Co. announced a plan to implement several initiatives in connection with the restructuring of its business over the next few years. In detail, Co. has suspended the writing of all new structured finance business for about six months and has ceased insuring new credit derivative contracts except in transactions related to the reduction of existing derivative exposure. As a result, Co. expects that its structured finance business written during 2008 should be less than 2007. Separately, while it expects to continue to insure transactions in the global public finance markets during 2008, Co. believes that its global public finance business written will be lower than 2007.

Financial Data
(US$ in Thousands)

	12/31/2007	12/31/2006	12/31/2005	12/31/2004	12/31/2003	12/31/2002	12/31/2001	12/31/2000
Earnings Per Share	(15.17)	5.99	5.18	5.63	5.61	3.92	3.82	3.55
Cash Flow Per Share	8.07	5.00	5.83	6.34	6.82	5.95	4.87	4.32
Tang Book Value Per Share	28.53	52.84	48.95	46.63	42.88	37.32	31.56	27.86
Dividends Per Share	1.360	1.240	1.120	0.960	0.800	0.680	0.600	0.547
Dividend Payout %	...	20.70	21.62	17.05	14.26	17.35	15.71	15.38
Income Statement								
Premium Income	824,017	835,593	842,742	822,467	732,997	588,509	523,870	446,353
Total Revenue	(282,554)	2,712,256	2,300,507	2,000,902	1,688,881	1,217,358	1,135,785	1,024,570
Benefits & Claims	900,345	80,889	84,274	81,880	72,888	61,688	56,651	51,291
Income Before Taxes	(3,065,692)	1,133,263	1,015,948	1,129,913	1,148,640	792,581	790,984	714,857
Income Taxes	(1,143,744)	320,080	303,869	317,185	335,055	205,763	207,826	186,220
Net Income	(1,921,948)	819,288	710,986	815,304	813,585	579,087	570,091	528,637
Average Shares	126,670	136,694	137,220	144,799	144,980	147,574	149,282	148,668
Balance Sheet								
Total Assets	47,415,074	39,763,030	34,561,394	33,027,410	30,267,734	18,852,101	16,199,685	13,894,338
Total Liabilities	43,759,269	32,558,776	27,969,750	26,448,339	24,008,719	13,358,750	11,417,047	9,670,925
Stockholders' Equity	3,655,805	7,204,254	6,591,644	6,579,071	6,259,015	5,493,351	4,782,638	4,223,413
Shares Outstanding	125,372	134,835	133,047	139,391	143,875	144,773	148,434	147,845
Statistical Record								
Return on Assets %	N.M.	2.20	2.10	2.57	3.31	3.30	3.79	4.03
Return on Equity %	N.M.	11.88	10.80	12.67	13.85	11.27	12.66	13.63
Loss Ratio %	109.26	9.68	10.00	9.96	9.94	10.48	10.81	11.49
Net Margin %	...	30.21	30.91	40.75	48.17	47.57	50.19	51.60
Price Range	73.02-18.63	73.31-56.50	63.83-50.50	67.13-53.67	60.08-34.64	59.65-35.32	57.25-39.21	49.96-24.42
P/E Ratio	...	12.24-9.43	12.32-9.75	11.92-9.53	10.71-6.17	15.22-9.01	14.99-10.26	14.07-6.88
Average Yield %	2.31	2.03	1.92	1.61	1.61	1.37	1.18	1.44

Address: 113 King Street, Armonk, NY 10504	**Web Site:** www.mbia.com	**Auditors:** PricewaterhouseCoopers LLP
Telephone: 914-273-4545	**Officers:** Joseph W. Brown Jr. - Chmn. Gary C. Dunton - Pres., C.E.O.	**Investor Contact:** 914-765-3190
Fax: 914-765-3163		**Transfer Agents:** Wells Fargo Shareowner Services, St. Paul, MN

MCAFEE INC

Exchange	Symbol	Price	52Wk Range	Yield	P/E
NYS	MFE	$33.09 (3/31/2008)	41.35-28.98	N/A	32.44

*7 Year Price Score 124.05 *NYSE Composite Index=100 *12 Month Price Score 102.74

Interim Earnings (Per Share)

Qtr.	Mar	Jun	Sep	Dec
2003	0.07	0.02	0.06	0.28
2004	0.32	0.06	0.70	0.23
2005	0.21	0.25	0.13	0.22
2006	0.25	0.16	0.21	0.20
2007	0.27	0.29	0.39	0.08

Interim Dividends (Per Share)

No Dividends Paid

Valuation Analysis		Institutional Holding	
Forecast P/E	19.30	No of Institutions	
	(1/10/2007)	224	
Market Cap	$5.3 Billion	Shares	
Book Value	1.9 Billion	146,305,168	
Price/Book	2.79	% Held	
Price/Sales	4.06	91.71	

Business Summary: IT & Technology (MIC: 10.2 SIC: 7372 NAIC: 511210)

McAfee is a security technology company that secures systems and networks from known and unknown threats. Co. develops, markets, distributes and supports computer security applications for large enterprises, governments, small and medium-sized businesses and consumers either directly or through a network of distribution partners. Co.'s applications protect systems and networks, blocking immediate threats while providing protection from future threats. Co. also provides software to manage and enforce security policies for organizations of any size. Co. incorporates its McAfee Expert Services, Foundstone services and technical support to ensure its applications meet its customers' needs.

Recent Developments: For the year ended Dec 31 2007, net income increased 21.5% to US$167.0 million from US$137.5 million in the prior year. Revenues were US$1.31 billion, up 14.2% from US$1.15 billion the year before. Operating income was US$159.8 million versus US$139.0 million in the prior year, an increase of 15.0%. Direct operating expenses rose 23.9% to US$305.7 million from US$246.8 million in the comparable period the year before. Indirect operating expenses increased 11.0% to US$842.7 million from US$759.3 million in the equivalent prior-year period.

Prospects: On Feb 7 2008, Co. announced that it has completed the acquisition of ScanAlert, Inc., the creator of the HACKER SAFE web site security certification service. Co. noted that the combination of HACKER SAFE®, which provides the reassurance needed to drive sales, and its safe search and surf technology, SiteAdvisor, is expected to significantly enhance e-commerce. Looking ahead to the first quarter of 2008, Co. is targeting net income of $0.24 to $0.29 per diluted share with net revenue in the range of $345.0 million to $360.0 million. Meanwhile, for full year 2008, Co. expects net income of $1.25 to $1.35 per diluted share on net revenue of $1.43 billion to $1.53 billion.

Financial Data

(US$ in Thousands)	12/31/2007	12/31/2006	12/31/2005	12/31/2004	12/31/2003	12/31/2002	12/31/2001	12/31/2000
Earnings Per Share	1.02	0.84	0.82	1.31	0.43	0.80	(0.73)	(0.74)
Cash Flow Per Share	2.46	1.80	2.54	2.23	0.97	1.31	1.06	0.19
Tang Book Value Per Share	5.82	4.90	5.58	4.04	2.09	2.55	1.85	2.16
Income Statement								
Total Revenue	1,308,220	1,145,158	987,299	910,542	936,336	1,043,044	834,478	745,692
EBITDA	313,677	254,075	246,451	383,167	135,931	183,802	41,368	(7,655)
Income Before Taxes	229,204	183,781	181,534	316,471	73,125	129,907	(91,383)	(97,751)
Income Taxes	62,224	46,310	42,706	91,406	13,220	(274)	11,409	9,924
Net Income	166,980	137,471	138,828	225,065	70,242	128,312	(100,650)	(102,721)
Average Shares	164,126	163,052	169,234	177,099	164,489	176,249	137,847	138,072
Balance Sheet								
Current Assets	1,407,746	1,176,632	1,567,661	965,750	961,253	1,194,146	1,082,787	620,692
Total Assets	3,414,103	2,800,270	2,642,624	2,237,676	2,120,498	2,045,487	1,627,132	1,384,848
Current Liabilities	1,177,601	1,030,379	868,991	705,880	545,485	881,943	541,034	423,699
Long-Term Obligations	...	...	...	...	347,397	356,013	578,850	395,969
Total Liabilities	1,508,778	1,373,021	1,187,591	1,036,428	1,232,409	1,275,319	1,165,034	855,130
Stockholders' Equity	1,905,325	1,427,249	1,455,033	1,201,248	888,089	770,168	444,787	518,651
Shares Outstanding	160,545	159,915	167,688	162,266	161,721	157,926	140,699	138,089
Statistical Record								
Return on Assets %	5.37	5.05	5.69	10.30	3.37	6.99	N.M.	N.M.
Return on Equity %	10.02	9.54	10.45	21.49	8.47	21.12	N.M.	N.M.
EBITDA Margin %	23.98	22.19	24.96	42.08	14.52	17.62	4.96	N.M.
Net Margin %	12.76	12.00	14.06	24.72	7.50	12.30	N.M.	N.M.
Asset Turnover	0.42	0.42	0.40	0.42	0.45	0.57	0.55	0.52
Current Ratio	1.20	1.14	1.80	1.37	1.76	1.35	2.00	1.46
Debt to Equity	...	...	...	...	0.39	0.46	1.30	0.76
Price Range	41.35-28.00	30.00-19.68	33.17-20.52	33.39-14.96	20.28-10.75	30.26-8.45	27.27-4.19	36.69-4.13
P/E Ratio	40.54-27.45	35.71-23.43	40.45-25.02	25.49-11.42	47.16-25.00	37.83-10.56	...	...

Address: 3965 Freedom Circle, Santa Clara, CA 95054 Telephone: 408-988-3832 Fax: 408-970-9727	Web Site: www.mcafee.com Officers: George Samenuk - Chmn., C.E.O. Gene Hodges - Pres.	Auditors: Deloitte & Touche LLP Transfer Agents: Mellon Investor Services

MCCLATCHY CO. (THE)

Exchange	Symbol	Price	52Wk Range	Yield	P/E
NYS	MNI	$10.70 (3/31/2008)	32.24-8.66	6.73	N/A

*7 Year Price Score 30.36   *NYSE Composite Index=100   *12 Month Price Score 55.33

Interim Earnings (Per Share)

Qtr.	Mar	Jun	Sep	Dec
2003	0.55	0.94	0.77	0.98
2004	0.62	0.86	0.83	1.02
2005	0.69	0.94	0.82	0.97
2006	0.59	0.94	0.64	(4.53)
2007	0.11	0.94	(16.42)	(17.48)

Interim Dividends (Per Share)

Amt	Decl	Ex	Rec	Pay
0.18Q	5/16/2007	6/11/2007	6/13/2007	7/2/2007
0.18Q	7/18/2007	9/10/2007	9/12/2007	10/1/2007
0.18Q	11/28/2007	12/10/2007	12/12/2007	1/2/2008
0.18Q	1/29/2008	3/10/2008	3/12/2008	4/1/2008
Indicated Div: $0.72				

Valuation Analysis

		Institutional Holding	
Forecast P/E	15.45	No of Institutions	
	(1/10/2007)	196	
Market Cap	$879.0 Million	Shares	
Book Value	425.5 Million	52,625,436	
Price/Book	2.07	% Held	
Price/Sales	0.39	64.20	

Business Summary: Media (MIC: 13.1 SIC: 2711 NAIC: 511110)

McClatchy is a newspaper company whose primary business is the publication of newspapers and related websites. As at Dec 31 2007, owned 30 daily newspapers, approximately 50 non-dailies and direct marketing and direct mail operations in 29 markets across the U.S. Co.-owned newspapers include, among others, The Miami Herald, The Sacramento Bee, the Fort Worth Star-Telegram, The Kansas City Star, The Charlotte Observer, and The (Raleigh) News & Observer. Co. also operates local websites in each of its markets which complement its newspapers and extend its audience reach in each market. Its local websites offer users information, comprehensive news, advertising, e-commerce and other services.

Recent Developments: For the year ended Dec 30 2007, loss from continuing operations was US$2.73 billion compared with income of US$183.5 million a year earlier. Net loss amounted to US$2.74 billion versus a net loss of US$155.6 million in the prior year. Revenues were US$2.26 billion, up 34.9% from US$1.68 billion the year before. Operating loss was US$2.57 billion versus an income of US$346.9 million in the prior year. Indirect operating expenses increased 263.4% to US$4.83 billion from US$1.33 billion in the equivalent prior-year period.

Prospects: On Jan 18 2008, Co. has entered into an agreement, along with the other general partners of SP Newsprint Co. (SP), to sell the partnership interests of SP for $350.0 million. The transaction is expected to generate after-tax proceeds of $40.0 million, which Co. plans to use for debt repayment and pre-tax gain on sale of between $30.0 million and $40.0 million. Co. expects the acquisition to close in the first four months of 2008. Meanwhile, Co. expects to be challenged by the anticipated increase in newsprint prices; as well as continuing advertising downturn, which it believes should lead to advertising results to likely be down in the low double-digit range in the first quarter of 2008.

Financial Data

(US$ in Thousands)	12/30/2007	12/31/2006	12/25/2005	12/26/2004	12/28/2003	12/29/2002	12/30/2001	12/31/2000
Earnings Per Share	(33.37)	(2.41)	3.42	3.33	3.23	2.84	1.27	1.97
Cash Flow Per Share	4.41	(9.17)	4.16	4.02	3.93	3.71	4.34	3.98
Tang Book Value Per Share	N.M.	N.M.	5.82	2.39	N.M.	N.M.	N.M.	N.M.
Dividends Per Share	0.720	0.720	0.670	0.500	0.440	0.400	0.400	0.400
Dividend Payout %	...	...	19.59	15.02	13.62	14.08	31.50	20.30
Income Statement								
Total Revenue	2,260,363	1,675,190	1,186,115	1,163,376	1,099,391	1,081,898	1,080,053	1,142,124
EBITDA	(2,536,878)	459,852	336,701	333,188	318,888	318,244	276,550	347,710
Income Before Taxes	(2,883,191)	270,885	263,227	257,561	230,659	216,885	120,702	171,020
Income Taxes	(156,582)	87,390	102,708	101,685	86,462	85,669	62,705	82,090
Net Income	(2,736,013)	(155,577)	160,519	155,876	150,222	131,216	57,997	88,930
Average Shares	82,000	64,645	46,996	46,815	46,456	46,178	45,616	45,243
Balance Sheet								
Current Assets	842,239	1,575,339	212,896	203,763	188,458	248,201	248,367	235,538
Total Assets	4,137,919	8,054,710	2,086,487	2,049,400	1,875,298	1,980,651	2,104,160	2,165,658
Current Liabilities	389,516	1,112,114	165,559	156,890	296,654	250,840	307,703	227,335
Long-Term Obligations	2,471,827	2,746,669	154,200	267,200	204,923	471,615	594,714	778,102
Total Liabilities	3,712,379	4,951,086	520,896	626,396	659,281	923,322	1,105,995	1,206,807
Stockholders' Equity	425,540	3,103,624	1,565,591	1,423,004	1,216,017	1,057,329	998,165	958,851
Shares Outstanding	82,153	81,911	46,750	46,464	46,280	46,015	45,593	45,244
Statistical Record								
Return on Assets %	N.M.	N.M.	7.78	7.97	7.81	6.44	2.72	4.00
Return on Equity %	N.M.	N.M.	10.77	11.85	13.25	12.80	5.94	9.52
EBITDA Margin %	N.M.	27.45	28.39	28.64	29.01	29.42	25.61	30.44
Net Margin %	N.M.	N.M.	13.53	13.40	13.66	12.13	5.37	7.79
Asset Turnover	0.37	0.33	0.58	0.59	0.57	0.53	0.51	0.51
Current Ratio	2.16	1.42	1.29	1.30	0.64	0.99	0.81	1.04
Debt to Equity	5.81	0.88	0.10	0.19	0.17	0.45	0.60	0.81
Price Range	41.67-12.43	59.40-39.00	75.47-56.53	73.75-67.31	68.25-51.59	64.25-46.25	48.96-37.50	44.88-28.94
P/E Ratio	...	...	22.07-16.53	22.15-20.21	21.13-15.97	22.62-16.29	38.55-29.53	22.78-14.69
Average Yield %	2.74	1.56	2.09	0.91	0.71	0.74	0.69	1.12

Address: 2100 Q Street, Sacramento, CA 95816	Web Site: www.mcclatchy.com	Auditors: Deloitte & Touche LLP
Telephone: 916-321-1846	Officers: Gary B. Pruitt - Chmn., Pres., C.E.O. Patrick J. Talamantes - V.P., Fin., C.F.O.	Investor Contact: 916-321-1846 Transfer Agents: Wells Fargo Shareowner Services, St. Paul, MN

MCCORMICK & CO., INC.

Exchange	Symbol	Price	52Wk Range	Yield	P/E	Div Achiever
NYS	MKC	$36.97 (3/31/2008)	38.99-33.55	2.38	20.65	21 Years

*7 Year Price Score 95.21 *NYSE Composite Index=100 *12 Month Price Score 104.62

Interim Earnings (Per Share)

Qtr.	Feb	May	Aug	Nov
2004-05	0.26	0.31	0.35	0.65
2005-06	0.11	0.46	0.32	0.62
2006-07	0.33	0.31	0.43	0.66
2007-08	0.39	...	...	...

Interim Dividends (Per Share)

Amt	Decl	Ex	Rec	Pay
0.20Q	6/26/2007	7/3/2007	7/6/2007	7/20/2007
0.20Q	9/26/2007	10/3/2007	10/5/2007	10/19/2007
0.22Q	11/27/2007	12/26/2007	12/20/2007	1/18/2008
0.22Q	4/2/2008	4/10/2008	4/14/2008	4/25/2008

Indicated Div: $0.88

Valuation Analysis **Institutional Holding**

Forecast P/E	N/A	No of Institutions
		341
Market Cap	$4.7 Billion	Shares
Book Value	1.2 Billion	86,108,720
Price/Book	4.10	% Held
Price/Sales	1.59	73.71

Business Summary: Food (MIC: 4 1 SIC: 2099 NAIC: 311942)

McCormick is specialty food company engaged in the manufacture, marketing and distribution of flavor products, such as spices, herbs, seasoning and flavorings, as well as other specialty food products to the food industry. Co.'s Consumer segment sells spices, herbs, extracts, seasoning blends, sauces, marinades and specialty foods to the consumer food market under a variety of brands, including McCormick, Zatarain's, Simply Asia and Thai Kitchens, Ducros, Vahine and Silvo, Club House and Schwartz. Co.'s Industrial segment sells seasoning blends, natural spices and herbs, wet flavors, coating systems and compound flavors to food manufacturers and the food service industry.

Recent Developments: For the quarter ended Feb 29 2008, net income increased 16.3% to US$51.4 million from US$44.2 million in the year-earlier quarter. Revenues were US$724.0 million, up 10.9% from US$652.6 million the year before. Operating income was US$77.4 million versus US$66.4 million in the prior-year quarter, an increase of 16.6%. Direct operating expenses rose 12.9% to US$438.2 million from US$388.3 million in the comparable period the year before. Indirect operating expenses increased 5.2% to US$208.4 million from US$198.0 million in the equivalent prior-year period.

Prospects: For the fiscal year ending Nov 30 2008, Co. now anticipates sales growth in the range of 5.0% to 7.0%, excluding sales related to the pending acquisition of the Lawry's business. In addition, Co. is forecasting earnings to range from $1.97 to $2.01 per share, reflecting an increase of 8.0% to 10.0% over its previous fiscal year's level. Separately, on Feb 20 2008, Co. announced the acquisition of Billy Bee Honey Products Ltd. for approximately US$75.0 million. Co. believes that this transaction should complement its savory products in Canada while strengthening its sweet products in Europe and the Asia/Pacific region. Co. expects this acquisition to be immediately accretive to its earnings.

Financial Data

(US$ in Thousands)	3 Mos	11/30/2007	11/30/2006	11/30/2005	11/30/2004	11/30/2003	11/30/2002	11/30/2001
Earnings Per Share	1.79	1.73	1.50	1.56	1.52	1.48	1.26	1.04
Cash Flow Per Share	2.53	1.74	2.36	2.52	2.54	1.40	1.60	1.48
Tang Book Value Per Share	N.M.	N.M.	N.M.	N.M.	0.45	0.28	0.62	N.M.
Dividends Per Share	0.820	0.800	0.720	0.640	0.560	0.460	0.420	0.400
Dividend Payout %	45.90	46.24	48.00	41.03	36.84	31.08	33.33	38.28
Income Statement								
Total Revenue	723,950	2,916,200	2,716,400	2,592,000	2,526,200	2,269,600	2,320,000	2,218,500
EBITDA	103,138	445,600	363,500	418,500	406,800	373,900	345,200	315,700
Depn & Amortn	22,449	...	...	...	...	...	...	...
Income Before Taxes	65,932	302,400	223,000	295,700	293,800	270,000	234,800	190,400
Income Taxes	19,873	92,200	64,700	96,700	89,000	83,400	74,300	62,900
Net Income	51,423	230,100	202,200	214,900	214,500	210,800	179,800	146,600
Average Shares	131,067	132,700	135,000	138,100	141,300	142,600	142,300	140,200
Balance Sheet								
Current Assets	951,344	983,100	899,400	800,200	864,000	762,100	724,600	635,800
Total Assets	2,858,276	2,787,500	2,568,000	2,272,700	2,369,600	2,148,200	1,930,800	1,772,000
Current Liabilities	737,726	861,300	780,500	699,000	772,700	712,700	673,400	713,700
Long-Term Obligations	676,665	573,500	569,600	463,900	465,000	448,600	453,900	454,100
Total Liabilities	1,693,778	1,692,500	1,631,100	1,443,600	1,448,900	1,370,800	1,338,500	1,308,900
Stockholders' Equity	1,155,372	1,085,100	933,300	799,900	889,700	755,200	592,300	463,100
Shares Outstanding	128,280	127,800	116,900	132,600	135,500	137,200	140,000	138,400
Statistical Record								
Return on Assets %	8.74	8.59	8.35	9.26	9.47	10.34	9.71	8.54
Return on Equity %	22.10	22.80	23.33	25.44	26.01	31.29	34.07	35.65
EBITDA Margin %	14.25	15.28	13.38	16.15	16.10	16.47	14.88	14.23
Net Margin %	7.10	7.89	7.44	8.29	8.49	9.29	7.75	6.61
Asset Turnover	1.10	1.09	1.12	1.12	1.12	1.11	1.25	1.29
Current Ratio	1.29	1.14	1.15	1.14	1.12	1.07	1.08	0.89
Debt to Equity	0.59	0.53	0.61	0.58	0.52	0.59	0.77	0.98
Price Range	39.18-33.55	39.58-34.16	38.78-29.82	39.06-29.24	37.41-28.84	30.21-22.10	26.93-20.36	23.00-17.13
P/E Ratio	21.89-18.74	22.88-19.75	25.85-19.88	25.04-18.74	24.61-18.97	20.41-14.93	21.37-16.16	22.11-16.47
Average Yield %	2.24	2.15	2.10	1.86	1.68	1.79	1.78	1.95

Address: 18 Loveton Circle, Sparks, MD 21152-6000	Web Site: www.mccormick.com	Auditors: SB & Co., LLC
Telephone: 410-771-7301	Officers: Robert J. Lawless - Chmn., Pres., C.E.O. Francis A. Contino - Exec. V.P., Strategic Planning, C.F.O.	Investor Contact: 410-771-7244
Fax: 410-771-7462		Transfer Agents: Wells Fargo Bank Minnesota, N.A., St. Paul, MN

MCDONALD'S CORP

Exchange	Symbol	Price	52Wk Range	Yield	P/E	Div Acheiver
NYS	MCD	$55.77 (3/31/2008)	63.13-44.82	2.69	28.17	31 Years

*7 Year Price Score 132.69 *NYSE Composite Index=100 ***12 Month Price Score 110.13**

Interim Earnings (Per Share)

Qtr.	Mar	Jun	Sep	Dec
2003	0.26	0.37	0.43	0.10
2004	0.40	0.47	0.61	0.31
2005	0.56	0.42	0.58	0.48
2006	0.49	0.67	0.68	1.00
2007	0.62	(0.60)	0.89	1.06

Interim Dividends (Per Share)

Amt	Decl	Ex	Rec	Pay
0.67Q	9/21/2005	11/10/2005	11/15/2005	12/1/2005
1.00Q	9/27/2006	11/13/2006	11/15/2006	12/1/2006
1.50Q	9/12/2007	11/13/2007	11/15/2007	12/3/2007
0.375Q	1/24/2008	2/28/2008	3/3/2008	3/17/2008

Indicated Div: $1.50 (Div. Reinv. Plan)

Valuation Analysis		Institutional Holding	
Forecast P/E	15.61	No of Institutions	
	(1/10/2007)	910	
Market Cap	$65.0 Billion	Shares	
Book Value	15.3 Billion	926,972,928	
Price/Book	4.25	% Held	
Price/Sales	2.85	77.02	

Business Summary: Food (MIC: 4.1 SIC: 5812 NAIC: 722211)

McDonald's primarily franchises and operates McDonald's restaurants. Co.'s business is operated in distinct geographic segments: U.S.; Europe; Asia/Pacific, Middle East and Africa; and Other Countries and Corporate that includes operations in Latin America and Canada. In addition, Co. has a minority ownership interest in U.K.-based Pret A Manger. As of Dec 31 2007, Co. had 31,377 McDonald's restaurants in 118 countries, with 20,505 operated by franchisees that include 2,781 which are operated by developmental licensees, 3,966 that are operated by affiliates as well as 6,906 that are Company-operated.

Recent Developments: For the year ended Dec 31 2007, income from continuing operations decreased 18.5% to US$2.34 billion from US$2.87 billion a year earlier. Net income decreased 32.4% to US$2.40 billion from US$3.54 billion in the prior year. Revenues were US$22.79 billion, up 9.1% from US$20.90 billion the year before. Operating income was US$3.88 billion versus US$4.43 billion in the prior year, a decrease of 12.5%. Direct operating expenses rose 7.3% to US$5.49 billion from US$5.11 billion in the comparable period the year before. Indirect operating expenses increased 18.2% to US$13.42 billion from US$11.35 billion in the equivalent prior-year period.

Prospects: Co. continues to execute its Plan to Win initiative targeting average annual Systemwide sales and revenue growth of 3.0% to 5.0% and average annual operating income growth of 6.0% to 7.0%. For 2008, Co. expects net restaurant additions to add slightly more than 1.0% to Systemwide sales growth (in constant currencies), most of which will be due to net traditional restaurant additions in 2007. Co. expects to open 1,000 restaurants in 2008 with net additions of about 600 restaurants. Separately, Co. recently agreed to sell its minority interest in Pret A Manger and expects to realize a non-operating gain upon the closing of the transaction in late first quarter or early second quarter of 2008.

Financial Data

(US$ in Thousands)	12/31/2007	12/31/2006	12/31/2005	12/31/2004	12/31/2003	12/31/2002	12/31/2001	12/31/2000
Earnings Per Share	1.98	2.83	2.04	1.79	1.15	0.70	1.25	1.46
Cash Flow Per Share	4.10	3.52	3.44	3.09	2.57	2.27	2.08	2.07
Tang Book Value Per Share	11.14	11.01	10.45	9.74	8.18	6.88	6.30	5.95
Dividends Per Share	1.500	1.000	0.670	0.550	0.400	0.235	0.225	0.215
Dividend Payout %	75.76	35.34	32.84	30.73	34.78	33.57	18.00	14.73
Income Statement								
Total Revenue	22,786,600	21,586,400	20,460,200	19,064,700	17,140,500	15,405,700	14,870,000	14,243,000
EBITDA	5,196,300	5,818,300	5,307,200	4,761,800	3,882,600	3,087,000	3,868,400	4,322,900
Income Before Taxes	3,572,100	4,166,400	3,701,600	3,202,400	2,346,400	1,662,100	2,329,700	2,882,300
Income Taxes	1,237,100	1,293,400	1,099,400	923,900	838,200	670,000	693,100	905,000
Net Income	2,395,100	3,544,200	2,602,200	2,278,500	1,471,400	893,500	1,636,600	1,977,300
Average Shares	1,211,800	1,251,700	1,274,200	1,273,700	1,276,500	1,281,500	1,309,300	1,356,500
Balance Sheet								
Current Assets	3,581,900	3,625,300	5,849,700	2,857,800	1,885,400	1,715,400	1,819,300	1,662,400
Total Assets	29,391,700	29,023,800	29,988,800	27,837,500	25,525,100	23,970,500	22,534,500	21,683,500
Current Liabilities	4,498,500	3,008,100	4,036,300	3,520,500	2,485,800	2,422,300	2,248,300	2,360,900
Long-Term Obligations	7,310,000	8,416,500	8,937,400	8,357,300	9,342,500	9,703,600	8,555,500	7,843,900
Total Liabilities	14,111,900	13,565,500	14,842,700	13,636,000	13,543,200	13,689,600	13,046,100	12,479,100
Stockholders' Equity	15,279,800	15,458,300	15,146,100	14,201,500	11,981,900	10,280,900	9,488,400	9,204,400
Shares Outstanding	1,165,300	1,203,700	1,263,200	1,269,900	1,261,900	1,268,200	1,280,700	1,304,900
Statistical Record								
Return on Assets %	8.20	12.01	9.00	8.52	5.95	3.84	7.40	9.24
Return on Equity %	15.58	23.16	17.73	17.36	13.22	9.04	17.51	20.93
EBITDA Margin %	22.80	26.95	25.94	24.98	22.65	20.04	26.01	30.35
Net Margin %	10.51	16.42	12.72	11.95	8.58	5.80	11.01	13.88
Asset Turnover	0.78	0.73	0.71	0.71	0.71	0.66	0.67	0.67
Current Ratio	0.80	1.21	1.45	0.81	0.76	0.71	0.81	0.70
Debt to Equity	0.48	0.54	0.59	0.59	0.78	0.94	0.90	0.85
Price Range	63.13-42.91	44.36-31.94	35.50-27.70	32.66-24.64	26.56-12.38	30.65-15.48	34.69-25.00	42.75-27.00
P/E Ratio	31.88-21.67	15.67-11.29	17.40-13.58	18.25-13.77	23.10-10.77	43.79-22.11	27.75-20.00	29.28-18.49
Average Yield %	2.94	2.72	2.10	1.98	1.98	0.97	0.79	0.64

Address: McDonald's Plaza, Oak Brook, IL 60523 Telephone: 630-623-3000 Fax: 630-623-5027	Web Site: www.mcdonalds.com Officers: Andrew J. McKenna - Chmn. Jim Skinner - Vice-Chmn., C.E.O.	Auditors: Ernst & Young LLP Investor Contact: 630-623-7428 Transfer Agents: First Chicago Trust Company, Jersey City, NJ

MCGRAW-HILL COS., INC. (THE)

Exchange	Symbol	Price	52Wk Range	Yield	P/E	Div Acheiver
NYS	MHP	$36.95 (3/31/2008)	71.96-35.20	2.38	12.57	34 Years

*7 Year Price Score 99.99 *NYSE Composite Index=100 *12 Month Price Score 81.66

Interim Earnings (Per Share)

Qtr.	Mar	Jun	Sep	Dec
2003	0.25	0.37	0.76	0.41
2004	0.20	0.43	0.84	0.49
2005	0.20	0.51	1.00	0.50
2006	0.20	0.60	1.06	0.56
2007	0.40	0.79	1.34	0.44

Interim Dividends (Per Share)

Amt	Decl	Ex	Rec	Pay
0.205Q	4/25/2007	5/24/2007	5/29/2007	6/12/2007
0.205Q	7/25/2007	8/24/2007	8/28/2007	9/12/2007
0.205Q	10/24/2007	11/28/2007	11/28/2007	12/12/2007
0.22Q	1/30/2008	2/25/2008	2/27/2008	3/12/2008

Indicated Div: $0.88 (Div. Reinv. Plan)

Valuation Analysis

		Institutional Holding	
Forecast P/E	19.87	No of Institutions	
	(1/10/2007)	668	
Market Cap	$11.9 Billion	Shares	
Book Value	1.6 Billion		276,819,520
Price/Book	7.41	% Held	
Price/Sales	1.76		77.99

Business Summary: Non-Media Publishing (MIC: 13.3 SIC: 2731 NAIC: 511130)

McGraw-Hill Companies is a global information services provider serving the financial services, education and business information markets with information products and services. Co.'s other markets also include energy, construction, aerospace and defense, and marketing information services. Co. operates through three business segments: Education; Financial Services; and Information and Media. Co. serves its customers through a range of distribution channels including printed books, magazines and newsletters; online via Internet Web sites and digital platforms; through wireless and traditional on-air broadcasting; and through a variety of conferences and trade shows.

Recent Developments: For the year ended Dec 31 2007, net income increased 14.9% to US$1.01 billion from US$882.2 million in the prior year. Revenues were US$6.77 billion, up 8.3% from US$6.26 billion the year before. Operating income was US$1.66 billion versus US$1.42 billion in the prior year, an increase of 17.2%. Direct operating expenses rose 5.9% to US$2.53 billion from US$2.39 billion in the comparable period the year before. Indirect operating expenses increased 5.4% to US$2.58 billion from US$2.45 billion in the equivalent prior-year period.

Prospects: For 2008, Co. expects revenue to grow 6.0% to 8.0% at its Education and Information and Media segments, and to grow 2.0% to 4.0% at its Financial Services segment. Specifically, Co. expects operating margin at Financial Services to decrease 125 and 225 basis points with operating margin at Education declining 50 to 100 basis points. However, Co. expects operating margin at Information and Media to improve. Hence, Co. expects earnings per share to increase by 3.0% to 5.0% although it expects net income to decline slightly. Co.'s guidance excludes a $0.08 per share restructuring charge in the fourth quarter of 2007 and a $0.03 gain from the divestiture of a mutual fund data business in 2007.

Financial Data

(US$ in Thousands)	12/31/2007	12/31/2006	12/31/2005	12/31/2004	12/31/2003	12/31/2002	12/31/2001	12/31/2000
Earnings Per Share	2.94	2.40	2.21	1.96	1.79	1.48	0.96	1.03
Cash Flow Per Share	5.11	4.23	4.16	2.79	3.63	2.96	2.76	1.81
Tang Book Value Per Share	N.M	1.00	2.04	2.72	2.24	0.94	0.09	0.16
Dividends Per Share	0.820	0.726	0.660	0.600	0.540	0.510	0.490	0.470
Dividend Payout %	27.89	30.25	29.86	30.61	30.17	34.46	51.04	45.63
Income Statement								
Total Revenue	6,772,281	6,255,138	6,003,642	5,250,538	4,827,857	4,787,668	4,645,535	4,280,968
EBITDA	1,824,102	1,580,041	1,516,149	1,299,428	1,255,066	1,055,960	850,485	973,891
Income Before Taxes	1,622,532	1,404,823	1,359,962	1,168,905	1,130,277	905,065	615,058	767,342
Income Taxes	608,973	522,592	515,656	412,495	442,466	328,305	238,027	295,426
Net Income	1,013,559	882,231	844,306	755,823	687,650	576,760	377,031	403,794
Average Shares	344,785	366,878	382,570	385,824	384,010	389,146	391,746	392,144
Balance Sheet								
Current Assets	2,333,035	2,257,938	2,590,939	2,447,830	2,256,152	1,674,307	1,812,947	1,801,690
Total Assets	6,357,336	6,042,890	6,395,808	5,862,989	5,394,068	5,032,182	5,161,191	4,931,444
Current Liabilities	2,656,860	2,468,016	2,224,826	1,968,662	1,993,734	1,775,291	1,876,393	1,780,785
Long-Term Obligations	1,197,425	314	339	513	39	458,923	833,571	817,529
Total Liabilities	4,750,686	3,363,272	3,282,660	2,878,476	2,837,017	2,866,360	3,307,306	3,170,400
Stockholders' Equity	1,606,650	2,679,618	3,113,148	2,984,513	2,557,051	2,165,822	1,853,885	1,761,044
Shares Outstanding	322,367	353,958	372,698	379,626	380,792	383,665	386,436	388,570
Statistical Record								
Return on Assets %	16.35	14.19	13.77	13.39	13.19	11.32	7.47	8.93
Return on Equity %	47.29	30.46	27.69	27.20	29.12	28.70	20.86	23.33
EBITDA Margin %	26.93	25.26	25.25	24.75	26.00	22.06	18.31	22.75
Net Margin %	14.97	14.10	14.06	14.40	14.24	12.05	8.12	9.43
Asset Turnover	1.09	1.01	0.98	0.93	0.93	0.94	0.92	0.95
Current Ratio	0.88	0.91	1.16	1.24	1.13	0.94	0.97	1.01
Debt to Equity	0.75	N.M.	N.M.	N.M.	N.M.	0.21	0.45	0.46
Price Range	71.96-43.81	69.10-47.06	53.52-40.56	45.93-34.75	34.96-26.25	34.45-25.57	35.23-24.65	33.56-21.38
P/E Ratio	24.48-14.90	28.79-19.61	24.22-18.35	23.43-17.73	19.53-14.66	23.27-17.28	36.69-25.68	32.58-20.75
Average Yield %	1.38	1.28	1.42	1.53	1.76	1.63	1.62	1.69

Address: 1221 Avenue Of The Americas, New York, NY 10020-1095 Telephone: 212-512-2000	Web Site: www.mcgraw-hill.com Officers: Harold McGraw III - Chmn., Pres., C.E.O. Robert J. Bahash - Exec. V.P., C.F.O.	Auditors: Ernst & Young LLP Transfer Agents: Mellon Investor Services, South Hackensack, NJ

MCKESSON CORP.

Exchange	Symbol	Price	52Wk Range	Yield	P/E
NYS	MCK	$52.37 (3/31/2008)	67.92-51.66	0.46	16.79

*7 Year Price Score 117.82 *NYSE Composite Index=100 *12 Month Price Score 102.38

Interim Earnings (Per Share)

Qtr.	Jun	Sep	Dec	Mar
2004-05	0.55	0.29	(2.26)	0.89
2005-06	0.55	0.53	0.61	0.64
2006-07	0.60	0.75	0.80	0.84
2007-08	0.77	0.83	0.68	...

Interim Dividends (Per Share)

Amt	Decl	Ex	Rec	Pay
0.06Q	5/23/2007	6/6/2007	6/8/2007	7/2/2007
0.06Q	7/25/2007	8/29/2007	9/3/2007	10/1/2007
0.06Q	10/26/2007	11/29/2007	12/3/2007	1/2/2008
0.06Q	1/23/2008	2/28/2008	3/3/2008	4/1/2008

Indicated Div: $0.24

Valuation Analysis

		Institutional Holding	
Forecast P/E	N/A		No of Institutions
			409
Market Cap	$15.1 Billion		Shares
Book Value	6.5 Billion		250,664,496
Price/Book	2.33		% Held
Price/Sales	0.15		84.86

TRADING VOLUME (thousand shares)

Business Summary: Pharmaceuticals (MIC: 9.1 SIC: 5122 NAIC: 424210)

McKesson provides supply, information and care management products and services via three business segments: Pharmaceutical Solutions, which distributes ethical and proprietary drugs, and health and beauty care products in North America; Medical-Surgical Solutions, which distributes medical-surgical supplies and first-aid products, and provides logistics and other services in the U.S. and Canada; and Provider Technologies, which delivers enterprise-wide patient care, clinical, financial, supply chain, and strategic management software applications, pharmacy automation for hospitals, and connectivity, outsourcing and other services in North America, the U.K. and other European countries.

Recent Developments: For the quarter ended Dec 31 2007, income from continuing operations decreased 16.3% to US$201.0 million from US$240.0 million in the year-earlier quarter. Net income decreased 17.3% to US$201.0 million from US$243.0 million in the year-earlier quarter. Revenues were US$26.49 billion, up 14.6% from US$23.11 billion the year before. Operating income was US$282.0 million versus US$318.0 million in the prior-year quarter, a decrease of 11.3%. Direct operating expenses rose 14.7% to US$25.29 billion from US$22.05 billion in the comparable period the year before. Indirect operating expenses increased 24.1% to US$922.0 million from US$743.0 million in the equivalent prior-year period.

Prospects: Co. believes that it will produce continued solid results in its distribution solutions segment as there is a robust pipeline of higher-margin generic product opportunities that are forecast for launch over the next several years. In its technology solutions segment, Co.'s integration of its Jan 2007 acquisition of Per-Se Technologies, Inc. continues to be ahead of schedule, and it expects to make solid progress toward its goal of low- to mid-teens operating margin for this segment in the fiscal year ending Mar 2008, solidly reaching double-digits. Overall, Co. expects to earn $3.22 to $3.32 per diluted share for the fiscal year, excluding adjustments to Securities Litigation reserves.

Financial Data

(US$ in Thousands)	9 Mos	6 Mos	3 Mos	03/31/2007	03/31/2006	03/31/2005	03/31/2004	03/31/2003
Earnings Per Share	3.12	3.24	3.16	2.99	2.38	(0.53)	2.19*	1.88
Cash Flow Per Share	3.23	7.26	5.64	5.16	8.97	5.24	1.94	2.40
Tang Book Value Per Share	7.87	8.88	8.98	9.10	13.36	12.47	12.66	10.57
Dividends Per Share	0.240	0.240	0.240	0.240	0.240	0.240	0.240	0.240
Dividend Payout %	7.69	7.41	7.59	8.03	10.08	...	10.96	12.77
Income Statement								
Total Revenue	75,472,000	48,978,000	24,528,000	92,977,000	88,050,000	80,514,600	69,506,100	57,120,800
EBITDA	1,372,000	966,000	482,000	1,588,000	1,414,000	88,100	1,235,200	1,155,700
Depn & Amortn	271,000	178,000	89,000	...	...	...	...	...
Income Before Taxes	993,000	716,000	357,000	1,297,000	1,158,000	(239,800)	911,400	861,600
Income Taxes	309,000	233,000	121,000	329,000	421,000	(83,100)	264,900	293,300
Net Income	683,000	482,000	235,000	913,000	751,000	(156,700)	646,500	555,400
Average Shares	297,000	299,000	304,000	305,000	316,000	293,500	298,600	298,800
Balance Sheet								
Current Assets	18,684,000	18,789,000	18,157,000	17,856,000	16,919,000	15,332,300	13,004,200	11,253,600
Total Assets	25,365,000	25,034,000	24,312,000	23,943,000	20,975,000	18,775,900	16,240,200	14,353,400
Current Liabilities	15,847,000	15,612,000	14,859,000	15,126,000	13,515,000	11,792,600	9,456,100	7,974,400
Long-Term Obligations	1,797,000	1,798,000	1,798,000	1,803,000	965,000	1,201,700	1,209,800	1,290,700
Total Liabilities	18,860,000	18,650,000	17,873,000	17,670,000	15,068,000	13,499,900	11,074,900	9,824,900
Stockholders' Equity	6,505,000	6,384,000	6,439,000	6,273,000	5,907,000	5,275,100	5,165,300	4,528,500
Shares Outstanding	289,000	289,000	296,000	295,000	304,000	299,300	290,300	291,200
Statistical Record								
Return on Assets %	3.93	4.22	4.22	4.07	3.78	N.M.	4.21	4.01
Return on Equity %	14.92	15.96	15.61	14.99	13.43	N.M.	13.30	13.12
EBITDA Margin %	1.82	1.97	1.97	1.71	1.61	0.11	1.78	2.02
Net Margin %	0.90	0.98	0.96	0.98	0.85	N.M.	0.93	0.97
Asset Turnover	4.16	4.14	4.13	4.14	4.43	4.60	4.53	4.13
Current Ratio	1.18	1.20	1.22	1.18	1.25	1.30	1.38	1.41
Debt to Equity	0.28	0.28	0.28	0.29	0.16	0.23	0.23	0.29
Price Range	67.06-51.13	63.71-48.00	63.71-45.67	58.82-45.00	54.77-35.08	38.41-22.98	36.94-23.60	41.81-22.99
P/E Ratio	21.49-16.39	19.66-14.81	20.16-14.45	19.67-15.05	23.01-14.74	...	16.87-10.78	22.24-12.23
Average Yield %	0.41	0.43	0.44	0.47	0.52	0.76	0.78	0.78

Address: One Post Street, San Francisco, CA 94104	Web Site: www.mckesson.com	Auditors: Deloitte & Touche LLP
Telephone: 415-983-8300	Officers: John H. Hammergren - Chmn., Pres., C.E.O. Jeffrey C. Campbell - Exec. V.P., C.F.O.	Investor Contact: 415-983-7153
Fax: 415-983-8453		Transfer Agents: The Bank of New York, New York, NY

494

M.D.C. HOLDINGS, INC.

Exchange	Symbol	Price	52Wk Range	Yield	P/E
NYS	MDC	$43.79 (3/31/2008)	54.73-32.15	2.28	N/A

*7 Year Price Score 79.01   *NYSE Composite Index=100   *12 Month Price Score 104.67

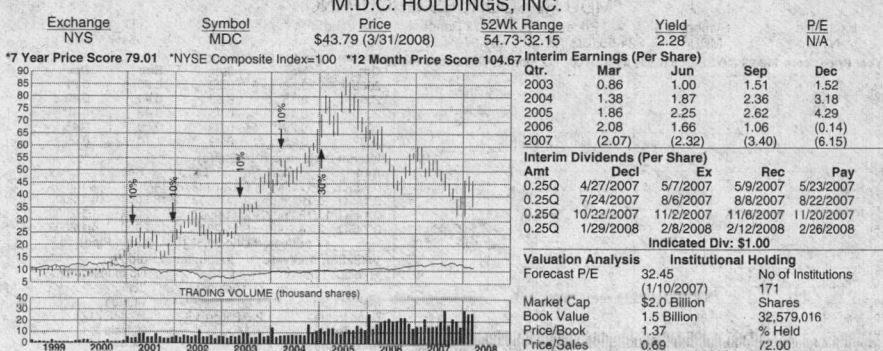

Interim Earnings (Per Share)

Qtr.	Mar	Jun	Sep	Dec
2003	0.86	1.00	1.51	1.52
2004	1.38	1.87	2.36	3.18
2005	1.86	2.25	2.62	4.29
2006	2.08	1.66	1.06	(0.14)
2007	(2.07)	(2.32)	(3.40)	(6.15)

Interim Dividends (Per Share)

Amt	Decl	Ex	Rec	Pay
0.25Q	4/27/2007	5/7/2007	5/9/2007	5/23/2007
0.25Q	7/24/2007	8/6/2007	8/8/2007	8/22/2007
0.25Q	10/22/2007	11/2/2007	11/6/2007	11/20/2007
0.25Q	1/29/2008	2/8/2008	2/12/2008	2/26/2008
Indicated Div: $1.00				

Valuation Analysis / **Institutional Holding**

Forecast P/E	32.45	No of Institutions
	(1/10/2007)	171
Market Cap	$2.0 Billion	Shares
Book Value	1.5 Billion	32,579,016
Price/Book	1.37	% Held
Price/Sales	0.69	72.00

Business Summary: Building & General Construction (MIC: 3.2 SIC: 1531 NAIC: 236117)

M.D.C. Holdings is a homebuilding company that operates through two segments: homebuilding, and financial services. Co.'s homebuilding segments build and sell homes under the name Richmond American Homes. Co.'s financial services operations consist of HomeAmerican Mortgage Corp., which originates mortgage loans for its homebuyers; American Home Insurance Agency, Inc., which offers third-party insurance products to its homebuyers; and American Home Title and Escrow Company (American Home Title), which provides title agency services to its homebuyers in Colorado, Delaware, Florida, Illinois, Nevada, Maryland, Virginia and West Virginia.

Recent Developments: For the year ended Dec 31 2007, net loss amounted to US$636.9 million versus net income of US$214.3 million in the prior year. Revenues were US$2.93 billion, down 38.9% from US$4.80 billion the year before. Direct operating expenses declined 33.2% to US$2.44 billion from US$3.65 billion in the comparable period the year before. Indirect operating expenses increased 53.3% to US$1.25 billion from US$815.5 million in the equivalent prior-year period.

Prospects: Co.'s results continued to be hurt by the downturn in the homebuilding and mortgage lending industries, which include on-going homebuyer concerns about declines in the market value of homes, as well as reduced availability of credit for homebuyers caused by tightening mortgage loan underwriting criteria and an overall reduction in liquidity in the mortgage industry. On a positive note, Co. is seeing a reduction in general and administrative expenses due to its continued efforts to right-size its homebuilding operations in view of the existing market conditions. In response, Co. will continue to assess the need for further adjustments to reduce such expenses as it moves through 2008.

Financial Data

(US$ in Thousands)	12/31/2007	12/31/2006	12/31/2005	12/31/2004	12/31/2003	12/31/2002	12/31/2001	12/31/2000
Earnings Per Share	(13.94)	4.66	10.99	8.79	4.90	3.83	3.64	2.95
Cash Flow Per Share	12.97	8.08	(9.65)	(0.56)	2.02	(3.95)	2.24	(1.55)
Tang Book Value Per Share	32.05	47.77	43.54	32.59	24.05	19.26	15.63	11.95
Dividends Per Share	1.000	1.000	0.760	0.434	0.283	0.197	0.153	0.126
Dividend Payout %	...	21.46	6.92	4.93	5.78	5.14	4.20	4.27
Income Statement								
Total Revenue	2,933,249	4,801,742	4,884,160	4,009,072	2,920,070	2,318,524	2,125,874	1,751,545
EBITDA	(709,122)	392,552	863,555	678,820	383,900	300,951	282,832	224,993
Income Before Taxes	(756,464)	333,137	808,763	636,914	348,223	274,044	255,387	203,201
Income Taxes	(119,524)	118,884	303,040	245,749	135,994	106,739	99,672	79,898
Net Income	(636,940)	214,253	505,723	391,165	212,229	167,305	155,715	123,303
Average Shares	45,687	45,971	46,036	44,498	43,333	43,657	42,835	41,772
Balance Sheet								
Current Assets	2,550,649	3,408,353	3,359,601	2,451,950	1,719,497	1,300,442	984,174	889,528
Total Assets	2,956,237	3,909,875	3,784,895	2,790,044	1,969,800	1,595,180	1,190,956	1,061,598
Current Liabilities	483,133	751,311	836,489	624,913	456,180	471,623	362,622	404,924
Long-Term Obligations	997,091	996,682	996,297	746,310	497,700	322,990	174,503	174,444
Total Liabilities	1,480,224	1,747,993	1,832,786	1,371,223	953,880	794,613	537,125	579,368
Stockholders' Equity	1,476,013	2,161,882	1,952,109	1,418,821	1,015,920	800,567	653,831	482,230
Shares Outstanding	46,053	45,165	44,630	43,224	42,233	41,572	41,819	40,366
Statistical Record								
Return on Assets %	N.M.	5.57	15.38	16.39	11.91	12.01	13.83	12.69
Return on Equity %	N.M.	10.42	30.00	32.04	23.37	23.01	27.41	28.23
EBITDA Margin %	N.M.	8.18	17.68	16.93	13.15	12.98	13.30	12.85
Net Margin %	N.M.	4.46	10.35	9.76	7.27	7.22	7.32	7.04
Asset Turnover	0.85	1.25	1.49	1.68	1.64	1.66	1.89	1.80
Current Ratio	5.28	4.54	4.02	3.92	3.77	2.76	2.71	2.20
Debt to Equity	0.68	0.46	0.51	0.53	0.49	0.40	0.27	0.36
Price Range	60.00-32.34	68.10-40.43	88.17-61.98	66.93-41.28	49.44-22.84	33.57-19.07	26.85-14.19	17.86-7.09
P/E Ratio	...	14.61-8.68	8.02-5.64	7.61-4.70	10.09-4.66	8.76-4.98	7.38-3.90	6.06-2.40
Average Yield %	2.12	1.84	1.04	0.84	0.82	0.74	0.76	1.13

Address: 4350 South Monaco Street, Suite 500, Denver, CO 80237
Telephone: 303-773-1100
Fax: 303-793-2760

Web Site: www.richmondamerican.com
Officers: Larry A. Mizel - Chmn., C.E.O. David D. Mandarich - Pres., C.O.O.

Auditors: Ernst & Young LLP
Investor Contact: 720-773-1100
Transfer Agents: Continental Stock Transfer & Trust Company, New York, NY

MDU RESOURCES GROUP INC.

Exchange	Symbol	Price	52Wk Range	Yield	P/E	Div Achiever
NYS	MDU	$24.55 (3/31/2008)	31.27-24.35	2.36	10.40	17 Years

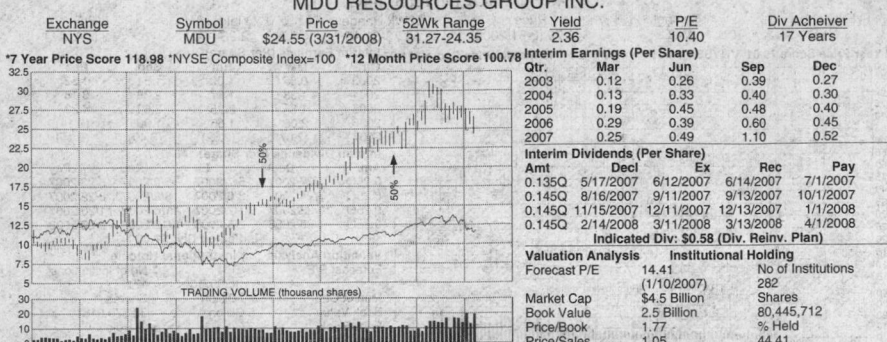

*7 Year Price Score 118.98 *NYSE Composite Index=100 *12 Month Price Score 100.78

Interim Earnings (Per Share)

Qtr.	Mar	Jun	Sep	Dec
2003	0.12	0.26	0.39	0.27
2004	0.13	0.33	0.40	0.30
2005	0.19	0.45	0.48	0.40
2006	0.29	0.39	0.60	0.45
2007	0.25	0.49	1.10	0.52

Interim Dividends (Per Share)

Amt	Decl	Ex	Rec	Pay
0.135Q	5/17/2007	6/12/2007	6/14/2007	7/1/2007
0.145Q	8/16/2007	9/11/2007	9/13/2007	10/1/2007
0.145Q	11/15/2007	12/11/2007	12/13/2007	1/1/2008
0.145Q	2/14/2008	3/11/2008	3/13/2008	4/1/2008

Indicated Div: $0.58 (Div. Reinv. Plan)

Valuation Analysis / **Institutional Holding**

Forecast P/E	14.41	No of Institutions
	(1/10/2007)	282
Market Cap	$4.5 Billion	Shares
Book Value	2.5 Billion	80,445,712
Price/Book	1.77	% Held
Price/Sales	1.05	44.41

Business Summary: Earth & Rock Mining (MIC: 14.5 SIC: 1429 NAIC: 212319)

MDU Resources Group is a diversified natural resource company. Through its Montana-Dakota Utilities Co. subsidiary, Co. generates, transmits and distributes electricity as well as distributes natural gas in Montana, North Dakota, South Dakota and Wyoming. Co.'s Great Plains Natural Gas Co. subsidiary distributes natural gas in western Minnesota and southeastern North Dakota. Co.'s Cascade Natural Gas Corp. indirect subsidiary distributes natural gas in Washington and Oregon. Through its Centennial Energy Holdings, Inc. subsidiary, Co. owns WBI Holdings Inc., Knife River Corp., MDU Construction Services Group, Inc., Centennial Energy Resources LLC and Centennial Holdings Capital LLC.

Recent Developments: For the year ended Dec 31 2007, income from continuing operations increased 4.9% to US$322.8 million from US$307.8 million a year earlier. Net income increased 36.9% to US$432.1 million from US$315.8 million in the prior year. Revenues were US$4.25 billion, up 6.1% from US$4.00 billion the year before. Operating income was US$557.1 million versus US$523.1 million in the prior year, an increase of 6.5%. Direct operating expenses rose 4.4% to US$3.24 billion from US$3.10 billion in the comparable period the year before. Indirect operating expenses increased 18.8% to US$455.3 million from US$383.3 million in the equivalent prior-year period.

Prospects: For the full year of 2008, Co. is projecting earnings to be in the range of $1.65 to $1.90 per share, while long-term compound annual growth goals on earnings per share from operations are forecasted to range from 7.0% to 10.0%. Meanwhile, Co. is encouraged by the acquisition of natural gas properties located in Rusk County, TX through its Fidelity Exploration & Production Co. subsidiary from EnerVest, Ltd. and certain of its affiliated parties and co-venturers for a total transaction value of about $235.0 million. Accordingly, Co. plans to drill about 25 wells in 2008 to further develop the properties. Co. expects the transaction to be accretive to its earnings per share in 2008.

Financial Data

(US$ in Thousands)	12/31/2007	12/31/2006	12/31/2005	12/31/2004	12/31/2003	12/31/2002	12/31/2001	12/31/2000
Earnings Per Share	2.36	1.74	1.53	1.17	1.03	0.92	1.02	0.80
Cash Flow Per Share	3.10	3.66	2.71	2.47	2.50	2.05	2.30	1.50
Tang Book Value Per Share	11.31	10.49	9.04	8.14	6.13	5.50	7.07	6.02
Dividends Per Share	0.560	0.523	0.493	0.467	0.440	0.418	0.400	0.382
Dividend Payout %	23.73	30.08	32.31	39.77	42.58	45.41	39.30	47.78
Income Statement								
Total Revenue	4,247,896	4,070,684	3,455,414	2,719,257	2,352,189	2,031,537	2,223,632	1,873,671
EBITDA	886,979	826,843	704,269	567,248	522,616	437,650	440,006	339,599
Income Before Taxes	512,810	483,165	420,862	301,041	281,485	234,674	254,190	180,678
Income Taxes	190,024	165,248	145,779	93,974	98,572	86,230	98,341	69,650
Net Income	432,120	315,757	275,083	207,067	175,324	148,444	155,849	111,028
Average Shares	182.902	181,392	179,490	176,116	168,690	160,294	152,705	138,127
Balance Sheet								
Net PPE	3,659,555	2,993,351	3,049,893	2,572,705	2,222,293	1,924,886	1,809,318	1,601,014
Total Assets	5,592,434	4,903,474	4,423,562	3,733,521	3,380,592	2,937,249	2,623,071	2,312,959
Long-Term Obligations	1,146,781	1,170,548	1,104,752	873,441	939,450	819,558	783,709	728,166
Total Liabilities	3,061,115	2,738,561	2,531,940	2,052,508	1,929,956	1,638,504	1,498,400	1,416,899
Stockholders' Equity	2,531,319	2,164,913	1,891,622	1,681,013	1,450,636	1,298,745	1,124,771	896,060
Shares Outstanding	182,407	181,018	179,856	177,341	170,036	166,595	156,998	146,313
Statistical Record								
Return on Assets %	8.23	6.77	6.74	5.81	5.55	5.34	6.31	5.43
Return on Equity %	18.40	15.57	15.40	13.19	12.75	12.25	15.42	14.01
EBITDA Margin %	20.88	20.31	20.38	20.86	22.22	21.54	19.79	18.12
Net Margin %	10.17	7.76	7.96	7.61	7.45	7.31	7.01	5.93
PPE Turnover	1.28	1.35	1.23	1.13	1.13	1.09	1.30	1.31
Asset Turnover	0.81	0.87	0.85	0.76	0.74	0.73	0.90	0.92
Debt to Equity	0.45	0.54	0.58	0.52	0.65	0.63	0.70	0.81
Price Range	31.27-24.80	26.90-21.99	24.47-17.07	18.31-14.71	16.17-11.13	14.82-8.31	17.88-10.13	14.67-8.00
P/E Ratio	13.25-10.51	15.46-12.64	15.99-11.15	15.65-12.57	15.70-10.80	16.11-9.03	17.53-9.93	18.33-10.00
Average Yield %	2.02	2.18	2.48	2.86	3.15	3.55	2.96	3.61

Address: 1200 West Century Avenue, Bismarck, ND 58506-5650	**Web Site:** www.mdu.com	**Auditors:** Deloite & Touche LLP
Telephone: 701-530-1000	**Officers:** Martin A. White - Chmn., C.E.O. Terry D. Hildestad - Pres., C.O.O.	**Investor Contact:** 800-437-8000x1020
Fax: 701-530-1731		**Transfer Agents:** Wells Fargo Bank Minnesota, N.A. Shareowner Services, St. Paul, MN

MEADWESTVACO CORP.

Exchange	Symbol	Price	52Wk Range	Yield	P/E
NYS	MWV	$27.22 (3/31/2008)	36.49-25.24	3.38	17.45

*7 Year Price Score 88.82   *NYSE Composite Index=100   *12 Month Price Score 91.86

Interim Earnings (Per Share)

Qtr.	Mar	Jun	Sep	Dec
2003	(0.38)	(0.04)	0.14	0.25
2004	(0.01)	0.24	0.52	(2.48)
2005	(0.03)	(0.41)	0.30	0.32
2006	0.02	(0.04)	0.31	0.23
2007	(0.09)	0.17	0.66	0.82

Interim Dividends (Per Share)

Amt	Decl	Ex	Rec	Pay
0.23Q	4/30/2007	5/8/2007	5/10/2007	6/1/2007
0.23Q	6/26/2007	8/1/2007	8/3/2007	9/4/2007
0.23Q	11/1/2007	11/7/2007	11/11/2007	12/3/2007
0.23Q	1/28/2008	2/5/2008	2/7/2008	3/3/2008

Indicated Div: $0.92

Valuation Analysis

	Institutional Holding	
Forecast P/E	19.21	No of Institutions
	(1/10/2007)	269
Market Cap	$4.7 Billion	Shares
Book Value	3.7 Billion	145,211,648
Price/Book	1.28	% Held
Price/Sales	0.69	79.58

Business Summary: Paper Products (MIC: 11.11 SIC: 2621 NAIC: 322130)

MeadWestvaco provides packaging applications in the food and beverage, media and entertainment, personal care, home and garden, cosmetics, and health care industries. Co.'s Packaging Resources segment produces Coated Natural Kraft® paperboard, linerboard and saturating kraft, and packaging for consumer products; while Consumer Solutions segment provides converting and consumer packaging applications for packaging media products. Consumer & Office Products segment manufactures, markets and distributes school and office products, time-management products and envelopes in North America and Brazil. Specialty Chemicals segment produces chemicals such as activated carbon and printing ink resins.

Recent Developments: For the year ended Dec 31 2007, income from continuing operations increased 206.5% to US$285.0 million from US$93.0 million a year earlier. Net income increased 206.5% to US$285.0 million from US$93.0 million in the prior year. Revenues were US$6.91 billion, up 5.8% from US$6.53 billion the year before. Direct operating expenses rose 5.8% to US$5.71 billion from US$5.40 billion in the comparable period the year before. Indirect operating expenses decreased 2.5% to US$882.0 million from US$905.0 million in the equivalent prior-year period.

Prospects: On Feb 15 2008, Co.'s Specialty Chemicals Division announced an agreement to acquire Eastman Chemical Co.'s pine chemicals product lines, which will expand its Performance Chemicals business. Notably, Co. projects the transaction to close by end of Feb 2008. Meanwhile, in 2008, Co. anticipates solid overall revenue growth in its Consumer Solutions segment, driven by personal care and healthcare business and by increased growth in emerging markets. In addition, Co. expects its Consumer Solutions segment growth to be led by new products, including Natralock®, a paperboard-based plastic clamshell replacement application and Shellpak™, an adherence application for prescription medications.

Financial Data

(US$ in Thousands)	12/31/2007	12/31/2006	12/31/2005	12/31/2004	12/31/2003	12/31/2002	12/31/2001	10/31/2001
Earnings Per Share	1.56	0.52	0.14	(1.73)	(0.03)	(7.02)	(0.21)	0.87
Cash Flow Per Share	3.51	3.14	1.18	4.65	2.31	2.57	0.29	2.49
Tang Book Value Per Share	13.16	11.51	14.25	16.47	17.95	18.42	17.11	17.21
Dividends Per Share	0.920	0.920	0.920	0.920	0.920	0.920	0.220	0.880
Dividend Payout %	58.97	176.92	657.14	...	...	...	...	101.15
Income Statement								
Total Revenue	6,906,000	6,530,000	6,170,000	8,227,000	7,553,000	7,242,000	600,400	3,983,632
EBITDA	1,119,000	806,000	801,000	538,000	974,000	956,000	55,000	673,593
Income Before Taxes	400,000	98,000	135,000	(454,000)	(29,000)	(15,000)	(38,600)	118,510
Income Taxes	115,000	5,000	16,000	(105,000)	(27,000)	(12,000)	(16,900)	30,300
Net Income	285,000	93,000	28,000	(349,000)	(6,000)	(389,000)	(21,700)	88,210
Average Shares	183,600	181,200	192,700	201,900	200,400	102,100	102,600	101,304
Balance Sheet								
Current Assets	2,167,000	2,015,000	2,030,000	2,562,000	2,426,000	2,431,000	1,033,600	1,015,670
Total Assets	9,837,000	9,285,000	8,908,000	11,681,000	12,487,000	12,921,000	6,828,300	6,786,989
Current Liabilities	1,455,000	1,465,000	1,042,000	1,751,000	1,501,000	1,620,000	725,800	701,051
Long-Term Obligations	2,375,000	2,372,000	2,417,000	3,427,000	3,969,000	4,233,000	2,697,200	2,660,467
Total Liabilities	6,129,000	5,752,000	5,425,000	7,364,000	7,719,000	8,090,000	4,513,100	4,446,136
Stockholders' Equity	3,708,000	3,533,000	3,483,000	4,317,000	4,768,000	4,831,000	2,315,200	2,340,853
Shares Outstanding	173,839	182,107	181,418	203,930	200,897	200,039	102,554	103,170
Statistical Record								
Return on Assets %	2.98	1.02	0.27	N.M.	N.M.	N.M.	N.M.	1.32
Return on Equity %	7.87	2.65	0.72	N.M.	N.M.	N.M.	N.M.	3.77
EBITDA Margin %	16.20	12.34	12.98	6.54	12.90	13.20	9.16	16.91
Net Margin %	4.13	1.42	0.45	N.M.	N.M.	N.M.	N.M.	2.21
Asset Turnover	0.72	0.72	0.60	0.68	0.59	0.73	0.08	0.60
Current Ratio	1.49	1.38	1.95	1.46	1.62	1.50	1.42	1.45
Debt to Equity	0.64	0.67	0.69	0.79	0.83	0.88	1.16	1.14
Price Range	36.49-28.69	30.80-24.81	33.89-25.28	34.23-25.60	29.75-21.69	36.40-15.70	29.08-24.55	31.92-22.90
P/E Ratio	23.39-18.39	59.23-47.71	242.07-180.57	...	...	...	...	36.69-26.32
Average Yield %	2.88	3.34	3.17	3.12	3.68	3.32	0.80	3.34

Address: One High Ridge Park, Stamford, CT 06905 **Telephone:** 203-461-7400	**Web Site:** www.meadwestvaco.com **Officers:** John A. Luke Jr. - Chmn., C.E.O. James A. Buzzard - Pres.	**Auditors:** PricewaterhouseCoopers LLP **Investor Contact:** 203-461-7616 **Transfer Agents:** The Bank of New York

MEDCO HEALTH SOLUTIONS, INC.

Exchange	Symbol	Price	52Wk Range	Yield	P/E
NYS	MHS	$43.79 (3/31/2008)	53.97-35.92	N/A	26.87

*7 Year Price Score N/A   *NYSE Composite Index=100   *12 Month Price Score 111.86

Interim Earnings (Per Share)

Qtr.	Mar	Jun	Sep	Dec
2003	0.19	0.20	0.19	0.22
2004	0.19	0.23	0.22	0.24
2005	0.23	0.24	0.27	0.28
2006	0.07	0.28	0.31	0.39
2007	0.47	0.38	0.39	0.39

Interim Dividends (Per Share)

No Dividends Paid

Valuation Analysis

		Institutional Holding	
Forecast P/E	14.76	No of Institutions	
	(1/10/2007)	581	
Market Cap	$23.5 Billion	Shares	
Book Value	6.9 Billion	220,239,312	
Price/Book	3.41	% Held	
Price/Sales	0.53	76.46	

Business Summary: Retail - Miscellaneous (MIC: 5.11 SIC: 5912 NAIC: 446110)

Medco Health Solutions is engaged in the provision of traditional and specialty prescription drug benefit programs and services. Co. provides prescription drug benefit programs and services, including plan design, clinical management, clinical services, pharmacy management, physician services, and Web-based services. In addition, Co. serves blue cross/blue shield plans; managed care organizations; insurance carriers; third-party benefit plan administrators; employers; federal, state, and local government agencies; and union-sponsored benefit plans. Co. provides its services through a network of retail pharmacies and mail-order pharmacies, as well as through specialty pharmacy operations.

Recent Developments: For the year ended Dec 29 2007, net income increased 44.7% to US$912.0 million from US$630.2 million in the prior year. Revenues were US$44.51 billion, up 4.6% from US$42.54 billion the year before. Direct operating expenses rose 3.5% to US$41.56 billion from US$40.14 billion in the comparable period the year before. Indirect operating expenses increased 3.5% to US$1.44 billion from US$1.39 billion in the equivalent prior-year period.

Prospects: For the full year of 2008, Co. is projecting earnings to be in the range of $2.07 to $2.11 per diluted share, compared with its previous earnings guidance of $1.95 to $2.01 per share, representing a growth rate of 27.0% to 29.0% over its 2007 level. In addition, Co. is estimating capital expenditures to be approximately $285.0 million, particularly for items such as capitalized software development for strategic initiatives and infrastructure enhancements. Specifically, Co. noted that the increase of capital expenditures over prior year is primarily associated with the construction of its third automated dispensing pharmacy in Indiana, which is expected to be operational in 2009.

Financial Data
(US$ in Thousands)

	12/29/2007	12/30/2006	12/31/2005	12/25/2004	12/27/2003	12/28/2002	12/29/2001	12/30/2000
Earnings Per Share	1.63	1.04	1.02	0.88	0.79	0.67	0.47	0.40
Cash Flow Per Share	2.49	2.09	1.78	1.31	2.09	0.87	1.22	...
Tang Book Value Per Share	N.M.	N.M.	N.M.	0.49	N.M.	1.69	0.85	...
Income Statement								
Total Revenue	44,506,200	42,543,700	37,870,900	35,351,900	34,264,500	32,958,500	29,070,600	22,266,300
EBITDA	1,900,300	1,403,900	1,310,400	1,183,800	1,012,000	877,700	841,200	736,700
Income Before Taxes	1,503,300	1,011,800	952,900	806,300	728,700	620,300	518,300	447,500
Income Taxes	591,300	381,600	350,900	324,700	302,900	258,700	261,700	230,700
Net Income	912,000	630,200	602,000	481,600	425,800	361,600	256,600	216,800
Average Shares	560,900	603,200	587,000	549,400	541,600	540,000	540,000	540,000
Balance Sheet								
Current Assets	6,302,700	5,855,000	5,060,900	4,320,400	3,760,300	3,226,400	2,533,800	...
Total Assets	16,217,900	14,388,100	13,703,000	10,541,500	10,263,000	9,922,500	9,251,800	...
Current Liabilities	5,129,200	4,826,800	3,760,800	2,644,500	2,605,300	2,054,900	1,809,400	...
Long-Term Obligations	2,894,400	866,400	943,900	1,092,900	1,346,100	...	...	...
Total Liabilities	9,342,600	6,884,600	5,978,800	4,822,100	5,183,000	3,286,900	2,983,500	...
Stockholders' Equity	6,875,300	7,503,500	7,724,200	5,719,400	5,080,000	6,635,600	6,268,300	...
Shares Outstanding	535,939	576,896	608,515	548,872	541,065	540,000	540,000	...
Statistical Record								
Return on Assets %	5.98	4.50	4.89	4.64	4.23	3.78	...	...
Return on Equity %	12.72	8.30	8.81	8.94	7.29	5.62	...	...
EBITDA Margin %	4.27	3.30	3.46	3.35	2.95	2.66	2.89	3.31
Net Margin %	2.05	1.48	1.59	1.36	1.24	1.10	0.88	0.97
Asset Turnover	2.92	3.04	3.07	3.41	3.40	3.45	...	...
Current Ratio	1.23	1.21	1.35	1.63	1.44	1.57	1.40	...
Debt to Equity	0.42	0.12	0.12	0.19	0.26	...	...	...
Price Range	51.57-26.59	32.00-23.91	28.78-20.27	20.13-15.00	18.88-10.25	...	...	...
P/E Ratio	31.64-16.32	30.76-22.99	28.22-19.87	22.87-17.05	23.89-12.97	...	...	...

Address: 100 Parsons Pond Drive, Franklin Lakes, NJ 07417-2603 **Telephone:** 201-269-3400	**Web Site:** www.medco.com **Officers:** David B. Snow Jr. - Chmn., Pres., C.E.O. Kenneth O. Klepper - Exec. V.P., C.O.O.	**Auditors:** PricewaterhouseCoopers LLP **Transfer Agents:** Bank of New York, New York, NY

MEDIA GENERAL, INC.

Exchange	Symbol	Price	52Wk Range	Yield	P/E	Div Acheiver
NYS	MEG	$14.02 (3/31/2008)	39.34-14.01	6.56	29.83	13 Years

*7 Year Price Score 43.13   *NYSE Composite Index=100   *12 Month Price Score 65.00

Interim Earnings (Per Share)

Qtr.	Mar	Jun	Sep	Dec
2003	0.30	0.75	0.16	1.29
2004	0.38	0.78	0.66	1.55
2005	(13.25)	1.61	0.41	1.04
2006	0.28	0.85	0.87	1.33
2007	(0.27)	0.22	0.11	0.42

Interim Dividends (Per Share)

Amt	Decl	Ex	Rec	Pay
0.23Q	4/26/2007	5/29/2007	5/31/2007	6/15/2007
0.23Q	7/26/2007	8/29/2007	8/31/2007	9/15/2007
0.23Q	9/27/2007	11/28/2007	11/30/2007	12/15/2007
0.23Q	1/31/2008	2/27/2008	2/29/2008	3/15/2008

Indicated Div: $0.92

Valuation Analysis   Institutional Holding

Forecast P/E	N/A	No of Institutions
		132
Market Cap	$317.0 Million	Shares
Book Value	913.0 Million	17,771,784
Price/Book	0.35	% Held
Price/Sales	0.34	75.40

Business Summary: Media (MIC: 13.1 SIC: 2711 NAIC: 511110)

Media General is a publicly owned communications company with interests in newspapers, television stations and interactive media. Co. operates in three segments: Publishing, which includes daily and Sunday newspaper operations in Virginia, North Carolina, South Carolina, Alabama, and Florida; Broadcast, which operates network-affiliated television stations in the U.S.; and Interactive Media, which operates in conjunction with its Publishing and Broadcast Divisions to provide online news, information and entertainment to its customers. As of Dec 30 2007, Co. owned 25 daily newspapers, over 150 other publications and 23 television stations, as well as operated more than 75 online enterprises.

Recent Developments: For the year ended Dec 30 2007, net income decreased 86.5% to US$10.7 million from US$79.0 million in the prior year. Revenues were US$932.2 million, down 3.4% from US$964.9 million the year before. Operating income was US$107.2 million versus US$137.7 million in the prior year, a decrease of 22.1%. Direct operating expenses rose 0.8% to US$417.1 million from US$413.6 million in the comparable period the year before. Indirect operating expenses decreased 1.4% to US$407.9 million from US$413.6 million in the equivalent prior-year period.

Prospects: For the fiscal year ending Dec 2008, Co. expects revenues at its Broadcast Division to more than offset any declines at its Publishing Division; which is expected to introduce several specialty products to supplement revenues from its traditional newspapers while exploring opportunities to further reduce expenses. Also, Co. expects its Interactive Media Division to achieve profitability by the end of 2008. Separately, Co. recently signed an agreement with NARAE Enterprises, Inc. to acquire DealTaker.com, an online social shopping portal, to drive revenue and audience growth. Co. expects the transaction to close in the second quarter of 2008 and be slightly accretive to earnings in 2008.

Financial Data
(US$ in Thousands)

	12/30/2007	12/31/2006	12/25/2005	12/26/2004	12/28/2003	12/29/2002	12/30/2001	12/31/2000
Earnings Per Share	0.47	3.32	(10.18)	3.38	2.50	(3.14)	0.79	2.22
Cash Flow Per Share	5.79	6.59	4.34	5.94	5.34	7.54	5.49	(15.33)
Dividends Per Share	0.920	0.880	0.840	0.800	0.760	0.720	0.680	0.640
Dividend Payout %	195.74	26.51	...	23.67	30.40		86.08	28.83
Income Statement								
Total Revenue	932,181	983,189	917,937	900,420	837,423	836,800	807,176	830,601
EBITDA	151,981	225,033	225,147	219,003	187,074	201,519	198,925	250,777
Income Before Taxes	13,954	103,895	133,143	127,278	93,846	88,150	30,946	102,926
Income Taxes	3,622	38,493	50,732	47,093	34,800	34,731	13,022	39,369
Net Income	10,687	79,042	(243,042)	80,185	58,685	(72,917)	18,204	53,719
Average Shares	22,827	23,784	23,884	23,729	23,408	23,236	22,956	24,189
Balance Sheet								
Current Assets	273,726	202,748	184,373	170,847	162,621	160,552	163,038	172,880
Total Assets	2,471,066	2,505,228	1,975,354	2,368,812	2,386,755	2,347,011	2,534,059	2,561,282
Current Liabilities	137,316	131,520	111,914	126,871	114,403	111,501	100,497	114,541
Long-Term Obligations	897,572	916,320	485,304	533,280	627,289	642,937	777,662	822,077
Total Liabilities	1,558,059	1,567,868	1,059,528	1,185,043	1,279,294	1,287,757	1,370,391	1,389,360
Stockholders' Equity	913,007	937,360	915,826	1,183,769	1,107,461	1,059,254	1,163,668	1,171,922
Shares Outstanding	22,611	24,112	24,046	23,786	23,545	23,208	22,976	22,714
Statistical Record								
Return on Assets %	0.43	3.47	N.M.	3.38	2.49	N.M.	0.72	2.16
Return on Equity %	1.16	8.39	N.M.	7.02	5.43	N.M.	1.56	4.22
EBITDA Margin %	16.30	22.89	24.53	24.32	22.34	24.08	24.64	30.19
Net Margin %	1.15	8.04	N.M.	8.91	7.01	N.M.	2.26	6.47
Asset Turnover	0.38	0.43	0.42	0.38	0.35	0.34	0.32	0.33
Current Ratio	1.99	1.54	1.65	1.35	1.42	1.44	1.62	1.51
Debt to Equity	0.98	0.98	0.53	0.45	0.57	0.61	0.67	0.70
Price Range	43.93-20.69	51.42-34.50	68.80-49.16	72.40-53.97	67.88-47.53	69.49-47.38	53.50-34.09	54.19-33.98
P/E Ratio	93.47-44.02	15.49-10.39	...	21.42-15.97	27.15-19.01	...	67.72-43.15	24.41-15.31
Average Yield %	2.80	2.13	1.38	1.27	1.31	1.26	1.45	1.36

Address: 333 East Franklin Street, Richmond, VA 23219 **Telephone:** 804-649-6000 **Fax:** 804-649-6898	**Web Site:** www.mediageneral.com **Officers:** J. Stewart Bryan III - Chmn. Marshall N. Morton - Pres., C.E.O.	**Auditors:** Ernst & Young LLP **Investor Contact:** 804-649-6000

MEDICIS PHARMACEUTICAL CORP.

Exchange	Symbol	Price	52Wk Range	Yield	P/E
NYS	MRX	$19.69 (3/31/2008)	34.15-18.62	0.81	17.27

*7 Year Price Score 73.35 *NYSE Composite Index=100 *12 Month Price Score 79.18

Interim Earnings (Per Share)

Qtr.	Mar	Jun	Sep	Dec
2005			0.76	
2006	(1.63)	0.25	(0.38)	0.33
2007	0.15	0.24	0.34	0.41

Interim Dividends (Per Share)

Amt	Decl	Ex	Rec	Pay
0.03Q	6/14/2007	6/28/2007	7/2/2007	7/31/2007
0.03Q	9/12/2007	9/27/2007	10/1/2007	10/31/2007
0.03Q	12/12/2007	12/28/2007	1/2/2008	1/31/2008
0.04Q	3/12/2008	3/28/2008	4/1/2008	4/30/2008

Indicated Div: $0.16

Valuation Analysis

Forecast P/E	23.00 (1/10/2007)
Market Cap	$1.1 Billion
Book Value	622.0 Million
Price/Book	1.78
Price/Sales	2.39

Institutional Holding

No of Institutions	195
Shares	62,531,960
% Held	N/A

Business Summary: Pharmaceuticals (MIC: 9.1 SIC: 2834 NAIC: 325412)

Medicis Pharmaceutical develops and markets products that are designed to treat dermatological, aesthetic and podiatric conditions. Co. provides products addressing various conditions, such as facial wrinkles, acne, fungal infections, rosacea, hyperpigmentation, photoaging, psoriasis, skin and skin-structure infections, seborrheic dermatitis and cosmesis. As of Dec 31 2006, Co. provided 17 branded products, including OMNICEF® (cefdinir), RESTYLANE® (hyaluronic acid), SOLODYN® (minocycline HCl, USP), TRIAZ® (benzoyl peroxide), VANOS™ (fluocinonide) Cream, and ZIANA™ (clindamycin phosphate and tretinoin) Gel.

Recent Developments: For the year ended Dec 31 2007, net income amounted to US$75.1 million versus a net loss of US$75.8 million in the prior year. Revenues were US$464.7 million, up 33.0% from US$349.2 million the year before. Operating income was US$97.7 million versus a loss of US$136.8 million in the prior year. Direct operating expenses rose 22.1% to US$51.0 million from US$41.7 million in the comparable period the year before. Indirect operating expenses decreased 28.9% to US$316.0 million from US$444.3 million in the equivalent prior-year period.

Prospects: Co. remains committed to business development opportunities as it is seeking approval of its RELOXIN® Biologics License Application for aesthetic, and the preservation of its SOLODYN®. Meanwhile, Co. will continue its design and implementation of an enterprise resource planning system in 2008 to integrate and improve the financial and operational aspects of its business. Accordingly, for 2008, Co. is targeting revenue of $528.0 million to $540.0 million and diluted earnings per share of $1.43 to $1.56, excluding the effect of a potential generic launch to SOLODYN®, revenue associated with a RELOXIN® approval, and charges related to the accounting for the Revance transaction.

Financial Data

(US$ in Thousands)	12/31/2007	12/31/2006	12/31/2005	06/30/2005	06/30/2004	06/30/2003	06/30/2002	06/30/2001
Earnings Per Share	1.14	(1.39)	0.76	1.01	0.52	0.91	0.80	0.64
Cash Flow Per Share	2.84	(0.75)	1.81	2.35	2.29	1.56	1.21	1.17
Tang Book Value Per Share	6.84	5.00	4.42	2.98	3.39	2.89	4.40	5.89
Dividends Per Share	0.120	0.120	0.120	0.120	0.100	0.025	...	...
Dividend Payout %	10.53	...	15.79	11.88	19.23	2.75	...	...
Income Statement								
Total Revenue	464,651	349,242	163,954	376,899	303,722	247,539	212,807	167,801
EBITDA	120,421	(113,759)	88,571	129,808	73,652	94,726	82,273	52,260
Income Before Taxes	126,095	(116,645)	80,223	99,102	46,157	77,660	78,984	59,325
Income Taxes	51,044	(40,796)	30,502	34,112	15,317	26,404	28,960	18,905
Net Income	75,051	(75,849)	49,721	64,990	30,840	51,256	50,024	40,420
Average Shares	71,246	54,688	69,772	70,909	59,258	56,422	62,810	63,387
Balance Sheet								
Current Assets	855,079	656,684	833,284	698,925	733,863	645,628	658,473	398,879
Total Assets	1,194,629	1,069,286	1,145,955	1,043,251	1,078,384	936,990	876,273	548,696
Current Liabilities	395,000	106,662	140,831	98,854	67,120	68,847	47,214	40,411
Long-Term Obligations	169,145	453,065	453,065	453,065	453,067	400,000	400,000	...
Total Liabilities	572,674	559,727	602,468	556,905	523,081	475,869	447,214	45,242
Stockholders' Equity	621,955	509,559	543,487	486,346	555,303	461,121	429,059	503,454
Shares Outstanding	56,348	55,394	54,404	54,386	66,177	63,267	55,485	60,486
Statistical Record								
Return on Assets %	5.63	N.M.	2.97	6.13	3.05	5.65	7.02	7.74
Return on Equity %	13.27	N.M.	6.02	12.48	6.05	11.52	10.73	8.59
EBITDA Margin %	25.92	N.M.	54.02	34.44	24.25	38.27	38.66	31.14
Net Margin %	16.15	N.M.	30.33	17.24	10.15	20.71	23.51	24.09
Asset Turnover	0.41	0.32	0.10	0.36	0.30	0.27	0.30	0.32
Current Ratio	2.16	6.16	5.92	7.07	10.93	9.38	13.95	9.87
Debt to Equity	0.27	0.89	0.83	0.93	0.82	0.87	0.93	...
Price Range	39.68-25.47	39.08-22.84	35.01-26.70	40.80-27.75	44.81-27.47	30.50-17.16	32.30-20.38	36.81-18.00
P/E Ratio	34.81-22.34	...	46.07-35.13	40.40-27.48	86.17-52.83	33.52-18.86	40.37-25.47	57.52-28.13
Average Yield %	0.39	0.38	0.37	0.35	0.28	0.10	...	...

Address: 8125 North Hayden Road, Scottsdale, AZ 85258
Telephone: 602-808-8800
Fax: 602-808-0822

Web Site: www.medicis.com
Officers: Jonah Shacknai - Chmn., C.E.O. Mark A. Prygocki Sr. - Exec. V.P., C.F.O., Treas., Sec.

Auditors: ERNST & YOUNG LLP
Transfer Agents: Wells Fargo Shareowner Services, St. Paul, MN

MEDTRONIC, INC.

Exchange	Symbol	Price	52Wk Range	Yield	P/E	Div Acheiver
NYS	MDT	$48.37 (3/31/2008)	57.86-45.25	1.03	24.81	30 Years

*7 Year Price Score 83.37   *NYSE Composite Index=100   *12 Month Price Score 102.24

Interim Earnings (Per Share)

Qtr.	Jul	Oct	Jan	Apr
2004-05	0.43	0.44	0.45	0.16
2005-06	0.26	0.67	0.55	0.61
2006-07	0.51	0.59	0.61	0.70
2007-08	0.59	0.58	0.07	...

Interim Dividends (Per Share)

Amt	Decl	Ex	Rec	Pay
0.125Q	6/22/2007	7/3/2007	7/6/2007	7/27/2007
0.125Q	8/23/2007	10/3/2007	10/5/2007	10/26/2007
0.125Q	10/19/2007	1/2/2008	1/4/2008	1/25/2008
0.125Q	2/21/2008	4/2/2008	4/4/2008	4/25/2008

Indicated Div: $0.50 (Div. Reinv. Plan)

Valuation Analysis

Forecast P/E	17.84
	(1/10/2007)
Market Cap	$61.3 Billion
Book Value	11.0 Billion
Price/Book	4.95
Price/Sales	4.19

Institutional Holding

No of Institutions	1078
Shares	870,963,392
% Held	75.63

Business Summary: Medical Instruments & Equipment (MIC: 9.6 SIC: 3845 NAIC: 334510)

Medtronic is a provider of enhanced products and therapies for use by medical professionals to address the healthcare needs of their patients. Co.'s primary products include those for cardiac rhythm disorders, cardiovascular disease, neurological disorders, spinal conditions and musculoskeletal trauma, urological and digestive disorders, diabetes, and ear, nose, and throat conditions. As of Apr 27 2007, Co. operated in eight operating segments that manufacture and sell device-based medical therapies: Cardiac Rhythm Disease Management, Spinal and Navigation, Vascular, Neurological, Diabetes, Cardiac Surgery, Ear, Nose, and Throat, as well as Physio-Control.

Recent Developments: For the quarter ended Jan 25 2008, net income decreased 89.2% to US$77.0 million from US$710.0 million in the year-earlier quarter. Revenues were US$3.41 billion, up 11.7% from US$3.05 billion the year before. Direct operating expenses rose 12.3% to US$870.0 million from US$775.0 million in the comparable period the year before. Indirect operating expenses increased 72.1% to US$2.29 billion from US$1.33 billion in the equivalent prior-year period.

Prospects: Going forward, Co. expects to benefit from the introduction of new products and the launch of existing products in new markets. For instance, Co. expects FDA approval and U.S. launch of its Talent AAA Stent Graft System in the first half of calendar year 2008, and of its Talent Thoracic device in the second half of the year. At the same time, Co. expects its ongoing restructuring plans, which are designed to, among others, drive manufacturing capabilities in its CardioVascular business and downsize its Physio-Control business, to be substantially completed by the end of Apr 2008. These actions should produce annual savings of about $125.0 million, driven by reduced compensation expense.

Financial Data

(US$ in Thousands)	9 Mos	6 Mos	3 Mos	04/27/2007	04/28/2006	04/29/2005	04/30/2004	04/25/2003
Earnings Per Share	1.95	2.49	2.50	2.41	2.09	1.48	1.60	1.30
Cash Flow Per Share	3.40	3.08	2.91	2.60	1.84	2.34	2.31	1.71
Tang Book Value Per Share	1.05	5.09	4.76	4.56	2.98	4.26	3.18	2.21
Dividends Per Share	0.485	0.470	0.455	0.440	0.385	0.335	0.290	0.250
Dividend Payout %	24.91	18.90	18.23	18.26	18.42	22.64	18.13	19.23
Income Statement								
Total Revenue	9,655,000	6,250,000	3,127,000	12,299,000	11,292,000	10,054,600	9,087,200	7,665,200
EBITDA	2,224,000	1,918,000	984,000	3,944,000	3,617,500	2,961,700	3,236,700	2,756,600
Depn & Amortn	457,000	276,000	149,000	...	...	...	...	...
Income Before Taxes	1,881,000	1,747,000	879,000	3,515,000	3,161,300	2,543,500	2,796,900	2,341,300
Income Taxes	463,000	406,000	204,000	713,000	614,600	739,600	837,600	741,500
Net Income	1,418,000	1,341,000	675,000	2,802,000	2,546,700	1,803,900	1,959,300	1,599,800
Average Shares	1,135,000	1,147,700	1,153,100	1,161,800	1,217,300	1,220,800	1,225,200	1,227,900
Balance Sheet								
Current Assets	6,681,000	10,541,000	7,668,000	7,918,000	10,376,600	7,421,500	5,312,700	4,605,500
Total Assets	21,412,000	20,586,000	19,660,000	19,512,000	19,664,800	16,617,400	14,110,800	12,320,800
Current Liabilities	3,536,000	2,651,000	2,040,000	2,563,000	4,405,800	3,380,000	4,240,600	1,813,300
Long-Term Obligations	5,656,000	5,494,000	5,576,000	5,578,000	5,486,300	1,973,200	1,100	1,980,300
Total Liabilities	10,446,000	9,111,000	8,517,000	8,535,000	10,282,300	6,167,900	5,033,800	4,414,400
Stockholders' Equity	10,966,000	11,475,000	11,143,000	10,977,000	9,382,500	10,449,500	9,077,000	7,906,400
Shares Outstanding	1,123,027	1,130,658	1,134,122	1,143,407	1,155,237	1,210,186	1,209,459	1,218,128
Statistical Record								
Return on Assets %	10.92	14.54	14.48	14.34	14.08	11.77	14.59	13.81
Return on Equity %	20.39	26.39	27.42	27.60	25.75	18.53	22.70	22.38
EBITDA Margin %	23.03	30.69	31.47	32.07	32.04	29.46	35.62	35.96
Net Margin %	14.69	21.46	21.59	22.78	22.55	17.94	21.56	20.87
Asset Turnover	0.63	0.64	0.63	0.63	0.62	0.66	0.68	0.66
Current Ratio	1.89	3.98	3.76	3.09	2.36	2.20	1.25	2.54
Debt to Equity	0.52	0.48	0.50	0.51	0.58	0.19	N.M.	0.25
Price Range	57.86-45.25	57.86-47.00	54.58-42.47	54.58-42.47	59.54-49.05	54.92-46.40	52.65-43.36	48.95-33.74
P/E Ratio	29.67-23.21	23.24-18.88	21.83-16.99	22.65-17.62	28.49-23.47	37.11-31.35	32.91-27.10	37.65-25.95
Average Yield %	0.94	0.90	0.90	0.88	0.71	0.66	0.60	0.57

Address: 710 Medtronic Parkway, Minneapolis, MN 55432-5604	**Web Site:** www.medtronic.com	**Auditors:** PricewaterhouseCoopers LLP
Telephone: 763-514-4000	**Officers:** Arthur D. Collins Jr. - Chmn., C.E.O.	**Investor Contact:** 763-505-2692
Fax: 763-514-4879	William A. Hawkins - Pres., C.O.O.	**Transfer Agents:** Wells Fargo Bank Minnesota N.A., St. Paul, MN

MEMC ELECTRONIC MATERIALS, INC.

Exchange	Symbol	Price	52Wk Range	Yield	P/E
NYS	WFR	$70.90 (3/31/2008)	94.02-53.69	N/A	19.92

*7 Year Price Score 233.55 *NYSE Composite Index=100 *12 Month Price Score 123.05

Interim Earnings (Per Share)

Qtr.	Mar	Jun	Sep	Dec
2003	0.09	0.13	0.16	0.15
2004	0.16	0.27	0.27	0.31
2005	0.34	0.26	0.45	0.22
2006	0.29	0.36	0.40	0.56
2007	0.58	0.70	0.65	1.62

Interim Dividends (Per Share)

No Dividends Paid

Valuation Analysis

		Institutional Holding	
Forecast P/E	13.15	No of Institutions	
	(1/10/2007)	398	
Market Cap	$16.3 Billion	Shares	
Book Value	2.0 Billion	180,741,952	
Price/Book	7.99	% Held	
Price/Sales	8.46	80.61	

TRADING VOLUME (thousand shares)

Business Summary: IT & Technology (MIC: 10.2 SIC: 3674 NAIC: 334413)

MEMC Electronic Materials is engaged in the design, manufacture and sale of silicon wafers. Co. provides wafers in sizes ranging from 100 millimeters to 300 millimeters. Co. offers wafers in three general categories: prime, epitaxial and test/monitor. Depending on market conditions, Co. also sells intermediate products, such as polysilicon, silane gas, partial ingots and scrap wafers to semiconductor device and equipment makers, solar customers, flat panel and other industries. The wafers are used as the starting material for the manufacture of various types of semiconductor devices, including microprocessor, memory, logic and power devices, as well as the starting material for solar cells.

Recent Developments: For the year ended Dec 31 2007, net income increased 123.7% to US$826.2 million from US$369.3 million in the prior year. Revenues were US$1.92 billion, up 24.7% from US$1.54 billion the year before. Operating income was US$849.9 million versus US$558.3 million in the prior year, an increase of 52.2%. Direct operating expenses rose 8.2% to US$921.3 million from US$851.6 million in the comparable period the year before. Indirect operating expenses increased 15.2% to US$150.6 million from US$130.7 million in the equivalent prior-year period.

Prospects: Looking ahead, Co. is targeting its first quarter of 2008 sales to be about US$560.0 million. Also, Co. estimates its 2008 first quarter margins to be about flat to slightly up compared with the 2007 fourth quarter. Further, Co. is expecting operating expenses to be about $42.0 million for the 2008 first quarter. Meanwhile, for 2008, Co. anticipates revenue of about $2.40 billion to $2.50 billion, representing sales growth of 25.0 % to 30.0% and assuming a reasonably healthy demand environment for the semiconductor and solar markets with no significant economic issues during 2008. Lastly, Co. expects to attain 8,000 metric tons of annualized polysilicon capacity by the end of year 2008.

Financial Data

(US$ in Thousands)	12/31/2007	12/31/2006	12/31/2005	12/31/2004	12/31/2003	12/31/2002	12/31/2001	11/13/2001
Earnings Per Share	3.56	1.61	1.10	1.02	0.53	(0.17)	(0.48)	(7.03)
Cash Flow Per Share	4.07	2.38	1.50	1.36	0.63	0.67	(0.07)	(0.33)
Tang Book Value Per Share	8.87	5.23	3.21	2.13	0.94	...	...	...
Income Statement								
Total Revenue	1,921,800	1,540,584	1,107,379	1,027,958	781,100	687,180	58,846	559,007
EBITDA	1,148,900	648,498	312,657	251,175	192,577	120,247	(28,664)	(18,649)
Income Before Taxes	1,111,800	590,486	252,375	198,531	155,887	19,567	(36,018)	(259,666)
Income Taxes	282,200	214,833	(2,808)	(40,119)	36,864	16,712	1,576	239,352
Net Income	826,200	369,288	249,353	226,201	116,617	(5,070)	(29,397)	(489,025)
Average Shares	232,300	229,743	226,449	221,047	218,719	129,810	69,612	69,612
Balance Sheet								
Current Assets	1,589,500	899,514	436,278	390,330	365,345	363,708	264,030	...
Total Assets	2,887,200	1,765,524	1,148,103	1,009,942	726,752	631,682	549,334	...
Current Liabilities	444,200	257,818	224,909	215,624	244,054	286,073	221,699	...
Long-Term Obligations	25,600	29,373	34,821	116,082	59,251	160,998	144,743	...
Total Liabilities	816,400	560,069	392,120	520,565	469,002	598,366	518,500	...
Stockholders' Equity	2,035,000	1,166,893	711,337	442,898	193,623	(24,680)	(20,249)	...
Shares Outstanding	229,300	223,257	221,517	208,393	207,002	195,532	69,612	...
Statistical Record								
Return on Assets %	35.51	25.35	23.11	25.98	17.17	N.M.	N.M.	...
Return on Equity %	51.61	39.32	43.21	70.88	138.05	...	N.M.	...
EBITDA Margin %	59.78	42.09	28.23	24.43	24.65	17.50	N.M.	N.M.
Net Margin %	42.99	23.97	22.52	22.00	14.93	N.M.	N.M.	N.M.
Asset Turnover	0.83	1.06	1.03	1.18	1.15	1.16	0.05	...
Current Ratio	3.58	3.49	1.94	1.81	1.50	1.27	1.19	...
Debt to Equity	0.01	0.03	0.05	0.26	0.31	...	...	...
Price Range	94.02-40.29	48.75-23.40	23.68-10.74	13.25-7.39	14.25-7.15	10.12-2.89	4.57-3.31	11.74-1.05
P/E Ratio	26.41-11.32	30.28-14.53	21.53-9.76	12.99-7.25	26.89-13.49	...	...	...

Address: 501 Pearl Drive (City of O'Fallon), St. Peters, MO 63376 **Telephone:** 636-474-5000 **Fax:** 636-474-5158	**Web Site:** www.memc.com **Officers:** John Marren - Chmn. Nabeel Gareeb - Pres., C.E.O.	**Auditors:** KPMG LLP **Investor Contact:** 636-279-5000 **Transfer Agents:** ComputerShare Investor Services, Chicago, IL

MERCK & CO., INC

Exchange	Symbol	Price	52Wk Range	Yield	P/E
NYS	MRK	$37.95 (3/31/2008)	60.77-37.95	4.01	25.47

*7 Year Price Score 88.95   *NYSE Composite Index=100   *12 Month Price Score 91.45

Interim Earnings (Per Share)

Qtr.	Mar	Jun	Sep	Dec
2003	0.76	0.83	0.82	0.62
2004	0.73	0.79	0.60	0.50
2005	0.62	0.33	0.65	0.51
2006	0.69	0.69	0.43	0.22
2007	0.78	0.77	0.70	(0.75)

Interim Dividends (Per Share)

Amt	Decl	Ex	Rec	Pay
0.38Q	5/22/2007	6/6/2007	6/8/2007	7/2/2007
0.38Q	7/24/2007	9/5/2007	9/7/2007	10/1/2007
0.38Q	11/27/2007	12/5/2007	12/7/2007	1/2/2008
0.38Q	2/26/2008	3/5/2008	3/7/2008	4/1/2008

Indicated Div: $1.52 (Div. Reinv. Plan)

Valuation Analysis   **Institutional Holding**

Forecast P/E	16.11	No of Institutions
	(1/10/2007)	1050
Market Cap	$82.4 Billion	Shares
Book Value	18.2 Billion	1,555,045,888
Price/Book	4.53	% Held
Price/Sales	3.41	71.78

Business Summary: Pharmaceuticals (MIC: 9.1 SIC: 2834 NAIC: 325412)

Merck & Co. is a pharmaceutical company engaged in discovering, developing, producing and marketing products designed to improve human and animal health, directly and through joint ventures. Co.'s products include therapeutic and preventive agents, generally sold by prescription, for the treatment of human disorders. Among these are Singulair (montelukast sodium), a leukotriene receptor antagonist for the chronic treatment of asthma and for the relief of symptoms of allergic rhinitis; Cozaar (losartan potassium), Hyzaar (losartan potassium and hydrochlorothiazide); Fosamax (alendronate sodium) and Fosamax Plus D (alendronate sodium/cholecalciferol).

Recent Developments: For the year ended Dec 31 2007, net income decreased 26.1% to US$3.28 billion from US$4.43 billion in the prior year. Revenues rose US$24.20 billion, up 6.9% from US$22.64 billion the year before. Direct operating expenses rose 2.3% to US$6.14 billion from US$6.00 billion in the comparable period the year before. Indirect operating expenses increased 35.6% to US$14.64 billion from US$10.80 billion in the equivalent prior-year period.

Prospects: Co. anticipates a significant decline in its U.S. sales of FOSAMAX and FOSAMAX PLUS D after each product's loss of market exclusivity in Feb and Apr 2008, respectively. However, Co. expects that the solid sales of its new products, coupled with continued strong growth from in-line products, particularly SINGULAIR, should allow it to offset the effect of the loss. Notably, Co. estimates its 2008 sales of SINGULAIR product of $4.60 billion to $4.80 billion, COZAAR/HYZAAR product of $3.20 billion to $3.40 billion, Vaccines product of $4.80 billion to $5.20 billion and FOSAMAX product of $1.10 billion to $1.40 billion. Consequently, Co. targets its 2008 earnings of $3.80 to $4.00 per share.

Financial Data

(US$ in Thousands)	12/31/2007	12/31/2006	12/31/2005	12/31/2004	12/31/2003	12/31/2002	12/31/2001	12/31/2000
Earnings Per Share	1.49	2.03	2.10	2.61	3.03	3.14	3.14	2.90
Cash Flow Per Share	3.22	3.11	3.46	3.95	3.77	4.22	3.97	3.32
Tang Book Value Per Share	7.37	7.00	7.48	7.03	6.13	4.88	3.77	3.23
Dividends Per Share	1.520	1.520	1.520	1.500	1.460	1.420	1.380	1.260
Dividend Payout %	102.01	74.88	72.38	57.47	48.18	45.22	43.95	43.45
Income Statement								
Total Revenue	24,197,700	22,636,000	22,011,900	22,938,600	22,485,900	51,790,300	47,715,700	40,363,200
EBITDA	5,002,100	8,100,600	8,976,600	9,418,800	10,408,000	11,673,400	11,841,000	11,115,200
Income Before Taxes	3,370,700	6,221,400	7,363,900	7,974,500	9,051,600	10,213,600	10,402,600	9,824,100
Income Taxes	95,300	1,787,600	2,732,600	2,161,100	2,462,000	3,064,100	3,120,800	3,002,400
Net Income	3,275,400	4,433,800	4,631,300	5,813,400	6,830,900	7,149,500	7,281,800	6,821,700
Average Shares	2,193,000	2,187,700	2,200,400	2,226,400	2,233,100	2,277,000	2,322,300	2,353,200
Balance Sheet								
Current Assets	15,045,400	15,230,200	21,049,300	13,475,200	11,527,200	14,833,900	12,961,600	13,353,400
Total Assets	48,350,700	44,569,800	44,845,800	42,572,800	40,587,500	47,561,200	44,006,700	39,910,400
Current Liabilities	12,258,200	12,722,700	13,303,500	11,744,100	9,569,600	12,375,200	11,544,200	9,709,600
Long-Term Obligations	3,915,800	5,551,000	5,125,600	4,691,500	5,096,000	4,879,000	4,798,600	3,600,700
Total Liabilities	30,166,000	27,010,100	26,929,200	25,284,600	25,011,100	29,360,700	27,956,600	25,078,000
Stockholders' Equity	18,184,700	17,559,700	17,916,600	17,288,200	15,576,400	18,200,500	16,050,100	14,832,400
Shares Outstanding	2,172,503	2,167,786	2,181,924	2,208,639	2,221,764	2,244,983	2,272,729	2,307,599
Statistical Record								
Return on Assets %	7.05	9.92	10.60	13.94	15.50	15.62	17.35	18.01
Return on Equity %	18.33	25.00	26.31	35.28	40.45	41.75	47.16	48.47
EBITDA Margin %	20.67	35.79	40.78	41.06	46.29	22.54	24.82	27.54
Net Margin %	13.54	19.59	21.04	25.34	30.38	13.80	15.26	16.90
Asset Turnover	0.52	0.51	0.50	0.55	0.51	1.13	1.14	1.07
Current Ratio	1.23	1.20	1.58	1.15	1.20	1.20	1.12	1.38
Debt to Equity	0.22	0.32	0.29	0.27	0.33	0.27	0.30	0.24
Price Range	60.77-42.94	46.21-32.75	34.93-25.85	49.08-26.00	59.85-40.60	60.92-36.96	88.02-54.11	89.80-51.05
P/E Ratio	40.79-28.82	22.76-16.13	16.63-12.31	18.80-9.96	19.75-13.40	19.40-11.77	28.03-17.23	30.96-17.60
Average Yield %	3.00	3.97	4.96	3.57	2.84	2.77	2.05	1.81

Address: One Merck Drive, P.O. Box 100, Whitehouse Station, NJ 08889-0100	Web Site: www.merck.com	Auditors: PricewaterhouseCoopers LLP
Telephone: 908-423-1000	Officers: Richard T. Clark - Pres., C.E.O. Judy C. Lewent - Exec. V.P., C.F.O.	Transfer Agents: Bank of New York
Fax: 908-735-1500		

MERCURY GENERAL CORP.

Exchange	Symbol	Price	52Wk Range	Yield	P/E	Div Acheiver
NYS	MCY	$44.31 (3/31/2008)	57.57-42.35	5.24	10.21	21 Years

*7 Year Price Score 84.47 *NYSE Composite Index=100 *12 Month Price Score 95.24

Interim Earnings (Per Share)

Qtr.	Mar	Jun	Sep	Dec
2003	0.77	0.80	0.91	0.90
2004	1.26	1.43	1.19	1.36
2005	1.10	1.35	1.33	0.85
2006	1.07	0.69	1.25	0.91
2007	1.10	1.27	1.15	0.82

Interim Dividends (Per Share)

Amt	Decl	Ex	Rec	Pay
0.52Q	5/7/2007	6/13/2007	6/15/2007	6/28/2007
0.52Q	8/6/2007	9/12/2007	9/14/2007	9/27/2007
0.52Q	11/5/2007	12/12/2007	12/14/2007	12/27/2007
0.58Q	2/11/2008	3/13/2008	3/17/2008	3/27/2008

Indicated Div: $2.32

Valuation Analysis — **Institutional Holding**

Forecast P/E	N/A	No of Institutions
		200
Market Cap	$2.4 Billion	Shares
Book Value	1.9 Billion	23,342,340
Price/Book	1.30	% Held
Price/Sales	0.76	42.70

TRADING VOLUME (thousand shares)

Business Summary: Insurance (MIC: 8.2 SIC: 6331 NAIC: 524126)

Mercury General and its subsidiaries are engaged primarily in writing automobile insurance in a number of states, principally California. Co. provides a range of coverage to automobile policyholders, including bodily injury liability, underinsured and uninsured motorist, personal injury protection, property damage liability, comprehensive, collision, and other hazards. Co. also provides homeowners, mechanical breakdown, commercial and dwelling fire, and commercial property insurance. As of Dec 31 2007, Co. sold its policies through more than 4,500 independent agents and brokers, of which approximately 1,000 are located in each of California and Florida.

Recent Developments: For the year ended Dec 31 2007, net income increased 10.7% to US$214.8 million in the prior year. Revenues were US$3.18 billion, up 0.3% from US$3.17 billion the year before. Net premiums earned were US$2.99 billion versus US$3.00 billion in the prior year, a decrease of 0.1%. Net investment income rose 5.2% to US$158.9 million from US$151.1 million a year ago.

Prospects: Co.'s near-term outlook appears constructive. Co. expects to implement its NextGen computer system to replace its existing underwriting, billings, claims and commissions systems in Georgia, Illinois, and Texas by the end of 2008. Also, Co. plans to introduce its Internet Business Strategy project in phases during the first quarter of 2008 and expects to complete the rollout by end of 2008. Meanwhile, for the 2008 and 2009 hurricane seasons, Co. intends to purchase the Temporary Increase in Coverage Limit options, which was created by the Florida Hurricane Catastrophe Trust Fund (FHCT) to provide coverage equal to approximately $20.0 million in addition to the mandatory coverage from FHCT.

Financial Data

(US$ in Thousands)	12/31/2007	12/31/2006	12/31/2005	12/31/2004	12/31/2003	12/31/2002	12/31/2001	12/31/2000
Earnings Per Share	4.34	3.92	4.63	5.24	3.38	1.21	1.94	2.02
Cash Flow Per Share	3.95	6.62	8.98	8.58	8.17	6.31	3.68	2.82
Tang Book Value Per Share	34.02	31.54	29.44	26.77	23.07	20.21	19.71	19.06
Dividends Per Share	2.080	1.920	1.720	1.480	1.320	1.200	1.060	0.960
Dividend Payout %	47.93	48.98	37.15	28.24	39.05	99.17	54.64	47.52
Income Statement								
Premium Income	2,993,877	2,997,023	2,847,733	2,528,636	2,145,047	1,741,527	1,380,561	1,249,259
Total Revenue	3,178,750	3,168,743	2,991,913	2,668,157	2,265,517	1,786,271	1,506,980	1,366,018
Benefits & Claims	2,036,644	2,021,646	1,862,936	1,582,254	1,452,051	1,268,243	1,010,439	901,781
Income Before Taxes	315,036	312,409	352,639	407,843	245,801	60,668	124,809	128,555
Income Taxes	77,204	97,592	99,380	121,635	61,480	(5,437)	19,470	19,189
Net Income	237,832	214,817	253,259	286,208	184,321	66,105	105,339	109,366
Average Shares	54,829	54,786	54,717	54,633	54,547	54,502	54,382	54,258
Balance Sheet								
Total Assets	4,414,496	4,301,062	4,041,551	3,609,743	3,119,766	2,645,296	2,316,540	2,142,263
Total Liabilities	2,552,498	2,576,932	2,433,714	2,150,195	1,864,263	1,546,510	1,246,829	1,109,358
Stockholders' Equity	1,861,998	1,724,130	1,607,837	1,459,548	1,255,503	1,098,786	1,069,711	1,032,905
Shares Outstanding	54,729	54,669	54,605	54,514	54,424	54,361	54,276	54,193
Statistical Record								
Return on Assets %	5.46	5.15	6.62	8.48	6.39	2.66	4.72	5.39
Return on Equity %	13.26	12.89	16.51	21.03	15.66	6.10	10.02	11.23
Loss Ratio %	68.03	67.46	65.42	62.57	67.69	72.82	73.19	72.19
Net Margin %	7.48	6.78	8.46	10.73	8.14	3.70	6.99	8.01
Price Range	57.57-49.17	59.52-49.02	60.45-51.62	59.98-46.44	48.58-34.30	50.63-37.37	43.85-32.21	43.88-21.25
P/E Ratio	13.26-11.33	15.18-12.51	13.06-11.15	11.45-8.86	14.37-10.15	41.84-30.88	22.60-16.60	21.72-10.52
Average Yield %	3.90	3.54	3.04	2.90	3.07	2.74	2.83	3.44

Address: 4484 Wilshire Boulevard, Los Angeles, CA 90010	Web Site: www.mercuryinsurance.com	Auditors: KPMG LLP
Telephone: 323-937-1060	Officers: George Joseph - Chmn., C.E.O. Gabriel Tirador - Pres., C.O.O.	Transfer Agents: The Bank of New York, New York, NY
Fax: 323-857-7116		

MEREDITH CORP.

Exchange	Symbol	Price	52Wk Range	Yield	P/E	Div Acheiver
NYS	MDP	$38.25 (3/31/2008)	63.25-37.35	2.25	11.25	14 Years

*7 Year Price Score 92.49   *NYSE Composite Index=100   *12 Month Price Score 84.28

Interim Earnings (Per Share)

Qtr.	Sep	Dec	Mar	Jun
2004-05	0.50	0.54	0.69	0.83
2005-06	0.52	0.58	0.80	0.96
2006-07	0.62	0.72	0.92	1.05
2007-08	0.68	0.75	...	...

Interim Dividends (Per Share)

Amt	Decl	Ex	Rec	Pay
0.185Q	5/9/2007	5/29/2007	5/31/2007	6/15/2007
0.185Q	8/8/2007	8/29/2007	8/31/2007	9/14/2007
0.185Q	11/7/2007	11/28/2007	11/30/2007	12/14/2007
0.215Q	2/4/2008	2/27/2008	2/29/2008	3/14/2008

Indicated Div: $0.86

Valuation Analysis

		Institutional Holding	
Forecast P/E	14.31 (1/10/2007)	No of Institutions	222
Market Cap	$1.0 Billion	Shares	34,458,992
Book Value	821.8 Million	% Held	
Price/Book	2.19		71.70
Price/Sales	1.12		

Business Summary: Media (MIC: 13.1 SIC: 2721 NAIC: 511120)

Meredith is engaged in the business of magazine and book publishing, television broadcasting, integrated marketing, and interactive media. As of June 30 2007, Co. conducted its businesses through two operating segments: Publishing and Broadcasting. The publishing segment focuses on the home and family market. In addition, Co. is a publisher of magazines serving women. The publishing segment also includes book publishing; integrated marketing, a consumer database; an internet presence; brand licensing activities; and other related operations. The broadcasting segment includes 13 network-affiliated television stations located across the U.S. and one AM radio station.

Recent Developments: For the quarter ended Dec 31 2007, income from continuing operations decreased 1.7% to US$35.2 million from US$35.8 million in the year-earlier quarter. Net income increased 2.9% to US$36.1 million from US$35.0 million in the year-earlier quarter. Revenues were US$396.2 million, down 0.8% from US$399.3 million the year before. Operating income was US$65.1 million versus US$66.0 million in the prior-year quarter, a decrease of 1.5%. Direct operating expenses rose 3.0% to US$166.1 million from US$161.4 million in the comparable period the year before. Indirect operating expenses decreased 4.0% to US$165.1 million from US$172.0 million in the equivalent prior-year period.

Prospects: Despite challenges due to an off-political year at its television stations and higher postal rates, Co. remains optimistic regarding its near-term outlook. For the fiscal year ending June 30 2008, Co. continues to anticipate earnings to be in the range of $3.50 to $3.55 per share. In addition, Co. expects to continue to absorb an annualized postal rate increase of more than $13.0 million. For the fiscal quarter ended Mar 31 2008, is projecting earnings to be approximately $0.98 per share. Meanwhile, Co.'s Meredith Books operations will continue to focus on its core content areas of cooking, gardening, remodeling, and decorating, with less emphasis on children's books and non-core titles.

Financial Data

(US$ in Thousands)	6 Mos	3 Mos	06/30/2007	06/30/2006	06/30/2005	06/30/2004	06/30/2003	06/30/2002
Earnings Per Share	3.40	3.37	3.31	2.86	2.52	2.14	0.10	1.79
Cash Flow Per Share	5.50	5.04	4.38	3.93	3.43	3.40	3.47	2.83
Dividends Per Share	0.740	0.715	0.690	0.600	0.520	0.430	0.370	0.350
Dividend Payout %	21.76	21.22	20.85	20.98	20.63	20.09	370.00	19.55
Income Statement								
Total Revenue	800,318	404,494	1,615,985	1,597,564	1,221,289	1,161,652	1,080,104	987,829
EBITDA	163,781	79,884	362,027	340,563	293,941	269,428	244,554	275,431
Depn & Amortn	38,052	19,368	...	...	...	...	...	...
Income Before Taxes	114,480	54,705	262,653	237,364	209,052	180,613	148,559	149,072
Income Taxes	45,799	21,335	93,823	92,572	80,903	69,897	57,491	57,691
Net Income	69,129	33,370	167,346	144,792	129,012	110,716	5,319	91,381
Average Shares	48,325	48,828	49,108	50,610	51,220	51,689	51,093	50,921
Balance Sheet								
Current Assets	453,385	466,869	452,640	431,520	304,495	314,014	268,429	272,211
Total Assets	2,105,880	2,086,129	2,089,951	2,040,675	1,491,308	1,465,927	1,436,721	1,460,264
Current Liabilities	564,527	529,757	487,029	463,946	439,080	370,961	297,199	307,406
Long-Term Obligations	295,000	325,000	375,000	515,000	125,000	225,000	375,000	385,000
Total Liabilities	1,284,065	1,273,628	1,256,750	1,342,571	839,481	877,197	935,956	952,547
Stockholders' Equity	821,815	812,501	833,201	698,104	651,827	588,730	500,765	507,717
Shares Outstanding	47,139	47,445	48,232	48,191	49,296	50,484	50,149	49,575
Statistical Record								
Return on Assets %	7.94	7.96	7.86	8.20	8.73	7.61	0.37	6.31
Return on Equity %	21.28	21.81	21.20	21.45	20.80	20.27	1.05	19.12
EBITDA Margin %	20.46	19.75	22.40	21.32	24.07	23.19	22.64	27.88
Net Margin %	8.68	8.25	10.05	9.06	10.57	9.53	0.49	9.25
Asset Turnover	0.77	0.78	0.78	0.90	0.83	0.80	0.75	0.68
Current Ratio	0.80	0.88	0.93	0.93	0.69	0.85	0.90	0.89
Debt to Equity	0.36	0.40	0.45	0.74	0.19	0.38	0.75	0.76
Price Range	63.25-50.49	63.25-49.50	63.25-46.18	56.48-47.65	55.13-44.81	55.75-44.00	47.58-34.09	44.75-27.20
P/E Ratio	18.60-14.85	18.77-14.69	19.11-13.95	19.75-16.66	21.88-17.78	26.05-20.56	475.80-340.90	25.00-15.20
Average Yield %	1.27	1.25	1.26	1.17	1.04	0.87	0.89	0.94

Address: 1716 Locust Street, Des Moines, IA 50309-3023 **Telephone:** 515-284-3000 **Fax:** 515-284-2700	**Web Site:** www.meredith.com **Officers:** William T. Kerr - Chmn., C.E.O. Stephen M. Lacy - Pres., C.O.O.	**Auditors:** KPMG LLP **Investor Contact:** 800-284-4236 **Transfer Agents:** Boston EquiServe, Boston, MA

MERRILL LYNCH & CO INC

Exchange	Symbol	Price	52Wk Range	Yield	P/E
NYS	MER	$40.74 (3/31/2008)	94.17-39.93	3.44	N/A

*7 Year Price Score 94.01 *NYSE Composite Index=100 *12 Month Price Score 76.79

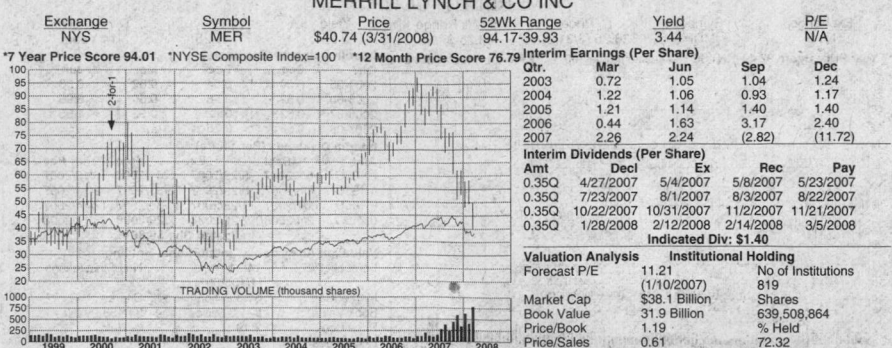

Interim Earnings (Per Share)

Qtr.	Mar	Jun	Sep	Dec
2003	0.72	1.05	1.04	1.24
2004	1.22	1.06	0.93	1.17
2005	1.21	1.14	1.40	1.40
2006	0.44	1.63	3.17	2.40
2007	2.26	2.24	(2.82)	(11.72)

Interim Dividends (Per Share)

Amt	Decl	Ex	Rec	Pay
0.35Q	4/27/2007	5/4/2007	5/8/2007	5/23/2007
0.35Q	7/23/2007	8/1/2007	8/3/2007	8/22/2007
0.35Q	10/22/2007	10/31/2007	11/2/2007	11/21/2007
0.35Q	1/28/2008	2/12/2008	2/14/2008	3/5/2008

Indicated Div: $1.40

Valuation Analysis   **Institutional Holding**

Forecast P/E	11.21 (1/10/2007)	No of Institutions 819
Market Cap	$38.1 Billion	Shares 639,508,864
Book Value	31.9 Billion	% Held
Price/Book	1.19	72.32
Price/Sales	0.61	

Business Summary: Finance Intermediaries & Services (MIC: 8.7 SIC: 6211 NAIC: 523999)

Merrill Lynch & Company is a holding company that, through its subsidiaries, is engaged in the provision of capital markets, advisory and wealth management products and services. As of Dec 28 2007, Co.'s operations were organized into two business segments: Global Markets and Investment Banking (GMI); and Global Wealth Management (GWM). GMI provides global markets and origination products and services to corporate, institutional, and government clients around the world. GWM creates and distributes investment products and services for individuals, small- and mid-size businesses, and employee benefit plans. As of Dec 28 2007, Co. had total assets of $1.02 trillion.

Recent Developments: For the year ended Dec 28 2007, loss from continuing operations was US$8.64 billion compared with income of US$7.10 billion a year earlier. Net loss amounted to US$7.78 billion versus net income of US$7.50 billion in the prior year. Revenues were US$62.68 billion, down 9.6% from US$69.35 billion the year before. Direct operating expenses rose 44.6% to US$51.43 billion from US$35.57 billion in the comparable period the year before. Indirect operating expenses increased 0.5% to US$24.08 billion from US$23.97 billion in the equivalent prior-year period.

Prospects: On Dec 31 2007, Co. has completed the sale of its Merrill Lynch Insurance Group, for $1.25 billion. As a result of the transaction, Co. has recorded an after-tax gain of $316.0 million in the fourth quarter of 2007, and anticipates the transaction to be slightly accretive to earnings per share and to have a positive effect on return on equity in 2008 after redeployment of proceeds. Meanwhile, on Feb 4 2008, Co. has completed the sale of its middle-market commercial finance business to GE Capital, as part of its strategic focus on divesting non-core assets and optimizing capital allocation, while enabling the redeployment of $1.30 billion of capital into other parts of its business.

Financial Data
(US$ in Thousands)

	12/28/2007	12/29/2006	12/30/2005	12/31/2004	12/26/2003	12/27/2002	12/28/2001	12/29/2000
Earnings Per Share	(9.69)	7.59	5.16	4.38	4.05	2.63	0.57	4.11
Cash Flow Per Share	(87.38)	(45.53)	(28.88)	(14.30)	10.56	22.61	7.68	1.64
Tang Book Value Per Share	23.99	38.67	29.26	26.48	23.69	20.76	18.39	16.67
Dividends Per Share	1.400	1.000	0.760	0.640	0.640	0.640	0.640	0.605
Dividend Payout %	...	13.18	14.73	14.61	15.80	24.33	112.28	14.72
Income Statement								
Interest Income	56,974,000	40,588,000	26,571,000	14,973,000	11,678,000	13,178,000	20,143,000	21,196,000
Commissions & Fees	12,866,000	10,632,000	8,965,000	8,138,000	7,024,000	7,070,000	8,805,000	11,026,000
Employee Costs	15,903,000	17,003,000	12,441,000	10,596,000	9,570,000	9,426,000	11,269,000	13,730,000
Interest Expense	51,425,000	35,932,000	21,774,000	10,444,000	7,591,000	9,645,000	16,877,000	18,085,000
Income Before Taxes	(12,831,000)	10,426,000	7,231,000	5,836,000	5,649,000	3,757,000	1,377,000	5,717,000
Income Taxes	(4,194,000)	2,927,000	2,115,000	1,400,000	1,470,000	1,053,000	609,000	1,738,000
Net Income	(7,777,000)	7,499,000	5,116,000	4,436,000	3,988,000	2,513,000	573,000	3,784,000
Average Shares	830,415	962,962	977,736	1,003,779	975,524	942,222	938,555	911,416
Balance Sheet								
Total Assets	1,020,050,000	841,299,000	681,015,000	648,059,000	494,518,000	447,928,000	419,419,000	407,200,000
Total Liabilities	988,118,000	802,261,000	645,415,000	616,689,000	464,197,000	422,395,000	396,716,000	386,182,000
Stockholders' Equity	31,932,000	39,038,000	35,600,000	31,370,000	27,651,000	22,875,000	20,008,000	18,304,000
Shares Outstanding	936,039	864,683	915,601	928,036	945,910	867,290	843,473	807,954
Statistical Record								
Return on Assets %	N.M.	0.99	0.77	0.76	0.85	0.58	0.14	1.03
Return on Equity %	N.M.	20.15	15.32	14.79	15.83	11.75	3.00	24.40
Net Interest Margin %	9.74	11.47	18.05	30.25	35.00	26.81	16.21	14.68
Price Range	97.53-51.23	93.56-65.41	69.02-52.48	64.25-47.53	59.86-31.57	58.36-28.43	80.00-36.01	72.94-36.72
P/E Ratio	...	12.33-8.62	13.38-10.17	14.67-10.85	14.78-7.80	22.19-10.81	140.35-63.18	17.75-8.93
Average Yield %	1.77	1.29	1.28	1.15	1.36	1.51	1.12	1.05

Address: 4 World Financial Center, New York, NY 10080
Telephone: 212-449-1000
Fax: 212-449-7461

Web Site: www.ml.com
Officers: E. Stanley O'Neal - Chmn., Pres., C.E.O.
Thomas H. Patrick - Exec. Vice-Chmn., Fin., Admin.

Auditors: DELOITTE & TOUCHE LLP
Investor Contact: 866-607-1234
Transfer Agents: Wells Fargo Bank, N.A., South St. Paul, MN

METLIFE INC

*7 Year Price Score 121.47 *NYSE Composite Index=100   *12 Month Price Score 99.54

Interim Earnings (Per Share)

Qtr.	Mar	Jun	Sep	Dec
2003	0.47	0.79	0.75	0.90
2004	0.69	1.25	0.92	0.68
2005	1.33	3.02	0.97	0.88
2006	0.93	0.80	1.29	4.96
2007	1.28	1.48	1.29	1.43

Interim Dividends (Per Share)

Amt	Decl	Ex	Rec	Pay
0.46A	9/28/2004	11/3/2004	11/5/2004	12/13/2004
0.52A	10/25/2005	11/3/2005	11/7/2005	12/15/2005
0.59A	10/24/2006	11/2/2006	11/6/2000	12/15/2006
0.74A	10/23/2007	11/2/2007	11/6/2007	12/14/2007

Indicated Div: $0.74

Valuation Analysis

		Institutional Holding	
Forecast P/E	N/A	No of Institutions	
		535	
Market Cap	$43.9 Billion	Shares	
Book Value	35.2 Billion	412,269,888	
Price/Book	1.25	% Held	
Price/Sales	0.83	54.77	

TRADING VOLUME (thousand shares)

Business Summary: Insurance (MIC: 8.2 SIC: 6411 NAIC: 524210)

MetLife is a provider of insurance and other financial services with operations throughout the U.S. and the regions of Latin America, Europe, and Asia Pacific. Through its domestic and international subsidiaries and affiliates, Co. provides life insurance, annuities, automobile and homeowners insurance, retail banking and other financial services to individuals, as well as group insurance, reinsurance and retirement and savings products and services to corporations and other institutions. Co. operates through five segments: Institutional, Individual, Auto & Home, International and Reinsurance, as well as Corporate & Other. As of Dec 31 2007, Co. had $558.56 billion of total assets.

Recent Developments: For the year ended Dec 31 2007, income from continuing operations increased 39.4% to US$4.28 billion from US$3.07 billion a year earlier. Net income decreased 31.4% to US$4.32 billion from US$6.29 billion in the prior year. Revenues were US$53.01 billion, up 9.8% from US$48.25 billion the year before. Net premiums earned were US$33.21 billion versus US$31.19 billion in the prior year, an increase of 6.5%. Net investment income rose 11.3% to US$19.01 billion from US$17.08 billion a year ago.

Prospects: Going forward, while the retrenchment of the mortgage market increases the downside risk to U.S. economic growth, Co. expects continued moderate U.S. growth over the next few quarters. Notably, a steady economy should provide for improving demand for group insurance and retirement, and savings-type products. However, Co. believes that investment income and the related yields on other limited partnership interests may decline in 2008 due to increased volatility in the equity and credit markets in 2007. Separately, on Aug 31 2007, Co.'s subsidiary, MetLife Insurance Ltd., completed the sale of its annuities and pension businesses to a third party for $25.0 million in cash consideration.

Financial Data

(US$ in Thousands)	12/31/2007	12/31/2006	12/31/2005	12/31/2004	12/31/2003	12/31/2002	12/31/2001	12/31/2000
Earnings Per Share	5.48	7.99	6.16	3.65	2.94	2.20	0.62	1.49
Cash Flow Per Share	13.39	8.67	10.69	10.73	9.98	7.09	6.48	1.71
Tang Book Value Per Share	41.51	38.43	32.08	31.16	27.93	24.83	22.45	22.31
Dividends Per Share	0.740	0.590	0.520	0.460	0.230	0.210	0.200	0.200
Dividend Payout %	13.50	7.38	8.44	12.60	7.82	9.55	32.26	13.42
Income Statement								
Premium Income	33,206,000	31,192,000	28,688,000	25,216,000	23,169,000	21,225,000	19,101,000	18,137,000
Total Revenue	53,007,000	48,396,000	44,776,000	39,014,000	35,789,000	33,147,000	31,928,000	31,947,000
Benefits & Claims	27,828,000	26,431,000	25,506,000	22,662,000	20,848,000	19,523,000	18,454,000	17,220,000
Income Before Taxes	6,039,000	4,221,000	4,399,000	3,779,000	2,630,000	1,671,000	739,000	1,416,000
Income Taxes	1,759,000	1,116,000	1,260,000	1,071,000	687,000	316,000	266,000	463,000
Net Income	4,317,000	6,293,000	4,714,000	2,758,000	2,217,000	1,605,000	473,000	953,000
Average Shares	762,263	770,704	755,336	754,833	746,844	729,201	767,017	788,508
Balance Sheet								
Total Assets	558,562,000	527,715,000	481,645,000	356,808,000	326,841,000	277,385,000	256,898,000	255,018,000
Total Liabilities	523,383,000	493,917,000	452,544,000	333,984,000	305,692,000	258,735,000	239,580,000	237,539,000
Stockholders' Equity	35,179,000	33,798,000	29,101,000	22,824,000	21,149,000	17,385,000	16,062,000	16,389,000
Shares Outstanding	729,223	751,984	757,537	732,487	757,186	700,278	715,507	734,597
Statistical Record								
Return on Assets %	0.79	1.25	1.12	0.80	0.73	0.60	0.18	0.40
Return on Equity %	12.52	20.01	18.16	12.51	11.51	9.60	2.92	6.32
Loss Ratio %	83.80	84.74	88.91	89.87	89.98	91.98	96.61	94.94
Net Margin %	8.14	13.00	10.53	7.07	6.19	4.84	1.48	2.98
Price Range	70.87-59.10	59.83-48.14	52.15-37.85	41.18-32.63	33.92-24.01	34.58-20.75	34.88-25.20	36.50-15.13
P/E Ratio	12.93-10.78	7.49-6.03	8.47-6.14	11.28-8.94	11.54-8.17	15.72-9.43	56.25-40.65	24.50-10.15
Average Yield %	1.14	1.11	1.15	1.27	0.80	0.74	0.67	0.85

Address: One Madison Avenue, New York, NY 10010-3690
Telephone: 212-578-2211

Web Site: www.metlife.com
Officers: Robert H. Benmosche - Chmn., Pres., C.E.O. Stewart G. Nagler - Vice-Chmn., C.F.O.

Auditors: Deloitte & Touche LLP

METTLER-TOLEDO INTERNATIONAL, INC.

Exchange	Symbol	Price	52Wk Range	Yield	P/E
NYS	MTD	$97.12 (3/31/2008)	118.54-86.59	N/A	20.66

*7 Year Price Score 145.37 *NYSE Composite Index=100 *12 Month Price Score 103.71

TRADING VOLUME (thousand shares)

Interim Earnings (Per Share)

Qtr.	Mar	Jun	Sep	Dec
2003	0.29	0.57	0.53	0.73
2004	0.41	0.62	0.54	0.80
2005	0.47	0.42	0.60	1.03
2006	0.57	0.84	1.16	1.30
2007	0.78	1.07	1.16	1.69

Interim Dividends (Per Share)

No Dividends Paid

Valuation Analysis		Institutional Holding	
Forecast P/E	17.44	No of Institutions	
	(1/10/2007)	204	
Market Cap	$3.5 Billion	Shares	
Book Value	581.3 Million	35,370,464	
Price/Book	5.95	% Held	
Price/Sales	1.93	92.47	

Business Summary: Instruments and Related Products (MIC: 11.15 SIC: 3826 NAIC: 334516)

Mettler-Toledo International is a supplier of precision instruments and services. Co. manufactures weighing instruments for use in laboratory, industrial and food retailing applications. Co. is also a provider of analytical instruments for use in life science, reaction engineering and real-time analytic systems used in drug and chemical compound development, and process analytics instruments used for in-line measurement in production processes. In addition, Co. is a supplier of end-of-line inspection systems used in production and packaging for food, pharmaceutical and other industries. Co.'s manufacturing facilities are primarily located in China, Germany, Switzerland, the U.K. and the U.S.

Recent Developments: For the year ended Dec 31 2007, net income increased 13.3% to US$178.5 million from US$157.5 million in the prior year. Revenues were US$1.79 billion, up 12.5% from US$1.59 billion the year before. Direct operating expenses rose 11.6% to US$897.6 million from US$804.5 million in the comparable period the year before. Indirect operating expenses increased 9.9% to US$633.2 million from US$576.0 million in the equivalent prior-year period.

Prospects: In 2008, Co. remains committed to pursue on its business growth strategies, including improving its sales and marketing programs, capitalizing on opportunities in emerging markets, utilizing its new product launches, and optimizing its costs and invested capital. In detail, in an effort to reduce costs, Co. is shifting more of its manufacturing to China where its three facilities manufacture for the local markets as well as for export. Meanwhile, Co. has raised its full-year 2008 earnings expectation in the range of $5.23 to $5.38 per share, assuming local currency sales growth of 4.0% to 6.0%, with estimated earnings of $0.94 to $0.96 per share for the first quarter of 2008.

Financial Data

(US$ in Thousands)	12/31/2007	12/31/2006	12/31/2005	12/31/2004	12/31/2003	12/31/2002	12/31/2001	12/31/2000
Earnings Per Share	4.70	3.86	2.52	2.37	2.11	2.21	1.68	1.66
Cash Flow Per Share	6.16	4.78	4.19	3.74	2.64	2.61	2.50	2.17
Tang Book Value Per Share	1.14	2.48	3.16	3.71	2.36	N.M.	N.M.	N.M.
Income Statement								
Total Revenue	1,793,748	1,594,912	1,482,472	1,404,454	1,304,431	1,213,707	1,148,022	1,095,547
EBITDA	295,034	252,908	205,141	197,880	179,950	162,343	172,568	161,893
Income Before Taxes	242,867	204,847	160,184	154,224	136,911	110,410	118,434	108,605
Income Taxes	64,360	47,315	51,282	46,267	41,073	9,989	46,170	38,510
Net Income	178,507	157,532	108,902	107,957	95,838	100,421	72,264	70,119
Average Shares	37,952	40,785	43,285	45,483	45,508	45,370	42,978	42,141
Balance Sheet								
Current Assets	683,209	669,770	800,659	552,357	505,537	475,727	431,758	423,339
Total Assets	1,678,214	1,587,085	1,669,773	1,480,072	1,387,276	1,303,393	1,189,412	887,582
Current Liabilities	447,773	384,379	353,456	348,246	327,909	367,664	347,587	349,153
Long-Term Obligations	385,072	345,705	443,795	196,290	223,239	262,093	309,479	237,807
Total Liabilities	1,096,928	956,223	1,010,771	759,186	733,280	801,007	801,228	708,742
Stockholders' Equity	581,286	630,862	659,002	720,886	653,996	502,386	388,184	178,840
Shares Outstanding	35,638	38,430	41,404	43,366	44,582	44,384	44,145	39,372
Statistical Record								
Return on Assets %	10.93	9.67	6.91	7.51	7.12	8.06	6.96	8.19
Return on Equity %	29.45	24.43	15.78	15.66	16.58	22.55	25.49	48.08
EBITDA Margin %	16.45	15.86	13.84	14.09	13.80	13.38	15.03	14.78
Net Margin %	9.95	9.88	7.35	7.69	7.35	8.27	6.29	6.40
Asset Turnover	1.10	0.98	0.94	0.98	0.97	0.97	1.11	1.28
Current Ratio	1.53	1.74	2.27	1.59	1.54	1.29	1.24	1.21
Debt to Equity	0.66	0.55	0.67	0.27	0.34	0.52	0.80	1.33
Price Range	118.54-77.78	80.80-55.62	58.20-45.24	51.97-40.50	42.73-28.90	51.85-25.77	53.06-37.90	55.63-31.88
P/E Ratio	25.22-16.55	20.93-14.41	23.10-17.95	21.93-17.09	20.25-13.70	23.46-11.66	31.58-22.56	33.51-19.20

Address: Im Langacher, P.O. Box MT-100, Greifensee, CH 8606	Web Site: www.mt.com	Auditors: PricewaterhouseCoopers LLP
Telephone: 449-442-211	Officers: Robert F. Spoerry - Chmn., Pres., C.E.O. William P. Donnelly - C.F.O.	Investor Contact: 614-438-4748
Fax: 194-424-70		Transfer Agents: Mellon Investor Services, Ridgefield Park, NJ

MGIC INVESTMENT CORP. (MILWAUKEE, WI)

Exchange	Symbol	Price	52Wk Range	Yield	P/E
NYS	MTG	$10.53 (3/31/2008)	66.53-10.04	0.95	N/A

*7 Year Price Score 48.78 *NYSE Composite Index=100 *12 Month Price Score 42.87

Interim Earnings (Per Share)

Qtr.	Mar	Jun	Sep	Dec
2003	1.42	1.46	1.06	1.05
2004	1.31	1.56	1.36	1.38
2005	1.90	1.87	1.55	1.45
2006	1.87	1.74	1.55	1.48
2007	1.12	0.93	(4.61)	(18.04)

Interim Dividends (Per Share)

Amt	Decl	Ex	Rec	Pay
0.25Q	5/10/2007	5/18/2007	5/22/2007	6/8/2007
0.25Q	7/26/2007	8/9/2007	8/13/2007	9/4/2007
0.025Q	10/25/2007	11/7/2007	11/9/2007	12/3/2007
0.025Q	1/24/2008	2/6/2008	2/8/2008	3/3/2008

Indicated Div: $0.10

Valuation Analysis

		Institutional Holding	
Forecast P/E	7.99 (1/10/2007)	No of Institutions	302
Market Cap	$861.3 Million	Shares	94,051,952
Book Value	2.6 Billion	% Held	N/A
Price/Book	0.33		
Price/Sales	0.51		

TRADING VOLUME (thousand shares)

Business Summary: Insurance (MIC: 8.2 SIC: 6351 NAIC: 524126)

MGIC Investment is a holding company, which, through its wholly owned subsidiary, Mortgage Guaranty Insurance Corporation, is a provider of private mortgage insurance to the home mortgage lending industry. Co. provides mortgage insurance to lenders throughout the U.S. and to government sponsored entities to protect against loss from defaults on low down payment residential mortgage loans. Co. also provides various services for the mortgage finance industry, such as contract underwriting and portfolio analysis and retention through certain other non-insurance subsidiaries. As of Dec 31 2007, Co. was licensed in all 50 states of the U.S., the District of Columbia, Puerto Rico and Guam.

Recent Developments: For the year ended Dec 31 2007, net loss amounted to US$1.67 billion versus net income of US$564.7 million in the prior year. Revenues were US$1.69 billion, up 15.2% from US$1.47 billion the year before. Net premiums earned were US$1.26 billion versus US$1.19 billion in the prior year, an increase of 6.3%. Net investment income rose 8.0% to US$259.8 million from US$240.6 million a year ago.

Prospects: For full-year 2008, Co. expects its average insurance in force to be higher compared to 2007, with its insurance in force balance to be stable throughout the year. At the same time, Co. believes that the anticipated decrease in the total mortgage origination market should be offset by its expectation that private mortgage insurance will be used on a greater percentage of mortgage originations. Additionally, Co. is seeing improving business fundamentals for mortgage insurance in the existing environment, including an increase in mortgage insurance penetration, increasing persistency and the favorable effect on the 2008 book of the underwriting and pricing changes it is implementing.

Financial Data

(US$ in Thousands)	12/31/2007	12/31/2006	12/31/2005	12/31/2004	12/31/2003	12/31/2002	12/31/2001	12/31/2000
Earnings Per Share	(20.54)	6.65	6.78	5.63	4.99	6.04	5.93	5.05
Cash Flow Per Share	7.77	5.90	5.54	5.72	6.95	5.91	5.85	5.17
Tang Book Value Per Share	31.72	51.88	47.31	43.05	38.58	33.87	28.47	23.07
Dividends Per Share	0.775	1.000	0.525	0.225	0.113	0.100	0.100	0.100
Dividend Payout %	...	15.04	7.74	4.00	2.25	1.66	1.69	1.98
Income Statement								
Premium Income	1,262,390	1,187,409	1,238,692	1,329,428	1,366,011	1,182,098	1,042,267	890,091
Total Revenue	1,693,206	1,469,169	1,526,530	1,612,693	1,685,411	1,565,803	1,357,841	1,110,341
Benefits & Claims	2,365,423	613,635	553,530	700,999	766,028	365,752	160,814	91,723
Income Before Taxes	(2,234,654)	525,328	656,493	591,777	575,797	897,642	931,910	788,801
Income Taxes	(833,977)	130,097	176,932	159,348	146,027	268,451	292,773	246,802
Net Income	(1,670,018)	564,739	626,873	553,186	493,879	629,191	639,137	541,999
Average Shares	81,294	84,950	92,443	98,245	99,022	104,214	107,795	107,260
Balance Sheet								
Total Assets	7,716,361	6,621,671	6,357,569	6,380,691	5,917,387	5,300,303	4,567,012	3,857,781
Total Liabilities	5,122,018	2,325,794	2,192,514	2,237,052	2,120,485	1,905,111	1,546,825	1,392,899
Stockholders' Equity	2,594,343	4,295,877	4,165,055	4,143,639	3,796,902	3,395,192	3,020,187	2,464,882
Shares Outstanding	81,793	82,799	88,046	96,260	98,412	100,251	106,086	106,825
Statistical Record								
Return on Assets %	N.M.	8.70	9.84	8.97	8.81	12.75	15.17	15.53
Return on Equity %	N.M.	13.35	15.09	13.90	13.73	19.62	23.30	25.49
Loss Ratio %	187.38	51.68	44.69	52.73	56.08	30.94	15.43	10.30
Net Margin %	(98.63)	38.44	41.07	34.30	29.30	40.18	47.07	48.81
Price Range	70.09-17.11	72.05-54.28	69.41-57.36	77.44-56.32	58.50-35.80	73.62-33.87	77.00-51.63	71.50-32.13
P/E Ratio	...	10.83-8.16	10.24-8.46	13.75-10.00	11.72-7.17	12.19-5.61	12.98-8.71	14.16-6.36
Average Yield %	1.66	1.58	0.83	0.33	0.23	0.17	0.16	0.19

Address: MGIC Plaza, 250 East Kilbourn Avenue, Milwaukee, WI 53202 **Telephone:** 414-347-6480 **Fax:** 414-347-6696	**Web Site:** www.mgic.com **Officers:** Curt S. Culver - Pres., C.E.O. J. Michael Lauer - Exec. V.P., C.F.O.	**Auditors:** PricewaterhouseCoopers LLP **Transfer Agents:** Firstar Trust Company

MGM MIRAGE

Exchange	Symbol	Price	52Wk Range	Yield	P/E
NYS	MGM	$58.77 (3/31/2008)	99.75-58.39	N/A	11.07

*7 Year Price Score 180.33 *NYSE Composite Index=100 *12 Month Price Score 88.73

Interim Earnings (Per Share)

Qtr.	Mar	Jun	Sep	Dec
2003	0.17	0.17	0.16	0.31
2004	0.36	0.36	0.45	0.26
2005	0.38	0.48	0.31	0.34
2006	0.49	0.50	0.54	0.69
2007	0.57	1.22	0.62	2.90

Interim Dividends (Per Share)

Amt	Decl	Ex	Rec	Pay
100%	...	5/19/2005	5/4/2005	5/18/2005

Valuation Analysis — **Institutional Holding**

Forecast P/E	N/A	No of Institutions
		228
Market Cap	$17.3 Billion	Shares
Book Value	6.1 Billion	116,760,184
Price/Book	2.85	% Held
Price/Sales	2.24	41.09

Business Summary: Hospitality & Tourism (MIC: 5.1 SIC: 7011 NAIC: 721120)

MGM Mirage is a holding company. Through its subsidiaries, Co. owns and operates hotel, casino and entertainment resorts. At Dec 31 2007, Co. owned and operated 17 casino resorts in Nevada and Mississippi and had investments in four other casino resorts in Nevada, New Jersey, Illinois and Mississippi. Co. owns and operates the following casino resorts on the Las Vegas Strip in Las Vegas: Bellagio, MGM Grand Las Vegas, Mandalay Bay, The Mirage, Luxor, Treasure Island, New York-New York, Excalibur, Monte Carlo, Slots-A-Fun and Circus Circus. In addition, Co. has a 50.0% interest in MGM Grand Macau, a hotel-casino resort in Macau, Special Administrative Region of the People's Republic of China.

Recent Developments: For the year ended Dec 31 2007, income from continuing operations increased 120.2% to US$1.40 billion from US$636.0 million a year earlier. Net income increased 144.4% to US$1.58 billion from US$648.3 million in the prior year. Revenues were US$7.69 billion, up 7.2% from US$7.18 billion the year before. Operating income was US$2.86 billion versus US$1.76 billion in the prior year, an increase of 62.9%. Direct operating expenses rose 8.5% to US$4.14 billion from US$3.81 billion in the comparable period the year before. Indirect operating expenses decreased 57.1% to US$688.6 million from US$1.60 billion in the equivalent prior-year period.

Prospects: Looking ahead, Co. believes that economic conditions in the U.S., including the downturn in the housing market and credit concerns to continue to have a negative effect on its operating results. Nonetheless, Co. believes that the strength of Las Vegas as a tourist destination should offset these negative factors. Further, Co. expects to continue to benefit from recent and ongoing strategic capital spending at its resorts. Specifically, based on its increased gaming capacity and extent of resort facilities, Co. expects significantly higher revenues at MGM Grand Detroit in 2008. Also, Co. anticipates that its share of income from MGM Grand Macau will positively affect its results for 2008.

Financial Data

(US$ in Thousands)	12/31/2007	12/31/2006	12/31/2005	12/31/2004	12/31/2003	12/31/2002	12/31/2001	12/31/2000
Earnings Per Share	5.31	2.22	1.50	1.43	0.81	0.92	0.53	0.55
Cash Flow Per Share	3.47	4.39	4.15	2.96	2.36	2.62	2.50	2.81
Tang Book Value Per Share	15.11	7.68	5.41	9.04	7.92	7.79	7.65	7.32
Dividends Per Share	...	...	...	...	...	...	...	0.050
Dividend Payout %	...	...	...	...	...	...	...	9.17
Income Statement								
Total Revenue	7,691,637	7,175,956	6,481,967	4,238,104	3,908,816	4,031,295	4,009,618	3,232,590
EBITDA	3,554,193	2,377,918	1,916,842	1,362,793	1,139,271	1,185,171	1,044,562	861,413
Income Before Taxes	2,158,428	977,926	678,900	555,815	353,704	466,314	277,589	275,040
Income Taxes	757,883	341,930	235,644	205,959	116,592	173,551	106,996	108,880
Net Income	1,584,419	648,264	443,256	412,332	243,697	292,435	169,815	160,744
Average Shares	298,284	291,747	296,334	289,332	303,184	319,880	321,644	295,802
Balance Sheet								
Current Assets	1,175,386	1,514,751	1,018,583	820,202	757,621	605,410	661,927	795,644
Total Assets	22,727,686	22,146,238	20,699,420	11,115,029	10,709,710	10,504,985	10,497,443	10,734,601
Current Liabilities	1,724,687	1,648,100	1,534,568	927,977	765,059	750,068	887,910	1,233,205
Long-Term Obligations	11,175,229	12,994,869	12,355,433	5,458,848	5,521,890	5,213,778	5,295,313	5,355,412
Total Liabilities	16,666,983	18,296,689	17,464,348	8,343,325	8,175,922	7,840,841	7,986,743	8,352,156
Stockholders' Equity	6,060,703	3,849,549	3,235,072	2,771,704	2,533,788	2,664,144	2,510,700	2,382,445
Shares Outstanding	293,768	283,909	285,069	280,739	286,192	309,148	314,792	318,260
Statistical Record								
Return on Assets %	7.06	3.03	2.79	3.77	2.30	2.78	1.60	2.38
Return on Equity %	31.98	18.30	14.76	15.50	9.38	11.30	6.94	9.38
EBITDA Margin %	46.21	33.14	29.57	32.16	29.15	29.40	26.05	26.65
Net Margin %	20.60	9.03	6.84	9.73	6.23	7.25	4.24	4.97
Asset Turnover	0.34	0.33	0.41	0.39	0.37	0.38	0.38	0.48
Current Ratio	0.68	0.92	0.66	0.88	0.99	0.81	0.75	0.65
Debt to Equity	1.84	3.38	3.82	1.97	2.18	1.96	2.11	2.25
Price Range	99.75-56.90	57.80-34.65	46.00-33.35	36.54-18.61	19.19-12.24	20.93-14.20	16.36-8.88	19.09-9.50
P/E Ratio	18.79-10.72	26.04-15.61	30.67-22.23	25.55-13.01	23.69-15.11	22.74-15.43	30.88-16.75	34.72-17.27
Average Yield %	...	...	...	...	...	...	...	0.34

Address: 3600 Las Vegas Boulevard South, Las Vegas, NV 89109
Telephone: 702-693-7120
Fax: 702-693-8626

Web Site: www.mgmmirage.com
Officers: J. Terrence Lanni - Chmn., C.E.O. James J. Murren - Pres., C.F.O., Treas.

Auditors: Deloitte & Touche LLP
Transfer Agents: Mellon Investor Services LLC, Ridgefield Park, NJ

MICRON TECHNOLOGY INC.

Exchange	Symbol	Price	52Wk Range	Yield	P/E
NYS	MU	$5.97 (3/31/2008)	13.98-5.46	N/A	N/A

7 Year Price Score 48.83 *NYSE Composite Index=100 **12 Month Price Score 73.34**

Interim Earnings (Per Share)

Qtr.	Nov	Feb	May	Aug
2004-05	0.23	0.17	(0.20)	0.07
2005-06	0.09	0.27	0.12	0.08
2006-07	0.15	(0.07)	(0.29)	(0.21)
2007-08	(0.34)	(1.01)	...	...

Interim Dividends (Per Share)

No Dividends Paid

Valuation Analysis		Institutional Holding	
Forecast P/E	12.96	No of Institutions	
	(1/10/2007)	356	
Market Cap	$4.5 Billion	Shares	
Book Value	6.7 Billion	626,382,076	
Price/Book	0.67	% Held	
Price/Sales	0.81	82.82	

Business Summary: IT & Technology (MIC: 10.2 SIC: 3674 NAIC: 334413)

Micron Technology is a global manufacturer and marketer of semiconductor devices, principally Dynamic Random Access Memory (DRAM), NAND Flash memory and Complementary Metal-Oxide Semiconductor (CMOS) image sensors. Co. operates in two segments. The Memory segment's primary products are DRAM and NAND Flash, which are used in personal computers, workstations, network servers, mobile phones, flash memory cards, Universal Storage Bus storage devices, MP3/4 players and other consumer electronics products. The Imaging segment's primary products are CMOS image sensors, which are used in mobile phones, digital still cameras, webcams as well as other consumer, security and automotive applications.

Recent Developments: For the quarter ended Feb 28 2008, net loss amounted to US$777.0 million versus a net loss of US$52.0 million in the year-earlier quarter. Revenues were US$1.36 billion, down 4.8% from US$1.43 billion the year before. Operating loss was US$772.0 million versus a loss of US$34.0 million in the prior-year quarter. Direct operating expenses rose 31.0% to US$1.40 billion from US$1.07 billion in the comparable period the year before. Indirect operating expenses increased 86.4% to US$729.0 million from US$391.0 million in the equivalent prior-year period.

Prospects: For the rest of fiscal year ending Aug 2008, Co. expects that its NAND Flash products will continue to grow significantly as it continues to ramp capacity at its 300mm wafer fabrication facilities and transitions to higher-density, advanced-geometry devices. Meanwhile, Co. intends to improve its focus on the semiconductor memory market by exploring business model alternatives for its Imaging business including partnering arrangements. Looking ahead, Co. will continue to reduce costs across its operations through several initiatives, including reducing workforce in certain areas as its business is realigned, and establishing certain operations closer in location to its global customers.

Financial Data
(US$ in Thousands)	6 Mos	3 Mos	08/30/2007	08/31/2006	09/01/2005	09/02/2004	08/28/2003	08/29/2002
Earnings Per Share	(1.85)	(0.91)	(0.42)	0.57	0.29	0.24	(2.11)	(1.51)
Cash Flow Per Share	1.01	1.02	1.22	2.93	1.92	1.78	0.47	0.96
Tang Book Value Per Share	8.28	8.67	9.02	9.64	9.07	8.73	7.68	9.93
Income Statement								
Total Revenue	2,894,000	1,535,000	5,688,000	5,272,000	4,880,200	4,404,200	3,091,300	2,589,000
EBITDA	(24,000)	243,000	1,447,000	1,638,000	1,476,200	1,469,400	27,100	141,600
Depn & Amortn	1,015,000	504,000	...	...	...			
Income Before Taxes	(1,027,000)	(252,000)	(168,000)	433,000	198,600	232,000	(1,200,200)	(998,500)
Income Taxes	3,000	7,000	30,000	18,000	10,600	74,800	73,000	(91,500)
Net Income	(1,039,000)	(262,000)	(320,000)	408,000	188,000	157,200	(1,273,200)	(907,000)
Average Shares	772,400	771,900	769,100	725,000	702,000	645,700	607,500	601,500
Balance Sheet								
Current Assets	4,304,000	4,652,000	5,234,000	5,101,000	2,925,600	2,638,700	2,037,000	2,118,800
Total Assets	13,785,000	14,498,000	14,818,000	12,221,000	8,006,400	7,760,600	7,158,200	7,555,400
Current Liabilities	1,720,000	1,852,000	2,026,000	1,661,000	978,600	972,100	993,000	752,700
Long-Term Obligations	2,162,000	1,936,000	1,987,000	405,000	1,020,200	1,027,900	997,100	360,800
Total Liabilities	4,239,000	4,237,000	4,459,000	2,539,000	2,159,600	2,145,200	2,120,700	1,188,800
Stockholders' Equity	6,738,000	7,501,000	7,752,000	8,114,000	5,846,800	5,614,800	4,971,000	6,306,400
Shares Outstanding	760,800	760,500	757,900	749,400	616,200	611,500	609,900	602,900
Statistical Record								
Return on Assets %	N.M.	N.M.	N.M.	4.05	2.39	2.07	N.M.	N.M.
Return on Equity %	N.M.	N.M.	N.M.	5.86	3.29	2.92	N.M.	N.M.
EBITDA Margin %	N.M.	15.83	25.44	31.07	30.25	33.36	0.88	5.47
Net Margin %	N.M.	N.M.	N.M.	7.74	3.85	3.57	N.M.	N.M.
Asset Turnover	0.42	0.41	0.42	0.52	0.62	0.58	0.42	0.33
Current Ratio	2.50	2.51	2.58	3.07	2.99	2.71	2.05	2.81
Debt to Equity	0.32	0.26	0.26	0.05	0.17	0.18	0.20	0.06
Price Range	13.98-5.75	14.93-7.94	18.57-10.60	17.52-11.62	12.76-9.41	17.96-11.06	18.76-6.76	39.50-17.25
P/E Ratio	...	...	...	30.74-20.39	44.00-32.45	74.83-46.08	...	...

Address: 8000 South Federal Way, P.O. Box 6, Boise, ID 83707-0006	Web Site: www.micron.com	Auditors: PricewaterhouseCoopers LLP
Telephone: 208-368-4000	Officers: Steven R. Appleton - Chmn., Pres., C.E.O.	Investor Contact: 208-368-4400
Fax: 208-368-4435	Wilbur G. Stover Jr. - V.P., Fin., C.F.O.	Transfer Agents: Wells Fargo Shareowner Services, South St. Paul, MN

MILLIPORE CORP

Exchange	Symbol	Price	52Wk Range	Yield	P/E
NYS	MIL	$67.41 (3/31/2008)	82.43-64.62	N/A	27.18

*7 Year Price Score 108.82 *NYSE Composite Index=100 *12 Month Price Score 100.30

Interim Earnings (Per Share)

Qtr.	Mar	Jun	Sep	Dec
2003	0.44	0.46	0.50	0.67
2004	0.55	0.57	0.50	0.49
2005	0.64	0.47	0.44	0.00
2006	0.64	0.54	0.27	0.34
2007	0.49	0.52	0.66	0.82

Interim Dividends (Per Share)

Dividend Payment Suspended

Valuation Analysis		Institutional Holding	
Forecast P/E	17.09	No of Institutions	
	(1/10/2007)	283	
Market Cap	$3.7 Billion	Shares	
Book Value	1.1 Billion	56,800,568	
Price/Book	3.25	% Held	
Price/Sales	2.41	N/A	

TRADING VOLUME (thousand shares)

Business Summary: Instruments and Related Products (MIC: 11.15 SIC: 3826 NAIC: 334516)

Millipore provides technologies, tools and services for the discovery, development and production of therapeutic drugs, vaccines and detection tools and other devices. Co.'s products and services are based various enabling technologies, such as filtration, chromatography, cell culture supplements, antibodies and cell lines. Co.'s Bioscience segment provides productsproducts and technologies for life science research. Co.'s Bioprocess Division provides tools and services for the commercial production of bioengineered and pharmaceutical substances, including biologics, vaccines and other biotherapeutic products.

Recent Developments: For the year ended Dec 31 2007, net income increased 40.7% to US$136.5 million from US$97.0 million in the prior year. Revenues were US$1.53 billion, up 22.0% from US$1.26 billion the year before. Operating income was US$216.7 million versus US$144.3 million in the prior year, an increase of 50.2%. Direct operating expenses rose 15.3% to US$721.1 million from US$625.6 million in the comparable period the year before. Indirect operating expenses increased 22.3% to US$593.7 million from US$485.5 million in the equivalent prior-year period.

Prospects: Despite the lower demand from biotechnology customers in the U.S., Co. believes that the overall biotechnology industry remains solid. Notably, Co. expects that growing levels of spending by private equity and large pharmaceutical companies, expected growth in commercially available antibodies, projected 2008 approvals of new biologic drugs and new indications of existing biologic drugs, and expected overall biotechnology market growth will result in higher sales of its products over the long term. Meanwhile, Co. anticipates its Bioscience division revenue growth to continue via its focus on marketing and re-branding programs, e-commerce sales channel and new products.

Financial Data

(US$ in Thousands)	12/31/2007	12/31/2006	12/31/2005	12/31/2004	12/31/2003	12/31/2002	12/31/2001	12/31/2000
Earnings Per Share	2.48	1.79	1.55	2.10	2.06	1.73	0.65	2.53
Cash Flow Per Share	4.09	2.77	3.63	3.38	2.72	2.23	1.31	2.15
Tang Book Value Per Share	N.M.	N.M.	12.74	12.24	8.72	5.16	7.60	5.25
Dividends Per Share	...	...	...	...	...	...	0.440	0.440
Dividend Payout %	...	...	...	...	...	...	67.69	17.39
Income Statement								
Total Revenue	1,531,555	1,255,371	991,031	883,263	799,622	704,251	656,898	953,771
EBITDA	344,265	243,549	191,435	182,331	167,105	156,183	131,888	223,247
Income Before Taxes	152,423	120,383	137,533	130,479	112,174	103,592	78,399	153,666
Income Taxes	12,424	21,462	57,365	24,923	11,378	22,791	14,913	34,472
Net Income	136,472	96,984	80,168	105,556	100,796	83,701	31,117	119,194
Average Shares	55,028	54,245	51,659	50,201	49,046	48,448	48,060	47,039
Balance Sheet								
Current Assets	690,089	709,355	1,067,101	540,856	516,362	390,211	311,995	465,483
Total Assets	2,777,257	2,771,491	1,646,665	1,013,819	951,273	786,230	915,767	874,925
Current Liabilities	282,241	401,830	242,599	163,010	222,392	134,429	134,319	234,647
Long-Term Obligations	1,260,043	1,316,256	552,285	147,000	216,000	334,000	320,000	300,130
Total Liabilities	1,634,446	1,818,000	855,102	374,969	490,232	498,726	521,811	569,557
Stockholders' Equity	1,136,568	948,411	791,563	638,850	461,041	287,504	393,956	305,368
Shares Outstanding	54,772	53,524	52,227	49,816	48,883	48,412	47,876	46,394
Statistical Record								
Return on Assets %	4.92	4.39	6.03	10.71	11.60	9.84	3.48	14.26
Return on Equity %	13.09	11.15	11.21	19.14	26.93	24.57	8.90	49.30
EBITDA Margin %	22.48	19.40	19.32	20.64	20.90	22.18	20.08	23.41
Net Margin %	8.91	7.73	8.09	11.95	12.61	11.89	4.74	12.50
Asset Turnover	0.55	0.57	0.75	0.90	0.92	0.83	0.73	1.14
Current Ratio	2.45	1.77	4.40	3.32	2.32	2.90	2.32	1.98
Debt to Equity	1.11	1.39	0.70	0.23	0.47	1.16	0.81	0.98
Price Range	82.43-65.81	75.25-60.26	67.40-42.60	56.37-42.50	48.91-30.25	53.68-27.68	58.95-38.17	67.48-32.39
P/E Ratio	33.24-26.54	42.04-33.66	43.48-27.48	26.84-20.24	23.74-14.68	31.03-16.00	90.70-58.72	26.67-12.80
Average Yield %	...	...	...	...	...	...	0.88	0.87

Address: 290 Concord Road, Billerica, MA 1821-3405
Telephone: 978-715-4321
Fax: 978-715-1380

Web Site: www.millipore.com
Officers: Martin Madaus - Chmn., Pres., C.E.O. Kathleen B. Allen - V.P., C.F.O.

Auditors: PricewaterhouseCoopers LLP
Investor Contact: 978-715-1527
Transfer Agents: American Stock Transfer & Trust Company, New York, NY

MINE SAFETY APPLIANCES CO

Exchange	Symbol	Price	52Wk Range	Yield	P/E	Div Acheiver
NYS	MSA	$41.19 (3/31/2008)	56.00-38.87	2.14	22.15	37 Years

*7 Year Price Score 122.56 *NYSE Composite Index=100   *12 Month Price Score 99.10

Interim Earnings (Per Share)

Qtr.	Mar	Jun	Sep	Dec
2003	0.33	0.36	0.66	0.40
2004	0.43	0.48	0.50	0.46
2005	0.57	0.52	0.46	0.65
2006	0.42	0.43	0.34	0.53
2007	0.44	0.48	0.46	0.48

Interim Dividends (Per Share)

Amt	Decl	Ex	Rec	Pay
0.22Q	5/11/2007	5/17/2007	5/21/2007	6/10/2007
0.22Q	8/2/2007	8/15/2007	8/17/2007	9/10/2007
0.22Q	11/6/2007	11/14/2007	11/16/2007	12/10/2007
0.22Q	1/15/2008	2/13/2008	2/15/2008	3/10/2008

Indicated Div: $0.88

Valuation Analysis   **Institutional Holding**

Forecast P/E	N/A	No of Institutions
		124
Market Cap	$1.5 Billion	Shares
Book Value	461.5 Million	21,522,140
Price/Book	3.18	% Held
Price/Sales	1.46	59.76

Business Summary: Medical Instruments & Equipment (MIC: 9.6 SIC: 3842 NAIC: 339112)

Mine Safety Appliances is engaged in the global development, manufacture and supply of enhanced products that protect people's health and safety. Co.'s line of safety products is used by workers around the world in the fire service, homeland security, construction and other industries, as well as the military. Co.'s product offering includes self-contained breathing apparatus, gas masks, gas detection instruments, head protection, respirators and thermal imaging devices. Co. also provides an offering of consumer and contractor safety products through retail channels. As of Dec 31 2007, Co. operated through three geographic segments: North America, Europe, and International.

Recent Developments: For the year ended Dec 31 2007, net income increased 5.7% to US$67.6 million from US$63.9 million in the prior year. Revenues were US$1.01 billion, up 9.6% from US$919.1 million the year before. Direct operating expenses rose 8.4% to US$616.2 million from US$568.4 million in the comparable period the year before. Indirect operating expenses increased 10.5% to US$285.3 million from US$258.0 million in the equivalent prior-year period.

Prospects: Looking ahead, Co. believes that the effects of the delay in utilization of U.S. Assistance to Firefighters Grant funding and in fire department evaluations of equipment meeting the new National Fire Protection Association standards that have recently constrained its U.S. Fire Service business are reducing and that it should benefit with better sales in the first half of 2008. Co. also expects that its North American military sales to be higher in 2008, while it pursues its long term goal of having its total sales, less North American military and U.S. Fire Service, growing at 10.0% annually. Meanwhile, Co. expects to complete the move to its new factory in Queretaro, Mexico during 2008.

Financial Data

(US$ in Thousands)	12/31/2007	12/31/2006	12/31/2005	12/31/2004	12/31/2003	12/31/2002	12/31/2001	12/31/2000
Earnings Per Share	1.86	1.73	2.19	1.86	1.75	0.95	0.87	0.63
Cash Flow Per Share	1.16	1.73	2.35	1.45	1.10	1.35	0.86	1.41
Tang Book Value Per Share	10.40	9.85	8.84	8.69	7.03	6.62	5.96	6.28
Dividends Per Share	0.840	0.680	0.520	0.370	1.717	0.217	0.180	0.158
Dividend Payout %	45.16	39.31	23.74	19.89	98.10	22.81	20.69	25.18
Income Statement								
Total Revenue	1,007,648	919,098	911,970	857,513	698,197	566,697	545,666	502,833
EBITDA	130,551	114,787	148,141	139,364	96,967	69,608	79,357	58,607
Income Before Taxes	106,188	92,640	123,796	113,868	73,759	48,083	52,886	34,050
Income Taxes	38,600	28,722	42,013	42,821	24,835	16,870	21,255	10,811
Net Income	67,588	63,918	81,783	71,047	65,267	35,077	31,631	23,239
Average Shares	36,240	36,928	37,301	38,130	37,264	36,885	36,237	37,068
Balance Sheet								
Current Assets	437,030	416,039	377,226	397,660	323,242	202,944	217,606	201,133
Total Assets	1,016,306	898,620	725,357	734,110	643,885	579,765	520,698	489,683
Current Liabilities	209,189	127,435	130,859	127,067	114,713	99,700	82,500	86,978
Long-Term Obligations	103,726	112,541	45,834	54,463	59,915	64,350	67,381	71,806
Total Liabilities	554,775	460,767	342,960	356,499	336,027	290,703	267,194	263,218
Stockholders' Equity	461,531	437,853	382,397	377,611	307,858	289,062	253,504	226,465
Shares Outstanding	35,661	36,015	36,545	37,341	36,927	36,621	36,302	35,482
Statistical Record								
Return on Assets %	7.06	7.87	11.21	10.28	10.67	6.37	6.26	4.92
Return on Equity %	15.03	15.59	21.52	20.67	21.87	12.93	13.18	9.88
EBITDA Margin %	12.96	12.49	16.24	16.25	13.89	12.28	14.54	11.66
Net Margin %	6.71	6.95	8.97	8.29	9.35	6.19	5.80	4.62
Asset Turnover	1.05	1.13	1.25	1.24	1.14	1.03	1.08	1.07
Current Ratio	2.38	3.27	2.88	3.13	2.82	2.84	2.64	2.31
Debt to Equity	0.22	0.26	0.12	0.14	0.19	0.22	0.27	0.32
Price Range	56.00-37.39	43.50-34.45	51.00-34.45	51.57-23.42	28.21-10.23	16.83-9.17	16.98-7.58	8.67-6.33
P/E Ratio	30.11-20.10	25.14-19.91	23.29-15.73	27.73-12.59	16.12-5.85	17.72-9.65	19.52-8.72	13.76-10.05
Average Yield %	1.88	1.76	1.23	1.06	10.91	1.70	1.49	2.13

Address: 121 Gamma Drive, RIDC Industrial Park, O'Hara Township, Pittsburgh, PA 15238
Telephone: 412-967-3000
Fax: 412-967-3451

Web Site: www.msanet.com
Officers: John T. Ryan III - Chmn., C.E.O. D. L. Zeitler - V.P., Treas., C.F.O.

Auditors: PricewaterhouseCoopers LLP
Transfer Agents: Wells Fargo Shareowner Services, South St.Paul, MN

MINERALS TECHNOLOGIES, INC.

Exchange	Symbol	Price	52Wk Range	Yield	P/E
NYS	MTX	$62.80 (3/31/2008)	70.91-52.29	0.32	N/A

*7 Year Price Score 96.32   *NYSE Composite Index=100   *12 Month Price Score 101.83

Interim Earnings (Per Share)

Qtr.	Mar	Jun	Sep	Dec
2003	0.57	0.70	1.18	0.63
2004	0.61	0.73	0.78	0.70
2005	0.73	0.63	0.60	0.63
2006	0.64	0.63	0.72	0.55
2007	0.56	0.74	(5.47)	0.88

Interim Dividends (Per Share)

Amt	Decl	Ex	Rec	Pay
0.05Q	4/26/2007	5/23/2007	5/25/2007	6/8/2007
0.05Q	7/26/2007	8/29/2007	9/3/2007	9/17/2007
0.05Q	10/25/2007	11/5/2007	11/7/2007	12/14/2007
0.05Q	1/31/2008	2/26/2008	2/28/2008	3/19/2008

Indicated Div: $0.20

Valuation Analysis

		Institutional Holding	
Forecast P/E	N/A	No of Institutions	119
Market Cap	$1.2 Billion	Shares	20,320,272
Book Value	751.2 Million	% Held	
Price/Book	1.60	N/A	
Price/Sales	1.11		

Business Summary: Chemicals (MIC: 11.1 SIC: 2819 NAIC: 325188)

Minerals Technologies develops, produces and markets specialty mineral, mineral-based and synthetic mineral products and supporting systems and services. Co.'s Specialty Minerals segment produces and sells the synthetic mineral product precipitated calcium carbonate and the processed mineral product quicklime, and mines, processes and sells other natural mineral products to the paper, building materials, paint and coatings, glass, ceramic, food and pharmaceutical industries. Co.'s Refractories segment produces and markets monolithic and shaped refractory materials and specialty products, services, applications and measurement equipment, and calcium metal and metallurgical wire products.

Recent Developments: For the year ended Dec 31 2007, loss from continuing operations was US$25.7 million compared with income of US$56.1 million a year earlier. Net loss amounted to US$63.5 million versus net income of US$50.0 million in the prior year. Revenues were US$1.08 billion, up 5.3% from US$1.02 billion the year before. Operating loss was US$8.5 million versus an income of US$92.4 million in the prior year. Direct operating expenses rose 5.8% to US$845.1 million from US$798.7 million in the comparable period the year before. Indirect operating expenses increased 82.1% to US$241.1 million from US$132.4 million in the equivalent prior-year period.

Prospects: Co. is experiencing some weakness in the paper industry, due to several paper machine shutdowns that is affecting its satellite precipitated calcium carbonate (PCC) product line as the paper industry continues to consolidate and reduce capacity. In addition, Co. is seeing softer residential construction and automotive markets, which is affecting its Processed Minerals product line. In response, for 2008, Co. intends to continue the development and potential commercial introduction of filler-fiber composite technology for the paper industry to increase the fill-rates of uncoated freesheet paper. Further, Co. plans to increase the market presence of PCC by expanding the satellite model.

Financial Data

(US$ in Thousands)	12/31/2007	12/31/2006	12/31/2005	12/31/2004	12/31/2003	12/31/2002	12/31/2001	12/31/2000
Earnings Per Share	(3.31)	2.53	2.59	2.82	3.09	2.61	2.48	2.58
Cash Flow Per Share	9.36	6.92	3.86	6.28	4.95	5.83	5.01	4.44
Tang Book Value Per Share	35.58	35.82	35.90	36.26	31.95	26.93	25.89	24.22
Dividends Per Share	0.200	0.200	0.200	0.200	0.100	0.100	0.100	0.100
Dividend Payout %	...	7.91	7.72	7.09	3.24	3.83	4.03	3.88
Income Statement								
Total Revenue	1,077,721	1,059,307	995,838	923,667	813,743	752,680	684,419	670,917
EBITDA	76,019	166,170	155,612	157,578	143,631	149,654	146,237	144,732
Income Before Taxes	(11,499)	79,579	78,285	84,572	72,344	75,734	72,670	79,772
Income Taxes	11,266	24,588	23,289	24,299	4,116	20,220	21,148	23,735
Net Income	(63,514)	49,951	53,264	58,563	63,220	53,752	49,793	54,208
Average Shares	19,190	19,738	20,567	20,769	20,431	20,569	20,063	21,004
Balance Sheet								
Current Assets	473,310	411,762	377,200	395,671	340,125	290,965	246,790	215,357
Total Assets	1,128,893	1,193,124	1,156,303	1,154,902	1,035,500	899,877	847,810	799,832
Current Liabilities	167,149	212,063	231,252	152,853	122,035	123,937	160,529	133,527
Long-Term Obligations	111,006	113,351	40,306	94,811	98,159	89,020	88,097	89,857
Total Liabilities	377,720	440,567	385,141	355,589	328,119	305,720	339,991	316,193
Stockholders' Equity	751,173	752,557	771,162	799,313	707,381	594,157	507,819	483,639
Shares Outstanding	19,090	19,085	19,986	20,561	20,491	20,155	19,613	19,966
Statistical Record								
Return on Assets %	N.M.	4.25	4.61	5.33	6.53	6.15	6.04	6.89
Return on Equity %	N.M.	6.56	6.78	7.75	9.71	9.76	10.04	11.16
EBITDA Margin %	7.05	15.69	15.63	17.06	17.65	19.88	21.37	21.57
Net Margin %	N.M.	4.72	5.35	6.34	7.77	7.14	7.28	8.08
Asset Turnover	0.93	0.90	0.86	0.84	0.84	0.86	0.83	0.85
Current Ratio	2.83	1.94	1.63	2.59	2.79	2.35	1.54	1.61
Debt to Equity	0.15	0.15	0.05	0.12	0.14	0.15	0.17	0.19
Price Range	70.91-56.80	61.27-48.01	68.83-51.59	67.67-51.56	60.75-35.45	53.91-33.17	47.66-33.06	53.25-29.38
P/E Ratio	...	24.22-18.98	26.58-19.92	24.00-18.28	19.66-11.47	20.66-12.71	19.22-13.33	20.64-11.39
Average Yield %	0.31	0.36	0.33	0.34	0.21	0.22	0.25	0.24

Address: The Chrysler Building, 405 Lexington Avenue, New York, NY 10174-0002 **Telephone:** 212-878-1800 **Fax:** 212-878-1801	**Web Site:** www.mineralstech.com **Officers:** Paul R. Saueracker - Chmn., Pres., C.E.O. John A. Sorel - Sr. V.P., Fin., C.F.O., Treas.	**Auditors:** KPMG LLP **Investor Contact:** 212-878-1831 **Transfer Agents:** EquiServe Trust Company, N.A., Providence, RI

514

MODINE MANUFACTURING CO

Exchange	Symbol	Price	52Wk Range	Yield	P/E
NYS	MOD	$14.49 (3/31/2008)	28.84-11.62	4.83	N/A

*7 Year Price Score 69.25   *NYSE Composite Index=100   *12 Month Price Score 68.34

TRADING VOLUME (thousand shares)

Interim Earnings (Per Share)

Qtr.	Jun	Sep	Dec	Mar
2004-05	0.40	0.41	0.55	0.43
2005-06	0.60	(1.14)	0.40	0.37
2006-07	0.51	0.38	0.51	(0.09)
2007-08	0.39	0.31	(1.48)	...

Interim Dividends (Per Share)

Amt	Decl	Ex	Rec	Pay
0.175Q	5/16/2007	5/23/2007	5/25/2007	6/8/2007
0.175Q	7/18/2007	8/21/2007	8/23/2007	9/7/2007
0.175Q	10/17/2007	11/19/2007	11/22/2007	12/7/2007
0.175Q	1/16/2008	2/13/2008	2/15/2008	3/3/2008

Indicated Div: $0.70

Valuation Analysis

		Institutional Holding	
Forecast P/E	15.92	No of Institutions	
	(1/10/2007)	123	
Market Cap	$466.6 Million	Shares	
Book Value	508.3 Million	23,272,384	
Price/Book	0.92	% Held	
Price/Sales	0.26	70.85	

Business Summary: Automotive (MIC: 15.1 SIC: 3714 NAIC: 336399)

Modine Manufacturing is engaged in providing thermal management technology, serving the vehicular, industrial, commercial, building HVAC&R (heating, ventilating, air conditioning and refrigeration) and electronics markets. Co. develops, manufactures, and markets thermal management products, components and systems for use in various original equipment manufacturer (OEM) applications and to an array of building and other commercial markets. Co. works with products, such as radiators, charge air coolers and oil coolers, that use a medium (air or liquid) to cool the heat that is produced by a vehicle engine.

Recent Developments: For the quarter ended Dec 26 2007, loss from continuing operations was US$47.5 million compared with income of US$16.4 million in the year-earlier quarter. Net loss amounted to US$47.4 million versus net income of US$16.3 million in the year-earlier quarter. Revenues were US$495.3 million, up 8.1% from US$458.1 million the year before. Operating loss was US$15.0 million versus an income of US$17.8 million in the prior-year quarter. Direct operating expenses rose 10.0% to US$418.3 million from US$380.3 million in the comparable period the year before. Indirect operating expenses increased 53.3% to US$92.0 million from US$60.0 million in the equivalent prior-year period.

Prospects: For the fiscal year ending Mar 31 2008, Co. now anticipates net sales of $1.80 billion, versus net sales of $1.73 billion in prior fiscal year. In addition, Co. is forecasting gross margin of 15.0%, while pre-tax earnings are estimated to be about $35.0 million. These expectations exclude charge of $10.0 million to reflect accruable costs related to the restructuring actions in the fourth fiscal quarter of 2008. Meanwhile, Co. plans to expand its gross margin through the implementation of its restructuring initiative, including closure of three U.S. manufacturing plants and the Tübingen facility in Europe, which should generate annualized savings of about $20.0 million to $25.0 million.

Financial Data

(US$ in Thousands)	9 Mos	6 Mos	3 Mos	03/31/2007	03/31/2006	03/31/2005	03/31/2004	03/31/2003
Earnings Per Share	(0.87)	1.12	1.19	1.31	0.22	1.79	1.19	0.38
Cash Flow Per Share	2.53	2.58	2.96	3.19	3.91	4.57	3.15	3.37
Tang Book Value Per Share	14.06	13.99	13.26	12.80	13.43	17.96	16.14	14.64
Dividends Per Share	0.700	0.700	0.700	0.700	0.700	0.630	0.550	0.500
Dividend Payout %	...	62.50	58.82	53.44	318.18	35.20	46.22	131.58
Income Statement								
Total Revenue	1,370,868	873,367	444,073	1,757,472	1,628,900	1,543,930	1,199,799	1,092,075
EBITDA	72,754	65,600	39,360	119,246	162,676	169,005	127,533	113,339
Depn & Amortn	58,445	38,473	19,225	...	...	...	...	...
Income Before Taxes	6,340	22,015	17,588	39,287	90,540	96,876	63,711	55,027
Income Taxes	31,513	(311)	5,192	(2,975)	29,788	35,214	23,274	20,669
Net Income	(24,638)	22,712	12,650	42,332	7,641	61,662	40,437	12,666
Average Shares	31,936	32,294	32,169	32,246	34,144	34,480	34,073	33,758
Balance Sheet								
Current Assets	573,384	502,897	501,199	456,857	412,195	509,330	442,362	417,366
Total Assets	1,223,807	1,168,963	1,147,254	1,101,573	1,052,095	1,152,155	979,192	910,818
Current Liabilities	364,621	325,856	309,882	307,953	294,949	345,094	213,218	193,263
Long-Term Obligations	232,825	202,755	195,843	175,856	151,706	40,724	84,885	98,556
Total Liabilities	715,498	640,916	640,758	608,306	546,670	492,375	392,651	380,431
Stockholders' Equity	508,309	528,047	506,496	493,267	505,425	659,780	586,541	530,387
Shares Outstanding	32,201	32,245	32,402	32,419	32,806	34,531	34,077	33,773
Statistical Record								
Return on Assets %	N.M.	3.17	3.40	3.93	0.69	5.79	4.27	1.40
Return on Equity %	N.M.	6.91	7.52	8.48	1.31	9.90	7.22	2.42
EBITDA Margin %	5.31	7.49	8.86	6.79	9.99	10.95	10.63	10.38
Net Margin %	N.M.	2.59	2.85	2.41	0.47	3.99	3.37	1.16
Asset Turnover	1.50	1.54	1.56	1.63	1.48	1.45	1.27	1.20
Current Ratio	1.57	1.54	1.62	1.48	1.40	1.48	2.07	2.16
Debt to Equity	0.46	0.38	0.39	0.36	0.30	0.06	0.14	0.19
Price Range	28.84-16.00	28.84-21.56	27.99-21.05	29.56-21.05	37.45-25.75	32.39-24.95	28.11-14.35	28.64-12.31
P/E Ratio	...	25.75-19.25	23.52-17.69	22.56-16.07	170.23-117.05	18.10-13.94	23.62-12.06	75.37-32.40
Average Yield %	2.86	2.81	2.91	2.83	2.22	2.15	2.40	2.52

Address: 1500 DeKoven Avenue, Racine, WI 53403-2552	**Web Site:** www.modine.com	**Auditors:** PricewaterhouseCoopers LLP
Telephone: 262-636-1200	**Officers:** David B. Rayburn - Pres., C.E.O. E. T. Thomas - Sr. V.P.	**Transfer Agents:** Wells Fargo Bank
Fax: 262-636-1424		

MOHAWK INDUSTRIES, INC.

Exchange	Symbol	Price	52Wk Range	Yield	P/E
NYS	MHK	$71.61 (3/31/2008)	103.32-66.14	N/A	6.94

*7 Year Price Score 96.22   *NYSE Composite Index=100   *12 Month Price Score 94.14

TRADING VOLUME (thousand shares)

Interim Earnings (Per Share)

Qtr.	Mar	Jun	Sep	Dec
2003	0.62	1.12	1.36	1.52
2004	0.98	1.29	1.67	1.52
2005	1.03	1.39	1.61	1.27
2006	1.04	1.76	1.88	1.90
2007	1.32	1.68	1.78	5.53

Interim Dividends (Per Share)

No Dividends Paid

Valuation Analysis / Institutional Holding

Valuation Analysis		Institutional Holding	
Forecast P/E	10.27	No of Institutions	
	(1/10/2007)	255	
Market Cap	$4.9 Billion	Shares	
Book Value	4.7 Billion	67,173,152	
Price/Book	1.04	% Held	
Price/Sales	0.65	98.82	

Business Summary: Textiles (MIC: 4.3 SIC: 2273 NAIC: 314110)

Mohawk Industries is a producer of floor covering products for residential and commercial applications in the U.S. and Europe. Co. operates in three business segments. The Mohawk segment designs, manufactures, sources, distributes and markets its floor covering product lines, which includes carpet, rug, carpet pad, ceramic tile, laminate, hardwood and resilient for residential and commercial applications. The Dal-Tile segment designs, manufactures, sources, distributes and markets a line of ceramic tile, porcelain tile, natural stone and other products used in the residential and commercial markets. The Unilin segment manufactures, distributes and markets laminate flooring in Europe and U.S.

Recent Developments: For the year ended Dec 31 2007, net income increased 55.1% to US$706.8 million from US$455.8 million in the prior year. Revenues were US$7.59 billion, down 4.0% from US$7.91 billion the year before. Operating income was US$750.1 million versus US$839.1 million in the prior year, a decrease of 10.6%. Direct operating expenses declined 3.6% to US$5.47 billion from US$5.67 billion in the comparable period the year before. Indirect operating expenses decreased 2.0% to US$1.36 billion from US$1.39 billion in the equivalent prior-year period.

Prospects: For the first quarter of 2008, Co. expects the U.S. flooring industry to continue its decline, the European building and remodeling sector to soften, and material costs to rise. As such, Co. has reduced production in the plants due to lower consumer demand, and is further reducing its infrastructure costs and increasing prices. Accordingly, Co. expects earnings to be $0.81 to $0.90 per share for the first quarter of 2008. However, Co. expects earnings to improve in the second quarter of 2008. Notably, Co. anticipates sales and earnings to benefit from higher seasonal sales rates, increases in selling prices, as well as reduced infrastructure costs.

Financial Data
(US$ in Thousands)

	12/31/2007	12/31/2006	12/31/2005	12/31/2004	12/31/2003	12/31/2002	12/31/2001	12/31/2000
Earnings Per Share	10.32	6.70	5.30	5.46	4.62	4.39	3.55	3.00
Cash Flow Per Share	12.84	11.56	8.39	3.63	4.67	8.62	6.32	4.02
Tang Book Value Per Share	10.80	N.M.	N.M.	14.48	9.07	8.42	15.93	12.28
Income Statement								
Total Revenue	7,586,018	7,905,842	6,620,099	5,880,372	5,005,053	4,522,336	3,445,945	3,255,846
EBITDA	1,065,023	1,124,960	773,141	753,869	650,624	614,543	405,370	388,019
Income Before Taxes	604,117	676,311	557,021	577,389	488,434	443,629	291,416	267,629
Income Taxes	(102,697)	220,478	198,826	208,767	178,285	159,140	102,824	105,030
Net Income	706,814	455,833	358,195	368,622	310,149	284,489	188,592	162,599
Average Shares	68,492	68,056	67,644	67,557	67,121	64,861	53,141	54,255
Balance Sheet								
Current Assets	2,449,720	2,378,911	2,340,487	1,783,325	1,533,218	1,298,579	1,031,222	1,024,114
Total Assets	8,680,050	8,178,394	7,991,523	4,403,118	4,163,575	3,596,743	1,768,485	1,792,641
Current Liabilities	1,211,500	1,595,763	1,111,914	814,402	886,735	616,710	581,861	596,922
Long-Term Obligations	2,021,395	2,207,547	3,194,561	700,000	763,618	793,000	150,067	365,437
Total Liabilities	3,972,693	4,463,131	4,964,403	1,736,781	1,865,774	1,613,864	819,934	1,038,281
Stockholders' Equity	4,707,357	3,715,263	3,027,120	2,666,337	2,297,801	1,982,879	948,551	754,360
Shares Outstanding	68,358	67,765	67,497	66,759	66,535	66,365	52,693	52,300
Statistical Record								
Return on Assets %	8.39	5.64	5.78	8.58	7.99	10.60	10.59	9.33
Return on Equity %	16.78	13.52	12.58	14.81	14.49	19.41	22.15	22.41
EBITDA Margin %	14.04	14.23	11.68	12.82	13.00	13.59	11.76	11.92
Net Margin %	9.32	5.77	5.41	6.27	6.20	6.29	5.47	4.99
Asset Turnover	0.90	0.98	1.07	1.37	1.29	1.69	1.94	1.87
Current Ratio	2.02	1.49	2.10	2.19	1.73	2.11	1.77	1.72
Debt to Equity	0.43	0.59	1.06	0.26	0.33	0.40	0.16	0.48
Price Range	103.32-74.40	90.14-65.00	93.66-75.22	91.57-69.41	75.38-44.26	69.80-42.86	55.01-27.25	29.00-19.19
P/E Ratio	10.01-7.21	13.45-9.70	17.67-14.19	16.77-12.71	16.32-9.58	15.90-9.76	15.50-7.68	9.67-6.40

Address: P.O. Box 12069, 160 S. Industrial Boulevard, Calhoun, GA 30701 Telephone: 706-629-7721 Fax: 706-625-3851	Web Site: www.mohawkind.com Officers: Jeffrey S. Lorberbaum - Chmn., Pres., C.E.O. Reid Batsel - V.P., Tech.	Auditors: KPMG LLP Investor Contact: 706-624-2247

MOLSON COORS BREWING CO.

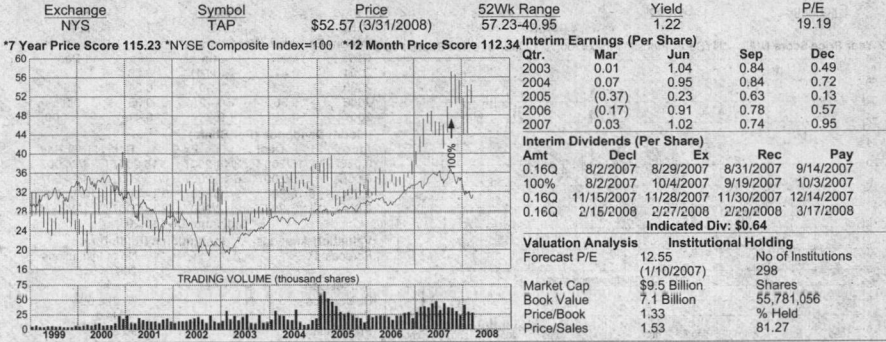

Exchange	Symbol	Price	52Wk Range	Yield	P/E
NYS	TAP	$52.57 (3/31/2008)	57.23-40.95	1.22	19.19

*7 Year Price Score 115.23 *NYSE Composite Index=100 *12 Month Price Score 112.34

Interim Earnings (Per Share)

Qtr.	Mar	Jun	Sep	Dec
2003	0.01	1.04	0.84	0.49
2004	0.07	0.95	0.84	0.72
2005	(0.37)	0.23	0.63	0.13
2006	(0.17)	0.91	0.78	0.57
2007	0.03	1.02	0.74	0.95

Interim Dividends (Per Share)

Amt	Decl	Ex	Rec	Pay
0.16Q	8/2/2007	8/29/2007	8/31/2007	9/14/2007
100%	8/2/2007	10/4/2007	9/19/2007	10/3/2007
0.16Q	11/15/2007	11/28/2007	11/30/2007	12/14/2007
0.16Q	2/15/2008	2/27/2008	2/29/2008	3/17/2008

Indicated Div: $0.64

Valuation Analysis / **Institutional Holding**

Forecast P/E	12.55	No of Institutions
	(1/10/2007)	298
Market Cap	$9.5 Billion	Shares
Book Value	7.1 Billion	55,781,056
Price/Book	1.33	% Held
Price/Sales	1.53	81.27

Business Summary: Food (MIC: 4.1 SIC: 2082 NAIC: 312120)

Molson Coors Brewing is engaged as a producer of beers. Co.'s brands are sold primarily in the U.S., Canada and the U.K. under the brand names: Coors Light®, Coors®, Coors® Non-Alcoholic, Pilsner®, Zima®, Keystone®, Keystone Light®, Keystone Ice®, Blue Moon™ Belgian White Ale, C2®, George Killian's® Irish Red™ Lager, Molson Canadian®, Molson Dry®, Molson Export®, Creemore Springs®, Rickard's Red Ale®, Carling®, Worthington's® ales, Caffrey's®, Reef®, Screamers® and Stones®. As of Dec 31 2007, Co. had six breweries in Canada, two breweries in the U.S., as well as three breweries in the U.K.

Recent Developments: For the year ended Dec 30 2007, income from continuing operations increased 37.8% to US$514.9 million from US$373.6 million a year earlier. Net income increased 37.7% to US$497.2 million from US$361.0 million in the prior year. Revenues were US$6.19 billion, up 5.9% from US$5.84 billion the year before. Operating income was US$641.1 million versus US$581.1 million in the prior year, an increase of 10.3%. Direct operating expenses rose 6.4% to US$3.70 billion from US$3.48 billion in the comparable period the year before. Indirect operating expenses increased 3.6% to US$1.85 billion from US$1.78 billion in the equivalent prior-year period.

Prospects: On Dec 21 2007, Co. and SABMiller plc announced that they have signed a definitive agreement for the combination of the US and Puerto Rico operations of their respective subsidiaries, Miller and Coors, into MillerCoors LLC, Co. expects to close the transaction in mid-2008. For full year 2008, Co. is focused on maintaining its strong volume and share momentum, while continuing to manage costs. Further, Co. plans to drive sales by growing its marketing and sales spending at a mid-single-digit rate, building its key retail account business, and furthering its alignment with its distributor network. Also, Co. expects its cost of goods per barrel in the US to increase at a low-single-digit rate.

Financial Data
(US$ in Thousands)

	12/30/2007	12/31/2006	12/25/2005	12/26/2004	12/28/2003	12/29/2002	12/30/2001	12/31/2000
Earnings Per Share	2.74	2.09	0.84	2.60	2.38	2.21	1.66	1.47
Cash Flow Per Share	3.46	4.76	2.67	6.75	7.51	3.60	2.63	3.82
Tang Book Value Per Share	N.M.	N.M.	N.M.	1.72	N.M.	N.M.	12.03	12.16
Dividends Per Share	0.640	0.640	0.640	0.410	0.410	0.410	0.400	0.360
Dividend Payout %	23.36	30.70	75.74	15.80	17.19	18.55	24.17	24.57
Income Statement								
Total Revenue	6,190,592	5,844,985	5,506,906	4,305,816	4,000,113	3,776,322	2,429,462	2,414,415
EBITDA	984,919	1,040,806	836,461	629,748	559,379	536,631	304,701	283,897
Income Before Taxes	534,378	472,050	295,201	308,182	253,818	256,600	198,013	169,525
Income Taxes	4,186	82,405	50,264	95,228	79,161	94,947	75,049	59,908
Net Income	497,192	361,031	134,944	196,736	174,657	161,653	122,964	109,617
Average Shares	181,437	173,312	160,072	75,818	73,192	73,132	74,354	74,900
Balance Sheet								
Current Assets	1,776,814	1,458,356	1,468,242	1,268,216	1,078,848	1,053,896	606,529	497,751
Total Assets	13,451,566	11,603,413	11,799,265	4,657,524	4,486,226	4,297,411	1,739,692	1,629,304
Current Liabilities	1,735,577	1,800,116	2,236,616	1,176,897	1,133,722	1,147,891	517,545	379,336
Long-Term Obligations	2,260,596	2,129,845	2,136,668	893,678	1,159,838	1,383,392	20,000	105,000
Total Liabilities	6,258,424	5,739,275	6,390,736	3,019,490	3,218,850	3,315,560	788,380	696,915
Stockholders' Equity	7,149,391	5,817,356	5,324,717	1,601,166	1,267,376	981,851	951,312	932,389
Shares Outstanding	180,752	174,049	171,306	75,304	72,827	72,681	71,898	74,262
Statistical Record								
Return on Assets %	3.98	3.04	1.64	4.32	3.99	5.38	7.32	6.79
Return on Equity %	7.69	6.38	3.91	13.75	15.57	16.82	13.09	12.16
EBITDA Margin %	15.91	17.81	15.19	14.63	13.98	14.21	12.54	11.76
Net Margin %	8.03	6.18	2.45	4.57	4.37	4.28	5.06	4.54
Asset Turnover	0.50	0.49	0.67	0.94	0.91	1.26	1.45	1.50
Current Ratio	1.02	0.81	0.66	1.08	0.95	0.92	1.17	1.31
Debt to Equity	0.32	0.37	0.40	0.56	0.92	1.41	0.02	0.11
Price Range	57.23-37.72	38.38-31.18	39.75-29.05	38.25-26.95	32.00-23.07	34.83-25.70	39.13-21.80	40.38-19.41
P/E Ratio	20.89-13.77	18.36-14.92	47.32-34.58	14.71-10.36	13.45-9.70	15.76-11.63	23.57-13.13	27.47-13.20
Average Yield %	1.37	1.87	1.91	1.22	1.54	1.33	1.45	1.23

Address: 1555 Notre Dame Street East, Montréal, 80401 Telephone: 514-521-1786 Fax: 303-425-7967	Web Site: www.coors.com Officers: Eric H. Molson - Chmn. Peter H. Coors - Vice-Chmn.	Auditors: PricewaterhouseCoopers LLP Investor Contact: 303-279-6565 Transfer Agents: Computershare Trust Company, N.A.

MONEYGRAM INTERNATIONAL INC

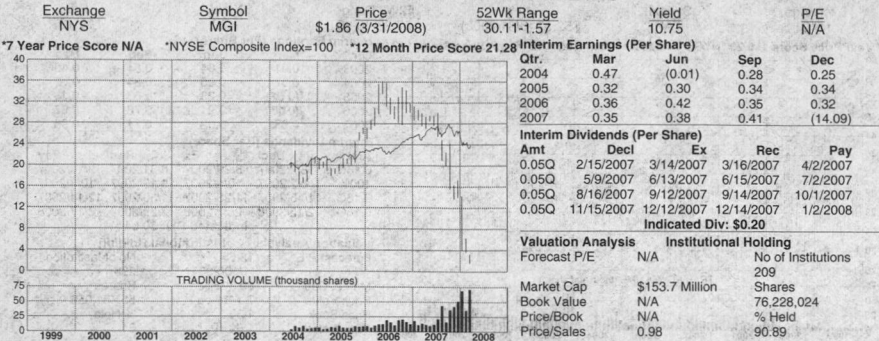

Exchange	Symbol	Price	52Wk Range	Yield	P/E
NYS	MGI	$1.86 (3/31/2008)	30.11-1.57	10.75	N/A

*7 Year Price Score N/A   *NYSE Composite Index=100   *12 Month Price Score 21.28

Interim Earnings (Per Share)

Qtr.	Mar	Jun	Sep	Dec
2004	0.47	(0.01)	0.28	0.25
2005	0.32	0.30	0.34	0.34
2006	0.36	0.42	0.35	0.32
2007	0.35	0.38	0.41	(14.09)

Interim Dividends (Per Share)

Amt	Decl	Ex	Rec	Pay
0.05Q	2/15/2007	3/14/2007	3/16/2007	4/2/2007
0.05Q	5/9/2007	6/13/2007	6/15/2007	7/2/2007
0.05Q	8/16/2007	9/12/2007	9/14/2007	10/1/2007
0.05Q	11/15/2007	12/12/2007	12/14/2007	1/2/2008

Indicated Div: $0.20

Valuation Analysis

		Institutional Holding	
Forecast P/E	N/A	No of Institutions	209
Market Cap	$153.7 Million	Shares	76,228,024
Book Value	N/A	% Held	90.89
Price/Book	N/A		
Price/Sales	0.98		

TRADING VOLUME (thousand shares)

Business Summary: Miscellaneous Business Services (MIC: 12.8 SIC: 7389 NAIC: 522320)

MoneyGram International is a global payment services company. Co. provides its products and services to consumers and businesses primarily through its network of agents and financial institution customers. Co.'s Global Funds Transfer segment provides money transfer services, money orders and bill payment services to consumers. Co.'s Payment Systems segment primarily provides financial institutions with payment processing services, specifically official check outsourcing services and money orders for sale to their customers as well as automated clearing house processing services. As of Dec 31 2007, Co. provided its ExpressPayment® bill payment services to over 1,900 billers.

Recent Developments: For the year ended Dec 31 2007, loss from continuing operations was US$1.07 billion compared with income of US$124.1 million a year earlier. Net loss amounted to US$1.07 billion versus net income of US$124.1 million in the prior year. Revenues were US$157.5 million, down 86.4% from US$1.16 billion the year before. Direct operating expenses rose 17.8% to US$663.9 million from US$563.7 million in the comparable period the year before. Indirect operating expenses increased 16.2% to US$486.9 million from US$419.1 million in the equivalent prior-year period.

Prospects: Co.'s near-term outlook appears to be somewhat mixed. For 2008, Co. expects to see lower money order fee and other revenue of approximately 5.0%. In addition, Co. foresees that its transaction expenses will increase due to marketing spend, investment in the agent network and development of its retail network in Western Europe. Nevertheless, Co. anticipates that money transfer revenue and money transfer volume growth percentages to remain in line, subject to volatility in the Euro exchange rate, pricing initiatives and product portfolio. Also, Co. will emphasize more on national television ads in conjunction with a new media campaign, and will also rely on radio and print advertising.

Financial Data

(US$ in Thousands)	12/31/2007	12/31/2006	12/31/2005	12/31/2004	12/31/2003	12/31/2002
Earnings Per Share	(12.94)	1.45	1.31	0.99	1.31	0.65
Cash Flow Per Share	(4.30)	(4.39)	1.20	5.12	(2.16)	...
Tang Book Value Per Share	...	2.76	2.41	1.76	5.14	...
Dividends Per Share	0.200	0.170	0.070	0.020	0.360	0.360
Dividend Payout %	...	11.72	5.34	2.02	27.48	55.38
Income Statement						
Total Revenue	157,537	1,159,559	971,236	826,530	737,223	707,690
EBITDA	(957,040)	207,543	186,486	137,657	153,708	108,230
Income Before Taxes	(993,267)	176,773	146,376	89,020	88,171	86,687
Income Taxes	78,481	52,719	34,170	23,891	12,485	11,923
Net Income	(1,071,997)	124,054	112,946	86,412	113,902	57,886
Average Shares	82,818	85,818	85,970	87,330	86,619	86,716
Balance Sheet						
Current Assets	7,210,658	8,568,713	2,192,013	1,699,008	1,814,592	...
Total Assets	7,935,011	9,276,137	9,075,164	8,630,735	9,222,154	...
Current Liabilities	7,762,470	8,209,789	8,059,309	7,640,581	7,421,481	...
Long-Term Obligations	345,000	150,000	150,000	150,000	201,351	...
Total Liabilities	8,423,528	8,607,074	8,451,035	8,065,544	8,353,371	...
Stockholders' Equity	(488,517)	669,063	624,129	565,191	868,783	...
Shares Outstanding	82,645	84,270	85,854	87,754	88,357	...
Statistical Record						
Return on Assets %	N.M.	1.35	1.28	0.97	...	...
Return on Equity %	N.M.	19.19	18.99	12.02	...	...
EBITDA Margin %	N.M.	17.90	19.20	16.65	20.85	15.29
Net Margin %	N.M.	10.70	11.63	10.45	15.45	8.18
Asset Turnover	0.02	0.13	0.11	0.09	...	...
Current Ratio	0.93	1.04	0.27	0.22	0.24	...
Debt to Equity	...	0.22	0.24	0.27	0.23	...
Price Range	31.33-13.71	36.20-24.97	27.24-17.94	22.75-16.40	...	...
P/E Ratio	...	24.97-17.22	20.79-13.69	22.98-16.57	...	...
Average Yield %	0.81	0.55	0.33	0.10	...	...

Address: 1550 Utica Avenue South, St. Louis Park, MN 55416	Web Site: www.moneygram.com	Auditors: DELOITTE & TOUCHE LLP
Telephone: 800-328-5678	Officers: Philip W. Milne - Pres., C.E.O. David J. Parrin - V.P., C.F.O.	Transfer Agents: Wells Fargo Shareowner Services, St. Paul, MN
Fax: 952-591-3000		

MONSANTO CO.

Exchange	Symbol	Price	52Wk Range	Yield	P/E
NYS	MON	$111.50 (3/31/2008)	127.25-55.01	0.63	35.74

*7 Year Price Score 209.60 *NYSE Composite Index=100 *12 Month Price Score 139.97

Interim Earnings (Per Share)

Qtr.	Nov	Feb	May	Aug
2004-05	(0.07)	0.69	0.09	(0.23)
2005-06	0.11	0.80	0.60	(0.26)
2006-07	0.16	0.98	1.03	(0.38)
2007-08	0.46	2.02	...	...

Interim Dividends (Per Share)

Amt	Decl	Ex	Rec	Pay
0.125Q	6/15/2007	7/3/2007	7/6/2007	7/27/2007
0.175Q	8/7/2007	10/3/2007	10/5/2007	10/26/2007
0.175Q	12/11/2007	1/2/2008	1/4/2008	1/25/2008
0.175Q	1/16/2008	4/2/2008	4/4/2008	4/25/2008
		Indicated Div: $0.70		

Valuation Analysis | **Institutional Holding**

Forecast P/E	N/A	No of Institutions	
		493	
Market Cap	$61.2 Billion	Shares	
Book Value	9.3 Billion	476,005,824	
Price/Book	6.58	% Held	
Price/Sales	5.96	87.58	

Business Summary: Chemicals (MIC: 11.1 SIC: 2879 NAIC: 325320)

Monsanto is engaged in providing agricultural products for farmers. Co. manages its business in two segments: Seeds and Genomics and Agricultural Productivity. Through the Seeds and Genomics segment, Co. produces seed brands, including DEKALB, Asgrow, D&PL, Deltapine and Seminis, and develops biotechnology traits that assist farmers in controlling insects and weeds. Through the Agricultural Productivity segment, Co. manufactures Roundup brand herbicides and other herbicides and provides lawn-and-garden herbicide products for the residential market and animal agricultural products focused on improving dairy cow productivity.

Recent Developments: For the quarter ended Feb 29 2008, income from continuing operations increased 106.8% to US$1.13 billion from US$546.0 million in the year-earlier quarter. Net income increased 107.9% to US$1.13 billion from US$543.0 million in the year-earlier quarter. Revenues were US$3.78 billion, up 44.8% from US$2.61 billion the year before. Operating income was US$1.47 billion versus US$832.0 million in the prior-year quarter, an increase of 77.2%. Direct operating expenses rose 33.5% to US$1.55 billion from US$1.16 billion in the comparable period the year before. Indirect operating expenses increased 22.6% to US$755.0 million from US$616.0 million in the equivalent prior-year period.

Prospects: On Mar 31 2008, Co. announced that it has signed a definitive agreement to acquire De Ruiter Seeds Group B.V. for a total value of about $800.0 million. Accordingly, Co. expects the acquisition to enhance its growth in the protected-culture segment. In addition, Co. foresees this acquisition to be accretive to its earnings per share and revenue growth by the second-full fiscal year of completion. The completion of this transaction is subject to review and approval by the appropriate regulatory authorities, including several European-based regulatory authorities. Separately, Co. is projecting earnings for the fiscal year ending Sep 30 2008 to be in the range of $3.38 to $3.48 per share.

Financial Data

(US$ in Thousands)	6 Mos	3 Mos	08/31/2007	08/31/2006	08/31/2005	08/31/2004	08/31/2003	12/31/2002
Earnings Per Share	3.12	2.09	1.79	1.25	0.47	0.50	(0.04)	(3.23)
Cash Flow Per Share	5.87	4.12	3.41	3.10	3.26	2.38	(0.61)	2.11
Tang Book Value Per Share	9.38	7.16	6.35	6.95	5.99	7.72	7.27	7.23
Dividends Per Share	0.600	0.550	0.475	0.385	0.328	0.268	0.245	0.240
Dividend Payout %	19.24	26.32	26.54	30.80	69.68	54.04	...	...
Income Statement								
Total Revenue	5,878,000	2,099,000	8,563,000	7,344,000	6,294,000	5,457,000	3,373,000	4,673,000
EBITDA	2,332,000	517,000	1,880,000	1,653,000	824,000	921,000	310,000	721,000
Depn & Amortn	281,000	143,000	...	...	...	...	...	...
Income Before Taxes	2,054,000	370,000	1,336,000	1,055,000	261,000	402,000	(38,000)	202,000
Income Taxes	662,000	107,000	402,000	340,000	104,000	131,000	(27,000)	73,000
Net Income	1,385,000	256,000	993,000	689,000	255,000	267,000	(23,000)	(1,693,000)
Average Shares	559,200	557,700	555,000	551,600	545,400	538,400	523,400	520,000
Balance Sheet								
Current Assets	7,676,000	6,562,000	5,084,000	5,461,000	4,644,000	4,931,000	4,962,000	4,424,000
Total Assets	16,593,000	15,313,000	12,983,000	11,728,000	10,579,000	9,164,000	9,461,000	8,890,000
Current Liabilities	4,087,000	4,127,000	3,075,000	2,279,000	2,159,000	1,894,000	1,944,000	1,810,000
Long-Term Obligations	1,155,000	1,153,000	1,150,000	1,639,000	1,458,000	1,075,000	1,258,000	851,000
Total Liabilities	7,294,000	7,254,000	5,480,000	5,203,000	4,966,000	3,906,000	4,305,000	3,710,000
Stockholders' Equity	9,299,000	8,059,000	7,503,000	6,525,000	5,613,000	5,258,000	5,156,000	5,180,000
Shares Outstanding	548,685	547,227	545,609	543,177	536,382	528,826	525,362	522,826
Statistical Record								
Return on Assets %	11.94	8.44	8.04	6.18	2.58	2.86	N.M.	N.M.
Return on Equity %	21.12	15.75	14.16	11.35	4.69	5.11	N.M.	N.M.
EBITDA Margin %	39.67	24.63	21.95	22.51	13.09	16.88	9.19	15.43
Net Margin %	23.56	12.20	11.60	9.38	4.05	4.89	N.M.	N.M.
Asset Turnover	0.70	0.67	0.69	0.66	0.64	0.58	0.55	0.46
Current Ratio	1.88	1.59	1.65	2.40	2.15	2.60	2.55	2.44
Debt to Equity	0.12	0.14	0.15	0.25	0.26	0.20	0.24	0.16
Price Range	127.25-50.80	99.37-47.72	70.06-42.99	47.44-28.45	33.92-17.30	19.25-11.62	12.86-7.04	16.90-6.90
P/E Ratio	40.79-16.28	47.55-22.83	39.14-24.02	37.95-22.76	72.17-36.81	38.50-23.24	...	...
Average Yield %	0.75	0.84	0.86	0.98	1.20	1.70	2.56	2.06

Address: 800 North Lindbergh Boulevard, St. Louis, MO 63167
Telephone: 314-694-1000
Fax: 314-694-1057

Web Site: www.monsanto.com
Officers: Hugh Grant - Chmn., Pres., C.E.O. Terrell K. Crews - Exec. V.P., C.F.O.

Auditors: Deloitte & Touche LLP
Investor Contact: 314-694-1000
Transfer Agents: Mellon Investor Services LLP

MOODY'S CORP.

Exchange	Symbol	Price	52Wk Range	Yield	P/E
NYS	MCO	$34.83 (3/31/2008)	72.56-32.06	1.15	13.50

*7 Year Price Score 101.49 *NYSE Composite Index=100   *12 Month Price Score 79.74

Interim Earnings (Per Share)

Qtr.	Mar	Jun	Sep	Dec
2003	0.30	0.33	0.28	0.28
2004	0.34	0.34	0.32	0.40
2005	0.39	0.47	0.48	0.50
2006	0.49	0.59	0.55	0.97
2007	0.62	0.95	0.51	0.50

Interim Dividends (Per Share)

Amt	Decl	Ex	Rec	Pay
0.08Q	4/24/2007	5/16/2007	5/20/2007	6/10/2007
0.08Q	7/30/2007	8/16/2007	8/20/2007	9/10/2007
0.08Q	10/24/2007	11/16/2007	11/20/2007	12/10/2007
0.10Q	12/18/2007	2/15/2008	2/20/2008	3/10/2008

Indicated Div: $0.40

Valuation Analysis		Institutional Holding	
Forecast P/E	24.13	No of Institutions	
	(1/10/2007)	488	
Market Cap	$8.8 Billion	Shares	
Book Value	N/A	247,952,640	
Price/Book	N/A	% Held	
Price/Sales	3.88	89.03	

TRADING VOLUME (thousand shares)

Business Summary: Miscellaneous Business Services (MIC: 12.8 SIC: 7323 NAIC: 561450)

Moody's provides credit ratings and related research, data and analytical tools; quantitative credit risk measures, risk scoring software and credit portfolio management products and services and; beginning in Jan 2008, fixed income pricing data and valuation models. Co.'s customers include corporate and governmental issuers of securities, institutional investors, depositors, creditors, investment banks, commercial banks and other financial intermediaries. At Dec 31 2007, Co. operated in two segments: Moody's Investors Service, which publishes credit ratings and associated opinions; and Moody's KMV, which develops and distributes quantitative credit risk assessment products and services.

Recent Developments: For the year ended Dec 31 2007, net income decreased 7.0% to US$701.5 million from US$753.9 million in the prior year. Revenues were US$2.26 billion, up 10.9% from US$2.04 billion the year before. Operating income was US$1.13 billion versus US$1.26 billion in the prior year, a decrease of 10.2%. Indirect operating expenses increased 45.1% to US$1.13 billion from US$777.6 million in the equivalent prior-year period.

Prospects: Co. anticipates a weak first half of 2008 with improvement in market liquidity and issuance conditions later in the year. Hence, Co. noted that its first half 2008 performance likely to reflect unusually weak market conditions, as well as challenging year-on-year comparisons against the stronger performance in the first half of 2007. As a result, Co. anticipates overall revenue to decline in the low double-digit percent range for full-year 2008, with earnings in a range from $2.17 to $2.25 per share. In addition, Co. expects full-year 2008 operating margin to decline to the mid- to high-forties percent range, excluding the 2007 restructuring charge, due primarily to lower ratings revenue.

Financial Data

(US$ in Thousands)	12/31/2007	12/31/2006	12/31/2005	12/31/2004	12/31/2003	12/31/2002	12/31/2001	12/31/2000
Earnings Per Share	2.58	2.58	1.84	1.40	1.20	0.92	0.66	0.48
Cash Flow Per Share	3.69	2.65	2.38	1.75	1.57	1.09	0.97	0.21
Tang Book Value Per Share	...	N.M.	0.30	0.39	...	...	...	...
Dividends Per Share	0.320	0.280	0.203	0.150	0.090	0.090	0.090	0.300
Dividend Payout %	12.40	10.85	11.01	10.75	7.53	9.84	13.64	61.86
Income Statement								
Total Revenue	2,259,000	2,037,100	1,731,600	1,438,300	1,246,600	1,023,300	796,700	602,300
EBITDA	1,183,900	1,297,000	964,900	821,600	710,800	563,200	415,400	304,200
Income Before Taxes	1,116,700	1,260,500	934,700	771,300	656,400	517,400	381,900	284,000
Income Taxes	415,200	506,600	373,900	346,200	292,500	228,500	169,700	125,500
Net Income	701,500	753,900	560,800	425,100	363,900	288,900	212,200	158,500
Average Shares	272,200	291,900	305,600	304,600	304,600	315,000	320,400	326,000
Balance Sheet								
Current Assets	989,100	1,001,900	1,051,800	1,022,600	569,000	272,300	371,200	277,600
Total Assets	1,714,600	1,497,700	1,457,200	1,376,000	941,400	630,800	505,400	398,300
Current Liabilities	1,349,200	700,000	578,900	837,200	432,100	462,000	359,300	253,100
Long-Term Obligations	600,000	300,000	300,000	...	300,000	300,000	300,000	300,000
Total Liabilities	2,498,200	1,330,300	1,147,800	1,058,500	973,500	957,800	809,500	680,800
Stockholders' Equity	(783,600)	167,400	309,400	317,500	(32,100)	(327,000)	(304,100)	(282,500)
Shares Outstanding	251,406	278,605	290,297	297,824	297,343	297,780	308,814	320,821
Statistical Record								
Return on Assets %	43.68	51.03	39.59	36.59	46.29	50.85	46.96	14.47
Return on Equity %	...	316.23	178.91	297.08	...	...	...	...
EBITDA Margin %	52.41	63.67	55.72	57.12	57.02	55.04	52.14	50.51
Net Margin %	31.05	37.01	32.39	29.56	29.19	28.23	26.63	26.32
Asset Turnover	1.41	1.38	1.22	1.24	1.59	1.80	1.76	0.55
Current Ratio	0.73	1.43	1.82	1.22	1.32	0.59	1.03	1.10
Debt to Equity	...	1.79	0.97	...	...	...	...	...
Price Range	74.84-35.39	72.45-50.30	62.30-40.01	43.60-29.95	30.28-20.13	25.79-18.32	20.45-13.13	13.78-9.48
P/E Ratio	29.01-13.72	28.08-19.50	33.86-21.74	31.14-21.39	25.23-16.77	28.03-19.92	30.98-19.89	28.71-19.76
Average Yield %	0.56	0.45	0.43	0.43	0.35	0.40	0.56	2.60

Address: 99 Church Street, New York, NY 10007
Telephone: 212-553-0300
Fax: 212-553-4820

Web Site: www.moodys.com
Officers: Raymond W. McDaniel Jr. - Chmn., C.E.O. Jeanne M. Dering - Sr. V.P., C.F.O.

Auditors: KPMG LLP
Transfer Agents: The Bank of New York

520

MORGAN STANLEY

Exchange	Symbol	Price	52Wk Range	Yield	P/E
NYS	MS	$45.70 (3/31/2008)	74.13-36.38	2.36	15.34

*7 Year Price Score 100.56 *NYSE Composite Index=100 *12 Month Price Score 79.56

TRADING VOLUME (thousand shares)

Interim Earnings (Per Share)

Qtr.	Feb	May	Aug	Nov
2002-03	0.82	0.55	1.15	0.93
2003-04	1.11	1.10	0.76	1.09
2004-05	1.29	0.86	0.13	2.28
2005-06	1.47	1.86	1.75	2.08
2006-07	2.51	2.45	1.44	(3.42)

Interim Dividends (Per Share)

Amt	Decl	Ex	Rec	Pay
0.27Q	6/20/2007	7/11/2007	7/13/2007	7/31/2007
0.27Q	9/19/2007	10/10/2007	10/12/2007	10/31/2007
0.27Q	12/19/2007	1/9/2008	1/11/2008	1/31/2008
0.27Q	3/19/2008	4/9/2008	4/11/2008	4/30/2008

Indicated Div: $1.08

Valuation Analysis

		Institutional Holding	
Forecast P/E	N/A	No of Institutions	907
Market Cap	$48.3 Billion	Shares	
Book Value	31.3 Billion	750,363,584	
Price/Book	1.54	% Held	
Price/Sales	0.57	70.36	

Business Summary: Finance Intermediaries & Services (MIC: 8.7 SIC: 6211 NAIC: 523120)

Morgan Stanley is a financial services firm that operates in three business segments: Institutional Securities, Global Wealth Management Group and Asset Management. Co.'s Institutional Securities includes capital raising; financial advisory services; corporate lending; benchmark indices and risk management analytics; research; and investment activities. Co.'s Global Wealth Management Group provides brokerage and investment advisory services covering various investment alternatives; financial and wealth planning services; retirement services; and trust and fiduciary services. Co.'s Asset Management provides global asset management products and services and engages in investment activities.

Recent Developments: For the year ended Nov 30 2007, net income decreased 57.1% to US$3.21 billion from US$7.47 billion in the prior year. Revenues were US$85.33 billion, up 20.6% from US$70.74 billion the year before. Direct operating expenses rose 40.1% to US$57.30 billion from US$40.90 billion in the comparable period the year before. Indirect operating expenses increased 18.6% to US$24.59 billion from US$20.74 billion in the equivalent prior-year period.

Prospects: On Jan 28 2008, Co. announced that it has reached an agreement to sell Morgan Stanley Wealth Management S.V., S.A.U., its Spanish onshore mass affluent wealth management business, to La Caixa for undisclosed terms. This transaction, which is part of Co.'s strategy to focus its international wealth management effort on the high net worth market segment, should close in the second quarter of the fiscal year ending Nov 2008. Meanwhile, on Feb 13 2008, Co. announced that in response to the deterioration of the mortgage markets, it plans to scale back its residential mortgage operations in the U.S. and discontinue its U.K.-based residential mortgage lending business, Advantage Home Loans.

Financial Data

(US$ in Thousands)	11/30/2007	11/30/2006	11/30/2005	11/30/2004	11/30/2003	11/30/2002	11/30/2001	11/30/2000
Earnings Per Share	2.98	7.07	4.57	4.06	3.45	2.69	3.11	4.73
Cash Flow Per Share	(22.05)	(60.19)	(29.86)	(22.63)	2.19	(4.67)	(22.18)	(2.17)
Tang Book Value Per Share	24.71	29.47	25.23	23.92	21.53	18.90	18.64	16.91
Dividends Per Share	1.080	1.080	1.080	1.000	0.920	0.920	0.920	0.800
Dividend Payout %	36.24	15.28	23.63	24.63	26.67	34.20	29.58	16.91
Income Statement								
Interest Income	60,083,000	45,216,000	28,175,000	18,590,000	15,744,000	15,866,000	24,127,000	21,234,000
Interest Expense	57,302,000	41,937,000	24,425,000	14,859,000	12,809,000	11,970,000	20,779,000	18,176,000
Net Interest Income	2,781,000	3,279,000	3,750,000	3,731,000	2,935,000	3,896,000	3,348,000	3,058,000
Provision for Losses	...	756,000	878,000	925,000	1,267,000	1,336,000	1,052,000	810,000
Non-Interest Income	25,245,000	31,335,000	23,906,000	20,959,000	19,189,000	16,549,000	19,600,000	24,179,000
Non-Interest Expense	24,585,000	22,858,000	19,417,000	17,080,000	15,090,000	14,389,000	16,212,000	17,936,000
Income Before Taxes	3,441,000	11,000,000	7,361,000	6,685,000	5,767,000	4,720,000	5,684,000	8,526,000
Income Taxes	831,000	3,275,000	1,858,000	1,803,000	1,517,000	1,615,000	2,074,000	3,070,000
Net Income	3,209,000	7,472,000	4,939,000	4,486,000	3,787,000	2,988,000	3,521,000	5,456,000
Average Shares	1,054,240	1,054,796	1,079,936	1,105,185	1,099,117	1,109,637	1,121,764	1,145,011
Balance Sheet								
Net Loans & Leases	...	24,173,000	22,916,000	20,226,000	19,382,000	23,404,000	20,108,000	21,090,000
Total Assets	1,045,409,000	1,120,645,000	898,523,000	775,410,000	602,843,000	529,499,000	482,628,000	426,794,000
Total Deposits	31,179,000	28,343,000	18,663,000	13,777,000	12,839,000	13,757,000	12,276,000	11,930,000
Total Liabilities	1,014,140,000	1,085,215,000	869,275,000	747,138,000	575,100,000	506,338,000	460,636,000	407,053,000
Stockholders' Equity	31,269,000	35,364,000	29,182,000	28,206,000	24,867,000	21,885,000	20,716,000	19,271,000
Shares Outstanding	1,056,289	1,048,877	1,057,677	1,087,087	1,084,696	1,081,417	1,093,006	1,107,270
Statistical Record								
Return on Assets %	0.30	0.74	0.59	0.65	0.67	0.59	0.77	1.37
Return on Equity %	9.63	23.15	17.21	16.86	16.20	14.03	17.61	29.99
Net Interest Margin %	4.63	7.25	13.31	20.07	18.64	24.56	13.88	14.40
Efficiency Ratio %	28.81	29.86	37.28	43.19	43.20	44.39	37.08	39.50
Loans to Deposits	...	0.85	1.23	1.47	1.51	1.70	1.64	1.77
Price Range	74.13-47.95	65.84-45.86	50.07-40.03	51.65-38.85	48.01-27.87	49.51-24.33	74.54-31.23	90.79-49.78
P/E Ratio	24.88-16.09	9.31-6.49	10.96-8.76	12.72-9.57	13.91-8.08	18.40-9.04	23.97-10.04	19.20-10.52
Average Yield %	1.64	2.01	2.42	2.24	2.43	2.38	1.78	1.21

Address: 1585 Broadway, New York, NY 10036	Web Site: www.morganstanley.com	Auditors: Deloitte & Touche LLP
Telephone: 212-761-4000	Officers: John J. Mack - Chmn., C.E.O. Zoe Cruz - Acting Pres.	Investor Contact: 212-762-8131
Fax: 212-761-0086		Transfer Agents: Mellon Investor Services LLC., South Hackensack, NJ

MOSAIC CO (THE)

Exchange	Symbol	Price	52Wk Range	Yield	P/E
NYS	MOS	$102.60 (3/31/2008)	117.06-26.85	N/A	47.94

*7 Year Price Score N/A   *NYSE Composite Index=100   *12 Month Price Score 182.32

Interim Earnings (Per Share)

Qtr.	Aug	Nov	Feb	May
2004-05	0.00	(0.03)	0.09	0.25
2005-06	0.18	0.13	(0.19)	(0.49)
2006-07	0.25	0.15	0.10	0.46
2007-08	0.69	0.89	...	...

Interim Dividends (Per Share)

No Dividends Paid

Valuation Analysis		Institutional Holding	
Forecast P/E	N/A	No of Institutions	176
Market Cap	$45.4 Billion	Shares	
Book Value	5.2 Billion		138,051,008
Price/Book	8.76	% Held	31.35
Price/Sales	6.35		

Business Summary: Chemicals (MIC: 11.1 SIC: 2874 NAIC: 325312)

Mosaic produces and markets phosphate and potash crop nutrients for the agriculture industry. Co. operates in four business segments. Co.'s phosphates business owns and operates mines and processing plants in Florida that produce phosphate fertilizer and feed phosphate, and processing plants in Louisiana that produce phosphate fertilizer. Co.'s potash business mines and processes potash in Canada and the U.S., while its offshore business consists of sales offices, fertilizer blending and bagging facilities, port terminals and warehouses in Brazil and other countries. Co.'s nitrogen business includes activities related to its North American distribution of nitrogen-based products.

Recent Developments: For the quarter ended Nov 30 2007, net income increased 497.9% to US$394.0 million from US$65.9 million in the year-earlier quarter. Revenues were US$2.20 billion, up 44.2% from US$1.52 billion the year before. Operating income was US$529.6 million versus US$90.7 million in the prior-year quarter, an increase of 483.9%. Direct operating expenses rose 15.5% to US$1.57 billion from US$1.36 billion in the comparable period the year before. Indirect operating expenses increased 34.0% to US$93.5 million from US$69.8 million in the equivalent prior-year period.

Prospects: Co.'s outlook appears constructive. Notably, Co. has several expansions underway at its potash mine sites such as the expansion at its Colonsay mine, which is expected to occur in two stages. In detail, Co. expects the first phase to expand capacity to 200,000 tonnes per year upon completion in 2010 at a capital cost of about $20.0 million, while the second phase should add 360,000 tonnes by 2012 at $120.0 million. Meanwhile, for the fiscal year ending May 2008, Co. continues to anticipate sales volumes for its phosphates business to range from 8.6 million tonnes to 9.1 million tonnes, while its potash sales volumes are projected to range from 8.5 million tonnes to 9.0 million tonnes.

Financial Data

(US$ in Thousands)	6 Mos	3 Mos	05/31/2007	05/31/2006	05/31/2005	05/31/2004	05/31/2003
Earnings Per Share	2.14	1.40	0.95	(0.35)	0.46	0.29	0.22
Cash Flow Per Share	3.16	2.26	1.63	0.73	1.02	0.48	...
Tang Book Value Per Share	6.84	5.30	4.31	3.04	2.74	...	...
Income Statement							
Total Revenue	4,198,700	2,003,300	5,773,700	5,305,800	4,396,700	2,374,000	1,662,700
EBITDA	908,600	430,200	968,600	276,600	516,200	173,900	158,000
Income Before Taxes	849,100	396,200	505,700	(160,100)	214,900	40,100	29,000
Income Taxes	201,700	100,800	123,400	5,300	98,300	2,200	3,800
Net Income	699,500	305,500	419,700	(121,400)	165,600	72,300	53,900
Average Shares	445,000	444,300	440,300	382,200	360,400	250,600	250,600
Balance Sheet							
Current Assets	2,277,800	2,170,000	1,955,500	1,580,400	1,731,900	668,500	...
Total Assets	9,694,100	9,313,100	9,163,600	8,720,600	8,444,000	1,870,500	...
Current Liabilities	1,444,000	1,604,300	1,629,700	1,126,100	1,107,300	458,200	...
Long-Term Obligations	1,382,600	1,585,700	1,818,100	2,388,100	2,463,700	350,800	...
Total Liabilities	4,504,000	4,764,900	4,979,700	5,189,800	5,230,500	1,028,100	...
Stockholders' Equity	5,190,100	4,548,200	4,183,900	3,530,800	3,213,500	842,400	...
Shares Outstanding	442,975	441,700	440,815	389,852	384,868	...	...
Statistical Record							
Return on Assets %	10.29	6.82	4.69	N.M.	3.21	...	...
Return on Equity %	21.37	15.04	10.88	N.M.	8.17	...	...
EBITDA Margin %	21.64	21.47	16.78	5.21	11.74	7.33	9.50
Net Margin %	16.66	15.25	7.27	N.M.	3.77	3.05	3.24
Asset Turnover	0.78	0.72	0.65	0.62	0.85	...	...
Current Ratio	1.58	1.35	1.20	1.40	1.56	1.46	...
Debt to Equity	0.27	0.35	0.43	0.68	0.77	0.42	...
Price Range	71.09-19.76	42.02-15.72	35.13-13.96	17.93-12.76	18.35-12.47	...	...
P/E Ratio	33.22-9.23	30.01-11.23	36.98-14.69	...	39.89-27.11	...	...

Address: 3033 Campus Drive, Suite E490, Plymouth, MN 55441 **Telephone:** 800-918-8270 **Fax:** 763-577-2990	**Web Site:** www.mosaicco.com **Officers:** Robert L. Lumpkins - Chmn. Fredric W. Corrigan - Pres., C.E.O.	**Auditors:** KPMG LLP **Investor Contact:** 763-577-2867 **Transfer Agents:** American Stock Transfer & Trust Company

MOTOROLA, INC.

Exchange	Symbol	Price	52Wk Range	Yield	P/E
NYS	MOT	$9.30 (3/31/2008)	19.34-9.21	2.15	N/A

*7 Year Price Score 81.86   *NYSE Composite Index=100   *12 Month Price Score 70.64

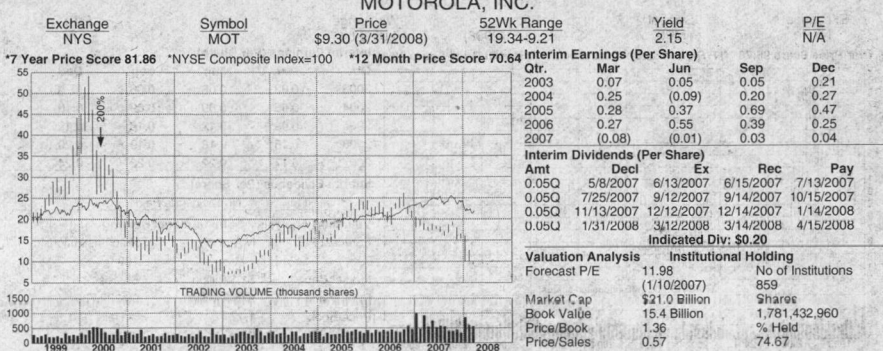

Interim Earnings (Per Share)

Qtr.	Mar	Jun	Sep	Dec
2003	0.07	0.05	0.05	0.21
2004	0.25	(0.09)	0.20	0.27
2005	0.28	0.37	0.69	0.47
2006	0.27	0.55	0.39	0.25
2007	(0.08)	(0.01)	0.03	0.04

Interim Dividends (Per Share)

Amt	Decl	Ex	Rec	Pay
0.05Q	5/8/2007	6/13/2007	6/15/2007	7/13/2007
0.05Q	7/25/2007	9/12/2007	9/14/2007	10/15/2007
0.05Q	11/13/2007	12/12/2007	12/14/2007	1/14/2008
0.05Q	1/31/2008	3/12/2008	3/14/2008	4/15/2008

Indicated Div: $0.20

Valuation Analysis / **Institutional Holding**

Forecast P/E	11.98	No of Institutions
	(1/10/2007)	859
Market Cap	$21.0 Billion	Shares
Book Value	15.4 Billion	1,781,432,960
Price/Book	1.36	% Held
Price/Sales	0.57	74.67

Business Summary: Communications (MIC: 10.1 SIC: 3663 NAIC: 334220)

Motorola is engaged in the design, manufacture, marketing, and sale of mobility products. As of Dec 31 2007, Co. had three operating business segments: Mobile Devices segment designs, manufactures, sells and services wireless handsets with integrated software and accessory products, and licenses intellectual property; Home and Networks Mobility segment designs, manufactures, sells, installs and services digital video, Internet Protocol video and wireless access systems; and Enterprise Mobility Solutions segment designs, manufactures, sells, installs and services analog and digital two-way radio, voice and data communications products and systems for private networks.

Recent Developments: For the year ended Dec 31 2007, loss from continuing operations was US$105.0 million compared with income of US$3.26 billion a year earlier. Net loss amounted to US$49.0 million versus net income of US$3.66 billion in the prior year. Revenues were US$36.62 billion, down 14.5% from US$42.85 billion the year before. Operating loss was US$553.0 million versus an income of US$4.09 billion in the prior year. Direct operating expenses declined 11.5% to US$26.67 billion from US$30.12 billion in the comparable period the year before. Indirect operating expenses increased 21.7% to US$10.51 billion from US$8.64 billion in the equivalent prior-year period.

Prospects: On Mar 2 2008, Co. announced a $335.0 million turnkey contract to deploy and manage a Second Generation/Third Generation mobile communications network for Zain in Saudi Arabia. Meanwhile, Co. expects its reorganization plans initiated in 2007 to provide annualized cost savings of $548.0 million, which include a saving of $251.0 million in research and development spending, beyond 2007. For the quarter ending Mar 2008, Co. projects a loss from continuing operations of $0.05 to $0.07 per share, excluding any reorganization of business charges related to its operating expense reduction plans. Going forward, Co. focuses on developing offering of 3G products for the Multimedia product segment.

Financial Data

(US$ in Thousands)	12/31/2007	12/31/2006	12/31/2005	12/31/2004	12/31/2003	12/31/2002	12/31/2001	12/31/2000
Earnings Per Share	(0.02)	1.46	1.81	0.64	0.38	(1.09)	(1.78)	0.58
Cash Flow Per Share	0.34	1.43	1.86	1.29	1.19	0.59	0.89	(0.53)
Tang Book Value Per Share	4.12	6.11	5.85	4.84	4.74	4.16	5.28	7.47
Dividends Per Share	0.200	0.190	0.160	0.160	0.160	0.160	0.160	0.160
Dividend Payout %	...	13.01	8.84	25.00	42.11	...	...	27.59
Income Statement								
Total Revenue	36,622,000	42,879,000	36,843,000	31,323,000	27,058,000	26,679,000	30,004,000	37,580,000
EBITDA	425,000	4,847,000	7,062,000	4,110,000	3,255,000	(982,000)	(2,522,000)	5,001,000
Income Before Taxes	(390,000)	4,610,000	6,520,000	3,252,000	1,293,000	(3,446,000)	(5,511,000)	2,231,000
Income Taxes	(285,000)	1,349,000	1,921,000	1,061,000	400,000	(961,000)	(1,574,000)	913,000
Net Income	(49,000)	3,661,000	4,578,000	1,532,000	893,000	(2,485,000)	(3,937,000)	1,318,000
Average Shares	2,312,700	2,504,200	2,527,000	2,472,000	2,351,200	2,282,300	2,213,300	2,256,600
Balance Sheet								
Current Assets	22,222,000	30,975,000	27,869,000	21,082,000	17,907,000	17,134,000	17,149,000	19,885,000
Total Assets	34,812,000	38,593,000	35,649,000	30,889,000	32,098,000	31,152,000	33,398,000	42,343,000
Current Liabilities	12,500,000	15,425,000	12,488,000	10,573,000	9,433,000	9,810,000	9,698,000	16,257,000
Long-Term Obligations	3,991,000	2,704,000	3,806,000	4,578,000	6,675,000	7,189,000	8,372,000	4,293,000
Total Liabilities	19,365,000	21,451,000	18,976,000	17,558,000	19,409,000	19,913,000	19,707,000	23,731,000
Stockholders' Equity	15,447,000	17,142,000	16,673,000	13,331,000	12,689,000	11,239,000	13,691,000	18,612,000
Shares Outstanding	2,263,100	2,397,400	2,501,100	2,447,800	2,338,700	2,315,300	2,254,000	2,191,200
Statistical Record								
Return on Assets %	N.M.	9.86	13.76	4.85	2.82	N.M.	N.M.	3.17
Return on Equity %	N.M.	21.65	30.52	11.74	7.46	N.M.	N.M.	7.05
EBITDA Margin %	1.16	11.30	19.17	13.12	12.03	N.M.	N.M.	13.31
Net Margin %	N.M.	8.54	12.43	4.89	3.30	N.M.	N.M.	3.51
Asset Turnover	1.00	1.16	1.11	0.99	0.86	0.83	0.79	0.90
Current Ratio	1.78	2.01	2.23	1.99	1.90	1.75	1.77	1.22
Debt to Equity	0.26	0.16	0.23	0.34	0.53	0.64	0.61	0.23
Price Range	20.57-15.24	26.20-18.69	24.77-14.61	18.63-12.59	12.76-6.93	15.24-6.99	22.20-10.34	54.15-15.74
P/E Ratio	...	17.95-12.80	13.69-8.07	29.11-19.67	33.58-18.25	...	...	93.35-27.13
Average Yield %	1.12	0.85	0.84	1.01	1.75	1.40	1.05	0.50

Address: 1303 E. Algonquin Road, Schaumburg, IL 60196
Telephone: 847-576-5000
Fax: 847-576-3477

Web Site: www.motorola.com
Officers: Edward J. Zander - Chmn., C.E.O. David W. Devonshire - Exec. V.P., C.F.O.

Auditors: KPMG LLP
Investor Contact: 800-262-8509
Transfer Agents: Mellon Investor Services LLC, Ridgefield Park, NJ

MPS GROUP, INC.

Exchange	Symbol	Price	52Wk Range	Yield	P/E
NYS	MPS	$11.82 (3/31/2008)	15.02-9.04	N/A	13.74

*7 Year Price Score 96.78 *NYSE Composite Index=100 *12 Month Price Score 98.31

TRADING VOLUME (thousand shares)

Interim Earnings (Per Share)

Qtr.	Mar	Jun	Sep	Dec
2003	0.03	0.06	0.06	(0.16)
2004	0.05	0.09	0.09	0.10
2005	0.09	0.12	0.16	0.19
2006	0.15	0.18	0.19	0.20
2007	0.17	0.22	0.23	0.24

Interim Dividends (Per Share)

No Dividends Paid

Valuation Analysis | **Institutional Holding**

Forecast P/E	N/A	No of Institutions
		159
Market Cap	$1.1 Billion	Shares
Book Value	976.3 Million	98,239,736
Price/Book	1.17	% Held
Price/Sales	0.53	95.86

Business Summary: Human Resources Services (MIC: 12.6 SIC: 7363 NAIC: 561330)

MPS Group is a provider of business services with over 230 offices throughout the U.S., Canada, the U.K., continental Europe, Australia, and Asia as of Dec 31 2007. Co. delivers specialty staffing, consulting and business services to a range of industries in the disciplines of Information Technology (IT) Services, Accounting and Finance, Engineering, Legal, IT Applications, Health Care, and Work Force Automation. Co. delivers these services through its primary brands that include Modis®, Badenoch & Clark®, Accounting Principals®, Entegee®, Special Counsel®, Idea Integration®, Soliant Health® and Beeline®.

Recent Developments: For the year ended Dec 31 2007, net income increased 15.8% to US$87.1 million from US$75.2 million in the prior year. Revenues were US$2.17 billion, up 15.7% from US$1.88 billion the year before. Operating income was US$133.6 million versus US$114.5 million in the prior year; an increase of 16.7%. Direct operating expenses rose 14.0% to US$1.55 billion from US$1.36 billion in the comparable period the year before. Indirect operating expenses increased 21.4% to US$488.7 million from US$402.5 million in the equivalent prior-year period.

Prospects: Co.'s near-term outlook appears encouraging, reflecting higher revenues from both of its Professional Services and Information Technology Services businesses. For full-year 2008, Co. anticipates capital expenditures for furniture and equipment, including improvements to its management information and operating systems to be about $15.0 million to $20.0 million. Meanwhile, for the first quarter of 2008, Co. expects revenue and diluted net income per common share to be in the range of $550.0 million to $580.0 million and $0.18 to $0.22, respectively. Going forward, Co. will continue to look for opportunities to increase its gross margin through acquiring companies with higher margins.

Financial Data

(US$ in Thousands)	12/31/2007	12/31/2006	12/31/2005	12/31/2004	12/31/2003	12/31/2002	12/31/2001	12/31/2000
Earnings Per Share	0.86	0.72	0.56	0.33	(0.01)	(5.62)	0.08	1.23
Cash Flow Per Share	1.33	1.05	0.90	0.49	0.69	1.15	1.78	1.99
Tang Book Value Per Share	3.08	3.53	3.23	2.96	2.98	2.64	1.47	1.07
Income Statement								
Total Revenue	2,171,835	1,876,622	1,684,699	1,426,842	1,096,030	1,154,970	1,500,615	1,827,686
EBITDA	160,664	136,404	106,102	69,325	53,363	23,016	63,697	110,535
Income Before Taxes	140,547	120,535	90,785	53,570	36,354	1,999	5,405	56,654
Income Taxes	53,459	45,321	31,188	18,150	14,519	14,591	3,102	(63,099)
Net Income	87,088	75,214	59,597	35,420	(1,235)	(566,304)	8,343	119,753
Average Shares	101,086	104,090	105,832	106,842	104,518	100,833	98,178	97,539
Balance Sheet								
Current Assets	463,704	479,922	416,428	338,782	303,468	272,561	300,696	372,307
Total Assets	1,209,651	1,142,279	1,028,006	954,604	893,151	897,983	1,543,622	1,653,560
Current Liabilities	198,554	161,043	136,569	106,649	86,589	100,630	95,974	123,919
Long-Term Obligations	...	...	...	...	...	...	101,000	194,000
Total Liabilities	233,306	178,981	151,966	118,941	99,689	116,424	232,811	350,342
Stockholders' Equity	976,345	963,298	876,040	835,663	793,462	781,559	1,310,811	1,303,218
Shares Outstanding	96,789	102,436	102,335	103,356	102,962	102,241	98,306	96,522
Statistical Record								
Return on Assets %	7.41	6.93	6.01	3.82	N.M.	N.M.	0.52	7.60
Return on Equity %	8.98	8.18	6.96	4.34	N.M.	N.M.	0.64	9.61
EBITDA Margin %	7.40	7.27	6.30	4.86	4.87	1.99	4.24	6.05
Net Margin %	4.01	4.01	3.54	2.48	N.M.	N.M.	0.56	6.55
Asset Turnover	1.85	1.73	1.70	1.54	1.22	0.95	0.94	1.16
Current Ratio	2.34	2.98	3.05	3.18	3.50	2.71	3.13	3.00
Debt to Equity	...	...	...	...	...	...	0.08	0.15
Price Range	15.69-10.30	17.21-11.92	14.21-7.99	12.38-7.87	10.60-4.85	9.79-4.51	8.00-3.70	18.44-3.50
P/E Ratio	18.24-11.98	23.90-16.56	25.38-14.27	37.52-23.85	...	...	100.00-46.25	14.99-2.85

Address: 1 Independent Drive, Jacksonville, FL 32202
Telephone: 904-360-2000
Fax: 904-360-2521

Web Site: www.mpsgroup.com
Officers: Derek E. Dewan - Chmn. Timothy D. Payne - Pres. C.E.O.

Auditors: PricewaterhouseCoopers LLP
Transfer Agents: Computershare Investor Services LLC, Providence, RI

MSC INDUSTRIAL DIRECT CO., INC.

Exchange	Symbol	Price	52Wk Range	Yield	P/E
NYS	MSM	$42.25 (3/31/2008)	57.33-35.13	1.70	15.88

*7 Year Price Score 120.85 *NYSE Composite Index=100   *12 Month Price Score 92.30

Interim Earnings (Per Share)

Qtr.	Nov	Feb	May	Aug
2004-05	0.37	0.39	0.44	0.42
2005-06	0.47	0.49	0.54	0.50
2006-07	0.60	0.61	0.69	0.70
2007-08	0.70	...	...	...

Interim Dividends (Per Share)

Amt	Decl	Ex	Rec	Pay
0.18Q	6/26/2007	7/6/2007	7/10/2007	7/24/2007
0.18Q	10/18/2007	10/30/2007	11/1/2007	11/15/2007
0.18Q	1/9/2008	1/17/2008	1/22/2008	2/5/2008
0.18Q	4/3/2008	4/15/2008	4/17/2008	5/1/2008

Indicated Div: $0.72

Valuation Analysis / **Institutional Holding**

Forecast P/E	15.12	No of Institutions
	(1/10/2007)	213
Market Cap	$2.8 Billion	Shares
Book Value	743.3 Million	44,669,400
Price/Book	3.73	% Held
Price/Sales	1.63	67.89

Business Summary: Machinery Supply Retail (MIC: 12.9 SIC: 5084 NAIC: 423830)

MSC Industrial Direct is a direct marketer of a range of industrial products designed to meet its customers' maintenance, repair and operations (MRO) supplies requirements. Co. provides over 590,000 stock-keeping units (SKUs) through its master catalogs; weekly, monthly and quarterly specialty and promotional catalogs, newspapers and brochures; and the Internet, including its website, MSCDirect.com. Co. serves primarily domestic markets through its distribution network of 95 branch offices and five customer fulfillment centers located near Harrisburg, PA; Elkhart, IN; Atlanta, GA; Reno, NV; and Wednesbury, U.K.

Recent Developments: For the quarter ended Dec 1 2007, net income increased 16.3% to US$46.9 million from US$40.3 million in the year-earlier quarter. Revenues were US$437.6 million, up 8.8% from US$402.0 million the year before. Operating income was US$78.0 million versus US$69.2 million in the prior-year quarter, an increase of 12.7%. Direct operating expenses rose 8.6% to US$235.0 million from US$216.3 million in the comparable period the year before. Indirect operating expenses increased 7.0% to US$124.6 million from US$116.5 million in the equivalent prior-year period.

Prospects: Looking ahead, Co. expects net sales for the second fiscal quarter ending Mar 2008 to be between $430.0 million and $436.0 million, which reflects growth over year ago levels despite the negative sales effect of the timing of the Christmas and New Year's holidays, which it believes would reduce sales by approximately $4.0 million to $5.0 million in the period. Furthermore, Co. expects diluted earnings per share for the fiscal 2008 second quarter to be between $0.68 and $0.70. Going forward, Co. will seek to continue to drive cost reduction throughout its business through cost saving strategies while continuing to provide additional procurement cost savings applications to its customers.

Financial Data

(US$ in Thousands)	3 Mos	09/01/2007	08/26/2006	08/27/2005	08/28/2004	08/30/2003	08/31/2002	09/01/2001
Earnings Per Share	2.66	2.59	2.00	1.61	1.17	0.77	0.51	0.58
Cash Flow Per Share	2.12	2.47	2.00	1.85	1.00	1.26	1.23	1.31
Tang Book Value Per Share	6.11	5.81	4.35	7.02	8.13	6.80	6.17	5.96
Dividends Per Share	0.680	0.640	0.540	1.940	0.290	0.050	...	...
Dividend Payout %	25.57	24.71	27.00	120.50	24.79	6.49	...	...
Income Statement								
Total Revenue	437,554	1,688,186	1,317,519	1,099,915	955,282	844,663	793,976	869,231
EBITDA	84,742	317,184	246,088	191,314	143,776	98,386	75,181	94,213
Depn & Amortn	6,711	...	...	...	...	...	...	...
Income Before Taxes	75,786	279,494	221,770	181,754	133,041	84,413	60,188	73,806
Income Taxes	28,920	105,564	85,381	69,484	51,886	32,321	23,773	33,260
Net Income	46,866	173,930	136,389	112,270	81,155	52,092	36,415	40,546
Average Shares	66,704	67,057	68,319	69,889	69,458	67,912	70,783	69,449
Balance Sheet								
Current Assets	616,321	589,802	527,473	431,996	411,389	432,584	370,892	351,852
Total Assets	1,095,943	1,075,327	1,014,298	651,598	729,387	618,970	562,948	553,908
Current Liabilities	189,066	173,287	152,727	92,802	85,013	78,644	71,632	63,745
Long-Term Obligations	131,910	142,200	192,986	830	997	1,132	1,308	1,517
Total Liabilities	352,689	347,450	375,025	121,182	111,181	108,615	88,269	81,331
Stockholders' Equity	743,254	727,877	639,273	530,416	618,206	510,355	474,679	472,577
Shares Outstanding	65,665	66,079	66,927	66,520	68,303	65,779	66,726	68,618
Statistical Record								
Return on Assets %	16.78	16.38	16.42	16.30	12.10	8.84	6.54	7.03
Return on Equity %	25.67	25.03	23.38	19.60	14.46	10.61	7.71	8.92
EBITDA Margin %	19.37	18.79	18.68	17.39	15.05	11.65	9.47	10.84
Net Margin %	10.71	10.30	10.35	10.21	8.50	6.17	4.59	4.66
Asset Turnover	1.60	1.59	1.59	1.60	1.42	1.43	1.43	1.51
Current Ratio	3.26	3.40	3.45	4.66	4.84	5.50	5.18	5.52
Debt to Equity	0.18	0.20	0.30	N.M.	N.M.	N.M.	N.M.	N.M.
Price Range	57.33-38.54	57.33-37.44	54.72-31.97	38.69-26.87	33.96-20.55	21.78-10.26	23.90-10.51	18.99-12.13
P/E Ratio	21.55-14.49	22.14-14.46	27.36-15.98	24.03-16.69	29.03-17.56	28.29-13.32	46.86-20.61	32.74-20.91
Average Yield %	1.42	1.40	1.26	5.91	1.04	0.30	...	...

Address: 75 Maxess Road, Melville, NY 11747	Web Site: www.mscdirect.com	Auditors: Ernst & Young LLP
Telephone: 516-812-2000	Officers: Mitchell Jacobson - Chmn, David K. Sandler - Pres., C.E.O.	Investor Contact: 516-812-2000
Fax: 516-349-7096		

MURPHY OIL CORP

Exchange	Symbol	Price	52Wk Range	Yield	P/E
NYS	MUR	$82.14 (3/31/2008)	85.85-53.16	0.91	20.48

*7 Year Price Score 137.58 *NYSE Composite Index=100 *12 Month Price Score 123.00

Interim Earnings (Per Share)

Qtr.	Mar	Jun	Sep	Dec
2003	0.47	0.43	0.37	0.32
2004	0.53	1.88	0.64	0.72
2005	0.60	1.85	1.23	0.82
2006	0.60	1.13	1.18	0.46
2007	0.58	1.32	1.04	1.07

Interim Dividends (Per Share)

Amt	Decl	Ex	Rec	Pay
0.188Q	8/1/2007	8/13/2007	8/15/2007	9/3/2007
0.188Q	10/3/2007	11/7/2007	11/12/2007	12/3/2007
0.188Q	2/6/2008	2/14/2008	2/19/2008	3/3/2008
0.188Q	4/2/2008	5/14/2008	5/16/2008	6/2/2008

Indicated Div: $0.75

Valuation Analysis   **Institutional Holding**

Forecast P/E	10.78	No of Institutions
	(1/10/2007)	299
Market Cap	$15.6 Billion	Shares
Book Value	5.1 Billion	150,327,424
Price/Book	3.08	% Held
Price/Sales	0.85	80.12

Business Summary: Oil and Gas (MIC: 14.2 SIC: 2911 NAIC: 324110)

Murphy Oil is an oil and gas exploration and production company with refining and marketing operations in the US and the UK. Co. produces oil and/or natural gas in the US, Canada, the UK, Malaysia and Ecuador and conducts oil and natural gas exploration activities worldwide. Co. has an interest in a Canadian synthetic oil operation, owns two petroleum refineries in the US and one refinery in the UK. Co.'s operations are classified into Exploration and Production, which are divided into six geographic segments, including the US, Canada, the UK, Malaysia, Ecuador and all other countries; and Refining and Marketing, which are divided into geographic segments for North America and UK.

Recent Developments: For the year ended Dec 31 2007, income from continuing operations increased 18.9% to US$766.5 million from US$644.7 million a year earlier. Net income increased 18.9% to US$766.5 million from US$644.7 million in the prior year. Revenues were US$18.44 billion, up 28.9% from US$14.31 billion the year before. Direct operating expenses rose 32.7% to US$14.88 billion from US$11.21 billion in the comparable period the year before. Indirect operating expenses increased 12.9% to US$2.32 billion from US$2.05 billion in the equivalent prior-year period.

Prospects: In Jan 2008, Co. sold its 80.0% interest in Berkana Energy Corp. for about C$103.8 million. Conversely, Co. has acquired about 80,000 acres of mineral rights in Tupper, located in northeastern British Columbia, which it expects to attain initial natural gas production in the fourth quarter 2008. Meanwhile, for 2008, Co. expects its production to average about 135,000 barrels of oil equivalent per day. The projected production increase is based on a full year of oil production along with continued volume growth at Co.'s Kikeh field. Further, Co. expects these improved volumes to offset projected field declines in the Gulf of Mexico, onshore South Louisiana and at Hibernia and Terra Nova.

Financial Data
(US$ in Thousands)

	12/31/2007	12/31/2006	12/31/2005	12/31/2004	12/31/2003	12/31/2002	12/31/2001	12/31/2000
Earnings Per Share	4.01	3.37	4.51	3.75	1.59	0.60	1.81	1.64
Cash Flow Per Share	9.26	5.17	6.65	5.95	3.55	2.91	3.51	4.14
Tang Book Value Per Share	26.43	21.37	18.38	14.16	10.26	8.41	7.98	6.72
Dividends Per Share	0.675	0.525	0.450	0.425	0.400	0.388	0.375	0.362
Dividend Payout %	16.83	15.58	9.98	11.32	25.24	64.05	20.66	22.10
Income Statement								
Total Revenue	18,439,098	14,307,387	11,877,151	8,359,839	5,345,238	3,984,327	4,478,509	4,639,165
EBITDA	1,782,391	1,434,954	1,791,753	1,142,797	774,852	476,331	761,404	692,949
Income Before Taxes	1,237,232	1,028,425	1,372,059	804,936	419,161	151,675	505,908	465,334
Income Taxes	470,703	390,146	534,156	308,541	117,977	54,165	175,005	159,773
Net Income	766,529	638,279	846,452	701,315	294,197	111,508	330,903	296,828
Average Shares	191,140	189,158	187,889	186,887	185,485	184,269	182,363	180,958
Balance Sheet								
Current Assets	2,886,792	2,107,091	1,838,946	1,629,363	1,038,855	854,160	598,661	816,937
Total Assets	10,535,849	7,445,727	6,368,511	5,458,243	4,712,647	3,885,775	3,259,099	3,134,353
Current Liabilities	2,109,262	1,311,105	1,287,008	1,204,991	810,326	717,892	560,057	745,227
Long-Term Obligations	1,516,156	840,275	609,574	613,355	1,090,307	862,808	520,785	524,759
Total Liabilities	5,469,675	3,393,051	2,907,521	2,809,087	2,761,764	2,292,222	1,760,936	1,874,793
Stockholders' Equity	5,066,174	4,052,676	3,460,990	2,649,156	1,950,883	1,593,553	1,498,163	1,259,560
Shares Outstanding	189,714	187,572	185,946	184,070	183,741	183,378	181,324	180,182
Statistical Record								
Return on Assets %	8.53	9.24	14.31	13.75	6.84	3.12	10.35	10.61
Return on Equity %	16.81	16.99	27.71	30.41	16.60	7.21	24.00	25.55
EBITDA Margin %	9.67	10.03	15.09	13.67	14.50	11.96	17.00	14.94
Net Margin %	4.16	4.46	7.13	8.39	5.50	2.80	7.39	6.40
Asset Turnover	2.05	2.07	2.01	1.64	1.24	1.12	1.40	1.66
Current Ratio	1.37	1.61	1.43	1.35	1.28	1.19	1.07	1.10
Debt to Equity	0.30	0.21	0.18	0.23	0.56	0.54	0.35	0.42
Price Range	85.38-45.93	59.15-45.12	55.98-38.05	43.38-29.04	34.13-19.42	24.83-16.24	21.90-13.91	17.06-12.19
P/E Ratio	21.29-11.45	17.55-13.39	12.41-8.44	11.57-7.74	21.47-12.21	41.39-27.06	12.10-7.68	10.40-7.43
Average Yield %	1.09	1.03	0.92	1.18	1.56	1.82	2.04	2.43

Address: 200 Peach Street, P.O. Box 7000, El Dorado, AR 71731-7000
Telephone: 870-862-6411
Fax: 870-864-3673

Web Site: www.murphyoilcorp.com
Officers: William C. Nolan Jr. - Chmn. Claiborne P. Deming - Pres., C.E.O.

Auditors: KPMG LLP
Investor Contact: 870-864-6496
Transfer Agents: Computershare Investor Services, L.L.C., Chicago, IL

MYERS INDUSTRIES INC.

Exchange	Symbol	Price	52Wk Range	Yield	P/E	Div Acheiver
NYS	MYE	$13.13 (3/31/2008)	22.55-10.18	1.83	8.47	31 Years

*7 Year Price Score 114.88 *NYSE Composite Index=100   *12 Month Price Score 75.25

Interim Earnings (Per Share)

Qtr.	Mar	Jun	Sep	Dec
2003	0.22	0.10	0.05	0.13
2004	0.26	0.18	0.11	0.20
2005	0.22	0.15	0.14	0.25
2006	0.31	(2.85)	0.17	0.40
2007	0.93	0.07	0.04	0.51

Interim Dividends (Per Share)

Amt	Decl	Ex	Rec	Pay
0.052Q	6/28/2007	6/29/2007	7/3/2007	7/20/2007
0.06Q	12/10/2007	12/18/2007	12/20/2007	1/2/2008
0.28Q	12/10/2007	12/18/2007	12/20/2007	1/2/2008
0.06Q	2/27/2008	3/6/2008	3/10/2008	4/4/2008

Indicated Div: $0.24 (Div. Reinv. Plan)

Valuation Analysis

		Institutional Holding	
Forecast P/E	10.96	No of Institutions	
	(1/10/2007)	127	
Market Cap	$461.0 Million	Shares	23,571,244
Book Value	317.3 Million	% Held	
Price/Book	1.46		66.96
Price/Sales	0.50		

TRADING VOLUME (thousand shares)

Business Summary: Plastics (MIC: 11.7 SIC: 3089 NAIC: 326199)

Myers Industries manufactures polymer products for industrial, agricultural, automotive, commercial, and consumer markets. Principal products include reusable plastic containers, plastic horticultural pots, trays, and flower planters. Other principal product lines include plastic storage and organization containers, plastic and rubber original equipment manufacturer parts, rubber tire repair products, and custom plastic and rubber products. Co. is also a wholesale distributor of tools, equipment, and supplies for the tire, wheel, and undervehicle service industry. Co.'s distribution products range from tire balancers and alignment systems to valve caps and other consumable service supplies.

Recent Developments: For the year ended Dec 31 2007, income from continuing operations increased 28.7% to US$36.9 million from US$28.7 million a year earlier. Net income amounted to US$54.7 million versus a net loss of US$69.0 million in the prior year. Revenues were US$918.8 million, up 17.8% from US$780.0 million the year before. Operating income was US$45.8 million versus US$60.9 million in the prior year, a decrease of 24.8%. Direct operating expenses rose 19.3% to US$683.1 million from US$572.4 million in the comparable period the year before. Indirect operating expenses increased 29.5% to US$189.9 million from US$146.6 million in the equivalent prior-year period.

Prospects: Co.'s net sales are benefiting from its Jan 2007 acquisition of ITML Horticultural Products, its Mar 2007 acquisition of material handling products from Schoeller Arca Systems, Inc. North America, and its focus on pricing, product and sales channel development to lessen the effect of soft market conditions. For 2008, Co. remains cautiously optimistic, despite current economic weakness in the U.S. Thus, in an effort to drive long-term, profitable growth, Co. will continue to invest in strategic growth initiatives, which include strategic acquisitions, exploring divestiture of non-strategic businesses, recovering raw material costs, controlling expenses, and improving productivity.

Financial Data
(US$ in Thousands)

	12/31/2007	12/31/2006	12/31/2005	12/31/2004	12/31/2003	12/31/2002	12/31/2001	12/31/2000
Earnings Per Share	1.55	(1.97)	0.76	0.76	0.49	0.73	0.47	0.73
Cash Flow Per Share	2.76	2.33	1.94	1.37	1.54	1.99	2.35	2.05
Tang Book Value Per Share	3.34	3.21	1.83	1.73	2.05	1.48	0.82	0.51
Dividends Per Share	0.498	0.205	0.200	0.191	0.182	0.178	0.167	0.151
Dividend Payout %	32.10	...	26.32	25.12	37.04	24.50	35.80	20.64
Income Statement								
Total Revenue	918,793	779,984	903,679	803,070	661,092	607,991	607,950	652,660
EBITDA	110,278	89,135	91,988	91,226	71,276	87,884	89,844	106,097
Income Before Taxes	57,051	45,074	40,407	38,729	24,647	40,361	27,240	40,910
Income Taxes	20,103	16,364	13,851	13,019	8,321	16,401	12,049	16,909
Net Income	54,736	(69,024)	26,556	25,710	16,326	23,960	15,191	24,001
Average Shares	35,249	35,044	34,724	33,846	33,138	32,969	32,727	32,811
Balance Sheet								
Current Assets	277,809	307,523	284,328	284,072	207,933	201,140	196,619	219,307
Total Assets	697,552	661,983	760,007	785,603	621,627	602,482	582,166	624,797
Current Liabilities	158,475	134,727	141,242	136,252	94,175	117,369	104,899	115,583
Long-Term Obligations	167,254	198,275	249,524	275,252	211,003	212,223	247,145	284,273
Total Liabilities	380,282	381,325	420,606	439,599	327,102	346,793	364,640	410,894
Stockholders' Equity	317,270	280,659	339,401	346,004	294,524	255,690	217,526	213,903
Shares Outstanding	35,180	35,067	34,806	34,645	33,201	33,078	32,790	32,654
Statistical Record								
Return on Assets %	8.05	N.M.	3.44	3.64	2.67	4.05	2.52	3.91
Return on Equity %	18.31	N.M.	7.75	8.01	5.93	10.13	7.04	11.35
EBITDA Margin %	12.00	11.43	10.18	11.36	10.78	14.45	14.78	16.26
Net Margin %	5.96	N.M.	2.94	3.20	2.47	3.94	2.50	3.68
Asset Turnover	1.35	1.10	1.17	1.14	1.08	1.03	1.01	1.06
Current Ratio	1.75	2.28	2.01	2.08	2.21	1.71	1.87	1.90
Debt to Equity	0.53	0.71	0.74	0.80	0.72	0.83	1.14	1.33
Price Range	22.55-13.57	18.62-14.24	14.70-9.36	13.50-10.06	12.05-8.00	13.16-8.51	10.41-7.60	9.59-6.45
P/E Ratio	14.55-8.75	...	19.34-12.32	17.76-13.24	24.60-16.33	18.03-11.66	22.16-16.18	13.13-8.83
Average Yield %	2.52	1.26	1.59	1.67	1.87	1.66	1.81	1.87

Address: 1293 South Main Street, Akron, OH 44301	Web Site: www.myersind.com	Auditors: KPMG LLP
Telephone: 330-253-5592	Officers: Stephen E. Myers - Chmn. Milton I. Wiskind - Vice-Chmn., Sec.	Investor Contact: 330-253-5592
Fax: 330-761-6156		Transfer Agents: National City Bank, Cleveland, Ohio

MYLAN INC

Exchange	Symbol	Price	52Wk Range	Yield	P/E
NYS	MYL	$11.60 (3/31/2008)	22.64-10.33	N/A	N/A

*7 Year Price Score 70.65 *NYSE Composite Index=100 *12 Month Price Score 82.39

Interim Earnings (Per Share)

Qtr.	Jun	Sep	Dec	Mar
2004-05	0.30	0.18	0.13	0.14
2005-06	0.16	0.16	0.22	0.26
2006-07	0.35	0.36	0.63	(5.83)

Interim Dividends (Per Share)

Amt	Decl	Ex	Rec	Pay
0.06Q	9/19/2006	9/27/2006	9/29/2006	10/16/2006
0.06Q	12/19/2006	12/27/2006	12/29/2006	1/16/2007
0.06Q	3/15/2007	3/28/2007	3/30/2007	4/16/2007
0.06Q	6/18/2007	6/27/2007	6/29/2007	7/16/2007

Valuation Analysis | **Institutional Holding**

Forecast P/E	N/A	No of Institutions 327
Market Cap	$2.9 Billion	Shares
Book Value	1.9 Billion	144,147,360
Price/Book	1.53	% Held
Price/Sales	1.16	58.89

Business Summary: Pharmaceuticals (MIC: 9.1 SIC: 2834 NAIC: 325412)

Mylan is engaged in the development, licensing, manufacture, marketing and distribution of generic, brand and branded generic pharmaceutical products for resale by others and active pharmaceutical ingredients. As of Dec 31 2007, Co. operated through two reportable segments: the Mylan Segment, which the principal markets for its products are proprietary and ethical pharmaceutical wholesalers and distributors, drug store chains, drug manufacturers, institutions, and public and governmental agencies within the U.S.; and the Matrix Segment, which the principal markets are regulated markets such as the U.S. and the European Union.

Recent Developments: For the nine months ended Dec 31 2007, net loss available to common shareholders amounted to $1.15 billion. Total revenues were $2.18 billion. Gross profit amounted to $874.4 million, or 40.1% of total revenues. Total operating expenses were $1.86 billion, which included acquired in-process research and development expenses of $1.27 billion and a net litigation settlement gain of $2.0 million.

Prospects: On Feb 27 2008, Co. has reached a definitive agreement with Forest Laboratories Holdings, Ltd. whereby it will sell its rights of Nebivolol, a U.S. Food and Drug Administration (FDA) approved product for the treatment of hypertension which is marketed by Forest under the brand name Bystolic™. Consequently, Co. will receive a one-time cash payment of $370.0 million and will retain royalties for the product through 2010. Separately, on Feb 1 2008, Co. announced that its Mylan Pharmaceuticals Inc. subsidiary has received final approval from the FDA for its Abbreviated New Drug Application for Granisetron Hydrochloride Tablets. Accordingly, this product is expected to be shipped immediately.

Financial Data

(US$ in Thousands)	12/31/2007	03/31/2007	03/31/2006	03/31/2005	03/31/2004	03/31/2003	03/31/2002	03/31/2001
Earnings Per Share	(4.49)	0.99	0.79	0.74	1.21	0.96	0.91	0.13
Cash Flow Per Share	0.37	1.81	1.82	0.76	0.84	1.12	1.23	0.24
Tang Book Value Per Share	N.M.	2.75	2.76	6.03	5.30	4.39	3.97	2.97
Dividends Per Share	0.120	0.240	0.240	0.120	0.104	0.080	0.071	0.071
Dividend Payout %	...	24.24	30.38	16.22	8.63	8.33	7.84	55.17
Income Statement								
Total Revenue	2,178,761	1,611,819	1,257,164	1,253,374	1,374,617	1,269,192	1,104,050	846,696
EBITDA	(743,854)	539,300	352,717	357,347	556,931	467,093	454,434	100,405
Income Before Taxes	(1,081,064)	425,512	274,605	312,247	512,608	426,513	408,323	58,013
Income Taxes	60,073	208,017	90,063	108,655	177,999	154,160	148,072	20,885
Net Income	(1,138,025)	217,284	184,542	203,592	334,609	272,353	260,251	37,128
Average Shares	257,150	219,120	234,209	273,621	276,318	282,330	286,578	285,185
Balance Sheet								
Current Assets	3,059,301	2,412,044	1,191,900	1,528,452	1,317,841	1,228,211	1,062,082	879,224
Total Assets	11,353,176	4,253,867	1,870,526	2,135,673	1,875,290	1,745,223	1,616,710	1,465,973
Current Liabilities	2,002,351	700,535	265,250	245,507	173,768	265,771	175,147	291,187
Long-Term Obligations	4,706,716	1,654,932	685,188	...	...	...	...	...
Total Liabilities	7,915,425	2,561,800	1,082,875	289,737	215,502	298,891	214,471	333,437
Stockholders' Equity	3,403,426	1,648,860	787,651	1,845,936	1,659,788	1,446,332	1,402,239	1,132,536
Shares Outstanding	304,375	248,412	210,178	269,305	268,423	271,760	284,371	281,155
Statistical Record								
Return on Assets %	N.M.	7.10	9.21	10.15	18.43	16.20	16.88	2.65
Return on Equity %	N.M.	17.84	14.01	11.61	21.49	19.12	20.53	3.18
EBITDA Margin %	N.M.	33.46	28.06	28.51	40.52	36.80	41.16	11.86
Net Margin %	N.M.	13.48	14.68	16.24	24.34	21.46	23.57	4.39
Asset Turnover	0.19	0.53	0.63	0.62	0.76	0.76	0.72	0.60
Current Ratio	1.53	3.44	4.49	6.23	7.58	4.62	6.06	3.02
Debt to Equity	1.38	1.00	0.87	...	...	...	...	...
Price Range	22.64-13.25	23.55-19.06	24.92-15.50	24.59-14.69	28.16-17.45	19.36-11.18	16.85-10.68	14.33-7.56
P/E Ratio	...	23.79-19.25	31.54-19.62	33.23-19.85	23.27-14.42	20.17-11.64	18.52-11.73	110.26-58.12
Average Yield %	0.70	1.15	1.23	0.64	0.45	0.54	0.50	0.65

Address: 1500 Corporate Drive, Suite 400, Canonsburg, PA 15317 Telephone: 724-514-1800	Web Site: www.mylan.com Officers: Milan Puskar - Chmn. Robert J. Coury - Vice-Chmn., C.E.O.	Auditors: Deloitte & Touche LLP Transfer Agents: American Stock Transfer & Trust Company, New York, NY

NABORS INDUSTRIES LTD.

Exchange	Symbol	Price	52Wk Range	Yield	P/E
NYS	NBR	$33.77 (3/31/2008)	36.08-25.12	N/A	10.02

*7 Year Price Score 96.44   *NYSE Composite Index=100   *12 Month Price Score 110.18

Interim Earnings (Per Share)

Qtr.	Mar	Jun	Sep	Dec
2003	0.16	0.10	0.17	0.21
2004	0.23	0.15	0.24	0.34
2005	0.40	0.41	0.56	0.64
2006	0.79	0.77	1.02	0.83
2007	0.92	0.79	0.76	0.90

Interim Dividends (Per Share)

No Dividends Paid

Valuation Analysis   Institutional Holding

Forecast P/E	N/A	No of Institutions
		N/A
Market Cap	$9.4 Billion	Shares
Book Value	4.5 Billion	N/A
Price/Book	2.09	% Held
Price/Sales	1.91	N/A

Business Summary: Oil and Gas (MIC: 14.2 SIC: 1381 NAIC: 213111)

Nabors Industries is a land drilling contractor. Co. conducts oil, gas and geothermal land drilling operations in the U.S. Lower 48 states, Alaska, Canada, South and Central America, the Middle East, the Far East and Africa. Co. is also a land well-servicing and workover contractors in the U.S. and Canada and is a provider of offshore platform workover and drilling rigs in the U.S. and international markets. As at Dec 31 2007, Co.'s marketed rigs consisted of approximately 535 land drilling rigs, 564 domestic and 173 international land workover and well-servicing rigs, 35 offshore platform rigs, 12 jack-up units, four barge rigs and a large component of trucks and fluid hauling vehicles.

Recent Developments: For the year ended Dec 31 2007, income from continuing operations decreased 9.8% to US$895.7 million from US$993.0 million a year earlier. Net income decreased 8.8% to US$930.7 million from US$1.02 billion in the prior year. Revenues were US$4.94 billion, up 2.3% from US$4.83 billion the year before. Direct operating expenses rose 10.1% to US$2.76 billion from US$2.51 billion in the comparable period the year before. Indirect operating expenses increased 16.9% to US$1.04 billion from US$890.5 million in the equivalent prior-year period.

Prospects: Co. expects a large number of expiring term contracts for older rigs to rollover in 2008 at lower margins in its U.S. Lower 48 Land Drilling operations, as well as projects a decline in both its North American natural gas driven operations and Canadian operations. However, Co. expects its International operations to grow due to the deployment of additional rigs under long-term contracts and renewal of existing contracts at higher market rates. Also, Co. is encouraged by the rising third-party sales in its manufacturing and technology businesses, ongoing market penetration by its directional drilling operation, and a healthy outlook in its Alaskan construction and logistics joint ventures.

Financial Data

(US$ in Thousands)	12/31/2007	12/31/2006	12/31/2005	12/31/2004	12/31/2003	12/31/2002	12/31/2001	12/31/2000
Earnings Per Share	3.37	3.40	2.00	0.96	0.63	0.41	1.12	0.45
Income Statement								
Total Revenue	4,940,681	4,942,714	3,551,009	2,448,152	1,922,846	1,519,012	2,225,337	1,409,316
EBITDA	1,720,627	1,971,592	1,243,529	662,546	440,887	372,101	770,169	385,745
Income Before Taxes	1,135,331	1,470,919	873,950	335,838	174,623	140,774	542,282	226,707
Income Taxes	239,664	450,183	225,255	33,381	(17,605)	19,285	194,490	91,233
Net Income	930,691	1,020,736	648,695	302,457	192,228	121,489	357,450	137,356
Average Shares	286,606	299,827	324,378	328,060	313,794	299,994	337,580	304,834
Balance Sheet								
Current Assets	2,205,112	2,504,856	2,617,308	1,580,974	1,515,647	1,369,908	1,030,946	1,018,318
Total Assets	10,103,382	9,142,303	7,230,407	5,862,609	5,602,692	5,063,872	4,151,915	3,136,868
Current Liabilities	1,494,132	854,360	1,352,456	1,199,316	598,373	751,454	330,130	279,179
Long-Term Obligations	3,306,433	4,004,074	1,251,751	1,201,686	1,985,553	1,614,656	1,567,616	854,777
Total Liabilities	5,589,261	5,605,650	3,472,267	2,933,216	3,112,417	2,905,417	2,294,049	1,330,400
Stockholders' Equity	4,514,121	3,536,653	3,758,140	2,929,393	2,490,275	2,158,455	1,857,866	1,806,468
Shares Outstanding	279,336	276,993	315,394	299,722	293,312	289,930	281,778	293,132
Statistical Record								
Price Range	36.08-26.42	41.16-27.69	39.44-23.50	26.82-20.15	22.75-16.25	24.35-13.26	31.25-9.33	29.79-14.41
P/E Ratio	10.71-7.84	12.10-8.14	19.72-11.75	27.94-20.99	36.11-25.79	59.39-32.34	27.91-8.33	66.20-32.01

Address: Mintflower Place, 8 Par-La-Ville Road, Hamilton, HM08 Telephone: 441-292-1510 Fax: 441-292-1334	Web Site: www.nabors.com Officers: Eugene M. Isenberg - Chmn., C.E.O. Anthony G. Petrello - Dep. Chmn., Pres., C.O.O.	Auditors: PricewaterhouseCoopers LLP Investor Contact: 713-874-0035 Transfer Agents: Computershare Trust Company, N.A.

NACCO INDUSTRIES INC.

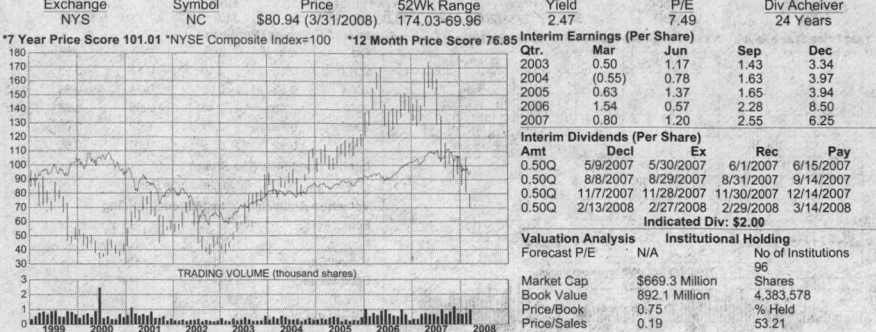

Exchange	Symbol	Price	52Wk Range	Yield	P/E	Div Achiever
NYS	NC	$80.94 (3/31/2008)	174.03-69.96	2.47	7.49	24 Years

*7 Year Price Score 101.01 *NYSE Composite Index=100 *12 Month Price Score 76.85

Interim Earnings (Per Share)

Qtr.	Mar	Jun	Sep	Dec
2003	0.50	1.17	1.43	3.34
2004	(0.55)	0.78	1.63	3.97
2005	0.63	1.37	1.65	3.94
2006	1.54	0.57	2.28	8.50
2007	0.80	1.20	2.55	6.25

Interim Dividends (Per Share)

Amt	Decl	Ex	Rec	Pay
0.50Q	5/9/2007	5/30/2007	6/1/2007	6/15/2007
0.50Q	8/8/2007	8/29/2007	8/31/2007	9/14/2007
0.50Q	11/7/2007	11/28/2007	11/30/2007	12/14/2007
0.50Q	2/13/2008	2/27/2008	2/29/2008	3/14/2008
		Indicated Div: $2.00		

Valuation Analysis   **Institutional Holding**

Forecast P/E	N/A	No of Institutions
		96
Market Cap	$669.3 Million	Shares
Book Value	892.1 Million	4,383,578
Price/Book	0.75	% Held
Price/Sales	0.19	53.21

TRADING VOLUME (thousand shares)

Business Summary: Industrial Machinery and Equipment (MIC: 11.5 SIC: 3537 NAIC: 333924)

NACCO Industries is a holding company with three principal businesses. Co.'s NACCO Materials Handling Group designs, engineers, manufactures, sells, services and leases a line of lift trucks and replacement parts marketed worldwide under the Hyster™ and Yale™ brand names. Co.'s NACCO Housewares Group consists of Hamilton Beach Brands, Inc., a designer, marketer and distributor of small electric household appliances, as well as commercial products for restaurants, bars and hotels; and The Kitchen Collection, Inc., a retailer of kitchenware and gourmet foods. Co.'s North American Coal Corporation subsidiary mines and markets lignite coal primarily as fuel for power generation.

Recent Developments: For the year ended Dec 31 2007, net income decreased 15.9% to US$89.3 million from US$106.2 million in the prior year. Revenues were US$3.60 billion, up 7.6% from US$3.35 billion the year before. Operating income was US$137.4 million versus US$172.6 million in the prior year, a decrease of 20.4%. Direct operating expenses rose 7.8% to US$3.00 billion from US$2.79 billion in the comparable period the year before. Indirect operating expenses increased 18.6% to US$461.9 million from US$389.6 million in the equivalent prior-year period.

Prospects: The economic environment appears uncertain for both the consumer markets in which Co.'s Hamilton Beach and Kitchen Collection subsidiaries participate, and the capital goods markets in the U.S. in which its NACCO Materials Handling Group (NMHG) participates. However, while NMHG expects a year-over-year decrease in the Americas lift truck markets in 2008, it expects continued growth in Europe and Asia-Pacific lift truck markets. As a result, Co. expects modest increases in unit booking and shipment levels for 2008 compared with 2007. Additionally, Hamilton Beach has new product introductions in the pipeline for 2008 and 2009, all of which are expected to favorably affect revenues.

Financial Data

(US$ in Thousands)	12/31/2007	12/31/2006	12/31/2005	12/31/2004	12/31/2003	12/31/2002	12/31/2001	12/31/2000
Earnings Per Share	10.80	12.89	7.60	5.83	6.44	5.17	(4.40)	8.29
Cash Flow Per Share	9.88	21.07	9.15	15.33	15.03	18.20	16.61	16.24
Tang Book Value Per Share	45.86	34.12	23.49	21.01	14.67	5.73	1.98	9.44
Dividends Per Share	1.980	1.905	1.847	1.675	1.260	0.970	0.930	0.890
Dividend Payout %	18.33	14.78	24.31	28.73	19.57	18.76	...	10.74
Income Statement								
Total Revenue	3,602,700	3,349,000	3,157,400	2,782,600	2,472,600	2,285,000	2,637,900	2,871,300
EBITDA	203,800	227,200	185,300	167,300	184,400	182,800	128,000	213,100
Income Before Taxes	112,300	120,500	70,800	52,300	65,000	59,700	(45,400)	60,000
Income Taxes	23,100	27,800	13,100	5,300	15,800	11,300	(9,900)	22,300
Net Income	89,300	106,200	62,500	47,900	52,800	42,400	(36,000)	67,700
Average Shares	8,272	8,242	8,226	8,214	8,204	8,198	8,190	8,167
Balance Sheet								
Current Assets	1,434,800	1,153,800	1,073,700	996,800	812,900	739,500	770,000	815,700
Total Assets	2,428,200	2,156,300	2,094,000	2,038,600	1,839,800	1,780,800	2,161,900	2,193,900
Current Liabilities	856,500	751,000	704,700	672,000	589,800	545,500	874,300	650,200
Long-Term Obligations	439,500	359,900	406,200	407,400	363,200	416,100	519,400	732,700
Total Liabilities	1,536,100	1,363,200	1,390,700	1,350,600	1,202,800	1,221,400	1,632,600	1,587,500
Stockholders' Equity	892,100	793,100	703,300	688,000	637,000	559,400	529,300	606,400
Shares Outstanding	8,268	8,237	8,226	8,214	8,206	8,201	8,195	8,171
Statistical Record								
Return on Assets %	3.90	5.00	3.02	2.46	2.92	2.15	N.M.	3.21
Return on Equity %	10.60	14.19	8.98	7.21	8.83	7.79	N.M.	11.55
EBITDA Margin %	5.66	6.78	5.87	6.01	7.46	8.00	4.85	7.42
Net Margin %	2.48	3.17	1.98	1.72	2.14	1.86	N.M.	2.36
Asset Turnover	1.57	1.58	1.53	1.43	1.37	1.16	1.21	1.36
Current Ratio	1.68	1.54	1.52	1.48	1.38	1.36	0.88	1.25
Debt to Equity	0.49	0.45	0.58	0.59	0.57	0.74	0.98	1.21
Price Range	174.03-90.57	170.70-119.85	122.44-94.95	111.70-77.15	93.77-37.99	75.25-36.65	81.47-42.63	55.56-33.75
P/E Ratio	16.11-8.39	13.24-9.30	16.11-12.49	19.16-13.23	14.56-5.90	14.56-7.09	...	6.70-4.07
Average Yield %	1.51	1.35	1.70	1.86	2.01	1.79	1.47	2.09

Address: 5875 Landerbrook Drive, Mayfield Heights, OH 44124-4017 Telephone: 440-449-9600 Fax: 440-449-9607	Web Site: www.naccoind.com Officers: Alfred M. Rankin Jr. - Chmn., Pres., C.E.O. J. C. Butler Jr. - V.P., Corp. Devel., Treas.	Auditors: ERNST & YOUNG LLP Transfer Agents: National City Bank, Cleveland, OH

NALCO HOLDING CO

Exchange	Symbol	Price	52Wk Range	Yield	P/E
NYS	NLC	$21.15 (3/31/2008)	30.62-18.95	0.66	24.03

*7 Year Price Score N/A   *NYSE Composite Index=100   *12 Month Price Score 92.06

TRADING VOLUME (thousand shares)

Interim Earnings (Per Share)

Qtr.	Mar	Jun	Sep	Dec
2004	(1.40)	0.03	0.00	0.00
2005	0.08	(0.04)	0.12	0.18
2006	0.06	0.15	0.21	0.25
2007	0.13	0.28	0.25	0.22

Interim Dividends (Per Share)

Amt	Decl	Ex	Rec	Pay
0.035Q	5/3/2007	6/13/2007	6/15/2007	7/2/2007
0.035Q	9/7/2007	9/14/2007	9/18/2007	10/2/2007
0.035Q	11/2/2007	12/10/2007	12/12/2007	1/2/2008
0.035Q	2/15/2008	3/17/2008	3/19/2008	4/2/2008

Indicated Div: $0.14

Valuation Analysis

		Institutional Holding	
Forecast P/E	N/A	No of Institutions	157
Market Cap	$3.0 Billion	Shares	
Book Value	1.1 Billion		112,358,864
Price/Book	2.64	% Held	
Price/Sales	0.76		78.37

Business Summary: Chemicals (MIC: 11.1 SIC: 2819 NAIC: 325998)

Nalco Holding is engaged in the worldwide manufacture and sale of specialized service chemical programs. This includes production and service related to the sale and application of chemicals and technology used in water treatment, pollution control, energy conservation, oil production and refining, steelmaking, papermaking, mining, and other industrial processes. Co. serves a broad range of end markets, including aerospace, paper, chemical, pharmaceutical, petroleum, steel, power, food and beverage, medium and light manufacturing, marine, metalworking and institutions such as hospitals, universities and hotels.

Recent Developments: For the year ended Dec 31 2007, net income increased 30.4% to US$129.0 million from US$98.9 million in the prior year. Revenues were US$3.91 billion, up 8.6% from US$3.60 billion the year before. Operating income was US$476.2 million versus US$433.0 million in the prior year, an increase of 10.0%. Direct operating expenses rose 8.1% to US$2.15 billion from US$1.99 billion in the comparable period the year before. Indirect operating expenses increased 8.9% to US$1.28 billion from US$1.18 billion in the equivalent prior-year period.

Prospects: Among Co.'s key areas of focus in 2008 are improving growth and profitability in its European business; additional price increases commensurate with any further raw material and freight cost increases; cost savings of at least $75.0 million. Separately, on Mar 14 2008, Co. and Evonik's Goldschmidt Industrial Specialties announced that they have expanded their agreement for Co. to be the exclusive distributor of Evonik's tissue additives in Central and South America. Tissue is a low-weight, thin paper often used to make facial and bathroom tissue. Evonik additives include softeners and debonders that help achieve the appropriate softness levels for the end use.

Financial Data

(US$ in Thousands)	12/31/2007	12/31/2006	12/31/2005	12/31/2004	12/31/2003
Earnings Per Share	0.88	0.67	0.33	(1.42)	...
Cash Flow Per Share	2.26	1.99	1.41	2.42	...
Dividends Per Share	0.140	...	...	...	...
Dividend Payout %	15.91	...	...	...	...
Income Statement					
Total Revenue	3,912,500	3,602,600	3,312,400	3,033,300	460,100
EBITDA	665,800	629,700	561,300	349,000	54,400
Income Before Taxes	206,500	165,700	96,800	(102,200)	(32,500)
Income Taxes	69,300	58,900	43,300	30,800	(8,300)
Net Income	129,000	98,900	47,800	(138,800)	(24,100)
Average Shares	146,700	146,700	146,600	97,700	...
Balance Sheet					
Current Assets	1,388,500	1,167,400	1,049,400	1,031,100	975,600
Total Assets	5,978,600	5,656,500	5,552,400	5,933,900	6,163,800
Current Liabilities	769,300	719,400	543,200	591,300	528,800
Long-Term Obligations	3,193,700	3,038,600	3,244,200	3,424,800	3,262,800
Total Liabilities	4,860,800	4,765,600	4,846,900	5,223,500	5,094,800
Stockholders' Equity	1,117,800	890,900	705,500	710,400	1,069,000
Shares Outstanding	139,788	143,055	142,737	141,663	...
Statistical Record					
Return on Assets %	2.22	1.76	0.83	N.M.	...
Return on Equity %	12.84	12.39	6.75	N.M.	...
EBITDA Margin %	17.02	17.48	16.95	11.51	11.82
Net Margin %	3.30	2.75	1.44	N.M.	N.M.
Asset Turnover	0.67	0.64	0.58	0.50	...
Current Ratio	1.80	1.62	1.93	1.74	1.84
Debt to Equity	2.86	3.41	4.60	4.82	3.05
Price Range	30.62-20.30	20.93-15.90	21.80-15.05	20.01-16.20	...
P/E Ratio	34.80-23.07	31.24-23.73	66.06-45.61	...	...
Average Yield %	0.56	...	...	...	...

Address: 1601 West Diehl Road, Naperville, IL 60563-1198 **Telephone:** 630-305-1000	**Web Site:** www.nalco.com **Officers:** William H. Joyce - Chmn., C.E.O. William J. Roe - Exec. V.P., C.O.O., Pres., Industrial & Institutional Serv. dvsn.	**Auditors:** Ernst & Young LLP **Investor Contact:** 630-305-1025 **Transfer Agents:** EquiServe Trust Company, N.A.

NATIONAL CITY CORP

Exchange	Symbol	Price	52Wk Range	Yield	P/E	Div Acheiver
NYS	NCC	$9.95 (3/31/2008)	37.90-7.52	8.44	19.51	15 Years

*7 Year Price Score 62.96   *NYSE Composite Index=100   *12 Month Price Score 61.15

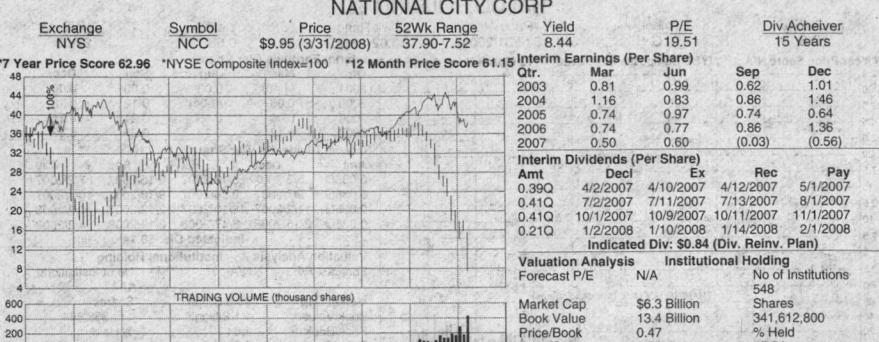

Interim Earnings (Per Share)

Qtr.	Mar	Jun	Sep	Dec
2003	0.81	0.99	0.62	1.01
2004	1.16	0.83	0.86	1.46
2005	0.74	0.97	0.74	0.64
2006	0.74	0.77	0.86	1.36
2007	0.50	0.60	(0.03)	(0.56)

Interim Dividends (Per Share)

Amt	Decl	Ex	Rec	Pay
0.39Q	4/2/2007	4/10/2007	4/12/2007	5/1/2007
0.41Q	7/2/2007	7/11/2007	7/13/2007	8/1/2007
0.41Q	10/1/2007	10/9/2007	10/11/2007	11/1/2007
0.21Q	1/2/2008	1/10/2008	1/14/2008	2/1/2008

Indicated Div: $0.84 (Div. Reinv. Plan)

Valuation Analysis   **Institutional Holding**

Forecast P/E	N/A	No of Institutions
		548
		Shares
Market Cap	$6.3 Billion	341,612,800
Book Value	13.4 Billion	% Held
Price/Book	0.47	55.54
Price/Sales	0.53	

Business Summary: Commercial Banking (MIC: 8.1 SIC: 6021 NAIC: 522110)

National City is a financial holding company. Co. operates through an extensive banking network in Ohio, Florida, Illinois, Indiana, Kentucky, Michigan, Missouri, Pennsylvania and Wisconsin, and also conducts selected lending and other financial services businesses on a nationwide basis. Co.'s primary businesses include commercial and retail banking, mortgage financing and servicing, consumer finance, and asset management. Co.'s businesses are organized by product and service offerings as well as the distribution channels. As of Dec 31 2007, Co. operated its business mainly through more than 1,400 branch banking offices located in nine-states and had total assets of $150.37 billion.

Recent Developments: For the year ended Dec 31 2007, net income decreased 86.3% to US$314.0 million from US$2.30 billion in the prior year. Net interest income decreased 4.5% to US$4.40 billion from US$4.60 billion in the prior year. Provision for loan losses was US$1.33 billion versus US$488.2 million in the prior year, an increase of 171.6%. Non-interest income fell 35.2% to US$2.61 billion from US$4.02 billion, while non-interest expense advanced 12.6% to US$5.31 billion.

Prospects: For 2008, Co. expects continuing weakness in the housing markets, reflecting higher nonperforming assets in loans secured by residential real estate. In addition, Co. expects its broker-sourced home equity portfolio to decline, given the stoppage of new production in late 2007. Co. also foresees production volume in 2008 to decline, due to the tightening of underwriting standards for residential construction loans in late 2006. Nevertheless, Co. believes that the restructuring actions to reduce costs and its efforts to transfer non-salable loans to its loan portfolio, and scaled back origination of certain products, should yield better performance in its mortgage business going forward.

Financial Data
(US$ in Thousands)

	12/31/2007	12/31/2006	12/31/2005	12/31/2004	12/31/2003	12/31/2002	12/31/2001	12/31/2000
Earnings Per Share	0.51	3.72	3.09	4.31	3.43	2.59	2.27	2.13
Cash Flow Per Share	(1.22)	10.17	10.20	7.78	20.92	(10.25)	(19.67)	1.94
Tang Book Value Per Share	8.05	13.42	11.41	12.03	11.33	10.70	12.15	11.06
Dividends Per Share	1.600	1.520	1.440	1.340	1.250	1.200	1.160	1.140
Dividend Payout %	313.73	40.86	46.60	31.09	36.44	46.33	51.10	53.52
Income Statement								
Interest Income	9,185,095	8,933,762	7,731,819	6,096,907	5,997,822	5,915,920	6,414,752	6,566,583
Interest Expense	4,789,362	4,330,159	3,036,071	1,593,335	1,629,816	1,910,541	2,975,903	3,608,221
Net Interest Income	4,395,733	4,603,603	4,695,748	4,503,572	4,368,006	4,005,379	3,438,849	2,958,362
Provision for Losses	1,325,903	482,593	283,594	323,272	638,418	681,918	605,295	286,795
Non-Interest Income	2,606,161	4,018,965	3,304,319	4,463,022	3,596,001	2,811,999	2,677,823	2,484,234
Non-Interest Expense	5,305,314	4,717,339	4,755,310	4,565,382	4,088,123	3,729,634	3,344,876	3,183,909
Income Before Taxes	370,677	3,422,636	2,961,163	4,077,940	3,237,466	2,405,826	2,166,501	1,971,892
Income Taxes	56,702	1,122,800	975,934	1,298,006	1,120,402	812,228	778,393	669,515
Net Income	313,975	2,299,836	1,985,229	2,779,934	2,117,064	1,593,598	1,388,108	1,302,377
Average Shares	612,236	617,671	641,600	645,510	616,410	616,174	611,936	612,625
Balance Sheet								
Net Loans & Leases	114,260,253	94,360,897	104,944,676	98,949,373	78,153,524	71,035,824	67,043,315	64,675,857
Total Assets	150,374,028	140,190,842	142,397,114	139,280,377	113,933,460	118,258,415	105,816,700	88,534,609
Total Deposits	97,555,495	87,233,590	83,985,991	85,954,607	63,930,030	65,118,768	63,129,932	55,256,422
Total Liabilities	136,966,200	125,609,839	129,784,243	126,476,848	104,604,789	109,950,403	98,435,477	81,764,788
Stockholders' Equity	13,407,828	14,581,003	12,612,871	12,803,529	9,328,671	8,308,012	7,381,223	6,769,821
Shares Outstanding	633,945	632,381	615,047	646,749	605,996	611,491	607,354	609,188
Statistical Record								
Return on Assets %	0.22	1.63	1.41	2.19	1.82	1.42	1.43	1.48
Return on Equity %	2.24	16.91	15.62	25.05	24.01	20.31	19.62	20.79
Net Interest Margin %	47.86	51.53	60.73	73.87	72.83	67.71	53.61	45.05
Efficiency Ratio %	44.99	36.42	43.09	43.23	42.61	42.73	36.79	35.18
Loans to Deposits	1.17	1.08	1.25	1.15	1.22	1.09	1.06	1.17
Price Range	38.49-16.13	37.75-33.36	37.75-31.01	39.44-32.36	34.58-26.75	33.69-24.68	32.51-24.50	29.38-16.00
P/E Ratio	75.47-31.63	10.15-8.97	12.22-10.04	9.15-7.51	10.08-7.80	13.01-9.53	14.32-10.79	13.79-7.51
Average Yield %	5.23	4.23	4.15	3.71	4.03	4.06	4.06	5.53

Address: 1900 East Ninth Street, Cleveland, OH 44114-3484	Web Site: www.nationalcity.com	Auditors: Ernst & Young LLP
Telephone: 216-222-2000	Officers: David A. Daberko - Chmn., C.E.O. Jeffrey D. Kelly - Vice-Chmn., C.F.O.	Investor Contact: 800-622-4204
Fax: 216-222-2353		Transfer Agents: National City Bank, Corporate Trust Operations, Cleveland, OH

NATIONAL FUEL GAS CO. (NJ)

Exchange	Symbol	Price	52Wk Range	Yield	P/E	Div Acheiver
NYS	NFG	$47.21 (3/31/2008)	49.75-39.55	2.63	11.40	36 Years

*7 Year Price Score 121.66 *NYSE Composite Index=100 *12 Month Price Score 108.74

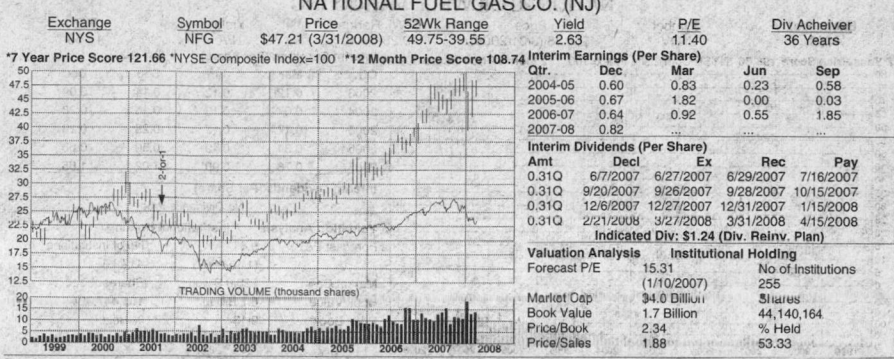

Interim Earnings (Per Share)

Qtr.	Dec	Mar	Jun	Sep
2004-05	0.60	0.83	0.23	0.58
2005-06	0.67	1.82	0.00	0.03
2006-07	0.64	0.92	0.55	1.85
2007-08	0.82	...	...	...

Interim Dividends (Per Share)

Amt	Decl	Ex	Rec	Pay
0.31Q	6/7/2007	6/27/2007	6/29/2007	7/16/2007
0.31Q	9/20/2007	9/26/2007	9/28/2007	10/15/2007
0.31Q	12/6/2007	12/27/2007	12/31/2007	1/15/2008
0.31Q	2/21/2008	3/27/2008	3/31/2008	4/15/2008

Indicated Div: $1.24 (Div. Reinv. Plan)

Valuation Analysis

		Institutional Holding	
Forecast P/E	15.31 (1/10/2007)	No of Institutions	255
Market Cap	34.0 Billion	Shares	44,140,164
Book Value	1.7 Billion	% Held	53.33
Price/Book	2.34		
Price/Sales	1.88		

Business Summary: Gas Utilities (MIC: 7.4 SIC: 4924 NAIC: 221210)

National Fuel Gas is a holding company consisting of five business segments. The Utility segment operations are carried out by National Fuel Gas Distribution Corporation; the Pipeline and Storage segment operations are carried out by National Fuel Gas Supply Corporation; the Exploration and Production segment operations are carried out by Seneca Resources Corporation; the Energy Marketing segment operations are carried out by National Fuel Resources, Inc.; while the Timber segment operations are carried out by Highland Forest Resources, Inc. As of Sep 30 2007, Co. had U.S. and Canadian reserves of 47,586 thousand barrels of oil and 205,389 million cubic feet equivalent of natural gas.

Recent Developments: For the quarter ended Dec 31 2007, income from continuing operations increased 39.3% to US$70.6 million from US$50.7 million in the year-earlier quarter. Net income increased 29.5% to US$70.6 million from US$54.5 million in the year-earlier quarter. Revenues were US$568.3 million, up 15.8% from US$490.7 million the year before. Operating income was US$126.0 million versus US$96.7 million in the prior-year quarter, an increase of 30.4%. Direct operating expenses rose 12.7% to US$380.5 million from US$337.6 million in the comparable period the year before. Indirect operating expenses increased 9.6% to US$61.8 million from US$56.4 million in the equivalent prior-year period.

Prospects: For the fiscal year ending Sep 30, 2008, Co. is increasing its consolidated earnings guidance by $0.10 per share to a new range of $2.60 to $2.80 per share. Co. believes that this increase is a result of higher than forecasted crude oil prices recently realized by its Seneca Resources Corporation subsidiary, along with the additional hedge contracts covering production for the remainder of this fiscal year at higher prices. Meanwhile, Co. will continue to explore various opportunities to expand its capabilities to transport gas to the East Coast, as exhibited by the ongoing construction of the Empire Connector, which is expected to be in-service by November 2008.

Financial Data

(US$ in Thousands)	3 Mos	09/30/2007	09/30/2006	09/30/2005	09/30/2004	09/30/2003	09/30/2002	09/30/2001
Earnings Per Share	4.14	3.96	1.61	2.23	2.01	2.20	1.46	0.82
Cash Flow Per Share	5.10	4.74	5.61	3.80	5.40	4.04	4.33	5.24
Tang Book Value Per Share	19.74	19.12	16.87	14.01	14.49	13.29	12.44	12.63
Dividends Per Share	1.230	1.220	1.180	1.140	1.100	1.060	1.025	0.985
Dividend Payout %	29.71	30.81	73.29	51.12	54.73	48.18	70.21	120.12
Income Statement								
Total Revenue	568,268	2,039,566	2,311,659	1,923,549	2,031,393	2,035,471	1,464,496	2,100,352
EBITDA	173,659	577,216	462,098	515,454	541,384	617,064	...	...
Depn & Amortn	44,121	...	...	...	...	...	...	...
Income Before Taxes	115,618	333,488	214,177	246,492	261,256	316,782	...	...
Income Taxes	45,014	131,813	76,086	92,978	92,737	128,161	...	...
Net Income	70,604	337,455	138,091	189,488	166,506	179,944	117,682	65,499
Average Shares	85,819	85,301	86,028	85,029	82,900	81,357	80,534	80,361
Balance Sheet								
Net PPE	2,909,120	2,878,405	2,877,726	2,839,300	3,006,764	2,999,087	2,844,745	2,780,713
Total Assets	4,031,423	3,888,412	3,734,331	3,722,652	3,711,798	3,727,915	3,401,309	3,445,566
Long-Term Obligations	799,000	799,000	1,095,675	1,119,012	1,133,317	1,147,779	1,145,341	1,046,694
Total Liabilities	2,340,436	2,258,293	2,290,769	2,493,069	2,458,097	2,590,525	2,394,451	2,442,911
Stockholders' Equity	1,690,987	1,630,119	1,443,562	1,229,583	1,253,701	1,137,390	1,006,858	1,002,655
Shares Outstanding	83,946	83,461	83,402	84,356	82,990	81,438	80,264	79,406
Statistical Record								
Return on Assets %	9.03	8.85	3.70	5.10	4.47	5.02	3.44	1.96
Return on Equity %	22.48	21.96	10.33	15.26	13.90	16.69	11.71	6.58
EBITDA Margin %	30.56	28.30	19.99	26.80	26.65	30.32	...	...
Net Margin %	12.42	16.55	5.97	9.85	8.20	8.79	8.04	3.12
PPE Turnover	0.72	0.71	0.81	0.66	0.67	0.70	0.52	0.77
Asset Turnover	0.54	0.54	0.62	0.52	0.54	0.57	0.43	0.63
Debt to Equity	0.47	0.49	0.76	0.91	0.90	1.01	1.14	1.04
Price Range	49.75-37.26	47.76-35.59	38.78-29.53	34.50-26.61	28.33-21.86	27.17-18.33	25.37-15.97	32.06-22.12
P/E Ratio	12.02-9.00	12.06-8.99	24.09-18.34	15.47-11.93	14.09-10.88	12.35-8.33	17.38-10.94	39.10-26.98
Average Yield %	2.75	2.89	3.49	3.98	4.41	4.73	4.54	3.68

Address: 6363 Main Street, Williamsville, NY 14221 Telephone: 716-857-7000	Web Site: www.nationalfuelgas.com Officers: Philip C. Ackerman - Chmn., Pres., C.E.O. Ronald J. Tanski - Treas.	Auditors: PricewaterhouseCoopers LLP Investor Contact: 716-857-6987 Transfer Agents: The Bank of New York, New York, NY

NATIONAL OILWELL VARCO INC

Exchange	Symbol	Price	52Wk Range	Yield	P/E
NYS	NOV	$58.38 (3/31/2008)	79.28-39.10	N/A	15.53

*7 Year Price Score 198.56 *NYSE Composite Index=100 *12 Month Price Score 106.21

Interim Earnings (Per Share)

Qtr.	Mar	Jun	Sep	Dec
2003	0.12	0.12	0.14	0.09
2004	0.07	0.13	0.16	0.28
2005	0.17	0.17	0.25	0.29
2006	0.34	0.42	0.50	0.68
2007	0.78	0.90	1.02	1.05

Interim Dividends (Per Share)

No Dividends Paid

Valuation Analysis

		Institutional Holding	
Forecast P/E	9.63	No of Institutions	
	(1/10/2007)	417	
Market Cap	$20.8 Billion	Shares	
Book Value	6.7 Billion	155,447,424	
Price/Book	3.13	% Held	
Price/Sales	2.13	88.42	

Business Summary: Oil and Gas (MIC: 14.2 SIC: 3533 NAIC: 333132)

National Oilwell Varco is a provider of equipment and components used in oil and gas drilling and production operations, oilfield services, and supply chain integration services to the upstream oil and gas industry. Co. designs, manufactures and services a range of drilling and well servicing equipment; sells and rents drilling motors, downhole tools, and rig instrumentation; executes inspection and internal coating of oilfield tubular products; provides drill cuttings separation, management and disposal systems and services; provides expendables and spare parts used in line with its installed base of equipment; and provides supply chain management services through its distribution network.

Recent Developments: For the year ended Dec 31 2007, net income increased 95.5% to US$1.34 billion from US$684.0 million in the prior year. Revenues were US$9.79 billion, up 39.3% from US$7.03 billion the year before. Operating income was US$2.04 billion versus US$1.11 billion in the prior year, an increase of 84.0%. Direct operating expenses rose 32.2% to US$6.96 billion from US$5.27 billion in the comparable period the year before. Indirect operating expenses increased 21.0% to US$785.8 million from US$649.5 million in the equivalent prior-year period.

Prospects: On Dec 16 2007, Co. and Grant Prideco Inc. entered into a definitive agreement under which Co. will acquire all of the outstanding shares of Grant Prideco for a combination of $23.20 cash per share and 0.4498 shares of Co.'s common stock. The transaction is expected to be accretive to Co.'s earnings in 2008 on a full-year basis and assuming a full year rate of estimated consolidation cost savings of $40.0 million. Further, Co. expects this transaction to advance its strategic goal of providing more products and services to its customers as it believes that Grant Prideco's product range will add to its growing market segments. The transaction should close in the second quarter of 2008.

Financial Data

(US$ in Thousands)	12/31/2007	12/31/2006	12/31/2005	12/31/2004	12/31/2003	12/31/2002	12/31/2001	12/31/2000
Earnings Per Share	3.76	1.94	0.91	0.64	0.45	0.45	0.64	0.08
Cash Flow Per Share	3.35	3.47	0.25	0.97	0.18	0.64	(0.22)	0.17
Tang Book Value Per Share	9.65	5.91	4.20	3.29	2.49	2.17	3.19	2.72
Income Statement								
Total Revenue	9,789,000	7,025,800	4,644,500	2,318,100	2,004,920	1,521,946	1,747,455	1,149,920
EBITDA	2,240,700	1,240,400	592,600	210,400	192,444	162,154	230,044	78,232
Income Before Taxes	2,028,900	1,049,200	430,000	131,500	116,651	112,465	168,017	27,037
Income Taxes	675,800	355,700	138,900	19,200	33,685	39,396	63,954	13,901
Net Income	1,337,100	684,000	286,900	110,200	76,821	73,069	104,063	13,136
Average Shares	355,400	353,600	316,600	173,000	169,970	163,418	163,466	161,520
Balance Sheet								
Current Assets	7,593,800	4,965,600	2,998,200	1,537,400	1,246,400	1,115,068	908,566	743,103
Total Assets	12,114,900	9,019,300	6,678,500	2,598,700	2,242,736	1,968,662	1,471,696	1,278,894
Current Liabilities	4,026,700	2,665,200	1,187,200	800,200	452,215	346,216	277,309	262,782
Long-Term Obligations	737,900	834,700	835,600	350,000	593,980	594,637	300,000	222,477
Total Liabilities	5,390,700	3,960,300	2,459,800	1,284,500	1,136,559	1,025,694	604,156	511,688
Stockholders' Equity	6,661,400	5,023,500	4,194,200	1,296,400	1,090,429	933,364	867,540	767,206
Shares Outstanding	356,867	351,143	348,724	171,990	170,249	162,029	161,805	161,017
Statistical Record								
Return on Assets %	12.65	8.71	6.19	4.54	3.65	4.25	7.57	1.27
Return on Equity %	22.89	14.84	10.45	9.21	7.59	8.11	12.73	2.25
EBITDA Margin %	22.89	17.65	12.76	9.08	9.60	10.65	13.16	6.80
Net Margin %	13.66	9.74	6.18	4.75	3.83	4.80	5.96	1.14
Asset Turnover	0.93	0.90	1.00	0.95	0.95	0.88	1.27	1.11
Current Ratio	1.89	1.86	2.53	1.92	2.76	3.22	3.28	2.83
Debt to Equity	0.11	0.17	0.20	0.27	0.54	0.64	0.35	0.29
Price Range	79.28-27.00	38.27-26.04	33.73-16.61	18.50-10.89	12.39-8.93	14.19-7.74	20.25-6.46	19.59-7.13
P/E Ratio	21.09-7.18	19.73-13.42	37.06-18.26	28.90-17.01	27.53-19.84	31.53-17.20	31.64-10.09	244.92-89.06

Address: 10000 Richmond Avenue, Houston, TX 77042-4200
Telephone: 713-346-7500
Fax: 713-960-5212

Web Site: www.natoil.com
Officers: Merrill A. Miller Jr. - Chmn., Pres., C.E.O. Steven W. Krablin - Sr. V.P., C.F.O.

Auditors: Ernst & Young LLP
Investor Contact: 713-346-7500
Transfer Agents: American Stock Transfer and Trust Company, New York, NY

NATIONAL RETAIL PROPERTIES INC

Exchange	Symbol	Price	52Wk Range	Yield	P/E	Div Acheiver
NYS	NNN	$22.05 (3/31/2008)	26.11-19.93	6.44	9.76	18 Years

*7 Year Price Score 99.83   *NYSE Composite Index=100   *12 Month Price Score 101.52

Interim Earnings (Per Share)

Qtr.	Mar	Jun	Sep	Dec
2003	0.23	0.28	0.32	0.30
2004	0.29	0.22	0.30	0.34
2005	0.47	0.51	0.28	0.30
2006	0.39	1.37	0.35	0.93
2007	0.41	0.70	0.68	0.44

Interim Dividends (Per Share)

Amt	Decl	Ex	Rec	Pay
0.355Q	4/12/2007	4/26/2007	4/30/2007	5/15/2007
0.355Q	7/13/2007	7/27/2007	7/31/2007	8/15/2007
0.355Q	10/15/2007	10/29/2007	10/31/2007	11/15/2007
0.355Q	1/15/2008	1/29/2008	1/31/2008	2/15/2008

Indicated Div: $1.42

Valuation Analysis

		Institutional Holding	
Forecast P/E	12.11	No of Institutions	
	(1/10/2007)	157	
Market Cap	31.0 Billion	Shares	
Book Value	1.4 Billion	37,744,752	
Price/Book	1.14	% Held	
Price/Sales	8.58	57.41	

Business Summary: Property, Real Estate & Development (MIC: 8.3 SIC: 6798 NAIC: 525930)

National Retail Properties is a real estate investment trust that operates through two primary business segments: investment assets, including real estate assets and mortgages and notes receivable (including structured finance) (collectively, Investment Assets); and inventory real estate assets (Inventory Assets). Co. acquires, owns, invests in, manages and develops properties that are leased primarily to retail tenants under long-term net leases (Investment Properties). As of Dec 31 2007, Co. owned 908 Investment Properties, with an aggregate leasable area of 10.6 million square feet, located in 44 states in the U.S.

Recent Developments: For the year ended Dec 31 2007, income from continuing operations increased 31.6% to US$85.2 million from US$64.7 million a year earlier. Net income decreased 13.9% to US$157.1 million from US$182.5 million in the prior year. Revenues were US$186.4 million, up 32.1% from US$141.2 million the year before. Revenues from property income rose 35.6% to US$181.5 million from US$133.9 million in the corresponding earlier year.

Prospects: Notwithstanding the existing cloudy economic and capital market environment, Co.'s results are benefiting from increased rental income primarily due to its acquisition of investment properties. For 2008, Co. believes that it will produce solid growth, with any significant increase in rental income expected to continue to come primarily from additional property acquisitions. Accordingly, Co. has increased its full-year guidance for funds from operations to a range of $1.95 to $2.00 per share, which represents a 4.0% to 7.0% increase over its 2007 results. This guidance equates to earnings before any gains or losses from the sale on investment properties of $1.45 to $1.50 per share.

Financial Data

(US$ in Thousands)	12/31/2007	12/31/2006	12/31/2005	12/31/2004	12/31/2003	12/31/2002	12/31/2001	12/31/2000
Earnings Per Share	2.26	3.05	1.56	1.15	1.13	1.09	0.91	1.26
Cash Flow Per Share	1.96	0.32	0.58	1.45	1.26	1.45	1.21	1.65
Tang Book Value Per Share	18.13	16.05	15.76	13.20	13.22	12.49	12.68	12.93
Dividends Per Share	1.400	1.320	1.300	1.290	1.280	1.270	1.260	1.245
Dividend Payout %	61.95	21.31	83.33	112.17	113.27	116.51	138.46	98.81
Income Statement								
Property Income	181,529	143,520	137,828	129,309	95,790	85,316	69,851	73,776
Non-Property Income	4,882	7,268	7,349	...	6,868	8,511	10,675	7,115
Total Revenue	186,411	150,788	145,177	129,309	102,658	93,827	80,526	80,891
Interest Expense	49,286	45,874	35,941	32,463	27,731	26,720	24,952	26,528
Income Before Taxes	76,374	52,299	50,014	44,589	...	...	...	...
Income Taxes	(8,537)	(11,143)	(2,776)	(2,542)	...	...	...	...
Net Income	157,110	182,505	89,400	64,934	53,473	48,058	28,963	38,251
Average Shares	66,407	58,079	54,640	51,742	43,896	40,588	31,717	30,407
Balance Sheet								
Total Assets	2,539,605	1,916,785	1,733,416	1,300,048	1,208,310	954,108	1,006,628	761,611
Long-Term Obligations	930,270	748,737	698,745	506,341	437,338	345,689	327,933	258,681
Total Liabilities	1,129,986	819,182	900,390	541,022	477,556	404,967	441,988	367,710
Stockholders' Equity	1,407,285	1,096,505	828,087	756,998	730,754	549,141	564,640	393,901
Shares Outstanding	72,527	59,823	55,130	52,077	50,001	40,403	40,599	30,456
Statistical Record								
Return on Assets %	7.05	10.00	5.89	5.16	4.95	4.90	3.28	5.05
Return on Equity %	12.55	18.97	11.28	8.71	8.36	8.63	6.04	9.72
Net Margin %	84.28	121.03	61.58	50.22	52.09	51.22	35.97	47.29
Price Range	26.11-20.77	23.97-18.90	21.53-18.16	21.20-15.49	18.30-14.37	16.34-13.00	14.25-10.25	11.31-9.69
P/E Ratio	11.55-9.19	7.86-6.20	13.80-11.64	18.43-13.47	16.19-12.72	14.99-11.93	15.66-11.26	8.98-7.69
Average Yield %	5.88	3.00	6.61	7.06	7.70	8.50	9.97	11.94

Address: 450 South Orange Avenue, Suite 900, Orlando, FL 32801
Telephone: 407-265-7348
Fax: 407-423-2894

Web Site: www.nnnreit.com
Officers: Clifford R. Hinkle - Chmn. Craig McNab - C.E.O.

Auditors: Ernst & Young LLP
Transfer Agents: American Stock Transfer & Trust Company, New York, N.Y.

NATIONAL SEMICONDUCTOR CORP.

Exchange	Symbol	Price	52Wk Range	Yield	P/E
NYS	NSM	$18.32 (3/31/2008)	29.58-16.34	1.31	15.39

*7 Year Price Score 102.44 *NYSE Composite Index=100 *12 Month Price Score 79.78

Interim Earnings (Per Share)

Qtr.	Aug	Nov	Feb	May
2004-05	0.31	0.24	0.21	0.35
2005-06	0.24	0.32	0.37	0.34
2006-07	0.35	0.27	0.22	0.27
2007-08	0.30	0.33	0.29	...

Interim Dividends (Per Share)

Amt	Decl	Ex	Rec	Pay
0.04Q	6/8/2007	6/14/2007	6/18/2007	7/9/2007
0.04Q	9/6/2007	9/13/2007	9/17/2007	10/9/2007
0.06Q	9/28/2007	12/13/2007	12/17/2007	1/7/2008
0.06Q	3/6/2008	3/13/2008	3/17/2008	4/7/2008

Indicated Div: $0.24

Valuation Analysis

		Institutional Holding	
Forecast P/E	14.31	No of Institutions	
	(1/10/2007)	314	
Market Cap	$4.4 Billion	Shares	
Book Value	259.3 Million	278,178,592	
Price/Book	17.13	% Held	
Price/Sales	2.36	88.73	

Business Summary: IT & Technology (MIC: 10.2 SIC: 3674 NAIC: 334413)

National Semiconductor is engaged in the business of designing, developing, manufacturing and marketing a range of semiconductor products, most of which are analog and mixed-signal integrated circuits. Co.'s product portfolio includes products such as power management circuits, audio and operational amplifiers, display drivers, communication interface products, and data conversion applications. Co.'s target markets and applications include wireless handsets, displays, networks, industrial markets, wireless basestations, portable, automotive, test and measurement as well as medical applications.

Recent Developments: For the quarter ended Feb 24 2008, net income decreased 1.1% to US$72.9 million from US$73.7 million in the year-earlier quarter. Revenues were US$453.4 million, up 5.2% from US$431.0 million the year before. Operating income was US$107.2 million versus US$85.7 million in the prior-year quarter, an increase of 25.1%. Direct operating expenses declined 6.7% to US$161.7 million from US$173.3 million in the comparable period the year before. Indirect operating expenses increased 7.3% to US$184.5 million from US$172.0 million in the equivalent prior-year period.

Prospects: Co. continues taking actions to improve its facilities and rationalize its capacity, including its disposition of certain manufacturing equipment and workforce reduction at its wafer fabrication facilities. Accordingly, Co. projects substantially all activities related to this action, which should benefit its gross margin, to be completed by end of fiscal quarter ending Aug 2008. Meanwhile, for the fiscal quarter ending May 2008, Co. estimates total orders to improve and resulting in its sales of $440.0 million to $460.0 million. Going forward, Co. believes that its growth will be driven by analog products that will be produced on 200 millimeter wafer technology.

Financial Data

(US$ in Thousands)	9 Mos	6 Mos	3 Mos	05/27/2007	05/28/2006	05/29/2005	05/30/2004	05/25/2003
Earnings Per Share	1.19	1.12	1.06	1.12	1.26	1.11	0.73	(0.09)
Cash Flow Per Share	2.88	2.56	2.26	1.94	2.35	1.50	1.30	0.61
Tang Book Value Per Share	0.82	0.84	1.43	5.43	5.57	5.65	4.21	4.17
Dividends Per Share	0.180	0.160	0.150	0.140	0.100	0.040	...	...
Dividend Payout %	15.10	14.25	14.10	12.50	7.94	3.60	...	...
Income Statement								
Total Revenue	1,423,900	970,500	471,500	1,929,900	2,158,100	1,913,100	1,983,100	1,672,500
EBITDA	475,600	339,500	163,700	636,400	829,700	588,400	533,200	191,100
Depn & Amortn	99,700	65,400	32,600	...	...	...	...	...
Income Before Taxes	339,000	252,100	122,700	530,600	695,200	409,900	333,700	(23,300)
Income Taxes	89,900	75,900	37,100	155,300	246,000	(5,400)	49,000	10,000
Net Income	249,100	176,200	85,600	375,300	449,200	415,300	282,800	(33,300)
Average Shares	255,500	271,500	283,900	334,200	357,000	373,900	388,500	363,600
Balance Sheet								
Current Assets	1,297,300	1,318,800	1,469,700	1,290,500	1,540,500	1,513,500	1,245,800	1,281,200
Total Assets	2,247,900	2,260,200	2,409,400	2,201,900	2,511,100	2,504,200	2,280,400	2,244,600
Current Liabilities	321,500	292,900	262,400	300,000	398,300	285,000	461,300	367,400
Long-Term Obligations	1,428,800	1,442,700	1,457,100	20,600	21,100	23,000	...	19,900
Total Liabilities	1,988,600	1,982,900	1,969,000	453,100	585,000	450,100	599,900	538,600
Stockholders' Equity	259,300	277,300	440,400	1,748,800	1,926,100	2,054,100	1,680,500	1,706,000
Shares Outstanding	242,512	254,887	264,007	310,292	335,680	347,952	357,611	367,144
Statistical Record								
Return on Assets %	15.22	15.18	14.46	15.97	17.96	17.41	12.30	N.M.
Return on Equity %	34.15	33.68	30.61	20.48	22.63	22.30	16.43	N.M.
EBITDA Margin %	33.40	34.98	34.72	32.98	38.45	30.76	26.89	11.43
Net Margin %	17.49	18.16	18.15	19.45	20.81	21.71	14.26	N.M.
Asset Turnover	0.84	0.83	0.79	0.82	0.86	0.80	0.86	0.74
Current Ratio	4.04	4.50	5.60	4.30	3.87	5.31	2.70	3.49
Debt to Equity	5.51	5.20	3.31	0.01	0.01	0.01	...	0.01
Price Range	29.58-16.87	29.58-21.88	29.58-21.88	27.79-20.69	30.70-19.84	22.35-12.00	24.27-9.79	16.30-5.25
P/E Ratio	24.86-14.18	26.41-19.54	27.91-20.64	24.81-18.47	24.37-15.75	20.14-10.81	33.25-13.41	...
Average Yield %	0.73	0.63	0.60	0.58	0.39	0.23	...	...

Address: 2900 Semiconductor Drive, P.O. BOX 58090, Santa Clara, CA 95052-8090 Telephone: 408-721-5000 Fax: 408-739-9803	Web Site: www.national.com Officers: Brian L. Halla - Chmn., Pres., C.E.O. Donald Macleod - Exec. V.P., C.O.O.	Auditors: KPMG LLP Investor Contact: 408-721-5800 Transfer Agents: EquiServe Trust Company, N.A., Providence, RI

NATIONWIDE FINANCIAL SERVICES INC.

Exchange	Symbol	Price	52Wk Range	Yield	P/E	Div Acheiver
NYS	NFS	$47.28 (3/31/2008)	64.59-37.93	2.45	10.82	10 Years

*7 Year Price Score 102.43 *NYSE Composite Index=100 *12 Month Price Score 89.43

Interim Earnings (Per Share)

Qtr.	Mar	Jun	Sep	Dec
2003	0.47	0.63	0.82	0.68
2004	0.78	0.68	0.89	0.92
2005	1.05	0.92	1.08	0.85
2006	0.93	1.72	1.06	1.03
2007	1.38	1.37	1.03	0.55

Interim Dividends (Per Share)

Amt	Decl	Ex	Rec	Pay
0.26Q	5/2/2007	6/28/2007	7/2/2007	7/16/2007
0.26Q	8/1/2007	9/27/2007	10/1/2007	10/15/2007
0.26Q	12/5/2007	12/28/2007	1/2/2008	1/14/2008
0.29Q	2/20/2008	3/28/2008	4/1/2008	4/14/2008

Indicated Div: $1.16

Valuation Analysis

		Institutional Holding	
Forecast P/E	11.51 (1/10/2007)	No of Institutions	193
Market Cap	90.5 Billion	Shares	35,418,576
Book Value	5.3 Billion	% Held	
Price/Book	1.23		24.25
Price/Sales	1.45		

Business Summary: Insurance (MIC: 8.2 SIC: 6311 NAIC: 524113)

Nationwide Financial Services is the holding company for Nationwide Life Insurance and other companies that comprise the domestic life insurance and retirement savings operations of the Nationwide group of companies. This group includes Nationwide Financial Network, which refers to Nationwide Life Insurance Company of America and its subsidiaries, including the affiliated distribution network. Co. develops and sells a range of products including individual annuities, private and public group retirement plans, other investment products sold to institutions, life insurance and advisory services. In addition, Co. provides a range of banking products and services through Nationwide Bank.

Recent Developments: For the year ended Dec 31 2007, income from continuing operations decreased 16.1% to US$609.7 million from US$727.1 million a year earlier. Net income decreased 13.4% to US$626.8 million from US$724.0 million in the prior year. Revenues were US$4.53 billion, down 0.7% from US$4.56 billion the year before. Net premiums earned were US$432.7 million versus US$441.5 million in the prior year, a decrease of 2.0%. Net investment income fell 1.0% to US$2.28 billion from US$2.30 billion a year ago.

Prospects: Co. is optimistic about its outlook for 2008 and believes that it is well positioned for growth. For example, Co. believes its increased product offerings, strong distribution relationships and diverse distribution network should position it to capitalize on the growing retirement savings market. Overall, Co. expects its enhanced core operations, combined with the addition of higher-return businesses, ongoing expense management and its improved capital structure, will result in further progress toward gaining its long-term financial targets. For full-year 2008, Co. expects interest spread margins of 185 to 190 basis points for both its Individual Investments and Retirement Plans segments.

Financial Data
(US$ in Thousands)

	12/31/2007	12/31/2006	12/31/2005	12/31/2004	12/31/2003	12/31/2002	12/31/2001	12/31/2000
Earnings Per Share	4.37	4.74	3.90	3.28	2.61	1.09	3.20	3.38
Cash Flow Per Share	15.62	16.28	12.78	13.68	9.19	11.19	9.75	10.44
Tang Book Value Per Share	36.27	35.47	32.40	31.37	29.07	26.25	26.73	23.29
Dividends Per Share	1.040	0.920	0.760	0.720	0.520	0.510	0.480	0.460
Dividend Payout %	23.80	19.41	19.49	21.95	19.92	46.79	15.00	13.61
Income Statement								
Premium Income	432,700	441,500	399,900	402,700	426,200	302,300	251,100	240,000
Total Revenue	4,528,900	4,415,500	4,339,900	4,180,200	3,935,400	3,287,800	3,179,000	3,170,300
Benefits & Claims	682,900	646,800	574,900	526,900	563,500	374,800	279,800	241,600
Income Before Taxes	800,400	778,900	755,800	674,600	517,800	133,500	562,700	623,900
Income Taxes	190,700	65,100	137,600	169,200	119,400	(7,300)	142,800	189,000
Net Income	626,800	713,800	598,700	502,000	397,800	144,200	412,800	434,900
Average Shares	143,500	150,700	153,600	152,900	152,300	132,600	129,200	128,900
Balance Sheet								
Total Assets	119,207,100	119,411,600	116,159,900	116,950,600	111,027,300	95,560,300	91,960,900	93,178,600
Total Liabilities	113,882,500	113,873,300	110,809,500	111,735,500	106,151,900	90,817,000	88,217,600	89,881,100
Stockholders' Equity	5,324,600	5,538,300	5,350,400	5,215,100	4,875,400	4,443,300	3,443,300	2,997,500
Shares Outstanding	138,500	146,000	152,500	152,500	151,900	151,800	128,800	128,700
Statistical Record								
Return on Assets %	0.53	0.61	0.51	0.44	0.39	0.15	0.45	0.47
Return on Equity %	11.54	13.11	11.33	9.92	8.54	3.66	12.82	15.82
Loss Ratio %	157.82	146.50	143.76	130.84	132.21	123.98	111.43	100.67
Net Margin %	13.84	16.17	13.80	12.01	10.11	4.39	12.99	13.72
Price Range	64.59-42.12	54.32-42.19	44.00-33.85	39.00-32.33	34.50-21.70	45.35-22.10	47.19-33.74	50.38-20.31
P/E Ratio	14.78-9.64	11.46-8.90	11.28-8.68	11.89-9.86	13.22-8.31	41.61-20.28	14.75-10.54	14.90-6.01
Average Yield %	1.91	1.99	1.97	2.00	1.74	1.43	1.17	1.35

Address: One Nationwide Plaza, Columbus, OH 43215 **Telephone:** 614-249-7111 **Fax:** 614-249-9071	**Web Site:** www.nationwidefinancial.com **Officers:** Arden L. Shisler - Chmn. Mark R. Thresher - Pres., C.O.O.	**Auditors:** KPMG LLP **Transfer Agents:** Mellon Investor Services, South Hackensack, NJ

NAVIGANT CONSULTING, INC.

Exchange	Symbol	Price	52Wk Range	Yield	P/E
NYS	NCI	$18.98 (3/31/2008)	20.93-11.19	N/A	28.76

*7 Year Price Score 85.37   *NYSE Composite Index=100   *12 Month Price Score 106.85

Interim Earnings (Per Share)

Qtr.	Mar	Jun	Sep	Dec
2003	0.08	0.09	0.13	0.11
2004	0.16	0.21	0.22	0.22
2005	0.25	0.24	0.25	0.22
2006	0.26	0.26	0.16	0.30
2007	0.20	0.21	0.10	0.13

Interim Dividends (Per Share)

No Dividends Paid

Valuation Analysis		Institutional Holding	
Forecast P/E	14.32	No of Institutions	
	(1/10/2007)	145	
Market Cap	$869.3 Million	Shares	
Book Value	342.8 Million	55,065,272	
Price/Book	2.54	% Held	
Price/Sales	1.13	95.04	

Business Summary: Accounting & Management Consulting Services (MIC: 12.2 SIC: 8742 NAIC: 541611)

Navigant Consulting is a consulting firm. Co. conducts its business through three operating segments: the North American Dispute and Investigative Services segment provides of services to clients facing the challenges of disputes, litigation, forensic investigation, discovery, and regulatory compliance; the North American Business Consulting Services segment provides strategic, operational, financial, regulatory and technical management consulting services to clients. Services are sold principally through vertical industry practices; the International Consulting Operations segment provides a mix of dispute and business consulting services to clients in Europe and Asia.

Recent Developments: For the year ended Dec 31 2007, net income decreased 37.0% to US$33.4 million from US$53.0 million in the prior year. Revenues were US$767.1 million, up 12.5% from US$681.7 million the year before. Operating income was US$73.3 million versus US$97.7 million in the prior year, a decrease of 25.0%. Direct operating expenses rose 19.1% to US$506.9 million from US$425.7 million in the comparable period the year before. Indirect operating expenses increased 18.1% to US$186.9 million from US$158.3 million in the equivalent prior-year period.

Prospects: Co. noted that its results reflect strong market demand as its revenues are being positively affected by improved utilization in its Disputes and Business Consulting segments. Further, revenue growth has been broad-based amongst Co.'s practices, particularly in the Business Consulting segment, while its Financial Services, Energy and Healthcare practices each experienced growth relative to its prior year's results. Overall, Co. believes that its strategy of selectively acquiring consulting businesses and consulting capabilities should continue to strengthen its platform, market share and operating results as a whole as it expects to see ongoing benefits going forward.

Financial Data
(US$ in Thousands)

	12/31/2007	12/31/2006	12/31/2005	12/31/2004	12/31/2003	12/31/2002	12/31/2001	12/31/2000
Earnings Per Share	0.66	0.97	0.95	0.80	0.40	0.21	(0.14)	(4.39)
Cash Flow Per Share	1.86	1.66	1.17	1.53	1.32	0.21	0.30	(0.87)
Tang Book Value Per Share	N.M.	1.64	1.30	1.33	1.71	1.11	1.98	2.29
Income Statement								
Total Revenue	767,058	681,745	575,492	482,119	317,782	258,020	235,580	244,629
EBITDA	107,776	122,012	110,463	85,520	43,291	25,072	5,223	(9,181)
Income Before Taxes	58,538	93,360	85,958	68,437	32,107	14,769	(7,595)	(20,551)
Income Taxes	25,142	40,386	36,102	28,062	13,399	5,908	(2,284)	(6,194)
Net Income	33,396	52,974	49,856	40,375	18,708	8,861	(5,311)	(179,553)
Average Shares	50,757	54,703	52,390	50,247	47,029	42,670	38,439	40,895
Balance Sheet								
Current Assets	228,559	200,245	179,907	166,358	116,663	78,401	98,777	111,413
Total Assets	778,697	652,358	542,863	418,807	255,316	201,204	158,826	163,482
Current Liabilities	126,519	129,742	143,642	117,885	64,797	52,491	45,221	47,757
Long-Term Obligations	5,348	5,786	...	...	...	...	...	...
Total Liabilities	435,944	165,782	158,415	130,133	66,558	56,909	46,721	47,757
Stockholders' Equity	342,753	486,576	384,448	288,674	188,758	144,295	112,105	115,725
Shares Outstanding	45,800	53,881	50,601	47,868	44,922	42,084	38,700	38,444
Statistical Record								
Return on Assets %	4.67	8.86	10.37	11.95	8.20	4.92	N.M.	N.M.
Return on Equity %	8.05	12.16	14.81	16.87	11.23	6.91	N.M.	N.M.
EBITDA Margin %	14.05	17.90	19.19	17.74	13.62	9.72	2.22	N.M.
Net Margin %	4.35	7.77	8.66	8.37	5.89	3.43	N.M.	N.M.
Asset Turnover	1.07	1.14	1.20	1.43	1.39	1.43	1.46	0.84
Current Ratio	1.81	1.54	1.25	1.41	1.80	1.49	2.18	2.33
Debt to Equity	0.02	0.01	...	...	...	...	...	...
Price Range	21.60-12.12	23.28-17.45	27.66-16.50	26.99-17.45	19.29-5.00	6.99-3.75	8.20-3.20	11.69-2.81
P/E Ratio	32.73-18.36	24.00-17.99	29.12-17.37	33.74-21.81	48.22-12.50	33.29-17.86	...	...

Address: 615 North Wabash Avenue, Chicago, IL 60611	Web Site: www.navigantconsulting.com	Auditors: KPMG LLP
Telephone: 312-573-5600	Officers: William M. Goodyear - Chmn., C.E.O. Ben W. Perks - Exec. V.P., C.F.O.	Investor Contact: 312-573-5630
Fax: 312-573-5675		

NCR CORP.

Exchange	Symbol	Price	52Wk Range	Yield	P/E
NYS	NCR	$22.83 (3/31/2008)	28.31-20.53	N/A	15.22

*7 Year Price Score 138.34 *NYSE Composite Index=100 *12 Month Price Score 99.71

Interim Earnings (Per Share)

Qtr.	Mar	Jun	Sep	Dec
2003	(0.14)	(0.07)	0.10	0.42
2004	(0.03)	0.64	0.23	0.67
2005	0.16	0.67	1.18	0.81
2006	0.22	0.42	0.49	0.96
2007	0.19	0.54	0.29	0.49

Interim Dividends (Per Share)

Amt	Decl	Ex	Rec	Pay
2-for-1	...	1/24/2005	12/31/2004	1/21/2005
0.000	...	10/1/2007	9/14/2007	10/1/2007

Valuation Analysis **Institutional Holding**

Forecast P/E	15.15	No of Institutions
	(1/10/2007)	292
Market Cap	$4.1 Billion	Shares
Book Value	1.8 Billion	141,967,952
Price/Book	2.32	% Held
Price/Sales	0.82	79.31

Business Summary: Office Equipment Supplies (MIC: 11.12 SIC: 3578 NAIC: 334119)

NCR is a global technology company that provides products and services that are designed to help businesses improve relationships with their customers. Co. provides applications for industries such as retail, financial, travel and hospitality, health care, entertainment and gaming, and public sector. Co. operates in the information technology industry and categorizes its operations into five reportable segments: Financial Self Service (which includes Co.'s automated-teller machines business), Retail Store Automation, Customer Services, Systemedia, and Payment & Imaging and Other. Each segment generally integrates hardware, software, and professional and installation-related services.

Recent Developments: For the year ended Dec 31 2007, income from continuing operations increased 13.2% to US$171.0 million from US$151.0 million a year earlier. Net income decreased 28.3% to US$274.0 million from US$382.0 million in the prior year. Revenues were US$4.97 billion, up 8.5% from US$4.58 billion the year before. Operating income was US$219.0 million versus US$154.0 million in the prior year, an increase of 42.2%. Direct operating expenses rose 7.5% to US$3.93 billion from US$3.66 billion in the comparable period the year before. Indirect operating expenses increased 6.2% to US$821.0 million from US$773.0 million in the equivalent prior-year period.

Prospects: For 2008, Co. expects higher operating income due to a more favorable mix of revenue as higher-margin, self-service technologies increase as a percent of the total revenue. Particularly, Co. expects 2008 earnings from continuing operations of $1.48 to $1.55 per share and year-over-year revenue growth from continuing operations in the range of 3.0% to 5.0%. Also, Co. noted that earnings expansion in 2008 should be more prevalent later in the year as it expects to launch new self-service products in the market. Meanwhile, in Sep 2007, Co. commenced a realignment program to improve operating efficiency and strengthen its position in Japan, and expects to realize the program benefits in 2008.

Financial Data

(US$ in Thousands)	12/31/2007	12/31/2006	12/31/2005	12/31/2004	12/31/2003	12/31/2002	12/31/2001	12/31/2000
Earnings Per Share	1.50	2.09	2.80	1.51	0.30	(1.11)	1.09	0.91
Cash Flow Per Share	0.84	2.68	3.29	2.32	2.32	1.26	0.75	0.90
Tang Book Value Per Share	9.50	9.68	10.49	10.51	9.35	6.30	8.06	6.44
Income Statement								
Total Revenue	4,970,000	6,142,000	6,028,000	5,984,000	5,598,000	5,585,000	5,917,000	5,959,000
EBITDA	311,000	626,000	645,000	539,000	404,000	468,000	555,000	618,000
Income Before Taxes	232,000	478,000	396,000	251,000	72,000	131,000	124,000	275,000
Income Taxes	61,000	96,000	(133,000)	(39,000)	14,000	3,000	(97,000)	97,000
Net Income	274,000	382,000	529,000	290,000	58,000	(220,000)	217,000	178,000
Average Shares	182,700	182,900	189,100	191,500	191,800	199,800	199,200	196,000
Balance Sheet								
Current Assets	3,088,000	3,332,000	2,693,000	2,633,000	2,422,000	2,186,000	1,963,000	2,234,000
Total Assets	4,780,000	5,227,000	5,287,000	5,554,000	5,480,000	4,672,000	4,855,000	5,106,000
Current Liabilities	1,530,000	1,770,000	1,645,000	1,724,000	1,579,000	1,417,000	1,518,000	1,836,000
Long-Term Obligations	307,000	306,000	305,000	307,000	307,000	306,000	10,000	11,000
Total Liabilities	3,023,000	3,346,000	3,252,000	3,468,000	3,605,000	3,347,000	2,828,000	3,348,000
Stockholders' Equity	1,757,000	1,881,000	2,035,000	2,086,000	1,875,000	1,325,000	2,027,000	1,758,000
Shares Outstanding	178,200	178,900	181,700	186,600	189,400	194,000	194,800	190,400
Statistical Record								
Return on Assets %	5.48	7.27	9.76	5.24	1.14	N.M.	4.36	3.55
Return on Equity %	15.06	19.51	25.67	14.60	3.63	N.M.	11.47	10.59
EBITDA Margin %	6.26	10.19	10.70	9.01	7.22	8.38	9.38	10.37
Net Margin %	5.51	6.22	8.78	4.85	1.04	N.M.	3.67	2.99
Asset Turnover	0.99	1.17	1.11	1.08	1.10	1.17	1.19	1.19
Current Ratio	2.02	1.88	1.64	1.53	1.53	1.54	1.29	1.22
Debt to Equity	0.17	0.16	0.15	0.15	0.16	0.23	N.M.	0.01
Price Range	28.31-20.20	21.23-15.19	18.76-13.94	16.71-9.24	9.35-4.10	10.82-4.50	11.90-6.89	12.62-7.90
P/E Ratio	18.87-13.46	10.16-7.27	6.70-4.98	11.07-6.12	31.17-13.66	...	10.92-6.33	13.87-8.69

Address: 1700 South Patterson Blvd., Dayton, OH 45479
Telephone: 937-445-1936

Web Site: www.ncr.com
Officers: James M. Ringler - Chmn. William Nuti - Pres., C.E.O.

Auditors: PricewaterhouseCoopers LLP
Transfer Agents: NCR Corporation c/o Mellon Investor Services LLC

NEUSTAR INC

Exchange	Symbol	Price	52Wk Range	Yield	P/E
NYS	NSR	$26.48 (3/31/2008)	36.12-21.50	N/A	22.63

*7 Year Price Score N/A   *NYSE Composite Index=100   *12 Month Price Score 93.04

Interim Earnings (Per Share)

Qtr.	Mar	Jun	Sep	Dec
2004	0.17	0.23	0.11	0.06
2005	0.19	0.18	0.17	0.18
2006	0.24	0.26	0.22	0.23
2007	0.23	0.24	0.32	0.38

Interim Dividends (Per Share)

No Dividends Paid

Valuation Analysis

		Institutional Holding	
Forecast P/E	N/A	No of Institutions	165
Market Cap	$2.0 Billion	Shares	
Book Value	480.5 Million	86,547,312	
Price/Book	4.25	% Held	
Price/Sales	4.76	N/A	

TRADING VOLUME (thousand shares)

Business Summary: Communications (MIC: 10.1 SIC: 4899 NAIC: 517910)

Neustar provides clearinghouse services to the communications industry. Co.'s customers use the databases it contractually maintains in its clearinghouse to obtain data required to route telephone calls in North America, to exchange information with other communications service providers (CSPs), and to manage technological changes in their own networks. Co. operates the authoritative directories that manage telephone area codes and numbers, and enables the routing of calls among CSPs in the U.S. and Canada. Co. provides its services to CSPs, including Internet service providers, mobile network operators, cable television operators, and voice over Internet protocol service providers.

Recent Developments: For the year ended Dec 31 2007, net income increased 24.9% to US$92.3 million from US$73.9 million in the prior year. Revenues were US$429.2 million, up 28.9% from US$333.0 million the year before. Operating income was US$149.6 million versus US$122.6 million in the prior year, an increase of 22.0%. Direct operating expenses rose 10.3% to US$94.9 million from US$86.1 million in the comparable period the year before. Indirect operating expenses increased 48.6% to US$184.6 million from US$124.2 million in the equivalent prior-year period.

Prospects: On Jan 15 2008, Co. announced that it has acquired San Diego, CA-based Webmetrics, a provider of web and network performance testing, monitoring and measurement services. The acquisition represents a strategic addition to Co.'s Ultra Services group, which focuses on providing web and network managed services to the enterprise and carrier markets. Separately, on Nov 26 2007, Co. announced that it has deployed network nodes in Sydney, Australia and Beijing, People's Republic of China, further expanding its global constellation of domain name systems (DNS) servers and improving the delivery of services of its Apr 2006 UltraDNS acquisition to the Asia-Pacific region.

Financial Data

(US$ in Thousands)	12/31/2007	12/31/2006	12/31/2005	12/31/2004	12/31/2003	12/31/2002
Earnings Per Share	1.17	0.94	0.72	0.57	0.31	(9.04)
Cash Flow Per Share	1.92	1.62	1.78	11.46	15.57	...
Tang Book Value Per Share	3.11	1.13	1.93	...	...	...
Income Statement						
Total Revenue	429,172	332,957	242,469	165,001	111,693	90,972
EBITDA	192,694	146,549	108,446	64,846	43,258	2,367
Income Before Taxes	153,111	125,252	92,649	46,542	24,854	(31,108)
Income Taxes	60,776	51,353	37,251	1,166	836	...
Net Income	92,335	73,899	55,398	45,376	24,028	(29,200)
Average Shares	79,235	78,267	77,046	80,237	76,520	4,236
Balance Sheet						
Current Assets	310,136	135,675	181,983	119,445	96,722	...
Total Assets	616,661	448,259	281,771	211,454	190,245	...
Current Liabilities	99,266	81,705	68,313	76,169	73,092	...
Long-Term Obligations	10,923	3,925	4,459	7,964	5,996	...
Total Liabilities	136,126	107,113	95,504	102,858	97,785	...
Stockholders' Equity	480,535	341,146	186,163	(31,858)	(68,581)	...
Shares Outstanding	77,086	74,369	68,349	6,159	5,548	4,447
Statistical Record						
Return on Assets %	17.34	20.25	22.46	22.53	...	...
Return on Equity %	22.47	28.03	71.80	...	...	...
EBITDA Margin %	44.90	44.01	44.73	39.30	38.73	2.60
Net Margin %	21.51	22.19	22.85	27.50	21.51	N.M.
Asset Turnover	0.81	0.91	0.98	0.82	...	...
Current Ratio	3.12	1.66	2.66	1.57	1.32	...
Debt to Equity	0.02	0.01	0.02	...	...	...
Price Range	36.12-26.69	37.25-26.67	32.51-25.60	...	...	...
P/E Ratio	30.87-22.81	39.63-28.37	45.15-35.56	...	...	...

Address: 46000 Center Oak Plaza, Sterling, VA 20166 Telephone: 571-434-5400	Web Site: www.neustar.biz Officers: Jeffrey E. Ganek - Chmn., C.E.O. Michael Lack - Pres., C.O.O.	Auditors: Ernst & Young LLP Investor Contact: 571-434-3443 Transfer Agents: Wachovia Bank, N.A.

NEW JERSEY RESOURCES CORP

Exchange	Symbol	Price	52Wk Range	Yield	P/E	Div Acheiver
NYS	NJR	$31.05 (3/31/2008)	37.00-29.81	3.61	19.41	12 Years

*7 Year Price Score 98.87   *NYSE Composite Index=100   *12 Month Price Score 101.91

Interim Earnings (Per Share)

Qtr.	Dec	Mar	Jun	Sep
2004-05	0.71	1.23	0.05	(0.17)
2005-06	0.82	1.43	(0.09)	(0.28)
2006-07	0.67	1.91	(0.12)	(0.91)
2007-08	0.72	...	...	...

Interim Dividends (Per Share)

Amt	Decl	Ex	Rec	Pay
0.253Q	8/11/2007	9/12/2007	9/15/2007	10/1/2007
0.267Q	11/15/2007	12/12/2007	12/15/2007	1/2/2008
3-for-2	1/23/2008	3/4/2008	2/8/2008	3/3/2008
0.28Q	1/23/2008	3/12/2008	3/14/2008	4/1/2008

Indicated Div: $1.12

Valuation Analysis

Forecast P/E	15.87
	(1/10/2007)
Market Cap	$1.3 Billion
Book Value	669.0 Million
Price/Book	1.94
Price/Sales	0.42

Institutional Holding

No of Institutions	159
Shares	15,685,096
% Held	56.35

Business Summary: Gas Utilities (MIC: 7.4 SIC: 4924 NAIC: 221210)

New Jersey Resources is an energy services holding company providing retail and wholesale energy services to customers in New Jersey, in states from the Gulf Coast to New England, and Canada. As of Sep 30 2007, Co. conducted its businesses through three operating segments. The Natural Gas Distribution segment consists of regulated energy and off-system, capacity and storage management operations. The Energy Services segment consists of unregulated wholesale energy operations. The Retail and Other segment consists of appliance repair, sales and installation services, natural gas and related investments, commercial real estate development and other corporate activities.

Recent Developments: For the quarter ended Dec 31 2007, net income increased 2.6% to US$30.2 million from US$29.4 million in the year-earlier quarter. Revenues were US$811.1 million, up 10.0% from US$737.4 million the year before. Operating income was US$54.5 million versus US$54.8 million in the prior-year quarter, a decrease of 0.5%. Direct operating expenses rose 10.2% to US$716.9 million from US$650.3 million in the comparable period the year before. Indirect operating expenses increased 22.9% to US$39.7 million from US$32.3 million in the equivalent prior-year period.

Prospects: For fiscal 2008 ending Sep 2008, Co. is raising its earnings guidance by $0.05 per share to range from $3.25 to $3.35 per share; assuming stable economic conditions; ongoing customer growth at its New Jersey Natural Gas subsidiary, which it expects to achieve a new customer growth rate of 1.6% to 1.8% in fiscal 2008; as well as continued volatility in the wholesale natural gas markets affecting its NJR Energy Services subsidiary. Meanwhile, Co. is progressing with the $250.0 million construction and development of Steckman Ridge natural gas storage facility under joint development with a partner in western Pennsylvania, which is expected to contribute to earnings beginning in fiscal 2010.

Financial Data

(US$ in Thousands)	3 Mos	09/30/2007	09/30/2006	09/30/2005	09/30/2004	09/30/2003	09/30/2002	09/30/2001
Earnings Per Share	1.60	1.55	1.87	1.81	1.70	1.87	1.39	1.30
Cash Flow Per Share	2.48	2.92	(0.55)	5.00	(1.18)	2.27	1.24	(0.76)
Tang Book Value Per Share	16.03	15.50	14.24	10.36	11.17	10.26	8.95	8.80
Dividends Per Share	1.027	1.013	0.960	0.907	0.867	0.827	0.800	0.782
Dividend Payout %	64.17	65.24	51.43	50.18	50.98	44.29	57.42	60.17
Income Statement								
Total Revenue	811,138	3,021,765	3,299,608	3,148,262	2,533,607	2,544,379	1,830,754	2,048,408
EBITDA	65,543	168,080	189,264	180,954	167,164	158,241	145,061	142,947
Depn & Amortn	9,478	...	...	...	...	...	...	...
Income Before Taxes	48,255	103,931	128,541	125,253	117,519	107,874	92,768	86,554
Income Taxes	18,494	40,312	50,022	48,913	45,945	42,462	35,924	32,891
Net Income	30,185	65,281	78,519	76,340	71,574	65,412	56,844	52,316
Average Shares	41,920	42,112	42,121	42,181	42,079	41,298	40,752	40,200
Balance Sheet								
Net PPE	978,707	970,871	934,939	905,130	880,389	852,604	756,397	743,949
Total Assets	2,367,755	2,230,745	2,398,928	2,209,828	1,855,600	1,570,979	1,319,304	1,192,192
Long-Term Obligations	359,165	383,184	332,332	317,204	315,887	257,899	370,628	353,799
Total Liabilities	1,698,786	1,585,948	1,777,266	1,771,776	1,387,683	1,152,038	957,851	840,123
Stockholders' Equity	668,969	644,797	621,662	438,052	467,917	418,941	361,453	352,069
Shares Outstanding	41,723	41,611	43,647	42,274	41,871	40,849	40,375	39,995
Statistical Record								
Return on Assets %	2.76	2.82	3.41	3.76	4.17	4.53	4.53	4.59
Return on Equity %	10.25	10.31	14.82	16.85	16.10	16.76	15.93	15.38
EBITDA Margin %	8.08	5.56	5.74	5.75	6.60	6.22	7.92	6.98
Net Margin %	3.72	2.16	2.38	2.42	2.82	2.57	3.10	2.55
PPE Turnover	3.22	3.17	3.59	3.53	2.92	3.16	2.44	2.78
Asset Turnover	1.26	1.31	1.43	1.55	1.47	1.76	1.46	1.80
Debt to Equity	0.54	0.59	0.53	0.72	0.68	0.62	1.03	1.00
Price Range	37.00-30.83	37.00-30.83	34.01-27.69	32.67-27.07	28.20-24.03	24.83-20.03	21.93-17.01	20.43-16.56
P/E Ratio	23.13-19.27	23.87-19.89	18.19-14.81	18.05-14.95	16.59-14.13	13.28-10.71	15.78-12.24	15.71-12.74
Average Yield %	3.08	3.01	3.04	3.06	3.34	3.70	3.90	4.23

Address: 1415 Wyckoff Road, P.O. Box 1468, Wall, NJ 07719 **Telephone:** 732-938-1480	**Web Site:** www.njliving.com **Officers:** Laurence M. Downes - Chmn., Pres., C.E.O. Glenn C. Lockwood - Sr. V.P., C.F.O.		**Auditors:** Deloitte & Touche LLP **Investor Contact:** 732-938-1229 **Transfer Agents:** Boston EquiServe, Boston, MA

NEW YORK COMMUNITY BANCORP INC.

Exchange	Symbol	Price	52Wk Range	Yield	P/E
NYS	NYB	$18.22 (3/31/2008)	19.42-15.06	5.49	20.24

*7 Year Price Score 77.36   *NYSE Composite Index=100   *12 Month Price Score 106.37

Interim Earnings (Per Share)

Qtr.	Mar	Jun	Sep	Dec
2003	0.37	0.40	0.40	0.50
2004	0.48	0.16	0.38	0.32
2005	0.35	0.33	0.30	0.14
2006	0.25	0.18	0.21	0.18
2007	0.22	0.12	0.35	0.21

Interim Dividends (Per Share)

Amt	Decl	Ex	Rec	Pay
0.25Q	4/25/2007	5/2/2007	5/4/2007	5/15/2007
0.25Q	7/25/2007	8/2/2007	8/6/2007	8/15/2007
0.25Q	10/19/2007	11/2/2007	11/6/2007	11/15/2007
0.25Q	1/29/2008	2/4/2008	2/6/2008	2/15/2008

Indicated Div: $1.00

Valuation Analysis

		Institutional Holding	
Forecast P/E	17.28 (1/10/2007)	No of Institutions	288
Market Cap	$5.9 Billion	Shares	150,582,256
Book Value	4.2 Billion	% Held	48.33
Price/Book	1.41		
Price/Sales	3.66		

Business Summary: Other Depository Banking (MIC: 8.5 SIC: 6036 NAIC: 522120)

New York Community Bancorp is a bank holding company for New York Community Bank (Community Bank) and New York Commercial Bank (Commercial Bank). As of Dec 31 2007, Community Bank had 179 locations that operated through ten divisional banks, and Commercial Bank had 38 branches. Community Bank provides a range of traditional and non-traditional products and services, while Commercial Bank focuses on personal service and addresses the needs of small and mid-size businesses, professional associations, and government agencies with a menu of services that include installment loans, revolving lines of credit, and cash management services. As of Dec 31 2007, Co. had total assets of $30.58 billion.

Recent Developments: For the year ended Dec 31 2007, net income increased 20.0% to US$279.1 million from US$232.6 million in the prior year. Net interest income increased 9.8% to US$616.5 million from US$561.6 million in the prior year. Non-interest income fell 50.8% to US$46.2 million from US$93.9 million, while non-interest expense advanced 6.6% to US$302.8 million.

Prospects: Co.'s results reflect improvements that include an increase in its net interest income as it increased the balance of its interest-earning assets, both organically and through acquisitions, and took actions to contain its cost of funds. Going forward, Co. believes that the downturn in the credit cycle could result in an increase in charge-offs and/or additional provisions for loan losses, which will negatively affect its future results. However, Co. remains encouraged with its near-term outlook as it believes that the nature of its multi-family lending niche and its underwriting standards will continue to support the performance of its loan portfolio during this difficult time.

Financial Data

(US$ in Thousands)	12/31/2007	12/31/2006	12/31/2005	12/31/2004	12/31/2003	12/31/2002	12/31/2001	12/31/2000
Earnings Per Share	0.90	0.81	1.11	1.33	1.65	1.25	0.75	0.32
Cash Flow Per Share	0.96	1.02	1.74	1.28	(7.12)	0.49	(3.12)	(1.36)
Tang Book Value Per Share	5.05	4.86	4.66	4.33	3.32	3.45	1.72	1.63
Dividends Per Share	1.000	1.000	1.000	0.960	0.658	0.428	0.303	0.250
Dividend Payout %	111.11	123.46	90.09	72.18	39.89	34.23	40.13	79.37
Income Statement								
Interest Income	1,566,745	1,408,700	1,155,654	1,172,159	749,160	599,507	423,304	174,832
Interest Expense	950,215	847,134	583,651	390,902	244,185	226,251	217,488	101,751
Net Interest Income	616,530	561,566	572,003	781,257	504,975	373,256	205,816	73,081
Non-Interest Income	46,173	93,887	112,026	102,158	98,135	84,834	90,615	21,645
Non-Interest Expense	302,765	283,971	236,621	193,632	169,373	133,062	112,757	49,330
Income Before Taxes	402,099	348,714	444,714	531,968	492,682	336,014	175,246	44,902
Income Taxes	123,017	116,129	152,629	176,882	169,311	106,784	70,779	20,425
Net Income	279,082	232,585	292,085	355,086	323,371	229,230	104,467	24,477
Average Shares	311,102	286,261	262,497	266,837	196,303	183,221	138,760	78,124
Balance Sheet								
Net Loans & Leases	20,270,454	19,567,502	16,948,697	13,317,987	10,422,078	5,443,572	5,361,187	3,616,386
Total Assets	30,579,822	28,482,370	26,283,705	24,037,826	23,441,337	11,313,092	9,202,635	4,710,785
Total Deposits	13,157,333	12,619,004	12,104,899	10,402,117	10,329,106	5,256,042	5,450,602	3,257,194
Total Liabilities	26,397,509	24,792,533	22,958,828	20,851,412	20,572,680	9,989,580	8,219,501	4,403,375
Stockholders' Equity	4,182,313	3,689,837	3,324,877	3,186,414	2,868,657	1,323,512	983,134	307,410
Shares Outstanding	323,812	295,350	269,776	265,190	256,649	187,843	181,053	115,884
Statistical Record								
Return on Assets %	0.95	0.85	1.16	1.49	1.86	2.23	1.50	0.74
Return on Equity %	7.09	6.63	8.97	11.70	15.43	19.88	16.19	10.98
Net Interest Margin %	39.35	39.86	49.50	66.65	67.41	62.26	48.62	41.80
Efficiency Ratio %	18.77	18.90	18.67	15.19	19.99	19.44	21.94	25.11
Loans to Deposits	1.54	1.55	1.40	1.28	1.01	1.04	0.98	1.11
Price Range	19.42-15.90	18.01-15.85	20.57-15.76	35.12-17.88	29.45-15.43	17.99-12.86	17.64-8.42	9.38-4.44
P/E Ratio	21.58-17.67	22.23-19.57	18.53-14.20	26.41-13.44	17.85-9.35	14.39-10.29	23.52-11.23	29.30-13.87
Average Yield %	5.70	6.00	5.67	4.03	3.05	2.20	2.41	4.24

<table>
<tr><td>Address: 615 Merrick Avenue,
Westbury, NY 11590
Telephone: 516-683-4100
Fax: 516-683-8385</td><td>Web Site: www.myNYCB.com
Officers: Michael F. Manzulli - Chmn. Joseph R.
Ficalora - Pres. C.E.O.</td><td>Auditors: KPMG LLP
Investor Contact: 516-683-4420
Transfer Agents: Registrar and
Transfer Company</td></tr>
</table>

NEW YORK TIMES CO.

Exchange	Symbol	Price	52Wk Range	Yield	P/E	Div Acheiver
NYS	NYT	$18.88 (3/31/2008)	26.55-14.48	4.87	13.02	12 Years

*7 Year Price Score 46.36 ***NYSE Composite Index=100** ***12 Month Price Score 97.48**

Interim Earnings (Per Share)

Qtr.	Mar	Jun	Sep	Dec
2003	0.45	0.47	0.33	0.73
2004	0.38	0.50	0.33	0.75
2005	0.76	0.42	0.16	0.45
2006	0.24	0.42	0.10	(4.52)
2007	0.17	0.82	0.09	0.37

Interim Dividends (Per Share)

Amt	Decl	Ex	Rec	Pay
0.23Q	3/22/2007	5/30/2007	6/1/2007	6/13/2007
0.23Q	6/21/2007	8/30/2007	9/4/2007	9/12/2007
0.23Q	11/15/2007	11/29/2007	12/3/2007	12/12/2007
0.23Q	2/21/2008	2/28/2008	3/3/2008	3/12/2008

Indicated Div: $0.92

Valuation Analysis | **Institutional Holding**

Forecast P/E	17.34	No of Institutions
	(1/10/2007)	269
Market Cap	$2.7 Billion	Shares
Book Value	978.2 Million	136,872,368
Price/Book	2.77	% Held
Price/Sales	0.85	95.65

TRADING VOLUME (thousand shares)

Business Summary: Media (MIC: 13.1 SIC: 2711 NAIC: 511110)

New York Times is a media company that includes newspapers, Internet businesses, a radio station, investments in paper mills and other investments. Co.'s operates through two segments, the News Media Group and the About Group. The News Media Group includes The New York Times, NYTimes.com, the International Herald Tribune, IHT.com, its New York City radio station, WQXR-FM, and The Boston Globe, Boston.com, the Worcester Telegram & Gazette, in Worcester, MA, as well as 14 daily newspapers in Alabama, California, Florida, Louisiana, North Carolina and South Carolina. The About Group is an online source that provides users with information and advice on various topics.

Recent Developments: For the year ended Dec 30 2007, income from continuing operations was US$108.9 million compared with a loss of US$568.2 million a year earlier. Net income amounted to US$208.7 million versus a net loss of US$543.4 million in the prior year. Revenues were US$3.20 billion, down 2.9% from US$3.29 billion the year before. Operating income was US$227.4 million versus a loss of US$520.6 million in the prior year. Direct operating expenses declined 6.6% to US$1.34 billion from US$1.44 billion in the comparable period the year before. Indirect operating expenses decreased 31.5% to US$1.63 billion from US$2.38 billion in the equivalent prior-year period.

Prospects: As part of its effort to reduce costs, Co. is consolidating its New York metro area printing into its newer facility in College Point, NY, and closing its older Edison, NJ, facility. Co. expects completing the plant consolidation in the first quarter of 2008, which is expected to save about $30.0 million in operating costs annually. Also, Co. believes that it can attain a reduction in costs from its year-end 2007 cost base of a total of about $230.0 million in 2008 and 2009, excluding the effects of inflation and certain one-time costs. About $130.0 million of these savings are expected in 2008. Moreover, Co. expects income from joint ventures of $12.0 million to $16.0 million in 2008.

Financial Data

(US$ in Thousands)	12/30/2007	12/31/2006	12/25/2005	12/26/2004	12/28/2003	12/29/2002	12/30/2001	12/31/2000
Earnings Per Share	1.45	(3.76)	1.70	1.96	1.98	1.94	2.78	2.32
Cash Flow Per Share	0.77	2.87	2.03	3.02	3.11	1.81	3.01	3.45
Tang Book Value Per Share	1.16	0.25	N.M.	N.M.	N.M.	N.M.	N.M.	N.M.
Dividends Per Share	0.865	0.690	0.650	0.610	0.570	0.530	0.490	0.450
Dividend Payout %	59.66	...	36.52	31.12	28.79	27.32	17.63	19.40
Income Statement								
Total Revenue	3,195,077	3,289,903	3,372,775	3,303,642	3,227,200	3,079,007	3,015,958	3,489,455
EBITDA	414,372	(331,418)	634,274	706,953	737,108	690,169	581,061	965,157
Income Before Taxes	184,969	(551,922)	446,104	476,645	499,847	491,387	339,854	673,086
Income Taxes	76,137	16,608	180,242	183,499	197,762	191,640	137,632	275,550
Net Income	208,704	(543,443)	259,753	292,557	302,655	299,747	444,672	397,536
Average Shares	144,158	144,579	145,877	149,357	152,840	154,805	160,081	171,597
Balance Sheet								
Current Assets	664,445	1,185,043	657,746	613,893	603,311	563,056	559,890	610,766
Total Assets	3,473,092	3,855,928	4,533,037	3,949,857	3,804,739	3,633,842	3,438,684	3,606,679
Current Liabilities	975,736	1,297,994	1,066,522	1,119,749	760,364	735,736	860,876	877,370
Long-Term Obligations	678,699	795,030	898,300	471,474	725,725	728,789	598,703	636,866
Total Liabilities	2,488,985	3,030,119	2,827,813	2,414,695	2,321,086	2,364,535	2,289,031	2,325,516
Stockholders' Equity	978,200	819,842	1,516,248	1,400,542	1,392,242	1,269,307	1,149,653	1,281,163
Shares Outstanding	143,727	143,859	145,215	146,105	149,878	152,216	151,456	162,373
Statistical Record								
Return on Assets %	5.71	N.M.	6.14	7.57	8.16	8.50	12.66	11.01
Return on Equity %	23.28	N.M.	17.86	21.01	22.81	24.85	36.69	28.65
EBITDA Margin %	12.97	N.M.	18.81	21.40	22.84	22.42	19.27	27.66
Net Margin %	6.53	N.M.	7.70	8.86	9.38	9.74	14.74	11.39
Asset Turnover	0.87	0.77	0.80	0.85	0.87	0.87	0.86	0.97
Current Ratio	0.68	0.91	0.62	0.55	0.79	0.77	0.65	0.70
Debt to Equity	0.69	0.97	0.59	0.34	0.52	0.57	0.52	0.50
Price Range	26.55-16.45	28.90-21.58	40.80-26.36	49.13-38.72	48.84-42.87	52.79-39.98	47.60-37.42	49.13-33.19
P/E Ratio	18.31-11.34	...	22.92-14.81	25.07-19.76	24.67-21.65	27.21-20.61	17.12-13.46	21.17-14.30
Average Yield %	3.86	2.81	1.98	1.40	1.25	1.13	1.15	1.11

Address: 229 West 43rd Street, New York, NY 10036
Telephone: 212-556-1234
Fax: 212-556-4647

Web Site: www.nytco.com
Officers: Arthur Sulzberger Jr. - Chmn. Janet L. Robinson - Exec. V.P., C.O.O.

Auditors: Ernst & Young
Investor Contact: 212-556-1981

NEWELL RUBBERMAID, INC.

Exchange	Symbol	Price	52Wk Range	Yield	P/E
NYS	NWL	$22.87 (3/31/2008)	31.84-22.00	3.67	13.61

*7 Year Price Score 82.76 *NYSE Composite Index=100 *12 Month Price Score 91.24

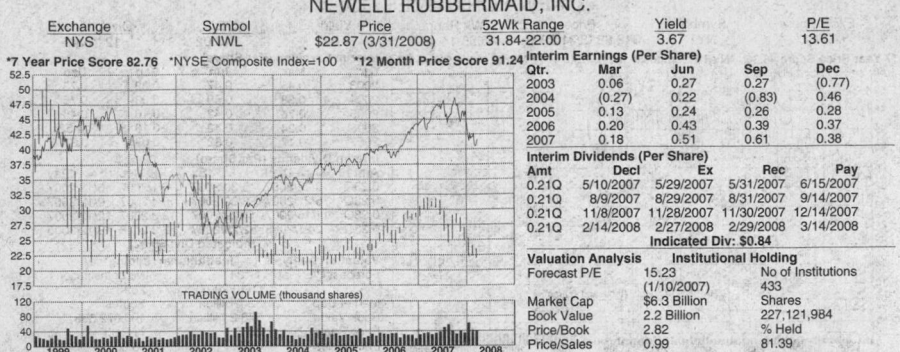

Interim Earnings (Per Share)

Qtr.	Mar	Jun	Sep	Dec
2003	0.06	0.27	0.27	(0.77)
2004	(0.27)	0.22	(0.83)	0.46
2005	0.13	0.24	0.26	0.28
2006	0.20	0.43	0.39	0.37
2007	0.18	0.51	0.61	0.38

Interim Dividends (Per Share)

Amt	Decl	Ex	Rec	Pay
0.21Q	5/10/2007	5/29/2007	5/31/2007	6/15/2007
0.21Q	8/9/2007	8/29/2007	8/31/2007	9/14/2007
0.21Q	11/8/2007	11/28/2007	11/30/2007	12/14/2007
0.21Q	2/14/2008	2/27/2008	2/29/2008	3/14/2008
		Indicated Div: $0.84		

Valuation Analysis

		Institutional Holding	
Forecast P/E	15.23	No of Institutions	
	(1/10/2007)	433	
Market Cap	$6.3 Billion	Shares	
Book Value	2.2 Billion	227,121,984	
Price/Book	2.82	% Held	
Price/Sales	0.99	81.39	

Business Summary: Plastics (MIC: 11.7 SIC: 3089 NAIC: 326199)

Newell Rubbermaid is a global marketer of consumer and commercial products. As of Dec 31 2007, Co.'s portfolio of brands includes Sharpie®, Paper Mate®, Dymo®, Expo®, Waterman®, Parker®, Rolodex®, Irwin®, Lenox®, BernzOmatic®, Rubbermaid®, Levolor®, Graco®, Calphalon® and Goody®. Co. categorizes its consumer and commercial products into four business segments: Cleaning, Organization & Décor; Office Products; Tools & Hardware, and Home & Family. Co.'s principal customers are large mass merchandisers, such as discount stores, home centers, warehouse clubs and office superstores, and commercial distributors.

Recent Developments: For the year ended Dec 31 2007, income from continuing operations increased 1.8% to US$479.2 million from US$470.7 million a year earlier. Net income increased 21.3% to US$467.1 million from US$385.0 million in the prior year. Revenues were US$6.41 billion, up 3.3% from US$6.20 billion the year before. Operating income was US$740.3 million versus US$656.6 million in the prior year, an increase of 12.7%. Direct operating expenses rose 0.5% to US$4.15 billion from US$4.13 billion in the comparable period the year before. Indirect operating expenses increased 7.3% to US$1.52 billion from US$1.41 billion in the equivalent prior-year period.

Prospects: On Feb 21 2008, Co. entered into a definitive agreement to acquire substantially all the assets of Aprica Childcare Institute Aprica Kassai, Inc., a manufacturer of strollers, car seats and other children's products in Osaka, Japan. The transaction compliments Co.'s Graco brand and its recent acquisition of Germany's Teutonia, and should provide it with distribution channels in Asia Pacific, Europe and North America. Separately, on Feb 27 2008, Co. announced its definitive agreement to acquire Technical Concepts Holdings, LLC, a provider of hygiene systems for the away-from-home washroom category, for about $445.0 million. Both transactions are expected to close in the first half of 2008.

Financial Data
(US$ in Thousands)

	12/31/2007	12/31/2006	12/31/2005	12/31/2004	12/31/2003	12/31/2002	12/31/2001	12/31/2000
Earnings Per Share	1.68	1.40	0.91	(0.42)	(0.17)	(0.76)	0.99	1.57
Cash Flow Per Share	2.37	2.34	2.34	2.40	2.82	3.25	3.25	2.32
Tang Book Value Per Share	N.M.	N.M.	N.M.	N.M.	N.M.	N.M.	0.44	0.97
Dividends Per Share	0.840	0.840	0.840	0.840	0.840	0.840	0.840	0.840
Dividend Payout %	50.00	60.00	92.31	...	...	...	84.85	53.50
Income Statement								
Total Revenue	6,407,300	6,201,000	6,342,500	6,748,400	7,750,000	7,453,900	6,909,319	6,934,747
EBITDA	910,000	840,200	759,000	454,700	432,600	859,800	882,093	1,108,096
Income Before Taxes	628,900	514,900	418,100	86,300	20,100	468,500	415,865	685,487
Income Taxes	149,700	44,200	61,700	105,400	66,700	157,000	151,230	263,912
Net Income	467,100	385,000	251,300	(116,100)	(46,600)	(203,400)	264,635	421,575
Average Shares	286,100	275,500	274,900	274,400	274,100	268,000	267,048	278,365
Balance Sheet								
Current Assets	2,651,700	2,476,900	2,472,800	3,012,400	3,000,200	3,080,000	2,850,652	2,896,652
Total Assets	6,682,900	6,310,500	6,445,800	6,665,900	7,480,700	7,388,900	7,266,122	7,261,825
Current Liabilities	2,563,800	1,896,600	1,797,500	1,871,300	2,022,000	2,614,400	2,533,852	1,550,826
Long-Term Obligations	1,197,400	1,972,300	2,429,700	2,424,300	2,868,600	1,856,600	1,365,001	2,314,774
Total Liabilities	4,435,600	4,420,300	4,802,600	4,901,700	5,464,400	5,325,400	4,832,746	4,813,184
Stockholders' Equity	2,247,300	1,890,200	1,643,200	1,764,200	2,016,300	2,063,500	2,433,376	2,448,641
Shares Outstanding	276,700	275,300	274,500	274,400	274,400	267,400	266,800	266,600
Statistical Record								
Return on Assets %	7.19	6.04	3.83	N.M.	N.M.	N.M.	3.64	6.01
Return on Equity %	22.58	21.79	14.75	N.M.	N.M.	N.M.	10.84	16.34
EBITDA Margin %	14.20	13.55	11.97	6.74	5.58	11.53	12.77	15.98
Net Margin %	7.29	6.21	3.96	N.M.	N.M.	N.M.	3.83	6.08
Asset Turnover	0.99	0.97	0.97	0.95	1.04	1.02	0.95	0.99
Current Ratio	1.03	1.31	1.38	1.61	1.48	1.18	1.13	1.87
Debt to Equity	0.53	1.04	1.48	1.37	1.42	0.90	0.56	0.95
Price Range	31.95-24.50	29.83-23.26	25.45-20.95	26.16-19.11	31.41-21.00	35.99-26.50	29.21-21.20	31.25-18.69
P/E Ratio	19.02-14.58	21.31-16.61	27.97-23.02	...	...	...	29.51-21.41	19.90-11.90
Average Yield %	2.90	3.16	3.66	3.68	3.20	2.64	3.30	3.40

Address: 10B Glenlake Parkway, Suite 300, Atlanta, GA 30328 Telephone: 800-424-1941	Web Site: www.newellrubbermaid.com Officers: William D. Marohn - Chmn. Mark D. Ketchum - Interim C.E.O.	Auditors: Ernst & Young LLP Transfer Agents: ComputerShare Investor Services, Providence, RI

NEWFIELD EXPLORATION CO.

Exchange	Symbol	Price	52Wk Range	Yield	P/E
NYS	NFX	$52.85 (3/31/2008)	57.22-41.84	N/A	15.36

*7 Year Price Score 125.34 *NYSE Composite Index=100 *12 Month Price Score 116.38

TRADING VOLUME (thousand shares)

Interim Earnings (Per Share)

Qtr.	Mar	Jun	Sep	Dec
2003	0.58	0.41	0.44	0.35
2004	0.69	0.59	0.64	0.72
2005	0.47	0.82	0.00	1.44
2006	1.17	0.73	2.06	0.63
2007	(0.75)	1.15	0.64	2.39

Interim Dividends (Per Share)

Amt	Decl	Ex	Rec	Pay
100%	5/5/2005	5/26/2005	5/16/2005	5/25/2005

Valuation Analysis **Institutional Holding**

Forecast P/E	10.03	No of Institutions	
	(1/10/2007)	300	
Market Cap	$6.9 Billion	Shares	
Book Value	3.6 Billion	117,720,248	
Price/Book	1.94	% Held	
Price/Sales	3.89	N/A	

Business Summary: Oil and Gas (MIC: 14.2 SIC: 1311 NAIC: 211111)

Newfield Exploration is an independent oil and gas company engaged in the exploration, development and acquisition of natural gas and crude oil properties. Co.'s domestic areas of operation include the Anadarko and Arkoma Basins of the Mid-Continent, the Rocky Mountains, onshore Texas and the Gulf of Mexico. In addition, Co. operates internationally in Malaysia and China. As of Dec 31 2007, Co. had proved reserves of 2.50 trillion cubic feet of gas equivalent. Of those reserves, 73.0% were natural gas, 63.0% were proved developed, 96.0% were located in Co.'s domestic areas of operation, and 4.0% were located internationally.

Recent Developments: For the year ended Dec 31 2007, income from continuing operations decreased 71.8% to US$172.0 million from US$610.0 million a year earlier. Net income decreased 23.9% to US$450.0 million from US$591.0 million in the prior year. Revenues were US$1.78 billion, up 6.6% from US$1.67 billion the year before. Operating income was US$531.0 million versus US$599.0 million in the prior year, a decrease of 11.4%. Direct operating expenses rose 23.1% to US$415.0 million from US$337.0 million in the comparable period the year before. Indirect operating expenses increased 13.6% to US$837.0 million from US$737.0 million in the equivalent prior-year period.

Prospects: For 2008, Co. plans to invest approximately $1.60 billion of capital, of which 40.0% will be allocated to the Mid-Continent, 20.0% to the Rocky Mountains, 15.0% to onshore Texas, 15.0% to the Gulf of Mexico and 10.0% to international projects in Malaysia and China. Co believes that the budget should enable it to deliver organic production growth of 13.0% to 21.0% and anticipates 2008 production to be 215.00 billion cubic feet equivalent (Bcfe) to 230.00 Bcfe versus 190.00 Bcfe from 2007. Further, for the first quarter of 2008, Co. expects natural gas production of 36.00 billion cubic feet (Bcf) to 40.00 Bcf and crude oil production of 23,000 barrels of oil per day (BOPD) to 25,200 BOPD.

Financial Data

(US$ in Thousands)	12/31/2007	12/31/2006	12/31/2005	12/31/2004	12/31/2003	12/31/2002	12/31/2001	12/31/2000
Earnings Per Share	3.44	4.58	2.73	2.63	1.78	0.81	1.28	1.47
Cash Flow Per Share	9.02	10.90	8.87	8.33	6.16	4.47	5.68	3.73
Tang Book Value Per Share	26.79	23.22	18.16	15.63	12.02	9.75	8.05	6.10
Income Statement								
Total Revenue	1,783,000	1,673,000	1,762,000	1,352,700	1,016,986	661,750	749,405	526,642
EBITDA	1,031,000	1,616,000	1,090,000	1,002,200	768,180	439,875	488,902	403,067
Income Before Taxes	294,000	949,000	543,000	498,900	331,619	110,885	191,360	204,689
Income Taxes	122,000	358,000	195,000	186,800	120,713	37,038	67,612	69,980
Net Income	450,000	591,000	348,000	312,100	199,489	73,847	118,954	132,349
Average Shares	131,000	129,000	128,000	118,600	113,488	99,178	97,787	94,155
Balance Sheet								
Current Assets	927,000	851,000	540,000	391,600	238,916	238,827	230,604	179,149
Total Assets	6,986,000	6,635,000	5,081,000	4,327,500	2,733,089	2,315,753	1,663,371	1,023,250
Current Liabilities	929,000	1,123,000	670,000	474,000	300,218	295,807	165,031	141,060
Long-Term Obligations	1,050,000	1,048,000	870,000	992,400	643,459	709,615	428,631	133,711
Total Liabilities	3,405,000	3,573,000	2,703,000	2,310,600	1,364,511	1,162,317	809,643	360,045
Stockholders' Equity	3,581,000	3,062,000	2,378,000	2,016,900	1,368,578	1,009,231	709,978	519,455
Shares Outstanding	131,335	129,183	127,540	124,837	112,511	103,461	88,203	85,214
Statistical Record								
Return on Assets %	6.61	10.09	7.40	8.82	7.90	3.71	8.86	14.63
Return on Equity %	13.55	21.73	15.84	18.39	16.78	8.59	19.35	29.51
EBITDA Margin %	57.82	96.59	61.86	74.09	75.53	66.47	65.24	76.54
Net Margin %	25.24	35.33	19.75	23.07	19.62	11.16	15.87	25.13
Asset Turnover	0.26	0.29	0.37	0.38	0.40	0.33	0.56	0.58
Current Ratio	1.00	0.76	0.81	0.83	0.80	0.81	1.40	1.27
Debt to Equity	0.29	0.34	0.37	0.49	0.47	0.70	0.60	0.26
Price Range	54.31-39.94	53.47-36.25	52.27-27.78	32.27-22.25	22.60-15.82	19.57-14.10	22.91-13.43	24.22-12.31
P/E Ratio	15.79-11.61	11.67-7.91	19.15-10.18	12.27-8.46	12.70-8.88	24.17-17.41	17.90-10.49	16.48-8.38

Address: 363 North Sam Houston Parkway East, Suite 2020, Houston, TX 77060
Telephone: 281-847-6000
Fax: 281-405-4242

Web Site: www.newfld.com
Officers: David A. Trice - Chmn., Pres., C.E.O. David F. Schaible - Exec. V.P., Opers., Acquisitions

Auditors: PricewaterhouseCoopers LLP
Transfer Agents: American Stock Transfer & Trust Company

NEWMONT MINING CORP. (HOLDING CO.)

Exchange	Symbol	Price	52Wk Range	Yield	P/E
NYS	NEM	$45.30 (3/31/2008)	56.22-38.53	0.88	N/A

*7 Year Price Score 95.87 ***NYSE Composite Index=100** ***12 Month Price Score 116.91**

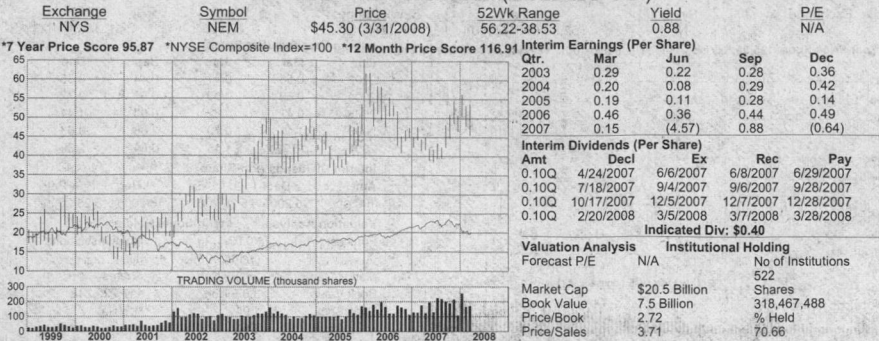

Interim Earnings (Per Share)

Qtr.	Mar	Jun	Sep	Dec
2003	0.29	0.22	0.28	0.36
2004	0.20	0.08	0.29	0.42
2005	0.19	0.11	0.28	0.14
2006	0.46	0.36	0.44	0.49
2007	0.15	(4.57)	0.88	(0.64)

Interim Dividends (Per Share)

Amt	Decl	Ex	Rec	Pay
0.10Q	4/24/2007	6/6/2007	6/8/2007	6/29/2007
0.10Q	7/18/2007	9/4/2007	9/6/2007	9/28/2007
0.10Q	10/17/2007	12/5/2007	12/7/2007	12/28/2007
0.10Q	2/20/2008	3/5/2008	3/7/2008	3/28/2008

Indicated Div: $0.40

Valuation Analysis | **Institutional Holding**

Forecast P/E	N/A	No of Institutions
		522
Market Cap	$20.5 Billion	Shares
Book Value	7.5 Billion	318,467,488
Price/Book	2.72	% Held
Price/Sales	3.71	70.66

Business Summary: Precious Metals (MIC: 14.1 SIC: 1041 NAIC: 212221)

Newmont Mining is a gold producer with assets/operations in the U.S., Australia, Peru, Indonesia, Ghana, Canada, Bolivia, New Zealand and Mexico. At Dec 31 2007, Co. had proven and probable gold reserves of 86.5 million equity ounces and an aggregate land position of about 42,680 square miles. Co. also produces copper, mainly at its Batu Hijau operation in Indonesia. Co. has operating segments of Nevada, Yanacocha in Peru, Australia/New Zealand, Batu Hijau in Indonesia, Africa and Other Operations comprised of smaller operations in Bolivia, Mexico and Canada. Co. also has an Exploration segment, which is responsible for activities related to its efforts to discover new mineralized material.

Recent Developments: For the year ended Dec 31 2007, loss from continuing operations was US$963.0 million compared with income of US$563.0 million a year earlier. Net loss amounted to US$1.89 billion versus net income of US$791.0 million in the prior year. Revenues were US$5.53 billion, up 13.2% from US$4.88 billion the year before. Direct operating expenses rose 21.4% to US$2.98 billion from US$2.45 billion in the comparable period the year before. Indirect operating expenses increased 159.2% to US$2.94 billion from US$1.13 billion in the equivalent prior-year period.

Prospects: On Dec 20 2007, Co. sold its royalty assets and certain other non-core investments to Franco-Nevada Corp. for about $1.19 billion, resulting in a $905.0 million pre-tax gain. Separately, in Jan 2008, Co. acquired about 40.0 million additional common shares of Miramar Mining Corp., a Canadian company that controls the Hope Bay Project, an undeveloped gold project in Nunavut, Canada, for C$6.25 per share, bringing its interest in Miramar to 96.0%. Meanwhile, for 2008, Co. expects consolidated gold sales of 5.9 million to 6.4 million ounces, primarily due to lower production from Australia and Batu Hijau, as well as expects consolidated copper sales of 345.0 million to 365.0 million pounds.

Financial Data

(US$ in Thousands)	12/31/2007	12/31/2006	12/31/2005	12/31/2004	12/31/2003	12/31/2002	12/31/2001	12/31/2000
Earnings Per Share	(4.17)	1.75	0.72	0.99	1.15	0.41	(0.16)	(0.11)
Cash Flow Per Share	1.47	2.72	2.79	3.50	1.43	1.81	1.95	3.02
Tang Book Value Per Share	16.25	14.04	12.28	11.02	5.99	2.44	7.49	8.58
Dividends Per Share	0.400	0.400	0.400	0.300	0.170	0.120	0.120	0.120
Dividend Payout %	...	22.86	55.56	30.30	14.78	29.27	...	...
Income Statement								
Total Revenue	5,526,000	4,987,000	4,406,000	4,524,185	3,214,059	2,745,007	1,664,101	1,566,673
EBITDA	398,000	2,291,000	1,691,000	1,873,864	1,541,949	759,119	305,916	519,387
Income Before Taxes	(352,000)	1,625,000	1,064,000	1,099,005	925,386	216,326	(43,228)	104,038
Income Taxes	200,000	424,000	314,000	275,882	206,950	19,900	(52,817)	11,310
Net Income	(1,886,000)	791,000	322,000	443,327	475,667	158,061	(23,279)	(18,947)
Average Shares	452,000	452,000	449,000	446,511	413,723	372,975	195,059	168,386
Balance Sheet								
Current Assets	2,672,000	2,642,000	3,036,000	2,721,149	2,360,468	1,113,256	709,460	511,902
Total Assets	15,598,000	15,601,000	13,992,000	12,770,688	11,050,173	10,154,518	4,062,405	3,510,704
Current Liabilities	1,500,000	1,739,000	1,350,000	1,101,005	834,020	693,463	485,811	290,668
Long-Term Obligations	2,683,000	1,752,000	1,733,000	1,311,260	886,633	1,701,282	1,089,718	976,446
Total Liabilities	6,601,000	5,166,000	4,685,000	4,057,968	3,318,720	4,380,712	2,330,878	1,856,262
Stockholders' Equity	7,548,000	9,337,000	8,376,000	7,937,660	7,384,935	5,419,248	1,480,048	1,466,388
Shares Outstanding	453,000	451,000	447,766	445,599	494,495	401,991	196,150	170,943
Statistical Record								
Return on Assets %	N.M.	5.35	2.41	3.71	4.49	2.22	N.M.	N.M.
Return on Equity %	N.M.	8.93	3.95	5.77	7.43	4.58	N.M.	N.M.
EBITDA Margin %	7.20	45.94	38.38	41.42	47.98	27.65	18.38	33.15
Net Margin %	N.M.	15.86	7.31	9.80	14.80	5.76	N.M.	N.M.
Asset Turnover	0.35	0.34	0.33	0.38	0.30	0.39	0.44	0.45
Current Ratio	1.78	1.52	2.25	2.47	2.83	1.61	1.46	1.76
Debt to Equity	0.36	0.19	0.21	0.17	0.12	0.31	0.74	0.67
Price Range	54.50-38.53	61.95-40.83	53.69-35.10	49.75-35.41	50.00-24.37	32.00-18.70	24.83-14.09	27.75-13.00
P/E Ratio	...	35.40-23.33	74.57-48.75	50.25-35.77	43.48-21.19	78.05-45.61	...	...
Average Yield %	0.91	0.79	0.95	0.70	0.49	0.47	0.62	0.60

Address: 1700 Lincoln Street, Denver, CO 80203 **Telephone:** 303-863-7414 **Fax:** 303-837-5837	**Web Site:** www.newmont.com **Officers:** Wayne W. Murdy - Chmn., C.E.O. Pierre Lassonde - Pres.	**Auditors:** PricewaterhouseCoopers LLP **Investor Contact:** 800-810-6463

NEWS CORP

Exchange	Symbol	Price	52Wk Range	Yield	P/E
NYS	NWS	$19.04 (3/31/2008)	25.27-18.28	0.58	17.47

*7 Year Price Score 101.29 *NYSE Composite Index=100 *12 Month Price Score 94.21

Interim Earnings (Per Share)

Qtr.	Sep	Dec	Mar	Jun
2004-05	0.22	0.14	0.14	0.23
2005-06	(0.14)	0.35	0.27	0.08
2006-07	0.28	0.27	0.29	0.30
2007-08	0.23	0.27	...	...

Interim Dividends (Per Share)

Amt	Decl	Ex	Rec	Pay
0.05S	...	9/11/2006	9/13/2006	10/18/2006
0.05S	...	3/12/2007	3/14/2007	4/18/2007
0.05S	...	9/10/2007	9/12/2007	10/17/2007
0.06S	...	3/10/2008	3/12/2008	4/16/2008

Indicated Div: $0.11

Valuation Analysis | **Institutional Holding**
Forecast P/E	16.98	No of Institutions
	(1/10/2007)	273
Market Cap	$59.5 Billion	Shares
Book Value	34.8 Billion	233,431,360
Price/Book	1.71	% Held
Price/Sales	1.95	23.66

Business Summary: Media (MIC: 13.1 SIC: 2711 NAIC: 511110)

News is an entertainment company with operations in eight industry segments: filmed entertainment; television; cable network programming; direct broadcast satellite television; magazines and inserts; newspapers; book publishing; and other. Co. is engaged in the production and acquisition of live-action and animated motion pictures for distribution and licensing in all formats in all entertainment media worldwide, and the production and licensing of television programming worldwide. Co.'s activities are conducted principally in the U.S., the U.K., Continental Europe, Australia, Asia and the Pacific Basin. Through HarperCollins Publishers, Co. publishes English language books.

Recent Developments: For the quarter ended Dec 31 2007, net income increased 1.2% to US$832.0 million from US$822.0 million in the year-earlier quarter. Revenues were US$8.59 billion, up 9.5% from US$7.84 billion the year before. Operating income was US$1.42 billion versus US$1.14 billion in the prior-year quarter, an increase of 24.0%. Direct operating expenses rose 1.9% to US$5.44 billion from US$5.34 billion in the comparable period the year before. Indirect operating expenses increased 27.2% to US$1.73 billion from US$1.36 billion in the equivalent prior-year period.

Prospects: On Dec 13 2007, Co. completed its $5.70 billion acquisition of all of the outstanding shares of Dow Jones & Co., including the assumption of net debt. Co. expects the purchase to strengthen its position in the financial news and information market and to enhance its ability to adapt to future challenges and opportunities within its Newspapers and Information Services segment and across its other related business segments. Meanwhile, on Dec 22 2007, Co. announced that it will sell eight of its owned-and-operated FOX network affiliated television stations to Oak Hill Capital Partners for approximately $1.10 billion. Co. expects to close the transaction in the third calendar quarter of 2008.

Financial Data
(US$ in Thousands)

	6 Mos	3 Mos	06/30/2007	06/30/2006	06/30/2005	06/30/2004	06/30/2003	06/30/2002
Earnings Per Share	1.09	1.09	1.14	0.76	0.73	0.41	0.34	(2.43)
Cash Flow Per Share	1.33	1.34	1.30	1.01	1.12	0.62	0.49	0.62
Tang Book Value Per Share	0.79	2.43	2.37	1.86	1.81	2.27	0.96	0.60
Dividends Per Share	0.100	0.100	0.100	0.130	0.065	0.078	0.059	0.053
Dividend Payout %	9.17	9.17	8.77	17.11	8.85	19.00	17.38	
Income Statement								
Total Revenue	15,657,000	7,067,000	28,655,000	25,327,000	23,859,000	29,428,000	29,913,000	29,014,000
EBITDA	3,492,000	1,627,000	6,786,000	5,828,000	4,862,000	...	...	...
Depn & Amortn	644,000	334,000	...	...	...	...	...	...
Income Before Taxes	2,568,000	1,180,000	5,306,000	4,405,000	3,561,000	...	...	...
Income Taxes	934,000	414,000	1,814,000	1,526,000	1,220,000	1,247,000	774,000	655,000
Net Income	1,564,000	732,000	3,426,000	2,314,000	2,128,000	2,312,000	1,808,000	(11,962,000)
Average Shares	3,139,000	3,139,000	3,178,000	3,228,000	3,082,000	5,595,999	5,144,999	4,940,999
Balance Sheet								
Current Assets	14,328,000	17,554,000	15,906,000	13,123,000	12,779,000	15,012,000	14,861,000	14,647,000
Total Assets	68,916,000	64,492,000	62,343,000	56,649,000	54,692,000	73,738,000	67,747,000	71,441,000
Current Liabilities	9,578,000	8,819,000	7,494,000	6,373,000	6,649,000	10,437,000	9,303,000	11,005,000
Long-Term Obligations	14,213,000	12,148,000	12,147,000	11,385,000	10,087,000	10,917,000	12,396,000	13,585,000
Total Liabilities	34,164,000	30,851,000	29,421,000	26,775,000	25,315,000	28,211,000	29,026,000	31,973,000
Stockholders' Equity	34,752,000	33,641,000	32,922,000	29,874,000	29,377,000	45,527,000	38,721,000	39,468,000
Shares Outstanding	3,126,846	3,125,274	3,126,107	3,155,716	3,266,650	5,969,605	5,327,498	5,303,106
Statistical Record								
Return on Assets %	5.19	5.43	5.76	4.16	3.31	3.26	2.60	N.M.
Return on Equity %	9.98	10.31	10.91	7.81	5.68	5.47	4.62	N.M.
EBITDA Margin %	22.30	23.02	23.68	23.01	20.38	...	...	...
Net Margin %	9.99	10.36	11.96	9.14	8.92	7.86	6.04	N.M.
Asset Turnover	0.48	0.49	0.48	0.45	0.37	0.41	0.43	0.37
Current Ratio	1.50	1.99	2.12	2.06	1.92	1.44	1.60	1.33
Debt to Equity	0.38	0.36	0.37	0.38	0.34	0.24	0.32	0.34
Price Range	25.34-20.49	25.34-20.30	25.34-18.96	20.47-14.97	19.22-15.38	19.74-14.94	16.20-9.02	19.53-10.99
P/E Ratio	23.25-18.80	23.25-18.62	22.23-16.63	26.93-19.70	26.33-21.07	48.15-36.43	47.63-26.51	...
Average Yield %	0.43	0.43	0.45	0.75	0.38	0.45	0.47	0.36

Address: 1211 Avenue of the Americas, New York, NY 10036 **Telephone:** 212-852-7000	**Web Site:** www.newscorp.com **Officers:** Keith Rupert Murdoch - Chmn., C.E.O. Peter Chernin - Pres., C.O.O.	**Auditors:** Ernst & Young LLP **Investor Contact:** 212-852-7070 **Transfer Agents:** Computershare Investor Services plc, Bristol, United Kingdom

NICOR INC.

Exchange	Symbol	Price	52Wk Range	Yield	P/E
NYS	GAS	$33.51 (3/31/2008)	53.22-32.74	5.55	11.21

*7 Year Price Score 87.77   *NYSE Composite Index=100   *12 Month Price Score 90.79

Interim Earnings (Per Share)

Qtr.	Mar	Jun	Sep	Dec
2003	1.04	0.54	0.01	0.79
2004	0.44	0.44	(0.26)	1.08
2005	0.99	0.75	(0.06)	1.40
2006	0.99	0.19	0.39	1.30
2007	1.04	0.40	0.32	1.23

Interim Dividends (Per Share)

Amt	Decl	Ex	Rec	Pay
0.465Q	4/26/2007	6/27/2007	6/29/2007	8/1/2007
0.465Q	7/26/2007	9/26/2007	9/28/2007	11/1/2007
0.465Q	11/29/2007	12/27/2007	12/31/2007	2/1/2008
0.465Q	3/27/2008	4/3/2008	4/7/2008	5/1/2008

Indicated Div: $1.86

Valuation Analysis

Forecast P/E	17.49 (1/10/2007)
Market Cap	$1.5 Billion
Book Value	945.2 Million
Price/Book	1.60
Price/Sales	0.48

Institutional Holding

No of Institutions	239
Shares	32,800,288
% Held	73.03

Business Summary: Gas Utilities (MIC: 7.4 SIC: 4924 NAIC: 221210)

NICOR is a holding company that is primarily engaged in the business of gas distribution. Co.'s subsidiaries include Nicor Gas, a distributor of natural gas, which had served 2.2 million customers at Dec 31 2007 mainly in the northern third of Illinois, excluding Chicago; and Tropical Shipping, a transporter of containerized freight in the Bahamas and the Caribbean region. Co. also owns several energy-related ventures, including Nicor Services, Nicor Solutions and Nicor Advanced Energy, which provides energy-related products and services to retail markets, and Nicor Enerchange, a wholesale natural gas marketing company. In addition, Co. has equity interests in energy-related businesses.

Recent Developments: For the year ended Dec 31 2007, net income increased 5.4% to US$135.2 million from US$128.3 million in the prior year. Revenues were US$3.18 billion, up 7.3% from US$2.96 billion the year before. Operating income was US$206.5 million versus US$202.5 million in the prior year, an increase of 2.0%. Direct operating expenses rose 8.0% to US$2.17 billion from US$2.01 billion in the comparable period the year before. Indirect operating expenses increased 7.0% to US$801.5 million from US$748.9 million in the equivalent prior-year period.

Prospects: Looking into 2008, Co. anticipates results to be negatively affected by lower operating results at its gas distribution business due to continued demand weakness and operating cost pressures. Therefore, Co. is under-recovering its allowed costs of delivery service, and thus, is evaluating the need for a general rate filing with the Illinois Commerce Commission (ICC). For 2008, based on lower expected results in each business segment and higher net interest expense, Co. is estimating diluted earnings per share of about $2.20 to $2.40, excluding any future effects associated with the ICC performance-based rate plan/purchased gas adjustment review, and other contingencies, among other things.

Financial Data

(US$ in Thousands)	12/31/2007	12/31/2006	12/31/2005	12/31/2004	12/31/2003	12/31/2002	12/31/2001	12/31/2000
Earnings Per Share	2.99	2.87	3.07	1.70	2.38	2.88	3.17	1.00
Cash Flow Per Share	5.58	10.02	4.67	7.18	(0.29)	6.08	10.89	4.97
Tang Book Value Per Share	20.94	19.43	18.36	16.99	17.13	16.55	16.39	15.56
Dividends Per Share	1.860	1.860	1.860	1.860	1.860	1.840	1.760	1.660
Dividend Payout %	62.21	64.81	60.59	109.41	78.15	63.89	55.52	166.00
Income Statement								
Total Revenue	3,176,300	2,960,000	3,357,800	2,739,700	2,662,700	1,897,400	2,544,100	2,298,100
EBITDA	397,600	392,300	384,200	310,800	366,500	379,100	410,800	254,000
Income Before Taxes	184,300	174,100	171,000	105,300	169,400	185,600	217,100	61,100
Income Taxes	49,100	45,800	34,700	30,200	59,600	57,600	73,400	14,400
Net Income	135,200	128,300	136,300	75,100	105,300	128,000	143,700	46,700
Average Shares	45,300	44,700	44,400	44,300	44,200	44,300	45,200	46,300
Balance Sheet								
Net PPE	2,757,300	2,714,700	2,659,100	2,549,800	2,484,200	1,796,800	1,768,600	1,729,600
Total Assets	4,252,000	4,090,100	4,391,200	3,975,200	3,797,200	2,899,400	2,574,800	2,885,400
Long-Term Obligations	422,800	497,500	485,800	495,300	495,100	396,200	446,400	347,100
Total Liabilities	3,306,800	3,217,500	3,579,900	3,226,100	3,042,600	2,171,000	1,847,200	2,177,600
Stockholders' Equity	945,200	872,600	811,300	749,100	754,600	728,400	727,600	707,800
Shares Outstanding	45,129	44,901	44,179	44,102	44,040	44,011	44,397	45,491
Statistical Record								
Return on Assets %	3.24	3.03	3.26	1.93	3.14	4.68	5.26	1.75
Return on Equity %	14.88	15.24	17.47	9.96	14.20	17.58	20.02	6.23
EBITDA Margin %	12.52	13.25	11.44	11.34	13.76	19.98	16.15	11.05
Net Margin %	4.26	4.33	4.06	2.74	3.95	6.75	5.65	2.03
PPE Turnover	1.16	1.10	1.29	1.09	1.24	1.06	1.45	1.32
Asset Turnover	0.76	0.70	0.80	0.70	0.80	0.69	0.93	0.86
Debt to Equity	0.45	0.57	0.60	0.66	0.66	0.54	0.61	0.49
Price Range	53.22-38.18	49.66-38.91	42.50-35.76	39.65-32.22	39.10-23.85	48.96-22.75	41.66-34.12	43.56-29.81
P/E Ratio	17.80-12.77	17.30-13.56	13.84-11.65	23.32-18.95	16.43-10.02	17.00-7.90	13.14-10.76	43.56-29.81
Average Yield %	4.15	4.33	4.74	5.28	5.58	4.89	4.58	4.75

Address: 1844 Ferry Road, Naperville, IL 60563-9600 **Telephone:** 630-305-9500 **Fax:** 630-983-9328	**Web Site:** www.nicor.com **Officers:** Russ M. Strobel - Chmn., Pres., C.E.O. Kathleen L. Halloran - Exec. V.P., Chief Risk Officer	**Auditors:** Deloitte & Touche LLP **Transfer Agents:** ComputerShare Investor Services, Chicago, IL

NIKE, INC

Exchange	Symbol	Price	52Wk Range	Yield	P/E
NYS	NKE	$68.00 (3/31/2008)	69.08-52.58	1.35	18.89

*7 Year Price Score 125.13 *NYSE Composite Index=100* ***12 Month Price Score 113.08**

TRADING VOLUME (thousand shares)

Interim Earnings (Per Share)

Qtr.	Aug	Nov	Feb	May
2004-05	0.60	0.48	0.51	0.65
2005-06	0.81	0.57	0.62	0.64
2006-07	0.73	0.64	0.68	0.86
2007-08	1.12	0.71	0.92	...

Interim Dividends (Per Share)

Amt	Decl	Ex	Rec	Pay
0.185Q	5/14/2007	6/7/2007	6/11/2007	7/2/2007
0.185Q	8/13/2007	9/6/2007	9/10/2007	10/1/2007
0.23Q	11/16/2007	12/6/2007	12/10/2007	1/2/2008
0.23Q	2/14/2008	3/6/2008	3/10/2008	4/1/2008

Indicated Div: $0.92

Valuation Analysis

		Institutional Holding	
Forecast P/E	13.05	No of Institutions	
	(1/10/2007)	551	
Market Cap	$34.4 Billion	Shares	
Book Value	7.6 Billion	312,456,896	
Price/Book	4.51	% Held	
Price/Sales	1.92	62.00	

Business Summary: Rubber Products (MIC: 11.6 SIC: 3021 NAIC: 316211)

Nike is engaged in the design, development and worldwide marketing of footwear, apparel, equipment, and accessory products. Co. sells its products to retail accounts, through NIKE-owned retail stores, and through a mix of independent distributors and licensees, in over 180 countries around the world. Co.'s footwear and apparel products are produced outside the U.S., while its equipment products are produced both in the U.S. and abroad. As of May 31 2007, Co. sold its line of products under trademarks and brand names that include NIKE®, Converse®, Chuck Taylor®, All Star®, One Star®, Jack Purcell®, Hurley®, Cole Haan®, G Series®, Bragano®, NIKE Bauer®, Starter brand name and S logo.

Recent Developments: For the quarter ended Feb 29 2008, net income increased 32.2% to US$463.8 million from US$350.8 million in the year-earlier quarter. Revenues were US$4.54 billion, up 15.7% from US$3.93 billion the year before. Direct operating expenses rose 13.9% to US$2.50 billion from US$2.19 billion in the comparable period the year before. Indirect operating expenses increased 13.3% to US$1.38 billion from US$1.22 billion in the equivalent prior-year period.

Prospects: Going forward, Co. will continue to evaluate its existing portfolio of businesses as well as new business opportunities as part of its long term growth strategy. In detail, on Feb 21 2008, Co. announced that it has reached a definitive agreement to divest its Bauer Hockey subsidiary to an investor group consisting of Kohlberg & Company and Canadian businessman W. Graeme Roustan for a total transaction value of approximately $200.0 million. Accordingly, Co. expects this transaction to be completed before the end of its fiscal year ending May 31 2008. Meanwhile, Co. is encouraged by the Mar 3 2008 acquisition of Umbro plc, which should expand its presence in the global football markets.

Financial Data

(US$ in Thousands)	9 Mos	6 Mos	3 Mos	05/31/2007	05/31/2006	05/31/2005	05/31/2004	05/31/2003
Earnings Per Share	3.60	3.37	3.30	2.93	2.64	2.24	1.75	0.89
Cash Flow Per Share	4.57	4.60	3.94	3.73	3.22	2.99	2.87	1.73
Tang Book Value Per Share	14.05	13.98	13.66	12.93	11.23	9.77	8.13	7.22
Dividends Per Share	0.785	0.740	0.710	0.680	0.560	0.450	0.340	0.260
Dividend Payout %	21.80	21.96	21.52	23.21	21.21	20.09	19.37	29.38
Income Statement								
Total Revenue	13,539,000	8,994,600	4,655,100	16,325,900	14,954,900	13,739,700	12,253,100	10,697,000
EBITDA	2,078,600	1,334,600	740,300	2,469,600	2,423,600	2,117,000	1,702,100	1,385,500
Depn & Amortn	224,000	148,700	70,000	...	...	...	...	...
Income Before Taxes	1,854,600	1,185,900	670,300	2,199,900	2,141,600	1,859,800	1,450,000	1,123,000
Income Taxes	461,700	256,800	100,600	708,400	749,600	648,200	504,400	382,900
Net Income	1,392,900	929,100	569,700	1,491,500	1,392,000	1,211,600	945,600	474,000
Average Shares	502,500	506,200	507,300	509,900	527,600	540,600	539,400	535,200
Balance Sheet								
Current Assets	8,904,700	8,687,400	8,341,500	8,076,500	7,359,000	6,351,100	5,512,000	4,679,900
Total Assets	11,788,200	11,454,600	11,013,500	10,688,300	9,869,600	8,793,600	7,891,600	6,713,900
Current Liabilities	2,913,200	2,788,900	2,615,400	2,584,000	2,623,300	1,999,200	2,009,000	2,015,200
Long-Term Obligations	446,700	436,300	420,900	409,900	410,700	687,300	682,400	551,600
Total Liabilities	4,175,000	3,962,400	3,658,900	3,662,900	3,584,400	3,149,400	3,109,900	2,723,200
Stockholders' Equity	7,613,200	7,492,200	7,354,600	7,025,400	6,285,200	5,644,200	4,781,700	3,990,700
Shares Outstanding	505,300	497,200	498,741	501,700	512,000	522,200	526,200	527,200
Statistical Record								
Return on Assets %	16.60	16.15	16.36	14.51	14.92	14.52	12.91	7.21
Return on Equity %	25.25	24.49	24.81	22.41	23.34	23.24	21.50	12.11
EBITDA Margin %	15.35	14.84	15.90	15.13	16.21	15.41	13.89	12.95
Net Margin %	10.29	10.33	12.24	9.14	9.31	8.82	7.72	4.43
Asset Turnover	1.62	1.63	1.63	1.59	1.60	1.65	1.67	1.63
Current Ratio	3.03	3.11	3.19	3.13	2.81	3.18	2.74	2.32
Debt to Equity	0.06	0.06	0.06	0.06	0.07	0.12	0.14	0.14
Price Range	67.00-51.23	66.26-47.60	59.83-40.30	56.75-38.10	45.72-38.51	45.85-34.64	39.04-24.85	28.38-19.66
P/E Ratio	18.61-14.23	19.66-14.12	18.13-12.21	19.37-13.00	17.32-14.59	20.47-15.46	22.31-14.20	31.89-22.09
Average Yield %	1.35	1.34	1.39	1.45	1.33	1.12	1.05	1.10

Address: One Bowerman Drive, Beaverton, OR 97005-6453 **Telephone:** 503-671-6453 **Fax:** 503-671-6300	**Web Site:** www.nikebiz.com **Officers:** Philip H. Knight - Chmn., C.E.O., Pres. William D. Perez - Pres., C.E.O.	**Auditors:** PricewaterhouseCoopers LLP **Transfer Agents:** EquiServe Trust Company

99 CENTS ONLY STORES

Exchange	Symbol	Price	52Wk Range	Yield	P/E
NYS	NDN	$9.89 (3/31/2008)	15.31-6.32	N/A	98.90

*7 Year Price Score 47.15   *NYSE Composite Index=100   *12 Month Price Score 91.00

TRADING VOLUME (thousand shares)

Interim Earnings (Per Share)

Qtr.	Jun	Sep	Dec	Mar
2005-06			0.16	
2006-07	0.03	0.00	0.13	(0.01)
2007-08	0.04	(0.07)	0.14	...

Interim Dividends (Per Share)

No Dividends Paid

Valuation Analysis

		Institutional Holding	
Forecast P/E	57.27	No of Institutions	
	(1/10/2007)	131	
Market Cap	$692.9 Million	Shares	
Book Value	530.2 Million	48,926,216	
Price/Book	1.31	% Held	
Price/Sales	0.58	69.96	

Business Summary: Retail - General (MIC: 5.2 SIC: 5331 NAIC: 452990)

99 Cents Only Stores is a retailer of consumable general merchandise with an emphasis on name-brand products. Co. also sells merchandise through its Bargain Wholesale division at prices generally below normal wholesale levels to retailers, distributors and exporters. Co. provides consumer items in each of the following product categories: food, beverages, health and beauty care, household products, housewares, hardware, stationery, party goods, seasonal goods, baby products, toys, giftware, pet products, plants and gardening, clothing, electronics and entertainment. As of Mar 31 2007, Co. operated 251 retail stores with 177 in California, 41 in Texas, 22 in Arizona, and 11 in Nevada.

Recent Developments: For the quarter ended Dec 31 2007, net income increased 6.5% to US$9.5 million from US$8.9 million in the year-earlier quarter. Revenues were US$325.0 million, up 7.6% from US$302.1 million the year before. Operating income was US$12.2 million versus US$10.6 million in the prior-year quarter, an increase of 14.6%. Direct operating expenses rose 7.5% to US$194.5 million from US$180.9 million in the comparable period the year before. Indirect operating expenses increased 7.1% to US$118.3 million from US$110.5 million in the equivalent prior-year period.

Prospects: Co. believes that near-term growth in sales for the remainder of fiscal 2008 ending Mar 2008 and in fiscal 2009 should result from new store openings in its existing states and increases in same store sales. As such, Co. intends to open approximately seven new stores during the fiscal fourth quarter ending Mar 2008, while expecting its store opening growth rate to be approximately 6.0% to 8.0% for fiscal 2009. Meanwhile, in fiscal 2009, Co. intends to continue to implement price changes on additional items that were previously sold in multiples for $0.99 to fewer multiples at price points less than $0.99, which has resulted in higher product margins for Co.

Financial Data

(US$ in Thousands)	9 Mos	6 Mos	3 Mos	03/31/2007	03/31/2006	03/31/2005	12/31/2004	12/31/2003
Earnings Per Share	0.10	0.09	0.16	0.14	0.16	0.01	0.39	0.78
Cash Flow Per Share	0.45	0.14	0.32	0.41	1.19	1.22	...	1.11
Tang Book Value Per Share	7.57	7.42	7.49	7.42	7.21	7.04	7.02	6.80
Income Statement								
Total Revenue	908,857	583,882	292,976	1,104,696	1,023,589	242,630	972,173	862,460
EBITDA	28,116	7,632	8,834	39,909	43,225	8,293	67,335	112,505
Depn & Amortn	24,761	16,464	8,207	...	...	...	...	...
Income Before Taxes	8,386	(5,361)	2,460	14,001	16,738	1,105	42,352	91,842
Income Taxes	1,071	(3,154)	(504)	4,239	5,316	306	14,521	35,313
Net Income	7,315	(2,207)	2,964	9,762	11,422	799	27,831	56,529
Average Shares	70,060	70,054	70,260	70,017	69,737	69,787	71,016	72,412
Balance Sheet								
Current Assets	326,798	315,944	336,619	313,534	310,536	271,923	287,619	275,127
Total Assets	658,008	648,621	660,471	643,135	628,708	588,418	600,204	553,238
Current Liabilities	112,835	114,356	123,020	103,644	109,061	86,885	100,202	57,225
Long-Term Obligations	599	614	629	7,930	6,874	752	774	1,553
Total Liabilities	127,808	128,598	136,306	123,908	127,182	99,010	111,920	63,352
Stockholders' Equity	530,200	520,023	524,165	519,227	501,526	489,408	488,284	489,886
Shares Outstanding	70,060	70,056	70,028	69,941	69,569	69,548	69,517	72,032
Statistical Record								
Return on Assets %	0.97	0.89	1.67	1.54	1.88	0.55	...	11.38
Return on Equity %	1.20	1.11	2.11	1.91	2.31	0.66	...	12.75
EBITDA Margin %	3.09	1.31	3.02	3.61	4.22	3.42	6.93	13.04
Net Margin %	0.80	N.M.	1.01	0.88	1.12	0.33	2.86	6.55
Asset Turnover	1.83	1.82	1.75	1.74	1.68	1.66	...	1.74
Current Ratio	2.90	2.76	2.74	3.03	2.85	3.13	2.87	4.81
Debt to Equity	N.M.	N.M.	N.M.	0.02	0.01	N.M.	N.M.	N.M.
Price Range	16.13-7.19	16.13-9.73	16.13-10.04	16.13-10.00	13.62-9.01	16.45-12.95	29.65-12.17	36.02-20.83
P/E Ratio	161.30-71.90	179.22-108.11	100.81-62.75	115.21-71.43	85.13-56.31	N.M.	76.03-31.21	46.18-26.71

Address: 4000 Union Pacific Avenue, City of Commerce, CA 90023
Telephone: 323-980-8145
Fax: 323-980-8160

Web Site: www.99only.com
Officers: David Gold - Chmn. Jeff Gold - Pres., C.O.O.

Auditors: BDO Seidman, LLP
Investor Contact: 323-980-8145
Transfer Agents: American Stock Transfer & Trust Co., New York, NY

NISOURCE INC. (HOLDING CO.)

Exchange	Symbol	Price	52Wk Range	Yield	P/E
NYS	NI	$17.24 (3/31/2008)	25.36-17.02	5.34	14.74

*7 Year Price Score 74.22   *NYSE Composite Index=100   *12 Month Price Score 96.40

Interim Earnings (Per Share)

Qtr.	Mar	Jun	Sep	Dec
2003	0.99	(1.23)	0.06	0.54
2004	0.81	0.13	0.11	0.59
2005	0.76	0.14	(0.03)	0.25
2006	0.63	0.08	0.10	0.22
2007	0.79	0.10	0.04	0.24

Interim Dividends (Per Share)

Amt	Decl	Ex	Rec	Pay
0.23Q	5/8/2007	7/27/2007	7/31/2007	8/20/2007
0.23Q	8/28/2007	10/29/2007	10/31/2007	11/20/2007
0.23Q	1/9/2008	1/29/2008	1/31/2008	2/20/2008
0.23Q	3/26/2008	4/28/2008	4/30/2008	5/20/2008

Indicated Div: $0.92

Valuation Analysis

Forecast P/E	16.8†
	(1/10/2007)
Market Cap	$4.7 Billion
Book Value	5.1 Billion
Price/Book	0.93
Price/Sales	0.60

Institutional Holding

No of Institutions	347
Shares	211,858,016
% Held	77.36

Business Summary: Electricity (MIC: 7.1 SIC: 4931 NAIC: 221121)

NiSource is an energy holding company that provides natural gas, electricity and other products and services to about 3.8 million customers from the Gulf Coast through the Midwest to New England. At Dec 31 2007, Co.'s natural gas distribution operations served over 3.3 million customers in nine states and operated about 58,000 miles of pipeline. Co.'s gas transmission and storage operations own and operate 16,000 miles of interstate pipelines and operate underground natural gas storage systems capable of storing 637.00 billion cubic feet of natural gas. Co.'s electric operations generate, transmit and distribute electricity to about 457,000 customers in 20 counties in northern Indiana.

Recent Developments: For the year ended Dec 31 2007, income from continuing operations decreased 0.5% to US$312.0 million from US$313.5 million a year earlier. Net income increased 13.9% to US$321.4 million from US$282.2 million in the prior year. Revenues were US$7.94 billion, up 6.0% from US$7.49 billion the year before. Operating income was US$931.9 million versus US$880.0 million in the prior year, an increase of 5.9%. Direct operating expenses rose 7.1% to US$4.68 billion from US$4.37 billion in the comparable period the year before. Indirect operating expenses increased 3.9% to US$2.33 billion from US$2.24 billion in the equivalent prior-year period.

Prospects: On Feb 15 2008, Co. has agreed to sell its Northern Utilities and Granite State Gas to Unitil Corporation for $160.0 million plus net working capital at the time of closing. The transaction should close by the end of 2008, and is expected to allow Co. to focus on commercial development and expansion of its natural gas pipeline and storage business, as well as investment-driven growth at its core regulated utility businesses, such as Bay State. For 2008, Co. expects earnings from continuing operations of $1.23 to $1.35 per share, assuming normal weather and excluding business dispositions, impairments, costs to retire debt and other significant items similar to those affecting 2007 results.

Financial Data

(US$ in Thousands)	12/31/2007	12/31/2006	12/31/2005	12/31/2004	12/31/2003	12/31/2002	12/31/2001	12/31/2000
Earnings Per Share	1.17	1.03	1.12	1.64	0.33	1.75	1.03	1.15
Cash Flow Per Share	2.77	4.24	2.63	3.87	1.82	5.56	5.08	(0.05)
Tang Book Value Per Share	3.36	3.29	2.79	2.14	...	...	N.M.	N.M.
Dividends Per Share	0.920	0.920	0.920	0.920	1.100	1.160	1.160	1.080
Dividend Payout %	78.63	89.32	82.14	56.10	333.33	66.29	112.62	93.91
Income Statement								
Total Revenue	7,939,800	7,490,000	7,899,100	6,666,200	6,246,600	6,492,300	9,458,700	6,030,700
EBITDA	1,439,000	1,419,800	1,393,100	1,596,900	1,625,700	1,759,700	1,664,700	955,900
Income Before Taxes	484,100	484,300	433,000	671,100	659,900	659,600	395,300	277,200
Income Taxes	172,100	170,800	149,400	240,900	234,200	233,900	183,200	130,100
Net Income	321,400	282,200	306,500	436,300	85,200	372,500	216,200	156,900
Average Shares	274,700	273,400	273,000	265,500	261,600	212,800	209,800	135,811
Balance Sheet								
Net PPE	10,031,800	9,694,500	9,554,300	9,384,700	9,304,900	10,068,000	9,554,700	9,546,700
Total Assets	18,004,800	18,156,500	17,958,500	16,988,000	16,623,800	16,896,900	17,374,100	19,696,800
Long-Term Obligations	5,594,400	5,146,200	5,271,200	4,835,900	5,993,400	5,018,000	5,780,800	5,802,700
Total Liabilities	12,928,200	13,142,900	12,944,400	12,119,800	12,126,800	12,292,100	13,471,100	15,803,900
Stockholders' Equity	5,076,600	5,013,600	4,933,000	4,787,100	...	...	3,469,400	3,415,200
Shares Outstanding	274,176	273,654	272,622	270,625	262,630	248,860	205,553	205,553
Statistical Record								
Return on Assets %	1.78	1.56	1.75	2.59	0.51	2.17	1.17	1.18
Return on Equity %	6.37	5.67	6.31	...	...	...	6.28	...
EBITDA Margin %	18.12	18.96	17.64	23.96	26.03	27.10	17.60	15.85
Net Margin %	4.05	3.77	3.88	6.54	1.36	5.74	2.29	2.60
PPE Turnover	0.80	0.78	0.83	0.71	0.64	0.66	0.99	0.81
Asset Turnover	0.44	0.41	0.45	0.40	0.37	0.38	0.51	0.45
Debt to Equity	1.10	1.03	1.07	1.01	...	...	1.67	1.70
Price Range	25.36-17.51	24.77-19.88	25.30-20.84	22.78-19.77	21.94-16.46	24.93-14.70	32.18-19.40	31.50-12.88
P/E Ratio	21.68-14.97	24.05-19.30	22.59-18.61	13.89-12.05	66.48-49.88	14.25-8.40	31.24-18.83	27.39-11.20
Average Yield %	4.28	4.22	3.97	4.35	5.65	5.66	4.39	5.23

Address: 801 East 86th Avenue,
Merrillville, IN 46410
Telephone: 219-647-5990
Fax: 219-647-6085

Web Site: www.nisource.com
Officers: Gary L. Neale - Chmn. Robert C. Skaggs Jr.
- Pres., C.E.O.

Auditors: Deloitte & Touche LLP
Investor Contact: 219-647-5200
Transfer Agents: Mellon Human
Resources & Investor Solutions, South
Hackensack, NJ

NOBLE CORP.

Exchange	Symbol	Price	52Wk Range	Yield	P/E
NYS	NE	$49.67 (3/31/2008)	57.01-39.53	0.32	11.09

*7 Year Price Score 141.45 *NYSE Composite Index=100 *12 Month Price Score 105.46

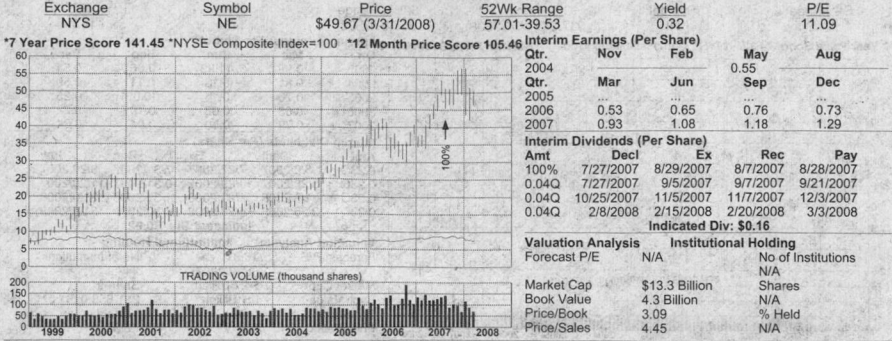

Interim Earnings (Per Share)

Qtr.	Nov	Feb	May	Aug
2004			0.55	
Qtr.	Mar	Jun	Sep	Dec
2005	...	...	...	...
2006	0.53	0.65	0.76	0.73
2007	0.93	1.08	1.18	1.29

Interim Dividends (Per Share)

Amt	Decl	Ex	Rec	Pay
100%	7/27/2007	8/29/2007	8/7/2007	8/28/2007
0.04Q	7/27/2007	9/5/2007	9/7/2007	9/21/2007
0.04Q	10/25/2007	11/5/2007	11/7/2007	12/3/2007
0.04Q	2/8/2008	2/15/2008	2/20/2008	3/3/2008

Indicated Div: $0.16

Valuation Analysis

		Institutional Holding	
Forecast P/E	N/A	No of Institutions	N/A
Market Cap	$13.3 Billion	Shares	N/A
Book Value	4.3 Billion	% Held	N/A
Price/Book	3.09		
Price/Sales	4.45		

Business Summary: Oil and Gas (MIC: 14.2 SIC: 1381 NAIC: 213111)

Noble is an offshore drilling contractor for the oil and gas industry. As of Dec 31 2007, Co. performed contract drilling services with its fleet of 62 mobile offshore drilling units located worldwide, which consisted of 13 semisubmersibles, three drillships, 43 jackups and three submersibles. Co. conducts its contract drilling operations principally in the Middle East, India, U.S. Gulf of Mexico, Mexico, the North Sea, Brazil, and West Africa. In addition, Co. performed services under labor contracts for drilling and workover activities covering 11 rigs operating in the U.K. sector of the North Sea and two rigs under a labor contract, the Hibernia Contract, off the east coast of Canada.

Recent Developments: For the year ended Dec 31 2007, net income increased 64.8% to US$1.21 billion from US$731.9 million in the prior year. Revenues were US$3.00 billion, up 42.6% from US$2.10 billion the year before. Operating income was US$1.49 billion versus US$927.4 million in the prior year, an increase of 60.8%. Direct operating expenses rose 28.2% to US$1.11 billion from US$867.1 million in the comparable period the year before. Indirect operating expenses increased 28.5% to US$392.8 million from US$305.7 million in the equivalent prior-year period.

Prospects: Co. is bolstered by its strong markets, robust demand, and deepwater rigs contracts that will roll over later in 2008 or in 2009. For example, on Mar 31 2008, Co. secured a memorandum of understanding for five deepwater rigs contracts with a total revenue potential of $4.0 billion over 29 rig years operating offshore Brazil for Petroleo Brasileiro S.A. (Petrobras). These contracts will boost Co.'s overall fleet backlog to over $10.00 billion and enable it to move forward with its planned upgrades on each of its three drillships. In addition, Co.'s newbuild deepwater semisubmersible, the Noble Dave Beard, is scheduled to commence its five-year contract with Petrobras offshore Brazil in 2009.

Financial Data

(US$ in Thousands)	12/31/2007	12/31/2006	12/31/2005	12/31/2004	12/31/2003	12/31/2002	12/31/2001	12/31/2000
Earnings Per Share	4.48	2.67	1.08	0.55	0.63	0.79	0.98	0.61
Dividends Per Share	0.120	0.080	0.050	...	...	...	...	...
Income Statement								
Total Revenue	2,995,311	2,100,239	1,382,137	1,066,231	987,380	986,356	1,002,329	882,600
Income Before Taxes	1,488,902	921,287	364,092	161,817	186,984	243,325	349,992	226,307
Income Taxes	282,891	189,421	67,396	15,731	20,568	33,822	86,082	60,753
Net Income	1,206,011	731,866	296,696	146,086	166,416	209,503	262,922	165,554
Average Shares	269,330	274,756	275,122	268,230	266,014	266,904	268,348	270,922
Balance Sheet								
Current Assets	860,191	569,980	522,455	425,283	421,959	465,643	494,049	379,132
Total Assets	5,876,006	4,585,914	4,346,367	3,307,973	3,189,633	3,065,714	2,750,740	2,595,531
Current Liabilities	492,772	426,260	259,335	214,166	244,023	280,660	207,549	205,428
Long-Term Obligations	774,182	684,469	1,129,325	503,288	541,907	589,562	550,131	650,291
Total Liabilities	1,573,280	1,364,269	1,614,633	923,539	1,011,208	1,076,504	972,421	1,018,812
Stockholders' Equity	4,308,322	3,228,993	2,731,734	2,384,434	2,178,425	1,989,210	1,778,319	1,576,719
Shares Outstanding	268,223	269,184	274,018	268,814	264,388	263,486	264,030	267,182
Statistical Record								
Price Range	56.85-33.87	42.63-29.97	37.77-23.66	25.20-16.98	18.70-15.36	22.90-14.07	26.60-10.90	26.28-13.94
P/E Ratio	12.69-7.56	15.96-11.22	34.97-21.90	45.81-30.86	29.67-24.38	28.98-17.82	27.14-11.12	43.08-22.85
Average Yield %	0.26	0.22	0.16	...	...	...	...	...

Address: 13135 South Dairy Ashford, Suite 800, Sugar Land, TX 77478
Telephone: 281-276-6100
Fax: 281-491-2091

Web Site: www.noblecorp.com
Officers: James C. Day - Chmn., C.E.O. Mark A. Jackson - Pres., C.O.O.

Auditors: PricewaterhouseCoopers LLP

NOBLE ENERGY, INC.

Exchange	Symbol	Price	52Wk Range	Yield	P/E
NYS	NBL	$72.80 (3/31/2008)	81.64-58.17	0.66	13.36

*7 Year Price Score 159.87 *NYSE Composite Index=100 ***12 Month Price Score 118.01**

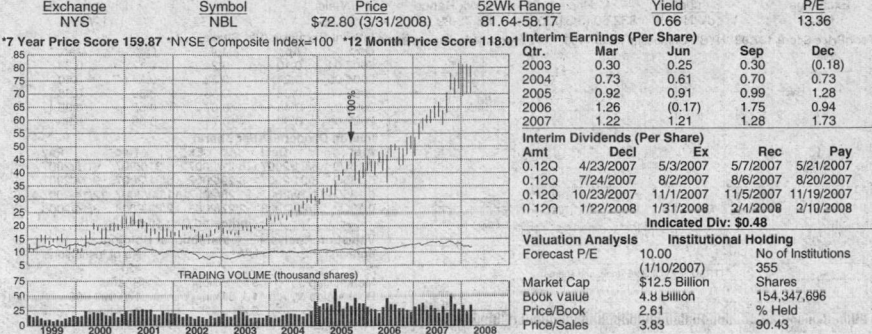

TRADING VOLUME (thousand shares)

Interim Earnings (Per Share)				
Qtr.	Mar	Jun	Sep	Dec
2003	0.30	0.25	0.30	(0.18)
2004	0.73	0.61	0.70	0.73
2005	0.92	0.91	0.99	1.28
2006	1.26	(0.17)	1.75	0.94
2007	1.22	1.21	1.28	1.73

Interim Dividends (Per Share)				
Amt	Decl	Ex	Rec	Pay
0.12Q	4/23/2007	5/3/2007	5/7/2007	5/21/2007
0.12Q	7/24/2007	8/2/2007	8/6/2007	8/20/2007
0.12Q	10/23/2007	11/1/2007	11/5/2007	11/19/2007
0.12Q	1/22/2008	1/31/2008	2/4/2008	2/10/2008
Indicated Div: $0.48				

Valuation Analysis		Institutional Holding	
Forecast P/E	10.00	No of Institutions	
	(1/10/2007)	355	
Market Cap	$12.5 Billion	Shares	
Book Value	4.8 Billion	154,347,696	
Price/Book	2.61	% Held	
Price/Sales	3.83	90.43	

Business Summary: Oil and Gas (MIC: 14.2 SIC: 1311 NAIC: 211111)

Noble Energy is engaged in the acquisition, exploration, development, production and marketing of crude oil and natural gas Co. operates throughout major basins in the U.S., including Colorado's Wattenberg field and Piceance basin, the Mid-continent area of western Oklahoma and the Texas Panhandle, the San Juan basin in New Mexico, the Gulf Coast and the deepwater Gulf of Mexico. Co. also conducts business internationally in China, Ecuador, the Mediterranean Sea, the North Sea, West Africa (Equatorial Guinea and Cameroon) and in other areas As of Dec 31 2007, Co. had estimated proved reserves of 3.307 trillion cubic feet of natural gas and 329.0 million barrels of crude oil.

Recent Developments: For the year ended Dec 31 2007, net income increased 39.1% to US$943.9 million from US$678.4 million in the prior year. Revenues were US$3.27 billion, up 11.3% from US$2.94 billion the year before. Direct operating expenses rose 5.4% to US$561.8 million from US$532.8 million in the comparable period the year before. Indirect operating expenses increased 19.6% to US$1.17 billion from US$974.4 million in the equivalent prior-year period.

Prospects: For 2008, Co. will invest $1.60 billion for its capital investment program, of which 74.0% will be designated for development activities, 24.0% on exploration efforts and the rest for corporate expenses and other items. Co. believes that such program should allow it to deliver 2008 sales volume of 205 to 216 thousand barrels of oil equivalents per day, up 6.0% over 2007. Notably, volumes in the U.S. should increase 5.0% due to active drilling programs in the Wattenberg, Piceance and Niobrara areas in the Rocky Mountain region. Also, the global volumes should be up 7.0% due to a full year of natural gas sales from the Alba field to the liquefied natural gas facility in Equatorial Guinea.

Financial Data
(US$ in Thousands)

	12/31/2007	12/31/2006	12/31/2005	12/31/2004	12/31/2003	12/31/2002	12/31/2001	12/31/2000
Earnings Per Share	5.45	3.79	4.12	2.77	0.68	0.16	1.17	1.69
Cash Flow Per Share	11.79	9.85	8.06	6.06	5.29	4.41	5.62	5.08
Tang Book Value Per Share	23.50	19.35	12.66	12.37	9.39	8.80	8.86	7.57
Dividends Per Share	0.435	0.275	0.150	0.100	0.085	0.080	0.080	0.080
Dividend Payout %	7.98	7.26	3.64	3.60	12.50	51.61	6.87	4.73
Income Statement								
Total Revenue	3,272,030	2,940,082	2,186,723	1,351,176	1,010,986	1,443,728	1,572,263	1,393,591
EBITDA	2,238,795	1,871,112	1,481,076	911,953	558,455	405,306	551,790	578,000
Income Before Taxes	1,367,567	1,096,217	968,660	516,041	141,639	42,599	224,610	299,483
Income Taxes	423,697	417,789	322,940	202,191	51,747	24,947	91,035	107,886
Net Income	943,870	678,428	645,720	328,710	77,992	17,652	133,575	191,597
Average Shares	173,344	179,044	156,759	118,452	115,078	115,526	114,606	113,510
Balance Sheet								
Current Assets	1,569,267	1,068,546	1,175,511	734,302	478,387	310,374	351,571	271,261
Total Assets	10,830,896	9,388,623	8,878,033	3,443,171	2,842,649	2,730,015	2,479,848	1,879,280
Current Liabilities	1,635,743	1,184,262	1,240,145	665,004	654,718	471,754	380,585	325,417
Long-Term Obligations	1,851,087	1,800,810	2,030,533	880,256	776,021	977,116	837,177	525,494
Total Liabilities	6,022,089	5,474,808	5,787,889	1,983,183	1,769,076	1,720,629	1,469,650	1,029,598
Stockholders' Equity	4,808,807	4,113,817	3,090,144	1,459,988	1,073,573	1,009,386	1,010,198	849,682
Shares Outstanding	172,233	172,233	175,624	118,044	114,389	114,725	114,011	112,181
Statistical Record								
Return on Assets %	9.24	7.35	10.48	10.43	2.80	0.68	6.13	11.48
Return on Equity %	21.16	18.83	28.38	25.88	7.49	1.75	14.36	24.92
EBITDA Margin %	68.42	63.64	67.73	67.49	55.24	28.07	35.10	41.48
Net Margin %	28.85	23.08	29.53	24.33	7.71	1.22	8.50	13.75
Asset Turnover	0.32	0.32	0.35	0.43	0.36	0.55	0.72	0.83
Current Ratio	0.96	0.90	0.95	1.10	0.73	0.66	0.92	0.83
Debt to Equity	0.38	0.44	0.66	0.60	0.72	0.97	0.83	0.62
Price Range	81.64-46.33	54.04-36.28	47.79-28.06	31.98-21.37	22.90-16.29	20.23-13.76	25.18-13.89	23.84-9.69
P/E Ratio	14.98-8.50	14.26-9.57	11.60-6.81	11.54-7.71	33.68-23.96	126.41-85.97	21.52-11.87	14.11-5.73
Average Yield %	0.68	0.60	0.40	0.39	0.46	0.45	0.42	0.47

Address: 100 Glenborough Drive, Suite 100, Houston, TX 77067-3610 Telephone: 281-872-3100 Fax: 281-872-3111	Web Site: www.nobleenergyinc.com Officers: Charles D. Davidson - Chmn., C.E.O. Susan M. Cunningham - Sr. V.P., Explor.	Auditors: KPMG LLP Investor Contact: 281-872-3100 Transfer Agents: Wachovia Bank N.A., Charlotte, NC

NORDSTROM, INC.

*7 Year Price Score 137.92 *NYSE Composite Index=100 *12 Month Price Score 89.02

Interim Earnings (Per Share)

Qtr.	Apr	Jul	Oct	Jan
2003-04	0.10	0.24	0.17	0.38
2004-05	0.24	0.38	0.27	0.50
2005-06	0.38	0.53	0.39	0.68
2006-07	0.48	0.67	0.52	0.88
2007-08	0.60	0.71	0.68	0.90

Interim Dividends (Per Share)

Amt	Decl	Ex	Rec	Pay
0.135Q	5/21/2007	5/29/2007	5/31/2007	6/15/2007
0.135Q	8/21/2007	8/29/2007	8/31/2007	9/14/2007
0.135Q	11/19/2007	11/28/2007	11/30/2007	12/14/2007
0.16Q	2/20/2008	2/27/2008	2/29/2008	3/14/2008

Indicated Div: $0.64

Valuation Analysis

		Institutional Holding	
Forecast P/E	N/A	No of Institutions	431
Market Cap	$7.2 Billion	Shares	179,020,608
Book Value	1.1 Billion	% Held	69.51
Price/Book	6.46		
Price/Sales	0.82		

TRADING VOLUME (thousand shares)

Business Summary: Retail - Apparel and Accessory Stores (MIC: 5.8 SIC: 5651 NAIC: 448140)

Nordstrom is a fashion specialty retailer of clothing, shoes and accessories for men, women and children. Co. provides several brand name and private label merchandise through multiple retail channels, including 103 Full-Line Nordstrom stores, 50 discount Nordstrom Rack stores, two Jeffrey boutiques, two Last Chance clearance stores, its catalogs and through its online store. Co.'s stores are located throughout the U.S., in addition to 37 Façonnable boutiques located in France, Portugal, and Belgium. Through its wholly owned federal savings bank, Nordstrom fsb, Co. also provides a private label card, two co-branded Nordstrom VISA credit cards and a debit card for Nordstrom purchases.

Recent Developments: For the year ended Feb 2 2008, net income increased 5.5% to US$715.0 million from US$678.0 million in the prior year. Revenues were US$8.83 billion, up 3.1% from US$8.56 billion the year before. Direct operating expenses rose 3.2% to US$5.53 billion from US$5.35 billion in the comparable period the year before. Indirect operating expenses remained unchanged at US$2.06 billion versus the equivalent prior-year period.

Prospects: For the fiscal year ending Jan 31 2009, Co. is targeting a flat to a 2.0% decrease in same-store sales and earnings of $2.75 to $2.90 per diluted share, while gross profit is projected to decline by 30 to 60 basis points. In addition, Co. intends to open six additional full-line stores and three Rack stores, which is expected to increase retail square footage by approximately 6.0%. For the fiscal quarter ended May 2008, Co. is anticipating a 3.0% to 5.0% decrease in same-store sales, while earnings are estimated to range from $0.49 to $0.54 per diluted share. Meanwhile, for the first half of fiscal year ending Jan 30 2010, Co. plans to open three new full-line stores and two Rack stores.

Financial Data

(US$ in Thousands)	02/02/2008	02/03/2007	01/28/2006	01/29/2005	01/31/2004	01/31/2003	01/31/2002	01/31/2001
Earnings Per Share	2.88	2.55	1.98	1.39	0.88	0.33	0.47	0.39
Cash Flow Per Share	0.66	4.31	2.86	2.18	2.10	1.03	1.54	0.68
Tang Book Value Per Share	4.81	7.90	7.26	6.09	5.40	4.55	4.37	4.06
Dividends Per Share	0.540	0.420	0.320	0.240	0.205	0.190	0.180	0.175
Dividend Payout %	18.75	16.47	16.16	17.33	23.30	57.58	38.71	44.87
Income Statement								
Total Revenue	8,828,000	8,560,698	7,722,860	7,131,388	6,491,673	5,975,076	5,634,130	5,528,537
EBITDA	1,480,000	1,396,638	1,173,503	958,100	712,064	489,297	488,707	421,666
Income Before Taxes	1,173,000	1,105,653	885,225	647,281	398,141	195,624	204,488	167,018
Income Taxes	458,000	427,654	333,886	253,831	155,300	92,041	79,800	65,100
Net Income	715,000	677,999	551,339	393,450	242,841	90,224	124,688	101,918
Average Shares	249,000	265,712	277,776	284,534	275,478	271,448	268,678	262,226
Balance Sheet								
Current Assets	3,361,000	2,742,193	2,874,157	2,572,444	2,455,430	2,072,618	2,054,598	1,812,982
Total Assets	5,600,000	4,821,578	4,921,349	4,605,390	4,465,688	4,096,376	4,048,779	3,608,503
Current Liabilities	1,635,000	1,433,143	1,623,312	1,341,152	1,049,549	870,091	947,738	950,568
Long-Term Obligations	2,236,000	623,652	627,776	929,010	1,227,410	1,341,826	1,351,044	1,099,710
Total Liabilities	4,485,000	2,653,057	2,828,668	2,816,396	2,831,679	2,724,319	2,734,291	2,378,935
Stockholders' Equity	1,115,000	2,168,521	2,092,681	1,788,994	1,634,009	1,372,057	1,314,488	1,229,568
Shares Outstanding	221,000	257,313	269,549	271,330	276,753	270,888	268,937	267,595
Statistical Record								
Return on Assets %	13.76	13.69	11.61	8.70	5.67	2.22	3.26	3.05
Return on Equity %	43.67	31.31	28.49	23.05	16.16	6.72	9.80	8.42
EBITDA Margin %	16.76	16.31	15.20	13.43	10.97	8.19	8.67	7.63
Net Margin %	8.10	7.92	7.14	5.52	3.74	1.51	2.21	1.84
Asset Turnover	1.70	1.73	1.63	1.58	1.52	1.47	1.47	1.65
Current Ratio	2.06	1.91	1.77	1.92	2.34	2.38	2.17	1.91
Debt to Equity	2.01	0.29	0.30	0.52	0.75	0.98	1.03	0.89
Price Range	59.66-29.04	56.94-32.36	42.28-24.13	24.38-17.72	20.18-7.93	13.19-7.75	12.65-7.05	16.88-7.16
P/E Ratio	20.72-10.08	22.33-12.69	21.35-12.18	17.54-12.75	22.93-9.01	39.95-23.47	26.91-15.00	43.27-18.35
Average Yield %	1.16	1.01	0.98	1.16	1.71	1.77	1.94	1.66

Address: 1617 Sixth Avenue, Suite 500, Seattle, WA 98101-1742 **Telephone:** 206-628-2111 **Fax:** 206-628-1795	**Web Site:** www.nordstrom.com **Officers:** Bruce A. Nordstrom - Chmn. Blake W. Nordstrom - Pres.	**Auditors:** Deloitte & Touche LLP **Transfer Agents:** Mellon Investor Services LLC

NORFOLK SOUTHERN CORP.

Exchange	Symbol	Price	52Wk Range	Yield	P/E
NYS	NSC	$54.32 (3/31/2008)	58.64-44.15	2.14	14.76

*7 Year Price Score 126.60 *NYSE Composite Index=100 *12 Month Price Score 110.71

Interim Earnings (Per Share)

Qtr.	Mar	Jun	Sep	Dec
2003	0.54	0.35	0.35	0.13
2004	0.40	0.54	0.72	0.65
2005	0.47	1.04	0.73	0.87
2006	0.72	0.89	1.02	0.95
2007	0.71	0.98	0.97	1.02

Interim Dividends (Per Share)

Amt	Decl	Ex	Rec	Pay
0.22Q	4/24/2007	5/2/2007	5/4/2007	6/11/2007
0.26Q	7/24/2007	8/1/2007	8/3/2007	9/10/2007
0.26Q	10/23/2007	10/31/2007	11/2/2007	12/10/2007
0.29Q	1/22/2008	1/30/2008	2/1/2008	3/10/2008

Indicated Div: $1.16

Valuation Analysis

		Institutional Holding	
Forecast P/E	10.85	No of Institutions	
	(1/10/2007)	625	
Market Cap	$20.6 Billion	Shares	
Book Value	9.7 Billion	280,127,744	
Price/Book	2.12	% Held	
Price/Sales	2.18	70.56	

Business Summary: Rail Transport (MIC: 15.5 SIC: 4011 NAIC: 482111)

Norfolk Southern is engaged principally in the rail transportation business. Through its main subsidiary, Norfolk Southern Railway Company, Co. is primarily engaged in the rail transportation of raw materials, intermediate products and finished goods primarily in the Southeast, East and Midwest and, via interchange with rail carriers, to and from the rest of the U.S. Co. also transports overseas freight through several Atlantic and Gulf Coast ports. As of Dec 31 2007, Co.'s railroads operated approximately 21,000 miles of road in 22 eastern states, the District of Columbia.

Recent Developments: For the year ended Dec 31 2007, net income decreased 1.1% to US$1.46 billion from US$1.48 billion in the prior year. Revenues were US$9.43 billion, up 0.3% from US$9.41 billion the year before. Operating income was US$2.59 billion versus US$2.56 billion in the prior year, an increase of 1.1%. Indirect operating expenses were unchanged at US$6.85 billion versus the equivalent prior-year period.

Prospects: Co. expects revenues to continue to grow, reflecting higher average revenue per unit and modestly higher traffic volume, particularly later in 2008 given the overall economy improves. In detail, while expecting utility inventories to be above normal stockpiles in the Southeast, Co. expects growth in demand for utility coal to be stimulated by a decline in utility inventories in the Northeast. Also, while expecting domestic metallurgical coal, coke and iron ore demand to be comparable with 2007 for the first half of 2008, Co. expects demand to increase in the second half of 2008 due to plant expansions. Co. also expects export coal tonnage to increase, reflecting higher global demand.

Financial Data

(US$ in Thousands)	12/31/2007	12/31/2006	12/31/2005	12/31/2004	12/31/2003	12/31/2002	12/31/2001	12/31/2000
Earnings Per Share	3.68	3.57	3.11	2.31	1.37	1.18	0.97	0.45
Cash Flow Per Share	5.99	5.43	5.21	4.20	2.70	2.07	1.70	3.49
Tang Book Value Per Share	25.64	24.19	22.66	19.95	17.83	16.71	15.78	15.16
Dividends Per Share	0.960	0.680	0.480	0.360	0.300	0.260	0.240	0.800
Dividend Payout %	26.09	19.05	15.43	15.58	21.90	22.03	24.74	177.78
Income Statement								
Total Revenue	9,432,000	9,407,000	8,527,000	7,312,000	6,468,000	6,270,000	6,170,000	6,159,000
EBITDA	3,419,000	3,380,000	2,937,000	2,387,000	1,611,000	1,753,000	1,633,000	1,318,000
Income Before Taxes	2,237,000	2,230,000	1,697,000	1,302,000	586,000	706,000	553,000	250,000
Income Taxes	783,000	758,000	425,000	387,000	175,000	246,000	191,000	78,000
Net Income	1,464,000	1,481,000	1,281,000	923,000	535,000	460,000	375,000	172,000
Average Shares	397,800	414,700	412,300	399,300	392,000	390,000	386,000	383,000
Balance Sheet								
Total Assets	26,144,000	26,028,000	25,861,000	24,750,000	20,596,000	19,956,000	19,418,000	18,976,000
Long-Term Obligations	5,999,000	6,109,000	6,616,000	6,863,000	6,800,000	7,006,000	7,027,000	7,339,000
Total Liabilities	16,417,000	16,413,000	16,572,000	16,760,000	13,620,000	13,456,000	13,328,000	13,152,000
Stockholders' Equity	9,727,000	9,615,000	9,289,000	7,990,000	6,976,000	6,500,000	6,090,000	5,824,000
Shares Outstanding	379,297	397,419	409,885	400,438	391,153	388,985	385,832	384,057
Statistical Record								
Return on Assets %	5.61	5.71	5.06	4.06	2.64	2.34	1.95	0.90
Return on Equity %	15.14	15.67	14.83	12.30	7.94	7.31	6.30	2.92
EBITDA Margin %	36.25	35.93	34.44	32.64	24.91	27.96	26.47	21.40
Net Margin %	15.52	15.74	15.02	12.62	8.27	7.34	6.08	2.79
Asset Turnover	0.36	0.36	0.34	0.32	0.32	0.32	0.32	0.32
Price Range	58.64-46.04	57.35-40.65	45.20-30.01	36.50-20.54	24.33-17.70	26.60-18.05	23.87-13.69	21.75-12.00
P/E Ratio	15.93-12.51	16.06-11.39	14.53-9.65	15.80-8.89	17.76-12.92	22.54-15.30	24.61-14.11	48.33-26.67
Average Yield %	1.84	1.38	1.31	1.34	1.50	1.22	1.31	4.98

Address: Three Commercial Place, Norfolk, VA 23510-2191 Telephone: 757-629-2680	Web Site: www.nscorp.com Officers: David R. Goode - Chmn. Henry C. Wolf - Vice-Chmn., C.F.O.	Auditors: KPMG LLP Investor Contact: 757-629-2861 Transfer Agents: The Bank of New York, New York, NY

NORTHEAST UTILITIES

Exchange	Symbol	Price	52Wk Range	Yield	P/E
NYS	NU	$24.54 (3/31/2008)	33.53-24.01	3.26	15.43

*7 Year Price Score 113.41 *NYSE Composite Index=100 *12 Month Price Score 94.96

TRADING VOLUME (thousand shares)

Interim Earnings (Per Share)

Qtr.	Mar	Jun	Sep	Dec
2003	0.47	0.21	0.31	(0.08)
2004	0.53	0.18	0.30	(0.10)
2005	(0.91)	(0.21)	(0.73)	(0.08)
2006	(0.07)	0.14	0.72	2.25
2007	0.49	0.31	0.32	0.47

Interim Dividends (Per Share)

Amt	Decl	Ex	Rec	Pay
0.188Q	4/11/2007	5/30/2007	6/1/2007	6/29/2007
0.20Q	5/8/2007	8/29/2007	9/1/2007	9/28/2007
0.20Q	11/13/2007	11/28/2007	12/1/2007	12/31/2007
0.20Q	2/12/2008	2/27/2008	3/1/2008	3/31/2008

Indicated Div: $0.80

Valuation Analysis / Institutional Holding

Forecast P/E	16.33	No of Institutions
	(1/10/2007)	223
Market Cap	$3.8 Billion	Shares
Book Value	2.9 Billion	113,592,816
Price/Book	1.31	% Held
Price/Sales	0.65	73.63

Business Summary: Electricity (MIC: 7.1 SIC: 4911 NAIC: 221122)

Northeast Utilities is a public utility holding company. Co. is engaged primarily in the energy delivery business through its wholly-owned regulated utility subsidiaries: The Connecticut Light and Power Company (CL&P), Public Service Company of New Hampshire (PSNH), Western Massachusetts Electric Company (WMECO), and Yankee Gas Services Company (Yankee Gas). The regulated companies operate through three business segments: the electric distribution segment (which includes PSNH's regulated generation activities), the natural gas distribution segment and the electric transmission segment. Co. also owns certain unregulated businesses through its wholly-owned subsidiary, NU Enterprises, Inc.

Recent Developments: For the year ended Dec 31 2007, net income decreased 47.6% to US$246.5 million from US$470.6 million in the prior year. Revenues were US$5.82 billion, down 15.3% from US$6.88 billion the year before. Operating income was US$539.5 million versus US$236.0 million in the prior year, an increase of 128.6%. Direct operating expenses declined 23.9% to US$4.52 billion from US$5.95 billion in the comparable period the year before. Indirect operating expenses increased 9.1% to US$759.2 million from US$695.7 million in the equivalent prior-year period.

Prospects: On Dec 20 2007, Co. and Quanta Services Inc. announced the completion of a master services agreement, in which Quanta will provide transmission infrastructure services related to Co.'s transmission build-out to strengthen electric reliability and reduce congestion in the New England region through upgrading the transmission infrastructure. The contract is expected to be valued at $750.0 million over six years beginning in 2008 through 2013. Meanwhile, for 2008, Co. expects consolidated earnings of $1.65 per share and $1.90 per share and an average compounded annual earnings per share growth rate of 8.0% to 11.0% for the period 2008 through 2012 based on its 2007 earnings of $1.59 per share.

Financial Data

(US$ in Thousands)	12/31/2007	12/31/2006	12/31/2005	12/31/2004	12/31/2003	12/31/2002	12/31/2001	12/31/2000
Earnings Per Share	1.59	3.05	(1.93)	0.91	0.91	1.18	1.79	(0.20)
Cash Flow Per Share	1.61	2.65	3.35	4.02	4.51	4.74	2.78	4.07
Tang Book Value Per Share	16.93	16.28	13.98	15.17	15.04	14.62	13.79	13.17
Dividends Per Share	0.775	0.725	0.675	0.625	0.575	0.525	0.450	0.400
Dividend Payout %	48.74	23.77	...	68.68	63.19	44.49	25.14	...
Income Statement								
Total Revenue	5,822,226	6,884,388	7,397,390	6,686,699	6,069,156	5,216,321	6,873,826	5,876,620
EBITDA	1,119,845	752,288	120,293	655,872	1,017,040	1,205,296	1,910,851	...
Income Before Taxes	360,875	50,280	(386,429)	173,903	186,573	239,972	447,143	...
Income Taxes	109,420	(81,429)	(162,765)	51,756	59,862	82,304	173,952	(68,306)
Net Income	246,483	470,578	(253,488)	116,588	116,411	152,109	243,510	(28,586)
Average Shares	155,304	154,146	131,638	128,396	127,240	129,341	135,917	141,967
Balance Sheet								
Net PPE	7,229,945	6,242,186	6,417,230	5,864,161	5,429,916	4,728,369	3,822,139	3,547,215
Total Assets	11,581,822	11,303,236	12,569,075	11,655,834	11,308,884	10,267,617	10,241,409	10,217,149
Long-Term Obligations	3,483,599	2,960,435	3,027,288	2,789,974	2,481,331	2,287,144	2,292,556	2,076,827
Total Liabilities	8,551,787	8,388,857	10,023,631	9,242,923	8,928,564	7,940,896	8,007,569	7,862,366
Stockholders' Equity	2,913,835	2,798,179	2,429,244	2,296,711	2,264,120	2,210,521	2,117,640	2,218,583
Shares Outstanding	155,079	154,233	153,225	129,034	127,695	127,562	130,132	143,820
Statistical Record								
Return on Assets %	2.15	3.94	N.M.	1.01	1.08	1.48	2.38	N.M.
Return on Equity %	8.63	18.00	N.M.	5.10	5.20	7.03	11.23	N.M.
EBITDA Margin %	19.23	10.93	1.63	9.81	16.76	23.11	27.80	...
Net Margin %	4.23	6.84	(3.43)	1.74	1.92	2.92	3.54	(0.49)
PPE Turnover	0.86	1.09	1.20	1.18	1.19	1.22	1.87	1.56
Asset Turnover	0.51	0.58	0.61	0.58	0.56	0.51	0.67	0.59
Debt to Equity	1.20	1.06	1.25	1.21	1.10	1.03	1.08	0.94
Price Range	33.53-26.93	28.81-19.24	21.79-17.61	20.17-17.30	20.17-13.38	20.57-13.20	23.75-16.80	24.25-18.25
P/E Ratio	21.09-16.94	9.45-6.31	...	22.16-19.01	22.16-14.70	17.43-11.19	13.27-9.39	...
Average Yield %	2.60	3.28	3.48	3.31	3.48	3.02	2.33	1.87

Address: P.O. Box 270, Hartford, CT 06141-0270	Web Site: www.nu.com	Auditors: Deloitte & Touche LLP
Telephone: 800-286-5000	Officers: Charles W. Shivery - Chmn., Pres., C.E.O. John P. Stack - V.P., Acctg., Contr.	Investor Contact: 800-286-5000
		Transfer Agents: The Bank of New York, New York, NY

NORTHROP GRUMMAN CORP

Exchange	Symbol	Price	52Wk Range	Yield	P/E
NYS	NOC	$77.81 (3/31/2008)	84.48-72.68	1.90	15.20

*7 Year Price Score 108.95 *NYSE Composite Index=100 *12 Month Price Score 109.54

Interim Earnings (Per Share)

Qtr.	Mar	Jun	Sep	Dec
2003	0.67	0.54	0.50	0.61
2004	0.64	0.81	0.76	0.74
2005	1.11	1.00	0.81	0.92
2006	1.02	1.23	0.86	1.28
2007	1.10	1.31	1.41	1.31

Interim Dividends (Per Share)

Amt	Decl	Ex	Rec	Pay
0.37Q	5/16/2007	5/24/2007	5/29/2007	6/9/2007
0.37Q	8/15/2007	8/23/2007	8/27/2007	9/8/2007
0.37Q	11/14/2007	11/21/2007	11/26/2007	12/8/2007
0.37Q	2/20/2008	2/28/2008	3/3/2008	3/15/2008

Indicated Div: $1.48

Valuation Analysis | **Institutional Holding**

Forecast P/E	12.84	No of Institutions	
	(1/10/2007)	493	
Market Cap	$26.3 Billion	Shares	
Book Value	17.7 Billion	303,197,568	
Price/Book	1.49	% Held	
Price/Sales	0.82	86.56	

Business Summary: Defense (MIC: 1.2 SIC: 3761 NAIC: 336414)

Northrop Grumman and its subsidiaries are engaged in the provision of products, services, and integrated solutions in information and services, aerospace, electronics, and shipbuilding. As a prime contractor, principal subcontractor, partner, or preferred supplier, Co. participates in high-priority defense and commercial technology programs in the U.S. and abroad. Co. conducts most of its business with the U.S. Government, principally the Department of Defense ("DoD"). Co. is aligned into seven segments: Mission Systems, Information Technology, Technical Services, Integrated Systems, Space Technology, Electronics, and Ships.

Recent Developments: For the year ended Dec 31 2007, income from continuing operations increased 14.6% to US$1.80 billion from US$1.57 billion a year earlier. Net income increased 16.1% to US$1.79 billion from US$1.54 billion in the prior year. Revenues were US$32.02 billion, up 6.3% from US$30.11 billion the year before. Operating income was US$3.01 billion versus US$2.46 billion in the prior year, an increase of 22.0%. Direct operating expenses rose 4.8% to US$25.80 billion from US$24.62 billion in the comparable period the year before. Indirect operating expenses increased 6.0% to US$3.21 billion from US$3.03 billion in the equivalent prior-year period.

Prospects: Despite the trend of slower growth rates in the US defense budget, Co. believes that its products, services, and integrated applications will continue generating revenue growth. Thus, based on total backlog of about $64.00 billion as of Dec 31 2007, Co. expects diluted earnings per share from continuing operations to be $5.50 to $5.75 on sales of about $33.00 billion in 2008. Meanwhile, on Feb 14 2008, the US Navy awarded Co. a $1.40 billion cost plus incentive fee contract for the construction of a Zumwalt-class destroyer, DDG 1001, and major components for the DDG 1000. Co. expects construction of DDG 1001 to begin in the fourth quarter of 2009, with an expected delivery date of 2014.

Financial Data

(US$ in Thousands)	12/31/2007	12/31/2006	12/31/2005	12/31/2004	12/31/2003	12/31/2002	12/31/2001	12/31/2000
Earnings Per Share	5.12	4.37	3.85	2.97	2.32	0.17	2.40	4.29
Cash Flow Per Share	8.46	5.08	7.37	5.37	2.18	7.31	4.84	7.13
Dividends Per Share	1.480	1.160	1.010	0.890	0.800	0.800	0.600	0.800
Dividend Payout %	28.91	26.54	26.23	29.97	34.48	470.59	25.00	18.65
Income Statement								
Total Revenue	32,018,000	30,148,000	30,721,000	29,853,000	26,206,000	17,206,000	13,558,000	7,618,000
EBITDA	3,713,000	3,270,000	3,151,000	2,722,000	2,250,000	1,916,000	1,684,000	1,502,000
Income Before Taxes	2,686,000	2,276,000	2,044,000	1,615,000	1,131,000	1,009,000	699,000	975,000
Income Taxes	883,000	709,000	661,000	522,000	323,000	312,000	272,000	350,000
Net Income	1,790,000	1,542,000	1,400,000	1,084,000	866,000	64,000	427,000	608,000
Average Shares	354,300	358,600	363,200	365,000	368,360	234,860	170,520	141,760
Balance Sheet								
Current Assets	6,772,000	6,719,000	7,549,000	6,907,000	5,745,000	15,835,000	4,589,000	2,526,000
Total Assets	33,373,000	32,009,000	34,214,000	33,361,000	33,009,000	42,266,000	20,886,000	9,622,000
Current Liabilities	6,432,000	6,753,000	7,974,000	6,223,000	6,361,000	11,373,000	5,132,000	2,688,000
Long-Term Obligations	3,918,000	3,992,000	3,881,000	5,116,000	5,410,000	9,398,000	5,033,000	1,605,000
Total Liabilities	15,686,000	15,394,000	17,386,000	16,661,000	17,224,000	27,944,000	13,495,000	5,703,000
Stockholders' Equity	17,687,000	16,615,000	16,828,000	16,700,000	15,785,000	14,322,000	7,391,000	3,919,000
Shares Outstanding	337,834	345,921	347,357	364,430	362,216	365,204	217,112	144,116
Statistical Record								
Return on Assets %	5.48	4.66	4.14	3.26	2.30	0.20	2.80	6.41
Return on Equity %	10.44	9.22	8.35	6.66	5.75	0.59	7.55	16.90
EBITDA Margin %	11.60	10.85	10.26	9.12	8.59	11.14	12.42	19.72
Net Margin %	5.59	5.11	4.56	3.63	3.30	0.37	3.15	7.98
Asset Turnover	0.98	0.91	0.91	0.90	0.70	0.54	0.89	0.80
Current Ratio	1.05	0.99	0.95	1.11	0.90	1.39	0.89	0.94
Debt to Equity	0.22	0.24	0.23	0.31	0.34	0.66	0.68	0.41
Price Range	84.48-66.95	71.23-59.63	60.11-51.25	57.75-47.34	50.22-39.50	66.25-43.73	54.48-38.50	46.25-21.78
P/E Ratio	16.50-13.08	16.30-13.65	15.61-13.31	19.44-15.94	21.64-17.03	389.71-257.24	22.70-16.04	10.78-5.08
Average Yield %	1.93	1.76	1.84	1.72	1.79	1.44	1.33	2.29

Address: 1840 Century Park East, Los Angeles, CA 90067	Web Site: www.northropgrumman.com	Auditors: Deloitte & Touche LLP
Telephone: 310-553-6262	Officers: Ronald D. Sugar - Chmn., Pres., C.E.O.	Transfer Agents: ComputerShare
Fax: 310-201-3023	Wesley G. Bush - V.P., C.F.O.	Investor Services, Providence, RI

NORTHWEST NATURAL GAS CO.

Exchange	Symbol	Price	52Wk Range	Yield	P/E	Div Acheiver
NYS	NWN	$43.44 (3/31/2008)	52.62-41.38	3.45	15.74	52 Years

*7 Year Price Score 111.21 *NYSE Composite Index=100 *12 Month Price Score 100.79

Interim Earnings (Per Share)

Qtr.	Mar	Jun	Sep	Dec
2003	1.01	0.17	(0.25)	0.83
2004	1.24	(0.03)	(0.30)	0.98
2005	1.43	0.04	(0.31)	0.94
2006	1.48	0.07	(0.35)	1.09
2007	1.76	0.10	(0.22)	1.11

Interim Dividends (Per Share)

Amt	Decl	Ex	Rec	Pay
0.355Q	7/2/2007	7/27/2007	7/31/2007	8/15/2007
0.375Q	10/3/2007	10/29/2007	10/31/2007	11/15/2007
0.375Q	1/3/2008	1/29/2008	1/31/2008	2/15/2008
0.375Q	4/4/2008	4/28/2008	4/30/2008	5/15/2008
		Indicated Div: $1.50		

Valuation Analysis / **Institutional Holding**

Forecast P/E	16.38	No of Institutions	
	(1/10/2007)	148	
Market Cap	$1.1 Billion	Shares	
Book Value	594.8 Million	14,112,024	
Price/Book	1.93	% Held	
Price/Sales	1.11	51.78	

Business Summary: Gas Utilities (MIC: 7.4 SIC: 4924 NAIC: 221210)

Northwest Natural Gas is principally engaged in the distribution of natural gas in Oregon and southwest Washington. Co.'s Local Gas Distribution segment involves in purchasing gas from producers, transporting the gas over interstate pipelines from the supply basins to service territory, and reselling the gas to customers. The Gas Storage segment offers underground natural gas storage services to large intrastate and interstate customers. Additionally, Co. has other investments, including assets in NNG Financial Corp., a Boeing 737-300 aircraft under lease to Continental Airlines but currently held for sale, and investments in development projects such as Gill Ranch and Palomar Pipeline.

Recent Developments: For the year ended Dec 31 2007, net income increased 17.5% to US$74.5 million from US$63.4 million in the prior year. Revenues were US$1.03 billion, up 2.0% from US$1.01 billion the year before. Operating income was US$154.9 million versus US$136.8 million in the prior year, an increase of 13.3%. Direct operating expenses declined 1.3% to US$664.2 million from US$673.0 million in the comparable period the year before. Indirect operating expenses increased 5.3% to US$214.1 million from US$203.4 million in the equivalent prior-year period.

Prospects: Looking ahead, Co. expects a slowdown in construction to continue through 2008, and estimates that a prolonged slowdown in residential new construction could hurt its future results of operations. However, Co. is expecting continued customer growth due to the growing market in the Pacific Northwest and projects full-year 2008 earnings per share to in the range of $2.48 to $2.63, assuming several factors which include normal weather and no significant changes in prevailing regulatory policies. Meanwhile, for 2008, Co. plans to focus on several areas, including advancing its key natural gas infrastructure investments, such as the Palomar Pipeline and Gill Ranch storage projects.

Financial Data

(US$ in Thousands)	12/31/2007	12/31/2006	12/31/2005	12/31/2004	12/31/2003	12/31/2002	12/31/2001	12/31/2000
Earnings Per Share	2.76	2.29	2.11	1.86	1.76	1.62	1.88	1.88
Cash Flow Per Share	6.85	5.39	2.87	3.98	4.15	4.87	2.84	3.45
Tang Book Value Per Share	22.52	21.97	21.28	20.64	19.52	18.88	18.56	17.92
Dividends Per Share	1.440	1.390	1.320	1.300	1.270	1.260	1.245	1.240
Dividend Payout %	52.17	60.70	62.56	69.89	72.16	77.78	66.22	65.96
Income Statement								
Total Revenue	1,033,193	1,013,172	910,486	707,604	611,256	641,376	650,252	532,110
EBITDA	224,174	203,331	189,797	170,225	158,671	153,458	161,185	155,642
Income Before Taxes	118,557	99,649	90,869	77,103	69,323	67,236	77,740	74,641
Income Taxes	44,060	36,234	32,720	26,531	23,340	23,444	27,553	26,829
Net Income	74,497	63,415	58,149	50,572	45,983	43,792	50,187	50,224
Average Shares	26,995	27,657	27,621	27,283	26,061	25,814	25,612	25,638
Balance Sheet								
Net PPE	1,495,873	1,425,141	1,373,423	1,318,405	1,205,913	995,595	964,976	934,030
Total Assets	2,014,183	1,956,856	2,042,031	1,732,195	1,591,332	1,342,791	1,435,022	1,278,713
Long-Term Obligations	512,000	517,000	521,500	484,027	500,319	445,945	378,377	400,790
Total Liabilities	1,419,432	1,357,311	1,455,100	1,163,678	1,085,016	859,688	966,861	826,404
Stockholders' Equity	594,751	599,545	586,931	568,517	506,316	483,103	468,161	452,309
Shares Outstanding	26,407	27,283	27,579	27,546	25,938	25,586	25,228	25,233
Statistical Record								
Return on Assets %	3.75	3.17	3.08	3.03	3.13	3.15	3.70	3.97
Return on Equity %	12.48	10.69	10.07	9.38	9.29	9.21	10.90	11.36
EBITDA Margin %	21.70	20.07	20.85	24.06	25.96	23.93	24.79	29.25
Net Margin %	7.21	6.26	6.39	7.15	7.52	6.83	7.72	9.44
PPE Turnover	0.71	0.72	0.68	0.56	0.56	0.65	0.68	0.58
Asset Turnover	0.52	0.51	0.48	0.42	0.42	0.46	0.48	0.42
Debt to Equity	0.86	0.86	0.89	0.85	0.99	0.92	0.81	0.89
Price Range	52.62-40.21	43.00-33.27	39.50-32.61	33.90-27.92	31.22-24.13	30.45-24.00	26.56-21.75	27.13-18.38
P/E Ratio	19.07-14.57	18.78-14.53	18.72-15.45	18.23-15.01	17.74-13.71	18.80-14.81	14.13-11.57	14.43-9.77
Average Yield %	3.12	3.74	3.67	4.19	4.58	4.52	5.14	5.61

Address: 220 N.W. Second Avenue,	Web Site: www.nwnatural.com	Auditors: PricewaterhouseCoopers LLP
Portland, OR 97209	Officers: Mark S. Dodson - Pres., C.E.O. Michael S.	Investor Contact: 503-226-4211
Telephone: 503-226-4211	McCoy - Exec. V.P., Customer & Utility Opers.	Transfer Agents: NW Natural,
Fax: 503-273-4824		Portland, OR

NSTAR

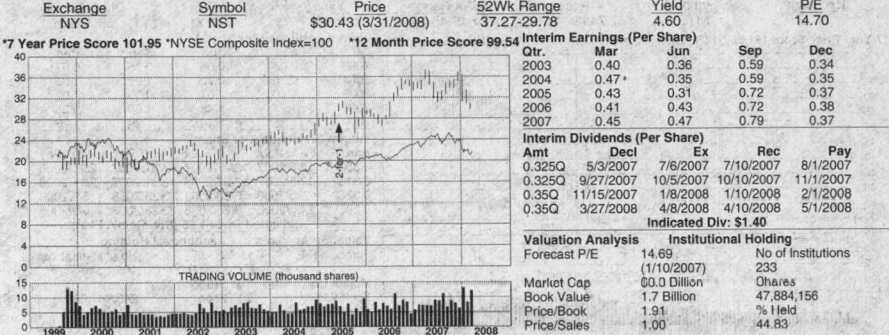

Exchange	Symbol	Price	52Wk Range	Yield	P/E
NYS	NST	$30.43 (3/31/2008)	37.27-29.78	4.60	14.70

*7 Year Price Score 101.95 *NYSE Composite Index=100 *12 Month Price Score 99.54

Interim Earnings (Per Share)

Qtr.	Mar	Jun	Sep	Dec
2003	0.40	0.36	0.59	0.34
2004	0.47 *	0.35	0.59	0.35
2005	0.43	0.31	0.72	0.37
2006	0.41	0.43	0.72	0.38
2007	0.45	0.47	0.79	0.37

Interim Dividends (Per Share)

Amt	Decl	Ex	Rec	Pay
0.325Q	5/3/2007	7/6/2007	7/10/2007	8/1/2007
0.325Q	9/27/2007	10/5/2007	10/10/2007	11/1/2007
0.35Q	11/15/2007	1/8/2008	1/10/2008	2/1/2008
0.35Q	3/27/2008	4/8/2008	4/10/2008	5/1/2008

Indicated Div: $1.40

Valuation Analysis | **Institutional Holding**

Forecast P/E	14.69 (1/10/2007)	No of Institutions 233
Market Cap	00.0 Dillion	Ohares
Book Value	1.7 Billion	47,884,156
Price/Book	1.91	% Held
Price/Sales	1.00	44.83

TRADING VOLUME (thousand shares)

Business Summary: Electricity (MIC: 7.1 SIC: 4911 NAIC: 221122)

NSTAR is a holding company engaged through its subsidiaries in the energy delivery business serving about 1.4 million customers in Massachusetts, including about 1.1 million electric distribution customers in 81 areas and around 300,000 natural gas customers in 51 areas. As of Dec 31 2007, Co.'s reportable segments are the electric and natural gas utility operations. At Dec 31 2007, the gas system of Co.'s NSTAR Gas Company subsidiary included about 3,080 miles of gas distribution lines, approximately 186,100 services and approximately 286,700 customer meters together with measuring and regulating equipment.

Recent Developments: For the year ended Dec 31 2007, net income increased 7.1% to US$221.5 million from US$206.8 million in the prior year. Revenues were US$3.26 billion, down 8.8% from US$3.58 billion the year before. Operating income was US$383.8 million versus US$374.5 million in the prior year, an increase of 2.5%. Direct operating expenses declined 13.5% to US$2.21 billion from US$2.56 billion in the comparable period the year before. Indirect operating expenses increased 3.3% to US$664.7 million from US$643.4 million in the equivalent prior-year period.

Prospects: Looking forward to full-year 2008, Co. is projecting earnings to be in a range of $2.16 to $2.26 per share, reflecting an anticipated 1.0% to 2.0% increase in electric sales assuming normal weather conditions. In addition, for 2008, Co. expects plant expenditures of approximately $440.0 million. These plant investments relate to system reliability and performance improvements, as well as capacity expansion. Notably, Co. expects to spend $75.0 million in 2008 and 2009 on phase two of its 345 kilovolt (kV) transmission project, which will add a third and final 345kV line to the project. Phase two of the project is expected to be in service in 2009.

Financial Data
(US$ in Thousands)

	12/31/2007	12/31/2006	12/31/2005	12/31/2004	12/31/2003	12/31/2002	12/31/2001	12/31/2000
Earnings Per Share	2.07	1.93	1.83	1.75	1.70	1.51	(0.03)	1.59
Cash Flow Per Share	4.60	4.99	(0.25)	4.11	3.97	5.53	3.07	1.55
Tang Book Value Per Share	15.95	14.82	14.37	9.52	8.70	7.99	7.53	8.17
Dividends Per Share	1.300	1.210	1.160	1.110	1.080	1.060	1.030	1.000
Dividend Payout %	62.80	62.69	63.39	63.25	63.53	69.97	...	62.89
Income Statement								
Total Revenue	3,261,784	3,577,702	3,243,120	2,954,332	2,914,131	2,719,067	3,191,836	2,699,506
Income Taxes	130,424	122,726	114,120	119,670	124,855	111,061	...	...
Net Income	221,515	206,774	196,135	188,481	181,574	163,667	3,201	180,962
Average Shares	107,122	107,125	107,100	107,292	106,678	106,594	106,432	110,090
Balance Sheet								
Net PPE	4,286,225	4,086,127	3,839,979	3,579,978	3,376,656	2,977,530	2,731,391	2,629,420
Total Assets	7,759,545	7,769,395	7,615,564	7,117,229	6,320,660	6,123,275	5,328,191	5,569,514
Long-Term Obligations	2,501,400	2,360,775	2,402,377	2,101,402	1,982,531	2,091,355	1,891,803	2,024,561
Total Liabilities	6,012,730	6,143,832	6,067,549	5,633,347	4,916,068	4,780,970	4,022,595	4,184,289
Stockholders' Equity	1,703,815	1,582,563	1,535,015	1,440,882	1,361,592	1,299,305	1,262,596	1,342,225
Shares Outstanding	106,808	106,808	106,808	106,550	106,065	106,065	106,065	106,065
Statistical Record								
Return on Assets %	2.85	2.68	2.66	2.80	2.92	2.86	0.06	3.27
Return on Equity %	13.48	13.27	13.18	13.41	13.65	12.78	0.25	12.51
Net Margin %	6.79	5.78	6.05	6.38	6.23	6.02	0.10	6.70
PPE Turnover	0.78	0.90	0.87	0.85	0.92	0.95	1.19	1.02
Asset Turnover	0.42	0.46	0.44	0.44	0.47	0.47	0.59	0.49
Debt to Equity	1.47	1.49	1.57	1.46	1.46	1.61	1.50	1.51
Price Range	37.27-31.02	35.79-26.55	31.40-25.05	27.19-22.70	24.34-19.50	24.00-17.41	22.59-17.72	22.53-18.56
P/E Ratio	18.00-14.99	18.54-13.76	17.16-13.69	15.54-12.97	14.32-11.47	15.89-11.53	...	14.17-11.67
Average Yield %	3.78	3.95	4.08	4.53	4.84	4.93	4.98	4.84

Address: 800 Boylston Street, Boston, MA 02199-8003	Web Site: www.nstar.com	Auditors: PricewaterhouseCoopers LLP
Telephone: 617-424-2000	Officers: Thomas J. May - Chmn., Pres., C.E.O.	Investor Contact: 617-424-2562
Fax: 617-424-4032	James J. Judge - Sr. V.P., C.F.O., Treas.	

NUCOR CORP.

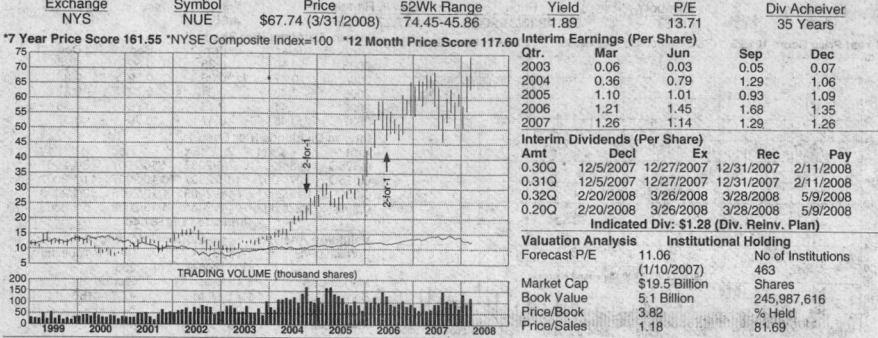

Exchange	Symbol	Price	52Wk Range	Yield	P/E	Div Acheiver
NYS	NUE	$67.74 (3/31/2008)	74.45-45.86	1.89	13.71	35 Years

*7 Year Price Score 161.55 *NYSE Composite Index=100 *12 Month Price Score 117.60

Interim Earnings (Per Share)

Qtr.	Mar	Jun	Sep	Dec
2003	0.06	0.03	0.05	0.07
2004	0.36	0.79	1.29	1.06
2005	1.10	1.01	0.93	1.09
2006	1.21	1.45	1.68	1.35
2007	1.26	1.14	1.29	1.26

Interim Dividends (Per Share)

Amt	Decl	Ex	Rec	Pay
0.30Q	12/5/2007	12/27/2007	12/31/2007	2/11/2008
0.31Q	12/5/2007	12/27/2007	12/31/2007	2/11/2008
0.32Q	2/20/2008	3/26/2008	3/28/2008	5/9/2008
0.20Q	2/20/2008	3/26/2008	3/28/2008	5/9/2008

Indicated Div: $1.28 (Div. Reinv. Plan)

Valuation Analysis

		Institutional Holding	
Forecast P/E	11.06 (1/10/2007)	No of Institutions	463
Market Cap	$19.5 Billion	Shares	245,987,616
Book Value	5.1 Billion	% Held	
Price/Book	3.82	81.69	
Price/Sales	1.18		

Business Summary: Metal Works (MIC: 11.3 SIC: 3312 NAIC: 331111)

Nucor produces and sells steel and steel products via its steel mills and steel products segments. Co.'s steel mills segment produces hot-rolled steel (angles, rounds, flats, channels, rebar, sheet, beams, pilings, billets, blooms, beam blanks and plate) and cold-rolled steel, while its steel products segment produces steel joists and joist girders, steel deck, cold finished steel, steel fasteners, metal building systems, light gauge steel framing, and wire and wire mesh. In the U.S., Co. sells hot- and cold-rolled steel to steel service centers, fabricators and manufacturers, and sells steel joists/ joist girders and steel deck to general contractors and fabricators.

Recent Developments: For the year ended Dec 31 2007, net income decreased 16.2% to US$1.47 billion from US$1.76 billion in the prior year. Revenues were US$16.59 billion, up 12.5% from US$14.75 billion the year before. Direct operating expenses rose 19.3% to US$13.46 billion from US$11.28 billion in the comparable period the year before. Indirect operating expenses decreased 2.5% to US$577.8 million from US$592.5 million in the equivalent prior-year period.

Prospects: On Feb 8 2008, Co. signed a Purchase Agreement to acquire the stock of SHV North America Corp., which owns 100.0% of The David J. Joseph Company, a broker and processor of ferrous scrap, its related affiliates and real estate, for approximately $1.44 billion. Co. expects the acquisition to provide it with global sourcing of key steelmaking raw materials, rail services and logistics capabilities for scrap transportation and to enable it to process approximately four million tons of ferrous scrap annually. Co. expects the transaction to close in the first quarter of 2008 and to be accretive in 2008. For the first quarter of 2008, Co. expects earnings of $1.20 to $1.30 per diluted share.

Financial Data

(US$ in Thousands)	12/31/2007	12/31/2006	12/31/2005	12/31/2004	12/31/2003	12/31/2002	12/31/2001	12/31/2000
Earnings Per Share	4.94	5.68	4.13	3.51	0.20	0.52	0.36	0.95
Cash Flow Per Share	6.54	7.34	6.80	3.24	1.58	1.59	1.59	2.50
Tang Book Value Per Share	13.18	16.04	13.80	10.83	7.45	7.43	7.08	6.87
Dividends Per Share	2.440	2.150	0.925	0.235	0.200	0.190	0.170	0.150
Dividend Payout %	49.39	37.85	22.40	6.70	100.00	36.71	46.90	15.79
Income Statement								
Total Revenue	16,592,976	14,751,270	12,700,999	11,376,828	6,265,823	4,801,777	4,139,249	4,586,146
EBITDA	2,686,340	3,020,389	2,395,623	2,136,933	455,616	551,440	469,449	736,857
Income Before Taxes	2,253,315	2,693,818	2,016,368	1,731,276	66,877	230,053	173,861	478,308
Income Taxes	781,368	936,137	706,084	609,791	4,096	67,973	60,900	167,400
Net Income	1,471,947	1,757,681	1,310,284	1,121,485	62,781	162,080	112,961	310,908
Average Shares	297,878	309,381	317,130	319,508	313,666	312,998	311,132	327,109
Balance Sheet								
Current Assets	5,073,249	4,675,036	4,071,553	3,174,948	1,620,560	1,424,139	1,373,666	1,381,447
Total Assets	9,826,122	7,884,989	7,138,787	6,133,207	4,492,353	4,381,001	3,759,348	3,721,788
Current Liabilities	1,582,036	1,450,028	1,255,699	1,065,790	629,595	591,536	484,159	558,068
Long-Term Obligations	2,250,300	922,300	922,300	923,550	903,550	878,550	460,450	460,450
Total Liabilities	4,713,205	3,059,000	2,858,999	2,677,222	2,150,275	2,058,012	1,557,888	1,590,836
Stockholders' Equity	5,112,917	4,825,989	4,279,788	3,455,985	2,342,078	2,322,989	2,201,460	2,130,952
Shares Outstanding	287,993	300,949	310,220	319,024	314,360	312,720	310,831	310,331
Statistical Record								
Return on Assets %	16.62	23.40	19.75	21.05	1.42	3.98	3.02	8.32
Return on Equity %	29.62	38.61	33.88	38.58	2.69	7.16	5.21	14.12
EBITDA Margin %	16.19	20.48	18.86	18.78	7.27	11.48	11.34	16.07
Net Margin %	8.87	11.92	10.32	9.86	1.00	3.38	2.73	6.78
Asset Turnover	1.87	1.96	1.91	2.14	1.41	1.18	1.11	1.23
Current Ratio	3.21	3.22	3.24	2.98	2.57	2.41	2.84	2.48
Debt to Equity	0.44	0.19	0.22	0.27	0.39	0.38	0.21	0.22
Price Range	69.25-45.86	65.84-34.23	34.62-22.81	27.54-13.34	14.48-8.99	17.29-9.47	14.00-8.63	13.98-7.50
P/E Ratio	14.02-9.28	11.59-6.03	8.38-5.52	7.85-3.80	72.38-44.97	33.25-18.22	38.89-23.96	14.72-7.89
Average Yield %	4.06	4.21	3.26	1.24	1.71	1.41	1.48	1.47

Address: 2100 Rexford Road, Charlotte, NC 28211	**Web Site:** www.nucor.com	**Auditors:** PricewaterhouseCoopers LLP
Telephone: 704-366-7000	**Officers:** Peter C. Browning - Chmn. Daniel R. DiMicco - Vice-Chmn., Pres., C.E.O.	**Transfer Agents:** American Stock Transfer & Trust Company, New York, NY
Fax: 704-362-4208		

NVR INC.

Interim Earnings (Per Share)

Qtr.	Mar	Jun	Sep	Dec
2003	10.10	10.90	12.55	14.86
2004	12.58	14.82	19.04	20.06
2005	14.38	21.42	24.33	29.74
2006	19.48	28.08	19.63	20.82
2007	12.96	14.14	15.26	11.89

Interim Dividends (Per Share)

No Dividends Paid

Valuation Analysis   **Institutional Holding**

Forecast P/E	14.81	No of Institutions
	(1/10/2007)	171
Market Cap	$3.1 Billion	Shares
Book Value	1.1 Billion	5,017,000
Price/Book	2.72	% Held
Price/Sales	0.60	93.66

TRADING VOLUME (thousand shares)

Business Summary: Building & General Construction (MIC: 3.2 SIC: 1531 NAIC: 236117)

NVR's primary business is the construction and sale of single-family detached homes, townhomes and condominium buildings. Co. also operates a mortgage banking business. Co. conducts its homebuilding activities directly, except for Rymarc Homes, which is operated as a wholly owned subsidiary, and its mortgage banking operations, which is operated primarily through a wholly owned subsidiary, NVR Mortgage Finance, Inc. As of Dec 31 2007, Co. operated in multiple locations in 12 states, primarily in the eastern part of the U.S. Co. operates its homebuilding operations under four trade names: Ryan Homes, NVHomes, Fox Ridge Homes and Rymarc Homes.

Recent Developments: For the year ended Dec 31 2007, net income decreased 43.1% to US$334.0 million from US$587.4 million in the prior year. Revenues were US$5.16 billion, down 16.2% from US$6.16 billion the year before. Direct operating expenses declined 10.1% to US$4.23 billion from US$4.70 billion in the comparable period the year before. Indirect operating expenses decreased 20.8% to US$389.9 million from US$492.5 million in the equivalent prior-year period.

Prospects: Co. expects the homebuilding and mortgage markets to remain challenging in 2008. As a result, Co. expects to see continued pricing pressure and in turn, continued pressure on gross profit margins in future periods. In view of that, Co. is working with its vendors to reduce material and labor costs incurred in the construction process, as well as continuing to work with its developers to reduce lot purchase prices and/or to defer scheduled lot purchases to coincide with its slower sales pace. Further, Co. is providing house types at lower sales price points by reducing the square footage of the products offered and by providing fewer upgraded features as standard options.

Financial Data
(US$ in Thousands)

	12/31/2007	12/31/2006	12/31/2005	12/31/2004	12/31/2003	12/31/2002	12/31/2001	12/31/2000
Earnings Per Share	54.14	88.05	89.61	66.42	48.39	36.05	24.86	14.98
Cash Flow Per Share	103.09	121.01	84.29	71.48	78.06	52.38	18.96	21.27
Tang Book Value Per Share	208.01	197.77	109.48	118.58	65.31	48.75	39.13	20.58
Income Statement								
Total Revenue	5,156,420	6,156,771	5,275,097	4,327,701	3,687,172	3,136,274	2,623,752	2,316,407
EBITDA	556,541	977,129	1,155,109	880,863	704,599	543,680	...	...
Income Before Taxes	539,505	962,971	1,144,419	872,005	696,172	536,023	...	...
Income Taxes	205,550	375,559	446,860	348,801	276,381	204,553	157,864	108,608
Net Income	333,955	587,412	697,559	523,204	419,791	331,470	236,794	158,246
Average Shares	6,168	6,672	7,784	7,877	8,674	9,193	9,525	10,564
Balance Sheet								
Current Assets	1,363,918	1,301,948	1,012,063	969,925	778,349	590,326	546,731	479,059
Total Assets	2,194,416	2,473,808	2,269,588	1,777,967	1,363,105	1,182,288	995,047	841,260
Current Liabilities	508,732	724,140	794,762	540,179	422,953	361,186	281,823	233,802
Long-Term Obligations	286,283	356,632	463,141	213,803	257,859	259,160	238,970	173,655
Total Liabilities	1,065,041	1,321,734	1,592,426	942,972	868,237	779,043	645,929	528,752
Stockholders' Equity	1,129,375	1,152,074	677,162	834,995	494,868	403,245	349,118	247,480
Shares Outstanding	5,137	5,517	5,628	6,574	6,727	7,022	7,475	8,858
Statistical Record								
Return on Assets %	14.31	24.77	34.47	33.22	32.98	30.45	25.79	19.62
Return on Equity %	29.28	64.22	92.26	78.47	93.48	88.11	79.38	70.43
EBITDA Margin %	10.79	15.87	21.90	20.35	19.11	17.34	...	...
Net Margin %	6.48	9.54	13.22	12.09	11.39	10.57	9.03	6.83
Asset Turnover	2.21	2.60	2.61	2.75	2.90	2.88	2.86	2.87
Current Ratio	2.68	1.80	1.27	1.80	1.84	1.63	1.94	2.05
Debt to Equity	0.25	0.31	0.68	0.26	0.52	0.64	0.68	0.70
Price Range	842.00-413.50	842.98-394.00	938.00-660.00	769.40-410.00	539.00-302.75	388.25-193.95	205.75-109.40	124.60-42.25
P/E Ratio	15.55-7.64	9.57-4.47	10.47-7.37	11.58-6.17	11.14-6.26	10.77-5.38	8.28-4.40	8.32-2.82

NYSE EURONEXT

Exchange	Symbol	Price	52Wk Range	Yield	P/E
NYS	NYX	$61.71 (3/31/2008)	101.00-56.46	1.94	22.86

*7 Year Price Score N/A   *NYSE Composite Index=100   *12 Month Price Score 91.36

Interim Earnings (Per Share)

Qtr.	Mar	Jun	Sep	Dec
2005	0.22	0.11	0.19	0.00
2006	0.24	0.39	0.43	0.28
2007	0.43	0.62	0.97	0.57

Interim Dividends (Per Share)

Amt	Decl	Ex	Rec	Pay
0.25Q	9/10/2007	9/12/2007	9/14/2007	9/28/2007
0.25Q	11/30/2007	3/12/2008	3/14/2008	3/31/2008
0.25Q	11/30/2007	12/11/2007	12/13/2007	12/28/2007
0.30Q	3/18/2008	6/11/2008	6/13/2008	6/30/2008

Indicated Div: $1.20

Valuation Analysis

		Institutional Holding	
Forecast P/E	N/A	No of Institutions	247
Market Cap	$16.4 Billion	Shares	84,626,864
Book Value	9.4 Billion	% Held	54.01
Price/Book	1.74		
Price/Sales	3.93		

Business Summary: Finance Intermediaries & Services (MIC: 8.7 SIC: 6211 NAIC: 523120)

NYSE Euronext is an exchange group providing financial products and services. As of Dec 31 2007, in the U.S., Co. operated the NYSE and NYSE Arca through NYSE Group; and in Europe, operated five European-based exchanges that comprise Euronext - the Paris, Amsterdam, Brussels and Lisbon stock exchanges, as well as the Liffe derivatives markets in London, Paris, Amsterdam, Brussels and Lisbon. Co. provides cash equities, exchange traded funds and other structured products, and equity and interest rate derivatives, and distributes market information related to trading in these products. Co. also operates a connectivity network and provide commercial trading and information technology systems.

Recent Developments: For the year ended Dec 31 2007, net income increased 213.7% to US$643.0 million from US$205.0 million in the prior year. Revenues were US$4.16 billion, up 75.0% from US$2.38 billion the year before. Operating income was US$909.0 million versus US$234.0 million in the prior year, an increase of 288.5%. Indirect operating expenses increased 51.7% to US$3.25 billion from US$2.14 billion in the equivalent prior-year period.

Prospects: On Jan 17 2008, Co. entered into an agreement to acquire the American Stock Exchange®, for $260.0 million. The transaction is expected to enhance Co.'s scale in U.S. options, exchange traded funds, closed-end funds, structured products and cash equities, provide annualized run rate cost savings of over $100.0 million within two years from closing, and close in the third quarter of 2008. Meanwhile, on Mar 7 2008, Co. announced that it has acquired Wombat Financial Software, Inc., for $200.0 million. The purchase should broaden Co.'s offering of market-agnostic connectivity, transaction and data management systems. Both acquisitions are expected to be accretive to Co.'s earnings in 2009.

Financial Data (US$ in Thousands)	12/31/2007	12/31/2006	12/31/2005
Earnings Per Share	2.70	1.36	...
Cash Flow Per Share	2.97	1.46	...
Tang Book Value Per Share	N.M.	3.51	100.00
Dividend Per Share	0.75	...	...
Income Statement			
Income Before Taxes	921,000	328,372	...
Income Taxes	253,000	120,566	...
Net Income	643,000	204,977	...
Average Shares	238,000	150,175	...
Balance Sheet			
Total Assets	16,618,000	3,465,542	200.00
Total Liabilities	7,003,000	1,796,523	...
Stockholders' Equity	9,384,000	1,669,019	200.00
Shares Outstanding	265,000	156,327	2.00
Statistical Record			
Return on Assets %	6.40	11.83	...
Return on Equity %	11.63	24.56	...
Price Range	108.21-69.30	108.96-49.98	...
P/E Ratio	40.08-25.67	80.12-36.75	...

Address: 11 Wall Street, New York, NY 10005
Telephone: 212-656-3000

Web Site: www.nysegroup.com
Officers: Jan-Michiel Hessels - Chmn. Marshall N. Carter - Deputy Chmn. Catherine R. Kinney - Pres., C.O.O.

Auditors: PricewaterhouseCoopers
Investor Contact: 212-656-5700

OCCIDENTAL PETROLEUM CORP

Exchange	Symbol	Price	52Wk Range	Yield	P/E
NYS	OXY	$73.17 (3/31/2008)	80.51-49.58	1.37	11.36

*7 Year Price Score 158.08 *NYSE Composite Index=100 *12 Month Price Score 123.23

Interim Earnings (Per Share)

Qtr.	Mar	Jun	Sep	Dec
2003	0.42	0.48	0.57	0.48
2004	0.61	0.73	0.94	0.92
2005	1.04	1.89	2.13	1.40
2006	1.43	0.98	1.36	1.09
2007	1.43	1.68	1.58	1.75

Interim Dividends (Per Share)

Amt	Decl	Ex	Rec	Pay
0.22Q	5/3/2007	6/6/2007	6/8/2007	7/15/2007
0.25Q	7/19/2007	9/6/2007	9/10/2007	10/15/2007
0.25Q	10/11/2007	12/6/2007	12/10/2007	1/15/2008
0.25Q	2/14/2008	3/6/2008	3/10/2008	4/15/2008

Indicated Div: $1.00

Valuation Analysis

		Institutional Holding	
Forecast P/E	10.07 (1/10/2007)	No of Institutions	606
Market Cap	$60.4 Billion	Shares	666,774,976
Book Value	22.8 Billion	% Held	79.56
Price/Book	2.65		
Price/Sales	3.02		

Business Summary: Oil and Gas (MIC: 14.2 SIC: 1311 NAIC: 211111)

Occidental Petroleum businesses consist of two industry segments operated by its subsidiaries: The oil and gas segment explores for, develops, produces and markets crude oil and natural gas. The chemical segment manufactures and markets basic chemicals, vinyls and performance chemicals. Co.'s domestic oil and gas operations are located in west Texas, New Mexico, California, Kansas, Oklahoma, Utah and western Colorado. International operations are located in Argentina, Bolivia, Colombia, Libya, Oman, Qatar, the United Arab Emirates and Yemen. As of Dec 31 2007, Co.'s total oil and natural gas proved reserves were 2.23 billion barrels and 3.843 trillion cubic feet, respectively.

Recent Developments: For the year ended Dec 31 2007, income from continuing operations increased 20.8% to US$5.08 billion from US$4.20 billion a year earlier. Net income increased 28.8% to US$5.40 billion from US$4.19 billion in the prior year. Revenues were US$20.01 billion, up 13.2% from US$17.67 billion the year before. Direct operating expenses rose 7.0% to US$6.63 billion from US$6.19 billion in the comparable period the year before. Indirect operating expenses increased 20.3% to US$4.81 billion from US$4.00 billion in the equivalent prior-year period.

Prospects: On Dec 17 2007, Co. announced the signing of a definitive purchase and sale agreement with Plains Exploration & Production (PXP) to purchase properties for $1.55 billion that consist of: 50.0% of PXP's working interests in oil and gas properties located in the Permian Basin, West Texas and New Mexico; and 50.0% of PXP's working interests in oil and gas properties located in the Piceance Basin in Colorado. Co. noted that this acquisition is consistent with its strategy of focusing on its Permian Basin core area and continuing to build a meaningful position in the Piceance Basin. The transaction, which is subject to government approvals, is expected to close in the first quarter of 2008.

Financial Data

(US$ in Thousands)	12/31/2007	12/31/2006	12/31/2005	12/31/2004	12/31/2003	12/31/2002	12/31/2001	12/31/2000
Earnings Per Share	6.44	4.86	6.46	3.20	1.97	1.30	1.54	2.13
Cash Flow Per Share	8.14	7.45	6.62	4.89	4.00	2.79	3.56	3.24
Tang Book Value Per Share	27.64	22.84	18.69	13.30	10.24	8.36	7.52	6.45
Dividends Per Share	0.940	0.800	0.645	0.550	0.520	0.500	0.500	0.500
Dividend Payout %	14.60	16.46	9.99	17.19	26.46	38.31	32.36	23.47
Income Statement								
Total Revenue	20,013,000	18,160,000	16,259,000	11,513,000	9,447,000	7,491,000	14,126,000	14,543,000
EBITDA	10,957,000	9,872,000	8,618,000	5,477,000	4,076,000	2,942,000	2,725,000	3,919,000
Income Before Taxes	8,578,000	7,830,000	7,133,000	4,155,000	2,893,000	1,923,000	1,749,000	3,011,000
Income Taxes	3,507,000	3,466,000	2,020,000	1,708,000	1,227,000	422,000	563,000	1,442,000
Net Income	5,400,000	4,182,000	5,281,000	2,568,000	1,527,000	989,000	1,154,000	1,570,000
Average Shares	839,100	860,400	818,200	802,200	777,200	759,000	748,400	738,400
Balance Sheet								
Current Assets	8,595,000	6,006,000	6,574,000	4,431,000	2,474,000	1,873,000	1,483,000	2,067,000
Total Assets	36,519,000	32,355,000	26,108,000	21,391,000	18,168,000	16,548,000	17,850,000	19,414,000
Current Liabilities	6,266,000	4,724,000	4,280,000	3,423,000	2,526,000	2,235,000	1,890,000	2,740,000
Long-Term Obligations	1,741,000	2,619,000	2,873,000	3,345,000	3,993,000	3,997,000	4,065,000	5,185,000
Total Liabilities	13,696,000	13,171,000	11,076,000	10,841,000	10,239,000	10,230,000	12,216,000	14,640,000
Stockholders' Equity	22,823,000	19,184,000	15,032,000	10,550,000	7,929,000	6,318,000	5,634,000	4,774,000
Shares Outstanding	825,735	839,918	804,430	793,454	774,095	755,720	749,550	739,968
Statistical Record								
Return on Assets %	15.68	14.31	22.24	12.95	8.80	5.75	6.19	9.34
Return on Equity %	25.71	24.44	41.29	27.72	21.44	16.55	22.18	37.74
EBITDA Margin %	54.75	54.36	53.00	47.57	43.15	39.27	19.29	26.95
Net Margin %	26.98	23.03	32.48	22.31	16.16	13.20	8.17	10.80
Asset Turnover	0.58	0.62	0.68	0.58	0.54	0.44	0.76	0.86
Current Ratio	1.37	1.27	1.54	1.29	0.98	0.84	0.78	0.75
Debt to Equity	0.08	0.14	0.19	0.32	0.50	0.63	0.72	1.09
Price Range	78.10-43.08	53.89-42.00	44.40-27.81	30.16-21.02	21.32-13.64	15.34-11.73	15.54-10.95	12.75-7.88
P/E Ratio	12.13-6.69	11.09-8.64	6.87-4.30	9.42-6.57	10.82-6.92	11.80-9.02	10.09-7.11	5.99-3.70
Average Yield %	1.64	1.65	1.73	2.20	3.14	3.56	3.83	4.76

Address: 10889 Wilshire Boulevard, Los Angeles, CA 90024-4201
Telephone: 310-208-8800
Fax: 310-443-6690

Web Site: www.oxy.com
Officers: Ray R. Irani - Chmn., C.E.O. Stephen I. Chazen - Exec. V.P., Corp. Devel., C.F.O.

Auditors: KPMG LLP
Investor Contact: 212-603-8111
Transfer Agents: Mellon Investor Services, Ridgefield Park, NJ

OCEANEERING INTERNATIONAL, INC.

Exchange	Symbol	Price	52Wk Range	Yield	P/E
NYS	OII	$63.00 (3/31/2008)	81.46-42.51	N/A	19.44

*7 Year Price Score 194.61 *NYSE Composite Index=100 ***12 Month Price Score 106.10**

TRADING VOLUME (thousand shares)

Interim Earnings (Per Share)

Qtr.	Mar	Jun	Sep	Dec
2003	0.13	0.17	0.19	0.13
2004	0.10	0.22	0.25	0.23
2005	0.20	0.28	0.33	0.36
2006	0.47	0.56	0.70	0.54
2007	0.60	0.86	0.96	0.82

Interim Dividends (Per Share)

Amt	Decl	Ex	Rec	Pay
100%	5/12/2006	6/19/2006	5/25/2006	6/16/2006

Valuation Analysis

		Institutional Holding	
Forecast P/E	13.98	No of Institutions	
	(1/10/2007)	225	
Market Cap	$3.5 Billion	Shares	
Book Value	915.3 Million	49,047,368	
Price/Book	3.79	% Held	
Price/Sales	1.99	88.46	

Business Summary: Oil and Gas (MIC: 14.2 SIC: 1389 NAIC: 213112)

Oceaneering International is an oilfield provider of engineered services and products mainly to the offshore oil and gas industry, with a focus on deepwater applications. Co. also serves the defense and aerospace industries. Co.'s services and products for the oil and gas industry include remotely operated vehicles, mobile offshore production systems, built-to-order specialty hardware, engineering and project management, subsea intervention services, nondestructive testing and inspection, and manned diving. Co.'s operations are divided into two segments: services and products provided to the oil and gas industry (Oil and Gas) and all other services and products (Advanced Technologies).

Recent Developments: For the year ended Dec 31 2007, net income increased 44.9% to US$180.4 million from US$124.5 million in the prior year. Revenues were US$1.74 billion, up 36.2% from US$1.28 billion the year before. Operating income was US$289.6 million versus US$194.3 million in the prior year, an increase of 49.0%. Direct operating expenses rose 35.1% to US$1.33 billion from US$984.1 million in the comparable period the year before. Indirect operating expenses increased 21.5% to US$123.7 million from US$101.8 million in the equivalent prior-year period.

Prospects: For 2008, Co. expects to benefit from its 2006 and 2007 Subsea Products investments, which increased its manufacturing capacity and rental service capabilities. In addition, for its Remotely Operated Vehicles (ROVs), Co. anticipates continued pricing improvement and expansion of its fleet to meet rising demand. Accordingly, for the full-year of 2008, Co. anticipates earnings per share in the range of $3.50 to $3.80, led by operating income improvements in Subsea Products and ROVs. Meanwhile for the first quarter of 2008, Co. expects earnings per share of $0.65 to $0.75. Looking beyond 2008, Co. anticipates demand for its deepwater services and products will continue to increase.

Financial Data

(US$ in Thousands)	12/31/2007	12/31/2006	12/31/2005	12/31/2004	12/31/2003	12/31/2002	12/31/2001	12/31/2000
Earnings Per Share	3.24	2.26	1:17	0.79	0.60	0.81	0.69	0.25
Cash Flow Per Share	3.81	2.80	1.80	1.99	1.98	2.56	1.27	0.51
Tang Book Value Per Share	14.59	11.20	8.43	7.58	6.58	6.11	5.00	4.24
Income Statement								
Total Revenue	1,743,080	1,280,198	998,543	780,181	639,249	547,467	523,820	307,730
EBITDA	385,409	283,541	183,660	133,931	109,280	116,808	108,280	53,583
Income Before Taxes	277,498	190,895	94,450	60,923	45,079	56,525	50,937	17,676
Income Taxes	97,124	66,401	31,770	20,623	15,778	16,392	17,828	6,363
Net Income	180,374	124,494	62,680	40,300	29,301	40,133	33,109	11,313
Average Shares	55,755	54,991	53,648	51,370	48,906	49,366	47,830	46,452
Balance Sheet								
Current Assets	670,569	523,645	394,233	276,876	224,765	233,070	205,218	144,347
Total Assets	1,531,440	1,242,022	989,568	819,664	662,856	590,348	579,611	512,684
Current Liabilities	338,975	279,706	222,667	170,672	132,972	116,031	113,834	94,024
Long-Term Obligations	200,000	194,000	174,000	142,172	122,324	112,800	170,000	180,000
Total Liabilities	616,130	545,258	453,450	365,227	303,481	276,483	328,178	305,790
Stockholders' Equity	915,310	696,764	536,118	454,437	359,375	313,865	251,433	206,894
Shares Outstanding	55,075	54,440	53,558	51,640	48,767	48,993	47,534	46,075
Statistical Record								
Return on Assets %	13.01	11.16	6.93	5.42	4.68	6.86	6.06	1.43
Return on Equity %	22.38	20.20	12.66	9.88	8.70	14.20	14.45	3.33
EBITDA Margin %	22.11	22.15	18.39	17.17	17.10	21.34	20.67	17.41
Net Margin %	10.35	9.72	6.28	5.17	4.58	7.33	6.32	3.68
Asset Turnover	1.26	1.15	1.10	1.05	1.02	0.94	0.96	0.39
Current Ratio	1.98	1.87	1.77	1.62	1.69	2.01	1.80	1.54
Debt to Equity	0.22	0.28	0.32	0.31	0.34	0.36	0.68	0.87
Price Range	81.46-35.58	47.15-25.59	27.44-16.41	19.40-13.85	14.13-10.37	16.08-9.47	13.38-7.10	10.56-6.69
P/E Ratio	25.14-10.98	20.86-11.32	23.45-14.02	24.56-17.53	23.55-17.28	19.85-11.69	19.38-10.29	42.25-26.75

Address: 11911 FM 529, Houston, TX 77041 **Telephone:** 713-329-4500 **Fax:** 713-329-4951	**Web Site:** www.oceaneering.com **Officers:** John R. Huff - Chmn., C.E.O. T. Jay Collins - Pres., C.O.O.	**Auditors:** Ernst & Young LLP **Transfer Agents:** EquiServe Trust Company, N.A., Kansas City, MO

OFFICE DEPOT, INC.

Exchange	Symbol	Price	52Wk Range	Yield	P/E
NYS	ODP	$11.05 (3/31/2008)	36.53-10.86	N/A	7.73

*7 Year Price Score 83.29   *NYSE Composite Index=100   *12 Month Price Score 60.45

Interim Earnings (Per Share)

Qtr.	Mar	Jun	Sep	Dec
2003	0.25	0.19	0.29	0.14
2004	0.37	0.25	0.28	0.16
2005	0.37	0.31	(0.15)	0.34
2006	0.43	0.41	0.47	0.48
2007	0.56	0.40	0.43	0.07

Interim Dividends (Per Share)

No Dividends Paid

Valuation Analysis

Forecast P/E	12.82
	(1/10/2007)
Market Cap	$3.0 Billion
Book Value	3.1 Billion
Price/Book	0.98
Price/Sales	0.19

Institutional Holding

No of Institutions	359
Shares	257,037,200
% Held	93.29

TRADING VOLUME (thousand shares)

Business Summary: Retail - Miscellaneous (MIC: 5.11 SIC: 5943 NAIC: 453210)

Office Depot is a global supplier of office products and services. Co. sells to consumers and businesses of all sizes through its three business segments: North American Retail Division, North American Business Solutions Division, and International Division. Sales are processed through multiple channels, consisting of office supply stores, a contract sales force, internet sites, direct marketing catalogs and call centers, all supported by its network of crossdocks, warehouses and delivery operations. Co. sells to customers in 43 countries throughout North America, Europe, Asia and Central America either through wholly-owned entities, majority-owned entities or other ventures and alliances.

Recent Developments: For the year ended Dec 29 2007, net income decreased 21.4% to US$395.6 million from US$503.5 million in the prior year. Revenues were US$15.53 billion, up 3.4% from US$15.01 billion the year before. Operating income was US$483.6 million versus US$713.2 million in the prior year, a decrease of 32.2%. Direct operating expenses rose 6.4% to US$11.02 billion from US$10.36 billion in the comparable period the year before. Indirect operating expenses increased 2.2% to US$4.02 billion from US$3.93 billion in the equivalent prior-year period.

Prospects: Co. believes the continued downturn in the U.S. economy in 2008 will negatively affect its sales and operating profit margin. However, while expecting continued challenges in its International Division in the first half of 2008, Co. expects improved performance in the second half of 2008 as it anticipates improvement in the U.K., and as it more fully realize the benefits of the investments it has made in its businesses in Europe and Asia. Meanwhile, Co. has reduced its 2008 capital expenditure estimates to $375.0 million, reflecting a reduction in planned new store openings from 150 stores to 75 stores, and investments in its global supply chain and information technology initiatives.

Financial Data
(US$ in Thousands)

	12/29/2007	12/30/2006	12/31/2005	12/25/2004	12/27/2003	12/28/2002	12/29/2001	12/30/2000
Earnings Per Share	1.43	1.79	0.87	1.06	0.88	0.98	0.66	0.16
Cash Flow Per Share	1.51	2.94	2.02	2.08	2.11	2.29	2.51	1.01
Tang Book Value Per Share	6.20	5.11	6.26	6.96	5.77	6.61	5.28	4.66
Income Statement								
Total Revenue	15,527,537	15,010,781	14,278,944	13,564,699	12,358,566	11,356,633	11,154,081	11,569,696
EBITDA	793,656	1,037,338	639,789	771,465	733,994	707,638	544,808	320,568
Income Before Taxes	458,633	727,331	361,515	461,233	445,040	479,205	314,130	92,459
Income Taxes	63,018	211,196	87,723	125,729	143,016	167,722	113,087	43,127
Net Income	395,615	516,135	273,792	335,504	276,295	310,708	201,043	49,332
Average Shares	275,940	287,722	315,242	315,625	313,688	322,200	316,424	311,231
Balance Sheet								
Current Assets	3,715,714	3,455,125	3,530,062	3,916,171	3,576,728	3,209,715	2,806,190	2,699,089
Total Assets	7,256,540	6,570,102	6,098,525	6,767,351	6,145,242	4,765,812	4,331,643	4,196,334
Current Liabilities	2,973,416	2,969,927	2,468,751	2,618,357	2,277,253	1,992,009	2,101,514	1,908,337
Long-Term Obligations	607,462	570,752	569,098	583,680	829,302	411,970	317,552	598,499
Total Liabilities	4,172,696	3,959,991	3,359,304	3,544,303	3,351,155	2,468,700	2,483,205	2,595,083
Stockholders' Equity	3,083,844	2,610,111	2,739,221	3,223,048	2,794,087	2,297,112	1,848,438	1,601,251
Shares Outstanding	272,958	276,399	297,025	312,301	310,193	308,515	303,095	296,497
Statistical Record								
Return on Assets %	5.74	8.17	4.19	5.21	5.08	6.85	4.73	1.15
Return on Equity %	13.93	19.35	9.04	11.18	10.88	15.03	11.69	2.77
EBITDA Margin %	5.11	6.91	4.48	5.69	5.94	6.23	4.88	2.77
Net Margin %	2.55	3.44	1.92	2.47	2.24	2.74	1.80	0.43
Asset Turnover	2.25	2.38	2.18	2.11	2.27	2.50	2.62	2.69
Current Ratio	1.25	1.16	1.43	1.50	1.57	1.61	1.34	1.41
Debt to Equity	0.20	0.22	0.21	0.18	0.30	0.18	0.17	0.37
Price Range	39.52-13.09	44.46-30.77	31.55-16.61	19.45-14.12	18.24-10.38	21.74-10.98	18.52-7.31	14.19-6.06
P/E Ratio	27.64-9.15	24.84-17.19	36.26-19.09	18.35-13.32	20.73-11.80	22.18-11.20	28.06-11.08	88.67-37.89

Address: 2200 Old Germantown Road, Delray Beach, FL 33445 **Telephone:** 561-438-4800 **Fax:** 561-265-4406	**Web Site:** www.officedepot.com **Officers:** Steve Odland - Chmn., C.E.O. Patricia A. McKay - Exec. V.P., C.F.O.	**Auditors:** Deloitte & Touche LLP **Investor Contact:** 561-438-4930 **Transfer Agents:** Mellon Investor Services, LLC

OFFICEMAX INC (DE)

Exchange	Symbol	Price	52Wk Range	Yield	P/E
NYS	OMX	$19.14 (3/31/2008)	53.76-17.90	3.13	7.20

*7 Year Price Score 79.89 *NYSE Composite Index=100 *12 Month Price Score 71.63

Interim Earnings (Per Share)

Qtr.	Mar	Jun	Sep	Dec
2003	(0.53)	(0.12)	0.48	0.06
2004	0.66	0.52	0.63	(0.04)
2005	(0.07)	(0.28)	(0.07)	(0.57)
2006	(0.37)	0.35	0.41	0.77
2007	0.76	0.35	0.64	0.92

Interim Dividends (Per Share)

Amt	Decl	Ex	Rec	Pay
0.15Q	4/26/2007	6/27/2007	7/1/2007	7/15/2007
0.15Q	7/26/2007	9/27/2007	10/1/2007	10/15/2007
0.15Q	12/19/2007	12/27/2007	1/1/2008	1/15/2008
0.15Q	2/15/2008	3/28/2008	4/1/2008	4/15/2008
		Indicated Div: $0.60		

Valuation Analysis

		Institutional Holding	
Forecast P/E	N/A	No of Institutions	
		252	
Market Cap	$1.4 Billion	Shares	
Book Value	2.3 Billion	74,274,424	
Price/Book	0.63	% Held	
Price/Sales	0.16	99.06	

Business Summary: Paper Products (MIC: 11.11 SIC: 5112 NAIC: 424120)

OfficeMax is a business-to-business and retail office products distributor. Co.'s OfficeMax, Contract segment markets and sells office supplies and paper, technology products and office furniture directly to large corporate and government offices, as well as to small and medium-sized offices through field salespeople, outbound telesales, catalogs, the Internet and through office products stores. Co.'s OfficeMax, Retail segment markets and sells office supplies and paper, print and document services, technology products and office furniture through a network of retail stores. As of Jan 26 2008, OfficeMax, Retail operated 981 stores in 48 states, Puerto Rico, the US Virgin Islands and Mexico.

Recent Developments: For the year ended Dec 29 2007, income from continuing operations increased 109.4% to US$207.4 million from US$99.1 million a year earlier. Net income increased 126.1% to US$207.4 million from US$91.7 million in the prior year. Revenues were US$9.08 billion, up 1.3% from US$8.97 billion the year before. Operating income was US$344.2 million versus US$165.9 million in the prior year, an increase of 107.5%. Direct operating expenses rose 1.7% to US$6.77 billion from US$6.66 billion in the comparable period the year before. Indirect operating expenses decreased 8.3% to US$1.97 billion from US$2.14 billion in the equivalent prior-year period.

Prospects: Going forward, Co. expects to pursue margin and cost management initiatives throughout 2008. Also, Co. will continue to focus on implementing numerous initiatives to further enhance its results. For instance, in its Retail segment, Co. expects to open up to 40 new stores featuring the Advantage store prototype, mostly in existing markets, and to remodel approximately 60 stores, featuring key elements of the Advantage store prototype during 2008. In view of that, Co. expects its capital investments in 2008 to range between $200.0 million and $220.0 million, excluding acquisitions.

Financial Data

(US$ in Thousands)	12/29/2007	12/30/2006	12/31/2005	12/31/2004	12/31/2003	12/31/2002	12/31/2001	12/31/2000
Earnings Per Share	2.66	1.19	(0.99)	1.77	(0.08)	(0.03)	(0.96)	2.73
Cash Flow Per Share	0.94	5.15	(0.73)	(5.18)	5.58	5.30	7.07	9.55
Tang Book Value Per Share	10.77	6.86	3.64	12.54	9.33	13.84	16.68	19.93
Dividends Per Share	0.600	0.600	0.600	0.600	0.600	0.600	0.600	0.600
Dividend Payout %	22.56	50.42	...	33.90	...	...	...	21.98
Income Statement								
Total Revenue	9,081,962	8,965,707	9,157,660	13,270,196	8,245,146	7,412,329	7,422,175	7,806,657
EBITDA	502,431	333,049	(6,384)	517,288	150,656	117,974	78,255	443,633
Income Before Taxes	337,527	171,878	(37,616)	379,442	19,297	1,005	(47,611)	298,331
Income Taxes	125,282	68,741	1,226	142,291	2,222	(18,403)	(5,494)	116,349
Net Income	207,373	91,721	(73,762)	173,058	8,272	11,340	(42,501)	178,574
Average Shares	76,374	73,713	78,745	91,654	60,093	58,216	57,680	61,413
Balance Sheet								
Current Assets	2,204,701	2,096,844	1,942,049	3,258,762	2,501,292	1,295,749	1,245,027	1,577,321
Total Assets	6,283,768	6,216,048	6,272,142	7,542,999	7,376,159	4,947,400	4,933,968	5,266,923
Current Liabilities	1,370,709	1,528,903	1,588,326	1,856,970	1,976,911	1,053,604	1,265,951	1,014,394
Long-Term Obligations	1,819,421	1,854,246	1,877,242	2,055,082	2,191,463	1,438,846	1,143,755	1,822,687
Total Liabilities	3,973,154	4,200,519	4,509,008	4,909,058	5,032,371	3,375,369	3,183,115	3,500,482
Stockholders' Equity	2,278,572	1,985,644	1,735,679	2,610,478	2,323,634	1,399,531	1,578,353	1,756,972
Shares Outstanding	75,397	74,903	70,804	93,575	87,137	58,283	58,061	57,337
Statistical Record								
Return on Assets %	3.33	1.47	N.M.	2.31	0.13	0.23	N.M.	3.42
Return on Equity %	9.75	4.94	N.M.	7.00	0.44	0.76	N.M.	10.57
EBITDA Margin %	5.53	3.71	N.M.	3.90	1.83	1.59	1.05	5.68
Net Margin %	2.28	1.02	N.M.	1.30	0.10	0.15	N.M.	2.29
Asset Turnover	1.46	1.44	1.33	1.77	1.34	1.50	1.46	1.50
Current Ratio	1.61	1.37	1.22	1.75	1.27	1.23	0.98	1.55
Debt to Equity	0.80	0.93	1.08	0.79	0.94	1.03	0.72	1.04
Price Range	54.54-20.54	51.17-24.84	34.50-24.35	37.73-29.01	32.86-20.99	38.51-19.61	37.63-27.76	43.50-22.19
P/E Ratio	20.50-7.72	43.00-20.87	...	21.32-16.39	...	...	...	15.93-8.13
Average Yield %	1.50	1.53	1.98	1.81	2.32	1.96	1.81	1.97

Address: 263 Shuman Boulevard, Naperville, IL 60563 **Telephone:** 630-438-7800	**Web Site:** www.officemax.com **Officers:** Sam K. Duncan - Chmn., Pres., C.E.O. Ryan Vero - Exec. V.P., Chief Merchandising Officer	**Auditors:** KPMG LLP **Investor Contact:** 630-864-6800 **Transfer Agents:** Wells Fargo Shareowner Services

OGE ENERGY CORP.

Exchange	Symbol	Price	52Wk Range	Yield	P/E
NYS	OGE	$31.17 (3/31/2008)	39.63-30.20	4.46	11.81

*7 Year Price Score 104.14 *NYSE Composite Index=100 *12 Month Price Score 99.33

Interim Earnings (Per Share)

Qtr.	Mar	Jun	Sep	Dec
2003	0.00	0.41	1.20	(0.05)
2004	0.12	0.44	1.07	0.10
2005	0.06	0.42	1.22	0.61
2006	0.27	1.02	1.31	0.23
2007	0.19	0.68	1.37	0.40

Interim Dividends (Per Share)

Amt	Decl	Ex	Rec	Pay
0.34Q	5/17/2007	7/6/2007	7/10/2007	7/30/2007
0.34Q	9/21/2007	10/5/2007	10/10/2007	10/30/2007
0.347Q	11/28/2007	1/8/2008	1/10/2008	1/30/2008
0.347Q	2/27/2008	4/8/2008	4/10/2008	4/30/2008
		Indicated Div: $1.39		

Valuation Analysis

Forecast P/E	N/A	
Market Cap	$2.9 Billion	
Book Value	1.7 Billion	
Price/Book	1.70	
Price/Sales	0.75	

Institutional Holding

No of Institutions	247
Shares	43,655,412
% Held	47.79

TRADING VOLUME (thousand shares)

Business Summary: Electricity (MIC: 7.1 SIC: 4911 NAIC: 221121)

OGE Energy is an energy and energy services provider offering physical delivery and related services for both electricity and natural gas primarily in the south central U.S. Co.'s Electric Utility segment generates, transmits, distributes and sells electric energy in Oklahoma and western Arkansas. The operations of the Electric Utility segment are conducted through Oklahoma Gas and Electric Company (OG&E). The operations of the Natural Gas Pipeline segment are conducted through Enogex Inc. and its subsidiaries, and consist of two related businesses: the transportation and storage of natural gas; as well as the gathering and processing of natural gas.

Recent Developments: For the year ended Dec 31 2007, income from continuing operations increased 8.0% to US$244.2 million from US$226.1 million a year earlier. Net income decreased 6.8% to US$244.2 million from US$262.1 million in the prior year. Revenues were US$3.80 billion, down 5.2% from US$4.01 billion the year before. Operating income was US$455.3 million versus US$432.7 million in the prior year, an increase of 5.2%. Direct operating expenses declined 9.2% to US$2.63 billion from US$2.90 billion in the comparable period the year before. Indirect operating expenses increased 5.5% to US$707.6 million from US$670.4 million in the equivalent prior-year period.

Prospects: On Jan 21 2008, Co.'s Oklahoma Gas and Electric Company (OG&E) subsidiary entered into definitive agreements with Kelson Holdings LLC, the Grand River Dam Authority and the Oklahoma Municipal Power Authority to purchase the natural gas-fired Redbud power plant near Luther, OK, for about $852.0 million. Subsequently, OG&E will acquire a 51.0% interest in the Redbud plant, and it will be in charge of operating the plant, which has four, 300-megawatt-plus generating units. Further, OG&E plans to continue focusing on reducing demand via conservation, efficiency and demand-side management initiatives going forward. Meanwhile, for 2008, Co. expects earnings of $2.40 to $2.60 per diluted share.

Financial Data
(US$ in Thousands)

	12/31/2007	12/31/2006	12/31/2005	12/31/2004	12/31/2003	12/31/2002	12/31/2001	12/31/2000
Earnings Per Share	2.64	2.84	2.32	1.73	1.58	1.16	1.29	1.89
Cash Flow Per Share	3.58	6.26	4.94	4.07	4.42	3.43	6.90	2.71
Tang Book Value Per Share	18.31	17.59	14.82	13.86	13.29	11.99	12.74	13.66
Dividends Per Share	1.360	1.330	1.330	1.330	1.330	1.330	1.330	1.330
Dividend Payout %	51.52	46.83	57.33	76.88	84.18	114.66	103.10	70.37
Income Statement								
Total Revenue	3,797,600	4,005,600	5,948,200	4,926,600	3,779,000	3,023,900	3,182,363	3,298,727
EBITDA	644,300	617,800	510,800	502,700	482,900	417,200	457,213	528,560
Income Before Taxes	360,900	346,600	237,900	233,200	209,300	125,600	153,154	223,540
Income Taxes	116,700	120,500	71,800	80,200	73,700	44,600	52,583	76,505
Net Income	244,200	262,100	211,000	153,500	129,800	90,800	100,571	147,035
Average Shares	92,500	92,100	90,800	88,500	82,100	78,200	77,929	77,688
Balance Sheet								
Net PPE	4,246,300	3,867,500	3,567,400	3,581,000	3,309,500	3,204,300	3,263,748	3,219,464
Total Assets	5,237,800	4,902,000	4,898,900	4,870,300	4,584,700	4,127,200	3,996,592	4,319,630
Long-Term Obligations	1,344,600	1,346,300	1,350,800	1,424,100	1,436,100	1,501,900	1,526,303	1,648,523
Total Liabilities	3,556,900	3,298,200	3,523,100	3,584,700	3,383,100	3,143,300	2,956,023	3,255,322
Stockholders' Equity	1,680,900	1,603,800	1,375,800	1,285,600	1,201,600	983,900	1,040,569	1,064,308
Shares Outstanding	91,800	91,200	90,600	90,000	87,400	78,500	77,991	77,921
Statistical Record								
Return on Assets %	4.82	5.35	4.32	3.24	2.98	2.24	2.42	3.56
Return on Equity %	14.87	17.59	15.86	12.31	11.88	8.97	9.56	14.07
EBITDA Margin %	16.97	15.42	8.59	10.20	12.78	13.80	14.37	16.02
Net Margin %	6.43	6.54	3.55	3.12	3.43	3.00	3.16	4.46
PPE Turnover	0.94	1.08	1.66	1.43	1.16	0.94	0.98	1.02
Asset Turnover	0.75	0.82	1.22	1.04	0.87	0.74	0.77	0.80
Debt to Equity	0.80	0.84	0.98	1.11	1.20	1.53	1.47	1.55
Price Range	41.01-31.03	40.41-26.42	30.38-24.67	26.79-23.08	24.30-16.51	24.02-14.04	24.13-20.73	24.75-16.56
P/E Ratio	15.53-11.75	14.23-9.30	13.09-10.63	15.49-13.34	15.38-10.45	20.71-12.10	18.70-16.07	13.10-8.76
Average Yield %	3.74	3.98	4.85	5.29	6.50	6.59	5.95	6.62

Address: 321 North Harvey, PO Box 321, Oklahoma City, OK 73101-0321 **Telephone:** 405-553-3000	**Web Site:** www.oge.com **Officers:** Steven E. Moore - Chmn., Pres., C.E.O. Peter B. Delaney - Exec. V.P., C.O.O.	**Auditors:** Ernst & Young LLP

OLD NATIONAL BANCORP (EVANSVILLE, IN)

Exchange	Symbol	Price	52Wk Range	Yield	P/E	Div Acheiver
NYS	ONB	$18.00 (3/31/2008)	19.26-13.26	5.11	15.79	24 Years

*7 Year Price Score 64.48   *NYSE Composite Index=100   *12 Month Price Score 109.87

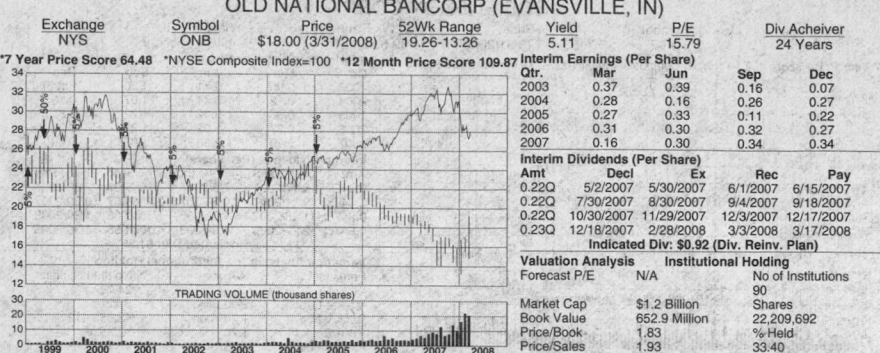

Interim Earnings (Per Share)

Qtr.	Mar	Jun	Sep	Dec
2003	0.37	0.39	0.16	0.07
2004	0.28	0.16	0.26	0.27
2005	0.27	0.33	0.11	0.22
2006	0.31	0.30	0.32	0.27
2007	0.16	0.30	0.34	0.34

Interim Dividends (Per Share)

Amt	Decl	Ex	Rec	Pay
0.22Q	5/2/2007	5/30/2007	6/1/2007	6/15/2007
0.22Q	7/30/2007	8/30/2007	9/4/2007	9/18/2007
0.22Q	10/30/2007	11/29/2007	12/3/2007	12/17/2007
0.23Q	12/18/2007	2/28/2008	3/3/2008	3/17/2008

Indicated Div: $0.92 (Div. Reinv. Plan)

TRADING VOLUME (thousand shares)

Valuation Analysis

Forecast P/E	N/A	Institutional Holding
		No of Institutions 90
Market Cap	$1.2 Billion	Shares
Book Value	652.9 Million	22,209,692
Price/Book	1.83	% Held
Price/Sales	1.93	33.40

Business Summary: Commercial Banking (MIC: 8.1 SIC: 6021 NAIC: 522110)

Old National Bancorp, with total assets of $7.85 billion and deposits of $5.66 billion as of Dec 31 2007, is a financial holding company headquartered in Evansville, IN. Co., through its wholly owned banking subsidiary, provides a range of services, including commercial and consumer loan and depository services, investment and brokerage services, lease financing and other traditional banking services. Through its non-bank affiliates, Co. provides services to supplement the banking business including fiduciary and wealth management services, insurance and other financial services. As of Dec 31 2007, Co. operated 115 banking financial centers primarily in Indiana, Illinois, and Kentucky.

Recent Developments: For the year ended Dec 31 2007, income from continuing operations decreased 5.6% to US$74.9 million from US$79.4 million a year earlier. Net income decreased 5.6% to US$74.9 million from US$79.4 million in the prior year. Net interest income increased 3.0% to US$219.2 million from US$212.7 million in the prior year. Provision for loan losses was US$4.1 million versus US$7.0 million in the prior year, a decrease of 41.2%. Non-interest income rose 0.8% to US$155.1 million from US$153.9 million, while non-interest expense advanced 5.0% to US$278.0 million.

Prospects: Looking ahead, Co. believes that the overall downturn of the banking industry led by significant declines in the values of financial assets backed by sub-prime mortgage loans will continue into 2008. Further, Co. expects that the conditions in the overall residential real estate and credit markets to remain uncertain for the foreseeable future. In the view of that, Co. has continued to tighten its underwriting standards, which has slowed potential loan growth. In addition, Co. plans to continue to monitor its asset quality closely in 2008 while staying focused on building its business presence in higher growth markets, including Indianapolis, Louisville, Lafayette and northern Indiana.

Financial Data

(US$ in Thousands)	12/31/2007	12/31/2006	12/31/2005	12/31/2004	12/31/2003	12/31/2002	12/31/2001	12/31/2000
Earnings Per Share	1.14	1.20	0.93	0.97	1.00	1.67	1.29	0.85
Cash Flow Per Share	1.13	1.81	1.35	1.27	2.91	0.99	1.48	1.44
Tang Book Value Per Share	6.98	7.64	7.59	7.48	7.58	8.40	9.03	8.54
Dividends Per Share	0.880	0.840	0.760	0.724	0.689	0.622	0.559	0.533
Dividend Payout %	77.19	70.00	81.72	74.62	68.93	37.27	43.46	62.87
Income Statement								
Interest Income	461,368	451,713	425,239	417,198	469,748	547,383	629,707	638,275
Interest Expense	242,177	238,996	206,087	166,391	197,741	257,954	338,408	368,404
Net Interest Income	219,191	212,717	219,152	250,807	272,007	289,429	291,299	269,871
Provision for Losses	4,118	7,000	23,100	22,400	85,000	33,500	28,700	29,803
Non-Interest Income	155,138	153,791	159,898	182,163	192,149	154,497	112,967	101,713
Non-Interest Expense	277,998	264,561	262,107	335,927	299,716	257,845	254,812	265,537
Income Before Taxes	92,213	94,947	93,843	74,643	79,440	152,581	120,754	76,244
Income Taxes	17,323	15,574	15,254	7,072	9,027	34,649	27,710	14,548
Net Income	74,890	79,373	63,764	67,571	70,413	117,932	93,044	61,696
Average Shares	65,750	66,261	68,256	70,024	70,173	70,673	72,037	73,173
Balance Sheet								
Net Loans & Leases	4,642,893	4,648,847	4,858,784	4,901,577	5,481,884	5,681,893	6,058,613	6,274,480
Total Assets	7,846,126	8,149,515	8,492,022	8,898,304	9,353,896	9,612,556	9,080,473	8,767,748
Total Deposits	5,663,383	6,321,494	6,465,636	6,414,263	6,493,092	6,439,280	6,616,440	6,583,906
Total Liabilities	7,193,245	7,507,146	7,842,124	8,195,096	8,638,406	8,871,846	8,441,238	8,141,407
Stockholders' Equity	652,881	642,369	649,898	703,208	715,490	740,710	639,235	626,341
Shares Outstanding	66,205	66,503	67,649	69,287	69,903	70,401	70,816	73,308
Statistical Record								
Return on Assets %	0.94	0.95	0.73	0.74	0.74	1.26	1.04	0.78
Return on Equity %	11.56	12.28	9.42	9.50	9.67	17.09	14.70	11.00
Net Interest Margin %	47.51	47.09	51.54	60.12	57.90	52.88	46.26	42.28
Efficiency Ratio %	45.09	43.69	44.79	56.05	45.28	36.74	34.31	35.88
Loans to Deposits	0.82	0.74	0.75	0.76	0.84	0.88	0.92	0.95
Price Range	19.42-14.03	21.90-18.27	24.63-18.71	25.41-20.02	21.73-19.22	22.89-19.70	23.51-16.92	27.23-18.46
P/E Ratio	17.04-12.31	18.25-15.23	26.48-20.12	26.20-20.64	21.73-19.22	13.71-11.80	18.22-13.12	32.03-21.72
Average Yield %	5.19	4.24	3.56	3.19	3.35	2.93	2.71	2.34

Address: 1 Main Street, Evansville, IN 47708	Web Site: www.oldnational.com	Auditors: Crowe Chizek and Co.
Telephone: 812-464-1294	Officers: Larry E. Dunigan - Chmn. Robert G. Jones - Pres., C.E.O.	Investor Contact: 812-464-1366
Fax: 812-464-1567		Transfer Agents: Old National Bancorp, Evansville, IN

OLD REPUBLIC INTERNATIONAL CORP.

Exchange	Symbol	Price	52Wk Range	Yield	P/E	Div Acheiver
NYS	ORI	$12.91 (3/31/2008)	22.38-12.31	4.96	11.03	26 Years

*7 Year Price Score 76.75   *NYSE Composite Index=100   *12 Month Price Score 84.83

Interim Earnings (Per Share)

Qtr.	Mar	Jun	Sep	Dec
2003	0.46	0.53	0.52	0.49
2004	0.46	0.52	0.47	0.44
2005	0.50	0.74	0.52	0.61
2006	0.51	0.54	0.50	0.44
2007	0.46	0.49	0.12	0.09

Interim Dividends (Per Share)

Amt	Decl	Ex	Rec	Pay
0.16Q	5/24/2007	6/1/2007	6/5/2007	6/15/2007
0.16Q	8/23/2007	8/31/2007	9/5/2007	9/14/2007
0.16Q	12/6/2007	12/3/2007	12/5/2007	12/14/2007
0.16Q	2/21/2008	3/3/2008	3/5/2008	3/14/2008

Indicated Div: $0.64 (Div. Reinv. Plan)

Valuation Analysis

		Institutional Holding	
Forecast P/E	13.20	No of Institutions	
	(1/10/2007)	265	
Market Cap	33.0 Billion	Shares	
Book Value	4.5 Billion	178,109,312	
Price/Book	0.66	% Held	
Price/Sales	0.73	77.05	

Business Summary: Insurance (MIC: 8.2 SIC: 6351 NAIC: 524126)

Old Republic International is a Chicago-based insurance holding company. As of Dec 31 2007, Co. operates through three major segments. Co.'s General Insurance Group segment is a commercial lines insurance business with a focus on liability insurance coverages. Co.'s Mortgage Guaranty Group insures only first mortgage loans, primarily on residential properties incorporating one-to-four family dwelling units. Co.'s title insurance business consists primarily of the issuance of policies to real estate purchasers and investors based upon searches of the public records, which contain information concerning interests in real property.

Recent Developments: For the year ended Dec 31 2007, net income decreased 41.4% to US$272.4 million from US$464.8 million in the prior year. Revenues were US$4.09 billion, up 7.8% from US$3.79 billion the year before. Net premiums earned were US$3.39 billion versus US$3.15 billion in the prior year, an increase of 7.4%. Net investment income rose 11.2% to US$379.8 million from US$341.5 million a year ago.

Prospects: Co.'s results are being hurt by continued difficult economic environments in the housing and mortgage lending industries, with higher incurred claims more than offsetting the strong premium revenue growth at its mortgage guaranty business, as well as lower premium and fee revenues at its title insurance business. On a positive note, Co. has experienced a favorable performance from its general insurance business. Additionally, Co. has redirected proceeds from the recent sale of its indexed stock portfolio to a more concentrated, select list of common stocks.

Financial Data

(US$ in Thousands)	12/31/2007	12/31/2006	12/31/2005	12/31/2004	12/31/2003	12/31/2002	12/31/2001	12/31/2000
Earnings Per Share	1.17	1.99	2.37	1.89	2.01	1.72	1.54	1.32
Cash Flow Per Share	3.73	4.35	3.83	3.62	3.33	2.97	2.36	1.53
Tang Book Value Per Share	19.71	18.91	17.53	16.68	15.41	13.60	12.15	10.71
Dividends Per Share	0.630	0.590	1.312	0.402	0.891	0.336	0.315	0.293
Dividend Payout %	53.85	29.65	55.36	21.31	44.36	19.50	20.49	22.27
Income Statement								
Premium Income	3,389,000	3,154,100	3,062,300	2,804,800	2,582,100	2,135,400	1,786,800	1,550,300
Total Revenue	4,091,000	3,794,200	3,805,900	3,491,600	3,285,800	2,756,400	2,373,400	2,070,600
Benefits & Claims	2,156,900	1,532,300	1,460,100	1,305,600	1,097,600	975,300	861,000	760,300
Income Taxes	105,900	215,200	195,900	713,900	218,900	107,700	139,700	131,000
Net Income	272,400	464,800	551,400	435,000	459,800	392,900	346,900	297,500
Average Shares	232,912	233,034	232,108	230,759	229,128	227,904	225,614	225,369
Balance Sheet								
Total Assets	13,290,600	12,612,200	11,543,200	10,570,800	9,712,300	8,715,400	7,920,200	7,281,400
Total Liabilities	8,749,000	8,243,000	7,519,100	6,705,100	6,158,600	5,559,500	5,136,100	4,842,000
Stockholders' Equity	4,541,600	4,369,200	4,024,000	3,865,600	3,553,600	3,155,800	2,783,700	2,438,700
Shares Outstanding	230,472	231,047	229,575	231,786	230,589	232,108	229,066	227,709
Statistical Record								
Return on Assets %	2.10	3.85	4.99	4.28	4.99	4.72	4.56	4.17
Return on Equity %	6.11	11.08	13.98	11.69	13.71	13.23	13.29	12.80
Loss Ratio %	63.64	48.58	47.68	46.55	42.51	45.67	48.19	49.04
Net Margin %	6.66	12.25	14.49	12.46	13.99	14.25	14.62	14.37
Price Range	23.51-13.73	23.50-20.20	22.44-17.85	21.75-17.10	20.63-13.22	18.52-13.48	16.03-12.08	17.07-5.73
P/E Ratio	20.09-11.74	11.81-10.15	9.47-7.53	11.51-9.05	10.26-6.58	10.77-7.84	10.41-7.84	12.93-4.34
Average Yield %	3.19	2.71	6.55	2.09	5.17	2.06	2.16	2.86

Address: 307 North Michigan Avenue, Chicago, IL 60601
Telephone: 312-346-8100
Fax: 312-726-0309

Web Site: www.oldrepublic.com
Officers: Aldo C. Zucaro - Chmn., Pres., C.E.O. Karl W. Mueller - Sr. V.P., C.F.O.

Auditors: PricewaterhouseCoopers LLP
Transfer Agents: EquiServe Trust Company, N.A.

OLIN CORP.

Exchange	Symbol	Price	52Wk Range	Yield	P/E
NYS	OLN	$19.76 (3/31/2008)	23.52-16.50	4.05	N/A

*7 Year Price Score 87.41   *NYSE Composite Index=100   *12 Month Price Score 105.85

Interim Earnings (Per Share)

Qtr.	Mar	Jun	Sep	Dec
2003	(0.67)	0.15	0.10	0.00
2004	0.04	0.15	0.27	0.33
2005	0.52	0.45	0.44	0.45
2006	0.47	0.45	0.77	0.37
2007	0.31	0.48	(1.12)	0.21

Interim Dividends (Per Share)

Amt	Decl	Ex	Rec	Pay
0.20Q	4/27/2007	5/8/2007	5/10/2007	6/11/2007
0.20Q	7/26/2007	8/8/2007	8/10/2007	9/10/2007
0.20Q	10/25/2007	11/7/2007	11/9/2007	12/10/2007
0.20Q	1/25/2008	2/7/2008	2/11/2008	3/10/2008

Indicated Div: $0.80

Valuation Analysis

		Institutional Holding	
Forecast P/E	N/A	No of Institutions	191
Market Cap	$1.5 Billion	Shares	52,810,144
Book Value	663.7 Million	% Held	71.86
Price/Book	2.22		
Price/Sales	1.15		

Business Summary: Chemicals (MIC: 11.1 SIC: 2812 NAIC: 325181)

Olin is a manufacturer concentrated in two business segments: Chlor Alkali Products and Winchester®. Chlor Alkali Products manufactures and sells chlorine and caustic soda, sodium hydrosulfite, hydrochloric acid, sodium hypochlorite, hydrogen, sodium hydrosulfite, sodium chlorate, bleach products and potassium hydroxide, while Winchester® produces sporting ammunition, reloading components, small caliber military ammunition and components, and industrial cartridges. Co. markets most of its products and services primarily through its sales force, and sells directly to various industrial customers, wholesalers, other distributors, and the U.S. Government and its prime contractors.

Recent Developments: For the year ended Dec 31 2007, income from continuing operations decreased 18.5% to US$100.8 million from US$123.7 million a year earlier. Net loss amounted to US$9.2 million versus net income of US$149.7 million in the prior year. Revenues were US$1.28 billion, up 22.8% from US$1.04 billion the year before. Operating income was US$114.0 million versus US$125.5 million in the prior year, a decrease of 9.2%. Direct operating expenses rose 30.5% to US$1.04 billion from US$795.7 million in the comparable period the year before. Indirect operating expenses increased 5.1% to US$124.5 million from US$118.5 million in the equivalent prior-year period.

Prospects: For the first quarter of 2008, Co.'s income from continuing operations is projected to be about $0.50 per diluted share. This forecast reflects a slight improvement in Electrochemical Unit pricing, driven by higher caustic soda prices. In addition, Co.'s Winchester results are expected to be about equal to the first quarter of 2007 as improved pricing and volumes are offset by higher commodity costs. Meanwhile, Co. forecasts its 2008 capital spending to be in the $200.0 million to $210.0 million range. This forecast reflects spending of about $120.0 million for Co.'s St. Gabriel facility conversion and expansion project, which is expected to be completed in the first quarter of 2009.

Financial Data

(US$ in Thousands)	12/31/2007	12/31/2006	12/31/2005	12/31/2004	12/31/2003	12/31/2002	12/31/2001	12/31/2000
Earnings Per Share	(0.12)	2.06	1.86	0.80	(0.42)	(0.63)	(0.22)	1.80
Cash Flow Per Share	2.76	0.89	3.91	(2.00)	2.04	0.63	1.74	4.02
Tang Book Value Per Share	4.86	6.37	4.89	3.94	1.63	2.59	6.24	7.48
Dividends Per Share	0.800	0.800	0.800	0.800	0.800	0.800	0.800	0.800
Dividend Payout %	...	38.83	43.01	100.00	...	...	...	44.44
Income Statement								
Total Revenue	1,276,800	3,151,800	2,357,700	1,997,000	1,586,000	1,301,000	1,271,000	1,549,000
EBITDA	209,200	282,000	299,700	170,000	106,000	84,000	90,000	226,000
Income Before Taxes	150,700	201,400	225,600	79,000	5,000	(27,000)	(13,000)	131,000
Income Taxes	49,900	51,700	85,900	28,000	4,000	4,000	(4,000)	50,000
Net Income	(9,200)	149,700	133,300	55,000	(24,000)	(31,000)	(9,000)	81,000
Average Shares	74,300	72,800	71,600	68,400	58,300	49,400	43,600	45,000
Balance Sheet								
Current Assets	671,000	919,200	873,400	713,000	681,000	638,000	616,000	528,000
Total Assets	1,701,400	1,636,500	1,797,200	1,618,000	1,445,000	1,424,000	1,219,000	1,123,000
Current Liabilities	408,200	407,800	367,100	322,000	311,000	257,000	335,000	275,000
Long-Term Obligations	249,200	252,200	257,200	261,000	301,000	328,000	329,000	228,000
Total Liabilities	1,037,700	1,093,200	1,370,600	1,262,000	1,269,000	1,193,000	948,000	794,000
Stockholders' Equity	663,700	543,300	426,600	356,000	176,000	231,000	271,000	329,000
Shares Outstanding	74,504	73,322	71,875	70,566	59,015	57,622	43,440	43,980
Statistical Record								
Return on Assets %	N.M.	8.72	7.81	3.58	N.M.	N.M.	N.M.	7.39
Return on Equity %	N.M.	30.87	34.07	20.62	N.M.	N.M.	N.M.	25.32
EBITDA Margin %	16.38	8.95	12.71	8.51	6.68	6.46	7.08	14.59
Net Margin %	N.M.	4.75	5.65	2.75	N.M.	N.M.	N.M.	5.23
Asset Turnover	0.77	1.84	1.38	1.30	1.11	0.98	1.09	1.41
Current Ratio	1.64	2.25	2.38	2.21	2.19	2.48	1.84	1.92
Debt to Equity	0.38	0.46	0.60	0.73	1.71	1.42	1.21	0.69
Price Range	23.52-16.14	22.51-14.46	25.00-17.15	22.79-15.50	20.47-15.30	22.15-14.01	22.53-12.21	23.06-14.50
P/E Ratio	...	10.93-7.02	13.44-9.22	28.49-19.38	...	...	...	12.81-8.06
Average Yield %	4.13	4.41	4.00	4.34	4.57	4.61	4.53	4.64

Address: 190 Carondelet Plaza, Suite 1530, Clayton, MO 63105-3443
Telephone: 314-480-1400

Web Site: www.olin.com
Officers: Randall W. Larrimore - Chmn. Joseph D. Rupp - Pres., C.E.O.

Auditors: KPMG LLP
Investor Contact: 203-750-3254

OMNICARE INC.

Exchange	Symbol	Price	52Wk Range	Yield	P/E
NYS	OCR	$18.16 (3/31/2008)	41.40-15.59	0.50	19.32

*7 Year Price Score 69.36   *NYSE Composite Index=100   *12 Month Price Score 73.28

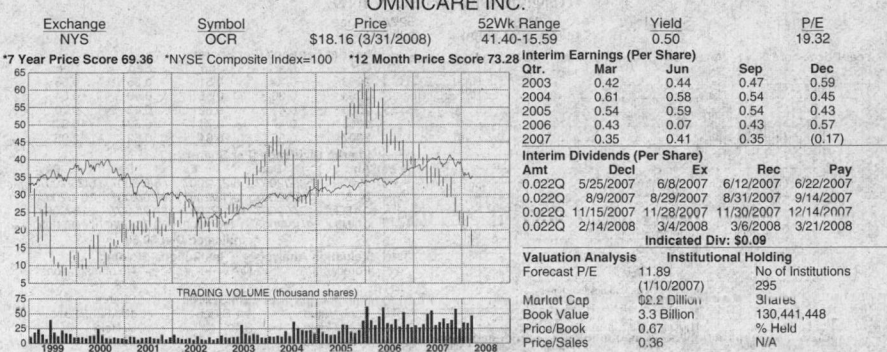

Interim Earnings (Per Share)

Qtr.	Mar	Jun	Sep	Dec
2003	0.42	0.44	0.47	0.59
2004	0.61	0.58	0.54	0.45
2005	0.54	0.59	0.54	0.43
2006	0.43	0.07	0.43	0.57
2007	0.35	0.41	0.35	(0.17)

Interim Dividends (Per Share)

Amt	Decl	Ex	Rec	Pay
0.022Q	5/25/2007	6/8/2007	6/12/2007	6/22/2007
0.022Q	8/9/2007	8/29/2007	8/31/2007	9/14/2007
0.022Q	11/15/2007	11/28/2007	11/30/2007	12/14/2007
0.022Q	2/14/2008	3/4/2008	3/6/2008	3/21/2008

Indicated Div: $0.09

Valuation Analysis

		Institutional Holding	
Forecast P/E	11.89	No of Institutions	
	(1/10/2007)	295	
Market Cap	02.2 Billion	Shares	
Book Value	3.3 Billion	130,441,448	
Price/Book	0.67	% Held	
Price/Sales	0.36	N/A	

Business Summary: Retail - Miscellaneous (MIC: 5.11 SIC: 5912 NAIC: 446110)

Omnicare is a geriatric pharmaceutical services company that provides pharmaceuticals and related ancillary pharmacy services to long-term healthcare institutions. Co. also provides operational software and support systems to long-term care pharmacy providers across the U.S. In addition, Co. provides pharmaceutical distribution and patient assistance services for specialty pharmaceuticals. Further, Co. provides product development and research services for the pharmaceutical, biotechnology, medical device and diagnostic industries in 30 countries worldwide. At Dec 31 2007, Co. operated in two business segments: Pharmacy Services and Contract Research Organization services.

Recent Developments: For the year ended Dec 31 2007, net income decreased 37.9% to US$114.1 million from US$183.6 million in the prior year. Revenues were US$6.22 billion, down 4.2% from US$6.49 billion the year before. Operating income was US$341.9 million versus US$480.3 million in the prior year, a decrease of 28.8%. Direct operating expenses declined 4.3% to US$4.68 billion from US$4.89 billion in the comparable period the year before. Indirect operating expenses increased 6.8% to US$1.20 billion from US$1.12 billion in the equivalent prior-year period.

Prospects: Going forward, Co. believes that the fundamentals in its business remain sound as it expects demand for pharmacy services for the senior population will continue to grow. In this respect, Co. intends continue to implement its Omnicare Full Potential Plan, which is slated to realign its pharmacy operating structure to increase efficiency and enhance customer growth. Upon the anticipated completion of this program by the end of 2008, Co. expects to generate annual pretax savings of $100.0 million to $120.0 million. Accordingly, Co. foresees that incremental capital expenditures related to this program will be approximately $45.0 million to $50.0 million throughout the implementation period.

Financial Data

(US$ in Thousands)	12/31/2007	12/31/2006	12/31/2005	12/31/2004	12/31/2003	12/31/2002	12/31/2001	12/31/2000
Earnings Per Share	0.94	1.50	2.10	2.17	1.93	1.33	0.79	0.53
Cash Flow Per Share	4.23	0.92	2.55	1.63	1.72	1.69	1.64	1.44
Tang Book Value Per Share	N.M.	N.M.	N.M.	N.M.	N.M.	0.91	0.27	N.M.
Dividends Per Share	0.090	0.090	0.090	0.090	0.090	0.090	0.090	0.090
Dividend Payout %	9.57	6.00	4.29	4.15	4.66	6.77	11.39	16.98
Income Statement								
Total Revenue	6,220,010	6,492,993	5,292,782	4,119,891	3,499,174	2,632,754	2,159,131	1,971,348
EBITDA	464,061	610,444	607,738	501,916	444,769	306,625	250,179	206,570
Income Before Taxes	186,498	320,496	361,806	375,199	310,449	203,051	119,785	77,523
Income Taxes	72,442	136,924	135,315	139,188	116,081	77,145	45,514	28,706
Net Income	114,056	183,572	226,491	236,011	194,368	125,906	74,271	48,817
Average Shares	121,258	122,336	108,804	112,819	103,243	94,905	93,758	92,012
Balance Sheet								
Current Assets	2,456,150	2,424,828	2,360,895	1,549,779	1,383,088	1,001,558	927,594	817,738
Total Assets	7,593,779	7,398,471	7,157,405	3,899,181	3,395,021	2,427,585	2,290,276	2,210,218
Current Liabilities	652,160	552,401	1,000,504	467,482	462,760	296,650	269,273	257,009
Long-Term Obligations	2,820,751	2,955,120	2,719,392	1,234,067	1,082,677	720,187	750,669	780,706
Total Liabilities	4,302,076	4,235,020	4,215,359	1,972,073	1,718,997	1,152,523	1,140,493	1,141,795
Stockholders' Equity	3,291,703	3,163,451	2,942,046	1,927,108	1,676,024	1,275,062	1,149,783	1,068,423
Shares Outstanding	121,772	121,464	119,882	104,496	103,187	94,301	94,671	92,156
Statistical Record								
Return on Assets %	1.52	2.52	4.10	6.45	6.68	5.34	3.30	2.22
Return on Equity %	3.53	6.01	9.30	13.06	13.17	10.38	6.70	4.64
EBITDA Margin %	7.46	9.40	11.48	12.18	12.71	11.65	11.59	10.48
Net Margin %	1.83	2.83	4.28	5.73	5.55	4.78	3.44	2.48
Asset Turnover	0.83	0.89	0.96	1.13	1.21	1.12	0.96	0.90
Current Ratio	3.77	4.39	2.36	3.32	2.99	3.38	3.44	3.18
Debt to Equity	0.86	0.93	0.92	0.64	0.65	0.56	0.65	0.73
Price Range	44.59-22.18	61.81-37.13	61.85-29.51	47.07-26.61	41.68-23.46	28.35-18.41	26.00-17.75	21.94-8.13
P/E Ratio	47.44-23.60	41.21-24.75	29.45-14.05	21.69-12.26	21.60-12.16	21.32-13.84	32.91-22.47	41.39-15.33
Average Yield %	0.26	0.20	0.20	0.24	0.29	0.38	0.42	0.65

Address: 1600 RiverCenter II, 100 East RiverCenter Boulevard, Covington, KY 41011 Telephone: 859-392-3300 Fax: 859-392-3333	Web Site: www.omnicare.com Officers: Edward L. Hutton - Chmn. Joel F. Gemunder - Pres., C.E.O.	Auditors: PricewaterhouseCoopers LLP Investor Contact: 606-392-3331 Transfer Agents: EquiServe Trust Company, N.A., Providence, RI

OMNICOM GROUP, INC.

Exchange	Symbol	Price	52Wk Range	Yield	P/E
NYS	OMC	$44.18 (3/31/2008)	54.84-42.32	1.36	14.98

*7 Year Price Score 95.41   *NYSE Composite Index=100   *12 Month Price Score 97.79

Interim Earnings (Per Share)

Qtr.	Mar	Jun	Sep	Dec
2003	0.34	0.51	0.36	0.58
2004	0.36	0.55	0.40	0.64
2005	0.41	0.62	0.45	0.70
2006	0.47	0.71	0.52	0.81
2007	0.55	0.84	0.62	0.95

Interim Dividends (Per Share)

Amt	Decl	Ex	Rec	Pay
100%	5/22/2007	6/26/2007	6/6/2007	6/25/2007
0.15Q	7/25/2007	9/18/2007	9/20/2007	10/4/2007
0.15Q	12/7/2007	12/13/2007	12/17/2007	1/4/2008
0.15Q	2/13/2008	3/5/2008	3/7/2008	4/4/2008

Indicated Div: $0.60

Valuation Analysis

		Institutional Holding
Forecast P/E	N/A	No of Institutions
		528
Market Cap	$14.3 Billion	Shares
Book Value	4.1 Billion	150,623,728
Price/Book	3.49	% Held
Price/Sales	1.12	90.14

Business Summary: Advertising, Marketing & PR (MIC: 12.4 SIC: 7311 NAIC: 541810)

Omnicom Group is a holding company engaged in providing advertising, marketing, and corporate communications services. Co.'s services include advertising, marketing research, brand consultancy, media planning and buying, crisis communications, mobile marketing services, database management, digital and interactive marketing, organizational communications, and direct marketing services. Co. also provides package design, directory advertising, product placement, entertainment marketing, public affairs, public relations, field marketing, recruitment communications, financial/corporate business-to-business advertising, reputation consulting, retail marketing and investor relations services.

Recent Developments: For the year ended Dec 31 2007, net income increased 12.9% to US$975.7 million from US$864.0 million in the prior year. Revenues were US$12.69 billion, up 11.6% from US$11.38 billion the year before. Operating income was US$1.66 billion versus US$1.48 billion in the prior year, an increase of 11.8%. Indirect operating expenses increased 11.5% to US$11.03 billion from US$9.89 billion in the equivalent prior-year period.

Prospects: Co.'s near-term outlook appears favorable. Looking ahead, Co. expects to continue to increase its investment in the Asian market and plans to focus on businesses that will complement as well as improve its existing strategic platforms and service capabilities to better serve its clients in various regions. For instance, Co. recently acquired a majority interest in Shift, a digital consultancy in New Zealand, which should add to Co.'s digital capabilities in the Asia Pacific region. In addition, Co.'s BBDO subsidiary recently announced a significant minority stake in China's Shunya Communications Group to further strengthen Co.'s position in China's communications industry.

Financial Data

(US$ in Thousands)	12/31/2007	12/31/2006	12/31/2005	12/31/2004	12/31/2003	12/31/2002	12/31/2001	12/31/2000
Earnings Per Share	2.95	2.50	2.18	1.94	1.79	1.72	1.35	1.37
Cash Flow Per Share	4.91	5.08	2.75	3.46	2.81	2.69	2.12	1.96
Dividends Per Share	0.575	0.500	0.463	0.450	0.400	0.400	0.388	0.350
Dividend Payout %	19.49	20.04	21.22	23.20	22.28	23.26	28.70	25.64
Income Statement								
Total Revenue	12,694,000	11,376,900	10,481,100	9,747,200	8,621,404	7,536,299	6,889,406	6,154,230
EBITDA	1,936,400	1,744,600	1,602,000	1,387,500	1,325,598	1,254,434	1,226,228	1,213,804
Income Before Taxes	1,585,100	1,391,900	1,280,600	1,178,800	1,121,849	1,073,623	895,385	911,617
Income Taxes	536,900	466,900	435,300	396,300	380,927	375,637	352,128	369,140
Net Income	975,700	864,000	790,700	723,500	675,883	643,459	503,142	498,795
Average Shares	330,400	346,200	363,555	373,174	377,312	375,205	380,579	378,075
Balance Sheet								
Current Assets	10,504,200	9,646,800	7,967,400	8,095,100	7,285,945	5,637,066	5,233,824	5,366,883
Total Assets	19,271,700	18,164,400	15,919,900	16,002,400	14,499,456	11,819,802	10,617,414	9,891,499
Current Liabilities	11,227,200	10,296,100	8,700,300	8,743,900	7,762,458	6,839,524	6,643,787	6,625,052
Long-Term Obligations	3,054,700	3,054,700	2,357,500	2,358,400	2,536,595	1,944,898	1,340,105	1,245,387
Total Liabilities	15,180,000	14,293,100	11,971,900	11,923,700	11,033,397	9,250,875	8,438,995	8,343,022
Stockholders' Equity	4,091,700	3,871,300	3,948,000	4,078,700	3,466,059	2,568,927	2,178,419	1,548,477
Shares Outstanding	323,000	337,600	356,588	374,150	380,849	376,803	381,257	368,158
Statistical Record								
Return on Assets %	5.21	5.07	4.95	4.73	5.14	5.74	4.91	5.26
Return on Equity %	24.51	22.10	19.70	19.13	22.40	27.11	27.00	32.08
EBITDA Margin %	15.25	15.33	15.28	14.23	15.38	16.65	17.80	19.72
Net Margin %	7.69	7.59	7.54	7.42	7.84	8.54	7.30	8.10
Asset Turnover	0.68	0.67	0.66	0.64	0.66	0.67	0.67	0.65
Current Ratio	0.94	0.94	0.92	0.93	0.94	0.82	0.79	0.81
Debt to Equity	0.75	0.79	0.60	0.58	0.73	0.76	0.62	0.80
Price Range	54.84-46.05	52.96-39.48	45.53-38.20	44.35-33.35	43.74-24.25	48.60-20.37	48.78-30.00	50.00-35.00
P/E Ratio	18.59-15.61	21.18-15.79	20.89-17.52	22.86-17.19	24.44-13.55	28.26-11.84	36.14-22.23	36.50-25.55
Average Yield %	1.13	1.10	1.10	1.16	1.15	1.11	0.92	0.81

Address: 437 Madison Ave, New York, NY 10022 **Telephone:** 212-415-3600 **Fax:** 212-415-3393	**Web Site:** www.omnicomgroup.com **Officers:** Bruce Crawford - Chmn. Peter Mead - Vice-Chmn.	**Auditors:** KPMG LLP **Investor Contact:** 212-415-3393

ONEOK INC.

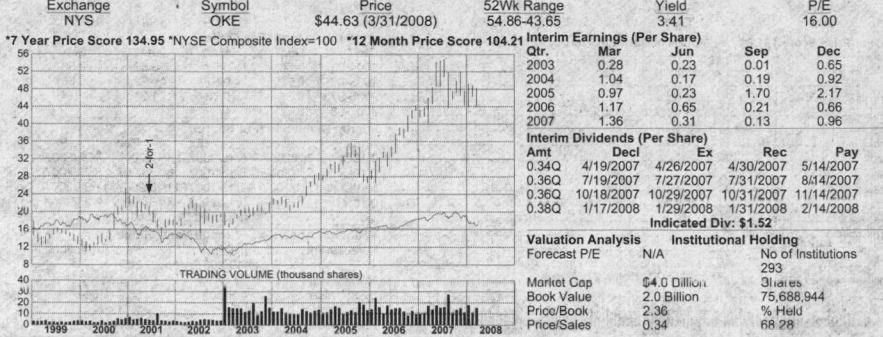

Exchange	Symbol	Price	52Wk Range	Yield	P/E
NYS	OKE	$44.63 (3/31/2008)	54.86-43.65	3.41	16.00

*7 Year Price Score 134.95 *NYSE Composite Index=100 *12 Month Price Score 104.21

Interim Earnings (Per Share)

Qtr.	Mar	Jun	Sep	Dec
2003	0.28	0.23	0.01	0.65
2004	1.04	0.17	0.19	0.92
2005	0.97	0.23	1.70	2.17
2006	1.17	0.65	0.21	0.66
2007	1.36	0.31	0.13	0.96

Interim Dividends (Per Share)

Amt	Decl	Ex	Rec	Pay
0.34Q	4/19/2007	4/26/2007	4/30/2007	5/14/2007
0.36Q	7/19/2007	7/27/2007	7/31/2007	8/14/2007
0.36Q	10/18/2007	10/29/2007	10/31/2007	11/14/2007
0.38Q	1/17/2008	1/29/2008	1/31/2008	2/14/2008

Indicated Div: $1.52

Valuation Analysis

		Institutional Holding
Forecast P/E	N/A	No of Institutions
		293
Market Cap	$4.0 Billion	Shares
Book Value	2.0 Billion	75,688,944
Price/Book	2.36	% Held
Price/Sales	0.34	68.28

Business Summary: Gas Utilities (MIC: 7.4 SIC: 4923 NAIC: 221210)

ONEOK purchases, transports, stores and distributes natural gas. Co.'s energy services operation is engaged in wholesale and retail natural gas and trading activities and provides services to customers in many states and Canada. Co. is the sole general partner of ONEOK Partners, L.P., a publicly traded limited partnership engaged in the gathering, processing, storing and transporting of natural gas in the U.S. and owns natural gas liquids (NGL) systems that connect much of the natural gas and NGL supply in the Mid-Continent and Gulf Coast regions with key market centers in Conway, KS, Mont Belvieu, TX, and Chicago, IL.

Recent Developments: For the year ended Dec 31 2007, income from continuing operations decreased 0.6% to US$304.9 million from US$306.7 million a year earlier. Net income decreased 0.5% to US$304.9 million from US$306.3 million in the prior year. Revenues were US$13.48 billion, up 13.1% from US$11.92 billion the year before. Operating income was US$822.5 million versus US$862.2 million in the prior year, a decrease of 4.6%. Direct operating expenses rose 13.6% to US$12.34 billion from US$10.86 billion in the comparable period the year before. Indirect operating expenses increased 58.3% to US$312.0 million from US$197.1 million in the equivalent prior-year period.

Prospects: On Feb 4 2008, Co.'s ONEOK Partners segment announced plans to construct a 78-mile natural gas liquids gathering pipeline to connect two natural gas processing plants in the Woodford Shale area in southeast Oklahoma to the partnership's Mid-Continent natural gas liquids gathering system for fractionation. The $25.0 million extension of 6- and 8-inch pipeline is scheduled for completion in the second quarter of 2008. Subsequently, Co. expects these plants to produce about 25,000 barrels per day of raw natural gas liquids (NGL). Meanwhile, for 2008, Co. expects its earnings to continue to be driven by its ONEOK Partners segment, and thus, targets earnings of $2.75 to $3.15 per diluted share.

Financial Data

(US$ in Thousands)	12/31/2007	12/31/2006	12/31/2005	12/31/2004	12/31/2003	12/31/2002	12/31/2001	12/31/2000
Earnings Per Share	2.79	2.68	5.06	2.30	1.22	1.39	0.85	1.48
Cash Flow Per Share	9.59	7.80	(1.79)	2.00	0.05	8.13	1.22	(1.62)
Tang Book Value Per Share	8.90	10.52	11.38	13.26	10.67	20.60	19.19	19.12
Dividends Per Share	1.400	1.220	1.090	0.880	0.675	0.620	0.620	0.620
Dividend Payout %	50.18	45.52	21.54	38.26	55.33	44.60	72.94	41.89
Income Statement								
Total Revenue	13,477,414	11,896,104	12,676,230	5,988,080	2,998,996	2,104,280	6,803,146	6,642,858
EBITDA	...	...	973,985	683,062	606,904	...	...	...
Income Before Taxes	...	...	645,669	392,145	344,819	...	...	...
Income Taxes	184,597	193,764	242,521	149,967	130,527	102,485	52,234	90,286
Net Income	304,921	306,312	546,545	242,178	112,488	166,624	101,565	145,607
Average Shares	109,298	114,477	108,006	105,461	96,999	100,528	99,671	98,388
Balance Sheet								
Net PPE	5,845,181	4,844,921	3,994,227	3,786,821	3,691,826	3,015,049	3,272,968	3,095,513
Total Assets	11,062,034	10,504,721	10,013,466	7,192,649	6,314,048	5,730,858	5,879,159	7,369,136
Long-Term Obligations	4,215,046	4,030,855	2,024,070	1,630,019	1,978,556	1,620,169	1,620,023	1,473,213
Total Liabilities	8,290,762	7,488,118	8,218,709	5,586,945	5,072,656	4,365,246	4,613,869	6,144,179
Stockholders' Equity	1,969,308	2,215,958	1,794,757	1,605,704	1,241,392	1,365,612	1,265,290	1,224,957
Shares Outstanding	103,987	110,678	97,654	104,106	95,194	60,761	60,002	59,176
Statistical Record								
Return on Assets %	2.83	2.99	6.35	3.58	1.87	2.87	1.53	2.74
Return on Equity %	14.57	15.27	32.15	16.97	8.63	12.67	8.16	12.22
EBITDA Margin %	...	...	7.68	11.41	20.24	...	...	...
Net Margin %	2.26	2.57	4.31	4.04	3.75	7.92	1.49	2.19
PPE Turnover	2.52	2.69	3.26	1.60	0.89	0.67	2.14	2.54
Asset Turnover	1.25	1.16	1.47	0.88	0.50	0.36	1.03	1.25
Debt to Equity	2.14	1.82	1.13	1.02	1.59	1.19	1.28	1.20
Price Range	54.86-40.12	44.26-26.56	35.72-26.63	28.90-19.80	22.22-16.44	22.77-15.21	24.16-14.42	25.28-10.88
P/E Ratio	19.66-14.38	16.51-9.91	7.06-5.26	12.57-8.61	18.21-13.48	16.38-10.94	28.42-16.96	17.08-7.35
Average Yield %	2.96	3.46	3.58	3.73	3.44	3.21	3.18	3.99

Address: 100 West Fifth Street, Tulsa, OK 74103 **Telephone:** 918-588-7000 **Fax:** 918-588-7273	**Web Site:** www.oneok.com **Officers:** David L. Kyle - Chmn., Pres., C.E.O. Jim C. Kneale - Exec. V.P., Fin., Admin., C.F.O.	**Auditors:** Pricewaterhouse Cooper LLP **Investor Contact:** 918-588-7950 **Transfer Agents:** UMB Bank, N.A.

OSHKOSH CORP

Exchange	Symbol	Price	52Wk Range	Yield	P/E
NYS	OSK	$36.28 (3/31/2008)	65.76-35.60	1.10	10.28

*7 Year Price Score 131.83 *NYSE Composite Index=100 *12 Month Price Score 81.76

Interim Earnings (Per Share)

Qtr.	Dec	Mar	Jun	Sep
2004-05	0.56	0.52	0.53	0.58
2005-06	0.72	0.67	0.72	0.66
2006-07	0.55	0.68	1.21	1.14
2007-08	0.50	...	...	...

Interim Dividends (Per Share)

Amt	Decl	Ex	Rec	Pay
0.10Q	5/3/2007	5/15/2007	5/17/2007	5/25/2007
0.10Q	8/1/2007	8/13/2007	8/15/2007	8/23/2007
0.10Q	11/1/2007	11/13/2007	11/15/2007	11/26/2007
0.10Q	2/1/2008	2/13/2008	2/15/2008	2/25/2008

Indicated Div: $0.40

TRADING VOLUME (thousand shares)

Valuation Analysis | **Institutional Holding**

Forecast P/E	10.19 (1/10/2007)	No of Institutions	265
Market Cap	$2.7 Billion	Shares	58,241,644
Book Value	1.4 Billion	% Held	78.78
Price/Book	1.88		
Price/Sales	0.40		

Business Summary: Automotive (MIC: 15.1 SIC: 3711 NAIC: 336120)

Oshkosh is a designer, manufacturer and marketer of a range of specialty vehicles and vehicle bodies, including access equipment, defense trucks, fire & emergency vehicles and concrete mixers and refuse collection vehicles. As a manufacturer of severe-duty, heavy- and medium-payload tactical trucks for the U.S. Department of Defense, Co. manufactures vehicles that perform various tasks such as hauling tanks, missile systems, ammunition, fuel and cargo for combat units. Co. also manufactures aerial work platforms under the JLG brand name. Co. operates in four segments: access equipment, defense, fire & emergency and commercial.

Recent Developments: For the quarter ended Dec 31 2007, net income decreased 9.5% to US$37.3 million from US$41.2 million in the year-earlier quarter. Revenues were US$1.50 billion, up 49.0% from US$1.01 billion the year before. Operating income was US$109.9 million versus US$83.6 million in the prior-year quarter, an increase of 31.5%. Direct operating expenses rose 49.6% to US$1.25 billion from US$834.1 million in the comparable period the year before. Indirect operating expenses increased 59.5% to US$142.1 million from US$89.1 million in the equivalent prior-year period.

Prospects: Co.'s outlook for the fiscal year ending Sep 2008 appears favorable. Notably, Co. expects consolidated net sales to be in a range of $7.10 billion to $7.30 billion excluding new acquisitions, representing an increase of 12.6% to 15.7% over the prior year. In addition, Co. has reaffirmed its earnings per share guidance range of $4.15 to $4.35, which represents an increase of between 16.0% and 22.0% over the prior year. These estimates reflect anticipated strong performance in the access equipment and defense segments, offset by weaker economic conditions negatively affecting the fire & emergency and commercial segments.

Financial Data

(US$ in Thousands)	3 Mos	09/30/2007	09/30/2006	09/30/2005	09/30/2004	09/30/2003	09/30/2002	09/30/2001
Earnings Per Share	3.53	3.58	2.76	2.18	1.56	1.08	0.86	0.75
Cash Flow Per Share	7.10	5.52	2.42	2.98	1.92	1.54	3.92	(0.13)
Tang Book Value Per Share	N.M.	N.M.	3.85	3.96	1.56	1.13	N.M.	N.M.
Dividends Per Share	0.400	0.400	0.367	0.221	0.130	0.093	0.086	0.086
Dividend Payout %	11.33	11.17	13.32	10.15	8.31	8.65	10.00	11.58
Income Statement								
Total Revenue	1,499,900	6,307,300	3,427,388	2,959,900	2,262,305	1,926,010	1,743,592	1,445,293
EBITDA	143,400	652,400	354,787	296,747	207,802	147,400	134,955	128,546
Depn & Amortn	35,600	...	...	...	...	...	...	...
Income Before Taxes	53,300	395,700	324,938	260,121	176,548	110,480	89,457	78,813
Income Taxes	18,100	135,200	121,194	102,267	65,892	37,131	32,285	29,361
Net Income	37,300	268,100	205,529	160,205	112,806	75,620	59,598	50,864
Average Shares	74,982	74,830	74,399	73,621	71,977	69,969	69,140	68,352
Balance Sheet								
Current Assets	2,065,600	2,194,900	1,003,394	954,384	710,707	466,558	427,036	503,150
Total Assets	6,284,400	6,399,800	2,110,908	1,718,303	1,452,414	1,083,132	1,024,329	1,089,268
Current Liabilities	1,343,600	1,548,000	882,074	775,539	679,681	467,994	393,072	379,201
Long-Term Obligations	2,956,300	2,975,600	2,176	2,589	3,209	1,510	131,713	282,249
Total Liabilities	4,850,300	5,006,200	1,049,003	899,633	816,321	564,269	614,569	742,242
Stockholders' Equity	1,430,500	1,393,600	1,061,905	818,670	636,093	518,863	409,760	347,026
Shares Outstanding	74,219	74,207	73,751	73,376	70,679	69,718	67,921	66,861
Statistical Record								
Return on Assets %	4.27	6.30	10.73	10.11	8.87	7.18	5.64	5.39
Return on Equity %	20.81	21.84	21.86	22.02	19.48	16.29	15.75	15.70
EBITDA Margin %	9.56	10.34	10.35	10.03	9.19	7.65	7.74	8.89
Net Margin %	2.49	4.25	6.00	5.41	4.99	3.93	3.42	3.52
Asset Turnover	1.10	1.48	1.79	1.87	1.78	1.83	1.65	1.53
Current Ratio	1.54	1.42	1.14	1.23	1.05	1.00	1.09	1.33
Debt to Equity	2.07	2.14	N.M.	N.M.	0.01	N.M.	0.32	0.81
Price Range	65.76-45.99	65.76-44.00	65.51-41.50	43.38-27.23	29.81-19.81	20.68-12.74	15.47-8.48	12.25-8.02
P/E Ratio	18.63-13.03	18.37-12.29	23.74-15.04	19.90-12.49	19.11-12.70	19.15-11.79	17.99-9.86	16.33-10.69
Average Yield %	0.72	0.73	0.73	0.60	0.50	0.60	0.66	0.86

Address: P.O. Box 2566, 2307 Oregon Street, Oshkosh, WI 54903-2566
Telephone: 920-235-9151

Web Site: www.oshkoshtruckcorporation.com
Officers: Robert G. Bohn - Chmn., Pres., C.E.O. Bryan J. Blankfield - Exec. V.P., Sec., Gen Couns.

Auditors: Deloitte & Touche LLP
Investor Contact: 920-235-9151x2296
Transfer Agents: Computershare Investor Services, LLC, Chicago, IL

OVERSEAS SHIPHOLDING GROUP, INC.

Exchange	Symbol	Price	52Wk Range	Yield	P/E
NYS	OSG	$70.04 (3/31/2008)	90.38-56.40	1.78	11.37

*7 Year Price Score 130.41 *NYSE Composite Index=100   ***12 Month Price Score 97.50**

TRADING VOLUME (thousand shares)

Interim Earnings (Per Share)

Qtr.	Mar	Jun	Sep	Dec
2003	1.28	1.20	0.40	0.60
2004	1.98	1.15	1.74	5.38
2005	4.18	2.89	1.82	2.88
2006	3.24	1.52	2.29	2.86
2007	2.16	2.28	0.83	0.77

Interim Dividends (Per Share)

Amt	Decl	Ex	Rec	Pay
0.25Q	4/19/2007	5/7/2007	5/9/2007	5/30/2007
0.313Q	6/6/2007	8/3/2007	8/7/2007	8/28/2007
0.313Q	9/26/2007	11/5/2007	11/7/2007	11/28/2007
0.313Q	1/23/2008	2/14/2008	2/19/2008	3/5/2008

Indicated Div: $1.25

Valuation Analysis

		Institutional Holding	
Forecast P/E	9.14 (1/10/2007)	No of Institutions	210
Market Cap	$2.2 Billion	Shares	34,657,112
Book Value	1.8 Billion	% Held	88.05
Price/Book	1.20		
Price/Sales	1.93		

Business Summary: Shipping (MIC: 15.3 SIC: 4412 NAIC: 483111)

Overseas Shipholding Group is an independent bulk shipping company engaged mainly in the ocean transportation of crude oil and petroleum products. At Dec 31 2007, Co. owned/operated a fleet of 112 vessels (aggregating 12.2 million deadweight tons and 432,400 cubic meters) of which 93 vessels operated in the international market and 19 operated in the U.S. Flag market. Co.'s newbuilding program of owned and chartered-in vessels totaled 44 and extends across each of its operating segments, bringing its total operating and newbuild fleet to 156 vessels at Dec 31 2007. Co.'s customers include independent and state-owned oil companies, oil traders, and U.S. and international government entities.

Recent Developments: For the year ended Dec 31 2007, net income decreased 46.2% to US$211.3 million from US$392.7 million in the prior year. Revenues were US$1.13 billion, up 7.8% from US$1.05 billion the year before. Operating income was US$216.4 million versus US$401.0 million in the prior year, a decrease of 46.0%. Direct operating expenses rose 32.1% to US$616.2 million from US$466.4 million in the comparable period the year before. Indirect operating expenses increased 64.8% to US$296.7 million from US$180.0 million in the equivalent prior-year period.

Prospects: Co. believes that the diversification of its crude oil and product fleets with Suezmax and LR1 tankers should increase its earnings going forward. Notably, Co. has two newbuilding Suezmaxes time chartered-in for three years commencing upon their delivery, which are expected in the fourth quarter of 2008, and expects to deliver six LR1 vessels in 2010 through 2011. Overall, charters-in for 21 vessels are scheduled to commence upon delivery of the vessels between 2008 and 2011 and 23 newbuilds (including one U.S. Flag Articulated Tug Barge that is being converted to a double hull configuration) are scheduled for delivery between 2008 and 2011.

Financial Data
(US$ in Thousands)

	12/31/2007	12/31/2006	12/31/2005	12/31/2004	12/31/2003	12/31/2002	12/31/2001	12/31/2000
Earnings Per Share	6.16	9.92	11.77	10.24	3.47	(0.51)	2.92	2.63
Cash Flow Per Share	4.91	11.29	11.46	9.49	6.43	0.38	5.32	2.95
Tang Book Value Per Share	52.47	52.27	47.56	36.20	25.54	22.76	23.73	22.07
Dividends Per Share	1.125	0.925	0.700	0.700	0.650	0.600	0.600	0.600
Dividend Payout %	18.26	9.32	5.95	6.84	18.73	...	20.55	22.81
Income Statement								
Total Revenue	1,129,305	1,047,403	961,662	789,581	431,136	266,725	381,018	370,081
EBITDA	393,049	529,065	684,401	645,012	308,265	96,995	255,617	217,529
Income Before Taxes	216,137	384,473	463,719	481,014	168,153	(20,864)	154,445	132,186
Income Taxes	4,827	(8,187)	(1,110)	79,778	46,844	(3,244)	53,004	46,520
Net Income	211,310	392,660	464,829	401,236	121,309	(17,620)	101,441	90,391
Average Shares	34,326	39,586	39,506	39,176	34,976	34,394	34,696	34,315
Balance Sheet								
Total Assets	4,158,917	4,230,669	3,348,680	2,680,798	2,000,686	2,034,842	1,964,275	1,823,913
Long-Term Obligations	1,531,334	1,306,947	965,655	906,183	787,588	985,035	854,929	836,497
Total Liabilities	2,208,422	2,023,358	1,472,652	1,254,426	1,083,611	1,250,693	1,150,849	1,073,746
Stockholders' Equity	1,818,025	2,207,311	1,876,028	1,426,372	917,075	784,149	813,426	750,167
Shares Outstanding	31,093	39,225	39,449	39,399	35,905	34,451	34,277	33,986
Statistical Record								
Return on Assets %	5.04	10.36	15.42	17.09	6.01	N.M.	5.36	5.09
Return on Equity %	10.50	19.23	28.15	34.15	14.26	N.M.	12.98	12.78
EBITDA Margin %	34.80	50.51	71.17	81.69	71.50	36.37	67.09	58.78
Net Margin %	18.71	37.49	48.34	50.82	28.14	(6.61)	26.62	24.42
Asset Turnover	0.27	0.28	0.32	0.34	0.21	0.13	0.20	0.21
Price Range	90.38-54.25	69.44-47.02	67.60-46.60	65.69-32.23	35.89-15.15	24.75-15.15	37.09-19.90	30.25-13.88
P/E Ratio	14.67-8.81	7.00-4.74	5.74-3.96	6.42-3.15	10.34-4.37	...	12.70-6.82	11.50-5.28
Average Yield %	1.60	1.64	1.22	1.58	2.91	3.03	2.25	2.60

Address: 666 Third Avenue, New York, NY 10017 Telephone: 212-953-4100 Fax: 212-578-1832	Web Site: www.osg.com Officers: Morton Arntzen - Pres., C.E.O. Myles R. Itkin - Sr. V.P., C.F.O., Treas.	Auditors: Ernst & Young LLP Investor Contact: 212-578-1699 Transfer Agents: Mellon Investor Services, Jersey City, NJ

OWENS-ILLINOIS, INC.

Exchange	Symbol	Price	52Wk Range	Yield	P/E
NYS	OI	$56.43 (3/31/2008)	57.97-26.12	N/A	7.06

*7 Year Price Score 173.99 *NYSE Composite Index=100 *12 Month Price Score 140.94

TRADING VOLUME (thousand shares)

Interim Earnings (Per Share)

Qtr.	Mar	Jun	Sep	Dec
2003	0.20	0.08	0.16	(7.33)
2004	0.29	0.52	0.42	0.20
2005	0.73	0.53	0.75	(5.86)
2006	0.12	0.24	0.02	(0.70)
2007	0.30	0.89	6.86	(0.14)

Interim Dividends (Per Share)

No Dividends Paid

Valuation Analysis

	Institutional Holding	
Forecast P/E	11.71	No of Institutions
	(1/10/2007)	191
Market Cap	$8.9 Billion	Shares
Book Value	2.2 Billion	160,156,688
Price/Book	4.06	% Held
Price/Sales	1.16	N/A

Business Summary: Stone, Clay, Glass, and Concrete Products (MIC: 11.2 SIC: 3221 NAIC: 327213)

Owens-Illinois is manufacturer of glass containers products. Co. produces glass containers for beer and ready-to-drink low alcohol refreshers, spirits, wine, food, tea, juice and pharmaceuticals. Co. also produces glass containers for soft drinks and other non-alcoholic beverages, principally outside the U.S. Co. sells most of its glass container products directly to customers under annual or multi-year supply agreements. Co. also sells some of its products through distributors. The principal markets for glass container products made by Co. are in Europe, North America, Asia Pacific, and South America.

Recent Developments: For the year ended Dec 31 2007, income from continuing operations was US$299.3 million compared with a loss of US$3.8 million a year earlier. Net income amounted to US$1.34 billion versus a net loss of US$27.5 million in the prior year. Revenues were US$7.68 billion, up 13.8% from US$6.75 billion the year before. Direct operating expenses rose 8.9% to US$5.97 billion from US$5.48 billion in the comparable period the year before. Indirect operating expenses increased 8.9% to US$1.20 billion from US$1.10 billion in the equivalent prior-year period.

Prospects: Co.'s recent improved bottom-line performance is attributable primarily to better operating profit driven by improvement in prices and product sales mix, lower warehouse, delivery and other cost of sales and a reduction in operating expenses. Favorable foreign currency translation also contributed to Co.'s earnings growth. Going forward, Co. plans to continue to focus on reducing capital spending and improving its return on invested capital by improving capital efficiency. In the meantime, Co. expects that the level of capital expenditures for continuing operations in 2008 will increase, but will not exceed 80.0% to 85.0% of its depreciation and amortization expense for the year.

Financial Data

(US$ in Thousands)	12/31/2007	12/31/2006	12/31/2005	12/31/2004	12/31/2003	12/31/2002	12/31/2001	12/31/2000
Earnings Per Share	7.99	(0.32)	(3.85)	1.43	(6.89)	(3.29)	2.30	(2.00)
Cash Flow Per Share	4.13	0.99	3.34	4.11	2.40	4.11	3.70	2.49
Income Statement								
Total Revenue	7,679,200	7,523,500	7,189,700	6,263,400	6,158,200	5,760,100	6,013,300	5,814,800
EBITDA	967,500	651,800	305,400	685,100	(565,500)	497,300	1,331,500	284,700
Income Before Taxes	506,600	142,600	(218,600)	210,300	(1,090,700)	16,600	667,200	(391,600)
Income Taxes	147,800	126,500	367,100	5,900	(125,700)	(18,300)	286,400	(143,900)
Net Income	1,340,600	(27,500)	(558,600)	235,500	(990,800)	(460,200)	356,600	(269,700)
Average Shares	167,767	152,071	150,909	149,679	146,913	146,615	145,660	145,983
Balance Sheet								
Current Assets	2,694,600	2,432,700	2,282,300	2,400,800	2,121,800	1,887,200	1,987,200	2,081,700
Total Assets	9,324,600	9,320,700	9,521,800	10,736,700	9,531,300	9,869,300	10,106,600	10,343,200
Current Liabilities	2,529,500	2,365,700	1,821,900	1,906,500	1,363,400	1,297,400	1,231,500	1,318,000
Long-Term Obligations	3,013,500	4,719,400	5,018,700	5,167,900	5,333,100	5,268,000	5,329,700	5,729,800
Total Liabilities	7,137,200	8,964,000	8,797,900	9,192,400	8,527,900	8,198,500	7,954,800	8,460,200
Stockholders' Equity	2,187,400	356,700	723,900	1,544,300	1,003,400	1,670,800	2,151,800	1,883,000
Shares Outstanding	157,350	154,235	152,911	150,916	147,853	147,351	146,478	144,954
Statistical Record								
Return on Assets %	14.38	N.M.	N.M.	2.32	N.M.	N.M.	3.49	N.M.
Return on Equity %	105.39	N.M.	N.M.	18.44	N.M.	N.M.	17.68	N.M.
EBITDA Margin %	12.60	8.66	4.25	10.94	N.M.	8.63	22.14	4.90
Net Margin %	17.46	N.M.	N.M.	3.76	N.M.	N.M.	5.93	N.M.
Asset Turnover	0.82	0.80	0.71	0.62	0.63	0.58	0.59	0.55
Current Ratio	1.07	1.03	1.25	1.26	1.56	1.45	1.61	1.58
Debt to Equity	1.38	13.23	6.93	3.35	5.32	3.15	2.48	3.04
Price Range	50.08-18.55	22.21-13.22	27.25-18.01	23.83-10.98	15.50-7.98	19.19-9.98	9.99-3.75	25.06-2.56
P/E Ratio	6.27-2.32	...	16.66-7.68	...	...	4.34-1.63	...

Address: One SeaGate, Toledo, OH 43666	Web Site: www.o-i.com	Auditors: Ernst & Young LLP
Telephone: 419-247-5000	Officers: Steven R. McCracken - Chmn., C.E.O. Thomas L. Young - C.F.O., Co-Chief Executive Officer	Investor Contact: 419-247-2400
Fax: 419-247-2839		

OWENS CORNING

Exchange	Symbol	Price	52Wk Range	Yield	P/E
NYSE	OC	$18.13 (3/31/2008)	36.06-16.76	N/A	N/A

*7 Year Price Score N/A   ***NYSE Composite Index=100**   ***12 Month Price Score 79.41** Interim Earnings (Per Share)

Qtr.	Mar	Jun	Sep	Dec
2006	1.05	4.19	1.04	(6.79)
2007	0.01	0.22	0.86	0.00

Interim Dividends (Per Share)

No Dividends Paid

Valuation Analysis   **Institutional Holding**

Forecast P/E	N/A	No of Institutions
		91
Market Cap	$2.4 Billion	Shares
Book Value	4.0 Billion	60,574,500
Price/Book	0.59	% Held
Price/Sales	0.48	52.39

Business Summary: General Construction Supplies & Services (MIC: 3.3 SIC: 5039 NAIC: 423390)

Owens Corning is a producer of residential and commercial building materials and glass fiber reinforcements and other similar materials for composite systems. Co. operates within two product categories: building materials, which includes Insulating Systems, Roofing and Asphalt, and Other Building Materials and Services reportable segments, and composites, which includes Co.'s Composite Solutions segment. Through Co.'s building materials product category, Co. manufactures and sells products in the United States, Canada, Asia and Latin America, and through Co.'s composites product category, Co. manufactures and sells products in the United States, Canada, Europe, Asia and Latin America.

Recent Developments: For the year ended Dec 31 2007, income from continuing operations was US$27.0 million compared with a loss of US$54.0 million a year earlier. Net income amounted to US$96.0 million versus a net loss of US$65.0 million in the prior year. Revenues were US$4.98 billion, up 544.8% from US$772.0 million the year before. Operating income was US$145.0 million versus a loss of US$44.0 million in the prior year. Direct operating expenses rose 540.4% to US$4.20 billion from US$656.0 million in the comparable period the year before. Indirect operating expenses increased 295.0% to US$632.0 million from US$160.0 million in the equivalent prior-year period.

Prospects: On Oct 31 2007, Co. closed the acquisition of Saint-Gobain's Reinforcements and Composite Fabrics businesses, which should accelerate Co.'s global growth strategy and strengthen its position in the glass reinforcements and composites markets. Co. expects global demand for composite products to grow for the rest of 2007 and into 2008. Also, Co. intends to expand its glass reinforcements and composite fabrics production capabilities beginning in 2008 to support growth in Asia and Eastern Europe, and specifically in China and Russia. Separately, Co. expects to reduce operating costs by about $100.0 million through its cost-reduction initiative that is expected to conclude by the end of 2007.

Financial Data

(US$ in Thousands)	12/31/2007	12/31/2006	10/31/2006	12/31/2005	12/31/2004	12/31/2003	12/31/2002	12/31/2001
Earnings Per Share	...	(0.51)	133.89	(74.08)	3.40	1.92	(51.02)	0.66
Cash Flow Per Share	1.42	0.12	(41.32)	13.49	8.10	5.91	6.48	8.68
Tang Book Value Per Share	12.26	8.22			...	...	...	...
Income Statement								
Total Revenue	4,978,000	909,000	5,552,000	6,323,000	5,675,000	4,996,000	4,872,000	4,762,000
EBITDA	488,000	9,000	9,615,000	(3,509,000)	658,000	473,000	(2,124,000)	339,000
Income Before Taxes	23,000	(89,000)	9,165,000	(4,482,000)	439,000	259,000	(2,329,000)	102,000
Income Taxes	(8,000)	(28,000)	1,025,000	(387,000)	227,000	145,000	31,000	57,000
Net Income	96,000	(65,000)	8,140,000	(4,099,000)	204,000	115,000	(2,009,000)	38,000
Average Shares	128,800	128,100	59,900	55,300	59,900	59,900	55,100	59,900
Balance Sheet								
Current Assets	1,852,000	2,552,000	...	2,705,000	2,128,000	1,888,000	1,774,000	1,649,000
Total Assets	7,872,000	8,470,000	...	8,735,000	7,639,000	7,358,000	6,920,000	7,041,000
Current Liabilities	1,246,000	2,560,000	...	1,786,000	951,000	864,000	861,000	849,000
Long-Term Obligations	1,993,000	1,296,000	...	36,000	38,000	73,000	71,000	5,000
Total Liabilities	3,884,000	4,784,000	...	16,882,000	11,719,000	11,686,000	11,388,000	8,658,000
Stockholders' Equity	3,988,000	3,686,000	...	(8,147,000)	(4,080,000)	(4,328,000)	(4,468,000)	(1,617,000)
Shares Outstanding	130,800	130,800	...	55,300	55,300	55,300	55,200	55,300
Statistical Record								
Return on Assets %	1.17	N.M.	...	N.M.	2.71	1.61	N.M.	0.56
Return on Equity %	2.50	...	...	...	...	...	...	...
EBITDA Margin %	9.80	0.99	173.18	N.M.	11.59	9.47	N.M.	7.12
Net Margin %	1.93	N.M.	146.61	N.M.	3.59	2.30	N.M.	0.82
Asset Turnover	0.61	0.11	...	0.77	0.75	0.70	0.70	0.68
Current Ratio	1.49	1.00	...	1.51	2.24	2.19	2.06	1.94
Debt to Equity	0.50	0.35	...	...	...	...	...	...
Price Range	36.06-19.90	31.65-25.98	28.75-27.60	...	...	...	...	...
P/E Ratio			0.21-0.20	...	...	...	...	...

Address: One Owens Corning Parkway, Toledo, OH 43659 **Telephone:** 419-248-8000 **Fax:** 419-248-8445	**Web Site:** www.owenscorning.com **Officers:** Michael H. Thaman - Chmn., C.F.O. Sheree L. Bargabos - V.P., Pres., Exterior Systems Business	**Auditors:** PricewaterhouseCoopers LLP

OWENS & MINOR, INC.

Exchange	Symbol	Price	52Wk Range	Yield	P/E	Div Acheiver
NYS	OMI	$39.34 (3/31/2008)	45.28-33.60	2.03	21.98	10 Years

*7 Year Price Score 118.91 *NYSE Composite Index=100 *12 Month Price Score 116.80

Interim Earnings (Per Share)

Qtr.	Mar	Jun	Sep	Dec
2003	0.35	0.37	0.34	0.36
2004	0.37	0.39	0.38	0.39
2005	0.40	0.40	0.42	0.39
2006	0.41	0.26	0.36	0.17
2007	0.27	0.45	0.52	0.56

Interim Dividends (Per Share)

Amt	Decl	Ex	Rec	Pay
0.17Q	4/26/2007	6/13/2007	6/15/2007	6/29/2007
0.17Q	7/19/2007	9/12/2007	9/14/2007	9/28/2007
0.17Q	10/18/2007	12/12/2007	12/14/2007	12/31/2007
0.20Q	2/4/2008	3/12/2008	3/14/2008	3/31/2008

Indicated Div: $0.80

Valuation Analysis / **Institutional Holding**

Forecast P/E	13.79
	(1/10/2007)
Market Cap	$1.6 Billion
Book Value	614.4 Million
Price/Book	2.62
Price/Sales	0.24

No of Institutions 167
Shares 36,975,100
% Held 91.78

Business Summary: Specialist Equipment Supplies (MIC: 12.10 SIC: 5047 NAIC: 423450)

Owens & Minor is a distributor of medical and surgical supplies to the acute-care market, a healthcare supply chain management company and a national direct-to-consumer supplier of testing and monitoring supplies for diabetics. As of Dec 31 2007, Co. distributed 180,000 finished medical and surgical products produced by over 1,200 suppliers to about 4,100 healthcare provider customers from 45 distribution centers. Most of Co.'s sales consist of consumable goods such as disposable gloves, dressings, endoscopic products, intravenous products, needles and syringes, sterile procedure trays, surgical products and gowns, urological products and wound closure products.

Recent Developments: For the year ended Dec 31 2007, net income increased 49.1% to US$72.7 million from US$48.8 million in the prior year. Revenues were US$6.80 billion, up 22.9% from US$5.53 billion the year before. Operating income was US$143.2 million versus US$102.8 million in the prior year, an increase of 39.4%. Direct operating expenses rose 23.3% to US$6.09 billion from US$4.94 billion in the comparable period the year before. Indirect operating expenses increased 15.7% to US$571.8 million from US$494.0 million in the equivalent prior-year period.

Prospects: Co.'s improved top-line performance is attributable to its Sep 2006 acquisition of McKesson Medical-Surgical Inc., greater sales volumes to existing healthcare provider customers and sales to new customers. For full-year 2008, Co. expects to attain revenue growth in the range of 5.0% to 7.0%, translating into earnings per diluted share in a range of $2.20 to $2.30, representing a 23.0% to 28.0% increase in earnings for the year. Co.'s 2008 outlook assumes gross margin to be consistent as a percentage of revenues, compared with the second half of 2007 and selling, general and administrative expenses to improve in the mid-single digit basis point, compared with the second half of 2007.

Financial Data

(US$ in Thousands)	12/31/2007	12/31/2006	12/31/2005	12/31/2004	12/31/2003	12/31/2002	12/31/2001	12/31/2000
Earnings Per Share	1.79	1.20	1.61	1.53	1.42	1.27	0.68	0.94
Cash Flow Per Share	5.46	(1.85)	3.43	1.50	2.70	(0.42)	0.05	1.32
Tang Book Value Per Share	7.59	5.84	6.29	6.57	5.45	2.15	1.12	0.24
Dividends Per Share	0.680	0.600	0.520	0.440	0.350	0.310	0.273	0.248
Dividend Payout %	37.99	50.00	32.30	28.76	24.65	24.41	40.07	26.33
Income Statement								
Total Revenue	6,800,466	5,533,736	4,822,414	4,525,105	4,244,067	3,959,781	3,814,994	3,503,583
EBITDA	168,913	111,153	128,932	124,752	112,475	94,123	87,046	81,675
Income Before Taxes	120,230	78,080	105,574	97,610	87,799	78,197	64,577	60,160
Income Taxes	47,520	29,328	41,154	37,110	34,158	30,980	34,474	27,072
Net Income	72,710	48,752	64,420	60,500	53,641	47,267	23,035	33,088
Average Shares	40,656	40,467	40,056	39,668	39,333	40,698	40,387	39,453
Balance Sheet								
Current Assets	1,089,857	1,266,770	894,552	864,476	781,375	729,753	679,452	594,291
Total Assets	1,515,080	1,685,750	1,239,850	1,131,833	1,045,748	1,009,477	953,853	867,548
Current Liabilities	568,464	670,503	488,868	430,531	395,632	344,730	367,674	360,654
Long-Term Obligations	283,845	433,133	204,418	207,476	209,499	240,185	203,449	152,872
Total Liabilities	900,721	1,138,296	727,852	671,577	635,393	612,890	585,610	522,776
Stockholders' Equity	614,359	547,454	511,998	460,256	410,355	271,437	236,243	212,772
Shares Outstanding	40,874	40,257	39,890	39,519	38,979	34,113	33,885	33,180
Statistical Record								
Return on Assets %	4.54	3.33	5.43	5.54	5.22	4.81	2.53	3.81
Return on Equity %	12.52	9.20	13.25	13.86	15.74	18.62	10.26	16.70
EBITDA Margin %	2.48	2.01	2.67	2.76	2.65	2.38	2.28	2.33
Net Margin %	1.07	0.88	1.34	1.34	1.26	1.19	0.60	0.94
Asset Turnover	4.25	3.78	4.07	4.14	4.13	4.03	4.19	4.03
Current Ratio	1.92	1.89	1.83	2.01	1.98	2.12	1.85	1.65
Debt to Equity	0.46	0.79	0.40	0.45	0.51	0.88	0.86	0.72
Price Range	43.77-30.40	34.72-27.96	33.28-26.35	29.34-21.91	26.80-15.86	20.86-13.40	20.96-14.35	18.00-8.31
P/E Ratio	24.45-16.98	28.93-23.30	20.67-16.37	19.18-14.32	18.87-11.17	16.43-10.55	30.82-21.10	19.15-8.84
Average Yield %	1.84	1.93	1.79	1.74	1.70	1.79	1.52	1.84

Address: 4800 Cox Road, Glen Allen, VA 23060	Web Site: www.owens-minor.com	Auditors: KPMG LLP
Telephone: 804-747-9794	Officers: G. Gilmer Minor III - Chmn. Craig R. Smith - Pres., C.E.O., C.O.O.	Investor Contact: 804-747-9794
Fax: 804-270-7281		Transfer Agents: The Bank of New York, New York, NY

PACKAGING CORP OF AMERICA

Exchange	Symbol	Price	52Wk Range	Yield	P/E
NYS	PKG	$22.33 (3/31/2008)	31.84-21.96	5.37	13.87

*7 Year Price Score 98.41 *NYSE Composite Index=100 *12 Month Price Score 95.20

Interim Earnings (Per Share)

Qtr.	Mar	Jun	Sep	Dec
2003	0.07	0.10	(0.31)	0.00
2004	(0.06)	0.13	0.24	0.34
2005	0.12	0.26	0.10	0.02
2006	0.09	0.31	0.42	0.39
2007	0.30	0.44	0.46	0.41

Interim Dividends (Per Share)

Amt	Decl	Ex	Rec	Pay
0.25Q	6/4/2007	6/13/2007	6/15/2007	7/13/2007
0.25Q	9/11/2007	9/12/2007	9/14/2007	10/15/2007
0.30Q	10/1/2007	12/12/2007	12/14/2007	1/15/2008
0.30Q	2/20/2008	3/12/2008	3/14/2008	4/15/2008

Indicated Div: $1.20

Valuation Analysis   **Institutional Holding**

Forecast P/E	19.52	No of Institutions	
	(1/10/2007)	208	
Market Cap	$2.3 Billion	Shares	
Book Value	760.9 Million	87,764,224	
Price/Book	3.08	% Held	
Price/Sales	1.01	83.66	

Business Summary: Paper Products (MIC: 11.11 SIC: 2653 NAIC: 322211)

Packaging Corporation of America produces containerboard and corrugated products in the U.S. Co.'s mill operations consist of two kraft linerboard mills located in Counce, TN, and Valdosta, GA, and two medium mills located in Filer City, MI, and Tomahawk, WI. At Dec 31 2007, Co. leased the cutting rights to approximately 102,000 acres of timberland. The mills operations transfer the majority of their containerboard produced to Co.'s corrugated products operations plants. Co.'s corrugated manufacturing operations consist of 67 plants; a technical and development center; five graphic design centers; a rotogravure printing operation as well as packaging supplies and distribution centers.

Recent Developments: For the year ended Dec 31 2007, net income increased 36.0% to US$170.1 million from US$125.0 million in the prior year. Revenues were US$2.32 billion, up 5.9% from US$2.19 billion the year before. Operating income was US$293.5 million versus US$225.9 million in the prior year, an increase of 29.9%. Direct operating expenses rose 2.7% to US$1.79 billion from US$1.74 billion in the comparable period the year before. Indirect operating expenses increased 6.2% to US$231.5 million from US$218.0 million in the equivalent prior-year period.

Prospects: Co.'s outlook seems favorable as results are benefiting primarily from higher pricing and volume of containerboard and corrugated products, partially offset by higher costs as well as the unplanned outage at the Counce mill. Looking into the first quarter of 2008, Co. expects a sequential increase in total corrugated products volume. However, Co. expects earnings in the first quarter 2008 to be lower than earnings in the fourth quarter 2007 of $0.42 per diluted share, primarily due to planned mill maintenance outages at both of its linerboard mills in Counce, TN and Valdosta, GA, as well as higher costs. Accordingly, Co. is estimating first quarter 2008 earnings of about $0.36 per share.

Financial Data

(US$ in Thousands)	12/31/2007	12/31/2006	12/31/2005	12/31/2004	12/31/2003	12/31/2002	12/31/2001	12/31/2000
Earnings Per Share	1.61	1.20	0.49	0.64	(0.14)	0.45	0.98	1.33
Cash Flow Per Share	2.87	2.38	2.26	2.02	2.34	2.28	2.95	3.22
Tang Book Value Per Share	6.76	6.12	5.96	7.43	7.50	7.58	7.25	6.45
Dividends Per Share	1.050	1.000	1.000	0.600	0.150	...	...	...
Dividend Payout %	65.22	83.33	204.08	93.75	...	...	...	...
Income Statement								
Total Revenue	2,316,006	2,187,046	1,993,658	1,890,085	1,735,534	1,735,858	1,789,956	1,921,868
EBITDA	439,122	377,027	268,826	292,591	255,678	298,693	395,822	553,050
Income Before Taxes	267,868	194,724	88,034	110,915	(24,874)	77,614	175,434	287,151
Income Taxes	97,802	69,692	35,430	42,185	(10,516)	29,435	67,912	114,190
Net Income	170,066	125,032	52,604	68,730	(14,358)	48,179	106,418	161,901
Average Shares	105,459	104,485	108,098	107,570	104,628	107,208	108,801	107,518
Balance Sheet								
Current Assets	733,037	646,718	553,489	677,061	567,077	509,554	448,217	403,709
Total Assets	2,035,857	1,986,976	1,973,298	2,082,774	1,985,126	1,982,551	1,971,780	1,942,112
Current Liabilities	562,577	388,338	372,094	335,104	342,977	296,806	191,895	218,548
Long-Term Obligations	398,501	567,770	577,173	585,724	585,198	629,119	795,163	869,175
Total Liabilities	1,274,996	1,295,205	1,291,878	1,265,204	1,187,646	1,186,676	1,201,946	1,254,688
Stockholders' Equity	760,861	691,771	681,420	817,570	797,480	795,875	769,834	687,424
Shares Outstanding	105,018	104,611	103,686	106,993	105,651	104,491	105,567	106,248
Statistical Record								
Return on Assets %	8.46	6.31	2.59	3.37	N.M.	2.44	5.44	7.89
Return on Equity %	23.41	18.21	7.02	8.49	N.M.	6.15	14.61	29.25
EBITDA Margin %	18.96	17.24	13.48	15.48	14.73	17.21	22.11	28.78
Net Margin %	7.34	5.72	2.64	3.64	N.M.	2.78	5.95	8.42
Asset Turnover	1.15	1.10	0.98	0.93	0.87	0.88	0.91	0.94
Current Ratio	1.30	1.67	1.49	2.02	1.65	1.72	2.34	1.85
Debt to Equity	0.52	0.82	0.85	0.72	0.73	0.79	1.03	1.26
Price Range	31.84-22.24	23.93-20.40	25.29-18.25	25.00-21.15	21.86-16.45	20.86-16.35	20.50-13.00	16.69-9.56
P/E Ratio	19.78-13.81	19.94-17.00	51.61-37.24	39.06-33.05	...	46.36-36.33	20.92-13.27	12.55-7.19
Average Yield %	4.00	4.43	4.54	2.61	0.79	...	...	...

Address: 1900 West Field Court, Lake Forest, IL 60045
Telephone: 847-482-3000

Web Site: www.packagingcorp.com.
Officers: Paul T. Stecko - Chmn., C.E.O. Richard B. West - Sr. V.P., C.F.O., Sec.

Auditors: Ernst & Young LLP

PACTIV CORP.

Exchange	Symbol	Price	52Wk Range	Yield	P/E
NYS	PTV	$26.21 (3/31/2008)	36.36-22.94	N/A	14.17

*7 Year Price Score 102.87 *NYSE Composite Index=100   *12 Month Price Score 96.75

Interim Earnings (Per Share)

Qtr.	Mar	Jun	Sep	Dec
2003	0.27	0.37	0.16	0.34
2004	0.00	0.33	0.37	0.31
2005	0.15	(0.28)	0.26	0.23
2006	0.35	0.49	0.73	0.39
2007	0.43	0.53	0.45	0.45

Interim Dividends (Per Share)

No Dividends Paid

Valuation Analysis		Institutional Holding	
Forecast P/E	19.76	No of Institutions	
	(1/10/2007)	288	
Market Cap	$3.4 Billion	Shares	
Book Value	1.2 Billion	118,456,992	
Price/Book	2.79	% Held	
Price/Sales	1.05	89.14	

TRADING VOLUME (thousand shares)

Business Summary: Paper Products (MIC: 11.11 SIC: 2673 NAIC: 322223)

Pactiv is a producer of consumer and foodservice/food packaging products. As of Dec 31 2007, Co. operated 44 manufacturing facilities in North America, and one in Germany. Co. operates in two segments: Consumer Products, which manufactures disposable plastic, foam, molded-fiber, pressed-paperboard, and aluminum packaging products, and sells them to customers such as grocery stores, mass merchandisers, and discount chains under trademarks such as Hefty®; Foodservice/Food Packaging, which manufactures foam, clear plastic, aluminum, pressed-paperboard, and molded-fiber packaging products, and sells them to customers in the food-distribution channel, who prepare and process food for consumption.

Recent Developments: For the year ended Dec 31 2007, income from continuing operations decreased 11.9% to US$244.0 million from US$277.0 million a year earlier. Net income decreased 10.6% to US$245.0 million from US$274.0 million in the prior year. Revenues were US$3.25 billion, up 11.5% from US$2.92 billion the year before. Operating income was US$472.0 million versus US$424.0 million in the prior year, an increase of 11.3%. Direct operating expenses rose 14.6% to US$2.32 billion from US$2.03 billion in the comparable period the year before. Indirect operating expenses decreased 1.5% to US$459.0 million from US$466.0 million in the equivalent prior-year period.

Prospects: For the first quarter of 2008, Co. expects earnings per share of $0.30 to $0.33, as it expects earnings to be hampered by higher resin cost. However, Co. has completed the implementation of cost pass-through pricing that should improve margins sequentially in the second quarter of 2008. Further, Co. has started its cost-reduction program, including the consolidation of two small facilities, asset rationalizations, and headcount reductions. This should increase Co.'s after-tax earnings by $7.0 million or $0.05 per share in 2008, and by $13.0 million or $0.10 per share on an annualized basis. Thus, for 2008, Co. expects sales to grow 10.0% to 14.0% with earnings per share of $2.00 to $2.10.

Financial Data

(US$ in Thousands)	12/31/2007	12/31/2006	12/31/2005	12/31/2004	12/31/2003	12/31/2002	12/31/2001	12/31/2000
Earnings Per Share	1.85	1.96	0.36	1.01	1.14	0.92	1.20	1.53
Cash Flow Per Share	3.33	2.70	1.81	2.42	2.13	2.42	2.34	1.79
Tang Book Value Per Share	N.M.	0.68	0.23	0.98	0.77	N.M.	4.90	3.79
Income Statement								
Total Revenue	3,253,000	2,917,000	2,756,000	3,382,000	3,138,000	2,880,000	2,812,000	3,134,000
EBITDA	638,000	603,000	...	...	...	...	...	...
Income Before Taxes	381,000	391,000	...	...	...	...	...	...
Income Taxes	135,000	114,000	81,000	90,000	118,000	146,000	118,000	91,000
Net Income	245,000	274,000	54,000	155,000	183,000	148,000	193,000	247,000
Average Shares	132,869	139,704	148,849	153,763	160,143	160,613	159,527	161,779
Balance Sheet								
Current Assets	797,000	838,000	820,000	1,079,000	982,000	904,000	740,000	900,000
Total Assets	3,765,000	2,758,000	2,820,000	3,741,000	3,706,000	3,412,000	4,060,000	4,341,000
Current Liabilities	460,000	549,000	456,000	984,000	474,000	501,000	459,000	512,000
Long-Term Obligations	1,574,000	771,000	869,000	869,000	1,336,000	1,224,000	1,211,000	1,560,000
Total Liabilities	2,539,000	1,905,000	2,000,000	2,658,000	2,645,000	2,515,000	2,371,000	2,802,000
Stockholders' Equity	1,226,000	853,000	820,000	1,083,000	1,061,000	897,000	1,689,000	1,539,000
Shares Outstanding	130,439	132,676	142,362	148,711	156,335	158,681	159,431	158,176
Statistical Record								
Return on Assets %	7.51	9.82	1.65	4.15	5.14	3.96	4.59	5.52
Return on Equity %	23.57	32.76	5.68	14.42	18.69	11.45	11.96	17.05
EBITDA Margin %	19.61	20.67	...	...	...	...	...	...
Net Margin %	7.53	9.39	1.96	4.58	5.83	5.14	6.86	7.88
Asset Turnover	1.00	1.05	0.84	0.91	0.88	0.77	0.67	0.70
Current Ratio	1.73	1.53	1.80	1.10	2.07	1.80	1.61	1.76
Debt to Equity	1.28	0.90	1.06	0.80	1.26	1.36	0.72	1.01
Price Range	36.65-22.94	36.33-21.60	25.48-16.81	25.68-20.49	23.90-17.92	24.10-15.75	18.10-11.43	13.13-7.63
P/E Ratio	19.81-12.40	18.54-11.02	70.78-46.69	25.43-20.29	20.96-15.72	26.20-17.12	15.08-9.55	8.58-4.98

Address: 1900 West Field Court, Lake Forest, IL 60045	Web Site: www.pactiv.com	Auditors: Ernst & Young LLP
Telephone: 847-482-2000	Officers: Richard L. Wambold - Chmn., Pres., C.E.O. Andrew A. Campbell - Sr. V.P., C.F.O.	Investor Contact: 847-482-2429
Fax: 847-482-4548		Transfer Agents: National City Bank, Cleveland, OH

PALL CORP.

Exchange	Symbol	Price	52Wk Range	Yield	P/E
NYS	PLL	$35.07 (3/31/2008)	48.87-34.83	1.48	33.08

*7 Year Price Score 118.86 *NYSE Composite Index=100 ***12 Month Price Score 101.75**

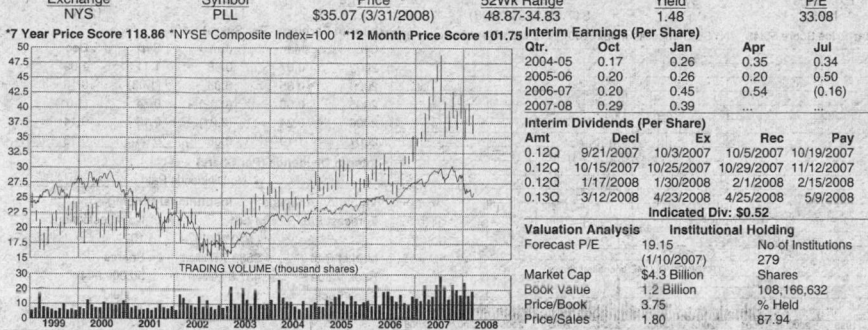

TRADING VOLUME (thousand shares)

Interim Earnings (Per Share)

Qtr.	Oct	Jan	Apr	Jul
2004-05	0.17	0.26	0.35	0.34
2005-06	0.20	0.26	0.20	0.50
2006-07	0.20	0.45	0.54	(0.16)
2007-08	0.29	0.39	...	...

Interim Dividends (Per Share)

Amt	Decl	Ex	Rec	Pay
0.12Q	9/21/2007	10/3/2007	10/5/2007	10/19/2007
0.12Q	10/15/2007	10/25/2007	10/29/2007	11/12/2007
0.12Q	1/17/2008	1/30/2008	2/1/2008	2/15/2008
0.13Q	3/12/2008	4/23/2008	4/25/2008	5/9/2008

Indicated Div: $0.52

Valuation Analysis   **Institutional Holding**

Forecast P/E	19.15	No of Institutions
	(1/10/2007)	279
Market Cap	$4.3 Billion	Shares
Book Value	1.2 Billion	108,166,632
Price/Book	3.75	% Held
Price/Sales	1.80	87.94

Business Summary: Industrial Machinery and Equipment (MIC: 11.5 SIC: 3569 NAIC: 333411)

Pall is engaged in the supplying of filtration, separation and purification technologies. Co.'s products are used to discover, develop and produce biotechnology drugs, vaccines and safe drinking water, protect hospital patients as in the case of its blood filters, bacterial detection systems and hospital water filters, enhance the quality and efficiency of manufacturing processes, keep equipment such as manufacturing equipment and airplanes running efficiently and to protect the environment. As of Jul 31 2007, Co. served its customers in two principal business groups: Life Sciences and Industrial.

Recent Developments: For the quarter ended Jan 31 2008, net income increased 8.2% to US$48.0 million from US$44.3 million in the year-earlier quarter. Revenues were US$625.7 million, up 14.8% from US$544.9 million the year before. Direct operating expenses rose 17.0% to US$337.5 million from US$288.5 million in the comparable period the year before. Indirect operating expenses increased 17.2% to US$210.8 million from US$179.8 million in the equivalent prior-year period.

Prospects: For the fiscal year ending Jul 31 2008, Co. expects its overall Medical sales to be slightly below its prior fiscal year's level. However, Co. is targeting double-digit growth in the BioPharmaceuticals market, while growth in the General Industrial markets are estimated to be in the high-single digit range, driven by improvements in the Municipal Water and Industrial Manufacturing markets. Also, Co. is estimating high-single digit growth in the Aerospace and Transportation market, while the Microelectronics markets are expected to grow in the low single-digit range. Lastly, Co. expects orders to be solid in the second half of fiscal 2008, mainly in the fuels and chemicals marketplace.

Financial Data

(US$ in Thousands)	6 Mos	3 Mos	07/31/2007	07/31/2006	07/31/2005	07/31/2004	08/02/2003	08/03/2002
Earnings Per Share	1.06	1.12	1.02	1.16	1.12	1.20	0.83	0.59
Cash Flow Per Share	0.88	1.09	2.70	1.75	1.30	1.53	1.82	1.24
Tang Book Value Per Share	6.82	6.51	6.14	7.21	6.73	6.21	5.16	4.21
Dividends Per Share	0.480	0.590	0.350	0.530	0.380	0.270	0.360	0.520
Dividend Payout %	45.28	52.68	34.31	45.69	33.93	22.50	43.37	88.14
Income Statement								
Total Revenue	1,186,754	561,007	2,249,905	2,016,830	1,902,284	1,770,747	1,613,635	1,290,820
EBITDA	142,145	64,665	391,381	327,728	296,231	304,716	250,609	188,309
Income Before Taxes	126,361	56,944	260,529	210,376	181,071	197,832	143,236	99,975
Income Taxes	42,271	20,842	133,032	64,883	40,255	46,259	40,034	26,741
Net Income	84,090	36,102	127,497	145,493	140,816	151,573	103,202	73,234
Average Shares	124,572	124,360	124,393	125,819	125,598	126,737	124,214	123,532
Balance Sheet								
Current Assets	1,626,777	1,594,036	1,606,377	1,376,981	1,160,392	1,069,815	938,434	915,982
Total Assets	2,878,696	2,843,460	2,708,846	2,552,858	2,265,301	2,140,383	2,016,726	2,027,222
Current Liabilities	586,120	567,657	832,190	530,813	457,139	418,774	421,496	438,171
Long-Term Obligations	692,430	711,406	591,591	640,015	510,161	488,686	489,870	619,705
Total Liabilities	1,728,606	1,731,069	1,648,245	1,374,162	1,125,324	1,085,944	1,082,190	1,207,502
Stockholders' Equity	1,150,090	1,112,391	1,060,601	1,178,696	1,139,977	1,054,439	934,536	819,720
Shares Outstanding	122,872	122,872	122,546	122,158	124,342	124,021	124,682	122,792
Statistical Record								
Return on Assets %	4.87	5.15	4.85	6.04	6.39	7.31	5.12	4.03
Return on Equity %	10.90	12.00	11.39	12.55	12.83	15.28	11.80	9.06
EBITDA Margin %	11.98	11.53	17.40	16.25	15.57	17.21	15.53	14.59
Net Margin %	7.09	6.44	5.67	7.21	7.40	8.56	6.40	5.67
Asset Turnover	0.89	0.86	0.86	0.84	0.86	0.85	0.80	0.71
Current Ratio	2.78	2.81	1.93	2.59	2.54	2.55	2.23	2.09
Debt to Equity	0.60	0.64	0.56	0.54	0.45	0.46	0.52	0.76
Price Range	48.87-34.52	48.87-30.73	48.87-25.36	32.38-25.26	31.46-22.32	27.78-21.82	24.48-15.00	24.90-16.32
P/E Ratio	46.10-32.57	43.63-27.44	47.91-24.86	27.91-21.78	28.09-19.93	23.15-18.18	29.49-18.07	42.20-27.66
Average Yield %	1.20	1.52	0.97	1.87	1.41	1.11	1.92	2.42

Address: 2200 Northern Boulevard, East Hills, NY 11548 Telephone: 516-484-5400 Fax: 516-484-3649	Web Site: www.pall.com Officers: Eric Krasnoff - Chmn., C.E.O. Marcus Wilson - Pres., C.F.O.	Auditors: KPMG LLP Investor Contact: 516-801-9848 Transfer Agents: EquiServe Trust Company, Providence, RI

PAR PHARMACEUTICAL COMPANIES INC

Exchange	Symbol	Price	52Wk Range	Yield	P/E
NYS	PRX	$17.39 (3/31/2008)	30.30-15.71	N/A	12.16

*7 Year Price Score 55.46   *NYSE Composite Index=100   *12 Month Price Score 87.77

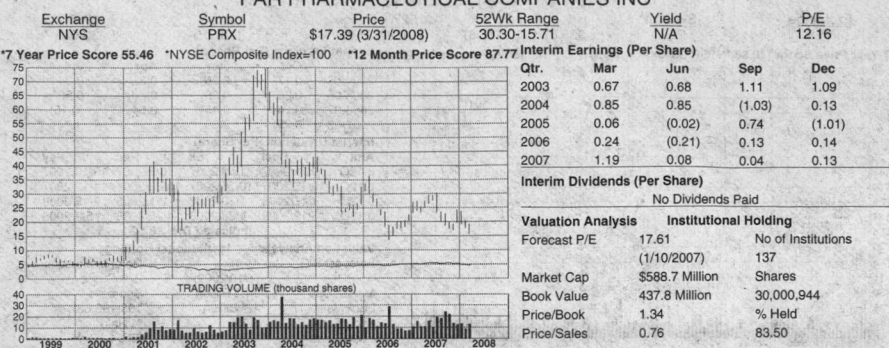

Interim Earnings (Per Share)

Qtr.	Mar	Jun	Sep	Dec
2003	0.67	0.68	1.11	1.09
2004	0.85	0.85	(1.03)	0.13
2005	0.06	(0.02)	0.74	(1.01)
2006	0.24	(0.21)	0.13	0.14
2007	1.19	0.08	0.04	0.13

Interim Dividends (Per Share)

No Dividends Paid

Valuation Analysis		Institutional Holding	
Forecast P/E	17.61	No of Institutions	
	(1/10/2007)	137	
Market Cap	$588.7 Million	Shares	
Book Value	437.8 Million	30,000,944	
Price/Book	1.34	% Held	
Price/Sales	0.76	83.50	

Business Summary: Pharmaceuticals (MIC: 9.1 SIC: 2834 NAIC: 325412)

Par Pharmaceutical is a holding company. Through its subsidiaries, Co. is engaged in developing, manufacturing and distributing generic and branded drugs in the U.S. Co.'s product line comprise of generic prescription drugs consisting of about 180 products representing various dosage strengths for more than 80 separate drugs. Co.'s products are manufactured mainly in the solid oral dosage form. In addition, Co. markets several oral suspension products, products in the semi-solid form of a cream. Co. conducts its businesses through two business segments: generic pharmaceuticals and brand pharmaceuticals.

Recent Developments: For the year ended Dec 31 2007, income from continuing operations increased 658.2% to US$51.1 million from US$6.7 million a year earlier. Net income increased 753.4% to US$49.9 million from US$5.8 million in the prior year. Revenues were US$769.7 million, up 6.1% from US$725.2 million the year before. Operating income was US$73.6 million versus US$7.7 million in the prior year, an increase of 853.0%. Direct operating expenses declined 1.2% to US$501.1 million from US$507.2 million in the comparable period the year before. Indirect operating expenses decreased 7.3% to US$194.9 million from US$210.2 million in the equivalent prior-year period.

Prospects: Co.'s business plan includes developing and marketing branded drugs as part of its effort to add products with longer life cycles and higher profitability to its product line. For example, on Jan 15 2008, Co. announced that it entered into a licensing agreement with Alfacell Corp. to acquire the commercialization rights in the U.S. and its territories for Onconase® (ranpirnase), which is in Phase III development for the treatment of inoperable malignant mesothelioma, a cancer affecting the lungs usually associated with exposure to asbestos. Onconase® was previously granted orphan drug status as well as fast-track development status by the FDA for the treatment of malignant mesothelioma.

Financial Data (US$ in Thousands)	12/31/2007	12/31/2006	12/31/2005	12/31/2004	12/31/2003	12/31/2002	12/31/2001	12/31/2000
Earnings Per Share	1.43	0.19	(0.24)	0.84	3.54	2.40	1.68	(0.03)
Cash Flow Per Share	2.92	1.77	1.38	1.55	3.53	0.98	2.40	(0.09)
Tang Book Value Per Share	9.98	8.84	9.75	8.38	9.76	4.89	4.06	2.03
Income Statement								
Total Revenue	769,666	725,168	433,194	690,016	661,688	381,603	271,035	85,022
EBITDA	97,162	29,184	34,386	60,697	211,055	135,424	79,723	...
Income Before Taxes	78,432	8,795	17,939	46,103	200,643	130,253	75,932	...
Income Taxes	27,322	2,054	(941)	16,857	78,110	50,799	22,010	...
Net Income	49,898	6,741	(8,250)	29,246	122,533	79,454	53,922	(929)
Average Shares	34,718	34,653	34,435	34,873	34,638	33,051	32,189	29,604
Balance Sheet								
Current Assets	523,307	514,577	523,509	493,982	626,975	210,984	175,850	46,800
Total Assets	781,523	810,418	787,017	769,004	762,812	301,457	216,926	89,150
Current Liabilities	312,793	389,409	157,413	154,744	167,173	74,679	72,983	28,288
Long-Term Obligations	...	...	200,068	200,275	200,211	2,426	1,060	163
Total Liabilities	343,768	389,409	358,042	355,414	367,731	80,667	78,503	29,065
Stockholders' Equity	437,755	421,009	428,975	413,590	395,081	220,790	138,423	60,085
Shares Outstanding	33,855	35,012	34,265	33,915	34,318	32,804	32,035	29,647
Statistical Record								
Return on Assets %	6.27	0.84	N.M.	3.81	23.03	30.65	35.23	N.M.
Return on Equity %	11.62	1.59	N.M.	7.21	39.79	44.24	54.33	N.M.
EBITDA Margin %	12.62	4.02	7.94	8.80	31.90	35.49	29.41	...
Net Margin %	6.48	0.93	N.M.	4.24	18.52	20.82	19.89	N.M.
Asset Turnover	0.97	0.91	0.56	0.90	1.24	1.47	1.77	0.99
Current Ratio	1.67	1.32	3.33	3.19	3.75	2.83	2.41	1.65
Debt to Equity	...	...	0.47	0.48	0.51	0.01	0.01	N.M.
Price Range	30.30-16.97	36.31-13.47	43.03-21.77	66.30-32.22	74.71-29.35	33.80-16.10	41.50-6.63	8.13-4.06
P/E Ratio	21.19-11.87	191.11-70.89	...	78.93-38.36	21.10-8.29	14.08-6.71	24.70-3.94	...

Address: 300 Tice Boulevard, Woodcliff Lake, NJ 07677
Telephone: 201-802-4000
Fax: 201-802-4600

Web Site: www.parpharm.com
Officers: Mark Auerbach - Exec.-Chmn. Scott L. Tarriff - Pres., C.E.O.

Auditors: Deloitte & Touche LLP

PARKER HANNIFIN CORP.

Exchange	Symbol	Price	52Wk Range	Yield	P/E	Div Achiever
NYS	PH	$69.27 (3/31/2008)	86.15-57.61	1.21	13.94	51 Years

*7 Year Price Score 129.45 *NYSE Composite Index=100 *12 Month Price Score 102.37

Interim Earnings (Per Share)

Qtr.	Sep	Dec	Mar	Jun
2004-05	0.74	0.94	0.77	0.89
2005-06	0.95	0.71	0.97	1.07
2006-07	1.17	1.09	1.19	1.23
2007-08	1.33	1.23	...	...

Interim Dividends (Per Share)

Amt	Decl	Ex	Rec	Pay
0.21Q	8/16/2007	8/23/2007	8/27/2007	9/7/2007
50%	8/16/2007	10/2/2007	9/17/2007	10/1/2007
0.21Q	10/24/2007	11/13/2007	11/15/2007	11/30/2007
0.21Q	1/25/2008	2/19/2008	2/21/2008	3/7/2008

Indicated Div: $0.84 (Div. Reinv. Plan)

Valuation Analysis

		Institutional Holding	
Forecast P/E	9.55	No of Institutions	
	(1/10/2007)	408	
Market Cap	$11.7 Billion	Shares	
Book Value	4.8 Billion	88,947,584	
Price/Book	2.44	% Held	
Price/Sales	1.04	76.83	

Business Summary: Metal Products (MIC: 11.4 SIC: 3491 NAIC: 332911)

Parker-Hannifin is engaged as a manufacturer of motion control products, including fluid power systems, electromechanical controls and related components. Co. is also a producer of fluid purification, fluid and fuel control, process instrumentation, air conditioning, refrigeration, electromagnetic shielding as well as thermal management products and systems. Co.'s motion control technology is used in the products of its three key business segments: Industrial; Aerospace; and Climate & Industrial Controls. The products are sold as original and replacement equipment, and are marketed through direct-sales employees, independent distributors, sales representatives and builder/dealers.

Recent Developments: For the quarter ended Dec 31 2007, net income increased 9.8% to US$211.9 million from US$193.0 million in the year-earlier quarter. Revenues were US$2.83 billion, up 12.7% from US$2.51 billion the year before. Direct operating expenses rose 13.2% to US$2.19 billion from US$1.94 billion in the comparable period the year before. Indirect operating expenses increased 8.9% to US$319.0 million from US$292.9 million in the equivalent prior-year period.

Prospects: For the fiscal year ending June 30 2008, Co. anticipates earnings of $5.15 to $5.40 per diluted share, versus prior earnings guidance of $5.05 to $5.35 per diluted share. Separately, on Jan 17 2008, Co.'s Aerospace segment has been selected by Airbus to supply fuel and hydraulic systems for its new A350 extra-widebody aircraft. Thus, Co. expects these contracts to yield over $2.00 billion over the life of the program. Meanwhile, the Dec 3 2007 acquisition of Texas Thermowell Industries business from Bravura, Ltd., with sales of about $5.0 million in 2007, is expected to bolster Co.'s presence in temperature sensing applications within chemical processing and petroleum refining markets.

Financial Data

(US$ in Thousands)	6 Mos	3 Mos	06/30/2007	06/30/2006	06/30/2005	06/30/2004	06/30/2003	06/30/2002
Earnings Per Share	4.97	4.84	4.67	3.71	3.35	1.94	1.12	0.75
Cash Flow Per Share	6.67	6.53	5.47	5.34	4.89	3.74	3.19	3.65
Tang Book Value Per Share	8.78	9.61	10.69	9.75	9.23	9.38	7.63	8.18
Dividends Per Share	0.767	0.730	0.693	0.613	0.520	0.507	0.493	0.480
Dividend Payout %	15.42	15.09	14.84	16.52	15.54	26.12	44.05	64.29
Income Statement								
Total Revenue	5,616,316	2,787,256	10,718,059	9,385,888	8,215,095	7,106,907	6,410,610	6,149,122
EBITDA	817,495	416,339	1,537,262	1,256,692	1,088,202	820,249	638,121	582,118
Depn & Amortn	155,146	76,176	...	...	...	...	...	...
Income Before Taxes	613,912	317,742	1,159,282	899,958	756,473	494,068	297,382	218,036
Income Taxes	172,452	88,145	329,236	261,682	208,500	148,285	101,110	87,886
Net Income	441,460	229,597	830,046	673,167	604,692	345,783	196,272	130,150
Average Shares	171,993	173,221	177,494	181,326	180,673	178,509	175,341	174,091
Balance Sheet								
Current Assets	3,621,580	3,524,424	3,386,175	3,138,978	2,785,872	2,536,933	2,396,807	2,235,618
Total Assets	9,217,506	8,692,993	8,441,413	8,173,432	6,898,961	6,256,904	5,985,633	5,752,583
Current Liabilities	2,496,488	2,244,939	1,925,245	1,681,105	1,335,927	1,259,741	1,423,727	1,359,837
Long Term Obligations	1,151,469	1,117,677	1,089,916	1,059,461	938,424	953,804	966,332	1,088,883
Total Liabilities	4,440,270	4,146,865	3,729,748	3,932,229	3,558,814	3,274,450	3,464,722	3,169,067
Stockholders' Equity	4,777,236	4,546,128	4,711,665	4,241,203	3,340,147	2,982,454	2,520,911	2,583,516
Shares Outstanding	168,499	168,222	174,238	180,472	179,540	179,225	177,247	177,036
Statistical Record								
Return on Assets %	9.82	9.98	9.99	8.93	9.19	5.63	3.34	2.35
Return on Equity %	19.09	19.26	18.54	17.76	19.13	12.53	7.69	5.09
EBITDA Margin %	14.56	14.94	14.34	13.39	13.25	11.54	9.95	9.47
Net Margin %	7.86	8.24	7.74	7.17	7.36	4.87	3.06	2.12
Asset Turnover	1.28	1.29	1.29	1.25	1.25	1.16	1.09	1.11
Current Ratio	1.45	1.57	1.76	1.87	2.09	2.01	1.68	1.64
Debt to Equity	0.24	0.25	0.23	0.25	0.28	0.32	0.38	0.42
Price Range	86.15-50.79	76.80-50.79	68.39-46.50	57.34-40.53	51.87-35.71	40.61-27.81	32.53-23.10	36.42-21.10
P/E Ratio	17.33-10.22	15.87-10.49	14.65-9.96	15.46-10.93	15.48-10.66	20.93-14.33	29.05-20.63	48.56-28.13
Average Yield %	1.15	1.21	1.25	1.28	1.22	1.43	1.77	1.59

Address: 6035 Parkland Boulevard, Cleveland, OH 44124-4141	**Web Site:** www.parker.com	**Auditors:** PricewaterhouseCoopers LLP
Telephone: 216-896-3000	**Officers:** Donald E. Washkewicz - Chmn., C.E.O.	**Investor Contact:** 216-896-2240
Fax: 216-383-9414	Nickolas W. Vande Steeg - Pres., C.O.O.	**Transfer Agents:** National City Bank, Cleveland, Ohio

PEABODY ENERGY CORP.

Exchange	Symbol	Price	52Wk Range	Yield	P/E
NYS	BTU	$51.00 (3/31/2008)	62.72-36.92	0.47	52.04

*7 Year Price Score N/A ***NYSE Composite Index=100** ***12 Month Price Score 118.04**

TRADING VOLUME (thousand shares)

Interim Earnings (Per Share)

Qtr.	Mar	Jun	Sep	Dec
2003	(0.05)	(0.01)	0.10	0.10
2004	0.10	0.16	0.17	0.26
2005	0.20	0.35	0.42	0.60
2006	0.48	0.57	0.53	0.65
2007	0.33	0.40	0.12	0.13

Interim Dividends (Per Share)

Amt	Decl	Ex	Rec	Pay
0.06Q	7/31/2007	8/10/2007	8/14/2007	9/4/2007
0.00Q	10/15/2007	11/1/2007	10/22/2007	10/31/2007
0.06Q	10/18/2007	11/5/2007	11/7/2007	11/23/2007
0.06Q	1/29/2008	2/8/2008	2/12/2008	3/4/2008

Indicated Div: $0.24

Valuation Analysis

		Institutional Holding	
Forecast P/E	9.17	No of Institutions	
	(1/10/2007)	449	
Market Cap	$13.8 Billion	Shares	
Book Value	2.5 Billion	211,377,168	
Price/Book	5.47	% Held	
Price/Sales	3.01	79.86	

Business Summary: Coal Mining (MIC: 14.4 SIC: 1221 NAIC: 212111)

Peabody Energy is a coal company selling coal to over 340 electricity generating and industrial plants in 19 countries as of Dec 31 2007. Co. owns, through its subsidiaries, majority interests in 31 coal mining operations located throughout all major U.S. coal-producing regions and in Australia. Co. also markets, brokers and trades coal. Co.'s other energy related commercial activities include the development of mine-mouth coal-fueled generating plants, the management of its coal reserve and real estate holdings, coalbed methane production, transportation services and British Thermal Unit (BTU) conversion. As of Dec 31 2007, Co. had 9.30 billion tons of proven and probable coal reserves.

Recent Developments: For the year ended Dec 31 2007, income from continuing operations decreased 23.8% to US$421.3 million from US$552.6 million a year earlier. Net income decreased 56.0% to US$264.3 million from US$600.7 million in the prior year. Revenues were US$4.57 billion, up 11.4% from US$4.11 billion the year before. Operating income was US$568.7 million versus US$590.9 million in the prior year, a decrease of 3.7%. Direct operating expenses rose 13.3% to US$3.57 billion from US$3.16 billion in the comparable period the year before. Indirect operating expenses increased 19.2% to US$431.2 million from US$361.8 million in the equivalent prior-year period.

Prospects: Looking ahead, Co. expects strong improvements in U.S. and Australia operating results from higher prices and increased volumes, partly offset by higher key supply costs and the effects of exchange rates. Notably, in Australia, Co. plans selling 23 million to 25 million tons in 2008, as much as 17.0% higher than 2007's level. In the U.S., Co. projects higher volumes in 2008 versus 2007 from all the coal basins it operates. In detail, the higher 2008 volume includes the mid-year startup of a new mine in the Southwestern U.S. Overall, Co. expects production of 220 million to 240 million tons with sales of 240 million to 260 million tons and earnings of $1.00 to $1.85 per share for 2008.

Financial Data
(US$ in Thousands)

	12/31/2007	12/31/2006	12/31/2005	12/31/2004	12/31/2003	12/31/2002	12/31/2001	03/31/2001
Earnings Per Share	0.98	2.23	1.58	0.69	0.14	0.49	(0.05)	0.78
Cash Flow Per Share	1.20	2.26	2.69	1.14	0.88	1.11	0.33	1.38
Tang Book Value Per Share	9.33	7.95	8.27	6.66	5.18	5.16	4.98	5.72
Dividends Per Share	0.240	0.240	0.170	0.131	0.113	0.100	0.050	...
Dividend Payout %	24.49	10.76	10.76	19.02	78.95	20.41	...	...
Income Statement								
Total Revenue	4,574,712	5,256,315	4,644,453	3,631,582	2,829,480	2,717,098	2,026,770	2,669,692
EBITDA	937,721	1,046,306	841,435	523,436	333,767	415,869	299,104	573,998
Income Before Taxes	340,835	530,962	426,085	153,071	(3,181)	78,804	29,000	152,894
Income Taxes	(78,112)	(81,515)	960	(26,437)	(47,708)	(40,007)	2,465	42,690
Net Income	264,285	600,697	422,653	175,387	31,348	105,519	(9,683)	107,060
Average Shares	269,166	269,166	268,013	254,812	219,342	215,287	202,099	110,098
Balance Sheet								
Current Assets	1,927,293	1,274,340	1,324,644	1,054,602	682,740	549,923	527,454	629,955
Total Assets	9,668,307	9,514,056	6,852,006	6,178,592	5,280,265	5,140,177	5,150,902	5,209,487
Current Liabilities	2,186,986	1,367,531	1,022,923	774,144	631,968	631,536	684,303	776,985
Long-Term Obligations	3,138,727	3,168,069	1,382,921	1,405,986	1,173,490	981,696	984,568	1,369,316
Total Liabilities	7,147,935	7,142,193	4,670,989	4,452,091	4,146,299	4,021,918	4,068,350	4,536,791
Stockholders' Equity	2,519,671	2,338,526	2,178,467	1,724,592	1,132,057	1,081,138	1,035,472	631,238
Shares Outstanding	270,066	263,846	263,357	259,135	218,587	209,601	208,040	110,442
Statistical Record								
Return on Assets %	2.76	7.34	6.49	3.05	0.60	2.05	N.M.	1.94
Return on Equity %	10.88	26.60	21.66	12.25	2.83	9.97	N.M.	18.79
EBITDA Margin %	20.50	19.91	18.12	14.41	11.80	15.31	14.76	21.50
Net Margin %	5.78	11.43	9.10	4.83	1.11	3.88	N.M.	4.01
Asset Turnover	0.48	0.64	0.71	0.63	0.54	0.53	0.21	0.48
Current Ratio	0.88	0.93	1.29	1.36	1.08	0.87	0.77	0.81
Debt to Equity	1.25	1.35	0.63	0.82	1.04	0.91	0.95	2.17
Price Range	62.28-34.17	68.94-32.67	40.31-17.35	19.66-8.57	10.01-5.77	7.11-4.38	8.88-5.44	...
P/E Ratio	63.55-34.87	30.92-14.65	25.52-10.98	28.50-12.42	71.47-41.21	14.52-8.93	...	...
Average Yield %	0.53	0.53	0.61	1.03	1.55	1.63	0.76	...

Address: 701 Market Street, St. Louis, MO 63101	Web Site: www.peabodyenergy.com	Auditors: Ernst & Young LLP
Telephone: 314-342-3400	Officers: Irl F. Engelhardt - Chmn. Gregory H. Boyce - Pres., C.E.O.	Transfer Agents: EquiServe, Canton MA

PENNEY (J.C.) CO.,INC. (HOLDING CO.)

Exchange	Symbol	Price	52Wk Range	Yield	P/E
NYS	JCP	$37.71 (3/31/2008)	84.06-34.57	2.12	7.65

*7 Year Price Score 116.73 *NYSE Composite Index=100   *12 Month Price Score 80.14

Interim Earnings (Per Share)

Qtr.	Apr	Jul	Oct	Jan
2003-04	0.20	(0.02)	0.27	(3.58)
2004-05	0.13	(0.02)	0.50	1.12
2005-06	0.63	0.50	0.94	2.21
2006-07	0.89	0.76	1.26	2.06
2007-08	1.04	0.81	1.17	1.92

Interim Dividends (Per Share)

Amt	Decl	Ex	Rec	Pay
0.20Q	5/18/2007	7/6/2007	7/10/2007	8/1/2007
0.20Q	9/21/2007	10/5/2007	10/10/2007	11/1/2007
0.20Q	12/12/2007	1/8/2008	1/10/2008	2/4/2008
0.20Q	3/27/2008	4/8/2008	4/10/2008	5/1/2008

Indicated Div: $0.80

Valuation Analysis

		Institutional Holding	
Forecast P/E	N/A	No of Institutions	521
Market Cap	$8.4 Billion	Shares	207,004,384
Book Value	5.3 Billion	% Held	
Price/Book	1.58		91.68
Price/Sales	0.42		

Business Summary: Retail - General (MIC: 5.2 SIC: 5311 NAIC: 452111)

J. C. Penney is a holding company. Co.'s business consists of selling merchandise and services to consumers through its department stores and Direct (Internet/catalog) channels, both of which serve the same type of customers and provide virtually the same mix of merchandise. The department stores also accept returns from sales made in the stores, via the Internet and through catalogs. Co. markets family apparel, jewelry, shoes, accessories and home furnishings. In addition, the department stores provide customers with services such as salon, optical, portrait photography and custom decorating. As of Feb 2 2008, Co. operated 1,067 department stores in 49 states in the U.S. and Puerto Rico.

Recent Developments: For the year ended Feb 2 2008, income from continuing operations decreased 2.6% to US$1.11 billion from US$1.13 billion a year earlier. Net income decreased 3.6% to US$1.11 billion from US$1.15 billion in the prior year. Revenues were US$19.86 billion, down 0.2% from US$19.90 billion the year before. Operating income was US$1.89 billion versus US$1.92 billion in the prior year, a decrease of 1.8%. Direct operating expenses rose 0.9% to US$12.19 billion from US$12.08 billion in the comparable period the year before. Indirect operating expenses decreased 2.0% to US$5.78 billion from US$5.90 billion in the equivalent prior-year period.

Prospects: For the fiscal year ending Jan 2009, Co. projects total sales growth in the low-single digits, comparable store sales to decline low-single digits and earnings per share to be in the range of $3.75 to $4.00. Further, Co. expects 2008 capital expenditures to be about $1.00 billion, relating principally to new stores and relocations, store renewals and updates, merchandise initiatives, technology and other support projects. Co. presently plans to open 36 new and relocated stores in 2008, of which 32 are expected to be off-mall, and to modernize about 20 existing stores. Lastly, net square footage growth is expected to increase about 2.8% for 2008, including relocations and store closures.

Financial Data
(US$ in Thousands)

	02/02/2008	02/03/2007	01/28/2006	01/29/2005	01/31/2004	01/25/2003	01/26/2002	01/27/2001
Earnings Per Share	4.93	4.96	4.26	1.76	(3.13)	1.37	0.26	(2.81)
Cash Flow Per Share	5.59	5.39	5.30	4.05	2.94	4.99	3.76	5.76
Tang Book Value Per Share	23.45	18.55	16.82	17.39	18.18	11.19	11.46	11.37
Dividends Per Share	0.800	0.720	0.500	0.500	0.500	0.500	...	0.825
Dividend Payout %	16.23	14.52	11.74	28.41	...	36.50	...	...
Income Statement								
Total Revenue	19,860,000	19,903,000	18,781,000	18,424,000	17,786,000	32,347,000	32,004,000	31,846,000
EBITDA	2,302,000	2,311,000	1,985,000	1,621,000	1,201,000	1,639,000	1,306,000	236,000
Income Before Taxes	1,723,000	1,792,000	1,444,000	1,020,000	546,000	584,000	203,000	(886,000)
Income Taxes	618,000	658,000	467,000	353,000	182,000	213,000	89,000	(318,000)
Net Income	1,111,000	1,153,000	1,088,000	524,000	(928,000)	405,000	98,000	(705,000)
Average Shares	225,000	232,000	255,000	307,000	297,000	293,000	267,000	262,000
Balance Sheet								
Current Assets	6,751,000	6,648,000	6,702,000	8,477,000	6,513,000	8,353,000	8,677,000	7,237,000
Total Assets	14,309,000	12,673,000	12,461,000	14,127,000	18,300,000	17,867,000	18,048,000	19,742,000
Current Liabilities	3,338,000	3,492,000	2,762,000	3,447,000	3,754,000	4,159,000	4,499,000	4,235,000
Long-Term Obligations	3,505,000	3,010,000	3,444,000	3,464,000	5,114,000	4,940,000	5,179,000	5,448,000
Total Liabilities	8,997,000	8,385,000	8,454,000	9,271,000	12,875,000	11,497,000	11,919,000	13,483,000
Stockholders' Equity	5,312,000	4,288,000	4,007,000	4,856,000	5,425,000	6,370,000	6,129,000	6,259,000
Shares Outstanding	222,000	226,000	233,000	271,000	274,000	269,000	264,000	263,000
Statistical Record								
Return on Assets %	8.26	9.03	8.21	3.24	N.M.	2.26	0.52	N.M.
Return on Equity %	23.21	27.35	24.62	10.22	N.M.	6.50	1.59	N.M.
EBITDA Margin %	11.59	11.61	10.57	8.80	6.75	5.07	4.08	0.74
Net Margin %	5.59	5.79	5.79	2.84	N.M.	1.25	0.31	N.M.
Asset Turnover	1.48	1.56	1.42	1.14	0.97	1.81	1.70	1.57
Current Ratio	2.02	1.90	2.43	2.44	1.73	2.01	1.93	1.71
Debt to Equity	0.66	0.70	0.86	0.71	0.94	0.78	0.84	0.87
Price Range	86.35-34.57	84.77-55.26	57.71-42.10	43.06-26.63	27.32-16.31	25.00-14.58	29.10-13.50	19.63-8.75
P/E Ratio	17.52-7.01	17.09-11.14	13.55-9.88	24.47-15.13	...	18.25-10.64	111.92-51.92	...
Average Yield %	1.21	1.06	0.99	1.36	2.42	2.42	...	5.74

Address: 6501 Legacy Drive, Plano, TX 75024	**Web Site:** www.jcpenney.net	**Auditors:** KPMG LLP
Telephone: 972-431-1000	**Officers:** Myron E. Ullman III - Chmn., C.E.O.	**Investor Contact:** 972-431-2217
Fax: 972-591-9322	Robert B. Cavanaugh - Exec. V.P., C.F.O.	**Transfer Agents:** Mellon Investor Services, L.L.C.

PENTAIR, INC.

Exchange	Symbol	Price	52Wk Range	Yield	P/E	Div Acheiver
NYS	PNR	$31.90 (3/31/2008)	39.21-27.78	2.13	15.19	31 Years

*7 Year Price Score 96.27 *NYSE Composite Index=100 *12 Month Price Score 102.01

Interim Earnings (Per Share)

Qtr.	Mar	Jun	Sep	Dec
2003	0.28	0.44	0.39	0.32
2004	0.40	0.55	0.47	0.26
2005	0.42	0.63	0.46	0.29
2006	0.41	0.67	0.34	0.39
2007	0.42	0.62	0.58	0.48

Interim Dividends (Per Share)

Amt	Decl	Ex	Rec	Pay
0.15Q	4/12/2007	4/25/2007	4/27/2007	5/11/2007
0.15Q	7/13/2007	7/25/2007	7/27/2007	8/10/2007
0.15Q	10/12/2007	10/24/2007	10/26/2007	11/9/2007
0.17Q	1/14/2008	1/23/2008	1/25/2008	2/8/2008

Indicated Div: $0.68 (Div. Reinv. Plan)

Valuation Analysis

		Institutional Holding	
Forecast P/E	12.67	No of Institutions	
	(1/10/2007)	254	
Market Cap	$3.2 Billion	Shares	
Book Value	1.9 Billion	69,965,048	
Price/Book	1.66	% Held	
Price/Sales	0.93	70.04	

Business Summary: Industrial Machinery and Equipment (MIC: 11.5 SIC: 3553 NAIC: 333210)

Pentair is an industrial manufacturing company comprised of two operating segments: Water and Technical Products. Co.'s Water Group is engaged in providing products and systems used in the movement, storage, treatment, and enjoyment of water. Co.'s Technical Products Group is engaged in designing and manufacturing standard, modified and custom enclosures that house and protect sensitive electronics and electrical components; thermal management products; and accessories. As of Dec 31 2007, Co.'s primary brand names for its Technical Products Group are: Hoffman®, Schroff®, Pentair Electronic Packaging™, Taunus™, McLean®, Electronic Solutions™, Birtcher™, Calmark™ and Aspen Motion™.

Recent Developments: For the year ended Dec 31 2007, income from continuing operations increased 14.5% to US$210.5 million from US$183.8 million a year earlier. Net income increased 14.8% to US$210.9 million from US$183.7 million in the prior year. Revenues were US$3.40 billion, up 7.7% from US$3.15 billion the year before. Operating income was US$378.0 million versus US$310.3 million in the prior year, an increase of 21.8%. Direct operating expenses rose 5.6% to US$2.37 billion from US$2.25 billion in the comparable period the year before. Indirect operating expenses increased 8.5% to US$646.7 million from US$595.9 million in the equivalent prior-year period.

Prospects: On Feb 21 2008, Co. announced that it has agreed to sell its National Pool Tile business to Pool Corporation in a cash transaction. The sale is subject to customary closing conditions and is expected to close in the first quarter 2008. Co. noted that the sale should enable it to focus on its growing, core global pool equipment business and it expects to use the cash proceeds from the transaction to pay down debt. Separately, for the first quarter of 2008, Co. is projecting earnings per share to be in the range of $0.46 to $0.48, an increase of 10.0% to 14.0% year-over-year. For full-year 2008, Co. is forecasting earnings per share to range from $2.25 to $2.40.

Financial Data
(US$ in Thousands)

	12/31/2007	12/31/2006	12/31/2005	12/31/2004	12/31/2003	12/31/2002	12/31/2001	12/31/2000
Earnings Per Share	2.10	1.81	1.80	1.68	1.42	1.30	0.34	0.57
Cash Flow Per Share	3.46	2.32	2.46	2.65	2.69	2.75	2.37	1.90
Dividends Per Share	0.600	0.560	0.522	0.430	0.410	0.370	0.350	0.330
Dividend Payout %	28.57	30.94	29.03	25.60	28.87	28.35	104.48	57.39
Income Statement								
Total Revenue	3,398,698	3,154,469	2,946,579	2,278,129	2,724,365	2,580,783	2,615,944	2,748,013
EBITDA	458,429	382,446	401,067	308,151	325,197	300,694	259,125	301,058
Income Before Taxes	303,643	255,469	283,518	210,032	218,618	192,447	93,288	127,131
Income Taxes	93,154	71,702	98,469	73,000	74,330	62,545	35,772	45,263
Net Income	210,927	183,731	185,049	171,225	141,352	129,902	32,869	55,887
Average Shares	100,205	101,371	102,618	101,706	99,620	99,488	98,594	97,290
Balance Sheet								
Current Assets	1,038,021	957,628	895,024	825,137	829,451	810,808	835,603	1,091,802
Total Assets	4,000,614	3,364,979	3,253,755	3,120,575	2,780,677	2,514,450	2,372,198	2,644,025
Current Liabilities	560,906	521,282	524,670	526,879	497,451	476,200	428,433	648,792
Long-Term Obligations	1,042,223	721,873	748,477	724,148	732,862	673,911	714,977	781,834
Total Liabilities	2,089,743	1,694,980	1,698,145	1,672,781	1,519,199	1,408,726	1,357,196	1,633,434
Stockholders' Equity	1,910,871	1,669,999	1,555,610	1,447,794	1,261,478	1,105,724	1,015,002	1,010,591
Shares Outstanding	99,221	99,777	101,202	100,967	99,005	98,444	98,221	97,423
Statistical Record								
Return on Assets %	5.73	5.55	5.81	5.79	5.34	5.32	1.31	2.05
Return on Equity %	11.78	11.39	12.32	12.61	11.94	12.25	3.25	5.56
EBITDA Margin %	13.49	12.12	13.61	13.53	11.94	11.65	9.91	10.96
Net Margin %	6.21	5.82	6.28	7.52	5.19	5.03	1.26	2.03
Asset Turnover	0.92	0.95	0.92	0.77	1.03	1.06	1.04	1.01
Current Ratio	1.85	1.84	1.71	1.57	1.67	1.70	1.95	1.68
Debt to Equity	0.55	0.43	0.48	0.50	0.58	0.61	0.70	0.77
Price Range	39.21-29.50	41.69-26.13	46.03-30.80	44.03-22.52	23.29-16.40	24.81-14.67	19.64-11.25	22.00-10.50
P/E Ratio	18.67-14.05	23.03-14.44	25.57-17.11	26.21-13.40	16.40-11.55	19.08-11.28	57.76-33.09	38.60-18.42
Average Yield %	1.77	1.65	1.32	1.35	2.09	1.85	2.19	2.00

Address: 5500 Wayzata Boulevard, Suite 800, Golden Valley, MN 55416-1261 Telephone: 763-545-1730	Web Site: www.pentair.com Officers: Randall J. Hogan - Chmn., Pres., C.E.O. Richard J. Cathcart - Vice-Chmn.	Auditors: Deloitte & Touche LLP Investor Contact: 651-639-5278 Transfer Agents: Wells Fargo Bank Minnesota, N.A.

PEPCO HOLDINGS INC.

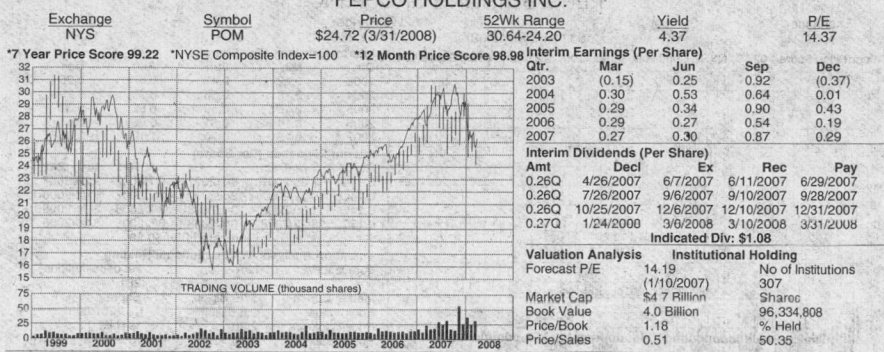

Exchange	Symbol	Price	52Wk Range	Yield	P/E
NYS	POM	$24.72 (3/31/2008)	30.64-24.20	4.37	14.37

*7 Year Price Score 99.22 *NYSE Composite Index=100 *12 Month Price Score 98.98

Interim Earnings (Per Share)

Qtr.	Mar	Jun	Sep	Dec
2003	(0.15)	0.25	0.92	(0.37)
2004	0.30	0.53	0.64	0.01
2005	0.29	0.34	0.90	0.43
2006	0.29	0.27	0.54	0.19
2007	0.27	0.30	0.87	0.29

Interim Dividends (Per Share)

Amt	Decl	Ex	Rec	Pay
0.26Q	4/26/2007	6/7/2007	6/11/2007	6/29/2007
0.26Q	7/26/2007	9/6/2007	9/10/2007	9/28/2007
0.26Q	10/25/2007	12/6/2007	12/10/2007	12/31/2007
0.27Q	1/24/2008	3/6/2008	3/10/2008	3/31/2008

Indicated Div: $1.08

Valuation Analysis

Forecast P/E	14.19 (1/10/2007)
Market Cap	$4.7 Billion
Book Value	4.0 Billion
Price/Book	1.18
Price/Sales	0.51

Institutional Holding

No of Institutions	307
Shares	96,334,808
% Held	50.35

TRADING VOLUME (thousand shares)

Business Summary: Electricity (MIC: 7.1 SIC: 4931 NAIC: 221122)

Pepco Holdings is an energy company engaged in two principal business operations: electricity and natural gas delivery (Power Delivery), and competitive energy generation, marketing and supply (Competitive Energy). Co.'s Power Delivery business is conducted by Potomac Electric Power Company, Delmarva Power & Light Company and Atlantic City Electric Company. Co.'s Competitive Energy operations are conducted by Conectiv Energy Holding Company and Pepco Energy Services, Inc. As of Dec 31 2007, Co.'s Power Delivery business delivered electricity to more than 1.8 million customers in the mid-Atlantic region and distributed natural gas to about 122,000 customers in Delaware.

Recent Developments: For the year ended Dec 31 2007, net income increased 34.6% to US$334.2 million from US$248.3 million in the prior year. Revenues were US$9.37 billion, up 12.0% from US$8.36 billion the year before. Operating income was US$806.6 million versus US$693.3 million in the prior year, an increase of 16.3%. Direct operating expenses rose 12.1% to US$8.17 billion from US$7.29 billion in the comparable period the year before. Indirect operating expenses increased 2.6% to US$393.1 million from US$383.2 million in the equivalent prior-year period.

Prospects: Co.'s outlook seems constructive as it remains committed to pursuing energy efficiency and demand-side management programs, investing in utility infrastructure, controlling costs in its power delivery business, as well as building on its improved competitive energy businesses. For example, on Dec 14 2007, Co.'s competitive energy subsidiary, Conectiv Energy Holding Co., announced a decision to construct a 545 megawatt natural gas and oil-fired combined-cycle electricity generation plant, the Delta Project, in Peach Bottom Township, PA. Co. is projecting total construction expenditures for the Delta Project to be $470.0 million, and the plant is expected to become operational by June 2011.

Financial Data

(US$ in Thousands)	12/31/2007	12/31/2006	12/31/2005	12/31/2004	12/31/2003	12/31/2002	12/31/2001	12/31/2000
Earnings Per Share	1.72	1.30	1.96	1.47	0.66	1.61	1.50	2.96
Cash Flow Per Share	4.10	1.06	5.22	4.14	3.87	6.14	...	...
Tang Book Value Per Share	13.59	11.48	11.34	10.28	9.13	9.20	17.00	...
Dividends Per Share	1.040	1.040	1.000	1.000	1.000	0.416	...	...
Dividend Payout %	60.47	80.00	51.02	68.03	151.52	25.82	...	...
Income Statement								
Total Revenue	9,366,400	8,362,900	8,065,500	7,221,800	7,271,300	4,324,500	2,400,500	2,989,300
EBITDA	1,227,800	1,162,000	1,377,600	1,246,000	...	...	...	...
Income Before Taxes	522,100	409,700	617,400	431,900	...	...	...	...
Income Taxes	187,900	161,400	255,200	173,200	65,900	124,100	83,500	341,200
Net Income	334,200	248,300	371,700	258,700	113,500	210,500	163,400	346,500
Average Shares	194,100	190,700	189,300	176,800	170,700	131,100	108,800	118,300
Balance Sheet								
Net PPE	7,876,700	7,576,600	7,312,000	7,088,000	6,964,900	6,798,000	2,753,400	...
Total Assets	15,111,000	14,243,500	14,017,800	13,349,400	13,434,400	12,861,700	5,285,900	...
Long-Term Obligations	4,734,600	4,367,400	4,839,300	5,072,800	5,372,800	4,832,400	1,722,400	...
Total Liabilities	11,086,400	10,606,900	10,387,800	9,928,200	10,412,900	9,465,200	3,252,900	...
Stockholders' Equity	4,018,400	3,612,200	3,584,100	3,366,300	3,003,300	2,995,800	1,823,200	...
Shares Outstanding	191,932	191,932	189,817	188,327	171,769	169,982	107,221	118,544
Statistical Record								
Return on Assets %	2.28	1.76	2.71	1.93	0.86	...	...	...
Return on Equity %	8.76	6.90	10.68	8.10	3.78	...	...	...
EBITDA Margin %	13.11	13.89	17.08	17.25	...	...	...	...
Net Margin %	3.57	2.97	4.60	3.58	1.56	4.87	6.81	11.59
PPE Turnover	1.21	1.12	1.12	1.02	1.06	...	...	...
Asset Turnover	0.64	0.59	0.59	0.54	0.55	...	...	...
Debt to Equity	1.18	1.21	1.35	1.51	1.79	1.61	0.94	...
Price Range	30.64-25.00	26.78-22.02	24.36-20.43	21.71-17.04	20.56-16.18	23.73-16.22	24.27-20.28	27.31-19.19
P/E Ratio	17.81-14.53	20.60-16.94	12.43-10.42	14.77-11.59	31.15-24.52	14.74-10.07	16.18-13.52	9.23-6.48
Average Yield %	3.75	4.33	4.50	5.05	5.54	1.98	...	...

Address: 701 Ninth Street N.W., Washington, DC 20068	Web Site: www.pepcoholdings.com	Auditors: PricewaterhouseCoopers LLP
Telephone: 202-872-2000	Officers: Dennis R. Wraase - Chmn., Pres., C.E.O. William T. Torgerson - Vice-Chmn., Gen. Couns.	Investor Contact: 302-429-3004 Transfer Agents: American Stock Transfer & Trust Company, Brooklyn, NY

PEPSI BOTTLING GROUP INC

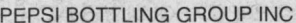

Exchange	Symbol	Price	52Wk Range	Yield	P/E
NYS	PBG	$33.91 (3/31/2008)	43.08-31.88	2.01	14.81

*7 Year Price Score 102.73 *NYSE Composite Index=100 *12 Month Price Score 101.36

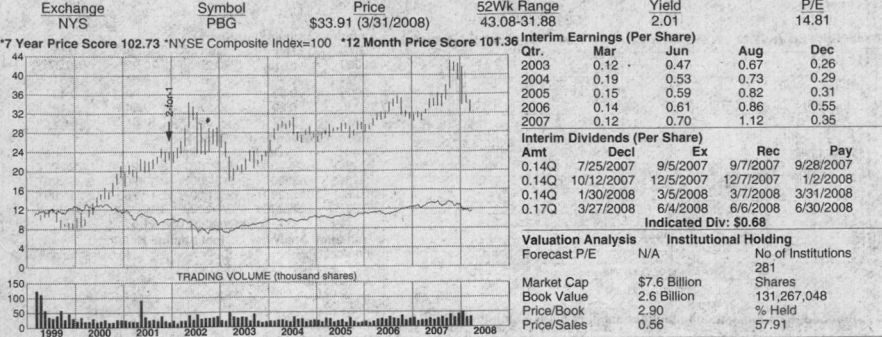

Interim Earnings (Per Share)

Qtr.	Mar	Jun	Aug	Dec
2003	0.12	0.47	0.67	0.26
2004	0.19	0.53	0.73	0.29
2005	0.15	0.59	0.82	0.31
2006	0.14	0.61	0.86	0.55
2007	0.12	0.70	1.12	0.35

Interim Dividends (Per Share)

Amt	Decl	Ex	Rec	Pay
0.14Q	7/25/2007	9/5/2007	9/7/2007	9/28/2007
0.14Q	10/12/2007	12/5/2007	12/7/2007	1/2/2008
0.14Q	1/30/2008	3/5/2008	3/7/2008	3/31/2008
0.17Q	3/27/2008	6/4/2008	6/6/2008	6/30/2008

Indicated Div: $0.68

Valuation Analysis | **Institutional Holding**

Forecast P/E	N/A	No of Institutions
		281
Market Cap	$7.6 Billion	Shares
Book Value	2.6 Billion	131,267,048
Price/Book	2.90	% Held
Price/Sales	0.56	57.91

Business Summary: Food (MIC: 4.1 SIC: 2086 NAIC: 312111)

Pepsi Bottling Group is a manufacturer, seller and distributor of Pepsi-Cola beverages including, Pepsi, Diet Pepsi, Mountain Dew, Aquafina, Lipton, Sierra Mist, Diet Mountain Dew, Tropicana juice drinks, SoBe and Starbucks Frappuccino®. In addition, in some of its territories, Co. has the right to manufacture, sell and distribute soft drink products of companies other than PepsiCo, such as Dr Pepper and Squirt. As of Dec 29 2007, Co. had the right to manufacture, sell and distribute Pepsi-Cola beverages in all or a portion of 41 states and the District of Columbia in the U.S., nine Canadian provinces, Spain, Greece, Russia, Turkey and all or a portion of 23 states in Mexico.

Recent Developments: For the year ended Dec 29 2007, net income increased 1.9% to US$532.0 million from US$522.0 million in the prior year. Revenues were US$13.59 billion, up 6.8% from US$12.73 billion the year before. Operating income was US$1.07 billion versus US$1.02 billion in the prior year, an increase of 5.3%. Direct operating expenses rose 6.8% to US$7.37 billion from US$6.90 billion in the comparable period the year before. Indirect operating expenses increased 7.0% to US$5.15 billion from US$4.81 billion in the equivalent prior-year period.

Prospects: Co.'s outlook appears constructive, as it plans to continue to pursue acquisitions of bottling assets and territories from PepsiCo's independent bottlers. For example, on Dec 11 2007, Co. announced that it has signed a Letter of Intent to acquire Pepsi-Cola Batavia Bottling Corp., a family owned and operated business based in Batavia, NY. The acquisition, which would expand Co.'s footprint in the upstate New York, is expected to close during the first quarter of 2008. Meanwhile, for full-year 2008, Co. expects to achieve top-line growth of about 6.0% to 7.0%. Concurrently, Co. projects operating profit growth of 4.0% to 6.0% and comparable diluted earnings of $2.30 to $2.38 per share.

Financial Data

(US$ in Thousands)	12/29/2007	12/30/2006	12/31/2005	12/25/2004	12/27/2003	12/28/2002	12/29/2001	12/30/2000
Earnings Per Share	2.29	2.16	1.86	1.73	1.50	1.46	1.03	0.77
Cash Flow Per Share	6.38	5.22	4.93	4.92	4.03	3.61	3.52	2.78
Dividends Per Share	0.530	0.410	0.290	0.160	0.040	0.040	0.040	0.040
Dividend Payout %	23.14	18.98	15.59	9.25	2.67	2.74	3.88	5.23
Income Statement								
Total Revenue	13,591,000	12,730,000	11,885,000	10,906,000	10,265,000	9,216,000	8,443,000	7,982,000
EBITDA	1,652,000	1,596,000	1,593,000	1,512,000	1,467,000	1,291,000	1,149,000	1,027,000
Income Before Taxes	709,000	681,000	713,000	689,000	660,000	649,000	441,000	364,000
Income Taxes	177,000	159,000	247,000	232,000	238,000	221,000	136,000	135,000
Net Income	532,000	522,000	466,000	457,000	416,000	428,000	305,000	229,000
Average Shares	233,000	242,000	250,213	263,000	277,000	293,000	296,000	298,000
Balance Sheet								
Current Assets	3,086,000	2,749,000	2,412,000	2,039,000	3,039,000	1,737,000	1,548,000	1,584,000
Total Assets	13,115,000	11,927,000	11,524,000	10,793,000	11,544,000	10,027,000	7,857,000	7,736,000
Current Liabilities	2,215,000	2,051,000	2,598,000	1,581,000	2,478,000	1,248,000	1,081,000	967,000
Long-Term Obligations	4,770,000	4,754,000	3,939,000	4,489,000	4,493,000	4,523,000	3,285,000	3,271,000
Total Liabilities	10,500,000	9,843,000	9,481,000	8,844,000	9,663,000	8,203,000	6,256,000	6,090,000
Stockholders' Equity	2,615,000	2,084,000	2,043,000	1,949,000	1,881,000	1,824,000	1,601,000	1,646,000
Shares Outstanding	224,000	230,000	239,000	249,000	261,100	281,100	281,100	290,176
Statistical Record								
Return on Assets %	4.26	4.46	4.11	4.10	3.87	4.80	3.92	2.93
Return on Equity %	22.71	25.37	22.97	23.93	22.52	25.06	18.84	14.04
EBITDA Margin %	12.16	12.54	13.40	13.86	14.29	14.01	13.61	12.87
Net Margin %	3.91	4.10	3.92	4.19	4.05	4.64	3.61	2.87
Asset Turnover	1.09	1.09	1.05	0.98	0.95	1.03	1.09	1.02
Current Ratio	1.39	1.34	0.93	1.29	1.23	1.39	1.43	1.64
Debt to Equity	1.82	2.28	1.93	2.30	2.39	2.48	2.05	1.99
Price Range	43.08-30.33	35.66-28.09	30.28-26.07	31.21-24.01	27.53-17.93	34.38-21.70	24.73-16.78	21.13-8.19
P/E Ratio	18.81-13.24	16.51-13.00	16.28-14.02	18.04-13.88	18.35-11.95	23.55-14.86	24.00-16.29	27.44-10.63
Average Yield %	1.50	1.29	1.02	0.57	0.18	0.15	0.19	0.29

Address: One Pepsi Way, Somers, NY 10589-2201	**Web Site:** www.pbg.com	**Auditors:** Deloitte & Touche LLP
Telephone: 914-767-6000	**Officers:** John T. Cahill - Chmn., C.E.O. L. Kevin Cox - Sr. V.P., Chief Personnel Officer	**Investor Contact:** 914-767-7216
Fax: 914-767-1313		**Transfer Agents:** Bank of New York, New York, NY

PEPSIAMERICAS, INC.

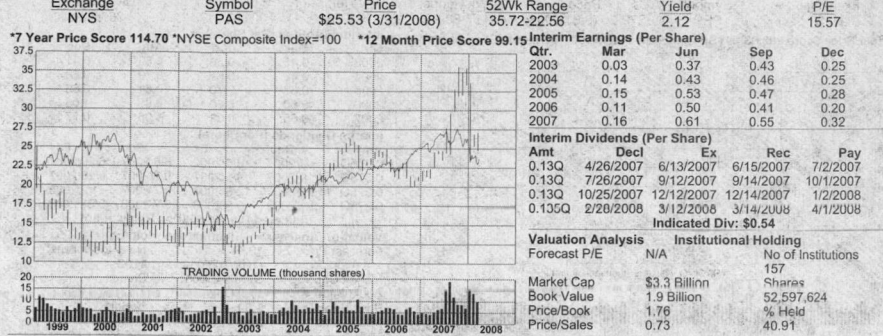

Exchange	Symbol	Price	52Wk Range	Yield	P/E
NYS	PAS	$25.53 (3/31/2008)	35.72-22.56	2.12	15.57

*7 Year Price Score 114.70 *NYSE Composite Index=100 *12 Month Price Score 99.15

Interim Earnings (Per Share)

Qtr.	Mar	Jun	Sep	Dec
2003	0.03	0.37	0.43	0.25
2004	0.14	0.43	0.46	0.25
2005	0.15	0.53	0.47	0.28
2006	0.11	0.50	0.41	0.20
2007	0.16	0.61	0.55	0.32

Interim Dividends (Per Share)

Amt	Decl	Ex	Rec	Pay
0.13Q	4/26/2007	6/13/2007	6/15/2007	7/2/2007
0.13Q	7/26/2007	9/12/2007	9/14/2007	10/1/2007
0.13Q	10/25/2007	12/12/2007	12/14/2007	1/2/2008
0.135Q	2/28/2008	3/12/2008	3/14/2008	4/1/2008

Indicated Div: $0.54

Valuation Analysis **Institutional Holding**

Forecast P/E	N/A	No of Institutions 157
Market Cap	$3.3 Billion	Shares 52,597,624
Book Value	1.9 Billion	% Held 40.91
Price/Book	1.76	
Price/Sales	0.73	

TRADING VOLUME (thousand shares)

Business Summary: Food (MIC: 4.1 SIC: 2086 NAIC: 312111)

PepsiAmericas manufactures, distributes and markets beverage products in the U.S., Central and Eastern Europe (CEE) and the Caribbean, as well as distributes snack foods and beer in certain markets. Co. sells a variety of brands under franchise agreements with various brand owners, the majority with PepsiCo, Inc. In some territories, Co. manufactures, packages, sells and distributes its own brands, such as Toma brands in CEE and the Caribbean and Sandora brands in Ukraine. As of Dec 29 2007, Co. operated in 19 states in the U.S. In CEE, Co. served Poland, Hungary, the Czech Republic, Republic of Slovakia, Romania and Ukraine, with distribution rights in Moldova, Estonia, Latvia and Lithuania.

Recent Developments: For the year ended Dec 29 2007, income from continuing operations increased 35.3% to US$214.2 million from US$158.3 million a year earlier. Net income increased 34.0% to US$212.1 million from US$158.3 million in the prior year. Revenues were US$4.48 billion, up 12.8% from US$3.97 billion the year before. Operating income was US$436.1 million versus US$356.0 million in the prior year, an increase of 22.5%. Direct operating expenses rose 12.3% to US$2.66 billion from US$2.36 billion in the comparable period the year before. Indirect operating expenses increased 10.8% to US$1.39 billion from US$1.25 billion in the equivalent prior-year period.

Prospects: Looking ahead to 2008, Co. expects worldwide volume to increase in the range of 13.0% to 14.0%. Co. also expects to improve average net selling price by 2.5% to 3.5% in order to cover anticipated higher cost of goods sold. In addition, Co. expects its 2007 acquisition of Sandora, LLC, a juice company in Ukraine, through a joint venture with PepsiCo, Inc., to broaden its product offerings and provide opportunities to further expand its portfolio. Additionally, the acquisition is anticipated to contribute 10.0% growth in volume and to raise Co.'s operating income by 5.0% to 6.0% in 2008. Overall, Co. is targeting diluted earnings per share of $1.77 to $1.83 for the full year.

Financial Data

(US$ in Thousands)	12/29/2007	12/30/2006	12/31/2005	01/01/2005	01/03/2004	12/28/2002	12/29/2001	12/30/2000
Earnings Per Share	1.64	1.22	1.42	1.28	1.09	0.85	0.12	0.58
Cash Flow Per Share	3.43	2.70	3.21	3.34	2.05	2.18	2.04	2.35
Dividends Per Share	0.520	0.500	0.340	0.300	0.040	0.040	0.040	0.040
Dividend Payout %	31.71	40.98	23.94	23.44	3.67	4.71	33.33	6.90
Income Statement								
Total Revenue	4,479,500	3,972,400	3,726,000	3,344,700	3,236,800	3,239,800	3,170,700	2,527,600
EBITDA	639,900	537,900	573,200	520,800	480,000	460,400	466,800	391,500
Income Before Taxes	326,300	243,200	298,600	282,300	240,200	220,200	173,900	141,100
Income Taxes	112,000	90,500	108,800	100,400	82,600	84,500	83,800	69,600
Net Income	212,100	158,300	194,700	181,900	157,600	129,700	18,900	80,400
Average Shares	129,200	129,800	137,200	141,800	144,100	153,000	156,600	170,100
Balance Sheet								
Current Assets	922,100	675,100	598,200	529,500	560,200	549,900	480,800	477,000
Total Assets	5,308,000	4,207,400	4,053,800	3,529,800	3,580,700	3,562,600	3,419,300	3,335,600
Current Liabilities	902,600	693,800	722,000	521,100	599,500	698,000	632,700	887,000
Long-Term Obligations	1,803,500	1,490,200	1,285,900	1,006,600	1,078,400	1,080,700	1,083,400	860,100
Total Liabilities	3,449,700	2,602,800	2,484,500	1,906,600	2,015,600	2,114,000	1,989,000	1,886,100
Stockholders' Equity	1,858,300	1,604,600	1,569,300	1,623,200	1,565,100	1,448,600	1,430,300	1,449,500
Shares Outstanding	128,100	127,000	133,000	138,600	143,800	147,600	153,600	155,600
Statistical Record								
Return on Assets %	4.47	3.84	5.15	5.13	4.34	3.73	0.56	2.59
Return on Equity %	12.28	10.00	12.23	11.44	10.29	9.04	1.32	6.20
EBITDA Margin %	14.29	13.54	15.38	15.57	14.83	14.21	14.72	15.49
Net Margin %	4.73	3.98	5.23	5.44	4.87	4.00	0.60	3.18
Asset Turnover	0.94	0.96	0.99	0.94	0.89	0.93	0.94	0.82
Current Ratio	1.02	0.97	0.83	1.02	0.93	0.79	0.74	0.54
Debt to Equity	0.97	0.93	0.82	0.62	0.69	0.75	0.76	0.59
Price Range	35.72-20.70	24.90-19.96	26.26-20.44	21.50-16.90	17.25-11.18	15.90-11.66	16.94-12.52	16.38-10.69
P/E Ratio	21.78-12.62	20.41-16.36	18.49-14.39	16.80-13.20	15.83-10.26	18.71-13.72	141.17-104.33	28.23-18.43
Average Yield %	1.93	2.22	1.44	1.51	0.29	0.28	0.27	0.31

Address: 4000 Dain Rauscher Plaza, 60 South Sixth Street, Minneapolis, MN 55402
Telephone: 612-661-3883
Fax: 612-483-6750

Web Site: www.pepsiamericas.com
Officers: Robert C. Pohlad - Chmn., C.E.O. Kenneth E. Keiser - Pres., C.O.O.

Auditors: KPMG LLP
Investor Contact: 612-661-4000
Transfer Agents: Wells Fargo Bank, N.A.

PEPSICO INC.

Exchange	Symbol	Price	52Wk Range	Yield	P/E	Div Acheiver
NYS	PEP	$72.20 (3/31/2008)	79.57-62.99	2.08	21.17	36 Years

*7 Year Price Score 103.93 *NYSE Composite Index=100 *12 Month Price Score 107.09

Interim Earnings (Per Share)

Qtr.	Mar	Jun	Aug	Dec
2003	0.45	0.58	0.62	0.41
2004	0.46	0.61	0.79	0.58
2005	0.53	0.70	0.51	0.65
2006	0.60	0.80	0.88	1.06
2007	0.65	0.94	1.06	0.77

Interim Dividends (Per Share)

Amt	Decl	Ex	Rec	Pay
0.375Q	5/2/2007	6/6/2007	6/8/2007	6/29/2007
0.375Q	7/19/2007	9/5/2007	9/7/2007	9/28/2007
0.375Q	11/16/2007	12/5/2007	12/7/2007	1/2/2008
0.375Q	2/1/2008	3/5/2008	3/7/2008	3/31/2008

Indicated Div: $1.50 (Div. Reinv. Plan)

Valuation Analysis | **Institutional Holding**

Forecast P/E	13.91	No of Institutions
	(1/10/2007)	1292
Market Cap	$115.9 Billion	Shares
Book Value	17.3 Billion	1,121,669,888
Price/Book	6.69	% Held
Price/Sales	2.94	68.49

Business Summary: Food (MIC: 4.1 SIC: 2086 NAIC: 312111)

PepsiCo is engaged in manufacturing, marketing and selling a range of salty, sweet and grain-based snacks as well as carbonated and non-carbonated beverages and foods. Co. is organized into four divisions: Frito-Lay North America (FLNA); PepsiCo Beverages North America (PBNA); PepsiCo International (PI); and Quaker Foods North America (QFNA). FLNA branded snacks include Lay's potato chips, Doritos tortilla chips and Rold Gold pretzels. PBNA's brands include Pepsi, Mountain Dew, Gatorade, Tropicana Pure Premium, and Lipton. PI's brands include Lay's, Walkers, Cheetos, Doritos, Ruffles, Gamesa and Sabritas. QFNA's brands include Quaker oatmeal, Rice-A-Roni and Near East side dishes.

Recent Developments: For the year ended Dec 29 2007, net income increased 0.3% to US$5.66 billion from US$5.64 billion in the prior year. Revenues were US$39.47 billion, up 12.3% from US$35.14 billion the year before. Operating income was US$7.17 billion versus US$6.50 billion in the prior year, an increase of 10.3%. Direct operating expenses rose 14.4% to US$18.04 billion from US$15.76 billion in the comparable period the year before. Indirect operating expenses increased 10.8% to US$14.27 billion from US$12.87 billion in the equivalent prior-year period.

Prospects: For the full year of 2008, Co. is projecting volume growth in the range of 3% to 5% and earnings to be about $3.72 per share, while net revenue growth is estimated in the mid-to-high single digit range. In addition, Co. is anticipating net capital spending of about $2.70 billion, which is expected to be within its net capital spending target of about 5% to 7% of net revenue. Specifically, planned capital spending in 2008 includes investments to increase capacity in Co.'s snack and beverage businesses to support growth in developing and potential markets, investments in North America to support growth in key brands, and investments in its ongoing business restructuring initiative.

Financial Data
(US$ in Thousands)

	12/29/2007	12/30/2006	12/31/2005	12/25/2004	12/27/2003	12/28/2002	12/29/2001	12/30/2000
Earnings Per Share	3.41	3.34	2.39	2.44	2.05	1.85	1.47	1.48
Cash Flow Per Share	4.29	3.70	3.45	2.99	2.53	2.65	2.39	2.66
Tang Book Value Per Share	6.30	5.50	5.20	4.84	3.82	4.93	2.17	1.91
Dividends Per Share	1.425	1.160	1.010	0.850	0.630	0.595	0.575	0.555
Dividend Payout %	41.79	34.73	42.26	34.84	30.73	32.16	39.12	37.50
Income Statement								
Total Revenue	39,474,000	35,137,000	32,562,000	29,261,000	26,971,000	25,112,000	26,935,000	20,438,000
EBITDA	9,092,000	8,399,000	7,732,000	6,848,000	6,269,000	6,077,000	5,189,000	4,209,000
Income Before Taxes	7,631,000	6,989,000	6,382,000	5,546,000	4,992,000	4,868,000	4,029,000	3,210,000
Income Taxes	1,973,000	1,347,000	2,304,000	1,372,000	1,424,000	1,555,000	1,367,000	1,027,000
Net Income	5,658,000	5,642,000	4,078,000	4,212,000	3,568,000	3,313,000	2,662,000	2,183,000
Average Shares	1,658,000	1,687,000	1,706,000	1,729,000	1,739,000	1,789,000	1,807,000	1,475,000
Balance Sheet								
Current Assets	10,151,000	9,130,000	10,454,000	8,639,000	6,930,000	6,413,000	5,853,000	4,604,000
Total Assets	34,628,000	29,930,000	31,727,000	27,987,000	25,327,000	23,474,000	21,695,000	18,339,000
Current Liabilities	7,753,000	6,860,000	9,406,000	6,752,000	6,415,000	6,052,000	4,998,000	3,935,000
Long-Term Obligations	4,203,000	2,550,000	2,313,000	2,397,000	1,702,000	2,187,000	2,651,000	2,346,000
Total Liabilities	17,394,000	14,562,000	17,476,000	14,464,000	13,453,000	14,183,000	13,021,000	11,090,000
Stockholders' Equity	17,325,000	15,447,000	14,320,000*	13,572,000	11,896,000	9,298,000	8,648,000	7,249,000
Shares Outstanding	1,605,000	1,638,000	1,656,000	1,679,000	1,705,000	1,722,000	1,756,000	1,446,000
Statistical Record								
Return on Assets %	17.58	18.35	13.44	15.84	14.66	14.71	13.34	11.97
Return on Equity %	34.62	38.01	28.77	33.17	33.76	37.02	33.58	30.40
EBITDA Margin %	23.03	23.90	23.75	23.40	23.24	24.20	19.26	20.59
Net Margin %	14.33	16.06	12.52	14.39	13.23	13.19	9.88	10.68
Asset Turnover	1.23	1.14	1.07	1.10	1.11	1.11	1.35	1.12
Current Ratio	1.31	1.33	1.11	1.28	1.08	1.06	1.17	1.17
Debt to Equity	0.24	0.17	0.16	0.18	0.14	0.24	0.31	0.32
Price Range	78.69-62.16	65.91-56.77	59.90-51.57	55.55-45.39	48.71-37.30	53.12-35.50	50.28-41.26	49.75-30.50
P/E Ratio	23.08-18.23	19.73-17.00	25.06-21.58	22.77-18.60	23.76-18.20	28.71-19.19	34.20-28.07	33.61-20.61
Average Yield %	2.09	1.90	1.82	1.66	1.43	1.29	1.25	1.35

Address: 700 Anderson Hill Road, Purchase, NY 10577-1444
Telephone: 914-253-2000
Fax: 914-253-2070

Web Site: www.pepsico.com
Officers: Steven S. Reinemund - Chmn., C.E.O. Indra K. Nooyi - Pres., C.F.O.

Auditors: KPMG LLP
Investor Contact: 914-253-3035
Transfer Agents: The Bank of New York

PERKINELMER, INC.

Exchange	Symbol	Price	52Wk Range	Yield	P/E
NYS	PKI	$24.25 (3/31/2008)	29.86-22.70	1.15	22.25

*7 Year Price Score 103.38 *NYSE Composite Index=100 *12 Month Price Score 101.02

Interim Earnings (Per Share)

Qtr.	Mar	Jun	Sep	Dec
2003	0.02	0.07	0.11	0.21
2004	0.10	0.16	0.19	0.29
2005	0.15	0.22	0.24	1.42
2006	0.18	0.19	0.24	0.34
2007	0.12	0.24	0.26	0.44

Interim Dividends (Per Share)

Amt	Decl	Ex	Rec	Pay
0.07Q	5/16/2007	7/18/2007	7/20/2007	8/10/2007
0.07Q	7/25/2007	10/17/2007	10/19/2007	11/9/2007
0.07Q	10/24/2007	1/16/2008	1/18/2008	2/8/2008
0.07Q	1/23/2008	4/16/2008	4/18/2008	5/9/2008

Indicated Div: $0.28

Valuation Analysis | **Institutional Holding**

Forecast P/E	15.22	No of Institutions
	(1/10/2007)	262
Market Cap	$2.9 Billion	Shares
Book Value	1.6 Billion	99,618,160
Price/Book	1.81	% Held
Price/Sales	1.60	81.77

TRADING VOLUME (thousand shares)

Business Summary: Instruments and Related Products (MIC: 11.15 SIC: 3826 NAIC: 334516)

PerkinElmer is a provider of technology, services and applications to the diagnostics, detection and analysis and photonics markets. Co. designs, manufactures, markets and services components, systems and products in two reporting segments. The Life and Analytical Sciences segment provides analysis tools, including instruments, reagents, software, and consumables, to the analytical sciences, genetic screening, BioDiscovery and laboratory services markets. The Optoelectronics segment provides a range of medical imaging, optical sensor and specialty lighting components used in medical, consumer products and other specialty end markets.

Recent Developments: For the year ended Dec 30 2007, income from continuing operations increased 13.1% to US$133.8 million from US$118.3 million a year earlier. Net income increased 10.1% to US$131.7 million from US$119.6 million in the prior year. Revenues were US$1.79 billion, up 15.6% from US$1.55 billion the year before. Operating income was US$168.2 million versus US$153.4 million in the prior year, an increase of 9.6%. Direct operating expenses rose 15.7% to US$1.06 billion from US$918.3 million in the comparable period the year before. Indirect operating expenses increased 17.3% to US$556.6 million from US$474.7 million in the equivalent prior-year period.

Prospects: For the full year of 2008, Co. is projecting revenue to increase in the low double digits to mid-teens range, with acquisitions and changes in foreign exchange rates contributing about 500 basis points. Going forward, Co. remains focused on expanding its products portfolio through strategic acquisitions. For instance, on Feb 29 2008, Co. announced that it has completed the acquisition of Pediatrix Medical Group, Inc.'s metabolic screening laboratory and the StepOne® newborn screening product for a total transaction value of about $66.0 million. Co. believes that this transaction would expand its capabilities to supply state laboratories with better newborn screening applications.

Financial Data

(US$ in Thousands)	12/30/2007	12/31/2006	01/01/2006	01/02/2005	12/28/2003	12/29/2002	12/30/2001	12/31/2000
Earnings Per Share	1.09	0.95	2.04	0.74	0.41	(1.21)	0.33	0.89
Cash Flow Per Share	1.73	1.02	1.61	1.33	1.33	0.81	1.19	1.49
Tang Book Value Per Share	N.M.	0.45	1.91	N.M.	N.M.	N.M.	N.M.	N.M.
Dividends Per Share	0.280	0.280	0.280	0.280	0.280	0.280	0.280	0.280
Dividend Payout %	25.69	29.47	13.73	37.84	68.29	...	84.85	31.64
Income Statement								
Total Revenue	1,787,331	1,546,358	1,473,831	1,687,231	1,535,222	1,504,981	1,330,054	1,695,267
EBITDA	239,926	219,703	157,628	248,586	211,128	96,965	149,992	260,554
Income Before Taxes	151,289	150,736	66,660	136,747	80,884	(8,550)	34,154	144,489
Income Taxes	17,455	32,412	128	38,495	25,871	(4,415)	34,774	58,422
Net Income	131,686	119,583	268,108	96,043	57,959	(151,938)	34,505	90,520
Average Shares	120,605	126,512	131,140	129,429	127,741	125,439	103,687	102,278
Balance Sheet								
Current Assets	842,948	744,766	998,889	747,630	766,298	991,343	997,439	893,061
Total Assets	2,949,337	2,510,322	2,693,461	2,575,507	2,607,719	2,836,239	2,919,129	2,260,179
Current Liabilities	547,598	476,533	494,539	445,967	452,015	697,674	708,210	717,599
Long-Term Obligations	516,078	151,781	243,282	364,874	544,307	614,053	598,125	583,337
Total Liabilities	1,374,060	932,592	1,042,948	1,115,422	1,258,669	1,583,895	1,555,572	1,531,790
Stockholders' Equity	1,575,277	1,577,730	1,650,513	1,460,085	1,349,050	1,252,344	1,363,557	728,389
Shares Outstanding	117,585	123,255	130,109	129,059	126,909	125,854	124,188	99,548
Statistical Record								
Return on Assets %	4.84	4.61	10.20	3.65	1.95	N.M.	1.34	4.57
Return on Equity %	8.38	7.43	17.29	6.73	4.08	N.M.	3.31	14.19
EBITDA Margin %	13.42	14.21	10.70	14.73	13.75	6.44	11.28	15.37
Net Margin %	7.37	7.73	18.19	5.69	3.45	N.M.	2.59	5.34
Asset Turnover	0.66	0.60	0.56	0.64	0.57	0.52	0.52	0.86
Current Ratio	1.54	1.56	2.02	1.68	1.70	1.42	1.41	1.24
Debt to Equity	0.33	0.10	0.15	0.25	0.40	0.49	0.44	0.80
Price Range	29.86-21.40	24.08-17.89	23.86-18.01	22.89-15.74	18.67-7.41	36.22-4.37	50.03-21.38	59.75-19.53
P/E Ratio	27.39-19.63	25.35-18.83	11.70-8.83	30.93-21.27	45.54-18.07	...	151.61-64.77	67.13-21.95
Average Yield %	1.08	1.32	1.33	1.44	2.17	2.15	0.87	0.75

Address: 45 William Street, Wellesley, MA 02481	**Web Site:** www.perkinelmer.com	**Auditors:** DELOITTE & TOUCHE
Telephone: 781-237-5100	**Officers:** Gregory L. Summe - Chmn., Pres., C.E.O.	
Fax: 781-431-4255	Robert F. Friel - Exec. V.P., C.F.O.	

PENSKE AUTOMOTIVE GROUP INC

Exchange	Symbol	Price	52Wk Range	Yield	P/E
NYS	PAG	$19.46 (3/31/2008)	22.49-14.14	1.85	14.41

*7 Year Price Score 108.69 *NYSE Composite Index=100 *12 Month Price Score 100.68

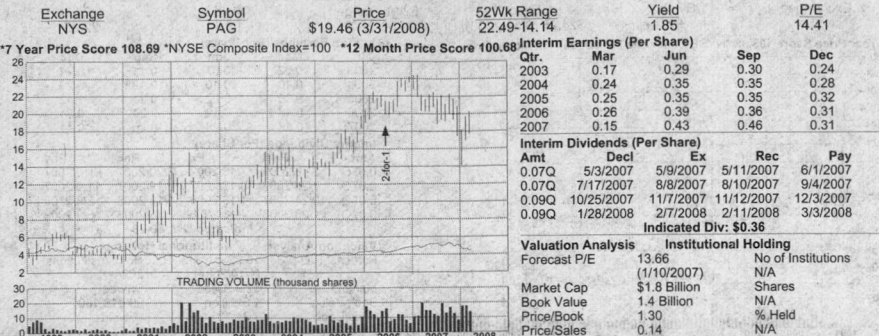

Interim Earnings (Per Share)

Qtr.	Mar	Jun	Sep	Dec
2003	0.17	0.29	0.30	0.24
2004	0.24	0.35	0.35	0.28
2005	0.25	0.35	0.35	0.32
2006	0.26	0.39	0.36	0.31
2007	0.15	0.43	0.46	0.31

Interim Dividends (Per Share)

Amt	Decl	Ex	Rec	Pay
0.07Q	5/3/2007	5/9/2007	5/11/2007	6/1/2007
0.07Q	7/17/2007	8/8/2007	8/10/2007	9/4/2007
0.09Q	10/25/2007	11/7/2007	11/12/2007	12/3/2007
0.09Q	1/28/2008	2/7/2008	2/11/2008	3/3/2008

Indicated Div: $0.36

Valuation Analysis

Forecast P/E	13.66
	(1/10/2007)
Market Cap	$1.8 Billion
Book Value	1.4 Billion
Price/Book	1.30
Price/Sales	0.14

Institutional Holding

No of Institutions	N/A
Shares	N/A
% Held	N/A
	N/A

TRADING VOLUME (thousand shares)

Business Summary: Retail - Automotive (MIC: 5.7 SIC: 5511 NAIC: 441110)

Penske Automotive Group is engaged as a retailer of both new and used vehicles. As of Feb 1 2008, Co. owned and operated 170 franchises in the U.S. and 145 franchises internationally, primarily in the U.K. Co. operates dealerships under franchise agreements with a number of automotive manufacturers. Co. provides a range of vehicle brands such as Audi, BMW, Honda, Lexus, Mercedes and Toyota. In addition, Co. provides maintenance and repair services, as well as facilitates the placement of third-party finance and insurance products, third-party extended service contracts and replacement and aftermarket automotive products.

Recent Developments: For the year ended Dec 31 2007, income from continuing operations decreased 3.3% to US$127.8 million from US$132.2 million a year earlier. Net income increased 2.4% to US$127.7 million from US$124.7 million in the prior year. Revenues were US$12.96 billion, up 16.5% from US$11.13 billion the year before. Operating income was US$342.6 million versus US$304.1 million in the prior year, an increase of 12.7%. Direct operating expenses rose 16.8% to US$11.03 billion from US$9.44 billion in the comparable period the year before. Indirect operating expenses increased 14.7% to US$1.58 billion from US$1.38 billion in the equivalent prior-year period.

Prospects: Looking forward, Co. expects earnings from continuing operations to be $1.63 to $1.71 per share for 2008. Also, Co. plans to grow its existing business by generating additional revenue at existing dealerships, with a particular focus on developing its higher-margin businesses such as finance, insurance, and parts and collision repair services. Meanwhile, retail deliveries have recently begun for the smart fortwo vehicle in the U.S., and Co. expects to distribute at least 20,000 smart fortwo vehicles in 2008. Separately, on Dec 21 2007, Co. announced that it has terminated the Nov 2007 agreement to acquire Rallye Motors, representing approximately $700.0 million in annualized revenue.

Financial Data
(US$ in Thousands)

	12/31/2007	12/31/2006	12/31/2005	12/31/2004	12/31/2003	12/31/2002	12/31/2001	12/31/2000
Earnings Per Share	1.35	1.32	1.26	1.23	1.00	0.76	0.66	0.51
Cash Flow Per Share	3.30	1.29	2.08	2.13	2.21	1.09	1.56	1.15
Dividends Per Share	0.300	0.270	0.225	0.205	0.050	...	...	...
Dividend Payout %	22.22	20.45	17.79	16.73	5.00	...	...	...
Income Statement								
Total Revenue	12,957,739	11,242,313	10,190,284	9,886,211	8,671,485	7,434,866	6,220,663	4,883,989
EBITDA	379,031	356,218	335,296	320,148	264,904	202,284	191,480	162,427
Income Before Taxes	197,080	200,617	192,235	182,478	145,452	105,796	80,635	61,070
Income Taxes	67,310	67,845	69,760	67,880	57,456	42,617	35,075	26,558
Net Income	127,739	124,701	118,973	111,687	82,929	62,241	44,745	30,031
Average Shares	94,558	94,178	93,932	91,226	82,868	82,322	68,392	58,830
Balance Sheet								
Current Assets	2,301,609	2,286,689	1,879,645	1,764,136	1,588,665	1,328,748	921,516	951,616
Total Assets	4,668,553	4,469,802	3,594,173	3,532,801	3,137,181	2,690,314	1,946,576	1,762,695
Current Liabilities	2,096,039	1,752,957	1,664,750	1,691,708	1,497,304	1,199,475	786,278	858,562
Long-Term Obligations	830,106	1,168,666	576,690	574,970	643,343	651,256	551,840	377,721
Total Liabilities	3,247,094	3,174,149	2,448,441	2,457,766	2,308,769	1,985,872	1,430,893	1,301,025
Stockholders' Equity	1,421,459	1,295,653	1,145,732	1,075,035	828,412	704,442	515,683	461,670
Shares Outstanding	95,020	89,162	92,966	92,966	83,444	81,196	39,438	37,112
Statistical Record								
Return on Assets %	2.80	3.09	3.34	3.34	2.85	2.68	2.41	1.97
Return on Equity %	9.40	10.22	10.71	11.70	10.82	10.20	9.16	6.71
EBITDA Margin %	2.93	3.17	3.29	3.24	3.05	2.72	3.08	3.33
Net Margin %	0.99	1.11	1.17	1.13	0.96	0.84	0.72	0.61
Asset Turnover	2.84	2.79	2.86	2.96	2.98	3.21	3.35	3.20
Current Ratio	1.10	1.30	1.13	1.04	1.06	1.11	1.17	1.11
Debt to Equity	0.58	0.90	0.50	0.53	0.78	0.92	1.07	0.82
Price Range	24.42-17.46	24.21-18.95	19.73-12.87	16.15-11.55	15.65-4.94	15.57-5.71	13.10-3.31	5.19-3.06
P/E Ratio	18.09-12.93	18.34-14.36	15.66-10.21	13.13-9.39	15.65-4.94	20.48-7.51	19.85-5.02	10.17-6.00
Average Yield %	1.43	1.25	1.41	1.46	0.50	...	...	...

Address: 2555 Telegraph Road,	Web Site: www.penskeautomotive.com	Auditors: Deloitte & Touche LLP
Bloomfield Hills, MI 48302-0954	Officers: Roger S. Penske - Chmn., C.E.O. Samuel X.	Investor Contact: 248-648-2540
Telephone: 248-648-2500	DiFeo - Pres., C.O.O.	Transfer Agents: ComputerShare
Fax: 248-648-2525		Investor Services, Providence, RI

PFIZER INC

Exchange	Symbol	Price	52Wk Range	Yield	P/E	Div Acheiver
NYS	PFE	$20.93 (3/31/2008)	27.68-20.50	6.12	17.89	40 Years

*7 Year Price Score 64.17 *NYSE Composite Index=100 *12 Month Price Score 97.90

Interim Earnings (Per Share)

Qtr.	Mar	Jun	Sep	Dec
2003	0.76	(0.48)	0.29	0.08
2004	0.30	0.38	0.44	0.37
2005	0.04	0.47	0.22	0.37
2006	0.56	0.33	0.46	1.31
2007	0.48	0.18	0.11	0.39

Interim Dividends (Per Share)

Amt	Decl	Ex	Rec	Pay
0.29Q	4/26/2007	5/9/2007	5/11/2007	6/5/2007
0.29Q	6/28/2007	8/8/2007	8/10/2007	9/5/2007
0.29Q	10/25/2007	11/7/2007	11/9/2007	12/4/2007
0.32Q	12/17/2007	2/6/2008	2/8/2008	3/4/2008

Indicated Div: $1.28 (Div. Reinv. Plan)

Valuation Analysis

		Institutional Holding	
Forecast P/E	11.42	No of Institutions	
	(1/10/2007)	1443	
Market Cap	$141.5 Billion	Shares	
Book Value	65.0 Billion	4,849,101,824	
Price/Book	2.18	% Held	
Price/Sales	2.92	68.42	

TRADING VOLUME (thousand shares)

Business Summary: Pharmaceuticals (MIC: 9.1 SIC: 2834 NAIC: 325412)

Pfizer discovers, develops, produces and markets prescription medicines for humans and animals. Co. has two segments: Pharmaceutical, which develops and produces products that treat cardiovascular and metabolic diseases, central nervous system disorders, arthritis and pain, infectious and respiratory diseases, urogenital conditions, cancer, eye disease, endocrine disorders and allergies; and Animal Health, which discovers, develops and sells products for the prevention and treatment of diseases in livestock and companion animals. Co. also operates several other businesses, such as the manufacture of empty soft-gelatin capsules, contract manufacturing and bulk pharmaceutical chemicals.

Recent Developments: For the year ended Dec 31 2007, income from continuing operations decreased 25.5% to US$8.21 billion from US$11.02 billion a year earlier. Net income decreased 57.9% to US$8.14 billion from US$19.34 billion in the prior year. Revenues were US$48.42 billion, up 0.1% from US$48.37 billion the year before. Direct operating expenses rose 47.1% to US$11.24 billion from US$7.64 billion in the comparable period the year before. Indirect operating expenses increased 3.7% to US$29.66 billion from US$28.61 billion in the equivalent prior-year period.

Prospects: On Feb 20 2008, Co. announced that it has agreed to acquire Encysive Pharmaceuticals Inc., a publicly held biopharmaceutical company, for $195.0 million. Co. expects the transaction, which should add growing, near-term revenue from the European market and expand its presence in the cardio-respitory arena, to close in the second quarter of 2008. Meanwhile, based on the projected affect of the loss of exclusivity in the U.S. of Norvasc in Mar 2007 and Zyrtec/Zyrtec D in Jan 2008, as well as the expiration of the U.S. basic patent for Camptosar in Feb 2008, Co. is expecting full-year 2008 revenue of $47.00 billion to $49.00 billion with diluted earnings of $1.78 to $1.93 per common share.

Financial Data

(US$ in Thousands)	12/31/2007	12/31/2006	12/31/2005	12/31/2004	12/31/2003	12/31/2002	12/31/2001	12/31/2000
Earnings Per Share	1.17	2.66	1.09	1.49	0.54	1.46	1.22	0.59
Cash Flow Per Share	1.93	2.43	2.00	2.16	1.63	1.60	1.49	0.99
Tang Book Value Per Share	3.41	3.65	1.89	1.48	0.85	3.04	2.64	2.26
Dividends Per Share	1.160	0.960	0.760	0.680	0.600	0.520	0.440	0.360
Dividend Payout %	99.15	36.09	69.72	45.64	111.11	35.62	36.07	61.02
Income Statement								
Total Revenue	48,418,000	48,371,000	51,298,000	52,516,000	45,188,000	32,373,000	32,259,000	29,574,000
EBITDA	13,379,000	17,884,000	16,841,000	19,101,000	7,265,000	12,701,000	11,124,000	6,577,000
Income Before Taxes	9,278,000	13,028,000	11,534,000	14,007,000	3,263,000	11,796,000	10,329,000	5,781,000
Income Taxes	1,023,000	1,992,000	3,424,000	2,665,000	1,621,000	2,609,000	2,561,000	2,049,000
Net Income	8,144,000	19,337,000	8,085,000	11,361,000	3,910,000	9,126,000	7,788,000	3,726,000
Average Shares	6,939,001	7,274,001	7,411,001	7,614,001	7,286,001	6,240,999	6,360,999	6,367,999
Balance Sheet								
Current Assets	46,849,000	46,949,000	41,896,000	39,694,000	29,741,000	24,781,000	18,450,000	17,187,000
Total Assets	115,268,000	114,837,000	117,565,000	123,684,000	116,775,000	46,356,000	39,153,000	33,510,000
Current Liabilities	21,835,000	21,389,000	28,448,000	26,458,000	23,657,000	18,555,000	13,640,000	11,981,000
Long-Term Obligations	7,314,000	5,546,000	6,347,000	7,279,000	5,755,000	3,140,000	2,609,000	1,123,000
Total Liabilities	50,144,000	43,479,000	51,938,000	55,406,000	51,398,000	26,406,000	20,860,000	17,434,000
Stockholders' Equity	65,010,000	71,358,000	65,627,000	68,278,000	65,377,000	19,950,000	18,293,000	16,076,000
Shares Outstanding	6,761,001	7,124,001	7,361,001	7,473,001	7,629,001	6,161,999	6,276,999	6,313,999
Statistical Record								
Return on Assets %	7.08	16.64	6.70	9.42	4.79	21.35	21.44	13.74
Return on Equity %	11.94	28.23	12.08	16.95	9.16	47.73	45.32	29.77
EBITDA Margin %	27.63	36.97	32.83	36.37	16.08	39.23	34.48	22.24
Net Margin %	16.82	39.98	15.76	21.63	8.65	28.19	24.14	12.60
Asset Turnover	0.42	0.42	0.43	0.44	0.55	0.76	0.89	1.09
Current Ratio	2.15	2.20	1.47	1.50	1.26	1.34	1.35	1.43
Debt to Equity	0.11	0.08	0.10	0.11	0.09	0.16	0.14	0.07
Price Range	27.68-22.30	28.47-22.41	28.90-20.60	38.85-24.29	36.18-28.56	42.15-25.92	46.31-35.67	49.00-30.00
P/E Ratio	23.66-19.06	10.70-8.42	26.51-18.90	26.07-16.30	67.00-52.89	28.87-17.75	37.81-29.24	83.05-50.85
Average Yield %	4.59	3.74	2.97	2.06	1.88	1.49	1.06	0.87

Address: 235 East 42nd Street, New York, NY 10017-5755
Telephone: 212-573-2323
Fax: 212-573-2641

Web Site: www.pfizer.com
Officers: Henry A. McKinnell - Chmn., Pres., C.E.O. Jeffery B. Kindler - Exec. V.P., Gen. Couns.

Auditors: KPMG LLP
Transfer Agents: EquiServe Trust Company, N.A., Jersey City, NJ

Exchange	Symbol	Price	52Wk Range	Yield	P/E
NYS	PCG	$36.82 (3/31/2008)	52.11-36.46	4.24	13.24

*7 Year Price Score 120.36   *NYSE Composite Index=100   *12 Month Price Score 92.27

Interim Earnings (Per Share)

Qtr.	Mar	Jun	Sep	Dec
2003	(0.93)	0.56	1.24	0.10
2004	7.21	0.88	0.53	2.02
2005	0.54	0.70	0.65	0.48
2006	0.60	0.65	1.09	0.43
2007	0.71	0.74	0.77	0.56

Interim Dividends (Per Share)

Amt	Decl	Ex	Rec	Pay
0.36Q	6/20/2007	6/28/2007	7/2/2007	7/15/2007
0.36Q	9/19/2007	9/27/2007	10/1/2007	10/15/2007
0.36Q	12/19/2007	12/27/2007	12/31/2007	1/15/2008
0.39Q	2/22/2008	3/27/2008	3/31/2008	4/15/2008

Indicated Div: $1.56

Valuation Analysis   **Institutional Holding**

Forecast P/E	N/A	No of Institutions
		371
Market Cap	$14.0 Billion	Shares
Book Value	8.6 Billion	229,176,016
Price/Book	1.63	% Held
Price/Sales	1.06	65.33

Business Summary: Electricity (MIC: 7.1 SIC: 4931 NAIC: 221122)

PG&E is an energy-based holding company that conducts its business principally through Pacific Gas and Electric Company (the Utility), a public utility operating in northern and central California. The Utility engages in the businesses of electricity and natural gas distribution, electricity generation, procurement and transmission, and natural gas procurement, transportation and storage. The Utility served approximately 5.1 million electricity distribution customers and approximately 4.3 million natural gas distribution customers as of Dec 31 2007. The Utility's revenues are generated mainly through the sale and delivery of electricity and natural gas.

Recent Developments: For the year ended Dec 31 2007, income from continuing operations increased 1.5% to US$1.01 billion from US$991.0 million a year earlier. Net income increased 1.5% to US$1.01 billion from US$991.0 million in the prior year. Revenues were US$13.24 billion, up 5.6% from US$12.54 billion the year before. Operating income was unchanged at US$2.11 billion versus the prior year. Direct operating expenses rose 6.6% to US$11.12 billion from US$10.43 billion in the comparable period the year before.

Prospects: For 2008, Co. is projecting earnings from operations in the range of $2.90 to $3.00 per share. Going forward, Co. expects its electric operating revenues for the period 2008 through 2010 to increase, as authorized by the California Public Utilities Commission in the 2007 General Rate Case and by the Federal Energy Regulatory Commission in future transmission owner rate cases. Moreover, Co. intends to obtain regulatory approval for potential investments in electric transmission projects including the proposed 500 kilovolt Central California Clean Energy Transmission project and a proposed new high voltage transmission line to run between Northern California and British Columbia, Canada.

Financial Data

(US$ in Thousands)	12/31/2007	12/31/2006	12/31/2005	12/31/2004	12/31/2003	12/31/2002	12/31/2001	12/31/2000
Earnings Per Share	2.78	2.76	2.37	10.57	1.06	(2.36)	3.02	(9.29)
Cash Flow Per Share	7.25	7.84	6.48	5.89	6.50	1.44	14.60	(2.14)
Tang Book Value Per Share	22.53	20.87	19.60	20.62	10.12	8.91	13.22	8.19
Dividends Per Share	1.440	1.320	1.230	...	...	...	...	0.900
Dividend Payout %	51.80	47.83	51.90	...	...	...	...	...
Income Statement								
Total Revenue	13,237,000	12,539,000	11,703,000	11,080,000	10,435,000	12,495,000	22,959,000	26,232,000
EBITDA	3,913,000	3,804,000	3,686,000	8,517,000	3,556,000	2,531,000	3,766,000	(1,171,000)
Income Before Taxes	1,545,000	1,545,000	1,448,000	6,286,000	1,249,000	(100,000)	1,698,000	(5,352,000)
Income Taxes	539,000	554,000	544,000	2,466,000	458,000	(43,000)	608,000	(2,028,000)
Net Income	1,006,000	991,000	917,000	4,504,000	420,000	(874,000)	1,099,000	(3,364,000)
Average Shares	353,000	349,000	397,000	426,000	413,000	371,000	363,000	362,000
Balance Sheet								
Net PPE	23,656,000	21,785,000	19,955,000	18,989,000	18,107,000	16,928,000	19,167,000	16,591,000
Total Assets	36,648,000	34,803,000	34,074,000	34,540,000	30,175,000	33,696,000	35,862,000	35,291,000
Long-Term Obligations	9,753,000	8,633,000	9,542,000	7,903,000	4,184,000	5,505,000	8,747,000	6,476,000
Total Liabilities	27,843,000	26,740,000	26,604,000	25,621,000	25,674,000	29,603,000	30,760,000	31,339,000
Stockholders' Equity	8,553,000	7,811,000	7,218,000	8,633,000	4,215,000	3,613,000	4,322,000	3,172,000
Shares Outstanding	379,646	374,181	368,268	418,616	416,520	405,486	326,926	387,193
Statistical Record								
Return on Assets %	2.82	2.88	2.67	13.88	1.32	N.M.	3.09	N.M.
Return on Equity %	12.30	13.19	11.57	69.92	10.73	N.M.	29.33	N.M.
EBITDA Margin %	29.56	30.34	31.50	76.87	34.08	20.26	16.40	N.M.
Net Margin %	7.60	7.90	7.84	40.65	4.02	(6.99)	4.79	(12.82)
PPE Turnover	0.58	0.60	0.60	0.60	0.60	0.69	1.28	1.57
Asset Turnover	0.37	0.36	0.34	0.34	0.33	0.36	0.65	0.80
Debt to Equity	1.14	1.11	1.32	0.92	0.99	1.52	2.02	2.04
Price Range	52.11-42.81	47.98-36.35	39.90-31.92	34.15-26.23	27.93-12.00	23.68-8.19	19.95-6.90	31.64-18.25
P/E Ratio	18.74-15.40	17.38-13.17	16.84-13.47	3.23-2.48	26.35-11.32	...	6.61-2.28	...
Average Yield %	3.07	3.23	3.40	...	...	...	...	3.61

Address: One Market, Spear Tower, Suite 2400, San Francisco, CA 94105 **Telephone:** 415-267-7000 **Fax:** 415-267-7265	**Web Site:** www.pgecorp.com **Officers:** Robert D. Glynn Jr. - Chmn, Peter A. Darbee - Pres., C.E.O.	**Auditors:** Deloitte & Touche LLP **Investor Contact:** 415-267-7080 **Transfer Agents:** Mellon Investor Services, South Hackensack, NJ

PHILLIPS-VAN HEUSEN CORP.

Exchange	Symbol	Price	52Wk Range	Yield	P/E
NYS	PVH	$37.92 (3/31/2008)	61.77-31.78	0.40	11.81

*7 Year Price Score 143.55 *NYSE Composite Index=100 *12 Month Price Score 83.17

Interim Earnings (Per Share)

Qtr.	Apr	Jul	Oct	Jan
2003-04	(0.22)	0.13	0.34	(0.48)
2004-05	(0.12)	0.24	0.52	0.35
2005-06	0.46	0.16	0.73	0.41
2006-07	0.87	0.33	0.89	0.45
2007-08	0.92	0.68	1.05	0.56

Interim Dividends (Per Share)

Amt	Decl	Ex	Rec	Pay
0.037Q	5/4/2007	5/21/2007	5/23/2007	6/19/2007
0.037Q	8/7/2007	8/21/2007	8/23/2007	9/13/2007
0.037Q	10/25/2007	11/16/2007	11/20/2007	12/13/2007
0.037Q	3/18/2008	3/19/2008	3/24/2008	3/31/2008

Indicated Div: $0.15

Valuation Analysis **Institutional Holding**

Forecast P/E	N/A	No of Institutions
		230
Market Cap	$1.9 Billion	Shares
Book Value	956.3 Million	55,016,580
Price/Book	2.03	% Held
Price/Sales	0.80	98.44

TRADING VOLUME (thousand shares)

Business Summary: Apparel (MIC: 4.4 SIC: 2321 NAIC: 315211)

Phillips-Van Heusen designs and markets branded dress shirts, sportswear, neckwear, and, to a lesser degree, footwear and other related products. As of Feb 3 2008, Co.'s portfolio of brands included its owned brands, Calvin Klein Collection, ck Calvin Klein, Calvin Klein, Van Heusen, IZOD, Arrow, G.H. Bass & Co., Bass and Eagle, and its licensed brands, Geoffrey Beene, BCBG Max Azria, BCBG Attitude, Chaps, Sean John, Donald J Trump Signature Collection, Kenneth Cole New York, Kenneth Cole Reaction, MICHAEL Michael Kors, Michael Kors Collection, DKNY, Tommy Hilfiger, Nautica, Perry Ellis Portfolio, Ted Baker, Ike Behar, Jones New York, Hart Schaffner Marx, and various private label brands.

Recent Developments: For the year ended Feb 3 2008, net income increased 18.1% to US$183.3 million from US$155.2 million in the prior year. Revenues were US$2.43 billion, up 16.0% from US$2.09 billion the year before. Direct operating expenses rose 16.3% to US$1.23 billion from US$1.06 billion in the comparable period the year before. Indirect operating expenses increased 15.0% to US$879.2 million from US$764.6 million in the equivalent prior-year period.

Prospects: For the fiscal year ending Feb 1 2009, Co. is forecasting total revenue to be approximately $2.60 billion, representing an increase of 7.0% to 8.0% over its previous fiscal year's level. Specifically, Co. is targeting revenue growth for its Calvin Klein licensing business to be about 10.0% and operating income to increase by 15.0% to 17.0%. In addition, Co. is anticipating revenue for its wholesale and retail businesses to improve in the range of 6.0% to 7.0% but foresees operating margin in this segment to decline by 150 to 200 basis points. In this respect, Co. is expecting earnings to be in the range of $3.30 to $3.40 per share, reflecting the ongoing challenging economic condition.

Financial Data
(US$ in Thousands)

	02/03/2008	02/04/2007	01/29/2006	01/30/2005	02/01/2004	02/02/2003	02/03/2002	02/04/2001
Earnings Per Share	3.21	2.64	1.85	1.14	(0.18)	1.08	0.38	1.10
Cash Flow Per Share	3.98	4.80	4.96	4.60	1.86	3.80	2.31	1.28
Tang Book Value Per Share	N.M.	N.M.	N.M.	N.M.	N.M.	5.73	5.53	5.67
Dividends Per Share	0.150	0.150	0.150	0.150	0.150	0.150	0.150	0.150
Dividend Payout %	4.67	5.68	8.11	13.16	...	13.89	39.47	13.64
Income Statement								
Total Revenue	2,425,175	2,090,648	1,908,848	1,641,428	1,582,011	1,404,973	1,431,892	1,455,548
EBITDA	358,420	303,208	242,327	161,901	87,848	94,713	66,873	90,588
Income Before Taxes	294,821	248,433	178,269	87,022	22,906	46,306	16,688	48,215
Income Taxes	111,502	93,204	66,581	28,407	8,200	15,869	6,008	18,115
Net Income	183,319	155,229	111,688	58,615	14,706	30,437	10,680	30,100
Average Shares	57,082	53,483	51,695	51,637	30,314	28,165	28,046	27,415
Balance Sheet								
Current Assets	836,219	785,003	663,648	491,692	488,912	451,127	405,300	436,381
Total Assets	2,172,394	1,998,485	1,747,439	1,549,582	1,439,283	771,700	708,933	724,364
Current Liabilities	360,148	283,166	224,616	208,193	182,864	127,439	114,358	138,095
Long-Term Obligations	399,552	399,538	399,525	399,512	399,097	249,012	248,935	248,851
Total Liabilities	1,216,111	1,056,328	974,851	920,810	878,380	499,473	443,206	455,803
Stockholders' Equity	956,283	942,157	610,662	364,026	296,157	272,227	265,727	268,561
Shares Outstanding	51,283	55,849	43,196	32,412	30,612	27,784	27,621	27,403
Statistical Record								
Return on Assets %	8.81	8.15	6.79	3.93	1.33	4.12	1.49	4.24
Return on Equity %	19.37	19.67	22.98	17.81	5.19	11.35	4.01	11.61
EBITDA Margin %	14.78	14.50	12.69	9.86	5.55	6.74	4.67	6.22
Net Margin %	7.56	7.42	5.85	3.57	0.93	2.17	0.75	2.07
Asset Turnover	1.17	1.10	1.16	1.10	1.43	1.90	2.00	2.05
Current Ratio	2.32	2.77	2.95	2.36	2.67	3.54	3.54	3.16
Debt to Equity	0.42	0.42	0.65	1.10	1.35	0.91	0.94	0.93
Price Range	61.77-32.63	55.66-33.05	36.59-24.37	27.50-16.61	18.12-11.20	16.06-10.43	18.45-8.50	14.05-5.88
P/E Ratio	19.24-10.17	21.08-12.52	19.78-13.17	24.12-14.57	...	14.87-9.66	48.55-22.37	12.77-5.34
Average Yield %	0.29	0.37	0.49	0.71	1.02	1.12	1.14	1.54

Address: 200 Madison Avenue, New York, NY 10016-3903	**Web Site:** www.pvh.com	**Auditors:** Ernst & Young LLP
Telephone: 212-381-3500	**Officers:** Bruce J. Klatsky - Chmn., C.E.O. Mark Weber - Pres., C.O.O.	**Transfer Agents:** The Bank of New York
Fax: 212-247-5309		

PIEDMONT NATURAL GAS CO., INC.

Exchange	Symbol	Price	52Wk Range	Yield	P/E	Div Acheiver
NYS	PNY	$26.26 (3/31/2008)	27.76-23.19	3.96	16.62	28 Years

*7 Year Price Score 95.01   *NYSE Composite Index=100   *12 Month Price Score 106.20

Interim Earnings (Per Share)

Qtr.	Jan	Apr	Jul	Oct
2004-05	0.93	0.52	(0.06)	(0.06)
2005-06	0.94	0.57	(0.16)	(0.08)
2006-07	0.94	0.69	(0.12)	(0.11)
2007-08	1.12	...	...	...

Interim Dividends (Per Share)

Amt	Decl	Ex	Rec	Pay
0.25Q	6/6/2007	6/20/2007	6/22/2007	7/13/2007
0.25Q	9/10/2007	9/20/2007	9/24/2007	10/15/2007
0.25Q	12/13/2007	12/20/2007	12/24/2007	1/15/2008
0.26Q	3/6/2008	3/20/2008	3/25/2008	4/15/2008

Indicated Div: $1.04 (Div. Reinv. Plan)

Valuation Analysis		Institutional Holding	
Forecast P/E	18.10	No of Institutions	
	(1/10/2007)	182	
Market Cap	$1.9 Billion	Shares	
Book Value	921.1 Million	33,236,368	
Price/Book	2.09	% Held	
Price/Sales	1.06	44.55	

Business Summary: Gas Utilities (MIC: 7.4 SIC: 4924 NAIC: 221210)

Piedmont Natural Gas Company is an energy services company primarily engaged in the distribution of natural gas to over 1.0 million residential, commercial and industrial customers in portions of North Carolina, South Carolina and Tennessee, including 62,000 customers served by municipalities who are Co.'s wholesale customers. Co. is also engaged in investing in joint venture, and energy-related businesses, including unregulated retail natural gas marketing, interstate natural gas storage and intrastate natural gas transportation. As of Oct 31 2007, Co. operated through two business segments, regulated utility and non-utility activities, both of which were conducted in the U.S.

Recent Developments: For the quarter ended Jan 31 2008, net income increased 16.3% to US$82.3 million from US$70.7 million in the year-earlier quarter. Revenues were US$788.5 million, up 16.4% from US$677.2 million the year before. Operating income was US$91.9 million versus US$81.7 million in the prior-year quarter, an increase of 12.5%. Direct operating expenses rose 19.8% to US$561.4 million from US$468.8 million in the comparable period the year before. Indirect operating expenses increased 6.5% to US$135.1 million from US$126.8 million in the equivalent prior-year period.

Prospects: Co.'s near-term outlook appears encouraging. In detail, Co.'s margin expansion is reflecting continued customer growth, colder weather structure as well as higher wholesale marketing and power generation margins. Also, Co. is benefiting from solid performance from its joint ventures, due to the start of commercial operations of Hardy Storage Company, LLC and strong results by SouthStar Energy Services LLC. Hence, for the fiscal year ending Oct 31 2008, Co. continues to anticipate earnings to be in the range of $1.45 to $1.55 per diluted share. Similarly, Co. is projecting gross utility construction expenditures to be approximately $168.5 million, primarily to address customer growth.

Financial Data
(US$ in Thousands)

	3 Mos	10/31/2007	10/31/2006	10/31/2005	10/31/2004	10/31/2003	10/31/2002	10/31/2001
Earnings Per Share	1.58	1.40	1.28	1.32	1.27	1.11	0.94	1.01
Cash Flow Per Share	2.89	3.14	1.37	2.39	2.07	1.49	1.66	2.49
Tang Book Value Per Share	11.88	11.18	11.07	10.91	10.52	8.61	8.91	8.63
Dividends Per Share	1.000	0.990	0.950	0.905	0.853	0.823	0.792	0.760
Dividend Payout %	63.29	70.71	74.22	68.56	67.13	74.10	83.86	75.25
Income Statement								
Total Revenue	788,470	1,711,292	1,924,628	1,761,091	1,529,739	1,220,822	832,028	1,107,856
Depn & Amortn	22,614	...	...	...	...	...	...	...
Income Taxes	54,587	66,494	63,498	63,408	63,147	48,617	39,794	41,875
Net Income	82,268	104,387	97,189	101,270	95,188	74,362	62,217	65,485
Average Shares	73,563	74,472	76,156	76,992	74,797	67,006	65,874	64,840
Balance Sheet								
Net PPE	2,159,896	2,142,544	2,076,464	1,939,806	1,850,796	1,813,414	1,159,601	1,115,862
Total Assets	3,079,438	2,820,318	2,733,939	2,602,490	2,335,877	2,296,406	1,445,088	1,393,658
Long-Term Obligations	824,773	824,887	825,000	625,000	660,000	460,000	462,000	509,000
Total Liabilities	2,158,313	1,941,944	1,851,014	1,718,298	1,480,979	1,666,211	855,492	833,279
Stockholders' Equity	921,125	878,374	882,925	884,192	854,898	630,195	589,596	560,379
Shares Outstanding	73,395	74,208	75,464	76,698	76,670	67,310	66,180	64,926
Statistical Record								
Return on Assets %	3.88	3.76	3.64	4.10	4.10	3.97	4.38	4.61
Return on Equity %	12.65	11.85	11.00	11.65	12.78	12.19	10.82	12.04
Net Margin %	10.43	6.10	5.05	5.75	6.22	6.09	7.48	5.91
PPE Turnover	0.86	0.81	0.96	0.93	0.83	0.82	0.73	1.01
Asset Turnover	0.61	0.62	0.72	0.71	0.66	0.65	0.59	0.78
Debt to Equity	0.90	0.94	0.93	0.71	0.77	0.73	0.78	0.91
Price Range	27.76-23.19	28.28-23.19	27.27-22.09	25.47-21.93	22.84-19.30	20.38-16.45	18.98-14.18	19.69-14.72
P/E Ratio	17.57-14.68	20.20-16.56	21.30-17.26	19.30-16.61	17.98-15.20	18.36-14.82	20.19-15.09	19.49-14.57
Average Yield %	3.86	3.78	3.86	3.83	4.06	4.44	4.56	4.51

Address: 4720 Piedmont Row Drive, Charlotte, NC 28210 Telephone: 704-364-3120 Fax: 704-731-4097	Web Site: www.piedmontng.com Officers: Thomas E. Skains - Chmn., Pres., C.E.O. David J. Dzuricky - Sr. V.P., C.F.O.	Auditors: Deloitte & Touche LLP Investor Contact: 704-731-4226 Transfer Agents: American Stock Transfer & Trust Company, New York, NY

PIER 1 IMPORTS INC.

Exchange	Symbol	Price	52Wk Range	Yield	P/E
NYS	PIR	$6.28 (3/31/2008)	8.93-3.28	N/A	N/A

*7 Year Price Score 35.28   *NYSE Composite Index=100   *12 Month Price Score 102.31

Interim Earnings (Per Share)

Qtr.	May	Aug	Nov	Feb
2004-05	0.13	0.12	0.22	0.21
2005-06	(0.14)	(0.12)	(0.08)	(0.12)
2006-07	(0.27)	(0.84)	(0.83)	(0.66)
2007-08	(0.64)	(0.49)	(0.11)	...

Interim Dividends (Per Share)

Amt	Decl	Ex	Rec	Pay
0.10Q	9/29/2005	10/31/2005	11/2/2005	11/16/2005
0.10Q	12/8/2005	1/30/2006	2/1/2006	2/15/2006
0.10Q	3/23/2006	5/1/2006	5/3/2006	5/17/2006
0.10Q	6/22/2006	7/31/2006	8/2/2006	8/16/2006

Valuation Analysis   Institutional Holding

Forecast P/E	N/A	No of Institutions
	(1/10/2007)	148
Market Cap	$555.8 Million	Shares
Book Value	253.7 Million	73,085,272
Price/Book	2.19	% Held
Price/Sales	0.37	83.29

TRADING VOLUME (thousand shares)

Business Summary: Retail - Furniture & Home Furnishings (MIC: 5.9 SIC: 5719 NAIC: 442299)

Pier 1 Imports is a retailer of decorative home furnishings, gifts and related items. Co. imports merchandise directly from over 40 countries and sells a variety of furniture collections, decorative accessories, bed and bath products, housewares and other seasonal assortments in its stores. Co. operates stores in the U.S. and Canada under the names Pier 1 Imports and Pier 1 Kids. Pier 1 Kids stores sell children's home furnishings and decorative accessories. As of Mar 3 2007, Co. operated 1,076 Pier 1 and 36 Pier 1 Kids stores in the U.S., 84 Pier 1 stores in Canada, and supported three franchised stores in the U.S.

Recent Developments: For the quarter ended Dec 1 2007, loss from continuing operations was US$10.0 million compared with a loss of US$72.7 million in the year-earlier quarter. Net loss amounted to US$10.0 million versus a net loss of US$72.7 million in the year-earlier quarter. Revenues were US$374.2 million, down 7.1% from US$402.7 million the year before. Operating loss was US$8.2 million versus a loss of US$71.0 million in the prior-year quarter. Direct operating expenses declined 10.7% to US$248.3 million from US$278.1 million in the comparable period the year before. Indirect operating expenses decreased 31.5% to US$134.0 million from US$195.6 million in the equivalent prior-year period.

Prospects: For the fiscal year ending Mar 1 2008, Co. expects to realize additional savings, and now anticipates savings to be at least $110.0 million. On an annualized basis, Co. is estimating on-going savings to be approximately $160.0 million. In addition, Co. foresees having approximately 1,025 stores in the U.S. and 83 stores in Canada, while approximately 90 to 100 stores is expected to be closed during fiscal 2008. Similarly, Co. is forecasting capital expenditures of about $10.0 million, mainly for existing stores. Meanwhile, for the fiscal quarter ended Mar 1 2008, Co. plans to close approximately 20 to 25 additional stores, while store openings in fiscal 2009 is projected to be minimal.

Financial Data

(US$ in Thousands)	9 Mos	6 Mos	3 Mos	03/03/2007	02/25/2006	02/26/2005	02/28/2004	03/01/2003
Earnings Per Share	(1.86)	(2.57)	(2.91)	(2.60)	(0.46)	0.68	1.29	1.36
Cash Flow Per Share	(1.27)	(0.68)	(1.06)	(1.18)	(0.74)	1.64	2.00	1.90
Tang Book Value Per Share	2.87	2.96	3.44	4.11	6.78	7.70	7.74	7.10
Dividends Per Share	...	...	0.100	0.200	0.400	0.400	0.300	0.210
Dividend Payout %	...	...	...	...	...	58.82	23.26	15.44
Income Statement								
Total Revenue	1,075,122	700,941	356,375	1,623,216	1,776,701	1,897,853	1,868,243	1,754,867
EBITDA	(54,462)	(62,686)	(38,747)	(148,511)	39,479	174,109	253,614	254,133
Depn & Amortn	41,248	27,172	13,577	...	...	...	...	...
Income Before Taxes	(107,426)	(97,815)	(56,281)	(228,123)	(41,912)	96,841	187,316	205,374
Income Taxes	2,323	1,972	97	(883)	(14,441)	36,384	69,315	75,988
Net Income	(109,749)	(99,787)	(56,378)	(227,645)	(39,804)	60,457	118,001	129,386
Average Shares	88,178	88,000	87,797	87,395	86,629	88,838	91,624	95,305
Balance Sheet								
Current Assets	604,901	579,334	590,521	633,968	774,923	660,690	698,151	663,601
Total Assets	853,576	838,481	861,138	916,170	1,169,861	1,075,749	1,052,173	967,487
Current Liabilities	317,417	295,012	290,124	284,585	288,848	289,009	279,888	243,589
Long-Term Obligations	184,000	184,000	184,000	184,000	184,000	19,000	19,000	25,000
Total Liabilities	599,908	576,333	557,742	555,353	579,879	411,380	368,542	323,551
Stockholders' Equity	253,668	262,148	303,396	361,117	589,982	664,369	683,631	643,936
Shares Outstanding	88,498	88,420	88,292	87,798	87,018	86,320	88,306	90,734
Statistical Record								
Return on Assets %	N.M.	N.M.	N.M.	N.M.	N.M.	5.70	11.72	14.18
Return on Equity %	N.M.	N.M.	N.M.	N.M.	N.M.	8.99	17.83	21.10
EBITDA Margin %	N.M.	N.M.	N.M.	N.M.	2.22	9.17	13.58	14.48
Net Margin %	N.M.	N.M.	N.M.	N.M.	N.M.	3.19	6.32	7.37
Asset Turnover	1.62	1.63	1.59	1.53	1.59	1.79	1.86	1.92
Current Ratio	1.91	1.96	2.04	2.23	2.68	2.29	2.49	2.72
Debt to Equity	0.73	0.70	0.61	0.51	0.31	0.03	0.03	0.04
Price Range	8.93-3.67	8.93-5.84	9.12-5.68	12.65-5.68	19.42-8.56	25.00-15.43	26.19-14.85	23.95-15.20
P/E Ratio	...	...	...	...	...	36.76-22.69	20.30-11.51	17.61-11.18
Average Yield %	...	...	1.45	2.57	2.99	2.11	1.46	1.08

Address: 100 Pier 1 Place, Fort Worth, TX 76102	**Web Site:** www.pier1.com	**Auditors:** Ernst & Young LLP
Telephone: 817-252-8000	**Officers:** Marvin J. Girouard - Chmn., C.E.O. Charles H. Turner - Exec. V.P., Fin., C.F.O., Treas.	**Transfer Agents:** Mellon Investor Services, Ridgefield Park, NJ
Fax: 817-334-0191		

PILGRIM'S PRIDE CORP.

Exchange	Symbol	Price	52Wk Range	Yield	P/E
NYS	PPC	$20.23 (3/31/2008)	40.59-20.23	0.44	57.80

*7 Year Price Score 112.03 *NYSE Composite Index=100   *12 Month Price Score 80.71

Interim Earnings (Per Share)

Qtr.	Dec	Mar	Jun	Sep
2004-05	0.73	0.85	1.28	1.12
2005-06	0.39	(0.48)	(0.31)	(0.11)
2006-07	(0.13)	(0.60)	0.94	0.50
2007-08	(0.49)	...	...	...

Interim Dividends (Per Share)

Amt	Decl	Ex	Rec	Pay
0.022Q	6/1/2007	6/13/2007	6/15/2007	6/29/2007
0.022Q	7/25/2007	9/12/2007	9/14/2007	9/28/2007
0.022Q	12/3/2007	12/12/2007	12/14/2007	12/28/2007
0.022Q	2/4/2008	3/12/2008	3/14/2008	3/28/2008

Indicated Div: $0.09

Valuation Analysis

		Institutional Holding	
Forecast P/E	12.81	No of Institutions	
	(1/10/2007)	147	
Market Cap	$1.3 Billion	Shares	
Book Value	1.1 Billion	42,715,120	
Price/Book	1.18	% Held	
Price/Sales	0.16	64.18	

Business Summary: Food (MIC: 4.1 SIC: 2015 NAIC: 311615)

Pilgrim's Pride is a producer of poultry in the U.S., Mexico and Puerto Rico. Co. has three segments: chicken products, turkey products and other products. Co.'s chicken products include prepared chicken parts that are sold either refrigerated or frozen and may be fully cooked, partially cooked or raw. Co. also sells fresh chicken, including prepackaged case-ready chicken, whole chickens and chicken parts in trays and bags, to the foodservice industry either pre-marinated or non-marinated. In addition, Co. sells turkey products such as fresh and frozen whole turkeys, as well as other products including other types of meat, table eggs, commercial feeds and related items and proteins.

Recent Developments: For the quarter ended Dec 29 2007, net loss amounted to US$32.3 million versus a net loss of US$8.7 million in the year-earlier quarter. Revenues were US$2.09 billion, up 56.5% from US$1.34 billion the year before. Operating income was US$2.4 million versus a loss of US$2.9 million in the prior-year quarter. Direct operating expenses rose 56.1% to US$1.99 billion from US$1.27 billion in the comparable period the year before. Indirect operating expenses increased 53.9% to US$105.3 million from US$68.4 million in the equivalent prior-year period.

Prospects: Co.'s results reflect the challenge posed by higher feed-ingredient costs, which has increased and is unlikely to decrease in 2008. Co. noted that these cost increases, coupled with labor shortages, higher production, freight and fuel costs, have offset most of the improvements in its market pricing and product mix. Nevertheless, Co. remains encouraged with its outlook as it continues to see growth in its consumer retail business due to increased penetration of supermarket meat and deli cases and new business from a number of large customers. Further, export demand remained solid and Co. has reduced its commodity pounds by upgrading product into higher-margin, value-added chicken items.

Financial Data

(US$ in Thousands)	3 Mos	09/29/2007	09/30/2006	10/01/2005	10/02/2004	09/27/2003	09/28/2002	09/29/2001
Earnings Per Share	0.35	0.71	(0.51)	3.98	2.05	1.36	0.35	1.00
Cash Flow Per Share	6.16	6.99	0.46	7.43	4.28	2.41	2.39	2.14
Tang Book Value Per Share	9.59	10.02	16.79	18.38	13.87	10.87	9.59	9.27
Dividends Per Share	0.090	0.090	1.090	0.060	0.060	0.060	0.060	0.060
Dividend Payout %	25.82	12.68	...	1.51	2.93	4.41	17.14	6.00
Income Statement								
Total Revenue	2,093,211	7,598,599	5,235,565	5,666,275	5,363,723	2,619,345	2,533,718	2,214,712
EBITDA	61,195	417,627	139,369	582,399	374,452	175,403	104,886	149,459
Depn & Amortn	55,923	...	...	...	...	...	...	...
Income Before Taxes	(24,555)	91,607	(36,317)	403,523	208,535	63,235	1,910	63,294
Income Taxes	7,774	44,590	(2,085)	138,544	80,195	7,199	(12,425)	21,263
Net Income	(32,329)	47,017	(34,232)	264,979	128,340	56,036	14,335	41,137
Average Shares	66,555	66,555	66,555	66,555	62,646	41,112	41,112	41,112
Balance Sheet								
Current Assets	1,365,996	1,284,334	1,105,674	999,415	1,017,228	490,708	443,918	443,272
Total Assets	3,836,712	3,774,236	2,426,868	2,511,903	2,245,989	1,257,484	1,227,890	1,215,695
Current Liabilities	925,661	905,202	576,837	594,814	633,502	279,589	264,881	239,922
Long-Term Obligations	1,404,062	1,318,558	554,876	518,863	535,866	415,965	450,161	467,242
Total Liabilities	2,698,484	2,602,015	1,309,540	1,288,305	1,323,033	810,788	833,566	834,763
Stockholders' Equity	1,138,228	1,172,221	1,117,328	1,223,598	922,956	446,696	394,324	380,932
Shares Outstanding	66,555	66,555	66,555	66,555	66,555	41,112	41,112	41,112
Statistical Record								
Return on Assets %	0.59	1.52	N.M.	11.17	7.21	4.52	1.18	4.29
Return on Equity %	2.07	4.12	N.M.	24.76	18.44	13.36	3.71	11.40
EBITDA Margin %	2.92	5.50	2.66	10.28	6.98	6.70	4.14	6.75
Net Margin %	N.M.	0.62	N.M.	4.68	2.39	2.14	0.57	1.86
Asset Turnover	2.12	2.46	2.13	2.39	3.01	2.11	2.08	2.31
Current Ratio	1.48	1.42	1.92	1.68	1.61	1.76	1.68	1.85
Debt to Equity	1.23	1.12	0.50	0.42	0.58	0.93	1.14	1.23
Price Range	40.59-23.73	40.59-23.64	37.60-21.00	39.36-26.03	31.67-12.50	13.80-5.28	14.84-8.50	15.35-6.06
P/E Ratio	115.97-67.80	57.17-33.30	...	9.89-6.54	15.45-6.10	10.15-3.88	42.40-24.29	15.35-6.06
Average Yield %	0.27	0.28	4.05	0.18	0.28	0.66	0.47	0.57

Address: 4845 U.S. Highway 271 North, P.O. Bos 93, Pittsburg, TX 75686 **Telephone:** 903-434-1000 **Fax:** 903-856-7505	**Web Site:** www.pilgrimspride.com **Officers:** Lonnie Pilgrim - Chmn. Clifford E. Butler - Vice-Chmn.	**Auditors:** Ernst & Young LLP **Transfer Agents:** Computershare Investor Services, LLC, Chicago, IL

PINNACLE WEST CAPITAL CORP.

Exchange	Symbol	Price	52Wk Range	Yield	P/E	Div Acheiver
NYS	PNW	$35.08 (3/31/2008)	50.52-34.61	5.99	11.50	14 Years

*7 Year Price Score 81.29   *NYSE Composite Index=100   *12 Month Price Score 94.34

TRADING VOLUME (thousand shares)

Interim Earnings (Per Share)

Qtr.	Mar	Jun	Sep	Dec
2003	0.28	0.61	1.20	0.54
2004	0.33	0.78	1.15	0.37
2005	0.27	0.28	1.05	0.20
2006	0.13	1.13	1.84	0.17
2007	0.16	0.78	2.07	0.03

Interim Dividends (Per Share)

Amt	Decl	Ex	Rec	Pay
0.525Q	4/18/2007	4/27/2007	5/1/2007	6/1/2007
0.525Q	7/18/2007	7/30/2007	8/1/2007	9/4/2007
0.525Q	10/18/2007	10/30/2007	11/1/2007	12/3/2007
0.525Q	1/23/2008	1/30/2008	2/1/2008	3/3/2008

Indicated Div: $2.10 (Div. Reinv. Plan)

Valuation Analysis | **Institutional Holding**

Forecast P/E	14.60	No of Institutions
	(1/10/2007)	303
Market Cap	£3.5 Billion	Shares
Book Value	3.5 Billion	84,380,728
Price/Book	1.00	% Held
Price/Sales	1.00	84.82

Business Summary: Electricity (MIC: 7.1 SIC: 4911 NAIC: 221121)

Pinnacle West Capital is a holding company that operates in two segments: regulated electricity and real estate. Co. owns all of the outstanding equity securities of Arizona Public Service Co. (APS), its key subsidiary. APS, a vertically-integrated electric utility, provides retail or wholesale electric service to most of the state of Arizona, with the major exceptions of about one-half of the Phoenix and Tucson metropolitan areas as well as Mohave County in northwestern Arizona. Co.'s other principal subsidiary include SunCor Development Co., while its other first-tier subsidiaries are APS Energy Services Co., Inc., El Dorado Investment Co. and Pinnacle West Marketing & Trading Co., LLC.

Recent Developments: For the year ended Dec 31 2007, income from continuing operations decreased 5.8% to US$298.8 million from US$317.1 million a year earlier. Net income decreased 6.1% to US$307.1 million from US$327.3 million in the prior year. Revenues were US$3.52 billion, up 3.6% from US$3.40 billion the year before. Operating income was US$619.3 million versus US$618.9 million in the prior year, an increase of 0.1%. Direct operating expenses rose 4.3% to US$2.36 billion from US$2.27 billion in the comparable period the year before. Indirect operating expenses increased 4.9% to US$540.6 million from US$515.5 million in the equivalent prior-year period.

Prospects: Going forward, Co. now anticipates customer growth to average about 1.0% to 2.0% per year for 2008 through 2010 due to factors reflecting the economic conditions both nationally and in Arizona. Co. also foresees total retail electricity sales in kilowatt-hours will grow 1.0% to 2.0% on average per year for 2008 through 2010, excluding the effects of weather variations. Further, Co. estimates retail sales growth in 2008 to be below average due to the potential effects on customer usage from the economic conditions. Lastly, Co. expects its SunCor subsidiary's net income in 2008 to be about $20.0 million, reflecting a continuation of the slowdown in the western U.S. real estate markets.

Financial Data

(US$ in Thousands)	12/31/2007	12/31/2006	12/31/2005	12/31/2004	12/31/2003	12/31/2002	12/31/2001	12/31/2000
Earnings Per Share	3.05	3.27	1.82	2.66	2.63	1.76	3.68	3.56
Cash Flow Per Share	6.56	3.96	7.57	9.19	9.88	10.26	6.74	8.23
Tang Book Value Per Share	35.15	34.48	34.58	32.14	31.00	18.99	29.46	28.09
Dividends Per Share	2.100	2.025	1.925	1.825	1.725	1.625	1.525	1.425
Dividend Payout %	68.85	61.93	105.77	68.61	65.59	92.33	41.44	40.03
Income Statement								
Total Revenue	3,523,620	3,401,748	2,987,955	2,899,725	2,817,852	2,637,279	4,551,373	3,690,175
EBITDA	1,010,302	1,002,979	878,140	962,819	955,630	953,567	1,125,127	1,100,278
Income Before Taxes	449,700	473,561	350,055	364,075	336,136	353,253	540,902	526,184
Income Taxes	150,920	156,418	126,892	128,857	105,560	138,100	213,535	223,852
Net Income	307,143	327,255	176,267	243,195	240,579	149,408	312,166	302,332
Average Shares	100,835	100,010	96,590	91,532	91,405	84,964	84,930	84,935
Balance Sheet								
Net PPE	8,436,389	7,881,928	7,577,083	7,535,487	7,480,090	6,479,398	5,907,315	5,133,193
Total Assets	11,243,712	11,455,943	11,322,645	9,896,747	9,536,378	8,425,806	7,981,748	7,149,151
Long-Term Obligations	3,127,125	3,232,633	2,608,455	2,584,985	2,897,725	2,881,695	2,673,078	1,955,083
Total Liabilities	7,712,101	8,009,827	7,897,681	6,946,551	6,706,599	5,739,653	5,482,425	4,766,437
Stockholders' Equity	3,531,611	3,446,116	3,424,964	2,950,196	2,829,779	1,732,900	2,499,323	2,382,714
Shares Outstanding	100,485	99,958	99,057	91,793	91,287	91,255	84,824	84,824
Statistical Record								
Return on Assets %	2.71	2.87	1.66	2.50	2.68	1.82	4.13	4.38
Return on Equity %	8.80	9.53	5.53	8.39	10.55	7.06	12.79	13.14
EBITDA Margin %	28.67	29.48	29.39	33.20	33.91	36.16	24.72	29.82
Net Margin %	8.72	9.62	5.90	8.39	8.54	5.67	6.86	8.19
PPE Turnover	0.43	0.44	0.40	0.39	0.40	0.43	0.82	0.74
Asset Turnover	0.31	0.30	0.28	0.30	0.31	0.32	0.60	0.53
Debt to Equity	0.89	0.94	0.76	0.88	1.02	1.66	1.07	0.82
Price Range	51.60-37.10	50.92-38.70	46.39-39.85	45.41-36.85	40.24-29.07	46.16-22.49	50.37-38.10	51.88-25.94
P/E Ratio	16.92-12.16	15.57-11.83	25.49-21.90	17.07-13.85	15.30-11.05	26.23-12.78	13.69-10.35	14.57-7.29
Average Yield %	4.74	4.69	4.46	4.48	4.90	4.46	3.45	3.77

Address: 400 North Fifth Street, P.O. Box 53999, Phoenix, AZ 85072-3999 Telephone: 602-250-1000 Fax: 602-379-2625	Web Site: www.pinnaclewest.com Officers: William J. Post - Chmn. Jack E. Davis - Pres., C.E.O	Auditors: Deloitte & Touche LLP Investor Contact: 602-250-5668 Transfer Agents: Pinnacle West Capital Corporation, Phoenix, AZ

PIONEER NATURAL RESOURCES CO

Exchange	Symbol	Price	52Wk Range	Yield	P/E
NYS	PXD	$49.12 (3/31/2008)	54.38-38.54	0.57	16.05

*7 Year Price Score 109.42 *NYSE Composite Index=100 *12 Month Price Score 104.61

Interim Earnings (Per Share)

Qtr.	Mar	Jun	Sep	Dec
2003	0.71	0.65	1.62	0.47
2004	0.50	0.58	0.67	0.71
2005	0.58	1.28	0.88	1.06
2006	4.28	0.69	0.64	0.28
2007	0.24	0.30	0.84	1.69

Interim Dividends (Per Share)

Amt	Decl	Ex	Rec	Pay
0.13S	8/25/2006	9/26/2006	9/28/2006	10/12/2006
0.13S	2/27/2007	3/28/2007	3/30/2007	4/13/2007
0.14S	8/22/2007	9/26/2007	9/28/2007	10/12/2007
0.14S	2/13/2008	3/27/2008	3/31/2008	4/14/2008

Indicated Div: $0.28

Valuation Analysis **Institutional Holding**

Forecast P/E	17.72	No of Institutions
	(1/10/2007)	269
Market Cap	$5.8 Billion	Shares
Book Value	3.0 Billion	95,258,560
Price/Book	1.90	% Held
Price/Sales	3.15	77.13

TRADING VOLUME (thousand shares)

Business Summary: Oil and Gas (MIC: 14.2 SIC: 1311 NAIC: 211111)

Pioneer Natural Resources is an independent oil and gas exploration and production company with operations in the U.S. South Africa and Tunisia. Co.'s asset base is anchored by the Spraberry oil field located in West Texas, the Hugoton gas field located in Southwest Kansas, the Raton gas field located in southern Colorado and the West Panhandle gas field located in the Texas Panhandle. Co. also has exploration and development opportunities and/or oil and gas production activities in South Texas, North Texas, the Gulf of Mexico shelf, Mississippi and Alaska, and internationally. As of Dec 31 2007, Co. had total proved reserves of approximately 963.8 million barrels of oil equivalent.

Recent Developments: For the year ended Dec 31 2007, income from continuing operations increased 61.1% to US$242.0 million from US$150.2 million a year earlier. Net income decreased 49.6% to US$372.7 million from US$739.7 million in the prior year. Revenues were US$1.83 billion, up 22.2% from US$1.50 billion the year before. Direct operating expenses rose 20.5% to US$420.7 million from US$349.1 million in the comparable period the year before. Indirect operating expenses increased 23.4% to US$918.0 million from US$743.9 million in the equivalent prior-year period.

Prospects: For the first quarter of 2008, Co. is projecting production of 103,000 barrels of oil per day (BOEPD) to 109,000 BOEPD, along with continuous consistent growth, driven by increasing production from its Spraberry, Raton, Edwards and Tunisia areas. In addition, Co. is anticipating production costs to average $11.75 per barrel of oil equivalent (BOE) to $12.75 per BOE. Meanwhile, Co. is encouraged by the three completed acquisitions in December 2007, which expands its presence in the Spraberry and Raton fields while gaining additional acreage in the Barnett Shale. Collectively, these transactions will add more than 1,000 drilling locations and about 140.0 million BOE of resource potential.

Financial Data

(US$ in Thousands)	12/31/2007	12/31/2006	12/31/2005	12/31/2004	12/31/2003	12/31/2002	12/31/2001	12/31/2000
Earnings Per Share	3.06	5.81	3.80	2.46	3.46	0.23	1.00	1.53
Cash Flow Per Share	6.45	6.07	9.45	8.80	6.52	2.95	4.83	4.32
Tang Book Value Per Share	23.20	22.01	14.82	17.37	14.75	11.73	12.37	9.19
Dividends Per Share	0.270	0.250	0.220	0.200	...	...	...	...
Dividend Payout %	8.82	4.30	5.79	8.13	...	...	...	...
Income Statement								
Total Revenue	1,833,349	1,632,881	2,373,223	1,846,776	1,312,195	717,434	876,481	912,697
EBITDA	738,397	622,107	1,370,224	1,178,187	797,434	360,503	471,044	535,389
Income Before Taxes	354,624	308,988	715,459	479,213	330,776	54,122	107,765	158,499
Income Taxes	112,645	136,666	291,728	166,359	(64,403)	5,063	4,016	(6,000)
Net Income	372,728	739,731	534,568	312,854	410,592	26,713	99,996	152,181
Average Shares	121,659	127,608	141,417	127,488	118,513	114,288	99,714	99,378
Balance Sheet								
Current Assets	765,055	536,558	623,804	312,199	205,115	147,093	255,643	191,391
Total Assets	8,616,981	7,355,399	7,329,234	6,647,241	3,951,572	3,455,116	3,271,053	2,954,435
Current Liabilities	994,169	886,979	1,033,355	544,459	429,752	274,592	228,209	216,514
Long-Term Obligations	2,755,491	1,497,162	2,058,412	2,385,950	1,555,461	1,668,536	1,577,304	1,578,776
Total Liabilities	5,574,259	4,370,728	5,112,132	3,815,461	2,191,800	2,080,219	1,985,664	2,049,530
Stockholders' Equity	3,042,722	2,984,671	2,217,102	2,831,780	1,759,772	1,374,897	1,285,389	904,905
Shares Outstanding	117,727	121,502	128,588	144,831	119,287	117,252	103,936	98,415
Statistical Record								
Return on Assets %	4.67	10.07	7.65	5.89	11.09	0.79	3.21	5.16
Return on Equity %	12.37	28.44	21.18	13.59	26.20	2.01	9.13	18.07
EBITDA Margin %	40.28	38.10	57.74	63.80	60.77	50.25	53.74	58.66
Net Margin %	20.33	45.30	22.52	16.94	31.29	3.72	11.41	16.67
Asset Turnover	0.23	0.22	0.34	0.35	0.35	0.21	0.28	0.31
Current Ratio	0.77	0.60	0.60	0.57	0.48	0.54	1.12	0.88
Debt to Equity	0.91	0.50	0.93	0.84	0.88	1.21	1.23	1.74
Price Range	54.38-37.55	53.81-36.53	56.19-33.15	36.92-29.70	32.75-22.82	27.11-16.11	23.00-12.76	20.19-6.88
P/E Ratio	17.77-12.27	9.26-6.29	14.79-8.72	15.01-12.07	9.47-6.60	117.87-70.04	23.00-12.76	13.19-4.49
Average Yield %	0.59	0.58	0.49	0.60	...	...	...	...

Address: 5205 N. O'Connor Blvd., Suite 900, Irving, TX 75039
Telephone: 972-444-9001
Fax: 972-969-3587

Web Site: www.pioneernrc.com
Officers: Scott D. Sheffield - Chmn., Pres., C.E.O., Asst. Sec. Richard P. Dealy - Exec. V.P., C.F.O.

Auditors: Ernst & Young LLP
Investor Contact: 972-444-9001

PITNEY BOWES INC

Exchange	Symbol	Price	52Wk Range	Yield	P/E	Div Acheiver
NYS	PBI	$35.02 (3/31/2008)	48.66-34.06	4.00	21.10	24 Years

*7 Year Price Score 82.30   ***NYSE Composite Index=100**   ***12 Month Price Score 92.23**

Interim Earnings (Per Share)

Qtr.	Mar	Jun	Sep	Dec
2003	0.48	0.50	0.50	0.62
2004	0.54	0.58	0.58	0.35
2005	0.64	0.60	0.62	0.41
2006	0.67	(1.59)	0.66	0.71
2007	0.65	0.68	0.58	(0.25)

Interim Dividends (Per Share)

Amt	Decl	Ex	Rec	Pay
0.33Q	4/9/2007	5/16/2007	5/18/2007	6/12/2007
0.33Q	7/9/2007	8/15/2007	8/17/2007	9/12/2007
0.33Q	11/12/2007	11/20/2007	11/23/2007	12/12/2007
0.35Q	11/15/2007	2/13/2008	2/18/2008	3/12/2008

Indicated Div: $1.40 (Div. Reinv. Plan)

Valuation Analysis   **Institutional Holding**

Forecast P/E	15.02	No of Institutions	
	(1/10/2007)	481	
Market Cap	€7.6 Billion	Shares	
Book Value	643.3 Million	176,692,320	
Price/Book	11.68	% Held	
Price/Sales	1.23	80.21	

TRADING VOLUME (thousand shares)

Business Summary: Office Equipment Supplies (MIC: 11.12 SIC: 3579 NAIC: 423420)

Pitney Bowes provides equipment, supplies, software and services for end-to-end mailstream applications that allow its customers to optimize the flow of physical and electronic mail, documents and packages across their operations. At Dec 31 2007, Co. operated in two business groups; Mailstream Solutions, which included its U.S. mailing, international mailing, production mail and software segments; and Mailstream Services, which included its management services, marketing services, and mail services segments. Co.'s products and services are marketed via a network of direct sales offices in the U.S. and through its subsidiaries and independent distributors and dealers worldwide.

Recent Developments: For the year ended Dec 31 2007, income from continuing operations decreased 36.1% to US$361.2 million from US$565.7 million a year earlier. Net income increased 248.2% to US$366.8 million from US$105.3 million in the prior year. Revenues were US$6.13 billion, up 7.0% from US$5.73 billion the year before. Direct operating expenses rose 8.7% to US$2.87 billion from US$2.64 billion in the comparable period the year before. Indirect operating expenses increased 19.9% to US$2.36 billion from US$1.97 billion in the equivalent prior-year period.

Prospects: For 2008, Co. expects revenue growth of 6.0% to 9.0% and diluted earnings from continuing operations of $2.45 to $2.82 per share. Specifically, Co. expects its mix of revenue to continue to change, with a greater portion of revenue coming from diversified revenue streams related to fully featured smaller systems and a smaller portion from larger system sales. Also, Co. anticipates increased revenue from its Software and Mail Services segments, and expects to derive further cost savings from its recent acquisitions. Further, Co. expects several of its efforts that include streamlining its process and reducing its costs structure to yield $70.0 million in pre-tax annual benefits in 2008.

Financial Data
(US$ in Thousands)

	12/31/2007	12/31/2006	12/31/2005	12/31/2004	12/31/2003	12/31/2002	12/31/2001	12/31/2000
Earnings Per Share	1.66	0.47	2.27	2.05	2.11	1.97	1.97	2.41
Cash Flow Per Share	4.85	(1.29)	2.36	4.08	3.64	2.10	4.22	3.39
Tang Book Value Per Share	N M	N M	N.M.	N.M.	N.M.	0.10	1.05	4.34
Dividends Per Share	1.320	1.280	1.240	1.220	1.200	1.180	1.160	1.140
Dividend Payout %	79.52	272.34	54.63	59.51	56.87	59.90	58.88	47.30
Income Statement								
Total Revenue	6,129,795	5,730,018	5,492,183	4,957,440	4,576,853	4,409,758	4,122,474	3,880,868
EBITDA	1,285,723	1,490,344	1,407,345	1,174,944	1,174,840	1,062,849	1,268,006	1,316,382
Income Before Taxes	660,711	914,490	867,124	699,448	721,091	619,445	766,384	802,848
Income Taxes	280,222	335,004	340,546	218,922	226,244	181,739	252,064	239,723
Net Income	366,781	105,341	526,578	480,526	498,111	475,750	488,343	622,546
Average Shares	221,219	225,443	231,771	234,133	236,165	241,483	247,615	258,602
Balance Sheet								
Current Assets	3,319,613	2,918,670	2,742,315	2,693,086	2,513,175	2,552,625	2,556,608	2,626,708
Total Assets	9,549,943	8,480,420	10,621,382	9,820,580	8,891,388	8,732,314	8,318,471	7,901,266
Current Liabilities	3,556,439	2,746,833	2,910,897	3,294,477	2,646,969	3,350,309	3,083,042	2,881,577
Long-Term Obligations	3,802,075	3,847,617	3,849,623	2,798,894	2,840,943	2,316,844	2,419,150	1,881,947
Total Liabilities	8,522,475	7,397,066	9,009,441	8,220,499	7,494,026	7,568,987	7,117,116	6,306,291
Stockholders' Equity	643,303	699,189	1,301,941	1,290,081	1,087,362	853,327	891,355	1,284,975
Shares Outstanding	214,514	220,613	226,707	230,318	232,288	235,373	242,028	248,800
Statistical Record								
Return on Assets %	4.07	1.10	5.15	5.12	5.65	5.58	6.02	7.70
Return on Equity %	54.64	10.53	40.63	40.31	51.33	54.54	44.88	42.66
EBITDA Margin %	20.97	26.01	25.62	23.70	25.67	24.10	30.76	33.92
Net Margin %	5.98	1.84	9.59	9.69	10.88	10.79	11.85	16.04
Asset Turnover	0.68	0.60	0.54	0.53	0.52	0.52	0.51	0.48
Current Ratio	0.93	1.06	0.94	0.82	0.95	0.76	0.83	0.91
Debt to Equity	5.91	5.50	2.96	2.17	2.61	2.72	2.71	1.46
Price Range	48.66-36.94	47.68-40.34	47.30-40.49	46.88-39.23	42.44-29.90	43.92-28.80	43.33-31.78	52.45-24.89
P/E Ratio	29.31-22.25	101.45-85.83	20.84-17.84	22.87-19.14	20.11-14.17	22.29-14.62	21.99-16.13	21.77-10.33
Average Yield %	2.92	2.94	2.84	2.83	3.26	3.11	3.09	3.01

Address: 1 Elmcroft Road, Stamford, CT 06926-0700 **Telephone:** 203-356-5000 **Fax:** 203-351-7336	**Web Site:** www.pb.com **Officers:** Michael J. Critelli - Chmn., C.E.O. Murray D. Martin - Pres., C.O.O.	**Auditors:** PricewaterhouseCoopers **Transfer Agents:** First Chicago Trust Company of New York, Jersey City, NJ

PLAINS ALL AMERICAN PIPELINE, L.P.

Exchange	Symbol	Price	52Wk Range	Yield	P/E
NYS	PAA	$47.54 (3/31/2008)	65.05-44.13	7.15	9.43

*7 Year Price Score 117.32 *NYSE Composite Index=100 *12 Month Price Score 93.06

Interim Earnings (Per Share)

Qtr.	Mar	Jun	Sep	Dec
2003	0.46	0.42	0.19	(0.05)
2004	0.49	0.54	0.59	0.31
2005	0.43	0.74	0.79	0.65
2006	0.71	0.81	0.89	0.45
2007	0.61	0.78	0.66	2.99

Interim Dividends (Per Share)

Amt	Decl	Ex	Rec	Pay
0.813Q	4/17/2007	5/2/2007	5/4/2007	5/15/2007
0.83Q	7/19/2007	8/1/2007	8/3/2007	8/14/2007
0.84Q	10/18/2007	10/31/2007	11/2/2007	11/14/2007
0.85Q	1/16/2008	1/31/2008	2/4/2008	2/14/2008
		Indicated Div: $3.40		

Valuation Analysis

		Institutional Holding	
Forecast P/E	15.38	No of Institutions	
	(1/10/2007)	163	
Market Cap	$5.5 Billion	Shares	
Book Value	N/A	39,305,728	
Price/Book	N/A	% Held	
Price/Sales	0.27	35.93	

Business Summary: Oil and Gas (MIC: 14.2 SIC: 4619 NAIC: 486990)

Plains All American Pipeline is engaged in transportation, storage, terminalling and marketing of crude oil, refined products and liquefied petroleum gas (LPG) and other natural gas-related petroleum products. Co. operates in three segments: transportation, marketing and facilities. As of Dec 31 2007, Co. owned approximately 20,000 miles of active gathering and mainline crude oil pipelines located throughout the U.S and Canada, and approximately 23.0 million barrels of above-ground crude oil terminalling and storage facilities, including 62 transport and storage barges and 32 transport tugs through its 50.0% interest in Settoon Towing, LLC.

Recent Developments: For the year ended Dec 31 2007, net income increased 28.1% to US$365.0 million from US$285.0 million in the prior year. Revenues were US$20.39 billion, down 9.1% from US$22.45 billion the year before. Operating income was US$518.0 million versus US$355.0 million in the prior year, an increase of 45.9%. Direct operating expenses declined 10.6% to US$19.53 billion from US$21.86 billion in the comparable period the year before. Indirect operating expenses increased 47.0% to US$344.0 million from US$234.0 million in the equivalent prior-year period.

Prospects: In 2008, Co. intends spending $330.0 million on internal growth projects and also to continue developing its inventory of projects for implementation beyond 2008. In particular, Co. anticipates its 3.0 million barrel crude oil storage and terminal facility at the Patoka Interchange in southern Illinois to become operational in the second half of 2008, for a total cost of $77.0 million. Co. will also commence a project on the Bumstead facility to increase capacity by about 1.0 million barrels, add rail car storage capacity and improve the operation of the rail rack in 2008. Notably, Co. estimates the cost of the project to be $14.0 million, of which $10.0 million will be incurred in 2008.

Financial Data

(US$ in Thousands)	12/31/2007	12/31/2006	12/31/2005	12/31/2004	12/31/2003	12/31/2002	12/31/2001	12/31/2000
Earnings Per Share	5.04	2.88	2.72	1.89	1.00	1.34	1.13	2.64
Cash Flow Per Share	7.04	(3.39)	0.35	1.64	1.30	3.82	(0.80)	(0.97)
Dividends Per Share	3.283	2.870	2.575	2.303	2.188	2.112	1.950	1.825
Dividend Payout %	65.13	99.65	94.67	121.83	218.75	157.65	172.57	69.13
Income Statement								
Total Revenue	20,394,000	22,444,400	31,177,300	20,975,470	12,589,849	8,384,223	6,868,215	6,641,187
EBITDA	723,000	...	...	...	...	...	...	145,863
Income Before Taxes	381,000	...	...	...	...	...	...	92,649
Income Taxes	16,000	300	...	...	...	...	...	...
Net Income	365,000	285,100	217,800	130,006	59,448	65,292	44,179	77,502
Average Shares	114,000	81,900	70,500	63,277	53,400	45,546	37,528	34,386
Balance Sheet								
Current Assets	3,673,000	3,157,600	1,805,200	1,101,202	732,974	602,935	558,082	397,904
Total Assets	9,906,000	8,714,900	4,120,300	3,160,411	2,095,631	1,666,575	1,261,251	885,801
Current Liabilities	3,729,000	3,024,700	1,793,300	1,113,717	801,919	637,249	505,160	350,793
Long-Term Obligations	2,624,000	2,626,300	951,700	949,024	518,991	509,736	351,677	320,000
Total Liabilities	6,482,000	5,738,100	2,789,600	2,090,207	1,348,904	1,154,965	858,454	671,802
Shares Outstanding	115,981	109,405	73,768	67,293	58,331	49,577	43,252	34,386
Statistical Record								
Return on Assets %	3.92	4.44	5.98	4.93	3.16	4.46	4.12	7.33
EBITDA Margin %	3.55	...	...	...	...	...	...	2.20
Net Margin %	1.79	1.27	0.70	0.62	0.47	0.78	0.64	1.17
Asset Turnover	2.19	3.50	8.56	7.96	6.69	5.73	6.40	6.28
Current Ratio	0.98	1.04	1.01	0.99	0.91	0.95	1.10	1.13
Price Range	65.05-49.16	52.45-40.42	47.52-36.70	37.75-30.30	32.53-24.24	27.10-21.35	29.50-19.50	20.00-13.00
P/E Ratio	12.91-9.75	18.21-14.03	17.47-13.49	19.97-16.03	32.53-24.24	20.22-15.93	26.11-17.26	7.58-4.92
Average Yield %	5.80	6.28	6.18	6.81	7.55	8.53	7.90	10.42

Address: 333 Clay Street, Suite 1600, Houston, TX 77002-4001	Web Site: www.paalp.com	Auditors: PricewaterhouseCoopers LLP
Telephone: 713-646-4100	Officers: Greg L. Armstrong - Chmn., C.E.O. Harry N. Pefanis - Pres., C.O.O.	Investor Contact: 713-646-4491
Fax: 713-646-4572		Transfer Agents: American Stock Transfer & Trust Company

PLAINS EXPLORATION & PRODUCTION CO. L.P.

Exchange	Symbol	Price	52Wk Range	Yield	P/E
NYS	PXP	$53.14 (3/31/2008)	56.11-35.51	N/A	26.70

*7 Year Price Score N/A   *NYSE Composite Index=100   *12 Month Price Score 116.56

TRADING VOLUME (thousand shares)

Interim Earnings (Per Share)

Qtr.	Mar	Jun	Sep	Dec
2003	0.86	0.25	0.33	0.46
2004	0.26	0.32	(0.62)	0.46
2005	(2.66)	(0.61)	(0.41)	0.92
2006	(0.66)	(0.09)	3.50	4.93
2007	0.28	0.35	0.45	0.92

Interim Dividends (Per Share)

No Dividends Paid

Valuation Analysis **Institutional Holding**

Forecast P/E	N/A	No of Institutions
		196
Market Cap	$6.0 Billion	Shares
Book Value	3.3 Billion	65,057,000
Price/Book	1.80	% Held
Price/Sales	4.71	90.96

Business Summary: Oil and Gas (MIC: 14.2 SIC: 1311 NAIC: 211111)

Plains Exploration & Production is an independent oil and gas company mainly engaged in the activities of acquiring, developing, exploring and producing oil and gas properties in the U.S. Co.'s core areas of operations are in the Los Angeles and San Joaquin Basins onshore California; the Santa Maria Basin offshore California; the Piceance and Wind River Basins in the Rocky Mountains; the Permian Basin in West Texas and New Mexico; the Anadarko Basin in the Texas Panhandle; and the South Texas and Gulf Coast regions. At Dec 31 2007, Co. had estimated total proved reserves of about 689.9 million barrels of oil equivalent, of which 63.0% was comprised of oil and 51.0% was proved developed.

Recent Developments: For the year ended Dec 31 2007, net income decreased 73.4% to US$158.8 million from US$597.5 million in the prior year. Revenues were US$1.27 billion, up 25.0% from US$1.02 billion the year before. Operating income was US$419.6 million versus US$1.35 billion in the prior year, a decrease of 68.9%. Indirect operating expenses amounted to US$853.2 million compared with an income of US$329.9 million in the equivalent prior-year period.

Prospects: On Feb 29 2008, Co. sold 50.0% of its working interest in both oil and gas properties located in the Permian Basin, West Texas and New Mexico, as well as in the Piceance Basin in Colorado to Occidental Petroleum Corp.'s subsidiary for $1.53 billion in cash. Also, on the same date, Co. announced an agreement in which one of its subsidiaries will acquire oil and gas producing properties covering 67,929 gross acres/34,509 net acres in South Texas for $335.0 million from a private company. Thus, Co. has raised its 2008 full year average sales volume to 92,000 barrels of oil equivalent per day (BOEPD) to 96,000 BOEPD, due to the pending acquisition, which should close in second quarter 2008.

Financial Data
(US$ in Thousands)

	12/31/2007	12/31/2006	12/31/2005	12/31/2004	12/31/2003	12/31/2002	12/31/2001	12/31/2000
Earnings Per Share	1.99	7.64	(2.75)	0.14	1.78	1.08	2.20	1.19
Cash Flow Per Share	7.48	8.74	5.96	5.70	3.53	3.26	...	...
Tang Book Value Per Share	24.84	13.42	6.94	9.07	5.14	7.18	...	...
Income Statement								
Total Revenue	1,272,840	1,018,503	944,420	671,706	304,090	188,563	204,139	142,451
EBITDA	653,485	1,266,064	(101,534)	187,302	156,801	92,705	130,597	80,258
Income Before Taxes	268,499	984,607	(344,870)	2,023	80,539	42,969	89,081	45,514
Income Taxes	109,748	384,897	(130,858)	(6,817)	33,452	16,732	34,388	16,765
Net Income	158,751	597,528	(214,012)	8,840	59,411	26,237	53,171	28,749
Average Shares	79,808	78,234	77,710	64,014	33,409	24,201	...	...
Balance Sheet								
Current Assets	674,920	184,796	293,332	258,167	60,325	38,739	42,811	37,452
Total Assets	9,693,351	2,463,228	2,741,942	2,633,245	1,184,112	550,880	516,755	401,035
Current Liabilities	818,046	460,192	363,998	426,395	155,086	86,175	41,879	44,313
Long-Term Obligations	3,305,000	235,500	797,375	635,468	487,906	233,166	236,183	226,529
Total Liabilities	6,355,104	1,332,545	2,023,605	1,762,870	829,856	377,060	336,668	290,003
Stockholders' Equity	3,338,247	1,130,683	718,337	870,375	354,256	173,820	180,087	111,032
Shares Outstanding	112,798	72,442	78,411	77,147	40,299	24,224	...	...
Statistical Record								
Return on Assets %	2.61	22.96	N.M.	0.46	6.85	4.91	11.59	...
Return on Equity %	7.10	64.63	N.M.	1.44	22.50	14.83	36.53	...
EBITDA Margin %	51.34	124.31	N.M.	27.88	51.56	49.16	63.97	56.34
Net Margin %	12.47	58.67	N.M.	1.32	19.54	13.91	26.05	20.18
Asset Turnover	0.21	0.39	0.35	0.35	0.35	0.35	0.44	...
Current Ratio	0.83	0.40	0.81	0.61	0.39	0.45	1.02	0.85
Debt to Equity	0.99	0.21	1.11	0.73	1.38	1.34	1.31	2.04
Price Range	55.98-35.51	49.18-31.70	45.68-24.25	28.03-14.87	15.68-8.11	10.00-9.10	...	...
P/E Ratio	28.13-17.84	6.44-4.15	...	200.21-106.21	8.81-4.56	9.26-8.43	...	...

Address: 700 Milam Street, Suite 3100, Houston, TX 77002 **Telephone:** 713-579-6000 **Fax:** 713-579-6500	**Web Site:** www.plainsxp.com **Officers:** James C. Flores - Chmn., Pres., C.E.O. Stephen A. Thorington - Exec. V.P., C.F.O.	**Auditors:** PricewaterhouseCoopers LLP **Transfer Agents:** American Stock Transfer & Trust, New York, NY

PLANTRONICS, INC.

Exchange	Symbol	Price	52Wk Range	Yield	P/E
NYS	PLT	$19.31 (3/31/2008)	32.71-17.82	1.04	15.45

*7 Year Price Score 74.94   *NYSE Composite Index=100   *12 Month Price Score 83.54

Interim Earnings (Per Share)

Qtr.	Jun	Sep	Dec	Mar
2004-05	0.44	0.49	0.48	0.51
2005-06	0.44	0.28	0.52	0.42
2006-07	0.25	0.26	0.32	0.21
2007-08	0.31	0.34	0.39	...

Interim Dividends (Per Share)

Amt	Decl	Ex	Rec	Pay
0.05Q	5/1/2007	5/16/2007	5/18/2007	6/8/2007
0.05Q	7/24/2007	8/8/2007	8/10/2007	9/10/2007
0.05Q	10/23/2007	11/7/2007	11/9/2007	12/10/2007
0.05Q	1/22/2008	2/7/2008	2/11/2008	3/10/2008

Indicated Div: $0.20

Valuation Analysis

Forecast P/E	15.09
	(1/10/2007)
Market Cap	$943.3 Million
Book Value	563.7 Million
Price/Book	1.67
Price/Sales	1.12

Institutional Holding

No of Institutions	148
Shares	47,318,960
% Held	98.80

Business Summary: Communications (MIC: 10.1 SIC: 3661 NAIC: 334210)

Plantronics is a designer, manufacturer and marketer of lightweight communications headsets, telephone headset systems and accessories for the business and consumer markets under the Plantronics brand. Co. also manufactures and markets computer and home entertainment sound systems, docking audio products, and a line of headsets and headphones for personal digital media under Co.'s Altec Lansing brand. In addition, Co. manufactures and markets under its Clarity brand specialty telephone products, such as telephones for the hearing impaired, and other related products for people with special communication needs.

Recent Developments: For the quarter ended Dec 31 2007, net income increased 25.8% to US$19.1 million from US$15.2 million in the year-earlier quarter. Revenues were US$232.8 million, up 8.1% from US$215.4 million the year before. Operating income was US$23.1 million versus US$16.8 million in the prior-year quarter, an increase of 37.6%. Direct operating expenses rose 3.3% to US$139.1 million from US$134.6 million in the comparable period the year before. Indirect operating expenses increased 10.3% to US$70.6 million from US$64.0 million in the equivalent prior-year period.

Prospects: On Nov 28 2007, Co. announced a plan to close and/or consolidate a number of facilities for its Audio Entertainment Group (AEG) to lower costs. Specifically, Co. plans to close AEG's manufacturing facility in Dongguan, China; shut down a Hong Kong research and development, sales and procurement office; and consolidate procurement, research and development activities for AEG in a new Shenzhen, China site, which it expects to complete by Mar 2008. In addition to these cost cutting activities, Co. believes a return to profitability for AEG is dependent on developing significant new products to refresh the product line. Co.'s goal remains to achieve profitability for AEG by the Dec 2008 quarter.

Financial Data

(US$ in Thousands)	9 Mos	6 Mos	3 Mos	03/31/2007	03/31/2006	03/31/2005	03/31/2004	03/31/2003
Earnings Per Share	1.25	1.18	1.10	1.04	1.66	1.92	1.31	0.89
Cash Flow Per Share	2.47	2.06	1.71	1.54	1.66	1.94	1.61	1.11
Tang Book Value Per Share	8.13	6.66	7.15	6.74	5.29	8.12	6.02	3.07
Dividends Per Share	0.200	0.200	0.200	0.200	0.200	0.150	...	...
Dividend Payout %	16.00	16.95	18.18	19.23	12.05	7.81	...	...
Income Statement								
Total Revenue	647,543	414,719	206,495	800,154	750,394	559,995	416,965	337,508
EBITDA	86,720	54,355	26,383	90,638	135,154	143,060	98,852	68,260
Depn & Amortn	21,012	13,974	7,102	...	...	...	...	...
Income Before Taxes	65,708	40,381	19,281	61,538	112,554	130,360	86,499	56,760
Income Taxes	15,103	8,884	4,306	11,395	31,404	32,840	24,220	15,284
Net Income	50,605	31,497	14,975	50,143	81,150	97,520	62,279	41,476
Average Shares	49,533	49,310	48,681	48,020	48,788	50,821	47,492	46,584
Balance Sheet								
Current Assets	463,135	374,861	399,523	374,861	328,349	406,694	310,627	153,017
Total Assets	733,845	651,304	675,278	651,304	612,249	487,929	368,252	205,209
Current Liabilities	120,912	116,457	109,627	116,457	126,929	71,171	61,230	49,412
Total Liabilities	170,139	154,497	159,441	154,497	176,628	82,210	68,949	58,279
Stockholders' Equity	563,706	496,807	515,837	496,807	435,621	405,719	299,303	146,930
Shares Outstanding	48,852	48,593	48,225	48,065	47,538	48,429	47,606	43,638
Statistical Record								
Return on Assets %	8.83	8.85	8.10	7.94	14.75	22.78	21.66	20.42
Return on Equity %	11.63	11.85	11.00	10.76	19.29	27.66	27.84	28.71
EBITDA Margin %	13.39	13.11	12.78	11.33	18.01	25.55	23.71	20.22
Net Margin %	7.81	7.59	7.25	6.27	10.81	17.41	14.94	12.29
Asset Turnover	1.22	1.29	1.24	1.27	1.36	1.31	1.45	1.66
Current Ratio	3.83	3.22	3.64	3.22	2.59	5.71	5.07	3.10
Price Range	32.71-19.45	29.92-17.62	26.22-14.83	38.62-14.83	39.46-27.05	47.57-32.95	43.38-14.61	23.64-12.78
P/E Ratio	26.17-15.56	25.36-14.93	23.84-13.48	37.13-14.26	23.77-16.30	24.78-17.16	33.11-11.15	26.56-14.36
Average Yield %	0.80	0.86	0.96	0.93	0.61	0.38	...	...

Address: 345 Encinal Street, Santa Cruz, CA 95060 **Telephone:** 831-426-5858 **Fax:** 831-426-6098	**Web Site:** www.plantronics.com **Officers:** Marv Tseu - Chmn. Kenneth Kannappan - Pres., C.E.O.	**Auditors:** PricewaterhouseCoopers LLP **Transfer Agents:** EquiServe

PLUM CREEK TIMBER CO., INC.

Exchange	Symbol	Price	52Wk.Range	Yield	P/E
NYS	PCL	$40.70 (3/31/2008)	48.22-38.44	4.13	25.28

*7 Year Price Score 102.13 *NYSE Composite Index=100 *12 Month Price Score 105.20

Interim Earnings (Per Share)

Qtr.	Mar	Jun	Sep	Dec
2003	0.18	0.31	0.25	0.30
2004	0.84	0.31	0.42	0.40
2005	0.66	0.37	0.52	0.36
2006	0.51	0.34	0.51	0.39
2007	0.25	0.34	0.34	0.68

Interim Dividends (Per Share)

Amt	Decl	Ex	Rec	Pay
0.42Q	5/1/2007	5/14/2007	5/16/2007	5/31/2007
0.42Q	7/31/2007	8/14/2007	8/16/2007	8/31/2007
0.42Q	10/31/2007	11/9/2007	11/14/2007	11/30/2007
0.42Q	2/5/2008	2/12/2008	2/14/2008	2/29/2008

Indicated Div: $1.68

Valuation Analysis / **Institutional Holding**

Forecast P/E	22.66 (1/10/2007)	No of Institutions	435
Market Cap	$7.0 Billion	Shares	96,915,368
Book Value	1.9 Billion	% Held	54.67
Price/Book	3.69		
Price/Sales	4.19		

Business Summary: Property, Real Estate & Development (MIC: 8.3 SIC: 6798 NAIC: 525930)

Plum Creek Timber Company is a private timberland owner in the U.S. Co. manages its timberlands in two segments: northern resources, consisting of timberlands in Maine, Michigan, Montana, New Hampshire, Oregon, Washington, West Virginia and Wisconsin; and southern resources, consisting of timberlands in Alabama, Arkansas, Florida, Georgia, Louisiana, Mississippi, North Carolina, Oklahoma, South Carolina and Texas. Co. also has a real estate segment that develops certain properties, internally and through joint ventures, and a manufactured products segment that converts logs to lumber, plywood and other wood products, and convert chips, sawdust and wood shavings to medium density fiberboard.

Recent Developments: For the year ended Dec 31 2007, income from continuing operations decreased 11.1% to US$280.0 million from US$315.0 million a year earlier. Net income decreased 11.0% to US$282.0 million from US$317.0 million in the prior year. Revenues were US$1.68 billion, up 3.0% from US$1.63 billion the year before. Revenues from property income rose 30.5% to US$402.0 million from US$308.0 million in the corresponding earlier year.

Prospects: During 2008, Co. anticipates that residential construction markets will remain weak and stabilize at recent levels with the potential for recovery in 2009. Meanwhile, Co. is seeing stable pricing and buyer interest levels within its rural real estate area. Thus, Co. expects its 2008 first quarter Real Estate segment sales to be between $75.0 million and $85.0 million and sales for the year 2008 to be between $320.0 million and $340.0 million. Overall, Co. projects its first quarter of 2008 earnings to be between $0.26 and $0.31 per share. For 2008, Co. plans to harvest between 18.5 million and 19.5 million tons of timber while estimating earnings to be between $1.15 and $1.40 per share.

Financial Data

(US$ in Thousands)	12/31/2007	12/31/2006	12/31/2005	12/31/2004	12/31/2003	12/31/2002	12/31/2001	12/31/2000
Earnings Per Share	1.61	1.75	1.92	1.97	1.04	1.26	2.58	1.91
Cash Flow Per Share	2.96	3.08	2.80	3.26	2.01	1.99	1.72	2.15
Tang Book Value Per Share	11.03	11.80	12.62	12.19	11.57	12.02	12.22	7.39
Dividends Per Share	1.680	1.600	1.520	1.420	1.400	1.490	2.850	2.280
Dividend Payout %	104.35	91.43	79.17	72.08	134.62	118.25	110.47	119.37
Income Statement								
Total Revenue	1,675,000	1,627,000	1,576,000	1,528,000	1,196,000	1,137,000	598,000	209,054
EBITDA	558,000	589,000	561,000	591,000	410,000	443,000	305,000	212,197
Income Before Taxes	277,000	328,000	339,000	366,000	186,000	235,000	196,000	131,254
Income Taxes	(3,000)	13,000	8,000	27,000	(6,000)	2,000	(142,000)	
Net Income	282,000	317,000	351,000	362,000	192,000	233,000	338,000	131,002
Average Shares	175,000	180,900	184,600	184,100	183,900	185,400	130,700	69,213
Balance Sheet								
Current Assets	456,000	513,000	574,000	499,000	405,000	378,000	306,000	194,635
Total Assets	4,664,000	4,661,000	4,812,000	4,378,000	4,387,000	4,289,000	4,122,000	1,250,068
Current Liabilities	303,000	281,000	375,000	184,000	168,000	155,000	149,000	179,705
Long-Term Obligations	2,376,000	2,198,000	2,019,000	1,853,000	2,031,000	1,839,000	1,667,000	559,798
Total Liabilities	2,763,000	2,572,000	2,487,000	2,138,000	2,268,000	2,067,000	1,875,000	743,400
Stockholders' Equity	1,901,000	2,089,000	2,325,000	2,240,000	2,119,000	2,222,000	2,247,000	506,668
Shares Outstanding	172,300	177,100	184,200	183,700	183,100	184,861	183,825	68,572
Statistical Record								
Return on Assets %	6.05	6.69	7.70	8.24	4.43	5.54	12.58	10.52
Return on Equity %	14.14	14.36	15.51	16.56	8.85	10.43	24.55	25.30
EBITDA Margin %	33.31	36.20	35.60	38.68	34.28	38.96	51.00	101.50
Net Margin %	16.84	19.48	22.46	23.69	16.05	20.49	56.52	63.09
Asset Turnover	0.36	0.34	0.34	0.35	0.28	0.27	0.22	0.17
Current Ratio	1.50	1.83	1.53	2.71	2.41	2.44	2.05	1.08
Debt to Equity	1.25	1.05	0.87	0.83	0.96	0.83	0.74	1.10
Price Range	48.22-37.59	39.75-33.51	39.34-34.19	39.32-28.50	30.54-21.15	31.80-19.11	29.99-23.35	29.50-22.06
P/E Ratio	29.95-23.35	22.71-19.15	20.49-17.81	19.96-14.47	29.37-20.34	25.24-15.17	11.62-9.05	15.45-11.55
Average Yield %	4.04	4.46	4.14	4.31	5.56	5.44	10.57	9.22

Address: 999 Third Avenue, Suite 4300, Seattle, WA 98104-4096 **Telephone:** 206-467-3600 **Fax:** 206-467-3795	**Web Site:** www.plumcreek.com **Officers:** David D. Leland - Chmn. Rick R. Holley - Pres., C.E.O.	**Auditors:** Ernst & Young LLP **Investor Contact:** 800-858-5347 **Transfer Agents:** Computershare Trust Company, N.A., Providence, RI

PMI GROUP, INC.

Exchange	Symbol	Price	52Wk Range	Yield	P/E
NYS	PMI	$5.82 (3/31/2008)	50.07-5.12	0.86	N/A

*7 Year Price Score 59.72   *NYSE Composite Index=100   *12 Month Price Score 29.29

Interim Earnings (Per Share)

Qtr.	Mar	Jun	Sep	Dec
2003	1.00	0.77	0.67	0.86
2004	1.23	0.99	1.05	0.59
2005	1.00	1.04	0.97	1.10
2006	1.09	1.14	1.16	1.19
2007	1.16	0.95	(1.04)	(11.95)

Interim Dividends (Per Share)

Amt	Decl	Ex	Rec	Pay
0.052Q	5/17/2007	6/27/2007	6/29/2007	7/16/2007
0.052Q	9/21/2007	9/26/2007	9/28/2007	10/15/2007
0.052Q	11/16/2007	12/27/2007	12/31/2007	1/15/2008
0.013Q	3/17/2008	3/27/2008	3/31/2008	4/15/2008

Indicated Div: $0.05

Valuation Analysis / Institutional Holding

Valuation Analysis		Institutional Holding	
Forecast P/E	N/A	No of Institutions	274
Market Cap	$472.1 Million	Shares	92,202,560
Book Value	2.5 Billion	% Held	
Price/Book	0.19		
Price/Sales	0.40	N/A	

TRADING VOLUME (thousand shares)

Business Summary: Insurance (MIC: 8.2 SIC: 6351 NAIC: 524130)

PMI Group is a global provider of financial products designed to reduce risk, lower costs and expand market access for residential mortgages, public finance obligations and asset-backed securities. Through its U.S., International and Financial Guaranty segments, Co. offers products that include: mortgage insurance and reinsurance; structured finance services, which may take the form of mortgage insurance; and financial guaranty. Co.'s U.S. customers are primarily mortgage lenders, depository institutions, commercial banks, investors (including the Fannie Mae and Freddie Mac), the Federal Home Loan Banks, and other capital market participants.

Recent Developments: For the year ended Dec 31 2007, net loss amounted to US$915.3 million versus net income of US$419.7 million in the prior year. Revenues were US$1.19 billion, up 9.9% from US$1.08 billion the year before. Net premiums earned were US$995.2 million versus US$860.5 million in the prior year, an increase of 15.6%.

Prospects: In light of the slowdown in the mortgage origination and secondary mortgage markets and the changes made to its pricing and underwriting guidelines, Co. expects new insurance written to be lower in 2008 than in 2007, and accordingly, should mitigate its premiums written and earned going forward. Also, the continued adverse loss development in its U.S. mortgage insurance operations could further weaken the perceived counterparty strength of Co.'s international insurance subsidiaries and limit new business opportunities. Further, while the size of the non-agency mortgage-backed securities market is expected to diminish in 2008, Co. anticipates claim rates and average claim sizes to increase.

Financial Data
(US$ in Thousands)

	12/31/2007	12/31/2006	12/31/2005	12/31/2004	12/31/2003	12/31/2002	12/31/2001	12/31/2000
Earnings Per Share	(10.81)	4.57	4.10	3.87	3.29	3.79	3.39	2.89
Cash Flow Per Share	6.60	4.54	4.21	4.08	6.19	4.71	3.39	2.50
Tang Book Value Per Share	30.98	41.14	36.42	33.37	29.26	24.39	20.04	16.92
Dividends Per Share	0.210	0.210	0.195	0.165	0.125	0.095	0.080	0.080
Dividend Payout %	...	4.60	4.76	4.26	3.80	2.51	2.36	2.77
Income Statement								
Premium Income	995,172	860,530	817,602	770,399	696,928	904,510	754,771	634,362
Total Revenue	1,185,164	1,206,037	1,117,783	1,038,236	891,721	1,121,362	936,963	762,572
Benefits & Claims	1,203,004	302,936	257,779	237,282	209,088	167,263	118,048	103,079
Income Before Taxes	(1,127,416)	559,715	540,831	478,991	393,122	470,790	446,966	373,866
Income Taxes	(212,090)	140,064	131,662	112,459	118,814	131,745	134,949	113,654
Net Income	(915,326)	419,651	409,169	399,333	299,433	346,217	307,212	260,212
Average Shares	84,645	92,866	101,620	105,231	91,045	91,380	90,667	90,037
Balance Sheet								
Total Assets	5,070,440	5,320,146	5,254,136	5,145,967	4,794,289	3,517,049	2,989,952	2,392,657
Total Liabilities	2,557,478	1,751,556	2,023,346	2,008,212	2,010,260	1,274,716	1,154,764	794,337
Stockholders' Equity	2,512,962	3,568,590	3,230,790	3,137,755	2,784,029	2,193,833	1,786,688	1,499,211
Shares Outstanding	81,120	86,747	88,713	94,025	95,161	89,943	89,162	88,619
Statistical Record								
Return on Assets %	N.M.	7.94	7.87	8.01	7.21	10.64	11.41	11.55
Return on Equity %	N.M.	12.34	12.85	13.45	12.03	17.40	18.70	19.11
Loss Ratio %	120.88	35.20	31.53	30.80	30.00	18.49	15.64	16.25
Net Margin %	(77.23)	34.80	36.61	38.46	33.58	30.87	32.79	34.12
Price Range	50.21-10.19	47.88-41.42	42.24-34.78	44.63-36.15	38.59-24.20	43.92-24.96	36.63-24.44	36.94-16.75
P/E Ratio	...	10.48-9.06	10.30-8.48	11.53-9.34	11.73-7.36	11.59-6.59	10.80-7.21	12.78-5.80
Average Yield %	0.57	0.48	0.50	0.41	0.40	0.27	0.26	0.29

Address: 3003 Oak Road, Walnut Creek, CA 94597-2098 Telephone: 925-658-7878	Web Site: www.pmigroup.com Officers: W. Roger Haughton - Chmn., C.E.O. L. Stephen Smith - Pres., C.O.O.	Auditors: Ernst & Young LLP Investor Contact: 888-641-4764

PNC FINANCIAL SERVICES GROUP (THE)

Exchange	Symbol	Price	52Wk Range	Yield	P/E
NYS	PNC	$65.57 (3/31/2008)	75.85-56.63	4.03	15.07

*7 Year Price Score 93.94   *NYSE Composite Index=100   *12 Month Price Score 99.59

Interim Earnings (Per Share)

Qtr.	Mar	Jun	Sep	Dec
2003	0.92	0.65	1.00	0.98
2004	1.15	1.07	0.91	1.08
2005	1.24	0.98	1.14	1.20
2006	1.19	1.28	5.01	1.27
2007	1.46	1.22	1.19	0.50

Interim Dividends (Per Share)

Amt	Decl	Ex	Rec	Pay
0.63Q	7/5/2007	7/11/2007	7/13/2007	7/24/2007
0.63Q	10/4/2007	10/10/2007	10/12/2007	10/24/2007
0.63Q	1/3/2008	1/9/2008	1/11/2008	1/24/2008
0.66Q	4/4/2008	4/10/2008	4/14/2008	4/24/2008

Indicated Div: $2.64

Valuation Analysis **Institutional Holding**

Forecast P/E	12.14	No of Institutions
	(1/10/2007)	555
Market Cap	$22.4 Billion	Shares
Book Value	14.9 Billion	197,205,248
Price/Book	1.51	% Held
Price/Sales	2.25	57.03

TRADING VOLUME (thousand shares)

Business Summary: Commercial Banking (MIC: 8.1 SIC: 6021 NAIC: 522110)

PNC Financial Services Group is a financial services company engaged in retail banking, corporate and institutional banking, asset management, and global fund processing services. Co. operates through four segments: Retail Banking, which provides deposit, lending, brokerage, trust, investment management, and cash management services; Corporate & Institutional Banking, which provides lending, treasury management, and capital markets products and services, BlackRock, which manages assets on behalf of institutions and individuals, and PFPC, which provides processing, technology and business systems. As of Dec 31 2007, Co. had total assets of $138.92 billion.

Recent Developments: For the year ended Dec 31 2007, net income decreased 43.5% to US$1.47 billion from US$2.60 billion in the prior year. Net interest income increased 29.8% to US$2.92 billion from US$2.25 billion in the prior year. Provision for loan losses was US$315.0 million versus US$124.0 million in the prior year, an increase of 154.0%. Non-interest income fell 40.1% to US$3.79 billion from US$6.33 billion, while non-interest expense declined 3.3% to US$4.30 billion.

Prospects: For 2008, Co. expects net interest income to be higher, and net interest margin to improve slightly versus 2007, based on its expectations that interest rates will remain low through most of 2008 and economic condition, although showing slower growth than in recent years, will avoid a recession. However, Co. believes that net interest margins for this industry will continue to be affected by competition from high quality loans and deposits, and customer migration from lower to higher rate deposit or other products. Also, given its projections for loan growth and continued credit deterioration, Co. expects nonperforming assets and the provision for credit losses to be higher versus 2007.

Financial Data

(US$ in Thousands)	12/31/2007	12/31/2006	12/31/2005	12/31/2004	12/31/2003	12/31/2002	12/31/2001	12/31/2000
Earnings Per Share	4.35	8.73	4.55	4.21	3.55	4.15	1.26	4.31
Cash Flow Per Share	(1.26)	9.08	(2.36)	1.55	5.96	9.37	4.41	10.48
Tang Book Value Per Share	15.55	23.02	13.98	14.55	14.22	14.78	12.19	14.42
Dividends Per Share	2.440	2.150	2.000	2.000	1.940	1.920	1.920	1.830
Dividend Payout %	56.09	24.63	43.96	47.51	54.65	46.27	152.38	42.46
Income Statement								
Interest Income	6,166,000	4,612,000	3,734,000	2,752,000	2,712,000	3,172,000	4,137,000	4,732,000
Interest Expense	3,251,000	2,367,000	1,580,000	783,000	716,000	975,000	1,875,000	2,568,000
Net Interest Income	2,915,000	2,245,000	2,154,000	1,969,000	1,996,000	2,197,000	2,262,000	2,164,000
Provision for Losses	315,000	124,000	21,000	52,000	177,000	309,000	903,000	136,000
Non-Interest Income	3,790,000	6,327,000	4,162,000	3,563,000	3,257,000	3,197,000	2,543,000	2,891,000
Non-Interest Expense	4,296,000	4,443,000	4,333,000	3,735,000	3,476,000	3,227,000	3,338,000	3,071,000
Income Before Taxes	2,094,000	4,005,000	1,962,000	1,745,000	1,600,000	1,858,000	564,000	1,848,000
Income Taxes	627,000	1,363,000	604,000	538,000	539,000	621,000	187,000	634,000
Net Income	1,467,000	2,595,000	1,325,000	1,197,000	1,001,000	1,184,000	377,000	1,279,000
Average Shares	335,157	296,522	289,840	284,000	281,000	285,000	290,000	292,800
Balance Sheet								
Net Loans & Leases	71,416,000	51,911,000	50,954,000	44,558,000	34,848,000	36,384,000	41,533,000	51,581,000
Total Assets	138,920,000	101,820,000	91,954,000	79,723,000	68,168,000	66,377,000	69,568,000	69,844,000
Total Deposits	82,696,000	66,301,000	60,275,000	53,269,000	45,241,000	44,982,000	47,304,000	47,664,000
Total Liabilities	122,412,000	90,147,000	82,801,000	71,746,000	61,061,000	58,400,000	62,727,000	62,340,000
Stockholders' Equity	14,854,000	10,788,000	8,563,000	7,473,000	6,645,000	6,859,000	5,823,000	6,656,000
Shares Outstanding	341,000	293,000	293,000	283,000	277,000	285,000	283,000	290,000
Statistical Record								
Return on Assets %	1.22	2.68	1.54	1.61	1.49	1.74	0.54	1.76
Return on Equity %	11.44	26.82	16.53	16.91	14.83	18.67	6.04	20.24
Net Interest Margin %	47.28	48.68	57.69	71.55	73.60	69.26	54.68	45.73
Efficiency Ratio %	43.15	40.62	54.88	59.14	58.23	50.67	49.97	40.29
Loans to Deposits	0.86	0.78	0.85	0.84	0.77	0.81	0.88	1.08
Price Range	76.23-64.09	74.98-62.41	65.00-49.38	58.70-49.42	55.03-41.90	62.63-36.00	75.15-52.42	75.00-36.63
P/E Ratio	17.52-14.73	8.59-7.15	14.29-10.85	13.94-11.74	15.50-11.80	15.09-8.67	59.64-41.60	17.40-8.50
Average Yield %	3.41	3.09	3.57	3.69	4.06	3.87	2.99	3.44

Address: One PNC Plaza, 249 Fifth Avenue, Pittsburgh, PA 15222-2707
Telephone: 412-762-2000
Fax: 412-762-5798

Web Site: www.pnc.com
Officers: James E. Rohr - Chmn., C.E.O. William S. Demchak - Vice-Chmn.

Auditors: PricewaterhouseCoopers LLP
Investor Contact: 412-762-8257
Transfer Agents: Computershare Investor Services, LLC, Chicago, IL

PNM RESOURCES INC

Exchange	Symbol	Price	52Wk Range	Yield	P/E
NYS	PNM	$12.47 (3/31/2008)	34.00-9.33	7.38	12.99

*7 Year Price Score 85.86   *NYSE Composite Index=100   *12 Month Price Score 62.03

Interim Earnings (Per Share)

Qtr.	Mar	Jun	Sep	Dec
2003	0.81	0.29	0.27	0.21
2004	0.41	0.28	0.45	0.30
2005	0.50	0.02	0.41	0.08
2006	0.38	0.23	0.62	0.49
2007	0.38	0.26	0.11	0.21

Interim Dividends (Per Share)

Amt	Decl	Ex	Rec	Pay
0.23Q	7/17/2007	7/30/2007	8/1/2007	8/17/2007
0.23Q	9/18/2007	10/30/2007	11/1/2007	11/16/2007
0.23Q	12/4/2007	1/30/2008	2/1/2008	2/15/2008
0.23Q	2/19/2008	4/7/2008	4/9/2008	5/2/2008

Indicated Div: $0.92

Valuation Analysis

		Institutional Holding	
Forecast P/E	N/A	No of Institutions	189
		Shares	71,974,960
Market Cap	$957.9 Million	% Held	95.48
Book Value	1.7 Billion		
Price/Book	0.56		
Price/Sales	0.50		

Business Summary: Electricity (MIC: 7.1 SIC: 4911 NAIC: 221121)

PNM Resources is an investor-owned holding company of energy and energy-related businesses. Co.'s primary subsidiaries are Public Service Company of New Mexico (PNM), Texas-New Mexico Power Company (TNMP) and First Choice. PNM is an integrated public utility with regulated operations engaged in the generation, transmission and distribution of electricity, transmission, distribution and sale of natural gas within New Mexico, and unregulated operations focused on the sale and marketing of electricity in the western U.S. TNMP is a regulated utility operating in Texas. First Choice is a retail electric provider operating in Texas.

Recent Developments: For the year ended Dec 31 2007, income from continuing operations decreased 45.0% to US$59.4 million from US$108.0 million a year earlier. Net income decreased 38.0% to US$74.9 million from US$120.8 million in the prior year. Revenues were US$1.91 billion, down 2.5% from US$1.96 billion the year before. Operating income was US$125.0 million versus US$249.8 million in the prior year, a decrease of 49.9%. Direct operating expenses rose 6.1% to US$1.38 billion from US$1.30 billion in the comparable period the year before. Indirect operating expenses decreased 0.9% to US$408.2 million from US$412.0 million in the equivalent prior-year period.

Prospects: On Jan 15 2008, Co. announced that it has reached a definitive agreement to sell its natural gas operations to a subsidiary of Continental Energy Systems for $620.0 million. In a separate transaction that is conditioned upon the sale of the natural gas operations, Co. will acquire Continental's regulated Texas electric delivery business for $202.5 million. Co. expects to use the net proceeds of these transactions to retire debt, fund future electric capital expenditures and for other corporate purposes. These transactions are expected to be slightly accretive to Co.'s ongoing earnings per diluted share in the first full year following both closings, expected to occur by year end 2008.

Financial Data
(US$ in Thousands)

	12/31/2007	12/31/2006	12/31/2005	12/31/2004	12/31/2003	12/31/2002	12/31/2001	12/31/2000
Earnings Per Share	0.96	1.73	1.00	1.43	1.58	1.07	2.51	1.69
Cash Flow Per Share	2.90	3.50	3.19	3.89	3.84	1.66	5.54	4.03
Tang Book Value Per Share	14.59	14.29	10.30	18.19	17.84	16.60	17.25	15.76
Dividends Per Share	0.910	0.860	0.770	0.633	0.607	0.573	0.533	0.533
Dividend Payout %	94.79	49.71	77.00	44.29	38.40	53.42	21.22	31.62
Income Statement								
Total Revenue	1,914,029	2,471,669	2,076,810	1,604,792	1,455,714	1,168,996	2,352,098	1,611,274
Income Taxes	3,226	17,772	13,411	13,185	2,710	12,144	(7,706)	20,382
Net Income	74,874	122,114	67,227	87,686	95,173	64,272	150,433	100,946
Average Shares	77,928	70,636	67,080	61,340	60,205	59,164	59,596	59,565
Balance Sheet								
Net PPE	2,942,353	3,769,424	2,988,306	2,326,023	2,195,890	1,868,799	1,782,741	1,620,972
Total Assets	5,872,136	6,165,624	5,124,709	3,487,635	3,378,629	3,026,907	2,934,638	2,894,233
Long-Term Obligations	1,231,859	1,765,907	1,746,395	987,823	987,210	980,092	953,884	953,823
Total Liabilities	4,168,196	4,460,799	3,826,721	2,376,527	2,288,525	2,040,058	1,909,814	1,956,806
Stockholders' Equity	1,703,940	1,704,825	1,297,988	1,111,108	1,090,104	986,849	1,024,824	937,427
Shares Outstanding	76,814	76,648	68,786	60,464	60,388	58,677	58,676	58,676
Statistical Record								
Return on Assets %	1.24	2.16	1.56	2.55	2.97	2.16	5.16	3.58
Return on Equity %	4.39	8.13	5.58	7.95	9.16	6.39	15.33	10.96
Net Margin %	3.91	4.94	3.24	5.46	6.54	5.50	6.40	6.26
PPE Turnover	0.57	0.73	0.78	0.71	0.72	0.64	1.38	1.00
Asset Turnover	0.32	0.44	0.48	0.47	0.45	0.39	0.81	0.57
Debt to Equity	0.72	1.04	1.35	0.89	0.91	0.99	0.93	1.02
Price Range	34.00-21.45	31.80-22.99	30.26-24.06	25.88-18.73	19.64-12.74	20.44-11.91	25.13-15.63	18.79-9.88
P/E Ratio	35.42-22.34	18.38-13.29	30.26-24.06	18.10-13.10	12.43-8.06	19.10-11.13	10.01-6.23	11.12-5.84
Average Yield %	3.34	3.22	2.84	2.96	3.59	3.55	2.78	4.08

Address: Alvarado Square, Albuquerque, NM 87158 **Telephone:** 505-241-2700 **Fax:** 505-241-2359	**Web Site:** www.pnm.com **Officers:** Jeff E. Sterba - Chmn., Pres., C.E.O. J. R. Loyack - Sr. V.P., C.F.O.	**Auditors:** Grant Thornton LLP **Transfer Agents:** PNM Shareholder Records Departement, Albuquerque, NM

POLARIS INDUSTRIES INC.

Exchange	Symbol	Price	52Wk Range	Yield	P/E	Div Acheiver
NYS	PII	$41.01 (3/31/2008)	57.74-36.45	3.71	13.36	12 Years

*7 Year Price Score 90.54 *NYSE Composite Index=100 *12 Month Price Score 91.85

Interim Earnings (Per Share)

Qtr.	Mar	Jun	Sep	Dec
2003	0.28	0.47	0.87	0.84
2004	0.32	0.54	0.42	1.05
2005	0.42	0.68	1.16	1.02
2006	0.27	0.48	1.03	0.82
2007	0.34	0.62	1.06	1.05

Interim Dividends (Per Share)

Amt	Decl	Ex	Rec	Pay
0.34Q	4/19/2007	4/27/2007	5/1/2007	5/15/2007
0.34Q	7/26/2007	7/30/2007	8/1/2007	8/15/2007
0.34Q	10/25/2007	10/30/2007	11/1/2007	11/15/2007
0.38Q	1/24/2008	1/30/2008	2/1/2008	2/15/2008

Indicated Div: $1.52

Valuation Analysis

		Institutional Holding	
Forecast P/E	14.20	No of Institutions	
	(1/10/2007)	192	
Market Cap	$1.1 Billion	Shares	
Book Value	173.0 Million	29,986,596	
Price/Book	8.11	% Held	
Price/Sales	0.77	84.42	

Business Summary: Automotive (MIC: 15.1 SIC: 3799 NAIC: 336999)

Polaris Industries designs and manufactures all-terrain vehicles (ATVs), snowmobiles and motorcycles, and markets them, together with replacement parts, garments and accessories, through dealers and distributors in the U.S., Canada and Europe, and on the Internet. Co.'s line of ATVs consists of 30 models, including general purpose, sport and four-wheel drive utility models. Co.'s snowmobiles consists of 33 models, ranging from youth models to utility and economy models to performance and competition models. Co. also manufactures V-twin cruiser motorcycles under the Victory™ brand consisting of nine models, including the Vegas™, Kingpin™, Hammer and Eight Ball.

Recent Developments: For the year ended Dec 31 2007, net income increased 4.4% to US$111.7 million from US$107.0 million in the prior year. Revenues were US$1.83 billion, up 7.1% from US$1.70 billion the year before. Operating income was US$176.0 million versus US$168.1 million in the prior year, an increase of 4.7%. Direct operating expenses rose 6.9% to US$1.39 billion from US$1.30 billion in the comparable period the year before. Indirect operating expenses increased 10.0% to US$262.3 million from US$238.4 million in the equivalent prior-year period.

Prospects: For first quarter 2008, Co. expects sales growth in the range of 15.0% to 18.0% over $317.7 million in the first quarter 2007 and earnings from continuing operations of $0.44 to $0.49 per diluted share, an increase of $0.05 per share. These increases are primarily due to operating performance from its parts, garments and accessories and its side-by-side vehicle businesses during the first two months of 2008 and the benefit from reduced interest rates during first quarter 2008. Meanwhile, for 2008, Co. expects sales growth in the range of 3.0% to 5.0% over 2007 and earnings from continuing operations in the range of $3.28 to $3.40 per diluted share, an increase of 6.0% to 10.0% over 2007.

Financial Data

(US$ in Thousands)	12/31/2007	12/31/2006	12/31/2005	12/31/2004	12/31/2003	12/31/2002	12/31/2001	12/31/2000
Earnings Per Share	3.07	2.58	3.27	2.32	2.46	2.19	1.94	1.75
Cash Flow Per Share	5.96	3.61	3.83	5.82	3.63	4.32	4.12	2.28
Tang Book Value Per Share	4.28	4.01	8.27	7.88	6.81	5.67	5.21	3.89
Dividends Per Share	1.360	1.240	1.120	0.920	0.620	0.560	0.500	0.440
Dividend Payout %	44.30	48.06	34.25	39.66	25.20	25.51	25.77	25.14
Income Statement								
Total Revenue	1,825,294	1,703,579	1,908,459	1,805,241	1,629,456	1,535,925	1,512,042	1,425,678
EBITDA	247,530	244,716	281,282	265,649	221,584	214,095	199,364	183,087
Income Before Taxes	170,336	163,779	208,633	204,199	164,339	154,171	139,563	128,386
Income Taxes	57,738	50,988	64,348	67,386	53,410	50,579	48,149	45,577
Net Income	111,650	106,985	113,278	101,501	110,929	103,592	91,414	82,809
Average Shares	36,324	41,451	43,881	45,035	45,056	47,232	47,134	47,332
Balance Sheet								
Current Assets	447,556	392,961	373,988	465,655	387,716	343,659	305,317	240,912
Total Assets	769,881	778,791	768,956	792,925	671,352	608,646	565,163	490,186
Current Liabilities	388,246	361,420	375,614	405,193	330,478	313,513	308,337	238,384
Long-Term Obligations	200,000	250,000	18,000	18,000	18,008	18,027	18,043	47,068
Total Liabilities	596,899	611,420	399,299	431,193	351,974	331,540	326,380	285,452
Stockholders' Equity	172,982	167,371	369,657	361,732	319,378	277,106	238,783	204,734
Shares Outstanding	34,212	35,455	41,687	42,741	43,362	44,600	45,854	47,084
Statistical Record								
Return on Assets %	14.42	13.82	18.35	14.23	17.33	17.65	17.32	17.72
Return on Equity %	65.61	39.84	39.18	30.60	37.19	40.16	41.22	44.28
EBITDA Margin %	13.56	14.36	14.74	14.72	13.60	13.94	13.19	12.84
Net Margin %	6.12	6.28	7.51	5.79	6.81	6.74	6.05	5.81
Asset Turnover	2.36	2.20	2.44	2.46	2.55	2.62	2.87	3.05
Current Ratio	1.15	1.09	1.00	1.15	1.17	1.10	0.99	1.01
Debt to Equity	1.16	1.49	0.05	0.05	0.06	0.07	0.08	0.23
Price Range	57.74-42.70	54.56-36.20	73.85-44.43	68.93-40.00	45.40-22.18	38.00-26.94	29.05-18.50	20.53-12.97
P/E Ratio	18.81-13.91	21.15-14.03	22.58-13.59	29.71-17.24	18.45-9.02	17.35-12.30	14.97-9.53	11.73-7.41
Average Yield %	2.76	2.74	1.97	1.85	1.85	1.73	2.16	2.70

Address: 2100 Highway 55, Medina, MN 55340
Telephone: 763-542-0500
Fax: 763-542-0599

Web Site: www.polarisindustries.com
Officers: Gregory A. Palen - Chmn. Thomas C. Tiller - Pres., C.E.O.

Auditors: Ernst & Young LLP
Investor Contact: 763-513-3477

POLO RALPH LAUREN CORP.

Exchange	Symbol	Price	52Wk Range	Yield	P/E
NYS	RL	$58.29 (3/31/2008)	102.30-51.33	0.34	15.80

*7 Year Price Score 140.75 *NYSE Composite Index=100   *12 Month Price Score 85.01

Interim Earnings (Per Share)

Qtr.	Jun	Sep	Dec	Mar
2004-05	0.13	0.78	0.72	0.20
2005-06	0.48	0.97	0.84	0.57
2006-07	0.74	1.28	1.03	0.69
2007-08	0.82	1.09	1.08	...

Interim Dividends (Per Share)

Amt	Decl	Ex	Rec	Pay
0.05Q	6/18/2007	6/27/2007	6/29/2007	7/13/2007
0.05Q	9/17/2007	9/26/2007	9/28/2007	10/12/2007
0.05Q	12/17/2007	12/26/2007	12/28/2007	1/11/2008
0.05Q	3/17/2008	3/26/2008	3/28/2008	4/11/2008

Indicated Div: $0.20

Valuation Analysis

		Institutional Holding	
Forecast P/E	17.38	No of Institutions	
	(1/10/2007)	251	
Market Cap	$5.9 Billion	Shares	
Book Value	2.4 Billion	57,186,740	
Price/Book	2.47	% Held	
Price/Sales	1.27	55.06	

Business Summary: Apparel (MIC: 4.4 SIC: 2329 NAIC: 315211)

Polo Ralph Lauren is engaged in the design, marketing and distribution of lifestyle products including men's, women's and children's apparel, accessories, fragrances and home furnishings through both of its wholesale and retail businesses worldwide, as well as via its online retail site, www.Polo.com. Co. also licenses the right to third parties to use its various trademarks. Co.'s brand names include Polo, Polo by Ralph Lauren, Ralph Lauren Purple Label, Ralph Lauren Black Label, RLX, Ralph Lauren, Blue Label, Lauren, RRL, Rugby, Chaps, Club Monaco and American Living. As of Mar 31 2007, Co. operated 147 full-price retail stores and 145 factory outlet stores worldwide.

Recent Developments: For the quarter ended Dec 29 2007, net income increased 2.0% to US$112.7 million from US$110.5 million in the year-earlier quarter. Revenues were US$1.27 billion, up 11.0% from US$1.14 billion the year before. Operating income was US$170.7 million versus US$184.2 million in the prior-year quarter, a decrease of 7.3%. Direct operating expenses rose 12.0% to US$593.3 million from US$529.7 million in the comparable period the year before. Indirect operating expenses increased 17.7% to US$505.8 million from US$429.8 million in the equivalent prior-year period.

Prospects: In the event that U.S. macroeconomic environment continues to be weak and/or spreads to markets outside U.S., Co. believes that these conditions could have a negative effect on its sales and margin growth rates for the rest of fiscal 2008 and into fiscal 2009. Notably, for the fiscal year ending Mar 2008, Co. expects its revenue to grow at a low double digit percentage, operating margins to decline by 250 basis points, with diluted earnings to be at the lower end of the range of $3.64 to $3.74 per share. Also, Co. projects its consolidated revenues for the fiscal year ending Mar 2009 to increase by a low-to-mid single digit percentage, with diluted earnings per share of $3.95 to $4.05.

Financial Data
(US$ in Thousands)

	9 Mos	6 Mos	3 Mos	03/31/2007	04/01/2006	04/02/2005	04/03/2004	03/29/2003
Earnings Per Share	3.69	3.64	3.83	3.73	2.87	1.83	1.69	1.76
Cash Flow Per Share	8.33	7.74	8.16	7.65	4.32	3.77	2.09	2.74
Tang Book Value Per Share	10.72	9.20	9.02	11.99	10.35	10.38	10.56	8.93
Dividends Per Share	0.200	0.200	0.200	0.200	0.200	0.200	0.200	...
Dividend Payout %	5.42	5.49	5.22	5.36	6.97	10.93	11.83	...
Income Statement								
Total Revenue	3,639,200	2,369,400	1,070,300	4,295,400	3,746,300	3,305,415	2,649,654	2,439,340
EBITDA	649,200	428,300	185,800	783,500	637,800	3,809,390	355,121	366,533
Depn & Amortn	147,600	94,600	43,100	...	...	...	...	...
Income Before Taxes	498,900	335,400	145,100	643,300	502,900	299,366	261,932	274,386
Income Taxes	182,600	131,800	56,800	242,400	194,900	107,336	95,055	100,151
Net Income	316,300	203,600	88,300	400,900	308,000	190,425	170,954	174,235
Average Shares	104,300	105,400	107,300	107,600	107,200	104,010	100,960	99,263
Balance Sheet								
Current Assets	1,925,700	1,812,100	1,706,200	1,685,900	1,378,500	1,413,763	1,271,319	1,166,007
Total Assets	4,344,700	4,187,500	3,995,400	3,758,000	3,088,700	2,726,669	2,270,241	2,038,822
Current Liabilities	909,900	909,100	792,700	640,300	843,500	622,410	501,130	500,347
Long-Term Obligations	438,500	424,400	403,100	445,900	24,200	290,960	277,345	248,494
Total Liabilities	1,944,600	1,944,700	1,767,300	1,423,100	1,039,100	1,050,961	848,168	830,055
Stockholders' Equity	2,400,100	2,242,800	2,228,100	2,334,900	2,049,600	1,675,708	1,422,073	1,208,767
Shares Outstanding	101,800	101,500	103,300	104,000	105,400	103,118	100,632	98,722
Statistical Record								
Return on Assets %	9.92	10.36	11.42	11.74	10.62	7.64	7.81	9.22
Return on Equity %	16.60	17.51	18.98	18.34	16.58	12.33	12.79	15.83
EBITDA Margin %	17.84	18.08	17.36	18.24	17.02	115.25	13.40	15.03
Net Margin %	8.69	8.59	8.25	9.33	8.22	5.76	6.45	7.14
Asset Turnover	1.19	1.21	1.23	1.26	1.29	1.33	1.21	1.29
Current Ratio	2.12	1.99	2.15	2.63	1.63	2.27	2.54	2.33
Debt to Equity	0.18	0.19	0.18	0.19	0.01	0.17	0.20	0.21
Price Range	102.30-61.45	102.30-64.69	99.42-46.50	89.64-46.50	61.47-35.10	42.60-31.04	35.13-22.41	30.64-16.57
P/E Ratio	27.72-16.65	28.10-17.77	25.96-12.14	24.03-12.47	21.42-12.23	23.28-16.96	20.79-13.26	17.41-9.41
Average Yield %	0.24	0.24	0.26	0.29	0.40	0.54	0.71	...

Address: 650 Madison Avenue, New York, NY 10022	Web Site: www.investor.polo.com	Auditors: Ernst & Young LLP
Telephone: 212-318-7000	Officers: Ralph Lauren - Chmn., C.E.O. F. Lance Isham - Vice-Chmn.	Investor Contact: 212-813-7862
Fax: 212-888-5780		Transfer Agents: The Bank of New York

POTLATCH CORP

Exchange	Symbol	Price	52Wk Range	Yield	P/E
NYS	PCH	$41.27 (3/31/2008)	48.17-38.56	4.94	28.86

*7 Year Price Score 91.15 ***NYSE Composite Index=100** ***12 Month Price Score 102.32**

Interim Earnings (Per Share)

Qtr.	Mar	Jun	Sep	Dec
2003	(0.33)	0.23	0.77	1.10
2004	0.74	1.68	7.05	(0.32)
2005	0.13	0.28	0.38	0.34
2006	2.11	0.21	0.62	1.14
2007	(0.76)	0.87	1.04	0.28

Interim Dividends (Per Share)

Amt	Decl	Ex	Rec	Pay
0.49Q	5/18/2007	5/25/2007	5/30/2007	6/15/2007
0.49Q	7/19/2007	8/29/2007	8/31/2007	9/17/2007
0.51Q	12/7/2007	12/13/2007	12/17/2007	12/31/2007
0.51Q	2/21/2008	3/3/2008	3/5/2008	3/19/2008

Indicated Div: $2.04

Valuation Analysis

		Institutional Holding	
Forecast P/E	N/A	No of Institutions	146
Market Cap	$1.6 Billion	Shares	30,211,284
Book Value	578.3 Million	% Held	77.69
Price/Book	2.80		
Price/Sales	0.98		

TRADING VOLUME (thousand shares)

Business Summary: Property, Real Estate & Development (MIC: 8.3 SIC: 6798 NAIC: 322121)

Potlatch is a real estate investment trust that owned and managed 1.7 million acres of timberlands located in Arkansas, Idaho, Minnesota and Oregon at Dec 31 2007. Through its subsidiary, Potlatch Forest Products Corporation, Co. also produces lumber and panel products and bleached pulp products, including paperboard and tissue products; as well as conducts a real estate sales and development business. The primary market for Co.'s products is the U.S., although it sells a significant amount of paperboard to countries in the Pacific Rim. As of Dec 31, 2007, Co. operated five business segments: Resource; Real Estate; Wood Products; Pulp and Paperboard; and Consumer Products.

Recent Developments: For the year ended Dec 31 2007, income from continuing operations decreased 40.3% to US$93.2 million from US$156.0 million a year earlier. Net income decreased 59.4% to US$56.4 million from US$139.1 million in the prior year. Revenues were US$1.65 billion, up 3.4% from US$1.60 billion the year before.

Prospects: Co.'s outlook seems mixed. For example, while overall pricing for timber is expected to decline by 10.0% in 2008, Co. expects the overall timber harvest from its lands of between 4.2 million and 4.4 million tons, rising to 4.9 million to 5.3 million tons by 2010 based on current market conditions, the ages of its timber stands and recent timberland acquisitions and sales. Meanwhile, Co.'s real estate business is performing well and it expects earnings growth in 2008, with the planned sale of 18,000 to 22,000 acres. Moreover, the outlook for pulp-based businesses appears solid due to price increases, and thus, Co. expects improvement in its Pulp and Paperboard and Consumer Products segments.

Financial Data

(US$ in Thousands)	12/31/2007	12/31/2006	12/31/2005	12/31/2004	12/31/2003	12/31/2002	12/31/2001	12/31/2000
Earnings Per Share	1.43	3.79	1.13	9.19	1.77	(8.23)	(2.81)	(1.16)
Cash Flow Per Share	3.73	4.99	2.29	(0.78)	6.32	(2.43)	3.01	3.28
Tang Book Value Per Share	14.73	14.88	24.01	23.22	16.33	15.07	24.98	28.69
Dividends Per Share	1.980	17.270	0.600	3.100	0.600	0.600	1.170	1.740
Dividend Payout %	138.46	455.67	53.10	33.73	33.90	...	...	...
Income Statement								
Total Revenue	1,654,021	1,607,827	1,496,144	1,351,472	1,506,634	1,286,217	1,751,996	1,808,770
EBITDA	195,689	208,298	74,179	67,543	114,637	(25,554)	(54,972)	4,989
Income Before Taxes	87,177	90,033	47,640	25,297	80,555	(83,497)	(130,238)	(54,449)
Income Taxes	(5,977)	(49,077)	14,676	9,967	27,334	(32,564)	(50,793)	(21,235)
Net Income	56,432	139,110	32,964	271,249	50,727	(234,381)	(79,445)	(33,214)
Average Shares	39,384	36,672	29,251	29,514	28,718	28,461	28,281	28,522
Balance Sheet								
Current Assets	333,959	356,519	402,590	407,370	330,619	347,764	511,668	483,839
Total Assets	1,517,204	1,457,607	1,628,797	1,594,672	1,597,377	1,616,326	2,487,146	2,542,445
Current Liabilities	284,707	196,264	146,992	152,305	169,817	245,071	356,452	439,099
Long Term Obligations	321,301	321,474	333,097	335,415	618,278	622,645	1,017,522	801,549
Total Liabilities	938,868	879,748	923,649	923,283	1,126,526	1,185,535	1,779,842	1,729,209
Stockholders' Equity	578,336	577,859	705,148	671,389	470,851	430,791	707,304	813,236
Shares Outstanding	39,256	38,824	29,367	28,919	28,840	28,578	28,311	28,346
Statistical Record								
Return on Assets %	3.79	9.01	2.05	16.95	3.16	N.M.	N.M.	N.M.
Return on Equity %	9.76	21.68	4.79	47.36	11.25	N.M.	N.M.	N.M.
EBITDA Margin %	11.83	12.96	4.96	5.00	7.61	N.M.	N.M.	0.28
Net Margin %	3.41	8.65	2.20	20.07	3.37	N.M.	N.M.	N.M.
Asset Turnover	1.11	1.04	0.93	0.84	0.94	0.63	0.70	0.72
Current Ratio	1.17	1.82	2.74	2.67	1.95	1.42	1.44	1.10
Debt to Equity	0.56	0.56	0.47	0.50	1.31	1.45	1.44	0.99
Price Range	48.17-41.21	54.10-33.99	58.64-44.18	51.90-34.77	35.95-18.75	36.13-23.88	36.22-24.90	44.63-28.94
P/E Ratio	33.69-28.82	14.27-8.97	51.89-39.10	5.65-3.78	20.31-10.59	...	...	...
Average Yield %	4.42	43.16	1.20	7.37	2.27	1.98	3.73	4.83

Address: 601 West 1st Ave., Suite 1600, Spokane, WA 99201
Telephone: 509-835-1500

Web Site: www.potlatchcorp.com
Officers: L. Pendleton Siegel - Chmn., C.E.O. Robert P. DeVleming - V.P., Consumer Products Div.

Auditors: KPMG LLP
Investor Contact: 509-835-1500
Transfer Agents: Computershare Investor Services, LLC

PPG INDUSTRIES, INC.

Exchange	Symbol	Price	52Wk Range	Yield	P/E	Div Acheiver
NYS	PPG	$60.51 (3/31/2008)	82.20-57.50	3.44	12.03	36 Years

*7 Year Price Score 95.06   *NYSE Composite Index=100   *12 Month Price Score 93.99

Interim Earnings (Per Share)

Qtr.	Mar	Jun	Sep	Dec
2003	0.46	0.89	0.83	0.71
2004	0.67	1.06	1.12	1.06
2005	0.55	1.34	0.92	0.68
2006	1.11	1.68	0.54	0.94
2007	1.17	1.50	1.15	1.21

Interim Dividends (Per Share)

Amt	Decl	Ex	Rec	Pay
0.50Q	4/19/2007	5/8/2007	5/10/2007	6/12/2007
0.52Q	7/19/2007	8/8/2007	8/10/2007	9/12/2007
0.52Q	10/18/2007	11/7/2007	11/12/2007	12/12/2007
0.52Q	1/17/2008	2/20/2008	2/22/2008	3/12/2008

Indicated Div: $2.08 (Div. Reinv. Plan)

Valuation Analysis

		Institutional Holding	
Forecast P/E	13.40	No of Institutions	
	(1/10/2007)	444	
Market Cap	$9.9 Billion	Shares	
Book Value	4.2 Billion	104,926,792	
Price/Book	2.39	% Held	
Price/Sales	0.88	63.99	

Business Summary: Chemicals (MIC: 11.1 SIC: 2851 NAIC: 325510)

PPG Industries is comprised of five reportable business segments: Performance Coatings, Industrial Coatings, Optical and Specialty Materials, Commodity Chemicals and Glass. Within these business segments, Co. has focused resources on industrial, aerospace, packaging, architectural, automotive original and refinish coatings; flat glass, automotive original and replacement glass, and continuous-strand fiber glass; and chlor-alkali and specialty chemicals. Co.'s coatings and chemicals businesses operate production facilities around the world. Co.'s principal glass production facilities are in North America and Europe.

Recent Developments: For the year ended Dec 31 2007, income from continuing operations increased 24.8% to US$815.0 million from US$653.0 million a year earlier. Net income increased 17.3% to US$834.0 million from US$711.0 million in the prior year. Revenues were US$11.21 billion, up 13.6% from US$9.86 billion the year before. Direct operating expenses rose 15.2% to US$7.09 billion from US$6.15 billion in the comparable period the year before. Indirect operating expenses increased 5.2% to US$2.94 billion from US$2.79 billion in the equivalent prior-year period.

Prospects: On Jan 2 2008, Co. completed the purchase of SigmaKalon Group, a coatings producer, for $3.20 billion. The acquisition is expected to be accretive to earnings in 2009, and is expected to add about $3.00 billion in sales annually. Further, the acquisition should expand Co.'s geographic footprint, extend its market presence in various end-use markets, and increase the proportion of sales coming from architectural or decorative coatings. Meanwhile, on Feb 11 2008, Co. has acquired the assets and intellectual property of NanoProducts Corporation, a producer and developer of nanoproduct materials and technology. As a result, the acquisition strengthens Co.'s nanotechnology patent portfolio.

Financial Data
(US$ in Thousands)

	12/31/2007	12/31/2006	12/31/2005	12/31/2004	12/31/2003	12/31/2002	12/31/2001	12/31/2000
Earnings Per Share	5.03	4.27	3.49	3.95	2.89	(0.41)	2.29	3.57
Cash Flow Per Share	6.05	6.82	6.28	5.91	6.61	5.16	6.30	5.04
Tang Book Value Per Share	12.59	7.63	8.46	10.81	7.37	3.48	9.12	8.61
Dividends Per Share	2.040	1.910	1.860	1.790	1.730	1.700	1.680	1.600
Dividend Payout %	40.56	44.73	53.30	45.32	59.86	...	73.36	44.82
Income Statement								
Total Revenue	11,206,000	11,037,000	10,201,000	9,513,000	8,756,000	8,067,000	8,169,000	8,629,000
EBITDA	1,696,000	1,509,000	1,387,000	1,529,000	1,334,000	489,000	1,267,000	1,629,000
Income Before Taxes	1,243,000	1,060,000	947,000	1,063,000	843,000	(28,000)	666,000	1,017,000
Income Taxes	355,000	278,000	282,000	322,000	293,000	(7,000)	247,000	369,000
Net Income	834,000	711,000	596,000	683,000	494,000	(69,000)	387,000	620,000
Average Shares	165,900	166,500	170,900	173,000	170,900	169,900	168,300	172,300
Balance Sheet								
Current Assets	7,136,000	4,592,000	4,019,000	4,054,000	3,537,000	2,945,000	2,703,000	3,093,000
Total Assets	12,629,000	10,021,000	8,681,000	8,932,000	8,424,000	7,863,000	8,452,000	9,125,000
Current Liabilities	4,661,000	2,787,000	2,349,000	2,221,000	2,139,000	1,920,000	1,955,000	2,543,000
Long-Term Obligations	1,201,000	1,155,000	1,169,000	1,184,000	1,339,000	1,699,000	1,699,000	1,810,000
Total Liabilities	8,345,000	6,639,000	5,520,000	5,264,000	5,376,000	5,582,000	5,250,000	5,900,000
Stockholders' Equity	4,151,000	3,234,000	3,053,000	3,572,000	2,911,000	2,150,000	3,080,000	3,097,000
Shares Outstanding	163,800	164,081	165,277	172,001	170,926	169,442	168,713	168,222
Statistical Record								
Return on Assets %	7.36	7.60	6.77	7.85	6.07	N.M.	4.40	6.86
Return on Equity %	22.59	22.62	17.99	21.01	19.52	N.M.	12.53	19.94
EBITDA Margin %	15.13	13.67	13.60	16.07	15.24	6.06	15.51	18.88
Net Margin %	7.44	6.44	5.84	7.18	5.64	N.M.	4.74	7.19
Asset Turnover	0.99	1.18	1.16	1.09	1.08	0.99	0.93	0.95
Current Ratio	1.53	1.65	1.71	1.83	1.65	1.53	1.38	1.22
Debt to Equity	0.29	0.36	0.38	0.33	0.46	0.79	0.55	0.58
Price Range	82.20-64.30	69.28-57.02	73.80-55.95	68.55-55.18	64.42-42.64	62.44-41.41	59.54-40.71	64.38-36.13
P/E Ratio	16.34-12.78	16.22-13.35	21.15-16.03	17.35-13.97	22.29-14.75	...	26.00-17.78	18.03-10.12
Average Yield %	2.82	2.98	2.88	2.94	3.31	3.24	3.27	3.39

Address: One PPG Place, Pittsburgh, PA 15272	**Web Site:** www.ppg.com	**Auditors:** Deloitte & Touche LLP
Telephone: 412-434-3131	**Officers:** Charles E. Bunch - Chmn., C.E.O. James C. Diggs - Sr. V.P., Sec., Gen. Couns.	**Investor Contact:** 412-434-3318
Fax: 412-434-2571		**Transfer Agents:** Mellon Investor Services LLC, Ridgefield Park, NJ

PPL CORP

Exchange	Symbol	Price	52Wk Range	Yield	P/E
NYS	PPL	$45.92 (3/31/2008)	55.16-42.08	2.92	13.71

*7 Year Price Score 137.67 *NYSE Composite Index=100 *12 Month Price Score 105.00

Interim Earnings (Per Share)

Qtr.	Mar	Jun	Sep	Dec
2003	0.71	0.34	0.48	0.59
2004	0.50	0.41	0.52	0.47
2005	0.44	0.34	0.51	0.48
2006	0.73	0.47	0.58	0.46
2007	0.52	0.88	0.84	1.10

Interim Dividends (Per Share)

Amt	Decl	Ex	Rec	Pay
0.305Q	5/23/2007	6/6/2007	6/8/2007	7/1/2007
0.305Q	8/24/2007	9/6/2007	9/10/2007	10/1/2007
0.305Q	11/15/2007	12/6/2007	12/10/2007	1/1/2008
0.335Q	2/22/2008	3/6/2008	3/10/2008	4/1/2000

Indicated Div: $1.34

Valuation Analysis

		Institutional Holding	
Forecast P/E	14.36 (1/10/2007)	No of Institutions	418
Market Cap	$17.1 Billion	Shares	237,750,976
Book Value	5.9 Billion	% Held	62.40
Price/Book	2.93		
Price/Sales	2.64		

Business Summary: Electricity (MIC: 7.1 SIC: 4911 NAIC: 221122)

PPL is an energy and utility holding company. Through its subsidiaries, Co. generates electricity from power plants in the northeastern and western U.S.; markets wholesale or retail energy mainly in the northeastern and western portions of the U.S.; delivers electricity to about 4.0 million customers in Pennsylvania and the U.K. Co. is organized into segments containing Supply, Pennsylvania Delivery and International Delivery. Co.'s PPL Energy Supply's segments consist of Supply and International Delivery. Co.'s PPL Electric operates in a single business segment, Pennsylvania Delivery.

Recent Developments: For the year ended Dec 31 2007, net income increased 48.9% to US$1.29 billion from US$865.0 million in the prior year. Revenues were US$6.50 billion, up 6.0% from US$6.13 billion the year before. Operating income was US$1.68 billion versus US$1.51 billion in the prior year, an increase of 11.5%. Direct operating expenses rose 1.4% to US$3.76 billion from US$3.70 billion in the comparable period the year before. Indirect operating expenses increased 15.3% to US$1.06 billion from US$919.0 million in the equivalent prior-year period.

Prospects: On Mar 6 2008, Co. announced that it has signed a definitive agreement to sell its natural gas distribution subsidiary, PPL Gas Utilities Corporation, and propane subsidiary, Penn Fuel Propane, LLC, to UGI Utilities, Inc. In particular, UGI Utilities has agreed to acquire these businesses for approximately $268.0 million in cash plus working capital. Co. expects this deal to close before the end of 2008. Meanwhile, Co. has reaffirmed its 2008 earnings forecast in the range of $2.35 to $2.45 per share. This forecast reflects the loss of earnings due to the expiration of the federal synfuel tax credit program at the end of 2007 and the sale of Co.'s Latin American businesses during 2007.

Financial Data

(US$ in Thousands)	12/31/2007	12/31/2006	12/31/2005	12/31/2004	12/31/2003	12/31/2002	12/31/2001	12/31/2000
Earnings Per Share	3.35	2.24	1.77	1.89	2.12	0.68	0.61	1.72
Cash Flow Per Share	4.13	4.62	3.66	3.89	3.88	2.61	3.11	2.99
Tang Book Value Per Share	11.33	9.35	7.72	7.50	5.53	4.66	6.33	6.94
Dividends Per Share	1.220	1.100	0.960	0.820	0.770	0.720	0.530	0.530
Dividend Payout %	36.42	49.11	54.24	43.50	36.32	105.88	86.89	30.81
Income Statement								
Total Revenue	6,498,000	6,899,000	6,219,000	5,812,000	5,587,000	5,429,000	5,725,000	5,683,000
EBITDA	2,608,000	2,381,000	2,073,000	2,043,000	2,024,000	1,760,000	1,345,000	1,569,000
Income Before Taxes	1,304,000	1,185,000	867,000	905,000	925,000	713,000	480,000	811,000
Income Taxes	270,000	275,000	121,000	195,000	170,000	210,000	261,000	294,000
Net Income	1,288,000	865,000	678,000	698,000	734,000	275,000	231,000	524,000
Average Shares	385,111	386,769	383,737	369,986	346,784	305,618	293,228	289,563
Balance Sheet								
Net PPE	12,605,000	12,069,000	10,916,000	11,209,000	10,446,000	9,566,000	6,135,000	5,948,000
Total Assets	19,972,000	19,747,000	17,926,000	17,761,000	17,123,000	15,569,000	12,574,000	12,360,000
Long-Term Obligations	6,890,000	6,728,000	6,044,000	6,881,000	8,145,000	5,901,000	5,081,000	4,467,000
Total Liabilities	14,115,000	14,324,000	13,457,000	13,471,000	13,813,000	13,263,000	10,635,000	10,251,000
Stockholders' Equity	5,857,000	5,423,000	4,469,000	4,290,000	3,310,000	2,306,000	1,939,000	2,109,000
Shares Outstanding	373,271	385,039	380,145	378,245	354,724	334,903	293,162	290,082
Statistical Record								
Return on Assets %	6.49	4.59	3.80	3.99	4.49	1.95	1.85	4.44
Return on Equity %	22.84	17.49	15.48	18.32	26.14	12.96	11.41	27.37
EBITDA Margin %	40.14	34.51	33.33	35.15	36.23	32.42	23.49	27.61
Net Margin %	19.82	12.54	10.90	12.01	13.14	5.07	4.03	9.22
PPE Turnover	0.53	0.60	0.56	0.54	0.56	0.69	0.95	0.98
Asset Turnover	0.33	0.37	0.35	0.33	0.34	0.39	0.46	0.48
Debt to Equity	1.18	1.24	1.35	1.60	2.46	2.56	2.62	2.12
Price Range	53.96-34.62	37.30-28.47	33.31-25.57	26.89-20.00	22.00-16.14	19.81-13.35	31.11-15.60	22.91-9.25
P/E Ratio	16.11-10.33	16.65-12.71	18.82-14.45	14.22-10.58	10.38-7.61	29.12-19.63	51.00-25.57	13.32-5.38
Average Yield %	2.69	3.41	3.30	3.52	3.95	4.25	2.40	3.63

Address: Two North Ninth Street, Allentown, PA 18101-1179 **Telephone:** 610-774-5151 **Fax:** 610-774-5106	**Web Site:** www.pplweb.com **Officers:** William F. Hecht - Chmn., C.E.O. James H. Miller - Pres.	**Auditors:** PricewaterhouseCoopers LLP **Investor Contact:** 800-345-3085 **Transfer Agents:** Wells Fargo Bank, N.A., South St. Paul, MN

PRAXAIR, INC.

Exchange	Symbol	Price	52Wk Range	Yield	P/E	Div Acheiver
NYS	PX	$84.23 (3/31/2008)	91.75-62.69	1.78	23.27	15 Years

*7 Year Price Score 139.30 *NYSE Composite Index=100 *12 Month Price Score 113.14

TRADING VOLUME (thousand shares)

Interim Earnings (Per Share)
Qtr.	Mar	Jun	Sep	Dec
2003	0.40	0.46	0.46	0.47
2004	0.49	0.53	0.53	0.54
2005	0.59	0.63	0.33	0.65
2006	0.68	0.75	0.75	0.82
2007	0.81	0.89	0.94	0.98

Interim Dividends (Per Share)
Amt	Decl	Ex	Rec	Pay
0.30Q	4/24/2007	6/5/2007	6/7/2007	6/15/2007
0.30Q	7/25/2007	9/5/2007	9/7/2007	9/17/2007
0.30Q	10/23/2007	12/5/2007	12/7/2007	12/17/2007
0.375Q	1/23/2008	3/5/2008	3/7/2008	3/17/2008

Indicated Div: $1.50 (Div. Reinv. Plan)

Valuation Analysis / Institutional Holding
Valuation Analysis		Institutional Holding	
Forecast P/E	15.81	No of Institutions	
	(1/10/2007)	618	
Market Cap	$26.6 Billion	Shares	
Book Value	5.1 Billion	266,799,968	
Price/Book	5.17	% Held	
Price/Sales	2.83	83.28	

Business Summary: Chemicals (MIC: 11.1 SIC: 2813 NAIC: 325120)

Praxair is an industrial gases supplier in North and South America, Asia, and Europe. Co.'s primary products include atmospheric gases (oxygen, nitrogen, argon, rare gases) and process gases (carbon dioxide, helium, hydrogen, electronic gases, specialty gases, acetylene). In addition, Co. designs, engineers, and builds equipment that produces industrial gases for internal use and external sale. In addition, Co.'s surface technologies segment, operated through Praxair Surface Technologies, Inc., supplies wear-resistant and high-temperature corrosion-resistant metallic and ceramic coatings and powders. As of Dec 31 2007, Co. served approximately 25 industries.

Recent Developments: For the year ended Dec 31 2007, net income increased 19.1% to US$1.18 billion from US$988.0 million in the prior year. Revenues were US$9.40 billion, up 13.0% from US$8.32 billion the year before. Operating income was US$1.79 billion versus US$1.52 billion in the prior year, an increase of 17.6%. Direct operating expenses rose 11.9% to US$5.56 billion from US$4.97 billion in the comparable period the year before. Indirect operating expenses increased 12.1% to US$2.06 billion from US$1.84 billion in the equivalent prior-year period.

Prospects: For the full year of 2008, Co. is targeting sales growth to be in the range of 10% to 14% and earnings of $4.00 to $4.20 per diluted share, excluding the effect of the first quarter pension settlement charge, which represents 10.0% to 16.0% growth from its 2007 levels. Specifically, the high end of Co.'s guidance assumes that the U.S. economy remains consistent with 2007, while the lower end of the range assumes the anticipated economic slowdown in the U.S. Co.'s expectations also assumes no significant changes in currency exchange rates. Lastly, Co. is projecting capital expenditures to be about $1.40 billion, mainly for supporting on-site production plants in all geographic segments.

Financial Data
(US$ in Thousands)

	12/31/2007	12/31/2006	12/31/2005	12/31/2004	12/31/2003	12/31/2002	12/31/2001	12/31/2000
Earnings Per Share	3.62	3.00	2.20	2.10	1.77	1.24	1.31	1.13
Cash Flow Per Share	6.14	5.42	4.56	3.80	3.48	3.07	3.16	2.82
Tang Book Value Per Share	9.64	8.94	7.06	6.08	6.00	4.02	4.00	3.95
Dividends Per Share	1.200	1.000	0.720	0.600	0.458	0.380	0.340	0.310
Dividend Payout %	33.15	33.33	32.73	28.57	25.85	30.65	25.86	27.56
Income Statement								
Total Revenue	9,402,000	8,324,000	7,656,000	6,594,000	5,613,000	5,128,000	5,158,000	5,043,000
EBITDA	2,560,000	2,215,000	1,958,000	1,681,000	1,439,000	1,406,000	1,299,000	1,178,000
Income Before Taxes	1,613,000	1,364,000	1,130,000	948,000	771,000	717,000	576,000	483,000
Income Taxes	419,000	355,000	376,000	232,000	174,000	158,000	135,000	103,000
Net Income	1,177,000	988,000	726,000	697,000	585,000	409,000	430,000	363,000
Average Shares	324,842	329,293	329,685	331,403	330,991	329,490	327,014	322,184
Balance Sheet								
Current Assets	2,408,000	2,059,000	2,133,000	1,744,000	1,449,000	1,286,000	1,276,000	1,361,000
Total Assets	13,382,000	11,102,000	10,491,000	9,878,000	8,305,000	7,401,000	7,715,000	7,762,000
Current Liabilities	2,650,000	1,758,000	2,001,000	1,875,000	1,117,000	1,100,000	1,194,000	1,439,000
Long-Term Obligations	3,364,000	2,981,000	2,926,000	2,876,000	2,661,000	2,510,000	2,725,000	2,641,000
Total Liabilities	7,919,000	6,326,000	6,387,000	6,045,000	5,022,000	4,897,000	5,077,000	5,247,000
Stockholders' Equity	5,142,000	4,554,000	3,902,000	3,608,000	3,088,000	2,340,000	2,477,000	2,357,000
Shares Outstanding	315,488	320,860	322,338	323,620	326,085	324,536	324,285	318,758
Statistical Record								
Return on Assets %	9.61	9.15	7.13	7.65	7.45	5.41	5.56	4.68
Return on Equity %	24.28	23.37	19.33	20.76	21.55	16.98	17.79	15.58
EBITDA Margin %	27.23	26.61	25.57	25.49	25.64	27.42	25.18	23.36
Net Margin %	12.52	11.87	9.48	10.57	10.42	7.98	8.34	7.20
Asset Turnover	0.77	0.77	0.75	0.72	0.71	0.68	0.67	0.65
Current Ratio	0.91	1.17	1.07	0.93	1.30	1.17	1.07	0.95
Debt to Equity	0.65	0.65	0.75	0.80	0.86	1.07	1.10	1.12
Price Range	91.75-58.85	63.54-50.95	54.08-41.07	45.97-34.70	38.20-25.33	30.30-22.81	27.64-18.65	27.25-15.84
P/E Ratio	25.35-16.26	21.18-16.98	24.58-18.67	21.89-16.52	21.58-14.31	24.43-18.39	21.10-14.24	24.12-14.02
Average Yield %	1.65	1.78	1.51	1.52	1.48	1.37	1.44	1.54

Address: 39 Old Ridgebury Rd., Danbury, CT 06810-5113 **Telephone:** 203-837-2000 **Fax:** 203-837-2450	**Web Site:** www.praxair.com **Officers:** Dennis H. Reilley - Chmn., Pres., C.E.O. Stephen F. Angel - Exec. V.P.	**Auditors:** PricewatehouseCoopers LLP **Investor Contact:** 203-837-2210 **Transfer Agents:** Registrar and Transfer Company, Cranford, NJ

614

PRECISION CASTPARTS CORP.

Exchange	Symbol	Price	52Wk Range	Yield	P/E
NYS	PCP	$102.08 (3/31/2008)	153.72-95.83	0.12	15.58

*7 Year Price Score 219.54 *NYSE Composite Index=100 *12 Month Price Score 92.45

Interim Earnings (Per Share)

Qtr.	Jun	Sep	Dec	Mar
2004-05	0.41	(1.38)	0.47	0.50
2005-06	0.57	0.58	0.69	0.73
2006-07	0.84	1.13	1.15	1.48
2007-08	1.62	1.68	1.76	...

Interim Dividends (Per Share)

Amt	Decl	Ex	Rec	Pay
0.03Q	5/25/2007	6/6/2007	6/8/2007	7/2/2007
0.03Q	8/16/2007	9/5/2007	9/7/2007	10/1/2007
0.03Q	11/16/2007	12/5/2007	12/7/2007	12/31/2007
0.03Q	2/15/2008	3/5/2008	3/7/2008	3/31/2008

Indicated Div: $0.12

Valuation Analysis

Forecast P/E	14.28 (1/10/2007)
Market Cap	$14.1 Billion
Book Value	3.7 Billion
Price/Book	3.86
Price/Sales	2.13

Institutional Holding

No of Institutions	386
Shares	119,389,184
% Held	87.07

Business Summary: Metal Works (MIC: 11.3 SIC: 3324 NAIC: 331512)

Precision Castparts manufactures metal components and products, provides investment castings, forgings and fasteners/fastener systems for critical aerospace and industrial gas turbine (IGT) applications. Co. also provides investment castings and forgings; nickel alloys and product forms, as well as cobalt alloys; fasteners; specialty alloys, waxes and metal processing solutions; refiner plates, screen cylinders and other products for the pulp and paper industry; metal injection molded and ThixoFormed™ parts; sewer systems; utility systems; and metalworking tools. Co. operates in three principal business segments: Investment Cast Products, Forged Products and Fastener Products.

Recent Developments: For the quarter ended Dec 30 2007, income from continuing operations increased 53.4% to US$242.2 million from US$157.9 million in the year-earlier quarter. Net income increased 55.3% to US$246.5 million from US$158.7 million in the year-earlier quarter. Revenues were US$1.70 billion, up 22.7% from US$1.38 billion the year before. Direct operating expenses rose 17.4% to US$1.23 billion from US$1.05 billion in the comparable period the year before. Indirect operating expenses increased 4.5% to US$90.8 million from US$86.9 million in the equivalent prior-year period.

Prospects: Co.'s outlook appears favorable. For instance, Co.'s investment cast and forged products sales are expected to continue to benefit from increased demand from commercial aerospace customers and renewed strength in the power generation market. In addition, Co. expects to benefit from the ongoing expansion of its manufacturing capacity, which includes the expansion of an industrial gas turbine (IGT) facility in Portland, OR and the construction of a new IGT plant in Painesville, OH that should open in early calendar 2009. Meanwhile, on Jan 3 2008, Co. completed the sale of Shape Memory Alloys, which it acquired through its May 2006 acquisition of Special Metals Corp., for $29.4 million.

Financial Data
(US$ in Thousands)

	9 Mos	6 Mos	3 Mos	04/01/2007	04/02/2006	04/03/2005	03/28/2004	03/30/2003
Earnings Per Share	6.55	5.94	5.39	4.59	2.58	(0.01)	1.02	1.18
Cash Flow Per Share	7.06	6.58	6.28	6.38	1.74	2.73	1.39	2.38
Tang Book Value Per Share	9.41	7.32	6.86	5.37	3.56	1.50	0.62	0.66
Dividends Per Share	0.120	0.120	0.120	0.120	0.105	0.060	0.060	0.060
Dividend Payout %	1.83	2.02	2.23	2.61	4.07		5.85	5.11
Income Statement								
Total Revenue	5,078,700	3,387,100	1,660,100	5,361,200	3,546,400	2,919,000	2,174,700	2,117,200
EBITDA	1,192,200	787,000	385,700	1,085,500	653,500	515,700	354,700	382,500
Depn & Amortn	97,800	64,600	32,100				...	...
Income Before Taxes	1,058,100	696,200	341,000	920,800	512,900	362,100	212,400	243,600
Income Taxes	356,200	235,900	115,300	304,700	162,200	121,300	75,800	83,400
Net Income	708,300	461,800	226,400	633,100	350,600	(1,700)	117,900	124,300
Average Shares	140,400	140,100	139,600	138,000	135,700	133,000	115,200	106,000
Balance Sheet								
Current Assets	2,254,600	2,298,900	2,259,000	2,036,900	1,233,800	1,213,100	1,187,500	785,900
Total Assets	5,842,200	5,878,500	5,603,100	5,258,700	3,751,200	3,625,000	3,756,200	2,467,200
Current Liabilities	1,240,500	1,294,700	1,336,500	1,658,200	768,400	779,700	912,800	624,800
Long-Term Obligations	476,100	741,600	723,100	319,200	599,800	798,700	823,000	532,100
Total Liabilities	2,179,800	2,505,400	2,493,700	2,422,500	1,610,700	1,844,600	2,041,600	1,405,500
Stockholders' Equity	3,662,400	3,373,100	3,109,400	2,836,200	2,140,500	1,780,400	1,714,600	1,061,700
Shares Outstanding	138,542	138,126	137,855	137,208	135,133	132,303	129,390	105,516
Statistical Record								
Return on Assets %	17.15	15.61	14.45	14.09	9.53	N.M.	3.80	4.95
Return on Equity %	28.85	28.35	27.70	25.51	17.93	N.M.	8.52	12.38
EBITDA Margin %	23.47	23.24	23.23	20.25	18.43	17.67	16.31	18.07
Net Margin %	13.95	13.63	13.64	11.81	9.89	N.M.	5.42	5.87
Asset Turnover	1.25	1.20	1.15	1.19	0.96	0.78	0.70	0.84
Current Ratio	1.82	1.78	1.69	1.23	1.61	1.56	1.30	1.26
Debt to Equity	0.13	0.22	0.23	0.11	0.28	0.45	0.48	0.50
Price Range	153.72-80.50	149.09-62.28	121.36-53.34	104.80-50.26	59.65-36.41	39.20-21.07	24.59-11.91	18.79-8.60
P/E Ratio	23.47-12.29	25.10-10.48	22.52-9.90	22.83-10.95	23.12-14.11	...	24.11-11.68	15.92-7.29
Average Yield %	0.10	0.12	0.14	0.17	0.22	0.20	0.32	0.45

Address: 4650 S.W. Macadam Avenue, Suite 440, Portland, OR 97239-4262
Telephone: 503-417-4800
Fax: 503-417-4817

Web Site: www.precast.com
Officers: Mark Donegan - Chmn., Pres., C.E.O.
Gregory M. Delaney - Exec. V.P., Special Projects

Auditors: Deloitte & Touche LLP
Investor Contact: 503-417-4850
Transfer Agents: The Bank of New York, New York, NY

PRIDE INTERNATIONAL, INC. (DE)

Exchange	Symbol	Price	52Wk Range	Yield	P/E
NYS	PDE	$34.95 (3/31/2008)	40.08-29.85	N/A	7.89

*7 Year Price Score 120.85 *NYSE Composite Index=100 *12 Month Price Score 105.55

TRADING VOLUME (thousand shares)

Interim Earnings (Per Share)

Qtr.	Mar	Jun	Sep	Dec
2003	0.03	(0.14)	0.19	(0.28)
2004	(0.05)	0.02	(0.13)	0.14
2005	0.11	0.01	0.41	0.25
2006	0.41	0.39	0.52	0.40
2007	0.58	0.83	2.25	0.76

Interim Dividends (Per Share)

No Dividends Paid

Valuation Analysis		Institutional Holding	
Forecast P/E	N/A	No of Institutions	254
Market Cap	$5.8 Billion	Shares	
Book Value	3.5 Billion		126,315,416
Price/Book	1.68	% Held	
Price/Sales	2.85		76.39

Business Summary: Oil and Gas (MIC: 14.2 SIC: 1389 NAIC: 213111)

Pride International is an international provider of contract drilling and related services, operating both offshore and on land. Co. also provides rig management services on a variety of rigs, consisting of technical drilling assistance, personnel, repair and maintenance services and drilling operation management services. As of Feb 27 2008, Co. owned a global fleet of 64 rigs, consisting of two deepwater drillships, 12 semisubmersible rigs, 28 jackup rigs, 10 platform rigs, five managed deepwater drilling rigs and seven Eastern Hemisphere-based land drilling rigs. Co. operates in South America, the Gulf of Mexico, the Mediterranean Sea, West Africa, the Middle East and Asia Pacific.

Recent Developments: For the year ended Dec 31 2007, income from continuing operations increased 128.8% to US$431.8 million from US$188.7 million a year earlier. Net income increased 164.5% to US$784.3 million from US$296.5 million in the prior year. Revenues were US$2.04 billion, up 26.9% from US$1.61 billion the year before. Operating income was US$679.0 million versus US$391.7 million in the prior year, an increase of 73.3%. Direct operating expenses rose 9.6% to US$1.03 billion from US$942.0 million in the comparable period the year before. Indirect operating expenses increased 19.8% to US$332.1 million from US$277.1 million in the equivalent prior-year period.

Prospects: Looking ahead, Co. believes that long-term market conditions for deepwater drilling services are favorable and that demand for deepwater rigs should continue to exceed supply for the next several years, producing opportunities for deepwater drilling rigs. Accordingly, on Feb 27 2008, Co. announced that it has been awarded contract extensions, representing six years per rig, from Petroleo Brasileiro S.A. for the deepwater, positioned semisubmersible rigs Pride Rio de Janeiro and Pride Portland. Estimated contract revenues that could be generated from each six-year contract extension, which are expected to commence during late 2010 to early 2011, are approximately $768.0 million.

Financial Data

(US$ in Thousands)	12/31/2007	12/31/2006	12/31/2005	12/31/2004	12/31/2003	12/31/2002	12/31/2001	12/31/2000
Earnings Per Share	4.43	1.72	0.80	(0.03)	(0.18)	(0.07)	0.68	0.01
Cash Flow Per Share	4.14	3.76	2.11	2.47	0.86	1.14	1.93	1.35
Tang Book Value Per Share	20.78	15.61	13.60	12.07	12.07	12.14	12.29	13.39
Income Statement								
Total Revenue	2,043,800	2,495,400	2,033,300	1,712,200	1,689,720	1,269,774	1,512,895	909,007
EBITDA	887,200	832,000	592,100	479,057	376,777	379,306	475,382	236,127
Income Before Taxes	615,000	475,800	248,700	98,316	(4,298)	11,355	154,613	16,889
Income Taxes	179,700	176,400	100,700	61,732	(1,130)	3,407	49,231	-5,341
Net Income	784,300	296,500	128,600	(3,459)	(23,933)	(8,947)	91,206	736
Average Shares	178,500	176,500	172,600	137,301	134,704	133,305	142,778	67,418
Balance Sheet								
Current Assets	1,532,600	963,200	688,300	559,551	726,924	669,384	632,140	478,148
Total Assets	5,613,900	5,097,500	4,086,500	4,038,324	4,378,430	4,324,995	4,205,690	2,676,928
Current Liabilities	644,600	670,100	474,500	425,926	643,803	546,845	537,085	387,616
Long-Term Obligations	1,115,700	1,294,700	1,187,300	1,686,251	1,815,078	1,804,130	1,639,885	1,162,320
Total Liabilities	2,143,500	2,463,600	1,827,100	2,322,262	2,675,651	2,625,290	2,508,584	1,718,832
Stockholders' Equity	3,470,400	2,633,900	2,259,400	1,716,062	1,702,779	1,699,705	1,697,106	958,096
Shares Outstanding	166,900	164,300	161,100	136,525	135,400	134,084	132,847	67,689
Statistical Record								
Return on Assets %	14.64	6.46	3.17	N.M.	N.M.	N.M.	2.65	0.03
Return on Equity %	25.70	12.12	6.47	N.M.	N.M.	N.M.	6.87	0.08
EBITDA Margin %	43.41	33.34	29.12	27.98	22.30	29.87	31.42	25.98
Net Margin %	38.37	11.88	6.32	N.M.	N.M.	N.M.	6.03	0.08
Asset Turnover	0.38	0.54	0.50	0.41	0.39	0.30	0.44	0.36
Current Ratio	2.38	1.44	1.45	1.31	1.13	1.22	1.18	1.23
Debt to Equity	0.32	0.49	0.53	0.98	1.07	1.06	0.97	1.21
Price Range	40.08-26.42	36.87-24.80	32.10-19.72	20.54-15.12	19.78-13.00	19.52-11.00	32.65-9.75	29.00-13.50
P/E Ratio	9.05-5.96	21.44-14.42	40.13-24.65	...	...	...	48.01-14.34	N.M.

Address: 5847 San Felipe, Suite 3300, Houston, TX 77057 **Telephone:** 713-789-1400 **Fax:** 713-789-1430	**Web Site:** www.prideinternational.com **Officers:** David A. B. Brown - Chmn. Louis A. Raspino - Pres., C.E.O.	**Auditors:** KPMG LLP **Investor Contact:** 713-789-1400 **Transfer Agents:** American Stock Transfer & Trust Company

PRINCIPAL FINANCIAL GROUP, INC.

Exchange	Symbol	Price	52Wk Range	Yield	P/E
NYS	PFG	$55.72 (3/31/2008)	70.72-48.57	1.62	18.03

*7 Year Price Score N/A   *NYSE Composite Index=100   *12 Month Price Score 97.61

Interim Earnings (Per Share)

Qtr.	Mar	Jun	Sep	Dec
2003	0.47	0.62	0.67	0.53
2004	0.60	0.37	0.95	0.70
2005	0.68	0.82	0.74	0.88
2006	1.01	0.76	0.92	1.04
2007	0.95	1.12	0.87	0.15

Interim Dividends (Per Share)

Amt	Decl	Ex	Rec	Pay
0.55A	10/22/2004	11/9/2004	11/12/2004	12/17/2004
0.65A	11/2/2005	11/15/2005	11/17/2005	12/16/2005
0.80A	11/7/2006	11/20/2006	11/22/2006	12/15/2006
0.90A	10/29/2007	11/14/2007	11/16/2007	12/7/2007

Indicated Div: $0.90

Valuation Analysis

	Institutional Holding
Forecast P/E 13.49 (1/10/2007)	No of Institutions 356
Market Cap $14.4 Billion	Shares 133,370,880
Book Value 7.4 Billion	% Held 49.79
Price/Book 1.95	
Price/Sales 1.32	

TRADING VOLUME (thousand shares)

Business Summary: Insurance (MIC: 8.2 SIC: 6321 NAIC: 524114)

Principal Financial Group is a provider of retirement savings, investment and insurance products and services, with $311.10 billion in assets under management as of Dec 31 2007. Co.'s U.S. and international operations concentrate primarily on asset management and accumulation. In addition, Co. provides a range of individual and group life insurance, group health insurance, and individual and group disability insurance. At Dec 31 2007, Co.'s businesses were organized into the following operating segments: U.S. Asset Accumulation; Global Asset Management; International Asset Management and Accumulation; and Life and Health Insurance.

Recent Developments: For the year ended Dec 31 2007, income from continuing operations decreased 18.9% to US$840.1 million from US$1.04 billion a year earlier. Net income decreased 19.2% to US$860.3 million from US$1.06 billion in the prior year. Revenues were US$10.91 billion, up 10.5% from US$9.87 billion the year before. Net premiums earned were US$4.63 billion versus US$4.31 billion in the prior year, an increase of 7.6%. Net investment income rose 9.6% to US$3.97 billion from US$3.62 billion a year ago.

Prospects: For 2008, Co. expects net income of $3.93 to $4.20 per diluted share, based on its estimate for 2008 mortgage and credit losses. Specifically, Co. expects results to be affected by difficult market conditions, including continued uncertainty around the U.S. economy, continued adverse credit conditions, and continued volatility in asset values and in the equity markets. However, Co. expects market conditions to improve over time, and is confident of achieving its longer-term performance objectives of 11.0% to13.0% average annual growth in earnings per share. Separately, Co. continues to focus on network discounts, claims costs and expense management in order to turnaround its health business.

Financial Data
(US$ in Thousands)

	12/31/2007	12/31/2006	12/31/2005	12/31/2004	12/31/2003	12/31/2002	12/31/2001	12/31/2000
Earnings Per Share	3.09	3.74	3.11	2.62	2.28	0.41	0.99	...
Cash Flow Per Share	11.15	8.35	8.28	7.18	11.39	16.64	10.89	...
Tang Book Value Per Share	23.31	24.28	26.09	23.67	16.03	14.78	10.39	...
Dividends Per Share	0.900	0.800	0.650	0.550	0.450	0.250	...	...
Dividend Payout %	29.13	21.39	20.90	20.99	19.74	60.98	...	...
Income Statement								
Premium Income	4,634,100	4,305,300	3,975,000	3,710,000	3,634,100	3,881,800	4,122,300	3,996,400
Total Revenue	10,906,500	9,870,500	9,007,700	8,303,700	9,404,200	8,822,500	8,817,500	8,884,900
Benefits & Claims	6,435,300	5,692,400	5,282,900	4,959,500	4,861,300	5,216,900	5,482,100	5,232,300
Income Before Taxes	1,048,200	1,328,700	1,124,300	881,600	935,700	663,800	448,300	860,300
Income Taxes	208,100	295,000	232,400	179,100	225,800	45,900	79,000	240,300
Net Income	860,300	1,064,300	919,000	825,600	746,300	142,300	358,800	620,200
Average Shares	268,100	275,500	289,900	314,700	326,800	350,200	362,400	...
Balance Sheet								
Total Assets	154,520,200	143,658,100	127,035,400	113,798,100	107,754,400	89,861,300	88,350,500	84,404,900
Total Liabilities	147,098,500	135,797,300	119,228,200	106,253,800	100,354,800	83,204,100	81,530,200	78,152,400
Stockholders' Equity	7,421,700	7,860,800	7,807,200	7,544,300	7,399,600	6,657,200	6,820,300	6,252,500
Shares Outstanding	259,100	268,400	280,600	300,600	320,700	334,400	360,100	...
Statistical Record								
Return on Assets %	0.58	0.79	0.76	0.74	0.76	0.16	0.42	0.73
Return on Equity %	11.26	13.59	11.97	11.02	10.62	2.11	5.49	10.48
Loss Ratio %	138.87	132.22	132.90	133.68	133.77	134.39	132.99	130.93
Net Margin %	7.89	10.78	10.20	9.94	7.94	1.61	4.07	6.98
Price Range	70.72-52.77	59.34-45.97	51.90-36.91	41.21-32.22	34.30-25.83	31.00-22.50	24.08-21.00	...
P/E Ratio	22.89-17.08	15.87-12.29	16.69-11.87	15.73-12.30	15.04-11.33	75.61-54.88	24.32-21.21	...
Average Yield %	1.47	1.51	1.50	1.54	1.46	0.91	...	...

Address: 711 High Street, Des Moines, IA 50392	Web Site: www.principal.com	Auditors: ERNST & YOUNG LLP
Telephone: 515-247-5111	Officers: J. Barry Griswell - Chmn., Pres., C.E.O. Michael H. Gersie - Exec. V.P., C.F.O.	Transfer Agents: ComputerShare Investor Services, Chicago, IL

PROCTER & GAMBLE CO.

Exchange	Symbol	Price	52Wk Range	Yield	P/E	Div Acheiver
NYS	PG	$70.07 (3/31/2008)	74.67-61.03	2.28	21.17	54 Years

*7 Year Price Score 102.57 *NYSE Composite Index=100 *12 Month Price Score 108.17

Interim Earnings (Per Share)

Qtr.	Sep	Dec	Mar	Jun
2004-05	0.73	0.74	0.63	0.56
2005-06	0.77	0.72	0.63	0.54
2006-07	0.79	0.84	0.74	0.67
2007-08	0.92	0.98	...	...

Interim Dividends (Per Share)

Amt	Decl	Ex	Rec	Pay
0.35Q	7/10/2007	7/18/2007	7/20/2007	8/15/2007
0.35Q	10/9/2007	10/17/2007	10/19/2007	11/15/2007
0.35Q	1/8/2008	1/16/2008	1/18/2008	2/15/2008
0.40Q	4/8/2008	4/16/2008	4/18/2008	5/15/2008

Indicated Div: $1.60 (Div. Reinv. Plan)

Valuation Analysis

		Institutional Holding	
Forecast P/E	16.33	No of Institutions	
	(1/10/2007)	1373	
Market Cap	$215.6 Billion	Shares	
Book Value	68.2 Billion	1,890,439,040	
Price/Book	3.16	% Held	
Price/Sales	2.70	59.91	

Business Summary: Chemicals (MIC: 11.1 SIC: 2841 NAIC: 325611)

Procter & Gamble is engaged as a global provider of branded consumer goods products. As of June 30 2007, Co.'s products were sold in more than 180 countries around the world principally through mass merchandisers, grocery stores, membership club stores and drug stores. Co. is organized into three Global Business Units (GBUs): Beauty and Health; Household Care; and Gillette GBU. Co. has seven reportable segments: Beauty; Health Care; Fabric Care and Home Care; Snacks, Coffee and Pet Care; Baby Care and Family Care; Blades and Razors; and Duracell and Braun.

Recent Developments: For the quarter ended Dec 31 2007, net income increased 14.3% to US$3.27 billion from US$2.86 billion in the year-earlier quarter. Revenues were US$21.58 billion, up 9.4% from US$19.73 billion the year before. Operating income was US$4.71 billion versus US$4.35 billion in the prior-year quarter, an increase of 8.4%. Direct operating expenses rose 11.9% to US$10.39 billion from US$9.29 billion in the comparable period the year before. Indirect operating expenses increased 6.2% to US$6.47 billion from US$6.09 billion in the equivalent prior-year period.

Prospects: On Jan 31 2008, Co. announced plans to separate its coffee business and create an independent company named The Folgers Coffee Company, to allow it to focus on its core businesses. Co. expects to determine the final deal structure, of either a spin-off or split-off transaction, during the Apr to June 2008 quarter and complete the transaction during the July to Dec 2008 quarter. Separately, Co. remains optimistic about the strength of its brand portfolio, initiative pipeline and productivity program, and thus, projects total sales for the fiscal year ending June 2008 to increase 7.0% to 9.0%, with organic sales growth of 4.0% to 6.0% and earnings estimate of $3.46 to $3.50 per share.

Financial Data

(US$ in Thousands)	6 Mos	3 Mos	06/30/2007	06/30/2006	06/30/2005	06/30/2004	06/30/2003	06/30/2002
Earnings Per Share	3.31	3.17	3.04	2.64	2.66	2.32	1.85	1.54
Cash Flow Per Share	4.98	4.40	4.25	3.72	3.47	3.62	3.35	2.98
Tang Book Value Per Share	N.M.	N.M.	N.M.	N.M.	N.M.	N.M.	0.42	N.M.
Dividends Per Share	1.360	1.320	1.280	1.150	1.030	0.933	0.820	0.760
Dividend Payout %	41.09	41.64	42.11	43.56	38.72	40.19	44.44	49.19
Income Statement								
Total Revenue	41,774,000	20,199,000	76,476,000	68,222,000	56,741,000	51,407,000	43,377,000	40,238,000
EBITDA	11,020,000	5,363,000	19,144,000	16,159,000	13,157,000	11,712,000	9,794,000	8,679,000
Depn & Amortn	1,503,000	752,000	...	...	...	...	...	...
Income Before Taxes	8,769,000	4,252,000	14,710,000	12,413,000	10,439,000	9,350,000	7,530,000	6,383,000
Income Taxes	2,420,000	1,173,000	4,370,000	3,729,000	3,182,000	2,869,000	2,344,000	2,031,000
Net Income	6,349,000	3,079,000	10,340,000	8,684,000	7,257,000	6,481,000	5,186,000	4,352,000
Average Shares	3,341,500	3,354,200	3,398,600	3,285,900	2,726,200	2,790,100	2,802,600	2,809,800
Balance Sheet								
Current Assets	26,960,000	25,182,000	24,031,000	24,329,000	20,329,000	17,115,000	15,220,000	12,166,000
Total Assets	144,401,000	141,791,000	138,014,000	135,695,000	61,527,000	57,048,000	43,706,000	40,776,000
Current Liabilities	31,479,000	30,874,000	30,717,000	19,985,000	25,039,000	22,147,000	12,358,000	12,704,000
Long-Term Obligations	23,528,000	22,172,000	23,375,000	35,976,000	12,887,000	12,554,000	11,475,000	11,201,000
Total Liabilities	76,158,000	74,144,000	71,254,000	72,787,000	44,050,000	39,770,000	27,520,000	27,070,000
Stockholders' Equity	68,243,000	67,559,000	66,760,000	62,908,000	17,477,000	17,278,000	16,186,000	13,706,000
Shares Outstanding	3,077,498	3,105,639	3,131,900	3,178,841	2,472,900	2,543,800	2,594,400	2,601,600
Statistical Record								
Return on Assets %	7.90	7.69	7.56	8.81	12.24	12.83	12.28	11.58
Return on Equity %	16.66	16.32	15.95	21.61	41.76	38.63	34.70	33.85
EBITDA Margin %	26.38	26.55	25.03	23.69	23.19	22.78	22.58	21.57
Net Margin %	15.20	15.24	13.52	12.73	12.79	12.61	11.96	10.82
Asset Turnover	0.57	0.56	0.56	0.69	0.96	1.02	1.03	1.07
Current Ratio	0.86	0.82	0.78	1.22	0.81	0.77	1.23	0.96
Debt to Equity	0.34	0.33	0.35	0.57	0.74	0.73	0.71	0.82
Price Range	74.67-61.03	70.51-61.03	66.09-55.60	62.25-52.16	56.73-50.97	55.96-43.35	46.50-37.23	47.20-32.00
P/E Ratio	22.56-18.44	22.24-19.25	21.74-18.29	23.58-19.76	21.33-19.16	24.12-18.69	25.14-20.12	30.65-20.78
Average Yield %	2.06	2.07	2.05	2.03	1.90	1.89	1.87	1.90

Address: One Procter & Gamble Plaza, Cincinnati, OH 45202
Telephone: 513-983-1100
Fax: 513-983-2062

Web Site: www.pg.com
Officers: Alan G. Lafley - Chmn., Pres., C.E.O. Bruce L. Byrnes - Vice-Chmn.

Auditors: Deloitte & Touche LLP
Investor Contact: 800-742-6253
Transfer Agents: The Procter and Gamble Company, Cincinnati, OH

PROGRESS ENERGY, INC.

Exchange	Symbol	Price	52Wk Range	Yield	P/E	Div Acheiver
NYS	PGN	$41.70 (3/31/2008)	52.55-41.32	5.90	21.28	19 Years

*7 Year Price Score 84.70 *NYSE Composite Index=100 *12 Month Price Score 98.74

TRADING VOLUME (thousand shares)

Interim Earnings (Per Share)

Qtr.	Mar	Jun	Sep	Dec
2003	0.89	0.64	1.34	0.41
2004	0.45	0.63	1.24	0.80
2005	0.38	(0.01)	1.81	0.62
2006	0.18	(0.19)	1.27	1.02
2007	1.08	(0.75)	1.24	0.40

Interim Dividends (Per Share)

Amt	Decl	Ex	Rec	Pay
0.61Q	5/9/2007	7/6/2007	7/10/2007	8/1/2007
0.61Q	9/21/2007	10/5/2007	10/10/2007	11/1/2007
0.615Q	12/12/2007	1/8/2008	1/10/2008	2/1/2008
0.615Q	3/19/2008	4/8/2008	4/10/2008	5/1/2008

Indicated Div: $2.46 (Div. Reinv. Plan)

Valuation Analysis / Institutional Holding

Forecast P/E	16.61 (1/10/2007)	No of Institutions 439
Market Cap	$10.8 Billion	Shares
Book Value	8.5 Billion	157,700,592
Price/Book	1.27	% Held
Price/Sales	1.18	61.34

Business Summary: Electricity (MIC: 7.1 SIC: 4911 NAIC: 221121)

Progress Energy is a utility holding company. Co.'s wholly owned regulated subsidiaries, Carolina Power & Light Company, and Florida Power Corporation, each a business segment, are primarily engaged in the generation, transmission, distribution and sale of electricity in portions of North Carolina, South Carolina and Florida. As of Dec 31 2007, Co. had more than 21,000 megawatts of regulated electric generation capacity, and served approximately 3.1 million retail electric customers as well as other load serving entities. Co.'s Corporate and Other segment primarily includes both the operations of Co. and its Progress Energy Service Company, LLC subsidiary.

Recent Developments: For the year ended Dec 31 2007, net income decreased 11.7% to US$504.0 million from US$571.0 million in the prior year. Revenues were US$9.15 billion, up 4.9% from US$8.72 billion the year before. Operating income was US$1.55 billion versus US$1.49 billion in the prior year, an increase of 4.0%. Direct operating expenses rose 8.3% to US$6.20 billion from US$5.73 billion in the comparable period the year before. Indirect operating expenses decreased 6.9% to US$1.41 billion from US$1.51 billion in the equivalent prior year period.

Prospects: Co.'s results are benefiting from favorable weather, increased wholesale sales and lower interest expense. As such, Co. reaffirms its full-year 2007 earnings guidance to be in the range of $2.70 to $2.90 per share, excluding the impacts from the contingent value obligations, mark-to-market adjustment, potential impairments, coal and synthetic fuels operations and discontinued operations of other businesses. Separately, on Oct 29 2007, Co. announced plans to invest about $700.0 million to $750.0 million in building new electric generation capability at its energy complex in Richmond County as well as new transmission capacity. Co. expects to complete these constructions by June 1 2011.

Financial Data

(US$ in Thousands)	12/31/2007	12/31/2006	12/31/2005	12/31/2004	12/31/2003	12/31/2002	12/31/2001	12/31/2000
Earnings Per Share	1.96	2.28	2.82	3.12	3.28	2.42	2.64	3.03
Cash Flow Per Share	4.89	7.64	5.98	6.62	7.54	7.36	7.06	5.46
Tang Book Value Per Share	18.33	18.09	15.94	14.48	13.78	12.43	10.58	8.60
Dividends Per Share	2.440	2.420	2.360	2.300	2.240	2.180	2.120	1.030
Dividend Payout %	124.49	106.14	83.69	73.72	68.29	90.08	80.30	33.99
Income Statement								
Total Revenue	9,153,000	9,570,000	10,108,000	9,772,000	8,743,000	7,945,120	8,461,459	4,118,873
EBITDA	2,616,000	1,928,000	1,870,000	2,137,000	2,467,000	2,112,404	2,241,745	1,751,386
Income Before Taxes	1,036,000	727,000	656,000	851,000	702,000	394,361	389,967	681,135
Income Taxes	334,000	204,000	(45,000)	115,000	(109,000)	(157,808)	(151,643)	202,774
Net Income	504,000	571,000	697,000	759,000	782,000	328,380	341,610	478,361
Average Shares	256,700	250,800	247,000	243,100	237,000	218,166	204,683	157,169
Balance Sheet								
Net PPE	16,605,000	15,276,000	16,322,000	16,373,000	16,592,000	12,540,505	11,987,961	11,166,360
Total Assets	26,286,000	25,701,000	27,023,000	25,993,000	26,202,000	21,352,704	20,739,791	20,091,012
Long-Term Obligations	8,976,000	8,835,000	10,446,000	9,521,000	9,934,000	9,747,293	9,483,715	5,890,099
Total Liabilities	17,771,000	17,322,000	18,892,000	18,267,000	18,665,000	14,582,864	14,643,427	14,573,980
Stockholders' Equity	8,515,000	8,379,000	8,131,000	7,726,000	7,537,000	6,769,840	6,096,364	5,517,032
Shares Outstanding	260,000	256,000	252,000	247,000	246,000	237,992	218,725	206,089
Statistical Record								
Return on Assets %	1.94	2.17	2.63	2.90	3.29	2.51	2.65	3.22
Return on Equity %	5.97	6.92	8.79	9.92	10.93	8.21	9.33	10.61
EBITDA Margin %	28.58	20.15	18.50	21.87	28.16	26.59	26.49	42.52
Net Margin %	5.51	5.97	6.90	7.77	8.94	6.65	6.40	11.61
PPE Turnover	0.57	0.61	0.62	0.59	0.60	0.65	0.73	0.45
Asset Turnover	0.35	0.36	0.38	0.38	0.37	0.38	0.41	0.28
Debt to Equity	1.05	1.05	1.28	1.23	1.32	1.44	1.56	1.07
Price Range	52.55-43.33	49.39-40.79	45.74-41.03	47.78-40.48	47.38-38.32	52.38-33.58	48.44-39.61	49.19-28.56
P/E Ratio	26.81-22.11	21.66-17.89	16.22-14.55	15.31-12.97	14.45-11.68	21.64-13.88	18.35-15.00	16.23-9.43
Average Yield %	5.07	5.48	5.42	5.27	5.29	4.79	4.98	2.88

Address: 410 South Wilmington Street, Raleigh, NC 27601-1748	**Web Site:** www.progress-energy.com	**Auditors:** Deloitte & Touche LLP
Telephone: 919-546-6111	**Officers:** Robert B. McGehee - Chmn., C.E.O.	**Investor Contact:** 919-546-6111
Fax: 919-549-7678	William D. Johnson - Pres., C.O.O.	**Transfer Agents:** EquiServe Trust Company, N.A., Providence, RI

PROGRESSIVE CORP. (OH)

Exchange	Symbol	Price	52Wk Range	Yield	P/E
NYS	PGR	$16.07 (3/31/2008)	24.70-15.47	0.90	9.74

*7 Year Price Score 83.93   *NYSE Composite Index=100   *12 Month Price Score 94.10

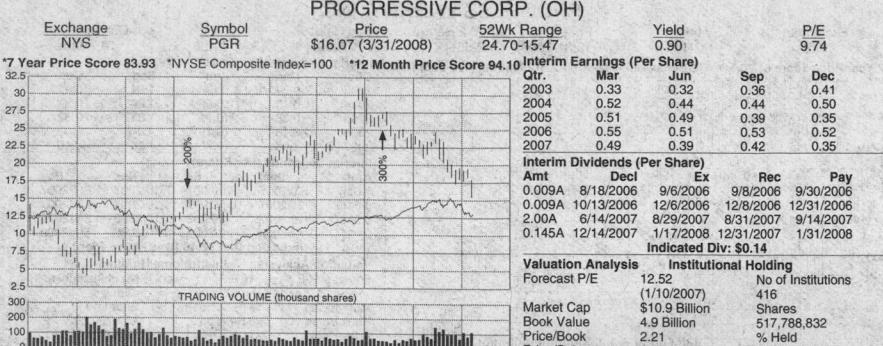

Interim Earnings (Per Share)

Qtr.	Mar	Jun	Sep	Dec
2003	0.33	0.32	0.36	0.41
2004	0.52	0.44	0.44	0.50
2005	0.51	0.49	0.39	0.35
2006	0.55	0.51	0.53	0.52
2007	0.49	0.39	0.42	0.35

Interim Dividends (Per Share)

Amt	Decl	Ex	Rec	Pay
0.009A	8/18/2006	9/6/2006	9/8/2006	9/30/2006
0.009A	10/13/2006	12/6/2006	12/8/2006	12/31/2006
2.00A	6/14/2007	8/29/2007	8/31/2007	9/14/2007
0.145A	12/14/2007	1/17/2008	12/31/2007	1/31/2008

Indicated Div: $0.14

Valuation Analysis / Institutional Holding

Forecast P/E	12.52 (1/10/2007)	No of Institutions 416
Market Cap	$10.9 Billion	Shares
Book Value	4.9 Billion	517,788,832
Price/Book	2.21	% Held
Price/Sales	0.74	69.55

Business Summary: Insurance (MIC: 8.2 SIC: 6331 NAIC: 524126)

Progressive is an insurance holding company. Co.'s insurance subsidiaries and affiliate provide personal and commercial automobile insurance and other specialty property-casualty insurance and related services throughout the U.S. Co.'s Personal Lines segment writes insurance for private passenger automobiles and recreational and other vehicles. In addition, Co.'s Commercial Auto Business writes primary liability and physical damage insurance for automobiles and trucks owned by small businesses. Co.'s service businesses include providing insurance-related services, primarily policy issuance and claims adjusting services in 27 states for Commercial Auto Insurance Procedures/Plans.

Recent Developments: For the year ended Dec 31 2007, net income decreased 28.2% to US$1.18 billion from US$1.65 billion in the prior year. Revenues were US$14.69 billion, down 0.7% from US$14.79 billion the year before. Net premiums earned were US$13.88 billion versus US$14.12 billion in the prior year, a decrease of 1.7%. Net investment income rose 5.1% to US$680.8 million from US$647.8 million a year ago.

Prospects: Co. appears to be closer to its targeted margins and has almost fully adjusted its pricing to reflect the favorable accident frequency of the past several years. Also, the reorganization of Co.'s Agency and Direct businesses under one Personal Lines organization should allow it to better execute its key strategies, lower its non-claims expense ratio and foster growth through competitive pricing, improved customer retention and greater focus on brand development. Meanwhile, Co. continues to implement internal retention measures through competitive pricing to grow its policies in force. In 2008, Co. plans to expand its Personal Lines and Personal Auto product offerings into Massachusetts.

Financial Data
(US$ in Thousands)

	12/31/2007	12/31/2006	12/31/2005	12/31/2004	12/31/2003	12/31/2002	12/31/2001	12/31/2000
Earnings Per Share	1.65	2.10	1.75	1.91	1.42	0.75	0.46	0.05
Cash Flow Per Share	2.52	2.61	2.53	3.12	2.81	2.18	1.40	0.93
Tang Book Value Per Share	7.26	9.15	7.74	6.43	5.81	4.32	3.69	3.25
Dividends Per Share	2.000	0.033	0.030	0.028	0.025	0.024	0.023	0.022
Dividend Payout %	121.21	1.55	1.72	1.44	1.76	3.23	5.11	43.54
Income Statement								
Premium Income	13,877,400	14,117,900	13,764,400	13,169,900	11,341,000	8,883,500	7,161,800	6,348,400
Total Revenue	14,686,800	14,786,400	14,303,400	13,782,100	11,892,000	9,294,400	7,488,200	6,771,000
Benefits & Claims	9,926,200	9,394,900	9,364,800	8,555,000	7,640,400	6,299,100	5,264,100	5,279,400
Income Before Taxes	1,693,000	2,433,200	2,058,900	2,450,800	1,859,700	981,400	587,600	31,800
Income Taxes	510,500	785,700	665,000	802,100	604,300	314,100	176,200	(14,300)
Net Income	1,182,500	1,647,500	1,393,900	1,648,700	1,255,400	667,300	411,400	46,100
Average Shares	718,500	783,800	799,300	864,800	882,000	892,800	901,198	891,600
Balance Sheet								
Total Assets	18,843,100	19,482,100	18,898,600	17,184,300	16,281,500	13,564,400	11,122,400	10,051,600
Total Liabilities	13,907,600	12,635,500	12,791,100	12,028,900	11,250,900	9,796,400	7,871,700	7,181,800
Stockholders' Equity	4,935,500	6,846,600	6,107,500	5,155,400	5,030,600	3,768,000	3,250,700	2,869,800
Shares Outstanding	680,200	748,000	789,200	801,600	865,600	872,000	880,800	882,000
Statistical Record								
Return on Assets %	6.17	8.59	7.73	9.83	8.41	5.41	3.89	0.47
Return on Equity %	20.07	25.44	24.75	32.28	28.54	19.01	13.44	1.64
Loss Ratio %	71.53	66.55	68.04	64.96	67.37	70.91	73.50	83.16
Net Margin %	8.05	11.14	9.75	11.96	10.56	7.18	5.49	0.68
Price Range	24.70-17.32	29.71-22.24	30.97-20.61	24.24-18.52	20.90-11.64	14.87-11.54	12.57-7.00	9.17-4.10
P/E Ratio	14.97-10.50	14.15-10.59	17.70-11.78	12.69-9.70	14.72-8.20	19.83-15.38	27.33-15.22	183.33-82.08
Average Yield %	9.30	0.13	0.12	0.13	0.15	0.18	0.23	0.35

Address: 6300 Wilson Mills Road, Mayfield Village, OH 44143
Telephone: 440-461-5000
Fax: 440-446-7168

Web Site: www.progressive.com
Officers: Peter B. Lewis - Chmn. Glenn M. Renwick - Pres., C.E.O.

Auditors: PricewaterhouseCoopers LLP
Investor Contact: 440-446-7165
Transfer Agents: Corporate Trust Customer Service, National City Bank, Cleveland, OH

PROLOGIS

Exchange	Symbol	Price	52Wk Range	Yield	P/E	Div Acheiver
NYS	PLD	$58.86 (3/31/2008)	72.42-51.66	3.52	14.94	13 Years

*7 Year Price Score 125.16 *NYSE Composite Index=100   *12 Month Price Score 98.81

Interim Earnings (Per Share)

Qtr.	Mar	Jun	Sep	Dec
2003	0.21	0.26	(0.04)	0.73
2004	0.23	0.42	0.42	0.00
2005	0.29	0.40	0.63	0.43
2006	0.72	0.66	0.65	1.28
2007	0.89	1.50	1.12	0.43

Interim Dividends (Per Share)

Amt	Decl	Ex	Rec	Pay
0.46Q	5/1/2007	5/14/2007	5/16/2007	5/31/2007
0.46Q	8/1/2007	8/14/2007	8/16/2007	8/31/2007
0.46Q	11/1/2007	11/9/2007	11/14/2007	11/30/2007
0.517Q	2/1/2008	2/13/2008	2/15/2008	2/29/2008

Indicated Div: $2.07

Valuation Analysis   **Institutional Holding**

Forecast P/E	N/A	No of Institutions
		398
Market Cap	$15.2 Billion	Shares
Book Value	7.4 Billion	238,811,632
Price/Book	2.04	% Held
Price/Sales	2.44	93.20

Business Summary: Property, Real Estate & Development (MIC: 8.3 SIC: 6798 NAIC: 525930)

ProLogis owns, manages and develops industrial distribution facilities. Co.'s business is organized into three segments: property operations, for direct ownership of distribution and retail properties; fund management, for investing management of property funds and the properties; and CDFS business, for development or acquisition of real estate properties. As of Dec 31 2007, Co.'s total portfolio of properties owned, managed and under development, including direct-owned properties and properties owned by property funds and CDFS joint ventures, consisted of 2,773 properties aggregating 510.2 million square feet and serving 4,912 customers in 118 markets in North America, Europe and Asia.

Recent Developments: For the year ended Dec 31 2007, income from continuing operations increased 38.5% to US$987.1 million from US$712.8 million a year earlier. Net income increased 22.9% to US$1.07 billion from US$874.4 million in the prior year. Revenues were US$6.20 billion, up 153.6% from US$2.45 billion the year before.

Prospects: For 2008, given its more cautious outlook for the U.S. market, Co. expects 80.0% to 85.0% of its development to be outside the U.S. Also, Co. noted that it has enhanced its focus for its U.S. operations on build-to-suit business and expects as much as 30.0% to 35.0% of its 2008 U.S. starts will be on permitted basis, which should minimize exposure to softer market conditions. Meanwhile, Co. expects absorption of available space in its global development pipeline during 2008 to continue to be robust as rents in most of its markets should continue to increase. Thus, Co. is expecting 2008 funds from operations of $4.65 to $4.85 per share with earnings of between $3.15 and $3.35 per share.

Financial Data

(US$ in Thousands)	12/31/2007	12/31/2006	12/31/2005	12/31/2004	12/31/2003	12/31/2002	12/31/2001	12/31/2000
Earnings Per Share	3.94	3.32	1.76	1.08	1.16	1.20	0.52	0.96
Cash Flow Per Share	4.77	2.93	2.45	2.63	1.82	2.12	2.01	2.05
Tang Book Value Per Share	27.50	24.11	21.08	14.82	14.35	13.96	12.94	13.53
Dividends Per Share	1.840	1.600	1.480	1.460	1.440	1.420	1.380	1.340
Dividend Payout %	46.70	48.19	84.09	135.19	124.14	118.33	265.38	139.58
Income Statement								
Property Income	6,204,666	2,463,909	1,868,041	598,139	674,939	576,252	570,213	558,191
Non-Property Income	...	...	...	...	59,166	98,749	(47,088)	85,330
Total Revenue	6,204,666	2,463,909	1,868,041	598,139	734,105	675,001	523,125	643,521
Interest Expense	368,065	294,403	178,369	153,334	155,475	152,958	163,629	172,191
Income Before Taxes	1,056,038	748,218	344,734	277,104	266,049	277,050	132,869	219,608
Income Taxes	68,899	30,528	26,892	43,562	15,374	28,169	4,725	5,130
Net Income	1,074,340	874,367	396,163	232,795	250,675	248,881	128,144	214,478
Average Shares	267,226	256,852	213,713	191,801	187,222	184,869	175,197	164,401
Balance Sheet								
Total Assets	19,724,034	15,903,525	13,114,096	7,097,799	6,369,202	5,923,525	5,603,941	5,946,334
Long-Term Obligations	8,550,930	5,924,090	4,437,826	2,453,959	2,291,201	2,186,072	2,202,465	2,237,914
Total Liabilities	12,208,975	9,452,678	7,567,429	3,929,033	3,270,757	2,994,571	2,882,303	2,972,333
Stockholders' Equity	7,436,398	6,398,579	5,488,023	3,102,493	3,060,668	2,886,487	2,675,999	2,927,371
Shares Outstanding	257,712	250,912	243,781	185,788	180,182	178,145	175,888	165,287
Statistical Record								
Return on Assets %	6.03	6.03	3.92	3.45	4.08	4.32	2.22	3.63
Return on Equity %	15.53	14.71	9.22	7.53	8.43	8.95	4.57	7.27
Net Margin %	17.32	35.49	21.21	38.92	34.15	36.87	24.50	33.33
Price Range	72.42-53.19	65.50-47.50	47.14-36.60	43.33-28.39	32.26-23.85	26.00-21.03	23.15-19.70	24.50-17.81
P/E Ratio	18.38-13.50	19.73-14.31	26.78-20.80	40.12-26.29	27.81-20.56	21.67-17.53	44.52-37.88	25.52-18.55
Average Yield %	2.87	2.92	3.56	4.21	5.20	5.98	6.47	6.36

Address: 4545 Airport Way, Denver, CO 80239	Web Site: www.prologis.com	Auditors: KPMG LLP
Telephone: 303-567-5000	Officers: K. Dane Brooksher - Chmn. Walter C. Rakowich - Pres., C.O.O.	Investor Contact: 303-576-2622
Fax: 303-375-8581		Transfer Agents: Equiserve Trust Company N.A.

PROTECTIVE LIFE CORP.

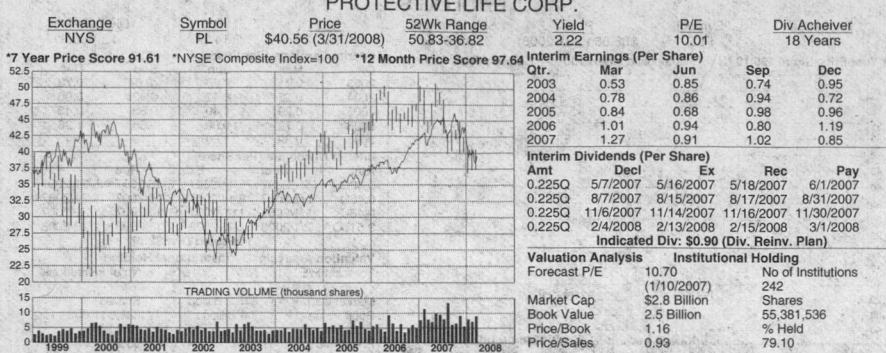

Exchange	Symbol	Price	52Wk Range	Yield	P/E	Div Acheiver
NYS	PL	$40.56 (3/31/2008)	50.83-36.82	2.22	10.01	18 Years

*7 Year Price Score 91.61 ***NYSE Composite Index=100** ***12 Month Price Score 97.64**

Interim Earnings (Per Share)
Qtr.	Mar	Jun	Sep	Dec
2003	0.53	0.85	0.74	0.95
2004	0.78	0.86	0.94	0.72
2005	0.84	0.68	0.98	0.96
2006	1.01	0.94	0.80	1.19
2007	1.27	0.91	1.02	0.85

Interim Dividends (Per Share)
Amt	Decl	Ex	Rec	Pay
0.225Q	5/7/2007	5/16/2007	5/18/2007	6/1/2007
0.225Q	8/7/2007	8/15/2007	8/17/2007	8/31/2007
0.225Q	11/6/2007	11/14/2007	11/16/2007	11/30/2007
0.225Q	2/4/2008	2/13/2008	2/15/2008	3/1/2008

Indicated Div: $0.90 (Div. Reinv. Plan)

Valuation Analysis
Forecast P/E	10.70
	(1/10/2007)
Market Cap	$2.8 Billion
Book Value	2.5 Billion
Price/Book	1.16
Price/Sales	0.93

Institutional Holding
No of Institutions	242
Shares	55,381,536
% Held	79.10

TRADING VOLUME (thousand shares)

Business Summary: Insurance (MIC: 8.2 SIC: 6311 NAIC: 524113)

Protective Life is a holding company whose subsidiaries provide financial services through the production, distribution, and administration of insurance and investment products. Co. markets individual life insurance, credit life and disability insurance, guaranteed investment contracts, guaranteed funding agreements, fixed and variable annuities, and extended service contracts throughout the U.S. Also, Co. maintains a separate division focused on the acquisition of insurance policies from other companies. Co.'s operating segments are Life Marketing, Acquisitions, Annuities, Stable Value Products and Asset Protection. As at Dec 31 2006, Co. had insurance in force of $765.18 billion.

Recent Developments: For the year ended Dec 31 2007, net income increased 2.8% to US$289.6 million from US$281.6 million in the prior year. Revenues were US$3.05 billion, up 13.9% from US$2.68 billion the year before. Net premiums earned were US$1.13 billion versus US$946.1 million in the prior year, an increase of 19.0%. Net investment income rose 18.0% to US$1.68 billion from US$1.42 billion a year ago.

Prospects: Co.'s results are being positively affected by robust net income growth, primarily reflecting increases in operating earnings in its Life Marketing, Acquisitions, Stable Value Products and Asset Protection segments, partially offset by a reduction in operating earnings for its Annuities segment attributable primarily to less favorable mortality and tighter spreads in the single premium immediate annuity line. Meanwhile, for full-year 2008, Co. expects operating income per diluted share to be in the range of $3.80 to $4.20, excluding any reserve adjustments or unusual or unpredictable benefits or charges that might occur during the year.

Financial Data
(US$ in Thousands)	12/31/2007	12/31/2006	12/31/2005	12/31/2004	12/31/2003	12/31/2002	12/31/2001	12/31/2000
Earnings Per Share	4.05	3.94	3.46	3.30	3.07	2.52	1.47	2.32
Cash Flow Per Share	12.12	6.90	13.04	10.60	11.22	12.90	17.02	13.28
Tang Book Value Per Share	33.35	31.62	30.62	30.52	28.33	24.37	19.72	13.38
Dividends Per Share	0.890	0.840	0.760	0.685	0.630	0.590	0.550	0.510
Dividend Payout %	21.98	21.32	21.97	20.76	20.52	23.41	37.41	21.98
Income Statement								
Premium Income	1,126,339	946,122	728,923	698,652	735,877	783,132	618,669	833,658
Total Revenue	3,051,700	2,679,133	2,109,204	1,988,575	1,957,525	1,920,678	1,614,217	1,733,967
Benefits & Claims	1,893,707	1,637,215	1,253,367	1,130,437	1,151,574	1,162,231	972,624	989,565
Income Before Taxes	436,088	431,908	377,013	385,201	325,412	267,203	209,596	253,795
Income Taxes	146,522	150,347	130,446	134,820	108,362	88,444	68,538	90,858
Net Income	289,566	281,561	246,567	234,580	217,050	177,355	102,943	153,476
Average Shares	71,478	71,390	71,350	71,064	70,644	70,462	69,950	66,281
Balance Sheet								
Total Assets	41,786,041	39,795,294	28,966,993	27,211,378	24,573,991	21,953,004	19,718,824	15,145,633
Total Liabilities	39,329,280	37,482,219	26,783,333	25,045,051	22,571,847	20,232,302	18,318,680	13,841,575
Stockholders' Equity	2,456,761	2,313,075	2,183,660	2,166,327	2,002,144	1,720,702	1,400,144	1,114,058
Shares Outstanding	70,149	69,964	69,694	69,449	68,991	68,675	68,555	64,557
Statistical Record								
Return on Assets %	0.71	0.82	0.88	0.90	0.93	0.85	0.59	1.09
Return on Equity %	12.14	12.52	11.34	11.22	11.66	11.37	8.19	15.47
Loss Ratio %	168.13	173.04	171.95	161.80	156.49	148.41	157.21	118.70
Net Margin %	9.49	10.51	11.69	11.80	11.09	9.23	6.38	8.85
Price Range	50.83-39.80	50.40-43.04	44.83-37.39	42.92-33.84	34.22-24.71	33.75-27.20	34.51-25.55	32.25-20.81
P/E Ratio	12.55-9.83	12.79-10.92	12.96-10.81	13.01-10.25	11.15-8.05	13.39-10.79	23.48-17.38	13.90-8.97
Average Yield %	1.98	1.81	1.83	1.81	2.16	1.93	1.82	1.90

Address: 2801 Highway 280 South, Birmingham, AL 35223
Telephone: 205-268-1000
Fax: 205-868-3541

Web Site: www.protective.com
Officers: John D. Johns - Chmn., Pres., C.E.O. Allen W. Ritchie - Exec. V.P., C.F.O.

Auditors: PricewaterhouseCoopers LLP
Investor Contact: 205-268-1000
Transfer Agents: Bank of New York, New York, NY

PRUDENTIAL FINANCIAL, INC.

Exchange	Symbol	Price	52Wk Range	Yield	P/E
NYS	PRU	$78.25 (3/31/2008)	103.17-67.36	1.47	10.28

*7 Year Price Score N/A   *NYSE Composite Index=100   *12 Month Price Score 88.70

TRADING VOLUME (thousand shares)

Interim Earnings (Per Share)

Qtr.	Mar	Jun	Sep	Dec
2003	0.39	0.25	0.44	0.91
2004	0.57	1.02	1.08	0.64
2005	1.49	1.48	2.59	0.80
2006	1.38	0.89	2.38	1.88
2007	2.18	1.80	1.88	1.75

Interim Dividends (Per Share)

Amt	Decl	Ex	Rec	Pay
0.625A	11/9/2004	11/19/2004	11/23/2004	12/20/2004
0.78A	11/8/2005	11/18/2005	11/22/2005	12/19/2005
0.95A	11/14/2006	11/22/2006	11/27/2006	12/21/2006
1.15A	11/13/2007	11/21/2007	11/26/2007	12/21/2007

Indicated Div: $1.15

Valuation Analysis   Institutional Holding

Forecast P/E	N/A	No of Institutions 482
Market Cap	$35.2 Billion	Shares
Book Value	23.5 Billion	249,253,168
Price/Book	1.50	% Held
Price/Sales	1.02	53.26

Business Summary: Insurance (MIC: 8.2 SIC: 6311 NAIC: 524113)

Prudential Financial is a holding company. Co. provides financial products and services, including life insurance, annuities, mutual funds, pension and retirement-related services and administration, investment management, real estate brokerage and relocation services, and, through a joint venture, retail securities brokerage services. Co.'s Financial Services Businesses consists of its Insurance, Investment and International Insurance and Investments divisions, and corporate and other operations. Co.'s Closed Block Business comprises the Closed Block assets and certain related assets and liabilities. At Dec 31 2007, Co. had about $648.00 billion of assets under management.

Recent Developments: For the year ended Dec 31 2007, income from continuing operations increased 9.8% to US$3.69 billion from US$3.36 billion a year earlier. Net income increased 8.1% to US$3.70 billion from US$3.43 billion in the prior year. Revenues were US$34.40 billion, up 6.6% from US$32.27 billion the year before. Net premiums earned were US$14.35 billion versus US$13.91 billion in the prior year, an increase of 3.2%. Net investment income rose 6.2% to US$12.02 billion from US$11.32 billion a year ago.

Prospects: Co.'s Financial Services Businesses are negatively affected by net realized investment losses including losses from impairments and sales of credit-impaired securities and disposals of asset-backed securities collateralized by sub-prime mortgages, as well as higher loss at Corporate and Other operations, partially offset by improved results at its Insurance division. In addition, Co. is seeing lower net income at its Closed Block Business and expects the decrease in premiums for this business to continue as its policies in force continue to mature or terminate. Co. also expects the proportion of its business represented by the Closed Block to decrease as it grows other businesses.

Financial Data
(US$ in Thousands)

	12/31/2007	12/31/2006	12/31/2005	12/31/2004	12/31/2003	12/31/2002	12/31/2001	12/31/2000
Earnings Per Share	7.61	6.50	6.34	3.31	1.98	1.25		
Cash Flow Per Share	12.98	9.04	7.90	13.64	(1.09)	17.31	...	
Tang Book Value Per Share	52.20	48.39	45.57	42.21	39.66	37.94	34.93	...
Dividends Per Share	1.150	0.950	0.780	0.625	0.500	0.400	...	...
Dividend Payout %	15.11	14.62	12.30	18.88	25.25	32.00	...	...
Income Statement								
Premium Income	14,351,000	13,908,000	13,685,000	12,580,000	13,233,000	13,531,000	12,477,000	10,221,000
Total Revenue	34,401,000	32,488,000	31,708,000	28,348,000	27,907,000	26,675,000	27,177,000	26,544,000
Benefits & Claims	14,749,000	14,283,000	13,840,000	12,896,000	13,424,000	13,658,000	12,752,000	10,640,000
Income Before Taxes	4,686,000	4,403,000	4,471,000	3,287,000	1,958,000	64,000	(227,000)	727,000
Income Taxes	1,245,000	1,248,000	869,000	955,000	650,000	(192,000)	(57,000)	406,000
Net Income	3,704,000	3,428,000	3,540,000	2,256,000	1,264,000	194,000	(134,000)	398,000
Average Shares	468,300	494,000	520,900	531,200	548,363	577,983	...	...
Balance Sheet								
Total Assets	485,814,000	454,266,000	417,776,000	401,058,000	321,274,000	292,746,000	293,030,000	272,753,000
Total Liabilities	462,357,000	431,374,000	395,013,000	378,714,000	299,982,000	270,726,000	271,887,000	252,145,000
Stockholders' Equity	23,457,000	22,892,000	22,763,000	22,344,000	21,292,000	21,330,000	20,453,000	20,608,000
Shares Outstanding	449,366	473,105	499,494	529,344	536,853	562,227	585,582	...
Statistical Record								
Return on Assets %	0.79	0.79	0.86	0.62	0.41	0.07	N.M.	0.14
Return on Equity %	15.98	15.02	15.70	10.31	5.93	0.93	N.M.	1.99
Loss Ratio %	102.77	102.70	101.13	102.51	101.44	100.94	102.20	104.10
Net Margin %	10.77	10.55	11.16	7.96	4.53	0.73	(0.57)	1.50
Price Range	103.17-84.28	86.84-71.47	77.96-52.62	55.09-41.05	42.19-27.56	35.75-25.50	33.19-29.30	...
P/E Ratio	13.56-11.07	13.36-11.00	12.30-8.30	16.64-12.40	21.31-13.92	28.60-20.40	...	...
Average Yield %	1.23	1.23	1.22	1.35	1.44	1.28	...	...

Address: 751 Broad Street, Newark, NJ 07102	**Web Site:** www.prudential.com	**Auditors:** PricewaterhouseCoopers LLP
Telephone: 973-802-6000	**Officers:** Arthur F. Ryan - Chmn., Pres., C.E.O. Mark B. Grier - Vice-Chmn., Financial Mgmt.	

PUBLIC SERVICE ENTERPRISE GROUP INC.

Exchange	Symbol	Price	52Wk Range	Yield	P/E
NYS	PEG	$40.19 (3/31/2008)	51.62-39.31	3.21	15.34

*7 Year Price Score 130.36 *NYSE Composite Index=100 *12 Month Price Score 106.26

Interim Earnings (Per Share)

Qtr.	Mar	Jun	Sep	Dec
2003	1.50	0.28	0.46	0.29
2004	0.57	0.26	0.52	0.18
2005	0.59	(0.17)	0.52	0.42
2006	0.41	0.41	0.74	(0.10)
2007	0.65	0.54	1.00	0.44

Interim Dividends (Per Share)

Amt	Decl	Ex	Rec	Pay
0.292Q	7/17/2007	9/6/2007	9/10/2007	9/28/2007
0.292Q	11/20/2007	12/5/2007	12/7/2007	12/31/2007
2-for-1	1/15/2008	2/5/2008	1/25/2008	2/4/2008
0.323Q	1/15/2008	3/6/2008	3/10/2008	3/31/2008

Indicated Div: $1.29

Valuation Analysis · **Institutional Holding**

Forecast P/E	11.78
	(1/10/2007)
Market Cap	$20.4 Billion
Book Value	7.3 Billion
Price/Book	2.80
Price/Sales	1.59

No of Institutions	359
Shares	147,243,184
% Held	58.38

Business Summary: Electricity (MIC: 7.1 SIC: 4931 NAIC: 221119)

Public Service Enterprise Group is an energy company with four principal direct wholly owned subsidiaries: PSEG Power, LLC., a wholesale energy supply company; Public Service Electric and Gas Company, an operating public utility engaged in the transmission of electric energy and distribution of electric energy and natural gas in certain areas of New Jersey; PSEG Energy Holdings, LLC., which focuses on investment opportunities in the domestic and international energy market; and PSEG Services Corporation, which provides management and administrative and general services to Co. and its subsidiaries.

Recent Developments: For the year ended Dec 31 2007, income from continuing operations increased 94.3% to US$1.32 billion from US$679.0 million a year earlier. Net income increased 80.6% to US$1.34 billion from US$739.0 million in the prior year. Revenues were US$12.85 billion, up 9.3% from US$11.76 billion the year before. Operating income was US$3.09 billion versus US$1.85 billion in the prior year, an increase of 67.3%. Direct operating expenses rose 1.9% to US$8.94 billion from US$8.77 billion in the comparable period the year before. Indirect operating expenses decreased 28.0% to US$822.0 million from US$1.14 billion in the equivalent prior-year period.

Prospects: Co. estimates a modest decline in its Public Service Electric and Gas Co. subsidiary's 2008 operating earnings, to $350.0 million to $370.0 million. Co. also projects its PSEG Energy Holdings, LLC., subsidiary's operating income to decline in 2008 to $45.0 million to $60.0 million attributable to the loss of earnings from the sale of Chilquinta and Luz del Sur in 2007. However, Co. expects its PSEG Power, LLC., subsidiary's 2008 operating earnings of $1.04 billion to $1.14 billion, reflecting the benefit of higher electric power pricing with the expiration of below market contracts. Consequently, Co. has reaffirmed its 2008 operating earnings guidance of $5.60 to $6.10 per share.

Financial Data

(US$ in Thousands)	12/31/2007	12/31/2006	12/31/2005	12/31/2004	12/31/2003	12/31/2002	12/31/2001	12/31/2000
Earnings Per Share	2.62	1.47	1.36	1.52	2.54	0.58	1.85	1.77
Cash Flow Per Share	3.78	3.83	1.96	3.39	3.17	3.66	3.22	2.63
Tang Book Value Per Share	14.23	12.19	10.78	10.70	10.42	7.39	8.47	9.61
Dividends Per Share	1.170	1.140	1.120	1.100	1.080	1.080	1.080	1.080
Dividend Payout %	44.66	77.82	82.66	72.13	42.60	184.62	58.38	60.85
Income Statement								
Total Revenue	12,853,000	12,164,000	12,430,000	10,996,000	11,116,000	8,390,000	9,815,000	6,848,000
EBITDA	4,005,000	2,961,000	3,052,000	2,806,000	2,767,000	2,107,000	2,462,000	2,320,000
Income Before Taxes	2,379,000	1,206,000	1,399,000	1,167,000	1,316,000	664,000	1,136,000	1,254,000
Income Taxes	1,060,000	454,000	541,000	446,000	464,000	248,000	373,000	490,000
Net Income	1,335,000	739,000	661,000	726,000	1,160,000	245,000	770,000	764,000
Average Shares	508,813	504,628	488,812	476,572	457,648	417,626	416,452	430,242
Balance Sheet								
Net PPE	13,275,000	13,002,000	13,336,000	13,750,000	12,422,000	11,449,000	10,064,000	7,702,000
Total Assets	28,392,000	28,570,000	29,815,000	29,207,000	28,055,000	25,742,000	25,397,000	20,796,000
Long-Term Obligations	8,662,000	10,370,000	11,279,000	12,925,000	12,945,000	10,991,000	10,301,000	5,297,000
Total Liabilities	21,013,000	21,743,000	23,713,000	23,388,000	22,446,000	20,355,000	20,500,000	15,592,000
Stockholders' Equity	7,299,000	6,747,000	6,022,000	5,739,000	5,529,000	3,987,000	4,137,000	3,996,000
Shares Outstanding	508,523	505,290	502,326	476,198	472,266	450,534	411,678	415,942
Statistical Record								
Return on Assets %	4.69	2.53	2.24	2.53	4.31	0.96	3.33	3.83
Return on Equity %	19.01	11.57	11.24	12.85	24.38	6.03	18.94	19.07
EBITDA Margin %	31.16	24.34	24.55	25.52	24.89	25.11	25.08	33.88
Net Margin %	10.39	6.08	5.32	6.60	10.44	2.92	7.85	11.16
PPE Turnover	0.98	0.92	0.92	0.84	0.93	0.78	1.10	0.92
Asset Turnover	0.45	0.42	0.42	0.38	0.41	0.33	0.42	0.34
Debt to Equity	1.19	1.54	1.87	2.25	2.34	2.76	2.49	1.33
Price Range	49.61-32.48	36.09-29.77	33.85-24.84	26.20-19.45	22.20-16.05	23.45-10.88	25.70-19.09	24.94-12.94
P/E Ratio	18.94-12.40	24.55-20.26	24.89-18.26	17.23-12.80	8.74-6.32	40.43-18.76	13.89-10.32	14.09-7.31
Average Yield %	2.74	3.47	3.80	5.08	5.46	5.76	4.88	5.89

Address: 80 Park Plaza, Newark, NJ 07101-1171	**Web Site:** www.pseg.com	**Auditors:** Deloitte & Touche LLP
Telephone: 973-430-7000	**Officers:** E. James Ferland - Chmn., C.E.O. Ralph Izzo - Pres., C.O.O.	**Investor Contact:** 877-773-4111
Fax: 973-430-5983		**Transfer Agents:** PSEG Services Corporation, Newark, NJ

PUBLIC STORAGE

Exchange	Symbol	Price	52Wk Range	Yield	P/E
NYS	PSA	$88.62 (3/31/2008)	97.56-66.78	2.48	75.74

*7 Year Price Score 114.42 *NYSE Composite Index=100 *12 Month Price Score 109.88

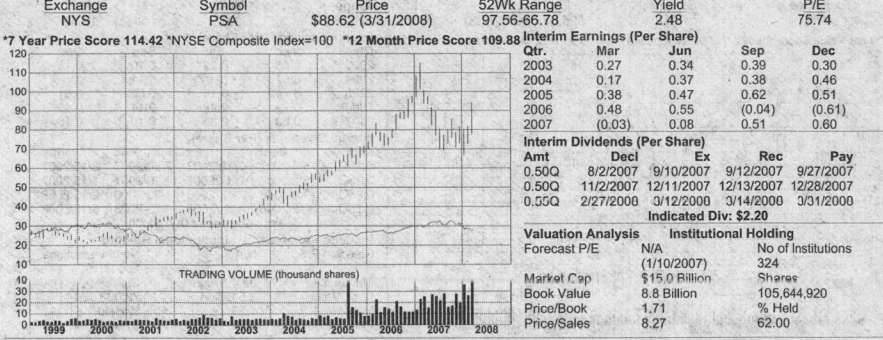

Interim Earnings (Per Share)

Qtr.	Mar	Jun	Sep	Dec
2003	0.27	0.34	0.39	0.30
2004	0.17	0.37	0.38	0.46
2005	0.38	0.47	0.62	0.51
2006	0.48	0.55	(0.04)	(0.61)
2007	(0.03)	0.08	0.51	0.60

Interim Dividends (Per Share)

Amt	Decl	Ex	Rec	Pay
0.50Q	8/2/2007	9/10/2007	9/12/2007	9/27/2007
0.50Q	11/2/2007	12/11/2007	12/13/2007	12/28/2007
0.55Q	2/27/2008	3/12/2008	3/14/2008	3/31/2008

Indicated Div: $2.20

Valuation Analysis | **Institutional Holding**

Forecast P/E	N/A	No of Institutions
	(1/10/2007)	324
Market Cap	$15.0 Billion	Shares
Book Value	8.8 Billion	105,644,920
Price/Book	1.71	% Held
Price/Sales	8.27	62.00

Business Summary: Property, Real Estate & Development (MIC: 8.3 SIC: 6798 NAIC: 525930)

Public Storage is engaged in acquiring, developing, owning and operating self-storage facilities. At Dec 31 2007, Co. had direct and indirect equity interests in 2,012 self-storage facilities in 38 states within the U.S. under the Public Storage name containing about 126.0 million net rentable square feet of space; and 174 self-storage facilities in seven Western European countries under the Shurgard Storage Centers name containing about 9.0 million net rentable square feet of space. Co. also has direct and indirect equity interests in about 21.0 million net rentable square feet of commercial space in 11 states in the U.S. operated under the PS Business Parks and Public Storage brands.

Recent Developments: For the year ended Dec 31 2007, income from continuing operations increased 45.8% to US$457.5 million from US$313.7 million a year earlier. Net income increased 45.7% to US$457.5 million from US$314.0 million in the prior year. Revenues were US$1.82 billion, up 31.5% from US$1.38 billion the year before. Revenues from property income rose 34.1% to US$1.66 billion from US$1.24 billion in the corresponding earlier year.

Prospects: Co. continues to focus on its acquisition and redevelopment efforts. For instance, Co. has entered into agreements to acquire two self-storage facilities in California for $31.0 million, which should close in the second quarter of 2008. Also, at Dec 31 2007, Co. had 29 projects that were either under construction or were expected to begin construction within the next year, comprised of 27 projects (1,105,000 net additional rentable square feet) at an estimated cost of $106.9 million, and two newly developed self-storage facilities (113,000 net rentable square feet) at an estimated cost of $14.7 million. Opening dates for these facilities are estimated through the next 24 months.

Financial Data
(US$ in Thousands)

	12/31/2007	12/31/2006	12/31/2005	12/31/2004	12/31/2003	12/31/2002	12/31/2001	12/31/2000
Earnings Per Share	1.17	0.33	1.97	1.38	1.28	1.19	1.51	1.41
Cash Flow Per Share	5.98	5.55	5.40	5.05	4.75	4.79	4.40	3.81
Tang Book Value Per Share	28.85	28.16	16.73	16.69	16.15	17.31	17.77	18.24
Dividends Per Share	1.000	2.000	1.900	1.800	1.800	1.800	1.690	1.480
Dividend Payout %	85.47	606.06	96.45	130.43	140.63	151.26	111.92	104.96
Income Statement								
Total Revenue	1,816,371	1,381,655	1,060,961	927,976	875,071	841,452	834,645	757,310
Net Income	457,535	314,026	456,393	366,213	336,653	318,738	324,208	297,088
Average Shares	170,147	143,715	128,819	128,681	126,517	124,571	123,577	131,657
Balance Sheet								
Current Assets	245,444	555,584	493,501	366,255	204,833	103,124	49,347	89,467
Total Assets	10,643,102	11,198,473	5,552,486	5,204,790	4,968,069	4,843,662	4,625,879	4,513,941
Current Liabilities	...	345,000	...	...	...	...	25,000	...
Long-Term Obligations	1,069,928	1,503,542	149,647	145,614	76,030	115,867	143,552	156,003
Total Liabilities	1,373,285	2,484,398	481,507	345,920	322,133	245,194	261,695	256,906
Stockholders' Equity	8,763,129	8,208,045	4,817,009	4,429,967	4,219,799	4,158,969	3,909,583	3,724,117
Shares Outstanding	169,422	169,144	128,089	128,526	133,986	123,991	121,961	130,703
Statistical Record								
Return on Assets %	4.19	3.75	8.49	7.18	6.86	6.73	7.09	6.79
Return on Equity %	5.39	4.82	9.87	8.44	8.04	7.90	8.49	7.99
Net Margin %	25.19	22.73	43.02	39.46	38.47	37.88	38.84	39.23
Asset Turnover	0.17	0.16	0.20	0.18	0.18	0.18	0.18	0.17
Current Ratio	...	1.61	...	...	...	...	1.97	...
Debt to Equity	0.12	0.18	0.03	0.03	0.02	0.03	0.04	0.04
Price Range	115.29-69.24	97.73-69.96	71.54-52.51	57.38-40.35	45.75-28.98	39.05-28.96	35.15-24.19	26.88-21.00
P/E Ratio	98.54-59.18	296.15-212.00	36.31-26.65	41.58-29.24	35.74-22.64	32.82-24.34	23.28-16.02	19.06-14.89
Average Yield %	1.16	2.46	3.05	3.70	4.97	5.23	5.68	6.39

Address: 701 Western Avenue,	Web Site: www.publicstorage.com	Auditors: Ernst & Young LLP
Glendale, CA 91201-2349	Officers: B. Wayne Hughes - Chmn. Ronald L.	
Telephone: 818-244-8080	Havner Jr. - Vice-Chmn. C.E.O.	
Fax: 818-244-0581		

PUGET ENERGY, INC. (HOLDING CO.)

Exchange	Symbol	Price	52Wk Range	Yield	P/E
NYS	PSD	$25.87 (3/31/2008)	28.25-22.61	3.87	16.58

*7 Year Price Score 90.62   *NYSE Composite Index=100   *12 Month Price Score 110.33

TRADING VOLUME (thousand shares)

Interim Earnings (Per Share)

Qtr.	Mar	Jun	Sep	Dec
2003	0.45	0.22	0.10	0.45
2004	0.67	(0.07)	0.11	(0.16)
2005	0.71	0.14	0.06	0.61
2006	0.79	0.46	0.14	0.49
2007	0.68	0.33	0.10	0.46

Interim Dividends (Per Share)

Amt	Decl	Ex	Rec	Pay
0.25Q	5/4/2007	7/18/2007	7/20/2007	8/15/2007
0.25Q	8/3/2007	10/17/2007	10/19/2007	11/15/2007
0.25Q	1/8/2008	1/18/2008	1/23/2008	2/15/2008
0.25Q	3/12/2008	4/21/2008	4/23/2008	5/15/2008

Indicated Div: $1.00

Valuation Analysis

		Institutional Holding	
Forecast P/E	N/A	No of Institutions	204
Market Cap	$3.4 Billion	Shares	72,003,520
Book Value	2.5 Billion	% Held	61.86
Price/Book	1.33		
Price/Sales	1.04		

Business Summary: Electricity (MIC: 7.1 SIC: 4911 NAIC: 221121)

Puget Energy is an energy services holding company. Through its Puget Sound Energy, Inc. (PSE) subsidiary, Co. is engaged in the business of electric transmission, distribution and generation and natural gas transmission and distribution, mainly in the Puget Sound region of Washington. As of Dec 31 2007, PSE had about 1.0 million electric customers, consisting of 933,200 residential, 116,400 commercial, 3,800 industrial and 3,100 other customers; and about 729,500 gas customers, consisting of 673,600 residential, 53,100 commercial, 2,600 industrial and 100 transportation customers. Co. also owns and operates Baker River, Electron, Snoqualmie Falls, and the Electron hydroelectric projects.

Recent Developments: For the year ended Dec 31 2007, income from continuing operations increased 10.4% to US$184.7 million from US$167.2 million a year earlier. Net income decreased 15.9% to US$184.5 million from US$219.2 million in the prior year. Revenues were US$3.22 billion, up 10.8% from US$2.91 billion the year before. Operating income was US$441.0 million versus US$420.9 million in the prior year, an increase of 4.8%. Direct operating expenses rose 11.8% to US$2.16 billion from US$1.94 billion in the comparable period the year before. Indirect operating expenses increased 11.9% to US$615.8 million from US$550.5 million in the equivalent prior-year period.

Prospects: On Dec 10 2007, Co.'s Puget Sound Energy, Inc. subsidiary has signed an agreement to acquire a 125-megawatt power plant in Sumas, WA from Sumas Cogeneration Company, L.P. to help meeting its customers' steadily growing electricity demands. This transaction now awaits review and approval from the Federal Energy Regulatory Commission and is expected to close in fall 2008. Separately, on Dec 3 2007, Co.'s Puget Sound Energy, Inc. subsidiary has filed a rate increase request with the Washington Utilities and Transportation Commission that would annually provide it with an additional $174.5 million in electric revenue and $56.8 million in natural gas revenue effective Nov 1 2008, if approved.

Financial Data

(US$ in Thousands)	12/31/2007	12/31/2006	12/31/2005	12/31/2004	12/31/2003	12/31/2002	12/31/2001	12/31/2000
Earnings Per Share	1.56	1.88	1.51	0.55	1.22	1.24	1.14	2.16
Cash Flow Per Share	4.79	1.60	2.49	4.58	3.41	8.19	3.45	3.74
Tang Book Value Per Share	19.45	18.15	17.52	15.64	15.17	14.73	14.55	16.61
Dividends Per Share	1.000	1.000	1.000	1.000	1.000	1.210	1.840	1.840
Dividend Payout %	64.10	53.19	66.23	181.82	81.97	97.58	161.40	85.19
Income Statement								
Total Revenue	3,220,147	2,905,693	2,573,210	2,568,813	2,491,523	2,392,322	3,373,991	3,441,672
EBITDA	770,701	...	...	...	...	...	...	...
Income Before Taxes	257,258	...	...	...	...	...	...	...
Income Taxes	72,582	97,277	89,715	76,150	73,639	60,582	...	...
Net Income	184,464	219,216	155,726	55,022	121,348	117,883	106,839	193,831
Average Shares	118,344	116,457	103,111	99,911	95,309	88,777	86,445	85,411
Balance Sheet								
Net PPE	5,642,639	5,181,046	4,630,918	4,228,358	4,080,227	3,916,229	3,887,981	3,838,409
Total Assets	7,598,736	7,066,039	6,609,951	5,833,369	5,674,685	5,657,491	5,546,977	5,556,669
Long-Term Obligations	2,678,860	2,646,110	2,421,110	2,492,782	2,249,739	2,149,733	2,127,054	2,170,797
Total Liabilities	5,076,782	4,950,010	4,576,088	4,206,445	4,007,950	4,063,075	4,124,253	4,070,029
Stockholders' Equity	2,521,954	2,116,029	2,027,047	1,622,276	1,655,046	1,583,787	1,422,724	1,486,640
Shares Outstanding	129,678	116,576	115,695	99,868	99,074	93,642	87,023	85,903
Statistical Record								
Return on Assets %	2.52	3.21	2.50	0.95	2.14	2.10	1.92	3.61
Return on Equity %	7.95	10.58	8.53	3.35	7.49	7.84	7.34	13.21
EBITDA Margin %	23.93	...	...	...	...	...	...	...
Net Margin %	5.73	7.54	6.05	2.14	4.87	4.93	3.17	5.63
PPE Turnover	0.60	0.59	0.58	0.62	0.62	0.61	0.87	0.90
Asset Turnover	0.44	0.42	0.41	0.45	0.44	0.43	0.61	0.64
Debt to Equity	1.06	1.25	1.19	1.54	1.36	1.36	1.50	1.46
Price Range	28.25-22.61	25.76-20.41	24.70-20.23	24.73-20.54	24.09-18.10	23.41-17.30	27.00-18.80	27.81-19.06
P/E Ratio	18.11-14.49	13.70-10.86	16.36-13.40	44.96-37.35	19.75-14.84	18.88-13.95	23.68-16.49	12.88-8.83
Average Yield %	3.95	4.52	4.46	4.44	4.53	5.73	7.94	7.89

Address: 10885 NE 4th Street, Suite 800, Bellevue, WA 98004-5591 Telephone: 425-454-6363	Web Site: www.pse.com Officers: Douglas P. Beighle - Chmn. Stephen P. Reynolds - Pres., C.E.O.	Auditors: PricewaterhouseCoopers LLP Investor Contact: 425-462-3808 Transfer Agents: Mellon Investor Services, Ridgefield Park, NJ

PULTE HOMES, INC.

Exchange	Symbol	Price	52Wk Range	Yield	P/E
NYS	PHM	$14.55 (3/31/2008)	28.82-8.66	1.10	N/A

*7 Year Price Score 61.48   *NYSE Composite Index=100   *12 Month Price Score 85.82

Interim Earnings (Per Share)

Qtr.	Mar	Jun	Sep	Dec
2003	0.35	0.48	0.67	0.98
2004	0.51	0.72	1.03	1.51
2005	0.83	1.15	1.50	2.19
2006	1.01	0.94	0.74	(0.03)
2007	(0.34)	(2.01)	(3.12)	(3.46)

Interim Dividends (Per Share)

Amt	Decl	Ex	Rec	Pay
0.04Q	5/10/2007	6/14/2007	6/18/2007	7/2/2007
0.04Q	9/12/2007	9/21/2007	9/25/2007	10/1/2007
0.04Q	12/6/2007	12/17/2007	12/19/2007	1/3/2008
0.04Q	2/7/2008	3/14/2008	3/18/2008	4/1/2008

Indicated Div: $0.16

Valuation Analysis

		Institutional Holding	
Forecast P/E	29.41	No of Institutions	
	(1/10/2007)	277	
Market Cap	$3.7 Billion	Shares	
Book Value	4.3 Billion	201,314,848	
Price/Book	0.87	% Held	
Price/Sales	0.40	78.63	

Business Summary: Building & General Construction (MIC: 3.2 SIC: 1531 NAIC: 236117)

Pulte Homes is a holding company. Through its subsidiaries, Co. is engaged in the homebuilding and financial services businesses. Co.'s Homebuilding segment focuses on the acquisition and development of land primarily for residential purposes within the continental U.S. and Puerto Rico, and the construction of housing on such land, targeted for the first-time, first and second move-up, and active adult home buyers. At Dec 31 2007, Co.'s Homebuilding operations provided homes for sale in 636 communities and operated in 51 markets spanning 26 states. Co.'s Financial Services segment consists of mortgage and title operations conducted through Pulte Mortgage and other subsidiaries.

Recent Developments: For the year ended Dec 31 2007, loss from continuing operations was US$2.27 billion compared with income of US$689.6 million a year earlier. Net loss amounted to US$2.26 billion versus net income of US$687.5 million in the prior year. Revenues were US$9.26 billion, down 35.1% from US$14.27 billion the year before. Direct operating expenses declined 11.8% to US$11.53 billion from US$13.08 billion in the comparable period the year before.

Prospects: Co. expects its business to continue to be affected by difficult market conditions for at least the near term. Co. expects decreases in its unit settlements and pricing to continue and the majority of the markets it serves to remain challenging throughout 2008. Also, Co. continues to shorten its land pipeline, limit land development expenditures, reduce production volumes, and balance home price and profitability with sales pace. For the first quarter of 2008, Co. expects a net loss from continuing operations of $0.15 to $0.30 per share, exclusive of a tax benefit and any additional impairments or land-related charges, reflecting the ongoing tough operating environment for homebuilding.

Financial Data

(US$ in Thousands)	12/31/2007	12/31/2006	12/31/2005	12/31/2004	12/31/2003	12/31/2002	12/31/2001	12/31/2000
Earnings Per Share	(8.94)	2.66	5.68	3.79	2.48	1.84	1.50	1.12
Cash Flow Per Share	4.83	(1.06)	0.07	(2.76)	(1.24)	0.67	(2.13)	0.14
Tang Book Value Per Share	16.35	23.82	21.49	15.95	11.97	9.41	7.63	7.51
Dividends Per Share	0.160	0.160	0.130	0.100	0.055	0.040	0.040	0.040
Dividend Payout %	...	6.02	2.29	2.64	2.21	2.18	2.67	3.58
Income Statement								
Total Revenue	9,263,094	14,274,408	14,694,535	11,711,216	9,048,926	7,471,819	5,381,920	4,159,051
EBITDA	(2,413,051)	1,166,403	2,338,526	1,646,833	1,035,816	728,822	491,787	355,096
Income Before Taxes	(2,496,903)	1,082,728	2,277,014	1,600,537	995,656	728,822	491,787	355,096
Income Taxes	(222,486)	393,082	840,126	602,529	378,334	284,221	189,362	136,712
Net Income	(2,255,755)	687,471	1,491,913	986,541	624,634	453,645	301,393	188,513
Average Shares	252,102	258,621	262,801	260,331	251,160	216,284	201,292	168,584
Balance Sheet								
Current Assets	8,087,822	9,925,627	9,758,361	7,705,425	5,932,502	4,906,765	3,905,907	2,064,248
Total Assets	10,225,703	13,176,874	13,048,174	10,406,897	8,063,352	6,888,455	5,714,276	2,886,483
Current Liabilities	1,118,726	1,657,773	2,293,945	1,770,061	1,383,833	1,292,100	1,699,742	960,950
Long-Term Obligations	3,478,230	3,537,947	3,386,527	2,861,550	2,150,972	1,913,268	1,737,869	677,602
Total Liabilities	5,905,510	6,599,513	7,090,832	5,884,623	4,615,229	4,128,029	3,437,611	1,638,552
Stockholders' Equity	4,320,193	6,577,361	5,957,342	4,522,274	3,448,123	2,760,426	2,276,665	1,247,931
Shares Outstanding	257,098	255,315	257,030	255,748	250,305	244,499	236,996	166,267
Statistical Record								
Return on Assets %	N.M.	5.24	12.72	10.65	8.36	7.20	7.01	6.86
Return on Equity %	N.M.	10.97	28.47	24.69	20.12	18.01	17.10	16.06
EBITDA Margin %	N.M.	8.17	15.91	14.06	11.45	9.75	9.14	8.54
Net Margin %	N.M.	4.82	10.15	8.42	6.90	6.07	5.60	4.53
Asset Turnover	0.79	1.09	1.25	1.26	1.21	1.19	1.25	1.51
Current Ratio	7.23	5.99	4.25	4.35	4.29	3.80	2.30	2.15
Debt to Equity	0.81	0.54	0.57	0.63	0.62	0.69	0.76	0.54
Price Range	35.10-9.08	44.65-26.56	47.92-30.17	32.49-21.42	24.49-11.38	14.73-9.15	12.39-6.75	10.94-3.92
P/E Ratio	...	16.79-9.98	8.44-5.31	8.57-5.65	9.88-4.59	8.01-4.97	8.26-4.50	9.77-3.50
Average Yield %	0.73	0.48	0.33	0.38	0.38	0.33	0.42	0.61

Address: 100 Bloomfield Hills Parkway, Suite 300, Bloomfield Hills, MI 48304	**Web Site:** www.pulte.com	**Auditors:** Ernst & Young LLP
Telephone: 248-647-2750	**Officers:** William J. Pulte - Chmn. Richard J. Dugas Jr. - Pres., C.E.O.	**Investor Contact:** 248-433-4597
Fax: 248-433-4598		**Transfer Agents:** Equiserve Trust Company, N.A., Canton, MA

QUANTA SERVICES, INC.

Exchange	Symbol	Price	52Wk Range	Yield	P/E
NYS	PWR	$23.17 (3/31/2008)	33.00-19.47	N/A	26.03

*7 Year Price Score 155.90 *NYSE Composite Index=100 *12 Month Price Score 91.36

Interim Earnings (Per Share)

Qtr.	Mar	Jun	Sep	Dec
2003	(0.04)	(0.08)	0.05	(0.24)
2004	(0.10)	(0.03)	0.04	0.02
2005	(0.04)	0.03	0.11	0.15
2006	0.07	0.14	0.17	(0.23)
2007	0.23	0.17	0.31	0.17

Interim Dividends (Per Share)

No Dividends Paid

Valuation Analysis

	Institutional Holding	
Forecast P/E	20.24	No of Institutions
	(1/10/2007)	210
Market Cap	$4.0 Billion	Shares
Book Value	2.2 Billion	123,596,840
Price/Book	1.81	% Held
Price/Sales	1.49	N/A

TRADING VOLUME (thousand shares)

Business Summary: Electrical (MIC: 11.14 SIC: 1731 NAIC: 238210)

Quanta Services is a specialized contracting services company, delivering end-to-end network services to the electric power, gas, telecommunications and cable television industries. Co.'s services include designing, installing, repairing and maintaining network infrastructure. Co. also provides various ancillary services to commercial, industrial and governmental entities. Co.'s services include installation, repair and maintenance of electric power transmission lines, installation of fiber optic, copper and coaxial cable and maintenance for video, data and voice transmission, and installation of cable and control systems for light rail lines, airports and highways.

Recent Developments: For the year ended Dec 31 2007, income from continuing operations increased 720.2% to US$133.1 million from US$16.2 million a year earlier. Net income increased 677.8% to US$136.0 million from US$17.5 million in the prior year. Revenues were US$2.66 billion, up 25.9% from US$2.11 billion the year before. Operating income was US$169.5 million versus US$74.1 million in the prior year, an increase of 128.8%. Direct operating expenses rose 24.0% to US$2.23 billion from US$1.80 billion in the comparable period the year before. Indirect operating expenses increased 8.6% to US$259.3 million from US$238.7 million in the equivalent prior-year period.

Prospects: Co.'s outlook appears favorable, reflecting robust customer spending on transmission and distribution systems due to the increasing demand for electricity. In addition, the integration of InfraSource Services, Inc., which was acquired in Aug 2007, is substantially completed and should contribute to revenue growth and margin improvement in 2008. For the first quarter of 2008, Co. expects revenues of $810.0 million to $840.0 million, with diluted earnings per share of approximately $0.10 to $0.11. Separately, on Feb 26 2008, Co. secured a contract with the Lower Colorado River Authority at an estimated value of up to $194.0 million over five years to provide transmission line construction.

Financial Data

(US$ in Thousands)	12/31/2007	12/31/2006	12/31/2005	12/31/2004	12/31/2002	12/31/2002	12/31/2001	12/31/2000
Earnings Per Share	0.89	0.15	0.25	(0.08)	(0.30)	(7.77)	1.10	1.42
Cash Flow Per Share	1.61	1.03	0.71	1.26	1.06	1.50	2.72	0.77
Tang Book Value Per Share	3.96	3.36	2.67	2.34	2.35	3.05	2.79	2.80
Income Statement								
Total Revenue	2,656,036	2,131,038	1,858,626	1,626,510	1,642,853	1,750,713	2,014,877	1,793,301
EBITDA	243,559	134,265	129,159	77,410	41,753	(97,402)	272,412	282,053
Income Before Taxes	167,362	65,126	52,247	(12,645)	(53,069)	(193,844)	156,966	199,051
Income Taxes	34,222	47,643	22,690	(3,451)	(18,080)	(19,710)	71,200	93,328
Net Income	135,977	17,483	29,557	(9,194)	(34,989)	(619,556)	85,766	105,723
Average Shares	167,260	117,863	116,634	114,441	110,906	80,815	78,238	76,583
Balance Sheet								
Current Assets	1,304,762	990,629	831,010	700,036	676,093	529,497	577,120	602,407
Total Assets	3,387,832	1,639,157	1,554,785	1,459,997	1,466,435	1,364,812	2,042,901	1,874,094
Current Liabilities	757,429	334,456	258,071	221,058	199,390	212,141	241,530	252,437
Long-Term Obligations	143,750	413,750	450,091	464,363	500,551	385,667	500,274	491,102
Total Liabilities	1,202,689	910,074	851,047	796,750	803,303	680,219	836,150	805,138
Stockholders' Equity	2,185,143	729,083	703,738	663,247	663,132	611,671	1,206,751	1,068,956
Shares Outstanding	171,015	118,533	118,164	117,139	116,567	70,790	60,760	58,166
Statistical Record								
Return on Assets %	5.41	1.09	1.96	N.M.	N.M.	N.M.	4.38	6.95
Return on Equity %	9.33	2.44	4.32	N.M.	N.M.	N.M.	7.54	11.55
EBITDA Margin %	9.17	6.30	6.95	4.76	2.54	N.M.	13.52	15.73
Net Margin %	5.12	0.82	1.59	N.M.	N.M.	N.M.	4.26	5.90
Asset Turnover	1.06	1.33	1.23	1.11	1.16	1.03	1.03	1.18
Current Ratio	1.72	2.96	3.22	3.17	3.39	2.50	2.39	2.39
Debt to Equity	0.07	0.57	0.64	0.70	0.75	0.63	0.41	0.46
Price Range	33.00-18.80	19.83-12.31	14.54-7.25	9.26-4.83	9.78-2.90	18.80-1.82	36.90-10.30	62.06-18.58
P/E Ratio	37.08-21.12	132.20-82.07	58.16-29.00	...	...	...	33.55-9.36	43.71-13.09

Address: 1360 Post Oak Boulevard, Suite 2100, Houston, TX 77056 **Telephone:** 713-629-7600 **Fax:** 713-629-7676	Web Site: www.quantaservices.com **Officers:** John R. Colson - C.E.O. Peter T. Dameris - Exec. V.P., C.O.O.	**Auditors:** PricewaterhouseCoopers LLP **Investor Contact:** 713-629-7600

QUEST DIAGNOSTICS, INC.

Exchange	Symbol	Price	52Wk Range	Yield	P/E
NYS	DGX	$45.27 (3/31/2008)	58.33-44.33	0.88	26.02

*7 Year Price Score 96.74   *NYSE Composite Index=100   *12 Month Price Score 98.24

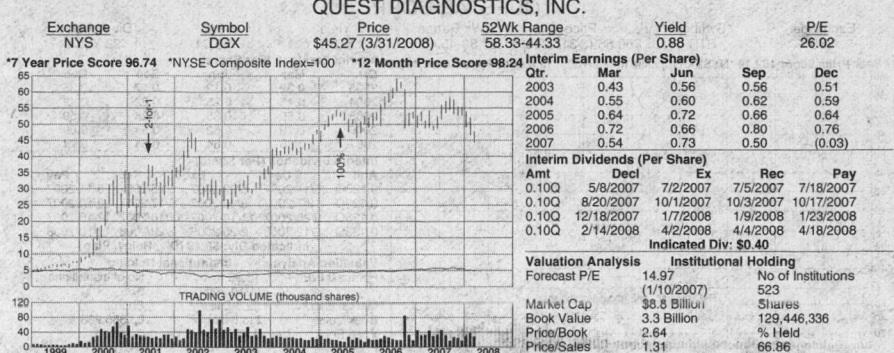

Interim Earnings (Per Share)

Qtr.	Mar	Jun	Sep	Dec
2003	0.43	0.56	0.56	0.51
2004	0.55	0.60	0.62	0.59
2005	0.64	0.72	0.66	0.64
2006	0.72	0.66	0.80	0.76
2007	0.54	0.73	0.50	(0.03)

Interim Dividends (Per Share)

Amt	Decl	Ex	Rec	Pay
0.10Q	5/8/2007	7/2/2007	7/5/2007	7/18/2007
0.10Q	8/20/2007	10/1/2007	10/3/2007	10/17/2007
0.10Q	12/18/2007	1/7/2008	1/9/2008	1/23/2008
0.10Q	2/14/2008	4/2/2008	4/4/2008	4/18/2008

Indicated Div: $0.40

Valuation Analysis   **Institutional Holding**

Forecast P/E	14.97	No of Institutions
	(1/10/2007)	523
Market Cap	$8.8 Billion	Shares
Book Value	3.3 Billion	129,446,336
Price/Book	2.64	% Held
Price/Sales	1.31	66.86

Business Summary: Diagnostic Services (MIC: 9.5 SIC: 8071 NAIC: 621511)

Quest Diagnostics is a provider of diagnostic testing, information and related services. Co. provides patients and physicians access to diagnostic laboratory services through its nationwide network of laboratories and patient service centers. Co. also provides interpretive consultation through its medical and scientific staff across the U.S. In addition, Co. provides gene-based testing and other esoteric testing, anatomic pathology services, including dermatopathology, and testing for drugs-of-abuse, as well as testing for clinical trials, and risk assessment services for the life insurance industry.

Recent Developments: For the year ended Dec 31 2007, income from continuing operations decreased 11.5% to US$553.8 million from US$625.7 million a year earlier. Net income decreased 42.0% to US$339.9 million from US$586.4 million in the prior year. Revenues were US$6.70 billion, up 7.0% from US$6.27 billion the year before. Operating income was US$1.09 billion versus US$1.13 billion in the prior year, a decrease of 3.3%. Direct operating expenses rose 7.4% to US$3.97 billion from US$3.70 billion in the comparable period the year before. Indirect operating expenses increased 13.8% to US$1.64 billion from US$1.44 billion in the equivalent prior-year period.

Prospects: Looking ahead, Co. expects solid revenue and earnings growth in 2008. Specifically, for the full year 2008, excluding potential special charges, Co. estimates its earnings of $3.00 to $3.20 per diluted share, revenue growth of 9.0%, and it also anticipates its operating income to approach 17.0% of revenues. In addition, Co. projects its investments of about $0.20 per share related to new information technology systems and its expansion into India. At the same time, Co. believes that it will be able to grow over the long term at a rate above U.S. clinical laboratory industry growth rate, to expand its margins and to increase its international revenues to 10.0% of consolidated revenues.

Financial Data

(US$ in Thousands)	12/31/2007	12/31/2006	12/31/2005	12/31/2004	12/31/2003	12/31/2002	12/31/2001	12/31/2000
Earnings Per Share	1.74	2.94	2.66	2.35	2.06	1.62	0.83	0.54
Cash Flow Per Share	4.80	4.83	4.22	3.91	3.20	3.09	2.50	2.06
Dividends Per Share	0.400	0.390	0.345	0.300	...	...	...	...
Dividend Payout %	22.99	13.27	12.97	12.79	...	...	...	...
Income Statement								
Total Revenue	6,704,907	6,268,659	5,503,711	5,126,601	4,737,958	4,108,051	3,627,771	3,421,162
EBITDA	1,328,595	1,320,385	1,144,049	1,061,801	951,489	727,441	550,854	448,369
Income Before Taxes	917,402	1,033,273	910,454	835,126	737,798	542,377	332,604	200,981
Income Taxes	358,574	407,581	364,177	335,931	301,081	220,223	148,692	96,033
Net Income	339,939	586,421	546,277	499,195	436,717	322,154	162,303	102,052
Average Shares	195,262	199,542	205,530	214,144	211,864	199,580	195,220	188,600
Balance Sheet								
Current Assets	1,374,357	1,191,018	1,069,497	931,080	995,786	824,443	876,514	980,689
Total Assets	8,565,693	5,661,482	5,306,115	4,203,788	4,301,418	3,324,197	2,930,555	2,864,536
Current Liabilities	1,288,297	1,150,870	1,101,292	1,043,788	723,800	635,977	658,623	954,990
Long Term Obligations	3,377,212	1,239,105	1,255,386	724,021	1,028,707	796,507	820,337	760,705
Total Liabilities	5,241,451	2,642,311	2,543,131	1,915,137	1,906,724	1,555,334	1,594,568	1,833,741
Stockholders' Equity	3,324,242	3,019,171	2,762,984	2,288,651	2,394,694	1,768,863	1,335,987	1,030,795
Shares Outstanding	194,040	193,949	198,455	196,220	205,628	195,926	192,048	186,164
Statistical Record								
Return on Assets %	4.78	10.69	11.49	11.71	11.45	10.30	5.60	3.54
Return on Equity %	10.72	20.28	21.63	21.26	20.98	20.75	13.72	10.75
EBITDA Margin %	19.82	21.06	20.79	20.71	20.08	17.71	15.18	13.11
Net Margin %	5.07	9.35	9.93	9.74	9.22	7.84	4.47	2.98
Asset Turnover	0.94	1.14	1.16	1.20	1.24	1.31	1.25	1.19
Current Ratio	1.07	1.03	0.97	0.89	1.38	1.30	1.33	1.03
Debt to Equity	1.02	0.41	0.45	0.32	0.43	0.45	0.61	0.74
Price Range	58.33-48.17	64.28-48.70	54.50-44.51	48.30-36.13	37.06-23.98	47.45-25.36	37.42-19.76	35.77-7.42
P/E Ratio	33.52-27.68	21.86-16.56	20.49-16.73	20.55-15.37	17.99-11.64	29.29-15.65	45.09-23.81	66.23-13.74
Average Yield %	0.76	0.71	0.68	0.70	...	...	...	...

Address: 1290 Wall Street West, Lyndhurst, NJ 07071
Telephone: 201-393-5000
Fax: 201-462-4169

Web Site: www.questdiagnostics.com
Officers: Surya N. Mohapatra Ph.D. - Chmn., Pres., C.E.O. Robert A. Hagemann - Sr. V.P., C.F.O.

Auditors: PricewaterhouseCoopers LLP
Transfer Agents: Computershare Investor Services, Chicago, IL

QUESTAR CORP.

Exchange	Symbol	Price	52Wk Range	Yield	P/E	Div Acheiver
NYS	STR	$56.56 (3/31/2008)	57.89-45.65	0.87	19.64	28 Years

*7 Year Price Score 152.19 *NYSE Composite Index=100 *12 Month Price Score 112.07

Interim Earnings (Per Share)

Qtr.	Mar	Jun	Sep	Dec
2003	0.39	0.12	0.17	0.35
2004	0.45	0.25	0.22	0.42
2005	0.55	0.35	0.38	0.59
2006	0.79	0.52	0.54	0.69
2007	0.86	0.64	0.64	0.74

Interim Dividends (Per Share)

Amt	Decl	Ex	Rec	Pay
0.123Q	5/14/2007	5/23/2007	5/25/2007	6/11/2007
0.123Q	8/7/2007	8/15/2007	8/17/2007	9/10/2007
0.123Q	10/23/2007	11/14/2007	11/16/2007	12/10/2007
0.123Q	2/12/2008	2/20/2008	2/22/2008	3/10/2008

Indicated Div: $0.49 (Div. Reinv. Plan)

Valuation Analysis **Institutional Holding**

Forecast P/E	13.30	No of Institutions
	(1/10/2007)	371
Market Cap	$9.8 Billion	Shares
Book Value	2.6 Billion	63,865,208
Price/Book	3.79	% Held
Price/Sales	3.58	74.31

Business Summary: Oil and Gas (MIC: 14.2 SIC: 1311 NAIC: 211111)

Questar is a natural gas-focused energy company with five major lines of business: gas and oil exploration and production; midstream field services; energy marketing; interstate gas transportation; and retail gas distribution. Co.'s operations are conducted through its Questar Market Resources, Inc., which acquires, explores for, develops and produces natural gas, oil and natural gas liquids, and provides midstream field services including natural gas-gathering and processing services; Questar Pipeline Company, which provides interstate natural gas transportation and storage services; and Questar Gas Company, which provides retail natural gas distribution services in Utah, WY and Idaho.

Recent Developments: For the year ended Dec 31 2007, net income increased 14.3% to US$507.4 million from US$444.1 million in the prior year. Revenues were US$2.73 billion, down 3.8% from US$2.84 billion the year before. Operating income was US$841.3 million versus US$756.4 million in the prior year, an increase of 11.2%. Direct operating expenses declined 19.5% to US$1.22 billion from US$1.51 billion in the comparable period the year before. Indirect operating expenses increased 17.7% to US$669.6 million from US$568.8 million in the equivalent prior-year period.

Prospects: On Jan 31 2008, Co. announced that its subsidiary, Questar Exploration and Production Company (Questar E&P), has entered into agreements to acquire two natural gas development properties in northwest Louisiana for an aggregate purchase price of $655.0 million. The acquired properties are expected to add 276.00 billion of cubic feet equivalent (Bcfe) of net proved reserves. Meanwhile, for full-year 2008, Co. expects its Questar E&P production to range from 148.00 Bcfe to 151.00 Bcfe. Concurrently, Co. is raising its previous earnings estimate of $2.85 to $3.00 per diluted share to a range of $2.90 to $3.05 per diluted share, excluding the effects of the acquisition mentioned above.

Financial Data

(US$ in Thousands)	12/31/2007	12/31/2006	12/31/2005	12/31/2004	12/31/2003	12/31/2002	12/31/2001	12/31/2000
Earnings Per Share	2.88	2.54	1.87	1.34	1.03	0.94	0.97	0.97
Cash Flow Per Share	6.63	5.65	4.12	3.46	2.70	2.84	2.30	1.61
Tang Book Value Per Share	14.51	12.43	8.60	8.03	7.06	6.40	6.07	6.00
Dividends Per Share	0.485	0.465	0.445	0.425	0.390	0.362	0.352	0.343
Dividend Payout %	16.84	18.34	23.80	31.84	37.86	38.56	36.34	35.31
Income Statement								
Total Revenue	2,726,600	2,835,600	2,724,888	1,901,431	1,463,188	1,200,667	1,439,350	1,266,153
EBITDA	1,246,000	1,089,300	842,633	587,148	485,609	456,388	405,498	389,723
Income Before Taxes	798,000	699,600	513,604	358,881	281,759	262,019	246,456	242,078
Income Taxes	290,600	255,500	187,923	129,580	102,563	91,126	88,270	85,367
Net Income	507,400	444,100	325,681	229,301	173,616	155,596	158,186	156,711
Average Shares	175,900	175,200	174,268	171,444	168,380	165,146	163,316	161,830
Balance Sheet								
Net PPE	5,098,600	4,091,400	3,427,542	2,984,660	2,768,529	2,617,798	2,565,098	1,953,993
Total Assets	5,944,200	5,064,700	4,357,073	3,646,658	3,309,055	3,067,850	3,235,711	2,539,045
Long-Term Obligations	1,021,200	1,022,400	983,200	933,195	950,189	1,145,180	997,423	714,537
Total Liabilities	3,366,300	2,859,200	2,807,270	2,207,100	2,047,790	1,929,089	2,154,930	1,547,979
Stockholders' Equity	2,577,900	2,205,500	1,549,803	1,439,558	1,261,265	1,138,761	1,080,781	991,066
Shares Outstanding	172,800	171,800	170,639	168,882	166,467	164,107	163,046	161,636
Statistical Record								
Return on Assets %	9.22	9.43	8.14	6.58	5.45	4.94	5.48	6.54
Return on Equity %	21.22	23.65	21.79	16.93	14.47	14.02	15.27	16.31
EBITDA Margin %	45.70	38.42	30.92	30.88	33.19	38.01	28.17	30.78
Net Margin %	18.61	15.66	11.95	12.06	11.87	12.96	10.99	12.38
PPE Turnover	0.59	0.75	0.85	0.66	0.54	0.46	0.64	0.68
Asset Turnover	0.50	0.60	0.68	0.55	0.46	0.38	0.50	0.53
Debt to Equity	0.40	0.46	0.63	0.65	0.75	1.01	0.92	0.72
Price Range	57.89-38.47	45.01-34.03	44.62-23.41	25.75-14.05	17.68-13.33	14.64-9.70	16.75-9.35	15.75-6.91
P/E Ratio	20.10-13.36	17.72-13.40	23.86-12.52	19.22-12.72	17.16-12.94	15.57-10.32	17.27-9.64	16.24-7.12
Average Yield %	0.98	1.17	1.33	2.10	2.49	2.91	2.73	3.23

Address: 180 East 100 South Street, P.O. Box 45433, Salt Lake City, UT 84145-0433 **Telephone:** 801-324-5000 **Fax:** 801-324-5483	**Web Site:** www.questar.com **Officers:** Keith O. Rattie - Chmn., Pres., C.E.O. Alan K. Allred - Exec. V.P.	**Auditors:** Ernst & Young LLP **Investor Contact:** 801-324-5497 **Transfer Agents:** Wells Fargo Bank Minnesota, N.A., South St. Paul, MN

QUICKSILVER RESOURCES, INC.

Exchange	Symbol	Price	52Wk Range	Yield	P/E
NYS	KWK	$36.53 (3/31/2008)	38.15-18.93	N/A	12.77

*7 Year Price Score 164.95 *NYSE Composite Index=100 ***12 Month Price Score 142.77**

TRADING VOLUME (thousand shares)

Interim Earnings (Per Share)

Qtr.	Mar	Jun	Sep	Dec
2003	0.03	0.01	0.04	0.04
2004	0.04	0.05	0.05	0.07
2005	0.07	0.11	0.16	0.21
2006	0.17	0.14	0.14	0.12
2007	0.14	0.19	0.17	2.36

Interim Dividends (Per Share)

Amt	Decl	Ex	Rec	Pay
100%	6/1/2004	7/1/2004	6/15/2004	6/30/2004
50%	6/1/2005	7/1/2005	6/15/2005	6/30/2005
100%	1/7/2008	2/1/2008	1/18/2008	1/31/2008

Valuation Analysis **Institutional Holding**

Forecast P/E	22.91	No of Institutions
	(1/10/2007)	182
Market Cap	$5.8 Billion	Shares
Book Value	1.1 Billion	61,090,032
Price/Book	5.40	% Held
Price/Sales	10.28	78.28

Business Summary: Oil and Gas (MIC: 14.2 SIC: 1311 NAIC: 211111)

Quicksilver Resources is an independent oil and gas company that is engaged in the development, exploitation, exploration, acquisition and production and sale of natural gas, natural gas liquids and crude oil as well as the marketing, processing and transmission of natural gas. Co. owns natural gas and oil properties in the U.S., principally in Texas, Wyoming and Montana, and in Canada, principally in Alberta, which in total had estimated proved reserves of approximately 1.50 trillion cubic feet of natural gas equivalents at Dec 31 2007. Also, as of Dec 31 2007, Co. owned approximately 73.0% of Quicksilver Gas Services LP, a publicly traded midstream master limited partnership

Recent Developments: For the year ended Dec 31 2007, income from continuing operations increased 411.5% to US$479.4 million from US$93.7 million a year earlier. Net income increased 411.5% to US$479.4 million from US$93.7 million in the prior year. Revenues were US$561.3 million, up 43.8% from US$390.4 million the year before. Operating income was US$803.6 million versus US$174.2 million in the prior year, an increase of 361.3%. Direct operating expenses rose 38.1% to US$153.0 million from US$110.8 million in the comparable period the year before. Indirect operating income amounted to US$395.3 million compared with an expense of US$105.4 million in the equivalent prior-year period.

Prospects: Co. intends to focus its capital spending program primarily on the continued development and exploration of its properties in Texas and Canada. For 2008, Co. has established a capital budget of $885.0 million, of which $650.0 million has been allocated for drilling activities. Notably, in the Fort Worth basin, Co. expects to drill 200 to 220 wells during 2008, and as a result, expects to achieve annual production growth of more than 100.0% from the basin in 2008. Also, Co. expects to drill about 265 (165 net) wells in the Horseshoe Canyon in Canada during 2008, and as a result, expects to achieve annual production growth in the range of 7.0% to 9.0% from its Canadian operations in 2008.

Financial Data

(US$ in Thousands)	12/31/2007	12/31/2006	12/31/2005	12/31/2004	12/31/2003	12/31/2002	12/31/2001	12/31/2000
Earnings Per Share	2.86	0.57	0.54	0.21	0.12	0.11	0.17	0.16
Cash Flow Per Share	2.05	1.44	0.95	0.66	0.47	0.37	0.52	0.43
Tang Book Value Per Share	6.76	3.71	2.52	2.02	1.63	1.02	0.84	0.78
Income Statement								
Total Revenue	561,258	390,362	310,448	179,729	140,949	121,979	143,088	120,018
EBITDA	932,404	256,891	206,356	103,048	83,388	72,570	...	75,481
Income Before Taxes	736,941	131,960	127,974	45,446	28,502	21,333	...	27,731
Income Taxes	256,508	38,150	40,702	14,174	9,997	7,498	10,800	10,113
Net Income	479,378	93,719	87,434	31,272	16,208	13,835	19,310	17,618
Average Shares	168,029	166,266	164,910	154,029	137,070	122,364	115,326	110,802
Balance Sheet								
Current Assets	190,401	170,964	113,584	66,196	49,711	44,776	35,294	47,449
Total Assets	2,775,846	1,882,912	1,243,094	888,334	666,934	529,538	469,244	440,111
Current Liabilities	358,575	199,389	212,190	83,451	80,514	68,454	52,074	46,514
Long-Term Obligations	813,817	919,117	506,039	399,134	249,097	248,493	248,425	239,986
Total Liabilities	1,677,153	1,299,815	859,479	584,058	425,118	400,633	374,857	353,353
Stockholders' Equity	1,068,355	575,666	383,615	304,276	241,816	128,905	94,387	86,758
Shares Outstanding	158,016	155,203	152,158	150,367	148,400	126,557	112,698	111,402
Statistical Record								
Return on Assets %	20.58	6.00	8.20	4.01	2.71	2.77	4.25	5.54
Return on Equity %	58.32	19.54	25.42	11.42	8.74	12.39	21.32	22.48
EBITDA Margin %	166.13	65.81	66.47	57.34	59.16	59.49	...	62.88
Net Margin %	85.41	24.01	28.16	17.40	11.50	11.34	13.50	14.68
Asset Turnover	0.24	0.25	0.29	0.23	0.24	0.24	0.31	0.38
Current Ratio	0.53	0.86	0.54	0.79	0.62	0.65	0.68	1.02
Debt to Equity	0.76	1.60	1.32	1.31	1.03	1.93	2.63	2.77
Price Range	30.36-16.72	25.14-14.84	24.55-11.25	12.42-5.36	5.59-3.33	4.38-2.82	3.40-1.54	1.63-0.60
P/E Ratio	10.61-5.85	44.10-26.03	45.45-20.84	59.13-25.52	46.54-27.75	39.82-25.61	20.00-9.07	10.16-3.78

Address: 777 West Rosedale Street, Suite 300, Fort Worth, TX 76104 **Telephone:** 817-665-5000 **Fax:** 817-665-5004	**Web Site:** www.qrinc.com **Officers:** Thomas F. Darden - Chmn. Glenn M. Darden - Pres., C.E.O.	**Auditors:** DELOITTE & TOUCHE **Investor Contact:** 817-665-4834 **Transfer Agents:** Mellon Investor Services, Ridgefield Park, NJ

QWEST COMMUNICATIONS INTERNATIONAL, INC.

Exchange	Symbol	Price	52Wk Range	Yield	P/E
NYS	Q	$4.53 (3/31/2008)	10.32-4.50	N/A	2.98

*7 Year Price Score 82.41   *NYSE Composite Index=100   *12 Month Price Score 71.83

TRADING VOLUME (thousand shares)

Interim Earnings (Per Share)

Qtr.	Mar	Jun	Sep	Dec
2003	0.09	(0.04)	1.05	(0.24)
2004	(0.17)	(0.43)	(0.31)	(0.08)
2005	0.03	(0.09)	(0.08)	(0.28)
2006	0.05	0.06	0.09	0.10
2007	0.12	0.13	1.08	0.21

Interim Dividends (Per Share)

Dividend Payment Suspended

Valuation Analysis		Institutional Holding	
Forecast P/E	19.30	No of Institutions	
	(1/10/2007)	357	
Market Cap	$8.1 Billion	Shares	
Book Value	563.0 Million	1,678,202,112	
Price/Book	14.38	% Held	
Price/Sales	0.59	89.87	

Business Summary: Communications (MIC: 10.1 SIC: 4813 NAIC: 517910)

Qwest Communications International is engaged in providing voice, data, internet and video services. Co. operates majority of its business within its local service area, which consists of the 14-state region of Arizona, Colorado, Idaho, Iowa, Minnesota, Montana, Nebraska, New Mexico, North Dakota, Oregon, South Dakota, Utah, Washington and Wyoming. Co.'s customers consist of consumers and small businesses, local, national and global businesses, governmental entities, public and private educational institutions as well as telecommunications providers. As of Dec 31 2007, Co. conducted its businesses through three segments: wireline services; wireless services; and other services.

Recent Developments: For the year ended Dec 31 2007, net income increased 391.9% to US$2.92 billion from US$593.0 million in the prior year. Revenues were US$13.78 billion, down 1.0% from US$13.92 billion the year before. Direct operating expenses declined 6.3% to US$5.26 billion from US$5.61 billion in the comparable period the year before. Indirect operating expenses increased 0.1% to US$6.77 billion from US$6.76 billion in the equivalent prior-year period.

Prospects: Co. continues to focus on products such as broadband services, private line, Multi-Protocol Label Switching -based services sold as iQ Networking™, Voice over Internet Protocol and video, as revenue increases from these more-advanced products have outpaced revenue declines from traditional data, Internet and video services. For instance, Co. continues to focus on improving penetration of broadband services by continually increasing connection speeds. As such, Co. is planning to reach 1.5 million homes with speeds up to 20 Mbps by the end of 2008. Co. expects broadband subscriber growth to continue despite expecting to face competition for these subscribers.

Financial Data

(US$ in Thousands)	12/31/2007	12/31/2006	12/31/2005	12/31/2004	12/31/2003	12/31/2002	12/31/2001	12/31/2000
Earnings Per Share	1.52	0.30	(0.42)	(1.00)	0.87	(22.87)	(2.42)	(0.06)
Cash Flow Per Share	1.65	1.48	1.26	1.02	1.25	1.39	2.43	2.89
Tang Book Value Per Share	N.M.	...	...	...	...	...	1.28	5.37
Dividends Per Share	...	...	...	...	...	...	0.050	0.310
Income Statement								
Total Revenue	13,778,000	13,923,000	13,903,000	13,809,000	14,288,000	15,385,000	19,695,000	16,610,000
EBITDA	4,218,000	4,496,000	3,788,000	2,948,000	3,092,000	(14,489,000)	2,819,000	4,509,000
Income Before Taxes	664,000	557,000	(760,000)	(1,706,000)	(1,832,000)	(20,125,000)	(3,958,000)	126,000
Income Taxes	(2,253,000)	(36,000)	(3,000)	88,000	(519,000)	(2,500,000)	...	207,000
Net Income	2,917,000	593,000	(779,000)	(1,794,000)	1,512,000	(38,468,000)	(4,023,000)	(81,000)
Average Shares	1,920,766	1,971,545	1,836,374	1,801,405	1,738,766	1,682,056	1,661,133	1,272,088
Balance Sheet								
Current Assets	3,573,000	3,654,000	3,164,000	4,218,000	4,416,000	6,420,000	5,757,000	5,376,000
Total Assets	22,532,000	21,239,000	21,497,000	24,324,000	26,216,000	29,345,000	73,781,000	73,501,000
Current Liabilities	4,209,000	5,160,000	4,235,000	4,286,000	5,548,000	6,895,000	9,989,000	9,893,000
Long-Term Obligations	13,650,000	13,206,000	14,968,000	16,690,000	15,639,000	19,754,000	20,197,000	15,421,000
Total Liabilities	21,969,000	22,684,000	24,714,000	26,936,000	27,232,000	32,175,000	37,126,000	32,197,000
Stockholders' Equity	563,000	(1,445,000)	(3,217,000)	(2,612,000)	(1,016,000)	(2,830,000)	36,655,000	41,304,000
Shares Outstanding	1,787,287	1,900,649	1,866,360	1,816,386	1,769,896	1,699,115	1,663,546	1,672,218
Statistical Record								
Return on Assets %	13.33	2.78	N.M.	N.M.	5.44	N.M.	N.M.	N.M.
EBITDA Margin %	30.61	32.29	27.25	21.35	21.64	N.M.	14.31	27.15
Net Margin %	21.17	4.26	N.M.	N.M.	10.58	N.M.	N.M.	N.M.
Asset Turnover	0.63	0.65	0.61	0.54	0.51	0.30	0.27	0.39
Current Ratio	0.85	0.71	0.75	0.98	0.80	0.93	0.58	0.54
Debt to Equity	24.25	...	...	...	...	...	0.55	0.37
Price Range	10.32-6.36	9.01-5.19	5.92-3.42	4.90-2.59	6.02-3.10	14.93-1.11	47.50-11.51	64.00-32.38
P/E Ratio	6.79-4.18	30.03-17.30	...	...	6.92-3.56	...	...	...
Average Yield %	...	...	...	...	...	...	0.18	0.67

Address: 1801 California Street, Denver, CO 80202 **Telephone:** 303-992-1400 **Fax:** 303-291-1724	**Web Site:** www.qwest.com **Officers:** Richard C. Notebaert - Chmn., C.E.O. Oren G. Shaffer - Vice-Chmn., C.F.O.	**Auditors:** KPMG LLP **Transfer Agents:** The Bank of New York, New York, NY

RADIAN GROUP, INC.

Exchange	Symbol	Price	52Wk Range	Yield	P/E
NYS	RDN	$6.57 (3/31/2008)	63.34-4.50	1.22	N/A

*7 Year Price Score 49.10   *NYSE Composite Index=100   *12 Month Price Score 29.46

Interim Earnings (Per Share)

Qtr.	Mar	Jun	Sep	Dec
2003	1.11	1.18	1.20	0.58
2004	1.26	1.27	1.31	1.49
2005	1.24	1.28	1.88	1.26
2006	1.96	1.79	1.36	1.96
2007	1.42	0.26	(8.82)	(9.06)

Interim Dividends (Per Share)

Amt	Decl	Ex	Rec	Pay
0.02Q	5/8/2007	5/16/2007	5/18/2007	6/19/2007
0.02Q	8/6/2007	8/15/2007	8/17/2007	9/18/2007
0.02Q	11/6/2007	11/14/2007	11/16/2007	12/18/2007
0.02Q	2/15/2008	2/20/2008	2/24/2008	3/27/2008

Indicated Div: $0.08

Valuation Analysis

Forecast P/E	7.60 (1/10/2007)
Market Cap	$528.3 Million
Book Value	2.7 Billion
Price/Book	0.19
Price/Sales	2.63

Institutional Holding

No of Institutions	280
Shares	82,944,528
% Held	N/A

Business Summary: Insurance (MIC: 8.2 SIC: 6351 NAIC: 524130)

Radian Group develops and delivers credit enhancement products. Co.'s mortgage insurance business provides credit protection for mortgage lenders and other financial services companies on residential mortgage assets, through traditional mortgage insurance and other mortgage-backed structured products. Co.'s financial guaranty business insures and reinsures credit-based risks and provides credit protection on various asset classes through credit default swaps. As at Dec 31 2007, Co.'s financial services business consists mainly of its 21.8% ownership interests in Sherman Financial Group LLC and 46.0% equity interest in Credit-Based Asset Servicing and Securitization LLC.

Recent Developments: For the year ended Dec 31 2007, net loss amounted to US$1.29 billion versus net income of US$582.2 million in the prior year. Revenues were US$201.1 million, down 84.9% from US$1.33 billion the year before. Net premiums earned were US$1.04 billion versus US$1.02 billion in the prior year, an increase of 2.2%. Net investment income rose 9.3% to US$256.1 million from US$234.3 million a year ago.

Prospects: Co. expects results in its traditional mortgage insurance business to continue to be hurt by the ongoing deteriorating domestic housing market. Accordingly, Co. expects incurred losses from its traditional mortgage insurance portfolio to be over 200.0% of earned premiums in 2008. Further, Co. expects to experience difficulties in writing international mortgage insurance business through its Radian Insurance, Inc. subsidiary due to the recent Standard & Poor's Ratings Service downgrade. Notwithstanding these negative projections, Co. noted that it is in the process of adjusting its pricing to improve its risk/reward posture and to generate appropriate returns on new business going forward.

Financial Data
(US$ in Thousands)

	12/31/2007	12/31/2006	12/31/2005	12/31/2004	12/31/2003	12/31/2002	12/31/2001	12/31/2000
Earnings Per Share	(16.22)	7.08	5.91	5.33	4.08	4.41	3.88	3.22
Cash Flow Per Share	3.79	6.01	6.66	3.50	5.72	6.22	5.32	3.71
Tang Book Value Per Share	33.83	51.23	44.11	39.98	34.31	29.43	24.54	17.97
Dividends Per Share	0.080	0.080	0.080	0.081	0.080	0.080	0.075	0.060
Dividend Payout %	...	1.13	1.35	1.51	1.96	1.81	1.93	1.86
Income Statement								
Premium Income	1,038,610	1,015,846	1,018,670	1,029,484	1,008,183	847,125	715,880	520,871
Total Revenue	201,051	1,327,946	1,298,151	1,364,053	1,363,144	1,152,090	947,201	615,434
Income Before Taxes	(2,068,915)	813,269	740,339	725,592	531,479	601,776	505,531	352,470
Income Taxes	(778,616)	231,097	217,485	206,939	145,578	174,107	145,112	103,532
Net Income	(1,290,299)	582,172	522,854	518,653	385,901	427,169	360,419	248,938
Average Shares	79,556	82,261	88,746	97,908	94,643	95,706	91,958	76,298
Balance Sheet								
Total Assets	8,210,189	7,928,671	7,230,610	7,000,820	6,445,767	5,393,405	4,438,626	2,272,811
Total Liabilities	5,489,453	3,861,114	3,567,730	3,311,765	3,219,923	2,639,970	2,092,298	870,614
Stockholders' Equity	2,720,736	4,067,557	3,662,880	3,689,055	3,225,844	2,753,435	2,306,328	1,362,197
Shares Outstanding	80,412	79,401	83,032	92,280	94,011	93,552	93,982	75,815
Statistical Record								
Return on Assets %	N.M.	7.68	7.35	7.69	6.52	8.69	10.74	12.26
Return on Equity %	N.M.	15.06	14.22	14.96	12.91	16.88	19.65	20.52
Net Margin %	(641.78)	43.84	40.28	38.02	28.31	37.08	38.05	40.45
Price Range	66.51-9.20	64.45-51.66	59.72-43.61	54.00-40.95	53.29-30.15	55.20-29.49	43.53-27.19	38.31-17.28
P/E Ratio	...	9.10-7.30	10.10-7.38	10.13-7.68	13.06-7.39	12.52-6.69	11.22-7.01	11.90-5.37
Average Yield %	0.20	0.14	0.16	0.17	0.19	0.18	0.20	0.22

Address: 1601 Market Street, Philadelphia, PA 19103 **Telephone:** 215-564-6600 **Fax:** 215-564-0129	**Web Site:** www.radiangroupinc.com **Officers:** Frank P. Filipps - Chmn. Roy J. Kasmar - Pres., C.O.O.	**Auditors:** PricewaterhouseCoopers LLP

RADIOSHACK CORP.

Exchange	Symbol	Price	52Wk Range	Yield	P/E
NYS	RSH	$16.25 (3/31/2008)	34.87-14.26	1.54	9.34

*7 Year Price Score 73.21   *NYSE Composite Index=100   *12 Month Price Score 77.69

Interim Earnings (Per Share)

Qtr.	Mar	Jun	Sep	Dec
2003	0.33	0.34	0.34	0.76
2004	0.41	0.42	0.43	0.82
2005	0.34	0.33	0.75	0.38
2006	0.06	(0.02)	(0.12)	0.62
2007	0.31	0.34	0.34	0.75

Interim Dividends (Per Share)

Amt	Decl	Ex	Rec	Pay
0.25A	9/24/2004	11/29/2004	12/1/2004	12/20/2004
0.25A	9/30/2005	11/29/2005	12/1/2005	12/19/2005
0.25A	11/6/2006	11/29/2006	12/1/2006	12/20/2006
0.25A	11/12/2007	11/27/2007	11/29/2007	12/19/2007

Indicated Div: $0.25

Valuation Analysis / Institutional Holding

Forecast P/E	15.63 (1/10/2007)	No of Institutions	238
Market Cap	$2.1 Billion	Shares	129,134,128
Book Value	769.7 Million	% Held	
Price/Book	2.77		94.81
Price/Sales	0.50		

TRADING VOLUME (thousand shares)

Business Summary: Retail - Appliances and Electrical (MIC: 5.10 SIC: 5731 NAIC: 443112)

RadioShack is primarily engaged in the retail sale of consumer electronics goods and services through its RadioShack store chain and non-RadioShack branded kiosk operations. As at Dec 31 2007, Co. operated 4,447 company-operated stores under the RadioShack brand located in shopping malls, strip centers and individual storefronts throughout the U.S., as well as in Puerto Rico and the U.S. Virgin Islands. In addition, Co. operated 739 kiosks primarily inside SAM'S CLUB locations, and stand-alone Sprint Nextel kiosks in shopping malls throughout the U.S., as well as a network of 1,484 RadioShack dealer outlets, including 36 located outside of North America.

Recent Developments: For the year ended Dec 31 2007, net income increased 222.6% to US$236.8 million from US$73.4 million in the prior year. Revenues were US$4.25 billion, down 11.0% from US$4.78 billion the year before. Operating income was US$381.9 million versus US$156.9 million in the prior year, an increase of 143.4%. Direct operating expenses declined 15.9% to US$2.23 billion from US$2.65 billion in the comparable period the year before. Indirect operating expenses decreased 16.7% to US$1.64 billion from US$1.97 billion in the equivalent prior-year period.

Prospects: Co.'s near-term outlook appears mixed. For instance, Co.'s consolidated net sales and gross profit are being negatively affected primarily by a decrease in comparable store sales driven by lower sales in postpaid wireless and satellite radio which reflects a challenging wireless industry environment, in addition to the closure of 481 Co.-operated stores during June and July 2006 as part of its 2006 restructuring. Nevertheless, Co. is encouraged by the improvement in bottom-line results, which is favorably affected by improved gross margin combined with a reduction in expenses. Separately, Co. noted that it will close its distribution center in Columbus, OH during the first half of 2008.

Financial Data
(US$ in Thousands)

	12/31/2007	12/31/2006	12/31/2005	12/31/2004	12/31/2003	12/31/2002	12/31/2001	12/31/2000
Earnings Per Share	1.74	0.54	1.79	2.08	1.77	1.45	0.85	1.84
Cash Flow Per Share	2.82	2.31	2.45	2.18	3.89	3.02	4.22	0.62
Tang Book Value Per Share	5.83	4.76	4.07	5.53	4.71	4.22	3.97	4.37
Dividends Per Share	0.250	0.250	0.250	0.250	0.250	0.220	0.165	0.220
Dividend Payout %	14.37	46.30	13.97	12.02	14.12	15.17	19.41	11.96
Income Statement								
Total Revenue	4,251,700	4,777,500	5,081,700	4,841,200	4,649,300	4,577,200	4,775,700	4,794,700
EBITDA	495,500	276,500	483,900	661,700	587,700	554,000	437,600	737,000
Income Before Taxes	366,600	111,400	321,500	542,100	472,800	424,900	291,500	593,600
Income Taxes	129,800	38,000	51,600	204,900	174,300	161,500	124,800	225,600
Net Income	236,800	73,400	267,000	337,200	298,500	263,400	166,700	368,000
Average Shares	135,900	136,200	148,800	162,500	168,900	179,300	191,200	197,700
Balance Sheet								
Current Assets	1,566,800	1,599,600	1,627,300	1,775,100	1,666,600	1,706,900	1,714,300	1,818,200
Total Assets	1,989,600	2,070,000	2,205,100	2,516,700	2,243,900	2,227,900	2,245,100	2,576,500
Current Liabilities	748,000	984,200	986,300	957,400	858,100	828,200	826,400	1,232,400
Long-Term Obligations	348,200	345,800	494,900	506,900	541,300	591,300	565,400	302,900
Total Liabilities	1,219,900	1,416,200	1,616,300	1,594,600	1,474,600	1,499,800	1,467,000	1,596,200
Stockholders' Equity	769,700	653,800	588,800	922,100	769,300	728,100	778,100	880,300
Shares Outstanding	131,093	135,837	134,962	158,198	162,552	171,727	176,800	185,764
Statistical Record								
Return on Assets %	11.67	3.43	11.31	14.13	13.35	11.78	6.91	15.56
Return on Equity %	33.27	11.81	35.34	39.76	39.87	34.98	20.10	42.90
EBITDA Margin %	11.65	5.79	9.52	13.67	12.64	12.10	9.16	15.37
Net Margin %	5.57	1.54	5.25	6.97	6.42	5.75	3.49	7.68
Asset Turnover	2.09	2.24	2.15	2.03	2.08	2.05	1.98	2.03
Current Ratio	2.09	1.63	1.65	1.85	1.94	2.06	2.07	1.48
Debt to Equity	0.45	0.53	0.84	0.55	0.70	0.81	0.73	0.34
Price Range	34.87-16.81	22.90-13.76	34.30-20.69	35.41-26.17	32.15-18.74	36.00-17.51	55.19-21.00	69.00-36.63
P/E Ratio	20.04-9.66	42.41-25.48	19.16-11.56	17.02-12.58	18.16-10.59	24.83-12.08	64.93-24.71	37.50-19.90
Average Yield %	1.01	1.38	0.97	0.82	0.98	0.83	0.52	0.42

Address: 100 Throckmorton Street, Suite 1800, Fort Worth, TX 76102 **Telephone:** 817-415-3700 **Fax:** 817-878-4887	**Web Site:** www.radioshackcorporation.com **Officers:** Leonard H. Roberts - Chmn. David J. Edmondson - Pres., C.E.O.	**Auditors:** PricewaterhouseCoopers LLP

RANGE RESOURCES CORP

Exchange	Symbol	Price	52Wk Range	Yield	P/E
NYS	RRC	$63.45 (3/31/2008)	65.16-34.01	0.25	41.20

*7 Year Price Score 209.37 *NYSE Composite Index=100 *12 Month Price Score 146.27

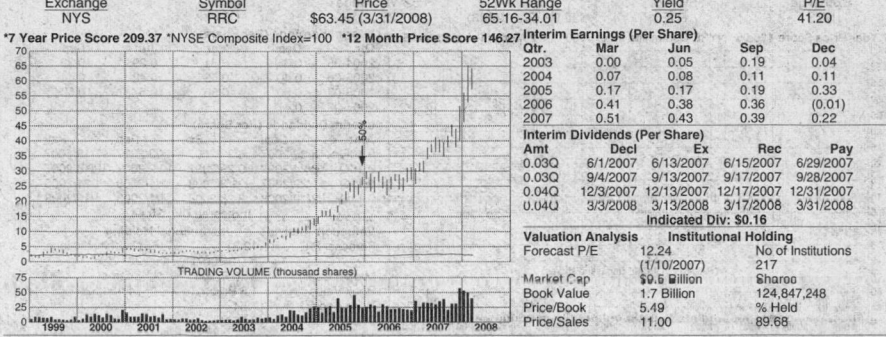

Interim Earnings (Per Share)

Qtr.	Mar	Jun	Sep	Dec
2003	0.00	0.05	0.19	0.04
2004	0.07	0.08	0.11	0.11
2005	0.17	0.17	0.19	0.33
2006	0.41	0.38	0.36	(0.01)
2007	0.51	0.43	0.39	0.22

Interim Dividends (Per Share)

Amt	Decl	Ex	Rec	Pay
0.03Q	6/1/2007	6/13/2007	6/15/2007	6/29/2007
0.03Q	9/4/2007	9/13/2007	9/17/2007	9/28/2007
0.04Q	12/3/2007	12/13/2007	12/17/2007	12/31/2007
0.04Q	3/3/2008	3/13/2008	3/17/2008	3/31/2008

Indicated Div: $0.16

Valuation Analysis

		Institutional Holding	
Forecast P/E	12.24 (1/10/2007)	No of Institutions	217
Market Cap	$9.5 Billion	Shares	124,847,248
Book Value	1.7 Billion	% Held	89.68
Price/Book	5.49		
Price/Sales	11.00		

Business Summary: Oil and Gas (MIC: 14.2 SIC: 1311 NAIC: 211111)

Range Resources is an oil and gas company engaged in the exploration, development and acquisition of oil and gas properties, primarily in the Southwestern, Appalachian and Gulf Coast regions of the U.S. As of Dec 31 2007, Co.'s proved reserves had the following characteristics: 2.20 trillion cubic feet equivalent of proved reserves, of which 82.0% were natural gas and 64.0% were proved developed; 77.0% operated; and a reserve life of 17.7 years (based on fourth quarter 2007 production). Also as of Dec 31 2007, Co. owned 3.4 million gross (2.7 million net) acres of leasehold, which included over 407,800 of acres associated with royalties.

Recent Developments: For the year ended Dec 31 2007, income from continuing operations decreased 13.9% to US$167.0 million from US$193.9 million a year earlier. Net income increased 45.3% to US$230.6 million from US$158.7 million in the prior year. Revenues were US$862.1 million, up 15.7% from US$744.8 million the year before. Direct operating expenses rose 33.8% to US$108.7 million from US$81.3 million in the comparable period the year before. Indirect operating expenses increased 40.2% to US$487.6 million from US$347.9 million in the equivalent prior-year period.

Prospects: Co.'s near-term outlook appears favorable. For 2008, Co. expects capital expenditures of $783.0 million to drill 968 gross (715 net) wells and undertake 82 (66 net) recompletions. Specifically, Co. expects to drill ten additional horizontal shale wells at its Huron shale in 2008. In addition, Co. noted that its Marcellus Shale play in the Appalachian Basin could represent as much as 10.00 trillion cubic feet equivalent (Tcfe) to 15.00 Tcfe in unproven unrisked reserve potential for Co. and plans to drill a total of 60 Marcellus shale wells, 40 of which are planned as horizontal wells in 2008. Hence, Co. expects production growth of 15.0% for 2008, including the effect of planned asset sales.

Financial Data
(US$ in Thousands)

	12/31/2007	12/31/2006	12/31/2005	12/31/2004	12/31/2003	12/31/2002	12/31/2001	12/31/2000
Earnings Per Share	1.54	1.14	0.86	0.38	0.41	0.31	0.13	0.66
Cash Flow Per Share	4.47	3.59	2.62	2.27	1.54	1.37	1.70	1.15
Tang Book Value Per Share	11.56	9.04	5.36	4.65	2.65	2.50	3.11	2.51
Dividends Per Share	0.130	0.090	0.060	0.033	0.007	...	...	...
Dividend Payout %	8.44	7.89	6.98	8.77	1.64			
Income Statement								
Income Before Taxes	265,737	321,340	177,379	66,776	49,413	19,310	4,994	18,624
Income Taxes	98,761	123,726	66,368	24,545	18,489	(4,442)	(51)	(1,574)
Net Income	230,569	158,702	111,011	42,231	35,415	25,766	8,996	37,961
Average Shares	149,911	138,711	129,126	97,998	86,775	81,627	77,043	64,495
Balance Sheet								
Total Assets	4,016,508	3,187,674	2,018,985	1,595,406	830,091	658,484	691,565	689,165
Total Liabilities	2,288,486	1,931,513	1,322,062	1,029,066	556,025	452,375	445,878	503,958
Stockholders' Equity	1,728,022	1,256,161	696,923	566,340	274,066	206,109	245,687	185,207
Shares Outstanding	149,511	138,931	129,907	121,829	84,614	82,487	78,964	73,781
Statistical Record								
Return on Assets %	6.40	6.10	6.14	3.47	4.76	3.82	1.30	5.25
Return on Equity %	15.45	16.25	17.58	10.02	14.75	11.41	4.18	24.24
Price Range	51.63-25.69	31.23-21.99	28.01-12.57	14.34-6.30	6.52-3.37	3.92-2.70	4.58-2.65	4.58-0.96
P/E Ratio	33.53-16.68	27.39-19.29	32.57-14.61	37.74-16.58	15.90-8.21	12.65-8.71	35.26-20.41	6.94-1.45
Average Yield %	0.35	0.34	0.31	0.35	0.15	...	...	...

Address: 777 Main Street, Suite 800, Fort Worth, TX 76102 **Telephone:** 817-870-2601 **Fax:** 817-870-2316	**Web Site:** www.rangeresources.com **Officers:** Charles L. Blackburn - Chmn. John H. Pinkerton - Pres., C.E.O.	**Auditors:** Ernst & Young LLP **Investor Contact:** 817-810-1938 **Transfer Agents:** Computershare Investor Services, LLC

RAYMOND JAMES FINANCIAL, INC.

Exchange	Symbol	Price	52Wk Range	Yield	P/E
NYS	RJF	$22.98 (3/31/2008)	37.25-20.65	1.91	11.10

*7 Year Price Score 120.06 *NYSE Composite Index=100 *12 Month Price Score 83.77

Interim Earnings (Per Share)

Qtr.	Dec	Mar	Jun	Sep
2004-05	0.35	0.31	0.29	0.39
2005-06	0.40	0.53	0.48	0.44
2006-07	0.50	0.50	0.57	0.53
2007-08	0.47	...	...	...

Interim Dividends (Per Share)

Amt	Decl	Ex	Rec	Pay
0.10Q	5/29/2007	6/29/2007	7/3/2007	7/19/2007
0.10Q	8/24/2007	9/28/2007	10/2/2007	10/18/2007
0.11Q	11/29/2007	1/2/2008	1/4/2008	1/21/2008
0.11Q	2/19/2008	3/28/2008	4/1/2008	4/16/2008

Indicated Div: $0.44

Valuation Analysis

		Institutional Holding	
Forecast P/E	12.31 (1/10/2007)	No of Institutions	207
Market Cap	$2.8 Billion	Shares	74,438,520
Book Value	1.8 Billion	% Held	62.74
Price/Book	1.54		
Price/Sales	0.86		

Business Summary: Finance Intermediaries & Services (MIC: 8.7 SIC: 6211 NAIC: 523110)

Raymond James Financial is a holding company whose subsidiaries are engaged in various financial services businesses, including the underwriting, distribution, trading and brokerage of equity and debt securities, as well as the sale of mutual funds and other investment products. As of Sep 30 2007, Co. had eight business segments: Private Client Group; Capital Markets; Asset Management; Raymond James Bank, FSB; Emerging Markets; Stock Loan/Borrow; Proprietary Capital and certain corporate activities combined in the Other segment. At Sep 30 2007, Co. had total assets of $16.25 billion.

Recent Developments: For the quarter ended Dec 31 2007, net income decreased 5.3% to US$56.2 million from US$59.4 million in the year-earlier quarter. Revenues were US$829.2 million, up 16.8% from US$709.6 million the year before. Direct operating expenses rose 35.6% to US$143.4 million from US$105.7 million in the comparable period the year before. Indirect operating expenses increased 15.9% to US$594.5 million from US$513.1 million in the equivalent prior-year period.

Prospects: Co. noted that it is currently operating in a challenging environment, with declining interest rates having a negative effect on near term spreads, and the current equity market conditions dampening investment banking activity. Specifically, results at Co.'s Capital Markets segment have been affected by slower underwriting activity due to the stock market's volatility and negative direction. However, Co.'s Private Client segment continues to benefit from the positive recruiting results of employee financial advisors and increased productivity, which in turn resulted in increases in assets under management. In addition, Co. is seeing loan growth at its Raymond James Bank subsidiary.

Financial Data

(US$ in Thousands)	3 Mos	09/30/2007	09/30/2006	09/30/2005	09/24/2004	09/26/2003	09/27/2002	09/28/2001
Earnings Per Share	2.07	2.11	1.85	1.33	1.15	0.78	0.71	0.88
Cash Flow Per Share	6.44	3.78	(0.35)	3.87	(1.67)	1.76	0.50	1.69
Tang Book Value Per Share	14.42	14.14	12.04	10.44	9.09	7.93	7.12	6.54
Dividends Per Share	0.300	0.400	0.320	0.213	0.220	0.160	0.160	0.160
Dividend Payout %	14.49	18.96	17.30	16.00	19.19	20.51	22.50	18.18
Income Statement								
Total Revenue	829,191	3,109,579	2,632,757	2,156,997	1,829,776	1,497,571	1,515,923	1,657,844
Income Before Taxes	90,757	392,224	342,066	245,453	204,121	138,275	131,516	157,468
Income Taxes	34,515	141,794	127,724	96,925	76,546	51,958	52,213	61,058
Net Income	56,242	250,430	214,342	151,046	127,575	86,317	79,303	96,410
Average Shares	120,241	118,693	115,738	113,047	111,603	110,218	111,665	109,797
Balance Sheet								
Total Assets	17,097,718	16,254,168	11,516,650	8,358,769	7,621,846	6,911,638	6,040,303	6,372,054
Total Liabilities	15,043,926	14,266,684	9,897,870	7,025,915	6,535,260	5,986,903	5,200,667	5,601,178
Stockholders' Equity	1,805,683	1,757,814	1,463,869	1,241,823	1,065,213	924,735	839,636	770,876
Shares Outstanding	120,918	119,897	116,385	112,966	110,340	108,654	109,129	107,989
Statistical Record								
Return on Assets %	1.68	1.80	2.16	1.86	1.76	1.34	1.28	1.52
Return on Equity %	14.83	15.55	15.84	12.88	12.86	9.81	9.88	13.60
Price Range	37.25-27.75	35.12-27.75	31.40-20.40	21.70-15.67	18.31-14.63	17.06-10.31	16.56-10.50	17.83-10.84
P/E Ratio	18.00-13.41	16.64-13.15	16.97-11.03	16.32-11.78	15.92-12.72	21.87-13.22	23.33-14.79	20.27-12.32
Average Yield %	0.94	1.27	1.17	1.10	1.32	1.18	1.15	1.14

Address: 880 Carillon Parkway, St. Petersburg, FL 33716	Web Site: www.raymondjames.com	Auditors: KPMG LLP
Telephone: 727-567-1000	Officers: Thomas A. James - Chmn., C.E.O. Chet B. Helck - Pres., C.O.O.	
Fax: 727-573-8365		

RAYONIER INC.

Exchange	Symbol	Price	52Wk Range	Yield	P/E
NYS	RYN	$43.44 (3/31/2008)	49.17-38.69	4.60	19.66

*7 Year Price Score 117.16 *NYSE Composite Index=100 *12 Month Price Score 104.08

Interim Earnings (Per Share)

Qtr.	Mar	Jun	Sep	Dec
2003	0.13	0.49	0.13	0.02
2004	0.99	0.57	0.31	0.17
2005	0.45	0.22	0.96	0.73
2006	0.30	0.55	0.70	0.71
2007	0.45	0.42	0.90	0.44

Interim Dividends (Per Share)

Amt	Decl	Ex	Rec	Pay
0.47Q	5/18/2007	6/6/2007	6/8/2007	6/29/2007
0.50Q	7/23/2007	9/5/2007	9/7/2007	9/28/2007
0.50Q	10/19/2007	12/6/2007	12/10/2007	12/31/2007
0.50Q	2/26/2008	3/6/2008	3/10/2008	3/31/2008

Indicated Div: $2.00

Valuation Analysis / **Institutional Holding**

Forecast P/E	21.82	No of Institutions
	(1/10/2007)	254
Market Cap	$3.4 Billion	Shares
Book Value	981.1 Million	48,820,232
Price/Book	3.46	% Held
Price/Sales	2.77	63.21

Business Summary: Property, Real Estate & Development (MIC: 8.3 SIC: 6798 NAIC: 525930)

Rayonier is an international forest products company primarily engaged in activities associated with timberland management, the sale, entitlement and development of real estate, and the production and sale of specialty cellulose fibers and fluff pulp. Co. has four operating segments: Timber, Real Estate, Performance Fibers and Wood Products. As of Dec 31 2007, Co. owned, leased or managed approximately 2.5 million acres of timberland and real estate located in the U.S. and New Zealand, including over 200,000 acres of real estate located primarily along the coastal corridor from Savannah, GA to Daytona Beach, FL. Co. also owns and operates two specialty cellulose mills in the U.S.

Recent Developments: For the year ended Dec 31 2007, income from continuing operations increased 1.8% to US$174.3 million from US$171.1 million a year earlier. Net income decreased 1.2% to US$174.3 million from US$176.5 million in the prior year. Revenues were US$1.22 billion, down 0.1% from US$1.23 billion the year before.

Prospects: For the full year of 2008, Co. is forecasting earnings to be slightly below its 2007 levels, given the soft housing market that is negatively affecting timber prices and volumes. Meanwhile, in its Timber segment, Co. will continue to improve its timber portfolio by selling non-strategic timberlands and pursuing potential acquisitions. In its Real Estate segment, Co. anticipates that interest in its rural properties will continue to be high among buyers with industrial, conservation or recreational land uses. Similarly, Co. is projecting better results from its Performance Fibers segment, and intends to increase capital investment to improve its capability and operational efficiencies.

Financial Data

(US$ in Thousands)	12/31/2007	12/31/2006	12/31/2005	12/31/2004	12/31/2003	12/31/2002	12/31/2001	12/31/2000
Earnings Per Share	2.21	2.26	2.36	2.05	0.77	0.85	0.93	1.25
Cash Flow Per Share	4.18	4.01	3.47	3.96	3.28	4.06	3.94	4.54
Tang Book Value Per Share	12.54	11.92	11.63	10.62	9.67	11.38	11.52	11.15
Dividends Per Share	1.940	1.880	1.710	1.493	0.700	0.640	0.640	0.640
Dividend Payout %	87.78	83.19	72.46	72.73	90.52	75.00	68.90	51.06
Income Statement								
Total Revenue	1,224,654	1,229,807	1,180,708	1,206,996	1,100,832	1,117,431	1,164,913	1,226,878
EBITDA	254,357	239,043	237,808	170,297	104,520	304,130	333,478	376,721
Income Before Taxes	198,028	190,138	190,847	123,448	55,778	69,797	82,562	108,645
Income Taxes	23,759	19,055	(16,948)	(33,453)	5,806	14,880	24,964	30,458
Net Income	174,269	176,418	182,839	156,901	49,972	54,172	57,598	78,187
Average Shares	78,920	78,159	77,644	76,533	64,609	63,334	61,164	62,331
Balance Sheet								
Current Assets	396,220	298,554	354,098	300,698	244,364	228,845	235,060	270,598
Total Assets	2,079,041	1,962,882	1,839,064	1,933,886	1,838,680	1,887,196	2,025,012	2,162,274
Current Liabilities	218,413	193,337	170,070	242,526	147,286	171,754	152,920	195,767
Long-Term Obligations	694,259	655,447	555,213	610,290	614,935	649,628	842,205	970,415
Total Liabilities	1,097,944	1,046,620	954,212	1,137,498	1,127,574	1,177,484	1,316,218	1,482,173
Stockholders' Equity	981,097	916,262	884,852	796,388	711,106	709,712	708,794	680,101
Shares Outstanding	78,216	76,879	76,092	74,966	73,527	62,368	61,527	60,985
Statistical Record								
Return on Assets %	8.62	9.28	9.69	8.30	2.68	2.77	2.75	3.51
Return on Equity %	18.37	19.59	21.75	20.76	7.03	7.64	8.29	11.70
EBITDA Margin %	20.77	19.44	20.14	14.11	9.49	27.22	28.63	30.71
Net Margin %	14.23	14.35	15.49	13.00	4.54	4.85	4.94	6.37
Asset Turnover	0.61	0.65	0.63	0.64	0.59	0.57	0.56	0.55
Current Ratio	1.81	1.54	2.08	1.24	1.66	1.33	1.54	1.38
Debt to Equity	0.71	0.72	0.63	0.77	0.86	0.92	1.19	1.43
Price Range	49.17-38.69	46.25-36.37	41.40-29.67	32.91-25.79	27.67-15.14	21.97-13.91	18.90-14.00	18.25-12.05
P/E Ratio	22.25-17.51	20.46-16.09	17.54-12.57	16.05-12.58	35.94-19.66	25.84-16.36	20.32-15.05	14.60-9.64
Average Yield %	4.37	4.63	4.85	5.10	3.49	3.52	3.91	4.28

| Address: 50 North Laura Street, Jacksonville, FL 32202 Telephone: 904-357-9100 | Web Site: www.rayonier.com Officers: W. Lee Nutter - Chmn., Pres., C.E.O. Paul G. Boynton - Sr. V.P., Performance Fibers | Auditors: DELOITTE & TOUCHE LLP Transfer Agents: The Bank of New York, New York , NY |

RAYTHEON CO.

Exchange	Symbol	Price	52Wk Range	Yield	P/E
NYS	RTN	$64.61 (3/31/2008)	67.11-52.71	1.73	11.16

*7 Year Price Score 120.30 *NYSE Composite Index=100 *12 Month Price Score 116.43

TRADING VOLUME (thousand shares)

Interim Earnings (Per Share)

Qtr.	Mar	Jun	Sep	Dec
2003	0.23	0.24	(0.08)	0.49
2004	0.30	(0.25)	0.34	0.55
2005	0.36	0.44	0.50	0.61
2006	0.64	0.69	0.71	0.81
2007	0.76	2.97	0.68	1.37

Interim Dividends (Per Share)

Amt	Decl	Ex	Rec	Pay
0.255Q	6/21/2007	6/29/2007	7/3/2007	8/2/2007
0.255Q	9/18/2007	9/28/2007	10/2/2007	11/1/2007
0.255Q	12/12/2007	12/31/2007	1/3/2008	1/31/2008
0.28Q	3/26/2008	3/28/2008	4/1/2008	4/29/2008
		Indicated Div: $1.12		

Valuation Analysis / **Institutional Holding**

Forecast P/E	N/A	No of Institutions
		515
Market Cap	$27.5 Billion	Shares
Book Value	12.5 Billion	348,062,976
Price/Book	2.20	% Held
Price/Sales	1.29	78.01

Business Summary: Instruments and Related Products (MIC: 11.15 SIC: 3812 NAIC: 334511)

Raytheon is engaged in the business of defense and government electronics, space, information technology and technical services. In addition, Co. is engaged in the design, development, manufacture, integration, support and provision of various products and services for governmental and commercial customers in the U.S. and abroad. As of Dec 31 2007, Co. conducted its businesses through six operating segments: Integrated Defense Systems; Intelligence and Information Systems; Missile Systems; Network Centric Systems; Space and Airborne Systems; and Technical Services.

Recent Developments: For the year ended Dec 31 2007, income from continuing operations increased 42.6% to US$1.69 billion from US$1.19 billion a year earlier. Net income increased 100.9% to US$2.58 billion from US$1.28 billion in the prior year. Revenues were US$21.30 billion, up 8.1% from US$19.71 billion the year before. Operating income was US$2.33 billion versus US$1.94 billion in the prior year, an increase of 19.8%. Direct operating expenses rose 6.6% to US$17.04 billion from US$15.98 billion in the comparable period the year before. Indirect operating expenses increased 8.4% to US$1.94 billion from US$1.79 billion in the equivalent prior-year period.

Prospects: Co.'s near-term outlook appears constructive, reflecting several recently attained milestones. For example, on Mar 8 2008, Co. has been awarded a U.S. Army contract modification worth $115.0 million to provide engineering services in support of the Patriot Air and Missile Defense program. Meanwhile, Co. expects its 2008 sales to be positively affected by the existing defense market. Thus, for 2008, Co. is raising its net sales guidance to $22.40 billion to $22.90 billion from its previous estimate of $22.10 billion to $22.60 billion. Concurrently, Co. is expecting earnings per share from continuing operations of $3.65 and $3.80 compared to its prior forecast of $3.45 to $3.65 per share.

Financial Data
(US$ in Thousands)

	12/31/2007	12/31/2006	12/31/2005	12/31/2004	12/31/2003	12/31/2002	12/31/2001	12/31/2000
Earnings Per Share	5.79	2.85	1.92	0.94	0.88	(1.57)	(2.11)	0.41
Cash Flow Per Share	2.77	6.21	5.63	4.71	3.80	2.59	0.37	2.83
Tang Book Value Per Share	1.15	N.M.	N.M.	N.M.	N.M.	N.M.	N.M.	N.M.
Dividends Per Share	1.020	0.960	0.880	0.800	0.800	0.800	0.200	0.800
Dividend Payout %	17.62	33.68	45.83	85.11	90.91	...	...	195.12
Income Statement								
Total Revenue	21,301,000	20,291,000	21,894,000	20,245,000	18,109,000	16,760,000	16,867,000	16,895,000
EBITDA	2,630,000	2,257,000	2,144,000	1,386,000	1,642,000	1,908,000	1,506,000	2,307,000
Income Before Taxes	2,225,000	1,688,000	1,440,000	579,000	762,000	1,074,000	117,000	877,000
Income Taxes	532,000	581,000	498,000	140,000	227,000	319,000	112,000	379,000
Net Income	2,578,000	1,283,000	871,000	417,000	365,000	(640,000)	(763,000)	141,000
Average Shares	445,659	450,875	453,302	442,201	415,429	408,031	361,323	341,118
Balance Sheet								
Current Assets	7,616,000	9,517,000	7,567,000	7,124,000	6,585,000	7,190,000	8,362,000	8,013,000
Total Assets	23,281,000	25,491,000	24,381,000	24,153,000	23,668,000	23,946,000	26,636,000	26,777,000
Current Liabilities	4,788,000	6,715,000	5,900,000	5,644,000	3,849,000	5,107,000	5,753,000	4,865,000
Long-Term Obligations	2,268,000	3,278,000	3,969,000	4,637,000	7,376,000	6,280,000	6,875,000	9,054,000
Total Liabilities	10,523,000	14,225,000	13,553,000	13,505,000	14,506,000	15,076,000	15,346,000	15,954,000
Stockholders' Equity	12,542,000	11,101,000	10,709,000	10,551,000	9,162,000	8,870,000	11,290,000	10,823,000
Shares Outstanding	426,196	445,870	446,373	453,096	418,136	408,209	395,432	340,620
Statistical Record								
Return on Assets %	10.57	5.15	3.59	1.74	1.53	N.M.	N.M.	0.51
Return on Equity %	21.81	11.77	8.19	4.22	4.05	N.M.	N.M.	1.29
EBITDA Margin %	12.35	11.12	9.79	6.85	9.07	11.38	8.93	13.65
Net Margin %	12.10	6.32	3.98	2.06	2.02	N.M.	N.M.	0.83
Asset Turnover	0.87	0.81	0.90	0.84	0.76	0.66	0.63	0.61
Current Ratio	1.59	1.42	1.28	1.26	1.71	1.41	1.45	1.65
Debt to Equity	0.18	0.30	0.37	0.44	0.81	0.71	0.61	0.84
Price Range	65.33-51.10	53.86-39.99	40.21-36.34	41.18-29.72	33.71-24.55	45.12-27.04	36.30-24.85	33.19-18.00
P/E Ratio	11.28-8.83	18.90-14.03	20.94-18.93	43.81-31.62	38.31-27.90	...	...	80.95-43.90
Average Yield %	1.78	2.08	2.29	2.34	2.69	2.26	0.66	3.27

Address: 870 Winter Street, Waltham, MA 02451	Web Site: www.raytheon.com	Auditors: PricewaterhouseCoopers LLP
Telephone: 781-522-3000	Officers: William H. Swanson - Chmn., Pres., C.E.O. Thomas M. Culligan - Exec. V.P., Bus. Devel.	Investor Contact: 781-522-5123

REGAL ENTERTAINMENT GROUP

Exchange	Symbol	Price	52Wk Range	Yield	P/E
NYS	RGC	$19.29 (3/31/2008)	23.01-17.03	6.22	8.46

*7 Year Price Score N/A   *NYSE Composite Index=100   *12 Month Price Score 100.57

TRADING VOLUME (thousand shares)

Interim Earnings (Per Share)

Qtr.	Mar	Jun	Sep	Dec
2003	0.26	0.33	0.30	0.41
2004	0.16	0.05	0.19	0.16
2005	0.09	0.18	0.11	0.22
2006	0.08	0.11	0.19	0.19
2007	1.46	0.33	0.36	0.15

Interim Dividends (Per Share)

Amt	Decl	Ex	Rec	Pay
0.30Q	4/26/2007	6/11/2007	6/13/2007	6/21/2007
0.30Q	7/26/2007	9/10/2007	9/12/2007	9/20/2007
0.30Q	10/25/2007	12/10/2007	12/12/2007	12/20/2007
0.30Q	2/7/2008	3/6/2008	3/10/2008	3/20/2008

Indicated Div: $1.20

Valuation Analysis   Institutional Holding

Forecast P/E	N/A	No of Institutions
		186
Market Cap	$3.0 Billion	Shares
Book Value	N/A	83,472,584
Price/Book	N/A	% Held
Price/Sales	1.11	55.31

Business Summary: Movies & Film (MIC: 13.2 SIC: 7832 NAIC: 512131)

Regal Entertainment Group develops, acquires and operates primarily multi-screen theatres mainly in mid-sized metropolitan markets and suburban growth areas of larger metropolitan markets in the U.S. As of Dec 27 2007, Co.'s theatre circuit in the U.S. included 6,388 screens in 527 theatres in 39 states and the District of Columbia. Co. primarily operates multi-screen theatres and has an average of 12.1 screens per location. In addition, majority of Co.'s theatre feature amenities such as wall to wall screens, digital stereo surround-sound, multi-station concessions stands, computerized ticketing systems, plush stadium seating, and video game areas adjacent to the theatre lobby.

Recent Developments: For the year ended Dec 27 2007, net income increased 320.6% to US$363.0 million from US$86.3 million in the prior year. Revenues were US$2.66 billion, up 2.4% from US$2.60 billion the year before. Operating income was US$322.2 million versus US$308.5 million in the prior year, an increase of 4.4%. Direct operating expenses rose 4.9% to US$1.06 billion from US$1.01 billion in the comparable period the year before. Indirect operating expenses were unchanged at US$1.28 billion versus the equivalent prior-year period.

Prospects: On Jan 15 2008, Co. announced that it has agreed to acquire Consolidated Theatres for $210.0 million. Co. expects the acquisition, which should be accretive to earnings, to add a total of 28 theatres with 400 screens in Georgia, Maryland, North Carolina, South Carolina, Tennessee and Virginia to its portfolio. The acquisition is expected to close in the quarter ending Mar 2008. Meanwhile, for the fiscal year ending Dec 2008, Co. expects to benefit from several factors, including modest increases in ticket prices and average concessions per patron. Notably, Co. estimates fiscal 2008 admission and concessions revenues to be supported by its continued focus on efficient theatre operations.

Financial Data

(US$ in Thousands)	12/27/2007	12/28/2006	12/29/2005	12/30/2004	01/01/2004	12/26/2002	01/03/2002
Earnings Per Share	2.28	0.56	0.59	0.55	1.30	0.79	...
Cash Flow Per Share	5.29	2.05	2.65	2.71	3.38	3.54	...
Tang Book Value Per Share	...	...	N.M.	N.M	4.21	7.92	...
Dividends Per Share	3.200	1.200	1.200	5.860	5.650	0.150	...
Dividend Payout %	140.35	214.29	203.39	1,065.45	434.62	18.99	...
Income Statement							
Total Revenue	2,661,200	2,598,100	2,516,700	2,468,000	2,489,900	2,140,200	556,900
EBITDA	902,200	466,300	474,800	417,800	542,400	407,400	72,900
Income Before Taxes	605,900	144,000	152,500	142,000	306,600	208,500	8,500
Income Taxes	242,900	57,700	60,700	59,500	121,200	89,800	3,600
Net Income	363,000	86,300	91,800	82,500	185,400	117,700	4,900
Average Shares	159,474	155,124	154,330	149,220	142,792	112,284	...
Balance Sheet							
Current Assets	525,500	241,000	262,600	321,100	376,600	389,800	132,700
Total Assets	2,634,900	2,468,800	2,532,800	2,542,400	2,471,800	2,310,200	1,122,700
Current Liabilities	527,500	556,300	693,600	644,200	412,800	304,000	196,400
Long-Term Obligations	1,819,000	1,841,700	1,724,100	1,745,600	1,196,100	661,400	423,300
Total Liabilities	2,753,700	2,489,100	2,501,100	2,471,400	1,673,000	1,036,600	656,100
Stockholders' Equity	(119,300)	(22,200)	29,900	69,000	794,900	1,270,800	383,000
Shares Outstanding	153,227	150,357	147,363	144,809	141,991	131,736	...
Statistical Record							
Return on Assets %	14.26	3.46	3.63	3.30	7.63	6.98	...
Return on Equity %	...	2,247.72	186.15	19.15	17.66	14.49	...
EBITDA Margin %	33.90	17.95	18.87	16.93	21.78	19.04	13.09
Net Margin %	13.64	3.32	3.65	3.34	7.45	5.48	0.88
Asset Turnover	1.05	1.04	0.99	0.99	1.02	1.27	...
Current Ratio	1.00	0.43	0.38	0.50	0.91	1.28	0.68
Debt to Equity	...	...	57.66	25.30	1.50	0.52	1.11
Price Range	23.01-17.85	21.55-17.95	21.35-18.20	23.13-17.50	23.73-17.25	24.25-16.20	...
P/E Ratio	10.09-7.83	38.48-32.05	36.19-30.85	42.05-31.82	18.25-13.27	30.70-20.51	...
Average Yield %	14.95	6.11	6.10	29.23	28.59	0.74	...

Address: 9110 East Nichols Avenue, Suite 200, Centennial, CO 80112 **Telephone:** 303-792-3600	**Web Site:** www.regalcinemas.com **Officers:** Michael L. Campbell - Co-Chmn., Co-C.E.O. Kurt C. Hall - Co-Chmn., Co-C.E.O.	**Auditors:** KPMG LLP **Transfer Agents:** Wells Fargo Bank Minnesota, National Association

REGENCY CENTERS CORP.

Exchange	Symbol	Price	52Wk Range	Yield	P/E	Div Achiever
NYS	REG	$64.76 (3/31/2008)	84.96-54.70	4.48	24.44	13 Years

*7 Year Price Score 114.27 *NYSE Composite Index=100 *12 Month Price Score 94.20

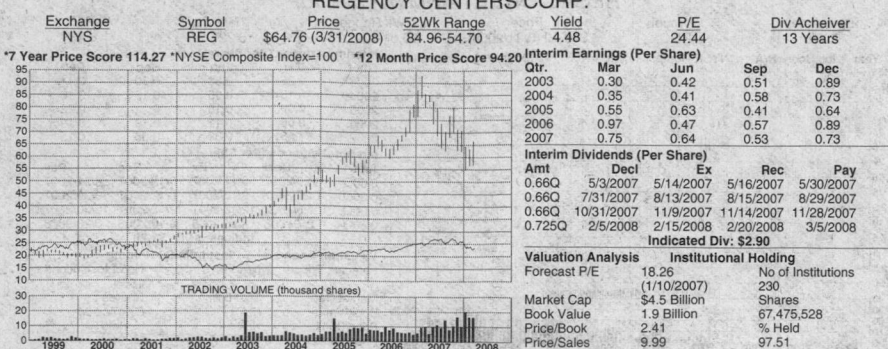

Interim Earnings (Per Share)

Qtr.	Mar	Jun	Sep	Dec
2003	0.30	0.42	0.51	0.89
2004	0.35	0.41	0.58	0.73
2005	0.55	0.63	0.41	0.64
2006	0.97	0.47	0.57	0.89
2007	0.75	0.64	0.53	0.73

Interim Dividends (Per Share)

Amt	Decl	Ex	Rec	Pay
0.66Q	5/3/2007	5/14/2007	5/16/2007	5/30/2007
0.66Q	7/31/2007	8/13/2007	8/15/2007	8/29/2007
0.66Q	10/31/2007	11/9/2007	11/14/2007	11/28/2007
0.725Q	2/5/2008	2/15/2008	2/20/2008	3/5/2008

Indicated Div: $2.90

Valuation Analysis / **Institutional Holding**

Forecast P/E	18.26	No of Institutions
	(1/10/2007)	230
Market Cap	$4.5 Billion	Shares
Book Value	1.9 Billion	67,475,528
Price/Book	2.41	% Held
Price/Sales	9.99	97.51

TRADING VOLUME (thousand shares)

Business Summary: Property, Real Estate & Development (MIC: 8.3 SIC: 6798 NAIC: 525930)

Regency Centers is a real-estate-investment-trust (REIT) engaged in the ownership, management, leasing, acquisition and development of shopping centers through its operating partnership, Regency Centers, L.P. (RCLP), in which it owned approximately 99.0% of the outstanding operating partnership units as of Dec 31 2007. As of such date, Co. operated and managed a real-estate investment portfolio of 451 shopping centers in 29 states and the District of Columbia, including 232 shopping centers owned by consolidated properties and 219 shopping centers owned by unconsolidated properties.

Recent Developments: For the year ended Dec 31 2007, income from continuing operations increased 13.5% to US$176.4 million from US$155.4 million a year earlier. Net income decreased 6.8% to US$203.7 million from US$218.5 million in the prior year. Revenues were US$451.5 million, up 8.3% from US$417.0 million the year before. Revenues from property income rose 8.6% to US$418.4 million from US$385.2 million in the corresponding earlier year.

Prospects: Looking ahead, Co. intends to continue to grow its portfolio by investing in shopping centers through ground up development of new centers or acquisition of existing centers. For instance, on Jan 7 2008, Co. and its co-investment partner Oregon Public Employees Retirement Fund announced the acquisition of seven grocery-anchored retail centers at a total cost of $76.7 million. Notably, Co. contributed $15.3 million of the cost and expects to own 20.0% of the properties. In addition, at Dec 31 2007, Co. had 50 projects under development for an estimated total net investment at completion of $1.10 billion and an expected return of 8.96% on net development costs after partner participation.

Financial Data
(US$ in Thousands)

	12/31/2007	12/31/2006	12/31/2005	12/31/2004	12/31/2003	12/31/2002	12/31/2001	12/31/2000
Earnings Per Share	2.65	2.89	2.23	2.08	2.12	1.84	1.69	1.49
Cash Flow Per Share	3.25	3.19	3.23	2.99	3.84	2.97	3.20	3.14
Tang Book Value Per Share	22.66	22.69	22.12	20.45	19.96	20.34	20.56	20.93
Dividends Per Share	2.640	2.380	2.200	2.120	2.080	2.040	2.000	1.920
Dividend Payout %	99.62	82.35	98.65	101.92	98.11	110.87	118.34	128.86
Income Statement								
Property Income	418,444	385,953	368,927	371,091	359,926	354,183	353,615	331,218
Non-Property Income	33,064	34,385	25,111	20,857	17,695	26,020	34,934	30,365
Total Revenue	451,508	420,338	394,038	391,948	377,621	380,203	388,550	361,583
Interest Expense	82,494	79,690	87,424	81,196	86,373	83,620	74,416	71,971
Income Before Taxes	164,465	165,727	111,517	135,613	144,146	117,873	137,417	122,336
Net Income	203,651	218,511	162,647	136,327	130,789	110,525	100,664	87,611
Average Shares	69,198	68,432	64,932	61,481	61,242	60,438	59,274	56,754
Balance Sheet								
Total Assets	4,143,012	3,671,785	3,616,215	3,243,824	3,098,229	3,061,859	3,109,314	3,035,144
Long-Term Obligations	2,007,975	1,575,386	1,613,942	1,493,090	1,452,777	1,333,524	1,396,721	1,307,072
Total Liabilities	2,194,244	1,734,572	1,739,225	1,610,743	1,562,530	1,419,280	1,478,812	1,390,795
Stockholders' Equity	1,870,386	1,853,317	1,788,825	1,498,717	1,280,978	1,221,720	1,219,051	1,225,415
Shares Outstanding	69,638	69,017	67,966	62,808	59,907	59,557	57,601	56,898
Statistical Record								
Return on Assets %	5.21	6.00	4.74	4.29	4.25	3.58	3.28	3.07
Return on Equity %	10.94	12.00	9.89	9.78	10.45	9.06	8.24	7.07
Net Margin %	45.10	51.98	41.28	34.78	34.64	29.07	25.91	24.23
Price Range	92.79-62.22	81.34-59.35	63.11-47.30	55.40-35.11	40.20-30.60	32.40-26.80	27.75-22.94	24.00-18.44
P/E Ratio	35.02-23.48	28.15-20.54	28.30-21.21	26.63-16.88	18.96-14.43	17.61-14.57	16.42-13.57	16.11-12.37
Average Yield %	3.50	3.59	4.00	4.79	5.94	6.84	8.02	8.92

Address: 121 West Forsyth Street, Suite 200, Jacksonville, FL 32202 **Telephone:** 904-598-7000 **Fax:** 904-634-3428	**Web Site:** www.regencycenters.com **Officers:** Martin E. Stein Jr. - Chmn., C.E.O. Mary Lou Fiala - Pres., C.O.O.	**Auditors:** KPMG LLP **Investor Contact:** 904-598-7000 **Transfer Agents:** American Stock Transfer & Trust Company, New York, NY

REGIONS FINANCIAL CORP

Exchange	Symbol	Price	52Wk Range	Yield	P/E
NYS	RF	$19.75 (3/31/2008)	36.49-19.19	7.70	11.22

*7 Year Price Score N/A   *NYSE Composite Index=100   *12 Month Price Score 83.05

Interim Earnings (Per Share)

Qtr.	Mar	Jun	Sep	Dec
2006	0.61	0.53	0.55	0.55
2006	0.64	0.75	0.77	0.51
2007	0.45	0.63	0.56	0.12

Interim Dividends (Per Share)

Amt	Decl	Ex	Rec	Pay
0.36Q	4/19/2007	6/14/2007	6/18/2007	7/2/2007
0.36Q	7/19/2007	9/13/2007	9/17/2007	10/1/2007
0.38Q	10/17/2007	12/17/2007	12/19/2007	1/2/2008
0.38Q	1/17/2008	3/14/2008	3/18/2008	4/1/2008

Indicated Div: $1.52

Valuation Analysis

		Institutional Holding	
Forecast P/E	N/A	No of Institutions	500
Market Cap	$13.7 Billion	Shares	285,803,008
Book Value	19.8 Billion	% Held	
Price/Book	0.69	39.06	
Price/Sales	1.25		

Business Summary: Commercial Banking (MIC: 8.1 SIC: 6021 NAIC: 522110)

Regions Financial is a financial holding company. Co.'s operations consist of banking, brokerage and investment services, mortgage banking, insurance brokerage, credit life insurance, leasing, commercial accounts receivable factoring and specialty financing. As of Dec 31 2007, Co. operated 1,965 full service banking offices in Alabama, Arkansas, Florida, Georgia, Illinois, Indiana, Iowa, Kentucky, Louisiana, Mississippi, Missouri, North Carolina, South Carolina, Tennessee, Texas and Virginia. As of Dec 31 2007, Co. had total consolidated assets of $141.04 billion, and total consolidated deposits of $94.77 billion.

Recent Developments: For the year ended Dec 31 2007, income from continuing operations increased 1.5% to US$1.39 billion from US$1.37 billion a year earlier. Net income decreased 7.5% to US$1.25 billion from US$1.35 billion in the prior year. Net interest income increased 32.9% to US$4.40 billion from US$3.31 billion in the prior year. Provision for loan losses was US$555.0 million versus US$142.4 million in the prior year, an increase of 289.8%. Non-interest income rose 40.7% to US$2.86 billion from US$2.03 billion, while non-interest expense advanced 45.5% to US$4.66 billion.

Prospects: Notwithstanding the challenging operating environment, particularly the weakening housing demand on residential builder loan portfolio, Co. believes that it is well positioned for 2008 and beyond. In detail, Co. remains focused on its business strategy to provide a mix of products and services, deliver customer service and maintain a branch distribution network with offices in convenient locations. In addition, Co. has completed the operational integration of AmSouth Bancorporation into Co. on Dec 10 2007. Accordingly, Co. estimates the integration will result in at least $500.0 million of ongoing annual cost savings and expects to achieve the full cost savings run rate by mid-2008.

Financial Data

(US$ in Thousands)	12/31/2007	12/31/2006	12/31/2005	12/31/2004	12/31/2003	12/31/2002
Earnings Per Share	1.76	2.67	2.15	2.19	2.35	2.19
Cash Flow Per Share	4.81	5.66	4.16	2.90	4.03	...
Tang Book Value Per Share	10.45	11.22	10.65	10.73	14.59	...
Dividends Per Share	1.460	1.760	1.360	0.667	1.000	0.940
Dividend Payout %	82.95	65.92	63.26	30.45	42.55	42.92
Income Statement						
Interest Income	8,074,663	5,694,258	4,310,375	2,955,685	2,219,130	2,536,989
Interest Expense	3,676,297	2,340,816	1,489,756	842,651	744,532	1,039,401
Net Interest Income	4,398,366	3,353,442	2,820,619	2,113,034	1,474,598	1,497,588
Provision for Losses	555,000	142,500	165,000	128,500	121,500	127,500
Non-Interest Income	2,833,833	2,062,104	1,813,432	1,654,354	1,352,313	1,223,287
Non-Interest Expense	4,660,351	3,314,031	3,046,956	2,463,306	1,793,839	1,724,135
Income Before Taxes	2,038,850	1,959,015	1,422,095	1,175,582	911,572	869,240
Income Taxes	645,687	605,870	421,551	351,817	259,731	249,338
Net Income	1,251,095	1,353,145	1,000,544	823,765	651,841	619,902
Average Shares	712,743	506,989	466,183	373,732	277,930	281,043
Balance Sheet						
Net Loans & Leases	94,778,527	98,414,950	59,153,041	58,555,564	32,972,118	...
Total Assets	141,041,717	143,369,021	84,785,600	84,106,438	48,597,996	...
Total Deposits	94,774,968	101,227,969	60,378,367	58,667,023	32,732,535	...
Total Liabilities	121,218,688	122,667,567	74,171,317	73,356,981	44,145,881	...
Stockholders' Equity	19,823,029	20,701,454	10,614,283	10,749,457	4,452,115	...
Shares Outstanding	693,635	730,075	456,347	466,241	221,967	...
Statistical Record						
Return on Assets %	0.88	1.19	1.18	1.24	...	...
Return on Equity %	6.17	8.64	9.37	10.81	...	...
Net Interest Margin %	54.47	58.89	65.44	71.49	66.45	59.03
Efficiency Ratio %	42.64	42.73	49.76	53.43	50.23	45.85
Loans to Deposits	1.00	0.97	0.98	1.00	1.01	...
Price Range	38.02-23.01	38.87-32.45	35.59-29.57	35.79-29.57	...	...
P/E Ratio	21.60-13.07	14.56-12.15	16.55-13.75	16.34-13.50	...	...
Average Yield %	4.53	4.93	4.10	2.01	...	...

Address: 417 North 20th Street, Birmingham, AL 35203
Telephone: 205-944-1300

Web Site: www.regions.com
Officers: Carl E. Jones Jr. - Chmn. Richard D. Horsley - Vice-Chmn., C.O.O.

Auditors: Ernst & Young LLP
Investor Contact: 205-801-0105
Transfer Agents: EquiServe

REGIS CORP.

Exchange	Symbol	Price	52Wk Range	Yield	P/E
NYS	RGS	$27.49 (3/31/2008)	41.59-22.67	0.58	16.17

*7 Year Price Score 77.20   ***NYSE Composite Index=100**   ***12 Month Price Score 86.23**

TRADING VOLUME (thousand shares)

Interim Earnings (Per Share)

Qtr.	Sep	Dec	Mar	Jun
2004-05	0.55	0.58	(0.37)	0.63
2005-06	0.48	0.59	0.40	0.89
2006-07	0.50	0.59	0.12	0.61
2007-08	0.46	0.51	...	...

Interim Dividends (Per Share)

Amt	Decl	Ex	Rec	Pay
0.04Q	4/27/2007	5/9/2007	5/11/2007	5/25/2007
0.04Q	8/23/2007	8/30/2007	9/4/2007	9/18/2007
0.04Q	10/24/2007	11/2/2007	11/6/2007	11/20/2007
0.04Q	1/24/2008	2/1/2008	2/5/2008	2/19/2008
		Indicated Div: $0.16		

Valuation Analysis

Forecast P/E	N/A
Market Cap	$1.2 Billion
Book Value	930.8 Million
Price/Book	1.27
Price/Sales	0.44

Institutional Holding

No of Institutions	179
Shares	37,927,584
% Held	84.43

Business Summary: Personal Services (MIC: 5.15 SIC: 7231 NAIC: 812112)

Regis primarily owns, operates and franchises hair and retail product salons. As at June 30 2007, Co. owned, franchised or held ownership interests in locations that consisted of 11,881 company-owned and franchise salons, 90 hair restoration centers, 56 beauty schools and 400 locations in which Co. maintains an ownership interest. Each of Co.'s salon concepts offer similar salon products and services and serve the mass market consumer marketplace; while its beauty school locations provide similar education services to students; and its hair restoration centers provide three hair restoration services: hair systems, hair transplants and hair therapy, targeting the mass-market consumer.

Recent Developments: For the quarter ended Dec 31 2007, net income decreased 16.1% to US$22.6 million from US$26.9 million in the year-earlier quarter. Revenues were US$682.2 million, up 3.8% from US$657.0 million the year before. Direct operating expenses rose 3.7% to US$419.9 million from US$404.7 million in the comparable period the year before. Indirect operating expenses increased 6.1% to US$217.5 million from US$205.0 million in the equivalent prior-year period.

Prospects: Co. remains focused on its growth strategy in seeking organic and acquisition growth to achieve long-term objective of 6.0% to 10.0% annual revenue growth. Co. also anticipates expanding its presence in North America. For fiscal year ending June 30 2008, Co. anticipates consolidated revenue to grow approximately 4.0% to $2.74 billion, with consolidated same-store sales in a range of 0.25% to 1.25%, as well as earnings to be in a range of $2.01 to $2.14 per diluted share. Also, Co. noted that its outlook for constructed salons in fiscal 2008 is approximately 350 units, and expects to add between 500 and 700 net locations through a combination of organic, acquisition and franchise growth.

Financial Data

(US$ in Thousands)	6 Mos	3 Mos	06/30/2007	06/30/2006	06/30/2005	06/30/2004	06/30/2003	06/30/2002
Earnings Per Share	1.70	1.78	1.82	2.36	1.39	2.29	1.92	1.63
Cash Flow Per Share	5.37	5.35	5.41	6.24	4.83	4.66	3.46	3.60
Tang Book Value Per Share	N.M.	N.M.	N.M.	N.M.	N.M.	3.42	2.89	1.98
Dividends Per Share	0.160	0.160	0.160	0.160	0.160	0.140	0.120	0.120
Dividend Payout %	9.41	8.99	8.79	6.78	11.51	6.11	6.25	7.36
Income Statement								
Total Revenue	1,349,766	667,525	2,626,588	2,430,864	2,194,294	1,923,143	1,684,530	1,454,191
EBITDA	153,298	77,803	287,053	312,612	232,595	257,420	227,394	194,392
Depn & Amortn	63,186	34,642	...	...	...	...	...	...
Income Before Taxes	67,774	32,583	127,956	170,153	116,457	164,809	138,601	115,650
Income Taxes	24,671	11,650	44,786	60,575	51,826	59,331	51,926	43,596
Net Income	43,155	20,599	83,170	109,578	64,631	105,478	86,675	72,054
Average Shares	43,915	44,579	45,623	46,400	46,380	46,145	45,229	44,172
Balance Sheet								
Current Assets	507,160	487,208	525,064	441,766	380,649	313,442	279,660	256,686
Total Assets	2,183,979	2,165,757	2,132,114	1,982,064	1,725,976	1,271,859	1,112,955	957,190
Current Liabilities	526,274	482,034	538,632	402,955	262,050	201,961	199,065	159,289
Long-Term Obligations	523,265	529,807	485,879	520,357	549,029	282,015	280,634	291,795
Total Liabilities	1,253,185	1,225,285	1,218,806	1,110,657	971,264	584,298	550,151	512,525
Stockholders' Equity	930,794	940,472	913,308	871,407	754,712	687,561	562,804	444,665
Shares Outstanding	42,881	44,175	44,164	45,303	44,952	44,283	43,527	43,040
Statistical Record								
Return on Assets %	3.57	3.82	4.04	5.91	4.31	8.82	8.37	8.51
Return on Equity %	8.33	8.88	9.32	13.48	8.96	16.83	17.21	18.38
EBITDA Margin %	11.36	11.66	10.93	12.86	10.60	13.39	13.50	13.37
Net Margin %	3.20	3.09	3.17	4.51	2.95	5.48	5.15	4.95
Asset Turnover	1.25	1.26	1.28	1.31	1.46	1.61	1.63	1.72
Current Ratio	0.96	1.01	0.97	1.10	1.45	1.55	1.40	1.61
Debt to Equity	0.56	0.56	0.53	0.60	0.73	0.41	0.50	0.66
Price Range	43.29-26.31	43.29-30.66	43.29-32.78	42.59-33.38	46.68-34.27	46.00-29.05	29.90-21.94	30.49-17.84
P/E Ratio	25.46-15.48	24.32-17.22	23.79-18.01	18.05-14.14	33.58-24.65	20.09-12.69	15.57-11.43	18.71-10.94
Average Yield %	0.44	0.42	0.41	0.42	0.42	0.39	0.36	0.49

Address: 7201 Metro Boulevard, Edina, MN 55439	Web Site: www.regiscorp.com	Auditors: PricewaterhouseCoopers LLP
Telephone: 952-947-7777	Officers: Paul D. Finkelstein - Chmn., Pres., C.E.O. Myron Kunin - Vice-Chmn.	Investor Contact: 952-947-7777
Fax: 952-947-7700		Transfer Agents: Wells Fargo Bank Minnesota, N.A., South St. Paul, MN

REINSURANCE GROUP OF AMERICA, INC.

Exchange	Symbol	Price	52Wk Range	Yield	P/E
NYS	RGA	$54.44 (3/31/2008)	64.43-48.50	0.66	11.91

*7 Year Price Score 106.98 *NYSE Composite Index=100   *12 Month Price Score 104.13

Interim Earnings (Per Share)

Qtr.	Mar	Jun	Sep	Dec
2003	0.66	0.85	0.83	1.02
2004	0.98	1.04	0.63	0.87
2005	1.04	0.34	1.06	1.07
2006	1.10	1.01	1.17	1.28
2007	1.19	1.20	1.19	0.98

Interim Dividends (Per Share)

Amt	Decl	Ex	Rec	Pay
0.09Q	4/23/2007	5/2/2007	5/4/2007	5/25/2007
0.09Q	7/23/2007	8/1/2007	8/3/2007	8/24/2007
0.09Q	10/22/2007	11/5/2007	11/7/2007	11/28/2007
0.09Q	1/23/2008	1/31/2008	2/4/2008	2/25/2008
		Indicated Div: $0.36		

Valuation Analysis / **Institutional Holding**

Forecast P/E	10.20 (1/10/2007)	No of Institutions	165
Market Cap	$3.4 Billion	Shares	33,093,588
Book Value	3.2 Billion	% Held	
Price/Book	1.06		53.89
Price/Sales	0.59		

Business Summary: Insurance (MIC: 8.2 SIC: 6321 NAIC: 524114)

Reinsurance Group of America is an insurance holding company. Co. is primarily engaged in traditional individual life, asset-intensive, critical illness and financial reinsurance. Co. has five main operational segments: U.S., Canada, Europe and South Africa, Asia Pacific, and Corporate and Other. These operating segments write reinsurance business that is wholly or partially retained in one or more of Co.'s reinsurance subsidiaries. As of Dec 31 2007, Co. had approximately $2.10 trillion of life reinsurance in force and $21.60 billion in consolidated assets.

Recent Developments: For the year ended Dec 31 2007, income from continuing operations increased 5.1% to US$308.3 million from US$293.3 million a year earlier. Net income increased 2.0% to US$293.8 million from US$288.2 million in the prior year. Revenues were US$5.72 billion, up 10.1% from US$5.19 billion the year before. Net premiums earned were US$4.91 billion versus US$4.35 billion in the prior year, an increase of 13.0%. Net investment income rose 16.4% to US$907.9 million from US$779.7 million a year ago.

Prospects: For full-year 2008, Co. expects operating income per diluted share to be within the range of $6.00 to $6.50, representing a 14.0% improvement at the midpoint of that range over the 2007 level. Moreover, Co. expects that net premiums will continue to grow, specifically in the range of 10.0% to 13.0% on a consolidated basis. At the segment level, Co. expects net premium growth of 7.0% to 9.0% in the U.S., 10.0% to 12.0% in Canada, 13.0% to 16.0% in Asia Pacific and 12.0% to 15.0% in Europe and South Africa. In addition, Co. will continue to capitalize on growth opportunities in select Asian markets such as Japan and South Korea, and will continue its expansion into European markets.

Financial Data

(US$ in Thousands)	12/31/2007	12/31/2006	12/31/2005	12/31/2004	12/31/2003	12/31/2002	12/31/2001	12/31/2000
Earnings Per Share	4.57	4.57	3.52	3.52	3.36	2.47	0.66	1.56
Cash Flow Per Share	15.48	13.82	9.58	11.44	11.15	3.26	4.89	3.88
Tang Book Value Per Share	51.42	45.85	41.38	36.50	31.33	24.72	20.30	17.51
Dividends Per Share	0.360	0.360	0.360	0.270	0.240	0.240	0.240	0.240
Dividend Payout %	7.88	7.88	10.23	7.67	7.14	9.72	36.36	15.38
Income Statement								
Premium Income	4,909,026	4,345,969	3,866,775	3,347,448	2,643,163	1,980,666	1,661,762	1,404,066
Total Revenue	5,718,361	5,193,691	4,584,765	4,038,919	3,174,333	2,381,963	1,968,284	1,725,735
Benefits & Claims	3,980,291	3,484,786	3,187,902	2,678,537	2,108,431	1,539,464	1,376,802	1,103,548
Income Before Taxes	474,918	451,388	356,346	369,193	271,610	193,978	66,150	175,345
Income Taxes	166,645	158,127	120,738	123,893	93,291	65,515	26,249	69,271
Net Income	293,834	288,210	224,100	221,891	173,141	122,800	33,040	77,669
Average Shares	64,231	63,062	63,724	62,964	51,598	49,648	49,905	49,920
Balance Sheet								
Total Assets	21,598,009	19,036,837	16,193,866	14,048,129	12,113,374	8,892,597	6,894,345	6,061,860
Total Liabilities	18,408,177	16,221,453	13,666,382	11,769,104	10,165,651	7,670,134	5,888,757	5,198,937
Stockholders' Equity	3,189,832	2,815,384	2,527,484	2,279,025	1,947,723	1,222,463	1,005,588	862,923
Shares Outstanding	62,031	61,410	61,075	62,445	62,160	49,456	49,526	49,293
Statistical Record								
Return on Assets %	1.45	1.64	1.48	1.69	1.65	1.56	0.51	1.38
Return on Equity %	9.79	10.79	9.33	10.47	10.92	11.02	3.54	9.71
Loss Ratio %	81.08	80.18	82.44	80.02	79.77	77.72	82.85	78.60
Net Margin %	5.14	5.55	4.89	5.49	5.45	5.16	1.68	4.50
Price Range	64.43-49.89	57.61-45.73	48.45-40.88	48.54-36.90	42.45-24.98	33.56-24.03	41.00-29.56	37.38-16.25
P/E Ratio	14.10-10.92	12.61-10.01	13.76-11.61	13.79-10.48	12.63-7.43	13.59-9.73	62.12-44.79	23.96-10.42
Average Yield %	0.63	0.72	0.80	0.66	0.73	0.82	0.68	0.83

Address: 1370 Timberlake Manor Parkway, Chesterfield, MO 63017 **Telephone:** 636-736-7439 **Fax:** 314-453-7307	**Web Site:** www.rgare.com **Officers:** Stewart G. Nagler - Chmn. A. Greig Woodring - Pres., C.E.O.	**Auditors:** Deloitte & Touche LLP **Investor Contact:** 636-736-7439

RELIANCE STEEL & ALUMINUM CO.

Exchange	Symbol	Price	52Wk Range	Yield	P/E
NYS	RS	$59.86 (3/31/2008)	63.76-43.33	0.67	11.17

*7 Year Price Score 171.98 *NYSE Composite Index=100 *12 Month Price Score 108.12

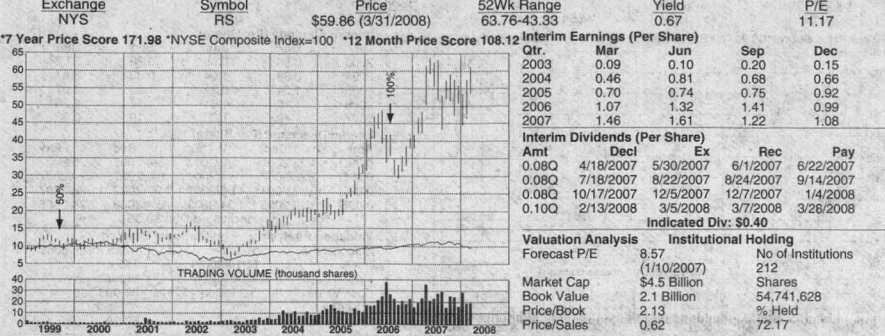

Interim Earnings (Per Share)

Qtr.	Mar	Jun	Sep	Dec
2003	0.09	0.10	0.20	0.15
2004	0.46	0.81	0.68	0.66
2005	0.70	0.74	0.75	0.92
2006	1.07	1.32	1.41	0.99
2007	1.46	1.61	1.22	1.08

Interim Dividends (Per Share)

Amt	Decl	Ex	Rec	Pay
0.08Q	4/18/2007	5/30/2007	6/1/2007	6/22/2007
0.08Q	7/18/2007	8/22/2007	8/24/2007	9/14/2007
0.08Q	10/17/2007	12/5/2007	12/7/2007	1/4/2008
0.10Q	2/13/2008	3/5/2008	3/7/2008	3/26/2008

Indicated Div: $0.40

Valuation Analysis | **Institutional Holding**

Forecast P/E	8.57	No of Institutions
	(1/10/2007)	212
Market Cap	$4.5 Billion	Shares
Book Value	2.1 Billion	54,741,628
Price/Book	2.13	% Held
Price/Sales	0.62	72.17

Business Summary: Specialist Equipment Supplies (MIC: 12.10 SIC: 5051 NAIC: 423510)

Reliance Steel & Aluminum is an operator of metals service centers. As of Dec 31 2007, Co.'s network of 28 divisions, 27 operating subsidiaries and two joint venture companies operates over 180 locations in 37 states, Belgium, Canada, China, South Korea and the U.K. Co. provides metals processing services and distributes a line of metal products, including alloy, aluminum, brass, copper, carbon steel, titanium, stainless steel and specialty steel products. A majority of Co.'s metals service centers process and distribute only specialty metals. Co.'s metals service centers acquire products from primary metals producers and processes carbon steel, aluminum, stainless steel and other metals.

Recent Developments: For the year ended Dec 31 2007, net income increased 15.1% to US$408.0 million from US$354.5 million in the prior year. Revenues were US$7.27 billion, up 26.4% from US$5.75 billion the year before. Operating income was US$654.7 million versus US$571.4 million in the prior year, an increase of 14.6%. Direct operating expenses rose 28.0% to US$5.42 billion from US$4.23 billion in the comparable period the year before. Indirect operating expenses increased 26.1% to US$1.19 billion from US$945.6 million in the equivalent prior-year period.

Prospects: On Jan 7 2008, Co. announced that it has sold certain assets and the business of the Encore Coils division of its Encore Group Limited subsidiary to Samuel Son & Co., Ltd. The Encore Coils division processed and distributed carbon steel flat-rolled products through four facilities located in Western Canada. Co. retained one of the Encore Coils operations that is now performing toll processing services. Meanwhile, based on the improved pricing environment, Co. expects some continued improvement in its gross profit margins during the 2008 first quarter compared with 2007 levels. As a result, Co. estimates earnings per diluted share for the 2008 first quarter in a range of $1.25 to $1.35.

Financial Data

(US$ in Thousands)	12/31/2007	12/31/2006	12/31/2005	12/31/2004	12/31/2003	12/31/2002	12/31/2001	12/31/2000
Earnings Per Share	5.36	4.82	3.11	2.60	0.54	0.47	0.64	1.14
Cash Flow Per Share	8.45	2.61	4.13	1.87	1.67	1.43	1.83	0.45
Tang Book Value Per Share	10.09	8.02	9.74	7.36	5.00	5.13	5.29	3.40
Dividends Per Share	0.320	0.220	0.190	0.130	0.120	0.120	0.120	0.110
Dividend Payout %	5.97	4.56	6.12	5.01	22.43	25.26	18.75	9.65
Income Statement								
Total Revenue	7,265,610	5,748,376	3,370,722	2,947,202	1,885,770	1,748,271	1,660,770	1,730,075
EBITDA	734,266	631,457	379,843	314,595	91,726	78,266	92,496	130,679
Income Before Taxes	654,393	571,132	333,212	269,968	54,856	49,720	60,159	102,587
Income Taxes	246,438	216,625	127,775	100,240	20,846	19,553	23,823	40,268
Net Income	407,955	354,507	205,437	169,728	34,010	30,167	36,336	62,319
Average Shares	76,064	73,599	66,194	65,350	63,732	63,597	56,939	54,578
Balance Sheet								
Current Assets	1,721,403	1,675,389	847,348	733,229	544,586	532,544	517,993	491,396
Total Assets	3,983,477	3,614,173	1,769,070	1,563,331	1,369,424	1,139,247	1,082,293	997,243
Current Liabilities	599,864	550,739	333,819	288,780	202,824	142,924	138,002	143,737
Long-Term Obligations	1,013,260	1,088,051	306,790	380,850	469,250	344,080	331,975	421,825
Total Liabilities	1,877,228	1,867,775	739,205	740,779	721,805	529,393	498,410	594,204
Stockholders' Equity	2,106,249	1,746,398	1,029,865	822,552	647,619	609,854	583,883	403,039
Shares Outstanding	74,906	75,702	66,217	65,339	64,451	63,504	63,145	50,263
Statistical Record								
Return on Assets %	10.74	13.17	12.33	11.54	2.71	2.72	3.49	6.55
Return on Equity %	21.18	25.54	22.18	23.03	5.41	5.05	7.36	15.47
EBITDA Margin %	10.11	10.98	11.27	10.67	4.86	4.48	5.57	7.55
Net Margin %	5.61	6.17	6.09	5.76	1.80	1.73	2.19	3.60
Asset Turnover	1.91	2.14	2.02	2.00	1.50	1.57	1.60	1.82
Current Ratio	2.87	3.04	2.54	2.54	2.69	3.73	3.75	3.42
Debt to Equity	0.48	0.62	0.30	0.46	0.72	0.56	0.57	1.05
Price Range	63.76-37.85	48.77-29.22	33.32-17.52	20.95-13.70	17.50-6.74	16.86-9.75	15.03-10.47	13.00-9.00
P/E Ratio	11.90-7.06	10.12-6.06	10.71-5.63	8.06-5.27	32.41-12.48	35.88-20.74	23.48-16.35	11.40-7.89
Average Yield %	0.61	0.58	0.82	0.72	1.11	0.93	0.93	1.01

Address: 350 South Grand Avenue, Suite 5100, Los Angeles, CA 90071
Telephone: 213-687-7700

Web Site: www.rsac.com
Officers: Joe D. Crider - Chmn. Gregg J. Mollins - Pres., C.O.O.

Auditors: Ernst & Young LLP
Investor Contact: 713-610-9937
Transfer Agents: EquiServe Trust Company, N.A., Providence, RI

RELIANT ENERGY INC

Exchange	Symbol	Price	52Wk Range	Yield	P/E
NYS	RRI	$23.65 (3/31/2008)	30.26-20.05	N/A	22.74

*7 Year Price Score N/A   *NYSE Composite Index=100   *12 Month Price Score 98.92

Interim Earnings (Per Share)

Qtr.	Mar	Jun	Sep	Dec
2003	(1.55)	(0.02)	(3.11)	0.13
2004	(0.13)	(0.24)	1.04	(0.87)
2005	(0.08)	0.30	(0.89)	(0.44)
2006	(0.44)	0.05	(0.50)	(0.18)
2007	0.74	(0.83)	0.46	0.65

Interim Dividends (Per Share)

No Dividends Paid

Valuation Analysis		Institutional Holding	
Forecast P/E	22.45	No of Institutions	
	(1/10/2007)	239	
Market Cap	$8.1 Billion	Shares	
Book Value	4.5 Billion	200,290,970	
Price/Book	1.82	% Held	
Price/Sales	0.73	76.72	

Business Summary: Electricity (MIC: 7.1 SIC: 4911 NAIC: 221122)

Reliant Energy is engaged in providing electricity and energy services to retail and wholesale customers through its retail energy and wholesale energy segments. In retail energy, Co. provides electricity and energy services to customers in Texas, including residential and small business customers and commercial, industrial and governmental/institutional customers. In wholesale energy, Co. provides electricity and energy services in the wholesale energy markets in the U.S. Co. also owns and operates or contracts for power generation capacity. At Dec 31 2007, Co. had 16,000 megawatt of owned or leased generation capacity in operation, and about 1.8 million retail electricity customers.

Recent Developments: For the year ended Dec 31 2007, income from continuing operations was US$358.0 million compared with a loss of US$326.7 million a year earlier. Net income amounted to US$365.1 million versus a net loss of US$327.8 million in the prior year. Revenues were US$11.21 billion, up 3.0% from US$10.88 billion the year before. Operating income was US$875.6 million versus a loss of US$23.8 million in the prior year. Direct operating expenses declined 7.1% to US$9.54 billion from US$10.27 billion in the comparable period the year before. Indirect operating expenses increased 25.5% to US$793.3 million from US$632.2 million in the equivalent prior-year period.

Prospects: On Feb 25 2008, Co. announced that it has agreed to sell its Channelview Cogeneration Plant and related contracts to an affiliate of Kelson Energy for $468.0 million. The transaction should close in the second or third quarter of 2008, pending closing conditions such as the approval of the bankruptcy court. The transaction is expected to resolve the bankruptcy proceedings that began in Aug 2007 when four subsidiaries related to the Channelview plant filed for Chapter 11 bankruptcy protection. Meanwhile, Co. expects its 2007 Smart Energy products, which were designed to help reduce customer electricity and energy consumption in peak usage periods, to lower its supply and operating costs.

Financial Data
(US$ in Thousands)

	12/31/2007	12/31/2006	12/31/2005	12/31/2004	12/31/2003	12/31/2002	12/31/2001	12/31/2000
Earnings Per Share	1.04	(1.07)	(1.09)	(0.10)	(4.57)	(1.93)	2.01	1.31
Cash Flow Per Share	2.22	4.15	(3.03)	0.97	2.96	2.11	(0.46)	1.35
Tang Book Value Per Share	10.71	9.31	9.73	11.13	10.76	11.62	17.53	4.54
Income Statement								
Total Revenue	11,208,724	10,877,385	9,711,995	8,735,538	11,000,319	11,557,998	36,545,739	19,791,922
EBITDA	1,282,190	349,053	143,208	700,982	77,964	584,527	1,096,893	677,746
Income Before Taxes	493,098	(448,621)	(693,827)	(269,000)	(822,075)	(112,107)	825,983	291,113
Income Taxes	135,115	(121,929)	(253,080)	(96,930)	80,082	214,105	271,594	88,593
Net Income	365,107	(327,812)	(330,556)	(29,370)	(1,342,117)	(559,812)	557,451	209,965
Average Shares	352,791	307,705	302,409	297,527	293,655	289,953	277,473	240,000
Balance Sheet								
Current Assets	2,784,667	3,173,249	4,730,451	2,629,277	2,689,270	5,071,503	4,745,290	7,162,736
Total Assets	9,456,530	10,567,133	13,568,806	12,146,865	13,308,259	17,636,820	12,253,556	13,591,709
Current Liabilities	1,603,184	2,693,243	3,406,230	2,070,015	1,998,409	3,925,944	3,586,611	8,574,845
Long-Term Obligations	2,903,000	3,178,000	4,317,000	4,577,000	5,709,000	6,045,000	867,712	1,539,235
Total Liabilities	4,975,456	6,615,922	9,704,686	7,760,654	8,936,349	11,983,852	6,149,674	11,259,259
Stockholders' Equity	4,477,034	3,949,873	3,863,693	4,386,354	4,371,799	5,652,888	6,103,882	2,332,450
Shares Outstanding	344,579	337,623	304,900	299,684	294,591	290,605	299,804	292,000
Statistical Record								
Return on Assets %	3.65	N.M.	N.M.	N.M.	N.M.	N.M.	4.31	2.18
Return on Equity %	8.67	N.M.	N.M.	N.M.	N.M.	N.M.	13.22	13.63
EBITDA Margin %	11.44	3.21	1.47	8.02	0.71	5.06	3.00	3.42
Net Margin %	3.26	N.M.	N.M.	N.M.	N.M.	N.M.	1.53	1.06
Asset Turnover	1.12	0.90	0.76	0.68	0.71	0.77	2.83	2.05
Current Ratio	1.74	1.18	1.39	1.27	1.35	1.29	1.32	0.84
Debt to Equity	0.65	0.80	1.12	1.04	1.31	1.07	0.14	0.66
Price Range	30.26-13.82	14.17-9.74	15.64-9.00	13.65-6.73	7.36-3.05	17.11-1.04	36.75-13.55	...
P/E Ratio	29.10-13.29	...	...	...	...	...	18.28-6.74	...

Address: 1000 Main Street, Houston, TX 77002	**Web Site:** www.reliant.com	**Auditors:** KPMG LLP
Telephone: 713-497-7000	**Officers:** Joel V. Staff - Chmn., C.E.O. Mark M. Jacobs - Exec. V.P., C.F.O.	

REPUBLIC SERVICES, INC.

Exchange	Symbol	Price	52Wk Range	Yield	P/E
NYS	RSG	$29.24 (3/31/2008)	34.85-27.19	N/A	19.36

*7 Year Price Score 119.94 *NYSE Composite Index=100 *12 Month Price Score 105.33

TRADING VOLUME (thousand shares)

Interim Earnings (Per Share)

Qtr.	Mar	Jun	Sep	Dec
2003	0.07	0.25	0.19	0.23
2004	0.24	0.26	0.27	0.25
2005	0.29	0.29	0.30	0.29
2006	0.31	0.35	0.39	0.34
2007	0.28	0.45	0.35	0.43

Interim Dividends (Per Share)

No Dividends Paid

Valuation Analysis | Institutional Holding

Forecast P/E	15.74	No of Institutions
	(1/10/2007)	278
Market Cap	$5.4 Billion	Shares
Book Value	1.3 Billion	172,633,856
Price/Book	4.16	% Held
Price/Sales	1.71	89.24

Business Summary: Sanitation Services (MIC: 7.3 SIC: 4953 NAIC: 562219)

Republic Services is engaged in the provision of services in the domestic non-hazardous solid waste industry. Co. provides non-hazardous solid waste collection services for commercial, industrial, municipal and residential customers through 136 collection companies in 21 states as of Dec 31 2007. In addition, Co.owns or operate 94 transfer stations, 58 solid waste landfills and 33 recycling facilities. As of Dec 31 2007, Co.'s operations were organized into five regions: Eastern, Central, Southern, Southwestern and Western. Each of Co.'s regions and substantially all its areas provide collection, transfer, recycling and disposal services.

Recent Developments: For the year ended Dec 31 2007, net income increased 3.8% to US$290.2 million from US$279.6 million in the prior year. Revenues were US$3.18 billion, up 3.4% from US$3.07 billion the year before. Operating income was US$536.0 million versus US$519.5 million in the prior year, an increase of 3.2%. Direct operating expenses rose 3.8% to US$2.00 billion from US$1.92 billion in the comparable period the year before. Indirect operating expenses increased 2.6% to US$642.9 million from US$626.7 million in the equivalent prior-year period.

Prospects: For the full year of 2008, Co. is projecting earnings in the range of $1.78 to $1.82 per share, while operating margins are forecasted to be 19.0%. In addition, Co. is targeting internal growth of about 2.0% to 3.5%, with about 3.5% to 4.0% growth from core price increases, while the change in volume is estimated to be down 0.5% to 1.5%. Separately, on Nov 27 2007, Co. announced the divestiture of its non-core, stand-alone business in Texas, Living Earth Technology Co. to Hunt Special Situations Group, L.P. for about $37.0 million. This transaction should allow Co. to better focus on its core business, including collection, recycling, transfer and disposal of municipal solid waste.

Financial Data

(US$ in Thousands)	12/31/2007	12/31/2006	12/31/2005	12/31/2004	12/31/2003	12/31/2002	12/31/2001	12/31/2000
Earnings Per Share	1.51	1.38	1.17	1.02	0.73	0.96	0.49	0.84
Cash Flow Per Share	3.48	2.61	3.59	2.90	2.50	2.28	1.79	1.75
Tang Book Value Per Share	N.M.	N.M.	0.07	1.24	1.36	1.27	0.80	0.91
Dividends Per Share	0.553	0.400	0.347	0.240	0.080	...	...	...
Dividend Payout %	36.65	28.99	29.71	23.53	10.91	...	...	...
Income Statement								
Total Revenue	3,176,200	3,070,600	2,863,900	2,708,100	2,517,800	2,365,100	2,257,500	2,103,300
EBITDA	855,600	819,700	757,600	712,900	655,000	658,800	500,400	633,700
Income Before Taxes	468,100	443,700	409,200	383,700	347,400	386,500	209,300	356,400
Income Taxes	177,900	164,100	155,500	145,800	132,000	146,900	83,800	135,400
Net Income	290,200	279,600	253,700	237,900	177,600	239,600	125,500	221,000
Average Shares	192,000	202,800	217,500	232,950	243,150	250,050	256,650	262,500
Balance Sheet								
Current Assets	413,800	393,400	482,300	496,500	556,000	452,300	324,800	405,800
Total Assets	4,467,800	4,429,400	4,550,500	4,464,600	4,554,100	4,209,100	3,856,300	3,561,500
Current Liabilities	628,700	602,200	667,000	446,600	672,000	392,200	386,400	381,800
Long-Term Obligations	1,565,500	1,544,600	1,472,100	1,351,900	1,289,200	1,439,300	1,334,100	1,200,200
Total Liabilities	3,164,000	3,007,300	2,944,700	2,592,100	2,649,600	2,328,000	2,100,400	1,886,600
Stockholders' Equity	1,303,800	1,422,100	1,605,800	1,872,500	1,904,500	1,881,100	1,755,900	1,674,900
Shares Outstanding	185,422	194,995	207,903	225,872	236,741	245,487	254,466	263,487
Statistical Record								
Return on Assets %	6.52	6.23	5.63	5.26	4.05	5.94	3.38	6.44
Return on Equity %	21.29	18.47	14.59	12.56	9.38	13.18	7.32	13.87
EBITDA Margin %	26.94	26.70	26.45	26.32	26.01	27.86	22.17	30.13
Net Margin %	9.14	9.11	8.86	8.78	7.05	10.13	5.56	10.51
Asset Turnover	0.71	0.68	0.64	0.60	0.57	0.59	0.61	0.61
Current Ratio	0.66	0.65	0.72	1.11	0.83	1.15	0.84	1.06
Debt to Equity	1.20	1.09	0.92	0.72	0.68	0.77	0.76	0.72
Price Range	34.85-26.61	29.34-24.65	25.39-20.23	22.65-16.55	17.30-12.50	14.74-11.11	13.87-9.17	11.50-6.71
P/E Ratio	23.08-17.62	21.26-17.86	21.70-17.29	22.21-16.23	23.70-17.12	15.35-11.57	28.30-18.71	13.69-7.99
Average Yield %	1.82	1.48	1.49	1.26	0.53	...	...	...

Address: 110 S.E. 6th Street, 28th Floor, Ft. Lauderdale, FL 33301 Telephone: 954-769-2400	Web Site: www.republicservices.com Officers: James E. O'Connor - Chmn., C.E.O. Harris W. Hudson - Vice-Chmn.	Auditors: Ernst & Young LLP

RESMED INC.

Exchange	Symbol	Price	52Wk Range	Yield	P/E
NYS	RMD	$42.18 (3/31/2008)	53.09-39.20	N/A	52.07

*7 Year Price Score 116.15 *NYSE Composite Index=100 *12 Month Price Score 103.54

Interim Earnings (Per Share)

Qtr.	Sep	Dec	Mar	Jun
2004-05	0.20	0.25	0.25	0.22
2005-06	0.23	0.30	0.34	0.29
2006-07	0.32	0.37	(0.20)	0.36
2007-08	0.31	0.34	...	...

Interim Dividends (Per Share)

No Dividends Paid

Valuation Analysis **Institutional Holding**

Forecast P/E	20.03	No of Institutions
	(1/10/2007)	212
Market Cap	$3.3 Billion	Shares
Book Value	1.0 Billion	51,067,216
Price/Book	3.23	% Held
Price/Sales	4.29	66.49

TRADING VOLUME (thousand shares)

Business Summary: Medical Instruments & Equipment (MIC: 9.6 SIC: 3841 NAIC: 339112)

ResMed is engaged in developing, manufacturing and distributing medical equipment for treating, diagnosing, and managing sleep-disordered breathing and other respiratory disorders. Sleep-disordered breathing (SDB) includes obstructive sleep apnea (OSA), and other respiratory disorders that occur during sleep. In addition to Co.'s nasal continuous positive airway pressure treatment for OSA, which delivers pressurized air typically through a nasal mask to prevent collapse of the upper airway during sleep, Co. has developed a number of products for SDB. As of June 30 2007, these products included airflow generators, diagnostic products, mask systems, headgear and other accessories.

Recent Developments: For the quarter ended Dec 31 2007, net income decreased 7.4% to US$26.9 million from US$29.0 million in the year-earlier quarter. Revenues were US$202.7 million, up 13.6% from US$178.4 million the year before. Operating income was US$36.8 million versus US$40.7 million in the prior-year quarter, a decrease of 9.5%. Direct operating expenses rose 22.0% to US$81.3 million from US$66.7 million in the comparable period the year before. Indirect operating expenses increased 18.9% to US$84.5 million from US$71.1 million in the equivalent prior-year period.

Prospects: Looking ahead, Co. is encouraged by its opportunities for growth as it remains focused on enhancing its product offerings. For instance, Co. plans to release a new version of its S8 flow generator platform for the U.S. market and an additional new mask in the quarter ending June 2008. Meanwhile, on Dec 10 2007, Co. agreed to sell and simultaneously leaseback real property in Poway, CA, where its offices and one of its U.S. distribution facilities are located, for $25.3 million. This transaction should close in Mar 2008 and generate a profit on sale of $6.5 million. Separately, Co. expects to complete the construction of its new corporate headquarters at Kearny Mesa, San Diego in Mar 2009.

Financial Data

(US$ in Thousands)	6 Mos	3 Mos	06/30/2007	06/30/2006	06/30/2005	06/30/2004	06/30/2003	06/30/2002
Earnings Per Share	0.81	0.84	0.85	1.16	0.91	0.81	0.67	0.55
Cash Flow Per Share	1.22	1.20	1.19	1.37	1.04	1.13	0.90	0.55
Tang Book Value Per Share	9.62	9.27	8.73	6.52	3.48	3.70	2.70	1.48
Income Statement								
Total Revenue	388,419	185,740	716,332	606,996	425,505	339,338	273,570	204,076
EBITDA	96,189	45,888	139,637	173,693	126,560	104,218	82,259	67,788
Depn & Amortn	28,198	14,390	...	...	...	...	...	...
Income Before Taxes	72,659	33,812	97,973	133,394	96,626	84,668	67,127	54,592
Income Taxes	21,673	9,687	31,671	45,183	31,841	27,384	21,398	17,086
Net Income	50,986	24,125	66,302	88,211	64,785	57,284	45,729	37,506
Average Shares	78,599	78,941	78,253	77,162	74,942	70,250	68,878	68,160
Balance Sheet								
Current Assets	689,798	672,702	660,799	510,204	360,210	277,829	241,903	193,713
Total Assets	1,319,379	1,287,843	1,252,042	1,007,221	774,146	544,159	459,595	376,191
Current Liabilities	162,653	181,141	202,403	129,000	218,551	60,591	50,583	49,047
Long-Term Obligations	106,533	90,540	87,648	116,212	58,934	113,250	113,250	123,250
Total Liabilities	304,628	305,858	320,820	269,073	300,081	182,660	173,162	183,261
Stockholders' Equity	1,014,751	981,985	931,222	738,148	474,065	361,499	286,433	192,930
Shares Outstanding	77,619	77,485	77,617	75,670	70,001	67,716	66,741	66,216
Statistical Record								
Return on Assets %	5.16	5.64	5.87	9.90	9.83	11.38	10.94	11.29
Return on Equity %	6.79	7.46	7.94	14.55	15.51	17.63	19.08	25.58
EBITDA Margin %	24.76	24.71	19.49	28.62	29.74	30.71	30.07	33.22
Net Margin %	13.13	12.99	9.26	14.53	15.23	16.88	16.72	18.38
Asset Turnover	0.62	0.64	0.63	0.68	0.65	0.67	0.65	0.61
Current Ratio	4.24	3.71	3.30	3.96	1.65	4.59	4.78	3.95
Debt to Equity	0.10	0.09	0.09	0.16	0.12	0.31	0.40	0.64
Price Range	54.26-39.65	54.26-39.53	54.26-38.52	48.50-32.20	33.14-21.73	25.78-19.02	20.98-12.45	30.88-12.35
P/E Ratio	66.99-48.95	64.60-47.06	63.84-45.32	41.81-27.76	36.42-23.88	31.83-23.49	31.31-18.57	56.14-22.45

Address: 14040 Danielson St., Poway, CA 92064-6857
Telephone: 858-746-2400

Web Site: www.resmed.com
Officers: Peter C. Farrell - Chmn., Pres., C.E.O. Adrian M. Smith - Sr. V.P., Fin., C.F.O.

Auditors: KPMG LLP
Investor Contact: 858-746-2280
Transfer Agents: American Stock Transfer & Trust Company, New York, NY

REYNOLDS AMERICAN INC

Exchange	Symbol	Price	52Wk Range	Yield	P/E
NYS	RAI	$59.03 (3/31/2008)	71.05-59.03	5.76	13.33

*7 Year Price Score 128.39 *NYSE Composite Index=100 *12 Month Price Score 105.20

Interim Earnings (Per Share)

Qtr.	Mar	Jun	Sep	Dec
2004			3.09	
2005	0.95	0.85	0.72	1.00
2006	1.17	1.27	1.05	0.61
2007	1.11	1.10	1.21	1.00

Interim Dividends (Per Share)

Amt	Decl	Ex	Rec	Pay
0.75Q	5/11/2007	6/7/2007	6/11/2007	7/2/2007
0.85Q	7/25/2007	9/6/2007	9/10/2007	10/1/2007
0.85Q	11/30/2007	12/7/2007	12/11/2007	1/2/2008
0.85Q	2/5/2008	3/6/2008	3/10/2008	4/1/2008

Indicated Div: $3.40

Valuation Analysis

Forecast P/E	14.56
	(1/10/2007)
Market Cap	$17.4 Billion
Book Value	7.5 Billion
Price/Book	2.33
Price/Sales	1.93

Institutional Holding

No of Institutions	317
Shares	196,016,736
% Held	66.31

TRADING VOLUME (thousand shares)

Business Summary: Tobacco Products (MIC: 4.2 SIC: 2111 NAIC: 312221)

Reynolds American is a holding company. Co.'s wholly owned subsidiaries include: RJR Tobacco, which sells the cigarette brands CAMEL, KOOL, DORAL, WINSTON and SALEM, PALL MALL, MISTY and CAPRI; Santa Fe, which manufactures and markets cigarettes and other tobacco products under the NATURAL AMERICAN SPIRIT brand; Lane, which manufactures or distributes cigars, roll-your-own, cigarette and pipe tobacco, including DUNHILL and CAPTAIN BLACK products; as well as Conwood, whose brands include GRIZZLY, KODIAK and LEVI GARRETT as well as dry snuff, plug and twist tobacco products.

Recent Developments: For the year ended Dec 31 2007, income from continuing operations increased 15.1% to US$1.31 billion from US$1.14 billion a year earlier. Net income increased 8.1% to US$1.31 billion from US$1.21 billion in the prior year. Revenues were US$9.02 billion, up 6.0% from US$8.51 billion the year before. Operating income was US$2.29 billion versus US$1.93 billion in the prior year, an increase of 18.5%. Direct operating expenses rose 3.3% to US$4.96 billion from US$4.80 billion in the comparable period the year before. Indirect operating expenses were unchanged at US$1.78 billion versus the equivalent prior-year period.

Prospects: Co.'s outlook appears positive, as it has raised its 2007 earnings guidance to a range of $4.55 to $4.65 per diluted share, representing a growth of 11.0% to 13.0% compared to 2006, excluding any potential effect of the annual assessment of intangible asset valuations. Notably, the guidance increase was driven by a cigarette price increase announced late in the third quarter of 2007. Also, Co. remains on track to attain productivity gains of $85.0 million for 2007, against a total goal of $500.0 million through 2011. Given the expected robust results in 2007, Co. believes that it is positioned to deliver mid-single digit earnings per share growth over the next several years.

Financial Data

(US$ in Thousands)	12/31/2007	12/31/2006	12/31/2005	12/31/2004	12/31/2003	12/31/2002	12/31/2001	12/31/2000
Earnings Per Share	4.43	4.10	3.53	3.09	(20.59)	(0.25)	2.19	8.97
Cash Flow Per Share	4.52	4.94	4.32	3.31	3.47	2.76	3.23	2.91
Dividends Per Share	3.200	2.750	2.100	0.950	1.900	1.865	1.650	1.550
Dividend Payout %	72.23	67.07	59.49	30.79	...	...	75.17	17.28
Income Statement								
Total Revenue	9,023,000	8,510,000	8,256,000	6,437,000	5,267,000	6,211,000	8,585,000	8,167,000
EBITDA	2,420,000	2,105,000	1,639,000	1,078,000	(3,670,000)	963,000	1,396,000	1,282,000
Income Before Taxes	2,073,000	1,809,000	1,416,000	829,000	(3,918,000)	683,000	892,000	748,000
Income Taxes	766,000	673,000	431,000	202,000	(229,000)	265,000	448,000	396,000
Net Income	1,308,000	1,210,000	1,042,000	688,000	(3,446,000)	(44,000)	435,000	1,827,000
Average Shares	294,889	295,384	295,172	222,872	167,394	180,350	197,972	203,714
Balance Sheet								
Current Assets	4,992,000	4,935,000	5,065,000	4,624,000	3,331,000	3,992,000	3,856,000	3,871,000
Total Assets	18,629,000	18,178,000	14,519,000	14,428,000	9,677,000	14,651,000	15,050,000	15,554,000
Current Liabilities	3,903,000	4,092,000	4,149,000	4,055,000	2,865,000	3,427,000	2,792,000	2,776,000
Long-Term Obligations	4,515,000	4,389,000	1,558,000	1,595,000	1,671,000	1,755,000	1,631,000	1,674,000
Total Liabilities	11,163,000	11,135,000	7,966,000	8,252,000	6,620,000	7,935,000	7,024,000	7,118,000
Stockholders' Equity	7,466,000	7,043,000	6,553,000	6,176,000	3,057,000	6,716,000	8,026,000	8,436,000
Shares Outstanding	295,007	295,624	295,465	294,728	170,206	172,096	188,470	202,530
Statistical Record								
Return on Assets %	7.11	7.40	7.20	5.69	N.M.	N.M.	2.84	12.17
Return on Equity %	18.03	17.80	16.37	14.86	N.M.	N.M.	5.28	23.51
EBITDA Margin %	26.82	24.74	19.85	16.75	N.M.	15.50	16.26	15.70
Net Margin %	14.50	14.22	12.62	10.69	N.M.	N.M.	5.07	22.37
Asset Turnover	0.49	0.52	0.57	0.53	0.43	0.42	0.56	0.54
Current Ratio	1.28	1.21	1.22	1.14	1.16	1.16	1.38	1.39
Debt to Equity	0.60	0.62	0.24	0.26	0.55	0.26	0.20	0.20
Price Range	71.05-58.63	66.17-48.25	48.70-38.56	40.16-26.86	29.78-14.02	35.67-17.55	30.86-22.84	24.56-7.88
P/E Ratio	16.04-13.23	16.14-11.77	13.80-10.92	13.00-8.69	...	...	14.09-10.43	2.74-0.88
Average Yield %	5.00	4.71	5.06	2.88	9.53	6.69	5.92	11.02

Address: 401 North Main Street, P.O. Box 2990, Winston-Salem, NC 27102-2990
Telephone: 336-741-2000
Fax: 336-728-8888

Web Site: www.ReynoldsAmerican.com
Officers: Andrew J. Schindler - Chmn., C.E.O. Lynn J. Beasley - Pres., C.O.O.

Auditors: KPMG LLP
Investor Contact: 336-741-5165
Transfer Agents: The Bank of New York, New York, NY

RITE AID CORP.

Exchange	Symbol	Price	52Wk Range	Yield	P/E
NYS	RAD	$2.94 (3/31/2008)	6.70-1.95	N/A	N/A

*7 Year Price Score 81.44   *NYSE Composite Index=100   *12 Month Price Score 66.12

TRADING VOLUME (thousand shares)

Interim Earnings (Per Share)

Qtr.	May	Aug	Nov	Feb
2004-05	0.10	0.00	(0.01)	0.38
2005-06	0.05	(0.03)	(0.02)	1.90
2006-07	0.01	(0.02)	(0.01)	0.01
2007-08	0.04	(0.10)	(0.12)	...

Interim Dividends (Per Share)

Dividend Payment Suspended

Valuation Analysis   Institutional Holding

Forecast P/E	58.28	No of Institutions
	(1/10/2007)	195
Market Cap	$2.3 Billion	Shares
Book Value	2.7 Billion	342,579,264
Price/Book	0.88	% Held
Price/Sales	0.11	64.29

Business Summary: Retail - Miscellaneous (MIC: 5.11 SIC: 5912 NAIC: 446110)

Rite Aid is a retail drugstore chain. Co. operates its drugstores in 27 states across the U.S. and in the District of Columbia. As of Mar 3 2007, Co. operated 3,333 stores. In its stores, Co. sells prescription drugs and an assortment of other merchandise, namely front-end products. Front end products include over-the-counter medications, health and beauty aids, personal care items, cosmetics, household items, beverages, convenience foods, greeting cards, seasonal merchandise and numerous other everyday and convenience products, as well as photo processing. Co. provides approximately 3,000 products under the Rite Aid private brand.

Recent Developments: For the quarter ended Dec 1 2007, net loss amounted to US$84.8 million versus net income of US$1.1 million in the year-earlier quarter. Revenues were US$6.52 billion, up 51.0% from US$4.32 billion the year before. Direct operating expenses rose 50.7% to US$4.77 billion from US$3.17 billion in the comparable period the year before. Indirect operating expenses increased 63.9% to US$1.89 billion from US$1.15 billion in the equivalent prior-year period.

Prospects: For the fiscal year ending Mar 2008, Co. has reduced its sales guidance to $24.30 billion to $24.60 billion, with same store sales improving 1.0% to 2.0% compared with prior guidance of $24.50 billion to $25.10 billion, with same store sales improving 1.3% to 3.3%. In addition, Co. is lowering its net loss guidance to $161.0 million to $192.0 million or $0.27 to $0.31 loss per diluted share from prior net loss guidance of $78.0 million to $161.0 million or $0.15 to $0.27 loss per diluted share. Meanwhile, Co. is encouraged by the integration of its June 2007 Brooks Eckerd acquisition and continues to expect cost-savings of $200.0 million in fiscal 2008 and $300.0 million in fiscal 2009.

Financial Data

(US$ in Thousands)	9 Mos	6 Mos	3 Mos	03/03/2007	03/04/2006	02/26/2005	02/28/2004	03/01/2003
Earnings Per Share	(0.17)	(0.06)	0.02	(0.01)	1.89	0.47	0.11	(0.28)
Cash Flow Per Share	(0.13)	0.28	0.71	0.59	0.78	1.00	0.44	0.59
Tang Book Value Per Share	N.M.	N.M.	0.70	0.62	0.53	...	...	...
Income Statement								
Total Revenue	17,580,559	11,057,015	4,457,810	17,507,719	17,270,968	16,816,439	16,600,449	15,800,920
EBITDA	117,051	117,835	94,288	559,108	570,026	675,620	612,302	447,710
Depn & Amortn	337,941	200,411	67,919	...	...	...	...	...
Income Before Taxes	(220,890)	(82,576)	26,369	13,582	43,254	134,007	34,516	(167,644)
Income Taxes	(94,080)	(40,612)	(1,265)	(13,244)	(1,229,752)	(168,471)	(48,795)	(41,940)
Net Income	(126,810)	(41,964)	27,634	26,826	1,273,006	302,478	83,311	(112,076)
Average Shares	783,312	781,805	550,338	524,460	676,666	634,062	525,831	515,129
Balance Sheet								
Current Assets	5,338,846	5,118,680	2,931,339	2,952,988	2,884,812	3,006,754	3,377,007	3,013,807
Total Assets	12,550,840	12,266,127	8,339,986	7,091,024	6,988,371	5,932,583	6,246,679	6,133,515
Current Liabilities	2,732,805	2,754,077	1,658,300	1,589,925	2,143,324	1,671,737	1,483,750	1,566,998
Long-Term Obligations	6,073,219	5,679,783	4,237,395	3,084,104	2,467,250	3,087,521	3,867,690	3,758,913
Total Liabilities	9,889,796	9,526,712	6,629,449	5,428,178	5,381,450	5,609,649	6,237,415	6,226,181
Stockholders' Equity	2,661,044	2,739,415	1,710,537	1,662,846	1,606,921	322,934	9,264	(112,329)
Shares Outstanding	795,352	795,430	539,510	536,686	527,667	520,438	516,496	515,115
Statistical Record								
Return on Assets %	N.M.	N.M.	0.57	0.38	19.39	4.98	1.35	N.M.
Return on Equity %	N.M.	N.M.	2.62	1.65	129.79	182.61	...	...
EBITDA Margin %	0.67	1.07	2.12	3.19	3.30	4.02	3.69	2.83
Net Margin %	N.M.	N.M.	0.62	0.15	7.37	1.80	0.50	N.M.
Asset Turnover	2.25	2.07	2.31	2.49	2.63	2.77	2.69	2.51
Current Ratio	1.95	1.86	1.77	1.86	1.35	1.80	2.28	2.07
Debt to Equity	2.28	2.07	2.48	1.85	1.54	9.56	417.50	...
Price Range	6.70-3.48	6.70-4.28	6.59-4.07	6.36-3.79	4.82-3.28	5.75-3.35	6.40-2.17	4.22-1.75
P/E Ratio	...	...	329.50-203.50	...	2.55-1.74	12.23-7.13	58.18-19.73	...

Address: 30 Hunter Lane, Camp Hill, PA 17011	Web Site: www.riteaid.com	Auditors: Deloitte & Touche LLP
Telephone: 717-761-2633	Officers: Robert G. Miller - Chmn. Mary F. Sammons - Pres., C.E.O.	Investor Contact: 717-975-5750
Fax: 717-975-5905		

Exchange	Symbol	Price	52Wk Range
NYS	RLI	$49.57 (3/31/2008)	60.82-48.48

Yield	P/E	Div Achiever
1.86	6.79	31 Years

*7 Year Price Score 113.44 *NYSE Composite Index=100 *12 Month Price Score 99.39

Interim Earnings (Per Share)

Qtr.	Mar	Jun	Sep	Dec
2003	0.56	0.60	0.98	0.62
2004	0.65	0.71	0.32	1.13
2005	1.12	1.31	0.96	0.68
2006	0.97	0.89	1.21	2.21
2007	1.32	2.04	2.56	1.39

Interim Dividends (Per Share)

Amt	Decl	Ex	Rec	Pay
0.22Q	5/4/2007	6/27/2007	6/29/2007	7/13/2007
0.22Q	8/23/2007	9/26/2007	9/28/2007	10/15/2007
0.23Q	11/14/2007	12/27/2007	12/31/2007	1/15/2008
0.23Q	2/7/2008	3/27/2008	3/31/2008	4/15/2008

Indicated Div: $0.92 (Div. Reinv. Plan)

Valuation Analysis

		Institutional Holding	
Forecast P/E	13.98	No of Institutions	
	(1/10/2007)	135	
Market Cap	$1.1 Billion	Shares	
Book Value	774.4 Million	19,824,568	
Price/Book	1.42	% Held	
Price/Sales	1.68	82.31	

Business Summary: Insurance (MIC: 8.2 SIC: 6331 NAIC: 524126)

RLI is a holding company that underwrites selected property and casualty insurance through its insurance subsidiaries. Co. conducts its operations principally through three insurance companies. RLI Insurance Company, Co.'s principal subsidiary, writes multiple lines insurance on an admitted basis in all 50 states, the District of Columbia and Puerto Rico. Mt. Hawley Insurance Company, a subsidiary of RLI Insurance, writes surplus lines insurance in all 50 states, the District of Columbia, Puerto Rico, the Virgin Islands and Guam. RLI Indemnity Company, a subsidiary of Mt. Hawley, has authority to write multiple lines insurance on an admitted basis in 49 states and the District of Columbia.

Recent Developments: For the year ended Dec 31 2007, net income increased 30.6% to US$175.9 million from US$134.6 million in the prior year. Revenues were US$652.3 million, up 3.1% from US$632.7 million the year before. Net premiums earned were US$544.5 million versus US$530.3 million in the prior year, an increase of 2.7%. Net investment income rose 10.6% to US$78.9 million from US$71.3 million a year ago.

Prospects: For 2008, Co. expects pricing in the overall insurance marketplace to continue to decline. However, Co. expects to see premium growth in selected products in 2008 and underwriting income in all three of its insurance segments absent any major catastrophe. Specifically, Co. will maintain its profit-focused strategy and look to broaden its production sources and product offerings to hold its market position and potentially growing its casualty segment. Co. also expects its marine business to grow moderately due to new product offerings and an increased focus on writing inland marine coverages. Within its investment portfolio, Co. expects investment income to be relatively flat.

Financial Data

(US$ in Thousands)	12/31/2007	12/31/2006	12/31/2005	12/31/2004	12/31/2003	12/31/2002	12/31/2001	12/31/2000
Earnings Per Share	7.30	5.27	4.07	2.80	2.76	1.75	1.55	1.45
Cash Flow Per Share	5.39	6.89	7.78	7.47	7.60	8.12	3.97	2.70
Tang Book Value Per Share	33.77	30.09	26.09	23.60	20.98	17.37	15.36	14.99
Dividends Per Share	0.870	0.750	0.630	0.510	0.400	0.345	0.315	0.295
Dividend Payout %	11.92	14.23	15.48	18.21	14.49	19.71	20.32	20.42
Income Statement								
Premium Income	544,478	530,338	491,307	511,348	463,597	348,065	273,008	231,603
Total Revenue	652,345	632,708	569,302	578,800	519,886	382,153	309,354	263,496
Benefits & Claims	190,868	256,889	251,170	306,131	278,990	203,122	155,876	124,586
Income Before Taxes	254,476	186,893	143,876	100,342	94,278	48,728	41,018	38,293
Income Taxes	78,609	52,254	36,742	27,306	22,987	12,876	10,771	9,600
Net Income	175,867	134,639	107,134	73,036	71,291	35,852	31,047	28,693
Average Shares	24,085	25,571	26,324	26,093	25,846	20,512	20,004	19,890
Balance Sheet								
Total Assets	2,626,523	2,771,296	2,735,870	2,468,775	2,134,364	1,719,327	1,390,970	1,281,323
Total Liabilities	1,852,101	2,014,776	2,042,929	1,845,114	1,580,230	1,262,772	1,055,538	954,669
Stockholders' Equity	774,422	756,520	692,941	623,661	554,134	456,555	335,432	326,654
Shares Outstanding	22,155	24,272	25,551	25,315	25,165	24,681	19,825	19,607
Statistical Record								
Return on Assets %	6.52	4.89	4.12	3.16	3.70	2.31	2.32	2.33
Return on Equity %	22.98	18.58	16.27	12.37	14.11	9.05	9.38	9.23
Loss Ratio %	35.06	48.44	51.12	59.87	60.18	58.36	57.10	53.79
Net Margin %	26.96	21.28	18.82	12.62	13.71	9.38	10.04	10.89
Price Range	60.82-51.00	57.41-45.16	55.68-40.28	43.20-33.55	38.10-25.40	29.60-22.25	23.00-19.40	22.34-13.25
P/E Ratio	8.33-6.99	10.89-8.57	13.68-9.90	15.43-11.98	13.80-9.20	16.91-12.71	14.84-12.52	15.41-9.14
Average Yield %	1.52	1.46	1.37	1.34	1.28	1.33	1.50	1.66

Address: 9025 N. Lindbergh Drive, Peoria, IL 61615-1499	Web Site: www.rlicorp.com	Auditors: KPMG LLP
Telephone: 309-692-1000	Officers: Jonathan E. Michael - Pres., C.E.O. Joseph E. Dondanville - Sr. V.P., C.F.O.	Investor Contact: 309-693-5846
Fax: 309-692-1068		Transfer Agents: Wells Fargo Shareholder Services, St. Paul, MN

ROBERT HALF INTERNATIONAL INC.

Exchange	Symbol	Price	52Wk Range	Yield	P/E
NYS	RHI	$25.74 (3/31/2008)	38.03-22.16	1.71	14.22

*7 Year Price Score 88.53   *NYSE Composite Index=100   *12 Month Price Score 92.17

Interim Earnings (Per Share)

Qtr.	Mar	Jun	Sep	Dec
2003	(0.02)	0.00	0.03	0.03
2004	0.09	0.18	0.24	0.27
2005	0.29	0.33	0.37	0.37
2006	0.38	0.39	0.43	0.45
2007	0.42	0.44	0.46	0.49

Interim Dividends (Per Share)

Amt	Decl	Ex	Rec	Pay
0.10Q	5/3/2007	5/23/2007	5/25/2007	6/15/2007
0.10Q	7/31/2007	8/22/2007	8/24/2007	9/14/2007
0.10Q	10/31/2007	11/21/2007	11/26/2007	12/14/2007
0.11Q	2/13/2008	2/21/2008	2/25/2008	3/14/2008
			Indicated Div: $0.44	

Valuation Analysis

Forecast P/E	17.09 (1/10/2007)
Market Cap	$4.1 Billion
Book Value	984.0 Million
Price/Book	4.13
Price/Sales	0.88

Institutional Holding

No of Institutions	281
Shares	136,945,040
% Held	81.46

TRADING VOLUME (thousand shares)

Business Summary: Human Resources Services (MIC: 12.6 SIC: 8742 NAIC: 541612)

Robert Half International provides staffing and risk consulting services through its Accountemps®, Robert Half® Finance & Accounting, OfficeTeam®, Robert Half® Technology, Robert Half® Management Resources, Robert Half® Legal, The Creative Group®, and Protiviti® divisions. Co. provides professionals in the fields of accounting and finance; temporary administrative support personnel; information technology professionals; temporary, project, and full time staffing of attorneys and support personnel in law firms and corporate legal departments; project staffing in the advertising, marketing, and web design fields; as well as business and technology risk consulting and internal audit services.

Recent Developments: For the year ended Dec 31 2007, net income increased 4.6% to US$296.2 million from US$283.2 million in the prior year. Revenues were US$4.65 billion, up 15.7% from US$4.01 billion the year before. Direct operating expenses rose 15.0% to US$2.67 billion from US$2.32 billion in the comparable period the year before. Indirect operating expenses increased 21.1% to US$1.49 billion from US$1.23 billion in the equivalent prior-year period.

Prospects: Co.'s temporary and permanent staffing services revenues is being positively affected by an improvement in both domestic and international markets, particularly in Continental Europe. Furthermore, Co. is experiencing an increase in its risk consulting and internal audit services revenues primarily attributable to higher international revenues, particularly in Asia. Looking ahead, Co.'s Protiviti division intends to expand the services and content on the Protiviti.com website and increase traffic through targeted Internet advertising. Additionally, Co. is anticipating its total revenue to continue to be affected by general macroeconomic conditions in 2008.

Financial Data

(US$ in Thousands)	12/31/2007	12/31/2006	12/31/2005	12/31/2004	12/31/2003	12/31/2002	12/31/2001	12/31/2000
Earnings Per Share	1.81	1.65	1.36	0.79	0.04	0.01	0.67	1.00
Cash Flow Per Share	2.57	2.27	1.95	0.95	0.73	0.96	1.58	1.50
Tang Book Value Per Share	4.99	5.15	4.72	4.30	3.65	3.41	3.69	3.13
Dividends Per Share	0.400	0.320	0.280	0.180	...	...	...	...
Dividend Payout %	22.10	19.39	20.59	22.78	...	...	...	...
Income Statement								
Total Revenue	4,645,666	4,013,546	3,338,439	2,675,696	1,974,991	1,904,951	2,452,850	2,699,319
EBITDA	561,845	527,287	443,503	283,178	77,619	75,805	269,400	358,266
Income Before Taxes	490,404	466,202	392,174	234,665	11,715	3,497	196,284	301,627
Income Taxes	194,192	183,024	154,304	94,061	5,325	1,329	75,177	115,524
Net Income	296,212	283,178	237,870	140,604	6,390	2,168	121,107	186,103
Average Shares	163,479	171,712	174,382	176,866	173,175	177,791	181,489	186,068
Balance Sheet								
Current Assets	1,059,638	1,112,355	1,016,908	916,316	698,619	643,172	686,006	671,610
Total Assets	1,450,298	1,459,021	1,318,686	1,198,657	979,903	935,671	994,162	971,029
Current Liabilities	447,952	402,740	336,701	280,345	188,899	184,215	176,647	237,156
Long-Term Obligations	3,753	3,831	2,698	2,266	2,343	2,414	2,480	2,541
Total Liabilities	466,249	416,350	347,813	286,787	191,242	190,705	188,466	252,490
Stockholders' Equity	984,049	1,042,671	970,873	911,870	788,661	744,966	805,696	718,539
Shares Outstanding	158,057	167,847	170,681	172,980	171,775	170,909	174,928	176,050
Statistical Record								
Return on Assets %	20.36	20.39	18.90	12.87	0.67	0.22	12.33	21.23
Return on Equity %	29.23	28.13	25.27	16.49	0.83	0.28	15.89	28.67
EBITDA Margin %	12.09	13.14	13.28	10.61	3.93	3.98	10.98	13.27
Net Margin %	6.38	7.06	7.13	5.25	0.32	0.11	4.94	6.89
Asset Turnover	3.19	2.89	2.65	2.45	2.06	1.97	2.50	3.08
Current Ratio	2.37	2.76	3.02	3.27	3.70	3.49	3.88	2.83
Price Range	41.62-24.58	43.90-30.05	39.29-24.23	30.70-20.84	24.58-11.74	30.81-12.06	30.47-18.77	37.63-12.69
P/E Ratio	22.99-13.58	26.61-18.21	28.89-17.82	38.86-26.38	614.50-293.50	N.M.	45.48-28.01	37.63-12.69
Average Yield %	1.18	0.86	0.91	0.69	...	...	...	...

Address: 2884 Sand Hill Road, Suite 200, Menlo Park, CA 94025 **Telephone:** 650-234-6000 **Fax:** 650-234-6999	**Web Site:** www.rhi.com **Officers:** Harold M. Messmer Jr. - Chmn., Pres., C.E.O. M. Keith Waddell - Vice-Chmn., C.F.O.	**Auditors:** PricewaterhouseCoopers LLP **Transfer Agents:** Mellon Investor Services L.L.C.

ROCKWELL AUTOMATION, INC.

Exchange	Symbol	Price	52Wk Range	Yield	P/E
NYS	ROK	$57.42 (3/31/2008)	75.52-51.75	2.02	7.46

*7 Year Price Score 124.76 *NYSE Composite Index=100   *12 Month Price Score 91.55

Interim Earnings (Per Share)

Qtr.	Dec	Mar	Jun	Sep
2004-05	0.71	0.79	0.68	0.70
2005-06	0.80	0.81	0.83	0.93
2006-07	2.50	4.45	1.05	1.16
2007-08	1.04	...	...	...

Interim Dividends (Per Share)

Amt	Decl	Ex	Rec	Pay
0.29Q	6/8/2007	8/9/2007	8/13/2007	9/4/2007
0.29Q	11/7/2007	11/15/2007	11/19/2007	12/10/2007
0.29Q	2/6/2008	2/14/2008	2/19/2008	3/10/2008
0.29Q	4/2/2008	5/8/2008	5/12/2008	6/2/2008

Indicated Div: $1.16

Valuation Analysis

Forecast P/E	13.79
	(1/10/2007)
Market Cap	$8.5 Billion
Book Value	1.8 Billion
Price/Book	4.78
Price/Sales	1.64

Institutional Holding

No of Institutions	410
Shares	103,787,960
% Held	62.65

Business Summary: Instruments and Related Products (MIC: 11.15 SIC: 3829 NAIC: 334519)

Rockwell Automation is engaged in the provision of industrial automation power, control and information applications. Co. operates through two business segments: Architecture and Software, which contains the elements of Co.'s integrated control and information architecture capable of connecting the customer's manufacturing enterprise; and Control Products and Solutions, which combines a portfolio of intelligent motor control and industrial control products with the customer support and application knowledge to implement an automation or information system on the plant floor. Co. has operations in the U.S., Canada, Italy, China, the U.K., Germany, Brazil, Australia, Korea, and France.

Recent Developments: For the quarter ended Dec 31 2007, income from continuing operations increased 19.6% to US$156.6 million from US$130.9 million in the year-earlier quarter. Net income decreased 63.5% to US$156.6 million from US$429.1 million in the year-earlier quarter. Revenues were US$1.33 billion, up 16.2% from US$1.15 billion the year before. Direct operating expenses rose 16.6% to US$756.4 million from US$648.7 million in the comparable period the year before. Indirect operating expenses increased 14.7% to US$356.5 million from US$310.7 million in the equivalent prior-year period.

Prospects: Despite the uncertainty in the economic environment, particularly in the U.S., customer capital spending and project activity appear to be solid. As a result, Co. has reaffirmed its guidance for the fiscal year ending Sep 2008, which calls for revenue growth of 10.0% to 12.0%, excluding the effects of currency translation, as well as earnings per share of $4.25 to $4.45. Meanwhile, Co. continues to expand its business through strategic acquisitions, as demonstrated by its Nov 2007 acquisition of Pavilion Technologies, Inc., a privately held company that provides enhanced process control, production optimization and environmental compliance applications for process and hybrid industries.

Financial Data

(US$ in Thousands)	3 Mos	09/30/2007	09/30/2006	09/30/2005	09/30/2004	09/30/2003	09/30/2002	09/30/2001
Earnings Per Share	7.70	9.23	3.37	2.88	2.17	1.51	0.64	1.65
Cash Flow Per Share	3.01	2.80	2.41	3.49	3.21	2.35	2.57	1.83
Tang Book Value Per Share	4.23	4.29	4.40	2.95	3.95	2.40	2.61	2.22
Dividends Per Share	1.160	1.160	0.900	0.780	0.660	0.660	0.660	0.930
Dividend Payout %	15.06	12.57	26.71	27.08	30.41	43.71	103.13	56.36
Income Statement								
Total Revenue	1,331,900	5,003,900	5,561,400	5,003,200	4,411,100	4,104,000	3,909,000	4,323,000
EBITDA	250,300	940,300	1,095,500	943,400	660,900	543,000	500,000	523,000
Depn & Amortn	31,300	...	...	...	...	...	...	...
Income Before Taxes	219,000	788,600	891,400	737,000	438,100	299,000	233,000	168,000
Income Taxes	62,400	219,300	263,300	218,600	84,000	17,000	7,000	43,000
Net Income	156,600	1,487,800	607,000	540,000	414,900	286,000	121,000	305,000
Average Shares	151,000	161,200	179,900	187,200	191,100	190,100	188,800	185,300
Balance Sheet								
Current Assets	2,667,100	2,382,000	2,188,000	2,186,500	2,026,100	1,736,000	1,775,000	1,697,000
Total Assets	4,941,000	4,545,800	4,735,400	4,525,100	4,201,200	3,986,000	4,024,000	4,074,000
Current Liabilities	1,541,500	1,744,500	1,293,300	940,800	863,600	820,000	966,000	867,000
Long-Term Obligations	903,900	405,700	748,200	748,200	757,700	764,000	767,000	922,000
Total Liabilities	3,157,200	2,803,000	2,817,400	2,876,000	2,340,200	2,399,000	2,415,000	2,474,000
Stockholders' Equity	1,783,800	1,742,800	1,918,200	1,649,100	1,861,000	1,587,000	1,609,000	1,600,000
Shares Outstanding	148,400	149,400	170,800	179,700	183,800	185,600	185,800	183,700
Statistical Record								
Return on Assets %	24.30	32.06	13.11	12.38	10.11	7.14	2.99	5.83
Return on Equity %	64.44	81.28	34.03	30.77	24.00	17.90	7.54	14.29
EBITDA Margin %	18.79	18.79	19.70	18.86	14.98	13.23	12.79	12.10
Net Margin %	11.76	29.73	10.91	10.79	9.41	6.97	3.10	7.06
Asset Turnover	1.04	1.08	1.20	1.15	1.07	1.02	0.97	0.83
Current Ratio	1.73	1.37	1.69	2.32	2.35	2.12	1.84	1.96
Debt to Equity	0.51	0.23	0.39	0.45	0.45	0.41	0.48	0.58
Price Range	75.52-57.69	75.52-57.45	78.55-50.72	62.30-38.00	39.69-26.25	28.55-15.02	22.66-13.40	18.63-11.47
P/E Ratio	9.81-7.49	8.18-6.22	23.31-15.05	21.63-13.19	18.29-12.10	18.91-9.95	35.41-20.94	11.29-6.95
Average Yield %	1.75	1.80	1.40	1.53	1.94	2.95	3.58	5.79

Address: 1201 South Second Street, Milwaukee, WI 53204 **Telephone:** 414-382-2000	**Web Site:** www.rockwellautomation.com **Officers:** Keith D. Nosbusch - Chmn., Pres., C.E.O. James V. Gelly - Sr. V.P., C.F.O.	**Auditors:** Deloitte & Touche LLP **Investor Contact:** 414-382-8510 **Transfer Agents:** Mellon Investor Services LLC, South Hackensack, NJ

ROCKWELL COLLINS, INC.

Exchange	Symbol	Price	52Wk Range	Yield	P/E
NYS	COL	$57.15 (3/31/2008)	75.86-54.76	1.12	16.14

*7 Year Price Score N/A   *NYSE Composite Index=100   *12 Month Price Score 93.19

TRADING VOLUME (thousand shares)

Interim Earnings (Per Share)

Qtr.	Dec	Mar	Jun	Sep
2004-05	0.50	0.52	0.56	0.62
2005-06	0.59	0.65	0.70	0.80
2006-07	0.84	0.82	0.86	0.93
2007-08	0.93	...	...	...

Interim Dividends (Per Share)

Amt	Decl	Ex	Rec	Pay
0.16Q	4/26/2007	5/10/2007	5/14/2007	6/4/2007
0.16Q	7/30/2007	8/9/2007	8/13/2007	9/4/2007
0.16Q	11/1/2007	11/7/2007	11/12/2007	12/3/2007
0.16Q	1/29/2008	2/7/2008	2/11/2008	3/3/2008

Indicated Div: $0.64

Valuation Analysis

		Institutional Holding	
Forecast P/E	18.10 (1/10/2007)	No of Institutions	363
Market Cap	$9.3 Billion	Shares	115,983,776
Book Value	1.5 Billion	% Held	68.94
Price/Book	6.20		
Price/Sales	2.06		

Business Summary: Aviation (MIC: 1.1 SIC: 3728 NAIC: 336413)

Rockwell Collins designs, produces and supports communications and aviation electronics for commercial and military customers worldwide. Co.'s Government Systems segment supplies defense communications and defense electronics systems, products and services to the U.S. Department of Defense, other government agencies, civil agencies, defense contractors and foreign ministries of defense. Its Commercial Systems segment supplies aviation electronics systems, products and services. Co. also provides services and support to its customers through its network of service centers, including equipment repair and overhaul, service parts, field service engineering, and aftermarket used equipment sales.

Recent Developments: For the quarter ended Dec 31 2007, net income increased 7.7% to US$154.0 million from US$143.0 million in the year-earlier quarter. Revenues were US$1.11 billion, up 12.0% from US$993.0 million the year before. Direct operating expenses rose 11.4% to US$769.0 million in the comparable period the year before. Indirect operating expenses increased 2.6% to US$118.0 million from US$115.0 million in the equivalent prior-year period.

Prospects: Co.'s outlook for the remainder of the fiscal year ending Sep 2008 appears encouraging, reflecting strong aerospace and defense market conditions. Particularly, in addition to the improving commercial aerospace market, Co. expects to benefit from its recent introduction of new aircraft models and strong order backlog for the production of new aircraft. As a result, Co. is raising its full fiscal 2008 total sales guidance to be approximately $4.75 billion compared with its previous range of $4.70 billion to $4.75 billion, along with earnings per share to be in the range of $3.85 to $4.00 compared with its previous guidance of $3.80 to $3.95.

Financial Data

(US$ in Thousands)	3 Mos	09/30/2007	09/30/2006	09/30/2005	09/30/2004	09/30/2003	09/30/2002	09/30/2001
Earnings Per Share	3.54	3.45	2.73	2.20	1.67	1.43	1.28	0.72
Cash Flow Per Share	3.43	3.63	3.46	3.24	2.25	2.09	2.47	1.06
Tang Book Value Per Share	4.91	5.32	3.30	2.13	3.29	2.21	2.93	4.49
Dividends Per Share	0.640	0.640	0.560	0.480	0.390	0.360	0.360	0.090
Dividend Payout %	18.08	18.55	20.51	21.82	23.35	25.17	28.13	12.50
Income Statement								
Total Revenue	1,112,000	4,415,000	3,863,000	3,445,000	2,930,000	2,542,000	2,492,000	2,820,000
EBITDA	261,000	992,000	824,000	638,000	545,000	474,000	450,000	358,000
Depn & Amortn	31,000	...	...	...	...	...	...	...
Income Before Taxes	232,000	843,000	689,000	547,000	430,000	368,000	341,000	224,000
Income Taxes	78,000	258,000	212,000	151,000	129,000	110,000	105,000	85,000
Net Income	154,000	585,000	477,000	396,000	301,000	258,000	236,000	139,000
Average Shares	165,300	169,700	174,500	180,200	180,000	180,100	184,100	185,500
Balance Sheet								
Current Assets	2,301,000	2,160,000	1,927,000	1,775,000	1,003,000	1,427,000	1,438,000	1,639,000
Total Assets	3,848,000	3,750,000	3,278,000	3,140,000	2,874,000	2,591,000	2,560,000	2,628,000
Current Liabilities	1,576,000	1,459,000	1,324,000	1,177,000	964,000	901,000	1,043,000	1,135,000
Long-Term Obligations	228,000	223,000	245,000	200,000	201,000	...	...	...
Total Liabilities	2,344,000	2,177,000	2,072,000	2,201,000	1,741,000	1,758,000	1,573,000	1,518,000
Stockholders' Equity	1,504,000	1,573,000	1,206,000	939,000	1,133,000	833,000	987,000	1,110,000
Shares Outstanding	163,200	165,800	167,100	172,500	177,000	177,800	181,000	183,600
Statistical Record								
Return on Assets %	16.47	16.65	14.86	13.17	10.99	10.02	9.10	5.88
Return on Equity %	42.45	42.10	44.48	38.22	30.54	28.35	22.51	13.78
EBITDA Margin %	23.47	22.47	21.33	18.52	18.60	18.65	18.06	12.70
Net Margin %	13.85	13.25	12.35	11.49	10.27	10.15	9.47	4.93
Asset Turnover	1.25	1.26	1.20	1.15	1.07	0.99	0.96	1.19
Current Ratio	1.40	1.49	1.46	1.51	1.73	1.58	1.38	1.44
Debt to Equity	0.15	0.14	0.20	0.21	0.18	...	...	...
Price Range	75.86-62.90	74.50-55.15	60.32-43.80	49.55-35.28	37.14-25.25	27.67-17.34	27.55-13.50	26.90-12.95
P/E Ratio	21.43-17.77	21.59-15.99	22.10-16.04	22.52-16.04	22.24-15.12	19.35-12.13	21.52-10.55	37.36-17.99
Average Yield %	0.92	0.97	1.09	1.08	1.25	1.60	1.67	0.45

Address: 400 Collins Road N.E., Cedar Rapids, IA 52498 Telephone: 319-295-1000	Web Site: www.rockwellcollins.com Officers: Clayton M. Jones - Chmn., Pres., C.E.O. Robert M. Chiusano - Exec. V.P., C.O.O., Commercial Systems	Auditors: Deloitte & Touche LLP Investor Contact: 319-295-7575 Transfer Agents: Wells Fargo Shareowner Services, St. Paul, MN

ROHM & HAAS CO.

Exchange	Symbol	Price	52Wk Range	Yield	P/E	Div Acheiver
NYS	ROH	$54.08 (3/31/2008)	61.27-47.21	2.74	17.28	30 Years

*7 Year Price Score 101.21 *NYSE Composite Index=100 *12 Month Price Score 107.52

Interim Earnings (Per Share)

Qtr.	Mar	Jun	Sep	Dec
2003	0.33	(0.02)	0.45	0.49
2004	0.51	0.52	0.61	0.58
2005	0.70	0.79	0.76	0.60
2006	0.93	0.75	0.85	0.80
2007	0.87	0.74	0.61	0.89

Interim Dividends (Per Share)

Amt	Decl	Ex	Rec	Pay
0.37Q	5/7/2007	5/16/2007	5/18/2007	6/1/2007
0.37Q	7/16/2007	8/8/2007	8/10/2007	9/4/2007
0.37Q	9/28/2007	10/31/2007	11/2/2007	12/1/2007
0.37Q	2/4/2008	2/13/2008	2/15/2008	3/1/2008

Indicated Div: $1.48 (Div. Reinv. Plan)

Valuation Analysis / **Institutional Holding**

Forecast P/E	13.10	No of Institutions
	(1/10/2007)	352
Market Cap	$10.6 Billion	Shares
Book Value	3.1 Billion	123,253,392
Price/Book	3.37	% Held
Price/Sales	1.19	56.29

TRADING VOLUME (thousand shares)

Business Summary: Chemicals (MIC: 11.1 SIC: 2821 NAIC: 325211)

Rohm & Haas is a specialty materials company that operates through seven reportable segments: Electronic Technologies, Display Technologies, Primary Materials, Paint and Coatings Materials, Packaging and Building Materials, Performance Materials Group, and Salt. In addition, Co. serves several market places, including building and construction, electronics, packaging and paper, industrial and other, transportation, household and personal care, water and food. In order to serve these markets, Co. had operations in about 96 manufacturing and 35 research facilities in 27 countries, as of Dec 31 2007.

Recent Developments: For the year ended Dec 31 2007, income from continuing operations decreased 12.6% to US$660.0 million from US$755.0 million a year earlier. Net income decreased 10.1% to US$661.0 million from US$735.0 million in the prior year. Revenues were US$8.90 billion, up 8.1% from US$8.23 billion the year before. Direct operating expenses rose 11.9% to US$6.43 billion from US$5.75 billion in the comparable period the year before. Indirect operating expenses increased 9.0% to US$1.54 billion from US$1.41 billion in the equivalent prior-year period.

Prospects: On Jan 15 2008, Co. agreed to acquire the FINNDISP division of OY Forcit AB, a Finnish paint emulsions operation, for $85.0 million. The acquisition strengthens Co.'s position mainly in Russia, and expands its technology products, mainly products for low-temperature climates. Co. also expects the FINNDISP division to add 2008 sales of Euro40.0 million to Euro50.0 million. The transaction is expected to close by the end of the first quarter of 2008. For 2008, Co. expects sales of about $10.00 billion, up 12.0% from 2007, with earnings per share from continuing operations of $3.80 to $4.00, excluding any potential new mergers and acquisitions or restructuring, up11.0% to 17.0% from 2007.

Financial Data

(US$ in Thousands)	12/31/2007	12/31/2006	12/31/2005	12/31/2004	12/31/2003	12/31/2002	12/31/2001	12/31/2000
Earnings Per Share	3.13	3.32	2.85	2.22	1.26	(2.57)	1.79	1.61
Cash Flow Per Share	4.63	3.84	4.27	3.95	4.51	4.41	3.17	3.50
Tang Book Value Per Share	N.M.	4.58	3.14	1.37	0.13	N.M.	N.M.	N.M.
Dividends Per Share	1.440	1.280	1.120	0.970	0.860	0.820	0.800	0.780
Dividend Payout %	46.01	38.55	39.30	43.69	68.25	...	44.69	48.45
Income Statement								
Total Revenue	8,897,000	8,230,000	7,994,000	7,300,000	6,421,000	5,727,000	5,666,000	6,879,000
EBITDA	1,451,000	1,570,000	1,453,000	1,319,000	1,014,000	903,000	672,000	1,428,000
Income Before Taxes	880,000	1,042,000	872,000	714,000	415,000	320,000	(64,000)	581,000
Income Taxes	206,000	274,000	224,000	207,000	127,000	102,000	6,000	227,000
Net Income	661,000	735,000	637,000	497,000	280,000	(570,000)	395,000	354,000
Average Shares	211,000	221,200	223,900	224,200	222,400	221,900	220,200	220,500
Balance Sheet								
Current Assets	3,527,000	3,411,000	3,205,000	3,247,000	2,527,000	2,543,000	2,421,000	2,781,000
Total Assets	10,208,000	9,553,000	9,727,000	10,095,000	9,445,000	9,706,000	10,350,000	11,267,000
Current Liabilities	1,870,000	1,988,000	1,694,000	1,740,000	1,797,000	1,621,000	1,624,000	2,194,000
Long-Term Obligations	3,139,000	1,688,000	2,074,000	2,563,000	2,468,000	2,872,000	2,720,000	3,225,000
Total Liabilities	6,847,000	5,400,000	5,699,000	6,294,000	6,075,000	6,576,000	6,517,000	7,591,000
Stockholders' Equity	3,146,000	4,031,000	3,917,000	3,697,000	3,357,000	3,119,000	3,815,000	3,653,000
Shares Outstanding	195,851	218,838	221,962	225,260	222,453	221,131	220,427	219,937
Statistical Record								
Return on Assets %	6.69	7.62	6.43	5.07	2.92	N.M.	3.65	3.13
Return on Equity %	18.42	18.50	16.73	14.05	8.65	N.M.	10.58	9.91
EBITDA Margin %	16.31	19.08	18.18	18.07	15.79	15.77	11.86	20.76
Net Margin %	7.43	8.93	7.97	6.81	4.36	N.M.	6.97	5.15
Asset Turnover	0.90	0.85	0.81	0.75	0.67	0.57	0.52	0.61
Current Ratio	1.89	1.72	1.89	1.87	1.41	1.57	1.49	1.27
Debt to Equity	1.00	0.42	0.53	0.69	0.74	0.92	0.71	0.88
Price Range	61.27-47.21	53.86-42.77	49.62-39.91	45.17-36.16	42.92-26.67	42.27-30.55	38.27-26.12	47.88-26.00
P/E Ratio	19.58-15.08	16.22-12.88	17.41-14.00	20.35-16.29	34.06-21.17	...	21.38-14.59	29.74-16.15
Average Yield %	2.69	2.61	2.48	2.39	2.53	...	2.25	2.35	2.26

Address: 100 Independence Mall West, Philadelphia, PA 19106-2399
Telephone: 215-592-3000
Fax: 215-592-3377

Web Site: www.rohmhaas.com
Officers: Raj L. Gupta - Chmn., C.E.O., Pres. Alan E. Barton - V.P., Coatings, Business Unit Director, Architectural Functional Coatings

Auditors: PricewaterhouseCoopers LLP
Transfer Agents: EquiServe Trust Company, N.A., Providence, RI

ROLLINS, INC.

Exchange	Symbol	Price	52Wk Range	Yield	P/E
NYS	ROL	$17.69 (3/31/2008)	20.57-14.72	1.41	27.64

*7 Year Price Score 125.34 *NYSE Composite Index=100 *12 Month Price Score 110.79

TRADING VOLUME (thousand shares)

Interim Earnings (Per Share)

Qtr.	Mar	Jun	Sep	Dec
2003	0.11	0.20	0.14	0.07
2004	0.13	0.34	0.17	0.11
2005	0.17	0.27	0.22	0.11
2006	0.16	0.28	0.25	0.15
2007	0.19	0.31	0.28	(0.14)

Interim Dividends (Per Share)

Amt	Decl	Ex	Rec	Pay
0.05Q	7/24/2007	8/8/2007	8/10/2007	9/10/2007
0.05Q	10/23/2007	11/7/2007	11/12/2007	12/10/2007
3-for-2	10/23/2007	12/11/2007	11/12/2007	12/10/2007
0.063Q	1/22/2008	2/6/2008	2/8/2008	3/10/2008

Indicated Div: $0.25

Valuation Analysis

		Institutional Holding	
Forecast P/E	N/A	No of Institutions	117
Market Cap	$1.8 Billion	Shares	
Book Value	233.6 Million	26,033,012	
Price/Book	7.62	% Held	
Price/Sales	1.99	38.17	

Business Summary: Miscellaneous Business Services (MIC: 12.8 SIC: 7342 NAIC: 561710)

Rollins provides pest control services to both residential and commercial customers in North America. Services are performed through a contract that specifies the pricing arrangement with the customer. Orkin, Inc. (Orkin), a wholly owned subsidiary of Co., provides customized services from over 400 locations to approximately 1.7 million customers as of Dec 31 2007. Orkin serves customers in the U.S., Canada, Mexico, Central America, the Caribbean, the Middle East and Asia providing pest control services and protection against termite damage, rodents and insects to homes and businesses, including hotels, food service establishments, food manufacturers, retailers and transportation companies.

Recent Developments: For the year ended Dec 31 2007, net income increased 12.0% to US$64.7 million from US$57.8 million in the prior year. Revenues were US$894.9 million, up 4.2% from US$858.9 million the year before. Direct operating expenses rose 2.4% to US$468.7 million from US$457.9 million in the comparable period the year before. Indirect operating expenses increased 5.1% to US$321.3 million from US$305.9 million in the equivalent prior-year period.

Prospects: Co.'s near-term outlook appears to be constructive, reflecting an increase in commercial revenue due to expanded sales force, improved customer retention in both its Orkin, Inc. (Orkin) and Western Pest Services operations, and strong growth at PCO Services, Inc., Orkin's Canadian business, which is fundamentally a commercial business. Meanwhile, on Feb 4 2008, Co. announced that it has expanded its international presence through the establishment of franchises in the city of Jeddah, Kingdom of Saudi Arabia and for the country of Qatar. Notably, this expansion adds to Co.'s presence internationally and increases its brand recognition, as well as adding its customers globally.

Financial Data

(US$ in Thousands)	12/31/2007	12/31/2006	12/31/2005	12/31/2004	12/31/2003	12/31/2002	12/31/2001	12/31/2000
Earnings Per Share	0.64	0.84	0.76	0.74	0.51	0.40	0.37	0.21
Cash Flow Per Share	0.88	1.27	1.14	1.05	0.92	0.80	0.65	0.25
Tang Book Value Per Share	0.34	0.14	N.M.	N.M.	0.53	N.M.	N.M.	N.M.
Dividends Per Share	0.200	0.167	0.133	0.107	0.089	0.059	0.059	0.059
Dividend Payout %	31.25	19.84	17.54	14.41	17.32	14.81	15.87	27.78
Income Statement								
Total Revenue	894,920	858,878	802,417	750,884	677,013	665,425	652,286	649,558
EBITDA	131,981	122,019	112,235	121,746	80,209	65,361	47,618	33,824
Income Before Taxes	104,913	95,159	87,955	98,712	60,030	43,726	27,326	15,403
Income Taxes	40,182	37,350	35,182	40,453	24,269	16,616	10,384	5,853
Net Income	64,731	57,809	52,773	52,055	35,761	27,110	16,942	9,550
Average Shares	101,409	68,876	69,772	70,167	69,309	68,113	45,399	45,069
Balance Sheet								
Current Assets	160,240	151,073	137,684	146,805	170,371	126,222	100,483	88,969
Total Assets	475,228	453,175	439,637	418,780	349,904	317,407	296,559	298,819
Current Liabilities	187,701	185,206	190,885	187,980	145,022	129,862	108,536	110,806
Long-Term Obligations	601	124	560	...	...	...	...	256
Total Liabilities	241,675	241,716	262,686	251,231	211,130	226,717	211,061	220,220
Stockholders' Equity	233,553	211,459	176,951	167,549	138,774	90,690	85,498	78,599
Shares Outstanding	100,635	67,891	68,011	68,504	67,735	67,199	45,104	45,054
Statistical Record								
Return on Assets %	13.94	12.95	12.30	13.51	10.72	8.83	5.69	3.11
Return on Equity %	29.09	29.77	30.64	33.89	31.17	30.77	20.65	12.67
EBITDA Margin %	14.75	14.21	13.99	16.21	11.85	9.82	7.30	5.21
Net Margin %	7.23	6.73	6.58	6.93	5.28	4.07	2.60	1.47
Asset Turnover	1.93	1.92	1.87	1.95	2.03	2.17	2.19	2.12
Current Ratio	0.85	0.82	0.72	0.78	1.17	0.97	0.93	0.80
Price Range	20.57-13.98	15.17-12.64	14.69-10.66	12.04-9.55	10.88-7.43	8.22-5.42	6.24-4.45	6.48-3.37
P/E Ratio	32.14-21.84	18.06-15.05	19.32-14.02	16.28-12.91	21.34-14.56	20.55-13.56	16.86-12.02	30.86-16.05
Average Yield %	1.20	1.21	1.04	0.98	0.99	0.96	1.07	1.29

Address: 2170 Piedmont Road, N.E., Atlanta, GA 30324	Officers: R. Randall Rollins - Chmn. Gary W. Rollins - Pres., C.E.O., C.O.O.	Auditors: Grant Thornton LLP
Telephone: 404-888-2000 Fax: 404-888-2670		Investor Contact: 404-888-2000

ROPER INDUSTRIES, INC

Exchange	Symbol	Price	52Wk Range	Yield	P/E	Div Achiever
NYS	ROP	$59.44 (3/31/2008)	70.81-50.05	0.49	22.18	15 Years

*7 Year Price Score 142.17 *NYSE Composite Index=100 *12 Month Price Score 101.33

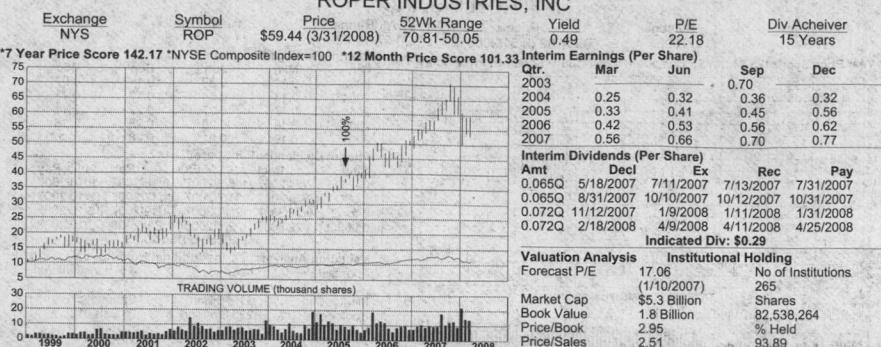

Interim Earnings (Per Share)

Qtr.	Mar	Jun	Sep	Dec
2003			0.70	
2004	0.25	0.32	0.36	0.32
2005	0.33	0.41	0.45	0.56
2006	0.42	0.53	0.56	0.62
2007	0.56	0.66	0.70	0.77

Interim Dividends (Per Share)

Amt	Decl	Ex	Rec	Pay
0.065Q	5/18/2007	7/11/2007	7/13/2007	7/31/2007
0.065Q	8/31/2007	10/10/2007	10/12/2007	10/31/2007
0.072Q	11/12/2007	1/9/2008	1/11/2008	1/31/2008
0.072Q	2/18/2008	4/9/2008	4/11/2008	4/25/2008

Indicated Div: $0.29

Valuation Analysis | **Institutional Holding**

Forecast P/E	17.06	No of Institutions
	(1/10/2007)	265
Market Cap	$5.3 Billion	Shares
Book Value	1.8 Billion	82,538,264
Price/Book	2.95	% Held
Price/Sales	2.51	93.89

Business Summary: Industrial Machinery and Equipment (MIC: 11.5 SIC: 3823 NAIC: 334513)

Roper Industries is engaged in the designing, manufacturing and distribution of energy systems and controls, scientific and industrial imaging products and software, radio frequency (RF) products and services, and industrial technology products. Co. markets its products and services to a range of markets, including RF applications, water, energy, research/medical and general industry. At Dec 31 2007, Co. operated in four segments: Industrial Technology, Energy Systems and Controls, Scientific and Industrial Imaging, and RF Technology. Co.'s products include fluid properties testing equipment, industrial pumps, digital imaging products and software, and radio frequency identification.

Recent Developments: For the year ended Dec 31 2007, net income increased 29.3% to US$250.0 million from US$193.3 million in the prior year. Revenues were US$2.10 billion, up 23.6% from US$1.70 billion the year before. Operating income was US$438.4 million versus US$337.7 million in the prior year, an increase of 29.8%. Direct operating expenses rose 24.3% to US$1.04 billion from US$839.4 million in the comparable period the year before. Indirect operating expenses increased 18.4% to US$620.0 million from US$523.7 million in the equivalent prior-year period.

Prospects: Co. is optimistic with its 2008 outlook as a result of its solid year end backlog and strong order growth. Specifically, Co. estimates its net earnings of at least US$294.0 million, with diluted earnings of $3.10 to $3.20 per share for the full year. Meanwhile, on Feb 21 2008, Co. announced its acquisition of CBORD Group, Inc., a provider of card systems and integrated security applications, in a transaction valued at $367.0 million. Accordingly, Co. anticipates the transaction to add $0.02 to $0.03 to its 2008 diluted earnings per share; and to increase its 2009 diluted earnings per share by up to $0.10, while enhancing the market presence of its Radio Frequency segment.

Financial Data
(US$ in Thousands)

	12/31/2007	12/31/2006	12/31/2005	12/31/2004	12/31/2003	12/31/2002	10/31/2002	10/31/2001
Earnings Per Share	2.68	2.13	1.74	1.24	0.70	0.01	0.63	0.89
Cash Flow Per Share	3.89	3.02	3.29	2.21	1.13	0.10	1.39	1.67
Dividends Per Share	0.260	0.235	0.212	0.193	0.175	0.165	0.165	0.150
Dividend Payout %	9.70	11.03	12.21	15.52	24.82	1,100.00	26.19	16.95
Income Statement								
Total Revenue	2,102,049	1,700,734	1,453,731	969,764	657,356	83,885	627,030	586,506
EBITDA	529,032	419,717	335,280	203,950	99,052	7,367	129,368	129,811
Income Before Taxes	383,657	292,872	220,567	133,716	66,290	1,769	95,686	86,439
Income Taxes	133,624	99,548	67,392	39,864	18,229	529	29,663	30,600
Net Income	250,033	193,324	153,175	93,852	45,239	853	40,053	55,839
Average Shares	93,229	90,880	87,884	75,664	63,984	63,708	63,630	62,986
Balance Sheet								
Current Assets	951,137	627,495	498,207	556,160	381,192	247,565	247,622	233,053
Total Assets	3,453,184	2,995,359	2,522,306	2,366,404	1,514,995	824,966	828,973	762,122
Current Liabilities	667,530	587,649	505,425	253,550	161,497	121,344	130,237	103,880
Long-Term Obligations	727,489	726,881	620,958	855,364	630,186	308,684	311,590	323,830
Total Liabilities	1,663,378	1,508,520	1,272,518	1,252,318	859,214	443,985	452,961	438,616
Stockholders' Equity	1,789,806	1,486,839	1,249,788	1,114,086	655,781	380,981	376,012	323,506
Shares Outstanding	88,773	87,779	85,960	84,832	72,084	62,740	62,726	61,758
Statistical Record								
Return on Assets %	7.75	7.01	6.27	4.82	3.87	0.09	5.03	8.22
Return on Equity %	15.26	14.13	12.96	10.58	8.73	0.21	11.45	18.81
EBITDA Margin %	25.17	24.68	23.06	21.03	15.07	8.78	20.63	22.13
Net Margin %	11.89	11.37	10.54	9.68	6.88	1.02	6.39	9.52
Asset Turnover	0.65	0.62	0.59	0.50	0.56	0.09	0.79	0.86
Current Ratio	1.42	1.07	0.99	2.19	2.36	2.04	1.90	2.24
Debt to Equity	0.41	0.49	0.50	0.77	0.96	0.81	0.83	1.00
Price Range	70.81-48.61	51.31-38.50	40.51-28.39	31.66-22.64	25.79-13.38	21.57-18.23	25.90-13.68	22.75-15.03
P/E Ratio	26.42-18.14	24.09-18.08	23.28-16.31	25.53-18.25	36.84-19.11	N.M.	41.11-21.71	25.56-16.89
Average Yield %	0.44	0.51	0.60	0.71	0.89		0.84	0.79

Address: 6901 Professional Parkway East, Suite 200, Sarasota, FL 34240 **Telephone:** 770-495-5100 **Fax:** 770-495-5150	**Web Site:** www.roperind.com **Officers:** Brian D. Jellison - Chmn., Pres., C.E.O. Shanler D. Cronk - V.P., Sec., Couns.	**Auditors:** PricewaterhouseCoopers LLP **Transfer Agents:** Wachovia Bank, N.A., Charlotte, NC

ROWAN COS., INC.

Exchange	Symbol	Price	52Wk Range	Yield	P/E
NYS	RDC	$41.18 (3/31/2008)	45.70-32.68	0.97	9.55

*7 Year Price Score 108.29 *NYSE Composite Index=100 *12 Month Price Score 108.15

Interim Earnings (Per Share)

Qtr.	Mar	Jun	Sep	Dec
2003	(0.18)	(0.07)	0.12	0.05
2004	(0.11)	(0.02)	0.09	0.02
2005	0.40	0.39	0.67	0.62
2006	0.53	0.98	0.78	0.56
2007	0.77	1.14	1.16	1.23

Interim Dividends (Per Share)

Amt	Decl	Ex	Rec	Pay
0.10Q	5/9/2007	5/18/2007	5/22/2007	6/6/2007
0.10Q	7/31/2007	8/10/2007	8/14/2007	8/29/2007
0.10Q	10/30/2007	11/9/2007	11/14/2007	11/30/2007
0.10Q	1/31/2008	2/12/2008	2/14/2008	2/29/2008

Indicated Div: $0.40

Valuation Analysis   **Institutional Holding**

Forecast P/E	5.67	No of Institutions
	(1/10/2007)	294
Market Cap	$4.6 Billion	Shares
Book Value	2.3 Billion	87,327,464
Price/Book	1.95	% Held
Price/Sales	2.19	79.03

TRADING VOLUME (thousand shares)

Business Summary: Oil and Gas (MIC: 14.2 SIC: 1381 NAIC: 213111)

Rowan Companies is engaged in the business of providing international and domestic contract drilling services. Co. also owns and operates a manufacturing division that produces equipment for the drilling, mining and timber industries. As of Dec 31 2007, Co. provided contract drilling services utilizing a fleet of 21 self-elevating mobile offshore drilling platforms (jack-up rigs) and 29 deep-well land drilling rigs. Co. conducts drilling operations primarily in the Gulf of Mexico, the Middle East, the North Sea, Trinidad, offshore eastern Canada, offshore West Africa, and onshore in the U.S.

Recent Developments: For the year ended Dec 31 2007, net income increased 52.0% to US$483.8 million from US$318.2 million in the prior year. Revenues were US$2.10 billion, up 38.7% from US$1.51 billion the year before. Operating income was US$733.9 million versus US$485.7 million in the prior year, an increase of 51.1%. Direct operating expenses rose 35.4% to US$1.19 billion from US$877.1 million in the comparable period the year before. Indirect operating expenses increased 17.1% to US$173.2 million from US$147.9 million in the equivalent prior-year period.

Prospects: On Jan 8 2008, Co. announced that it has signed a drilling contract for one of its rigs for approximately six months of work offshore eastern Canada that should begin in mid 2009, over which Co. expects total revenues, including mobilization and modification fees, of approximately $56.0 million. Separately, on Feb 21 2008, Co. announced that it has been awarded a term drilling contract for work offshore Saudi Arabia. The contract provides for a three-year term, over which Co. expects total revenues of approximately $201.0 million, and contains an option for a fourth year. The rig is expected to commence drilling operations in the second quarter of 2008.

Financial Data

(US$ in Thousands)	12/31/2007	12/31/2006	12/31/2005	12/31/2004	12/31/2003	12/31/2002	12/31/2001	12/31/2000
Earnings Per Share	4.31	2.85	2.08	(0.01)	(0.08)	0.90	0.80	0.74
Cash Flow Per Share	3.90	2.65	3.06	1.11	0.51	1.26	2.99	1.12
Tang Book Value Per Share	21.11	16.97	14.75	13.12	12.08	12.09	11.84	11.17
Dividends Per Share	0.400	0.550	0.500	...	...	0.250	...	...
Dividend Payout %	9.28	19.30	24.04	...	...	27.78	...	...
Income Statement								
Total Revenue	2,095,021	1,510,734	1,068,782	708,501	679,088	617,258	731,064	645,959
EBITDA	852,895	575,867	431,917	152,743	89,660	222,727	193,394	...
Income Before Taxes	739,086	493,354	345,470	42,785	(11,952)	132,819	120,207	...
Income Taxes	255,286	176,377	127,633	16,414	(4,178)	46,541	43,209	40,650
Net Income	483,800	318,246	229,800	(1,273)	(7,774)	86,278	76,998	70,213
Average Shares	112,265	111,775	110,304	107,133	93,820	95,392	95,811	94,637
Balance Sheet								
Current Assets	1,302,967	1,102,849	1,208,132	814,693	444,224	469,902	506,682	483,357
Total Assets	3,875,305	3,435,398	2,975,183	2,492,286	2,190,809	2,054,504	1,938,955	1,678,426
Current Liabilities	495,589	516,706	340,613	234,800	150,365	115,975	201,494	104,354
Long-Term Obligations	420,482	485,404	550,326	574,350	569,067	512,844	438,484	372,212
Total Liabilities	1,526,867	1,561,352	1,355,444	1,083,402	1,053,979	922,727	830,868	625,669
Stockholders' Equity	2,348,438	1,874,046	1,619,739	1,408,884	1,136,830	1,131,777	1,108,087	1,052,757
Shares Outstanding	111,263	110,461	109,776	107,408	94,110	93,606	93,567	94,234
Statistical Record								
Return on Assets %	13.24	9.93	8.41	N.M.	N.M.	4.32	4.26	4.62
Return on Equity %	22.92	18.22	15.18	N.M.	N.M.	7.70	7.13	7.88
EBITDA Margin %	40.71	38.12	40.41	21.56	13.20	36.08	26.45	...
Net Margin %	23.09	21.07	21.50	N.M.	N.M.	13.98	10.53	10.87
Asset Turnover	0.57	0.47	0.39	0.30	0.32	0.31	0.40	0.42
Current Ratio	2.63	2.13	3.55	3.47	2.95	4.05	2.51	4.63
Debt to Equity	0.18	0.26	0.34	0.41	0.50	0.45	0.40	0.35
Price Range	45.70-29.72	47.95-29.64	38.88-24.83	27.05-20.62	26.38-17.93	26.84-16.11	33.42-11.75	33.63-19.44
P/E Ratio	10.60-6.90	16.82-10.40	18.69-11.94	...	...	29.82-17.90	41.78-14.69	45.44-26.27
Average Yield %	1.09	1.47	1.59	...	...	1.19	...	...

Address: 2800 Post Oak Blvd., Suite 5450, Houston, TX 77056-6127 **Telephone:** 713-621-7800 **Fax:** 713-960-7660	**Web Site:** www.rowancompanies.com **Officers:** D. F. McNease - Chmn., Pres., C.E.O. C. R. Palmer - Chmn. Emeritus	**Auditors:** Deloitte & Touche LLP **Investor Contact:** 713-960-7575 **Transfer Agents:** Computershare Trust Co., Inc., Golden, CO

RPM INTERNATIONAL INC (DE)

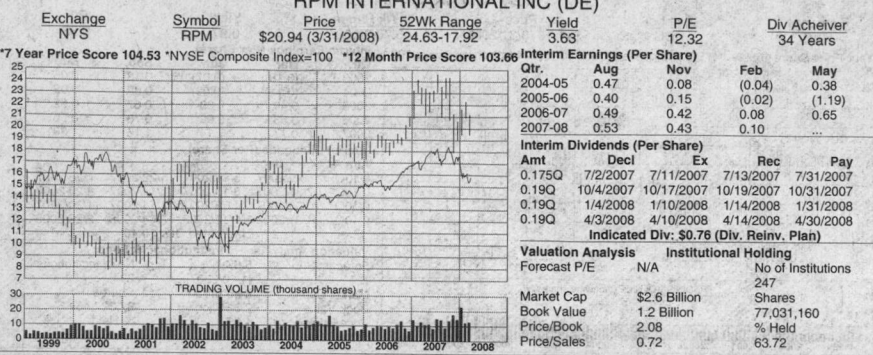

Exchange	Symbol	Price	52Wk Range	Yield	P/E	Div Acheiver
NYS	RPM	$20.94 (3/31/2008)	24.63-17.92	3.63	12.32	34 Years

*7 Year Price Score 104.53 *NYSE Composite Index=100 *12 Month Price Score 103.66

Interim Earnings (Per Share)

Qtr.	Aug	Nov	Feb	May
2004-05	0.47	0.08	(0.04)	0.38
2005-06	0.40	0.15	(0.02)	(1.19)
2006-07	0.49	0.42	0.08	0.65
2007-08	0.53	0.43	0.10	...

Interim Dividends (Per Share)

Amt	Decl	Ex	Rec	Pay
0.175Q	7/2/2007	7/11/2007	7/13/2007	7/31/2007
0.19Q	10/4/2007	10/17/2007	10/19/2007	10/31/2007
0.19Q	1/4/2008	1/10/2008	1/14/2008	1/31/2008
0.19Q	4/3/2008	4/10/2008	4/14/2008	4/30/2008

Indicated Div: $0.76 (Div. Reinv. Plan)

Valuation Analysis

			Institutional Holding	
Forecast P/E	N/A		No of Institutions	247
Market Cap	$2.6 Billion		Shares	77,031,160
Book Value	1.2 Billion		% Held	63.72
Price/Book	2.08			
Price/Sales	0.72			

Business Summary: Chemicals (MIC: 11.1 SIC: 2851 NAIC: 325510)

RPM International manufactures, markets and sells chemical product lines, including paints, protective coatings, roofing systems, sealants and adhesives, to the industrial and consumer markets. Co.'s products include those marketed under brand names such as CARBOLINE, DAP, DAY-GLO, DRYVIT, EUCO, FLECTO, ILLBRUCK, RUST-OLEUM, STONHARD, TREMCO and ZINSSER. As of May 31 2007, Co.'s subsidiaries marketed products in 149 countries and territories and operated manufacturing facilities in about 90 locations in the U.S., Argentina, Belgium, Canada, China, Colombia, The Czech Republic, Germany, Italy, Mexico, The Netherlands, New Zealand, Poland, South Africa, the United Arab Emirates and the U.K.

Recent Developments: For the quarter ended Feb 29 2008, net income increased 20.9% to US$12.2 million from US$10.1 million in the year-earlier quarter. Revenues were US$731.8 million, up 7.7% from US$679.5 million the year before. Direct operating expenses rose 5.9% to US$440.5 million from US$416.0 million in the comparable period the year before. Indirect operating expenses increased 10.5% to US$266.2 million from US$241.0 million in the equivalent prior-year period.

Prospects: On Nov 9 2007, Co. sold its Bondo auto body repair products subsidiary to 3M's Automotive Aftermarket Division for proceeds of $45.0 million, which generated a one-time, pre-tax gain of $2.2 million. Meanwhile, Co. continues to expand its business through acquisitions. For instance, in Dec 2007, Co.'s Euclid Chemical Company subsidiary acquired Productos Cave S.A., a Santiago, Chile-based manufacturer of restoration, waterproofing and concrete admixture products, with annual sales of approximately $5.0 million at Dec 31 2006. Separately, for the fiscal year ending May 2008, Co. expects sales and earnings growth in the 8.0% range, excluding the effect of asbestos-related items.

Financial Data

(US$ in Thousands)	9 Mos	6 Mos	3 Mos	05/31/2007	05/31/2006	05/31/2005	05/31/2004	05/31/2003
Earnings Per Share	1.70	1.69	1.68	1.64	(0.65)	0.86	1.22	0.30
Cash Flow Per Share	1.91	1.79	1.47	1.71	1.59	1.35	1.32	1.39
Tang Book Value Per Share	0.20	0.27	N.M.	N.M.	N.M.	0.91	0.38	N.M.
Dividends Per Share	0.730	0.715	0.700	0.685	0.630	0.590	0.550	0.515
Dividend Payout %	42.87	42.31	41.67	41.77	...	68.60	45.08	171.67
Income Statement								
Total Revenue	2,567,820	1,836,047	930,339	3,338,764	3,008,338	2,555,735	2,341,572	2,083,489
EBITDA	293,714	247,662	133,745	431,324	(9,369)	261,947	322,638	145,143
Depn & Amortn	62,402	41,775	20,878	...	...	...	...	...
Income Before Taxes	196,685	181,062	100,149	307,535	(122,475)	163,728	217,616	47,853
Income Taxes	61,412	57,939	31,881	99,246	(46,270)	58,696	75,730	12,526
Net Income	135,273	123,123	68,268	208,289	(76,205)	105,032	141,886	35,327
Average Shares	130,223	130,608	130,026	128,711	116,837	126,364	116,710	115,986
Balance Sheet								
Current Assets	1,678,497	1,510,718	1,546,252	1,570,249	1,369,218	1,271,495	994,617	928,094
Total Assets	3,433,852	3,259,681	3,297,820	3,333,149	2,980,218	2,656,245	2,353,119	2,247,211
Current Liabilities	744,393	738,450	764,676	864,740	713,500	575,339	477,493	427,650
Long-Term Obligations	1,031,740	840,564	921,734	886,416	870,415	837,948	718,929	724,846
Total Liabilities	2,207,022	2,028,580	2,154,457	2,246,279	2,054,277	1,609,736	1,377,827	1,370,203
Stockholders' Equity	1,226,830	1,231,101	1,143,363	1,086,870	925,941	1,046,509	975,292	877,008
Shares Outstanding	121,819	121,782	121,299	120,906	118,743	117,554	116,122	115,496
Statistical Record								
Return on Assets %	6.81	6.90	6.85	6.60	N.M.	4.19	6.15	1.65
Return on Equity %	19.35	19.24	20.33	20.70	N.M.	10.39	15.28	4.07
EBITDA Margin %	11.43	13.49	14.38	12.92	N.M.	10.25	13.78	6.97
Net Margin %	5.27	6.71	7.34	6.24	N.M.	4.11	6.06	1.70
Asset Turnover	1.11	1.12	1.09	1.06	1.07	1.02	1.02	0.97
Current Ratio	2.25	2.04	2.02	1.82	1.92	2.21	2.08	2.17
Debt to Equity	0.84	0.68	0.81	0.82	0.94	0.80	0.74	0.83
Price Range	24.63-17.92	24.63-17.92	24.63-18.57	24.18-17.64	19.46-17.11	19.83-14.02	17.10-12.55	16.06-9.20
P/E Ratio	14.49-10.54	14.57-10.60	14.66-11.05	14.74-10.76	...	23.06-16.30	14.02-10.29	53.53-30.67
Average Yield %	3.33	3.22	3.23	3.35	3.43	3.43	3.73	3.88

Address: 2628 Pearl Road, P.O. Box 777, Medina, OH 44258
Telephone: 330-273-5090
Fax: 330-225-8743

Web Site: www.rpminc.com
Officers: Thomas C. Sullivan - Chmn. Frank C. Sullivan - Pres., C.E.O.

Auditors: Ernst & Young LLP
Transfer Agents: National City Bank, Cleveland, OH

RUBY TUESDAY, INC.

Exchange	Symbol	Price	52Wk Range	Yield	P/E
NYS	RT	$7.50 (3/31/2008)	28.59-5.74	6.67	7.89

*7 Year Price Score 62.15   *NYSE Composite Index=100   *12 Month Price Score 43.90

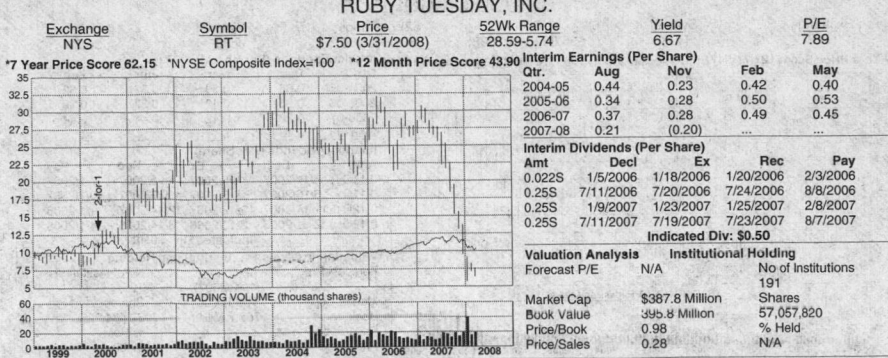

Interim Earnings (Per Share)

Qtr.	Aug	Nov	Feb	May
2004-05	0.44	0.23	0.42	0.40
2005-06	0.34	0.28	0.50	0.53
2006-07	0.37	0.28	0.49	0.45
2007-08	0.21	(0.20)	...	...

Interim Dividends (Per Share)

Amt	Decl	Ex	Rec	Pay
0.022S	1/5/2006	1/18/2006	1/20/2006	2/3/2006
0.25S	7/11/2006	7/20/2006	7/24/2006	8/8/2006
0.25S	1/9/2007	1/23/2007	1/25/2007	2/8/2007
0.25S	7/11/2007	7/19/2007	7/23/2007	8/7/2007

Indicated Div: $0.50

Valuation Analysis

Forecast P/E	N/A
Market Cap	$387.8 Million
Book Value	395.8 Million
Price/Book	0.98
Price/Sales	0.28

Institutional Holding

No of Institutions	191
Shares	57,057,820
% Held	N/A

Business Summary: Hospitality & Tourism (MIC: 5.1 SIC: 5812 NAIC: 722110)

Ruby Tuesday owns and operates the Ruby Tuesday concept in the bar and grill segment of casual dining. Co. also provides franchises for the Ruby Tuesday concept in domestic and international markets. In addition, Co. provides American dining emphasizing 13 appetizers, handcrafted burgers, a garden bar, which provides up to 46 items, fresh chicken, steaks, crab cakes, salmon, tilapia, ribs, and more. As of June 5 2007, Co. owned and operated 680 casual dining restaurants, located in 28 states and the District of Columbia. Also, as of June 5 2007, Co.'s franchise partnerships operated 154 restaurants and traditional franchisees operated 45 domestic and 54 international restaurants.

Recent Developments: For the quarter ended Dec 4 2007, net loss amounted to US$10.4 million versus net income of US$16.7 million in the year-earlier quarter. Revenues were US$320.9 million, down 4.7% from US$336.8 million the year before. Direct operating expenses rose 4.3% to US$158.8 million from US$152.2 million in the comparable period the year before. Indirect operating expenses increased 11.0% to US$177.3 million from US$159.7 million in the equivalent prior-year period.

Prospects: For the fiscal year ending June 3 2008, Co. expects earnings of $0.40 to $0.60 per diluted share, based on several factors, including same-restaurant sales of down 6.0% to 8.5% as well as about 20 Company-owned openings and 15 to 20 franchise openings. Also, Co. estimates capital expenditures of US$65.0 million to US$75.0 million and US$50.0 million to US$55.0 million for new restaurants and improvements at existing restaurants as well as for the remodeling of Company-owned restaurants, respectively. For the rest of fiscal 2008, Co. plans to open 11 additional Company-owned Ruby Tuesday restaurants as well as 8 to 13 additional Ruby Tuesday restaurants of domestic and international franchisees.

Financial Data

(US$ in Thousands)	6 Mos	3 Mos	06/05/2007	06/06/2006	05/31/2005	06/01/2004	06/03/2003	06/04/2002
Earnings Per Share	0.95	1.43	1.59	1.65	1.56	1.64	1.36	0.88
Cash Flow Per Share	3.70	3.45	3.24	3.12	2.85	3.12	2.31	2.29
Tang Book Value Per Share	7.29	7.43	7.93	8.77	8.58	7.97	6.31	5.00
Dividends Per Share	0.500	0.500	0.500	0.045	0.045	0.045	0.045	0.045
Dividend Payout %	52.46	34.87	31.45	2.73	2.88	2.74	3.31	5.11
Income Statement								
Total Revenue	667,720	346,797	1,410,227	1,306,240	1,110,294	1,041,359	913,784	833,181
EBITDA	49,705	39,554	230,151	235,292	226,160	229,376	184,112	116,229
Depn & Amortn	49,050	23,733	...	...	...	...		
Income Before Taxes	655	15,821	132,398	150,958	154,946	170,816	135,710	88,146
Income Taxes	(84)	4,731	40,730	49,981	52,648	60,807	47,226	29,870
Net Income	739	11,090	91,668	100,977	102,298	110,009	88,484	58,218
Average Shares	51,380	52,429	57,633	61,301	65,524	67,076	65,093	65,912
Balance Sheet								
Current Assets	98,370	85,660	100,446	78,340	62,414	59,679	50,463	88,876
Total Assets	1,283,054	1,230,055	1,229,856	1,171,568	1,074,067	918,533	805,067	520,327
Current Liabilities	696,135	124,930	123,758	107,998	99,813	90,542	80,554	93,283
Long-Term Obligations	43,673	550,645	512,559	375,639	247,222	168,087	207,064	7,626
Total Liabilities	887,213	827,218	790,530	644,410	510,844	391,749	390,539	185,921
Stockholders' Equity	395,841	402,837	439,326	527,158	563,223	526,784	414,528	334,406
Shares Outstanding	51,713	51,690	53,240	58,191	63,687	65,549	64,404	64,188
Statistical Record								
Return on Assets %	4.37	6.71	7.66	8.85	10.30	12.80	13.39	12.09
Return on Equity %	11.15	17.33	19.02	18.22	18.82	23.44	23.69	18.87
EBITDA Margin %	7.44	11.41	16.32	18.01	20.37	22.03	20.15	13.95
Net Margin %	0.11	3.20	6.50	7.73	9.21	10.56	9.68	6.99
Asset Turnover	1.13	1.17	1.18	1.14	1.12	1.21	1.38	1.73
Current Ratio	0.14	0.69	0.81	0.73	0.63	0.66	0.63	0.95
Debt to Equity	0.11	1.37	1.17	0.71	0.44	0.32	0.50	0.02
Price Range	30.75-12.47	30.75-21.70	30.75-21.39	32.10-20.75	29.55-22.50	33.00-21.10	24.21-15.99	25.96-15.06
P/E Ratio	32.37-13.13	21.50-15.17	19.34-13.45	19.45-12.58	18.94-14.42	20.12-12.87	17.80-11.76	29.50-17.11
Average Yield %	2.05	1.84	1.85	0.17	0.17	0.17	0.24	0.22

Address: 150 West Church Avenue, Maryville, TN 37801
Telephone: 865-379-5700
Fax: 865-379-6817

Web Site: www.rubytuesday.com
Officers: Samuel E. Beall III - Chmn., Pres., C.E.O.
Marguerite N. Duffy - Sr. V.P., C.F.O.

Auditors: KPMG LLP
Transfer Agents: The Bank of New York

RUDDICK CORP.

Exchange	Symbol	Price	52Wk Range	Yield	P/E
NYS	RDK	$36.86 (3/31/2008)	37.65-27.80	1.30	20.71

*7 Year Price Score 121.71 *NYSE Composite Index=100 *12 Month Price Score 112.95

Interim Earnings (Per Share)

Qtr.	Dec	Mar	Jun	Sep
2004-05	0.35	0.39	0.37	0.32
2005-06	0.36	0.42	0.37	0.38
2006-07	0.38	0.42	0.44	0.44
2007-08	0.48	...	...	...

Interim Dividends (Per Share)

Amt	Decl	Ex	Rec	Pay
0.11Q	5/17/2007	6/6/2007	6/8/2007	7/1/2007
0.11Q	8/16/2007	9/5/2007	9/7/2007	10/1/2007
0.12Q	11/15/2007	12/12/2007	12/14/2007	1/1/2008
0.12Q	2/21/2008	3/12/2008	3/14/2008	4/1/2008

Indicated Div: $0.48

Valuation Analysis / Institutional Holding

Valuation Analysis		Institutional Holding	
Forecast P/E	13.47 (1/10/2007)	No of Institutions	125
Market Cap	$1.8 Billion	Shares	32,484,926
Book Value	757.7 Million	% Held	67.83
Price/Book	2.35		
Price/Sales	0.48		

Business Summary: Retail - Food & Beverage (MIC: 5.3 SIC: 5411 NAIC: 445110)

Ruddick is a holding company. Through its subsidiaries, Co. is engaged in two businesses; Harris Teeter, Inc., which operates a regional chain of supermarkets in seven southeastern states; and American & Efird, Inc. (A&E), which manufactures and distributes industrial sewing thread, embroidery thread and technical textiles on a global basis. Harris Teeter, Inc. provides groceries, produce, meat and seafood, delicatessen items, bakery items, wines and non-food items such as health and beauty care, and floral, as well as operates pharmacies in their supermarkets, while A&E provides its products to manufacturers of apparel, automotive materials, home furnishings, medical supplies and footwear.

Recent Developments: For the quarter ended Dec 30 2007, net income increased 27.6% to US$23.3 million from US$18.3 million in the year-earlier quarter. Revenues were US$976.7 million, up 10.9% from US$880.8 million the year before. Operating income was US$42.9 million versus US$33.8 million in the prior-year quarter, an increase of 26.8%. Direct operating expenses rose 10.7% to US$685.7 million from US$619.4 million in the comparable period the year before. Indirect operating expenses increased 9.0% to US$248.1 million from US$227.6 million in the equivalent prior-year period.

Prospects: Co. remains cautious with its outlook for the remainder of the fiscal year ending Sep 2008 due to the competitive retail grocery market and difficult textile and apparel environment. In addition, Co. believes that it will be challenged by the pre-opening and start-up costs associated with new store openings in fiscal 2007 and fiscal 2008. Specifically, Co.'s subsidiary, Harris Teeter, Inc., plans to open 13 new stores and complete the major remodeling on six more stores for the balance of fiscal 2008, resulting in a 9.0% increase in retail square footage for the fiscal year. Overall, Harris Teeter's capital expenditures for the fiscal year are estimated at approximately US$202.0 million.

Financial Data
(US$ in Thousands)

	3 Mos	09/30/2007	10/01/2006	10/02/2005	10/03/2004	09/28/2003	09/29/2002	09/30/2001
Earnings Per Share	1.78	1.68	1.52	1.44	1.38	1.29	1.12	(0.02)
Cash Flow Per Share	4.16	4.48	3.39	3.14	2.87	3.25	3.10	3.74
Tang Book Value Per Share	14.93	14.56	13.24	11.98	11.46	10.44	9.85	9.61
Dividends Per Share	0.450	0.440	0.440	0.440	0.400	0.360	0.360	0.360
Dividend Payout %	25.22	26.19	28.95	30.56	28.99	27.91	32.14	...
Income Statement								
Total Revenue	976,743	3,639,208	3,265,856	2,964,655	2,868,597	2,724,739	2,644,198	2,743,290
EBITDA	69,384	248,636	215,802	195,552	189,246	180,297	168,588	125,230
Depn & Amortn	26,639	...	...	...	...	...	...	...
Income Before Taxes	37,874	130,491	113,397	107,558	101,164	92,092	81,592	31,013
Income Taxes	14,526	49,803	41,061	38,960	36,505	32,210	29,609	31,740
Net Income	23,348	80,688	72,336	68,598	64,659	59,882	51,983	(727)
Average Shares	48,363	48,139	47,687	47,730	46,851	46,463	46,577	46,276
Balance Sheet								
Current Assets	466,097	456,264	425,445	425,330	445,886	440,869	425,714	341,251
Total Assets	1,586,598	1,529,689	1,362,936	1,203,640	1,111,992	1,067,203	1,038,947	939,988
Current Liabilities	349,273	382,770	327,326	291,203	257,915	279,248	259,596	228,979
Long-Term Obligations	316,347	255,857	228,269	155,120	157,639	157,499	185,165	156,437
Total Liabilities	828,868	793,079	692,419	594,698	562,282	571,938	581,259	494,635
Stockholders' Equity	757,730	736,610	670,517	608,942	549,710	495,265	457,688	445,353
Shares Outstanding	48,404	48,127	47,557	47,488	46,730	46,223	46,454	46,319
Statistical Record								
Return on Assets %	5.77	5.59	5.65	5.94	5.84	5.70	5.27	N.M.
Return on Equity %	11.89	11.50	11.34	11.87	12.18	12.60	11.54	N.M.
EBITDA Margin %	7.10	6.83	6.61	6.60	6.60	6.62	6.38	4.56
Net Margin %	2.39	2.22	2.21	2.31	2.25	2.20	1.97	N.M.
Asset Turnover	2.51	2.52	2.55	2.57	2.59	2.59	2.68	2.81
Current Ratio	1.33	1.19	1.30	1.46	1.73	1.58	1.64	1.49
Debt to Equity	0.42	0.35	0.34	0.25	0.29	0.32	0.40	0.35
Price Range	37.65-26.88	35.00-25.65	26.43-19.60	28.24-19.46	22.45-15.54	17.15-11.98	17.81-14.90	16.95-10.44
P/E Ratio	21.15-15.10	20.83-15.27	17.39-12.89	19.61-13.51	16.27-11.26	13.29-9.29	15.90-13.30	...
Average Yield %	1.43	1.48	1.90	1.91	2.09	2.47	2.21	2.61

Address: 301 S. Tryon St., Suite 1800, Charlotte, NC 28202	Web Site: www.ruddickcorp.com	Auditors: KPMG LLP
Telephone: 704-372-5404	Officers: Alan T. Dickson - Chmn. Thomas W. Dickson - Pres., C.E.O.	
Fax: 704-372-6409		

RYDER SYSTEM, INC.

Exchange	Symbol	Price	52Wk Range	Yield	P/E
NYS	R	$60.91 (3/31/2008)	63.60-38.99	1.51	14.37

*7 Year Price Score 109.83 *NYSE Composite Index=100 *12 Month Price Score 122.60

TRADING VOLUME (thousand shares)

Interim Earnings (Per Share)

Qtr.	Mar	Jun	Sep	Dec
2003	0.31	0.55	0.58	0.61
2004	0.53	0.97	0.83	0.95
2005	0.64	0.98	0.98	0.92
2006	0.77	1.13	1.06	1.07
2007	0.84	1.07	1.11	1.23

Interim Dividends (Per Share)

Amt	Decl	Ex	Rec	Pay
0.21Q	5/7/2007	5/17/2007	5/21/2007	6/15/2007
0.21Q	7/13/2007	8/16/2007	8/20/2007	9/14/2007
0.21Q	10/12/2007	11/15/2007	11/19/2007	12/14/2007
0.23Q	2/8/2008	2/15/2008	2/20/2008	3/14/2008

Indicated Div: $0.92

Valuation Analysis / **Institutional Holding**

Forecast P/E	10.58	No of Institutions
	(1/10/2007)	254
Market Cap	$3.5 Billion	Shares
Book Value	1.9 Billion	59,904,152
Price/Book	1.87	% Held
Price/Sales	0.54	98.66

Business Summary: Road Transport (MIC: 15.2 SIC: 7513 NAIC: 532120)

Ryder System is engaged in providing transportation and supply chain management services and products. Co.'s business is divided into three segments: Fleet Management Solutions, which provides full service leasing, contract maintenance, contract-related maintenance and commercial rental of trucks, tractors and trailers to customers in the U.S., Canada and the U.K.; Supply Chain Solutions, which provides comprehensive supply chain applications including distribution and transportation services throughout North America and in Latin America, Europe and Asia; and Dedicated Contract Carriage, which provides vehicles and drivers as part of a dedicated transportation service in the U.S.

Recent Developments: For the year ended Dec 31 2007, income from continuing operations increased 2.0% to US$253.9 million from US$249.0 million a year earlier. Net income increased 2.0% to US$253.9 million from US$249.0 million in the prior year. Revenues were US$6.57 billion, up 4.1% from US$6.31 billion the year before. Indirect operating expenses increased 4.2% to US$6.16 billion from US$5.91 billion in the equivalent prior-year period.

Prospects: On Jan 18 2008, Co. announced that it has acquired substantially all the assets of the Full Service Truck Leasing, Commercial Truck Rental and Contract Maintenance businesses of Lily Transportation Corp. The acquisition, which should be immediately accretive to earnings due to cost savings and operational improvements, is expected to add $30.0 million in annualized revenue to Co.'s Fleet Management Solutions business. Meanwhile, despite the soft overall economic and transportation environment, Co. is expecting 2008 earnings of $4.50 to $4.65 per diluted share and operating revenue growth of 3.0% to 6.0%. However, Co. projects total revenue of $6.18 billion, a decline of 6.0% from 2007.

Financial Data

(US$ in Thousands)	12/31/2007	12/31/2006	12/31/2005	12/31/2004	12/31/2003	12/31/2002	12/31/2001	12/31/2000
Earnings Per Share	4.24	4.04	3.52	3.28	2.06	1.50	0.31	1.49
Cash Flow Per Share	18.59	14.02	12.22	13.70	12.75	10.28	5.14	17.00
Tang Book Value Per Share	29.32	25.48	21.81	20.65	18.09	17.75	20.24	20.86
Dividends Per Share	0.840	0.720	0.640	0.600	0.600	0.600	0.600	0.600
Dividend Payout %	19.81	17.82	18.18	18.29	29.13	40.00	193.55	40.27
Income Statement								
Total Revenue	6,565,995	6,306,643	5,740,847	5,150,278	4,802,294	4,776,265	5,006,123	5,336,792
EBITDA	1,222,426	1,137,261	1,098,503	1,038,150	837,055	728,374	576,191	721,677
Income Before Taxes	405,464	392,973	357,088	331,122	212,475	175,883	30,706	141,321
Income Taxes	151,603	144,014	129,460	115,513	76,916	63,318	12,028	52,289
Net Income	253,861	248,959	226,929	215,609	131,436	93,666	18,678	89,032
Average Shares	59,845	61,578	64,560	65,671	63,871	62,587	60,665	59,759
Balance Sheet								
Current Assets	1,222,062	1,261,816	1,163,755	1,227,669	1,107,100	1,024,171	982,493	978,776
Total Assets	6,834,649	6,828,923	6,033,264	5,637,933	5,278,603	4,766,982	4,923,611	5,474,923
Current Liabilities	1,019,361	1,267,622	1,253,495	1,454,856	1,074,077	862,076	1,013,926	1,302,304
Long Term Obligations	2,553,431	2,484,198	1,915,928	1,393,666	1,449,489	1,389,099	1,391,597	1,604,242
Total Liabilities	4,967,060	5,108,144	4,505,808	4,127,745	3,934,218	3,658,767	3,692,942	4,222,215
Stockholders' Equity	1,887,589	1,720,779	1,527,456	1,510,188	1,344,385	1,108,215	1,230,669	1,252,708
Shares Outstanding	58,041	60,721	61,869	64,310	64,487	62,440	60,809	60,044
Statistical Record								
Return on Assets %	3.71	3.87	3.89	3.94	2.62	1.93	0.36	1.58
Return on Equity %	14.07	15.33	14.94	15.06	10.72	8.01	1.50	7.23
EBITDA Margin %	18.62	18.03	19.13	20.16	17.43	15.25	11.51	13.52
Net Margin %	3.87	3.95	3.95	4.19	2.74	1.96	0.37	1.67
Asset Turnover	0.96	0.98	0.98	0.94	0.96	0.99	0.96	0.95
Current Ratio	1.20	1.00	0.93	0.84	1.03	1.19	0.97	0.71
Debt to Equity	1.35	1.44	1.25	0.92	1.08	1.25	1.13	1.28
Price Range	56.81-38.99	58.56-40.32	47.77-32.09	55.11-33.67	34.30-20.14	30.84-21.29	23.19-16.19	25.13-15.31
P/E Ratio	13.40-9.20	14.50-9.98	13.57-9.12	16.80-10.27	16.65-9.78	20.56-14.19	74.81-52.22	16.86-10.28
Average Yield %	1.65	1.44	1.63	1.42	2.25	2.31	3.00	3.02

Address: 11690 N.W. 105th Street, Miami, FL 33178 Telephone: 305-500-3726 Fax: 305-500-4129	Web Site: www.ryder.com Officers: Gregory T. Swieton - Chmn., Pres., C.E.O. Tracy A. Leinbach - Exec. V.P., C.F.O.	Auditors: PricewaterhouseCoopers LLP Transfer Agents: EquiServe Trust Company, N.A.

RYLAND GROUP, INC.

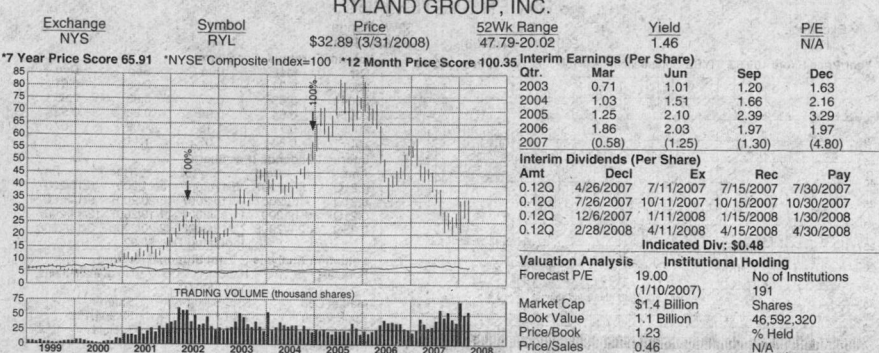

Exchange	Symbol	Price	52Wk Range	Yield	P/E
NYS	RYL	$32.89 (3/31/2008)	47.79-20.02	1.46	N/A

*7 Year Price Score 65.91 ***NYSE Composite Index=100** ***12 Month Price Score 100.35**

Interim Earnings (Per Share)

Qtr.	Mar	Jun	Sep	Dec
2003	0.71	1.01	1.20	1.63
2004	1.03	1.51	1.66	2.16
2005	1.25	2.10	2.39	3.29
2006	1.86	2.03	1.97	1.97
2007	(0.58)	(1.25)	(1.30)	(4.80)

Interim Dividends (Per Share)

Amt	Decl	Ex	Rec	Pay
0.12Q	4/26/2007	7/11/2007	7/15/2007	7/30/2007
0.12Q	7/26/2007	10/11/2007	10/15/2007	10/30/2007
0.12Q	12/6/2007	1/11/2008	1/15/2008	1/30/2008
0.12Q	2/28/2008	4/11/2008	4/15/2008	4/30/2008

Indicated Div: $0.48

Valuation Analysis

		Institutional Holding	
Forecast P/E	19.00 (1/10/2007)	No of Institutions	191
Market Cap	$1.4 Billion	Shares	46,592,320
Book Value	1.1 Billion	% Held	N/A
Price/Book	1.23		
Price/Sales	0.46		

Business Summary: Building & General Construction (MIC: 3.2 SIC: 1531 NAIC: 236117)

Ryland Group is engaged in the homebuilding and mortgage-financing business. Co.'s homebuilding operations builds single-family detached homes, as well as attached homes, such as town homes and condominiums, including some mid-rise buildings, which share common walls and roofs. At Dec 31 2007, Co.'s homes are built on-site and marketed in four major geographic regions: North, Southeast, Texas and West. Co.'s financial services segment provides mortgage-related products and services, as well as insurance services, to its homebuyers and subcontractors. In addition, Co. has a corporate segment, which is a non-operating business segment to support its existing operations.

Recent Developments: For the year ended Dec 31 2007, net loss amounted to US$333.5 million versus net income of US$359.9 million in the prior year. Revenues were US$3.03 billion, down 36.3% from US$4.76 billion the year before. Direct operating expenses declined 16.7% to US$3.03 billion from US$3.64 billion in the comparable period the year before. Indirect operating expenses decreased 24.7% to US$387.4 million from US$514.4 million in the equivalent prior-year period.

Prospects: Co.'s earnings are being hampered by a decline in revenues and lower margins resulting from inventory valuation adjustments and other write-offs, as well as from a competitive sales environment. In addition, new orders for sales contracts decreased primarily due to slowing demand. Further, Co.'s financial services segment is seeing lower earnings primarily attributable to a decline in the number of mortgages originated due to a slowdown in the homebuilding market and a decrease in average loan size. Looking ahead, Co. will remain focused on its liquidity and balance sheet, while seeking to optimize its earnings and to position itself for a return to a favorable economic environment.

Financial Data

(US$ in Thousands)	12/31/2007	12/31/2006	12/31/2005	12/31/2004	12/31/2003	12/31/2002	12/31/2001	12/31/2000
Earnings Per Share	(7.92)	7.83	9.03	6.36	4.55	3.32	2.31	1.48
Cash Flow Per Share	5.41	0.33	4.60	(1.64)	2.87	1.65	3.25	2.11
Tang Book Value Per Share	26.68	35.04	29.28	21.94	16.61	13.10	10.30	8.18
Dividends Per Share	0.480	0.480	0.240	0.200	0.040	0.040	0.040	0.040
Dividend Payout %	...	6.13	2.66	3.14	0.88	1.20	1.73	2.70
Income Statement								
Total Revenue	3,032,594	4,757,216	4,817,566	3,951,821	3,444,129	2,877,213	2,741,784	2,331,645
EBITDA	(334,131)	649,440	795,799	586,556	432,653	342,010	262,648	163,329
Income Before Taxes	(420,098)	567,108	721,051	521,212	396,217	309,340	225,580	134,840
Income Taxes	(86,572)	207,166	273,999	200,667	154,525	123,736	89,104	52,588
Net Income	(333,526)	359,942	447,052	320,545	241,692	185,604	132,093	82,252
Average Shares	42,136	45,944	49,490	50,378	53,044	55,918	57,022	55,573
Balance Sheet								
Current Assets	2,056,207	2,986,522	3,041,050	2,112,521	1,713,356	1,369,457	1,197,699	1,030,606
Total Assets	2,542,179	3,416,697	3,386,873	2,424,970	2,007,590	1,657,751	1,510,869	1,361,341
Current Liabilities	509,454	773,665	914,230	701,419	415,761	367,031	346,613	360,112
Long-Term Obligations	839,080	950,117	921,970	558,942	540,500	490,500	490,500	471,250
Total Liabilities	1,348,534	1,723,782	1,836,200	1,260,361	1,126,397	977,672	948,007	907,712
Stockholders' Equity	1,124,726	1,511,166	1,376,021	1,056,834	824,542	680,079	562,862	453,629
Shares Outstanding	42,151	42,612	46,368	47,348	48,552	50,520	52,867	52,995
Statistical Record								
Return on Assets %	N.M.	10.58	15.38	14.42	13.19	11.72	9.20	6.29
Return on Equity %	N.M.	24.93	36.75	33.98	32.13	29.87	25.99	19.53
EBITDA Margin %	N.M.	13.65	16.52	14.84	12.56	11.89	9.58	7.00
Net Margin %	N.M.	7.57	9.28	8.11	7.02	6.45	4.82	3.53
Asset Turnover	1.02	1.40	1.66	1.78	1.88	1.82	1.91	1.78
Current Ratio	4.04	3.86	3.33	3.01	4.12	3.73	3.46	2.86
Debt to Equity	0.75	0.63	0.67	0.53	0.66	0.72	0.87	1.04
Price Range	59.29-20.02	82.37-34.82	83.13-53.97	57.63-34.69	47.07-16.68	28.98-15.81	18.60-8.95	10.39-3.81
P/E Ratio	...	10.52-4.45	9.21-5.98	9.06-5.45	10.35-3.66	8.73-4.76	8.05-3.87	7.02-2.58
Average Yield %	1.28	0.88	0.35	0.47	0.12	0.19	0.32	0.65

Address: 24025 Park Sorrento, Suite 400, Calabasas, CA 91302 Telephone: 818-223-7500	Web Site: www.ryland.com Officers: R. Chad Dreier - Chmn., Pres., C.E.O. Kipling W. Scott - Exec. V.P.	Auditors: Ernst & Young LLP

SAFECO CORPORATION

Exchange	Symbol	Price	52Wk Range	Yield	P/E
NYS	SAF	$43.88 (3/31/2008)	67.20-42.40	3.65	6.30

*7 Year Price Score 100.89 *NYSE Composite Index=100 *12 Month Price Score 87.05

Interim Earnings (Per Share)

Qtr.	Mar	Jun	Sep	Dec
2003	0.65	0.81	(0.21)	1.19
2004	1.70	1.77	(0.76)	1.38
2005	1.65	1.46	0.80	1.52
2006	1.69	1.68	2.20	1.95
2007	1.71	1.75	1.93	1.58

Interim Dividends (Per Share)

Amt	Decl	Ex	Rec	Pay
0.40Q	5/2/2007	7/3/2007	7/6/2007	7/23/2007
0.40Q	8/1/2007	10/3/2007	10/5/2007	10/22/2007
0.40Q	10/30/2007	1/9/2008	1/11/2008	1/28/2008
0.40Q	1/30/2008	4/9/2008	4/11/2008	4/28/2008

Indicated Div: $1.60

Valuation Analysis

		Institutional Holding	
Forecast P/E	10.62 (1/10/2007)	No of Institutions	337
Market Cap	$3.9 Billion	Shares	82,695,184
Book Value	3.4 Billion	% Held	78.33
Price/Book	1.16		
Price/Sales	0.63		

TRADING VOLUME (thousand shares)

Business Summary: Insurance (MIC: 8.2 SIC: 6331 NAIC: 524126)

Safeco sells property and casualty insurance to drivers, homeowners and owners of small- and mid-sized businesses through independent agents. Co. has four business segments which include: Safeco Personal Insurance, which provides auto, property and specialty insurance products for individuals; Safeco Business Insurance, which provides business owner policies, commercial auto, commercial multi-peril, workers compensation, commercial property and general liability policies; Surety, which provides surety bonds primarily for construction and commercial businesses; and Property and Casualty Other, which includes assumed reinsurance and commercial business accounts in runoff.

Recent Developments: For the year ended Dec 31 2007, net income decreased 19.6% to US$707.8 million from US$880.0 million in the prior year. Revenues were US$6.21 billion, down 1.3% from US$6.29 billion the year before. Net premiums earned were US$5.58 billion versus US$5.61 billion in the prior year, a decrease of 0.6%. Net investment income fell 4.4% to US$486.7 million from US$509.1 million a year ago.

Prospects: For 2008, Co. expects improving auto profitability and continued strong performance of its property, small commercial and surety lines. Notably, Co. expects to see an improvement in auto profitability by the second half of 2008, due to improved pricing and claims management resulting from the roll-out of its Safeco True Pricing™ multi-variate pricing segmentation model in 2007. However, Co. anticipates a challenging market for premium growth in its Safeco Business Insurance Regular segment in 2008. Meanwhile, Co. is targeting an additional $25.0 million to $50.0 million reduction in its annualized expense run rate by the end of 2008.

Financial Data

(US$ in Thousands)	12/31/2007	12/31/2006	12/31/2005	12/31/2004	12/31/2003	12/31/2002	12/31/2001	12/31/2000
Earnings Per Share	6.97	7.51	5.43	4.16	2.44	2.33	(7.75)	0.90
Cash Flow Per Share	7.55	6.27	8.11	7.36	11.31	6.62	4.14	5.14
Tang Book Value Per Share	37.81	37.30	33.37	30.88	34.92	30.69	27.71	26.54
Dividends Per Share	1.400	1.100	0.940	0.775	0.740	0.740	0.925	1.480
Dividend Payout %	20.09	14.65	17.31	18.63	30.33	31.76	...	164.44
Income Statement								
Premium Income	5,576,000	5,608,300	5,805,400	5,529,100	5,769,900	5,299,600	5,109,800	5,066,100
Total Revenue	6,208,800	6,289,900	6,351,100	6,195,400	7,358,100	7,065,100	6,862,500	7,118,400
Benefits & Claims	3,520,500	3,279,800	3,635,000	3,495,200	...	...	...	...
Income Before Taxes	952,100	1,239,500	985,700	892,900	441,100	462,500	(1,413,300)	158,600
Income Taxes	244,300	359,500	294,600	272,700	101,900	116,600	(412,800)	(800)
Net Income	707,800	880,000	691,100	562,400	339,200	301,100	(989,200)	114,600
Average Shares	101,600	117,100	127,200	135,200	138,900	129,300	127,700	127,800
Balance Sheet								
Total Assets	12,640,400	14,199,000	14,887,000	14,586,100	35,845,100	34,656,000	30,092,500	31,511,500
Total Liabilities	9,226,300	10,254,800	10,762,400	10,665,200	30,821,800	29,380,600	25,614,500	25,972,700
Stockholders' Equity	3,392,600	3,927,900	4,124,600	3,920,900	5,023,300	4,431,600	3,634,600	4,695,800
Shares Outstanding	89,731	105,300	123,584	126,958	138,600	138,195	127,733	127,649
Statistical Record								
Return on Assets %	5.27	6.05	4.69	2.22	0.96	0.93	N.M.	0.37
Return on Equity %	19.34	21.86	17.18	12.54	7.18	7.47	N.M.	2.54
Loss Ratio %	63.14	58.48	62.61	63.21	...	...	...	...
Net Margin %	11.40	13.99	10.88	9.08	4.61	4.26	(14.41)	1.61
Price Range	68.91-53.68	64.22-49.12	57.85-45.44	52.24-38.23	39.17-32.35	36.55-26.31	32.79-21.75	35.69-18.56
P/E Ratio	9.89-7.70	8.55-6.54	10.65-8.37	12.56-9.19	16.05-13.26	15.69-11.29	...	39.65-20.63
Average Yield %	2.28	1.96	1.79	1.72	2.07	2.27	3.24	6.14

Address: Safeco Plaza, Seattle, WA 98185	**Web Site:** www.safeco.com/ir	**Auditors:** Ernst & Young LLP
Telephone: 206-545-5000	**Officers:** Michael S. McGavick - Chmn. Christine B. Mead - Sr. V.P., C.F.O., Sec.	**Investor Contact:** 206-545-3399
Fax: 206-545-5995		**Transfer Agents:** The Bank of New York, New York, NY

SAFEWAY INC.

Exchange	Symbol	Price	52Wk Range	Yield	P/E
NYS	SWY	$29.35 (3/31/2008)	38.00-28.27	0.94	14.75

*7 Year Price Score 92.56   *NYSE Composite Index=100   *12 Month Price Score 96.41

Interim Earnings (Per Share)

Qtr.	Mar	Jun	Sep	Dec
2004	0.10	0.35	0.35	0.45
2005	0.29	0.30	0.27	0.39
Qtr.	Mar	Jun	Aug	Dec
2006	0.32	0.55	0.39	0.69
2007	0.39	0.49	0.44	0.67

Interim Dividends (Per Share)

Amt	Decl	Ex	Rec	Pay
0.069Q	5/16/2007	6/27/2007	6/29/2007	7/19/2007
0.069Q	8/29/2007	9/25/2007	9/27/2007	10/18/2007
0.069Q	12/5/2007	12/24/2007	12/27/2007	1/17/2008
0.069Q	3/7/2008	3/25/2008	3/27/2008	4/17/2008

Indicated Div: $0.28

Valuation Analysis

Forecast P/E	15.26
	(1/10/2007)
Market Cap	$12.9 Billion
Book Value	6.7 Billion
Price/Book	1.93
Price/Sales	0.31

Institutional Holding

No of Institutions	378
Shares	401,433,952
% Held	91.13

Business Summary: Retail - Food & Beverage (MIC: 5.3 SIC: 5411 NAIC: 445110)

Safeway operates as a food and drug retailers, with 1743 stores as of Dec 29 2007. Co.'s U.S. retail operations are located principally in California, Oregon, Washington, Alaska, Colorado, Arizona, Texas, the Chicago metropolitan area and the Mid-Atlantic region. Co.'s Canadian retail operations are located principally in British Columbia, Alberta and Manitoba/Saskatchewan. Co.'s stores provide dry grocery items tailored to local preferences, with most of its stores offering food and general merchandise, as well as feature specialty departments such as bakery, delicatessen, floral and pharmacy.

Recent Developments: For the year ended Dec 29 2007, net income increased 2.0% to US$888.4 million from US$870.6 million in the prior year. Revenues were US$42.29 billion, up 5.2% from US$40.19 billion the year before. Operating income was US$1.77 billion versus US$1.60 billion in the prior year, an increase of 10.8%. Direct operating expenses rose 5.3% to US$30.13 billion from US$28.60 billion in the comparable period the year before. Indirect operating expenses increased 4.0% to US$10.38 billion from US$9.98 billion in the equivalent prior-year period.

Prospects: Co. has confirmed its 2008 guidance for earnings of $2.25 to $2.35 per diluted share. Co. also expects its 2008 identical-store sales, excluding fuel, to grow 3.0% to 3.2%. At the same time, Co. plans to spend $1.70 billion to $1.75 billion in capital expenditures, open 20 to 25 new Lifestyle stores and to remodel 250 to 255 stores into the Lifestyle format. In particular, Co. targets to have 75.0% of its store base in the Lifestyle format by end of 2008 and 90.0% by end of 2009. Separately, in order to grow or maintain its profit margins, Co. develops strategies to reduce costs, including productivity improvements, and distribution center enhancements.

Financial Data
(US$ in Thousands)

	12/29/2007	12/30/2006	12/31/2005	01/01/2005	01/03/2004	12/28/2002	12/29/2001	12/30/2000
Earnings Per Share	1.99	1.94	1.25	1.25	(0.38)	(1.75)	2.44	2.13
Cash Flow Per Share	4.99	4.90	4.21	5.01	3.58	4.16	4.45	3.83
Tang Book Value Per Share	9.76	7.44	5.60	4.24	2.79	1.77	1.67	1.35
Dividends Per Share	0.265	0.223	0.150	...	...	...	...	...
Dividend Payout %	13.29	11.47	12.00	...	...	...	...	...
Income Statement								
Total Revenue	42,286,000	40,185,000	38,416,000	35,822,900	35,552,700	32,399,200	34,301,000	31,976,900
EBITDA	2,869,000	2,633,300	2,191,800	2,107,500	1,455,100	2,509,100	3,487,600	3,161,400
Income Before Taxes	1,403,600	1,240,000	849,000	793,900	141,100	1,320,200	2,095,000	1,866,500
Income Taxes	515,200	369,400	287,900	233,700	310,900	751,700	841,100	774,600
Net Income	888,400	870,600	561,100	560,200	(169,800)	(828,100)	1,253,900	1,091,900
Average Shares	445,700	447,800	449,800	449,100	441,900	473,800	513,200	511,600
Balance Sheet								
Current Assets	4,007,500	3,565,700	3,702,400	3,597,700	3,507,700	4,259,100	3,311,800	3,223,500
Total Assets	17,651,000	16,273,800	15,756,900	15,377,400	15,096,700	16,047,300	17,462,600	15,965,300
Current Liabilities	5,136,400	4,601,400	4,263,900	3,792,100	3,464,300	3,936,300	3,882,600	3,779,500
Long-Term Obligations	4,657,700	5,036,600	5,605,300	6,123,700	7,072,300	7,521,500	6,712,300	5,822,100
Total Liabilities	10,949,200	10,606,900	10,837,200	11,070,500	11,452,400	12,419,800	11,573,000	10,575,500
Stockholders' Equity	6,701,800	5,666,900	4,919,700	4,306,900	3,644,300	3,627,500	5,889,600	5,389,800
Shares Outstanding	440,100	440,100	449,400	447,700	444,200	441,000	488,100	504,100
Statistical Record								
Return on Assets %	5.25	5.45	3.61	3.69	N.M.	N.M.	7.52	7.09
Return on Equity %	14.40	16.49	12.20	14.13	N.M.	N.M.	22.29	23.11
EBITDA Margin %	6.78	6.55	5.71	5.88	4.09	7.74	10.17	9.89
Net Margin %	2.10	2.17	1.46	1.56	N.M.	N.M.	3.66	3.41
Asset Turnover	2.50	2.52	2.47	2.36	2.25	1.94	2.06	2.08
Current Ratio	0.78	0.77	0.87	0.95	1.01	1.08	0.85	0.85
Debt to Equity	0.69	0.89	1.14	1.42	1.94	2.07	1.14	1.08
Price Range	38.00-30.56	35.31-22.37	26.05-17.92	25.40-17.34	25.80-16.45	46.09-19.08	60.44-38.50	62.50-31.50
P/E Ratio	19.10-15.36	18.20-11.53	20.84-14.34	20.32-13.87	...	...	24.77-15.78	29.34-14.79
Average Yield %	0.77	0.82	0.68	...	...	...	...	...

Address: 5918 Stoneridge Mall Rd., Pleasanton, CA 94588-3229
Telephone: 925-467-3000
Fax: 925-467-3323

Web Site: www.safeway.com
Officers: Steven A. Burd - Chmn., Pres., C.E.O. Brian C. Cornell - Exec. V.P., Chief Mktg. Officer

Auditors: Deloitte & Touche LLP

ST. JOE CO. (THE)

Exchange	Symbol	Price	52Wk Range	Yield	P/E
NYS	JOE	$42.93 (3/31/2008)	59.45-27.23	N/A	81.00

*7 Year Price Score 74.40   *NYSE Composite Index=100   *12 Month Price Score 106.67

TRADING VOLUME (thousand shares)

Interim Earnings (Per Share)

Qtr.	Mar	Jun	Sep	Dec
2003	0.18	0.13	0.30	0.37
2004	0.17	0.30	0.34	0.36
2005	0.20	0.50	0.47	0.49
2006	0.05	0.25	0.08	0.30
2007	0.27	0.34	(0.09)	0.02

Interim Dividends (Per Share)

Amt	Decl	Ex	Rec	Pay
0.16Q	11/30/2006	12/13/2006	12/15/2006	12/29/2006
0.16Q	2/13/2007	3/13/2007	3/15/2007	3/30/2007
0.16Q	5/16/2007	6/13/2007	6/15/2007	6/29/2007
0.16Q	8/29/2007	9/12/2007	9/14/2007	9/28/2007

Valuation Analysis / Institutional Holding

Forecast P/E	39.66 (1/10/2007)	No of Institutions 223
Market Cap	$3.2 Billion	Shares 72,795,328
Book Value	480.3 Million	% Held 97.88
Price/Book	6.67	
Price/Sales	8.49	

Business Summary: Property, Real Estate & Development (MIC: 8.3 SIC: 6552 NAIC: 237210)

St. Joe is a real estate development company that is primarily engaged in town and resort development, commercial and industrial development and rural land sales. In addition, Co. has significant interests in timber. Most of its real estate operations, as well as its timber operations, are within the state of Florida. As of Dec 31 2007, Co. owned approximately 700,000 acres, approximately 310,000 acres of which are within 10 miles of the coast of the Gulf of Mexico. Co. has four operating segments: residential real estate, commercial real estate, rural land sales and forestry.

Recent Developments: For the year ended Dec 31 2007, income from continuing operations decreased 67.6% to US$11.1 million from US$34.3 million a year earlier. Net income decreased 23.2% to US$39.2 million from US$51.0 million in the prior year. Revenues were US$377.0 million, down 28.1% from US$524.3 million the year before. Revenues from property income fell 32.1% to US$312.9 million from US$461.1 million in the corresponding earlier year.

Prospects: While the markets for residential real estate and Northwest Florida resort remains weak, Co.'s outlook seems constructive. For instance, Co. expects significant interest to develop in the near future for its commercial and industrial properties that surround the site of its new Bay County International Airport, Panama City, which is under construction and is estimated to open as early as 2010, subject to the resolution of any legal challenges and other construction delays. Meanwhile, Co. remains focused on its restructuring plan, which include the divestiture of certain non-core assets, reduction in capital expenditures, and an increased focus on the use of strategic business partners.

Financial Data

(US$ in Thousands)	12/31/2007	12/31/2006	12/31/2005	12/31/2004	12/31/2003	12/31/2002	12/31/2001	12/31/2000
Earnings Per Share	0.53	0.69	1.66	1.17	0.98	2.14	0.83	1.15
Cash Flow Per Share	(2.84)	(1.95)	2.57	1.80	1.67	0.47	0.69	(0.07)
Tang Book Value Per Share	6.15	5.29	5.42	5.22	5.27	5.59	4.71	5.14
Dividends Per Share	0.480	0.640	0.600	0.520	0.320	0.080	0.080	0.080
Dividend Payout %	90.57	92.75	36.14	44.44	32.65	3.74	9.64	6.96
Income Statement								
Total Revenue	377,037	748,192	938,192	951,503	760,630	646,352	868,411	880,830
EBITDA	...	...	...	...	...	282,887	160,758	231,105
Income Before Taxes	...	...	...	...	...	242,064	113,074	166,920
Income Taxes	869	25,157	64,332	53,258	42,626	89,561	42,345	56,643
Net Income	39,207	51,020	126,658	90,100	75,915	174,363	70,205	100,323
Average Shares	74,300	74,419	76,208	76,908	77,825	81,340	81,788	86,367
Balance Sheet								
Current Assets	89,370	88,803	261,510	184,629	133,095	122,987	92,412	140,946
Total Assets	1,203,966	1,360,393	1,391,948	1,403,629	1,275,730	1,169,887	1,340,559	1,115,021
Current Liabilities	152,305	250,611	214,396	212,341	165,867	151,215	108,503	114,443
Long-Term Obligations	541,181	627,056	554,446	421,110	382,176	320,915	498,015	263,807
Total Liabilities	777,349	1,088,782	1,084,754	897,825	780,227	689,794	822,486	545,937
Stockholders' Equity	480,341	461,080	488,998	495,411	487,315	480,093	518,073	569,084
Shares Outstanding	74,597	74,272	74,928	75,893	76,030	76,004	79,509	83,926
Statistical Record								
Return on Assets %	2.78	3.24	8.46	6.71	6.21	13.89	5.72	6.81
Return on Equity %	8.33	10.74	25.73	18.29	15.69	34.94	12.92	13.25
EBITDA Margin %	...	...	...	...	...	43.77	18.51	26.24
Net Margin %	10.40	6.82	13.50	9.47	9.98	26.98	8.08	11.39
Asset Turnover	0.27	0.47	0.63	0.71	0.62	0.51	0.71	0.60
Current Ratio	0.59	0.35	1.22	0.87	0.80	0.81	0.85	1.23
Debt to Equity	1.13	1.36	1.13	0.85	0.78	0.67	0.96	0.46
Price Range	61.06-27.23	67.99-41.92	84.73-59.89	64.20-35.75	37.97-26.33	33.65-25.09	29.55-21.07	22.00-15.81
P/E Ratio	115.21-51.38	98.54-60.75	51.04-36.08	54.87-30.56	38.74-26.87	15.72-11.72	35.60-25.39	19.13-13.75
Average Yield %	1.08	1.19	0.84	1.18	1.03	0.27	0.32	0.41

Address: 245 Riverside Avenue, Suite 500, Jacksonville, FL 32202
Telephone: 904-301-4200
Fax: 904-396-4042

Web Site: www.st-joe.com
Officers: Peter S. Rummell - Chmn., C.E.O. Kevin M. Twomey - Pres., C.F.O., C.O.O.

Auditors: KPMG LLP
Transfer Agents: Wachovia Bank, Charlotte, NC

ST. JUDE MEDICAL, INC.

Exchange	Symbol	Price	52Wk Range	Yield	P/E
NYS	STJ	$43.19 (3/31/2008)	48.10-37.13	N/A	27.16

*7 Year Price Score 104.00 *NYSE Composite Index=100   *12 Month Price Score 107.45

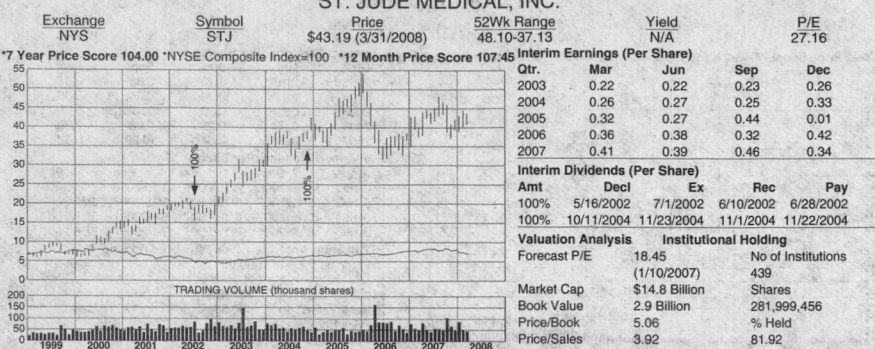

Interim Earnings (Per Share)

Qtr.	Mar	Jun	Sep	Dec
2003	0.22	0.22	0.23	0.26
2004	0.26	0.27	0.25	0.33
2005	0.32	0.27	0.44	0.01
2006	0.36	0.38	0.32	0.42
2007	0.41	0.39	0.46	0.34

Interim Dividends (Per Share)

Amt	Decl	Ex	Rec	Pay
100%	5/16/2002	7/1/2002	6/10/2002	6/28/2002
100%	10/11/2004	11/23/2004	11/1/2004	11/22/2004

Valuation Analysis **Institutional Holding**

Forecast P/E	18.45	No of Institutions	
	(1/10/2007)	439	
Market Cap	$14.8 Billion	Shares	
Book Value	2.9 Billion	281,999,456	
Price/Book	5.06	% Held	
Price/Sales	3.92	81.92	

Business Summary: Medical Instruments & Equipment (MIC: 9.6 SIC: 3845 NAIC: 334510)

St. Jude Medical is engaged in the development, manufacturing and distribution of cardiovascular medical devices for the cardiac rhythm management, cardiology and cardiac surgery and atrial fibrillation therapy areas and implantable neurostimulation devices for the management of chronic pain. Co,'s four operating segments are Cardiac Rhythm Management, Cardiovascular, Atrial Fibrillation, and Advanced Neuromodulation Systems. Co markets and sells its products through both a direct sales force and independent distributors. The principal geographic markets for Co.'s products are the U.S., Europe, Japan and Asia Pacific.

Recent Developments: For the year ended Dec 29 2007, net income increased 2.0% to US$559.0 million from US$548.3 million in the prior year. Revenues were US$3.78 billion, up 14.4% from US$3.30 billion the year before. Operating income was US$793.5 million versus US$743.1 million in the prior year, an increase of 6.8%. Direct operating expenses rose 14.0% to US$1.04 billion from US$913.5 million in the comparable period the year before. Indirect operating expenses increased 18.1% to US$1.94 billion from US$1.65 billion in the equivalent prior-year period.

Prospects: Looking ahead, Co. expects cost containment pressure on healthcare systems as well as competitive pressures in the industry to continue to place downward pressure on prices for its products. Nevertheless, Co. plans to focus on improving its operating margins through the enhancement of its existing products and continuous improvement of its manufacturing processes. Hence, for the first quarter of 2008, Co. is projecting consolidated earnings of $0.50 to $0.52 per diluted share, while consolidated earnings for full-year 2008 are expected to be in the range of $2.08 to $2.13. In addition, Co. expects research and development expense as a percentage of net sales of 12.0% to 13.0% for 2008.

Financial Data

(US$ in Thousands)	12/29/2007	12/30/2006	12/31/2005	12/31/2004	12/31/2003	12/31/2002	12/31/2001	12/31/2000
Earnings Per Share	1.59	1.47	1.04	1.10	0.92	0.76	0.48	0.38
Cash Flow Per Share	2.54	1.81	1.97	1.70	1.34	1.18	0.90	0.60
Tang Book Value Per Share	2.25	2.14	1.84	4.27	3.01	3.26	2.28	1.49
Income Statement								
Total Revenue	3,779,277	3,302,447	2,915,280	2,294,173	1,932,514	1,589,929	1,347,356	1,178,806
EBITDA	975,825	912,070	742,118	617,664	532,035	444,551	327,583	295,587
Income Before Taxes	744,305	720,641	621,404	537,192	458,637	373,358	227,978	177,309
Income Taxes	185,267	172,390	227,914	127,258	119,246	97,073	55,386	48,215
Net Income	559,038	548,251	393,490	409,934	339,391	276,285	172,592	129,094
Average Shares	352,444	372,830	379,106	370,992	370,754	366,004	357,536	343,268
Balance Sheet								
Current Assets	2,128,183	1,690,165	1,941,141	1,863,217	1,492,337	1,114,317	797,546	704,642
Total Assets	5,329,404	4,789,794	4,844,840	3,230,747	2,556,094	1,951,379	1,628,727	1,532,716
Current Liabilities	1,849,229	676,207	1,534,382	605,393	510,315	374,652	321,854	297,367
Long-Term Obligations	182,493	859,376	176,970	234,865	351,813	...	123,128	294,500
Total Liabilities	2,401,394	1,820,807	1,961,795	896,819	951,847	374,652	444,982	591,867
Stockholders' Equity	2,928,010	2,968,987	2,883,045	2,333,928	1,604,247	1,576,727	1,183,745	940,849
Shares Outstanding	342,846	353,932	367,904	358,760	346,028	356,056	348,837	341,345
Statistical Record								
Return on Assets %	11.08	11.41	9.75	14.13	15.06	15.43	10.92	8.34
Return on Equity %	19.01	18.79	15.08	20.76	21.34	20.02	16.25	14.84
EBITDA Margin %	25.82	27.62	25.46	26.92	27.53	27.96	24.31	25.08
Net Margin %	14.79	16.60	13.50	17.87	17.56	17.38	12.81	10.95
Asset Turnover	0.75	0.69	0.72	0.79	0.86	0.89	0.85	0.76
Current Ratio	1.15	2.50	1.27	3.08	2.92	2.97	2.48	2.37
Debt to Equity	0.06	0.29	0.06	0.10	0.22	...	0.10	0.31
Price Range	48.10-35.00	54.20-31.62	51.91-35.06	42.55-29.94	31.68-19.84	21.38-15.54	19.42-11.75	15.36-5.98
P/E Ratio	30.25-22.01	36.87-21.51	49.91-33.71	38.68-27.22	34.43-21.57	28.13-20.45	40.46-24.48	40.42-15.75

Address: One Lillehei Plaza, St. Paul, MN 55117 Telephone: 651-483-2000 Fax: 651-490-4310	Web Site: www.sjm.com Officers: Daniel J. Starks - Chmn. John C. Heinmiller - Exec. V.P., C.F.O.	Auditors: Ernst & Young LLP Investor Contact: 180-055-27664 Transfer Agents: Computershare Trust Company, N.A., Providence, RI

ST. MARY LAND & EXPLORATION CO.

Exchange	Symbol	Price	52Wk Range	Yield	P/E
NYS	SM	$38.50 (3/31/2008)	44.07-31.80	0.26	13.10

*7 Year Price Score 125.71 *NYSE Composite Index=100 *12 Month Price Score 104.51

Interim Earnings (Per Share)

Qtr.	Mar	Jun	Sep	Dec
2003	0.48	0.35	0.20	0.30
2004	0.33	0.34	0.35	0.41
2005	0.54	0.59	0.42	0.78
2006	0.76	0.61	0.88	0.69
2007	0.63	0.91	0.89	0.51

Interim Dividends (Per Share)

Amt	Decl	Ex	Rec	Pay
0.05S	4/21/2006	5/3/2006	5/5/2006	5/15/2006
0.05S	10/18/2006	11/1/2006	11/3/2006	11/13/2006
0.05S	4/25/2007	5/2/2007	5/4/2007	5/14/2007
0.05S	10/17/2007	10/31/2007	11/2/2007	11/12/2007
		Indicated Div: $0.10		

Valuation Analysis

		Institutional Holding	
Forecast P/E	N/A	No of Institutions	201
Market Cap	$2.4 Billion	Shares	
Book Value	863.3 Million		50,678,036
Price/Book	2.81	% Held	
Price/Sales	2.45		92.13

Business Summary: Oil and Gas (MIC: 14.2 SIC: 1311 NAIC: 211111)

St. Mary Land & Exploration is an oil and gas company engaged in the exploration, exploitation, development, acquisition and production of natural gas and crude oil. Co.'s U.S. operations are focused in five core areas in the Rocky Mountain region, Mid-Continent in Oklahoma and northern Texas, the ArkLaTex region spanning northern Louisiana, southern Arkansas, Mississippi, and eastern Texas, the Permian Basin region in western Texas and eastern New Mexico, and the Gulf Coast region of onshore Texas. As of Dec 31 2007, Co. had estimated proved reserves of 78.8 million barrels of oil and 613.50 billion cubic feet of natural gas, totaling 1,086.50 billion cubic feet of natural gas equivalent.

Recent Developments: For the year ended Dec 31 2007, net income decreased 0.2% to US$189.7 million from US$190.0 million in the prior year. Revenues were US$990.1 million, up 25.7% from US$787.7 million the year before. Operating income was US$319.4 million versus US$302.3 million in the prior year, an increase of 5.7%. Direct operating expenses rose 23.6% to US$218.2 million from US$176.6 million in the comparable period the year before. Indirect operating expenses increased 46.5% to US$452.5 million from US$308.8 million in the equivalent prior-year period.

Prospects: On Jan 31 2008, Co. closed the divestiture of non-core oil and gas properties located mainly in the Rocky Mountain and Mid-Continent regions to Abraxas Petroleum Corp. and Abraxas Operating, LLC, for $131.1 million in cash, before commission costs. Meanwhile, for full year 2008, Co. projects oil and gas production to be 107.00 billion cubic feet equivalent (Bcfe) to 111.00 Bcfe. Co. also has a $626.0 million capital investment plan for 2008, which is weighted towards the second half of the year. As a result of this and the effects of the divestiture, Co. expects production volumes in the second quarter of 2008 to dip slightly and then ramp up through the remainder of 2008.

Financial Data

(US$ in Thousands)	12/31/2007	12/31/2006	12/31/2005	12/31/2004	12/31/2003	12/31/2002	12/31/2001	12/31/2000
Earnings Per Share	2.94	2.94	2.33	1.44	1.40	0.40	0.71	0.98
Cash Flow Per Share	10.70	8.31	7.19	4.10	3.27	2.54	2.28	1.66
Tang Book Value Per Share	13.55	13.34	9.86	8.51	6.92	5.35	5.15	4.38
Dividends Per Share	0.100	0.100	0.100	0.050	0.050	0.050	0.050	0.050
Dividend Payout %	3.40	3.40	4.29	3.47	3.57	10.31	7.04	5.08
Income Statement								
Total Revenue	990,094	787,701	739,590	433,099	393,934	196,394	207,469	195,666
EBITDA	319,411	302,266	245,994	151,915	153,311	45,689	61,912	88,550
Income Before Taxes	300,262	295,321	238,237	146,228	146,070	42,579	62,288	89,287
Income Taxes	110,550	105,306	86,301	53,749	55,930	18,019	21,829	33,667
Net Income	189,712	190,015	151,936	92,479	95,575	27,560	40,459	55,620
Average Shares	64,850	65,962	66,894	66,894	71,068	56,782	57,110	56,542
Balance Sheet								
Current Assets	269,941	226,940	203,931	126,927	107,923	59,547	72,221	63,984
Total Assets	2,571,680	1,899,097	1,268,747	945,460	735,854	537,139	436,989	321,895
Current Liabilities	362,545	204,070	198,994	114,892	104,822	57,497	38,221	23,345
Long-Term Obligations	572,500	433,980	99,885	136,791	110,696	113,601	64,000	22,000
Total Liabilities	1,708,335	1,155,723	699,427	461,005	345,201	236,981	150,161	71,152
Stockholders' Equity	863,345	743,374	569,320	484,455	390,653	299,513	286,117	250,136
Shares Outstanding	63,001	55,001	56,761	56,958	56,484	55,946	55,539	57,107
Statistical Record								
Return on Assets %	8.49	12.00	13.72	10.97	15.02	5.66	10.66	20.08
Return on Equity %	23.61	28.95	28.84	21.08	27.70	9.41	15.09	25.28
EBITDA Margin %	32.26	38.37	33.26	35.08	38.92	23.26	29.84	45.26
Net Margin %	19.16	24.12	20.54	21.35	24.26	14.03	19.50	28.43
Asset Turnover	0.44	0.50	0.67	0.51	0.62	0.40	0.55	0.71
Current Ratio	0.74	1.11	1.02	1.10	1.03	1.04	1.89	2.74
Debt to Equity	0.66	0.58	0.18	0.28	0.28	0.38	0.22	0.09
Price Range	44.07-31.80	45.28-34.34	40.28-19.57	21.50-14.02	14.85-11.91	13.50-9.72	17.31-7.39	16.91-5.63
P/E Ratio	14.99-10.82	15.40-11.68	17.29-8.40	14.93-9.73	10.60-8.51	28.13-20.26	24.38-10.42	17.25-5.74
Average Yield %	0.27	0.25	0.34	0.28	0.38	0.43	0.45	0.53

Address: 1776 Lincoln Street, Suite 700, Denver, CO 80203 **Telephone:** 303-861-8140 **Fax:** 303-861-0934	**Web Site:** www.stmaryland.com **Officers:** Mark A. Hellerstein - Chmn., Pres., C.E.O. Douglas W. York - Exec. V.P., C.O.O.	**Auditors:** Deloitte & Touche, LLP **Investor Contact:** 303-863-4377 **Transfer Agents:** Computershare Investor Services, Golden, Co

SAKS, INC.

Exchange	Symbol	Price	52Wk Range	Yield	P/E
NYS	SKS	$12.47 (3/31/2008)	22.69-11.71	N/A	40.23

*7 Year Price Score 101.83 *NYSE Composite Index=100 *12 Month Price Score 87.52

Interim Earnings (Per Share)

Qtr.	Apr	Jul	Oct	Jan
2003-04	0.10	(0.18)	0.09	0.57
2004-05	0.15	(0.20)	(0.18)	0.65
2005-06	0.11	0.06	0.00	(0.01)
2006-07	0.57	(0.38)	0.05	0.16
2007-08	0.07	(0.17)	0.14	0.26

Interim Dividends (Per Share)

Amt	Decl	Ex	Rec	Pay
2.00U	3/15/2004	4/28/2004	4/30/2004	5/17/2004
4.00U	3/6/2006	5/2/2006	4/14/2006	5/1/2006
4.00U	10/3/2006	12/1/2006	11/15/2006	11/30/2006

Valuation Analysis   Institutional Holding

Forecast P/E	N/A	No of Institutions
		199
Market Cap	$1.8 Billion	Shares
Book Value	1.2 Billion	141,074,496
Price/Book	1.50	% Held
Price/Sales	0.54	99.77

Business Summary: Retail - General (MIC: 5.2 SIC: 5311 NAIC: 452111)

Saks is a fashion retail organization providing an assortment of luxury fashion apparel, shoes, accessories, jewelry, cosmetics and gifts. Co.'s Saks Fifth Avenue (SFA) stores are principally free-standing stores in shopping destinations or anchor stores in regional malls. Customers may also purchase SFA products by catalog or online at www.saks.com.Co.'s Off Fifth stores are primarily located in mixed-use and off-price centers, providing luxury apparel, shoes, and accessories. Co.'s Club Libby Lu (CLL) consists of mall-based specialty stores, targeting girls aged 4 to 12 years old. As of Feb 2 2008, Co. operated 54 SFA stores, 48 Off Fifth units and 95 CLL specialty stores.

Recent Developments: For the year ended Feb 2 2008, income from continuing operations was US$47.5 million compared with a loss of US$7.3 million a year earlier. Net income decreased 11.7% to US$47.5 million from US$53.7 million in the prior year. Revenues were US$3.28 billion, up 11.7% from US$2.94 billion the year before. Operating income was US$98.0 million versus a loss of US$20.4 million in the prior year. Direct operating expenses rose 10.8% to US$2.00 billion from US$1.80 billion in the comparable period the year before. Indirect operating expenses increased 2.5% to US$1.19 billion from US$1.16 billion in the equivalent prior-year period.

Prospects: For the fiscal year ending Jan 31 2009, Co. is projecting comparable store sales growth of mid-single digits, assuming low-to-mid single digit comparable store sales growth in the first half of fiscal 2009 and mid-single digit comparable store sales growth in the second half of fiscal 2009. In addition, Co. foresees inventory levels to be in-line with its sales growth guidance by the beginning of the third fiscal quarter. Also, Co. plans to open or remodel over 100 vendor shops while focusing on seven major store projects. However, Co. is forecasting a modest decrease in gross margin rate, with challenges during the first half of fiscal 2009 due to the existing economic environment.

Financial Data

(US$ in Thousands)	02/02/2008	02/03/2007	01/28/2006	01/29/2005	01/31/2004	02/01/2003	02/02/2002	02/03/2001
Earnings Per Share	0.31	0.40	0.16	0.42	0.58	0.17	...	0.53
Cash Flow Per Share	0.51	0.40	1.36	2.58	3.34	1.94	2.64	3.37
Tang Book Value Per Share	8.29	7.80	13.37	12.57	14.08	13.46	13.27	12.56
Dividends Per Share	...	8.000	...	2.000	...	...	...	...
Dividend Payout %	...	2,000.00	...	476.19	...	...	...	...
Income Statement								
Total Revenue	3,282,640	2,940,003	5,953,352	6,437,277	6,055,055	5,911,122	6,070,568	6,581,236
EBITDA	251,929	136,533	390,532	427,204	440,942	450,059	325,225	479,693
Income Before Taxes	74,980	(42,125)	94,638	84,238	109,879	109,985	(25,587)	115,599
Income Taxes	27,507	(34,783)	72,290	23,153	27,052	40,148	(9,851)	40,383
Net Income	47,473	53,742	22,348	61,085	82,827	24,244	322	75,216
Average Shares	153,530	135,880	143,571	144,034	142,921	146,707	141,988	142,718
Balance Sheet								
Current Assets	1,126,135	1,250,841	1,644,651	2,079,015	2,043,163	1,918,525	1,769,929	1,916,238
Total Assets	2,371,024	2,544,303	3,850,725	4,704,079	4,654,869	4,579,356	4,595,521	5,050,611
Current Liabilities	781,038	862,780	845,050	940,020	966,410	794,692	786,778	830,282
Long-Term Obligations	253,346	450,010	722,736	1,346,222	1,125,637	1,327,381	1,356,580	1,801,657
Total Liabilities	1,195,418	1,448,164	1,851,342	2,619,662	2,332,701	2,312,084	2,324,084	2,756,782
Stockholders' Equity	1,175,606	1,096,139	1,999,383	2,084,417	2,322,168	2,267,272	2,271,437	2,293,829
Shares Outstanding	141,784	140,480	136,005	140,115	141,835	144,960	143,989	141,897
Statistical Record								
Return on Assets %	1.94	1.65	0.52	1.31	1.80	0.53	0.01	1.46
Return on Equity %	4.19	3.42	1.10	2.78	3.62	1.07	0.01	3.29
EBITDA Margin %	7.67	4.64	6.56	6.64	7.28	7.61	5.36	7.29
Net Margin %	1.45	1.83	0.38	0.95	1.37	0.41	0.01	1.14
Asset Turnover	1.34	0.90	1.40	1.38	1.32	1.29	1.26	1.28
Current Ratio	1.44	1.45	1.95	2.21	2.11	2.41	2.25	2.31
Debt to Equity	0.22	0.41	0.36	0.65	0.48	0.59	0.60	0.79
Price Range	22.69-15.09	20.63-14.26	24.43-14.23	17.85-11.81	17.27-6.91	15.48-8.75	13.80-5.00	14.94-7.81
P/E Ratio	73.19-48.68	51.57-35.65	152.69-88.94	42.50-28.12	29.78-11.91	91.06-51.47	...	28.18-14.74
Average Yield %	...	45.46	...	13.96	...	...	...	...

Address: 750 Lakeshore Parkway, Birmingham, AL 35211
Telephone: 205-940-4000
Fax: 205-940-4987

Web Site: www.saksincorporated.com
Officers: R. Brad Martin - Chmn., C.E.O. Stephen I. Sadove - Vice-Chmn., C.O.O.

Auditors: PricewaterhouseCoopers LLP
Investor Contact: 865-981-6243

SALESFORCE.COM INC

Exchange	Symbol	Price	52Wk Range	Yield	P/E
NYS	CRM	$57.87 (3/31/2008)	64.99-38.86	N/A	385.80

*7 Year Price Score N/A   *NYSE Composite Index=100   *12 Month Price Score 121.91

Interim Earnings (Per Share)

Qtr.	Apr	Jul	Oct	Jan
2003-04	0.00	0.00	0.04	0.00
2004-05	0.00	0.01	0.02	0.04
2005-06	0.04	0.04	0.11	0.05
2006-07	0.00	0.00	0.00	0.00
2007-08	0.01	0.03	0.05	0.06

Interim Dividends (Per Share)

No Dividends Paid

Valuation Analysis — **Institutional Holding**

Forecast P/E	N/A	No of Institutions
		184
Market Cap	$6.9 Billion	Shares
Book Value	452.1 Million	01,132,544
Price/Book	15.27	% Held
Price/Sales	9.22	70.55

Business Summary: IT & Technology (MIC: 10.2 SIC: 7372 NAIC: 511210)

Salesforce.Com is a provider of application services that allow organizations to share customer information on demand. Co. provides customer relationship management (CRM) service to businesses of all sizes and industries worldwide. Co. delivers its service through a standard Web browser. Most of the features of Co.'s service can be accessed through a variety of devices, including laptop computers and mobile devices. Co.'s service helps customers more effectively manage and share their sales, support, marketing and partner information on-demand. Co. markets its service to businesses on a subscription basis, primarily through its direct sales efforts and also indirectly through partners.

Recent Developments: For the year ended Jan 31 2008, net income increased to US$18.4 million from US$481,000 in the prior year. Revenues were US$748.7 million, up 50.6% from US$497.1 million the year before. Operating income was US$20.3 million versus a loss of US$3.6 million in the prior year. Direct operating expenses rose 44.3% to US$171.6 million from US$118.9 million in the comparable period the year before. Indirect operating expenses increased 45.8% to US$556.8 million from US$381.8 million in the equivalent prior-year period.

Prospects: For the fiscal year ending Jan 31 2008, Co. now anticipates revenues of $737.0 million to $739.0 million and earnings of $0.12 to $0.13 per diluted share. For the fourth fiscal quarter of 2008, Co. is targeting revenues of $206.0 million to $208.0 million, while earnings are forecasted to range from $0.03 to $0.04 per diluted share. Meanwhile, for the fiscal year ending Jan 31 2009, Co. is estimating revenues of $1.00 billion to $1.02 billion. Looking ahead, Co. intends to continue to add substantial numbers of paying subscriptions and upgrade its customers to better versions, such as its Unlimited Edition, in order to increase its revenues and capitalize on its market potential.

Financial Data

(US$ in Thousands)	01/31/2008	01/31/2007	01/31/2006	01/31/2005	01/31/2004	01/31/2003	01/31/2002
Earnings Per Share	0.15	...	0.24	0.07	0.04	(0.37)	(1.36)
Cash Flow Per Share	1.75	0.99	0.89	0.74	0.74	0.20	...
Tang Book Value Per Share	3.51	2.30	1.76	1.38	...	...	...
Income Statement							
Total Revenue	748,700	497,098	309,857	176,375	96,023	50,991	22,409
EBITDA	41,303	33,597	41,174	9,679	6,473	(7,738)	(26,873)
Income Before Taxes	46,213	12,496	28,198	9,153	4,239	(10,008)	(29,034)
Income Taxes	23,385	9,795	(1,310)	1,217	541	...	...
Net Income	18,356	481	28,474	7,346	3,514	(9,716)	(28,609)
Average Shares	122,422	120,154	118,737	110,874	95,409	26,375	21,039
Balance Sheet							
Current Assets	740,011	419,096	303,217	178,713	74,146	29,907	...
Total Assets	1,089,593	664,832	434,749	280,499	87,511	39,673	...
Current Liabilities	605,917	376,999	234,625	131,671	70,006	28,795	...
Long-Term Obligations	...	6	184	721	...	78	...
Total Liabilities	637,534	383,041	238,378	135,368	72,611	34,411	...
Stockholders' Equity	452,059	281,791	196,371	145,131	(46,237)	(55,875)	...
Shares Outstanding	119,305	114,537	110,513	104,990	31,530	30,480	29,254
Statistical Record							
Return on Assets %	2.09	0.09	7.96	3.98	5.53	...	...
Return on Equity %	5.00	0.20	16.68	14.82	...	...	...
EBITDA Margin %	5.52	6.76	13.29	5.49	6.74	N.M.	N.M.
Net Margin %	2.45	0.10	9.19	4.16	3.66	N.M.	N.M.
Asset Turnover	0.85	0.90	0.87	0.96	1.51	...	...
Current Ratio	1.22	1.11	1.29	1.36	1.06	1.04	...
Price Range	64.99-38.86	44.00-21.85	42.65-13.07	21.96-9.59	...	...	...
P/E Ratio	433.27-259.07	N.M.	177.71-54.46	313.71-137.00	...	...	...

Address: The Landmark @ One Market, Suite 300, San Francisco, CA 94105 **Telephone:** 415-901-7000	**Web Site:** www.salesforce.com **Officers:** Marc Benioff - Chmn., C.E.O. Jim Steele - Pres.	**Auditors:** Ernst & Young LLP **Transfer Agents:** Computershare Investor Services, LLC

SARA LEE CORP.

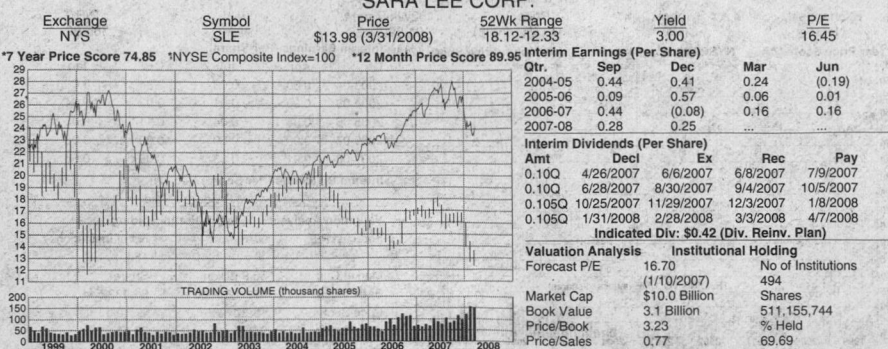

Exchange	Symbol	Price	52Wk Range	Yield	P/E
NYS	SLE	$13.98 (3/31/2008)	18.12-12.33	3.00	16.45

*7 Year Price Score 74.85 ¹NYSE Composite Index=100 *12 Month Price Score 89.95

Interim Earnings (Per Share)

Qtr.	Sep	Dec	Mar	Jun
2004-05	0.44	0.41	0.24	(0.19)
2005-06	0.09	0.57	0.06	0.01
2006-07	0.44	(0.08)	0.16	0.16
2007-08	0.28	0.25	...	...

Interim Dividends (Per Share)

Amt	Decl	Ex	Rec	Pay
0.10Q	4/26/2007	6/6/2007	6/8/2007	7/9/2007
0.10Q	6/28/2007	8/30/2007	9/4/2007	10/5/2007
0.105Q	10/25/2007	11/29/2007	12/3/2007	1/8/2008
0.105Q	1/31/2008	2/28/2008	3/3/2008	4/7/2008

Indicated Div: $0.42 (Div. Reinv. Plan)

Valuation Analysis / **Institutional Holding**

Forecast P/E	16.70	No of Institutions
	(1/10/2007)	494
Market Cap	$10.0 Billion	Shares
Book Value	3.1 Billion	511,155,744
Price/Book	3.23	% Held
Price/Sales	0.77	69.69

Business Summary: Food (MIC: 4.1 SIC: 2013 NAIC: 311613)

Sara Lee is engaged as a global manufacturer and marketer of brand-name products for consumers throughout the world. As of June 30 2007, Co. had business operations organized around six business segments: North American Retail Meats, North American Retail Bakery, Foodservice, International Beverage, International Bakery, and Household and Body Care. In addition, Co. owned approximately 28,000 active trademark registrations and applications in countries around the world. Further, Co. operated more than 300 food processing and consumer product manufacturing plants, warehouses and distribution facilities that each contains more than 20,000 square feet in building area.

Recent Developments: For the quarter ended Dec 29 2007, income from continuing operations was US$182.0 million compared with a loss of US$57.0 million in the year-earlier quarter. Net income amounted to US$182.0 million versus a net loss of US$62.0 million in the year-earlier quarter. Revenues were US$3.49 billion, up 9.7% from US$3.18 billion the year before. Direct operating expenses rose 9.8% to US$2.17 billion from US$1.97 billion in the comparable period the year before. Indirect operating expenses decreased 7.3% to US$1.09 billion from US$1.17 billion in the equivalent prior-year period.

Prospects: For the fiscal year ending June 30 2008, Co. currently anticipates earnings from continuing operations of $1.03 to $1.09 per diluted share, versus earnings from continuing operations of $0.57 per diluted share in the prior fiscal year. In addition, Co. is projecting net sales to be $13.40 billion, versus its previous fiscal year's level of $12.30 billion, reflecting growth of 9.0%. Similarly, Co. is targeting operating margin of 8.2% to 8.6% over its prior fiscal year's level of 4.5%, an improvement of 3.7 to 4.1 basis points. Going forward, Co. intends to offset commodity price increases with pricing actions and mitigate any operating cost increases with continuous improvement savings.

Financial Data

(US$ in Thousands)	6 Mos	3 Mos	06/30/2007	07/01/2006	07/02/2005	07/03/2004	06/28/2003	06/29/2002
Earnings Per Share	0.85	0.52	0.68	0.72	0.90	1.59	1.50	1.23
Cash Flow Per Share	0.92	0.86	0.67	1.61	1.72	2.55	2.34	2.22
Dividends Per Share	0.405	0.400	0.400	0.790	0.780	0.563	0.615	0.595
Dividend Payout %	47.70	76.21	58.82	109.72	86.67	35.38	41.00	48.37
Income Statement								
Total Revenue	6,622,000	3,131,000	12,278,000	15,944,000	19,254,000	19,566,000	18,291,000	17,628,000
EBITDA	780,000	419,000	1,095,000	1,612,000	1,857,000	2,457,000	2,356,000	1,975,000
Depn & Amortn	253,000	125,000	...	...	...	...	...	...
Income Before Taxes	469,000	265,000	419,000	683,000	934,000	1,542,000	1,484,000	1,185,000
Income Taxes	87,000	65,000	(7,000)	273,000	203,000	270,000	263,000	175,000
Net Income	382,000	200,000	504,000	555,000	719,000	1,272,000	1,221,000	1,010,000
Average Shares	722,000	727,000	743,000	768,000	796,000	798,000	812,000	818,000
Balance Sheet								
Current Assets	5,112,000	4,975,000	5,643,000	6,774,000	5,811,000	5,746,000	5,953,000	4,986,000
Total Assets	12,079,000	11,601,000	12,190,000	14,522,000	14,412,000	14,883,000	15,084,000	13,753,000
Current Liabilities	3,802,000	3,414,000	4,301,000	6,277,000	4,968,000	5,423,000	5,199,000	5,463,000
Long-Term Obligations	2,481,000	2,792,000	2,803,000	3,807,000	4,115,000	4,171,000	5,157,000	4,326,000
Total Liabilities	8,997,000	8,715,000	9,575,000	12,073,000	11,474,000	11,935,000	13,032,000	12,011,000
Stockholders' Equity	3,082,000	2,886,000	2,615,000	2,449,000	2,938,000	2,948,000	2,052,000	1,742,000
Shares Outstanding	712,174	724,191	724,432	760,980	785,894	793,924	777,347	784,720
Statistical Record								
Return on Assets %	5.21	3.19	3.78	3.85	4.92	8.35	8.49	8.47
Return on Equity %	22.01	13.37	19.96	20.66	24.50	50.06	64.54	70.72
EBITDA Margin %	11.78	13.38	8.92	10.11	9.64	12.56	12.88	11.20
Net Margin %	5.77	6.39	4.10	3.48	3.73	6.50	6.68	5.73
Asset Turnover	1.09	1.07	0.92	1.11	1.32	1.28	1.27	1.48
Current Ratio	1.34	1.46	1.31	1.08	1.17	1.06	1.15	0.91
Debt to Equity	0.80	0.97	1.07	1.55	1.40	1.41	2.51	2.48
Price Range	18.12-15.43	18.12-15.43	18.12-13.75	17.77-13.60	21.25-16.44	19.96-15.64	20.23-14.05	19.62-16.13
P/E Ratio	21.32-18.15	34.85-29.67	26.65-20.23	24.69-18.89	23.61-18.27	12.55-9.83	13.48-9.37	15.95-13.11
Average Yield %	2.42	2.37	2.45	5.06	4.09	3.16	3.61	3.30

Address: 3500 Lacey Road, Downers Grove, IL 60515-5424
Telephone: 630-598-6000
Fax: 312-558-4913

Web Site: www.saralee.com
Officers: C. Steven McMillan - Chmn. Brenda C. Barnes - Pres., C.E.O.

Auditors: PricewaterhouseCoopers LLP
Investor Contact: 630-598-8100
Transfer Agents: Sara Lee Corporation, Chicago, IL

SCANA CORP

Exchange	Symbol	Price	52Wk Range	Yield	P/E
NYS	SCG	$36.58 (3/31/2008)	45.26-36.21	5.03	13.35

*7 Year Price Score 90.49   ***NYSE Composite Index=100**   ***12 Month Price Score 101.20**

TRADING VOLUME (thousand shares)

Interim Earnings (Per Share)

Qtr.	Mar	Jun	Sep	Dec
2003	0.75	0.67	0.76	0.36
2004	0.91	0.54	0.48	0.37
2005	0.89	0.39	0.88	0.65
2006	0.85	0.50	0.76	0.57
2007	0.73	0.47	0.79	0.75

Interim Dividends (Per Share)

Amt	Decl	Ex	Rec	Pay
0.44Q	4/26/2007	6/7/2007	6/11/2007	7/1/2007
0.44Q	8/2/2007	9/6/2007	9/10/2007	10/1/2007
0.44Q	10/24/2007	12/6/2007	12/10/2007	1/1/2008
0.46Q	2/14/2008	3/6/2008	3/10/2008	4/1/2008

Indicated Div: $1.84

Valuation Analysis   **Institutional Holding**

Forecast P/E	N/A	No of Institutions
		285
Market Cap	$4.3 Billion	Shares
Book Value	3.1 Billion	48,287,008
Price/Book	1.40	% Held
Price/Sales	0.93	41.62

Business Summary: Electricity (MIC: 7.1 SIC: 4931 NAIC: 221122)

SCANA, through its wholly owned regulated subsidiaries, is primarily engaged in the generation, transmission, distribution and sale of electricity in parts of South Carolina and the purchase, transmission and sale of natural gas in portions of North Carolina and South Carolina. Through its wholly owned nonregulated subsidiary, Co. markets natural gas to retail customers in Georgia and to wholesale customers primarily in the southeast. Co's other wholly owned nonregulated subsidiaries provide fiber optic and other telecommunications services, and provides service contracts to homeowners on certain home appliances and heating and air conditioning units.

Recent Developments: For the year ended Dec 31 2007, net income increased 3.2% to US$310.0 million in the prior year. Revenues were US$4.62 billion, up 1.3% from US$4.56 billion the year before. Operating income was US$633.0 million versus US$603.0 million in the prior year, an increase of 5.0%. Direct operating expenses rose 0.8% to US$3.50 billion from US$3.48 billion in the comparable period the year before. Indirect operating expenses decreased 0.2% to US$484.0 million from US$485.0 million in the equivalent prior-year period.

Prospects: On Nov 28 2007, Co. announced that its South Carolina Electric & Gas Co. subsidiary has received approval from the South Carolina Public Service Commission for an overall increase in its retail electric revenues of about $76.9 million. Meanwhile, Co. has affirmed its 2008 earnings guidance of $2.90 to $3.05 per share, excluding any potential effects from changes in accounting principles and gains or losses from certain investing activities, litigation and sales of assets. Also, Co. expects an average annual earnings growth rate of 4.0% to 6.0% over the next three to five years. Separately, Co. estimates its 2008 capital expenditures for construction and nuclear fuel of $823.0 million.

Financial Data

(US$ in Thousands)	12/31/2007	12/31/2006	12/31/2005	12/31/2004	12/31/2003	12/31/2002	12/31/2001	12/31/2000
Earnings Per Share	2.74	2.68	2.81	2.30	2.54	(1.34)	5.15	2.40
Cash Flow Per Share	6.26	6.50	4.10	5.05	3.03	4.88	4.74	3.73
Tang Book Value Per Share	25.30	24.32	23.35	21.71	20.82	19.64	20.95	19.40
Dividends Per Share	1.760	1.680	1.560	1.460	1.380	1.300	1.200	1.150
Dividend Payout %	64.23	62.69	55.52	63.48	54.33	...	23.30	47.92
Income Statement								
Total Revenue	4,621,000	4,563,000	4,777,000	3,885,000	3,416,000	2,954,000	3,451,000	3,433,000
EBITDA	1,028,000	1,012,000	1,022,000	885,000	896,000	587,000	1,330,000	841,000
Income Before Taxes	473,000	439,000	274,000	387,000	426,000	135,000	855,000	373,000
Income Taxes	140,000	119,000	(118,000)	123,000	135,000	36,000	405,000	141,000
Net Income	320,000	310,000	320,000	257,000	282,000	(142,000)	539,000	250,000
Average Shares	116,700	115,800	113,800	111,600	110,800	106,000	104,700	104,500
Balance Sheet								
Net PPE	7,669,000	7,139,000	6,842,000	6,866,000	6,513,000	5,569,000	5,356,000	5,028,000
Total Assets	10,165,000	9,817,000	9,519,000	8,996,000	8,456,000	7,754,000	7,822,000	7,420,000
Long-Term Obligations	2,879,000	3,067,000	2,948,000	3,186,000	3,225,000	2,834,000	2,646,000	2,850,000
Total Liabilities	7,099,000	6,865,000	6,736,000	6,439,000	6,044,000	5,421,000	5,472,000	5,232,000
Stockholders' Equity	3,066,000	2,952,000	2,783,000	2,557,000	2,412,000	2,283,000	2,300,000	2,138,000
Shares Outstanding	117,000	117,000	114,671	112,909	110,735	110,831	104,728	104,729
Statistical Record								
Return on Assets %	3.20	3.21	3.46	2.94	3.48	N.M.	7.07	3.71
Return on Equity %	10.63	10.81	11.99	10.32	12.01	N.M.	24.29	11.48
EBITDA Margin %	22.25	22.18	21.39	22.78	26.23	19.87	38.54	24.50
Net Margin %	6.92	6.79	6.70	6.62	8.26	(4.81)	15.62	7.28
PPE Turnover	0.62	0.65	0.70	0.58	0.57	0.54	0.66	0.77
Asset Turnover	0.46	0.47	0.52	0.44	0.42	0.38	0.45	0.51
Debt to Equity	0.94	1.04	1.06	1.25	1.34	1.24	1.15	1.33
Price Range	45.26-36.70	41.99-37.16	43.40-37.10	39.62-33.09	35.52-28.21	31.98-24.25	29.25-24.57	30.89-22.56
P/E Ratio	16.52-13.39	15.67-13.87	15.44-13.20	17.23-14.39	13.98-11.11	...	5.68-4.77	12.87-9.40
Average Yield %	4.29	4.21	3.88	4.03	4.23	4.49	4.43	4.33

Address: 1426 Main Street, Columbia, SC 29201	**Web Site:** www.scana.com	**Auditors:** Deloitte & Touche LLP
Telephone: 803-217-9000	**Officers:** William B. Timmerman - Chmn., C.E.O.	**Investor Contact:** 803-217-9240
Fax: 803-343-2389	Kevin B. Marsh - Sr. V.P., C.F.O.	**Transfer Agents:** Scana Corp.; Stockholder Records Department

SCHERING-PLOUGH CORP.

Exchange	Symbol	Price	52Wk Range	Yield	P/E
NYS	SGP	$14.41 (3/31/2008)	33.34-14.41	1.80	N/A

*7 Year Price Score 95.26   *NYSE Composite Index=100   *12 Month Price Score 75.17

Interim Earnings (Per Share)

Qtr.	Mar	Jun	Sep	Dec
2003	0.12	0.12	(0.18)	(0.12)
2004	(0.05)	(0.04)	0.01	(0.59)
2005	0.07	(0.05)	0.03	0.07
2006	0.24	0.16	0.19	0.12
2007	0.36	0.35	0.45	(2.19)

Interim Dividends (Per Share)

Amt	Decl	Ex	Rec	Pay
0.065Q	6/26/2007	8/1/2007	8/3/2007	8/28/2007
0.065Q	9/19/2007	10/31/2007	11/2/2007	11/27/2007
0.065Q	12/14/2007	1/30/2008	2/1/2008	2/26/2008
0.065Q	2/29/2008	4/30/2008	5/2/2008	5/27/2008
		Indicated Div: $0.26		

Valuation Analysis   **Institutional Holding**

Forecast P/E	18.94	No of Institutions
	(1/10/2007)	700
Market Cap	$23.4 Billion	Shares
Book Value	10.4 Billion	1,152,842,496
Price/Book	2.25	% Held
Price/Sales	1.84	77.49

TRADING VOLUME (thousand shares)

Business Summary: Pharmaceuticals (MIC: 9.1 SIC: 2834 NAIC: 325412)

Schering-Plough is a science-centered health care company operating through three business segments. Co.'s Human Prescription Pharmaceuticals segment discovers, develops, manufactures and markets human pharmaceutical products. Co.'s Consumer Health Care segment develops, manufactures and markets over-the-counter, foot care and sun care products. Co.'s Animal Health segment discovers, develops, manufactures and markets animal health products including vaccines. As of Dec 31 2007, Co. had subsidiaries in more than 55 countries outside the U.S. In addition, as of Dec 31 2007, Co. had business operations in more than 140 countries.

Recent Developments: For the year ended Dec 31 2007, net loss amounted to US$1.47 billion versus net income of US$1.14 billion in the prior year. Revenues were US$12.69 billion, up 19.8% from US$10.59 billion the year before. Direct operating expenses rose 19.2% to US$4.41 billion from US$3.70 billion in the comparable period the year before. Indirect operating expenses increased 75.9% to US$12.15 billion from US$6.91 billion in the equivalent prior-year period.

Prospects: Moving ahead, Co. is planning additional investments to enhance its infrastructure and is in the process of building a pharmaceutical sciences center in New Jersey. Specifically, Co. is projecting capital expenditures of approximately $175.0 million over the next two years for this center, which should allow it to streamline its drug development process, where products are moved from the drug discovery pipeline to market. Meanwhile, Co. expects its Nov 2007 acquisition of Organon BioSciences N.V., a company that discovers, develops and manufactures human prescription and animal health products to be accretive to its stand-alone earnings per share by about $0.10 in the first full year.

Financial Data

(US$ in Thousands)	12/31/2007	12/31/2006	12/31/2005	12/31/2004	12/31/2003	12/31/2002	12/31/2001	12/31/2000
Earnings Per Share	(1.04)	0.71	0.12	(0.67)	(0.06)	1.35	1.32	1.64
Cash Flow Per Share	1.71	1.46	0.60	(0.10)	0.41	1.35	1.72	1.71
Tang Book Value Per Share	N.M.	4.02	3.64	3.75	4.57	5.10	4.41	3.75
Dividends Per Share	0.250	0.220	0.220	0.220	0.565	0.670	0.620	0.545
Dividend Payout %	...	30.99	183.33	...	...	49.63	46.97	33.23
Income Statement								
Total Revenue	12,690,000	10,594,000	9,508,000	8,272,000	8,334,000	10,180,000	9,802,000	9,815,000
EBITDA	(504,000)	1,926,000	970,000	373,000	395,000	2,888,000	2,843,000	3,487,000
Income Before Taxes	(1,215,000)	1,483,000	497,000	(168,000)	(46,000)	2,563,000	2,523,000	3,188,000
Income Taxes	258,000	362,000	228,000	779,000	46,000	589,000	580,000	765,000
Net Income	(1,473,000)	1,143,000	269,000	(947,000)	(92,000)	1,974,000	1,943,000	2,423,000
Average Shares	1,536,000	1,491,000	1,484,000	1,472,000	1,469,000	1,470,000	1,470,000	1,476,000
Balance Sheet								
Current Assets	10,846,000	10,423,000	9,732,000	10,003,000	9,147,000	8,272,000	6,519,000	5,720,000
Total Assets	29,156,000	16,071,000	15,469,000	15,911,000	15,102,000	14,136,000	12,174,000	10,805,000
Current Liabilities	6,043,000	4,162,000	4,659,000	5,208,000	4,609,000	4,729,000	3,917,000	3,645,000
Long-Term Obligations	9,019,000	2,414,000	2,399,000	2,392,000	2,410,000	...	...	...
Total Liabilities	18,771,000	8,163,000	8,082,000	8,355,000	7,765,000	5,994,000	5,049,000	4,686,000
Stockholders' Equity	10,385,000	7,908,000	7,387,000	7,556,000	7,337,000	8,142,000	7,125,000	6,119,000
Shares Outstanding	1,621,000	1,487,000	1,480,000	1,475,000	1,471,000	1,468,000	1,465,000	1,463,000
Statistical Record								
Return on Assets %	N.M.	7.25	1.71	N.M.	N.M.	15.01	16.91	23.95
Return on Equity %	N.M.	14.95	3.60	N.M.	N.M.	25.86	29.34	42.83
EBITDA Margin %	N.M.	18.18	10.20	4.51	4.74	28.37	29.00	35.53
Net Margin %	N.M.	10.79	2.83	N.M.	N.M.	19.39	19.82	24.69
Asset Turnover	0.56	0.67	0.61	0.53	0.57	0.77	0.85	0.97
Current Ratio	1.79	2.50	2.09	1.92	1.98	1.75	1.66	1.57
Debt to Equity	0.87	0.31	0.32	0.32	0.33	...	...	...
Price Range	33.34-22.75	23.90-18.00	22.45-17.68	21.12-15.96	23.68-14.52	36.00-17.30	54.25-32.65	59.13-30.50
P/E Ratio	...	33.66-25.35	187.08-147.33	...	...	26.67-12.81	41.10-24.73	36.05-18.60
Average Yield %	0.87	1.09	1.10	1.23	3.24	2.57	1.57	1.21

Address: 2000 Galloping Hill Road, Kenilworth, NJ 07033	Web Site: www.schering-plough.com	Auditors: Deloitte & Touche LLP
Telephone: 908-298-4000	Officers: Fred Hassan - Chmn., Pres., C.E.O. Robert J. Bertolini CPA - Exec. V.P., C.F.O.	
Fax: 908-822-7048		

SCHLUMBERGER LTD. (NETHERLANDS ANTILLES)

Exchange	Symbol	Price	52Wk Range	Yield	P/E
NYS	SLB	$87.00 (3/31/2008)	112.09-70.82	0.97	20.71

*7 Year Price Score 163.63 *NYSE Composite Index=100 *12 Month Price Score 100.62

Interim Earnings (Per Share)

Qtr.	Mar	Jun	Sep	Dec
2003	0.13	0.10	(0.04)	0.15
2004	...	...	0.27	0.28
2005	0.43	0.40	0.45	0.55
2006	0.59	0.69	0.81	0.92
2007	0.96	1.02	1.09	1.12

Interim Dividends (Per Share)

Amt	Decl	Ex	Rec	Pay
0.175Q	4/19/2007	6/4/2007	6/6/2007	7/6/2007
0.175Q	7/19/2007	8/31/2007	9/5/2007	10/5/2007
0.175Q	10/18/2007	12/3/2007	12/5/2007	1/4/2008
0.21Q	1/17/2008	2/15/2008	2/20/2008	4/4/2008

Indicated Div: $0.84

Valuation Analysis

Forecast P/E	N/A
Market Cap	$104.0 Billion
Book Value	14.9 Billion
Price/Book	6.99
Price/Sales	4.39

Institutional Holding

No of Institutions	1037
Shares	930,141,696
% Held	78.92

Business Summary: Oil and Gas (MIC: 14.2 SIC: 1389 NAIC: 213112)

Schlumberger is an oilfield services company that operates through two business segments: Schlumberger Oilfield Services, which provides technology, project management and information applications to the international oil and gas exploration and production industry; and WesternGeco, which provides reservoir imaging, monitoring and development services with seismic crews and data processing centers in the industry as well as multiclient seismic library. Co.'s services in its WesternGeco segment range from three dimensional and time-lapse (four dimensional) seismic surveys to multi-component surveys for delineating prospects and reservoir management.

Recent Developments: For the year ended Dec 31 2007, income from continuing operations increased 39.5% to US$5.18 billion from US$3.71 billion a year earlier. Net income increased 39.5% to US$5.18 billion from US$3.71 billion in the prior year. Revenues were US$23.71 billion, up 21.5% from US$19.52 billion the year before. Direct operating expenses rose 17.4% to US$15.48 billion from US$13.18 billion in the comparable period the year before. Indirect operating expenses increased 15.5% to US$1.60 billion from US$1.39 billion in the equivalent prior year period.

Prospects: In the near-term, Co. believes that natural gas drilling in North America will not vary much in the absence of the winter weather. Co. also believes that its growth and operating capabilities will be restricted by high utilization of the existing offshore rig fleet and the projected limited new builds entering the market. However, growth in land activity outside North America should remain strong, and seismic exploration services worldwide should remain in high demand on both land and offshore as the industry gears up for the expanding exploration cycle. In the longer term, Co. believes that growth will be driven by, among others, plans to increase its research and development spending.

Financial Data

(US$ in Thousands)	12/31/2007	12/31/2006	12/31/2005	12/31/2004	12/31/2003	12/31/2002	12/31/2001	12/31/2000
Earnings Per Share	4.20	3.01	1.82	1.02	0.33	(2.00)	0.46	0.64
Cash Flow Per Share	5.27	1.05	2.55	1.56	1.81	1.89	1.37	
Tang Book Value Per Share	7.39	3.84	3.69	2.53	1.87	0.70	1.13	5.87
Dividends Per Share	0.700	0.500	0.420	0.375	0.375	0.375	0.375	0.375
Dividend Payout %	16.67	16.61	23.08	36.76	113.64	...	82.42	59.06
Income Statement								
Total Revenue	23,708,037	19,517,194	14,716,951	11,608,863	14,059,097	13,612,730	13,988,064	10,034,717
EBITDA	8,578,436	6,509,568	4,322,699	2,635,368	2,138,594	(685,233)	3,022,305	960,681
Income Before Taxes	6,624,449	4,948,158	2,971,730	1,327,437	567,743	(2,230,286)	1,126,186	960,681
Income Taxes	1,447,933	1,189,568	681,927	276,949	209,386	279,127	575,474	229,248
Net Income	5,176,516	3,709,851	2,206,967	1,223,870	383,002	(2,319,995)	522,217	734,596
Average Shares	1,238,675	1,242,196	1,229,716	1,225,744	1,172,982	1,157,176	1,160,428	1,160,152
Balance Sheet								
Current Assets	11,055,383	9,185,662	8,553,913	7,059,749	10,369,121	7,185,440	7,704,890	7,493,211
Total Assets	27,853,372	22,832,138	18,077,492	16,000,777	20,041,326	19,435,195	22,326,367	17,172,731
Current Liabilities	7,504,851	6,454,795	5,514,736	4,701,200	6,794,730	6,450,918	6,217,785	3,990,905
Long-Term Obligations	3,794,466	4,663,942	3,591,338	3,944,180	6,097,418	6,028,549	6,215,709	3,573,047
Total Liabilities	12,915,603	12,412,255	9,980,725	9,467,602	13,761,707	13,275,530	13,310,987	8,877,515
Stockholders' Equity	14,875,888	10,419,883	7,591,585	6,116,737	5,881,289	5,606,138	8,378,481	8,295,216
Shares Outstanding	1,195,616	1,178,543	1,177,604	1,178,516	1,171,896	1,164,346	1,151,780	1,145,449
Statistical Record								
Return on Assets %	20.43	18.14	12.95	6.77	1.94	N.M.	2.64	4.54
Return on Equity %	40.93	41.19	32.20	20.35	6.67	N.M.	6.26	9.15
EBITDA Margin %	36.18	33.35	29.37	22.70	15.21	N.M.	21.61	9.57
Net Margin %	21.83	19.01	15.00	10.54	2.72	N.M.	3.73	7.32
Asset Turnover	0.94	0.95	0.86	0.64	0.71	0.65	0.71	0.62
Current Ratio	1.47	1.42	1.55	1.50	1.53	1.11	1.24	1.88
Debt to Equity	0.26	0.45	0.47	0.64	1.04	1.08	0.74	0.43
Price Range	112.09-56.52	73.37-51.68	51.44-31.73	34.63-26.34	27.84-18.04	30.75-17.14	40.88-20.97	43.94-27.03
P/E Ratio	26.69-13.46	24.38-17.17	28.26-17.44	33.95-25.83	84.35-54.65	...	88.86-45.59	68.65-42.24
Average Yield %	0.84	0.80	1.07	1.20	1.66	1.56	1.30	1.00

Address: Parkstraat 83, The Hague, 2514 JG
Telephone: 713-513-2000

Web Site: www.slb.com
Officers: Andrew Gould - Chmn., C.E.O. Jean-Marc Perraud - Exec. V.P., C.F.O.

Auditors: PricewaterhouseCoopers LLP
Transfer Agents: Computershare Trust Company, N.A., Providence, RI

SCOTTS MIRACLE-GRO CO (THE)

Exchange	Symbol	Price	52Wk Range	Yield	P/E
NYS	SMG	$32.42 (3/31/2008)	48.93-32.00	1.54	18.85

*7 Year Price Score 98.49   *NYSE Composite Index=100   *12 Month Price Score 93.78

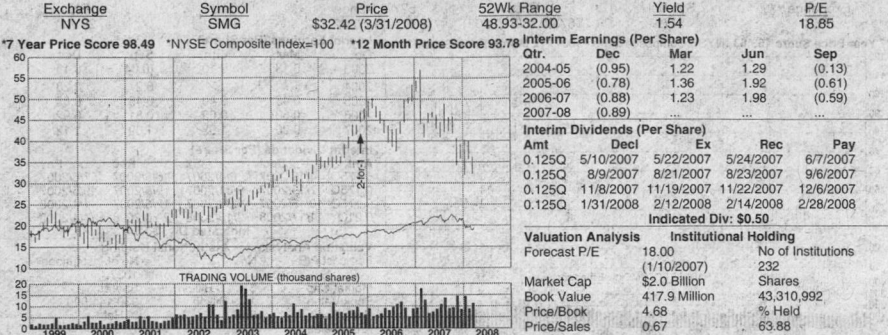

Interim Earnings (Per Share)

Qtr.	Dec	Mar	Jun	Sep
2004-05	(0.95)	1.22	1.29	(0.13)
2005-06	(0.78)	1.36	1.92	(0.61)
2006-07	(0.88)	1.23	1.98	(0.59)
2007-08	(0.89)	...	...	...

Interim Dividends (Per Share)

Amt	Decl	Ex	Rec	Pay
0.125Q	5/10/2007	5/22/2007	5/24/2007	6/7/2007
0.125Q	8/9/2007	8/21/2007	8/23/2007	9/6/2007
0.125Q	11/8/2007	11/19/2007	11/22/2007	12/6/2007
0.125Q	1/31/2008	2/12/2008	2/14/2008	2/28/2008

Indicated Div: $0.50

Valuation Analysis

	Institutional Holding	
Forecast P/E	18.00 (1/10/2007)	No of Institutions 232
Market Cap	$2.0 Billion	Shares
Book Value	417.9 Million	43,310,992
Price/Book	4.68	% Held
Price/Sales	0.67	63.88

Business Summary: Chemicals (MIC: 11.1 SIC: 2879 NAIC: 325320)

Scotts Miracle-Gro and its subsidiaries are engaged in the manufacturing and marketing of consumer branded products for lawn and garden care, and horticulture in North America and Europe. Co.'s operates through four reportable segments; North America, Scotts LawnService®, International, and Corporate & Other. Co.'s portfolio of consumer brands include Scotts®, Turf Builder®, Miracle-Gro®, Osmocote®, Hyponex®, LiquaFeed®, Bug-B-Gon®, Weed-B-Gon®, Earthgro®, SuperSoil®, Ortho®, Smith & Hawken®, Morning Song® and Roundup®. Co. also has a presence in Australia, the Far East, Latin America and South America.

Recent Developments: For the quarter ended Dec 29 2007, net loss amounted to US$56.8 million versus a net loss of US$59.4 million in the year-earlier quarter. Revenues were US$308.7 million, up 13.8% from US$271.2 million the year before. Operating loss was US$69.8 million versus a loss of US$84.6 million in the prior-year quarter. Direct operating expenses rose 10.0% to US$237.4 million from US$215.9 million in the comparable period the year before. Indirect operating expenses increased 0.9% to US$141.1 million from US$139.9 million in the equivalent prior-year period.

Prospects: Co. remains focused on making strategic investments in technology and innovation, as well as targeted marketing and selling spending, to support its long-term growth initiatives. Hence, with the launch of new products and further investment in both marketing and sales support, Co. is optimistic about its outlook for fiscal 2008 ending Sep 2007, and thus, projects net sales to grow about 6.0% to 8.0% and operating profits to improve by as much as 6.0%. However, Co. anticipates gross profit for fiscal 2008 as a percentage of net sales to closely approximate fiscal 2007, as price increases, product mix and cost savings measures are expected to mostly be offset by volatile commodity costs.

Financial Data

(US$ in Thousands)	3 Mos	09/30/2007	09/30/2006	09/30/2005	09/30/2004	09/30/2003	09/30/2002	09/30/2001
Earnings Per Share	1.72	1.69	1.91	1.47	1.51	1.62	1.30	0.26
Cash Flow Per Share	4.18	3.78	2.70	3.39	3.31	3.53	3.83	1.16
Tang Book Value Per Share	N.M.	N.M.	2.99	2.27	0.39	N.M.	N.M.	N.M.
Dividends Per Share	8.500	8.500	0.500	0.125	...	...	...	...
Dividend Payout %	494.09	502.96	26.18	8.50	...	...	...	...
Income Statement								
Total Revenue	308,700	2,871,800	2,697,100	2,369,300	2,037,900	1,910,100	1,760,600	1,747,700
EBITDA	(52,600)	326,300	319,500	266,800	261,700	281,400	279,300	176,700
Depn & Amortn	17,200	...	...	...	...	...	...	...
Income Before Taxes	(88,800)	188,100	212,900	158,100	158,500	163,300	162,900	28,700
Income Taxes	(32,000)	74,700	80,200	57,700	58,000	59,500	61,900	13,200
Net Income	(56,800)	113,400	132,700	100,600	100,900	103,800	82,500	15,500
Average Shares	64,200	67,000	69,400	68,600	66,600	64,200	63,400	60,800
Balance Sheet								
Current Assets	1,134,400	999,300	942,000	787,800	830,300	810,200	730,100	694,200
Total Assets	2,409,000	2,277,200	2,217,600	2,018,900	2,047,800	2,027,900	1,901,400	1,843,000
Current Liabilities	519,700	586,600	496,200	486,200	433,600	445,800	451,800	445,100
Long-Term Obligations	1,286,600	1,031,400	475,200	382,400	608,500	702,200	731,200	816,500
Total Liabilities	1,991,100	1,797,900	1,135,900	992,700	1,173,200	1,299,700	1,307,500	1,336,800
Stockholders' Equity	417,900	479,300	1,081,700	1,026,200	874,600	728,200	593,900	506,200
Shares Outstanding	60,300	64,100	66,600	67,800	65,600	64,000	60,200	57,400
Statistical Record								
Return on Assets %	4.87	5.05	6.26	4.95	4.94	5.28	4.41	0.86
Return on Equity %	15.81	14.53	12.59	10.59	12.56	15.70	15.00	3.15
EBITDA Margin %	N.M.	11.36	11.85	11.26	12.84	14.73	15.86	10.11
Net Margin %	N.M.	3.95	4.92	4.25	4.95	5.43	4.69	0.89
Asset Turnover	1.23	1.28	1.27	1.17	1.00	0.97	0.94	0.97
Current Ratio	2.18	1.70	1.90	1.62	1.91	1.82	1.62	1.56
Debt to Equity	3.08	2.15	0.44	0.37	0.70	0.96	1.23	1.61
Price Range	57.04-34.18	57.04-40.86	50.24-37.57	43.97-30.95	34.27-27.35	28.85-20.84	25.18-17.23	23.55-14.44
P/E Ratio	33.16-19.87	33.75-24.18	26.30-19.67	29.91-21.05	22.70-18.11	17.81-12.87	19.37-13.25	90.58-55.53
Average Yield %	19.14	18.18	1.13	0.35	...	...	...	...

Address: 14111 Scottslawn Road, Marysville, OH 43041	Web Site: www.investor.scotts.com	Auditors: Deloitte & Touche LLP
Telephone: 937-644-0011	Officers: James Hagedorn - Chmn., Pres., C.E.O.	Investor Contact: 614-719-5500
Fax: 937-644-7614	Robert F. Bernstock - Exec. V.P., Pres. North America	

SCRIPPS (E.W.) CO.

Exchange	Symbol	Price	52Wk Range	Yield	P/E
NYS	SSP	$42.01 (3/31/2008)	47.20-38.25	1.33	N/A

*7 Year Price Score 79.38   ***NYSE Composite Index=100**   ***12 Month Price Score 105.50**

Interim Earnings (Per Share)

Qtr.	Mar	Jun	Sep	Dec
2003	0.33	0.40	0.32	0.62
2004	0.43	0.53	0.34	0.55
2005	0.42	0.59	0.50	0.00
2006	0.45	0.43	0.44	0.81
2007	0.42	0.59	0.54	(1.56)

Interim Dividends (Per Share)

Amt	Decl	Ex	Rec	Pay
0.14Q	5/10/2007	5/23/2007	5/25/2007	6/8/2007
0.14Q	8/1/2007	8/29/2007	8/31/2007	9/10/2007
0.14Q	11/7/2007	11/28/2007	11/30/2007	12/10/2007
0.14Q	2/15/2008	2/27/2008	2/29/2008	3/10/2008

Indicated Div: $0.56

Valuation Analysis / Institutional Holding

Forecast P/E	N/A
	No of Institutions 265
Market Cap	$6.8 Billion
Book Value	2.5 Billion
	Shares 86,056,128
Price/Book	2.79
	% Held 67.71
Price/Sales	2.72

TRADING VOLUME (thousand shares)

Business Summary: Media (MIC: 13.1 SIC: 2711 NAIC: 511110)

Scripps (E.W.) is a media company with interests in national television networks (Scripps Networks), newspaper publishing, broadcast television, interactive media and licensing and syndication. Scripps Networks includes five national lifestyle television networks and their affiliated Web sites, Home & Garden Television, Food Network, DIY Network, Fine Living and Great American Country. As of Dec 31 2007, Co. operated daily and community newspapers in 17 U.S. markets. Co. also owned and operated the Washington-based Scripps Media Center, home to the Scripps Howard News Service, a supplemental wire service covering stories in the capital, other parts of the U.S. and abroad.

Recent Developments: For the year ended Dec 31 2007, loss from continuing operations was US$5.6 million compared with income of US$397.2 million a year earlier. Net loss amounted to US$1.6 million versus net income of US$353.2 million in the prior year. Revenues were US$2.52 billion, up 0.8% from US$2.50 billion the year before. Operating income was US$210.1 million versus US$686.2 million in the prior year, a decrease of 69.4%. Indirect operating expenses increased 27.3% to US$2.31 billion from US$1.81 billion in the equivalent prior-year period.

Prospects: For the first quarter of 2008, Co. expects its Scripps Networks revenue to grow 10.0% to 12.0%, while revenue at its broadcast television stations is expected to be flat to up 4.0% and revenue in its newspapers business is expected to decline 5.0% to 7.0% due primarily to weakness in classified and local advertising. In view of that, Co. is targeting earnings per share from continuing operations of $0.38 to $0.42 for the quarter. Meanwhile, Co. continues to make progress in its plans to pursue a separation of its organization into two publicly traded companies, one focused on national brands and the other focused on local media. This transaction is expected to be completed in June 2008.

Financial Data

(US$ in Thousands)	12/31/2007	12/31/2006	12/31/2005	12/31/2004	12/31/2003	12/31/2002	12/31/2001	12/31/2000
Earnings Per Share	(0.01)	2.14	1.51	1.84	1.66	1.17	0.86	1.03
Cash Flow Per Share	3.65	3.40	2.74	2.37	2.04	1.34	1.31	1.63
Tang Book Value Per Share	1.19	N.M.	N.M.	0.72	1.21	N.M.	N.M.	N.M.
Dividends Per Share	0.540	0.470	0.430	0.388	0.300	0.300	0.300	0.280
Dividend Payout %	...	21.96	28.48	21.06	18.07	25.64	34.68	27.18
Income Statement								
Total Revenue	2,517,140	2,498,077	2,513,890	2,167,503	1,874,845	1,618,909	1,437,131	1,719,359
EBITDA	424,179	861,268	602,366	642,535	522,742	399,491	379,706	437,101
Income Before Taxes	254,647	690,204	472,371	542,653	423,062	308,922	241,382	276,002
Income Taxes	177,765	219,761	191,794	105,773	137,974	115,619	99,622	108,090
Net Income	(1,621)	333,220	249,153	303,811	270,815	188,297	137,963	163,453
Average Shares	164,267	164,849	165,435	164,917	162,938	161,238	159,940	158,322
Balance Sheet								
Current Assets	926,793	875,319	796,569	643,298	562,437	500,011	450,658	523,985
Total Assets	4,005,292	4,344,334	4,032,628	3,424,849	3,009,402	2,870,337	2,643,760	2,572,866
Current Liabilities	346,802	399,268	348,424	375,346	330,959	426,073	905,511	532,976
Long-Term Obligations	504,663	766,381	825,775	532,686	509,117	649,801	109,966	501,781
Total Liabilities	1,554,931	1,762,899	1,745,549	1,328,728	1,186,871	1,354,872	1,291,860	1,295,056
Stockholders' Equity	2,450,361	2,581,435	2,287,079	2,096,121	1,822,531	1,515,465	1,351,900	1,277,810
Shares Outstanding	162,989	163,542	163,662	163,190	161,936	160,074	158,401	157,477
Statistical Record								
Return on Assets %	N.M.	8.43	6.68	9.42	9.21	6.83	5.29	6.40
Return on Equity %	N.M.	14.51	11.37	15.46	16.23	13.13	10.49	13.35
EBITDA Margin %	16.85	34.48	23.96	29.64	27.88	24.71	26.42	25.42
Net Margin %	N.M.	14.14	9.91	14.02	14.44	11.63	9.60	9.51
Asset Turnover	0.60	0.60	0.67	0.67	0.64	0.59	0.55	0.67
Current Ratio	2.67	2.19	2.29	1.71	1.70	1.17	0.50	0.98
Debt to Equity	0.21	0.30	0.36	0.25	0.28	0.43	0.08	0.39
Price Range	53.07-38.25	50.85-40.90	52.35-44.92	54.28-45.40	47.42-37.56	43.63-32.88	35.63-28.23	31.44-21.25
P/E Ratio	...	23.76-19.11	34.67-29.75	29.50-24.67	28.57-22.62	37.29-28.10	41.44-32.83	30.52-20.63
Average Yield %	1.21	1.00	0.88	0.78	0.70	0.80	0.93	1.12

Address: 312 Walnut Street, Cincinnati, OH 45202	Web Site: www.scripps.com	Auditors: Deloitte & Touche, LLP
Telephone: 513-977-3000	Officers: William R. Burleigh - Chmn. Kenneth W. Lowe - Pres., C.E.O.	Investor Contact: 513-977-3825
Fax: 513-977-3721		Transfer Agents: Mellon Investor Services, South Hackensack, NJ

SEALED AIR CORP.

Exchange	Symbol	Price	52Wk Range	Yield	P/E
NYS	SEE	$25.25 (3/31/2008)	33.56-20.33	1.90	13.36

*7 Year Price Score 90.59   ***NYSE Composite Index=100**   ***12 Month Price Score 100.14**

Interim Earnings (Per Share)

Qtr.	Mar	Jun	Sep	Dec
2003	0.26	0.28	0.20	0.25
2004	0.32	0.33	0.34	0.14
2005	0.29	0.33	0.34	0.39
2006	0.30	0.31	0.41	0.45
2007	0.67	0.40	0.39	0.43

Interim Dividends (Per Share)

Amt	Decl	Ex	Rec	Pay
0.10Q	4/12/2007	5/30/2007	6/1/2007	6/15/2007
0.10Q	8/9/2007	9/5/2007	9/7/2007	9/21/2007
0.10Q	11/16/2007	12/5/2007	12/7/2007	12/21/2007
0.12Q	2/19/2008	3/5/2008	3/7/2008	3/21/2008

Indicated Div: $0.48

Valuation Analysis / Institutional Holding

Forecast P/E	N/A	No of Institutions
		292
Market Cap	$4.1 Billion	Shares
Book Value	2.0 Billion	142,439,232
Price/Book	2.02	% Held
Price/Sales	0.88	88.28

TRADING VOLUME (thousand shares)

Business Summary: Paper Products (MIC; 11.11 SIC: 2671 NAIC: 326112)

Sealed Air, through its subsidiaries, manufactures a range of packaging and performance-based materials and equipment systems that serve an array of food, industrial, medical and consumer applications. As of Dec 31 2007, Co. conducted its business through four operating segments. The Food Packaging segments focuses on industrial food packaging. The Food Solutions segment targets enhancement in food packaging technologies. The Protective Packaging segment includes core protective packaging technologies and services for traditional industrial applications. The Other segment focuses on growth into new market though new ventures, such as products sourced from renewable materials.

Recent Developments: For the year ended Dec 31 2007, net income increased 28.8% to US$353.0 million from US$274.1 million in the prior year. Revenues were US$4.65 billion, up 7.5% from US$4.33 billion the year before. Operating income was US$549.3 million versus US$526.1 million in the prior year, an increase of 4.4%. Direct operating expenses rose 8.5% to US$3.35 billion from US$3.09 billion in the comparable period the year before. Indirect operating expenses increased 5.3% to US$751.8 million from US$714.0 million in the equivalent prior-year period.

Prospects: Despite the anticipated softness in the U.S. economy as well as unfavorable comparisons in raw materials and energy costs in the first half of 2008, Co. expects to grow revenue and improve margins in 2008. Hence, Co. is forecasting net earnings for the full year of 2008 to be in the range of $1.75 to $1.85 per diluted share, excluding charges of $0.11 per share, which is estimated to be incurred relating to its global manufacturing strategy. Specifically, Co.'s guidance assumes a slight increase in average raw material costs compared with 2007, as well as a unit volume growth rate comparable to the 2007 rate, consistent with projections for moderate growth in the global economy.

Financial Data

(US$ in Thousands)	12/31/2007	12/31/2006	12/31/2005	12/31/2004	12/31/2003	12/31/2002	12/31/2001	12/31/2000
Earnings Per Share	1.89	1.47	1.35	1.13	1.00	(2.15)	0.61	0.96
Cash Flow Per Share	2.36	2.67	2.16	2.58	2.77	1.93	3.46	1.96
Tang Book Value Per Share	0.31	N.M.	N.M.	N.M.	N.M.	N.M.	N.M.	N.M.
Dividends Per Share	0.400	0.300	...	...	...	...	...	...
Dividend Payout %	21.16	20.48	...	...	...	...	...	...
Income Statement								
Total Revenue	4,651,200	4,327,900	4,085,100	3,798,100	3,531,900	3,204,256	3,067,482	3,067,714
EBITDA	765,400	718,900	704,100	659,300	684,800	(160,919)	595,027	697,901
Income Before Taxes	456,000	400,100	376,600	322,900	376,900	(391,933)	297,452	413,429
Income Taxes	103,000	126,000	120,800	107,300	136,500	(82,864)	140,755	188,110
Net Income	353,000	274,100	255,800	215,600	240,400	(309,069)	156,697	225,319
Average Shares	191,300	192,600	196,000	198,720	187,380	168,580	167,800	175,902
Balance Sheet								
Current Assets	1,936,100	1,756,700	1,695,400	1,611,200	1,427,800	1,056,258	776,352	877,080
Total Assets	5,438,300	5,020,900	4,864,200	4,855,000	4,704,100	4,260,766	3,907,909	4,048,098
Current Liabilities	1,741,600	1,406,100	1,533,500	1,303,800	1,190,400	1,152,754	626,980	674,568
Long-Term Obligations	1,531,600	1,826,600	1,813,050	2,088,000	2,259,800	868,030	788,111	944,453
Total Liabilities	3,418,700	3,366,100	3,472,100	3,521,500	3,580,500	2,120,801	1,691,603	1,902,596
Stockholders' Equity	2,019,600	1,654,800	1,392,100	1,333,500	1,123,600	812,960	850,152	753,129
Shares Outstanding	161,627	161,330	162,903	167,248	170,170	168,081	167,553	167,292
Statistical Record								
Return on Assets %	6.75	5.55	5.26	4.50	5.36	N.M.	3.94	5.69
Return on Equity %	19.21	17.99	18.77	17.50	24.83	N.M.	19.55	34.46
EBITDA Margin %	16.46	16.61	17.24	17.36	19.39	N.M.	19.40	22.75
Net Margin %	7.59	6.33	6.26	5.68	6.81	N.M.	5.11	7.34
Asset Turnover	0.89	0.88	0.84	0.79	0.79	0.78	0.77	0.77
Current Ratio	1.11	1.25	1.11	1.24	1.20	0.92	1.24	1.30
Debt to Equity	0.76	1.10	1.30	1.57	2.01	1.07	0.93	1.25
Price Range	33.72-22.41	32.77-22.91	28.22-23.01	27.27-22.14	27.23-17.71	24.07-6.58	23.45-15.41	30.38-13.38
P/E Ratio	17.84-11.86	22.30-15.58	20.90-17.04	24.14-19.59	27.23-17.71	...	38.44-25.26	31.64-13.93
Average Yield %	1.38	1.09	...	...	...	...	...	...

Address: Park 80 East, Saddle Brook, NJ 07663-5291	Web Site: www.sealedair.com	Auditors: KPMG LLP
Telephone: 201-791-7600	Officers: William V. Hickey - Pres., C.E.O. David H. Kelsey - Sr. V.P., C.F.O.	Investor Contact: 201-791-7600
Fax: 201-703-4205		Transfer Agents: Mellon Investor Services, South Hackensack, NJ

SEMPRA ENERGY

Exchange	Symbol	Price	52Wk Range	Yield	P/E
NYS	SRE	$53.28 (3/31/2008)	66.29-49.52	2.40	12.81

*7 Year Price Score 123.35 *NYSE Composite Index=100   *12 Month Price Score 98.32

Interim Earnings (Per Share)

Qtr.	Mar	Jun	Sep	Dec
2003	0.42	0.55	1.00	1.05
2004	0.85	0.52	0.98	1.47
2005	0.92	0.48	0.86	1.39
2006	0.98	1.43	2.49	0.46
2007	0.86	1.05	1.15	1.10

Interim Dividends (Per Share)

Amt	Decl	Ex	Rec	Pay
0.31Q	9/11/2007	9/25/2007	9/27/2007	10/15/2007
0.31Q	12/4/2007	12/18/2007	12/20/2007	1/15/2008
0.32Q	2/13/2008	3/18/2008	3/20/2008	4/15/2008
0.35Q	4/2/2008	6/25/2008	6/27/2008	7/15/2008

Indicated Div: $1.28

Valuation Analysis | **Institutional Holding**

Forecast P/E	13.75	No of Institutions
	(1/10/2007)	380
Market Cap	$13.9 Billion	Shares
Book Value	8.3 Billion	175,397,488
Price/Book	1.67	% Held
Price/Sales	1.22	66.71

Business Summary: Electricity (MIC: 7.1 SIC: 4932 NAIC: 221210)

Sempra Energy, together with its business units, provides electric, natural gas and other energy products and services to its customers. As of Dec 31 2007, Co.'s operations were divided into: Sempra Utilities, which consists of San Diego Gas and Electric and Southern California Gas Co., serves 23 million consumers from California's Central Valley to the Mexican border; and Sempra Global, which is a holding company for most of the Co.'s subsidiaries that are not subject to California utility regulation. Sempra Global's principal subsidiaries include Sempra Commodities, Sempra Generation, Sempra LNG and Sempra Pipelines and Storage.

Recent Developments: For the year ended Dec 31 2007, income from continuing operations increased 3.1% to US$1.13 billion from US$1.09 billion a year earlier. Net income decreased 21.8% to US$1.10 billion from US$1.41 billion in the prior year. Revenues were US$11.44 billion, down 2.7% from US$11.76 billion the year before. Operating income was US$1.68 billion versus US$1.79 billion in the prior year, a decrease of 5.9%. Direct operating expenses declined 6.7% to US$5.75 billion from US$6.17 billion in the comparable period the year before. Indirect operating expenses increased 5.2% to US$4.01 billion from US$3.81 billion in the equivalent prior-year period.

Prospects: Co. will complete several of its natural gas infrastructure projects in 2008. For instance, Co. expects its Energia Costa Azul receipt terminal in Baja California, Mexico, to receive start-up liquefied natural gas cargoes and begin commercial operation in the second quarter of 2008. Also, Co. expects the Cameron liquefied natural gas receipt terminal in Louisiana to be ready for commercial operations by the end of 2008. Further, Co. anticipates launching its global commodities-marketing joint venture with The Royal Bank of Scotland in 2008, which will expand the global footprint of its commodities business. Hence, Co. reaffirmed its earnings-per-share guidance of $3.65 to $3.85 for 2008.

Financial Data

(US$ in Thousands)	12/31/2007	12/31/2006	12/31/2005	12/31/2004	12/31/2003	12/31/2002	12/31/2001	12/31/2000
Earnings Per Share	4.16	5.38	3.65	3.83	3.03	2.87	2.52	2.06
Cash Flow Per Share	8.03	6.53	2.12	4.13	5.29	6.69	3.60	4.23
Tang Book Value Per Share	31.92	28.67	23.95	20.77	17.17	13.79	13.17	12.35
Dividends Per Share	1.240	1.200	1.160	1.000	1.000	1.000	1.000	1.000
Dividend Payout %	29.81	22.30	31.78	26.11	33.00	34.84	39.68	48.54
Income Statement								
Total Revenue	11,438,000	11,761,000	11,737,000	9,410,000	7,887,000	6,020,000	8,029,000	7,143,000
EBITDA	2,449,000	2,822,000	1,804,000	1,987,000	1,561,000	1,611,000	1,633,000	1,548,000
Income Before Taxes	1,550,000	1,914,000	916,000	1,113,000	742,000	721,000	731,000	699,000
Income Taxes	524,000	641,000	42,000	193,000	47,000	146,000	213,000	270,000
Net Income	1,099,000	1,406,000	920,000	895,000	649,000	591,000	518,000	429,000
Average Shares	264,004	261,368	252,088	233,852	214,482	206,062	205,338	208,345
Balance Sheet								
Net PPE	14,884,000	13,175,000	12,101,000	11,086,000	10,474,000	6,832,000	6,217,000	5,726,000
Total Assets	30,091,000	28,949,000	29,213,000	23,643,000	22,009,000	17,757,000	15,156,000	15,612,000
Long-Term Obligations	4,553,000	4,525,000	4,823,000	4,192,000	3,841,000	4,083,000	3,436,000	3,268,000
Total Liabilities	21,752,000	21,438,000	23,053,000	18,778,000	18,119,000	14,932,000	12,464,000	13,118,000
Stockholders' Equity	8,339,000	7,511,000	6,160,000	4,865,000	3,890,000	2,825,000	2,692,000	2,494,000
Shares Outstanding	261,214	262,005	257,187	234,175	226,598	204,912	204,475	201,927
Statistical Record								
Return on Assets %	3.72	4.83	3.48	3.91	3.26	3.59	3.37	3.18
Return on Equity %	13.87	20.57	16.69	20.39	19.33	21.42	19.98	15.61
EBITDA Margin %	21.41	23.99	15.37	21.12	19.79	26.76	20.34	21.67
Net Margin %	9.61	11.95	7.84	9.51	8.23	9.82	6.45	6.01
PPE Turnover	0.82	0.93	1.01	0.87	0.91	0.92	1.34	1.28
Asset Turnover	0.39	0.40	0.44	0.41	0.40	0.37	0.52	0.53
Debt to Equity	0.55	0.60	0.78	0.86	0.99	1.45	1.28	1.31
Price Range	66.29-52.21	56.78-43.36	47.49-35.75	37.80-29.74	30.67-22.50	26.01-16.00	28.39-18.19	24.50-16.63
P/E Ratio	15.94-12.55	10.55-8.06	13.01-9.79	9.87-7.77	10.12-7.43	9.06-5.57	11.27-7.22	11.89-8.07
Average Yield %	2.08	2.47	2.79	2.95	3.70	4.58	4.27	5.18

Address: 101 Ash Street, San Diego, CA 92101-3017	Web Site: www.sempra.com	Auditors: Deloitte & Touche LLP
Telephone: 619-696-2034	Officers: Stephen L. Baum - Chmn., Pres., C.E.O. M. Javade Chaudhri - Exec. V.P., Gen. Couns.	Transfer Agents: EquiServe Trust Company, N.A., Providence, RI
Fax: 619-696-2374		

SENSIENT TECHNOLOGIES CORP.

Exchange	Symbol	Price	52Wk Range	Yield	P/E
NYS	SXT	$29.49 (3/31/2008)	30.26-24.09	2.44	17.87

*7 Year Price Score 99.95   *NYSE Composite Index=100   *12 Month Price Score 109.07

Interim Earnings (Per Share)

Qtr.	Mar	Jun	Sep	Dec
2003	0.43	0.46	0.44	0.40
2004	0.32	0.39	0.46	0.41
2005	0.27	0.34	0.30	0.03
2006	0.34	0.40	0.37	0.33
2007	0.37	0.45	0.44	0.39

Interim Dividends (Per Share)

Amt	Decl	Ex	Rec	Pay
0.16Q	4/27/2007	5/8/2007	5/10/2007	6/1/2007
0.18Q	7/19/2007	8/7/2007	8/9/2007	9/4/2007
0.18Q	10/18/2007	11/6/2007	11/8/2007	12/3/2007
0.18Q	1/18/2008	2/6/2008	2/8/2008	3/3/2008

Indicated Div: $0.72

Valuation Analysis | **Institutional Holding**

Forecast P/E	N/A	No of Institutions
		174
Market Cap	$1.4 Billion	Shares
Book Value	814.4 Million	41,219,144
Price/Book	1.71	% Held
Price/Sales	1.18	88.14

Business Summary: Food (MIC: 4.1 SIC: 2869 NAIC: 311930)

Sensient Technologies manufactures and markets colors, flavors and fragrances through two segments: Flavors and Fragrances Group and Colors Group. Co. develops specialty food and beverage systems, cosmetic and pharmaceutical systems, inkjet and specialty inks and colors, and other specialty chemicals. Co.'s principal products include: flavors, flavor enhancers and bio-nutrients; fragrances and aroma chemicals; dehydrated vegetables and other food ingredients; natural and synthetic food colors, cosmetic and pharmaceutical additives, inkjet inks, technical colors and specialty dyes and pigments as well as chemicals for laser printing and flat screen displays.

Recent Developments: For the year ended Dec 31 2007, net income increased 17.1% to US$77.8 million from US$66.4 million in the prior year. Revenues were US$1.18 billion, up 7.8% from US$1.10 billion the year before. Operating income was US$147.4 million versus US$129.3 million in the prior year, an increase of 14.0%. Direct operating expenses rose 7.3% to US$822.5 million from US$766.5 million in the comparable period the year before. Indirect operating expenses increased 5.9% to US$214.9 million from US$203.0 million in the equivalent prior-year period.

Prospects: Co.'s near-term outlook appears favorable. For instance, Co. is seeing an increase in revenues primarily driven by increased volumes and prices at its Flavors and Fragrances Group and Color Group as well as the effect of foreign currency translation. In addition, Co. is seeing an increase in gross margin due to higher selling prices partially offset by higher raw material cost. Looking ahead, Co. expects to continue to pursue a strategy that emphasizes product development, new technologies and global expansion. For full-year 2008, Co. has increased its diluted earnings per share guidance to be within a range of $1.74 to $1.78 from the range of $1.73 and $1.77 announced previously.

Financial Data

(US$ in Thousands)	12/31/2007	12/31/2006	12/31/2005	12/31/2004	12/31/2003	12/31/2002	12/31/2001	12/31/2000
Earnings Per Share	1.65	1.44	0.94	1.58	1.73	1.69	1.54	1.26
Cash Flow Per Share	2.25	2.16	2.36	2.69	1.21	1.99	1.25	1.87
Tang Book Value Per Share	6.82	5.16	4.04	4.00	2.86	2.16	2.65	2.54
Dividends Per Share	0.680	0.610	0.600	0.600	0.600	0.537	0.530	0.530
Dividend Payout %	41.21	42.36	63.83	37.97	34.68	31.80	34.42	42.06
Income Statement								
Total Revenue	1,184,778	1,098,774	1,023,930	1,047,133	987,408	939,886	816,947	809,163
EBITDA	191,682	172,321	140,983	175,399	180,582	187,785	167,780	157,747
Income Before Taxes	111,243	93,529	58,477	97,891	108,344	116,972	89,959	78,028
Income Taxes	33,457	27,104	14,282	23,973	26,912	36,282	24,996	21,681
Net Income	77,786	66,425	44,195	73,918	81,432	80,690	73,602	62,043
Average Shares	47,257	46,204	47,067	46,877	47,041	47,788	47,926	49,166
Balance Sheet								
Current Assets	610,044	551,702	520,344	536,244	536,730	475,578	415,222	491,398
Total Assets	1,564,182	1,454,067	1,398,273	1,488,578	1,453,528	1,289,971	1,104,820	1,164,248
Current Liabilities	229,273	260,610	442,087	255,225	282,420	209,330	192,188	252,132
Long-Term Obligations	449,621	441,306	283,123	525,153	525,924	511,707	423,137	417,141
Total Liabilities	749,761	749,963	776,045	829,880	873,410	790,613	674,004	747,190
Stockholders' Equity	814,421	704,104	622,228	658,698	580,118	499,358	430,816	417,058
Shares Outstanding	47,351	46,569	46,334	47,067	46,724	47,208	47,409	48,551
Statistical Record								
Return on Assets %	5.15	4.66	3.06	5.01	5.94	6.74	6.49	5.39
Return on Equity %	10.24	10.02	6.90	11.90	15.09	17.35	17.36	14.59
EBITDA Margin %	16.18	15.68	13.77	16.75	18.29	19.98	20.54	19.50
Net Margin %	6.57	6.05	4.32	7.06	8.25	8.59	9.01	7.67
Asset Turnover	0.79	0.77	0.71	0.71	0.72	0.78	0.72	0.70
Current Ratio	2.66	2.12	1.18	2.10	1.90	2.27	2.16	1.95
Debt to Equity	0.55	0.63	0.46	0.80	0.91	1.02	0.98	1.00
Price Range	30.26-23.83	25.18-17.11	23.99-16.84	24.19-18.15	24.18-18.00	25.85-18.07	23.81-15.60	23.06-16.06
P/E Ratio	18.34-14.44	17.49-11.88	25.52-17.91	15.31-11.49	13.98-10.40	15.30-10.69	15.46-10.13	18.30-12.75
Average Yield %	2.55	2.99	3.00	2.88	2.85	2.41	2.64	2.73

Address: 777 East Wisconsin Avenue,	Web Site: www.sensient-tech.com	Auditors: Ernst & Young LLP
Milwaukee, WI 53202-5304	Officers: Kenneth P. Manning - Chmn., Pres., C.E.O.	Transfer Agents: Wells Fargo Bank
Telephone: 414-271-6755	Richard Carney - V.P., Admin.	Minnesota, N.A., St. Paul, MN
Fax: 414-347-4795		

SERVICE CORP. INTERNATIONAL

Exchange	Symbol	Price	52Wk Range	Yield	P/E
NYS	SCI	$10.14 (3/31/2008)	14.47-9.48	1.58	11.93

*7 Year Price Score 137.70 *NYSE Composite Index=100 *12 Month Price Score 92.95

Interim Earnings (Per Share)

Qtr.	Mar	Jun	Sep	Dec
2003	0.13	0.05	(0.02)	0.11
2004	0.09	0.15	0.04	0.08
2005	(0.49)	0.04	(0.03)	0.08
2006	0.08	0.09	0.01	0.00
2007	0.13	0.05	0.10	0.58

Interim Dividends (Per Share)

Amt	Decl	Ex	Rec	Pay
0.03Q	5/9/2007	7/12/2007	7/16/2007	7/31/2007
0.03Q	8/8/2007	10/11/2007	10/15/2007	10/31/2007
0.04Q	11/14/2007	1/11/2008	1/15/2008	1/31/2008
0.04Q	2/13/2008	4/11/2008	4/15/2008	4/30/2008

Indicated Div: $0.16

Valuation Analysis

		Institutional Holding
Forecast P/E	N/A	No of Institutions 169
Market Cap	$2.7 Billion	Shares
Book Value	1.5 Billion	227,824,144
Price/Book	1.79	% Held
Price/Sales	1.17	77.63

TRADING VOLUME (thousand shares)

Business Summary: Personal Services (MIC: 5.15 SIC: 7261 NAIC: 812210)

Service Corporation International provides deathcare products and services. At Dec 31 2007, Co. operated 1,329 funeral service locations and 366 cemeteries, (including 202 combination locations) in North America, which are geographically expanded across 43 states, eight Canadian provinces, the District of Columbia, and Puerto Rico. Co.'s funeral service and cemetery operations consist of funeral service locations, cemeteries, funeral service/cemetery combination locations, crematoria, and related businesses. Co. also provide services relating to funerals and cremations, including the use of funeral facilities and motor vehicles, and preparation and embalming services.

Recent Developments: For the year ended Dec 31 2007, net income increased 338.4% to US$247.7 million from US$56.5 million in the prior year. Revenues were US$2.29 billion, up 30.4% from US$1.75 billion the year before. Operating income was US$346.2 million versus US$196.7 million in the prior year, an increase of 76.0%. Direct operating expenses rose 29.5% to US$1.82 billion from US$1.40 billion in the comparable period the year before. Indirect operating expenses decreased 20.3% to US$122.3 million from US$153.6 million in the equivalent prior year period.

Prospects: For the full year of 2008, Co. is forecasting funeral revenues of $1.45 billion to $1.50 billion, while funeral gross margin percentage is anticipated to range from 20.0% to 24.0%. In addition, Co. is targeting cemetery revenues of $710.0 million to $750.0 million, while cemetery gross margin percentage is projected to range from 18.0% to 22.0%. Similarly, Co. is expecting total capital expenditures of $165.0 million to $195.0 million, consisting of $85.0 million to $95.0 million for capital improvements at existing facilities, $55.0 million to $60.0 million to develop cemetery property, and $25.0 million to $40.0 million for new construction and expansion of market presence projects.

Financial Data

(US$ in Thousands)	12/31/2007	12/31/2006	12/31/2005	12/31/2004	12/31/2003	12/31/2002	12/31/2001	12/31/2000
Earnings Per Share	0.85	0.19	(0.41)	0.35	0.28	(0.79)	(2.10)	(4.93)
Cash Flow Per Share	1.25	1.11	1.03	0.74	1.25	1.20	1.24	1.55
Tang Book Value Per Share	0.45	0.32	1.33	1.87	0.83	0.40	0.08	N.M.
Dividends Per Share	0.120	0.100	0.075	...	...	...	...	...
Dividend Payout %	14.12	52.63	...	...	...	...	...	...
Income Statement								
Total Revenue	2,285,303	1,747,295	1,715,605	1,859,308	2,341,651	2,272,423	2,510,343	2,564,730
EBITDA	988,643	511,181	395,898	374,279	418,817	149,077	(129,865)	(59,894)
Income Before Taxes	386,987	97,449	90,807	110,798	114,333	(140,963)	(535,428)	(516,978)
Income Taxes	143,670	44,845	34,122	(6,213)	29,251	(39,740)	61,199	(91,455)
Net Income	247,729	56,511	(126,730)	113,699	85,082	(231,880)	(597,796)	(1,343,251)
Average Shares	290,444	297,371	306,745	344,675	300,790	294,533	285,127	272,544
Balance Sheet								
Current Assets	421,327	238,337	630,383	533,497	673,324	754,899	829,953	907,299
Total Assets	8,932,244	9,729,389	7,536,692	8,199,196	11,202,669	10,723,785	11,579,937	12,898,469
Current Liabilities	426,440	407,947	271,956	311,913	668,947	464,283	710,602	684,280
Long-Term Obligations	1,820,106	1,912,696	1,175,463	1,178,885	1,528,883	1,884,508	2,313,973	3,114,515
Total Liabilities	7,440,161	8,134,614	5,948,206	6,345,620	9,675,711	9,420,014	10,147,076	10,922,648
Stockholders' Equity	1,492,083	1,594,775	1,588,486	1,853,576	1,526,958	1,303,771	1,432,861	1,975,821
Shares Outstanding	262,858	293,222	294,808	323,225	302,039	297,010	292,153	272,507
Statistical Record								
Return on Assets %	2.65	0.65	N.M.	1.17	0.78	N.M.	N.M.	N.M.
Return on Equity %	16.05	3.55	N.M.	6.71	6.01	N.M.	N.M.	N.M.
EBITDA Margin %	43.26	29.26	23.08	20.13	17.89	6.56	N.M.	N.M.
Net Margin %	10.84	3.23	N.M.	6.12	3.63	N.M.	N.M.	N.M.
Asset Turnover	0.24	0.20	0.22	0.19	0.21	0.20	0.21	0.19
Current Ratio	0.99	0.58	2.39	1.71	1.01	1.63	1.17	1.33
Debt to Equity	1.22	1.20	0.74	0.64	1.00	1.45	1.61	1.58
Price Range	14.47-10.31	10.45-7.37	8.85-6.58	7.69-5.39	5.58-2.67	5.50-2.25	7.90-1.56	7.00-1.69
P/E Ratio	17.02-12.13	55.00-38.79	...	21.97-15.40	19.93-9.54	...	...	...
Average Yield %	0.96	1.17	0.96	...	...	...	...	...

Address: 1929 Allen Parkway, Houston, TX 77019 Telephone: 713-522-5141	Web Site: www.sci.com Officers: Robert L. Waltrip - Chmn. Thomas L. Ryan - Pres., C.E.O.	Auditors: PricewaterhouseCoopers LLP Transfer Agents: The Bank of New York

SHAW GROUP INC.

Exchange	Symbol	Price	52Wk Range	Yield	P/E
NYS	SGR	$47.14 (3/31/2008)	76.61-29.32	N/A	N/A

*7 Year Price Score 161.33 *NYSE Composite Index=100 *12 Month Price Score 117.87

TRADING VOLUME (thousand shares)

Interim Earnings (Per Share)

Qtr.	Nov	Feb	May	Aug
2004-05	0.16	0.15	(0.31)	0.25
2005-06	0.41	0.31	(0.21)	0.16
2006-07	(0.26)	(0.78)	0.67	0.04
2007-08	0.03	...	...	...

Interim Dividends (Per Share)

No Dividends Paid

Valuation Analysis

	Institutional Holding	
Forecast P/E	17.03	No of Institutions
(1/10/2007)		182
Market Cap	$3.9 Billion	Shares
Book Value	1.3 Billion	78,675,272
Price/Book	3.00	% Held
Price/Sales	0.62	97.42

Business Summary: Metal Products (MIC: 11.4 SIC: 3498 NAIC: 332996)

Shaw Group consists of six operating segments. Fossil & Nuclear offers project-related services to the global fossil and nuclear power generation industries. Environmental and Infrastructure designs applications involving contaminants in soil, air and water. Energy and Chemicals provides project-related services to oil and gas, refinery, petrochemical, and chemical industries. Maintenance performs routine and outage/turnaround maintenance. Fabrication and Manufacturing provides piping systems and services for construction, site expansion and retrofit projects for energy and chemical plants. Westinghouse supplies nuclear plant designs, licensing, engineering services, equipment and fuel.

Recent Developments: For the quarter ended Nov 30 2007, net income amounted to US$2.2 million versus a net loss of US$12.3 million in the year-earlier quarter. Revenues were US$1.71 billion, up 34.2% from US$1.28 billion the year before. Operating income was US$66.1 million versus US$25.7 million in the prior-year quarter, an increase of 157.2%. Direct operating expenses rose 33.0% to US$1.58 billion from US$1.19 billion in the comparable period the year before. Indirect operating expenses increased 7.0% to US$68.9 million from US$64.4 million in the equivalent prior-year period.

Prospects: For the rest of the fiscal year ending Aug 2008, Co. expects revenues to continue to increase as compared to fiscal year ended Aug 31 2007 as it progresses on its major power generation, chemical and petrochemical contracts. For instance, Co. anticipates that fiscal 2008 revenues for its Fossil & Nuclear segment will be higher than fiscal year 2007, reflecting the number of major projects that it is executing as well as the increasing activity related to its nuclear business. In addition, Co. expects global energy and petrochemical markets to remain strong, while estimating the improvements in federal government contracting to further support expected backlog growth during fiscal 2008.

Financial Data

(US$ in Thousands)	3 Mos	08/31/2007	08/31/2006	08/31/2005	08/31/2004	08/31/2003	08/31/2002	08/31/2001
Earnings Per Share	(0.04)	(0.24)	0.63	0.23	(0.53)	0.54	2.26	1.46
Cash Flow Per Share	5.39	5.77	(0.95)	0.99	(0.43)	(5.33)	7.72	0.28
Tang Book Value Per Share	9.23	8.56	8.77	7.65	5.68	3.99	4.73	5.60
Income Statement								
Total Revenue	1,712,160	5,723,712	4,775,615	3,265,916	3,076,945	3,306,762	3,170,696	1,538,932
EBITDA	20,144	100,711	131,793	85,718	53,354	114,554	200,199	152,083
Depn & Amortn	10,383	...	...	...	...	...	...	...
Income Before Taxes	3,520	33,166	87,705	38,531	(35,224)	35,590	151,012	99,894
Income Taxes	2,116	10,747	20,540	20,610	(11,624)	11,745	54,348	38,366
Net Income	2,230	(19,000)	50,850	16,376	(30,975)	20,866	98,367	60,997
Average Shares	83,575	79,857	80,289	69,792	58,005	38,355	48,238	41,828
Balance Sheet								
Current Assets	2,041,465	1,852,090	1,678,660	1,254,820	1,137,783	1,113,561	1,450,354	1,096,041
Total Assets	4,093,654	3,874,852	2,529,134	2,070,655	2,029,936	1,986,115	2,304,200	1,701,854
Current Liabilities	1,551,801	1,453,114	1,040,659	781,161	853,737	1,028,115	1,072,470	574,997
Long-Term Obligations	1,153,499	1,096,765	173,534	65,541	261,173	251,745	522,147	512,867
Total Liabilities	2,808,184	2,638,331	1,285,927	926,102	1,145,165	1,323,825	1,611,943	1,103,461
Stockholders' Equity	1,285,470	1,236,521	1,243,207	1,144,553	884,771	662,290	692,257	598,393
Shares Outstanding	81,736	81,197	80,475	78,957	63,769	37,790	40,841	41,012
Statistical Record								
Return on Assets %	N.M.	N.M.	2.21	0.80	N.M.	0.97	4.91	4.02
Return on Equity %	N.M.	N.M.	4.26	1.61	N.M.	3.08	15.24	12.50
EBITDA Margin %	1.18	1.76	2.76	2.62	1.73	3.46	6.31	9.88
Net Margin %	0.13	N.M.	1.06	0.50	N.M.	0.63	3.10	3.96
Asset Turnover	1.63	1.79	2.08	1.59	1.53	1.54	1.58	1.01
Current Ratio	1.32	1.27	1.61	1.61	1.33	1.08	1.35	1.91
Debt to Equity	0.90	0.89	0.14	0.06	0.30	0.38	0.75	0.86
Price Range	76.61-28.60	60.69-23.64	35.81-19.73	23.01-10.29	13.85-8.75	18.65-6.97	35.50-14.80	62.37-24.59
P/E Ratio	...	...	56.84-31.32	100.04-44.74	...	34.54-12.91	15.71-6.55	42.72-16.84

Address: 4171 Essen Lane, Baton Rouge, LA 70809	**Web Site:** www.shawgrp.com	**Auditors:** KPMG LLC
Telephone: 225-932-2500	**Officers:** J. M. Bernhard Jr. - Chmn., C.E.O. T. A. Barfield Jr. - Pres., C.O.O.	**Investor Contact:** 225-932-2500
Fax: 225-296-1199		**Transfer Agents:** Wachovia Bank, N.A., Charlotte, North Carolina

SHERWIN-WILLIAMS CO.

Exchange	Symbol	Price	52Wk Range	Yield	P/E	Div Achelver
NYS	SHW	$51.04 (3/31/2008)	72.99-50.13	2.74	10.86	28 Years

*7 Year Price Score 120.80 *NYSE Composite Index=100   *12 Month Price Score 92.19

Interim Earnings (Per Share)

Qtr.	Mar	Jun	Sep	Dec
2003	0.21	0.75	0.82	0.49
2004	0.35	0.87	0.92	0.58
2005	0.58	1.08	1.07	0.55
2006	0.82	1.33	1.30	0.73
2007	0.83	1.52	1.55	0.82

Interim Dividends (Per Share)

Amt	Decl	Ex	Rec	Pay
0.315Q	4/18/2007	5/16/2007	5/18/2007	6/8/2007
0.315Q	7/18/2007	8/22/2007	8/24/2007	9/14/2007
0.315Q	10/19/2007	11/14/2007	11/16/2007	12/7/2007
0.35Q	2/20/2008	2/27/2008	2/29/2008	3/14/2008

Indicated Div: $1.40 (Div. Reinv. Plan)

Valuation Analysis / **Institutional Holding**

Forecast P/E	12.83	No of Institutions
	(1/10/2007)	363
Market Cap	$6.3 Billion	Sharos
Book Value	1.8 Billion	97,286,008
Price/Book	3.51	% Held
Price/Sales	0.78	72.36

Business Summary: Retail - Hardware (MIC: 5.6 SIC: 5231 NAIC: 444120)

Sherwin-Williams develops, manufactures, distributes and sell paint, coatings and related products to professional, industrial, commercial and retail customers primarily in North and South America with additional operations in the U.K., Europe, India and China. As of Dec 31 2007, Co.'s reportable operating segments are: Paint Stores Group, which consists of 3,325 company-operated specialty paint stores and seven manufacturing/distribution facilities; Consumer Group, which develops, manufactures and distributes a variety of paint, coatings and related products; and Global Group, which develops, licenses, manufactures, distributes and sells a variety of paint, coatings and related products.

Recent Developments: For the year ended Dec 31 2007, net income increased 6.9% to US$615.6 million from US$576.1 million in the prior year. Revenues were US$8.01 billion, up 2.5% from US$7.81 billion the year before. Direct operating expenses rose 0.3% to US$4.41 billion from US$4.40 billion in the comparable period the year before. Indirect operating expenses increased 3.7% to US$2.63 billion from US$2.54 billion in the equivalent prior-year period.

Prospects: Co. is cautiously positive of its 2008 outlook despite anticipating ongoing weakness in the domestic coatings market; with the demand for architectural coatings used in new residential construction to remain soft and its residential repaint business to remain somewhat weak due to the decline in existing home turnover, which is affecting its Paint Stores Group. Also, sales momentum in the Do-It-Yourself market could remain slow, hampering results of Co.'s Consumer Group. However, Co. believes that the market segments it serves will show improvement in 2008, and projects a low-to-mid single digit percentage growth in total net sales over 2007 with diluted earnings per share of $5.00 to $5.15.

Financial Data

(US$ in Thousands)	12/31/2007	12/31/2006	12/31/2005	12/31/2004	12/31/2003	12/31/2002	12/31/2001	12/31/2000
Earnings Per Share	4.70	4.19	3.28	2.72	2.26	0.84	1.68	0.10
Cash Flow Per Share	6.87	6.11	5.24	3.86	3.86	3.72	3.61	2.84
Tang Book Value Per Share	0.93	2.67	3.03	1.90	2.93	3.77	2.39	5.18
Dividends Per Share	1.260	1.000	0.820	0.680	0.620	0.600	0.580	0.540
Dividend Payout %	26.81	23.87	25.00	25.00	27.43	71.43	34.52	540.00
Income Statement								
Total Revenue	8,005,292	7,809,759	7,190,661	6,113,789	5,407,764	5,184,788	5,066,005	5,211,624
EBITDA	1,148,052	1,047,391	849,318	745,785	678,232	653,298	627,174	361,638
Income Before Taxes	912,943	834,312	656,215	580,195	522,926	497,164	424,449	143,406
Income Taxes	297,365	258,254	191,601	185,662	190,868	186,463	161,291	127,380
Net Income	615,578	576,058	463,258	393,254	332,058	127,565	263,158	16,026
Average Shares	130,924	137,342	141,078	144,735	147,005	152,435	156,893	162,693
Balance Sheet								
Current Assets	2,069,580	2,450,281	1,894,385	1,721,028	1,718,144	1,808,993	1,806,945	1,551,539
Total Assets	4,855,340	4,995,087	4,369,195	4,274,151	3,682,608	3,432,312	3,627,925	3,750,670
Current Liabilities	2,141,385	2,074,815	1,554,371	1,520,137	1,154,170	1,083,496	1,141,353	1,115,243
Long-Term Obligations	293,454	291,876	486,996	488,239	502,992	506,682	503,517	623,587
Total Liabilities	3,069,613	3,002,727	2,638,583	2,626,905	2,223,751	2,090,422	2,140,161	2,278,806
Stockholders' Equity	1,785,727	1,992,360	1,730,612	1,647,246	1,458,857	1,341,890	1,487,764	1,471,864
Shares Outstanding	122,814	133,565	135,139	140,777	143,406	148,910	153,978	159,558
Statistical Record								
Return on Assets %	12.50	12.30	10.72	9.86	9.33	3.61	7.13	0.41
Return on Equity %	32.59	30.95	27.43	25.25	23.71	9.02	17.78	1.01
EBITDA Margin %	14.34	13.41	11.81	12.20	12.54	12.60	12.38	6.94
Net Margin %	7.69	7.38	6.44	6.43	6.14	2.46	5.19	0.31
Asset Turnover	1.63	1.67	1.66	1.53	1.52	1.47	1.37	1.33
Current Ratio	0.97	1.18	1.22	1.17	1.49	1.39	1.32	1.39
Debt to Equity	0.16	0.15	0.28	0.30	0.34	0.38	0.34	0.42
Price Range	72.99-57.65	64.61-41.29	48.63-40.75	45.48-33.06	34.74-24.82	33.00-22.06	28.02-20.31	27.00-17.44
P/E Ratio	15.53-12.27	15.42-9.85	14.83-12.42	16.72-12.15	15.37-10.98	39.29-26.26	16.68-12.09	270.00-174.38
Average Yield %	1.92	1.92	1.84	1.72	2.12	2.14	2.42	2.45

Address: 101 Prospect Avenue, N.W., Cleveland, OH 44115-1075
Telephone: 216-566-2000
Fax: 216-566-3310

Web Site: www.sherwin.com
Officers: Christopher M. Connor - Chmn., Pres., C.E.O. Sean P. Hennessy - Sr. V.P., Fin., C.F.O.

Auditors: Ernst & Young LLP
Investor Contact: 216-566-2000
Transfer Agents: The Bank of New York, New York, NY

SIERRA PACIFIC RESOURCES

Exchange	Symbol	Price	52Wk Range	Yield	P/E
NYS	SRP	$12.63 (3/31/2008)	19.29-12.09	N/A	14.19

*7 Year Price Score 112.58 *NYSE Composite Index=100 ***12 Month Price Score 88.54**

Interim Earnings (Per Share)

Qtr.	Mar	Jun	Sep	Dec
2003	(0.15)	(1.48)	0.28	(0.32)
2004	(0.38)	(0.38)	0.50	0.15
2005	(0.08)	0.05	0.33	0.11
2006	0.01	0.14	1.05	0.10
2007	0.07	0.12	0.69	0.02

Interim Dividends (Per Share)

Dividend Payment Suspended

Valuation Analysis   Institutional Holding

Forecast P/E	16.52	No of Institutions
	(1/10/2007)	209
Market Cap	$3.0 Billion	Shares
Book Value	3.0 Billion	159,259,648
Price/Book	0.99	% Held
Price/Sales	0.82	72.08

Business Summary: Electricity (MIC: 7.1 SIC: 4931 NAIC: 221111)

Sierra Pacific Resources is a holding company. Co. has six primary, wholly-owned subsidiaries: Nevada Power Company (NPC), Sierra Pacific Power Company (SPPC), Tuscarora Gas Pipeline Company, Sierra Pacific Communications, Sierra Pacific Energy Company, and Lands of Sierra. NPC and SPPC provides electric service to Las Vegas and surrounding Clark County, northern Nevada and the Lake Tahoe area of California, and also provides natural gas service in the Reno-Sparks area of Nevada. As of Dec 31 2007, NPC served approximately 826,000 electric customers, while SPPC served about 366,000 electric customers and about 149,000 natural gas customers.

Recent Developments: For the year ended Dec 31 2007, revenues were US$3.60 billion, up 7.3% from US$3.36 billion the year before. Operating income was US$414.6 million versus US$488.8 million in the prior year, a decrease of 15.2%. Direct operating expenses rose 13.1% to US$2.83 billion from US$2.50 billion in the comparable period the year before. Indirect operating expenses decreased 2.1% to US$360.8 million from US$368.5 million in the equivalent prior-year period.

Prospects: Co. is seeing a continued rise in the cost of energy and natural gas with increased demand and the decline in the ability to meet those demands. Accordingly, Co. is focused on reducing dependence on purchased power by the use of energy efficiency and conservation programs and diversifying fuel mix, including renewable energy and owning more generating facilities. Notably, Co. anticipates the 619 megawatts (MWs) of natural gas-fired combustion turbine peaking units at the Clark Generating Station to be in service in 2008. Furthermore, Co. expects the 541 MW gas fired generator at the Tracy Plant to be in-service in mid 2008.

Financial Data

(US$ in Thousands)	12/31/2007	12/31/2006	12/31/2005	12/31/2004	12/31/2003	12/31/2002	12/31/2001	12/31/2000
Earnings Per Share	0.89	1.33	0.44	0.16	(1.21)	(3.01)	0.65	(0.51)
Cash Flow Per Share	3.39	2.06	1.26	1.81	2.32	4.49	(11.94)	2.36
Tang Book Value Per Share	12.82	11.86	10.15	12.56	9.60	9.95	13.61	13.25
Dividends Per Share	0.160	...	...	...	...	0.200	0.650	1.000
Dividend Payout %	17.98	...	...	...	...	...	100.00	...
Income Statement								
Total Revenue	3,600,960	3,355,950	3,030,219	2,823,839	2,789,158	2,991,703	4,588,730	2,334,254
Income Taxes	87,555	145,605	43,173	20,631	(57,337)	(164,440)	(1,230)	(31,022)
Net Income	...	279,792	86,137	32,471	(136,629)	(303,621)	56,733	(39,780)
Average Shares	222,554	209,020	185,932	183,400	115,774	102,126	87,542	78,435
Balance Sheet								
Net PPE	7,010,998	6,086,998	5,397,605	4,926,926	4,642,650	4,308,696	4,109,235	3,981,134
Total Assets	9,464,750	8,832,076	7,870,546	7,528,467	7,063,758	6,896,244	8,181,314	5,639,484
Long-Term Obligations	4,137,864	4,001,542	3,817,122	4,081,281	3,579,674	3,062,883	3,376,105	2,133,679
Total Liabilities	6,468,175	6,209,779	5,760,392	5,979,851	5,578,364	5,519,078	6,435,978	4,229,772
Stockholders' Equity	2,996,575	2,622,297	2,060,154	1,498,616	1,435,394	1,327,166	1,702,322	1,359,712
Shares Outstanding	233,739	221,030	200,792	117,469	117,236	102,177	102,111	78,475
Statistical Record								
Return on Assets %	...	3.35	1.12	0.44	N.M.	N.M.	0.82	N.M.
Return on Equity %	...	11.95	4.84	2.21	N.M.	N.M.	3.71	N.M.
Net Margin %	...	8.34	2.84	1.15	(4.90)	(10.15)	1.24	(1.70)
PPE Turnover	0.55	0.58	0.59	0.59	0.62	0.71	1.13	0.58
Asset Turnover	0.39	0.40	0.39	0.39	0.40	0.40	0.66	0.43
Debt to Equity	1.38	1.53	1.85	2.72	2.49	2.31	1.98	1.57
Price Range	19.29-14.63	17.48-12.78	15.22-9.30	10.54-6.57	7.37-2.92	16.73-4.88	17.02-10.80	19.25-12.25
P/E Ratio	21.67-16.44	13.14-9.61	34.59-21.14	65.88-41.06	...	...	26.18-16.62	...
Average Yield %	0.94	...	...	...	...	...	2.24	4.36	6.50

Address: 6100 Neil Road, Reno, NV 89511	Web Site: www.sierrapacificresources.com	Auditors: Deloitte & Touche LLP
Telephone: 775-834-4011	Officers: Walter M. Higgins - Chmn., Pres., C.E.O.	Investor Contact: 702-367-5624
Fax: 775-834-3614	Michael W. Yackira CPA - Exec. V.P., C.F.O.	Transfer Agents: Wells Fargo Shareowner Services, South St. Paul, MN

SIMON PROPERTY GROUP, INC.

Exchange	Symbol	Price	52Wk Range	Yield	P/E
NYS	SPG	$92.91 (3/31/2008)	117.10-77.38	3.87	47.65

*7 Year Price Score 125.43 *NYSE Composite Index=100 *12 Month Price Score 99.83

Interim Earnings (Per Share)

Qtr.	Mar	Jun	Sep	Dec
2003	0.29	0.26	0.22	0.87
2004	0.24	0.34	0.36	0.50
2005	0.26	0.70	0.34	0.52
2006	0.47	0.37	0.43	0.92
2007	0.44	0.27	0.74	0.50

Interim Dividends (Per Share)

Amt	Decl	Ex	Rec	Pay
0.84Q	4/27/2007	5/15/2007	5/17/2007	5/31/2007
0.84Q	7/30/2007	8/15/2007	8/17/2007	8/31/2007
0.84Q	10/29/2007	11/14/2007	11/16/2007	11/30/2007
0.90Q	2/1/2008	2/13/2008	2/15/2008	2/29/2008

Indicated Div: $3.60

Valuation Analysis | **Institutional Holding**

Forecast P/E	50.12 (1/10/2007)	No of Institutions	450
Market Cap	$20.7 Billion	Shares	200,082,960
Book Value	3.6 Billion	% Held	
Price/Book	5.82		90.30
Price/Sales	5.68		

Business Summary: Property, Real Estate & Development (MIC: 8.3 SIC: 6798 NAIC: 525930)

Simon Property Group is as a self-administered and self-managed real estate investment trust company. Co. owns, develops, and manages retail real estate properties, primarily regional malls, Premium Outlet® centers, The Mills®, and community/lifestyle centers. As of Dec 31 2007, Co. owned or held an interest in 168 regional malls, 38 Premium Outlet centers, 67 community/lifestyle centers, 37 properties acquired in the Mills acquisition, and 10 other shopping or outlet centers in 41 states and Puerto Rico. Co. also owns 51 shopping centers in France, Italy and Poland, six Premium Outlet centers in Japan, one Premium Outlet center in Mexico, and one Premium Outlet center in South Korea.

Recent Developments: For the year ended Dec 31 2007, income from continuing operations decreased 7.8% to US$519.3 million from US$563.4 million a year earlier. Net income decreased 12.9% to US$491.2 million from US$563.8 million in the prior year. Revenues were US$3.65 billion, up 9.6% from US$3.33 billion the year before. Revenues from property income rose 7.3% to US$3.29 billion from US$3.06 billion in the corresponding earlier year.

Prospects: For full year 2008, Co. has six development projects scheduled to open, including Hamilton Town Center in Noblesville, IN; Houston Premium Outlets in Cypress (Houston), TX; Jersey Shore Premium Outlets in Tinton Falls, NJ; Pier Park in Panama City Beach, FL; and hypermarket-anchored shopping centers in Argine (Naples), Italy and Changshu, China. Accordingly, Co. expects comparable property net operating income growth of 3.0% to 4.0% from its regional malls; 4.0% to 6.0% from its Premium Outlet Centers®; and 2.0% to 3.0% from its Community/Lifestyle Centers. As such, Co. is targeting diluted funds from operations of $6.25 to $6.45 per share and earnings of $1.93 to $2.13 per diluted share.

Financial Data

(US$ in Thousands)	12/31/2007	12/31/2006	12/31/2005	12/31/2004	12/31/2003	12/31/2002	12/31/2001	12/31/2000
Earnings Per Share	1.95	2.19	1.82	1.44	1.65	1.99	0.85	1.11
Cash Flow Per Share	6.53	5.76	5.32	5.19	5.02	4.91	4.66	4.08
Tang Book Value Per Share	12.02	13.15	13.54	16.25	14.71	14.10	13.23	14.23
Dividends Per Share	3.360	3.040	2.800	2.600	2.400	2.175	2.080	2.020
Dividend Payout %	172.31	138.81	153.85	180.56	145.45	109.30	244.71	181.98
Income Statement								
Property Income	3,287,880	3,063,177	2,920,094	2,411,416	2,098,252	2,044,799	1,926,192	1,887,124
Non-Property Income	362,919	268,977	246,759	230,335	215,401	141,003	122,643	125,613
Total Revenue	3,650,799	3,332,154	3,166,853	2,641,751	2,313,653	2,185,802	2,048,835	2,012,737
Interest Expense	945,852	821,858	799,092	662,090	602,510	602,972	607,625	637,173
Net Income	491,239	563,840	475,749	342,993	368,715	422,588	199,149	228,911
Average Shares	223,776	221,921	221,130	208,857	190,298	181,500	173,027	172,994
Balance Sheet								
Total Assets	23,605,662	22,084,455	21,131,039	22,070,019	15,684,721	14,904,502	13,810,954	13,911,407
Long-Term Obligations	17,218,674	15,394,489	14,106,117	14,586,393	10,266,388	9,546,081	8,841,378	8,728,582
Total Liabilities	19,003,160	16,909,517	15,556,451	16,049,369	11,228,824	10,412,992	9,625,172	9,458,153
Stockholders' Equity	3,563,383	3,979,642	4,307,296	4,642,606	3,338,627	3,467,733	3,214,691	3,054,012
Shares Outstanding	223,034	221,431	220,361	220,306	201,977	185,539	173,802	174,040
Statistical Record								
Return on Assets %	2.15	2.61	2.20	1.81	2.41	2.94	1.44	1.62
Return on Equity %	13.02	13.61	10.63	8.57	10.83	12.65	6.35	7.26
Net Margin %	13.46	16.92	15.02	12.98	15.94	19.33	9.72	11.37
Price Range	123.78-84.90	103.59-76.95	80.53-59.03	65.35-45.11	47.93-31.79	36.84-29.31	30.90-24.31	26.88-21.69
P/E Ratio	63.48-43.54	47.30-35.14	44.25-32.43	45.38-31.33	29.05-19.27	18.51-14.73	36.35-28.60	24.21-19.54
Average Yield %	3.29	3.41	4.01	4.79	5.97	6.52	7.59	8.43

Address: National City Center, 115 West Washington Street, Suite 15 East, Indianapolis, IN 46204 **Telephone:** 317-636-1600 **Fax:** 317-685-7336	**Web Site:** www.simon.com **Officers:** Melvin Simon - Co-Chmn. Herbert Simon - Co-Chmn.	**Auditors:** Ernst & Young LLP **Investor Contact:** 317-685-7330 **Transfer Agents:** Mellon Investor Services LLC, South Hackensack, NJ

SJW CORP.

Exchange	Symbol	Price	52Wk Range	Yield	P/E	Div Acheiver
NYS	SJW	$28.59 (3/31/2008)	40.10-28.05	2.26	27.49	40 Years

*7 Year Price Score 125.69 *NYSE Composite Index=100   *12 Month Price Score 98.48

Interim Earnings (Per Share)
Qtr.	Mar	Jun	Sep	Dec
2003	0.29	0.24	0.33	0.16
2004	0.10	0.27	0.30	0.41
2005	0.14	0.31	0.50	0.23
2006	0.23	0.35	0.48	1.03
2007	0.11	0.29	0.43	0.20

Interim Dividends (Per Share)
Amt	Decl	Ex	Rec	Pay
0.151Q	4/26/2007	5/3/2007	5/7/2007	6/1/2007
0.151Q	7/26/2007	8/2/2007	8/6/2007	9/1/2007
0.151Q	10/25/2007	11/1/2007	11/5/2007	12/1/2007
0.161Q	1/31/2008	2/7/2008	2/11/2008	3/1/2008

Indicated Div: $0.65

Valuation Analysis   Institutional Holding
Forecast P/E	N/A	No of Institutions
		72
Market Cap	$525.0 Million	Shares
Book Value	236.9 Million	7,364,379
Price/Book	2.22	% Held
Price/Sales	2.54	40.26

Business Summary: Water Utilities (MIC: 7.2 SIC: 4941 NAIC: 221310)

SJW is a holding company with three subsidiaries: San Jose Water Company, SJWTX, Inc. (doing business as Canyon Lake Water Service Company) and SJW Land Company. San Jose Water Company is a public utility that provides water service to approximately 1.0 million people in an area comprising approximately 138 square miles in the metropolitan San Jose area. SJWTX, Inc. provides service to approximately 36,000 residents in a service area comprising more than 78 square miles in the region between San Antonio and Austin, TX. SJW Land Company operates commercial buildings throughout the states of California, Florida, Connecticut, Texas, Arizona and Tennessee.

Recent Developments: For the year ended Dec 31 2007, net income decreased 49.9% to US$19.3 million from US$38.6 million in the prior year. Revenues were US$206.6 million, up 9.2% from US$189.2 million the year before. Operating income was US$29.8 million versus US$31.6 million in the prior year, a decrease of 5.7%. Direct operating expenses rose 17.3% to US$135.1 million from US$115.2 million in the comparable period the year before. Indirect operating expenses decreased 1.8% to US$41.7 million from US$42.5 million in the equivalent prior-year period.

Prospects: Despite experiencing a decline in net income, Co.'s near-term outlook appears to be constructive. For the full year of 2008, Co. is estimating total capital expenditures to be approximately $49.5 million for its Water Utility Services, primarily focusing on main replacements, including an allocation of approximately $21.0 million to replace that segment's pipes and mains. In addition, Co. intends to invest about $29.0 million for distribution systems, $5.6 million for equipment and other, $4.0 million for pump stations and equipment, $4.0 million for facility plan projects, $3.2 million for reservoirs and tanks, $3.0 million for source of supply, with the remainder for water treatment.

Financial Data
(US$ in Thousands)

	12/31/2007	12/31/2006	12/31/2005	12/31/2004	12/31/2003	12/31/2002	12/31/2001	12/31/2000
Earnings Per Share	1.04	2.08	1.18	1.08	1.02	0.78	0.77	0.58
Cash Flow Per Share	2.29	2.44	2.33	2.25	2.30	1.59	1.39	1.31
Tang Book Value Per Share	12.72	12.31	10.55	9.93	8.92	8.11	7.88	7.60
Dividends Per Share	0.605	0.565	0.535	0.510	0.485	0.460	0.429	0.410
Dividend Payout %	58.17	27.16	45.34	47.44	47.55	59.10	55.92	70.29
Income Statement								
Total Revenue	206,601	189,238	180,105	166,911	149,732	145,652	136,083	123,157
Income Taxes	12,549	...	...	...	12,629	9,658	7,391	...
Net Income	19,323	38,581	21,840	19,786	18,677	14,232	14,017	10,665
Average Shares	18,552	18,528	18,480	18,394	18,296	18,270	18,270	18,270
Balance Sheet								
Net PPE	645,480	546,811	490,058	462,356	436,353	390,830	367,815	333,475
Total Assets	767,326	705,864	587,709	552,152	511,717	453,223	431,017	391,930
Long-Term Obligations	216,312	163,648	145,281	143,604	139,614	110,000	110,000	90,000
Total Liabilities	530,392	477,682	391,801	367,461	345,349	299,724	281,663	247,605
Stockholders' Equity	236,934	228,182	195,908	184,691	166,368	153,499	149,354	144,325
Shares Outstanding	18,361	18,281	18,270	18,270	18,270	18,270	18,270	18,270
Statistical Record								
Return on Assets %	2.62	5.97	3.83	3.71	...	...	3.41	2.78
Return on Equity %	8.31	18.19	11.48	11.24	...	...	9.55	7.38
Net Margin %	9.35	20.39	12.13	11.85	12.47	9.77	10.30	8.66
PPE Turnover	0.35	0.37	0.38	0.37	...	...	0.39	0.38
Asset Turnover	0.28	0.29	0.32	0.31	...	...	0.33	0.32
Debt to Equity	0.91	0.72	0.74	0.78	0.84	0.72	0.74	0.62
Price Range	43.00-28.19	39.50-21.56	27.69-16.15	19.45-14.65	14.95-12.57	14.83-12.71	17.75-11.98	20.29-16.33
P/E Ratio	41.35-27.11	18.99-10.37	23.47-13.68	18.01-13.56	14.66-12.32	19.02-16.29	23.05-15.56	34.99-28.16
Average Yield %	1.74	2.04	2.43	2.98	3.46	3.42	3.04	2.13

Address: 374 West Santa Clara Street, San Jose, CA 95196 Telephone: 408-279-7800 Fax: 408-279-7934	Web Site: www.sjwater.com Officers: Drew Gibson - Chmn. W. Richard Roth - Pres., C.E.O.	Auditors: KPMG LLP Transfer Agents: Boston Equiserve, Boston, MA

SL GREEN REALTY CORP.

Exchange	Symbol	Price	52Wk Range	Yield	P/E
NYS	SLG	$81.47 (3/31/2008)	143.47-76.78	3.87	7.56

*7 Year Price Score 137.91 *NYSE Composite Index=100 ***12 Month Price Score 84.73**

TRADING VOLUME (thousand shares)

Interim Earnings (Per Share)

Qtr.	Mar	Jun	Sep	Dec
2003	1.01	0.49	0.59	0.57
2004	0.40	1.13	0.49	2.72
2005	0.54	1.31	0.87	0.45
2006	0.54	0.65	2.53	0.60
2007	2.53	4.38	1.64	2.16

Interim Dividends (Per Share)

Amt	Decl	Ex	Rec	Pay
0.70Q	6/14/2007	6/27/2007	6/29/2007	7/13/2007
0.70Q	9/19/2007	9/26/2007	9/28/2007	10/15/2007
0.787Q	11/28/2007	12/27/2007	12/31/2007	1/15/2008
0.787Q	3/19/2008	3/27/2008	3/31/2008	4/15/2008

Indicated Div: $3.15

Valuation Analysis

		Institutional Holding	
Forecast P/E	N/A	No of Institutions	246
Market Cap	$4.8 Billion	Shares	
Book Value	3.8 Billion	54,527,488	
Price/Book	1.25	% Held	
Price/Sales	4.54	92.15	

Business Summary: Property, Real Estate & Development (MIC: 8.3 SIC: 6798 NAIC: 525930)

SL Green Realty is a self-managed real estate investment trust, with in-house capabilities in property management, acquisitions, financing, development, construction and leasing. As of Dec 31 2007, Co. owned or held interests in 23 consolidated and nine unconsolidated commercial office properties encompassing approximately 14.6 million rentable square feet and 10.0 million rentable square feet, respectively, located primarily in midtown Manhattan. At such date, Co.'s portfolio also included ownership interests in 30 consolidated and six unconsolidated commercial office properties located in Brooklyn, Queens, Long Island, Westchester County, Connecticut and New Jersey.

Recent Developments: For the year ended Dec 31 2007, net income increased 199.2% to US$660.4 million from US$220.7 million in the prior year. Revenues were US$1.05 billion, up 113.5% from US$493.8 million the year before. Revenues from property income rose 119.3% to US$696.9 million from US$317.8 million in the corresponding earlier year.

Prospects: Co.'s top-line results are being positively affected by an increase in rental revenue due to increases in rental rates on new leases signed in 2007. However, Co. believes that rental rates will moderate during 2008. Co. also believes that occupancy rates will moderate at its Same-Store Properties in 2008. Meanwhile, on Mar 4 2008, Co. announced the sale of 1250 Broadway in Manhattan to Murray Hill Properties, for $310.0 million. As a result, Co. expects to recognize an incentive fee of at least $15.0 million upon consummation of the sale. The sale is expected to close during the second quarter of 2008, subject to customary closing conditions.

Financial Data

(US$ in Thousands)	12/31/2007	12/31/2006	12/31/2005	12/31/2004	12/31/2003	12/31/2002	12/31/2001	12/31/2000
Earnings Per Share	10.78	4.38	3.20	4.75	2.66	2.09	1.94	2.93
Cash Flow Per Share	6.92	5.06	3.31	2.96	2.43	3.55	2.99	2.20
Tang Book Value Per Share	60.90	43.07	28.53	26.90	22.18	20.60	20.45	18.56
Dividends Per Share	2.888	2.500	2.220	2.040	1.895	1.793	1.605	1.475
Dividend Payout %	26.79	57.08	69.38	42.95	71.24	85.77	82.73	50.34
Income Statement								
Property Income	696,919	365,135	298,495	244,886	234,001	188,946	206,184	191,185
Non-Property Income	357,604	187,142	141,687	104,102	74,956	57,209	51,501	39,138
Total Revenue	1,054,523	552,277	440,182	348,988	308,957	246,155	257,685	230,323
Interest Expense	265,073	96,049	77,333	62,710	45,493	36,656	46,238	40,431
Net Income	660,410	220,719	157,419	209,430	98,159	74,331	63,001	86,217
Average Shares	61,885	48,405	45,504	43,078	38,970	37,788	29,808	31,818
Balance Sheet								
Total Assets	11,430,078	4,632,227	3,309,777	2,751,881	2,261,841	1,473,170	1,371,577	1,161,154
Long-Term Obligations	5,739,624	1,831,773	1,558,512	1,166,818	1,135,617	557,365	520,405	476,019
Total Liabilities	6,888,796	2,109,451	1,751,275	1,328,937	1,256,268	690,086	601,008	551,981
Stockholders' Equity	3,826,875	2,394,883	1,459,441	1,347,880	950,782	626,645	612,908	455,073
Shares Outstanding	58,759	49,840	42,456	40,876	36,016	30,422	29,978	24,516
Statistical Record								
Return on Assets %	8.22	5.56	5.19	8.33	5.26	5.23	4.97	7.70
Return on Equity %	21.23	11.45	11.21	18.17	12.45	11.99	11.80	19.97
Net Margin %	62.63	39.97	35.76	60.01	31.77	30.20	24.45	37.43
Price Range	156.10-89.43	139.50-77.70	77.14-52.70	60.55-40.24	41.05-29.05	36.50-27.65	31.52-25.30	30.19-21.06
P/E Ratio	14.48-8.30	31.85-17.74	24.11-16.47	12.75-8.47	15.43-10.92	17.46-13.23	16.25-13.04	10.30-7.19
Average Yield %	2.29	2.35	3.48	4.22	5.49	5.53	5.52	5.73

Address: 420 Lexington Avenue, New York, NY 10170
Telephone: 212-594-2700
Fax: 212-216-1785

Web Site: www.slgreen.com
Officers: Stephen L. Green - Chmn. Marc Holliday - Pres., C.E.O.

Auditors: Ernst & Young LLP
Transfer Agents: The Bank of New York, New York, NY

SLM CORP.

Exchange	Symbol	Price	52Wk Range	Yield	P/E
NYS	SLM	$15.35 (3/31/2008)	57.98-15.16	N/A	N/A

*7 Year Price Score 79.39   *NYSE Composite Index=100   *12 Month Price Score 51.65

Interim Earnings (Per Share)

Qtr.	Mar	Jun	Sep	Dec
2003	0.88	0.80	1.04	0.58
2004	0.64	1.36	0.80	1.24
2005	0.49	0.66	0.95	0.95
2006	0.34	1.52	0.60	0.07
2007	0.26	1.03	(0.85)	(3.95)

Interim Dividends (Per Share)

Amt	Decl	Ex	Rec	Pay
0.25Q	5/18/2006	5/31/2006	6/2/2006	6/16/2006
0.25Q	7/27/2006	8/30/2006	9/1/2006	9/15/2006
0.25Q	10/26/2006	11/29/2006	12/1/2006	12/15/2006
0.25Q	1/25/2007	2/28/2007	3/2/2007	3/16/2007

Valuation Analysis | **Institutional Holding**

Forecast P/E	N/A	No of Institutions
		489
Market Cap	$7.2 Billion	Shares
Book Value	5.2 Billion	366,886,912
Price/Book	1.37	% Held
Price/Sales	0.78	89.38

Business Summary: Credit & Lending (MIC: 8.6 SIC: 6141 NAIC: 522291)

SLM is a holding company. Through its subsidiaries, Co. is engaged in originating and holding student loans by providing funding, delivery and servicing support for education loans in the U.S. through its participation in the Federal Family Education Loan Program (FFELP) and through its own non-federally guaranteed Private Education Loan programs. Co. primarily markets its FFELP Stafford and Private Education Loans through on-campus financial aid offices. Co. has also expanded into direct-to-consumer marketing, primarily for Private Education Loans, to reach those students and families that choose not to consult with the financial aid office.

Recent Developments: For the year ended Dec 31 2007, net loss amounted to US$896.4 million versus net income of US$1.16 billion in the prior year. Net interest income increased 9.2% to US$1.59 billion from US$1.45 billion in the prior year. Provision for loan losses was US$1.02 billion versus US$287.0 million in the prior year, an increase of 253.8%. Non-interest income fell 77.1% to US$497.1 million from US$2.17 billion, while non-interest expense advanced 15.3% to US$1.55 billion.

Prospects: Going forward, Co. plans to decrease less profitable student loan origination and acquisition activities that have less strategic value, including originations of Private Education Loans for high default rate and lower-tier credit borrowers, as well as spot purchases and Wholesale Consolidation Loan purchases, all of which will reduce Co.'s funding needs. Also, Co. plans to focus on higher-margin Private Education Loans, both through school channel and direct-to-consumer channel, with particular attention to continuing more stringent underwriting standards. Moreover, Co. is targeting to reduce operating expenses by up to 20.0% compared with 2007 operating expenses by year-end 2009.

Financial Data

(US$ in Thousands)	12/31/2007	12/31/2006	12/31/2005	12/31/2004	12/31/2003	12/31/2002	12/31/2001	12/31/2000
Earnings Per Share	(2.26)	2.63	3.05	4.04	3.29	1.64	0.76	0.92
Cash Flow Per Share	(0.12)	1.97	(1.67)	(0.73)	1.49	1.65	1.76	1.55
Tang Book Value Per Share	5.05	5.90	5.13	4.42	4.18	2.72	3.23	2.54
Dividends Per Share	0.250	0.970	0.850	0.740	0.593	0.283	0.242	0.058
Dividend Payout %	...	36.88	27.87	18.32	18.03	17.24	31.80	6.34
Income Statement								
Interest Income	8,674,022	6,576,972	4,510,163	2,732,995	2,348,275	2,211,761	2,997,531	3,478,659
Interest Expense	7,085,772	5,122,855	3,058,718	1,433,696	1,021,906	1,202,620	2,124,115	2,836,871
Net Interest Income	1,588,250	1,454,117	1,451,445	1,299,299	1,326,369	1,009,141	873,416	641,788
Provision for Losses	1,015,308	286,962	203,006	111,066	147,480	116,624	65,991	32,119
Non-Interest Income	497,109	2,174,271	2,007,352	2,484,532	1,811,951	1,020,654	517,617	687,632
Non-Interest Expense	1,551,847	1,346,152	1,138,328	1,115,780	807,871	689,772	707,654	585,710
Income Before Taxes	(481,796)	1,995,274	2,117,463	2,556,985	2,182,969	1,223,399	617,388	711,591
Income Taxes	412,283	834,311	728,767	642,689	779,380	431,403	223,322	235,880
Net Income	(896,394)	1,156,956	1,382,284	1,913,270	1,533,560	791,996	383,996	465,017
Average Shares	412,323	451,170	460,260	475,787	463,335	474,519	490,200	493,065
Balance Sheet								
Net Loans & Leases	125,326,640	97,228,593	83,741,549	67,028,795	51,078,136	43,541,720	42,769,017	39,485,817
Total Assets	155,564,991	116,135,732	99,338,684	84,093,526	64,610,651	53,175,005	52,873,959	48,791,788
Total Liabilities	150,330,096	111,766,575	95,538,077	80,919,589	61,980,605	51,177,055	51,201,497	47,162,569
Stockholders' Equity	5,223,535	4,360,042	3,791,425	3,102,304	2,630,046	1,997,950	1,672,462	1,415,336
Shares Outstanding	466,542	410,617	413,137	423,632	447,678	457,740	466,485	492,434
Statistical Record								
Return on Assets %	N.M.	1.07	1.51	2.57	2.60	1.49	0.76	1.00
Return on Equity %	N.M.	28.39	40.10	66.57	66.27	43.16	24.87	41.11
Net Interest Margin %	18.31	22.11	32.18	47.54	56.48	45.63	29.14	18.45
Efficiency Ratio %	16.92	15.38	17.47	21.39	19.42	21.34	20.13	14.06
Price Range	57.98-19.65	58.12-44.99	55.82-46.08	54.24-36.99	42.64-33.85	35.63-26.38	29.13-19.38	22.67-9.44
P/E Ratio	...	22.10-17.11	18.30-15.11	13.43-9.16	12.96-10.29	21.73-16.09	38.33-25.49	24.64-10.26
Average Yield %	0.54	1.87	1.66	1.76	1.55	0.90	0.96	0.42

Address: 12061 Bluemont Way,	Web Site: www.salliemae.com	Auditors: PricewaterhouseCoopers LLP
Reston, VA 20190	Officers: Edward A. Fox - Chmn. Thomas J.	Investor Contact: 703-984-6746
Telephone: 703-810-3000	Fitzpatrick - Vice-Chmn., C.E.O.	Transfer Agents: The Bank of New
Fax: 703-810-5074		York, New York, NY

SMITH (A.O.) CORP

Exchange	Symbol	Price	52Wk Range	Yield	P/E	Div Achiever
NYS	AOS	$32.87 (3/31/2008)	51.15-30.43	2.19	11.53	15 Years

*7 Year Price Score 100.70 *NYSE Composite Index=100 *12 Month Price Score 96.94

TRADING VOLUME (thousand shares)

Interim Earnings (Per Share)

Qtr.	Mar	Jun	Sep	Dec
2003	0.46	0.67	0.20	0.43
2004	0.36	0.58	0.10	0.14
2005	0.48	0.22	0.32	0.53
2006	0.50	0.81	0.55	0.61
2007	0.63	0.87	0.79	0.56

Interim Dividends (Per Share)

Amt	Decl	Ex	Rec	Pay
0.17Q	4/10/2007	4/26/2007	4/30/2007	5/15/2007
0.18Q	7/10/2007	7/27/2007	7/31/2007	8/15/2007
0.18Q	10/9/2007	10/29/2007	10/31/2007	11/15/2007
0.18Q	1/15/2008	1/29/2008	1/31/2008	2/15/2008

Indicated Div: $0.72 (Div. Reinv. Plan)

Valuation Analysis

		Institutional Holding	
Forecast P/E	N/A	No of Institutions	144
Market Cap	$987.8 Million	Shares	20,497,700
Book Value	757.8 Million	% Held	66.71
Price/Book	1.30		
Price/Sales	0.43		

Business Summary: Electrical (MIC: 11.14 SIC: 3621 NAIC: 335312)

A. O. Smith is engaged as a manufacturer of water heating equipment and electric motors, serving a range of residential, commercial and industrial end markets principally in the U.S. As of Dec 31 2007, Co. conducted its businesses through two operating segments. Co.'s Water Products business manufactures and markets an array of residential gas and electric water heaters, standard and specialty commercial water heating equipment, high efficiency copper-tube boilers and water systems tanks. Co.'s Electrical Products business manufactures and markets a range of hermetic motors, fractional horsepower alternating current and direct current motors.

Recent Developments: For the year ended Dec 31 2007, income from continuing operations increased 15.7% to US$88.2 million from US$76.2 million a year earlier. Net income increased 15.3% to US$88.2 million from US$76.5 million in the prior year. Revenues were US$2.31 billion, up 7.0% from US$2.16 billion the year before. Direct operating expenses rose 6.0% to US$1.80 billion from US$1.70 billion in the comparable period the year before. Indirect operating expenses increased 16.2% to US$387.7 million from US$333.6 million in the equivalent prior-year period.

Prospects: Co.'s near-term outlook appears to be somewhat uncertain. On one hand, Co. is forecasting lower unit sales in its residential businesses in 2008. Furthermore, Co. believes that the weakness in construction could continue and negatively affect its commercial businesses later in 2008. Accordingly, Co. is projecting commercial sales to be flat to down in the North American market for the full year of 2008. On the other hand, Co. expects its businesses in China to continue to generate favorable results during 2008. In this respect, Co. is projecting full-year 2008 earnings to be in the range of $2.70 and $2.90 per share, which includes restructuring expense of approximately $0.25 per share.

Financial Data

(US$ in Thousands)	12/31/2007	12/31/2006	12/31/2005	12/31/2004	12/31/2003	12/31/2002	12/31/2001	12/31/2000
Earnings Per Share	2.85	2.47	1.54	1.18	1.76	1.86	0.61	1.26
Cash Flow Per Share	6.23	4.24	6.29	2.29	0.87	4.16	2.11	3.27
Tang Book Value Per Share	5.27	3.16	9.52	9.35	9.07	6.95	6.30	8.64
Dividends Per Share	0.700	0.660	0.640	0.620	0.580	0.540	0.520	0.500
Dividend Payout %	24.56	26.72	41.56	52.54	32.95	29.03	85.25	39.68
Income Statement								
Total Revenue	2,312,100	2,161,300	1,689,200	1,653,100	1,530,700	1,469,100	1,151,156	1,247,945
EBITDA	194,100	190,600	134,500	114,900	143,500	143,291	92,936	139,181
Income Before Taxes	99,900	104,800	68,700	47,500	79,000	78,390	22,486	65,088
Income Taxes	11,700	28,600	22,200	12,100	26,800	27,045	7,984	23,432
Net Income	88,200	76,500	46,500	35,400	52,200	51,345	14,502	29,753
Average Shares	30,973	31,003	30,281	29,912	29,710	27,649	23,914	23,691
Balance Sheet								
Current Assets	767,600	760,000	576,000	585,000	547,700	488,251	477,574	406,099
Total Assets	1,854,400	1,839,900	1,292,700	1,312,800	1,279,900	1,224,857	1,293,923	1,059,176
Current Liabilities	472,600	437,300	307,600	245,200	338,600	261,679	255,950	170,431
Long-Term Obligations	379,600	432,100	162,400	272,500	170,100	239,084	390,385	316,732
Total Liabilities	1,096,600	1,155,300	679,800	722,200	703,700	713,805	842,045	610,781
Stockholders' Equity	757,800	684,600	612,900	590,600	576,200	511,052	451,878	448,395
Shares Outstanding	30,053	30,684	30,413	29,665	29,246	29,039	23,786	23,549
Statistical Record								
Return on Assets %	4.77	4.88	3.57	2.72	4.17	4.08	1.23	2.80
Return on Equity %	12.23	11.79	7.73	6.05	9.60	10.66	3.22	6.75
EBITDA Margin %	8.39	8.82	7.96	6.95	9.37	9.75	8.07	11.15
Net Margin %	3.81	3.54	2.75	2.14	3.41	3.49	1.26	2.38
Asset Turnover	1.25	1.38	1.30	1.27	1.22	1.17	0.98	1.17
Current Ratio	1.62	1.74	1.87	2.39	1.62	1.87	1.87	2.38
Debt to Equity	0.50	0.63	0.26	0.46	0.30	0.47	0.86	0.71
Price Range	51.15-32.79	56.66-34.05	37.13-25.13	35.49-23.20	36.50-23.80	32.10-19.15	20.00-14.68	22.63-11.75
P/E Ratio	17.95-11.51	22.94-13.79	24.11-16.32	30.08-19.66	20.74-13.52	17.26-10.30	32.79-24.07	17.96-9.33
Average Yield %	1.73	1.55	2.16	2.13	1.91	2.02	2.96	2.83

Address: 11270 West Park Place, P.O. Box 245008, Milwaukee, WI 53224-9508 Telephone: 414-359-4000 Fax: 414-359-4180	Web Site: www.aosmith.com Officers: Robert J. O'Toole - Chmn., C.E.O. Paul W. Jones - Pres., C.O.O.	Auditors: Ernst & Young LLP Investor Contact: 414-359-4009 Transfer Agents: Wells Fargo Bank Minnesota, N.A., St. Paul, MN

SMITH INTERNATIONAL, INC.

Exchange	Symbol	Price	52Wk Range	Yield	P/E
NYS	SII	$64.23 (3/31/2008)	75.50-49.00	0.75	20.07

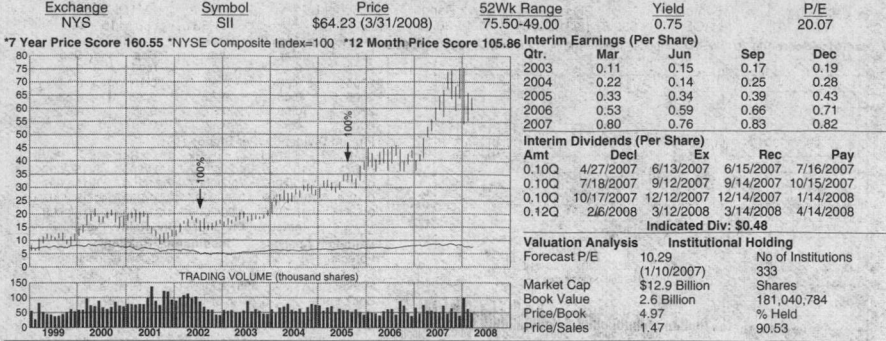

*7 Year Price Score 160.55 *NYSE Composite Index=100 *12 Month Price Score 105.86

Interim Earnings (Per Share)

Qtr.	Mar	Jun	Sep	Dec
2003	0.11	0.15	0.17	0.19
2004	0.22	0.14	0.25	0.28
2005	0.33	0.34	0.39	0.43
2006	0.53	0.59	0.66	0.71
2007	0.80	0.76	0.83	0.82

Interim Dividends (Per Share)

Amt	Decl	Ex	Rec	Pay
0.10Q	4/27/2007	6/13/2007	6/15/2007	7/16/2007
0.10Q	7/18/2007	9/12/2007	9/14/2007	10/15/2007
0.10Q	10/17/2007	12/12/2007	12/14/2007	1/14/2008
0.12Q	2/6/2008	3/12/2008	3/14/2008	4/14/2008

Indicated Div: $0.48

Valuation Analysis

Forecast P/E	10.29
	(1/10/2007)
Market Cap	$12.9 Billion
Book Value	2.6 Billion
Price/Book	4.97
Price/Sales	1.47

Institutional Holding

No of Institutions	333
Shares	181,040,784
% Held	90.53

Business Summary: Oil and Gas (MIC: 14.2 SIC: 3533 NAIC: 333132)

Smith International is a worldwide supplier of products and services to the oil and gas exploration and production industry. Co. provides a line of products and engineering services that include drilling and completion fluid systems, solids-control and separation equipment, waste-management services, oilfield production chemicals, three-cone and diamond drill bits, turbine products, tubulars, fishing services, drilling tools, underreamers, casing exit and multilateral systems, packers and liner hangers. In addition, Co. provides supply-chain management through a North American branch network that provides pipe, valves and fittings, as well as mill, safety and other maintenance products.

Recent Developments: For the year ended Dec 31 2007, net income increased 28.9% to US$647.1 million from US$502.0 million in the prior year. Revenues were US$8.76 billion, up 19.5% from US$7.33 billion the year before. Operating income was US$1.37 billion versus US$1.08 billion in the prior year, an increase of 26.8%. Direct operating expenses rose 18.4% to US$5.91 billion from US$4.99 billion in the comparable period the year before. Indirect operating expenses increased 17.5% to US$1.49 billion from US$1.26 billion in the equivalent prior-year period.

Prospects: For the near-term, Co. expects its North American activity to remain relatively flat. Nonetheless, Co. believes that markets outside North America will continue to expand as the increased number of drilling programs in the Eastern Hemisphere, combined with the addition of a number of newbuild offshore rigs scheduled for delivery in 2008 and beyond, contribute to increased customer spending levels. Thus, Co. now expects full-year 2008 earnings to be between $3.70 and $3.80 per share as its margins in the oilfield segment should improve from the existing levels. Meanwhile, Co. plans to continue to offset the affect of future cost inflation via productivity gains and pricing initiatives.

Financial Data

(US$ in Thousands)	12/31/2007	12/31/2006	12/31/2005	12/31/2004	12/31/2003	12/31/2002	12/31/2001	12/31/2000
Earnings Per Share	3.20	2.49	1.48	0.89	0.61	0.47	0.76	0.36
Cash Flow Per Share	3.44	1.43	1.09	0.90	0.71	1.63	1.03	0.29
Tang Book Value Per Share	7.82	4.89	3.80	3.06	2.72	2.24	1.90	1.83
Dividends Per Share	0.400	0.320	0.240	...	...	...	...	...
Dividend Payout %	12.50	12.85	16.22	...	...	...	...	...
Income Statement								
Total Revenue	8,764,330	7,333,559	5,579,003	4,419,015	3,594,828	3,170,080	3,551,209	2,761,014
EBITDA	1,563,093	1,230,465	788,283	545,257	430,456	345,475	464,405	279,714
Income Before Taxes	1,303,875	1,020,096	627,807	401,302	289,756	217,799	329,046	164,131
Income Taxes	408,471	326,674	202,743	129,721	93,334	66,632	106,397	54,998
Net Income	647,051	502,006	302,305	182,451	123,480	93,189	152,145	72,800
Average Shares	201,947	202,008	204,522	205,138	201,806	200,182	200,896	201,208
Balance Sheet								
Current Assets	3,727,735	3,271,027	2,437,231	2,019,632	1,679,796	1,426,914	1,523,031	1,310,003
Total Assets	6,061,880	5,335,475	4,059,914	3,506,778	3,097,047	2,749,545	2,735,828	2,295,287
Current Liabilities	1,173,300	1,379,468	933,153	887,357	630,924	595,096	666,004	642,804
Long-Term Obligations	845,624	800,928	610,857	387,798	488,548	441,967	538,842	374,716
Total Liabilities	3,466,983	3,348,538	2,481,409	2,105,967	1,861,271	1,686,010	1,786,669	1,477,806
Stockholders' Equity	2,594,897	1,986,937	1,578,505	1,400,811	1,235,776	1,063,535	949,159	817,481
Shares Outstanding	200,761	199,916	200,969	202,150	200,672	198,324	197,608	199,052
Statistical Record								
Return on Assets %	11.35	10.69	7.99	5.51	4.22	3.40	6.05	3.47
Return on Equity %	28.24	28.16	20.29	13.80	10.74	9.26	17.22	9.44
EBITDA Margin %	17.83	16.78	14.13	12.34	11.97	10.90	13.08	10.13
Net Margin %	7.38	6.85	5.42	4.13	3.43	2.94	4.28	2.64
Asset Turnover	1.54	1.56	1.47	1.33	1.23	1.16	1.41	1.31
Current Ratio	3.18	2.37	2.61	2.28	2.66	2.40	2.29	2.04
Debt to Equity	0.33	0.40	0.39	0.28	0.40	0.42	0.57	0.46
Price Range	75.34-36.21	45.97-35.96	39.59-25.95	31.25-20.14	21.26-14.93	19.04-11.68	20.97-8.36	21.88-11.59
P/E Ratio	23.54-11.32	18.46-14.44	26.75-17.54	35.11-22.62	34.85-24.47	40.50-24.84	27.60-11.00	60.76-32.20
Average Yield %	0.70	0.79	0.75	...	...	...	...	...

Address: 411 North Sam Houston Parkway, Suite 600, Houston, TX 77060
Telephone: 281-443-3370
Fax: 281-233-5199

Web Site: www.smith.com
Officers: Douglas L. Rock - Chmn., Pres., C.E.O., C.O.O. John J. Kennedy - Pres., C.E.O., Wilson

Auditors: Deloitte & Touche LLP
Investor Contact: 800-877-6424

SMITHFIELD FOODS, INC.

Exchange	Symbol	Price	52Wk Range	Yield	P/E
NYS	SFD	$25.76 (3/31/2008)	34.95-24.45	N/A	19.97

*7 Year Price Score 95.12 *NYSE Composite Index=100 *12 Month Price Score 98.16

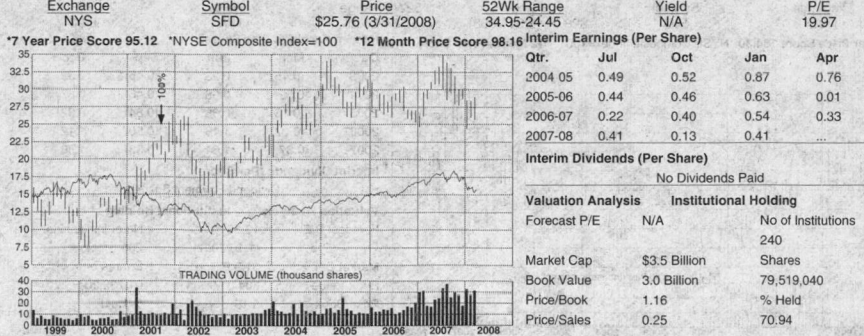

Interim Earnings (Per Share)

Qtr.	Jul	Oct	Jan	Apr
2004-05	0.49	0.52	0.87	0.76
2005-06	0.44	0.46	0.63	0.01
2006-07	0.22	0.40	0.54	0.33
2007-08	0.41	0.13	0.41	...

Interim Dividends (Per Share)

No Dividends Paid

Valuation Analysis | Institutional Holding

Forecast P/E	N/A	No of Institutions
		240
Market Cap	$3.5 Billion	Shares
Book Value	3.0 Billion	79,519,040
Price/Book	1.16	% Held
Price/Sales	0.25	70.94

Business Summary: Food (MIC: 4.1 SIC: 2011 NAIC: 311615)

Smithfield Foods is engaged in the production of hog, as well as the processing of pork and beef worldwide. Co.'s Pork segment produces domestically a variety of fresh pork and processed meat products and markets them to foreign markets. The Beef segment produces boxed beef and ground beef, while Co.'s International segment is engaged in the production of internationally a variety of fresh and processed meat products. The HP segment develops breeding stock, optimizes diets for its hogs at each stage of the growth process, processes feed for its hogs and designs and builds hog confinement facilities. The Other segment is comprised of Co.'s turkey production and hatchery operations.

Recent Developments: For the quarter ended Jan 27 2008, income from continuing operations decreased 4.8% to US$59.1 million from US$62.1 million in the year-earlier quarter. Net income decreased 9.6% to US$54.6 million from US$60.4 million in the year-earlier quarter. Revenues were US$3.79 billion, up 15.6% from US$3.28 billion the year before. Direct operating expenses rose 13.4% to US$3.38 billion from US$2.99 billion in the comparable period the year before. Indirect operating expenses increased 33.1% to US$316.4 million from US$237.8 million in the equivalent prior-year period.

Prospects: Looking ahead, Co. expects hog supplies to solid strong and foresees that the softer U.S. currency and robust international demand should continue to support strong export markets. For its International segment, Co. is anticipating higher raw material costs due to the escalating grain prices. In response, Co. plans to mitigate these challenges through price increases and overall operating performance. Separately, on Mar 5 2008, Co. announced a definitive agreement to divest Smithfield Beef Group, Inc., its beef processing and cattle feeding operation, to JBS S.A. for about US$565.0 million. The completion of the transaction is based on customary regulatory review and closing conditions.

Financial Data

(US$ in Thousands)	9 Mos	6 Mos	3 Mos	04/29/2007	04/30/2006	05/01/2005	05/02/2004	04/27/2003
Earnings Per Share	1.29	1.41	1.68	1.49	1.54	2.64	2.03	0.24
Cash Flow Per Share	0.69	1.50	1.54	1.87	4.54	0.91	2.77	0.76
Tang Book Value Per Share	12.52	12.60	12.21	11.06	11.76	11.66	10.07	7.27
Income Statement								
Total Revenue	10,617,900	6,828,400	3,364,200	11,911,100	11,403,600	11,354,200	9,267,000	7,904,500
EBITDA	436,000	266,500	164,500	653,000	628,700	780,900	543,200	305,900
Depn & Amortn	208,100	141,600	69,200	...	...	...	...	...
Income Before Taxes	227,900	124,900	95,300	252,700	271,300	447,000	246,800	39,200
Income Taxes	88,100	44,200	33,300	64,300	91,000	150,800	84,100	12,900
Net Income	126,500	71,900	54,500	166,800	172,700	296,200	227,100	26,300
Average Shares	134,500	134,500	133,000	111,900	112,000	112,300	111,700	109,800
Balance Sheet								
Current Assets	3,240,200	3,278,300	3,095,300	2,733,700	2,119,600	2,527,300	2,025,600	1,658,800
Total Assets	8,504,400	8,434,100	8,129,200	6,968,600	6,176,500	5,704,800	4,813,700	4,210,600
Current Liabilities	1,586,600	1,474,600	1,446,300	1,361,200	1,241,800	1,081,900	967,000	817,500
Long-Term Obligations	3,324,100	3,407,500	3,170,100	2,838,600	2,313,900	2,151,700	1,696,800	1,599,100
Total Liabilities	5,505,700	5,479,500	5,208,000	4,713,900	4,130,000	3,780,500	3,183,300	2,898,600
Stockholders' Equity	2,982,100	2,941,100	2,907,700	2,240,800	2,028,200	1,901,400	1,617,200	1,299,200
Shares Outstanding	134,397	134,297	134,230	112,423	111,167	111,249	110,978	109,460
Statistical Record								
Return on Assets %	2.14	2.22	2.73	2.54	2.92	5.65	4.95	0.65
Return on Equity %	6.34	6.73	7.94	7.84	8.81	16.88	15.32	1.98
EBITDA Margin %	4.11	3.90	4.89	5.48	5.51	6.88	5.86	3.87
Net Margin %	1.19	1.05	1.62	1.40	1.51	2.61	2.45	0.33
Asset Turnover	1.78	1.72	1.74	1.82	1.92	2.16	2.02	1.96
Current Ratio	2.04	2.22	2.14	2.01	1.95	2.34	2.09	2.02
Debt to Equity	1.11	1.16	1.09	1.27	1.14	1.13	1.05	1.23
Price Range	34.95-24.45	34.95-24.61	34.95-24.61	31.08-24.61	31.39-25.98	34.39-23.55	27.95-19.14	21.32-14.80
P/E Ratio	27.09-18.95	24.79-17.45	20.80-14.65	20.86-16.52	20.38-16.87	13.03-8.92	13.77-9.43	88.83-61.67

Address: 200 Commerce Street, Smithfield, VA 23430
Telephone: 757-365-3000

Web Site: www.smithfieldfoods.com
Officers: Joseph W. Luter III - Chmn., C.E.O. C. Larry Pope - Pres., C.O.O.

Auditors: Ernst & Young LLP
Investor Contact: 212-758-2100
Transfer Agents: Computershare Investor Services LLC

SOTHEBY'S

Exchange	Symbol	Price	52Wk Range	Yield	P/E
NYS	BID	$28.91 (3/31/2008)	57.64-26.26	N/A	8.90

*7 Year Price Score 164.30 *NYSE Composite Index=100 *12 Month Price Score 78.63

Interim Earnings (Per Share)

Qtr.	Mar	Jun	Sep	Dec
2003	(0.45)	0.23	(0.45)	0.32
2004	0.59	0.68	(0.46)	0.57
2005	(0.16)	0.66	(0.34)	0.82
2006	(0.07)	1.16	(0.50)	1.12
2007	0.37	1.64	(0.33)	1.56

Interim Dividends (Per Share)

Dividend Payment Suspended

Valuation Analysis | **Institutional Holding**

Forecast P/E	13.35	No of Institutions
	(1/10/2007)	204
Market Cap	$1.9 Billion	Shares
Book Value	604.0 Million	61,733,204
Price/Book	3.19	% Held
Price/Sales	2.10	93.91

Business Summary: Retail - Miscellaneous (MIC: 5.11 SIC: 7389 NAIC: 453920)

Sotheby's and its subsidiaries are auctioneers of authenticated fine art, antiques and decorative art, jewelry and collectibles. Co.'s main role as an auctioneer is to identify, evaluate and appraise works of art; to stimulate purchaser interest; and to match sellers and buyers through the auction process. In addition to auctioneering, Co.'s Auction segment is engaged in a number of related activities, such as the brokering of private purchases and sales of fine art, jewelry and collectibles. Co. also operates as a dealer in works of art via its Dealer segment, conducts art-related financing activities via its Finance segment and is engaged, to a lesser extent, in licensing activities.

Recent Developments: For the year ended Dec 31 2007, income from continuing operations increased 98.5% to US$213.1 million from US$107.4 million a year earlier. Net income increased 99.1% to US$213.1 million from US$107.0 million in the prior year. Revenues were US$917.7 million, up 38.0% from US$664.8 million the year before. Operating income was US$275.8 million versus US$197.2 million in the prior year, an increase of 39.9%. Direct operating expenses rose 86.8% to US$129.6 million from US$69.4 million in the comparable period the year before. Indirect operating expenses increased 28.6% to US$512.4 million from US$398.3 million in the equivalent prior-year period.

Prospects: Co.'s outlook appears favorable as its top- and bottom-line results are being driven by growth in its auction commission revenues. Separately, on Jan 9 2008, Co.'s International Realty Affiliates LLC announced that it has signed a 25-year licensing agreement with Indochina Land to develop Co.'s International Realty® brand in Vietnam. Notably, Co. believes that this agreement will contribute to its overall international growth plans going forward due to Vietnam's gross domestic product growth of about 8.0% annually for the last three years, and projected growth of 8.0% to 8.5% over the next several years. Accordingly, Co. expects its first office in Vietnam to open in April 2008.

Financial Data

(US$ in Thousands)	12/31/2007	12/31/2006	12/31/2005	12/31/2004	12/31/2003	12/31/2002	12/31/2001	12/31/2000
Earnings Per Share	3.25	1.72	1.00	1.38	(0.34)	(0.89)	(0.69)	(3.22)
Cash Flow Per Share	(0.58)	4.48	0.97	2.35	(0.74)	(0.28)	(0.34)	(0.73)
Tang Book Value Per Share	8.56	3.92	1.95	3.48	1.85	2.02	2.75	2.81
Dividends Per Share	0.500	0.200	...	...	...	...	...	...
Dividend Payout %	15.38	11.63	...	...	...	...	...	...
Income Statement								
Total Revenue	917,722	664,809	513,508	496,720	319,599	345,095	336,163	397,788
EBITDA	320,227	218,393	144,718	155,638	18,102	(27,009)	(24,415)	(213,901)
Income Before Taxes	283,019	165,783	90,913	96,653	(37,576)	(71,461)	(71,546)	(250,127)
Income Taxes	72,512	60,050	28,573	35,000	(11,093)	(16,706)	(29,850)	(60,433)
Net Income	213,139	107,049	61,602	86,679	(20,656)	(54,755)	(41,696)	(189,694)
Average Shares	65,600	62,100	61,900	61,900	61,600	61,500	60,700	58,900
Balance Sheet								
Current Assets	1,565,602	1,047,827	686,956	832,297	480,011	457,868	511,324	726,568
Total Assets	2,020,104	1,477,165	1,060,752	1,225,346	901,470	875,705	864,111	1,074,158
Current Liabilities	1,074,862	789,191	545,245	619,937	387,888	447,929	475,202	687,053
Long-Term Obligations	267,078	268,777	304,849	271,663	271,708	199,466	99,398	99,334
Total Liabilities	1,416,087	1,175,478	934,476	989,427	774,062	735,337	678,241	886,104
Stockholders' Equity	604,017	301,687	126,276	235,919	127,408	140,368	185,870	188,054
Shares Outstanding	66,563	64,795	57,847	63,774	61,573	61,305	61,305	58,842
Statistical Record								
Return on Assets %	12.19	8.44	5.39	8.13	N.M.	N.M.	N.M.	N.M.
Return on Equity %	47.07	50.03	34.02	47.58	N.M.	N.M.	N.M.	N.M.
EBITDA Margin %	34.89	32.85	28.18	31.33	5.66	N.M.	N.M.	N.M.
Net Margin %	23.22	16.10	12.00	17.45	N.M.	N.M.	N.M.	N.M.
Asset Turnover	0.52	0.52	0.45	0.47	0.36	0.40	0.35	0.37
Current Ratio	1.46	1.33	1.26	1.34	1.24	1.02	1.08	1.06
Debt to Equity	0.44	0.89	2.41	1.15	2.13	1.42	0.53	0.53
Price Range	57.64-30.71	38.00-18.55	19.43-13.52	18.90-12.21	14.10-6.49	17.00-6.57	27.31-10.76	30.00-14.75
P/E Ratio	17.74-9.45	22.09-10.78	19.43-13.52	13.70-8.85	...	...	...	...
Average Yield %	1.14	0.71	...	...	...	...	...	...

Address: 38500 Woodward Avenue, Suite 100, Bloomfield Hills, MI 48304 **Telephone:** 248-646-2400	**Web Site:** www.sothebys.com **Officers:** Michael I. Sovern - Chmn. Max M. Fisher - Vice-Chmn.	**Auditors:** Deloitte & Touche LLP **Investor Contact:** 800-700-6321 **Transfer Agents:** Mellon Investor Services LLC

SMUCKER (J.M.) CO.

Exchange	Symbol	Price	52Wk Range	Yield	P/E
NYS	SJM	$50.61 (3/31/2008)	63.66-44.66	2.37	16.43

*7 Year Price Score 99.95   ***NYSE Composite Index=100**   ***12 Month Price Score 100.43**

Interim Earnings (Per Share)

Qtr.	Jul	Oct	Jan	Apr
2004-05	0.60	0.65	0.61	0.38
2005-06	0.51	0.79	0.54	0.62
2006-07	0.50	0.80	0.71	0.75
2007-08	0.71	0.87	0.75	...

Interim Dividends (Per Share)

Amt	Decl	Ex	Rec	Pay
0.30Q	4/17/2007	5/11/2007	5/15/2007	6/1/2007
0.30Q	7/24/2007	8/14/2007	8/16/2007	9/4/2007
0.30Q	10/25/2007	11/13/2007	11/15/2007	12/3/2007
0.30Q	1/22/2008	2/13/2008	2/15/2008	3/3/2008

Indicated Div: $1.20

Valuation Analysis

Forecast P/E	14.68 (1/10/2007)
Market Cap	$2.8 Billion
Book Value	1.9 Billion
Price/Book	1.53
Price/Sales	1.17

Institutional Holding

No of Institutions	294
Shares	30,640,496
% Held	54.12

Business Summary: Food (MIC: 4.1 SIC: 2033 NAIC: 311421)

Smucker (J.M.) is engaged in the manufacture and marketing of branded food products on a worldwide basis. Co.'s U.S. retail market segment includes the consumer and consumer oils and baking businesses. Co.'s special markets segment represents the aggregation of the foodservice, beverage, Canada, and international businesses. As of Apr 30 2007, Co.'s principal products were peanut butter, shortening and oils, flour and baking ingredients, fruit spreads, baking mixes and ready-to-spread frostings, fruit and vegetable juices, beverages, dessert toppings, syrups, frozen sandwiches, pickles and condiments, and potato side dishes as well as canned milk.

Recent Developments: For the quarter ended Jan 31 2008, net income increased 4.9% to US$42.4 million from US$40.4 million in the year-earlier quarter. Revenues were US$665.4 million, up 27.2% from US$523.1 million the year before. Operating income was US$68.9 million versus US$64.4 million in the prior-year quarter, an increase of 7.1%. Direct operating expenses rose 34.2% to US$469.9 million from US$350.1 million in the comparable period the year before. Indirect operating expenses increased 16.5% to US$126.5 million from US$108.6 million in the equivalent prior-year period.

Prospects: Despite the escalating commodity costs, Co.'s near-term outlook appears solid as it continues to implement its strategy of owning and marketing core North American food brands. For instance, on Mar 4 2008, Co. announced that it has signed an agreement to acquire Europe's Best, Inc., a privately owned company in Montreal, Quebec. Co. expects this transaction, which is projected to close by end of March 2008, to add about $70.0 million in net sales and slightly accretive to its earnings for the fiscal year ending Apr 30 2009. Also, Co. expects Europe's Best's administrative functions in Montreal to be integrated to its Canadian operations in Markham, Ontario, by the end of October 2008.

Financial Data

(US$ in Thousands)	9 Mos	6 Mos	3 Mos	04/30/2007	04/30/2006	04/30/2005	04/30/2004	04/30/2003
Earnings Per Share	3.08	3.02	2.97	2.76	2.45	2.24	2.21	2.02
Cash Flow Per Share	4.25	3.58	3.92	4.85	3.43	3.41	2.52	3.51
Tang Book Value Per Share	2.64	3.63	3.05	5.75	5.52	4.61	7.10	5.58
Dividends Per Share	1.180	1.160	1.140	1.120	1.080	1.000	0.920	0.600
Dividend Payout %	38.31	38.35	38.38	40.58	44.08	44.64	41.63	29.70
Income Statement								
Total Revenue	1,934,776	1,269,403	561,513	2,148,017	2,154,726	2,043,877	1,417,011	1,311,744
EBITDA	269,047	183,577	85,312	314,016	304,049	278,534	221,672	199,854
Depn & Amortn	46,468	30,189	14,891	...	...	...	...	...
Income Before Taxes	201,859	139,699	63,823	241,004	215,570	204,614	178,819	155,390
Income Taxes	68,531	48,772	23,062	83,785	72,216	74,154	67,469	59,048
Net Income	133,328	90,927	40,761	157,219	143,354	129,073	111,350	96,342
Average Shares	56,823	57,531	57,265	57,056	58,425	57,748	50,395	47,764
Balance Sheet								
Current Assets	854,317	943,697	915,194	639,366	571,495	555,851	425,258	466,660
Total Assets	3,162,253	3,283,407	3,202,232	2,693,823	2,649,744	2,635,894	1,684,125	1,615,407
Current Liabilities	243,923	293,171	283,885	236,468	235,440	308,292	174,883	167,274
Long-Term Obligations	790,424	791,164	791,903	392,643	428,602	431,560	135,000	135,000
Total Liabilities	1,311,649	1,365,466	1,356,543	898,166	921,685	945,094	473,432	491,236
Stockholders' Equity	1,850,604	1,917,941	1,845,689	1,795,657	1,728,059	1,690,800	1,210,693	1,124,171
Shares Outstanding	55,901	57,532	57,513	56,779	56,949	58,540	50,174	49,767
Statistical Record								
Return on Assets %	6.04	5.79	5.72	5.88	5.42	5.98	6.73	9.00
Return on Equity %	9.75	9.42	9.43	8.92	8.39	8.90	9.51	13.72
EBITDA Margin %	13.91	14.46	15.19	14.62	14.11	13.63	15.64	15.24
Net Margin %	6.89	7.16	7.26	7.32	6.65	6.32	7.86	7.34
Asset Turnover	0.83	0.76	0.74	0.80	0.82	0.95	0.86	1.23
Current Ratio	3.50	3.22	3.22	2.70	2.43	1.80	2.43	2.79
Debt to Equity	0.43	0.41	0.43	0.22	0.25	0.26	0.11	0.12
Price Range	63.66-44.66	63.66-46.80	63.66-43.22	56.88-39.53	50.87-37.78	53.09-41.28	53.38-35.95	41.75-29.55
P/E Ratio	20.67-14.50	21.08-15.50	21.43-14.55	20.61-14.32	20.76-15.42	23.70-18.43	24.15-16.27	20.67-14.63
Average Yield %	2.20	2.17	2.21	2.36	2.38	2.37	2.13	1.66

Address: Strawberry Lane, Orrville, OH 44667	**Web Site:** www.smuckers.com	**Auditors:** Ernst & Young LLP
Telephone: 330-682-3000	**Officers:** Timothy P. Smucker - Chmn., Co-C.E.O.	**Investor Contact:** 330-684-3838
Fax: 330-682-3370	Richard K. Smucker - Pres., Co-C.E.O.	**Transfer Agents:** Computershare Investor Services, LLC, Chicago, IL

Exchange	Symbol	Price	52Wk Range	Yield	P/E
NYS	SNA	$50.85 (3/31/2008)	56.20-39.78	2.36	16.46

*7 Year Price Score 111.92 *NYSE Composite Index=100 *12 Month Price Score 108.00

Interim Earnings (Per Share)

Qtr.	Mar	Jun	Sep	Dec
2003	0.37	0.38	0.30	0.30
2004	0.22	0.38	0.39	0.41
2005	0.31	0.46	0.36	0.47
2006	0.37	0.20	0.48	0.64
2007	0.66	0.74	0.70	0.98

Interim Dividends (Per Share)

Amt	Decl	Ex	Rec	Pay
0.27Q	4/30/2007	5/17/2007	5/21/2007	6/11/2007
0.27Q	8/2/2007	8/16/2007	8/20/2007	9/10/2007
0.30Q	11/1/2007	11/15/2007	11/19/2007	12/10/2007
0.30Q	2/13/2008	2/21/2008	2/25/2008	3/10/2008

Indicated Div: $1.20

Valuation Analysis / **Institutional Holding**

Forecast P/E	17.35	No of Institutions
	(1/10/2007)	248
Market Cap	$2.9 Billion	Shares
Book Value	1.3 Billion	51,180,016
Price/Book	2.28	% Held
Price/Sales	1.01	86.89

Business Summary: Metal Products (MIC: 11.4 SIC: 3429 NAIC: 332510)

Snap-on is a global manufacturer and marketer of tools, diagnostics, equipment, software and service applications designed for professional users. Co.'s products and services include hand and power tools, tool storage, diagnostics software, information and management systems, shop equipment and other applications for vehicle dealerships and repair centers, as well as customers in industry, government, agriculture, aviation and natural resources. Co. also derives income from various financing programs to facilitate the sales of its products. At Dec 29 2007, Co. marketed its products and brands through multiple distribution sales channels in more than 130 countries.

Recent Developments: For the year ended Dec 29 2007, income from continuing operations increased 93.3% to US$189.2 million from US$97.9 million a year earlier. Net income increased 81.0% to US$181.2 million from US$100.1 million in the prior year. Revenues were US$2.90 billion, up 16.0% from US$2.50 billion the year before. Operating income was US$324.8 million versus US$162.8 million in the prior year, an increase of 99.5%. Direct operating expenses rose 14.4% to US$1.62 billion from US$1.41 billion in the comparable period the year before. Indirect operating expenses increased 3.7% to US$964.2 million from US$930.0 million in the equivalent prior-year period.

Prospects: Looking ahead, Co. will continue to invest in its growth initiatives which include investing in growing market, such as China, India and Eastern Europe, in order to penetrate new and adjacent segments as well as to extend its presence in the emerging markets of Asia/Pacific and Eastern Europe. Co. also expects to continue implementing its Rapid Continuous Improvement and low-cost sourcing initiatives to provide higher levels of growth and profitability. Meanwhile, Co. is projecting 2008 restructuring costs of $15.0 million to $20.0 million, down from the $26.0 million incurred in 2007. Moreover, Co. anticipates full-year 2008 sales and operating earnings to improve over the 2007 levels.

Financial Data

(US$ in Thousands)	12/29/2007	12/30/2006	12/31/2005	01/01/2005	01/03/2004	12/28/2002	12/29/2001	12/30/2000
Earnings Per Share	3.09	1.69	1.59	1.40	1.35	1.81	0.33	2.53
Cash Flow Per Share	4.00	3.50	3.84	2.54	2.99	3.86	2.84	3.27
Tang Book Value Per Share	3.94	0.72	8.17	9.67	8.29	6.27	6.01	6.95
Dividends Per Share	1.110	1.080	1.000	1.000	1.000	0.970	0.960	0.940
Dividend Payout %	35.92	63.91	62.89	71.43	74.07	53.59	290.91	37.15
Income Statement								
Total Revenue	2,904,200	2,522,400	2,362,200	2,407,200	2,233,200	2,109,100	2,095,700	2,175,700
EBITDA	406,000	218,400	221,900	206,900	203,500	243,400	151,100	299,500
Income Before Taxes	284,200	145,900	148,000	120,400	116,700	161,200	47,600	192,600
Income Taxes	92,500	45,800	55,100	38,700	38,000	58,000	26,100	69,500
Net Income	181,200	100,100	92,900	81,700	78,700	106,000	19,000	148,500
Average Shares	58,600	59,200	58,400	58,300	58,400	58,500	58,100	58,600
Balance Sheet								
Current Assets	1,187,400	1,113,200	1,072,900	1,192,600	1,131,700	1,051,000	1,139,400	1,186,400
Total Assets	2,765,100	2,654,500	2,008,400	2,290,100	2,138,500	1,994,100	1,974,300	2,050,400
Current Liabilities	639,200	682,000	506,100	674,200	567,200	552,400	549,400	538,000
Long-Term Obligations	502,000	505,600	201,700	203,200	303,000	304,300	445,500	473,000
Total Liabilities	1,485,000	1,578,200	1,046,200	1,179,400	1,127,600	1,163,700	1,198,500	1,206,400
Stockholders' Equity	1,280,100	1,076,300	962,200	1,110,700	1,010,900	830,400	775,800	844,000
Shares Outstanding	57,429	58,578	61,162	62,030	63,181	63,571	63,923	60,346
Statistical Record								
Return on Assets %	6.71	4.31	4.33	3.70	3.75	5.36	0.95	7.09
Return on Equity %	15.42	9.85	8.99	7.72	8.41	13.24	2.35	17.84
EBITDA Margin %	13.98	8.66	9.39	8.60	9.11	11.54	7.21	13.77
Net Margin %	6.24	3.97	3.93	3.39	3.52	5.03	0.91	6.83
Asset Turnover	1.07	1.08	1.10	1.09	1.06	1.07	1.04	1.04
Current Ratio	1.86	1.63	2.12	1.77	2.00	1.90	2.07	2.21
Debt to Equity	0.39	0.47	0.21	0.18	0.30	0.37	0.57	0.56
Price Range	56.20-44.59	48.31-36.39	38.54-30.70	34.36-27.26	32.34-22.90	34.96-21.50	34.21-21.65	31.94-21.19
P/E Ratio	18.19-14.43	28.59-21.53	24.24-19.31	24.54-19.47	23.96-16.96	19.31-11.88	103.67-65.61	12.62-8.37
Average Yield %	2.23	2.59	2.88	3.12	3.52	3.29	3.42	3.56

Address: 2801 80th Street, Kenosha, WI 53143
Telephone: 262-656-5200
Fax: 262-656-5577

Web Site: www.snapon.com
Officers: Jack D. Michaels - Chmn., Pres., C.E.O. Martin M. Ellen - Sr. V.P., Fin., C.F.O.

Auditors: Deloitte & Touche LLP
Investor Contact: 262-656-6488
Transfer Agents: EquiServe Trust Company, N.A., Providence, RI

SONIC AUTOMOTIVE, INC.

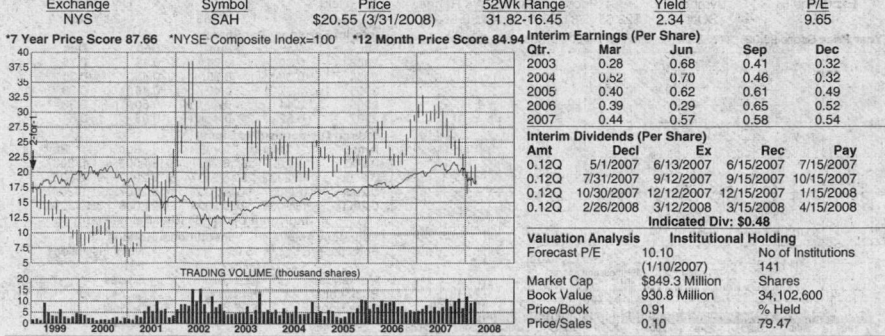

Exchange	Symbol	Price	52Wk Range	Yield	P/E
NYS	SAH	$20.55 (3/31/2008)	31.82-16.45	2.34	9.65

*7 Year Price Score 87.66 *NYSE Composite Index=100 *12 Month Price Score 84.94

Interim Earnings (Per Share)

Qtr.	Mar	Jun	Sep	Dec
2003	0.28	0.68	0.41	0.32
2004	0.52	0.70	0.46	0.32
2005	0.40	0.62	0.61	0.49
2006	0.39	0.29	0.65	0.52
2007	0.44	0.57	0.58	0.54

Interim Dividends (Per Share)

Amt	Decl	Ex	Rec	Pay
0.12Q	5/1/2007	6/13/2007	6/15/2007	7/15/2007
0.12Q	7/31/2007	9/12/2007	9/15/2007	10/15/2007
0.12Q	10/30/2007	12/12/2007	12/15/2007	1/15/2008
0.12Q	2/26/2008	3/12/2008	3/15/2008	4/15/2008

Indicated Div: $0.48

Valuation Analysis

		Institutional Holding	
Forecast P/E	10.10	No of Institutions	
	(1/10/2007)	141	
Market Cap	$849.3 Million	Shares	
Book Value	930.8 Million	34,102,600	
Price/Book	0.91	% Held	
Price/Sales	0.10	79.47	

Business Summary: Retail - Automotive (MIC: 5.7 SIC: 5511 NAIC: 441110)

Sonic Automotive is engaged as an automotive retailer in the U.S. As of Feb 22 2008, Co. operated 169 dealership franchises at approximately 144 dealership locations, representing 33 different brands of cars and light trucks, and 34 collision repair centers in 15 states. As of Dec 31 2007, each of Co.'s dealerships provided comprehensive services including sales of both new and used cars and light trucks; sales of replacement parts and performance of vehicle maintenance; warranty, paint and repair services; and arrangement of extended service contracts, financing and insurance as well as other aftermarket products for its automotive customers.

Recent Developments: For the year ended Dec 31 2007, income from continuing operations increased 18.6% to US$114.8 million from US$96.8 million a year earlier. Net income increased 17.7% to US$95.5 million from US$81.1 million in the prior year. Revenues were US$8.34 billion, up 4.4% from US$7.99 billion the year before. Operating income was US$296.6 million versus US$262.2 million in the prior year, an increase of 13.1%. Direct operating expenses rose 4.3% to US$7.05 billion from US$6.76 billion in the comparable period the year before. Indirect operating expenses increased 3.0% to US$995.0 million from US$966.1 million in the equivalent prior-year period.

Prospects: Going forward, Co. expects to see continued softness in new vehicle sales in 2008, which it believes that will be largely offset by growth in its used vehicle, as well as parts and service revenue. In addition, as part of its ongoing portfolio enhancement and capital allocation strategies, Co. is considering changes to its group of stores held for sale, including the potential sale of a number of stores that no longer fit its business model. Accordingly, Co. anticipates this change, when enacted, to reduce its earnings from continuing operations in 2008 by about $0.09, resulting in its 2008 earnings per share from continuing operations target of $2.35 to $2.50.

Financial Data
(US$ in Thousands)

	12/31/2007	12/31/2006	12/31/2005	12/31/2004	12/31/2003	12/31/2002	12/31/2001	12/31/2000
Earnings Per Share	2.13	1.85	2.12	2.00	1.69	2.47	1.91	1.69
Cash Flow Per Share	0.80	(1.46)	2.05	5.06	3.37	3.33	3.61	2.49
Dividends Per Share	0.480	0.480	0.480	0.440	0.200	...	...	...
Dividend Payout %	22.54	25.95	22.64	22.00	11.83	...	...	...
Income Statement								
Total Revenue	8,336,933	7,972,074	7,884,842	7,394,937	7,034,215	7,071,015	6,337,358	6,052,476
EBITDA	330,507	294,114	275,092	240,431	206,219	248,347	227,204	231,938
Income Before Taxes	189,213	165,357	164,181	152,569	134,045	175,330	130,044	119,872
Income Taxes	74,377	66,791	62,390	56,858	46,210	66,821	50,715	45,700
Net Income	95,502	81,117	91,861	86,071	71,560	106,564	79,329	74,172
Average Shares	46,941	46,265	45,333	43,217	42,421	43,158	41,609	43,826
Balance Sheet								
Current Assets	1,580,061	1,613,132	1,616,700	1,591,543	1,554,197	1,301,627	956,296	1,037,403
Total Assets	3,282,744	3,124,764	3,025,501	2,901,611	2,686,229	2,375,308	1,805,926	1,789,248
Current Liabilities	1,426,117	1,431,693	1,320,494	1,333,375	1,196,929	1,038,384	737,253	818,321
Long-Term Obligations	697,800	598,627	712,311	668,826	694,898	637,545	511,877	485,212
Total Liabilities	2,351,916	2,220,924	2,194,703	2,131,924	1,987,896	1,738,130	1,288,665	1,338,326
Stockholders' Equity	930,828	903,840	830,798	769,687	698,333	637,178	517,261	450,922
Shares Outstanding	41,327	42,720	41,975	41,661	41,221	41,140	40,549	41,965
Statistical Record								
Return on Assets %	2.98	2.64	3.10	3.07	2.83	5.10	4.41	4.50
Return on Equity %	10.41	9.35	11.48	11.69	10.72	18.46	16.39	17.33
EBITDA Margin %	3.96	3.69	3.49	3.25	2.93	3.51	3.59	3.83
Net Margin %	1.15	1.02	1.17	1.16	1.02	1.51	1.25	1.23
Asset Turnover	2.60	2.59	2.66	2.64	2.78	3.38	3.53	3.67
Current Ratio	1.11	1.13	1.22	1.19	1.30	1.25	1.30	1.27
Debt to Equity	0.75	0.66	0.86	0.87	1.00	1.00	0.99	1.08
Price Range	32.86-19.36	29.50-21.08	24.80-19.23	26.10-18.40	28.65-13.65	38.60-14.05	23.86-6.00	12.13-6.00
P/E Ratio	15.43-9.09	15.95-11.39	11.70-9.07	13.05-9.20	16.95-8.08	15.63-5.69	12.49-3.14	7.17-3.55
Average Yield %	1.75	1.94	2.15	1.97	0.97	...	...	...

Address: 6415 Idlewild Road, Suite 109, Charlotte, NC 28212 **Telephone:** 704-566-2400 **Fax:** 704-536-5116	**Web Site:** www.sonicautomotive.com **Officers:** O. Bruton Smith - Chmn., C.E.O. B. Scott Smith - Vice-Chmn., Chief Strategic Officer	**Auditors:** Deloitte & Touche LLP **Investor Contact:** 888-766-4218 **Transfer Agents:** Wachovia Bank, N.A.

Exchange	Symbol	Price	52Wk Range	Yield	P/E	Div Achiever
NYS	SON	$28.63 (3/31/2008)	44.89-26.46	3.63	13.63	24 Years

*7 Year Price Score 99.02   *NYSE Composite Index=100   *12 Month Price Score 88.79

Interim Earnings (Per Share)

Qtr.	Mar	Jun	Sep	Dec
2003	0.30	0.24	0.14	0.75
2004	0.38	0.35	0.42	0.35
2005	0.37	0.40	0.46	0.38
2006	0.44	0.49	0.60	0.38
2007	0.52	0.41	0.63	0.54

Interim Dividends (Per Share)

Amt	Decl	Ex	Rec	Pay
0.26Q	4/18/2007	5/16/2007	5/18/2007	6/8/2007
0.26Q	7/18/2007	8/15/2007	8/17/2007	9/10/2007
0.26Q	10/16/2007	11/14/2007	11/16/2007	12/10/2007
0.26Q	2/6/2008	2/20/2008	2/22/2008	3/10/2008

Indicated Div: $1.04 (Div. Reinv. Plan)

Valuation Analysis

		Institutional Holding	
Forecast P/E	15.05	No of Institutions	
	(1/10/2007)	261	
Market Cap	$2.8 Billion	Shares	
Book Value	1.4 Billion	59,740,940	
Price/Book	1.97	% Held	
Price/Sales	0.70	60.04	

Business Summary: Paper Products (MIC: 11.11 SIC: 2631 NAIC: 322130)

Sonoco Products manufactures industrial and consumer packaging products and provides packaging services. Co.'s Consumer Packaging segment includes round and shaped rigid packaging; printed flexible packaging; and metal and plastic ends and closures. The Tubes and Cores/Paper segment includes paper and composite paperboard tubes and cores; fiber-based construction tubes and forms; recycled paperboard; linerboard and recovered paper. The Packaging Services segment provides point-of-purchase displays; brand management and supply chain management; while its All Other Sonoco segment offers wooden, metal and composite reels, molded and extruded plastics, and protective packaging.

Recent Developments: For the year ended Dec 31 2007, net income increased 9.8% to US$214.2 million from US$195.1 million in the prior year. Revenues were US$4.04 billion, up 10.5% from US$3.66 billion the year before. Operating income was US$307.9 million versus US$320.1 million in the prior year, a decrease of 3.8%. Direct operating expenses rose 11.3% to US$3.29 billion from US$2.95 billion in the comparable period the year before. Indirect operating expenses increased 15.8% to US$445.9 million from US$384.9 million in the equivalent prior-year period.

Prospects: Looking into 2008, Co. remains cautious about the North American economy given the weak overall demand for tubes and cores. Co. also noted that the high cost of old corrugated containers, other raw materials, and energy is expected to continue at least into the first half of 2008, which will pressure margins further. Meanwhile, in Dec 2007, Co. announced a five-year plan to grow revenue, improve margins and increase assets utilization, by increasing organic sales, geographic expansion, providing total packaging applications for customers, developing new products and making strategic acquisitions. Accordingly, Co. expects to grow sales to about $5.50 billion to $6.00 billion by end of 2012.

Financial Data

(US$ in Thousands)	12/31/2007	12/31/2006	12/31/2005	12/31/2004	12/31/2003	12/31/2002	12/31/2001	12/31/2000
Earnings Per Share	2.10	1.92	1.61	1.53	1.43	1.39	0.96	1.66
Cash Flow Per Share	4.42	4.82	2.29	2.57	3.43	2.82	3.82	3.62
Tang Book Value Per Share	4.76	4.53	6.16	5.00	6.48	5.26	4.64	5.94
Dividends Per Share	1.020	0.950	0.910	0.870	0.840	0.830	0.800	0.790
Dividend Payout %	48.57	49.48	56.52	56.86	58.74	59.71	83.33	47.59
Income Statement								
Total Revenue	4,039,992	3,656,839	3,528,574	3,155,433	2,758,326	2,812,150	2,606,276	2,711,493
EBITDA	489,223	484,981	437,821	403,333	321,778	410,296	382,772	477,221
Income Before Taxes	255,626	274,808	231,126	197,342	108,333	198,493	175,781	270,595
Income Taxes	-55,186	93,329	84,174	-58,858	37,698	70,614	82,958	111,999
Net Income	214,156	195,081	161,877	151,229	138,949	135,316	91,609	166,298
Average Shares	101,875	101,534	100,418	98,947	97,129	97,178	95,807	99,900
Balance Sheet								
Current Assets	1,027,679	942,798	885,500	922,112	755,265	663,267	665,169	695,793
Total Assets	3,340,243	2,916,678	2,981,740	3,041,319	2,520,633	2,390,094	2,352,197	2,212,611
Current Liabilities	758,081	659,824	620,486	639,886	679,594	600,027	460,270	437,080
Long-Term Obligations	804,339	712,089	657,075	813,207	473,220	699,346	885,961	812,085
Total Liabilities	1,898,706	1,697,610	1,718,426	1,888,440	1,506,473	1,522,669	1,548,075	1,411,140
Stockholders' Equity	1,441,537	1,219,068	1,263,314	1,152,879	1,014,160	867,425	804,122	801,471
Shares Outstanding	99,431	100,550	99,988	98,793	97,217	96,640	95,713	95,006
Statistical Record								
Return on Assets %	6.85	6.61	5.38	5.42	5.66	5.71	4.01	7.36
Return on Equity %	16.10	15.72	13.40	13.92	14.77	16.19	11.41	19.48
EBITDA Margin %	12.11	13.26	12.41	12.78	11.67	14.59	14.69	17.60
Net Margin %	5.30	5.33	4.59	4.79	5.04	4.81	3.51	6.13
Asset Turnover	1.29	1.24	1.17	1.13	1.12	1.19	1.14	1.20
Current Ratio	1.36	1.43	1.43	1.44	1.11	1.11	1.45	1.59
Debt to Equity	0.56	0.58	0.52	0.71	0.47	0.81	1.10	1.01
Price Range	44.89-28.51	38.64-29.25	30.48-25.68	29.70-22.86	24.73-19.47	29.70-19.81	26.58-19.69	23.00-16.88
P/E Ratio	21.38-13.58	20.13-15.23	18.93-15.95	19.41-14.94	17.29-13.62	21.37-14.25	27.69-20.51	13.86-10.17
Average Yield %	2.77	2.86	3.27	3.39	3.78	3.25	3.36	3.97

Address: One North Second Street,	Web Site: www.sonoco.com	Auditors: PricewaterhouseCoopers LLP
Hartsville, SC 29550-3305	Officers: Harris E. DeLoach Jr. - Chmn., Pres., C.E.O.	Investor Contact: 843-383-7524
Telephone: 843-383-7000	Charles L. Sullivan Jr. - Exec. V.P.	Transfer Agents: EquiServe Trust
Fax: 843-383-7008		Company, NA Providence, RI

SOUTHERN COMPANY (THE)

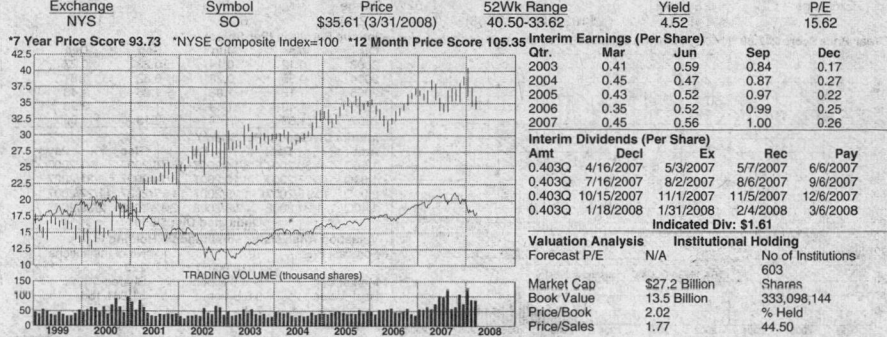

Exchange	Symbol	Price	52Wk Range	Yield	P/E
NYS	SO	$35.61 (3/31/2008)	40.50-33.62	4.52	15.62

*7 Year Price Score 93.73   *NYSE Composite Index=100   *12 Month Price Score 105.35

Interim Earnings (Per Share)

Qtr.	Mar	Jun	Sep	Dec
2003	0.41	0.59	0.84	0.17
2004	0.45	0.47	0.87	0.27
2005	0.43	0.52	0.97	0.22
2006	0.35	0.52	0.99	0.25
2007	0.45	0.56	1.00	0.26

Interim Dividends (Per Share)

Amt	Decl	Ex	Rec	Pay
0.403Q	4/16/2007	5/3/2007	5/7/2007	6/6/2007
0.403Q	7/16/2007	8/2/2007	8/6/2007	9/6/2007
0.403Q	10/15/2007	11/1/2007	11/5/2007	12/6/2007
0.403Q	1/18/2008	1/31/2008	2/4/2008	3/6/2008

Indicated Div: $1.61

Valuation Analysis · **Institutional Holding**

Forecast P/E	N/A	No of Institutions	603
Market Cap	$27.2 Billion	Shares	333,098,144
Book Value	13.5 Billion	% Held	
Price/Book	2.02		44.50
Price/Sales	1.77		

Business Summary: Electricity (MIC: 7.1 SIC: 4911 NAIC: 221119)

Southern owns Alabama Power Co., Georgia Power Co., Gulf Power Co., and Mississippi Power Co., each of which is an operating public utility company. In addition, Co. owns Southern Power, an operating public utility company, which constructs, acquires, owns, and manages generation assets and sells electricity at market-based rates in the wholesale market; SouthernLINC Wireless, which provides digital wireless communications services; Southern Nuclear that operates and provides services to Alabama Power's and Georgia Power's nuclear plants; SCS, a system service company; and Southern Holdings, a holding for its investments in synthetic fuels and leases and other energy-related businesses.

Recent Developments: For the year ended Dec 31 2007, net income increased 10.2% to US$1.73 billion from US$1.57 billion in the prior year. Revenues were US$15.35 billion, up 6.9% from US$14.36 billion the year before. Operating income was US$3.33 billion versus US$3.22 billion in the prior year, an increase of 3.2%. Direct operating expenses rose 9.0% to US$10.04 billion from US$9.21 billion in the comparable period the year before. Indirect operating expenses increased 3.5% to US$1.99 billion from US$1.92 billion in the equivalent prior-year period.

Prospects: Co.'s outlook appears to be encouraging as bottom-line results are being positively affected by the state regulatory actions, as well as warm summer and the resilient economy, partially offset by higher non-fuel operations and higher expenses. Going forward, Co. remains focused on business strategies such as business combinations, acquisitions involving other utility or non-utility businesses or properties, disposition of certain assets, and internal restructuring, to adapt to a less regulated, and more competitive environment. Meanwhile, assuming normal weather, Co. anticipates sales to retail customers to grow approximately 1.9% annually on average during 2008 through 2012.

Financial Data

(US$ in Thousands)	12/31/2007	12/31/2006	12/31/2005	12/31/2004	12/31/2003	12/31/2002	12/31/2001	12/31/2000
Earnings Per Share	2.28	2.10	2.13	2.06	2.02	1.85	1.82	2.01
Cash Flow Per Share	4.49	3.80	3.40	3.63	4.22	4.00	3.46	4.30
Tang Book Value Per Share	16.22	15.23	14.42	13.86	13.13	12.15	11.42	15.67
Dividends Per Share	1.595	1.535	1.475	1.415	1.385	1.355	1.340	1.340
Dividend Payout %	69.96	73.10	69.25	68.69	68.56	73.24	73.63	66.67
Income Statement								
Total Revenue	15,353,000	14,356,000	13,554,000	11,902,000	11,251,000	10,549,000	10,155,000	10,066,000
EBITDA	4,896,000	4,601,000	4,295,000	3,910,000	3,740,000	3,474,000	3,565,000	3,527,000
Income Before Taxes	2,569,000	2,355,000	2,186,000	2,119,000	2,086,000	1,846,000	1,677,000	1,582,000
Income Taxes	835,000	781,000	595,000	587,000	612,000	528,000	358,000	388,000
Net Income	1,734,000	1,573,000	1,591,000	1,532,000	1,474,000	1,318,000	1,262,000	1,313,000
Average Shares	761,000	748,000	749,000	743,000	732,000	714,000	694,000	654,194
Balance Sheet								
Net PPE	33,327,000	31,092,000	29,480,000	28,361,000	27,534,000	24,642,000	23,084,000	21,622,000
Total Assets	45,789,000	42,858,000	39,877,000	36,962,000	35,045,000	31,799,000	29,824,000	31,362,000
Long-Term Obligations	14,143,000	12,503,000	12,846,000	12,449,000	10,164,000	8,658,000	8,297,000	7,843,000
Total Liabilities	32,324,000	30,743,000	28,592,000	26,123,000	24,974,000	22,791,000	21,472,000	20,304,000
Stockholders' Equity	13,465,000	12,115,000	11,285,000	10,839,000	10,071,000	9,008,000	8,352,000	11,058,000
Shares Outstanding	763,600	746,400	741,448	741,800	734,800	716,900	699,000	682,000
Statistical Record								
Return on Assets %	3.91	3.80	4.14	4.24	4.41	4.28	4.13	3.75
Return on Equity %	13.56	13.44	14.38	14.61	15.45	15.18	13.00	12.69
EBITDA Margin %	31.89	32.05	31.69	32.85	33.24	32.93	35.11	35.04
Net Margin %	11.29	10.96	11.74	12.87	13.10	12.49	12.43	13.04
PPE Turnover	0.48	0.47	0.47	0.42	0.43	0.44	0.45	0.43
Asset Turnover	0.35	0.35	0.35	0.33	0.34	0.34	0.33	0.29
Debt to Equity	1.05	1.03	1.14	1.15	1.01	0.96	0.99	0.71
Price Range	39.20-33.62	37.34-30.49	36.16-31.25	33.92-27.86	31.81-27.71	30.85-23.89	25.87-16.63	20.75-12.52
P/E Ratio	17.19-14.75	17.78-14.52	16.98-14.67	16.47-13.52	15.75-13.72	16.68-12.91	14.21-9.14	10.32-6.23
Average Yield %	4.39	4.53	4.34	4.68	4.74	5.01	6.03	8.29

Address: 30 Ivan Allen Jr. Boulevard, N.W., Atlanta, GA 30308
Telephone: 404-506-5000
Fax: 404-506-0455

Web Site: www.southerncompany.com
Officers: H. Allen Franklin - Chmn., C.E.O. David M. Ratcliffe - Pres.

Auditors: Deloitte & Touche LLP
Investor Contact: 404-506-5195
Transfer Agents: SCS Stockholder Services, Atlanta, GA

SOUTHERN COPPER CORP

Exchange	Symbol	Price	52Wk Range	Yield	P/E
NYS	PCU	$103.83 (3/31/2008)	141.35-72.64	6.26	13.79

*7 Year Price Score 247.08 *NYSE Composite Index=100 *12 Month Price Score 110.93

Interim Earnings (Per Share)

Qtr.	Mar	Jun	Sep	Dec
2003	0.12	0.14	0.23	0.27
2004	0.55	0.76	0.82	1.61
2005	1.15	1.06	1.25	1.43
2006	1.43	1.49	1.77	2.23
2007	1.87	2.46	2.13	1.06

Interim Dividends (Per Share)

Amt	Decl	Ex	Rec	Pay
1.50Q	4/30/2007	5/14/2007	5/16/2007	6/1/2007
1.60Q	7/27/2007	8/10/2007	8/14/2007	8/31/2007
2.00Q	10/18/2007	11/5/2007	11/7/2007	11/27/2007
1.40Q	1/24/2008	2/8/2008	2/12/2008	2/29/2008

Indicated Div: $6.50

Valuation Analysis

		Institutional Holding	
Forecast P/E	10.13	No of Institutions	
	(1/10/2007)	229	
Market Cap	$30.6 Billion	Shares	51,231,156
Book Value	3.8 Billion	% Held	
Price/Book	7.96		17.40
Price/Sales	5.03		

Business Summary: Non-Precious Metals (MIC: 14.3 SIC: 1021 NAIC: 212234)

Southern Copper is an integrated producer of copper, molybdenum, zinc and silver. All of Co.'s mining, smelting and refining facilities are located in Peru and in Mexico and it conducts exploration activities in those countries and Chile. Co.'s Peruvian copper operations involve mining, milling and flotation of copper ore to produce copper concentrates and molybdenum concentrates; the smelting of copper concentrates to produce anode and blister copper; and the refining of blister/anode copper to produce copper cathodes. In addition, Co. produces refined copper using solvent extraction/electrowinning technology.

Recent Developments: For the year ended Dec 31 2007, net income increased 8.8% to US$2.22 billion from US$2.04 billion in the prior year. Revenues were US$6.09 billion, up 11.5% from US$5.46 billion the year before. Operating income was US$3.50 billion versus US$3.05 billion in the prior year, an increase of 14.5%. Direct operating expenses rose 5.1% to US$2.12 billion from US$2.02 billion in the comparable period the year before. Indirect operating expenses increased 20.8% to US$466.2 million from US$386.0 million in the equivalent prior-year period.

Prospects: Despite the decrease in earnings due to a strike at its Cananea mine in Mexico, Co.'s near-term outlook appears favorable. Specifically, Co. expects to focus its expansion program on the Tia Maria solvent extraction/electrowinning (SX-EW) project, expansions of the Toquepala and Cuajone Concentrators, and the expansion of the Ilo smelter and copper refinery, all in Peru, which will increase its copper production by 270,000 tons per year by 2011, representing an increase of 39.0% over existing production capacity. Also, Co. expects new facilities that began operations in 2007 at its Toquepala SX-EW plant to reduce long-term haulage cost and to increase copper recovery in 2009.

Financial Data

(US$ in Thousands)	12/31/2007	12/31/2006	12/31/2005	12/31/2004	12/31/2003	12/31/2002	12/31/2001	12/31/2000
Earnings Per Share	7.53	6.92	4.75	3.73	0.75	0.38	0.29	0.58
Cash Flow Per Share	9.18	6.99	5.58	4.47	1.19	0.89	1.24	1.14
Tang Book Value Per Share	12.66	12.03	10.89	10.09	7.54	7.76	7.56	7.45
Dividends Per Share	6.800	5.130	2.900	1.195	0.285	0.180	0.180	0.170
Dividend Payout %	90.31	74.13	60.99	32.04	38.26	47.37	62.07	29.31
Income Statement								
Total Revenue	6,085,672	5,460,221	4,112,629	1,715,919	798,406	664,650	657,521	711,057
EBITDA	3,765,726	3,316,345	2,350,280	998,944	290,280	188,397	170,281	229,334
Income Before Taxes	3,411,860	3,006,029	2,002,367	916,737	206,899	109,947	71,548	139,534
Income Taxes	1,185,261	959,087	589,744	315,237	84,969	39,999	22,142	44,648
Net Income	2,216,370	2,037,640	1,400,148	596,773	119,231	60,555	46,551	92,917
Average Shares	294,466	294,461	294,456	160,032	160,034	160,018	160,008	160,006
Balance Sheet								
Current Assets	2,635,509	2,442,877	1,714,354	1,013,553	475,951	310,872	426,645	441,847
Total Assets	6,580,558	6,376,414	5,687,574	2,597,130	1,930,752	1,752,246	1,821,417	1,770,558
Current Liabilities	927,190	859,571	795,632	461,447	187,197	100,794	220,953	132,380
Long-Term Obligations	1,289,700	1,518,100	1,162,100	256,700	289,000	299,000	273,100	322,900
Total Liabilities	2,715,753	2,695,820	2,348,802	864,947	607,436	503,195	597,941	564,438
Stockholders' Equity	3,848,120	3,666,605	3,326,077	1,720,899	1,315,403	1,241,375	1,209,455	1,191,655
Shares Outstanding	294,865	294,865	294,456	160,035	160,027	160,016	160,007	160,001
Statistical Record								
Return on Assets %	34.21	33.78	33.80	26.29	6.47	3.39	2.59	5.59
Return on Equity %	58.99	58.28	55.48	39.20	9.33	4.94	3.88	8.00
EBITDA Margin %	61.88	60.74	57.15	58.22	36.36	28.35	25.90	32.25
Net Margin %	36.42	37.32	34.05	34.78	14.93	9.11	7.08	13.07
Asset Turnover	0.94	0.91	0.99	0.76	0.43	0.37	0.37	0.43
Current Ratio	2.84	2.84	2.15	2.20	2.54	3.08	1.93	3.34
Debt to Equity	0.34	0.41	0.35	0.15	0.22	0.24	0.23	0.27
Price Range	141.35-50.52	58.12-34.65	35.30-20.82	27.05-13.27	24.43-7.20	7.77-5.41	7.55-4.40	8.22-5.50
P/E Ratio	18.77-6.71	8.40-5.01	7.43-4.38	7.25-3.56	32.57-9.60	20.45-14.24	26.03-15.17	14.17-9.48
Average Yield %	7.24	11.27	11.00	5.82	2.71	2.64	2.90	2.55

Address: 2575 East Camelback Rd., Phoenix, AZ 85016
Telephone: 602-977-6595

Web Site: www.southernperu.com
Officers: German Larrea Mota-Velasco - Chmn.
Oscar Gonzalez Rocha - Pres., C.E.O.

Auditors: PricewaterhouseCoopers
Investor Contact: 800-223-2064
Transfer Agents: The Bank of New York, New York, NY

SOUTHWEST AIRLINES CO

Exchange	Symbol	Price	52Wk Range	Yield	P/E
NYS	LUV	$12.40 (3/31/2008)	16.60-11.27	0.15	14.76

*7 Year Price Score 71.65   *NYSE Composite Index=100   *12 Month Price Score 94.43

Interim Earnings (Per Share)

Qtr.	Mar	Jun	Sep	Dec
2003	0.03	0.30	0.13	0.08
2004	0.03	0.14	0.15	0.06
2005	0.09	0.20	0.28	0.10
2006	0.07	0.40	0.06	0.08
2007	0.12	0.36	0.22	0.15

Interim Dividends (Per Share)

Amt	Decl	Ex	Rec	Pay
0.004Q	5/16/2007	6/5/2007	6/7/2007	6/28/2007
0.004Q	7/19/2007	8/28/2007	8/30/2007	9/20/2007
0.004Q	11/15/2007	12/4/2007	12/6/2007	1/3/2008
0.004Q	1/17/2008	2/26/2008	2/28/2008	3/20/2008

Indicated Div: $0.02

Valuation Analysis / **Institutional Holding**

Forecast P/E	15.78 (1/10/2007)	No of Institutions 423
Market Cap	$9.1 Billion	Shares
Book Value	6.9 Billion	589,788,992
Price/Book	1.31	% Held
Price/Sales	0.92	74.81

Business Summary: Aviation (MIC: 1.1 SIC: 4512 NAIC: 481111)

Southwest Airlines is a domestic airline that provides point-to-point, low-fare service. Co. serves 411 nonstop city pairs. In addition, Co. leases terminal passenger service facilities at each of the airports it serves, by which it leases land on a long-term basis for its maintenance centers at Dallas Love Field, Houston Hobby, Phoenix Sky Harbor, and Chicago Midway, its training center near Love Field, which houses seven 737 simulators, and its corporate headquarters, also located near Love Field. As of Dec 31 2007, Co. operated 520 Boeing 737 aircraft and provided service to 64 cities in 32 states throughout the U.S.

Recent Developments: For the year ended Dec 31 2007, net income increased 29.3% to US$645.0 million from US$499.0 million in the prior year. Revenues were US$9.86 billion, up 8.5% from US$9.09 billion the year before. Operating income was US$791.0 million versus US$934.0 million in the prior year, a decrease of 15.3%. Direct operating expenses rose 18.7% to US$3.87 billion from US$3.26 billion in the comparable period the year before. Indirect operating expenses increased 6.3% to US$5.20 billion from US$4.89 billion in the equivalent prior-year period.

Prospects: For 2008, Co. intends to overcome the affect of higher anticipated fuel prices and other cost pressures through continued focus on non-fuel costs and improved revenues. Specifically, Co. expects to grow its available seat mile capacity 4.0% to 5.0% by adding 29 new 737-700 aircraft from Boeing and reducing its fleet by 22 aircraft, bringing its fleet total to 527 crafts by the end of 2008. Also, for the first quarter of 2008, Co. expects an increase in total freight revenues due to an increase in capacity and higher rates charged. Concurrently, Co. expects its other revenues to increase as a result of higher commissions earned, and at a somewhat comparable rate to the 2007 increase.

Financial Data
(US$ in Thousands)

	12/31/2007	12/31/2006	12/31/2005	12/31/2004	12/31/2003	12/31/2002	12/31/2001	12/31/2000
Earnings Per Share	0.84	0.61	0.67	0.38	0.54	0.30	0.63	0.76
Cash Flow Per Share	3.76	1.77	2.83	1.47	1.71	0.67	1.95	1.73
Tang Book Value Per Share	9.43	8.23	8.33	7.04	6.40	5.69	5.23	4.56
Dividends Per Share	0.018	0.018	0.018	0.018	0.018	0.018	0.018	0.015
Dividend Payout %	2.14	2.95	2.69	4.74	3.33	6.00	2.86	1.93
Income Statement								
Total Revenue	9,861,000	9,086,000	7,584,000	6,530,000	5,937,000	5,521,771	5,555,174	5,649,560
EBITDA	1,624,000	1,282,000	1,412,000	984,000	1,159,000	832,455	1,180,120	1,322,056
Income Before Taxes	1,058,000	790,000	874,000	489,000	708,000	392,682	827,659	1,017,364
Income Taxes	413,000	291,000	326,000	176,000	266,000	151,713	316,512	397,140
Net Income	645,000	499,000	548,000	313,000	442,000	240,969	511,147	603,093
Average Shares	768,000	824,000	814,000	815,000	822,000	809,420	807,115	796,317
Balance Sheet								
Total Assets	16,772,000	13,460,000	14,218,000	11,337,000	9,878,000	8,953,750	8,997,141	6,669,572
Long-Term Obligations	2,050,000	1,567,000	1,394,000	1,700,000	1,332,000	1,552,781	1,327,158	760,992
Total Liabilities	9,831,000	7,011,000	7,543,000	5,813,000	4,826,000	4,532,133	4,983,088	3,218,252
Stockholders' Equity	6,941,000	6,449,000	6,675,000	5,524,000	5,052,000	4,421,617	4,014,053	3,451,320
Shares Outstanding	734,797	783,309	801,641	784,982	789,390	776,663	766,774	756,243
Statistical Record								
Return on Assets %	4.27	3.61	4.29	2.94	4.69	2.68	6.53	9.76
Return on Equity %	9.63	7.60	8.98	5.90	9.33	5.71	13.69	19.13
EBITDA Margin %	16.47	14.11	18.62	15.07	19.52	15.08	21.24	23.40
Net Margin %	6.54	5.49	7.23	4.79	7.44	4.36	9.20	10.68
Asset Turnover	0.65	0.66	0.59	0.61	0.63	0.62	0.71	0.91
Price Range	16.60-12.20	18.15-14.62	16.82-13.14	17.00-13.21	19.54-12.04	21.99-11.60	23.27-12.83	22.67-10.08
P/E Ratio	19.76-14.52	29.75-23.97	25.10-19.61	44.74-34.76	36.19-22.30	73.30-38.67	36.93-20.37	29.83-13.27
Average Yield %	0.12	0.11	0.12	0.12	0.11	0.11	0.10	0.10

Address: P.O. Box 36611, Dallas, TX 75235-1611 Telephone: 214-792-4000 Fax: 214-792-5015	Web Site: www.southwest.com Officers: Herbert D. Kelleher - Chmn, Gary C. Kelly - Vice-Chmn., C.E.O.	Auditors: Ernst & Young LLP Transfer Agents: Continental Stock Transfer & Trust Co., New York, NY

SOUTHWESTERN ENERGY COMPANY

Exchange	Symbol	Price	52Wk Range	Yield	P/E
NYS	SWN	$33.69 (3/31/2008)	34.06-18.00	0.09	52.64

*7 Year Price Score 204.69 *NYSE Composite Index=100 *12 Month Price Score 136.55

TRADING VOLUME (thousand shares)

Interim Earnings (Per Share)

Qtr.	Mar	Jun	Sep	Dec
2003	0.06	0.03	0.04	0.05
2004	0.08	0.07	0.09	0.11
2005	0.11	0.09	0.13	0.15
2006	0.17	0.11	0.10	0.00
2007	0.15	0.14	0.15	0.20

Interim Dividends (Per Share)

Amt	Decl	Ex	Rec	Pay
2-for-1	5/11/2005	6/6/2005	5/20/2005	6/3/2005
2-for-1	10/25/2005	11/18/2005	11/3/2005	11/17/2005
2-for-1	2/28/2008	3/26/2008	3/14/2008	3/25/2008
		Indicated Div: $0.03		

Valuation Analysis   Institutional Holding

Forecast P/E	18.97	No of Institutions	
	(1/10/2007)	301	
Market Cap	$11.5 Billion	Shares	
Book Value	1.6 Billion	152,767,872	
Price/Book	6.98	% Held	
Price/Sales	9.16	90.34	

Business Summary: Oil and Gas (MIC: 14.2 SIC: 1311 NAIC: 211111)

Southwestern Energy is an independent energy company primarily engaged in exploring for and production of natural gas. Co. operates in three key segments: Exploration and Production, which is engaged in natural gas and oil exploration, development and production within the U.S., with operations mainly in Arkansas, Oklahoma and Texas; Natural Gas Distribution, which operates integrated natural gas distribution systems in northern Arkansas; and Midstream Services, which transports natural gas to market and markets its own gas production and some third-party natural gas. At Dec 31 2007, Co. had estimated proved natural gas and oil reserves of 1,450 billion cubic feet of gas equivalent.

Recent Developments: For the year ended Dec 31 2007, net income increased 36.0% to US$221.2 million from US$162.6 million in the prior year. Revenues were US$1.26 billion, up 64.5% from US$763.1 million the year before. Operating income was US$381.5 million versus US$246.3 million in the prior year, an increase of 54.9%. Direct operating expenses rose 74.1% to US$477.6 million from US$274.3 million in the comparable period the year before. Indirect operating expenses increased 63.3% to US$396.1 million from US$242.5 million in the equivalent prior-year period.

Prospects: On Dec 19 2007, Co. announced a planned capital investment program for 2008 of $1.46 billion, including $1.33 billion for its Exploration and Production segment, $101.0 million for its Midstream Services segment, and $25.0 million for its Natural Gas Distribution segment and other corporate purposes. Also, for 2008, Co. expects gas and oil production of 148.00 billion of cubic feet equivalent (Bcfe) to 152.00 Bcfe, and net income of $245.0 million to $250.0 million, assuming NYMEX commodity prices of $7.00 per thousand cubic feet of gas and $70.00 per barrel of oil. Meanwhile, Co. expects to close the sale of its utility subsidiary for $224.0 million plus working capital by mid-2008.

Financial Data

(US$ in Thousands)	12/31/2007	12/31/2006	12/31/2005	12/31/2004	12/31/2003	12/31/2002	12/31/2001	12/31/2000
Earnings Per Share	0.64	0.47	0.47	0.35	0.18	0.07	0.17	(0.23)
Cash Flow Per Share	...	...	1.01	0.83	0.41	0.38	0.72	(0.26)
Tang Book Value Per Share	4.82	4.25	3.32	1.54	1.19	0.86	0.90	0.70
Dividends Per Share	...	...	...	...	...	...	...	0.015
Income Statement								
Total Revenue	1,255,131	763,112	676,329	477,137	327,401	261,502	344,927	363,883
EBITDA	676,234	415,233	348,789	257,696	154,747	100,884	135,445	(4,245)
Income Before Taxes	357,029	262,035	234,191	163,354	78,648	23,019	57,241	(74,702)
Income Taxes	135,855	99,399	86,431	59,778	28,896	8,708	21,917	(28,905)
Net Income	221,174	162,636	147,760	103,576	48,897	14,311	35,324	(46,687)
Average Shares	347,442	342,575	312,618	295,702	273,903	208,417	204,808	200,348
Balance Sheet								
Net PPE	3,077,630	2,016,500	1,370,397	984,156	762,284	632,161	619,830	564,107
Total Assets	3,622,716	2,379,069	1,868,524	1,146,144	890,710	740,162	743,123	705,378
Long-Term Obligations	977,600	136,600	100,000	325,000	278,800	342,400	350,000	225,000
Total Liabilities	1,976,216	944,426	758,220	698,467	549,149	562,674	560,037	564,087
Stockholders' Equity	1,646,500	1,434,643	1,110,304	447,677	341,561	177,488	183,086	141,291
Shares Outstanding	341,358	337,907	334,470	291,232	287,340	207,557	203,810	201,449
Statistical Record								
Return on Assets %	...	...	9.80	10.14	6.00	1.93	4.88	N.M.
Return on Equity %	...	...	18.97	26.18	18.84	7.94	21.78	N.M.
EBITDA Margin %	53.88	54.41	51.57	54.01	47.27	38.58	39.27	N.M.
Net Margin %	17.62	21.31	21.85	21.71	14.93	5.47	10.24	(12.83)
PPE Turnover	...	...	0.57	0.54	0.47	0.42	0.58	0.64
Asset Turnover	...	...	0.45	0.47	0.40	0.35	0.48	0.53
Debt to Equity	0.59	0.10	0.09	0.73	0.82	1.93	1.91	1.59
Price Range	28.27-16.43	21.71-12.40	20.57-5.61	6.86-2.42	3.10-1.40	1.90-1.24	1.99-1.10	1.30-0.68
P/E Ratio	44.16-25.68	46.19-26.38	43.78-11.93	19.61-6.91	17.21-7.76	27.12-17.68	11.73-6.44	...
Average Yield %	...	...	...	...	...	...	...	1.57

Address: 2350 N. Sam Houston Parkway East, Suite 300, Houston, TX 77032	Web Site: www.swn.com	Auditors: PricewaterhouseCoopers LLP
Telephone: 281-618-4700	Officers: Harold M. Korell - Chmn., Pres., C.E.O. Gregory D. Kerley - Exec. V.P., C.F.O.	Investor Contact: 501-521-1141
Fax: 281-618-4757		Transfer Agents: EquiServe

SOVEREIGN BANCORP INC

Exchange	Symbol	Price	52Wk Range	Yield	P/E
NYS	SOV	$9.32 (3/31/2008)	25.16-9.28	N/A	N/A

*7 Year Price Score 75.23   *NYSE Composite Index=100   *12 Month Price Score 71.75

Interim Earnings (Per Share)

Qtr.	Mar	Jun	Sep	Dec
2003	0.26	0.35	0.35	0.35
2004	0.31	0.40	0.23	0.35
2005	0.36	0.45	0.46	0.42
2006	0.36	(0.15)	0.37	(0.32)
2007	0.09	0.29	0.11	(3.36)

Interim Dividends (Per Share)

Amt	Decl	Ex	Rec	Pay
0.08Q	1/23/2007	1/31/2007	2/2/2007	2/15/2007
0.08Q	4/17/2007	4/27/2007	5/1/2007	5/15/2007
0.08Q	7/17/2007	7/30/2007	8/1/2007	8/15/2007
0.08Q	10/18/2007	10/30/2007	11/1/2007	11/15/2007

Valuation Analysis

		Institutional Holding	
Forecast P/E	15.27	No of Institutions	
	(1/10/2007)	347	
Market Cap	$4.5 Billion	Shares	
Book Value	7.0 Billion	224,522,832	
Price/Book	0.64	% Held	
Price/Sales	0.90	47.25	

Business Summary: Other Depository Banking (MIC: 8.5 SIC: 6035 NAIC: 522120)

Sovereign Bancorp is the parent company of Sovereign Bank, a federally chartered savings bank. Co. had approximately 750 community banking offices and over 2,300 automatic teller machines as of Dec 31 2007 with principal markets in the Northeastern US. Co.'s primary business consists of attracting deposits from its network of community banking offices, and originating small business and middle market commercial loans, multifamily loans, residential mortgage loans, home equity loans and lines of credit, and auto and other consumer loans in the communities served by those offices. As of Dec 31 2007, Co. had total assets of $84.75 billion.

Recent Developments: For the year ended Dec 31 2007, net loss amounted to US$1.35 billion versus net income of US$136.9 million in the prior year. Net interest income increased 2.3% to US$1.86 billion from US$1.82 billion in the prior year. Provision for loan losses was US$407.7 million versus US$484.5 million in the prior year, a decrease of 15.8%. Non-interest income rose 24.1% to US$354.4 million from US$285.6 million, while non-interest expense advanced 108.0% to US$3.12 billion.

Prospects: Co. continues to focus on its core businesses and markets and execute on its strategic initiatives. In view of this, Co. has ceased originating new loans in the Southeast and Southwest production offices while strengthening its underwriting standards on its auto loan portfolio. Accordingly, Co. expects to see lower loss rates going forward; however losses should remain at elevated levels in the first half of 2008 as the newly originated loans continue to season. For 2008, Co. expects the opening or relocation of up to 20 branch offices and expects its net interest margin to be influenced by the interest rate yield environment and its ability to originate loans and grow low cost deposits.

Financial Data
(US$ in Thousands)

	12/31/2007	12/31/2006	12/31/2005	12/31/2004	12/31/2003	12/31/2002	12/31/2001	12/31/2000
Earnings Per Share	(2.85)	0.30	1.69	1.30	1.31	1.17	0.43	(0.12)
Cash Flow Per Share	1.32	2.28	2.82	1.74	4.75	0.12	(1.08)	(0.79)
Tang Book Value Per Share	6.23	6.18	7.60	7.11	6.31	5.02	3.24	2.03
Dividends Per Share	0.320	0.293	0.162	0.110	0.005	0.005	0.005	0.005
Dividend Payout %	...	97.78	9.60	8.46	7.25	8.13	22.22	...
Income Statement								
Interest Income	4,656,236	4,326,404	2,918,779	2,224,144	1,929,751	2,059,540	2,222,475	2,269,735
Interest Expense	2,792,234	2,504,856	1,330,498	819,327	724,123	899,924	1,168,193	1,414,924
Net Interest Income	1,864,022	1,821,548	1,588,281	1,404,817	1,205,628	1,159,616	1,054,282	854,811
Provision for Losses	407,692	484,461	90,000	127,000	161,957	146,500	97,100	56,500
Non-Interest Income	354,396	285,574	646,472	482,298	522,223	432,526	426,066	108,561
Non-Interest Expense	3,118,836	1,499,138	1,198,977	1,083,661	981,157	979,087	990,232	893,224
Income Before Taxes	(1,409,712)	19,131	892,120	581,222	554,899	466,555	149,945	(106,232)
Income Taxes	(60,450)	(117,780)	215,960	127,670	153,048	124,570	26,575	(65,215)
Net Income	(1,349,262)	136,911	676,160	453,552	401,851	341,985	116,821	(30,747)
Average Shares	478,726	433,908	415,996	367,810	305,000	292,990	269,739	237,175
Balance Sheet								
Net Loans & Leases	57,070,335	62,117,566	43,384,248	36,222,363	25,820,765	22,828,575	20,134,917	21,655,889
Total Assets	84,746,396	89,641,849	63,678,726	54,471,313	43,505,329	39,524,193	35,474,838	33,457,797
Total Deposits	49,915,905	52,384,554	37,977,706	32,555,518	27,344,008	26,784,980	23,297,574	24,498,917
Total Liabilities	77,607,641	80,841,065	57,662,367	49,279,035	40,042,787	36,162,918	32,664,557	31,050,698
Stockholders' Equity	6,992,325	8,644,399	5,810,699	4,988,372	3,260,406	2,764,318	2,202,481	1,948,884
Shares Outstanding	481,404	476,515	379,024	366,514	311,494	278,214	264,891	242,620
Statistical Record								
Return on Assets %	N.M.	0.18	1.14	0.92	0.97	0.91	0.34	N.M.
Return on Equity %	N.M.	1.89	12.52	10.97	13.34	13.77	5.63	N.M.
Net Interest Margin %	40.03	42.10	54.42	63.16	62.48	56.30	47.44	37.66
Efficiency Ratio %	62.24	32.51	33.63	40.04	40.01	39.29	37.39	37.56
Loans to Deposits	1.14	1.19	1.14	1.11	0.94	0.85	0.86	0.88
Price Range	26.42-10.08	25.90-19.57	23.54-19.17	23.34-18.58	23.80-12.11	14.83-10.77	12.59-7.29	9.40-6.13
P/E Ratio	...	86.33-65.24	13.93-11.34	17.96-14.29	18.17-9.25	12.67-9.21	29.28-16.96	...
Average Yield %	1.58	1.36	0.75	0.53	0.58	0.72	0.97	1.31

Address: 1500 Market Street, Philadelphia, PA 19103 **Telephone:** 215-557-4630 **Fax:** 610-320-8448	**Web Site:** www.sovereignbank.com **Officers:** Jay S. Sidhu - Chmn., Pres., C.E.O. Lawrence M. Thompson Jr. - Vice-Chmn., Chief Admin. Officer	**Auditors:** Ernst & Young LLP **Investor Contact:** 610-208-6426 **Transfer Agents:** Mellon Investor Services L.L.C., Ridgefield Park, NJ

SOVRAN SELF STORAGE, INC.

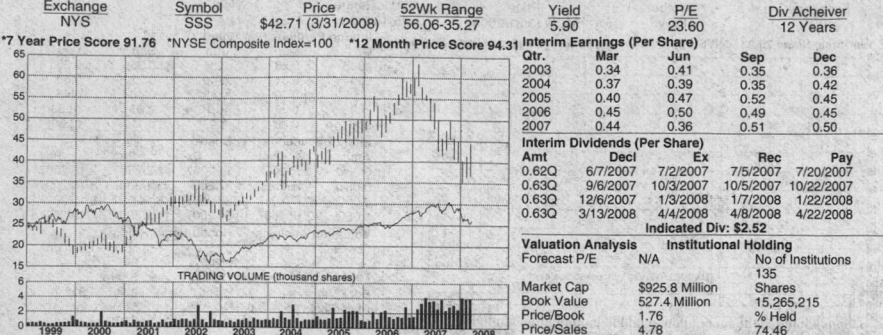

Exchange	Symbol	Price	52Wk Range	Yield	P/E	Div Acheiver
NYS	SSS	$42.71 (3/31/2008)	56.06-35.27	5.90	23.60	12 Years

*7 Year Price Score 91.76 *NYSE Composite Index=100 *12 Month Price Score 94.31

Interim Earnings (Per Share)

Qtr.	Mar	Jun	Sep	Dec
2003	0.34	0.41	0.35	0.36
2004	0.37	0.39	0.35	0.42
2005	0.40	0.47	0.52	0.45
2006	0.45	0.50	0.49	0.45
2007	0.44	0.36	0.51	0.50

Interim Dividends (Per Share)

Amt	Decl	Ex	Rec	Pay
0.62Q	6/7/2007	7/2/2007	7/5/2007	7/20/2007
0.63Q	9/6/2007	10/3/2007	10/5/2007	10/22/2007
0.63Q	12/6/2007	1/3/2008	1/7/2008	1/22/2008
0.63Q	3/13/2008	4/4/2008	4/8/2008	4/22/2008

Indicated Div: $2.52

Valuation Analysis

		Institutional Holding	
Forecast P/E	N/A	No of Institutions	135
Market Cap	$925.8 Million	Shares	15,265,215
Book Value	527.4 Million	% Held	74.46
Price/Book	1.76		
Price/Sales	4.78		

TRADING VOLUME (thousand shares)

Business Summary: Property, Real Estate & Development (MIC: 8.3 SIC: 6798 NAIC: 525930)

Sovran Self Storage is a self-administered and self-managed real estate investment trust that acquires, owns and manages self-storage properties throughout the U.S. As of Dec 31 2007, Co. owned and/or managed 358 properties situated in 22 states. Co.'s properties conduct business under the trade name Uncle Bob's Self-Storage®. All of Co.'s assets are owned by, and all its operations are conducted through, Sovran Acquisition Limited Partnership (the Operating Partnership). Co. is a limited partner of the Operating Partnership, and thereby controls the operations of the Operating Partnership, holding a 98.1% ownership interest at Dec 31 2007.

Recent Developments: For the year ended Dec 31 2007, net income increased 7.1% to US$39.2 million from US$36.6 million in the prior year. Revenues were US$193.8 million, up 16.5% from US$166.3 million the year before. Revenues from property income rose 16.5% to US$187.5 million from US$160.9 million in the corresponding earlier year.

Prospects: Co. is continuing with its program of expanding and enhancing its properties. Accordingly, Co. expects to spend about $50.0 million in 2008 to add up to 700,000 square feet of climate and/or humidity controlled space, and acquire several parcels of land contiguous to its existing stores. Further, Co. plans to acquire self-storage facilities, and is forecasting accretive acquisitions of $50.0 million in 2008. Meanwhile, for 2008, Co. expects conditions in most of its markets to remain relatively stable, and estimates growth in net operating income on a same store basis to be approximately 3.0% to 3.5%. Also, Co. expects funds from operations of $3.50 to $3.56 per share for 2008.

Financial Data
(US$ in Thousands)

	12/31/2007	12/31/2006	12/31/2005	12/31/2004	12/31/2003	12/31/2002	12/31/2001	12/31/2000
Earnings Per Share	1.81	1.89	1.84	1.53	1.46	1.64	1.74	1.89
Cash Flow Per Share	4.06	3.59	3.65	3.54	3.90	3.57	3.35	3.26
Tang Book Value Per Share	24.33	24.67	20.92	20.30	19.11	19.03	20.12	20.68
Dividends Per Share	2.490	2.465	2.430	2.413	2.402	2.370	2.330	2.290
Dividend Payout %	137.57	130.42	132.07	157.68	164.55	144.51	133.91	121.16
Income Statement								
Net Income	39,214	36,610	34,790	32,004	28,423	26,301	24,189	25,707
Average Shares	21,004	18,021	16,633	15,295	13,473	12,945	12,316	12,068
Balance Sheet								
Total Assets	1,164,636	1,053,210	784,376	719,573	683,457	652,337	567,838	547,139
Total Liabilities	610,805	495,352	365,037	315,108	285,876	278,755	255,999	246,309
Stockholders' Equity	527,389	530,911	394,085	377,451	368,197	342,774	277,164	277,398
Shares Outstanding	21,676	20,443	17,563	15,972	14,259	12,984	12,354	12,028
Statistical Record								
Return on Assets %	3.54	3.98	4.63	4.55	4.26	4.31	4.34	4.76
Return on Equity %	7.41	7.92	9.02	8.56	8.00	8.49	8.72	9.07
Price Range	63.32-40.10	59.94-45.78	50.24-38.31	43.53-33.25	37.40-25.62	34.17-27.22	31.44-20.00	22.94-18.00
P/E Ratio	34.98-22.15	31.71-24.22	27.30-20.82	28.45-21.73	25.62-17.55	20.84-16.60	18.07-11.49	12.14-9.52
Average Yield %	4.95	4.70	5.44	6.24	7.79	7.82	9.11	11.55

Address: 6467 Main Street, Buffalo, NY 14221 **Telephone:** 716-633-1850 **Fax:** 716-633-1860	**Web Site:** www.sovranss.com **Officers:** Robert J. Attea - Chmn., C.E.O. Kenneth F. Myszka - Pres., C.O.O.	**Auditors:** Ernst & Young LLP **Investor Contact:** 716-633-1850 **Transfer Agents:** American Stock Transfer & Trust Co., New York, NY

SPECTRA ENERGY CORP

Exchange	Symbol	Price	52Wk Range	Yield	P/E
NYS	SE	$22.75 (3/31/2008)	27.42-21.92	4.04	15.07

*7 Year Price Score N/A   *NYSE Composite Index=100   *12 Month Price Score 101.14

Interim Earnings (Per Share)

Qtr.	Mar	Jun	Sep	Dec
2007	0.37	0.31	0.37	0.46

Interim Dividends (Per Share)

Amt	Decl	Ex	Rec	Pay
0.22Q	7/2/2007	8/15/2007	8/17/2007	9/17/2007
0.22Q	11/1/2007	11/14/2007	11/16/2007	12/17/2007
0.23Q	1/4/2008	2/13/2008	2/15/2008	3/17/2008
0.23Q	4/4/2008	5/14/2008	5/16/2008	6/16/2008

Indicated Div: $0.92

Valuation Analysis		Institutional Holding	
Forecast P/E	N/A	No of Institutions	
		48	
Market Cap	$14.4 Billion	Shares	
Book Value	6.9 Billion	38,023,970	
Price/Book	2.10	% Held	
Price/Sales	3.03	6.12	

Business Summary: Gas Utilities (MIC: 7.4 SIC: 4923 NAIC: 486210)

Spectra Energy operates in three areas of the natural gas industry: transmission and storage, distribution and gathering and processing. Co. provides transportation and storage of natural gas to customers in various regions of the Eastern and Southeastern U.S., the Maritimes Provinces and the Pacific Northwest in the U.S. and Canada and in the province of Ontario in Canada. Additionally, Co. provides natural gas sales and distribution service to retail customers in Ontario, and natural gas gathering and processing services to customers in Western Canada. As of Dec 31 2006, Co. pipeline systems consisted of approximately 17,500 miles of transmission pipelines.

Recent Developments: For the year ended Dec 31 2007, income from continuing operations increased 0.9% to US$944.0 million from US$936.0 million a year earlier. Net income decreased 23.1% to US$957.0 million from US$1.24 billion in the prior year. Revenues were US$4.74 billion, up 4.6% from US$4.53 billion the year before. Operating income was US$1.44 billion versus US$1.25 billion in the prior year, an increase of 15.8%. Direct operating expenses declined 2.3% to US$2.58 billion from US$2.64 billion in the comparable period the year before. Indirect operating expenses increased 11.2% to US$723.0 million from US$650.0 million in the equivalent prior-year period.

Prospects: For 2008, Co. plans to bring into service $1.50 billion in new pipeline, gas processing, storage and distribution projects. In addition, such plan will also involve planned investments of over $1.00 billion in projects per year through 2010. Meanwhile, Co. expects its 2007 expansion projects that include Northeast Gateway, Time II - Phase I, Dawn-Trafalgar - Phase II, Pine River, Cape Cod and Egan, to fuel revenue and earnings growth in 2008. Also, Co. has placed into demand 13 projects that include the expanded capacity of Spectra Energy's North American natural gas transmission system by 1.60 billion cubic feet per day in time to meet the demands of the 2008 winter heating season.

Financial Data

(US$ in Thousands)	12/31/2007	12/31/2006	12/31/2005
Earnings Per Share	1.51	...	...
Tang Book Value Per Share	4.60	...	...
Dividends Per Share	0.880	...	...
Dividend Payout %	58.28	...	...
Income Statement			
Total Revenue	4,742,000	4,532,000	9,454,000
EBITDA	2,528,000	2,510,000	3,743,000
Income Before Taxes	1,387,000	1,331,000	2,335,000
Income Taxes	443,000	395,000	926,000
Net Income	957,000	1,244,000	674,000
Average Shares	635,000	...	...
Balance Sheet			
Current Assets	1,379,000	1,625,000	...
Total Assets	22,970,000	20,345,000	...
Current Liabilities	2,422,000	2,358,000	...
Long-Term Obligations	8,345,000	7,726,000	...
Total Liabilities	15,307,000	14,141,000	...
Stockholders' Equity	6,857,000	5,639,000	...
Shares Outstanding	632,000	1,000.00	...
Statistical Record			
EBITDA Margin %	53.31	55.38	39.59
Net Margin %	20.18	27.45	7.13
Current Ratio	0.57	0.69	...
Debt to Equity	1.22	1.37	...
Price Range	29.05-21.92	28.67-27.75	...
P/E Ratio	19.24-14.52	...	...
Average Yield %	3.45	...	...

Address: 5400 Westheimer Court, Houston, TX 77056	Web Site: www.spectraenergy.com	Auditors: DELOITTE & TOUCHE LLP
Telephone: 713-627-5400	Officers: Paul M. Anderson - Chmn. Fred J. Fowler Pres., C.E.O.	

SPRINT NEXTEL CORP

Exchange	Symbol	Price	52Wk Range	Yield	P/E
NYS	S	$6.69 (3/31/2008)	23.34-5.63	N/A	N/A

*7 Year Price Score 76.49 *NYSE Composite Index=100 *12 Month Price Score 49.96

Interim Earnings (Per Share)

Qtr.	Mar	Jun	Sep	Dec
2003	0.00	0.00	0.00	0.00
2004	0.15	0.16	(1.32)	0.31
2005	0.31	0.40	0.23	(0.04)
2006	0.14	0.12	0.08	0.10
2007	(0.07)	0.01	0.02	(10.27)

Interim Dividends (Per Share)

Amt	Decl	Ex	Rec	Pay
0.025Q	2/27/2007	3/7/2007	3/9/2007	3/30/2007
0.025Q	5/8/2007	6/6/2007	6/8/2007	6/29/2007
0.025Q	8/7/2007	9/5/2007	9/7/2007	9/28/2007
0.025Q	11/5/2007	12/5/2007	12/7/2007	12/28/2007

Valuation Analysis | **Institutional Holding**

Forecast P/E	N/A	No of Institutions	702
Market Cap	$19.0 Billion	Shares	2,525,404,416
Book Value	22.0 Billion	% Held	87.01
Price/Book	0.87		
Price/Sales	0.47		

TRADING VOLUME (thousand shares)

Business Summary: Communications (MIC: 10.1 SIC: 4813 NAIC: 517110)

Sprint Nextel is a global communications company providing a range of wireless and wireline communications products and services. As of Dec 31 2007, Co. had two reportable segments: Wireless and Wireline. Co., together with its PCS Affiliates, provides digital wireless services in all 50 states, Puerto Rico and the U.S. Virgin Islands under the Sprint® brand name utilizing wireless code division multiple access (CDMA) technology. In addition, Co. provides digital wireless services under the Nextel® and Boost Mobile® brand names using Digital Enhanced Network (iDEN®) technology. Co. is also a provider of long distance services and a carrier of Internet traffic in the nation.

Recent Developments: For the year ended Dec 31 2007, loss from continuing operations was US$29.58 billion compared with income of US$995.0 million a year earlier. Net loss amounted to US$29.58 billion versus net income of US$1.33 billion in the prior year. Revenues were US$40.15 billion, down 2.1% from US$41.00 billion the year before. Operating loss was US$28.91 billion versus an income of US$2.48 billion in the prior year. Direct operating expenses rose 2.6% to US$17.19 billion from US$16.76 billion in the comparable period the year before. Indirect operating expenses increased 138.4% to US$51.87 billion from US$21.76 billion in the equivalent prior-year period.

Prospects: For the first quarter of 2008, Co. expects a sequential increase in post-paid churn and a decline in Wireless post-paid subscribers of approximately 1.2 million customers, which is unlikely to improve in the second quarter of 2008. Co. also expects continued downward pressure on postpaid average revenue per user. Separately, Co. recently announced initial plans to streamline the business through job reductions, reduced utilization of outsourced services and contractors, reduction in third-party distribution points and the closure of certain company-owned retail locations. Co. expects these actions to reduce its labor costs by $700.0 million to $800.0 million annually by the end of 2008.

Financial Data
(US$ in Thousands)

	12/31/2007	12/31/2006	12/31/2005	12/31/2004	12/31/2003	12/31/2002	12/31/2001	12/31/2000
Earnings Per Share	(10.31)	0.45	0.87	(0.71)	...	...	...	...
Cash Flow Per Share	3.22	3.71	5.25	4.58	3.39	3.25	2.50	2.33
Tang Book Value Per Share	N.M.	N.M.	0.88	3.85	2.79	1.68	1.86	2.63
Dividends Per Share	0.100	0.100	0.300	0.500	0.500	0.500	0.500	0.500
Dividend Payout %	...	22.22	34.48	...	...	...	...	...
Income Statement								
Total Revenue	40,146,000	41,028,000	34,680,000	27,428,000	26,197,000	26,634,000	26,071,000	23,613,000
EBITDA	(19,640,000)	12,307,000	10,288,000	4,365,000	5,756,000	6,747,000	3,754,000	4,432,000
Income Before Taxes	(29,945,000)	1,483,000	2,906,000	(1,603,000)	(623,000)	429,000	(2,026,000)	(702,000)
Income Taxes	(365,000)	488,000	1,105,000	(591,000)	(256,000)	(39,000)	(624,000)	(126,000)
Net Income	(29,580,000)	1,329,000	1,785,000	(1,012,000)	1,215,000	630,000	(1,401,000)	93,000
Average Shares	2,868,000	2,972,000	2,054,000	1,443,400	1,931,900	1,909,100	1,876,500	1,858,900
Balance Sheet								
Net PPE	26,496,000	25,868,000	31,133,000	22,628,000	27,276,000	28,745,000	28,977,000	25,316,000
Total Assets	64,109,000	97,161,000	102,580,000	41,321,000	42,850,000	45,293,000	45,793,000	42,601,000
Long-Term Obligations	20,469,000	21,011,000	20,632,000	15,916,000	16,841,000	18,405,000	16,501,000	17,514,000
Total Liabilities	42,110,000	44,030,000	50,396,000	27,553,000	29,379,000	32,444,000	32,921,000	28,638,000
Stockholders' Equity	21,999,000	53,131,000	51,937,000	13,521,000	13,224,000	12,294,000	12,616,000	13,963,000
Shares Outstanding	2,845,000	2,897,000	2,961,000	1,474,800	1,939,700	1,938,000	1,914,200	1,817,300
Statistical Record								
Return on Assets %	N.M.	1.33	2.48	N.M.	2.76	1.38	N.M.	0.23
Return on Equity %	N.M.	2.53	5.45	N.M.	9.52	5.06	N.M.	0.67
EBITDA Margin %	N.M.	30.00	29.67	15.91	21.97	25.33	14.40	18.77
Net Margin %	(73.68)	3.24	5.15	(3.69)	4.64	2.37	(5.37)	0.39
PPE Turnover	1.53	1.44	1.29	1.10	0.94	0.92	0.96	1.00
Asset Turnover	0.50	0.41	0.48	0.65	0.59	0.58	0.59	0.58
Debt to Equity	0.93	0.40	0.40	1.18	1.27	1.50	1.31	1.25
Price Range	23.34-13.13	24.23-16.08	24.41-19.68	22.78-14.82	15.17-9.69	18.22-6.40	25.58-17.22	61.09-18.15
P/E Ratio	...	53.85-35.73	28.06-22.63	...	...	...	...	...
Average Yield %	0.53	0.50	1.37	2.85	3.92	4.05	2.50	1.21

Address: P.O. Box 7997, Shawnee Mission, KS 66207-0997	**Web Site:** www.sprint.com	**Auditors:** KPMG LLP
Telephone: 913-624-3000	**Officers:** Gary D. Forsee - Chmn., C.E.O. Len J. Lauer - Pres., C.O.O.	**Investor Contact:** 913-624-2541
Fax: 913-624-3496		**Transfer Agents:** UMB Bank, N.A.

SPX CORP.

Exchange	Symbol	Price	52Wk Range	Yield	P/E
NYS	SPW	$104.90 (3/31/2008)	114.04-69.11	0.95	20.10

*7 Year Price Score 131.81 *NYSE Composite Index=100 *12 Month Price Score 122.72

Interim Earnings (Per Share)

Qtr.	Mar	Jun	Sep	Dec
2003	0.11	0.69	0.98	1.29
2004	0.49	0.72	0.03	(1.47)
2005	9.17	4.26	0.49	1.10
2006	0.35	1.83	(0.82)	1.44
2007	0.49	1.12	1.71	1.97

Interim Dividends (Per Share)

Amt	Decl	Ex	Rec	Pay
0.25Q	6/1/2007	6/13/2007	6/15/2007	7/2/2007
0.25Q	8/30/2007	9/12/2007	9/14/2007	10/1/2007
0.25Q	11/30/2007	12/12/2007	12/14/2007	1/2/2008
0.25Q	2/21/2008	3/12/2008	3/14/2008	4/1/2008

Indicated Div: $1.00

Valuation Analysis

Forecast P/E	15.14
	(1/10/2007)
Market Cap	$5.5 Billion
Book Value	2.0 Billion
Price/Book	2.76
Price/Sales	1.15

Institutional Holding

No of Institutions	212
Shares	53,477,792
% Held	89.57

TRADING VOLUME (thousand shares)

Business Summary: Industrial Machinery and Equipment (MIC: 11.5 SIC: 3541 NAIC: 333512)

SPX is a multi-industry manufacturing company with operations in over 35 countries and sales in over 150 countries around the world as of Dec 31 2007. Co.'s infrastructure-related products and services include wet and dry cooling systems, thermal service and repair work, heat exchangers and power transformers into the global power market. In addition, Co. provides pumps, metering systems and valves into the global oil and gas, chemical and petrochemical exploration, refinement and distribution markets. Co.'s infrastructure-related products also include packaged cooling towers, boilers, heating and ventilation equipment and filters.

Recent Developments: For the year ended Dec 31 2007, income from continuing operations increased 33.1% to US$300.3 million from US$225.7 million a year earlier. Net income increased 72.3% to US$294.2 million from US$170.7 million in the prior year. Revenues were US$4.82 billion, up 15.7% from US$4.17 billion the year before. Operating income was US$425.6 million versus US$320.9 million in the prior year, an increase of 32.6%. Direct operating expenses rose 14.4% to US$3.43 billion from US$3.00 billion in the comparable period the year before. Indirect operating expenses increased 14.0% to US$967.5 million from US$848.5 million in the equivalent prior-year period.

Prospects: For the full year of 2008, Co. is projecting revenue growth in the range of 25.0% to 30.0% to approximately $6.10 billion. In addition, Co. is targeting earnings from continuing operations to range from $6.00 to $6.20 per share, reflecting an improvement of 26.0% to 31.0% over its 2007 levels. Similarly, Co. is forecasting strong revenue and profit growth in its Flow Technology segment as a result of the Dec 31 2007 acquisition of APV and anticipated organic growth within the end markets. Lastly, Co. is projecting moderate revenue and profit growth in its Test and Measurement segment, driven primarily by the acquisitions of Johnson Controls and Matra in the second half of 2007.

Financial Data
(US$ in Thousands)

	12/31/2007	12/31/2006	12/31/2005	12/31/2004	12/31/2003	12/31/2002	12/31/2001	12/31/2000
Earnings Per Share	5.22	2.83	15.33	(0.23)	3.04	1.54	2.34	2.98
Cash Flow Per Share	8.02	1.03	(1.85)	2.41	8.15	5.39	6.78	2.77
Dividends Per Share	1.000	1.000	1.000	1.000	...	...	...	...
Dividend Payout %	19.16	35.34	6.52	...	...	...	...	...
Income Statement								
Total Revenue	4,822,300	4,313,300	4,292,200	4,372,000	5,081,500	5,045,800	4,114,300	2,678,900
EBITDA	534,700	400,300	165,200	76,800	735,700	762,000	608,600	541,500
Income Before Taxes	389,800	276,800	27,300	(172,300)	416,200	453,200	314,000	335,600
Income Taxes	89,500	56,300	70,400	(31,600)	151,600	177,200	141,000	137,300
Net Income	294,200	170,700	1,090,000	(17,100)	236,000	127,400	173,000	189,500
Average Shares	56,307	60,774	71,084	74,271	77,684	82,959	74,120	63,502
Balance Sheet								
Current Assets	2,629,400	2,458,500	2,228,300	3,870,800	2,661,700	2,573,100	2,429,000	1,062,900
Total Assets	6,237,400	5,437,100	5,308,400	7,388,300	7,823,000	7,091,300	7,080,100	3,104,000
Current Liabilities	2,157,000	1,723,400	1,470,700	1,814,100	1,530,300	1,620,100	1,532,800	637,100
Long-Term Obligations	1,240,700	753,600	720,900	2,414,300	2,530,200	2,414,600	2,450,800	1,295,600
Total Liabilities	4,221,000	3,324,200	3,193,300	5,456,800	5,555,400	5,387,400	5,339,800	2,528,200
Stockholders' Equity	2,006,000	2,109,400	2,111,200	2,127,800	2,067,200	1,692,400	1,715,300	608,200
Shares Outstanding	52,792	58,766	62,563	74,242	74,315	80,626	80,786	60,644
Statistical Record								
Return on Assets %	5.04	3.18	16.91	N.M.	3.21	1.80	3.38	6.29
Return on Equity %	14.30	8.09	51.43	N.M.	12.55	7.48	14.89	32.57
EBITDA Margin %	11.09	9.28	3.85	1.76	14.48	15.10	14.79	20.21
Net Margin %	6.10	3.96	25.39	N.M.	4.64	2.52	4.20	7.07
Asset Turnover	0.83	0.80	0.67	0.57	0.69	0.71	0.80	0.89
Current Ratio	1.22	1.43	1.52	2.13	1.74	1.59	1.58	1.67
Debt to Equity	0.62	0.36	0.34	1.13	1.22	1.43	1.43	2.13
Price Range	109.88-60.98	62.48-45.91	50.09-38.10	61.66-33.30	59.00-30.83	74.75-36.50	68.45-38.50	89.86-37.00
P/E Ratio	21.05-11.68	22.08-16.22	3.27-2.49	...	19.41-10.14	48.54-23.70	29.25-16.45	30.15-12.42
Average Yield %	1.19	1.85	2.26	2.29	...	...	...	...

Address: 13515 Ballantyne Corporate Place, Charlotte, NC 28277
Telephone: 704-752-4400
Fax: 704-752-4505

Web Site: www.spx.com
Officers: Charles E. Johnson II - Chmn. Christopher J. Kearney - Pres., C.E.O.

Auditors: Deloitte & Touche LLP
Investor Contact: 231-724-5194
Transfer Agents: EquiServe Trust Company, N.A., Providence, RI

SRA INTERNATIONAL INC

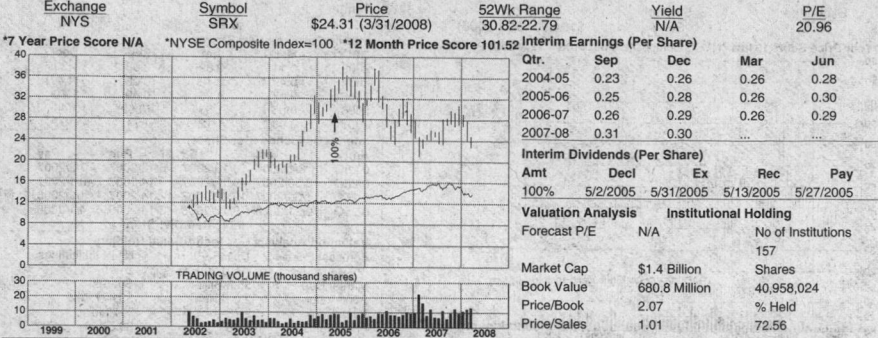

Exchange	Symbol	Price	52Wk Range	Yield	P/E
NYS	SRX	$24.31 (3/31/2008)	30.82-22.79	N/A	20.96

*7 Year Price Score N/A   *NYSE Composite Index=100   *12 Month Price Score 101.52

Interim Earnings (Per Share)

Qtr.	Sep	Dec	Mar	Jun
2004-05	0.23	0.26	0.26	0.28
2005-06	0.25	0.28	0.26	0.30
2006-07	0.26	0.29	0.26	0.29
2007-08	0.31	0.30	...	...

Interim Dividends (Per Share)

Amt	Decl	Ex	Rec	Pay
100%	5/2/2005	5/31/2005	5/13/2005	5/27/2005

Valuation Analysis   **Institutional Holding**

Forecast P/E	N/A	No of Institutions
		157
Market Cap	$1.4 Billion	Shares
Book Value	680.8 Million	40,958,024
Price/Book	2.07	% Held
Price/Sales	1.01	72.56

Business Summary: IT & Technology (MIC: 10.2 SIC: 7374 NAIC: 518210)

SRA International is engaged in providing technology and strategic consulting services and applications to clients in national security, civil government, and health care and public health. One of Co.'s markets, national security, includes the Department of Defense, the National Guard, the Department of Homeland Security, the intelligence agencies, and other federal organizations with homeland security missions. Co. provides a range of services that spans the information technology life-cycle: strategic consulting; systems design, development, and integration; and outsourcing and managed services.

Recent Developments: For the quarter ended Dec 31 2007, net income increased 7.8% to US$18.0 million from US$16.7 million in the year-earlier quarter. Revenues were US$382.0 million, up 19.0% from US$321.0 million the year before. Operating income was US$29.7 million versus US$22.1 million in the prior-year quarter, an increase of 34.6%. Direct operating expenses rose 16.9% to US$286.0 million from US$244.7 million in the comparable period the year before. Indirect operating expenses increased 22.2% to US$66.3 million from US$54.2 million in the equivalent prior-year period.

Prospects: For the fiscal year ending June 30 2008, Co. is projecting revenues to be in the range of $1.51 billion to $1.54 billion, while earnings are forecasted to range from $1.22 to $1.25 per diluted share. Meanwhile, for the third quarter ended Mar 31 2008, Co. is targeting revenues in the range of $380.0 million to $395.0 million, while earnings are estimated to range from $0.30 to $0.31 per diluted share. Lastly, for the fourth fiscal quarter of 2008, Co. is anticipating revenues to be in the range of $385.0 million to $400.0 million, while earnings are anticipated to range from $0.31 to $0.33 per diluted share. Specifically, these expectations exclude any effect from future acquisitions.

Financial Data

(US$ in Thousands)	6 Mos	3 Mos	06/30/2007	06/30/2006	06/30/2005	06/30/2004	06/30/2003	06/30/2002
Earnings Per Share	1.16	1.15	1.09	1.08	1.02	0.71	0.63	0.33
Cash Flow Per Share	1.89	1.73	2.17	1.58	1.25	0.85	1.01	0.31
Tang Book Value Per Share	4.33	3.85	5.92	6.05	5.96	5.09	4.81	3.73
Income Statement								
Total Revenue	746,142	364,127	1,268,872	1,179,267	881,770	615,802	450,375	361,197
EBITDA	72,154	36,040	117,686	115,168	102,251	72,265	56,746	28,448
Depn & Amortn	12,591	6,167	...	...	...	...	...	...
Income Before Taxes	60,446	30,619	102,775	101,199	92,552	63,228	49,091	20,554
Income Taxes	23,996	12,160	39,345	38,679	34,829	24,291	19,431	9,277
Net Income	36,450	18,459	63,430	62,520	57,723	38,937	29,660	11,277
Average Shares	59,599	59,152	58,381	57,738	56,549	54,738	47,459	34,061
Balance Sheet								
Current Assets	488,112	464,541	506,673	477,779	416,561	344,100	296,335	193,855
Total Assets	990,218	964,031	847,684	721,974	569,117	461,893	364,711	226,293
Current Liabilities	231,749	234,925	209,588	178,212	131,485	114,304	76,680	62,286
Long-Term Obligations	50,000	50,000	...	...	...	...	...	400
Total Liabilities	309,400	310,566	222,229	188,677	140,025	122,625	81,696	66,849
Stockholders' Equity	680,818	653,465	625,455	533,297	429,092	339,268	283,015	159,444
Shares Outstanding	57,894	57,516	57,064	55,863	54,047	51,775	50,076	41,422
Statistical Record								
Return on Assets %	7.62	7.79	8.08	9.68	11.20	9.40	10.04	6.38
Return on Equity %	10.80	11.06	10.95	12.99	15.02	12.48	13.41	11.13
EBITDA Margin %	9.67	9.90	9.27	9.77	11.60	11.74	12.60	7.88
Net Margin %	4.89	5.07	5.00	5.30	6.55	6.32	6.59	3.12
Asset Turnover	1.56	1.55	1.62	1.83	1.71	1.49	1.52	2.04
Current Ratio	2.11	1.98	2.42	2.68	3.17	3.01	3.86	3.11
Debt to Equity	0.07	0.08	...	...	...	...	...	N.M.
Price Range	30.82-20.99	32.10-20.99	32.10-20.99	38.16-26.63	35.70-19.92	22.15-15.32	16.72-10.73	13.55-10.75
P/E Ratio	26.57-18.09	27.91-18.25	29.45-19.26	35.33-24.66	35.00-19.53	31.20-21.58	26.54-17.02	41.06-32.58

Address: 4300 Fair Lakes Court, Fairfax, VA 22033
Telephone: 703-803-1500
Fax: 703-803-1793

Web Site: www.sra.com
Officers: Ernst Volgenau - Chmn. Renato A. DiPentima - Pres., C.E.O.

Auditors: Deloitte & Touche LLP
Transfer Agents: American Stock Transfer & Trust Company, New York, NY

STANCORP FINANCIAL GROUP INC

Exchange	Symbol	Price	52Wk Range	Yield	P/E
NYS	SFG	$47.71 (3/31/2008)	55.13-41.44	1.51	10.97

*7 Year Price Score 106.93 *NYSE Composite Index=100 *12 Month Price Score 104.78

Interim Earnings (Per Share)

Qtr.	Mar	Jun	Sep	Dec
2003	0.55	0.64	0.72	0.76
2004	0.74	0.91	0.91	0.90
2005	0.76	0.95	1.00	1.05
2006	0.70	0.78	1.01	1.25
2007	0.90	0.97	1.29	1.21

Interim Dividends (Per Share)

Amt	Decl	Ex	Rec	Pay
0.625A	11/14/2005	11/22/2005	11/25/2005	12/9/2005
100%	11/14/2005	12/12/2005	11/25/2005	12/9/2005
0.65A	11/6/2006	11/15/2006	11/17/2006	12/8/2006
0.72A	11/5/2007	11/14/2007	11/16/2007	12/7/2007

Indicated Div: $0.72

Valuation Analysis   **Institutional Holding**

Forecast P/E	9.64	No of Institutions
	(1/10/2007)	176
Market Cap	$2.3 Billion	Shares
Book Value	1.4 Billion	35,984,124
Price/Book	1.64	% Held
Price/Sales	0.87	67.17

TRADING VOLUME (thousand shares)

Business Summary: Insurance (MIC: 8.2 SIC: 6321 NAIC: 524114)

StanCorp Financial Group is a provider of insurance products and services serving the life and disability insurance needs of employer groups and individuals. Through its subsidiaries, Co. has the authority to underwrite insurance products in 50 states. Co. also provides accidental death and dismemberment insurance, dental insurance, annuity products, retirement plan products and services and investment advisory services. Co.'s mortgage business originates and services fixed-rate commercial mortgage loans for the investment portfolios of its insurance subsidiaries and for participation to institutional investors. Co. has two operating segments: Insurance Services and Asset Management.

Recent Developments: For the year ended Dec 31 2007, net income increased 11.6% to US$227.5 million from US$203.8 million in the prior year. Revenues were US$2.71 billion, up 8.7% from US$2.49 billion the year before. Net premiums earned were US$2.08 billion versus US$1.94 billion in the prior year, an increase of 7.4%. Net investment income rose 7.8% to US$516.3 million from US$478.9 million a year ago.

Prospects: Co.'s results are benefiting from increased net income due mainly to premium growth and comparatively favorable claims experience in its group insurance and individual disability businesses. Meanwhile, for full-year 2008, Co. is expecting premium growth in the range of 6.0% to 8.0% while targeting its earnings per share, excluding after-tax net capital gains and losses, to increase by approximately 10.0% to 15.0%. At the same time, Co. believes that it should be able to meet or exceed its annual return on average equity target, which excludes after-tax net capital gains and losses from net income and accumulated other comprehensive income and losses from equity, of 14.0% to 15.0%.

Financial Data
(US$ in Thousands)

	12/31/2007	12/31/2006	12/31/2005	12/31/2004	12/31/2003	12/31/2002	12/31/2001	12/31/2000
Earnings Per Share	4.35	3.73	3.76	3.45	2.67	1.87	1.72	1.48
Cash Flow Per Share	9.37	7.21	7.34	7.06	5.82	6.46	4.33	11.48
Tang Book Value Per Share	29.07	27.33	25.84	24.63	22.35	19.75	16.35	14.64
Dividends Per Share	0.720	0.650	0.625	0.500	0.350	0.200	0.150	0.135
Dividend Payout %	16.55	17.43	16.62	14.49	13.13	10.72	8.72	9.15
Income Statement								
Premium Income	2,078,300	1,935,000	1,826,500	1,678,700	1,609,300	1,383,300	1,231,700	1,102,000
Total Revenue	2,709,200	2,492,900	2,337,200	2,149,700	2,066,800	1,750,300	1,585,400	1,462,700
Benefits & Claims	1,591,800	1,513,100	1,392,300	1,291,200	1,297,800	1,117,100	1,017,000	929,500
Income Before Taxes	341,700	309,700	325,600	292,000	239,800	177,000	164,500	141,100
Income Taxes	114,200	105,900	114,500	92,600	83,500	61,000	58,500	46,400
Net Income	227,500	203,800	211,100	199,400	156,300	111,000	106,000	94,700
Average Shares	52,344	54,688	56,076	57,838	58,669	59,544	61,671	64,251
Balance Sheet								
Total Assets	14,982,900	13,638,600	12,450,700	11,212,000	9,981,700	8,742,700	7,277,000	6,859,600
Total Liabilities	13,553,900	12,174,100	11,036,900	9,810,900	8,672,200	7,590,100	6,303,300	5,935,200
Stockholders' Equity	1,429,000	1,464,500	1,413,800	1,401,100	1,309,500	1,152,600	973,700	924,400
Shares Outstanding	49,155	53,592	54,712	56,889	58,601	58,370	59,566	63,130
Statistical Record								
Return on Assets %	1.59	1.56	1.78	1.88	1.67	1.39	1.50	1.49
Return on Equity %	15.72	14.16	15.00	14.67	12.70	10.44	11.17	10.71
Loss Ratio %	76.59	78.20	76.23	76.92	80.64	80.76	82.57	84.35
Net Margin %	8.40	8.18	9.03	9.28	7.56	6.34	6.69	6.47
Price Range	55.13-41.44	55.75-42.07	52.95-36.05	41.59-29.93	31.74-23.31	30.55-23.20	24.20-18.50	24.56-11.88
P/E Ratio	12.67-9.53	14.95-11.28	14.08-9.59	12.05-8.67	11.89-8.73	16.34-12.41	14.07-10.76	16.60-8.02
Average Yield %	1.46	1.34	1.45	1.48	1.45	1.28	0.74	0.81

Address: 1100 SW Sixth Avenue, Portland, OR 97204 Telephone: 503-321-7000	Web Site: www.stancorpfinancial.com Officers: Eric E. Parsons - Chmn., Pres., C.E.O. Cindy J. McPike - Sr. V.P., C.F.O.	Auditors: Deloitte & Touche LLP Investor Contact: 503-321-7529

STANLEY WORKS (THE)

Exchange	Symbol	Price	52Wk Range	Yield	P/E	Div Acheiver
NYS	SWK	$47.62 (3/31/2008)	63.92-44.35	2.60	11.90	40 Years

*7 Year Price Score 100.43 *NYSE Composite Index=100 *12 Month Price Score 96.59

TRADING VOLUME (thousand shares)

Interim Earnings (Per Share)

Qtr.	Mar	Jun	Sep	Dec
2003	0.22	0.14	0.51	0.41
2004	1.84	0.73	0.76	1.04
2005	0.78	0.78	0.90	0.70
2006	0.45	0.90	1.09	1.03
2007	0.80	1.01	1.09	1.11

Interim Dividends (Per Share)

Amt	Decl	Ex	Rec	Pay
0.30Q	4/25/2007	6/4/2007	6/6/2007	6/26/2007
0.31Q	7/20/2007	9/5/2007	9/7/2007	9/25/2007
0.31Q	10/19/2007	12/5/2007	12/7/2007	12/18/2007
0.31Q	2/20/2008	3/3/2008	3/5/2008	3/25/2008

Indicated Div: $1.24 (Div. Reinv. Plan)

Valuation Analysis **Institutional Holding**

Forecast P/E	11.38	No of Institutions
	(1/10/2007)	280
Market Cap	$3.8 Billion	Shares
Book Value	1.7 Billion	61,954,196
Price/Book	2.21	% Held
Price/Sales	0.85	74.81

Business Summary: Metal Products (MIC: 11.4 SIC: 3423 NAIC: 332212)

Stanley Works supplies tools and engineered applications. Co.'s Construction & Do-It-Yourself segment manufactures and markets hand tools, consumer mechanics tools, storage systems, pneumatic tools, fasteners, and electronic leveling and measuring tools. Co.'s Industrial segment manufactures and markets: professional mechanics tools and storage systems; plumbing, heating, air conditioning and roofing tools; hydraulic tools and accessories; assembly tools and systems; and specialty tools. Co.'s Security segment provides access and security applications mainly for retailers, educational, financial and healthcare institutions, as well as commercial, governmental and industrial customers.

Recent Developments: For the year ended Dec 29 2007, income from continuing operations increased 15.8% to US$336.6 million from US$290.7 million a year earlier. Net income increased 16.3% to US$336.6 million from US$289.5 million in the prior year. Revenues were US$4.48 billion, up 11.6% from US$4.02 billion the year before. Direct operating expenses rose 9.0% to US$2.79 billion from US$2.56 billion in the comparable period the year before. Indirect operating expenses increased 13.7% to US$1.24 billion from US$1.09 billion in the equivalent prior-year period.

Prospects: For full-year 2008, Co. is targeting earnings per share to be in the range of $4.20 to $4.40 per fully-diluted share, an increase of 5.0% to 10.0% over $4.00 earned in 2007. Additionally, Co. expects organic sales growth of flat to 1.0%, with its Construction and Do-It-Yourself segment modestly negative, its Industrial segment modestly positive and its Security segment up 2.0% to 3.0%. This 2008 revenue outlook reflects Co.'s expectation of a subdued economic environment, including a possible mild and short-lived U.S. recession, as well as continued deterioration of North American markets associated with homebuilding and remodeling.

Financial Data

(US$ in Thousands)	12/29/2007	12/30/2006	12/31/2005	01/01/2005	01/03/2004	12/28/2002	12/29/2001	12/30/2000
Earnings Per Share	4.00	3.46	3.16	4.36	1.27	2.10	1.81	2.22
Cash Flow Per Share	6.63	5.38	4.36	4.54	5.43	3.31	2.59	2.71
Tang Book Value Per Share	N.M.	N.M.	4.59	3.56	2.65	5.05	7.04	6.58
Dividends Per Share	1.220	1.180	1.140	1.080	1.030	0.990	0.940	0.900
Dividend Payout %	30.50	34.10	36.08	24.77	81.10	47.14	51.93	40.54
Income Statement								
Total Revenue	4,483,800	4,018,600	3,285,300	3,043,400	2,678,100	2,593,000	2,624,400	2,748,900
EBITDA	613,300	488,300	454,700	424,100	219,500	343,700	319,600	377,000
Income Before Taxes	451,100	367,100	358,200	329,100	133,000	272,500	236,700	293,700
Income Taxes	114,500	76,400	86,500	88,900	36,300	87,500	78,400	99,300
Net Income	336,600	289,500	269,600	366,900	107,900	185,000	158,300	194,400
Average Shares	84,045	83,704	85,405	84,243	84,839	88,246	87,467	87,667
Balance Sheet								
Current Assets	1,768,400	1,638,500	1,825,600	1,371,900	1,200,700	1,190,400	1,141,400	1,094,300
Total Assets	4,779,900	3,935,400	3,545,100	2,850,600	2,423,800	2,418,200	2,055,700	1,884,800
Current Liabilities	1,277,500	1,251,100	875,300	818,800	753,500	680,900	825,500	707,300
Long-Term Obligations	1,212,100	679,200	895,300	481,800	534,500	564,300	196,800	248,700
Total Liabilities	3,051,400	2,383,400	2,100,200	1,629,300	1,565,200	1,434,400	1,223,400	1,148,300
Stockholders' Equity	1,728,500	1,552,000	1,444,900	1,221,300	858,600	983,800	832,300	736,500
Shares Outstanding	80,378	81,841	83,791	82,407	81,276	86,835	84,658	85,188
Statistical Record								
Return on Assets %	7.75	7.76	8.45	13.95	4.38	8.29	8.06	10.33
Return on Equity %	20.58	19.37	20.28	35.38	11.52	20.43	20.24	26.49
EBITDA Margin %	13.68	12.15	13.84	13.94	8.20	13.25	12.18	13.71
Net Margin %	7.51	7.20	8.21	12.06	4.03	7.13	6.03	7.07
Asset Turnover	1.03	1.08	1.03	1.16	1.09	1.16	1.34	1.46
Current Ratio	1.38	1.31	2.09	1.68	1.59	1.75	1.38	1.55
Debt to Equity	0.70	0.44	0.62	0.39	0.62	0.57	0.24	0.34
Price Range	63.92-47.46	54.33-41.95	51.17-42.20	48.99-36.50	37.87-21.00	51.98-28.38	46.60-28.50	31.19-19.25
P/E Ratio	15.98-11.87	15.70-12.12	16.19-13.35	11.24-8.37	29.82-16.54	24.75-13.51	25.75-15.75	14.05-8.67
Average Yield %	2.17	2.40	2.46	2.53	3.57	2.48	2.46	3.45

Address: 1000 Stanley Drive, New Britain, CT 06053 **Telephone:** 860-225-5111 **Fax:** 860-827-3895	**Web Site:** www.stanleyworks.com **Officers:** John F. Lundgren - Chmn., C.E.O. Donald R. McIlnay - Pres.	**Auditors:** Ernst & Young LLP **Investor Contact:** 860-827-3833 **Transfer Agents:** EquiServe Limited Partnership, Boston, MA

708

STARWOOD HOTELS & RESORTS WORLDWIDE INC

Exchange	Symbol	Price	52Wk Range	Yield	P/E
NYS	HOT	$51.75 (3/31/2008)	75.09-38.22	1.74	20.14

*7 Year Price Score N/A   *NYSE Composite Index=100   *12 Month Price Score 92.05

TRADING VOLUME (thousand shares)

Interim Earnings (Per Share)

Qtr.	Mar	Jun	Sep	Dec
2003	(0.58)	1.41	0.23	0.42
2004	0.16	0.72	0.50	0.46
2005	0.36	0.65	0.17	0.70
2006	0.02	3.01	0.71	0.95
2007	0.56	0.67	0.61	0.73

Interim Dividends (Per Share)

Amt	Decl	Ex	Rec	Pay
0.42A	12/19/2006	12/27/2006	12/31/2006	1/19/2007
0.90A	11/8/2007	12/27/2007	12/31/2007	1/11/2008

Indicated Div: $0.90

Valuation Analysis   Institutional Holding

Forecast P/E	20.97	No of Institutions
	(1/10/2007)	391
Market Cap	$9.9 Billion	Shares
Book Value	2.1 Billion	108,082,006
Price/Book	4.76	% Held
Price/Sales	1.61	92.20

Business Summary: Hospitality & Tourism (MIC: 5.1 SIC: 7011 NAIC: 721110)

Starwood Hotels & Resorts Worldwide is a hotel and leisure company. Co.'s hotel segment represents a worldwide network of owned, leased and consolidated joint venture hotels and resorts primarily under its proprietary brand names including: Sheraton, Westin, The Luxury Collection, St. Regis, Le Meridien, W brands, Four Points by Sheraton and Element. The vacation ownership segment includes the development, ownership and operation of vacation ownership resorts, marketing and selling vacation ownership interests and providing financing for customers who purchase those interests. As of Dec 31 2007, Co. owned, leased, managed or franchised 897 hotels with about 275,000 rooms.

Recent Developments: For the year ended Dec 31 2007, income from continuing operations decreased 51.3% to US$543.0 million from US$1.12 billion a year earlier. Net income decreased 48.0% to US$542.0 million from US$1.04 billion in the prior year. Revenues were US$6.15 billion, up 2.9% from US$5.98 billion the year before. Operating income rose US$858.0 million versus US$839.0 million in the prior year, an increase of 2.3%. Direct operating expenses rose 1.8% to US$4.42 billion from US$4.34 billion in the comparable period the year before. Indirect operating expenses increased 9.5% to US$872.0 million from US$796.0 million in the equivalent prior-year period.

Prospects: For full-year 2008, Co. has revised its outlook to reflect the uncertainty surrounding the U.S. economic environment and the possibility of a slowdown in U.S. lodging demand. As a result, Co. now expects earnings per share before special items of $2.32 to $2.57, assuming a revenue per available room (REVPAR) growth range at same-store company operated hotels worldwide of 4.0% to 7.0% and a REVPAR growth range at branded same-store company owned hotels in North America of 3.0% to 6.0%. In addition, Co. expects to open approximately 80 to 100 hotels (representing approximately 20,000 rooms) in 2008 and is targeting signing more than 200 hotel management and franchise contracts in 2008.

Financial Data
(US$ in Thousands)

	12/31/2007	12/31/2006	12/31/2005	12/31/2004	12/31/2003	12/31/2002	12/31/2001	12/31/2000
Earnings Per Share	2.57	4.69	1.88	1.84	1.50	1.73	0.70	1.97
Cash Flow Per Share	4.41	2.35	3.52	2.78	3.80	3.51	3.79	4.35
Tang Book Value Per Share	N.M.	3.31	13.57	10.75	9.11	7.15	4.71	4.99
Dividends Per Share	0.900	0.420	0.840	0.840	0.840	0.840	0.800	0.690
Dividend Payout %	35.02	8.96	44.68	45.65	56.00	48.55	114.29	35.03
Income Statement								
Total Revenue	6,153,000	5,979,000	5,977,000	5,368,000	4,630,000	4,659,000	3,967,000	4,345,000
EBITDA	1,109,000	1,208,000	1,300,000	1,109,000	700,000	1,101,000	1,084,000	1,511,000
Income Before Taxes	733,000	682,000	642,000	412,000	(11,000)	252,000	200,000	610,000
Income Taxes	189,000	(434,000)	219,000	43,000	(113,000)	4,000	46,000	201,000
Net Income	542,000	1,043,000	422,000	395,000	309,000	355,000	145,000	403,000
Average Shares	211,000	223,000	225,000	215,000	207,000	205,000	206,000	205,000
Balance Sheet								
Current Assets	1,824,000	1,810,000	2,283,000	1,683,000	1,245,000	950,000	897,000	1,048,000
Total Assets	9,622,000	9,280,000	12,454,000	12,298,000	11,894,000	12,259,000	12,461,000	12,660,000
Current Liabilities	2,101,000	2,461,000	2,879,000	2,128,000	1,644,000	2,199,000	1,587,000	1,805,000
Long-Term Obligations	3,590,000	1,827,000	2,926,000	3,823,000	4,393,000	4,449,000	5,227,000	4,957,000
Total Liabilities	7,520,000	6,247,000	7,218,000	7,483,000	7,509,000	8,172,000	8,622,000	8,644,000
Stockholders' Equity	2,076,000	3,008,000	5,211,000	4,788,000	4,326,000	3,997,000	3,756,000	3,851,000
Shares Outstanding	190,998	213,484	217,218	208,730	201,812	199,579	197,718	194,485
Statistical Record								
Return on Assets %	5.73	9.60	3.41	3.26	2.56	2.87	1.15	3.14
Return on Equity %	21.32	25.38	8.44	8.64	7.43	9.16	3.81	10.66
EBITDA Margin %	18.02	20.20	21.75	20.66	15.12	23.63	27.33	34.78
Net Margin %	8.81	17.44	7.06	7.36	6.67	7.62	3.66	9.28
Asset Turnover	0.65	0.55	0.48	0.44	0.38	0.38	0.32	0.34
Current Ratio	0.87	0.74	0.79	0.79	0.76	0.43	0.57	0.58
Debt to Equity	1.73	0.61	0.56	0.80	1.02	1.11	1.39	1.29
Price Range	75.09-43.30	65.61-56.79	...	...	...	...	...	...
P/E Ratio	29.22-16.85	13.99-12.11	...	...	...	...	...	...
Average Yield %	1.44	0.68	...	...	...	...	...	...

Address: 1111 Westchester Avenue, White Plains, NY 10604 **Telephone:** 914-640-8100 **Fax:** 914-640-8310	**Web Site:** www.starwoodhotels.com **Officers:** Bruce W. Duncan - Chmn. Robert F. Cotter - Pres., C.O.O.	**Auditors:** Ernst & Young LLP **Transfer Agents:** American Stock Transfer & Trust Company, New York, NY

STATE STREET CORP.

Exchange	Symbol	Price	52Wk Range	Yield	P/E	Div Acheiver
NYS	STT	$79.00 (3/31/2008)	85.37-59.48	1.16	22.90	27 Years

*7 Year Price Score 109.15 *NYSE Composite Index=100   *12 Month Price Score 118.42

Interim Earnings (Per Share)

Qtr.	Mar	Jun	Sep	Dec
2003	0.29	(0.07)	0.60	1.33
2004	0.63	0.65	0.52	0.55
2005	0.67	0.66	0.43	0.74
2006	0.87	0.68	0.83	0.91
2007	0.93	1.07	0.91	0.54

Interim Dividends (Per Share)

Amt	Decl	Ex	Rec	Pay
0.22Q	6/21/2007	6/27/2007	6/29/2007	7/16/2007
0.22Q	9/19/2007	9/27/2007	10/1/2007	10/15/2007
0.23Q	12/13/2007	12/28/2007	1/2/2008	1/15/2008
0.23Q	3/20/2008	3/28/2008	4/1/2008	4/15/2008

Indicated Div: $0.92 (Div. Reinv. Plan)

Valuation Analysis

Forecast P/E	16.46
	(1/10/2007)
Market Cap	$30.5 Billion
Book Value	11.3 Billion
Price/Book	2.70
Price/Sales	2.58

Institutional Holding

No of Institutions	635
Shares	269,602,080
% Held	80.76

Business Summary: Commercial Banking (MIC: 8.1 SIC: 6022 NAIC: 522110)

State Street is a financial holding company. Through its subsidiaries, including its principal banking subsidiary, State Street Bank and Trust Company, Co. provides a range of products and services for institutional investors worldwide. Co. has two reportable lines of business: Investment Servicing and Investment Management. Co.'s customers include mutual funds and other collective investment funds, corporate and public retirement plans, insurance companies, foundations, endowments and other investment pools, and investment managers. As of Dec 31 2007, Co. had total assets of $142.54 billion and total deposits of $95.79 billion.

Recent Developments: For the year ended Dec 31 2007, income from continuing operations increased 15.1% to US$1.26 billion from US$1.10 billion a year earlier. Net income increased 14.0% to US$1.26 billion from US$1.11 billion in the prior year. Net interest income increased 55.9% to US$1.73 billion from US$1.11 billion in the prior year. Non-interest income rose 27.0% to US$6.61 billion from US$5.20 billion, while non-interest expense advanced 41.7% to US$6.43 billion.

Prospects: Co. is experiencing significant top-line growth as well as substantial earnings improvement on an operating basis. Specifically, Co. is benefiting from investment servicing and investment management escalation, while revenue from trading services and securities finance capitalized on the continuing market volatility, mainly in the fixed-income markets. For 2008, Co. is projecting revenue growth to range from 14.0% to 17.0%, up from its long-term objective of 8.0% to 12.0%, due to the Jul 2 2007 acquisition of Investors Financial Services Corp. Also, Co. is targeting earnings per share growth of 10.0% to 15.0%.

Financial Data

(US$ in Thousands)	12/31/2007	12/31/2006	12/31/2005	12/31/2004	12/31/2003	12/31/2002	12/31/2001	12/31/2000
Earnings Per Share	3.45	3.29	2.50	2.35	2.15	3.10	1.90	1.81
Cash Flow Per Share	8.15	2.96	7.52	1.24	4.57	3.10	1.44	1.98
Tang Book Value Per Share	12.28	16.35	13.70	12.49	11.65	12.92	11.88	10.09
Dividends Per Share	0.880	0.800	0.720	0.640	0.560	0.480	0.405	0.345
Dividend Payout %	25.51	24.32	28.80	27.23	26.05	15.48	21.32	19.01
Income Statement								
Interest Income	5,212,000	4,324,000	2,930,000	1,787,000	1,539,000	1,974,000	2,855,000	3,256,000
Interest Expense	3,482,000	3,214,000	2,023,000	928,000	729,000	995,000	1,830,000	2,362,000
Net Interest Income	1,730,000	1,110,000	907,000	859,000	810,000	979,000	1,025,000	894,000
Provision for Losses	...	...	...	(18,000)	...	4,000	10,000	9,000
Non-Interest Income	6,606,000	5,201,000	4,566,000	4,074,000	3,924,000	3,421,000	2,782,000	2,665,000
Non-Interest Expense	6,433,000	4,540,000	4,041,000	3,759,000	3,622,000	2,841,000	2,867,000	2,644,000
Income Before Taxes	1,903,000	1,771,000	1,432,000	1,192,000	1,112,000	1,555,000	930,000	906,000
Income Taxes	642,000	675,000	487,000	394,000	390,000	540,000	302,000	311,000
Net Income	1,261,000	1,106,000	838,000	798,000	722,000	1,015,000	628,000	595,000
Average Shares	365,488	335,732	334,636	339,605	335,326	327,477	330,492	328,088
Balance Sheet								
Net Loans & Leases	15,784,000	8,928,000	6,464,000	4,611,000	4,960,000	4,113,000	5,283,000	5,216,000
Total Assets	142,543,000	107,353,000	97,968,000	94,040,000	87,534,000	85,794,000	69,896,000	69,298,000
Total Deposits	95,789,000	65,646,000	59,646,000	55,129,000	47,516,000	45,468,000	38,559,000	37,937,000
Total Liabilities	131,244,000	100,101,000	91,601,000	87,881,000	81,787,000	81,007,000	66,051,000	66,036,000
Stockholders' Equity	11,299,000	7,252,000	6,367,000	6,159,000	5,747,000	4,787,000	3,845,000	3,262,000
Shares Outstanding	386,284	332,438	333,625	333,645	334,474	324,927	323,670	323,422
Statistical Record								
Return on Assets %	1.01	1.08	0.87	0.88	0.83	1.30	0.90	0.91
Return on Equity %	13.59	16.24	13.38	13.37	13.71	23.52	17.67	20.07
Net Interest Margin %	33.19	25.67	30.96	48.07	52.63	49.59	35.90	27.46
Efficiency Ratio %	54.43	47.66	53.91	64.14	66.30	52.66	50.86	44.65
Loans to Deposits	0.16	0.14	0.11	0.08	0.10	0.09	0.14	0.14
Price Range	82.24-59.48	68.36-54.49	59.29-40.68	56.45-41.07	53.18-31.63	57.59-32.38	62.75-38.66	66.93-31.69
P/E Ratio	23.84-17.24	20.78-16.56	23.72-16.27	24.02-17.48	24.73-14.71	18.58-10.45	33.03-20.35	36.98-17.51
Average Yield %	1.26	1.30	1.47	1.33	1.32	1.04	0.80	0.66

Address: One Lincoln Street, Boston, MA 02111-2900
Telephone: 617-786-3000
Fax: 617-985-8055

Web Site: www.statestreet.com
Officers: Ronald E. Logue - Chmn., C.E.O. John R. Towers - Vice Chmn.

Auditors: Ernst & Young LLP
Investor Contact: 617-664-3477
Transfer Agents: EquiServe Trust Company, N.A., Providence, RI

STEELCASE, INC.

Exchange	Symbol	Price	52Wk Range	Yield	P/E
NYS	SCS	$11.06 (3/31/2008)	20.31-11.06	5.42	12.29

*7 Year Price Score 94.74   *NYSE Composite Index=100   *12 Month Price Score 87.52

Interim Earnings (Per Share)

Qtr.	May	Aug	Nov	Feb
2004-05	(0.04)	0.05	0.07	0.01
2005-06	0.05	0.09	0.13	0.06
2006-07	0.12	0.18	0.22	0.19
2007-08	0.23	0.26	0.22	

Interim Dividends (Per Share)

Amt	Decl	Ex	Rec	Pay
0.15Q	10/5/2007	10/11/2007	10/15/2007	10/24/2007
0.15Q	12/19/2007	12/28/2007	1/2/2008	1/15/2008
1.75Q	12/19/2007	12/28/2007	1/2/2008	1/15/2008
0.15Q	3/19/2008	4/10/2008	4/14/2008	4/28/2008

Indicated Div: $0.60

TRADING VOLUME (thousand shares)

Valuation Analysis

Forecast P/E	13.21 (1/10/2007)
Market Cap	$1.6 Billion
Book Value	1.2 Billion
Price/Book	1.31
Price/Sales	0.47

Institutional Holding

No of Institutions	154
Shares	65,544,388
% Held	44.14

Business Summary: Furniture and Fixtures (MIC: 11.10 SIC: 2522 NAIC: 337214)

Steelcase designs, markets and manufactures office furniture. Co. has two segments: North America, which consists of the design, sales and marketing, and manufacturing operations of its Steelcase Group, Turnstone and Nurture by Steelcase that serve customers through independent dealers in the U.S. and Canada; and International, which includes all design, sales and marketing, and manufacturing operations of the Steelcase brand outside the U.S. and Canada. As of Feb 23 2007, Co. operated manufacturing and distribution center facilities in 29 main locations, and distributed products through various channels, including independent and company-owned dealers in over 800 locations globally.

Recent Developments: For the quarter ended Nov 23 2007, net income decreased 4.6% to US$31.3 million from US$32.8 million in the year-earlier quarter. Revenues were US$885.9 million, up 10.5% from US$802.0 million the year before. Operating income was US$52.7 million versus US$40.5 million in the prior-year quarter, an increase of 30.1%. Direct operating expenses rose 6.2% to US$589.0 million from US$554.7 million in the comparable period the year before. Indirect operating expenses increased 18.1% to US$244.2 million from US$206.8 million in the equivalent prior-year period.

Prospects: Notwithstanding the slight reduction in its net income, Co. is benefiting from strong revenue growth in both its North America and International segments. Moreover, Co. is encouraged by its $14.0 million acquisition of Ultra Group Co. Ltd. in the third quarter of the fiscal year ending Feb 2008, which expands its operations in China and enhances its sales and distribution capabilities throughout Asia. Hence, for the fiscal 2008 fourth quarter, Co. is expecting revenue growth of 10.0% to 14.0% over the prior year quarter, and earnings of $0.23 to $0.28 per share. Co. has also updated its three-year plan, and as such, is targeting operating income of 10.0% to 11.0% of sales by fiscal 2011.

Financial Data
(US$ in Thousands)

	9 Mos	6 Mos	3 Mos	02/23/2007	02/24/2006	02/25/2005	02/27/2004	02/28/2003
Earnings Per Share	0.90	0.90	0.82	0.71	0.33	0.09	(0.16)	(1.80)
Cash Flow Per Share	1.82	1.83	1.82	1.89	1.19	0.78	0.60	0.28
Tang Book Value Per Share	6.57	6.40	6.42	6.54	6.15	6.10	6.13	6.43
Dividends Per Share	0.580	0.550	0.500	0.450	0.330	0.240	0.240	0.240
Dividend Payout %	64.27	60.98	60.88	63.38	100.00	266.67	...	...
Income Statement								
Total Revenue	2,519,500	1,633,600	808,500	3,097,400	2,868,900	2,613,800	2,345,600	2,586,900
EBITDA	229,400	153,400	71,300	218,600	202,800	146,800	64,800	114,900
Depn & Amortn	70,100	44,700	22,100	...	...	...	...	...
Income Before Taxes	165,200	113,200	51,300	124,600	76,400	5,000	(92,000)	(59,200)
Income Taxes	62,600	41,900	17,700	17,700	27,500	(6,700)	(30,600)	(22,200)
Net Income	102,600	71,300	33,600	106,900	48,900	12,700	(23,200)	(266,100)
Average Shares	141,900	143,800	146,500	149,800	148,700	148,200	148,000	147,700
Balance Sheet								
Current Assets	1,269,000	1,173,600	1,155,600	1,229,600	1,128,100	1,057,300	942,000	814,100
Total Assets	2,430,800	2,330,200	2,317,100	2,399,400	2,344,500	2,364,600	2,350,400	2,342,200
Current Liabilities	687,000	614,700	590,800	644,100	836,200	609,500	543,300	502,500
Long-Term Obligations	251,200	249,900	249,900	250,000	2,200	258,100	319,600	294,200
Total Liabilities	1,236,800	1,145,300	1,111,600	1,161,500	1,139,600	1,168,000	1,145,100	1,087,100
Stockholders' Equity	1,194,000	1,184,900	1,205,500	1,237,900	1,204,900	1,196,600	1,205,300	1,255,100
Shares Outstanding	141,439	142,197	144,339	146,845	149,489	148,575	147,979	147,612
Statistical Record								
Return on Assets %	5.45	5.41	5.27	4.52	2.08	0.54	N.M.	N.M.
Return on Equity %	10.90	11.08	10.04	8.78	4.08	1.06	N.M.	N.M.
EBITDA Margin %	9.10	9.39	8.82	7.06	7.07	5.62	2.76	4.44
Net Margin %	4.07	4.36	4.16	3.45	1.70	0.49	N.M.	N.M.
Asset Turnover	1.36	1.30	1.37	1.31	1.22	1.11	1.00	0.96
Current Ratio	1.85	1.91	1.96	1.91	1.35	1.73	1.73	1.62
Debt to Equity	0.21	0.21	0.21	0.20	N.M.	0.22	0.27	0.23
Price Range	20.41-14.71	20.41-13.82	20.41-13.30	20.07-13.30	17.34-12.40	14.65-11.40	14.50-8.64	17.65-8.55
P/E Ratio	22.68-16.34	22.68-15.36	24.89-16.22	28.27-18.73	52.55-37.58	162.78-126.67	...	...
Average Yield %	3.13	3.03	2.86	2.62	2.28	1.81	2.05	1.88

Address: 901 44th Street SE, Grand Rapids, MI 49508 Telephone: 616-247-2710 Fax: 616-475-2270	Web Site: www.steelcase.com Officers: Robert C. Pew III - Chmn. James P. Hackett - Pres., C.E.O.	Auditors: BDO Seidman, LLP Transfer Agents: Computershare Trust Company, N.A., Providence, RI

STEPAN CO.

Exchange	Symbol	Price	52Wk Range	Yield	P/E	Div Acheiver
NYS	SCL	$38.23 (3/31/2008)	38.25-25.88	2.20	25.49	40 Years

*7 Year Price Score 94.62   *NYSE Composite Index=100   *12 Month Price Score 117.82

Interim Earnings (Per Share)

Qtr.	Mar	Jun	Sep	Dec
2003	0.23	0.49	0.12	(0.40)
2004	0.42	0.39	0.19	0.05
2005	0.33	0.64	0.43	(0.05)
2006	0.31	0.31	0.61	(0.60)
2007	0.56	0.47	0.31	0.16

Interim Dividends (Per Share)

Amt	Decl	Ex	Rec	Pay
0.205Q	4/24/2007	5/29/2007	5/31/2007	6/15/2007
0.205Q	7/31/2007	8/29/2007	8/31/2007	9/14/2007
0.21Q	10/16/2007	11/28/2007	11/30/2007	12/14/2007
0.21Q	2/12/2008	2/27/2008	2/29/2008	3/14/2008

Indicated Div: $0.84

Valuation Analysis | **Institutional Holding**

Forecast P/E	N/A	No of Institutions
		55
Market Cap	$355.9 Million	Shares
Book Value	206.1 Million	4,105,625
Price/Book	1.73	% Held
Price/Sales	0.27	44.44

Business Summary: Chemicals (MIC: 11.1 SIC: 2843 NAIC: 325613)

Stepan produces specialty and intermediate chemicals. Co. has three segments: surfactants, polymers and specialty products. Surfactants refer to chemical agents that affect the interaction amid two surfaces, providing actions such as detergency, wetting and foaming, dispersing, emulsification, demulsification, viscosity modifications and biocidal disinfectants. Polymers, which include phthalic anhydride, polyols and polyurethane foam systems, are used in plastics, building materials and refrigeration industries. Polymers are also used in coating, adhesive, sealant and elastomer applications. Specialty products include chemicals used in food, flavoring and pharmaceutical applications.

Recent Developments: For the year ended Dec 31 2007, net income increased 126.7% to US$15.1 million in the prior year. Revenues were US$1.33 billion, up 13.4% from US$1.17 billion the year before. Operating income was US$35.1 million versus US$15.9 million in the prior year, an increase of 121.4%. Direct operating expenses rose 13.5% to US$1.19 billion from US$1.05 billion in the comparable period the year before. Indirect operating expenses decreased 3.3% to US$106.3 million from US$109.9 million in the equivalent prior-year period.

Prospects: Co.'s near-term outlook appears constructive, reflecting recent capacity additions and restructuring activities coupled with strong operating results from across its three business groups. With respect to raw material costs, Co. noted that increased raw material costs are passed on to customers as quickly as the marketplace allows; however, it has arrangements with certain customers that allow for price changes only on a quarterly basis, and competitive pressures sometimes prevent cost increases from being passed on to customers. Consequently, Co. stated that it may take time to recover raw material cost increases for some product lines or market segments.

Financial Data

(US$ in Thousands)	12/31/2007	12/31/2006	12/31/2005	12/31/2004	12/31/2003	12/31/2002	12/31/2001	12/31/2000
Earnings Per Share	1.50	0.63	1.35	1.05	0.45	2.05	1.59	1.47
Cash Flow Per Share	5.05	4.25	4.67	4.88	5.13	5.20	5.79	5.71
Tang Book Value Per Share	19.40	16.43	15.07	15.05	14.31	13.98	15.41	15.47
Dividends Per Share	0.825	0.805	0.785	0.772	0.762	0.738	0.708	0.662
Dividend Payout %	55.00	127.78	58.15	73.57	169.44	35.98	44.50	45.07
Income Statement								
Total Revenue	1,329,901	1,172,583	1,078,377	935,816	784,855	748,539	711,517	698,937
EBITDA	70,621	54,658	64,216	61,039	54,758	77,773	73,066	72,008
Income Before Taxes	23,715	7,389	17,646	14,633	5,271	30,268	25,926	24,403
Income Taxes	8,687	900	4,170	4,320	360	10,139	9,774	9,395
Net Income	15,118	6,670	13,159	10,324	4,911	20,129	16,152	15,008
Average Shares	10,113	9,284	9,725	9,038	9,086	9,802	10,133	10,236
Balance Sheet								
Current Assets	293,932	268,469	259,248	235,484	204,460	185,112	185,194	177,213
Total Assets	573,185	546,055	516,159	492,776	464,217	439,667	435,488	415,049
Current Liabilities	200,978	180,495	162,904	157,602	132,939	105,017	109,730	108,341
Long-Term Obligations	96,939	107,403	108,945	94,018	92,004	104,304	109,588	96,466
Total Liabilities	366,458	364,518	348,420	323,601	302,150	280,838	275,759	260,873
Stockholders' Equity	206,051	180,786	166,834	168,241	162,067	158,829	159,729	154,176
Shares Outstanding	9,309	9,207	9,040	8,993	8,933	8,880	9,420	9,024
Statistical Record								
Return on Assets %	2.70	1.26	2.61	2.15	1.09	4.60	3.80	3.61
Return on Equity %	7.82	3.84	7.85	6.23	3.06	12.64	10.29	9.68
EBITDA Margin %	5.31	4.66	5.95	6.52	6.98	10.39	10.27	10.30
Net Margin %	1.14	0.57	1.22	1.10	0.63	2.69	2.27	2.15
Asset Turnover	2.38	2.21	2.14	1.95	1.74	1.71	1.67	1.68
Current Ratio	1.46	1.49	1.59	1.49	1.54	1.76	1.69	1.64
Debt to Equity	0.47	0.59	0.65	0.56	0.57	0.66	0.69	0.63
Price Range	34.90-25.40	33.00-25.05	27.48-20.80	26.15-21.70	26.80-21.55	29.21-23.55	26.38-17.80	25.00-18.50
P/E Ratio	23.27-16.93	52.38-39.76	20.36-15.41	24.90-20.67	59.56-47.89	14.25-11.49	16.59-11.19	17.01-12.59
Average Yield %	2.73	2.74	3.26	3.19	3.12	2.77	3.05	3.07

Address: Edens & Winnetka Road, Northfield, IL 60093
Telephone: 847-446-7500
Fax: 847-501-2443

Web Site: www.stepan.com
Officers: F. Quinn Stepan - Chmn., C.E.O. F. Quinn Stepan Jr. - Pres., C.O.O.

Auditors: Deloitte & Touche LLP
Investor Contact: 847-446-7500
Transfer Agents: Computershare Investor Services, Chicago, IL

STERIS CORP.

Exchange	Symbol	Price	52Wk Range	Yield	P/E
NYS	STE	$26.83 (3/31/2008)	31.21-23.20	0.89	21.64

*7 Year Price Score 93.45   *NYSE Composite Index=100   *12 Month Price Score 97.73

Interim Earnings (Per Share)

Qtr.	Jun	Sep	Dec	Mar
2004-05	0.25	0.27	0.35	0.36
2005-06	0.25	0.24	0.41	0.13
2006-07	0.22	0.25	0.33	0.45
2007-08	0.20	0.25	0.34	...

Interim Dividends (Per Share)

Amt	Decl	Ex	Rec	Pay
0.05Q	4/25/2007	5/14/2007	5/16/2007	6/13/2007
0.06Q	7/26/2007	8/13/2007	8/15/2007	9/12/2007
0.06Q	10/24/2007	11/9/2007	11/14/2007	12/12/2007
0.06Q	1/22/2008	2/8/2008	2/12/2008	3/11/2008

Indicated Div: $0.24

Valuation Analysis — **Institutional Holding**

Forecast P/E	15.04	No of Institutions
	(1/10/2007)	199
Market Cap	$1.7 Billion	Shares
Book Value	753.9 Million	58,580,640
Price/Book	2.22	% Held
Price/Sales	1.35	90.30

TRADING VOLUME (thousand shares)

Business Summary: Medical Instruments & Equipment (MIC: 9.6 SIC: 3842 NAIC: 339113)

STERIS is engaged in the provision of infection prevention as well as surgical products and services, with a primary focus on the markets of healthcare, pharmaceutical and research. Co. provides its customers a mix of capital products, which include sterilizers and surgical tables; consumable products, such as detergents and skin care products; and services which include equipment installation and maintenance, as well as the bulk sterilization of single-use medical devices. As of Mar 31 2007, Co. managed its business in three market-focused business segments: Healthcare, Life Sciences, and STERIS Isomedix Services.

Recent Developments: For the quarter ended Dec 31 2007, income from continuing operations increased 4.4% to US$21.8 million from US$20.9 million in the year-earlier quarter. Net income increased 2.2% to US$21.8 million from US$21.3 million in the year-earlier quarter. Revenues were US$314.0 million, up 5.0% from US$299.0 million the year before. Operating income was US$33.5 million versus US$33.9 million in the prior-year quarter, a decrease of 1.1%. Direct operating expenses rose 7.3% to US$183.8 million from US$171.3 million in the comparable period the year before. Indirect operating expenses increased 3.1% to US$96.7 million from US$93.9 million in the equivalent prior-year period.

Prospects: For the fiscal year ending Mar 31 2008, Co. is revising its outlook and now projects revenue growth to be in the range of 4.0% to 5.0%, while earnings are estimated to range from $1.30 to $1.35 per diluted share. Specifically, these expectations reflect the effects of the slower than anticipated ramp in production levels at Co.'s manufacturing facility in Monterrey, Mexico. Meanwhile, Co. will continue to focus its research and development efforts on enhancing capabilities of delivery systems in the defense and industrial areas, sterile processing combination technologies, surgical tables and accessories, and the areas of infectious agents such as Prions and Nanobacteria.

Financial Data

(US$ in Thousands)	9 Mos	6 Mos	3 Mos	03/31/2007	03/31/2006	03/31/2005	03/31/2004	03/31/2003
Earnings Per Share	1.24	1.23	1.23	1.25	1.02	1.23	1.33	1.12
Cash Flow Per Share	2.36	2.03	1.87	1.47	2.37	2.19	1.77	1.92
Tang Book Value Per Share	6.75	6.81	6.81	6.79	6.04	5.82	6.43	5.41
Dividends Per Share	0.220	0.210	0.190	0.180	0.160	...	...	...
Dividend Payout %	17.74	17.07	15.45	14.40	15.69	...	...	...
Income Statement								
Total Revenue	889,920	575,946	280,944	1,197,407	1,160,285	1,119,745	1,087,012	972,087
EBITDA	130,633	80,575	37,611	200,398	170,972	196,185	189,039	172,284
Depn & Amortn	47,499	31,484	15,582	...	...	...	...	...
Income Before Taxes	78,905	46,378	20,794	132,930	108,118	141,941	138,084	124,118
Income Taxes	27,908	17,157	7,591	51,833	45,172	55,961	43,841	44,682
Net Income	50,997	29,221	13,203	87,155	70,289	85,980	94,243	79,436
Average Shares	63,836	65,047	65,909	65,731	68,939	70,022	70,742	70,870
Balance Sheet								
Current Assets	473,211	481,364	466,669	484,720	460,315	420,132	462,678	354,432
Total Assets	1,194,795	1,204,030	1,187,876	1,209,170	1,188,973	1,185,722	1,069,810	894,992
Current Liabilities	199,285	189,709	184,095	217,399	234,146	221,815	190,428	191,051
Long-Term Obligations	132,225	124,890	109,780	100,800	114,480	104,274	109,090	59,704
Total Liabilities	440,854	435,530	415,221	434,878	458,146	430,084	389,111	325,462
Stockholders' Equity	753,941	768,500	772,655	774,292	730,827	755,638	680,699	569,530
Shares Outstanding	62,350	63,739	64,741	64,982	66,976	69,627	69,946	69,741
Statistical Record								
Return on Assets %	6.84	6.78	6.77	6.85	5.92	7.62	9.57	9.15
Return on Equity %	10.77	10.82	10.93	10.92	9.46	11.97	15.03	15.04
EBITDA Margin %	14.68	13.99	13.39	16.74	14.74	17.52	17.39	17.72
Net Margin %	5.73	5.07	4.70	6.86	6.06	7.68	8.67	8.17
Asset Turnover	1.05	1.03	1.02	1.00	0.98	0.99	1.10	1.12
Current Ratio	2.37	2.54	2.53	2.23	1.97	1.89	2.43	1.86
Debt to Equity	0.18	0.16	0.14	0.13	0.16	0.14	0.16	0.10
Price Range	31.21-24.65	31.21-23.74	31.21-21.94	27.20-21.33	27.58-21.62	27.44-19.97	27.21-19.99	27.00-16.30
P/E Ratio	25.17-19.88	25.37-19.30	25.37-17.84	21.76-17.06	27.04-21.20	22.31-16.24	20.46-15.03	24.11-14.55
Average Yield %	0.79	0.78	0.74	0.74	0.64	...	...	...

Address: 5960 Heisley Road, Mentor, OH 44060-1834
Telephone: 440-354-2600
Fax: 440-639-4457

Web Site: www.steris.com
Officers: John P. Wareham - Chmn. Les C. Vinney - Pres., C.E.O.

Auditors: Ernst & Young LLP
Investor Contact: 440-392-7607
Transfer Agents: National City Bank, Cleveland, OH

STRYKER CORP.

Exchange	Symbol	Price	52Wk Range	Yield	P/E	Div Acheiver
NYS	SYK	$65.05 (3/31/2008)	76.48-59.74	0.51	26.66	15 Years

*7 Year Price Score 122.07 *NYSE Composite Index=100 *12 Month Price Score 103.33

Interim Earnings (Per Share)

Qtr.	Mar	Jun	Sep	Dec
2003	0.26	0.27	0.27	0.33
2004	0.33	0.37	0.04	0.40
2005	0.42	0.45	0.32	0.45
2006	0.36	0.52	0.46	0.55
2007	0.59	0.65	0.55	0.66

Interim Dividends (Per Share)

Amt	Decl	Ex	Rec	Pay
0.09A	12/10/2004	12/29/2004	12/31/2004	1/31/2005
0.11A	12/7/2005	12/28/2005	12/30/2005	1/31/2006
0.22A	12/6/2006	12/27/2006	12/29/2006	1/31/2007
0.33A	12/6/2007	12/27/2007	12/31/2007	1/31/2008

Indicated Div: $0.33

Valuation Analysis / **Institutional Holding**

Forecast P/E	19.48	No of Institutions
	(1/10/2008)	658
Market Cap	$26.7 Billion	Shares
Book Value	5.4 Billion	198,275,664
Price/Book	4.97	.% Held
Price/Sales	4.46	48.54

Business Summary: Medical Instruments & Equipment (MIC: 9.6 SIC: 3841 NAIC: 339112)

Stryker is a medical technology company with a range of products in orthopaedics and other medical specialties. Co. operates through two reportable business segments: Orthopaedic Implants and MedSurg Equipment. The Orthopaedic Implants segment sells orthopaedic reconstructive (hip, knee and shoulder), trauma, spinal and craniomaxillofacial implant systems; bone cement; and the bone growth factor OP-1. The MedSurg Equipment segment sells surgical equipment; surgical navigation systems; endoscopic, communications and digital imaging systems as well as patient handling and emergency medical equipment.

Recent Developments: For the year ended Dec 31 2007, income from continuing operations increased 27.9% to US$986.7 million from US$771.4 million a year earlier. Net income increased 30.8% to US$1.02 billion from US$777.7 million in the prior year. Revenues were US$6.00 billion, up 16.6% from US$5.15 billion the year before. Operating income was US$1.31 billion versus US$1.06 billion in the prior year, an increase of 22.9%. Direct operating expenses rose 15.4% to US$1.87 billion from US$1.62 billion in the comparable period the year before. Indirect operating expenses increased 14.6% to US$2.83 billion from US$2.47 billion in the equivalent prior-year period.

Prospects: Co. is optimistic with its 2008 outlook regarding the growth rates in orthopaedic procedures and sales growth rates in its orthopaedics products and other medical specialties, despite the potential for continued pricing pressure in certain markets. Thus, for 2008, Co. estimates diluted net earnings per share of $2.88, representing a 22.0% increase over 2007, with a constant currency net sales increase of 11.0% to 13.0% due to growth in shipments at its Orthopaedic Implants and MedSurg Equipment segments. Meanwhile, Co. expects completion of the development and initial commercialization of the spinal disc implant technologies beginning in 2008 and the sterilization technology in 2010.

Financial Data

(US$ in Thousands)	12/31/2007	12/31/2006	12/31/2005	12/31/2004	12/31/2003	12/31/2002	12/31/2001	12/31/2000
Earnings Per Share	2.44	1.89	1.64	1.14	1.12	0.85	0.66	0.55
Cash Flow Per Share	2.51	2.13	2.14	1.47	1.63	1.28	1.19	0.85
Tang Book Value Per Share	10.83	7.98	5.75	4.44	2.98	1.42	0.65	0.04
Dividends Per Share	0.330	0.220	0.110	0.090	0.070	0.060	0.050	0.040
Dividend Payout %	13.52	11.64	6.71	7.89	6.28	7.06	7.58	7.27
Income Statement								
Total Revenue	6,000,500	5,405,600	4,871,500	4,262,300	3,625,300	3,011,600	2,602,300	2,289,400
EBITDA	1,548,600	1,270,900	1,158,200	874,300	817,700	604,400	509,700	471,500
Income Before Taxes	1,370,100	1,103,800	1,003,300	717,000	652,500	506,700	405,700	334,900
Income Taxes	383,400	326,100	328,100	251,300	199,000	161,100	133,900	113,900
Net Income	1,017,400	777,700	675,200	465,700	453,500	345,600	267,000	221,000
Average Shares	417,200	411,800	411,600	410,300	406,800	407,600	406,000	402,200
Balance Sheet								
Current Assets	4,904,900	3,534,300	2,870,100	2,142,600	1,397,600	1,151,300	993,100	997,000
Total Assets	7,354,000	5,873,800	4,944,100	4,083,800	3,159,100	2,815,500	2,423,600	2,430,800
Current Liabilities	1,333,000	1,351,500	1,248,800	1,113,500	850,500	707,500	533,400	617,400
Long-Term Obligations	...	...	184,200	700	18,800	491,000	720,900	876,500
Total Liabilities	1,975,500	1,682,800	1,692,300	1,331,800	1,004,300	1,317,300	1,367,400	1,575,900
Stockholders' Equity	5,378,500	4,191,000	3,251,800	2,752,000	2,154,800	1,498,200	1,056,200	854,900
Shares Outstanding	411,000	407,900	405,200	402,500	399,400	396,200	393,400	391,800
Statistical Record								
Return on Assets %	15.38	14.38	14.96	12.82	15.18	13.19	11.00	8.80
Return on Equity %	21.26	20.90	22.49	18.93	24.83	27.06	27.94	28.88
EBITDA Margin %	25.81	23.51	23.78	20.51	22.56	20.07	19.59	20.59
Net Margin %	16.96	14.39	13.86	10.93	12.51	11.48	10.26	9.65
Asset Turnover	0.91	1.00	1.08	1.17	1.21	1.15	1.07	0.91
Current Ratio	3.68	2.62	2.30	1.92	1.64	1.63	1.86	1.61
Debt to Equity	...	...	0.06	N.M.	0.01	0.33	0.68	1.03
Price Range	76.48-55.12	55.45-40.88	56.10-39.80	57.33-41.75	42.51-30.12	33.62-22.72	30.75-22.06	27.00-12.75
P/E Ratio	31.34-22.59	29.34-21.63	34.21-24.27	50.29-36.62	37.95-26.89	39.55-26.73	46.60-33.42	49.09-23.18
Average Yield %	0.49	0.46	0.23	0.19	0.19	0.21	0.19	0.20

Address: 2725 Fairfield Road, Kalamazoo, MI 49002
Telephone: 269-385-2600
Fax: 269-385-1062

Web Site: www.stryker.com
Officers: John W. Brown - Chmn. Stephen P. MacMillan - Pres., C.E.O.

Auditors: Ernst & Young LLP
Investor Contact: 616-385-2600
Transfer Agents: National City Bank, Cleveland, OH

STUDENT LOAN CORP. (THE)

Exchange	Symbol	Price	52Wk Range	Yield	P/E
NYS	STU	$98.90 (3/31/2008)	211.02-92.60	5.78	10.83

*7 Year Price Score 87.88 *NYSE Composite Index=100 *12 Month Price Score 72.90

Interim Earnings (Per Share)

Qtr.	Mar	Jun	Sep	Dec
2003	3.08	2.31	2.58	0.00
2004	3.64	3.48	3.48	0.00
2005	3.31	4.05	4.15	3.95
2006	2.31	5.09	3.89	3.05
2007	2.20	3.53	1.25	2.15

Interim Dividends (Per Share)

Amt	Decl	Ex	Rec	Pay
1.43Q	4/13/2007	5/11/2007	5/15/2007	6/1/2007
1.43Q	7/18/2007	8/13/2007	8/15/2007	9/4/2007
1.43Q	10/11/2007	11/13/2007	11/15/2007	12/3/2007
1.43Q	1/14/2008	2/13/2008	2/15/2008	3/3/2008

Indicated Div: $5.72

Valuation Analysis

Forecast P/E	N/A
Market Cap	$2.0 Billion
Book Value	1.6 Billion
Price/Book	1.22
Price/Sales	1.16

Institutional Holding

No of Institutions	112
Shares	19,801,516
% Held	99.01

TRADING VOLUME (thousand shares)

Business Summary: Credit & Lending (MIC: 8.6 SIC: 6141 NAIC: 522298)

The Student Loan is engaged in the origination management and services of loans that are guaranteed under the Federal Family Education Loan (FFEL) Program, authorized by the US Department of Education through a trust agreement with Citibank, N.A. (CBNA), an indirect wholly owned subsidiary of Citigroup Inc. Co. is also eligible four types of FFEL Program loans: subsidized Federal Stafford, unsubsidized Federal Stafford, Federal PLUS and Federal Consolidation Loans. Co. originates loans through CBNA and holds private education loans that are not insured under the FFEL Program, including CitiAssist Loans and Private Consolidation loans. As of Dec 31 2007, Co. had total assets of $23.8 million.

Recent Developments: For the year ended Dec 31 2007, net income decreased 36.3% to US$182.7 million from US$286.8 million in the prior year. Net interest income decreased 5.6% to US$388.6 million from US$411.5 million in the prior year. Provision for loan losses was US$59.9 million versus US$26.2 million in the prior year, an increase of 129.0%. Non-interest income fell 39.5% to US$148.2 million from US$244.7 million, while non-interest expense advanced 8.3% to US$179.5 million.

Prospects: Looking ahead, Co. expects market conditions to remain challenging, resulting from the decrease in its securitization volume due to dislocation and illiquidity in the asset-backed securities and credit markets. As a result, gains on loans securitized under such conditions will be reduced significantly or possibly eliminated. Further, such conditions may increase Co.'s cost of funds under the Omnibus Credit Agreement with CBNA, which is negotiated on a borrowing by borrowing basis. In addition, Co. expects that losses from the uninsured private education loan portfolio will continue to increase during 2008 as a larger percentage of the portfolio moves into repayment.

Financial Data

(US$ in Thousands)	12/31/2007	12/31/2006	12/31/2005	12/31/2004	12/31/2003	12/31/2002	12/31/2001	12/31/2000
Earnings Per Share	9.13	14.34	15.45	14.25	10.61	8.77	6.77	5.24
Cash Flow Per Share	(8.97)	10.06	10.56	21.30	17.63	12.37	19.74	...
Tang Book Value Per Share	81.21	77.67	68.09	57.35	46.57	38.25	32.59	29.61
Dividends Per Share	5.590	4.980	4.320	3.600	3.080	2.800	2.800	2.400
Dividend Payout %	61.23	34.73	27.96	25.26	29.03	31.93	41.36	45.80
Income Statement								
Interest Income	1,563,811	1,624,563	1,300,849	939,187	833,593	974,590	1,151,632	1,093,728
Interest Expense	1,175,164	1,213,033	807,808	378,191	379,078	581,242	835,115	835,465
Net Interest Income	388,647	411,530	493,041	560,996	454,515	393,348	316,517	258,263
Provision for Losses	59,920	-26,170	13,157	7,989	9,277	11,214	7,324	5,587
Non-Interest Income	148,159	244,691	155,821	41,478	19,237	22,367	10,599	6,365
Non-Interest Expense	179,518	165,739	148,955	132,262	115,051	108,879	91,804	79,600
Income Before Taxes	297,368	464,292	486,750	462,223	349,424	295,622	227,988	179,441
Income Taxes	114,677	177,480	183,255	177,267	137,220	120,131	92,627	74,560
Net Income	182,691	286,812	308,960	284,956	212,204	175,491	135,361	104,881
Average Shares	20,000	20,000	20,000	20,000	20,000	20,000	20,000	20,000
Balance Sheet								
Net Loans & Leases	21,991,804	21,274,360	25,140,816	24,883,549	23,221,754	20,530,382	18,233,382	15,771,419
Total Assets	23,779,859	22,636,603	25,987,697	25,452,841	23,705,143	21,005,604	18,717,096	16,243,231
Total Liabilities	22,155,636	21,083,302	24,625,852	24,305,934	22,773,819	20,240,568	18,065,394	15,670,969
Stockholders' Equity	1,624,223	1,553,301	1,361,845	1,146,907	931,324	765,036	651,702	572,262
Shares Outstanding	20,000	20,000	20,000	20,000	20,000	20,000	20,000	20,000
Statistical Record								
Return on Assets %	0.79	1.18	1.20	...	0.95	0.88	0.77	...
Return on Equity %	11.50	19.68	24.63	...	25.02	24.77	22.12	...
Net Interest Margin %	24.85	25.33	37.90	59.73	54.52	40.36	27.48	23.61
Efficiency Ratio %	10.49	8.87	10.23	13.49	13.49	10.92	7.90	7.24
Price Range	214.62-110.00	239.99-161.70	241.50-162.50	186.69-130.31	146.00-90.91	101.15-74.90	83.20-52.50	56.00-37.19
P/E Ratio	23.51-12.05	16.74-11.28	15.63-10.52	13.10-9.14	13.76-8.57	11.53-8.54	12.29-7.75	10.69-7.10
Average Yield %	3.04	2.49	2.04	2.40	2.64	3.08	4.01	5.28

Address: 750 Washington Boulevard, Stamford, CT 06901 **Telephone:** 203-975-6320	**Web Site:** www.studentloan.com **Officers:** Bill Beckmann - Chmn. Sue F. Roberts - Pres.	**Auditors:** KPMG LLP **Investor Contact:** 203-975-6320 **Transfer Agents:** Citibank Stockholder Services, Providence, RI

SUNOCO, INC.

Exchange	Symbol	Price	52Wk Range	Yield	P/E
NYS	SUN	$52.47 (3/31/2008)	85.84-48.92	2.29	7.06

*7 Year Price Score 130.13 *NYSE Composite Index=100   *12 Month Price Score 90.31

TRADING VOLUME (thousand shares)

Interim Earnings (Per Share)

Qtr.	Mar	Jun	Sep	Dec
2003	0.56	0.52	0.70	0.23
2004	0.58	1.53	0.69	1.23
2005	0.83	1.75	2.39	2.11
2006	0.59	3.22	2.76	1.06
2007	1.44	4.20	1.81	(0.03)

Interim Dividends (Per Share)

Amt	Decl	Ex	Rec	Pay
0.275Q	7/3/2007	8/6/2007	8/8/2007	9/7/2007
0.275Q	10/4/2007	11/5/2007	11/7/2007	12/7/2007
0.275Q	1/3/2008	2/6/2008	2/8/2008	3/10/2008
0.30Q	2/7/2008	5/7/2008	5/9/2008	6/10/2008
		Indicated Div: $1.20		

Valuation Analysis   **Institutional Holding**

Forecast P/E	8.50	No of Institutions	
	(1/10/2007)	391	
Market Cap	$6.2 Billion	Shares	
Book Value	2.5 Billion	90,762,208	
Price/Book	2.44	% Held	
Price/Sales	0.14	74.80	

Business Summary: Oil and Gas (MIC: 14.2 SIC: 2911 NAIC: 324110)

Sunoco is a holding company, which through its subsidiaries, operates as a petroleum refiner and marketer, as well as a chemicals manufacturer with interests in logistics and cokemaking. Co.'s petroleum refining and marketing operations include the manufacture and marketing of various petroleum products, such as fuels, lubricants and petrochemicals. Co.'s chemical operations comprise the manufacturing, distribution and marketing of commodity and intermediate petrochemicals. Co.'s petroleum refining and marketing, and chemicals and logistics operations are conducted in the eastern half of the U.S., while its cokemaking operations are conducted in Virginia, Indiana, Ohio and Vitória, Brazil.

Recent Developments: For the year ended Dec 31 2007, net income decreased 9.0% to US$891.0 million from US$979.0 million in the prior year. Revenues were US$44.73 billion, up 15.5% from US$38.72 billion the year before. Direct operating expenses rose 16.9% to US$41.60 billion from US$35.58 billion in the comparable period the year before. Indirect operating expenses increased 10.6% to US$1.62 billion from US$1.47 billion in the equivalent prior-year period.

Prospects: For 2008, Co. estimates capital expenditures to be about $1.20 billion, with $406.0 million for income improvement projects, $365.0 million for base infrastructure, $151.0 million for turnarounds at its refineries, $273.0 million for its Philadelphia and Toledo refineries projects and $154.0 million for other environmental projects, including $73.0 million related to a project at its Tulsa refinery to enable the production of diesel fuel that meets new product requirements. Meanwhile, Co. is progressing towards the construction of an additional cokemaking facility and associated cogeneration power plant at its Haverhill site, which it expects to be operational in the second half of 2008.

Financial Data

(US$ in Thousands)	12/31/2007	12/31/2006	12/31/2005	12/31/2004	12/31/2003	12/31/2002	12/31/2001	12/31/2000
Earnings Per Share	7.43	7.59	7.08	4.04	2.02	(0.31)	2.42	2.41
Cash Flow Per Share	19.77	7.67	15.15	11.76	6.47	3.59	4.81	4.46
Tang Book Value Per Share	20.47	16.08	15.40	11.59	10.32	9.12	10.87	10.03
Dividends Per Share	1.075	0.950	0.750	0.575	0.512	0.500	0.500	0.500
Dividend Payout %	14.47	12.52	10.59	14.23	25.43	...	20.62	20.75
Income Statement								
Total Revenue	44,728,000	38,715,000	33,764,000	25,508,000	17,929,000	14,384,000	14,143,000	14,300,000
EBITDA	1,990,000	2,128,000	2,078,000	1,501,000	969,000	364,000	1,011,000	972,000
Income Before Taxes	1,409,000	1,580,000	1,580,000	995,000	495,000	(73,000)	587,000	596,000
Income Taxes	518,000	601,000	606,000	390,000	183,000	(26,000)	189,000	185,000
Net Income	891,000	979,000	974,000	605,000	312,000	(47,000)	398,000	422,000
Average Shares	120,000	129,000	137,500	149,800	155,000	152,400	164,000	175,000
Balance Sheet								
Current Assets	4,638,000	4,015,000	3,687,000	2,551,000	2,068,000	1,898,000	1,510,000	1,683,000
Total Assets	12,426,000	10,982,000	9,931,000	8,079,000	6,922,000	6,441,000	5,932,000	5,426,000
Current Liabilities	5,640,000	4,755,000	4,210,000	3,022,000	2,170,000	1,776,000	1,778,000	1,646,000
Long-Term Obligations	1,724,000	1,705,000	1,234,000	1,379,000	1,350,000	1,453,000	1,142,000	933,000
Total Liabilities	9,893,000	8,907,000	7,880,000	6,472,000	5,366,000	5,047,000	4,290,000	3,724,000
Stockholders' Equity	2,533,000	2,075,000	2,051,000	1,607,000	1,556,000	1,394,000	1,642,000	1,702,000
Shares Outstanding	117,606	121,300	133,149	138,655	150,760	152,878	151,058	169,664
Statistical Record								
Return on Assets %	7.61	9.36	10.82	8.04	4.67	N.M.	7.01	7.92
Return on Equity %	38.67	47.46	53.25	38.15	21.15	N.M.	23.80	26.24
EBITDA Margin %	4.45	5.50	6.15	5.88	5.40	2.53	7.15	6.80
Net Margin %	1.99	2.53	2.88	2.37	1.74	N.M.	2.81	2.95
Asset Turnover	3.82	3.70	3.75	3.39	2.68	2.33	2.49	2.69
Current Ratio	0.82	0.84	0.88	0.84	0.95	1.07	0.85	1.02
Debt to Equity	0.68	0.82	0.60	0.86	0.87	1.04	0.70	0.55
Price Range	85.84-57.12	96.21-58.64	83.82-38.33	42.20-25.40	26.10-14.99	20.95-13.65	21.25-14.69	16.94-11.16
P/E Ratio	11.55-7.69	12.68-7.73	11.84-5.41	10.44-6.29	12.92-7.42	...	8.78-6.07	7.03-4.63
Average Yield %	1.51	1.32	1.24	1.75	2.62	2.86	2.81	3.57

Address: 1735 Market Street, Suite LL, Philadelphia, PA 19103-7583	**Web Site:** www.Sunocoinc.com	**Auditors:** Ernst & Young LLP
Telephone: 215-977-3000	**Officers:** John G. Drosdick - Chmn., Pres., C.E.O.	**Investor Contact:** 215-977-6082
Fax: 215-977-3409	Thomas W. Hofmann - Sr. V.P., C.F.O.	**Transfer Agents:** Computershare Trust Company, N.A.

SUNTRUST BANKS, INC.

Exchange	Symbol	Price	52Wk Range	Yield	P/E	Div Acheiver
NYS	STI	$55.14 (3/31/2008)	90.61-54.23	5.59	12.12	22 Years

*7 Year Price Score 85.72 *NYSE Composite Index=100 *12 Month Price Score 88.05

Interim Earnings (Per Share)

Qtr.	Mar	Jun	Sep	Dec
2003	1.17	1.17	1.18	1.21
2004	1.26	1.29	1.30	1.25
2005	1.36	1.28	1.40	1.43
2006	1.46	1.49	1.47	(1.60)
2007	1.44	1.89	1.18	0.03

Interim Dividends (Per Share)

Amt	Decl	Ex	Rec	Pay
0.73Q	4/17/2007	5/30/2007	6/1/2007	6/15/2007
0.73Q	8/14/2007	8/29/2007	9/1/2007	9/14/2007
0.73Q	11/15/2007	11/28/2007	11/30/2007	12/14/2007
0.77Q	2/12/2008	2/27/2008	2/29/2008	3/14/2008

Indicated Div: $3.08 (Div. Reinv. Plan)

Valuation Analysis / **Institutional Holding**

Forecast P/E	12.30 (1/10/2007)	No of Institutions 565
Market Cap	$19.2 Billion	Shares
Book Value	18.1 Billion	207,800,480
Price/Book	1.06	% Held
Price/Sales	1.43	58.49

Business Summary: Commercial Banking (MIC: 8.1 SIC: 6021 NAIC: 522110)

SunTrust Banks is a financial services holding company. Through its SunTrust Bank subsidiary, Co. provides deposit, credit, and trust and investment services. Through its other subsidiaries, Co. provides banking, asset management, securities' brokerage, capital market services and credit-related insurance. Co. operates mainly within Florida, Georgia, Maryland, North Carolina, South Carolina, Tennessee, Virginia, and the District of Columbia. Co. conducted its businesses through five segments: Retail, Commercial, Corporate and Investment Banking, Mortgage, and Wealth and Investment Management. As of Dec 31 2007, Co. had total assets of $179.6 billion and total deposits of $117.8 billion.

Recent Developments: For the year ended Dec 31 2007, net income decreased 22.8% to US$1.63 billion from US$2.12 billion in the prior year. Net interest income increased 1.3% to US$4.72 billion from US$4.66 billion in the prior year. Provision for loan losses was US$664.9 million versus US$262.5 million in the prior year, an increase of 153.3%. Non-interest income fell 1.1% to US$3.43 billion from US$3.47 billion, while non-interest expense advanced 7.3% to US$5.23 billion.

Prospects: Co.'s recent operating results reflect the downturn in the consumer credit cycle, primarily the residential housing market. In addition, Co. is seeing lower market values of several investment products and loans as a result of the deterioration in the credit markets. Meanwhile, Co. continues to progress with its Excellence in Execution Efficiency and Productivity Program. Specifically, Co. expects to attain total cost savings of approximately $530.0 million during 2009 through initiatives identified in corporate real estate, supplier management, off-shoring, and process/organizational reviews.

Financial Data

(US$ in Thousands)	12/31/2007	12/31/2006	12/31/2005	12/31/2004	12/31/2003	12/31/2002	12/31/2001	12/31/2000
Earnings Per Share	4.55	2.82	5.47	5.19	4.73	4.66	4.72	4.30
Cash Flow Per Share	10.63	10.82	(13.14)	3.77	14.85	(5.54)	(4.49)	1.72
Tang Book Value Per Share	26.60	26.04	24.67	22.50	28.43	26.56	26.67	25.07
Dividends Per Share	2.920	2.440	2.200	2.000	1.800	1.720	1.600	1.480
Dividend Payout %	64.18	86.52	40.22	38.54	38.05	36.91	33.90	34.42
Income Statement								
Interest Income	10,035,920	9,792,020	7,731,309	5,218,382	4,768,842	5,135,197	6,279,574	6,845,419
Interest Expense	5,316,376	5,131,555	3,152,343	1,533,227	1,448,539	1,891,488	3,026,974	3,736,981
Net Interest Income	4,719,544	4,660,465	4,578,966	3,685,155	3,320,303	3,243,709	3,252,600	3,108,438
Provision for Losses	664,922	262,536	176,886	135,537	313,550	469,792	275,165	133,974
Non-Interest Income	3,428,684	3,468,372	3,155,044	2,604,446	2,303,001	2,391,675	2,155,823	1,773,625
Non Interest Expense	5,317,980	4,879,690	4,691,935	3,898,857	3,400,616	3,342,268	3,113,530	2,820,533
Income Before Taxes	2,249,529	2,986,441	2,866,395	2,257,026	1,909,138	1,823,324	2,019,720	1,919,556
Income Taxes	615,514	868,970	879,156	684,125	576,841	491,515	650,501	625,456
Net Income	1,634,015	2,117,471	1,987,239	1,572,901	1,332,297	1,331,809	1,375,537	1,294,100
Average Shares	352,688	362,802	363,454	303,309	281,434	286,052	291,584	300,956
Balance Sheet								
Net Loans & Leases	129,888,185	132,199,934	127,222,380	106,956,371	85,342,459	79,985,614	72,411,757	73,124,554
Total Assets	179,573,933	182,161,609	179,712,841	158,869,784	125,393,153	117,322,523	104,740,644	103,496,380
Total Deposits	117,842,650	124,021,629	122,053,178	103,361,251	81,189,519	79,706,628	67,536,422	69,533,337
Total Liabilities	161,521,415	164,348,003	162,825,446	142,882,885	115,661,987	108,553,027	96,381,076	95,257,172
Stockholders' Equity	18,052,518	17,813,606	16,887,395	15,986,899	9,731,166	8,769,496	8,359,568	8,239,208
Shares Outstanding	348,411	354,902	361,984	360,840	281,923	270,843	283,040	296,266
Statistical Record								
Return on Assets %	0.90	1.17	1.17	1.10	1.10	1.20	1.32	1.30
Return on Equity %	9.11	12.20	12.09	12.20	14.40	15.55	16.57	16.27
Net Interest Margin %	47.03	47.59	59.23	70.62	69.62	63.17	51.80	45.41
Efficiency Ratio %	38.75	36.80	43.10	49.84	48.09	44.40	36.91	32.82
Loans to Deposits	1.10	1.07	1.04	1.03	1.05	1.00	1.07	1.05
Price Range	90.61-61.09	85.45-70.34	75.73-65.80	76.41-61.80	71.55-51.56	70.00-51.79	71.81-58.10	68.81-42.56
P/E Ratio	19.91-13.43	30.30-24.94	13.84-12.03	14.72-11.91	15.13-10.90	15.02-11.11	15.21-12.31	16.00-9.90
Average Yield %	3.65	3.18	3.05	2.90	2.96	2.71	2.48	2.80

Address: 303 Peachtree Street, NE, Atlanta, GA 30308	**Web Site:** www.suntrust.com	**Auditors:** PricewaterhouseCoopers
Telephone: 404-588-7711	**Officers:** L. Phillip Humann - Chmn., Pres., C.E.O. James M. Wells III - Vice-Chmn., Pres., C.O.O.	**Investor Contact:** 404-658-4879
Fax: 404-827-6173		**Transfer Agents:** SunTrust Bank Atlanta, Atlanta, GA

SUPERIOR ENERGY SERVICES, INC.

Exchange	Symbol	Price	52Wk Range	Yield	P/E
NYS	SPN	$39.62 (3/31/2008)	45.14-31.95	N/A	11.62

*7 Year Price Score 163.70 *NYSE Composite Index=100 *12 Month Price Score 112.57

Interim Earnings (Per Share)

Qtr.	Mar	Jun	Sep	Dec
2003	0.10	0.11	0.12	0.08
2004	0.05	0.12	0.15	0.16
2005	0.22	0.32	0.12	0.20
2006	0.40	0.48	0.68	0.77
2007	0.78	0.85	0.91	0.88

Interim Dividends (Per Share)

No Dividends Paid

Valuation Analysis   **Institutional Holding**

Forecast P/E	7.81	No of Institutions
	(1/10/2007)	240
Market Cap	$3.2 Billion	Shares
Book Value	980.7 Million	73,500,704
Price/Book	3.26	% Held
Price/Sales	2.03	91.15

Business Summary: Oil and Gas (MIC: 14.2 SIC: 1389 NAIC: 213112)

Superior Energy Services provides oilfield services and equipment. Co.'s business segments include: Well Intervention Services, which provides well intervention services designed to stimulate oil and gas production; Rental Tools, which manufactures, sells and rents equipment for use with offshore and onshore oil and gas well drilling, completion, production and workover activities; Marine Services, owns and operates a fleet of liftboats, which are self-propelled, self-elevating work platforms with legs, cranes and living accommodations; as well as Oil and Gas Operations, in which Co. acquires mature oil and gas properties in the Gulf of Mexico through its subsidiary, SPN Resources, LLC.

Recent Developments: For the year ended Dec 31 2007, net income increased 49.3% to US$281.1 million from US$188.2 million in the prior year. Revenues were US$1.57 billion, up 43.8% from US$1.09 billion the year before. Operating income was US$465.8 million versus US$316.9 million in the prior year, an increase of 47.0%. Direct operating expenses rose 40.3% to US$698.1 million from US$497.5 million in the comparable period the year before. Indirect operating expenses increased 46.2% to US$408.5 million from US$279.4 million in the equivalent prior-year period.

Prospects: Going forward, Co. continues to implement its growth strategy of increasing its scope of services through both internal growth and strategic acquisitions as well as to continue its geographic diversification strategy. In detail, on Feb 26 2008, Co. announced a purchase agreement to sell 75.0% of its interest in SPN Resources LLC to Dynamic Offshore LLC for $165.0 million in cash. The transaction is expected to close during the first quarter of 2008. Meanwhile, on Jan 2 2008, Co. announced contracts with subsidiaries of BP plc, Chevron Corp., and Apache Corp. to decommission seven downed platforms and related well facilities located offshore Louisiana for a fixed sum of $750.0 million.

Financial Data
(US$ in Thousands)

	12/31/2007	12/31/2006	12/31/2005	12/31/2004	12/31/2003	12/31/2002	12/31/2001	12/31/2000
Earnings Per Share	3.41	2.32	0.85	0.47	0.41	0.30	0.77	0.28
Cash Flow Per Share	6.55	3.51	2.02	1.22	1.36	1.20	1.30	0.47
Tang Book Value Per Share	6.15	3.30	3.83	2.70	2.21	2.37	1.74	1.35
Income Statement								
Total Revenue	1,572,467	1,093,821	735,334	564,339	500,625	443,147	449,042	257,502
EBITDA	654,257	422,516	216,107	145,842	120,969	99,567	139,668	65,991
Income Before Taxes	432,492	291,846	106,031	56,908	48,822	35,587	86,758	33,179
Income Taxes	151,372	103,605	38,172	21,056	18,308	13,701	35,571	13,298
Net Income	281,120	188,241	67,859	35,852	30,514	21,886	53,776	18,324
Average Shares	82,389	81,289	79,735	75,900	74,648	73,872	69,592	65,921
Balance Sheet								
Current Assets	471,005	419,787	304,302	212,024	165,840	129,582	135,479	88,770
Total Assets	2,257,249	1,874,478	1,097,250	1,003,913	832,863	727,620	665,520	430,676
Current Liabilities	292,431	243,095	149,184	130,708	104,211	68,611	78,921	53,732
Long-Term Obligations	711,151	711,505	216,596	244,906	255,516	256,334	269,633	146,393
Total Liabilities	1,276,570	1,163,790	572,876	570,034	464,734	392,278	395,944	224,429
Stockholders' Equity	980,679	710,688	524,374	433,879	368,129	335,342	269,576	206,247
Shares Outstanding	80,671	80,617	79,499	76,766	74,099	73,819	69,322	67,803
Statistical Record								
Return on Assets %	13.61	12.67	6.46	3.89	3.91	3.14	9.81	5.13
Return on Equity %	33.24	30.48	14.16	8.92	8.68	7.24	22.60	11.15
EBITDA Margin %	41.61	38.63	29.39	25.84	24.16	22.47	31.10	25.63
Net Margin %	17.88	17.21	9.23	6.35	6.10	4.94	11.98	7.12
Asset Turnover	0.76	0.74	0.70	0.61	0.64	0.64	0.82	0.72
Current Ratio	1.61	1.73	2.04	1.62	1.59	1.89	1.72	1.65
Debt to Equity	0.73	1.00	0.41	0.56	0.69	0.76	1.00	0.71
Price Range	41.37-28.51	35.98-21.95	23.62-14.26	15.66-8.76	11.58-6.90	11.65-6.03	13.70-5.60	12.19-6.00
P/E Ratio	12.13-8.36	15.51-9.46	27.79-16.78	33.32-18.64	28.24-16.83	38.83-20.10	17.79-7.27	43.53-21.43

Address: 1105 Peters Road, Harvey, LA 70058	Web Site: www.superiorenergy.com	Auditors: KPMG LLP
Telephone: 504-362-4321	Officers: Terence E. Hall - Chmn., Pres., C.E.O.	Investor Contact: 504-362-4321
Fax: 504-362-4966	Kenneth Blanchard - Exec. V.P., C.O.O.	Transfer Agents: American Stock Transfer & Trust Company, New York, NY

SUPERVALU INC

Exchange	Symbol	Price	52Wk Range	Yield	P/E	Div Acheiver
NYS	SVU	$29.98 (3/31/2008)	49.67-26.25	2.27	11.44	35 Years

*7 Year Price Score 109.52 *NYSE Composite Index=100 *12 Month Price Score 79.48

Interim Earnings (Per Share)

Qtr.	Jun	Sep	Nov	Feb
2005-06	0.64	0.24	0.53	0.05

Qtr.	Jun	Aug	Nov	Feb
2006-07	0.57	0.61	0.54	0.57
2007-08	0.69	0.69	0.66	

Interim Dividends (Per Share)

Amt	Decl	Ex	Rec	Pay
0.165Q	4/18/2007	5/30/2007	6/1/2007	6/15/2007
0.17Q	8/8/2007	8/29/2007	9/3/2007	9/17/2007
0.17Q	10/5/2007	11/29/2007	12/3/2007	12/17/2007
0.17Q	2/6/2008	2/28/2008	3/3/2008	3/17/2008

Indicated Div: $0.68 (Div. Reinv. Plan)

Valuation Analysis   **Institutional Holding**

Forecast P/E	12.60	No of Institutions
	(1/10/2007)	346
Market Cap	$6.4 Billion	Shares
Book Value	5.8 Billion	181,666,848
Price/Book	1.10	% Held
Price/Sales	0.14	87.42

Business Summary: Retail - Food & Beverage (MIC: 5.3 SIC: 5141 NAIC: 424410)

SUPERVALU is a grocery company operating in two segments of the grocery industry, Retail food stores, and Supply chain services. As of Feb 24 2007, Co. operated 2,478 stores, including 858 licensed limited assortment stores, under several banners including Albertsons, Save-A-Lot, Shaw's Supermarkets, Jewel-Osco, Acme Markets, Shoppers Food & Pharmacy, Cub Foods, Farm Fresh, Lucky, Shop 'n Save, Scott's, Star Markets, Bristol Farms, bigg's, Hornbacher's and Sunflower Market. In addition, Co. provides supply chain services, such as food distribution and related logistics support services primarily across the U.S. retail grocery channel.

Recent Developments: For the quarter ended Dec 1 2007, net income increased 24.8% to US$141.0 million from US$113.0 million in the year-earlier quarter. Revenues were US$10.21 billion, down 4.2% from US$10.66 billion the year before. Operating income was US$395.0 million versus US$367.0 million in the prior-year quarter, an increase of 7.6%. Direct operating expenses declined 3.4% to US$7.94 billion from US$8.22 billion in the comparable period the year before. Indirect operating expenses decreased 9.5% to US$1.88 billion from US$2.07 billion in the equivalent prior-year period.

Prospects: For the fiscal year ending Feb 23 2008, Co. now anticipates earnings of $2.71 to $2.77 per diluted share. Specifically, Co.'s updated earnings guidance assumes are based on several factors, including, but not limited to, projected net sales of about $44.00 billion, forecasted identical store sales growth, excluding fuel for the combined retail network, of 0.5% to 1.0% and sales attrition, excluding new business, in the traditional food distribution business to be about 4.0% to 5.0%. Co.'s guidance also assumes expected store development plans of about 30 standard size and 55 limited assortment stores while major and minor remodels are estimated at about 125 and 25 stores, respectively.

Financial Data
(US$ in Thousands)

	9 Mos	6 Mos	3 Mos	02/24/2007	02/25/2006	02/26/2005	02/28/2004	02/22/2003
Earnings Per Share	2.62	2.50	2.42	2.32	1.46	2.71	2.07	1.91
Cash Flow Per Share	6.93	6.59	4.90	4.25	4.97	5.88	6.11	4.30
Tang Book Value Per Share	N.M.	N.M.	N.M.	N.M.	7.37	6.52	4.84	3.24
Dividends Per Share	0.670	0.665	0.660	0.655	0.477	0.603	0.578	0.565
Dividend Payout %	25.61	26.63	27.33	28.23	32.71	22.23	27.90	29.58
Income Statement								
Total Revenue	33,661,000	23,450,000	13,292,000	37,406,000	19,863,599	19,543,240	20,209,679	19,160,368
EBITDA	2,055,000	1,424,000	790,000	2,146,000	745,836	1,018,685	902,987	866,999
Depn & Amortn	788,000	552,000	324,000	...	...	...	...	...
Income Before Taxes	717,000	486,000	243,000	747,000	329,148	600,864	454,880	408,004
Income Taxes	280,000	190,000	95,000	295,000	122,979	215,041	174,742	150,962
Net Income	437,000	296,000	148,000	452,000	206,169	385,823	280,138	257,042
Average Shares	214,000	216,000	216,000	196,000	145,699	144,924	135,418	134,877
Balance Sheet								
Current Assets	4,571,000	4,276,000	4,361,000	4,460,000	2,168,040	2,126,500	2,037,092	1,647,366
Total Assets	21,356,000	21,065,000	21,140,000	21,702,000	6,038,271	6,278,342	6,152,938	5,896,245
Current Liabilities	4,723,000	4,659,000	4,458,000	4,705,000	1,506,669	1,631,591	1,871,972	1,525,307
Long-Term Obligations	8,781,000	8,590,000	8,936,000	9,192,000	1,405,971	1,578,867	1,633,721	2,019,658
Total Liabilities	15,558,000	15,375,000	15,485,000	16,396,000	3,418,818	3,767,781	3,943,364	3,887,005
Stockholders' Equity	5,798,000	5,690,000	5,655,000	5,306,000	2,619,453	2,510,561	2,209,574	2,009,240
Shares Outstanding	212,000	211,000	213,000	209,000	136,437	135,478	134,760	133,688
Statistical Record								
Return on Assets %	2.54	2.44	2.33	3.27	3.36	6.22	4.57	4.40
Return on Equity %	10.12	9.77	9.50	11.44	8.06	16.39	13.07	13.13
EBITDA Margin %	6.10	6.07	5.94	5.74	3.75	5.21	4.47	4.52
Net Margin %	1.30	1.26	1.11	1.21	1.04	1.97	1.39	1.34
Asset Turnover	2.00	2.04	2.04	2.70	3.23	3.15	3.30	3.28
Current Ratio	0.97	0.92	0.98	0.95	1.44	1.30	1.09	1.08
Debt to Equity	1.51	1.51	1.58	1.73	0.54	0.63	0.74	1.01
Price Range	49.67-34.12	49.67-29.39	48.64-26.21	38.95-26.21	35.80-29.85	34.88-25.95	29.43-12.60	30.50-14.32
P/E Ratio	18.96-13.02	19.87-11.76	20.10-10.83	16.79-11.30	24.52-20.45	12.87-9.58	14.22-6.09	15.97-7.50
Average Yield %	1.65	1.70	1.85	2.07	1.46	1.99	2.55	2.63

Address: 11840 Valley View Road, Eden Prairie, MN 55344	**Web Site:** www.supervalu.com	**Auditors:** KPMG LLP
Telephone: 952-828-4000	**Officers:** Jeffrey Noddle - Chmn., C.E.O. Michael L. Jackson - Pres., C.O.O.	**Investor Contact:** 952-828-4000
Fax: 952-828-8998		**Transfer Agents:** Wells Fargo Shareowner Services, St. Paul, MN

SYBASE, INC.

Exchange	Symbol	Price	52Wk Range	Yield	P/E
NYS	SY	$26.30 (3/31/2008)	28.60-22.07	N/A	16.34

*7 Year Price Score 106.59 *NYSE Composite Index=100 *12 Month Price Score 114.52

Interim Earnings (Per Share)

Qtr.	Mar	Jun	Sep	Dec
2003	0.13	0.15	0.23	0.38
2004	0.13	0.13	0.19	0.25
2005	0.14	0.17	0.30	0.30
2006	0.19	0.29	0.27	0.28
2007	0.16	0.28	0.37	0.80

Interim Dividends (Per Share)

No Dividends Paid

Valuation Analysis / Institutional Holding

Forecast P/E	14.62	No of Institutions
	(1/10/2007)	208
Market Cap	$2.3 Billion	Shares
Book Value	930.8 Million	94,516,848
Price/Book	2.46	% Held
Price/Sales	2.24	N/A

Business Summary: IT & Technology (MIC: 10.2 SIC: 7372 NAIC: 511210)

Sybase is a global enterprise software and services company, primarily focused on managing and mobilizing information from the data-center to the point of action. Co. provides open, cross-platform applications that are designed to securely deliver information anytime, anywhere. Co. operates in three business segments: Infrastructure Platform Group, which focuses on enterprise class database servers, integration and development products; iAnywhere Solutions, which provides mobile database and mobile enterprise solutions; and Sybase 365, which provides global services for mobile messaging interoperability and the management and distribution of mobile content.

Recent Developments: For the year ended Dec 31 2007, net income increased 56.6% to US$148.9 million from US$95.1 million in the prior year. Revenues were US$1.03 billion, up 17.0% from US$876.2 million the year before. Operating income was US$168.6 million versus US$133.8 million in the prior year, an increase of 26.0%. Direct operating expenses rose 36.8% to US$293.5 million from US$214.6 million in the comparable period the year before. Indirect operating expenses increased 6.8% to US$563.5 million from US$527.8 million in the equivalent prior-year period.

Prospects: For full-year 2008, Co. is projecting earnings per share of $1.50 to $1.55, with total revenue of $1.08 billion to $1.09 billion driven by the increasing acceptance of its IQ product and the Data Integration Suite. Further, Co. expects its inter-carrier messaging business revenue will be driven by continuing growth in Short Messaging Services and Multimedia Messaging Services traffic levels, and the acquisition of new carriers, mainly in new territories. Meanwhile, reflecting further growth in the application messaging industry, Co. plans to expand its data center capacity and disaster-recovery capabilities, add connectors from its new customers to its network and develop new services.

Financial Data

(US$ in Thousands)	12/31/2007	12/31/2006	12/31/2005	12/31/2004	12/31/2003	12/31/2002	12/31/2001	12/31/2000
Earnings Per Share	1.61	1.03	0.92	0.69	0.89	(0.95)	(0.27)	0.78
Cash Flow Per Share	2.82	2.40	1.88	1.84	2.13	1.65	0.98	1.95
Tang Book Value Per Share	2.21	0.90	3.39	4.33	5.10	3.49	2.91	3.53
Income Statement								
Total Revenue	1,025,530	876,163	818,695	788,536	778,062	829,861	926,086	960,458
EBITDA	211,331	164,255	154,908	123,597	143,766	99,435	79,685	165,959
Income Before Taxes	189,952	161,317	136,715	100,966	118,095	71,209	978	107,586
Income Taxes	41,102	66,253	51,132	33,016	30,829	33,428	26,500	35,461
Net Income	148,850	95,064	85,583	67,950	87,266	(94,669)	(25,522)	72,125
Average Shares	92,598	92,251	93,257	98,001	97,582	99,584	94,592	92,150
Balance Sheet								
Current Assets	1,027,726	871,561	933,950	668,882	644,482	504,619	514,378	574,113
Total Assets	1,913,483	1,787,550	1,570,614	1,183,522	1,151,356	992,749	1,133,242	915,040
Current Liabilities	422,998	416,418	360,703	378,645	389,728	396,705	405,807	416,627
Long-Term Obligations	460,000	460,000	460,000	...	...	...	...	...
Total Liabilities	982,673	944,419	871,784	426,966	409,887	412,375	416,723	424,288
Stockholders' Equity	930,810	843,131	698,830	756,556	741,469	580,374	716,519	490,752
Shares Outstanding	87,210	91,281	90,531	95,518	98,525	94,660	98,725	87,656
Statistical Record								
Return on Assets %	8.04	5.66	6.21	5.80	8.14	N.M.	N.M.	8.71
Return on Equity %	16.78	12.33	11.76	9.05	13.20	N.M.	N.M.	17.40
EBITDA Margin %	20.61	18.75	18.92	15.67	18.48	11.98	8.60	17.28
Net Margin %	14.51	10.85	10.45	8.62	11.22	N.M.	N.M.	7.51
Asset Turnover	0.55	0.52	0.59	0.67	0.73	0.78	0.90	1.16
Current Ratio	2.43	2.09	2.59	1.77	1.65	1.27	1.27	1.38
Debt to Equity	0.49	0.55	0.66	...	...	...	...	...
Price Range	28.60-22.07	26.00-19.40	23.82-17.12	22.66-12.80	22.10-11.49	19.00-9.35	25.88-8.58	29.75-16.50
P/E Ratio	17.76-13.71	25.24-18.83	25.89-18.61	32.84-18.55	24.83-12.91	...	...	38.14-21.15

Address: One Sybase Drive, Dublin, CA 94568-7902	Web Site: www.sybase.com	Auditors: ERNST & YOUNG LLP
Telephone: 925-236-5000	Officers: John S. Chen - Chmn., Pres., C.E.O. Thomas Volk - Exec. V.P., Worldwide Field Organization	Investor Contact: 510-922-3500
Fax: 925-236-4468		Transfer Agents: American Stock Transfer and Trust Co.

SYNOVUS FINANCIAL CORP.

Exchange	Symbol	Price	52Wk Range	Yield	P/E	Div Acheiver
NYS	SNV	$11.06 (3/31/2008)	14.57-9.86	6.15	6.91	31 Years

*7 Year Price Score 85.39   *NYSE Composite Index=100   *12 Month Price Score 105.26

TRADING VOLUME (thousand shares)

Interim Earnings (Per Share)

Qtr.	Mar	Jun	Sep	Dec
2003	0.30	0.32	0.33	0.34
2004	0.34	0.34	0.35	0.38
2005	0.37	0.41	0.43	0.44
2006	0.43	0.47	0.47	0.53
2007	0.45	0.49	0.41	0.25

Interim Dividends (Per Share)

Amt	Decl	Ex	Rec	Pay
0.205Q	9/5/2007	9/18/2007	9/20/2007	10/1/2007
0.00Q	11/30/2007	1/2/2008	12/18/2007	12/31/2007
0.205Q	11/30/2007	12/14/2007	12/18/2007	1/2/2008
0.17Q	3/10/2008	3/18/2008	3/20/2008	4/1/2008

Indicated Div: $0.68 (Div. Reinv. Plan)

Valuation Analysis

		Institutional Holding	
Forecast P/E	14.28	No of Institutions	
	(1/10/2007)	309	
Market Cap	$3.8 Billion	Shares	
Book Value	3.4 Billion	166,883,328	
Price/Book	1.06	% Held	
Price/Sales	1.39	51.10	

Business Summary: Commercial Banking (MIC: 8.1 SIC: 6021 NAIC: 522110)

Synovus Financial, with assets of $33.02 billion as of Dec 31 2007, is a registered bank-holding company. Co. provides integrated financial services including banking, financial management, insurance, mortgage and leasing services via 37 wholly-owned bank subsidiaries in five southeastern states as of Dec 31 2007. Co.'s bank subsidiaries provide commercial banking services, including commercial, financial, agricultural and real estate loans, and retail banking services, including demand and savings deposits; making individual, consumer, installment and mortgage loans; safe deposit; leasing; automated banking; automated fund transfers; Internet based banking; and bank credit card services.

Recent Developments: For the year ended Dec 31 2007, income from continuing operations decreased 17.4% to US$342.9 million from US$415.1 million a year earlier. Net income decreased 14.7% to US$526.3 million from US$616.9 million in the prior year. Net interest income increased 2.1% to US$1.15 billion from US$1.13 billion in the prior year. Provision for loan losses was US$170.2 million versus US$75.1 million in the prior year, an increase of 126.5%. Non-interest income rose 8.2% to US$389.0 million from US$359.4 million, while non-interest expense advanced 9.9% to US$840.1 million.

Prospects: Co. is seeing continued weakness in its residential construction and residential development portfolios. Accordingly, Co. plans to take actions to manage these portfolios, such as increasing special asset resources and regional credit support. Meanwhile, on Dec 21 2007, Co. announced plans to merge its Naples-based First Florida Bank into Synovus Bank of Tampa Bay, FL. Co. expects the transaction to enhance its ability to serve customers and expend the growth potential on the west coast of Florida. The newly expanded Synovus Bank of Tampa Bay, with a total asset of $1.68 billion, should continue providing a range of banking products, as well as mortgage, insurance and investments services.

Financial Data

(US$ in Thousands)	12/31/2007	12/31/2006	12/31/2005	12/31/2004	12/31/2003	12/31/2002	12/31/2001	12/31/2000
Earnings Per Share	1.60	1.90	1.04	1.41	1.28	1.21	1.03	0.92
Cash Flow Per Share	2.04	2.43	1.99	2.60	2.40	2.43	0.61	1.60
Tang Book Value Per Share	8.77	7.96	6.44	5.75	5.23	5.32	5.75	4.98
Dividends Per Share	0.820	0.780	0.730	0.693	0.660	0.590	0.510	0.440
Dividend Payout %	51.25	41.05	44.51	49.16	51.56	48.76	48.57	47.83
Income Statement								
Interest Income	2,238,404	2,016,466	1,496,225	1,159,070	1,061,492	1,055,040	1,130,888	1,097,805
Interest Expense	1,089,456	882,592	527,378	298,341	298,428	337,536	501,097	535,473
Net Interest Income	1,148,948	1,133,874	968,847	860,679	763,064	717,504	629,791	562,332
Provision for Losses	170,208	75,148	82,532	75,319	71,777	65,327	51,673	44,341
Non-Interest Income	389,028	2,133,386	1,918,479	1,321,011	1,369,329	1,234,822	937,697	833,513
Non-Interest Expense	840,094	2,170,677	1,943,391	1,588,366	1,422,143	1,299,470	1,005,963	923,274
Income Before Taxes	527,671	973,533	824,022	689,281	611,501	563,880	489,993	411,738
Income Taxes	184,739	356,616	307,576	252,248	222,576	198,533	178,377	149,178
Net Income	526,305	616,917	516,446	437,033	388,925	365,347	311,616	262,557
Average Shares	329,863	324,232	314,815	310,330	304,928	301,197	295,850	286,882
Balance Sheet								
Net Loans & Leases	26,130,972	24,340,093	21,102,735	19,214,651	16,238,855	14,264,068	12,247,148	10,604,020
Total Assets	33,018,452	31,854,773	27,620,672	25,050,178	21,632,629	19,036,246	16,657,947	14,908,092
Total Deposits	24,959,816	24,294,447	20,784,365	18,577,468	15,941,609	13,928,834	12,146,198	11,161,710
Total Liabilities	29,576,862	27,909,414	24,474,370	22,241,605	19,245,752	16,878,294	14,864,363	13,410,031
Stockholders' Equity	3,441,590	3,708,650	2,949,329	2,641,289	2,245,039	2,040,853	1,694,946	1,417,171
Shares Outstanding	329,867	325,552	312,639	309,974	302,090	300,397	294,673	284,642
Statistical Record								
Return on Assets %	1.62	2.07	1.96	1.87	1.91	2.05	1.97	1.91
Return on Equity %	14.72	18.53	18.48	17.84	18.15	19.56	20.03	19.81
Net Interest Margin %	51.33	56.23	64.75	74.26	71.89	68.01	55.69	51.22
Efficiency Ratio %	31.97	52.30	56.91	59.27	58.50	56.75	48.63	47.81
Loans to Deposits	1.05	1.00	1.02	1.03	1.02	1.02	1.01	0.95
Price Range	14.60-9.86	13.55-11.27	13.10-11.58	12.65-9.91	12.70-7.57	13.88-7.35	15.07-10.07	11.89-6.34
P/E Ratio	9.13-6.16	7.13-5.93	7.99-7.06	8.97-7.03	9.92-5.91	11.47-6.08	14.35-9.59	12.92-6.89
Average Yield %	6.34	6.32	5.94	6.16	6.57	5.72	4.16	5.15

Address: 901 Front Avenue, P.O. Box 120, Columbus, GA 31902	Web Site: www.synovus.com	Auditors: KPMG LLP
Telephone: 706-649-2401	Officers: James H. Blanchard - Chmn. Richard E. Anthony - Pres., C.E.O.	Investor Contact: 706-649-5220
Fax: 706-641-6555		Transfer Agents: State Street Bank and Trust Company, Boston, MA

SYSCO CORP.

Exchange	Symbol	Price	52Wk Range	Yield	P/E	Div Acheiver
NYS	SYY	$29.02 (3/31/2008)	35.84-27.48	3.03	17.07	31 Years

*7 Year Price Score 80.95   *NYSE Composite Index=100   *12 Month Price Score 96.95

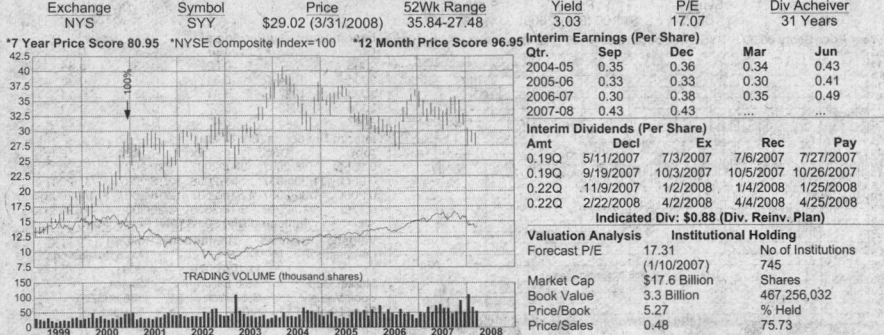

Interim Earnings (Per Share)

Qtr.	Sep	Dec	Mar	Jun
2004-05	0.35	0.36	0.34	0.43
2005-06	0.33	0.33	0.30	0.41
2006-07	0.30	0.38	0.35	0.49
2007-08	0.43	0.43	...	...

Interim Dividends (Per Share)

Amt	Decl	Ex	Rec	Pay
0.19Q	5/11/2007	7/3/2007	7/6/2007	7/27/2007
0.19Q	9/19/2007	10/3/2007	10/5/2007	10/26/2007
0.22Q	11/9/2007	1/2/2008	1/4/2008	1/25/2008
0.22Q	2/22/2008	4/2/2008	4/4/2008	4/25/2008

Indicated Div: $0.88 (Div. Reinv. Plan)

Valuation Analysis / Institutional Holding

Forecast P/E	17.31 (1/10/2007)	No of Institutions	745
Market Cap	$17.6 Billion	Shares	467,256,032
Book Value	3.3 Billion	% Held	75.73
Price/Book	5.27		
Price/Sales	0.48		

Business Summary: Retail - Food & Beverage (MIC: 5.3 SIC: 5141 NAIC: 424410)

Sysco is engaged in the distribution of food and related products to the foodservice or 'food-prepared-away-from-home' industry. As of June 30 2007, Co. provided these services to about 391,000 customers, including restaurants, healthcare and educational facilities, lodging establishments and other foodservice customers. Co.'s Broadline segment distributes a line of food products and non-food products to both traditional and chain restaurant customers. Co.'s SYGMA segment distributes a line of food products and non-food products to certain chain restaurant customer locations. The Other segment includes Co.'s specialty produce, custom-cut meat and lodging industry products segments.

Recent Developments: For the quarter ended Dec 29 2007, net income increased 7.1% to US$264.1 million from US$246.5 million in the year-earlier quarter. Revenues were US$9.24 billion, up 7.8% from US$8.57 billion the year before. Direct operating expenses rose 8.0% to US$7.47 billion from US$6.92 billion in the comparable period the year before. Indirect operating expenses increased 7.1% to US$1.32 billion from US$1.23 billion in the equivalent prior-year period.

Prospects: Co.'s near-term outlook appears to be constructive as it continues to implement its business initiatives. Specifically, Co. is progressing towards its National Supply Chain project, which entails the utilization of redistribution centers (RDC). As part of this project, Co. is constructing its second RDC site in Alachua, FL, which is expected to be operational in the fourth fiscal quarter ended June 30 2008. Meanwhile, Co. estimates that fuel costs for the second half of fiscal 2008 will be higher over the prior year by $30.0 million to $40.0 million, based upon both ongoing market prices for diesel and the cost agreed to in its forward fuel purchase agreements currently in place.

Financial Data

(US$ in Thousands)	6 Mos	3 Mos	06/30/2007	07/01/2006	07/02/2005	07/03/2004	06/28/2003	06/29/2002
Earnings Per Share	1.70	1.65	1.60	1.36	1.47	1.37	1.18	1.01
Cash Flow Per Share	2.08	2.33	2.28	1.81	1.88	1.82	2.12	1.64
Tang Book Value Per Share	3.03	2.98	2.99	2.67	2.35	2.11	1.68	1.85
Dividends Per Share	0.760	0.740	0.720	0.640	0.560	0.480	0.400	0.320
Dividend Payout %	44.60	44.76	45.00	47.06	38.10	35.04	33.90	31.68
Income Statement								
Total Revenue	18,645,349	9,405,844	35,042,075	32,628,438	30,281,914	29,335,403	26,140,337	23,350,504
EBITDA	1,095,660	548,121	2,088,776	1,849,108	1,906,116	1,828,619	1,605,763	1,442,018
Depn & Amortn	180,640	90,456	...	...	...	...	...	...
Income Before Taxes	859,734	431,294	1,621,215	1,394,946	1,525,436	1,475,144	1,260,387	1,100,870
Income Taxes	328,597	164,305	620,139	548,906	563,979	567,930	482,099	421,083
Net Income	531,137	266,989	1,001,076	855,325	961,457	907,214	778,288	679,787
Average Shares	614,620	617,108	626,366	628,800	653,157	661,919	661,535	673,445
Balance Sheet								
Current Assets	4,884,480	5,029,827	4,675,546	4,399,694	4,001,786	3,851,411	3,629,534	3,185,289
Total Assets	9,952,827	10,017,944	9,518,931	8,992,025	8,267,902	7,847,632	6,936,521	5,989,753
Current Liabilities	3,268,683	3,374,745	3,415,089	3,226,403	3,457,570	3,126,634	2,701,129	2,239,357
Long-Term Obligations	2,135,547	1,969,804	1,758,227	1,627,127	956,177	1,231,493	1,249,467	1,176,307
Total Liabilities	6,622,764	6,720,489	6,240,531	5,939,741	5,509,063	5,283,126	4,738,990	3,857,234
Stockholders' Equity	3,330,063	3,297,455	3,278,400	3,052,284	2,758,839	2,564,506	2,197,531	2,132,519
Shares Outstanding	605,048	608,917	611,840	618,895	628,567	636,535	643,657	653,540
Statistical Record								
Return on Assets %	11.01	10.65	10.85	9.94	11.96	12.07	12.08	11.90
Return on Equity %	32.48	31.97	31.71	29.52	36.22	37.49	36.05	31.85
EBITDA Margin %	5.88	5.83	5.96	5.67	6.29	6.23	6.14	6.18
Net Margin %	2.85	2.84	2.86	2.62	3.18	3.09	2.98	2.91
Asset Turnover	3.80	3.71	3.80	3.79	3.77	3.90	4.06	4.09
Current Ratio	1.49	1.49	1.37	1.36	1.16	1.23	1.34	1.42
Debt to Equity	0.64	0.60	0.54	0.53	0.35	0.48	0.57	0.55
Price Range	36.72-30.30	36.95-30.30	36.95-26.91	37.20-29.25	38.20-29.89	40.90-28.75	32.34-21.81	30.15-22.22
P/E Ratio	21.60-17.82	22.39-18.36	23.09-16.82	27.35-21.51	25.99-20.33	29.85-20.99	27.41-18.48	29.85-22.00
Average Yield %	2.28	2.19	2.17	1.67	1.64	1.38	1.39	1.17

Address: 1390 Enclave Parkway, Houston, TX 77077-2099
Telephone: 281-584-1390
Fax: 281-584-2880

Web Site: www.sysco.com
Officers: Richard J. Schnieders - Chmn., Pres., C.E.O.
Larry J. Accardi - Exec. V.P., Merchandising Services & Multi-Unit Sales

Auditors: Ernst & Young LLP
Investor Contact: 281-584-1308
Transfer Agents: EquiServe Trust Company, N.A., Providence, RI

TALBOTS, INC.

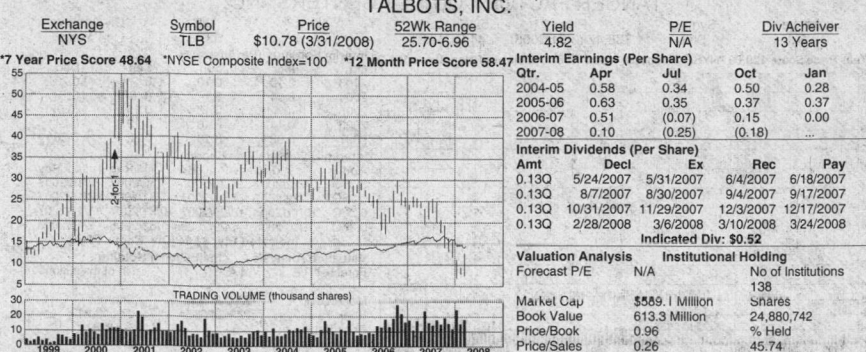

Exchange	Symbol	Price	52Wk Range	Yield	P/E	Div Achiever
NYS	TLB	$10.78 (3/31/2008)	25.70-6.96	4.82	N/A	13 Years

*7 Year Price Score 48.64 *NYSE Composite Index=100 *12 Month Price Score 58.47

Interim Earnings (Per Share)

Qtr.	Apr	Jul	Oct	Jan
2004-05	0.58	0.34	0.50	0.28
2005-06	0.63	0.35	0.37	0.37
2006-07	0.51	(0.07)	0.15	0.00
2007-08	0.10	(0.25)	(0.18)	...

Interim Dividends (Per Share)

Amt	Decl	Ex	Rec	Pay
0.13Q	5/24/2007	5/31/2007	6/4/2007	6/18/2007
0.13Q	8/7/2007	8/30/2007	9/4/2007	9/17/2007
0.13Q	10/31/2007	11/29/2007	12/3/2007	12/17/2007
0.13Q	2/28/2008	3/6/2008	3/10/2008	3/24/2008

Indicated Div: $0.52

Valuation Analysis | **Institutional Holding**

Forecast P/E	N/A	No of Institutions
		138
Market Cap	$589.1 Million	Shares
Book Value	613.3 Million	24,880,742
Price/Book	0.96	% Held
Price/Sales	0.26	45.74

TRADING VOLUME (thousand shares)

Business Summary: Retail - Apparel and Accessory Stores (MIC: 5.8 SIC: 5621 NAIC: 448120)

Talbots is an international specialty retailer and cataloger of women's, children's, and men's apparel, accessories and shoes sold under the Talbots and J. Jill brand names. As of Feb 3 2007, Co. operated 1,364 stores in 47 states, the District of Columbia, Canada and the U.K., with 1,125 stores under the Talbots brand name and 239 stores under the J. Jill brand name. Co.'s 1,364 stores consisted of the following: 554 Talbots Misses stores, 297 Talbots Petites stores, 39 Talbots Accessories & Shoes stores, 67 Talbots Kids stores, 131 Talbots Woman stores, 12 Talbots Mens stores, two Talbots Collection stores, 23 Talbots Outlet stores, 231 J. Jill stores, and eight J. Jill Outlet stores.

Recent Developments: For the quarter ended Nov 3 2007, net loss amounted to US$9.4 million versus net income of US$8.1 million in the year-earlier quarter. Revenues were US$556.0 million, down 2.2% from US$568.6 million the year before. Operating loss was US$8.3 million versus an income of US$20.9 million in the prior-year quarter. Direct operating expenses rose 2.1% to US$366.3 million from US$358.7 million in the comparable period the year before. Indirect operating expenses increased 4.8% to US$198.0 million from US$189.1 million in the equivalent prior-year period.

Prospects: On Apr 1 2008, Co. announced its strategic plan for long-term growth. Components of the plan include adding about 35 new Talbots Womans stores over the next 5 years; higher Accessories segment penetration; while tightening its shoe assortment; clearly differentiating its Collection offering; pursuing Premium Outlet opportunities; and improving J. Jill brand's existing store network through improved merchandise, prospecting to increase customer acquisition and marketing to build greater brand awareness. For fiscal 2008, Co. sees Talbots brand same store sales decreasing 1.0% and the J. Jill brand growing 1.0%, with earnings from continuing operations of $0.47 to $0.52 per diluted share.

Financial Data

(US$ in Thousands)	9 Mos	6 Mos	3 Mos	02/03/2007	01/28/2006	01/29/2005	01/31/2004	02/01/2003
Earnings Per Share	(0.33)	(0.01)	0.18	0.59	1.72	1.70	1.81	2.01
Cash Flow Per Share	2.39	2.81	2.48	2.51	4.01	2.83	3.75	3.80
Tang Book Value Per Share	2.33	2.54	2.79	2.76	9.66	8.82	8.91	7.93
Dividends Per Share	0.520	0.520	0.520	0.510	0.470	0.430	0.390	0.350
Dividend Payout %	...	...	281.67	86.44	27.33	25.29	21.55	17.41
Income Statement								
Total Revenue	1,701,899	1,145,887	573,556	2,231,033	1,808,606	1,697,843	1,624,339	1,595,325
EBITDA	95,030	71,139	50,593	196,569	250,692	229,752	237,097	255,180
Depn & Amortn	98,267	66,046	33,279	...	...	...	...	...
Income Before Taxes	(29,558)	(12,420)	8,031	50,522	149,042	140,005	167,493	193,214
Income Taxes	(12,095)	(4,344)	2,791	18,946	55,891	44,639	62,810	72,455
Net Income	(17,463)	(8,076)	5,240	31,576	93,151	95,366	104,683	120,759
Average Shares	53,032	52,980	53,908	53,485	54,103	56,252	57,901	60,191
Balance Sheet								
Current Assets	723,772	615,258	679,151	692,409	620,661	527,397	496,154	435,898
Total Assets	1,742,314	1,643,629	1,720,118	1,748,688	1,146,144	1,062,130	958,392	871,925
Current Liabilities	481,854	343,605	381,411	429,800	244,457	202,638	166,142	147,941
Long-Term Obligations	328,542	348,705	369,012	389,174	100,000	100,000	100,000	100,000
Total Liabilities	1,129,036	1,016,757	1,076,739	1,105,377	519,176	473,542	342,266	304,249
Stockholders' Equity	613,278	626,872	643,379	643,311	626,968	588,588	616,126	567,676
Shares Outstanding	54,645	54,329	54,417	53,999	53,359	54,123	56,675	57,505
Statistical Record								
Return on Assets %	N.M.	N.M.	0.58	2.15	8.46	9.47	11.47	14.22
Return on Equity %	N.M.	N.M.	1.50	4.89	15.37	15.88	17.73	21.33
EBITDA Margin %	5.58	6.21	8.82	8.81	13.86	13.53	14.60	16.00
Net Margin %	N.M.	N.M.	0.91	1.42	5.15	5.62	6.44	7.57
Asset Turnover	1.31	1.39	1.39	1.52	1.64	1.69	1.78	1.88
Current Ratio	1.50	1.79	1.78	1.61	2.54	2.60	2.99	2.95
Debt to Equity	0.54	0.56	0.57	0.60	0.16	0.17	0.16	0.18
Price Range	26.89-13.66	30.00-19.58	30.00-17.38	30.00-17.38	34.85-24.52	39.81-24.79	38.15-23.02	41.02-22.90
P/E Ratio	...	...	166.67-96.56	50.85-29.46	20.26-14.26	23.42-14.58	21.08-12.72	20.41-11.39
Average Yield %	2.30	2.15	2.19	2.12	1.59	1.38	1.23	1.09

Address: One Talbots Drive, Hingham, MA 02043-1586
Telephone: 781-749-7600
Fax: 781-741-4369

Web Site: www.talbots.com
Officers: Arnold B. Zetcher - Chmn., Pres., C.E.O. Harold B. Bosworth - Exec. V.P., Chief Merchandise Off.

Auditors: DELOITTE & TOUCHE
Investor Contact: 781-741-7775
Transfer Agents: Computershare Trust Company, N.A., Providence, RI

TANGER FACTORY OUTLET CENTERS, INC.

Exchange	Symbol	Price	52Wk Range	Yield	P/E	Div Acheiver
NYS	SKT	$38.47 (3/31/2008)	44.04-33.21	3.74	53.43	14 Years

*7 Year Price Score 129.09 *NYSE Composite Index=100 *12 Month Price Score 103.24

Interim Earnings (Per Share)

Qtr.	Mar	Jun	Sep	Dec
2003	0.10	0.10	0.17	0.23
2004	0.04	0.14	(0.07)	0.16
2005	(0.11)	0.13	0.15	(0.02)
2006	0.44	0.16	0.19	0.24
2007	0.06	0.16	0.22	0.28

Interim Dividends (Per Share)

Amt	Decl	Ex	Rec	Pay
0.36Q	4/12/2007	4/26/2007	4/30/2007	5/15/2007
0.36Q	7/12/2007	7/27/2007	7/31/2007	8/15/2007
0.36Q	10/11/2007	10/29/2007	10/31/2007	11/15/2007
0.36Q	1/10/2008	1/29/2008	1/31/2008	2/15/2008

Indicated Div: $1.44 (Div. Reinv. Plan)

Valuation Analysis | **Institutional Holding**

Forecast P/E	N/A	No of Institutions
		136
Market Cap	$1.2 Billion	Shares
Book Value	249.2 Million	27,018,212
Price/Book	4.84	% Held
Price/Sales	5.27	87.04

TRADING VOLUME (thousand shares)

Business Summary: Property, Real Estate & Development (MIC: 8.3 SIC: 6798 NAIC: 525930)

Tanger Factory Outlet Centers and subsidiaries owns and operates factory outlet centers in the U.S. Co. is a fully-integrated, self-administered and self-managed real estate investment trust that develops, acquires, owns, operates and manages factory outlet shopping centers. As of Dec 31 2007, Co. owned 29 outlet centers, with a total gross leasable area (GLA), of approximately 8.4 million square feet. These factory outlet centers were 98.0% occupied and contained over 1,800 stores, representing approximately 370 store brands. In addition, Co. owns a 50.0% interest in two outlet centers with a GLA of approximately 667,000 square feet.

Recent Developments: For the year ended Dec 31 2007, income from continuing operations increased 11.8% to US$28.5 million from US$25.5 million a year earlier. Net income decreased 23.4% to US$28.6 million from US$37.3 million in the prior year. Revenues were US$228.8 million, up 8.4% from US$211.0 million the year before. Revenues from property income rose 7.1% to US$155.6 million from US$145.3 million in the corresponding earlier year.

Prospects: Co.'s outlook remains constructive. For example, in response to the strong tenant demand for space, Co. increased the size of the initial phase of its Pittsburgh center from 308,000 square feet to 370,000 square feet, with leases for 63.0% of the first phase signed and another 20.0% under negotiation or out for signature. Co. now expects delivery of the initial phase in the second quarter of 2008, with stores opening by the end of the third quarter of 2008. Meanwhile, for 2008, Co. expects net income of $0.93 to $1.01 per share, excluding the affect of any potential sales or acquisitions of properties. Concurrently, Co. is projecting funds from operations of $2.60 to $2.68 per share.

Financial Data
(US$ in Thousands)

	12/31/2007	12/31/2006	12/31/2005	12/31/2004	12/31/2003	12/31/2002	12/31/2001	12/31/2000
Earnings Per Share	0.72	1.03	0.16	0.26	0.58	0.54	0.34	0.16
Cash Flow Per Share	3.20	2.89	2.96	3.13	2.23	2.35	2.82	2.42
Tang Book Value Per Share	3.21	3.94	3.84	5.87	6.46	5.00	4.82	5.74
Dividends Per Share	1.420	1.343	1.280	1.245	1.229	1.224	1.219	1.214
Dividend Payout %	197.22	130.34	800.00	478.85	210.04	226.62	363.81	783.06
Income Statement								
Property Income	155,581	145,884	139,238	135,222	84,229	79,313	78,089	74,710
Non-Property Income	73,184	65,827	63,561	59,331	37,743	33,854	32,979	34,111
Total Revenue	228,765	211,711	202,799	194,553	121,972	113,167	111,068	108,821
Interest Expense	40,066	40,775	42,927	35,117	26,486	28,460	30,134	27,565
Net Income	28,576	37,309	5,089	7,046	12,849	11,007	7,112	4,312
Average Shares	31,668	31,081	28,646	27,261	20,566	17,028	15,896	15,844
Balance Sheet								
Total Assets	1,060,280	1,040,877	1,000,605	936,378	987,437	477,675	476,272	487,408
Long-Term Obligations	706,345	678,579	663,607	488,007	540,319	345,005	358,195	346,843
Total Liabilities	777,343	727,177	701,025	516,951	562,689	363,410	378,395	369,434
Stockholders' Equity	249,204	274,676	250,214	161,133	167,418	90,635	76,371	90,877
Shares Outstanding	31,329	31,041	30,748	27,443	25,921	18,122	15,859	15,837
Statistical Record								
Return on Assets %	2.72	3.66	0.53	0.73	1.75	2.31	1.48	0.88
Return on Equity %	10.91	14.22	2.47	4.28	9.96	13.18	8.50	4.33
Net Margin %	12.49	17.62	2.51	3.62	10.53	9.73	6.40	3.96
Price Range	44.04-33.21	40.09-29.48	29.86-21.64	26.48-17.68	21.18-14.43	15.60-10.43	11.66-9.90	12.44-9.25
P/E Ratio	61.17-46.13	38.92-28.62	186.63-135.25	101.87-67.98	36.52-24.87	28.89-19.31	34.28-29.13	77.73-57.81
Average Yield %	3.56	3.95	4.94	5.77	7.16	9.02	11.27	11.19

Address: 3200 Northline Avenue, Suite 360, Greensboro, NC 27408 Telephone: 336-292-3010 Fax: 336-852-2096	Web Site: www.tangeroutlet.com Officers: Stanley K. Tanger - Chmn., C.E.O. Steven B. Tanger - Pres., C.O.O.	Auditors: PricewaterhouseCoopers LLP Investor Contact: 336-292-3010 Transfer Agents: EquiServe Trust Company NA, Providence, RI

TARGET CORP

Exchange	Symbol	Price	52Wk Range	Yield	P/E	Div Acheiver
NYS	TGT	$50.68 (3/31/2008)	70.14-48.08	1.10	15.22	36 Years

*7 Year Price Score 101.98 *NYSE Composite Index=100 *12 Month Price Score 95.97

Interim Earnings (Per Share)

Qtr.	Apr	Jul	Oct	Jan
2003-04	0.38	0.39	0.33	0.91
2004-05	0.48	1.54	0.60	0.89
2005-06	0.55	0.61	0.49	1.06
2006-07	0.63	0.70	0.59	1.29
2007-08	0.75	0.80	0.56	1.22

Interim Dividends (Per Share)

Amt	Decl	Ex	Rec	Pay
0.14Q	6/14/2007	8/16/2007	8/20/2007	9/10/2007
0.14Q	9/12/2007	11/16/2007	11/20/2007	12/10/2007
0.14Q	1/10/2008	2/15/2008	2/20/2008	3/10/2008
0.14Q	3/13/2008	5/16/2008	5/20/2008	6/10/2008

Indicated Div: $0.56 (Div. Reinv. Plan)

Valuation Analysis | **Institutional Holding**

Forecast P/E	N/A	No of Institutions
		863
Market Cap	$41.5 Billion	Shares
Book Value	15.3 Billion	758,414,464
Price/Book	2.71	% Held
Price/Sales	0.65	88.33

TRADING VOLUME (thousand shares)

Business Summary: Retail - General (MIC: 5.2 SIC: 5331 NAIC: 452990)

Target operates large-format general merchandise discount stores in the U.S., which include Target and SuperTarget stores. Co. also maintains REDcard, its credit card operation and operates Target.com, an online business. Target provides a range of general merchandise and a more limited assortment of food items in its stores. SuperTarget stores provide an array of food items along with general merchandise items. As of Feb 2 2008, Co. owned 1,352 stores, leased 73 stores, and operated 166 owned buildings on leased land (combined)stores for a total of 1,591 locations. Co. also owned 26, leased 5 and operated 1 combined distribution centers for a total of 32 locations.

Recent Developments: For the year ended Feb 2 2008, net income increased 2.2% to US$2.85 billion from US$2.79 billion in the prior year. Revenues were US$63.37 billion, up 6.5% from US$59.49 billion the year before. Operating income was US$5.27 billion versus US$5.07 billion in the prior year, an increase of 4.0%. Direct operating expenses rose 6.3% to US$41.90 billion from US$39.40 billion in the comparable period the year before. Indirect operating expenses increased 7.8% to US$16.20 billion from US$15.02 billion in the equivalent prior year period.

Prospects: Despite the challenging economic conditions, Co. remains focused on implementing its core strategies. Hence, for the fiscal year ending Jan 31 2009, Co. foresees sales to increase in the range of 8.0% to 9.0%, reflecting the ongoing contribution from new stores and an expected comparable store sales increase of 2.0% to 3.0%. In addition, Co. intends to invest about $4.50 billion to $4.70 billion in capital expenditures, including investments in about 116 new stores, adding about 95 new locations, net of relocations and closings, and two distribution centers that will open this fiscal year. However, Co. expects its gross margin rate to decrease modestly from its prior fiscal year.

Financial Data

(US$ in Thousands)	02/02/2008	02/03/2007	01/28/2006	01/29/2005	01/31/2004	02/01/2003	02/02/2002	02/03/2001
Earnings Per Share	3.33	3.21	2.71	3.51	2.01	1.81	1.50	1.38
Cash Flow Per Share	4.89	5.55	5.06	4.24	3.48	1.76	2.22	2.07
Tang Book Value Per Share	18.44	17.94	16.04	14.40	12.14	10.38	8.68	7.15
Dividends Per Share	0.520	0.440	0.360	0.300	0.260	0.240	0.220	0.210
Dividend Payout %	15.62	13.71	13.28	8.55	12.94	13.26	14.67	15.22
Income Statement								
Total Revenue	63,367,000	59,490,000	52,620,000	46,839,000	48,163,000	43,917,000	39,888,000	36,903,000
EBITDA	6,931,000	6,565,000	5,732,000	4,860,000	4,839,000	4,476,000	3,759,000	3,418,000
Income Before Taxes	4,625,000	4,497,000	3,860,000	3,031,000	2,960,000	2,676,000	2,216,000	2,053,000
Income Taxes	1,776,000	1,710,000	1,452,000	1,146,000	1,119,000	1,022,000	842,000	789,000
Net Income	2,849,000	2,787,000	2,408,000	3,198,000	1,841,000	1,654,000	1,368,000	1,264,000
Average Shares	850,800	868,600	889,200	917,100	917,100	914,000	909,800	913,000
Balance Sheet								
Current Assets	18,906,000	14,706,000	14,405,000	13,922,000	12,928,000	11,935,000	9,648,000	7,304,000
Total Assets	44,560,000	37,349,000	34,995,000	32,293,000	31,392,000	28,603,000	24,154,000	19,490,000
Current Liabilities	11,782,000	11,117,000	9,588,000	8,220,000	8,314,000	7,523,000	7,054,000	6,301,000
Long-Term Obligations	15,126,000	8,675,000	9,119,000	9,034,000	10,217,000	10,186,000	8,088,000	5,634,000
Total Liabilities	29,253,000	21,716,000	20,790,000	19,264,000	20,327,000	19,160,000	16,294,000	12,971,000
Stockholders' Equity	15,307,000	15,633,000	14,205,000	13,029,000	11,065,000	9,443,000	7,860,000	6,519,000
Shares Outstanding	818,737	859,771	874,074	890,643	911,808	909,802	905,165	911,682
Statistical Record								
Return on Assets %	6.98	7.58	7.18	10.07	6.15	6.29	6.29	6.79
Return on Equity %	18.47	18.38	17.73	26.62	18.00	19.17	19.08	20.09
EBITDA Margin %	10.94	11.04	10.89	10.38	10.05	10.19	9.42	9.26
Net Margin %	4.50	4.68	4.58	6.83	3.82	3.77	3.43	3.43
Asset Turnover	1.55	1.62	1.57	1.48	1.61	1.67	1.83	1.98
Current Ratio	1.60	1.32	1.50	1.69	1.55	1.59	1.37	1.16
Debt to Equity	0.99	0.55	0.64	0.69	0.92	1.08	1.03	0.86
Price Range	70.14-48.08	62.35-45.28	59.98-46.28	52.43-38.59	41.54-26.06	45.72-26.15	44.41-26.68	38.59-22.75
P/E Ratio	21.06-14.44	19.42-14.11	22.13-17.08	14.94-10.99	20.67-12.97	25.26-14.45	29.61-17.79	27.97-16.49
Average Yield %	0.86	0.82	0.68	0.65	0.65	0.72	0.66	0.69

Address: 1000 Nicollet Mall, Minneapolis, MN 55403
Telephone: 612-304-6073
Fax: 612-370-5502

Web Site: www.target.com
Officers: Robert J. Ulrich - Chmn., C.E.O. Douglas A. Scovanner - Exec. V.P., C.F.O., Chief Acctg. Officer

Auditors: Ernst & Young LLP
Investor Contact: 612-370-6736
Transfer Agents: EquiServe, Jersey City, NJ

TAUBMAN CENTERS, INC.

Exchange	Symbol	Price	52Wk Range	Yield	P/E	Div Acheiver
NYS	TCO	$52.10 (3/31/2008)	60.37-43.93	3.19	57.89	11 Years

*7 Year Price Score 140.75 *NYSE Composite Index=100 *12 Month Price Score 103.60

TRADING VOLUME (thousand shares)

Interim Earnings (Per Share)

Qtr.	Mar	Jun	Sep	Dec
2003	(0.14)	(0.26)	(0.21)	1.01
2004	0.07	(0.08)	(0.06)	(0.03)
2005	0.05	(0.09)	(0.18)	1.09
2006	0.10	(0.05)	0.03	0.32
2007	0.19	0.16	0.15	0.40

Interim Dividends (Per Share)

Amt	Decl	Ex	Rec	Pay
0.375Q	5/9/2007	6/27/2007	6/29/2007	7/20/2007
0.375Q	9/6/2007	9/26/2007	9/28/2007	10/22/2007
0.415Q	12/11/2007	12/27/2007	12/31/2007	1/22/2008
0.415Q	2/27/2008	3/27/2008	3/31/2008	4/21/2008

Indicated Div: $1.66

Valuation Analysis / **Institutional Holding**

Forecast P/E	50.54 (1/10/2007)	No of Institutions 180
Market Cap	$2.7 Billion	Shares 52,246,956
Book Value	N/A	% Held 97.49
Price/Book	N/A	
Price/Sales	4.37	

Business Summary: Property, Real Estate & Development (MIC: 8.3 SIC: 6798 NAIC: 525930)

Taubman Centers, a real estate investment trust, is the managing general partner of The Taubman Realty Group Ltd. Partnership (the Operating Partnership). The Operating Partnership is an operating subsidiary that engages in the ownership, management, leasing, acquisition, development, and expansion of regional and super-regional retail shopping centers. Co.'s centers are located in metropolitan areas including Atlantic City, Charlotte, Dallas, Denver, Detroit, Los Angeles, Miami, New York City, Orlando, Phoenix, San Francisco, Tampa, and Washington, D.C. As of Dec 31 2007, The Operating Partnership's owned portfolio included 23 urban and suburban shopping centers in 10 states.

Recent Developments: For the year ended Dec 31 2007, income from continuing operations increased 22.2% to US$116.2 million from US$95.1 million a year earlier. Net income increased 39.9% to US$63.1 million from US$45.1 million in the prior year. Revenues were US$626.8 million, up 8.2% from US$579.3 million the year before. Revenues from property income rose 5.6% to US$344.2 million from US$325.9 million in the corresponding earlier year.

Prospects: For full year 2008, Co. now anticipates Funds From Operations to be in the range of $3.05 to $3.12 per diluted share. In addition, Co. is targeting net income allocable to common shareholders to range from $0.60 to $0.83 per share. Also, Co. is forecasting total capital expenditures to be about $105.4 million, with allocations of $24.2 million for new development projects, $79.4 million for existing centers and $1.8 million for corporate office improvements and equipment. Looking ahead, Co. expects occupancy to be flat to modestly down in the first half of 2008 but foresees a slight increase in the second half of 2008.

Financial Data

(US$ in Thousands)	12/31/2007	12/31/2006	12/31/2005	12/31/2004	12/31/2003	12/31/2002	12/31/2001	12/31/2000
Earnings Per Share	0.90	0.40	0.87	(0.10)	0.41	(0.05)	(0.18)	1.64
Cash Flow Per Share	4.87	4.24	3.66	2.68	2.65	2.76	2.39	2.25
Tang Book Value Per Share	...	1.94	6.12	6.53	6.32	7.17	8.40	9.66
Dividends Per Share	1.540	1.290	1.160	1.095	1.050	1.025	1.005	0.985
Dividend Payout %	171.11	322.50	133.33	...	256.10	...	...	60.06
Income Statement								
Property Income	344,237	325,887	271,941	241,402	212,360	201,197	181,640	160,853
Non-Property Income	282,585	253,397	201,497	190,051	176,123	171,755	159,788	230,086
Total Revenue	626,822	579,284	473,438	431,453	388,483	372,952	341,428	390,939
Interest Expense	131,700	128,643	121,612	95,934	84,194	83,667	68,150	57,329
Net Income	63,124	45,117	71,735	12,378	37,836	14,426	7,657	103,020
Average Shares	53,622	52,979	50,530	49,021	50,387	51,239	50,500	52,463
Balance Sheet								
Total Assets	3,151,307	2,826,622	2,797,580	2,526,067	2,186,970	2,269,707	2,141,439	1,907,563
Long-Term Obligations	2,700,980	2,319,538	2,089,948	1,930,439	1,495,777	1,543,693	1,423,241	1,173,973
Total Liabilities	3,119,438	2,688,763	2,442,205	2,167,662	1,768,196	1,798,250	1,618,090	1,317,918
Stockholders' Equity	(15,842)	108,642	326,158	329,188	321,499	374,182	426,074	492,370
Shares Outstanding	52,624	52,931	51,866	48,745	49,936	52,207	50,734	50,984
Statistical Record								
Return on Assets %	2.11	1.60	2.69	0.52	1.70	0.65	0.38	5.86
Return on Equity %	136.04	20.75	21.89	3.79	10.88	3.61	1.67	21.09
Net Margin %	10.07	7.79	15.15	2.87	9.74	3.87	2.24	26.35
Price Range	63.22-47.07	50.65-35.61	36.04-26.60	30.33-19.30	21.25-15.94	16.99-12.58	15.80-10.75	12.63-9.75
P/E Ratio	70.24-52.30	126.63-89.03	41.43-30.57	...	51.83-38.88	...	...	7.70-5.95
Average Yield %	2.81	3.08	3.68	4.46	5.55	6.85	7.71	8.85

Address: 200 East Long Lake Rd, Suite 300, P.O. Box 200, Bloomfield Hills, MI 48303-0200
Telephone: 248-258-6800

Web Site: www.taubman.com
Officers: Robert S. Taubman - Chmn., Pres., C.E.O. Lisa A. Payne - Vice-Chmn., C.F.O.

Auditors: KPMG LLP
Investor Contact: 248-258-7367
Transfer Agents: Mellon Investor Services, South Hackensack, NJ

TCF FINANCIAL CORP.

Exchange	Symbol	Price	52Wk Range	Yield	P/E	Div Acheiver
NYS	TCB	$17.92 (3/31/2008)	28.98-15.53	5.58	8.45	16 Years

*7 Year Price Score 75.25 *NYSE Composite Index=100 *12 Month Price Score 90.74

Interim Earnings (Per Share)

Qtr.	Mar	Jun	Sep	Dec
2003	0.41	0.42	0.26	0.42
2004	0.44	0.47	0.45	0.50
2005	0.47	0.53	0.50	0.50
2006	0.45	0.52	0.51	0.42
2007	0.65	0.49	0.48	0.50

Interim Dividends (Per Share)

Amt	Decl	Ex	Rec	Pay
0.242Q	4/16/2007	4/25/2007	4/27/2007	5/31/2007
0.242Q	7/16/2007	7/25/2007	7/27/2007	8/31/2007
0.242Q	10/15/2007	10/24/2007	10/26/2007	11/30/2007
0.25Q	1/21/2008	1/30/2008	2/1/2008	2/29/2008

Indicated Div: $1.00 (Div. Reinv. Plan)

Valuation Analysis   **Institutional Holding**

Forecast P/E	12.35	No of Institutions
	(1/10/2008)	260
Market Cap	$2.3 Billion	Shares
Book Value	1.1 Billion	81,592,376
Price/Book	2.06	% Held
Price/Sales	1.50	62.55

Business Summary: Commercial Banking (MIC: 8.1 SIC: 6021 NAIC: 522110)

TCF Financial is a financial holding company. Co.'s principal subsidiaries are TCF National Bank and TCF National Bank Arizona. Co.'s core businesses include retail banking; commercial banking; small business banking; consumer lending; leasing and equipment finance; and investments and insurance services. As of Dec 31 2007, Co. had 453 retail banking branches, consisting of 194 traditional branches, 244 supermarket branches and 15 campus branches, with 109 branches located in Minnesota, 202 in Illinois, 56 in Michigan, 46 in Colorado, 31 in Wisconsin, five in Indiana and four in Arizona. At such dated, Co. had total assets of $15.98 billion and total deposits of $9.58 billion.

Recent Developments: For the year ended Dec 31 2007, net income increased 8.9% to US$266.8 million from US$244.9 million in the prior year. Net interest income increased 2.4% to US$550.2 million from US$537.5 million in the prior year. Provision for loan losses was US$57.0 million versus US$20.7 million in the prior year, an increase of 175.5%. Non-interest income rose 10.6% to US$541.5 million from US$489.5 million, while non-interest expense advanced 2.0% to US$662.1 million.

Prospects: For 2008, Co. intends to focus on optimizing existing branches in target market areas to improve convenience and service to customers and enhance branch performance, and plans to remodel 19 supermarket branches and one campus branch, as well as to relocate two traditional branches and one supermarket branch. Concurrently, Co. expects to open 10 new branches, consisting of five traditional branches and five supermarket branches, and to close and consolidate three traditional branches into nearby branches. Looking ahead, Co. anticipates its residential loan portfolio to continue to decline, which will provide it funding for expected growth in other loan, lease or investment categories.

Financial Data

(US$ in Thousands)	12/31/2007	12/31/2006	12/31/2005	12/31/2004	12/31/2003	12/31/2002	12/31/2001	12/31/2000
Earnings Per Share	2.12	1.90	2.00	1.86	1.52	1.58	1.35	1.18
Cash Flow Per Share	2.85	2.80	1.16	3.23	3.10	2.21	0.96	1.28
Tang Book Value Per Share	7.48	6.75	6.04	5.50	5.09	5.15	4.95	4.64
Dividends Per Share	0.970	0.920	0.850	0.750	0.650	0.575	0.500	0.412
Dividend Payout %	45.75	48.42	42.50	40.32	42.62	36.51	37.04	35.11
Income Statement								
Interest Income	968,023	886,138	732,022	622,809	641,519	733,363	826,609	826,681
Interest Expense	417,846	348,608	214,332	130,918	160,374	234,138	345,387	388,145
Net Interest Income	550,177	537,530	517,690	491,891	481,145	499,225	481,222	438,536
Provision for Losses	56,992	20,689	5,022	10,947	12,532	22,006	20,878	14,772
Non-Interest Income	541,457	489,464	478,330	490,466	419,279	418,842	354,941	325,197
Non-Interest Expense	662,124	649,197	610,588	586,934	560,109	538,360	501,006	463,528
Income Before Taxes	372,518	357,108	380,410	384,476	327,783	357,692	329,834	302,838
Income Taxes	105,710	112,165	115,278	129,483	111,905	124,761	122,512	116,593
Net Income	266,808	244,943	265,132	254,993	215,878	232,931	207,322	186,245
Average Shares	125,830	129,225	132,741	137,174	141,540	147,881	153,685	158,777
Balance Sheet								
Net Loans & Leases	12,413,429	11,419,711	10,363,976	9,461,058	8,606,531	8,520,595	8,620,783	8,707,809
Total Assets	15,977,054	14,669,734	13,365,360	12,340,567	11,319,015	12,202,069	11,358,715	11,197,462
Total Deposits	9,576,549	9,769,250	9,110,694	7,962,195	7,611,749	7,709,988	7,098,958	6,891,824
Total Liabilities	14,878,042	13,636,360	12,366,888	11,382,149	10,398,157	11,225,049	10,441,682	10,287,242
Stockholders' Equity	1,099,012	1,033,374	998,472	958,418	920,858	977,020	917,033	910,220
Shares Outstanding	126,602	130,418	133,776	137,186	140,952	147,711	153,863	160,578
Statistical Record								
Return on Assets %	1.74	1.75	2.06	2.15	1.84	1.98	1.84	1.70
Return on Equity %	25.02	24.11	27.10	27.06	22.75	24.60	22.69	21.61
Net Interest Margin %	56.84	60.66	70.72	78.98	75.00	68.07	58.22	53.05
Efficiency Ratio %	43.86	47.19	50.45	52.72	52.80	46.73	42.49	40.15
Loans to Deposits	1.30	1.17	1.14	1.19	1.13	1.11	1.21	1.26
Price Range	28.98-17.32	28.11-24.48	32.14-24.84	32.53-24.15	26.78-18.52	27.20-17.61	25.35-16.85	22.66-9.31
P/E Ratio	13.67-8.17	14.79-12.88	16.07-12.42	17.49-12.98	17.62-12.19	17.21-11.14	18.78-12.48	19.20-7.89
Average Yield %	3.86	3.50	3.12	2.65	2.91	2.43	2.36	2.78

Address: 200 Lake Street East, Mail Code EX0-03-A, Wayzata, MN 55391-1693
Telephone: 952-745-2760

Web Site: www.tcfexpress.com
Officers: William A. Cooper - Chmn., C.E.O. Lynn A. Nagorske - Pres., C.O.O.

Auditors: KPMG LLP
Investor Contact: 952-745-2755
Transfer Agents: EquiServe Trust Company, N.A., Providence, RI

TECO ENERGY INC.

Exchange	Symbol	Price	52Wk Range	Yield	P/E
NYS	TE	$15.95 (3/31/2008)	18.50-14.88	4.89	8.10

*7 Year Price Score 75.91 *NYSE Composite Index=100 *12 Month Price Score 101.57

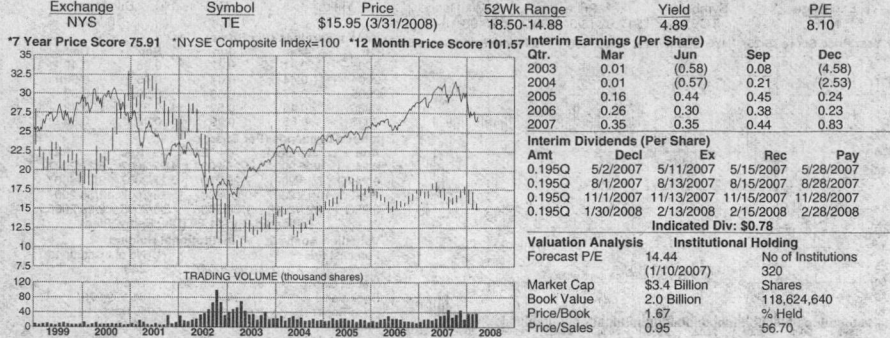

Interim Earnings (Per Share)

Qtr.	Mar	Jun	Sep	Dec
2003	0.01	(0.58)	0.08	(4.58)
2004	0.01	(0.57)	0.21	(2.53)
2005	0.16	0.44	0.45	0.24
2006	0.26	0.30	0.38	0.23
2007	0.35	0.35	0.44	0.83

Interim Dividends (Per Share)

Amt	Decl	Ex	Rec	Pay
0.195Q	5/2/2007	5/11/2007	5/15/2007	5/28/2007
0.195Q	8/1/2007	8/13/2007	8/15/2007	8/28/2007
0.195Q	11/1/2007	11/13/2007	11/15/2007	11/28/2007
0.195Q	1/30/2008	2/13/2008	2/15/2008	2/28/2008

Indicated Div: $0.78

Valuation Analysis

		Institutional Holding	
Forecast P/E	14.44	No of Institutions	
	(1/10/2007)	320	
Market Cap	$3.4 Billion	Shares	
Book Value	2.0 Billion	118,624,640	
Price/Book	1.67	% Held	
Price/Sales	0.95	56.70	

Business Summary: Electricity (MIC: 7.1 SIC: 4911 NAIC: 221122)

TECO Energy is a diversified energy-related holding company with businesses consisting of regulated electric and gas utility operations in Florida and other operating companies engaged in coal mining and synthetic fuel production, and unregulated electric generation with long-term contracts and regulated electricity distribution. Co.'s subsidiary, Tampa Electric Co., provides retail electric service through its Tampa Electric division; and purchases, distributes and sells natural gas through its Peoples Gas System division. Co.'s other energy-related operating companies included TECO Coal Corp. and TECO Guatemala, Inc.

Recent Developments: For the year ended Dec 31 2007, income from continuing operations increased 63.2% to US$398.9 million from US$244.4 million a year earlier. Net income increased 67.8% to US$413.2 million from US$246.3 million in the prior year. Revenues were US$3.54 billion, up 2.6% from US$3.45 billion the year before. Operating income was US$636.6 million versus US$418.2 million in the prior year, an increase of 52.2%. Direct operating expenses rose 3.4% to US$2.64 billion from US$2.55 billion in the comparable period the year before. Indirect operating expenses decreased 45.6% to US$260.7 million from US$479.0 million in the equivalent prior-year period.

Prospects: In 2008, Co. expects about 2.0% customer growth in its Tampa Electric Co. subsidiary to drive 2.0% energy sales growth reflecting a weakened Florida housing market. Also, based on Co.'s projected growth from continued population increases and business expansion, Tampa Electric expects average annual customer and retail energy sales growth of 2.1% and 2.3%, respectively, over the next five years. This energy sales growth projection is lower than previous projections, reflecting changes in usage patterns and in population trends. These growth projections assume continued local area economic growth, a recovery in the housing market, and a continuation of the energy market structure.

Financial Data
(US$ in Thousands)

	12/31/2007	12/31/2006	12/31/2005	12/31/2004	12/31/2003	12/31/2002	12/31/2001	12/31/2000
Earnings Per Share	1.97	1.18	1.31	(2.87)	(5.05)	2.15	2.24	1.97
Cash Flow Per Share	2.65	2.73	0.84	0.72	1.83	4.28	3.81	3.02
Tang Book Value Per Share	9.28	7.97	7.36	6.13	8.55	13.75	12.94	11.93
Dividends Per Share	0.775	0.760	0.760	0.760	0.925	1.410	1.370	1.330
Dividend Payout %	39.34	64.41	58.02	...	...	65.58	61.16	67.51
Income Statement								
Total Revenue	3,536,100	3,448,100	3,010,100	2,669,100	2,740,000	2,675,800	2,648,600	2,295,100
EBITDA	1,052,400	865,500	802,200	(137,600)	508,700	753,500	782,100	713,700
Income Before Taxes	530,900	293,500	225,800	(749,000)	(198,700)	259,800	293,600	269,400
Income Taxes	214,200	118,700	101,900	(265,100)	(135,200)	(38,400)	(10,100)	18,500
Net Income	413,200	246,300	274,500	(552,000)	(909,400)	330,100	303,700	250,900
Average Shares	209,900	208,700	208,200	192,600	179,900	153,300	135,400	126,300
Balance Sheet								
Net PPE	4,888,200	4,766,900	4,566,900	4,657,900	5,679,000	5,464,000	4,838,300	3,970,100
Total Assets	6,765,200	7,361,800	7,170,100	9,476,500	10,462,300	8,637,800	6,722,100	5,676,200
Long-Term Obligations	3,158,400	3,212,600	3,709,200	3,880,000	4,392,600	3,324,300	1,842,500	1,374,600
Total Liabilities	4,748,200	5,632,800	5,578,400	8,192,600	8,784,600	6,026,100	4,750,500	4,169,300
Stockholders' Equity	2,017,000	1,729,000	1,591,700	1,283,900	1,677,700	2,611,700	1,971,600	1,506,900
Shares Outstanding	210,900	209,500	208,200	199,700	187,800	175,800	139,600	126,300
Statistical Record								
Return on Assets %	5.85	3.39	3.30	N.M.	N.M.	4.30	4.90	4.83
Return on Equity %	22.06	14.83	19.09	N.M.	N.M.	14.40	17.46	17.11
EBITDA Margin %	29.76	25.10	26.65	N.M.	18.57	28.16	29.53	31.10
Net Margin %	11.69	7.14	9.12	(20.68)	(33.19)	12.34	11.47	10.93
PPE Turnover	0.73	0.74	0.65	0.52	0.49	0.52	0.60	0.60
Asset Turnover	0.50	0.47	0.36	0.27	0.29	0.35	0.43	0.44
Debt to Equity	1.57	1.86	2.33	3.02	2.62	1.27	0.93	0.91
Price Range	18.50-15.13	17.67-14.50	19.21-14.94	15.42-11.38	16.94-9.88	28.72-10.49	32.62-24.94	32.94-17.38
P/E Ratio	9.39-7.68	14.97-12.29	14.66-11.40	...	...	13.36-4.88	14.56-11.13	16.72-8.82
Average Yield %	4.57	4.72	4.44	5.54	7.38	6.59	4.76	5.70

Address: 702 N. Franklin Street, Tampa, FL 33602 Telephone: 813-228-1111 Fax: 813-228-1670	Web Site: www.tecoenergy.com Officers: Sherrill W. Hudson - Chmn., C.E.O. John B. Ramil - Pres., C.O.O.	Auditors: PricewaterhouseCoopers Investor Contact: 813-228-1111

TELEFLEX INCORPORATED

Exchange	Symbol	Price	52Wk Range	Yield	P/E	Div Acheiver
NYS	TFX	$47.71 (3/31/2008)	86.19-47.71	2.68	12.79	30 Years

*7 Year Price Score 101.44 *NYSE Composite Index=100 *12 Month Price Score 86.85

TRADING VOLUME (thousand shares)

Interim Earnings (Per Share)

Qtr.	Mar	Jun	Sep	Dec
2003	0.74	0.80	0.45	0.74
2004	0.73	0.84	0.43	(1.76)
2005	0.95	0.71	0.82	0.92
2006	0.72	0.90	0.91	0.96
2007	1.12	2.37	(1.45)	1.68

Interim Dividends (Per Share)

Amt	Decl	Ex	Rec	Pay
0.32Q	5/4/2007	5/23/2007	5/25/2007	6/15/2007
0.32Q	7/30/2007	8/13/2007	8/15/2007	9/14/2007
0.32Q	10/23/2007	11/13/2007	11/15/2007	12/14/2007
0.32Q	2/26/2008	3/3/2008	3/5/2008	3/17/2008

Indicated Div: $1.28 (Div. Reinv. Plan)

Valuation Analysis / Institutional Holding

Valuation Analysis		Institutional Holding	
Forecast P/E	14.98 (1/10/2007)	No of Institutions	226
Market Cap	$1.9 Billion	Shares	30,275,108
Book Value	1.3 Billion	% Held	77.39
Price/Book	1.42		
Price/Sales	0.97		

Business Summary: Medical Instruments & Equipment (MIC: 9.6 SIC: 3841 NAIC: 339112)

Teleflex designs, manufactures and distributes specialty-engineered products. Co. operates its business in three segments: Medical, which designs, manufactures and distributes medical devices primarily used in critical care, surgical applications and cardiac care; Aerospace, which provides engine repair products and services for flight turbine engines and cargo handling systems and equipment for wide body and narrow body aircraft; and Commercial, which designs, manufactures and distributes driver controls and engine and drive assemblies for the marine market, power and fuel systems for truck, rail, automotive and industrial vehicles and rigging products and services.

Recent Developments: For the year ended Dec 31 2007, loss from continuing operations was US$42.4 million compared with income of US$96.1 million a year earlier. Net income increased 5.1% to US$146.5 million from US$139.4 million in the prior year. Revenues were US$1.93 billion, up 14.4% from US$1.69 billion the year before. Operating income was US$173.7 million versus US$187.1 million in the prior year, a decrease of 7.2%. Direct operating expenses rose 13.4% to US$1.25 billion from US$1.11 billion in the comparable period the year before. Indirect operating expenses increased 27.3% to US$506.6 million from US$398.0 million in the equivalent prior-year period.

Prospects: On Dec 28 2007, Co. completed the sale of its business units that manufacture automotive and industrial driver controls and fluid handling systems in a cash transaction valued at $560.0 million, which is expected to result in an estimated after tax gain on sale of assets of about $90.0 million. Separately, for 2008, Co. expects its portfolio to deliver overall segment operating profit margins in the mid teens with Medical segment operating margins returning to the 20.0% range and segment operating margin growth in Aerospace and Commercial. Hence, Co. expects 2008 total revenues of approximately $2.40 billion and diluted earnings per share from continuing operations of $3.70 to $3.90.

Financial Data

(US$ in Thousands)	12/31/2007	12/31/2006	12/25/2005	12/26/2004	12/28/2003	12/29/2002	12/30/2001	12/31/2000
Earnings Per Share	3.73	3.49	3.39	0.24	2.73	3.15	2.86	2.83
Cash Flow Per Share	7.21	8.51	8.31	6.35	5.70	5.12	4.87	4.88
Tang Book Value Per Share	N.M.	17.31	15.79	14.49	19.42	16.61	19.99	18.01
Dividends Per Share	1.245	1.105	0.970	0.860	0.780	0.710	0.660	0.580
Dividend Payout %	33.38	31.66	28.61	358.33	28.57	22.54	23.08	20.49
Income Statement								
Total Revenue	1,934,332	2,646,757	2,514,552	2,485,378	2,282,435	2,076,229	1,905,004	1,764,482
EBITDA	273,358	367,568	362,772	254,081	282,180	267,605	252,096	235,631
Income Before Taxes	109,348	219,027	207,915	102,368	151,491	172,488	159,695	158,214
Income Taxes	122,767	54,140	47,806	14,351	42,388	47,222	47,384	48,990
Net Income	146,484	139,430	138,817	9,517	109,103	125,266	112,311	109,224
Average Shares	39,759	39,988	40,958	40,495	39,942	39,786	39,280	38,633
Balance Sheet								
Current Assets	1,009,810	1,139,529	1,168,576	1,148,442	1,006,187	837,895	747,477	662,038
Total Assets	4,187,997	2,359,052	2,506,385	2,634,436	2,110,613	1,813,384	1,635,020	1,401,288
Current Liabilities	690,682	470,775	589,677	535,247	612,671	498,483	495,426	383,872
Long-Term Obligations	1,499,130	487,370	505,272	685,912	229,882	240,123	228,180	220,557
Total Liabilities	2,816,971	1,127,574	1,346,911	1,459,225	1,048,311	901,103	856,877	710,866
Stockholders' Equity	1,328,843	1,189,421	1,142,074	1,109,733	1,062,302	912,281	778,143	690,422
Shares Outstanding	39,451	39,018	40,357	40,424	39,795	39,398	38,932	38,344
Statistical Record								
Return on Assets %	4.47	5.64	5.42	0.40	5.58	7.29	7.42	8.07
Return on Equity %	11.63	11.77	12.36	0.88	11.08	14.86	15.34	16.62
EBITDA Margin %	14.13	13.89	14.43	10.22	12.36	12.89	13.23	13.35
Net Margin %	7.57	5.27	5.52	0.38	4.78	6.03	5.90	6.19
Asset Turnover	0.59	1.07	0.98	1.05	1.17	1.21	1.26	1.30
Current Ratio	1.46	2.42	1.98	2.15	1.64	1.68	1.51	1.72
Debt to Equity	1.13	0.41	0.44	0.62	0.22	0.26	0.29	0.32
Price Range	86.19-57.25	71.80-50.50	71.80-48.62	54.82-40.72	49.95-34.24	58.57-40.92	50.98-35.71	44.69-26.94
P/E Ratio	23.11-15.35	20.57-14.47	21.18-14.34	228.42-169.67	18.30-12.54	18.59-12.99	17.83-12.49	15.79-9.52
Average Yield %	1.74	1.79	1.63	1.82	1.83	1.44	1.44	1.49

Address: 155 South Limerick Road, Limerick, PA 19468 Telephone: 610-948-5100 Fax: 610-834-8228	Web Site: www.teleflex.com Officers: Lennox K. Black - Chmn. John J. Sickler - Vice-Chmn.	Auditors: PricewaterhouseCoopers LLP Investor Contact: 610-834-6362 Transfer Agents: American Stock Transfer & Trust Company, New York, NY

729

TEMPLE-INLAND INC.

Exchange	Symbol	Price	52Wk Range	Yield	P/E
NYS	TIN	$12.72 (3/31/2008)	38.53-12.10	3.14	1.05

*7 Year Price Score 110.39 *NYSE Composite Index=100 *12 Month Price Score 56.38

Interim Earnings (Per Share)

Qtr.	Mar	Jun	Sep	Dec
2003	(0.16)	1.44	(0.03)	(0.36)
2004	0.12	0.50	0.36	0.48
2005	0.39	0.60	0.33	0.22
2006	0.67	1.71	0.87	0.97
2007	0.35	0.62	0.33	10.78

Interim Dividends (Per Share)

Amt	Decl	Ex	Rec	Pay
10.25Q	12/7/2007	12/10/2007	12/12/2007	12/21/2007
0.00Q	12/7/2007	12/31/2007	12/14/2007	12/28/2007
0.00Q	12/7/2007	12/31/2007	12/14/2007	12/28/2007
0.10Q	2/1/2008	2/27/2008	2/29/2008	3/14/2008

Indicated Div: $0.40

Valuation Analysis

Forecast P/E	16.02
	(1/10/2007)
Market Cap	$1.4 Billion
Book Value	780.0 Million
Price/Book	1.73
Price/Sales	0.34

Institutional Holding

No of Institutions	301
Shares	88,104,504
% Held	83.79

TRADING VOLUME (thousand shares)

Business Summary: Paper Products (MIC: 11.11 SIC: 2631 NAIC: 322130)

Temple-Inland is engaged in the manufacturing of corrugated packaging and building products, which it reported as separate operating segments as of Dec 29 2007. The corrugated packaging segment is a vertically integrated corrugated packaging operation, which includes five linerboard mills, one corrugating medium mill, and 64 converting facilities. Through its corrugated packaging segment, Co. manufactures containerboard and converts it into a line of corrugated packaging. Meanwhile, through its building products segment, Co. manufactures a range of building products, including lumber, gypsum wallboard, particleboard, medium density fiberboard, and fiberboard.

Recent Developments: For the year ended Dec 29 2007, income from continuing operations increased 318.8% to US$1.20 billion from US$287.0 million a year earlier. Net income increased 178.8% to US$1.31 billion from US$468.0 million in the prior year. Revenues were US$3.93 billion, down 6.2% from US$4.19 billion the year before. Operating income was US$2.09 billion versus US$420.0 million in the prior year, an increase of 397.9%. Direct operating expenses declined 2.5% to US$3.39 billion from US$3.48 billion in the comparable period the year before. Indirect operating income amounted to US$1.56 billion compared with an expense of US$289.0 million in the equivalent prior-year period.

Prospects: Going forward, with the Dec 2007 completion of its transformation plan, Co. is committed to maximizing return on investment and profitably growing its business. For instance, in its corrugated packaging segment, Co. will further improve asset utilization in its box plants in 2008, and expects to attain an additional $63.0 million in business improvement through 2009 by focusing on manufacturing and sales quality within its box plant and mill systems. Meanwhile, Co. expects demand for most building products to continue to be hampered by the challenging market conditions in the housing industry in 2008. Thus, Co. remains focused on lowering costs and matching its production to its demand.

Financial Data
(US$ in Thousands)

	12/29/2007	12/30/2006	12/31/2005	01/01/2005	01/03/2004	12/28/2002	12/29/2001	12/31/2000
Earnings Per Share	12.08	4.22	1.54	1.46	0.89	0.51	1.11	1.92
Cash Flow Per Share	2.80	8.88	5.74	4.14	8.16	2.52	(1.78)	4.71
Tang Book Value Per Share	3.91	15.80	14.90	15.19	14.51	14.42	17.32	18.64
Dividends Per Share	11.370	1.000	0.900	1.220	0.680	0.640	0.640	0.640
Dividend Payout %	94.12	23.70	58.44	83.56	76.84	125.49	57.66	33.42
Income Statement								
Total Revenue	3,926,000	5,558,000	4,888,000	4,750,000	4,653,000	4,518,000	4,172,000	4,286,000
EBITDA	2,270,000	1,080,000	638,000	670,000	390,000	551,000	530,000	677,000
Income Before Taxes	1,955,000	677,000	262,000	233,000	(97,000)	107,000	177,000	320,000
Income Taxes	753,000	208,000	86,000	71,000	(194,000)	42,000	66,000	125,000
Net Income	1,305,000	468,000	176,000	165,000	96,000	53,000	109,000	195,000
Average Shares	108,100	110,800	114,500	112,400	108,400	104,800	98,600	101,800
Balance Sheet								
Current Assets	1,277,000	1,292,000	1,280,000	1,178,000	1,088,000	1,145,000	1,136,000	884,000
Total Assets	5,942,000	20,413,000	21,633,000	20,119,000	21,143,000	21,760,000	18,687,000	18,142,000
Current Liabilities	890,000	9,479,000	9,201,000	9,751,000	10,025,000	12,110,000	10,137,000	10,423,000
Long-Term Obligations	852,000	6,947,000	8,601,000	6,408,000	6,842,000	5,450,000	4,988,000	4,460,000
Total Liabilities	5,162,000	18,224,000	19,553,000	18,027,000	19,175,000	19,811,000	16,791,000	16,309,000
Stockholders' Equity	780,000	2,189,000	2,080,000	2,092,000	1,968,000	1,949,000	1,896,000	1,833,000
Shares Outstanding	106,141	104,850	110,974	112,186	109,194	107,612	98,718	98,348
Statistical Record								
Return on Assets %	9.93	2.23	0.85	0.80	0.44	0.26	0.60	1.14
Return on Equity %	88.15	21.99	8.46	8.15	4.82	2.76	5.88	10.37
EBITDA Margin %	57.82	19.43	13.05	14.11	8.38	12.20	12.70	15.80
Net Margin %	33.24	8.42	3.60	3.47	2.06	1.17	2.61	4.55
Asset Turnover	0.30	0.27	0.23	0.23	0.21	0.22	0.23	0.25
Current Ratio	1.43	0.14	0.14	0.12	0.11	0.09	0.11	0.08
Debt to Equity	1.09	3.17	4.14	3.06	3.48	2.80	2.63	2.43
Price Range	38.53-17.60	27.90-22.34	26.34-18.68	20.55-16.88	18.41-10.98	17.56-9.69	18.22-12.22	19.66-10.26
P/E Ratio	3.19-1.46	6.61-5.29	17.11-12.13	14.08-11.56	20.68-12.34	34.43-19.01	16.42-11.01	10.24-5.34
Average Yield %	35.51	3.97	4.05	6.49	4.87	4.26	4.16	4.57

Address: 1300 South MoPac Expressway, Austin, TX 78746	**Web Site:** www.templeinland.com	**Auditors:** Ernst & Young LLP
Telephone: 512-434-5800	**Officers:** Kenneth M. Jastrow II - Chmn., C.E.O. M. Richard Warner - Pres.	**Investor Contact:** 409-829-1378
		Transfer Agents: EquiServe Trust Company, N.A., Providence, RI

TENET HEALTHCARE CORP.

Exchange	Symbol	Price	52Wk Range	Yield	P/E
NYS	THC	$5.66 (3/31/2008)	7.63-3.10	N/A	N/A

*7 Year Price Score 24.28   *NYSE Composite Index=100   *12 Month Price Score 102.03

Interim Earnings (Per Share)

Qtr.	Mar	Jun	Sep	Dec
2003	(0.04)	(0.42)	(0.66)	(2.05)
2004	(0.26)	(0.91)	(0.15)	(4.33)
2005	(0.01)	(0.04)	(0.87)	(0.62)
2006	0.15	(0.85)	(0.19)	(0.82)
2007	0.16	(0.06)	(0.12)	(0.16)

Interim Dividends (Per Share)

No Dividends Paid

Valuation Analysis **Institutional Holding**

Forecast P/E	125.09	No of Institutions
	(1/10/2007)	238
Market Cap	$2.7 Billion	Shares
Book Value	54.0 Million	464,774,080
Price/Book	49.72	% Held
Price/Sales	0.30	98.55

Business Summary: Hospitals & Health Care (MIC: 9.3 SIC: 8062 NAIC: 622110)

Tenet Healthcare is a health care services company whose subsidiaries and affiliates operate general hospitals and related health care facilities, and also hold investments in other companies. At Dec 31 2007, Co.'s subsidiaries operated 57 general hospitals, a cancer hospital and a critical access hospital, with a combined total of 15,244 licensed beds, serving urban and rural communities in 12 states. Co. also owned interests in two health maintenance organizations and operate; related health care facilities, including rehabilitation hospital, acute care hospital, and skilled nursing facility; physician practices; captive insurance companies; and other ancillary health care businesses.

Recent Developments: For the year ended Dec 31 2007, loss from continuing operations was US$49.0 million compared with a loss of US$815.0 million a year earlier. Net loss amounted to US$89.0 million versus a net loss of US$803.0 million in the prior year. Revenues were US$8.85 billion, up 4.7% from US$8.45 billion the year before. Operating income was US$269.0 million versus a loss of US$732.0 million in the prior year. Indirect operating expenses decreased 6.6% to US$8.58 billion from US$9.19 billion in the equivalent prior-year period.

Prospects: Going forward, Co. expects the stabilizing volumes, pricing improvement with its key commercial managed care payers, as well as its ongoing progress in cost control efforts to drive a strengthening earnings performance. For 2008, Co. is forecasting same-hospital admission growth of approximately 1.0% to 2.0%, and same-hospital outpatient visit growth of 2.0% to 3.0%. Accordingly, based on these volume assumptions, Co. anticipates growth in net operating revenues to be in the range of 5.0% to 6.0%, or approximately $9.30 billion to $9.40 billion for 2008. Co. is also projecting a loss of $0.10 per share to earnings of $0.05 per share per share for income from continuing operations in 2008.

Financial Data
(US$ in Thousands)

	12/31/2007	12/31/2006	12/31/2005	12/31/2004	12/31/2003	12/31/2002	05/31/2002	05/31/2001
Earnings Per Share	(0.19)	(1.71)	(1.54)	(5.66)	(3.17)	0.93	1.56	1.31
Cash Flow Per Share	0.69	(0.98)	1.63	(0.18)	1.80	1.46	4.73	3.70
Tang Book Value Per Share	N.M.	N.M.	N.M.	1.63	4.85	4.81	4.39	3.44
Income Statement								
Total Revenue	8,852,000	8,701,000	9,614,000	9,919,000	13,212,000	8,743,000	13,913,000	12,053,000
EBITDA	674,000	(382,000)	79,000	(892,000)	(1,074,000)	1,207,000	2,692,000	2,152,000
Income Before Taxes	(107,000)	(1,133,000)	(708,000)	(1,613,000)	(1,841,000)	758,000	1,761,000	1,142,000
Income Taxes	(58,000)	(262,000)	(87,000)	184,000	(437,000)	299,000	736,000	464,000
Net Income	(89,000)	(803,000)	(724,000)	(2,640,000)	(1,477,000)	459,000	785,000	643,000
Average Shares	473,405	470,847	468,898	466,226	465,927	493,530	502,899	490,728
Balance Sheet								
Current Assets	2,560,000	3,025,000	3,508,000	3,992,000	4,248,000	3,792,000	3,394,000	3,226,000
Total Assets	8,393,000	8,539,000	9,812,000	10,078,000	12,298,000	13,780,000	13,814,000	12,995,000
Current Liabilities	2,048,000	1,925,000	2,292,000	2,130,000	2,394,000	2,381,000	2,584,000	2,166,000
Long-Term Obligations	4,771,000	4,760,000	4,784,000	4,395,000	4,039,000	3,872,000	3,919,000	4,202,000
Total Liabilities	8,339,000	8,275,000	8,791,000	8,346,000	7,937,000	8,057,000	8,195,000	7,916,000
Stockholders' Equity	54,000	264,000	1,021,000	1,732,000	4,361,000	5,723,000	5,619,000	5,079,000
Shares Outstanding	474,379	471,585	469,709	467,236	464,786	473,738	488,541	488,201
Statistical Record								
Return on Assets %	N.M.	N.M.	N.M.	N.M.	N.M.	2.16	5.86	4.92
Return on Equity %	N.M.	N.M.	N.M.	N.M.	N.M.	5.36	14.68	14.06
EBITDA Margin %	7.61	N.M.	0.82	N.M.	N.M.	13.81	19.35	17.85
Net Margin %	N.M.	N.M.	N.M.	N.M.	N.M.	5.25	5.64	5.33
Asset Turnover	1.05	0.95	0.97	0.88	1.01	0.41	1.04	0.92
Current Ratio	1.25	1.57	1.53	1.87	1.77	1.59	1.31	1.49
Debt to Equity	88.35	18.03	4.69	2.54	0.93	0.68	0.70	0.83
Price Range	7.63-3.10	9.04-5.81	12.90-7.31	18.20-9.81	18.98-11.45	52.20-14.00	49.85-30.28	31.32-16.79
P/E Ratio	...	...	...	...	...	56.13-15.05	31.96-19.41	23.91-12.82

Address: 3820 State Street, Santa Barbara, CA 93105
Telephone: 805-563-7000
Fax: 888-896-9016

Web Site: www.tenethealth.com
Officers: Jeffrey C. Barbakow - Chmn., C.E.O. Barry P. Schochet - Vice-Chmn.

Auditors: Deloitte & Touche LLP
Transfer Agents: Bank of New York, NY

TENNANT CO.

Exchange	Symbol	Price	52Wk Range	Yield	P/E	Div Acheiver
NYS	TNC	$39.81 (3/31/2008)	49.32-31.16	1.31	19.14	35 Years

*7 Year Price Score 134.69 *NYSE Composite Index=100 *12 Month Price Score 100.00

Interim Earnings (Per Share)

Qtr.	Mar	Jun	Sep	Dec
2003	0.14	0.18	0.18	0.28
2004	0.14	0.20	0.06	0.33
2005	0.20	0.37	0.34	0.35
2006	0.23	0.48	0.42	0.43
2007	0.31	0.55	0.57	0.66

Interim Dividends (Per Share)

Amt	Decl	Ex	Rec	Pay
0.12Q	5/3/2007	5/29/2007	5/31/2007	6/15/2007
0.12Q	8/15/2007	8/29/2007	8/31/2007	9/17/2007
0.12Q	11/9/2007	11/28/2007	11/30/2007	12/17/2007
0.13Q	2/21/2008	2/27/2008	2/29/2008	3/17/2008

Indicated Div: $0.52 (Div. Reinv. Plan)

Valuation Analysis / **Institutional Holding**

Forecast P/E	N/A	No of Institutions 110
Market Cap	$736.5 Million	Shares
Book Value	252.4 Million	14,315,188
Price/Book	2.92	% Held
Price/Sales	1.11	76.21

Business Summary: Purpose Machinery (MIC: 11.13 SIC: 3589 NAIC: 333319)

Tennant designs, manufactures and markets cleaning products. Co.'s floor maintenance equipment, outdoor cleaning equipment, coatings and related products are used to clean factories, office buildings, parking lots and streets, airports, hospitals, schools, warehouses and shopping centers, among others. Customers include the building service contract cleaners to whom organizations outsource facilities maintenance, as well as user corporations, healthcare facilities, schools and federal, state and local governments that handle facilities maintenance themselves. Co. sells its products through its direct sales and service organization and through a network of authorized distributors worldwide.

Recent Developments: For the year ended Dec 31 2007, net income increased 33.7% to US$39.9 million from US$29.8 million in the prior year. Revenues were US$664.2 million, up 10.9% from US$599.0 million the year before. Operating income was US$54.8 million versus US$40.0 million in the prior year, an increase of 37.2%. Direct operating expenses rose 10.9% to US$385.2 million from US$347.4 million in the comparable period the year before. Indirect operating expenses increased 5.9% to US$224.1 million from US$211.6 million in the equivalent prior-year period.

Prospects: For full-year 2008, Co. anticipates organic growth in net sales of 5.0% to 9.0%, fueled by a new product pipeline and market expansion, with earnings per diluted share of $2.25 to $2.40 versus $2.08 in 2007, and saving of $9.0 million to $12.0 million through its global low-cost sourcing and lean manufacturing initiatives. Meanwhile, as part of its strategy to increasing its global market coverage and expanding its product offering, on Feb 29 2008, Co. announced that it has completed its acquisition of Applied Sweepers, maker of Green Machines® brand cleaning equipment, for about $68.0 million. The acquisition complements Co.'s existing outdoor offerings, particularly in Europe.

Financial Data
(US$ in Thousands)

	12/31/2007	12/31/2006	12/31/2005	12/31/2004	12/31/2003	12/31/2002	12/31/2001	12/31/2000
Earnings Per Share	2.08	1.57	1.26	0.73	0.78	0.46	0.26	1.54
Cash Flow Per Share	2.13	2.17	2.45	2.03	1.70	1.07	1.88	2.13
Tang Book Value Per Share	11.78	10.60	9.21	8.28	8.22	7.59	7.59	7.58
Dividends Per Share	0.480	0.460	0.440	0.430	0.420	0.410	0.400	0.390
Dividend Payout %	23.08	29.30	34.92	58.90	53.85	90.11	153.85	25.24
Income Statement								
Total Revenue	664,218	598,981	552,908	507,785	453,962	424,183	422,970	454,044
EBITDA	74,810	55,662	46,906	34,019	35,754	31,335	31,916	61,628
Income Before Taxes	57,712	43,302	34,994	21,379	22,483	14,898	13,749	44,044
Income Taxes	17,845	13,493	12,058	7,999	8,328	6,633	8,945	15,794
Net Income	39,867	29,809	22,936	13,380	14,155	8,265	4,804	28,250
Average Shares	19,146	18,989	18,210	18,300	18,128	18,096	18,406	18,270
Balance Sheet								
Current Assets	240,724	235,404	211,601	188,631	176,370	162,901	152,387	171,628
Total Assets	382,070	354,250	311,472	285,792	258,873	256,237	246,619	263,285
Current Liabilities	96,673	94,804	88,965	81,853	59,507	70,349	55,648	67,255
Long-Term Obligations	2,470	1,907	1,608	1,029	6,295	5,000	10,000	10,000
Total Liabilities	129,639	124,586	118,370	111,758	93,257	102,092	92,291	108,337
Stockholders' Equity	252,431	229,664	193,102	174,034	165,616	154,145	154,328	154,948
Shares Outstanding	18,499	18,753	18,382	18,006	17,989	17,962	18,072	18,105
Statistical Record								
Return on Assets %	10.83	8.96	7.68	4.90	5.50	3.29	1.88	10.82
Return on Equity %	16.54	14.10	12.49	7.86	8.85	5.36	3.11	19.37
EBITDA Margin %	11.26	9.29	8.48	6.70	7.88	7.39	7.55	13.57
Net Margin %	6.00	4.98	4.15	2.63	3.12	1.95	1.14	6.22
Asset Turnover	1.80	1.80	1.85	1.86	1.76	1.69	1.66	1.74
Current Ratio	2.49	2.48	2.38	2.30	2.96	2.32	2.74	2.55
Debt to Equity	0.01	0.01	0.01	0.01	0.04	0.03	0.06	0.06
Price Range	49.32-27.84	29.88-21.70	26.00-17.41	22.10-18.41	22.50-14.64	22.00-13.31	24.44-16.45	26.16-15.06
P/E Ratio	23.71-13.38	19.03-13.82	20.63-13.82	30.27-25.22	28.84-18.77	47.83-28.93	93.99-63.27	16.98-9.78
Average Yield %	1.27	1.79	2.20	2.15	2.30	2.24	2.01	2.06

Address: 701 North Lilac Drive, P.O. Box 1452, Minneapolis, MN 55440
Telephone: 763-540-1208
Fax: 612-513-2142

Web Site: www.tennantco.com
Officers: Eric A. Blanchard - V.P., Gen. Couns., Sec. Chris Killingstad - Pres., C.E.O.

Auditors: KPMG LLP
Investor Contact: 763-540-1553
Transfer Agents: Wells Fargo Bank Minnesota, N.A., St. Paul, MN

TENNECO INC

Exchange	Symbol	Price	52Wk Range	Yield	P/E
NYS	TEN	$27.94 (3/31/2008)	37.16-21.36	N/A	N/A

*7 Year Price Score 167.25 *NYSE Composite Index=100 *12 Month Price Score 95.94

Interim Earnings (Per Share)

Qtr.	Mar	Jun	Sep	Dec
2003	0.02	0.58	0.10	(0.05)
2004	(0.05)	0.69	0.14	(0.47)
2005	0.16	0.71	0.23	0.18
2006	0.14	0.53	0.12	0.31
2007	0.07	0.85	0.45	(1.53)

Interim Dividends (Per Share)

No Dividends Paid

Valuation Analysis   Institutional Holding

Forecast P/E	10.70	No of Institutions
	(1/10/2007)	146
Market Cap	$1.3 Billion	Shares
Book Value	400.0 Million	39,109,896
Price/Book	3.25	% Held
Price/Sales	0.21	85.90

Business Summary: Automotive (MIC: 15.1 SIC: 3714 NAIC: 336399)

Tenneco is engaged in the design, manufacture and sell automotive emission control and ride control systems and products. Co. serves both original equipment manufacturers (OEMs) and replacement markets worldwide through brands, including Monroe®, Rancho®, Clevite®, Elastomers, and FricRot™ ride control products and Walker®, Fonos™, and Gillet™ emission control products. As an automotive parts supplier, Co. produces individual component parts for vehicles as well as groups of components that are combined as modules or systems within vehicles. These parts, modules and systems are sold globally to OEMs and throughout all aftermarket distribution channels.

Recent Developments: For the year ended Dec 31 2007, net loss amounted to US$5.0 million versus net income of US$49.0 million in the prior year. Revenues were US$6.18 billion, up 32.1% from US$4.68 billion the year before. Direct operating expenses rose 35.8% to US$5.21 billion from US$3.84 billion in the comparable period the year before. Indirect operating expenses increased 11.3% to US$718.0 million from US$645.0 million in the equivalent prior-year period.

Prospects: Despite the expected ongoing industry volatility, Co.'s outlook seems positive. Notably, given its strong technology and engineering capabilities, favorable geographic and customer balance, cost flexibility and ongoing focus on managing costs and improving operations, Co. believes that it is well-positioned to address the industry challenges in 2008 while capturing additional new business opportunities, which will fuel its growth globally going forward. Meanwhile, as part of its five year strategic vision, Co. is projecting an average compounded annual original equipment revenue growth rate of 11.0% to 13.0% between 2008 and 2012, driven by tightening emission control regulations globally.

Financial Data

(US$ in Thousands)	12/31/2007	12/31/2006	12/31/2005	12/31/2004	12/31/2003	12/31/2002	12/31/2001	12/31/2000
Earnings Per Share	(0.11)	1.10	1.29	0.31	0.65	(4.74)	(3.43)	(1.20)
Cash Flow Per Share	3.60	4.46	3.11	4.80	6.95	4.72	3.73	6.72
Tang Book Value Per Share	3.56	0.20	N.M.	N.M.	N.M.	...	N.M.	N.M.
Dividends Per Share	...	...	...	...	...	...	...	0.200
Income Statement								
Total Revenue	6,184,000	4,685,000	4,441,000	4,213,000	3,766,000	3,459,000	3,364,000	3,549,000
EBITDA	...	...	...	...	339,000	313,000	245,000	271,000
Income Before Taxes	...	...	...	...	27,000	28,000	(78,000)	(66,000)
Income Taxes	83,000	3,000	25,000	(25,000)	(6,000)	(7,000)	51,000	(27,000)
Net Income	(5,000)	51,000	58,000	13,000	27,000	(187,000)	(130,000)	(42,000)
Average Shares	45,809	46,755	45,321	44,180	41,767	41,667	38,001	34,906
Balance Sheet								
Current Assets	1,641,000	1,422,000	1,197,000	1,278,000	1,105,000	966,000	941,000	1,109,000
Total Assets	3,590,000	3,263,000	2,940,000	3,110,000	2,795,000	2,504,000	2,681,000	2,886,000
Current Liabilities	1,358,000	1,133,000	979,000	1,047,000	893,000	1,016,000	876,000	809,000
Long-Term Obligations	1,328,000	1,350,000	1,356,000	1,401,000	1,410,000	1,217,000	1,324,000	1,135,000
Total Liabilities	3,190,000	3,042,000	2,811,000	2,960,000	2,737,000	2,598,000	2,607,000	2,556,000
Stockholders' Equity	400,000	221,000	129,000	150,000	58,000	(94,000)	74,000	330,000
Shares Outstanding	46,597	45,790	44,249	42,980	40,872	40,052	40,060	36,498
Statistical Record								
Return on Assets %	N.M.	1.64	1.92	0.44	1.02	N.M.	N.M.	N.M.
Return on Equity %	N.M.	29.14	41.58	12.47	...	...	N.M.	N.M.
EBITDA Margin %	...	...	...	...	9.00	9.05	7.28	7.64
Net Margin %	N.M.	1.09	1.31	0.31	0.72	N.M.	N.M.	N.M.
Asset Turnover	1.80	1.51	1.47	1.42	1.42	1.33	1.21	1.21
Current Ratio	1.21	1.26	1.22	1.22	1.24	0.95	1.07	1.37
Debt to Equity	3.32	6.11	10.51	9.34	24.31	...	17.89	4.35
Price Range	37.16-23.25	27.45-19.92	20.03-12.00	17.34-6.69	7.34-2.06	8.16-1.95	5.45-1.35	10.88-2.63
P/E Ratio	...	24.95-18.11	15.53-9.30	55.94-21.58	11.29-3.17	...	...	...
Average Yield %	...	...	...	...	...	...	...	2.98

Address: 500 North Field Drive, Lake Forest, IL 60045
Telephone: 847-482-5000
Fax: 847-482-5940

Web Site: www.tenneco-automotive.com
Officers: Mark P. Frissora - Chmn., Pres., C.E.O.
Timothy R. Donovan - Exec. V.P., Strategy & Bus.
Devel., Gen. Couns.

Auditors: Deloitte & Touche LLP
Investor Contact: 847-482-5042
Transfer Agents: Wells Fargo Bank, N.A., South St. Paul, MN

Exchange	Symbol	Price	52Wk Range	Yield	P/E	Div Acheiver
NYS	TPP	$34.49 (3/31/2008)	46.15-33.22	8.06	13.27	15 Years

*7 Year Price Score 89.12   ***NYSE Composite Index=100**   ***12 Month Price Score 97.60**

Interim Earnings (Per Share)

Qtr.	Mar	Jun	Sep	Dec
2003	0.43	0.43	0.36	0.31
2004	0.46	0.43	0.29	0.43
2005	0.55	0.45	0.31	0.42
2006	0.63	0.42	0.39	0.53
2007	1.29	0.44	0.44	0.43

Interim Dividends (Per Share)

Amt	Decl	Ex	Rec	Pay
0.685Q	4/13/2007	4/26/2007	4/30/2007	5/7/2007
0.685Q	7/16/2007	7/27/2007	7/31/2007	8/7/2007
0.695Q	10/12/2007	10/29/2007	10/31/2007	11/7/2007
0.695Q	1/14/2008	1/29/2008	1/31/2008	2/7/2008

Indicated Div: $2.78

Valuation Analysis | **Institutional Holding**

Forecast P/E	21.11	No of Institutions
	(1/10/2007)	169
Market Cap	$3.1 Billion	Shares
Book Value	N/A	14,978,791
Price/Book	N/A	% Held
Price/Sales	0.32	16.68

Business Summary: Oil and Gas (MIC: 14.2 SIC: 4922 NAIC: 486210)

TEPPCO Partners is engaged as a common carrier pipeline of refined products and liquefied petroleum gases in the U.S. Co.'s downstream segment includes transportation, marketing and storage of refined products, liquefied petroleum gases and petrochemicals. The upstream segment includes gathering, transportation, marketing, and storage of crude oil, and distribution of lubrication oils and specialty chemicals. The midstream segment includes natural gas gathering services, fractionation of natural gas liquids (NGLs) and transportation of NGLs. Texas Eastern Products Pipeline Company, LLC serves as Co.'s general partner and owns a 2.0% general partner interest in Co.

Recent Developments: For the year ended Dec 31 2007, income from continuing operations increased 52.8% to US$279.2 million from US$182.7 million a year earlier. Net income increased 38.2% to US$279.2 million from US$202.1 million in the prior year. Revenues were US$9.66 billion, up 0.5% from US$9.61 billion the year before. Operating income was US$249.6 million versus US$229.8 million in the prior year, an increase of 8.6%. Direct operating expenses rose 0.5% to US$9.27 billion from US$9.23 billion in the comparable period the year before. Indirect operating expenses decreased 7.9% to US$138.2 million from US$150.2 million in the equivalent prior-year period.

Prospects: On Feb 1 2008, Co. has acquired transportation assets and certain intangible assets of Cenac Towing Co., Inc. and Cenac Offshore, LLC for around $500.0 million. The transaction, which consists of 42 push boats, 89 barges and the economic benefit of certain related commercial agreements, will enable Co. to enter the marine transportation business for refined products, crude oil and lube products. This business serves refineries and storage terminals along the Mississippi, Illinois and Ohio rivers, as well as the Intracoastal Waterway between Texas and Florida. Also, these assets gather crude oil from production facilities and platforms along the Gulf Coast and in the Gulf of Mexico.

Financial Data

(US$ in Thousands)	12/31/2007	12/31/2006	12/31/2005	12/31/2004	12/31/2003	12/31/2002	12/31/2001	12/31/2000
Earnings Per Share	2.60	1.96	1.71	1.61	1.52	1.79	2.18	1.89
Cash Flow Per Share	3.90	3.71	3.78	4.21	4.00	4.77	4.31	3.21
Dividends Per Share	2.740	2.700	2.675	2.638	2.500	2.350	2.150	2.000
Dividend Payout %	105.38	137.76	156.43	163.82	164.47	131.28	98.62	105.82
Income Statement								
Total Revenue	9,658,060	9,607,485	8,618,488	5,958,192	4,255,832	3,242,163	3,556,413	3,087,941
EBITDA	485,339	375,680	...	...	...	...	...	...
Income Before Taxes	279,737	183,334	...	...	...	...	...	...
Income Taxes	557	652	...	...	...	...	...	...
Net Income	279,180	202,051	162,551	142,381	125,769	117,862	109,131	77,376
Average Shares	89,850	73,657	67,397	62,999	59,765	49,202	39,258	33,594
Balance Sheet								
Net PPE	1,793,634	1,642,095	1,960,068	1,703,702	1,619,163	1,587,824	1,180,461	949,705
Total Assets	4,750,057	3,922,092	3,680,538	3,197,705	2,940,992	2,770,642	2,065,348	1,622,810
Long-Term Obligations	1,511,083	1,603,287	1,525,021	1,480,226	1,339,650	1,377,692	730,472	835,784
Total Liabilities	3,485,430	2,601,762	2,479,168	2,176,257	1,831,671	1,878,800	1,522,167	1,307,753
Shares Outstanding	89,911	89,804	69,963	62,998	62,998	53,809	40,500	32,700
Statistical Record								
Return on Assets %	6.44	5.32	4.73	4.63	4.40	4.87	5.92	5.79
EBITDA Margin %	5.03	3.91	...	...	...	...	...	...
Net Margin %	2.89	2.10	1.89	2.39	2.96	3.64	3.07	2.51
PPE Turnover	5.62	5.33	4.70	3.58	2.65	2.34	3.34	3.69
Asset Turnover	2.23	2.53	2.51	1.94	1.49	1.34	1.93	2.31
Price Range	46.15-37.40	41.74-35.18	45.29-33.55	42.16-34.79	41.15-27.75	33.00-26.10	35.90-24.75	26.63-19.31
P/E Ratio	17.75-14.38	21.30-17.95	26.49-19.62	26.19-21.61	27.07-18.26	18.44-14.58	16.47-11.35	14.09-10.22
Average Yield %	6.53	7.22	6.59	6.73	7.26	7.80	7.32	8.72

Address: 2929 Allen Parkway, P.O. Box 2521, Houston, TX 77252-2521 Telephone: 713-759-3636 Fax: 713-759-3957	Web Site: www.teppco.com Officers: Jim W. Mogg - Chmn. Barry R. Pearl - Pres., C.E.O., C.O.O.	Auditors: DELOITTE & TOUCHE Investor Contact: 800-659-0059 Transfer Agents: ChaseMellon Shareholder Services, L.L.C., Ridgefield Park, NJ

TERADATA CORP (DE)

Exchange	Symbol	Price	52Wk Range	Yield	P/E
NYS	TDC	$22.06 (3/31/2008)	29.08-21.75	N/A	20.05

*7 Year Price Score N/A   *NYSE Composite Index=100   *12 Month Price Score N/A

Interim Earnings (Per Share)

Qtr.	Mar	Jun	Sep	Dec
2007	0.24	0.27	0.16	0.43

Interim Dividends (Per Share)

No Dividends Paid

Valuation Analysis   **Institutional Holding**

Forecast P/E	N/A	No of Institutions
		N/A
Market Cap	$4.0 Billion	Shares
Book Value	631.0 Million	N/A
Price/Book	6.33	% Held
Price/Sales	2.35	N/A

TRADING VOLUME (thousand shares)

Business Summary: IT & Technology (MIC: 10.2 SIC: 3571 NAIC: 334111)

Teradata provides integrated enterprise data warehousing technology, including enterprise analytic technologies and services. Co.'s data warehousing solutions are comprised of software, hardware, and related business consulting and support services. Co.'s services include Teradata Professional Services, Teradata Customer Services, and training services. Co.'s products include Teradata Database Software, Teradata Servers, Teradata Logical Data Models, and Teradata Analytic Applications and Tools. As of Dec 31 2007, Co. had sales and services offices located in approximately 40 countries and a client base of over 850 customers worldwide.

Recent Developments: For the year ended Dec 31 2007, net income increased 4.2% to US$200.0 million from US$192.0 million in the prior year. Revenues were US$1.70 billion, up 10.0% from US$1.55 billion the year before. Operating income was US$320.0 million versus US$302.0 million in the prior year, an increase of 6.0%. Direct operating expenses rose 9.5% to US$786.0 million from US$718.0 million in the comparable period the year before. Indirect operating expenses increased 13.1% to US$596.0 million from US$527.0 million in the equivalent prior-year period.

Prospects: Co.'s consolidated revenue is benefiting from increases in both its product and service revenues. Specifically, Co. is seeing higher product revenue due to capacity expansions and technology upgrades by existing customers and sales to new customers from its increased investments in demand creation resources. Co. is also seeing higher service revenue due to solid growth in both professional services and annuity support services. Looking ahead, Co. believes that demand for its applications should continue to increase due to the growing use of new data elements and more real-time analytics, thus adding to the scale and complexity of business requirements and to data volumes over time.

Financial Data

(US$ in Thousands)	12/31/2007	12/31/2006	12/31/2005
Earnings Per Share	1.10	1.06	1.14
Cash Flow Per Share	2.14	1.91	...
Tang Book Value Per Share	2.65	...	...
Income Statement			
Total Revenue	1,702,000	1,547,000	1,467,000
EBITDA	388,000	357,000	339,000
Income Before Taxes	322,000	302,000	284,000
Income Taxes	122,000	110,000	78,000
Net Income	200,000	192,000	206,000
Average Shares	181,300	180,700	180,700
Balance Sheet			
Current Assets	873,000	502,000	...
Total Assets	1,294,000	1,003,000	...
Current Liabilities	572,000	393,000	...
Total Liabilities	663,000	412,000	...
Stockholders' Equity	631,000	591,000	...
Shares Outstanding	181,000	...	...
Statistical Record			
Return on Assets %	17.41	...	...
Return on Equity %	32.73	...	...
EBITDA Margin %	22.80	23.08	23.11
Net Margin %	11.75	12.41	14.04
Asset Turnover	1.48	...	...
Current Ratio	1.53	1.28	...
Price Range	29.08-23.13	...	...
P/E Ratio	26.44-21.03	...	...

Address: 1700 South Patterson Blvd., Dayton, OH 45479
Telephone: 937-445-5000

Officers: James M. Ringler - Chmn. Michael Koehler - Pres., C.E.O.

Auditors: PricewaterhouseCoopers LLP

TERADYNE, INC.

Exchange	Symbol	Price	52Wk Range	Yield	P/E
NYS	TER	$12.42 (3/31/2008)	18.30-8.94	N/A	29.57

*7 Year Price Score 59.59   *NYSE Composite Index=100   *12 Month Price Score 91.76

Interim Earnings (Per Share)

Qtr.	Mar	Jun	Sep	Dec
2003	(0.41)	(0.28)	(0.28)	(0.05)
2004	0.20	0.39	0.21	0.03
2005	(0.27)	(0.23)	(0.18)	1.14
2006	0.23	0.40	0.31	0.05
2007	(0.04)	0.14	0.22	0.10

Interim Dividends (Per Share)

No Dividends Paid

Valuation Analysis

		Institutional Holding	
Forecast P/E	16.48	No of Institutions	
	(1/10/2007)	254	
Market Cap	$2.1 Billion	Shares	
Book Value	1.2 Billion	191,211,568	
Price/Book	1.75	% Held	
Price/Sales	1.95	N/A	

Business Summary: Instruments and Related Products (MIC: 11.15 SIC: 3825 NAIC: 334515)

Teradyne is a global supplier of automatic test equipment. Co.'s products and services include semiconductor test; circuit-board test and inspection systems; military/aerospace test instrumentation and systems; and automotive diagnostic and test systems (Systems Test Group). The test systems that Co. provides are used both for wafer level and device package testing. These chips are used in automotive, communications, consumer, computer and electronic game applications, among others. As of Dec 31 2007, Co.'s Systems Test Group segment is comprised of three business units: Military/Aerospace (Mil/Aero) Test, Commercial Board Test, and Diagnostic Solutions.

Recent Developments: For the year ended Dec 31 2007, income from continuing operations decreased 65.5% to US$71.9 million from US$208.2 million a year earlier. Net income decreased 60.9% to US$77.7 million from US$198.8 million in the prior year. Revenues were US$1.10 billion, down 18.7% from US$1.36 billion the year before. Operating income was US$42.2 million versus US$202.5 million in the prior year, a decrease of 79.2%. Direct operating expenses declined 16.4% to US$588.8 million from US$704.4 million in the comparable period the year before. Indirect operating expenses increased 4.9% to US$471.2 million from US$449.4 million in the equivalent prior-year period.

Prospects: On Jan 24 2008, Co. has completed the acquisition of Nextest Systems Corporation, a designer and manufacturer of flash memory products, for an estimated net purchase price of $325.0 million. The acquisition, which should enable Co. to enter the fast-growing flash memory test segment, is expected to be slightly dilutive to full-year 2008 earnings per share. Meanwhile, Co. expects the restructuring actions taken during 2007 to generate quarterly cost savings of approximately $3.5 million across all segments. Also, Co. anticipates its Feb 2008 reduction-in-force activities across all reportable segments, functions and geographies to result in annual savings of approximately $25.0 million

Financial Data
(US$ in Thousands)

	12/31/2007	12/31/2006	12/31/2005	12/31/2004	12/31/2003	12/31/2002	12/31/2001	12/31/2000
Earnings Per Share	0.42	1.01	0.46	0.84	(1.03)	(3.93)	(1.15)	2.51
Cash Flow Per Share	0.70	2.31	0.07	1.31	0.18	(0.02)	(0.45)	2.71
Tang Book Value Per Share	6.70	6.84	5.96	5.24	4.33	4.80	8.44	9.89
Income Statement								
Total Revenue	1,102,280	1,376,818	1,075,232	1,791,880	1,352,867	1,222,236	1,440,581	3,043,946
EBITDA	111,534	270,371	9,470	315,647	(26,835)	(396,426)	(206,137)	812,627
Income Before Taxes	79,243	230,395	(80,137)	187,974	(186,193)	(560,945)	(326,153)	739,648
Income Taxes	7,360	27,752	(19,680)	22,737	7,800	157,524	(123,938)	221,894
Net Income	77,711	198,757	90,648	165,237	(193,993)	(718,469)	(202,215)	453,616
Average Shares	185,374	204,414	196,283	197,432	187,845	182,861	175,828	181,011
Balance Sheet								
Current Assets	944,933	889,410	1,094,942	805,826	769,277	809,273	1,207,022	1,377,834
Total Assets	1,555,288	1,721,055	1,859,732	1,922,562	1,785,362	1,894,677	2,542,391	2,355,868
Current Liabilities	223,234	259,716	515,495	276,558	280,815	279,365	296,131	619,288
Long-Term Obligations	...	...	1,819	398,932	407,658	450,561	451,682	8,352
Total Liabilities	326,114	359,868	617,066	788,998	835,792	866,204	778,007	648,897
Stockholders' Equity	1,229,174	1,361,187	1,242,666	1,133,564	949,570	1,028,473	1,764,384	1,706,971
Shares Outstanding	173,088	188,952	197,011	194,253	191,973	183,196	181,119	172,559
Statistical Record								
Return on Assets %	4.74	11.10	4.79	8.89	N.M.	N.M.	N.M.	23.06
Return on Equity %	6.00	15.27	7.63	15.82	N.M.	N.M.	N.M.	31.63
EBITDA Margin %	10.12	19.64	0.88	17.62	N.M.	N.M.	N.M.	26.70
Net Margin %	7.05	14.44	8.43	9.22	N.M.	N.M.	N.M.	14.90
Asset Turnover	0.67	0.77	0.57	0.96	0.74	0.55	0.59	1.55
Current Ratio	4.23	3.42	2.12	2.91	2.74	2.90	4.08	2.22
Debt to Equity	...	...	N.M.	0.35	0.43	0.44	0.26	N.M.
Price Range	18.30-10.06	17.90-11.90	17.10-10.95	30.69-12.71	25.60-9.58	39.49-7.22	47.19-19.00	110.00-24.31
P/E Ratio	43.57-23.95	17.72-11.78	37.17-23.80	36.54-15.13	...	...	...	43.82-9.69

Address: 321 Harrison Avenue, Boston, MA 02118
Telephone: 617-482-2700
Fax: 617-422-2910

Web Site: www.teradyne.com
Officers: George W. Chamillard - Chmn., C.E.O.
Michael A. Bradley - Pres., , C.E.O.

Auditors: PricewaterhouseCoopers LLP
Investor Contact: 617-422-2425
Transfer Agents: EquiServe Trust Company, N.A., Providence, RI

TEREX CORP.

Exchange	Symbol	Price	52Wk Range	Yield	P/E
NYS	TEX	$62.50 (3/31/2008)	94.13-49.19	N/A	10.68

*7 Year Price Score 204.01 *NYSE Composite Index=100 *12 Month Price Score 92.52

Interim Earnings (Per Share)

Qtr.	Mar	Jun	Sep	Dec
2003	0.13	(0.51)	0.14	(0.04)
2004	0.17	0.58	0.44	1.93
2005	0.30	0.70	0.51	0.34
2006	0.77	1.16	0.98	0.97
2007	1.09	1.66	1.45	1.65

Interim Dividends (Per Share)

No Dividends Paid

Valuation Analysis

		Institutional Holding	
Forecast P/E	N/A	No of Institutions	295
Market Cap	$6.3 Billion	Shares	
Book Value	2.3 Billion	91,616,311	
Price/Book	2.68	% Held	
Price/Sales	0.69	92.12	

TRADING VOLUME (thousand shares)

Business Summary: Industrial Machinery and Equipment (MIC: 11.5 SIC: 3537 NAIC: 333924)

Terex is a global manufacturer of capital equipment focused on delivering products for the construction, infrastructure, quarrying, surface mining, shipping, transportation, refining and utility industries. Co. operates five segments: Terex Aerial Work Platforms, Terex Construction, Terex Cranes, Terex Materials Processing & Mining, and Terex Roadbuilding, Utility Products and Other. Co.'s products include aerial work platform equipment, construction trailers, mobile telescopic cranes, tower cranes, crushing and screening equipment, hydraulic mining excavators, surface mining trucks, drilling equipment, asphalt and concrete equipment, and related components and replacement parts.

Recent Developments: For the year ended Dec 31 2007, income from continuing operations increased 54.8% to US$613.9 million from US$396.5 million a year earlier. Net income increased 53.5% to US$613.9 million from US$399.9 million in the prior year. Revenues were US$9.14 billion, up 19.5% from US$7.65 billion the year before. Operating income was US$961.4 million versus US$709.5 million in the prior year, an increase of 35.5%. Direct operating expenses rose 16.9% to US$7.26 billion from US$6.20 billion in the comparable period the year before. Indirect operating expenses increased 25.5% to US$920.6 million from US$733.6 million in the equivalent prior-year period.

Prospects: On Mar 4 2008, Co. announced that it has completed the acquisition of A.S.V., Inc., a manufacturer of compact rubber track loaders and related accessories, undercarriages and traction products, for a total value of about $488.0 million. Co. believes that the acquisition is a strategic and cultural fit, which expands its product offerings as it continues to grow as a global construction equipment manufacturer. Co. also expects that ASV will add about $220.0 million to $250.0 million in sales on a 2008 full-year basis and enhances its future earnings growth potential. Meanwhile, Co. projects total revenue of $10.00 billion to $10.50 billion and earnings per share of $6.65 to $7.15 for 2008.

Financial Data
(US$ in Thousands)

	12/31/2007	12/31/2006	12/31/2005	12/31/2004	12/31/2003	12/31/2002	12/31/2001	12/31/2000
Earnings Per Share	5.85	3.88	1.85	3.17	(0.27)	(1.53)	0.22	1.71
Cash Flow Per Share	3.53	4.81	2.75	1.67	4.03	0.81	(0.10)	3.68
Tang Book Value Per Share	16.39	11.06	6.14	4.80	2.80	1.54	N.M.	N.M.
Income Statement								
Total Revenue	9,137,700	7,647,600	6,380,400	5,019,800	3,897,100	2,797,400	1,812,500	2,068,700
EBITDA	1,044,300	766,100	460,100	304,600	133,400	109,400	147,700	298,900
Income Before Taxes	919,300	614,700	289,800	147,400	(35,300)	(25,800)	24,600	159,600
Income Taxes	305,400	218,200	101,300	(176,700)	(9,800)	(8,300)	7,900	55,700
Net Income	613,000	399,000	188,500	324,100	(25,500)	(137,500)	12,800	95,100
Average Shares	104,900	103,000	102,200	102,200	95,400	86,400	57,800	55,800
Balance Sheet								
Current Assets	4,776,900	3,432,800	2,903,500	2,647,100	2,194,000	2,221,100	1,383,000	1,242,400
Total Assets	6,316,300	4,785,900	4,200,300	4,179,100	3,723,800	3,625,700	2,387,000	1,983,700
Current Liabilities	2,175,300	2,027,200	1,524,600	1,529,500	1,159,400	1,106,200	627,100	575,600
Long-Term Obligations	1,319,500	536,100	1,075,800	1,114,200	1,274,800	1,487,100	1,020,700	882,000
Total Liabilities	3,973,100	3,034,900	3,039,300	3,043,900	2,847,100	2,856,500	1,791,600	1,532,200
Stockholders' Equity	2,343,200	1,751,000	1,161,000	1,135,200	876,700	769,200	595,400	451,500
Shares Outstanding	100,300	101,100	98,600	97,600	97,600	94,800	72,800	53,600
Statistical Record								
Return on Assets %	11.06	8.90	4.50	8.18	N.M.	N.M.	0.59	4.56
Return on Equity %	29.99	27.47	16.42	32.13	N.M.	N.M.	2.45	21.45
EBITDA Margin %	11.43	10.02	7.21	6.07	3.42	3.91	8.15	14.45
Net Margin %	6.72	5.23	2.95	6.46	N.M.	N.M.	0.71	4.60
Asset Turnover	1.65	1.70	1.52	1.27	1.06	0.93	0.83	0.99
Current Ratio	2.20	1.69	1.90	1.73	1.89	2.01	2.21	2.16
Debt to Equity	0.56	0.31	0.93	0.98	1.45	1.93	1.71	1.95
Price Range	94.13-56.57	66.29-30.42	31.16-18.65	23.82-14.07	14.73-4.85	13.36-5.25	12.13-7.78	14.31-5.81
P/E Ratio	16.09-9.67	17.09-7.84	16.85-9.81	7.52-4.44	...	...	55.11-35.37	8.37-3.40

Address: 200 Nyala Farm Road, Westport, CT 06880
Telephone: 203-222-7170
Fax: 203-222-7976

Web Site: www.terex.com
Officers: Ronald M. DeFeo - Chmn., C.E.O. Phillip C. Widman - Sr. V.P., C.F.O.

Auditors: PricewaterhouseCoopers LLP
Transfer Agents: American Stock Transfer & Trust Company, New York, NY

737

TESORO CORPORATION

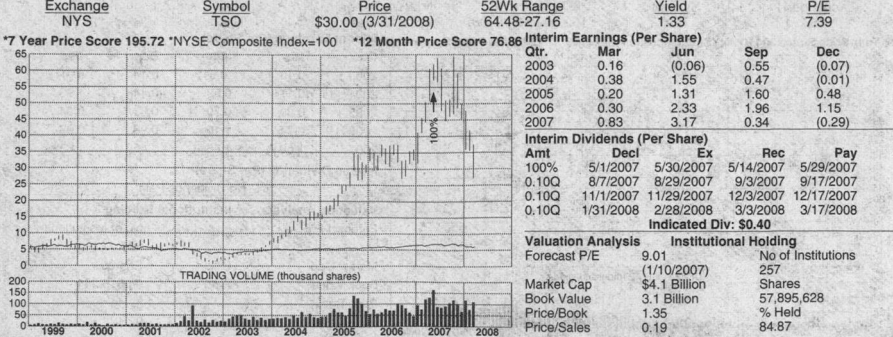

Exchange	Symbol	Price	52Wk Range	Yield	P/E
NYS	TSO	$30.00 (3/31/2008)	64.48-27.16	1.33	7.39

*7 Year Price Score 195.72 *NYSE Composite Index=100 *12 Month Price Score 76.86

Interim Earnings (Per Share)

Qtr.	Mar	Jun	Sep	Dec
2003	0.16	(0.06)	0.55	(0.07)
2004	0.38	1.55	0.47	(0.01)
2005	0.20	1.31	1.60	0.48
2006	0.30	2.33	1.96	1.15
2007	0.83	3.17	0.34	(0.29)

Interim Dividends (Per Share)

Amt	Decl	Ex	Rec	Pay
100%	5/1/2007	5/30/2007	5/14/2007	5/29/2007
0.10Q	8/7/2007	8/29/2007	9/3/2007	9/17/2007
0.10Q	11/1/2007	11/29/2007	12/3/2007	12/17/2007
0.10Q	1/31/2008	2/28/2008	3/3/2008	3/17/2008

Indicated Div: $0.40

Valuation Analysis

Forecast P/E	9.01
	(1/10/2007)
Market Cap	$4.1 Billion
Book Value	3.1 Billion
Price/Book	1.35
Price/Sales	0.19

Institutional Holding

No of Institutions	257
Shares	57,895,628
% Held	84.87

Business Summary: Oil and Gas (MIC: 14.2 SIC: 2911 NAIC: 324110)

Tesoro is an independent petroleum refiner and marketer, engaged in refining crude oil and other feedstocks at its seven refineries in the western and mid-continental U.S. and selling refined products in bulk and wholesale markets, as well as selling motor fuels and convenience products in the retail market. Co.'s refining segment produces refined products, mainly gasoline and gasoline blendstocks, jet fuel, diesel fuel and heavy fuel oils for sale to commercial customers in the western and mid-continental U.S. Co.'s retail segment distributes motor fuels through a network of retail stations, primarily under the Tesoro® Mirastar®, Shell® and USA Gasoline™ brands.

Recent Developments: For the year ended Dec 31 2007, net income decreased 29.3% to US$566.0 million from US$801.0 million in the prior year. Revenues were US$21.92 billion, up 21.1% from US$18.10 billion the year before. Operating income was US$967.0 million versus US$1.32 billion in the prior year, a decrease of 26.6%. Direct operating expenses rose 24.5% to US$20.31 billion from US$16.31 billion in the comparable period the year before. Indirect operating expenses increased 35.3% to US$640.0 million from US$473.0 million in the equivalent prior-year period.

Prospects: Co.'s near-term outlook appears encouraging. For example, Co. believes that factors such as the increased seasonal demand, the lower planned industry production runs combined with the effect of planned turnarounds, as well as the seasonal reductions of gasoline inventories due to the transition into summer-grade gasoline, should have a positive affect on industry refining margins beginning in the first quarter of 2008. Looking ahead, Co. anticipates realizing annual recurring cost savings of approximately $100.0 million in connection with its acquisitions through its crude purchasing and shipping logistics as well as by maximizing the production of clean fuels for the California market.

Financial Data

(US$ in Thousands)	12/31/2007	12/31/2006	12/31/2005	12/31/2004	12/31/2003	12/31/2002	12/31/2001	12/31/2000
Earnings Per Share	4.06	5.73	3.60	2.38	0.58	(0.96)	1.05	0.88
Cash Flow Per Share	9.74	8.38	5.57	5.22	3.46	0.48	2.96	1.44
Tang Book Value Per Share	19.48	16.94	12.11	8.31	5.70	5.00	9.14	8.19
Dividends Per Share	0.350	0.200	0.100	...	...	...	...	...
Dividend Payout %	8.62	3.49	2.78	...	...	...	...	...
Income Statement								
Total Revenue	21,915,000	18,104,000	16,581,000	12,262,200	8,845,700	7,119,300	5,217,800	5,104,400
EBITDA	1,369,000	1,625,000	1,245,000	885,000	502,300	112,000	278,600	198,900
Income Before Taxes	905,000	1,286,000	831,000	546,600	123,100	(181,300)	146,900	123,500
Income Taxes	339,000	485,000	324,000	218,700	47,000	(64,300)	58,900	50,200
Net Income	566,000	801,000	507,000	327,900	76,100	(117,000)	88,000	73,300
Average Shares	139,500	139,800	140,800	137,800	130,200	121,000	83,800	83,600
Balance Sheet								
Current Assets	2,600,000	2,811,000	2,215,000	1,393,400	1,024,000	1,054,200	878,000	630,200
Total Assets	8,128,000	5,904,000	5,097,000	4,075,100	3,661,300	3,758,800	2,662,300	1,543,600
Current Liabilities	2,494,000	1,672,000	1,502,000	992,700	687,000	608,300	538,500	382,400
Long-Term Obligations	1,657,000	1,029,000	1,044,000	1,214,900	1,605,300	1,906,700	1,112,500	306,800
Total Liabilities	5,076,000	3,402,000	3,210,000	2,748,000	2,695,900	2,871,200	1,905,300	873,700
Stockholders' Equity	3,052,000	2,502,000	1,887,000	1,327,100	965,400	887,600	757,000	669,900
Shares Outstanding	137,044	135,813	138,604	133,646	129,512	129,216	82,827	61,638
Statistical Record								
Return on Assets %	8.07	14.56	11.06	8.45	2.05	N.M.	4.18	4.82
Return on Equity %	20.38	36.50	31.55	28.53	8.21	N.M.	12.33	11.31
EBITDA Margin %	6.25	8.98	7.51	7.22	5.68	1.57	5.34	3.90
Net Margin %	2.58	4.42	3.06	2.67	0.86	N.M.	1.69	1.44
Asset Turnover	3.12	3.29	3.62	3.16	2.38	2.22	2.48	3.36
Current Ratio	1.04	1.68	1.47	1.40	1.49	1.73	1.63	1.65
Debt to Equity	0.54	0.41	0.55	0.92	1.66	2.15	1.47	0.46
Price Range	64.48-31.73	37.52-27.11	34.93-14.52	16.86-7.01	7.56-1.83	7.63-0.67	8.10-5.05	6.38-4.50
P/E Ratio	15.88-7.81	6.55-4.73	9.70-4.03	7.08-2.95	13.03-3.15	...	7.71-4.81	7.24-5.11
Average Yield %	0.69	0.60	0.42	...	...	...	...	...

Address: 300 Concord Plaza Drive, San Antonio, TX 78216-6999
Telephone: 210-283-2000

Web Site: www.tsocorp.com
Officers: Bruce A. Smith - Chmn., Pres., C.E.O.
Gregory A. Wright - Exec. V.P., C.F.O.

Auditors: Ernst and Young LLP
Transfer Agents: American Stock Transfer & Trust Company, New York, NY

TETRA TECHNOLOGIES, INC.

Exchange	Symbol	Price	52Wk Range	Yield	P/E
NYS	TTI	$15.84 (3/31/2008)	30.14-13.92	N/A	41.68

*7 Year Price Score 136.85 *NYSE Composite Index=100   *12 Month Price Score 86.46

TRADING VOLUME (thousand shares)

Interim Earnings (Per Share)

Qtr.	Mar	Jun	Sep	Dec
2003	0.01	0.09	0.15	0.00
2004	0.02	0.07	0.07	0.08
2005	0.08	0.21	0.09	0.15
2006	0.27	0.39	0.39	0.32
2007	0.28	0.30	0.05	(0.24)

Interim Dividends (Per Share)

Amt	Decl	Ex	Rec	Pay
50%	8/1/2003	8/22/2003	8/15/2003	8/21/2003
50%	8/8/2005	8/29/2005	8/19/2005	8/26/2005
100%	5/4/2006	5/23/2006	5/15/2006	5/22/2006

Valuation Analysis   **Institutional Holding**

Forecast P/E	N/A	No of Institutions
		200
Market Cap	$1.2 Billion	Shares
Book Value	447.9 Million	71,767,288
Price/Book	2.63	% Held
Price/Sales	1.20	98.95

Business Summary: Oil and Gas (MIC: 14.2 SIC: 1389 NAIC: 213112)

TETRA Technologies is an oil and gas services company with an integrated calcium chloride and brominated products manufacturing operation that supplies feedstocks to energy and other markets. Co.'s Fluids division manufactures and markets clear brine fluids, additives and other related products and services. Co.'s Well Abandonment & Decommissioning division provides various services for the abandonment of depleted oil and gas wells and the decommissioning of platforms, pipelines and other related equipment. Co.'s Production Enhancement division provides production testing services to the Texas, New Mexico, Colorado, Louisiana, offshore Gulf of Mexico, and certain international markets.

Recent Developments: For the year ended Dec 31 2007, income from continuing operations decreased 98.8% to US$1.2 million from US$99.9 million a year earlier. Net income decreased 71.8% to US$28.8 million from US$101.9 million in the prior year. Revenues were US$982.5 million, up 28.0% from US$767.8 million the year before. Operating income was US$16.5 million versus US$160.8 million in the prior year, a decrease of 89.7%. Direct operating expenses rose 68.2% to US$866.1 million from US$515.0 million in the comparable period the year before. Indirect operating expenses increased 8.6% to US$99.9 million from US$92.0 million in the equivalent prior-year period.

Prospects: On Dec 24 2007, Co. sold its process services operation, which it identified as not a strategic part of its core operations, for total cash proceeds of approximately $58.7 million. Separately, in Jan 2008, Co. noted that its Maritech Resources, Inc. subsidiary has closed on three acquisitions involving 38 properties for an aggregate cash purchase price of approximately $46.0 million. These acquisitions should allow Co. to increase its production to approximately 85.0 million cubic feet per day equivalent (MMCF/DE) by late 2008 from its current volumes of about 60.0 MMCF/DE. For 2008, Co. expects net income of $100.0 million to $119.3 million and earnings per share of $1.30 to $1.55.

Financial Data

(US$ in Thousands)	12/31/2007	12/31/2006	12/31/2005	12/31/2004	12/31/2003	12/31/2002	12/31/2001	12/31/2000
Earnings Per Share	0.38	1.36	0.53	0.25	0.31	0.13	0.36	(0.11)
Cash Flow Per Share	2.84	0.76	0.77	0.84	0.56	0.39	0.92	0.37
Tang Book Value Per Share	4.00	3.87	2.49	1.79	2.82	2.45	2.33	1.93
Income Statement								
Total Revenue	982,483	784,868	531,019	353,186	318,669	242,606	303,438	224,505
EBITDA	149,161	253,208	108,681	60,586	58,469	37,521	58,611	31,218
Income Before Taxes	2,162	156,899	57,208	26,359	29,331	13,827	38,269	12,409
Income Taxes	941	54,209	18,878	8,303	9,931	4,928	14,396	4,672
Net Income	28,771	101,878	38,062	17,699	21,664	8,899	23,873	(6,722)
Average Shares	75,921	74,824	72,136	71,199	69,015	67,027	66,766	61,272
Balance Sheet								
Current Assets	423,491	408,097	249,479	157,896	136,801	112,743	136,347	118,084
Total Assets	1,295,536	1,086,190	726,850	508,988	309,599	308,817	309,809	278,940
Current Liabilities	242,050	161,758	134,796	60,844	44,689	40,923	66,891	52,525
Long-Term Obligations	358,024	336,381	157,270	143,754	4	37,220	41,473	50,610
Total Liabilities	847,617	665,810	442,703	272,807	98,830	124,665	142,159	135,186
Stockholders' Equity	447,919	420,380	284,147	236,181	210,769	184,152	167,650	143,754
Shares Outstanding	74,370	71,931	69,537	67,542	66,324	62,682	61,156	61,315
Statistical Record								
Return on Assets %	2.42	11.24	6.16	4.31	7.01	2.88	8.11	N.M.
Return on Equity %	6.63	28.92	14.63	7.90	10.97	5.06	15.33	N.M.
EBITDA Margin %	15.18	32.26	20.47	17.15	18.35	15.47	19.32	13.91
Net Margin %	2.93	12.98	7.17	5.01	6.80	3.67	7.87	N.M.
Asset Turnover	0.83	0.87	0.86	0.86	1.04	0.78	1.03	0.79
Current Ratio	1.75	2.52	1.85	2.60	3.06	2.76	2.04	2.25
Debt to Equity	0.80	0.80	0.55	0.61	N.M.	0.20	0.25	0.35
Price Range	30.14-14.72	31.22-16.67	16.30-8.43	10.72-7.02	8.44-4.00	6.59-3.83	6.46-3.10	3.69-1.61
P/E Ratio	79.32-38.74	22.96-12.26	30.75-15.91	42.89-28.09	27.24-12.90	50.68-29.49	17.95-8.60	..

Address: 25025 I-45 North, The Woodlands, TX 77380
Telephone: 281-367-1983
Fax: 281-364-2240

Web Site: www.tetratec.com
Officers: J. Taft. Symonds - Chmn. Geoffrey M. Hertel - Pres., C.E.O.

Auditors: Ernst & Young LLP
Investor Contact: 281-367-1983

TEXAS INSTRUMENTS INC.

Exchange	Symbol	Price	52Wk Range	Yield	P/E
NYS	TXN	$28.27 (3/31/2008)	39.18-28.11	1.41	15.36

*7 Year Price Score 95.55   *NYSE Composite Index=100   *12 Month Price Score 95.93

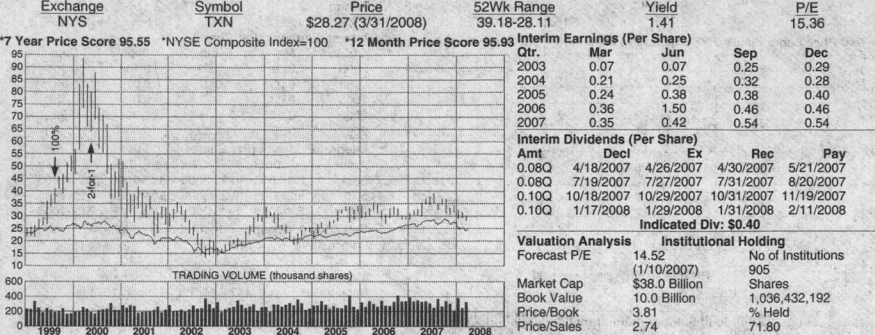

Interim Earnings (Per Share)

Qtr.	Mar	Jun	Sep	Dec
2003	0.07	0.07	0.25	0.29
2004	0.21	0.25	0.32	0.28
2005	0.24	0.38	0.38	0.40
2006	0.36	1.50	0.46	0.46
2007	0.35	0.42	0.54	0.54

Interim Dividends (Per Share)

Amt	Decl	Ex	Rec	Pay
0.08Q	4/18/2007	4/26/2007	4/30/2007	5/21/2007
0.08Q	7/19/2007	7/27/2007	7/31/2007	8/20/2007
0.10Q	10/18/2007	10/29/2007	10/31/2007	11/19/2007
0.10Q	1/17/2008	1/29/2008	1/31/2008	2/11/2008
Indicated Div: $0.40				

Valuation Analysis

		Institutional Holding	
Forecast P/E	14.52	No of Institutions	
	(1/10/2007)	905	
Market Cap	$38.0 Billion	Shares	
Book Value	10.0 Billion	1,036,432,192	
Price/Book	3.81	% Held	
Price/Sales	2.74	71.80	

Business Summary: IT & Technology (MIC: 10.2 SIC: 3674 NAIC: 334413)

Texas Instruments makes, markets and sells technology components through two business segments. Co.'s Semiconductor segment designs, manufactures and sells integrated circuits, and its key products are analog semiconductors and digital signal processors. Co. also designs and manufactures other types of semiconductors, such as DLP® products that are used in projectors and high-definition televisions. Co.'s Education Technology segment supplies graphing handheld calculators. This segment also provides business and scientific calculators and a range of classroom tools and development resources designed to help students and teachers explore math and science.

Recent Developments: For the year ended Dec 31 2007, income from continuing operations was unchanged at US$2.64 billion compared with the year before. Net income decreased 38.8% to US$2.66 billion from US$4.34 billion in the prior year. Revenues were US$13.84 billion, down 2.9% from US$14.26 billion the year before. Operating income was US$3.50 billion versus US$3.37 billion in the prior year, an increase of 3.9%. Direct operating expenses declined 7.1% to US$6.50 billion from US$7.00 billion in the comparable period the year before. Indirect operating expenses decreased 1.4% to US$3.84 billion from US$3.89 billion in the equivalent prior-year period.

Prospects: For the first quarter of 2008, Co. expects year-over-year growth to accelerate in its semiconductor operations. Notably, Co. expects revenue at its semiconductor segment to be in a range of $3.20 billion to $3.46 billion, while expecting revenue at its education technology segment to range between $70.0 million and $90.0 million. Overall, Co. is expecting total revenues of $3.27 billion to $3.55 billion along with earnings per share ranging from $0.43 to $0.49 for the first quarter of 2008. Separately, Co. noted that its assembly/test facility in the Philippines is currently under construction, with initial production planned in the second half of 2008.

Financial Data

(US$ in Thousands)	12/31/2007	12/31/2006	12/31/2005	12/31/2004	12/31/2003	12/31/2002	12/31/2001	12/31/2000
Earnings Per Share	1.84	2.78	1.39	1.05	0.68	(0.20)	(0.12)	1.71
Cash Flow Per Share	3.11	1.61	2.30	1.81	1.24	1.15	1.05	1.27
Tang Book Value Per Share	6.55	7.08	6.84	6.95	6.35	5.73	6.42	6.16
Dividends Per Share	0.300	0.130	0.105	0.089	0.085	0.085	0.085	0.085
Dividend Payout %	16.30	4.68	7.55	8.45	12.50	...	...	4.97
Income Statement								
Total Revenue	13,835,000	14,255,000	13,392,000	12,580,000	9,834,000	8,383,000	8,201,000	11,875,000
EBITDA	4,606,000	4,598,000	4,334,000	3,855,000	2,708,000	1,279,000	1,279,000	5,733,000
Income Before Taxes	3,692,000	3,625,000	2,988,000	2,421,000	1,250,000	(346,000)	(426,000)	4,578,000
Income Taxes	1,051,000	987,000	664,000	560,000	52,000	(2,000)	(225,000)	1,491,000
Net Income	2,657,000	4,341,000	2,324,000	1,861,000	1,198,000	(344,000)	(201,000)	3,058,000
Average Shares	1,446,000	1,560,000	1,671,000	1,768,000	1,766,400	1,733,343	1,734,506	1,791,630
Balance Sheet								
Current Assets	6,918,000	7,854,000	9,185,000	10,190,000	7,709,000	6,126,000	5,775,000	8,115,000
Total Assets	12,667,000	13,930,000	15,063,000	16,299,000	15,510,000	14,679,000	15,779,000	17,720,000
Current Liabilities	2,025,000	2,078,000	2,346,000	1,925,000	2,200,000	1,934,000	1,580,000	2,813,000
Long-Term Obligations	...	...	360,000	368,000	395,000	833,000	1,211,000	1,216,000
Total Liabilities	2,692,000	2,570,000	3,126,000	3,236,000	3,646,000	3,945,000	3,900,000	5,132,000
Stockholders' Equity	9,975,000	11,360,000	11,937,000	13,063,000	11,864,000	10,734,000	11,879,000	12,588,000
Shares Outstanding	1,343,210	1,450,030	1,596,589	1,718,115	1,732,337	1,730,588	1,733,933	1,732,052
Statistical Record								
Return on Assets %	19.98	29.95	14.82	11.67	7.94	N.M.	N.M.	18.62
Return on Equity %	24.91	37.27	18.59	14.89	10.60	N.M.	N.M.	27.92
EBITDA Margin %	33.29	32.26	32.36	30.64	27.54	15.26	15.60	48.28
Net Margin %	19.20	30.45	17.35	14.79	12.18	N.M.	N.M.	25.75
Asset Turnover	1.04	0.98	0.85	0.79	0.65	0.55	0.49	0.72
Current Ratio	3.42	3.78	3.92	5.29	3.50	3.17	3.66	2.88
Debt to Equity	...	...	0.03	0.03	0.03	0.08	0.10	0.10
Price Range	39.18-28.32	35.56-27.00	34.11-20.77	33.65-18.40	30.92-14.15	35.71-13.23	52.06-21.73	93.81-36.88
P/E Ratio	21.29-15.39	12.79-9.71	24.54-14.94	32.05-17.52	45.47-20.81	...	...	54.86-21.56
Average Yield %	0.89	0.42	0.37	0.35	0.40	0.35	0.25	0.13

Address: 12500 TI Boulevard, P.O. Box 660199, Dallas, TX 75266-0199 Telephone: 972-995-3773 Fax: 972-995-4360	Web Site: www.ti.com Officers: Thomas J. Engibous - Chmn. Richard K. Templeton - Pres., C.E.O.	Auditors: Ernst & Young LLP Investor Contact: 972-995-3773

TEXTRON INC.

Exchange	Symbol	Price	52Wk Range	Yield	P/E
NYS	TXT	$55.42 (3/31/2008)	73.38-45.34	1.66	15.39

*7 Year Price Score 135.68 *NYSE Composite Index=100 *12 Month Price Score 101.09

TRADING VOLUME (thousand shares)

Interim Earnings (Per Share)

Qtr.	Mar	Jun	Sep	Dec
2003	0.24	0.23	0.17	0.30
2004	0.13	0.35	0.36	0.45
2005	0.46	0.45	(0.61)	0.44
2006	0.63	0.27	0.66	0.76
2007	0.77	0.83	1.00	1.00

Interim Dividends (Per Share)

Amt	Decl	Ex	Rec	Pay
100%	7/19/2007	8/27/2007	8/3/2007	8/24/2007
0.23Q	7/19/2007	9/12/2007	9/14/2007	10/1/2007
0.23Q	10/24/2007	12/12/2007	12/14/2007	1/1/2008
0.23Q	2/27/2008	3/12/2008	3/14/2008	4/1/2008

Indicated Div: $0.92

Valuation Analysis / **Institutional Holding**

Forecast P/E	13.04 (1/10/2007)	No of Institutions 429
Market Cap	$13.0 Billion	Shares
Book Value	3.5 Billion	87,667,928
Price/Book	3.95	% Held
Price/Sales	1.05	69.98

Business Summary: Aviation (MIC: 1.1 SIC: 3721 NAIC: 336411)

Textron is a global multi-industry company with operations in four business segments: Bell, Cessna, Industrial, and Finance. Co.'s Bell segment comprises of Bell Helicopter and Textron Systems, while its Cessna segment is engaged in the manufacture of general aviation aircraft and has four primary product lines: Citation business jets, single engine turboprop Caravans, Cessna single engine piston aircraft and aftermarket parts and services. Co.'s Industrial segment consists of E-Z-GO, Jacobsen, Kautex, Greenlee and Fluid & Power businesses, while its Finance segment includes Textron Financial Corporation and its subsidiaries.

Recent Developments: For the year ended Dec 29 2007, income from continuing operations increased 29.6% to US$915.0 million from US$706.0 million a year earlier. Net income increased 52.6% to US$917.0 million from US$601.0 million in the prior year. Revenues were US$13.23 billion, up 15.1% from US$11.49 billion the year before. Direct operating expenses rose 13.9% to US$9.72 billion from US$8.53 billion in the comparable period the year before. Indirect operating expenses increased 11.2% to US$2.21 billion from US$1.99 billion in the equivalent prior-year period.

Prospects: Despite the expected softening as well as a temporary downturn in the U.S. economy in 2008, Co. anticipates jet orders to exceed the existing year deliveries. Accordingly, for full-year 2008, Co. expects revenues to increase by 13.0% to about $15.00 billion and projects earnings to be between $3.75 and $3.95 per share. In addition, Co. is expecting earnings of $0.75 to $0.85 per share for the first quarter of 2008. Meanwhile, on Jan 16 2008, Co.'s Bell Helicopter segment announced the acquisition of SkyBOOKS, an aviation management applications business, which should further advance its strategy in delivering broader and more integrated applications to the worldwide aviation industry.

Financial Data

(US$ in Thousands)	12/29/2007	12/30/2006	12/31/2005	01/01/2005	01/03/2004	12/28/2002	12/29/2001	12/30/2000
Earnings Per Share	3.60	2.31	0.75	1.30	0.94	(0.44)	0.58	0.75
Cash Flow Per Share	4.21	3.91	3.80	3.46	3.07	2.51	3.49	3.30
Tang Book Value Per Share	4.81	4.83	8.01	7.35	7.47	6.46	6.93	5.83
Dividends Per Share	0.848	0.775	0.700	0.662	0.650	0.650	0.650	0.650
Dividend Payout %	23.54	33.55	93.96	50.77	68.78	...	112.07	87.25
Income Statement								
Total Revenue	13,225,000	11,490,000	10,043,000	10,242,000	9,859,000	10,658,000	12,321,000	13,090,000
EBITDA	1,636,000	1,265,000	1,042,000	881,000	757,000	858,000	933,000	1,105,000
Income Before Taxes	1,300,000	975,000	739,000	528,000	401,000	490,000	419,000	611,000
Income Taxes	385,000	269,000	223,000	155,000	107,000	100,000	227,000	308,000
Net Income	917,000	601,000	203,000	303,000	259,000	(124,000)	166,000	218,000
Average Shares	254,826	260,444	272,892	280,338	274,434	280,504	285,874	292,300
Balance Sheet								
Current Assets	4,846,000	4,287,000	4,975,000	4,168,000	3,592,000	3,887,000	4,017,000	3,914,000
Total Assets	19,956,000	17,550,000	16,499,000	15,875,000	15,090,000	15,505,000	16,052,000	16,370,000
Current Liabilities	4,122,000	2,994,000	3,147,000	2,975,000	2,256,000	2,239,000	3,075,000	3,263,000
Long-Term Obligations	9,104,000	8,582,000	7,079,000	6,141,000	6,118,000	6,526,000	5,959,000	6,136,000
Total Liabilities	16,449,000	14,901,000	13,223,000	12,223,000	11,400,000	11,587,000	11,605,000	11,864,000
Stockholders' Equity	3,507,000	2,649,000	3,276,000	3,652,000	3,690,000	3,406,000	3,934,000	3,994,000
Shares Outstanding	250,100	251,191	260,369	270,746	274,476	273,000	282,502	281,866
Statistical Record								
Return on Assets %	4.90	3.54	1.26	2.36	1.67	N.M.	1.03	1.33
Return on Equity %	29.87	20.34	5.88	9.97	7.18	N.M.	4.20	5.22
EBITDA Margin %	12.37	11.01	10.38	8.60	7.68	8.05	7.57	8.44
Net Margin %	6.93	5.23	2.02	3.56	2.63	N.M.	1.35	1.67
Asset Turnover	0.71	0.68	0.62	0.66	0.63	0.68	0.76	0.80
Current Ratio	1.18	1.43	1.58	1.40	1.59	1.74	1.31	1.20
Debt to Equity	2.60	3.24	2.16	1.68	1.66	1.92	1.51	1.54
Price Range	73.38-44.08	49.19-37.88	40.02-32.92	37.31-25.42	28.85-13.43	26.59-16.25	29.95-15.82	38.34-20.72
P/E Ratio	20.38-12.24	21.29-16.40	53.37-43.90	28.70-19.55	30.69-14.28	...	51.63-27.28	51.13-27.63
Average Yield %	1.51	1.74	1.88	2.18	3.19	3.01	2.63	2.30

Address: 40 Westminster Street, Providence, RI 02903	**Web Site:** www.textron.com	**Auditors:** Ernst & Young LLP
Telephone: 401-421-2800	**Officers:** Lewis B. Campbell - Chmn., Pres., C.E.O. John D. Butler - Exec. V.P., Admin., Chief Human Res. Officer	**Investor Contact:** 401-421-2800
Fax: 401-421-2878		

THE GAP, INC.

Exchange	Symbol	Price	52Wk Range	Yield	P/E
NYS	GPS	$19.68 (3/31/2008)	21.87-15.66	1.73	18.74

*7 Year Price Score 80.72 *NYSE Composite Index=100 *12 Month Price Score 113.13

Interim Earnings (Per Share)

Qtr.	Apr	Jul	Oct	Jan
2003-04	0.22	0.22	0.28	0.37
2004-05	0.32	0.21	0.28	0.40
2005-06	0.31	0.30	0.24	0.38
2006-07	0.28	0.15	0.23	0.27
2007-08	0.22	0.19	0.30	0.35

Interim Dividends (Per Share)

Amt	Decl	Ex	Rec	Pay
0.08Q	6/6/2007	7/6/2007	7/10/2007	7/31/2007
0.08Q	10/2/2007	10/12/2007	10/16/2007	10/30/2007
0.08Q	11/27/2008	1/7/2008	1/9/2008	1/30/2008
0.085Q	3/26/2009	4/4/2008	4/8/2008	4/29/2008

Indicated Div: $0.34

Valuation Analysis

Forecast P/E	N/A
Market Cap	$14.4 Billion
Book Value	4.3 Billion
Price/Book	3.38
Price/Sales	0.92

Institutional Holding

No of Institutions	379
Shares	482,309,792
% Held	59.13

TRADING VOLUME (thousand shares)

Business Summary: Retail - Apparel and Accessory Stores (MIC: 5.8 SIC: 5651 NAIC: 448140)

The Gap is a global specialty retailer operating retail and outlet stores selling casual apparel, accessories, and personal care products for men, women and children under the Gap, Old Navy, Banana Republic and Piperlime brands. Co. operates its stores in the U.S., Canada, the U.K., France, Ireland and Japan. In addition, Co.'s U.S. customers may shop online at www.gap.com, www.bananarepublic.com, www.oldnavy.com and www.piperlime.com. Co. designs most of its products, which are manufactured by independent sources, and sell them under its brands. Co.'s stores provide a shopper-friendly environment with an assortment of casual apparel and accessories.

Recent Developments: For the year ended Feb 2 2008, income from continuing operations increased 7.2% to US$867.0 million from US$809.0 million a year earlier. Net income increased 7.1% to US$833.0 million from US$778.0 million in the prior year. Revenues were US$15.76 billion, down 1.0% from US$15.92 billion the year before. Direct operating expenses declined 1.9% to US$10.07 billion from US$10.27 billion in the comparable period the year before. Indirect operating expenses decreased 1.2% to US$4.38 billion from US$4.43 billion in the equivalent prior-year period.

Prospects: Looking ahead into fiscal year ending Feb 2009, Co. estimates its capital spending to be about $500 million. Further, Co. plans to open about 115 new store locations and to close about 100 store locations. These openings and closings include 15 store repositions. As a result, Co. expects net square footage to grow less than half a percent for fiscal 2008. Also, Co. projects its diluted earnings to be in the range of $1.20 to $1.27 per share for fiscal 2008. Meanwhile, Co. will focus on driving earnings through inventory discipline which supports improved gross margin, continuing cost management, improving return on invested capital, and continuing to focus on product across all brands.

Financial Data

(US$ in Thousands)	02/02/2008	02/03/2007	01/28/2006	01/29/2005	01/31/2004	02/01/2003	02/02/2002	02/03/2001
Earnings Per Share	1.05	0.93	1.24	1.21	1.09	0.54	(0.01)	1.00
Cash Flow Per Share	2.64	1.48	1.77	1.82	2.44	1.42	1.54	1.49
Tang Book Value Per Share	5.82	6.36	6.33	5.74	5.33	4.12	3.48	3.43
Dividends Per Share	0.320	0.320	0.202	0.089	0.089	0.089	0.089	0.089
Dividend Payout %	30.48	34.41	16.31	7.34	8.15	16.44	...	8.88
Income Statement								
Total Revenue	15,763,000	15,943,000	16,023,000	16,267,000	15,854,000	14,454,709	13,847,873	13,673,460
EBITDA	1,862,000	1,704,000	2,370,000	2,600,000	2,543,000	1,793,505	1,148,002	2,035,126
Income Before Taxes	1,406,000	1,264,000	1,793,000	1,872,000	1,683,000	800,875	241,641	1,381,885
Income Taxes	539,000	486,000	680,000	722,000	653,000	323,418	249,405	504,388
Net Income	833,000	778,000	1,113,000	1,150,000	1,030,000	477,457	(7,764)	877,497
Average Shares	794,000	835,973	902,305	991,121	988,177	881,477	860,255	879,137
Balance Sheet								
Current Assets	4,086,000	5,029,000	5,239,000	6,304,000	6,689,000	5,739,725	3,044,550	2,648,050
Total Assets	7,838,000	8,544,000	8,821,000	10,048,000	10,343,000	9,902,004	7,591,326	7,012,908
Current Liabilities	2,433,000	2,272,000	1,942,000	2,242,000	2,492,000	2,726,574	2,056,233	2,799,144
Long-Term Obligations	50,000	188,000	513,000	1,886,000	2,487,000	2,895,794	1,961,397	780,246
Total Liabilities	3,564,000	3,370,000	3,396,000	5,112,000	5,560,000	6,243,792	4,581,745	4,084,669
Stockholders' Equity	4,274,000	5,174,000	5,425,000	4,936,000	4,783,000	3,658,212	3,009,581	2,928,239
Shares Outstanding	734,000	813,870	856,986	860,559	897,202	887,322	865,726	853,996
Statistical Record								
Return on Assets %	10.20	8.82	11.83	11.31	10.20	5.47	N.M.	14.15
Return on Equity %	17.68	14.44	21.54	23.73	24.47	14.36	N.M.	33.45
EBITDA Margin %	11.81	10.69	14.79	15.98	16.04	12.41	8.29	14.88
Net Margin %	5.28	4.88	6.95	7.07	6.50	3.30	N.M.	6.42
Asset Turnover	1.93	1.81	1.70	1.60	1.57	1.66	1.90	2.20
Current Ratio	1.68	2.21	2.70	2.81	2.68	2.11	1.48	0.95
Debt to Equity	0.01	0.04	0.09	0.38	0.52	0.79	0.65	0.27
Price Range	21.87-15.66	21.09-16.22	22.58-16.00	25.66-18.65	23.24-12.70	16.89-8.84	34.90-11.40	52.88-18.75
P/E Ratio	20.83-14.91	22.68-17.44	18.21-12.90	21.21-15.41	21.32-11.65	31.28-16.37	...	52.88-18.75
Average Yield %	1.71	1.74	1.03	0.41	0.49	0.65	0.41	0.27

Address: Two Folsom Street, San Francisco, CA 94105	Web Site: www.gapinc.com	Auditors: Deloitte & Touche LLP
Telephone: 650-952-4400	Officers: Paul S. Pressler - Pres., C.E.O. Byron H. Pollitt Jr. - Exec. V.P., C.F.O.	Transfer Agents: Wells Fargo Bank, N.A., South St. Paul, MN
Fax: 650-952-4407		

THERMO FISHER SCIENTIFIC INC

Exchange	Symbol	Price	52Wk Range	Yield	P/E
NYS	TMO	$56.84 (3/31/2008)	59.51-46.30	N/A	33.05

*7 Year Price Score 141.49 *NYSE Composite Index=100 *12 Month Price Score 107.67

TRADING VOLUME (thousand shares)

Interim Earnings (Per Share)

Qtr.	Mar	Jun	Sep	Dec
2003	0.22	0.32	0.29	0.37
2004	0.26	0.54	0.65	0.74
2005	0.30	0.37	0.35	0.34
2006	0.28	0.29	0.30	(0.04)
2007	0.31	0.37	0.49	0.55

Interim Dividends (Per Share)

No Dividends Paid

Valuation Analysis   **Institutional Holding**

Forecast P/E	15.06	No of Institutions
	(1/10/2007)	589
Market Cap	$23.6 Billion	Shares
Book Value	14.5 Billion	388,954,816
Price/Book	1.63	% Held
Price/Sales	2.42	92.60

Business Summary: Instruments and Related Products (MIC: 11.15 SIC: 3829 NAIC: 334519)

Thermo Fisher Scientific provides analytical instruments, equipment, reagents and consumables, software and services for research, manufacturing, analysis, discovery and diagnostics. Co. operates through two principal segments: Analytical Technologies and Laboratory Products and Services. Co.'s portfolio of products includes technologies for mass spectrometry, elemental analysis, molecular spectroscopy, sample preparation, informatics, fine and high-purity chemistry production, cell culture, ribonuclele acid interference analysis and immunodiagnostic testing, as well as air and water quality monitoring and process control.

Recent Developments: For the year ended Dec 31 2007, income from continuing operations increased 368.8% to US$779.6 million from US$166.3 million a year earlier. Net income increased 350.6% to US$761.1 million from US$168.9 million in the prior year. Revenues were US$9.75 billion, up 157.1% from US$3.79 billion the year before. Operating income was US$974.4 million versus US$242.0 million in the prior year, an increase of 302.6%. Direct operating expenses rose 167.2% to US$5.94 billion from US$2.22 billion in the comparable period the year before. Indirect operating expenses increased 113.4% to US$2.83 billion from US$1.33 billion in the equivalent prior year period.

Prospects: On Dec 20 2007, Co. announced that it has acquired La-Pha-Pack, a producer of chromatography consumables and related accessories, based in Langerwehe, Germany. The acquisition should allow Co. to strengthen its chromatography offering in Europe by complementing its existing specialty brand, Chromacol, which is manufactured in the U.K. Also, Co. plans to take advantage of La-Pha-Pack's manufacturing and assembly processes to improve its production capabilities as well as the efficiency of its consumable products. Meanwhile, Co. expects 2008 revenues, excluding any future acquisitions or divestitures, to be between $10.50 billion and $10.60 billion, up 8.0% to 9.0% over its 2007 results.

Financial Data
(US$ in Thousands)

	12/31/2007	12/31/2006	12/31/2005	12/31/2004	12/31/2003	12/28/2002	12/29/2001	12/30/2000
Earnings Per Share	1.72	0.84	1.36	2.17	1.20	1.73	...	(0.22)
Cash Flow Per Share	3.32	2.07	1.88	1.82	1.32	0.61	1.05	1.20
Tang Book Value Per Share	N.M.	N.M.	2.32	6.19	5.00	3.79	3.17	6.34
Income Statement								
Total Revenue	9,746,400	3,791,617	2,633,027	2,205,995	2,097,135	2,086,355	2,188,210	2,280,522
EBITDA	1,731,400	485,654	424,316	327,318	276,180	337,404	172,481	325,308
Income Before Taxes	881,300	209,370	285,898	259,219	218,633	287,986	70,681	184,831
Income Taxes	101,700	43,054	87,597	40,852	45,936	92,987	26,929	112,217
Net Income	761,100	168,935	223,218	361,837	200,009	309,730	(781)	(36,111)
Average Shares	443,700	203,672	165,334	167,641	170,730	186,611	183,916	170,519
Balance Sheet								
Current Assets	3,665,300	3,659,536	1,353,900	1,469,654	1,395,756	1,771,559	1,965,210	2,465,529
Total Assets	21,207,400	21,262,238	4,251,569	3,576,725	3,388,969	3,647,062	3,825,070	4,862,977
Current Liabilities	1,901,600	2,152,321	791,662	578,728	684,793	1,103,720	1,142,039	728,551
Long-Term Obligations	2,045,900	2,180,705	468,620	226,070	229,509	451,341	727,502	1,528,483
Total Liabilities	6,719,100	7,350,411	1,458,257	911,175	1,006,163	1,613,739	1,916,928	2,329,001
Stockholders' Equity	14,488,300	13,911,827	2,793,312	2,665,550	2,382,806	2,033,323	1,908,142	2,533,976
Shares Outstanding	415,237	416,605	162,482	160,549	165,063	162,853	176,357	182,168
Statistical Record								
Return on Assets %	3.58	1.32	5.70	10.36	5.64	8.31	N.M.	N.M.
Return on Equity %	5.36	2.02	8.18	14.30	8.98	15.76	N.M.	N.M.
EBITDA Margin %	17.76	12.81	16.12	14.84	13.17	16.17	7.88	14.26
Net Margin %	7.81	4.46	8.48	16.40	9.54	14.85	N.M.	N.M.
Asset Turnover	0.46	0.30	0.67	0.63	0.59	0.56	0.51	0.46
Current Ratio	1.93	1.70	1.71	2.54	2.04	1.61	1.72	3.38
Debt to Equity	0.14	0.16	0.17	0.08	0.10	0.22	0.38	0.60
Price Range	59.51-44.16	46.16-30.28	31.78-24.24	31.00-24.21	25.37-17.02	24.37-14.50	26.25-15.56	26.76-12.26
P/E Ratio	34.60-25.67	54.95-36.05	23.37-17.82	14.29-11.16	21.14-14.18	14.09-8.38	N.M.	...

Address: 81 Wyman Street, P.O. Box 9046, Waltham, MA 02454-9046
Telephone: 781-622-1000
Fax: 781-933-4476

Web Site: www.thermofisher.com
Officers: Jim P. Manzi - Chmn. Marijn E. Dekkers - Pres., C.E.O.

Auditors: PricewaterhouseCoopers LLP
Investor Contact: 781-622-1111
Transfer Agents: American Stock Transfer & Trust Co., New York, NY

THOMAS & BETTS CORP.

Exchange	Symbol	Price	52Wk Range	Yield	P/E
NYS	TNB	$36.37 (3/31/2008)	63.31-34.27	N/A	11.66

*7 Year Price Score 131.23 *NYSE Composite Index=100 *12 Month Price Score 81.94

TRADING VOLUME (thousand shares)

Interim Earnings (Per Share)

Qtr.	Mar	Jun	Sep	Dec
2003	0.09	0.12	0.20	0.33
2004	0.27	0.34	0.56	0.40
2005	0.40	0.47	0.57	0.42
2006	0.62	0.66	0.74	0.84
2007	0.63	0.80	0.88	0.82

Interim Dividends (Per Share)

No Dividends Paid

Valuation Analysis — **Institutional Holding**

Forecast P/E	13.17	No of Institutions
	(1/10/2007)	237
Market Cap	$2.1 Billion	Shares
Book Value	1.2 Billion	52,661,724
Price/Book	1.72	% Held
Price/Sales	0.99	89.14

Business Summary: Electrical (MIC: 11.14 SIC: 3678 NAIC: 334417)

Thomas & Betts is engaged in the designing and manufacturing of electrical components used in industrial, commercial, communications, and utility markets. As of Dec 31 2007, Co. operated in three business segments: Electrical, which designs, manufactures and markets different connectors, components and other products for electrical, utility and communications applications; Steel Structures, which designs, manufactures and markets engineered tubular steel transmission and distribution poles; and Heating, Ventilation and Air-Conditioning, which designs, manufactures and markets heating and ventilation products for commercial and industrial buildings.

Recent Developments: For the year ended Dec 31 2007, income from continuing operations increased 4.9% to US$183.7 million from US$175.1 million a year earlier. Net income increased 4.6% to US$183.2 million from US$175.1 million in the prior year. Revenues were US$2.14 billion, up 14.4% from US$1.87 billion the year before. Operating income was US$289.4 million versus US$245.8 million in the prior year, an increase of 17.7%. Direct operating expenses rose 13.6% to US$1.48 billion from US$1.30 billion in the comparable period the year before. Indirect operating expenses increased 14.9% to US$371.9 million from US$323.6 million in the equivalent prior-year period.

Prospects: On Jan 17 2008, Co. announced that it has acquired The Homac Manufacturing Company, a privately held manufacturer of components used in utility distribution and substation markets, as well as industrial and telecommunications markets, for $75.0 million. Separately, for 2008, Co. expects sales growth of approximately 25.0% when compared with 2007. In addition, Co. expects its recently completed acquisitions to contribute approximately 20.0% to the sales growth, with the balance of the sales growth coming from existing businesses. Also, Co. expects diluted per share earnings from continuing operations to be in the range of $3.80 to $3.95 for 2008.

Financial Data
(US$ in Thousands)

	12/31/2007	12/31/2006	12/31/2005	12/31/2004	12/31/2003	12/29/2002	12/30/2001	12/31/2000
Earnings Per Share	3.12	2.85	1.86	1.57	0.73	(0.91)	(2.52)	(0.77)
Cash Flow Per Share	4.51	3.66	3.22	1.09	1.65	1.38	1.83	(4.30)
Tang Book Value Per Share	0.89	9.72	9.65	7.39	4.73	3.21	3.58	6.34
Dividends Per Share	...	...	...	...	0.005	...	0.560	1.120
Dividend Payout %	...	...	...	...	0.68	...	...	...
Income Statement								
Total Revenue	2,136,888	1,868,689	1,695,383	1,516,292	1,322,297	1,345,857	1,497,491	1,756,083
EBITDA	345,178	296,124	249,478	210,243	134,951	83,259	(48,860)	(111,585)
Income Before Taxes	263,891	233,442	175,860	127,830	47,745	(2,210)	(187,039)	(272,230)
Income Taxes	80,215	58,312	62,452	34,575	4,932	6,002	(48,162)	(78,847)
Net Income	183,216	175,130	113,408	93,255	42,813	(53,027)	(146,390)	(44,570)
Average Shares	58,720	61,447	61,065	59,357	58,447	58,273	58,116	57,950
Balance Sheet								
Current Assets	905,915	868,370	950,142	778,895	812,279	704,931	770,303	968,561
Total Assets	2,567,786	1,830,223	1,920,396	1,755,752	1,782,625	1,619,756	1,761,610	2,087,763
Current Liabilities	468,973	248,529	404,411	238,409	364,960	297,159	355,709	419,260
Long-Term Obligations	695,048	386,912	387,155	543,085	551,972	559,982	618,035	669,983
Total Liabilities	1,338,852	761,864	867,806	854,033	1,051,198	995,620	1,078,325	1,181,853
Stockholders' Equity	1,228,934	1,068,359	1,052,590	901,719	731,427	624,136	683,285	905,910
Shares Outstanding	57,988	59,473	61,089	59,353	58,475	58,296	58,158	58,148
Statistical Record								
Return on Assets %	8.33	9.34	6.17	5.26	2.50	N.M.	N.M.	N.M.
Return on Equity %	15.95	16.51	11.61	11.39	6.28	N.M.	N.M.	N.M.
EBITDA Margin %	16.15	15.85	14.72	13.87	10.21	6.19	N.M.	N.M.
Net Margin %	8.57	9.37	6.69	6.15	3.24	N.M.	N.M.	N.M.
Asset Turnover	0.97	1.00	0.92	0.85	0.77	0.80	0.78	0.74
Current Ratio	1.93	3.49	2.35	3.27	2.23	2.37	2.17	2.31
Debt to Equity	0.57	0.36	0.37	0.60	0.75	0.90	0.90	0.74
Price Range	63.31-45.46	60.48-41.79	42.82-27.59	32.09-19.72	23.15-13.75	24.48-12.26	23.63-15.50	33.69-13.50
P/E Ratio	20.29-14.57	21.22-14.66	23.02-14.83	20.44-12.56	31.71-18.84	...	...	...
Average Yield %	...	...	...	...	0.03	...	2.81	5.03

Address: 8155 T & B Boulevard,	Web Site: www.tnb.com	Auditors: KPMG LLP
Memphis, TN 38125	Officers: Dominic J. Pileggi - Pres., C.E.O. Kenneth	Investor Contact: 901-252-8266
Telephone: 901-252-8000	W. Fluke - Sr. V.P., C.F.O.	
Fax: 901-685-1988		

THOR INDUSTRIES, INC.

Exchange	Symbol	Price	52Wk Range	Yield	P/E
NYS	THO	$29.77 (3/31/2008)	52.00-28.60	0.94	11.41

*7 Year Price Score 111.53 *NYSE Composite Index=100   *12 Month Price Score 85.69

Interim Earnings (Per Share)

Qtr.	Oct	Jan	Apr	Jul
2004-05	0.61	0.36	0.58	0.58
2005-06	0.76	0.56	0.90	0.81
2006-07	0.58	0.33	0.64	0.90
2007-08	0.68	0.39	...	...

Interim Dividends (Per Share)

Amt	Decl	Ex	Rec	Pay
0.07Q	8/6/2007	9/25/2007	9/27/2007	10/8/2007
2.00Q	8/6/2007	9/25/2007	9/27/2007	10/8/2007
0.07Q	11/16/2007	12/5/2007	12/7/2007	1/4/2008
0.07Q	3/11/2008	3/18/2008	3/20/2008	4/7/2008

Indicated Div: $0.28

Valuation Analysis

Institutional Holding		
Forecast P/E	15.29	No of Institutions
	(1/10/2007)	212
Market Cap	$1.7 Billion	Shares
Book Value	681.1 Million	38,271,648
Price/Book	2.43	% Held
Price/Sales	0.57	68.70

Business Summary: Automotive (MIC: 15.1 SIC: 3716 NAIC: 336213)

Thor Industries produces and sells recreation vehicles as well as small and mid-size buses in the U.S. and Canada, as well as related parts and accessories. Co. has three reportable segments: towable recreation vehicles, motorized recreation vehicles, and buses. As of Jul 31 2007, Co. produced several types of recreation vehicles, including travel trailers and motorhomes, conventional travel trailers and fifth wheels, Class C and Class A motorhomes and truck campers. Co. also sells small and mid-size commercial buses consisting of buses for transit, airport car rental and hotel/motel shuttles, paramedical transit for hospitals and nursing homes, tour and charter operations.

Recent Developments: For the quarter ended Jan 31 2008, net income increased 18.4% to US$21.6 million from US$18.3 million in the year-earlier quarter. Revenues were US$599.2 million, up 2.6% from US$584.0 million the year before. Direct operating expenses rose 1.3% to US$529.5 million from US$522.9 million in the comparable period the year before. Indirect operating expenses increased 0.2% to US$37.5 million from US$37.4 million in the equivalent prior-year period.

Prospects: Co.'s outlook appears favorable reflecting increases in its top- and bottom-line results. Specifically, Co is seeing revenue growth in its Towable Recreation Vehicles segment primarily from an increase in its average price per unit and product offerings, coupled with higher unit shipments, partly offset by a lower revenues in its Motorized Recreation Vehicles segment due to reduced unit shipment. Looking ahead, Co. remains focused on increasing its profitability in North America in the recreation vehicle industry and in its bus business by enriching its product portfolio, improving its customer service, manufacturing capabilities, and its facilities, as well as via strategic acquisitions.

Financial Data

(US$ in Thousands)	6 Mos	3 Mos	07/31/2007	07/31/2006	07/31/2005	07/31/2004	07/31/2003	07/31/2002
Earnings Per Share	2.61	2.55	2.41	3.03	2.13	1.84	1.37	0.94
Cash Flow Per Share	3.03	3.43	4.18	2.43	2.32	1.45	0.80	2.46
Tang Book Value Per Share	9.01	8.86	10.49	9.53	7.31	6.21	5.49	3.35
Dividends Per Share	2.280	2.280	1.280	0.240	0.370	0.090	0.025	0.020
Dividend Payout %	87.36	89.41	53.11	7.92	17.37	4.89	1.82	2.14
Income Statement								
Total Revenue	1,362,906	763,736	2,856,308	3,066,276	2,558,351	2,187,739	1,571,404	1,245,300
EBITDA	96,147	60,210	200,163	276,697	201,810	175,042	130,934	85,836
Depn & Amortn	7,105	3,566	...	...	...	...	...	...
Income Before Taxes	95,686	60,480	196,860	270,423	193,610	168,220	126,244	81,827
Income Taxes	35,875	22,271	62,129	97,959	71,843	62,134	47,613	30,646
Net Income	59,811	38,209	134,731	172,464	121,767	106,085	78,631	51,182
Average Shares	55,910	55,966	55,923	56,897	57,107	57,590	57,449	54,685
Balance Sheet								
Current Assets	653,101	663,176	705,528	659,833	524,040	497,966	378,632	291,238
Total Assets	1,006,854	1,018,071	1,059,297	1,011,843	857,879	762,587	608,941	497,503
Current Liabilities	278,043	295,728	277,199	285,827	248,812	241,768	187,943	156,920
Total Liabilities	325,750	341,948	292,966	298,738	260,492	250,983	194,120	162,884
Stockholders' Equity	681,104	676,123	766,331	713,104	597,387	511,604	414,822	334,619
Shares Outstanding	55,497	55,870	55,780	55,699	56,677	57,146	49,561	56,965
Statistical Record								
Return on Assets %	14.74	14.31	13.01	18.45	15.03	15.43	14.21	12.69
Return on Equity %	21.32	20.91	18.21	26.32	21.96	22.84	20.98	18.46
EBITDA Margin %	7.05	7.88	7.01	9.02	7.89	8.00	8.33	6.89
Net Margin %	4.39	5.00	4.72	5.62	4.76	4.85	5.00	4.11
Asset Turnover	2.94	2.91	2.76	3.28	3.16	3.18	2.84	3.09
Current Ratio	2.35	2.24	2.55	2.31	2.11	2.06	2.01	1.86
Price Range	52.00-30.24	52.00-38.90	47.52-38.90	55.94-30.96	37.91-24.92	34.34-21.25	22.65-10.90	18.36-5.63
P/E Ratio	19.92-11.59	20.39-15.25	19.72-16.14	18.46-10.22	17.80-11.70	18.66-11.55	16.53-7.96	19.53-5.98
Average Yield %	5.49	5.24	2.99	0.57	1.19	0.31	0.15	0.17

Address: 419 West Pike Street, Jackson Center, OH 45334	Web Site: www.thorindustries.com	Auditors: Deloitte & Touche LLP
Telephone: 937-596-6849	Officers: Wade F. B. Thompson - Chmn., Pres., C.E.O. Peter B. Orthwein - Vice-Chmn., Treas.	Transfer Agents: Computershare Investor Services
Fax: 937-596-6539		

THORNBURG MORTGAGE INC

Exchange	Symbol	Price	52Wk Range	Yield	P/E
NYS	TMA	$1.21 (3/31/2008)	28.11-0.71	N/A	N/A

*7 Year Price Score 56.06   *NYSE Composite Index=100   *12 Month Price Score 47.03

TRADING VOLUME (thousand shares)

Interim Earnings (Per Share)

Qtr.	Mar	Jun	Sep	Dec
2003	0.67	0.67	0.68	0.69
2004	0.70	0.71	0.69	0.71
2005	0.72	0.70	0.70	0.68
2006	0.66	0.61	0.64	0.67
2007	0.62	0.66	(8.94)	0.59

Interim Dividends (Per Share)

Amt	Decl	Ex	Rec	Pay
0.68Q	12/14/2006	12/27/2006	12/29/2006	1/26/2007
0.68Q	4/19/2007	5/2/2007	5/4/2007	5/15/2007
0.68Q	7/19/2007	8/1/2007	8/3/2007	9/17/2007
0.25Q	12/18/2007	12/27/2007	12/31/2007	1/30/2008

Valuation Analysis — **Institutional Holding**

Forecast P/E	N/A	No of Institutions 182
Market Cap	$169.3 Million	Shares
Book Value	2.0 Billion	27,416,920
Price/Book	0.08	% Held
Price/Sales	0.11	24.05

Business Summary: Property, Real Estate & Development (MIC: 8.3 SIC: 6798 NAIC: 525930)

Thornburg Mortgage is a single-family residential mortgage lender that originates, acquires and retains investments in adjustable-rate mortgage (ARM) assets, thereby providing capital to the single-family residential housing market. Co.'s ARM assets consist of Purchased ARM Assets and ARM Loans. Purchased ARM Assets are mortgage backed securities that represent interests in pools of ARM loans, which are publicly rated and issued by third parties. ARM Loans are either loans that Co. has securitized from its own loan origination or acquisition activities, loans that it uses as collateral to support the issuance of collateralized mortgage debt or loans pending securitization.

Recent Developments: For the year ended Dec 31 2007, net loss amounted to US$874.9 million versus net income of US$297.7 million in the prior year. Revenues were US$1.52 billion, down 39.7% from US$2.53 billion the year before.

Prospects: While the mortgage industry is projected to remain challenging, Co. expects its interest spread and portfolio margin to increase in the coming quarters as borrowing costs react to lower market interest rates while relatively slow prepayments preserve the yield on its Adjustable Rate Mortgage (ARM) assets at present level. Co. also expects to benefit from its focus on providing jumbo and super-jumbo ARM loans to key borrowers with better credit directly and via its lending partners, as well as from the expansion of its lending partner network as it builds and retains relationships with its existing client base. Accordingly, Co. expects to originate $6.10 billion in mortgage loans in 2008.

Financial Data

(US$ in Thousands)	12/31/2007	12/31/2006	12/31/2005	12/31/2004	12/31/2003	12/31/2002	12/31/2001	12/31/2000
Earnings Per Share	(7.48)	2.58	2.79	2.80	2.71	2.59	2.09	1.05
Cash Flow Per Share	1.83	1.99	2.25	3.40	3.30	3.01	3.25	2.27
Tang Book Value Per Share	8.36	18.92	20.00	19.47	16.75	14.54	14.02	11.67
Dividends Per Share	1.610	2.720	2.720	2.660	2.490	2.285	2.000	0.940
Dividend Payout %	...	105.43	97.49	95.00	91.88	88.22	95.69	89.52
Income Statement								
Interest Income	2,623,503	2,474,487	1,511,334	930,062	589,615	401,967	278,594	289,973
Interest Expense	2,307,242	2,127,803	1,166,877	635,794	355,662	244,038	199,829	253,343
Net Interest Income	316,261	346,684	344,457	294,268	233,953	157,929	78,765	36,630
Provision for Losses	6,728	3,149	1,212	1,436	3,137	...	653	1,158
Non-Interest Income	(1,100,147)	50,714	26,734	17,264	7,888	1,495	50	287
Non-Interest Expense	67,334	96,552	87,135	77,057	62,200	39,408	19,500	6,594
Income Before Taxes	(857,948)	297,697	282,844	233,039	...	...	...	...
Income Taxes	17,000	...	...	475	...	...	...	...
Net Income	(874,948)	297,697	282,844	232,564	176,504	120,016	58,460	29,165
Average Shares	122,303	111,055	99,187	83,001	65,217	46,350	24,803	21,506
Balance Sheet								
Net Loans & Leases	24,739,298	23,221,639	14,349,521	10,087,016	7,331,425	999,570	569,518	780,109
Total Assets	36,521,162	52,705,052	42,507,741	29,189,618	19,118,799	10,512,932	5,803,648	4,190,167
Total Liabilities	34,518,477	50,327,980	40,300,655	27,400,434	17,879,695	9,679,890	5,270,990	3,872,629
Stockholders' Equity	2,002,685	2,377,072	2,207,086	1,789,184	1,239,104	833,042	532,658	317,538
Shares Outstanding	139,936	113,775	104,775	91,904	73,985	52,763	33,305	21,572
Statistical Record								
Return on Assets %	N.M.	0.63	0.79	0.96	1.19	1.47	1.17	0.68
Return on Equity %	N.M.	12.99	14.16	15.32	17.04	17.58	13.75	9.26
Net Interest Margin %	12.05	14.01	22.79	31.64	39.68	39.29	28.27	12.63
Efficiency Ratio %	4.42	3.82	5.67	8.13	10.41	9.77	7.00	2.27
Price Range	28.11-7.61	28.91-22.55	30.82-22.72	31.28-23.75	27.90-19.70	21.20-17.10	21.03-9.44	9.75-7.06
P/E Ratio	...	11.21-8.74	11.05-8.14	11.17-8.48	10.30-7.27	8.19-6.60	10.06-4.52	9.29-6.73
Average Yield %	7.93	10.47	9.78	9.45	10.35	11.34	13.61	11.11

Address: 150 Washington Avenue, Suite 302, Santa Fe, NM 87501	Web Site: www.thornburgmortgage.com	Auditors: KPMG LLP
Telephone: 505-989-1900	Officers: Garrett Thornburg - Chmn., C.E.O. Larry A. Goldstone - Pres., C.O.O.	Investor Contact: 505-989-1900
Fax: 505-989-8156		Transfer Agents: American Stock Transfer & Trust Company

3M CO

Exchange	Symbol	Price	52Wk Range	Yield	P/E	Div Acheiver
NYS	MMM	$79.15 (3/31/2008)	95.85-74.91	2.53	14.13	49 Years

*7 Year Price Score 92.82 *NYSE Composite Index=100 *12 Month Price Score 100.64

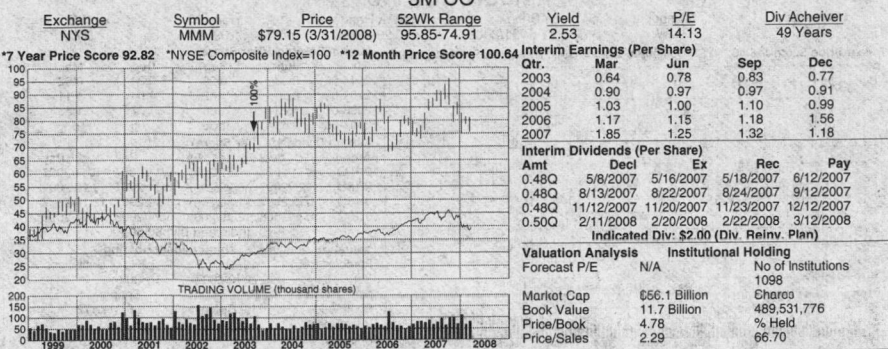

Interim Earnings (Per Share)

Qtr.	Mar	Jun	Sep	Dec
2003	0.64	0.78	0.83	0.77
2004	0.90	0.97	0.97	0.91
2005	1.03	1.00	1.10	0.99
2006	1.17	1.15	1.18	1.56
2007	1.85	1.25	1.32	1.18

Interim Dividends (Per Share)

Amt	Decl	Ex	Rec	Pay
0.48Q	5/8/2007	5/16/2007	5/18/2007	6/12/2007
0.48Q	8/13/2007	8/22/2007	8/24/2007	9/12/2007
0.48Q	11/12/2007	11/20/2007	11/23/2007	12/12/2007
0.50Q	2/11/2008	2/20/2008	2/22/2008	3/12/2008

Indicated Div: $2.00 (Div. Reinv. Plan)

Valuation Analysis   **Institutional Holding**

Forecast P/E	N/A
	No of Institutions 1098
Market Cap	$56.1 Billion
Book Value	11.7 Billion
Price/Book	4.78
Price/Sales	2.29

	Shares
	489,531,776
% Held	
	66.70

Business Summary: Medical Instruments & Equipment (MIC: 9.6 SIC: 3841 NAIC: 339112)

3M is a technology company with a global presence in the following markets: industrial and transportation; health care; display and graphics; consumer and office; safety, security and protection services; and electro and communications. As of Dec 31 2007, Co. had 157 sales offices, with 9 in the U.S. and 148 internationally. Co.'s products are sold through distribution channels, including directly to users and via wholesalers, retailers, jobbers, distributors and dealers around the world. Co.'s products include: Scotch® Brand Products, such as Scotch® Magic™ Tape, Scotch® Glue Stick and Scotch® Cushioned Mailer, and Post-it® Products, such as Post-it® Flags, and Post-it® Labels.

Recent Developments: For the year ended Dec 31 2007, net income increased 6.4% to US$4.10 billion from US$3.85 billion in the prior year. Revenues were US$24.46 billion, up 6.7% from US$22.92 billion the year before. Operating income was US$6.19 billion versus US$5.70 billion in the prior year, an increase of 8.7%. Direct operating expenses rose 8.7% to US$12.74 billion from US$11.71 billion in the comparable period the year before. Indirect operating expenses increased 0.4% to US$5.53 billion from US$5.51 billion in the equivalent prior-year period.

Prospects: For the full year of 2008, Co. continues to anticipate earnings to grow by 10.0% over its 2007 earnings per share level of $4.98, excluding special items. In addition, Co. is projecting sales to improve at double-digit rates, with organic local currency growth of 5.0% to 8.0% and acquisitions adding more than 3.0%. Also, Co. is targeting foreign currency effects to add about two to three points of growth at ongoing exchange rates. Going forward, Co. will continue to implement its growth initiatives, including reinvesting in its core businesses, developing potential business opportunities, expanding on its capabilities internationally, and acquiring companies in complementary industries.

Financial Data

(US$ in Thousands)	12/31/2007	12/31/2006	12/31/2005	12/31/2004	12/31/2003	12/31/2002	12/31/2001	12/31/2000
Earnings Per Share	5.60	5.06	4.12	3.75	3.02	2.50	1.79	2.23
Cash Flow Per Share	5.95	5.14	5.57	5.47	4.81	3.84	3.90	3.93
Tang Book Value Per Share	8.96	7.04	8.14	9.63	6.62	4.90	6.18	7.17
Dividends Per Share	1.920	1.840	1.680	1.440	1.320	1.240	1.200	1.160
Dividend Payout %	34.29	36.36	40.78	38.40	43.71	49.70	67.04	52.13
Income Statement								
Total Revenue	24,462,000	22,923,000	21,167,000	20,011,000	18,232,000	16,332,000	16,054,000	16,724,000
EBITDA	7,265,000	6,775,000	5,995,000	5,577,000	4,677,000	4,000,000	3,362,000	4,110,000
Income Before Taxes	6,115,000	5,625,000	4,983,000	4,555,000	3,657,000	3,005,000	2,186,000	2,974,000
Income Taxes	1,964,000	1,723,000	1,694,000	1,503,000	1,202,000	966,000	702,000	1,025,000
Net Income	4,096,000	3,851,000	3,199,000	2,990,000	2,403,000	1,974,000	1,430,000	1,782,000
Average Shares	732,000	761,000	776,900	796,500	795,300	791,000	799,800	799,800
Balance Sheet								
Current Assets	9,838,000	8,946,000	7,115,000	8,720,000	7,720,000	6,059,000	6,296,000	6,379,000
Total Assets	24,694,000	21,294,000	20,513,000	20,708,000	17,600,000	15,329,000	14,606,000	14,522,000
Current Liabilities	5,362,000	7,323,000	5,238,000	6,071,000	5,082,000	4,457,000	4,509,000	4,754,000
Long-Term Obligations	4,088,000	1,112,000	1,368,000	798,000	1,805,000	2,140,000	1,520,000	971,000
Total Liabilities	12,947,000	11,335,000	10,413,000	10,330,000	9,715,000	9,336,000	8,520,000	7,991,000
Stockholders' Equity	11,747,000	9,959,000	10,100,000	10,378,000	7,885,000	5,993,000	6,086,000	6,531,000
Shares Outstanding	709,156	734,362	754,538	773,518	784,117	780,391	782,607	792,170
Statistical Record								
Return on Assets %	17.81	18.42	15.52	15.57	14.60	13.19	9.82	12.51
Return on Equity %	37.74	38.40	31.24	32.65	34.63	32.68	22.67	27.72
EBITDA Margin %	29.70	29.56	28.32	27.87	25.65	24.49	20.94	24.58
Net Margin %	16.74	16.80	15.11	14.94	13.18	12.09	8.91	10.66
Asset Turnover	1.06	1.10	1.03	1.04	1.11	1.09	1.10	1.17
Current Ratio	1.83	1.22	1.36	1.44	1.52	1.36	1.40	1.34
Debt to Equity	0.35	0.11	0.14	0.08	0.23	0.36	0.25	0.15
Price Range	95.85-73.01	88.13-68.11	86.80-70.07	90.01-74.87	85.25-60.51	65.49-51.85	62.75-43.49	60.97-39.50
P/E Ratio	17.12-13.04	17.42-13.46	21.07-17.01	24.00-19.97	28.23-20.03	26.20-20.74	35.06-24.30	27.34-17.71
Average Yield %	2.29	2.39	2.16	1.76	1.92	2.04	2.16	2.52

Address: 3M Center, St. Paul, MN 55144-1000	**Web Site:** www.3m.com	**Auditors:** PricewaterhouseCoopers LLP
Telephone: 651-733-1110	**Officers:** Robert S. Morrison - Interim Chmn., C.E.O.	**Investor Contact:** 651-733-8206
Fax: 651-733-9973	Joe E. Harlan - Exec. V.P., Electro & Communications Business	**Transfer Agents:** Wells Fargo Shareowner Services, St. Paul, MN

TIDEWATER INC.

Exchange	Symbol	Price	52Wk Range	Yield	P/E
NYS	TDW	$55.11 (3/31/2008)	79.29-46.91	1.09	8.71

*7 Year Price Score 118.46 *NYSE Composite Index=100   *12 Month Price Score 96.03

Interim Earnings (Per Share)

Qtr.	Jun	Sep	Dec	Mar
2004-05	0.23	0.29	0.34	0.92
2005-06	0.50	1.42	1.04	1.11
2006-07	1.23	1.86	1.67	1.56
2007-08	1.55	1.56	1.66	...

Interim Dividends (Per Share)

Amt	Decl	Ex	Rec	Pay
0.15Q	5/31/2007	6/7/2007	6/11/2007	6/21/2007
0.15Q	8/21/2007	8/29/2007	8/31/2007	9/10/2007
0.15Q	11/15/2007	11/30/2007	12/4/2007	12/14/2007
0.15Q	1/31/2008	2/29/2008	3/4/2008	3/14/2008

Indicated Div: $0.60

TRADING VOLUME (thousand shares)

Valuation Analysis

		Institutional Holding	
Forecast P/E	12.04 (1/10/2007)	No of Institutions	303
Market Cap	$2.9 Billion	Shares	
Book Value	1.9 Billion		58,311,172
Price/Book	1.55	% Held	
Price/Sales	2.35	N/A	

Business Summary: Shipping (MIC: 15.3 SIC: 4412 NAIC: 483111)

Tidewater provides offshore supply vessels and marine support services to the offshore energy industry through the operation of offshore marine service vessels. With a fleet of over 463 vessels at Mar 31 2007, Co. operated in oil and gas exploration and production markets and provided services supporting various phases of offshore exploration, development and production, including: towing of and anchor handling of mobile drilling rigs and equipment; transporting supplies and personnel necessary to sustain drilling, workover and production activities; assisting in offshore construction activities; and a range of other services, including pipe laying and cable laying .

Recent Developments: For the quarter ended Dec 31 2007, net income decreased 4.3% to US$89.4 million from US$93.4 million in the year-earlier quarter. Revenues were US$314.2 million, up 9.1% from US$287.9 million the year before. Operating income was US$102.2 million versus US$111.3 million in the prior-year quarter, a decrease of 8.2%. Direct operating expenses rose 15.3% to US$150.5 million from US$130.5 million in the comparable period the year before. Indirect operating expenses increased 33.8% to US$61.6 million from US$46.0 million in the equivalent prior-year period.

Prospects: Co. is seeing lower U.S.-based vessel revenues due mainly to the transfer of vessels to international markets, the sale of its U.S.-based offshore tugs in the second and third quarters of fiscal year ending Mar 2007 and lower utilization and average day rates. However, Co. is benefiting from higher average day rates on all vessel classes operating in global markets and an increase in the number of vessels operating internationally. Meanwhile, subsequent to Dec 31 2007, Co. is committed to construct eight additional deepwater platform supply vessels for about US$202.0 million. The vessels should be delivered to the market beginning in Sep 2010 with final delivery anticipated in June 2012.

Financial Data

(US$ in Thousands)	9 Mos	6 Mos	3 Mos	03/31/2007	03/31/2006	03/31/2005	03/31/2004	03/31/2003
Earnings Per Share	6.33	6.34	6.64	6.31	4.07	1.78	0.73	1.57
Cash Flow Per Share	8.45	7.93	8.17	7.78	4.94	2.82	2.28	3.58
Tang Book Value Per Share	29.25	28.82	27.86	27.09	22.88	19.37	18.19	18.06
Dividends Per Share	0.600	0.600	0.600	0.600	0.600	0.600	0.600	0.600
Dividend Payout %	9.48	9.46	9.04	9.51	14.74	33.71	82.19	38.22
Income Statement								
Total Revenue	938,743	624,528	305,482	1,125,260	877,617	692,150	652,630	635,823
EBITDA	410,349	275,718	139,115	576,676	440,112	206,295	156,696	211,275
Depn & Amortn	89,156	58,033	28,197	...	...	...	...	...
Income Before Taxes	321,193	213,507	108,076	450,835	323,512	99,795	54,503	127,710
Income Taxes	57,815	39,499	20,534	94,189	87,756	(1,544)	12,841	39,080
Net Income	263,378	174,008	87,542	356,646	235,756	101,339	41,662	88,630
Average Shares	53,814	55,558	56,519	56,508	57,966	57,068	56,688	56,602
Balance Sheet								
Current Assets	600,333	666,718	687,078	731,549	529,043	227,956	224,637	213,492
Total Assets	2,710,698	2,744,394	2,703,148	2,649,298	2,364,540	2,213,173	2,081,790	1,849,578
Current Liabilities	219,611	214,128	193,378	146,680	115,754	92,242	72,052	72,266
Long-Term Obligations	300,000	300,000	309,776	319,712	300,000	380,000	325,000	139,000
Total Liabilities	843,713	834,675	821,131	763,288	705,419	770,471	715,680	498,183
Stockholders' Equity	1,866,985	1,909,719	1,882,017	1,886,010	1,659,121	1,442,702	1,366,110	1,351,395
Shares Outstanding	52,585	54,865	55,758	57,476	58,143	57,516	57,032	56,637
Statistical Record								
Return on Assets %	13.39	13.75	14.75	14.23	10.30	4.72	2.11	5.04
Return on Equity %	19.18	19.69	21.18	20.12	15.20	7.22	3.06	6.72
EBITDA Margin %	43.71	44.15	45.54	51.25	50.15	29.80	24.01	33.23
Net Margin %	28.06	27.86	28.66	31.69	26.86	14.64	6.38	13.94
Asset Turnover	0.47	0.47	0.46	0.45	0.38	0.32	0.33	0.36
Current Ratio	2.73	3.11	3.55	4.99	4.57	2.47	3.12	2.95
Debt to Equity	0.16	0.16	0.16	0.17	0.18	0.26	0.24	0.10
Price Range	79.29-43.78	79.29-41.44	71.68-41.44	62.32-41.44	58.42-32.67	42.68-25.81	34.09-25.82	45.18-23.54
P/E Ratio	12.53-6.92	12.51-6.54	10.80-6.24	9.88-6.57	14.35-8.03	23.98-14.50	46.70-35.37	28.78-14.99
Average Yield %	1.00	1.02	1.12	1.20	1.36	1.86	2.05	1.88

Address: 601 Poydras Street, Suite 1900, New Orleans, LA 70130
Telephone: 504-568-1010
Fax: 504-566-4582

Web Site: www.tdw.com
Officers: Dean E. Taylor - Chmn., Pres., C.E.O. Cliffe F. Laborde - Exec. V.P., Gen. Couns.

Auditors: Deloitte & Touche LLP
Investor Contact: 504-568-1010
Transfer Agents: EquiServe Trust Company

TIFFANY & CO.

Exchange	Symbol	Price	52Wk Range	Yield	P/E
NYS	TIF	$41.84 (3/31/2008)	56.83-34.04	1.43	19.02

*7 Year Price Score 105.84 *NYSE Composite Index=100 *12 Month Price Score 90.16

Interim Earnings (Per Share)

Qtr.	Apr	Jul	Oct	Jan
2003-04	0.24	0.28	0.19	0.74
2004-05	0.27	0.25	0.14	1.39
2005-06	0.27	0.35	0.16	0.96
2006-07	0.30	0.29	0.21	1.00
2007-08	0.36	0.26	0.71	0.87

Interim Dividends (Per Share)

Amt	Decl	Ex	Rec	Pay
0.12Q	5/17/2007	6/18/2007	6/20/2007	7/10/2007
0.15Q	8/16/2007	9/18/2007	9/20/2007	10/10/2007
0.15Q	11/15/2007	12/18/2007	12/20/2007	1/10/2008
0.15Q	2/21/2008	3/18/2008	3/20/2008	4/10/2008

Indicated Div: $0.60

Valuation Analysis | **Institutional Holding**

Forecast P/E	N/A	No of Institutions
		382
Market Cap	$5.3 Billion	Shares
Book Value	1.6 Billion	129,153,032
Price/Book	3.24	% Held
Price/Sales	1.80	94.75

TRADING VOLUME (thousand shares)

Business Summary: Retail - Miscellaneous (MIC: 5.11 SIC: 5944 NAIC: 448310)

Tiffany & Co. is a holding company that operates through its subsidiary companies. Co.'s principal subsidiary, Tiffany and Company, is a jeweler and specialty retailer whose principal merchandise offering is fine jewelry. In addition, Tiffany and Company is engaged in the business of selling timepieces, sterling silverware, china, crystal, stationery, fragrances and accessories. Through Tiffany and Company and other subsidiaries, Co. is also engaged in product design, manufacturing and retailing activities. As of Jan 31 2008, Co. had 69 branch stores in the U.S in addition to its New York Flagship store.

Recent Developments: For the year ended Jan 31 2008, income from continuing operations increased 23.3% to US$331.3 million from US$268.7 million a year earlier. Net income increased 19.6% to US$303.8 million from US$253.9 million in the prior year. Revenues were US$2.94 billion, up 14.8% from US$2.56 billion the year before. Operating income was US$530.3 million versus US$430.8 million in the prior year, an increase of 23.1%. Direct operating expenses rose 16.9% to US$1.31 billion from US$1.12 billion in the comparable period the year before. Indirect operating expenses increased 8.8% to US$1.10 billion from US$1.01 billion in the equivalent prior-year period.

Prospects: Despite experiencing slight comparable store sales growth, Co. remains cautious about its outlook for the U.S. and expects a slight decline in comparable U.S. store sales in the first half of the year 2008. For the full fiscal year ending Jan 31 2009, Co. anticipates net sales growth of about 10.0%, including comparable store sales increasing by low-single-digits in the U.S. and mid-single-digits internationally, assuming the opening of six new U.S. stores and approximately 20 international locations, operating margin approximately equal to the prior year, net earnings growth of 5.0% to 9.0% and net earnings per diluted share increasing by 11.0% to 15.0% to a range of $2.75 to $2.85.

Financial Data
(US$ in Thousands)

	01/31/2008	01/31/2007	01/31/2006	01/31/2005	01/31/2004	01/31/2003	01/31/2002	01/31/2001
Earnings Per Share	2.20	1.80	1.75	2.05	1.45	1.28	1.15	1.26
Cash Flow Per Share	2.90	1.69	1.84	0.89	1.95	1.52	1.66	0.75
Tang Book Value Per Share	12.92	13.28	12.85	11.77	10.01	8.34	7.15	6.34
Dividends Per Share	0.520	0.380	0.300	0.230	0.190	0.160	0.160	0.150
Dividend Payout %	23.64	21.11	17.14	11.22	13.10	12.50	13.91	11.90
Income Statement								
Total Revenue	2,938,771	2,648,321	2,395,153	2,204,831	2,000,045	1,706,602	1,606,535	1,668,056
EBITDA	669,077	548,324	500,485	602,336	448,011	392,774	373,773	380,583
Income Before Taxes	522,202	404,435	367,974	472,148	342,685	299,637	289,312	317,641
Income Taxes	190,883	150,508	113,319	167,849	127,168	109,743	115,725	127,057
Net Income	303,772	253,927	254,655	304,299	215,517	189,894	173,587	190,584
Average Shares	138,140	140,841	145,578	148,093	148,472	148,591	150,517	151,816
Balance Sheet								
Current Assets	1,843,567	1,706,644	1,698,843	1,607,889	1,348,082	1,070,388	954,414	1,004,845
Total Assets	2,922,156	2,845,510	2,777,272	2,666,118	2,391,088	1,923,586	1,629,868	1,568,340
Current Liabilities	584,861	452,671	364,610	399,821	395,159	299,907	341,436	337,198
Long-Term Obligations	343,465	406,383	426,548	397,606	392,991	297,107	179,065	242,157
Total Liabilities	1,284,789	1,040,615	946,359	964,958	922,888	715,537	592,923	642,857
Stockholders' Equity	1,637,367	1,804,895	1,830,913	1,701,160	1,468,200	1,208,049	1,036,945	925,483
Shares Outstanding	126,753	135,875	142,509	144,548	146,735	144,865	145,001	145,897
Statistical Record								
Return on Assets %	10.53	9.03	9.36	12.00	9.99	10.69	10.86	13.05
Return on Equity %	17.65	13.97	14.42	19.15	16.11	16.92	17.69	22.59
EBITDA Margin %	22.77	20.70	20.90	27.32	22.40	23.01	23.27	22.82
Net Margin %	10.34	9.59	10.63	13.80	10.78	11.13	10.81	11.43
Asset Turnover	1.02	0.94	0.88	0.87	0.93	0.96	1.00	1.14
Current Ratio	3.15	3.77	4.66	4.02	3.41	3.57	2.80	2.98
Debt to Equity	0.21	0.23	0.23	0.23	0.27	0.25	0.17	0.26
Price Range	56.83-34.04	40.28-29.93	42.90-29.30	42.70-27.10	48.72-22.01	40.20-20.41	37.59-20.76	45.38-27.50
P/E Ratio	25.83-15.47	22.38-16.63	24.51-16.74	20.83-13.22	33.60-15.18	31.41-15.95	32.69-18.05	36.01-21.83
Average Yield %	1.09	1.08	0.85	0.67	0.54	0.54	0.52	0.42

Address: 727 Fifth Avenue, New York, NY 10022	**Web Site:** www.tiffany.com	**Auditors:** PricewaterhouseCoopers LLP
Telephone: 212-755-8000	**Officers:** Michael J. Kowalski - Chmn., C.E.O. James E. Quinn - Pres.	**Investor Contact:** 212-230-5301
Fax: 212-605-4465		**Transfer Agents:** Mellon Investor Services LLC

TIM HORTONS INC

Exchange	Symbol	Price	52Wk Range	Yield	P/E
NYS	THI	$34.05 (3/31/2008)	39.73-30.38	1.06	23.81

*7 Year Price Score N/A   *NYSE Composite Index=100   *12 Month Price Score 108.35

Interim Earnings (Per Share) Can$

Qtr.	Mar	Jun	Sep	Dec
2005	0.30	0.38	0.41	0.10
2006	0.39	0.39	0.27	0.35
2007	0.31	0.36	0.36	0.41

Interim Dividends (Per Share)

Amt	Decl	Ex	Rec	Pay
0.07Q	5/3/2007	5/10/2007	5/14/2007	5/30/2007
0.07Q	8/3/2007	8/13/2007	8/15/2007	8/27/2007
0.07Q	10/26/2007	11/2/2007	11/6/2007	11/20/2007
0.09Q	2/20/2008	2/28/2008	3/3/2008	3/17/2008

Indicated Div: C$0.36

Valuation Analysis

		Institutional Holding	
Forecast P/E	N/A	No of Institutions	200
Market Cap	C$6.3 Billion	Shares	113,622,024
Book Value	1.0 Billion	% Held	59.68
Price/Book	6.32		
Price/Sales	3.34		

TRADING VOLUME (thousand shares)

Business Summary: Hospitality & Tourism (MIC: 5.1 SIC: 5812 NAIC: 722410)

Tim Hortons is engaged in the development and franchising of quick-service restaurants that serve food such as hot and cold coffee, baked goods, sandwiches and soups. As of Dec 30 2007, Co. and its franchisees operated 2,823 restaurants in Canada and 398 restaurants in the U.S. under the name Tim Hortons. Co.'s menu consists of products such as blend coffee, flavoured hot and iced cappuccinos, specialty and steeped teas, cold beverages, flavour shots in hot and cold beverages, home-style soups (including chili), sandwiches, wraps, yogurt and berries and baked goods, including donuts, bagels, muffins, cookies, croissants, danishes, and pastries.

Recent Developments: For the year ended Dec 31 2007, net income increased 3.8% to C$269.6 million from C$259.6 million in the prior year. Revenues were C$1.90 billion, up 14.2% from C$1.66 billion the year before. Operating income was C$425.1 million versus C$379.2 million in the prior year, an increase of 12.1%. Direct operating expenses rose 16.7% to C$1.10 billion from C$941.9 million in the comparable period the year before. Indirect operating expenses increased 9.8% to C$371.5 million from C$338.4 million in the equivalent prior-year period.

Prospects: Co. remains focused on its growth strategies including new menu and operational initiatives, such as its new cashless payment systems. For 2008, Co. is expecting operating income growth of 10.0% while targeting same-store sales growth of 4.0% to 6.0% in Canada and 2.0% to 4.0% in the U.S. Also, Co. estimates its total capital spending for the year to be $200.0 million to $250.0 million, including capital spending for new restaurant development, remodelling, technology initiatives and other capital needs. Specifically, Co. plans to open 120 to 140 new restaurants in Canada and 90 to 110 new restaurants in the U.S. Further, Co. expects to close 20 to 40 restaurants on a systemwide basis.

Financial Data

(Can$ in Thousands)	12/31/2007	12/31/2006	01/01/2006	01/02/2005	12/28/2003
Earnings Per Share	1.43	1.40	1.19	1.28	0.98
Cash Flow Per Share	2.09	1.41	2.37	2.46	...
Tang Book Value Per Share	5.37	5.31	0.22	6.16	...
Dividends Per Share	0.280	0.140	...	...	...
Dividend Payout %	19.58	10.00	...	...	...
Income Statement					
Income Before Taxes	408,402	360,758	275,530	305,786	262,863
Income Taxes	138,851	101,162	84,439	100,735	106,601
Net Income	269,551	259,596	191,091	205,051	156,262
Average Shares	188,759	185,401	159,952	159,952	159,952
Balance Sheet					
Total Assets	1,797,131	1,744,987	1,596,863	1,756,869	...
Total Liabilities	795,048	726,583	1,557,485	735,180	...
Stockholders' Equity	1,002,083	1,018,404	39,378	1,021,689	...
Shares Outstanding	186,131	191,106	159,952	159,952	159,952
Statistical Record					
Return on Assets %	15.22	15.58	11.43	...	...
Return on Equity %	26.68	49.22	36.12	...	...
Price Range	39.73-28.78	30.88-23.94	...	...	...
P/E Ratio	27.78-20.13	22.06-17.10	...	...	...
Average Yield %	0.85	0.52	...	...	...

Address: 874 Sinclair Road, Oakville, L6K 2Y1 **Telephone:** 945-845-6511	**Web Site:** www.timhortons.com **Officers:** P.D. House - Chmn., Pres., C.E.O. C.J. Devine - Exec. V.P., C.F.O.	**Auditors:** PricewaterhouseCoopers LLP **Transfer Agents:** Computershare Investor Services, LLC, Chicago, IL

TIMBERLAND CO. (THE)

Exchange	Symbol	Price	52Wk Range	Yield	P/E
NYS	TBL	$13.73 (3/31/2008)	27.60-13.12	N/A	21.12

*7 Year Price Score 64.07   *NYSE Composite Index=100   *12 Month Price Score 79.59

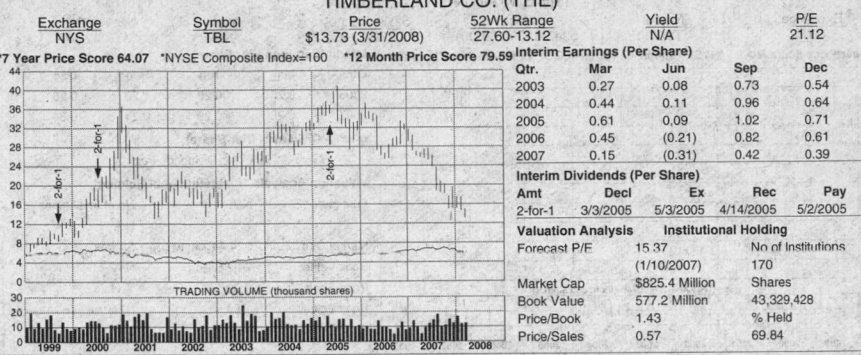

Interim Earnings (Per Share)

Qtr.	Mar	Jun	Sep	Dec
2003	0.27	0.08	0.73	0.54
2004	0.44	0.11	0.96	0.64
2005	0.61	0,09	1.02	0.71
2006	0.45	(0.21)	0.82	0.61
2007	0.15	(0.31)	0.42	0.39

Interim Dividends (Per Share)

Amt	Decl	Ex	Rec	Pay
2-for-1	3/3/2005	5/3/2005	4/14/2005	5/2/2005

Valuation Analysis   **Institutional Holding**

Forecast P/E	15.37	No of Institutions	
	(1/10/2007)	170	
Market Cap	$825.4 Million	Shares	
Book Value	577.2 Million	43,329,428	
Price/Book	1.43	% Held	
Price/Sales	0.57	69.84	

Business Summary: Leather and Leather Products (MIC: 4.5 SIC: 3143 NAIC: 316213)

Timberland designs, develops, engineers, markets and distributes under the Timberland®, Timberland PRO®, SmartWool®, Timberland Boot Company™, Mion™, GoLite®, Howies® and IPATH® brands, footwear, apparel and accessory products for men, women and children. Co.'s products are sold via independent retailers, department stores, athletic stores and other national retailers in the U.S., Canada, Europe, Asia, Latin America, South Africa and the Middle East. Co.'s products are also sold via Timberland® specialty stores, Timberland® factory outlet stores, franchised retail stores in Europe, in the U.S. online at timberland.com and smartwool.com, and in the U.K. online at timberlandonline.co.uk.

Recent Developments: For the year ended Dec 31 2007, net income decreased 60.5% to US$40.0 million from US$101.2 million in the prior year. Revenues were US$1.44 billion, down 8.4% from US$1.57 billion the year before. Operating income was US$59.2 million versus US$162.6 million in the prior year, a decrease of 63.6%. Direct operating expenses declined 6.3% to US$771.7 million from US$823.4 million in the comparable period the year before. Indirect operating expenses increased 4.1% to US$605.5 million from US$581.5 million in the equivalent prior-year period.

Prospects: In Feb 2008, Co. had taken several actions to streamline its global operations that should result in incremental operating expense savings of $30.0 million. These actions, when combined with Co.'s decisions to license its U.S. apparel business, close underperforming retail stores and reorganize its U.S. sales and global product organizations in 2007, are expected to result in $65.0 million of annual operating expense savings. For 2008, Co. expects low-single digit revenue declines; operating expenses of $550.0 million for marketing, international expansion and other growth initiatives; and flat to modest operating margin improvement excluding restructuring costs, compared with 2007 results.

Financial Data
(US$ in Thousands)

	12/31/2007	12/31/2006	12/31/2005	12/31/2004	12/31/2003	12/31/2002	12/31/2001	12/31/2000
Earnings Per Share	0.65	1.67	2.43	2.14	1.62	1.25	1.33	1.43
Cash Flow Per Share	0.63	1.79	2.75	2.65	2.80	1.85	1.14	1.76
Tang Book Value Per Share	7.95	7.64	6.93	7.20	5.86	4.89	4.50	3.80
Income Statement								
Total Revenue	1,436,451	1,567,619	1,565,681	1,500,580	1,342,123	1,190,896	1,183,623	1,091,478
EBITDA	90,197	190,660	270,193	260,929	207,440	162,156	183,193	211,591
Income Before Taxes	59,725	163,741	249,053	236,733	182,757	138,769	161,729	186,652
Income Taxes	19,726	57,309	84,429	84,040	64,878	48,569	54,988	62,528
Net Income	39,999	106,432	164,624	152,693	117,879	95,113	106,741	121,998
Average Shares	61,659	63,690	67,744	71,310	72,950	76,284	80,494	85,294
Balance Sheet								
Current Assets	617,157	635,516	615,606	649,047	539,560	441,783	405,543	381,760
Total Assets	836,345	843,105	788,654	757,510	641,716	538,671	504,612	476,311
Current Liabilities	218,035	269,224	243,346	226,192	196,991	155,756	128,502	145,073
Total Liabilities	259,185	282,288	260,467	246,003	213,253	165,886	145,374	159,560
Stockholders' Equity	577,160	560,817	528,187	511,507	428,463	372,785	359,238	316,751
Shares Outstanding	60,113	61,980	64,627	68,362	70,041	72,612	76,668	79,231
Statistical Record								
Return on Assets %	4.76	13.05	21.29	21.77	19.97	18.23	21.76	25.10
Return on Equity %	7.03	19.55	31.67	32.40	29.42	25.99	31.58	41.30
EBITDA Margin %	6.28	12.16	17.26	17.39	15.46	13.62	15.48	19.39
Net Margin %	2.78	6.79	10.51	10.18	8.78	7.99	9.02	11.18
Asset Turnover	1.71	1.92	2.03	2.14	2.27	2.28	2.41	2.25
Current Ratio	2.83	2.36	2.53	2.87	2.74	2.84	3.16	2.63
Price Range	31.65-15.05	37.13-25.35	40.75-27.40	33.56-24.73	29.32-15.34	22.95-13.54	36.63-13.07	34.59-9.25
P/E Ratio	48.69-23.15	22.23-15.18	16.77-11.28	15.68-11.55	18.10-9.47	18.36-10.83	27.54-9.83	24.19-6.47

Address: 200 Domain Drive, Stratham, NH 03885	**Web Site:** www.timberland.com	**Auditors:** Deloitte & Touche LLP
Telephone: 603-772-9500	**Officers:** Sidney W. Swartz - Chmn. Jeffrey B. Swartz - Pres., C.E.O.	**Transfer Agents:** Computershare Trust Company, N.A., Providence, RI
Fax: 603-773-1640		

TIME WARNER CABLE INC

Exchange	Symbol	Price	52Wk Range	Yield	P/E
NYS	TWC	$24.98 (3/31/2008)	41.85-23.65	N/A	21.72

*7 Year Price Score N/A   *NYSE Composite Index=100   *12 Month Price Score 87.67

Interim Earnings (Per Share)

Qtr.	Mar	Jun	Sep	Dec
2006	0.23	0.29	1.20	0.28
2007	0.28	0.28	0.25	0.34

Interim Dividends (Per Share)

No Dividends Paid

Valuation Analysis   **Institutional Holding**

Forecast P/E	N/A	No of Institutions
		N/A
Market Cap	$24.4 Billion	Shares
Book Value	24.7 Billion	N/A
Price/Book	0.99	% Held
Price/Sales	1.53	N/A

Business Summary: Communications (MIC: 10.1 SIC: 4841 NAIC: 515210)

Time Warner Cable is a U.S. cable operator, with clustered systems located mainly in five geographic areas: New York state (including New York City), the Carolinas, Ohio, southern California (including Los Angeles) and Texas. As of Dec 31 2007, Co. served approximately 14.6 million customers who subscribed to one or more of its video, high-speed data and voice services, representing approximately 32.1 million revenue generating units (RGUs), which reflects the total of all Time Warner Cable basic video, digital video, high-speed data and voice service subscribers.

Recent Developments: For the year ended Dec 31 2007, income from continuing operations increased 20.0% to US$1.12 billion from US$936.0 million a year earlier. Net income decreased 43.2% to US$1.12 billion from US$1.98 billion in the prior year. Revenues were US$15.96 billion, up 35.6% from US$11.77 billion the year before. Operating income was US$2.77 billion versus US$2.18 billion in the prior year, an increase of 26.9%. Direct operating expenses rose 40.8% to US$7.54 billion from US$5.36 billion in the comparable period the year before. Indirect operating expenses increased 33.4% to US$5.65 billion from US$4.23 billion in the equivalent prior-year period.

Prospects: Looking ahead, Co. foresees continued strong growth in residential high-speed data subscribers and revenues, but projects the rate of growth of both subscribers and revenues to slow as high-speed data services become well-penetrated. Also, Co. estimates video programming costs to continue to increase, given the contractual rate increases, subscriber growth and the expansion of service offerings. Hence, Co. intends to improve video revenues through better digital video services as well as price escalation and digital video subscriber expansion. Over the longer term, Co. expects its video service margins to decline as increases in programming costs overcome growth in video revenues.

Financial Data
(US$ in Thousands)

	12/31/2007	12/31/2006	12/31/2005	12/31/2004
Earnings Per Share	1.15	2.00	1.25	0.73
Cash Flow Per Share	4.67	3.63	2.54	...
Income Statement				
Total Revenue	15,955,000	11,767,000	8,812,000	7,861,000
EBITDA	5,733,000	4,252,000	3,303,000	2,951,000
Income Before Taxes	1,863,000	1,556,000	1,302,000	1,085,000
Income Taxes	740,000	620,000	153,000	454,000
Net Income	1,123,000	1,976,000	1,253,000	726,000
Average Shares	977,200	990,000	1,000,000	1,000,000
Balance Sheet				
Current Assets	1,163,000	910,000	487,000	...
Total Assets	56,600,000	55,743,000	43,677,000	...
Current Liabilities	2,536,000	2,490,000	1,696,000	...
Long-Term Obligations	13,577,000	14,428,000	4,463,000	...
Total Liabilities	31,894,000	32,179,000	22,346,000	...
Stockholders' Equity	24,706,000	23,564,000	20,347,000	...
Shares Outstanding	977,000	977,000	957,000	...
Statistical Record				
Return on Assets %	2.00	3.98	...	...
Return on Equity %	4.65	9.00	...	...
EBITDA Margin %	35.93	36.13	37.48	37.54
Net Margin %	7.04	16.79	14.22	9.24
Asset Turnover	0.28	0.24	...	...
Current Ratio	0.46	0.37	0.29	...
Debt to Equity	0.55	0.61	0.22	...
Price Range	41.85-24.03	...	...	...
P/E Ratio	36.39-20.90	...	...	...

Address: 290 Harbor Drive, Stamford, CT 06902-7441 **Telephone:** 203-328-0600	**Web Site:** www.timewarnercable.com **Officers:** Don Logan - Chmn. Glenn A. Britt - Pres., C.E.O.	**Auditors:** Ernst & Young LLP **Transfer Agents:** The Bank of New York, New York, NY

TIME WARNER INC

Exchange	Symbol	Price	52Wk Range	Yield	P/E
NYS	TWX	$14.02 (3/31/2008)	21.91-13.87	1.78	11.98

*7 Year Price Score 73.47   *NYSE Composite Index=100   *12 Month Price Score 90.38

Interim Earnings (Per Share)

Qtr.	Mar	Jun	Sep	Dec
2003	0.09	0.23	0.12	0.14
2004	0.20	0.17	0.11	0.24
2005	0.20	(0.07)	0.19	0.29
2006	0.32	0.24	0.57	0.43
2007	0.31	0.28	0.29	0.29

Interim Dividends (Per Share)

Amt	Decl	Ex	Rec	Pay
0.055Q	4/26/2007	5/29/2007	5/31/2007	6/15/2007
0.063Q	7/26/2007	8/29/2007	8/31/2007	9/15/2007
0.063Q	10/25/2007	11/28/2007	11/30/2007	12/15/2007
0.063Q	1/31/2008	2/27/2008	2/29/2008	3/15/2008

Indicated Div: $0.25

Valuation Analysis

Forecast P/E	N/A
Market Cap	$50.4 Billion
Book Value	58.5 Billion
Price/Book	0.86
Price/Sales	1.08

Institutional Holding

No of Institutions	861
Shares	2,995,543,552
% Held	78.51

TRADING VOLUME (thousand shares)

Business Summary: Movies & Film (MIC: 13.2 SIC: 7812 NAIC: 512110)

Time Warner is a media and entertainment company whose businesses encompass of media brands such as HBO, CNN, AOL, People, Sports Illustrated, Time and Time Warner Cable. At Dec 31 2007, Co. classified its business into five reporting segments: America Online (AOL), consisting principally of interactive consumer and advertising services; Cable, consisting of cable systems that provide video, high-speed data and voice services; Filmed Entertainment, consisting primarily of feature film, television and home video production and distribution; Networks, consisting principally of cable television networks that provide programming; and Publishing, consisting principally of magazine publishing.

Recent Developments: For the year ended Dec 31 2007, income from continuing operations decreased 20.1% to US$4.05 billion from US$5.07 billion a year earlier. Net income decreased 33.0% to US$4.39 billion from US$6.55 billion in the prior year. Revenues were US$46.48 billion, up 6.4% from US$43.69 billion the year before. Operating income was US$8.95 billion versus US$7.30 billion in the prior year, an increase of 22.5%. Direct operating expenses rose 10.3% to US$27.43 billion from US$24.88 billion in the comparable period the year before. Indirect operating expenses decreased 12.2% to US$10.11 billion from US$11.51 billion in the equivalent prior-year period.

Prospects: Looking ahead, Co. plans to drive strong results by implementing key initiatives such as strengthening its creative and entrepreneurial focus to accelerate business growth, and controlling costs to fund its investments in future growth. For 2008, Co. anticipates earnings from continuing operations of $1.07 to $1.11 per diluted share, excluding the effect of any future merger or unidentified restructuring charges, sales and acquisitions of operating assets and investments. Meanwhile, on Feb 6 2008, Co. has begun separating the AOL Access and Global Web Services businesses to provide better operational focus and increase the strategic options available, and expects to complete during 2008.

Financial Data
(US$ in Thousands)

	12/31/2007	12/31/2006	12/31/2005	12/31/2004	12/31/2003	12/31/2002	12/31/2001	12/31/2000
Earnings Per Share	1.17	1.55	0.62	0.72	0.57	(22.15)	(1.11)	0.45
Cash Flow Per Share	2.28	2.06	1.07	1.45	1.46	1.58	1.20	0.56
Tang Book Value Per Share	N M	N M	N M	N M	N M	N M	N M	2.51
Dividends Per Share	0.235	0.210	0.100	...	...	...	...	...
Dividend Payout %	20.09	13.55	16.13	...	...	...	...	...
Income Statement								
Total Revenue	46,482,000	44,224,000	43,652,000	42,089,000	39,565,000	40,961,000	38,234,000	7,703,000
EBITDA	19,174,000	11,705,000	8,635,000	9,647,000	9,501,000	(37,056,000)	8,187,000	2,265,000
Income Before Taxes	6,387,000	6,451,000	4,092,000	4,907,000	4,517,000	(44,434,000)	(4,775,000)	1,884,000
Income Taxes	2,336,000	1,337,000	1,187,000	1,698,000	1,371,000	140,000	146,000	732,000
Net Income	4,387,000	6,552,000	2,905,000	3,364,000	2,639,000	(98,696,000)	(4,921,000)	1,152,000
Average Shares	3,762,300	4,224,800	4,709,999	4,694,699	4,623,699	4,521,799	4,429,099	2,595,000
Balance Sheet								
Current Assets	12,451,000	10,851,000	13,463,000	14,639,000	12,268,000	11,155,000	10,274,000	4,671,000
Total Assets	133,830,000	131,669,000	122,475,000	123,339,000	121,783,000	115,450,000	208,559,000	10,827,000
Current Liabilities	12,193,000	12,780,000	12,588,000	14,624,000	15,518,000	13,395,000	12,972,000	2,328,000
Long-Term Obligations	37,004,000	34,933,000	20,238,000	20,703,000	23,458,000	27,354,000	22,792,000	1,411,000
Total Liabilities	75,294,000	71,280,000	59,760,000	62,568,000	65,745,000	62,633,000	56,488,000	4,049,000
Stockholders' Equity	58,536,000	60,389,000	62,715,000	60,771,000	56,038,000	52,817,000	152,071,000	6,778,000
Shares Outstanding	3,593,000	3,882,400	4,585,199	4,588,699	4,536,199	4,476,199	4,429,199	2,378,601
Statistical Record								
Return on Assets %	3.30	5.16	2.36	2.74	2.22	N.M.	N.M.	9.45
Return on Equity %	7.38	10.64	4.70	5.74	4.85	N.M.	N.M.	15.58
EBITDA Margin %	41.25	26.47	19.78	22.92	24.01	N.M.	21.41	29.40
Net Margin %	9.44	14.82	6.65	7.99	6.67	N.M.	N.M.	14.96
Asset Turnover	0.35	0.35	0.36	0.34	0.33	0.25	0.35	0.63
Current Ratio	1.02	0.85	1.07	1.00	0.79	0.83	0.79	2.01
Debt to Equity	0.63	0.58	0.32	0.34	0.42	0.52	0.15	0.21
Price Range	22.96-16.29	22.22-15.77	19.45-16.25	19.55-15.60	18.10-10.06	32.68-9.64	56.60-29.25	83.00-34.80
P/E Ratio	19.62-13.92	14.34-10.17	31.37-26.21	27.15-21.67	31.75-17.65	...	...	184.44-77.33
Average Yield %	1.19	1.18	0.57	...	...	...	...	...

Address: OneTime Warner Center, New York, NY 10019-8016 **Telephone:** 212-484-8000 **Fax:** 212-489-6183	**Web Site:** www.timewarner.com **Officers:** Richard D. Parsons - Chmn., C.E.O. Edward I. Adler - Exec. V.P., Corp. Communications	**Auditors:** Ernst & Young LLP **Transfer Agents:** Computershare Trust Company, N.A., Providence, RI

753

TIMKEN CO. (THE)

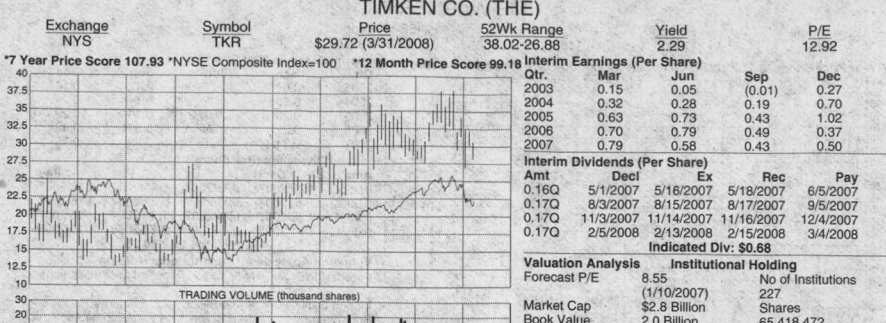

Exchange	Symbol	Price	52Wk Range	Yield	P/E
NYS	TKR	$29.72 (3/31/2008)	38.02-26.88	2.29	12.92

*7 Year Price Score 107.93 *NYSE Composite Index=100   *12 Month Price Score 99.18

Interim Earnings (Per Share)

Qtr.	Mar	Jun	Sep	Dec
2003	0.15	0.05	(0.01)	0.27
2004	0.32	0.28	0.19	0.70
2005	0.63	0.73	0.43	1.02
2006	0.70	0.79	0.49	0.37
2007	0.79	0.58	0.43	0.50

Interim Dividends (Per Share)

Amt	Decl	Ex	Rec	Pay
0.16Q	5/1/2007	5/16/2007	5/18/2007	6/5/2007
0.17Q	8/3/2007	8/15/2007	8/17/2007	9/5/2007
0.17Q	11/3/2007	11/14/2007	11/16/2007	12/4/2007
0.17Q	2/5/2008	2/13/2008	2/15/2008	3/4/2008

Indicated Div: $0.68

Valuation Analysis

		Institutional Holding	
Forecast P/E	8.55	No of Institutions	
	(1/10/2007)	227	
Market Cap	$2.8 Billion	Shares	
Book Value	2.0 Billion	65,418,472	
Price/Book	1.45	% Held	
Price/Sales	0.54	69.46	

Business Summary: Industrial Machinery and Equipment (MIC: 11.5 SIC: 3562 NAIC: 332991)

Timken is engaged as a manufacturer of engineered bearings, alloy and specialty steel and related components. As of Dec 31 2007, Co. manufactured two basic product lines: anti-friction bearings and steel products. These two product lines are differentiated by bearing type or steel type, as well as by the applications of bearings and steel. Co.'s Industrial and Automotive Groups design, manufacture, and distribute a range of bearings and related products and services. Co.'s Steel Group products include steels of low and intermediate alloy as well as some carbon grades. As of the date stated above, Co. had facilities in 28 countries on six continents.

Recent Developments: For the year ended Dec 31 2007, net income decreased 1.1% to US$220.1 million from US$222.5 million in the prior year. Revenues were US$5.24 billion, up 5.3% from US$4.97 billion the year before. Operating income was US$317.6 million versus US$218.6 million in the prior year, an increase of 45.3%. Direct operating expenses rose 5.4% to US$4.18 billion from US$3.97 billion in the comparable period the year before. Indirect operating expenses decreased 6.4% to US$736.2 million from US$786.5 million in the equivalent prior-year period.

Prospects: For 2008, Co. expects the continued strength in industrial markets to drive year-over-year volume increases. However, Co. expects the estimated improvements in its operating performance to be partially constrained by restructuring and strategic initiatives, which include its Asian growth and Project O.N.E. initiatives. Notably, the objective of Co.'s Asian growth initiatives is to expand its network of sources of globally competitive friction management products, while its Project O.N.E. is designed to improve its business processes and systems. Meanwhile, Co. expects earnings per diluted share for full-year 2008, excluding special items, to be $2.75 to $2.95 compared to $2.40 in 2007.

Financial Data
(US$ in Thousands)

	12/31/2007	12/31/2006	12/31/2005	12/31/2004	12/31/2003	12/31/2002	12/31/2001	12/31/2000
Earnings Per Share	2.30	2.36	2.81	1.49	0.44	0.62	(0.69)	0.76
Cash Flow Per Share	3.56	3.61	3.48	1.54	2.44	3.37	3.00	2.52
Tang Book Value Per Share	15.95	12.43	11.92	9.96	8.07	5.52	8.28	12.75
Dividends Per Share	0.660	0.620	0.600	0.520	0.520	0.520	0.670	0.720
Dividend Payout %	28.70	26.27	21.35	34.90	118.18	83.87	...	94.74
Income Statement								
Total Revenue	5,236,020	4,973,365	5,168,434	4,513,671	3,788,097	2,550,075	2,447,178	2,643,008
EBITDA	536,249	495,608	656,753	458,647	316,931	262,205	156,876	250,087
Income Before Taxes	282,257	254,234	390,546	199,779	60,802	85,518	(26,883)	70,597
Income Taxes	62,868	77,795	130,265	64,123	24,321	34,067	14,783	24,709
Net Income	220,054	222,527	260,281	135,656	36,481	38,749	(41,666)	45,888
Average Shares	95,612	94,294	92,537	90,759	83,159	61,635	59,947	60,723
Balance Sheet								
Current Assets	2,045,251	1,900,280	1,983,309	1,733,291	1,377,105	968,292	828,380	898,542
Total Assets	4,379,237	4,031,533	3,993,734	3,938,500	3,689,789	2,748,356	2,533,084	2,564,105
Current Liabilities	904,422	835,569	1,074,475	1,041,327	1,054,556	634,070	641,156	587,452
Long-Term Obligations	580,587	547,390	561,747	620,634	613,446	350,085	368,151	305,181
Total Liabilities	2,418,568	2,555,353	2,496,667	2,668,652	2,600,162	2,139,270	1,751,349	1,559,423
Stockholders' Equity	1,960,669	1,476,180	1,497,067	1,269,848	1,089,627	609,086	781,735	1,004,682
Shares Outstanding	95,808	94,164	93,005	90,504	89,065	63,411	59,856	59,965
Statistical Record								
Return on Assets %	5.23	5.55	6.56	3.55	1.13	1.47	N.M.	1.83
Return on Equity %	12.81	14.97	18.81	11.47	4.30	5.57	N.M.	4.46
EBITDA Margin %	10.24	9.97	12.71	10.16	8.37	10.28	6.41	9.46
Net Margin %	4.20	4.47	5.04	3.01	0.96	1.52	N.M.	1.74
Asset Turnover	1.25	1.24	1.30	1.18	1.18	0.97	0.96	1.05
Current Ratio	2.26	2.27	1.85	1.66	1.31	1.53	1.29	1.53
Debt to Equity	0.30	0.37	0.38	0.49	0.56	0.57	0.47	0.30
Price Range	38.02-27.63	36.18-26.77	32.63-22.90	27.14-19.49	20.30-14.84	27.35-14.92	18.60-12.49	21.50-12.75
P/E Ratio	16.53-12.01	15.33-11.34	11.61-8.15	18.21-13.08	46.14-33.73	44.11-24.06	...	28.29-16.78
Average Yield %	2.02	1.96	2.21	2.21	3.06	2.61	4.25	4.35

Address: 1835 Dueber Ave., S.W., Canton, OH 44706-2798
Telephone: 330-438-3000
Fax: 330-471-3452

Web Site: www.timken.com
Officers: Ward J. Timken Jr. - Chmn. James W. Griffith - Pres., C.E.O.

Auditors: ERNST & YOUNG LLP
Investor Contact: 330-471-7446
Transfer Agents: National City Bank Shareholder Services, Cleveland, OH

TITANIUM METALS CORP.

Exchange	Symbol	Price	52Wk Range	Yield	P/E
NYS	TIE	$15.05 (3/31/2008)	39.76-13.68	1.99	10.31

*7 Year Price Score 210.64 *NYSE Composite Index=100   *12 Month Price Score 72.62

TRADING VOLUME (thousand shares)

Interim Earnings (Per Share)

Qtr.	Mar	Jun	Sep	Dec
2003	(0.11)	(0.05)	(0.02)	0.08
2004	(0.01)	0.01	0.17	0.08
2005	0.23	0.20	0.20	0.23
2006	0.32	0.31	0.29	0.61
2007	0.41	0.42	0.29	0.33

Interim Dividends (Per Share)

Amt	Decl	Ex	Rec	Pay
100%	1/13/2006	2/17/2006	2/6/2006	2/16/2006
100%	4/20/2006	5/16/2006	5/5/2006	5/15/2006
0.075Q	11/27/2007	12/13/2007	12/17/2007	12/21/2007
0.075Q	2/21/2008	3/7/2008	3/11/2008	3/25/2008

Indicated Div: $0.30

Valuation Analysis

		Institutional Holding	
Forecast P/E	N/A	No of Institutions	167
Market Cap	$2.8 Billion	Shares	
Book Value	1.1 Billion	53,413,156	
Price/Book	2.43	% Held	
Price/Sales	2.15	2.46	

Business Summary: Metal Works (MIC: 11.3 SIC: 3341 NAIC: 331492)

Titanium Metals produces titanium melted and mill products, which include titanium sponge, melted products, mill products, and industrial fabrications. Co.'s titanium sponge is the basic form of titanium metal used in processed titanium products. Co.'s melted products include ingot, electrodes, and slab, which are the result of melting sponge and titanium scrap either alone or with various alloys. Co.'s mill products that are forged and rolled from ingot or slab include billets and bars, plates, sheets, strips, and pipes. Co.'s fabrication products include spools, pipefittings, manifolds, and vessels that are cut, formed, welded, and assembled from titanium mill products.

Recent Developments: For the year ended Dec 31 2007, net income decreased 4.7% to US$268.2 million from US$281.3 million in the prior year. Revenues were US$1.28 billion, up 8.1% from US$1.18 billion the year before. Operating income was US$372.0 million versus US$382.8 million in the prior year, a decrease of 2.8%. Direct operating expenses rose 11.3% to US$831.5 million from US$747.1 million in the comparable period the year before. Indirect operating expenses increased 41.5% to US$75.4 million from US$53.3 million in the equivalent prior-year period.

Prospects: Going forward, in anticipation of a significant increase in the availability of titanium scrap and moderation in its cost, Co. is increasing its capacity to recycle scrap and use electron beam (EB) melt capacity to use a combination of sponge and scrap to produce melted titanium products. For example, Co. recently completed an 8,500 metric ton expansion of its EB capacity, and it has commenced construction of other EB and vacuum arc remelting (VAR) capacity additions, all of which are expected to be completed during 2008 and 2009. As a result of these additions, Co. expects to more than double its EB melt capacity and to increase its VAR melt capacity by approximately one-third.

Financial Data

(US$ in Thousands)	12/31/2007	12/31/2006	12/31/2005	12/31/2004	12/31/2003	12/31/2002	12/31/2001	12/31/2000
Earnings Per Share	1.46	1.53	0.86	0.28	(0.10)	(0.88)	(0.33)	(0.31)
Cash Flow Per Share	1.18	0.51	0.56	(0.18)	0.52	(0.11)	0.49	0.50
Tang Book Value Per Share	6.17	4.98	3.02	1.58	1.20	1.18	1.91	2.35
Dividends Per Share	0.075	...	...	...	...	...	...	...
Dividend Payout %	5.14	...	...	...	...	...	...	...
Income Statement								
Total Revenue	1,278,900	1,183,168	749,777	501,828	385,304	366,501	568,660	434,310
EBITDA	437,300	455,884	220,835	84,304	41,710	(14,056)	48,665	6,513
Income Before Taxes	393,600	418,403	185,340	39,025	(11,281)	(54,535)	4,471	(43,133)
Income Taxes	116,900	128,363	24,496	(2,132)	1,207	(1,952)	31,112	(15,097)
Net Income	268,200	281,277	155,945	39,938	(13,057)	(111,530)	(41,766)	(38,902)
Average Shares	184,300	183,812	181,712	143,000	126,760	126,440	127,704	125,492
Balance Sheet								
Current Assets	897,800	757,566	550,270	343,626	275,978	262,526	308,687	248,205
Total Assets	1,419,900	1,216,873	907,264	665,549	567,409	563,778	699,383	759,146
Current Liabilities	177,700	211,131	166,850	162,172	78,505	92,625	122,360	115,842
Long-Term Obligations	...	...	51,359	175	9,766	15,976	19,310	27,595
Total Liabilities	263,300	316,677	331,573	273,326	397,521	192,771	191,301	192,537
Stockholders' Equity	1,132,700	878,872	562,168	379,684	158,757	159,350	298,114	357,515
Shares Outstanding	183,000	161,535	141,930	127,344	127,240	127,400	127,424	125,484
Statistical Record								
Return on Assets %	20.34	26.48	19.83	6.46	N.M.	N.M.	N.M.	N.M.
Return on Equity %	26.67	39.04	33.11	14.79	N.M.	N.M.	N.M.	N.M.
EBITDA Margin %	34.19	38.53	29.45	16.80	10.83	N.M.	8.56	1.50
Net Margin %	20.97	23.77	20.80	7.96	N.M.	N.M.	N.M.	N.M.
Asset Turnover	0.97	1.11	0.95	0.81	0.68	0.58	0.78	0.53
Current Ratio	5.05	3.59	3.30	2.12	3.52	2.83	2.52	2.14
Debt to Equity	...	...	0.09	N.M.	0.06	0.10	0.06	0.08
Price Range	39.76-25.59	44.87-16.46	18.63-2.94	3.26-1.09	1.46-0.42	1.35-0.23	3.60-0.63	2.19-0.84
P/E Ratio	27.23-17.53	29.32-10.76	21.67-3.42	11.63-3.88	...	...	...	...
Average Yield %	0.23	...	...	...	...	...	...	...

Address: 1999 Broadway, Suite 4300, Denver, CO 80202	Web Site: www.timet.com	Auditors: PricewaterhouseCoopers LLP
Telephone: 303-296-5600	Officers: J. Landis Martin - Chmn., Pres., C.E.O.	Transfer Agents: American Stock
Fax: 303-296-5650	Harold C. Simmons - Vice-Chmn.	Transfer and Trust Company, New York, NY

TJX COMPANIES, INC.

Exchange	Symbol	Price	52Wk Range	Yield	P/E	Div Acheiver
NYS	TJX	$33.07 (3/31/2008)	34.45-26.59	1.33	19.92	11 Years

*7 Year Price Score 102.72 *NYSE Composite Index=100 *12 Month Price Score 117.60

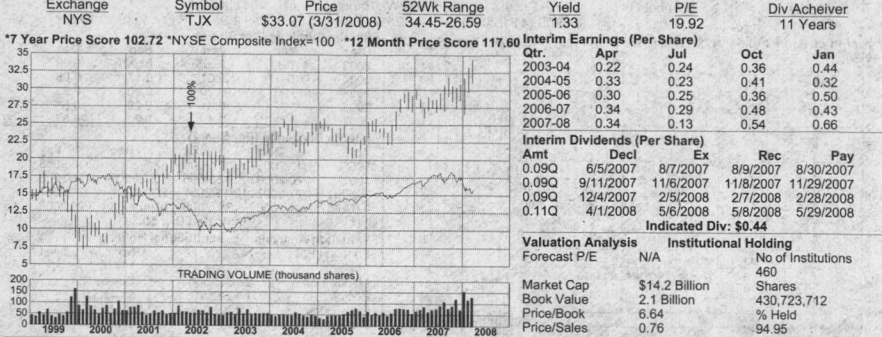

Interim Earnings (Per Share)

Qtr.	Apr	Jul	Oct	Jan
2003-04	0.22	0.24	0.36	0.44
2004-05	0.33	0.23	0.41	0.32
2005-06	0.30	0.25	0.36	0.50
2006-07	0.34	0.29	0.48	0.43
2007-08	0.34	0.13	0.54	0.66

Interim Dividends (Per Share)

Amt	Decl	Ex	Rec	Pay
0.09Q	6/5/2007	8/7/2007	8/9/2007	8/30/2007
0.09Q	9/11/2007	11/6/2007	11/8/2007	11/29/2007
0.09Q	12/4/2007	2/5/2008	2/7/2008	2/28/2008
0.11Q	4/1/2008	5/6/2008	5/8/2008	5/29/2008

Indicated Div: $0.44

Valuation Analysis

Forecast P/E	N/A
Market Cap	$14.2 Billion
Book Value	2.1 Billion
Price/Book	6.64
Price/Sales	0.76

Institutional Holding

No of Institutions	460
Shares	430,723,712
% Held	94.95

TRADING VOLUME (thousand shares)

Business Summary: Retail - Apparel and Accessory Stores (MIC: 5.8 SIC: 5651 NAIC: 448140)

TJX Companies is an off-price retailer of apparel and home fashions. Co.'s T.J. Maxx, Marshalls and A.J. Wright chains in the U.S., its Winners chain in Canada, and its T.K. Maxx chain in Europe sell off-price family apparel and home fashions. Co.'s HomeGoods chain in the U.S. and its HomeSense chain, operated by Winners in Canada, sell off-price home fashions. Co.'s Bob's Stores chain is a branded apparel chain based in the Northeastern U.S. that provides casual, family apparel. As of Jan 26 2008, Co. operated 847 T.J. Maxx stores, 776 Marshalls stores, 191 Winners stores, 226 T.K. Maxx stores, 289 HomeGoods stores, 129 A.J. Wright stores, 71 HomeSense stores, and 34 Bob's Stores.

Recent Developments: For the year ended Jan 26 2008, income from continuing operations decreased 0.6% to US$771.8 million from US$776.8 million a year earlier. Net income increased 4.6% to US$771.8 million from US$738.0 million in the prior year. Revenues were US$18.65 billion, up 7.1% from US$17.40 billion the year before. Direct operating expenses rose 6.6% to US$14.08 billion from US$13.21 billion in the comparable period the year before. Indirect operating expenses increased 12.8% to US$3.32 billion from US$2.94 billion in the equivalent prior-year period.

Prospects: For the fiscal year ending Jan 31 2009, Co. is forecasting earnings in the range of $2.20 to $2.25 per share, excluding an expected $0.09 per share benefit from the 53rd week in its fiscal 2009 calendar. Specifically, this range is based upon estimated consolidated comparable store sales growth of 2.0% to 3.0%, of which about 0.5 percentage points is due to the effects of foreign currency exchange rates. For the fiscal quarter ending April 2008, Co. is projecting earnings to range from $0.40 to $0.41 per share, based upon estimated consolidated comparable store sales growth of 4.0% to 5.0%, of which about two percentage points is due to the effects of foreign currency exchange rates.

Financial Data

(US$ in Thousands)	01/26/2008	01/27/2007	01/28/2006	01/29/2005	01/31/2004	01/25/2003	01/26/2002	01/27/2001
Earnings Per Share	1.66	1.55	1.41	1.30	1.25	1.08	0.90	0.93
Cash Flow Per Share	3.08	2.64	2.49	2.22	1.49	1.71	1.66	0.97
Tang Book Value Per Share	4.56	4.65	3.71	3.06	2.74	2.36	2.14	1.84
Dividends Per Share	0.340	0.270	0.225	0.170	0.135	0.113	0.087	0.077
Dividend Payout %	20.48	17.42	15.96	13.08	10.80	10.42	9.72	8.33
Income Statement								
Total Revenue	18,647,126	17,404,637	16,057,935	14,913,483	13,327,938	11,981,207	10,708,998	9,579,006
EBITDA	1,669,455	1,669,762	1,414,802	1,368,131	1,316,919	1,145,600	1,078,125	1,040,723
Income Before Taxes	1,242,689	1,246,848	1,009,327	1,079,693	1,068,326	937,724	874,044	864,942
Income Taxes	470,939	470,092	318,904	415,549	409,961	359,336	333,647	326,876
Net Income	771,750	738,039	690,423	664,144	658,365	578,388	500,397	538,066
Average Shares	468,046	480,045	491,500	512,649	512,874	537,740	556,267	578,392
Balance Sheet								
Current Assets	3,992,294	3,748,813	3,140,127	2,905,120	2,451,748	2,240,540	2,115,926	1,721,947
Total Assets	6,599,934	6,085,700	5,496,305	5,075,473	4,396,767	3,940,489	3,595,743	2,932,283
Current Liabilities	2,760,993	2,382,980	2,251,851	2,204,112	1,690,520	1,566,345	1,315,010	1,228,759
Long-Term Obligations	853,460	808,027	807,150	598,540	692,321	693,764	702,379	319,372
Total Liabilities	4,468,689	3,795,579	3,603,651	3,421,991	2,844,379	2,531,342	2,255,045	1,713,571
Stockholders' Equity	2,131,245	2,290,121	1,892,654	1,653,482	1,552,388	1,409,147	1,340,698	1,218,712
Shares Outstanding	427,949	453,649	460,967	480,699	499,181	520,515	543,075	560,757
Statistical Record								
Return on Assets %	12.20	12.78	13.10	14.06	15.54	15.39	15.37	18.81
Return on Equity %	35.01	35.39	39.05	41.55	43.74	42.18	39.21	46.16
EBITDA Margin %	8.95	9.59	8.81	9.17	9.88	9.56	10.07	10.86
Net Margin %	4.14	4.24	4.30	4.45	4.94	4.83	4.67	5.62
Asset Turnover	2.95	3.01	3.05	3.16	3.15	3.19	3.29	3.35
Current Ratio	1.45	1.57	1.39	1.32	1.45	1.43	1.61	1.40
Debt to Equity	0.40	0.35	0.43	0.36	0.45	0.49	0.52	0.26
Price Range	31.87-26.00	30.04-22.23	25.89-20.26	26.35-20.95	23.59-15.93	22.18-16.02	20.31-13.88	15.16-7.06
P/E Ratio	19.20-15.66	19.38-14.34	18.36-14.37	20.27-16.12	18.87-12.74	20.53-14.83	22.56-15.42	16.30-7.59
Average Yield %	1.19	1.03	0.97	0.72	0.68	0.57	0.52	0.73

Address: 770 Cochituate Road, Framingham, MA 01701 **Telephone:** 508-390-1000 **Fax:** 508-390-2091	**Web Site:** www.tjx.com **Officers:** Bernard Cammarata - Chmn., Acting Pres., C.E.O. Donald G. Campbell - Sr. Exec. V.P., Chief Admin. & Bus. Devel. Officer	**Auditors:** PricewaterhouseCoopers LLP **Investor Contact:** 508-390-2323 **Transfer Agents:** The Bank of New York, New York, NY

TOLL BROTHERS INC.

Exchange	Symbol	Price	52Wk Range	Yield	P/E
NYS	TOL	$23.48 (3/31/2008)	30.59-16.04	N/A	N/A

*7 Year Price Score 82.48   ***NYSE Composite Index=100**   ***12 Month Price Score 100.70**

TRADING VOLUME (thousand shares)

Interim Earnings (Per Share)

Qtr.	Jan	Apr	Jul	Oct
2004-05	0.66	1.00	1.27	1.84
2005-06	0.98	1.06	1.07	1.07
2006-07	0.33	0.22	0.16	(0.50)
2007-08	(0.61)	...	...	...

Interim Dividends (Per Share)

Amt	Decl	Ex	Rec	Pay
100%	3/4/2002	4/1/2002	3/14/2002	3/28/2002
100%	6/9/2005	7/11/2005	6/21/2005	7/8/2005

Valuation Analysis   Institutional Holding

Forecast P/E	N/A	No of Institutions 290
Market Cap	$3.7 Billion	Shares
Book Value	3.4 Billion	116,686,488
Price/Book	1.09	% Held
Price/Sales	0.85	75.45

Business Summary: Building & General Construction (MIC: 3.2 SIC: 1531 NAIC: 236117)

Toll Brothers designs, builds, markets and arranges financings for single-family detached and attached homes in luxury residential communities. Co. is also involved, directly and through joint ventures, in projects where it is building, or converting existing rental apartment buildings into, high-, mid- and low-rise luxury homes. In addition, Co. develops, owns and operates golf courses and country clubs associated with several of its master planned communities. As of Oct 31 2007, Co. operated from 368 communities containing approximately 27,900 home sites that it owned or controlled through options.

Recent Developments: For the quarter ended Jan 31 2008, net loss amounted to US$96.0 million versus net income of US$54.3 million in the year-earlier quarter. Revenues were US$842.9 million, down 22.7% from US$1.09 billion the year before. Operating loss was US$147.0 million versus an income of US$51.4 million in the prior-year quarter. Direct operating expenses declined 3.0% to US$847.5 million from US$873.3 million in the comparable period the year before. Indirect operating expenses decreased 14.2% to US$142.3 million from US$165.8 million in the equivalent prior-year period.

Prospects: Co.'s results continue to be hampered by the overall softening of demand for new homes, an oversupply of homes available for sale, and the inability of some home buyers to sell their current home. Specifically, Co.'s backlog of homes under contract has declined due to lower value and number of new contracts signed. Further, the decline in the average sales price of contracts signed in the fiscal 2008 period was due to, among others, the higher average value of the contracts cancelled, and a shift in the number of contracts signed to less expensive areas and/or product. For the fiscal year ending Oct 2008, Co. expects to sell about 300 communities, compared with 315 communities at Oct 2007.

Financial Data
(US$ in Thousands)

	3 Mos	10/31/2007	10/31/2006	10/31/2005	10/31/2004	10/31/2003	10/31/2002	10/31/2001
Earnings Per Share	(0.73)	0.22	4.17	4.78	2.52	1.72	1.46	1.38
Cash Flow Per Share	3.21	2.13	(0.68)	2.17	0.75	(0.33)	(0.67)	(1.04)
Tang Book Value Per Share	21.54	22.47	22.20	17.84	12.83	10.07	8.04	6.56
Income Statement								
Total Revenue	842,852	4,646,979	6,123,453	5,793,425	3,893,093	2,775,241	2,328,972	2,229,605
EBITDA	(144,994)	101,920	1,158,930	1,347,475	762,502	496,473	422,342	405,492
Depn & Amortn	6,961	...	...	...	...	...	...	...
Income Before Taxes	(151,955)	70,680	1,126,616	1,323,128	647,432	411,153	347,318	337,889
Income Taxes	(55,998)	35,029	439,403	517,018	238,321	151,333	127,431	124,216
Net Income	(95,957)	35,651	687,213	806,110	409,111	259,820	219,887	213,673
Average Shares	157,813	164,166	164,852	168,552	162,330	151,082	150,960	154,732
Balance Sheet								
Current Assets	6,333,361	6,689,414	6,898,337	5,757,843	4,459,123	3,505,600	2,653,398	2,366,381
Total Assets	7,020,619	7,220,316	7,583,541	6,343,840	4,905,578	3,787,391	2,895,365	2,532,200
Current Liabilities	2,039,027	1,419,221	1,812,106	1,746,075	1,257,493	812,458	644,003	562,570
Long-Term Obligations	1,560,196	2,265,850	2,347,806	1,830,254	1,728,098	1,498,305	1,121,853	1,057,047
Total Liabilities	3,599,223	3,685,071	4,159,912	3,576,329	2,985,591	2,310,763	1,765,856	1,619,617
Stockholders' Equity	3,413,382	3,527,234	3,415,926	2,763,571	1,919,987	1,476,628	1,129,509	912,583
Shares Outstanding	158,493	157,008	153,899	154,943	149,642	146,644	140,434	139,108
Statistical Record								
Return on Assets %	N.M.	0.48	9.87	14.33	9.39	7.78	8.10	9.37
Return on Equity %	N.M.	1.03	22.24	34.42	24.02	19.94	21.54	25.78
EBITDA Margin %	N.M.	2.19	18.93	23.26	19.59	17.89	18.13	18.19
Net Margin %	N.M.	0.77	11.22	13.91	10.51	9.36	9.44	9.58
Asset Turnover	0.61	0.63	0.88	1.03	0.89	0.83	0.86	0.98
Current Ratio	3.11	4.71	3.81	3.30	3.55	4.31	4.12	4.21
Debt to Equity	0.46	0.64	0.69	0.66	0.90	1.01	0.99	1.16
Price Range	35.35-16.04	35.35-19.57	39.90-22.67	58.25-23.47	23.90-18.42	18.45-8.88	15.69-7.79	11.00-6.75
P/E Ratio	...	160.68-88.95	9.57-5.44	12.19-4.91	9.48-7.31	10.73-5.16	10.75-5.34	7.97-4.89

Address: 250 Gibraltar Road, Horsham, PA 19044	**Web Site:** www.tollbrothers.com	**Auditors:** Ernst & Young LLP
Telephone: 215-938-8000	**Officers:** Robert I. Toll - Chmn., C.E.O. Bruce E. Toll - Vice-Chmn.	**Investor Contact:** 215-938-8045
Fax: 215-938-8023		**Transfer Agents:** American Stock Transfer & Trust Co., New York, NY

TOOTSIE ROLL INDUSTRIES INC

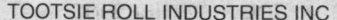

Exchange	Symbol	Price	52Wk Range	Yield	P/E	Div Acheiver
NYS	TR	$25.20 (3/31/2008)	29.95-21.80	1.27	27.69	44 Years

*7 Year Price Score 71.76   *NYSE Composite Index=100   *12 Month Price Score 99.75

Interim Earnings (Per Share)

Qtr.	Mar	Jun	Sep	Dec
2003	0.18	0.21	0.45	0.28
2004	0.20	0.20	0.46	0.24
2005	0.21	0.24	0.48	0.43
2006	0.22	0.23	0.51	0.21
2007	0.17	0.18	0.42	0.15

Interim Dividends (Per Share)

Amt	Decl	Ex	Rec	Pay
0.078Q	9/25/2007	10/3/2007	10/5/2007	10/15/2007
0.078Q	12/5/2007	12/13/2007	12/17/2007	1/4/2008
0.078Q	2/26/2008	3/6/2008	3/10/2008	3/31/2008
3%	2/26/2008	3/6/2008	3/10/2008	4/10/2008

Indicated Div: $0.32

Valuation Analysis   **Institutional Holding**

Forecast P/E	N/A	No of Institutions
		140
Market Cap	$1.4 Billion	Shares
Book Value	638.2 Million	14,605,817
Price/Book	2.21	% Held
Price/Sales	2.83	26.38

Business Summary: Food (MIC: 4.1 SIC: 2064 NAIC: 311340)

Tootsie Roll Industries manufactures and sells confectionery products. The majority of Co.'s products are sold under the registered trademarks Tootsie Roll, Tootsie Roll Pops, Child's Play, Caramel Apple Pops, Charms, Blow-Pop, Blue Razz, Zip-A-Dee Pops, Cella's, Mason Dots, Mason Crows, Junior Mint, Charleston Chew, Sugar Daddy, Sugar Babies, Andes, Fluffy Stuff, Dubble Bubble, Razzles, Cry Baby and Nik-L-Nip. As of Dec 31 2007, Co.'s products were distributed through about 100 candy and grocery brokers and by Co. itself to customers, including wholesale distributors of candy and groceries, supermarkets, and chain grocers, in the U.S. Co.'s key markets are in the U.S., Canada and Mexico.

Recent Developments: For the year ended Dec 31 2007, net income decreased 21.7% to US$51.6 million from US$65.9 million in the prior year. Revenues were US$497.7 million, down 0.7% from US$501.1 million the year before. Operating income was US$70.9 million versus US$87.5 million in the prior year, a decrease of 19.1%. Direct operating expenses rose 5.3% to US$329.0 million from US$312.6 million in the comparable period the year before. Indirect operating expenses decreased 3.2% to US$97.8 million from US$101.0 million in the equivalent prior-year period.

Prospects: Co.'s outlook appears to be challenging as earnings continue to be hurt by higher input costs relating to key ingredients, packaging materials, freight and distribution, and products manufactured in Canada due to less favorable foreign exchange rates. Nonetheless, Co. is encouraged by the recent slight increase in sales that benefited from its marketing programs and the timing of shipments. Meanwhile, Co. continues to maintain a bottom line focus and remains committed to reviewing its operations to increase efficiency. Also, in view of the higher input costs, Co. has adjusted selling prices or package weights on some items and will continue to take other steps to increase profitability.

Financial Data
(US$ in Thousands)

	12/31/2007	12/31/2006	12/31/2005	12/31/2004	12/31/2003	12/31/2002	12/31/2001	12/31/2000
Earnings Per Share	0.91	1.15	1.36	1.09	1.12	1.11	1.12	1.32
Cash Flow Per Share	1.59	0.97	1.45	1.29	1.43	1.19	1.39	1.48
Tang Book Value Per Share	6.73	6.45	6.28	5.15	7.27	6.93	6.69	5.94
Dividends Per Share	0.308	0.299	0.264	0.247	0.240	0.233	0.226	0.214
Dividend Payout %	33.79	26.04	19.41	22.60	21.42	20.92	20.15	16.19
Income Statement								
Total Revenue	497,717	495,990	487,739	420,110	392,656	393,185	423,496	427,054
EBITDA	94,082	112,166	132,556	109,165	107,568	107,798	112,513	124,527
Income Before Taxes	77,167	94,715	113,652	94,688	97,947	100,688	100,787	117,808
Income Taxes	25,542	28,796	36,425	30,514	32,933	34,300	35,100	42,071
Net Income	51,625	65,919	77,227	64,174	65,014	66,388	65,687	75,737
Average Shares	56,629	57,495	56,802	58,938	58,283	59,740	58,486	57,307
Balance Sheet								
Current Assets	199,726	190,917	246,596	192,693	243,705	224,948	246,096	203,211
Total Assets	812,725	791,639	813,696	811,753	665,297	646,080	618,676	562,442
Current Liabilities	57,972	62,211	113,656	82,317	62,887	63,096	57,846	57,446
Long-Term Obligations	7,500	7,500	7,500	93,167	7,500	7,500	7,500	7,500
Total Liabilities	174,495	160,958	196,291	241,574	128,716	119,340	110,215	103,746
Stockholders' Equity	638,230	630,681	617,405	570,179	536,581	526,740	508,461	458,696
Shares Outstanding	55,859	56,961	56,434	58,770	57,656	59,067	58,433	56,834
Statistical Record								
Return on Assets %	6.44	8.21	9.50	8.67	9.92	10.50	11.12	13.84
Return on Equity %	8.14	10.56	13.01	11.57	12.23	12.83	13.58	16.99
EBITDA Margin %	18.90	22.61	27.18	25.98	27.39	27.42	26.57	29.16
Net Margin %	10.37	13.29	15.83	15.28	16.56	16.88	15.51	17.73
Asset Turnover	0.62	0.62	0.60	0.57	0.60	0.62	0.72	0.78
Current Ratio	3.45	3.07	2.17	2.34	3.88	3.57	4.25	3.54
Debt to Equity	0.01	0.01	0.01	0.16	0.01	0.01	0.01	0.02
Price Range	30.81-22.86	31.35-24.84	30.77-26.48	33.42-25.84	31.86-22.86	40.17-24.71	40.34-28.52	37.74-22.18
P/E Ratio	33.86-25.13	27.26-21.60	22.62-19.47	30.66-23.70	28.45-20.41	36.19-22.27	36.02-25.47	28.59-16.80
Average Yield %	1.14	1.08	0.94	0.84	0.84	0.90	0.74	0.66	0.76

Address: 7401 South Cicero Avenue, Chicago, IL 60629
Telephone: 773-838-3400
Fax: 773-838-3534

Web Site: www.tootsie.com
Officers: Melvin J. Gordon - Chmn., C.E.O. Ellen R. Gordon - Pres., C.O.O.

Auditors: PricewaterhouseCoopers LLP
Transfer Agents: Mellon Investor Services, LLC, Ridgefield Park, NJ

TORCHMARK CORP.

Exchange	Symbol	Price	52Wk Range	Yield	P/E
NYS	TMK	$60.11 (3/31/2008)	70.32-57.85	0.93	10.93

*7 Year Price Score 101.13 *NYSE Composite Index=100 *12 Month Price Score 102.74

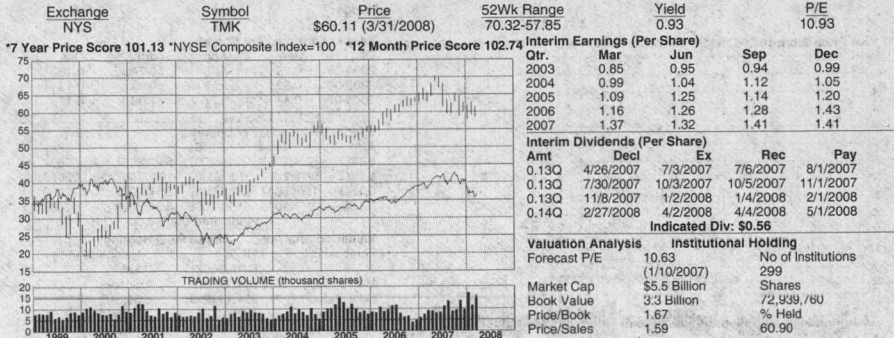

Interim Earnings (Per Share)

Qtr.	Mar	Jun	Sep	Dec
2003	0.85	0.95	0.94	0.99
2004	0.99	1.04	1.12	1.05
2005	1.09	1.25	1.14	1.20
2006	1.16	1.26	1.28	1.43
2007	1.37	1.32	1.41	1.41

Interim Dividends (Per Share)

Amt	Decl	Ex	Rec	Pay
0.13Q	4/26/2007	7/3/2007	7/6/2007	8/1/2007
0.13Q	7/30/2007	10/3/2007	10/5/2007	11/1/2007
0.13Q	11/8/2007	1/2/2008	1/4/2008	2/1/2008
0.14Q	2/27/2008	4/2/2008	4/4/2008	5/1/2008

Indicated Div: $0.56

Valuation Analysis | **Institutional Holding**

Forecast P/E	10.63 (1/10/2007)	No of Institutions 299
Market Cap	$5.5 Billion	Shares
Book Value	3.3 Billion	72,939,760
Price/Book	1.67	% Held
Price/Sales	1.59	60.90

Business Summary: Insurance (MIC: 8.2 SIC: 6311 NAIC: 524113)

Torchmark is an insurance holding company that operates through its American Income Life Insurance Company, Liberty National Life Insurance Company, Globe Life & Accident Insurance Company, United American Insurance Company and United Investors Life Insurance Company subsidiaries. Co.'s insurance subsidiaries write a range of nonparticipating ordinary life insurance products including, traditional and interest-sensitive whole-life insurance, term life insurance, as well as other life insurance. Additionally Co. also provides supplemental health insurance products classified as Medicare Supplement, cancer and other health policies.

Recent Developments: For the year ended Dec 31 2007, net income increased 1.7% to US$527.5 million from US$518.6 million in the prior year. Revenues were US$3.49 billion, up 1.9% from US$3.42 billion the year before. Net premiums earned were US$2.83 billion versus US$2.78 billion in the prior year, an increase of 1.5%. Net investment income rose 3.2% to US$648.8 million from US$628.7 million a year ago.

Prospects: Looking ahead, Co. does not expect significant growth in its Medicare Part D business in future periods, as majority of the Part D enrollees selected a plan in 2006. Nevertheless, Co. remains optimistic regarding its near-term outlook. For instance, Co. anticipates its January 2007 acquisition of Direct Marketing and Advertising Distributors, Inc. will increase distribution opportunities while reducing per unit acquisition costs for the insert media component of the Direct Response group. Meanwhile, for the full-year of 2008, Co. projects net operating income per share will range from $5.88 to $5.94.

Financial Data
(US$ in Thousands)

	12/31/2007	12/31/2006	12/31/2005	12/31/2004	12/31/2003	12/31/2002	12/31/2001	12/31/2000
Earnings Per Share	5.50	5.13	4.68	4.19	3.73	3.18	2.83	2.82
Cash Flow Per Share	9.01	8.68	8.19	6.95	6.45	5.41	5.29	4.15
Tang Book Value Per Share	31.47	31.40	29.49	28.18	25.39	20.91	17.24	14.34
Dividends Per Share	0.520	0.480	0.440	0.440	0.380	0.360	0.360	0.360
Dividend Payout %	9.45	9.36	9.40	10.50	10.19	11.32	12.72	12.77
Income Statement								
Premium Income	2,827,231	2,784,713	2,508,074	2,471,900	2,375,783	2,279,033	2,215,169	2,046,210
Total Revenue	3,486,697	3,421,178	3,125,910	3,071,500	2,930,638	2,737,966	2,707,042	2,515,894
Benefits & Claims	1,902,428	1,863,531	1,661,186	1,645,700	1,590,072	1,524,074	1,454,636	1,339,482
Income Before Taxes	796,805	773,570	731,521	720,800	658,935	584,320	601,429	562,958
Income Taxes	269,270	254,939	236,131	245,100	225,009	197,037	205,967	190,841
Net Income	527,535	518,631	495,390	468,600	430,141	383,433	356,513	362,035
Average Shares	95,845	101,112	105,751	111,907	115,377	120,669	125,860	128,353
Balance Sheet								
Total Assets	15,241,428	14,980,355	14,768,903	14,252,200	13,460,886	12,360,722	12,428,153	12,962,558
Total Liabilities	11,916,801	11,521,162	11,336,135	10,832,400	10,220,787	9,364,842	9,786,469	10,566,803
Stockholders' Equity	3,324,627	3,459,193	3,432,768	3,419,800	3,240,099	2,851,453	2,497,127	2,202,360
Shares Outstanding	92,175	98,114	103,568	107,943	112,714	118,267	122,887	126,389
Statistical Record								
Return on Assets %	3.49	3.49	3.41	3.37	3.33	3.09	2.81	2.88
Return on Equity %	15.55	15.05	14.46	14.03	14.12	14.34	15.17	17.21
Loss Ratio %	67.29	66.92	66.23	66.58	66.93	66.87	65.67	65.46
Net Margin %	15.13	15.16	15.85	15.26	14.68	14.00	13.17	14.39
Price Range	70.32-58.78	64.23-54.25	57.14-50.42	57.51-45.11	45.54-33.32	41.86-31.00	43.05-33.25	40.88-19.00
P/E Ratio	12.79-10.69	12.52-10.58	12.21-10.77	13.73-10.77	12.21-8.93	13.16-9.75	15.21-11.75	14.49-6.74
Average Yield %	0.81	0.80	0.83	0.84	0.96	0.95	0.94	1.32

Address: 2001 3rd Avenue South, Birmingham, AL 35233 **Telephone:** 205-325-4200 **Fax:** 205-325-4157	**Web Site:** www.torchmarkcorp.com **Officers:** C. B. Hudson - Chmn. Mark S. McAndrew - C.E.O.	**Auditors:** DELOITTE & TOUCHE LLP **Investor Contact:** 972-569-3627 **Transfer Agents:** The Bank of New York

TORO CO. (THE)

Exchange	Symbol	Price	52Wk Range	Yield	P/E
NYS	TTC	$41.39 (3/31/2008)	62.21-41.02	1.45	12.07

7 Year Price Score 132.96 *NYSE Composite Index=100 **12 Month Price Score 93.23**

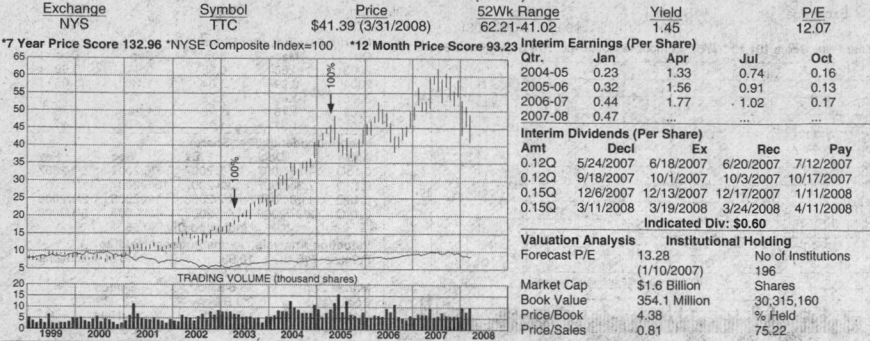

Interim Earnings (Per Share)

Qtr.	Jan	Apr	Jul	Oct
2004-05	0.23	1.33	0.74	0.16
2005-06	0.32	1.56	0.91	0.13
2006-07	0.44	1.77	1.02	0.17
2007-08	0.47	...	...	...

Interim Dividends (Per Share)

Amt	Decl	Ex	Rec	Pay
0.12Q	5/24/2007	6/18/2007	6/20/2007	7/12/2007
0.12Q	9/18/2007	10/1/2007	10/3/2007	10/17/2007
0.15Q	12/6/2007	12/13/2007	12/17/2007	1/11/2008
0.15Q	3/11/2008	3/19/2008	3/24/2008	4/11/2008

Indicated Div: $0.60

Valuation Analysis

		Institutional Holding	
Forecast P/E	13.28	No of Institutions	196
	(1/10/2007)		
Market Cap	$1.6 Billion	Shares	30,315,160
Book Value	354.1 Million	% Held	75.22
Price/Book	4.38		
Price/Sales	0.81		

Business Summary: Industrial Machinery and Equipment (MIC: 11.5 SIC: 3524 NAIC: 333112)

Toro designs, manufactures and markets turf maintenance equipment and services, turf and agricultural irrigation systems, landscaping equipment, and residential yard products. Co. operates via two key segments: professional and residential. A third segment, other, consists of domestic company-owned distributorships, corporate functions, and Co.'s financing subsidiary, Toro Credit Company. Co. sells its products through a network of distributors, dealers, hardware retailers, home centers, mass retailers, and over the Internet, mainly through Internet retailers. Co.'s products are sold at under the primary trademarks of Toro®, Exmark®, Irritrol®, Lawn-Boy®, Hayter®, Pope®, and Lawn Genie®.

Recent Developments: For the quarter ended Feb 1 2008, net income increased 1.0% to US$18.6 million from US$18.5 million in the year-earlier quarter. Revenues were US$405.8 million, up 7.0% from US$379.1 million the year before. Operating income was US$32.0 million versus US$27.8 million in the prior-year quarter, an increase of 15.2%. Direct operating expenses rose 7.4% to US$256.7 million from US$239.0 million in the comparable period the year before. Indirect operating expenses increased 4.3% to US$117.1 million from US$112.3 million in the equivalent prior-year period.

Prospects: Co. is cautiously optimistic that results for fiscal 2008 ending Oct 2008 would be higher compared to the prior fiscal year due to continued growth in international markets and new products introduced during the past two years, somewhat tempered by uncertain domestic economic conditions and outlook. Also, Co. intends to mitigate the effects of anticipated increases in commodity costs and other inflationary pressures by engaging in vendor negotiations and cost reduction efforts, reviewing alternative sourcing options, and moderately increasing prices on some products. For fiscal 2008, Co. expects an 8.0% to 10.0% increase in net earnings per share on revenue growth of 2.0% to 4.0%.

Financial Data
(US$ in Thousands)

	3 Mos	10/31/2007	10/31/2006	10/31/2005	10/31/2004	10/31/2003	10/31/2002	10/31/2001
Earnings Per Share	3.43	3.40	2.91	2.45	2.02	1.56	0.68	0.96
Cash Flow Per Share	5.82	4.51	4.44	3.89	3.79	2.35	2.88	1.38
Tang Book Value Per Share	6.71	7.10	7.57	7.24	7.00	7.31	5.86	4.77
Dividends Per Share	0.510	0.480	0.360	0.240	0.120	0.120	0.120	0.120
Dividend Payout %	14.85	14.12	12.37	9.80	5.94	7.69	17.58	12.44
Income Statement								
Total Revenue	405,799	1,876,904	1,835,991	1,779,387	1,652,508	1,496,588	1,399,273	1,353,083
EBITDA	44,704	271,629	251,557	229,315	203,717	169,763	137,478	139,251
Depn & Amortn	10,986	...	...	...	...	...	...	...
Income Before Taxes	28,835	213,227	192,754	170,272	153,233	120,918	86,799	80,077
Income Taxes	10,208	70,791	63,609	56,190	50,567	39,298	26,868	29,629
Net Income	18,627	142,436	129,145	114,082	102,666	81,620	35,317	50,448
Average Shares	39,395	41,864	44,344	46,539	50,766	52,298	51,744	52,268
Balance Sheet								
Current Assets	741,863	664,928	657,093	647,074	665,175	673,915	592,141	564,193
Total Assets	1,031,109	950,837	921,983	916,737	928,747	927,432	846,140	835,674
Current Liabilities	431,644	341,470	345,539	341,202	340,775	303,136	293,750	292,567
Long-Term Obligations	228,241	227,598	175,000	175,000	175,046	175,091	178,756	194,565
Total Liabilities	676,971	580,399	529,954	526,703	533,133	490,230	480,850	494,281
Stockholders' Equity	354,138	370,438	392,029	390,034	395,614	437,202	365,290	341,393
Shares Outstanding	37,450	37,950	40,355	41,898	45,036	48,777	48,684	49,064
Statistical Record								
Return on Assets %	13.83	15.21	14.05	12.36	11.03	9.20	4.20	6.25
Return on Equity %	38.60	37.36	33.03	29.04	24.59	20.34	10.00	15.32
EBITDA Margin %	11.02	14.47	13.70	12.89	12.33	11.34	9.82	10.29
Net Margin %	4.59	7.59	7.03	6.41	6.21	5.45	2.52	3.73
Asset Turnover	1.85	2.00	2.00	1.93	1.78	1.69	1.66	1.68
Current Ratio	1.72	1.95	1.90	1.90	1.95	2.22	2.02	1.93
Debt to Equity	0.64	0.61	0.45	0.45	0.44	0.40	0.49	0.57
Price Range	62.21-43.01	62.21-42.59	52.36-36.51	48.50-33.94	35.55-22.58	24.85-15.14	15.97-10.51	12.38-8.20
P/E Ratio	18.14-12.54	18.30-12.53	17.99-12.55	19.80-13.85	17.60-11.18	15.93-9.70	23.48-15.46	12.89-8.54
Average Yield %	0.93	0.90	0.81	0.60	0.41	0.63	0.90	1.15

Address: 8111 Lyndale Avenue South, Bloomington, MN 55420-1196 **Telephone:** 952-888-8801	**Web Site:** www.thetorocompany.com **Officers:** Kendrick B. Melrose - Chmn. Michael J. Hoffman - Pres., C.E.O.	**Auditors:** KPMG LLP **Transfer Agents:** Wells Fargo Bank, N.A., St. Paul, MN

TOTAL SYSTEM SERVICES, INC.

Exchange	Symbol	Price	52Wk Range	Yield	P/E	Div Acheiver
NYS	TSS	$23.66 (3/31/2008)	34.33-20.23	1.18	19.72	10 Years

*7 Year Price Score 95.59   *NYSE Composite Index=100   *12 Month Price Score 87.53

Interim Earnings (Per Share)

Qtr.	Mar	Jun	Sep	Dec
2003	0.16	0.17	0.18	0.20
2004	0.17	0.18	0.20	0.21
2005	0.23	0.26	0.24	0.26
2006	0.26	0.29	0.28	0.44
2007	0.29	0.33	0.35	0.23

Interim Dividends (Per Share)

Amt	Decl	Ex	Rec	Pay
0.07Q	9/6/2007	9/18/2007	9/20/2007	10/1/2007
3.031Q	11/30/2007	12/19/2007	12/17/2007	12/31/2007
0.07Q	11/30/2007	12/19/2007	12/17/2007	1/2/2008
0.07Q	3/10/2008	3/18/2008	3/20/2008	4/1/2008

Indicated Div: $0.28

Valuation Analysis

		Institutional Holding	
Forecast P/E	20.38	No of Institutions	
	(1/10/2007)	122	
Market Cap	$4.7 Billion	Shares	
Book Value	844.5 Million	14,068,591	
Price/Book	5.55	% Held	
Price/Sales	2.59	7.13	

Business Summary: Miscellaneous Business Services (MIC: 12.8 SIC: 7389 NAIC: 561499)

Total System Services is a provider of electronic payment processing and related services to financial and non-financial institutions. Services include processing consumer, retail, commercial, government services, and debit cards. Co. provides merchant acquiring services to financial institutions and other organizations in the U.S. through its wholly-owned subsidiary, TSYS Acquiring Solutions, L.L.C., and in Japan through its majority owned subsidiary, GP Network Corp. Co. also provides optional products and services, such as credit evaluation, fraud detection and prevention, behavior analysis tools, loyalty programs and bonus rewards, to support its core processing services.

Recent Developments: For the year ended Dec 31 2007, net income decreased 4.7% to US$237.4 million from US$249.2 million in the prior year. Revenues were US$1.81 billion, up 1.0% from US$1.79 billion the year before. Operating income was US$353.5 million versus US$357.1 million in the prior year, a decrease of 1.0%. Indirect operating expenses increased 1.6% to US$1.45 billion from US$1.43 billion in the equivalent prior-year period.

Prospects: Co. believes that its spin-off from Synovus Financial Corporation in Dec 2007, which enables it to become a fully independent company, will allow for additional investment in strategic growth opportunities and potential acquisitions going forward. Accordingly, for 2008, Co. expects its net income to increase between 7.0% and 9.0% to a range of $254.0 million to $259.0 million. This guidance is based on several assumptions, including estimated total revenues in a range of $1.93 billion to $1.96 billion in 2008, representing growth of 7.0% to 9.0% versus 2007. The guidance also assumes that there will be no significant movement in foreign currency exchange rates related to Co.'s business.

Financial Data

(US$ in Thousands)	12/31/2007	12/31/2006	12/31/2005	12/31/2004	12/31/2003	12/31/2002	12/31/2001	12/31/2000
Earnings Per Share	1.20	1.26	0.99	0.76	0.71	0.64	0.53	0.44
Cash Flow Per Share	1.70	1.96	1.21	1.68	1.35	1.00	0.45	0.85
Tang Book Value Per Share	1.67	3.45	2.30	1.97	1.62	1.41	1.31	1.02
Dividends Per Share	3.311	0.270	0.220	0.140	0.077	0.068	0.060	0.048
Dividend Payout %	275.91	21.43	22.22	18.42	10.92	10.55	11.32	10.80
Income Statement								
Total Revenue	1,805,836	1,787,171	1,602,931	1,187,008	1,053,466	955,133	650,408	601,293
EBITDA	506,367	543,208	437,503	310,964	290,037	235,189	210,508	178,272
Income Before Taxes	377,691	371,854	291,927	204,291	194,369	163,286	155,793	131,708
Income Taxes	143,668	126,182	103,286	77,210	70,868	57,908	52,891	46,065
Net Income	237,443	249,163	194,520	150,558	140,973	125,805	102,902	85,643
Average Shares	197,103	197,077	197,343	197,236	197,437	197,497	195,604	195,265
Balance Sheet								
Current Assets	586,578	744,716	512,289	448,156	274,363	265,979	206,354	210,955
Total Assets	1,479,020	1,634,241	1,410,897	1,281,943	1,001,236	782,868	652,277	604,393
Current Liabilities	273,795	295,787	277,012	277,903	146,971	113,982	102,553	147,301
Long-Term Obligations	256,593	3,625	3,555	4,508	29,748	67	...	...
Total Liabilities	625,967	410,652	394,443	413,517	265,263	177,918	149,107	192,795
Stockholders' Equity	844,473	1,217,360	1,012,772	864,612	732,534	602,206	500,812	409,014
Shares Outstanding	197,965	196,912	197,283	196,849	196,815	197,049	194,778	194,738
Statistical Record								
Return on Assets %	15.25	16.36	14.45	13.15	15.80	17.53	16.38	16.09
Return on Equity %	23.03	22.35	20.72	18.80	21.12	22.81	22.62	22.98
EBITDA Margin %	28.04	30.39	27.29	26.20	27.53	24.62	32.37	29.65
Net Margin %	13.15	13.94	12.14	12.68	13.38	13.17	15.82	14.24
Asset Turnover	1.16	1.17	1.19	1.04	1.18	1.33	1.04	1.13
Current Ratio	2.14	2.52	1.85	1.61	1.87	2.33	2.01	1.43
Debt to Equity	0.30	N.M.	N.M.	0.01	0.04	N.M.	...	...
Price Range	34.33-25.50	26.54-18.07	25.38-18.91	31.13-19.57	31.13-13.50	29.00-11.67	35.54-19.25	22.38-15.19
P/E Ratio	28.61-21.25	21.06-14.34	25.64-19.10	40.96-25.92	43.85-19.01	45.31-18.23	67.06-36.32	50.85-34.52
Average Yield %	11.14	1.26	0.94	0.60	0.35	0.36	0.24	0.27

Address: 1600 First Avenue, Columbus, GA 31901	Web Site: www.tsys.com	Auditors: KPMG LLP
Telephone: 706-649-5220	Officers: Richard W. Ussery - Chmn. M. Troy Woods - Pres., C.O.O.	Investor Contact: 706-649-5220
Fax: 706-649-2456		

TRANE, INC.

Exchange	Symbol	Price	52Wk Range	Yield	P/E
NYS	TT	$45.90 (3/31/2008)	46.71-32.98	1.39	32.79

*7 Year Price Score 124.10 *NYSE Composite Index=100 *12 Month Price Score 121.17

Interim Earnings (Per Share)

Qtr.	Mar	Jun	Sep	Dec
2003	0.29	0.61	0.55	0.38
2004	0.38	0.73	0.71	(0.39)
2005	0.57	0.95	0.74	0.30
2006	0.40	0.93	0.74	0.56
2007	0.84	0.84	0.30	(0.59)

Interim Dividends (Per Share)

Amt	Decl	Ex	Rec	Pay
0.00Q	7/12/2007	8/1/2007	7/19/2007	7/31/2007
0.16Q	7/12/2007	8/30/2007	9/4/2007	9/20/2007
0.16Q	10/4/2007	11/29/2007	12/3/2007	12/20/2007
0.16Q	2/7/2008	2/28/2008	3/3/2008	3/20/2008

Indicated Div: $0.64

Valuation Analysis

Forecast P/E	N/A
Market Cap	$8.9 Billion
Book Value	538.2 Million
Price/Book	16.58
Price/Sales	1.20

Institutional Holding

No of Institutions	N/A
Shares	N/A
% Held	N/A

Business Summary: Purpose Machinery (MIC: 11.13 SIC: 3585 NAIC: 333415)

Trane is a global manufacturer of commercial and residential heating, ventilation and air conditioning equipment (HVAC) and provides systems and services that enhance the quality and comfort of the air in homes and buildings. Co. offers customers a broad range of energy-efficient HVAC systems; dehumidifying and air cleaning products; service and parts support and advanced building controls. Co.'s operations are organized and managed as two divisions: Commercial Systems, a global business, and Residential Systems, a North American regional business. Co. has operations in North America, Europe, the Middle East, Asia and Central and South America.

Recent Developments: For the year ended Dec 31 2007, income from continuing operations increased 3.7% to US$400.2 million from US$385.9 million a year earlier. Net income decreased 47.1% to US$286.3 million from US$541.0 million in the prior year. Revenues were US$7.45 billion, up 10.2% from US$6.76 billion the year before. Operating income was US$717.5 million versus US$650.0 million in the prior year, an increase of 10.4%. Direct operating expenses rose 11.2% to US$5.33 billion from US$4.80 billion in the comparable period the year before. Indirect operating expenses increased 6.7% to US$1.40 billion from US$1.31 billion in the equivalent prior-year period.

Prospects: On Dec 15 2007, Co. entered into an agreement with Ingersoll-Rand Company Ltd. (Ingersoll), global diversified industrial firm, pursuant to which Co. will be acquired by Ingersoll for about $10.10 billion, including transaction fees and the assumption of debt. Accordingly, Co. will become a wholly-owned subsidiary of Ingersoll, and the integration of both companies should provide Co. with the opportunity to participate in a strong global diversified industrial company in the future. Co. expects to close the transaction in the second quarter of 2008. Meanwhile, Co. expects full-year 2008 sales growth of 5.0% to 6.0% and income from continuing operations of $473.5 million to $503.5 million.

Financial Data

(US$ in Thousands)	12/31/2007	12/31/2006	12/31/2005	12/31/2004	12/31/2003	12/31/2002	12/31/2001	12/31/2000
Earnings Per Share	1.40	2.62	2.56	1.42	1.83	1.68	1.35	1.45
Cash Flow Per Share	3.36	3.50	3.88	3.55	3.00	2.87	2.31	2.17
Tang Book Value Per Share	1.13	N.M.	N.M.	N.M.	N.M.	N.M.	...	...
Dividends Per Share	0.680	0.720	0.600	...	...	...	...	...
Dividend Payout %	48.57	27.48	23.44	...	...	...	...	...
Income Statement								
Total Revenue	7,449,600	11,208,200	10,264,400	9,508,800	8,567,600	7,795,400	7,465,300	7,598,370
EBITDA	820,000	1,024,200	990,200	615,700	794,400	767,500	706,400	719,224
Income Before Taxes	602,400	746,200	725,900	362,900	549,200	556,200	476,300	509,433
Income Taxes	202,200	205,200	169,600	49,500	144,000	185,200	181,300	194,201
Net Income	286,300	541,000	556,300	313,400	405,200	371,000	295,000	315,232
Average Shares	204,500	206,265	216,969	220,584	221,150	220,924	219,353	216,593
Balance Sheet								
Current Assets	3,052,400	3,436,700	3,066,200	2,889,800	2,490,700	2,014,400	1,896,400	1,878,496
Total Assets	5,097,300	7,413,100	6,867,800	6,841,800	5,878,700	5,143,800	4,831,400	4,744,660
Current Liabilities	2,239,100	2,568,100	2,228,900	2,346,700	2,033,500	1,665,600	1,688,300	1,806,566
Long-Term Obligations	687,200	1,600,700	1,676,100	1,429,100	1,626,800	1,918,400	2,142,000	2,375,566
Total Liabilities	4,559,100	6,489,600	5,945,300	5,911,500	5,164,900	4,914,000	4,921,500	5,137,563
Stockholders' Equity	538,200	923,500	922,500	930,300	713,800	229,800	(90,100)	(392,903)
Shares Outstanding	194,464	199,891	206,741	214,947	217,914	217,841	216,215	208,597
Statistical Record								
Return on Assets %	4.58	7.58	8.12	4.91	7.35	7.44	6.16	6.67
Return on Equity %	39.17	58.61	60.05	38.02	85.88	531.14	...	...
EBITDA Margin %	11.01	9.14	9.65	6.48	9.27	9.85	9.46	9.47
Net Margin %	3.84	4.83	5.42	3.30	4.73	4.76	3.95	4.15
Asset Turnover	1.19	1.57	1.50	1.49	1.55	1.56	1.56	1.61
Current Ratio	1.36	1.34	1.38	1.23	1.22	1.21	1.12	1.04
Debt to Equity	1.28	1.73	1.82	1.54	2.28	8.35	...	...
Price Range	46.71-32.00	33.09-25.34	33.81-25.34	29.31-23.34	23.82-15.04	18.47-13.73	16.57-11.12	11.57-8.13
P/E Ratio	33.36-22.85	12.63-9.67	13.21-9.90	20.64-16.44	13.02-8.22	10.99-8.17	12.27-8.23	7.98-5.60
Average Yield %	1.79	2.44	1.97	...	...	...	...	...

Address: One Centennial Avenue, P.O. Box 6820, Piscataway, NJ 08855-6820
Telephone: 732-980-6000
Fax: 732-980-6300

Web Site: www.americanstandard.com
Officers: Frederic M. Poses - Chmn., C.E.O. G. Peter D'Aloia - Sr. V.P., C.F.O.

Auditors: Ernst & Young LLP
Transfer Agents: Bank of New York, New York, NY

TRANSATLANTIC HOLDINGS, INC.

Exchange	Symbol	Price	52Wk Range	Yield	P/E	Div Acheiver
NYS	TRH	$66.35 (3/31/2008)	75.78-58.84	0.96	9.08	17 Years

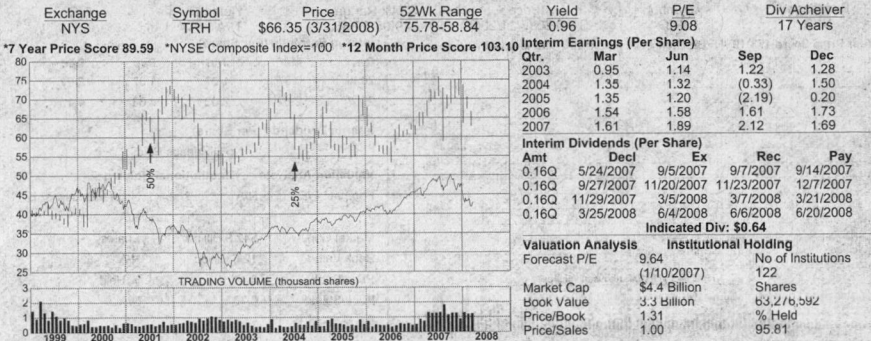

*7 Year Price Score 89.59   *NYSE Composite Index=100   *12 Month Price Score 103.10

Interim Earnings (Per Share)

Qtr.	Mar	Jun	Sep	Dec
2003	0.95	1.14	1.22	1.28
2004	1.35	1.32	(0.33)	1.50
2005	1.35	1.20	(2.19)	0.20
2006	1.54	1.58	1.61	1.73
2007	1.61	1.89	2.12	1.69

Interim Dividends (Per Share)

Amt	Decl	Ex	Rec	Pay
0.16Q	5/24/2007	9/5/2007	9/7/2007	9/14/2007
0.16Q	9/27/2007	11/20/2007	11/23/2007	12/7/2007
0.16Q	11/29/2007	3/5/2008	3/7/2008	3/21/2008
0.16Q	3/25/2008	6/4/2008	6/6/2008	6/20/2008

Indicated Div: $0.64

Valuation Analysis

		Institutional Holding	
Forecast P/E	9.64	No of Institutions	
	(1/10/2007)	122	
Market Cap	$4.4 Billion	Shares	
Book Value	3.3 Billion	63,276,592	
Price/Book	1.31	% Held	
Price/Sales	1.00	95.81	

Business Summary: Insurance (MIC: 8.2 SIC: 6331 NAIC: 524126)

Transatlantic Holdings, through its wholly-owned subsidiaries Transatlantic Reinsurance Company, Trans Re Zurich and Putnam Reinsurance Company, provides reinsurance capacity for property and casualty products on a treaty and facultative basis, directly and through brokers, to insurance and reinsurance companies, in both the domestic and international markets. As of Dec 31 2007, Co.'s principal lines of reinsurance included ocean marine and aviation, medical malpractice, auto liability (including non-standard risks), accident and health and surety and credit in the casualty lines, and fire, allied lines, auto physical damage and homeowners multiple peril lines in the property lines.

Recent Developments: For the year ended Dec 31 2007, net income increased 13.8% to US$487.1 million from US$428.2 million in the prior year. Revenues were US$4.38 billion, up 8.2% from US$4.05 billion the year before. Net premiums earned were US$3.90 billion versus US$3.60 billion in the prior year, an increase of 8.3%. Net investment income rose 8.1% to US$469.8 million from US$434.5 million a year ago

Prospects: Co. is seeing increased net premiums written, primarily reflecting several factors which include premiums generated by domestic regional offices which were opened in 2006 but generated minimal premium volume in that year, and higher international other liability business. In addition, Co. is benefiting from increased net investment income due to an increase in fixed maturity income, resulting mostly from investment returns from continued positive operating cash flows. Meanwhile, Co. is addressing the weakened market pricing in many regions and classes through several initiatives, including capitalizing on opportunities in less saturated sectors of the global reinsurance marketplace.

Financial Data

(US$ in Thousands)	12/31/2007	12/31/2006	12/31/2005	12/31/2004	12/31/2003	12/31/2002	12/31/2001	12/31/2000
Earnings Per Share	7.31	6.46	0.57	3.85	4.60	2.57	0.29	3.23
Cash Flow Per Share	15.53	12.82	9.57	13.73	14.06	9.15	3.71	(0.23)
Tang Book Value Per Share	50.56	44.80	38.60	39.30	36.24	31.03	28.26	28.47
Dividends Per Share	0.590	0.510	0.440	0.376	0.336	0.314	0.298	0.277
Dividend Payout %	8.07	7.89	77.19	9.77	7.30	12.21	103.33	8.60
Income Statement								
Premium Income	3,902,669	3,604,094	3,384,994	3,661,090	3,171,226	2,369,452	1,790,339	1,631,536
Total Revenue	4,381,830	4,049,496	3,768,125	3,990,057	3,452,140	2,615,527	2,030,182	1,866,021
Benefits & Claims	2,638,033	2,462,666	2,877,042	2,754,560	2,233,447	1,796,352	1,561,529	1,196,896
Income Before Taxes	595,752	539,900	(46,000)	276,212	386,674	188,320	(34,107)	267,982
Income Taxes	108,611	111,756	(84,000)	21,628	83,030	19,002	(52,999)	56,344
Net Income	487,141	428,152	37,910	254,584	303,644	169,318	18,892	211,638
Average Shares	66,654	66,266	66,169	66,189	65,952	65,943	65,920	65,595
Balance Sheet								
Total Assets	15,484,327	14,268,464	12,364,676	10,605,292	8,707,758	7,286,525	6,741,303	5,522,672
Total Liabilities	12,135,285	11,310,194	9,820,725	8,018,163	6,331,171	5,255,758	4,895,293	3,666,307
Stockholders' Equity	3,349,042	2,958,270	2,543,951	2,587,129	2,376,587	2,030,767	1,846,010	1,856,365
Shares Outstanding	66,233	66,037	65,911	65,827	65,585	65,451	65,319	65,200
Statistical Record								
Return on Assets %	3.27	3.22	0.33	2.63	3.80	2.41	0.31	3.84
Return on Equity %	15.45	15.56	1.48	10.23	13.78	8.73	1.02	12.06
Loss Ratio %	67.60	68.33	84.99	75.24	70.43	75.81	87.22	73.36
Net Margin %	11.12	10.57	1.01	6.38	8.80	6.47	0.93	11.34
Price Range	75.78-58.84	68.00-53.28	70.94-54.60	73.49-53.80	64.64-49.18	72.80-48.44	73.60-50.54	56.47-36.77
P/E Ratio	10.37-8.05	10.53-8.25	124.46-95.79	19.09-13.97	14.05-10.69	28.33-18.85	253.79-174.29	17.48-11.38
Average Yield %	0.85	0.85	0.72	0.59	0.59	0.51	0.48	0.61

Address: 80 Pine Street, New York, NY 10005
Telephone: 212-770-2000
Fax: 212-785-7230

Web Site: www.transre.com
Officers: Robert F. Orlich - Interim Chmn., Pres., C.E.O. Steven S. Skalicky - Exec. V.P., C.F.O.

Auditors: PricewaterhouseCoopers LLP
Investor Contact: 212-770-2040
Transfer Agents: American Stock Transfer & Trust Company

TRANSOCEAN INC (NEW)

Exchange	Symbol	Price	52Wk Range	Yield	P/E
NYS	RIG	$135.20 (3/31/2008)	149.05-80.85	N/A	9.56

*7 Year Price Score 173.19 *NYSE Composite Index=100 *12 Month Price Score 125.53

Interim Earnings (Per Share)

Qtr.	Mar	Jun	Sep	Dec
2006	0.87	1.07	1.37	2.92
2007	2.62	2.63	4.63	4.17

Interim Dividends (Per Share)

No Dividends Paid

Valuation Analysis		Institutional Holding	
Forecast P/E	N/A	No of Institutions	N/A
Market Cap	$42.9 Billion	Shares	
Book Value	12.6 Billion	N/A	
Price/Book	3.41	% Held	N/A
Price/Sales	6.73		

TRADING VOLUME (thousand shares)

Business Summary: Oil and Gas (MIC: 14.2 SIC: 1381 NAIC: 213111)

Transocean is an international provider of offshore contract drilling services for oil and gas wells. Co.'s primary business is to contract drilling rigs, related equipment and work crews primarily on a dayrate basis to drill oil and gas wells. In addition, Co. provides oil and gas drilling management services on either a dayrate basis or a completed-project, fixed-price basis, as well as drilling engineering and drilling project management services. Co. also participates in oil and gas exploration and production activities. As of Feb 20 2008, Co. owned, had partial ownership interests in or operated 139 mobile offshore drilling units.

Recent Developments: For the year ended Dec 31 2007, net income increased 126.1% to US$3.13 billion from US$1.39 billion in the prior year. Revenues were US$6.38 billion, up 64.3% from US$3.88 billion the year before. Operating income was US$3.24 billion versus US$1.64 billion in the prior year, an increase of 97.4%. Direct operating expenses rose 29.0% to US$2.78 billion from US$2.15 billion in the comparable period the year before. Indirect operating expenses increased 315.1% to US$357.0 million from US$86.0 million in the equivalent prior-year period.

Prospects: On Feb 15 2008, Co. announced that it has agreed to sell three U.S. Gulf of Mexico jackup drilling rigs and related equipment to Hercules Offshore, Inc. for $320.0 million. The sale will allow Co. to focus on more strategic assets as it exits the shallow-water area of the U.S. Gulf of Mexico. Meanwhile, in 2008, Co. expects its revenues to grow due to its Nov 2007 acquisition of the operations of GlobalSantaFe Corp. and the commencement of new contracts with higher dayrates. Co. also expects revenues to be driven by the commencement of its Sedco 702 and Sedco 706 contracts at the end of the rigs' deepwater upgrade shipyard projects in the first and fourth quarters of 2008, respectively.

Financial Data

(US$ in Thousands)	12/31/2007	12/31/2006	12/31/2005
Earnings Per Share	14.14	6.10	3.03
Cash Flow Per Share	14.36	5.65	...
Tang Book Value Per Share	13.70	22.68	...
Income Statement			
Total Revenue	6,377,000	3,882,000	2,892,000
EBITDA	3,438,000	2,102,000	1,301,000
Income Before Taxes	3,384,000	1,607,000	803,000
Income Taxes	253,000	222,000	87,000
Net Income	3,131,000	1,385,000	716,000
Average Shares	222,000	228,000	238,000
Balance Sheet			
Current Assets	4,296,000	1,656,000	...
Total Assets	34,364,000	11,476,000	...
Current Liabilities	7,902,000	1,039,000	...
Long-Term Obligations	11,085,000	3,203,000	...
Total Liabilities	21,793,000	4,636,000	...
Stockholders' Equity	12,566,000	6,836,000	...
Shares Outstanding	317,222	204,609	227,000
Statistical Record			
Return on Assets %	13.66	...	...
Return on Equity %	32.28	...	...
EBITDA Margin %	53.91	54.15	44.99
Net Margin %	49.10	35.68	24.76
Asset Turnover	0.28	...	...
Current Ratio	0.54	1.59	...
Debt to Equity	0.88	0.47	...
Price Range	149.05-72.75	88.97-65.05	70.65-39.80
P/E Ratio	10.54-5.14	14.59-10.66	23.32-13.14

Address: 70 Harbour Drive, Grand Cayman, KYI-1003 Telephone: 345-745-4500	Web Site: www.deepwater.com Officers: Robert L. Long - C.E.O John A. Marshall - Pres., C.O.O	Auditors: Ernst & Young LLP

TRAVELERS COMPANIES INC (THE)

Exchange	Symbol	Price	52Wk Range	Yield	P/E
NYS	TRV	$47.85 (3/31/2008)	56.76-44.92	2.42	6.98

*7 Year Price Score 97.35   *NYSE Composite Index=100   *12 Month Price Score 98.84

Interim Earnings (Per Share)

Qtr.	Mar	Jun	Sep	Dec
2003	0.75	0.89	0.88	0.21
2004	1.34	(0.42)	0.50	0.44
2005	0.31	1.52	0.23	0.26
2006	1.41	1.36	1.47	1.68
2007	1.56	1.86	1.81	1.64

Interim Dividends (Per Share)

Amt	Decl	Ex	Rec	Pay
0.29Q	5/2/2007	6/6/2007	6/8/2007	6/29/2007
0.29Q	8/1/2007	9/6/2007	9/10/2007	9/28/2007
0.29Q	11/6/2007	12/6/2007	12/10/2007	12/31/2007
0.29Q	2/6/2008	3/6/2008	3/10/2008	3/31/2008

Indicated Div: $1.16

Valuation Analysis

		Institutional Holding	
Forecast P/E	9.05	No of Institutions	
	(1/10/2007)	622	
Market Cap	$30.0 Billion	Shares	
Book Value	26.6 Billion	574,404,096	
Price/Book	1.13	% Held	
Price/Sales	1.15	85.02	

TRADING VOLUME (thousand shares)

Business Summary: Insurance (MIC: 8.2 SIC: 6331 NAIC: 524126)

The Travelers Companies is a holding company engaged, through its subsidiaries, in providing commercial and personal property and casualty insurance products and services to businesses, government units, associations and individuals. As of Dec 31 2007, Co. had three operating segments: Business Insurance, Financial, Professional & International Insurance and Personal Insurance. The Business Insurance segment includes property and casualty insurance and insurance-related services. The Financial, Professional & International Insurance segment includes surety and financial liability coverages. The Personal Insurance segment writes property and casualty insurance covering personal risks.

Recent Developments: For the year ended Dec 31 2007, income from continuing operations increased 9.3% to US$4.60 billion from US$4.21 billion a year earlier. Net income increased 9.3% to US$4.60 billion from US$4.21 billion in the prior year. Revenues were US$26.02 billion, up 3.7% from US$25.09 billion the year before. Net premiums earned were US$21.47 billion versus US$20.76 billion in the prior year, an increase of 3.4%. Net investment income rose 6.9% to US$3.76 billion from US$3.52 billion a year ago.

Prospects: For 2008, Co. expects continuous competitive property casualty market conditions, mainly for new business. In addition, Co. foresees renewal price changes in its Business Insurance as well as the Financial, Professional & International Insurance segments to decline modestly from its 2007 levels. Also, Co. projects automobile and homeowners renewal price changes in the Personal Insurance segment to increase slightly versus its 2007 levels. However, Co. believes that these expectations, along with anticipated modestly increased loss costs, will result in reduced underwriting profitability over its 2007 levels. Hence, Co. is projecting operating income of $5.40 to $5.75 per diluted share.

Financial Data
(US$ in Thousands)

	12/31/2007	12/31/2006	12/31/2005	12/31/2004	12/31/2003	12/31/2002	12/31/2001	12/31/2000
Earnings Per Share	6.86	5.91	2.33	1.53	2.72	0.92	(5.22)	4.24
Cash Flow Per Share	0.10	6.95	5.34	0.59	0.50	0.60	4.66	(2.59)
Tang Book Value Per Share	35.56	30.67	25.66	20.93	22.26	20.58	21.03	30.54
Dividends Per Share	0.260	1.010	0.910	1.160	1.160	1.160	1.120	1.080
Dividend Payout %	3.79	17.09	39.06	75.82	42.65	126.09	...	25.47
Income Statement								
Premium Income	21,470,000	20,760,000	20,341,000	19,038,000	7,039,000	7,390,000	7,296,000	5,898,000
Total Revenue	26,017,000	25,090,000	24,365,000	22,934,000	8,854,000	8,918,000	8,943,000	8,608,000
Benefits & Claims	12,397,000	12,244,000	14,927,000	15,439,000	5,188,000	5,995,000	7,479,000	4,407,000
Income Before Taxes	6,216,000	5,723,000	2,671,000	1,128,000	836,000	176,000	(1,431,000)	1,453,000
Income Taxes	1,615,000	1,517,000	610,000	138,000	137,000	(73,000)	(422,000)	440,000
Net Income	4,601,000	4,208,000	1,622,000	955,000	661,000	218,000	(1,088,000)	993,000
Average Shares	672,300	716,700	712,800	628,300	240,000	227,000	212,000	233,000
Balance Sheet								
Total Assets	115,224,000	113,761,000	113,187,000	111,815,000	39,563,000	39,920,000	38,321,000	41,075,000
Total Liabilities	88,608,000	88,626,000	90,884,000	90,614,000	33,338,000	33,285,000	32,314,000	33,511,000
Stockholders' Equity	26,616,000	25,135,000	22,303,000	21,201,000	6,225,000	5,746,000	5,114,000	7,227,000
Shares Outstanding	627,800	678,300	693,400	670,300	228,393	226,798	207,624	218,308
Statistical Record								
Return on Assets %	4.02	3.71	1.44	1.26	1.66	0.56	N.M.	2.48
Return on Equity %	17.78	17.74	7.46	6.95	11.04	4.01	N.M.	14.46
Loss Ratio %	57.74	58.98	73.38	81.10	73.70	81.12	102.51	74.72
Net Margin %	17.68	16.77	6.66	4.16	7.47	2.44	(12.17)	11.54
Price Range	56.76-48.38	54.23-40.75	46.70-33.71	43.35-30.99	39.65-29.33	50.12-24.20	52.12-35.50	56.38-21.75
P/E Ratio	8.27-7.05	9.18-6.90	20.04-14.47	28.33-20.25	14.58-10.78	54.48-26.30	...	13.30-5.13
Average Yield %	0.49	2.20	2.24	3.03	3.30	3.01	2.44	2.73

Address: 385 Washington Street, St. Paul, MN 55102	Web Site: www.stpaultravelers.com	Auditors: KPMG LLP
Telephone: 651-310-7911	Officers: Jay S. Fishman - Chmn., Pres., C.E.O. John A. MacColl - Vice-Chmn., Gen. Couns.	Transfer Agents: Wells Fargo Bank, Minnesota, N.A., St. Paul, MN
Fax: 651-310-3386		

TRINITY INDUSTRIES, INC.

Exchange	Symbol	Price	52Wk Range	Yield	P/E
NYS	TRN	$26.65 (3/31/2008)	47.94-22.34	1.05	7.30

*7 Year Price Score 120.70 *NYSE Composite Index=100 *12 Month Price Score 85.31

Interim Earnings (Per Share)

Qtr.	Mar	Jun	Sep	Dec
2003	(0.21)	0.05	0.01	(0.02)
2004	(0.17)	0.04	0.00	(0.05)
2005	0.07	0.29	0.43	0.33
2006	0.47	1.08	0.64	0.71
2007	0.74	0.85	1.08	0.98

Interim Dividends (Per Share)

Amt	Decl	Ex	Rec	Pay
0.06Q	5/7/2007	7/11/2007	7/13/2007	7/31/2007
0.07Q	9/10/2007	10/11/2007	10/15/2007	10/31/2007
0.07Q	12/31/2007	1/11/2008	1/15/2008	1/31/2008
0.07Q	3/4/2008	4/11/2008	4/15/2008	4/30/2008

Indicated Div: $0.28

Valuation Analysis

		Institutional Holding	
Forecast P/E	10.65 (1/10/2007)	No of Institutions	236
Market Cap	$2.2 Billion	Shares	77,583,800
Book Value	1.7 Billion	% Held	97.00
Price/Book	1.26		
Price/Sales	0.57		

Business Summary: Rail Transport (MIC: 15.5 SIC: 3743 NAIC: 336510)

Trinity Industries is a multi-industry company that owns a variety of businesses which provides products and services for the industrial, energy, transportation, and construction sectors. As of Dec 31 2007, Co. operated in five business segments: the Rail Group, Construction Products Group, Inland Barge Group, Energy Equipment Group, and Railcar Leasing and Management Services Group. In addition, Co. also reports All Other segment which includes its captive insurance and transportation companies, legal and environmental costs associated with non-operating facilities, other peripheral businesses, as well as the change in market valuation related to ineffective commodity hedges.

Recent Developments: For the year ended Dec 31 2007, income from continuing operations increased 36.3% to US$293.8 million from US$215.5 million a year earlier. Net income increased 27.4% to US$293.1 million from US$230.1 million in the prior year. Revenues were US$3.83 billion, up 19.1% from US$3.22 billion the year before. Operating income was US$512.8 million versus US$382.6 million in the prior year, an increase of 34.0%. Direct operating expenses rose 17.6% to US$3.09 billion from US$2.63 billion in the comparable period the year before. Indirect operating expenses increased 10.0% to US$228.9 million from US$208.1 million in the equivalent prior-year period.

Prospects: Co.'s results are benefiting from increased total revenue due to higher total sales across its business segments. Also, Co. is being driven by an increase in the size of its lease fleet and higher average lease rates, and increased sales of cars from the lease fleet. Meanwhile, for the first quarter of 2008, Co. is expecting earnings from continuing operations in the range of $0.69 to $0.74 per common diluted share. Moreover, Co. anticipates earnings from continuing operations of between $3.20 and $3.50 per common diluted share for full-year 2008. Looking ahead, Co. expects to deliver a majority of its backlog for new railcars, Inland Barge products and structural wind towers in 2008.

Financial Data
(US$ in Thousands)

	12/31/2007	12/31/2006	12/31/2005	12/31/2004	12/31/2003	12/31/2002	12/31/2001	03/31/2001
Earnings Per Share	3.65	2.90	1.13	(0.18)	(0.17)	(0.29)	(0.60)	(1.32)
Cash Flow Per Share	4.38	1.70	2.40	(1.18)	1.68	1.78	1.97	1.62
Tang Book Value Per Share	15.03	11.75	9.19	8.26	7.71	7.73	8.91	15.91
Dividends Per Share	0.250	0.213	0.167	0.160	0.160	0.240	0.480	0.480
Dividend Payout %	6.85	7.36	14.79	...	...	...	...	...
Income Statement								
Total Revenue	3,832,800	3,218,900	2,902,000	2,198,100	1,432,800	1,487,300	1,347,800	1,904,300
EBITDA	646,100	485,400	271,400	104,800	105,500	101,400	44,900	(5,200)
Income Before Taxes	463,200	348,500	143,600	(15,100)	(14,300)	(24,400)	(40,500)	(116,300)
Income Taxes	169,400	133,000	57,300	(5,800)	(4,300)	(4,800)	(5,800)	(41,900)
Net Income	293,100	230,100	86,300	(9,300)	(10,000)	(19,600)	(34,700)	(74,400)
Average Shares	80,400	79,300	76,650	69,750	68,400	67,950	58,050	56,250
Balance Sheet								
Current Assets	1,172,800	1,092,900	845,200	798,800	502,100	450,600	501,700	611,700
Total Assets	4,043,200	3,425,600	2,586,500	2,210,200	2,007,900	1,942,900	1,952,000	1,825,900
Current Liabilities	684,300	655,800	629,900	511,700	460,200	396,000	424,900	858,000
Long-Term Obligations	1,374,200	1,198,900	689,000	518,000	395,200	488,900	476,300	44,000
Total Liabilities	2,316,500	2,022,100	1,413,400	1,139,100	946,300	941,300	942,600	946,900
Stockholders' Equity	1,726,700	1,403,500	1,114,400	1,012,900	1,003,800	1,001,600	1,009,400	879,000
Shares Outstanding	81,400	80,000	74,100	71,700	76,350	76,350	66,600	55,264
Statistical Record								
Return on Assets %	7.85	7.65	3.60	N.M.	N.M.	N.M.	N.M.	N.M.
Return on Equity %	18.73	18.28	8.11	N.M.	N.M.	N.M.	N.M.	N.M.
EBITDA Margin %	16.86	15.08	9.35	4.77	7.36	6.82	3.33	N.M.
Net Margin %	7.65	7.15	2.97	N.M.	N.M.	N.M.	N.M.	N.M.
Asset Turnover	1.03	1.07	1.21	1.04	0.73	0.76	0.42	1.07
Current Ratio	1.71	1.67	1.34	1.56	1.09	1.14	1.18	0.71
Debt to Equity	0.80	0.85	0.62	0.51	0.39	0.49	0.47	0.05
Price Range	47.94-24.32	47.49-29.30	29.83-15.49	23.86-16.90	21.17-10.15	18.11-9.95	18.69-11.67	17.75-12.25
P/E Ratio	13.13-6.66	16.38-10.10	26.40-13.71	...	...	...	...	...
Average Yield %	0.65	0.59	0.74	0.79	1.12	1.77	3.07	3.26

Address: 2525 Stemmons Freeway, Dallas, TX 75207-2401
Telephone: 214-631-4420
Fax: 214-589-8501

Web Site: www.trin.net
Officers: Timothy R. Wallace - Chmn., Pres., C.E.O.
John L. Adams - Vice-Chmn.

Auditors: Ernst & Young LLP
Investor Contact: 214-631-4420
Transfer Agents: Wachovia Bank, N.A.

TRW AUTOMOTIVE HOLDINGS CORP

Exchange	Symbol	Price	52Wk Range	Yield	P/E
NYS	TRW	$23.37 (3/31/2008)	41.90-19.67	N/A	26.56

*7 Year Price Score N/A   *NYSE Composite Index=100   *12 Month Price Score 84.30

TRADING VOLUME (thousand shares)

Interim Earnings (Per Share)

Qtr.	Mar	Jun	Sep	Dec
2003	(0.53)	(0.23)	(0.39)	(0.01)
2004	0.02	0.74	0.13	(0.62)
2005	0.50	0.83	0.10	0.57
2006	0.46	0.88	0.05	0.33
2007	(0.87)	0.94	0.22	0.55

Interim Dividends (Per Share)
No Dividends Paid

Valuation Analysis   Institutional Holding

Forecast P/E	N/A	No of Institutions
		121
Market Cap	$2.4 Billion	Shares
Book Value	3.2 Billion	46,718,532
Price/Book	0.74	% Held
Price/Sales	0.16	47.53

Business Summary: Automotive (MIC: 15.1 SIC: 3714 NAIC: 336340)

TRW Automotive Holdings, through its subsidiaries, supplies automotive systems, modules and components to global automotive original equipment manufacturers (OEMs), as well as other related aftermarkets. Co.'s primary operations include the design, manufacture and sale of active and passive safety related products. Active safety related products primarily refer to vehicle dynamic controls (mainly braking and steering), and passive safety related products primarily refer to occupant restraints (mainly air bags and seat belts) as well as crash sensors. Co. conducts its businesses in three operating segments: Chassis Systems, Occupant Safety Systems, and Automotive Components.

Recent Developments: For the year ended Dec 31 2007, net income decreased 48.9% to US$90.0 million from US$176.0 million in the prior year. Revenues were US$14.70 billion, up 11.9% from US$13.14 billion the year before. Operating income was US$624.0 million versus US$636.0 million in the prior year, a decrease of 1.9%. Direct operating expenses rose 12.9% to US$13.49 billion from US$11.96 billion in the comparable period the year before. Indirect operating expenses increased 5.8% to US$584.0 million from US$552.0 million in the equivalent prior-year period.

Prospects: Co.'s 2008 outlook appears challenging, primarily in North America where customer production volumes are anticipated to be down significantly during the first half of the year. However, Co. believes that the stability provided by having 70.0% of its sales derived from the combined regions of Europe, Asia and South America, and a robust level of demand for its products in all markets, will help to mitigate such challenges. Meanwhile, Co. expects full-year 2008 sales to be in the range of $15.60 billion to $16.00 billion, including projected first quarter 2008 sales of around $4.00 billion. Concurrently, Co. expects 2008 net earnings per diluted share to be in the range of $2.15 to $2.45.

Financial Data
(US$ in Thousands)

	12/31/2007	12/31/2006	12/31/2005	12/31/2004	12/31/2003	02/28/2003	12/31/2002	12/31/2001
Earnings Per Share	0.88	1.71	1.99	0.29	(1.16)	...	...	...
Cash Flow Per Share	7.30	6.49	5.07	0.03	9.73	...	...	...
Tang Book Value Per Share	2.38	N.M.	N.M.	N.M.	N.M.	...	...	...
Income Statement								
Total Revenue	14,702,000	13,144,000	12,643,000	12,011,000	9,435,000	1,916,000	10,630,000	10,091,000
EBITDA	1,030,000	1,106,000	1,065,000	913,000	691,000	181,000	1,105,000	830,000
Income Before Taxes	245,000	342,000	328,000	164,000	(3,000)	50,000	302,000	(66,000)
Income Taxes	155,000	166,000	124,000	135,000	98,000	19,000	138,000	(30,000)
Net Income	90,000	176,000	204,000	29,000	(101,000)	31,000	164,000	(25,000)
Average Shares	102,800	103,100	102,300	100,500	86,804	...	...	...
Balance Sheet								
Current Assets	4,126,000	3,676,000	3,500,000	3,516,000	3,315,000	...	2,363,000	...
Total Assets	12,290,000	11,133,000	10,230,000	10,114,000	9,907,000	...	10,948,000	...
Current Liabilities	3,715,000	3,675,000	3,590,000	3,480,000	3,126,000	...	2,755,000	...
Long-Term Obligations	3,150,000	2,862,000	3,101,000	3,122,000	3,708,000	...	3,581,000	...
Total Liabilities	8,964,000	8,627,000	8,916,000	8,944,000	9,129,000	...	8,476,000	...
Stockholders' Equity	3,192,000	2,397,000	1,208,000	1,105,000	728,000	...	2,391,000	...
Shares Outstanding	100,629	98,204	99,245	98,970	86,845	...	...	...
Statistical Record								
Return on Assets %	0.77	1.65	2.01	0.29	N.M.	...	...	...
Return on Equity %	3.22	9.76	17.64	3.16	N.M.	...	...	...
EBITDA Margin %	7.01	8.41	8.42	7.60	7.32	9.45	10.40	8.23
Net Margin %	0.61	1.34	1.61	0.24	N.M.	1.62	1.54	N.M.
Asset Turnover	1.26	1.23	1.24	1.20	0.90	...	...	...
Current Ratio	1.16	1.00	1.00	1.01	1.06	...	0.86	...
Debt to Equity	0.99	1.19	2.57	2.83	5.09	...	1.50	...
Price Range	41.90-20.90	28.34-22.18	29.58-17.81	27.10-16.68	...	...	...	...
P/E Ratio	47.61-23.75	16.57-12.97	14.86-8.95	93.45-57.52	...	...	...	...

Address: 12001 Tech Center Drive, Livonia, MI 48150 **Telephone:** 734-855-2600	**Web Site:** www.trwauto.com **Officers:** Neil P. Simpkins - Chmn. John C. Plant - Pres., C.E.O.	**Auditors:** Ernst & Young LLP **Transfer Agents:** National City Bank

TUPPERWARE BRANDS CORP

Exchange	Symbol	Price	52Wk Range	Yield	P/E
NYS	TUP	$38.68 (3/31/2008)	39.00-24.77	2.28	20.68

*7 Year Price Score 119.08 *NYSE Composite Index=100 *12 Month Price Score 125.62

Interim Earnings (Per Share)

Qtr.	Mar	Jun	Sep	Dec
2003	0.11	0.24	0.00	0.47
2004	0.25	0.40	0.22	0.61
2005	0.40	0.46	0.04	0.51
2006	0.26	0.41	0.22	0.65
2007	0.32	0.56	0.11	0.88

Interim Dividends (Per Share)

Amt	Decl	Ex	Rec	Pay
0.22Q	5/16/2007	6/12/2007	6/14/2007	7/6/2007
0.22Q	8/22/2007	9/10/2007	9/12/2007	10/1/2007
0.22Q	11/2/2007	12/5/2007	12/7/2007	1/7/2008
0.22Q	2/20/2008	3/11/2008	3/13/2008	4/3/2008

Indicated Div: $0.88

Valuation Analysis

		Institutional Holding	
Forecast P/E	10.36	No of Institutions	
	(1/10/2007)	180	
Market Cap	$2.4 Billion	Shares	
Book Value	522.7 Million	52,091,924	
Price/Book	4.55	% Held	
Price/Sales	1.20	85.33	

Business Summary: Chemicals (MIC: 11.1 SIC: 3089 NAIC: 326199)

Tupperware Brands is a global direct seller of consumer products for the manufacture and sale of food storage, preparation and serving items and beauty and personal care products. The core of Co.'s product line consists of food storage, serving and preparation products through the Tupperware® brand. Co. also has a line of kitchen tools, children's educational toys, microwave products and gifts. Co.'s beauty businesses manufacture and distribute skin care products, cosmetics, bath and body care, toiletries, fragrances, nutritional products, apparel and related products through its Avroy Shlain®, BeautiControl®, Fuller®, NaturCare®, Nutrimetics®, Nuvo® and Swissgarde® brands.

Recent Developments: For the year ended Dec 29 2007, net income increased 24.1% to US$116.9 million from US$94.2 million in the prior year. Revenues were US$1.98 billion, up 13.6% from US$1.74 billion the year before. Operating income was US$194.1 million versus US$152.1 million in the prior year, an increase of 27.6%. Direct operating expenses rose 13.1% to US$695.4 million from US$615.0 million in the comparable period the year before. Indirect operating expenses increased 11.8% to US$1.09 billion from US$976.6 million in the equivalent prior-year period.

Prospects: For full year 2008, Co. is projecting sales growth of 8.0% to 10.0%, while earnings are forecasted to range from $2.37 to $2.47 per diluted share, including a $0.10 to $0.12 per share benefit from stronger foreign currencies. In addition, Co. is targeting sales in the Tupperware brand segments to increase the mid-single-digit range, while sales in the Beauty brand segments are estimated to improve in the high-single-digit range. Meanwhile, for the first quarter of 2008, Co. is anticipating sales growth of 13.0% to 15.0%, while earnings is expected to range from $0.44 to $0.49 per diluted share, versus earnings of $0.36 per diluted share in 2007, excluding certain adjustment items diluted.

Financial Data

(US$ in Thousands)	12/29/2007	12/30/2006	12/31/2005	12/25/2004	12/27/2003	12/28/2002	12/29/2001	12/30/2000
Earnings Per Share	1.87	1.54	1.41	1.48	0.82	1.54	1.04	1.29
Cash Flow Per Share	2.92	2.88	2.77	2.08	1.81	2.21	1.88	1.47
Tang Book Value Per Share	N.M.	N.M.	N.M.	3.99	2.94	2.08	1.21	1.14
Dividends Per Share	0.880	0.880	0.880	0.880	0.880	0.880	0.880	0.880
Dividend Payout %	47.06	57.14	62.41	59.46	107.32	57.14	84.62	68.22
Income Statement								
Total Revenue	1,981,400	1,743,700	1,279,300	1,224,300	1,174,800	1,155,100	1,114,400	1,073,100
EBITDA	240,500	198,600	159,900	165,800	123,000	190,200	153,800	174,200
Income Before Taxes	141,400	103,800	65,700	102,000	56,600	117,400	82,200	101,100
Income Taxes	24,500	9,600	(20,500)	15,100	8,700	27,300	20,700	26,200
Net Income	116,900	94,200	85,400	86,900	47,900	90,100	61,500	74,900
Average Shares	62,614	61,171	60,617	58,800	58,440	58,716	58,900	58,000
Balance Sheet								
Current Assets	699,500	586,600	672,700	466,000	411,400	360,100	366,100	372,400
Total Assets	1,868,700	1,712,100	1,740,200	983,200	889,900	830,600	845,700	849,400
Current Liabilities	450,300	381,600	454,700	292,100	274,200	283,000	352,300	275,800
Long-Term Obligations	589,800	680,500	750,500	246,500	263,500	265,100	276,100	358,100
Total Liabilities	1,346,000	1,311,600	1,404,700	692,300	661,700	653,100	719,100	725,500
Stockholders' Equity	522,700	400,500	335,500	290,900	228,200	177,500	126,600	123,900
Shares Outstanding	61,521	60,561	60,431	58,825	58,516	58,360	58,134	57,884
Statistical Record								
Return on Assets %	6.55	5.47	6.17	9.30	5.58	10.78	7.28	8.96
Return on Equity %	25.39	25.67	26.83	33.57	23.68	59.42	49.24	54.75
EBITDA Margin %	12.14	11.39	12.50	13.54	10.47	16.47	13.80	16.23
Net Margin %	5.90	5.40	6.68	7.10	4.08	7.80	5.52	6.98
Asset Turnover	1.11	1.01	0.92	1.31	1.37	1.38	1.32	1.28
Current Ratio	1.55	1.54	1.48	1.60	1.50	1.27	1.04	1.35
Debt to Equity	1.13	1.70	2.24	0.85	1.15	1.49	2.18	2.89
Price Range	36.10-22.30	23.41-17.11	24.37-19.70	20.27-16.06	17.03-12.18	24.73-14.85	25.14-17.81	23.88-14.63
P/E Ratio	19.30-11.93	15.20-11.11	17.28-13.97	13.70-10.85	20.77-14.85	16.06-9.64	24.17-17.12	18.51-11.34
Average Yield %	3.05	4.31	4.02	4.89	5.90	4.56	3.97	4.75

Address: 14901 South Orange Blossom Trail, Orlando, FL 32837
Telephone: 407-826-5050
Fax: 407-826-8849

Web Site: www.tupperware.com
Officers: E. V. Goings - Chmn., C.E.O. Michael S. Poteshman - Exec.V.P, C.F.O.

Auditors: PricewaterhouseCoopers LLP
Investor Contact: 407-826-4522
Transfer Agents: Wells Fargo Bank Minnesota, N.A.

TYSON FOODS, INC.

Exchange	Symbol	Price	52Wk Range	Yield	P/E
NYS	TSN	$15.95 (3/31/2008)	24.08-13.26	1.00	23.12

*7 Year Price Score 98.08 *NYSE Composite Index=100 *12 Month Price Score 88.77

Interim Earnings (Per Share)

Qtr.	Dec	Mar	Jun	Sep
2004-05	0.14	0.21	0.36	0.28
2005-06	0.11	(0.37)	(0.15)	(0.17)
2006-07	0.16	0.19	0.31	0.09
2007-08	0.10	...	...	...

Interim Dividends (Per Share)

Amt	Decl	Ex	Rec	Pay
0.04Q	5/8/2007	8/29/2007	9/1/2007	9/15/2007
0.04Q	8/3/2007	11/28/2007	12/1/2007	12/15/2007
0.04Q	11/20/2007	2/27/2008	3/1/2008	3/15/2008
0.04Q	2/5/2008	5/28/2008	6/1/2008	6/15/2008

Indicated Div: $0.16

Valuation Analysis

Forecast P/E	13.57 (1/10/2007)
Market Cap	$5.7 Billion
Book Value	4.8 Billion
Price/Book	1.19
Price/Sales	0.21

Institutional Holding

No of Institutions	239
Shares	227,657,056
% Held	64.07

Business Summary: Food (MIC: 4.1 SIC: 2015 NAIC: 311615)

Tyson Foods produces, distributes and markets chicken, beef, pork, prepared foods and related allied products. As of Sep 29 2007, Co. had four operating segments. Chicken operations include breeding and raising chickens, as well as processing live chickens into fresh, frozen and other chicken products. Beef operations include processing live fed cattle and fabrication of dressed beef carcasses into primal and sub-primal meat cuts and case ready products. Pork operations include processing live market hogs and fabricating pork carcasses into primal and sub-primal cuts and case-ready products. Prepared Foods operations manufacture and market frozen and refrigerated food products.

Recent Developments: For the quarter ended Dec 29 2007, net income decreased 40.4% to US$34.0 million from US$57.0 million in the year-earlier quarter. Revenues were US$6.77 billion, up 3.2% from US$6.56 billion the year before. Operating income was US$84.0 million versus US$145.0 million in the prior-year quarter, a decrease of 42.1%. Direct operating expenses rose 3.9% to US$6.46 billion from US$6.22 billion in the comparable period the year before. Indirect operating expenses increased 15.1% to US$221.0 million from US$192.0 million in the equivalent prior-year period.

Prospects: Co.'s outlook seems challenging. For instance, in the fiscal year ending Sep 2008, Co. expects an increase in grain costs in its chicken segment to exceed $500.0 million, which it will be working to mitigate mainly through price increases. Also, as a result of the difficult conditions in the beef segment, on Jan 25 2008, Co. announced plans to cease slaughter operations at its beef plant in Emporia, KS in the second quarter of fiscal 2008, which will result in the elimination of 1,700 to 1,800 jobs. While it expects this segment to improve in the second quarter of fiscal 2008, Co. expects the difficult environment to persist until cattle supplies are more balanced with slaughter capacity.

Financial Data
(US$ in Thousands)

	3 Mos	09/29/2007	09/30/2006	10/01/2005	10/02/2004	09/27/2003	09/28/2002	09/29/2001
Earnings Per Share	0.69	0.75	(0.58)	0.99	1.13	0.96	1.08	0.40
Cash Flow Per Share	1.55	1.95	0.83	2.90	2.66	2.38	3.38	2.32
Tang Book Value Per Share	6.01	5.96	5.05	5.66	4.49	3.17	2.92	1.71
Dividends Per Share	0.160	0.160	0.160	0.160	0.160	0.160	0.160	0.160
Dividend Payout %	23.13	21.33	...	16.16	14.16	16.67	14.81	40.00
Income Statement								
Total Revenue	6,766,000	26,900,000	25,559,000	26,014,000	26,441,000	24,549,000	23,367,000	10,751,000
EBITDA	230,000	1,119,000	429,000	1,223,000	1,376,000	1,254,000	1,365,000	644,000
Depn & Amortn	127,000	...	...	...	...	...	...	...
Income Before Taxes	52,000	410,000	(293,000)	528,000	635,000	523,000	593,000	165,000
Income Taxes	18,000	142,000	(102,000)	175,000	232,000	186,000	210,000	58,000
Net Income	34,000	268,000	(196,000)	353,000	403,000	337,000	383,000	88,000
Average Shares	355,000	355,000	345,000	357,000	357,000	352,000	355,000	222,000
Balance Sheet								
Current Assets	3,641,000	3,596,000	4,187,000	3,485,000	3,532,000	3,371,000	3,144,000	3,290,000
Total Assets	10,250,000	10,227,000	11,121,000	10,504,000	10,464,000	10,486,000	10,372,000	10,632,000
Current Liabilities	2,127,000	2,115,000	2,846,000	2,157,000	2,293,000	2,475,000	2,093,000	2,416,000
Long-Term Obligations	2,574,000	2,642,000	2,987,000	2,869,000	3,024,000	3,114,000	3,733,000	4,016,000
Total Liabilities	5,498,000	5,496,000	6,681,000	5,852,000	6,172,000	6,532,000	6,710,000	7,278,000
Stockholders' Equity	4,752,000	4,731,000	4,440,000	4,652,000	4,292,000	3,954,000	3,662,000	3,354,000
Shares Outstanding	356,000	356,000	355,000	355,000	353,000	353,000	353,000	349,000
Statistical Record								
Return on Assets %	2.40	2.52	N.M.	3.38	3.79	3.24	3.66	1.14
Return on Equity %	5.30	5.86	N.M.	7.92	9.62	8.87	10.95	3.19
EBITDA Margin %	3.40	4.16	1.68	4.70	5.20	5.11	5.84	5.99
Net Margin %	0.50	1.00	N.M.	1.36	1.52	1.37	1.64	0.82
Asset Turnover	2.66	2.53	2.37	2.49	2.48	2.36	2.23	1.39
Current Ratio	1.71	1.70	1.47	1.62	1.54	1.36	1.50	1.36
Debt to Equity	0.54	0.56	0.67	0.62	0.70	0.79	1.02	1.20
Price Range	24.08-14.11	24.08-14.20	18.70-12.92	19.47-14.12	21.06-12.59	14.42-7.28	15.56-8.75	14.38-8.35
P/E Ratio	34.90-20.45	32.11-18.93	...	19.67-14.26	18.64-11.14	15.02-7.58	14.41-8.10	35.94-20.88
Average Yield %	0.84	0.84	1.04	0.92	0.95	1.52	1.30	1.36

Address: 2210 West Oaklawn Drive, Springdale, AR 72762-6999. **Telephone:** 479-290-4000 **Fax:** 479-290-7984	**Web Site:** www.tyson.com **Officers:** John Tyson - Chmn., C.E.O. Richard L. Bond - Pres., C.O.O.	**Auditors:** Ernst & Young LLP **Investor Contact:** 479-290-4235 **Transfer Agents:** EquiServe, Trust Co., N.A. Providence RI

UDR INC

Exchange	Symbol	Price	52Wk Range	Yield	P/E	Div Acheiver
NYS	UDR	$24.52 (3/31/2008)	31.07-19.24	5.38	16.03	22 Years

*7 Year Price Score 93.96   *NYSE Composite Index=100   *12 Month Price Score 102.01

Interim Earnings (Per Share)

Qtr.	Mar	Jun	Sep	Dec
2003	0.06	0.02	0.01	0.12
2004	0.07	0.17	0.17	0.16
2005	0.08	0.36	0.08	0.50
2006	0.06	0.21	0.42	0.16
2007	0.21	0.01	0.56	0.75

Interim Dividends (Per Share)

Amt	Decl	Ex	Rec	Pay
0.33Q	7/3/2007	7/11/2007	7/13/2007	7/31/2007
0.33Q	10/3/2007	10/10/2007	10/12/2007	10/31/2007
0.33Q	1/2/2008	1/9/2008	1/11/2008	1/31/2008
0.33Q	4/3/2008	4/9/2008	4/11/2008	4/30/2008

Indicated Div: $1.32

Valuation Analysis

		Institutional Holding	
Forecast P/E	204.87	No of Institutions	
	(1/10/2007)	259	
Market Cap	$3.3 Billion	Shares	
Book Value	1.0 Billion	113,066,600	
Price/Book	3.21	% Held	
Price/Sales	6.54	83.42	

TRADING VOLUME (thousand shares)

Business Summary: Property, Real Estate & Development (MIC: 8.3 SIC: 6798 NAIC: 525930)

UDR is a self-administered real estate investment trust (REIT) that is engaged in the ownership, acquisition, renovation, development and management of apartment communities nationwide. As of Dec 31 2007, Co.'s apartment portfolio included 234 communities located in 30 markets, with a total of 65,867 completed apartment homes. As of such date, Co.'s subsidiaries included two operating partnerships, Heritage Communities L.P., a Delaware limited partnership, and United Dominion Realty L.P., a Delaware limited partnership, and RE3, its subsidiary that focuses on development, land entitlement and short-term hold investments.

Recent Developments: For the year ended Dec 31 2007, income from continuing operations was US$13.2 million compared with a loss of US$85.5 million a year earlier. Net income increased 72.1% to US$221.3 million from US$128.6 million in the prior year. Revenues were US$500.2 million, up 7.0% from US$467.3 million the year before. Revenues from property income rose 7.3% to US$497.5 million from US$463.7 million in the corresponding earlier year.

Prospects: On Jan 29 2008, Co. announced that it has entered into a contract to sell 25,684 apartment homes in 86 communities for $1.70 billion to DRA Advisors LLC. Upon completion of the transaction, which should be on or about Mar 3 2008, Co. will own 40,183 homes in 146 communities. The portfolio sale should allow Co. to focus on markets that have the best growth prospects based on favorable job formation and low single-family home affordability. Meanwhile, Co. expects that its 2008 financial results will be affected by several factors, including credit market volatility. Thus, for 2008, Co. is expecting same-store revenue growth of 4.0% to 4.5% and net operating income growth of 5.0% to 5.5%.

Financial Data

(US$ in Thousands)	12/31/2007	12/31/2006	12/31/2005	12/31/2004	12/31/2003	12/31/2002	12/31/2001	12/31/2000
Earnings Per Share	1.53	0.85	1.02	0.56	0.21	0.24	0.27	0.41
Cash Flow Per Share	1.87	1.72	1.82	1.96	2.05	2.14	2.24	2.17
Tang Book Value Per Share	6.28	6.47	6.91	7.43	7.28	6.48	7.10	7.91
Dividends Per Share	1.303	1.238	1.192	1.163	1.133	1.103	1.077	1.067
Dividend Payout %	85.13	145.59	116.91	207.59	539.29	459.38	399.07	260.37
Income Statement								
Property Income	497,474	694,473	680,553	604,270	603,367	594,314	618,590	616,825
Non-Property Income	2,720	3,585	20,664	2,608	1,068	1,806	4,593	5,326
Total Revenue	500,194	698,058	701,217	606,878	604,435	596,120	623,183	622,151
Interest Expense	174,677	182,285	162,508	124,087	117,185	130,956	144,379	156,040
Net Income	221,349	128,605	155,166	97,152	70,404	53,229	61,828	76,615
Average Shares	134,016	133,732	137,013	129,080	115,648	106,952	101,037	103,208
Balance Sheet								
Total Assets	4,801,121	4,675,875	4,541,593	4,332,001	3,543,643	3,276,136	3,348,091	3,453,957
Long-Term Obligations	3,502,676	3,338,785	3,159,777	2,879,982	2,132,037	2,057,640	2,064,197	1,992,330
Total Liabilities	3,719,679	3,531,787	3,350,050	3,052,957	2,286,001	2,205,649	2,229,701	2,146,739
Stockholders' Equity	1,019,393	1,055,255	1,107,724	1,195,451	1,163,436	1,001,271	1,042,725	1,218,892
Shares Outstanding	133,317	135,029	134,012	136,429	127,295	106,605	103,133	102,219
Statistical Record								
Return on Assets %	4.67	2.79	3.50	2.46	2.06	1.61	1.82	2.14
Return on Equity %	21.34	11.89	13.47	8.21	6.50	5.21	5.47	6.04
Net Margin %	44.25	18.42	22.13	16.01	11.65	8.93	9.92	12.31
Price Range	33.95-19.64	33.66-23.93	25.85-20.64	24.80-17.52	19.37-15.22	16.70-13.95	14.72-10.75	11.75-9.44
P/E Ratio	22.19-12.84	39.60-28.15	25.34-20.24	44.29-31.29	92.24-72.48	69.58-58.13	54.52-39.81	28.66-23.02
Average Yield %	4.86	4.33	5.21	5.80	6.53	7.18	8.10	10.22

Address: 400 East Cary St., Richmond, VA 23219
Telephone: 720-283-6120

Web Site: www.udrt.com
Officers: Robert C. Larson - Chmn. James D. Klingbeil - Vice-Chmn.

Auditors: Ernst & Young LLP
Transfer Agents: ChaseMellon Shareholder Services, LLC, Pittsburgh, PA

UGI CORP.

Exchange	Symbol	Price	52Wk Range	Yield	P/E	Div Achiever
NYS	UGI	$24.92 (3/31/2008)	29.30-23.78	2.97	12.10	20 Years

*7 Year Price Score 112.63 *NYSE Composite Index=100 *12 Month Price Score 104.89

Interim Earnings (Per Share)

Qtr.	Dec	Mar	Jun	Sep
2004-05	0.75	1.12	0.01	(0.09)
2005-06	0.54	0.98	0.18	(0.04)
2006-07	0.58	1.12	0.11	0.09
2007-08	0.74	...	...	...

Interim Dividends (Per Share)

Amt	Decl	Ex	Rec	Pay
0.185Q	4/25/2007	6/13/2007	6/15/2007	7/1/2007
0.185Q	7/31/2007	9/12/2007	9/15/2007	10/1/2007
0.185Q	11/27/2007	12/12/2007	12/15/2007	1/1/2008
0.185Q	1/29/2008	3/12/2008	3/14/2008	4/1/2008

Indicated Div: $0.74 (Div. Reinv. Plan)

Valuation Analysis / **Institutional Holding**

Forecast P/E	13.36	No of Institutions
	(1/10/2007)	213
Market Cap	$2.9 Billion	Shares
Book Value	1.4 Billion	74,018,728
Price/Book	2.04	% Held
Price/Sales	0.50	69.80

Business Summary: Electricity (MIC: 7.1 SIC: 4932 NAIC: 221210)

UGI is a holding company that distributes and markets energy products and related services via its subsidiaries and joint venture affiliates. Co. is a domestic and international distributor of propane and butane (liquefied petroleum gases); a provider of natural gas and electric service through regulated local distribution utilities; a generator of electricity through its ownership interests in electric generation facilities; a regional marketer of energy commodities; and a provider of heating, air conditioning, refrigeration and electrical services. Co.'s subsidiaries operate in five key segments: AmeriGas Propane, International Propane, Gas Utility, Electric Utility, and Energy Services.

Recent Developments: For the quarter ended Dec 31 2007, net income increased 29.2% to US$80.0 million from US$61.9 million in the year-earlier quarter. Revenues were US$1.76 billion, up 20.6% from US$1.46 billion the year before. Operating income was US$196.2 million versus US$167.3 million in the prior-year quarter, an increase of 17.3%. Direct operating expenses rose 24.9% to US$1.24 billion from US$994.4 million in the comparable period the year before. Indirect operating expenses increased 8.3% to US$326.5 million from US$301.5 million in the equivalent prior-year period.

Prospects: Co.'s operating results are benefiting from double-digit increases in operating income in all of its operating units other than domestic propane. Specifically, the growth in Co.'s international businesses is mainly due to the return of normal weather conditions, while growth in its utility and energy services businesses reflect contributions from prior investments in those businesses. However, results in Co.'s domestic propane unit are being hurt by lower retail gallons sold principally reflecting customer conservation in response to increasing propane product costs, which more than offset the benefits of acquisitions made in the fiscal year ended Sep 2007.

Financial Data
(US$ in Thousands)

	3 Mos	09/30/2007	09/30/2006	09/30/2005	09/30/2004	09/30/2003	09/30/2002	09/30/2001
Earnings Per Share	2.06	1.89	1.65	1.77	1.16	1.15	0.90	0.69
Cash Flow Per Share	3.49	4.29	2.65	4.21	2.72	2.95	2.99	2.50
Dividends Per Share	0.731	0.723	0.690	0.650	0.598	0.565	0.542	0.525
Dividend Payout %	35.50	38.23	41.82	36.72	51.73	49.34	60.19	76.46
Income Statement								
Total Revenue	1,764,700	5,476,900	5,221,000	4,888,700	3,784,700	3,026,100	2,213,700	2,468,100
EBITDA	240,400	745,000	594,400	611,500	426,100	373,000	326,600	309,000
Depn & Amortn	44,900	...	...	...	...	...	...	...
Income Before Taxes	159,400	437,900	323,400	336,600	176,000	160,800	124,000	99,000
Income Taxes	48,500	126,700	98,500	119,200	64,400	60,700	46,900	45,400
Net Income	80,000	204,300	176,200	187,900	111,600	98,900	75,500	56,500
Average Shares	108,318	107,941	106,727	105,723	96,682	86,472	83,814	82,119
Balance Sheet								
Net PPE	2,419,000	2,397,400	2,214,700	1,802,700	1,781,900	1,336,800	1,271,900	1,268,000
Total Assets	6,068,100	5,502,700	5,080,500	4,571,500	4,235,400	2,781,700	2,614,400	2,550,200
Long Term Obligations	2,052,500	2,038,800	1,965,000	1,392,500	1,547,300	1,158,500	1,127,000	1,196,900
Total Liabilities	4,451,100	3,988,600	3,841,400	3,367,600	3,222,900	2,077,300	2,001,100	2,028,400
Stockholders' Equity	1,403,300	1,321,900	1,099,600	997,600	834,100	569,800	317,300	255,600
Shares Outstanding	115,152	106,646	105,454	104,849	102,422	85,398	83,103	81,889
Statistical Record								
Return on Assets %	3.89	3.86	3.65	4.26	3.17	3.67	2.92	2.34
Return on Equity %	17.37	16.87	16.80	20.47	15.86	22.30	26.36	22.47
EBITDA Margin %	13.62	13.60	11.38	12.51	11.26	12.33	14.75	12.52
Net Margin %	4.53	3.73	3.37	3.84	2.95	3.27	3.41	2.29
PPE Turnover	2.48	2.38	2.60	2.73	2.42	2.32	1.74	2.11
Asset Turnover	1.01	1.04	1.08	1.11	1.08	1.12	0.86	1.02
Debt to Equity	1.46	1.54	1.79	1.40	1.86	2.03	3.55	4.68
Price Range	29.30-23.78	29.30-23.78	28.15-20.46	29.74-18.55	18.63-14.47	17.45-11.74	12.22-8.87	9.70-7.23
P/E Ratio	14.22-11.54	15.50-12.58	17.06-12.40	16.80-10.48	16.06-12.47	15.17-10.21	13.57-9.85	14.05-10.48
Average Yield %	2.74	2.70	2.99	2.74	3.68	3.92	5.26	6.24

Address: 460 North Gulph Road, King of Prussia, PA 19406
Telephone: 610-337-1000

Web Site: www.ugicorp.com
Officers: Lon R. Greenberg - Chmn., C.E.O. John L. Walsh - Pres., C.O.O.

Auditors: PricewaterhouseCoopers LLP
Investor Contact: 610-337-1000
Transfer Agents: Mellon Investor Services LLC, Ridgefield Park, NJ

UNION PACIFIC CORP.

Exchange	Symbol	Price	52Wk Range	Yield	P/E
NYS	UNP	$125.38 (3/31/2008)	135.26-101.97	1.40	18.14

*7 Year Price Score 128.15 *NYSE Composite Index=100 *12 Month Price Score 112.92

Interim Earnings (Per Share)

Qtr.	Mar	Jun	Sep	Dec
2003	1.67	1.10	1.21	2.10
2004	0.63	0.60	0.77	0.30
2005	0.48	0.88	1.38	1.10
2006	1.15	1.44	1.54	1.78
2007	1.41	1.65	2.00	1.85

Interim Dividends (Per Share)

Amt	Decl	Ex	Rec	Pay
0.35Q	5/3/2007	5/25/2007	5/30/2007	7/2/2007
0.35Q	7/26/2007	8/28/2007	8/30/2007	10/1/2007
0.44Q	11/15/2007	11/27/2007	11/29/2007	1/2/2008
0.44Q	2/28/2008	3/10/2008	3/12/2008	4/1/2008

Indicated Div: $1.76

Valuation Analysis

		Institutional Holding	
Forecast P/E	11.98	No of Institutions	
	(1/10/2007)	583	
Market Cap	$32.7 Billion	Shares	
Book Value	15.6 Billion	218,964,672	
Price/Book	2.10	% Held	
Price/Sales	2.01	80.74	

Business Summary: Rail Transport (MIC: 15.5 SIC: 4011 NAIC: 482111)

Union Pacific operates primarily as a rail transportation provider. Through Union Pacific Railroad Company, its principal operating company, Co. have 32,205 route miles, linking Pacific Coast and Gulf Coast ports with the Midwest and eastern U.S. gateways and providing several corridors to key Mexican gateways. Co. serves the western two-thirds of the country and maintains coordinated schedules with other rail carriers to move freight to and from the Atlantic Coast, the Pacific Coast, the Southeast, the Southwest, Canada, and Mexico. Co.'s business mix includes agricultural products, automotive, chemicals, energy, industrial products, and intermodal.

Recent Developments: For the year ended Dec 31 2007, net income increased 15.5% to US$1.86 billion from US$1.61 billion in the prior year. Revenues were US$16.28 billion, up 4.5% from US$15.58 billion the year before. Operating income was US$3.38 billion versus US$2.88 billion in the prior year, an increase of 17.0%. Direct operating expenses rose 1.4% to US$9.89 billion from US$9.76 billion in the comparable period the year before. Indirect operating expenses increased 2.7% to US$3.02 billion from US$2.94 billion in the equivalent prior-year period.

Prospects: Although cautious about the economic environment, Co. expects revenue growth and continued network improvement in 2008, and targets earnings of $7.75 to $8.25 per diluted share. Specifically, Co. expects higher revenue in 2008 based on existing economic indicators, forecasted demand, improved customer service and opportunities to reprice certain of its business, with yield increases and fuel surcharges driving commodity revenue growth. Co. also expects overall volume to be 1.0% higher than to 1.0% lower than 2007, with continued softness in some market sectors. Meanwhile, Co. will continue to reduce the effect of fuel price on earnings through its fuel surcharge programs and conservation efforts.

Financial Data

(US$ in Thousands)	12/31/2007	12/31/2006	12/31/2005	12/31/2004	12/31/2003	12/31/2002	12/31/2001	12/31/2000
Earnings Per Share	6.91	5.91	3.85	2.30	6.04	5.05	3.77	3.34
Cash Flow Per Share	12.32	10.69	9.85	8.61	9.52	8.93	8.03	7.92
Tang Book Value Per Share	59.74	56.68	51.41	48.58	47.85	41.99	38.26	35.09
Dividends Per Share	1.490	1.200	1.200	1.200	0.990	0.830	0.800	0.800
Dividend Payout %	21.56	20.30	31.17	52.17	16.39	16.44	21.22	23.95
Income Statement								
Total Revenue	16,283,000	15,578,000	13,578,000	12,215,000	11,551,000	12,491,000	11,973,000	11,878,000
EBITDA	4,762,000	4,210,000	3,098,000	2,484,000	3,270,000	3,855,000	3,408,000	3,173,000
Income Before Taxes	3,009,000	2,525,000	1,436,000	856,000	1,637,000	2,016,000	1,533,000	1,310,000
Income Taxes	1,154,000	919,000	410,000	252,000	581,000	675,000	567,000	468,000
Net Income	1,855,000	1,606,000	1,026,000	604,000	1,585,000	1,341,000	966,000	842,000
Average Shares	268,400	272,000	266,500	262,200	268,000	276,800	271,900	269,450
Balance Sheet								
Total Assets	38,033,000	36,515,000	35,620,000	34,589,000	33,460,000	32,764,000	31,551,000	30,499,000
Long-Term Obligations	7,543,000	6,000,000	6,760,000	7,981,000	7,822,000	7,428,000	7,886,000	8,144,000
Total Liabilities	22,448,000	21,203,000	21,913,000	21,934,000	21,106,000	22,113,000	21,976,000	21,837,000
Stockholders' Equity	15,585,000	15,312,000	13,707,000	12,655,000	12,354,000	10,651,000	9,575,000	8,662,000
Shares Outstanding	260,869	270,172	266,634	260,519	258,160	253,659	250,290	246,820
Statistical Record								
Return on Assets %	4.98	4.45	2.92	1.77	4.79	4.17	3.11	2.78
Return on Equity %	12.01	11.07	7.78	4.82	13.78	13.26	10.59	10.08
EBITDA Margin %	29.25	27.03	22.82	20.34	28.31	30.86	28.46	26.71
Net Margin %	11.39	10.31	7.56	4.94	13.72	10.74	8.07	7.09
Asset Turnover	0.44	0.43	0.39	0.36	0.35	0.39	0.39	0.39
Price Range	135.26-90.13	97.21-78.58	81.00-58.61	69.48-55.09	69.49-51.34	65.05-54.75	60.60-44.77	52.63-35.06
P/E Ratio	19.57-13.04	16.45-13.30	21.04-15.22	30.21-23.95	11.50-8.50	12.88-10.84	16.07-11.88	15.76-10.50
Average Yield %	1.31	1.35	1.77	1.98	1.65	1.39	1.49	1.90

Address: 1400 Douglas Street, Omaha, NE 68179	Web Site: www.up.com	Auditors: Deloitte & Touche LLP
Telephone: 402-544-5000	Officers: Richard K. Davidson - Chmn., Pres., C.E.O. Robert M. Knight Jr. - Exec. V.P., Fin., C.F.O.	Transfer Agents: Computershare Investor Services, LLC, Providence, RI

UNIONBANCAL CORP.

Exchange	Symbol	Price	52Wk Range	Yield	P/E
NYS	UB	$49.08 (3/31/2008)	63.87-41.64	4.24	11.23

*7 Year Price Score 83.30   *NYSE Composite Index=100   *12 Month Price Score 94.51

Interim Earnings (Per Share)

Qtr.	Mar	Jun	Sep	Dec
2003	0.89	0.96	1.02	1.03
2004	1.05	1.54	1.09	1.19
2005	1.21	1.27	1.26	2.10
2006	1.18	1.26	1.20	1.59
2007	1.07	1.19	0.92	1.19

Interim Dividends (Per Share)

Amt	Decl	Ex	Rec	Pay
0.52Q	5/24/2007	5/31/2007	6/4/2007	7/6/2007
0.52Q	7/25/2007	9/5/2007	9/7/2007	10/5/2007
0.52Q	10/24/2007	12/5/2007	12/7/2007	1/4/2008
0.52Q	1/23/2008	3/5/2008	3/7/2008	4/4/2008

Indicated Div: $2.08

Valuation Analysis

		Institutional Holding	
Forecast P/E	N/A	No of Institutions	175
Market Cap	$0.0 Billion	Shares	0
Book Value	4.7 Billion		128,589,136
Price/Book	1.43	% Held	
Price/Sales	1.75		92.46

Business Summary: Commercial Banking (MIC: 8.1 SIC: 6021 NAIC: 522110)

UnionBanCal, through its banking subsidiary, Union Bank of California, N.A., provides a range of financial services to consumers, small businesses, middle-market companies and corporations, primarily in California, Oregon and Washington, and nationally and internationally as well. Co.'s operations are divided into two primary segments: the Retail Banking, provides its customers a range of financial products; and the Wholesale Banking, offers a variety of commercial financial services. As of Dec 31 2007, Co. had total assets of $55.73 billion and total deposits of $42.68 billion.

Recent Developments: For the year ended Dec 31 2007, income from continuing operations decreased 25.1% to US$569.9 million from US$761.3 million a year earlier. Net income decreased 19.2% to US$608.1 million from US$753.0 million in the prior year. Net interest income decreased 6.3% to US$1.72 billion from US$1.83 billion in the prior year. Provision for loan losses was US$81.0 million versus a credit for loan losses of US$5.0 million in the prior year. Non-interest income rose 4.5% to US$868.3 million from US$830.9 million, while non-interest expense was unchanged at US$1.64 billion:

Prospects: Co.'s bottom-line results are being tempered by lower net interest income due mainly to a deposit mix shift from non-interest bearing and low-cost deposits into higher-cost deposits, partially offset by strong loan growth and higher yields on its earning assets as a result of the higher interest rate environment. Looking ahead, Co. anticipates that the growth rate in residential mortgage loans will decline with the slowdown in the housing market. Meanwhile, for the first quarter of 2008, Co. estimates that its fully diluted earnings per share will be in the range of $0.94 to $0.99. For 2008, Co. expects that its fully diluted earnings per share to be in the range of $4.05 to $4.30.

Financial Data

(US$ in Thousands)	12/31/2007	12/31/2006	12/31/2005	12/31/2004	12/31/2003	12/31/2002	12/31/2001	12/31/2000
Earnings Per Share	4.37	5.24	5.84	4.87	3.90	3.38	3.04	2.72
Cash Flow Per Share	3.46	6.18	7.31	5.12	3.22	6.79	6.90	3.70
Tang Book Value Per Share	30.98	29.39	28.18	23.48	23.77	23.68	22.66	20.17
Dividends Per Share	2.030	1.820	1.590	1.390	1.210	1.090	1.000	1.000
Dividend Payout %	46.45	34.73	27.23	28.54	31.03	32.25	32.89	36.76
Income Statement								
Interest Income	2,992,416	2,681,485	2,223,981	1,844,902	1,769,663	1,855,972	2,195,311	2,501,080
Interest Expense	1,273,764	843,330	384,867	199,679	200,597	294,003	671,269	916,640
Net Interest Income	1,718,652	1,838,155	1,839,114	1,645,223	1,569,066	1,561,969	1,524,042	1,584,440
Provision for Losses	81,000	(5,000)	(50,683)	(35,000)	75,000	175,000	285,000	440,000
Non-Interest Income	868,302	878,499	804,787	989,305	794,253	735,976	716,404	647,180
Non-Interest Expense	1,643,405	1,686,288	1,617,746	1,524,182	1,408,353	1,347,666	1,240,174	1,130,185
Income Before Taxes	862,549	1,035,366	1,087,338	1,145,346	879,966	775,279	715,272	661,435
Income Taxes	292,683	271,623	356,698	412,812	292,827	247,376	233,844	221,535
Net Income	608,094	752,996	862,933	732,534	587,139	527,903	481,428	439,900
Average Shares	139,052	143,755	147,791	150,303	150,645	156,415	158,623	161,989
Balance Sheet								
Net Loans & Leases	40,801,462	36,340,646	32,744,063	30,309,800	25,401,783	25,828,893	24,359,521	25,396,496
Total Assets	55,727,748	52,619,576	49,416,002	48,098,021	42,498,467	40,169,773	36,039,089	35,162,475
Total Deposits	42,680,191	41,969,368	40,082,239	40,175,836	35,532,283	32,840,815	28,556,199	27,283,183
Total Liabilities	50,989,767	48,048,175	44,856,302	43,805,777	38,758,031	36,411,584	32,492,847	31,950,910
Stockholders' Equity	4,737,981	4,571,401	4,559,700	4,292,244	3,740,436	3,758,189	3,546,242	3,211,565
Shares Outstanding	137,836	139,107	144,207	148,359	145,758	150,702	156,483	159,234
Statistical Record								
Return on Assets %	1.12	1.48	1.77	1.61	1.42	1.39	1.35	1.27
Return on Equity %	13.06	16.49	19.50	18.19	15.66	14.45	14.25	14.15
Net Interest Margin %	57.43	68.55	82.69	89.18	88.66	84.16	69.42	63.35
Efficiency Ratio %	42.57	47.37	53.07	53.78	54.93	51.99	42.59	35.90
Loans to Deposits	0.96	0.87	0.82	0.75	0.71	0.79	0.85	0.93
Price Range	64.93-48.25	71.30-56.40	71.64-58.24	64.78-49.51	58.45-37.77	49.60-34.98	39.14-24.81	39.44-18.38
P/E Ratio	14.86-11.04	13.61-10.76	12.27-9.97	13.30-10.17	14.99-9.68	14.67-10.35	12.88-8.16	14.50-6.76
Average Yield %	3.45	2.83	2.43	2.43	2.64	2.55	3.09	3.84

Address: 400 California Street, San Francisco, CA 94104	**Web Site:** www.uboc.com	**Auditors:** Deloitte & Touche LLP
Telephone: 415-765-2969	**Officers:** Tetsuo Shimura - Chmn. Philip B. Flynn - Vice-Chmn., C.O.O.	**Investor Contact:** 415-765-2969
Fax: 415-765-2950		**Transfer Agents:** Computershare Investor Services LLC, Chicago, IL

UNISYS CORP.

Exchange	Symbol	Price	52Wk Range	Yield	P/E
NYS	UIS	$4.43 (3/31/2008)	9.60-3.23	N/A	N/A

*7 Year Price Score 56.19   *NYSE Composite Index=100   *12 Month Price Score 69.94

Interim Earnings (Per Share)

Qtr.	Mar	Jun	Sep	Dec
2003	0.12	0.16	0.17	0.34
2004	0.09	0.06	0.07	(0.11)
2005	(0.13)	(0.08)	(4.78)	(0.08)
2006	(0.08)	(0.57)	(0.23)	0.06
2007	0.01	(0.19)	(0.09)	0.04

Interim Dividends (Per Share)

No Dividends Paid

Valuation Analysis   Institutional Holding

Forecast P/E	11.13	No of Institutions	
	(1/10/2007)	233	
Market Cap	$1.6 Billion	Shares	
Book Value	366.6 Million	286,443,296	
Price/Book	4.27	% Held	
Price/Sales	0.28	82.97	

Business Summary: IT & Technology (MIC: 10.2 SIC: 7373 NAIC: 541512)

Unisys is an information technology services and applications company. Co. has two business segments: Services, which consists of systems integration and consulting, outsourcing, infrastructure services and core maintenance; and Technology segment, which develops servers and related products that operate in transaction-intensive, mission-critical environments. Co.'s offerings include enterprise-class servers based on its Cellular MultiProcessing architecture; operating system software and middleware to power high-end servers as well as enhanced technologies such as payment systems and third-party technology products.

Recent Developments: For the year ended Dec 31 2007, net loss amounted to US$79.1 million versus a net loss of US$278.7 million in the prior year. Revenues were US$5.65 billion, down 1.8% from US$5.76 billion the year before. Operating income was US$85.9 million versus a loss of US$326.8 million in the prior year. Direct operating expenses declined 8.0% to US$4.37 billion from US$4.75 billion in the comparable period the year before. Indirect operating expenses decreased 10.1% to US$1.20 billion from US$1.34 billion in the equivalent prior-year period.

Prospects: On Feb 24 2008, Co. announced that its Australian subsidiary has signed a contract with the Australian Department of Defence to provide a range of Information Technology support services to 460 Defence locations across Australia. The contract, with an initial term of five years following a transition period of an estimated 18 months duration, has a value estimated at about $225.0 million, with the potential for two future contract extensions, each of two years duration. Meanwhile, Co. had firm order backlog of $6.90 billion in its services segment at Dec 31 2007 compared $6.60 billion at the same period in 2006. About $3.10 billion of Co.'s 2007 backlog is expected to be filled in 2008.

Financial Data

(US$ in Thousands)	12/31/2007	12/31/2006	12/31/2005	12/31/2004	12/31/2003	12/31/2002	12/31/2001	12/31/2000
Earnings Per Share	(0.23)	(0.81)	(5.09)	0.11	0.78	0.69	(0.21)	0.71
Cash Flow Per Share	0.50	0.08	0.83	1.40	1.61	1.00	0.64	1.34
Tang Book Value Per Share	N.M.	...	...	2.90	2.67	1.18	5.20	5.99
Income Statement								
Total Revenue	5,652,500	5,757,200	5,758,700	5,820,700	5,911,200	5,607,400	6,018,100	6,885,000
EBITDA	581,900	347,700	268,000	387,000	792,700	697,100	325,700	729,800
Income Before Taxes	3,500	(250,900)	(170,900)	(76,000)	380,500	332,800	(46,500)	379,000
Income Taxes	82,600	27,800	1,561,000	(114,600)	121,800	109,800	3,400	134,200
Net Income	(79,100)	(278,700)	(1,731,900)	38,600	258,700	223,000	(67,100)	225,000
Average Shares	349,661	343,747	340,216	338,217	332,948	323,526	318,207	316,651
Balance Sheet								
Current Assets	2,212,200	2,238,500	2,153,300	2,417,600	2,258,000	1,946,000	2,204,100	2,587,000
Total Assets	4,137,100	4,037,900	4,028,900	5,620,900	5,474,600	4,981,400	5,769,100	5,717,700
Current Liabilities	1,896,000	1,931,700	1,814,800	2,022,800	2,053,500	2,184,500	2,323,100	2,685,800
Long-Term Obligations	1,058,300	1,049,100	1,049,000	898,400	1,048,300	748,000	745,000	536,300
Total Liabilities	3,770,500	4,102,100	4,061,500	4,114,400	4,079,400	4,125,400	3,656,400	3,531,600
Stockholders' Equity	366,600	(64,200)	(32,600)	1,506,500	1,395,200	856,000	2,112,700	2,186,100
Shares Outstanding	353,408	345,254	341,966	337,298	331,780	326,202	320,493	315,439
Statistical Record								
Return on Assets %	N.M.	N.M.	N.M.	0.69	4.95	4.15	N.M.	3.87
Return on Equity %	N.M.	...	N.M.	2.65	22.98	15.02	N.M.	10.84
EBITDA Margin %	10.29	6.04	4.65	6.65	13.41	12.43	5.41	10.60
Net Margin %	N.M.	N.M.	N.M.	0.66	4.38	3.98	N.M.	3.27
Asset Turnover	1.38	1.43	1.19	1.05	1.13	1.04	1.05	1.18
Current Ratio	1.17	1.16	1.19	1.20	1.10	0.89	0.95	0.96
Debt to Equity	2.89	...	...	0.60	0.75	0.87	0.35	0.25
Price Range	9.60-4.47	7.76-4.77	10.18-4.50	15.69-9.55	16.70-8.47	13.67-6.08	18.91-8.00	35.06-9.38
P/E Ratio	...	...	...	142.64-86.82	21.41-10.86	19.81-8.81	...	49.38-13.20

Address: Unisys Way, Blue Bell, PA 19424	**Web Site:** www.unisys.com	**Auditors:** KPMG LLP
Telephone: 215-986-4011	**Officers:** Lawrence A. Weinbach - Chmn., Pres., C.E.O. George R. Gazerwitz - Vice-Chmn.	**Investor Contact:** 215-986-6999
Fax: 215-986-6850		

UNIT CORP.

Exchange	Symbol	Price	52Wk Range	Yield	P/E
NYS	UNT	$56.65 (3/31/2008)	64.99-43.93	N/A	9.92

*7 Year Price Score 121.46 *NYSE Composite Index=100 *12 Month Price Score 110.71

TRADING VOLUME (thousand shares)

Interim Earnings (Per Share)

Qtr.	Mar	Jun	Sep	Dec
2003	0.32	0.27	0.29	0.27
2004	0.34	0.44	0.54	0.66
2005	0.67	0.86	1.25	1.82
2006	1.61	1.61	1.75	1.74
2007	1.39	1.41	1.37	1.55

Interim Dividends (Per Share)

No Dividends Paid

Valuation Analysis

		Institutional Holding	
Forecast P/E	5.77	No of Institutions	
	(1/10/2007)	200	
Market Cap	$2.7 Billion	Shares	
Book Value	1.4 Billion	38,425,912	
Price/Book	1.86	% Held	
Price/Sales	2.30	83.01	

Business Summary: Oil and Gas (MIC: 14.2 SIC: 1311 NAIC: 211111)

Unit is primarily engaged in the land contract drilling of natural gas and oil wells, the exploration, development, acquisition and production of oil and natural gas properties, as well as the buying, selling, gathering, processing and treating of natural gas through its three principal wholly owned subsidiaries: Unit Drilling Company, Unit Petroleum Company, and Superior Pipeline Company, LLC. Co.'s operations are located principally in the U.S. As of Dec 31 2007, Co. had total proved reserves 514,569.0 million cubic feet of natural gas equivalent.

Recent Developments: For the year ended Dec 31 2007, net income decreased 14.7% to US$266.3 million from US$312.2 million in the prior year. Revenues were US$1.16 billion, unchanged from the year before. Indirect operating expenses increased 10.6% to US$745.3 million from US$674.1 million in the equivalent prior-year period.

Prospects: On Jan 18 2008, Co. purchased a 50.0% interest in a 6,800 gross-acre leasehold at its Segno area in Hardin County, TX, for $16.8 million. The purchase includes five producing wells with 4.90 billion cubic feet of natural gas equivalent (Bcfe) of estimated proved reserves and production of 2.8 million cubic feet of natural gas per day and 88.2 barrels of natural gas liquids. Meanwhile, for 2008, Co. plans to participate in the drilling of about 280 wells, an increase of 11.0% over 2007, and expects annual production of 59.00 Bcfe to 61.00 Bcfe. At its contract drilling business, Co. plans to place two new drilling rigs into service in its Rocky Mountain division in May 2008.

Financial Data

(US$ in Thousands)	12/31/2007	12/31/2006	12/31/2005	12/31/2004	12/31/2003	12/31/2002	12/31/2001	12/31/2000
Earnings Per Share	5.71	6.72	4.60	1.97	1.15	0.47	1.73	0.95
Cash Flow Per Share	12.46	10.96	6.92	4.43	2.79	1.82	3.70	1.88
Tang Book Value Per Share	28.88	23.41	17.27	12.63	10.79	9.72	7.76	6.00
Income Statement								
Total Revenue	1,150,754	1,162,383	883,608	519,203	302,584	187,636	259,179	201,264
EBITDA	609,522	655,322	448,967	226,155	129,534	66,453	135,321	86,218
Income Before Taxes	413,411	488,256	334,673	143,130	77,751	27,796	98,679	55,272
Income Taxes	147,153	176,079	122,231	53,458	28,887	9,552	35,913	20,928
Net Income	266,258	312,177	212,442	90,275	50,189	18,244	62,766	34,344
Average Shares	46,653	46,451	46,189	45,934	43,773	39,112	36,258	36,132
Balance Sheet								
Current Assets	197,015	232,940	223,685	118,601	72,742	51,399	40,394	46,017
Total Assets	2,199,819	1,874,096	1,456,195	1,023,136	712,925	578,163	417,253	346,288
Current Liabilities	156,404	160,942	172,512	77,176	51,811	34,532	29,011	33,673
Long-Term Obligations	120,600	174,300	145,000	95,500	400	30,500	31,000	54,000
Total Liabilities	765,002	716,060	619,233	414,867	197,157	156,791	138,091	131,748
Stockholders' Equity	1,434,817	1,158,036	836,962	608,269	515,768	421,372	279,162	214,540
Shares Outstanding	47,035	46,283	46,178	45,745	45,592	43,339	35,976	35,768
Statistical Record								
Return on Assets %	13.07	18.75	17.14	10.37	7.77	3.67	16.44	10.88
Return on Equity %	20.54	31.30	29.40	16.02	10.71	5.21	25.43	17.73
EBITDA Margin %	52.60	56.38	50.70	43.56	42.81	35.42	52.21	42.84
Net Margin %	22.98	26.86	23.99	17.39	16.59	9.72	24.22	17.06
Asset Turnover	0.57	0.70	0.71	0.60	0.47	0.38	0.68	0.64
Current Ratio	1.26	1.45	1.30	1.54	1.40	1.49	1.60	1.41
Debt to Equity	0.08	0.15	0.17	0.16	N.M.	0.07	0.11	0.25
Price Range	64.99-43.93	63.46-42.50	59.21-34.10	40.40-23.32	24.35-16.59	20.15-10.53	22.81-7.55	19.25-6.81
P/E Ratio	11.38-7.69	9.44-6.32	12.87-7.41	20.51-11.84	21.17-14.43	42.87-22.40	13.18-4.36	20.26-7.17

Address: 1000 Kensington Tower I, 7130 South Lewis Ave., Tulsa, OK 74136 **Telephone:** 918-493-7700 **Fax:** 918-493-7711	**Web Site:** www.unitcorp.com **Officers:** John G. Nikkel - Chmn. Larry D. Pinkston - Pres., C.E.O.	**Auditors:** PricewaterhouseCoopers LLP **Investor Contact:** 918-493-7700

UNITED PARCEL SERVICE INC

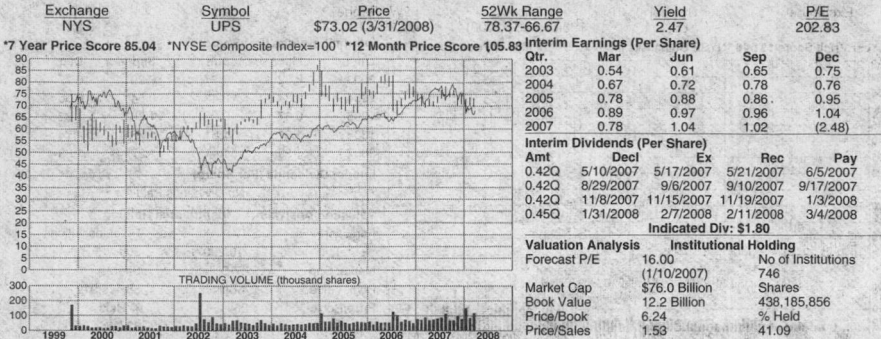

Exchange	Symbol	Price	52Wk Range	Yield	P/E
NYS	UPS	$73.02 (3/31/2008)	78.37-66.67	2.47	202.83

*7 Year Price Score 85.04   *NYSE Composite Index=100   *12 Month Price Score 105.83

Interim Earnings (Per Share)

Qtr.	Mar	Jun	Sep	Dec
2003	0.54	0.61	0.65	0.75
2004	0.67	0.72	0.78	0.76
2005	0.78	0.88	0.86	0.95
2006	0.89	0.97	0.96	1.04
2007	0.78	1.04	1.02	(2.48)

Interim Dividends (Per Share)

Amt	Decl	Ex	Rec	Pay
0.42Q	5/10/2007	5/17/2007	5/21/2007	6/5/2007
0.42Q	8/29/2007	9/6/2007	9/10/2007	9/17/2007
0.42Q	11/8/2007	11/15/2007	11/19/2007	1/3/2008
0.45Q	1/31/2008	2/7/2008	2/11/2008	3/4/2008

Indicated Div: $1.80

Valuation Analysis / **Institutional Holding**

Forecast P/E	16.00	No of Institutions	
	(1/10/2007)	746	
Market Cap	$76.0 Billion	Shares	
Book Value	12.2 Billion	438,185,856	
Price/Book	6.24	% Held	
Price/Sales	1.53	41.09	

Business Summary: Road Transport (MIC: 15.2 SIC: 4215 NAIC: 492110)

United Parcel Service is a package delivery company. As of Dec 31 2007, Co. delivered packages for 1.8 million shipping customers to 6.1 million consignees in over 200 countries and territories. Co. operates a ground fleet of 100,000 vehicles, and utilizes about 600 airplanes. Co.'s service portfolio includes less-than-truckload transportation and supply chain services. Co.'s U.S. Domestic Package operations include the delivery of letters, documents, and packages in the U.S.; International Package operations include delivery to over 200 countries and territories; and Supply Chain & Freight operations include its forwarding and logistics operations, UPS Freight, and other business units.

Recent Developments: For the year ended Dec 31 2007, net income decreased 90.9% to US$382.0 million from US$4.20 billion in the prior year. Revenues were US$49.69 billion, up 4.5% from US$47.55 billion the year before. Operating income was US$578.0 million versus US$6.64 billion in the prior year, a decrease of 91.3%. Direct operating expenses rose 7.8% to US$10.03 billion from US$9.31 billion in the comparable period the year before. Indirect operating expenses increased 23.7% to US$39.08 billion from US$31.61 billion in the equivalent prior-year period.

Prospects: Going forward, Co. anticipates higher package shipments due to just-in-time inventory management, greater use of the Internet for ordering goods, and direct-to-consumer business models. Further, Co. is constructing a package and freight air hub in Shanghai, China that should open in 2008. Notably, this hub will link Shanghai to Co.'s international air network, with direct service to Europe, Asia, and the Americas. Meanwhile, Co. expects lower profitability in the first quarter of 2008 due to an early Easter and additional interest expense from labor contract benefits, resulting in earnings per share of $0.94 to $0.98. For full year 2008, Co. expects earnings per share of $4.30 to $4.50.

Financial Data

(US$ in Thousands)	12/31/2007	12/31/2006	12/31/2005	12/31/2004	12/31/2003	12/31/2002	12/31/2001	12/31/2000
Earnings Per Share	0.36	3.86	3.47	2.93	2.55	2.81	2.10	2.50
Cash Flow Per Share	1.06	5.15	5.20	4.71	4.12	5.02	3.46	2.37
Tang Book Value Per Share	8.62	11.46	12.44	12.84	12.05	11.10	9.15	8.58
Dividends Per Share	1.680	1.520	1.320	1.120	0.920	0.760	0.760	0.680
Dividend Payout %	466.67	39.38	38.04	38.23	36.08	27.05	36.19	27.20
Income Statement								
Total Revenue	49,692,000	47,547,000	42,581,000	36,582,000	33,485,000	31,272,000	30,646,000	29,771,000
EBITDA	2,422,000	8,469,000	7,891,000	6,614,000	6,040,000	6,646,000	5,517,000	6,212,000
Income Before Taxes	431,000	6,510,000	6,075,000	4,922,000	4,370,000	5,009,000	3,937,000	4,834,000
Income Taxes	49,000	2,308,000	2,205,000	1,589,000	1,472,000	1,755,000	1,512,000	1,900,000
Net Income	382,000	4,202,000	3,870,000	3,333,000	2,898,000	3,182,000	2,399,000	2,934,000
Average Shares	1,063,000	1,089,000	1,116,000	1,137,000	1,138,000	1,134,000	1,144,000	1,175,000
Balance Sheet								
Total Assets	39,042,000	33,210,000	35,222,000	33,026,000	28,909,000	26,357,000	24,636,000	21,662,000
Long-Term Obligations	7,506,000	3,133,000	3,159,000	3,261,000	3,149,000	3,495,000	4,648,000	2,981,000
Total Liabilities	26,859,000	17,728,000	18,338,000	16,642,000	14,057,000	13,902,000	14,388,000	11,927,000
Stockholders' Equity	12,183,000	15,482,000	16,884,000	16,384,000	14,852,000	12,455,000	10,248,000	9,735,000
Shares Outstanding	1,041,000	1,070,000	1,097,000	1,126,000	1,127,000	1,122,000	1,120,508	1,134,693
Statistical Record								
Return on Assets %	1.06	12.28	11.34	10.73	10.49	12.48	10.36	13.09
Return on Equity %	2.76	25.97	23.27	21.28	21.23	28.03	24.01	26.35
EBITDA Margin %	4.87	17.81	18.53	18.08	18.04	21.25	18.00	20.87
Net Margin %	0.77	8.84	9.09	9.11	8.65	10.18	7.83	9.86
Asset Turnover	1.38	1.39	1.25	1.18	1.21	1.23	1.32	1.33
Price Range	78.37-69.26	83.35-65.92	85.46-66.86	87.53-67.98	74.81-53.18	67.00-54.46	61.90-47.95	69.06-50.63
P/E Ratio	217.69-192.39	21.59-17.08	24.63-19.27	29.87-23.20	29.34-20.85	23.84-19.38	29.48-22.83	27.63-20.25
Average Yield %	2.29	1.99	1.80	1.51	1.44	1.24	1.42	1.15

Address: 55 Glenlake Parkway, NE, Atlanta, GA 30328 Telephone: 404-828-6000 Fax: 404-828-6562	Web Site: www.ups.com Officers: Michael L. Eskew - Chmn., C.E.O. D. Scott Davis - Sr. V.P., C.F.O., Treas.	Auditors: DELOITTE & TOUCHE Investor Contact: 404-828-6977

UNITED RENTALS, INC.

Exchange	Symbol	Price	52Wk Range	Yield	P/E
NYS	URI	$18.84 (3/31/2008)	34.70-15.54	N/A	5.80

*7 Year Price Score 104.49 *NYSE Composite Index=100   *12 Month Price Score 73.72

TRADING VOLUME (thousand shares)

Interim Earnings (Per Share)

Qtr.	Mar	Jun	Sep	Dec
2003	(0.11)	0.25	0.34	(3.85)
2004	(1.38)	0.36	(0.83)	0.68
2005	0.11	0.48	0.71	0.48
2006	0.19	0.51	0.85	0.50
2007	0.28	0.60	0.98	1.38

Interim Dividends (Per Share)

No Dividends Paid

Valuation Analysis		Institutional Holding	
Forecast P/E	N/A	No of Institutions	
		203	
Market Cap	$1.6 Billion	Shares	
Book Value	2.0 Billion	80,655,232	
Price/Book	0.81	% Held	
Price/Sales	0.44	99.28	

Business Summary: General Construction Supplies & Services (MIC: 3.3 SIC: 7359 NAIC: 532412)

United Rentals is an equipment rental company. Co. provides for rent over 2,900 classes of rental equipment to customers such as construction and industrial companies, manufacturers, utilities, municipalities, homeowners and others. Co. also sells new and used rental equipment as well as related contractor supplies, parts and service. As of Dec 31 2007, Co.'s fleet of rental equipment included over 260,000 units consisting of general construction and industrial equipment, aerial work platforms, general tools and light equipment as well as trench safety equipment for underground work. As of Dec 31 2007, Co.'s network consisted of 697 rental locations in the U.S., Canada and Mexico.

Recent Developments: For the year ended Dec 31 2007, income from continuing operations increased 45.8% to US$363.0 million from US$249.0 million a year earlier. Net income increased 61.6% to US$362.0 million from US$224.0 million in the prior year. Revenues were US$3.73 billion, up 2.5% from US$3.64 billion the year before. Operating income was US$659.0 million versus US$626.0 million in the prior year, an increase of 5.3%. Direct operating expenses rose 3.1% to US$2.42 billion from US$2.35 billion in the comparable period the year before. Indirect operating expenses decreased 2.1% to US$649.0 million from US$663.0 million in the equivalent prior-year period.

Prospects: Looking ahead, as part of its strategy to refocus its contractor supplies business and position it as a complementary offering to its equipment rental business, Co. intends to close two distribution centers in the first half of 2008. Thus, in line with this strategy and its efforts to improve time utilization, Co. expects contractor supplies and used equipment sales to decline by 40.0% and 35.0%, respectively, in 2008 versus 2007. For 2008, Co. reaffirms its earnings per share outlook of $2.80 to $3.00 based on expected total revenue of $3.53 billion, and rental revenue growth of 3.0%, which reflects improved time utilization and modest growth in non-residential construction activity.

Financial Data

(US$ in Thousands)	12/31/2007	12/31/2006	12/31/2005	12/31/2004	12/31/2003	12/31/2002	12/31/2001	12/31/2000
Earnings Per Share	3.25	2.06	1.80	(1.07)	(3.35)	(5.25)	1.18	1.89
Cash Flow Per Share	8.64	8.88	6.78	9.47	4.45	6.83	9.66	7.19
Tang Book Value Per Share	7.11	2.00	N.M.	N.M.	N.M.	N.M.	N.M.	N.M.
Income Statement								
Total Revenue	3,731,000	3,640,000	3,563,000	3,094,000	2,867,236	2,820,989	2,886,605	2,918,861
EBITDA	1,286,000	1,129,000	971,000	549,000	311,132	490,870	870,015	944,707
Income Before Taxes	578,000	405,000	310,000	(88,000)	(326,521)	(101,384)	214,550	301,496
Income Taxes	215,000	156,000	123,000	(4,000)	(67,940)	8,102	91,977	125,121
Net Income	362,000	224,000	187,000	(84,000)	(258,581)	(397,825)	111,256	176,375
Average Shares	113,722	113,793	110,036	77,610	90,115	96,730	94,387	99,253
Balance Sheet								
Current Assets	1,120,000	1,005,000	1,216,000	1,032,000	803,014	708,518	696,580	741,851
Total Assets	5,842,000	5,366,000	5,274,000	4,882,000	4,722,141	4,690,557	5,061,516	5,123,933
Current Liabilities	520,000	599,000	631,000	540,000	377,576	394,117	379,460	396,380
Long-Term Obligations	2,701,000	2,665,000	3,152,000	3,167,000	3,038,638	2,512,798	2,459,522	2,675,367
Total Liabilities	3,824,000	3,828,000	4,045,000	3,856,000	3,581,266	3,132,502	3,136,006	3,277,990
Stockholders' Equity	2,018,000	1,538,000	1,229,000	1,026,000	1,140,875	1,331,505	1,625,510	1,545,943
Shares Outstanding	86,329	81,178	77,302	77,869	77,150	76,657	73,361	71,065
Statistical Record								
Return on Assets %	6.46	4.21	3.68	N.M.	N.M.	N.M.	2.18	3.66
Return on Equity %	20.36	16.19	16.59	N.M.	N.M.	N.M.	7.02	11.95
EBITDA Margin %	34.47	31.02	27.25	17.74	10.85	17.40	30.14	32.37
Net Margin %	9.70	6.15	5.25	N.M.	N.M.	N.M.	3.85	6.04
Asset Turnover	0.67	0.68	0.70	0.64	0.61	0.58	0.57	0.61
Current Ratio	2.15	1.68	1.93	1.91	2.13	1.80	1.84	1.87
Debt to Equity	1.34	1.73	2.56	3.09	2.66	1.89	1.51	1.73
Price Range	34.70-17.91	37.57-20.30	24.42-16.22	23.20-14.30	19.85-8.29	30.54-6.04	26.25-13.19	24.31-12.00
P/E Ratio	10.68-5.51	18.24-9.85	13.57-9.01	...	...	...	22.25-11.18	12.86-6.35

Address: Five Greenwich Office Park, Greenwich, CT 06830 Telephone: 203-622-3131 Fax: 203-622-6080	Web Site: www.unitedrentals.com Officers: Bradley S. Jacobs - Chmn. Wayland R. Hicks - C.E.O.	Auditors: Ernst & Young LLP Investor Contact: 203-622-3131

UNITED STATES STEEL CORP.

Exchange	Symbol	Price	52Wk Range	Yield	P/E
NYS	X	$126.87 (3/31/2008)	126.87-80.42	0.79	17.14

*7 Year Price Score 184.37 *NYSE Composite Index=100 *12 Month Price Score 113.23

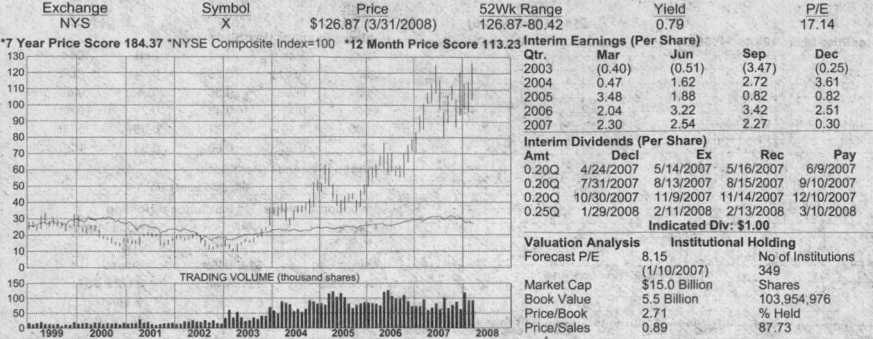

Interim Earnings (Per Share)

Qtr.	Mar	Jun	Sep	Dec
2003	(0.40)	(0.51)	(3.47)	(0.25)
2004	0.47	1.62	2.72	3.61
2005	3.48	1.88	0.82	0.82
2006	2.04	3.22	3.42	2.51
2007	2.30	2.54	2.27	0.30

Interim Dividends (Per Share)

Amt	Decl	Ex	Rec	Pay
0.20Q	4/24/2007	5/14/2007	5/16/2007	6/9/2007
0.20Q	7/31/2007	8/13/2007	8/15/2007	9/10/2007
0.20Q	10/30/2007	11/9/2007	11/14/2007	12/10/2007
0.25Q	1/29/2008	2/11/2008	2/13/2008	3/10/2008

Indicated Div: $1.00

Valuation Analysis / **Institutional Holding**

Forecast P/E	8.15	No of Institutions
	(1/10/2007)	349
Market Cap	$15.0 Billion	Shares
Book Value	5.5 Billion	103,954,976
Price/Book	2.71	% Held
Price/Sales	0.89	87.73

TRADING VOLUME (thousand shares)

Business Summary: Metal Works (MIC: 11.3 SIC: 3312 NAIC: 331513)

U.S. Steel is a steel producer with production operations in North America and Central Europe. Co. uses iron ore and coke as primary raw materials for steel production. Co. is also engaged in several other business activities, most of which are related to steel manufacturing. These include the production of coke in both North America and Central Europe; and the production of iron ore pellets from taconite, transportation services (railroad and barge operations), real estate operations, and engineering and consulting services in North America. Co.'s three reportable operating segments include Flat-rolled Products, U. S. Steel Europe, and Tubular Products.

Recent Developments: For the year ended Dec 31 2007, net income decreased 36.0% to US$879.0 million from US$1.37 billion in the prior year. Revenues were US$16.87 billion, up 7.4% from US$15.72 billion the year before. Operating income was US$1.21 billion versus US$1.79 billion in the prior year, a decrease of 32.0%. Direct operating expenses rose 12.8% to US$14.63 billion from US$12.97 billion in the comparable period the year before. Indirect operating expenses increased 6.8% to US$1.03 billion from US$962.0 million in the equivalent prior-year period.

Prospects: For the first quarter of 2008, Co. expects a sequential improvement at its Flat-rolled segment due to expected increases in shipments and operating rates, with the full quarter inclusion of U.S. Steel Canada Inc. acquired in Oct 2007 and the completion of the blast furnace projects. At its U.S. Steel Europe segment, Co. expects higher euro-based prices, and shipments to increase due to higher facility availability in the quarter. However, Co. expects both segments to experience escalating raw material costs. Meanwhile, as 2008 progresses, Co. expects to benefit from the new galvanizing line at its U.S. Steel Kosice subsidiary, which is in the process of being ramped up to full capacity.

Financial Data

(US$ in Thousands)	12/31/2007	12/31/2006	12/31/2005	12/31/2004	12/31/2003	12/31/2002	12/31/2001	12/31/2000
Earnings Per Share	7.40	11.18	7.00	8.48	(4.64)	0.62	(2.45)	(0.33)
Cash Flow Per Share	14.78	14.67	10.73	12.48	5.59	2.86	7.50	(7.06)
Tang Book Value Per Share	28.81	36.82	26.00	32.60	3.76	15.74	28.09	21.60
Dividends Per Share	0.800	0.600	0.380	0.200	0.200	0.200	0.100	1.000
Dividend Payout %	10.81	5.37	5.43	2.36	...	32.26	...	...
Income Statement								
Total Revenue	16,873,000	15,715,000	14,039,000	14,108,000	9,458,000	7,054,000	6,375,000	6,132,000
EBITDA	1,687,000	2,213,000	1,717,000	2,001,000	(357,000)	486,000	(88,000)	452,000
Income Before Taxes	1,108,000	1,723,000	1,312,000	1,461,000	(860,000)	13,000	(546,000)	(1,000)
Income Taxes	218,000	324,000	365,000	351,000	(454,000)	(48,000)	(328,000)	20,000
Net Income	879,000	1,374,000	910,000	1,091,000	(463,000)	61,000	(218,000)	(21,000)
Average Shares	118,815	122,918	129,970	128,643	103,179	97,428	89,200	88,613
Balance Sheet								
Current Assets	4,959,000	5,196,000	4,831,000	4,243,000	3,107,000	2,440,000	2,073,000	2,717,000
Total Assets	15,632,000	10,586,000	9,822,000	10,956,000	7,838,000	7,977,000	8,337,000	8,711,000
Current Liabilities	3,003,000	2,702,000	2,749,000	2,531,000	2,130,000	1,372,000	1,259,000	1,391,000
Long-Term Obligations	3,147,000	943,000	1,363,000	1,363,000	1,890,000	1,408,000	1,434,000	2,236,000
Total Liabilities	10,013,000	6,183,000	6,466,000	6,958,000	6,745,000	5,950,000	5,831,000	6,792,000
Stockholders' Equity	5,531,000	4,365,000	3,324,000	3,970,000	1,093,000	2,027,000	2,506,000	1,919,000
Shares Outstanding	117,995	118,545	108,786	114,003	103,663	102,485	89,197	88,767
Statistical Record								
Return on Assets %	6.71	13.47	8.76	11.58	N.M.	0.75	N.M.	N.M.
Return on Equity %	17.76	35.74	24.95	42.98	N.M.	2.69	N.M.	N.M.
EBITDA Margin %	10.00	14.08	12.23	14.18	N.M.	6.89	N.M.	7.37
Net Margin %	5.21	8.74	6.48	7.73	N.M.	0.86	N.M.	N.M.
Asset Turnover	1.29	1.54	1.35	1.50	1.20	0.86	0.75	0.75
Current Ratio	1.65	1.92	1.76	1.68	1.46	1.78	1.65	1.95
Debt to Equity	0.57	0.22	0.41	0.34	1.73	0.69	0.57	1.17
Price Range	125.05-69.72	78.75-49.44	63.12-34.10	53.43-25.78	36.83-9.83	21.71-10.92	21.74-13.36	33.00-12.94
P/E Ratio	16.90-9.42	7.04-4.42	9.02-4.87	6.30-3.04	...	35.02-17.61	...	...
Average Yield %	0.81	0.95	0.85	0.54	1.15	1.23	0.58	4.94

Address: 600 Grant Street, Pittsburgh, PA 15219-2800	**Web Site:** www.ussteel.com	**Auditors:** PricewaterhouseCoopers LLP
Telephone: 412-433-1121	**Officers:** Thomas J. Usher - Chmn. Dan D. Sandman - Vice-Chmn., Chief Legal & Admin. Officer, Sec., Gen. Couns.	**Investor Contact:** 412-433-1139
Fax: 412-433-4818		**Transfer Agents:** United States Steel Corporation

UNITEDHEALTH GROUP INC

Exchange	Symbol	Price	52Wk Range	Yield	P/E
NYS	UNH	$34.36 (3/31/2008)	58.99-33.84	0.09	10.05

*7 Year Price Score 110.39 *NYSE Composite Index=100   *12 Month Price Score 94.33

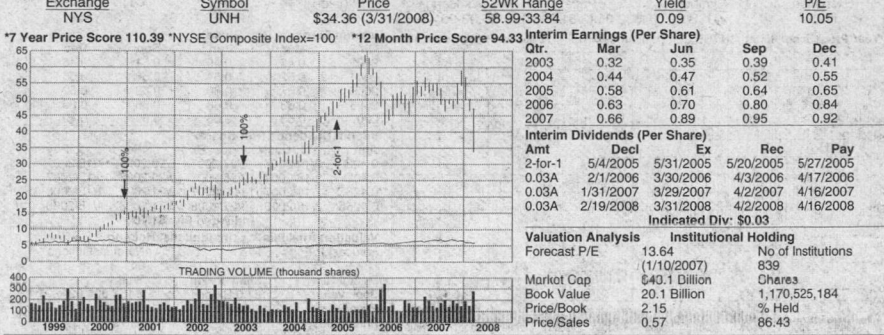

Interim Earnings (Per Share)

Qtr.	Mar	Jun	Sep	Dec
2003	0.32	0.35	0.39	0.41
2004	0.44	0.47	0.52	0.55
2005	0.58	0.61	0.64	0.65
2006	0.63	0.70	0.80	0.84
2007	0.66	0.89	0.95	0.92

Interim Dividends (Per Share)

Amt	Decl	Ex	Rec	Pay
2-for-1	5/4/2005	5/31/2005	5/20/2005	5/27/2005
0.03A	2/1/2006	3/30/2006	4/3/2006	4/17/2006
0.03A	1/31/2007	3/29/2007	4/2/2007	4/16/2007
0.03A	2/19/2008	3/31/2008	4/2/2008	4/16/2008

Indicated Div: $0.03

Valuation Analysis | **Institutional Holding**

Forecast P/E	13.64	No of Institutions
	(1/10/2007)	839
Market Cap	540.1 Billion	Shares
Book Value	20.1 Billion	1,170,525,184
Price/Book	2.15	% Held
Price/Sales	0.57	86.43

Business Summary: Insurance (MIC: 8.2 SIC: 6324 NAIC: 524114)

Unitedhealth Group is a health and well-being company that operates through four segments as of Dec 31 2007. The Health Care Services segment includes Co.'s Commercial Markets (UnitedHealthcare and Uniprise), Ovations and AmeriChoice businesses. The OptumHealth segment provides health, financial and ancillary benefit services and products. The Ingenix segment provides database and data management services, software products, publications, consulting and outsourced services as well as pharmaceutical consulting and research services. The Prescription Solutions segment provides integrated pharmacy benefit management services through retail network pharmacies and mail service facilities.

Recent Developments: For the year ended Dec 31 2007, net income increased 11.9% to US$4.65 billion from US$4.16 billion in the prior year. Revenues were US$75.43 billion, up 5.4% from US$71.54 billion the year before. Net premiums earned were US$68.78 billion versus US$65.67 billion in the prior year, an increase of 4.7%.

Prospects: For the full year of 2008, Co. is targeting earnings to be in the range of $3.95 to $4.00 per share. Meanwhile, Co. is forecasting earnings for the first quarter of 2008 to range from $0.82 to $0.84 per share. Separately, on Jan 8 2008, Co. announced that its AmeriChoice subsidiary has signed a definitive agreement to acquire Unison Health Plans. Co. believes that this transaction complements AmeriChoice's services in Pennsylvania and Tennessee, while expanding AmeriChoice's presence in the Delaware, Ohio and South Carolina markets. The transaction, which is projected to close by mid-2008, is expected to be marginally accretive to Co.'s earnings per share for the first year after closing.

Financial Data

(US$ in Thousands)	12/31/2007	12/31/2006	12/31/2005	12/31/2004	12/31/2003	12/31/2002	12/31/2001	12/31/2000
Earnings Per Share	3.42	2.97	2.48	1.97	1.48	1.06	0.70	0.55
Cash Flow Per Share	4.48	4.86	3.42	3.29	2.55	2.00	1.48	1.17
Tang Book Value Per Share	1.17	1.55	N.M.	0.03	1.23	0.79	0.88	0.61
Dividends Per Share	0.030	0.030	0.015	0.015	0.007	0.007	0.007	0.004
Dividend Payout %	0.88	1.01	0.60	0.76	0.51	0.71	1.08	0.68
Income Statement								
Premium Income	68,781,000	65,666,000	41,058,000	33,495,000	25,448,000	21,906,000	20,683,000	18,926,000
Total Revenue	75,431,000	71,542,000	45,365,000	37,218,000	28,823,000	25,020,000	23,454,000	21,122,000
Benefits & Claims	55,435,000	53,308,000	32,725,000	27,000,000	20,714,000	18,192,000	17,644,000	16,155,000
Income Before Taxes	7,305,000	6,528,000	5,132,000	3,973,000	2,840,000	2,096,000	1,472,000	1,155,000
Income Taxes	2,651,000	2,369,000	1,832,000	1,386,000	1,015,000	744,000	559,000	419,000
Net Income	4,654,000	4,159,000	3,300,000	2,587,000	1,825,000	1,352,000	913,000	736,000
Average Shares	1,361,000	1,402,000	1,330,000	1,312,000	1,234,000	1,272,400	1,307,200	1,346,000
Balance Sheet								
Total Assets	50,899,000	48,320,000	41,374,000	27,879,000	17,634,000	14,164,000	12,486,000	11,053,000
Total Liabilities	30,836,000	27,510,000	23,641,000	17,162,000	12,506,000	9,736,000	8,595,000	7,365,000
Stockholders' Equity	20,063,000	20,810,000	17,733,000	10,717,000	5,128,000	4,428,000	3,891,000	3,688,000
Shares Outstanding	1,253,000	1,345,000	1,358,000	1,286,000	1,166,000	1,197,832	1,234,504	1,268,940
Statistical Record								
Return on Assets %	9.38	9.27	9.53	11.34	11.48	10.15	7.76	6.88
Return on Equity %	22.77	21.58	23.20	32.56	38.20	32.50	24.09	19.44
Loss Ratio %	80.60	81.18	79.70	80.61	81.40	83.05	85.31	85.36
Net Margin %	6.17	5.81	7.27	6.95	6.33	5.40	3.89	3.48
Price Range	58.99-46.33	62.90-42.09	63.79-42.87	44.02-28.10	29.09-19.94	25.09-17.03	18.05-12.89	15.63-5.95
P/E Ratio	17.25-13.55	21.18-14.17	25.72-17.28	22.34-14.26	19.66-13.47	23.67-16.07	25.78-18.42	28.41-10.82
Average Yield %	0.06	0.06	0.03	0.04	0.03	0.04	0.05	0.04

Address: 9900 Bren Road East, Minnetonka, MN 55343
Telephone: 952-936-1300
Fax: 952-936-0044

Web Site: www.unitedhealthgroup.com
Officers: William W. McGuire M.D. - Chmn., C.E.O.
Stephen J. Hemsley - Pres., C.O.O.

Auditors: Deloitte & Touche LLP
Transfer Agents: Wells Fargo Shareowner Services, St. Paul, MN

U.S. BANCORP (DE)

Exchange	Symbol	Price	52Wk Range	Yield	P/E	Div Achiever
NYS	USB	$32.36 (3/31/2008)	35.03-28.44	5.25	13.32	36 Years

*7 Year Price Score 95.59   *NYSE Composite Index=100   *12 Month Price Score 108.21

Interim Earnings (Per Share)

Qtr.	Mar	Jun	Sep	Dec
2003	0.47	0.49	0.51	0.46
2004	0.52	0.54	0.56	0.56
2005	0.57	0.60	0.62	0.62
2006	0.63	0.66	0.66	0.66
2007	0.63	0.65	0.67	0.49

Interim Dividends (Per Share)

Amt	Decl	Ex	Rec	Pay
0.40Q	6/19/2007	6/27/2007	6/29/2007	7/16/2007
0.40Q	9/18/2007	9/26/2007	9/28/2007	10/15/2007
0.425Q	12/11/2007	12/27/2007	12/31/2007	1/15/2008
0.425Q	3/18/2008	3/27/2008	3/31/2008	4/15/2008

Indicated Div: $1.70

Valuation Analysis

		Institutional Holding	
Forecast P/E	N/A	No of Institutions	841
		Shares	
Market Cap	$55.9 Billion	1,157,802,624	
Book Value	21.0 Billion	% Held	
Price/Book	2.66	65.79	
Price/Sales	2.75		

TRADING VOLUME (thousand shares)

Business Summary: Commercial Banking (MIC: 8.1 SIC: 6021 NAIC: 522110)

U.S. Bancorp is a financial holding and bank holding company. Co. provides a range of financial services, including lending and depository services, cash management, foreign exchange and trust and investment management services. Co. also engages in credit card services, merchant and ATM processing, mortgage banking, insurance, brokerage and leasing. Co.'s banking subsidiaries are engaged in the general banking business in domestic markets. Co.'s non-banking subsidiaries provide investment and insurance products within its markets and mutual fund processing services to a range of mutual funds. As of Dec 31 2007, Co. had total assets of $237.62 billion and total deposits of $131.45 billion.

Recent Developments: For the year ended Dec 31 2007, net income decreased 9.0% to US$4.32 billion from US$4.75 billion in the prior year. Net interest income decreased 0.8% to US$6.69 billion from US$6.74 billion in the prior year. Provision for loan losses was US$792.0 million versus US$544.0 million in the prior year, an increase of 45.6%. Non-interest income rose 4.8% to US$7.17 billion from US$6.85 billion, while non-interest expense advanced 11.0% to US$6.86 billion.

Prospects: Co.'s near-term outlook appears mixed. While net income is expected to improve moderately in 2008, Co. remains focused on its financial objectives to attain 10.0% long-term growth in earnings per share. In addition, Co. will continue to stringently manage its credit quality while maintaining an acceptable level of credit and earnings volatility. However, Co. anticipates that the nonperforming assets will increase moderately over the next several quarters due to continued stress in residential mortgages and residential construction. In this respect, Co. continues to expect its net interest margin to stabilize in the mid 3.40 range due to the projected growth in its balance sheet portfolio.

Financial Data

(US$ in Thousands)	12/31/2007	12/31/2006	12/31/2005	12/31/2004	12/31/2003	12/31/2002	12/31/2001	12/31/2000
Earnings Per Share	2.43	2.61	2.42	2.18	1.93	1.71	0.88	2.13
Cash Flow Per Share	1.50	3.05	1.86	2.76	4.51	1.98	1.13	3.46
Tang Book Value Per Share	5.41	5.34	5.62	5.87	5.77	4.93	4.64	7.11
Dividends Per Share	1.625	1.390	1.230	1.020	0.855	0.780	0.750	...
Dividend Payout %	66.87	53.26	50.83	46.79	44.30	45.61	85.23	...
Income Statement								
Interest Income	13,136,000	12,263,000	10,551,000	9,186,500	9,258,000	9,553,700	11,083,600	6,707,100
Interest Expense	6,447,000	5,522,000	3,496,000	2,075,200	2,068,700	2,714,000	4,674,800	3,235,800
Net Interest Income	6,689,000	6,741,000	7,055,000	7,111,300	7,189,300	6,839,700	6,408,800	3,471,300
Provision for Losses	792,000	544,000	666,000	669,600	1,254,000	1,349,000	2,528,800	670,000
Non-Interest Income	7,172,000	6,846,000	6,045,000	5,519,200	5,313,000	5,868,600	5,359,400	3,258,400
Non-Interest Expense	6,862,000	6,180,000	5,863,000	5,784,500	5,596,900	6,256,600	6,605,200	3,598,400
Income Before Taxes	6,207,000	6,863,000	6,571,000	6,176,400	5,651,400	5,102,700	2,634,200	2,461,300
Income Taxes	1,883,000	2,112,000	2,082,000	2,009,600	1,941,300	1,776,300	927,700	869,300
Net Income	4,324,000	4,751,000	4,489,000	4,166,800	3,732,600	3,289,200	1,706,500	1,592,000
Average Shares	1,758,000	1,804,000	1,857,000	1,912,900	1,936,200	1,926,100	1,939,500	747,900
Balance Sheet								
Net Loans & Leases	156,588,000	144,831,000	137,451,000	125,674,000	117,299,000	117,988,000	114,768,000	68,024,000
Total Assets	237,615,000	219,232,000	209,465,000	195,104,000	189,286,000	180,027,000	171,390,000	87,336,000
Total Deposits	131,445,000	124,882,000	124,709,000	120,741,000	119,052,000	115,534,000	105,219,000	53,257,000
Total Liabilities	216,569,000	198,035,000	189,379,000	175,565,000	170,044,000	161,926,000	154,929,000	78,696,000
Stockholders' Equity	21,046,000	21,197,000	20,086,000	19,539,000	19,242,000	18,101,000	16,461,000	8,640,000
Shares Outstanding	1,727,856	1,764,714	1,814,954	1,857,622	1,922,920	1,916,956	1,951,709	752,059
Statistical Record								
Return on Assets %	1.89	2.22	2.22	2.16	2.02	1.87	1.32	1.88
Return on Equity %	20.47	23.02	22.66	21.43	19.99	19.03	13.60	19.51
Net Interest Margin %	50.92	54.97	66.87	77.41	77.66	71.59	57.82	51.76
Efficiency Ratio %	33.79	32.34	35.33	39.34	38.41	40.57	40.17	36.11
Loans to Deposits	1.19	1.16	1.10	1.04	0.99	1.02	1.09	1.28
Price Range	36.68-29.26	36.69-29.03	31.32-27.16	31.53-25.13	29.35-18.71	24.10-16.02	25.25-16.57	27.35-15.40
P/E Ratio	15.09-12.04	14.06-11.12	12.94-11.22	14.46-11.53	15.21-9.69	14.09-9.37	28.70-18.83	12.84-7.23
Average Yield %	4.84	4.35	4.17	3.60	3.64	3.70	3.48	...

Address: 800 Nicollet Mall, Minneapolis, MN 55402 Telephone: 651-466-3000	Web Site: www.usbank.com Officers: Jerry A. Grundhofer - Chmn. David M. Moffett - Vice-Chmn., C.F.O.	Auditors: Ernst & Young LLP Investor Contact: 612-303-0783 Transfer Agents: Mellon Investor Services

UNITED TECHNOLOGIES CORP.

Exchange	Symbol	Price	52Wk Range	Yield	P/E	Div Acheiver
NYS	UTX	$68.82 (3/31/2008)	82.07-64.08	1.86	16.12	14 Years

*7 Year Price Score 119.05 *NYSE Composite Index=100 *12 Month Price Score 104.02

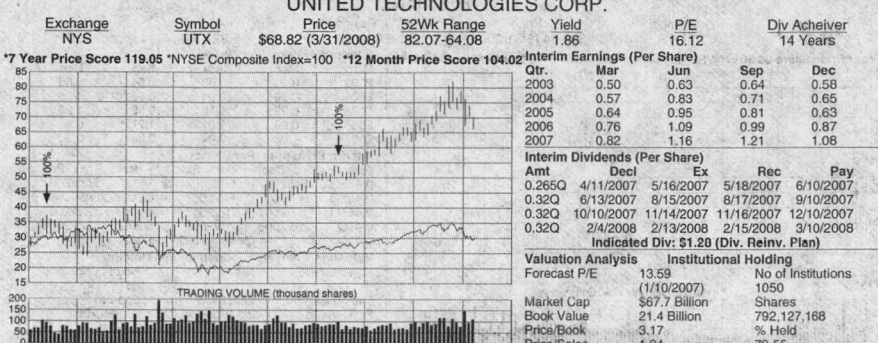

Interim Earnings (Per Share)

Qtr.	Mar	Jun	Sep	Dec
2003	0.50	0.63	0.64	0.58
2004	0.57	0.83	0.71	0.65
2005	0.64	0.95	0.81	0.63
2006	0.76	1.09	0.99	0.87
2007	0.82	1.16	1.21	1.08

Interim Dividends (Per Share)

Amt	Decl	Ex	Rec	Pay
0.265Q	4/11/2007	5/16/2007	5/18/2007	6/10/2007
0.32Q	6/13/2007	8/15/2007	8/17/2007	9/10/2007
0.32Q	10/10/2007	11/14/2007	11/16/2007	12/10/2007
0.32Q	2/4/2008	2/13/2008	2/15/2008	3/10/2008

Indicated Div: $1.28 (Div. Reinv. Plan)

Valuation Analysis / **Institutional Holding**

Forecast P/E	13.59	No of Institutions
	(1/10/2007)	1050
Market Cap	$67.7 Billion	Shares
Book Value	21.4 Billion	792,127,168
Price/Book	3.17	% Held
Price/Sales	1.24	79.55

Business Summary: Aviation (MIC: 1.1 SIC: 3724 NAIC: 336412)

United Technologies has six principal segments: Otis, which is an elevator and escalator manufacturing, installation and service company; Carrier, a manufacturer and distributor of heating, ventilation, and air conditioning and refrigeration systems; UTC Fire & Security, which provides security and fire safety products and services; Pratt & Whitney, which is engaged as a supplier of commercial, general aviation and military aircraft engines; Hamilton Sundstrand, which supplies aerospace and industrial products and aftermarket services; and Sikorsky, which is a manufacturer of military and commercial helicopters and a provider of aftermarket helicopter and aircraft parts and services.

Recent Developments: For the year ended Dec 31 2007, net income increased 13.2% to US$4.22 billion from US$3.73 billion in the prior year. Revenues were US$54.76 billion, up 14.5% from US$47.83 billion the year before. Operating income was US$7.05 billion versus US$6.10 billion in the prior year, an increase of 15.6%. Direct operating expenses rose 14.9% to US$39.92 billion from US$34.74 billion in the comparable period the year before. Indirect operating expenses increased 11.4% to US$7.79 billion from US$6.99 billion in the equivalent prior-year period.

Prospects: Although the U.S. economic outlook appears mixed, Co. believes that its geographic and product market mix should allow for double digit earnings per share growth in 2008. Notably, for 2008, Co. is projecting earnings per share to be in a range of $4.65 to $4.85, reflecting an increase of between 9.0% and 14.0%. In addition, Co. expects mid-single digit organic revenue growth in 2008. Meanwhile, on Dec 27 2007, Co. completed its purchase of Rentokil Initial's Electronic Security business unit in France, Initial Securite Holdings SAS. Co. believes that the acquisition should strengthen its global electronic security presence as well as position it for further growth and expansion.

Financial Data

(US$ in Thousands)	12/31/2007	12/31/2006	12/31/2005	12/31/2004	12/31/2003	12/31/2002	12/31/2001	12/31/2000
Earnings Per Share	4.27	3.71	3.03	2.76	2.35	2.21	1.92	1.77
Cash Flow Per Share	5.53	4.90	4.37	3.72	3.03	3.02	3.07	2.79
Tang Book Value Per Share	1.50	N.M.	0.91	1.84	2.31	1.46	1.66	0.95
Dividends Per Share	1.170	1.015	0.880	0.700	0.568	0.490	0.450	0.412
Dividend Payout %	27.40	27.36	29.04	25.36	24.20	22.17	23.50	23.24
Income Statement								
Total Revenue	54,759,000	47,829,000	42,725,000	37,445,000	31,034,000	28,212,000	27,897,000	26,583,000
EBITDA	8,223,000	7,131,000	6,166,000	5,448,000	4,644,000	4,384,000	4,138,000	3,999,000
Income Before Taxes	6,384,000	5,492,000	4,684,000	4,107,000	3,470,000	3,276,000	2,807,000	2,758,000
Income Taxes	1,836,000	1,494,000	1,253,000	1,085,000	941,000	887,000	755,000	853,000
Net Income	4,224,000	3,732,000	3,069,000	2,788,000	2,361,000	2,236,000	1,938,000	1,808,000
Average Shares	988,800	1,005,700	1,014,500	1,010,858	1,005,800	1,011,158	1,010,800	1,016,020
Balance Sheet								
Current Assets	22,071,000	18,844,000	17,200,000	13,522,000	12,364,000	11,751,000	11,263,000	10,662,000
Total Assets	54,575,000	47,141,000	45,925,000	40,035,000	34,648,000	29,090,000	26,969,000	25,364,000
Current Liabilities	17,469,000	15,208,000	15,345,000	12,947,000	10,295,000	7,903,000	8,371,000	9,344,000
Long-Term Obligations	8,015,000	7,037,000	5,935,000	4,231,000	4,257,000	4,632,000	4,237,000	3,476,000
Total Liabilities	32,308,000	29,008,000	28,156,000	26,027,000	22,941,000	20,735,000	18,600,000	17,702,000
Stockholders' Equity	21,355,000	17,297,000	16,991,000	14,008,000	11,707,000	8,355,000	8,369,000	7,662,000
Shares Outstanding	983,547	955,700	1,013,853	1,022,196	1,028,124	939,240	944,318	940,612
Statistical Record								
Return on Assets %	8.31	8.02	7.14	7.45	7.41	7.98	7.41	7.25
Return on Equity %	21.86	21.77	19.80	21.62	23.54	26.74	24.18	24.40
EBITDA Margin %	15.02	14.91	14.43	14.55	14.96	15.54	14.83	15.04
Net Margin %	7.71	7.80	7.18	7.45	7.61	7.93	6.95	6.80
Asset Turnover	1.08	1.03	0.99	1.00	0.97	1.01	1.07	1.07
Current Ratio	1.26	1.24	1.12	1.20	1.20	1.49	1.35	1.14
Debt to Equity	0.38	0.41	0.35	0.30	0.36	0.55	0.51	0.45
Price Range	82.07-62.47	66.79-54.47	58.03-48.77	52.76-40.75	47.77-27.07	38.63-24.59	43.60-20.82	39.88-24.03
P/E Ratio	19.22-14.63	18.00-14.68	19.15-16.10	19.12-14.76	20.33-11.52	17.48-11.13	22.71-10.84	22.53-13.58
Average Yield %	1.64	1.65	1.70	1.52	1.56	1.50	1.29	1.33

Address: One Financial Plaza, Hartford, CT 06103 Telephone: 860-728-7000 Fax: 860-728-7028	Web Site: www.utc.com Officers: George David - Chmn., Pres., C.E.O. William H. Trachsel - Sr. V.P., Gen. Couns	Auditors: PricewaterhouseCoopers LLP Transfer Agents: EquiServe Trust Company, N.A. of Providence, RI

UNITRIN, INC.

*7 Year Price Score 88.50   *NYSE Composite Index=100   *12 Month Price Score 88.03

TRADING VOLUME (thousand shares)

Interim Earnings (Per Share)

Qtr.	Mar	Jun	Sep	Dec
2003	0.20	0.33	0.64	0.65
2004	0.70	0.91	0.82	1.06
2005	0.98	1.12	0.32	1.25
2006	0.96	1.01	1.27	0.92
2007	1.08	0.94	0.98	0.30

Interim Dividends (Per Share)

Amt	Decl	Ex	Rec	Pay
0.455Q	5/2/2007	5/9/2007	5/11/2007	5/25/2007
0.455Q	8/1/2007	8/8/2007	8/10/2007	8/24/2007
0.455Q	11/7/2007	11/14/2007	11/16/2007	12/3/2007
0.47Q	2/6/2008	2/13/2008	2/15/2008	3/3/2008
		Indicated Div: $1.88		

Valuation Analysis

		Institutional Holding	
Forecast P/E	N/A	No of Institutions	201
		Shares	
Market Cap	$2.3 Billion		21,866,700
Book Value	2.3 Billion	% Held	
Price/Book	0.99		32.64
Price/Sales	0.78		

Business Summary: Insurance (MIC: 8.2 SIC: 6331 NAIC: 524126)

Unitrin, through its subsidiaries, is engaged in the property and casualty insurance, life and health insurance and automobile finance businesses. Co.'s property and casualty businesses provides automobile, homeowners, fire, and other types of property and casualty insurance, while its life and health insurance business provide ordinary life insurance and Medicare Supplement insurance. Co.'s automobile business includes the financing of used automobiles through the purchase of retail installment contracts from automobile dealers. Co. conducts its operations through five operating segments: Kemper, Unitrin Specialty, Unitrin Direct, Life and Health Insurance and Fireside Bank.

Recent Developments: For the year ended Dec 31 2007, income from continuing operations decreased 28.5% to US$189.0 million from US$264.2 million a year earlier. Net income decreased 23.1% to US$217.8 million from US$283.1 million in the prior year. Revenues were US$2.92 billion, up 2.2% from US$2.86 billion the year before. Net premiums earned were unchanged at US$2.29 billion versus the prior year. Net investment income rose 9.2% to US$306.7 million from US$280.8 million a year ago.

Prospects: On Dec 7 2007, Co. has agreed to sell its Unitrin Business Insurance operations to AmTrust Financial Services, Inc. for undisclosed terms. AmTrust will acquire the renewal rights to Co.'s Unitrin Business Insurance book of business, and certain legal entities and selected other assets upon closure, which is slated to occur by end of the first quarter of 2008. Separately, Co. expects to close its $96.0 million acquisition of Primesco of Decatur, Alabama in the first quarter of 2008. Subsequently, Co. plans to combine the products, distribution network and back-office operations of their Career Agency Companies and Mutual Savings and Mutual Savings Fire businesses into a single business unit.

Financial Data
(US$ in Thousands)

	12/31/2007	12/31/2006	12/31/2005	12/31/2004	12/31/2003	12/31/2002	12/31/2001	12/31/2000
Earnings Per Share	3.30	4.15	3.67	3.48	1.82	(0.12)	5.60	1.32
Cash Flow Per Share	3.84	4.51	5.46	4.35	8.66	5.85	2.84	1.14
Tang Book Value Per Share	30.86	28.95	26.46	24.61	21.75	21.56	23.27	19.93
Dividends Per Share	1.820	1.760	1.700	1.660	1.660	1.660	1.600	1.500
Dividend Payout %	55.15	42.41	46.32	47.70	91.21	...	28.57	113.64
Income Statement								
Premium Income	2,286,900	2,478,700	2,478,300	2,485,200	2,457,200	1,878,000	1,568,000	1,447,900
Total Revenue	2,919,800	3,075,500	3,048,100	3,040,800	2,943,800	2,298,200	2,533,800	1,953,200
Income Before Taxes	243,600	391,300	332,900	335,500	158,900	(24,600)	542,500	152,200
Income Taxes	55,800	117,400	82,700	98,900	34,100	(18,300)	190,300	54,400
Net Income	217,800	283,100	255,500	240,200	123,600	(8,200)	380,900	91,000
Average Shares	65,900	68,200	69,500	68,900	67,700	67,700	67,900	68,800
Balance Sheet								
Total Assets	9,405,000	9,321,400	9,198,300	8,790,300	8,536,800	7,705,600	7,133,700	6,164,800
Total Liabilities	7,107,200	7,037,400	7,040,600	6,751,600	6,717,900	5,903,200	5,216,900	4,463,600
Stockholders' Equity	2,297,800	2,284,000	2,157,700	2,038,700	1,818,900	1,802,400	1,916,800	1,701,200
Shares Outstanding	64,254	66,991	68,516	68,828	67,778	67,596	67,547	67,648
Statistical Record								
Return on Assets %	2.33	3.06	2.84	2.76	1.52	N.M.	5.73	1.50
Return on Equity %	9.51	12.75	12.18	12.42	6.83	N.M.	21.06	5.31
Net Margin %	7.46	9.21	8.38	7.90	4.20	(0.36)	15.03	4.66
Price Range	52.60-40.47	50.96-40.00	53.69-41.09	49.87-37.13	42.20-22.29	42.40-28.00	40.19-31.88	38.16-25.89
P/E Ratio	15.94-12.26	12.28-9.64	14.63-11.20	14.33-10.67	23.19-12.25	...	7.18-5.69	28.91-19.61
Average Yield %	3.84	3.83	3.61	3.88	5.64	4.69	4.48	4.88

Address: One East Wacker Drive, Chicago, IL 60601
Telephone: 312-661-4600
Fax: 312-661-4690

Web Site: www.unitrin.com
Officers: Richard C. Vie - Chmn., C.E.O. Donald G. Southwell - Pres., C.O.O.

Auditors: Deloitte & Touche LLP
Investor Contact: 312-661-4930
Transfer Agents: Wachovia Bank, N.A., Charlotte, NC

782

US AIRWAYS GROUP INC

Exchange	Symbol	Price	52Wk Range	Yield	P/E
NYS	LCC	$8.91 (3/31/2008)	47.87-7.45	N/A	1.97

*7 Year Price Score N/A   *NYSE Composite Index=100   *12 Month Price Score 50.79

TRADING VOLUME (thousand shares)

Interim Earnings (Per Share)

Qtr.	Mar	Jun	Sep	Dec
2005	(6.58)	(0.20)	(5.74)	0.48
2006	0.76	3.25	(0.88)	0.12
2007	0.70	2.77	1.87	(0.81)

Interim Dividends (Per Share)

No Dividends Paid

Valuation Analysis   Institutional Holding

Forecast P/E	N/A	No of Institutions
		198
Market Cap	$818.5 Million	Shares
Book Value	1.4 Billion	87,441,856
Price/Book	0.57	% Held
Price/Sales	0.07	95.67

Business Summary: Aviation (MIC: 1.1 SIC: 4512 NAIC: 481111)

US Airways Group is a holding company. Co. is engaged in the operation of a network air carrier through its subsidiaries. Co., through its subsidiaries, operates a hub-and-spoke network with major hubs in Charlotte, Philadelphia and Phoenix and secondary hubs/focus cities in Las Vegas, New York, Washington, D.C. and Boston. As of Dec 31 2007, Co. offered scheduled passenger service on approximately 3,800 flights daily to 230 communities in the U.S., Hawaii, Alaska, Canada, the Caribbean, Latin America and Europe, and operated 356 mainline jets that are supported by its regional airline subsidiaries and affiliates operating as US Airways Express.

Recent Developments: For the year ended Dec 31 2007, net income increased 40.5% to US$427.0 million from US$304.0 million in the prior year. Revenues were US$11.70 billion, up 1.2% from US$11.56 billion the year before. Operating income was US$533.0 million versus US$558.0 million in the prior year, a decrease of 4.5%. Direct operating expenses rose 1.1% to US$4.49 billion from US$4.44 billion in the comparable period the year before. Indirect operating expenses increased 1.8% to US$6.68 billion from US$6.56 billion in the equivalent prior-year period.

Prospects: Going forward, Co. remains committed to maintaining a low cost structure, which it believes is necessary to compete effectively with other airlines. Accordingly, Co. will continue to exercise tight cost controls and minimize unnecessary capital expenditures to drive down expenses. Separately, Co. noted that it has a $50.0 million aircraft appearance initiative underway to refurbish the interiors of nearly 300 mainline aircraft, including common interior branding. Meanwhile, Co. noted that the recent increase in fuel price is expected to adversely affect its operating costs. Hence, Co. expects to post a loss for the first quarter of 2008.

Financial Data

(US$ in Thousands)	12/31/2007	12/31/2006	12/31/2005	12/31/2004	12/31/2003
Earnings Per Share	4.52	3.33	(17.06)	(5.99)	3.07
Cash Flow Per Share	4.83	7.15	1.46	1.41	...
Tang Book Value Per Share	2.87	N.M.	N.M.	1.66	...
Income Statement					
Total Revenue	11,700,000	11,557,000	5,077,000	2,748,000	2,572,000
EBITDA	721,000	727,000	(86,000)	169,000	350,000
Income Before Taxes	434,000	404,000	(335,000)	(89,000)	57,000
Income Taxes	7,000	101,000	...	...	...
Net Income	427,000	304,000	(537,000)	(89,000)	57,000
Average Shares	95,603	93,821	31,487	14,860	23,146
Balance Sheet					
Total Assets	8,040,000	7,576,000	6,964,000	1,475,000	...
Long-Term Obligations	3,031,000	2,907,000	2,749,000	640,000	...
Total Liabilities	6,601,000	6,606,000	6,544,000	1,439,000	...
Stockholders' Equity	1,439,000	970,000	420,000	36,000	...
Shares Outstanding	91,865	91,283	81,664	21,731	...
Statistical Record					
Return on Assets %	5.47	4.18	N.M.	...	...
Return on Equity %	35.45	43.74	N.M.	...	...
EBITDA Margin %	6.16	6.29	N.M.	6.15	13.61
Net Margin %	3.65	2.63	(10.58)	(3.24)	2.22
Asset Turnover	1.50	1.59	1.20	...	...
Price Range	61.96-14.71	62.95-28.89	37.73-19.30	...	...
P/E Ratio	13.71-3.25	18.90-8.68	...	...	...

Address: 111 West Rio Salado Parkway, Tempe, AZ 85281 **Telephone:** 480-693-0800	**Web Site:** www.usairways.com **Officers:** W. Douglas Parker - Chmn., C.E.O. J. Scott Kirby - Pres.	**Auditors:** KPMG LLP

UNIVERSAL CORP.

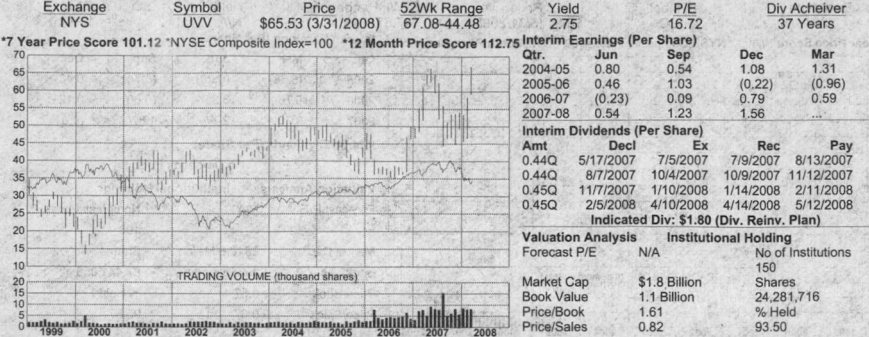

Exchange	Symbol	Price	52Wk Range	Yield	P/E	Div Acheiver
NYS	UVV	$65.53 (3/31/2008)	67.08-44.48	2.75	16.72	37 Years

*7 Year Price Score 101.12 *NYSE Composite Index=100 *12 Month Price Score 112.75

Interim Earnings (Per Share)

Qtr.	Jun	Sep	Dec	Mar
2004-05	0.80	0.54	1.08	1.31
2005-06	0.46	1.03	(0.22)	(0.96)
2006-07	(0.23)	0.09	0.79	0.59
2007-08	0.54	1.23	1.56	...

Interim Dividends (Per Share)

Amt	Decl	Ex	Rec	Pay
0.44Q	5/17/2007	7/5/2007	7/9/2007	8/13/2007
0.44Q	8/7/2007	10/4/2007	10/9/2007	11/12/2007
0.45Q	11/7/2007	1/10/2008	1/14/2008	2/11/2008
0.45Q	2/5/2008	4/10/2008	4/14/2008	5/12/2008

Indicated Div: $1.80 (Div. Reinv. Plan)

Valuation Analysis | **Institutional Holding**

Forecast P/E	N/A	No of Institutions
		150
Market Cap	$1.8 Billion	Shares
Book Value	1.1 Billion	24,281,716
Price/Book	1.61	% Held
Price/Sales	0.82	93.50

Business Summary: Tobacco Products (MIC: 4.2 SIC: 5159 NAIC: 424590)

Universal is a holding company. Through its subsidiaries, Co. is engaged as an independent leaf tobacco merchant and processor. Co.'s primary subsidiary is Universal Leaf Tobacco Company, Inc., who generally conducts Co.'s tobacco business. Co.'s tobacco business includes selecting, buying, processing, packing, storing, shipping, and financing of leaf tobacco in tobacco growing countries for sale to, or for the account of, manufacturers of consumer tobacco products throughout the world. Co.'s tobacco sales consist primarily of flue-cured and burley tobaccos, which, along with oriental tobaccos, are the major ingredients in American-blend cigarettes.

Recent Developments: For the quarter ended Dec 31 2007, income from continuing operations increased 41.8% to US$50.8 million from US$35.8 million in the year-earlier quarter. Net income increased 110.5% to US$50.8 million from US$24.1 million in the year-earlier quarter. Revenues were US$573.1 million, up 12.0% from US$511.7 million the year before. Operating income was US$79.1 million versus US$66.8 million in the prior-year quarter, an increase of 18.4%. Direct operating expenses rose 17.9% to US$446.1 million from US$378.3 million in the comparable period the year before. Indirect operating expenses decreased 28.0% to US$47.9 million from US$66.5 million in the equivalent prior-year period.

Prospects: Despite the existing difficult supply shortages and rising costs, Co.'s results are reflecting higher earnings in its Other Regions segment of the flue-cured and burley operations, as well as Other Tobacco Operations, coupled with lower net interest expense. Conversely, Co. noted that the smaller crops in Africa and Canada and increasing shipment of leaf has resulted in substantial reduction in inventories, and thus, is projecting lower shipments in future quarters. Nevertheless, Co. believes that it is well-positioned for long-term growth given its ongoing efforts to improve its performance such as working with its customers to mitigate the effect of the weak dollar on its unit costs.

Financial Data

(US$ in Thousands)	9 Mos	6 Mos	3 Mos	03/31/2007	03/31/2006	03/31/2005	03/31/2004	06/30/2003
Earnings Per Share	3.92	3.15	2.01	1.13	0.31	3.73	3.94	4.34
Cash Flow Per Share	12.23	9.48	7.10	9.48	2.46	(3.41)	(1.39)	(1.76)
Tang Book Value Per Share	29.01	27.70	26.62	26.47	24.67	26.66	-24.57	19.56
Dividends Per Share	1.760	1.750	1.740	1.730	1.690	1.590	1.470	1.400
Dividend Payout %	44.90	55.56	86.57	153.10	545.16	42.63	37.31	32.26
Income Statement								
Total Revenue	1,678,641	1,105,547	450,217	2,007,272	3,511,332	3,276,057	2,271,152	2,636,776
EBITDA	224,896	126,567	42,106	226,131	187,755	298,338	246,537	271,758
Depn & Amortn	32,625	21,909	11,206	...	...	...	...	...
Income Before Taxes	173,314	91,562	23,797	134,877	38,323	165,953	162,638	172,984
Income Taxes	62,937	33,733	9,156	61,126	34,403	68,197	59,329	53,094
Net Income	109,258	58,506	18,708	44,352	7,940	96,013	99,636	110,594
Average Shares	27,357	32,430	27,126	26,051	25,957	25,717	25,277	25,499
Balance Sheet								
Current Assets	1,512,295	1,552,587	1,602,455	1,545,365	1,802,598	1,788,808	1,526,669	1,374,997
Total Assets	2,322,834	2,308,120	2,377,842	2,328,822	2,901,341	2,885,324	2,482,773	2,243,074
Current Liabilities	586,129	605,962	711,293	692,974	937,806	969,761	739,110	824,281
Long-Term Obligations	400,644	399,272	398,122	398,952	762,201	838,687	770,296	614,994
Total Liabilities	1,206,218	1,227,226	1,330,024	1,292,267	1,918,671	2,027,691	1,722,940	1,622,796
Stockholders' Equity	1,109,631	1,075,775	1,045,532	1,030,733	964,871	822,388	759,833	620,278
Shares Outstanding	27,299	27,374	27,356	26,948	25,748	25,668	25,446	24,920
Statistical Record								
Return on Assets %	5.54	4.20	2.39	1.70	0.27	3.58	5.60	5.41
Return on Equity %	12.26	9.97	6.46	4.44	0.89	12.14	19.16	18.31
EBITDA Margin %	13.40	11.45	9.35	11.27	5.35	9.11	10.86	10.31
Net Margin %	6.51	5.29	4.16	2.21	0.23	2.93	4.39	4.19
Asset Turnover	0.94	0.87	0.76	0.77	1.21	1.22	1.28	1.29
Current Ratio	2.58	2.56	2.25	2.23	1.92	1.84	2.07	1.67
Debt to Equity	0.36	0.37	0.38	0.39	0.79	1.02	1.01	0.99
Price Range	66.60-44.48	66.60-36.14	66.60-35.02	61.35-35.02	48.21-36.17	53.01-42.25	52.32-40.78	43.01-31.81
P/E Ratio	16.99-11.35	21.14-11.47	33.13-17.42	54.29-30.99	155.52-116.68	14.21-11.33	13.28-10.35	9.91-7.33
Average Yield %	3.21	3.32	3.57	4.12	3.97	3.34	3.27	3.73

Address: 1501 North Hamilton Street,	Web Site: www.universalcorp.com	Auditors: Ernst & Young LLP
Richmond, VA 23230	Officers: Allen B. King - Chmn., Pres., C.E.O.,	Investor Contact: 804-359-9311
Telephone: 804-359-9311	C.O.O. Hartwell H. Roper - V.P., C.F.O.	Transfer Agents: Wells Fargo Bank
Fax: 804-254-3594		Minnesota, N.A., St. Paul, MN

UNIVERSAL HEALTH REALTY INCOME TRUST

Exchange	Symbol	Price	52Wk Range	Yield	P/E	Div Acheiver
NYS	UHT	$33.30 (3/31/2008)	38.76-29.23	6.97	17.81	20 Years

*7 Year Price Score 91.21   *NYSE Composite Index=100   *12 Month Price Score 107.26

Interim Earnings (Per Share)

Qtr.	Mar	Jun	Sep	Dec
2003	0.48	0.45	0.45	0.68
2004	0.43	0.54	0.47	0.56
2005	0.64	0.52	0.54	0.44
2006	0.42	0.58	1.32	0.60
2007	0.49	0.67	0.37	0.34

Interim Dividends (Per Share)

Amt	Decl	Ex	Rec	Pay
0.575Q	6/1/2007	6/13/2007	6/15/2007	6/29/2007
0.575Q	9/6/2007	9/13/2007	9/17/2007	9/28/2007
0.58Q	12/3/2007	12/13/2007	12/17/2007	12/31/2007
0.58Q	3/7/2008	3/13/2008	3/17/2008	3/31/2008

Indicated Div: $2.32 (Div. Reinv. Plan)

Valuation Analysis

		Institutional Holding	
Forecast P/E	N/A	No of Institutions	83
Market Cap	$394.3 Million	Shares	
Book Value	160.3 Million		4,908,936
Price/Book	2.46	% Held	
Price/Sales	14.10		41.63

Business Summary: Property, Real Estate & Development (MIC: 8.3 SIC: 6798 NAIC: 525930)

Universal Health Realty Income Trust is an organized Maryland real estate investment trust (REIT). As of Dec 31 2007, Co. had 46 real estate investments or commitments located in 14 states in the U.S. consisting of: six hospital facilities including three acute care, one behavioral healthcare, one rehabilitation and one sub-acute; 36 medical office buildings (including three being constructed); and; four preschool and childcare centers. Four of Co.'s hospital facilities are leased to subsidiaries of Universal Health Services, Inc. (UHS). As of Dec 31 2007, UHS owned 6.7% of Co.'s outstanding shares of beneficial interest.

Recent Developments: For the year ended Dec 31 2007, income from continuing operations decreased 42.9% to US$19.7 million from US$34.4 million a year earlier. Net income decreased 36.0% to US$22.2 million from US$34.7 million in the prior year. Revenues were US$28.0 million, down 11.8% from US$31.7 million the year before.

Prospects: Co.'s outlook appears constructive. For instance, at Dec 31 2007, Co. held 95.0%, non-controlling ownership interests in Limited Liability Companies that own the following medical office buildings that are presently under construction and scheduled to be completed and opened during 2008, notably Palmdale Medical Plaza located in Palmdale, CA; Deer Valley Medical Office Building III located in Phoenix, AZ, and Summerlin Medical Office Building III located in Las Vegas, NV. Separately, in Feb 2008, Co. has acquired Kindred Hospital; Corpus Christi, an unaffiliated 74-bed long-term acute care hospital located in Corpus Christi, TX for a total purchase price of $8.1 million.

Financial Data
(US$ in Thousands)

	12/31/2007	12/31/2006	12/31/2005	12/31/2004	12/31/2003	12/31/2002	12/31/2001	12/31/2000
Earnings Per Share	1.87	2.92	2.15	2.00	2.07	1.84	1.74	1.81
Cash Flow Per Share	1.93	2.10	2.15	2.29	2.48	2.25	2.17	2.22
Tang Book Value Per Share	13.54	13.92	13.20	13.10	12.97	12.73	12.85	11.05
Dividends Per Share	2.300	2.260	2.175	2.000	1.960	1.920	1.875	1.840
Dividend Payout %	122.99	77.40	101.16	100.00	94.69	104.35	107.76	101.66
Income Statement								
Property Income	27,960	32,509	33,338	31,777	28,313	28,429	27,574	27,315
Total Revenue	27,960	32,509	33,338	31,777	28,313	28,429	27,574	27,315
Interest Expense	1,749	2,283	3,298	3,357	2,497	2,403	3,896	6,114
Net Income	22,191	34,697	25,423	23,671	24,475	21,673	18,349	16,256
Average Shares	11,875	11,866	11,841	11,813	11,779	11,750	10,536	9,003
Balance Sheet								
Total Assets	199,749	194,139	196,889	204,583	194,291	185,117	187,904	183,658
Long-Term Obligations	36,617	26,337	35,548	46,210	...	...	1,446	1,359
Total Liabilities	39,357	29,873	41,137	50,291	42,093	36,255	37,870	84,401
Stockholders' Equity	160,305	164,197	155,450	154,053	152,198	148,862	150,034	99,257
Shares Outstanding	11,841	11,791	11,777	11,755	11,736	11,698	11,678	8,980
Statistical Record								
Return on Assets %	11.27	17.75	12.66	11.84	12.88	11.59	9.88	8.94
Return on Equity %	13.68	21.71	16.43	15.42	16.23	14.47	14.72	16.30
Net Margin %	79.37	106.73	76.26	74.49	86.27	76.06	66.54	59.51
Price Range	42.05-29.23	40.24-29.72	40.80-27.47	34.50-24.82	30.55-25.30	28.50-22.69	25.70-18.94	19.88-14.31
P/E Ratio	22.49-15.63	13.78-10.18	18.98-12.78	17.25-12.41	14.76-12.22	15.49-12.33	14.77-10.88	10.98-7.91
Average Yield %	6.48	6.50	6.56	6.66	7.19	7.59	8.48	10.90

Address: Universal Corporate Center, 367 South Gulph Road, King of Prussia, PA 19406-0958
Telephone: 610-265-0688
Fax: 610-768-3336

Web Site: www.uhrit.com
Officers: Alan B. Miller - Chmn., Pres., C.E.O. Charles F. Boyle - V.P., C.F.O., Contr.

Auditors: KPMG LLP
Transfer Agents: EquiServe Trust Company, N.A., Providence, RI

UNIVERSAL HEALTH SERVICES, INC.

Exchange	Symbol	Price	52Wk Range	Yield	P/E
NYS	UHS	$53.69 (3/31/2008)	63.00-46.73	0.60	16.88

*7 Year Price Score 88.53   *NYSE Composite Index=100   *12 Month Price Score 103.30

Interim Earnings (Per Share)

Qtr.	Mar	Jun	Sep	Dec
2003	0.84	0.82	0.79	0.75
2004	0.74	0.78	0.62	0.61
2005	0.99	2.53	0.15	0.27
2006	0.88	1.04	2.00	0.67
2007	0.92	0.97	0.54	0.75

Interim Dividends (Per Share)

Amt	Decl	Ex	Rec	Pay
0.08Q	5/17/2007	5/30/2007	6/1/2007	6/15/2007
0.08Q	7/19/2007	8/29/2007	8/31/2007	9/17/2007
0.08Q	11/20/2007	11/29/2007	12/3/2007	12/17/2007
0.08Q	1/16/2008	2/28/2008	3/3/2008	3/17/2008

Indicated Div: $0.32

Valuation Analysis   **Institutional Holding**

Forecast P/E	N/A	No of Institutions
		210
Market Cap	$2.8 Billion	Shares
Book Value	1.5 Billion	47,703,880
Price/Book	1.86	% Held
Price/Sales	0.59	88.54

Business Summary: Hospitals & Health Care (MIC: 9.3 SIC: 8062 NAIC: 622110)

Universal Health Services owns and operates acute care hospitals, behavioral health centers, surgical hospitals, ambulatory surgery centers and radiation oncology centers. As of Feb 28 2008, Co. owned and/or operated or had under construction, 31 acute care hospitals and 113 behavioral health centers located in 32 states, Washington, DC and Puerto Rico; and managed and/or owned outright or in partnerships with physicians, 11 surgical hospitals and surgery and radiation oncology centers located in six states and Puerto Rico. Co.'s hospitals provide services such as general and specialty surgery, internal medicine, obstetrics, emergency room care, and behavioral health services.

Recent Developments: For the year ended Dec 31 2007, income from continuing operations decreased 34.3% to US$170.5 million from US$259.6 million a year earlier. Net income decreased 34.3% to US$170.4 million from US$259.5 million in the prior year. Revenues were US$4.75 billion, up 13.4% from US$4.19 billion the year before. Operating income was US$370.1 million versus US$323.3 million in the prior year, an increase of 14.5%. Indirect operating expenses increased 13.3% to US$4.38 billion from US$3.87 billion in the equivalent prior-year period.

Prospects: For 2008, Co. is estimating earnings per diluted share from continuing operations of approximately $3.37 to $3.42 on projected net revenues of $5.13 billion. Also, Co. expects to spend about $400.0 million to $425.0 million on capital expenditures in 2008, including $240.0 million related to expenditures for capital equipment, renovations, new projects at existing hospitals and completion of construction projects. For instance, Co. is progressing with the construction of a new 171-bed acute care facility located in Palmdale, CA, which is expected to be completed and opened in 2009 and; a new 220-bed replacement acute care facility in Denison, TX, which is expected to complete by Jan 2010.

Financial Data

(US$ in Thousands)	12/31/2007	12/31/2006	12/31/2005	12/31/2004	12/31/2003	12/31/2002	12/31/2001	12/31/2000
Earnings Per Share	3.18	4.56	4.00	2.75	3.20	2.74	1.60	1.50
Cash Flow Per Share	6.53	3.10	7.64	6.80	6.53	5.55	5.21	3.02
Tang Book Value Per Share	14.59	12.67	9.61	10.42	11.17	8.59	7.27	6.68
Dividends Per Share	0.320	0.320	0.320	0.320	0.080	...	...	...
Dividend Payout %	10.06	7.02	8.00	11.64	2.50	...	...	...
Income Statement								
Total Revenue	4,751,005	4,191,300	3,935,480	3,938,320	3,643,566	3,258,898	2,840,491	2,242,444
EBITDA	509,976	608,724	368,791	470,621	500,398	401,865	285,420	258,917
Income Before Taxes	275,069	412,472	172,144	271,143	317,699	277,071	157,897	146,108
Income Taxes	104,550	152,878	62,301	101,137	118,430	101,710	57,147	52,746
Net Income	170,381	259,458	240,845	169,492	199,269	175,361	99,742	93,362
Average Shares	53,569	57,908	62,647	64,865	65,089	67,075	67,220	64,820
Balance Sheet								
Current Assets	774,847	728,506	608,298	808,925	645,791	606,576	548,262	476,455
Total Assets	3,608,657	3,277,042	2,858,709	3,022,843	2,772,730	2,323,229	2,114,584	1,742,377
Current Liabilities	487,711	502,451	524,170	469,656	395,753	370,413	322,716	248,840
Long-Term Obligations	1,008,786	821,363	637,654	852,229	868,566	680,514	718,830	548,064
Total Liabilities	2,091,458	1,874,578	1,653,611	1,802,257	1,681,808	1,405,770	1,306,684	1,025,803
Stockholders' Equity	1,517,199	1,402,464	1,205,098	1,220,586	1,090,922	917,459	807,900	716,574
Shares Outstanding	52,563	53,873	53,971	57,750	58,072	59,041	59,879	59,830
Statistical Record								
Return on Assets %	4.95	8.46	8.19	5.83	7.82	7.90	5.17	5.75
Return on Equity %	11.67	19.90	19.86	14.62	19.84	20.33	13.09	13.71
EBITDA Margin %	10.73	14.52	9.37	11.95	13.73	12.33	10.05	11.55
Net Margin %	3.59	6.19	6.12	4.30	5.47	5.38	3.51	4.16
Asset Turnover	1.38	1.37	1.34	1.36	1.43	1.47	1.47	1.38
Current Ratio	1.59	1.45	1.16	1.72	1.63	1.64	1.70	1.91
Debt to Equity	0.66	0.59	0.53	0.70	0.80	0.74	0.89	0.76
Price Range	63.00-48.45	60.07-45.27	63.20-42.42	56.51-39.87	54.30-34.77	56.20-37.80	52.60-37.81	55.88-18.00
P/E Ratio	19.81-15.24	13.17-9.93	15.80-10.61	20.55-14.50	16.97-10.87	20.51-13.80	32.88-23.63	37.25-12.00
Average Yield %	0.57		0.61	0.62	0.70	0.18	...	...

Address: Universal Corporate Center, 367 South Gulph Road, King Of Prussia, PA 19406 **Telephone:** 610-768-3300 **Fax:** 610-768-3336	**Web Site:** www.uhsinc.com **Officers:** Alan B. Miller - Chmn., Pres., C.E.O. Steve G. Filton - Sr. V.P., C.F.O., Sec.	**Auditors:** PricewaterhouseCoopers LLP **Investor Contact:** 610-768-3300

UNUM GROUP

*7 Year Price Score 95.70   *NYSE Composite Index=100   *12 Month Price Score 100.26

TRADING VOLUME (thousand shares)

Interim Earnings (Per Share)

Qtr.	Mar	Jun	Sep	Dec
2003	(1.02)	0.36	0.36	(1.25)
2004	(1.91)	0.02	0.55	0.45
2005	0.49	0.55	0.17	0.43
2006	0.23	0.38	(0.19)	0.82
2007	0.51	0.43	0.52	0.45

Interim Dividends (Per Share)

Amt	Decl	Ex	Rec	Pay
0.075Q	4/16/2007	4/26/2007	4/30/2007	5/18/2007
0.075Q	7/16/2007	7/26/2007	7/30/2007	8/17/2007
0.075Q	10/15/2007	10/25/2007	10/29/2007	11/16/2007
0.075Q	1/14/2008	1/24/2008	1/28/2008	2/15/2008

Indicated Div: $0.30

Valuation Analysis

		Institutional Holding	
Forecast P/E	9.83	No of Institutions	326
	(1/10/2007)	Shares	338,853,632
Market Cap	$7.9 Billion	% Held	98.87
Book Value	8.0 Billion		
Price/Book	0.99		
Price/Sales	0.76		

Business Summary: Insurance (MIC: 8.2 SIC: 6321 NAIC: 524114)

Unum Group provides group and individual income protection insurance products in the U.S. and the U.K. Co. also provides a complementary portfolio of other insurance products, such as long-term care insurance, life insurance, employer- and employee-paid group benefits, and other related services. Co.'s principal operating subsidiaries in the U.S. are Unum Life Insurance Company of America, Provident Life and Accident Insurance Company, The Paul Revere Life Insurance Company, and Colonial Life & Accident Insurance Company, and in the U.K., Unum Limited. Co.'s business segments include Unum US, Unum UK, Colonial, Individual Income Protection - Closed Block, Other, and Corporate.

Recent Developments: For the year ended Dec 31 2007, income from continuing operations increased 66.6% to US$672.4 million from US$403.6 million a year earlier. Net income increased 65.3% to US$679.3 million from US$411.0 million in the prior year. Revenues were US$10.52 billion, down 0.1% from US$10.54 billion the year before. Net premiums earned were US$7.90 billion versus US$7.95 billion in the prior year, a decrease of 0.6%. Net investment income rose 3.8% to US$2.41 billion from US$2.32 billion a year ago.

Prospects: For 2008, Co. continues to anticipate operating earnings to range from $2.35 and $2.40 per diluted share. In addition, Co. foresees that its portfolio yield will continue to gradually decline until the market rates on new purchases increase above the level of the overall yield in its portfolio. Going forward, Co. remains focused on continuously develop its businesses. Within its Unum U.S. segment, Co. intends to launch its Simply Unum platform in the small to mid sized employer marketplace. Co. also plans to capitalize on the introduction of several health related products for its Colonial Life segment, as well as the launch of a pilot voluntary benefits program in its Unum U.K. business.

Financial Data

(US$ in Thousands)	12/31/2007	12/31/2006	12/31/2005	12/31/2004	12/31/2003	12/31/2002	12/31/2001	12/31/2000
Earnings Per Share	1.91	1.23	1.64	(0.86)	(1.40)	1.65	2.38	2.33
Cash Flow Per Share	4.96	4.41	5.08	2.52	4.87	7.38	7.32	5.02
Tang Book Value Per Share	21.71	21.93	23.75	23.45	22.94	25.57	21.74	20.29
Dividends Per Share	0.075	0.300	0.300	0.300	0.373	0.590	0.590	0.590
Dividend Payout %	3.93	24.39	18.29	...	...	35.76	24.79	25.32
Income Statement								
Premium Income	7,901,100	7,948,200	7,815,600	7,839,600	7,615,700	7,453,100	7,078,200	7,057,000
Total Revenue	10,519,900	10,535,300	10,437,200	10,464,900	9,991,600	9,613,000	9,394,800	9,432,300
Benefits & Claims	6,988,200	7,577,200	7,083,200	7,248,400	7,868,100	6,582,400	6,234,300	6,407,500
Income Before Taxes	997,200	465,400	709,600	(259,500)	(435,200)	610,900	825,100	865,600
Income Taxes	324,800	61,800	196,000	(67,300)	(170,600)	202,600	243,000	301,400
Net Income	679,300	411,000	513,600	(253,000)	(386,400)	401,200	579,200	564,200
Average Shares	355,776	334,361	312,512	295,224	276,132	243,070	243,608	242,061
Balance Sheet								
Total Assets	52,432,700	52,823,300	51,866,800	50,832,300	49,718,300	45,259,500	42,442,700	40,363,900
Total Liabilities	44,392,800	45,104,500	44,502,900	43,608,200	42,447,300	38,116,300	36,202,800	34,488,400
Stockholders' Equity	8,039,900	7,718,800	7,363,900	7,224,100	7,271,000	6,843,200	5,939,900	5,575,500
Shares Outstanding	360,893	342,627	298,557	296,545	296,143	241,587	242,218	241,134
Statistical Record								
Return on Assets %	1.29	0.79	1.00	N.M.	N.M.	0.91	1.40	1.43
Return on Equity %	8.62	5.45	7.04	N.M.	N.M.	6.28	10.06	10.66
Loss Ratio %	88.45	95.33	90.63	92.46	103.31	88.32	88.08	90.80
Net Margin %	6.46	3.90	4.92	(2.42)	(3.87)	4.17	6.17	5.98
Price Range	27.57-19.93	24.05-16.23	22.76-15.98	18.14-12.19	19.40-5.97	29.45-16.58	33.75-22.43	32.06-12.06
P/E Ratio	14.43-10.43	19.55-13.20	13.88-9.74	...	...	17.85-10.05	14.18-9.42	13.76-5.18
Average Yield %	0.31	1.53	1.59	1.97	2.70	2.50	2.12	2.65

Address: 1 Fountain Square, Chattanooga, TN 37402
Telephone: 423-294-1011

Web Site: www.unum.com
Officers: C. William Pollard - Co-Chmn. Lawrence R. Pugh - Co-Chmn.

Auditors: Ernst & Young LLP
Investor Contact: 207-770-4330
Transfer Agents: Computershare Trust Company, N.A., Providence, RI

USG CORP

Exchange	Symbol	Price	52Wk Range	Yield	P/E
NYS	USG	$36.82 (3/31/2008)	52.06-31.05	N/A	47.21

*7 Year Price Score 104.47 *NYSE Composite Index=100 *12 Month Price Score 94.28

Interim Earnings (Per Share)

Qtr.	Mar	Jun	Sep	Dec
2003	0.13	0.73	0.89	1.07
2004	1.33	1.86	2.10	1.98
2005	1.77	2.53	3.57	(40.82)
2006	(3.15)	3.03	1.71	1.30
2007	0.45	0.56	0.07	(0.29)

Interim Dividends (Per Share)

Dividend Payment Suspended

Valuation Analysis		Institutional Holding	
Forecast P/E	9.27	No of Institutions	
	(1/10/2007)	224	
Market Cap	$3.6 Billion	Shares	
Book Value	2.2 Billion		69,245,192
Price/Book	1.66	% Held	
Price/Sales	0.70		70.59

TRADING VOLUME (thousand shares)

Business Summary: Stone, Clay, Glass, and Concrete Products (MIC: 11.2 SIC: 3275 NAIC: 327420)

USG, through its subsidiaries, is engaged as a manufacturer and distributor of building materials, producing a range of products for use in new residential, new nonresidential, and repair and remodel construction as well as products used in certain industrial processes. As of Dec 31 2007, Co.'s operations were divided into three segments. Co.'s North American Gypsum segment manufactures and markets gypsum and related products in the U.S., Canada and Mexico. Co.'s Worldwide Ceilings segment manufactures and markets interior systems products worldwide, while its Building Products Distribution segment consists of L&W Supply, a U.S. specialty building products distribution business.

Recent Developments: For the year ended Dec 31 2007, net income decreased 73.6% to US$76.0 million from US$288.0 million in the prior year. Revenues were US$5.20 billion, down 10.5% from US$5.81 billion the year before. Operating income was US$165.0 million versus US$985.0 million in the prior year, a decrease of 83.2%. Direct operating expenses rose 3.7% to US$4.60 billion from US$4.44 billion in the comparable period the year before. Indirect operating expenses increased 12.7% to US$434.0 million from US$385.0 million in the equivalent prior-year period.

Prospects: For 2008, Co. expects continued challenging housing market conditions due to the downturn in new residential construction that began in 2006. Specifically, Co. expects that residential repair and remodeling expenditures will continue to decline as a result of lower sales of existing homes and weakness in housing prices. However, Co. anticipates the non-residential market to remain stable in 2008, but believes that sales and operating profit will continue to be negatively affected by reduced demand for its products. Meanwhile, Co. expects industry demand for gypsum wallboard in 2008 to be down approximately 10.0% to 15.0%, as industry capacity utilization rate should be below 70.0%.

Financial Data

(US$ in Thousands)	12/31/2007	12/31/2006	12/31/2005	12/31/2004	12/31/2003	12/31/2002	12/31/2001	12/31/2000
Earnings Per Share	0.78	4.33	(32.92)	7.26	2.82	1.00	0.36	(5.62)
Cash Flow Per Share	13.46	(55.70)	11.60	9.92	5.78	10.28	5.46	7.90
Tang Book Value Per Share	19.86	15.36	...	22.65	15.10	12.37	11.30	10.69
Dividends Per Share	...	...	...	...	...	...	0.025	0.600
Dividend Payout %	...	...	...	...	...	...	6.94	...
Income Statement								
Total Revenue	5,202,000	5,810,000	5,139,000	4,509,000	3,666,000	3,468,000	3,296,000	3,781,000
EBITDA	345,000	1,126,000	(2,229,000)	628,000	331,000	366,000	187,000	(277,000)
Income Before Taxes	86,000	476,000	(2,349,000)	509,000	217,000	256,000	52,000	(420,000)
Income Taxes	10,000	188,000	(924,000)	197,000	79,000	117,000	36,000	(161,000)
Net Income	76,000	288,000	(1,436,000)	312,000	122,000	43,000	16,000	(259,000)
Average Shares	97,303	66,563	43,622	43,025	43,076	43,282	43,435	45,972
Balance Sheet								
Current Assets	1,251,000	2,707,000	2,179,000	1,790,000	1,498,000	1,393,000	1,197,000	876,000
Total Assets	4,621,000	5,365,000	6,142,000	4,278,000	3,799,000	3,617,000	3,464,000	3,214,000
Current Liabilities	567,000	1,764,000	600,000	570,000	414,000	438,000	321,000	896,000
Long-Term Obligations	1,238,000	1,439,000	...	...	1,000	2,000	2,000	564,000
Total Liabilities	2,428,000	3,831,000	6,444,000	3,254,000	3,110,000	3,082,000	2,973,000	2,750,000
Stockholders' Equity	2,193,000	1,534,000	(302,000)	1,024,000	689,000	535,000	491,000	464,000
Shares Outstanding	99,051	89,865	44,637	43,309	43,049	43,238	43,457	43,401
Statistical Record								
Return on Assets %	1.52	5.01	N.M.	7.70	3.29	1.21	0.48	N.M.
Return on Equity %	4.08	46.75	N.M.	36.33	19.93	8.38	3.35	N.M.
EBITDA Margin %	6.63	19.38	N.M.	13.93	9.03	10.55	5.67	N.M.
Net Margin %	1.46	4.96	N.M.	6.92	3.33	1.24	0.49	N.M.
Asset Turnover	1.04	1.01	0.99	1.11	0.99	0.98	0.99	1.26
Current Ratio	2.21	1.53	3.63	3.14	3.62	3.18	3.73	0.98
Debt to Equity	0.56	0.94	...	...	N.M.	N.M.	N.M.	1.22
Price Range	58.03-34.96	115.76-44.69	69.31-27.72	40.72-12.60	23.20-4.03	8.71-3.43	23.88-3.65	47.13-13.75
P/E Ratio	74.40-44.82	26.73-10.32	...	5.61-1.74	8.23-1.43	8.71-3.43	66.32-10.14	...
Average Yield %	...	...	...	...	...	...	0.26	1.92

Address: 550 W. Adams Street, Chicago, IL 60661-3676
Telephone: 312-436-4000

Web Site: www.usg.com
Officers: William C. Foote - Chmn., Pres., C.E.O. Edward M. Bosowski - Exec. V.P., Mktg. & Corporate Strategy

Auditors: Deloitte & Touche LLP

UST, INC.

Exchange	Symbol	Price	52Wk Range	Yield	P/E
NYS	UST	$54.52 (3/31/2008)	60.07-47.74	4.62	16.67

*7 Year Price Score 103.87 *NYSE Composite Index=100 *12 Month Price Score 110.15

Interim Earnings (Per Share)

Qtr.	Mar	Jun	Sep	Dec
2003	0.66	0.77	0.75	(0.27)
2004	0.73	0.89	0.80	0.77
2005	0.73	0.82	0.80	0.88
2006	0.71	0.83	0.73	0.85
2007	0.67	0.87	0.84	0.90

Interim Dividends (Per Share)

Amt	Decl	Ex	Rec	Pay
0.60Q	5/1/2007	6/13/2007	6/15/2007	6/29/2007
0.60Q	8/2/2007	9/12/2007	9/14/2007	9/28/2007
0.60Q	11/1/2007	12/12/2007	12/14/2007	12/28/2007
0.63Q	2/21/2008	3/12/2008	3/14/2008	3/31/2008

Indicated Div: $2.52

Valuation Analysis

Institutional Holding	
Forecast P/E	16.51	No. of Institutions
(1/10/2007)	348
Market Cap	$8.2 Billion	Shares
Book Value	N/A	157,581,024
Price/Book	N/A	% Held
Price/Sales	4.22	98.11

Business Summary: Tobacco Products (MIC: 4.2 SIC: 2131 NAIC: 312229)

UST is a holding company. Through its direct and indirect subsidiaries, Co. is engaged in the manufacture and marketing of consumer products in three segments: smokeless tobacco products, wine, and all other operations. Co. manufactures and markets smokeless tobacco, including such brand names as: Moist: Copenhagen, Skoal, Red Seal, and Husky; and Dry: Bruton, CC and Red Seal. Co.'s principal wine brand names include: Table (produced): Chateau Ste. Michelle, Columbia Crest, Conn Creek, Villa Mt. Eden, Northstar, Red Diamond, Distant Bay, Spring Valley and 14 Hands; Table (imported): Tignanello, Solaia, Tormaresca, Villa Antinori and Peppoli; and Sparkling (produced): Domaine Ste. Michelle.

Recent Developments: For the year ended Dec 31 2007, net income increased 2.9% to US$520.3 million from US$505.9 million in the prior year. Revenues were US$1.95 billion, up 5.4% from US$1.85 billion the year before. Operating income was US$853.6 million versus US$834.8 million in the prior year, an increase of 2.3%. Direct operating expenses rose 12.5% to US$524.6 million from US$466.1 million in the comparable period the year before. Indirect operating expenses increased 4.1% to US$572.6 million from US$550.0 million in the equivalent prior-year period.

Prospects: Co.'s outlook for seems positive as it plans to further increase its focus on building its brands to sustain growth and solid position in the moist smokeless tobacco category. Also, Co. expects its wine segment revenues and operating profit to benefit from its strong product name and from the 2007 acquired Stag's Leap Wine Cellars labels, which it began selling late in the third quarter of 2007. For 2008, Co. expects diluted earnings per share of $3.60 to $3.70, excluding any additional restructuring charges associated with Project Momentum. Co. is targeting to realize $150.0 million in annual savings within the planned three-year period of the Project Momentum, which commenced in 2006.

Financial Data

(US$ in Thousands)	12/31/2007	12/31/2006	12/31/2005	12/31/2004	12/31/2003	12/31/2002	12/31/2001	12/31/2000
Earnings Per Share	3.27	3.12	3.23	3.19	1.90	(1.61)	2.97	2.70
Cash Flow Per Share	3.62	3.71	3.42	3.40	(4.26)	4.72	3.45	3.34
Tang Book Value Per Share	...	0.37	0.45	0.03	...	...	2.86	1.66
Dividends Per Share	2.400	2.280	2.200	2.080	2.000	1.920	1.840	1.760
Dividend Payout %	73.39	73.08	68.11	65.20	105.26	...	61.95	65.19
Income Statement								
Total Revenue	1,950,779	1,850,911	1,851,885	1,838,238	1,742,629	1,682,877	1,670,315	1,547,644
EBITDA	899,237	880,650	924,633	960,256	633,160	(348,570)	876,224	792,326
Income Before Taxes	813,037	793,026	827,617	837,590	514,675	(444,363)	799,268	718,435
Income Taxes	292,764	291,060	293,349	299,538	195,886	(172,894)	307,666	276,549
Net Income	520,273	505,856	534,268	530,837	318,789	(271,469)	491,602	441,886
Average Shares	159,295	162,280	165,497	166,622	167,376	168,786	165,682	163,506
Balance Sheet								
Current Assets	846,274	998,110	889,554	1,173,133	1,247,966	2,291,267	891,959	691,405
Total Assets	1,487,078	1,440,348	1,366,983	1,659,483	1,726,494	2,765,275	2,011,702	1,646,399
Current Liabilities	400,174	300,077	258,778	618,873	521,093	1,462,442	222,462	169,572
Long-Term Obligations	1,090,000	840,000	840,000	840,000	1,140,000	1,140,000	862,575	869,175
Total Liabilities	1,779,280	1,374,522	1,291,885	1,649,918	1,841,681	2,812,265	1,430,640	1,375,827
Stockholders' Equity	(320,202)	65,826	75,098	9,565	(115,187)	(46,990)	581,062	270,572
Shares Outstanding	150,936	160,592	162,571	164,606	165,491	168,019	203,420	162,921
Statistical Record								
Return on Assets %	35.54	36.04	35.31	31.27	14.19	N.M.	26.88	33.11
Return on Equity %	...	717.91	1,262.11	...	...	N.M.	115.45	186.98
EBITDA Margin %	46.10	47.58	49.93	52.24	36.33	N.M.	52.46	51.20
Net Margin %	26.67	27.33	28.85	28.88	18.29	N.M.	29.43	28.55
Asset Turnover	1.33	1.32	1.22	1.08	0.78	0.70	0.91	1.16
Current Ratio	2.11	3.33	3.44	1.90	2.39	1.57	4.01	4.08
Debt to Equity	...	12.76	11.19	87.82	...	...	1.48	3.21
Price Range	60.71-47.74	58.45-38.04	56.48-37.65	48.90-34.53	37.72-27.42	41.06-25.36	35.90-24.81	28.69-14.00
P/E Ratio	18.57-14.60	18.73-12.19	17.49-11.66	15.33-10.82	19.85-14.43	...	12.09-8.35	10.63-5.19
Average Yield %	4.40	4.78	4.83	5.36	6.06	5.64	6.02	8.81

Address: 100 West Putnam Avenue, Greenwich, CT 06830 Telephone: 203-661-1100 Fax: 203-661-1129	Web Site: www.ustinc.com Officers: Vincent A. Gierer Jr. - Chmn., C.E.O. Murray S. Kessler - Pres., C.O.O.	Auditors: Ernst & Young LLP Investor Contact: 800-730-4001 Transfer Agents: EquiServe Trust Company, N.A.

VALASSIS COMMUNICATIONS, INC.

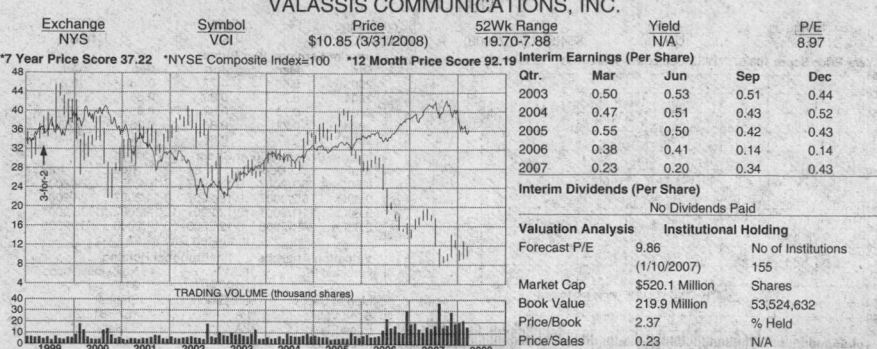

Exchange	Symbol	Price	52Wk Range	Yield	P/E
NYS	VCI	$10.85 (3/31/2008)	19.70-7.88	N/A	8.97

*7 Year Price Score 37.22   *NYSE Composite Index=100   *12 Month Price Score 92.19

Interim Earnings (Per Share)

Qtr.	Mar	Jun	Sep	Dec
2003	0.50	0.53	0.51	0.44
2004	0.47	0.51	0.43	0.52
2005	0.55	0.50	0.42	0.43
2006	0.38	0.41	0.14	0.14
2007	0.23	0.20	0.34	0.43

Interim Dividends (Per Share)

No Dividends Paid

Valuation Analysis

		Institutional Holding	
Forecast P/E	9.86	No of Institutions	
	(1/10/2007)	155	
Market Cap	$520.1 Million	Shares	
Book Value	219.9 Million	53,524,632	
Price/Book	2.37	% Held	
Price/Sales	0.23	N/A	

Business Summary: Advertising, Marketing & PR (MIC: 12.4 SIC: 7319 NAIC: 541870)

Valassis Communications is engaged as a marketing services company. Co.'s products and services portfolio includes shared and solo mail programs, preprinted inserts, newspaper-delivered product sampling and polybag advertising, door hangers, advertising brokering, cooperative free-standing inserts, coupon clearing, promotion information management products and marketing services, promotion security and consulting services, in-store promotions joint venture, direct mail advertising/sampling, software and analytics as well as internet-delivered promotions. Co. has five segments; Shared Mail, Neighborhood Targeted, Free-standing Inserts, International & Services and Household Targeted.

Recent Developments: For the year ended Dec 31 2007, net income increased 13.1% to US$58.0 million from US$51.3 million in the prior year. Revenues were US$2.24 billion, up 114.9% from US$1.04 billion the year before. Operating income was US$165.8 million versus US$102.0 million in the prior year, an increase of 62.5%. Direct operating expenses rose 117.1% to US$1.71 billion from US$789.6 million in the comparable period the year before. Indirect operating expenses increased 138.4% to US$362.2 million from US$151.9 million in the equivalent prior-year period.

Prospects: For full year 2008, Co. is projecting integration costs to increase to $38.0 million, based on the annualization of integration costs in 2007 to $34.0 million and the anticipated $4.0 million in additional cost savings. In addition, Co. is forecasting lower free-standing inserts margin due to the competitive environment and higher paper costs. Also, Co. estimates capital expenditures to be about $35.0 million to improve technology and replace equipment. Meanwhile, Co. believes that the shift of its products and services to the acquired 13,000 shared mail clients, as well as selling shared mail to its existing 2,000 clients, should drive revenue growth beginning in the second half of 2008.

Financial Data

(US$ in Thousands)	12/31/2007	12/31/2006	12/31/2005	12/31/2004	12/31/2003	12/31/2002	12/31/2001	12/31/2000
Earnings Per Share	1.21	1.07	1.90	1.93	1.98	1.77	2.17	2.27
Cash Flow Per Share	3.29	1.04	2.35	1.48	2.36	3.65	2.52	2.09
Tang Book Value Per Share	N.M.	0.71	N.M.	0.11	N.M.	...	...	...
Income Statement								
Total Revenue	2,242,171	1,043,491	1,131,043	1,044,069	916,520	853,019	849,529	863,121
EBITDA	230,934	123,261	173,126	183,685	190,840	162,308	204,822	216,497
Income Before Taxes	88,860	83,538	146,225	156,805	162,833	149,197	187,689	202,117
Income Taxes	30,858	32,256	50,829	56,058	59,125	53,943	68,545	76,418
Net Income	58,002	51,282	95,396	100,747	103,708	95,254	117,859	125,699
Average Shares	47,885	47,780	50,183	52,214	52,269	53,752	54,406	55,478
Balance Sheet								
Current Assets	710,252	542,492	450,916	501,183	456,623	241,976	183,547	167,659
Total Assets	2,190,453	801,426	697,683	737,965	692,754	386,079	363,025	325,717
Current Liabilities	541,396	362,220	323,451	315,395	349,175	161,794	173,067	171,050
Long-Term Obligations	1,279,640	259,931	259,896	273,703	259,819	257,280	252,383	325,490
Total Liabilities	1,970,562	633,852	594,158	597,459	616,695	419,366	428,709	498,221
Stockholders' Equity	219,891	167,574	103,525	140,506	76,059	(33,287)	(65,684)	(172,504)
Shares Outstanding	47,935	47,783	47,629	51,191	52,072	51,995	53,698	53,562
Statistical Record								
Return on Assets %	3.88	6.84	13.29	14.04	19.23	25.43	34.22	43.76
Return on Equity %	29.94	37.83	78.18	92.79	484.93	...	...	...
EBITDA Margin %	10.30	11.81	15.31	17.59	20.82	19.03	24.11	25.08
Net Margin %	2.59	4.91	8.43	9.65	11.32	11.17	13.87	14.56
Asset Turnover	1.50	1.39	1.58	1.46	1.70	2.28	2.47	3.00
Current Ratio	1.31	1.50	1.39	1.59	1.31	1.50	1.06	0.98
Debt to Equity	5.82	1.55	2.51	1.95	3.42	...	...	...
Price Range	19.70-7.88	30.67-14.28	40.57-28.89	35.77-27.59	30.57-21.71	41.00-25.26	37.25-28.30	42.31-21.69
P/E Ratio	16.28-6.51	28.66-13.35	21.35-15.21	18.53-14.30	15.44-10.96	23.16-14.27	17.17-13.04	18.64-9.55

Address: 19975 Victor Parkway, Livonia, MI 48152	Web Site: www.valassis.com	Auditors: Deloitte & Touche LLP
Telephone: 734-591-3000	Officers: Alan F. Schultz - Chmn., Pres., C.E.O. John Lieblang - V.P., Chief Tech. Officer	Investor Contact: 734-591-7374
Fax: 734-591-4994		Transfer Agents: National City Bank, Cleveland, OH

VALEANT PHARMACEUTICALS INTERNATIONAL

Exchange	Symbol	Price	52Wk Range	Yield	P/E
NYS	VRX	$12.83 (3/31/2008)	18.69-10.65	N/A	N/A

*7 Year Price Score 60.24 *NYSE Composite Index=100 *12 Month Price Score 95.15

Interim Earnings (Per Share)

Qtr.	Mar	Jun	Sep	Dec
2003	0.16	0.18	(0.99)	(0.03)
2004	(0.16)	(0.49)	(0.19)	(1.18)
2005	(1.57)	(0.01)	(0.04)	(0.48)
2006	(0.07)	(0.49)	0.14	(0.24)
2007	0.09	0.17	(0.13)	(0.21)

Interim Dividends (Per Share)

Amt	Decl	Ex	Rec	Pay
0.077Q	11/3/2005	11/15/2005	11/17/2005	12/1/2005
0.077Q	2/28/2006	3/14/2006	3/16/2006	3/30/2006
0.077Q	5/4/2006	5/16/2006	5/18/2006	6/1/2006
0.077Q	8/3/2006	8/15/2006	8/17/2006	8/31/2006

Valuation Analysis

		Institutional Holding	
Forecast P/E	13.89	No of Institutions	
	(1/10/2007)	156	
Market Cap	$1.1 Billion	Shares	
Book Value	414.1 Million	94,148,800	
Price/Book	2.77	% Held	
Price/Sales	1.31	99.46	

TRADING VOLUME (thousand shares)

Business Summary: Pharmaceuticals (MIC: 9.1 SIC: 2834 NAIC: 325412)

Valeant Pharmaceuticals is a pharmaceutical company that develops, manufactures and markets a range of pharmaceutical products which are sold in more than 100 markets around the world. Co.'s products are sold through three pharmaceutical segments comprising: North America, International (Latin America, Asia, and Australasia) and EMEA (Europe, Middle East, and Africa). Co.'s products are focused on neurology, dermatology, and Infectious disease. Co.'s prescription pharmaceutical products also treat, among other things, neuromuscular disorders, cancer, cardiovascular disease, diabetes and psychiatric disorders.

Recent Developments: For the year ended Dec 31 2007, income from continuing operations was US$26.1 million compared with a loss of US$56.8 million a year earlier. Net loss amounted to US$6.2 million versus a net loss of US$57.6 million in the prior year. Revenues were US$872.2 million, up 1.1% from US$862.8 million the year before. Operating income was US$75.3 million versus US$8.0 million in the prior year, an increase of 844.5%. Direct operating expenses declined 2.1% to US$233.1 million from US$238.1 million in the comparable period the year before. Indirect operating expenses decreased 8.6% to US$563.8 million from US$616.7 million in the equivalent prior-year period.

Prospects: On Mar 3 2008, Co. completed the sale of its Asia Pacific operations, including its existing licensing rights and commercial operations in Asia Pacific for the products marketed in twelve Asian markets, to Invida Pharmaceutical Holdings Pte. Ltd. for approximately $37.8 million in cash as part of Co.'s effort to simplify its business. Also, Co. recently reported positive results for its retigabine product candidate in RESTORE 1, the first of two Phase III pivotal trials, for the treatment of epilepsy. Hence, Co. expects to file a New Drug Application for retigabine with the FDA and a Marketing Authorization Application to the European Medicines Evaluation Agency before the end of 2008.

Financial Data

(US$ in Thousands)	12/31/2007	12/31/2006	12/31/2005	12/31/2004	12/31/2003	12/31/2002	12/31/2001	12/31/2000
Earnings Per Share	(0.07)	(0.61)	(2.05)	(2.02)	(0.67)	(1.61)	0.77	1.10
Cash Flow Per Share	0.99	1.34	0.70	0.21	2.26	0.27	1.70	2.28
Tang Book Value Per Share	N.M.	N.M.	N.M.	0.28	2.05	3.80	4.46	3.99
Dividends Per Share	...	0.233	0.310	0.310	0.310	0.308	0.297	0.287
Dividend Payout %	...	...	...	...	...	...	38.64	26.14
Income Statement								
Total Revenue	872,222	907,238	822,681	682,520	685,953	737,074	858,104	800,304
EBITDA	164,343	93,625	(6,911)	71,548	78,304	270,392	261,531	241,908
Income Before Taxes	51,289	(29,837)	(131,419)	(52,423)	(13,760)	176,938	144,357	129,554
Income Taxes	25,233	34,219	54,187	83,597	39,463	74,963	58,609	37,683
Net Income	(6,186)	(56,565)	(188,759)	(169,797)	(55,640)	(134,834)	64,134	90,180
Average Shares	93,976	93,251	91,696	83,887	83,602	83,988	83,166	82,264
Balance Sheet								
Current Assets	794,672	781,975	595,739	770,667	1,142,152	576,573	772,929	565,416
Total Assets	1,494,262	1,505,437	1,530,877	1,521,875	1,976,937	1,488,549	1,754,365	1,477,072
Current Liabilities	205,661	252,208	234,927	192,205	166,784	179,503	161,480	158,777
Long-Term Obligations	782,552	778,196	788,439	793,139	1,119,802	481,548	734,933	510,781
Total Liabilities	1,080,159	1,070,184	1,091,626	1,013,596	1,356,878	736,791	943,648	719,878
Stockholders' Equity	414,103	435,253	439,251	476,223	605,361	703,690	810,717	757,194
Shares Outstanding	89,286	94,416	92,760	84,219	83,185	84,066	81,689	80,197
Statistical Record								
Return on Assets %	N.M.	N.M.	N.M.	N.M.	N.M.	N.M.	3.97	6.10
Return on Equity %	N.M.	N.M.	N.M.	N.M.	N.M.	N.M.	8.18	12.48
EBITDA Margin %	18.84	10.32	N.M.	10.48	11.42	36.68	30.48	30.23
Net Margin %	N.M.	N.M.	N.M.	N.M.	N.M.	N.M.	7.47	11.27
Asset Turnover	0.58	0.60	0.54	0.39	0.40	0.45	0.53	0.54
Current Ratio	3.86	3.10	2.54	4.01	6.85	3.21	4.79	3.56
Debt to Equity	1.89	1.79	1.79	1.67	1.85	0.68	0.91	0.67
Price Range	18.69-10.65	20.46-15.81	26.35-16.46	27.09-17.06	25.50-7.87	33.50-6.88	34.26-21.60	40.19-19.75
P/E Ratio	...	...	...	...	...	...	44.49-28.05	36.53-17.95
Average Yield %	...	1.30	1.51	1.37	2.04	1.57	1.07	1.01

Address: One Enterprise, Aliso Viejo, CA 92656	Web Site: www.valeant.com	Auditors: PricewaterhouseCoopers LLP
Telephone: 949-461-6000	Officers: Robert W. O'Leary - Chmn. Timothy C. Tyson - Pres., C.E.O.	Investor Contact: 949-461-6002
Fax: 949-461-6609		Transfer Agents: American Stock Transfer and Trust Corporation, Brooklyn, NY

VALERO ENERGY CORP.

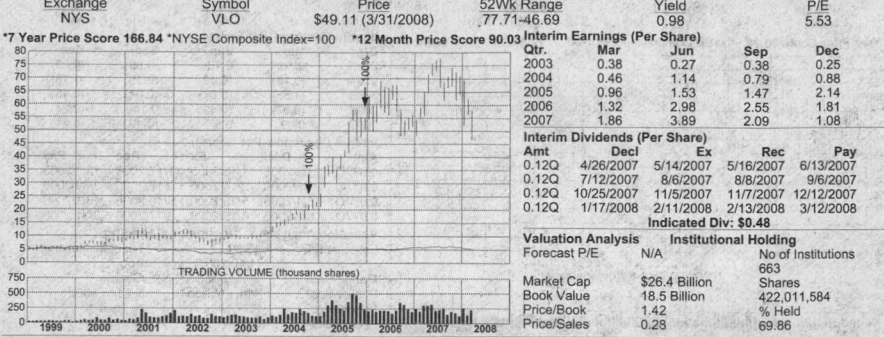

Exchange	Symbol	Price	52Wk Range	Yield	P/E
NYS	VLO	$49.11 (3/31/2008)	77.71-46.69	0.98	5.53

*7 Year Price Score 166.84 *NYSE Composite Index=100 *12 Month Price Score 90.03

Interim Earnings (Per Share)

Qtr.	Mar	Jun	Sep	Dec
2003	0.38	0.27	0.38	0.25
2004	0.46	1.14	0.79	0.88
2005	0.96	1.53	1.47	2.14
2006	1.32	2.98	2.55	1.81
2007	1.86	3.89	2.09	1.08

Interim Dividends (Per Share)

Amt	Decl	Ex	Rec	Pay
0.12Q	4/26/2007	5/14/2007	5/16/2007	6/13/2007
0.12Q	7/12/2007	8/6/2007	8/8/2007	9/6/2007
0.12Q	10/25/2007	11/5/2007	11/7/2007	12/12/2007
0.12Q	1/17/2008	2/11/2008	2/13/2008	3/12/2008
			Indicated Div: $0.48	

Valuation Analysis   Institutional Holding

Forecast P/E	N/A	No of Institutions
		663
Market Cap	$26.4 Billion	Shares
Book Value	18.5 Billion	422,011,584
Price/Book	1.42	% Held
Price/Sales	0.28	69.86

Business Summary: Oil and Gas (MIC: 14.2 SIC: 2911 NAIC: 324110)

Valero Energy owns and operates refineries in the U.S., Canada, and Aruba. At Dec 31 2007, Co. owned and operated 17 refineries that produce conventional gasolines, distillates, jet fuel, asphalt, petrochemicals, lubricants, and other refined products, as well as reformulated gasoline blendstock for oxygenate blending, gasoline meeting the specifications of the California Air Resources Board (CARB), CARB diesel fuel, low-sulfur and ultra-low-sulfur diesel fuel, and oxygenates. Co. markets branded and unbranded refined products on a wholesale basis in the U.S. and Canada, and sells refined products through retail and wholesale branded outlets in the U.S., Canada, and Aruba.

Recent Developments: For the year ended Dec 31 2007, income from continuing operations decreased 13.7% to US$4.57 billion from US$5.29 billion a year earlier. Net income decreased 4.2% to US$5.23 billion from US$5.46 billion in the prior year. Revenues were US$95.33 billion, up 8.8% from US$87.64 billion the year before. Operating income was US$6.92 billion versus US$7.72 billion in the prior year, a decrease of 10.4%. Direct operating expenses rose 10.5% to US$81.65 billion in the comparable period the year before. Indirect operating expenses increased 11.7% to US$6.76 billion from US$6.06 billion in the equivalent prior-year period.

Prospects: On Feb 28 2008, Co. announced the approval of its $2.40 billion capital investment project, which includes an expansion at its refinery in Port Arthur, TX that involves the construction of a 50,000 barrel-per-day hydrocracker, a 45,000 barrel-per-day coker, and a revamp and expansion of other units. This project is expected to boost the refinery's overall throughput capacity to 415,000 barrels per day, giving it more capacity to process heavy, sour feedstocks. The hydrocracker project and the coker project should be completed in the fourth quarter of 2010 and in the second quarter of 2011, respectively. Meanwhile, Co.'s outlook for refined product margins for 2008 remains positive.

Financial Data

(US$ in Thousands)	12/31/2007	12/31/2006	12/31/2005	12/31/2004	12/31/2003	12/31/2002	12/31/2001	12/31/2000
Earnings Per Share	8.88	8.64	6.10	3.27	1.27	0.21	2.21	1.40
Cash Flow Per Share	9.31	10.33	10.56	5.78	3.81	0.64	3.73	2.56
Tang Book Value Per Share	26.38	23.34	15.80	9.55	5.85	3.24	3.90	6.28
Dividends Per Share	0.480	0.300	0.190	0.145	0.105	0.100	0.085	0.080
Dividend Payout %	5.41	3.47	3.11	4.44	8.25	48.19	3.85	5.71
Income Statement								
Total Revenue	95,327,000	91,833,000	82,162,000	54,618,600	37,968,600	26,976,200	14,988,339	14,671,087
EBITDA	8,461,000	9,554,000	6,428,000	3,588,200	1,758,400	884,700	1,235,715	777,521
Income Before Taxes	6,726,000	8,189,000	5,287,000	2,710,100	986,600	149,700	894,853	528,220
Income Taxes	2,161,000	2,726,000	1,697,000	906,300	365,100	58,200	331,300	189,100
Net Income	5,234,000	5,463,000	3,590,000	1,803,800	621,500	91,500	563,553	339,120
Average Shares	579,000	632,000	588,000	552,200	488,000	440,400	255,212	242,100
Balance Sheet								
Current Assets	14,792,000	10,760,000	8,276,000	5,264,400	3,817,300	3,536,400	4,113,144	1,285,067
Total Assets	42,722,000	37,753,000	32,728,000	19,391,600	15,664,200	14,465,200	14,377,096	4,307,704
Current Liabilities	11,914,000	8,822,000	7,305,000	4,533,500	3,064,300	3,006,700	4,730,246	1,038,992
Long-Term Obligations	6,521,000	4,722,000	5,208,000	3,945,700	4,299,700	4,494,100	2,805,247	1,042,417
Total Liabilities	24,215,000	19,148,000	17,678,000	11,593,600	9,929,000	10,156,900	10,174,533	2,780,649
Stockholders' Equity	18,507,000	18,605,000	15,050,000	7,798,000	5,735,200	4,308,300	4,202,563	1,527,055
Shares Outstanding	536,659	603,763	617,422	510,951	481,065	428,549	416,789	243,353
Statistical Record								
Return on Assets %	13.01	15.50	13.78	10.26	4.13	0.63	6.03	9.28
Return on Equity %	28.21	32.46	31.43	26.58	12.38	2.15	19.67	25.90
EBITDA Margin %	8.88	10.40	7.82	6.57	4.63	3.28	8.24	5.30
Net Margin %	5.49	5.95	4.37	3.30	1.64	0.34	3.76	2.31
Asset Turnover	2.37	2.61	3.15	3.11	2.52	1.87	1.60	4.02
Current Ratio	1.24	1.22	1.13	1.16	1.25	1.18	0.87	1.24
Debt to Equity	0.35	0.25	0.35	0.51	0.75	1.04	0.67	0.68
Price Range	77.71-48.21	69.10-48.15	58.06-21.08	23.82-11.51	11.70-8.28	12.38-5.87	12.96-8.19	9.59-4.73
P/E Ratio	8.75-5.43	8.00-5.57	9.52-3.46	7.28-3.52	9.21-6.52	58.95-27.93	5.87-3.70	6.85-3.38
Average Yield %	0.72	0.52	0.46	0.83	1.08	1.05	0.89	1.08

Address: One Valero Way, San Antonio, TX 78249	**Web Site:** www.valero.com	**Auditors:** KPMG LLP
Telephone: 210-345-2000	**Officers:** William E. Greehey - Chmn., C.E.O.	**Investor Contact:** 800-531-7911
Fax: 210-246-2646	Gregory C. King - Pres.	**Transfer Agents:** ComputerShare Investor Services, Chicago, IL

VALLEY NATIONAL BANCORP

Exchange	Symbol	Price	52Wk Range	Yield	P/E	Div Acheiver
NYS	VLY	$19.21 (3/31/2008)	24.89-17.55	4.37	15.13	16 Years

*7 Year Price Score 78.36   *NYSE Composite Index=100   *12 Month Price Score 96.94

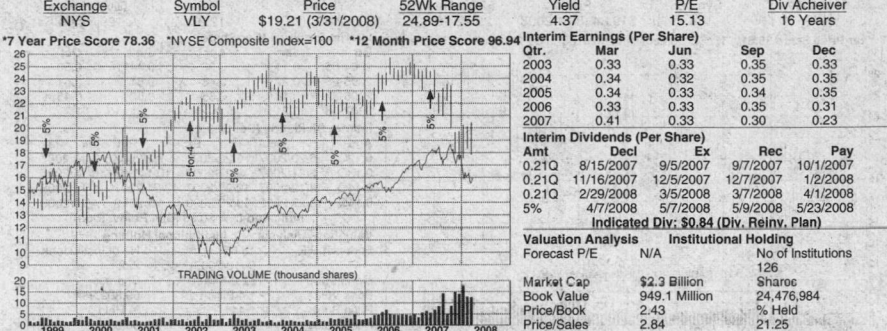

Interim Earnings (Per Share)

Qtr.	Mar	Jun	Sep	Dec
2003	0.33	0.33	0.35	0.33
2004	0.34	0.32	0.35	0.35
2005	0.34	0.33	0.34	0.35
2006	0.33	0.33	0.35	0.31
2007	0.41	0.33	0.30	0.23

Interim Dividends (Per Share)

Amt	Decl	Ex	Rec	Pay
0.21Q	8/15/2007	9/5/2007	9/7/2007	10/1/2007
0.21Q	11/16/2007	12/5/2007	12/7/2007	1/2/2008
0.21Q	2/29/2008	3/5/2008	3/7/2008	4/1/2008
5%	4/7/2008	5/7/2008	5/9/2008	5/23/2008

Indicated Div: $0.84 (Div. Reinv. Plan)

Valuation Analysis

		Institutional Holding	
Forecast P/E	N/A	No of Institutions	126
Market Cap	$2.3 Billion	Shares	24,476,984
Book Value	949.1 Million	% Held	21.25
Price/Book	2.43		
Price/Sales	2.84		

Business Summary: Commercial Banking (MIC: 8.1 SIC: 6021 NAIC: 522110)

Valley National Bancorp is a bank holding company. Co.'s principal subsidiary, Valley National Bank, provides a range of commercial and retail banking services, including: the acceptance of demand, savings and time deposits; extension of consumer, real estate, Small Business Administration loans and other commercial credits; equipment leasing; and personal and corporate trust, as well as pension and fiduciary services. In addition, Co. owns 100.0% of the voting shares of VND Capital Trust I, through which it issued trust preferred securities. As of Dec 31 2007, Co. had total assets of $12.75 billion, and total deposits of $8.09 billion.

Recent Developments: For the year ended Dec 31 2007, net income decreased 6.4% to US$153.2 million from US$163.7 million in the prior year. Net interest income decreased 2.4% to US$381.7 million from US$391.1 million in the prior year. Provision for loan losses was US$11.9 million versus US$9.3 million in the prior year, an increase of 28.1%. Non-interest income rose 19.7% to US$86.3 million from US$72.1 million, while non-interest expense advanced 0.3% to US$251.2 million.

Prospects: Going forward, Co. anticipates continued pressure on the net interest margin due to the asset sensitivity of its balance sheet, as well as the potential continuation of high deposit rates within its primary markets. In addition, Co. noted that the competitive pricing of deposits and the current decline in market rates for loans and investments could negatively affect net interest income during the first half of 2008. Meanwhile, in view of its focus on branch expansion plan and increasing its geographic presence, Co. anticipates opening another eight de novo branches throughout 2008.

Financial Data

(US$ in Thousands)	12/31/2007	12/31/2006	12/31/2005	12/31/2004	12/31/2003	12/31/2002	12/31/2001	12/31/2000
Earnings Per Share	1.27	1.33	1.35	1.35	1.33	1.29	1.08	1.04
Cash Flow Per Share	8.16	1.88	0.97	1.41	1.95	0.96	1.31	1.15
Tang Book Value Per Share	6.21	6.09	5.82	5.78	5.26	5.47	5.56	5.42
Dividends Per Share	0.035	0.014	0.793	0.760	0.732	0.693	0.034	0.013
Dividend Payout %	65.73	61.04	58.68	57.01	54.89	53.76	60.27	58.72
Income Statement								
Interest Income	725,007	707,371	625,084	518,926	497,498	517,419	553,486	460,853
Interest Expense	343,322	316,250	226,659	146,607	148,922	157,723	218,653	202,756
Net Interest Income	381,685	391,121	398,425	372,319	348,576	359,696	334,833	258,097
Provision for Losses	11,875	9,270	4,340	8,003	7,345	13,644	15,706	6,130
Non-Interest Income	86,280	72,064	73,708	84,328	108,197	81,238	68,476	50,883
Non-Interest Expense	251,164	250,340	237,566	220,049	216,278	207,994	188,248	141,013
Income Before Taxes	204,926	203,575	230,227	228,595	233,150	219,296	199,355	161,837
Income Taxes	51,698	39,884	66,778	74,197	79,735	64,680	64,151	55,064
Net Income	153,228	162,601	162,440	154,398	153,415	154,616	135,204	106,773
Average Shares	120,616	122,868	120,560	114,811	114,863	119,553	124,499	102,364
Balance Sheet								
Net Loans & Leases	8,426,541	8,261,641	8,058,766	6,868,616	6,107,759	5,757,353	5,324,229	4,625,606
Total Assets	12,748,959	12,395,027	12,436,102	10,763,391	9,880,740	9,134,674	8,583,765	6,425,837
Total Deposits	8,091,004	8,487,651	8,570,001	7,518,739	7,162,968	6,683,387	6,306,974	5,123,717
Total Liabilities	11,799,899	11,445,437	11,504,192	10,055,793	9,227,951	8,302,936	7,705,390	5,880,763
Stockholders' Equity	949,060	949,590	931,910	707,598	652,789	631,738	678,375	545,074
Shares Outstanding	119,851	121,125	122,737	114,437	114,148	115,533	121,992	100,570
Statistical Record								
Return on Assets %	1.22	1.32	1.41	1.49	1.61	1.75	1.80	1.67
Return on Equity %	16.14	17.40	19.94	22.64	23.89	23.60	22.10	19.39
Net Interest Margin %	52.65	55.29	63.74	71.75	70.07	69.52	60.50	56.00
Efficiency Ratio %	30.96	32.12	34.00	36.48	35.71	34.74	30.27	27.56
Loans to Deposits	1.04	0.97	0.94	0.91	0.85	0.86	0.84	0.90
Price Range	25.18-17.73	25.71-21.01	24.03-19.98	24.57-20.86	24.66-18.80	22.68-19.16	20.65-15.31	20.00-12.29
P/E Ratio	19.83-13.96	19.33-15.79	17.80-14.80	18.20-15.45	18.54-14.14	17.58-14.85	19.12-14.17	19.23-11.82
Average Yield %	3.69	3.43	3.63	3.39	3.31	3.25	3.68	3.98

Address: 1455 Valley Road, Wayne, NJ 07470	**Web Site:** www.valleynationalbank.com	**Auditors:** Ernst & Young LLP
Telephone: 973-305-8800	**Officers:** Gerald H. Lipkin - Chmn., Pres., C.E.O. Peter Crocitto - Exec. V.P.	**Investor Contact:** 973-305-8800
Fax: 973-305-1605		**Transfer Agents:** American Stock Transfer & Trust Company

VALSPAR CORP.

Exchange	Symbol	Price	52Wk Range	Yield	P/E	Div Acheiver
NYS	VAL	$19.84 (3/31/2008)	29.22-18.13	2.82	12.97	29 Years

*7 Year Price Score 86.51   *NYSE Composite Index=100   *12 Month Price Score 90.05

TRADING VOLUME (thousand shares)

Interim Earnings (Per Share)

Qtr.	Jan	Apr	Jul	Oct
2004-05	0.11	0.38	0.44	0.50
2005-06	0.22	0.46	0.51	0.51
2006-07	0.18	0.35	0.52	0.45
2007-08	0.21	...	...	...

Interim Dividends (Per Share)

Amt	Decl	Ex	Rec	Pay
0.13Q	6/20/2007	6/28/2007	7/2/2007	7/13/2007
0.13Q	8/21/2007	9/27/2007	10/1/2007	10/15/2007
0.14Q	12/12/2007	12/27/2007	12/31/2007	1/14/2008
0.14Q	2/27/2008	3/28/2008	4/1/2008	4/15/2008

Indicated Div: $0.56 (Div. Reinv. Plan)

Valuation Analysis

		Institutional Holding	
Forecast P/E	13.65	No of Institutions	
	(1/10/2007)	222	
Market Cap	$2.0 Billion	Shares	
Book Value	1.4 Billion	69,802,944	
Price/Book	1.44	% Held	
Price/Sales	0.60	68.08	

Business Summary: Chemicals (MIC: 11.1 SIC: 2851 NAIC: 325510)

Valspar is engaged in the business of manufacturing and distributing a portfolio of coatings, paints and related products globally. In addition, Co. manufactures and sells specialty polymers, colorants and gelcoats, as well as sells furniture protection plans. As of Oct 26 2007, Co. conducted its businesses through two operating segments. Co.'s Coatings segment includes a range of decorative and protective coatings for metal, wood, plastic and glass, primarily for sale to original equipment manufacturer customers. Co.'s Paint segment provides a portfolio of interior and exterior paints, stains, primers, varnishes, high performance floor paints and specialty decorative products.

Recent Developments: For the quarter ended Jan 25 2008, net income increased 1.8% to US$24.0 million from US$23.6 million in the year-earlier quarter. Revenues were US$765.1 million, up 10.2% from US$694.5 million the year before. Operating income was US$55.0 million versus US$51.2 million in the prior-year quarter, an increase of 7.3%. Direct operating expenses rose 12.0% to US$554.7 million from US$495.4 million in the comparable period the year before. Indirect operating expenses increased 5.2% to US$155.5 million from US$147.9 million in the equivalent prior-year period.

Prospects: Although the U.S. residential construction market remains weak, Co.'s results are benefiting from increased packaging, industrial and architectural product lines, growing international business, and acquisitions. Separately, in Dec 2007, Co. acquired Aries Coil Coatings S.A. de C.V., a privately owned manufacturer of coil and packaging coatings based in Monterrey, Mexico, for undisclosed terms. Co. expects the acquisition to build on its growing international presence and boost its market position in coil and packaging coatings in the Americas; and will be slightly accretive to earnings in 2008. For full-year 2008, Co. anticipates net income per diluted share of between $1.52 and $1.62.

Financial Data

(US$ in Thousands)	3 Mos	10/26/2007	10/27/2006	10/28/2005	10/29/2004	10/31/2003	10/25/2002	10/26/2001
Earnings Per Share	1.53	1.50	1.71	1.42	1.36	1.09	1.17	0.55
Cash Flow Per Share	2.36	1.89	2.82	2.27	2.40	2.44	2.16	2.15
Dividends Per Share	0.530	0.520	0.440	0.400	0.360	0.300	0.280	0.270
Dividend Payout %	34.60	34.67	25.73	28.17	26.57	27.65	23.93	49.09
Income Statement								
Total Revenue	765,124	3,249,287	2,978,062	2,713,950	2,440,692	2,247,926	2,126,853	1,920,970
EBITDA	71,776	393,244	372,354	338,637	330,473	282,939	298,402	236,759
Depn & Amortn	19,429	...	...	...	...	...	...	...
Income Before Taxes	36,664	259,771	257,432	225,720	228,537	181,474	198,548	91,150
Income Taxes	12,649	87,656	82,180	78,102	85,701	68,960	78,427	39,650
Net Income	24,015	172,115	175,252	147,618	142,836	112,514	120,121	51,500
Average Shares	100,940	102,617	102,726	104,149	105,418	103,848	102,740	93,315
Balance Sheet								
Current Assets	1,049,314	1,029,642	967,123	865,204	802,315	738,831	701,788	661,494
Total Assets	3,545,120	3,452,281	3,188,253	2,761,163	2,634,258	2,496,524	2,419,552	2,226,070
Current Liabilities	923,613	1,029,147	1,195,683	625,631	718,211	531,063	503,895	475,067
Long-Term Obligations	801,695	648,988	350,267	706,415	549,073	749,199	885,819	1,006,217
Total Liabilities	2,121,318	2,034,142	1,929,467	1,700,071	1,633,895	1,627,207	1,682,299	1,571,505
Stockholders' Equity	1,383,546	1,380,797	1,240,063	1,061,092	1,000,363	869,317	737,253	654,565
Shares Outstanding	100,169	100,634	101,904	100,432	102,608	101,461	100,208	98,963
Statistical Record								
Return on Assets %	5.06	5.20	5.91	5.49	5.58	4.50	5.19	3.08
Return on Equity %	12.95	13.17	15.27	14.36	15.32	13.78	17.31	9.46
EBITDA Margin %	9.38	12.10	12.50	12.48	13.54	12.59	14.03	12.32
Net Margin %	3.14	5.30	5.88	5.44	5.85	5.01	5.65	2.68
Asset Turnover	0.97	0.98	1.00	1.01	0.95	0.90	0.92	1.15
Current Ratio	1.14	1.00	0.81	1.38	1.12	1.39	1.39	1.39
Debt to Equity	0.58	0.47	0.28	0.67	0.55	0.86	1.20	1.54
Price Range	29.22-18.13	29.22-24.57	29.42-21.80	25.38-20.57	25.68-22.43	23.98-18.84	24.95-16.61	18.75-12.50
P/E Ratio	19.10-11.85	19.48-16.38	17.20-12.75	17.87-14.49	18.88-16.50	22.00-17.29	21.33-14.19	34.08-22.73
Average Yield %	2.01	1.88	1.68	1.71	1.48	1.37	1.33	1.69

Address: 1101 Third Street South,	Web Site: www.valsparglobal.com	Auditors: Ernst & Young LLP
Minneapolis, MN 55415	Officers: Thomas R. McBurney - Chmn. William L.	Transfer Agents: Mellon Investor
Telephone: 612-332-7371	Mansfield - Pres., C.E.O.	Services LLC, Ridgefield Park, NJ
Fax: 612-375-7723		

VARIAN MEDICAL SYSTEMS, INC.

Exchange	Symbol	Price	52Wk Range	Yield	P/E
NYS	VAR	$46.84 (3/31/2008)	54.26-37.82	N/A	24.78

*7 Year Price Score 102.64 *NYSE Composite Index=100 *12 Month Price Score 118.04

Interim Earnings (Per Share)

Qtr.	Dec	Mar	Jun	Sep
2004-05	0.29	0.39	0.37	0.45
2005-06	0.30	0.41	0.49	0.61
2006-07	0.37	0.46	0.39	0.61
2007-08	0.43	...	...	...

Interim Dividends (Per Share)

Amt	Decl	Ex	Rec	Pay
100%	11/19/2001	1/16/2002	12/10/2001	1/15/2002
2-for-1	6/14/2004	8/2/2004	6/30/2004	7/30/2004

Valuation Analysis   Institutional Holding

Forecast P/E	21.84	No of Institutions
	(1/10/2007)	381
Market Cap	$5.9 Billion	Shares
Book Value	862.0 Million	108,182,768
Price/Book	6.81	% Held
Price/Sales	3.17	84.46

Business Summary: Medical Instruments & Equipment (MIC: 9.6 SIC: 3845 NAIC: 334510)

Varian Medical Systems designs, produces and sells equipment and software products for treating cancer with focused energy beams, or radiation. Co. also designs, manufactures, sells and services X-ray tubes; replacement X-ray tubes; flat panel digital image detectors for filmless X-rays for medical, dental, veterinary, scientific and industrial applications; linear accelerators, image detectors, image processing software and image detection systems for security and inspection purposes; proton therapy systems for cancer treatment; and scientific instruments used in fundamental and applied physics research. Co. has two reportable business segments: Oncology Systems and X-ray Products.

Recent Developments: For the quarter ended Dec 28 2007, net income increased 12.1% to US$55.5 million from US$49.5 million in the year-earlier quarter. Revenues were US$458.5 million, up 18.2% from US$387.9 million the year before. Operating income was US$84.3 million versus US$70.0 million in the prior-year quarter, an increase of 20.4%. Direct operating expenses rose 17.6% to US$267.7 million from US$227.7 million in the comparable period the year before. Indirect operating expenses increased 18.2% to US$106.5 million from US$90.1 million in the equivalent prior year period.

Prospects: On Dec 26 2007, Co. has completed its approximately $2.0 million acquisition of Pan-Pacific Enterprises, Inc., an independent distributor of medical X-ray tubes, for the purpose of marketing, sales, and distribution of its X-ray imaging products in China. Meanwhile, Co. anticipates that net orders and revenue in its Oncology Systems business segment to continue to benefit mainly from image guided radiation therapy products, its radiosurgical device, Novalis Tx, as well as from its Dec 2007 approved RapidArc™ radiotherapy technology in the long-term. For full fiscal year ending Sep 2008, Co. expects revenue to grow by about 14.0% with earnings of between $2.05 and $2.07 per diluted share.

Financial Data (US$ in Thousands)	3 Mos	09/28/2007	09/29/2006	09/30/2005	10/01/2004	09/26/2003	09/27/2002	09/28/2001
Earnings Per Share	1.89	1.83	1.81	1.50	1.18	0.93	0.67	0.40
Cash Flow Per Share	2.72	2.36	1.54	1.91	1.69	1.55	1.16	0.90
Tang Book Value Per Share	5.21	4.92	5.21	4.11	3.74	3.71	3.04	2.93
Income Statement								
Total Revenue	458,533	1,776,624	1,597,820	1,382,557	1,235,523	1,041,557	873,092	773,643
EBITDA	92,982	367,322	338,979	332,134	281,152	218,632	164,826	125,015
Depn & Amortn	8,646	...	...	...	...	...	...	...
Income Before Taxes	85,850	342,539	318,682	308,326	257,303	201,368	146,259	107,040
Income Taxes	30,371	103,083	75,120	101,750	90,060	70,480	52,650	39,070
Net Income	55,479	239,456	245,091	206,576	167,243	130,888	93,609	54,250
Average Shares	127,793	130,622	135,439	137,835	142,215	142,152	140,478	136,912
Balance Sheet								
Current Assets	1,217,724	1,160,229	1,156,049	1,016,895	885,136	805,524	651,359	619,503
Total Assets	1,764,195	1,684,375	1,511,751	1,317,402	1,170,192	1,053,487	910,277	759,199
Current Liabilities	727,354	781,687	643,990	543,933	461,339	409,416	358,083	285,354
Long-Term Obligations	40,329	40,386	49,356	57,318	53,250	58,500	58,500	58,500
Total Liabilities	901,312	862,920	714,498	658,375	556,478	489,811	437,474	364,803
Stockholders' Equity	862,883	821,455	797,253	659,027	613,714	563,676	472,803	394,396
Shares Outstanding	125,486	125,215	129,721	130,715	134,045	135,942	135,580	134,720
Statistical Record								
Return on Assets %	15.11	15.03	17.37	16.65	14.80	13.37	11.24	7.99
Return on Equity %	29.60	29.67	33.75	32.55	27.95	25.33	21.65	16.37
EBITDA Margin %	20.28	20.68	21.22	24.02	22.76	20.99	18.88	16.16
Net Margin %	12.10	13.48	15.34	14.94	13.54	12.57	10.72	7.01
Asset Turnover	1.14	1.11	1.13	1.11	1.09	1.06	1.05	1.14
Current Ratio	1.67	1.48	1.80	1.87	1.92	1.97	1.82	2.17
Debt to Equity	0.05	0.05	0.06	0.09	0.09	0.10	0.12	0.15
Price Range	53.01-37.82	54.86-37.82	60.63-36.79	43.57-32.63	46.06-28.25	31.15-21.00	23.45-15.04	19.20-10.64
P/E Ratio	28.05-20.01	29.98-20.67	33.50-20.33	29.05-21.75	39.04-23.94	33.86-22.83	35.00-22.44	47.99-26.60

Address: 3100 Hansen Way, Palo Alto, CA 94304-1038
Telephone: 650-493-4000
Fax: 650-493-0307

Web Site: www.varian.com
Officers: Richard M. Levy - Chmn., C.E.O. Timothy E. Guertin - Pres., C.O.O.

Auditors: PricewaterhouseCoopers LLP
Transfer Agents: First Chicago Trust Company of New York, Jersey City, NJ

VECTREN CORP

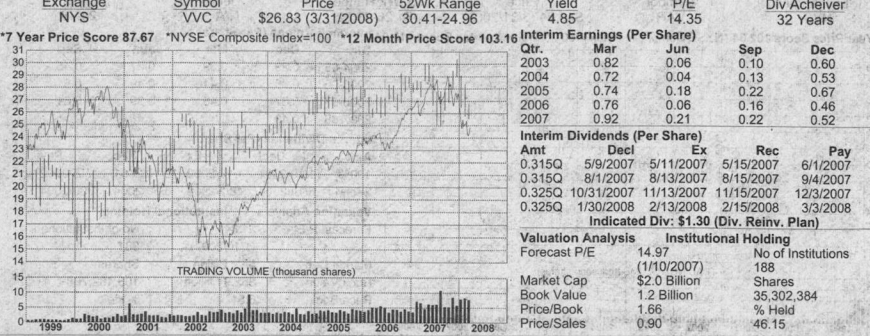

Exchange	Symbol	Price	52Wk Range	Yield	P/E	Div Acheiver
NYS	VVC	$26.83 (3/31/2008)	30.41-24.96	4.85	14.35	32 Years

*7 Year Price Score 87.67 ***NYSE Composite Index=100** ***12 Month Price Score 103.16**

Interim Earnings (Per Share)

Qtr.	Mar	Jun	Sep	Dec
2003	0.82	0.06	0.10	0.60
2004	0.72	0.04	0.13	0.53
2005	0.74	0.18	0.22	0.67
2006	0.76	0.06	0.16	0.46
2007	0.92	0.21	0.22	0.52

Interim Dividends (Per Share)

Amt	Decl	Ex	Rec	Pay
0.315Q	5/9/2007	5/11/2007	5/15/2007	6/1/2007
0.315Q	8/1/2007	8/13/2007	8/15/2007	9/4/2007
0.325Q	10/31/2007	11/13/2007	11/15/2007	12/3/2007
0.325Q	1/30/2008	2/13/2008	2/15/2008	3/3/2008

Indicated Div: $1.30 (Div. Reinv. Plan)

Valuation Analysis — **Institutional Holding**

Forecast P/E	14.97 (1/10/2007)	No of Institutions 188
Market Cap	$2.0 Billion	Shares
Book Value	1.2 Billion	35,302,384
Price/Book	1.66	% Held
Price/Sales	0.90	46.15

TRADING VOLUME (thousand shares)

Business Summary: Electricity (MIC: 7.1 SIC: 4932 NAIC: 221210)

Vectren is an energy holding company. Co.'s wholly owned subsidiary, Vectren Utility Holdings, Inc. (Utility Holdings), serves as the intermediate holding company for three operating public utilities: Indiana Gas Company, Inc., which provides energy delivery services to natural gas customers in central and southern Indiana; Southern Indiana Gas and Electric Co., which provides energy delivery services to electric and gas customers in southwestern Indiana; and the Ohio operations, which provide energy delivery services to natural gas customers in west central Ohio. Utility Holdings also has other assets that provide information technology and other services to the three utilities.

Recent Developments: For the year ended Dec 31 2007, net income increased 31.5% to US$143.1 million from US$108.8 million in the prior year. Revenues were US$2.28 billion, up 11.8% from US$2.04 billion the year before. Operating income was US$260.5 million versus US$220.5 million in the prior year, an increase of 18.1%. Direct operating expenses rose 5.5% to US$1.31 billion from US$1.24 billion in the comparable period the year before. Indirect operating expenses increased 22.8% to US$711.7 million from US$579.4 million in the equivalent prior-year period.

Prospects: Looking ahead, Co. expects continued earnings growth due to several factors which include the anticipation that its utility business should benefit from its Aug 2007 rate relief plan. Co. also believes that its nonutility businesses are well-positioned for long-term growth, reflecting the growing markets for its infrastructure services and its earnings reinvestment in firm gas storage capacity and new coal mine reserves. Meanwhile, Co. is projecting 2008 earnings of $1.85 to $2.05 per share, based on the expected normal weather in its electric and Ohio service territories and slightly lower volatility in the wholesale natural gas markets affecting its ProLiance Holdings, LLC affiliate.

Financial Data

(US$ in Thousands)	12/31/2007	12/31/2006	12/31/2005	12/31/2004	12/31/2003	12/31/2002	12/31/2001	12/31/2000
Earnings Per Share	1.87	1.43	1.80	1.42	1.57	1.68	0.95	1.17
Cash Flow Per Share	3.93	4.10	3.55	3.18	2.51	4.32	2.75	0.66
Tang Book Value Per Share	13.05	12.30	12.32	11.70	11.46	9.83	9.68	8.69
Dividends Per Share	1.270	1.230	1.190	1.150	1.110	1.070	1.030	0.740
Dividend Payout %	67.91	86.01	66.11	80.99	70.70	63.69	108.42	63.25
Income Statement								
Total Revenue	2,281,900	2,041,600	2,028,000	1,689,800	1,587,700	1,804,300	2,170,000	1,648,690
EBITDA	495,800	397,800	416,700	357,200	344,200	341,100	293,700	270,070
Income Before Taxes	219,200	139,200	181,000	147,000	149,000	153,400	87,400	107,276
Income Taxes	76,000	30,300	44,100	39,000	37,700	38,900	18,600	34,232
Net Income	143,100	108,800	136,800	107,900	111,200	114,000	63,600	72,040
Average Shares	76,600	76,200	76,100	75,900	70,800	67,900	66,900	61,380
Balance Sheet								
Net PPE	2,860,000	2,679,900	2,492,200	2,385,400	2,226,000	1,876,100	1,776,700	1,659,238
Total Assets	4,296,400	4,091,600	3,868,100	3,586,900	3,353,400	2,926,500	2,856,800	2,909,187
Long-Term Obligations	1,245,400	1,208,000	1,198,000	1,016,600	1,072,800	954,200	1,014,000	631,954
Total Liabilities	3,062,700	2,917,400	2,724,800	2,492,000	2,281,500	2,056,300	2,007,700	2,160,538
Stockholders' Equity	1,233,700	1,174,200	1,143,300	1,094,800	1,071,700	869,900	848,600	731,684
Shares Outstanding	76,300	76,100	76,000	75,900	75,600	67,900	67,700	61,419
Statistical Record								
Return on Assets %	3.41	2.73	3.67	3.10	3.54	3.94	2.21	2.94
Return on Equity %	11.89	9.39	12.22	9.93	11.45	13.27	8.05	9.97
EBITDA Margin %	21.73	19.48	20.55	21.14	21.68	18.90	13.53	16.38
Net Margin %	6.27	5.33	6.75	6.39	7.00	6.32	2.93	4.37
PPE Turnover	0.82	0.79	0.83	0.73	0.77	0.99	1.26	1.07
Asset Turnover	0.54	0.51	0.54	0.49	0.51	0.62	0.75	0.67
Debt to Equity	1.01	1.03	1.05	0.93	1.00	1.10	1.19	0.86
Price Range	30.41-24.96	29.25-25.61	29.32-25.39	27.08-22.90	26.00-20.01	25.87-18.69	24.19-19.90	26.50-15.13
P/E Ratio	16.26-13.35	20.45-17.91	16.29-14.11	19.07-16.13	16.56-12.75	15.40-11.13	25.46-20.95	22.65-12.93
Average Yield %	4.52	4.52	4.35	4.61	4.81	4.49	4.70	3.79

Address: One Vectren Square, Evansville, IN 47708	**Web Site:** www.vectren.com	**Auditors:** Deloitte & Touche LLP
Telephone: 812-491-4000	**Officers:** Niel C. Ellerbrook - Chmn., Pres., C.E.O. Jerome A. Benkert Jr. - Exec. V.P., C.F.O.	**Investor Contact:** 800-227-8625
Fax: 812-491-4149		**Transfer Agents:** National City Bank, Cleveland, OH

VENTAS, INC.

Exchange	Symbol	Price	52Wk Range	Yield	P/E
NYS	VTR	$44.91 (3/31/2008)	46.80-31.51	4.56	19.96

*7 Year Price Score 129.15 *NYSE Composite Index=100 *12 Month Price Score 113.47

TRADING VOLUME (thousand shares)

Interim Earnings (Per Share)

Qtr.	Mar	Jun	Sep	Dec
2003	0.47	0.20	0.40	0.96
2004	0.28	0.30	0.30	0.55
2005	0.32	0.30	0.28	0.46
2006	0.28	0.28	0.31	0.38
2007	0.42	1.48	0.21	0.18

Interim Dividends (Per Share)

Amt	Decl	Ex	Rec	Pay
0.475Q	6/6/2007	6/14/2007	6/18/2007	6/29/2007
0.475Q	9/5/2007	9/13/2007	9/17/2007	9/28/2007
0.475Q	11/27/2007	12/5/2007	12/7/2007	12/28/2007
0.512Q	2/13/2008	3/4/2008	3/6/2008	3/28/2008

Indicated Div: $2.05

Valuation Analysis

	Institutional Holding
Forecast P/E N/A	No of Institutions 204
Market Cap $6.0 Billion	Shares
Book Value 1.8 Billion	99,208,144
Price/Book 3.29	% Held
Price/Sales 7.78	93.36

Business Summary: Property, Real Estate & Development (MIC: 8.3 SIC: 6798 NAIC: 525930)

Ventas is a real estate investment trust (REIT) with portfolio of seniors housing and healthcare-related properties, which include 253 seniors housing communities, 197 skilled nursing facilities, 42 hospitals and 27 medical office and other properties in 43 states and two Canadian provinces, including 77 seniors housing communities acquired from Sunrise REIT in Apr 2007. Excluding Co.'s medical office buildings and 79 of its seniors housing communities that are managed by Sunrise pursuant to long-term management agreements, Co. leases its properties to healthcare operating companies under triple-net or absolute-net leases that require the tenants to pay all property-related expenses.

Recent Developments: For the year ended Dec 31 2007, income from continuing operations increased 16.5% to US$146.7 million from US$126.0 million a year earlier. Net income increased 114.8% to US$282.3 million from US$131.4 million in the prior year. Revenues were US$771.8 million, up 85.6% from US$415.9 million the year before. Revenues from property income rose 88.7% to US$766.2 million from US$406.0 million in the corresponding earlier year.

Prospects: Co. remains committed with its efforts to expand its real estate portfolio by operator, property type, geography and reimbursement source through investments in, and acquisitions and/or development of, additional seniors housing and/or healthcare-related assets across a wide spectrum. For example, in Jan 2008, Co. purchased one seniors housing community located in Texas for $5.1 million and leased it to an affiliate of Capital Senior Living Corp. The lease provides Co. with an initial cash yield of 7.8% and an expected unlevered yield over the life of the lease of 8.6%. Meanwhile, for 2008, Co. expects net income of $1.36 to $1.43 per share and funds from operations of $1.70 per share.

Financial Data

(US$ in Thousands)	12/31/2007	12/31/2006	12/31/2005	12/31/2004	12/31/2003	12/31/2002	12/31/2001	12/31/2000
Earnings Per Share	2.25	1.25	1.36	1.43	2.03	0.93	0.73	(0.96)
Cash Flow Per Share	3.26	2.29	2.35	1.79	1.73	1.68	1.17	1.25
Tang Book Value Per Share	13.64	6.69	6.45	1.89	0.70	...	...	...
Dividends Per Share	1.900	1.580	1.440	1.300	1.070	0.950	0.920	0.910
Dividend Payout %	84.44	126.40	105.88	90.91	52.71	102.15	126.03	...
Income Statement								
Property Income	766,211	418,449	324,719	232,911	191,232	189,517	185,152	232,841
Non-Property Income	5,580	9,900	8,269	3,945	13,771	7,187	19,429	9,481
Total Revenue	771,791	428,349	332,988	236,856	205,003	196,704	204,581	242,322
Interest Expense	204,218	141,094	105,581	66,817	66,733	81,985	91,624	95,319
Income Before Taxes	120,351	...	...	100,173	96,734	50,688	54,283	(62,202)
Income Taxes	(28,042)	...	...	...	...	(2,200)	2,685	...
Net Income	282,318	131,430	130,583	120,900	162,753	65,706	50,566	(65,452)
Average Shares	123,012	104,731	95,775	84,352	80,094	70,290	69,363	68,131
Balance Sheet								
Total Assets	5,716,628	3,253,800	2,639,118	1,126,935	812,850	895,780	941,859	981,145
Long-Term Obligations	3,360,499	2,329,053	1,802,564	843,178	640,562	707,709	848,368	886,385
Total Liabilities	3,861,520	2,543,924	1,971,799	966,711	756,535	949,407	1,032,933	1,098,659
Stockholders' Equity	1,823,654	709,876	667,319	160,224	56,315	(53,627)	(91,074)	(117,514)
Shares Outstanding	133,651	106,137	103,523	84,599	80,791	78,878	68,885	68,436
Statistical Record								
Return on Assets %	6.29	4.46	6.93	12.43	19.05	7.15	5.26	N.M.
Return on Equity %	22.29	19.09	31.56	111.36	12,109.60	...	...	...
Net Margin %	36.58	30.68	39.22	51.04	79.39	33.40	24.72	(27.01)
Price Range	47.70-31.51	41.94-29.98	32.67-24.67	29.10-21.10	22.68-11.20	13.70-10.12	12.70-5.88	5.69-2.81
P/E Ratio	21.20-14.00	33.55-23.98	24.02-18.14	20.35-14.76	11.17-5.52	14.73-10.88	17.40-8.05	...
Average Yield %	4.60	4.50	4.97	5.13	6.95	7.58	9.11	21.53

Address: 10350 Ormsby Park Place, Suite 300, Louisville, KY 40223
Telephone: 502-357-9000
Fax: 502-569-7499

Web Site: www.ventasreit.com
Officers: Debra A. Cafaro - Chmn., Pres., C.E.O. Richard A. Schweinhart - Sr. V.P., C.F.O.

Auditors: Ernst & Young LLP
Transfer Agents: National City Bank, Cleveland, OH

VERIZON COMMUNICATIONS INC

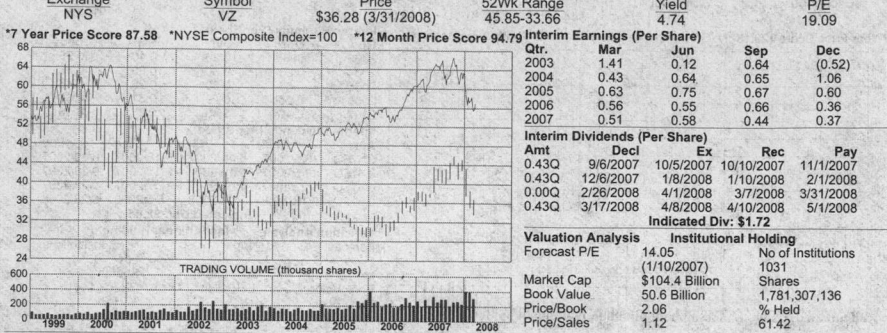

Exchange	Symbol	Price	52Wk Range	Yield	P/E
NYS	VZ	$36.28 (3/31/2008)	45.85-33.66	4.74	19.09

*7 Year Price Score 87.58   *NYSE Composite Index=100   *12 Month Price Score 94.79

Interim Earnings (Per Share)

Qtr.	Mar	Jun	Sep	Dec
2003	1.41	0.12	0.64	(0.52)
2004	0.43	0.64	0.65	1.06
2005	0.63	0.75	0.67	0.60
2006	0.56	0.55	0.66	0.36
2007	0.51	0.58	0.44	0.37

Interim Dividends (Per Share)

Amt	Decl	Ex	Rec	Pay
0.43Q	9/6/2007	10/5/2007	10/10/2007	11/1/2007
0.43Q	12/6/2007	1/8/2008	1/10/2008	2/1/2008
0.00Q	2/26/2008	4/1/2008	3/7/2008	3/31/2008
0.43Q	3/17/2008	4/8/2008	4/10/2008	5/1/2008

Indicated Div: $1.72

Valuation Analysis

		Institutional Holding	
Forecast P/E	14.05 (1/10/2007)	No of Institutions	1031
Market Cap	$104.4 Billion	Shares	1,781,307,136
Book Value	50.6 Billion	% Held	
Price/Book	2.06	61.42	
Price/Sales	1.12		

TRADING VOLUME (thousand shares)

Business Summary: Communications (MIC: 10.1 SIC: 4813 NAIC: 517110)

Verizon Communications is engaged in providing communications services. As of Dec 31 2007, Co. had two reportable segments: wireline and domestic wireless. Co.'s wireline business provides communications services, including voice, broadband video and data, Internet Protocol (IP) network services, network access, long distance and other services to consumers, carriers, businesses and government customers both domestically and globally. Co.'s wireline business also owns and operates IP networks. Co.'s domestic wireless business, which operates as Verizon Wireless, provides wireless voice and data products and services across the U.S.

Recent Developments: For the year ended Dec 31 2007, income from continuing operations increased 0.5% to US$5.51 billion from US$5.48 billion a year earlier. Net income decreased 10.9% to US$5.52 billion from US$6.20 billion in the prior year. Revenues were US$93.47 billion, up 6.0% from US$88.18 billion the year before. Operating income was US$15.58 billion versus US$13.37 billion in the prior year, an increase of 16.5%. Direct operating expenses rose 6.3% to US$37.55 billion from US$35.31 billion in the comparable period the year before. Indirect operating expenses increased 2.1% to US$40.34 billion from US$39.50 billion in the equivalent prior-year period.

Prospects: Co.'s recent improved top-line results are mainly due continued strong revenue growth within its Domestic Wireless segment. However, Co. is experiencing lower revenue in its Wireline segment driven by lower demand and usage of its basic local exchange and accompanying services. Moving forward, Co. anticipates devoting more resources to higher growth markets such as wireless, including wireless data, wireline broadband connections, including its fiber optics to the premises network, digital subscriber lines and other data services, as well as expanded strategic services to business markets, rather than to the traditional wireline voice market as part of its emphasis to grow its revenue.

Financial Data
(US$ in Thousands)

	12/31/2007	12/31/2006	12/31/2005	12/31/2004	12/31/2003	12/31/2002	12/31/2001	12/31/2000
Earnings Per Share	1.90	2.12	2.65	2.79	1.11	1.49	0.14	4.31
Cash Flow Per Share	8.88	8.28	7.96	7.86	8.16	8.10	7.30	5.82
Dividends Per Share	1.645	1.620	1.600	1.155	1.540	1.540	1.540	1.540
Dividend Payout %	86.58	76.42	60.38	41.40	138.74	103.36	1,100.00	35.73
Income Statement								
Total Revenue	93,469,000	88,144,000	75,112,000	71,283,000	67,752,000	67,625,000	67,190,000	64,707,000
EBITDA	25,530,000	24,847,000	26,714,000	26,290,000	21,079,000	22,862,000	19,792,000	33,570,000
Income Before Taxes	9,492,000	8,154,000	10,607,000	10,112,000	4,761,000	6,202,000	2,766,000	17,819,000
Income Taxes	3,982,000	2,674,000	3,210,000	2,851,000	1,252,000	1,618,000	2,176,000	7,009,000
Net Income	5,521,000	6,197,000	7,397,000	7,831,000	3,077,000	4,079,000	389,000	11,797,000
Average Shares	2,902,000	2,938,000	2,817,000	2,831,000	2,789,000	2,745,000	2,730,000	2,737,000
Balance Sheet								
Current Assets	18,698,000	22,538,000	16,448,000	19,479,000	18,293,000	20,921,000	23,187,000	22,121,000
Total Assets	186,959,000	188,804,000	168,130,000	165,958,000	165,968,000	167,468,000	170,795,000	164,735,000
Current Liabilities	24,741,000	32,280,000	25,063,000	23,129,000	26,570,000	27,047,000	38,020,000	34,236,000
Long-Term Obligations	28,203,000	28,646,000	31,869,000	35,674,000	39,413,000	44,791,000	45,657,000	42,491,000
Total Liabilities	136,378,000	140,269,000	128,450,000	128,398,000	132,502,000	134,852,000	138,256,000	130,157,000
Stockholders' Equity	50,581,000	48,535,000	39,680,000	37,560,000	33,466,000	32,616,000	32,539,000	34,578,000
Shares Outstanding	2,876,824	2,967,596	2,763,409	2,769,652	2,767,760	2,743,027	2,716,478	2,702,436
Statistical Record								
Return on Assets %	2.94	3.47	4.43	4.71	1.85	2.41	0.23	10.35
Return on Equity %	11.14	14.05	19.15	21.99	9.31	12.52	1.16	46.63
EBITDA Margin %	27.31	28.19	35.57	36.88	31.11	33.81	29.46	51.88
Net Margin %	5.91	7.03	9.85	10.99	4.54	6.03	0.58	18.23
Asset Turnover	0.50	0.49	0.45	0.43	0.41	0.40	0.40	0.57
Current Ratio	0.76	0.70	0.66	0.84	0.69	0.77	0.61	0.65
Debt to Equity	0.56	0.59	0.80	0.95	1.18	1.37	1.40	1.23
Price Range	45.85-35.51	37.24-29.13	38.84-27.99	40.48-32.72	42.25-30.20	48.52-26.30	54.80-44.10	62.50-38.71
P/E Ratio	24.13-18.69	17.56-13.74	14.66-10.56	14.51-11.73	38.06-27.21	32.56-17.65	391.43-315.01	14.50-8.98
Average Yield %	4.01	4.94	4.93	3.15	4.49	4.06	3.09	3.03

Address: 1095 Avenue of the Americas, New York, NY 10036
Telephone: 212-395-2121
Fax: 212-921-2917

Web Site: www.verizon.com
Officers: Ivan G. Seidenberg - Chmn., C.E.O.
Lawrence T. Babbio Jr. - Vice-Chmn., Pres.

Auditors: Ernst & Young LLP
Investor Contact: 212-395-1525

VF CORP.

Exchange	Symbol	Price	52Wk Range	Yield	P/E	Div Acheiver
NYS	VFC	$77.51 (3/31/2008)	95.65-63.79	2.99	14.85	35 Years

*7 Year Price Score 121.59 *NYSE Composite Index=100 *12 Month Price Score 100.66

Interim Earnings (Per Share)

Qtr.	Mar	Jun	Sep	Dec
2003	0.83	0.68	1.14	0.96
2004	0.93	0.80	1.38	1.10
2005	1.07	0.88	1.59	0.89
2006	1.14	0.88	1.75	0.95
2007	1.20	0.72	1.84	1.46

Interim Dividends (Per Share)

Amt	Decl	Ex	Rec	Pay
0.55Q	4/24/2007	6/6/2007	6/8/2007	6/18/2007
0.55Q	7/19/2007	9/6/2007	9/10/2007	9/20/2007
0.58Q	10/18/2007	12/6/2007	12/10/2007	12/20/2007
0.58Q	2/5/2008	3/6/2008	3/10/2008	3/20/2008

Indicated Div: $2.32 (Div. Reinv. Plan)

Valuation Analysis

		Institutional Holding
Forecast P/E	12.99	No of Institutions
	(1/10/2007)	357
Market Cap	$8.5 Billion	Shares
Book Value	3.6 Billion	100,652,064
Price/Book	2.38	% Held
Price/Sales	1.18	89.42

Business Summary: Apparel (MIC: 4.4 SIC: 2329 NAIC: 315228)

VF is an apparel company that is engaged in designing and manufacturing or sourcing from independent contractors a range of apparel and footwear for all ages. As of Dec 31 2007, Co. had five product categories that comprised of Jeanswear, Outdoor, Imagewear, Sportswear and Contemporary Brands. Co.'s products are marketed to consumers shopping in specialty stores, upscale and traditional department stores, national chains and mass merchants. Co.'s brand include. Lee®, Rustler®, Wrangler®, Wrangler Hero®, Timber Creek by Wrangler®, Riders®, JanSport®, The North Face®, Eastpak®, Vans®, Napapijri®, Reef®, Eagle Creek®, Kipling®, Red Kap®, John Varvatos®, and Nautica®.

Recent Developments: For the year ended Dec 29 2007, income from continuing operations increased 14.6% to US$613.2 million from US$535.1 million a year earlier. Net income increased 10.9% to US$591.6 million from US$533.5 million in the prior year. Revenues were US$7.22 billion, up 16.1% from US$6.22 billion the year before. Operating income was US$965.4 million versus US$826.1 million in the prior year, an increase of 16.9%. Direct operating expenses rose 16.1% to US$4.08 billion from US$3.52 billion in the comparable period the year before. Indirect operating expenses increased 16.0% to US$2.17 billion from US$1.87 billion in the equivalent prior-year period.

Prospects: For 2008, Co. expects revenues to increase 9.0% with organic growth in all of its segments. In detail, Co. expects Outdoor segment revenues to increase at a mid-teen percentage rate, with mid single-digit revenue growth in Imagewear segment and slightly lower growth in both Sportswear and Jeanswear segments. In addition, Co. expects Contemporary Brands segment revenues to be about $415.0 million in 2008. Moreover, Co. expects earnings per share from continuing operations to increase 10.0% in 2008, driven by top-line growth and margin expansion, particularly in its Outdoor and Jeanswear segments, while Sportswear segment margins are expected to remain relatively stable with 2007 levels.

Financial Data

(US$ in Thousands)	12/29/2007	12/30/2006	12/31/2005	01/01/2005	01/03/2004	01/04/2003	12/29/2001	12/30/2000
Earnings Per Share	5.22	4.72	4.44	4.21	3.61	(1.38)	1.19	2.21
Cash Flow Per Share	7.45	4.45	5.06	6.66	5.06	5.82	6.18	3.90
Tang Book Value Per Share	7.38	12.62	7.77	6.57	8.61	10.91	9.97	9.71
Dividends Per Share	2.230	1.940	1.100	1.050	1.010	0.970	0.930	0.890
Dividend Payout %	42.72	41.10	24.77	24.94	27.98		78.15	40.27
Income Statement								
Total Revenue	7,219,359	6,215,794	6,502,377	6,054,536	5,207,459	5,083,523	5,518,805	5,747,879
EBITDA	1,090,028	936,880	949,470	921,773	756,437	735,330	518,289	685,987
Income Before Taxes	905,570	777,238	770,813	712,120	598,506	561,728	262,801	431,533
Income Taxes	292,324	242,187	252,278	237,418	200,573	197,300	124,971	164,417
Net Income	591,621	533,516	506,702	474,702	397,933	(154,543)	137,830	260,334
Average Shares	113,348	113,040	114,192	112,730	110,323	112,336	114,764	117,218
Balance Sheet								
Current Assets	2,645,129	2,578,010	2,365,376	2,378,568	2,208,531	2,074,540	2,031,420	2,110,096
Total Assets	6,446,685	5,465,693	5,171,071	5,004,278	4,245,552	3,503,151	4,103,016	4,358,156
Current Liabilities	1,134,387	1,014,848	1,152,143	1,372,214	871,857	874,844	813,833	1,006,200
Long-Term Obligations	1,144,810	635,359	647,728	556,639	956,383	602,287	904,035	905,036
Total Liabilities	2,869,856	2,200,521	2,339,532	2,464,984	2,264,258	1,808,401	1,944,589	2,117,860
Stockholders' Equity	3,576,829	3,265,172	2,808,213	2,513,241	1,951,307	1,657,848	2,112,796	2,191,813
Shares Outstanding	109,797	112,184	110,107	111,388	108,170	108,525	109,998	112,258
Statistical Record								
Return on Assets %	9.96	10.06	9.99	10.29	10.30	N.M.	3.27	6.23
Return on Equity %	17.34	17.62	19.10	21.32	22.11	N.M.	6.42	11.99
EBITDA Margin %	15.10	15.07	14.60	15.22	14.53	14.46	9.39	11.93
Net Margin %	8.19	8.58	7.79	7.84	7.64	N.M.	2.50	4.53
Asset Turnover	1.22	1.17	1.28	1.31	1.35	1.32	1.31	1.37
Current Ratio	2.33	2.54	2.05	1.73	2.53	2.37	2.50	2.10
Debt to Equity	0.32	0.19	0.23	0.22	0.49	0.36	0.43	0.41
Price Range	95.65-68.90	82.60-53.66	61.52-50.85	55.38-42.36	44.05-32.85	45.33-32.09	41.99-28.61	36.56-22.00
P/E Ratio	18.32-13.20	17.50-11.37	13.86-11.45	13.15-10.06	12.20-9.10	...	35.29-24.04	16.54-9.95
Average Yield %	2.68	2.93	1.93	2.17	2.64	2.43	2.56	3.37

Address: 105 Corporate Center Boulevard, Greensboro, NC 27408	**Web Site:** www.vfc.com	**Auditors:** PricewaterhouseCoopers LLP
Telephone: 336-424-6000	**Officers:** Mackey J. McDonald - Chmn., Pres., C.E.O. Robert K. Shearer - Sr. V.P., Fin., C.F.O.	**Transfer Agents:** EquiServe Trust Company, Jersey City, NJ
Fax: 336-547-7634		

VIACOM INC

*7 Year Price Score N/A   *NYSE Composite Index=100   *12 Month Price Score 105.55

Interim Earnings (Per Share)

Qtr.	Mar	Jun	Sep	Dec
2005	0.47	0.47	0.56	0.17
2006	0.43	0.61	0.50	0.68
2007	0.29	0.63	0.96	0.85

Interim Dividends (Per Share)

No Dividends Paid

Valuation Analysis   **Institutional Holding**

Forecast P/E	N/A	No of Institutions
		96
Market Cap	$25.5 Billion	Shares
Book Value	7.1 Billion	8,898,305
Price/Book	3.59	% Held
Price/Sales	1.90	15.01

TRADING VOLUME (thousand shares)

Business Summary: Media (MIC: 13.1 SIC: 4841 NAIC: 515210)

Viacom is a worldwide entertainment content company, which operated its business through two reportable operating segments as of Dec 31 2007. Co.'s Media Networks segment consists of the businesses of MTV Networks (MTV) and the businesses of BET Networks (BET). Through MTV and BET, Co.'s media networks businesses own and operate program services, websites and other digital media services in the U.S. and abroad. Co.'s Filmed Entertainment segment produces, finances and distributes motion pictures under the Paramount Pictures, DreamWorks Pictures, Paramount Vantage, Paramount Classics, MTV Films and Nickelodeon Movies brands.

Recent Developments: For the year ended Dec 31 2007, income from continuing operations increased 4.0% to US$1.63 billion from US$1.57 billion a year earlier. Net income increased 15.5% to US$1.84 billion from US$1.59 billion in the prior year. Revenues were US$13.42 billion, up 18.1% from US$11.36 billion the year before. Operating income was US$2.94 billion versus US$2.77 billion in the prior year, an increase of 6.1%. Indirect operating expenses increased 22.0% to US$10.49 billion from US$8.59 billion in the equivalent prior-year period.

Prospects: Co. is focused on expanding its Media Networks segment brands through the introduction of hit programming and other content, including games, as well as the expansion of its online and wireless platforms portfolio. Also, Co. plans to increase its market presence and profitability in its Filmed Entertainment segment through the development of franchise and branded films, as well as the improvement of revenue streams, such as making library product available online, while capitalizing on its Paramount, DreamWorks, and Paramount Vantage labels as well as on various media networks brands. Hence, Co. expects to deliver low, double-digit annual growth in net earnings from 2008 through 2010.

Financial Data
(US$ in Thousands)

	12/31/2007	12/31/2006	12/31/2005	12/31/2004	12/31/2003
Earnings Per Share	2.72	2.22	1.67	0.39	0.45
Cash Flow Per Share	2.63	3.17	2.17	2.64	...
Income Statement					
Total Revenue	13,423,100	11,466,500	9,609,600	8,132,200	7,304,400
EBITDA	7,183,200	5,848,500	2,596,400	2,516,700	2,175,100
Income Before Taxes	2,579,200	2,314,800	2,318,300	2,244,200	1,956,200
Income Taxes	929,000	737,800	1,020,000	808,200	787,600
Net Income	1,838,100	1,592,100	1,256,900	293,700	338,500
Average Shares	675,600	716,200	751,600	751,600	751,600
Balance Sheet					
Current Assets	4,832,600	4,211,100	3,512,800	2,626,300	...
Total Assets	22,904,100	21,796,700	19,115,600	18,440,800	...
Current Liabilities	5,273,400	4,616,800	3,268,600	2,785,600	...
Long-Term Obligations	8,059,500	7,584,000	5,702,100	291,700	...
Total Liabilities	15,756,200	14,603,500	11,325,300	4,964,200	...
Stockholders' Equity	7,111,200	7,166,200	7,787,900	13,465,200	...
Shares Outstanding	644,800	693,200	751,600	...	...
Statistical Record					
Return on Assets %	8.22	7.78	6.69	...	...
Return on Equity %	25.75	21.29	11.83	...	...
EBITDA Margin %	53.51	51.01	27.02	30.95	29.78
Net Margin %	13.69	13.88	13.08	3.61	4.63
Asset Turnover	0.60	0.56	0.51	...	...
Current Ratio	0.92	0.91	1.07	0.94	...
Debt to Equity	1.13	1.06	0.73	0.02	...
Price Range	44.95-37.12	43.57-33.10	44.90-40.00	...	...
P/E Ratio	16.53-13.65	19.63-14.91	26.89-23.95	...	...

Address: 1515 Broadway, New York, NY 10036 Telephone: 212-258-6000	Web Site: www.viacom.com Officers: Sumner M. Redstone - Exec. Chmn. Philippe P. Bauman - Pres., C.E.O.	Auditors: PricewaterhouseCoopers LLP

VISHAY INTERTECHNOLOGY, INC.

Exchange	Symbol	Price	52Wk Range	Yield	P/E
NYS	VSH	$9.06 (3/31/2008)	18.17-8.50	N/A	13.13

*7 Year Price Score 68.30   *NYSE Composite Index=100   *12 Month Price Score 76.81

Interim Earnings (Per Share)

Qtr.	Mar	Jun	Sep	Dec
2003	0.04	0.02	0.04	0.07
2004	0.20	0.22	0.13	(0.28)
2005	0.03	0.05	0.11	0.14
2006	0.20	0.22	0.17	0.14
2007	0.25	0.22	0.19	0.03

Interim Dividends (Per Share)

No Dividends Paid

Valuation Analysis

		Institutional Holding	
Forecast P/E	N/A	No of Institutions	242
Market Cap	$1.7 Billion	Shares	
Book Value	3.4 Billion		149,995,472
Price/Book	0.50	% Held	
Price/Sales	0.60		81.31

TRADING VOLUME (thousand shares)

Business Summary: Electrical (MIC: 11.14 SIC: 3676 NAIC: 334415)

Vishay Intertechnology is an international manufacturer and supplier of semiconductors and passive electronic components. Co. has two reportable segments: the Semiconductors segment includes diodes, transistors, rectifiers, power integrated circuits (ICs), infrared (IR) transceivers, IR sensors and optocouplers; and, the Passive Components segment includes resistors, capacitors, transducers and inductors. Electronic components manufactured by Co. are used in all types of electronic products, including those in the computer, telecommunications, military/aerospace, industrial, automotive, medical, and consumer electronics industries.

Recent Developments: For the year ended Dec 31 2007, income from continuing operations increased 0.4% to US$140.4 million from US$139.7 million a year earlier. Net income decreased 6.4% to US$130.8 million from US$139.7 million in the prior year. Revenues were US$2.83 billion, up 9.8% from US$2.58 billion the year before. Operating income was US$218.4 million versus US$209.2 million in the prior year, an increase of 4.4%. Direct operating expenses rose 11.2% to US$2.14 billion from US$1.92 billion in the comparable period the year before. Indirect operating expenses increased 5.9% to US$476.5 million from US$449.9 million in the equivalent prior-year period.

Prospects: Co. expects its revenues of $720.0 million to $740.0 million for the quarter ending Mar 2008, with higher margins. Meanwhile, Co. anticipates some restructuring projects in 2008, which should result in higher profitability through improved gross margins and lower selling, general and administrative expenses. Specifically, Co. projects annual pretax savings resulting from its Apr 2005 restructuring projects to be $50.0 million, of which it estimates to begin attaining an additional $10.0 million of savings from these programs in 2008. As part of its growth strategy, Co. continues to seek acquisition targets in niche businesses for passive components, semiconductors and weighing systems.

Financial Data
(US$ in Thousands)

	12/31/2007	12/31/2006	12/31/2005	12/31/2004	12/31/2003	12/31/2002	12/31/2001	12/31/2000
Earnings Per Share	0.69	0.73	0.34	0.27	0.17	(0.58)	...	3.77
Cash Flow Per Share	1.91	1.90	1.14	1.42	1.60	2.30	1.14	4.00
Tang Book Value Per Share	7.98	7.85	6.77	7.29	5.74	5.51	7.57	11.15
Income Statement								
Total Revenue	2,833,266	2,581,477	2,296,521	2,413,576	2,170,597	1,822,813	1,655,346	2,465,066
EBITDA	429,588	398,327	286,382	298,147	271,084	101,512	172,274	843,504
Income Before Taxes	205,664	191,550	77,772	70,017	46,426	(100,045)	10,103	690,225
Income Taxes	64,133	50,836	11,737	13,729	11,528	(16,900)	5,695	148,186
Net Income	130,764	139,736	62,274	44,696	26,842	(92,614)	513	517,864
Average Shares	198,226	210,316	189,321	165,938	160,443	159,413	142,514	137,063
Balance Sheet								
Current Assets	1,742,801	1,727,247	1,606,632	1,682,420	1,637,253	1,473,693	1,574,627	1,474,874
Total Assets	4,995,233	4,691,896	4,527,591	4,638,590	4,572,513	4,315,159	3,951,523	2,783,658
Current Liabilities	596,928	534,414	470,166	517,738	587,361	576,237	478,593	417,674
Long-Term Obligations	607,237	608,434	751,553	752,145	836,606	706,316	605,031	140,467
Total Liabilities	1,638,460	1,611,083	1,671,739	1,865,255	2,058,479	1,956,372	1,584,978	949,803
Stockholders' Equity	3,356,775	3,080,813	2,855,852	2,773,335	2,514,034	2,358,787	2,366,545	1,833,855
Shares Outstanding	186,342	184,463	184,141	166,102	160,050	159,680	159,291	137,926
Statistical Record								
Return on Assets %	2.70	3.03	1.36	0.97	0.60	N.M.	0.02	20.22
Return on Equity %	4.06	4.71	2.21	1.69	1.10	N.M.	0.02	36.27
EBITDA Margin %	15.16	15.43	12.47	12.35	12.49	5.57	10.41	34.22
Net Margin %	4.62	5.41	2.71	1.85	1.24	N.M.	0.03	21.01
Asset Turnover	0.58	0.56	0.50	0.52	0.49	0.44	0.49	0.96
Current Ratio	2.92	3.23	3.42	3.25	2.79	2.56	3.29	3.53
Debt to Equity	0.18	0.20	0.26	0.27	0.33	0.30	0.26	0.08
Price Range	18.17-11.23	17.41-12.69	15.02-10.55	24.88-11.57	22.90-8.90	26.00-7.03	27.75-14.44	61.17-14.00
P/E Ratio	26.33-16.28	23.85-17.38	44.18-31.03	92.15-42.85	134.71-52.35	...	N.M.	16.22-3.71

Address: 63 Lincoln Highway, Malvern, PA 19355-2143
Telephone: 610-644-1300
Fax: 610-296-0657

Web Site: www.vishay.com
Officers: Felix Zandman - Chmn., Chief Tech. & Bus. Devel. Officer   Marc Zandman - Vice-Chmn.

Auditors: Ernst & Young LLP
Investor Contact: 610-644-1300
Transfer Agents: American Stock Transfer & Trust Co., New York, NY

VISTEON CORP.

Exchange	Symbol	Price	52Wk Range	Yield	P/E
NYS	VC	$3.76 (3/31/2008)	10.08-3.25	N/A	N/A

*7 Year Price Score 52.49 *NYSE Composite Index=100 *12 Month Price Score 69.02

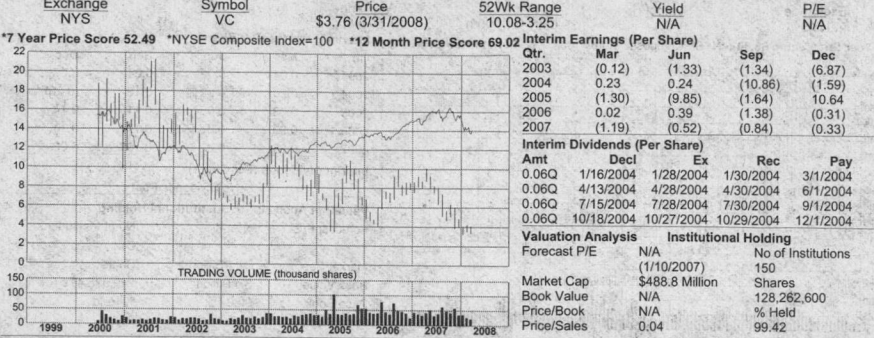

Interim Earnings (Per Share)

Qtr.	Mar	Jun	Sep	Dec
2003	(0.12)	(1.33)	(1.34)	(6.87)
2004	0.23	0.24	(10.86)	(1.59)
2005	(1.30)	(9.85)	(1.64)	10.64
2006	0.02	0.39	(1.38)	(0.31)
2007	(1.19)	(0.52)	(0.84)	(0.33)

Interim Dividends (Per Share)

Amt	Decl	Ex	Rec	Pay
0.06Q	1/16/2004	1/28/2004	1/30/2004	3/1/2004
0.06Q	4/13/2004	4/28/2004	4/30/2004	6/1/2004
0.06Q	7/15/2004	7/28/2004	7/30/2004	9/1/2004
0.06Q	10/18/2004	10/27/2004	10/29/2004	12/1/2004

Valuation Analysis / **Institutional Holding**

Forecast P/E	N/A	No of Institutions
	(1/10/2007)	150
Market Cap	$488.8 Million	Shares
Book Value	N/A	128,262,600
Price/Book	N/A	% Held
Price/Sales	0.04	99.42

TRADING VOLUME (thousand shares)

Business Summary: Automotive (MIC: 15.1 SIC: 3714 NAIC: 336399)

Visteon is a global supplier of automotive systems, modules and components to global vehicle manufacturers and the automotive aftermarket. Co. operates through four product groups: Climate, which includes facilities that manufacture climate products, including air handling modules and power train cooling modules; Electronics, which includes facilities that manufacture electronics products, including audio systems, infotainment systems, and electronic control modules; Interior, which includes facilities that manufacture interior products, including instrument panels and cockpit modules; and Other, which includes facilities that manufacture fuel products and power train products.

Recent Developments: For the year ended Dec 31 2007, net loss amounted to US$372.0 million versus a net loss of US$163.0 million in the prior year. Revenues were US$11.27 billion, up 0.1% from US$11.25 billion the year before. Operating loss was US$168.0 million versus an income of US$29.0 million in the prior year. Direct operating expenses rose 1.8% to US$10.69 billion from US$10.50 billion in the comparable period the year before. Indirect operating expenses increased 2.3% to US$741.0 million from US$724.0 million in the equivalent prior-year period.

Prospects: On Feb 1 2008, Co. announced the sale of its non-core North American-based aftermarket underhood and remanufacturing operations, including a manufacturing plant in Sparta, TN. and two Reynosa, Mexico. The Sparta facility manufactures starters and alternators for aftermarket customers and the two Reynosa facilities manufacture aftermarket climate products including radiators, compressors and condensers. This transaction reflects another step in Co.'s plan to restructure, improve and grow its business by focusing on strategic product lines, including enhanced climate, interiors and electronics products. Meanwhile, Co. anticipates product sales of about $9.70 billion in 2008.

Financial Data

(US$ in Thousands)	12/31/2007	12/31/2006	12/31/2005	12/31/2004	12/31/2003	12/31/2002	12/31/2001	12/31/2000
Earnings Per Share	(2.87)	(1.28)	(2.14)	(11.96)	(9.65)	(2.75)	(0.91)	2.08
Cash Flow Per Share	2.26	2.20	3.31	3.33	2.94	8.97	3.33	(4.04)
Tang Book Value Per Share	...	...	...	3.13	14.40	22.73	25.12	26.76
Dividends Per Share	...	...	...	0.240	0.240	0.240	0.240	0.120
Dividend Payout %	...	...	...	...	...	...	...	5.77
Income Statement								
Total Revenue	11,266,000	11,418,000	16,976,000	18,657,000	17,660,000	18,395,000	17,843,000	19,467,000
EBITDA	351,000	478,000	554,000	271,000	(399,000)	594,000	573,000	1,173,000
Income Before Taxes	(285,000)	(111,000)	(173,000)	(499,000)	(1,150,000)	(117,000)	(169,000)	439,000
Income Taxes	20,000	25,000	64,000	965,000	34,000	(58,000)	(72,000)	143,000
Net Income	(372,000)	(163,000)	(270,000)	(1,499,000)	(1,213,000)	(352,000)	(118,000)	270,000
Average Shares	129,400	127,900	126,000	125,300	125,800	127,700	131,000	130,000
Balance Sheet								
Current Assets	4,072,000	3,565,000	3,345,000	4,444,000	4,410,000	4,737,000	4,753,000	5,005,000
Total Assets	7,205,000	6,938,000	6,736,000	10,309,000	10,964,000	11,170,000	11,078,000	11,325,000
Current Liabilities	2,528,000	2,568,000	2,959,000	3,843,000	3,572,000	3,466,000	3,435,000	3,804,000
Long-Term Obligations	2,745,000	2,128,000	1,509,000	1,513,000	1,467,000	1,298,000	1,293,000	1,397,000
Total Liabilities	7,295,000	7,126,000	6,784,000	9,902,000	9,106,000	8,192,000	7,787,000	7,820,000
Stockholders' Equity	(90,000)	(188,000)	(48,000)	407,000	1,858,000	2,978,000	3,291,000	3,505,000
Shares Outstanding	130,000	129,000	129,000	130,000	129,000	131,000	131,000	131,000
Statistical Record								
Return on Assets %	N.M.	N.M.	N.M.	N.M.	N.M.	N.M.	N.M.	2.27
Return on Equity %	...	...	N.M.	N.M.	N.M.	N.M.	N.M.	10.76
EBITDA Margin %	3.12	4.19	3.26	1.45	N.M.	3.23	3.21	6.03
Net Margin %	N.M.	N.M.	N.M.	N.M.	N.M.	N.M.	N.M.	1.39
Asset Turnover	1.59	1.67	1.99	1.75	1.60	1.65	1.59	1.63
Current Ratio	1.61	1.39	1.13	1.16	1.23	1.37	1.38	1.32
Debt to Equity	...	...	...	3.72	0.79	0.44	0.39	0.40
Price Range	10.08-3.84	9.99-4.07	10.86-3.40	12.35-6.61	10.43-5.60	16.55-6.57	21.32-10.99	19.25-9.81
P/E Ratio	...	...	...	...	...	...	...	9.25-4.72
Average Yield %	...	...	...	2.46	3.50	2.00	1.54	0.81

Address: 17000 Rotunda Drive, Dearborn, MI 48120
Telephone: 313-755-3699
Fax: 313-755-2776

Web Site: www.visteon.com
Officers: Michael F. Johnston - Chmn., C.E.O.
Donald J. Stebbins - Pres., C.O.O.

Auditors: PricewaterhouseCoopers LLP
Transfer Agents: Bank of New York

VORNADO REALTY TRUST

Exchange	Symbol	Price	52Wk Range	Yield	P/E	Div Achiever
NYS	VNO	$86.21 (3/31/2008)	122.55-78.74	4.18	26.69	14 Years

*7 Year Price Score 117.30 *NYSE Composite Index=100 *12 Month Price Score 90.84

Interim Earnings (Per Share)

Qtr.	Mar	Jun	Sep	Dec
2003	0.77	0.71	0.60	1.71
2004	0.59	1.21	0.79	1.76
2005	1.39	1.25	0.19	0.71
2006	0.91	0.99	0.76	0.69
2007	0.96	0.96	0.74	0.58

Interim Dividends (Per Share)

Amt	Decl	Ex	Rec	Pay
0.85Q	2/22/2007	4/27/2007	5/1/2007	5/21/2007
0.85Q	5/17/2007	8/7/2007	8/9/2007	8/22/2007
0.90Q	7/26/2007	10/10/2007	10/12/2007	10/26/2007
0.90Q	1/16/2008	1/28/2008	1/30/2008	2/20/2008

Indicated Div: $3.60

Valuation Analysis

		Institutional Holding	
Forecast P/E	49.85	No of Institutions	379
	(1/10/2007)		
Market Cap	$13.2 Billion	Shares	128,729,848
Book Value	6.1 Billion	% Held	84.91
Price/Book	2.16		
Price/Sales	4.03		

Business Summary: Property, Real Estate & Development (MIC: 8.3 SIC: 6798 NAIC: 525930)

Vornado Realty Trust is a fully-integrated real estate investment trust. As of Dec 31 2007, Co. owned directly or indirectly all or portions of 111 office properties aggregating about 33.6 million square feet in the New York City metropolitan area and in the Washington, DC and Northern Virginia areas; 177 retail properties in 21 states, Washington, DC and Puerto Rico; nine properties in five states and Washington, DC aggregating about 9.1 million square feet of showroom and office space; a 47.6% interest in Americold Realty Trust; a 32.7% interest in Toys "R" Us, Inc.; 32.8% of the common stock of Alexander's, Inc.; as well as various other interests in other real estate.

Recent Developments: For the year ended Dec 31 2007, income from continuing operations decreased 4.3% to US$577.0 million from US$603.1 million a year earlier. Net income increased 1.6% to US$568.9 million from US$560.1 million in the prior year. Revenues were US$3.27 billion, up 21.1% from US$2.70 billion the year before. Revenues from property income rose 27.2% to US$2.31 billion from US$1.82 billion in the corresponding earlier year.

Prospects: Going forward, Co. remains focused on developing and redeveloping its existing properties. For instance, Co. expects to complete the expansion of 60,000 square feet of free-standing retail space in the Monmouth Mall in Eatontown, NJ, in 2008, of which Co. owns a 50.0% interest. In addition, Co. plans to redevelop the South Hills Mall in Poughkeepsie, NY into a 575,000 square foot strip shopping center, which is expected to be completed in 2009. Additionally, Co. intends to redevelop, reposition and re-tenant the Springfield Mall in Springfield, VA.

Financial Data
(US$ in Thousands)

	12/31/2007	12/31/2006	12/31/2005	12/31/2004	12/31/2003	12/31/2002	12/31/2001	12/31/2000
Earnings Per Share	3.23	3.35	3.50	4.35	3.80	1.91	2.47	2.20
Cash Flow Per Share	4.59	5.80	5.70	5.29	4.71	4.72	4.35	2.81
Tang Book Value Per Share	34.58	35.22	31.38	26.95	23.90	21.74	21.22	18.40
Dividends Per Share	3.450	3.790	3.900	3.030	2.910	2.660	2.629	1.970
Dividend Payout %	106.81	113.13	111.43	70.11	76.58	139.27	106.44	89.55
Income Statement								
Property Income	2,313,312	1,829,359	1,605,812	1,535,871	1,440,256	1,408,881	975,113	815,134
Non-Property Income	957,317	882,736	941,816	171,391	62,799	26,189	10,660	11,398
Total Revenue	3,270,629	2,712,095	2,547,628	1,707,262	1,503,055	1,435,070	985,773	826,532
Income Before Taxes	587,502	...	...	...	...	...	...	...
Income Taxes	10,530							
Net Income	568,906	560,140	539,604	592,917	460,703	232,903	263,738	233,991
Average Shares	138,338	130,411	141,012	133,133	118,831	109,809	92,072	88,892
Balance Sheet								
Total Assets	22,478,935	17,954,281	13,637,163	11,580,517	9,518,928	9,018,179	6,777,343	6,370,314
Long-Term Obligations	12,951,812	9,554,798	6,254,883	4,936,633	4,064,385	4,071,320	2,477,173	2,656,897
Total Liabilities	14,866,776	10,675,307	7,117,212	5,619,905	4,520,069	4,353,465	2,727,313	2,835,435
Stockholders' Equity	6,118,399	6,150,770	5,263,510	4,012,741	3,077,573	2,627,356	2,570,372	2,078,720
Shares Outstanding	153,076	151,093	141,153	127,478	118,247	108,629	99,035	86,803
Statistical Record								
Return on Assets %	2.81	3.55	4.28	5.60	4.97	2.95	4.01	3.94
Return on Equity %	9.27	9.81	11.63	16.68	16.15	8.96	11.35	11.29
Net Margin %	17.39	20.65	21.18	34.73	30.65	16.23	26.75	28.31
Price Range	135.75-84.52	129.49-85.62	88.64-68.70	76.40-48.09	55.66-33.30	47.10-34.41	41.65-34.56	40.75-29.88
P/E Ratio	42.03-26.17	38.65-25.56	25.33-19.63	17.56-11.06	14.65-8.76	24.66-18.02	16.86-13.99	18.52-13.58
Average Yield %	3.08	3.72	4.92	5.04	6.67	6.44	6.89	5.57

Address: 888 Seventh Avenue, New York, NY 10019 **Telephone:** 212-894-7000 **Fax:** 212-587-0600	**Web Site:** www.vno.com **Officers:** Steven Roth - Chmn., C.E.O. Michael D. Fascitelli - Pres.	**Auditors:** Deloitte & Touche LLP **Transfer Agents:** American Stock Transfer & Trust Co., New York, NY

VULCAN MATERIALS CO (HOLDING COMPANY)

Exchange	Symbol	Price	52Wk Range	Yield	P/E	Div Acheiver
NYS	VMC	$66.40 (3/31/2008)	123.67-63.15	2.95	14.63	15 Years

*7 Year Price Score 121.03 *NYSE Composite Index=100   *12 Month Price Score 81.32

Interim Earnings (Per Share)

Qtr.	Mar	Jun	Sep	Dec
2003	(0.17)	0.55	0.96	0.56
2004	0.14	0.85	0.96	0.82
2005	0.52	1.17	1.17	0.87
2006	0.68	1.45	1.39	1.18
2007	0.91	1.45	1.38	0.80

Interim Dividends (Per Share)

Amt	Decl	Ex	Rec	Pay
0.46Q	11/16/2007	11/21/2007	11/26/2007	12/10/2007
0.49Q	2/8/2008	2/21/2008	2/25/2008	3/10/2008

Indicated Div: $1.96 (Div. Reinv. Plan)

Valuation Analysis   Institutional Holding

Forecast P/E	15.19	No of Institutions
	(1/10/2007)	342
Market Cap	$7.2 Billion	Shares
Book Value	3.8 Billion	74,827,424
Price/Book	1.91	% Held
Price/Sales	2.16	78.76

Business Summary: Earth & Rock Mining (MIC: 14.5 SIC: 1422 NAIC: 212312)

Vulcan Materials produces construction aggregates as well as asphalt mix and concrete. Co. is engaged in the production, distribution and sale of construction aggregates and other construction materials and related services. Construction aggregates include crushed stone, sand and gravel, rock asphalt and recrushed asphalt and concrete. Aggregates are widely used as railroad track ballast and are employed in virtually all types of construction, such as highway construction and maintenance, and in the production of asphaltic and portland cement concrete mixes. As of Dec 31 2007, Co. operated 183 crushed stone plants, 51 sand and gravel plants and 16 plants producing other aggregates.

Recent Developments: For the year ended Dec 31 2007, income from continuing operations decreased 3.6% to US$463.1 million from US$480.2 million a year earlier. Net income decreased 4.1% to US$450.9 million from US$470.2 million in the prior year. Revenues were US$3.33 billion, down 0.4% from US$3.34 billion the year before. Operating income was US$714.4 million versus US$695.1 million in the prior year, an increase of 2.8%. Direct operating expenses declined 1.4% to US$2.38 billion from US$2.41 billion in the comparable period the year before. Indirect operating expenses decreased 0.1% to US$236.5 million from US$236.8 million in the equivalent prior-year period.

Prospects: Co.'s near term outlook is clouded by uncertain market conditions, due to weakness in residential construction and some softening in certain categories of private nonresidential construction. However, Co.'s future prospects appear solid, owing in part to the broad use of aggregates in construction and the multi-year nature of highway and infrastructure projects. For 2008, including its Florida Rock operations that were acquired on Nov 16 2007, Co. expects an increase in aggregates shipments of 9.0% to 12.0%. Also, Co. sees 2008 prices improving 8.0% to 10.0%. Thus, Co. anticipates 2008 consolidated earnings from continuing operations in the range of $4.75 to $5.15 per diluted share.

Financial Data

(US$ in Thousands)	12/31/2007	12/31/2006	12/31/2005	12/31/2004	12/31/2003	12/31/2002	12/31/2001	12/31/2000
Earnings Per Share	4.54	4.69	3.73	2.77	1.90	1.66	2.17	2.16
Cash Flow Per Share	7.30	5.94	4.63	5.65	5.10	4.54	5.03	4.13
Tang Book Value Per Share	N.M.	14.60	15.05	13.77	12.01	11.04	10.02	9.00
Dividends Per Share	1.840	1.480	1.160	1.040	0.980	0.940	0.900	0.840
Dividend Payout %	40.53	31.56	31.10	37.55	51.58	56.63	41.47	38.89
Income Statement								
Total Revenue	3,327,787	3,342,475	2,895,327	2,454,335	2,892,186	2,796,577	3,019,990	2,491,744
EBITDA	968,477	935,874	709,319	643,898	638,108	576,805	659,098	588,012
Income Before Taxes	667,502	703,461	480,237	375,566	311,425	257,660	324,053	312,238
Income Taxes	204,416	225,963	136,402	114,353	87,971	67,247	101,373	92,345
Net Income	450,910	467,534	388,757	287,385	194,952	169,876	222,680	219,893
Average Shares	99,403	99,777	104,085	103,664	102,710	102,515	102,497	102,012
Balance Sheet								
Current Assets	1,157,229	731,379	1,164,722	1,417,959	1,050,242	789,688	729,952	694,504
Total Assets	8,936,310	3,424,225	3,588,884	3,665,133	3,636,860	3,448,221	3,398,224	3,228,574
Current Liabilities	2,528,187	493,687	579,014	426,689	542,952	297,709	344,495	572,231
Long-Term Obligations	1,529,828	322,064	323,392	604,522	607,654	857,757	906,299	685,361
Total Liabilities	5,176,770	1,423,114	1,462,343	1,651,158	1,742,037	1,658,577	1,793,950	1,757,078
Stockholders' Equity	3,759,600	2,001,111	2,126,541	2,013,975	1,802,836	1,696,986	1,604,274	1,471,496
Shares Outstanding	108,234	94,606	100,326	102,659	101,811	101,557	101,320	101,043
Statistical Record								
Return on Assets %	7.30	13.33	10.72	7.85	5.50	4.96	6.72	7.23
Return on Equity %	15.65	22.65	18.78	15.02	11.14	10.29	14.48	15.69
EBITDA Margin %	29.10	28.00	24.50	26.24	22.06	20.63	21.82	23.60
Net Margin %	13.55	13.99	13.43	11.71	6.74	6.07	7.37	8.82
Asset Turnover	0.54	0.95	0.80	0.67	0.82	0.82	0.91	0.82
Current Ratio	0.46	1.48	2.01	3.32	1.93	2.65	2.12	1.21
Debt to Equity	0.41	0.16	0.15	0.30	0.34	0.51	0.56	0.47
Price Range	123.67-77.43	93.49-66.97	75.79-52.44	54.95-42.35	48.25-29.06	49.55-32.37	55.10-38.15	48.50-36.69
P/E Ratio	27.24-17.06	19.93-14.28	20.32-14.06	19.84-15.29	25.39-15.29	29.85-19.50	25.39-17.58	22.45-16.98
Average Yield %	1.83	1.85	1.84	2.16	2.56	2.23	1.91	1.95

Address: 1200 Urban Center Drive, Birmingham, AL 35242-2545	**Web Site:** www.vulcanmaterials.com	**Auditors:** Deloitte & Touche LLP
Telephone: 205-298-3000	**Officers:** Donald M. James - Chmn., C.E.O. Daniel F. Sansone - Sr. V.P., C.F.O., Treas.	**Investor Contact:** 205-298-3220
Fax: 205-298-2963		**Transfer Agents:** The Bank of New York, New York, NY

WACHOVIA CORP

Exchange	Symbol	Price	52Wk Range	Yield	P/E
NYS	WB	$27.00 (3/31/2008)	56.81-25.60	9.48	8.28

*7 Year Price Score 80.57   *NYSE Composite Index=100   *12 Month Price Score 75.44

Interim Earnings (Per Share)

Qtr.	Mar	Jun	Sep	Dec
2003	0.76	0.77	0.83	0.83
2004	0.94	0.95	0.96	0.96
2005	1.01	1.04	1.06	1.09
2006	1.09	1.17	1.17	1.20
2007	1.20	1.22	0.85	0.00

Interim Dividends (Per Share)

Amt	Decl	Ex	Rec	Pay
0.56Q	4/17/2007	5/29/2007	5/31/2007	6/15/2007
0.64Q	8/21/2007	8/29/2007	8/31/2007	9/17/2007
0.64Q	10/16/2007	11/28/2007	11/30/2007	12/17/2007
0.64Q	2/19/2008	2/27/2008	2/29/2008	3/17/2008

Indicated Div: $2.56

Valuation Analysis

		Institutional Holding	
Forecast P/E	N/A	No of Institutions	973
Market Cap	$52.9 Billion	Shares	1,079,961,728
Book Value	76.9 Billion	% Held	
Price/Book	0.69		56.63
Price/Sales	0.95		

TRADING VOLUME (thousand shares)

1999 2000 2001 2002 2003 2004 2005 2006 2007 2008

Business Summary: Commercial Banking (MIC: 8.1 SIC: 6021 NAIC: 522110)

Wachovia is a bank holding company with total assets of $782.90 billion and deposits of $449.13 billion at Dec 31 2007. Co. provides various commercial and retail banking and trust services through full-service banking offices in Alabama, Arizona, California, Colorado, Connecticut, Delaware, Florida, Georgia, Illinois, Kansas, Maryland, Mississippi, Nevada, New Jersey, New York, North Carolina, Pennsylvania, South Carolina, Tennessee, Texas, Virginia and Washington, D.C. Co. also provides other financial services, such as mortgage banking, investment banking, investment advisory, home equity lending, asset-based lending, leasing, insurance, international and securities brokerage services.

Recent Developments: For the year ended Dec 31 2007, income from continuing operations decreased 18.5% to US$6.31 billion from US$7.75 billion a year earlier. Net income decreased 19.0% to US$6.31 billion from US$7.79 billion in the prior year. Net interest income increased 18.9% to US$18.13 billion from US$15.25 billion in the prior year. Provision for loan losses was US$2.26 billion versus US$434.0 million in the prior year, an increase of 421.0%. Non-interest income fell 9.3% to US$13.30 billion from US$14.67 billion, while non-interest expense advanced 12.7% to US$19.82 billion.

Prospects: For 2008, Co. expects net interest income growth to be driven by loan and deposit growth and spread widening. In particular, Co. expects deposits to grow as it, among others, expands product distribution in its Wachovia Mortgage, FSB branches, and increases productivity in its de novo branches. Co. also expects solid fee income growth in service charges, interchange fees, fiduciary and asset management fees and commissions, global rates, high grade, treasury and trade finance, merger and acquisition advisory services, and equities. These projections exclude any merger-related and restructuring expenses, as well as assume a slowing U.S. economy and declining short-term interest rates.

Financial Data
(US$ in Thousands)

	12/31/2007	12/31/2006	12/31/2005	12/31/2004	12/31/2003	12/31/2002	12/31/2001	12/31/2000
Earnings Per Share	3.26	4.63	4.19	3.81	3.18	2.60	1.45	0.07
Cash Flow Per Share	(4.96)	1.18	3.67	(5.82)	(4.35)	0.37	6.65	8.12
Tang Book Value Per Share	14.06	15.60	15.76	15.25	15.27	14.48	11.30	11.92
Dividends Per Share	2.400	2.140	1.940	1.660	1.250	1.000	0.240	1.920
Dividend Payout %	73.62	46.22	46.30	43.57	39.31	38.46	16.55	2,742.86
Income Statement								
Interest Income	42,231,000	32,265,000	23,689,000	17,288,000	15,080,000	15,586,000	16,100,000	17,534,000
Interest Expense	24,101,000	17,016,000	10,008,000	5,327,000	4,473,000	5,763,000	8,325,000	10,097,000
Net Interest Income	18,130,000	15,249,000	13,681,000	11,961,000	10,607,000	9,823,000	7,775,000	7,437,000
Provision for Losses	2,261,000	434,000	249,000	257,000	586,000	1,479,000	1,947,000	1,736,000
Non-Interest Income	13,297,000	14,545,000	12,219,000	10,779,000	9,394,000	8,005,000	6,296,000	6,712,000
Non-Interest Expense	19,822,000	17,476,000	15,117,000	14,666,000	13,092,000	11,602,000	9,831,000	11,710,000
Income Before Taxes	8,773,000	11,470,000	9,462,000	7,633,000	6,080,000	4,667,000	2,293,000	703,000
Income Taxes	2,461,000	3,725,000	3,033,000	2,419,000	1,833,000	1,088,000	674,000	565,000
Net Income	6,312,000	7,791,000	6,643,000	5,214,000	4,264,000	3,579,000	1,619,000	92,000
Average Shares	1,934,000	1,681,000	1,585,000	1,370,000	1,340,000	1,369,000	1,105,000	974,172
Balance Sheet								
Net Loans & Leases	474,219,000	429,366,000	262,696,000	234,071,000	163,067,000	160,299,000	160,806,000	122,038,000
Total Assets	782,896,000	707,121,000	520,755,000	493,324,000	401,032,000	341,839,000	330,452,000	254,170,000
Total Deposits	449,129,000	407,458,000	324,894,000	295,053,000	221,225,000	191,518,000	187,453,000	142,668,000
Total Liabilities	702,689,000	634,304,000	470,294,000	443,189,000	366,094,000	309,761,000	301,997,000	238,823,000
Stockholders' Equity	76,872,000	69,716,000	47,561,000	47,317,000	32,428,000	32,078,000	28,455,000	15,347,000
Shares Outstanding	1,960,000	1,904,000	1,557,000	1,588,000	1,312,000	1,357,000	1,362,000	980,000
Statistical Record								
Return on Assets %	0.85	1.27	1.31	1.16	1.15	1.06	0.55	0.04
Return on Equity %	8.61	13.29	14.00	13.04	13.22	11.82	7.39	0.57
Net Interest Margin %	42.93	47.26	57.75	69.19	70.34	63.02	48.29	42.41
Efficiency Ratio %	35.70	37.33	44.13	52.25	53.90	49.52	43.90	48.30
Loans to Deposits	1.06	1.05	0.81	0.79	0.74	0.84	0.86	0.86
Price Range	58.77-38.03	59.85-51.09	56.01-46.49	54.52-43.56	46.59-32.72	39.50-28.75	36.38-27.81	38.88-24.00
P/E Ratio	18.03-11.67	12.93-11.03	13.37-11.10	14.31-11.43	14.65-10.29	15.19-11.06	25.09-19.18	555.36-342.86
Average Yield %	4.71	3.88	3.79	3.50	3.08	2.84	0.75	6.29

Address: One Wachovia Center, Charlotte, NC 28288-0013 **Telephone:** 704-374-6161 **Fax:** 704-374-4609	**Web Site:** www.wachovia.com **Officers:** G. Kennedy Thompson - Chmn., Pres., C.E.O. Robert P. Kelly - Sr. Exec. V.P., C.F.O.	**Auditors:** KPMG LLP **Investor Contact:** 704-374-6782 **Transfer Agents:** Wachovia Bank, N.A., Charlotte, NC

WADDELL & REED FINANCIAL, INC.

Exchange	Symbol	Price	52Wk Range	Yield	P/E
NYS	WDR	$32.13 (3/31/2008)	37.34-22.24	2.37	21.14

*7 Year Price Score 96.18   *NYSE Composite Index=100   *12 Month Price Score 119.77

Interim Earnings (Per Share)

Qtr.	Mar	Jun	Sep	Dec
2003	0.02	0.27	0.03	0.34
2004	0.34	0.31	0.29	0.32
2005	0.28	(0.09)	0.30	0.24
2006	0.30	(0.40)	0.30	0.36
2007	0.35	0.36	0.39	0.42

Interim Dividends (Per Share)

Amt	Decl	Ex	Rec	Pay
0.17Q	6/18/2007	7/5/2007	7/9/2007	8/1/2007
0.17Q	9/14/2007	10/3/2007	10/5/2007	11/1/2007
0.17Q	12/14/2007	1/2/2008	1/4/2008	2/1/2008
0.19Q	2/26/2008	4/2/2008	4/4/2008	5/1/2008
		Indicated Div: $0.76		

Valuation Analysis

Forecast P/E	15.52
	(1/10/2007)
Market Cap	$2.8 Billion
Book Value	381.6 Million
Price/Book	7.29
Price/Sales	3.32

Institutional Holding

No of Institutions	217
Shares	71,337,232
% Held	85.07

Business Summary: Finance Intermediaries & Services (MIC: 8.7 SIC: 6211 NAIC: 523120)

Waddell & Reed Financial provides investment management, investment product underwriting and distribution, and shareholder services administration to mutual funds and institutional and separately managed accounts. Co. operates its business via three distribution channels. Co.'s retail products are distributed through its sales force of registered financial advisors (the Advisors channel) or through third-parties such as other broker/dealers, registered investment advisors, and various retirement platforms (collectively, the Wholesale channel). Co. also markets its investment advisory services to institutional investors, either directly or through consultants (the Institutional channel).

Recent Developments: For the year ended Dec 31 2007, net income increased 172.2% to US$125.5 million from US$46.1 million in the prior year. Revenues were US$837.6 million, up 16.5% from US$718.7 million the year before. Operating income was US$194.6 million versus US$88.9 million in the prior year, an increase of 118.9%. Direct operating expenses rose 18.4% to US$422.3 million from US$356.5 million in the comparable period the year before. Indirect operating expenses decreased 19.2% to US$220.6 million from US$273.2 million in the equivalent prior-year period.

Prospects: Co.'s near-term outlook appears encouraging, as it continues to benefit from improved sales attributable primarily to higher sales volume as well as continued industry low redemption rate. Looking ahead, Co. is anticipating operating margin pressure in 2008 as a result of the strong sales growth in its Wholesale channel, which has a higher cost to gather assets. Consequently, Co. believes that such situation requires it to manage its Wholesale channel growth by adding additional resources and infrastructure. Meanwhile, Co. will continue to invest in its Advisors channel by providing support to its advisors through training, wholesaling efforts and enhanced technology tools.

Financial Data
(US$ in Thousands)

	12/31/2007	12/31/2006	12/31/2005	12/31/2004	12/31/2003	12/31/2002	12/31/2001	12/31/2000
Earnings Per Share	1.52	0.55	0.73	1.25	0.66	1.07	1.28	1.60
Cash Flow Per Share	1.59	1.22	1.29	1.42	1.21	1.26	1.76	2.08
Tang Book Value Per Share	1.77	0.19	N.M.	N.M.	N.M.	N.M.	N.M.	N.M.
Dividends Per Share	0.660	0.600	0.600	0.600	0.548	0.486	0.354	0.354
Dividend Payout %	43.42	109.09	82.19	48.00	83.00	45.44	27.63	22.10
Income Statement								
Total Revenue	837,554	718,655	622,080	504,077	451,182	439,125	482,562	520,702
Income Before Taxes	199,160	89,200	95,950	158,210	84,934	132,598	171,120	227,946
Income Taxes	73,663	43,088	35,829	56,045	30,669	45,173	63,953	88,941
Net Income	125,497	46,112	60,121	102,165	54,265	87,425	107,167	139,005
Average Shares	82,824	83,212	82,045	81,924	82,590	81,874	83,423	86,895
Balance Sheet								
Total Assets	893,750	662,714	632,271	619,907	565,804	560,492	433,105	422,186
Total Liabilities	512,132	418,014	384,897	401,030	390,399	411,187	319,307	280,576
Stockholders' Equity	381,618	244,700	247,374	218,877	175,405	149,305	113,798	141,610
Shares Outstanding	86,630	84,660	83,804	82,798	82,048	80,637	80,204	83,410
Statistical Record								
Return on Assets %	16.13	7.12	9.60	17.19	9.64	17.60	25.06	36.61
Return on Equity %	40.07	18.74	25.79	51.68	33.42	66.46	83.92	103.47
Price Range	37.34-22.24	27.67-19.40	23.90-16.79	27.21-19.01	27.41-16.01	32.69-15.43	36.01-24.03	40.00-16.63
P/E Ratio	24.57-14.63	50.31-35.27	32.74-23.00	21.77-15.21	41.53-24.26	30.55-14.42	28.13-18.77	25.00-10.39
Average Yield %	2.44	2.60	3.02	2.64	2.48	2.07	1.17	1.22

Address: 6300 Lamar Avenue, Overland Park, KS 66202 Telephone: 913-236-2000 Fax: 913-236-2017	Web Site: www.waddell.com Officers: Alan W. Kosloff - Chmn. Henry J. Herrmann - Pres., C.E.O.	Auditors: KPMG LLP Investor Contact: 913-236-1880 Transfer Agents: Equiserve Trust Company NA

WAL-MART STORES, INC.

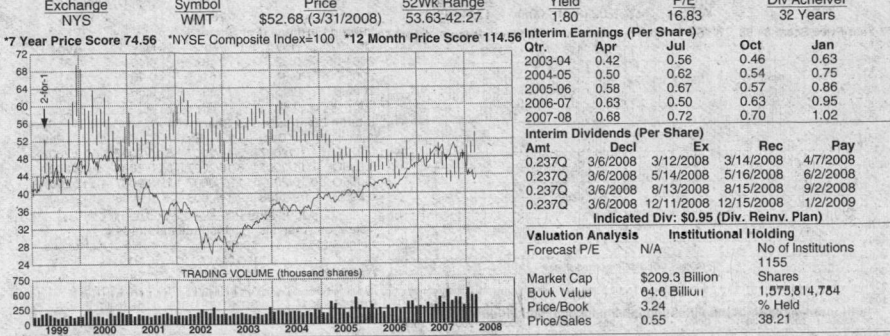

Exchange	Symbol	Price	52Wk Range	Yield	P/E	Div Achiever
NYS	WMT	$52.68 (3/31/2008)	53.63-42.27	1.80	16.83	32 Years

*7 Year Price Score 74.56 *NYSE Composite Index=100 *12 Month Price Score 114.56

Interim Earnings (Per Share)

Qtr.	Apr	Jul	Oct	Jan
2003-04	0.42	0.56	0.46	0.63
2004-05	0.50	0.62	0.54	0.75
2005-06	0.58	0.67	0.57	0.86
2006-07	0.63	0.50	0.63	0.95
2007-08	0.68	0.72	0.70	1.02

Interim Dividends (Per Share)

Amt	Decl	Ex	Rec	Pay
0.237Q	3/6/2008	3/12/2008	3/14/2008	4/7/2008
0.237Q	3/6/2008	5/14/2008	5/16/2008	6/2/2008
0.237Q	3/6/2008	8/13/2008	8/15/2008	9/2/2008
0.237Q	3/6/2008	12/11/2008	12/15/2008	1/2/2009

Indicated Div: $0.95 (Div. Reinv. Plan)

Valuation Analysis

		Institutional Holding	
Forecast P/E	N/A	No of Institutions	1155
Market Cap	$209.3 Billion	Shares	1,575,814,784
Book Value	64.6 Billion	% Held	38.21
Price/Book	3.24		
Price/Sales	0.55		

TRADING VOLUME (thousand shares)

Business Summary: Retail - General (MIC: 5.2 SIC: 5331 NAIC: 452990)

Wal-Mart Stores operates in three business segments: Wal-Mart Stores, Sam's Club and International. Co.'s Wal-Mart Stores retail formats include: Supercenters, Discount Stores and Neighbourhood Markets. Co.'s Sam's Club segment consists of membership warehouse clubs, which operate in the U.S., and the segment's online retail format, samsclub.com. As of Jan 31 2008, Co.'s International segment consisted of retail operations in Argentina, Brazil, Canada, China, Costa Rica, El Salvador, Guatemala, Honduras, Japan, Mexico, Nicaragua, Puerto Rico, and the U.K. As of Jan 31 2008, Co. operated 971 discount stores, 2,447 supercenters, 591 Sam's Clubs and 132 Neighborhood Markets in the U.S.

Recent Developments: For the year ended Jan 31 2008, income from continuing operations increased 5.8% to US$12.88 billion from US$12.18 billion a year earlier. Net income increased 12.8% to US$12.73 billion from US$11.28 billion in the prior year. Revenues were US$378.80 billion, up 8.6% from US$348.65 billion the year before. Operating income was US$22.00 billion versus US$20.50 billion in the prior year, an increase of 7.3%. Direct operating expenses rose 8.5% to US$286.52 billion from US$264.15 billion in the comparable period the year before. Indirect operating expenses increased 9.8% to US$70.29 billion from US$64.00 billion in the equivalent prior-year period.

Prospects: For the fiscal year ending Jan 31 2009, Co. is targeting earnings from continuing operations to range from $3.30 and $3.43 per diluted share. In addition, Co. intends to open, relocate or expand 170 supercenters and 25 neighborhood markets within its Wal-Mart Stores segment, as well as 25 units in its Sam's Club segment, while 400 units are scheduled in its International segment. Thus, Co. is estimating capital expenditures of $13.50 billion to 15.20 billion, with 65.8% for its U.S. operations and 34.2% for its International segment. Meanwhile, for the fiscal quarter ended Apr 30 2008, Co. is forecasting earnings from continuing operations in the range of $0.70 and $0.74 per diluted share.

Financial Data

(US$ in Thousands)	01/31/2008	01/31/2007	01/31/2006	01/31/2005	01/31/2004	01/31/2003	01/31/2002	01/31/2001
Earnings Per Share	3.13	2.71	2.68	2.41	2.07	1.81	1.49	1.40
Cash Flow Per Share	5.01	4.84	4.22	3.52	3.67	2.83	2.30	2.15
Tang Book Value Per Share	12.22	11.57	9.84	9.12	7.83	6.78	5.95	4.99
Dividends Per Share	0.880	0.670	0.600	0.520	0.360	0.300	0.280	0.240
Dividend Payout %	28.12	24.72	22.39	21.58	17.39	16.57	18.79	17.14
Income Statement								
Total Revenue	378,799,000	348,650,000	315,654,000	287,989,000	258,681,000	246,525,000	219,812,000	193,295,000
EBITDA	28,313,000	25,956,000	23,247,000	21,496,000	18,877,000	17,076,000	15,367,000	14,358,000
Income Before Taxes	20,198,000	18,968,000	17,358,000	16,105,000	14,193,000	12,719,000	10,751,000	10,116,000
Income Taxes	6,908,000	6,365,000	5,803,000	5,589,000	5,118,000	4,487,000	3,897,000	3,692,000
Net Income	12,731,000	11,284,000	11,231,000	10,267,000	9,054,000	8,039,000	6,671,000	6,295,000
Average Shares	4,072,000	4,168,000	4,188,000	4,266,000	4,372,999	4,445,999	4,480,999	4,483,999
Balance Sheet								
Current Assets	47,585,000	46,588,000	43,824,000	38,491,000	34,421,000	30,483,000	28,246,000	26,555,000
Total Assets	163,514,000	151,193,000	138,187,000	120,223,000	104,912,000	94,685,000	83,451,000	78,130,000
Current Liabilities	58,454,000	51,754,000	48,826,000	42,888,000	37,418,000	32,617,000	27,282,000	28,949,000
Long-Term Obligations	33,402,000	30,735,000	30,171,000	23,669,000	20,099,000	19,608,000	18,732,000	15,655,000
Total Liabilities	98,906,000	89,620,000	85,016,000	70,827,000	61,289,000	55,348,000	48,349,000	46,787,000
Stockholders' Equity	64,608,000	61,573,000	53,171,000	49,396,000	43,623,000	39,337,000	35,102,000	31,343,000
Shares Outstanding	3,973,000	4,131,000	4,165,000	4,234,000	4,310,999	4,394,999	4,452,999	4,469,999
Statistical Record								
Return on Assets %	8.09	7.80	8.69	9.10	9.07	9.03	8.26	8.46
Return on Equity %	20.18	19.67	21.90	22.01	21.83	21.60	20.08	21.96
EBITDA Margin %	7.47	7.44	7.36	7.46	7.30	6.93	6.99	7.43
Net Margin %	3.36	3.24	3.56	3.57	3.50	3.26	3.03	3.26
Asset Turnover	2.41	2.41	2.44	2.55	2.59	2.77	2.72	2.60
Current Ratio	0.81	0.90	0.90	0.90	0.92	0.93	1.04	0.92
Debt to Equity	0.52	0.50	0.57	0.48	0.46	0.50	0.53	0.50
Price Range	51.21-42.27	51.75-43.02	53.51-42.49	61.05-51.33	60.08-46.74	63.75-44.60	59.98-44.00	63.56-43.25
P/E Ratio	16.36-13.50	19.10-15.87	19.97-15.85	25.33-21.30	29.02-22.58	35.22-24.64	40.26-29.53	45.40-30.89
Average Yield %	1.87	1.43	1.25	0.95	0.66	0.55	0.53	0.45

Address: 702 S.W. Eighth Street, Bentonville, AR 72716
Telephone: 479-273-4000
Fax: 479-273-1986

Web Site: www.wal-mart.com
Officers: S. Robson Walton - Chmn. Michael T. Duke - Vice-Chmn.

Auditors: Ernst & Young LLP
Transfer Agents: EquiServe Trust Company, N.A., Providence, RI

WALGREEN CO.

Exchange	Symbol	Price	52Wk Range	Yield	P/E	Div Achiever
NYS	WAG	$38.09 (3/31/2008)	47.93-33.01	1.00	18.14	32 Years

*7 Year Price Score 84.98   *NYSE Composite Index=100   *12 Month Price Score 95.52

Interim Earnings (Per Share)

Qtr.	Nov	Feb	May	Aug
2004-05	0.32	0.48	0.40	0.32
2005-06	0.34	0.51	0.46	0.41
2006-07	0.43	0.65	0.56	0.40
2007-08	0.46	0.69	...	...

Interim Dividends (Per Share)

Amt	Decl	Ex	Rec	Pay
0.077Q	4/10/2007	5/16/2007	5/18/2007	6/12/2007
0.095Q	7/11/2007	8/16/2007	8/20/2007	9/12/2007
0.095Q	10/10/2007	11/7/2007	11/12/2007	12/12/2007
0.095Q	1/9/2008	2/14/2008	2/19/2008	3/12/2008

Indicated Div: $0.38 (Div. Reinv. Plan)

Valuation Analysis		Institutional Holding	
Forecast P/E	19.64	No of Institutions	
	(1/10/2007)		919
Market Cap	$37.7 Billion	Shares	643,207,808
Book Value	12.1 Billion	% Held	
Price/Book	3.13		64.27
Price/Sales	0.67		

TRADING VOLUME (thousand shares)

Business Summary: Retail - Miscellaneous (MIC: 5.11 SIC: 5912 NAIC: 446110)

Walgreen is principally engaged in the retail drugstore business. Co.'s drugstores are engaged in the retail sale of prescription and non-prescription drugs and general merchandise. General merchandise includes, among other things, beauty care, personal care, household items, candy, photofinishing, greeting cards, seasonal items and convenience foods. Co.'s customers can have prescriptions filled at its drugstore counter, as well as through the mail, by telephone and via the Internet. Co. markets products under various trademarks, trade dress and trade names and holds assorted business licenses. As of Aug 31 2007, Co. operated retail stores at 5,997 locations in 48 states and Puerto Rico.

Recent Developments: For the quarter ended Feb 29 2008, net income increased 5.2% to US$685.9 million from US$651.9 million in the year-earlier quarter. Revenues were US$15.39 billion, up 10.5% from US$13.93 billion the year before. Direct operating expenses rose 10.7% to US$10.96 billion from US$9.90 billion in the comparable period the year before. Indirect operating expenses increased 11.0% to US$3.35 billion from US$3.02 billion in the equivalent prior-year period.

Prospects: For the fiscal year ending Sep 2 2008, Co. is anticipating capital expenditures to be in excess of $2.00 billion. In detail, Co. intends to use the capital expenditures for store relocation and expansion activities, with plans of 550 new store openings. Also, expenditures are planned for technology and distribution centers, with a new distribution center in Windsor, CT slated to open in fiscal 2009. Going forward, Co. will continue to expand into new markets and increase presence in existing markets. For instance, Co. is encouraged by the Jan 17 2008 announced acquisition of 20 drugstores in Puerto Rico from Farmacias El Amal, a family-owned chain of 61 drugstores based on the island.

Financial Data

(US$ in Thousands)	6 Mos	3 Mos	08/31/2007	08/31/2006	08/31/2005	08/31/2004	08/31/2003	08/31/2002
Earnings Per Share	2.10	2.07	2.03	1.72	1.52	1.32	1.14	0.99
Cash Flow Per Share	2.51	2.27	2.36	2.41	1.34	1.61	1.46	1.44
Tang Book Value Per Share	11.09	10.51	10.13	10.04	8.77	8.04	7.02	6.08
Dividends Per Share	0.362	0.345	0.328	0.273	0.223	0.182	0.156	0.145
Dividend Payout %	17.23	16.67	16.13	15.84	14.64	13.78	13.65	14.65
Income Statement								
Total Revenue	29,421,500	14,027,900	53,762,000	47,409,000	42,201,600	37,508,200	32,505,400	28,681,100
EBITDA	2,212,900	923,500	3,826,600	3,273,700	2,906,100	2,562,100	2,224,000	1,937,700
Depn & Amortn	396,900	195,700	...	...	...	...	...	...
Income Before Taxes	1,813,900	728,200	3,189,100	2,754,100	2,455,600	2,176,300	1,888,700	1,637,300
Income Taxes	672,500	272,700	1,147,800	1,003,500	896,100	816,100	713,000	618,100
Net Income	1,141,400	455,500	2,041,300	1,750,600	1,559,500	1,360,200	1,175,700	1,019,200
Average Shares	995,000	997,500	1,006,340	1,019,400	1,028,333	1,031,798	1,031,580	1,032,270
Balance Sheet								
Current Assets	10,143,200	10,335,100	9,510,500	9,705,400	8,316,500	7,764,400	6,358,100	5,166,500
Total Assets	20,748,300	20,475,600	19,313,600	17,131,100	14,608,800	13,342,100	11,405,900	9,878,800
Current Liabilities	7,230,500	7,545,400	6,744,300	5,755,300	4,481,000	4,077,900	3,420,500	2,955,200
Total Liabilities	8,685,000	8,985,500	8,209,300	7,015,300	5,719,100	5,114,100	4,210,200	3,648,600
Stockholders' Equity	12,063,300	11,490,100	11,104,300	10,115,800	8,889,700	8,228,000	7,195,700	6,230,200
Shares Outstanding	990,456	991,380	991,141	1,007,862	1,013,512	1,023,292	1,024,908	1,024,908
Statistical Record								
Return on Assets %	10.90	10.73	11.20	11.03	11.16	10.96	11.05	10.89
Return on Equity %	18.50	19.08	19.24	18.42	18.22	17.59	17.51	17.82
EBITDA Margin %	7.52	6.58	7.12	6.91	6.89	6.83	6.84	6.76
Net Margin %	3.88	3.25	3.80	3.69	3.70	3.63	3.62	3.55
Asset Turnover	2.94	2.86	2.95	2.99	3.02	3.02	3.05	3.07
Current Ratio	1.40	1.37	1.41	1.69	1.86	1.90	1.86	1.75
Price Range	47.93-33.01	47.93-36.59	51.48-40.10	49.69-39.80	48.34-35.41	37.74-30.57	35.96-27.35	40.24-30.98
P/E Ratio	22.82-15.72	23.15-17.68	25.36-19.75	28.89-23.14	31.80-23.30	28.59-23.16	31.54-23.99	40.65-31.29
Average Yield %	0.87	0.78	0.73	0.61	0.53	0.52	0.50	0.40

Address: 200 Wilmot Road, Deerfield, IL 60015	Web Site: www.walgreens.com	Auditors: Deloitte & Touche LLP
Telephone: 847-940-2500	Officers: David W. Bernauer - Chmn., C.E.O. Jeffrey A. Rein - Pres., C.O.O.	Investor Contact: 847-914-2972
Fax: 847-914-2804		Transfer Agents: Computershare Investor Services, Chicago, IL

WARNER MUSIC GROUP CORP

Exchange	Symbol	Price	52Wk Range	Yield	P/E
NYS	WMG	$4.98 (3/31/2008)	17.49-4.75	10.44	N/A

*7 Year Price Score N/A   *NYSE Composite Index=100   *12 Month Price Score 62.34

Interim Earnings (Per Share)

Qtr.	Dec	Mar	Jun	Sep
2004-05	0.00	(0.28)	(1.41)	(0.18)
2005-06	0.46	(0.05)	(0.10)	0.08
2006-07	0.12	(0.19)	(0.12)	0.04
2007-08	(0.11)	...	...	...

Interim Dividends (Per Share)

Amt	Decl	Ex	Rec	Pay
0.13Q	3/8/2007	3/26/2007	3/28/2007	4/27/2007
0.13Q	6/5/2007	6/21/2007	6/25/2007	7/25/2007
0.13Q	9/4/2007	9/20/2007	9/24/2007	10/24/2007
0.13Q	2/6/2008	2/19/2008	2/21/2008	2/29/2008

Indicated Div: $0.52

Valuation Analysis | **Institutional Holding**

Forecast P/E	N/A	No of Institutions 112
Market Cap	$744.6 Million	Shares
Book Value	N/A	120,348,664
Price/Book	N/A	% Held
Price/Sales	0.22	80.56

TRADING VOLUME (thousand shares)

Business Summary: Sporting & Recreational (MIC: 13.5 SIC: 7929 NAIC: 711510)

Warner Music Group, through its subsidiaries, offers recorded music and music publishing services worldwide. Co.'s recorded music operations consist of the discovery and development of artists as well as related marketing and distribution of recorded music produced by such artists. Co.'s recorded products are sold to consumers primarily in the compact disc format through distributors, sub-distributors, wholesalers as well and digital formats through online physical retailers and mobile full-track download stores. Co.'s music publishing business involves the ownership and acquisition rights to pop hits, American standards, folk songs and motion picture as well as theatrical compositions.

Recent Developments: For the quarter ended Dec 31 2007, net loss amounted to US$16.0 million versus net income of US$18.0 million in the year-earlier quarter. Revenues were US$989.0 million, or 6.6% from US$928.0 million the year before. Operating income was US$44.0 million versus US$80.0 million in the prior-year quarter, a decrease of 45.0%. Direct operating expenses rose 7.3% to US$545.0 million from US$508.0 million in the comparable period the year before. Indirect operating expenses increased 17.6% to US$400.0 million from US$340.0 million in the equivalent prior-year period.

Prospects: Looking ahead, Co. expects sales of compact disc (CD) to continue to decline industry-wide, despite generating most of the recorded music revenues. In addition, Co. believes that the creation of new formats for selling recorded music product, including the legal downloading of digital music using the Internet and the distribution of music on mobile devices, could not offset the declines in sales of CD. Hence, Co. anticipates that a declining recorded music industry could continue to negatively affect its operating results as its Music Publishing business generates a portion of its revenues from mechanical royalties received from the sale of music in recorded music formats such as the CD.

Financial Data

(US$ in Thousands)	3 Mos	09/30/2007	09/30/2006	09/30/2005	09/30/2004	02/29/2004	11/30/2003	11/30/2002
Earnings Per Share	(0.38)	(0.14)	0.40	(1.40)	...	...	...	...
Cash Flow Per Share	1.56	2.07	2.13	1.70	...	...	...	...
Dividends Per Share	0.520	0.520	0.650	...	...	...	...	...
Dividend Payout %	...	...	162.50	...	...	...	...	...
Income Statement								
Total Revenue	989,000	3,385,000	3,516,000	3,502,000	1,769,000	779,000	3,376,000	3,290,000
EBITDA	109,000	456,000	523,000	307,000	12,000	59,000	(984,000)	(1,298,000)
Depn & Amortn	67,000	...	...	...	...	...	...	...
Income Before Taxes	(6,000)	28,000	107,000	(114,000)	(208,000)	(15,000)	(1,317,000)	(1,570,000)
Income Taxes	10,000	49,000	47,000	55,000	30,000	17,000	36,000	(340,000)
Net Income	(16,000)	(21,000)	60,000	(169,000)	(230,000)	(32,000)	(1,353,000)	(6,026,000)
Average Shares	147,200	146,200	150,900	120,900	...	...	...	...
Balance Sheet								
Current Assets	1,149,000	1,195,000	1,300,000	1,242,000	1,538,000	...	1,506,000	...
Total Assets	4,599,000	4,572,000	4,520,000	4,498,000	5,090,000	...	4,484,000	...
Current Liabilities	1,913,000	1,887,000	1,799,000	1,748,000	2,180,000	...	1,645,000	...
Long-Term Obligations	2,254,000	2,256,000	2,239,000	2,229,000	1,828,000	...	120,000	...
Total Liabilities	4,646,000	4,608,000	4,462,000	4,409,000	4,810,000	...	2,897,000	...
Stockholders' Equity	(47,000)	(36,000)	58,000	89,000	280,000	...	1,587,000	...
Shares Outstanding	149,522	149,524	149,156	148,455	114,115	...	...	...
Statistical Record								
Return on Assets %	N.M.	N.M.	1.33	N.M.	N.M.	...	...	...
Return on Equity %	N.M.	N.M.	81.63	N.M.	N.M.	...	...	...
EBITDA Margin %	11.02	13.47	14.87	8.77	0.68	7.57	N.M.	N.M.
Net Margin %	N.M.	N.M.	1.71	N.M.	N.M.	N.M.	N.M.	N.M.
Asset Turnover	0.75	0.74	0.78	0.73	0.44	...	...	...
Current Ratio	0.60	0.63	0.72	0.71	0.71	...	0.92	...
Debt to Equity	...	...	38.60	25.04	6.53	...	0.08	...
Price Range	23.60-5.97	26.94-9.74	30.08-15.25	18.71-14.75	...	...	...	...
P/E Ratio	...	...	75.20-38.13	...	...	...	...	...
Average Yield %	3.67	2.82	2.90	...	...	...	...	...

Address: 75 Rockefeller Plaza, New York, NY 10019	Web Site: www.wmg.com	Auditors: Ernst & Young LLP
Telephone: 212-275-2000	Officers: Edgar Bronfman Jr. - Chmn., C.E.O. Michael D. Fleisher - Exec. V.P., C.F.O.	Investor Contact: 212-275-2000 Transfer Agents: American Stock Transfer and Trust Company

W & T OFFSHORE INC

Exchange	Symbol	Price	52Wk Range	Yield	P/E
NYS	WTI	$34.11 (3/31/2008)	38.84-21.19	0.35	17.95

*7 Year Price Score N/A   *NYSE Composite Index=100   *12 Month Price Score 127.65

Interim Earnings (Per Share)
Qtr.	Mar	Jun	Sep	Dec
2004			2.27	
2005	0.60	0.69	0.80	0.78
2006	0.85	0.58	0.91	0.49
2007	0.17	0.60	0.48	0.65

Interim Dividends (Per Share)
Amt	Decl	Ex	Rec	Pay
0.03Q	9/6/2007	10/11/2007	10/15/2007	11/1/2007
0.03Q	12/6/2007	12/19/2007	12/21/2007	1/11/2008
0.394Q	12/6/2007	12/19/2007	12/21/2007	1/11/2008
0.03Q	2/25/2008	3/14/2008	3/18/2008	4/4/2008

Indicated Div: $0.12

Valuation Analysis
Forecast P/E N/A

Market Cap $2.6 Billion
Book Value 1.2 Billion
Price/Book 2.26
Price/Sales 2.33

Institutional Holding
No of Institutions 114
Shares 24,479,758
% Held 32.26

TRADING VOLUME (thousand shares)
1999 2000 2001 2002 2003 2004 2005 2006 2007 2008

Business Summary: Oil and Gas (MIC: 14.2 SIC: 1311 NAIC: 211111)

W & T Offshore is engaged in oil and natural gas acquisition, exploitation, exploration and production activities, primarily in the Gulf of Mexico. As of Dec 31 2006, Co. had working interests in leases covering approximately 2.0 million acres spanning across the outer continental shelf off the coast of Louisiana, Texas, Mississippi and Alabama. In addition, Co. owned interests in approximately 523 offshore structures at Dec 31 2006. As of the above date, Co. had proved reserves of 735.2 billions of cubic feet equivalent of oil and natural gas.

Recent Developments: For the year ended Dec 31 2007, net income decreased 27.5% to US$144.3 million from US$199.1 million in the prior year. Revenues were US$1.11 billion, up 39.1% from US$800.5 million the year before. Operating income was US$249.2 million versus US$317.6 million in the prior year, a decrease of 21.5%. Direct operating expenses rose 21.2% to US$21.4 million from US$17.7 million in the comparable period the year before. Indirect operating expenses increased 81.2% to US$843.1 million from US$465.2 million in the equivalent prior-year period.

Prospects: On Dec 24 2007, Co. announced an agreement to acquire Apache's Corp. interest in Ship Shoal 349 field, located off the coast of Louisiana, and covering two federal offshore lease blocks, Ship Shoal Blocks 349 and 359 for $116.0 million. The transaction is expected to close on Apr 30 2008. Meanwhile, Co. anticipated 2008 production for its Jan 2006 commodity swap and option contracts to be 11.0 billion cubic feet of natural gas equivalent. Also, Co. estimates 2008 budget of $800.0 million, an increase of 77.0% over 2007. The budget includes capital to drill 44 exploration and six development wells. Of these wells, 40 are on the conventional shelf and 10 are in the deep shelf or deepwater.

Financial Data
(US$ in Thousands)	12/31/2007	12/31/2006	12/31/2005	12/31/2004	12/31/2003	12/31/2002	12/31/2001
Earnings Per Share	1.90	2.84	2.87	2.27	1.79	...	...
Cash Flow Per Share	9.09	8.14	6.83	7.15	5.09	...	...
Tang Book Value Per Share	15.11	13.74	8.24	5.98	3.22	1.73	...
Dividends Per Share	0.543	0.120	0.060	0.070	...	...	...
Dividend Payout %	28.61	4.23 *	2.09	3.08	...		
Income Statement							
Income Before Taxes	215,759	306,354	290,026	229,490	177,594	54,457	63,569
Income Taxes	71,459	107,250	101,003	80,008	61,156	52,408	
Net Income	144,300	199,104	189,023	149,482	116,582	2,049	63,569
Average Shares	75,939	70,217	65,971	65,942	65,037	...	...
Balance Sheet							
Total Assets	2,822,334	2,609,685	1,064,520	760,784	546,729	341,194	...
Total Liabilities	1,670,994	1,566,768	521,137	400,906	332,274	207,864	...
Stockholders' Equity	1,151,340	1,042,917	543,383	359,878	214,455	133,330	...
Shares Outstanding	76,175	75,900	65,979	52,611	52,516	50,695	...
Statistical Record							
Return on Assets %	5.31	10.84	20.71	22.80	26.26	...	...
Return on Equity %	13.15	25.10	41.85	51.91	67.04	...	...
Price Range	31.88-21.19	48.12-27.70	33.15-18.19	...	...	...	...
P/E Ratio	16.78-11.15	16.94-9.75	11.55-6.34	...	...	...	...
Average Yield %	1.98	0.34	0.24	...	...	...	...

Address: Eight Greenway Plaza, Suite 1330, Houston, TX 77046, Houston, TX 77046
Telephone: 713-626-8525
Fax: 713-626-8527

Web Site: www.wtoffshore.com
Officers: Tracy W. Krohn - Chmn., Pres., C.E.O., Treas. Jerome F. Freel - Chmn. Emeritus, Sec.

Auditors: Ernst & Young LLP
Transfer Agents: Computershare Investor Services L.L.C.

WASHINGTON MUTUAL INC.

Exchange	Symbol	Price	52Wk Range	Yield	P/E	Div Acheiver
NYS	WM	$10.30 (3/31/2008)	44.41-9.24	5.83	N/A	18 Years

*7 Year Price Score 62.13   *NYSE Composite Index=100   *12 Month Price Score 54.09

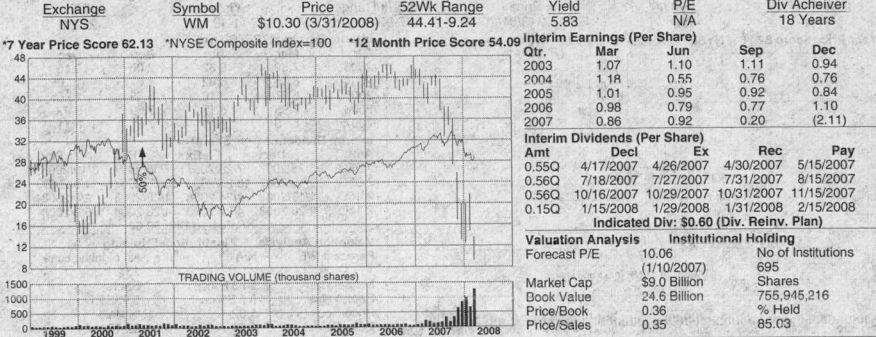

Interim Earnings (Per Share)

Qtr.	Mar	Jun	Sep	Dec
2003	1.07	1.10	1.11	0.94
2004	1.18	0.55	0.76	0.76
2005	1.01	0.95	0.92	0.84
2006	0.98	0.79	0.77	1.10
2007	0.86	0.92	0.20	(2.11)

Interim Dividends (Per Share)

Amt	Decl	Ex	Rec	Pay
0.55Q	4/17/2007	4/26/2007	4/30/2007	5/15/2007
0.56Q	7/18/2007	7/27/2007	7/31/2007	8/15/2007
0.56Q	10/16/2007	10/29/2007	10/31/2007	11/15/2007
0.15Q	1/15/2008	1/29/2008	1/31/2008	2/15/2008

Indicated Div: $0.60 (Div. Reinv. Plan)

Valuation Analysis

		Institutional Holding	
Forecast P/E	10.06	No of Institutions	
	(1/10/2007)	695	
Market Cap	$9.0 Billion	Shares	
Book Value	24.6 Billion	755,945,216	
Price/Book	0.36	% Held	
Price/Sales	0.35	85.03	

TRADING VOLUME (thousand shares)

Business Summary: Other Depository Banking (MIC: 8.5 SIC: 6035 NAIC: 522120)

Washington Mutual is a thrift holding company providing financial services to consumers and small businesses. Co. has four operating segments for management reporting purposes: the Retail Banking Group, which as of Dec 31 2007, operated a retail bank network of 2,257 stores across 15 states throughout the U.S.; the Card Services Group, which operates a nationwide credit card lending business; the Commercial Group, which conducts a multi-family and commercial real estate lending business in certain markets; as well as the Home Loans Group, which engages in single-family residential real estate lending, servicing and capital markets activities.

Recent Developments: For the year ended Dec 31 2007, loss from continuing operations was US$67.0 million compared with income of US$3.11 billion a year earlier. Net loss amounted to US$67.0 million versus net income of US$3.56 billion in the prior year. Net interest income increased 0.7% to US$8.18 billion from US$8.12 billion in the prior year. Provision for loan losses was US$3.11 billion versus US$816.0 million in the prior year, an increase of 280.8%. Non-interest income fell 5.3% to US$6.04 billion from US$6.38 billion, while non-interest expense advanced 20.4% to US$10.60 billion.

Prospects: On Dec 10 2007, Co. announced plans to adjust and resize its Home Loans business, and reduce corporate support expense, by implementing several actions, including discontinuing all remaining lending through its subprime mortgage channel, closing various home loan centers and sales offices, as well as closing its institutional broker-dealer business and its mortgage banker finance warehouse lending operation. Accordingly, these actions are expected to generate about $500.0 million of expense savings in 2008. Meanwhile, Co. plans to continue to exploit its Retail Bank's distribution network by opening additional stores and adding more than 1.0 million net new checking accounts in 2008.

Financial Data

(US$ in Thousands)	12/31/2007	12/31/2006	12/31/2005	12/31/2004	12/31/2003	12/31/2002	12/31/2001	12/31/2000
Earnings Per Share	(0.12)	3.64	3.73	3.26	4.21	4.05	3.59	2.36
Cash Flow Per Share	8.91	7.66	1.97	(22.78)	13.84	0.03	(12.68)	3.76
Tang Book Value Per Share	8.33	11.31	10.66	10.21	7.88	9.03	6.29	9.96
Dividends Per Share	2.210	2.060	1.900	1.740	1.400	1.060	0.897	0.760
Dividend Payout %	...	56.59	50.94	53.37	33.25	26.17	24.98	32.20
Income Statement								
Interest Income	19,489,000	19,907,000	15,588,000	11,350,000	12,163,000	14,247,000	15,065,000	13,783,000
Interest Expense	11,312,000	11,786,000	7,702,000	4,234,000	4,534,000	5,906,000	8,189,000	9,472,000
Net Interest Income	8,177,000	8,121,000	7,886,000	7,116,000	7,629,000	8,341,000	6,876,000	4,311,000
Provision for Losses	3,107,000	816,000	316,000	209,000	42,000	595,000	575,000	185,000
Non-Interest Income	6,042,000	6,377,000	5,738,000	4,612,000	5,850,000	4,790,000	2,627,000	1,984,000
Non-Interest Expense	10,600,000	8,807,000	7,870,000	7,533,000	7,400,000	6,302,000	4,617,000	3,126,000
Income Before Taxes	309,000	4,770,000	5,438,000	3,984,000	6,029,000	6,154,000	4,311,000	2,984,000
Income Taxes	376,000	1,656,000	2,006,000	1,505,000	2,236,000	2,258,000	1,579,000	1,085,000
Net Income	(67,000)	3,558,000	3,432,000	2,878,000	3,880,000	3,896,000	3,114,000	1,899,000
Average Shares	866,183	975,406	919,238	884,050	921,757	960,152	864,700	804,694
Balance Sheet								
Net Loans & Leases	247,218,000	268,300,000	261,519,000	248,513,000	194,737,000	179,871,000	155,429,000	122,016,000
Total Assets	327,913,000	346,288,000	343,839,000	307,918,000	275,178,000	268,298,000	242,506,000	194,716,000
Total Deposits	181,926,000	213,956,000	193,167,000	173,658,000	153,181,000	155,516,000	107,182,000	79,574,000
Total Liabilities	303,329,000	319,319,000	316,223,000	286,692,000	255,436,000	248,164,000	228,341,000	184,550,000
Stockholders' Equity	24,584,000	26,969,000	27,616,000	21,226,000	19,742,000	20,134,000	14,063,000	10,166,000
Shares Outstanding	869,036	944,478	993,913	874,261	880,985	944,046	873,089	809,783
Statistical Record								
Return on Assets %	N.M.	1.03	1.05	0.98	1.43	1.53	1.42	0.99
Return on Equity %	N.M.	13.04	14.05	14.01	19.46	22.79	25.70	19.71
Net Interest Margin %	41.96	40.79	50.59	62.70	62.72	58.55	45.64	31.28
Efficiency Ratio %	41.52	33.51	36.90	47.21	41.13	33.52	26.10	19.83
Loans to Deposits	1.36	1.25	1.35	1.43	1.27	1.16	1.45	1.53
Price Range	45.56-13.07	46.48-41.47	44.54-36.92	45.28-37.63	46.55-32.98	39.45-28.41	42.69-28.56	37.25-14.54
P/E Ratio	...	12.77-11.39	11.94-9.90	13.89-11.54	11.06-7.83	9.74-7.01	11.89-7.96	15.78-6.16
Average Yield %	6.04	4.69	4.63	4.27	3.57	3.00	2.55	3.50

Address: 1201 Third Avenue, Seattle, WA 98101	Web Site: www.wamu.com	Auditors: Deloitte & Touche LLP
Telephone: 206-461-2000	Officers: Kerry K. Killinger - Chmn., C.E.O. William A. Longbrake - Vice-Chmn.	Investor Contact: 206-461-3186
Fax: 206-554-2778		Transfer Agents: Mellon Investor Services, L.L.C., Ridgefield Park, NJ

WASHINGTON POST CO.

Exchange	Symbol	Price	52Wk Range	Yield	P/E
NYS	WPO	$661.50 (3/31/2008)	857.92-641.00	1.30	21.91

*7 Year Price Score 82.76   *NYSE Composite Index=100   *12 Month Price Score 99.45

Interim Earnings (Per Share)

Qtr.	Mar	Jun	Sep	Dec
2003	7.59	6.32	2.06	9.15
2004	6.15	8.82	8.57	11.05
2005	6.87	8.16	6.89	10.66
2006	7.95	8.17	7.60	9.97
2007	6.70	7.19	7.60	8.71

Interim Dividends (Per Share)

Amt	Decl	Ex	Rec	Pay
2.05Q	6/28/2007	7/26/2007	7/30/2007	8/10/2007
2.05Q	9/13/2007	10/25/2007	10/29/2007	11/9/2007
2.15Q	1/17/2008	1/24/2008	1/28/2008	2/8/2008
2.15Q	2/26/2008	4/24/2008	4/28/2008	5/9/2008

Indicated Div: $8.60

Valuation Analysis

		Institutional Holding	
Forecast P/E	N/A	No of Institutions	237
Market Cap	$6.3 Billion	Shares	5,932,717
Book Value	3.5 Billion	% Held	62.15
Price/Book	1.82		
Price/Sales	1.51		

Business Summary: Vocational Education Services (MIC: 6.2 SIC: 8299 NAIC: 611699)

Washington Post is an education and media company. Co.'s Kaplan subsidiary provides a variety of educational services, both domestically and outside the U.S. Co. divides Kaplan's various businesses into three categories: Test Prep and Admissions; Professional; and Higher Education. Co.'s media operations consist of newspaper publishing (principally The Washington Post), television broadcasting (through the ownership and operation of six television broadcast stations), magazine publishing (principally Newsweek) and the ownership and operation of cable television systems.

Recent Developments: For the year ended Dec 30 2007, net income decreased 11.0% to US$288.6 million from US$324.5 million in the prior year. Revenues were US$4.18 billion, up 7.1% from US$3.90 billion the year before. Operating income was US$477.0 million versus US$459.8 million in the prior year, an increase of 3.7%. Direct operating expenses rose 8.3% to US$1.88 billion from US$1.74 billion in the comparable period the year before. Indirect operating expenses increased 6.7% to US$1.82 billion from US$1.71 billion in the equivalent prior-year period.

Prospects: Co.'s revenue benefited from solid growth in its education and cable divisions despite lower revenues at its newspaper publishing, magazine publishing and television broadcasting divisions due to weak advertising demand. As a result, Co. recently announced that a Voluntary Retirement Incentive Program will be offered in 2008 to some employees of The Washington Post newspaper and Newsweek and the corporate office. The Post will also close its College Park, MD, printing plant in early 2010. Separately, Co.'s Kaplan subsidiary recently agreed to acquire Pacific Language Institute, an English language instruction provider in Canada, thus expanding into the Canadian English language markets.

Financial Data

(US$ in Thousands)	12/30/2007	12/31/2006	01/01/2006	01/02/2005	12/28/2003	12/29/2002	12/30/2001	12/31/2000
Earnings Per Share	30.19	33.68	32.59	34.59	25.12	21.34	24.06	14.32
Cash Flow Per Share	61.40	62.33	54.64	57.79	35.53	52.49	36.87	39.13
Tang Book Value Per Share	144.13	143.63	103.67	92.76	64.70	61.18	50.32	50.03
Dividends Per Share	8.200	7.800	7.400	7.000	5.800	5.600	5.600	5.400
Dividend Payout %	27.16	23.16	22.71	20.24	23.09	26.24	23.28	37.71
Income Statement								
Total Revenue	4,180,406	3,904,927	3,553,887	3,300,104	2,838,911	2,584,203	2,416,673	2,412,150
EBITDA	732,625	746,384	721,034	753,514	584,723	559,718	652,245	464,216
Income Before Taxes	481,107	519,134	499,644	542,432	382,588	353,668	387,539	229,870
Income Taxes	192,500	189,600	185,300	209,700	141,500	137,300	157,900	93,400
Net Income	288,607	324,459	314,344	332,732	241,088	204,268	229,639	136,470
Average Shares	9,528	9,605	9,615	9,591	9,554	9,522	9,499	9,459
Balance Sheet								
Current Assets	994,970	934,825	818,326	754,367	495,836	382,955	396,857	405,067
Total Assets	6,004,509	5,381,372	4,584,773	4,316,641	3,901,558	3,583,894	3,559,098	3,200,743
Current Liabilities	1,013,473	803,200	694,721	688,161	711,873	736,112	434,090	408,797
Long-Term Obligations	400,519	401,571	403,635	425,889	422,471	405,547	883,078	873,267
Total Liabilities	2,531,524	2,209,738	1,934,083	1,891,892	1,814,077	1,733,685	1,862,481	1,706,588
Stockholders' Equity	3,461,159	3,159,514	2,638,423	2,412,482	2,074,941	1,837,293	1,683,485	1,481,007
Shares Outstanding	9,516	9,536	9,601	9,576	9,541	9,510	9,494	9,460
Statistical Record								
Return on Assets %	5.08	6.53	7.08	7.97	6.46	5.74	6.81	4.42
Return on Equity %	8.74	11.22	12.48	14.59	12.36	11.64	14.55	9.61
EBITDA Margin %	17.53	19.11	20.29	22.83	20.60	21.66	26.99	19.24
Net Margin %	6.90	8.31	8.85	10.08	8.49	7.90	9.50	5.66
Asset Turnover	0.74	0.79	0.80	0.79	0.76	0.73	0.72	0.78
Current Ratio	0.98	1.16	1.18	1.10	0.70	0.52	0.91	0.99
Debt to Equity	0.12	0.13	0.15	0.18	0.20	0.22	0.52	0.59
Price Range	857.92-742.45	813.02-710.65	963.50-717.00	996.74-790.23	814.78-657.40	738.50-518.00	632.76-491.65	620.75-472.00
P/E Ratio	28.42-24.59	24.14-21.10	29.56-22.00	28.82-22.85	32.44-26.17	34.61-24.27	26.30-20.43	43.35-32.96
Average Yield %	1.05	1.03	0.88	0.77	0.81	0.89	0.99	1.05

Address: 1150 15th Street N.W., Washington, DC 20071	Web Site: www.washpostco.com	Auditors: PricewaterhouseCoopers LLP
Telephone: 202-334-6000	Officers: Donald E. Graham - Chmn., C.E.O. Diana M. Daniels - V.P., Gen. Couns., Sec.	Investor Contact: 202-334-6000
Fax: 202-334-1031		Transfer Agents: EquiServe Trust Company, N.A., Providence, RI

WASHINGTON REAL ESTATE INVESTMENT TRUST

Exchange	Symbol	Price	52Wk Range	Yield	P/E	Div Acheiver
NYS	WRE	$33.42 (3/31/2008)	39.16-26.91	5.06	24.94	38 Years

*7 Year Price Score 87.64   *NYSE Composite Index=100   *12 Month Price Score 103.85

Interim Earnings (Per Share)

Qtr.	Mar	Jun	Sep	Dec
2003	0.28	0.29	0.28	0.28
2004	0.27	0.26	0.26	0.30
2005	1.01	0.26	0.32	0.26
2006	0.25	0.18	0.23	0.22
2007	0.24	0.18	0.73	0.18

Interim Dividends (Per Share)

Amt	Decl	Ex	Rec	Pay
0.422Q	5/4/2007	6/12/2007	6/14/2007	6/29/2007
0.422Q	8/7/2007	9/12/2007	9/14/2007	9/28/2007
0.422Q	11/28/2007	12/12/2007	12/14/2007	12/31/2007
0.422Q	2/21/2008	3/13/2008	3/17/2008	3/31/2008

Indicated Div: $1.69 (Div. Reinv. Plan)

Valuation Analysis

		Institutional Holding	
Forecast P/E	31.99 (1/10/2007)	No of Institutions	166
Market Cap	$1.6 Billion	Shares	25,153,120
Book Value	486.5 Million	% Held	55.84
Price/Book	3.21		
Price/Sales	6.10		

Business Summary: Property, Real Estate & Development (MIC: 8.3 SIC: 6798 NAIC: 525930)

Washington Real Estate Investment Trust is a self-administered, self-managed, equity real estate investment trust. Co.'s business consists of the ownership and development of income-producing real properties in the greater Washington metro region. Co. owns a portfolio of office buildings, medical office buildings, industrial/flex properties, multifamily buildings and retail centers. As of Dec 31 2007, Co. owned a portfolio of 89 properties, consisting of 14 retail centers, 25 office properties, 17 medical office properties, 23 industrial/flex properties, 10 multifamily properties encompassing in the aggregate 12.8 million net rentable square feet, and land for development.

Recent Developments: For the year ended Dec 31 2007, income from continuing operations decreased 9.8% to US$32.1 million from US$35.6 million a year earlier. Net income increased 60.1% to US$61.9 million from US$38.7 million in the prior year. Revenues were US$255.7 million, up 22.5% from US$208.7 million the year before.

Prospects: Going forward, Co. continues to focus on investing in additional income producing properties. For instance, on Dec 5 2007, Co. acquired the leasehold interest for an eight-story, Class A office building with a three-level parking garage in Washington, D.C. for $73.5 million. Subsequently, on Feb 25 2008, Co. acquired a 150,000 square foot industrial warehouse in Landover, MD for $11.2 million. Meanwhile, for 2008, Co. is projecting net operating income for overall portfolio to increase 7.0% to 9.0% over 2007, while funds from operations per diluted share excluding non-recurring items is expected to be in the range of $2.29 to $2.39.

Financial Data
(US$ in Thousands)

	12/31/2007	12/31/2006	12/31/2005	12/31/2004	12/31/2003	12/31/2002	12/31/2001	12/31/2000
Earnings Per Share	1.34	0.88	1.84	1.09	1.13	1.32	1.38	1.26
Cash Flow Per Share	2.52	1.98	2.08	1.91	1.94	1.80	1.98	1.73
Tang Book Value Per Share	10.42	9.81	9.03	8.71	9.10	8.33	8.33	7.24
Dividends Per Share	1.600	1.640	1.600	1.550	1.470	1.390	1.310	1.230
Dividend Payout %	125.37	186.36	86.96	142.20	130.09	105.30	94.93	97.62
Income Statement								
Property Income	255,655	219,662	190,046	172,067	163,405	152,929	148,424	134,732
Non-Property Income	...	...	...	327	414	680	...	...
Total Revenue	255,655	219,662	190,046	172,394	163,819	153,609	148,424	134,732
Interest Expense	61,906	47,846	37,743	34,500	30,040	27,849	27,071	25,531
Net Income	61,881	38,661	77,638	45,561	44,887	51,836	52,351	45,139
Average Shares	46,115	43,874	42,203	41,863	39,600	39,281	37,951	35,872
Balance Sheet								
Total Assets	1,898,326	1,531,265	1,141,285	1,012,393	927,129	755,997	707,935	632,047
Long-Term Obligations	1,131,607	965,328	689,617	493,429	517,182	351,951	359,726	351,260
Total Liabilities	1,408,006	1,087,595	759,310	644,755	546,780	428,266	382,717	371,833
Stockholders' Equity	486,544	441,931	380,305	366,009	378,748	326,177	323,607	258,656
Shares Outstanding	46,682	45,042	42,139	42,000	41,607	39,168	38,829	35,740
Statistical Record								
Return on Assets %	3.61	2.89	7.21	4.69	5.33	7.08	7.81	7.26
Return on Equity %	13.33	9.40	20.81	12.20	12.74	15.95	17.98	17.45
Net Margin %	24.20	17.60	40.85	26.43	27.40	33.75	35.27	33.50
Price Range	43.20-29.65	43.30-31.26	33.87-28.15	34.43-25.80	31.04-24.10	30.15-21.96	25.45-21.27	25.00-14.31
P/E Ratio	32.24-22.13	49.20-35.52	18.41-15.30	31.59-23.67	27.47-21.33	22.84-16.64	18.44-15.41	19.84-11.36
Average Yield %	4.72	4.40	5.24	5.16	5.33	5.31	5.59	6.89

Address: 6110 Executive Boulevard, Suite 800, Rockville, MD 20852-3927
Telephone: 301-984-9400
Fax: 301-984-9610

Web Site: www.writ.com
Officers: Edmund B. Cronin Jr. - Chmn., Pres., C.E.O. George F. McKenzie - Exec. V.P., Real Estate

Auditors: Ernst & Young LLP
Transfer Agents: EquiServe Trust Company N.A., Providence, RI

WASTE MANAGEMENT, INC. (DE)

Exchange	Symbol	Price	52Wk Range	Yield	P/E
NYS	WMI	$33.56 (3/31/2008)	40.30-29.15	3.22	15.05

*7 Year Price Score 96.40 *NYSE Composite Index=100 *12 Month Price Score 100.06

Interim Earnings (Per Share)

Qtr.	Mar	Jun	Sep	Dec
2003	0.10	0.30	0.35	0.31
2004	0.26	0.37	0.52	0.46
2005	0.26	0.92	0.38	0.52
2006	0.34	0.76	0.55	0.45
2007	0.42	0.64	0.54	0.61

Interim Dividends (Per Share)

Amt	Decl	Ex	Rec	Pay
0.24Q	5/11/2007	5/31/2007	6/4/2007	6/22/2007
0.24Q	8/24/2007	8/30/2007	9/4/2007	9/21/2007
0.24Q	11/13/2007	11/29/2007	12/3/2007	12/19/2007
0.27Q	2/27/2008	3/6/2008	3/10/2008	3/21/2008

Indicated Div: $1.08

Valuation Analysis

		Institutional Holding	
Forecast P/E	N/A	No of Institutions	509
Market Cap	$16.8 Billion	Shares	450,807,232
Book Value	5.8 Billion	% Held	84.57
Price/Book	2.90		
Price/Sales	1.26		

Business Summary: Sanitation Services (MIC: 7.3 SIC: 4953 NAIC: 562211)

Waste Management is a holding company. Through its subsidiaries, Co. provides collection, transfer, recycling, disposal and waste-to-energy services. Co.'s customers include commercial, industrial, municipal and residential customers, other waste management companies, electric utilities and governmental entities. Co. operates six operating Groups, of which four are organized by geographic area and two are organized by function. The geographic Groups include its Eastern, Midwest, Southern and Western Groups, and the two functional Groups are its Wheelabrator Group, which provides waste-to-energy services, and its WM Recycle America Group, which provides recycling services.

Recent Developments: For the year ended Dec 31 2007, net income increased 1.2% to US$1.16 billion from US$1.15 billion in the prior year. Revenues were US$13.31 billion, down 0.4% from US$13.36 billion the year before. Operating income was US$2.25 billion versus US$2.03 billion in the prior year, an increase of 11.1%. Direct operating expenses declined 2.2% to US$8.40 billion from US$8.59 billion in the comparable period the year before. Indirect operating expenses decreased 3.4% to US$2.65 billion from US$2.75 billion in the equivalent prior-year period.

Prospects: Looking ahead, Co. remains focused on growing earnings, expanding its operating margins, and increasing its return on invested capital by utilizing its disciplined pricing approach. Furthermore, Co. plans to apply its strategy of utilizing standard tools and processes, particularly in the areas of labor capability, maintenance and safety, to improve and reduce operating costs. Accordingly, for full year 2008, Co. expects income from operations as a percentage of revenue to increase approximately 18.0%. In addition, Co. expects its capital expenditures to be approximately $1.50 billion, which includes higher spending on its truck fleet and on renewable energy power plants at its landfills.

Financial Data

(US$ in Thousands)	12/31/2007	12/31/2006	12/31/2005	12/31/2004	12/31/2003	12/31/2002	12/31/2001	12/31/2000
Earnings Per Share	2.23	2.10	2.09	1.61	1.06	1.33	0.80	(0.16)
Cash Flow Per Share	4.71	4.70	4.26	3.84	3.27	3.51	3.76	3.41
Tang Book Value Per Share	0.52	1.52	1.10	0.91	0.24	0.21	0.43	N.M.
Dividends Per Share	0.960	0.880	0.800	0.750	0.010	0.010	0.010	0.010
Dividend Payout %	43.05	41.90	38.28	46.58	0.94	0.75	1.25	...
Income Statement								
Total Revenue	13,310,000	13,363,000	13,074,000	12,516,000	11,574,000	11,142,000	11,322,000	12,492,000
EBITDA	3,436,000	3,284,000	2,918,000	2,899,000	2,815,000	2,910,000	2,662,000	2,467,000
Income Before Taxes	1,703,000	1,474,000	1,092,000	1,178,000	1,123,000	1,247,000	787,000	321,000
Income Taxes	540,000	325,000	(90,000)	247,000	404,000	424,000	284,000	418,000
Net Income	1,163,000	1,149,000	1,182,000	939,000	630,000	822,000	503,000	(97,000)
Average Shares	521,800	546,100	565,100	581,100	592,500	617,500	630,800	621,257
Balance Sheet								
Current Assets	2,480,000	3,182,000	3,451,000	2,819,000	2,588,000	2,700,000	3,124,000	2,457,000
Total Assets	20,175,000	20,600,000	21,135,000	20,905,000	20,656,000	19,631,000	19,490,000	18,565,000
Current Liabilities	2,598,000	3,268,000	3,257,000	3,205,000	3,332,000	3,173,000	3,721,000	2,937,000
Long-Term Obligations	8,008,000	7,495,000	8,165,000	8,182,000	7,997,000	8,062,000	7,709,000	8,372,000
Total Liabilities	14,073,000	14,103,000	14,733,000	14,652,000	14,843,000	14,304,000	14,085,000	13,749,000
Stockholders' Equity	5,792,000	6,222,000	6,121,000	5,971,000	5,563,000	5,308,000	5,392,000	4,801,000
Shares Outstanding	500,118	533,683	552,253	570,212	576,118	594,600	628,017	622,650
Statistical Record								
Return on Assets %	5.70	5.51	5.62	4.51	3.13	4.20	2.64	N.M.
Return on Equity %	19.36	18.62	19.55	16.24	11.59	15.36	9.87	N.M.
EBITDA Margin %	25.82	24.58	22.32	23.16	24.32	26.12	23.51	19.75
Net Margin %	8.74	8.60	9.04	7.50	5.44	7.38	4.44	N.M.
Asset Turnover	0.65	0.64	0.62	0.60	0.57	0.57	0.60	0.60
Current Ratio	0.95	0.97	1.06	0.88	0.78	0.85	0.84	0.84
Debt to Equity	1.38	1.20	1.33	1.37	1.44	1.52	1.43	1.74
Price Range	40.30-32.67	38.52-30.27	31.01-27.04	31.10-26.17	29.60-19.72	31.91-20.87	32.38-23.01	27.94-13.06
P/E Ratio	18.07-14.65	18.34-14.41	14.84-12.94	19.32-16.25	27.92-18.60	23.99-15.69	40.48-28.76	
Average Yield %	2.62	2.49	2.76	2.61	0.04	0.04	0.04	0.05

Address: 1001 Fannin Street, Suite 4000, Houston, TX 77002
Telephone: 713-512-6200
Fax: 713-512-6299

Web Site: www.wm.com
Officers: A. Maurice Myers - Chmn., Pres., C.E.O.
David P. Steiner - Exec. V.P., C.F.O.

Auditors: Ernst & Young LLP

WATERS CORP.

Exchange	Symbol	Price	52Wk Range	Yield	P/E
NYS	WAT	$55.70 (3/31/2008)	80.77-52.59	N/A	21.26

*7 Year Price Score 125.64 *NYSE Composite Index=100   *12 Month Price Score 97.43

TRADING VOLUME (thousand shares)

Interim Earnings (Per Share)

Qtr.	Mar	Jun	Sep	Dec
2003	0.26	0.33	0.29	0.47
2004	0.33	0.49	0.42	0.58
2005	0.38	0.46	0.22	0.67
2006	0.42	0.46	0.49	0.77
2007	0.54	0.59	0.52	0.97

Interim Dividends (Per Share)

No Dividends Paid

Valuation Analysis   Institutional Holding

Forecast P/E	17.27	No of Institutions
	(1/10/2007)	336
Market Cap	$5.6 Billion	Shares
Book Value	586.1 Million	88,394,856
Price/Book	9.60	% Held
Price/Sales	3.82	87.06

Business Summary: Instruments and Related Products (MIC: 11.15 SIC: 3826 NAIC: 334516)

Waters is an analytical instrument manufacturer. Co. designs, manufactures, sells and services high performance liquid chromatography, ultra performance liquid chromatography and mass spectrometry instrument systems and associated service and support products including chromatography columns and other consumable products. Also, Co. designs, manufactures, sells and services thermal analysis and rheometry instruments that are used in predicting the suitability of fine chemicals and polymers for various industrial, consumer goods and health care products. Co. also develops and supplies software based products that interface with its instruments and other instrument manufacturers' instruments.

Recent Developments: For the year ended Dec 31 2007, net income increased 20.6% to US$268.1 million from US$222.2 million in the prior year. Revenues were US$1.47 billion, up 15.1% from US$1.28 billion the year before. Operating income was US$348.9 million versus US$295.2 million in the prior year, an increase of 18.2%. Direct operating expenses rose 17.7% to US$631.1 million from US$536.2 million in the comparable period the year before. Indirect operating expenses increased 9.8% to US$493.0 million from US$448.9 million in the equivalent prior-year period.

Prospects: Going forward, Co. is continuing on its growth strategies, which include introducing new products. For instance, on Mar 3 2008, Co. expands its platform technologies by introducing its Waters® PATROL™ ultra performance liquid chromatography™ Process Analyzer, a real-time liquid chromatography online process analytical technology system, its Waters SYNAPT™ mass spectrometry (MS) system, an improved quadrupole orthogonal acceleration time- of-flight MS platform, and Waters SDMS™ VP's Intelligent Procedure Manager, a workflow software package to guide analysts through laboratory procedures.

Financial Data

(US$ in Thousands)	12/31/2007	12/31/2006	12/31/2005	12/31/2004	12/31/2003	12/31/2002	12/31/2001	12/31/2000
Earnings Per Share	2.62	2.13	1.74	1.82	1.34	1.09	0.83	1.06
Cash Flow Per Share	3.69	2.57	2.61	2.16	1.27	1.68	1.45	1.37
Tang Book Value Per Share	1.70	N.M.	N.M.	3.05	2.67	3.42	3.19	2.21
Income Statement								
Total Revenue	1,473,048	1,280,229	1,158,236	1,104,536	958,205	889,967	859,208	795,071
EBITDA	402,196	335,463	323,737	325,770	252,770	227,608	176,412	235,284
Income Before Taxes	323,192	262,959	274,563	285,671	223,686	195,411	147,426	210,962
Income Taxes	55,120	40,759	72,588	61,618	52,795	43,193	32,883	54,849
Net Income	268,072	222,200	201,975	224,053	170,891	147,712	114,543	145,342
Average Shares	102,505	104,240	115,045	123,069	127,579	135,762	137,509	136,743
Balance Sheet								
Current Assets	1,237,062	999,680	912,992	973,884	715,399	636,456	522,744	343,796
Total Assets	1,881,055	1,617,313	1,428,931	1,460,426	1,130,861	1,010,947	886,911	692,345
Current Liabilities	658,434	685,834	603,891	492,990	378,521	320,215	281,006	220,533
Long-Term Obligations	500,000	500,000	500,000	250,000	125,000	...	...	...
Total Liabilities	1,294,979	1,254,930	1,145,299	781,740	540,384	345,637	305,166	240,564
Stockholders' Equity	586,076	362,383	283,632	678,686	590,477	665,310	581,745	451,781
Shares Outstanding	100,975	101,371	105,336	119,835	120,691	128,104	130,918	129,811
Statistical Record								
Return on Assets %	15.33	14.59	13.98	17.25	15.96	15.57	14.51	22.70
Return on Equity %	56.53	68.79	41.98	35.21	27.22	23.69	22.17	38.97
EBITDA Margin %	27.30	26.20	27.95	29.49	26.38	25.57	20.53	29.59
Net Margin %	18.20	17.36	17.44	20.28	17.83	16.60	13.33	18.28
Asset Turnover	0.84	0.84	0.80	0.85	0.89	0.94	1.09	1.24
Current Ratio	1.88	1.46	1.51	1.98	1.89	1.99	1.86	1.56
Debt to Equity	0.85	1.38	1.76	0.37	0.21	...	...	...
Price Range	80.07-48.67	51.38-37.26	51.11-34.43	48.88-33.12	33.20-20.10	38.89-17.97	78.88-22.65	90.38-22.00
P/E Ratio	30.56-18.58	24.12-17.49	29.37-19.79	26.86-18.20	24.78-15.00	35.68-16.49	95.03-27.29	85.26-20.75

Address: 34 Maple Street, Milford, MA 01757	Web Site: www.waters.com	Auditors: PricewaterhouseCoopers LLP
Telephone: 508-478-2000	Officers: Douglas A. Berthiaume - Chmn., Pres.,	Investor Contact: 508-482-2349
Fax: 508-872-1990	C.E.O. Arthur G. Caputo - Exec. V.P.	Transfer Agents: EquiServe Trust Company, N.A., Kansas City , MO

WATSON PHARMACEUTICALS, INC.

Exchange	Symbol	Price	52Wk Range	Yield	P/E
NYS	WPI	$29.32 (3/31/2008)	33.69-25.74	N/A	23.09

*7 Year Price Score 71.47   *NYSE Composite Index=100   *12 Month Price Score 101.48

Interim Earnings (Per Share)

Qtr.	Mar	Jun	Sep	Dec
2003	0.44	0.47	0.47	0.48
2004	0.42	0.32	0.13	0.40
2005	0.33	0.35	0.36	0.18
2006	0.23	(0.15)	0.31	(4.80)
2007	0.29	0.33	0.31	0.34

Interim Dividends (Per Share)

No Dividends Paid

Valuation Analysis   **Institutional Holding**

Forecast P/E	13.48	No of Institutions
	(1/10/2007)	248
Market Cap	$3.0 Billion	Shares
Book Value	1.8 Billion	86,745,784
Price/Book	1.64	% Held
Price/Sales	1.22	84.63

Business Summary: Pharmaceuticals (MIC: 9.1 SIC: 2834 NAIC: 325412)

Watson Pharmaceuticals is engaged in the development, manufacture, marketing, sale and distribution of brand and off-patent (generic) pharmaceutical products. Co.'s portfolio of generic products includes products that it has internally developed, products that it has licensed from third parties, and products that it distributes for third parties. In addition, Co. markets a number of patented products to physicians, hospitals, and other markets that it serves. As of Dec 31 2007, Co. marketed 150 generic pharmaceutical product families and 27 brand pharmaceutical product families.

Recent Developments: For the year ended Dec 31 2007, net income amounted to US$141.0 million versus a net loss of US$445.0 million in the prior year. Revenues were US$2.50 billion, up 26.1% from US$1.98 billion the year before. Operating income was US$255.7 million versus a loss of US$422.1 million in the prior year. Direct operating expenses rose 22.0% to US$1.50 billion from US$1.23 billion in the comparable period the year before. Indirect operating expenses decreased 37.0% to US$736.2 million from US$1.17 billion in the equivalent prior-year period.

Prospects: Co. continues to make progress on the development of its product pipeline, including the completion of Phase 3 program on its topical gel formulation of oxybutynin for overactive bladder. Specifically, Co. believes that it is on target to file new drug application in quarter ending June 2008. Meanwhile, for the full year ending Dec 2008, Co. targets its total net revenue of $2.50 billion, with net revenue of $1.45 billion to $1.55 billion in generic segment, $420.0 million to $440.0 million in brand segment and $580.0 million to $610.0 million in distribution segment. Accordingly, Co. estimates its 2008 earnings of $1.68 to $1.78 per diluted share.

Financial Data

(US$ in Thousands)	12/31/2007	12/31/2006	12/31/2005	12/31/2004	12/31/2003	12/31/2002	12/31/2001	12/31/2000
Earnings Per Share	1.27	(4.37)	1.21	1.27	1.86	1.64	1.07	1.52
Cash Flow Per Share	4.18	4.63	3.10	2.82	2.44	2.89	1.89	(0.40)
Tang Book Value Per Share	3.56	0.10	8.81	7.97	5.54	4.33	3.79	0.98
Income Statement								
Total Revenue	2,496,651	1,979,244	1,646,203	1,640,551	1,457,722	1,223,198	1,160,676	811,524
EBITDA	513,430	(198,939)	421,345	350,258	438,766	387,747	327,989	451,095
Income Before Taxes	224,284	(410,949)	219,416	236,878	318,112	279,090	198,952	355,402
Income Taxes	83,254	34,056	81,183	85,545	115,248	103,294	82,591	184,678
Net Income	141,030	(445,005)	138,233	151,333	202,864	175,796	116,361	157,495
Average Shares	117,039	101,761	120,021	124,727	108,927	107,367	108,340	103,575
Balance Sheet								
Current Assets	1,173,776	1,261,676	1,360,430	1,370,186	1,323,489	920,781	889,738	831,345
Total Assets	3,472,027	3,760,577	3,080,033	3,243,683	3,282,600	2,663,464	2,528,334	2,579,898
Current Liabilities	444,927	689,929	245,670	255,629	338,685	375,465	245,125	280,440
Long-Term Obligations	899,408	1,124,145	587,935	587,653	722,535	331,877	415,703	483,272
Total Liabilities	1,622,562	2,080,189	975,792	1,000,534	1,225,254	865,180	856,284	1,031,929
Stockholders' Equity	1,849,465	1,680,388	2,104,241	2,243,149	2,057,346	1,798,284	1,672,050	1,547,969
Shares Outstanding	103,658	102,467	101,805	109,719	108,330	106,878	106,458	105,600
Statistical Record								
Return on Assets %	3.90	N.M.	4.37	4.62	6.82	6.77	4.56	7.82
Return on Equity %	7.99	N.M.	6.36	7.02	10.52	10.13	7.23	12.07
EBITDA Margin %	20.56	N.M.	25.59	21.35	30.10	31.70	28.26	55.59
Net Margin %	5.65	N.M.	8.40	9.22	13.92	14.37	10.03	19.41
Asset Turnover	0.69	0.58	0.52	0.50	0.49	0.47	0.45	0.40
Current Ratio	2.64	1.83	5.54	5.36	3.91	2.45	3.63	2.96
Debt to Equity	0.49	0.67	0.28	0.26	0.35	0.18	0.25	0.31
Price Range	33.69-25.28	34.76-21.42	36.61-28.11	49.11-24.70	48.80-27.02	32.81-18.62	65.85-27.88	69.72-33.88
P/E Ratio	26.53-19.91	...	30.26-23.23	38.67-19.45	26.24-14.53	20.01-11.35	61.54-26.06	45.87-22.29

Address: 311 Bonnie Circle, Corona, CA 92880 **Telephone:** 909-493-5300 **Fax:** 909-270-1096	**Web Site:** www.watsonpharm.com **Officers:** Allen Chao Ph.D. - Chmn., Pres., C.E.O. Charles P. Slacik - Exec. V.P., C.F.O.	**Auditors:** PricewaterhouseCoopers LLP **Transfer Agents:** American Stock Transfer and Trust Company, New York, NY

WEATHERFORD INTERNATIONAL, LTD.

Exchange	Symbol	Price	52Wk Range	Yield	P/E
NYS	WFT	$72.47 (3/31/2008)	72.47-46.42	N/A	23.53

*7 Year Price Score 151.24 *NYSE Composite Index=100 ***12 Month Price Score 118.76**

Interim Earnings (Per Share)

Qtr.	Mar	Jun	Sep	Dec
2004		1.15		
2005	0.28	0.32	0.16	0.72
2006	0.57	0.52	0.66	0.78
2007	0.81	0.48	0.84	0.95

Interim Dividends (Per Share)

No Dividends Paid

Valuation Analysis | **Institutional Holding**

Forecast P/E	9.10	No of Institutions
	(1/10/2007)	N/A
Market Cap	$24.6 Billion	Shares
Book Value	7.4 Billion	N/A
Price/Book	3.32	% Held
Price/Sales	3.14	N/A

TRADING VOLUME (thousand shares)

1999 2000 2001 2002 2003 2004 2005 2006 2007 2008

Business Summary: Oil and Gas (MIC: 14.2 SIC: 1381 NAIC: 213111)

Weatherford International is a provider of equipment and services used for the drilling, evaluation, completion and production and intervention of oil and natural gas wells. Co.'s product offerings are grouped into ten service lines: artificial lift systems; drilling services; well construction; drilling tools; completion systems; wireline and evaluation services; re-entry and fishing; stimulation and chemicals; integrated drilling; and pipeline and specialty services. As of Dec 31 2007, Co. operated in approximately 100 countries through four business segments: North America; Latin America; Europe/West Africa/the Commonwealth of Independent States; and Middle East/North Africa/Asia.

Recent Developments: For the year ended Dec 31 2007, income from continuing operations increased 20.5% to US$1.09 billion from US$906.1 million a year earlier. Net income increased 19.4% to US$1.07 billion from US$896.4 million in the prior year. Revenues were US$7.83 billion, up 19.0% from US$6.58 billion the year before. Operating income was US$1.62 billion versus US$1.35 billion in the prior year, an increase of 19.9%. Direct operating expenses rose 20.1% to US$5.06 billion from US$4.21 billion in the comparable period the year before. Indirect operating expenses increased 13.7% to US$1.15 billion from US$1.01 billion in the equivalent prior-year period.

Prospects: Co.'s outlook appears favorable. Notably, Co. believes that the acceleration of decline rates and growing complexity of reservoirs should increase customers' requirements for technologies that improve productivity and efficiency, assuming the demand for hydrocarbons does not weaken. As a result, Co. expects its newer technologies to continue to gain traction. Furthermore, in 2008, Co. expects average worldwide rig activity to grow versus fourth quarter of 2007 levels, and it expects its business to grow at a faster rate than the underlying rig count, led by robust growth in the Eastern Hemisphere, followed by the Latin America market.

Financial Data

(US$ in Thousands)	12/31/2007	12/31/2006	12/31/2005	12/31/2004	12/31/2003	12/31/2002	12/31/2001	12/31/2000
Earnings Per Share	3.08	2.53	1.47	1.15	0.55	(0.03)	0.88	(0.20)
Cash Flow Per Share	2.58	3.14	1.68	1.87	1.13	1.12	1.09	0.60
Tang Book Value Per Share	10.18	7.56	6.45	4.95	2.11	0.90	1.97	1.30
Income Statement								
Total Revenue	7,832,062	6,578,928	4,333,227	3,131,774	2,591,408	2,328,930	2,328,715	1,814,261
EBITDA	2,221,967	1,810,244	1,029,627	746,363	501,839	287,747	633,495	325,906
Income Before Taxes	1,444,486	1,224,223	626,192	430,747	194,617	(9,835)	338,587	71,275
Income Taxes	332,760	316,524	159,166	92,672	50,601	(4,356)	123,048	109,450
Net Income	1,070,606	896,369	467,420	330,146	143,352	(6,030)	214,651	(42,350)
Average Shares	347,758	354,832	322,286	297,368	263,522	240,116	266,510	218,914
Balance Sheet								
Current Assets	4,471,769	3,359,997	2,638,873	1,943,178	1,436,024	1,259,239	1,231,333	1,241,587
Total Assets	13,190,957	10,139,240	8,500,304	5,543,402	5,000,212	4,191,989	4,396,363	3,461,670
Current Liabilities	2,202,365	2,043,145	1,998,141	660,006	782,342	877,477	759,597	462,716
Long-Term Obligations	3,066,335	1,564,600	632,071	1,404,431	1,379,611	1,513,907	1,499,794	1,132,676
Total Liabilities	5,784,238	3,964,449	2,913,487	2,230,093	2,292,144	2,520,493	2,458,122	2,123,121
Stockholders' Equity	7,406,719	6,174,799	5,666,817	3,313,389	2,708,068	1,974,496	1,838,240	1,338,458
Shares Outstanding	339,093	339,789	347,114	272,470	262,628	241,258	236,650	219,920
Statistical Record								
Return on Assets %	9.18	9.58	6.62	6.25	3.02	N.M.	5.53	N.M.
Return on Equity %	15.77	15.14	10.41	10.94	6.12	N.M.	13.51	N.M.
EBITDA Margin %	28.37	27.52	23.76	23.83	19.37	12.36	27.20	17.96
Net Margin %	13.67	13.62	10.79	10.54	5.53	N.M.	9.22	N.M.
Asset Turnover	0.67	0.70	0.61	0.59	0.55	0.53	0.60	0.52
Current Ratio	2.03	1.64	1.32	2.94	1.84	1.44	1.62	2.68
Debt to Equity	0.41	0.25	0.11	0.42	0.51	0.77	0.82	0.85
Price Range	71.58-36.92	58.14-38.12	37.65-24.25	27.38-18.00	23.27-15.73	26.66-16.36	29.84-11.89	24.81-11.92
P/E Ratio	23.24-11.99	22.98-15.07	25.61-16.50	23.80-15.65	42.31-28.61	...	33.91-13.51	...

Address: 515 Post Oak Boulevard, Suite 600, Houston, TX 77027-3415	**Web Site:** www.weatherford.com	**Auditors:** Ernst & Young LLP
Telephone: 713-693-4000	**Officers:** Bernard J. Duroc-Danner - Chmn., Pres., C.E.O. E. Lee Colley - Sr. V.P., Pres., Completion & Production Systems	**Investor Contact:** 713-693-4000
Fax: 713-297-8488		**Transfer Agents:** American Stock Transfer & Trust Co, New York, NY

WEBSTER FINANCIAL CORP (WATERBURY, CONN)

Exchange	Symbol	Price	52Wk Range	Yield	P/E	Div Acheiver
NYS	WBS	$27.87 (3/31/2008)	47.76-26.03	4.31	15.84	15 Years

*7 Year Price Score 73.75   *NYSE Composite Index=100   *12 Month Price Score 83.57

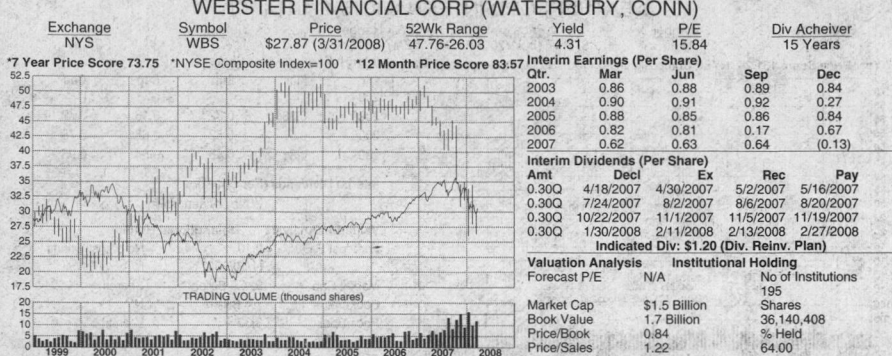

Interim Earnings (Per Share)

Qtr.	Mar	Jun	Sep	Dec
2003	0.86	0.88	0.89	0.84
2004	0.90	0.91	0.92	0.27
2005	0.88	0.85	0.86	0.84
2006	0.82	0.81	0.17	0.67
2007	0.62	0.63	0.64	(0.13)

Interim Dividends (Per Share)

Amt	Decl	Ex	Rec	Pay
0.30Q	4/18/2007	4/30/2007	5/2/2007	5/16/2007
0.30Q	7/24/2007	8/2/2007	8/6/2007	8/20/2007
0.30Q	10/22/2007	11/1/2007	11/5/2007	11/19/2007
0.30Q	1/30/2008	2/11/2008	2/13/2008	2/27/2008

Indicated Div: $1.20 (Div. Reinv. Plan)

Valuation Analysis   **Institutional Holding**

Forecast P/E	N/A	No of Institutions
		195
Market Cap	$1.5 Billion	Shares
Book Value	1.7 Billion	36,140,408
Price/Book	0.84	% Held
Price/Sales	1.22	64.00

Business Summary: Commercial Banking (MIC: 8.1 SIC: 6021 NAIC: 522110)

Webster Financial, through its Webster Bank subsidiary and various non-banking financial services subsidiaries, delivers financial services to individuals, families and businesses throughout southern New England and eastern New York State. Co. also offers equipment financing, commercial real estate lending, asset-based lending, and insurance premium financing on a regional or national basis. Also, through Webster Bank, Co. provides commercial banking, retail banking, consumer financing, mortgage banking, trust and investment services through 181 banking offices, 343 automatic teller machines and its internet website As of Dec 31 2007, Co. had total assets of $17.20 billion.

Recent Developments: For the year ended Dec 31 2007, income from continuing operations decreased 17.2% to US$110.7 million from US$133.7 million a year earlier. Net income decreased 27.7% to US$96.8 million from US$133.8 million in the prior year. Net interest income decreased 0.1% to US$508.2 million from US$508.6 million in the prior year. Provision for loan losses was US$67.8 million versus US$11.0 million in the prior year, an increase of 515.9%. Non-interest income rose 53.7% to US$202.3 million from US$131.6 million, while non-interest expense advanced 10.9% to US$484.0 million.

Prospects: On Dec 11 2007, Co. announced that its Webster Bank, National Association subsidiary has entered into an agreement to place its brand on 158 automated teller machines in select Walgreens' pharmacy stores in Massachusetts, Rhode Island and Connecticut. This branding agreement complements Co.'s branch expansion program and establishes another distribution platform for future growth in Rhode Island and the Boston market. The project is scheduled to begin and reach completion in the first quarter of 2008. Meanwhile, Co. is planning to open new branch locations in Greenwich, CT and North Kingston, RI and a downtown Boston flagship branch by the end of 2008.

Financial Data

(US$ in Thousands)	12/31/2007	12/31/2006	12/31/2005	12/31/2004	12/31/2003	12/31/2002	12/31/2001	12/31/2000
Earnings Per Share	1.76	2.47	3.43	3.00	3.52	3.16	2.68	2.55
Cash Flow Per Share	5.61	2.95	1.08	7.08	10.93	(1.76)	0.23	4.63
Tang Book Value Per Share	18.46	18.65	17.68	15.85	17.76	16.18	13.97	11.53
Dividends Per Share	1.170	1.060	0.980	0.900	0.820	0.740	0.670	0.620
Dividend Payout %	66.48	42.91	28.57	30.00	23.30	23.42	25.00	24.31
Income Statement								
Interest Income	995,595	1,014,738	871,847	732,108	658,718	692,034	757,235	738,911
Interest Expense	487,403	506,188	354,506	263,947	245,199	286,306	389,756	412,395
Net Interest Income	508,192	508,550	517,341	468,161	413,519	405,728	367,479	326,516
Provision for Losses	67,750	11,000	9,500	5,000	18,000	25,000	29,000	14,400	11,800
Non-Interest Income	202,312	170,471	220,885	219,707	232,483	185,572	162,098	128,821
Non-Interest Expense	483,970	474,948	455,570	447,137	377,982	328,323	308,932	267,130
Income Before Taxes	158,784	193,073	273,156	222,731	243,020	233,977	206,245	176,407
Income Taxes	48,088	59,283	87,301	68,898	79,772	73,965	69,430	58,116
Net Income	96,773	133,790	185,855	153,833	163,248	152,732	133,188	118,291
Average Shares	54,996	54,065	54,236	51,352	46,362	48,392	42,742	46,427
Balance Sheet								
Net Loans & Leases	12,509,425	13,130,570	12,406,719	11,709,874	9,180,965	8,200,992	6,869,911	6,819,209
Total Assets	17,201,960	17,097,471	17,836,562	17,020,597	14,568,690	13,468,004	11,857,382	11,249,508
Total Deposits	12,354,158	12,458,396	11,631,145	10,571,288	8,372,135	7,606,122	7,066,471	6,941,522
Total Liabilities	15,455,751	15,211,031	16,179,759	15,467,046	13,406,218	12,301,714	10,691,338	10,159,557
Stockholders' Equity	1,736,632	1,876,863	1,647,226	1,543,974	1,152,895	1,035,458	1,006,467	890,374
Shares Outstanding	52,475	56,388	53,661	53,628	46,276	45,625	49,149	48,939
Statistical Record								
Return on Assets %	0.56	0.77	1.07	0.97	1.16	1.21	1.15	1.11
Return on Equity %	5.36	7.59	11.65	11.38	14.92	14.96	14.04	15.46
Net Interest Margin %	51.04	50.12	59.34	63.95	62.78	58.63	48.53	44.19
Efficiency Ratio %	40.40	40.07	41.69	46.98	42.41	37.41	33.60	30.78
Loans to Deposits	1.01	1.05	1.07	1.11	1.10	1.08	0.97	0.98
Price Range	51.13-30.93	49.38-45.36	50.64-43.67	51.65-42.56	46.50-33.93	39.96-30.65	37.06-26.44	29.63-20.13
P/E Ratio	29.05-17.57	19.99-18.36	14.76-12.73	17.22-14.19	13.21-9.64	12.65-9.70	13.83-9.86	11.62-7.89
Average Yield %	2.72	2.23	2.11	1.87	2.11	2.09	2.15	2.68

Address: Webster Plaza, Waterbury, CT 06702 Telephone: 203-578-2476	Web Site: www.websteronline.com Officers: James C. Smith - Chmn., C.E.O. William T. Bromage - Pres., C.O.O.	Auditors: KPMG LLP Investor Contact: 203-578-2318 Transfer Agents: American Stock Transfer & Trust Co, New York, NY

WEIGHT WATCHERS INTERNATIONAL, INC.

Exchange	Symbol	Price	52Wk Range	Yield	P/E
NYS	WTW	$46.33 (3/31/2008)	57.75-41.85	N/A	18.68

*7 Year Price Score N/A *NYSE Composite Index=100 *12 Month Price Score 101.13

TRADING VOLUME (thousand shares)

Interim Earnings (Per Share)

Qtr.	Mar	Jun	Sep	Dec
2003	0.37	0.49	0.10	0.35
2004	0.34	0.49	0.47	0.41
2005	0.49	0.33	0.47	0.37
2006	0.56	0.58	0.52	0.45
2007	0.63	0.73	0.62	0.50

Interim Dividends (Per Share)
No Dividends Paid

Valuation Analysis

		Institutional Holding	
Forecast P/E	N/A	No of Institutions	145
Market Cap	$3.7 Billion	Shares	
Book Value	N/A		43,360,108
Price/Book	N/A	% Held	
Price/Sales	2.51		55.15

Business Summary: Personal Services (MIC: 5.15 SIC: 7299 NAIC: 812191)

Weight Watchers International is a global provider of weight management services. Co. has two operating segments: Weight Watchers International and WeightWatchers.com. Co. derives its revenues principally from meeting fees; product sales, which include proprietary products that complement its weight management plans, such as bars, snacks, cookbooks, POINTS value guides, Weight Watchers magazines and POINTS calculators, primarily to members in its meetings and to its franchisees; Internet revenues from its Internet subscription products and from the sale of Internet advertising; and licensing, franchise royalties and other.

Recent Developments: For the year ended Dec 29 2007, net income decreased 4.1% to US$201.2 million from US$209.8 million in the prior year. Revenues were US$1.47 billion, up 19.0% from US$1.23 billion the year before. Operating income was US$435.6 million versus US$380.0 million in the prior year, an increase of 14.6%. Direct operating expenses rose 17.2% to US$653.2 million from US$557.2 million in the comparable period the year before. Indirect operating expenses increased 27.8% to US$378.3 million from US$296.1 million in the equivalent prior year period.

Prospects: Co.'s near-term outlook appears favorable, reflecting an increase in net revenues driven primarily by increases in meeting fees and product sales, both as a result of attendance growth and higher average sales per attendee, supported by growth in Internet and licensing revenues. Thus, for the fiscal year ending Jan 2009, Co. expects earnings of between $2.80 and $3.00 per fully diluted share. Separately, on Feb 5 2008, Co. announced the signing of a joint venture agreement with Groupe DANONE to establish a weight management business in China. Co. expects the joint venture, 51.0% owned by Co. and 49.0% owned by Groupe DANONE, to commence retail operations in China within the next year.

Financial Data

(US$ in Thousands)	12/29/2007	12/31/2006	12/31/2005	01/01/2005	01/03/2004	12/28/2002	12/29/2001	12/30/2000
Earnings Per Share	2.48	2.11	1.67	1.71	1.31	1.31	1.31	0.13
Cash Flow Per Share	3.97	2.69	2.90	2.42	2.15	1.56	1.12	0.15
Dividends Per Share	0.700	0.700	...	...	...	...	...	...
Dividend Payout %	28.23	33.18	...	...	...	...	...	...
Income Statement								
Total Revenue	1,467,167	1,233,325	1,151,251	1,024,919	943,932	809,644	623,870	273,175
EBITDA	456,514	395,054	313,980	316,549	273,069	283,885	194,751	64,748
Income Before Taxes	326,491	330,642	279,315	289,547	232,229	235,535	126,971	21,023
Income Taxes	125,311	120,817	104,913	94,522	88,288	91,807	(23,198)	5,857
Net Income	201,180	209,825	174,402	183,084	143,941	143,694	147,187	15,019
Average Shares	81,107	99,426	104,203	106,985	109,724	109,663	110,975	112,171
Balance Sheet								
Current Assets	186,336	154,746	127,710	125,816	114,625	145,438	83,879	93,440
Total Assets	1,046,221	1,002,392	835,491	816,186	769,688	609,903	482,848	346,217
Current Liabilities	358,431	236,532	165,888	152,622	134,170	123,381	108,010	83,241
Long-Term Obligations	1,602,500	830,237	741,425	466,125	454,320	436,319	458,320	456,530
Total Liabilities	1,972,551	1,070,759	916,142	619,747	588,500	563,355	570,369	542,999
Stockholders' Equity	(926,330)	(68,367)	(80,651)	196,439	181,188	46,548	(113,517)	(222,778)
Shares Outstanding	79,410	111,988	111,988	111,988	106,349	106,277	100,587	111,988
Statistical Record								
Return on Assets %	19.75	22.83	21.18	23.15	20.53	26.37	35.60	2.48
Return on Equity %	...	...	302.07	97.23	124.37	...	...	68.01
EBITDA Margin %	31.12	32.03	27.27	30.89	28.93	35.06	31.22	23.70
Net Margin %	13.71	17.01	15.15	17.86	15.25	17.75	23.59	5.50
Asset Turnover	1.44	1.34	1.40	1.30	1.35	1.49	1.51	0.45
Current Ratio	0.52	0.65	0.77	0.82	0.85	1.18	0.78	1.12
Debt to Equity	...	...	...	2.37	2.51	9.37	...	...
Price Range	57.75-44.95	53.87-38.24	58.03-40.58	44.24-32.57	48.10-35.34	49.61-31.95	35.28-29.50	...
P/E Ratio	23.29-18.13	25.53-18.12	34.75-24.30	25.87-19.05	36.72-26.98	37.87-24.39	26.93-22.52	...
Average Yield %	1.38	1.53	...	...	...	...	...	...

Address: 175 Crossways Park West, Woodbury, NY 11797-2055 Telephone: 516-390-1400	Web Site: www.WeightWatchers.com Officers: Raymond Debbane - Chmn. Linda Huett - Pres., C.E.O.	Auditors: PricewaterhouseCoopers LLP Investor Contact: 212-589-2700 Transfer Agents: Computershare, Canton, MA

WEINGARTEN REALTY INVESTORS

Exchange	Symbol	Price	52Wk Range	Yield	P/E	Div Acheiver
NYS	WRI	$34.44 (3/31/2008)	49.00-28.37	6.10	14.11	19 Years

*7 Year Price Score 94.47   *NYSE Composite Index=100   *12 Month Price Score 91.09

Interim Earnings (Per Share)

Qtr.	Mar	Jun	Sep	Dec
2003	0.32	0.27	0.36	0.29
2004	0.32	0.42	0.33	0.47
2005	0.38	0.74	0.65	0.54
2006	0.57	0.95	1.15	0.60
2007	0.53	0.79	0.44	0.67

Interim Dividends (Per Share)

Amt	Decl	Ex	Rec	Pay
0.495Q	5/3/2007	6/6/2007	6/8/2007	6/15/2007
0.495Q	7/27/2007	9/5/2007	9/7/2007	9/14/2007
0.495Q	...	12/5/2007	12/7/2007	12/17/2007
0.525Q	2/26/2008	3/5/2008	3/7/2008	3/17/2008

Indicated Div: $2.10 (Div. Reinv. Plan)

Valuation Analysis

		Institutional Holding	
Forecast P/E	14.76	No of Institutions	
	(1/10/2007)	280	
Market Cap	$2.9 Billion	Shares	
Book Value	1.5 Billion	49,260,284	
Price/Book	1.99	% Held	
Price/Sales	4.90	56.99	

TRADING VOLUME (thousand shares)

Business Summary: Property, Real Estate & Development (MIC: 8.3 SIC: 6798 NAIC: 525930)

Weingarten Realty Investors is a real estate investment trust engaged in the management, acquisition and development of real estate, primarily anchored neighborhood, community shopping centers and industrial properties. As of Dec 31 2007, Co. owned or operated under long-term leases, either directly or through its interest in joint ventures or partnerships, 383 developed income-producing properties, including 335 neighborhood and community shopping centers located in Arizona, Arkansas, California, Colorado, Florida, Georgia, Illinois, Kansas, Kentucky, Louisiana, Maine, Missouri, Nevada, New Mexico, North Carolina, Oklahoma, Oregon, Tennessee, Utah, Texas, South Carolina and Washington.

Recent Developments: For the year ended Dec 31 2007, income from continuing operations increased 6.2% to US$151.2 million from US$142.5 million a year earlier. Net income decreased 22.0% to US$238.0 million from US$305.0 million in the prior year. Revenues were US$599.1 million, up 11.3% from US$538.2 million the year before. Revenues from property income rose 10.2% to US$585.7 million from US$531.4 million in the corresponding earlier year.

Prospects: Co. continues to progress in the execution of its long-term growth strategy, which focuses on new development, acquisitions and dispositions. Notably, Co. is projecting that six of its 32 projects currently under development will be stabilized by the end of 2008 and these centers are 93.0% leased. By the end of 2009, Co. is projecting that 16 of the 32 projects currently under development will be stabilized and these projects are 73.0% leased. Overall, Co. expects $300.0 million in annual new development completions starting in 2009. Meanwhile, for 2008, Co. expects that it can achieve Funds from Operations per share in the range of $3.21 to $3.27, representing growth of 5.0% to 7.0%.

Financial Data
(US$ in Thousands)

	12/31/2007	12/31/2006	12/31/2005	12/31/2004	12/31/2003	12/31/2002	12/31/2001	12/31/2000
Earnings Per Share	2.44	3.27	2.31	1.54	1.24	1.43	1.23	0.97
Cash Flow Per Share	2.61	2.77	2.25	2.44	2.08	2.16	2.03	2.20
Tang Book Value Per Share	17.29	13.13	12.87	12.30	10.03	11.95	11.92	10.39
Dividends Per Share	1.980	1.860	1.760	1.660	1.560	1.480	1.404	1.333
Dividend Payout %	81.15	56.88	76.19	107.79	125.81	103.26	114.49	136.99
Income Statement								
Property Income	585,702	554,361	534,495	492,036	410,490	359,044	309,457	264,552
Non-Property Income	13,352	7,019	9,550	10,255	8,670	6,366	5,435	8,822
Total Revenue	599,054	561,380	544,045	502,291	419,160	365,410	314,892	273,374
Interest Expense	148,829	146,943	130,761	115,506	88,871	65,863	54,473	45,545
Income Taxes	4,073	1,366	...	...	...	...	...	...
Net Income	238,017	305,010	219,653	141,381	116,280	131,867	108,542	79,001
Average Shares	88,893	91,779	93,166	89,511	81,574	80,040	72,553	60,594
Balance Sheet								
Total Assets	4,993,343	4,375,540	3,737,741	3,470,318	2,923,794	2,423,889	2,095,747	1,646,011
Long-Term Obligations	3,165,059	2,900,952	2,299,855	2,105,948	1,810,706	1,330,369	1,070,835	869,627
Total Liabilities	3,424,635	3,162,079	2,504,097	2,300,428	2,052,427	1,435,493	1,170,789	943,451
Stockholders' Equity	1,471,823	1,125,781	1,150,286	1,095,960	821,563	933,413	921,072	629,867
Shares Outstanding	85,146	85,765	89,403	89,066	81,888	78,114	77,280	60,572
Statistical Record								
Return on Assets %	5.08	7.52	6.09	4.41	4.35	5.84	5.80	5.33
Return on Equity %	18.33	26.80	19.56	14.71	13.25	14.22	14.00	12.35
Net Margin %	39.73	54.33	40.37	28.15	27.74	36.09	34.47	28.90
Price Range	52.16-31.44	47.83-37.10	40.50-33.49	40.90-27.55	30.70-23.80	25.76-20.57	22.40-17.80	19.89-15.42
P/E Ratio	21.38-12.89	14.63-11.35	17.53-14.50	26.56-17.89	24.76-19.19	18.01-14.38	18.21-14.48	20.50-15.89
Average Yield %	4.60	4.50	4.73	5.03	5.59	6.26	6.99	7.47

Address: 2600 Citadel Plaza Drive, P.O. Box 924133, Houston, TX 77292-4133 Telephone: 713-866-6000 Fax: 713-866-6049	Web Site: www.weingarten.com Officers: Stanford Alexander - Chmn. Martin Debrovner - Vice-Chmn.	Auditors: Deloitte & Touche LLP Investor Contact: 713-866-6050 Transfer Agents: Mellon Investor Services, LLC, Ridgefield Park, NJ

WELLPOINT INC

Exchange	Symbol	Price	52Wk Range	Yield	P/E
NYS	WLP	$44.13 (3/31/2008)	89.72-43.23	N/A	7.94

*7 Year Price Score N/A *NYSE Composite Index=100 *12 Month Price Score 90.40

TRADING VOLUME (thousand shares)

Interim Earnings (Per Share)

Qtr.	Mar	Jun	Sep	Dec
2003	0.68	0.63	0.69	0.73
2004	1.04	0.83	0.85	0.34
2005	0.98	0.90	1.02	1.04
2006	1.09	1.17	1.29	1.28
2007	1.26	1.35	1.45	1.50

Interim Dividends (Per Share)

Amt	Decl	Ex	Rec	Pay
2-for-1	4/27/2005	6/1/2005	5/13/2005	5/31/2005

Valuation Analysis — **Institutional Holding**

Forecast P/E	N/A	No of Institutions 671
Market Cap	$24.5 Billion	Shares 515,636,180
Book Value	20.0 Billion	% Held 84.20
Price/Book	1.07	
Price/Sales	0.40	

Business Summary: Insurance (MIC: 8.2 SIC: 6324 NAIC: 524114)

WellPoint is a health benefits company, serving 34.8 million medical members at Dec 31 2007. Co. is also an independent licensee of the Blue Cross and Blue Shield Association, an association of independent health benefit plans. Co. provides network-based managed care plans, including preferred provider organizations; health maintenance organizations; point-of-service plans; traditional indemnity plans and other hybrid plans; hospital only and limited benefit products. Co. also provides managed care services to self-funded customers; and an array of specialty and other products and services including life and disability insurance benefits, pharmacy benefit management, and specialty pharmacy.

Recent Developments: For the year ended Dec 31 2007, net income increased 8.1% to US$3.35 billion from US$3.09 billion in the prior year. Revenues were US$61.13 billion, up 7.2% from US$57.04 billion the year before. Net premiums earned were US$55.87 billion versus US$51.97 billion in the prior year, an increase of 7.5%. Net investment income rose 13.9% to US$1.00 billion from US$878.7 million a year ago.

Prospects: Co. expects the termination of its participation in the Ohio Covered Families & Children's Medicaid program by Mar 31 2008 to result in a membership reduction of approximately 145,000 during the first quarter of 2008. However, Co. remains encouraged with its outlook as it expects to begin providing services in South Carolina in the second quarter of 2008. Accordingly, Co.'s year-end medical enrollment is projected to be about 35.6 million members, representing growth for the year of approximately 800,000 members. Co. is also targeting 2008 operating revenue of approximately $62.60 billion as well as net income for the year of $6.41 per share, which represents growth of 15.3% over 2007.

Financial Data

(US$ in Thousands)	12/31/2007	12/31/2006	12/31/2005	12/31/2004	12/31/2003	12/31/2002	12/31/2001	12/31/2000
Earnings Per Share	5.56	4.82	3.94	3.05	2.73	2.25	1.65	...
Cash Flow Per Share	7.32	6.44	5.33	4.26	4.13	4.16	3.17	...
Tang Book Value Per Share	0.60	2.92	2.78	4.06	8.44	5.75	7.71	...
Income Statement								
Premium Income	55,865,000	51,971,900	41,216,700	18,771,600	15,170,200	11,941,000	9,244,800	7,737,300
Total Revenue	61,134,300	56,953,000	45,136,000	20,815,100	16,771,400	13,282,300	10,444,700	8,771,000
Benefits & Claims	46,036,100	42,218,800	33,219,900	15,387,800	12,263,900	9,839,400	7,814,700	6,551,000
Income Before Taxes	5,257,900	4,914,400	3,890,300	1,443,300	1,219,100	807,600	524,600	329,800
Income Taxes	1,912,500	1,819,500	1,426,500	483,200	440,100	255,200	183,400	102,200
Net Income	3,345,400	3,094,900	2,463,800	960,100	774,300	549,100	342,200	226,000
Average Shares	602,000	642,100	625,800	314,600	284,040	243,596	207,644	...
Balance Sheet								
Total Assets	52,060,000	51,759,800	51,405,200	39,738,400	13,438,600	12,293,100	6,276,600	5,708,500
Total Liabilities	29,069,600	27,184,000	26,412,100	20,279,400	7,438,700	6,930,800	4,216,600	3,788,700
Stockholders' Equity	22,990,400	24,575,800	24,993,100	19,459,000	5,999,900	5,362,300	2,060,000	1,919,800
Shares Outstanding	556,212	615,500	660,424	302,626	275,282	278,664	206,591	...
Statistical Record								
Return on Assets %	6.44	6.00	5.41	3.60	6.02	5.91	5.71	4.28
Return on Equity %	14.07	12.49	11.09	7.52	13.63	14.80	17.20	12.59
Loss Ratio %	82.41	81.23	80.60	81.97	80.84	82.40	84.53	84.67
Net Margin %	5.47	5.43	5.46	4.61	4.62	4.13	3.28	2.58
Price Range	89.72-74.45	79.77-67.50	80.00-55.50	58.50-36.50	41.01-27.11	37.30-23.51	25.75-20.45	...
P/E Ratio	16.14-13.39	16.55-14.00	20.30-14.09	19.18-11.97	15.02-9.93	16.58-10.45	15.61-12.39	...

Address: 120 Monument Circle, Indianapolis, IN 46204 Telephone: 317-488-6000	Web Site: www.wellpoint.com Officers: Larry C. Glasscock - Chmn., Pres., C.E.O. David C. Colby - Exec. V.P., C.F.O.	Auditors: Ernst & Young LLP Investor Contact: 317-488-6390

WELLS FARGO & CO.

Exchange	Symbol	Price	52Wk Range	Yield	P/E	Div Achiever
NYS	WFC	$29.10 (3/31/2008)	37.47-25.48	4.26	12.23	20 Years

*7 Year Price Score 92.96   *NYSE Composite Index=100   *12 Month Price Score 98.94

Interim Earnings (Per Share)

Qtr.	Mar	Jun	Sep	Dec
2003	0.44	0.45	0.46	0.47
2004	0.52	0.50	0.51	0.52
2005	0.54	0.56	0.58	0.57
2006	0.59	0.61	0.64	0.64
2007	0.66	0.67	0.68	0.37

Interim Dividends (Per Share)

Amt	Decl	Ex	Rec	Pay
0.28Q	4/24/2007	5/2/2007	5/4/2007	6/1/2007
0.31Q	7/24/2007	8/8/2007	8/10/2007	9/1/2007
0.31Q	10/23/2007	11/7/2007	11/9/2007	12/1/2007
0.31Q	1/22/2008	2/6/2008	2/8/2008	3/1/2008

Indicated Div: $1.24 (Div. Reinv. Plan)

Valuation Analysis

Forecast P/E	N/A
Market Cap	$95.9 Billion
Book Value	47.6 Billion
Price/Book	2.01
Price/Sales	1.79

Institutional Holding

No of Institutions	1159
Shares	2,348,558,848
% Held	69.51

Business Summary: Commercial Banking (MIC: 8.1 SIC: 6021 NAIC: 522110)

Wells Fargo is a financial holding company that provides retail, commercial and corporate banking services through banking stores in 23 states. Co. also provides other financial services through subsidiaries engaged in various businesses, mainly: wholesale banking, mortgage banking, consumer finance, equipment leasing, agricultural finance, commercial finance, securities brokerage and investment banking, insurance agency and brokerage services, computer and data processing services, trust services, investment advisory services, mortgage-backed securities servicing and venture capital investment. As of Dec 31 2007, Co. had assets of about $575.00 billion and deposits of about $344.00 billion.

Recent Developments: For the year ended Dec 31 2007, net income decreased 4.3% to US$8.06 billion from US$8.42 billion in the prior year. Net interest income increased 5.1% to US$20.97 billion from US$19.95 billion in the prior year. Provision for loan losses was US$4.94 billion versus US$2.20 billion in the prior year, an increase of 124.1%. Non-interest income rose 17.0% to US$18.42 billion from US$15.74 billion, while non-interest expense advanced 9.5% to US$22.82 billion.

Prospects: On Feb 27 2008, Co.'s Wells Fargo Insurance Services, Inc. subsidiary has acquired St. Louis-based Insurance Brokers of America. Co. believes that this acquisition should establish a good base to grow its presence in the St. Louis marketplace. Meanwhile, on Jan 15 2008, Co. and United Bancorporation of Wyoming Inc. announced that they have signed a definitive agreement for Co. to acquire United Bancorporation of Wyoming's five banking operations in Wyoming and eastern Idaho. This deal is expected to be completed in the second quarter of 2008. Separately, Co. anticipates making capital expenditures of about $1.00 billion in 2008 for its stores, relocation and remodeling of its facilities.

Financial Data

(US$ in Thousands)	12/31/2007	12/31/2006	12/31/2005	12/31/2004	12/31/2003	12/31/2002	12/31/2001	12/31/2000
Earnings Per Share	2.38	2.49	2.25	2.04	1.83	1.58	0.98	1.17
Cash Flow Per Share	2.71	9.53	(2.77)	5.92	9.28	(4.11)	(3.28)	0.26
Tang Book Value Per Share	4.98	4.70	4.93	5.43	4.78	4.45	3.01	2.92
Dividends Per Share	1.180	1.080	1.000	0.930	0.750	0.550	0.500	0.450
Dividend Payout %	49.58	43.37	44.44	45.48	41.10	34.81	50.76	38.63
Income Statement								
Interest Income	35,177,000	32,239,000	25,962,000	20,967,000	19,418,000	18,832,000	19,201,000	18,725,000
Interest Expense	14,203,000	12,288,000	7,458,000	3,817,000	3,411,000	3,977,000	6,741,000	7,860,000
Net Interest Income	20,974,000	19,951,000	18,504,000	17,150,000	16,007,000	14,855,000	12,460,000	10,865,000
Provision for Losses	4,939,000	2,204,000	2,383,000	1,717,000	1,722,000	1,733,000	1,780,000	1,329,000
Non-Interest Income	18,416,000	15,740,000	14,445,000	12,909,000	12,382,000	9,641,000	7,690,000	8,843,000
Non-Interest Expense	22,824,000	20,742,000	19,018,000	17,573,000	17,190,000	13,857,000	12,912,000	11,888,000
Income Before Taxes	11,627,000	12,745,000	11,548,000	10,769,000	9,477,000	8,854,000	5,479,000	6,549,000
Income Taxes	3,570,000	4,263,000	3,877,000	3,755,000	3,275,000	3,144,000	2,056,000	2,523,000
Net Income	8,057,000	8,482,000	7,671,000	7,014,000	6,202,000	5,434,000	3,423,000	4,026,000
Average Shares	3,382,800	3,410,100	3,411,000	3,426,800	3,395,000	3,436,000	3,453,800	3,436,800
Balance Sheet								
Net Loans & Leases	377,836,000	316,073,000	307,578,000	292,563,000	256,679,000	199,437,000	173,483,000	161,944,000
Total Assets	575,442,000	481,996,000	481,741,000	427,849,000	387,798,000	349,259,000	307,569,000	272,426,000
Total Deposits	344,460,000	310,243,000	314,450,000	274,858,000	247,527,000	216,916,000	187,266,000	169,559,000
Total Liabilities	527,814,000	436,120,000	441,081,000	389,983,000	353,329,000	279,040,903	280,355,000	245,938,000
Stockholders' Equity	47,628,000	45,876,000	40,660,000	37,866,000	34,469,000	30,358,000	27,214,000	26,488,000
Shares Outstanding	3,297,102	3,377,150	3,355,166	3,389,183	3,396,219	3,371,813	3,390,990	3,429,292
Statistical Record								
Return on Assets %	1.52	1.76	1.69	1.72	1.68	1.65	1.18	1.64
Return on Equity %	17.23	19.60	19.54	19.34	19.13	18.88	12.75	16.52
Net Interest Margin %	59.62	61.88	71.27	81.80	82.43	78.88	64.89	58.02
Efficiency Ratio %	42.59	43.23	47.07	51.87	54.06	48.67	48.02	43.12
Loans to Deposits	1.10	1.02	0.98	1.06	1.04	0.92	0.93	0.96
Price Range	37.47-29.49	36.81-30.52	32.17-28.89	31.63-27.40	29.47-22.07	26.61-21.32	26.97-19.43	27.88-15.50
P/E Ratio	15.74-12.39	14.78-12.26	14.30-12.84	15.50-13.43	16.10-12.06	16.84-13.49	27.52-19.82	23.82-13.25
Average Yield %	3.40	3.17	3.30	3.18	2.97	2.26	2.17	2.11

Address: 420 Montgomery Street, San Francisco, CA 94104
Telephone: 800-333-0343
Fax: 651-450-4033

Web Site: www.wellsfargo.com
Officers: Richard M. Kovacevich - Chmn., C.E.O. John G. Stumpf - Pres., C.O.O.

Auditors: KPMG LLP
Investor Contact: 415-396-0523
Transfer Agents: Wells Fargo Shareowners Services, St. Paul, MN

WENDY'S INTERNATIONAL, INC.

Exchange	Symbol	Price	52Wk Range	Yield	P/E
NYS	WEN	$23.06 (3/31/2008)	40.58-22.54	2.17	23.77

*7 Year Price Score 119.68 *NYSE Composite Index=100 ***12 Month Price Score 81.39**

Interim Earnings (Per Share)

Qtr.	Mar	Jun	Sep	Dec
2003	0.38	0.53	0.58	0.56
2004	0.45	0.62	0.60	(1.22)
2005	0.45	0.61	0.61	0.25
2006	0.44	(0.25)	0.58	0.04
2007	0.15	0.33	0.34	0.16

Interim Dividends (Per Share)

Amt	Decl	Ex	Rec	Pay
0.125Q	4/25/2007	5/3/2007	5/7/2007	5/21/2007
0.125Q	7/27/2007	8/2/2007	8/6/2007	8/20/2007
0.125Q	10/25/2007	11/1/2007	11/5/2007	11/19/2007
0.125Q	2/4/2008	2/12/2008	2/14/2008	2/29/2008
		Indicated Div: $0.50		

Valuation Analysis | **Institutional Holding**

Forecast P/E	23.62	No of Institutions	
	(1/10/2007)	255	
Market Cap	$2.0 Billion	Shares	
Book Value	804.1 Million	81,527,736	
Price/Book	2.51	% Held	
Price/Sales	0.82	85.28	

Business Summary: Hospitality & Tourism (MIC: 5.1 SIC: 5812 NAIC: 722211)

Wendy's International is primarily engaged in the operation, development and franchising of quick-service restaurants. As of Dec 31 2007, Co. and its franchisees operated 6,645 restaurants under the name Wendy's in the U.S., and in 19 other countries and territories. Of these restaurants, 1,414 were operated by Co. and 5,231 by its franchisees. The New Bakery Co. of Ohio, Inc., a wholly owned subsidiary of Co., is a producer of buns for Wendy's restaurants, and to a lesser extent for outside parties. At Dec 31 2007, The New Bakery Co. supplied 637 restaurants operated by Co. and 2,366 restaurants operated by franchisees.

Recent Developments: For the year ended Dec 30 2007, income from continuing operations increased 133.8% to US$86.6 million from US$37.0 million a year earlier. Net income decreased 6.8% to US$87.9 million from US$94.3 million in the prior year. Revenues were US$2.45 billion, up 0.4% from US$2.44 billion the year before. Operating income was US$157.0 million versus US$40.3 million in the prior year, an increase of 289.4%. Direct operating expenses declined 2.9% to US$1.94 billion from US$2.00 billion in the comparable period the year before. Indirect operating expenses decreased 11.7% to US$351.0 million in the equivalent prior year period.

Prospects. Co. continues to implement its strategic initiatives that include growing average same-store sales, improving store level productivity to strengthen margins, improving underperforming operations, developing profitable new restaurants and executing new technology initiatives. Accordingly, in 2008, Co. plans to open 70 and 90 new company operated and franchised restaurants versus 92 in 2007, concentrating in North America. At the same time, Co. has launched its Phase 2 strategic plan, which focuses on further growth in same-store sales and earnings, through the introduction of new product lineup and new advertising strategy, and by focusing more on restaurant operations.

Financial Data

(US$ in Thousands)	12/30/2007	12/31/2006	01/01/2006	01/02/2005	12/28/2003	12/29/2002	12/30/2001	12/31/2000
Earnings Per Share	0.97	0.82	1.92	0.45	2.05	1.89	1.65	1.44
Cash Flow Per Share	2.85	2.38	4.16	4.34	3.79	3.90	2.73	2.65
Tang Book Value Per Share	8.21	9.64	16.03	13.41	12.15	9.84	9.40	9.48
Dividends Per Share	0.460	0.595	0.575	0.480	0.240	0.240	0.240	0.240
Dividend Payout %	47.42	72.56	29.95	106.67	11.71	12.70	14.55	16.67
Income Statement								
Total Revenue	2,450,244	2,439,277	3,783,147	3,635,438	3,148,912	2,730,261	2,391,197	2,236,946
EBITDA	272,336	164,014	581,525	408,779	586,286	488,672	430,618	384,928
Income Before Taxes	125,756	42,479	338,064	184,063	377,598	345,899	307,380	271,437
Income Taxes	39,131	5,433	113,997	132,028	141,599	127,118	113,731	101,789
Net Income	87,096	94,312	224,067	52,035	235,999	218,781	193,649	169,618
Average Shares	90,190	115,325	116,819	115,685	115,021	116,558	121,144	122,483
Balance Sheet								
Current Assets	366,166	656,732	756,566	458,844	462,665	330,819	266,353	319,099
Total Assets	1,789,397	2,060,347	3,440,318	3,197,544	3,164,013	2,667,361	2,076,043	1,957,716
Current Liabilities	321,005	394,666	583,352	688,387	528,473	360,075	296,687	296,416
Long-Term Obligations	543,023	556,102	615,833	593,607	692,632	681,679	451,246	248,384
Total Liabilities	985,266	1,048,670	1,381,729	1,481,855	1,405,407	1,218,756	1,046,264	831,573
Stockholders' Equity	804,131	1,011,677	2,058,589	1,715,689	1,758,606	1,448,605	1,029,779	1,126,143
Shares Outstanding	87,397	95,704	117,809	112,409	114,697	114,692	105,175	114,210
Statistical Record								
Return on Assets %	4.58	3.44	6.77	1.61	8.12	9.25	9.63	8.86
Return on Equity %	9.71	6.16	11.91	2.95	14.76	17.70	18.01	15.52
EBITDA Margin %	11.11	6.72	15.37	11.24	18.62	17.90	18.01	17.21
Net Margin %	3.59	3.87	5.92	1.43	7.49	8.01	8.10	7.58
Asset Turnover	1.28	0.89	1.14	1.12	1.08	1.15	1.19	1.17
Current Ratio	1.14	1.66	1.30	0.67	0.88	0.92	0.90	1.08
Debt to Equity	0.68	0.55	0.30	0.35	0.39	0.47	0.44	0.22
Price Range	40.58-26.01	35.76-25.41	26.10-17.45	19.84-14.88	18.93-11.36	19.35-12.38	14.12-9.52	12.64-6.61
P/E Ratio	41.84-26.81	43.61-30.99	13.59-9.09	44.10-33.07	9.23-5.54	10.24-6.55	8.56-5.77	8.77-4.59
Average Yield %	1.37	2.00	2.74	2.77	1.67	1.52	1.98	2.55

Address: P.O. Box 256, 4288 West Dublin-Granville Road, Dublin, OH 43017-0256
Telephone: 614-764-3100
Fax: 614-764-3330

Web Site: www.wendys.com
Officers: John T. Schuessler - Chmn., Pres., C.E.O. Kerrii B. Anderson - Exec. V.P., C.F.O.

Auditors: PricewaterhouseCoopers LLP
Investor Contact: 614-764-3019

WESCO INTERNATIONAL, INC.

Exchange	Symbol	Price	52Wk Range	Yield	P/E
NYS	WCC	$36.49 (3/31/2008)	66.29-32.89	N/A	7.31

*7 Year Price Score 140.66 *NYSE Composite Index=100 *12 Month Price Score 86.37

TRADING VOLUME (thousand shares)

Interim Earnings (Per Share)

Qtr.	Mar	Jun	Sep	Dec
2003	0.10	0.16	0.18	0.21
2004	0.23	0.44	0.43	0.37
2005	0.23	0.56	0.51	0.80
2006	0.86	1.05	1.13	1.10
2007	0.93	1.22	1.54	1.34

Interim Dividends (Per Share)

No Dividends Paid

Valuation Analysis

		Institutional Holding	
Forecast P/E	10.18	No of Institutions	
	(1/10/2007)	249	
Market Cap	$1.6 Billion	Shares	
Book Value	608.5 Million	49,697,924	
Price/Book	2.59	% Held	
Price/Sales	0.26	N/A	

Business Summary: Specialist Equipment Supplies (MIC: 12.10 SIC: 5063 NAIC: 444190)

WESCO International is a provider of electrical construction products and electrical and industrial maintenance, repair and operating supplies. Co.'s products include electrical supplies, industrial supplies, power distribution, lighting, control, automation and motors as well as data communications. In conjunction with product sales, Co. offer customers a range of services, including national accounts programs, integrated supply programs and major project programs. As of Dec 31 2007, Co. had over 400 branches and seven distribution centers in the U.S., Canada, Mexico, U.K., Nigeria, United Arab Emirates and Singapore.

Recent Developments: For the year ended Dec 31 2007, net income increased 10.7% to US$240.6 million from US$217.3 million in the prior year. Revenues were US$6.00 billion, up 12.8% from US$5.32 billion the year before. Operating income was US$394.2 million versus US$365.0 million in the prior year, an increase of 8.0%. Direct operating expenses rose 12.9% to US$4.78 billion from US$4.23 billion in the comparable period the year before. Indirect operating expenses increased 14.7% to US$827.9 million from US$721.5 million in the equivalent prior-year period.

Prospects: Co. expects acquisitions made in 2007 to position it well for 2008. For instance, on Dec 4 2007, Co. announced that it has acquired the assets of Monti Electric Supply, Inc., a construction oriented electrical distributor. Co. expects the transaction to provide it an opportunity to benefit from the long-term hurricane- related reconstruction of the Gulf Coast region, and to be immediately accretive to earnings. However, Co. noted that activity levels in its major end markets may be somewhat softer. Meanwhile, in 2008, Co. expects its capital spending to grow by $5.9 million from $16.1 million in 2007, due to higher information technology and facility improvement spending.

Financial Data
(US$ in Thousands)

	12/31/2007	12/31/2006	12/31/2005	12/31/2004	12/31/2003	12/31/2002	12/31/2001	12/31/2000
Earnings Per Share	4.99	4.14	2.10	1.47	0.65	0.49	0.43	0.70
Cash Flow Per Share	5.74	4.25	6.27	0.52	0.80	0.45	3.59	1.03
Income Statement								
Total Revenue	6,003,452	5,320,603	4,421,103	3,741,253	3,286,766	3,325,780	3,658,033	3,881,096
EBITDA	435,175	373,368	197,851	158,946	104,681	89,667	110,648	126,094
Income Before Taxes	331,028	317,566	150,884	99,498	39,091	25,970	33,368	56,713
Income Taxes	90,397	100,246	47,358	34,566	9,085	2,847	13,143	23,275
Net Income	240,631	217,320	103,526	64,932	30,006	23,123	20,225	33,438
Average Shares	48,250	52,463	49,238	44,109	46,349	46,820	46,901	47,746
Balance Sheet								
Current Assets	1,680,499	1,618,012	908,863	854,916	656,288	577,057	718,035	764,225
Total Assets	2,859,887	2,823,983	1,651,159	1,356,855	1,161,205	1,015,118	1,157,958	1,170,033
Current Liabilities	1,291,925	1,153,672	719,886	564,245	479,710	398,475	529,479	523,842
Long-Term Obligations	811,311	743,887	352,232	386,173	420,042	412,196	446,436	482,740
Total Liabilities	2,251,411	2,060,756	1,159,709	1,003,302	993,517	845,830	1,013,307	1,045,046
Stockholders' Equity	608,476	763,227	491,450	353,553	167,688	169,288	144,651	124,987
Shares Outstanding	43,144	49,545	47,711	42,076	40,938	45,103	44,890	44,769
Statistical Record								
Return on Assets %	8.47	9.71	6.88	5.14	2.76	2.13	1.74	3.03
Return on Equity %	35.09	34.64	24.50	24.85	17.81	14.73	15.00	27.53
EBITDA Margin %	7.25	7.02	4.48	4.25	3.18	2.70	3.02	3.25
Net Margin %	4.01	4.08	2.34	1.74	0.91	0.70	0.55	0.86
Asset Turnover	2.11	2.38	2.94	2.96	3.02	3.06	3.14	3.52
Current Ratio	1.30	1.40	1.26	1.52	1.37	1.45	1.36	1.46
Debt to Equity	1.33	0.97	0.72	1.09	2.50	2.43	3.09	3.86
Price Range	69.35-38.25	79.85-43.49	43.76-23.47	29.94-8.85	9.13-3.44	7.40-3.14	11.00-4.05	10.69-6.63
P/E Ratio	13.90-7.67	19.29-10.50	20.84-11.18	20.37-6.02	14.05-5.29	15.10-6.41	25.58-9.42	15.27-9.46

Address: Suite 700, 225 West Station Square Drive, Pittsburgh, PA 15219-1122 **Telephone:** 412-454-2200 **Fax:** 412-454-2595	**Web Site:** www.wescodist.com **Officers:** Roy W. Haley - Chmn., C.E.O. Stephen A. Van Oss - Sr. V.P., C.F.O., Chief Admin. Officer	**Auditors:** PricewaterhouseCoopers LLP

WEST PHARMACEUTICAL SERVICES, INC.

Exchange	Symbol	Price	52Wk Range	Yield	P/E	Div Acheiver
NYS	WST	$44.23 (3/31/2008)	51.95-36.12	1.27	21.58	15 Years

*7 Year Price Score 139.36 *NYSE Composite Index=100 *12 Month Price Score 102.12

Interim Earnings (Per Share)

Qtr.	Mar	Jun	Sep	Dec
2003	0.13	0.24	0.14	0.58
2004	0.23	0.25	0.14	0.01
2005	0.42	0.40	0.24	0.35
2006	0.55	0.62	0.39	0.45
2007	0.77	0.73	0.36	0.20

Interim Dividends (Per Share)

Amt	Decl	Ex	Rec	Pay
0.13Q	7/10/2007	7/16/2007	7/18/2007	8/1/2007
0.14Q	9/20/2007	10/22/2007	10/24/2007	11/7/2007
0.14Q	12/14/2007	1/18/2008	1/23/2008	2/6/2008
0.14Q	2/27/2008	4/21/2008	4/23/2008	5/7/2008

Indicated Div: $0.56 (Div. Reinv. Plan)

Valuation Analysis

		Institutional Holding	
Forecast P/E	21.39	No of Institutions	
	(1/10/2007)	175	
Market Cap	$1.4 Billion	Shares	
Book Value	485.3 Million	26,413,882	
Price/Book	2.93	% Held	
Price/Sales	1.40	79.94	

Business Summary: Rubber Products (MIC: 11.6 SIC: 3069 NAIC: 326299)

West Pharmaceutical Services manufactures components and systems for injectable drug delivery and plastic packaging and delivery system components for the healthcare, personal care and consumer products markets. Co.'s Pharmaceutical Systems segment designs, manufactures and sells a range of elastomer, metal and plastic components used in parenteral drug delivery for the branded pharmaceutical, generic and biopharmaceutical industries. Co.'s Tech Group segment provides custom contract-manufacturing applications utilizing plastic injection molding and manual and automated assembly processes targeted to the healthcare and consumer products industries.

Recent Developments: For the year ended Dec 31 2007, income from continuing operations increased 15.8% to US$71.2 million from US$61.5 million a year earlier. Net income increased 5.4% to US$70.7 million from US$67.1 million in the prior year. Revenues were US$1.02 billion, up 11.7% from US$913.3 million the year before. Operating income was US$94.9 million versus US$101.0 million in the prior year, a decrease of 6.0%. Direct operating expenses rose 12.3% to US$728.3 million from US$648.5 million in the comparable period the year before. Indirect operating expenses increased 20.2% to US$196.9 million from US$163.8 million in the equivalent prior-year period.

Prospects: On Dec 12 2007, Co. approved a restructuring plan for its Tech Group segment. In detail, Co. plans to reduce spending in the Tech Group segment by consolidating two tool production operations into one facility, in Scottsdale, AZ, and by reductions and consolidations at other production and administrative operations in North America. The plan is expected to be completed in Dec 2008 with the Tech Group workforce will be reduced by approximately 13.0%. As a result, Co. expects to realize $3.0 million of cost savings in 2008 and annual operating savings thereafter are expected to be about $7.0 million. Meanwhile, Co. expects 2008 sales growth of 3.0% to 5.0% over reported 2007 sales.

Financial Data

(US$ in Thousands)	12/31/2007	12/31/2006	12/31/2005	12/31/2004	12/31/2003	12/31/2002	12/31/2001	12/31/2000
Earnings Per Share	2.06	2.00	1.40	0.63	1.10	0.64	(0.18)	0.06
Cash Flow Per Share	3.95	4.33	2.75	2.70	2.38	1.58	1.08	1.68
Tang Book Value Per Share	9.97	7.46	5.49	8.38	7.15	5.42	5.03	5.32
Dividends Per Share	0.530	0.490	0.450	0.425	0.405	0.385	0.365	0.345
Dividend Payout %	25.85	24.50	32.14	67.46	36.99	60.16	...	627.27
Income Statement								
Total Revenue	1,020,100	913,300	699,700	541,600	490,700	419,700	396,900	430,100
EBITDA	151,500	147,800	114,800	81,500	87,500	59,700	73,300	52,200
Income Before Taxes	86,400	84,500	60,200	41,200	47,000	17,200	27,800	2,100
Income Taxes	17,200	24,600	17,300	11,100	16,700	4,100	8,600	1,500
Net Income	70,700	67,100	45,600	19,400	31,900	18,400	(5,200)	1,600
Average Shares	36,200	33,600	32,525	30,842	29,092	28,868	28,696	28,818
Balance Sheet								
Current Assets	412,300	281,700	237,200	226,500	216,700	161,300	158,500	173,100
Total Assets	1,185,600	918,200	823,600	658,700	623,600	536,800	511,300	557,400
Current Liabilities	182,900	156,900	124,800	116,500	118,900	87,700	75,300	79,300
Long-Term Obligations	394,600	235,800	280,700	150,800	167,000	159,200	184,300	195,800
Total Liabilities	694,700	498,900	486,000	357,600	366,000	335,300	334,500	352,600
Stockholders' Equity	485,300	414,500	333,500	301,100	257,600	201,500	176,800	204,800
Shares Outstanding	32,200	32,900	31,772	30,709	29,264	28,960	28,688	28,620
Statistical Record								
Return on Assets %	6.72	7.70	6.15	3.02	5.50	3.51	N.M.	0.29
Return on Equity %	15.71	17.94	14.37	6.93	13.90	9.73	N.M.	0.73
EBITDA Margin %	14.85	16.18	16.41	15.05	17.83	14.22	18.47	12.14
Net Margin %	6.93	7.35	6.52	3.58	6.50	4.38	N.M.	0.37
Asset Turnover	0.97	1.05	0.94	0.84	0.85	0.80	0.74	0.77
Current Ratio	2.25	1.80	1.90	1.94	1.82	1.84	2.10	2.18
Debt to Equity	0.81	0.57	0.84	0.50	0.65	0.79	1.04	0.96
Price Range	52.14-36.12	52.13-25.30	29.83-23.10	25.03-16.55	17.80-8.50	16.05-8.28	14.03-11.45	15.84-9.94
P/E Ratio	25.43-17.62	26.07-12.65	21.31-16.50	39.73-26.26	16.18-7.73	25.07-12.93	...	264.06-165.63
Average Yield %	1.19	1.31	1.70	2.13	3.06	3.01	2.86	2.86

Address: 101 Gordon Drive, P.O. Box 645, Lionville, PA 19341-0645	Web Site: www.westpharma.com	Auditors: PricewaterhouseCoopers LLP
Telephone: 610-594-2900	Officers: Donald E. Morel Jr. - Chmn., C.E.O. Steven A. Ellers - Pres., C.O.O.	Investor Contact: 610-594-3345
Fax: 610-594-3000		Transfer Agents: American Stock Transfer and Trust Company, New York, NY

WESTAR ENERGY INC

Exchange	Symbol	Price	52Wk Range	Yield	P/E
NYS	WR	$22.77 (3/31/2008)	28.40-22.06	5.09	12.44

*7 Year Price Score 99.10   *NYSE Composite Index=100   *12 Month Price Score 99.87

Interim Earnings (Per Share)

Qtr.	Mar	Jun	Sep	Dec
2003	1.71	0.38	(1.11)	0.19
2004	0.21	0.16	0.69	1.05
2005	0.18	0.32	0.96	0.08
2006	0.30	0.40	1.02	0.15
2007	0.34	0.36	0.99	0.13

Interim Dividends (Per Share)

Amt	Decl	Ex	Rec	Pay
0.27Q	5/17/2007	6/6/2007	6/8/2007	7/2/2007
0.27Q	8/28/2007	9/5/2007	9/7/2007	10/1/2007
0.27Q	11/27/2007	12/5/2007	12/7/2007	1/2/2008
0.29Q	2/20/2008	3/5/2008	3/7/2008	4/1/2008

Indicated Div: $1.16

Valuation Analysis

		Institutional Holding	
Forecast P/E	N/A	No of Institutions	204
Market Cap	$2.2 Billion	Shares	69,212,136
Book Value	1.8 Billion	% Held	
Price/Book	1.18		79.10
Price/Sales	1.26		

TRADING VOLUME (thousand shares)

Business Summary: Electricity (MIC: 7.1 SIC: 4931 NAIC: 221121)

Westar Energy is an electric utility company. As of Dec 31 2007, Co. provided electric generation, transmission and distribution services to approximately 674,000 customers in Kansas. Co. provides these services in central and northeastern Kansas, including the cities of Topeka, Lawrence, Manhattan, Salina and Hutchinson. Kansas Gas and Electric Company (KGE), Co.'s wholly owned subsidiary, provides these services in south-central and southeastern Kansas, including the city of Wichita. Both Co. and KGE conduct business using the name Westar Energy. As of Dec 31 2007, Co. had 6,178 megawatts (MW) of accredited generating capacity, of which 2,575 MW is owned or leased by KGE.

Recent Developments: For the year ended Dec 31 2007, income from continuing operations increased 1.8% to US$168.4 million from US$165.3 million a year earlier. Net income increased 1.8% to US$168.4 million from US$165.3 million in the prior year. Revenues were US$1.73 billion, up 7.5% from US$1.61 billion the year before. Operating income was US$337.4 million versus US$306.8 million in the prior year, an increase of 10.0%. Direct operating expenses rose 7.4% to US$1.02 billion from US$947.7 million in the comparable period the year before. Indirect operating expenses increased 5.8% to US$371.5 million from US$351.2 million in the equivalent prior-year period.

Prospects: Going forward, Co. continues to make significant investments in new generation, new transmission and air emission controls at existing fossil-fueled power plants. For example, on Jan 11 2008, Co. announced an agreement with developers to build three wind farms in Kansas totaling about 300 megawatts. Under the terms of the agreements, Co. plans to own half of the wind generators and purchase energy produced by the wind farms under 20 year supply contracts for the other half. All three wind farms are expected to produce energy by the end of 2008. Meanwhile, for 2008, Co. expects of $1.50 to $1.65 per share, excluding the affects of settlements of open prior period income tax audits.

Financial Data

(US$ in Thousands)	12/31/2007	12/31/2006	12/31/2005	12/31/2004	12/31/2003	12/31/2002	12/31/2001	12/31/2000
Earnings Per Share	1.83	1.87	1.54	2.13	1.15	(11.06)	(0.31)	1.96
Cash Flow Per Share	2.72	2.93	4.07	4.26	1.60	5.20	3.18	4.14
Tang Book Value Per Share	19.14	17.61	16.31	16.13	13.98	12.79	13.15	13.28
Dividends Per Share	1.080	1.000	0.920	0.800	0.760	1.200	1.200	1.435
Dividend Payout %	59.02	53.48	59.74	37.56	66.09	...	...	73.21
Income Statement								
Total Revenue	1,726,834	1,605,743	1,583,278	1,464,489	1,461,143	1,771,118	2,186,262	2,368,476
EBITDA	553,895	524,191	476,092	467,915	589,808	236,475	526,437	841,220
Income Before Taxes	232,193	221,621	195,381	133,523	244,683	(323,647)	(143,601)	137,111
Income Taxes	63,839	56,312	60,513	33,443	81,768	(157,605)	(80,875)	46,061
Net Income	168,354	165,309	135,610	178,870	85,010	(793,001)	(20,876)	136,481
Average Shares	91,260	88,099	87,409	82,941	73,354	71,731	70,649	68,962
Balance Sheet								
Net PPE	4,803,672	4,071,607	3,947,732	3,910,987	3,909,500	3,995,371	4,042,852	3,993,438
Total Assets	6,395,430	5,455,175	5,210,069	5,085,711	5,734,505	6,443,099	7,513,065	7,767,208
Long-Term Obligations	2,013,635	1,563,265	1,562,990	1,639,901	2,069,132	3,058,323	2,978,382	3,237,849
Total Liabilities	4,541,726	3,887,609	3,772,630	3,676,389	4,697,745	5,464,977	5,669,004	5,835,788
Stockholders' Equity	1,848,480	1,560,895	1,437,439	1,409,322	1,036,760	978,122	1,844,061	1,931,420
Shares Outstanding	95,463	87,394	86,835	86,029	72,636	71,506	71,107	70,082
Statistical Record								
Return on Assets %	2.84	3.10	2.63	3.30	1.40	N.M.	N.M.	1.73
Return on Equity %	9.88	11.03	9.53	14.59	8.44	N.M.	N.M.	7.10
EBITDA Margin %	32.08	32.64	30.07	31.95	40.37	13.35	24.08	35.52
Net Margin %	9.75	10.29	8.57	12.21	5.82	(44.77)	(0.95)	5.76
PPE Turnover	0.39	0.40	0.40	0.37	0.37	0.44	0.54	0.60
Asset Turnover	0.29	0.30	0.31	0.27	0.24	0.25	0.29	0.30
Debt to Equity	1.09	1.00	1.09	1.16	2.00	3.13	1.62	1.68
Price Range	28.40-23.02	27.12-20.16	24.75-21.15	22.87-18.25	20.39-9.88	17.96-8.50	25.65-15.68	25.75-14.94
P/E Ratio	15.52-12.58	14.50-10.78	16.07-13.73	10.74-8.57	17.73-8.59	...	...	13.14-7.62
Average Yield %	4.15	4.39	4.00	3.92	4.79	8.58	5.81	7.83

Address: 818 S. Kansas Avenue, Topeka, KS 66612-1203 Telephone: 785-575-6300 Fax: 785-575-6596	Web Site: www.wr.com Officers: Charles Q. Chandler IV - Chmn. James S. Haines Jr. - Pres., C.E.O.	Auditors: Deloitte & Touche LLP Investor Contact: 785-575-8227 Transfer Agents: Continental Stock Transfer & Trust Company, New York, NY

WESTERN DIGITAL CORP.

Exchange	Symbol	Price	52Wk Range	Yield	P/E
NYS	WDC	$27.04 (3/31/2008)	33.99-16.50	N/A	8.61

*7 Year Price Score 149.64 *NYSE Composite Index=100 *12 Month Price Score 133.69

TRADING VOLUME (thousand shares)

Interim Earnings (Per Share)

Qtr.	Sep	Dec	Mar	Jun
2004-05	0.14	0.26	0.32	0.18
2005-06	0.31	0.47	0.45	0.52
2006-07	0.46	0.57	0.53	0.94
2007-08	0.31	1.35	...	...

Interim Dividends (Per Share)

No Dividends Paid

Valuation Analysis

	Institutional Holding	
Forecast P/E	8.97	No of Institutions
	(1/10/2007)	284
Market Cap	$6.1 Billion	Shares
Book Value	2.1 Billion	189,149,936
Price/Book	2.86	% Held
Price/Sales	0.90	85.20

Business Summary: IT & Technology (MIC: 10.2 SIC: 3572 NAIC: 334112)

Western Digital designs, develops, manufactures and sells hard drives. A hard drive is a device that uses one or more rotating magnetic disks to store and allow fast access to data. Co.'s hard drives are used in desktop computers, notebook computers, and enterprise applications such as servers, workstations, network attached storage, storage area networks and video surveillance equipment. Co.'s hard drives are also used in consumer electronics applications such as digital video recorders, and satellite and cable set-top boxes. Co. sells its products worldwide to original equipment manufacturers and original design manufacturers, as well as to distributors, resellers and retailers.

Recent Developments: For the quarter ended Dec 28 2007, net income increased 138.3% to US$305.0 million in the year-earlier quarter. Revenues were US$2.20 billion, up 54.3% from US$1.43 billion the year before. Operating income was US$332.0 million versus US$122.0 million in the prior-year quarter, an increase of 172.1%. Direct operating expenses rose 44.2% to US$1.69 billion from US$1.17 billion in the comparable period the year before. Indirect operating expenses increased 36.1% to US$181.0 million from US$133.0 million in the equivalent prior-year period.

Prospects: Co.'s improved results are being driven by a significant increase in hard drive revenue, aided by strong demand for hard drives and a more favorable pricing environment. However, Co. expects its revenue and gross margin for the quarter ending Mar 2008 to decline sequentially from an unusually strong December quarter. Nevertheless, Co.'s operating expenses are anticipated to remain consistent as it continues to invest in new products and technology. For the fiscal year ending June 2008, Co.'s capital additions are expected to be about $700.0 million, including approximately $200.0 million for expansion of its head wafer fabrication facility and $100.0 million for its media operations.

Financial Data

(US$ in Thousands)	6 Mos	3 Mos	06/29/2007	06/30/2006	07/01/2005	07/02/2004	06/27/2003	06/28/2002
Earnings Per Share	3.14	2.36	2.50	1.76	0.91	0.70	0.89	0.34
Cash Flow Per Share	4.81	3.23	2.83	1.97	2.23	0.91	1.44	0.44
Tang Book Value Per Share	8.68	7.10	7.73	5.24	3.29	2.37	1.61	0.54
Income Statement								
Total Revenue	3,970,000	1,766,000	5,468,000	4,341,300	3,638,800	3,046,700	2,718,500	2,151,152
EBITDA	626,000	207,000	621,000	522,000	328,400	254,500	235,000	101,981
Depn & Amortn	189,000	78,000	...	...	...	...	...	...
Income Before Taxes	454,000	138,000	443,000	381,700	202,300	155,200	188,400	52,095
Income Taxes	80,000	69,000	(121,000)	(12,900)	3,900	3,900	7,600	(1,140)
Net Income	374,000	69,000	564,000	394,600	198,400	151,300	182,100	65,428
Average Shares	226,000	224,000	226,000	223,600	216,900	216,700	205,500	193,708
Balance Sheet								
Current Assets	2,653,000	2,447,000	2,029,000	1,492,200	1,181,200	857,300	744,100	527,509
Total Assets	4,600,000	4,374,000	2,901,000	2,073,300	1,588,600	1,159,200	866,200	636,680
Current Liabilities	2,352,000	2,463,000	1,130,000	859,000	818,500	586,900	505,700	492,676
Long-Term Obligations	4,000	7,000	10,000	19,400	32,600	52,700	...	...
Total Liabilities	2,473,000	2,587,000	1,185,000	916,100	886,500	671,600	538,800	533,818
Stockholders' Equity	2,127,000	1,787,000	1,716,000	1,157,200	702,100	487,600	327,400	102,862
Shares Outstanding	225,000	225,300	222,000	221,000	213,700	206,100	202,900	192,143
Statistical Record								
Return on Assets %	19.84	15.89	22.74	21.61	14.48	14.70	24.30	11.47
Return on Equity %	39.89	34.80	39.37	42.56	33.44	36.53	84.88	119.65
EBITDA Margin %	15.77	11.72	11.36	12.02	9.02	8.35	8.64	4.74
Net Margin %	9.42	3.91	10.31	9.09	5.45	4.97	6.70	3.04
Asset Turnover	1.89	1.79	2.20	2.38	2.66	2.96	3.63	3.77
Current Ratio	1.13	0.99	1.80	1.74	1.44	1.46	1.47	1.07
Debt to Equity	N.M.	N.M.	0.01	0.02	0.05	0.11	...	...
Price Range	31.51-16.50	25.80-16.50	21.64-16.05	24.18-11.35	15.95-6.52	14.83-7.89	12.82-3.05	7.50-2.05
P/E Ratio	10.04-5.25	10.93-6.99	8.66-6.42	13.74-6.45	17.53-7.16	21.19-11.27	14.40-3.43	22.06-6.03

Address: 20511 Lake Forest Drive, Lake Forest, CA 92630 Telephone: 949-672-7000 Fax: 949-932-5612	Web Site: www.westerndigital.com Officers: Matthew E. Massengill - Chmn. Arif Shakeel - Pres., C.E.O.	Auditors: KPMG LLP Transfer Agents: American Stock Transfer & Trust Company

WESTERN REFINING INC

Exchange	Symbol	Price	52Wk Range	Yield	P/E
NYS	WNR	$13.47 (3/31/2008)	65.16-13.07	1.78	3.82

*7 Year Price Score N/A   *NYSE Composite Index=100   *12 Month Price Score 56.18

Interim Earnings (Per Share)

Qtr.	Mar	Jun	Sep	Dec
2006	(0.32)	1.29	1.30	0.75
2007	0.93	2.29	0.69	(0.38)

Interim Dividends (Per Share)

Amt	Decl	Ex	Rec	Pay
0.04Q	2/20/2007	3/29/2007	4/2/2007	4/25/2007
0.06Q	5/16/2007	6/28/2007	7/2/2007	7/25/2007
0.06Q	8/16/2007	9/27/2007	10/1/2007	10/24/2007
0.06Q	12/7/2007	12/28/2007	1/2/2008	1/23/2008
		Indicated Div: $0.24		

Valuation Analysis

		Institutional Holding	
Forecast P/E	N/A	No of Institutions	99
Market Cap	$912.6 Million	Shares	24,457,428
Book Value	756.5 Million	% Held	35.83
Price/Book	1.21		
Price/Sales	0.12		

TRADING VOLUME (thousand shares)

Business Summary: Oil and Gas (MIC: 14.2 SIC: 2911 NAIC: 324110)

Western Refining is a holding company. Through its subsidiary, Western Refining Company, L.P., Co. is a crude oil refiner and marketer of refined products based in El Paso, TX and operates primarily in Arizona, New Mexico and West Texas. Co.'s refinery is located in El Paso and had a crude oil refining capacity of 124,000 barrels per day (bpd) at Dec 31 2006. Over 90.0% of products produced at Co.'s refinery consist of light transportation fuels, including gasoline, diesel and jet fuel. Co.'s refinery also has around 4.3 million barrels of storage capacity and a 45,000 bpd product marketing terminal, where Co.'s refined products are loaded into tanker trucks for local deliveries.

Recent Developments: For the year ended Dec 31 2007, net income increased 16.5% to US$238.6 million from US$204.8 million in the prior year. Revenues were US$7.31 billion, up 74.0% from US$4.20 billion the year before. Operating income was US$389.2 million versus US$301.8 million in the prior year, an increase of 29.0%. Direct operating expenses rose 76.7% to US$6.76 billion from US$3.82 billion in the comparable period the year before. Indirect operating expenses increased 116.1% to US$157.5 million from US$72.9 million in the equivalent prior-year period.

Prospects: Co. is continuing to improve its operations at its May 2007 acquisition of Giant refineries that it believes should aid improved returns going forward. For instance, Co. has recently increased crude oil throughput at its Four Corners refineries and at its Yorktown refinery by 70.0% and 8.0%, respectively, compared with operations immediately prior to the acquisition. Meanwhile, Co. expects its sour and heavy crude oil processing capability to reach approximately 45.0% by the end of 2009, following the completion of its acid and sulfur gas facilities and its gasoline desulfurization projects at its El Paso refinery.

Financial Data

(US$ in Thousands)	12/31/2007	12/31/2006	12/31/2005	09/19/2005
Earnings Per Share	3.53	3.11	...	...
Cash Flow Per Share	1.69	3.75	...	...
Tang Book Value Per Share	5.68	7.79	...	...
Dividends Per Share	0.220	0.160	...	...
Dividend Payout %	6.23	5.14	...	...
Income Statement				
Income Before Taxes	340,503	317,153	(51)	...
Income Taxes	101,892	112,373	(18)	...
Net Income	238,611	204,780	(33)	...
Average Shares	67,597	65,774	...	...
Balance Sheet				
Total Assets	3,559,716	908,523	37	2
Total Liabilities	2,803,231	386,922	68	...
Stockholders' Equity	756,485	521,601	(31)	2
Shares Outstanding	67,750	66,896	100.00	...
Statistical Record				
Return on Assets %	10.68	45.08	...	...
Return on Equity %	37.34	78.52	...	...
Price Range	65.16-24.01	28.89-14.55	...	...
P/E Ratio	18.46-6.80	9.29-4.68	...	...
Average Yield %	0.55	0.74	...	...

Address: 6500 Trowbridge Drive, El Paso, TX 79905 **Telephone:** 915-775-3300 **Fax:** 915-775-5587	**Web Site:** www.wnr.com **Officers:** Paul L. Foster - Pres., C.E.O. Jeff A. Stevens - Exec. Vice-Pres., C.O.O.	**Auditors:** Deloitte and Touche LLP **Transfer Agents:** American Stock Transfer & Trust Company

WESTERN UNION CO.

Exchange	Symbol	Price	52Wk Range	Yield	P/E
NYS	WU	$21.27 (3/31/2008)	24.72-18.36	0.19	19.16

*7 Year Price Score N/A   *NYSE Composite Index=100   *12 Month Price Score 108.75

Interim Earnings (Per Share)

Qtr.	Mar	Jun	Sep	Dec
2006	0.29	0.29	0.34	0.28
2007	0.25	0.26	0.28	0.32

Interim Dividends (Per Share)

Amt	Decl	Ex	Rec	Pay
0.01A	12/5/2006	12/13/2006	12/15/2006	12/28/2006
0.04A	12/4/2007	12/12/2007	12/14/2007	12/28/2007

Indicated Div: $0.04

Valuation Analysis   **Institutional Holding**

Forecast P/E	N/A	No of Institutions
		686
Market Cap	$15.9 Billion	Shares
Book Value	50.7 Million	598,044,100
Price/Book	314.56	% Held
Price/Sales	3.25	77.47

TRADING VOLUME (thousand shares)

Years: 1999 2000 2001 2002 2003 2004 2005 2006 2007 2008

Business Summary: Miscellaneous Business Services (MIC: 12.8 SIC: 7389 NAIC: 522320)

Western Union is a provider of money transfer services. Co. operates in two business segments. Co. provides consumer-to-consumer money transfer services through a global network of third-party agents using its multi-currency, real-time money transfer processing systems. This service is available for both international cross-border transfers from one country to another and intra-country transfers from one location to another in the same country. Also, Co. provides consumer-to-business payment services, which provide consumers with options for making one-time or recurring payments.

Recent Developments: For the year ended Dec 31 2007, net income decreased 6.2% to US$857.3 million from US$914.0 million in the prior year. Revenues were US$4.90 billion, up 9.6% from US$4.47 billion the year before. Operating income was US$1.31 billion versus US$1.31 billion in the prior year, an increase of 0.8%. Direct operating expenses rose 15.5% to US$2.81 billion from US$2.43 billion in the comparable period the year before. Indirect operating expenses increased 5.7% to US$769.8 million from US$728.3 million in the equivalent prior-year period.

Prospects: Looking to 2008, Co. expects the international consumer-to-consumer business to remain robust, the Mexico business to have modest growth, and the U.S. domestic and U.S. outbound businesses to be challenged in light of the current economic conditions in the U.S. As such, for full-year 2008, Co. is targeting revenue growth in the range of 9.0% to 11.0%, along with earnings per share of $1.24 to $1.28. Meanwhile, Co. intends to further develop services such as mobile phone money transfer, microlending and new business-to-business offerings. Also, Co. has recently received the required approvals to resume service in South Africa and expects to be offering services later in 2008.

Financial Data

(US$ in Thousands)	12/31/2007	12/31/2006	12/31/2005	12/31/2004	12/31/2003
Earnings Per Share	1.11	1.19	...	...	...
Cash Flow Per Share	1.45	1.45	...	...	...
Tang Book Value Per Share	N M	...	10,134,000.00	...	...
Income Statement					
Total Revenue	4,900,200	4,470,200	3,987,900	3,547,600	3,151,600
EBITDA	1,455,900	1,416,200	1,399,300	1,168,700	1,041,000
Income Before Taxes	1,222,400	1,335,100	1,344,100	1,098,600	962,600
Income Taxes	365,100	421,100	416,700	347,000	328,900
Net Income	857,300	914,000	927,400	751,600	633,700
Average Shares	772,900	768,600			
Balance Sheet					
Current Assets	1,857,900	1,518,200	1,488,300	819,200	
Total Assets	5,784,200	5,321,100	4,606,400	3,330,200	...
Current Liabilities	1,805,800	1,240,500	573,800	504,800	...
Long-Term Obligations	2,499,800	2,995,900	163,500	9,900	...
Total Liabilities	5,733,500	5,635,900	1,794,600	1,395,700	...
Stockholders' Equity	50,700	(314,800)	2,811,800	1,934,500	...
Shares Outstanding	749,800	771,100	100.00	...	...
Statistical Record					
Return on Assets %	15.44	18.41	23.37	...	...
Return on Equity %	...	73.21	39.08	...	...
EBITDA Margin %	29.71	31.68	35.09	32.94	33.03
Net Margin %	17.50	20.45	23.26	21.19	20.11
Asset Turnover	0.88	0.90	1.00	...	...
Current Ratio	1.03	1.22	2.59	1.62	...
Debt to Equity	49.31	...	0.06	0.01	...
Price Range	24.72-18.36	24.12-17.35	...	...	...
P/E Ratio	22.27-16.54	20.27-14.58	...	...	...

Address: 12500 East Belford Avenue, Englewood, CO 80112
Telephone: 866-405-5012

Web Site: www.westernunion.com
Officers: Christina A. Gold - Pres., C.E.O.
Scott Scheirman - Exec. Vice-Pres., C.F.O.

Auditors: Ernst & Young LLP
Transfer Agents: Wells Fargo Bank, National Association, South St. Paul, MN

WESTLAKE CHEMICAL CORP

Exchange	Symbol	Price	52Wk Range	Yield	P/E
NYS	WLK	$13.05 (3/31/2008)	31.47-13.01	1.53	7.41

*7 Year Price Score N/A ***NYSE Composite Index=100** ***12 Month Price Score 76.67**

Interim Earnings (Per Share)

Qtr.	Mar	Jun	Sep	Dec
2004	0.22	0.00	0.50	0.77
2005	0.94	0.74	0.67	1.13
2006	0.79	1.03	0.95	0.22
2007	0.30	0.58	0.59	0.29

Interim Dividends (Per Share)

Amt	Decl	Ex	Rec	Pay
0.04Q	5/21/2007	5/30/2007	6/1/2007	6/15/2007
0.05Q	8/17/2007	8/28/2007	8/30/2007	9/14/2007
0.05Q	11/16/2007	11/27/2007	11/29/2007	12/13/2007
0.05Q	2/18/2008	2/27/2008	2/29/2008	3/17/2008
		Indicated Div: $0.20		

Valuation Analysis / **Institutional Holding**

Forecast P/E	N/A	No of Institutions
		117
Market Cap	$854.6 Million	Shares
Book Value	1.3 Billion	26,624,828
Price/Book	0.66	% Held
Price/Sales	0.27	40.79

TRADING VOLUME (thousand shares)

Business Summary: Chemicals (MIC: 11.1 SIC: 2865 NAIC: 325110)

Westlake Chemical is a manufacturer and marketer of basic chemicals, vinyls, polymers and fabricated products. Co. operates in two principal business segments, Olefins and Vinyls. In the Olefins segment, Co. manufactures ethylene, polyethylene, styrene and associated co-products at its manufacturing facilities in Lake Charles, LA and polyethylene and Epolene® at its Longview facilities. Products in Co.'s integrated Vinyls segment include polyvinyl chloride (PVC), chlorine, caustic soda and ethylene. Co. also manufactures and sells products fabricated from the PVC it produces, including pipe, fence and deck, and window and patio door components.

Recent Developments: For the year ended Dec 31 2007, net income decreased 41.0% to US$114.7 million from US$194.6 million in the prior year. Revenues were US$3.19 billion, up 28.5% from US$2.48 billion the year before. Operating income was US$174.7 million versus US$313.3 million in the prior year, a decrease of 44.2%. Direct operating expenses rose 39.9% to US$2.92 billion from US$2.09 billion in the comparable period the year before. Indirect operating expenses increased 16.2% to US$96.7 million from US$83.2 million in the equivalent prior-year period.

Prospects: On Oct 29 2007, Co. announced that it is improving the level of integration in its vinyls segment by expanding its chlor-alkali and polyvinyl chloride (PVC) resin units and building a large diameter PVC pipe plant at its Calvert City, KY facility. Co. expects this to improve the vertical integration of its business, further strengthen its position in the large diameter pipe market and increase its ability to serve its customers through an improved overall product mix. Meanwhile, Co. is concerned with the effects that the recent increase in crude oil prices may have on the economy, as vinyls selling prices and margins continue under pressure due to the weakness in the domestic housing market.

Financial Data

(US$ in Thousands)	12/31/2007	12/31/2006	12/31/2005	12/31/2004	12/31/2003	12/31/2002	12/31/2001
Earnings Per Share	1.76	2.98	3.48	2.18	0.30	(0.14)	(1.45)
Cash Flow Per Share	0.95	3.64	4.90	2.72	1.58	(0.43)	...
Tang Book Value Per Share	18.66	16.83	15.00	11.22	7.69	7.65	...
Dividends Per Share	0.180	0.135	0.098	0.021	...	...	...
Dividend Payout %	10.23	4.53	2.80	0.97	...	...	...
Income Statement							
Total Revenue	3,192,178	2,484,366	2,441,105	1,985,353	1,423,034	1,072,627	1,087,033
EBITDA	278,761	376,106	447,425	312,213	149,149	106,881	(1,950)
Income Before Taxes	158,957	282,549	345,328	190,662	23,503	(14,203)	(117,339)
Income Taxes	44,228	87,990	118,511	69,940	8,747	(7,141)	(45,353)
Net Income	114,729	194,559	226,817	120,722	14,756	(7,062)	(71,986)
Average Shares	65,324	65,254	65,251	55,355	49,499	49,499	49,499
Balance Sheet							
Current Assets	1,092,185	849,787	902,863	671,938	412,847	336,573	...
Total Assets	2,569,335	2,082,098	1,827,189	1,592,453	1,370,113	1,309,245	...
Current Liabilities	441,262	321,912	305,849	250,215	215,132	177,580	...
Long-Term Obligations	511,414	260,156	265,689	296,889	509,089	491,677	...
Total Liabilities	1,282,665	908,557	833,083	823,056	902,410	858,626	...
Stockholders' Equity	1,286,670	1,173,541	994,106	769,397	445,603	428,519	...
Shares Outstanding	65,487	65,268	65,121	64,896	49,499	49,499	...
Statistical Record							
Return on Assets %	4.93	9.95	13.27	8.13	1.10	...	...
Return on Equity %	9.33	17.95	25.72	19.82	3.38	...	...
EBITDA Margin %	8.73	15.14	18.33	15.73	10.48	9.96	N.M.
Net Margin %	3.59	7.83	9.29	6.08	1.04	N.M.	N.M.
Asset Turnover	1.37	1.27	1.43	1.34	1.06	...	...
Current Ratio	2.48	2.64	2.95	2.69	1.92	1.90	...
Debt to Equity	0.40	0.22	0.27	0.39	1.14	1.15	...
Price Range	37.11-18.50	36.75-26.38	37.03-22.29	34.02-14.65	...	...	...
P/E Ratio	21.09-10.51	12.33-8.85	10.64-6.41	15.61-6.72	...	...	...
Average Yield %	0.67	0.43	0.33	0.09	...	...	...

Address: 2801 Post Oak Boulevard, Suite 600, Houston, TX 77056 **Telephone:** 713-960-9111	**Web Site:** www.westlakechemical.com **Officers:** James Chao - Chmn. Albert Chao - Pres., C.E.O.	**Auditors:** PricewaterhouseCoopers **Transfer Agents:** American Stock Transfer & Trust Company

WESTWOOD ONE, INC.

Exchange	Symbol	Price	52Wk Range	Yield	P/E
NYS	WON	$2.10 (3/31/2008)	8.16-1.51	N/A	7.00

*7 Year Price Score 14.67   *NYSE Composite Index=100   *12 Month Price Score 50.75

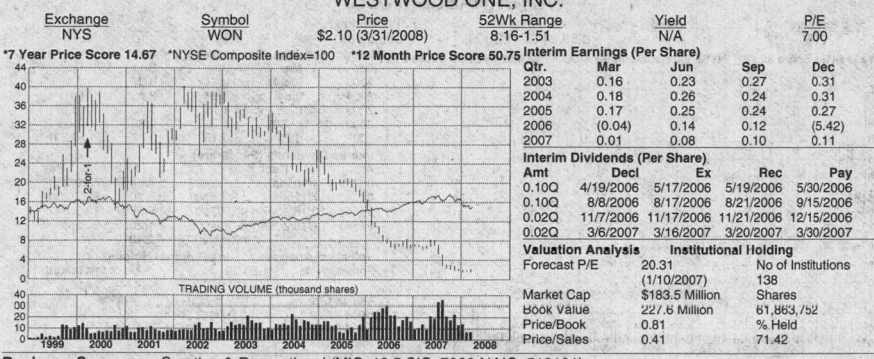

Interim Earnings (Per Share)

Qtr.	Mar	Jun	Sep	Dec
2003	0.16	0.23	0.27	0.31
2004	0.18	0.26	0.24	0.31
2005	0.17	0.25	0.24	0.27
2006	(0.04)	0.14	0.12	(5.42)
2007	0.01	0.08	0.10	0.11

Interim Dividends (Per Share)

Amt	Decl	Ex	Rec	Pay
0.10Q	4/19/2006	5/17/2006	5/19/2006	5/30/2006
0.10Q	8/8/2006	8/17/2006	8/21/2006	9/15/2006
0.02Q	11/7/2006	11/17/2006	11/21/2006	12/15/2006
0.02Q	3/6/2007	3/16/2007	3/20/2007	3/30/2007

Valuation Analysis / **Institutional Holding**

Forecast P/E	20.31	No of Institutions
	(1/10/2007)	138
Market Cap	$183.5 Million	Shares
Book Value	227.6 Million	61,863,752
Price/Book	0.81	% Held
Price/Sales	0.41	71.42

Business Summary: Sporting & Recreational (MIC: 13.5 SIC: 7922 NAIC: 512191)

Westwood One supplies radio and television stations with information services and programming. Co. is a domestic outsource provider of traffic reporting services, and a radio network that produces and distributes national news, sports, talk, music and special event programs, besides local news, sports, weather, video news as well as other information. Co. derives substantially all of its revenues from the sales of 10 second, 30 second and 60 second commercial airtime to advertisers. Co. receives the commercial airtime it sells to advertisers from radio and television affiliates, or other distribution partners, in exchange for the programming or information services it provides to them.

Recent Developments: For the year ended Dec 31 2007, net income amounted to US$24.4 million versus a net loss of US$469.5 million in the prior year. Revenues were US$451.4 million, down 11.9% from US$512.1 million the year before. Operating income was US$63.3 million versus a loss of US$436.0 million in the prior year. Direct operating expenses declined 11.3% to US$350.4 million from US$395.2 million in the comparable period the year before. Indirect operating expenses decreased 93.2% to US$37.6 million from US$552.9 million in the equivalent prior-year period.

Prospects: On Mar 3 2008, Co. closed its previously announced agreement with CBS Radio, Inc. As part of the new arrangement, certain CBS Radio stations will broadcast Co.'s local/regional and national commercial inventory through Mar 31 2017. Going forward, Co. will manage its business directly and separately from CBS Radio. For 2008, Co. anticipates higher operating costs due to increased clearance levels by CBS Radio, additional investments in new program offerings, and growing RADAR audience levels. Nonetheless, Co. expects revenue in 2008 to increase low single digits compared with 2007 due to new program launches, increasing RADAR audiences, as well as investment in a new distribution system.

Financial Data

(US$ in Thousands)	12/31/2007	12/31/2006	12/31/2005	12/31/2004	12/31/2003	12/31/2002	12/31/2001	12/31/2000
Earnings Per Share	0.30	(5.20)	0.93	0.97	0.97	1.00	0.38	0.36
Cash Flow Per Share	0.32	1.21	1.31	1.31	1.07	1.39	1.35	1.41
Dividends Per Share	0.020	0.320	0.300	...	...	...	...	...
Dividend Payout %	6.67	...	32.26	...	...	...	...	...
Income Statement								
Total Revenue	451,384	493,995	557,830	562,246	539,226	550,751	515,940	553,693
EBITDA	83,558	(413,939)	177,863	185,663	182,225	190,471	165,075	166,257
Income Before Taxes	40,092	(460,644)	138,389	154,614	159,945	172,052	88,759	93,368
Income Taxes	15,724	8,809	53,706	59,124	59,906	62,937	45,564	51,085
Net Income	24,368	(469,453)	84,683	95,490	100,039	109,115	43,195	42,283
Average Shares	86,718	86,305	91,488	98,454	103,625	109,101	112,265	115,864
Balance Sheet								
Current Assets	138,154	149,222	172,245	174,346	165,495	153,628	138,482	153,881
Total Assets	669,757	696,701	1,230,877	1,246,279	1,262,034	1,266,312	1,207,972	1,285,556
Current Liabilities	90,860	119,909	100,151	81,341	79,873	90,086	105,515	138,202
Long-Term Obligations	345,244	366,860	427,514	359,439	300,366	232,135	152,000	168,000
Total Liabilities	442,126	493,770	546,236	461,786	426,084	363,272	292,601	335,664
Stockholders' Equity	227,631	202,931	684,641	784,493	835,950	903,040	915,371	949,892
Shares Outstanding	87,397	86,287	86,965	94,645	99,760	104,692	107,565	130,003
Statistical Record								
Return on Assets %	3.57	N.M.	6.84	7.59	7.91	8.82	3.46	3.22
Return on Equity %	11.32	N.M.	11.53	11.75	11.51	12.00	4.63	4.28
EBITDA Margin %	18.51	N.M.	31.88	33.02	33.79	34.58	31.99	30.03
Net Margin %	5.40	N.M.	15.18	16.98	18.55	19.81	8.37	7.64
Asset Turnover	0.66	0.51	0.45	0.45	0.43	0.45	0.41	0.42
Current Ratio	1.52	1.24	1.72	2.14	2.07	1.71	1.31	1.11
Debt to Equity	1.52	1.81	0.62	0.46	0.36	0.26	0.17	0.18
Price Range	8.16-1.83	16.58-6.44	26.93-16.02	34.66-19.21	39.15-29.30	40.20-25.66	36.85-18.31	39.81-14.25
P/E Ratio	27.20-6.10	...	28.96-17.23	35.73-19.80	40.36-30.21	40.20-25.66	96.97-48.19	110.59-39.58
Average Yield %	0.39	3.50	1.48	...	...	...	...	...

Address: 40 West 57th Street, 5th Floor, New York, NY 10019	Web Site: www.westwoodone.com	Auditors: PricewaterhouseCoopers
Telephone: 212-641-2000	Officers: Norman J. Pattiz - Chmn. Shane Coppola - Pres., C.E.O.	
Fax: 212-840-4052		

WEYERHAEUSER CO.

Exchange	Symbol	Price	52Wk Range	Yield	P/E
NYS	WY	$65.04 (3/31/2008)	84.05-58.99	3.69	18.12

*7 Year Price Score 92.62   *NYSE Composite Index=100   *12 Month Price Score 95.57

Interim Earnings (Per Share)

Qtr.	Mar	Jun	Sep	Dec
2003	(0.24)	0.71	0.37	0.42
2004	0.54	1.57	2.45	0.81
2005	0.98	1.71	1.16	(0.87)
2006	(2.36)	1.26	0.85	2.06
2007	3.24	0.15	0.47	(0.39)

Interim Dividends (Per Share)

Amt	Decl	Ex	Rec	Pay
0.60Q	4/19/2007	5/2/2007	5/4/2007	5/29/2007
0.60Q	7/12/2007	8/1/2007	8/3/2007	8/27/2007
0.60Q	10/18/2007	11/7/2007	11/9/2007	12/3/2007
0.60Q	1/10/2008	1/30/2008	2/1/2008	2/25/2008

Indicated Div: $2.40

Valuation Analysis   **Institutional Holding**

Forecast P/E	20.79	No of Institutions	
	(1/10/2007)	474	
Market Cap	$13.7 Billion	Shares	
Book Value	8.0 Billion	190,376,384	
Price/Book	1.72	% Held	
Price/Sales	0.84	80.43	

TRADING VOLUME (thousand shares)

Business Summary: Wood Products (MIC: 11.9 SIC: 2499 NAIC: 423310)

Weyerhaeuser is engaged in the growing and harvesting of timber; the manufacture, distribution and sale of forest products; as well as real estate development and construction. Co.'s business segments consists of: Timberlands, which includes logs, minerals and oil and gas; Wood Products, which includes softwood lumber, plywood, veneer, composite panels, oriented strand board, hardwood lumber, engineered lumber, raw materials and building materials distribution; Cellulose Fiber and Fine Papers, which includes pulp, paper and liquid packaging board; Containerboard, Packaging and Recycling; Real Estate and Related Assets; as well as Corporate and Other.

Recent Developments: For the year ended Dec 30 2007, income from continuing operations decreased 95.2% to US$51.0 million from US$1.06 billion a year earlier. Net income increased 74.4% to US$790.0 million from US$453.0 million in the prior year. Revenues were US$16.31 billion, down 12.7% from US$18.67 billion the year before. Operating income was US$406.0 million versus US$1.81 billion in the prior year, a decrease of 77.6%. Direct operating expenses declined 9.6% to US$13.13 billion from US$14.52 billion in the comparable period the year before. Indirect operating expenses increased 18.7% to US$2.78 billion from US$2.34 billion in the equivalent prior-year period.

Prospects: On Feb 29 2008, Co. and Chevron Corp., an energy company, announced the creation of a 50-50 joint venture company, Catchlight Energy LLC. The joint venture, which will research and develop technology for converting cellulose-based biomass into economical, low-carbon biofuels, represents the first milestone of a biofuels alliance of Co. and Chevron. Meanwhile, Co. anticipates that the existing unfavorable market conditions for its Timberlands, Wood Products and Real Estate businesses to persist due to the continuing erosion of the U.S. housing market. However, Co. remains focused on managing through the downturn and positioning it to capitalize on stronger markets once conditions improve.

Financial Data
(US$ in Thousands)

	12/30/2007	12/31/2006	12/25/2005	12/26/2004	12/28/2003	12/29/2002	12/30/2001	12/31/2000
Earnings Per Share	3.59	1.84	2.98	5.43	1.25	1.09	1.61	3.72
Cash Flow Per Share	2.89	6.46	7.17	9.37	8.21	6.85	5.10	6.24
Tang Book Value Per Share	27.35	28.91	27.81	24.79	17.40	15.78	25.47	25.92
Dividends Per Share	2.400	2.200	1.900	1.600	1.600	1.600	1.600	1.600
Dividend Payout %	66.85	119.57	63.76	29.47	128.00	146.79	99.38	43.01
Income Statement								
Total Revenue	16,308,000	21,896,000	22,629,000	22,665,000	19,873,000	18,521,000	14,545,000	15,980,000
EBITDA	1,489,000	2,640,000	2,973,000	4,096,000	2,550,000	2,367,000	1,736,000	2,533,000
Income Before Taxes	59,000	826,000	906,000	1,945,000	436,000	371,000	516,000	1,323,000
Income Taxes	8,000	471,000	324,000	662,000	148,000	130,000	162,000	483,000
Net Income	790,000	453,000	733,000	1,283,000	277,000	241,000	354,000	840,000
Average Shares	220,277	245,707	245,559	236,546	222,000	221,456	219,957	225,608
Balance Sheet								
Current Assets	3,035,000	4,141,000	5,162,000	5,446,000	4,052,000	3,895,000	3,063,000	3,296,000
Total Assets	23,806,000	26,862,000	28,229,000	29,954,000	28,109,000	28,219,000	18,293,000	18,195,000
Current Liabilities	2,607,000	3,129,000	3,255,000	3,149,000	2,525,000	2,994,000	1,863,000	2,704,000
Long-Term Obligations	6,834,000	7,675,000	8,262,000	10,146,000	12,397,000	12,784,000	6,073,000	5,114,000
Total Liabilities	15,825,000	17,777,000	18,429,000	20,699,000	21,000,000	21,596,000	11,598,000	11,363,000
Stockholders' Equity	7,981,000	9,085,000	9,800,000	9,255,000	7,109,000	6,623,000	6,695,000	6,832,000
Shares Outstanding	211,146	238,008	245,183	242,471	222,493	221,253	219,863	219,213
Statistical Record								
Return on Assets %	3.13	1.62	2.53	4.43	0.99	1.04	1.95	4.52
Return on Equity %	9.28	4.72	7.71	15.72	4.05	3.63	5.25	11.80
EBITDA Margin %	9.13	12.06	13.14	18.07	12.83	12.78	11.94	15.85
Net Margin %	4.84	2.07	3.24	5.66	1.39	1.30	2.43	5.26
Asset Turnover	0.65	0.78	0.78	0.78	0.71	0.80	0.80	0.86
Current Ratio	1.16	1.32	1.59	1.73	1.60	1.30	1.64	1.22
Debt to Equity	0.86	0.84	0.84	1.10	1.74	1.93	0.91	0.75
Price Range	86.20-62.97	75.09-55.35	71.52-61.12	67.86-56.04	63.01-45.80	67.83-38.04	62.05-45.70	74.13-36.69
P/E Ratio	24.01-17.54	40.81-30.08	24.00-20.51	12.50-10.32	50.41-36.64	62.23-34.90	38.54-28.39	19.93-9.86
Average Yield %	3.18	3.37	2.89	2.53	2.96	2.86	2.98	3.22

Address: 33663 Weyerhaeuser Way South, Federal Way, WA 98063-9777 **Telephone:** 253-924-2345 **Fax:** 253-924-3332	**Web Site:** www.weyerhaeuser.com **Officers:** Steven R. Rogel - Chmn., Pres., C.E.O. Richard J. Taggart - Exec. V.P., C.F.O.	**Auditors:** KPMG LLP **Investor Contact:** 253-924-2058 **Transfer Agents:** Mellon Investor Services LLC

WGL HOLDINGS, INC.

Exchange	Symbol	Price	52Wk Range	Yield	P/E	Div Achiever
NYS	WGL	$32.06 (3/31/2008)	35.46-29.94	4.43	14.38	31 Years

*7 Year Price Score 90.46   *NYSE Composite Index=100   *12 Month Price Score 104.78

Interim Earnings (Per Share)

Qtr.	Dec	Mar	Jun	Sep
2004-05	0.88	1.63	(0.17)	(0.24)
2005-06	0.91	1.16	(0.04)	(0.24)
2006-07	0.92	1.29	0.26	(0.27)
2007-08	0.95	...	...	...

Interim Dividends (Per Share)

Amt	Decl	Ex	Rec	Pay
0.343Q	6/28/2007	7/6/2007	7/10/2007	8/1/2007
0.343Q	9/26/2007	10/5/2007	10/10/2007	11/1/2007
0.343Q	12/14/2007	1/8/2008	1/10/2008	2/1/2008
0.355Q	3/6/2008	4/8/2008	4/10/2008	5/1/2008

Indicated Div: $1.42 (Div. Reinv. Plan)

Valuation Analysis		Institutional Holding	
Forecast P/E	16.03	No of Institutions	
	(1/10/2007)	185	
Market Cap	$1.6 Billion	Shares	
Book Value	1.0 Billion	30,413,174	
Price/Book	1.57	% Held	
Price/Sales	0.60	62.21	

Business Summary: Gas Utilities (MIC: 7.4 SIC: 4924 NAIC: 221210)

WGL Holdings is a holding company. Through its subsidiaries, Co. sells and delivers natural gas, and provides energy-related products and services to customers in Washington, D.C., and the surrounding metropolitan areas in Maryland and Virginia. Co.'s subsidiary, Washington Gas, is engaged in the delivery and sale of natural gas that is predominantly regulated by state regulatory commissions. Through wholly owned subsidiaries of Washington Gas Resources, Co. also offers energy related products and services that are closely related to its core business. Co. has three operating segments: regulated utility; retail energy marketing; and commercial heating, ventilating and air conditioning.

Recent Developments: For the quarter ended Dec 31 2007, income from continuing operations increased 4.7% to US$47.2 million from US$45.1 million in the year-earlier quarter. Net income increased 4.7% to US$47.2 million from US$45.1 million in the year-earlier quarter. Revenues were US$751.6 million, up 2.5% from US$733.0 million the year before. Operating income was US$89.9 million versus US$87.8 million in the prior-year quarter, an increase of 2.5%. Direct operating expenses rose 2.4% to US$634.4 million from US$619.8 million in the comparable period the year before. Indirect operating expenses increased 7.1% to US$27.2 million from US$25.4 million in the equivalent prior-year period.

Prospects: For the fiscal year ending Sep 2008, Co. believes that the favorable regulatory outcomes, the expansion of its asset management program, ongoing customer growth and improving unregulated results should continue to drive earnings growth. As a result, Co. anticipates earnings of $2.30 to $2.40 per share for fiscal 2008, including earnings of $1.99 to $2.05 per share from its regulated utility segment and $0.31 to $0.35 per share from its unregulated business segments. Meanwhile, Co. noted that its Washington Gas subsidiary is planning to construct a third HHC injection facility and expects the facility to be operational prior to the planned Cove Point terminal expansion by end of 2008.

Financial Data

(US$ in Thousands)	3 Mos	09/30/2007	09/30/2006	09/30/2005	09/30/2004	09/30/2003	09/30/2002	09/30/2001
Earnings Per Share	2.23	2.19	1.79	2.11	1.98	2.30	0.80	1.75
Cash Flow Per Share	3.43	4.34	1.76	4.78	4.97	2.96	4.23	1.70
Tang Book Value Per Share	20.48	19.89	18.86	18.36	17.54	16.83	15.78	16.24
Dividends Per Share	1.365	1.360	1.340	1.315	1.290	1.275	1.265	1.250
Dividend Payout %	61.21	62.10	74.86	62.32	65.15	55.43	158.13	71.43
Income Statement								
Total Revenue	751,626	2,646,008	2,637,883	2,186,302	2,089,603	2,064,248	1,569,969	1,933,024
EBITDA	115,328	320,161	300,258	...	...	...	...	...
Depn & Amortn	25,135	...	...	...	...	...	...	...
Income Before Taxes	77,456	178,037	156,007	...	...	...	...	...
Income Taxes	57,502	70,137	61,313	102,096	97,182	106,642	64,755	97,239
Net Income	47,107	107,900	87,378	104,813	97,957	113,667	40,441	83,765
Average Shares	49,645	49,377	48,905	49,008	48,847	48,756	48,563	47,120
Balance Sheet								
Net PPE	2,161,612	2,150,441	2,067,895	1,969,683	1,915,551	1,874,923	1,606,843	1,519,747
Total Assets	3,458,888	3,046,361	2,791,406	2,600,600	2,504,908	2,436,052	2,113,664	2,081,113
Long-Term Obligations	593,513	616,419	576,139	584,150	590,164	636,650	667,951	584,370
Total Liabilities	2,417,460	2,037,421	1,841,426	1,678,435	1,623,311	1,589,661	1,319,088	1,264,687
Stockholders' Equity	1,013,255	1,008,940	949,980	922,165	881,597	846,391	794,576	816,426
Shares Outstanding	49,464	49,316	48,878	48,704	48,652	48,611	48,564	48,542
Statistical Record								
Return on Assets %	3.33	3.70	3.25	4.11	3.95	5.00	1.93	4.17
Return on Equity %	11.15	11.02	9.36	11.62	11.31	13.85	5.02	10.77
EBITDA Margin %	15.34	12.10	11.38	...	...	...	...	...
Net Margin %	6.28	4.08	3.32	4.79	4.69	5.51	2.58	4.33
PPE Turnover	1.25	1.25	1.31	1.13	1.10	1.19	1.00	1.30
Asset Turnover	0.81	0.91	0.98	0.86	0.84	0.91	0.75	0.96
Debt to Equity	0.59	0.61	0.61	0.63	0.67	0.75	0.84	0.72
Price Range	35.46-29.94	35.46-29.94	32.31-27.38	34.52-27.80	30.28-26.27	28.64-22.38	29.45-20.16	31.44-25.19
P/E Ratio	15.90-13.43	16.19-13.67	18.05-15.30	16.36-13.18	15.29-13.27	12.45-9.73	36.81-25.20	17.96-14.39
Average Yield %	4.16	4.17	4.47	4.20	4.58	4.97	4.82	4.55

Address: 101 Constitution Avenue, N.W., Washington, DC 20080	Web Site: www.wglholdings.com	Auditors: Deloitte & Touche LLP
Telephone: 703-750-2000	Officers: James H. DeGraffenreidt Jr. - Chmn., C.E.O. Terry D. McCallister - Pres., C.O.O.	Transfer Agents: The Bank of New York, New York, NY

WHIRLPOOL CORP

Exchange	Symbol	Price	52Wk Range	Yield	P/E
NYS	WHR	$86.78 (3/31/2008)	116.85-69.80	1.98	10.83

*7 Year Price Score 102.34 *NYSE Composite Index=100   *12 Month Price Score 99.48

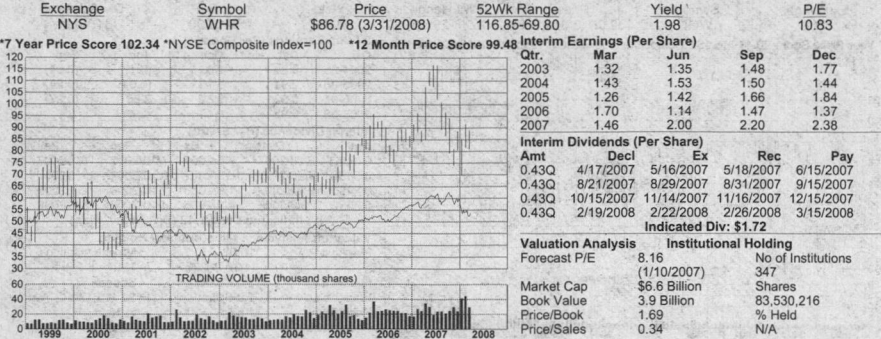

Interim Earnings (Per Share)

Qtr.	Mar	Jun	Sep	Dec
2003	1.32	1.35	1.48	1.77
2004	1.43	1.53	1.50	1.44
2005	1.26	1.42	1.66	1.84
2006	1.70	1.14	1.47	1.37
2007	1.46	2.00	2.20	2.38

Interim Dividends (Per Share)

Amt	Decl	Ex	Rec	Pay
0.43Q	4/17/2007	5/16/2007	5/18/2007	6/15/2007
0.43Q	8/21/2007	8/29/2007	8/31/2007	9/15/2007
0.43Q	10/15/2007	11/14/2007	11/16/2007	12/15/2007
0.43Q	2/19/2008	2/22/2008	2/26/2008	3/15/2008
				Indicated Div: $1.72

Valuation Analysis   **Institutional Holding**

Forecast P/E	8.16	No of Institutions
	(1/10/2007)	347
Market Cap	$6.6 Billion	Shares
Book Value	3.9 Billion	83,530,216
Price/Book	1.69	% Held
Price/Sales	0.34	N/A

Business Summary: Electrical (MIC: 11.14 SIC: 3639 NAIC: 335228)

Whirlpool is a manufacturer and marketer of a line of appliances and related products, primarily for home use. Co.'s principal products are laundry appliances, refrigerators, cooking appliances, dishwashers, and mixers and other small household appliances. Co. also produces hermetic compressors for refrigeration systems. In the U.S., Co. markets and distributes products under the Whirlpool, Maytag, KitchenAid, Jenn-Air, Roper, Estate, Admiral, Magic Chef, Amana, and Inglis brand names primarily to retailers, distributors, and builders. In addition, Co. is a supplier to Sears of laundry, refrigerator, dishwasher, and trash compactor home appliances.

Recent Developments: For the year ended Dec 31 2007, income from continuing operations increased 33.1% to US$647.0 million from US$486.0 million a year earlier. Net income increased 47.8% to US$640.0 million from US$433.0 million in the prior year. Revenues were US$19.41 billion, up 7.3% from US$18.08 billion the year before. Operating income was US$1.06 billion versus US$823.0 million in the prior year, an increase of 29.2%. Direct operating expenses rose 7.1% to US$16.52 billion from US$15.42 billion in the comparable period the year before. Indirect operating expenses decreased 0.5% to US$1.83 billion from US$1.84 billion in the equivalent prior-year period.

Prospects: For 2008, Co. expects prices for material- and oil-related costs to increase by approximately $350.0 million, mainly driven by increases in component parts, base metals, such as copper, aluminum, zinc and nickel, as well as steel. Nevertheless, Co. expects these higher costs to be offset by productivity improvements, new product introductions, including the revitalization of its Maytag branded products and recently implemented cost-based price adjustments. Meanwhile, Co. is projecting earnings per diluted share from continuing operations to be in the range of $8.50 to $9.00 for full-year 2008.

Financial Data

(US$ in Thousands)	12/31/2007	12/31/2006	12/31/2005	12/31/2004	12/31/2003	12/31/2002	12/31/2001	12/31/2000
Earnings Per Share	8.01	5.67	6.19	5.90	5.91	(5.68)	0.31	5.20
Cash Flow Per Share	11.81	11.72	13.13	11.75	10.83	11.96	15.35	6.32
Tang Book Value Per Share	3.91	N.M.	21.49	19.85	15.23	5.82	11.10	13.91
Dividends Per Share	1.720	1.720	1.720	1.720	1.360	1.360	1.360	1.360
Dividend Payout %	21.47	30.34	27.79	29.15	23.01	...	438.71	26.15
Income Statement								
Total Revenue	19,408,000	18,080,000	14,317,000	13,220,000	12,176,000	11,016,000	10,343,000	10,325,000
EBITDA	1,600,000	1,371,000	1,169,000	1,189,000	1,216,000	1,043,000	651,000	1,157,000
Income Before Taxes	804,000	619,000	597,000	616,000	652,000	495,000	93,000	577,000
Income Taxes	117,000	126,000	171,000	209,000	228,000	193,000	43,000	200,000
Net Income	640,000	433,000	422,000	406,000	414,000	(394,000)	21,000	367,000
Average Shares	79,900	76,500	68,300	68,900	70,100	69,300	68,000	70,600
Balance Sheet								
Current Assets	6,555,000	6,476,000	4,710,000	4,514,000	3,865,000	3,327,000	3,311,000	3,237,000
Total Assets	14,009,000	13,878,000	8,248,000	8,181,000	7,361,000	6,631,000	6,967,000	6,902,000
Current Liabilities	5,893,000	6,002,000	4,301,000	3,985,000	3,589,000	3,505,000	3,082,000	3,303,000
Long-Term Obligations	1,668,000	1,798,000	745,000	1,160,000	1,134,000	1,092,000	1,295,000	795,000
Total Liabilities	10,029,000	10,547,000	6,411,000	6,507,000	5,997,000	5,814,000	5,382,000	5,071,000
Stockholders' Equity	3,911,000	3,283,000	1,745,000	1,606,000	1,301,000	739,000	1,458,000	1,684,000
Shares Outstanding	76,000	78,000	68,000	67,000	69,000	68,000	68,000	66,265
Statistical Record								
Return on Assets %	4.59	3.91	5.14	5.21	5.92	N.M.	0.30	5.33
Return on Equity %	17.79	17.22	25.19	27.86	40.59	N.M.	1.34	20.61
EBITDA Margin %	8.24	7.58	8.17	8.99	9.99	9.47	6.29	11.21
Net Margin %	3.30	2.39	2.95	3.07	3.40	N.M.	0.20	3.55
Asset Turnover	1.39	1.63	1.74	1.70	1.74	1.62	1.49	1.50
Current Ratio	1.11	1.08	1.10	1.13	1.08	0.95	1.07	0.98
Debt to Equity	0.43	0.55	0.43	0.72	0.87	1.48	0.89	0.47
Price Range	116.85-73.86	95.95-75.00	85.65-61.13	79.38-55.04	72.67-42.91	79.66-40.60	73.54-47.25	67.25-34.81
P/E Ratio	14.59-9.22	16.92-13.23	13.84-9.88	13.45-9.33	12.30-7.26	...	237.23-152.42	12.93-6.69
Average Yield %	1.83	2.02	2.38	2.61	2.23	2.19	2.27	2.72

Address: 2000 North M-63, Benton Harbor, MI 49022-2692	Web Site: www.whirlpoolcorp.com	Auditors: Ernst & Young LLP
Telephone: 269-923-5000	Officers: Jeff M. Fettig - Chmn., Pres., C.E.O.	Investor Contact: 269-923-4678
Fax: 269-923-3978	Michael D. Thieneman - Exec. V.P., Chief Tech. Officer	

WILEY (JOHN) & SONS INC.

Exchange	Symbol	Price	52Wk Range	Yield	P/E	Div Acheiver
NYS	JW A	$39.70 (3/31/2008)	49.35-35.98	1.11	17.72	14 Years

*7 Year Price Score 105.79 *NYSE Composite Index=100   *12 Month Price Score 99.27

Interim Earnings (Per Share)

Qtr.	Jul	Oct	Jan	Apr
2004-05	0.32	0.42	0.53	0.08
2005-06	0.46	0.45	0.69	0.26
2006-07	0.38	0.52	0.57	0.24
2007-08	0.68	0.65	0.67	...

Interim Dividends (Per Share)

Amt	Decl	Ex	Rec	Pay
0.11Q	6/21/2007	7/2/2007	7/5/2007	7/16/2007
0.11Q	9/20/2007	9/28/2007	10/2/2007	10/15/2007
0.11Q	12/13/2007	12/24/2007	12/27/2007	1/15/2008
0.11Q	3/12/2008	3/28/2008	4/1/2008	4/15/2008

Indicated Div: $0.44

Valuation Analysis | **Institutional Holding**

Forecast P/E	N/A	No of Institutions
		180
Market Cap	$2.3 Billion	Shares
Book Value	632.7 Million	36,368,080
Price/Book	3.66	% Held
Price/Sales	1.42	76.54

Business Summary: Non-Media Publishing (MIC: 13.3 SIC: 2731 NAIC: 511130)

Wiley (John) & Sons is a global publisher of print and electronic products via three core businesses: the Professional/Trade business which produces professional and consumer books and subscription products; the Scientific, Technical and Medical business which produces scientific, technical and medical journals, encyclopedias, books and online products; and the Higher Education business which publishes textbooks and educational materials, including integrated online teaching and learning resources, for undergraduate and graduate students, teachers and lifelong learners. In addition, Co. maintains publishing, marketing and distribution centers in the U.S., Canada, Europe, Asia and Australia.

Recent Developments: For the quarter ended Jan 31 2008, net income increased 19.7% to US$40.0 million from US$33.4 million in the year-earlier quarter. Revenues were US$429.3 million, up 44.7% from US$296.7 million the year before. Operating income was US$68.0 million versus US$50.7 million in the prior-year quarter, an increase of 34.2%. Direct operating expenses rose 48.5% to US$139.7 million from US$94.0 million in the comparable period the year before. Indirect operating expenses increased 45.8% to US$221.6 million from US$152.0 million in the equivalent prior year period.

Prospects: For the fiscal year ending Apr 30 2008; Co. expects revenue growth of mid single digits and earnings improvements of low double digits, excluding the Feb 2 2007 Blackwell Publishing Ltd. acquisition and one-time tax benefits. Also, Co. now anticipates revenue from Blackwell to be about $470.0 million and to be accretive to its earnings by at least $0.20 per share. Meanwhile, Co. is implementing its initiative to launch a new online platform to replace Wiley InterScience and Blackwell's Synergy. Further, Co. is reducing maintenance, support and licensing expenses, while discontinuing some third party relationships in its efforts to consolidate systems and integrate activities globally.

Financial Data

(US$ in Thousands)	9 Mos	6 Mos	3 Mos	04/30/2007	04/30/2006	04/30/2005	04/30/2004	04/30/2003
Earnings Per Share	2.01	2.14	2.01	1.71	1.85	1.35	1.41	1.38
Cash Flow Per Share	5.09	2.77	3.37	3.87	4.18	4.01	3.43	2.75
Dividends Per Share	0.430	0.420	0.410	0.400	0.360	0.300	0.260	0.200
Dividend Payout %	19.20	19.63	20.40	23.39	19.46	22.22	18.44	14.49
Income Statement								
Total Revenue	1,240,769	811,608	388,562	1,234,936	1,044,185	974,048	922,962	853,971
EBITDA	265,368	166,974	75,023	215,292	199,333	232,121	211,412	193,106
Depn & Amortn	85,865	56,601	27,761	...	...	...	...	...
Income Before Taxes	126,907	74,791	29,773	139,502	143,844	135,663	125,110	112,559
Income Taxes	8,364	(3,768)	(10,396)	39,883	33,516	51,822	36,270	25,284
Net Income	118,543	78,559	40,169	99,619	110,328	83,841	88,840	87,275
Average Shares	59,280	59,147	59,086	58,287	59,792	62,093	63,226	63,086
Balance Sheet								
Current Assets	619,100	444,111	473,364	405,437	326,308	338,918	324,006	283,844
Total Assets	2,766,996	2,614,998	2,616,645	2,531,115	1,026,009	1,032,569	1,014,582	955,972
Current Liabilities	712,089	482,209	498,329	598,883	362,109	341,311	306,365	323,265
Long-Term Obligations	988,106	1,067,355	1,104,905	977,721	160,496	196,214	200,000	200,000
Total Liabilities	2,134,280	1,962,983	2,029,369	2,001,607	624,169	635,995	599,518	611,968
Stockholders' Equity	632,716	652,015	587,276	529,508	401,840	396,574	415,064	344,004
Shares Outstanding	58,366	58,434	58,027	57,552	57,145	59,331	61,694	61,630
Statistical Record								
Return on Assets %	6.95	6.96	6.50	5.60	10.72	8.19	8.99	9.42
Return on Equity %	23.40	22.71	23.17	21.39	27.64	20.66	23.34	28.12
EBITDA Margin %	21.39	20.57	19.31	17.43	19.09	23.83	22.91	22.61
Net Margin %	9.55	9.68	10.34	8.07	10.57	8.61	9.63	10.22
Asset Turnover	0.85	0.83	0.75	0.69	1.01	0.95	0.93	0.92
Current Ratio	0.87	0.92	0.95	0.68	0.90	0.99	1.06	0.88
Debt to Equity	1.56	1.64	1.88	1.85	0.40	0.49	0.48	0.58
Price Range	49.35-35.98	49.35-35.12	49.35-31.86	41.00-31.86	44.90-35.73	36.91-29.27	31.58-24.07	27.30-19.61
P/E Ratio	22.03-16.06	23.06-16.41	24.55-15.85	23.98-18.63	24.27-19.31	27.34-21.68	22.40-17.07	19.78-14.21
Average Yield %	1.03	1.02	1.05	1.11	0.91	0.90	0.97	0.87

Address: 111 River Street, Hoboken, NJ 07030-5774
Telephone: 201-748-6000
Fax: 201-748-6088

Web Site: www.wiley.com
Officers: Peter Booth Wiley - Chmn. William J. Pesce - Pres., C.E.O.

Auditors: KPMG LLP
Transfer Agents: Registrar and Transfer Company

WILLIAMS COS INC (THE)

Exchange	Symbol	Price	52Wk Range	Yield	P/E
NYS	WMB	$32.98 (3/31/2008)	37.16-28.20	1.21	20.23

*7 Year Price Score 135.46 *NYSE Composite Index=100 *12 Month Price Score 111.93

Interim Earnings (Per Share)

Qtr.	Mar	Jun	Sep	Dec
2003	(1.59)	0.46	0.20	(0.12)
2004	0.02	(0.03)	0.19	0.14
2005	0.34	0.07	0.01	0.11
2006	0.22	(0.13)	0.18	0.24
2007	0.22	0.71	0.33	0.38

Interim Dividends (Per Share)

Amt	Decl	Ex	Rec	Pay
0.10Q	4/10/2007	5/23/2007	5/25/2007	6/11/2007
0.10Q	7/19/2007	8/22/2007	8/24/2007	9/10/2007
0.10Q	11/15/2007	12/12/2007	12/14/2007	12/31/2007
0.10Q	1/25/2008	3/12/2008	3/14/2008	3/31/2008

Indicated Div: $0.40

Valuation Analysis

Institutional Holding	
Forecast P/E	14.90
	(1/10/2007)
Market Cap	$19.3 Billion
Book Value	6.4 Billion
Price/Book	3.03
Price/Sales	1.83

No of Institutions 500
Shares 448,853,344
% Held 75.01

TRADING VOLUME (thousand shares)

Business Summary: Gas Utilities (MIC: 7.4 SIC: 4922 NAIC: 486210)

Williams Companies is a natural gas company that primarily discovers, produces, gathers, processes and transports natural gas. Co.'s operations are concentrated in the Pacific Northwest, Rocky Mountains, Gulf Coast, Southern California and Eastern Seaboard. Co.'s business segments include Gas Pipeline, Exploration & Production, Midstream Gas & Liquids, and Gas Marketing Services. As of Dec 31 2007, Co. owned and operated, through Williams Gas Pipeline Company, LLC and its subsidiaries, a combined total of approximately 14,200 miles of pipelines with a total annual throughput of approximately 2,700.00 trillion British Thermal Units of natural gas.

Recent Developments: For the year ended Dec 31 2007, income from continuing operations increased 144.1% to US$847.0 million from US$347.0 million a year earlier. Net income increased 220.4% to US$990.0 million from US$309.0 million in the prior year. Revenues were US$10.56 billion, up 12.6% from US$9.38 billion the year before. Operating income was US$1.87 billion versus US$1.09 billion in the prior year, an increase of 71.4%. Direct operating expenses rose 6.8% to US$8.08 billion from US$7.57 billion in the comparable period the year before. Indirect operating expenses decreased 15.0% to US$614.0 million from US$722.0 million in the equivalent prior-year period.

Prospects: Co. continues to invest in its natural gas businesses and expects capital expenditures of about $2.60 billion to $2.90 billion in 2008. Notably, Co.'s Exploration & Production segment plans to maintain its development drilling program in the Piceance, Powder River, San Juan, Arkoma, and Fort Worth basins, and expects to grow average daily domestic production level with a goal of about 10.0% to 15.0% annual growth. Co.'s Gas Pipeline segment is also expanding its system, with the 34 mile pipeline extension within Florida which should be completed in Jul 2008. Also, Co.'s Midstream segment plans to continue pursuing deepwater production commitments and expand capacity in the western U.S.

Financial Data

(US$ in Thousands)	12/31/2007	12/31/2006	12/31/2005	12/31/2004	12/31/2003	12/31/2002	12/31/2001	12/31/2000
Earnings Per Share	1.63	0.51	0.53	0.31	(1.01)	(1.63)	(0.95)	1.17
Cash Flow Per Share	3.75	3.18	2.54	2.80	1.49	(1.05)	3.59	1.21
Tang Book Value Per Share	9.15	8.48	7.70	7.06	5.96	7.15	9.43	13.26
Dividends Per Share	0.390	0.345	0.250	0.080	0.040	0.420	0.680	0.600
Dividend Payout %	23.93	67.65	47.17	25.81	...	...	...	51.28
Income Statement								
Total Revenue	10,558,000	11,812,900	12,583,600	12,461,300	16,834,100	5,608,400	11,034,700	10,398,000
EBITDA	3,176,000	2,107,400	1,948,500	1,735,200	2,138,600	1,514,200	3,010,100	3,052,600
Income Before Taxes	1,371,000	539,100	531,300	224,500	51,600	(696,500)	1,465,600	1,427,200
Income Taxes	524,000	206,300	213,900	131,300	36,400	(195,000)	630,200	554,000
Net Income	990,000	308,500	313,600	163,700	(492,200)	(754,700)	(477,700)	524,300
Average Shares	609,866	608,627	605,847	535,611	518,137	516,793	500,567	449,320
Balance Sheet								
Current Assets	5,538,000	6,322,000	9,697,300	6,043,600	8,795,000	12,886,100	12,938,000	15,476,700
Total Assets	25,061,000	25,402,400	29,442,600	23,993,000	27,021,800	34,988,500	38,906,200	40,197,000
Current Liabilities	4,431,000	4,693,600	8,450,900	5,145,900	6,270,100	11,308,500	13,494,500	16,803,500
Long-Term Obligations	7,757,000	7,622,000	7,590,500	7,711,900	11,039,800	11,896,400	9,500,700	10,342,400
Total Liabilities	18,686,000	19,329,200	24,015,100	19,037,100	22,919,700	29,939,500	32,862,200	34,305,000
Stockholders' Equity	6,375,000	6,073,200	5,427,500	4,955,900	4,102,100	5,049,000	6,044,000	5,892,000
Shares Outstanding	586,000	597,100	573,400	558,000	518,200	516,700	515,500	444,300
Statistical Record								
Return on Assets %	3.92	1.12	1.17	0.64	N.M.	N.M.	N.M.	1.60
Return on Equity %	15.91	5.36	6.04	3.60	N.M.	N.M.	N.M.	9.11
EBITDA Margin %	30.08	17.84	15.48	13.92	12.70	27.00	27.28	29.36
Net Margin %	9.38	2.61	2.49	1.31	N.M.	N.M.	N.M.	5.04
Asset Turnover	0.42	0.43	0.47	0.49	0.54	0.15	0.28	0.32
Current Ratio	1.25	1.35	1.15	1.17	1.40	1.14	0.96	0.92
Debt to Equity	1.22	1.26	1.40	1.56	2.69	2.36	1.57	1.76
Price Range	37.16-25.32	27.95-19.49	25.40-15.29	17.10-8.75	10.62-2.60	25.97-0.88	43.45-22.10	44.69-27.83
P/E Ratio	22.80-15.53	54.80-38.22	47.92-28.85	55.16-28.23	...	...	...	38.20-23.78
Average Yield %	1.25	1.47	1.25	0.67	0.56	4.03	2.01	1.59

Address: One Williams Center, Tulsa, OK 74172	**Web Site:** www.williams.com	**Auditors:** ERNST & YOUNG LLP
Telephone: 918-573-2000	**Officers:** Steven J. Malcolm - Chmn., Pres., C.E.O. Donald R. Chappel - Sr. V.P., C.F.O.	**Investor Contact:** 918-573-3679
Fax: 918-588-2334		**Transfer Agents:** EquiServe Trust Company, N.A., Providence, RI

WILLIAMS-SONOMA, INC.

Exchange	Symbol	Price	52Wk Range	Yield	P/E
NYS	WSM	$24.24 (3/31/2008)	36.52-20.01	1.98	13.77

*7 Year Price Score 79.19   *NYSE Composite Index=100   *12 Month Price Score 88.97

Interim Earnings (Per Share)

Qtr.	Apr	Jul	Oct	Jan
2003-04	0.11	0.15	0.20	0.86
2004-05	0.18	0.23	0.24	0.95
2005-06	0.22	0.26	0.31	1.02
2006-07	0.20	0.30	0.25	1.04
2007-08	0.16	0.23	0.25	1.12

Interim Dividends (Per Share)

Amt	Decl	Ex	Rec	Pay
0.115Q	6/22/2007	7/25/2007	7/27/2007	8/24/2007
0.115Q	9/21/2007	10/24/2007	10/26/2007	11/23/2007
0.115Q	12/21/2007	1/23/2008	1/25/2008	2/27/2008
0.12Q	3/27/2008	4/23/2008	4/25/2008	5/23/2008

Indicated Div: $0.48

Valuation Analysis

Institutional Holding		
Forecast P/E	12.87	No of Institutions
	(1/10/2007)	243
Market Cap	$2.6 Billion	Shares
Book Value	1.2 Billion	99,480,576
Price/Book	2.19	% Held
Price/Sales	0.65	90.53

TRADING VOLUME (thousand shares)

Business Summary: Retail - Furniture & Home Furnishings (MIC: 5.9 SIC: 5719 NAIC: 442299)

Williams-Sonoma is a retailer of products for the home. Co.'s retail segment sells its products through its five retail store concepts: Williams-Sonoma, Pottery Barn, Pottery Barn Kids, West Elm and Williams-Sonoma Home. Co.'s direct-to-customer segment sells similar products through its seven direct-mail catalogs: Williams-Sonoma, Pottery Barn, Pottery Barn Kids, Pottery Barn Bed and Bath, PBteen, West Elm and Williams-Sonoma Home, as well as six e-commerce websites. williams-sonoma.com, potterybarn.com, potterybarnkids.com, pbteen.com, westelm.com and wshome.com. As of Feb 3 2008, Co. operated 600 retail stores, located in 44 states, Washington, D.C. and Canada.

Recent Developments: For the year ended Feb 3 2008, net income decreased 6.3% to US$195.8 million from US$208.9 million in the prior year. Revenues were US$3.94 billion, up 5.8% from US$3.73 billion the year before. Direct operating expenses rose 7.5% to US$2.41 billion from US$2.24 billion in the comparable period the year before. Indirect operating expenses increased 5.4% to US$1.22 billion from US$1.16 billion in the equivalent prior-year period.

Prospects: For the fiscal year ending Feb 1 2009, Co. is projecting net revenues to be in the range of $3.80 billion to $3.90 billion, while retail net revenues are forecasted to range from $2.25 billion to $2.30 billion. In addition, Co. is targeting comparable store sales to decline in the range of 3.0% to 5.5%, excluding the results from its West Elm and Williams-Sonoma Home stores. Nevertheless, Co. continues to expect retail leased and selling square footage to increase in the range of 7.5% to 8.5%. Lastly, Co. intends to add approximately 29 net new retail stores as well as expand or remodel an additional 20 stores in order to support future growth and to continue the expansion of its brands.

Financial Data

(US$ in Thousands)	02/03/2008	01/28/2007	01/29/2006	01/30/2005	02/01/2004	02/02/2003	02/03/2002	01/28/2001
Earnings Per Share	1.76	1.79	1.81	1.60	1.32	1.04	0.65	0.50
Cash Flow Per Share	2.21	2.72	3.02	2.63	1.82	2.70	1.79	1.63
Tang Book Value Per Share	11.07	10.48	0.80	8.30	6.95	5.63	4.65	3.83
Dividends Per Share	0.460	0.400	...	...	...	...	...	...
Dividend Payout %	26.14	22.35	...	...	...	...	...	...
Income Statement								
Total Revenue	3,944,934	3,727,513	3,538,947	3,136,931	2,754,368	2,360,830	2,086,662	1,829,483
EBITDA	424,699	433,849	443,380	399,063	335,058	285,014	199,845	151,047
Income Before Taxes	316,340	337,186	348,798	310,205	255,638	202,282	122,106	92,329
Income Taxes	120,583	128,318	133,932	118,971	98,427	77,879	47,010	35,547
Net Income	195,757	208,868	214,866	191,234	157,211	124,403	75,096	56,782
Average Shares	111,447	116,773	118,427	119,347	119,016	119,550	115,440	114,920
Balance Sheet								
Current Assets	1,049,775	1,100,963	1,083,164	873,765	687,889	625,384	417,239	392,909
Total Assets	2,093,854	2,048,331	1,981,620	1,745,545	1,470,735	1,264,455	994,903	891,928
Current Liabilities	611,534	627,734	590,392	522,157	442,884	424,828	297,179	311,286
Long-Term Obligations	11,238	12,822	14,490	19,154	28,389	18,071	24,625	23,189
Total Liabilities	928,131	896,900	856,302	787,883	666,144	620,477	462,372	464,470
Stockholders' Equity	1,165,723	1,151,431	1,125,318	957,662	804,591	643,978	532,531	427,458
Shares Outstanding	105,349	109,868	114,779	115,372	115,827	114,317	114,486	111,605
Statistical Record								
Return on Assets %	9.30	10.39	11.56	11.92	11.53	11.04	7.83	6.98
Return on Equity %	16.62	18.40	20.69	21.76	21.77	21.21	15.39	14.05
EBITDA Margin %	10.77	11.64	12.53	12.72	12.16	12.07	9.58	8.26
Net Margin %	4.96	5.60	6.07	6.10	5.71	5.27	3.60	3.10
Asset Turnover	1.87	1.85	1.90	1.96	2.02	2.10	2.18	2.25
Current Ratio	1.72	1.75	1.83	1.67	1.55	1.47	1.40	1.26
Debt to Equity	0.01	0.01	0.01	0.02	0.04	0.03	0.05	0.05
Price Range	36.52-20.01	44.33-28.57	45.09-33.49	41.21-28.79	37.15-20.37	32.80-19.96	23.00-10.87	22.38-8.09
P/E Ratio	20.75-11.37	24.77-15.96	24.91-18.50	25.76-17.99	28.14-15.43	31.54-19.19	35.38-16.72	44.75-16.19
Average Yield %	1.46	1.12	...	...	...	...	...	...

Address: 3250 Van Ness Avenue, San Francisco, CA 94109	**Web Site:** www.williams-sonoma.com	**Auditors:** Deloitte & Touche LLP
Telephone: 415-421-7900	**Officers:** W. Howard Lester - Chmn. Edward A. Mueller - C.E.O.	**Transfer Agents:** Wells Fargo Shareowner Services, St. Paul, MN
Fax: 415-434-0881		

WILMINGTON TRUST CORP. (DE)

Exchange	Symbol	Price	52Wk Range	Yield	P/E	Div Acheiver
NYS	WL	$31.10 (3/31/2008)	43.11-28.18	4.31	11.78	26 Years

*7 Year Price Score 84.63   *NYSE Composite Index=100   *12 Month Price Score 92.52

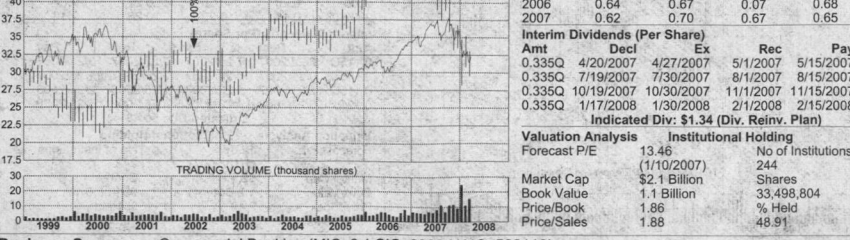

Interim Earnings (Per Share)

Qtr.	Mar	Jun	Sep	Dec
2003	0.44	0.49	0.52	0.57
2004	0.53	0.54	0.50	0.52
2005	0.59	0.59	0.65	0.70
2006	0.64	0.67	0.07	0.68
2007	0.62	0.70	0.67	0.65

Interim Dividends (Per Share)

Amt	Decl	Ex	Rec	Pay
0.335Q	4/20/2007	4/27/2007	5/1/2007	5/15/2007
0.335Q	7/19/2007	7/30/2007	8/1/2007	8/15/2007
0.335Q	10/19/2007	10/30/2007	11/1/2007	11/15/2007
0.335Q	1/17/2008	1/30/2008	2/1/2008	2/15/2008

Indicated Div: $1.34 (Div. Reinv. Plan)

Valuation Analysis

	Institutional Holding	
Forecast P/E	13.46	No of Institutions
	(1/10/2007)	244
Market Cap	$2.1 Billion	Shares
Book Value	1.1 Billion	33,498,804
Price/Book	1.86	% Held
Price/Sales	1.88	48.91

Business Summary: Commercial Banking (MIC: 8.1 SIC: 6022 NAIC: 522110)

Wilmington Trust is a financial holding company. Co.'s Regional Banking business is engaged in lending, deposit-taking, and other banking activities in Delaware, Maryland, New Jersey, and Pennsylvania. Co.'s Wealth Advisory Services' activities encompass a range of financial planning, investment management, fiduciary, and family office services for individuals and families. Co.'s Corporate Client Services business provides a variety of trustee, agency, and administrative services in jurisdictions in the U.S., the Caribbean, and Europe with legal, tax, and creditor protections, while its affiliate Money Managers segment comprises of Cramer Rosenthal McGlynn and Roxbury Capital Management.

Recent Developments: For the year ended Dec 31 2007, net income increased 26.6% to US$182.0 million from US$143.8 million in the prior year. Net interest income increased 1.6% to US$368.9 million from US$363.1 million in the prior year. Provision for loan losses was US$28.2 million versus US$21.3 million in the prior year, an increase of 32.4%. Non-interest income rose 11.5% to US$386.0 million from US$346.1 million, while non-interest expense declined 5.8% to US$444.1 million.

Prospects: On Jan 31 2008, Co. announced that its Wilmington Trust FSB subsidiary has signed an agreement to acquire AST Capital Trust Co., a provider of trust and administrative services for retirement plans, institutional investors, and individuals and families. The purchase should enhance Co.'s presence and service capabilities in the retirement plan services market, and nearly double the amount of retirement plan assets Wilmington Trust administers and double the number of plans Co. serves, to $41.00 billion and 3,000, respectively. The transaction is expected to be completed in summer 2008, and is estimated to add about $27.0 million of revenue and to be non-dilutive to Co.'s earnings in 2008.

Financial Data

(US$ in Thousands)	12/31/2007	12/31/2006	12/31/2005	12/31/2004	12/31/2003	12/31/2002	12/31/2001	12/31/2000
Earnings Per Share	2.64	2.06	2.52	2.09	2.02	2.01	1.90	1.85
Cash Flow Per Share	3.28	3.94	3.10	2.97	2.99	2.66	4.14	2.28
Tang Book Value Per Share	11.21	10.70	9.26	7.78	8.08	7.31	7.25	6.48
Dividends Per Share	1.320	1.245	1.185	1.125	1.065	1.005	0.945	0.885
Dividend Payout %	50.00	60.44	47.02	53.83	52.72	50.00	49.74	47.84
Income Statement								
Interest Income	722,200	674,800	516,600	386,500	368,800	392,871	468,798	530,454
Interest Expense	353,300	311,700	187,700	92,100	91,700	116,341	209,985	275,315
Net Interest Income	368,900	363,100	328,900	294,400	277,100	276,530	258,813	255,139
Provision for Losses	28,200	21,300	11,800	15,600	21,600	22,013	19,850	21,900
Non-Interest Income	386,000	346,100	313,300	286,700	264,200	262,159	228,003	216,210
Non-Interest Expense	444,100	471,600	363,500	344,000	312,000	309,892	276,917	264,682
Income Before Taxes	282,600	216,300	266,900	221,500	207,700	206,784	190,049	184,767
Income Taxes	99,700	72,700	93,600	78,700	72,200	73,002	66,009	63,828
Net Income	182,000	143,800	173,000	141,900	134,400	133,157	125,170	120,939
Average Shares	68,851	69,707	68,570	67,755	66,536	66,301	65,942	65,360
Balance Sheet								
Net Loans & Leases	8,374,700	8,000,700	7,306,300	6,673,300	6,135,400	5,939,947	5,407,175	5,111,670
Total Assets	11,485,700	11,157,000	10,228,100	9,510,200	8,820,200	8,131,275	7,518,462	7,321,564
Total Deposits	7,857,500	8,329,100	7,289,200	6,871,900	6,577,200	6,337,093	5,590,785	5,286,016
Total Liabilities	10,365,300	10,097,700	9,214,900	8,604,800	8,019,200	7,390,001	6,835,932	6,729,716
Stockholders' Equity	1,120,300	1,059,300	1,013,000	905,300	800,800	741,269	682,530	591,900
Shares Outstanding	67,086	68,459	67,903	67,405	66,063	65,627	65,400	64,786
Statistical Record								
Return on Assets %	1.61	1.34	1.75	1.54	1.59	1.70	1.69	1.66
Return on Equity %	16.70	13.88	18.04	16.59	17.43	18.70	19.64	22.13
Net Interest Margin %	51.08	53.81	63.67	76.17	75.14	70.39	55.21	48.10
Efficiency Ratio %	40.07	46.19	43.80	51.10	49.29	47.31	39.74	35.45
Loans to Deposits	1.07	0.96	1.00	0.97	0.93	0.94	0.97	0.97
Price Range	44.54-33.16	45.32-39.37	40.69-33.01	38.30-33.95	36.21-26.35	34.58-25.30	33.42-25.65	31.56-20.75
P/E Ratio	16.87-12.56	22.00-19.11	16.15-13.10	18.33-16.24	17.93-13.04	17.20-12.59	17.59-13.50	17.06-11.22
Average Yield %	3.30	2.90	3.26	3.11	3.47	3.24	3.24	3.58

Address: Rodney Square North, 1100 North Market Street, Wilmington, DE 19890-0001 Telephone: 302-651-1000 Fax: 302-651-8010	Web Site: www.wilmingtontrust.com Officers: Ted T. Cecala - Chmn., C.E.O. Robert V. A. Harra Jr. - Pres., C.O.O., Treas.	Auditors: KPMG LLP Investor Contact: 302-651-8069 Transfer Agents: Wells Fargo Shareowner Services, St. Paul, MN

WINDSTREAM CORP

Exchange	Symbol	Price	52Wk Range	Yield	P/E
NYS	WIN	$11.95 (3/31/2008)	15.21-10.96	8.37	6.16

*7 Year Price Score N/A   *NYSE Composite Index=100   *12 Month Price Score 94.31

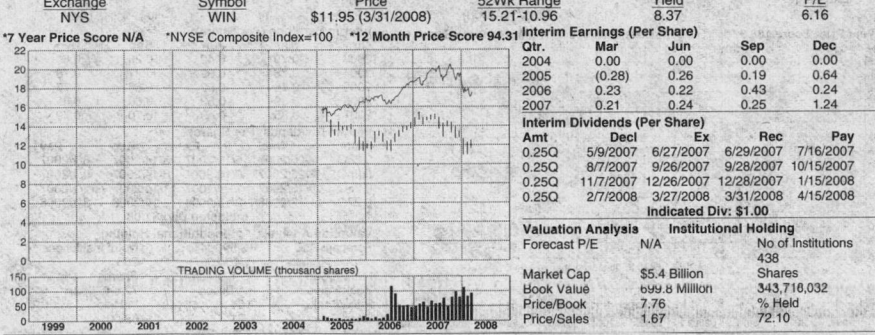

Interim Earnings (Per Share)

Qtr.	Mar	Jun	Sep	Dec
2004	0.00	0.00	0.00	0.00
2005	(0.28)	0.26	0.19	0.64
2006	0.23	0.22	0.43	0.24
2007	0.21	0.24	0.25	1.24

Interim Dividends (Per Share)

Amt	Decl	Ex	Rec	Pay
0.25Q	5/9/2007	6/27/2007	6/29/2007	7/16/2007
0.25Q	8/7/2007	9/26/2007	9/28/2007	10/15/2007
0.25Q	11/7/2007	12/26/2007	12/28/2007	1/15/2008
0.25Q	2/7/2008	3/27/2008	3/31/2008	4/15/2008

Indicated Div: $1.00

Valuation Analysis

		Institutional Holding	
Forecast P/E	N/A	No of Institutions	438
Market Cap	$5.4 Billion	Shares	343,716,032
Book Value	699.8 Million	% Held	72.10
Price/Book	7.76		
Price/Sales	1.67		

Business Summary: Communications (MIC: 10.1 SIC: 4813 NAIC: 517310)

Windstream is a provider of telecommunications services in rural communities in the U.S. Through its subsidiaries, Co. provides local telephone, high-speed Internet, as well as long distance services in 16 states. In addition to its wireline, high-speed Internet and long distance service offerings, Co. also provides network access, video services and wireless products and services in select markets. As of Dec 31 2007, Co. served more than 3.2 million communications customers in 16 states, as well as provided data services to more than 871,000 high speed Internet customers.

Recent Developments: For the year ended Dec 31 2007, net income increased 68.2% to US$917.1 million from US$545.3 million in the prior year. Revenues were US$3.26 billion, up 7.5% from US$3.03 billion the year before. Operating income was US$1.15 billion versus US$898.8 million in the prior year, an increase of 28.1%. Direct operating expenses rose 3.2% to US$1.18 billion from US$1.14 billion in the comparable period the year before. Indirect operating expenses decreased 6.1% to US$933.5 million from US$994.3 million in the equivalent prior-year period.

Prospects: Co. expects the number of access lines served by its wireline operations to continue to be hampered by fixed line and wireless substitution in 2008. Thus, Co. will continue to focus on sales of additional services by bundling its various product offerings, including Internet and digital satellite television. For 2008, Co. estimates revenue of $3.16 billion to $3.29 billion, with capital expenditure of $340.0 million to $370.0 million. Separately, on Nov 30 2007, Co. completed the split off of its directory publishing business in a tax-free transaction with entities affiliated with Welsh, Carson, Anderson & Stowe, a private equity investment firm and Co.'s shareholder, for $506.7 million.

Financial Data

(US$ in Thousands)	12/31/2007	12/31/2006	12/31/2005	12/31/2004	12/31/2003	12/31/2002
Earnings Per Share	1.94	1.25	0.82	(0.09)	0.73	0.17
Cash Flow Per Share	2.19	2.59	2.75	2.07	...	...
Dividends Per Share	1.000	0.790	1.200	...	...	...
Dividend Payout %	51.55	63.20	153.66	...	...	...
Income Statement						
Total Revenue	3,260,800	3,033,300	505,894	507,310	497,334	479,883
EBITDA	2,121,000	1,349,200	227,584	177,315	271,898	241,212
Income Before Taxes	1,169,100	721,900	50,413	(26,948)	60,857	21,425
Income Taxes	252,000	276,300	14,329	665	2,478	1,649
Net Income	917,100	545,300	35,347	(27,755)	58,233	16,302
Average Shares	473,000	435,400	69,666	69,358	...	...
Balance Sheet						
Net PPE	4,042,300	3,939,800	717,529	749,984	769,570	...
Total Assets	8,210,700	8,030,700	1,962,781	1,971,167	2,039,043	...
Long-Term Obligations	5,331,200	5,456,200	1,180,555	1,599,177	1,426,655	...
Total Liabilities	7,510,900	7,560,900	1,391,013	1,964,696	1,988,804	...
Stockholders' Equity	699,800	469,800	571,768	6,471	49,862	...
Shares Outstanding	454,500	476,800	71,130	70,833	...	...
Statistical Record						
Return on Assets %	11.29	10.91	1.80	N.M.	...	...
Return on Equity %	156.82	104.71	12.23	N.M.	...	...
EBITDA Margin %	65.05	44.48	44.99	34.95	54.67	50.26
Net Margin %	28.13	17.98	6.99	(5.47)	11.71	3.40
PPE Turnover	0.82	1.30	0.69	0.67	...	...
Asset Turnover	0.40	0.61	0.26	0.25	...	...
Debt to Equity	7.62	11.61	2.06	247.13	28.61	...
Price Range	15.44-12.70	14.35-11.35	16.00-11.40	...	...	...
P/E Ratio	7.96-6.55	11.48-9.08	19.51-13.90	...	...	...
Average Yield %	7.02	8.18	9.24	...	...	...

Address: 201 E. John Carpenter Freeway, Suite 200, Irving, TX 75062 **Telephone:** 972-373-1000	**Web Site:** www.valortelecom.com **Officers:** Anthony J. de Nicola - Chmn. Kenneth R. Cole - Vice-Chmn.	**Auditors:** PricewaterhouseCoopers LLP

WISCONSIN ENERGY CORP.

Exchange	Symbol	Price	52Wk Range	Yield	P/E
NYS	WEC	$43.99 (3/31/2008)	50.00-41.82	2.46	15.54

*7 Year Price Score 108.32 *NYSE Composite Index=100 *12 Month Price Score 103.26

Interim Earnings (Per Share)

Qtr.	Mar	Jun	Sep	Dec
2003	0.79	0.42	0.26	0.60
2004	0.76	0.32	0.71	0.78
2005	0.76	0.52	0.56	0.77
2006	0.89	0.53	0.60	0.65
2007	0.85	0.49	0.70	0.79

Interim Dividends (Per Share)

Amt	Decl	Ex	Rec	Pay
0.25Q	4/26/2007	5/10/2007	5/14/2007	6/1/2007
0.25Q	7/26/2007	8/10/2007	8/14/2007	9/1/2007
0.25Q	10/18/2007	11/9/2007	11/14/2007	12/1/2007
0.27Q	1/17/2008	2/12/2008	2/14/2008	3/1/2008

Indicated Div: $1.08

Valuation Analysis / **Institutional Holding**

Forecast P/E	16.59 (1/10/2007)	No of Institutions 288
Market Cap	$5.1 Billion	Shares 72,546,832
Book Value	3.1 Billion	% Held
Price/Book	1.64	62.03
Price/Sales	1.21	

Business Summary: Electricity (MIC: 7.1 SIC: 4931 NAIC: 221121)

Wisconsin Energy is a holding company. Co. conducts its operations mainly in two segments: a utility energy segment and a non-utility energy segment. Co.'s utility energy segment consists of Wisconsin Electric, Wisconsin Gas and Edison Sault, which as of Dec 31 2007, served about 1.1 million electric customers in Wisconsin and the Upper Peninsula of Michigan, approximately 1.0 million gas customers in Wisconsin, 470 steam customers in metro Milwaukee, and 3,040 water customers in suburban Milwaukee. Co.'s non-utility energy segment consists primarily of We Power, which designs, constructs, owns and leases generating capacity to Wisconsin Electric.

Recent Developments: For the year ended Dec 31 2007, income from continuing operations increased 7.7% to US$336.5 million from US$312.5 million a year earlier. Net income increased 6.1% to US$335.6 million from US$316.4 million in the prior year. Revenues were US$4.24 billion, up 6.0% from US$4.00 billion the year before. Operating income was US$628.5 million versus US$568.5 million in the prior year, an increase of 10.6%. Direct operating expenses rose 6.0% to US$3.18 billion from US$3.00 billion in the comparable period the year before. Indirect operating expenses increased 0.2% to US$424.9 million from US$423.9 million in the equivalent prior-year period.

Prospects: On Jan 17 2008, the Public Service Commission of Wisconsin approved pricing increases for Co.'s Wisconsin Electric and Wisconsin Gas subsidiaries. Notably, this included increases of $73.2 million in electric rates for Wisconsin Electric; $4.0 million for natural gas service from Wisconsin Electric; $3.6 million for steam service from Wisconsin Electric; and $20.1 million for natural gas service from Wisconsin Gas. Co. expects its gas margins to increase in 2008 due to the pricing increases. However, while expecting higher electric utility operating revenues in 2008, Co. does not expect a material increase in earnings as the primary driver for the pricing increase is increased costs.

Financial Data

(US$ in Thousands)	12/31/2007	12/31/2006	12/31/2005	12/31/2004	12/31/2003	12/31/2002	12/31/2001	12/31/2000
Earnings Per Share	2.83	2.67	2.61	2.57	2.06	1.44	1.86	1.27
Cash Flow Per Share	4.56	6.24	4.93	5.07	5.33	6.16	4.75	3.81
Tang Book Value Per Share	22.72	20.92	19.13	17.53	12.86	11.26	10.60	10.03
Dividends Per Share	1.000	0.920	0.880	0.830	0.800	0.800	0.800	1.370
Dividend Payout %	35.34	34.46	33.72	32.30	38.83	55.56	43.01	107.87
Income Statement								
Total Revenue	4,237,800	3,996,400	3,815,500	3,431,100	4,054,300	3,736,200	3,928,500	3,354,700
EBITDA	1,081,700	1,025,700	999,200	780,100	992,000	870,300	982,200	889,900
Income Before Taxes	552,900	487,500	452,800	202,500	379,400	272,700	358,900	280,100
Income Taxes	216,400	175,000	149,200	80,300	135,100	105,700	150,400	125,900
Net Income	335,600	316,400	308,700	306,400	244,300	167,000	219,000	154,200
Average Shares	118,500	118,400	118,400	119,100	118,400	116,300	117,900	121,200
Balance Sheet								
Net PPE	7,681,200	7,052,500	6,362,900	5,903,100	5,926,100	4,398,800	4,188,000	4,152,400
Total Assets	11,720,300	11,130,200	10,462,000	9,565,400	10,025,700	8,364,900	8,328,700	8,406,100
Long-Term Obligations	3,172,500	3,073,400	3,031,000	3,239,500	3,574,300	3,030,500	3,237,300	2,732,700
Total Liabilities	8,590,700	8,210,800	7,751,500	7,042,600	7,636,700	6,195,100	6,242,200	6,358,900
Stockholders' Equity	3,129,600	2,919,400	2,710,500	2,522,800	2,389,000	2,169,800	2,086,500	2,047,200
Shares Outstanding	116,943	116,969	116,980	116,985	118,425	116,027	115,420	118,645
Statistical Record								
Return on Assets %	2.94	2.93	3.08	3.12	2.66	2.00	2.62	2.10
Return on Equity %	11.10	11.24	11.80	12.44	10.72	7.85	10.60	7.53
EBITDA Margin %	25.53	25.67	26.19	22.74	24.47	23.29	25.00	26.53
Net Margin %	7.92	7.92	8.09	8.93	6.03	4.47	5.57	4.60
PPE Turnover	0.58	0.60	0.62	0.58	0.79	0.87	0.94	0.84
Asset Turnover	0.37	0.37	0.38	0.35	0.44	0.45	0.47	0.46
Debt to Equity	1.01	1.05	1.12	1.28	1.50	1.40	1.55	1.33
Price Range	50.00-41.82	48.57-38.40	40.41-33.45	34.49-29.65	33.46-22.67	26.36-20.75	24.37-19.44	23.00-16.81
P/E Ratio	17.67-14.78	18.19-14.38	15.48-12.82	13.42-11.54	16.24-11.00	18.31-14.41	13.10-10.45	18.11-13.24
Average Yield %	2.14	2.19	2.38	2.56	2.85	3.30	3.61	6.81

Address: 231 West Michigan Street, Milwaukee, WI 53201 **Telephone:** 414-221-2345 **Fax:** 414-221-2172	**Web Site:** www.wisconsinenergy.com **Officers:** Gale E. Klappa - Chmn., Pres., C.E.O. Richard R. Grigg - Exec. V.P.	**Auditors:** Deloitte & Touche LLP **Investor Contact:** 414-221-2592 **Transfer Agents:** The Bank of New York, New York, NY

WOLVERINE WORLD WIDE, INC.

Exchange	Symbol	Price	52Wk Range	Yield	P/E	Div Acheiver
NYS	WWW	$29.01 (3/31/2008)	30.34-20.21	1.52	17.06	14 Years

*7 Year Price Score 116.34 *NYSE Composite Index=100 *12 Month Price Score 108.65

Interim Earnings (Per Share)

Qtr.	Mar	Jun	Sep	Dec
2004	0.20	0.18	0.37	0.34
2005	0.27	0.22	0.42	0.36
Qtr.	Mar	Jun	Aug	Dec
2006	0.34	0.25	0.46	0.42
2007	0.39	0.28	0.54	0.49

Interim Dividends (Per Share)

Amt	Decl	Ex	Rec	Pay
0.09Q	4/19/2007	6/28/2007	7/2/2007	8/1/2007
0.09Q	7/13/2007	9/27/2007	10/1/2007	11/1/2007
0.09Q	12/19/2007	12/28/2007	1/2/2008	2/1/2008
0.11Q	2/12/2008	3/28/2008	4/1/2008	5/1/2008

Indicated Div: $0.44

Valuation Analysis — **Institutional Holding**

Forecast P/E	14.97	No of Institutions
	(1/10/2007)	190
Market Cap	$1.5 Billion	Shares
Book Value	478.8 Million	49,443,088
Price/Book	3.10	% Held
Price/Sales	1.24	88.98

Business Summary: Leather and Leather Products (MIC: 4.5 SIC: 3149 NAIC: 316219)

Wolverine World Wide is a designer, manufacturer and marketer of a line of casual shoes, rugged outdoor and work footwear. Co.'s products are marketed worldwide under several brand names including Bates®, Cat® Footwear, Harley-Davidson® Footwear, Hush Puppies®, HyTest®, Merrell®, Patagonia®, Sebago® and Wolverine®. At Dec 29 2007, Co.'s footwear was distributed domestically through 90 Company-owned retail stores and to numerous accounts such as department stores, footwear chains, catalogs, specialty retailers, mass merchants and Internet retailers. Co.'s products are marketed worldwide in nearly 200 countries through Company-owned wholesale operations, licensees and distributors.

Recent Developments: For the year ended Dec 29 2007, net income increased 11.0% to US$92.9 million from US$83.6 million in the prior year. Revenues were US$1.20 billion, up 5.0% from US$1.14 billion the year before. Direct operating expenses rose 3.8% to US$727.0 million from US$700.3 million in the comparable period the year before. Indirect operating expenses increased 4.5% to US$332.5 million from US$318.0 million in the equivalent prior-year period.

Prospects: Co.'s results are benefiting from expanding operating margins, as well as robust year-end order backlog. For instance, Co. attributed its revenue growth to several factors, such as increases in unit volume, changes in product mix and changes in selling price for the branded footwear, apparel and licensing segment operations. Thus, for full-year 2008, Co. is expecting revenue of $1.23 billion to $1.26 billion and is increasing its earnings per share estimate of $1.78 to $1.84 to a range of $1.80 to $1.88. Co. anticipates shipping substantially all of the backlog of $389.0 million at Feb 16 2008, which relates to demand for products, in 2008.

Financial Data

(US$ in Thousands)	12/29/2007	12/30/2006	12/31/2005	01/01/2005	01/03/2004	12/28/2002	12/29/2001	12/30/2000
Earnings Per Share	1.70	1.47	1.27	1.09	0.85	0.77	0.71	0.17
Cash Flow Per Share	2.35	1.98	2.14	1.86	1.71	1.47	0.87	1.14
Tang Book Value Per Share	8.40	8.24	7.45	7.16	6.56	5.59	5.76	5.18
Dividends Per Share	0.360	0.300	0.260	0.195	0.147	0.120	0.107	0.093
Dividend Payout %	21.18	20.41	20.47	17.89	17.32	15.58	14.95	53.85
Income Statement								
Total Revenue	1,198,972	1,141,887	1,060,999	991,909	888,926	827,106	720,066	701,291
EBITDA	161,362	142,914	131,287	116,141	93,095	88,514	86,168	32,710
Income Before Taxes	138,571	122,292	111,247	97,070	75,148	71,654	68,547	15,015
Income Taxes	45,685	38,645	36,780	30,879	23,262	23,599	23,307	4,325
Net Income	92,886	83,647	74,467	65,938	51,716	47,912	45,240	10,690
Average Shares	54,487	56,931	58,675	60,474	61,081	62,689	63,673	62,692
Balance Sheet								
Current Assets	445,641	485,313	420,748	430,855	386,636	363,345	374,802	325,086
Total Assets	638,378	671,092	626,580	639,571	578,881	531,994	543,678	494,568
Current Liabilities	122,632	120,915	104,037	110,251	85,766	80,177	74,521	54,004
Long-Term Obligations	...	10,741	21,439	32,169	43,903	57,885	75,818	87,878
Total Liabilities	159,599	166,533	164,259	180,714	148,473	162,754	169,526	157,330
Stockholders' Equity	478,779	504,559	462,321	458,291	430,094	369,097	374,152	337,238
Shares Outstanding	51,234	55,462	56,129	57,898	59,179	59,955	62,333	62,329
Statistical Record								
Return on Assets %	14.23	12.93	11.80	10.85	9.16	8.93	8.74	2.08
Return on Equity %	18.94	17.35	16.22	14.89	12.73	12.93	12.75	3.20
EBITDA Margin %	13.46	12.52	12.37	11.71	10.47	10.70	11.97	4.66
Net Margin %	7.75	7.33	7.02	6.65	5.82	5.79	6.28	1.52
Asset Turnover	1.84	1.76	1.68	1.63	1.57	1.54	1.39	1.37
Current Ratio	3.63	4.01	4.04	3.91	4.51	4.53	5.03	6.02
Debt to Equity	...	0.02	0.05	0.07	0.10	0.16	0.20	0.26
Price Range	30.77-23.72	29.39-20.44	25.25-19.50	21.48-13.57	14.19-9.59	12.83-8.60	12.80-8.37	11.04-5.75
P/E Ratio	18.10-13.95	19.99-13.90	19.88-15.35	19.71-12.45	16.69-11.29	16.66-11.17	18.03-11.79	64.95-33.82
Average Yield %	1.31	1.21	1.19	1.14	1.19	1.12	1.00	1.27

Address: 9341 Courtland Drive, Rockford, MI 49351	**Web Site:** www.wolverineworldwide.com	**Auditors:** Ernst & Young LLP
	Officers: Timothy J. O'Donovan - Chmn., C.E.O.	**Investor Contact:** 616-866-5589
Telephone: 616-866-5500	Blake W. Krueger - Pres., C.O.O.	**Transfer Agents:** Computershare
Fax: 616-866-0257		Investor Services, Chicago, IL

WORLD FUEL SERVICES CORP.

Exchange	Symbol	Price	52Wk Range	Yield	P/E
NYS	INT	$28.07 (3/31/2008)	48.23-24.42	0.53	12.59

*7 Year Price Score 126.19 *NYSE Composite Index=100 *12 Month Price Score 82.16

Interim Earnings (Per Share)

Qtr.	Mar	Jun	Sep	Dec
2003	0.24	0.25	0.25	0.25
2004	0.26	0.29	0.29	0.38
2005	0.31	0.40	0.44	0.42
2006	0.52	0.50	0.59	0.59
2007	0.51	0.58	0.51	0.63

Interim Dividends (Per Share)

Amt	Decl	Ex	Rec	Pay
0.037Q	6/8/2007	6/20/2007	6/22/2007	7/11/2007
0.037Q	9/7/2007	9/19/2007	9/21/2007	10/10/2007
0.037Q	12/7/2007	12/19/2007	12/21/2007	1/9/2008
0.037Q	3/7/2008	3/18/2008	3/21/2008	4/9/2008

Indicated Div: $0.15

Valuation Analysis — **Institutional Holding**

Forecast P/E	13.24	No of Institutions
	(1/10/2007)	169
Market Cap	$802.2 Million	Shares
Book Value	483.9 Million	26,092,316
Price/Book	1.66	% Held
Price/Sales	0.06	91.52

Business Summary: Retail - Fuel & Oil (MIC: 5.5 SIC: 5172 NAIC: 424720)

World Fuel Services is engaged in the marketing and sale of marine, aviation and land fuel products and related services on a worldwide basis. In its marine segment, Co. provides marine fuel and related services to maritime customers as well as to the U.S. and foreign governments. In its aviation segment, Co. provides fuel and related services to commercial airlines, second and third-tier airlines, cargo carriers, regional and low cost carriers, corporate fleets, fractional operators, private aircraft, military fleets and to the U.S. and foreign governments. In its land segment, Co. provides fuel and related services to petroleum-distributors operating in the land transportation market.

Recent Developments: For the year ended Dec 31 2007, net income increased 1.3% to US$64.8 million from US$63.9 million in the prior year. Revenues were US$13.73 billion, up 27.3% from US$10.79 billion the year before. Operating income was US$85.9 million versus US$76.6 million in the prior year, an increase of 12.1%. Direct operating expenses rose 27.6% to US$13.48 billion from US$10.57 billion in the comparable period the year before. Indirect operating expenses increased 16.0% to US$159.4 million from US$137.4 million in the equivalent prior-year period.

Prospects: Co.'s results are being positively affected by net revenue growth due to increased results across its segments, primarily reflecting increased sales volume to both new and existing customers. Also, Co. is benefiting from several other factors that include an increase in the average price per metric ton sold as a result of higher world oil prices in 2007, and an increase in the average price per gallon sold in its land segment. Meanwhile, on Dec 3 2007, Co. announced that it has completed the previously announced acquisition of AVCARD, a global provider of contract fuel sales and charge card services to the aviation industry. The transaction should be $0.02 to $0.04 accretive in 2008.

Financial Data

(US$ in Thousands)	12/31/2007	12/31/2006	12/31/2005	12/31/2004	12/31/2003	12/31/2002	03/31/2002	03/31/2001
Earnings Per Share	2.23	2.21	1.57	1.22	0.98	0.46	0.81	0.50
Cash Flow Per Share	(2.77)	2.47	(0.17)	(1.30)	1.26	0.17	1.65	1.32
Tang Book Value Per Share	14.18	13.22	11.15	6.07	5.25	4.31	3.89	3.81
Dividends Per Share	0.150	0.150	0.150	0.150	0.150	0.150	0.200	0.100
Dividend Payout %	6.73	6.79	9.55	12.30	15.31	32.97	24.69	20.00
Income Statement								
Total Revenue	13,729,555	10,785,136	8,733,947	5,654,373	2,661,790	1,546,897	1,365,065	1,529,242
EBITDA	88,457	80,676	56,869	39,848	31,550	13,114	23,887	17,076
Income Before Taxes	86,586	81,399	55,828	35,528	27,618	11,756	23,226	16,343
Income Taxes	21,235	17,353	15,475	6,969	5,744	1,884	5,991	4,557
Net Income	64,773	63,948	39,609	28,559	21,874	9,872	17,235	10,634
Average Shares	29,062	28,923	25,214	23,454	22,338	21,800	21,292	21,326
Balance Sheet								
Current Assets	1,665,308	1,196,091	948,310	648,068	311,021	262,580	213,139	188,225
Total Assets	1,798,046	1,277,400	1,014,001	712,171	357,678	312,287	257,923	222,165
Current Liabilities	1,231,111	826,761	635,556	466,985	204,762	180,359	133,851	112,439
Long-Term Obligations	45,191	20,062	20,006	50,467	...	...	...	...
Total Liabilities	1,314,169	851,431	660,654	523,668	209,299	184,557	141,484	118,305
Stockholders' Equity	483,877	425,969	353,347	188,503	148,379	127,730	116,439	103,860
Shares Outstanding	28,579	28,488	27,370	22,846	21,584	21,388	20,754	20,806
Statistical Record								
Return on Assets %	4.21	5.58	4.59	5.32	6.53	2.11	7.18	4.74
Return on Equity %	14.24	16.41	14.62	16.91	15.84	4.86	15.65	10.45
EBITDA Margin %	0.64	0.75	0.65	0.70	1.19	0.85	1.75	1.12
Net Margin %	0.47	0.59	0.45	0.51	0.82	0.64	1.26	0.70
Asset Turnover	8.93	9.41	10.12	10.54	7.95	3.30	5.69	6.81
Current Ratio	1.35	1.45	1.49	1.39	1.52	1.46	1.59	1.67
Debt to Equity	0.09	0.05	0.06	0.27	...	...	...	...
Price Range	48.23-28.91	51.87-30.30	37.05-22.68	24.90-16.34	17.00-9.84	12.20-9.35	9.98-4.36	4.85-3.09
P/E Ratio	21.63-12.96	23.47-13.71	23.60-14.45	20.41-13.39	17.35-10.04	26.52-20.33	12.33-5.38	9.70-6.19
Average Yield %	0.37	0.34	0.52	0.77	1.22	1.47	2.48	2.55

Address: 9800 Northwest 41st Street, Suite 400, Miami, FL 33178
Telephone: 305-428-8000
Fax: 305-392-5621

Web Site: www.wfscorp.com
Officers: Paul H. Stebbins - Chmn., C.E.O. Michael J. Kasbar - Pres., C.O.O.

Auditors: PricewaterhouseCoopers LLP
Investor Contact: 305-428-8000
Transfer Agents: American Stock Transfer & Trust Company, New York, NY

WORTHINGTON INDUSTRIES, INC.

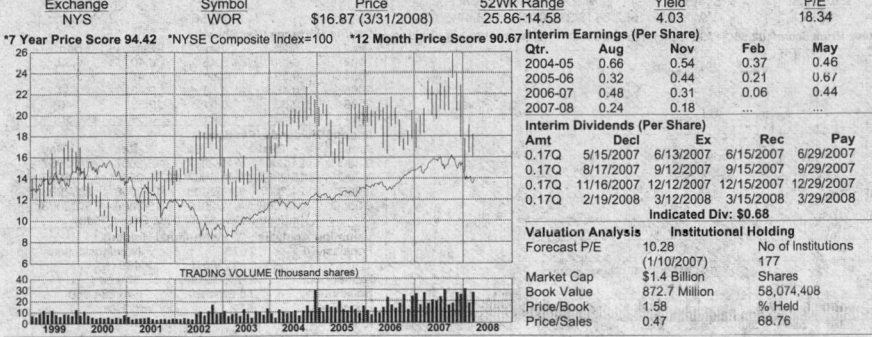

Exchange	Symbol	Price	52Wk Range	Yield	P/E
NYS	WOR	$16.87 (3/31/2008)	25.86-14.58	4.03	18.34

*7 Year Price Score 94.42   *NYSE Composite Index=100   *12 Month Price Score 90.67

Interim Earnings (Per Share)

Qtr.	Aug	Nov	Feb	May
2004-05	0.66	0.54	0.37	0.46
2005-06	0.32	0.44	0.21	0.67
2006-07	0.48	0.31	0.06	0.44
2007-08	0.24	0.18	...	...

Interim Dividends (Per Share)

Amt	Decl	Ex	Rec	Pay
0.17Q	5/15/2007	6/13/2007	6/15/2007	6/29/2007
0.17Q	8/17/2007	9/12/2007	9/15/2007	9/29/2007
0.17Q	11/16/2007	12/12/2007	12/15/2007	12/29/2007
0.17Q	2/19/2008	3/12/2008	3/15/2008	3/29/2008

Indicated Div: $0.68

Valuation Analysis

		Institutional Holding	
Forecast P/E	10.28	No of Institutions	
	(1/10/2007)	177	
Market Cap	$1.4 Billion	Shares	
Book Value	872.7 Million	58,074,408	
Price/Book	1.58	% Held	
Price/Sales	0.47	68.76	

Business Summary: Metal Works (MIC: 11.3 SIC: 3316 NAIC: 331221)

Worthington Industries is a metal processing company, focused on steel processing and manufactured metal products such as metal framing, pressure cylinders, automotive part stampings and, through joint ventures, metal ceiling grid systems and laser-welded blanks. As of May 31 2007, Co. operated 48 manufacturing facilities worldwide and held equity positions in seven joint ventures, which operated an additional 16 manufacturing facilities worldwide. Co. operates through three business segments: Steel Processing, Metal Framing and Pressure Cylinders.

Recent Developments: For the quarter ended Nov 30 2007, net income decreased 45.3% to US$14.7 million from US$26.9 million in the year-earlier quarter. Revenues were US$713.7 million, down 2.1% from US$729.3 million the year before. Operating income was US$11.5 million versus US$30.6 million in the prior-year quarter, a decrease of 62.4%. Direct operating expenses declined 0.2% to US$643.7 million from US$645.2 million in the comparable period the year before. Indirect operating expenses increased 9.3% to US$58.5 million from US$53.5 million in the equivalent prior-year period.

Prospects: Going forward, Co. is pursuing a company-wide cost reduction plan focused on lowering overhead and administrative expenses, which is expected to generate annual savings in excess of $35.0 million. In detail, realized cost savings are expected to increase for the balance of fiscal year ending May 2008 and into fiscal year 2009, reaching the full $35.0 million annual savings run rate in fiscal 2010. Meanwhile, on Nov 13 2007, Co. announced that its Worthington Steelpac Systems, LLC subsidiary has acquired a 49.0% interest in LEFCO Industries, LLC to form a joint venture to produce steel rack systems. This investment gives Co. the opportunity to expand its customer base and its rack business.

Financial Data
(US$ in Thousands)

	6 Mos	3 Mos	05/31/2007	05/31/2006	05/31/2005	05/31/2004	05/31/2003	05/31/2002
Earnings Per Share	0.92	1.05	1.31	1.64	2.03	1.00	0.87	0.08
Cash Flow Per Share	4.55	4.27	2.09	2.57	0.37	0.92	2.11	1.58
Tang Book Value Per Share	8.47	8.39	8.91	8.65	7.47	6.48	6.04	6.21
Dividends Per Share	0.680	0.680	0.680	0.680	0.650	0.640	0.640	0.640
Dividend Payout %	73.91	64.76	51.91	41.46	32.02	64.00	73.56	800.00
Income Statement								
Total Revenue	1,472,619	758,955	2,971,808	2,897,179	3,078,884	2,379,104	2,219,891	1,744,961
EBITDA	89,280	49,567	249,381	298,144	371,104	216,964	212,583	101,867
Depn & Amortn	31,222	15,486	...	...	...	...	...	...
Income Before Taxes	48,050	29,443	166,017	212,749	288,469	127,464	118,398	10,240
Income Taxes	13,142	9,275	52,112	66,759	109,057	40,712	43,215	3,738
Net Income	34,908	20,168	113,905	145,990	179,412	86,752	75,183	6,502
Average Shares	82,358	85,001	87,002	88,976	88,503	86,950	86,537	85,929
Balance Sheet								
Current Assets	933,452	966,205	969,383	996,241	938,333	833,110	506,248	490,340
Total Assets	1,814,240	1,804,669	1,814,182	1,900,397	1,830,005	1,643,139	1,478,069	1,457,314
Current Liabilities	487,636	491,183	420,494	490,786	545,443	475,060	318,171	339,351
Long-Term Obligations	245,000	245,000	245,000	245,000	245,000	288,422	289,689	289,250
Total Liabilities	896,503	897,592	878,181	955,091	1,009,169	962,764	841,775	851,058
Stockholders' Equity	872,662	859,178	936,001	945,306	820,836	680,374	636,294	606,256
Shares Outstanding	81,567	81,034	84,908	88,691	87,933	86,855	85,948	85,512
Statistical Record								
Return on Assets %	4.21	4.80	6.13	7.83	10.33	5.54	5.12	0.44
Return on Equity %	8.76	9.92	12.11	16.53	23.90	13.14	12.10	1.04
EBITDA Margin %	6.06	6.53	8.39	10.29	12.05	9.12	9.58	5.84
Net Margin %	2.37	2.66	3.83	5.04	5.83	3.65	3.39	0.37
Asset Turnover	1.57	1.56	1.60	1.55	1.77	1.52	1.51	1.19
Current Ratio	1.91	1.97	2.31	2.03	1.72	1.75	1.59	1.44
Debt to Equity	0.28	0.29	0.26	0.26	0.30	0.42	0.46	0.48
Price Range	25.86-16.84	23.25-16.64	23.25-16.36	21.19-15.56	22.71-15.36	19.37-12.47	19.88-11.93	16.20-10.30
P/E Ratio	28.11-18.30	22.14-15.85	17.75-12.49	12.92-9.49	11.19-7.57	19.37-12.47	22.85-13.71	202.50-128.75
Average Yield %	3.25	3.44	3.53	3.59	3.29	4.04	4.01	4.55

Address: 200 Old Wilson Bridge Road,	Web Site: www.worthingtonindustries.com	Auditors: KPMG LLP
Columbus, OH 43085	Officers: John P. McConnell - Chmn., C.E.O. John S.	Transfer Agents: National City Bank,
Telephone: 614-438-3210	Christie - Pres., C.F.O.	Department 5352
Fax: 614-438-3256		

WRIGLEY (WILLIAM) JR. CO.

Exchange	Symbol	Price	52Wk Range	Yield	P/E	Div Acheiver
NYS	WWY	$62.84 (3/31/2008)	68.44-50.84	2.13	27.56	27 Years

*7 Year Price Score 102.56 *NYSE Composite Index=100 *12 Month Price Score 107.20

Interim Earnings (Per Share)

Qtr.	Mar	Jun	Sep	Dec
2003	0.34	0.45	0.40	0.39
2004	0.39	0.50	0.45	0.42
2005	0.46	0.58	0.46	0.34
2006	0.32	0.51	0.53	0.46
2007	0.52	0.61	0.59	0.56

Interim Dividends (Per Share)

Amt	Decl	Ex	Rec	Pay
0.29Q	5/24/2007	7/11/2007	7/13/2007	8/1/2007
0.29Q	8/15/2007	10/11/2007	10/15/2007	11/1/2007
0.29Q	10/24/2007	1/11/2008	1/15/2008	2/1/2008
0.335Q	2/1/2008	4/11/2008	4/15/2008	5/1/2008

Indicated Div: $1.34 (Div. Reinv. Plan)

Valuation Analysis | **Institutional Holding**

Forecast P/E	21.73	No of Institutions	
	(1/10/2007)	489	
Market Cap	$17.3 Billion	Shares	
Book Value	2.8 Billion	148,384,960	
Price/Book	6.14	% Held	
Price/Sales	3.21	53.74	

Business Summary: Food (MIC: 4.1 SIC: 2067 NAIC: 311340)

William Wrigley Jr. is engaged as a manufacturer and marketer of chewing gum and other confectionery products, both in the U.S. and abroad. Co. markets chewing gum and other confectionery products primarily through distributors, wholesalers, corporate chains and cooperative buying groups. As of Dec 31 2007, Co.'s brands were sold in more than 180 countries and territories, under various brand names which include, among others, Doublemint®, Orbit®, Wrigley's Spearmint®, Winterfresh®, Airwaves®, Cool Air™, Excel®, Freedent®, Juicy Fruit®, Hubba Bubba®, Solano®, Altoids®, Wrigley's 5®, Life Savers®, Crème Savers® and P.K.™.

Recent Developments: For the year ended Dec 31 2007, net income increased 19.4% to US$632.0 million from US$529.4 million in the prior year. Revenues were US$5.39 billion, up 15.1% from US$4.68 billion the year before. Operating income was US$962.8 million versus US$821.5 million in the prior year, an increase of 17.2%. Direct operating expenses rose 12.9% to US$2.55 billion from US$2.26 billion in the comparable period the year before. Indirect operating expenses increased 17.0% to US$1.88 billion from US$1.61 billion in the equivalent prior-year period.

Prospects: For 2008, Co. intends to focus on accelerating sales growth, and also plans to continue to emphasize on retail execution, particularly at the check out, while investing in areas such as category management, consumer insights and retail coverage. Moreover, Co. plans to focus on controlling non-sales-related operating expenses as well as managing gross margins through procurement efforts, cost reduction and price increases, in order to manage against inflationary pressures, including rising costs for energy and various commodities, as well as new product development.

Financial Data

(US$ in Thousands)	12/31/2007	12/31/2006	12/31/2005	12/31/2004	12/31/2003	12/31/2002	12/31/2001	12/31/2000
Earnings Per Share	2.28	1.90	1.83	1.75	1.58	1.42	1.29	1.16
Cash Flow Per Share	3.65	2.60	2.70	2.57	2.30	1.33	1.39	1.58
Tang Book Value Per Share	3.31	2.98	2.55	7.00	6.48	5.41	4.54	3.90
Dividends Per Share	1.126	1.112	1.075	0.925	0.865	0.805	0.745	0.700
Dividend Payout %	49.39	58.53	58.68	52.80	54.61	56.53	57.84	60.34
Income Statement								
Total Revenue	5,389,100	4,686,011	4,159,306	3,648,592	3,069,088	2,746,318	2,429,646	2,145,706
EBITDA	1,215,945	1,030,980	961,593	862,347	771,581	668,989	595,692	537,192
Income Before Taxes	932,163	769,047	754,660	720,496	651,541	583,421	527,366	479,312
Income Taxes	300,158	239,670	237,408	227,542	205,647	181,896	164,380	150,370
Net Income	632,005	529,377	517,252	492,954	445,894	401,525	362,986	328,942
Average Shares	277,413	278,399	282,283	281,841	281,203	281,431	281,686	283,795
Balance Sheet								
Current Assets	1,549,778	1,481,227	1,306,094	1,505,910	1,290,591	1,006,292	913,843	828,715
Total Assets	5,231,512	4,661,598	4,460,201	3,166,703	2,520,410	2,108,296	1,765,648	1,574,740
Current Liabilities	1,101,120	1,027,129	980,811	717,970	464,794	386,087	332,324	288,210
Long-Term Obligations	1,000,000	1,000,000	1,000,000	...	...	...	...	...
Total Liabilities	2,414,032	2,273,506	2,245,779	988,019	699,589	585,720	489,451	441,843
Stockholders' Equity	2,817,480	2,388,092	2,214,422	2,178,684	1,820,821	1,522,576	1,276,197	1,132,897
Shares Outstanding	275,375	276,907	278,512	280,963	281,075	281,320	281,187	290,552
Statistical Record								
Return on Assets %	12.78	11.61	13.56	17.29	19.27	20.73	21.73	21.01
Return on Equity %	24.28	23.00	23.55	24.58	26.67	28.69	30.13	28.88
EBITDA Margin %	22.56	22.00	23.12	23.64	25.14	24.36	24.52	25.04
Net Margin %	11.73	11.30	12.44	13.51	14.53	14.62	14.94	15.33
Asset Turnover	1.09	1.03	1.09	1.28	1.33	1.42	1.45	1.37
Current Ratio	1.41	1.44	1.33	2.10	2.78	2.61	2.75	2.88
Debt to Equity	0.35	0.42	0.45	...	...	...	...	...
Price Range	68.44-48.89	53.23-43.16	53.98-47.13	51.74-40.98	43.12-37.98	43.30-33.04	39.27-32.16	35.55-22.49
P/E Ratio	30.02-21.44	28.02-22.72	29.50-25.75	29.57-23.42	27.29-24.04	30.49-23.26	30.44-24.93	30.64-19.39
Average Yield %	1.97	2.34	2.10	2.01	2.10	2.03	2.08	2.43

Address: 410 North Michigan Avenue, Chicago, IL 60611	**Web Site:** www.wrigley.com	**Auditors:** Ernst & Young LLP
Telephone: 312-644-2121	**Officers:** William Wrigley Jr. - Chmn., Pres., C.E.O. Peter R. Hempstead - Sr. V.P.., Worldwide Strategy & New Bus.	**Investor Contact:** 180-087-40474. **Transfer Agents:** EquiServe Trust
Fax: 312-645-4083		Company, N.A., Providence, RI

WYETH

Exchange	Symbol	Price	52Wk Range	Yield	P/E
NYS	WYE	$41.76 (3/31/2008)	58.42-39.00	2.68	12.36

*7 Year Price Score 83.38   *NYSE Composite Index=100   *12 Month Price Score 91.86

Interim Earnings (Per Share)

Qtr.	Mar	Jun	Sep	Dec
2003	0.96	0.65	(0.32)	0.25
2004	0.56	0.62	1.06	(1.33)
2005	0.80	0.72	0.64	0.54
2006	0.82	0.78	0.85	0.63
2007	0.92	0.87	0.84	0.75

Interim Dividends (Per Share)

Amt	Decl	Ex	Rec	Pay
0.26Q	4/26/2007	5/9/2007	5/11/2007	6/1/2007
0.26Q	6/28/2007	8/9/2007	8/13/2007	9/4/2007
0.28Q	9/27/2007	11/8/2007	11/13/2007	12/3/2007
0.28Q	1/25/2008	2/11/2008	2/13/2008	3/3/2008

Indicated Div: $1.12

Valuation Analysis

		Institutional Holding	
Forecast P/E	13.38 (1/10/2007)	No of Institutions	1075
Market Cap	$55.9 Billion	Shares	1,067,679,040
Book Value	18.2 Billion	% Held	79.31
Price/Book	3.07		
Price/Sales	2.49		

Business Summary: Pharmaceuticals (MIC: 9.1 SIC: 2834 NAIC: 325412)

Wyeth is engaged in the discovery, development, manufacture, distribution and sale of a line of products in three primary businesses: Wyeth Pharmaceuticals (Pharmaceuticals), Wyeth Consumer Healthcare (Consumer Healthcare) and Fort Dodge Animal Health (Animal Health). Co.'s Pharmaceutical products include branded human ethical pharmaceuticals, biotechnology products, vaccines and nutrition products, while its Consumer Healthcare products include analgesics, cough/cold/allergy remedies, nutritional supplements, and hemorrhoidal, asthma and personal care items sold over-the-counter, and its Animal Health products include vaccines, pharmaceuticals, parasite control and growth implants.

Recent Developments: For the year ended Dec 31 2007, net income increased 10.0% to US$4.62 billion from US$4.20 billion in the prior year. Revenues were US$22.40 billion, up 10.1% from US$20.35 billion the year before. Direct operating expenses rose 13.0% to US$6.31 billion from US$5.59 billion in the comparable period the year before. Indirect operating expenses increased 4.2% to US$10.01 billion from US$9.61 billion in the equivalent prior-year period.

Prospects: Co. continues to progress with the development and commercialization of its product candidates. For instance, on Feb 29 2008, Co. announced that the U.S. FDA has approved PRISTIQ™ (desvenlafaxine), its once-daily serotonin-norepinephrine reuptake inhibitor for the treatment of major depressive disorder in adult patients, which it expects to begin shipping to wholesalers in the second quarter of 2008. Meanwhile, in 2008, Co. will begin Project Impact, a program designed to aid long-term growth and address short-term fiscal challenges by stressing on its productivity initiatives. In view of that, Co. expects net revenue for the year to be comparable with its 2007 levels of $22.40 billion.

Financial Data

(US$ in Thousands)	12/31/2007	12/31/2006	12/31/2005	12/31/2004	12/31/2003	12/31/2002	12/31/2001	12/31/2000
Earnings Per Share	3.38	3.08	2.70	0.91	1.54	3.33	1.72	(1.81)
Cash Flow Per Share	4.38	2.42	1.76	2.15	2.19	0.14	(3.38)	0.42
Tang Book Value Per Share	10.23	7.71	5.86	4.33	4.01	3.22	0.17	N.M.
Dividends Per Share	1.060	1.010	0.940	0.920	0.920	0.920	0.920	0.920
Dividend Payout %	31.36	32.79	34.81	101.10	59.74	27.63	53.49	...
Income Statement								
Total Revenue	22,399,798	20,350,655	18,755,790	17,358,028	15,850,632	14,584,035	11,128,514	13,262,754
EBITDA	7,360,871	6,267,658	5,679,945	602,825	3,002,635	6,783,997	3,622,834	(508,429)
Income Before Taxes	6,456,682	5,429,904	4,780,589	(129,847)	2,361,612	6,097,245	2,868,747	(1,101,040)
Income Taxes	1,840,722	1,233,198	1,124,291	(1,363,844)	310,420	1,650,040	583,453	(200,000)
Net Income	4,615,960	4,196,706	3,656,298	1,233,997	2,051,192	4,447,205	2,285,294	(2,370,687)
Average Shares	1,374,342	1,374,053	1,365,417	1,354,489	1,333,910	1,334,127	1,330,809	1,306,474
Balance Sheet								
Current Assets	22,985,398	17,314,241	18,044,841	14,430,029	14,902,242	11,595,082	9,766,753	10,180,811
Total Assets	42,717,282	36,478,715	35,841,126	33,629,704	31,031,922	25,994,949	22,967,922	21,092,466
Current Liabilities	7,324,279	7,221,848	9,947,961	8,535,542	8,429,510	5,475,659	7,257,181	9,742,059
Long-Term Obligations	11,492,881	9,096,743	9,231,479	7,792,311	8,076,429	7,546,041	7,357,277	2,394,790
Total Liabilities	24,506,747	21,825,960	23,846,757	23,781,801	21,737,541	17,839,037	18,895,349	18,274,373
Stockholders' Equity	18,210,535	14,652,755	11,994,369	9,847,903	9,294,381	8,155,912	4,072,573	2,818,093
Shares Outstanding	1,337,786	1,345,249	1,343,349	1,335,091	1,332,451	1,326,055	1,320,570	1,311,774
Statistical Record								
Return on Assets %	11.66	11.61	10.53	3.81	7.19	18.17	10.37	N.M.
Return on Equity %	28.09	31.50	33.48	12.86	23.51	72.74	66.33	N.M.
EBITDA Margin %	32.86	30.80	30.28	3.47	18.94	46.52	25.64	N.M.
Net Margin %	20.61	20.62	19.49	7.11	12.94	30.49	16.18	N.M.
Asset Turnover	0.57	0.56	0.54	0.54	0.56	0.60	0.64	0.59
Current Ratio	3.14	2.43	1.81	1.69	1.77	2.12	1.35	1.05
Debt to Equity	0.63	0.62	0.77	0.79	0.87	0.93	1.81	0.85
Price Range	58.42-44.17	53.19-42.37	47.48-38.69	44.65-33.80	49.16-33.57	66.21-29.75	63.65-53.10	64.50-39.25
P/E Ratio	17.28-13.07	17.27-13.76	17.59-14.33	49.07-37.14	31.92-21.80	19.88-8.93	37.01-30.87	...
Average Yield %	2.09	2.09	2.15	2.38	2.20	1.87	1.57	1.69

Address: Five Giralda Farms, Madison, NJ 07940-0874	Web Site: www.wyeth.com	Auditors: PricewaterhouseCoopers LLP
Telephone: 973-660-5000	Officers: Robert Essner - Chmn., Pres., C.E.O.	Investor Contact: 973-660-5706
Fax: 973-660-5012	Kenneth J. Martin - Exec. V.P., C.F.O.	Transfer Agents: The Bank of New York, New York, NY

WYNDHAM WORLDWIDE CORP

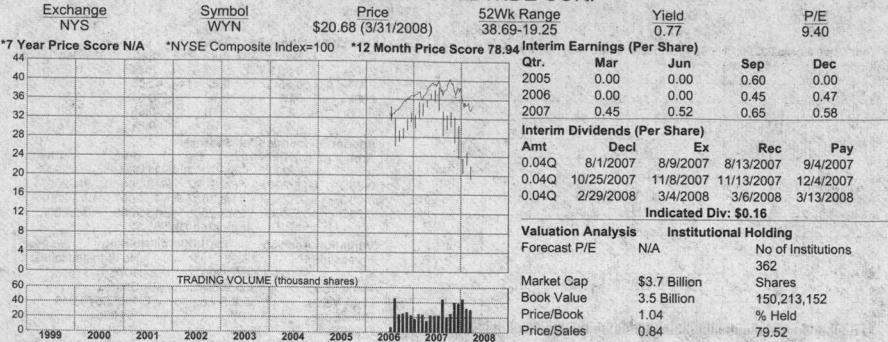

Exchange	Symbol	Price	52Wk Range	Yield	P/E
NYS	WYN	$20.68 (3/31/2008)	38.69-19.25	0.77	9.40

*7 Year Price Score N/A   *NYSE Composite Index=100   *12 Month Price Score 78.94

Interim Earnings (Per Share)

Qtr.	Mar	Jun	Sep	Dec
2005	0.00	0.00	0.60	0.00
2006	0.00	0.00	0.45	0.47
2007	0.45	0.52	0.65	0.58

Interim Dividends (Per Share)

Amt	Decl	Ex	Rec	Pay
0.04Q	8/1/2007	8/9/2007	8/13/2007	9/4/2007
0.04Q	10/25/2007	11/8/2007	11/13/2007	12/4/2007
0.04Q	2/29/2008	3/4/2008	3/6/2008	3/13/2008

Indicated Div: $0.16

Valuation Analysis | **Institutional Holding**

Forecast P/E	N/A	No of Institutions
		362
Market Cap	$3.7 Billion	Shares
Book Value	3.5 Billion	150,213,152
Price/Book	1.04	% Held
Price/Sales	0.84	79.52

Business Summary: Hospitality & Tourism (MIC: 5.1 SIC: 7011 NAIC: 721110)

Wyndham Worldwide is a hospitality company. Co. operates its business in three segments: lodging, which franchises hotels in the lodging industry and provides property management services to owners of hotels; vacation exchange and rental, which provides vacation exchange products and services to owners of intervals of vacation ownership interests and markets vacation rental properties primarily on behalf of independent owners; and vacation ownership, which markets and sells vacation ownership interests (VOIs) to individual consumers, provides consumer financing in connection with the sale of VOIs and provides property management services at resorts.

Recent Developments: For the year ended Dec 31 2007, net income increased 40.4% to US$403.0 million from US$287.0 million in the prior year. Revenues were US$4.36 billion, up 13.5% from US$3.84 billion the year before. Operating income was US$710.0 million versus US$577.0 million in the prior year, an increase of 23.1%. Direct operating expenses rose 18.6% to US$376.0 million from US$317.0 million in the comparable period the year before. Indirect operating expenses increased 11.1% to US$3.27 billion from US$2.95 billion in the equivalent prior-year period.

Prospects: For 2008, Co. believes that it is positioned to take advantage of favorable demographics as the baby-boomer generation begins to retire and spends more time on leisure travel. Thus, Co. is expecting 2008 revenues of $4.80 billion to $4.90 billion and earnings of $2.23 to $2.38 per share. Moreover, Co. is projecting earnings of $0.30 to $0.35 per share for the first quarter of 2008. Looking ahead, Co. will continue to focus on several long-term plans, such as investing in its Wyndham Hotels and Resorts brand though enhanced marketing efforts. Co. will also continue to invest in capital improvements and the development of its vacation ownership, vacation rentals and mixed-use properties.

Financial Data
(US$ in Thousands)

	12/31/2007	12/31/2006	12/31/2005	12/31/2004	12/31/2003
Earnings Per Share	2.20	1.44	...	...	...
Cash Flow Per Share	0.06	0.83	...	...	...
Income Statement					
Total Revenue	4,360,000	3,842,000	3,470,000	3,014,000	2,652,000
EBITDA	883,000	725,000	746,000	719,000	602,000
Income Before Taxes	655,000	542,000	621,000	587,000	500,000
Income Taxes	252,000	190,000	193,000	234,000	186,000
Net Income	403,000	287,000	428,000	349,000	299,000
Average Shares	183,000	199,000	...	...	...
Balance Sheet					
Current Assets	2,056,000	2,052,000	2,569,000	2,075,000	...
Total Assets	10,459,000	9,520,000	9,164,000	8,343,000	...
Current Liabilities	2,180,000	1,977,000	1,295,000	1,179,000	...
Long-Term Obligations	3,195,000	2,607,000	1,687,000	1,478,000	...
Total Liabilities	6,943,000	5,961,000	4,134,000	3,664,000	...
Stockholders' Equity	3,516,000	3,559,000	5,030,000	4,679,000	...
Shares Outstanding	177,217	190,417	...	...	...
Statistical Record					
Return on Assets %	4.03	3.07	4.89	...	...
Return on Equity %	11.39	6.68	8.82	...	...
EBITDA Margin %	20.25	18.87	21.50	23.86	22.70
Net Margin %	9.24	7.47	12.33	11.58	11.27
Asset Turnover	0.44	0.41	0.40	...	...
Current Ratio	0.94	1.04	1.98	1.76	...
Debt to Equity	0.91	0.73	0.34	0.32	...
Price Range	38.69-23.56	34.41-26.07	...	...	...
P/E Ratio	17.59-10.71	23.90-18.10	...	...	...

Address: Seven Sylvan Way, Parsippany, NJ 07054
Telephone: 973-496-8900
Fax: 973-496-8906

Web Site: www.wyndhamworldwide.com
Officers: Stephen P. Holmes - Chmn., C.E.O.
Virginia M. Wilson - Exec. Vice-Pres., C.F.O.

Auditors: Deloitte & Touche LLP
Transfer Agents: Mellon Investor Services LLC, Jersey City, NJ

XCEL ENERGY, INC.

Exchange	Symbol	Price	52Wk Range	Yield	P/E
NYS	XEL	$19.95 (3/31/2008)	24.99-19.65	4.61	14.78

*7 Year Price Score 89.77   *NYSE Composite Index=100   *12 Month Price Score 100.41

Interim Earnings (Per Share)

Qtr.	Mar	Jun	Sep	Dec
2003	0.35	(0.71)	0.69	1.14
2004	0.36	0.21	0.12	0.18
2005	0.29	0.20	0.47	0.27
2006	0.36	0.24	0.53	0.24
2007	0.28	0.18	0.58	0.30

Interim Dividends (Per Share)

Amt	Decl	Ex	Rec	Pay
0.23Q	5/23/2007	6/26/2007	6/28/2007	7/20/2007
0.23Q	8/21/2007	9/25/2007	9/27/2007	10/20/2007
0.23Q	12/12/2007	12/24/2007	12/27/2007	1/20/2008
0.23Q	2/20/2008	3/25/2008	3/27/2008	4/20/2008

Indicated Div: $0.92

Valuation Analysis

	Institutional Holding
Forecast P/E 15.63 (1/10/2007)	No of-Institutions 374
Market Cap $8.6 Billion	Shares 207,004,002
Book Value 6.4 Billion	% Held 65.68
Price/Book 1.34	
Price/Sales 0.85	

Business Summary: Electricity (MIC: 7.1 SIC: 4931 NAIC: 221121)

Xcel Energy is a holding company. As of Dec 31 2007, Co. directly owned four utility subsidiaries that serve electric and natural gas customers in eight states. These utility subsidiaries are Northern States Power Co.-Minnesota, Northern States Power Co.-Wisconsin, Public Service Company of Colorado and Southwestern Public Service Co. These utilities serve customers in portions of Colorado, Michigan, Minnesota, New Mexico, North Dakota, South Dakota, Texas and Wisconsin. Along with WestGas Interstate, Inc., an interstate natural gas pipeline company, these companies comprise the continuing regulated utility operations.

Recent Developments: For the year ended Dec 31 2007, income from continuing operations increased 1.3% to US$575.9 million from US$568.7 million a year earlier. Net income increased 1.0% to US$577.3 million from US$571.8 million in the prior year. Revenues were US$10.03 billion, up 2.0% from US$9.84 billion the year before. Operating income was US$1.35 billion versus US$1.18 billion in the prior year, an increase of 14.8%. Direct operating expenses rose 0.4% to US$7.58 billion from US$7.55 billion in the comparable period the year before. Indirect operating expenses decreased 1.1% to US$1.10 billion from US$1.12 billion in the equivalent prior-year period.

Prospects: Going forward, Co. expects to gain regulatory approval of various riders related to Metropolitan Emissions Reduction Project, Minnesota and Colorado transmission and Minnesota renewable energy, which should increase its revenue by $60.0 million to $70.0 million over 2007 levels. Further, Co. expects weather-adjusted retail electric utility sales to grow by 1.8% to 2.2% while weather-adjusted retail firm natural gas sales should grow by 0.0% to 1.0%. Co. also expects short-term wholesale and commodity trading margins of $20.0 million to $30.0 million. Accordingly, for full year 2008, Co. reaffirms its earnings from continuing operations guidance in the range of $1.45 to $1.55 per share.

Financial Data

(US$ in Thousands)	12/31/2007	12/31/2006	12/31/2005	12/31/2004	12/31/2003	12/31/2002	12/31/2001	12/31/2000
Earnings Per Share	1.35	1.36	1.23	0.87	1.50	(5.82)	2.30	1.54
Cash Flow Per Share	3.78	4.74	2.94	2.04	3.46	4.49	4.62	4.16
Tang Book Value Per Share	14.70	14.28	13.37	12.99	12.95	11.44	17.91	16.32
Dividends Per Share	0.912	0.882	0.853	0.810	0.750	1.125	1.500	1.482
Dividend Payout %	67.59	64.89	69.31	93.10	50.00		65.22	96.21
Income Statement								
Total Revenue	10,034,170	9,840,304	9,625,477	8,345,259	7,937,516	9,524,372	15,028,204	11,591,796
EBITDA	2,297,353	2,108,298	1,941,101	1,896,236	1,898,112	(408,656)	2,950,925	2,366,034
Income Before Taxes	870,383	750,092	672,577	686,515	668,662	(2,306,426)	1,193,910	850,653
Income Taxes	294,484	181,411	173,539	159,586	158,642	(627,985)	336,723	304,865
Net Income	577,348	571,754	512,972	355,961	622,392	(2,217,991)	794,966	526,828
Average Shares	433,131	429,605	425,671	423,334	418,912	382,051	343,742	338,111
Balance Sheet								
Net PPE	16,675,689	15,548,658	14,696,310	14,095,955	13,667,116	18,815,794	21,165,117	13,272,914
Total Assets	23,184,727	21,958,346	21,648,316	20,304,843	20,205,380	27,257,842	28,735,062	21,768,843
Long-Term Obligations	6,342,160	6,449,638	5,897,789	6,493,020	6,518,853	6,550,248	12,117,516	7,583,441
Total Liabilities	16,778,745	16,036,544	16,148,081	14,996,945	14,933,960	22,487,538	22,435,265	16,101,739
Stockholders' Equity	6,405,982	5,921,802	5,500,235	5,307,898	5,271,420	4,770,304	6,299,797	5,667,104
Shares Outstanding	428,782	407,296	403,387	400,461	398,964	398,714	345,801	340,834
Statistical Record								
Return on Assets %	2.56	2.62	2.45	1.75	2.62	N.M.	3.15	3.33
Return on Equity %	9.37	10.01	9.49	6.71	12.40	N.M.	13.29	12.61
EBITDA Margin %	22.90	21.43	20.17	22.72	23.91	N.M.	19.64	20.41
Net Margin %	5.75	5.81	5.33	4.27	7.84	(23.29)	5.29	4.54
PPE Turnover	0.62	0.65	0.67	0.60	0.49	0.48	0.82	1.17
Asset Turnover	0.44	0.45	0.46	0.41	0.33	0.34	0.60	0.73
Debt to Equity	0.99	1.09	1.07	1.22	1.24	1.37	1.92	1.34
Price Range	24.99-19.80	23.47-17.89	19.90-16.57	18.73-15.67	17.34-10.59	28.34-5.66	31.64-24.56	29.75-16.25
P/E Ratio	18.51-14.67	17.26-13.15	16.18-13.47	21.53-18.01	11.56-7.06		13.76-10.68	19.32-10.55
Average Yield %	4.05	4.43	4.62	4.67	5.27	6.57	5.32	6.47

Address: 414 Nicollet Mall, Minneapolis, MN 55401 **Telephone:** 612-330-5500 **Fax:** 612-330-5688	**Web Site:** www.xcelenergy.com **Officers:** Wayne H. Brunetti - Chmn., C.E.O. Richard C. Kelly - Pres., C.O.O.	**Auditors:** Deloitte & Touche LLP **Investor Contact:** 303-294-2362 **Transfer Agents:** The Bank of New York, New York, NY

847

XEROX CORP

Exchange	Symbol	Price	52Wk Range	Yield	P/E
NYS	XRX	$14.97 (3/31/2008)	19.90-13.10	N/A	12.58

*7 Year Price Score 105.54 *NYSE Composite Index=100   *12 Month Price Score 95.50

Interim Earnings (Per Share)

Qtr.	Mar	Jun	Sep	Dec
2003	(0.01)	0.09	0.11	0.25
2004	0.25	0.21	0.17	0.23
2005	0.20	0.40	0.05	0.28
2006	0.20	0.26	0.54	0.23
2007	0.24	0.28	0.27	0.40

Interim Dividends (Per Share)

Dividend Payment Suspended

Valuation Analysis   **Institutional Holding**

Forecast P/E	13.50	No of Institutions
	(1/10/2007)	405
Market Cap	$13.7 Billion	Shares
Book Value	8.6 Billion	795,783,424
Price/Book	1.60	% Held
Price/Sales	0.80	83.89

TRADING VOLUME (thousand shares)

Business Summary: Office Equipment Supplies (MIC: 11.12 SIC: 3577 NAIC: 333315)

Xerox develops, manufactures, markets, services and finances document equipment, software, applications and services. Co.'s production segment provides digital monochrome and color systems designed for customers in the graphic communications industry and for enterprises. Co.'s office segment serves global, national, and small to medium-size commercial customers. Co.'s Developing Markets Operations segment markets, sells and services Xerox products, supplies, and services in Latin America, Brazil, the Middle East, India, Eurasia and Central-Eastern Europe and Africa. Co.'s other segment consists of revenue from paper sales, services and wide-format systems.

Recent Developments: For the year ended Dec 31 2007, income from continuing operations decreased 6.2% to US$1.14 billion from US$1.21 billion a year earlier. Net income decreased 6.2% to US$1.14 billion from US$1.21 billion in the prior year. Revenues were US$17.23 billion, up 8.4% from US$15.90 billion the year before. Direct operating expenses rose 9.1% to US$9.96 billion from US$9.13 billion in the comparable period the year before. Indirect operating expenses decreased 2.2% to US$5.81 billion from US$5.94 billion in the equivalent prior-year period.

Prospects: For 2008, Co. expects revenue to grow moderately driven by continued increases in annuity revenue, excluding currency affects. At the same time, Co. anticipates that new launches combined with products and applications launched during the prior two years, as well as the businesses acquired in 2007, will enable it to further strengthen its market position. Moreover, Co. believes that growth in its post sale and other revenue will be driven by several factors, including growth in its document management services. Meanwhile, Co. is projecting earnings of $0.25 to $0.28 per share for the first quarter of 2008, and expects full-year 2008 to be in the range of $1.31 to $1.35 per share.

Financial Data

(US$ in Thousands)	12/31/2007	12/31/2006	12/31/2005	12/31/2004	12/31/2003	12/31/2002	12/31/2001	12/31/2000
Earnings Per Share	1.19	1.22	0.94	0.86	0.36	0.02	(0.12)	(0.44)
Cash Flow Per Share	2.00	1.71	1.48	2.09	2.44	2.57	2.22	(0.99)
Tang Book Value Per Share	4.93	5.04	4.68	4.29	1.57	N.M.	N.M.	N.M.
Dividends Per Share	0.043	...	...	...	...	...	0.050	0.650
Dividend Payout %	3.57	...	...	...	...	...	...	...
Income Statement								
Total Revenue	17,228,000	15,895,000	15,701,000	15,722,000	15,701,000	15,849,000	17,008,000	18,701,000
EBITDA	2,015,000	1,360,000	1,357,000	1,518,000	1,041,000	1,037,000	1,518,000	651,000
Income Before Taxes	1,438,000	808,000	830,000	965,000	436,000	252,000	365,000	(384,000)
Income Taxes	400,000	(288,000)	(5,000)	340,000	134,000	60,000	485,000	(109,000)
Net Income	1,135,000	1,210,000	978,000	859,000	360,000	91,000	(71,000)	(257,000)
Average Shares	952,941	996,522	1,045,353	1,046,947	828,387	807,444	704,181	667,581
Balance Sheet								
Current Assets	8,540,000	8,754,000	8,736,000	10,928,000	10,335,000	11,019,000	12,600,000	13,022,000
Total Assets	23,543,000	21,709,000	21,953,000	24,884,000	24,591,000	25,458,000	27,689,000	29,475,000
Current Liabilities	4,077,000	4,698,000	4,346,000	6,300,000	7,569,000	7,787,000	10,260,000	6,268,000
Long-Term Obligations	6,939,000	5,660,017	12,278,000	14,100,000	13,860,000	19,588,000	10,128,000	15,404,000
Total Liabilities	14,955,000	14,629,000	14,745,000	17,751,000	19,912,000	21,283,000	23,639,000	24,745,000
Stockholders' Equity	8,588,000	7,080,000	7,208,000	7,133,000	4,679,000	2,401,000	2,290,000	3,249,000
Shares Outstanding	917,177	946,205	931,189	955,997	793,884	738,273	722,314	665,156
Statistical Record								
Return on Assets %	5.02	5.54	4.18	3.46	1.44	0.34	N.M.	N.M.
Return on Equity %	14.49	16.94	13.64	14.50	10.17	3.88	N.M.	N.M.
EBITDA Margin %	11.70	8.56	8.64	9.66	6.63	6.54	8.93	3.48
Net Margin %	6.59	7.61	6.23	5.46	2.29	0.57	N.M.	N.M.
Asset Turnover	0.76	0.73	0.67	0.63	0.63	0.60	0.60	0.64
Current Ratio	2.09	1.86	2.01	1.73	1.37	1.42	1.23	2.08
Debt to Equity	0.81	0.80	1.70	1.98	2.96	8.16	4.42	4.74
Price Range	19.90-15.79	17.22-13.28	17.01-12.41	17.12-12.66	13.80-8.05	11.45-4.30	11.35-4.95	29.75-4.44
P/E Ratio	16.72-13.27	14.11-10.89	18.10-13.20	19.91-14.72	38.33-22.36	572.50-215.00	...	...
Average Yield %	0.24	...	...	...	...	...	0.63	3.55

Address: P.O. Box 4505, 45 Glover Avenue, Norwalk, CT 06856-4505	Web Site: www.xerox.com	Auditors: PricewaterhouseCoopers LLP
Telephone: 203-968-3000	Officers: Anne M. Mulcahy - Chmn., C.E.O. Lawrence A. Zimmerman - Sr. V.P., C.F.O.	Investor Contact: 800-828-6396

XL CAPITAL LTD.

Exchange	Symbol	Price	52Wk Range	Yield	P/E
NYS	XL	$29.55 (3/31/2008)	85.03-29.18	5.14	25.70

*7 Year Price Score 70.72   ***NYSE Composite Index=100**   ***12 Month Price Score 60.70**

Interim Earnings (Per Share)

Qtr.	Mar	Jun	Sep	Dec
2003	1.74	2.51	0.71	0.00
2004	3.25	2.62	0.16	0.00
2005	3.18	0.97	(7.53)	0.00
2006	2.56	2.10	2.32	0.00
2007	3.06	3.00	1.82	0.00

Interim Dividends (Per Share)

Amt	Decl	Ex	Rec	Pay
0.38Q	4/27/2007	6/7/2007	6/11/2007	6/29/2007
0.38Q	7/27/2007	9/6/2007	9/10/2007	9/28/2007
0.38Q	11/2/2007	12/6/2007	12/10/2007	12/28/2007
0.38Q	1/25/2008	3/12/2008	3/14/2008	3/31/2008

Indicated Div: $1.52

Valuation Analysis

		Institutional Holding	
Forecast P/E	N/A	No of Institutions	N/A
Market Cap	$5.3 Billion	Shares	N/A
Book Value	9.9 Billion	% Held	N/A
Price/Book	0.53		
Price/Sales	N/A		

TRADING VOLUME (thousand shares)

Business Summary: Insurance (MIC: 8.2 SIC: 6351 NAIC: 524126)

XL Capital is a provider of insurance and reinsurance coverages to industrial, commercial and professional service firms, insurance companies and other enterprises on a global basis. Co. operates through several segments. Co.'s Insurance and Reinsurance segments are engaged in managing its structured indemnity products through its financial systems operations; political risk products; weather and energy management products; and legacy financial guarantee business. Co.'s Corporate segment includes its investment in Primus Guaranty Ltd. and other financial operating affiliates, while its Other Financial Lines segment includes its guaranteed investment contract and funding agreement businesses.

Recent Developments: For the year ended Dec 31 2007, net income decreased 84.3% to $275.9 million from $1.76 billion in the previous year. Total revenues dropped 7.1% to $9.14 billion from $9.83 billion a year earlier. Net premiums earned amounted to $7.21 billion, a decline of 4.8% compared with $7.57 billion in the previous year. Net investment income advanced 13.7% to $2.25 billion from $1.98 billion in the prior year. Co.'s combined ratio was 88.8% versus 89.5% a year earlier.

Prospects: Co.'s near-term outlook appears to be challenging. For instance, despite expectation of a stable net investment income from its property and casualty operations in 2008, Co. is seeing a decline in premium rates across most major lines of business in its Reinsurance segment, as the reinsurance industry continues to experience pricing erosion, increased competition and increased retentions by cedants. In its Insurance segment, market competition continues to increase in most lines of business, and Co. believes that it may be more difficult to gain new business and/or retain previously written business, particularly within certain casualty and professional lines of business, going forward.

Financial Data
(US$ in Thousands)

	12/31/2007	12/31/2006	12/31/2005	12/31/2004	12/31/2003	12/31/2002	12/31/2001	12/31/2000
Earnings Per Share	1.15	9.60	(9.14)	8.13	2.69	2.88	(4.55)	4.03
Cash Flow Per Share	12.55	13.64	30.05	31.62	25.06	22.39	11.35	2.10
Income Statement								
Premium Income	...	7,569,518	9,365,495	8,549,533	6,969,150	5,989,810	3,475,522	...
Income Before Taxes	1,593,587	1,895,758	(1,261,908)	1,112,169	457,071	457,565	(758,636)	451,089
Income Taxes	233,922	219,645	49,284	84,526	30,049	22,647	(189,914)	(56,356)
Net Income	275,889	1,762,767	(1,251,976)	1,166,613	411,979	405,571	(576,135)	506,352
Average Shares	179,693	179,450	141,406	138,582	138,187	137,388	126,676	125,697
Balance Sheet								
Total Assets	57,762,264	59,308,870	58,454,901	49,014,632	40,764,215	35,647,369	27,963,075	16,941,952
Total Liabilities	47,811,703	48,615,583	49,983,090	41,275,937	33,827,300	29,077,780	22,525,891	11,368,284
Stockholders' Equity	9,948,142	10,131,166	8,471,811	7,738,695	6,936,915	6,569,589	5,437,184	5,573,668
Shares Outstanding	177,910	180,983	179,528	138,932	137,343	136,063	134,734	125,020
Statistical Record								
Return on Assets %	0.47	2.99	N.M.	2.59	1.08	1.28	N.M.	3.15
Return on Equity %	2.75	18.95	N.M.	15.86	6.10	6.76	N.M.	9.06
Price Range	85.03-49.23	72.55-60.25	79.16-60.26	81.54-67.62	88.00-64.57	97.38-61.00	96.12-62.00	88.56-39.56
P/E Ratio	73.94-42.81	7.56-6.28	...	10.03-8.32	32.71-24.00	33.81-21.18	...	21.98-9.82

Address: XL House, One Bermudiana Road, Hamilton, HM 11
Telephone: 292-851-5
Fax: 292-528-0

Web Site: www.xlcapital.com
Officers: Brian M. O'Hara - Pres., C.E.O. Fiona E. Luck - Exec. V.P., Corp. Serv., Asst. Sec.

Auditors: PricewaterhouseCoopers LLP

XTO ENERGY, INC.

Exchange	Symbol	Price	52Wk Range	Yield	P/E
NYS	XTO	$61.86 (3/31/2008)	63.13-41.98	0.78	17.52

*7 Year Price Score 175.36 *NYSE Composite Index=100 *12 Month Price Score 126.02

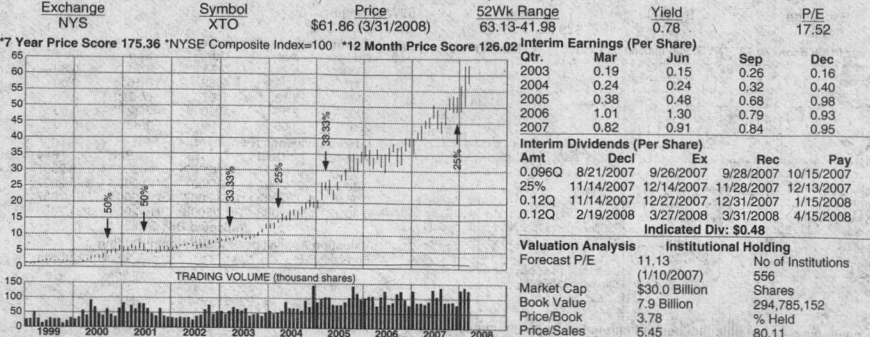

Interim Earnings (Per Share)

Qtr.	Mar	Jun	Sep	Dec
2003	0.19	0.15	0.26	0.16
2004	0.24	0.24	0.32	0.40
2005	0.38	0.48	0.68	0.98
2006	1.01	1.30	0.79	0.93
2007	0.82	0.91	0.84	0.95

Interim Dividends (Per Share)

Amt	Decl	Ex	Rec	Pay
0.096Q	8/21/2007	9/26/2007	9/28/2007	10/15/2007
25%	11/14/2007	12/14/2007	11/28/2007	12/13/2007
0.12Q	11/14/2007	12/27/2007	12/31/2007	1/15/2008
0.12Q	2/19/2008	3/27/2008	3/31/2008	4/15/2008

Indicated Div: $0.48

Valuation Analysis

Forecast P/E	11.13
	(1/10/2007)
Market Cap	$30.0 Billion
Book Value	7.9 Billion
Price/Book	3.78
Price/Sales	5.45

Institutional Holding

No of Institutions	556
Shares	294,785,152
% Held	80.11

Business Summary: Oil and Gas (MIC: 14.2 SIC: 1311 NAIC: 211111)

XTO Energy acquires, develops, exploits and explores producing oil and gas properties, and produces, processes, markets and transports oil and natural gas. Co.'s proved reserves are principally located in relatively long-lived fields concentrated in the following areas: Eastern Region, including the East Texas Basin, northwestern Louisiana and Mississippi; North Texas Region, including the Barnett Shale; San Juan Region; Permian and South Texas Region; and Mid-Continent and Rocky Mountain Region, including the Fayetteville and Woodford Shales. As of Dec31 2007, Co.'s estimated proved reserves totaled 9.44 trillion cubic feet of natural gas and 241.2 million barrels of oil.

Recent Developments: For the year ended Dec 31 2007, net income decreased 9.1% to US$1.69 billion from US$1.86 billion in the prior year. Revenues were US$5.51 billion, up 20.5% from US$4.58 billion the year before. Operating income was US$2.89 billion versus US$2.67 billion in the prior year, an increase of 8.2%. Direct operating expenses rose 25.3% to US$615.0 million from US$491.0 million in the comparable period the year before. Indirect operating expenses increased 42.0% to US$2.01 billion from US$1.41 billion in the equivalent prior-year period.

Prospects: On Feb 12 2008, Co. announced its definitive agreements with multiple parties to acquire producing properties in the Eastern and San Juan Regions and to purchase acreage positions in the Woodford, Fayetteville and Barnett shales for about $1.00 billion. From the producing property transactions, Co. estimates proved reserves to be 212.0 billion cubic feet of gas equivalent of which about 60.0% are proved developed. These acquisitions will add about 35.0 million cubic feet of natural gas equivalent per day to Co.'s growing production base while adding 76,000 net acres in the emerging shale plays to expand its drilling inventory. The acquisitions should close in the first quarter of 2008.

Financial Data

(US$ in Thousands)	12/31/2007	12/31/2006	12/31/2005	12/31/2004	12/31/2003	12/31/2002	12/31/2001	12/31/2000
Earnings Per Share	3.53	4.02	2.52	1.21	0.76	0.53	0.72	0.37
Cash Flow Per Share	7.71	6.27	4.67	2.92	2.12	1.41	1.59	1.27
Tang Book Value Per Share	15.69	12.03	8.50	5.99	3.75	2.57	2.39	1.45
Dividends Per Share	0.408	0.252	0.180	0.072	0.019	0.014	0.013	0.008
Dividend Payout %	11.56	6.26	7.14	5.96	2.52	2.73	1.83	2.15
Income Statement								
Total Revenue	5,513,000	4,576,000	3,519,000	1,947,601	1,189,555	810,163	838,748	600,851
EBITDA	4,079,000	4,016,000	2,618,000	1,326,030	792,285	544,413	665,280	385,153
Income Before Taxes	2,642,000	2,961,000	1,810,000	825,620	444,510	286,749	455,357	176,432
Income Taxes	951,000	1,101,000	658,000	317,738	158,009	100,690	161,952	59,380
Net Income	1,691,000	1,860,000	1,152,000	507,882	288,279	186,059	248,816	116,993
Average Shares	479,000	462,250	448,000	419,601	379,689	351,358	346,174	315,433
Balance Sheet								
Current Assets	1,287,000	1,585,000	943,000	436,965	261,163	244,790	239,367	193,437
Total Assets	18,922,000	12,885,000	9,857,000	6,110,372	3,611,134	2,648,193	2,132,327	1,591,904
Current Liabilities	1,537,000	1,240,000	884,000	500,966	320,557	285,896	201,843	218,751
Long-Term Obligations	6,320,000	3,451,000	3,109,000	2,042,732	1,252,000	1,118,170	856,000	769,000
Total Liabilities	10,981,000	7,020,000	5,648,000	3,510,999	2,145,492	1,740,407	1,311,277	1,094,537
Stockholders' Equity	7,941,000	5,865,000	4,209,000	2,599,373	1,465,642	907,786	821,050	497,367
Shares Outstanding	485,293	459,442	454,456	433,972	390,418	352,713	343,804	323,141
Statistical Record								
Return on Assets %	10.63	16.36	14.43	10.42	9.21	7.78	13.36	7.60
Return on Equity %	24.50	36.93	33.84	24.92	24.29	21.52	37.74	30.10
EBITDA Margin %	73.99	87.76	74.40	68.09	66.60	67.20	79.32	64.10
Net Margin %	30.67	40.65	32.74	26.08	24.23	22.97	29.67	19.47
Asset Turnover	0.35	0.40	0.44	0.40	0.38	0.34	0.45	0.39
Current Ratio	0.84	1.28	1.07	0.87	0.81	0.86	1.19	0.88
Debt to Equity	0.80	0.59	0.74	0.79	0.85	1.23	1.04	1.55
Price Range	53.66-35.48	40.48-29.58	36.13-18.41	20.97-12.01	13.45-7.95	9.01-5.10	7.36-4.26	6.48-1.16
P/E Ratio	15.20-10.05	10.07-7.36	14.34-7.31	17.33-9.92	17.70-10.46	16.99-9.62	10.23-5.91	17.51-3.14
Average Yield %	0.89	0.72	0.66	0.44	0.20	0.21	0.24	0.25

Address: 810 Houston Street, Suite 2000, Fort Worth, TX 76102 **Telephone:** 817-870-2800 **Fax:** 817-870-1671	**Web Site:** www.xtoenergy.com **Officers:** Bob R. Simpson - Chmn., C.E.O. Keith A. Hutton - Pres.	**Auditors:** KPMG LLP **Transfer Agents:** Mellon Investor Services LLC

YUM! BRANDS, INC.

Exchange	Symbol	Price	52Wk Range	Yield	P/E
NYS	YUM	$37.21 (3/31/2008)	40.27-29.11	1.61	22.15

*7 Year Price Score 130.54 *NYSE Composite Index=100 *12 Month Price Score 111.87

Interim Earnings (Per Share)
Qtr.	Mar	Jun	Aug	Dec
2003	0.20	0.20	0.27	0.35
2004	0.23	0.29	0.30	0.38
2005	0.27	0.31	0.36	0.34
2006	0.29	0.34	0.42	0.41
2007	0.35	0.39	0.50	0.44

Interim Dividends (Per Share)
Amt	Decl	Ex	Rec	Pay
100%	5/17/2007	6/27/2007	6/1/2007	6/26/2007
0.15Q	9/20/2007	10/10/2007	10/12/2007	11/2/2007
0.15Q	11/16/2007	1/9/2008	1/11/2008	2/1/2008
0.15Q	3/14/2008	4/9/2008	4/11/2008	5/2/2008

Indicated Div: $0.60

Valuation Analysis
	Institutional Holding	
Forecast P/E	16.22	No of Institutions
	(1/10/2007)	452
Market Cap	$18.6 Billion	Shares
Book Value	1.1 Billion	217,534,496
Price/Book	16.30	% Held
Price/Sales	1.78	82.52

Business Summary: Hospitality & Tourism (MIC: 5.1 SIC: 5812 NAIC: 722211)

Yum! Brands is a worldwide quick service restaurant company. Through its five concepts of KFC, Pizza Hut, Taco Bell, Long John Silver's Inc. , and A&W All-American Food Restaurants, Co. develops, operates, franchises and licenses a worldwide system of restaurants which prepare, package and sell a menu of food items. As of Dec 31 2007, Co. had more than 30,000 system units in its U.S. operations, operated more than 12,000 restaurants, primarily KFC's and Pizza Huts In over 100 countries outside the U.S. through its International division which is based in Dallas, TX; and managed more than 3,000 system restaurants, predominately KFCs, through its China division.

Recent Developments: For the year ended Dec 29 2007, net income increased 10.3% to US$909.0 million from US$824.0 million in the prior year. Revenues were US$10.42 billion, up 8.9% from US$9.56 billion the year before. Operating income was US$1.36 billion versus US$1.26 billion in the prior year, an increase of 7.5%. Direct operating expenses rose 9.6% to US$7.77 billion from US$7.09 billion in the comparable period the year before. Indirect operating expenses increased 6.7% to US$1.29 billion from US$1.21 billion in the equivalent prior-year period.

Prospects: For 2008, Co. projects earnings growth of at least 10.0% and anticipates its China Division's operating-profit growth to be about 20.0%, driven by new-unit development in mainland China, while operating-profit growth at its YUM Restaurants International Division is estimated to be about 10.0%, driven by new-unit development, measured by system-sales growth of at least 5.0%. Similarly, Co. is projecting U.S. operating-profit growth of about 5.0%, along with same-store-sales improvement of 2.0% to 3.0%. Meanwhile, Co. expects the expansion of its U.S. refranchising to generate pre-tax sales proceeds about $1.10 billion, margin expansion of about 2.5%, and earnings accretion of about 2.0%.

Financial Data
(US$ in Thousands)	12/29/2007	12/30/2006	12/31/2005	12/25/2004	12/27/2003	12/28/2002	12/29/2001	12/30/2000
Earnings Per Share	1.68	1.46	1.27	1.21	1.01	0.94	0.81	0.69
Cash Flow Per Share	3.01	2.39	2.13	1.95	1.80	1.84	1.42	0.82
Tang Book Value Per Share	0.27	0.81	1.04	1.20	0.41	N.M.	N.M.	...
Income Statement								
Total Revenue	10,416,000	9,561,000	9,349,000	9,011,000	8,380,000	7,757,000	6,953,000	7,093,000
EBITDA	1,899,000	1,741,000	1,622,000	1,603,000	1,460,000	1,400,000	1,245,000	1,214,000
Income Before Taxes	1,191,000	1,108,000	1,026,000	1,026,000	886,000	858,000	733,000	684,000
Income Taxes	282,000	284,000	264,000	286,000	268,000	275,000	241,000	271,000
Net Income	909,000	824,000	762,000	740,000	617,000	583,000	492,000	413,000
Average Shares	541,000	564,000	596,000	610,000	612,000	620,000	608,000	596,000
Balance Sheet								
Current Assets	1,481,000	901,000	837,000	747,000	806,000	730,000	547,000	688,000
Total Assets	7,242,000	6,353,000	5,898,000	5,890,000	5,620,000	5,400,000	4,388,000	4,149,000
Current Liabilities	2,062,000	1,724,000	1,605,000	1,376,000	1,461,000	1,520,000	1,805,000	1,216,000
Long-Term Obligations	2,924,000	2,045,000	1,649,000	1,731,000	2,056,000	2,299,000	1,552,000	2,397,000
Total Liabilities	6,103,000	4,916,000	4,249,000	4,101,000	4,500,000	4,806,000	4,284,000	4,471,000
Stockholders' Equity	1,139,000	1,437,000	1,449,000	1,595,000	1,120,000	594,000	104,000	(322,000)
Shares Outstanding	499,000	530,000	556,000	580,000	584,000	588,000	584,000	588,000
Statistical Record								
Return on Assets %	13.41	13.71	13.16	13.11	11.23	11.95	11.56	10.02
Return on Equity %	70.77	57.26	49.26	54.66	72.19	167.51	...	...
EBITDA Margin %	18.23	18.21	17.35	17.79	17.42	18.05	17.91	17.12
Net Margin %	8.73	8.62	8.15	8.21	7.36	7.52	7.08	5.82
Asset Turnover	1.54	1.59	1.61	1.60	1.53	1.59	1.63	1.72
Current Ratio	0.72	0.52	0.52	0.54	0.55	0.48	0.30	0.57
Debt to Equity	2.57	1.42	1.14	1.09	1.84	3.87	14.92	...
Price Range	40.27-27.69	31.73-22.47	26.66-22.56	23.48-16.28	17.57-11.03	16.45-10.65	13.27-7.98	9.66-5.94
P/E Ratio	23.97-16.48	21.74-15.39	20.99-17.76	19.40-13.45	17.39-10.92	17.49-11.34	16.38-9.86	13.99-8.61

Address: 1411 Gardiner Lane, Louisville, KY 40213
Telephone: 502-874-8300
Fax: 502-874-8790

Web Site: www.yum.com
Officers: David C. Novak - Chmn., Pres., C.E.O.
Christian L. Campbell - Sr. V.P., Sec., Gen. Couns., Chief Franchise Policy Officer

Auditors: KPMG LLP
Investor Contact: 502-874-2543
Transfer Agents: American Stock Transfer & Trust Company

ZIMMER HOLDINGS, INC.

Exchange	Symbol	Price	52Wk Range	Yield	P/E
NYS	ZMH	$77.86 (3/31/2008)	91.87-63.48	N/A	23.88

*7 Year Price Score N/A   *NYSE Composite Index=100   *12 Month Price Score 105.44

Interim Earnings (Per Share)

Qtr.	Mar	Jun	Sep	Dec
2003	0.68	0.45	0.43	0.09
2004	0.40	0.47	0.52	0.81
2005	0.70	0.76	0.67	0.80
2006	0.82	0.81	0.76	1.01
2007	0.98	0.97	0.19	1.12

Interim Dividends (Per Share)

No Dividends Paid

Valuation Analysis

		Institutional Holding	
Forecast P/E	17.79	No of Institutions	
	(1/10/2007)	716	
Market Cap	$18.1 Billion	Shares	
Book Value	5.4 Billion	186,486,272	
Price/Book	3.33	% Held	
Price/Sales	4.65	78.73	

Business Summary: Medical Instruments & Equipment (MIC: 9.6 SIC: 3842 NAIC: 339113)

Zimmer Holdings designs, develops, manufactures and markets reconstructive orthopaedic implants, including joint and dental, spinal implants, trauma products and related orthopaedic surgical products. Co. manages its operations through three reportable geographic segments: the Americas, Europe and Asia Pacific. In addition, Co. markets and sells its products through three principal channels: direct to healthcare institutions, such as hospitals, or direct channel accounts; through stocking distributors and, in the Asia Pacific region, healthcare dealers; and directly to dental practices and dental laboratories.

Recent Developments: For the year ended Dec 31 2007, net income decreased 7.3% to US$773.2 million from US$834.5 million in the prior year. Revenues were US$3.90 billion, up 11.5% from US$3.50 billion the year before. Operating income was US$1.13 billion versus US$1.17 billion in the prior year, a decrease of 3.2%. Direct operating expenses rose 12.3% to US$875.9 million from US$780.1 million in the comparable period the year before. Indirect operating expenses increased 22.2% to US$1.89 billion from US$1.55 billion in the equivalent prior-year period.

Prospects: On Feb 5 2008, Co. announced that it will expand its global manufacturing network by adding a 100,000 square foot plant in Shannon, Ireland. Specifically, Co. expects to invest between $70.0 million and $75.0 million over the next two years in this new facility and plans to begin manufacturing operations in late 2008. At start-up, the facility will produce knee replacement implants, although other products could be added in the future. Meanwhile, Co. expects the general availability of its LPS-Flex Mobile knee in the U.S. in mid-2008. For the full-year of 2008, Co. is projecting net sales to be approximately 10.0% to 11.0% over 2007.

Financial Data
(US$ in Thousands)

	12/31/2007	12/31/2006	12/31/2005	12/31/2004	12/31/2003	12/31/2002	12/31/2001	12/31/2000
Earnings Per Share	3.26	3.40	2.93	2.19	1.64	1.31	0.77	0.91
Cash Flow Per Share	4.60	4.28	3.55	3.52	2.38	1.13	0.89	1.20
Tang Book Value Per Share	8.95	7.14	6.04	2.52	0.38	1.88	0.41	...
Income Statement								
Total Revenue	3,897,500	3,495,400	3,286,100	2,980,900	1,901,000	1,372,400	1,178,600	1,041,000
EBITDA	1,357,600	1,362,600	1,240,700	944,500	554,000	426,200	271,700	291,000
Income Before Taxes	1,131,600	1,169,000	1,040,700	731,500	437,500	388,900	240,900	268,000
Income Taxes	357,900	334,000	307,300	189,600	146,800	131,100	91,100	92,000
Net Income	773,200	834,500	732,500	541,800	346,300	257,800	149,800	176,000
Average Shares	237,500	245,400	249,800	247,800	211,200	196,800	194,300	193,600
Balance Sheet								
Current Assets	2,082,700	1,746,200	1,575,600	1,560,900	1,338,700	612,400	508,600	419,000
Total Assets	6,633,700	5,974,400	5,721,900	5,695,500	5,156,000	858,900	745,000	597,000
Current Liabilities	748,600	628,200	606,900	701,000	645,300	400,800	373,100	336,000
Long-Term Obligations	104,300	99,600	81,600	624,000	1,007,800	...	213,900	...
Total Liabilities	1,181,300	1,051,200	1,036,800	1,745,900	2,005,700	492,600	666,300	336,000
Stockholders' Equity	5,449,600	4,920,500	4,682,800	3,942,500	3,143,300	366,300	78,700	261,000
Shares Outstanding	232,900	236,800	247,740	245,500	242,400	195,200	193,900	...
Statistical Record								
Return on Assets %	12.27	14.27	12.83	9.96	11.51	32.15	22.32	29.18
Return on Equity %	14.91	17.38	16.98	15.25	19.73	115.87	88.20	53.84
EBITDA Margin %	34.83	38.98	37.76	31.69	29.14	31.06	23.05	27.95
Net Margin %	19.84	23.87	22.29	18.18	18.22	18.78	12.71	16.91
Asset Turnover	0.62	0.60	0.58	0.55	0.63	1.71	1.76	1.73
Current Ratio	2.78	2.78	2.60	2.23	2.07	1.53	1.36	1.25
Debt to Equity	0.02	0.02	0.02	0.16	0.32	...	2.72	...
Price Range	91.87-63.48	78.66-53.05	87.40-61.70	89.15-67.90	71.17-38.16	42.60-29.37	32.85-25.02	...
P/E Ratio	28.18-19.47	23.14-15.60	29.83-21.06	40.71-31.00	43.40-23.27	32.52-22.42	42.66-32.49	...

Address: 345 East Main Street, Warsaw, IN 46580	**Web Site:** www.zimmer.com	**Auditors:** PricewaterhouseCoopers LLP
Telephone: 574-267-6131	**Officers:** J. Raymond Elliott - Chmn., Pres., C.E.O. David C. Dvorak - Exec. V.P., Corp. Services, Sec., Chief Couns.	**Investor Contact:** 157-437-18515 **Transfer Agents:** Bank of New York, New York, NY

CONDENSED

STATISTICAL

TABULATION

The tab section consists of statistical highlights for all U.S. companies listed on the New York Stock Exchange.

Statistics for companies whose fiscal year ends prior to June 30 are listed under the prior calendar year. Statistics for companies whose fiscal year ends June 30 or after are listed under the current calendar year. Dividends and price ranges are on a calendar year basis.

Because of editorial constraints a column for fourth quarter results was not included. At fiscal year-end, full fiscal year per share earnings are listed and quarterly figures are eliminated. Quarterly per share earnings are inserted as the company reports in the current fiscal year.

NOTE: Figures listed under "Earnings Per Share" for investment companies are net asset value per share.

For abbreviations, see the blue section of the Handbook.

SYMBOL	COMPANY	NATURE OF BUSINESS	FISCAL YEAR-END	TOTAL REV. $MILL	NET INCOME $MILL	TOTAL ASSETS $MILL	NET STK EQUITY $MILL	NO OF INST	INST. HOLDINGS (SHARES)
MMM	3M Co (United States)	Medical Instruments & Equipment	12/31/07	24462.0	4096.0	24694.0	11747.0	980	534312540
KDE	4 Kids Entertainment Inc.	Miscellaneous	12/31/07	55.6	-23.3	151.1	128.1	88	12524234
CFD	40/86 Strategic Income Fund	Trusts & Holding Entities	6/30/07	8.0	5.2	103.2	74.9	11	354664
NDN	99 Cents Only Stores	Retail - General	3/31/07	1104.7	9.8	643.1	519.2	129	48448673
AIR	AAR Corp (United States)	Aviation	5/31/07	1061.2	58.7	1067.6	494.2	99	28872045
RNT	Aaron Rents, Inc. (United States)	General Construction Supplies & Ser	12/31/07	1494.9	80.3	1113.2	673.4	135	34353116
ABB	ABB Ltd	Accounting & Management Consulti	12/31/07	29183.0	3757.0	31001.0	10957.0	57	36898011
ABT	Abbott Laboratories	Pharmaceuticals	12/31/07	25914.2	3606.3	39713.9	17778.5	1043	946894596
ANF	Abercrombie & Fitch Co.	Retail - Apparel and Accessory Store	2/2/08	3749.8	475.7	2567.6	1618.3	295	75830506
ABH	AbitibiBowater Inc	Paper Products	12/31/07	3876.0	-490.0	10319.0	1899.0	-	-
ABM	ABM Industries, Inc. (United States)	Miscellaneous Business Services	10/31/07	2842.8	52.4	1120.7	605.8	135	33982238
ABN	ABN AMRO Holding N.V.	Commercial Banking	12/31/04	36873.0	3865.0	727454.0	16552.0	98	36724140
AKR	Acadia Realty Trust	Property, Real Estate & Developmen	12/31/07	101.6	27.3	999.0	240.7	75	24953768
ACN	Accenture Ltd.	Miscellaneous Business Services	8/31/07	21452.7	1243.1	10747.2	2063.3	258	349605043
ABD	Acco Brands Corp	Retail - Miscellaneous	12/31/07	1938.9	-0.9	1898.5	438.3	-	-
ACW	Accuride Corp	Automotive	12/31/07	1013.7	-8.6	1113.6	273.8	-	-
ACE	ACE, Ltd.	Insurance	12/31/07	14154.0	2578.0	72090.0	16677.0	317	244357270
ADF	ACM Managed Dollar Income Fund	Trusts & Holding Entities	9/30/07	-	10.8	192.6	161.3	13	304388
ATV	Acorn International Inc	Office Equipment Supplies	12/31/06	-	3.9	-	51.2	-	-
ATU	Actuant Corp.	Automotive	8/31/07	1458.7	105.0	1500.8	499.9	145	27865431
AYI	Acuity Brands Inc (Holding Compan	Chemicals	8/31/07	2530.7	148.1	1612.5	672.0	145	34394487
ADX	Adams Express Co.	Trusts & Holding Entities	12/31/07	32.1	25.9	1421.2	1378.5	49	3493696
ASF	Administaff, Inc.	Human Resources Services	12/31/07	1570.0	47.5	560.7	198.7	114	19564162
PVD	Administradora de Fondos de Pensi	Wealth Management	-	-	-	-	-	15	1735040
AEA	Advance America Cash Advance C	Credit & Lending	12/31/07	709.6	54.4	471.7	250.3	61	20282727
AAP	Advance Auto Parts Inc (United Stat	Retail - Automotive	12/29/07	4844.4	238.3	2805.6	1023.8	227	67033421
EYE	Advanced Medical Optics Inc	Medical Instruments & Equipment	12/31/07	1090.8	-192.9	2748.3	598.7	261	80847491
AMD	Advanced Micro Devices, Inc.	IT & Technology	12/29/07	6013.0	-3379.0	11550.0	2990.0	259	299282591
ASX	Advanced Semiconductor Engineeri	IT & Technology	12/31/06	100423.6	17416.2	137040.9	77126.8	34	14993858
AAV	Advantage Energy Income Fund	Oil and Gas	12/31/06	353.5	49.8	1981.6	1164.6	2	23415
ATE	Advantest Corp.	Instruments and Related Products	3/31/07	235012.0	35556.0	366374.0	294797.0	-	-
LCM	Advent / Claymore Enhanced Growt	Trusts & Holding Entities	-	-	-	-	-	5	149011
AVK	Advent Claymore Convertible Secur	Trusts & Holding Entities	10/31/07	53.4	-46.5	906.9	627.4	15	570233
AGC	Advent/Claymore Global Convertibl	Trusts & Holding Entities	5/2/07	-	-	-	0.1	-	-
ACM	Aecom Technology Corp (DE)	Engineering Services	9/30/07	4237.3	100.3	2491.8	1278.5	-	-
AEG	AEGON N.V.	Insurance	12/31/04	36518.0	2256.0	268692.0	17759.0	-	-
AER	Aercap Holdings NV	Aviation	12/31/06	814.4	88.0	3923.0	729.9	-	-
ARO	Aeropostale Inc (United States)	Retail - Apparel and Accessory Store	2/2/08	1590.9	129.2	514.2	197.3	196	49724403
AES	AES Corp.	Electricity	12/31/07	13588.0	-95.0	34453.0	3164.0	332	483399742
AET	Aetna Inc. (New)	Insurance	12/31/07	27599.6	1831.0	50724.7	10038.4	463	259352231
ACS	Affiliated Computer Services, Inc.	IT & Technology	6/30/07	5772.5	253.1	5982.4	2066.2	390	116035610
AMG	Affiliated Managers Group Inc. (Unit	Wealth Management	12/31/07	1369.9	182.0	3395.7	469.2	241	44091099
AFL	AFLAC Inc.	Insurance	12/31/07	15393.0	1634.0	65805.0	8795.0	-	-
AG	AGCO Corp.	Industrial Machinery and Equipment	12/31/07	6828.1	246.3	4787.6	2043.0	222	84982572
A	Agilent Technologies, Inc.	Instruments and Related Products	10/31/07	5420.0	638.0	7554.0	3234.0	387	339579687
ATG	AGL Resources Inc.	Gas Utilities	12/31/07	2494.0	211.0	6268.0	1661.0	220	48632477
AEM	Agnico-Eagle Mines Ltd	Precious Metals	12/31/06	510.5	161.3	1521.5	1252.4	98	36298697
ADC	Agree Realty Corp.	Property, Real Estate & Developmen	12/31/07	34.5	15.5	239.3	131.6	42	2185574
AGU	Agrium, Inc.	Chemicals	12/31/07	4193.0	33.0	3265.0	1233.0	150	77079041
AKH	Air France-KLM	Aviation	3/31/05	18983.0	1710.0	23194.0	6020.0	20	7610181
APD	Air Products & Chemicals, Inc. (Unit	Chemicals	9/30/07	10037.8	1035.6	12659.5	5495.6	-	-
AYR	Aircastle Ltd.	Aviation	12/31/06	189.3	51.2	1918.7	637.2	-	-
ARG	Airgas Inc.	Machinery Supply Retail	3/31/07	3205.1	154.4	3333.5	1125.4	173	55250813
AAI	AirTran Holdings, Inc.	Aviation	12/31/07	2310.0	52.7	2048.5	446.3	141	70814914
AKS	AK Steel Holding Corp.	Metal Works	12/31/07	7003.0	387.7	5197.4	874.7	169	86368227
ALG	Alamo Group, Inc.	Industrial Machinery and Equipment	12/31/07	504.4	12.4	350.6	198.7	37	5346642
ALK	Alaska Air Group, Inc.	Aviation	12/31/07	3506.0	125.0	4490.9	1024.0	144	28828619
AIN	Albany International Corp (New)	Textiles	12/31/07	1093.0	17.8	1527.0	599.7	142	25723446
ALB	Albemarle Corp.	Chemicals	12/31/07	2336.2	229.7	2830.4	1278.3	152	28216271
ACV	Alberto-Culver Co (New)	Chemicals	9/30/07	1541.6	78.3	1487.6	973.4	-	-
ALU	Alcatel-Lucent	Communications	12/31/04	12244.0	576.0	20629.0	5293.0	95	89036650
AA	Alcoa, Inc.	Metal Works	12/31/07	30748.0	2564.0	38803.0	16016.0	0	0
ACL	Alcon, Inc. (Switzerland)	Pharmaceuticals	12/31/07	5599.6	1586.4	7015.6	-	178	67424724
AFN	Alesco Financial Inc	Property, Real Estate & Developmen	12/31/07	99.8	-1261.3	8935.4	-2399.5	-	-
ALX	Alexander's, Inc.	Property, Real Estate & Developmen	12/31/07	208.0	114.3	1532.4	135.1	57	1614124
ARE	Alexandria Real Estate Equities, Inc	Property, Real Estate & Developmen	12/31/07	405.4	93.7	4642.1	1503.8	129	19523813
Y	Alleghany Corp.	Insurance	12/31/07	1432.0	305.3	6733.0	2793.9	125	4441490
AYE	Allegheny Energy, Inc.	Electricity	12/31/07	3307.0	412.2	9906.6	2535.4	239	123711628
ATI	Allegheny Technologies, Inc (United	Metal Works	12/31/07	5452.5	747.1	4095.6	2223.5	206	65891389
AGN	Allergan, Inc.	Pharmaceuticals	12/31/07	3938.9	499.3	6579.3	3738.6	321	119303047
ALE	Allete Inc.	Electricity	12/31/07	841.7	87.6	1644.2	742.6	134	16164644
AKP	Alliance California Municipal Income	Trusts & Holding Entities	10/31/06	-	9.2	213.2	130.7	5	61779
ADS	Alliance Data Systems Corp.	Miscellaneous Business Services	12/31/07	2291.2	164.1	4103.6	1197.0	193	66038870
AIQ	Alliance Imaging, Inc. (United State	Diagnostic Services	12/31/07	444.9	16.2	849.8	3.7	64	15008918
AYN	Alliance New York Municipal Incom	Trusts & Holding Entities	10/31/06	-	5.0	119.9	74.5	5	39490
AOI	Alliance One International Inc	Tobacco Products	3/31/07	1979.1	-21.6	1653.9	225.5	1	16250
AWF	AllianceBernstein Global High Inco	Trusts & Holding Entities	3/31/07	-	61.8	1142.7	1027.3	33	4915713
AB	AllianceBernstein Holding L P.	Wealth Management	12/31/07	-	376.2	1575.2	-	-	-
ACG	AllianceBernstein Income Fund Inc	Trusts & Holding Entities	12/31/06	207.3	138.6	3196.8	2084.4	-	-
AFB	AllianceBernstein National Municipa	Trusts & Holding Entities	10/31/06	-	23.2	520.5	319.7	10	141977

T2

| EARNINGS PER SHARE | | | | | | P/E RATIO | DIVIDENDS PER SHARE | | | AV. YLD % | DIV. DECLARED | | PRICE RANGE |
| QUARTERLY | | | ANNUAL | | | | | | | | | | 2007 |
1st	2nd	3rd	2007	2006	2005		2007	2006	2005		AMOUNT	PAYABLE	
1.85	1.25	1.32	5.60	5.06	4.12	16.1 - 13.4	1.92	1.84	1.68	2.3	0.5Q	3/12/08	90.0 - 74.9
-0.02	-0.17	-0.31	-1.77	-0.08	0.37								29.8 - 15.5
-	-	-	0.76	0.83	0.86	14.9 - 11.9	0.75	0.85	0.86	7.3	0.0625M	3/7/08	11.4 - 9.1
0.04	-0.07	0.14	0.14	0.16	0.01	211.8 - 86.9	-	-	-	-	-	-	29.6 - 12.2
0.36	-	-	1.40	0.94	0.46	11.6 - 6.2	-	-	-	-	0.025Q	9/4/02	16.2 - 8.7
0.53	0.36	0.29	1.46	1.47	1.14	17.2 - 9.3	0.06	0.06	0.05	0.3	0.016Q	4/3/08	25.1 - 13.6
-	-	-	1.63	0.63	0.36	4.1 - 3.0	-	-	-	-	-	-	6.7 - 4.9
0.45	0.63	0.46	2.31	1.12	2.16	20.3 - 15.9	1.27	1.16	1.09	3.1	0.36Q	5/15/08	47.0 - 36.8
0.65	0.88	1.29	4.59	3.66	2.28	10.3 - 5.2	0.70	0.60	0.50	2.0	0.175Q	3/18/08	47.1 - 23.6
-	-	-	-14.11	-4.64	-4.05		1.15	1.54	1.54	-	-	-	-
0.13	-	-	1.04	1.88	1.15	21.5 - 16.3	0.48	0.44	0.42	2.5	0.125Q	5/5/08	22.4 - 16.9
-	-	-	5.32	2.49	2.42	4.9 - 3.6	-	-	-	-	-	-	25.9 - 19.2
0.20	0.09	0.25	0.82	1.18	0.64	20.0 - 14.2	1.03	0.76	0.70	7.4	0.21Q	4/15/08	16.4 - 11.6
0.60	-	-	1.97	1.59	1.56	14.2 - 11.2	0.35	0.30	-	1.4	0.42A	11/15/07	27.9 - 22.0
-	0.08	0.16	-0.02	0.13	1.40		-	-	-	-	-	-	-
-0.05	0.14	-0.03	-0.25	1.88	1.70		-	-	-	-	-	-	-
2.10	1.93	1.95	7.66	6.91	3.31	6.0 - 4.3	1.06	0.98	0.90	2.6	0.27Q	4/14/08	45.7 - 33.1
-	-	-	0.54	0.58	0.65	15.9 - 12.7	-	-	-	-	0.0465M	3/20/08	0.0 - 0.9
-	-	-	-	0.05	0.12		-	-	0.02	-	-	-	-
0.41	0.31	0.47	1.69	1.50	1.21	15.5 - 9.6	0.04	0.04	-	0.2	0.08A	10/15/07	26.3 - 16.3
0.77	0.55	0.88	3.37	2.34	1.17	7.9 - 5.3	0.60	0.60	0.60	2.8	0.13Q	5/1/08	26.5 - 18.0
-	-	-	0.30	0.23	0.22	46.4 - 40.2	1.03	0.90	0.86	8.1	0.03Q	3/1/08	13.9 - 12.1
0.30	0.50	0.45	1.74	1.64	1.12	10.5 - 5.4	0.44	0.36	0.28	3.1	0.11Q	3/19/08	18.3 - 9.5
-	-	-	-	-	-		-	-	-	-	-	-	29.9 - 24.3
0.28	0.19	0.07	0.70	0.87	0.76	33.4 - 29.3	0.50	0.44	0.38	2.3	0.125Q	3/7/08	23.4 - 20.5
0.71	0.64	0.57	2.28	2.16	2.13	19.4 - 9.7	0.24	0.24	-	0.9	0.06Q	4/1/08	20.6 - 22.1
0.20	-2.78	-0.43	-3.22	1.21	-8.28		-	-	-	-	-	-	43.0 - 20.4
-1.11	-1.09	-0.71	-6.06	-0.34	0.40		-	-	-	-	-	-	24.9 - 10.9
-	-	-	-	-	-		-	-	-	-	-	-	4.5 - 2.4
-	-	-	0.61	1.32			-	2.66	3.12	-	0.12M	2/15/08	18.6 - 12.1
-	-	-	188.85	443.96	388.51	0.2 - 0.2	-	-	-	-	-	-	44.3 - 28.4
-	-	-	-	0.58	0.47		-	1.60	0.80	-	0.4Q	2/29/08	-
-	-	-	-	1.99	2.33		-	2.58	2.49	-	0.1710M	1/31/08	27.1 - 22.2
-	-	-	-	-	-		-	-	-	-	0.1458M	1/31/08	-
0.29	-	-	1.15	0.74	0.84								-
-	-	-	-	1.62	1.63								-
-	-	-	-	1.11	0.63								-
0.17	0.19	0.48	1.32	1.00	0.98	17.0 - 8.8	-	-	-	-	-	-	22.5 - 11.6
-0.67	0.36	0.15	-0.14	0.39	0.95		-	-	-	-	-	-	13.7 - 7.7
0.81	0.85	0.95	3.47	2.99	2.70	9.1 - 4.8	0.04	0.04	0.02	0.2	0.04A	11/30/07	31.7 - 16.5
0.65	0.81	-	2.49	2.87	3.19	24.4 - 18.7	-	-	-	-	-	-	60.8 - 46.6
0.93	1.04	1.07	4.58	3.74	2.81	14.8 - 9.5	-	-	-	-	-	-	67.7 - 43.4
0.84	0.84	0.85	3.31	2.95	2.92		0.80	0.55	0.44	-	0.24Q	3/3/08	-
0.76	0.67	0.80	2.55	-0.71	0.35	8.9 - 6.4	-	-	-	-	0.01Q	3/1/01	22.8 - 16.3
0.31	-	-	1.57	7.50	0.65	22.5 - 11.8	-	-	-	-	-	-	18.3 - 18.0
1.30	0.40	0.17	2.72	2.72	2.48	12.3 - 9.9	1.64	1.48	1.30	5.5	0.42Q	3/1/08	33.6 - 26.8
0.20	0.27	0.08	1.04	1.35	0.42	15.9 - 11.2	0.12	0.03	0.03	0.9	0.18A	3/28/08	16.5 - 11.7
0.47	0.47	0.47	2.01	1.83	2.14	16.5 - 11.3	1.97	1.96	1.96	7.0	0.5Q	4/15/08	00.1 - 22.0
-0.08	1.70	-	0.25	2.12			-	0.11	0.11	-	0.055S	1/10/08	18.6 - 11.9
-	-	-	3.05	3.25	6.60	6.5 - 4.7	-	-	-	-	-	-	19.7 - 14.4
1.19	-	-	4.64	3.18	3.08		1.48	1.34	1.25	-	0.44Q	5/12/08	-
0.36	0.57	-	-	1.11	0.01		-	-	-	-	0.7Q	1/15/08	-
0.63	0.60	0.67	1.92	1.57	1.20	14.1 - 10.3	0.28	0.24	0.18	1.2	0.12Q	3/31/08	27.1 - 19.9
0.03	0.42	0.11	0.58	0.17	0.02	26.2 - 16.7	-	-	-	-	-	-	15.2 - 9.7
0.50	0.90	0.07	3.16	0.11	-0.02	4.6 - 1.2	-	-	-	-	0.09Q	3/10/08	18.8 - 4.8
0.08	0.41	0.42	1.24	1.16	1.14	21.9 - 11.6	0.24	0.24	0.24	1.4	0.06Q	2/1/08	27.2 - 14.4
0.26	1.13	2.11	3.09	-1.39	-0.01	10.8 - 6.1	-	-	-	-	-	-	33.5 - 18.9
0.01	0.16	0.12	0.60	1.92	2.72	NR.R - 44.0	0.43	0.39	0.31	1.4	0.11Q	4/7/08	35.2 - 26.4
0.60	0.55	0.61	2.36	1.47	1.21	8.5 - 5.8	0.42	0.34	0.31	2.6	0.12Q	4/1/08	20.2 - 13.7
0.31	-	-	0.80	2.20	2.27		25.16	0.49	0.45	-	0.065Q	2/20/08	-
-	-	-	-1.56	-0.12	0.68		-	-	-	-	-	-	17.9 - 10.9
0.75	0.81	0.63	2.95	2.57	1.40	29.1 - 24.2	0.68	0.60	0.60	0.9	0.9375Q	7/1/08	85.9 - 71.5
-	-	-	5.25	4.37	2.98	16.6 - 11.2	-	-	-	-	0.2255U	6/4/03	87.2 - 58.9
0.21	-0.86	-8.36	-22.48	1.48	-0.45		1.23	0.59	0.44	11.6	0.25Q	4/10/08	12.9 - 9.4
6.32	3.85	5.62	22.44	-14.92	16.19	10.2 - 5.6	-	-	-	-	-	-	230.0 - 125.7
0.52	0.73	0.68	2.63	2.25	2.22	28.5 - 19.6	3.04	2.86	2.72	4.9	0.5234Q	1/15/08	74.9 - 51.6
11.90	7.03	7.87	33.40	29.72	6.38	8.3 - 6.0	-	-	-	-	3.8036Q	3/17/08	276.9 - 199.5
0.65	0.45	0.67	2.43	1.89	0.40	8.3 - 5.0	0.15	-	-	1.0	0.15Q	3/24/08	20.1 - 12.0
1.92	2.00	1.88	7.26	5.59	3.57	3.2 - 1.2	0.57	0.43	0.28	3.7	0.18Q	3/28/08	22.9 - 8.7
0.14	0.45	0.51	1.62	-0.44	1.50	28.4 - 20.9	0.20	0.20	0.20	0.5	0.05Q	3/7/08	46.0 - 33.8
0.93	0.80	0.58	3.08	2.74	0.48	13.9 - 10.1	1.64	1.45	1.25	4.4	0.43Q	3/1/08	42.9 - 31.1
-	-	-	-	1.08	1.07		-	0.96	0.96	-	0.0615M	3/20/08	14.7 - 12.5
0.70	0.55	0.36	2.03	2.32	1.64	23.9 - 13.3	-	-	-	-	-	-	48.5 - 26.9
0.12	0.09	0.08	0.31	0.38	0.39	36.7 - 11.2	-	-	-	-	-	-	11.4 - 3.5
-	-	-	-	1.04	1.03		-	0.77	0.91	-	0.059M	3/20/08	14.7 - 12.2
-	-	-	-	-	-		-	0.11	0.30	-	0.03Q	9/23/05	7.6 - 5.0
0.07	0.20	0.18	-0.25	-5.51	0.29		-	-	-	-	0.085M	3/20/08	13.4 - 9.8
-	-	-	0.91	0.90	0.87	14.7 - 10.8	0.82	0.90	0.83	6.9	1.06Q	2/14/08	42.0 - 31.7
0.91	1.16	1.20	4.32	3.82	3.02	9.7 - 7.3	4.33	1.02	2.80	12.0	0.05M	3/20/08	8.9 - 7.2
-	-	-	0.57	0.60	0.66	15.6 - 12.6	0.05	0.61	0.68	0.6	0.066M	3/20/08	14.9 - 12.6
-	-	-	-	1.13	1.13		-	1.00	1.00	-	-	-	-

T3

SYMBOL	COMPANY	NATURE OF BUSINESS	FISCAL YEAR-END	TOTAL REV. $MILL	NET INCOME $MILL	TOTAL ASSETS $MILL	NET STK EQUITY $MILL	NO OF INST	INST. HOLDINGS (SHARES)
LNT	Alliant Energy Corp.	Electricity	12/31/07	3437.6	425.3	7189.7	2681.2	213	51759419
ATK	Alliant Techsystems Inc.	Aerospace & Defense	3/31/07	3564.9	184.1	2874.7	557.9	225	32569063
AZ	Allianz SE	Insurance	12/31/05	96027.0	4380.0	997881.0	47102.0	55	37638727
ALD	Allied Capital Corp. (New)	Venture Capital	12/31/07	461.7	153.3	5214.6	2771.8	186	41406603
AIB	Allied Irish Banks Plc	Commercial Banking	12/31/04	5451.0	1129.0	102819.0	7683.0	89	12034913
AW.	Allied Waste Industries, Inc.	Sanitation Services	12/31/07	6068.7	273.6	13948.7	3904.2	206	222114783
AWH	Allied World Assurance Company H	Insurance	12/31/06	1467.7	442.8	7620.6	2220.1		
ALY	Allis-Chalmers Energy Inc	Oil and Gas	12/31/07	571.0	50.4	1053.6	414.3	6	2056338
ALL	Allstate Corp.	Insurance	12/31/07	36769.0	4636.0	156408.0	21851.0	702	449166161
ALJ	Alon USA Energy Inc	Oil and Gas	12/31/07	4542.2	103.9	1581.4	387.8		
ANR	Alpha Natural Resources Inc	Coal Mining	12/31/07	1877.6	27.7	1210.9	380.8	111	28981597
ALO	Alpharma, Inc.	Pharmaceuticals	12/31/07	722.4	-13.6	1288.2	731.1	144	42734441
AGD	Alpine Global Dynamic Dividend Fu	Trusts & Holding Entities	10/31/06		11.9	484.1	475.7		
AWP	Alpine Global Premier Properties Fu	Finance & Investment							
AOD	Alpine Total Dynamic Dividend Fun	Finance & Investment	12/15/06			0.4	0.1		
MO	Altria Group Inc	Tobacco Products	12/31/07	73801.0	9786.0	57211.0	18554.0	922	1447470381
AWC	Alumina Ltd	Precious Metals	12/31/04	292.4	316.4	1823.2	1411.9	20	10144657
ACH	Aluminum Corp of China Ltd.	Metal Works	12/31/05	37110.3	7022.4	59009.9	32644.4	38	2802914
AMB	AMB Property Corp.	Property, Real Estate & Developmen	12/31/07	669.7	314.3	7262.4	2764.0		
ABK	Ambac Financial Group, Inc.	Insurance	12/31/07	-4214.9	-3248.2	23565.0	2279.9	374	105569194
ACO	AMCOL International Corp.	Earth & Rock Mining	12/31/07	744.3	56.7	652.1	352.3	83	16166954
DOX	Amdocs Ltd.	IT & Technology	9/30/07	2836.2	364.9	4344.6	2600.2	205	160740248
AEE	Ameren Corp.	Electricity	12/31/07	7546.0	618.0	20728.0	6752.0	339	99380144
AMX	America Movil, S.A.B. de C.V.	Communications	12/31/06	234221.6	42816.3	320698.6	108976.1	272	215193891
AXL	American Axle & Manufacturing Hol	Automotive	12/31/07	3248.2	37.0	2914.7	890.7	126	48260788
ACC	American Campus Communities Inc	Property, Real Estate & Developmen	12/31/07	147.1	-1.7	1076.3	444.4	44	10496102
AEO	American Eagle Outfitters, Inc. (Ne	Retail - Apparel and Accessory Store	2/2/08	3055.4	400.0	1867.7	1340.5	275	117769531
AEP	American Electric Power Company,	Electricity	12/31/07	13380.0	1089.0	40366.0	10079.0	390	259408491
AEL	American Equity Investment Life Ho	Insurance	12/31/07	714.5	29.0	16394.4	611.6	85	26536814
AXP	American Express Co.	Credit & Lending	12/31/07	27731.0	4012.0	149830.0	11029.0	961	968347273
AFG	American Financial Group, Inc (Hol	Insurance	12/31/07	4404.7	383.2	25807.5	3046.1	163	35408855
AIG 09G	American General Finance Corp.	Credit & Lending							
AM	American Greetings Corp.	Printing	2/28/07	1744.6	42.4	1778.2	1012.6	176	82460274
MRF	American Income Fund Inc	Trusts & Holding Entities						8	1279659
AIG	American International Group Inc	Insurance	12/31/07	110064.0	6200.0	1060505.0	95801.0	1142	1584452931
ANL	American Land Lease, Inc.	Property, Real Estate & Developmen	12/31/07	66.2	14.4	436.5	139.0	29	2069765
XAA	American Municipal Income Portfoli	Trusts & Holding Entities						7	160335
AOB	American Oriental Bioengineering In	Pharmaceuticals	12/31/07	160.5	43.3	353.7	313.1	0	0
ARL	American Realty Investors, Inc.	Property, Real Estate & Developmen	12/31/06	182.3	13.1	1493.7	160.5	10	132658
ARP	American Reprographics Co	Advertising, Marketing & PR	12/31/07	688.4	69.1	722.6	251.7	39	12326527
ASI	American Safety Insurance Holding	Insurance	12/31/06	171.4	20.5	847.1	196.2	15	1961446
SLA	American Select Portfolio, Inc.	Trusts & Holding Entities						12	2072876
AWR	American States Water Co. (United	Water Utilities	12/31/07	301.4	28.0	963.9	302.1	103	6246152
ASP	American Strategic Income Portfolio	Trusts & Holding Entities						10	1378525
BSP	American Strategic Income Portfolio	Trusts & Holding Entities						13	4546308
CSP	American Strategic Income Portfolio	Trusts & Holding Entities	8/31/07		25.1	323.5	257.5	14	3543987
AMT	American Tower Corp.	Communications	12/31/07	1456.6	56.3	8130.5	3022.1	225	231346460
AVD	American Vanguard Corp.	Chemicals	12/31/07	216.7	18.7	248.6	139.7	48	7862652
ACF	AmeriCredit Corp. (United States)	Credit & Lending	6/30/07	2339.9	360.2	17811.0	2075.2	207	148742569
APU	AmeriGas Partners, L.P. (United St	Retail - Fuel & Oil	9/30/07	2277.4	190.8	1696.8		53	1718517
AGP	Amerigroup Corp	Insurance	12/31/07	3945.5	116.4	2088.6	913.9	179	48038199
AMP	Ameriprise Financial Inc	Wealth Management	12/31/07	8909.0	814.0	109230.0	7810.0		
ABC	AmerisourceBergen Corp. (United S	Pharmaceuticals	9/30/07	66074.3	469.2	12310.1	3099.7	299	97941585
AMN	Ameron International Corp.	Stone, Clay, Glass, and Concrete Pr	11/30/07	631.0	67.2	705.8	445.4	59	4768015
AME	Ametek, Inc. (New)	Electrical	12/31/07	2136.8	228.0	2745.7	1240.7	225	53719932
AHS	AMN Healthcare Services, Inc.	Diagnostic Services	12/31/07	1164.0	36.5	633.6	276.1	74	18338111
AP	Ampco-Pittsburgh Corp.	Industrial Machinery and Equipment	12/31/07	346.8	39.2	404.4	187.7	26	5137360
APH	Amphenol Corp. (New)	Electrical	12/31/07	2851.0	353.2	2675.7	1264.9	233	81432609
AMR	AMR Corp. (DE)	Aviation	12/31/07	22935.0	504.0	28571.0	2657.0	179	157505404
AXR	AMREP Corp.	Miscellaneous Business Services	4/30/07	204.8	45.1	292.7	160.0	14	750527
APC	Anadarko Petroleum Corp	Oil and Gas	12/31/07	15892.0	3781.0	48481.0	16364.0	621	183877742
ADI	Analog Devices, Inc.	IT & Technology	11/3/07	2546.1	496.9	2971.9	2338.1	417	304231758
AGL	Angelica Corp. (United States)	Personal Services	1/27/07	425.7	3.6	336.3	147.5	76	8344440
AU	AngloGold Ashanti Ltd	Precious Metals	12/31/04	14788.0	728.0	46296.0	18117.0	115	27003020
BUD	Anheuser-Busch Cos., Inc.	Food	12/31/07	16685.7	2115.3	17155.0	-3151.6	749	433191785
AXE	Anixter International Inc	Specialist Equipment Supplies	12/28/07	5852.9	253.5	3016.2	1047.8	158	33259026
NLY	Annaly Capital Management Inc	Property, Real Estate & Developmen	12/31/07	2416.7	414.4	53903.5	5204.9		
ANN	AnnTaylor Stores Corp.	Retail - Apparel and Accessory Store	2/2/08	2396.5	97.2	1393.8	839.5	185	65296554
AHR	Anthracite Capital, Inc.	Property, Real Estate & Developmen	12/31/07	358.5	84.0	5247.7	451.4	100	29887464
ANH	Anworth Mortgage Asset Corp.	Property, Real Estate & Developmen	12/31/07	225.2	-156.5	4797.5	401.4		
AOC	Aon Corp.	Insurance	12/31/07	7471.0	864.0	24948.0	6221.0	285	265843872
APA	Apache Corp.	Oil and Gas	12/31/07	9977.9	2812.4	28634.7	15378.0	697	258202171
AIV	Apartment Investment & Manageme	Property, Real Estate & Developmen	12/31/07	1721.2	29.9	10606.5	1749.7	219	84199359
ABI	Applera Corp.	Instruments and Related Products	6/30/06	1949.4	212.5	3013.0	2204.3	250	175199921
ABI	Applera Corp.	Instruments and Related Products	6/30/06	1911.2	275.1	2245.8	1477.7	250	175199921
CRA	Applera Corp.	Diagnostic Services	6/30/06	46.2	-62.7	773.7	726.4	129	57121839
AIT	Applied Industrial Technologies, Inc.	Machinery Supply Retail	6/30/07	2014.1	86.0	777.4	451.0	129	22635236
AHG	Apria Healthcare Group Inc.	Diagnostic Services	12/31/07	1631.8	86.0	1597.8	512.0	182	49376092
ATS	APT Satellite Holdings Ltd.	Communications	12/31/05	336.5	-135.6	3614.3	2061.6	3	311896
ATR	AptarGroup Inc.	Plastics	12/31/07	1892.2	141.7	1911.9	1119.0	179	31196945

1st	2nd	3rd	ANNUAL 2007	2006	2005	P/E RATIO		DIV 2007	2006	2005	AV. YLD %	AMOUNT	PAYABLE	PRICE 2007	
0.55	0.43	1.08	3.78	2.69	-0.07	7.6 -	6.3	1.27	1.15	1.05	4.9	0.35Q	2/15/08	28.8 -	23.8
1.50	1.44	1.65	5.32	4.11	4.03	12.7 -	10.1	-	-	-	-	-	-	67.5 -	53.9
-	-	-	17.71	16.78	11.14	0.8 -	0.5	-	-	-	-	-	-	14.0 -	9.0
0.87	0.57	-0.62	0.99	1.68	6.36	31.2 -	22.4	2.64	2.47	2.33	9.9	0.65Q	3/27/08	30.9 -	22.2
-	-	-	-	2.45	1.50	-		-	-	-	-	-	-	41.5 -	28.0
0.08	0.21	0.05	0.63	0.33	0.46	22.8 -	12.7	-	-	-	-	-	-	14.4 -	8.0
1.83	1.96	1.72	-	7.75	-3.19	-		-	-	-	-	0.18Q	12/20/07	-	
0.37	0.55	0.37	1.45	1.66	0.44	7.1 -	1.2	-	-	-	-	-	-	10.3 -	1.8
2.41	2.30	1.70	7.77	7.84	2.64	6.7 -	5.5	1.52	1.40	1.28	3.2	0.41Q	4/1/08	51.8 -	42.7
0.76	2.00	0.26	2.16	3.37	2.61	-		0.16	3.03		-	0.04Q	3/14/08	-	
0.13	0.07	0.14	0.43	2.00	0.38	-		-	-	-	-	-	-	-	
0.28	0.30	0.34	-0.32	1.52	2.52	-		0.00	0.18	0.18	0.0	0.045Q	10/27/06	24.0 -	12.4
-	-	-	-	0.51	-	-		-	-	-	-	0.17M	3/28/08	-	
-	-	-	-	-	-	-		-	-	-	-	0.1267M	1/25/08	-	
-	-	-	-	-	-	-		-	-	-	-	0.54M	12/31/07	-	
1.30	1.05	1.24	4.62	5.71	4.99	3.1 -	2.3	3.05	3.32	3.06	25.2	0.75Q	4/10/08	14.3 -	10.4
-	-	-	-	0.44	0.27	-		-	-	-	-	-	-	20.9 -	13.9
-	-	-	-	-	-	-		-	-	-	-	-	-	32.9 -	10.7
0.23	1.10	0.69	2.96	2.30	2.85	-		2.00	1.84	1.76	-	0.4281Q	4/15/08	-	
2.02	1.67	-3.53	-31.56	8.15	6.87	-		0.78	0.66	0.55	1.0	0.07Q	3/5/08	84.4 -	64.0
0.35	0.48	0.65	1.83	1.62	1.33	13.3 -	8.3	0.60	0.49	0.38	3.3	0.16Q	4/4/08	24.4 -	15.3
-	-	-	1.65	1.48	1.35	18.2 -	11.1	-	-	-	-	-	-	30.0 -	18.3
0.59	0.69	1.18	2.98	2.66	3.02	16.8 -	13.7	2.54	2.54	2.54	5.5	0.635Q	3/31/08	50.1 -	40.8
-	-	-	-	-	-	-		-	-	-	-	-	-	17.5 -	9.4
0.30	0.64	0.25	0.70	-4.42	1.10	60.0 -	38.4	0.60	0.60	0.60	1.7	0.15Q	3/28/08	42.0 -	26.9
-0.20	-0.03	-0.10	-0.07	1.17	0.65	-		1.35	1.35	1.35	6.9	0.3375Q	2/29/08	22.5 -	17.1
0.35	0.37	0.45	1.70	1.26	0.95	9.3 -	3.2	0.28	0.18	0.04	2.7	0.1Q	4/11/08	15.8 -	5.4
0.68	0.45	1.02	2.72	2.53	2.08	13.0 -	10.7	1.58	1.50	1.42	4.9	0.41Q	3/10/08	35.2 -	29.0
0.17	0.41	0.13	0.50	1.27	0.99	25.9 -	18.0	0.06	0.05	0.04	0.6	0.06A	12/21/07	12.9 -	9.0
0.87	0.88	0.90	3.36	2.99	2.97	14.8 -	12.4	0.60	0.54	0.48	1.3	0.18Q	2/8/08	49.8 -	41.8
0.92	0.54	0.93	3.10	3.75	1.75	6.9 -	5.7	0.40	0.37	0.33	2.0	0.125Q	1/25/08	21.5 -	17.6
0.54	0.15	0.52	0.71	1.16	1.25	39.3 -	27.4	0.32	0.32	0.12	1.4	0.1Q	1/14/08	27.9 -	19.4
-	-	-	-	-	-	-		-	-	-	-	0.0425Q	2/20/08	8.9 -	7.9
1.58	1.64	1.19	2.39	5.36	3.99	32.1 -	22.9	0.73	0.63	0.55	1.1	0.2Q	6/20/08	76.8 -	54.7
0.16	0.13	1.26	1.57	1.24	1.35	14.4 -	10.8	1.00	1.00	1.00	5.1	0.4844Q	2/29/08	22.5 -	16.9
-	-	-	-	-	-	-		-	-	-	-	0.062M	2/20/08	15.5 -	13.1
-	-	-	-	-	-	-		-	-	-	-	-	-	4.9 -	1.2
0.10	0.15	0.16	0.61	0.46	0.31	8.0 -	2.0	-	-	-	-	-	-	-	
-0.89	-2.28	-0.33	2.35	1.04	4.42	4.7 -	3.1	1.00	1.00	1.45	11.5	-	-	11.1 -	7.2
0.37	0.43	0.35	1.51	1.13	1.40	-		-	-	-	-	0.12Q	1/6/03	17.5 -	10.0
0.65	0.66	0.64	-	2.26	2.05	-		-	-	-	-	0.065M	2/20/08	14.3 -	11.8
-	-	-	-	-	-	-		-	-	-	-	0.25Q	3/1/08	26.8 -	21.4
0.40	0.42	0.44	1.61	1.33	1.57	16.6 -	13.3	0.95	0.91	0.90	3.9	0.065M	2/20/08	13.6 -	10.9
-	-	-	-	-	-	-		-	-	-	-	0.065M	2/20/08	11.2 -	11.0
-	-	-	1.18	1.01	0.98	11.4 -	9.3	1.25	0.79	1.00	10.1	0.075M	2/20/08	13.5 -	10.9
-	-	-	-	-	-	142.7 -	79.5	-	-	-	-	-	-	18.6 -	10.3
0.05	-0.05	0.14	0.13	0.06	-0.57	-		-	-	-	-	-	-	15.4 -	0.4
0.08	0.13	0.20	0.68	0.57	0.73	22.6 -	12.4	0.07	0.08	0.00	0.0	0.05Q	4/15/00	24.6 -	15.8
0.49	-0.17	-	2.73	2.08	1.73	9.0 -	5.8	-	-	-	-	-	-	30.5 -	26.2
0.87	-	-	3.15	1.59	1.10	9.7 -	8.0	2.03	2.20	2.22	9.3	0.61Q	2/18/08	38.3 -	18.5
0.40	0.61	0.58	2.16	2.02	1.02	17.7 -	0.6	-	-	-	-	0.15Q	2/18/08	-	
0.68	0.81	0.83	3.39	2.54	2.32	-		0.56	0.44	-	-	0.075Q	3/3/08	30.9 -	24.2
0.66	-	-	2.50	2.25	1.24	12.4 -	9.7	0.20	0.10	0.05	0.7	0.25Q	2/19/08	40.0 -	28.6
0.94	1.74	2.32	7.40	5.88	3.80	5.4 -	3.9	0.90	0.80	0.80	2.6	0.06Q	3/31/08	23.9 -	15.4
0.48	0.54	0.53	2.12	1.71	1.33	11.3 -	7.3	0.24	0.18	0.16	1.2	-	-	21.4 -	11.1
0.23	0.26	0.29	1.05	1.02	0.69	20.3 -	10.6	-	-	-	-	-	-	-	
0.95	1.01	0.92	3.88	1.67	1.53	3.8 -	3.2	0.55	0.40	0.40	4.2	0.15Q	1/31/08	14.7 -	12.6
0.43	0.48	0.50	1.99	1.40	1.18	8.0 -	7.7	0.00	0.00	0.00	0.1	0.010Q	1/0/00	10.0 -	11.1
0.30	1.08	0.61	1.78	0.98	-5.21	9.0 -	3.6	-	-	-	-	-	-	17.4 -	6.5
0.94	0.55	0.57	-6.78	3.93	2.35	3.5 -	2.3	0.85	4.05	0.40	4.8	1.U	8/24/07	23.9 -	15.4
0.23	1.39	1.07	8.08	10.46	5.20	4.4 -	3.0	0.36	0.36	0.36	1.2	13.65Q	3/31/08	35.5 -	24.3
1.22	-	-	1.50	1.48	1.08	34.3 -	22.4	0.70	0.56	0.32	1.6	0.18Q	3/26/08	51.4 -	33.6
-0.12	-0.16	0.50	0.39	0.03	0.70	70.9 -	54.6	0.44	0.44	0.44	1.8	0.11Q	1/3/08	27.6 -	21.3
-	-	-	-	-2.15	-4.77	-		-	-	-	-	-	-	47.8 -	30.1
-	-	-	2.79	2.53	2.35	19.5 -	17.7	1.25	1.13	1.03	2.4	0.33Q	3/10/08	54.3 -	49.5
1.27	1.53	1.51	6.00	4.86	2.22	6.5 -	4.3	-	-	4.00	-	4.U	10/31/05	39.0 -	25.8
0.28	0.30	0.32	1.31	0.44	-0.19	-		1.04	0.24	1.04	-	0.48Q	4/29/08	-	
0.46	0.50	0.66	1.98	1.13	0.88	15.8 -	10.3	-	-	-	-	-	-	31.3 -	20.4
0.41	0.34	0.19	1.18	1.31	1.20	11.0 -	8.9	1.19	1.15	1.12	10.3	0.5156Q	4/30/08	13.0 -	10.5
0.05	0.05	-3.47	-3.47	-0.40	0.53	-		0.27	0.08	0.55	-	0.3906Q	4/15/08	-	
0.66	0.75	0.64	2.69	2.13	2.17	10.8 -	7.1	0.60	0.60	0.60	2.3	0.15Q	2/14/08	29.0 -	19.2
1.47	1.89	1.83	8.39	7.64	7.84	6.4 -	4.4	0.60	0.45	0.34	1.3	1.42Q	4/30/08	54.1 -	37.2
0.09	0.03	-0.22	-0.36	1.00	-0.18	-		4.31	2.40	3.00	13.0	0.4922Q	4/15/08	38.8 -	27.9
-0.41	0.38	0.33	-	1.43	1.19	-		-	0.17	0.17	-	0.0425Q	4/1/08	23.8 -	18.1
-0.32	0.39	0.39	-	1.43	1.19	-		-	0.17	0.17	-	0.0425Q	10/1/07	23.8 -	18.1
-0.09	-0.01	-0.06	-	-0.83	-1.05	-		-	-	-	-	0.0425Q	7/2/07	16.3 -	10.4
0.56	0.52	-	1.93	1.57	1.20	10.6 -	4.6	0.48	0.40	0.28	3.6	0.15Q	2/29/08	20.5 -	8.8
0.44	0.47	0.48	1.95	1.75	1.37	17.4 -	13.6	-	-	-	-	-	-	34.0 -	26.6
-	-	-	-	-0.19	-0.33	-		-	-	-	-	-	-	3.0 -	1.3
0.41	0.52	0.56	1.98	1.44	1.39	13.7 -	9.4	0.50	0.42	0.35	2.3	0.13Q	2/21/08	27.2 -	18.7

T5

SYMBOL	COMPANY	NATURE OF BUSINESS	FISCAL YEAR-END	TOTAL REV. $MILL	NET INCOME $MILL	TOTAL ASSETS $MILL	NET STK EQUITY $MILL	NO OF INST	INST. HOLDINGS (SHARES)
WTR	Aqua America Inc	Water Utilities	12/31/07	602.5	95.0	3226.9	976.3	197	25933112
ILA	Aquila Inc (New) (DE)	Electricity	12/31/07	1466.6	-5.4	2993.6	1355.7	174	185077514
ARA	Aracruz Celulose S.A. (Brazil)	Paper Products	12/31/07	3846.9	1042.2	9930.7	5361.0	97	28843100
ARB	Arbitron Inc. (United States)	Research Support Services	12/31/07	338.5	40.2	180.5	48.2	132	31739541
ABR	Arbor Realty Trust Inc	Property, Real Estate & Developmen	12/31/07	274.0	84.5	2901.5	395.3	63	11116879
MT	ArcelorMittal SA (New)	Metal Works	12/31/05	32963.0	3873.0	35864.0	17430.0	-	-
ARJ	Arch Chemicals Inc (United States)	Chemicals	12/31/07	1487.6	35.3	1194.2	474.4	103	19360862
ACI	Arch Coal, Inc.	Coal Mining	12/31/07	2413.6	174.9	3594.6	1531.7	258	65349468
ADM	Archer Daniels Midland Co.	Food	6/30/07	44018.0	2162.0	25118.0	11253.0	444	442016728
ARD	Arena Resources Inc	Oil and Gas	12/31/07	100.1	34.4	349.3	257.8	4	158601
ATB	Arlington Tankers Ltd	Shipping	12/31/06	69.4	21.5	363.4	130.6	-	-
AWI	Armstrong World Industry Inc (New)	Building & General Construction	12/31/07	3549.7	145.3	4649.9	2437.2	-	-
ARW	Arrow Electronics, Inc.	Retail - Appliances and Electrical	12/31/07	15985.0	407.8	8059.9	3551.9	194	107826639
ARM	ArvinMeritor, Inc.	Automotive	9/30/07	6449.0	-219.0	4789.0	543.0	-	-
ASA	ASA Limited	Trusts & Holding Entities	11/30/06	11.5	184.0	720.5	-	43	2633653
ABG	Asbury Automotive Group, Inc	Retail - Automotive	12/31/07	5713.0	51.0	2016.3	584.2	51	6373483
AHT	Ashford Hospitality Trust Inc	Property, Real Estate & Developmen	12/31/07	1128.8	30.2	4381.3	1285.0	-	-
ASH	Ashland Inc (New)	Chemicals	9/30/07	7834.0	230.0	5686.0	3154.0	283	54169224
APB	Asia Pacific Fund, Inc. (The)	Trusts & Holding Entities	3/31/07	-	0.8	251.1	248.5	30	1204531
SAT	Asia Satellite Telecommunications	Communications	12/31/05	879.7	366.2	4683.5	4109.7	9	617971
GRR	Asia Tigers Fund, Inc. (The)	Trusts & Holding Entities	10/31/06	-	-0.0	96.6	95.0	27	1318066
ALC	Assisted Living Concepts Inc (Neva	Hospitals & Health Care	12/31/07	229.3	17.2	476.2	294.5	-	-
AEC	Associated Estates Realty Corp.	Property, Real Estate & Developmen	12/31/07	151.4	10.2	686.8	89.8	52	8773280
AIZ	Assurant Inc	Insurance	12/31/07	8453.5	653.7	26750.3	4088.9	186	118035985
AGO	Assured Guaranty Ltd	Miscellaneous Business Services	12/31/06	322.1	159.7	2935.3	1650.8	-	-
AF	Astoria Financial Corp. (United Stat	Other Depository Banking	12/31/07	1181.1	124.8	21719.4	1211.3	210	68276661
AZN	AstraZeneca Plc	Pharmaceuticals	12/31/04	21426.0	3664.0	25652.0	14497.0	141	130150681
T	AT&T Inc	Communications	12/31/07	118928.0	11951.0	275644.0	115367.0	-	-
ATN	Atlas Energy Resources LLC	Oil and Gas	12/31/07	577.9	117.5	1891.2	836.1	-	-
AHD	Atlas Pipeline Holdings LP	Oil and Gas	12/31/07	668.8	-15.6	2877.5	-	-	-
APL	Atlas Pipeline Partners LP	Gas Utilities	12/31/07	668.8	-144.3	2877.6	-	26	859122
ATO	Atmos Energy Corp.	Gas Utilities	9/30/07	5898.4	168.5	5896.9	1965.8	186	43541478
ATW	Atwood Oceanics, Inc. (United State	Oil and Gas	9/30/07	403.0	139.0	717.7	615.9	146	12179526
AUO	AU Optronics Corp.	Electrical	12/31/06	293106.8	9093.4	578126.0	231076.3	105	69077757
ALV	Autoliv Inc. (United States)	Automotive	12/31/07	6769.0	287.9	5305.4	2349.1	222	60048744
ADP	Automatic Data Processing Inc.	IT & Technology	6/30/07	7800.0	1138.7	26648.9	5147.9	773	417425111
AN	AutoNation, Inc.	Retail - Automotive	12/31/07	17691.5	278.7	8479.6	3473.5	222	208898183
AZO	AutoZone, Inc.	Retail - Automotive	8/25/07	6169.8	595.7	4804.7	403.2	312	71533483
AVB	AvalonBay Communities, Inc.	Property, Real Estate & Developmen	12/31/07	812.7	358.2	6736.5	3026.7	208	67208488
AVR	Aventine Renewable Energy Holdin	Chemicals	12/31/07	1571.6	33.8	762.2	343.9	-	-
AVY	Avery Dennison Corp.	Paper Products	12/29/07	6307.8	303.5	6244.8	1989.4	-	-
CAR	Avis Budget Group Inc	Hospitality & Tourism	12/31/07	5986.0	-916.0	12474.0	1465.0	-	-
AVA	Avista Corp.	Electricity	12/31/07	1417.8	38.5	3189.8	914.0	133	27689062
AVT	Avnet Inc	Electrical	6/30/07	15681.1	393.1	7355.1	3400.6	204	114317617
AVP	Avon Products, Inc.	Consumer Products Manufacturing	12/31/07	9938.7	530.7	5716.2	711.6	485	396059324
AVX	AVX Corp.	Electrical	3/31/07	1498.5	153.9	1899.5	1635.3	84	38327841
AXA	AXA S.A.	Insurance	12/31/04	92879.0	3798.0	504367.0	30834.0	110	36835196
AZZ	AZZ Inc	Electrical	2/28/07	260.3	21.6	200.9	111.1	20	3154983
BGS	B&G Foods Inc (New)	Food	12/29/07	471.3	17.8	847.6	174.6	41	15366846
FLY	Babcock & Brown Air Ltd	Aviation	12/31/06	-	-7.5	-	27.7	-	-
BHI	Baker Hughes Inc.	Oil and Gas	12/31/07	10428.2	1513.9	9856.6	6305.6	429	309418195
BEZ	Baldor Electric Co.	Electrical	12/29/07	1824.9	94.1	2821.6	810.8	115	18101410
BLL	Ball Corp	Metal Products	12/31/07	7389.7	281.3	6020.6	1342.5	-	-
BYI	Bally Technologies Inc	Sporting & Recreational	6/30/07	682.3	22.3	824.9	199.5	-	-
BBV	Banco Bilbao Vizcaya Argentaria S	Commercial Banking	12/31/04	21361.7	2922.6	329441.2	13805.3	71	53847926
BBD	Banco Bradesco S.A.	Commercial Banking	12/31/07	41604.5	8009.7	341184.4	30357.3	62	33692319
BPC RT	Banco Comercial Portugues, S.A. (	Commercial Banking	12/31/04	4427.6	513.0	71678.5	3605.3	-	-
BCH	Banco de Chile	Commercial Banking	12/31/06	1010841.1	195247.7	12760285.9	834630.6	11	536352
BTO MC	Banco Espanol de Credito S.A.	Commercial Banking	12/31/04	4268.1	458.4	69582.0	3628.8	-	-
ITU	Banco Itau Holding Financeira SA	Commercial Banking	12/31/07	32129.7	8473.6	294876.3	28969.1	78	8546081
BLX	Banco Latinoamericano de Exporta	Other Depository Banking						67	17713657
BMA	Banco Macro S.A.	Commercial Banking	12/31/07	2552.7	495.2	19781.2	2707.7	-	-
SAN	Banco Santander Chile (New)	Commercial Banking	12/31/06	1350044.0	285582.0	14843439.0	1245339.0	64	14775679
STD	Banco Santander SA (New)	Commercial Banking	12/31/04	29477.5	3605.9	664486.3	36500.3	93	85796862
CIB	BanColombia, S.A.	Commercial Banking						48	12785501
BXS	BancorpSouth Inc.	Commercial Banking	12/31/07	1033.0	137.9	13189.8	1196.6	95	15060361
BAC	Bank of America Corp.	Commercial Banking	12/31/07	119190.0	14982.0	1715746.0	146803.0	1221	2359901886
BOH	Bank of Hawaii Corp	Commercial Banking	12/31/07	842.4	183.7	10472.9	750.3	198	34648790
IRE	Bank of Ireland (Ireland)	Credit & Lending	3/31/05	8157.0	1054.0	127780.0	4412.0	56	3868624
BMO	Bank of Montreal	Commercial Banking	10/31/07	20344.0	2131.0	366524.0	15298.0	-	-
BK	Bank of New York Mellon Corp	Finance & Investment						-	-
BNS	Bank of Nova Scotia Halifax	Commercial Banking	10/31/07	26427.0	4045.0	411510.0	18804.0	80	343165625
BBX	BankAtlantic Bancorp, Inc.	Other Depository Banking	12/31/07	523.5	-22.2	6378.8	459.3	146	31322691
BCS	Barclays PLC	Commercial Banking	12/31/04	23177.0	3254.0	538181.0	16764.0	115	27505581
BCR	Bard (C.R.), Inc.	Health	12/31/07	2202.0	406.4	2475.5	1848.0	397	85188075
BKS	Barnes & Noble Inc	Retail - Miscellaneous	2/2/08	5410.8	135.8	3249.8	1074.7	198	49570487
B	Barnes Group Inc.	Metal Products	12/31/07	1439.5	101.3	1539.3	653.9	-	-
BRL	Barr Pharmaceuticals Inc	Pharmaceuticals	12/31/07	2500.6	128.3	4761.6	1866.3	295	74551959
BBG	Barrett (Bill) Corp	Oil and Gas	12/31/07	390.3	26.8	1329.7	773.5	81	24670977
ABX	Barrick Gold Corp.	Precious Metals	12/31/06	5636.0	1506.0	21373.0	14199.0	198	273486392

EARNINGS PER SHARE						P/E RATIO	DIVIDENDS PER SHARE			AV. YLD %	DIV. DECLARED		PRICE RANGE 2007
QUARTERLY			ANNUAL										
1st	2nd	3rd	2007	2006	2005		2007	2006	2005	%	AMOUNT	PAYABLE	
0.13	0.18	0.22	0.71	0.70	0.71	26.0 - 20.0	0.48	0.44	0.40	3.0	0.125Q	3/1/08	18.4 - 14.2
-0.06	-0.04	0.11	-0.01	0.06	-0.60						0.175Q	9/12/02	4.8 - 2.3
													39.2 - 28.4
0.52	0.13	0.58	1.35	1.68	2.14	33.3 - 23.7	0.40	0.40	0.40	1.0	0.1Q	4/1/08	45.0 - 31.9
0.97	1.75	1.02	4.44	2.93	2.98	5.6 - 4.2	2.46	2.57	2.24	11.9	0.62Q	2/26/08	24.8 - 18.5
				4.71	5.94								
0.60	0.93	-0.51	1.43	0.58	1.70	21.4 - 16.6	0.80	0.80	0.80	2.9	0.2Q	3/14/08	30.6 - 23.7
-0.20	0.26	0.19	1.21	1.80	0.17	15.8 - 11.0	0.27	0.22	0.16	1.7	0.07Q	3/14/08	19.1 - 13.3
0.68	0.73	-	3.30	2.00	1.59	6.8 - 4.5	0.43	0.37	0.32	2.5	0.13Q	3/11/08	22.4 - 14.9
0.19	0.25	0.32	1.02	0.78	0.38	4.7 - 2.9							4.8 - 2.9
0.25	0.55	0.00	-	1.38	1.41		-	2.29	1.97		0.56Q	2/12/08	
0.46	0.91	0.85	2.56	0.04	-						4.5U	3/31/08	
0.77	0.79	0.79	3.28	3.16	2.09	8.7 - 6.4							28.5 - 20.8
-0.17	-	-	-3.11	-2.52	0.17		0.40	0.40	0.40		0.1Q	3/10/08	
											2.S	11/30/07	45.6 - 40.3
0.01	0.62	0.57	1.53	1.78	1.86	12.6 - 8.2	0.85	0.40		5.6	0.225Q	2/29/08	19.4 - 12.6
0.12	0.13	-0.05	0.06	0.43	-		0.84	0.80	0.71		0.5281Q	4/15/08	
0.52	-	-	3.60	5.64	26.83		11.30	1.10	0.20		0.275Q	3/15/00	
-	-	-	0.08	0.11	0.18	185.9 - 133.3	2.96	0.68	0.15	22.4	4.04A	1/14/08	14.9 - 10.7
-	-	-	-	1.16	0.94								22.1 - 15.2
-	-	-	-	-	0.06						0.52A	1/14/08	11.6 - 8.3
0.07	0.06	0.06	0.25	0.13	0.18								
-0.05	-0.51	-0.24	0.30	1.29	1.51	35.0 - 24.0	0.68	0.51	0.85	7.7	0.17Q	5/1/08	10.5 - 7.2
1.45	1.36	1.56	5.38	5.57	3.50	5.8 - 4.4	0.46	0.30	0.31	1.8	0.12Q	3/10/08	31.0 - 23.7
0.57	0.47	-1.70	-	2.15	2.53		-	0.14	0.12		0.04Q	12/10/07	
0.38	0.37	0.39	1.36	1.80	2.26	20.6 - 16.5	1.04	0.96	0.80	4.2	0.26Q	3/3/08	28.0 - 22.5
-	-	-	3.73	3.85	2.91	13.6 - 9.8							50.9 - 35.9
0.45	0.47	0.50	1.94	1.89	1.42		1.47	1.35	1.29		0.4Q	5/1/08	
0.53	1.08	0.98	2.29	0.08	-						0.57Q	2/14/08	
0.13	-0.06	-0.12	-0.06	0.30	-						0.34Q	2/19/08	
-0.14	-2.20	-0.90	-6.75	1.27	1.84		3.50	3.37	2.33	9.4	0.93Q	2/14/08	42.8 - 32.8
0.82	-	-	1.92	1.82	1.72	14.3 - 12.3	1.28	1.26	1.24	5.0	0.325Q	3/10/08	27.4 - 23.7
1.20	-	-	4.37	2.74	0.83	6.1 - 3.6							20.9 - 15.0
													23.2 - 8.5
0.91	0.72	0.81	3.68	4.88	3.26	13.3 - 10.3	1.54	1.36	1.17	3.6	0.39Q	6/5/08	48.8 - 37.9
0.55	0.55	-	2.04	2.68	1.79	20.6 - 17.1	0.88	0.71	0.60	2.3	0.29Q	4/1/08	42.1 - 34.9
0.37	0.37	0.37	1.39	1.38	1.85	13.8 - 10.9							19.2 - 15.2
2.02	1.67	-	8.53	7.50	7.18	10.7 - 8.5							91.3 - 72.3
0.56	0.61	1.58	4.38	3.57	4.21	17.2 - 10.7	3.40	3.12	2.84	5.9	0.5437Q	6/16/08	75.3 - 46.9
0.35	0.30	0.07	0.80	1.39	0.89								
0.80	0.87	0.59	3.07	3.66	2.25		1.61	1.57	1.53		0.41Q	3/19/08	
0.12	0.23	0.99	-8.88	-19.82	12.60		-	1.10	4.00				31.8 - 25.4
0.26	0.26	0.07	0.72	1.47	0.02	26.6 - 21.6	0.69	0.67	0.55	3.3	0.165Q	3/14/08	19.2 - 15.5
0.69	0.93	-	2.63	1.39	1.39	10.0 - 6.0					0.075Q	1/2/02	26.4 - 15.8
0.34	0.26	0.32	1.21	1.06	1.81	38.1 - 25.5	0.74	0.70	0.00	1.0	0.2Q	3/3/00	40.1 - 30.9
0.23	0.22	0.22	0.89	0.47	0.32	21.4 - 12.6	0.15	0.15	0.15	1.1	0.04Q	3/3/08	19.0 - 11.2
-	-	-	-	2.56	2.19								24.8 - 19.2
0.34	0.66	0.66	1.82	0.69	0.44	4.7 - 3.7					0.16A	4/27/01	8.6 - 6.7
0.20	0.17	0.13	0.62	0.65	0.53	24.3 - 23.4	1.71	1.71	1.71	11.5	0.212Q	1/30/08	15.0 - 14.5
1.17	1.09	1.22	4.73	7.27	2.57	9.5 - 6.7	0.52	0.52	0.47	1.3	0.13Q	2/15/08	44.9 - 31.8
0.50	0.54	0.53	2.08	1.46	1.28	13.8 - 10.3	0.68	0.67	0.62	2.9	0.17Q	3/31/08	28.8 - 21.4
0.78	1.03	0.59	2.74	3.14	2.38		0.40	0.40	0.40		0.1Q	3/17/08	
0.37	0.42	-	0.40	-0.88	-0.49	85.0 - 22.8							34.0 - 9.1
-	-	-	1.70	1.39	1.12	10.5 - 7.3							17.8 - 12.5
													6.3 - 2.9
													55.3 - 14.5
													7.6 - 3.5
-	-	-	-	-	-		-	-	-		0.22Q	10/5/07	19.9 - 14.7
				1.52	1.20			1.31	1.46				33.9 - 23.6
				1.21	0.99								12.5 - 9.4
													14.1 - 5.3
0.42	0.43	0.44	1.69	1.57	1.47	14.9 - 11.7	0.83	0.79	0.76	3.7	0.21Q	4/1/08	25.2 - 19.8
1.16	1.28	0.82	3.30	4.59	4.04	14.4 - 11.8	2.40	2.12	1.90	5.6	1.75Q	4/25/08	47.4 - 39.0
0.94	0.95	0.96	3.69	3.52	3.41	13.8 - 11.3	1.67	1.52	1.36	3.6	0.44Q	3/14/08	51.0 - 41.7
-	-	-	1.71	1.35	1.10	39.1 - 27.6							66.8 - 47.1
1.13	1.29	1.28	4.11	5.15	4.64		3.33	2.13	1.80		0.3281Q	5/26/08	
-	0.62	0.56	-	-	-						0.24Q	2/1/08	33.9 - 26.5
1.01	1.03	1.02	4.01	3.55	3.15	8.6 - 5.9	1.74	1.50	1.32	6.2	0.392U	1/29/07	34.4 - 23.9
0.09	0.19	-0.52	-0.38	0.25	0.92		0.26	0.32	0.29	1.5	0.005Q	4/18/08	20.0 - 14.2
-	-	-	0.67	0.70	0.53	68.2 - 49.3							45.7 - 33.1
0.95	0.91	0.96	3.84	2.55	3.12	16.8 - 10.5	0.58	0.54	0.50	1.1	0.15Q	2/1/08	64.6 - 40.2
-0.03	0.26	0.07	2.17	2.03	1.93	14.9 - 9.4	0.60	0.30	-	2.4	0.15Q	3/31/08	32.4 - 20.3
0.50	0.49	0.47	1.76	1.39	1.24		0.55	0.48	0.42		0.14Q	3/10/08	
0.49	0.41	0.36	1.18	-3.18	2.03	45.3 - 27.5							53.5 - 32.4
0.32	0.22	0.01	0.60	1.40	0.55	55.8 - 48.0							33.5 - 28.8
-0.18	0.45	0.39	-	1.77	0.75		-	0.22	0.22		0.15S	12/17/07	25.4 - 18.2

SYMBOL	COMPANY	NATURE OF BUSINESS	FISCAL YEAR-END	TOTAL REV. $MILL	NET INCOME $MILL	TOTAL ASSETS $MILL	NET STK EQUITY $MILL	NO OF INST	INST. HOLDINGS (SHARES)
BAS	Basic Energy Services Inc (New)	Oil and Gas	12/31/07	877.2	87.7	1143.6	524.8	-	
BAX	Baxter International Inc.	Medical Instruments & Equipment	12/31/07	11263.0	1707.0	15294.0	6916.0	594	489551170
BTE	Baytex Energy Trust	Oil and Gas	12/31/06	471.4	147.1	1079.6	459.1	3	205285
BBT	BB&T Corp.	Commercial Banking	12/31/07	10668.0	1734.0	132618.0	12632.0	412	156794525
BFR	BBVA Banco Frances S.A. (Argenti	Commercial Banking	12/31/07	3087.0	235.0	22023.0	2056.8	22	1933667
BSC	Bear Stearns Cos., Inc. (The)	Finance Intermediaries & Services	11/30/07	16151.0	233.0	395362.0	11793.0	4	619910
BE	Bearingpoint Inc	Accounting & Management Consulti	12/31/07	3455.6	-362.7	1981.4	-469.3	143	202664262
BZH	Beazer Homes USA, Inc. (United St	Building & General Construction	9/30/06	5462.0	388.8	4559.4	1701.9	173	44749675
BEC	Beckman Coulter, Inc.	Instruments and Related Products	12/31/07	2761.3	211.3	3594.3	1441.7	313	51823813
BDX	Becton, Dickinson and Co.	Medical Instruments & Equipment	9/30/07	6359.7	890.0	7329.4	4362.0	523	212973407
BDC	Belden Inc	Metal Works	12/31/06	1495.8	65.9	1356.0	843.9	145	48211105
BLC	Belo Corp.	Media	12/31/07	1515.6	-262.8	3179.1	1251.7	180	75715252
BMS	Bemis Co Inc	Paper Products	12/31/07	3649.3	181.6	3191.4	1562.3	-	
BHE	Benchmark Electronics, Inc.	Electrical	12/31/07	2915.9	93.3	1762.8	1288.5	179	43536210
BNT	Bentley Pharmaceuticals Inc (New)	Pharmaceuticals	12/31/07	124.7	2.7	173.1	116.0	40	8487156
BER	Berkley (W. R.) Corp.	Insurance	12/31/07	5553.6	743.6	16832.2	3569.8	252	63144663
BRK B	Berkshire Hathaway Inc.	Insurance	12/31/07	118245.0	13213.0	273160.0	120733.0	638	3848361
BRY	Berry Petroleum Co	Oil and Gas	12/31/07	583.5	129.9	1452.1	460.0	105	10156734
BBY	Best Buy Inc	Retail - Appliances and Electrical	3/3/07	35934.0	1377.0	13570.0	6201.0	526	233630124
BHP	BHP Billiton Ltd.	Oil and Gas						206	67345297
BBL	BHP Billiton Plc	Non-Precious Metals	6/30/05	26722.0	6396.0	41843.0	17916.0	17	3087475
BIG	Big Lots, Inc.	Retail - General	2/2/08	4656.3	158.5	1443.8	638.5	159	122193365
BMR	Biomed Realty Trust Inc	Property, Real Estate & Developmen	12/31/07	266.1	72.5	3057.3	1386.9	80	28259379
BVF	Biovail Corp (Canada)	Pharmaceuticals	12/31/06	1067.7	211.6	2192.4	1302.3	114	56495567
BJS	BJ Services Co.	Oil and Gas	9/30/07	4802.4	753.6	4715.2	2851.4	370	147026460
BJ	BJ's Wholesale Club Inc	Retail - General	2/2/08	9005.0	122.9	2046.5	980.5	220	71111884
BDK	Black & Decker Corp.	Industrial Machinery and Equipment	12/31/07	6563.2	518.1	5410.9	1458.7	354	68293922
BKH	Black Hills Corporation	Electricity	12/31/07	695.9	98.8	2472.9	969.9	141	18295832
APX	BlackRock Apex Municipal Fund, In	Trusts & Holding Entities	6/30/07	13.0	11.4	200.3	196.8	-	
BFC	BlackRock California Insured Munici	Trusts & Holding Entities						16	972000
BCK	Blackrock California Insured Munici	Trusts & Holding Entities	8/31/07		5.2	124.5	77.3	4	7979
BJZ	Blackrock California Municipal 2018	Trusts & Holding Entities	12/31/07	7.7	6.8	151.2	95.3	2	5000
BZA	Blackrock California Municipal Bond	Trusts & Holding Entities	8/31/07		3.8	82.4	52.0	3	1491
BFZ	BlackRock California Municipal Inco	Trusts & Holding Entities	10/31/06		16.8	380.0	236.6	7	356799
CII	Blackrock Capital & Income Strategi	Trusts & Holding Entities	12/31/07	9.4	3.8	265.7	260.4	-	
BHK	Blackrock Core Bond Trust	Trusts & Holding Entities						20	615467
CYE	BlackRock Corporate High Yield Fu	Trusts & Holding Entities	5/31/07	37.5	26.6	471.1	335.5	-	
COY	BlackRock Corporate High Yield Fu	Trusts & Holding Entities	5/31/07	35.0	25.2	445.6	313.8	-	
HYV	BlackRock Corporate High Yield Fu	Trusts & Holding Entities	8/31/07		39.7	586.0	455.7	-	
HYT	BlackRock Corporate High Yield Fu	Trusts & Holding Entities	8/31/07		41.5	625.9	487.3	-	
BHL	Blackrock Defined Opportunity Cred	Trusts & Holding Entities	11/13/07		-0.0	0.1	0.1	-	
DVF	BlackRock Diversified Income Strat	Trusts & Holding Entities	8/31/07		22.1	287.8	212.8	-	
BDV	BlackRock Dividend Achievers Trus	Trusts & Holding Entities						20	968561
BQR	Blackrock Ecosolutions Investment	Trusts & Holding Entities	7/16/07		-0.0		0.1	-	
BDJ	Blackrock Enhanced Dividend Achie	Trusts & Holding Entities	10/31/06		27.1	1103.7	1033.1	-	
ECV	BlackRock Enhanced Equity Yield &	Trusts & Holding Entities						-	
EEF	BlackRock Enhanced Equity Yield F	Trusts & Holding Entities						-	
EGF	BlackRock Enhanced Government	Trusts & Holding Entities						-	
FRB	BlackRock Floating Rate Income Str	Trusts & Holding Entities	2/28/07		16.2	261.2	202.4	-	
FRA	BlackRock Floating Rate Income Str	Trusts & Holding Entities	8/31/07		28.1	448.3	334.1	-	
BRF	BlackRock Florida Insured Municipa	Trusts & Holding Entities	12/31/07	5.5	4.7	129.8	129.5	13	395271
BAF	Blackrock Florida Insured Municipal	Trusts & Holding Entities	8/31/07		8.9	206.4	128.2	7	64277
BFO	BlackRock Florida Municipal 2020 T	Trusts & Holding Entities	12/31/07	6.5	5.5	131.0	81.9	4	31847
BIE	Blackrock Florida Municipal Bond Tr	Trusts & Holding Entities	8/31/07		3.8	82.5	51.4	3	54897
BBF	Blackrock Florida Municipal Incom	Trusts & Holding Entities	10/31/06		7.4	165.3	104.5	5	28716
BGR	BlackRock Global Energy & Resour	Trusts & Holding Entities	10/31/06		22.0	888.7	883.1	11	293849
BFD	BlackRock Global Equity Income Tr	Trusts & Holding Entities	2/22/07		-0.0	0.1	0.1	-	
BGT	Blackrock Global Floating Rate Inco	Trusts & Holding Entities	12/31/07	53.8	47.9	683.8	417.1	16	731744
BOE	BlackRock Global Opportunities Eq	Trusts & Holding Entities	10/31/06		7.7	351.5	331.7	-	
BME	BlackRock Health Sciences Trust	Trusts & Holding Entities	10/31/06		-0.2	216.0	208.2	1	13000
HIS	BlackRock High Income Shares	Trusts & Holding Entities	12/31/07	18.0	12.9	183.5	135.1	2	41950
BHY	Blackrock High Yield Trust	Trusts & Holding Entities						8	100588
BNA	BlackRock Income Opportunity Trus	Trusts & Holding Entities	10/31/06		19.5	463.2	384.9	20	4703479
BKT	Blackrock Income Trust Inc. (The)	Trusts & Holding Entities	10/31/06		20.4	585.9	414.5	28	772862
BRM	Blackrock Insured Municipal 2008	Trusts & Holding Entities	12/31/07	20.5	18.0	414.0	413.2	25	1995210
BYM	Blackrock Insured Municipal Income	Trusts & Holding Entities	8/31/07		27.1	639.8	388.3	14	186409
BMT	Blackrock Insured Municipal Term	Trusts & Holding Entities	12/31/07	15.8	13.6	333.5	267.9	27	1090685
BGY	BlackRock International Growth & In	Trusts & Holding Entities	4/18/07		-0.0		0.1	-	
BKN	Blackrock Investment Quality Muni	Trusts & Holding Entities	10/31/06		18.4	418.7	263.9	21	860738
BLW	Blackrock Limited Duration Income	Trusts & Holding Entities						16	1365223
BTA	BlackRock Long-Term Municipal Ad	Trusts & Holding Entities	10/31/06		6.0	378.9	198.1	-	
MUI	BlackRock Muni Intermediate Durati	Trusts & Holding Entities	5/31/07	45.2	39.0	945.4	574.2	-	
MNE	BlackRock Muni New York Intermed	Trusts & Holding Entities	5/31/07	4.5	3.8	94.5	62.7	-	
MUA	BlackRock MuniAssets Fund, Inc.	Trusts & Holding Entities	5/31/07	18.9	17.0	292.2	287.4	-	
BPK	Blackrock Municipal 2018 Term Tru	Trusts & Holding Entities	12/31/07	20.9	18.7	381.1	239.6	7	97424
BKK	Blackrock Municipal 2020 Term Tr	Trusts & Holding Entities	12/31/07	25.8	22.6	480.0	299.4	8	145612
BBK	Blackrock Municipal Bond Trust	Trusts & Holding Entities	8/31/07		12.3	252.1	159.9	9	128113
BFK	BlackRock Municipal Income Trust	Trusts & Holding Entities	10/31/06		50.1	1068.8	674.1	15	349527
MEN	BlackRock MuniEnhanced Fund Inc	Trusts & Holding Entities						-	
MUC	BlackRock MuniHoldings California	Trusts & Holding Entities	6/30/07	50.9	41.2	1064.2	592.1	-	

EARNINGS PER SHARE — QUARTERLY			ANNUAL			P/E RATIO		DIVIDENDS PER SHARE			AV. YLD %	DIV. DECLARED		PRICE RANGE 2007
1st	2nd	3rd	2007	2006	2005			2007	2006	2005		AMOUNT	PAYABLE	
0.56	0.52	0.59	2.13	2.56	1.35	-					-			-
0.61	0.65	0.61	2.61	2.13	1.52	13.3 -	11.0	0.72	0.58	0.58	2.3	0.2175Q	4/1/08	34.6 - 28.8
-	-	-	-	1.91	1.15	-		-	2.16	1.80	-	0.18M	2/15/08	11.4 - 7.4
0.77	0.83	0.80	3.14	2.81	3.00	13.8 -	10.6	1.76	1.60	1.46	4.6	0.46Q	5/1/08	43.3 - 33.3
														10.2 - 4.7
3.82	2.52	1.16	1.52	14.27	10.31	35.2 -	30.4	1.28	1.12	1.00	2.5	0.6863Q	4/15/08	53.5 - 46.3
-0.29	-0.30	-0.32	-1.68	-1.01	-3.59									11.3 - 7.3
-1.54	-1.12	-	-	8.89	5.87			-	0.40	0.33	-	0.1Q	9/21/07	49.3 - 29.4
0.59	1.09	0.93	3.30	2.92	2.32	20.5 -	15.1	0.64	0.60	0.56	1.1	0.17Q	3/7/08	67.7 - 50.0
1.07	-	-	3.49	2.93	2.77	16.6 -	11.8	0.98	0.86	0.72	2.0	0.285Q	3/31/08	57.8 - 41.0
0.44	0.60	0.99	-	1.37	0.96	-		-	0.20	0.20	-	0.05Q	4/2/08	24.1 - 15.6
0.15	0.35	0.18	-2.57	1.26	1.12	-		0.50	0.45	0.40	2.4	0.075Q	6/6/08	23.6 - 17.0
0.45	0.47	0.40	1.74	1.65	1.51	-		0.84	0.76	0.72	-	0.22Q	3/3/08	-
0.34	0.35	0.30	1.28	1.71	1.25	20.6 -	12.7	-						26.4 - 16.2
0.10	0.03	-0.03	0.12	0.04	0.48	120.8 -	70.8	-						14.5 - 8.5
0.93	0.93	0.93	3.78	3.46	2.72	5.5 -	4.1	0.20	0.16	0.13	1.1	-		21.0 - 15.7
0.42	1.16	0.60	2.89	2.41	2.50	8.6 -	3.2	0.30	0.30	0.30	1.9	0.075Q	3/28/08	24.8 - 9.3
0.39	0.55	0.53	2.79	2.27	1.96	14.8 -	10.6	0.36	0.31	0.28	1.0	0.13Q	1/30/08	41.3 - 29.5
														24.3 - 15.7
-	-	-	2.29	1.72	1.04	10.3 -	6.7	-						23.7 - 15.3
0.26	0.22	0.14	1.11	-0.09	0.21	14.0 -	10.2	-						15.5 - 11.3
0.25	0.22	0.19	0.85	0.62	0.44	26.9 -	18.7	1.24	1.16	1.08	6.7	0.4609Q	1/15/08	22.8 - 15.9
0.58	0.42	0.41	-	1.32	1.48	-		-	0.50	0.50	-	0.375Q	11/30/07	25.5 - 14.7
0.58	-	-	2.55	2.52	1.38	10.6 -	6.9	0.20	0.20	0.17	0.9	0.05Q	4/15/08	27.0 - 17.6
0.01	0.66	0.06	1.00	1.07	1.00	20.7 -	10.0	-						31.0 - 20.3
1.61	1.75	1.59	7.85	6.55	6.69	11.4 -	6.1	1.68	1.52	1.12	2.5	0.42Q	3/28/08	89.2 - 48.3
0.91	0.66	0.46	2.64	2.42	1.00	12.2 -	10.1	1.37	1.32	1.28	4.6	0.35Q	3/1/08	32.3 - 26.7
-	-	-	0.58	0.58	0.58	15.6 -	13.7	0.15	0.58	0.58	1.7	0.0465M	4/1/08	9.1 - 8.0
-	-	-	-	-	0.90	-		-	-	0.78	-	0.0525Q	2/1/08	17.4 - 15.6
-	-	-	0.99	0.98	0.99	14.9 -	12.5	0.70	0.71	0.90	5.1	0.058M	3/3/08	14.8 - 12.4
-	-	-	1.04	1.02	0.97	14.1 -	12.4	0.75	0.73	0.73	5.4	0.0612M	4/1/08	14.6 - 12.9
-	-	-	1.13	1.14	1.13	13.0 -	11.0	0.94	0.96	0.96	6.8	0.077M	3/3/08	14.6 - 12.4
-	-	-	-	1.11	1.12	-		-	0.91	0.91	-	0.0761M	3/3/08	14.2 - 12.1
-	-	-	0.31	0.37	0.46	64.5 -	52.9	-	0.90	1.20	-	0.485Q	3/31/08	20.0 - 16.4
-	-	-	-	-	0.78	-		-	-	1.36	-	0.062M	1/9/08	14.5 - 12.6
-	-	-	0.71	0.72	0.85	13.1 -	10.4	-				0.06M	3/31/08	9.3 - 7.4
-	-	-	0.73	0.74	0.87	14.1 -	10.4	0.22	0.77	0.89	2.4	0.061M	3/31/08	10.3 - 7.6
-	-	-	1.22	1.22	1.47	13.6 -	11.3	0.10	1.81	2.62	0.7	0.1M	12/18/07	16.6 - 13.8
-	-	-	1.18	1.16	1.37	13.1 -	10.9	-				0.1M	12/18/07	15.4 - 12.9
-	-	-	-	-	-	-		-				0.1125M	3/31/08	
-	-	-	1.83	1.77	0.84	-		0.15	1.70	0.75	-	0.15M	12/18/07	
-	-	-	-	0.42	0.43	-		-	0.00	0.00	-	0.225Q	12/31/07	15.2 - 12.7
-	-	-	-	-	-	-		-				0.4Q	3/31/08	
-	-	-	-	0.37	0.08	-		-	1.22	0.10	-	0.1019M	1/9/08	
-	-	-	-	0.27	0.19	-		-	1.02	1.02	-	1.025S	12/31/07	
-	-	-	-	0.27	0.23	-		-	1.67	1.00	-	0.5Q	5/31/08	
-	-	-	-	0.78	0.13	-		-	-	-	-	0.105M	3/31/08	
-	-	-	1.55	1.33	0.58	13.0 -	11.8	0.78	1.37	0.48	4.0	0.1234M	12/10/07	20.2 - 10.2
-	-	-	1.54	1.40	1.23	12.9 -	11.9	0.12	1.37	1.12	0.6	0.1248M	12/18/07	19.9 - 18.4
-	-	-	0.54	0.72	0.78	31.0 -	27.9	0.47	0.50	0.76	3.0	0.02M	4/1/08	16.7 - 15.1
-	-	-	1.01	1.02	1.02	15.0 -	12.3	0.70	0.71	0.90	5.0	0.05M	3/3/08	15.1 - 12.4
-	-	-	0.99	0.98	0.98	15.7 -	13.1	0.65	0.66	0.81	4.4	0.051M	4/1/08	15.5 - 13.0
-	-	-	1.15	1.17	1.16	13.2 -	11.2	0.93	0.93	0.93	6.5	0.0778M	3/3/08	15.2 - 12.9
-	-	-	1.11	1.11	-			-	0.90	0.90	-	0.0729M	3/3/08	14.9 - 12.5
-	-	-	-	0.75	0.56	-		-	2.84	1.13	-	1.9105Q	12/31/07	25.0 - 25.0
-	-	-	-	-	-	-		-				0.475Q	11/30/07	
-	-	-	2.03	1.99	1.64	9.9 -	9.0	1.63	1.46	1.22	8.4	0.125M	3/31/08	20.0 - 18.3
-	-	-	-	0.50	0.37	-		-	2.27	0.57	-	0.8028Q	12/31/07	
-	-	-	-	-0.01	-0.03	-		-	1.92	0.77	-	0.5346Q	12/31/07	
-	-	-	0.24	0.22	0.24	12.8 -	10.3	0.24	0.23	0.27	8.6	0.0182M	3/31/08	3.1 - 2.5
-	-	-	-	-	0.68	-		-	-	0.79	-	0.051M	1/9/08	11.8 - 9.1
-	-	-	-	0.57	0.72	-		-	0.97	1.09	-	0.051M	1/9/08	11.6 - 10.0
-	-	-	-	0.32	0.44	-		-	0.43	0.56	-	0.024M	1/9/08	8.0 - 6.4
-	-	-	0.66	0.88	0.91	26.9 -	24.0	0.76	0.81	0.80	4.6	0.0475M	4/1/08	17.8 - 15.9
-	-	-	1.03	1.03	1.03	14.5 -	12.0	0.78	0.75	0.94	5.6	0.061M	12/31/07	14.9 - 12.4
-	-	-	0.53	0.59	0.59	22.2 -	19.8	0.37	0.46	0.59	3.3	0.0304M	4/1/08	11.7 - 10.5
-	-	-	-	-	-	-		-				0.1517M	1/9/08	
-	-	-	-	1.10	1.14	-		-	1.06	0.96	-	0.08M	2/1/08	15.4 - 13.1
-	-	-	-	-	1.46	-		-	-	1.48	-	0.125M	1/9/08	20.4 - 17.9
-	-	-	-	0.45	-			-				0.055M	2/1/08	
-	-	-	1.03	1.04	1.02	14.5 -	12.1	0.25	1.07	1.05	1.8	0.061M	4/1/08	14.9 - 12.5
-	-	-	0.90	0.87	0.85	16.7 -	13.5	0.22	0.69	0.72	1.6	0.053M	4/1/08	15.1 - 12.1
-	-	-	0.82	0.81	0.81	15.4 -	13.0	0.28	0.83	0.81	2.4	0.0675M	4/1/08	12.6 - 10.7
-	-	-	1.17	1.15	1.19	13.0 -	11.6	0.93	0.91	0.84	6.3	0.0755M	4/1/08	15.2 - 13.6
-	-	-	1.12	1.10	1.11	13.8 -	12.0	0.80	0.80	0.87	5.4	0.0623M	4/1/08	15.5 - 13.4
-	-	-	1.02	1.21	1.21	15.1 -	12.8	1.03	1.13	1.04	7.1	0.0765M	3/3/08	15.4 - 13.1
-	-	-	-	1.14	1.18	-		-	0.99	0.98	-	0.0775M	3/3/08	14.8 - 12.4
-	-	-	-	-	-	-		-				0.043M	3/3/08	11.5 - 9.9
-	-	-	1.01	1.05	-	14.9 -	12.5	0.20	0.91	-	1.4	0.0555M	4/1/08	15.0 - 12.7

SYMBOL	COMPANY	NATURE OF BUSINESS	FISCAL YEAR-END	TOTAL REV. $MILL	NET INCOME $MILL	TOTAL ASSETS $MILL	NET STK EQUITY $MILL	NO OF INST	INST. HOLDINGS (SHARES)
MFL	BlackRock MuniHoldings Florida Ins	Trusts & Holding Entities	-	-	-	-	-	-	-
MUH	BlackRock MuniHoldings Fund II Inc	Trusts & Holding Entities	-	-	-	-	-	-	-
MHD	BlackRock MuniHoldings Fund Inc	Trusts & Holding Entities	4/30/07	-	16.2	387.3	229.4	-	-
MUS	BlackRock MuniHoldings Insured F	Trusts & Holding Entities	4/30/07	-	12.0	335.5	181.6	-	-
MUE	BlackRock Muniholdings Insured Fu	Trusts & Holding Entities	9/30/06	-	11.6	252.8	165.6	-	-
MUJ	BlackRock MuniHoldings New Jerse	Trusts & Holding Entities	-	-	-	-	-	-	-
MHN	BlackRock MuniHoldings New York	Trusts & Holding Entities	-	-	-	-	-	-	-
MVT	BlackRock MuniVest Fund II Inc	Trusts & Holding Entities	10/30/06	-	23.4	535.0	310.0	-	-
MYC	BlackRock MuniYield California Fun	Trusts & Holding Entities	10/31/06	-	20.5	563.2	321.7	-	-
MCA	BlackRock MuniYield California Insu	Trusts & Holding Entities	10/31/06	-	32.9	898.6	518.7	-	-
MYF	BlackRock MuniYield Florida Fund	Trusts & Holding Entities	10/31/06	-	13.4	338.5	204.9	-	-
MFT	BlackRock MuniYield Florida Insure	Trusts & Holding Entities	10/31/06	-	8.2	212.0	126.0	-	-
MYD	BlackRock MuniYield Fund Inc	Trusts & Holding Entities	10/31/06	-	48.1	1052.9	672.4	-	-
MYI	BlackRock MuniYield Insured Fund,	Trusts & Holding Entities	10/31/06	-	65.9	1821.7	1030.0	-	-
MYM	BlackRock MuniYield Michigan Insu	Trusts & Holding Entities	10/31/06	-	11.7	302.9	176.2	-	-
MIY	BlackRock MuniYield Michigan Insu	Trusts & Holding Entities	10/31/06	-	18.9	491.0	281.3	-	-
MJI	BlackRock MuniYield New Jersey In	Trusts & Holding Entities	10/31/06	-	8.6	222.0	135.8	-	-
MYN	BlackRock MuniYield New York Ins	Trusts & Holding Entities	10/31/06	-	36.3	960.7	568.0	-	-
MYJ	BlackRock MuniYield NJ Fund Inc	Trusts & Holding Entities	11/30/07	17.2	14.4	340.2	215.6	-	-
MPA	BlackRock MuniYield Pennsylvania	Trusts & Holding Entities	10/31/06	-	11.6	314.3	182.4	-	-
MQT	BlackRock MuniYield Quality Fund I	Trusts & Holding Entities	10/31/06	-	19.3	519.4	305.1	-	-
MQY	BlackRock MuniYield Quality Fund I	Trusts & Holding Entities	10/31/06	-	30.2	806.7	466.0	-	-
BNJ	Blackrock New Jersey Municipal Inc	Trusts & Holding Entities	10/31/06	-	8.7	189.5	122.0	7	82632
BLN	BlackRock New York Insured Munic	Trusts & Holding Entities	12/31/07	8.7	7.7	171.6	171.2	9	60003
BSE	Blackrock New York Insured Munici	Trusts & Holding Entities	8/31/07	-	6.4	156.3	94.3	3	37439
BLH	Blackrock New York Municipal 2018	Trusts & Holding Entities	12/31/07	4.9	4.3	89.7	58.0	1	1574
BQH	Blackrock New York Municipal Bond	Trusts & Holding Entities	8/31/07	-	3.1	66.7	42.2	5	39126
BNY	Blackrock New York Municipal Inco	Trusts & Holding Entities	10/31/06	-	14.3	312.8	199.7	7	104492
PSW	BlackRock Preferred & Corporate In	Trusts & Holding Entities	10/31/06	-	22.0	373.6	228.7	-	-
PSY	BlackRock Preferred Income Strate	Trusts & Holding Entities	10/31/06	-	82.6	1490.1	907.9	-	-
BPP	Blackrock Preferred Opportunity Tru	Trusts & Holding Entities	12/31/07	43.9	37.7	582.0	358.0	19	447352
BCF	Blackrock Real Asset Equity Trust	Finance & Investment	10/31/06	-	1.9	843.8	820.3	-	-
ARK	BlackRock Senior High Income Fun	Trusts & Holding Entities	-	-	-	-	-	-	-
BHD	Blackrock Strategic Bond Trust (Uni	Trusts & Holding Entities	-	-	-	-	-	5	47430
BDT	Blackrock Strategic Dividend Achiev	Trusts & Holding Entities	10/31/06	-	10.7	434.6	433.9	12	357646
BSD	Blackrock Strategic Municipal Trust	Trusts & Holding Entities	12/31/07	9.0	7.8	166.8	103.9	7	401722
BLK	BlackRock, Inc.	Finance Intermediaries & Services	12/31/07	4844.7	995.3	22561.5	11597.0	109	15276392
BX	Blackstone Group LP	Wealth Management	12/31/07	3050.1	1623.2	13174.2	-	-	-
HRB	Block (H & R), Inc.	Personal Services	4/30/07	4021.3	-433.7	7499.5	1414.5	387	144696540
BBI	Blockbuster, Inc.	Movies & Film	1/6/08	5542.4	-73.8	2733.6	655.7	177	124944304
BLT	Blount International, Inc. (New)	Metal Products	12/31/07	515.5	42.9	411.9	-54.1	84	43373949
BLU	Blue Chip Value Fund, Inc.	Trusts & Holding Entities	12/31/07	2.6	0.4	168.6	152.1	14	148690
BSI	Blue Square - Israel Ltd. (Israel)	Retail - General	12/31/06	6515.0	213.9	4071.7	992.9	3	229003
BXG	Bluegreen Corp. (United States)	Property, Real Estate & Developmen	12/31/07	691.5	31.9	1039.6	385.1	89	16359319
BXC	BlueLinx Holdings Inc	General Construction Supplies & Ser	12/29/07	3833.9	-27.9	883.4	154.8	40	26517812
BTH	Blyth, Inc. (United States)	Consumer Accessories	1/31/07	1220.6	-103.2	774.6	363.7	148	23716076
BMC	BMC Software, Inc.	IT & Technology	3/31/07	1580.4	215.9	3260.0	1049.1	254	182524525
BWP	Boardwalk Pipeline Partners LP	Oil and Gas	12/31/07	643.3	227.8	4157.3	-	-	-
BA	Boeing Co. (The)	Aviation	12/31/07	66387.0	4074.0	58986.0	9004.0	633	533721912
BDE	Bois D' Arc Energy Inc	Oil and Gas	12/31/07	355.5	78.7	956.6	602.5	-	-
BZ	Boise, Inc.	Miscellaneous	12/31/07	10.4	5.5	407.6	233.1	-	-
BGP	Borders Group, Inc.	Retail - Miscellaneous	2/3/07	4113.5	-151.3	2613.4	642.0	189	74078393
BWA	Borg Warner Inc	Automotive	12/31/07	5328.6	288.5	4958.5	2321.1	223	50629923
SAM	Boston Beer Co., Inc	Food	12/29/07	341.6	22.5	195.9	133.6	69	6384438
BXP	Boston Properties, Inc.	Property, Real Estate & Developmen	12/31/07	1482.3	1324.7	11192.6	3668.8	250	97442226
BSX	Boston Scientific Corp.	Medical Instruments & Equipment	12/31/07	8357.0	-495.0	31197.0	15097.0	528	450074086
BIF	Boulder Growth & Income Fund Inc.	Trusts & Holding Entities	11/30/07	5.9	3.0	161.1	135.8	8	470330
BTF	Boulder Total Return Fund Inc	Trusts & Holding Entities	11/30/07	10.4	4.3	386.0	307.9	16	1529214
BNE	Bowne & Co., Inc.	Printing	12/31/07	850.6	27.1	509.4	250.5	107	32102173
BYD	Boyd Gaming Corp.	Sporting & Recreational	12/31/07	1997.1	303.0	4487.6	1385.4	167	29655919
BP	BP p.l.c.	Oil and Gas	-	-	-	-	-	968	558745379
BPT	BP Prudhoe Bay Royalty Trust	Oil and Gas	12/31/07	177.4	175.7	7.0	6.6	71	1540483
BRC	Brady Corp.	Consumer Accessories	7/31/07	1362.6	109.4	1698.9	891.0	132	35389736
BDN	Brandywine Realty Trust	Property, Real Estate & Developmen	12/31/07	684.0	56.5	5214.1	1743.2	141	50821099
BRP	Brasil Telecom Participacoes S.A. (	Communications	12/31/07	11058.5	671.3	17429.3	5246.5	79	25537122
BTM	Brasil Telecom S.A.	Communications	12/31/07	11058.5	797.3	15575.7	5583.9	7	1460303
BAK	Braskem S A	Oil and Gas	12/31/07	17679.4	547.6	20892.0	5757.0	40	9310966
BRE	BRE Properties, Inc.	Property, Real Estate & Developmen	12/31/07	345.2	128.1	2953.7	923.2	149	37399263
BGG	Briggs & Stratton Corp.	Industrial Machinery and Equipment	7/1/07	2157.2	0.1	1887.2	846.1	223	43788487
EAT	Brinker International, Inc.	Hospitality & Tourism	6/27/07	4376.9	230.0	2318.0	805.1	239	80260229
BCO	Brinks Co (The)	Stone, Clay, Glass, and Concrete Pr	12/31/07	3219.0	137.3	2394.3	1046.3	196	44682767
BMY	Bristol-Myers Squibb Co.	Pharmaceuticals	12/31/07	19348.0	2165.0	26172.0	10562.0	2	65
BRS	Bristow Group Inc	Aviation	3/31/07	897.9	74.2	1505.8	871.7	-	-
BSY	British Sky Broadcasting Group plc (	Media	6/30/05	3842.0	578.0	2456.0	187.0	37	3050262
BR	Broadridge Financial Solutions Inc	Finance Intermediaries & Services	6/30/07	2137.9	197.1	2678.2	531.1	-	-
BKD	Brookdale Senior Living Inc	Hospitals & Health Care	12/31/07	1839.3	-162.0	4811.6	1419.5	-	-
BAM	Brookfield Asset Management Inc	Property, Real Estate & Developmen	12/31/06	3195.0	1170.0	40708.0	7739.0	-	-
BHS	Brookfield Homes Corp	Building & General Construction	12/31/07	583.4	15.6	1350.7	379.6	90	13189460
BPO	Brookfield Properties Corp.	Property, Real Estate & Developmen	12/31/06	1028.0	135.0	19314.0	3112.0	95	125143301
BRO	Brown & Brown, Inc.	Insurance	12/31/07	959.7	191.0	1960.7	1097.5	182	45053007

EARNINGS PER SHARE QUARTERLY 1st	2nd	3rd	ANNUAL 2007	2006	2005	P/E RATIO 2007	DIVIDENDS PER SHARE 2007	2006	2005	AV. YLD %	DIV. DECLARED AMOUNT	PAYABLE	PRICE RANGE 2007
-	-	-	-	-	-	-	-	-	-	-	0.0555M	3/3/08	15.6 - 13.0
-	-	-	-	1.04	1.08	-	-	0.91	1.04	-	0.063M	3/3/08	14.8 - 12.4
-	-	1.17	-	1.16	1.20	13.8 - 11.7	0.39	1.08	1.15	2.5	0.071M	3/3/08	16.2 - 13.7
-	-	0.93	-	0.97	1.01	15.6 - 13.2	0.27	0.83	0.91	2.0	0.0485M	2/1/08	14.5 - 12.3
-	-	-	-	1.04	0.97	-	-	0.75	0.88	-	0.05M	3/3/08	14.2 - 12.0
-	-	-	-	-	-	-	-	-	-	-	0.053M	3/3/08	15.2 - 13.0
-	-	-	-	-	-	-	-	-	-	-	0.0545M	3/3/08	15.2 - 12.9
-	-	-	-	1.16	1.19	-	-	0.93	1.10	-	0.071M	3/3/08	15.7 - 13.1
-	-	-	-	0.96	0.93	-	-	0.64	0.86	-	0.055M	3/3/08	15.1 - 12.9
-	-	-	-	0.96	0.95	-	-	0.74	0.88	-	0.056M	3/3/08	14.4 - 12.4
-	-	-	-	0.99	0.98	-	-	0.75	0.92	-	0.058M	3/3/08	15.0 - 12.5
-	-	-	-	0.97	0.98	-	-	0.69	0.90	-	0.0535M	3/3/08	15.4 - 12.7
-	-	-	-	1.08	1.11	-	-	0.87	0.99	-	0.068M	3/3/08	14.1 - 12.0
-	-	-	-	0.98	1.04	-	-	1.06	0.97	-	0.056M	3/3/08	15.4 - 12.9
-	-	-	-	0.97	0.99	-	-	0.71	0.91	-	0.056M	3/3/08	14.8 - 12.8
-	-	-	-	1.04	1.08	-	-	0.77	0.98	-	0.059M	3/3/08	15.6 - 13.6
-	-	-	-	0.97	0.96	-	-	0.67	0.92	-	0.054M	3/3/08	15.8 - 12.8
-	-	-	-	0.92	0.94	-	-	0.70	0.84	-	0.054M	3/3/08	14.0 - 11.9
-	-	1.01	-	1.00	1.01	15.3 - 12.8	-	0.64	0.91	-	0.058M	4/1/08	15.4 - 12.9
-	-	-	-	1.01	1.05	-	-	0.72	0.96	-	0.056M	3/3/08	16.0 - 13.3
-	-	-	-	0.86	0.89	-	-	0.65	0.85	-	0.05M	3/3/08	13.2 - 11.3
-	-	-	-	0.99	0.99	-	-	0.73	0.96	-	0.057M	3/3/08	15.3 - 12.8
-	-	-	-	1.17	1.17	-	-	0.96	0.92	-	0.0796M	3/3/08	15.1 - 12.7
-	-	0.68	-	0.85	0.90	25.5 - 22.8	0.74	0.63	0.76	4.5	0.045M	4/1/08	17.4 - 15.5
-	-	0.99	-	1.00	1.00	15.2 - 12.3	0.75	0.71	0.90	5.4	0.058M	3/3/08	15.0 - 12.2
-	-	1.18	-	1.11	1.08	12.9 - 11.7	0.80	0.73	0.73	5.5	0.0688M	4/1/08	15.2 - 13.8
-	-	1.14	-	1.13	1.13	13.0 - 11.0	0.93	0.93	0.93	6.7	0.0771M	3/3/08	14.8 - 12.6
-	-	-	-	1.13	1.14	-	-	0.90	0.90	-	0.0753M	3/3/08	14.8 - 12.4
-	-	-	-	2.14	2.16	-	-	1.55	2.00	-	0.1033M	1/0/08	24.5 - 20.6
-	-	-	-	2.03	2.09	-	-	1.48	2.00	-	0.1146M	2/29/08	24.6 - 20.8
-	-	2.05	-	2.05	2.11	12.4 - 10.4	1.77	2.00	2.35	7.3	0.125M	3/31/08	25.5 - 21.3
-	-	-	-	0.04	-	-	-	-	-	-	0.0906M	1/9/08	-
-	-	-	-	-	-	-	-	-	-	-	0.047M	12/18/07	6.7 - 5.2
-	-	-	-	-	1.10	-	-	-	1.39	-	0.077M	1/9/08	17.2 - 13.7
-	-	-	-	0.37	0.46	-	-	0.90	0.90	-	0.225Q	12/31/07	15.1 - 12.9
-	-	1.07	-	1.07	1.14	14.6 - 12.2	1.02	1.10	1.03	7.1	0.075M	4/1/08	15.6 - 13.0
1.48	1.69	1.94	7.53	3.87	3.50	10.3 - 7.2	2.68	1.68	1.20	4.1	0.78Q	3/24/08	77.5 - 54.0
-	-	-0.44	-1.29	-	-	-	-	-	-	-	0.3Q	4/11/08	-
-0.93	-1.55	-0.14	-1.33	1.47	1.89	-	-	0.53	0.48	0.43	0.1425Q	4/1/08	30.4 - 22.4
-0.26	-0.20	-0.20	-0.45	0.23	-3.20	-	-	-	0.04	-	18.75Q	2/15/08	19.1 - 6.8
0.10	0.23	0.20	0.89	0.89	2.24	20.6 - 8.7	-	-	-	-	-	-	18.3 - 7.8
-	-	0.01	0.02	0.01	-	692.0 - 570.0	0.58	0.58	0.57	9.1	0.14Q	1/11/08	6.9 - 5.7
-	-	-	4.92	2.32	-	-	-	-	-	-	-	-	13.1 - 9.3
0.17	0.13	0.45	1.02	0.96	1.49	19.7 - 6.1	-	-	-	-	-	-	20.1 - 6.3
-0.01	0.18	0.03	-0.91	0.51	1.46	-	0.50	0.50	0.50	3.7	0.125Q	12/28/07	14.5 - 13.1
0.30	0.08	0.17	-2.58	0.60	2.22	-	-	0.50	0.44	0.36	0.27S	11/15/07	35.8 - 28.5
0.28	0.39	0.45	1.03	0.47	0.34	21.0 - 13.4	-	-	-	-	-	-	21.6 - 13.8
0.61	0.35	0.35	1.87	1.85	0.35	-	1.74	-	-	-	0.46Q	2/25/08	-
1.13	1.35	1.44	5.20	2.05	3.20	10.5 - 7.0	1.40	1.20	1.00	2.9	0.4Q	3/7/00	55.0 - 30.7
0.18	0.26	0.32	1.17	0.84	-0.89	-	-	-	-	-	-	-	-
0.00	0.02	0.05	0.16	-	-	-	-	-	-	-	-	-	-
-0.61	-0.43	-2.74	-2.44	1.42	1.69	-	0.41	0.37	0.33	1.8	0.11Q	2/10/08	25.4 - 21.3
0.50	0.65	0.70	2.45	1.83	2.09	11.1 - 7.8	0.34	0.32	0.28	1.5	0.11Q	2/15/08	27.1 - 19.2
0.40	0.46	0.21	1.53	1.27	1.07	18.1 - 10.9	-	-	-	-	-	-	27.7 - 16.7
6.55	6.84	1.95	10.54	7.46	3.86	5.0 - 4.0	8.70	8.12	5.19	16.3	5.98Q	1/30/08	54.0 - 44.0
0.08	0.08	-0.18	-0.33	-2.81	0.75	-	-	-	-	-	-	-	45.8 - 32.1
-	-	-	0.25	0.40	0.04	28.5 - 22.3	1.35	0.72	-	21.3	0.115M	4/30/08	7.1 - 5.6
-	-	-	0.35	0.30	0.15	53.6 - 43.3	1.03	0.74	-	6.2	0.273M	4/30/08	18.8 - 15.1
0.03	0.49	0.03	0.89	-0.06	-0.02	19.9 - 13.6	0.22	0.22	0.22	1.5	0.055Q	2/15/08	17.7 - 12.1
2.46	0.25	0.36	3.42	1.30	1.60	12.4 - 4.6	0.58	0.53	0.46	2.2	0.15Q	3/3/08	42.3 - 15.8
-	-	-	1.08	1.09	1.06	57.1 - 43.8	-	-	-	-	-	-	61.7 - 17.3
-	-	-	-	-	-	-	8.21	8.59	7.10	23.3	0.0553Q	10/20/08	50.0 - 23.2
0.66	0.48	-	2.00	2.07	1.64	16.1 - 8.7	0.56	0.52	0.44	2.5	0.15Q	4/30/08	32.1 - 17.4
0.19	-0.01	0.00	0.55	0.03	0.62	56.0 - 44.2	1.76	1.30	1.78	6.3	0.4609Q	4/15/08	30.8 - 24.3
-	-	-	-	-	-	-	-	-	-	-	-	-	45.5 - 25.7
-	-	-	-	-	-	-	-	-	-	-	-	-	19.2 - 8.5
-	-	-	-	-	-	-	-	-	-	-	-	-	25.5 - 6.3
0.23	0.29	0.99	2.11	1.96	1.22	20.1 - 14.6	2.15	2.05	2.00	6.0	0.4219Q	3/31/08	42.3 - 30.8
-0.41	0.11	-	0.00	1.98	2.63	-	0.88	0.88	0.68	2.3	0.22Q	4/1/08	44.2 - 31.7
0.34	0.52	-	1.85	1.62	1.15	21.4 - 15.9	0.34	0.20	-	1.0	0.11Q	3/26/08	39.5 - 29.5
0.61	0.60	0.55	2.92	11.64	2.50	13.7 - 7.9	0.36	0.21	0.10	1.2	0.1Q	3/3/08	39.9 - 22.9
0.35	0.36	0.43	1.09	0.81	1.52	481.7 - 445.0	1.12	1.12	1.12	0.2	0.31Q	5/1/08	525.0 - 485.0
0.75	1.12	0.66	2.74	2.45	2.21	13.9 - 7.5	-	-	-	-	0.6875Q	3/17/08	38.0 - 20.5
-	-	-	0.28	0.30	0.30	211.6 - 120.6	-	-	-	-	-	-	59.2 - 33.8
0.26	0.21	-	1.42	-	-	-	-	-	-	-	0.06Q	4/1/08	-
-0.35	-0.18	-0.58	-1.60	-1.34	-0.41	-	1.95	1.55	-	-	0.5Q	1/14/08	-
0.31	0.24	-	1.95	2.72	-	-	-	0.15	0.59	-	0.1213M	2/12/08	17.2 - 9.0
1.07	0.35	0.06	0.58	5.45	7.04	64.7 - 42.0	0.40	0.40	0.32	1.4	0.2S	6/30/08	37.5 - 24.4
0.13	0.20	-	-	0.37	0.46	-	-	0.50	0.43	-	0.325Q	12/31/07	16.9 - 12.0
0.42	0.37	0.33	1.35	1.22	1.08	17.3 - 11.9	0.25	0.21	0.17	1.2	0.07Q	2/20/08	23.3 - 16.0

SYMBOL	COMPANY	NATURE OF BUSINESS	FISCAL YEAR-END	TOTAL REV. $MILL	NET INCOME $MILL	TOTAL ASSETS $MILL	NET STK EQUITY $MILL	NO OF INST	INST. HOLDINGS (SHARES)
BWS	Brown Shoe Co., Inc.	Leather and Leather Products	2/2/08	2359.9	60.4	1099.8	558.6	117	14539879
BF B	Brown-Forman Corp.	Food	4/30/07	2218.0	389.0	3551.0	1573.0	219	49445659
BRT	BRT Realty Trust	Property, Real Estate & Developmen	9/30/07	42.9	35.1	328.1	235.2	15	256979
BC	Brunswick Corp.	Industrial Machinery and Equipment	12/31/07	5671.2	111.6	4365.6	1892.9	281	77817246
BW	Brush Engineered Materials Inc (Hol	Metal Works	12/31/07	955.7	53.3	550.6	353.7	92	15309131
BT	BT Group Plc	Communications	3/31/05	18429.0	1829.0	27533.0	95.0	82	25294921
BGH	Buckeye GP Holdings LP	Misc. Transportation Services	12/31/07	-	22.9	-	-	-	-
BPL	Buckeye Partners, L.P.	Oil and Gas	12/31/07	519.3	155.4	2133.7	-	130	4872658
BKI	Buckeye Technologies Inc.	Paper Products	6/30/07	769.3	30.1	951.8	347.2	101	28588283
BKE	Buckle, Inc. (The)	Retail - Apparel and Accessory Store	2/3/07	530.1	55.7	368.2	286.6	59	5944398
BBW	Build-A-Bear Workshop Inc	Retail - Sporting, Toys & Hobby	12/29/07	474.4	22.5	339.5	193.6	75	10101514
BLG	Building Materials Holding Corp	Retail - Hardware	12/31/07	2285.0	-312.7	874.8	253.7	131	10977060
BG	Bunge Ltd.	Food	12/31/06	26274.0	521.0	14347.0	5668.0	203	59875384
BKC	Burger King Holdings Inc	Hospitality & Tourism	6/30/07	2234.0	148.0	2517.0	716.0	-	-
BNI	Burlington Northern Santa Fe Corp.	Rail Transport	12/31/07	15802.0	1829.0	33583.0	11144.0	530	283359161
BWY	Bway Holding Co	Metal Products							
CHP	C&D Technologies Inc.	Electrical	1/31/07	524.6	-46.1	400.2	83.9	108	23955133
CA	CA Inc	IT & Technology	3/31/07	3943.0	118.0	10585.0	3690.0	-	-
CAB	Cabelas Inc	Retail - Sporting, Toys & Hobby	12/29/07	2349.6	87.9	2212.8	828.6	81	16072167
CVC	Cablevision Systems Corp.	Media	12/31/07	6484.5	218.5	9140.6	-5098.8	240	194841325
CBT	Cabot Corp.	Chemicals	9/30/07	2616.0	129.0	2636.0	1194.0	200	49030379
COG	Cabot Oil & Gas Corp.	Oil and Gas	12/31/07	732.2	167.4	2208.6	1070.3	146	45720427
CAI	Caci International Inc.	IT & Technology	6/30/07	1938.0	78.5	1791.9	813.8	185	26764625
CSG	Cadbury Schweppes PLC (United K	Food	1/2/05	6085.0	525.0	9880.0	2300.0	166	60804655
CGT	CAE Inc.	Electrical	3/31/07	1250.7	127.4	1956.2	829.9	54	86678255
CAP	CAI International Inc	Misc. Transportation Services	12/31/07	64.9	19.2	359.1	131.1	-	-
DVR	Cal Dive International Inc	Oil and Gas	12/31/07	623.6	105.6	1274.1	587.9	-	-
CHY	Calamos Convertible & High Incom	Trusts & Holding Entities	10/31/06	-	85.4	1620.1	1030.7	24	1163510
CHI	Calamos Convertible Opportunities	Trusts & Holding Entities	10/31/06	-	70.1	1311.1	772.0	31	1455575
CHW	Calamos Global Dynamic Income F	Trusts & Holding Entities		-		-	-	-	-
CGO	Calamos Global Total Return Fund	Trusts & Holding Entities	10/31/06	-	6.9	204.3	130.6	-	-
CSQ	Calamos Strategic Total Return Fun	Trusts & Holding Entities	10/31/06	-	137.6	4044.0	2427.6	32	3571984
CCC	Calgon Carbon Corp.	Chemicals	12/31/07	351.1	15.3	348.1	172.2	77	26938130
CWT	California Water Service Group (DE	Water Utilities	12/31/07	367.1	31.2	1184.5	389.2	81	4586514
ELY	Callaway Golf Co. (DE)	Consumer Accessories	12/31/07	1124.6	54.6	857.0	568.2	150	58657491
CPE	Callon Petroleum Co. (DE)	Oil and Gas	12/31/07	170.8	15.2	792.5	287.1	76	10705890
CBM	Cambrex Corp (United States)	Pharmaceuticals	12/31/07	252.5	209.2	373.5	102.1	114	23347354
CPT	Camden Property Trust	Property, Real Estate & Development	12/31/07	634.1	148.5	4890.8	1531.3	162	40677825
CCJ	Cameco Corp.	Mining	12/31/07	2309.7	416.1	5371.4	2743.9	163	93248396
CAM	Cameron International Corp	Oil and Gas	12/31/07	4666.4	500.9	4730.8	2095.0	-	-
CPB	Campbell Soup Co.	Food	7/29/07	7867.0	854.0	6445.0	1295.0	310	164726332
CM	Canadian Imperial Bank of Commer	Commercial Banking	10/31/07	23289.0	3296.0	342178.0	13489.0	-	-
CNI	Canadian National Railway Co.	Rail Transport	12/31/07	7897.0	2158.0	23460.0	10177.0	194	161492249
CNQ	Canadian Natural Resources Ltd.	Oil and Gas	12/31/07	11152.0	2608.0	36114.0	13321.0	172	287798324
CP	Canadian Pacific Railway Ltd.	Rail Transport	12/31/06	4583.2	796.3	11415.9	4856.5	143	56165215
CAJ	Canon, Inc.	Office Equipment Supplies	12/31/07	4481346.0	488332.0	4512625.0	2922336.0	176	33641172
CMN	Cantel Medical Corp (United States)	Specialist Equipment Supplies	7/31/95	31.1	1.0	17.4	6.4	67	6871436
COF	Capital One Financial Corp	Commercial Banking	12/31/07	19132.4	1570.3	150590.4	24294.1	490	199020637
CSU	Capital Senior Living Corp. (United	Hospitals & Health Care	12/31/07	189.1	4.4	390.1	150.2	27	12235322
CT	Capital Trust, Inc. (MD)	Property, Real Estate & Development	12/31/07	102.5	84.4	3211.5	408.2	61	6618503
CSE	CapitalSource Inc	Finance Intermediaries & Services	12/31/07	1537.3	176.3	18040.3	2582.3	125	99695430
CBC	Capitol Bancorp Ltd. (United States)	Commercial Banking	12/31/07	354.8	21.9	4901.8	389.1	62	3146245
LSE	CapLease Inc	Property, Real Estate & Development	12/31/07	172.2	-2.3	2158.3	349.7	57	20454124
CMO	Capstead Mortgage Corp.	Property, Real Estate & Development	12/31/07	43.8	24.7	7208.9	560.9	52	4849958
CRR	Carbo Ceramics Inc.	Stone, Clay, Glass, and Concrete Pr	12/31/06	312.1	54.3	404.7	342.9	135	12400934
CAH	Cardinal Health, Inc.	Medical & Health Related Services	6/30/07	86852.0	1931.1	23153.8	7376.9	492	342057939
CRE	Care Investment Trust Inc	Property, Real Estate & Development	12/31/07	12.9	-1.6	328.4	293.3	-	-
CSL	Carlisle Companies Inc.	Rubber Products	12/31/07	2876.4	215.6	1988.8	1118.9	155	23640574
KMX	Carmax Inc.	Retail - Automotive	2/28/07	-7465.7	198.6	1885.6	1247.4	202	96983663
CCL	Carnival Corp.	Shipping	11/30/07	13033.0	2408.0	34181.0	19963.0	463	449989225
CUK	Carnival Plc	Hospitality & Tourism	11/30/07	13033.0	2408.0	34181.0	19963.0	25	2625192
CRS	Carpenter Technology Corp.	Metal Works	6/30/07	1944.8	227.2	2025.7	1067.7	159	19759248
CSV	Carriage Services, Inc.	Personal Services	12/31/07	167.8	8.3	610.8	106.9	31	9139933
CRI	Carter's Inc	Apparel	12/29/07	1412.2	-70.6	974.7	382.1	90	20563509
CAE	Cascade Corp.	Industrial Machinery and Equipment	1/31/07	478.8	45.5	397.4	271.6	89	8497172
CSH	Cash America International, Inc.	Retail - Miscellaneous	12/31/07	929.4	79.3	904.6	496.6	138	25224868
CAS	Castle (A.M.) & Co.	Specialist Equipment Supplies	12/31/07	1420.4	51.8	677.0	385.1	63	8684441
CAT	Caterpillar Inc.	Industrial Machinery and Equipment	12/31/07	44958.0	3541.0	56132.0	8883.0	678	492830470
CTR	Cato Corp.	Retail - Apparel and Accessory Store	2/3/07	875.9	51.4	432.3	276.8	125	27937434
CBG	CB Richard Ellis Group Inc	Property, Real Estate & Development	12/31/07	6034.2	390.5	6242.6	988.5	135	64558611
CBZ	CBIZ Inc	Miscellaneous Business Services	12/31/07	643.9	34.8	578.0	226.4	72	28917686
CBL	CBL & Associates Properties, Inc.	Property, Real Estate & Development	12/31/07	1040.6	89.1	8105.0	920.5	166	47598722
CBF	CBRE Realty Finance Inc	Property, Real Estate & Development	12/31/07	141.0	-70.8	2069.3	212.8	-	-
CBS	CBS Corp	Media	12/31/07	14072.9	1247.0	40430.2	21472.4	-	-
CDI	CDI Corp.	Human Resources Services	12/31/07	1187.3	34.2	450.1	335.0	74	10538211
CEC	CEC Entertainment, Inc.	Hospitality & Tourism	12/30/07	785.3	55.9	737.9	218.0	146	33538767
FUN	Cedar Fair, L.P.	Sporting & Recreational	12/31/07	987.0	-4.5	2418.7	-	124	11576233
CDR	Cedar Shopping Centers Inc	Property, Real Estate & Development	12/31/07	152.9	22.0	1595.0	558.2	60	12810198
CE	Celanese Corp (DE)	Chemicals	12/31/07	6444.0	426.0	8058.0	1062.0	60	39331902
CLS	Celestica, Inc.	Electrical	12/31/07	8070.4	-13.7	4470.5	2118.2	122	96434542

T12

| EARNINGS PER SHARE QUARTERLY | | | EARNINGS PER SHARE ANNUAL | | | P/E RATIO | DIVIDENDS PER SHARE | | | AV. YLD % | DIV. DECLARED | | PRICE RANGE |
1st	2nd	3rd	2007	2006	2005		2007	2006	2005		AMOUNT	PAYABLE	2007
0.22	0.22	0.61	1.51	0.97	1.02	12.3 - 7.2	0.21	0.18	0.18	1.4	0.07Q	4/1/08	18.6 - 10.8
0.77	1.04	0.94	3.14	2.60	2.52	15.9 - 13.9	2.82	1.05	0.92	6.0	0.34Q	4/1/08	50.0 - 43.5
0.28	-	-	3.33	2.52	2.08	8.8 - 5.7	2.44	2.14	1.96	11.2	0.62Q	4/3/08	29.2 - 19.1
0.50	0.63	0.02	1.24	1.41	3.90	40.2 - 25.3	0.60	0.60	0.60	1.5	0.6A	12/14/07	49.8 - 31.4
1.12	0.38	0.48	2.59	2.45	0.92	8.8 - 5.8	-	-	-	-	0.12Q	7/6/01	22.7 - 14.9
-	-	-	0.34	0.18	0.21	117.9 - 89.2	-	-	-	-	-	-	40.1 - 30.3
0.21	0.15	0.18	0.81	0.09	-	-	-	-	-	-	0.285Q	2/29/08	-
0.77	0.70	0.71	3.03	2.64	2.69	15.1 - 11.8	3.23	3.02	2.83	7.8	0.8375Q	2/29/08	45.6 - 35.8
0.34	0.35	-	0.79	0.05	0.54	16.5 - 10.3	-	-	-	-	-	-	13.0 - 8.1
0.40	0.38	0.72	1.86	1.69	1.29	11.4 - 7.8	2.56	0.41	0.29	14.1	0.25Q	1/28/08	21.3 - 14.5
0.39	0.08	0.15	1.10	1.44	1.35	32.0 - 21.4	-	-	-	-	-	-	35.1 - 23.6
-0.17	0.66	0.14	-10.86	3.45	4.41	-	0.40	0.40	0.24	3.6	0.1Q	1/11/08	19.5 - 7.5
0.05	1.30	2.70	-	4.28	4.43	-	-	0.62	0.56	-	1.2188Q	12/1/07	57.1 - 33.0
0.35	0.36	-	1.08	0.24	0.44	-	0.13	-	-	-	0.0625Q	12/27/07	-
0.96	1.20	1.48	5.10	5.10	4.01	9.5 - 5.9	1.14	0.90	0.74	3.2	0.32Q	4/1/08	48.7 - 30.1
0.10	-0.12	-0.36	-1.80	-2.39	-2.35	-	0.01	0.06	0.06	0.1	0.0138Q	5/12/06	21.3 - 13.8
0.24	0.26	0.31	0.22	0.27	0.02	143.3 - 102.8	0.16	0.12	0.08	0.6	0.04Q	3/28/08	31.5 - 22.6
0.11	0.17	0.20	1.31	1.29	1.10	22.4 - 16.0	-	-	-	-	-	-	29.4 - 21.0
-0.09	1.08	-0.27	0.74	-0.45	0.33	37.0 - 22.5	-	10.00	-	-	10.U	4/24/06	27.4 - 16.7
0.56	-	-	1.90	1.28	-0.84	21.4 - 16.0	0.72	0.64	0.64	2.0	0.18Q	3/14/08	40.7 - 30.3
0.50	0.42	0.36	1.71	3.25	1.50	9.4 - 5.6	0.11	0.08	0.07	0.9	0.03Q	2/21/08	16.1 - 9.6
0.60	0.63	-	2.51	2.72	2.79	27.4 - 14.8	-	-	-	-	-	-	68.7 - 37.1
-	-	-	0.19	0.56	0.37	198.7 - 153.4	-	-	-	-	-	-	37.8 - 29.1
0.15	-	-	0.50	0.26	-0.81	10.2 - 7.3	0.04	0.04	0.10	0.9	0.01Q	3/31/08	5.1 - 3.6
-0.19	0.23	0.32	0.85	0.36	0.44	-	-	-	-	-	-	-	-
0.36	0.14	0.45	1.24	1.91	-	-	-	-	-	-	-	-	-
-	-	-	1.34	1.49	-	-	-	1.55	1.46	-	0.1052M	1/4/08	17.2 - 14.0
-	-	-	1.50	1.65	-	-	-	2.09	2.86	-	0.0336M	1/4/08	21.9 - 16.6
-	-	-	-	-	-	-	-	-	-	-	0.11M	1/4/08	-
-	-	-	-	0.86	-	-	-	-	-	-	0.115M	1/4/08	-
-	-	-	-	0.89	0.93	-	-	1.15	0.99	-	0.0398M	1/4/08	15.2 - 12.6
0.05	0.09	0.10	0.31	0.20	-0.19	30.2 - 17.7	-	-	0.09	-	0.03Q	9/1/05	9.4 - 5.5
0.07	0.37	0.67	1.50	1.34	1.47	25.1 - 17.5	1.16	1.15	1.14	4.0	0.275Q	2/15/08	37.7 - 26.2
0.48	0.53	0.02	0.81	0.34	0.19	24.6 - 11.5	0.28	0.28	0.28	2.0	0.07Q	4/3/08	19.9 - 9.3
0.27	0.12	0.11	0.71	1.90	1.28	20.5 - 12.5	-	-	-	-	-	-	14.6 - 8.9
7.31	0.08	0.05	7.30	-1.12	-4.18	3.8 - 2.8	14.03	0.12	0.12	58.0	14.0	5/3/07	28.1 - 20.6
0.22	0.71	0.20	2.51	3.96	3.58	20.3 - 16.0	2.76	2.64	2.54	6.1	0.7Q	4/17/08	51.0 - 40.0
0.16	0.55	0.25	1.13	1.02	0.60	15.5 - 6.4	0.20	0.16	0.12	1.9	0.05Q	1/15/08	17.5 - 7.2
0.44	0.54	0.66	2.16	1.36	0.76	6.5 - 4.8	-	-	-	-	-	-	14.1 - 10.3
0.70	0.71	-	2.16	1.85	1.71	14.0 - 11.6	0.80	0.72	0.68	3.0	0.22Q	1/28/08	30.3 - 25.1
2.11	2.27	2.31	9.21	7.43	-0.46	-	3.11	2.76	2.66	-	0.2813Q	1/28/08	-
0.63	1.01	0.96	4.25	3.91	2.77	7.2 - 4.3	0.84	0.65	0.50	3.7	0.23Q	3/31/08	30.7 - 18.4
0.50	1.56	1.30	4.84	4.70	1.95	4.5 - 2.5	0.34	0.30	0.24	2.1	0.085Q	1/1/08	22.0 - 12.1
0.81	1.09	1.81	5.02	3.39	-	-	-	0.75	0.58	-	0.225Q	1/28/08	34.4 - 21.0
-	-	-	377.53	341.84	432.55	0.1 - 0.1	-	-	-	-	-	-	36.2 - 29.9
0.12	0.13	-	0.52	1.46	0.96	48.3 - 19.7	-	-	-	-	-	-	25.1 - 10.2
1.60	1.00	-0.21	0.97	7.02	6.73	21.2 - 15.2	0.11	0.11	0.11	0.2	0.375Q	2/20/08	64.2 - 60.2
0.03	0.03	0.05	0.16	-0.10	-0.21	45.0 - 23.2	-	-	-	-	-	-	7.2 - 3.7
0.84	1.43	0.87	4.77	0.40	2.00	7.2 - 4.7	5.10	3.45	2.45	19.3	0.80	4/15/08	34.2 - 22.4
0.43	0.45	0.15	0.91	1.65	1.33	28.3 - 21.1	2.38	2.02	2.50	10.7	0.6Q	3/31/08	25.8 - 19.2
0.36	0.37	0.35	1.27	2.57	2.34	28.0 - 19.0	1.00	0.95	0.72	3.5	0.25Q	3/3/08	35.8 - 24.1
0.00	-0.10	0.00	-0.13	0.14	0.16	-	0.40	0.80	0.74	3.7	0.5078Q	1/15/08	13.4 - 9.1
0.06	0.04	-0.43	0.19	-0.87	1.96	98.1 - 54.8	0.34	0.08	0.32	2.4	0.52Q	4/21/08	18.6 - 10.4
0.64	0.50	0.37	-	2.23	1.93	-	-	0.44	0.55	-	0.14Q	2/15/08	61.8 - 00.5
0.82	0.89	-	4.77	2.33	2.41	15.9 - 7.9	0.39	0.27	0.15	0.7	0.12Q	4/15/08	76.0 - 37.6
-0.43	0.18	-	-0.07	-	-	-	-	-	-	-	0.17U	11/30/07	-
0.90	0.96	1.01	0.11	0.40	1.71	3.7 - 6.0	0.56	0.52	0.48	1.9	0.145Q	3/1/08	33.5 - 27.4
0.30	0.29	0.14	0.92	0.69	0.54	19.2 - 10.0	-	-	-	-	-	-	17.7 - 9.2
0.30	-	-	2.95	2.77	2.70	19.9 - 13.5	1.38	1.02	0.80	3.0	0.4Q	3/14/08	58.7 - 39.8
0.05	0.48	1.67	2.95	2.77	2.70	21.0 - 13.7	1.38	1.02	0.80	2.8	-	-	62.0 - 40.4
1.12	1.14	-	4.32	4.04	2.69	7.2 - 3.0	0.49	0.30	0.20	2.5	0.15Q	3/6/08	30.9 - 12.9
0.18	0.10	0.04	0.43	-0.08	-1.19	12.4 - 8.9	-	-	-	-	-	-	5.3 - 3.8
0.16	-2.48	0.58	-1.22	1.42	0.78	-	-	-	-	-	-	-	17.6 - 12.5
1.90	1.21	1.00	3.48	3.27	2.24	11.8 - 5.6	0.61	0.54	0.45	2.3	0.18Q	1/9/08	41.0 - 19.5
0.63	0.43	0.68	2.61	2.00	1.49	11.5 - 7.4	0.14	0.10	0.10	0.6	0.035Q	2/20/08	30.1 - 19.2
0.81	0.78	0.57	2.41	2.89	2.11	5.7 - 2.9	0.24	0.24	-	2.5	0.06Q	3/7/08	13.7 - 6.9
1.23	1.24	1.40	5.37	5.17	4.04	9.2 - 6.5	1.32	1.10	0.91	3.3	0.36Q	2/20/08	49.2 - 34.8
0.59	0.39	0.09	1.62	1.41	1.11	12.1 - 7.8	0.58	0.51	0.46	3.9	0.165Q	3/24/08	19.6 - 12.6
0.05	0.59	0.48	1.66	1.35	0.95	6.8 - 3.7	-	-	-	-	-	-	11.3 - 6.1
0.21	0.15	0.07	0.53	0.33	0.24	9.6 - 7.6	-	-	-	-	-	-	5.1 - 4.0
0.26	0.17	0.26	0.90	1.33	2.03	42.6 - 26.3	2.06	1.88	1.77	6.9	0.4609Q	3/31/08	38.3 - 23.7
0.05	-0.15	-1.64	-2.33	0.60	0.05	-	0.80	0.82	0.19	-	0.15Q	4/14/08	-
0.28	0.55	0.48	1.73	2.15	-8.98	-	0.94	0.74	0.28	-	0.25Q	4/1/08	-
0.42	0.41	0.47	1.68	1.16	0.69	21.0 - 9.5	0.46	0.44	0.44	1.7	0.13Q	3/27/08	35.2 - 15.9
0.95	0.26	0.50	1.76	2.04	2.01	23.8 - 16.5	-	-	-	-	-	-	42.0 - 29.0
-1.02	0.10	0.98	-0.08	1.59	2.93	-	1.90	1.87	1.83	6.0	0.475Q	2/15/08	35.7 - 28.9
0.08	0.07	0.09	0.32	0.23	0.25	44.7 - 34.7	0.90	0.90	0.90	6.9	0.5547Q	2/20/08	14.3 - 11.1
1.15	-0.76	0.76	2.49	2.36	1.67	-	1.06	1.06	0.81	-	0.2656Q	2/1/08	-
-0.15	0.11	0.22	-0.06	-0.66	-0.21	-	-	-	-	-	-	-	21.1 - 12.3

SYMBOL	COMPANY	NATURE OF BUSINESS	FISCAL YEAR-END	TOTAL REV. $MILL	NET INCOME $MILL	TOTAL ASSETS $MILL	NET STK EQUITY $MILL	NO OF INST	INST. HOLDINGS (SHARES)
CEL	Cellcom Israel Ltd	Communications						-	-
CX	Cemex S.A.B. de C.V.	Stone, Clay, Glass, and Concrete Pr	12/31/06	197093.0	25682.0	323698.0	138878.0	189	126872715
CNC	Centene Corp	Hospitals & Health Care	12/31/07	2919.3	73.4	1119.1	415.0	182	41910669
CHC	Centerline Holding Co	Property, Real Estate & Developmen	12/31/07	572.9	-60.1	9491.6	542.0	-	-
CNP	Centerpoint Energy, Inc (United Stat	Electricity	12/31/07	9623.0	399.0	17872.0	-1810.0	2	295000
CTX	Centex Corp.	Building & General Construction	3/31/07	12014.6	268.4	13205.8	5112.3	330	109904690
CEE	Central Europe and Russia Fund In	Trusts & Holding Entities	10/31/06		7.2	817.3	772.7	30	1533286
CPF	Central Pacific Financial Corp	Commercial Banking	12/31/07	392.0	5.8	5680.4	674.4	87	20435047
CV	Central Vermont Public Service Cor	Electricity	12/31/07	329.1	15.8	540.3	198.9	70	5574053
CTL	CenturyTel, Inc.	Communications	12/31/07	2656.2	418.4	8184.6	3409.2	312	111063517
CVO	Cenveo Inc	Paper Products	12/31/07	2046.7	40.8	2002.7	99.3	44	29473815
CF	CF Industries Holdings Inc	Chemicals	12/31/07	2756.7	372.7	2012.5	1187.0	-	-
CGV	CGG Veritas	Oil and Gas	12/31/04	687.8	-6.4	971.2	402.3	7	812811
GIB	CGI Group, Inc.	Accounting & Management Consulti	9/30/05	3686.0	216.5	3986.7	2494.7	53	73729547
CHG	CH Energy Group, Inc.	Electricity	12/31/07	1196.8	42.6	1494.7	544.8	104	7411824
CHB	Champion Enterprises, Inc (United	Wood Products	12/29/07	1273.5	7.2	1022.2	319.8	135	76359753
CRL	Charles River Laboratories Internati	Miscellaneous Business Services	12/29/07	1230.6	154.4	2805.5	1860.5	249	62645444
CWF	Chartwell Dividend & Income Fund I	Trusts & Holding Entities	11/30/07	19.3	13.5	194.5	138.0	2	148423
FLI	CHC Helicopter Corp	Aviation	4/30/07	1149.1	44.0	2102.2	551.3	-	-
CKP	Checkpoint Systems Inc (United Sta	Communications	12/30/07	834.2	58.8	1031.0	588.3	115	32736170
CHE	Chemed Corp (New)	Diagnostic Services	12/31/07	1100.1	64.0	772.3	364.3	141	21456004
CEM	Chemtura Corp	Chemicals	12/31/07	3747.0	-3.0	4416.0	1853.0	-	-
CSK	Chesapeake Corp.	Paper Products	12/30/07	1059.6	-15.5	1213.7	281.2	106	14146945
CHK	Chesapeake Energy Corp.	Oil and Gas	12/31/07	7800.0	1451.0	30734.0	12130.0	340	197614346
CPK	Chesapeake Utilities Corp.	Gas Utilities	12/31/07	258.3	13.2	381.6	119.6	41	1150483
CVX	Chevron Corporation	Oil and Gas	12/31/07	220904.0	18688.0	148786.0	77088.0	1143	1248386226
CBI	Chicago Bridge & Iron Co., N.V. (Ne	Building & General Construction	12/31/06	3125.3	117.0	1835.0	542.4	145	91072626
CHS	Chico's FAS Inc	Retail - Apparel and Accessory Store	2/2/08	1714.3	88.9	1250.1	912.5	297	161783796
CIM	Chimera Investment Corp	Finance & Investment	12/31/07	3.1	-2.9	1565.6	538.9	-	-
CEA	China Eastern Airlines Corp., Ltd.	Aviation	12/31/05	27454.4	-467.3	58899.3	6918.5	7	596590
CHN	China Fund, Inc. (The)	Trusts & Holding Entities	10/31/06		4.4	457.9	455.2	34	768622
LFC	China Life Insurance Co Ltd	Insurance	12/31/05	98212.0	9306.0	559219.0	80809.0	40	3810331
CHL	China Mobile Limited	Communications	12/31/05	243041.0	53549.0	421027.0	273107.0	118	30722619
CN	China Netcom Group Corp Hong Ko	Communications	12/31/05	87232.0	13888.0	202840.0	63010.0	23	4867147
SNP	China Petroleum & Chemical Corp.	Oil and Gas	12/31/05	823117.0	40920.0	537321.0	223556.0	98	18544133
CSR	China Security & Surveillance Tech	Miscellaneous Business Services	12/31/07	240.2	35.3	377.4	199.7	-	-
ZNH	China Southern Airlines Co Ltd	Aviation	12/31/05	38293.0	-1848.0	71402.0	10000.0	11	736819
CHA	China Telecom Corp Ltd	Communications	12/31/05	169310.0	27912.0	417136.0	181517.0	46	4550236
CHU	China Unicom Ltd.	Communications	12/31/05	87048.8	4931.1	142630.0	76284.3	36	3504128
CYD	China Yuchai International Ltd.	Industrial Machinery and Equipment						38	1450237
CMG	Chipotle Mexican Grill Inc	Hospitality & Tourism	12/31/07	1085.8	70.6	722.1	562.1	-	-
CQB	Chiquita Brands International, Inc.	Agricultural Crop Production	12/31/07	4662.8	-49.0	2677.6	895.5	153	42159385
CHH	Choice Hotels International, Inc. (Ne	Hospitality & Tourism	12/31/07	615.5	111.3	328.4	-157.1	122	13674065
CPS	ChoicePoint, Inc.	IT & Technology	12/31/07	982.0	32.4	1214.8	309.9	242	74810435
CBK	Christopher & Banks Corp.	Retail - Apparel and Accessory Store	3/3/07	547.3	33.7	307.3	225.8	123	35762101
CB	Chubb Corp.	Insurance	12/31/07	14107.0	2807.0	50574.0	14445.0	500	168274149
CHT	Chunghwa Telecom Co Ltd	Communications	12/31/06	186342.0	42072.0	398781.0	320047.0	-	-
CHD	Church & Dwight Co., Inc.	Chemicals	12/31/07	2220.9	169.0	2532.5	1080.3	200	42075397
CBR	CIBER, Inc.	IT & Technology	12/31/07	1082.0	29.0	849.1	454.6	122	46082215
CI	CIGNA Corp.	Insurance	12/31/07	17623.0	1115.0	40065.0	4748.0	398	106382513
XEC	Cimarex Energy Co	Oil and Gas	12/31/07	1431.2	346.5	5362.8	3259.3	270	74368768
CBB	Cincinnati Bell Inc (New)	Communications	12/31/07	1348.6	73.2	2019.6	-667.6	174	198985494
CNK	Cinemark Holdings Inc	Movies & Film	12/31/07	1682.8	88.9	3296.9	1019.2	-	-
CIR	Circor International Inc	Metal Products	12/31/07	665.7	37.9	676.5	420.4	67	11836199
CC	Circuit City Stores, Inc.	Retail - Appliances and Electrical	2/28/07	12429.8	-8.3	4007.3	1791.2	245	167976659
CC	Circuit City Stores, Inc.	Retail - Appliances and Electrical	2/28/05	10472.4	61.7	3789.4	2087.4	245	167976659
CIT	CIT Group, Inc. (New)	Credit & Lending	12/31/07	7024.9	-81.0	90248.0	6960.6	336	192611816
CDL	Citadel Broadcasting Corp	Media	12/31/07	719.8	-1285.2	3843.4	627.2	99	54242206
C	Citigroup Inc	Commercial Banking	12/31/07	159229.0	3617.0	2187631.0	113598.0	-	-
CZN	Citizens Communications Co	Communications	12/31/07	2288.0	214.7	7256.1	997.9	286	248842138
CIA	Citizens, Inc. (Austin, TX)	Insurance	12/31/07	173.8	16.6	787.9	176.2	-	-
CYN	City National Corp. (Beverly Hills, C	Commercial Banking	12/31/07	1197.3	222.7	15889.3	1655.6	219	29371402
CKR	CKE Restaurants, Inc. (United State	Hospitality & Tourism						133	42220892
CLC	Clarcor Inc.	Industrial Machinery and Equipment	12/1/07	921.2	90.7	739.1	555.7	172	42117914
GOF	Claymore/Guggenheim Strategic O	Trusts & Holding Entities						-	-
RYJ	Claymore/Raymond James SB-1 Eq	Trusts & Holding Entities	8/31/07		-0.6	243.4	241.0	-	-
CCU	Clear Channel Communications Inc	Media	12/31/07	6816.9	938.5	18805.5	8797.5	384	424785657
CCO	Clear Channel Outdoor Holdings Inc	Advertising, Marketing & PR	12/31/07	3281.8	246.0	5935.6	1982.7	-	-
CNL	Cleco Corp. (New)	Electricity	12/31/07	1030.6	151.8	2710.7	1011.4	144	27806425
CLF	Cleveland-Cliffs Inc.	Non-Precious Metals	12/31/07	2275.2	270.0	3075.8	1163.7	185	25651023
CLX	Clorox Co.	Chemicals	6/30/07	4847.0	501.0	3666.0	171.0	430	113300539
CME	CME Group Inc	Finance Intermediaries & Services	12/31/07	1756.1	658.5	20306.2	13205.6	-	-
CMS	CMS Energy Corp	Electricity	12/31/07	6464.0	-215.0	14196.0	2424.0	258	182467444
CNA	CNA Financial Corp.	Insurance	12/31/07	9885.0	851.0	56732.0	10150.0	114	254107349
SUR	CNA Surety Corp.	Insurance	12/31/07	465.7	92.5	1507.7	667.7	59	42374218
CNH	CNH Global N.V.	Industrial Machinery and Equipment	12/31/07	12998.0	292.0	18274.0	5120.0	42	16783585
CEO	Cnooc Ltd.	Oil and Gas	12/31/06	88947.3	30926.9	155268.0	107813.9	86	6667846
COH	Coach, Inc.	Leather and Leather Products	6/30/07	2612.5	663.7	2449.5	1910.4	434	322837894
COA	Coachmen Industries, Inc.	Automotive	12/31/07	480.8	-38.8	207.7	121.1	60	13560876
KO	Coca-Cola Co (The) (United States)	Food	12/31/07	28857.0	5981.0	43269.0	21744.0	1006	1418033939

T14

EARNINGS PER SHARE QUARTERLY 1st	2nd	3rd	ANNUAL 2007	2006	2005	P/E RATIO 2007		DIVIDENDS PER SHARE 2007	2006	2005	AV. YLD %	DIV. DECLARED AMOUNT	PAYABLE	PRICE RANGE 2007	
												2.63Q	12/3/07		
				1.19	1.08									18.3 -	13.1
0.85	0.40	0.36	1.64	-1.01	1.24	18.2 -	8.0							29.9 -	13.1
-0.27	0.06	0.17	-1.19	0.62	0.98			0.42	1.68	1.65	1.9	0.15Q	6/15/08	25.4 -	10.0
0.38	0.20	0.27	1.17	1.33	0.75	32.1 -	25.6	0.68	0.60	0.40	2.0	0.1825Q	3/10/08	37.5 -	30.0
-1.05	-5.26	-7.94	2.23	9.71	7.64	26.8 -	18.5	0.16	0.16	0.16	0.3	0.04Q	3/26/08	59.7 -	41.2
				0.55	0.27				3.05	0.17		0.4648A	12/31/07	28.0 -	18.9
0.65	0.68	0.30	0.19	2.57	2.38	192.9 -	120.4	0.98	0.88	0.73	3.5	0.25Q	3/14/08	36.7 -	22.9
0.55	0.04	0.41	1.49	1.66	0.48	16.1 -	12.6	0.92	0.92	0.92	4.3	1.16Q	4/1/08	24.0 -	18.8
0.68	1.00	1.01	3.72	3.07	2.49	9.5 -	7.1	0.26	0.25	0.24	0.8	0.0675Q	3/24/08	35.5 -	26.3
0.34	0.05	0.06	0.75	2.23	-2.70	6.6 -	3.3							4.9 -	2.5
1.02	1.65	1.52	6.57	0.60	-2.04			0.08	0.08	0.02		0.1Q	2/29/08		
				8.86	-0.64							1.2961U	12/27/05	14.0 -	7.8
			0.71	0.40	0.49	9.8 -	8.0							7.0 -	5.7
1.37	0.33	0.27	2.70	2.73	2.81	18.3 -	16.0	2.16	2.16	2.16	4.7	0.54Q	5/1/08	49.5 -	43.3
-0.09	0.10	0.17	0.09	1.78	0.48	135.2 -	72.4							12.2 -	6.5
0.54	0.55	0.62	2.25	-0.80	1.96	21.7 -	15.0							48.9 -	33.8
			0.80	0.63	0.61	13.4 -	10.3	0.89	0.93	1.00	9.1	0.075M	3/31/08	10.7 -	8.3
0.61			0.97	1.97	1.37			0.47	0.38	0.29		0.125Q	5/7/08		
0.12	0.37	0.35	1.44	0.89	1.01	15.1 -	10.0					0.005U	4/8/97	21.8 -	14.4
0.62	0.38	0.74	2.55	1.90	1.36	13.2 -	8.4	0.24	0.24	0.24	0.9	0.06Q	3/10/08	33.7 -	21.4
-0.05	-0.01	0.01	-0.01	-0.85	-1.05			0.20	0.20	0.20	2.6	0.05Q	3/7/08	11.8 -	5.4
0.04	-0.65	0.16	-0.80	-2.04	-16.20			0.44	0.88	0.88	1.8	0.22Q	5/15/07	27.8 -	20.7
0.50	1.01	0.72	2.62	4.35	2.51	6.9 -	4.5	0.26	0.23	0.20	1.8	3.9063Q	6/16/08	18.1 -	11.9
1.18	0.22	-0.05	1.94	1.72	1.77	13.9 -	10.6	1.18	1.16	1.14	4.8	0.205Q	4/7/08	27.0 -	20.6
2.18	2.52	1.75	8.77	7.80	6.54	6.3 -	1.0	2.20	2.01	1.75	4.7	0.58U	3/10/08	55.4 -	42.2
0.38	0.27	0.61		1.19	0.16				0.12	0.11		0.04Q	12/28/07	20.5 -	12.4
0.27	0.22	0.13	0.93	1.06	0.78	25.5 -	18.2							23.7 -	17.0
			-0.08					0.03				0.025Q	1/25/08		
				-0.68	-0.10									23.3 -	16.7
				0.30	0.21				2.51	3.57		2.84A	1/25/08	47.9 -	23.4
			1.38	0.75	0.35	9.4 -	5.4							13.0 -	7.5
				3.29	2.70									18.1 -	12.3
				1.94	2.10									20.8 -	23.6
														49.9 -	32.1
0.13	0.11	0.29	0.91	0.85	0.39										
				0.04										29.7 -	16.2
														44.5 -	28.3
				0.29	0.39									13.2 -	6.8
														32.2 -	10.1
0.38	0.60	0.62	2.13	1.28	1.43										
-0.08	0.20	-0.66	-1.22	-2.28	2.92				0.20	0.40		0.1Q	7/14/06	24.3 -	15.7
0.24	0.43	0.59	1.70	1.68	1.32	17.6 -	10.1	0.62	0.54	0.47	2.6	0.17Q	4/18/08	29.8 -	17.2
0.40	0.43	0.02	0.44	0.20	1.53	105.3 -	82.7							10.0 -	06.4
0.32	0.09		0.89	0.84	0.73	25.4 -	16.7	0.20	0.10	0.10	1.1	0.06Q	1/9/08	22.6 -	14.9
1.71	1.75	1.87	7.01	5.98	4.47	5.5 -	4.6	1.16	1.00	0.86	3.3	0.33Q	4/15/08	00.5 -	32.0
0.66	0.59	0.75	2.46	2.07	1.83	13.7 -	10.5	0.30	0.26	0.24	1.0	0.08Q	3/3/08	33.6 -	25.0
0.11	0.13	0.12	0.47	0.40	0.38	24.0 -	13.7							11.3 -	6.4
0.98	0.68	1.28	3.87	3.43	4.17	7.1 -	4.6	0.04	0.03	0.03	0.2	0.04A	4/10/08	27.4 -	17.7
0.77	0.93	0.87	4.09	4.11	4.90	10.0 -	6.0	0.16	0.16		0.5	0.06Q	8/2/08	41.0 -	24.5
0.08	0.09	0.09	0.24	0.30	-0.30	24.5 -	13.0					0.8438Q	4/1/08	5.9 -	3.3
1.25	0.45	-0.22	0.85	0.01	-0.31							0.18Q	3/14/08		
0.45	0.60	0.62	2.27	1.80	1.27	10.6 -	7.5	0.15	0.15	0.15	0.7	0.0375Q	3/21/08	24.1 -	17.1
-0.33			-0.05	0.77	0.31			0.07	0.00	0.07	0.5	0.04Q	1/15/08	17.5 -	8.8
					0.31							0.04Q	1/15/08	17.5 -	8.8
1.01	-0.70	-0.24	-0.58	5.00	4.44			1.00	0.80	0.61	2.6	1.2973Q	3/17/08	45.8 -	33.3
0.00	0.03	-1.71	-6.51	-0.43	0.55			2.64	0.54	0.18	16.5	2.46Q	6/12/07	22.3 -	12.4
1.01	1.24	0.44	0.72	4.31	4.75			2.16	1.96	1.76		0.1128Q	2/15/08		
0.21	0.12	0.14	0.65	1.06	0.60	22.7 -	18.0	1.00	1.00	1.00	7.6	0.25Q	3/31/08	14.8 -	11.7
0.05	0.07	0.10	0.35	0.16	0.13										
1.15	1.19	1.22	4.52	4.66	4.60	15.7 -	12.8	1.84	1.64	1.44	2.9	0.48Q	2/20/08	70.8 -	57.9
0.23	0.15	0.11	0.72	2.70	0.30	20.5 -	8.8	0.16	0.16		1.4	0.06Q	6/10/08	14.8 -	6.3
0.32			1.78	1.59	1.46	15.4 -	11.5	0.30	0.28	0.26	1.3	0.08Q	1/25/08	27.4 -	20.4
												0.154M	2/29/08		
			-0.05	0.00								0.11U	12/29/06		
0.21	0.48	0.56	1.89	1.38	1.71	24.0 -	15.3	0.75	0.75	0.69	2.1	0.1875Q	1/15/08	45.4 -	29.0
0.05	0.19	0.15	0.69	0.43	0.19										
0.14	1.05	1.13	2.54	1.36	3.53	8.1 -	6.5	0.90	0.90	0.90	5.0	1.125Q	3/1/08	20.5 -	16.5
0.62	1.66	1.08	5.14	5.20	4.99	5.2 -	1.9	0.50	0.47	0.30	3.1	8.125Q	4/15/08	26.8 -	9.9
0.76	0.65		3.26	2.90	6.11	18.1 -	14.4	1.20	1.14	1.10	2.3	0.4Q	5/15/08	59.2 -	46.8
3.69	3.57	3.87	14.93	11.60	8.81	15.3 -	4.9	1.72	2.52	1.84	1.3	1.15Q	3/25/08	228.7 -	72.9
-0.97	0.15	0.34	-1.02	-0.41	-0.44			0.20			2.2	0.5625Q	3/3/08	10.5 -	7.9
1.09	0.80	0.64	3.13	4.05	0.76	9.7 -	7.1	0.35			1.3	0.15Q	3/20/08	30.5 -	22.2
0.47	0.50	0.63	2.09	1.89	0.89	6.7 -	4.6					0.15Q	10/7/02	13.9 -	9.5
			1.23	0.70					0.19	0.19		0.55A	6/11/99	21.4 -	16.2
				0.73	0.61									58.7 -	35.0
0.41	0.69		1.76	1.27	1.00	16.2 -	9.7							28.5 -	17.1
-0.67	-0.64	-0.28	-2.46	-2.03	-1.69			0.06	0.18	0.24	0.4	0.03Q	6/14/07	20.0 -	13.3
0.54	0.80	0.71	2.57	2.16	2.04	20.6 -	15.0	1.36	1.24	1.12	2.9	0.38Q	4/1/08	53.0 -	38.6

SYMBOL	COMPANY	NATURE OF BUSINESS	FISCAL YEAR-END	TOTAL REV. $MILL	NET INCOME $MILL	TOTAL ASSETS $MILL	NET STK EQUITY $MILL	NO OF INST	INST. HOLDINGS (SHARES)
CCE	Coca-Cola Enterprises Inc.	Food	12/31/07	20936.0	711.0	24046.0	5689.0	244	176789181
KOF	Coca-Cola FEMSA, S.A.B. de C.V.	Trusts & Holding Entities	12/31/05	50198.0	4586.0	67148.0	34727.0	61	24424834
CCH	Coca-Cola Hellenic Bottling Co SA	Food	12/31/05	4780.3	308.1	5584.9	2447.9	18	513417
CDE	Coeur d'Alene Mines Corp (Idaho)	Precious Metals	12/31/07	215.3	43.9	2651.7	1727.4	126	77750175
CSA	Cogdell Spencer Inc	Property, Real Estate & Development	12/31/06	55.8	-9.1	393.1	59.7	-	-
RLF	Cohen & Steers Advantage Income	Trusts & Holding Entities	12/31/07	33.6	26.8	720.5	407.7	27	1317060
FOF	Cohen & Steers Closed-End Opport	Finance & Investment						-	-
DVM	Cohen & Steers Dividend Majors Fu	Trusts & Holding Entities		-		-	-	5	40715
INB	Cohen & Steers Global Income Buil	Trusts & Holding Entities	8/31/07	1.8	1.3	442.3	435.2	-	-
CNS	Cohen & Steers Inc	Wealth Management	12/31/07		75.5	332.2	281.9	42	7672855
RPF	Cohen & Steers Premium Income R	Trusts & Holding Entities	12/31/07	38.8	30.4	892.5	503.6	22	1220852
RQI	Cohen & Steers Quality Income Re	Trusts & Holding Entities	12/31/07	46.7	36.6	1060.3	609.1	29	1720725
RNP	Cohen & Steers Reit & Preferred In	Trusts & Holding Entities	12/31/07	107.2	89.3	1829.8	1055.6	-	-
RTU	Cohen & Steers Reit And Utilities In	Trusts & Holding Entities	12/31/07	97.7	78.9	2116.7	1302.5	29	3391905
UTF	Cohen & Steers Select Utilities Fun	Trusts & Holding Entities	12/31/07	81.4	65.1	1948.8	1280.7	23	2714113
RFI	Cohen & Steers Total Return Realty	Trusts & Holding Entities	12/31/07	5.7	4.2	131.3	128.8	19	299878
RWF	Cohen & Steers Worldwide Realty I	Trusts & Holding Entities						-	-
KCP	Cole (Kenneth) Productions, Inc.	Leather and Leather Products	12/31/07	510.7	7.1	354.5	242.0	80	10561219
CL	Colgate-Palmolive Co.	Chemicals	12/31/07	13789.7	1737.4	10112.0	2286.2	746	335659526
PSS	Collective Brands Inc	Retail - Apparel and Accessory Store	2/2/08	3035.4	42.7	2415.2	702.9	-	-
CNB	Colonial BancGroup Inc.	Commercial Banking	12/31/07	1742.7	180.9	25976.0	2273.6	190	60239022
CLP	Colonial Properties Trust (AL)	Property, Real Estate & Development	12/31/07	401.5	355.9	3229.8	1140.8	133	18825805
CCZ	Comcast Holdings Corp	Media	12/31/04	8586.0	986.0	41942.0	19912.0	2	123125
CMA	Comerica, Inc.	Commercial Banking	12/31/07	4618.0	686.0	62331.0	5117.0	382	112710326
FIX	Comfort Systems USA, Inc.	Building & General Construction	12/31/07	1109.5	32.5	547.1	262.6	79	27456232
CGI	Commerce Group Inc (MA)	Insurance	12/31/07	1982.4	190.9	3914.7	1316.9	107	11688040
CMC	Commercial Metals Co.	Metal Works	8/30/07	8329.0	355.4	3472.7	1548.6	180	44027218
CTV	Commscope, Inc.	Communications	12/31/07	1930.8	204.8	5106.6	1280.0	148	59371687
CBU	Community Bank System, Inc.	Commercial Banking	12/31/97	129.4	15.6	1633.7	118.0	93	11856116
CYH	Community Health Systems, Inc. (N	Hospitals & Health Care	12/31/07	7127.5	30.3	13493.6	1710.8	238	86647260
CBD	Companhia Brasileira de Distribuica	Retail - Food & Beverage	12/31/07	14902.9	210.9	12746.1	5012.0	47	14148905
ABV	Companhia de Bebidas das Americ	Food	12/31/07	19648.2	2816.4	35475.8	17420.0	77	68267428
SBS	Companhia de Saneamento Basico	Water Utilities	12/31/06	5527.3	872.7	18093.7	9112.2	40	16861587
CIG	Companhia Energetica de Minas G	Electricity	12/31/06	9681.3	1718.8	23208.7	7522.5	61	12867819
ELP	Companhia Paranaense De Energia	Electricity	12/31/06	5384.6	1242.7	11934.6	6376.3	37	27567053
SID	Companhia Siderurgica Nacional	Metal Works	12/31/06	9040.4	1167.5	25028.3	6124.1	65	24834299
RIO	Companhia Vale Do Rio Doce	Non-Precious Metals	12/31/07	64764.0	20006.0	132899.0	57030.0	190	182732717
CU	Compania Cervecerias Unidas S.A.	Food	12/31/06	545797.1	55832.7	702407.0	349227.5	18	1689944
BVN	Compania de Minas Buenaventura	Precious Metals	12/31/06	646.9	428.1	1735.8	1300.5	92	47036915
CTC	Compania de Telecomunicaciones	Communications	12/31/06	577203.5	23353.0	1616776.2	900760.9	54	20387520
CMP	Compass Minerals International Inc	Earth & Rock Mining	12/31/07	857.3	80.0	820.0	-4.6	94	29559083
CPX	Complete Production Services Inc	Oil and Gas	12/31/07	1655.2	161.6	2054.8	930.3	-	-
CMZ	Compton Petroleum Corp	Oil and Gas	12/31/06	533.7	127.4	2147.5	734.1	10	1867900
CSC	Computer Sciences Corp.	IT & Technology	3/30/07	14856.6	388.8	13730.5	5885.5	422	153197312
CIX	CompX International, Inc.	Metal Products	12/31/07	177.7	9.0	187.7	104.1	37	1929061
CRK	Comstock Resources, Inc.	Oil and Gas	12/31/07	687.1	68.9	2354.4	771.6	138	36464851
CAG	ConAgra Foods, Inc.	Food	5/27/07	12028.2	764.6	11835.5	4582.9	481	307917589
COP	ConocoPhillips	Oil and Gas	12/31/07	194495.0	11891.0	177557.0	88983.0	901	1095205440
CNO	Conseco Inc	Insurance	12/31/07	4572.3	-179.9	33514.8	4235.9	181	145484258
CNX	Consol Energy Inc	Coal Mining	12/31/07	3762.2	267.8	6208.1	1214.4	239	74916394
ED	Consolidated Edison, Inc.	Electricity	12/31/07	13120.0	929.0	28343.0	9076.0	369	105282475
CGX	Consolidated Graphics, Inc.	Printing	3/31/07	1006.2	50.7	724.0	365.5	116	10557469
STZ	Constellation Brands Inc	Food	2/28/07	5216.4	331.9	9438.2	3417.5	313	151043358
CEG	Constellation Energy Group, Inc.	Electricity	12/31/07	21193.2	821.5	21945.7	5340.2	342	115560037
CMS PRA	Consumers Energy Co.	Electricity	12/31/07	6064.0	312.0	13401.0	3691.0	-	-
CAL	Continental Airlines Inc (United Stat	Aviation	12/31/07	14232.0	459.0	12105.0	1550.0	140	65401821
CLR	Continental Resources Inc.	Oil and Gas	12/31/07	582.2	28.6	1365.2	623.1	-	-
CVG	Convergys Corp.	IT & Technology	12/31/07	2844.3	169.5	2564.2	1521.7	217	102890068
CNW	Con-Way Inc	Road Transport	12/31/07	4387.4	152.9	3017.7	909.1	-	-
COO	Cooper Companies, Inc. (United Sta	Medical Instruments & Equipment	10/31/07	950.6	-11.2	2560.3	1423.6	245	39849015
CBE	Cooper Industries, Ltd.	Electrical	12/31/07	5903.1	692.3	6133.5	2841.9	247	73619749
CTB	Cooper Tire & Rubber Co.	Rubber Products	12/31/07	2932.6	119.6	2296.9	792.3	175	56864914
CPA	Copa Holdings S.A.	Transport & Automotive	12/31/06	851.2	133.8	1255.0	371.7	-	-
CLB	Core Laboratories N.V. (Netherland	Oil and Gas	12/31/06	575.7	82.7	501.2	71.8	-	-
CPO	Corn Products International Inc	Food	12/31/07	3391.0	198.0	3103.0	1605.0	209	61118817
CRN	Cornell Companies Inc	Miscellaneous Business Services	12/31/06	360.9	11.9	523.5	181.6	39	10764161
GLW	Corning, Inc.	Metal Works	12/31/07	5860.0	2150.0	15215.0	9496.0	513	960952289
BCA	Corpbanca	Commercial Banking	12/31/06	271835.0	39104.0	3695822.0	433249.0	15	2038993
CXP	Corporate Express N.V.	Retail - General	12/31/03	8053.0	-132.0	3677.0		-	-
OFC	Corporate Office Properties Trust	Property, Real Estate & Development	12/31/07	410.2	34.8	2931.9	822.6	-	-
CXW	Corrections Corporation of America	Miscellaneous Business Services	12/31/07	1478.8	133.4	2485.7	1222.0	124	25113289
CJR	Corus Entertainment, Inc.	Media	8/31/07	768.7	107.0	1937.0	975.9	25	16663886
COT	Cott Corp. (Canada)	Food	12/30/06	1771.8	-17.5	1139.5	488.7	95	54390315
CFC	Countrywide Financial Corp	Finance Intermediaries & Services	2/28/97	1530.5	257.4	8089.3	1611.5	425	505109245
CUZ	Cousins Properties (United Sta	Property, Real Estate & Development	12/31/07	165.4	32.9	1509.6	552.5	5	300600
CVD	Covance Inc.	Biotechnology	12/31/07	1631.5	175.9	1560.2	1110.2	232	53288620
CVA	Covanta Holding Corp	Electricity	12/31/06	1268.5	105.8	4437.8	739.2	-	-
CVH	Coventry Health Care Inc.	Insurance	12/31/07	9879.5	626.1	7158.8	3301.5	313	92512633
COV	Covidien Ltd	Medical Instruments & Equipment	9/28/07	10170.0	-342.0	18328.0	6742.0	-	-
CXR	Cox Radio Inc.	Media	12/31/07	444.9	1.9	1997.4	1154.2	111	38789720

1st	2nd	3rd	2007	2006	2005	P/E RATIO		2007	2006	2005	AV. YLD %	AMOUNT	PAYABLE	PRICE RANGE 2007	
0.03	0.56	0.55	1.46	-2.41	1.08	19.9 -	12.8	0.24	0.24	0.16	1.0	0.07Q	3/27/08	29.0 -	18.6
-	-	-	-	-	-	-	-	-	-	-	-	-	-	25.0 -	19.5
-	-	-	1.38	1.29	-	-	-	-	-	-	-	-	-	18.7 -	14.0
0.05	0.04	0.01	0.14	0.30	0.04	54.8 -	22.1	-	-	-	-	-	-	7.7 -	3.1
-0.23	-0.12	-0.13	-	-1.14	-0.70	-	-	-	1.40	0.23	-	0.35Q	1/21/08	-	-
-	-	-	1.13	1.18	0.97	19.7 -	13.2	3.86	4.36	2.87	20.9	0.16M	6/30/08	22.3 -	14.9
-	-	-	-	-	-	-	-	-	-	-	-	0.1175M	6/30/08	-	-
-	-	-	0.49	0.43	-	-	-	-	2.30	1.00	-	0.105M	6/30/08	-	-
-	-	-	0.06	-	-	-	-	-	-	-	-	0.17M	6/30/08	-	-
0.52	0.44	0.37	1.77	0.08	0.79	10.1 -	7.3	0.80	0.48	0.42	5.1	0.22Q	3/28/08	17.9 -	13.0
-	-	-	1.18	1.20	1.06	18.6 -	12.8	3.71	4.70	3.03	19.9	0.16M	6/30/08	22.0 -	15.1
-	-	-	1.06	1.10	0.82	19.5 -	13.8	3.19	3.81	2.70	18.0	0.15M	6/30/08	20.6 -	14.6
-	-	-	2.03	1.92	1.76	-	-	3.79	4.02	3.42	-	0.2M	6/30/08	-	-
-	-	-	1.50	1.43	1.17	13.5 -	9.8	1.99	2.35	1.60	11.2	0.1375M	6/30/08	20.3 -	14.7
-	-	-	1.61	1.56	1.42	12.5 -	10.1	3.04	1.55	1.16	16.7	0.185M	6/30/08	20.1 -	16.2
-	-	-	0.52	0.52	0.49	38.7 -	28.7	2.69	2.95	2.87	15.1	0.1125M	6/30/08	20.1 -	14.9
-	-	-	1.35	1.06	-	-	-	-	2.93	1.38	-	0.12M	6/30/08	-	-
0.17	0.10	0.17	0.35	1.31	1.65	105.5 -	72.3	0.72	0.72	0.66	2.3	0.09Q	3/28/08	36.9 -	25.3
0.89	0.76	0.77	3.20	2.46	2.43	18.4 -	13.5	1.40	1.25	1.11	2.7	0.4Q	5/15/08	58.9 -	43.1
0.59	0.38	0.39	1.82	0.98	-0.03	9.2 -	5.1	-	-	-	-	-	-	16.8 -	9.3
0.24	0.43	0.45	1.17	1.72	1.52	19.2 -	14.1	0.75	0.68	0.61	4.0	0.19Q	2/8/08	22.4 -	16.5
0.69	6.51	0.03	7.28	3.92	5.13	5.8 -	4.7	13.29	2.72	2.70	34.0	0.5070Q	4/30/08	42.4 -	33.9
1.19	1.25	1.18	4.43	5.49	5.11	14.3 -	11.5	2.56	2.36	2.20	4.5	0.66Q	4/1/08	63.5 -	51.0
0.04	0.25	0.28	0.79	0.70	-0.16	9.9 -	6.7	0.15	0.14	0.03	2.2	0.045Q	3/20/08	7.8 -	5.3
1.11	0.63	0.88	2.97	3.55	3.61	10.5 -	9.6	1.00	0.07	0.73	4.8	0.3Q	3/7/08	31.1 -	19.7
0.71	0.54	0.82	2.92	2.89	2.31	4.4 -	2.2	0.33	0.17	0.12	3.9	0.12Q	1/24/08	12.9 -	6.3
0.63	0.83	0.81	2.78	1.84	0.78	8.1 -	5.7	-	-	-	-	-	-	22.5 -	16.0
0.32	0.34	0.37	1.42	1.26	1.65	20.0 -	13.6	0.82	0.78	0.74	3.4	0.21Q	4/10/08	28.4 -	19.3
0.58	0.57	0.11	0.32	1.75	1.79	96.0 -	73.1	-	-	-	-	-	-	30.7 -	23.4
-	-	-	-	-	-	-	-	-	-	-	-	-	-	27.7 -	13.4
-	-	-	-	-	-	-	-	-	-	-	-	-	-	22.8 -	13.0
-	-	-	-	-	-	-	-	-	-	-	-	-	-	16.1 -	9.2
-	-	-	-	-	-	-	-	-	-	-	-	-	-	8.3 -	3.8
-	-	-	-	-	-	-	-	-	-	-	-	-	-	4.9 -	2.6
-	-	-	-	-	-	-	-	-	-	-	-	-	-	6.4 -	3.2
-	-	-	-	-	-	-	-	-	-	-	-	-	-	7.3 -	3.5
-	-	-	-	-	-	-	-	-	-	-	-	-	-	25.8 -	17.9
-	-	-	-	-	-	-	-	-	-	-	-	0.0899S	4/21/97	30.0 -	19.9
-	-	-	-	-	-	-	-	-	-	-	-	-	-	16.8 -	9.4
0.80	-0.10	0.20	2.43	1.69	0.97	10.0 -	5.8	1.28	1.22	1.10	6.6	0.335Q	3/14/08	24.3 -	14.2
0.65	0.60	0.57	2.20	2.04	1.06	-	-	-	-	-	-	-	-	-	-
-	-	-	0.05	0.62	-	-	-	-	-	-	-	-	-	9.5 -	4.7
0.61	0.43	1.05	2.16	3.38	4.22	26.7 -	18.1	-	-	-	-	0.0017U	1/10/08	55.7 -	35.0
0.20	0.17	0.18	0.61	0.76	0.03	28.9 -	10.4	0.50	0.50	0.50	3.6	0.125Q	3/21/08	17.6 -	6.3
0.28	0.41	0.37	1.54	1.61	1.47	15.4 -	10.9	-	-	-	-	-	-	23.0 -	16.8
0.36	0.50	0.63	1.51	1.03	1.23	19.5 -	16.9	0.72	1.00	1.08	2.7	0.19Q	2/29/08	39.4 -	26.6
2.12	0.18	2.23	7.22	9.88	9.55	6.3 -	4.5	1.64	1.44	1.18	4.3	0.47Q	3/3/08	45.5 -	32.4
0.01	-0.38	-0.20	1.12	0.08	1.70	-	-	-	-	-	-	-	-	23.8 -	15.7
0.01	0.83	-0.03	1.45	2.20	3.13	14.8 -	7.5	0.31	0.28	0.28	1.9	0.1Q	2/22/08	21.5 -	10.9
0.99	0.58	1.15	3.47	2.95	2.94	13.1 -	10.7	2.32	2.30	2.28	6.5	0.505Q	3/15/08	45.6 -	37.3
0.96	0.98	1.58	3.65	2.73	2.31	13.0 -	8.8	-	-	-	-	-	-	47.5 -	32.3
0.13	0.33	-	1.38	1.36	1.19	17.3 -	11.1	-	-	-	-	-	-	23.9 -	15.4
1.07	0.61	1.38	4.50	5.10	0.47	8.8 -	8.1	1.74	1.51	1.04	4.3	0.4775Q	4/1/08	11.0 -	68.4
-	-	-	-	-	-	-	-	4.50	4.50	4.50	6.0	1.125Q	4/1/08	81.5 -	70.5
0.21	2.03	2.15	4.18	3.30	-0.97	4.4 -	1.9	-	-	-	-	-	-	18.3 -	7.8
0.34	-0.87	0.33	0.17	1.59	1.22	-	-	0.33	0.55	0.01	-	-	-	-	-
0.01	0.10	0.30	1.23	1.17	0.86	15.8 -	10.1	-	-	-	-	-	-	19.5 -	12.4
0.65	0.96	0.78	3.04	4.98	3.85	16.6 -	10.0	0.40	0.10	0.40	1.0	0.1Q	3/14/08	50.5 -	30.5
0.15	-	-	-0.25	1.44	2.04	-	-	0.06	0.06	0.06	0.1	0.03S	1/4/00	74.4 -	46.4
0.71	1.12	0.93	3.73	2.48	0.86	9.1 -	6.9	0.84	0.74	0.74	2.9	0.25Q	4/1/08	34.1 -	25.8
0.33	0.28	0.48	1.91	-1.28	-0.15	12.4 -	9.3	0.42	0.42	0.42	2.0	0.105Q	3/31/08	23.7 -	17.8
-	-	-	-	3.10	1.94	-	-	-	-	-	-	0.31A	6/15/07	-	-
1.04	1.18	1.29	-	3.07	1.11	-	-	-	-	-	-	-	-	-	-
0.66	0.66	0.66	2.59	1.63	1.19	10.7 -	6.7	0.38	0.24	0.28	1.7	0.11Q	1/25/08	27.8 -	17.3
0.05	0.24	0.17	-	0.84	0.02	-	-	-	-	-	-	-	-	15.3 -	11.2
0.20	0.30	0.38	1.34	1.16	0.38	10.3 -	7.1	0.10	-	-	0.9	0.05Q	3/31/08	13.8 -	9.6
-	-	-	-	0.17	0.24	-	-	-	-	-	-	-	-	28.8 -	26.4
-	-	-	0.93	0.65	0.01	12.6 -	7.8	-	-	-	-	-	-	11.7 -	7.3
0.03	0.08	0.15	0.39	0.69	0.63	-	-	1.30	1.18	1.07	-	0.7Q	4/15/08	-	-
0.26	0.26	0.26	1.06	0.85	0.42	12.7 -	8.8	-	-	-	-	-	-	13.5 -	9.3
-	-	-	1.24	0.41	0.82	9.3 -	6.8	0.53	0.13	0.04	5.3	0.0496M	4/30/08	11.5 -	8.4
0.07	0.07	-0.08	-	-0.24	0.34	-	-	-	-	-	-	0.025Q	6/30/98	33.4 -	23.8
0.72	0.81	-2.85	-2.03	4.30	4.11	-	-	0.60	0.60	0.59	1.8	0.15Q	2/29/08	39.4 -	23.4
0.27	0.01	0.15	0.34	4.14	0.67	74.3 -	73.5	1.48	4.88	1.48	5.9	0.4688Q	2/15/08	25.3 -	25.0
0.60	0.64	0.69	2.71	2.24	1.88	15.3 -	9.7	-	-	-	-	-	-	41.4 -	26.3
-0.12	0.24	0.25	-	0.72	0.46	-	-	-	-	-	-	-	-	10.3 -	2.9
0.76	0.96	1.08	3.98	3.47	3.10	9.0 -	6.4	-	-	-	-	-	-	36.0 -	25.6
0.84	-	-	-0.69	2.33	2.08	-	-	-	-	-	-	0.16Q	2/11/08	-	-
0.14	0.21	0.21	0.02	-0.25	0.61	1267.5 -	695.0	-	-	-	-	-	-	25.4 -	13.9

T17

SYMBOL	COMPANY	NATURE OF BUSINESS	FISCAL YEAR-END	TOTAL REV. $MILL	NET INCOME $MILL	TOTAL ASSETS $MILL	NET STK EQUITY $MILL	NO OF INST	INST. HOLDINGS (SHARES)
CPL	CPFL Energia SA	Electricity	12/31/06	8914.0	1404.1	14048.8	4866.3	18	7863501
CPY	CPI Corp.	Personal Services	2/3/07	293.8	16.3	90.3	10.3	40	4654314
CR	Crane Co.	Metal Products	12/31/07	2619.2	-62.3	2877.3	884.8	160	38238693
CRD B	Crawford & Co.	Insurance	12/31/07	1051.3	16.1	902.8	254.2	43	17665016
BAP	CrediCorp Ltd.	Finance Intermediaries & Services	12/31/05	1097.4	181.9	11029.6	1292.0	-	-
CS	Credit Suisse Group	Commercial Banking	12/31/06	-	11327.0	1255956.0	-	84	31385940
CRH	CRH Plc	Stone, Clay, Glass, and Concrete Pr	12/31/04	12754.5	866.1	13072.0	4979.4	33	3596271
CRT	Cross Timbers Royalty Trust	Miscellaneous	12/31/07	20.2	19.8	20.1	18.4	58	861215
CCI	Crown Castle International Corp	Communications	12/31/07	1385.5	-222.8	10488.1	3166.9	196	197518753
CCK	Crown Holdings Inc	Metal Products	12/31/07	7727.0	528.0	6979.0	15.0	203	125178886
CRY	CryoLife, Inc.	Medical Instruments & Equipment	12/31/07	94.8	7.2	92.7	62.6	67	12754466
CRZ	Crystal River Capital Inc	Property, Real Estate & Developmen	12/31/07	236.1	-345.9	2479.4	110.6	-	-
CAO	CSK Auto Corp.	Retail - Automotive	2/4/07	1907.8	6.3	1151.8	171.5	114	44979030
CSS	CSS Industries, Inc.	Printing	3/31/07	530.7	23.9	343.1	261.1	51	6363597
CSX	CSX Corp.	Rail Transport	12/28/07	10030.0	1336.0	25534.0	8685.0	337	162465537
CTS	CTS Corp.	Electrical	12/31/07	685.9	25.4	543.7	324.2	107	30630579
CFR	Cullen/Frost Bankers, Inc.	Commercial Banking	12/31/07	1037.1	212.1	13485.0	1477.1	190	34370503
CFI	Culp Inc.	Textiles	4/29/07	250.5	-1.3	159.9	79.1	29	5650151
CMI	Cummins, Inc.	Industrial Machinery and Equipment	12/31/07	13048.0	739.0	8195.0	3409.0	267	40227328
CW	Curtiss-Wright Corp.	Metal Products	12/31/07	1592.1	104.3	1985.6	914.8	145	15055271
SRV	Cushing MLP Total Return Fund	Trusts & Holding Entities	7/31/07	-	-	0.5	0.1	-	-
CVS	CVS Caremark Corporation	Retail - Miscellaneous	12/29/07	76329.5	2637.0	54721.9	31321.9	627	664410806
CY	Cypress Semiconductor Corp. (Unit	IT & Technology	12/30/07	1596.4	394.3	3725.9	1720.4	217	102660697
CYT	Cytec Industries, Inc.	Chemicals	12/31/07	3503.8	206.5	4061.7	1929.9	190	34315683
DAI	Daimler AG	Automotive	12/31/06	99222.0	3744.0	217634.0	37346.0	126	207525534
DAN	Dana Holding Corp	Automotive	12/31/07	8721.0	-551.0	6425.0	-782.0	-	-
DHR	Danaher Corp.	Instruments and Related Products	12/31/07	11025.9	1369.9	17471.9	9085.7	523	214124147
DAC	Danaos Corp	Shipping						-	-
DRI	Darden Restaurants, Inc.	Hospitality & Tourism	5/27/07	5567.1	201.4	2880.8	1094.5	318	116268158
DAR	Darling International Inc.	Food	12/29/07	645.3	45.5	351.3	201.0	75	53913553
DR	Darwin Professional Underwriters In	Insurance	12/31/07	203.4	32.2	827.1	254.2	-	-
DVA	Davita Inc.	Professional Health Care Services	12/31/07	5264.2	381.8	6944.0	1732.3	210	87994054
DPM	DCP Midstream Partners LP	Gas Utilities	12/31/07	873.3	-15.8	1120.7		-	-
DCT	DCT Industrial Trust Inc	Property, Real Estate & Developmen	12/31/07	260.2	40.1	2779.0	1162.7	-	-
DF	Dean Foods Co.	Food	12/31/07	11821.9	131.4	7033.4	51.3	284	120367467
DE	Deere & Co.	Industrial Machinery and Equipment	10/31/07	24082.2	1821.7	38575.7	7155.8	468	194811249
DFR	Deerfield Capital Corp	Property, Real Estate & Developmen	12/31/07	494.4	-96.2	7788.0	468.6	-	-
DSF	Defined Strategy Fund Inc	Trusts & Holding Entities	9/30/07	-	2.4	193.4	98.8	2	27050
DLM	Del Monte Foods Co. (United States	Food	4/29/07	3414.9	112.6	4561.5	1452.2	239	174622425
DEX	Delaware Enhanced Global Dividen	Trusts & Holding Entities	5/18/07				0.1	-	-
DDF	Delaware Investments Dividend & I	Trusts & Holding Entities	11/30/07	8.5	4.4	185.6	123.9	14	204985
DGF	Delaware Investments Global Divid	Trusts & Holding Entities	11/30/07	3.7	1.5	97.4	63.3	8	55859
DK	Delek US Holdings Inc	Retail - Fuel & Oil	12/31/07	4097.1	96.4	1237.8	512.5	-	-
DFG	Delphi Financial Group, Inc.	Insurance	12/31/07	1570.6	164.5	6094.8	1141.4	-	-
DAL	Delta Air Lines, Inc. (DE)	Aviation	12/31/07	13358.0	314.0	32423.0	10113.0	-	-
DEL	Deltic Timber Corp.	Wood Products	12/31/07	128.3	11.1	328.7	218.1	87	8297490
DLX	Deluxe Corp.	Printing	12/31/07	1606.4	143.5	1210.8	41.1	195	38889598
DNY	Denali Fund Inc (The)	Trusts & Holding Entities	10/31/06	-	4.6	188.6	133.9	-	-
DNR	Denbury Resources, Inc. (DE)	Oil and Gas	12/31/07	971.9	253.1	2771.1	1404.4	159	49134520
HXM	Desarrolladora Homex SA De CV	Building & General Construction	12/31/06	12952.6	1340.9	18909.3	7317.4	50	11961741
DB	Deutsche Bank AG (Germany)	Commercial Banking	12/31/06	76636.0	5986.0	1126230.0	32808.0	84	81431302
DT	Deutsche Telekom AG	Communications	12/31/05	59604.0	5589.0	128468.0	48599.0	103	105723147
DDR	Developers Diversified Realty Corp.	Property, Real Estate & Developmen	12/31/07	944.9	276.0	9089.8	2998.8	229	78382189
DVN	Devon Energy Corp. (New)	Oil and Gas	12/31/07	11362.0	3606.0	41456.0	22006.0	576	369182434
DV	DeVRY Inc.	Vocational Education Services	6/30/07	933.5	76.2	844.1	642.0	145	58687704
DEO	Diageo Plc	Food	6/30/05	6677.0	1344.0	13921.0	4626.0	223	68092645
DO	Diamond Offshore Drilling, Inc.	Oil and Gas	12/31/07	2567.7	846.5	4341.5	2877.1	194	134078121
DRH	DiamondRock Hospitality Co.	Property, Real Estate & Developmen	12/31/07	710.9	68.3	2131.6	1080.3	1	20000
DSX	Diana Shipping Inc	Shipping	12/31/05	103.1	65.0	341.9	324.2	15	2131297
DHX	Dice Holdings Inc	Miscellaneous	12/31/07	142.3	15.5	341.6	120.6	-	-
DKS	Dick's Sporting Goods, Inc	Retail - Sporting, Toys & Hobby	2/2/08	3888.4	155.0	2035.6	888.5	132	36159910
DBD	Diebold, Inc.	Office Equipment Supplies	12/31/06	2906.2	86.5	2514.3	1091.4	325	54231152
DLR	Digital Realty Trust, Inc.	Property, Real Estate & Developmen	12/31/07	395.2	40.6	2809.5	1043.9	47	19176346
DDS	Dillard's Inc. (United States)	Retail - General	2/2/08	7370.8	53.8	5338.1	2514.1	207	70591202
DFS	Discover Financial Services	Credit & Lending	11/30/07	-	588.6	37376.1	5599.4	-	-
DIS	Disney (Walt) Co. (The)	Media	9/30/06	34285.0	3374.0	59998.0	31820.0	877	1372503248
DIS	Disney (Walt) Co. (The)	IT & Technology	9/30/00	368.5	-1016.3	1955.2	1550.8	877	1372503248
DYS	Distribucion y Servicio (D & S) S.A.	Retail - Food & Beverage	12/31/06	1696664.8	39652.6	1205405.1	519710.9	12	3718278
DCA	Dividend Capital Realty Income Allo	Trusts & Holding Entities	9/30/07	22.5	14.1	225.2	154.0	2	25350
DCW	Dividend Capital Strategic Global R	Trusts & Holding Entities						-	-
DNP	DNP Select Income Fund Inc (Unite	Trusts & Holding Entities	12/31/07	154.1	101.9	3944.3	2331.8	101	6577081
DLB	Dolby Laboratories Inc	Communications	9/28/07	482.0	142.8	991.9	797.2	103	27383218
DTG	Dollar Thrifty Automotive Group, Inc	Hospitality & Tourism	12/31/07	1760.8	1.2	3891.5	578.9	102	25274921
DOM	Dominion Resources Black Warrior	Trusts & Holding Entities	12/31/07	22.0	20.9	26.7	26.4	24	340812
D	Dominion Resources Inc	Electricity	12/31/07	15674.0	2539.0	39123.0	9406.0	561	213632396
DPZ	Dominos Pizza Inc.	Hospitality & Tourism	12/30/07	1462.9	37.9	473.2	-1450.1	86	55534281
UFS	Domtar Corp	Paper Products	12/31/06	3989.0	328.0	4955.0	1941.0	-	-
DCI	Donaldson Co. Inc.	Industrial Machinery and Equipment	7/31/07	1918.8	150.7	1319.0	624.7	211	53057375
RHD	Donnelley (R.H.) Corp.	Advertising, Marketing & PR	12/31/07	2680.3	46.9	16089.1	1822.7	165	30393941
RRD	Donnelley (R.R.) & Sons Co.	Printing	12/31/07	11587.1	-48.9	12086.7	3907.3	370	173708445

EARNINGS PER SHARE QUARTERLY 1st	2nd	3rd	ANNUAL 2007	2006	2005	P/E RATIO	DIVIDENDS PER SHARE 2007	2006	2005	AV. YLD %	DIV. DECLARED AMOUNT	PAYABLE	PRICE RANGE 2007	
-	-	-	-	-	-	-	-	-	-	-	-	-	20.0 -	15.7
0.40	-0.53	-1.57	2.56	0.81	-2.35	8.7 - 4.5	0.64	0.64	0.64	4.0	0.16Q	12/3/07	22.3 -	11.4
0.71	0.75	-3.29	-1.04	2.67	2.25	-	0.66	0.55	0.45	2.2	0.18Q	3/10/08	34.3 -	25.9
0.07	0.12	0.07	0.32	0.30	0.26	25.9 - 14.2	-	0.18	0.24	-	0.06Q	8/25/06	8.3 -	4.5
-	-	-	-	-	2.28	-	-	-	-	-	0.2A	4/30/99	-	
-	-	-	-	9.83	5.02	-	-	-	-	-	-		42.5 -	30.0
-	-	-	-	2.22	1.85	-	-	-	-	-	-		26.9 -	19.9
0.76	0.85	0.83	3.30	4.24	3.38	12.6 - 7.5	3.30	4.24	3.38	10.6	0.3191M	4/14/08	41.5 -	24.8
-0.18	-0.13	-0.26	-0.87	-0.30	-2.07	-	-	-	-	-	0.7813Q	2/15/08	17.3 -	11.0
0.10	0.53	0.56	3.19	1.82	-2.18	4.4 - 2.5	-	-	-	-	-		14.0 -	8.1
0.04	0.05	0.07	0.26	-0.02	-0.85	31.5 - 17.6	-	-	-	-	-		8.2 -	4.6
0.30	-0.36	-3.76	-13.86	2.27	0.80	-	2.72	2.71	1.55	-	0.68Q	4/29/08	-	
0.04	0.12	-0.13	0.14	1.29	0.80	143.1 - 82.5	-	-	-	-	-		20.0 -	11.6
-0.41	1.22	2.07	2.19	2.00	2.45	16.9 - 13.3	0.48	0.48	0.40	1.5	0.14Q	12/14/07	37.0 -	29.0
0.52	0.71	0.91	2.99	2.82	2.52	6.7 - 4.9	0.54	0.33	0.22	3.3	0.15Q	3/14/08	20.2 -	14.6
0.11	0.15	0.20	0.66	0.63	0.57	23.9 - 15.5	0.12	0.12	0.12	0.9	0.03Q	5/2/08	15.8 -	10.2
0.78	0.89	0.95	3.55	3.42	3.07	13.8 - 11.0	1.54	1.32	1.17	3.5	0.4Q	3/14/08	49.0 -	38.9
0.07	0.12	0.07	-0.11	-1.02	-1.55	-	-	-	-	-	0.035Q	1/9/01	12.2 -	5.0
0.71	1.06	0.92	3.70	3.55	2.75	5.7 - 3.3	0.43	0.33	0.30	2.7	0.125Q	3/3/08	21.1 -	12.2
0.44	0.48	0.56	2.32	1.82	1.72	12.9 - 9.5	0.28	0.24	0.20	1.1	0.08Q	4/18/08	30.0 -	22.1
-	-	-	-	-	-	-	-	-	-	-	0.309Q	3/10/08	-	
0.43	0.47	0.45	1.92	1.60	1.45	12.2 - 8.9	0.05	0.16	0.14	0.2	0.06Q	5/2/08	23.4 -	17.1
-0.01	2.29	0.18	2.30	0.25	-0.69	10.3 - 3.7	-	-	-	-	-		23.7 -	8.6
1.05	1.11	1.06	4.20	4.01	1.27	12.3 - 7.8	0.40	0.40	0.40	0.9	0.125Q	2/25/08	51.7 -	33.0
-	-	-	3.80	3.64	2.80	13.0 - 10.6	-	-	0.37	-	-		49.3 -	40.2
-0.61	-0.89	-0.46	-0.97	4.02	10.70	-	-	-	-	-	-		-	
0.78	0.96	1.48	4.19	3.48	2.76	14.0 - 10.5	0.11	0.08	0.07	0.2	0.03Q	4/25/08	58.6 -	44.0
-	-	-	-	-	-	-	-	-	-	-	0.465Q	2/14/08	-	
0.72	0.30	0.88	1.05	2.10	1.78	20.8 - 14.1	0.46	-	0.08	2.0	0.18Q	5/1/08	28.1 -	19.0
0.12	0.12	0.15	0.56	0.07	0.12	8.5 - 4.6	-	-	-	-	-		4.8 -	2.6
0.31	0.45	0.49	1.89	0.95	0.46	-	-	-	-	-	-		-	
0.72	1.17	0.88	3.55	2.74	2.20	11.2 - 7.1	-	-	-	-	-		39.6 -	25.3
0.58	0.01	0.29	-1.05	1.90	0.20	-	1.98	-	-	-	0.57Q	2/14/08	-	
0.09	0.05	0.07	0.24	-1.05	-0.12	-	0.64	0.64	-	-	0.10Q	4/10/08	-	
0.47	0.21	0.05	0.96	1.61	2.13	33.1 - 25.2	15.00	-	-	52.4	15.U	4/2/07	31.8 -	24.2
0.83	-	-	4.00	3.59	2.94	9.4 - 7.2	0.91	0.78	0.60	2.8	0.25Q	5/1/08	37.4 -	28.8
0.44	0.28	-0.45	-1.87	1.39	1.17	-	1.68	1.56	0.65	-	0.42Q	1/29/08	-	
-	-	-	0.52	0.54	0.40	38.5 - 38.5	0.54	0.55	0.26	2.7	0.6356Q	12/31/07	20.0 -	20.0
0.02	0.13	0.26	0.55	0.83	0.56	21.1 - 18.0	0.16	0.08	-	1.5	0.04Q	1/31/08	11.6 -	9.9
-	-	-	-	-	-	-	-	-	-	-	0.142M	1/25/08	-	
-	-	-	0.41	0.47	0.62	30.9 - 24.8	2.12	1.07	0.96	18.2	0.00M	3/28/08	12.7 -	10.2
-	-	-	0.27	0.27	0.38	47.3 - 37.6	2.16	2.53	0.96	18.3	0.08M	3/28/08	12.8 -	10.2
0.40	1.29	0.38	1.82	1.94	1.63	-	0.54	0.38	-	-	0.0375Q	3/7/08	-	
0.76	0.83	0.79	3.19	2.79	2.25	-	0.35	0.31	0.24	-	0.09Q	0/5/00	-	
-0.66	0.42	0.56	0.79	-31.58	-23.75	-	-	-	-	-	-		-	
0.53	0.20	0.02	0.89	0.89	1.17	51.7 - 34.5	0.30	0.30	0.28	0.8	0.075Q	3/17/08	40.0 -	30.7
0.68	0.69	0.62	2.76	1.96	3.09	16.2 - 13.5	1.00	1.30	1.60	2.4	0.25Q	3/3/08	44.7 -	37.3
-	-	-	-	1.10	0.36	-	-	1.82	1.77	-	0.115M	2/29/08	21.6 -	15.5
0.07	0.25	0.27	1.00	0.82	0.69	7.3 - 3.4	-	-	-	-	-		7.3 -	3.4
-	-	-	-	3.99	3.07	-	-	-	-	-	-		23.6 -	16.4
-	-	-	-	11.55	6.95	-	-	-	-	-	-		93.5 -	65.4
-	-	-	0.13	0.74	1.01	174.7 - 119.8	-	-	-	-	-		22.7 -	15.6
0.42	0.89	0.26	1.85	1.81	2.08	24.8 - 17.0	2.64	2.36	2.16	7.0	0.5Q	3/17/08	45.9 -	31.5
1.44	2.00	1.63	8.00	6.34	6.26	5.2 - 3.3	0.56	0.45	0.30	1.7	1.6225Q	3/31/08	41.4 -	26.6
0.37	0.49	-	1.07	0.61	0.40	30.1 - 18.0	0.10	-	-	0.4	0.065	1/4/08	32.2 -	14.2
-	-	-	0.55	0.67	0.45	105.2 - 88.3	-	-	-	-	-		57.9 -	48.6
1.64	1.81	1.48	6.12	5.12	1.91	6.6 - 3.3	5.75	2.00	0.38	21.2	1.25Q	3/3/08	40.2 -	30.4
0.07	0.21	0.17	0.72	0.51	-0.19	-	0.96	0.72	0.38	-	0.25Q	4/1/08	-	
-	-	-	-	-	1.72	-	-	-	1.60	-	0.58Q	12/6/07	-	
-1082.87	0.03	0.07	-3.26	-47.74	-18.67	-	-	-	-	-	-		-	
0.19	0.41	0.10	1.01	0.68	0.65	18.8 - 12.1	-	-	-	-	-		19.0 -	12.3
-0.09	-	-	-	1.29	1.36	-	-	0.86	0.82	-	0.235Q	12/7/07	56.1 -	44.9
0.32	0.04	-	0.34	0.47	0.25	41.0 - 35.3	1.17	1.08	1.00	9.1	0.2101Q	3/31/08	13.9 -	12.0
0.53	-0.31	-0.15	3.05	1.49	1.41	8.8 - 5.1	0.16	0.16	0.16	0.8	0.04Q	2/4/08	26.9 -	15.5
-	0.44	0.42	1.23	-	-	-	-	-	-	-	0.06Q	1/22/08	-	
0.79	-	-	1.64	1.22	-	-	-	0.27	0.24	-	0.35A	1/11/08	27.5 -	20.5
-	-	-	-	-	-	-	-	-	-	-	0.35A	1/11/08	27.5 -	20.5
-	-	-	-	-	-	-	-	-	-	-	-		21.9 -	13.4
-	-	-	1.02	0.99	0.63	-	-	-	-	-	0.11M	6/30/08	-	
-	-	-	-	-	-	-	-	-	-	-	0.15M	6/30/08	-	
-	-	-	0.48	0.47	0.41	24.8 - 20.4	0.78	0.78	0.79	7.1	0.065M	6/10/08	11.9 -	9.8
0.42	-	-	1.26	0.80	0.50	-	-	-	-	-	-		-	
0.21	0.63	0.48	0.05	2.04	2.21	604.0 - 458.0	-	-	-	-	-		30.2 -	22.9
0.69	0.65	0.74	2.66	3.88	3.95	14.6 - 10.0	2.68	3.88	3.96	8.6	0.6515Q	3/10/08	38.8 -	26.6
0.65	-0.76	3.62	3.88	1.97	1.50	8.8 - 7.9	1.46	1.38	1.34	4.6	0.395Q	3/20/08	34.2 -	30.6
0.13	0.04	0.17	0.59	1.65	1.58	31.6 - 21.6	-	-	-	-	13.5Q	5/4/07	18.6 -	12.8
-0.10	-0.04	-	-	1.42	-1.69	-	-	-	0.18	-	-		-	
0.53	0.42	-	1.83	1.55	1.27	18.6 - 13.8	0.36	0.32	0.23	1.3	0.11Q	3/10/08	34.0 -	25.2
0.22	0.34	0.25	0.65	-3.14	-9.10	90.9 - 61.2	-	0.01	-	-	0.01Q	5/30/06	59.1 -	39.8
0.63	-0.32	0.80	-0.22	1.83	0.63	-	1.04	1.04	1.04	3.3	0.26Q	3/3/08	35.3 -	27.9

SYMBOL	COMPANY	NATURE OF BUSINESS	FISCAL YEAR-END	TOTAL REV. $MILL	NET INCOME $MILL	TOTAL ASSETS $MILL	NET STK EQUITY $MILL	NO OF INST	INST. HOLDINGS (SHARES)
DRL	Doral Financial Corp.	Finance Intermediaries & Services	12/31/07	503.6	-170.9	9304.4	1346.7	-	-
DHT	Double Hull Tankers	Shipping	8/31/05	-	-	0.0	0.0	-	-
DEI	Douglas Emmett Inc	Property, Real Estate & Developmen	12/31/07	518.2	-13.0	6190.0	1829.8	-	-
DOV	Dover Corp	Industrial Machinery and Equipment	12/31/07	7226.1	661.1	8069.8	3946.2	404	159878518
DDE	Dover Downs Gaming & Entertainm	Sporting & Recreational	12/31/07	242.4	26.1	225.2	89.6	51	7869275
DVD	Dover Motorsports, Inc.	Sporting & Recreational	12/31/07	86.1	3.7	167.7	76.1	41	8835472
DPO	Dow 30 Enhanced Premuim & Inco	Trusts & Holding Entities	-	-	-	-	-	-	-
DPD	Dow 30 Premium & Dividend Incom	Trusts & Holding Entities	-	-	-	-	-	-	-
DOW	Dow Chemical Co.	Chemicals	12/31/07	53513.0	2887.0	48801.0	19389.0	831	626475777
DSL	Downey Financial Corp. (DE)	Other Depository Banking	12/31/07	1026.6	-56.6	13409.1	1334.4	131	13587314
DPL	DPL Inc.	Electricity	12/31/07	1515.7	221.8	3566.6	895.6	202	58972189
RDY	Dr. Reddy's Laboratories Ltd.	Pharmaceuticals	3/31/07	66417.6	9658.9	-	-	43	13297999
DWA	DreamWorks Animation SKG Inc	Movies & Film	12/31/07	767.2	218.4	1327.8	1018.6	119	27811057
DCS	Dreman/Claymore Dividend & Inco	Trusts & Holding Entities	10/31/07	85.1	69.7	1529.6	1034.6	17	477925
DRC	Dresser-Rand Group Inc	Industrial Machinery and Equipment	12/31/07	1665.0	106.7	1950.9	805.2	-	-
DW	Drew Industries, Inc.	Automotive	12/31/07	668.6	39.8	345.7	251.5	66	6885294
DHF	Dreyfus High Yield Strategies Fund	Trusts & Holding Entities	3/31/07	-	23.4	494.6	337.6	19	614836
DSM	Dreyfus Strategic Municipal Bond F	Trusts & Holding Entities	11/30/07	35.8	30.3	627.7	417.2	23	559369
LEO	Dreyfus Strategic Municipals, Inc.	Trusts & Holding Entities	-	-	-	-	-	32	1354117
DRQ	Dril-Quip, Inc.	Oil and Gas	12/31/07	495.6	107.9	699.8	592.5	97	6658265
DRS	DRS Technologies Inc	Instruments and Related Products	3/31/07	2821.1	127.1	4214.7	1502.5	177	24768786
DST	DST Systems Inc. (DE)	IT & Technology	12/31/07	2302.5	874.7	3395.9	1159.1	229	60397194
DSW	DSW Inc	Retail - Apparel and Accessory Store	2/3/07	1279.1	65.5	608.3	374.6	-	-
DTE	DTE Energy Co.	Electricity	12/31/07	8506.0	971.0	23754.0	5853.0	284	104617786
DTF	DTF Tax-Free Income, Inc. (United	Trusts & Holding Entities	10/31/06	-	8.1	204.8	139.3	11	77441
DD	Du Pont (E.I.) de Nemours & Co (U	Chemicals	12/31/07	30653.0	2988.0	34131.0	11136.0	882	612711823
DCO	Ducommun Inc.	Aviation	12/31/07	367.3	19.6	332.5	214.1	46	7834169
DUF	Duff & Phelps Corp (New)	Finance & Investment	6/30/07	-	-	0.0	-	-	-
DUC	Duff & Phelps Utility & Corporate Bo	Trusts & Holding Entities	12/31/07	29.4	25.1	506.2	315.4	22	252825
DUK	Duke Energy Corp	Electricity	12/31/07	12720.0	1500.0	49704.0	21199.0	-	-
DRE	Duke Realty Corp.	Property, Real Estate & Developmen	12/31/07	1170.1	279.5	7662.0	2750.0	271	84902557
DNB	Dun & Bradstreet Corp (DE)	Miscellaneous Business Services	12/31/07	1599.2	298.1	1658.8	-440.1	270	57113579
DEP	Duncan Energy Partners L.P.	Oil and Gas	12/31/07	797.0	19.2	982.4	-3.6	-	-
DFT	Dupont Fabros Technology Inc	Property, Real Estate & Developmen	12/31/07	25.9	-99.3	1454.2	557.6	-	-
DHG	DWS Dreman Value Income Edge F	Trusts & Holding Entities	9/30/07	-	71.9	-	937.0	-	-
GCS	DWS Global Commodities Stock Fu	Trusts & Holding Entities	6/30/07	7.3	2.6	495.7	473.1	-	-
LBF	DWS Global High Income Fund	Trusts & Holding Entities	10/31/06	-	6.0	123.6	95.9	-	-
KHI	DWS High Income Trust	Trusts & Holding Entities	11/30/07	21.9	16.4	254.6	175.2	-	-
KMM	DWS Multi Market Income Trust	Trusts & Holding Entities	11/30/07	20.2	15.4	287.0	233.0	-	-
KTF	DWS Municipal Income Trust	Trusts & Holding Entities	11/30/07	39.7	33.3	796.2	459.3	-	-
DRP	DWS RREEF World Real Estate &	Trusts & Holding Entities	-	-	-	-	-	-	-
KST	DWS Strategic Income Trust	Trusts & Holding Entities	11/30/07	5.1	3.6	75.7	61.5	-	-
KSM	DWS Strategic Municipal Income Tr	Trusts & Holding Entities	11/30/07	12.3	10.1	237.2	132.6	-	-
DY	Dycom Industries, Inc.	Construction - Public Infrastructure	7/28/07	1137.8	41.9	789.8	444.6	169	44125593
DCP	Dyncorp International Inc	Government Services	3/30/07	2082.3	27.0	1362.9	379.7	-	-
DYN	Dynegy Inc (DE)	Electricity	12/31/07	3103.0	264.0	13221.0	4506.0	-	-
DX	Dynex Capital, Inc.	Property, Real Estate & Developmen	12/31/07	30.8	8.9	374.8	141.9	14	992770
EXP	Eagle Materials Inc	Stone, Clay, Glass, and Concrete Pr	3/31/07	922.4	202.7	971.4	546.0	158	12394229
NGT	Eastern American Natural Gas Trus	Miscellaneous	12/31/07	14.7	12.0	25.0	21.8	14	250081
EGP	EastGroup Properties, Inc.	Property, Real Estate & Developmen	12/31/07	150.7	29.7	1055.8	402.4	97	14981689
EMN	Eastman Chemical Co.	Chemicals	12/31/07	6830.0	300.0	6009.0	2082.0	283	62079504
EK	Eastman Kodak Co.	Consumer Accessories	12/31/07	10301.0	676.0	13659.0	3029.0	410	272497043
ETN	Eaton Corp.	Industrial Machinery and Equipment	12/31/07	13033.0	994.0	13430.0	5172.0	377	115827834
EV	Eaton Vance Corp	Wealth Management	10/31/07	1084.1	142.8	966.8	229.2	208	83464270
EOE	Eaton Vance Credit Opportunities F	Trusts & Holding Entities	4/30/07	-	14.6	223.0	139.0	-	-
EOI	Eaton Vance Enhanced Equity Inco	Trusts & Holding Entities	9/30/07	-	3.2	-914.7	837.6	10	257282
EOS	Eaton Vance Enhanced Equity Inco	Trusts & Holding Entities	-	-	-	-	-	8	186398
EFT	Eaton Vance Floating Rate Income	Trusts & Holding Entities	5/31/07	89.1	81.1	1182.6	708.8	14	1479966
EVN	Eaton Vance Municipal Income Trus	Trusts & Holding Entities	11/30/07	26.5	18.5	466.4	247.0	12	109669
ETJ	Eaton Vance Risk-Managed Diversif	Trusts & Holding Entities	-	-	-	-	-	-	-
EFR	Eaton Vance Senior Floating Rate T	Trusts & Holding Entities	10/31/06	-	68.8	1021.9	625.9	15	1602806
EVF	Eaton Vance Senior Income Trust	Trusts & Holding Entities	6/30/07	43.1	29.2	562.4	320.9	15	2688061
EVG	Eaton Vance Short Duration Diversif	Trusts & Holding Entities	10/31/06	-	19.1	496.0	347.2	3	145350
EVT	Eaton Vance Tax Advantaged Divid	Trusts & Holding Entities	8/31/07	-	157.2	2954.6	2208.0	26	1816163
ETW	Eaton Vance Tax Managed Global	Trusts & Holding Entities	-	-	-	-	-	-	-
ETG	Eaton Vance Tax-Advantage Global	Trusts & Holding Entities	10/31/06	-	124.7	2773.5	1998.9	21	1312673
ETO	Eaton Vance Tax-Advantaged Glob	Trusts & Holding Entities	10/31/06	-	21.1	575.7	430.1	8	246083
ETB	Eaton Vance Tax-Managed Buy-Wri	Trusts & Holding Entities	-	-	-	-	-	-	-
ETV	Eaton Vance Tax-Managed Buy-Wri	Trusts & Holding Entities	-	-	-	-	-	-	-
EXG	Eaton Vance Tax-Managed Global	Finance & Investment	1/11/07	-	-	0.6	0.1	-	-
ETY	Eaton Vance Tax-Managed Premiu	Trusts & Holding Entities	11/9/06	-	-	0.6	0.1	-	-
ECL	Ecolab, Inc.	Chemicals	12/31/07	5469.6	427.2	4722.8	1935.7	350	133280793
EIX	Edison International	Electricity	12/31/07	13113.0	1098.0	37562.0	8444.0	310	232410144
EDR	Education Realty Trust Inc	Property, Real Estate & Developmen	12/31/07	120.0	-5.4	767.5	297.8	59	15930045
EW	Edwards Lifesciences Corp	Medical Instruments & Equipment	12/31/07	1091.1	113.0	1345.1	835.0	210	53558600
EJ	E-House China Holdings, Ltd	Property, Real Estate & Developmen	12/31/06	-	18.1	-	32.4	-	-
EP	El Paso Corp.	Gas Utilities	12/31/07	4648.0	1110.0	24579.0	5280.0	362	504124925
EE	El Paso Electric Company (United S	Electricity	12/31/07	877.4	74.8	1853.9	666.5	143	46595274
EPB	El Paso Pipeline Partners LP	Gas Utilities	12/31/07	110.0	66.0	902.0	-	-	-
ELN	Elan Corp Plc	Pharmaceuticals	12/31/06	560.4	-267.3	2746.3	85.1	173	109687330

T20

EARNINGS PER SHARE QUARTERLY			EARNINGS PER SHARE ANNUAL			P/E RATIO		DIVIDENDS PER SHARE			AV. YLD %	DIV. DECLARED AMOUNT	DIV. DECLARED PAYABLE	PRICE RANGE 2007	
1st	2nd	3rd	2007	2006	2005			2007	2006	2005					
-8.40	-8.40	-1.59	-7.45	-47.60	-3.80	-		0.00	1.60	12.40	0.0	2.9688Q	3/15/08	985.0 -	597.4
-	-	-	-	-	-	-		-	-	-	-	0.37Q	12/12/07	-	
-0.03	-0.01	-0.03	-0.12	-0.18	-	-		0.70	-	-	-	0.175Q	1/15/08	-	
0.63	0.84	0.86	3.26	2.73	2.50	13.5 -	11.1	0.77	0.71	0.66	1.9	0.2Q	3/14/08	44.0 -	36.0
0.21	0.20	0.23	0.80	0.77	0.73	10.9 -	7.5	0.19	0.17	0.16	2.7	0.05Q	3/10/08	8.7 -	6.0
-0.10	0.16	0.14	0.10	-0.98	0.12	60.7 -	35.6	0.06	0.06	0.05	1.4	0.015Q	3/10/08	6.1 -	3.6
-	-	-	-	-	-	-		-	-	-	-	0.1667M	3/31/08	-	
-	-	-	-	0.25	0.19	-		-	1.80	1.06	-	0.15M	3/31/08	-	
1.00	1.07	0.42	2.99	3.82	4.62	17.1 -	12.3	1.64	1.50	1.34	3.9	0.42Q	4/30/08	51.0 -	36.9
1.54	1.17	-0.84	-2.03	7.36	7.80	-		0.48	0.40	0.40	0.9	0.12Q	2/22/08	59.3 -	47.5
0.47	0.49	0.53	1.88	1.15	1.35	13.5 -	9.2	1.04	1.00	0.96	5.1	0.275Q	3/1/08	25.4 -	17.2
-	-	-	60.52	19.07	4.29	0.3 -	0.1	-	-	-	-	-	-	16.5 -	7.5
0.15	0.60	0.47	2.17	0.15	1.01	19.3 -	16.4	-	-	-	-	-	-	42.0 -	35.5
-	-	-	1.54	1.42	1.20	13.2 -	10.6	1.30	1.30	1.30	7.2	0.326Q	2/20/00	20.4 -	10.4
0.18	0.31	0.25	1.25	0.92	0.56	-		-	-	-	-	-	-	-	
0.44	0.57	0.50	1.80	1.42	1.56	11.6 -	7.6	-	-	-	-	-	-	20.8 -	13.6
-	-	-	0.33	0.37	0.45	18.0 -	12.2	-	-	-	-	0.0285M	12/27/07	5.0 -	4.0
-	-	-	0.62	0.64	0.63	14.9 -	12.3	0.50	0.52	0.59	5.9	0.0385M	3/31/08	9.2 -	7.6
-	-	-	-	-	-	-		-	-	-	-	0.042M	1/31/08	10.2 -	7.9
0.59	0.59	0.67	2.63	2.15	0.90	4.8 -	2.8	-	-	-	-	-	-	12.6 -	7.5
0.04	1.04	1.03	3.12	2.67	2.18	14.5 -	8.6	0.12	0.12	-	0.4	0.03Q	3/31/08	45.1 -	26.8
0.90	1.01	9.62	12.35	3.78	5.39	4.2 -	3.3	-	-	-	-	-	-	52.0 -	41.3
0.54	0.15	0.51	1.48	1.00	.			-	-	-	-	-	-	-	
0.76	2.20	1.19	5.70	2.43	3.05	7.9 -	6.7	2.12	2.08	2.06	5.2	0.53Q	4/15/08	45.3 -	38.1
-	-	-	-	0.95	0.94	-		-	0.78	0.96	-	0.05M	1/31/08	16.8 -	14.0
1.01	1.01	0.60	0.11	3.36	3.07	19.5 -	12.5	4.50	4.50	4.50	10.3	0.41Q	3/14/08	49.1 -	40.2
0.37	0.44	0.55	1.88	1.39	1.57	13.5 -	9.8	-	-	-	-	-	-	25.4 -	18.4
-	-	-	0.93	0.71	0.73	16.5 -	13.2	0.78	0.84	1.02	5.5	0.065M	3/31/08	15.4 -	12.3
0.28	0.23	0.48	1.18	1.57	1.88	12.8 -	9.4	0.86	0.31	1.17	6.7	0.22Q	3/17/08	15.1 -	11.1
0.49	0.27	0.39	1.55	1.07	2.17	23.1 -	18.6	1.91	1.89	2.92	5.9	0.2268Q	3/31/08	35.8 -	28.8
0.87	1.46	0.94	4.99	3.70	3.19	12.1 -	9.7	1.00	-	-	1.8	0.3Q	3/17/08	60.4 -	48.2
0.19	0.22	0.22	0.93	-	-	-		-	-	-	-	0.41Q	2/7/00	-	
-	-	-	-2.80	-	-	-		-	-	-	-	0.1875Q	1/11/08	-	
-	-	-	1.38	-	-	-		-	-	-	-	0.1167M	1/2/08	-	
-	-	-	0.11	0.20	0.12	138.2 -	120.0	-	1.82	0.03	-	1.3057A	1/10/08	15.2 -	13.2
-	-	-	-	0.60	0.48	-		-	0.14	0.56	-	0.15Q	1/10/08	8.1 -	5.8
-	-	-	0.51	0.54	0.60	14.8 -	11.0	-	0.11	0.66	-	0.042M	3/31/08	7.6 -	5.0
-	-	-	0.68	0.72	0.78	13.9 -	10.8	-	0.13	0.78	-	0.065M	3/31/08	9.4 -	7.3
-	-	-	0.85	0.86	0.87	14.9 -	12.3	-	0.14	0.81	-	0.048M	3/31/08	12.7 -	10.5
-	-	-	-	-	-	-		-	-	-	-	0.134M	3/31/08	-	
-	-	-	0.87	0.95	1.16	15.9 -	12.6	-	0.76	1.08	-	0.08M	3/31/08	13.9 -	11.0
-	-	-	0.93	0.93	0.95	14.4 -	12.1	-	0.15	0.90	-	0.055M	3/31/08	13.4 -	11.3
0.36	-0.08	-	1.03	0.43	0.49	34.4 -	20.7	-	-	-	-	-	-	36.4 -	21.3
0.22	0.24	0.21	0.49	-6.21				-	-	-	-	-	-	-	
0.03	0.09	0.26	0.35	-0.75	0.21	16.7 -	9.9	-	-	-	-	-	-	5.9 -	3.5
0.08	0.14	0.14	0.40	0.07	0.35	19.6 -	15.4	-	-	-	-	0.2375Q	4/30/08	7.8 -	6.2
0.80	0.73	0.50	4.07	3.02	1.91	7.1 -	4.3	0.70	0.47	0.40	3.2	0.2Q	4/18/08	28.9 -	17.6
0.48	0.53	0.52	2.04	2.40	2.47	13.4 -	10.3	2.07	2.70	2.27	8.5	0.3631Q	12/15/90	27.4 -	20.9
0.25	0.23	0.30	1.14	1.17	0.89	33.9 -	24.6	2.00	1.96	1.94	5.9	0.4969Q	4/15/08	38.6 -	28.0
0.91	1.22	0.24	3.58	4.91	6.81	16.2 -	10.6	1.76	1.77	1.76	3.9	0.44Q	4/1/08	58.0 -	00.0
-0.53	2.00	0.13	2.35	-2.09	-4.73	14.6 -	10.6	0.50	0.50	0.50	1.8	0.255	12/14/07	34.3 -	24.8
1.56	1.64	1.71	6.62	6.22	5.23	10.9 -	8.0	1.72	1.48	1.24	2.8	0.5Q	2/22/08	72.4 -	53.2
0.46	-	-	1.06	1.17	1.13	24.6 -	15.5	0.63	0.40	0.24	3.2	0.15Q	2/11/08	26.1 -	16.5
-	-	-	2.06	-	-	-		-	-	-	-	0.17M	1/31/08	-	
-	-	-	0.08	0.09	0.05	253.1 -	246.9	1.64	1.64	1.23	8.2	0.137M	11/30/07	20.3 -	19.8
-	-	-	0.20	-0.01	-	-		-	1.73	1.44	-	0.144M	3/31/00	-	
-	-	-	2.17	1.83	1.10	9.2 -	8.6	1.62	1.39	0.95	8.4	0.113M	3/31/08	20.0 -	18.6
-	-	-	1.08	1.10	1.17	15.4 -	12.8	0.79	0.88	1.11	5.0	0.0658M	3/17/08	16.6 -	13.8
-	-	-	-	-	-	-		-	-	-	-	0.45Q	1/31/08	-	
-	-	-	2.05	1.55		-		-	1.52	1.23	-	0.119M	1/31/08	20.1 -	19.2
-	-	-	0.80	0.70	0.53	12.5 -	10.6	0.65	0.57	0.46	7.0	0.051M	3/19/08	10.0 -	8.5
-	-	-	-	1.01	0.54	-		-	1.40	0.78	-	0.1183M	1/31/08	-	
-	-	-	2.16	2.12	1.76	10.0 -	7.8	1.69	1.56	1.35	8.5	0.1524M	11/30/07	21.7 -	16.9
-	-	-	-	0.24	0.03	-		-	-	-	-	0.45Q	3/31/08	-	
-	-	-	-	1.64	1.62	-		-	1.50	1.31	-	0.1438M	1/7/08	20.3 -	15.9
-	-	-	-	1.93	1.67	-		-	1.70	1.10	-	0.1795M	1/7/08	20.4 -	16.9
-	-	-	-	0.23	0.14	-		-	1.80	0.90	-	0.45Q	1/31/08	-	
-	-	-	-	0.10	0.05	-		-	-	-	-	0.475Q	3/31/08	-	
-	-	-	-	-	-	-		-	-	-	-	0.475Q	2/29/08	-	
-	-	-	-	-	-	-		-	-	-	-	0.4625Q	11/30/07	-	
0.35	0.44	0.46	1.70	1.43	1.23	20.7 -	15.4	0.47	0.41	0.36	1.5	0.13Q	4/15/08	35.3 -	26.2
1.01	0.28	1.39	3.31	3.57	3.43	9.8 -	6.5	1.18	1.10	1.02	4.6	0.305Q	4/30/08	32.4 -	21.5
-0.02	-0.01	-0.20	-0.20	-0.46	-0.67	-		0.82	1.10	0.79	-	0.205Q	2/5/08	-	
0.54	0.57	0.48	1.87	2.10	1.27	22.6 -	15.8	-	-	-	-	-	-	42.3 -	29.6
0.06	-	-	-	0.27	0.22	-		-	0.08	0.07	-	-	-	-	
0.89	0.22	0.20	1.53	0.64	-0.98	7.5 -	4.3	0.16	0.16	0.16	2.0	0.04Q	7/1/08	11.5 -	6.6
0.33	0.21	0.79	1.63	1.40	0.74	11.7 -	8.0	-	-	-	-	-	-	19.0 -	13.1
-	-	-	0.13	-	-	-		-	-	-	-	0.1281Q	2/14/08	-	
-0.08	-0.21	-0.27	-	-0.62	-0.93	-		-	-	-	-	-	-	30.1 -	7.1

SYMBOL	COMPANY	NATURE OF BUSINESS	FISCAL YEAR-END	TOTAL REV. $MILL	NET INCOME $MILL	TOTAL ASSETS $MILL	NET STK EQUITY $MILL	NO OF INST	INST. HOLDINGS (SHARES)
EDS	Electronic Data Systems Corp. (Ne	IT & Technology	12/31/07	22134.0	716.0	19224.0	9691.0	331	462482966
EQ	Embarq Corp	Communications	12/31/07	6365.0	683.0	8901.0	264.0	-	-
AKO B	Embotelladora Andina S.A. (Chile)	Food	12/31/06	546731.8	74355.1	513599.1	274733.3	23	7793778
ERJ	Embraer-Empresa Brasileira de Aer	Aviation	12/31/07	9983.4	657.0	15659.7	5262.3	115	75708034
EMC	EMC Corp. (MA)	IT & Technology	12/31/07	13230.2	1665.7	22284.7	12521.3	760	1558923500
EME	EMCOR Group, Inc.	Building & General Construction	12/31/07	5927.2	126.8	2871.6	885.0	117	15715415
EMS	Emergency Medical Services Corp	Urban Transport	12/31/07	2107.0	59.8	1479.6	449.5	-	-
EBS	Emergent BioSolutions Inc	Pharmaceuticals	12/31/07	182.9	22.9	273.5	171.2	-	-
EMR	Emerson Electric Co.	Electrical	9/30/07	22572.0	2136.0	19680.0	8772.0	813	297522436
EDE	Empire District Electric Co.	Electricity	12/31/07	490.2	33.2	1471.8	539.2	71	6983368
EIG	Employers Holdings Inc	Insurance	12/31/07	429.9	120.3	3191.2	379.5	-	-
EDN	Empresa Distribuidora y Comerciali	Electricity	12/31/06	1378.3	293.1	3534.7	1670.3	-	-
EOC	Empresa Nacional de Electricidad S	Electricity	12/31/05	1123038.9	110623.0	4874470.9	1642258.8	38	9264714
ICA	Empresas ICA S.A. de C.V.	Construction - Public Infrastructure	12/31/06	21395.7	645.0	36257.1	14092.0	-	-
ERI	Emrise Corp	Instruments and Related Products	12/31/06	46.4	-3.6	44.8	25.2	6	5461165
ELX	Emulex Corporation (United States)	Office Equipment Supplies	7/1/07	470.2	29.4	659.3	581.9	155	71034509
EEQ	Enbridge Energy Management LLC	Oil and Gas			31.4	462.0	414.0	47	5578923
EEP	Enbridge Energy Partners, L.P.	Oil and Gas	12/31/07	7282.6	249.5	6891.6		118	9414997
ENB	Enbridge Inc	Oil and Gas	12/31/07	11919.4	707.1	19907.4	5275.2	-	-
ECA	EnCana Corp	Oil and Gas	12/31/07	21446.0	3959.0	46974.0	20704.0	293	390755400
EAC	Encore Acquisition Co.	Oil and Gas	12/31/07	754.9	17.2	2784.6	948.2	116	43697960
ENP	Encore Energy Partners LP	Oil and Gas						-	-
ENH	Endurance Specialty Holdings Ltd	Insurance	12/31/06	1877.1	498.1	6925.6	2297.9	107	42182580
EN	ENEL S.p.A.	Electricity	12/31/03	32374.0	2509.0	69839.0	21315.0	57	13485070
EGN	Energen Corp.	Gas Utilities	12/31/07	1435.1	309.2	3079.7	1378.7	212	47851220
ENR	Energizer Holdings, Inc.	Electrical	9/30/07	3365.1	321.4	3553.0	653.9	242	50000547
EAS	Energy East Corp.	Electricity	12/31/07	5178.1	251.3	11878.7	3207.1	211	69771034
EPL	Energy Partners Ltd.	Oil and Gas	12/31/07	454.6	-80.0	814.9	102.0	150	33332053
ETE	Energy Transfer Equity L P	Oil and Gas	8/31/07	6792.0	319.4	8183.1		-	-
ETP	Energy Transfer Partners L P	Gas Utilities	8/31/07	6792.0	676.1	7708.4		68	21742441
ES	EnergySolutions Inc	Sanitation Services	12/31/06	427.1	26.9	1157.2	149.0	-	-
ERF	Enerplus Resources Fund	Trusts & Holding Entities	12/31/06	1301.4	544.8	4203.8	2733.1	118	11461182
ENI	Enersis S A. (Chile)	Electricity	12/31/06	3892064.7	285960.4	11062409.3	2869881.9	53	55042005
ENS	Enersys	Specialist Equipment Supplies	3/31/07	1504.5	45.2	1409.0	542.1	39	43995664
BEO	Enhanced S&P 500 Covered Call F	Trusts & Holding Entities						-	-
E	ENI S.p.A.	Petroleum and Coal Products	12/31/04	58922.0	7059.0	72853.0	35540.0	132	19734302
EBF	Ennis Inc	Printing	2/28/07	584.7	41.6	478.2	316.4	80	11578012
NPO	EnPro Industries Inc	Rubber Products	12/31/07	1030.0	40.2	1470.3	475.1	108	18467413
ESV	ENSCO International Inc.	Oil and Gas	12/31/07	2143.8	992.0	4968.8	3752.0	290	126877419
ETM	Entercom Communications Corp	Media	12/31/07	468.4	-8.4	1919.4	660.8	148	32002239
ETR	Entergy Corp.	Electricity	12/31/07	11484.4	1134.8	33643.0	7862.7	-	-
EHL	Entergy Lousiana LLC	Electricity & Utilities	12/31/07	2737.6	143.3	5723.1		-	-
EPE	Enterprise GP Holdings LP	Gas Utilities	12/31/07		109.0	23724.1		-	-
EPD	Enterprise Products Partners L.P.	Oil and Gas	12/31/07	16950.1	533.7	16608.0	6009.4	205	52741557
ENT	Enterra Energy Trust	Trusts & Holding Entities	12/31/06	196.1	-64.2	795.4	402.0	24	4480790
EPR PRC	Entertainment Properties Trust	Property, Real Estate & Developmen	12/31/07	235.7	104.7	2171.6	1007.9	-	-
EVC	Entravision Communications Corp.	Media	12/31/07	250.0		1366.1	657.8	96	49043404
ENZ	Enzo Biochem, Inc.	Diagnostic Services	7/31/07	52.9	-13.3	159.0	141.9	81	11520780
EOG	EOG Resources, Inc.	Oil and Gas	12/31/07	4190.8	1089.9	12088.9	6990.1	366	223910989
EFX	Equifax, Inc.	Miscellaneous Business Services	12/31/07	1843.0	272.7	3523.9	1399.2	290	96865877
EQT	Equitable Resources, Inc.	Gas Utilities	12/31/07	1361.4	257.5	3937.0	1097.5	265	43194346
ELS	Equity Lifestyle Properties Inc	Property, Real Estate & Developmen	12/31/07	413.5	32.1	2033.7	70.9	100	19572659
EQY	Equity One, Inc.	Property, Real Estate & Developmen	12/31/07	246.6	69.4	2174.4	915.9	114	20814881
EQR	Equity Residential	Property, Real Estate & Developmen	12/31/07	2038.1	989.6	15689.8	5062.5	341	241879106
EQS	Equus Total Return, Inc.	Trusts & Holding Entities	12/31/06		-0.1	125.9	93.2	8	521772
ESE	ESCO Technologies, Inc.	Instruments and Related Products	9/30/07	527.5	33.7	576.1	415.5	125	11291199
ESS	Essex Property Trust, Inc.	Property, Real Estate & Developmen	12/31/07	388.5	115.6	2980.3	790.3	-	-
ESL	Esterline Technologies Corp	Instruments and Related Products	10/26/07	1266.6	92.3	2050.3	1121.8	134	23088907
DEG	Etablissements Delhaize Freres et	Retail - Food & Beverage	12/31/04	17875.1	295.7	8702.1	2880.6	42	1782718
ETH	Ethan Allen Interiors, Inc.	Furniture and Fixtures	6/30/07	1005.3	69.2	802.6	409.6	169	32822867
EEA	European Equity Fund Inc (The)	Trusts & Holding Entities	12/31/07	3.9	1.9	168.2	165.7	-	-
EVR	Evercore Partners Inc	Finance Intermediaries & Services	12/31/07	321.6	-34.5	689.1	173.0	-	-
RE	Everest Re Group Ltd	Insurance	12/31/06	4517.3	840.8	17107.6	5107.7	239	46128917
EBI	Evergreen International Balanced In	Trusts & Holding Entities	4/30/07		9.6	255.3	249.6	-	-
EXM	Excel Maritime Carriers Ltd.	Shipping	12/31/05	118.6	67.8	561.0	288.0	34	4155940
XCO	Exco Resources Inc.	Oil and Gas	12/31/07	906.5	49.7	5955.8	1115.7	-	-
EXC	Exelon Corp.	Electricity	12/31/07	18916.0	2736.0	45894.0	10137.0	536	429635128
XJT	ExpressJet Holdings Inc. (United Sta	Aviation	12/31/07	1685.5	-70.2	597.6	232.4	101	44274996
EXH	Exterran Holdings Inc	General Construction Supplies & Ser	12/31/07	2540.5	34.6	6863.5	3162.3	-	-
EXR	Extra Space Storage Inc	Property, Real Estate & Developmen	12/31/07	238.9	36.1	2054.1	619.9	53	18797336
XOM	Exxon Mobil Corp.	Oil and Gas	12/31/07	404552.0	40610.0	242082.0	121762.0	1345	3276498721
FNB	F.N.B. Corp (PA)	Commercial Banking	12/31/07	450.5	69.7	6088.0	544.4	79	18441262
FDS	FactSet Research Systems Inc.	IT & Technology	8/31/07	475.8	109.6	523.8	409.3	176	34551016
FIC	Fair Isaac Corp	Miscellaneous Business Services	9/30/07	822.2	104.6	1275.8	566.3	233	54773193
FA	Fairchild Corp. (The)	Miscellaneous	9/30/07	356.0	-0.3	357.4	92.9	-	-
FCS	Fairchild Semiconductor Internation	IT & Technology	12/31/07	1670.2	64.0	2132.6	1218.5	205	113847086
FFH	Fairfax Financial Holdings, Ltd.	Insurance	12/31/06	6803.7	227.5	26576.5	2856.9	67	13554342
FRP	FairPoint Communications Inc	Communications	12/31/07	283.5	6.0	896.5	161.9	59	19977389
FDO	Family Dollar Stores, Inc.	Retail - General	9/1/07	6834.3	242.9	2624.2	1174.6	271	146749976
FNM	Fannie Mae (United States)	Credit & Lending	12/31/07	43355.0	-2050.0	882547.0	44011.0	3	227300

T22

____ QUARTERLY ____ EARNINGS PER SHARE ____ ANNUAL ____						P/E RATIO		DIVIDENDS PER SHARE			AV. YLD	DIV. DECLARED		PRICE RANGE	
1st	2nd	3rd	2007	2006	2005	2007		2007	2006	2005	%	AMOUNT	PAYABLE	2007	
0.31	0.26	0.42	1.35	0.89	0.28	18.7 -	11.7	0.20	0.20	0.20	1.0	0.05Q	3/10/08	25.2 -	15.8
1.05	1.15	1.01	4.44	-	-	-	-	2.38	-	-	-	0.6875Q	3/31/08	-	
														13.4 -	10.5
														36.8 -	23.3
0.15	0.16	0.23	0.77	0.54	0.47	20.2 -	12.2							15.6 -	9.4
0.18	0.39	0.57	1.90	1.33	0.94	6.2 -	4.5							11.7 -	8.6
0.39	0.35	0.34	1.39	0.92	0.55										
-0.10	-0.17	-0.10	0.77	0.93	0.69			-	-	0.26					
0.71	-	-	2.66	2.24	1.70	13.2 -	10.6	1.05	0.89	0.83	3.3	0.3Q	3/10/08	35.2 -	28.3
0.15	0.19	0.76	1.09	1.39	0.92	21.5 -	17.9	1.28	1.28	1.28	6.0	0.32Q	3/15/08	23.5 -	19.5
0.40	0.58	0.58										0.06Q	3/27/08	-	
														18.6 -	11.5
														9.0 -	6.1
-	-	-	1.60	1.44											
-0.02	-0.02	-	-	-0.10	0.03										
0.12	0.21	-	0.34	0.46	0.80	90.0 -	27.4							30.6 -	9.3
0.26	1.26	0.48	2.40	2.35	1.10	20.7 -	16.6							49.7 -	39.9
0.40	0.69	0.75	2.45	3.62	1.06	21.0 -	17.1	3.73	3.70	3.70	7.7	0.95Q	2/14/08	51.6 -	41.8
0.64	0.41	0.22	1.95	1.79	1.63			1.23	1.15	1.04		0.3438Q	12/1/07		
0.64	1.89	1.24	5.18	6.76	3.85	5.5 -	3.7	0.80	0.38	0.28	3.6	0.2Q	12/31/07	28.5 -	19.2
-0.55	0.28	0.22	0.32	1.75	2.09	75.0 -	49.8							24.0 -	15.9
-	-	-0.33	-	-	-							0.3875Q	2/14/08	37.2 -	30.5
1.36	1.85	1.81	-	6.73	-3.60			-	1.00	1.00		0.4844Q	12/17/07	49.4 -	34.4
-	-	-	-	0.50	0.67										
1.44	0.94	0.80	4.28	3.73	2.35	7.0 -	4.7	0.46	0.44	0.40	1.9	0.12Q	3/3/08	29.9 -	20.0
1.71	-	-	5.01	4.14	3.30	9.1 -	0.7							49.9 -	35.9
0.90	0.12	0.16	1.61	1.76	1.74	16.8 -	13.8	1.21	1.17	1.12	5.0	0.31Q	2/15/08	27.0 -	22.1
0.09	-0.18	-0.12	-2.32	-1.32	1.79									20.5 -	12.9
0.20	0.67	0.40	1.55	0.79	0.60							0.55Q	2/19/08		
0.15	1.33	0.71	3.31	3.15	2.60	8.9 -	5.4	3.11	2.31	1.80	14.5	1.125Q	2/14/08	29.6 -	17.9
-	-	-	-	-	-							0.025Q	3/13/08	-	
-	-	-	4.47	3.95								0.42M	2/20/08	36.3 -	23.7
														8.5 -	5.6
0.15	0.35	0.33	0.95	0.66	0.65	16.3 -	12.5							16.6 -	11.0
-	-	-	0.25	0.06				-	2.20	0.55		1.1S	12/31/07		
-	-	-	2.49	2.34										50.6 -	36.9
0.42	0.43	0.45	1.62	1.58	1.19	13.6 -	9.2	0.62	0.62	0.62	3.5	0.155Q	2/1/08	22.0 -	14.9
0.56	0.61	0.54	1.80	-7.60	2.75	16.7 -	8.1							30.0 -	14.6
1.54	1.72	1.82	6.73	5.04	1.93	5.0 -	3.7	0.10	0.10	0.10	0.3	0.025Q	3/21/08	33.8 -	25.1
-0.01	-0.32	0.37	-0.22	1.19	1.50			1.52	1.52		3.8	0.38Q	3/28/08	53.8 -	30.4
1.03	1.32	2.30	5.60	5.36	4.19			2.58	2.16	2.16		0.75Q	3/3/08		
-	-	-	-	-	-							1.7375Q	3/15/08	27.8 -	24.8
0.29	0.21	0.10	0.97	1.12	0.69			1.49	1.22	0.09		0.41Q	2/8/08		
0.20	0.26	0.20	0.96	1.22	0.91	26.9 -	20.8	1.92	1.79	1.66	8.5	0.5Q	2/7/08	25.9 -	20.0
1.12	0.13	0.78	-	1.46	0.03			-	1.00	1.90		0.00M	9/15/07	19.0 -	10.2
0.67	0.78	0.77	2.99	2.65	2.26			3.04	2.75	2.50		0.4609Q	1/15/08		
-0.03	0.08	-0.01	-0.42	-1.27	-0.08									11.5 -	6.8
-0.03	-0.11	-	-0.38	-0.49	0.09									20.4 -	11.2
0.88	1.24	0.82	4.37	5.24	5.13	8.7 -	4.9	0.33	0.22	0.15	1.2	0.12Q	4/30/08	37.9 -	21.4
0.54	0.51	0.48	2.02	2.12	1.86	14.0 -	11.5	0.16	0.16	0.15	0.6	0.04Q	3/14/08	28.4 -	23.3
0.46	0.87	0.27	2.10	1.80	2.10	14.5 -	10.0	0.88	0.87	0.82	3.5	0.22Q	3/1/08	30.4 -	21.1
0.00	0.07	0.39	1.31	0.09	-0.10	28.8 -	22.1	0.60	0.30	0.10	1.8	0.2Q	4/11/08	37.8 -	28.9
0.27	0.17	0.14	0.95	2.38	1.24	25.1 -	16.6	1.20	2.20	1.17	6.2	0.3Q	3/31/08	23.8 -	15.8
0.40	0.95	1.62	3.39	3.50	2.79	10.8 -	8.1	1.76	1.76	1.75	5.7	0.405Q	4/15/00	30.0 -	27.3
0.00	-	-	-	-0.01	0.45				2.50			0.125Q	12/17/07	9.5 -	7.3
0.11	-	-	1.28	1.19	1.66	30.4 -	16.6							38.9 -	21.3
1.46	0.39	0.39	4.24	2.45	3.32			3.72	3.36	3.24		0.3047Q	1/30/08		
1.04	-	-	3.52	2.15	2.29	10.3 -	6.5							36.3 -	22.8
-	-	-	-	3.55	3.71									79.3 -	43.5
0.57	0.70	-	2.15	2.51	2.19	21.4 -	15.7	0.78	0.69	0.55	2.0	0.22Q	4/25/08	46.1 -	33.7
-	-	-	0.16	0.10	0.06	50.9 -	39.4					1.S	12/31/07	8.1 -	6.3
0.64	-4.68	0.19	-3.38	0.76				0.41	-	-		0.12Q	3/14/08		
4.59	4.45	3.90	-	12.87	-3.79			-	0.60	0.44		0.48Q	12/21/07	90.1 -	70.0
-	-	-	0.84	-	-							0.1458M	3/3/08		
-	-	-	-	-	3.64							0.2Q	12/11/07	59.3 -	4.0
-0.85	0.30	0.10	-0.00	1.41	-										
1.02	1.03	1.15	4.05	2.35	1.36	11.0 -	7.7	1.76	1.60	1.60	4.9	0.5Q	3/10/08	44.7 -	31.3
0.18	-0.49	-0.41	-1.31	1.56	1.65									15.6 -	9.7
0.46	0.81	-1.55	0.75	2.82	1.69										
0.10	0.13	0.15	0.53	0.27	-0.14	27.1 -	23.6	0.93	0.91	0.91	6.9	0.25Q	3/31/08	14.4 -	12.5
1.62	1.83	1.70	7.28	6.62	5.71	7.1 -	5.5	1.37	1.28	1.14	3.0	0.35Q	3/10/08	52.0 -	40.1
0.29	0.29	0.29	1.15	1.14	0.98	19.8 -	16.5	0.95	0.94	0.93	4.5	0.24Q	3/15/08	22.8 -	19.0
0.58	-	-	2.14	1.64	1.43	18.4 -	11.1	0.36	0.22	0.20	1.2	0.12Q	3/18/08	39.4 -	23.8
0.39	-	-	1.82	1.59	1.86	22.7 -	13.2	0.08	0.08	0.08	0.2	0.02Q	3/5/08	41.3 -	24.0
0.28	-	-	-0.01	-1.48	-0.84										
0.05	0.03	0.16	0.51	0.67	-2.01	54.9 -	23.5							28.0 -	12.0
5.88	8.92	13.47	58.38	11.92	-30.72	3.2 -	2.1	2.75	1.40	1.40	1.8	5.A	2/11/08	185.4 -	120.8
0.00	0.88	-0.15	0.17	0.89	0.91			1.59	1.59	1.42		0.3978Q	4/16/08		
0.37	0.45	-	1.62	1.26	1.30	24.3 -	15.8	0.44	0.40	0.36	1.4	0.125Q	4/15/08	39.4 -	25.6
0.85	1.86	-1.56	-2.63	7.30	6.01			1.90	1.18	1.04	3.7	0.6302Q	3/31/08	53.3 -	47.8

SYMBOL	COMPANY	NATURE OF BUSINESS	FISCAL YEAR-END	TOTAL REV. $MILL	NET INCOME $MILL	TOTAL ASSETS $MILL	NET STK EQUITY $MILL	NO OF INST	INST. HOLDINGS (SHARES)
FFG	FBL Financial Group, Inc.	Insurance	12/31/07	914.6	86.3	14003.0	902.9	56	8570380
AGM A	Federal Agricultural Mortgage Corp.	Credit & Lending	12/31/07	284.5	6.7	4977.6	223.6	63	7839106
FRT	Federal Realty Investment Trust (M	Property, Real Estate & Developmen	12/31/07	485.9	195.5	2989.3	1114.6	158	40924994
FSS	Federal Signal Corp. (United States	Automotive	12/31/07	1268.1	54.9	1177.1	445.3	133	38277513
FII	Federated Investors Inc (PA)	Wealth Management	12/31/07	1127.6	217.5	841.0	574.0	205	60638677
FPT	Federated Premier Intermediate Mu	Trusts & Holding Entities	11/30/07	7.9	6.9	162.2	98.3	-	-
FMN	Federated Premier Municipal Incom	Trusts & Holding Entities	11/30/07	7.8	6.9	144.7	89.5	5	38786
FDX	FedEx Corp	Aviation	5/31/07	35214.0	2016.0	24000.0	12656.0	618	219062574
FCH	FelCor Lodging Trust, Inc.	Property, Real Estate & Developmen	12/31/06	991.0	51.0	2583.2	1010.9	119	43646333
FGP	Ferrellgas Partners, L.P.	Retail - Fuel & Oil	7/31/07	1992.4	34.8	1503.4	-	41	4386743
FOE	Ferro Corp.	Chemicals	12/31/07	2204.8	-94.5	1638.3	476.3	120	35219807
FNF	Fidelity National Financial Inc	Insurance	12/31/07	5524.0	129.8	7556.4	3244.1	-	-
FIS	Fidelity National Information Service	Credit & Lending	12/31/07	4758.0	561.2	9794.6	3781.2	-	-
HCE	Fiduciary / Claymore Dynamic Equit	Trusts & Holding Entities	-	-	-	-	-	-	-
FMO	Fiduciary / Claymore MLP Opportun	Trusts & Holding Entities	-	-	-	-	-	4	87693
FIF	Financial Federal Corp. (United Stat	Credit & Lending	7/31/07	191.3	50.0	2120.1	387.8	102	17822253
FAC	First Acceptance Corp	Insurance	6/30/07	347.6	-16.7	498.9	239.5	48	8040560
FAF	First American Corp (The)	Insurance	12/31/07	8195.6	-3.1	8647.9	2984.8	223	58117403
FBP	First Bancorp (PR)	Commercial Banking	12/31/07	1256.4	68.1	17186.9	1421.6	123	34933428
FCF	First Comnmonwealth Financial Corp	Commercial Banking	12/31/07	380.0	46.3	5883.6	568.8	84	13741744
FF	First Financial Fund, Inc.	Trusts & Holding Entities	3/31/06	-	6.4	442.4	439.7	20	1686422
FHN	First Horizon National Corp	Commercial Banking	12/31/07	3165.9	-170.1	37015.5	2135.6	303	56506195
FR	First Industrial Realty Trust, Inc.	Property, Real Estate & Developmen	12/31/07	434.9	155.1	3258.0	923.9	161	27516122
FMD	First Marblehead Corp	Credit & Lending	6/30/07	880.7	371.3	1214.5	842.6	149	28941849
FMR	First Mercury Financial Corp	Insurance	12/31/07	202.6	41.7	747.3	229.4	-	-
FPO	First Potomac Realty Trust	Property, Real Estate & Developmen	12/31/07	124.6	0.5	1052.3	330.8	53	12878062
FEO	First Trust / Aberdeen Emerging Op	Trusts & Holding Entities	-	-	-	-	-	-	-
FAM	First Trust / Aberdeen Global Oppor	Trusts & Holding Entities	12/31/07	38.0	23.4	471.6	322.0	7	113917
FAV	First Trust Active Dividend Income	Trusts & Holding Entities	7/19/07	-	-	0.5	-	-	-
FFA	First Trust Enhanced Equity Income	Trusts & Holding Entities	12/31/07	7.5	2.9	371.3	367.0	10	427963
FCT	First Trust Four Corners Senior Floa	Trusts & Holding Entities	12/31/07	58.8	41.9	800.1	478.2	16	945623
FHI	First Trust Strategic High Income Fu	Trusts & Holding Entities	10/31/06	-	18.4	178.2	176.4	-	-
FHY	First Trust Strategic High Income Fu	Trusts & Holding Entities	10/31/06	-	11.1	254.2	190.1	-	-
FMY	First Trust/FIDAC Mortgage Income	Trusts & Holding Entities	10/31/06	-	4.2	97.0	74.5	-	-
FGB	First Trust/Gallatin Specialty Financ	Trusts & Holding Entities	-	-	-	-	-	-	-
FE	FirstEnergy Corp.	Electricity	12/31/07	12802.0	1309.0	32068.0	8977.0	303	225294433
FED	Firstfed Financial Corp.	Other Depository Banking	12/31/07	608.9	92.9	7223.0	654.5	137	13330516
FBC	Flagstar Bancorp, Inc. (United State	Other Depository Banking	12/31/07	1022.6	-39.2	15792.7	693.0	135	23786829
FSR	Flagstone Reinsurance Holdings Lt	Insurance	12/31/06	244.6	152.3	1144.5	864.5	-	-
FLC	Flaherty & Crumrine / Claymore Tot	Trusts & Holding Entities	11/30/06	-	20.0	360.2	227.7	8	193883
PFD	Flaherty & Crumrine Preferred Inco	Trusts & Holding Entities	11/30/07	16.5	14.2	217.7	135.6	14	319617
PFO	Flaherty & Crumrine Preferred Inco	Trusts & Holding Entities	11/30/07	14.6	12.4	191.4	119.1	12	331328
FFC	Flaherty & Crumrine/Claymore Pref	Trusts & Holding Entities	11/30/07	106.4	95.3	1368.2	821.2	18	506995
FLE	Fleetwood Enterprises Inc	Automotive	4/29/07	2007.9	-90.0	703.2	84.2	120	67645800
FTK	Flotek Industries Inc	Chemicals	12/31/07	158.0	16.7	160.8	77.5	2	25950
FLO	Flowers Foods, Inc. (United States)	Food	12/29/07	2036.7	94.6	987.5	656.2	117	36112520
FLS	Flowserve Corp.	Industrial Machinery and Equipment	12/31/07	3762.7	255.8	3520.4	1293.0	161	50500591
FLR	Fluor Corp. (New)	Construction - Public Infrastructure	12/31/07	16691.0	533.3	5796.2	2274.5	264	83101222
FMC	FMC Corp.	Chemicals	12/31/07	2632.9	132.4	2733.4	1064.3	180	33230094
FTI	FMC Technologies, Inc.	Oil and Gas	12/31/07	4615.4	302.8	3211.1	1021.7	178	63499888
FMX	Fomento Economico Mexicano, S.A	Food	12/31/06	126427.0	6622.0	145390.0	74228.0	112	38547188
FL	Foot Locker, Inc.	Retail - Apparel and Accessory Store	2/3/07	5750.0	251.0	3249.0	2295.0	244	129901771
F	Ford Motor Co. (DE)	Automotive	12/31/07	172455.0	-2723.0	285727.0	5628.0	445	764778098
FCZ	Ford Motor Credit Company LLC	Credit & Lending	12/31/07	3820.0	775.0	169023.0	13394.0	3	502420
FDG	Fording Canadian Coal Trust	Mining	12/31/07	1427.3	333.3	1086.8	311.8	108	21743999
FCE A	Forest City Enterprises, Inc.	Property, Real Estate & Developmen	1/31/07	1168.8	177.3	8981.6	1025.8	3	851500
FRX	Forest Laboratories, Inc.	Pharmaceuticals	3/31/07	3441.8	454.1	3653.4	3024.8	406	310394145
FST	Forest Oil Corp.	Oil and Gas	12/31/07	1083.9	169.3	5695.5	2411.8	190	55715522
FOR	Forestar Real Estate Group Inc	Building & General Construction	12/29/07	178.0	24.8	748.7	433.2	-	-
FDI	Fort Dearborn Income Securities Inc	Trusts & Holding Entities	-	-	-	-	-	11	238072
FIG	Fortress Investment Group LLC	Finance & Investment	-	-	-	-	-	-	-
FO	Fortune Brands Inc	Metal Products	12/31/07	8563.1	762.6	13956.9	5685.5	7	1326
FCL	Foundation Coal Holdings Inc	Coal Mining	12/31/07	1489.7	32.6	1908.2	336.3	95	18976892
FGC	FPL Group Capital Inc.	Media	-	-	-	-	-	-	-
FPL	FPL Group, Inc.	Electricity	12/31/07	15263.0	1312.0	40123.0	10735.0	554	256054487
FTE	France Telecom S.A.	Communications	12/31/04	46158.0	3017.0	98693.0	17683.0	59	29211196
FC	Franklin Covey Co.	Accounting & Management Consulti	8/31/07	284.1	7.6	196.6	100.9	14	3944882
BEN	Franklin Resources, Inc.	Wealth Management	9/30/07	6205.8	1772.9	9943.3	7332.3	380	117174906
FT	Franklin Universal Trust	Trusts & Holding Entities	-	-	-	-	-	21	2496001
FRE	Freddie Mac	Credit & Lending	12/31/06	44002.0	2211.0	813081.0	28301.0	1	10000
FCX	Freeport-McMoRan Copper & Gold	Non-Precious Metals	12/31/07	16939.0	2977.0	40661.0	18234.0	347	166159681
FMT	Fremont General Corp.	Commercial Banking	12/31/06	736.6	-202.3	12890.5	1114.0	152	45550475
FMS	Fresenius Medical Care AG & Co K	Medical Instruments & Equipment	12/31/06	8499.0	536.7	13044.7	4870.2	64	9842017
FDP	Fresh Del Monte Produce Inc.	Retail - Food & Beverage	12/29/06	3214.3	-145.1	2082.2	1011.7	87	20669686
FBR	Friedman Billings Ramsey Group In	Property, Real Estate & Developmen	12/31/07	582.9	-660.3	2945.0	393.7	198	79158576
FTO	Frontier Oil Corp.	Oil and Gas	12/31/07	5188.7	449.1	1863.8	1038.6	136	42590646
FRO	Frontline Ltd	Shipping	12/31/06	1583.9	516.0	4589.9	668.6	97	13723790
FCN	FTI Consulting Inc.	Accounting & Management Consulti	12/31/06	707.9	42.0	1391.2	565.1	110	44277877
FUL	Fuller (H.B.) Company	Chemicals	12/1/07	1400.3	102.2	1364.6	799.0	128	22399910
FRM	Furmanite Corp	Building & General Construction	12/31/07	290.3	12.5	172.1	78.3	-	-

EARNINGS PER SHARE QUARTERLY 1st	2nd	3rd	ANNUAL 2007	2006	2005	P/E RATIO		DIVIDENDS PER SHARE 2007	2006	2005	AV. YLD %	DIV. DECLARED AMOUNT	PAYABLE	PRICE RANGE 2007	
0.80	1.12	0.54	2.84	3.01	2.47	10.4 -	8.5	0.48	0.46	0.42	1.8	0.125Q	3/31/08	29.6 -	24.3
0.37	1.74	-0.82	0.42	2.68	2.37	74.3 -	40.8	0.40	0.40	0.40	1.7	0.8Q	3/31/08	31.2 -	17.1
0.41	0.47	0.41	3.45	1.92	1.94	15.2 -	10.1	2.37	2.46	2.37	5.4	0.61Q	4/15/08	52.5 -	34.7
0.64	0.23	0.09	1.15	0.47	-0.10	17.8 -	13.9	0.24	0.24	0.24	1.3	0.06Q	4/4/08	20.4 -	16.0
0.50	0.54	0.57	2.12	1.86	1.48	15.8 -	12.7	0.81	0.69	0.57	2.7	0.21Q	2/15/08	33.6 -	26.9
-	-	-	0.99	0.96	0.92	-		0.69	0.69	0.76	-	0.0575M	4/1/08	-	
-	-	-	1.12	1.12	1.12	13.4 -	11.4	0.80	0.87	0.97	5.7	0.067M	4/1/08	15.0 -	12.8
1.58	1.54	1.26	6.48	5.83	4.72	15.5 -	10.0	0.36	0.32	0.28	0.5	0.1Q	4/1/08	100.5 -	64.9
0.32	0.73	-	-	0.20	-5.01	-		-	0.80	0.15	-	0.5Q	1/31/08	14.8 -	9.7
-0.36	0.76	-	0.55	0.41	1.50	46.9 -	35.3	2.00	2.00	2.00	9.1	0.5Q	3/14/08	25.8 -	19.4
0.14	0.10	0.12	-2.23	0.44	0.35	-		0.58	0.58	0.58	2.4	0.145Q	3/10/08	27.4 -	18.5
0.37	0.38	0.03	0.59	2.39	3.11	-		-	-	-	-	0.3Q	3/27/08	-	
0.30	0.75	1.25	2.86	1.37	2.06	13.9 -	11.0	-	3.75	0.20	-	0.05Q	3/27/08	39.6 -	31.4
-	-	-	-	-0.07	-0.02	-		-	1.70	0.85	-	0.425Q	2/29/08	-	
-	-	-	-	-0.33	-0.26	-		-	1.25	0.94	-	0.36Q	1/31/08	20.1 -	20.0
0.50	0.51	-	1.90	1.65	1.41	13.8 -	10.4	0.55	0.37	0.20	2.4	0.15Q	4/10/08	26.3 -	19.7
0.04	-0.25	-	-0.35	0.57	0.53	-		-	-	-	-	0.006U	6/28/02	9.2 -	6.0
0.84	-0.68	0.49	-0.03	2.92	4.97	-		0.88	0.72	0.72	3.0	0.22Q	4/15/08	35.1 -	24.6
0.15	0.16	0.05	0.32	0.53	0.90	101.3 -	54.9	0.28	0.28	0.28	1.2	0.07Q	3/31/08	32.4 -	17.6
0.15	0.16	0.17	0.63	0.74	0.83	25.0 -	19.1	0.68	0.68	0.67	4.8	0.17Q	1/15/08	15.8 -	12.0
-	-	-	-	0.15	0.38	-		-	4.12	5.10	-	0.18A	12/31/07	24.0 -	18.4
0.55	0.17	-0.11	-1.35	3.62	3.40	-		1.80	1.80	1.74	4.1	0.2Q	4/1/08	48.0 -	41.8
0.66	0.67	0.66	2.99	2.04	1.80	14.1 -	10.9	2.85	2.81	2.79	7.6	0.4531Q	3/31/08	42.1 -	32.7
1.80	-1.26	-	3.92	2.45	1.59	9.8 -	3.8	0.62	0.32	-	2.3	0.12Q	12/21/07	38.6 -	15.0
0.55	0.58	0.59	2.25	1.58	0.80	-		-	-	-	-	-	-	-	
-0.01	-	0.01	0.02	0.45	0.08	1162.5 -	846.0	1.36	1.24	1.13	6.7	0.34Q	2/8/08	23.3 -	16.9
-	-	-	-	0.29	-	-		-	-	-	-	0.39Q	3/31/08	-	
-	-	-	1.34	1.38	1.34	14.9 -	14.3	1.70	2.03	1.30	8.6	0.13M	4/15/08	20.0 -	19.2
-	-	-	-	-	-	-		-	-	-	-	0.24Q	1/18/08	-	
-	-	-	0.14	0.02	0.01	144.1 -	136.4	1.26	1.60	1.60	6.4	0.4Q	3/31/08	20.2 -	19.1
-	-	-	1.66	1.48	0.95	12.2 -	10.8	1.50	1.30	0.91	7.8	0.1078M	3/17/08	20.2 -	18.0
-	-	-	-	2.08	0.39	-		-	2.15	0.15	-	0.16M	4/15/08	-	
-	-	-	-	1.18	-	-		-	-	-	-	0.1667M	4/15/08	-	
-	-	-	-	1.03	0.36	-		-	1.06	0.31	-	0.085M	4/15/08	-	
-	-	-	-	-	-	-		-	-	-	-	0.37Q	2/29/08	-	
0.92	1.10	1.34	4.22	3.81	2.61	10.2 -	8.4	2.00	1.80	1.67	5.1	0.55Q	3/1/08	43.1 -	35.3
1.92	1.74	1.57	6.00	7.65	5.43	8.9 -	6.5	-	-	-	-	-	-	53.5 -	38.9
0.12	0.25	-0.53	-0.64	1.17	1.25	-		0.35	0.60	0.90	1.6	0.05Q	12/31/07	27.6 -	18.8
-	-	-	-	2.16	-0.22	-		-	-	-	-	0.04Q	3/12/08	-	
-	-	-	-	2.04	1.94	-		-	1.57	1.83	-	0.13M	3/31/08	26.6 -	21.8
-	-	-	1.35	1.29	1.22	14.7 -	11.1	1.03	1.05	1.17	5.8	0.0775M	3/31/08	19.8 -	14.9
-	-	-	1.06	1.02	0.96	14.2 -	11.5	0.79	0.80	0.91	5.8	0.068M	3/31/08	15.1 -	12.2
-	-	-	2.24	2.04	1.96	12.4 -	10.2	1.53	1.57	2.09	6.0	0.1325M	3/31/08	27.8 -	22.8
0.04	0.05	0.70	1.41	0.40	0.00	-		-	-	-	-	0.00U	11/19/01	10.0 -	10.3
0.20	0.25	0.26	0.88	0.61	0.47	2.8 -	0.4	-	-	-	-	-	-	2.5 -	0.4
0.01	0.24	0.24	1.02	0.07	0.04	10.9 -	9.2	0.40	0.32	0.20	4.0	0.120Q	3/7/08	14.2 -	9.4
0.59	1.11	1.10	4.46	2.02	0.21	6.2 -	4.2	0.60	-	-	2.6	0.26Q	4/0/08	07.6 -	10.0
0.94	1.05	1.02	5.05	2.95	2.62	9.3 -	6.3	0.80	0.80	0.64	1.9	0.25Q	4/2/08	54.5 -	36.8
0.58	0.11	0.48	1.71	1.67	1.49	14.6 -	9.7	0.41	0.36	-	1.9	0.105Q	4/17/08	25.0 -	16.6
0.45	0.55	0.59	2.26	1.97	0.75	7.6 -	5.1	-	-	-	-	-	-	17.2 -	11.5
-	-	-	-	-	-	-		-	-	-	-	-	-	17.6 -	12.3
0.11	-0.12	-0.22	1.60	1.68	1.88	17.0 -	12.5	0.40	0.32	0.26	1.7	0.15Q	5/2/08	27.2 -	20.1
-0.15	0.31	-0.19	-1.38	-6.72	1.05	-		-	0.25	0.40	-	0.05Q	9/1/06	17.1 -	12.7
-	-	-	-	-	-	-		-	-	-	-	-	-	26.8 -	23.7
0.52	0.79	-	2.25	3.39	5.67	11.4 -	4.7	2.43	4.15	4.77	15.2	0.53Q	1/15/08	25.7 -	10.7
-0.17	0.03	-0.11	1.70	0.01	0.03	15.1 -	13.5	0.26	0.22	0.29	1.1	0.08Q	3/17/08	25.6 -	22.9
0.83	0.71	0.06	1.41	2.08	2.25	55.0 -	36.1	-	-	-	-	-	-	17.0 -	00.0
0.11	1.08	0.65	2.18	2.66	2.41	10.5 -	7.2	-	-	-	-	-	-	22.8 -	15.7
-	-	-	0.70	1.47	0.99	-		-	-	-	-	-	-	-	
-	-	-	-	-	-	-		-	-	-	-	0.0947Q	12/31/07	15.6 -	13.7
-0.87	-0.66	-	-	-	-	-		-	-	-	-	0.225Q	10/12/07	-	
0.77	1.48	1.33	4.87	5.42	4.13	100.8 -	86.0	1.62	1.50	1.38	0.4	0.6675Q	3/10/08	491.0 -	419.0
0.53	-0.08	0.04	0.70	0.67	1.92	33.4 -	30.7	0.20	0.20	0.18	0.9	0.05Q	3/27/08	23.4 -	21.5
0.38	1.01	1.33	3.27	3.23	2.29	11.6 -	9.3	1.64	1.50	1.42	4.9	0.445Q	3/17/08	38.0 -	30.5
-	-	-	-	1.57	2.20	-		-	-	-	-	-	-	33.5 -	22.3
0.10	-	-	0.27	1.18	-0.34	10.8 -	6.1	-	-	-	-	-	-	2.9 -	1.6
2.12	-	-	7.03	4.86	4.06	10.1 -	6.7	0.57	0.36	2.40	1.0	0.2Q	4/11/08	70.8 -	47.4
-	-	-	-	-	-	-		-	-	-	-	0.038M	3/14/08	6.1 -	5.2
-	-	-	-	2.84	2.75	-		-	1.91	1.52	-	0.4185Q	12/31/07	47.4 -	46.2
2.02	2.62	1.87	7.50	6.63	4.67	5.9 -	3.8	1.38	4.75	2.50	3.8	1.6875Q	5/1/08	44.5 -	28.4
-7.74	-3.45	0.23	-	-2.72	4.37	-		-	0.45	0.33	-	0.12Q	1/31/07	30.8 -	16.3
-	-	-	-	5.44	4.64	-		-	1.29	1.18	-	-	-	27.2 -	20.4
-	-	-	-	-2.51	1.84	-		-	0.50	0.80	-	0.05Q	12/13/06	29.6 -	22.9
-1.08	0.06	-1.28	-3.95	-0.39	-1.01	-		0.15	0.50	1.22	0.7	0.05Q	10/31/07	28.0 -	15.9
0.68	2.23	1.28	4.62	3.37	2.40	1.4 -	0.9	0.18	0.11	0.57	3.5	0.05Q	4/16/08	6.7 -	4.0
-	-	-	-	6.90	8.11	-		-	-	-	-	-	-	47.3 -	16.1
0.36	0.53	0.50	-	1.04	1.35	-		-	-	-	-	-	-	24.1 -	13.7
0.32	-	1.68	-	2.23	1.05	9.0 -	7.4	0.26	0.25	0.24	1.9	0.0645Q	2/21/08	15.1 -	12.4
0.04	0.11	0.10	0.35	-0.10	-0.13	8.7 -	6.4	-	-	-	-	-	-	3.0 -	2.3

SYMBOL	COMPANY	NATURE OF BUSINESS	FISCAL YEAR-END	TOTAL REV. $MILL	NET INCOME $MILL	TOTAL ASSETS $MILL	NET STK EQUITY $MILL	NO OF INST	INST. HOLDINGS (SHARES)
FBN	Furniture Brands International Inc. (	Furniture and Fixtures	12/31/07	2082.1	-45.6	1463.1	844.8	158	55642347
GCV	Gabelli Convertible and Income Sec	Trusts & Holding Entities	12/31/07	6.9	5.1	150.1	99.6	12	1368355
GDV	Gabelli Dividend & Income Trust	Trusts & Holding Entities	12/31/07	72.4	44.3	2485.3	1975.8	-	
GAB	Gabelli Equity Trust Inc.	Trusts & Holding Entities	12/31/07	42.9	19.1	2001.5	1586.4	36	1380830
GDL	Gabelli Global Deal Fund	Finance & Investment						-	
GGT	Gabelli Global Multimedia Trust Inc.	Trusts & Holding Entities	12/31/07	4.4	1.0	252.3	201.5	-	
GUT	Gabelli Utility Trust	Trusts & Holding Entities	12/31/07	9.0	5.0	301.8	245.6	1	34885
GFA	Gafisa S.A.	Property, Real Estate & Developmen	12/31/07	1172.2	113.6	2950.5	1530.8	-	
AJG	Gallagher (Arthur J.) & Co.	Insurance	12/31/07	1623.3	138.8	3556.8	715.5	221	64171619
GBL	GAMCO Investors Inc	Finance Intermediaries & Services	12/31/07	292.4	79.6	757.6	501.3	-	
GME	GameStop Corp (New)	Retail - Appliances and Electrical	2/2/08	7094.0	288.3	3775.9	1862.4	-	
GCI	Gannett Co Inc	Media	12/26/99	5260.2	957.9	9006.4	4629.6	635	200922938
GDI	Gardner Denver, Inc.	Industrial Machinery and Equipment	12/31/07	1868.8	205.1	1905.6	1159.7	128	17985763
IT	Gartner, Inc.	Accounting & Management Consulti	12/31/07	1189.2	73.6	1133.2	17.5	113	52606027
GHS	Gatehouse Media Inc	Media	12/31/07	588.9	-231.4	1875.0	454.0	-	
GMT	GATX Corp.	Rail Transport	12/31/07	1346.0	203.7	4725.6	1149.5	200	47193444
GET	Gaylord Entertainment Co. (New)	Media	12/31/07	747.7	111.9	2336.9	941.5	122	34149270
GNK	Genco Shipping & Trading Ltd	Misc. Transportation Services	12/31/06	133.2	63.5	578.3	353.5	-	
GY	GenCorp Inc. (United States)	Defense	11/30/07	745.4	69.0	995.2	-52.0	147	56545992
DNA	Genentech, Inc.	Pharmaceuticals	12/31/07	11724.0	2769.0	18940.0	11905.0	451	414337903
GAM	General American Investors Co., In	Trusts & Holding Entities	12/31/07	2.8	9.8	1419.4	1202.9	1	1400
BGC	General Cable Corp. (DE) (New)	Metal Works	12/31/07	4614.8	208.6	3798.0	651.3	-	
GD	General Dynamics Corp.	Shipping	12/31/07	27240.0	2072.0	25733.0	11768.0	576	157563739
GEJ	General Electric Capital Corp.	Credit & Lending	12/31/07	67249.0	9815.0	620386.0	61230.0	-	
GE	General Electric Co	Electrical	12/31/07	172738.0	22208.0	795337.0	115559.0	1391	5783708095
GGP	General Growth Properties, Inc. (DE	Property, Real Estate & Developmen	12/31/07	3261.8	288.0	28814.3	1456.7	281	188810930
GMR	General Maritime Corp. (Marshall Isl	Shipping	12/31/06	326.0	156.8	843.7	763.9	-	
GIS	General Mills, Inc. (United States)	Food	5/27/07	12442.0	1144.0	18184.0	5319.0	586	252571605
GM	General Motors Corp	Automotive	12/31/07	207349.0	-1978.0	186192.0	-5441.0	440	475333989
GM	General Motors Corp	Communications	12/31/94	10052.4	821.9	8786.5	4232.5	4	467791
GM	General Motors Corp	Communications	12/31/02	8934.9	-893.8	17885.1	9977.1	4	467791
GCO	Genesco Inc. (United States)	Retail - Apparel and Accessory Store	2/2/08	1502.1	6.9	804.6	421.4	139	24102846
GWR	Genesee & Wyoming Inc.	Rail Transport	12/31/07	516.2	55.2	1077.8	431.0	122	21942715
GLS	Genesis Lease Ltd	Aviation	12/31/06	-	28.8	-	476.7	-	
GPC	Genuine Parts Co.	Retail - Automotive	12/31/07	10843.2	506.3	4774.1	2716.7	341	123327135
GNW	Genworth Financial Inc	Insurance	12/31/07	11125.0	1220.0	114315.0	13478.0	192	219765011
GEO	Geo Group Inc	Miscellaneous Business Services	12/30/07	1024.8	41.8	1192.6	527.7	70	7865641
GGC	Georgia Gulf Corp.	Chemicals	12/31/07	3157.3	-266.0	2201.7	196.8	180	27980840
GPJ	Georgia Power Co.	Electricity						3	1401662
TGP	Georgia-Pacific Corp.	Forestry	12/30/00	394.0	162.0	1619.0	145.0	337	203688468
GRB	Gerber Scientific Inc.	Industrial Machinery and Equipment	4/30/07	574.8	13.5	336.0	144.5	65	15420777
GNA	Gerdau Ameristeel Corp	Metal Works	12/31/06	4464.2	378.6	3176.4	1852.1	45	36700543
GGB	Gerdau S.A. (Brazil)	Metal Works	12/31/06	23516.8	2880.9	26929.5	9964.6	64	14559230
GYI	Getty Images, Inc.	Advertising, Marketing & PR	12/31/07	857.6	125.9	2012.2	1427.9	221	54304866
GTY	Getty Realty Corp. (New)	Property, Real Estate & Developmen	12/31/07	78.5	33.9	396.9	212.2	84	6613310
GIL	Gildan Activewear Inc.	Apparel	9/30/07	964.4	130.0	874.5	663.6	53	15422371
GLT	Glatfelter	Paper Products	12/31/07	1157.8	63.5	1287.1	476.1	132	36176285
GSK	GlaxoSmithKline Plc	Pharmaceuticals	12/31/04	19986.0	3908.0	22944.0	5937.0	455	266004941
GLG	GLG Partners Inc	Miscellaneous	12/31/07	1040.1	59.3	984.1	91.9	-	
GRT	Glimcher Realty Trust	Property, Real Estate & Developmen	12/31/07	302.2	38.4	1830.9	189.1	100	24372525
GCA	Global Cash Access Holdings Inc	Trusts & Holding Entities	12/31/07	600.9	23.7	539.3	138.3	-	
GCF	Global Currency Strategy Income F	Trusts & Holding Entities						-	
GHI	Global High Income Fund Inc	Trusts & Holding Entities	10/31/06	-	16.8	341.1	320.5	13	442413
GLP	Global Partners LP	Petroleum and Coal Products	12/31/07	6757.8	47.0	1159.2	-	-	
GPN	Global Payments, Inc.	Miscellaneous Business Services	5/31/07	1061.5	143.0	1200.6	957.8	180	37064195
GAI	Global Tech Appliances, Inc.	Electrical	3/31/00	-	8.7	-	122.9	-	
GMA	GMAC LLC	Credit & Lending	12/31/07	31490.0	-2332.0	247710.0	15565.0	-	
GCT	GMH Communities Trust	Property, Real Estate & Developmen	12/31/07	332.5	31.4	1488.8	267.1	53	24266614
GNC	GNC Corp	Retail - Food & Beverage	12/31/05	1317.7	18.4	1023.8	212.1	-	
GOL	Gol Linhas Aereas Inteligentes SA	Aviation	12/31/07	4967.3	268.5	5764.8	2411.0	48	16730121
GFI	Gold Fields Ltd. (New)	Precious Metals	6/30/05	11756.3	127.7	23997.4	16534.1	106	66628300
GG	Goldcorp Inc (New)	Precious Metals	12/31/06	1710.0	408.3	17965.9	12475.0	149	129935760
GS	Goldman Sachs Group, Inc.	Finance Intermediaries & Services	11/30/07	87968.0	11599.0	1119796.0	42800.0	722	316151898
GR	Goodrich Corp.	Aviation	12/31/07	6392.2	482.6	7534.0	2579.4	252	100747952
GDP	Goodrich Petroleum Corp. (Holding	Oil and Gas	12/31/07	111.3	-45.0	590.1	283.6	48	4461794
GT	Goodyear Tire & Rubber Co.	Rubber Products	12/31/07	19644.0	602.0	17191.0	2850.0	237	137521453
GOT	Gottschalks, Inc.	Retail - General	2/3/07	687.5	2.6	350.1	124.6	26	3443286
GPX	GP Strategies Corp.	Vocational Education Services	12/31/07	248.4	9.7	147.4	90.4	23	7203384
GRA	Grace (W.R.) Co. (DE) (New)	Chemicals	12/31/07	3115.2	80.3	3869.0	-386.6	122	59493350
GGG	Graco Inc.	Industrial Machinery and Equipment	12/28/07	841.3	152.8	536.7	244.7	211	51955322
GTI	Graftech International Ltd.	Electrical	12/31/07	1004.8	153.7	866.7	112.7	113	101426048
GWW	Grainger (W.W.) Inc.	Engineering Services	12/31/07	6418.0	420.1	3094.0	2098.1	357	60286651
GKK	Gramercy Capital Corp	Property, Real Estate & Developmen	12/31/07	327.3	161.6	4205.1	748.7	53	10554003
GVA	Granite Construction Inc.	Construction - Public Infrastructure	12/31/07	2737.9	112.1	1786.4	700.2	137	27006060
GRP	Grant Prideco Inc	Oil and Gas	12/31/07	1908.6	519.2	2350.7	1709.8	217	112650015
GPK	Graphic Packaging Holding Co	Paper Products	12/31/07	2421.2	-74.6	2777.3	144.0	-	
GTN	Gray Television Inc	Media	12/31/07	307.3	-23.2	1626.0	337.8	84	40107153
GAP	Great Atlantic & Pacific Tea Compa	Retail - Food & Beverage	2/24/07	6850.3	26.9	2111.6	430.7	87	18181382
GNI	Great Northern Iron Ore Properties	Property, Real Estate & Developmen	12/31/07	17.2	14.5	17.5	12.0	24	70194
GXP	Great Plains Energy, Inc.	Industrial Machinery and Equipment	12/31/07	3267.1	159.2	4826.7	1606.9	201	28809692

EARNINGS PER SHARE QUARTERLY — 1st	2nd	3rd	ANNUAL — 2007	2006	2005	P/E RATIO	DIVIDENDS PER SHARE — 2007	2006	2005	AV. YLD %	DIV. DECLARED AMOUNT	PAYABLE	PRICE RANGE 2007
0.06	0.12	-0.28	-0.94	1.13	1.18	-	0.64	0.64	0.60	2.4	0.04Q	2/29/08	35.0 - 21.0
-	-	-	0.42	0.45	0.40	27.6 - 21.4	0.80	0.80	0.80	7.8	0.375Q	3/26/08	11.6 - 9.0
-	-	-	0.53	0.87	0.55	-	1.66	1.54	1.20	-	0.375Q	3/26/08	-
-	-	-	0.14	0.18	0.09	63.5 - 52.9	0.90	0.88	0.85	11.0	0.3875Q	3/26/08	8.9 - 7.4
-	-	-	-	-	-	-	-	-	-	-	0.4Q	3/25/08	-
-	-	-	0.10	0.29	0.16	259.9 - 222.0	0.75	0.63	0.60	3.0	0.375Q	3/26/08	26.0 - 22.2
-	-	-	0.19	0.17	0.18	138.2 - 115.8	0.72	0.72	0.72	2.9	0.3516Q	3/26/08	26.3 - 22.0
0.20	0.44	0.54	1.43	1.31	0.32	23.7 - 18.9	1.24	1.20	1.12	3.9	0.32Q	4/15/08	34.0 - 27.1
0.67	0.63	0.64	2.79	2.40	2.09	18.0 - 13.4	1.12	0.12	0.09	2.6	0.03Q	3/28/08	50.1 - 37.3
0.15	0.13	0.31	1.00	0.81	0.53	11.8 - 7.3	-	-	-	-			11.8 - 7.3
0.90	1.56	1.01	4.52	4.90	5.05	20.1 - 17.5	1.42	1.20	1.12	1.7	0.4Q	4/1/08	91.0 - 79.0
0.80	0.83	0.99	3.80	2.49	1.37	5.0 - 3.2	-	-	-	-			18.9 - 12.1
0.08	0.13	0.11	0.68	0.50	-0.02	19.7 - 16.2	-	-	-	-			13.4 - 11.0
-0.16	-0.05	-0.17	-4.99	-0.06	0.43	-	1.57	0.64	-	-	0.2Q	4/15/08	-
0.62	0.77	1.62	3.76	2.00	-0.29	8.0 - 5.5	0.96	0.84	0.80	3.8	0.27Q	3/31/08	30.1 - 20.5
0.08	2.52	-0.05	2.65	-1.96	-0.85	15.8 - 10.0	-	-	-	-	0.2Q	12/20/99	42.0 - 26.6
0.78	0.54	0.64	-	2.51	2.90	-	-	2.40	0.60	-	0.66Q	11/30/07	-
0.51	0.20	0.24	1.14	-0.69	-4.21	16.3 - 8.9	-	-	-	-	0.03Q	5/28/04	18.6 - 10.2
0.66	0.70	0.64	2.59	1.97	1.18	25.5 - 16.6	-	-	-	-			66.0 - 42.9
-	-	-	0.31	0.34	0.19	82.9 - 71.3	5.75	3.14	2.12	23.3	0.3719Q	3/24/08	25.7 - 22.1
0.71	1.15	1.11	3.82	2.00	0.41	-	-	-	-	-	0.7108Q	2/22/08	-
1.06	1.26	1.34	5.08	4.56	3.61	10.8 - 8.5	1.10	0.89	0.78	2.3	0.35Q	5/9/08	54.9 - 43.0
0.44	0.53	0.54	2.17	2.00	1.54	17.3 - 13.4	1.15	1.03	0.01	3.5	0.31Q	4/25/08	37.5 - 20.2
0.84	0.03	-0.04	1.16	0.24	0.32	31.0 - 21.6	1.65	1.68	1.49	6.0	0.5U	1/31/08	36.6 - 25.5
0.53	0.37	0.35	-	4.87	5.61	-	-	4.80	2.86	-	0.5Q	11/30/07	-
0.81	1.14	1.23	3.18	2.90	3.08	15.7 - 13.6	1.44	1.34	1.24	3.1	0.4Q	5/1/08	49.8 - 43.3
0.11	-	-	-	-3.50	-18.69	-	-	1.00	2.00	-	0.25Q	3/10/08	55.0 - 37.0
-	-	0.55	-	-	-	-	-	-	-	-	0.25Q	12/10/07	26.3 - 23.0
-	-	-	-	-	-	-	-	-	-	-	0.25Q	12/10/07	26.3 - 23.0
0.10	-0.19	0.23	2.59	2.38	1.91	12.0 - 5.9	-	-	-	-	0.375Q	1/30/08	31.1 - 15.4
0.04	0.27	0.42	1.41	3.10	1.20	13.5 - 10.1	-	-	-	-			19.0 - 14.2
			2673.07										
0.71	0.76	0.76	2.98	2.76	2.50	14.8 - 10.8	1.46	1.35	1.25	3.9	0.39Q	4/1/08	44.1 - 32.1
0.71	0.84	0.76	2.73	2.83	2.52	10.0 - 7.1	0.37	0.32	0.27	1.6	0.6563Q	3/3/08	27.3 - 19.5
0.13	-0.24	0.25	0.85	0.84	0.23	10.4 - 6.8	-	-	-	-			8.9 - 5.8
-1.01	-0.12	0.00	-7.75	1.41	2.79	-	0.32	0.32	0.32	0.9	0.08Q	10/10/07	57.6 - 24.9
-	0.44	-	-	-	-	-	-	-	-	-	0.3828Q	4/1/08	25.9 - 21.1
-	-	-	-	-	-	-	-	-	-	-	0.175Q	8/19/05	37.9 - 26.7
0.12	0.11	0.13	0.58	0.12	-0.25	14.5 - 9.5	-	-	-	-	0.08Q	2/28/01	8.4 - 5.5
0.44	0.45	0.40	-	1.24	0.97	-	-	0.30	0.22	-	0.02Q	3/13/08	7.2 - 3.1
-	-	-	-	-	-	-	-	-	-	-			8.1 - 3.5
0.62	0.56	0.43	2.10	2.11	2.29	22.0 - 22.6	-	-	-	-			60.3 - 17.5
0.42	0.40	0.52	1.37	1.73	1.84	21.8 - 15.7	1.85	1.81	1.76	7.2	0.465Q	4/10/08	29.9 - 21.5
0.13	0.17	0.43	1.07	0.88	0.71	8.0 - 6.1	-	-	-	-			8.5 - 6.5
0.07	0.04	0.17	1.40	-0.27	0.87	11.1 - 7.6	0.36	0.36	0.36	2.9	0.09Q	5/1/08	15.5 - 10.6
-	-	-	0.94	0.94	0.82	50.5 - 41.5	-	-	-	-			47.5 - 39.0
0.04	0.03	0.04	0.23	0.01	-	-	-	-	-	-	0.025Q	4/21/08	-
0.03	-0.14	1.23	0.56	-2.58	0.09	51.3 - 35.4	1.92	1.92	1.92	7.9	0.5078Q	4/15/08	28.7 - 19.9
0.10	0.10	0.07	0.29	0.02	0.00	-	-	-	-	-			-
-	-	-	-	0.71	-	-	-	-	-	-	0.3625Q	3/31/08	-
-	-	-	-	0.79	1.02	-	-	2.55	2.89	-	0.1073M	1/31/08	20.0 - 13.9
1.75	1.28	0.19	1.38	2.46	0.70	-	1.87	1.72	-	-	0.4875Q	3/14/08	-
0.53	0.48	-	1.73	1.53	1.17	17.0 - 12.0	0.08	0.08	0.08	0.3	0.02Q	2/29/08	29.7 - 20.9
-	-	-	-	-	-	-	-	-	-	-	1.35U	6/16/00	-
-	-	-	-	-	-	-	-	1.07	1.00	-			20.2 - 24.9
0.00	0.58	0.11	0.76	-0.12	0.18	18.6 - 15.8	0.66	0.85	0.91	5.1	0.165Q	1/15/08	14.1 - 12.0
-	0.17	0.18	-	-	-	-	-	-	-	-			16.4 - 8.2
-	-	-	3.98	2.70	0.26	3.8 - 2.3	-	-	-	-			14.9 - 9.3
0.18	0.00	0.11	-	0.93	0.83	-	-	-	-	-	0.015M	3/25/08	16.3 - 10.5
3.23	-	-	24.73	19.69	11.21	4.5 - 3.4	1.40	1.30	1.00	1.4	0.35Q	5/29/08	110.5 - 83.9
0.78	0.98	0.99	3.78	3.81	2.13	8.9 - 7.1	0.82	0.80	0.80	2.7	0.225Q	4/1/08	33.5 - 26.8
-0.02	-0.19	-0.94	-1.76	0.06	-0.75	-	-	-	-	-	0.6719Q	3/17/08	16.5 - 5.1
-0.96	0.26	2.75	2.65	-1.86	1.16	5.7 - 2.7	-	-	-	-	0.12Q	12/16/02	15.0 - 7.1
-0.34	-0.35	-0.30	0.19	0.38	0.40	48.0 - 17.9	-	-	-	-			9.1 - 3.4
0.12	0.14	0.15	0.56	0.40	0.38	5.4 - 3.8	-	-	-	-			3.0 - 2.1
0.07	0.29	0.23	1.12	0.27	1.00	13.3 - 2.2	-	-	-	-			14.9 - 2.5
0.50	0.66	0.60	2.32	2.17	1.80	16.3 - 11.4	0.66	0.58	0.52	2.1	0.185Q	5/7/08	37.7 - 26.4
0.17	0.55	0.30	1.37	0.86	-1.28	11.3 - 5.8	-	-	-	-			15.5 - 8.0
1.17	1.21	1.29	4.94	4.24	3.78	13.5 - 9.1	1.34	1.11	0.92	2.5	0.35Q	3/1/08	66.6 - 45.2
0.62	0.73	3.43	5.28	2.15	1.51	4.0 - 2.7	4.45	2.08	1.50	26.7	0.5078Q	4/15/08	21.3 - 14.0
-0.05	1.05	1.28	2.71	1.94	2.02	10.3 - 6.4	0.43	0.40	0.40	1.9	0.13Q	4/15/08	27.9 - 17.3
1.01	1.04	0.96	4.01	3.50	1.45	5.5 - 3.2	-	-	-	-			22.3 - 13.0
-0.19	-0.11	-0.07	-0.37	-0.50	-0.46	-	-	-	-	-			8.7 - 4.1
-0.24	-0.23	-0.09	-0.52	0.17	-0.05	-	0.12	0.12	0.12	1.0	0.03Q	4/25/08	14.1 - 10.0
-1.03	-2.18	1.35	0.64	9.64	-4.88	16.0 - 8.8	7.25	-	-	97.4	7.25Q	4/25/06	10.3 - 5.6
1.76	3.04	3.08	9.63	9.85	10.48	12.9 - 8.8	10.00	10.30	10.40	9.9	2.Q	4/30/08	124.5 - 85.0
0.28	0.29	0.72	1.85	1.61	2.15	19.1 - 15.2	1.66	1.66	1.66	5.4	1.125Q	6/1/08	35.3 - 28.2

SYMBOL	COMPANY	NATURE OF BUSINESS	FISCAL YEAR-END	TOTAL REV. $MILL	NET INCOME $MILL	TOTAL ASSETS $MILL	NET STK EQUITY $MILL	NO OF INST	INST. HOLDINGS (SHARES)
GB	GreatBatch Inc	Electrical	12/28/07	318.7	15.0	663.9	322.7	-	-
GCH	Greater China Fund, Inc. (The)	Trusts & Holding Entities	12/31/07	9.1	0.1	715.1	486.5	39	2549841
GBX	Greenbrier Companies Inc (The)	Rail Transport	8/31/07	1223.8	22.0	1072.7	243.6	77	6932445
GHL	Greenhill & Co Inc	Miscellaneous Business Services	12/31/07	400.4	115.3	374.2	143.1	74	5711940
GEF	Greif Inc	Paper Products	10/31/07	3322.3	156.4	2652.7	999.9	120	9728809
GFF	Griffon Corp.	Metal Products	9/30/07	1616.6	22.1	959.9	466.9	142	27553247
GPI	Group 1 Automotive, Inc.	Retail - Automotive	12/31/07	6393.0	68.0	2505.3	684.5	97	17409652
GBE	Grubb & Ellis Co	Property, Real Estate & Developmen	12/31/07	231.4	20.8	969.4	408.6	5	703976
GMK	Gruma S.A.B. de C.V.	Agricultural Crop Production	12/31/06	30654.2	1524.7	30237.5	17048.1	11	178319
PAC	Grupo Aeroportuario del Pacifico, S.	Aviation							
ASR	Grupo Aeroportuario del Sureste SA	Aviation	12/31/06	2239.0	528.1	14941.4	13785.1	68	16130268
SAB	Grupo Casa Saba, S.A. de C.V.	Pharmaceuticals	12/31/06	23599.4	883.4	10388.5	5343.2	5	846953
RC	Grupo Radio Centro S.A.B. de C.V.	Media	12/31/06	795.7	418.9	1659.8	1337.2	6	470405
TV	Grupo Televisa, S.A.	Media	12/31/06	37931.8	8586.2	83030.5	36604.4	140	77875084
TMM	Grupo TMM, S.A.B.	Shipping	12/31/06	224.1	69.9	635.5	182.7	31	17365546
GNV	GSC Investment Corp	Finance & Investment	2/28/07	-	-0.1	-	-0.1	-	-
GSH	Guangshen Railway Co., Ltd.	Rail Transport	12/31/05	3276.9	647.0	11856.5	9844.8	15	805838
GFG	Guaranty Financial Group Inc	Commercial Banking	12/31/07	1153.0	78.0	16796.0	1138.0	-	-
GES	GUESS ?, Inc. (United States)	Apparel	2/2/08	1749.9	186.5	1186.2	657.0	87	15340177
GLF	Gulfmark Offshore, Inc.	Oil and Gas	12/31/07	306.0	99.0	934.0	676.1	78	14323522
HQH	H&Q HealthCare Investors	Trusts & Holding Entities	9/30/07	-	-4.1	444.7	444.0	31	2545837
HQL	H&Q Life Sciences Investors	Trusts & Holding Entities	9/30/07	-	-1.7	309.1	308.0	27	921110
HAE	Haemonetics Corp.	Medical Instruments & Equipment	3/31/07	449.6	49.1	572.7	479.6	148	23507527
HAL	Halliburton Company	Oil and Gas	12/31/07	15264.0	3499.0	13135.0	6866.0	484	425130204
HPS	Hancock John Preferred Income Fd	Trusts & Holding Entities	5/31/07	72.4	64.8	1082.9	731.6	23	1174675
HPF	Hancock John Preferred Income Fu	Trusts & Holding Entities	7/31/07	-	47.2	745.9	487.5	23	782837
HTD	Hancock John Tax-Advantaged Divi	Trusts & Holding Entities	12/31/07	62.2	53.0	1221.7	840.9	17	1044534
HBI	Hanesbrands Inc	Apparel	12/29/07	4474.5	126.1	3439.5	288.9	-	-
HGR	Hanger Orthopedic Group, Inc.	Diagnostic Services	12/31/07	637.4	19.3	759.7	190.5	69	15357555
THG	Hanover Insurance Group Inc	Insurance	12/31/07	2786.8	253.1	9815.6	2299.0	-	-
HOG	Harley-Davidson Inc	Automotive	12/31/07	6143.0	933.8	5656.6	2375.5	597	206455935
HAR	Harman International Industries, Inc	Electrical	6/30/07	3551.1	314.0	2508.9	1494.0	258	60560785
HMY	Harmony Gold Mining Co. Ltd.	Precious Metals	6/30/05	7822.0	-3214.0	33815.0	23218.0	98	80627759
HRS	Harris Corp.	Instruments and Related Products	6/29/07	4243.0	480.4	4406.0	1903.8	280	109012889
HWD	Harry Winston Diamond Corp	Precious Metals	1/31/07	558.8	104.3	1287.9	501.7	-	-
HSC	Harsco Corp.	Metal Products	12/31/07	3688.2	299.5	3905.4	1566.1	204	26963706
HHS	Harte-Hanks, Inc. (United States)	Advertising, Marketing & PR	12/31/07	1162.9	92.6	951.9	408.5	166	47958296
HIG	Hartford Financial Services Group I	Insurance	12/31/07	25916.0	2949.0	360361.0	19204.0	484	264198596
HSF	Hartford Income Shares Fund, Inc. (	Trusts & Holding Entities	7/31/07	7.9	7.1	103.1	102.1	12	203374
HLGF S09	Hartford Life Insurance Co	Insurance	12/31/06	6089.0	731.0	241150.0	7660.0	-	-
HMX	Hartmarx Corp.	Apparel	11/30/07	564.9	-4.2	459.9	228.0	96	19794190
HNR	Harvest Natural Resources Inc (Unit	Oil and Gas	12/31/07	11.2	57.2	413.5	313.8	97	28768962
HAS	Hasbro, Inc. (United States)	Consumer Accessories	12/30/07	3837.6	333.0	3237.1	1385.1	224	151514975
HVT	Haverty Furniture Cos., Inc.	Retail - Furniture & Home Furnishing	12/31/07	784.6	1.8	421.9	278.8	85	12540353
HE	Hawaiian Electric Industries, Inc.	Electricity	12/31/07	2536.4	84.8	10293.9	1275.4	185	24988511
HCC	HCC Insurance Holdings, Inc.	Insurance	12/31/07	2388.4	395.4	8074.6	2440.4	205	65243241
HCP	HCP, Inc.	Property, Real Estate & Developmen	12/31/07	982.5	589.0	12521.8	4103.7	-	-
HDB	HDFC Bank Ltd	Commercial Banking	3/31/07	84052.5	11414.5	-	-	82	16971375
HED	Head N.V.	Consumer Accessories	12/31/05	359.6	6.7	432.3	166.5	5	6968407
HW	Headwaters Inc	Petroleum and Coal Products	9/30/07	1207.8	20.1	1655.9	830.3	202	34157033
HCN	Health Care REIT Inc.	Property, Real Estate & Developmen	12/31/07	486.0	141.4	5213.9	2404.4	143	24418011
HMA	Health Management Associates, Inc	Hospitals & Health Care	12/31/07	4392.1	119.9	4643.9	81.0	360	233273149
HNT	Health Net, Inc.	Insurance	12/31/07	14108.3	193.7	4933.1	1875.6	194	111177960
HR	Healthcare Realty Trust, Inc.	Property, Real Estate & Developmen	12/31/07	212.6	60.1	1495.5	632.0	162	27446114
HLS	HealthSouth Corp.	Diagnostic Services	12/31/07	1752.5	653.4	2050.6	-1554.5	-	-
HS	HealthSpring Inc	Insurance	12/31/07	1574.8	86.5	1351.1	671.4	-	-
HTV	Hearst-Argyle Television Inc.	Media	12/31/07	755.7	64.7	3959.0	1952.4	102	22969661
HPY	Heartland Payment Systems Inc	Miscellaneous Business Services	12/31/07	1313.8	35.9	329.2	165.7	-	-
HL	Hecla Mining Co.	Earth & Rock Mining	12/31/06	217.4	69.1	346.3	224.7	-	-
HEI	Heico Corp. (New)	Aviation	10/31/07	507.9	39.0	631.3	371.6	45	4984001
HNZ	Heinz (H.J.) Co. (United States)	Food	5/2/07	9001.6	785.7	10033.0	1841.7	1	2
HLX	Helix Energy Solutions Group Inc	Oil and Gas	12/31/07	1767.4	320.5	5452.4	1846.6	-	-
OTE	Hellenic Telecommunications Organ	Communications	12/31/04	5219.3	117.1	10404.0	4831.4	27	11996373
HP	Helmerich & Payne, Inc.	Oil and Gas	9/30/07	1629.7	449.3	2885.4	1815.5	210	41611384
HLF	Herbalife Ltd.	Medical & Health Related Services	12/31/06	1885.5	143.1	1016.9	353.9	29	38538739
HPC	Hercules Inc.	Chemicals	12/31/07	2136.2	178.9	2678.4	478.0	193	97931633
HSY	Hershey Company (The)	Food	12/31/07	4946.7	214.2	4247.1	592.9	-	-
HTZ	Hertz Global Holdings Inc	Miscellaneous	12/31/07	8685.6	264.6	19255.7	2913.4	-	-
HES	Hess Corp	Oil and Gas	12/31/07	31924.0	1832.0	26131.0	9774.0	-	-
HEW	Hewitt Associates Inc	Accounting & Management Consulti	9/30/07	2990.3	-175.1	2755.5	1038.0	113	46380709
HPQ	Hewlett-Packard Co	IT & Technology	10/31/07	104286.0	7264.0	88699.0	38526.0	836	1968469579
HXL	Hexcel Corp. (New)	Chemicals	12/31/07	1171.1	61.3	1060.5	427.6	98	44660236
HF	HFF Inc	Property, Real Estate & Developmen	12/31/07	255.7	14.4	240.5	38.0	-	-
HGG	hhgregg Inc	Electrical	3/31/07	1059.4	21.4	290.5	16.3	-	-
HYI	High Yield Income Fund, Inc.	Trusts & Holding Entities	-	-	-	-	-	11	95956
HYP	High Yield Plus Fund, Inc.	Trusts & Holding Entities	-	-	-	-	-	4	11702
HCF	Highland Credit Strategies Fund	Trusts & Holding Entities	-	-	-	-	-	-	-
HCD	Highland Distressed Opportunities, I	Finance & Investment	12/31/07	31.3	17.1	346.9	182.0	-	-
HIW	Highwoods Properties, Inc.	Property, Real Estate & Developmen	12/31/07	437.1	90.7	2927.0	1022.0	155	40422086
HRH	Hilb Rogal & Hobbs Co	Insurance	12/31/07	799.7	78.1	1817.4	683.2	137	36025615

	EARNINGS PER SHARE					P/E RATIO	DIVIDENDS PER SHARE			AV. YLD %	DIV. DECLARED		PRICE RANGE
1st	2nd	3rd	2007	2006	2005		2007	2006	2005		AMOUNT	PAYABLE	2007
0.43	-0.15	0.22	0.67	0.73	0.46	66.7 - 21.7	-	-	-	-	-	-	44.7 - 14.5
-	-	-	-	0.13	0.19		13.14	2.65	2.68	85.8	3.49S	1/11/08	20.3 - 11.8
0.16	-	-	1.37	2.48	1.92	27.0 - 10.4	0.32	0.32	0.26	1.5	0.08Q	2/13/08	37.0 - 14.3
0.29	1.47	1.25	4.01	2.55	1.81	7.4 - 4.6	1.26	0.70	0.44	5.6	0.45Q	3/19/08	29.6 - 18.6
1.03	-	-	2.65	2.42	1.78	10.7 - 5.9	0.92	0.60	0.40	4.6	0.42Q	4/1/08	28.5 - 15.7
-0.05	-	-	0.71	1.65	1.55	38.1 - 27.8	-	-	-	-	-	-	27.1 - 19.7
0.72	1.01	0.90	2.90	3.62	2.24	13.2 - 9.2	0.56	0.55	-	1.8	0.14Q	3/17/08	38.3 - 26.7
-0.06	-	-	-4.00	0.40	0.81		0.03	-	-	1.2	0.1025Q	4/15/08	5.0 - 0.9
-	-	-	-	-	-		-	-	-	-	-	-	9.5 - 5.4
-	-	-	-	-	-		-	-	-	-	-	-	28.0 - 17.4
-	-	-	-	-	-		-	-	-	-	-	-	14.9 - 10.9
-	-	-	-	-	-		-	-	-	-	-	-	7.1 - 4.0
-	-	-	-	-	-		-	-	-	-	-	-	16.7 - 9.8
-	-	-	-	-	-		-	-	-	-	-	-	4.6 - 2.0
0.44	-0.09	-	-	-	-		-	-	-	-	0.18Q	1/28/08	-
-	-	-	-	0.17	0.15		-	-	-	-	-	-	20.6 - 11.8
-	-	-	2.16	-	-		-	-	-	-	-	-	-
0.38	0.40	0.62	0.09	1.34	0.66	107.8 - 62.1	-	-	-	-	0.08Q	1/4/08	9.7 - 5.6
1.06	1.32	1.35	4.29	4.28	1.86	5.3 - 3.1	-	-	-	-	-	-	22.8 - 13.3
-	-	-	-0.18	-0.13	-0.21		1.44	1.61	1.44	7.7	0.38Q	12/31/07	21.5 - 16.2
-	-	-	-0.09	-0.10	-0.21		1.14	2.05	1.29	7.0	0.31Q	12/31/07	18.4 - 13.8
0.46	0.42	0.54	1.78	2.51	1.52	20.8 - 13.3	-	-	-	-	-	-	37.0 - 23.7
0.54	1.62	0.79	3.68	2.23	2.27	5.6 - 3.5	0.34	0.30	0.25	2.1	0.09Q	3/20/08	20.7 - 13.0
-	-	-	2.07	2.16	2.16	12.4 - 9.9	1.66	1.80	2.03	7.0	0.132M	3/31/08	25.6 - 20.5
-	-	-	2.24	2.33	2.33	12.1 - 8.3	2.23	2.10	2.01	8.2	0.133M	2/23/08	27.1 - 21.2
-	-	-	1.26	1.43	1.22	15.9 - 12.5	1.78	1.69	1.25	10.1	0.125M	3/31/08	20.1 - 15.8
0.12	0.26	0.40	1.30	0.77	-		-	-	-	-	-	-	-
0.06	0.17	0.18	0.64	-0.19	0.53	29.8 - 6.7	-	-	-	-	-	-	19.1 - 4.3
1.22	1.14	1.03	4.83	3.27	-6.02	7.9 - 5.3	0.40	0.30	0.25	1.2	0.4A	12/12/07	30.3 - 25.4
0.74	1.14	1.07	3.74	3.93	3.41	16.8 - 12.3	1.06	0.81	0.63	1.9	0.3Q	3/18/08	63.0 - 46.0
0.55	0.68	-	4.72	3.75	3.31	27.7 - 14.5	0.05	0.05	0.05	0.1	0.0125Q	2/20/08	130.7 - 68.3
-	-	-	0.85	1.33	8.88	20.5 - 10.7	-	-	-	-	-	-	17.4 - 0.1
0.73	0.83	-	3.43	1.71	1.46	9.9 - 5.6	0.44	0.32	0.24	1.7	0.15Q	3/14/08	34.1 - 19.2
-	-	-	1.76	1.39	0.90	23.4 - 15.7	1.00	0.90	0.15	3.0	0.05Q	1/21/08	41.1 - 27.7
0.56	0.98	0.91	3.53	2.33	1.86	7.9 - 5.7	0.71	0.65	0.60	3.1	0.195Q	5/15/08	28.0 - 20.2
0.27	0.31	0.30	1.26	1.39	1.34	21.3 - 17.1	0.28	0.24	0.20	1.2	0.075Q	3/14/08	26.9 - 21.5
2.71	1.96	2.68	9.24	8.69	7.44	7.5 - 5.8	2.03	1.70	1.17	3.2	0.53Q	4/1/08	69.3 - 53.3
-	-	-	0.55	0.56	0.56	14.6 - 12.5	0.55	0.55	0.55	7.2	0.045M	4/15/08	8.1 - 6.9
-0.09	0.15	0.01	-0.12	0.20	0.63		-	-	-	-	-	-	8.7 - 4.1
-0.17	-0.18	0.14	1.51	-1.57	1.32	12.1 - 6.3	-	-	-	-	-	-	18.3 - 9.5
0.19	0.03	0.95	1.97	1.29	1.09	11.8 - 8.6	0.60	0.45	0.33	3.1	0.2Q	5/15/08	23.3 - 17.0
0.04	-0.06	0.03	0.15	1.37	1.29	156.3 - 107.0	0.27	0.27	0.26	1.4	0.0675Q	3/18/08	23.4 - 16.1
0.00	0.21	0.24	1.03	1.30	1.50	20.7 - 22.4	1.24	1.24	1.24	4.8	0.31Q	3/11/08	29.5 - 23.1
0.83	0.86	0.84	3.38	2.93	1.79	6.8 - 5.5	0.42	0.38	0.28	2.0	0.11Q	1/14/08	23.0 - 18.6
0.68	0.32	1.53	2.71	2.66	1.12	10.1 - 8.3	1.34	1.70	1.68	5.2	0.4531Q	3/31/08	27.4 - 22.4
-	-	-	36.06	26.66	21.64	1.3 - 0.6	-	-	-	-	-	-	45.4 - 22.9
-	-	-	-	0.12	0.18		-	-	-	-	-	-	3.9 - 2.5
0.23	-	-	0.47	2.10	2.70	72.4 - 42.5	-	-	-	-	-	-	34.0 - 20.0
0.32	0.32	0.30	1.46	1.31	1.15	27.9 - 19.9	2.28	2.88	2.46	6.6	0.1766Q	4/16/08	40.7 - 20.0
0.27	0.05	0.12	0.49	0.75	1.42	51.7 - 38.7	10.00	0.24	0.16	46.0	10.Q	3/1/07	25.3 - 18.9
0.77	0.80	-0.93	1.70	2.78	1.99	19.7 - 13.1	-	-	-	-	-	-	33.5 - 22.2
0.76	0.20	0.12	1.24	0.84	1.11	35.2 - 26.5	6.84	2.64	2.63	17.7	0.005Q	9/9/08	49.7 - 32.9
-0.80	5.87	3.13	7.10	-8.14	-5.80	4.4 - 2.7	-	-	-	-	18.25Q	1/15/08	30.9 - 16.3
0.25	0.42	0.39	1.51	1.44	0.34		-	-	-	-	-	-	-
0.05	0.18	0.10	0.69	1.06	1.08	42.0 - 32.8	0.28	0.28	0.28	1.1	0.07Q	1/16/08	28.0 - 22.6
0.17	0.26	0.30	0.90	0.71	0.50		0.25	0.05	-	-	0.09Q	3/15/08	-
0.07	0.20	-	-	0.57	-0.22		-	-	-	-	1.8597Q	4/1/08	-
0.37	-	-	1.45	1.20	0.87	16.0 - 9.1	0.08	0.08	0.05	0.5	0.05S	1/23/08	23.1 - 13.2
0.63	0.71	0.68	2.36	1.89	2.13		1.40	1.20	1.14	-	0.38Q	1/10/08	-
0.60	0.61	0.88	3.34	3.87	1.86	6.4 - 3.4	-	-	-	-	-	-	21.5 - 11.5
-	-	-	-	1.17	-0.44		-	-	-	-	-	-	8.9 - 5.8
1.02	-	-	4.27	2.77	1.23	4.0 - 2.8	0.18	0.17	0.17	1.3	0.045Q	12/3/07	17.1 - 12.0
0.53	0.49	1.37	-	1.92	1.28		-	-	-	-	0.2Q	12/14/07	16.5 - 14.6
0.64	0.30	0.37	1.56	2.14	-0.38	9.7 - 6.4	0.10	-	-	0.8	0.05Q	4/18/08	15.1 - 10.0
0.40	0.01	0.27	0.93	2.34	1.99		1.14	1.03	0.93	-	0.2678Q	3/14/08	-
-0.20	0.26	0.50	0.81	0.48	-0.09		-	1.12	-	-	-	-	-
1.17	1.75	1.23	5.74	6.07	3.98	5.4 - 3.1	0.40	0.10	0.40	1.6	0.1Q	3/31/08	31.0 - 17.9
0.59	-	-	-1.62	-1.08	1.19		-	-	-	-	-	-	35.5 - 24.5
0.80	-	-	2.68	2.18	0.82	9.7 - 6.2	0.32	0.32	0.32	1.5	0.08Q	4/2/08	26.1 - 16.5
0.24	0.09	0.18	0.64	0.69	1.51	27.7 - 10.6	-	-	-	-	-	-	17.8 - 6.8
0.13	0.31	0.24	0.84	-	-		-	-	-	-	-	-	-
0.10	-0.22	0.45	0.73	0.78	0.51		-	-	-	-	0.035M	1/31/08	6.4 - 5.0
-	-	-	-	-	-		-	-	-	-	0.025M	3/14/08	5.0 - 3.5
-	-	-	-	0.71	-		-	-	-	-	0.15M	3/31/08	-
0.07	0.42	-	-	-	-		-	-	-	-	0.2625Q	3/31/08	-
0.85	0.07	0.17	1.31	0.62	0.58	21.3 - 15.9	1.70	1.70	1.70	6.8	0.5Q	3/17/08	27.9 - 20.9
0.69	0.60	0.53	2.11	2.39	1.55	18.4 - 14.9	0.51	0.47	0.45	1.5	0.13Q	3/31/08	38.8 - 31.5

T29

SYMBOL	COMPANY	NATURE OF BUSINESS	FISCAL YEAR-END	TOTAL REV. $MILL	NET INCOME $MILL	TOTAL ASSETS $MILL	NET STK EQUITY $MILL	NO OF INST	INST. HOLDINGS (SHARES)
HIL	Hill International Inc	Miscellaneous Business Services	-	-	-	-	-	-	-
HB	Hill-Rom Holdings, Inc.	Hospitals & Health Care	9/30/07	2023.7	190.6	2117.0	1277.8	205	33242270
HTH	Hilltop Holdings, Inc.	Property, Real Estate & Developmen	12/31/07	131.3	293.2	1085.5	824.2	-	-
HIT	Hitachi, Ltd.	Industrial Machinery and Equipment	3/31/07	102479030	-32799.0	10644259.0	2442797.0	73	20096609
HNI	HNI Corp	Furniture and Fixtures	12/29/07	2570.5	120.4	1207.0	458.9	140	27852821
HOC	Holly Corp.	Oil and Gas	12/31/07	4791.7	334.1	1663.9	593.8	109	22651873
HEP	Holly Energy Partners LP	Oil and Gas	12/31/07	105.4	39.3	238.9	-	31	3036591
HD	Home Depot Inc	Retail - Hardware	2/3/08	77349.0	4395.0	44324.0	17714.0	1078	1334759224
HME	Home Properties Inc	Property, Real Estate & Developmen	12/31/07	505.2	61.5	3216.4	668.1	137	25506180
HMC	Honda Motor Co., Ltd.(Honda Giken	Automotive	3/31/07	1087140.0	592322.0	12036500.0	4482611.0	146	65624241
HON	Honeywell International, Inc.	Automotive	12/31/07	34589.0	2444.0	33805.0	9222.0	689	632891917
HMN	Horace Mann Educators Corp.	Insurance	12/31/07	887.0	82.8	6259.3	693.3	119	42243199
HRZ	Horizon Lines Inc	Shipping	12/23/07	1206.5	28.9	926.4	154.6	-	-
HRL	Hormel Foods Corp.	Food	10/28/07	6193.0	301.9	3393.6	1884.8	197	38590396
HOS	Hornbeck Offshore Services Inc (Ne	Shipping	12/31/07	339.0	94.8	1262.1	562.3	77	9458037
DHI	Horton (D.R.) Inc.	Building & General Construction	9/30/07	11296.5	-712.5	11556.3	5586.9	334	288165673
HSP	Hospira Inc	Pharmaceuticals	12/31/07	3436.2	136.8	5084.7	1745.2	388	99296233
HPT	Hospitality Properties Trust	Property, Real Estate & Developmen	12/31/07	1285.5	331.0	5679.3	2786.4	217	31995531
HST	Host Hotels & Resorts Inc	Property, Real Estate & Developmen	12/31/07	5426.0	727.0	11812.0	5441.0	2	260000
HOV	Hovnanian Enterprises, Inc.	Building & General Construction	10/31/07	4798.9	-627.1	4540.5	1321.8	192	31981053
HRP	HRPT Properties Trust	Property, Real Estate & Developmen	12/31/07	840.0	124.3	5859.3	2902.9	181	103564393
HTB	HSBC Finance Corp	Credit & Lending	12/31/07	-	-4906.0	165504.0	13584.0	2	1452118
HBC	HSBC Holdings Plc	Commercial Banking	12/31/04	78582.0	12918.0	1279974.0	99197.0	252	57626015
HBA PRH	HSBC USA, Inc. (New)	Commercial Banking	12/31/07	10885.0	138.0	188373.0	11237.0	-	-
HNP	Huaneng Power International, Inc.	Electricity	12/31/05	40076.5	4871.8	99439.7	46144.2	52	2590883
HUB B	Hubbell Inc.	Electrical	12/31/07	2533.9	208.3	1863.4	1082.6	217	40319510
HGT	Hugoton Royalty Trust (TX)	Miscellaneous	12/31/07	70.6	69.4	161.0	155.8	57	3937332
HUM	Humana Inc.	Insurance	12/31/07	25290.0	833.7	12879.1	4028.9	291	123910289
HUN	Huntsman Corp	Chemicals	12/31/07	9650.8	-172.1	8165.6	1826.6	126	63710124
HTX	Hutchison Telecommunications Inte	Communications	12/31/05	24356.0	-768.0	59591.0	19822.0	15	30161625
HBP	Huttig Building Products, Inc.	General Construction Supplies & Ser	12/31/07	874.8	-8.2	212.7	104.3	47	7218184
HYC	Hypercom Corp	Office Equipment Supplies	12/31/07	293.8	-7.5	250.2	174.5	79	42181475
HSM	Hyperion Brookfield Strategic Mortg	Trusts & Holding Entities	12/31/07	12.8	9.9	154.5	113.6	6	74404
HTR	Hyperion Brookfield Total Return Fu	Trusts & Holding Entities	11/30/07	27.9	21.8	308.3	241.4	13	354792
IAG	IAMGold Corp	Precious Metals	12/31/06	303.3	72.5	2278.7	1773.4	58	64967859
IEP	Icahn Enterprises L P	Property, Real Estate & Developmen	12/31/07	2487.6	308.3	12433.6	-	-	-
IBN	ICICI Bank Ltd (India)	Other Depository Banking	3/31/07	413637.9	27606.3	-	-	131	76313501
IDA	Idacorp, Inc. (United States)	Electricity	12/31/07	879.4	82.3	3653.3	1207.3	164	21028568
IAR	Idearc Inc	Non-Media Publishing	12/31/07	3189.0	429.0	1667.0	-8600.0	-	-
IEX	IDEX Corporation	Industrial Machinery and Equipment	12/31/07	1358.6	155.1	1989.6	1162.7	172	48822072
IDT C	IDT Corp.	IT & Technology	7/31/07	2012.7	58.6	1367.3	630.2	91	41134962
IHP	IHOP Corp. (New)	Miscellaneous	12/31/07	484.6	-0.5	3831.2	209.4	115	19799362
IHS	IHS Inc	Communications	11/30/07	688.4	83.8	1323.8	840.9	-	-
IKN	Ikon Office Solutions, Inc.	IT & Technology	9/30/07	4168.3	114.5	3278.1	1710.8	128	122358602
ITW	Illinois Tool Works, Inc.	Industrial Machinery and Equipment	12/31/07	16170.6	1869.9	15525.9	9351.3	623	229831889
IMN	Imation Corp.	Electrical	12/31/06	1584.7	76.4	1382.9	946.3	163	28927302
IMH	IMPAC Mortgage Holdings, Inc.	Property, Real Estate & Developmen	12/31/06	1396.9	-75.3	23599.0	1009.5	110	17656308
IMP	Imperial Capital Bancorp Inc	Commercial Banking	12/31/07	254.4	15.6	3551.2	227.6	-	-
ITY	Imperial Tobacco Group Plc	Retail - Alcohol & Tobacco	-	-	-	-	-	39	22640352
RX	IMS Health, Inc.	IT & Technology	12/31/07	2192.6	234.0	2244.2	-40.3	327	202444229
IHC	Independence Holding Co.	Insurance	12/31/07	402.3	-2.3	1308.1	222.9	31	2204733
IFN	India Fund, Inc. (The)	Trusts & Holding Entities	12/31/07	21.2	-6.3	3110.5	2754.1	74	6979631
IJD	Indiana Michigan Power Co	Electricity	12/31/07	2043.2	136.9	5750.7	1385.7	0	0
IBA	Industrias Bachoco S.A.B. de C.V.	Retail - Food & Beverage	12/31/06	14987.6	873.4	16923.1	13592.0	13	4157563
IMB	IndyMac Bancorp Inc	Other Depository Banking	12/31/07	2020.1	-614.8	32734.5	1343.8	11	1447071
IFX	Infineon Technologies AG	Electrical	9/30/07	7682.0	-368.0	10679.0	4914.0	35	23362175
IGR	ING Clarion Global Real Estate Inco	Trusts & Holding Entities	12/31/07	150.2	119.6	2598.4	1659.2	27	2784132
IIA	ING Clarion Real Estate Income Fu	Trusts & Holding Entities	12/31/07	20.6	17.0	302.3	184.6	14	595255
IGA	ING Global Advantage & Premium	Trusts & Holding Entities	2/28/07	-	4.8	389.2	385.4	-	-
ING	ING Groep N.V.	Insurance	12/31/04	86746.0	5755.0	876391.0	27550.0	-	-
IID	ING International High Dividend Eq	Trusts & Holding Entities	-	-	-	-	-	-	-
PPR	ING Prime Rate Trust (United State	Trusts & Holding Entities	-	-	-	-	-	39	10284958
IRR	ING Risk Managed Natural Resourc	Finance & Investment	2/28/07	-	1.3	439.3	433.6	-	-
IR	Ingersoll-Rand Co. Ltd.	Industrial Machinery and Equipment	12/31/07	8763.1	3966.7	14376.2	7907.9	522	129768534
IM	Ingram Micro Inc.	IT & Technology	12/29/07	35047.1	275.9	8975.0	3426.9	160	116793004
IRC	Inland Real Estate Corp	Property, Real Estate & Developmen	12/31/07	189.4	43.8	1321.3	363.4	61	20592320
PIF	Insured Municipal Income Fund	Trusts & Holding Entities	-	-	-	-	-	24	1055946
TEG	Integrys Energy Group Inc	Electricity	12/31/07	10292.4	254.4	11234.4	3286.9	-	-
IDC	Interactive Data Corp. (United State	Finance Intermediaries & Services	12/31/07	689.6	126.0	1228.2	963.5	89	28720482
IAB 07O	Inter-American Development Bank	Other Depository Banking	12/31/05	-	762.0	-	18727.0	-	-
ICE	IntercontinentalExchange Inc	Finance Intermediaries & Services	12/31/07	574.3	240.6	2796.3	1476.9	-	-
IBI	Interline Brands Inc	Retail - Hardware	12/28/07	1239.0	51.0	936.8	377.4	50	19758372
IN	Intermec Inc	Office Equipment Supplies	12/31/07	849.2	23.1	900.6	484.1	-	-
IBM	International Business Machines Co	IT & Technology	12/31/07	98786.0	10418.0	120431.0	28470.0	1190	873552081
ICO	International Coal Group (New)	Coal Mining	12/31/07	849.2	-147.0	1303.6	514.4	-	-
OPT WS	International Finance Corp. (World	Central Banking	6/30/05	-	2015.0	-	9798.0	-	-
IFF	International Flavors & Fragrances	Chemicals	12/31/07	2276.6	247.1	2726.8	617.2	251	70823464
IGT	International Game Technology	Consumer Accessories	9/30/07	2621.4	508.2	4167.5	1452.7	354	263480090
AIG 09	International Lease Finance Corp.	General Construction Supplies & Ser	12/31/07	-	604.4	-	7028.8	1	100
IP	International Paper Co.	Paper Products	12/31/07	21890.0	1168.0	24159.0	8672.0	469	430892180

EARNINGS PER SHARE QUARTERLY 1st	2nd	3rd	ANNUAL 2007	2006	2005	P/E RATIO	DIV PER SHARE 2007	2006	2005	AV. YLD %	DIV DECLARED AMOUNT	PAYABLE	PRICE RANGE 2007
0.08	0.10	0.13	-	0.46	0.03	-	-	-	-	-	-	-	5.1 - 4.7
0.72	-	-	3.07	3.59	-1.52	-	1.14	1.13	1.12	-	-	-	
-0.17	-0.18	5.12	5.02	-0.63	-4.76	3.8 - 2.5	-	0.00	0.50	-	0.5156Q	1/30/08	19.0 - 12.5
-	-	-	-9.87	10.84	15.15	-	-	-	-	-	-	-	81.3 - 58.0
0.43	0.57	0.76	2.57	2.45	2.50	17.8 - 13.8	0.78	0.72	0.62	1.9	0.215Q	2/29/08	45.7 - 35.4
1.20	2.84	1.04	5.98	4.58	2.65	2.4 - 1.1	0.46	0.29	0.19	4.7	0.15Q	4/2/08	14.2 - 6.8
0.43	0.64	0.61	2.26	1.60	1.70	15.3 - 10.9	2.79	2.59	2.23	9.4	0.725Q	2/14/08	34.5 - 24.6
0.53	0.81	0.60	2.79	2.72	2.26	15.7 - 11.8	0.68	0.40	0.33	1.8	0.225Q	3/27/08	43.8 - 32.9
0.15	0.26	0.84	1.73	3.15	2.33	25.4 - 21.3	2.61	2.57	2.53	6.5	0.66Q	2/29/08	43.9 - 36.9
-	-	-	-	648.67	520.68	-	-	-	-	-	-	-	26.1 - 19.6
0.66	0.78	0.81	3.16	2.52	1.94	12.1 - 10.0	1.00	0.91	0.82	2.8	0.275Q	3/10/08	38.1 - 31.8
0.52	0.52	0.41	1.86	2.19	1.67	10.4 - 7.6	0.42	0.42	0.42	2.5	0.105Q	3/31/08	19.3 - 14.1
0.21	0.28	0.05	0.85	2.14	-1.05	-	0.44	0.44	0.11	-	0.11Q	3/15/08	
0.64	-	-	2.17	2.05	1.82	14.7 - 11.5	0.60	0.56	0.52	2.1	0.185Q	2/15/08	31.0 - 25.0
0.67	0.85	1.09	3.58	2.76	1.64	5.9 - 2.8	-	-	-	-	-	-	21.2 - 10.2
-0.41	-	-	-2.27	3.90	4.62	-	0.60	0.44	0.31	2.6	0.15Q	2/20/08	31.0 - 19.2
-0.19	0.20	0.37	0.85	1.48	1.46	39.9 - 28.6	-	-	-	-	-	-	33.9 - 24.4
0.43	0.50	1.52	3.27	2.20	1.75	13.4 - 10.4	3.03	2.94	2.17	7.6	0.5547Q	4/15/08	44.0 - 33.9
0.35	0.27	0.18	1.33	1.48	0.38	21.1 - 18.6	1.00	0.14	0.41	3.7	0.5547Q	4/15/08	28.1 - 24.8
-2.07	-	-	-10.11	2.14	7.16	-	-	-	-	-	0.4766Q	10/15/07	49.5 - 29.3
0.08	0.08	0.08	0.28	0.94	0.60	46.3 - 31.6	0.63	0.84	0.84	5.9	0.4063Q	2/15/08	13.0 - 8.8
-	-	-	-	-	-	-	-	-	-	2.23	0.3075Q	3/17/00	27.3 - 23.5
-	-	-	1.39	1.35	-	-	-	-	-	-	-	-	87.8 - 70.0
-	-	-	-	-	-	-	1.13	1.13	1.13	-	0.4063Q	4/1/08	
-	-	-	-	0.50	0.40	-	-	-	-	-	-	-	43.5 - 27.3
0.69	0.90	1.10	2.50	0.50	0.07	14.0 - 10.0	1.00	1.00	1.00	3.0	0.33Q	4/11/08	52.3 - 38.1
0.41	0.52	0.44	1.73	2.27	2.62	17.2 - 10.1	1.73	2.27	2.62	7.2	0.1948M	3/14/08	29.8 - 17.5
0.42	1.28	1.70	4.91	2.90	1.87	6.1 - 3.2	-	-	-	-	-	-	30.0 - 15.6
0.20	-0.30	-0.68	-0.74	0.99	-0.35	-	2.50	2.50	1.88	-	0.1Q	3/31/08	
-	-	-	-	0.08	-0.26	-	-	-	-	-	-	-	13.6 - 10.1
-0.17	0.05	-	-0.40	-0.38	0.90	-	-	-	-	-	-	-	10.4 - 3.3
-0.05	-0.11	0.01	-0.14	0.13	-0.64	-	-	-	-	-	-	-	8.5 - 4.5
-	-	-	0.97	0.92	1.16	15.5 - 12.8	0.72	1.08	1.21	5.1	0.09M	3/27/08	15.0 - 12.4
-	-	-	0.71	0.66	0.79	14.9 - 12.1	0.68	0.72	0.82	6.9	0.065M	3/27/08	10.6 - 8.6
0.04	-0.28	-	-	0.39	0.14	-	-	0.07	0.07	-	0.06A	1/11/08	8.5 - 4.5
1.53	-0.40	0.53	1.58	12.69	-0.40	4.6 - 4.1	0.40	0.40	0.20	5.8	0.25Q	4/1/08	7.2 - 6.5
-	-	-	30.75	30.64	25.25	0.7 - 0.4	-	-	-	-	-	-	20.4 - 11.3
0.56	0.42	0.65	1.86	2.51	1.50	17.6 - 13.7	1.20	1.20	1.20	4.1	0.3Q	2/29/08	32.8 - 25.5
0.71	0.75	0.80	2.94	5.29	7.03	-	1.37	-	-	-	0.3425Q	3/13/08	
0.45	0.51	0.47	1.89	1.81	1.39	14.4 - 9.4	0.46	0.38	0.32	2.1	0.12Q	1/31/08	27.1 - 17.8
0.08	-0.83	-	0.71	-1.86	-0.45	33.5 - 19.0	0.38	-	-	2.2	0.125Q	7/31/07	23.8 - 13.5
0.63	0.82	-0.69	-0.13	2.43	2.24	-	1.00	1.00	1.00	2.7	0.25Q	2/22/08	43.2 - 33.2
0.32	0.32	0.35	1.39	0.99	0.75	-	-	-	-	-	-	-	
0.13	-	-	0.91	0.80	0.43	14.5 - 11.2	0.16	0.16	0.16	1.4	0.04Q	3/10/08	13.2 - 10.2
0.71	0.90	0.89	3.36	3.01	2.60	14.3 - 10.9	0.90	0.75	0.61	2.2	0.28Q	4/14/08	48.0 - 36.7
0.44	-0.04	0.24	-	2.17	2.54	-	-	0.54	0.46	-	0.16Q	3/31/08	43.6 - 29.8
-1.65	-2.05	-15.66	-	-1.18	3.35	-	-	0.95	1.95	-	0.5703Q	3/31/08	27.8 - 18.3
1.19	1.08	0.31	2.81	4.71	4.04	20.9 - 13.6	0.48	0.60	-	1.0	0.16Q	1/15/08	58.8 - 38.2
-	-	-	-	-	-	-	-	-	-	-	-	-	56.1 - 39.3
0.43	0.36	0.29	1.18	1.53	1.22	22.5 - 17.7	0.12	0.12	0.08	0.5	0.03Q	3/28/08	26.6 - 20.9
0.30	0.26	-0.55	-0.15	0.93	1.21	-	0.05	0.05	0.05	0.3	0.0258	1/22/08	22.9 - 10.3
-	-	-	-0.14	-0.14	0.04	-	9.61	5.12	4.46	39.3	0.73A	1/14/08	31.3 - 19.6
-	-	-	-	-	-	-	-	-	-	-	1.14Q	1/2/08	26.6 - 22.1
-	-	-	-	-	-	-	-	-	-	-	-	-	14.2 - 8.8
0.70	0.60	-2.77	-9.29	4.92	4.61	-	1.75	1.00	1.50	0.0	0.75Q	2/1/08	63.5 - 52.9
-	-	-	-0.49	-0.36	-0.42	-	-	-	-	-	-	-	15.9 - 9.4
-	-	-	1.17	0.98	1.09	13.1 - 9.8	3.22	3.27	1.55	23.6	0.115M	3/31/08	15.0 - 11.4
-	-	-	1.13	1.20	1.15	14.4 - 11.1	2.36	3.30	1.79	16.3	0.115M	3/31/08	16.3 - 12.6
-	-	-	0.26	0.06	-	-	-	-	-	-	0.465Q	10/15/07	
-	-	-	4.28	3.53	3.32	-	-	-	-	-	-	-	
-	-	-	-	-	-	-	-	-	-	-	0.163M	3/17/08	
-	-	-	-	-	-	-	-	-	-	-	0.046M	2/25/08	8.3 - 7.2
-	-	-	0.06	-	-	-	-	-	-	-	0.425Q	10/15/07	
0.70	3.17	0.92	13.43	3.20	3.09	3.1 - 2.3	0.72	0.68	0.57	2.1	0.18Q	3/3/08	41.0 - 30.5
0.21	0.30	0.41	1.56	1.56	1.32	13.3 - 7.6	-	-	-	-	-	-	20.8 - 11.9
0.18	0.16	0.15	0.07	0.07	0.70	23.8 - 22.7	0.98	0.96	0.95	6.3	0.081/M	3/17/08	15.9 - 15.2
-	-	-	-	-	-	-	-	-	-	-	0.0475M	1/31/08	14.6 - 12.4
2.41	-0.22	0.56	3.50	3.67	4.07	14.4 - 12.4	0.58	2.28	2.24	1.2	0.67Q	3/20/08	50.3 - 43.5
0.27	0.30	0.40	1.30	0.98	0.98	17.0 - 12.6	0.50	0.80	0.80	2.7	0.15Q	3/31/08	22.1 - 16.3
0.80	0.75	0.93	3.39	2.40	-0.39	-	-	-	-	-	-	-	
0.29	0.37	0.49	1.56	0.95	0.89	11.5 - 10.9	-	-	-	-	-	-	17.9 - 17.1
-0.07	0.11	0.07	0.38	0.50	0.98	69.7 - 36.3	-	-	-	-	-	-	26.5 - 13.8
1.21	1.55	1.68	7.18	6.11	4.87	14.0 - 11.4	1.50	1.10	0.78	1.7	0.4Q	3/10/08	100.2 - 82.2
-0.05	-0.07	-0.01	-0.97	-0.06	0.29	-	-	-	-	-	-	-	12.1 - 7.6
-	-	-	-	-	-	-	-	-	-	-	-	-	10.0 - 8.9
0.69	0.87	0.67	2.82	2.48	2.04	15.3 - 11.8	0.88	0.77	0.73	2.3	0.23Q	4/3/08	43.0 - 33.3
0.36	-	-	1.51	1.20	1.20	31.0 - 19.0	0.52	0.50	0.48	1.4	0.14Q	4/2/08	46.8 - 28.7
-	-	-	-	-	-	-	-	-	-	-	-	-	
0.97	0.44	0.51	2.70	2.18	2.21	16.7 - 14.0	1.00	1.00	1.00	2.4	0.25Q	3/14/08	45.0 - 37.8

SYMBOL	COMPANY	NATURE OF BUSINESS	FISCAL YEAR-END	TOTAL REV. $MILL	NET INCOME $MILL	TOTAL ASSETS $MILL	NET STK EQUITY $MILL	NO OF INST	INST. HOLDINGS (SHARES)
IRF	International Rectifier Corp.	IT & Technology	6/30/06	1171.1	107.2	2505.0	1604.3	225	52931004
ISH	International Shipholding Corp.	Shipping	12/31/07	197.1	17.4	440.7	173.7	23	2491242
IPG	Interpublic Group of Companies Inc.	Advertising, Marketing & PR	12/31/07	6554.2	167.6	12458.1	2332.2	296	433877198
IHR	Interstate Hotels & Resorts, Inc	Hospitality & Tourism	12/31/07	800.1	22.8	470.9	189.5	44	16881826
IPL PRB	Interstate Power & Light Co (United	Electricity	12/31/07	1695.9	290.3	3362.0	1111.3	4	2097100
ITP	Intertape Polymer Group Inc.	Paper Products	12/31/06	812.3	-166.7	692.4	273.7	40	24573324
IVC	Invacare Corp	Medical Instruments & Equipment	12/31/07	1602.2	1.2	1500.0	554.0	124	25259534
IVZ	Invesco Ltd	Wealth Management	12/31/04	2124.5	-36.2	7419.6	3543.0	-	-
PPM	Investment Grade Municipal Income	Trusts & Holding Entities						13	420014
ITG	Investment Technology Group Inc. (	Finance Intermediaries & Services	12/31/07	731.0	111.1	2100.9	704.3	125	34240285
IOM	Iomega Corp. (United States)	IT & Technology	12/31/07	336.6	10.1	205.2	101.2	69	27827516
IO	ION Geophysical Corp	Instruments and Related Products	12/31/07	713.1	42.6	709.1	476.2	-	-
IWA	Iowa Telecommunications Services	Communications	12/31/07	251.4	29.3	831.6	243.0	80	18702429
IRM	Iron Mountain Inc	Miscellaneous Business Services	12/31/07	2730.0	153.1	6307.9	1795.5	182	116988348
IRS	IRSA Inversiones y Representacion	Property, Real Estate & Developmen	6/30/07	738.8	107.1	4144.9	1646.7	50	11850266
IFC	Irwin Financial Corp. (Columbus, IN	Commercial Banking	12/31/07	540.4	-54.7	6166.1	459.3	99	12692492
EZA	iShares Inc MSCI France Index Fun	Trusts & Holding Entities						-	-
EWU	iShares Inc.	Trusts & Holding Entities	8/31/06	-	31.3	877.5	872.4	40	8029166
EWI	iShares Inc.	Trusts & Holding Entities	8/31/06	-	3.3	171.5	146.3	14	352477
EWJ	iShares Inc.	Trusts & Holding Entities	8/31/06	-	60.4	13946.7	13724.6	225	230134129
EWT	iShares Inc.	Trusts & Holding Entities	8/31/06	-	45.1	1932.5	1893.8	62	25695087
EWH	iShares Inc.	Trusts & Holding Entities	8/31/06	-	21.4	915.7	882.7	67	16372294
JKJ	iShares Trust	Trusts & Holding Entities	4/30/07	-	0.7	162.4	157.9	3	9928
JKL	iShares Trust	Trusts & Holding Entities	4/30/07	-	2.3	138.7	136.0	5	50779
CFT	iShares Trust	Trusts & Holding Entities						-	-
EFV	iShares Trust	Trusts & Holding Entities	7/31/07	-	23.5	1205.6	1196.7	-	-
ICF	iShares Trust - Cohen & Steers Rea	Trusts & Holding Entities						-	-
JKD	iShares Trust - Large Core Index Fu	Trusts & Holding Entities						-	-
IWR	iShares Trust - Russell Midcap Inde	Trusts & Holding Entities						-	-
IYH	iShares Trust (United States)	Trusts & Holding Entities						59	4115434
IYR	iShares Trust (United States)	Trusts & Holding Entities						77	12754513
TIP	iShares Trust (United States)	Trusts & Holding Entities						-	-
IJS	iShares Trust (United States)	Trusts & Holding Entities						-	-
IYZ	iShares Trust (United States)	Trusts & Holding Entities						40	5490849
NYC	iShares Trust (United States)	Trusts & Holding Entities						-	-
IJT	iShares Trust (United States)	Trusts & Holding Entities						-	-
IOO	iShares Trust (United States)	Trusts & Holding Entities						-	-
IYM	iShares Trust (United States)	Trusts & Holding Entities						48	2132693
IVV	iShares Trust (United States)	Trusts & Holding Entities						163	49890204
IYT	iShares Trust (United States)	Trusts & Holding Entities						-	-
IWV	iShares Trust (United States)	Trusts & Holding Entities						58	5673321
IYJ	iShares Trust (United States)	Trusts & Holding Entities						-	-
IYC	iShares Trust (United States)	Trusts & Holding Entities						31	1196000
IYK	iShares Trust (United States)	Trusts & Holding Entities						32	2233564
IDU	iShares Trust (United States)	Trusts & Holding Entities						46	1804699
IWZ	iShares Trust (United States)	Trusts & Holding Entities						16	551676
IYE	iShares Trust (United States)	Trusts & Holding Entities						-	-
IGN	iShares Trust Goldman Sachs Netw	Trusts & Holding Entities						-	-
IGW	iShares Trust Goldman Sachs Semi	Trusts & Holding Entities						-	-
IWW	iShares Trust Russell 3000 Value In	Trusts & Holding Entities						-	-
IXC	iShares Trust S&P Global Energy S	Trusts & Holding Entities						-	-
IXJ	iShares Trust S&P Global Healthcar	Trusts & Holding Entities						-	-
IXP	iShares Trust S&P Global Telecom	Trusts & Holding Entities						-	-
SFI	iStar Financial Inc	Property, Real Estate & Development	12/31/07	1425.6	239.0	15848.3	2899.5	205	80255988
ITC	ITC Holdings Corp	Electricity	12/31/07	426.2	73.3	3213.3	563.1	-	-
ITT	ITT Corporation	Industrial Machinery and Equipment	12/31/07	9003.3	742.1	11552.7	3944.8	371	75506022
ESI	ITT Educational Services, Inc. (Unit	Schools and Universities	12/31/07	869.5	151.6	541.0	70.6	176	45727280
IVN	Ivanhoe Mines Ltd	Precious Metals	12/31/06		-198.7	703.2	653.9	51	95942530
JCG	J Crew Group Inc	Retail - Apparel and Accessory Store	2/2/08	1334.7	97.1	535.6	140.3	-	-
JBL	Jabil Circuit, Inc.	Electrical	8/31/07	12290.6	73.2	6295.2	2443.0	316	165247721
JBX	Jack in the Box, Inc.	Hospitality & Tourism	9/30/07	2876.0	126.3	1382.8	414.6	151	35784448
JTX	Jackson Hewitt Tax Services Inc	Personal Services	4/30/07	293.2	65.4	573.5	303.5	87	32221885
JEC	Jacobs Engineering Group, Inc. (Un	Construction - Public Infrastructure	9/30/07	8474.0	287.1	3389.4	1843.7	280	46024589
JHX	James Hardie Industries NV (Nether	Stone, Clay, Glass, and Concrete Pr	3/31/06	1488.5	-506.7	1445.4	94.9	8	114228
JNS	Janus Capital Group Inc	Wealth Management	12/31/07	1117.0	116.3	3564.1	1723.5	231	198322903
JEQ	Japan Equity Fund, Inc. (The)	Trusts & Holding Entities	10/31/06	-	0.2	123.9	123.8	26	2178491
JOF	Japan Smaller Capitalization Fund I	Trusts & Holding Entities						23	3373130
JAH	Jarden Corp.	Plastics	12/31/07	4660.1	28.1	5868.1	1538.6	141	47384446
JEF	Jefferies Group, Inc. (New) (United	Finance Intermediaries & Services	12/31/07	2718.9	144.7	29793.8	1761.5	143	35022457
JRT	JER Investors Trust Inc	Property, Real Estate & Developmen	12/31/06		31.7	1368.0	370.0	-	-
JFC	JF China Region Fund Inc	Trusts & Holding Entities	12/31/07	2.5	0.5	139.2	138.6	10	763325
JMP	JMP Group Inc	Finance Intermediaries & Services	12/31/07	65.5	6.5	184.7	115.6	-	-
JAS	Jo-Ann Stores, Inc.	Retail - Miscellaneous	2/3/07	1850.6	-1.9	856.7	409.8	112	15653369
BTO	John Hancock Bank and Thrift Opp	Trusts & Holding Entities	10/31/06		13.4	999.6	892.5	45	10826327
JHS	John Hancock Income Securities Tr	Trusts & Holding Entities	12/31/07	17.1	15.1	257.9	164.8	17	620902
JHI	John Hancock Investors Trust	Trusts & Holding Entities	12/31/07	17.5	15.6	251.7	159.6	19	88143
PDT	John Hancock Patriot Premium Divi	Trusts & Holding Entities	10/31/07		13.3	294.4	193.7	13	62379
HPI	John Hancock Preferred Income Fu	Trusts & Holding Entities	7/31/07		55.1	881.3	596.5	24	890283
JNJ	Johnson & Johnson	Health	12/30/07	61095.0	10576.0	80954.0	43319.0	1368	1880668712
JCI	Johnson Controls Inc	Automotive	9/30/07	34624.0	1252.0	24105.0	8907.0	465	128792286

T32

| EARNINGS PER SHARE | | | | | | P/E RATIO | | DIVIDENDS PER SHARE | | | AV. YLD | DIV. DECLARED | | PRICE RANGE | |
| QUARTERLY | | | ANNUAL | | | | | | | | | | | 2007 | |
1st	2nd	3rd	2007	2006	2005			2007	2006	2005	%	AMOUNT	PAYABLE		
0.47	0.99	-	-	1.49	1.91	-	-	-	-	-	-	-	-	54.5 -	31.4
0.58	0.84	0.27	2.08	2.39	0.75	8.1 -	6.3	-	-	-	-	0.0625Q	6/15/01	16.8 -	13.1
-0.29	0.24	-0.06	0.26	-0.19	-0.68	66.1 -	40.4	-	-	-	-	13.125Q	4/15/08	17.2 -	10.5
0.54	0.05	0.06	0.71	0.94	0.42	8.7 -	5.7	-	-	-	-	-	-	8.2 -	4.0
-	-	-	-	-	-	-	-	2.09	2.09	2.09	6.4	0.4437Q	3/14/08	34.0 -	31.0
-0.01	-0.20	-	-	-4.07	0.67	-	-	-	-	-	-	0.16A	6/8/00	13.3 -	6.4
-0.55	0.00	0.36	0.04	-10.00	1.51	1300.0 -	983.5	0.05	0.05	0.05	0.1	0.0114Q	4/11/08	52.0 -	39.3
-	-	-	-	-	0.26	-	-	-	-	-	-	-	-	17.3 -	9.8
-	-	-	-	-	-	-	-	-	-	-	-	0.0525M	1/31/08	15.6 -	12.9
0.55	0.60	0.65	2.48	2.21	1.60	8.1 -	4.8	-	-	-	-	-	-	20.0 -	12.0
0.02	0.02	0.02	0.18	-0.17	-0.44	38.3 -	21.2	-	-	-	-	5.U	10/1/03	6.9 -	3.8
0.04	0.08	0.14	0.45	0.33	0.21	24.4 -	10.3	-	-	-	-	-	-	11.0 -	4.7
0.33	0.20	0.20	0.91	1.06	1.46	24.0 -	22.6	1.62	1.62	1.62	7.6	0.405Q	4/15/08	21.8 -	20.6
0.17	0.19	0.25	0.76	0.64	0.56	30.7 -	22.9	-	-	-	-	-	-	23.4 -	17.4
-	-	-	-	-	-	-	-	-	-	-	-	-	-	11.5 -	6.5
-0.36	-0.03	-0.64	-1.94	0.05	0.66	-	-	0.48	0.44	0.40	1.8	0.12Q	12/28/07	36.0 -	23.2
-	-	-	-	0.97	-	-	-	-	-	-	-	0.007U	12/28/00	-	
-	-	-	-	1.07	-	-	-	-	-	-	-	0.007U	12/28/00	-	
-	-	-	-	0.06	-	-	-	-	-	-	-	0.007U	12/28/00	-	
-	-	-	-	0.34	-	-	-	-	-	-	-	0.007U	12/28/00	-	
-	-	-	-	0.38	-	-	-	-	-	-	-	0.007U	12/28/00	-	
-	-	-	0.53	0.73	-	-	-	-	-	-	-	0.124U	10/2/07	-	
-	-	-	1.85	1.55	-	-	-	-	-	-	-	0.124U	10/2/07	-	
-	-	-	-	-	-	-	-	-	-	-	-	0.7111Q	1/3/08	-	
-	-	-	2.16	3.61	-	-	-	-	-	-	-	0.124U	10/2/07	-	
-	-	-	-	-	-	-	-	-	-	-	-	-	-	-	
-	-	-	-	-	-	-	-	-	-	-	-	0.0885Q	7/6/07	-	
-	-	-	-	-	-	-	-	-	-	-	-	0.0885Q	7/6/07	-	
-	-	-	-	-	-	-	-	-	-	-	-	-	-	-	
-	-	-	-	-	-	-	-	-	-	-	-	0.0885Q	7/6/07	-	
-	-	-	-	-	-	-	-	-	-	-	-	-	-	-	
-	-	-	-	-	-	-	-	-	-	-	-	0.0885Q	7/6/07	-	
-	-	-	-	-	-	-	-	-	-	-	-	-	-	-	
-	-	-	-	-	-	-	-	-	-	-	-	0.3343Q	12/28/06	-	
-	-	-	-	-	-	-	-	-	-	-	-	0.0885Q	7/6/07	-	
-	-	-	-	-	-	-	-	-	-	-	-	0.0885Q	7/6/07	-	
-	-	-	-	-	-	-	-	-	-	-	-	0.0885Q	7/6/07	-	
-	-	-	-	-	-	-	-	-	-	-	-	0.0885Q	7/6/07	-	
-	-	-	-	-	-	-	-	-	-	-	-	-	-	-	
-	-	-	-	-	-	-	-	-	-	-	-	-	-	-	
0.64	0.75	0.73	1.51	2.70	2.11	30.2 -	22.8	3.60	3.08	2.93	8.9	0.87Q	4/30/08	45.6 -	34.5
0.39	0.46	0.48	1.68	0.92	1.06	-	-	1.13	1.09	0.63	-	0.20Q	0/17/00	-	
0.76	1.16	1.25	4.03	3.10	1.91	10.7 -	8.8	0.56	0.22	0.36	1.4	0.175Q	4/1/08	43.2 -	35.7
0.66	0.87	0.98	3.71	2.72	2.33	16.0 -	7.6	-	-	-	-	-	-	59.5 -	28.3
-0.13	-0.20	-	-	-0.59	-0.29	-	-	-	-	-	-	-	-	8.6 -	3.8
0.39	0.32	0.42	1.49	-0.39	-4.82	-	-	-	-	-	-	-	-	-	
0.30	-0.12	-	-	0.35	0.77	1.12	-	92.4 -	55.7	0.28	0.14	-	1.1	0.07Q	3/3/08	32.4 -	19.5
0.60	-	-	1.88	1.50	1.24	10.3 -	5.7	-	-	-	-	-	-	19.4 -	10.7
-0.65	-0.78	0.61	1.93	1.59	1.32	13.2 -	8.6	0.48	0.32	0.21	2.4	0.18Q	4/15/08	25.5 -	16.6
0.79	-	-	2.35	1.64	1.28	10.2 -	7.9	-	-	-	-	-	-	24.0 -	18.6
-	-	-	-	-1.10	0.28	-	-	-	0.38	0.11	-	-	-	27.6 -	18.1
0.19	0.27	0.07	0.65	0.66	0.40	27.2 -	19.6	0.04	0.04	0.04	0.3	0.04A	5/31/07	17.7 -	12.7
-	-	-	-	0.01	-	-	-	-	0.06	-	-	0.09A	12/27/06	7.7 -	5.8
-	-	-	-	-	-	-	-	-	-	-	-	0.0035S	1/15/08	14.6 -	10.2
0.02	0.23	0.28	0.38	1.59	0.22	77.1 -	49.7	-	-	-	-	-	-	29.3 -	18.9
0.42	0.45	0.26	0.97	1.42	1.16	22.1 -	14.6	0.50	0.45	0.26	2.8	0.125Q	3/14/08	21.5 -	14.2
0.38	0.39	0.41	-	1.23	1.08	-	-	-	1.81	0.63	-	0.45Q	1/30/08	-	
-	-	-	0.11	0.07	0.13	179.7 -	89.8	5.23	0.09	0.06	40.8	1.1791A	12/14/07	19.8 -	9.9
0.17	0.12	0.05	-23.84	0.89	1.04	-	-	-	-	-	-	0.05Q	4/11/08	-	
-0.07	-0.76	0.32	-0.08	-1.01	2.02	-	-	-	-	-	-	-	-	30.3 -	20.0
-	-	-	-	0.16	0.14	-	-	-	1.07	1.13	-	0.0815Q	12/28/07	10.8 -	8.7
-	-	-	1.34	1.26	1.20	12.1 -	10.5	0.92	0.93	1.03	6.0	0.2551Q	3/31/08	16.2 -	14.0
-	-	-	1.89	1.74	1.70	11.9 -	9.9	1.31	1.30	1.47	6.2	0.32Q	12/31/07	22.6 -	18.7
-	-	-	-	0.99	0.85	-	-	-	0.65	0.77	-	0.048M	2/29/08	11.9 -	9.4
-	-	-	2.13	2.24	2.30	12.6 -	9.8	2.07	2.06	2.01	8.3	0.155M	2/29/08	26.9 -	20.8
0.88	1.05	0.88	3.63	3.73	3.46	17.6 -	13.6	1.62	1.46	1.27	2.9	0.415Q	3/11/08	63.8 -	49.5
0.39	-	-	2.09	1.74	1.56	10.2 -	8.2	0.44	0.37	0.33	2.3	0.13Q	4/2/08	21.3 -	17.1

T33

SYMBOL	COMPANY	NATURE OF BUSINESS	FISCAL YEAR-END	TOTAL REV. $MILL	NET INCOME $MILL	TOTAL ASSETS $MILL	NET STK EQUITY $MILL	NO OF INST	INST. HOLDINGS (SHARES)
JNY	Jones Apparel Group, Inc.	Apparel	12/31/07	3848.5	311.1	3236.6	1996.8	284	113025819
JLL	Jones Lang LaSalle Inc	Property, Real Estate & Development	12/31/07	2652.1	257.8	2291.9	1010.5	130	27649020
JRN	Journal Communications Inc	Media	12/30/07	582.7	110.1	857.0	487.6	92	26102776
JRC	Journal Register Co.	Media	12/30/07	463.2	-102.5	932.5	91.1	99	41227502
JPM	JPMorgan Chase & Co.	Commercial Banking	12/31/07	116353.0	15365.0	1562147.0	123221.0	-	-
KAI	Kadant Inc	Industrial Machinery and Equipment	12/29/07	366.5	22.7	437.1	278.8	81	12421192
KSU	Kansas City Southern (United State	Rail Transport	12/31/07	1742.8	153.8	4928.2	1726.3	158	59903112
KDN	Kaydon Corp.	Industrial Machinery and Equipment	12/31/07	451.4	77.7	786.6	483.4	140	26915766
KED	Kayne Anderson Energy Developm	Finance & Investment	11/30/07	-	3.6	355.4	245.1	-	-
KYE	Kayne Anderson Energy Total Retur	Finance & Investment							
KYN	Kayne Anderson MLP Investment C	Trusts & Holding Entities	11/30/07	18.3	-30.0	2239.8	1300.0	21	1780041
KBH	KB HOME	Building & General Construction	11/30/07	6416.5	-929.4	5706.0	1850.7	300	71681744
KBR	KBR Inc	Construction - Public Infrastructure	12/31/07	8745.0	302.0	5203.0	2267.0	-	-
KBW	KBW Inc	Finance Intermediaries & Services	12/31/07	427.5	27.3	864.4	448.4	-	-
KEI	Keithley Instruments, Inc.	Instruments and Related Products	9/30/07	143.7	-0.3	146.4	113.0	71	8854291
K	Kellogg Co	Food	12/29/07	11776.0	1103.0	11397.0	2526.0	405	324341994
KEM	KEMET Corp.	Electrical	3/31/07	658.7	6.9	943.5	535.8	134	73421641
KMT	Kennametal Inc.	Industrial Machinery and Equipment	6/30/07	2385.5	174.2	2606.2	1484.5	203	33343733
KEG	Key Energy Services, Inc.	Oil and Gas	12/31/06	1546.2	171.0	1541.4	730.5	177	119337752
KEY	KeyCorp (New)	Commercial Banking	12/31/07	7873.0	919.0	99983.0	7746.0	433	210373233
KHD	KHD Humboldt Wedag International	Engineering Services	12/31/06	458.5	35.5	748.0	318.5	-	-
KRC	Kilroy Realty Corp	Property, Real Estate & Development	12/31/07	258.5	113.8	2068.7	693.3	118	26641018
KMB	Kimberly-Clark Corp.	Paper Products	12/31/07	18266.0	1822.9	18439.7	5223.7	770	350674382
KIM	Kimco Realty Corp.	Property, Real Estate & Development	12/31/07	681.6	442.8	9097.8	3894.6	2	442180
KMP	Kinder Morgan Energy Partners, L.	Gas Utilities	12/31/07	9217.7	590.3	15177.8	-	276	27022672
KMR	Kinder Morgan Management, LLC	Oil and Gas	12/31/07	65.4	50.4	2213.8	2183.0	118	29805146
KND	Kindred Healthcare Inc	Hospitals & Health Care	12/31/07	4220.3	-46.9	2079.6	862.1	163	43683954
KCI	Kinetic Concepts Inc (New)	Specialist Equipment Supplies	12/31/07	1609.9	237.1	1057.6	677.0	189	50351252
KG	King Pharmaceuticals, Inc.	Pharmaceuticals	12/31/07	2136.9	183.0	3426.8	2510.8	233	175017279
KFS	Kingsway Financial Services Inc.	Insurance	12/31/06	1916.4	123.3	4048.3	901.0	36	22828219
KGC	Kinross Gold Corp.	Precious Metals	12/31/06	905.6	165.8	2053.5	1468.0	106	123714290
KEX	Kirby Corp.	Shipping	12/31/07	1172.6	123.3	1430.5	769.8	124	19048386
KRG	Kite Realty Group Trust	Property, Real Estate & Development	12/31/07	138.8	13.5	1048.2	259.6	54	15104750
KFN	KKR Financial Holdings LLC	Property, Real Estate & Development	12/31/07	727.5	-100.2	19046.0	1644.5	-	-
KNX	Knight Transportation Inc.	Road Transport	12/31/06	664.4	73.0	570.2	426.1	143	37228958
KNL	Knoll Inc (New)	Furniture and Fixtures	12/31/07	1055.8	71.4	717.4	74.7	45	15003096
KSS	Kohl's Corp.	Retail - General	1/31/04	10282.1	591.2	6698.4	4191.3	479	280512301
KNM	Konami Corp	Office Equipment Supplies	3/31/07	280279.0	16211.0	304657.0	174662.0	5	58811
KPN	KONINKLIJKE KPN NV	Communications	12/31/04	11746.0	1707.0	23661.0	6556.0	32	4692370
PHG	Koninklijke Philips Electronics N.V.	Electrical	12/31/04	29346.0	2836.0	30723.0	15143.0	179	109752898
KB	Kookmin Bank (New) (South Korea)	Commercial Banking	12/31/06	4284562.0	3090566.0	92978245.0	14772176.0	124	40545795
KOP	Koppers Holdings Inc	Wood Products	12/31/07	1327.9	63.3	669.3	-23.3	-	-
KEP	Korea Electric Power Corp. (Korea)	Electricity	12/31/06	27408813.3	2225560.3	77435486.1	-	123	130645422
KEF	Korea Equity Fund, Inc.	Trusts & Holding Entities	10/31/06	-	0.2	97.5	97.2	15	3804200
KF	Korea Fund, Inc. (The)	Trusts & Holding Entities	6/30/07	18.9	9.6	1113.2	1033.2	57	24299496
KFY	Korn/Ferry International (DE)	Human Resources Services	4/30/07	689.2	55.5	761.5	433.0	144	31109978
KFT	Kraft Foods, Inc.	Food	12/31/07	37241.0	2590.0	67993.0	27295.0	301	222369000
KKD	Krispy Kreme Doughnuts Inc	Retail - Food & Beverage	1/28/07	461.2	-42.2	349.5	79.0	127	30878044
KR	Kroger Co.	Retail - Food & Beverage	2/2/08	70235.0	1181.0	22299.0	4914.0	346	569258333
KRO	Kronos Worldwide Inc	Chemicals	12/31/07	1310.3	-66.7	1455.0	411.0	51	2116004
KSP	K-Sea Transportation Partners LP	Shipping	6/30/07	226.6	15.8	429.8	-	22	1305693
KTC	KT Corp (Korea)	Communications	12/31/06	7756156.0	1291863.0	24222036.0	-	112	199646186
KUB	Kubota Corp. (Japan)	Industrial Machinery and Equipment	3/31/07	1127456.0	76457.0	1502532.0	659637.0	19	1308310
KV A	KV Pharmaceutical Co.	Pharmaceuticals	3/31/07	443.6	58.1	707.8	364.8	105	32891661
KYO	Kyocera Corp. (Japan)	Electrical	3/31/07	1283897.0	106504.0	2130464.0	1514560.0	56	2221117
ID	L-1 Identity Solutions Inc (Holding C	IT & Technology	12/31/06	164.4	-31.0	1227.2	1067.1	-	-
LLL	L-3 Communications Holdings, Inc.	Communications	12/31/07	13960.5	756.1	14390.7	5988.9	490	90546076
LH	Laboratory Corp. of America Holdin	Diagnostic Services	12/31/07	4068.2	476.8	4368.2	1725.3	388	119140817
LAB	LaBranche & Co., Inc.	Finance Intermediaries & Services	12/31/07	145.6	-350.5	5343.7	527.9	118	48765292
LG	Laclede Group Inc	Gas Utilities	9/30/07	2021.6	49.8	1641.2	428.3	103	6428362
LFL	Lan Airlines SA	Aviation	12/31/06	3034.0	241.3	2928.8	626.3	37	6657990
LFG	Landamerica Financial Group, Inc.	Insurance	12/31/07	3705.8	-54.1	3853.7	1200.7	147	19050467
LDR	Landauer, Inc.	Instruments and Related Products	9/30/07	83.7	19.3	97.3	59.5	82	5919671
LNY	Landry's Restaurants, Inc.	Hospitality & Tourism	12/31/07	1171.9	18.1	1503.0	316.9	127	19423183
LVS	Las Vegas Sands Corp	Hospitality & Tourism	12/31/07	2950.6	116.7	11466.5	2260.3	119	23840248
LHO	LaSalle Hotel Properties	Property, Real Estate & Development	12/31/07	662.4	89.8	2111.3	1038.1	99	26392846
LDF	Latin American Discovery Fund, Inc.	Trusts & Holding Entities	12/31/07	6.0	2.7	289.9	247.9	17	2935404
EL	Lauder (Estee) Cos., Inc. (The)	Chemicals	6/30/07	7037.5	449.2	4125.7	1199.0	1	3182
LGI	Lazard Global Total Return & Incom	Trusts & Holding Entities	12/31/07	7.7	4.0	284.8	234.1	10	215259
LAZ	Lazard Ltd	Wealth Management	12/31/06	1597.8	93.0	3208.7	-240.4	-	-
LOR	Lazard World Dividend & Income Fu	Trusts & Holding Entities							
LZB	La-Z-Boy Inc.	Chemicals	4/28/07	1617.3	4.1	878.7	485.3	141	39516099
LDK	LDK Solar Co., Ltd.	IT & Technology	12/31/06	-	30.2	-	57.2	-	-
LF	Leapfrog Enterprises Inc	Consumer Accessories	12/31/07	442.3	-101.3	380.2	243.5	106	32179962
LEA	Lear Corp.	Furniture and Fixtures	12/31/07	15995.0	241.5	7800.4	1090.7	212	62582041
LEE	Lee Enterprises, Inc.	Media	9/30/07	1127.7	81.0	3261.0	1086.4	153	31534103
LM	Legg Mason, Inc.	Finance Intermediaries & Services	3/31/07	4343.7	646.8	9604.5	6541.5	335	84138904
LEG	Leggett & Platt, Inc.	Furniture and Fixtures	12/31/07	4306.4	-11.2	4072.5	2132.7	270	124609634
LBC	Lehman Brothers First Trust Income	Trusts & Holding Entities	12/31/07	23.0	20.4	255.7	162.1	8	433656
LEH	Lehman Brothers Holdings Inc	Finance Intermediaries & Services	11/30/07	59003.0	4192.0	691063.0	22490.0	-	-

T34

EARNINGS PER SHARE QUARTERLY			ANNUAL			P/E RATIO		DIVIDENDS PER SHARE			AV. YLD %	DIV. DECLARED		PRICE RANGE 2007	
1st	2nd	3rd	2007	2006	2005			2007	2006	2005		AMOUNT	PAYABLE		
0.44	-0.44	3.97	3.07	-1.30	2.30	12.9 -	10.9	0.56	0.50	0.44	1.5	0.14Q	3/14/08	39.7 -	33.5
0.81	2.32	1.38	7.64	5.24	3.12	5.0 -	2.7	0.85	0.60	0.25	3.0	0.5S	12/14/07	38.0 -	20.5
1.05	0.21	0.21	1.65	0.89	0.88	12.2 -	9.5	0.30	0.26	0.26	1.7	0.08Q	3/7/08	20.1 -	15.7
0.74	0.14	0.28	-2.62	-0.02	1.12			0.06	0.08	0.04	0.3	0.02Q	10/8/07	21.8 -	18.0
1.34	1.20	0.97	4.38	4.04	2.38			1.44	1.36	1.36		0.38Q	4/30/08	-	
0.30	0.35	0.40	1.59	1.21	0.49	14.6 -	11.2							23.2 -	17.9
0.21	0.30	0.48	1.57	1.08	1.10	11.3 -	8.1	1.00	1.00	1.00	6.7	0.25Q	4/1/08	17.8 -	12.7
0.57	0.61	0.54	2.41	2.17	2.30	14.0 -	10.3	0.54	0.48	0.48	1.9	0.15Q	3/31/08	33.9 -	24.9
												0.41Q	1/17/08	-	
			1.17	0.23								0.495Q	4/11/08	-	
			-0.73	-0.62	-0.17			1.93	1.75	1.50	7.7	0.4975Q	4/11/08	25.7 -	24.4
-3.47			-12.04	5.82	9.53			1.00	1.00	0.75	2.7	0.25Q	2/21/08	52.8 -	30.5
0.17	0.83	0.37	1.79	1.20	1.76							0.05Q	4/15/08	-	
0.24	0.33	0.18	0.86	1.93	0.64									-	
0.05			-0.02	0.50	0.61			0.15	0.15	0.15	0.8	0.03Q	3/31/08	25.6 -	16.1
0.80	0.75	0.76	2.76	2.51	2.36	16.4 -	13.5	1.20	1.14	1.06	2.9	0.31Q	3/18/08	45.2 -	37.2
0.08	0.05	-0.10	0.08	0.00	-2.01	207.8 -	94.8							16.6 -	7.6
0.44	0.64		2.22	3.24	1.56	11.8 -	8.7	0.41	0.38	0.34	1.9	0.12Q	2/20/08	26.3 -	19.3
0.39	0.36			1.28	0.34									13.8 -	8.7
0.87	0.84	0.54	2.32	2.57	2.73	14.9 -	12.3	1.46	1.38	1.30	4.7	0.375Q	3/14/08	34.5 -	28.4
														12.6 -	7.7
0.51	0.40	0.28	3.20	2.30	0.84	13.7 -	9.6	2.22	2.12	2.04	6.2	0.4688Q	5/15/08	43.9 -	30.6
0.98	1.00	1.04	4.09	3.25	3.28	16.4 -	13.6	2.12	1.96	1.80	3.4	0.58Q	4/2/08	67.0 -	55.5
0.59	0.49	0.29	1.65	1.70	1.52	16.5 -	13.6	1.52	1.38	1.27	5.9	0.4844Q	4/15/08	27.3 -	22.5
0.33	0.36	0.24	-0.09	2.04	1.58			3.39	3.23	3.07	7.6	0.92Q	2/14/08	49.0 -	38.3
0.20	0.10	0.16	-0.65	1.21	1.00									44.2 -	34.3
0.20	-1.52	-0.23	-1.17	1.92	3.20									23.6 -	17.6
0.75	0.81	0.82	3.31	2.69	1.67	23.3 -	12.1							77.1 -	40.0
0.48	0.26	-0.17	0.75	1.19	0.49	26.6 -	13.8							20.0 -	10.4
0.35	0.74	0.42		2.17	2.37				0.26	0.20		0.076Q	12/28/07	15.0 -	10.4
0.15	0.09		0.47	-0.63										8.5 -	5.0
0.46	0.56	0.64	2.29	1.79	1.34	10.0 -	6.7							23.0 -	15.4
0.06	0.09	0.13	0.46	0.35	0.62	33.6 -	27.7	0.79	0.76	0.56	5.8	0.205Q	4/17/08	15.4 -	12.8
0.60	0.66	-2.98	-1.11	1.71	0.92			0.54	1.86	0.32		0.5Q	2/29/08	-	
0.19	0.21	0.17		0.84	0.71				0.10	0.04		0.03Q	12/28/07	17.2 -	9.9
0.30	0.35	0.37	1.45	1.14	0.68	12.6 -	11.8	0.45	0.41	0.25	2.5	0.12Q	3/31/08	18.3 -	17.1
0.64	0.83	0.61	3.31	2.43	2.12	16.1 -	12.4							53.2 -	41.0
			118.09	175.80	87.41	0.3 -	0.2							31.0 -	20.5
			1.42	0.79	0.65	6.8 -	5.0							9.7 -	7.0
			3.80	4.55	2.29	8.8 -	5.8							33.3 -	22.0
			-9188.00	6411.00										44.2 -	27.1
0.50	1.07	1.22	3.03	0.75	-6.58			0.68	1.30	3.19		0.22Q	4/2/08	-	
			-3389.00	3766.00								0.0882U	4/20/97	13.9 -	8.8
				0.03	-0.05									6.2 -	4.3
			0.38	0.33	0.40	63.6 -	13.0	7.12	0.85	0.65	05.0	0.1715A	1/10/00	24.2 -	10.7
0.36	0.37	0.37	1.24	1.32	0.90	17.4 -	9.7							21.6 -	12.2
0.43	0.44	0.38	1.62	1.85	1.55	22.2 -	18.2	1.04	0.96	0.87	3.2	0.27Q	4/4/08	35.9 -	29.6
-0.12	-0.42	-0.01	-0.68	-2.20	-3.22									39.7 -	9.6
0.47	0.38	0.37	1.54	1.31	-0.14	12.6 -	9.6	0.20			1.2	0.075Q	3/1/08	19.5 -	14.7
0.26		-1.66	-1.36	1.67	1.45			1.00	1.00	1.00	3.0	0.25Q	3/25/08	48.5 -	22.2
0.62	0.68		1.55	0.60	0.95	22.5 -	15.6	2.60	2.32	2.15	9.0	0.74Q	2/14/08	34.9 -	24.1
			6148.00	1066.00										22.7 -	16.6
			59.01	61.67	86.83	0.5 -	0.3							27.5 -	19.6
			1.96	0.31	0.63	14.0 -	7.8							27.5 -	15.3
			564.79	371.43	244.81	0.2 -	0.1							00.0 -	00.0
-0.12	-0.02	0.02		-0.71	-0.37									33.1 -	9.5
1.29	1.49	1.56	5.98	4.22	4.20	12.9 -	8.3	1.00	0.75	0.50	1.6	0.3Q	3/17/08	76.9 -	49.8
0.98	1.05	0.92	3.93	3.24	2.71	12.7 -	9.4							50.0 -	36.8
0.08	0.00	0.10	-5.71	2.22	0.61							0.08Q	8/14/03	12.1 -	7.1
0.97			2.31	2.30	1.90	14.0 -	11.3	1.46	1.41	1.38	5.0	0.285Q	3/31/08	32.4 -	26.2
														6.6 -	3.4
0.26	0.42	-1.28	-3.31	5.61	9.29			1.04	0.80	0.66	2.3	0.3Q	3/14/08	57.1 -	36.3
0.57			2.10	2.09	1.90	24.0 -	18.6	1.90	1.80	1.70	4.3	0.5Q	4/4/08	50.3 -	39.1
1.01	0.33	-0.25	0.93	-0.99	1.95	36.0 -	26.9					0.05Q	1/31/08	33.5 -	25.1
0.26	0.10	-0.14	0.33	1.24	0.80	160.6 -	141.1							53.0 -	46.6
0.39	0.48	0.50	1.53	1.85	0.67	21.5 -	12.5	1.05	1.56	1.00	7.7	0.17M	4/15/08	32.9 -	19.1
			0.34	0.29	0.45	54.0 -	31.5	7.80	9.00	6.24	55.5	0.5805S	1/7/08	18.4 -	10.7
0.20	1.14		2.16	1.12	1.78			0.50	0.40	0.40		0.55A	12/27/07	-	
			0.42	0.40	0.23	47.6 -	38.5	1.66	2.34	1.25	9.1	0.1042M	4/23/08	20.0 -	16.2
0.47	0.52			2.31	1.45				1.66	0.85		0.1Q	2/29/08	-	
			1.11	0.26					3.26	0.72		0.1167M	4/23/08	-	
-0.17	-0.19	0.18	0.08	-0.06	0.71	293.8 -	161.9	0.48	0.44	0.44	2.7	0.04Q	3/10/08	23.5 -	12.9
			0.35	-0.01										-	
-0.48	-0.44	-0.16	-1.60	-2.31	0.28									31.8 -	12.0
0.64	1.58	0.52	3.09	-10.31	-20.57	22.3 -	16.1		0.25	1.00		0.25Q	3/13/08	68.9 -	49.7
0.48			1.77	1.56	1.70	28.1 -	24.6	0.72	0.72	0.72	1.5	0.19Q	4/1/08	49.7 -	43.5
1.32	1.23	1.07	4.48	8.80	3.53	16.4 -	10.9	0.81	0.69	0.55	1.4	0.24Q	4/7/08	73.3 -	49.0
0.41	0.33	0.37	-0.06	1.61	1.30			0.78	0.67	0.63	3.0	0.25Q	4/15/08	30.6 -	21.4
			1.67	1.65	1.71	10.0 -	8.2	1.74	1.35	1.60	11.1	0.11M	3/31/08	16.7 -	13.8
0.81			7.26	6.81	5.43			0.60	0.48	0.40		0.17Q	2/22/08	-	

SYMBOL	COMPANY	NATURE OF BUSINESS	FISCAL YEAR-END	TOTAL REV. $MILL	NET INCOME $MILL	TOTAL ASSETS $MILL	NET STK EQUITY $MILL	NO OF INST	INST. HOLDINGS (SHARES)
LEN	Lennar Corp.	Building & General Construction	11/30/07	10186.8	-1941.1	9102.7	3822.1	75	10030328
LII	Lennox International Inc	Purpose Machinery	12/31/07	3749.7	169.0	1814.6	808.5	115	34320430
LNX	Lenox Group Inc	Stone, Clay, Glass, and Concrete Pr	12/29/07	452.1	-15.8	352.1	136.1	-	-
LUK	Leucadia National Corp.	Communications	12/31/07	1154.9	484.3	8126.6	5570.5	203	62330361
LEV	Levitt Corp (Fla)	Building & General Construction	12/31/07	415.9	-234.6	712.9	261.1	99	12081253
LXP	Lexington Realty Trust	Property, Real Estate & Developmen	12/31/07	431.7	76.9	5265.2	939.1	-	-
LXK	Lexmark International, Inc.	Office Equipment Supplies	12/31/07	4973.9	300.8	3121.1	1278.3	367	112649128
LPL	LG Display Co Ltd	Electrical	12/31/06	10624200.0	-769313.0	13487787.0	-	39	25414376
LBY	Libbey Inc.	Stone, Clay, Glass, and Concrete Pr	12/31/07	816.4	-2.3	899.1	93.1	86	12508954
USA	Liberty All-Star Equity Fund	Trusts & Holding Entities	12/31/07	24.0	10.5	1474.1	1442.5	35	4645029
ASG	Liberty All-Star Growth Fund Inc.	Trusts & Holding Entities	12/31/07	1.3	-0.8	175.1	171.7	16	242640
LRY	Liberty Property Trust	Property, Real Estate & Developmen	12/31/07	698.7	164.8	5638.7	1837.0	225	67486588
LTM	Life-Time Fitness Inc	Sporting & Recreational	12/31/07	655.8	68.0	1386.5	572.6	75	13757089
LLY	Lilly (Eli) & Co.	Pharmaceuticals	12/31/07	18633.5	2953.0	26787.8	13664.4	777	775235952
LTD	Limited Brands Inc.	Retail - Apparel and Accessory Store	2/2/08	10134.0	718.0	7437.0	2219.0	324	306322731
TVL	LIN TV Corp	Media	12/31/07	395.9	53.7	1982.0	656.1	85	26687128
LNC	Lincoln National Corp. (ID)	Insurance	12/31/07	10594.0	1215.0	191435.0	11718.0	-	-
LNN	Lindsay Corp	Industrial Machinery and Equipment	8/31/07	281.9	15.6	242.2	141.0	71	10261433
LGF	Lions Gate Entertainment Corp.	Movies & Film	3/31/07	976.7	27.5	1137.1	247.9	125	99845215
LAD	Lithia Motors, Inc.	Retail - Automotive	12/31/06	3172.9	37.3	1579.4	493.4	72	15077612
LYV	Live Nation Inc	Media	12/31/07	4185.0	-11.9	2752.1	867.1	-	-
LIZ	Liz Claiborne, Inc. (United States)	Apparel	12/29/07	4577.3	-372.8	3268.5	1515.6	307	92479908
LRT	LL&E Royalty Trust Co.	Miscellaneous	12/31/06	3.1	2.1	2.6	2.6	22	1631187
LYG	Lloyds TSB Group Plc	Commercial Banking						76	19198212
SCD	LMP Capital & Income Fund Inc	Trusts & Holding Entities	10/31/06		14.9	870.8	633.9	-	-
TLI	LMP Corporate Loan Fund Inc	Trusts & Holding Entities	9/30/07		14.9	228.3	133.5	-	-
RIT	LMP Real Estate Income Fund Inc	Trusts & Holding Entities		15.4	12.6	276.8	179.8	-	-
LMT	Lockheed Martin Corp.	Defense	12/31/07	41862.0	3033.0	28926.0	9805.0	466	454066703
LTR	Loews Corp.	Insurance	12/31/06	17911.0	2491.3	76880.9	16501.8	315	110799614
CG	Loews Corp.	Tobacco Products						133	57187435
LDG	Longs Drug Stores Corp. (United St	Retail - Miscellaneous	1/31/08	5262.6	96.2	1846.7	827.9	-	-
LPX	Louisiana-Pacific Corp. (United Stat	Wood Products	12/31/07	1704.9	-179.9	3229.3	1819.5	249	89691273
LOW	Lowe's Companies Inc	Retail - Hardware	2/1/08	48283.0	2809.0	30869.0	16098.0	770	617627071
LSI	LSI Corp	IT & Technology	12/31/07	2603.6	-2486.8	4396.4	2485.0	267	215292323
LTC	LTC Properties, Inc.	Property, Real Estate & Developmen	12/31/07	74.8	47.8	544.1	479.2	69	11682444
LZ	Lubrizol Corp	Chemicals	12/31/07	4499.0	283.4	4643.8	1951.3	231	56699639
LUB	Luby's, Inc. (United States)	Hospitality & Tourism	8/29/07	320.4	10.9	219.6	178.3	35	7613538
LL	Lumber Liquidators Inc	Retail - Hardware	12/31/07	405.3	11.3	128.4	92.2	-	-
LUM	Luminent Mortgage Capital Inc	Property, Real Estate & Developmen	12/31/07	-175.5	-721.0	4721.9	-310.0	72	18686409
LMC	Lundin Mining Corp	Earth & Rock Mining	12/31/06	539.7	152.9	2829.6	2129.8	1	140000
LUX	Luxottica Group S.P.A.	Medical Instruments & Equipment	12/31/06	4676.2	424.3	4915.0	2215.8	53	21856508
LDL	Lydall, Inc.	Industrial Machinery and Equipment	12/31/07	338.9	9.1	258.6	180.5	58	12958780
MFW	M & F Worldwide Corp.	Food	12/31/07	1472.8	-4.2	3811.7	405.5	59	7452973
MTB	M & T Bank Corp	Commercial Banking	12/31/07	4477.8	654.3	64875.6	6485.3	276	73539599
MDC	M.D.C. Holdings, Inc. (United States	Building & General Construction	12/31/07	2933.2	-636.9	2956.2	1476.0	201	31266702
MHO	M/I Homes Inc	Building & General Construction	12/31/07	1016.5	-128.1	1117.6	581.3	98	11564651
MAC	Macerich Co. (The)	Property, Real Estate & Developmen	12/31/07	896.4	96.5	8121.1	1312.6	180	53724096
TUC	Mac-Gray Corp.	Personal Services	12/31/07	295.9	2.5	383.5	97.8	18	2888133
CLI	Mack Cali Realty Corp	Property, Real Estate & Developmen	12/31/07	808.3	110.5	4593.2	1642.6	207	51605530
MGU	Macquarie Global Infrastructure Tot	Trusts & Holding Entities						-	-
MIC	Macquarie Infrastructure Co LLC	Trusts & Holding Entities	12/31/06		49.9	2097.5	864.4	-	-
MFD	Macquarie/First Trust Global Infrastr	Trusts & Holding Entities	11/30/07	21.3	12.0	360.4	225.5	12	151770
M	Macys Inc	Retail - General	2/2/08	26313.0	893.0	27789.0	9907.0	-	-
MAD	Madeco S.A.	Metal Works	12/31/06	559141.5	30204.0	416781.8	251555.2	4	121102
MSP	Madison Strategic Sector Premium	Trusts & Holding Entities						-	-
MCN	Madison/Claymore Covered Call &	Trusts & Holding Entities	12/31/07	6.8	3.3	263.9	250.8	1	15419
MGG	Magellan Midstream Holdings LP	Oil and Gas	12/31/07	1319.1	57.0	2416.9		-	-
MMP	Magellan Midstream Partners LP	Oil and Gas	12/31/07	1318.1	242.8	2101.2		114	20695676
MGA	Magna International Inc.	Automotive	12/31/06	24180.0	528.0	13154.0	7157.0	136	57346473
MAG	MagneTek, Inc.	Electrical	7/1/07	103.8	-8.0	104.7	41.5	81	23376570
MPG	Maguire Properties Inc	Property, Real Estate & Developmen	12/31/07	548.0	19.3	5749.8	343.3	119	31314772
MTA	Magyar Telekom Telecommunicatio	Communications	12/31/04	601438.0	34641.0	1029558.0	576664.0	51	22621491
MTE	Mahanagar Telephone Nigam Ltd. (I	Communications	3/31/07	45475.0	11302.0			33	19421192
MFB	Maidenform Brands Inc	Retail - Apparel and Accessory Store	12/29/07	422.2	34.2	279.7	99.6	-	-
MAY	Malaysia Fund, Inc.	Trusts & Holding Entities	12/31/07	2.8	1.5	119.2	117.3	11	546083
HYF	Managed High Yield Plus Fund Inc	Commercial Banking	5/31/07	43.4	32.0	439.3	299.3	22	5025030
MTW	Manitowoc Co., Inc.	Industrial Machinery and Equipment	12/31/07	4005.0	336.7	2868.7	1349.9	159	23534936
MAN	Manpower Inc. (WI)	Human Resources Services	12/31/07	20500.3	484.7	7224.4	2669.3	261	79554054
MFC	Manulife Financial Corp.	Insurance	12/31/06	34194.0	3970.0	186169.0	25656.0	-	-
MRO	Marathon Oil Corp.	Oil and Gas	12/31/07	65207.0	3956.0	42746.0	19223.0	465	260475910
MCS	Marcus Corp. (The)	Hospitality & Tourism	5/31/07	327.6	33.3	698.4	319.5	-	-
MPX	Marine Products Corp.	Shipping	12/31/07	244.3	16.4	118.7	93.8	53	9095408
HZO	MarineMax, Inc.	Retail - Automotive	9/30/07	1256.0	20.1	825.9	373.6	106	15646345
ME	Mariner Energy Inc.	Oil and Gas	12/31/07	874.7	143.9	3083.6	1391.0	-	-
MKL	Markel Corp (Holding Co)	Insurance	12/31/07	2483.3	405.7	10134.4	2641.2	-	-
MWE	Markwest Energy Partners L.P.	Oil and Gas	12/31/07	602.9	17.2	1392.8		29	2598686
MAR	Marriott International, Inc. (New)	Hospitality & Tourism	12/28/07	12990.0	696.0	8942.0	1429.0	361	130995473
MMC	Marsh & McLennan Companies Inc.	Insurance	12/31/07	11350.0	2475.0	17359.0	7822.0	438	418742146
MI	Marshall & Ilsley Corp (New)	Commercial Banking	12/31/07	4398.2	1150.9	59848.6	7032.7	-	-
MSO	Martha Stewart Living Omnimedia, I	Media	12/31/07	327.9	10.3	255.3	155.5	74	5898874

1st	2nd	3rd	2007	2006	2005	P/E RATIO	DIV 2007	DIV 2006	DIV 2005	AV. YLD %	AMOUNT	PAYABLE	PRICE RANGE 2007
-0.56	-	-	-12.31	3.69	8.23	-	0.64	0.64	0.57	1.5	0.16Q	2/19/08	53.4 - 38.0
0.12	0.85	0.88	2.43	2.26	2.11	8.4 - 5.8	0.53	0.46	0.41	3.1	0.14Q	4/11/08	20.5 - 14.0
-0.94	-0.82	0.29	-1.15	-3.58	1.10	-	-	-	-	-	-	-	17.3 - 12.9
0.04	0.12	0.02	2.10	0.85	7.13	11.1 - 7.3	0.25	0.25	0.13	1.4	0.25A	12/28/07	23.4 - 15.2
0.06	-2.93	-8.37	-6.00	-0.47	2.74	-	0.02	0.08	0.08	0.1	0.02	2/16/07	31.1 - 16.8
-0.05	0.34	0.12	0.77	-0.17	0.33	-	-	2.06	1.44	-	0.4719Q	4/15/08	-
0.95	0.67	0.48	3.14	3.27	2.91	30.7 - 24.3	-	-	-	-	-	-	96.5 - 76.3
-	-	-	-2150.00	1523.00		-	-	-	-	-	-	-	18.2 - 13.3
-0.12	0.27	0.03	-0.16	-1.47	-1.39	-	0.10	0.10	0.40	0.4	0.025Q	3/4/08	30.6 - 17.2
-	-	-	0.07	0.04	0.02	148.6 - 115.4	0.23	0.88	0.87	2.5	0.19Q	3/17/08	10.4 - 8.1
-	-	-	-0.50	-0.04	-0.04	-	0.15	0.59	0.58	2.3	-	-	7.6 - 5.6
0.43	0.57	0.41	1.80	2.95	2.82	25.3 - 19.5	2.49	2.47	2.45	6.2	0.625Q	4/15/08	45.5 - 35.0
0.38	0.44	0.48	1.78	1.37	1.13	15.2 - 11.8	-	-	-	-	-	-	27.0 - 21.0
0.47	0.61	0.85	2.71	2.45	1.81	28.1 - 18.6	1.70	1.60	1.52	2.6	0.47Q	3/10/08	76.3 - 50.4
0.13	0.67	0.03	1.68	1.66	1.47	16.6 - 10.5	0.60	0.60	1.71	2.9	0.15Q	3/14/08	27.8 - 17.6
0.42	0.07	0.03	1.01	-4.78	-0.51	26.4 - 17.3	-	-	-	-	-	-	26.7 - 17.5
1.42	1.37	1.21	4.43	5.13	4.72	-	3.00	3.00	3.00	-	0.415Q	5/1/08	-
0.36	-	-	1.31	1.00	0.41	22.5 - 17.3	0.07	0.25	0.23	0.3	0.07Q	2/29/08	29.5 - 22.7
-0.45	-0.47	-	0.25	0.06	0.20	45.6 - 18.0	-	-	-	-	-	-	11.4 - 4.5
0.34	0.38	0.53	-	1.77	2.37	-	-	0.52	0.40	-	0.14Q	1/30/08	30.5 - 20.5
-0.69	0.15	0.55	-0.17	-0.48	-1.96	-	-	-	-	-	-	-	-
0.16	0.13	0.33	-3.74	2.16	2.94	-	0.23	0.23	0.23	0.6	0.0563Q	3/17/08	42.2 - 33.2
0.03	-	-	-	0.10	0.32	-	-	0.10	0.32	-	0.0334M	10/15/07	6.8 - 4.4
-	-	-	0.58	0.50	0.44	63.6 - 50.8	-	-	-	-	-	-	36.9 - 29.5
-	-	-	0.48	0.69		-	1.20	1.20	-		1.53M	12/28/07	20.2 - 15.4
-	-	-	1.51	1.00	0.00	10.5 - 9.0	-	0.83	0.70	-	0.003M	1/25/00	13.9 - 13.6
-	-	-	1.13	0.99	0.89	16.5 - 12.4	-	1.29	1.71	-	0.19M	5/30/08	18.6 - 14.0
1.60	1.82	1.80	7.10	5.80	4.10	8.7 - 6.2	1.47	1.25	1.05	2.8	0.42Q	3/28/08	61.6 - 43.8
1.20	-	-	-	3.75	1.72	-	-	0.24	0.20	-	0.455U	3/14/08	23.6 - 16.4
											0.455U	9/13/07	20.7 - 22.7
0.34	0.69	0.51	1.95	1.93	0.97	-	0.56	0.56	0.56	-	0.14Q	4/14/08	-
-0.36	-0.22	-0.65	-1.73	1.17	4.15	-	0.60	0.60	0.47	2.5	0.15Q	3/3/08	28.0 - 18.3
0.48	0.67	0.43	1.99	1.73	1.36	15.1 - 11.7	0.18	0.11	0.08	0.7	0.08Q	2/1/08	30.1 - 23.2
0.07	-0.50	-0.20	-3.87	0.42	-0.01	-	-	-	-	-	-	-	11.4 - 4.0
0.35	0.36	0.31	1.32	2.51	1.56	15.3 - 11.0	1.50	1.44	1.29	8.7	0.5Q	4/15/08	20.1 - 14.5
1.02	1.16	1.02	4.05	1.52	2.75	9.2 - 7.4	1.16	1.04	1.04	3.5	0.3Q	3/10/08	37.4 - 29.9
0.17	0.01	-	0.40	0.71	0.15	20.1 - 8.5	-	-	-	-	0.1Q	9/25/00	8.1 - 3.4
-	-	-	0.48	0.56	0.46	-	-	-	-	-	-	-	-
0.30	0.20	-12.17	-16.21	1.14	-2.13	-	0.30	0.93	0.77	2.4	0.3Q	5/9/07	15.3 - 10.6
-	-	-	-	1.01	0.26	-	-	-	-	-	-	-	2.8 - 1.4
-	-	-	-	0.93	0.76	-	-	-	-	-	-	-	20.4 - 15.2
0.08	0.21	0.11	0.55	0.63	0.32	21.6 - 15.7	-	-	-	-	-	-	11.9 - 8.7
0.44	-1.68	0.47	-0.20	1.78	1.21	-	-	-	-	-	-	-	14.9 - 12.4
1.57	1.95	1.83	5.95	7.37	6.73	18.2 - 14.0	2.60	2.25	1.75	7.7	0.70Q	3/31/08	108.0 - 83.4
-2.07	-2.32	-3.40	-13.94	4.00	10.99	-	1.00	1.00	0.70	1.9	0.25Q	2/20/00	66.9 - 41.3
0.16	-3.05	-1.73	-9.69	2.74	6.93	-	0.10	0.10	0.10	0.2	0.6094Q	3/17/08	55.1 - 36.0
0.04	0.19	0.24	1.00	3.19	0.88	64.7 - 39.8	2.93	2.75	2.63	5.7	0.8Q	3/7/08	64.7 - 39.8
0.09	0.06	0.01	0.18	0.06	0.91	44.9 - 28.7	-	-	-	-	-	-	8.1 - 5.2
0.28	0.75	0.34	1.61	2.28	1.51	29.2 - 21.9	2.56	2.53	2.52	6.1	0.5Q	4/15/08	47.0 - 35.2
-	-	-	-	1.29	0.46	-	-	-	1.55	-	0.4Q	3/31/08	-
0.21	-	-	-	1.73	0.56	-	-	2.08	1.59	-	0.62Q	12/10/07	29.4 - 26.9
-	-	-	1.33	0.90	1.23	16.8 - 12.6	6.54	3.96	1.69	34.8	0.425Q	2/29/08	22.3 - 16.8
0.08	0.16	0.08	1.81	3.24	1.93	16.0 - 11.9	0.51	0.39	0.27	2.1	0.13Q	4/1/08	28.9 - 21.6
-	-	-	-	-	-	-	-	-	-	-	0.0276U	12/12/05	10.9 - 5.8
-	-	-	0.06	0.00		-	1.00	0.00	-		0.46Q	3/31/08	-
-	-	-	0.17	0.01	-0.02	89.4 - 85.9	1.32	1.32	1.32	8.8	0.33Q	2/29/08	15.2 - 14.6
-	-	-	-	-	-	-	-	-	-	-	0.307Q	2/14/08	-
0.19	0.26	0.26	0.98	0.53	-	-	-	-	-	-	-	-	-
0.55	0.66	0.65	2.60	2.24	2.03	11.4 - 9.0	2.49	2.29	1.97	9.4	0.6575Q	2/14/08	29.7 - 23.4
1.96	2.35	-	-	4.78	5.90	-	-	1.52	1.52	-	0.36Q	12/14/07	85.2 - 68.8
0.02	0.09	-	-0.27	-1.62	-0.94	-	-	-	-	-	-	-	8.4 - 5.4
-0.27	-0.52	1.74	0.01	1.09	-0.99	2790.0 - 2160.0	1.60	1.60	1.60	6.5	0.4766Q	1/31/08	27.9 - 21.6
-	-	-	-	72.51	75.60	-	-	-	-	-	-	-	24.8 - 18.7
-	-	-	17.94	1.69	5.41	0.5 - 0.3	-	-	-	-	-	-	8.8 - 5.8
0.44	0.39	0.32	1.43	1.15	-0.39	-	-	-	-	-	-	-	-
-	-	-	0.16	0.07	0.11	43.8 - 30.1	0.18	0.08	0.13	3.1	0.1782A	1/7/08	7.0 - 4.8
-	-	-	0.53	0.57	0.61	11.9 - 9.2	0.50	0.56	0.65	8.7	0.04M	3/31/08	6.3 - 4.9
0.51	0.77	0.59	2.64	1.33	0.54	3.7 - 2.6	0.07	0.07	0.07	0.8	0.02Q	3/17/08	9.8 - 6.9
0.69	1.86	1.57	5.73	4.54	2.87	8.9 - 6.8	0.69	0.59	0.47	1.5	0.37S	12/14/07	50.8 - 38.7
0.63	0.71	0.70	-	0.51	2.04	-	-	0.72	0.58	-	0.2813Q	12/19/07	-
1.03	2.25	1.49	5.69	7.25	4.22	3.7 - 2.7	0.92	0.77	0.61	5.1	0.24Q	3/10/08	21.1 - 15.4
0.38	0.10	-	2.09	0.91	3.25	-	0.32	7.26	0.22	-	0.0773Q	2/15/08	-
0.10	0.14	0.08	0.43	0.52	0.65	44.1 - 18.8	0.24	0.20	0.16	2.1	0.065Q	3/10/08	19.0 - 8.1
-0.35	-	-	1.04	2.08	1.88	30.0 - 17.6	-	-	-	-	-	-	31.2 - 18.3
0.45	0.38	0.26	1.67	1.58	1.20	-	-	-	-	-	-	-	-
9.88	12.15	9.26	40.64	39.40	14.80	-	-	-	-	-	-	-	-
0.14	0.17	0.47	0.12	2.44	0.01	202.6 - 147.8	2.09	1.79	1.60	10.1	0.57Q	2/14/08	24.3 - 17.7
0.44	0.51	0.33	1.75	1.41	1.45	18.2 - 11.7	0.29	0.24	0.20	1.2	0.075Q	5/1/08	31.8 - 20.4
0.47	0.31	3.60	4.53	1.76	0.74	10.9 - 5.3	0.76	0.68	0.68	1.8	0.2Q	5/15/08	49.3 - 24.1
-	-	-	4.34	3.17	2.99	-	1.20	1.05	0.93	-	0.31Q	3/14/08	-
-0.23	-0.13	-0.08	0.20	-0.33	-1.49	154.7 - 42.7	-	0.50	-	-	0.5U	9/14/06	30.9 - 8.5

SYMBOL	COMPANY	NATURE OF BUSINESS	FISCAL YEAR-END	TOTAL REV. $MILL	NET INCOME $MILL	TOTAL ASSETS $MILL	NET STK EQUITY $MILL	NO OF INST	INST. HOLDINGS (SHARES)
MLM	Martin Marietta Materials, Inc.	Earth & Rock Mining	12/31/07	2207.1	262.7	2683.8	946.0	191	43083775
MVL	Marvel Entertainment Inc	Miscellaneous	12/31/07	485.8	139.8	817.4	181.5	-	-
MAS	Masco Corp.	Wood Products	12/31/07	11770.0	386.0	10907.0	4025.0	463	332087919
MYS	Masisa S.A.	Wood Products							
MEE	Massey Energy Co.	Coal Mining	12/31/07	2413.5	94.1	2860.7	784.0	219	79235035
MCI	MassMutual Corporate Investors Inc	Trusts & Holding Entities	12/31/07	29.1	23.6	292.4	251.2	19	293572
MPV	MassMutual Participation Investors	Trusts & Holding Entities	12/31/07	14.5	12.1	144.8	126.6	10	738981
MTZ	MasTec Inc. (FL)	Construction - Public Infrastructure	12/31/07	1037.8	-7.3	710.7	314.6	61	20217323
MA	MasterCard Inc	Miscellaneous Business Services	12/31/07	4067.6	1085.9	6260.0	3027.3	-	-
MSC	Material Sciences Corp.	Metal Products	2/28/07	262.6	6.1	187.4	126.3	74	11471509
MC	Matsushita Electric Industrial Co., Ltd	Electrical	3/31/07	9108170.0	217185.0	7896958.0	3916741.0	83	155828525
MAT	Mattel Inc	Consumer Accessories	12/31/07	5970.1	600.0	4805.5	2306.7	346	361802194
MMS	Maximus Inc.	Accounting & Management Consulti	9/30/07	738.6	-8.3	564.5	409.4	111	20470735
MZF	MBIA Capital / Claymore Managed	Trusts & Holding Entities	7/31/07		7.5	187.5	112.8	8	235680
MBI	MBIA Inc.	Insurance	12/31/07	-282.6	-1921.9	47415.1	3655.8	394	138092088
MFE	McAfee Inc.	IT & Technology	12/31/07	1308.2	167.0	3414.1	1905.3	226	128835890
MNI	McClatchy Co. (The)	Media	12/30/07	2260.4	-2736.0	4137.9	425.5	108	17879642
MKC V	McCormick & Co., Inc.	Food	11/30/07	2916.2	230.1	2787.5	1085.1	315	84754856
MDR	McDermott International, Inc. (Pana	Metal Products	12/31/06	4120.1	342.3	3594.2	388.4	116	46230837
MCD	McDonald's Corp	Food	12/31/07	22786.6	2395.1	29391.7	15279.8	769	895819655
MHP	McGraw-Hill Cos., Inc. (The)	Non-Media Publishing	12/31/07	6772.3	1013.6	6357.3	1606.6	559	277859688
MCK	McKesson Corp. (New)	Pharmaceuticals	3/31/07	92977.0	913.0	23943.0	6273.0	351	243577908
MMR	McMoran Exploration Co	Oil and Gas	12/31/07	481.2	-59.7	1715.3	372.2	87	20666206
MDZ	MDS Inc	Diagnostic Services	10/31/07	1210.0	773.0	3018.0	1897.0	46	76245220
MDU	MDU Resources Group Inc.	Earth & Rock Mining	12/31/07	4247.9	432.1	5592.4	2531.3	-	-
MIG	Meadowbrook Insurance Group Inc	Insurance	12/31/07	340.7	28.0	1114.0	301.9	56	20110786
MWV	MeadWestvaco Corp.	Paper Products	12/31/07	6906.0	285.0	9837.0	3708.0	294	148189262
MTL	Mechel OAO	Metal Works	12/31/07	4397.8	603.2	4449.1	2865.0	32	7535391
MHS	Medco Health Solutions, Inc.	Retail - Miscellaneous	12/29/07	44506.2	912.0	16217.9	6875.3	517	208462303
MEG	Media General, Inc.	Media	12/30/07	932.2	10.7	2471.1	913.0	147	16936480
MPW	Medical Properties Trust Inc	Property, Real Estate & Developmen	12/31/07	96.3	41.2	1051.7	513.1	-	-
MRN	Medical Staffing Network Holdings, I	Human Resources Services	12/30/07	482.3	-1.1	319.9	119.8	47	11263761
MRX	Medicis Pharmaceutical Corp. (Unit	Pharmaceuticals	12/31/07	464.7	75.1	1194.6	622.0	196	57411819
MED	Medifast Inc	Food	12/31/07	83.8	3.8	43.7	32.4	9	362757
MDT	Medtronic, Inc. (United States)	Medical Instruments & Equipment	4/27/07	12299.0	2802.0	19512.0	10977.0	993	845018811
WFR	MEMC Electronic Materials, Inc. (U	IT & Technology	12/31/07	1921.8	826.2	2887.2	2035.0	-	-
MW	Men's Wearhouse, Inc. (The) (Unite	Retail - Apparel and Accessory Store	2/3/07	1882.1	148.6	1097.0	753.8	185	49204596
MNT	Mentor Corp. (MN)	Medical Instruments & Equipment	3/31/07	302.0	290.6	709.8	434.9	144	34925708
MRK	Merck & Co., Inc	Pharmaceuticals	12/31/07	24197.7	3275.4	48350.7	18184.7	987	1337989149
MCY	Mercury General Corp.	Insurance	12/31/07	3178.8	237.8	4414.5	1862.0	171	21635059
MDP	Meredith Corp. (United States)	Media	6/30/07	1616.0	162.3	2090.0	833.2	2	2513949
TMR	Meridian Resource Corp. (The) (Uni	Oil and Gas	12/31/07	152.2	7.1	483.8	325.4	98	38580565
MTH	Meritage Homes Corp	Building & General Construction	12/31/07	2343.6	-288.9	1748.4	730.2	163	20537434
MER	Merrill Lynch & Co Inc	Finance Intermediaries & Services	12/28/07	62675.0	-7777.0	1020050.0	31932.0	-	-
MTR	Mesa Royalty Trust	Miscellaneous	12/31/06	9.8	9.8	9.8	8.1	18	554983
MSB	Mesabi Trust	Trusts & Holding Entities	1/31/07	17.9	17.1	5.4	1.1	38	2876532
MV	Metavante Technologies Inc	Miscellaneous Business Services	12/31/07	1598.1	49.5	3100.0	299.4	-	-
MEI	Methode Electronics, Inc.	Electrical	4/28/07	450.0	26.1	411.7	324.2	126	31766046
MET	MetLife Inc	Insurance	12/31/07	53007.0	4317.0	558562.0	35179.0	404	325115301
MPR	Met-Pro Corp.	Industrial Machinery and Equipment	1/31/07	91.4	7.2	97.2	72.6	26	3566734
MGS	MetroGas S.A. (Argentina)	Gas Utilities	12/31/06	873.9	292.6	2032.8	973.7	2	1884
PCS	MetroPCS Communications Inc	Communications	12/31/07	2235.7	100.4	5806.1	1848.7	-	-
MTD	Mettler-Toledo International, Inc.	Instruments and Related Products	12/31/07	1793.7	178.5	1678.2	581.3	163	37303247
MXE	Mexico Equity & Income Fund, Inc.	Trusts & Holding Entities						8	677926
MXF	Mexico Fund, Inc.	Trusts & Holding Entities	10/31/06		5.0	647.7	647.0	28	4788936
MFA	MFA Mortgage Investments Inc	Property, Real Estate & Developmen	12/31/07		30.2	8605.9	927.3	94	35543895
MCR	MFS Charter Income Trust	Trusts & Holding Entities	11/30/07	29.5	25.7	529.8	527.3	31	4802705
MGF	MFS Government Markets Income	Trusts & Holding Entities	11/30/07	18.9	15.7	236.4	235.7	31	14476487
CXE	MFS High Income Municipal Trust	Trusts & Holding Entities	11/30/07	19.5	16.4	308.6	187.7	-	-
CMU	MFS High Yield Municipal Trust	Trusts & Holding Entities	11/30/07	14.9	12.6	239.3	148.4	-	-
CMK	MFS Intermarket Income Trust I	Trusts & Holding Entities	11/30/07	6.2	5.2	100.3	99.4	-	-
CIF	MFS Intermediate High Income Fun	Trusts & Holding Entities	11/30/07	8.6	6.1	103.9	72.8	-	-
MIN	MFS Intermediate Income Trust	Trusts & Holding Entities	10/31/06		32.7	849.1	811.9	37	10623492
CXH	MFS Investment-Grade Municipal Tr	Trusts & Holding Entities	10/31/07	10.8	9.1	183.4	121.6	-	-
MMT	MFS Multimarket Income Trust	Trusts & Holding Entities	10/31/06		26.3	576.6	533.1	28	6029402
MFM	MFS Municipal Income Trust	Trusts & Holding Entities	10/31/06		23.2	466.1	323.1	23	455939
MFV	MFS Special Value Trust	Trusts & Holding Entities	10/31/06		3.8	75.2	65.0	5	23809
MTG	MGIC Investment Corp. (Milwaukee	Insurance	12/31/07	1693.2	-1670.0	7716.4	2594.3	-	-
MGM 16	MGM Mirage	Hospitality & Tourism	12/31/07	7691.6	1584.4	22727.7	6060.7	-	-
MIM	MI Developments Inc	Property, Real Estate & Developmen	12/31/06	866.5	59.9	2822.3	1677.3	-	-
MU	Micron Technology Inc.	IT & Technology	8/30/07	5688.0	-320.0	14818.0	7752.0	279	493055212
MAA	Mid-America Apartment Communiti	Property, Real Estate & Developmen	12/31/07	353.0	39.9	1783.8	401.0	95	11424618
MDS	Midas, Inc.	Retail - Automotive	12/29/07	180.0	13.3	216.6	27.2	78	12374915
MWY	Midway Games Inc. (United States)	IT & Technology	12/31/07	157.2	-99.6	213.4	29.1	57	6844401
MZ	Milacron Inc.	Industrial Machinery and Equipment	12/31/07	807.9	-87.1	602.9	-49.4	-	-
MLR	Miller Industries Inc. (TN) (United St	Automotive	12/31/07	400.0	16.3	189.0	132.5	19	4353933
MIL	Millipore Corp	Instruments and Related Products	12/31/07	1531.6	135.5	2777.3	1136.6	220	45843687
MR	Mindray Medical International Ltd	Medical Instruments & Equipment	12/31/06	1515.0	361.8	2557.1	2182.9	-	-
MSA	Mine Safety Appliances Co	Medical Instruments & Equipment	12/31/07	1007.6	67.6	1016.3	461.5	118	17026043
MTX	Minerals Technologies, Inc.	Chemicals	12/31/07	1077.7	-63.5	1128.9	751.2	133	21018668

T38

| EARNINGS PER SHARE | | | | | | P/E RATIO | DIVIDENDS PER SHARE | | | AV. YLD | DIV. DECLARED | | PRICE RANGE 2007 | |
| QUARTERLY | | | ANNUAL | | | | | | | % | | | | |
1st	2nd	3rd	2007	2006	2005	2007	2007	2006	2005		AMOUNT	PAYABLE		
0.73	1.92	2.12	6.06	5.29	4.08	8.9 - 6.9	1.24	1.01	0.86	2.7	0.345Q	3/31/08	53.7 -	41.7
0.56	0.34	0.45	1.70	0.67	0.97	13.9 - 7.3	-	-	-	-	-	-	23.6 -	12.4
0.37	0.51	0.56	1.03	1.22	2.19	35.7 - 25.3	0.91	0.86	0.78	2.9	0.23Q	2/4/08	36.8 -	26.0
0.40	0.43	0.27	1.17	0.50	-1.33	30.9 - 16.3	0.17	0.16	0.16	0.7	0.05Q	4/8/08	36.2 -	19.1
0.53	-	-	2.56	2.27	2.03	11.5 - 8.8	2.57	2.48	2.29	10.4	0.43Q	1/11/08	29.4 -	22.5
0.25	-	-	1.23	1.10	0.99	11.0 - 8.9	1.25	1.19	1.01	10.5	0.25Q	1/11/08	13.5 -	11.0
0.03	0.24	-0.48	-0.11	-0.77	-0.29	-	-	-	-	-	-	-	16.1 -	3.9
1.57	1.85	2.31	8.00	0.37	2.67	-	0.60	0.18	-	-	0.15Q	5/9/08		
-0.02	-	-	0.42	0.35	0.06	43.2 - 20.9	-	-	-	-	0.01U	5/16/03	18.2 -	8.8
-	-	-	99.50	69.48	25.49	0.2 - 0.1	-	-	-	-	-	-	16.1 -	12.7
0.03	0.06	0.61	1.54	1.53	1.01	12.7 - 10.4	0.75	0.65	0.50	4.2	0.75A	12/14/07	19.5 -	16.0
0.51	-	-	-0.38	0.11	1.67	-	0.40	0.40	0.30	1.2	0.1Q	2/29/08	41.0 -	26.5
-	-	-	0.95	0.90	0.92	16.8 - 13.5	-	-	-	-	0.0525M	12/17/07	16.0 -	12.8
1.46	1.61	-0.30	-15.17	5.99	5.18	-	1.36	1.24	1.12	2.3	0.34Q	1/15/08	67.1 -	53.7
0.27	0.29	0.39	1.02	0.84	0.82	32.7 - 14.7	-	-	-	-	-	-	33.4 -	15.0
0.11	0.43	-16.42	-33.37	-2.41	3.42	-	0.72	0.72	0.67	1.0	0.18Q	4/1/08	73.8 -	67.3
0.39	-	-	1.73	1.50	1.56	22.5 - 16.7	0.80	0.72	0.64	2.4	0.22Q	1/18/08	38.9 -	28.8
0.69	0.66	0.61	-	1.50	0.91	-	-	-	-	-	0.05U	7/1/00	6.1 -	2.3
0.62	-0.60	0.89	1.98	2.83	2.04	16.5 - 12.4	1.50	1.00	0.67	5.4	0.375Q	3/17/08	32.7 -	24.6
0.40	0.79	1.34	2.94	2.40	2.21	15.6 - 11.8	0.82	0.73	0.66	2.1	0.22Q	3/12/08	45.9 -	34.8
0.77	0.83	0.68	2.99	2.38	-0.53	12.0 - 7.7	0.24	0.24	0.24	0.8	0.06Q	4/1/08	35.8 -	23.0
-0.53	-0.23	-1.50	-1.86	-1.76	-1.68	-	-	-	-	-	1.8375Q	2/15/08	19.2 -	12.6
0.10	5.34	0.06	5.86	1.01	0.30	3.0 - 2.4	0.03	0.13	0.13	0.2	0.0325Q	1/8/07	17.3 -	13.9
0.25	0.49	1.10	2.36	1.74	1.53	-	0.56	0.52	0.49	-	1.275Q	4/1/08		
0.20	0.10	0.21	0.86	0.75	0.60	8.8 - 5.6	-	-	-	-	0.02U	9/31/08	5.8 -	4.2
-0.09	0.17	0.66	1.56	0.52	0.14	21.9 - 16.4	0.92	0.92	0.92	3.1	0.23Q	3/3/08	34.2 -	25.6
-	-	-	-	1.48	0.95	-	-	-	-	-	-	-	22.4 -	15.8
0.47	0.38	0.39	1.63	1.04	1.02	12.8 - 9.2	-	-	-	-	-	-	20.8 -	15.0
-0.27	0.22	0.11	0.47	3.32	-10.18	154.0 - 114.8	0.92	0.88	0.84	1.5	0.23Q	3/15/08	72.4 -	54.0
0.24	0.23	0.24	0.86	0.76	0.61	-	1.08	0.99	0.35	-	0.27Q	4/11/08		
-	0.06	-0.06	-0.03	-0.89	-0.03	-	-	-	-	-	-	-	12.0 -	5.3
0.15	0.21	0.34	1.14	-1.30	1.01	30.3 - 20.0	0.12	0.12	0.12	0.3	0.03Q	1/31/08	44.8 -	33.1
0.10	0.07	0.07	0.28	0.38	0.19	50.2 - 10.9	-	-	-	-	-	-	14.1 -	3.0
0.59	0.58	0.07	2.41	2.09	1.48	22.1 - 19.3	0.44	0.39	0.34	0.9	0.125Q	4/25/08	53.3 -	46.4
0.58	0.70	0.65	3.56	1.61	1.10	-	-	-	-	-	-	-		
0.75	1.00	0.69	2.71	1.88	1.29	8.3 - 5.5	0.20	0.05	-	1.1	0.07Q	3/28/08	22.6 -	14.8
0.48	0.26	0.32	5.99	1.29	1.17	6.0 - 4.0	0.74	0.71	0.66	2.4	0.2Q	4/17/08	35.9 -	23.9
0.78	0.77	0.70	1.49	2.03	2.10	32.9 - 17.4	1.52	1.52	1.52	3.6	0.38Q	4/1/08	49.1 -	26.0
1.10	1.27	1.15	4.34	3.92	4.63	13.8 - 10.7	2.08	1.92	1.72	4.1	0.58Q	3/27/08	60.0 -	46.4
0.68	0.75	-	3.31	2.86	2.52	14.5 - 13.6	0.69	0.60	0.52	1.5	0.215Q	3/14/08	48.0 -	45.0
0.02	0.03	0.01	0.08	-0.84	0.31	112.1 - 65.1	-	-	-	-	-	-	9.0 -	5.2
0.57	-2.16	-4.52	-11.01	8.32	8.88	-	-	-	-	-	-	-	56.5 -	29.9
2.26	2.24	-2.82	-9.69	7.59	5.16	-	1.40	1.00	0.76	-	0.3906Q	3/28/08		
1.00	1.42	-	-	5.24	5.05	-	-	5.24	5.05	-	0.4717M	4/30/00	71.3 -	52.2
0.13	0.32	0.50	1.31	1.50	0.99	10.8 - 4.5	1.60	1.53	0.77	18.4	0.515Q	2/20/08	14.1 -	6.0
-	-	-	0.41	-	-	-	-	-	-	-	-	-		
0.22	0.24	0.26	0.71	0.47	0.71	20.8 - 15.1	0.20	0.20	0.20	1.6	0.05Q	5/2/08	14.8 -	10.7
1.28	1.48	1.29	5.48	7.99	6.16	7.5 - 6.0	0.74	0.59	0.52	2.0	0.1063Q	3/17/08	41.2 -	32.6
0.26	0.17	0.18	0.47	0.49	0.32	21.5 - 15.4	0.19	0.18	0.17	2.2	0.055Q	3/11/08	10.1 -	7.2
-	-	-	-	0.51	0.05	-	-	-	-	-	-	-	7.2 -	3.3
0.11	0.17	0.15	0.28	0.10	0.62	-	-	-	-	-	-	-		
0.78	1.07	1.16	4.70	3.86	2.52	11.1 - 8.6	-	-	-	-	-	-	52.0 -	40.5
-	-	-	-	-	-	-	-	-	-	-	-	-	17.3 -	10.4
-	-	-	-	0.30	0.23	-	-	2.01	0.71	-	0.2480A	1/22/08	22.0 -	16.7
0.10	0.10	-0.15	0.24	0.01	-0.02	44.9 - 33.6	0.41	0.21	0.41	4.4	0.5313Q	3/31/08	10.8 -	8.1
-	-	-	0.46	0.44	0.45	20.3 - 17.9	0.48	0.49	0.51	5.5	0.041M	3/31/08	9.3 -	8.2
-	-	-	0.32	0.31	0.31	21.7 - 19.6	0.38	0.35	0.32	5.7	0.0441M	3/31/08	6.9 -	6.3
-	-	-	0.52	0.52	0.53	13.0 - 11.0	0.24	0.40	0.46	3.8	0.028M	3/31/08	6.8 -	5.7
-	-	-	0.45	0.45	0.45	13.4 - 11.3	0.19	0.35	0.38	3.4	0.027M	3/31/08	6.0 -	5.1
-	-	-	0.47	0.50	0.55	19.7 - 16.5	0.32	0.68	0.74	3.7	0.041M	3/31/08	9.3 -	7.8
-	-	-	0.29	0.29	0.33	13.1 - 10.4	0.17	0.34	0.32	4.9	0.024M	3/31/08	3.8 -	3.0
-	-	-	-	0.28	0.29	-	-	0.35	0.36	-	0.0498M	1/31/08	7.0 -	6.2
-	-	-	0.79	0.75	0.75	13.9 - 11.7	0.33	0.58	0.66	3.3	0.046M	3/31/08	11.0 -	9.2
-	-	-	-	0.33	0.34	-	-	0.38	0.39	-	0.031M	1/31/08	6.5 -	5.7
-	-	-	-	0.58	0.59	-	-	0.49	0.55	-	0.038M	1/31/08	8.2 -	6.8
-	-	-	-	0.56	0.60	-	-	0.96	1.02	-	0.0713M	1/31/08	12.4 -	10.4
1.12	0.93	-4.61	-20.54	6.65	6.78	-	0.78	1.00	0.53	-	0.025Q	3/3/08		
0.57	1.22	0.62	5.31	2.22	1.50	-	-	-	-	-	0.1Q	3/3/08		
-	-	-	-	1.24	0.14	-	-	0.60	0.54	-	0.15Q	4/15/08		
-0.34	-1.01	-	-0.42	0.57	0.29	-	-	-	-	-	-	-	18.0 -	11.1
0.31	0.22	0.33	1.01	0.29	0.25	41.3 - 31.3	2.42	2.38	2.35	6.5	0.615Q	4/30/08	41.7 -	31.6
0.14	0.21	0.21	0.91	0.67	0.13	22.2 - 15.4	-	-	-	-	0.08A	4/1/01	20.2 -	14.0
-0.22	-0.16	-0.37	-1.09	-0.86	-1.30	-	-	-	-	-	-	-	12.9 -	3.6
-2.68	-0.50	-1.36	-19.25	-10.20	-4.20	-	-	-	-	-	-	-	44.8 -	23.0
0.46	0.42	0.31	1.40	3.91	1.62	8.2 - 5.3	-	-	-	-	-	-	11.5 -	7.3
0.49	0.52	0.66	2.48	1.79	1.55	22.7 - 17.1	-	-	-	-	-	-	56.4 -	42.5
-	-	-	-	3.75	2.31	-	-	-	-	-	-	-		
0.44	0.48	0.46	1.86	1.73	2.19	27.7 - 12.6	0.84	0.68	0.52	2.4	0.22Q	3/10/08	51.6 -	23.4
0.56	0.74	-5.47	-3.31	2.53	2.59	-	0.20	0.20	0.20	0.3	0.05Q	3/19/08	67.7 -	51.6

SYMBOL	COMPANY	NATURE OF BUSINESS	FISCAL YEAR-END	TOTAL REV. $MILL	NET INCOME $MILL	TOTAL ASSETS $MILL	NET STK EQUITY $MILL	NO OF INST	INST. HOLDINGS (SHARES)
MIR	Mirant Corp (New)	Electricity	12/31/06	3103.0	1864.0	11536.0	4443.0	-	-
MPJ	Mississippi Power Co.	Electricity	-	-	-	-	-	1	400
MTU	Mitsubishi UFJ Financial Group Inc	Trusts & Holding Entities	3/31/07	6226156.0	880997.0	87281022.0	10523700.0	-	-
MFG	Mizuho Financial Group Inc	Trusts & Holding Entities	3/31/07	4622470.0	620965.0	49880031.0	4911292.0	-	-
NUT	ML Macadamia Orchards, L.P.	Agricultural Crop Production	12/31/06	17.1	0.8	54.0	-	11	360031
MTP	MLP & Strategic Equity Fund Inc	Trusts & Holding Entities	5/18/07	-	-	-	0.1	-	-
MBT	Mobile Telesystems OJSC	Communications	12/31/06	6384.3	1075.7	8573.9	3751.8	156	95634762
MOD	Modine Manufacturing Co	Automotive	3/31/07	1757.5	42.3	1101.6	493.3	115	22506781
MHK	Mohawk Industries, Inc. (United Stat	Textiles	12/31/07	7586.0	706.8	8680.0	4707.4	252	60076323
MOH	Molina Healthcare Inc	Insurance	12/31/06	2005.0	45.7	864.5	420.2	106	10845928
TAP	Molson Coors Brewing Co.	Food	12/30/07	6190.6	497.2	13451.6	7149.4	237	42034458
MNC	Monaco Coach Corp. (United States	Automotive	12/29/07	1272.1	12.0	563.8	325.9	117	26801500
MGI	MoneyGram International Inc	Miscellaneous Business Services	12/31/07	157.5	-1072.0	7935.0	-488.5	161	69428182
MON	Monsanto Co. (New)	Chemicals	8/31/05	6294.0	255.0	10579.0	5613.0	397	222210080
MTS	Montgomery Street Income Securiti	Trusts & Holding Entities	12/31/07	12.2	10.9	228.3	187.6	18	725885
MRH	Montpelier Re Holdings Ltd.	Insurance	12/31/06	735.7	302.9	3898.8	1492.9	116	53704709
MCO	Moody's Corp.	Miscellaneous Business Services	12/31/07	2259.0	701.5	1714.6	-783.6	405	268055912
MOG A	Moog, Inc.	Purpose Machinery	9/29/07	1558.1	100.9	2006.2	877.2	131	29779956
MS	Morgan Stanley	Commercial Banking	11/30/07	85328.0	3209.0	1045409.0	31269.0	769	698681712
APF	Morgan Stanley Asia-Pacific Fund, I	Trusts & Holding Entities	12/31/07	14.5	5.2	893.0	808.6	50	10203627
CAF	Morgan Stanley China A Share Fun	Finance & Investment	-	-	-	-	-	-	-
RNE	Morgan Stanley Eastern Europe Fu	Trusts & Holding Entities	12/31/07	2.0	-1.5	215.3	161.8	15	544173
MSD	Morgan Stanley Emerging Markets	Trusts & Holding Entities	12/31/07	18.4	15.2	260.0	245.8	21	1126548
MSF	Morgan Stanley Emerging Markets	Trusts & Holding Entities	12/31/07	9.2	1.0	643.3	491.7	23	5273307
YLT	Morgan Stanley Funds	Trusts & Holding Entities	7/31/02	-	6.2	34.5	34.2	-	-
YLH	Morgan Stanley Funds	Trusts & Holding Entities	1/31/02	-	3.1	16.5	16.1	-	-
IMT	Morgan Stanley Funds	Trusts & Holding Entities	10/31/02	-	22.0	451.0	320.3	12	331025
IQC	Morgan Stanley Funds	Trusts & Holding Entities	10/31/02	-	9.5	208.5	149.2	7	39951
ICS	Morgan Stanley Funds	Trusts & Holding Entities	10/31/02	-	2.8	62.5	60.9	4	224615
IIM	Morgan Stanley Funds	Trusts & Holding Entities	10/31/02	-	27.0	571.6	551.5	17	459073
IQN	Morgan Stanley Funds	Trusts & Holding Entities	10/31/02	-	4.3	93.5	69.4	7	73587
IQM	Morgan Stanley Funds	Trusts & Holding Entities	10/31/02	-	16.0	347.8	245.8	15	316477
IMS	Morgan Stanley Funds	Trusts & Holding Entities	10/31/02	-	5.8	123.0	122.9	9	160595
MGB	Morgan Stanley Global Opportunity	Trusts & Holding Entities	12/31/07	2.8	2.1	36.9	33.3	7	51224
MSY	Morgan Stanley High Yield Fund, In	Trusts & Holding Entities	12/31/07	6.9	5.6	88.4	76.1	13	513221
IIF	Morgan Stanley India Investment Fu	Trusts & Holding Entities	12/31/07	10.5	-3.5	1342.7	1108.4	38	3104676
ICB	Morgan Stanley Trusts	Trusts & Holding Entities	9/30/02	-	11.9	183.2	182.5	18	214820
OIB	Morgan Stanley Trusts	Trusts & Holding Entities	2/28/03	-	9.3	150.8	150.5	14	128633
IQT	Morgan Stanley Trusts	Trusts & Holding Entities	10/31/02	-	18.0	360.0	254.6	15	196925
IIC	Morgan Stanley Trusts	Trusts & Holding Entities	10/31/02	-	12.3	259.7	248.6	8	73627
OIA	Morgan Stanley Trusts	Trusts & Holding Entities	5/31/02	-	11.6	165.3	165.0	11	225763
PIA	Morgan Stanley Trusts	Trusts & Holding Entities	5/31/02	-	14.6	307.2	306.8	17	880068
OIC	Morgan Stanley Trusts	Trusts & Holding Entities	3/31/03	-	5.2	87.4	86.6	11	145242
IMC	Morgan Stanley Trusts	Trusts & Holding Entities	10/31/02	-	4.8	103.9	73.7	6	80875
IQI	Morgan Stanley Trusts	Trusts & Holding Entities	10/31/02	-	32.4	664.1	658.6	23	495688
MRT	Morton's Restaurant Group Inc (Ne	Retail - Food & Beverage	12/30/07	353.8	13.0	310.1	158.4	-	-
MOT	Motorola, Inc.	Communications	12/31/07	36622.0	-49.0	34812.0	15447.0	687	1600041265
MOV	Movado Group, Inc.	Consumer Accessories	1/31/08	559.5	60.8	646.2	463.2	79	15425411
MPS	MPS Group, Inc. (United States)	Human Resources Services	12/31/07	2171.8	87.1	1209.7	976.3	146	87018412
MSM	MSC Industrial Direct Co., Inc.	Machinery Supply Retail	9/1/07	1688.2	173.9	1075.3	727.9	153	46242483
MXB	MSCI Inc	Media	11/30/07	369.9	81.1	904.7	200.0	-	-
MLI	Mueller Industries, Inc.	Metal Works	12/29/07	2697.8	115.5	1449.2	710.5	141	29939092
MWA	Mueller Water Products Inc	Metal Products	9/30/07	1849.0	48.2	3009.2	1311.0	-	-
MUR	Murphy Oil Corp	Oil and Gas	12/31/07	18439.1	766.5	10535.8	5066.2	289	132473874
MVO	MV Oil Trust	Oil and Gas	-	-	-	-	-	-	-
MVC	MVC Capital Inc	Trusts & Holding Entities	10/31/07	27.0	2.1	470.5	369.1	27	11355345
MYE	Myers Industries Inc.	Plastics	12/31/07	918.8	54.7	697.6	317.3	101	19087132
MYL	Mylan Inc	Pharmaceuticals	12/31/07	2178.8	-1138.0	11353.2	3403.4	304	181545740
NBR	Nabors Industries Ltd.	Oil and Gas	12/31/07	4940.7	930.7	10103.4	4514.1	-	-
NC	NACCO Industries Inc.	Industrial Machinery and Equipment	12/31/07	3602.7	89.3	2428.2	892.1	75	4430911
NLC	Nalco Holding Co	Chemicals	12/31/07	3912.5	129.0	5978.6	1117.8	73	47805904
NTE	Nam Tai Electronics, Inc.	Electrical	12/31/07	780.8	69.5	544.8	330.2	79	10963785
NTG	Natco Group Inc	Metal Products	12/31/07	570.1	46.3	423.7	249.5	27	8293066
NBG	National Bank Greece S A	Commercial Banking	-	-	-	-	-	26	14747475
NCC	National City Corp	Commercial Banking	12/31/07	11791.3	314.0	150374.0	13407.8	-	-
NFP	National Financial Partners Corp	Insurance	12/31/07	1194.3	54.2	1560.1	763.2	116	16618113
NFG	National Fuel Gas Co. (NJ)	Gas Utilities	9/30/07	2039.6	337.5	3888.4	1630.1	233	36170504
NGG	National Grid plc	Electricity	3/31/05	7382.0	1424.0	27560.0	2121.0	-	-
NHI	National Health Investors, Inc.	Property, Real Estate & Developmen	12/31/07	62.3	96.4	500.7	446.1	78	10004975
NOV	National Oilwell Varco Inc	Oil and Gas	12/31/07	9789.0	1337.1	12114.9	6661.4	343	158926232
NPK	National Presto Industries, Inc.	Electrical	12/31/07	420.7	38.6	374.7	294.6	62	3202494
NNN	National Retail Properties Inc	Property, Real Estate & Developmen	12/31/07	186.4	157.1	2539.6	1407.3	-	-
NRN	National Rural Utilities Cooperative	Credit & Lending	5/31/07	57.5	11.7	18575.2	710.0	2	18650
NSM	National Semiconductor Corp.	IT & Technology	5/27/07	1929.9	375.3	2201.9	1748.8	297	298218263
NFS	Nationwide Financial Services Inc.	Insurance	12/31/07	4528.9	626.8	119207.1	5324.6	173	33814775
NHP	Nationwide Health Properties, Inc.	Property, Real Estate & Developmen	12/31/07	329.2	224.5	3144.4	1482.7	134	44852240
NRP	Natural Resources Partners L.P.	Coal Mining	12/31/07	215.0	102.5	1320.0	-	57	3132414
NTZ	Natuzzi S.p.A.	Chemicals	12/31/06	735.4	12.3	674.7	478.8	35	18693360
NLS	Nautilus Inc	Consumer Accessories	12/31/07	501.5	-55.6	390.8	196.5	148	32445115
NCI	Navigant Consulting, Inc.	Accounting & Management Consulti	12/31/07	767.1	33.4	778.7	342.8	156	46200672

EARNINGS PER SHARE — *QUARTERLY* (1st, 2nd, 3rd) / *ANNUAL* (2007, 2006, 2005) | **P/E RATIO** | **DIVIDENDS PER SHARE** (2007, 2006, 2005) | **AV. YLD %** | **DIV. DECLARED** (AMOUNT, PAYABLE) | **PRICE RANGE 2007**

1st	2nd	3rd	Ann. 2007	Ann. 2006	Ann. 2005	P/E Ratio	Div. 2007	Div. 2006	Div. 2005	Av. Yld %	Amount	Payable	Price Range 2007
-0.20				6.28	-4.36						1.3125Q	4/1/08	26.5 - 21.0
													10.4 - 7.3
			86.27	89.84		0.1 -			0.1				
			48803.0	6234.5	37719.13								
0.05	-0.05			0.11	0.10			0.20	0.20		0.03Q	2/15/08	5.9 - 3.5
											0.1M	3/31/08	
				0.54	0.57				0.86				38.5 - 21.2
0.39	0.31	-1.48	1.31	0.22	1.79	24.7 - 17.9	0.70	0.70	0.63	2.5	0.175Q	3/3/08	32.4 - 23.5
1.32	1.68	1.78	10.32	6.70	5.30	8.9 - 6.7							91.6 - 69.4
0.34	0.47	0.62		1.62	0.98								49.2 - 23.6
0.03	1.02	0.74	2.74	2.09	0.84	14.0 - 9.8	0.64	0.64	0.64	1.9	0.16Q	3/17/08	38.3 - 26.9
0.05	0.15	0.12	0.40	0.03	0.09	76.7 - 43.3	0.24	0.24	0.24	1.0	0.06Q	3/14/08	30.7 - 17.3
0.35	0.38	0.41	-12.94	1.45	1.31		0.20	0.17	0.07	1.0	0.05Q	1/2/08	22.8 - 16.4
0.46	2.02		1.79	1.25	0.47	15.7 - 7.9	0.47	0.39	0.33	2.5	0.175Q	4/25/08	28.1 - 14.1
			1.05	0.90	1.00	18.5 - 15.8	1.12	1.05	1.14	6.1	0.28Q	12/31/07	19.4 - 16.6
0.76	0.53	1.06		3.23	-10.49			0.30	6.66		0.075Q	1/15/08	39.1 - 32.9
0.62	0.95	0.51	2.58	2.58	1.84	16.9 - 11.6	0.32	0.28	0.20	0.9	0.1Q	3/10/08	43.6 - 29.9
0.64			2.34	1.97	1.64	13.2 - 8.7							31.0 - 20.5
1.45			2.98	7.07	4.57	17.3 - 13.0	1.08	1.08	1.08	2.4	0.3133Q	4/15/08	51.6 - 38.8
			0.15	0.13	0.11	85.9 - 63.7	2.50	0.24	0.18	21.8	2.0431S	1/7/08	12.9 - 9.6
				-0.05							8.973A	1/31/08	
			-0.06	-0.21	0.32		12.11	7.48	10.54	42.0	2.3859S	1/7/08	35.3 - 24.5
			0.69	0.67	0.91	14.6 - 11.3	0.66	0.77	0.94	7.2	0.1966Q	1/7/08	10.1 - 7.8
			0.05	0.12	0.22	357.4 - 237.0	10.79	5.47	1.40	72.6	1.3861S	1/7/08	17.9 - 11.9
													15.2 - 12.9
													14.5 - 13.2
													14.3 - 13.1
													15.3 - 13.1
													14.7 - 12.4
													15.0 - 12.9
													15.0 - 13.0
		0.61	0.19	0.61		30.1 - 12.4	0.56	0.55	0.67	6.8	0.2313Q	1/7/08	10.3 - 6.3
		0.48	0.45	0.55		14.2 - 11.9	0.47	0.46	0.52	7.4	0.035M	3/14/08	6.8 - 5.7
		-0.18	-0.06	0.06			16.81	5.30	3.88	70.7	0.3696S	1/7/08	31.4 - 19.2
											0.0375M	12/21/07	18.8 - 14.7
											0.04M	6/22/07	8.2 - 7.3
											0.0375M	12/21/07	15.0 - 12.7
											0.1359M	12/21/07	14.4 - 12.2
											0.1359M	12/23/05	7.7 - 6.8
											0.0375M	12/21/07	10.1 - 8.4
											0.1359M	12/23/05	9.2 - 0.0
											0.04M	6/22/07	15.5 - 13.1
											0.04M	6/22/07	14.7 - 12.9
0.29	0.14	-0.04	0.77	-0.84	0.07								18.6 - 12.7
-0.08	-0.01	0.03	-0.02	1.46	1.81		0.20	0.19	0.16	1.3	0.05Q	4/15/08	19.0 - 12.8
0.09	0.45	0.97	1.87	1.02	1.03	10.2 - 6.8	0.24	0.20	0.16	1.5	0.08Q	4/30/08	12.4 - 7.9
0.17	0.22	0.23	0.86	0.72	0.56	14.4 - 9.2							
0.60	0.61	0.09	2.59	2.00	1.61	14.1 - 10.3	0.64	0.54	1.94	2.1	0.18Q	2/5/08	36.6 - 26.8
			0.06	0.86	0.65								
0.51	0.98	0.84	3.10	4.00	2.49	14.4 - 8.4	0.40	0.40	0.40	1.2	0.1Q	3/14/08	44.6 - 26.0
-0.01			0.42	0.05	0.20						0.0175Q	2/20/08	
0.58	1.32	1.04	4.01	3.37	4.51	10.8 - 7.2	0.68	0.53	0.45	1.9	0.1875Q	3/3/08	43.4 - 29.0
1.01	0.53										0.6367Q	1/25/08	
			2.92	2.48	1.45	3.3 - 2.8	0.54	0.48	0.24	6.0	0.12Q	1/9/08	9.7 - 8.2
0.89	0.07	0.04	1.55	1.97	0.76	8.7 - 6.5	0.50	0.20	0.20	4.4	0.06Q	4/4/08	13.5 - 10.1
0.32	0.60		0.99	0.79	0.74	26.1 - 14.8	0.24	0.24	0.12	1.2	15.5277Q	2/15/08	25.8 - 14.7
0.92	0.79	0.76	3.37	3.40	2.00								
0.80	1.20	2.55	10.80	12.89	7.60	10.3 - 7.1	1.98	1.91	1.85	2.2	0.5Q	3/14/08	111.7 - 77.2
0.13	0.28	0.25	0.88	0.67	0.33	22.7 - 18.4	0.14			0.8	0.035Q	4/2/08	20.0 - 16.2
			1.55	0.93	1.19	21.8 - 9.1	0.84	1.52	1.32	3.8	0.22Q	1/21/09	33.8 - 14.1
0.45	0.62	0.63	2.36	1.97	0.77	3.9 - 2.9							9.2 - 6.9
				2.20	1.96								6.8 - 3.8
0.50	0.60	-0.03	0.51	3.72	3.09		1.60	1.52	1.44		0.21Q	2/1/08	
0.21	0.26	0.40	1.35	1.43	1.48	29.1 - 20.3	0.75	0.03	0.51	2.2	0.21Q	1/7/08	29.3 - 27.4
0.82			3.96	1.61	2.23	7.3 - 6.0	1.22	1.18	1.14	4.7	0.31Q	4/15/08	28.9 - 23.8
			0.51	1.35	0.46	94.2 - 69.8							48.0 - 35.6
0.56	0.54	1.31	3.47	2.49	1.96	8.9 - 6.4	2.85	2.37	1.80	10.4	0.08Q	5/9/08	30.8 - 22.4
0.78	0.90	1.02	3.76	1.94	0.91	4.9 - 2.9							18.5 - 10.9
			5.65	4.09	2.78	8.2 - 6.4	3.80	2.12	1.67	9.4	3.25A	3/14/08	46.5 - 36.0
0.41	0.70	0.68	2.26	3.05	1.56		1.40	0.65	1.30		0.4609Q	3/14/08	
													27.0 - 21.9
0.30	0.33		1.12	1.26	1.11	21.7 - 10.7	0.14	0.10	0.04	0.8	0.06Q	4/7/08	24.3 - 12.0
1.38	1.37	1.03	4.37	4.74	3.90	8.9 - 7.4	1.04	0.92	0.76	2.9	0.29Q	4/14/08	39.0 - 32.3
0.25	0.93	0.58	2.32	2.19	0.79	10.2 - 7.3	1.64	1.54	1.48	8.0	1.9375Q	3/31/08	38.3 - 16.9
0.28	0.28	0.35	1.26	1.74	1.70	22.9 - 13.7	1.84	1.61	1.40	8.9	0.485Q	2/14/08	28.8 - 17.2
				0.23	-0.27								11.6 - 9.2
0.08	0.04	-0.43	-1.76	0.90	0.68		0.30	0.40	0.40	1.6	0.1Q	9/10/07	25.3 - 13.4
0.20	0.21	0.10	0.66	0.97	0.95	40.9 - 26.4							27.0 - 17.4

SYMBOL	COMPANY	NATURE OF BUSINESS	FISCAL YEAR-END	TOTAL REV. $MILL	NET INCOME $MILL	TOTAL ASSETS $MILL	NET STK EQUITY $MILL	NO OF INST	INST. HOLDINGS (SHARES)
NVT	Navteq Corp	IT & Technology	12/31/07	853.4	172.9	1321.8	1006.6	134	49318274
NBD	NB Capital Corp.	Property, Real Estate & Developmen	-	-	-	-	-	3	16350
NTY	NBTY Inc.	Pharmaceuticals	9/30/07	2014.5	207.9	1534.9	1056.0	164	50811354
NCS	NCI Building Systems, Inc. (United	Metal Products	10/28/07	1624.3	63.7	1343.1	539.7	132	21686197
NCR	NCR Corp. (New)	Office Equipment Supplies	12/31/07	4970.0	274.0	4780.0	1757.0	308	138808629
NP	Neenah Paper Inc	Paper Products	12/31/07	990.5	10.2	932.8	288.0	214	10595303
NNI	Nelnet Inc	Credit & Lending	12/31/07	2123.6	32.9	29162.8	608.9	81	15052405
N	Netsuite Inc	IT & Technology							
NWK	Network Equipment Technologies, I	IT & Technology	3/30/07	84.1	-16.2	134.0	81.6	76	18872563
NSR	Neustar Inc	Communications	12/31/07	429.2	92.3	616.7	480.5	-	
HYB	New America High Income Fund, In	Trusts & Holding Entities	12/31/07	28.1	25.2	360.4	223.8	23	1473696
GF	New Germany Fund, Inc.	Trusts & Holding Entities	12/31/07	8.8	4.2	562.6	480.7	30	6255416
IRL	New Ireland Fund, Inc. (The)	Trusts & Holding Entities	10/31/06		1.1	153.2	151.1	14	1295420
NJR	New Jersey Resources Corp (Unite	Gas Utilities	9/30/07	3021.8	65.3	2230.7	644.8	146	12762215
EDU	New Oriental Education & Technolo	Education, Social & Public Services	5/31/07	1044.0	226.7	2418.4	1889.6	-	
NWY	New York & Company Inc	Retail - Apparel and Accessory Store	2/3/07	1193.2	46.2	469.8	240.8	53	11420211
NYB	New York Community Bancorp Inc.	Other Depository Banking	12/31/07	1612.9	279.1	30579.8	4182.3	261	106251547
NYT	New York Times Co.	Media	12/30/07	3195.1	208.7	3473.1	978.2	-	
NAL	NewAlliance Bancshares Inc	Commercial Banking	12/31/07	374.8	48.8	7247.7	1362.3	122	49386446
NCT	Newcastle Investment Corp (New)	Property, Real Estate & Developmen	12/31/07	688.1	-65.5	8037.8	447.6	113	31230601
NWL	Newell Rubbermaid, Inc.	Plastics	12/31/07	6407.3	467.1	6682.9	2247.3	370	232085993
NFX	Newfield Exploration Co.	Oil and Gas	12/31/07	1783.0	450.0	6986.0	3581.0	289	110735364
NEU	NewMarket Corp	Chemicals	12/31/07	1374.9	95.3	770.9	317.0	74	6991060
NEM	Newmont Mining Corp. (Holding Co.	Precious Metals	12/31/07	5526.0	-1886.0	15598.0	7548.0	487	294609414
NR	Newpark Resources, Inc.	Oil and Gas	12/31/07	612.8	26.7	641.8	360.7	111	77008840
NWS A	News Corp	Media	6/30/07	28655.0	3426.0	62343.0	32922.0	455	1386223602
NXY	Nexen Inc.	Oil and Gas	12/31/07	6604.0	1086.0	18075.0	5610.0	93	167367450
NFJ	NFJ Dividend Interest & Premium St	Trusts & Holding Entities	1/31/07		71.3	2469.2	2431.6	11	278054
NCV	Nicholas-Applegate Convertible & In	Trusts & Holding Entities	2/28/07	129.1	116.2	1643.0	1050.1	23	1399244
NCZ	Nicholas-Applegate Convertible & In	Trusts & Holding Entities	2/28/07		98.9	1447.9	879.0	16	810735
NIE	Nicholas-Applegate Equity & Conve	Finance & Investment	2/15/07			0.1	0.1	-	
NGZ	Nicholas-Applegate Global Equity &	Trusts & Holding Entities							
NAI	Nicholas-Applegate International &	Trusts & Holding Entities	2/28/07		3.1	284.1	277.9	-	
GAS	NICOR Inc.	Gas Utilities	12/31/07	3176.3	135.2	4252.0	945.2	-	
NJ	Nidec Corp. (Japan)	Electrical	3/31/07	629667.0	39932.0	662623.0	305016.0	29	1411797
NKE	NIKE, Inc	Rubber Products	5/31/07	16325.9	1491.5	10688.3	7025.4	463	160436929
NTT	Nippon Telegraph & Telephone Cor	Communications	3/31/07	10760550.0	476907.0	18365775.0	7172610.0	86	58884522
NIS	NIS Group Co Ltd	Credit & Lending	3/31/07		8.0	403880.0	82664.0	-	
NI	NiSource Inc. (Holding Co.)	Electricity	12/31/07	7939.8	321.4	18004.8	5076.6	317	192289047
NL	NL Industries, Inc.	Chemicals	12/31/07	177.7	-1.7	524.8	246.5	61	4701293
NED	Noah Education Holdings Ltd	Education, Social & Public Services	6/30/07		66.4		104.7	-	
NE	Noble Corp.	Oil and Gas	12/31/07	2995.3	1206.0	5876.0	4308.3	338	122515916
NBL	Noble Energy, Inc.	Oil and Gas	12/31/07	3272.0	943.9	10830.9	4808.8	274	67318708
NOK	Nokia Corp.	Communications	12/31/05	34191.0	3616.0	22452.0	12514.0	567	717061396
NMR	Nomura Holdings Inc	Venture Capital	3/31/07	2049101.0	175828.0	35873374.0	2185919.0	68	48698543
NAT	Nordic American Tanker Shipping Lt	Shipping	12/31/06	175.5	67.4	800.2	611.9	-	
JWN	Nordstrom, Inc.	Retail - Apparel and Accessory Store	2/2/08	8828.0	715.0	5600.0	1115.0	343	178871836
NSC	Norfolk Southern Corp.	Rail Transport	12/31/07	9432.0	1464.0	26144.0	9727.0	533	268392308
NTL	Nortel Inversora S.A. (Argentina)	Communications	12/31/06	7437.0	129.0	8719.0	1167.0	20	17071602
NT	Nortel Networks Corp (New)	Communications	12/31/07	10948.0	-957.0	17068.0	2758.0	-	
NOA	North American Energy Partners Inc	Oil and Gas	3/31/07	629.4	21.1	710.7	244.3	-	
NRT	North European Oil Royalty Trust	Trusts & Holding Entities	10/31/07	27.7	26.7	5.9	0.0	32	918759
NU	Northeast Utilities	Electricity	12/31/07	5822.2	246.5	11581.8	2913.8	171	87577857
NOC	Northrop Grumman Corp	Defense	12/31/07	32018.0	1790.0	33373.0	17687.0	491	306096681
NRF	Northstar Realty Financial Corp	Property, Real Estate & Developmen	12/31/07	415.3	47.8	4792.8	618.0	42	15914314
NWN	Northwest Natural Gas Co. (United	Gas Utilities	12/31/07	1033.2	74.5	2014.2	594.8	130	12974713
NCX	Nova Chemicals Corp.	Chemicals	12/31/06	6519.0	-703.0	4155.0	546.0	125	46226481
NVS	Novartis AG Basel	Pharmaceuticals	12/31/05	31319.0	6130.0	57732.0	33164.0	318	184136878
NVO	Novo-Nordisk A/S (Denmark)	Pharmaceuticals	12/31/04	29031.0	5013.0	37433.0	26504.0	86	8645849
NRG	NRG Energy Inc (New)	Electricity	12/31/07	5989.0	586.0	19274.0	5504.0	175	82059184
NST	NSTAR	Electricity	12/31/07	3261.8	221.5	7759.5	1703.8	210	43816472
DCM	NTT DoCoMo Inc.	Communications	3/31/07	4788093.0	457278.0	6116215.0	4161303.0	52	9118107
NUS	NU Skin Enterprises, Inc.	Pharmaceuticals	12/31/07	1157.7	43.9	683.2	275.0	126	41989314
NUE	Nucor Corp.	Metal Works	12/31/07	16593.0	1471.9	9826.1	5112.9	397	137380021
NS	NuStar Energy L.P.	Oil and Gas	12/31/07	1475.0	150.3	3783.1		-	
NSH	NuStar Group Holdings LLC	Petroleum and Coal Products	12/31/07	46.2	43.3	573.8	553.8	-	
NAZ	Nuveen Arizona Premium Income M	Trusts & Holding Entities	7/31/07		3.7	97.5	62.5	6	61655
NAC	Nuveen California Dividend Advanta	Trusts & Holding Entities						11	124670
NQC	Nuveen California Investment Qualit	Trusts & Holding Entities						8	55405
NCO	Nuveen California Municipal Market	Trusts & Holding Entities						5	60041
NCA	Nuveen California Municipal Value	Trusts & Holding Entities						13	430688
NCP	Nuveen California Performance Plu	Trusts & Holding Entities						6	66423
NUC	Nuveen California Quality Income M	Trusts & Holding Entities						15	134796
NVC	Nuveen California Select Quality Mu	Trusts & Holding Entities						14	183664
NXC	Nuveen California Select Tax-Free I	Trusts & Holding Entities	3/31/07		4.0	93.3	92.2	2	13314
NTC	Nuveen Connecticut Premium Inco	Trusts & Holding Entities	5/31/07	5.4	4.4	115.9	77.2	10	86108
JDD	Nuveen Diversified Dividend and In	Trusts & Holding Entities	12/31/07	27.0	20.6	496.5	325.1	11	267207
NAD	Nuveen Dividend Advantage Munici	Trusts & Holding Entities	10/31/06		41.0	917.1	610.3	23	516641
JPG	Nuveen Equity Premium & Growth	Trusts & Holding Entities							
JLA	Nuveen Equity Premium Advantage	Trusts & Holding Entities							

EARNINGS PER SHARE						P/E RATIO		DIVIDENDS PER SHARE			AV. YLD %	DIV. DECLARED		PRICE RANGE 2007	
QUARTERLY			ANNUAL					2007	2006	2005		AMOUNT	PAYABLE		
1st	2nd	3rd	2007	2006	2005										
0.31	0.41	0.40	1.73	1.15	1.81	27.7 -	14.6	-	-	-	-	-	-	47.9 -	25.3
12.00	16.00	10.00		61164.08	2725.00	-		-	60000.00	65000.00	-	0.5219Q	3/30/01	28.6 -	25.9
0.67	-	-	3.00	1.62	1.13	13.0 -	6.6	-	-	-	-	-	-	39.0 -	19.7
0.39	-	-	3.06	3.45	2.68	12.8 -	7.4	-	-	-	-	-	-	39.1 -	22.7
0.19	0.54	0.29	1.50	2.09	2.80	11.1 -	6.2	-	-	-	-	-	-	16.7 -	9.2
0.98	0.17	1.01	0.67	4.21	-2.02	56.6 -	45.5	0.40	0.40	0.40	1.2	0.1Q	3/4/08	38.0 -	30.5
0.29	0.30	-0.32	0.66	1.27	3.37	40.8 -	25.7	0.28	-	-	1.3	0.07Q	3/15/08	26.9 -	17.0
-	-	-	-	-6.42	-27.99	-		-	-	-	-	-	-		
0.05	0.06	-	-0.65	-1.10	-0.26	-		-	-	-	-	-	-	14.7 -	6.2
0.23	0.24	0.32	1.17	0.94	0.72	-		-	-	-	-	-	-		
-	-	-	0.25	0.25	0.25	9.1 -	7.4	0.20	0.21	0.22	9.5	0.013M	3/31/08	2.3 -	1.9
-	-	-	0.17	0.04	-0.01	53.4 -	39.8	0.59	0.20	0.55	7.7	0.255S	1/10/08	9.1 -	6.8
-	-	-	-	0.23	0.16	-		-	1.93	0.03	-	0.2A	12/28/07	21.5 -	13.8
0.72	-	-	1.55	1.87	1.81	18.9 -	15.7	1.01	0.96	0.91	3.8	0.28Q	4/3/08	29.3 -	24.4
-	-	-	1.60	0.21	1.35	-		-	-	-	-	-	-	23.9 -	16.5
0.01	0.06	-0.27	0.77	1.02	0.33	31.0 -	21.4	-	-	-	-	-	-		
0.22	0.12	0.35	0.90	0.81	1.11	39.0 -	19.9	1.00	1.00	1.00	4.2	0.25Q	2/15/08	35.1 -	17.9
0.17	0.82	0.09	1.45	-3.76	1.78	-		0.86	0.69	0.65	-	0.23Q	3/12/08		
0.09	-0.04	0.07	-	0.49	0.50	-		-	0.23	0.21	-	0.065Q	2/19/08	15.6 -	13.1
0.70	0.64	-0.74	-1.52	2.67	2.51	-		2.85	2.62	2.50	9.7	0.5234Q	1/31/08	33.7 -	25.2
0.18	0.51	0.61	1.68	1.40	0.91	15.6 -	11.4	0.84	0.84	0.84	3.7	0.21Q	3/14/08	26.2 -	19.1
-0.75	1.15	0.64	3.44	4.58	2.73	9.4 -	6.5	-	-	-	-	-	-	32.3 -	22.2
0.93	1.78	1.25	5.62	3.30	2.45	4.5 -	3.1	0.57	0.50	-	2.8	0.2Q	4/1/08	25.3 -	17.4
0.15	-4.57	0.88	-4.17	1.75	0.72	-		0.40	0.40	0.40	0.9	0.1Q	3/28/08	49.8 -	35.4
0.08	0.06	0.08	0.29	-0.36	0.25	23.4 -	14.8	-	-	-	-	-	-	6.8 -	4.3
0.23	0.17	•	1.14	0.70	0.73	10.4 -	15.0	0.10	0.10	0.00	0.0	-	-	10.7 -	11.0
0.23	0.68	0.75	2.02	1.12	2.17	5.7 -	4.3	0.10	0.10	0.10	1.0	0.025Q	4/1/08	11.5 -	8.6
-	-	-	0.75	0.70		-		2.10	1.65	-	-	0.525Q	9/28/07		
-	-	-	1.66	1.51	1.48	10.5 -	8.5	1.69	2.14	2.32	10.5	0.125M	12/31/07	17.4 -	14.2
-	-	-	1.69	1.04	1.59	9.4 -	7.6	1.67	1.77	1.56	11.2	0.1187M	12/31/07	15.9 -	12.8
-	-	-	-	-	-	-		-	-	-	-	0.5625Q	9/28/07		
-	-	-	-	-	-	-		-	-	-	-	0.6405Q	12/28/07	-	
-	-	-	-	-	-	-		-	-	-	-	1.5124Q	12/5/07	-	
-	-	-	0.33	0.16		-		3.93	1.45	-	-	0.465Q	2/1/08	-	
1.04	0.40	0.32	2.99	2.87	3.07	-		1.86	1.86	1.86	-	-	-	-	
-	-	-	268.25	275.05	456.58	0.1 -	0.0	-	-	-	-	-	-	15.4 -	11.0
1.12	0.71	0.92	2.93	2.64	2.24	15.6 -	11.3	0.68	0.56	0.45	1.8	0.23Q	4/1/08	45.9 -	33.0
-	-	-	-	-	-	-		-	-	-	-	-	-	30.2 -	19.6
-	-	-	0.00	6.50	11.53	-		-	-	-	-	-	-	5.3 -	2.3
0.79	0.10	0.04	1.17	1.03	1.12	19.5 -	16.9	0.92	0.92	0.92	4.4	0.23Q	11/20/07	22.8 -	19.8
0.12	-0.03	-0.33	-0.04	0.54	0.68	-		0.50	0.50	0.75	3.2	0.125Q	3/27/08	32.1 -	11.0
-	-	-	4.31	1.76	2.64	-		-	-	-	-	-	-		
0.93	1.08	1.18	4.48	2.67	1.08	5.6 -	3.8	0.12	0.08	0.05	0.6	0.04Q	3/3/08	25.2 -	17.0
1.22	1.21	1.28	5.45	3.79	4.12	5.9 -	3.9	0.44	0.26	0.15	1.7	0.12Q	2/10/08	32.0 -	21.4
-	-	-	1.83	1.05	0.83	12.7 -	6.0	-	-	-	-	-	-	23.2 -	11.0
-	-	-	92.00	158.78	48.77	0.2 -	0.1	-	-	-	-	-	-	16.5 -	12.1
-	-	-	3.14	3.03		-		5.85	4.21	-	-	0.4Q	12/4/07		
0.60	0.71	0.68	2.55	1.98	1.39	9.2 -	6.5	0.42	0.32	0.24	2.1	0.16Q	3/14/08	23.5 -	16.6
0.71	0.98	0.97	3.68	3.57	3.11	9.9 -	5.6	0.96	0.68	0.48	3.6	0.29Q	3/10/08	36.5 -	20.5
-	-	-	-	-	-	-		-	-	-	-	-	-	7.8 -	4.5
-0.23	-0.07	0.05	-1.98	0.06	-5.90	-		-	-	-	-	-	-	83.9 -	30.3
-	-	-	0.83	-1.18	-2.28	-		•	-	-	-	-	-		
0.76	-	-	2.91	3.29	2.20	8.9 -	7.2	3.05	2.92	2.13	12.9	0.76Q	2/27/08	25.9 -	20.9
0.49	0.31	0.32	1.59	3.05	-1.93	12.6 -	10.9	0.78	0.72	0.68	4.1	0.2Q	3/31/08	20.1 -	17.3
1.10	1.31	1.41	5.12	4.37	3.85	11.3 -	9.2	1.48	1.16	1.01	2.9	0.37Q	3/15/08	57.8 -	47.3
0.10	0.18	0.14	0.51	0.94	1.74	22.5 -	16.7	1.43	1.21	0.53	14.5	0.515MQ	2/15/08	11.5 -	8.5
1.76	0.10	-0.22	2.76	2.29	2.11	12.3 -	10.1	1.44	1.39	1.32	4.6	0.375Q	2/15/08	33.9 -	27.9
0.53	0.96	-	-	-8.52	-1.26	-		-	0.40	0.40	-	0.1Q	5/15/08	47.5 -	23.9
-	-	-	-	3.04	2.62	-		-	-	-	-	-	-	50.6 -	41.3
-	-	-	-	19.99	17.83	-		-	-	-	-	-	-	27.5 -	19.6
0.20	0.51	0.93	2.01	2.04	0.38	9.0 -	4.6	-	-	-	-	10.Q	3/17/08	18.0 -	9.2
0.45	0.47	0.79	2.07	1.93	1.83	13.1 -	11.0	1.30	1.21	1.16	5.3	0.35Q	5/1/08	27.2 -	22.7
-	-	-		13491.2	5771.01	-		-	-	-	-	-	-	23.6 -	16.2
0.16	0.21	0.21	0.67	0.47	1.04	41.3 -	24.6	0.42	0.40	0.36	1.9	0.11Q	3/19/08	27.7 -	16.5
1.26	1.14	1.29	4.94	5.68	4.13	5.6 -	2.7	2.44	2.15	0.93	12.8	0.32Q	5/9/08	27.5 -	13.3
0.57	0.74	0.97	2.74	2.83	2.86	22.3 -	16.3	0.92	3.54	3.31	1.7	0.985Q	2/14/08	61.0 -	44.6
0.21	0.26	0.33	1.02	0.72	-	-		-	-	-	-	0.36Q	2/19/08		
-	-	-	0.83	0.83	0.86	21.0 -	17.4	0.61	0.69	0.84	3.8	0.051M	2/1/06	17.4 -	14.4
-	-	-	-	-	-	-		-	-	-	-	0.0357M	12/31/07	15.7 -	13.1
-	-	-	-	-	-	-		-	-	-	-	0.0585M	2/1/08	15.6 -	13.2
-	-	-	-	-	-	-		-	-	-	-	0.0575M	2/1/08	15.6 -	13.0
-	-	-	-	-	-	-		-	-	-	-	0.0365M	2/1/08	10.0 -	8.6
-	-	-	-	-	-	-		-	-	-	-	0.0565M	2/1/08	15.1 -	12.9
-	-	-	-	-	-	-		-	-	-	-	0.0595M	2/1/08	16.0 -	13.4
-	-	-	-	-	-	-		-	-	-	-	0.058M	2/1/08	15.7 -	13.0
-	-	-	0.64	0.65	0.66	22.3 -	19.6	0.66	0.71	0.71	4.9	0.053M	2/1/08	14.2 -	12.5
-	-	-	0.83	0.84	0.88	20.4 -	16.6	0.72	0.97	0.88	4.6	0.049M	4/1/08	16.9 -	13.8
-	-	-	1.02	0.99	0.83	15.8 -	12.5	1.54	1.36	1.61	10.4	0.37Q	4/1/08	16.1 -	12.7
-	-	-	-	1.04	1.06	-		-	0.86	1.00	-	0.0635M	4/1/08	16.4 -	13.4
-	-	-	-	0.49	0.04	-		-	-	-	-	0.405Q	4/1/08		
-	-	-	-	0.20	0.10	-		-	1.81	0.91	-	0.425Q	4/1/08	-	

SYMBOL	COMPANY	NATURE OF BUSINESS	FISCAL YEAR-END	TOTAL REV. $MILL	NET INCOME $MILL	TOTAL ASSETS $MILL	NET STK EQUITY $MILL	NO OF INST	INST. HOLDINGS (SHARES)
JPZ	Nuveen Equity Premium Income Fu	Trusts & Holding Entities	12/31/07	21.6	17.0	724.1	707.9	14	276171
JSN	Nuveen Equity Premium Opportunit	Trusts & Holding Entities						11	349538
JFR	Nuveen Floating Rate Income Fund	Trusts & Holding Entities	7/31/07	-	73.7	1038.8	619.8	14	2860562
JRO	Nuveen Floating Rate Income Oppo	Trusts & Holding Entities	7/31/07	-	46.0	625.8	373.4	9	519177
NQF	Nuveen Florida Investment Quality	Trusts & Holding Entities	4/30/07	-	13.1	438.1	251.5	18	292267
NUF	Nuveen Florida Quality Income Mun	Trusts & Holding Entities	4/30/07	-	11.2	379.1	219.4	19	288874
JGG	Nuveen Global Government Enhanc	Trusts & Holding Entities							
JGV	Nuveen Global Value Opportunities	Trusts & Holding Entities							
NCL	Nuveen Insured California Premium	Trusts & Holding Entities						8	72069
NPC	Nuveen Insured California Premium	Trusts & Holding Entities						7	18795
NFL	Nuveen Insured Florida Premium In	Trusts & Holding Entities	4/30/07	-	11.4	351.3	222.1	16	316000
NIO	Nuveen Insured Municipal Opportun	Trusts & Holding Entities	10/31/06	-	79.5	1992.0	1263.2	44	1227106
NNF	Nuveen Insured New York Premium	Trusts & Holding Entities	9/30/07	-	7.3	195.5	124.0	6	64087
NPX	Nuveen Insured Premium Income M	Trusts & Holding Entities	10/31/06	-	32.0	832.4	529.0	27	542155
NQI	Nuveen Insured Quality Municipal F	Trusts & Holding Entities	10/31/06	-	37.8	930.0	589.9	24	428756
NQM	Nuveen Investment Quality Municip	Trusts & Holding Entities	10/31/06	-	37.6	867.8	561.5	25	587021
NMY	Nuveen Maryland Premium Income	Trusts & Holding Entities	5/31/07	11.3	9.3	238.3	155.0	6	75702
NMT	Nuveen Massachusetts Premium In	Trusts & Holding Entities	5/31/07	5.0	4.2	105.0	69.3	5	33500
NMP	Nuveen Michigan Premium Income	Trusts & Holding Entities	7/31/07	-	7.0	178.3	113.6	7	92966
NUM	Nuveen Michigan Quality Income M	Trusts & Holding Entities						8	208576
JGT	Nuveen Multi-Currency Short-Term	Trusts & Holding Entities							
JPC	Nuveen Multi-Strategy Income and	Trusts & Holding Entities	12/31/07	111.3	96.9	1958.9	1230.3	32	1133647
JQC	Nuveen Multi-Strategy Income and	Trusts & Holding Entities	12/31/07	156.3	136.5	2738.0	1741.0	31	2122252
NMA	Nuveen Municipal Advantage Fund,	Trusts & Holding Entities	10/31/06	-	46.6	1098.0	683.7	29	736317
NMD	Nuveen Municipal High Income Opp	Trusts & Holding Entities	10/16/07				0.1		
NMI	Nuveen Municipal Income Fund, Inc	Trusts & Holding Entities	10/31/06	-	4.3	89.8	89.6	12	146959
NMO	Nuveen Municipal Market Opportuni	Trusts & Holding Entities	10/31/06	-	46.5	1083.5	701.6	25	631850
NUV	Nuveen Municipal Value Fund, Inc.	Trusts & Holding Entities	10/31/04	-	93.8	1978.0	1971.9	56	6089535
NQJ	Nuveen New Jersey Investment Qu	Trusts & Holding Entities	4/30/07	-	15.4	469.6	306.4	12	191038
NNJ	Nuveen New Jersey Premium Inco	Trusts & Holding Entities	4/30/07	-	8.9	275.4	183.5	12	156313
NAN	Nuveen New York Dividend Advant	Trusts & Holding Entities	9/30/07	-	9.0	209.8	138.5	6	41218
NQN	Nuveen New York Investment Quali	Trusts & Holding Entities	9/30/07	-	15.8	418.2	260.2	13	95277
NNY	Nuveen New York Municipal Value	Trusts & Holding Entities	9/30/07	-	6.6	151.5	150.3	11	220422
NNP	Nuveen New York Performance Plu	Trusts & Holding Entities	9/30/07	-	15.0	363.0	233.3	9	71450
NUN	Nuveen New York Quality Income	Trusts & Holding Entities	9/30/07	-	21.4	569.6	353.6	11	72512
NVN	Nuveen New York Select Quality M	Trusts & Holding Entities	9/30/07	-	21.5	562.2	349.4	15	161780
NXN	Nuveen New York Select Tax-Free I	Trusts & Holding Entities	3/31/07	-	2.4	57.6	55.8	2	4330
NNC	Nuveen North Carolina Premium Inc	Trusts & Holding Entities	5/31/07	6.5	5.4	144.1	91.2	4	88085
NUO	Nuveen Ohio Quality Income Munici	Trusts & Holding Entities						10	209560
NQP	Nuveen Pennsylvania Investment Q	Trusts & Holding Entities	4/30/07	-	12.5	418.9	247.6	17	246362
NPY	Nuveen Pennsylvania Premium Inc	Trusts & Holding Entities	4/30/07	-	11.8	395.7	232.6	15	224152
NPP	Nuveen Performance Plus Municipa	Trusts & Holding Entities	10/31/06	-	59.8	1428.0	945.2	37	1370122
NIF	Nuveen Premier Insured Municipal I	Trusts & Holding Entities	10/31/06	-	19.0	461.3	299.0	19	244432
NPF	Nuveen Premier Municipal Income	Trusts & Holding Entities	10/31/06	-	18.9	501.2	309.1	15	578546
NPM	Nuveen Premium Income Municipal	Trusts & Holding Entities	10/31/06	47.3	39.9	1005.2	635.0	24	545928
NPT	Nuveen Premium Income Municipal	Trusts & Holding Entities	10/31/06	-	38.9	962.7	591.9	30	914393
NPI	Nuveen Premium Income Municipal	Trusts & Holding Entities	10/31/06	-	63.7	1554.0	977.6	37	1544509
NQU	Nuveen Quality Income Municipal F	Trusts & Holding Entities	10/31/06	-	54.8	1295.6	839.8	38	1179081
JTP	Nuveen Quality Preferred Income F	Trusts & Holding Entities	12/31/07	92.7	83.3	1156.5	1153.9	28	1884333
JPS	Nuveen Quality Preferred Income F	Trusts & Holding Entities	12/31/07	176.2	159.8	2189.2	1386.1		
JHP	Nuveen Quality Preferred Income F	Trusts & Holding Entities	12/31/07	34.3	30.8	427.6	427.1	13	257442
NIM	Nuveen Select Maturities Municipal	Trusts & Holding Entities	3/31/07	-	5.6	126.4	126.3	17	250567
NQS	Nuveen Select Quality Municipal Fu	Trusts & Holding Entities	10/31/06	-	36.2	812.0	530.0	24	466142
NXQ	Nuveen Select Tax Free Income Po	Trusts & Holding Entities	3/31/07	-	11.5	258.7	257.0	21	496030
NXP	Nuveen Select Tax-Free Income Po	Trusts & Holding Entities	3/31/07	-	11.5	242.1	241.1	16	186117
NXR	Nuveen Select Tax-Free Income Po	Trusts & Holding Entities	3/31/07	-	8.3	187.9	187.0	10	147808
NSL	Nuveen Senior Income Fund	Trusts & Holding Entities	7/31/07	-	23.4	392.7	238.8	14	1202332
JTD	Nuveen Tax-Advantaged Dividend	Trusts & Holding Entities							
JFP	Nuveen Tax-Advantaged Floating R	Trusts & Holding Entities	6/30/07	19.1	17.2	281.4	203.1	2	391410
JTA	Nuveen Tax-Advantaged Total Retu	Trusts & Holding Entities	12/31/07	22.1	12.5	489.3	328.6	11	313220
NTX	Nuveen Texas Quality Income Muni	Trusts & Holding Entities						5	128944
NPV	Nuveen Virginia Premium Income M	Trusts & Holding Entities	5/31/07	9.4	7.8	202.0	132.9	8	140387
NVR	NVR Inc.	Building & General Construction	12/31/07	5156.4	334.0	2194.4	1129.4	180	4438920
NYM	NYMAGIC, Inc.	Insurance	12/31/07	190.4	13.4	1108.0	279.4	41	5162669
NMX	Nymex Holdings Inc	Finance & Investment	12/31/07	673.6	224.0	2227.2	925.6		
NYX	NYSE Euronext	Trusts & Holding Entities	12/31/07	4158.0	643.0	16618.0	9384.0		
OXY	Occidental Petroleum Corp	Oil and Gas	12/31/07	20013.0	5400.0	36519.0	22823.0	512	315169384
OII	Oceaneering International, Inc.	Oil and Gas	12/31/07	1743.1	180.4	1531.4	915.3	146	22702258
OZM	Och-Ziff Capital Management Grou	Wealth Management							
OCN	Ocwen Financial Corp.	Finance'Intermediaries & Services	12/31/07	-	38.6	2394.7	586.1		
ORH	Odyssey Re Holdings Corp.	Insurance	12/31/07	2989.1	595.6	9501.0	2654.7	92	17745301
ODP	Office Depot, Inc.	Retail - Miscellaneous	12/29/07	15527.5	395.6	7256.5	3083.8	346	252856721
OMX	OfficeMax Inc (DE)	Paper Products	12/29/07	9082.0	207.4	6283.8	2278.6	215	89600401
OGE	OGE Energy Corp.	Electricity	12/31/07	3797.6	244.2	5237.8	1680.9	194	35968622
OIS	Oil States International, Inc.	Oil and Gas	12/31/07	2088.2	203.4	1929.6	1084.8	128	37718020
ODC	Oil-Dri Corp. of America	Consumer Accessories	7/31/07	212.1	7.7	142.1	80.2	21	2772194
OLA	Old Mutual/Claymore Long-Short Fu	Trusts & Holding Entities							
ONB	Old National Bancorp (Evansville, I	Commercial Banking	12/31/07	616.5	74.9	7846.1	652.9	86	19653755
ORI	Old Republic International Corp.	Insurance	12/31/07	4091.0	272.4	13290.6	4541.6	259	132578687
OLN	Olin Corp.	Chemicals	12/31/07	1276.8	-9.2	1701.4	663.7	184	53449339

EARNINGS PER SHARE						P/E RATIO		DIVIDENDS PER SHARE			AV. YLD	DIV. DECLARED		PRICE RANGE	
QUARTERLY			ANNUAL								%	AMOUNT	PAYABLE	2007	
1st	2nd	3rd	2007	2006	2005	2007		2007	2006	2005					
-	-	-	0.44	0.43	0.42	46.0 -	45.3	1.70	1.70	1.70	8.5	0.4Q	4/1/08	20.3 -	19.9
-	-	-	-	0.32	0.30	-		-	1.78	1.48	-	0.4175Q	4/1/08	-	
-	-	-	1.56	1.31	1.00	9.9 -	8.8	1.17	0.99	0.86	8.0	0.097M	12/31/07	15.4 -	13.7
-	-	-	1.62	1.38	1.00	9.3 -	8.5	1.22	1.03	0.84	8.3	0.102M	12/31/07	15.0 -	13.8
-	-	-	0.79	0.94	0.96	21.8 -	17.1	0.69	0.80	0.97	4.4	0.054M	2/1/08	17.2 -	13.5
-	-	-	0.78	0.92	0.94	21.8 -	17.3	0.67	0.77	0.95	4.4	0.055M	2/1/08	17.0 -	13.5
-	-	-	0.38	-	-	-		-	-	-	-	0.405Q	4/1/08	-	
-	-	-	0.16	-	-	-		-	-	-	-	0.43Q	4/1/08	-	
-	-	-	-	-	-	-		-	-	-	-	0.053M	2/1/08	15.9 -	13.1
-	-	-	-	-	-	-		-	-	-	-	0.0605M	2/1/08	16.8 -	13.3
-	-	-	0.79	0.96	0.99	22.2 -	17.6	0.77	0.97	1.06	4.9	0.0575M	2/1/08	17.5 -	13.9
-	-	-	-	0.98	1.01	-		-	0.94	0.95	-	0.058M	2/1/08	16.7 -	13.3
-	-	-	0.87	0.88	0.91	19.2 -	15.4	0.71	1.06	1.07	4.7	0.0505M	2/1/08	16.7 -	13.4
-	-	-	0.86	0.89	-	-		-	0.68	0.83	-	0.0515M	2/1/08	15.1 -	12.1
-	-	-	0.99	1.03	-	-		-	0.88	1.02	-	0.0605M	2/1/08	17.1 -	13.8
-	-	-	1.05	1.05	-	-		-	0.99	1.06	-	0.0645M	4/1/08	16.1 -	13.2
-	-	-	0.88	0.89	0.92	19.5 -	15.9	0.67	0.81	0.90	4.2	0.0495M	4/1/08	17.1 -	13.9
-	-	-	0.88	0.88	0.91	18.7 -	15.8	0.67	0.86	0.88	4.4	0.0515M	4/1/08	16.4 -	13.9
-	-	-	0.90	0.91	0.93	18.1 -	15.1	0.81	0.94	0.95	5.4	0.055M	2/1/08	16.3 -	13.6
-	-	-	-	-	-	-		-	-	-	-	0.0555M	2/1/08	16.7 -	14.3
-	-	-	-	-	-	-		-	-	-	-	0.451Q	4/1/08	-	
-	-	-	0.97	1.02	1.13	16.3 -	12.7	0.28	1.10	1.31	1.9	0.285Q	4/1/08	15.8 -	12.3
-	-	-	0.97	1.04	0.52	15.6 -	12.4	0.28	1.10	1.17	2.0	0.285Q	4/1/08	15.2 -	12.1
-	-	-	-	1.08	1.09	-		-	0.92	1.02	-	0.064M	2/1/08	16.4 -	13.6
-	-	-	-	-	-	-		-	-	-	-	0.0785M	4/1/08	-	
-	-	-	-	0.52	0.51	-		-	0.51	0.53	-	0.042M	2/1/08	10.6 -	9.1
-	-	-	-	1.02	1.03	-		-	0.83	0.92	-	0.0605M	2/1/08	15.4 -	12.7
-	-	-	-	-	-	-		-	-	-	-	0.039M	2/1/08	9.7 -	8.7
-	-	-	0.75	0.91	0.95	22.4 -	18.0	0.70	1.03	1.05	4.6	0.0545M	2/1/08	16.8 -	13.5
-	-	-	0.74	0.90	0.94	23.1 -	18.6	0.72	1.10	1.14	4.7	0.0545M	2/1/08	17.1 -	13.7
-	-	-	0.97	0.98	1.03	17.2 -	14.0	0.85	1.08	0.99	5.6	0.0682M	12/31/07	16.7 -	13.6
-	-	-	0.89	0.90	0.95	19.0 -	15.7	0.74	1.28	1.21	4.8	0.052M	2/1/08	16.9 -	13.9
-	-	-	0.43	0.44	0.45	22.1 -	19.8	0.43	0.43	0.43	4.7	0.0355M	2/1/08	9.5 -	8.5
-	-	-	0.99	1.01	1.05	17.5 -	13.9	0.83	1.19	1.07	5.3	0.061M	2/1/08	17.3 -	13.8
-	-	-	0.89	0.90	0.93	18.1 -	14.7	0.69	1.03	0.97	4.7	0.051M	2/1/08	16.1 -	13.1
-	-	-	0.92	0.93	0.97	18.3 -	14.8	0.73	1.03	1.04	4.8	0.053M	2/1/08	16.8 -	13.6
-	-	-	0.61	0.62	0.64	24.3 -	20.7	0.65	0.68	0.73	4.8	0.051M	2/1/08	14.8 -	12.6
-	-	-	0.85	0.88	0.91	20.6 -	16.4	0.67	0.95	0.89	4.1	0.049M	4/1/08	17.5 -	13.9
-	-	-	-	-	-	-		-	-	-	-	0.055M	2/1/08	18.8 -	15.3
-	-	-	0.77	0.90	0.92	20.8 -	17.0	0.63	0.81	1.03	4.3	0.055M	2/1/08	16.0 -	13.1
-	-	-	0.74	0.89	0.92	21.9 -	17.7	0.67	0.98	1.11	4.5	0.0495M	2/1/08	16.2 -	13.1
-	-	-	-	1.00	1.02	-		-	0.86	0.96	-	0.0575M	2/1/08	15.9 -	13.1
-	-	-	-	0.98	1.01	-		-	0.89	1.01	-	0.053M	2/1/08	16.9 -	13.5
-	-	-	-	0.94	0.94	-		-	0.70	1.01	-	0.056M	2/1/08	15.7 -	12.9
-	-	-	0.97	0.97	0.98	16.0 -	13.3	0.71	0.82	1.03	5.0	0.0575M	2/1/08	15.5 -	12.9
-	-	-	-	0.90	0.91	-		-	0.69	0.81	-	0.0485M	2/1/08	13.7 -	11.2
-	-	-	-	1.00	0.98	-		-	0.75	0.91	-	0.059M	2/1/08	15.4 -	12.5
-	-	-	-	1.01	1.02	-		-	0.82	0.92	-	0.0605M	2/1/08	15.5 -	12.7
-	-	-	1.29	1.28	1.30	12.5 -	9.7	1.02	1.08	1.13	7.0	0.0775M	4/1/08	16.2 -	12.6
-	-	-	1.34	1.33	1.34	-		1.12	1.12	1.35	-	0.082M	4/1/08	-	
-	-	-	1.31	1.31	1.32	12.3 -	9.4	1.05	1.10	1.26	7.1	0.0795M	4/1/08	16.1 -	12.3
-	-	-	0.46	0.48	0.40	21.7 -	10.6	0.17	0.48	0.48	4.9	0.0365M	2/1/08	10.0 -	9.0
-	-	-	-	1.07	1.06	-		-	0.88	0.97	-	0.067M	2/1/08	15.7 -	13.0
-	-	-	0.66	0.66	0.67	21.0 -	18.7	0.64	0.67	0.72	4.9	0.053M	2/1/08	13.9 -	12.4
-	-	-	0.70	0.70	0.70	20.6 -	18.0	0.66	0.66	0.81	5.0	0.057M	2/1/08	14.4 -	12.6
-	-	-	0.64	0.65	0.66	21.5 -	19.1	0.64	0.65	0.71	4.9	0.0535M	2/1/08	13.8 -	12.2
-	-	-	0.79	0.69	0.66	12.8 -	11.1	0.71	0.62	0.58	7.4	0.058M	12/31/07	10.2 -	8.7
-	-	-	-	-	-	-		-	-	-	-	0.405Q	4/1/08	-	
-	-	-	1.24	1.10	0.15	-		1.00	0.80	0.20	-	0.0825Q	4/1/08	-	
-	-	-	0.90	0.89	0.83	22.3 -	17.8	1.95	1.59	1.69	10.7	0.5075Q	4/1/08	20.1 -	16.0
-	-	-	-	-	-	-		-	-	-	-	0.057M	2/1/08	16.0 -	12.9
-	-	-	0.88	0.88	0.93	21.4 -	16.2	0.72	1.04	0.90	4.3	0.053M	4/1/08	18.8 -	14.3
-	-	-	-	-	-	14.2 -	7.6	-	-	-	-	-	-	769.4 -	410.0
12.96	14.14	15.26	54.14	88.05	89.61	-		-	-	-	-	-	-	-	
0.82	1.12	0.41	1.46	3.25	1.09	19.4 -	13.6	0.32	0.30	0.24	1.3	0.08Q	4/3/08	28.3 -	19.9
0.59	0.44	0.66	2.36	2.38	7167.00	-		1.362	32844.18	108824.00	-	0.1Q	3/28/08	-	
0.40	0.02	0.97	2.70	1.36	-	-		-	-	-	-	0.3Q	6/30/08	-	
1.43	1.68	1.58	6.44	4.86	6.46	4.7 -	3.3	0.94	0.80	0.65	3.8	0.25Q	4/15/08	30.2 -	21.0
0.60	0.86	0.96	3.24	2.26	1.17	6.0 -	4.3	-	-	-	-	-	-	19.4 -	13.8
-	-	-	-	-	-	-		-	-	-	-	1.2Q	2/12/08	-	
0.18	0.39	0.09	0.58	2.91	0.24	21.7 -	12.9	-	-	-	-	-	-	12.6 -	7.5
1.20	2.02	1.57	8.23	6.93	-1.62	3.3 -	2.5	0.25	0.13	0.13	1.0	0.4485Q	4/20/08	27.5 -	20.5
0.56	0.40	0.43	1.43	1.79	0.87	13.6 -	9.9	-	-	-	-	-	-	19.4 -	14.1
0.76	0.35	0.64	2.66	1.19	-0.99	14.2 -	10.9	0.60	0.60	0.60	1.8	0.15Q	4/15/08	37.7 -	29.0
0.19	0.68	1.37	2.64	2.84	2.32	10.1 -	8.7	1.36	1.33	1.33	5.4	0.3475Q	4/30/08	26.8 -	23.1
1.05	1.03	0.97	3.99	3.89	2.41	5.2 -	3.3	-	-	-	-	-	-	20.6 -	13.0
0.35	0.29	-	1.09	0.73	0.88	13.4 -	9.4	0.48	0.38	0.34	3.7	0.0975Q	6/6/08	14.6 -	10.2
-	-	-	-	0.07	0.04	-		-	-	-	-	0.4Q	3/31/08	-	
0.16	0.30	0.34	1.14	1.20	0.93	22.3 -	17.6	0.88	0.84	0.76	3.9	0.23Q	3/17/08	25.4 -	20.0
0.46	0.49	0.12	1.17	1.99	2.37	18.6 -	14.6	0.63	0.59	1.31	3.3	0.16Q	3/14/08	21.8 -	17.1
0.31	0.48	-1.12	-0.12	2.06	1.86	-		0.80	0.80	0.80	4.3	0.2Q	3/10/08	22.8 -	15.5

T45

SYMBOL	COMPANY	NATURE OF BUSINESS	FISCAL YEAR-END	TOTAL REV. $MILL	NET INCOME $MILL	TOTAL ASSETS $MILL	NET STK EQUITY $MILL	NO OF INST	INST. HOLDINGS (SHARES)
OMG	OM Group, Inc.	Metal Works	12/31/07	1021.5	246.9	1469.2	1028.4	139	25144776
OHI	Omega Healthcare Investors, Inc.	Property, Real Estate & Developmen	12/31/07	159.6	69.4	1182.3	586.1	88	33684698
OME	Omega Protein Corp.	Food	12/31/07	157.1	12.1	207.8	118.5	31	8934635
OCR	Omnicare Inc.	Retail - Miscellaneous	12/31/07	6220.0	114.1	7593.8	3291.7	252	93788427
OMC	Omnicom Group, Inc.	Advertising, Marketing & PR	12/31/07	12694.0	975.7	19271.7	4091.7	479	154138075
OMN	Omnova Solutions, Inc.	Rubber Products	11/30/07	745.5	-6.7	326.4	65.3	75	30414667
OLP	One Liberty Properties, Inc. (United	Property, Real Estate & Developmen	12/31/07	36.8	10.6	406.6	171.2	40	4432645
OB	OneBeacon Insurance Group Ltd	Insurance	12/31/06	2470.1	246.7	9869.4	1777.2		
OKE	Oneok Inc. (New)	Gas Utilities	12/31/07	13477.4	304.9	11062.0	1969.3	227	77880511
OKS	ONEOK Partners LP	Gas Utilities	12/31/07	5831.6	407.7	6112.1			
VIP	Open Joint Stock Co.-Vimpel Comm	Communications	12/31/06	4868.0	811.5	8436.5	3942.9	113	44383503
OPY	Oppenheimer Holdings Inc	Finance Intermediaries & Services	12/31/07	914.4	75.4	2138.2	444.0	20	4480457
ORB	Orbital Sciences Corp.	Communications	12/31/07	1084.1	56.7	788.3	433.1	109	46550559
OWW	Orbitz Worldwide Inc	Misc. Transportation Services	12/31/07	859.0	-85.0	1925.0	738.0		
OEH	Orient Express Hotels Ltd.	Hospitality & Tourism	12/31/06	492.8	39.8	1751.7	807.0	86	38947262
OFG	Oriental Financial Group, Inc.	Commercial Banking	12/31/07	331.9	41.3	5999.9	359.5		
IX	Orix Corp. (Japan)	Credit & Lending	3/31/07	1176461.0	196506.0	8207187.0	1194234.0	37	2029833
ORA	Ormat Technologies Inc	Electricity	12/31/07	295.9	27.4	1274.9	618.1	35	5149951
OSP	OSG America LP	Shipping	12/31/07	31.1	3.6	651.1			
OSK	Oshkosh Corp	Automotive	9/30/07	6307.3	268.1	6399.8	1393.6	206	30668861
OSG	Overseas Shipholding Group, Inc.	Shipping	12/31/07	1129.3	211.3	4158.9	1818.0	200	25702622
OMI	Owens & Minor, Inc.	Specialist Equipment Supplies	12/31/07	6800.5	72.7	1515.1	614.4	158	33694600
OC	Owens Corning (New)	General Construction Supplies & Ser	12/31/07	4978.0	96.0	7872.0	3988.0		
OI	Owens-Illinois, Inc.	Stone, Clay, Glass, and Concrete Pr	12/31/07	7679.2	1340.6	9324.6	2187.4	190	139854224
OXM	Oxford Industries, Inc.	Apparel	2/2/08	695.8	19.2	910.3	407.5	113	15230332
TLK	P.T. Telekomunikasi Indonesia (Per	Communications	12/31/06	1294008.0	1005577.0	75135745.0		74	24858093
PKG	Packaging Corp of America	Paper Products	12/31/07	2316.0	170.1	2035.9	760.9	146	65178734
PTV	Pactiv Corp.	Paper Products	12/31/07	3253.0	245.0	3765.0	1226.0	273	123491538
PLL	Pall Corp.	Industrial Machinery and Equipment	7/31/07	2249.9	127.5	2708.8	1060.6	274	105459958
PRX	Par Pharmaceutical Companies Inc	Pharmaceuticals	12/31/07	769.7	49.9	781.5	437.8	182	32381551
PTC	Par Technology Corp.	Office Equipment Supplies	12/31/07	209.5	-2.7	146.5	85.0	17	1423059
PKE	Park Electrochemical Corp.	Electrical	2/25/07	257.4	39.8	321.9	264.2	87	14403809
PKD	Parker Drilling Co. (United States)	Oil and Gas	12/31/07	654.6	104.1	1077.0	534.7	107	53943814
PH	Parker Hannifin Corp.	Metal Products	6/30/07	10718.1	830.0	8441.4	4711.7	327	87726111
PKY	Parkway Properties Inc. (United Sta	Property, Real Estate & Developmen	12/31/07	248.3	19.7	1535.8	439.9	2	24400
PRE	PartnerRe Ltd.	Insurance	12/31/06	4187.4	749.3	14948.2	3785.8	155	50802666
PTI	Patni Computer Systems Ltd	IT & Technology							
PCX	Patriot Coal Corp	Coal Mining	12/31/07	1073.4	-106.9	1199.8	82.3		
PCM	PCM Fund Inc	Trusts & Holding Entities	12/31/07	14.4	9.1	230.9	128.1		
BTU	Peabody Energy Corp	Coal Mining	12/31/07	4574.7	264.3	9668.3	2519.7	329	110035186
PSO	Pearson Plc (United Kingdom)	Non-Media Publishing	12/31/04	3696.0	284.0	6578.0	3014.0	42	11173705
PDX	Pediatrix Medical Group, Inc.	Hospitals & Health Care	12/31/07	917.6	142.7	1302.8	959.1	161	21329431
PGH	Pengrowth Energy Trust	Trusts & Holding Entities	12/31/06	991.4	262.3	4670.0	3049.7		
PTA	Penn Treaty American Corp	Insurance	12/31/06	366.0	-33.2	1314.8	207.6	36	2754575
PVA	Penn Virginia Corp.	Oil and Gas	12/31/07	852.9	50.8	2253.5	810.1	111	15485129
PVG	Penn Virginia GP Holdings LP	Coal Mining	12/31/07	549.4	29.2	942.3	220.4		
PVR	Penn Virginia Resource Partners, L.	Coal Mining	12/31/07	549.4	56.6	931.3		76	2863386
PWE	Penn West Energy Trust	Trusts & Holding Entities	12/31/06	1770.4	665.6	8069.7	5188.3		
JCP	Penney (J.C.) Co.,Inc. (Holding Co.)	Retail - General	2/2/08	19860.0	1111.0	14309.0	5312.0	449	232572747
PEI	Pennsylvania Real Estate Investme	Property, Real Estate & Developmen	12/31/07	466.6	23.2	3264.1	757.6	130	20352033
PAG	Penske Automotive Group Inc	Retail - Automotive	12/31/07	12957.7	127.7	4668.6	1421.5		
PNR	Pentair, Inc.	Industrial Machinery and Equipment	12/31/07	3398.7	210.9	4000.6	1910.9	250	72436025
PBY	Pep Boys-Manny, Moe & Jack (Unit	Retail - Automotive	2/3/07	2272.2	-2.5	1767.2	567.8	135	50575854
POM	Pepco Holdings Inc.	Electricity	12/31/07	9366.4	334.2	15111.0	4018.4	245	83297752
PBG	Pepsi Bottling Group Inc	Food	12/29/07	13591.0	532.0	13115.0	2615.0	230	145775885
PAS	PepsiAmericas, Inc. (New)	Food	12/29/07	4479.5	212.1	5308.0	1858.3	168	53179784
PEP	PepsiCo Inc.	Food	12/29/07	39474.0	5658.0	34628.0	17325.0	1122	1108465396
PDA	Perdigao S.A.	Food	12/31/07	6633.4	321.3	6543.3	3226.0	8	381761
PCR	Perini Corp.	Building & General Construction	12/31/07	4628.4	97.1	1654.1	368.3	77	16570499
PKI	PerkinElmer, Inc.	Instruments and Related Products	12/30/07	1787.3	131.7	2949.3	1575.3	267	95720209
PBT	Permian Basin Royalty Trust	Miscellaneous	12/31/07	68.5	67.6	9.5	1.3	23	6293465
PER	Perot Systems Corp.	IT & Technology	12/31/07	2612.0	115.0	1900.0	1243.0	124	59021777
PZE	Petrobras Energia Participaciones S	Oil and Gas	12/31/06	11745.0	1064.0	20457.0	6220.0	33	10823271
PCZ	Petro-Canada	Oil and Gas	12/31/07	21250.0	2733.0	23852.0	11870.0	125	114274973
PTR	PetroChina Co Ltd	Oil and Gas	12/31/05	552229.0	133362.0	778067.0	543667.0	121	15457877
HK	Petrohawk Energy Corp	Oil and Gas	12/31/07	883.4	52.9	4672.4	2008.9	56	21490654
PBR	Petroleo Brasileiro S.A.	Oil and Gas	12/31/06	158238.8	25918.9	210538.1	97530.6	206	159478853
PEO	Petroleum & Resources Corp.	Trusts & Holding Entities	12/31/07	15.0	10.1	1020.6	978.9	27	2999739
PQ	PetroQuest Energy Inc	Oil and Gas	12/31/07	263.7	40.6	644.3	302.3	56	21024864
PFB	PFF Bancorp Inc.	Other Depository Banking	3/31/07	361.0	55.9	4553.5	397.1	92	17388327
PFE	Pfizer Inc	Pharmaceuticals	12/31/07	48418.0	8144.0	115268.0	65010.0	1411	4464162091
PCG	PG&E Corp. (Holding Co.)	Electricity	12/31/07	13237.0	1006.0	36648.0	8553.0	326	237161085
PMC	PharMerica Corp	Health	12/31/07	1217.8	-24.1	680.1	309.2		
PHH	PHH Corp (New)	Credit & Lending	12/31/07	2240.0	-12.0	9357.0	1529.0	211	41644076
PHI	Philippine Long Distance Telephone	Communications	12/31/07	126044.0	34112.0	250197.0	74369.0	66	22724202
PVH	Phillips-Van Heusen Corp. (United	Apparel	2/3/08	2425.2	183.3	2172.4	956.3	123	24549066
PNX	Phoenix Companies, Inc. (The)	Insurance	12/31/07	2572.8	123.9	30206.9	2289.9	1	416349
PNY	Piedmont Natural Gas Co., Inc.	Gas Utilities	10/31/07	1711.3	104.4	2820.3	878.4	180	30785621
PIR	Pier 1 Imports Inc.	Retail - Furniture & Home Furnishing	3/3/07	1623.2	-227.6	916.5	361.1	180	72830454
PPC	Pilgrim's Pride Corp.	Food	9/29/07	7598.6	47.0	3774.2	1172.2	146	30843332

EARNINGS PER SHARE						P/E RATIO		DIVIDENDS PER SHARE			AV. YLD %	DIV. DECLARED		PRICE RANGE	
QUARTERLY			ANNUAL											2007	
1st	2nd	3rd	2007	2006	2005			2007	2006	2005	%	AMOUNT	PAYABLE		
3.85	1.52	1.26	8.15	7.31	1.35	4.6 -	3.0	-	-	-	-	0.14Q	8/30/02	37.4 -	24.3
0.30	0.20	0.19	0.90	0.78	0.45	14.1 -	9.7	1.08	0.96	0.85	10.4	0.5234Q	2/15/08	12.7 -	8.7
-0.14	0.14	0.41	0.70	0.18	-0.29	15.9 -	9.5	-	-	-	-			11.2 -	6.7
0.35	0.41	0.35	0.94	1.50	2.10	50.1 -	28.3	0.09	0.09	0.09	0.2	0.0225Q	3/21/08	47.1 -	26.6
0.55	0.84	0.62	2.95	2.50	2.18	15.0 -	11.3	0.57	0.50	0.46	1.5	0.15Q	4/4/08	44.4 -	33.4
-0.12	-0.23	0.11	-0.16	0.51	-0.04	-		-	-	-	-	0.05Q	5/31/01	6.4 -	4.5
0.31	0.25	0.26	1.05	3.67	2.16	22.9 -	15.7	2.11	1.35	1.32	10.8	0.36Q	4/2/08	24.0 -	16.5
-	-	-	-	2.47	2.33	-		-	-	-	-	0.21Q	3/26/08		
1.36	0.31	0.13	2.79	2.68	5.06	10.4 -	7.1	1.40	1.22	1.09	5.9	0.38Q	2/14/08	28.9 -	19.8
1.00	0.97	0.98	4.21	5.01	2.93	11.7 -	8.6	3.98	1.68	3.20	9.5	1.025Q	2/14/08	49.3 -	36.2
-	-	-		15.93	12.04	-		-	-	-	-			8.4 -	4.7
1.26	1.16	1.19	5.57	2.76	1.36	6.2 -	3.9	0.42	0.40	0.36	1.5	0.11Q	11/23/07	34.4 -	21.5
0.19	0.23	0.26	0.93	0.56	0.45	15.1 -	10.5	-	-	-	-			14.1 -	9.8
-0.09	0.46	0.53	-	0.97	1.06	-		-	0.10	0.10	-	0.025Q	11/5/07	22.4 -	14.5
0.40	0.21	0.30	1.50	-0.40	2.05	17.8 -	16.6	0.56	0.56	0.55	2.2	0.14Q	4/15/08	26.8 -	24.9
-	-	-	2100.93	1790.30	1002.18	0.0 -	0.0	-	-	-	-			68.6 -	41.9
-0.15	0.22	0.41	0.70	0.99	0.48	26.1 -	22.4	0.22	0.15	0.12	1.0	0.05Q	3/27/08	18.3 -	15.7
-	-	-	285.20	2434.93	1873.81	-		-	-	-	-	0.1875Q	2/14/08		
0.50	-	-	3.58	2.76	2.18	9.6 -	6.8	0.40	0.37	0.22	1.4	0.1Q	2/25/08	34.4 -	24.3
2.16	2.28	0.83	6.16	9.92	11.77	10.7 -	5.2	1.13	0.93	0.70	2.6	0.3125Q	3/5/08	65.7 -	32.2
0.27	0.45	0.52	1.79	1.20	1.61	16.4 -	12.6	0.68	0.60	0.52	2.7	0.2Q	3/31/08	29.3 -	22.5
0.01	0.22	0.86	-	-0.51	-74.08	-		-	-	-	-				
0.30	0.89	6.86	7.99	-0.32	-3.85	3.0 -	1.4	-	-	-	-	0.5938Q	2/15/08	23.8 -	11.0
0.27	0.71	-	2.92	3.96	2.87	16.0 -	11.7	0.66	0.57	0.51	1.6	0.18Q	2/29/08	46.8 -	34.2
-	-	-	-	-	-	-		-	-	-	-			23.3 -	14.1
0.30	0.44	0.46	1.61	1.20	0.49	15.5 -	13.1	1.05	1.00	1.00	4.6	0.3Q	4/15/08	25.0 -	21.1
0.43	0.53	0.45	1.85	1.96	0.36	13.9 -	11.1	-	-	-	-			25.7 -	20.5
0.29	0.39	-	1.02	1.16	1.12	28.9 -	21.8	0.35	0.53	0.38	1.4	0.13Q	5/9/08	29.5 -	22.3
1.19	0.08	0.04	1.43	0.19	-0.24	46.4 -	22.5	-	-	-	-			66.3 -	32.2
-0.09	-0.07	-0.06	-0.19	0.39	0.64	-		-	-	-	-			8.2 -	5.2
0.37	0.45	0.43	1.96	1.33	1.08	15.4 -	10.1	1.32	1.32	1.26	5.6	0.08Q	5/8/08	30.2 -	19.9
0.27	0.15	0.20	0.94	0.75	1.02	4.6 -	2.8	-	-	-	-			4.4 -	2.6
1.33	1.23	-	4.67	3.71	3.35	11.1 -	7.5	0.69	0.61	0.52	1.7	0.21Q	3/7/08	51.9 -	35.1
-0.05	1.14	-0.14	0.95	1.32	0.96	29.4 -	26.1	2.60	2.60	2.60	9.9	0.65Q	3/26/08	27.9 -	24.8
2.76	1.66	4.44	-	12.37	-1.56	-		-	1.60	1.52	-	0.46Q	3/3/08	62.6 -	50.3
-	-	-	-4.61	-	-	-		-	-	-	-				
-	-	-	0.80	0.90	0.98	18.7 -	15.1	0.40	1.13	1.13	2.9	0.07M	3/13/08	15.0 -	12.1
0.33	0.40	0.12	0.98	2.23	1.58	20.1 -	8.7	0.24	0.24	0.17	1.9	0.06Q	3/4/08	19.7 -	8.6
-	-	-	-	0.56	0.78	-		-	-	-	-			12.7 -	10.7
0.51	0.72	0.79	2.86	2.52	1.86	12.5 -	9.2	-	-	-	-			35.8 -	26.3
-	-	-	-	1.49	2.07	-		-	-	-	-	0.225M	1/15/08		
-	-	-	-	-1.42	-0.96	-		-	-	-	-			9.0 -	5.7
0.12	0.63	0.45	1.32	2.01	1.66	16.9 -	10.3	0.23	0.23	0.23	1.3	0.0563Q	3/19/08	22.4 -	13.0
0.20	0.21	0.23	0.75	0.98	0.65	-		-	-	-	-	0.32Q	2/19/08		
0.30	0.30	0.29	0.96	1.56	1.22	27.9 -	16.6	1.66	1.48	1.24	8.6	0.44Q	2/14/08	26.8 -	15.9
-	-	-	-	3.27	3.48	-		-	-	-	-	0.34M	2/15/00		
1.04	0.81	1.17	4.90	4.26	1.76	8.3 -	5.2	0.72	0.50	0.50	2.0	0.2Q	2/4/08	41.4 -	25.0
0.15	0.01	0.35	0.73	0.37	1.17	59.7 -	42.2	2.28	2.28	2.25	6.2	0.57Q	3/17/08	43.6 -	30.8
0.15	0.43	0.46	1.35	1.32	1.26	12.0 -	8.6	0.14	0.27	0.23	1.0	0.09Q	3/3/08	16.1 -	11.6
0.42	0.62	0.58	2.10	1.81	1.80	21.0 -	10.7	0.60	0.56	0.52	1.9	0.17Q	2/8/08	44.0 -	22.5
0.06	-	-0.54	-0.05	-0.69	0.41	-		0.27	0.27	0.27	1.3	0.0675Q	4/28/08	29.3 -	12.0
0.27	0.30	0.87	1.72	1.30	1.96	12.6 -	9.9	1.04	1.04	1.00	5.3	0.27Q	3/31/08	21.7 -	17.0
0.12	0.70	1.12	2.29	2.16	1.86	13.6 -	10.5	0.53	0.41	0.29	1.8	0.17Q	6/30/08	31.2 -	24.1
0.16	0.61	0.55	1.64	1.22	1.42	13.1 -	10.3	0.52	0.50	0.34	2.6	0.135Q	4/1/08	21.5 -	16.9
0.65	0.94	1.06	3.41	3.34	2.39	16.3 -	13.3	1.43	1.16	1.01	2.8	0.375Q	3/31/08	55.5 -	45.4
-	-	-	-	-	-	-		-	-	-	-			41.7 -	6.1
0.84	1.01	0.87	3.54	1.54	0.20	5.6 -	2.5	-	-	-	-			19.9 -	8.8
0.12	0.28	0.26	1.09	0.95	2.04	21.0 -	14.4	0.28	0.28	0.28	1.4	0.07Q	5/9/08	22.9 -	15.7
0.20	0.28	0.38	1.45	1.41	1.34	10.3 -	5.3	1.45	1.41	1.34	14.1	0.1828M	4/14/08	15.0 -	7.7
0.19	0.18	0.20	0.92	0.66	0.91	18.3 -	12.8	-	-	-	-			16.8 -	11.8
-	-	-	-	-	-	-		-	-	-	-			14.1 -	8.8
1.18	1.70	1.58	5.53	3.41	3.41	5.2 -	3.8	0.52	0.40	0.35	2.2	0.13Q	4/1/08	28.6 -	20.9
-	-	-	0.81	0.79	0.75	78.6 -	51.4	-	-	-	-			63.7 -	41.6
-0.12	0.27	0.16	0.31	0.92	-0.31	31.8 -	13.5	-	-	-	-			9.8 -	4.2
-	-	-	-	-	-	-		-	-	-	-			20.2 -	12.2
-	-	-	0.46	0.47	0.53	59.5 -	47.7	4.31	3.80	1.78	17.6	0.05Q	3/1/08	27.4 -	21.9
0.22	0.19	0.16	0.79	0.49	0.44	7.0 -	3.2	-	-	-	-	0.8594Q	4/15/08	5.6 -	2.5
0.02	-0.33	-0.65	2.25	2.10	1.81	13.9 -	10.3	0.70	0.62	0.55	2.7	0.19Q	12/27/07	31.2 -	23.2
0.48	0.18	0.11	1.17	2.66	1.09	33.2 -	20.8	1.16	0.96	0.76	3.5	0.32Q	3/4/08	38.9 -	24.3
0.71	0.74	0.77	2.78	2.76	2.37	12.3 -	9.4	1.44	1.32	1.23	4.9	0.39Q	4/15/08	34.1 -	26.2
-	-	-	-1.13	-	-	-		-	-	-	-				
0.27	-0.02	-0.69	-0.23	-0.29	1.34	-		0.16	-	-	-				
-	-	-		-187.81	185.72	-		-	-	-	-			27.0 -	14.7
0.92	0.68	1.05	2.64	1.85	1.14	10.4 -	6.3	0.15	0.15	0.15	0.7	0.0375Q	3/31/08	27.5 -	16.6
0.44	0.29	0.31	1.07	0.88	1.06	24.6 -	21.5	0.16	0.16	0.16	0.6	0.16A	7/11/07	26.3 -	23.0
1.12	-	-	1.40	1.28	1.32	17.1 -	13.8	0.99	0.95	0.91	4.6	0.26Q	4/15/08	23.9 -	19.3
-0.64	-0.49	-0.11	-2.60	-0.46	0.68	-		0.20	0.40	0.40	1.0	0.1Q	8/16/06	25.0 -	15.4
-0.49	-	-	0.71	-0.51	3.98	49.3 -	23.7	0.09	1.09	0.06	0.3	0.0225Q	3/28/08	35.0 -	16.8

SYMBOL	COMPANY	NATURE OF BUSINESS	FISCAL YEAR-END	TOTAL REV. $MILL	NET INCOME $MILL	TOTAL ASSETS $MILL	NET STK EQUITY $MILL	NO OF INST	INST. HOLDINGS (SHARES)
PCQ	Pimco California Municipal Income	Trusts & Holding Entities	4/30/07	-	19.8	436.0	267.1	12	125135
PCK	Pimco California Municipal Income	Trusts & Holding Entities	5/31/07	46.0	33.0	943.0	455.3	10	280625
PZC	Pimco California Municipal Income	Trusts & Holding Entities	9/30/07	-	23.1	644.2	312.0		-
PCN	Pimco Corporate Income Fund	Trusts & Holding Entities	10/31/06	-	51.3	898.3	535.1	17	1129633
PTY	Pimco Corporate Opportunity Fund	Trusts & Holding Entities	11/30/07	110.2	98.6	1819.7	946.9	28	2926572
PFL	Pimco Floating Rate Income Fund	Trusts & Holding Entities	7/31/07	-	38.5	598.7	316.3	15	1182803
PGP	PIMCO Global StocksPLUS & Inco	Trusts & Holding Entities	3/31/07	16.3	9.7	426.4	258.8		-
PHK	Pimco High Income Fund	Trusts & Holding Entities	3/31/07	-	193.2	3031.1	1756.3	38	6543162
MAF	PIMCO Municipal Advantage Fund I	Trusts & Holding Entities	10/31/07	-	5.9	162.1	106.6		-
PMF	Pimco Municipal Income Fund	Trusts & Holding Entities	4/30/07	-	26.3	599.1	366.0	16	211817
PML	Pimco Municipal Income Fund II (U	Trusts & Holding Entities	5/31/07	78.7	65.7	1514.4	886.8	20	449936
PMX	Pimco Municipal Income Fund III (U	Trusts & Holding Entities	9/30/07	-	36.9	926.1	457.9		-
PNI	Pimco New York Municipal Fund II (	Trusts & Holding Entities	5/31/07	14.8	11.5	288.9	156.2	2	12022
PNF	Pimco New York Municipal Income	Trusts & Holding Entities	4/30/07	-	7.2	186.5	103.0	10	141988
PYN	Pimco New York Municipal Income	Trusts & Holding Entities	9/30/07	-	5.7	167.7	80.4		-
RCS	PIMCO Strategic Global Governme	Trusts & Holding Entities	1/31/07	-	24.2	1452.8	378.4	22	1123309
PNK	Pinnacle Entertainment Inc	Sporting & Recreational	12/31/07	923.7	-1.4	2193.5	1052.4	122	35006245
PNW	Pinnacle West Capital Corp.	Electricity	12/31/07	3523.6	307.1	11243.7	3531.6	247	66869973
PHD	Pioneer Floating Rate Trust	Trusts & Holding Entities	11/30/07	62.8	56.2	694.3	441.5	6	375034
PHT	Pioneer High Income Trust	Trusts & Holding Entities	3/31/07	-	50.7	640.1	450.4	16	849101
PBF	Pioneer Municipal & Equity Income	Trusts & Holding Entities	11/30/07	33.7	27.9	609.4	425.4		-
MAV	Pioneer Municipal High Income Adv	Trusts & Holding Entities	3/31/07	-	26.4	513.9	361.9	7	137540
MHI	Pioneer Municipal High Income Tru	Trusts & Holding Entities	4/30/07	-	22.6	460.3	354.5	11	164841
PXD	Pioneer Natural Resources Co	Oil and Gas	12/31/07	1833.3	372.7	8617.0	3042.7	282	116806348
PJC	Piper Jaffray Companies	Wealth Management	12/31/07	498.9	42.2	1723.2	912.6	189	14679799
PBI	Pitney Bowes Inc	Office Equipment Supplies	12/31/07	6129.8	366.8	9549.9	643.3	466	175790126
PAA	Plains All American Pipeline, L.P.	Oil and Gas	12/31/07	20394.0	365.0	9906.0	-	97	15443845
PXP	Plains Exploration & Production Co.	Oil and Gas	12/31/07	1272.8	158.8	9693.4	3338.2	216	65263597
PLT	Plantronics, Inc.	Communications	3/31/07	800.2	50.1	651.3	496.8	188	45041052
PTP	Platinum Underwriters Holdings, Ltd	Insurance	12/31/06	1522.9	329.7	5099.6	1858.1		-
PLA	Playboy Enterprises, Inc.	Media	12/31/07	339.8	4.9	445.2	171.3	71	21577032
PCL	Plum Creek Timber Co., Inc.	Property, Real Estate & Developmen	12/31/07	1675.0	282.0	4664.0	1901.0	429	87835759
PMI	PMI Group, Inc.	Insurance	12/31/07	1185.2	-915.3	5070.4	2513.0	252	93191861
PNC	PNC Financial Services Group (The	Commercial Banking	12/31/07	9956.0	1467.0	138920.0	14854.0	462	166166776
PNM	PNM Resources Inc	Electricity	12/31/07	1914.0	74.9	5872.1	1703.9	171	57317650
PII	Polaris Industries Inc.	Automotive	12/31/07	1825.3	111.6	769.9	173.0	217	28470574
RL	Polo Ralph Lauren Corp.	Apparel	3/31/07	4295.4	400.9	3758.0	2334.9	174	56721889
POL	PolyOne Corp.	Chemicals	12/31/07	2642.7	11.4	1583.0	649.4	157	74974985
PPO	Polypore International Inc	Chemicals	12/29/07	537.1	0.5	1429.0	335.3		-
POR	Portland General Electric Co.	Electricity	12/31/07	1743.0	145.0	4108.0	1316.0		-
PT	Portugal Telecom, SGPS, S.A.	Communications	12/31/04	5967.4	623.2	13928.7	2254.2	60	58458400
PKX	POSCO (South Korea)	Metal Works	12/31/06	25842326.1	3314181.0	31149073.4	-	180	53852891
PPS	Post Properties, Inc.	Property, Real Estate & Developmen	12/31/07	307.5	178.7	2268.1	1058.5	137	33491612
POT	Potash Corp. of Saskatchewan Inc.	Chemicals	12/31/07	5234.2	1103.6	9716.6	6018.7	150	77329943
PCH	Potlatch Corp (New)	Property, Real Estate & Developmen	12/31/07	1654.0	56.4	1517.2	578.3		-
PPG	PPG Industries, Inc.	Chemicals	12/31/07	11206.0	834.0	12629.0	4151.0	444	102059586
PPL	PPL Corp	Electricity	12/31/07	6498.0	1288.0	19972.0	5857.0	339	117120506
PPL PRA	PPL Electric Utilities Corp	Electricity	12/31/07	3410.0	163.0	4986.0	1586.0	1	28740
PLS	PPL Energy Supply, LLC	Electricity	12/31/06	5272.0	698.0	14655.0	4534.0		-
PX	Praxair, Inc.	Chemicals	12/31/07	9402.0	1177.0	13382.0	5142.0	506	263014390
PCP	Precision Castparts Corp.	Metal Works	4/1/07	5361.2	633.1	5258.7	2836.2	255	56494266
PGI	Premiere Global Services Inc	Miscellaneous Business Services	12/31/07	559.7	33.4	624.1	242.2	111	53989648
PPD	Pre-Paid Legal Services Inc	Personal Services	12/31/06	444.0	51.8	188.5	30.9	101	11290648
PDE	Pride International, Inc. (DE)	Oil and Gas	12/31/07	2043.8	784.3	5613.9	3470.4	226	120328412
PRM	Primedia, Inc	Media	12/31/07	314.8	491.4	256.9	-143.8		-
PRS	Primus Guaranty Ltd	Trusts & Holding Entities	12/31/06	147.9	94.9	902.5	462.1		-
PFG	Principal Financial Group, Inc.	Insurance	12/31/07	10906.5	860.3	154520.2	7421.7	278	153839060
PRA	ProAssurance Corp.	Insurance	12/31/07	706.1	168.2	4439.8	1255.1	140	19947640
PG	Procter & Gamble Co.	Chemicals	6/30/07	76476.0	10340.0	138014.0	66760.0		-
PGN	Progress Energy, Inc.	Electricity	12/31/07	9153.0	504.0	26286.0	8515.0	394	142507263
PGR	Progressive Corp. (OH)	Insurance	12/31/07	14686.8	1182.5	18843.1	4935.5	345	145451044
PLD	ProLogis	Property, Real Estate & Developmen	12/31/07	6204.7	1074.3	19724.0	7436.4	297	165340583
PRO	Pros Holdings Inc	IT & Technology	12/31/07	62.1	10.5	69.0	33.7		-
PHY	Prospect Street High Income Portfol	Trusts & Holding Entities	10/31/06	-	11.2	167.7	104.5	11	197979
CNN	Prospect Street Income Shares, Inc.	Trusts & Holding Entities	12/31/07	7.5	6.5	103.1	58.3	10	34053
PL	Protective Life Corp.	Insurance	12/31/07	3051.7	289.6	41786.0	2456.8	223	54557943
PL 09	Protective Life Insurance Co	Insurance	12/31/06	2483.6	264.9	39157.9	3253.5		-
PVX	Provident Energy Trust	Trusts & Holding Entities						62	3306481
PFS	Provident Financial Services Inc	Other Depository Banking	12/31/07	338.1	37.4	6359.4	1000.8	92	31361436
PRU	Prudential Financial, Inc.	Insurance	12/31/07	34401.0	3704.0	485814.0	23457.0	436	268364877
PUK	Prudential Plc	Insurance	12/31/04	33904.0	517.0	180006.0	4626.0	23	1667400
IIT	PT Indosat Tbk	Communications	12/31/06	12239407.0	1410093.0	34228658.0	-	28	7684184
POH	Public Service Company of Oklahoma	Electricity	12/31/07	1395.6	-24.1	2844.1	646.2	4	71500
PEG	Public Service Enterprise Group Inc	Electricity	12/31/07	12853.0	1335.0	28392.0	7299.0	335	135353060
PSA	Public Storage	Property, Real Estate & Developmen	12/31/07	1816.4	457.5	10643.1	8763.1	196	63237551
PSD	Puget Energy, Inc. (Holding Co.)	Electricity	12/31/07	3220.1	184.5	7598.7	2522.0	181	47834726
PHM	Pulte Homes, Inc.	Building & General Construction	12/31/07	9263.1	-2255.8	10225.7	4320.2	339	92573148
PCF	Putnam High Income Securities Fun	Trusts & Holding Entities						16	1402724
PMM	Putnam Managed Municipal Income	Trusts & Holding Entities	10/31/06	-	24.1	558.8	373.8	27	1115398
PIM	Putnam Master Intermediate Incom	Trusts & Holding Entities						41	5258350

\	EARNINGS PER SHARE	\	\	\	\	P/E RATIO	\	DIVIDENDS PER SHARE	\	\	AV. YLD %	DIV. DECLARED	\	PRICE RANGE	\
QUARTERLY			ANNUAL					PER SHARE						2007	
1st	2nd	3rd	2007	2006	2005			2007	2006	2005	%	AMOUNT	PAYABLE		
-	-	1.10	1.05	1.07		12.9 -	11.6	0.92	0.92	0.92	6.7	0.077M	2/1/08	14.2 -	12.7
-	-	1.08	1.05	1.04		13.4 -	11.7	0.84	0.93	0.97	6.1	0.07M	4/1/08	14.5 -	12.6
-	-	1.07	1.11	1.14		-		0.87	0.96	0.96	-	0.06M	12/31/07	-	
-	-	-	1.42	1.30		-		-	1.34	1.55	-	0.1063M	4/1/08	16.2 -	12.8
-	-	1.50	1.57	1.50		12.0 -	9.9	1.69	1.66	2.29	10.1	0.115M	4/1/08	10.1 -	14.8
-	-	2.13	1.91	1.36		10.2 -	9.2	2.01	1.66	1.33	9.8	0.1527M	12/7/07	21.6 -	19.6
-	-	1.04	0.80	-		-		2.44	2.11	-	-	0.1834M	4/1/08	-	
-	-	1.68	1.66	1.67		9.2 -	7.7	1.79	1.50	1.96	12.3	0.1219M	12/31/07	15.4 -	12.9
-	-	-	0.81	0.85		-		-	0.58	0.92	-	0.06M	3/3/08	14.8 -	11.9
-	-	1.07	1.10	1.15		13.9 -	12.1	0.97	0.97	0.97	6.9	0.0813M	2/1/08	14.9 -	12.9
-	-	1.13	1.08	1.11		13.2 -	11.5	0.81	0.95	1.01	5.7	0.065M	4/1/08	15.0 -	13.0
-	-	1.17	1.12	1.14		-		0.84	0.89	1.00	-	0.07M	12/31/07	-	
-	-	1.10	1.07	1.06		13.5 -	11.4	0.80	0.92	0.97	5.7	0.0663M	4/1/08	14.8 -	12.5
-	-	0.97	0.98	1.01		14.8 -	12.3	0.79	0.89	0.90	5.9	0.057M	2/1/08	14.4 -	11.9
-	-	1.03	1.07	1.13		-		0.78	0.88	0.96	-	0.0525M	12/31/07	-	
-	-	0.65	0.75	0.82		19.8 -	14.6	0.83	0.89	0.99	7.2	0.065M	2/14/08	12.9 -	9.5
														20.3 -	9.4
0.05	0.16	0.08	-0.02	1.56	0.14	-		-	-	-	-	-		-	
0.16	0.78	2.07	3.05	3.27	1.82	14.9 -	12.1	2.10	2.02	1.93	5.2	0.525Q	0/3/00	48.4 -	36.9
-	-	-	2.30	2.20	1.33	8.7 -	8.7	1.91	1.67	0.92	9.5	0.145M	3/31/08	20.0 -	20.0
-	-	1.88	1.88	1.90		9.2 -	7.7	1.74	1.88	1.78	10.7	0.0507M	12/20/07	17.4 -	14.5
-	-	0.97	0.98	0.95		15.6 -	11.7	0.89	0.75	0.79	6.9	0.112M	3/31/08	15.2 -	11.3
-	-	1.16	1.17	1.26		13.0 -	11.0	0.86	0.99	1.21	6.1	0.075M	12/20/07	15.1 -	12.8
-	-	1.02	1.02	1.14		14.9 -	12.8	0.77	0.89	1.16	5.4	0.07M	1/31/08	15.2 -	13.1
0.24	0.30	0.84	3.06	5.81	3.80	12.1 -	9.7	0.27	0.25	0.22	0.8	0.14S	4/14/08	36.9 -	29.7
0.74	0.52	0.26	2.43	12.40	2.10	23.7 -	15.5	-	-	-	-	-		57.6 -	37.6
0.05	0.09	0.58	1.66	0.47	2.37	28.7 -	23.0	1.00	1.00	1.04	3.1	0.75Q	3/12/08	46.9 -	39.2
0.61	0.78	0.66	5.04	2.88	2.72	7.5 -	6.0	3.28	2.87	2.58	9.7	0.85Q	2/14/08	37.8 -	30.3
0.28	0.35	0.45	1.99	7.64	-2.75	14.1 -	7.5	-	-	-	-	-		28.0 -	14.9
0.31	0.34	0.39	1.04	1.66	1.92	45.7 -	31.7	0.20	0.20	0.15	0.5	0.05Q	3/10/08	47.6 -	33.0
1.08	1.34	1.37	-	4.96	-3.01	-		-	0.32	0.32	-	0.08Q	3/31/08	-	
0.04	0.06	0.08	0.15	0.07	-0.02	107.6 -	53.3	-	-	-	-	-		16.1 -	8.0
0.25	0.34	0.34	1.61	1.75	1.92	24.4 -	17.7	1.68	1.60	1.52	5.1	0.42Q	2/29/08	39.3 -	28.5
1.16	0.95	-1.04	-10.81	4.57	4.10	-		0.21	0.21	0.20	0.5	0.0126Q	4/15/08	44.6 -	36.1
1.46	1.22	1.19	4.35	8.73	4.55	13.5 -	11.4	2.44	2.15	2.00	4.5	0.45Q	4/1/08	58.7 -	49.4
0.38	0.26	0.11	0.96	1.73	1.00	27.0 -	19.7	0.91	0.86	0.77	4.2	0.23Q	5/2/08	25.9 -	15.8
0.34	0.62	1.06	3.07	2.58	3.27	22.5 -	13.0	1.36	1.24	1.12	2.7	0.38Q	2/15/08	68.9 -	40.0
0.82	1.09	1.08	3.73	2.87	1.83	11.4 -	7.4	0.20	0.20	0.20	0.6	0.05Q	1/11/08	42.0 -	27.5
0.08	-0.06	0.02	0.12	1.33	0.51	79.7 -	45.0	-	-	-	-	0.0625Q	12/16/02	9.6 -	5.4
0.08	-0.04	-0.36	0.02	-1.17	-0.12	-		-	-	-	-	-		-	
0.88	0.73	0.32	2.33	1.14	-	-		0.93	0.68	-	-	0.235Q	4/15/08	-	
-	-	-	-	-	0.56	-		-	-	-	-	-		10.7 -	8.5
				42115.0	60790.00	-		-	-	-	-	-		47.5 -	28.0
0.51	1.40	0.21	3.88	2.15	3.34	9.2 -	6.8	1.80	1.80	1.80	6.0	0.4766Q	3/31/08	35.6 -	26.3
0.62	0.88	0.75	3.40	1.98	1.63	8.2 -	3.8	0.30	0.20	0.20	1.7	0.1Q	5/8/08	28.0 -	12.8
-0.76	0.87	1.04	1.43	3.79	1.13	36.3 -	24.3	1.90	1.70	1.60	4.7	0.81Q	3/19/08	-	-
1.17	1.50	1.15	5.03	4.27	3.49	13.6 -	11.0	2.04	1.91	1.86	3.3	0.52Q	3/12/08	68.5 -	55.2
0.52	0.88	0.84	3.35	2.24	1.77	8.0 -	6.0	1.22	1.10	0.96	5.2	0.335Q	4/1/08	26.9 -	20.0
-	-	-	-	-	-	-		4.50	4.50	4.50	5.7	0.0900Q	4/1/08	86.0	73.3
-	-	-	-	-	-	-		-	-	-	-	0.4375Q	10/15/07	-	
0.81	0.89	0.94	3.62	3.00	2.20	12.7 -	9.6	1.20	1.00	0.72	3.0	0.375Q	3/17/08	46.0 -	34.7
1.62	1.68	1.76	4.59	2.58	-0.01	7.3 -	4.6	0.12	0.11	0.06	0.5	0.03Q	3/31/08	33.7 -	21.0
0.13	0.09	0.15	0.52	0.37	0.66	23.3 -	14.7	-	-	-	-	-		12.1 -	7.6
1.08	0.99	0.88	-	3.51	2.29	-		-	-	0.60	-	0.3U	1/13/06	38.4 -	22.1
0.58	0.83	2.25	4.43	1.72	0.80	4.6 -	3.4	-	-	-	-	-		20.5 -	15.1
2.40	0.17	8.92	11.14	0.90	12.90	2.1 -	0.9	2.15	-	-	13.0	0.07Q	6/01/08	29.0 -	10.0
-0.22	-0.48	-2.85	-	2.13	0.09	-		-	-	-	-	0.4375Q	9/27/07	-	
0.95	1.12	0.87	3.09	3.74	3.11	13.3 -	10.4	0.90	0.80	0.65	2.5	0.4040Q	3/31/08	41.2 -	32.2
1.02	1.05	1.23	4.78	6.85	3.54	5.5 -	5.3	-	-	-	-	-		10.W	90.9
0.92	0.98	-	3.04	2.64	2.66	-		1.28	1.15	1.03	-	0.35Q	2/15/08	-	
1.08	-0.75	1.24	1.96	2.28	2.82	24.4 -	20.7	2.44	2.42	2.36	5.6	0.615Q	2/1/08	47.8 -	40.5
0.49	0.39	0.42	1.65	2.10	1.75	14.7 -	11.2	2.00	0.03	0.03	9.4	0.145A	1/31/08	24.2 -	10.5
0.89	1.50	1.12	3.94	3.32	1.76	11.0 -	7.2	1.84	1.60	1.48	5.3	0.4219Q	3/31/08	43.3 -	28.4
0.11	0.06	0.13	0.45	0.32	0.16	-		-	-	-	-	-		-	
-	-	-	-	0.35	0.36	-		-	0.26	0.29	-	0.0235M	2/29/08	3.6 -	2.7
-	-	-	0.66	0.63	0.58	10.1 -	8.2	0.45	0.45	0.46	7.4	0.1125Q	4/15/08	6.7 -	5.4
1.27	0.91	1.02	1.05	3.94	3.46	10.6 -	8.4	0.89	0.84	0.76	2.3	0.225Q	3/1/08	42.9 -	33.9
-	-	-	-	-	-	-		-	-	-	-	0.12M	4/15/08	9.6 -	7.6
0.18	0.22	0.14	0.63	0.87	0.88	31.3 -	26.3	0.42	0.39	0.32	2.3	0.11Q	2/28/08	19.7 -	16.6
2.18	1.80	1.88	7.61	6.50	6.34	7.2 -	5.4	1.15	0.95	0.78	2.5	1.15A	12/21/07	55.1 -	41.0
-	-	-	-	0.36	0.32	-		-	-	-	-	-		20.3 -	14.7
-	-	-	-	258.82	309.04	-		-	-	-	-	-		33.3 -	17.8
-	-	-	-	-	-	-		4.00	4.00	4.00	15.7	1.0	1/2/08	26.6 -	22.1
0.65	0.54	1.00	2.62	1.47	1.36	10.0 -	7.4	1.17	1.14	1.12	5.4	0.3225Q	3/31/08	26.2 -	19.5
-0.03	0.08	0.51	1.17	0.33	1.97	49.0 -	34.5	1.00	2.00	1.90	2.1	0.4375Q	3/31/08	57.4 -	40.4
0.68	0.33	0.10	1.56	1.88	1.51	15.9 -	13.2	1.00	1.00	1.00	4.4	0.25Q	2/15/08	24.7 -	20.5
-0.34	-2.01	-3.12	-8.94	2.66	5.68	-		0.16	0.16	0.13	0.6	0.04Q	4/1/08	32.5 -	21.4
-	-	-	-	-	-	-		-	-	-	-	0.0459M	1/2/08	8.2 -	7.0
-	-	-	-	0.53	0.51	-		-	0.41	0.45	-	0.0341M	3/3/08	7.8 -	6.6
-	-	-	-	-	-	-		-	-	-	-	0.033M	3/3/08	6.9 -	6.2

SYMBOL	COMPANY	NATURE OF BUSINESS	FISCAL YEAR-END	TOTAL REV. $MILL	NET INCOME $MILL	TOTAL ASSETS $MILL	NET STK EQUITY $MILL	NO OF INST	INST. HOLDINGS (SHARES)
PMO	Putnam Municipal Opportunities Tru	Trusts & Holding Entities	4/30/07		13.7	322.7	200.2	16	225388
PPT	Putnam Premier Income Trust	Trusts & Holding Entities						48	9593943
QXM	Qiao Xing Mobile Communication C	Communications	12/31/06		-19.5		1040.3		
QI	Qimonda AG	IT & Technology	9/30/06	3815.0		5861.0	3871.0		
KWR	Quaker Chemical Corp.	Petroleum and Coal Products	12/31/07	545.6	15.5	399.0	130.4	60	5196534
NX	Quanex Corp	Metal Works	10/31/07	2049.0	134.6	1334.8	883.1	159	24240631
PWR	Quanta Services, Inc.	Electrical	12/31/07	2656.0	136.0	3387.8	2185.1	141	96239231
QTM	Quantum Corp.	IT & Technology	3/31/07	1016.2	-64.1	1125.8	254.4	99	154371092
DGX	Quest Diagnostics, Inc.	Diagnostic Services	12/31/07	6704.9	339.9	8565.7	3324.2	468	142921982
STR	Questar Corp.	Oil and Gas	12/31/07	2726.6	507.4	5944.2	2577.9	308	56410985
KWK	Quicksilver Resources, Inc.	Oil and Gas	12/31/07	561.3	479.4	2775.8	1068.4	138	58879697
ZQK	Quiksilver, Inc.	Apparel	10/31/07	2426.0	-121.1	2641.5	886.6	198	90978684
LQU	Quilmes Industrial S.A. (Quinsa), So	Food	12/31/04	765.2	81.7	1312.5	576.7	24	2131530
Q	Qwest Communications Internation	Communications	12/31/07	13778.0	2917.0	22532.0	563.0	298	1319856348
RDN	Radian Group, Inc.	Insurance	12/31/07	201.1	-1290.3	8210.2	2720.7	252	77592675
RSH	RadioShack Corp.	Retail - Appliances and Electrical	12/31/07	4251.7	236.8	1989.6	769.7	260	114382151
RAS	RAIT Financial Trust	Property, Real Estate & Developmen	12/31/07	205.9	-367.5	11057.6	579.2	82	12100605
RAH	Ralcorp Holdings, Inc. (New) (Unite	Food	9/30/07	2233.4	31.9	1853.1	483.4	173	24607839
RPT	Ramco-Gershenson Properties Trus	Property, Real Estate & Developmen	12/31/07	153.3	38.7	1088.5	281.4	82	13213064
RRC	Range Resources Corp	Oil and Gas	12/31/07	862.1	230.6	4016.5	1728.0	160	72185885
RJF	Raymond James Financial, Inc.	Finance Intermediaries & Services	9/30/07	3109.6	250.4	16254.2	1757.8	181	45634002
RYN	Rayonier Inc.	Property, Real Estate & Developmen	12/31/07	1224.7	174.3	2079.0	981.1	203	31259008
RTN	Raytheon Co.	Instruments and Related Products	12/31/07	21301.0	2578.0	23281.0	12542.0	465	331149860
O	Realty Income Corp.	Property, Real Estate & Developmen	12/31/07	296.5	140.4	3077.4	1538.1	115	20819846
RHT	Red Hat Inc	IT & Technology	2/28/07	400.6	59.9	1785.9	821.2	152	142488821
RLH	Red Lions Hotels Corp	Hospitality & Tourism	12/31/06	170.4	-0.6	351.4	183.8		
FRZ	Reddy Ice Holdings Inc	Food	12/31/07	339.0	10.3	607.6	140.0		
RWT	Redwood Trust Inc.	Property, Real Estate & Developmen	12/31/07		-1108.6	9938.5	-718.3	139	18666681
ENL	Reed Elsevier N.V.	Non-Media Publishing	12/31/04		338.0	1245.0	1173.0		
RUK	Reed Elsevier Plc (New)	Non-Media Publishing	12/31/04	4812.0	459.0	7952.0	1677.0		
RGC	Regal Entertainment Group	Movies & Film	12/27/07	2661.2	363.0	2634.9	-119.3	147	70576422
RBC	Regal-Beloit Corp.	Electrical	12/29/07	1802.5	118.3	1862.2	858.0	125	24708540
REG	Regency Centers Corp.	Property, Real Estate & Developmen	12/31/07	451.5	203.7	4143.0	1870.4	181	65086237
RF	Regions Financial Corp (New)	Commercial Banking	12/31/07	10930.5	1251.1	141041.7	19823.0	355	134618838
RGS	Regis Corp.	Personal Services	6/30/07	2626.6	83.2	2132.1	913.3	202	37040836
RHB	RehabCare Group Inc.	Hospitals & Health Care	12/31/07	711.7	12.7	408.6	244.0	120	15870712
RGA	Reinsurance Group of America, Inc.	Insurance	12/31/07	5718.4	293.8	21598.0	3189.8	16	2585540
RS	Reliance Steel & Aluminum Co.	Specialist Equipment Supplies	12/31/07	7265.6	408.0	3983.5	2106.2	136	21824055
RRI	Reliant Energy Inc (New)	Electricity	12/31/07	11208.7	365.1	9456.5	4477.0	210	228932701
RNR	RenaissanceRe Holdings Ltd.	Insurance	12/31/06	1840.7	797.1	7769.0	3280.5	146	60688436
SOL	Renesola Ltd.	Electrical							
REP	Repsol YPF, S.A.	Oil and Gas	12/31/03	37206.0	2020.0	38033.0		105	29620315
RSG	Republic Services, Inc.	Sanitation Services	12/31/07	3176.2	290.2	4467.8	1303.8	236	130449092
RMD	ResMed Inc.	Medical Instruments & Equipment	6/30/07	716.3	66.3	1252.0	931.2	176	25552764
RSO	Resource Capital Corp	Property, Real Estate & Developmen	12/31/07	177.0	8.9	2072.1	271.6		
RVI	Retail Ventures Inc	Retail - General	2/3/07	3067.7	-150.9	1267.2	91.6	70	12297004
REV	Revlon Inc	Chemicals	12/31/07	1400.1	-16.1	889.3	-1082.0	87	110543846
RSC	Rex Stores Corp.	Retail - Appliances and Electrical	1/31/07	347.3	11.4	335.2	230.8	47	8002775
RAI	Reynolds American Inc	Tobacco Products	12/31/07	9023.0	1308.0	18629.0	7466.0	265	84398999
RTP	Rio Tinto Plc	Non-Precious Metals	12/31/04	12954.0	-53.0	26308.0	12591.0	134	28051753
RMG	RiskMetrics Group Inc	Miscellaneous Business Services	12/31/07	240.3	2.4	743.2	136.1		
RBA	Ritchie Bros. Auctioneers, Inc.	Miscellaneous Business Services	12/31/07	261.0	57.2	554.2	368.6	52	16519026
RAD	Rite Aid Corp.	Retail - Miscellaneous	3/3/07	17507.7	26.8	7091.0	1662.8	164	167077341
BDF	Rivus Bond Fund	Trusts & Holding Entities							
RLI	RLI Corp. (United States)	Insurance	12/31/07	652.3	175.9	2626.5	774.4	122	20093931
RMA	RMK Advantage Income Fund Inc	Trusts & Holding Entities	3/31/07		50.9	572.7	417.0	7	493132
RMH	RMK High Income Fund Inc	Trusts & Holding Entities	3/31/07		39.8	422.0	303.3	6	100297
RHY	RMK Multi-Sector High Income Fun	Trusts & Holding Entities	3/31/07		58.5	644.9	468.9		
RSF	RMK Strategic Income Fund Inc	Trusts & Holding Entities	3/31/07		44.2	504.6	359.2	3	117543
RBN	Robbins & Myers, Inc.	Industrial Machinery and Equipment	8/31/07	695.4	50.7	816.1	412.5	83	10127074
RHI	Robert Half International Inc.	Human Resources Services	12/31/07	4645.7	296.2	1450.3	984.0	256	147578109
RKT	Rock-Tenn Co. (United States)	Paper Products	9/30/07	2315.8	81.7	1800.7	589.0	92	19292635
ROK	Rockwell Automation, Inc.	Instruments and Related Products	9/30/07	5003.9	1487.8	4545.8	1742.8	396	112449266
COL	Rockwell Collins, Inc.	Aviation	9/30/07	4415.0	585.0	3750.0	1573.0	301	108462083
ROC	Rockwood Holdings Inc	Chemicals	12/31/07	3136.4	317.1	5514.9	1571.6		
RCI	Rogers Communications Inc.	Communications	12/31/07	10123.0	637.0	15325.0	4624.0	74	104818635
ROG	Rogers Corp.	Chemicals	12/31/07	431.4	22.1	470.9	364.0	99	14319108
ROH	Rohm & Haas Co.	Chemicals	12/31/07	8897.0	661.0	10208.0	3146.0	295	125716329
ROL	Rollins, Inc.	Miscellaneous Business Services	12/31/07	894.9	64.7	475.2	233.6	111	24753423
ROP	Roper Industries, Inc (New)	Industrial Machinery and Equipment	12/31/07	2102.0	250.0	3453.2	1789.8	203	40282427
ROS	Rostelecom Open Joint Stock Co of	Communications	12/31/04	37318.0	4266.0	64420.0	50838.0	45	10809576
RDC	Rowan Cos., Inc.	Oil and Gas	12/31/07	2095.0	483.8	3875.3	2348.4	252	90196015
RY	Royal Bank of Canada	Commercial Banking	10/31/07	41307.0	5492.0	600346.0	24439.0	111	189459386
RBS	Royal Bank of Scotland Group Plc	Commercial Banking	12/31/04	32878.0	4856.0	588122.0	37397.0		
RCL	Royal Caribbean Cruises Ltd.	Hospitality & Tourism	12/31/06	5229.6	633.9	13393.1	6091.6	220	114880895
RDS A	Royal Dutch Shell Plc	Oil and Gas							
RMT	Royce Micro-Cap Trust, Inc.	Trusts & Holding Entities	12/31/07	5.3	-0.2	441.5	331.5		
RVT	Royce Value Trust, Inc.	Trusts & Holding Entities						0	0
RES	RPC, Inc.	Oil and Gas	12/31/07	690.2	87.0	701.0	409.3	80	11247129
RPM	RPM International Inc (DE)	Chemicals	5/31/07	3338.8	208.3	3333.1	1086.9	232	63650333

EARNINGS PER SHARE QUARTERLY			ANNUAL			P/E RATIO		DIVIDENDS PER SHARE			AV. YLD %	DIV. DECLARED		PRICE RANGE 2007
1st	2nd	3rd	2007	2006	2005			2007	2006	2005	%	AMOUNT	PAYABLE	
-	-	-	0.89	0.86	0.91	15.5 -	13.3	0.57	0.68	0.87	4.5	0.0479M	3/3/08	13.8 - 11.9
-	-	-	-	-	-	-	-	-	-	-	-	0.033M	2/1/08	6.8 - 6.0
-	-	-	-	7.65	5.77	-	-	-	-	-	-	-	-	
-	-	-	-	0.24	0.06	-	-	-	-	-	-	-	-	
0.35	0.41	0.31	1.53	1.18	0.17	19.8 -	14.4	0.86	0.86	0.86	3.4	0.23Q	4/30/08	30.4 - 22.1
0.08	-	-	3.41	4.08	3.95	9.1 -	5.2	0.56	0.48	0.37	2.6	0.14Q	3/28/08	31.1 - 17.7
0.23	0.17	0.31	0.89	0.15	0.25	-10.4 -	5.4	-	-	-	-	-	-	9.3 - 4.8
-0.11	-0.10	-0.01	-0.33	-0.23	-0.02	-	-	-	-	-	-	-	-	4.2 - 2.1
0.54	0.73	0.50	1.74	2.94	2.66	27.8 -	20.8	0.40	0.39	0.34	0.9	0.1Q	4/18/08	48.3 - 36.1
0.86	0.64	0.64	2.88	2.54	1.87	8.9 -	5.9	0.48	0.47	0.45	2.4	0.1225Q	3/10/08	25.8 - 17.0
0.14	0.19	0.17	2.86	0.57	0.54	4.3 -	1.9	-	-	-	-	-	-	12.4 - 5.4
-0.18	-	-	-0.98	0.73	0.86	-	-	-	-	-	-	-	-	15.6 - 8.2
-	-	-	-	1.69	1.29	-	-	-	-	-	-	-	-	20.2 - 14.8
0.12	0.13	1.08	1.52	0.30	-0.42	3.2 -	1.7	-	-	-	-	0.08A	2/21/08	4.9 - 2.6
1.42	0.26	-8.82	-16.22	7.08	5.91	-	-	0.08	0.08	0.08	0.2	0.02Q	3/27/08	54.0 - 41.0
0.31	0.34	0.34	1.74	0.54	1.79	20.4 -	15.0	0.25	0.25	0.25	0.8	0.25A	12/19/07	35.4 - 26.2
0.34	0.45	-4.02	-6.26	2.30	2.57	-	-	2.56	1.95	2.43	9.7	0.5547Q	3/31/08	29.6 - 22.8
1.61	-	-	1.17	2.41	2.34	36.1 -	25.2	-	-	1.00	-	1.U	10/22/04	42.0 - 20.6
1.25	0.56	0.15	1.91	1.73	0.70	17.2 -	11.8	1.85	1.79	1.75	6.8	0.4625Q	4/1/08	32.9 - 22.5
0.51	0.43	0.39	1.54	1.14	0.86	9.3 -	4.1	0.13	0.09	0.06	1.4	0.04Q	3/31/08	14.3 - 6.3
0.47	-	-	2.11	1.85	1.33	9.9 -	6.9	0.40	0.32	0.21	2.3	0.11Q	4/16/08	20.8 - 14.6
0.45	0.42	0.90	2.21	2.26	2.36	14.9 -	11.7	1.04	1.88	1.71	6.6	0.5Q	3/31/08	32.9 - 25.8
0.76	2.97	0.68	5.79	2.85	1.92	7.1 -	5.1	1.02	0.96	0.88	3.0	0.28Q	4/29/08	41.2 - 29.7
0.30	0.31	0.28	1.16	1.11	1.12	22.5 -	15.6	1.57	1.45	1.35	7.2	0.1406M	3/17/08	26.1 - 18.1
0.00	0.00	0.10	0.20	0.41	0.24	99.1 -	39.1	-	-	-	-	-	-	28.7 - 11.3
-	-	-	-	-	-	-	-	-	-	-	-	-	-	8.4 - 4.7
-0.10	0.11	0.36	-	-0.03	0.34	-	-	-	-	-	-	0.42Q	4/15/08	
-0.47	0.48	0.75	0.47	0.68	-0.72	-	-	1.66	1.58	0.59	-	0.75Q	4/21/08	66.0 - 43.5
0.66	0.41	-2.18	-39.70	4.85	7.96	-	-	5.00	5.80	5.80	8.9	-	-	33.7 - 28.4
-	-	-	-	0.59	0.43	-	-	-	-	-	-	-	-	45.9 - 38.5
-	-	-	-	0.25	0.18	-	-	-	-	-	-	-	-	
1.48	0.33	0.36	2.28	0.56	0.59	10.1 -	7.7	3.20	1.20	1.20	16.0	0.3Q	3/20/08	23.1 - 17.5
0.80	1.06	0.92	3.49	3.28	2.25	8.4 -	5.5	0.59	0.55	0.51	2.6	0.15Q	4/18/08	29.2 - 19.3
0.75	0.64	0.53	2.65	2.89	2.23	20.9 -	13.2	2.64	2.38	2.20	6.0	0.4188Q	3/31/08	55.4 - 35.1
0.45	0.63	0.56	1.76	2.67	2.15	20.3 -	16.8	1.46	1.76	1.36	4.4	0.38Q	4/1/08	35.8 - 29.6
0.46	0.51	-	1.82	2.36	1.39	25.6 -	21.2	0.16	0.16	0.16	0.4	0.04Q	2/19/08	46.7 - 38.5
0.12	0.09	0.22	0.73	0.42	-1.01	39.5 -	25.8	-	-	-	-	-	-	28.8 - 18.8
1.19	1.20	1.19	4.57	4.57	3.52	13.7 -	12.3	0.36	0.36	0.36	0.6	0.09Q	2/25/08	62.5 - 58.1
1.46	1.61	1.22	5.36	4.82	3.11	3.9 -	2.6	0.32	0.22	0.19	1.8	0.1Q	3/28/08	20.9 - 13.7
0.74	-0.83	0.46	1.04	-1.07	-1.09	13.1 -	6.5	-	-	-	-	-	-	13.7 - 6.7
2.63	2.53	1.85	-	10.57	-3.99	-	-	-	0.84	0.80	-	0.22Q	12/31/07	56.3 - 46.8
-	-	-	-	-	-	-	-	-	-	-	-	-	-	26.1 - 19.3
-	-	-	-	2.56	2.50	-	-	-	-	-	-	-	-	
0.28	0.45	0.35	1.51	1.38	1.17	15.0 -	11.0	0.55	0.40	0.35	2.9	0.17Q	4/15/08	22.7 - 16.6
0.31	0.34	-	0.85	1.16	0.51	00.0 -	22.0	-	-	-	-	-	-	25.8 - 20.3
0.38	0.39	-0.56	0.36	0.87	0.71	-	-	1.62	1.49	0.86	-	0.41Q	4/28/08	
0.05	1.81	1.20	-3.35	-2.94	-0.57	-	-	-	-	-	-	-	-	9.7 - 4.7
-0.07	-0.02	-0.02	-0.03	-0.00	0.23	-	-	-	-	-	-	-	-	3.7 - 2.1
0.64	0.48	1.25	0.98	2.31	2.17	18.5 -	11.5	-	-	-	-	-	-	10.1 - 11.3
1.11	1.10	1.21	4.40	4.10	3.53	9.1 -	6.1	3.20	2.75	2.10	9.7	0.85Q	4/1/08	40.2 - 20.9
-	-	-	5.66	5.56	3.81	21.1 -	15.3	-	-	-	-	-	-	110.4 - 86.4
-	-	-	0.04	0.33	0.32	-	-	-	-	-	-	-	-	
0.50	0.76	0.42	-	1.64	1.54	-	-	-	0.78	0.58	-	0.24Q	3/14/08	33.2 - 25.1
0.04	-0.10	-0.12	-0.01	1.89	0.47	-	-	-	-	-	-	0.3438Q	2/1/08	6.1 - 3.4
-	-	-	-	-	-	-	-	-	-	-	-	0.2875Q	11/1/07	19.9 - 16.9
1.32	2.04	2.56	7.30	5.27	4.07	5.9 -	4.6	0.07	0.75	0.63	2.3	0.25Q	4/18/08	43.8 - 00.6
-	-	-	1.66	1.90	0.57	9.7 -	9.2	1.76	2.10	0.48	11.2	0.1M	2/19/08	16.1 - 15.3
-	-	-	1.70	1.09	2.15	10.6 -	0.5	1.76	2.58	2.68	10.5	0.1M	2/19/08	18.6 - 14.9
-	-	-	1.81	0.21	-	-	-	-	-	-	-	0.11M	2/20/08	
-	-	-	1.63	1.78	1.76	10.7 -	8.7	1.76	2.27	1.68	11.2	0.1M	2/20/08	17.4 - 14.3
0.40	0.47	-	1.48	-0.00	-0.01	8.3 -	5.9	0.13	0.11	0.11	1.2	0.0375Q	5/8/08	12.2 - 8.7
0.42	0.44	0.46	1.81	1.65	1.36	17.0 -	11.5	0.40	0.32	0.28	1.5	0.11Q	3/14/08	30.7 - 20.0
0.46	-	-	2.07	0.77	0.49	8.6 -	6.4	0.39	0.36	0.36	2.5	0.1Q	2/18/08	17.8 - 13.3
1.04	-	-	9.23	3.37	2.88	5.4 -	3.1	1.16	0.90	0.78	3.1	0.29Q	3/10/08	49.5 - 28.6
0.84	0.82	0.86	3.45	2.73	2.20	11.8 -	8.5	0.64	0.56	0.48	1.9	0.16Q	3/3/08	40.9 - 29.4
1.93	0.37	0.32	4.16	1.37	1.52	-	-	-	-	-	-	-	-	
0.26	-0.09	0.42	0.99	0.97	-0.07	13.2 -	8.4	0.41	0.08	0.06	4.2	0.25Q	4/1/08	13.1 - 8.3
0.54	-0.26	0.51	1.32	2.69	0.98	53.6 -	30.4	-	-	-	-	-	-	70.8 - 40.1
0.87	0.74	0.61	3.13	3.32	2.85	14.4 -	11.6	1.44	1.28	1.12	3.6	0.37Q	3/1/08	46.3 - 36.2
0.19	0.31	0.28	0.64	0.84	0.76	18.8 -	14.9	0.20	0.17	0.13	1.8	0.0625Q	3/10/08	12.0 - 9.6
0.56	0.66	0.70	2.68	2.13	1.74	11.8 -	8.4	0.26	0.23	0.21	1.0	0.0725Q	4/25/08	31.7 - 22.6
-	-	-	-	1.50	1.01	-	-	-	-	-	-	-	-	15.8 - 10.1
0.77	1.14	1.16	4.31	2.85	2.08	6.3 -	4.8	0.40	0.55	0.50	1.7	0.1Q	2/29/08	27.1 - 20.6
1.14	0.98	1.06	4.19	3.59	2.56	6.4 -	5.0	1.82	1.44	1.18	7.7	0.2938Q	2/22/08	26.9 - 21.1
-	-	-	0.76	1.93	1.68	-	-	-	-	-	-	-	-	
0.04	0.60	1.84	-	2.94	3.26	-	-	-	0.60	0.56	-	0.15Q	1/8/08	55.4 - 35.0
-	-	-	4.99	0.40	3.78	-	-	-	-	-	-	-	-	
-	-	-	0.00	0.01	0.01	-	-	1.35	1.55	1.85	5.5	0.375Q	3/24/08	26.3 - 21.5
-	-	-	0.13	0.01	0.01	-	-	-	1.78	1.61	-	0.3688Q	3/24/08	25.6 - 21.4
0.29	0.24	0.15	0.89	1.13	0.67	9.2 -	3.6	0.20	0.13	0.07	4.3	0.06Q	3/10/08	8.2 - 3.2
0.53	0.43	0.10	1.64	-0.65	0.86	12.1 -	8.2	0.69	0.63	0.59	4.2	0.19Q	1/31/08	19.8 - 13.5

SYMBOL	COMPANY	NATURE OF BUSINESS	FISCAL YEAR-END	TOTAL REV. $MILL	NET INCOME $MILL	TOTAL ASSETS $MILL	NET STK EQUITY $MILL	NO OF INST	INST. HOLDINGS (SHARES)
RRR	RSC Holdings Inc	General Construction Supplies & Ser	12/31/07	1769.2	123.3	3460.3	-44.1	-	-
RTI	RTI International Metals, Inc. (Unite	Metal Works	12/31/07	626.8	92.6	755.3	575.8	100	19902906
RT	Ruby Tuesday, Inc.	Hospitality & Tourism	6/5/07	1410.2	91.7	1229.9	439.3	197	63298457
RDK	Ruddick Corp.	Retail - Food & Beverage	9/30/07	3639.2	80.7	1529.7	736.6	133	26781755
RUS	Russ Berrie & Co., Inc.	Consumer Accessories	12/31/06	294.8	-9.4	303.8	190.7	81	11087894
R	Ryder System, Inc.	Road Transport	12/31/07	6566.0	253.9	6854.6	1887.6	244	61801305
RYL	Ryland Group, Inc. (United States)	Building & General Construction	12/31/07	3032.6	-333.5	2542.2	1124.7	213	44428227
BEP	S&P 500 Covered Call Fund Inc	Trusts & Holding Entities							
GRE	S&P 500 Geared Fund Inc	Trusts & Holding Entities	12/31/07	1.9	0.8	81.1	69.0	1	21295
SBR	Sabine Royalty Trust	Miscellaneous	12/31/07	59.3	57.1	6.6	5.8	42	857461
SDA	Sadia S.A. (New)	Food	12/31/07	8623.2	689.0	8181.4	2910.5	7	160019
SAF	SAFECO Corporation	Insurance	12/31/07	6208.8	707.8	12640.4	3392.6	301	91689396
SFE	Safeguard Scientifics, Inc.	Commercial Banking	12/31/07	176.1	-64.8	391.9	154.6	97	32859727
SWY	Safeway Inc.	Retail - Food & Beverage	12/29/07	42286.0	888.4	17651.0	6701.8	314	404959882
SGA	Saga Communications, Inc.	Media	12/31/07	144.0	11.0	337.6	149.1	63	15773423
SAI	SAIC Inc	Industrial Services	1/31/08	8935.0	415.0	4981.0	1901.0	-	-
SKS	Saks, Inc.	Retail - General	2/2/08	3282.6	47.5	2371.0	1175.6	179	98306022
CRM	Salesforce.Com Inc	IT & Technology	1/31/08	748.7	18.4	1089.6	452.1	91	41861933
SBH	Sally Beauty Holdings Inc	Retail - Miscellaneous	9/30/07	2513.8	44.5	1404.5	-767.7	-	-
SJT	San Juan Basin Royalty Trust	Miscellaneous	12/31/07	115.2	113.2	28.9	19.9	115	10021711
SNY	Sanofi-Aventis	Pharmaceuticals	12/31/04	15733.0	1986.0	85407.0	41523.0	205	122965947
SBP	Santander Bancorp (Holding Co)	Commercial Banking	12/31/07	822.3	-36.2	9160.2	536.5	54	3167969
SAP	Sap AG	IT & Technology	12/31/07	10242.0	1919.0	10366.0	6502.0	205	82967875
SPP	Sappi Ltd. (South Africa)	Wood Products	9/30/05	5018.0	-184.0	5889.0	1589.0	68	45499466
SLE	Sara Lee Corp.	Food	6/30/07	12278.0	504.0	12190.0	2615.0	584	466948802
SSL	Sasol Ltd.	Coal Mining	6/30/05	52497.0	9437.0	87869.0	43786.0	86	22404193
SAY	Satyam Computer Services Ltd	IT & Technology	3/31/07	66683.6	14046.2			71	15393718
SHS	Sauer-Danfoss Inc.	Purpose Machinery	12/31/07	1972.5	47.2	1500.4	525.5	64	7247083
BFS	Saul Centers, Inc.	Property, Real Estate & Developmen	12/31/07	150.6	36.7	727.4	148.8	2	127125
SCG	SCANA Corp (New)	Electricity	12/31/07	4621.0	320.0	10165.0	3066.0	244	48990623
SGK	Schawk, Inc.	Printing	12/31/06	548.4	28.4	538.2	268.9	43	2718304
SGP	Schering-Plough Corp.	Pharmaceuticals	12/31/07	12690.0	-1473.0	29156.0	10385.0	649	1109603200
WNI	Schiff Nutrition International Inc	Pharmaceuticals	5/31/07	172.7	12.4	145.1	124.1	-	-
SLB	Schlumberger Ltd. (Netherlands Ant	Oil and Gas	12/31/07	23708.0	5176.5	27853.4	14875.9	808	440426517
SWM	Schweitzer-Mauduit International, In	Paper Products	12/31/07	714.8	3.4	775.0	341.8	112	12737146
SCT	Scottish Re Group Ltd	Insurance	12/31/04	811.8	71.4	9021.1	862.7	-	-
SCT PRB	Scottish Re Group Ltd	Insurance	12/31/06	2451.5	-366.7	13436.1	1057.2	-	-
SMG	Scotts Miracle-Gro Co (The)	Chemicals	9/30/07	2871.8	113.4	2277.2	479.3	190	20124968
SKP	SCPIE Holdings Inc.	Insurance	12/31/07	143.7	17.9	672.7	232.0	34	3364028
SSP	Scripps (E.W.) Co. (New)	Media	12/31/07	2517.1	-1.6	4005.3	2450.4	177	87475535
CKH	SEACOR Holdings Inc	Shipping	12/31/07	1359.2	241.6	3568.7	1621.8	134	18914685
STX	Seagate Technology (New)	Office Equipment Supplies	6/29/07	11360.0	913.0	9472.0	4737.0	198	226300795
SEE	Sealed Air Corp. (New)	Paper Products	12/31/07	4651.2	353.0	5438.3	2019.6	284	71144055
ZZ	Sealy Corp.	Furniture and Fixtures	12/2/07	1702.1	79.4	1025.1	-129.4	-	-
SSW	Seaspan Corp	Misc. Transportation Services	12/31/04	35.9	6.1	476.3	-9.6	-	-
SCA	Security Capital Assurance Ltd	Insurance	12/31/06	238.6	117.4	2496.8	1366.5	-	-
SLS	Seligman Lasalle International Real	Trusts & Holding Entities							
SEL	Seligman Select Municipal Fund, In	Trusts & Holding Entities	12/31/06		6.4	228.1	152.9	13	472067
SMI	Semiconductor Manufacturing Inter	IT & Technology	12/31/06	1465.3	-44.1	4541.3	3007.4	30	5552787
SRE	Sempra Energy	Electricity	12/31/07	11438.0	1099.0	30091.0	8339.0	330	142317866
SNH	Senior Housing Properties Trust	Property, Real Estate & Developmen	12/31/07	188.0	85.3	1701.9	1249.4	129	32955896
SXT	Sensient Technologies Corp.	Food	12/31/07	1184.8	77.8	1564.2	814.4	162	41216122
SCI	Service Corp. International	Personal Services	12/31/07	2285.3	247.7	8932.2	1492.1	157	182130653
SGR	Shaw Group Inc.	Metal Products	8/31/07	5723.7	-19.0	3874.9	1236.5	150	64634758
SHW	Sherwin-Williams Co.	Retail - Hardware	12/31/07	8005.3	615.6	4855.3	1785.7	359	91807507
SHG	Shinhan Financial Group Co. Ltd.	Finance & Investment	12/31/06	9383971.0	1832718.0	77725169.0		32	1320896
SFL	Ship Finance International Ltd	Shipping	12/31/05	437.5	209.5	2393.9	561.5	103	16240203
SI	Siemens AG (Germany)	Electrical	9/30/05	75445.0	2248.0	86117.0	27678.0	130	19245824
SRP	Sierra Pacific Resources (New)	Electricity	12/31/07	3601.0		9464.8	2996.6	175	117804609
SIG	Signet Group Plc	Consumer Accessories	1/29/05	1615.5	134.8	1310.3	771.7	23	67377476
SLW	Silver Wheaton Corp	Mining							
SCR	Simcere Pharmaceutical Group	Pharmaceuticals	12/31/06		172.3		442.7	-	-
SPG	Simon Property Group, Inc. (New)	Property, Real Estate & Developmen	12/31/07	3650.8	491.2	23605.7	3563.4	1	7398
SSD	Simpson Manufacturing Co., Inc. (D	General Construction Supplies & Ser	12/31/07	817.0	68.7	817.7	723.4	139	30645178
SGF	Singapore Fund, Inc.	Trusts & Holding Entities	10/31/06		3.2	135.4	134.5	17	1920443
SHI	Sinopec Shanghai Petrochemical C	Petroleum and Coal Products	12/31/05	45823.0	1850.4	26810.4	19177.4	19	307723
SIX	Six Flags Inc	Sporting & Recreational	12/31/07	972.8	-253.2	2945.3	-252.6	123	68434333
SJW	SJW Corp.	Water Utilities	12/31/07	206.6	19.3	767.3	236.9	47	2223103
SKM	SK Telecom Co., Ltd. (South Korea	Communications	12/31/06	1027977.3	1451491.0	16239967.8		138	134788350
SKX	Skechers U S A, Inc.	Leather and Leather Products	12/31/07	1398.4	75.7	828.0	626.7	92	18690169
SKH	Skilled Healthcare Group Inc	Health	12/31/07	634.6	17.1	970.1	374.5	-	-
SKY	Skyline Corp.	Wood Products	5/31/07	365.5	2.6	214.9	177.8	62	5910840
SLG	SL Green Realty Corp.	Property, Real Estate & Developmen	12/31/07	1054.5	660.4	11430.1	3826.9	168	38370098
SLM	SLM Corp.	Credit & Lending	12/31/07	9171.1	-896.4	155565.0	5223.5	427	407649948
RCC	Small Cap Premium & Dividend Inc	Trusts & Holding Entities							
SNN	Smith & Nephew Plc (United Kingdo	Medical Instruments & Equipment	12/31/04	1249.0	138.0	1522.0	702.0	53	5216948
AOS	Smith (A.O.) Corp	Electrical	12/31/07	2312.1	88.2	1854.4	757.8	115	18633910
SII	Smith International, Inc. (United Stat	Oil and Gas	12/31/07	8764.3	647.1	6061.9	2594.9	267	93817213
SFD	Smithfield Foods, Inc.	Food	4/29/07	11911.1	166.8	6968.6	2240.8	242	66512561
SJM	Smucker (J.M.) Co. (United States)	Food	4/30/07	2148.0	157.2	2693.8	1795.7	277	32184071

1st	2nd	3rd	2007	2006	2005	P/E RATIO		2007	2006	2005	AV. YLD %	AMOUNT	PAYABLE	PRICE RANGE 2007	
-	-	-	1.24	0.58	0.45	-	-	-	-	-	-	-	-	21.6 -	13.2
0.95	0.90	1.06	4.00	3.29	1.73	5.4 -	3.3	-	-	-	-	-	-	33.0 -	23.4
0.21	-0.20	-	1.59	1.65	1.56	20.8 -	14.7	0.50	0.04	0.04	1.8	0.25S	8/7/07	22.5 -	17.8
0.48	-	-	1.68	1.52	1.44	13.4 -	10.6	0.44	0.44	0.44	2.2	0.12Q	4/1/08	36.8 -	18.5
0.12	0.02	0.67	-	-0.45	-1.69	-	-	-	-	0.10	-	0.1Q	4/21/05	55.1 -	33.7
0.84	1.07	1.11	4.24	4.04	3.52	13.0 -	7.9	0.84	0.72	0.64	2.0	0.23Q	3/14/08	57.6 -	34.7
-0.58	-1.25	-1.30	-7.92	7.83	9.03	-	-	0.48	0.48	0.24	1.1	0.12Q	4/30/08	-	-
-	-	-	0.17	0.13	-	-	-	-	2.00	2.00	-	1.S	12/31/07	-	-
-	-	-	0.20	0.16	0.20	100.5 -	98.0	2.78	2.64	0.09	13.9	0.4441A	12/31/07	20.1 -	19.6
0.84	0.96	1.12	3.91	4.10	3.61	10.8 -	7.0	3.85	4.24	3.43	11.2	0.3739M	3/31/08	42.3 -	27.4
-	-	-	-	-	-	-	-	-	-	-	-	-	-	6.7 -	3.4
1.71	1.75	1.93	6.97	7.51	5.43	7.5 -	5.5	1.40	1.10	0.94	3.1	0.4Q	4/28/08	52.2 -	38.2
-0.10	-0.11	-0.20	-0.53	0.38	-0.27	-	-	-	-	-	-	-	-	6.0 -	1.5
0.39	0.49	0.44	1.99	1.94	1.25	12.8 -	8.7	0.26	0.22	0.15	1.2	0.069Q	4/17/08	25.4 -	17.3
0.04	0.19	0.17	0.55	0.61	0.51	36.8 -	30.1	-	-	-	-	-	-	20.2 -	16.6
0.19	0.31	0.25	1.07	-	1.09	-	-	15.00	-	-	-	-	-	-	-
0.07	-0.17	0.14	0.40	0.16	0.42	44.6 -	29.5	8.00	-	2.00	55.2	4.U	11/30/06	17.9 -	11.8
0.01	0.03	0.05	0.00	0.24	0.07	-	-	-	-	-	-	-	-	22.0 -	9.6
0.08	-	-	0.24	-	-	-	-	-	-	-	-	-	-	-	-
0.52	0.55	0.80	2.43	2.92	3.25	13.8 -	7.4	2.43	2.92	3.25	9.7	0.236M	3/14/08	33.5 -	17.9
-	-	-	3.89	2.95	1.68	10.4 -	7.5	-	-	-	-	-	-	40.5 -	29.4
0.25	0.09	-1.07	-0.78	0.93	1.71	-	-	0.64	0.64	0.64	2.5	0.1Q	4/1/08	30.4 -	21.7
-	-	-	1.59	1.52	1.60	28.6 -	22.3	-	-	-	-	-	-	45.5 -	35.5
-	-	-	-	-0.02	-0.81	-	-	-	-	-	-	-	-	16.0 -	12.6
0.20	0.05	0.68	0.72	0.90	-	30.7 -	25.4	0.40	0.79	0.78	2.1	0.105Q	4/7/08	20.9 -	17.3
-	-	-	27.02	16.42	15.11	0.8 -	0.5	-	-	-	-	-	-	21.8 -	13.9
-	-	-	-	-	-	-	-	-	-	-	-	-	-	15.5 -	11.4
-	-	-	20.98	34.10	21.93	0.8 -	0.4	-	-	-	-	-	-	-	-
0.32	0.37	0.11	0.98	1.11	0.81	22.5 -	12.7	0.72	0.60	0.48	4.3	0.18Q	1/15/08	22.1 -	12.4
0.39	0.39	0.43	1.62	1.43	1.27	17.3 -	15.2	1.77	1.68	1.60	6.7	0.5Q	4/15/08	28.0 -	24.6
0.73	0.47	0.79	2.74	2.68	2.81	14.5 -	12.1	1.76	1.68	1.56	4.9	0.46Q	4/1/08	39.6 -	33.1
0.26	0.38	0.15	-	1.04	1.13	-	-	-	0.13	0.13	-	0.0325Q	12/31/07	18.5 -	12.7
0.36	0.35	0.45	-1.04	0.71	0.12	-	-	0.25	0.22	0.22	1.4	3.75Q	5/15/08	21.1 -	16.0
0.06	-	-	0.45	0.59	0.25	11.6 -	6.7	-	-	-	-	1.5Q	8/13/07	5.2 -	3.0
0.96	1.02	1.09	4.20	3.01	1.82	8.2 -	6.3	0.70	0.50	0.42	2.2	0.21Q	4/4/08	34.6 -	26.3
0.27	0.06	-0.27	0.22	-0.05	1.26	161.7 -	127.0	0.60	0.60	0.60	1.9	0.15Q	3/17/08	35.6 -	27.9
-	-	-	-	-	-	-	-	-	-	-	-	0.4531Q	7/15/06	-	-
-	-	-	-	-	-	-	-	-	-	-	-	0.4531Q	1/15/08	-	-
-0.55	0.63	-1.60	-	-6.70	2.64	-	-	-	-	-	-	0.125Q	2/28/08	36.8 -	28.0
-0.89	-	-	1.89	1.91	1.47	21.8 -	16.6	8.50	0.50	0.13	26.6	0.1Q	12/31/03	10.1 -	7.1
0.38	0.38	0.44	1.82	1.27	0.36	5.5 -	3.9	-	-	-	-	0.14Q	3/10/08	54.3 -	45.4
0.42	0.59	0.54	-0.01	2.14	1.51	-	-	0.54	0.47	0.43	1.1	-	-	55.8 -	37.4
1.40	2.41	2.66	9.04	8.44	6.95	6.2 -	4.1	-	-	-	-	-	-	21.5 -	10.3
0.64	-	-	1.50	1.60	1.41	13.8 -	6.6	0.38	0.32	0.26	2.6	0.1Q	11/16/07	27.3 -	22.1
0.67	0.40	0.39	1.89	1.47	1.35	14.4 -	11.7	0.40	0.30	-	1.8	0.12Q	3/21/08	-	-
0.26	0.17	0.00	0.92	0.83	0.91	-	-	-	-	-	-	0.075Q	2/1/08	-	-
-	-	-	-	-	-	-	-	-	-	-	-	0.4462Q	11/14/07	-	-
0.58	0.40	-1.40	-	2.18	1.74	-	-	-	-	-	-	0.02Q	12/31/07	-	-
-	-	-	-	-	-	-	-	-	-	-	-	0.4375Q	3/24/08	-	-
-	-	-	-	0.48	0.61	-	-	-	0.48	0.61	-	0.036M	1/22/08	11.4 -	9.9
-	-	-	-	0.00	-0.01	-	-	-	-	-	-	-	-	15.6 -	9.4
0.86	1.05	1.15	4.16	5.38	3.65	9.1 -	7.1	1.24	1.20	1.10	3.7	0.32Q	4/15/08	37.8 -	29.7
0.22	0.25	0.25	1.03	0.91	0.85	19.7 -	14.1	1.37	1.30	1.28	7.7	0.35Q	2/15/08	20.3 -	14.5
0.37	0.45	0.44	1.65	1.44	0.94	14.7 -	11.0	0.68	0.61	0.60	3.3	0.18Q	3/3/08	24.2 -	18.1
0.13	0.05	0.10	0.85	0.19	-0.41	9.0 -	6.4	0.12	0.10	0.07	1.8	0.04Q	4/30/08	7.7 -	5.5
0.03	-	-	-0.54	0.67	0.23	-	-	-	-	-	-	-	-	17.9 -	9.2
0.83	1.52	1.55	4.70	4.19	3.28	9.7 -	7.0	1.26	1.00	0.82	3.1	0.31Q	3/14/08	45.5 -	33.1
-	-	-	-	-	-	-	-	-	-	-	-	-	-	15.6 -	26.5
-	-	-	4770.00	4100.00	-	-	-	-	-	2.00	-	0.55Q	12/10/07	25.8 -	13.1
-	-	-	-	-	2.04	-	-	-	-	-	-	-	-	87.5 -	65.5
-	-	-	4.10	3.26	2.42	21.3 -	16.0	-	-	-	-	-	-	10.5 -	6.6
0.07	0.12	0.69	0.89	1.33	0.44	11.8 -	7.4	0.16	-	-	1.9	0.08Q	3/12/08	22.3 -	17.3
-	-	-	0.00	0.07	0.08	278.5 -	216.8	-	-	-	-	-	-	15.6 -	2.7
-	-	-	-	1.86	1.49	-	-	-	-	-	-	-	-	57.1 -	51.5
0.44	0.27	0.74	1.95	2.19	1.82	29.3 -	26.4	3.36	3.04	2.80	6.1	1.0469Q	3/31/08	35.6 -	22.4
0.35	0.58	0.46	1.40	2.10	2.02	25.4 -	16.0	0.38	0.32	0.20	1.4	0.1Q	4/24/08	9.4 -	6.8
-	-	-	-	0.34	0.16	-	-	-	0.17	0.22	-	0.15A	1/18/08	53.1 -	25.1
-1.86	-0.54	0.61	-2.90	-3.48	-1.43	-	-	-	-	-	-	0.574Q	5/15/01	8.3 -	3.5
0.11	0.29	0.43	1.04	2.08	1.18	18.7 -	14.1	0.60	0.56	0.54	3.5	0.1613Q	3/1/08	19.4 -	14.6
-	-	-	19523.00	25036.00	-	-	-	-	-	-	-	-	-	25.0 -	17.3
0.52	0.32	0.53	1.63	1.59	1.06	9.2 -	4.6	-	-	-	-	-	-	15.0 -	7.5
-0.01	-0.18	0.19	0.35	-0.09	25.73	-	-	-	-	-	-	-	-	-	-
0.08	-0.22	-	0.31	1.70	0.65	144.4 -	111.8	2.72	0.72	1.72	7.0	0.18Q	1/2/08	44.8 -	34.7
2.53	4.38	1.64	10.78	4.38	3.20	5.6 -	3.7	2.89	2.50	2.22	6.0	0.4922Q	1/15/08	60.5 -	40.2
0.26	1.03	-0.85	-2.26	2.63	3.05	-	-	0.25	0.97	0.85	0.6	0.8712Q	4/30/08	54.2 -	37.0
-	-	-	-	0.08	0.04	-	-	-	2.00	0.83	-	1.S	12/31/07	-	-
-	-	-	0.34	0.79	0.20	170.6 -	120.0	-	-	-	-	-	-	58.0 -	40.8
0.63	0.87	0.79	2.85	2.47	1.54	12.5 -	8.1	0.70	0.66	0.64	2.4	0.18Q	2/15/08	35.5 -	23.2
0.80	0.76	0.83	3.20	2.49	1.48	9.8 -	6.3	0.40	0.32	0.24	1.5	0.12Q	4/14/08	31.3 -	20.1
0.41	0.13	0.41	1.49	1.54	2.64	20.3 -	13.6	-	-	-	-	-	-	30.2 -	20.3
0.71	0.87	0.75	2.76	2.45	2.24	19.3 -	15.0	1.12	1.08	1.00	2.4	0.3Q	3/3/08	53.4 -	41.3

T53

SYMBOL	COMPANY	NATURE OF BUSINESS	FISCAL YEAR-END	TOTAL REV. $MILL	NET INCOME $MILL	TOTAL ASSETS $MILL	NET STK EQUITY $MILL	NO OF INST	INST. HOLDINGS (SHARES)
SNA	Snap-On, Inc.	Metal Products	12/29/07	2904.2	181.2	2765.1	1280.1	216	48553040
SQM	Sociedad Quimica y Minera de Chil	Chemicals	12/31/06	1042.9	141.3	1871.2	1085.9	37	1790971
SLH	Solera Holdings Inc	Insurance	6/30/07	472.0	-80.9	1224.0	401.3	-	-
SOA	Solutia, Inc.	Chemicals	12/31/07	3535.0	-208.0	2640.0	-1595.0	-	-
SAH	Sonic Automotive, Inc.	Retail - Automotive	12/31/07	8336.9	95.5	3282.7	930.8	116	25865538
SON	Sonoco Products Co.	Paper Products	12/31/07	4040.0	214.2	3340.2	1441.5	223	54505427
SNE	Sony Corp	Electrical	3/31/07	8295695.0	126328.0	11716362.0	3370704.0	217	119766712
BID	Sotheby's	Retail - Miscellaneous	12/31/07	917.7	213.1	2020.1	604.0	130	43749781
SOR	Source Capital, Inc.	Trusts & Holding Entities	12/31/07	9.9	4.7	615.2	614.6	20	81348
SJI	South Jersey Industries, Inc.	Gas Utilities	12/31/07	956.4	62.3	1529.4	481.1	94	12728954
SO	Southern Company (The)	Electricity	12/31/07	15353.0	1734.0	45789.0	13465.0	537	297233534
PCU	Southern Copper Corp	Non-Precious Metals	12/31/07	6085.7	2216.4	6580.6	3848.1	-	-
SUG	Southern Union Co. (New)	Gas Utilities	12/31/07	2616.7	228.7	7397.9	2205.8	6	2293300
LUV	Southwest Airlines Co	Aviation	12/31/07	9861.0	645.0	16772.0	6941.0	393	525677039
SWX	Southwest Gas Corporation	Gas Utilities	12/31/07	2152.1	83.2	3670.2	983.7	122	22404066
SWN	Southwestern Energy Company	Oil and Gas	12/31/07	1255.1	221.2	3622.7	1646.5	212	60022772
SOV	Sovereign Bancorp Inc	Other Depository Banking	12/31/07	5010.7	-1349.3	84746.4	6992.3	360	234379256
SSS	Sovran Self Storage, Inc. (United St	Property, Real Estate & Developmen	12/31/07	193.8	39.2	1164.6	527.4	106	8617421
SNF	Spain Fund, Inc.	Trusts & Holding Entities	11/30/07	2.9	1.3	136.0	135.7	8	81864
SEH	Spartech Corp.	Plastics	11/3/07	1452.0	33.8	1110.9	439.3	97	30563809
SPA	Sparton Corp.	Electrical	6/30/07	200.1	-7.8	137.0	86.5	16	1873489
SE	Spectra Energy Corp	Gas Utilities	12/31/07	4742.0	957.0	22970.0	6857.0	-	-
SEP	Spectra Energy Partners LP	Gas Utilities						-	-
SPC	Spectrum Brands Inc	Electrical	9/30/07	1994.5	-596.7	3211.4	-103.8	161	45829707
TRK	Speedway Motorsports, Inc.	Sporting & Recreational	12/31/07	561.6	38.4	1578.3	827.7	82	13051218
SFN	Spherion Corp.	Human Resources Services	12/30/07	2017.1	25.3	844.8	500.7	105	53714063
SPR	Spirit AeroSystems Holdings Inc	Aviation	12/31/07	3860.8	296.9	3339.9	1266.6	-	-
S	Sprint Nextel Corp	Communications	12/31/07	40146.0	-29580.0	64109.0	21999.0	594	1285351222
SPW	SPX Corp.	Industrial Machinery and Equipment	12/31/07	4822.3	294.2	6237.4	2006.0	215	68178979
SRX	SRA International Inc (United States	IT & Technology	6/30/07	1268.9	63.4	847.7	625.5	117	34164500
JOE	St. Joe Co. (The) (United States)	Property, Real Estate & Developmen	12/31/07	377.0	39.2	1264.0	480.3	238	53189561
STJ	St. Jude Medical, Inc.	Medical Instruments & Equipment	12/29/07	3779.3	559.0	5329.4	2928.0	378	287108541
SM	St. Mary Land & Exploration Co.	Oil and Gas	12/31/07	990.1	189.7	2571.7	863.3	152	49306276
SSI	Stage Stores Inc.	Retail - Apparel and Accessory Store	2/3/07	1550.2	55.3	825.0	571.4	129	20284060
SFG	Stancorp Financial Group Inc	Insurance	12/31/07	2709.2	227.5	14982.9	1429.0	184	18116795
SMP	Standard Motor Products, Inc.	Electrical	12/31/07	790.2	2.3	678.1	188.4	64	11213285
SPF	Standard Pacific Corp. (New)	Building & General Construction	12/31/07	2905.5	-767.3	3400.7	995.0	219	28585254
SR	Standard Register Co.	Printing	12/30/07	865.4	-7.3	419.5	110.0	78	13248353
SXI	Standex International Corp.	Purpose Machinery	6/30/07	621.2	21.2	539.9	204.4	86	7410971
SXE	Stanley Inc	Engineering Services	3/31/07	409.4	10.7	238.0	134.2	-	-
SWK	Stanley Works (The)	Metal Products	12/29/07	4483.8	336.6	4779.9	1728.5	-	-
SXC	Stantec Inc	Miscellaneous Business Services	12/31/06	707.9	60.2	630.5	410.9	0	0
SGU	Star Gas Partners L.P.	Retail - Miscellaneous	9/30/07	1267.2	38.2	602.1	-	32	9402389
SCX	Starrett (L.S.) Co.	Instruments and Related Products	6/30/07	222.4	6.7	234.0	178.0	27	2651569
SRT	Startek, Inc.	Miscellaneous Business Services	12/31/07	245.3	-2.8	155.5	118.2	77	7487022
HOT	Starwood Hotels & Resorts Worldwi	Hospitality & Tourism	12/31/07	6153.0	542.0	9622.0	2076.0	-	-
STT	State Street Corp.	Commercial Banking	12/31/07	11818.0	1261.0	142543.0	11299.0	540	260660551
STO	StatoilHydro ASA	Oil and Gas	12/31/06	425166.0	40615.0	315468.0	-	91	27663946
SNS	Steak n Shake Co. (The)	Hospitality & Tourism	9/26/07	654.1	11.8	565.2	303.9	96	16835620
SCS	Steelcase, Inc.	Furniture and Fixtures	2/23/07	3097.4	106.9	2399.4	1237.9	103	54005374
LVB	Steinway Musical Instruments Inc.	Consumer Accessories	12/31/07	406.3	15.4	457.7	163.8	64	5185975
SCL	Stepan Co.	Chemicals	12/31/07	1329.9	15.1	573.2	206.1	1	9987
STE	Steris Corp.	Medical Instruments & Equipment	3/31/07	1197.4	82.2	1209.2	774.3	184	59952529
STL	Sterling Bancorp (N.Y.)	Commercial Banking	12/31/07	157.2	14.6	2012.6	121.1	60	9054238
SLT	Sterlite Industries (India) Ltd.	Metal Works	3/31/07	243497.0	47432.0	225881.0	96960.0	-	-
STC	Stewart Information Services Corp.	Insurance	12/31/07	2106.7	-40.2	1442.0	754.1	136	15338292
SF	Stifel Financial Corp.	Finance Intermediaries & Services	12/31/07	793.1	32.2	1499.4	424.6	37	4182122
SWC	Stillwater Mining Co.	Non-Precious Metals	12/31/07	619.2	-14.3	742.4	517.4	88	29065584
STM	STMicroelectronics N.V.	IT & Technology	12/31/07	10001.0	-477.0	14272.0	9573.0	98	24472640
SGY	Stone Energy Corp.	Oil and Gas	12/31/07	753.3	181.4	1889.6	885.8	165	23415837
SRI	Stoneridge Inc.	Automotive	12/31/07	727.1	16.7	527.8	206.2	52	10068862
SGL	Strategic Global Income Fund, Inc.	Trusts & Holding Entities	11/30/07	10.7	8.1	215.0	208.1	18	455090
BEE	Strategic Hotels & Resorts, Inc.	Property, Real Estate & Developmen	12/31/07	1008.0	69.2	3366.3	1236.8	57	23577918
SYK	Stryker Corp.	Medical Instruments & Equipment	12/31/07	6000.5	1017.4	7354.0	5378.5	551	181130017
STU	Student Loan Corp. (The)	Credit & Lending	12/31/07	1712.0	182.7	23779.9	1624.2	115	19247659
RGR	Sturm, Ruger & Co., Inc.	Metal Products	12/31/07	156.5	10.3	101.9	76.1	75	8428150
SPH	Suburban Propane Partners L.P.	Retail - Fuel & Oil	9/29/07	1439.6	127.3	975.2	-	70	4252843
SUI	Sun Communities, Inc.	Property, Real Estate & Developmen	12/31/07	236.0	-16.6	1245.8	21.0	89	14342026
SLF	Sun Life Financial Inc	Insurance	12/31/06	24287.0	2144.0	117831.0	17184.0	-	-
FGF	SunAmerica Focused Alpha Growth	Trusts & Holding Entities						-	-
FGI	SunAmerica Focused Alpha Large-	Trusts & Holding Entities						-	-
SU	Suncor Energy Inc	Oil and Gas	12/31/07	17933.0	2832.0	24167.0	11613.0	283	219247056
SXL	Sunoco Logistics Partners L.P. (Unit	Oil and Gas	12/31/07	7405.8	120.9	2504.6	-	46	2441031
SUN	Sunoco, Inc.	Oil and Gas	12/31/07	44728.0	891.0	12426.0	2533.0	310	53437139
SRZ	Sunrise Senior Living Inc	Hospitals & Health Care	12/31/06	1648.4	20.4	1817.4	647.3	139	14855181
SHO	Sunstone Hotel Investors Inc (New)	Property, Real Estate & Developmen	12/31/07	1056.7	125.7	3049.2	1093.9	71	20668268
STP	Suntech Power Holdings Co Ltd	IT & Technology	12/31/06	598.9	106.0	1098.0	652.5	-	-
SVN	Sun-Times Media Group Inc	Media	12/31/07	372.3	271.6	791.6	-75.0	-	-
STI	SunTrust Banks, Inc.	Commercial Banking	12/31/07	13464.6	1634.0	179573.9	18052.5	500	192072374
SPN	Superior Energy Services, Inc.	Oil and Gas	12/31/07	1572.5	281.1	2257.2	980.7	183	65995087

T54

EARNINGS PER SHARE						P/E RATIO		DIVIDENDS PER SHARE			AV. YLD %	DIV. DECLARED		PRICE RANGE	
QUARTERLY			ANNUAL											2007	
1st	2nd	3rd	2007	2006	2005			2007	2006	2005		AMOUNT	PAYABLE		
0.66	0.74	0.70	3.09	1.69	1.59	11.1 -	8.8	1.11	1.08	1.00	3.5	0.3Q	3/10/08	34.4 -	27.3
-	-	-	-	-	-	-	-	-	-	-	-	-	-	6.3 -	3.3
0.06	0.17	-	-2.82	-6.34	-0.07	-	-	-	-	-	-	-	-	-	-
-0.08	0.54	-1.06	-1.99	0.11	0.08	-	-	-	-	-	-	-	-	-	-
0.44	0.57	0.58	2.13	1.85	2.12	12.3 -	8.6	0.48	0.48	0.48	2.1	0.12Q	4/15/08	20.1 -	18.4
0.52	0.41	0.63	2.10	1.92	1.61	14.1 -	10.9	1.02	0.95	0.91	4.0	0.26Q	3/10/08	29.7 -	22.9
-	-	-	120.29	116.88	158.07	0.4 -	0.3	-	-	-	-	-	-	43.7 -	32.5
0.37	1.64	-0.33	3.25	1.72	1.00	5.8 -	3.8	0.50	0.20	-	3.3	0.15Q	3/15/08	18.9 -	12.2
-	-	-	0.55	0.44	0.42	130.1 -	108.6	4.00	4.74	5.47	6.1	1.Q	3/15/08	71.5 -	59.8
0.92	0.36	0.29	2.10	2.44	1.69	12.6 -	9.5	1.00	0.92	0.86	4.5	0.27Q	4/2/08	26.4 -	19.9
0.45	0.56	1.00	2.28	2.10	2.13	14.9 -	12.2	1.60	1.53	1.48	5.3	0.4025Q	3/6/08	33.9 -	27.9
1.87	2.46	2.13	7.53	6.92	4.75	3.6 -	1.8	6.80	5.13	2.90	33.2	1.4Q	2/29/08	27.1 -	13.3
0.62	0.39	0.34	1.75	0.40	0.03	16.1 -	14.5	0.45	0.40	-	1.7	0.15Q	4/11/08	28.1 -	25.4
0.12	0.36	0.22	0.84	0.61	0.67	20.2 -	15.7	0.02	0.02	0.02	0.1	0.0045Q	3/20/08	17.0 -	13.2
1.17	-0.01	-0.22	1.95	2.05	1.14	13.3 -	11.1	0.85	0.82	0.82	3.6	0.225Q	6/2/08	25.9 -	21.6
0.30	0.28	0.30	1.27	0.95	0.95	5.4 -	1.9	-	-	-	-	0.06Q	5/5/00	6.9 -	2.4
0.09	0.29	0.11	-2.85	0.30	1.69	-	-	0.32	0.29	0.16	1.5	0.4562Q	2/15/08	23.3 -	18.6
0.44	0.36	0.51	1.81	1.89	1.84	24.0 -	18.4	2.49	2.46	2.43	6.4	0.63Q	1/22/08	43.5 -	33.3
-	-	-	0.15	0.12	0.14	90.7 -	60.7	1.50	1.06	0.98	13.7	0.3Q	1/4/08	13.6 -	9.1
-0.12	-	-	1.05	1.20	0.38	26.8 -	20.6	0.54	0.50	0.48	2.2	0.135Q	5/7/08	28.2 -	21.7
-0.14	-0.19	-	-0.79	0.01	0.83	-	-	-	0.09	-	-	0.1A	10/5/05	9.0 -	7.0
0.37	0.31	0.37	1.51	-	-	-	-	0.88	-	-	-	0.23Q	3/17/08	-	-
-	-	-	-	-	-	-	-	-	-	-	-	0.32Q	2/14/08	-	-
-0.85	-	-	-11.72	-8.77	1.03	-	-	-	-	-	-	-	-	31.3 -	20.2
0.72	0.92	-0.31	0.87	2.53	2.45	45.0 -	33.1	0.34	0.33	0.32	1.0	0.335A	10/31/07	39.2 -	28.8
0.03	0.00	0.17	0.14	0.05	0.20	25.0 -	15.6	-	-	-	-	-	-	11.0 -	6.9
0.50	0.49	0.60	2.13	0.14	-0.80	-	-	-	-	-	-	-	-	-	-
-0.07	0.01	0.02	-10.31	0.45	0.87	-	-	0.10	0.10	0.30	0.6	0.025Q	12/28/07	22.8 -	14.8
0.49	1.12	1.71	5.22	2.83	15.33	11.0 -	6.4	1.00	1.00	1.00	2.3	0.25Q	4/1/08	61.7 -	33.3
0.31	0.00	-	1.09	1.08	1.02	30.0 -	16.1	-	-	-	-	-	-	32.6 -	17.6
0.27	0.34	-0.09	0.53	0.69	1.66	121.1 -	67.5	0.48	0.64	0.60	1.1	0.16Q	9/28/07	64.2 -	35.8
0.41	0.39	0.46	1.59	1.47	1.04	26.8 -	18.8	-	-	-	-	-	-	42.5 -	29.9
0.60	0.01	0.89	2.94	2.94	2.33	7.3 -	4.8	0.10	0.10	0.10	0.6	0.06S	11/12/07	21.5 -	14.0
0.20	0.23	0.06	1.25	1.27	1.15	14.9 -	9.9	-	0.17	-	-	0.05Q	3/26/08	18.7 -	12.4
0.90	0.97	1.29	4.35	3.73	3.76	9.6 -	6.9	0.72	0.65	0.63	2.1	0.72A	12/7/07	41.6 -	29.9
0.14	0.28	0.14	0.12	0.51	-0.18	137.1 -	102.1	0.36	0.36	0.36	2.5	0.09Q	3/3/08	16.4 -	12.3
-0.63	-2.56	-1.85	-11.85	1.85	6.30	-	-	0.12	0.16	0.16	0.5	0.04Q	8/23/07	32.5 -	22.5
-0.03	-0.16	0.08	-0.25	-0.41	0.05	-	-	0.92	0.92	0.92	6.8	0.23Q	3/7/08	20.0 -	10.2
0.48	0.45	-	1.71	1.85	1.91	17.4 -	12.6	0.84	0.84	0.84	3.2	0.21Q	2/23/08	29.8 -	21.6
0.23	0.27	0.29	0.55	0.51	0.70	-	-	-	-	-	-	-	-	-	-
0.80	1.01	1.09	4.00	3.46	3.16	-	-	1.22	1.18	1.14	-	0.31Q	3/25/08	-	-
-	-	-	-	1.31	0.99	-	-	-	-	-	-	-	-	11.1 -	8.8
0.33	-	-	0.50	-1.02	-0.72	51.2 -	8.6	-	-	-	-	0.575Q	8/13/04	25.6 -	4.3
0.35	0.52	-	1.00	-0.57	0.61	20.9 -	14.2	0.40	0.40	0.40	2.5	0.1Q	12/28/07	20.9 -	14.2
-0.01	-0.23	0.03	-0.19	0.30	0.88	-	-	-	1.11	1.50	-	0.25Q	11/27/00	43.1 -	27.4
0.56	0.67	0.61	2.57	4.69	1.88	-	-	0.90	0.42	0.84	-	0.9A	1/11/08	-	-
0.93	1.07	0.91	3.45	3.29	2.50	16.4 -	11.9	0.88	0.80	0.72	1.8	0.23Q	4/15/08	56.5 -	41.1
-	-	-	-	18.79	14.19	-	-	-	-	-	-	-	-	16.0	10.9
-0.04	-	-	0.42	1.00	1.08	51.7 -	39.0	-	-	-	-	-	-	21.7 -	16.4
0.23	0.26	0.22	0.71	0.33	0.09	20.6 -	16.1	0.45	0.33	0.24	3.4	1.75Q	1/15/08	14.7 -	11.4
0.17	0.36	0.35	1.78	-0.08	1.67	20.4 -	13.1	3.00	-	-	10.0	3.U	3/9/07	36.3 -	23.4
0.56	0.47	0.31	1.50	0.63	1.35	10.9 -	17.7	0.82	0.81	0.79	2.9	0.3438Q	2/29/08	29.8 -	26.5
0.20	0.25	0.34	1.25	1.02	1.23	22.0 -	16.0	0.18	0.16	-	0.8	0.06Q	3/11/08	27.4 -	20.0
0.18	0.20	0.17	0.79	0.56	1.22	34.1 -	25.3	0.76	0.76	0.73	3.4	0.19Q	3/31/08	26.9 -	20.0
-	-	-	84.03	-	-	-	-	0.08	-	-	-	-	-	-	-
-0.26	0.55	-0.79	-2.21	2.36	4.86	-	-	0.75	0.75	0.75	2.0	0.75A	12/21/07	47.3 -	31.3
0.58	0.08	0.45	1.88	1.11	1.56	12.9 -	7.4	-	-	-	-	0.03Q	6/6/02	24.2 -	13.9
-0.01	-0.03	-0.12	-0.15	0.09	-0.15	-	-	-	-	-	-	-	-	19.1 -	9.3
-	-	-	-0.53	0.83	0.29	-	-	0.30	0.12	0.12	1.4	-	-	29.9 -	16.4
0.38	2.60	1.23	6.54	-9.29	5.02	7.7 -	6.0	-	-	-	-	-	-	50.5 -	39.0
0.21	0.11	0.11	0.71	0.63	0.04	24.2 -	18.0	-	-	-	-	-	-	17.2 -	12.8
-	-	-	0.45	0.51	0.54	35.3 -	25.6	0.93	0.93	1.91	6.7	0.0775M	3/31/08	15.9 -	11.5
-0.13	-0.34	0.91	0.52	1.39	0.66	31.8 -	25.4	0.96	0.92	0.88	6.6	0.5313Q	12/31/07	16.6 -	13.2
0.59	0.65	0.55	2.44	1.89	1.64	23.5 -	17.1	0.33	0.22	0.11	0.7	0.33A	1/31/08	57.3 -	41.8
2.20	3.53	1.25	9.13	14.34	15.45	20.4 -	14.3	5.59	4.98	4.32	3.7	1.43Q	3/3/08	186.7 -	130.3
0.36	0.22	-0.03	0.46	0.04	0.03	30.4 -	18.0	0.00	0.00	0.30	0.0	0.1Q	9/15/05	14.0 -	8.3
2.60	-	-	3.89	2.83	-0.26	9.1 -	7.4	2.76	2.48	2.45	8.4	0.7625Q	2/12/08	35.5 -	28.9
0.00	-0.12	-0.24	-0.93	-1.42	-0.31	-	-	2.52	2.52	2.50	6.5	0.63Q	1/22/08	42.8 -	34.0
0.86	1.02	1.00	-	3.58	3.12	-	-	-	1.15	0.99	-	0.2813Q	3/31/08	-	-
-	-	-	-	0.01	-0.02	-	-	-	1.20	0.50	-	0.35Q	3/27/08	-	-
-	-	-	0.00	-	-	-	-	-	-	-	-	0.35Q	3/27/08	-	-
1.17	1.36	1.43	6.02	6.32	2.67	5.9 -	3.9	0.19	0.15	0.12	0.7	0.1Q	12/24/07	35.5 -	23.6
0.70	0.76	0.97	3.37	2.85	2.35	12.8 -	9.3	3.33	3.02	2.56	8.8	0.87Q	2/14/08	43.0 -	31.5
1.44	4.20	1.81	7.43	7.59	7.08	5.7 -	3.4	1.08	0.95	0.75	3.3	0.3Q	6/10/08	42.2 -	25.4
-	-	-	0.40	1.67	-	-	-	-	-	-	-	-	-	23.2 -	15.6
-0.01	1.09	0.19	1.75	0.58	0.47	11.9 -	9.5	1.31	1.22	1.16	7.1	0.5Q	4/15/08	20.8 -	16.7
-	-	-	0.68	0.26	-	-	-	-	-	-	-	-	-	-	-
-0.06	6.56	-2.39	3.37	-0.66	-0.13	6.0 -	4.4	-	0.10	3.20	-	0.05Q	10/13/06	20.4 -	14.8
1.44	1.89	1.18	4.55	2.82	5.47	16.8 -	13.6	2.92	2.44	2.20	4.2	0.3489Q	3/17/08	76.4 -	61.8
0.78	0.85	0.91	3.41	2.32	0.85	4.6 -	2.6	-	-	-	-	-	-	15.7 -	8.8

T55

SYMBOL	COMPANY	NATURE OF BUSINESS	FISCAL YEAR-END	TOTAL REV. $MILL	NET INCOME $MILL	TOTAL ASSETS $MILL	NET STK EQUITY $MILL	NO OF INST	INST. HOLDINGS (SHARES)
SUP	Superior Industries International, Inc	Automotive	12/31/06	789.9	-9.3	712.0	560.2	121	28899634
SVU	SUPERVALU INC	Retail - Food & Beverage	2/24/07	37406.0	452.0	21702.0	5306.0	289	112064140
SFY	Swift Energy Company (New)	Oil and Gas	12/31/07	654.1	21.3	1969.1	836.1	139	26571832
SWZ	Swiss Helvetia Fund, Inc. (The)	Trusts & Holding Entities	12/31/07	7.3	0.7	672.0	621.9	32	5648022
SWS	SWS Group, Inc.	Finance Intermediaries & Services	6/29/07	273.6	37.6	5074.6	306.4	87	10757445
SY	Sybase, Inc.	IT & Technology	12/31/07	1025.5	148.8	1913.5	930.8	198	83123137
SMA	Symmetry Medical Inc.	Medical Instruments & Equipment	12/30/06	253.6	24.1	410.1	290.9	61	10312328
SYT	Syngenta AG	Chemicals	12/31/05	8104.0	622.0	11404.0	5431.0	84	52952064
SVR	Syniverse Holdings Inc	Communications	12/31/07	377.5	52.4	1107.6	470.8	39	17337177
SNX	Synnex Corp	IT & Technology	11/30/07	7004.1	63.1	1887.1	604.6	48	7975811
SNV	Synovus Financial Corp.	Commercial Banking	12/31/07	2627.4	526.3	33018.5	3441.6	244	145135134
SYY	Sysco Corp.	Retail - Food & Beverage	6/30/07	35042.1	1001.1	9518.9	3278.4	741	417070548
SYX	Systemax, Inc.	Advertising, Marketing & PR	12/31/07	2779.9	69.5	673.9	335.8	30	3372887
TWN	Taiwan Fund, Inc. (The)	Trusts & Holding Entities						18	4249056
TFC	Taiwan Greater China Fund	Trusts & Holding Entities						23	7426548
TSM	Taiwan Semiconductor Manufacturi	IT & Technology	12/31/06	317407.2	127009.7	587485.2	507981.3	247	480889479
TAL	Tal International Group Inc	General Construction Supplies & Ser	12/31/07	343.3	38.8	1705.9	393.5		
TLB	Talbots, Inc. (United States)	Retail - Apparel and Accessory Store	2/3/07	2231.0	31.6	1748.7	643.3	109	22018790
TLM	Talisman Energy, Inc.	Oil and Gas	12/31/07	7919.0	2078.0	21443.0	7963.0		
TAM	Tam S.A.	Aviation	12/31/06	7344.6	556.0	5168.3	1449.4		
SKT	Tanger Factory Outlet Centers, Inc.	Property, Real Estate & Developmen	12/31/07	228.8	28.6	1060.3	249.2	108	17385545
TGT	Target Corp	Retail - General	2/2/08	63367.0	2849.0	44560.0	15307.0	788	759009511
TCL	Tata Communications Ltd	Communications	3/31/07	88566.0	16.7				
TCO	Taubman Centers, Inc.	Property, Real Estate & Developmen	12/31/07	626.8	63.1	3151.3	-15.8	124	47070489
TCB	TCF Financial Corp.	Commercial Banking	12/31/07	1509.5	266.8	15977.1	1099.0	257	84202915
TSI	TCW Strategic Income Fund Inc	Trusts & Holding Entities	12/31/07	21.1	18.3	265.0	203.3	30	1816909
TDK	TDK Corp. (Japan)	Electrical	3/31/07	862025.0	70125.0	989304.0	762712.0	28	1370003
TNL	Technitrol, Inc.	Electrical	12/28/07	1026.6	61.7	821.4	561.1	119	29390966
TCK	Teck Cominco Ltd.	Mining	12/31/06	6539.0	2431.0	11447.0	6549.0		
TE	TECO Energy Inc.	Electricity	12/31/07	3536.1	413.2	6765.2	2017.0	280	98000935
TK	Teekay Corp	Shipping	12/31/05	1954.6	570.9	5294.1	2236.5	129	46259490
TGP	Teekay LNG Partners LP	Trusts & Holding Entities	12/31/06		-9.6		-49.5		
TFR	Tefron Ltd. (Israel)	Consumer Accessories							
TRC	Tejon Ranch Co.	Property, Real Estate & Developmen	12/31/07	32.3	7.3	175.5	165.1	62	9081756
TCN	Tele Norte Celular Participacoes S	Communications						6	546323
TNE	Tele Norte Leste Participacoes S.A.	Communications	12/31/07	17584.3	2358.5	30252.7	10664.8	108	90044588
TEO	Telecom Argentina SA	Communications	12/31/06	7437.0	244.0	8715.0	2129.0	61	39471578
NZT	Telecom Corp. of New Zealand Ltd	Communications	6/30/05	5804.0	967.0	7504.0	2471.0	84	16089601
TI	Telecom Italia SPA (New)	Communications	12/31/04	29032.0	2834.0	81834.0	20798.0	8	4448951
TBH	Telecomunicacoes Brasileiras S.A. (	Communications	12/31/07		-24.2	229.9	-163.6	40	20980339
TSP	Telecomunicacoes de Sao Paulo S.	Communications	12/31/06	14643.0	2816.2	18145.9	10610.1	23	2215784
TDY	Teledyne Technologies, Inc.	Engineering Services	12/30/07	1622.3	98.5	1159.4	530.2	142	24155956
TFX	Teleflex Incorporated	Medical Instruments & Equipment	12/31/07	1934.3	146.5	4188.0	1328.8	213	29482938
TAR	Telefonica de Argentina S.A. (Argen	Communications	12/31/06	3747.0	222.0	6437.0	2129.0	7	188115
TEF RT	Telefonica, S.A.	Communications	12/31/06	30280.9	3175.7	60078.9	12342.5	165	59627602
TMX	Telefonos de Mexico SAB de CV	Communications	12/31/06	175006.1	527.9	264030.0	105955.9	232	389715128
TMB	Telemig Celular Participacoes S.A. (	Communications	12/31/07	1377.4	148.4	2339.2	1229.8	27	3092773
TKG	Telkom SA Ltd	Communications	3/31/05	43160.0	6751.0	57597.0	26361.0	12	377599
TIN	Temple-Inland Inc.	Paper Products	12/29/07	3926.0	1305.0	5942.0	780.0	283	97500124
TDF	Templeton Dragon Fund, Inc.	Trusts & Holding Entities	12/31/07	39.4	22.0	1326.7	1315.4	53	3914563
EMF	Templeton Emerging Markets Fund	Trusts & Holding Entities						30	1636875
TEI	Templeton Emerging Markets Inco	Trusts & Holding Entities						37	2077599
GIM	Templeton Global Income Fund (DE	Trusts & Holding Entities						63	9709104
TRF	Templeton Russia and East Europe	Trusts & Holding Entities	3/31/07		-1.3	369.6	368.8	19	166110
TPX	Tempur-Pedic International Inc	Furniture and Fixtures	12/31/07	1106.7	141.5	806.4	48.1	160	87279188
TS	Tenaris SA	Metal Works	12/31/05	6209.8	1277.5	6706.0	3775.9	101	17380493
THC	Tenet Healthcare Corp.	Hospitals & Health Care	12/31/07	8852.0	-89.0	8393.0	54.0	243	447501562
TNC	Tennant Co.	Purpose Machinery	12/31/07	664.2	39.9	382.1	252.4	66	6066154
TEN	Tenneco Inc	Automotive	12/31/07	6184.0	-5.0	3590.0	400.0	135	30462740
TVC	Tennessee Valley Authority	Electricity						9	264865
TPP	TEPPCO Partners, L.P.	Oil and Gas	12/31/07	9658.1	279.2	4750.1		148	13675542
TDC	Teradata Corp (DE)	IT & Technology	12/31/07	1702.0	200.0	1294.0	631.0		
TER	Teradyne, Inc.	Instruments and Related Products	12/31/07	1102.3	77.7	1555.3	1229.2	238	181349775
TEX	Terex Corp.	Industrial Machinery and Equipment	12/31/07	9137.7	613.9	6316.3	2343.2	181	39892697
TX	Ternium S A	Metal Works							
TRA	Terra Industries, Inc.	Chemicals	12/31/07	2360.1	201.9	1888.3	620.4	127	90956090
TNH	Terra Nitrogen Co., L.P.	Chemicals	12/31/07	636.3	205.8	413.8		23	753417
TSO	Tesoro Corporation	Oil and Gas	12/31/07	21915.0	566.0	8128.0	3052.0	193	58176846
TTI	TETRA Technologies, Inc.	Oil and Gas	12/31/07	982.5	28.8	1295.5	447.9	128	21392822
TXI	Texas Industries Inc.	Metal Works	5/31/07	996.3	100.9	1262.2	728.5	178	19467868
TXN	Texas Instruments Inc.	IT & Technology	12/31/07	13835.0	2657.0	12667.0	9975.0	794	1160608480
TPL	Texas Pacific Land Trust	Property, Real Estate & Development	12/31/07	15.5	8.2	32.7	24.9	34	307287
TXT	Textron Inc.	Aviation	12/29/07	13225.0	917.0	19956.0	3507.0	4	409
TTF	Thai Fund, Inc. (The)	Trusts & Holding Entities	12/31/07	5.7	3.1	208.0	204.1	15	2358391
GPS	The Gap, Inc.	Retail - Apparel and Accessory Store	2/2/08	15763.0	833.0	7838.0	4274.0	404	544220227
TGX	Theragenics Corp.	Medical Instruments & Equipment	12/31/07	62.2	5.6	148.8	132.6	60	13869200
TMO	Thermo Fisher Scientific Inc	Instruments and Related Products	12/31/07	9746.4	761.1	21207.4	14488.3	297	132790558
TNB	Thomas & Betts Corp.	Electrical	12/31/07	2136.9	183.2	2567.8	1228.9	196	55267770
TC	Thompson Creek Metals Co., Inc.	Miscellaneous Business Services	12/31/06	150.8	-20.6	935.7	224.1		
TMS	Thomson	Electrical	12/31/04	6036.0	-559.0	8555.0	2493.0	41	12358639

T56

1st	2nd	3rd	2007	2006	2005	P/E High	P/E Low	Div 2007	Div 2006	Div 2005	AV. YLD %	AMOUNT	PAYABLE	Price High 2007	Price Low 2007
0.07	0.11	-0.02	0.35	-0.35	-0.22	124.8 -	75.3	0.64	0.64	0.63	2.0	0.16Q	1/18/08	43.7 -	26.4
0.69	0.69	-	2.32	1.46	2.71	15.0 -	11.2	0.66	0.48	0.60	2.2	0.17Q	12/17/07	34.9 -	25.9
0.90	1.03	1.38	0.69	5.38	3.95	44.0 -	23.0							30.3 -	15.9
-	-	-	0.02	0.02	0.05	757.5 -	611.0	1.95	1.98	1.61	14.7	0.261S	1/29/08	15.2 -	12.2
0.28	0.26	-	1.38	1.55	1.20	11.0 -	6.3	1.31	0.95	0.27	11.6	0.09Q	4/1/08	15.2 -	8.7
0.16	0.28	0.37	1.61	1.03	0.92	14.1 -	8.0							22.7 -	12.8
0.11	0.13	-	-	0.69	0.92									21.1 -	18.1
-	-	-	11.42	6.35	6.13	1.9 -	1.2							21.4 -	13.2
0.11	0.17	0.24	0.78	1.33	0.09										
0.43	0.45	0.44	1.93	1.61	1.70	12.5 -	7.1							24.1 -	13.8
0.45	0.49	0.41	1.60	1.90	1.64	7.9 -	6.2	0.82	0.78	0.73	7.3	0.17Q	4/1/08	12.6 -	9.9
0.43	0.43	-	1.60	1.36	1.47	25.6 -	18.7	0.72	0.49	0.58	2.0	0.22Q	4/25/08	40.9 -	29.9
0.37	0.37	0.47	1.84	1.22	0.31	4.3 -	2.7	1.00	-	-	16.2	1.U	4/2/08	8.0 -	4.9
												0.4285A	1/25/08	14.5 -	10.0
												0.37U	1/26/01	5.2 -	3.9
														9.4 -	6.1
0.33	0.62	0.11	1.16	1.26	-0.68			1.43	0.45	-		0.375Q	4/10/08		
0.10	-0.25	-0.18	0.59	1.72	1.70	67.5 -	42.0	0.51	0.47	0.43	1.6	0.13Q	3/24/08	39.8 -	24.8
0.48	0.52	0.34	1.97	1.79	1.38			0.17	0.15	0.11		0.0875S	12/31/07		
0.06	0.16	0.22	0.72	1.03	0.16	36.8 -	24.5	1.42	1.34	1.28	6.6	0.4688Q	2/15/08	26.5 -	17.7
0.75	0.80	0.56	3.21	2.71	3.51	16.3 -	11.5	0.44	0.36	0.30	1.0	0.14Q	6/10/08	52.4 -	37.0
-	-	-	0.54	2.45	24.86	19.6 -	10.3							10.6 -	5.5
0.19	0.16	0.15	0.90	0.40	0.87	33.7 -	21.4	1.54	1.29	1.16	6.3	0.4766Q	3/31/08	30.3 -	19.3
0.65	0.49	0.48	2.12	1.90	2.00	15.3 -	11.4	0.97	0.92	0.85	3.4	0.25Q	2/29/08	32.5 -	24.1
-	-	-	0.29	0.20	0.21	14.3 -	11.6	-	0.09	0.40		0.075Q	4/11/08	5.4 -	4.4
-	-	-	529.29	333.20	339.55	0.2 -	0.1							80.0 -	62.0
0.12	0.51	0.47	1.51	1.41	-0.63	15.2 -	10.7	0.35	0.35	0.26	1.8	0.0875Q	4/18/08	23.0 -	16.1
0.83	1.13	-	-	5.60	3.11			-	1.00	0.40		0.5S	1/3/08		
0.35	0.35	0.44	1.97	1.18	1.31	7.8 -	5.8	0.78	0.76	0.76	5.7	0.195Q	2/28/08	15.4 -	11.4
-	-	-	-	-	6.83			-	-	0.62		0.275Q	1/25/08	54.5 -	27.9
-	-	-	-	-0.28	1.28			-	1.80	0.65		0.53Q	2/14/08		
0.03	-0.02	0.35	0.42	-0.16	0.09	102.1 -	76.7					0.025S	12/10/99	42.9 -	32.2
														13.0 -	8.5
														18.2 -	10.0
														11.1 -	7.3
-	-	-	1.52	-0.22	0.49	16.4 -	12.4							24.9 -	18.9
-	-	-	-	0.16	0.18									34.0 -	20.8
														17.6 -	10.4
														19.4 -	12.4
0.57	0.67	0.75	2.72	2.26	1.85	11.4 -	6.3							30.9 -	17.1
1.12	2.37	-1.45	3.73	3.49	3.39	14.7 -	10.9	1.25	1.11	0.97	2.6	0.32Q	3/17/08	54.8 -	40.7
														12.8 -	6.2
-	-	-	-	1.30	0.91									54.5 -	39.0
-	-	-	-	1.36	1.23									19.3 -	15.1
														47.2 -	24.8
-	-	-	12.45	17.35	12.44	5.6 -	2.8							70.3 -	35.0
0.35	0.62	0.33	12.08	4.22	1.54	1.7 -	1.4	11.37	1.00	0.90	00.5	0.1Q	3/14/08	26.0 -	16.9
-	-	-	0.58	0.38	0.59	34.0 -	20.5	3.24	2.35	0.77	20.7	0.3/25S	12/31/07	19.7 -	11.9
												0.0524A	12/31/07	16.5 -	10.9
												0.3395Q	12/31/07	14.1 -	10.9
												0.042M	1/31/08	10.0 -	7.3
-	-	-	-0.24	0.26	-0.01			14.10	8.92	3.57	36.9	0.059A	12/31/07	47.9 -	31.8
0.35	0.39	0.49	1.74	1.28	0.97	12.2 -	6.6	0.80			1.9	0.08U	3/14/08	21.2 -	11.6
-	-	-	-	1.65	1.08									10.3 -	5.6
0.16	-0.06	-0.12	-0.19	-1.71	-1.54							0.01U	3/24/00	18.2 -	9.8
0.31	0.55	0.57	2.08	1.57	1.26	10.5 -	8.9	0.48	0.46	0.44	2.4	0.13U	3/17/08	22.1 -	16.4
0.07	0.85	0.45	-0.11	1.10	1.29							0.05U	12/5/00	17.3 -	6.7
												0.4219Q	3/1/99	26.5 -	22.0
1.29	0.44	0.44	2.60	1.96	1.71	16.2 -	13.4	2.74	2.70	2.67	7.0	0.695Q	2/7/08	42.2 -	34.8
-	-	0.16	1.10	1.06	1.14									30.7 -	12.7
-0.04	0.14	0.22	0.42	1.01	0.46	73.1 -	30.3							23.8 -	14.1
1.09	1.66	1.45	5.85	3.88	1.85	4.1 -	2.4								
-	-	-	-	0.41	0.58										
0.06	0.66	0.51	1.00	0.01	0.18	4.0 -	1.8					0.02Q	6/11/99	9.2 -	3.4
1.87	3.02	2.42	10.90	2.45	2.95	2.3 -	0.5	7.64	1.92	2.95	55.1	4.45Q	2/27/08	25.4 -	5.0
0.83	3.17	0.34	4.06	5.73	3.60	4.2 -	1.7	0.35	0.20	0.10	2.9	0.1Q	3/17/08	16.9 -	7.0
0.28	0.30	0.05	0.38	1.36	0.53	28.2 -	18.5							10.7 -	7.0
0.64	1.05	0.53	3.80	0.35	5.12	12.7 -	6.1	0.30	0.30	0.30	0.9	0.075Q	2/29/08	48.1 -	23.1
0.35	0.42	0.54	1.84	2.78	1.39	18.3 -	10.0	0.30	0.13	0.11	1.2	0.1Q	2/11/08	33.6 -	18.4
0.15	0.19	0.24	0.78	1.08	0.78	34.6 -	14.2	0.16	0.55	0.11	1.1	0.18A	3/17/08	27.0 -	11.1
0.77	0.83	1.00	3.60	2.31	0.75	71.7 -	52.1	0.85	0.78	0.70	0.4	0.23Q	4/1/08	258.0 -	187.5
-	-	-	0.19	0.24	0.23	62.1 -	37.4	0.24	0.26	0.22	2.8	0.2115A	1/31/08	11.8 -	7.1
0.22	0.19	0.30	0.93	1.24	1.21	27.6 -	19.8	0.32	0.20	0.09	1.5	0.085Q	4/29/08	25.7 -	18.4
0.04	0.05	0.05	0.17	0.21	-0.93	36.5 -	20.6							6.2 -	3.5
0.31	0.37	0.49	1.72	0.84	1.36	18.0 -	14.1							31.0 -	24.2
0.63	0.80	0.88	3.12	2.85	1.86	10.3 -	6.3					0.28Q	7/2/01	32.1 -	19.7
-	-	-	-	-0.36	-0.15									0.4 -	0.0
-	-	-	-	0.15	-2.48									26.6 -	17.4

SYMBOL	COMPANY	NATURE OF BUSINESS	FISCAL YEAR-END	TOTAL REV. $MILL	NET INCOME $MILL	TOTAL ASSETS $MILL	NET STK EQUITY $MILL	NO OF INST	INST. HOLDINGS (SHARES)
TOC	Thomson Corp.	Communications	12/31/06	6641.0	1120.0	20132.0	10481.0	-	-
THO	Thor Industries, Inc.	Automotive	7/31/07	2856.3	134.7	1059.3	766.3	166	31535308
TMA	Thornburg Mortgage Inc	Property, Real Estate & Developmen	12/31/07	1523.4	-874.9	36521.2	2002.7	153	17999528
TDW	Tidewater Inc.	Shipping	3/31/07	1125.3	356.6	2649.3	1886.0	245	52202026
TIF	Tiffany & Co.	Retail - Miscellaneous	1/31/08	2938.8	303.8	2922.2	1637.4	340	134426504
THI	Tim Hortons Inc	Hospitality & Tourism	12/31/07	1895.8	269.6	1797.1	1002.1	-	-
TSU	TIM Participacoes S.A.	Communications	12/31/07	10116.1	-301.7	14200.1	7886.4	61	22422381
TBL	Timberland Co. (The)	Leather and Leather Products	12/31/07	1436.5	40.0	836.3	577.2	194	56212692
TWC	Time Warner Cable Inc	Communications	12/31/07	15955.0	1123.0	56600.0	24706.0	-	-
TWX	Time Warner Inc (New)	Movies & Film	12/31/07	46482.0	4387.0	133830.0	58536.0	878	3313593058
TKR	Timken Co. (The)	Industrial Machinery and Equipment	12/31/07	5236.0	220.1	4379.2	1960.7	185	57395924
TWI	Titan International, Inc. (IL)	Rubber Products	12/31/07	837.0	-7.2	590.5	272.5	63	12530495
TIE	Titanium Metals Corp.	Metal Works	12/31/07	1278.9	268.2	1419.9	1132.7	63	5396945
TJX	TJX Companies, Inc. (New)	Retail - Apparel and Accessory Store	1/26/08	18647.1	771.8	6599.9	2131.2	383	438570704
TNS	TNS Inc	Miscellaneous Business Services	12/31/07	325.6	-2.8	383.1	92.3	61	11621472
TOD	Todd Shipyards Corp.	Shipping	4/1/07	125.5	3.2	120.5	64.0	13	1014197
TOL	Toll Brothers Inc. (United States)	Building & General Construction	10/31/07	4647.0	35.7	7220.3	3527.2	284	106700402
TKS	Tomkins Plc (United Kingdom)	Industrial Machinery and Equipment	12/31/05	3182.4	192.2	2578.3	712.9	26	8190294
TCM	Tongjitang Chinese Medicines Co	Pharmaceuticals	12/31/06	-	134.3	-	377.1	-	-
TR	Tootsie Roll Industries Inc	Food	12/31/07	497.7	51.6	812.7	638.2	134	11420302
TRU	Torch Energy Royalty Trust	Miscellaneous	12/31/06	8.3	7.3	18.4	18.2	7	30252
TMK	Torchmark Corp.	Insurance	12/31/07	3486.7	527.5	15241.4	3324.6	294	75112812
TTC	Toro Co. (The)	Industrial Machinery and Equipment	10/31/07	1876.9	142.4	950.8	370.4	189	14730196
TD	Toronto Dominion Bank	Commercial Banking	10/31/07	25209.0	3997.0	422124.0	21404.0	0	0
TYY	Tortoise Energy Capital Corp	Trusts & Holding Entities							
TYG	Tortoise Energy Infrastructure Corp	Trusts & Holding Entities	11/30/07	9.9	-12.5	1261.6	618.4	33	2917139
TYN	Tortoise North American Energy Co	Trusts & Holding Entities							
TOT	Total S.A. (New)	Oil and Gas	12/31/04	100481.0	10868.0	86767.0	32418.0	249	90859955
TSS	Total System Services, Inc.	Miscellaneous Business Services	12/31/07	1805.8	237.4	1479.0	844.5	75	12717305
TM	Toyota Motor Corp. (Japan)	Automotive	3/31/07	23948091.0	1644032.0	32574779.0	11836092.0	183	22348043
TT	Trane, Inc.	Purpose Machinery	12/31/07	7449.6	286.3	5097.3	538.2	-	-
TAC	TransAlta Corp.	Industrial Machinery and Equipment	12/31/06	2796.5	44.9	7460.1	2427.9	42	39582430
TAI	Transamerica Income Shares, Inc. (	Trusts & Holding Entities						14	91872
TRH	Transatlantic Holdings, Inc.	Insurance	12/31/07	4381.8	487.1	15484.3	3349.0	96	62663462
TRP	TransCanada Corp	Gas Utilities	12/31/07	8828.0	1223.0	30330.0	9785.0	105	142550383
TCI	Transcontinental Realty Investors, I	Property, Real Estate & Developmen	12/31/07	134.5	11.1	1521.2	285.5	11	43752
TDG	Transdigm Group Inc	Aviation	9/30/07	592.8	88.6	2061.1	487.6	-	-
TLP	Transmontaigne Partners L.P.	Oil and Gas	12/31/07	131.7	25.1	460.8	-	-	-
RIG	Transocean Inc (New)	Mining						-	-
TGS	Transportadora de Gas del Sur S.A.	Gas Utilities	12/31/07	1257.3	147.5	5001.7	2929.5	11	4422209
TRV	Travelers Companies Inc (The)	Insurance	12/31/07	26017.0	4601.0	115224.0	26616.0	-	-
TRR	TRC Companies, Inc.	Engineering Services	6/30/07	264.8	-3.6	486.0	161.7	47	5954476
TG	Tredegar Corp. (United States)	Metal Works	12/31/07	924.4	15.2	784.5	491.3	102	16717377
THS	TreeHouse Foods Inc	Food	12/31/07	1157.9	41.6	1456.0	629.3	-	-
TWP	Trex Co., Inc.	Plastics	12/31/07	329.0	-75.9	328.7	94.0	94	9245483
TRY B	Triarc Companies, Inc. (United Stat	Hospitality & Tourism	12/30/07	1263.7	16.1	1454.6	448.9	96	28762527
TY	Tri-Continental Corp.	Trusts & Holding Entities	12/31/07	103.9	86.2	2472.0	2411.1	-	-
TRS	Trimas Corp (New)	Metal Products	12/31/07	1068.3	-158.4	1128.0	208.5	-	-
TSL	Trina Solar Ltd	Electrical	12/31/06	-	12.4	-	157.2	-	-
TRN	Trinity Industries, Inc.	Rail Transport	12/31/07	3832.8	293.1	4043.2	1726.7	156	48737912
TGI	Triumph Group Inc.	Aviation	3/31/07	954.7	47.1	1229.2	627.4	85	14474330
TRX B	Tronox Inc	Chemicals	12/31/07	1426.3	-106.4	1723.4	429.6	-	-
TBI	TrueBlue Inc	Human Resources Services	12/28/07	1385.7	66.2	545.2	283.8	-	-
TRW	TRW Automotive Holdings Corp	Automotive	12/31/07	14702.0	90.0	12290.0	3192.0	76	28838887
TNP	Tsakos Energy Navigation Ltd.	Shipping	12/31/06	427.7	196.4	1969.9	755.3	82	7964310
TUP	Tupperware Brands Corp	Chemicals	12/29/07	1981.4	116.9	1868.7	522.7	185	44755934
TKC	Turkcell Iletisim Hizmetleri AS	Communications	12/31/05	4528.0	747.5	5215.1	3690.3	64	30997857
TKF	Turkish Investment Fund, Inc. (The)	Trusts & Holding Entities	10/31/06	-	0.9	139.8	139.4	15	383575
TWB	Tween Brands Inc	Apparel	2/3/07	883.7	64.8	569.7	371.3	-	-
TEL	Tyco Electronics Ltd	Communications	9/28/07	13460.0	-554.0	23688.0	11377.0	-	-
TYC	Tyco International Ltd (Bermuda)	Miscellaneous	9/28/07	18781.0	-1742.0	32815.0	15624.0	-	-
TYC	Tyco International Ltd.	Electrical	9/28/07	18781.0	-1742.0	32815.0	15624.0	-	-
TYL	Tyler Technologies, Inc.	IT & Technology	12/31/07	219.8	17.5	241.5	137.2	78	26614643
TSN	Tyson Foods, Inc.	Food	9/29/07	26900.0	268.0	10227.0	4731.0	-	-
USB PRH	U.S. Bancorp (DE)	Commercial Banking	12/31/07	20308.0	4324.0	237615.0	21046.0	-	-
USS	U.S. Shipping Partners LP	Shipping	12/31/07	176.7	4.8	683.0	131.0	21	2797751
UBS	UBS AG (Switzerland)	Trusts & Holding Entities	12/31/04	69654.0	8470.0	1737118.0	39367.0	-	-
UDR	UDR Inc	Property, Real Estate & Developmen	12/31/07	500.2	221.3	4801.1	1019.4	-	-
UGI	UGI Corp. (New)	Electricity	9/30/07	5476.9	204.3	5502.7	1321.9	192	67776162
UIL	UIL Holding Corp	Electricity	12/31/07	982.0	44.7	1775.8	464.3	96	6122609
UPL	Ultra Petroleum Corp.	Oil and Gas	12/31/07	566.6	263.0	1776.2	853.6	173	67100352
UGP	Ultrapar Participacoes S.A.	Retail - Fuel & Oil	12/31/07	19921.3	181.9	9224.5	4600.8	23	4116851
UA	Under Armour Inc	Apparel	12/31/07	606.6	52.6	390.6	280.5	-	-
UBB	Unibanco-Uniao de Bancos Brasileir	Commercial Banking	12/31/07	17252.0	3447.8	149596.9	11837.3	91	54762173
UFI	Unifi, Inc.	Textiles	6/24/07	690.3	-116.3	660.9	299.9	70	28916665
UNF	Unifirst Corp.	Personal Services	8/25/07	902.1	45.2	874.5	497.3	89	7929567
UN	Unilever N.V.	Food	12/31/04	38566.0	2755.0	36858.0	7629.0	221	101329220
UL	Unilever Plc (United Kingdom)	Food	12/31/04	38566.0	2755.0	36858.0	7629.0	119	44389667
UNP	Union Pacific Corp. (United States)	Rail Transport	12/31/07	16283.0	1855.0	38033.0	15585.0	514	210599219
UB	UnionBanCal Corp. (United States)	Commercial Banking	12/31/07	3860.7	608.1	55727.7	4738.0	164	132454434

EARNINGS PER SHARE QUARTERLY 1st	2nd	3rd	ANNUAL 2007	2006	2005	P/E RATIO		DIVIDENDS PER SHARE 2007	2006	2005	AV. YLD %	DIV. DECLARED AMOUNT	PAYABLE	PRICE RANGE 2007	
0.35	0.58	4.61	-	1.73	1.42				0.88	0.79		0.3175Q	5/1/08		
0.68	0.39	-	2.41	3.03	2.13	15.7 -	9.7	1.28	0.24	0.37	4.3	0.07Q	1/4/08	37.9 -	23.4
0.62	0.66	-8.94	-7.48	2.58	2.79	-		1.61	2.72	2.72	5.7	0.6372Q	2/15/08	31.3 -	23.8
1.55	1.56	1.66	6.31	4.07	1.78	5.7 -	4.1	0.60	0.60	0.60	2.0	0.15Q	3/14/08	36.3 -	25.8
0.36	0.26	0.71	1.80	1.75	2.05	24.3 -	15.1	0.38	0.30	0.23	1.1	0.15Q	4/10/08	43.7 -	27.1
0.31	0.36	0.36	1.43	1.40	1.19	-		0.28	0.14	-	-	0.09Q	3/17/08	-	
														16.7 -	11.1
0.15	-0.31	0.42	0.65	1.67	2.43	51.6 -	38.0							33.6 -	24.7
0.28	0.28	0.25	1.15	2.00	1.25	-								-	
0.31	0.28	0.29	1.17	1.55	0.62	16.7 -	13.3	0.23	0.21	0.10	1.3	0.0625Q	3/15/08	19.6 -	15.6
0.79	0.58	0.43	2.30	2.36	2.81	11.8 -	8.5	0.66	0.62	0.60	2.8	0.17Q	3/4/08	27.1 -	19.5
-0.12	0.18	-0.03	-0.28	0.26	0.60	-		0.02	0.02	0.02	0.2	0.005Q	4/15/08	15.1 -	3,1
0.41	0.42	0.29	1.46	1.53	0.86	2.2 -	0.7	0.07	-	-	2.9	8.8438Q	3/17/08	3.3 -	1.1
0.34	0.13	0.54	1.55	1.41	1.30	17.0 -	13.5	0.27	0.23	0.17	1.1	0.09Q	2/28/08	26.4 -	20.9
-0.13	0.02	0.02	-0.12	-0.41	0.23	4.00		-	-	-	19.2	4.U	4/12/07	23.3 -	18.0
0.08	-0.05	0.50	0.57	1.47	1.62	31.8 -	26.2	4.60	0.40	0.40	27.6	0.05Q	3/20/08	18.1 -	14.9
-0.61	-	-	0.22	4.17	4.78	155.9 -	83.8	-	-	-	-			34.3 -	18.4
-	-	-	0.17	0.22	0.24	120.8 -	105.6	-	-	-	-			20.5 -	18.0
-	-	-	-	1.47	1.39									-	
0.17	0.18	0.42	0.91	1.15	1.36	36.7 -	28.4	0.31	0.30	0.26	1.1	0.08Q	3/31/08	33.4 -	25.8
0.10	0.10	0.13	-	0.84	0.65	-		-	0.84	0.65		0.156Q	12/10/07	7.6 -	5.6
1.37	1.32	1.41	5.50	5.13	4.68	10.5 -	8.2	0.52	0.48	0.44	1.0	0.14Q	5/1/08	57.5 -	45.1
0.47	-	-	3.40	2.91	2.45	12.1 -	6.7	0.48	0.36	0.24	1.5	0.15Q	4/11/08	41.0 -	22.6
1.26	1.20	1.51	5.48	6.34	3.20	-		2.11	1.78	1.58	-	0.3031Q	4/30/08	-	
-	-	-	-	-0.36	0.04	-		-	1.50	0.57	-	0.4175Q	3/3/08	-	
-	-	0.61	0.32	-0.16		-		2.19	2.02	1.79	0.0	0.5550	0/0/00	07.7 -	00.0
-	-	-	0.61	0.02								0.3725Q	3/3/08	-	
-	-	5.80	5.09	5.20		9.3 -	7.5	-	-	-	-			54.2 -	43.4
0.29	0.33	0.35	1.20	1.26	0.99	25.8 -	16.4	3.31	0.27	0.22	14.1	0.07Q	4/1/08	30.9 -	19.7
-	-	-	511.80	421.62	355.28	0.2 -	0.1	-	-	-	-			82.9 -	64.7
0.84	0.84	0.30	1.40	2.62	2.56	20.9 -	16.7	0.68	0.72	0.60	2.6	0.16Q	3/20/08	29.3 -	23.3
0.33	0.28	0.33	-	0.22	1.01	-		-	1.00	1.00	-	0.27Q	4/1/08	15.3 -	11.7
-	-	-	-	-	-	-		-	-	-	-	0.11M	1/16/06	25.4 -	21.5
1.61	1.89	2.12	7.31	6.46	0.57	10.1 -	7.4	0.59	0.51	0.44	0.9	0.16Q	3/21/08	73.5 -	53.8
0.52	0.48	0.60	2.30	2.20	2.47	10.8 -	8.2	1.36	1.28	1.22	6.4	0.36Q	4/30/08	24.9 -	18.9
-0.85	-1.66	-0.58	1.24	0.40	1.12	14.0 -	8.9	-	-	-	-	0.18Q	9/29/00	17.3 -	11.0
0.54	-	-	1.83	0.53	111.49	-		-	-	-	-			-	
0.33	0.15	0.41	1.42	0.44	0.13	-		1.90	1.69	0.55	-	0.52Q	2/5/08	-	
														43.0 -	23.9
														5.7 -	3.6
1.56	1.86	1.81	6.86	5.91	2.33	6.3 -	4.5	0.26	1.01	0.91	0.7	0.29Q	3/31/08	43.4 -	31.0
0.01	0.27	-0.04	-0.33	-1.62	-0.57	-		-	-	-	-			23.1 -	14.2
0.26	0.25	-0.47	0.39	0.98	0.42	51.9 -	33.3	0.16	0.16	0.16	1.0	0.04Q	4/1/08	20.3 -	13.0
0.24	0.30	0.34	1.33	1.43	0.37	-		-	-	-	-			-	
0.25	0.17	2.77	-5.10	0.16	0.17	-		-	-	-	-			53.5 -	32.0
0.07	-0.30	0.04	0.16	-0.13	-0.79	78.3 -	59.2	0.32	0.77	0.29	3.0	0.09Q	3/14/08	12.5 -	9.5
-	-0.12	0.20	-5.56	-6.37	-2.21	58.3 -	51.2	2.50	2.50	2.50	5.5	0.633Q	3/26/08	49.0 -	43.0
-	-	-	-	0.01	0.00	-		-	-	-	-			-	
0.74	0.85	1.08	3.65	2.90	1.13	6.5 -	4.6	0.25	0.21	0.17	1.2	0.07Q	4/30/08	23.9 -	16.9
0.81	0.97	0.93	2.87	2.15	0.72	14.3 -	10.1	0.12	-	-	0.4	0.04Q	3/15/08	41.0 -	29.0
-0.23	-0.52	-0.47	-2.61	-	0.77	-		0.20	0.20	-	-	0.050	4/1/08	-	
0.21	0.41	0.51	1.44	1.45	1.18	11.8 -	7.7	-	-	-	-			17.0 -	11.1
-0.87	0.94	0.22	0.88	1.71	1.99	30.8 -	19.0	-	-	-	-			27.1 -	16.7
-	-	-	-	5.15	4.09	-		-	1.18	0.97	-	1.855	10/26/07	21.7 -	9.3
0.32	0.56	0.11	1.87	1.54	1.41	11.1 -	8.6	0.88	0.88	0.88	4.9	0.22Q	4/3/08	20.8 -	16.1
-	-	-	-	0.40	0.35	-		-	-	-	-			12.1 -	5.4
-	-	-	-	0.16	0.21	-		-	1.43	0.08	-	2.2736A	1/7/08	17.9 -	8.8
0.39	0.07	0.46	1.95	1.60	1.19	13.6 -	6.9	-	-	-	-			26.6 -	13.4
1.90	-	-	-1.11	2.40	2.30	-		-	-	-	-	0.14Q	2/4/08	-	
-	-	-	-3.52	6.95	5.85	-		-	-	-	-	0.15Q	2/1/08	56.9 -	41.5
0.73	-	-	-3.52	7.20	5.72	-		1.60	1.20	1.60	3.3	0.15Q	5/1/08	56.9 -	41.5
0.06	0.09	0.12	0.42	0.34	0.19	26.2 -	18.3	-	-	-	-			11.0 -	7.7
0.10	-	-	0.75	-0.58	0.99	-		0.16	0.16	0.16	-	0.036Q	6/15/08	-	
0.63	0.65	0.67	2.43	2.61	2.42	-		1.63	1.39	1.23	-	0.307Q	4/15/08	-	
0.31	0.13	-0.11	0.26	0.37	1.28	105.0 -	89.4	1.80	1.80	1.64	7.2	0.45Q	2/15/08	27.3 -	23.2
-	-	-	-2.28	5.95	13.36	-		-	-	-	-			42.2 -	32.5
0.21	0.01	0.56	1.53	0.85	1.02	16.2 -	11.5	0.31	1.24	1.19	1.5	0.4219Q	1/30/08	24.8 -	17.5
0.74	-	-	1.89	1.65	1.77	10.9 -	7.9	0.72	0.69	0.65	4.2	0.185Q	4/1/08	20.6 -	14.9
0.21	0.39	0.83	1.77	-2.63	1.28	18.3 -	14.2	1.73	1.73	1.73	6.0	0.432Q	4/1/08	32.4 -	25.2
0.42	0.31	0.24	1.66	1.43	1.41	16.5 -	6.7	-	-	-	-			27.4 -	11.1
														17.4 -	7.6
0.20	0.11	0.40	1.05	0.79	0.36	-		-	-	-	-			-	
														31.7 -	17.0
-0.15	-0.13	-	-2.07	-0.28	-0.79	-		-	-	-	-	0.14Q	5/8/98	6.6 -	1.9
0.85	-	-	2.34	2.03	2.24	12.8 -	10.4	0.15	0.15	0.15	0.5	0.03Q	4/3/08	29.9 -	24.4
-	-	-	-	1.60	3.76	-		-	-	-	-			24.8 -	18.9
-	-	-	1.31	1.60	0.56	18.5 -	13.9	-	-	-	-			24.2 -	18.2
1.41	1.65	2.00	6.91	5.91	3.85	10.0 -	8.0	1.49	1.20	1.20	2.5	0.44Q	4/1/08	69.3 -	55.1
1.07	1.19	0.92	4.37	5.24	5.84	14.8 -	11.3	2.03	1.82	1.59	3.6	0.52Q	4/4/08	64.8 -	49.5

SYMBOL	COMPANY	NATURE OF BUSINESS	FISCAL YEAR-END	TOTAL REV. $MILL	NET INCOME $MILL	TOTAL ASSETS $MILL	NET STK EQUITY $MILL	NO OF INST	INST. HOLDINGS (SHARES)
UNS	UniSource Energy Corp.	Electricity	12/31/07	1381.4	58.4	3185.7	690.1	123	29856523
UIS	Unisys Corp.	IT & Technology	12/31/07	5652.5	-79.1	4137.1	366.6	244	238031037
UNT	Unit Corp.	Oil and Gas	12/31/07	1158.8	266.3	2199.8	1434.8	172	36519552
UMC	United Microelectronics Corp.	IT & Technology	12/31/06	112003.8	32619.3	367653.5	297402.9	-	-
UPS	United Parcel Service Inc	Road Transport	12/31/07	49692.0	382.0	39042.0	12183.0	638	395035310
URI	United Rentals, Inc.	General Construction Supplies & Ser	12/31/07	3731.0	362.0	5842.0	2018.0	162	65027538
X	United States Steel Corp. (New)	Metal Works	12/31/07	16873.0	879.0	15632.0	5531.0	330	116302868
UTX	United Technologies Corp.	Aviation	12/31/07	54759.0	4224.0	54575.0	21355.0	882	814925370
UNH	UnitedHealth Group Inc	Insurance	12/31/07	75431.0	4654.0	50899.0	20063.0	692	1091525338
UTR	Unitrin, Inc.	Insurance	12/31/07	2919.8	217.8	9405.0	2297.8	156	19705933
UAM	Universal American Corp	Insurance	12/31/07	3034.6	84.1	4089.8	1351.1	98	18505972
UVV	Universal Corp.	Tobacco Products	3/31/07	2007.3	44.4	2328.8	1030.7	141	22173140
UHT	Universal Health Realty Income Tru	Property, Real Estate & Developmen	12/31/07	28.0	22.2	199.7	160.3	77	4206528
UHS	Universal Health Services, Inc.	Hospitals & Health Care	12/31/07	4751.0	170.4	3608.7	1517.2	218	52490696
UTI	Universal Technical Institute, Inc.	Vocational Education Services	9/30/07	353.4	15.6	232.8	124.5	79	20369660
UNM	Unum Group	Insurance	12/31/07	10519.9	679.3	52432.7	8039.9	314	309987970
URS	URS Corp	Engineering Services	12/28/07	5383.0	132.2	6930.0	3478.6	132	39032318
UBA	Urstadt Biddle Properties Inc	Property, Real Estate & Developmen	10/31/07	81.9	44.4	471.8	294.2	67	8730906
LCC	US Airways Group Inc (New)	Aviation	12/31/07	11700.0	427.0	8040.0	1439.0	-	-
USU	USEC, Inc.	Earth & Rock Mining	12/31/07	1928.0	96.6	3087.8	1309.5	122	56276108
USG	USG Corp	Stone, Clay, Glass, and Concrete Pr	12/31/07	5202.0	76.0	4621.0	2193.0	163	39619995
UST	UST, Inc.	Tobacco Products	12/31/07	1950.8	520.3	1487.1	-320.2	309	135550997
YSI	U-Store-It Trust	Property, Real Estate & Developmen	12/31/07	229.2	-13.1	1687.8	555.6	69	25087060
EGY	VAALCO Energy, Inc.	Oil and Gas	12/31/07	125.0	19.1	186.6	142.3	38	25750504
MTN	Vail Resorts Inc.	Sporting & Recreational	7/31/07	940.5	61.4	1909.1	714.0	94	26657085
VCI	Valassis Communications, Inc.	Advertising, Marketing & PR	12/31/07	2242.2	58.0	2190.5	219.9	155	51112823
VRX	Valeant Pharmaceuticals Internation	Pharmaceuticals	12/31/07	872.2	-6.2	1494.3	414.1	167	90284266
VLO	Valero Energy Corp. (New)	Oil and Gas	12/31/07	95327.0	5234.0	42722.0	18507.0	473	191740410
VHI	Valhi, Inc.	Chemicals	12/31/07	1563.1	-45.7	2603.0	618.4	46	4527051
VLY	Valley National Bancorp	Commercial Banking	12/31/07	811.3	153.2	12749.0	949.1	99	12551957
VMI	Valmont Industries, Inc. (United Stat	Metal Products	12/29/07	1499.8	94.7	1052.6	510.6	87	9970585
VAL	Valspar Corp.	Chemicals	10/26/07	3249.3	172.1	3452.3	1380.8	182	37189416
VBF	Van Kampen Bond Fund	Trusts & Holding Entities	6/30/07	11.5	10.2	251.4	211.4	18	649723
VCV	Van Kampen California Value Munic	Trusts & Holding Entities	10/31/06	-	23.6	580.8	365.7	7	48437
VTA	Van Kampen Dynamic Credit Oppor	Trusts & Holding Entities	7/31/07	-	6.0	-	1379.8	-	-
VLT	Van Kampen High Income Trust II	Trusts & Holding Entities	12/31/07	11.0	9.6	145.0	77.0	6	66823
VMO	Van Kampen Municipal Opportunity	Trusts & Holding Entities	10/31/06	-	32.8	1021.9	567.5	14	180383
VKQ	Van Kampen Municipal Trust	Trusts & Holding Entities	10/31/06	-	40.3	1087.8	643.1	27	950776
VOQ	Van Kampen Ohio Quality Municipal	Trusts & Holding Entities	10/31/06	-	6.0	179.4	97.9	7	33038
VPV	Van Kampen Pennsylvania Value M	Trusts & Holding Entities	10/31/06	-	22.8	635.8	393.4	6	20682
VVR	Van Kampen Senior Income Trust	Trusts & Holding Entities	7/31/07	233.1	166.7	2727.0	1450.1	57	15454754
VIM	Van Kampen Trust for Insured Muni	Trusts & Holding Entities	10/31/06	-	9.8	285.2	157.2	15	160411
VGM	Van Kampen Trust for Investment G	Trusts & Holding Entities	10/31/06	-	48.7	1335.3	743.4	30	1182517
VTJ	Van Kampen Trust for Investment G	Trusts & Holding Entities	10/31/06	-	7.1	195.7	109.0	7	61913
VTN	Van Kampen Trust for Investment G	Trusts & Holding Entities	10/31/06	-	16.2	498.5	262.6	8	109274
VAR	Varian Medical Systems, Inc.	Medical Instruments & Equipment	9/28/07	1776.6	239.5	1684.4	821.5	330	108129745
VGR	Vector Group Ltd	Tobacco Products	12/31/07	555.4	73.8	785.3	100.9	64	16021175
VVC	Vectren Corp	Electricity	12/31/07	2281.9	143.1	4296.4	1233.7	179	30949151
VQ	Venoco Inc	Oil and Gas	12/31/07	233.9	-73.4	1265.5	245.6	-	-
VTR	Ventas, Inc.	Property, Real Estate & Developmen	12/31/07	771.8	282.3	5716.6	1823.7	135	71014370
VE	Veolia Environnement	Water Utilities	12/31/04	22500.3	391.5	35825.9	4948.3	14	612689
VSE	VeraSun Energy Corp	Chemicals	12/31/07	848.3	26.6	1863.5	755.7	-	-
VZ	Verizon Communications Inc	Communications	12/31/07	93469.0	5521.0	186959.0	50581.0	991	1532059539
VFC	VF Corp. (United States)	Apparel	12/29/07	7219.4	591.6	6446.7	3576.8	300	98327724
VIA B	Viacom Inc (New)	Media	12/31/07	13423.1	1838.1	22904.1	7111.2	-	-
VVI	Viad Corp.	Miscellaneous Business Services	12/31/07	1003.7	44.6	781.4	469.8	120	19096038
VCO	Vina Concha y Toro S.A. (Chile)	Food	12/31/07	285790.0	34058.7	393905.8	222715.3	20	362554
VM	Virgin Mobile USA Inc	Communications	12/31/07	1312.9	4.2	282.0	-415.2	-	-
D 37A	Virginia Electric & Power Co.	Electricity	12/31/07	6181.0	448.0	17057.0	5798.0	-	-
V	Visa Inc	Miscellaneous Business Services	10/1/07	-	-	27069.3	16285.6	-	-
VSH	Vishay Intertechnology, Inc.	Electrical	12/31/07	2833.3	130.8	4995.2	3356.8	-	-
VC	Visteon Corp.	Automotive	12/31/07	11266.0	-372.0	7205.0	-90.0	191	107969400
VTO	Vitro, S.A de C.V. (New)	Stone, Clay, Glass, and Concrete Pr	12/31/06	26562.0	373.0	27104.0	8875.0	6	199891
VIV	Vivo Participacoes S.A.	Communications	12/31/06	10936.7	16.3	17542.1	8372.2	-	-
VMW	VMWARE, Inc.	Information Technologies & Commu	12/31/07	1325.8	218.1	2695.7	1340.6	-	-
VOD	Vodafone Group Plc (New)	Communications	3/31/05	26678.0	6410.0	147197.0	113648.0	-	-
VOL	Volt Information Sciences, Inc. (Unit	Human Resources Services	10/28/07	2353.1	39.3	840.2	352.5	77	6364459
VG	Vonage Holdings Corp	Communications	12/31/07	828.2	-267.4	462.3	-75.1	-	-
VNO	Vornado Realty Trust	Property, Real Estate & Developmen	12/31/07	3270.6	568.9	22478.9	6118.4	254	92718554
VCP	Votorantim Celulose e Papel S.A.	Paper Products	12/31/06	3795.2	655.8	10206.8	5114.1	66	39415891
VMC	Vulcan Materials Co (Holding Comp	Earth & Rock Mining	12/31/95	1461.0	166.2	1215.8	796.6	254	75102998
WTI	W & T Offshore Inc	Oil and Gas	12/31/07	1113.7	144.3	2822.3	1151.3	52	7336838
WHI	W Holding Co Inc	Trusts & Holding Entities	12/31/06	1037.3	100.5	17154.7	1227.9	-	-
WPC	W.P. Carey & Co. LLC	Property, Real Estate & Developmen	12/31/07	263.1	79.3	1153.3	634.3	68	2741877
WPL	W.P. Stewart & Co. Ltd.	Wealth Management	12/31/06	142.1	37.5	146.6	112.8	47	12796448
WNC	Wabash National Corp	Automotive	12/31/07	1102.5	16.3	483.6	279.9	139	37291881
WBC	WABCO Holdings Inc	Specialist Equipment Supplies	12/31/07	2415.9	125.4	1794.2	607.6	-	-
WAB	Wabtec Corp.	Rail Transport	12/31/07	1360.1	109.6	1158.7	617.3	131	40448926
WB	Wachovia Corp (New)	Commercial Banking	12/31/07	55528.0	6312.0	782896.0	76872.0	856	825764500
WNA PR	Wachovia Preferred Funding Corp (	Property, Real Estate & Developmen						9	1096549

T60

1st	2nd	3rd	2007	2006	2005	P/E High	P/E Low	Div 2007	Div 2006	Div 2005	AV. YLD %	Amount	Payable	Price High 2007	Price Low 2007
0.14	0.32	0.66	1.57	1.80	1.28	15.9-	14.8	0.90	0.84	0.76	3.7	0.24Q	3/21/08	24.9-	23.3
0.01	-0.19	-0.09	-0.23	-0.81	-5.09	-		-	-	-	-	-	-	15.7-	9.6
1.39	1.41	1.37	5.71	6.72	4.60	7.1-	4.1	-	-	-	-	-	-	40.4-	23.3
0.78	1.04	1.02	0.36	3.86	3.47	243.1-	188.8	1.68	1.52	1.32	2.3	0.45Q	3/4/08	87.5-	68.0
0.28	0.60	0.98	3.25	2.06	1.80	7.1-	4.4	-	-	-	-	-	-	23.2-	14.3
2.30	2.54	2.27	7.40	11.18	7.00	7.2-	3.5	0.80	0.60	0.38	2.2	0.25Q	3/10/08	53.4-	25.8
0.82	1.16	1.21	4.27	3.71	3.03	12.4-	9.5	1.17	1.01	0.88	2.5	0.32Q	3/10/08	52.8-	40.8
0.66	0.89	0.95	3.42	2.97	2.48	12.9-	8.2	0.03	0.03	0.01	0.1	0.03A	4/16/08	44.0-	28.1
1.08	0.94	0.98	3.30	4.15	3.67	15.1-	11.3	1.82	1.76	1.70	4.3	0.47Q	3/3/08	49.9-	37.1
0.07	0.35	0.40	1.18	1.99	0.91	13.5-	8.1	-	-	-	-	-	-	15.9-	9.5
0.54	1.23	1.56	1.13	0.31	3.73	46.9-	37.4	1.73	1.69	1.59	3.6	16.875Q	3/17/08	53.0-	42.3
0.49	0.67	0.37	1.87	2.92	2.15	18.4-	13.3	2.30	2.26	2.17	7.7	0.58Q	3/31/08	34.5-	24.8
0.92	0.97	0.54	3.18	4.56	4.00	17.8-	12.5	0.32	0.32	0.32	0.7	0.08Q	3/17/08	56.5-	39.9
0.24	-	-	0.57	0.97	1.26	82.9-	42.9	-	-	-	-	-	-	47.2-	24.4
0.51	0.43	0.52	1.91	1.23	1.64	9.5-	6.4	0.07	0.30	0.30	0.5	0.075Q	2/15/08	18.1-	12.2
0.58	0.70	0.73	2.35	2.19	1.72	13.7-	9.5	-	-	-	-	-	-	32.1-	22.4
0.16	-	-	1.25	0.57	0.87	14.2-	10.1	0.83	0.81	0.80	5.5	2.2475Q	4/30/08	17.8-	12.6
0.70	2.77	1.87	4.52	3.33	-17.06	-		-	-	-	-	-	-	-	
0.45	-0.15	0.51	0.94	1.22	0.26	11.8-	7.3	-	-	0.55	-	0.1375Q	12/15/05	11.1-	6.9
0.45	0.56	0.07	0.78	4.33	-32.02	52.2-	16.2	-	-	-	-	0.025Q	3/21/01	40.7-	12.6
0.67	0.87	0.84	3.27	3.12	3.23	15.0-	10.0	2.40	2.28	2.20	6.2	0.63Q	3/31/08	48.9-	34.5
-0.06	-	-0.07	-0.22	-0.15	0.07	-		1.16	1.16	1.04	6.8	0.18Q	4/22/08	17.4-	16.5
0.08	0.06	0.15	0.32	0.67	0.50	17.2-	4.8	-	-	-	-	-	-	5.5-	1.6
-0.63	1.31	-	1.50	1.19	0.64	15.1-	8.0	-	-	-	-	-	-	23.5-	13.9
0.23	0.20	0.34	1.21	1.07	1.90	29.6-	22.8	-	-	-	-	-	-	05.0	07.0
0.09	0.17	-0.13	-0.07	-0.61	-2.05	-		-	0.23	0.31	-	0.0775Q	8/31/06	27.1-	17.1
1.86	3.89	2.09	8.88	8.64	6.10	2.7-	1.3	0.48	0.30	0.19	2.8	0.12Q	3/12/08	23.8-	11.5
0.22	-0.04	-0.46	-0.40	1.20	0.68	-		0.40	0.40	0.40	7.3	0.1Q	3/31/08	6.6-	4.1
0.41	0.33	0.30	1.27	1.33	1.35	19.3-	16.4	0.83	0.81	0.79	3.7	0.21Q	4/1/08	24.6-	20.9
0.72	1.03	0.99	3.63	2.38	1.54	7.0-	5.4	0.41	0.37	0.34	1.9	0.105Q	4/15/08	25.4-	19.7
0.21	-	-	1.50	1.71	1.42	17.1-	15.0	0.52	0.44	0.40	2.1	0.14Q	4/15/08	25.7-	22.4
-	-	0.90	0.89	0.96		20.5-	18.5	0.94	0.90	1.02	5.3	0.23Q	3/31/08	18.1-	16.6
-	-	-	1.09	1.04		-		-	1.01	1.03	-	0.07M	1/31/08	17.2-	14.1
-	-	0.08	-	-		-		-	-	-	-	0.1517M	12/31/07	-	
-	-	0.51	0.49	0.52		10.2-	7.9	0.33	0.36	0.44	6.9	0.025M	3/31/08	5.2-	4.0
-	-	-	1.11	1.12		-		-	1.16	0.94	-	0.068M	1/31/08	17.6-	14.1
-	-	-	1.02	1.02		-		-	1.03	0.88	-	0.067M	1/31/08	15.7-	13.3
-	-	-	1.03	1.01		-		-	0.84	0.93	-	0.065M	1/31/08	17.3-	14.0
-	-	-	1.00	1.03		-		-	0.76	0.94	-	0.0615M	1/31/08	17.2-	13.9
-	-	0.93	0.79	0.60		9.8-	8.8	0.77	0.62	0.47	8.8	0.0578M	3/31/08	9.1-	8.2
-	-	-	1.00	1.03		-		-	1.00	0.87	-	0.0625M	1/31/08	17.4-	13.7
-	-	-	1.11	1.09		-		-	1.06	0.93	-	0.0685M	1/31/08	16.6-	13.9
-	-	-	1.10	1.19		-		-	1.02	1.05	-	0.069M	1/31/08	18.2-	14.9
-	-	-	1.05	1.07		-		-	1.05	0.98	-	0.065M	1/31/08	18.5-	14.2
0.43	-		1.83	1.81	1.50	25.2-	17.1	-	-	-	-	-	-	46.1-	31.4
0.16	0.32	0.23	1.13	0.68	0.96	13.0-	11.1	1.54	1.47	1.40	11.4	0.4Q	3/28/08	14.7-	12.5
0.92	0.21	0.22	1.87	1.43	1.80	14.5-	12.2	1.27	1.23	1.19	5.1	0.325Q	3/3/08	27.1-	22.9
-0.24	-0.07	0.01	-1.58	0.69	0.49	-		-	-	-	-	-	-	-	
0.42	1.48	0.21	2.25	1.25	1.36	12.9-	9.4	1.90	1.58	1.44	7.5	0.5125Q	3/28/08	29.1-	21.1
-	-	-	1.91	1.59		-		-	-	-	-	-	-	36.5-	25.2
-	0.19	0.09	0.31	1.03	0.01	-		-	-	-	-	-	-	-	
0.51	0.58	0.44	1.90	2.12	2.65	21.3-	17.2	1.65	1.62	1.60	4.5	0.43Q	5/1/08	40.5-	32.7
1.20	0.72	1.84	5.22	4.72	4.44	10.6-	8.1	2.23	1.94	1.10	4.6	0.58Q	3/20/08	56.4-	42.4
0.29	0.63	0.96	2.72	2.22	1.67	-		-	-	-	-	-	-	-	
0.00	0.00	0.41	2.14	2.81	1.70	13.5-	10.0	0.16	0.16	0.16	0.7	0.04Q	4/1/08	28.8-	21.5
-	-	-	-	-		-		-	-	-	-	-	-	29.6-	16.0
-	-	-	0.08	-1.45	-4.49	-		4.80	4.80	4.80	-	1.745Q	3/20/08	-	
0.55	-	-	-	-		-		-	-	-	-	-	-	-	
0.25	0.22	0.19	0.69	0.73	0.34	-		-	-	-	-	-	-	-	
-1.19	-0.52	-0.84	-2.87	-1.28	-2.14							0.06Q	12/1/04	12.4-	6.6
-	-	-	-	-								-	-	4.0-	2.5
-	-	-	-	-								-	-	9.7-	5.8
0.12	0.10	0.18	0.61	0.26	0.20							-	-	-	
-	-	-	-0.10	-0.40	0.11							-	-	-	
-0.59	-	-	1.71	1.31	0.74	12.4-	8.3	-	-	-	-	-	-	21.2-	14.1
-0.47	-0.22	-1.04	-1.72	-3.59	-189.67							-	-	-	
0.96	0.96	0.74	3.23	3.35	3.50	23.7-	14.9	3.45	3.79	3.90	5.7	0.4141Q	4/1/08	76.4-	48.1
-	-	-	-	-								-	-	16.4-	10.8
0.91	1.45	1.38	4.54	4.69	3.73	12.1-	9.3	1.38	1.48	1.16	2.9	0.49Q	3/10/08	55.0-	42.4
0.17	0.60	0.48	1.90	2.84	2.87	-		0.54	0.12	0.06	-	0.03Q	4/4/08	-	
0.12	-	-	0.38	0.74		-		-	0.19	0.19	-	0.0158M	6/15/05	-	
0.27	1.10	0.53	2.05	2.22	1.25	17.3-	12.4	2.15	1.82	1.79	7.1	0.27Q	1/15/08	35.5-	25.5
0.28	0.21	-	-	0.82	0.87	-		-	1.13	1.20	-	0.15Q	8/3/07	23.7-	18.7
0.03	0.18	0.12	0.52	0.30	3.06	58.7-	43.3	0.18	0.18	0.18	0.7	0.045Q	4/4/08	30.5-	22.5
-	-	-	1.81	-		-		0.14	-	-	-	0.07Q	3/20/08	-	
0.52	0.57	0.55	2.23	1.73	1.17	10.0-	6.2	0.04	0.04	0.04	0.2	0.01Q	2/29/08	22.4-	13.8
1.20	1.22	0.85	3.26	4.63	4.19	16.7-	13.4	2.40	2.14	1.94	5.1	0.4667Q	3/17/08	54.5-	43.6
1.69	1.67	1.76	-	6.71	4.40	-		-	1.81	1.81	-	0.4531Q	3/31/08	29.2-	25.3

SYMBOL	COMPANY	NATURE OF BUSINESS	FISCAL YEAR-END	TOTAL REV. $MILL	NET INCOME $MILL	TOTAL ASSETS $MILL	NET STK EQUITY $MILL	NO OF INST	INST. HOLDINGS (SHARES)
WDR	Waddell & Reed Financial, Inc.	Finance Intermediaries & Services	12/31/07	837.6	125.5	893.8	381.6	174	62521494
WAG	Walgreen Co.	Retail - Miscellaneous	8/31/07	53762.0	2041.3	19313.6	11104.3	-	-
WMT	Wal-Mart Stores, Inc.	Retail - General	1/31/08	378799.0	12731.0	163514.0	64608.0	1120	1518101118
WLT	Walter Industries Inc	Building & General Construction	12/31/07	1241.4	112.0	2767.3	114.7	170	44068373
WMG	Warner Music Group Corp	Sporting & Recreational	9/30/07	3385.0	-21.0	4572.0	-36.0	-	-
WM	Washington Mutual Inc.	Other Depository Banking	12/31/07	25531.0	-67.0	327913.0	24584.0	692	651776846
WPO	Washington Post Co.	Vocational Education Services	12/30/07	4180.4	288.6	6004.5	3461.2	245	6088753
WRE	Washington Real Estate Investment	Property, Real Estate & Developmen	12/31/07	255.7	61.9	1898.3	486.5	140	16660724
WCN	Waste Connections, Inc.	Sanitation Services	12/31/07	958.5	99.1	1982.0	775.1	167	46133183
WMI	Waste Management, Inc. (DE)	Sanitation Services	12/31/07	13310.0	1163.0	20175.0	5792.0	421	484996055
WAT	Waters Corp.	Instruments and Related Products	12/31/07	1473.0	268.1	1881.1	586.1	324	100617445
WSO	Watsco Inc.	Machinery Supply Retail	12/31/07	1758.0	65.6	748.2	550.0	112	21300154
WPI	Watson Pharmaceuticals, Inc.	Pharmaceuticals	12/31/07	2496.7	141.0	3472.0	1849.5	254	87223437
WW	Watson Wyatt Worldwide Inc	Accounting & Management Consulti	6/30/07	1486.5	116.3	1529.7	787.5	114	23078630
WTS	Watts Water Technologies Inc	Metal Products	12/31/07	1382.3	77.4	1729.3	915.5	133	22909885
WPP	Wausau Paper Corp	Paper Products	12/31/07	1240.4	-1.8	744.2	280.9	128	35889871
WCI	WCI Communities Inc	Building & General Construction	12/31/07	936.4	-578.5	2891.2	420.0	153	38235899
WFT	Weatherford International, Ltd.	Oil and Gas	12/31/07	7832.1	1070.6	13191.0	7406.7	288	125249596
WBS	Webster Financial Corp (Waterbury,	Commercial Banking	12/31/07	1197.9	96.8	17202.0	1736.6	185	33348906
WTW	Weight Watchers International, Inc.	Personal Services	12/29/07	1467.2	201.2	1046.2	-926.3	157	48380341
WRI	Weingarten Realty Investors	Property, Real Estate & Developmen	12/31/07	599.1	238.0	4993.3	1471.8	231	41098812
WMK	Weis Markets, Inc.	Retail - Food & Beverage	12/29/07	2318.6	51.0	840.1	648.2	81	5554983
WCG	WellCare Health Plans Inc	Insurance	12/31/06	3762.9	139.2	1664.0	563.1	86	32587741
WLP	WellPoint Inc	Insurance	12/31/07	61134.3	3345.4	52060.0	22990.4	624	251593473
WFC	Wells Fargo & Co. (New)	Commercial Banking	12/31/07	53593.0	8057.0	575442.0	47628.0	1038	1117285835
WEN	Wendy's International, Inc.	Hospitality & Tourism	12/30/07	2450.2	87.9	1789.4	804.1	-	-
WCC	Wesco International, Inc.	Specialist Equipment Supplies	12/31/07	6003.5	240.6	2859.9	608.5	150	29541083
WST	West Pharmaceutical Services, Inc.	Rubber Products	12/31/07	1020.1	70.7	1185.6	485.3	104	23857937
WR	Westar Energy Inc	Electricity	12/31/07	1726.8	168.4	6395.4	1848.5	-	-
WAL	Western Alliance Bancorporation	Commercial Banking	12/31/07	333.1	32.9	5016.1	501.5	-	-
SBG	Western Asset 2008 Worldwide Doll	Trusts & Holding Entities	-	-	-	-	-	-	-
ESD	Western Asset Emerging Markets D	Trusts & Holding Entities	10/31/06	-	31.5	628.9	584.4	-	-
EFL	Western Asset Emerging Markets F	Trusts & Holding Entities	-	-	-	-	-	-	-
EDF	Western Asset Emerging Markets In	Trusts & Holding Entities	5/31/07	24.3	19.7	382.6	366.4	-	-
EMD	Western Asset Emerging Markets In	Trusts & Holding Entities	-	-	-	-	-	-	-
EHI	Western Asset Global High Income	Trusts & Holding Entities	5/31/07	38.1	25.5	864.9	449.1	-	-
GDF	Western Asset Global Partners Inco	Trusts & Holding Entities	-	-	-	-	-	-	-
HIF	Western Asset High Income Fund In	Trusts & Holding Entities	12/31/07	4.7	4.1	52.7	52.4	-	-
HIO	Western Asset High Income Opport	Trusts & Holding Entities	9/30/07	-	40.5	530.6	519.9	-	-
PAI	Western Asset Income Fund	Trusts & Holding Entities	12/31/07	10.1	8.9	156.7	142.0	-	-
IMF	Western Asset Inflation Manageme	Trusts & Holding Entities	10/31/06	-	8.1	230.1	155.1	-	-
MHY	Western Asset Managed High Inco	Trusts & Holding Entities	2/28/07	-	24.0	331.0	328.2	-	-
MMU	Western Asset Managed Municipals	Trusts & Holding Entities	5/31/07	37.8	32.4	759.0	504.5	-	-
MHF	Western Asset Municipal High Inco	Trusts & Holding Entities	10/31/06	-	8.9	173.0	172.6	-	-
MNP	Western Asset Municipal Partners F	Trusts & Holding Entities	12/31/07	8.4	6.7	241.9	156.7	-	-
WEA	Western Asset Premier Bond Fund (	Trusts & Holding Entities	12/31/07	17.5	14.6	259.7	163.5	8	543822
GFY	Western Asset Variable Rate Strate	Trusts & Holding Entities	9/30/07	-	8.9	192.0	156.9	-	-
SBW	Western Asset Worldwide Income F	Trusts & Holding Entities	10/31/06	-	11.1	210.9	199.9	-	-
ZIF	Western Asset Zenix Income Fund	Trusts & Holding Entities	3/31/07	-	6.6	96.2	59.5	-	-
WIW	Western Asset/Claymore Inflation-Li	Trusts & Holding Entities	12/31/07	51.3	43.9	1045.0	827.8	20	2572949
WIA	Western Asset/Claymore Inflation-Li	Trusts & Holding Entities	12/31/07	23.9	20.5	491.0	390.0	19	1774650
WDC	Western Digital Corp.	IT & Technology	6/29/07	5468.0	564.0	2901.0	1716.0	206	157833521
WNR	Western Refining Inc	Oil and Gas	12/31/07	7305.0	238.6	3559.7	756.5	-	-
WU	Western Union Co.	Miscellaneous Business Services	12/31/07	4900.2	857.3	5784.2	50.7	-	-
WLK	Westlake Chemical Corp	Chemicals	12/31/07	3192.2	114.7	2569.3	1286.7	93	11201854
WBK	Westpac Banking Corp. (Australia)	Commercial Banking	9/30/05	18998.0	2698.0	266263.0	16893.0	50	2723709
WHG	Westwood Holdings Group, Inc. (Un	Wealth Management	12/31/07	36.3	7.9	39.0	29.3	20	2921605
WON	Westwood One, Inc.	Sporting & Recreational	12/31/07	451.4	24.4	669.8	227.6	161	70475111
WY	Weyerhaeuser Co.	Wood Products	12/30/07	16308.0	790.0	23806.0	7981.0	463	186344752
WGL	WGL Holdings, Inc.	Gas Utilities	9/30/07	2646.0	107.9	3046.4	1008.9	179	26112524
WHQ	W-H Energy Services Inc.	Oil and Gas	12/31/07	1127.0	146.4	1007.0	655.5	125	24730138
WHR	Whirlpool Corp	Electrical	12/31/07	19408.0	640.0	14009.0	3911.0	289	64787440
WTM	White Mountains Insurance Group,	Insurance	12/31/06	4794.2	673.2	19443.7	4455.3	-	-
WLL	Whiting Petroleum Corp (New)	Oil and Gas	12/31/07	818.7	130.6	2952.0	1490.8	122	26050892
JW A	Wiley (John) & Sons Inc.	Non-Media Publishing	4/30/07	1234.9	99.6	2531.1	529.5	129	32926669
WG	Willbros Group Inc.	Oil and Gas	12/31/06	543.3	-105.4	588.3	97.9	81	21665603
WTU	Williams Coal Seam Gas Royalty Tr	Miscellaneous	12/31/07	9.5	8.5	6.9	6.9	13	342325
WMB	Williams Cos Inc (The)	Gas Utilities	12/31/07	10558.0	990.0	25061.0	6375.0	442	371830033
WPZ	Williams Partners L.P.	Gas Utilities	12/31/07	572.8	164.6	1283.5	1471.3	-	-
WMZ	Williams Pipeline Partners L.P.	Gas Utilities	12/31/07	-	-	1.7	-	-	-
WSM	Williams-Sonoma, Inc. (United State	Retail - Furniture & Home Furnishing	2/3/08	3944.9	195.8	2093.9	1165.7	242	90260717
WSH	Willis Group Holdings Ltd.	Insurance	12/31/07	2428.0	449.0	13378.0	1454.0	-	-
WL	Wilmington Trust Corp. (DE) (United	Commercial Banking	12/31/07	1108.2	182.0	11485.7	1120.3	203	28141094
WBD	Wimm-Bill-Dann Foods OJSC	Food	12/31/07	1762.1	95.4	1175.9	497.5	30	7864692
WIN	Windstream Corp	Communications	12/31/07	3260.8	917.1	8210.7	699.8	-	-
WGO	Winnebago Industries, Inc.	Automotive	8/25/07	870.2	41.6	366.5	208.4	156	35724219
FUR	Winthrop Realty Trust	Property, Real Estate & Developmen	12/31/07	51.3	2.5	745.4	291.8	-	-
WIT	Wipro Ltd	IT & Technology	3/31/07	152945.0	29120.0	-	-	52	9625191
WEC 36	Wisconsin Electric Power Company	Electricity	12/31/07	3321.6	288.9	8312.8	2686.6	-	-
WEC	Wisconsin Energy Corp.	Electricity	12/31/07	4237.8	335.6	11720.3	3129.6	256	68101829

| EARNINGS PER SHARE | | | | | | P/E RATIO | DIVIDENDS PER SHARE | | | AV. YLD % | DIV. DECLARED | | PRICE RANGE |
| QUARTERLY | | | ANNUAL | | | | PER SHARE | | | | | | 2007 |
1st	2nd	3rd	2007	2006	2005		2007	2006	2005	%	AMOUNT	PAYABLE	
0.35	0.36	0.39	1.52	0.55	0.73	17.9 - 12.5	0.66	0.60	0.60	2.9	0.19Q	5/1/08	27.2 - 19.0
0.46	0.69	-	2.03	1.72	1.52		0.33	0.27	0.22	-	0.095Q	3/12/08	-
0.68	0.72	0.70	2.71	2.68	2.41	22.5 - 18.9	0.67	0.60	0.52	1.2	0.2375Q	1/2/09	61.0 - 51.3
0.56	0.34	0.46	2.13	3.87	0.18	8.1 - 2.4	0.20	0.16	0.16	2.6	0.05Q	3/14/08	17.2 - 5.1
-0.11	-	-	-0.14	0.40	-1.40		0.52	0.65	-		0.13Q	2/29/08	-
0.86	0.92	0.20	-0.12	3.64	3.73		2.21	2.06	1.90	5.4	19.1597Q	3/17/08	45.3 - 37.6
6.70	7.19	7.60	30.19	33.68	32.59	33.0 - 26.2	8.20	7.80	7.40	0.9	2.15Q	5/9/08	996.7 - 790.2
0.24	0.18	0.73	1.34	0.88	1.84	25.7 - 19.3	1.68	1.64	1.60	5.6	0.4225Q	3/31/08	34.4 - 25.8
0.32	0.36	0.41	1.42	1.10	1.16	16.8 - 11.6	-	-	-		-		23.9 - 16.4
0.42	0.64	0.54	2.23	2.10	2.09	13.9 - 11.7	0.96	0.88	0.80	3.3	0.27Q	3/21/08	31.1 - 26.2
0.54	0.59	0.52	2.62	2.13	1.74	18.7 - 12.6	-	-	-		-		48.9 - 33.1
0.39	0.82	0.90	2.36	2.96	2.52	14.9 - 9.5	1.31	0.95	0.62	4.6	0.4Q	1/31/08	35.2 - 22.4
0.29	0.33	0.31	1.27	-4.37	1.21	38.7 - 19.4	-	-	-		-		49.1 - 24.7
0.77	0.82	-	2.60	2.01	1.58	10.5 - 8.7	-	0.15	0.30		0.075Q	4/15/08	27.5 - 22.7
0.51	0.46	0.46	1.99	2.19	1.66	16.2 - 10.8	0.40	0.36	0.32	1.6	0.11Q	3/7/08	32.2 - 21.4
0.29	0.09	0.12	-0.04	0.34	-0.38		0.34	0.34	0.34	2.2	0.085Q	2/15/08	19.1 - 12.3
-0.38	-0.79	-1.66	-13.77	0.21	4.00		-	-	-		-		29.6 - 19.4
0.81	0.48	0.84	3.08	2.53	1.47	8.9 - 5.9	-	-	-		-		27.4 - 18.0
0.62	0.63	0.64	1.76	2.47	3.43	29.3 - 24.2	1.17	1.06	0.98	2.4	0.3Q	2/27/08	51.6 - 42.6
0.63	0.73	0.62	2.48	2.11	1.67	17.8 - 13.1	0.70	0.70	-	1.8	0.175Q	4/11/08	44.2 - 32.6
0.53	0.79	0.44	2.44	3.27	2.31	16.8 - 11.3	1.98	1.86	1.76	6.0	0.384Q	3/17/08	40.9 - 27.6
0.50	0.67	0.40	1.89	2.07	2.35	20.8 - 16.6	1.16	1.16	1.12	3.3	0.29Q	2/29/08	39.3 - 31.4
0.60	1.30	-	-	3.43	1.32		-	-	-		-		34.6 - 17.9
1.26	1.35	1.45	5.56	4.82	3.94	10.5 - 6.6	-	-	-		-		58.5 - 36.5
0.00	0.67	0.00	2.30	2.49	2.25	13.3 - 11.5	1.18	1.08	1.00	4.0	0.31Q	3/1/08	31.0 - 27.4
0.15	0.33	0.34	0.97	0.82	1.92		0.46	0.59	0.57		0.125Q	2/29/08	-
0.93	1.22	1.54	4.99	4.14	2.10	6.0 - 1.8	-	-	-		-		29.9 - 9.2
0.77	0.73	0.36	2.05	2.00	1.40	12.2 - 8.1	0.53	0.49	0.45	2.7	0.14Q	5/7/08	25.0 - 16.5
0.34	0.36	0.99	1.83	1.87	1.54		1.08	1.00	0.92		1.25Q	4/1/08	-
0.39	0.25	0.35	1.06	1.41	1.24		-	-	-		-		-
-	-	-	-	-	-		-	-	-		0.063M	2/29/08	11.4 - 10.2
-	-	-	-	1.12	1.49		-	-	-		0.14M	2/29/08	20.3 - 14.6
-	-	-	-	-	-		-	-	-		0.085M	2/29/08	14.0 - 11.0
-	-	-	0.01	0.90	1.15	21.0 - 15.5	0.52	1.71	1.05	0.4	0.29Q	3/20/08	17.0 - 12.5
-	-	-	-	-	-		-	-	-		0.315Q	12/28/07	20.3 - 14.1
-	-	-	0.83	0.06	1.02	18.7 - 14.0	0.61	1.62	1.27	3.6	0.086M	5/30/08	16.6 - 13.4
-	-	-	-	-	-		-	-	-		0.079M	12/28/07	15.7 - 12.0
-	-	-	0.79	0.72	0.70	15.4 - 12.7	-	0.63	0.71		0.07M	5/30/08	12.2 - 10.0
-	-	-	0.55	0.54	0.52	13.7 - 11.1	0.09	0.50	0.55	1.3	0.047M	12/28/07	7.5 - 6.1
-	-	-	0.95	0.91	0.88	16.5 - 14.4	1.12	0.94	1.07	7.5	0.0775M	3/31/08	15.7 - 13.7
-	-	-	-	0.06	1.00		-	1.08	1.18		0.07M	2/29/08	20.0 - 18.0
-	-	-	0.54	0.50	0.53	13.4 - 10.9	0.37	0.50	0.58	5.5	0.045M	2/29/08	7.2 - 5.9
-	-	-	0.77	0.75	0.72	15.5 - 13.4	0.28	0.55	0.65	2.5	0.045M	5/30/08	11.9 - 10.4
-	-	-	0.19	0.16			-	0.11	0.16		0.001M	10/00/07	0.1 - 7.0
-	-	-	0.89	0.90	0.92	16.5 - 14.0	-	0.71	0.86		0.05M	5/30/08	14.7 - 12.4
-	-	-	1.27	1.37	1.37	12.8 - 10.8	1.22	1.30	1.20	8.1	0.0938M	3/31/08	16.3 - 13.7
-	-	-	1.07	1.04	0.86	18.8 - 18.1	0.20	1.19	0.90	1.0	0.095M	2/29/08	20.1 - 19.4
-	-	-	-	0.85	1.20		-	2.78	1.37		0.095M	5/30/08	17.4 - 12.1
-	-	-	0.35	0.35	0.37	11.9 - 9.8	0.18	0.30	0.37	4.7	0.021M	2/29/08	4.2 - 3.4
-	-	-	0.72	0.71	1.15	21.5 - 16.8	0.44	0.66	0.94	3.3	0.0625M	3/31/08	15.5 - 12.1
-	-	-	0.70	0.72	1.15	22.4 - 18.0	0.42	0.63	0.93	3.0	0.0575M	3/31/08	15.7 - 12.6
0.31	1.35	-	2.50	1.76	0.91	5.3 - 2.6	-	-	-		-		13.3 - 6.5
0.93	2.29	0.69	3.53	3.11	-		0.22	0.16	-		0.06Q	1/23/08	-
0.25	0.26	0.28	1.11	1.19	-		-	-	-		0.04A	12/28/07	-
0.30	0.58	0.59	1.76	2.98	3.48	19.3 - 8.3	0.18	0.14	0.10	0.8	0.05Q	3/17/08	34.0 - 14.7
-	-	-	1.85	1.66	1.47	41.1 - 31.2	-	-	-		-		76.0 - 57.7
0.25	0.24	0.27	1.28	0.79	0.90	15.0 - 12.9	1.15	1.33	1.09	8.4	0.30	4/1/08	20.0 - 18.5
0.01	0.08	0.10	0.30	-5.20	0.93	115.5 - 64.0	0.02	0.32	0.30	0.1	0.016Q	3/30/07	34.7 - 19.2
3.24	0.15	0.47	3.59	1.84	2.98	18.9 - 15.6	2.40	2.20	1.90	3.8	0.6Q	2/25/08	67.9 - 56.0
0.95	-	-	2.19	1.79	2.11	14.3 - 12.2	1.36	1.34	1.31	4.7	0.355Q	5/1/08	31.2 - 26.8
1.16	1.25	1.11	4.70	3.76	1.68	4.9 - 3.0	-	-	-		-		23.2 - 14.3
1.46	2.00	2.20	8.01	5.67	6.19	9.9 - 6.9	1.72	1.72	1.72	2.6	0.43Q	3/15/08	79.4 - 55.0
8.54	9.49	10.32	-	62.32	26.56		-	8.00	8.00		2.Q	3/26/08	-
0.29	0.72	1.13	3.29	4.25	3.88	10.3 - 5.6	-	-	-		-		34.0 - 18.6
0.68	0.65	0.67	1.71	1.85	1.35	20.5 - 15.3	0.40	0.36	0.30	1.3	0.11Q	4/15/08	35.1 - 26.1
-	-	-	-	-	-		-	-	-		-		23.1 - 11.9
0.20	0.22	0.27	0.88	1.34	1.40	21.0 - 14.8	0.88	1.34	1.41	5.8	0.1796Q	2/29/08	18.5 - 13.0
0.22	0.71	0.33	1.63	0.51	0.53	10.5 - 5.4	0.39	0.34	0.25	3.3	0.1Q	3/31/08	17.1 - 8.8
0.31	0.56	0.62	1.97	1.62	0.44		2.04	1.61	0.15		0.575Q	2/14/08	-
0.16	0.23	0.25	1.79	1.81	1.60	23.0 - 16.1	0.40	-	-	1.2	0.12Q	5/23/08	41.2 - 28.8
1.10	0.54	0.46	-	2.84	1.83		-	0.94	0.86		0.26Q	4/14/08	-
0.62	0.70	0.67	2.64	2.06	2.52	14.5 - 12.9	1.32	1.25	1.19	3.7	0.335Q	2/15/08	38.3 - 34.0
-	-	-	-	2.17	0.69		-	0.47	-		-		20.0 - 12.5
0.21	0.24	0.25	1.94	1.25	0.82		1.00	0.79	1.26		0.25Q	4/15/08	-
0.25	0.24	0.35	1.32	1.37	1.92	30.6 - 19.8	0.40	0.36	0.28	1.2	0.12Q	4/7/08	40.4 - 26.1
0.12	0.16	0.08	0.04	0.71	0.53	103.5 - 54.8	0.43	0.30	-	13.9	0.065Q	4/15/08	4.1 - 2.2
-	-	-	20.41	14.48	23.19	0.6 - 0.3	-	-	-		-		12.8 - 6.3
-	-	-	-	-	-		3.60	3.60	3.60		0.9Q	3/1/08	-
0.85	0.49	0.70	2.83	2.67	2.61	12.2 - 10.5	1.00	0.92	0.88	3.1	0.27Q	3/1/08	34.5 - 29.6

SYMBOL	COMPANY	NATURE OF BUSINESS	FISCAL YEAR-END	TOTAL REV. $MILL	NET INCOME $MILL	TOTAL ASSETS $MILL	NET STK EQUITY $MILL	NO OF INST	INST. HOLDINGS (SHARES)
DBU	WisdomTree Trust	Trusts & Holding Entities		-	-	-	-	-	-
DWM	WisdomTree Trust	Trusts & Holding Entities		-	-	-	-	-	-
DLN	WisdomTree Trust	Trusts & Holding Entities		-	-	-	-	-	-
DTD	WisdomTree Trust	Trusts & Holding Entities		-	-	-	-	-	-
DHS	WisdomTree Trust	Trusts & Holding Entities		-	-	-	-	-	-
WMS	WMS Industries Inc.	Consumer Accessories	6/30/07	539.8	48.9	655.7	433.6	111	34992451
WNS	WNS (Holdings) Ltd	Research Support Services	3/31/07	-	26.6	-	205.5	-	-
WWW	Wolverine World Wide, Inc. (United	Leather and Leather Products	12/29/07	1199.0	92.9	638.4	478.8	164	45050053
WF	Woori Finance Holdings Co., Ltd	Trusts & Holding Entities	12/31/06	9227033.0	2029319.0	11997330.0	-	5	138396
INT	World Fuel Services Corp. (United	Retail - Fuel & Oil	12/31/07	13729.6	64.8	1798.0	483.9	97	16611027
WWE	World Wrestling Entertainment Inc (	Movies & Film	12/31/07	485.7	52.1	470.1	383.4	68	15541803
WOR	Worthington Industries, Inc. (United	Metal Works	5/31/07	2971.8	113.9	1814.2	936.0	193	43023986
WXS	Wright Express Corp	Automotive Repair Services	12/31/07	336.1	51.6	1785.1	204.3	83	34408381
WWY	Wrigley (William) Jr. Co.	Food	12/31/07	5389.1	632.0	5231.5	2817.5	2	10800
WYE	Wyeth	Pharmaceuticals	12/31/07	22399.8	4616.0	42717.3	18210.5	914	977385457
WYN	Wyndham Worldwide Corp	Hospitality & Tourism	12/31/07	4360.0	403.0	10459.0	3516.0	-	-
XEL	Xcel Energy, Inc.	Electricity	12/31/07	10034.2	577.3	23184.7	6406.0	-	-
XRM	Xerium Technologies Inc	Paper Products	12/31/06	601.4	29.5	990.7	116.6	-	-
XRX	Xerox Corp	Office Equipment Supplies	12/31/07	17228.0	1135.0	23543.0	8588.0	373	745339183
XL	XL Capital Ltd.	Insurance	12/31/07	9135.7	275.9	57762.3	9948.1	-	-
XTO	XTO Energy, Inc.	Oil and Gas	12/31/07	5513.0	1691.0	18922.0	7941.0	405	282801984
AUY	Yamana Gold, Inc.	Precious Metals	12/31/06	169.2	-70.2	2181.2	1716.6	36	41622215
YZC	Yanzhou Coal Mining Co., Ltd.	Coal Mining	12/31/06	13224.3	1749.3	22894.1	18027.0	19	278380
YGE	Yingli Green Energy Holding Co., Lt	IT & Technology	12/31/06	-	450.0	-	68.5	-	-
YPF	YPF SA	Oil and Gas	12/31/06	25635.0	4457.0	35394.0	24345.0	13	153024
YUM	Yum! Brands, Inc.	Hospitality & Tourism	12/29/07	10416.0	909.0	7242.0	1139.0	432	229530042
ZLC	Zale Corp. (New)	Retail - Miscellaneous	7/31/07	2437.1	59.3	1613.9	902.6	159	51116537
ZAP	Zapata Corp. (NV)	Food	12/31/07	-	2.6	165.4	162.1	18	845773
ZNT	Zenith National Insurance Corp.	Insurance	12/31/07	873.7	233.9	2773.0	1073.4	135	15019623
ZEP	Zep Inc	Chemicals	8/31/07	-	14.1	-	74.8	-	-
ZMH	Zimmer Holdings, Inc.	Medical Instruments & Equipment	12/31/07	3897.5	773.2	6633.7	5449.6	678	194721424
ZF	Zweig Fund, Inc. (The)	Trusts & Holding Entities	12/31/07	9.0	3.8	525.0	519.1	32	9281766
ZTR	Zweig Total Return Fund, Inc. (The)	Trusts & Holding Entities	12/31/07	18.1	13.0	609.8	569.7	25	8305497

1st	2nd	3rd	ANNUAL 2007	2006	2005	P/E RATIO	DIV 2007	2006	2005	AV. YLD %	AMOUNT	PAYABLE	PRICE RANGE 2007
-	-	-	-	-	-	-	-	-	-	-	0.1876Q	9/28/07	-
-	-	-	-	-	-		-	-	-	-	0.0481U	12/21/07	-
-	-	-	-	-	-		-	-	-	-	0.1876Q	9/28/07	-
-	-	-	-	-	-		-	-	-	-	0.1876Q	9/28/07	-
-	-	-	-	-	-	-	-	-	-	-	0.0481U	12/21/07	-
0.19	0.27	-	0.86	0.63	0.41	26.0 - 15.3	-	-	-		-		22.4 - 13.1
-	-	-	0.65	0.52	-0.19		-	-	-		-		
0.39	0.28	0.54	1.70	1.47	1.27	12.6 - 8.0	0.36	0.30	0.26	2.1	0.11Q	5/1/08	21.5 - 13.6
-	-	-			-2095.00		-	-	-		-		25.3 - 16.4
0.51	0.58	0.51	2.23	2.21	1.57	11.2 - 7.3	0.15	0.15	0.15	0.8	0.0375Q	4/9/08	24.9 - 16.3
0.16	0.10	0.12	0.72	0.44	0.56	21.3 - 15.9	0.96	0.96	0.36	7.5	0.24Q	3/25/08	15.4 - 11.4
0.24	0.18	0.23	1.31	1.64	2.03	17.3 - 12.1	0.68	0.68	0.65	3.5	0.17Q	3/29/08	22.7 - 15.9
0.20	0.45	0.55	1.27	1.81	0.46		-	-	-		-		
0.52	0.61	0.59	2.28	1.90	1.83	24.9 - 19.1	1.13	1.11	1.08	2.3	0.335Q	5/1/08	56.8 - 43.6
0.92	0.87	0.84	3.38	3.08	2.70	13.2 - 10.0	1.06	1.01	0.94	2.7	0.5Q	4/1/08	44.6 - 33.8
0.45	0.52	0.65	2.20	1.44	-		-	-	-		0.04Q	3/13/08	
0.28	0.18	0.58	1.35	1.36	1.23		0.91	0.88	0.85		1.14Q	4/15/08	
0.09	0.17	0.16	-	0.67	-0.05		-	0.90	0.33		0.1125Q	12/17/07	
0.24	0.28	0.27	1.19	1.22	0.94	14.4 - 10.6	0.04	-	-	0.3	0.0425Q	4/30/08	17.1 - 12.7
3.06	3.00	1.82	1.15	9.60	-9.14		-	-	-		0.38Q	3/31/08	
0.82	0.91	0.84	3.53	4.02	2.52	5.9 - 3.4	0.41	0.25	0.18	2.5	0.12Q	4/15/08	21.0 - 12.0
-	-	-	-	-0.25	-0.03		-	0.02	-		0.01Q	1/14/08	3.4 - 1.8
0.12	0.15	0.09	-	0.36	0.51		-	-	-		-		49.4 - 21.8
-	-	-	-	0.36	-		-	-	-		-		44.0 - 36.0
0.30	0.39	0.00	1.68	1.48	1.27	14.0 - 9.7	-	-	-		0.15Q	5/2/08	23.8 - 16.3
-0.58	1.34	-	1.21	1.09	2.05	25.7 - 20.4	-	-	-		-		31.1 - 24.7
0.02	0.04	0.03	0.13	-0.24	-0.48	66.3 - 48.8	-	-	-		-		8.6 - 6.3
1.73	1.75	1.73	6.27	6.96	4.32	5.4 - 3.4	2.69	1.16	0.88	9.4	0.5Q	5/14/08	34.0 - 21.4
-	-	-	0.64	0.93	-		-	-	-		0.04Q	2/4/08	
0.98	0.97	0.19	3.26	3.40	2.93	27.3 - 20.8	-	-	-		-		89.2 - 67.9
-	-	-	0.05	-	0.08	111.6 - 93.6	0.59	0.58	0.59	11.6	0.142Q	1/10/08	5.6 - 4.7
-	-	-	0.12	0.13	0.12	45.4 - 40.5	0.50	0.52	0.54	9.7	0.04M	3/26/08	5.4 - 4.9